OTHER TITLES OF INTEREST

CODING AND REIMBURSEMENT

Collections Made Easy!
CPT Coders Choice®, Thumb Indexed
CPT TimeSaver®, Ring Binder, Tab Indexed
CPT & HCPCS Coding Made Easy!
HCPCS Coders Choice®
Health Insurance Carrier Directory
ICD-9-CM, Coders Choice®, Thumb Indexed
ICD-9-CM, TimeSaver® Ring Binder, Tab Indexed
ICD-9-CM Coding Made Easy!
Physicians Fees
Medicare Rules and Regulations
Reimbursement Manual for the Medical Office

PRACTICE MANAGEMENT

365 Ways to Manage the Business Called Private Practice
Computerizing Your Medical Office
Designing and Building Your Professional Office
Effective Laboratory Supervision
Encyclopedia of Practice and Financial Management
Health Information Management
Hospital and Health Facilities Directory
Managing Medical Office Personnel
Marketing Healthcare
Marketing Strategies for Physicians
Medical Practice Handbook
Medical Risk Management
Medical Staff Privileges
On-Line Systems: How to Access and Use Databases
Patient Satisfaction
Performance Standards for the Laboratory
Physician's Office Laboratory
Professional and Practice Development
Promoting Your Medical Practice
Remodeling Your Professional Office
Software, Systems and Services Directory
Starting in Medical Practice

**AVAILABLE FROM YOUR LOCAL MEDICAL
BOOK STORE OR CALL 1-800-MED-SHOP**

OTHER TITLES OF INTEREST

FINANCIAL MANAGEMENT

A Physician's Guide to Financial Independence
Business Ventures for Physicians
Financial Planning Workbook for Physicians
Financial Valuation of Your Practice
Personal Money Management for Physicians
Personal Pension Plan Strategies for Physicians
Securing Your Assets
Selling or Buying a Medical Practice

RISK MANAGEMENT

Belli: For Your Malpractice Defense
Law, Liability and Ethics
Malpractice Depositions
Malpractice: Managing Your Defense
Preventing Emergency Malpractice
Testifying in Court

DICTIONARIES AND OTHER REFERENCE

Drug Interactions Index
Isler's Pocket Dictionary
Medical Acronyms and Abbreviations
Medical Phrase Index
Medico-Legal Glossary
Spanish/English Handbook

MEDICAL REFERENCE AND CLINICAL

Gastroenterology: Problems in Primary Care
Medical Procedures for Referral
Neurology: Problems in Primary Care
Orthopaedics: Problems in Primary Care
Patient Care Emergency Handbook
Patient Care Flowchart Manual
Patient Care Procedures for Your Practice
Sexually Transmitted Diseases

**AVAILABLE FROM YOUR LOCAL MEDICAL
BOOK STORE OR CALL 1-800-MED-SHOP**

ICD·9·CM

International Classification of Diseases
9th Revision

Clinical Modification
Fifth Edition

Color Coded

1997

Volumes 1 & 2

ISBN 1-57066-058-1 (Soft cover)
ISBN 1-57066-060-3 (Hard cover)

Volumes 1, 2, & 3

ISBN 1-57066-059-X (Soft cover)
ISBN 1-57066-057-3 (Timesaver Binder)

Practice Management Information Corporation [PMIC]
4727 Wilshire Boulevard, Suite 300
Los Angeles, California 90010
1-800-MED-SHOP

Printed in the United States of America

Preface

Health care professionals have long used coding systems to describe procedures, services, and supplies. However, most described the reason for the procedure, service or supply with a diagnostic statement. Of those health care professionals who do code the diagnosis, either due to a requirement for a computer billing system and/or electronic claims filing, many do not code completely or accurately. With the passage of the Medicare Catastrophic Coverage Act of 1988, diagnostic coding using *ICD-9-CM* became mandatory for Medicare claims. In the area of health care reimbursement rules and regulations, the typical progression is that changes required for Medicare are followed shortly by similar changes for Medicaid and private insurance carriers.

To some professionals, the requirement to use diagnostic coding may seem a burden or simply another excuse for Medicare intermediaries to delay or deny payment. However, it is important to understand that the proper use of coding systems for both procedures and diagnoses gives the professional absolute control over his or her billing and reimbursement. Accurate diagnosis coding is not easy. It requires a good working knowledge of medical terminology and a fundamental understanding of *ICD-9-CM*. In addition, the coder must know the rules and regulations required to comply with Medicare requirements for coding.

This edition of the *International Classification of Diseases, 9th Revision, Clinical Modification (ICD-9-CM)* is published by Practice Management Information Corporation in recognition of its responsibility to promulgate this classification throughout the United States for morbidity coding and billing purposes. The *International Classification of Diseases, 9th Revision*, originally published by the World Health Organization (WHO) is the foundation of the *ICD-9-CM* and continues to be the classification employed in cause-of-death coding in the United States.

The *ICD-9-CM* is recommended for use in all clinical settings, but is required for reporting diagnoses and diseases to all U.S. Public Health Service and Health Care Financing Administration programs. This version faithfully follows and contains the same information found in the U.S. Public Health Service and Health Care Financing Administration version of the *ICD-9-CM*.

All official authorized addenda effective October 1, 1996 have been included in this edition. A new revision will be available approximately September 15th of each year. Revised editions may be purchased from:

Practice Management Information Corporation
4727 Wilshire Boulevard., Suite 300
Los Angeles, California 90010
1-800-MED-SHOP

Disclaimer

This publication is identical in content to U.S. Department of Health and Human Services Publication No. (PHS) 91-1260 with the exception that this publication includes special symbols to indicate additions and revisions from the previous edition and special symbols to facilitate identification of diagnostic codes that require 4th or 5th digit specificity, the use of color coding to alert the user to special coding considerations, and thumb indexing to make locating codes easier. This publication is revised annually so that we may present the most current information possible. Though all of the information is carefully researched and checked for accuracy and completeness, the publisher accepts no responsibility with regard to errors, omissions, misuse or misinterpretation.

Table of Contents

Table of Contents

Table of Contents

Table of Contents

(1) These listings appear only in the three volume edition

Introduction to ICD-9-CM

ICD-9-CM is an acronym for *International Classification of Diseases, 9th Revision, Clinical Modification*, published under different names since 1900. *ICD-9-CM* is a statistical classification system that arranges diseases and injuries into groups according to established criteria. Most *ICD-9-CM* codes are numeric and consist of three, four or five numbers and a description. The codes are revised approximately every 10 years by the World Health Organization and annual updates are published by HCFA.

HISTORICAL PERSPECTIVE

The *International Classification of Diseases, 9th Revision, Clinical Modification* (*ICD-9-CM*) is based on the official version of the *World Health Organization's (WHO) 9th Revision, International Classification of Diseases* (*ICD-9*). *ICD-9* is designed for the classification of morbidity and mortality information for statistical purposes, and for the indexing of medical records by disease and operations, and for data storage and retrieval. *ICD-9-CM* replaced the Eighth Revision International Classification of Diseases, Adapted for Use in the United States commonly referred to as *ICDA*.

The concept of extending the International Classification of Diseases for use in hospital indexing was originally developed in response to a need for a more efficient basis for storage and retrieval of diagnostic data. In 1950, the U.S. Public Health Service and the Veterans Administration began independent tests of the International Classification of Diseases for hospital indexing purposes. In the following year, the Columbia Presbyterian Medical Center in New York City adopted the International Classification of Diseases, 6th Revision for use in its medical record department. A few years later, the Commission on Professional and Hospital Activities adopted the International Classification of Diseases for use in hospitals participating in the Professional Activity Study (PAS).

In view of the growing interest in the use of the International Classification of Diseases for hospital indexing, a study was undertaken in 1956 by the American Medical Association and the American Medical Record Association of the relative efficiencies of coding systems for diagnostic indexing. Following this study, the major uses of the International Classification of Diseases for hospital indexing purposes consolidated their experiences and an adaptation was published in December 1959. A revision containing the first "Classification of Operations and Treatments" was published in 1962.

In 1968, following a study by the American Hospital Association, the United States Public Health Service published the Eighth Revision International Classification of Diseases, Adapted for Use in the United States. This publication became commonly known as ICDA, and served as the basis for coding diagnostic data for official morbidity and mortality statistics in the United States.

ICD-9-CM Background

In February 1977, a committee was convened by the National Center for Health Statistics to provide advice and counsel for the development of clinical modification of the ICD-9. The organizations represented on the committee included:

American Association of Health Data Systems
American Hospital Association
American Medical Record Association
Association for Health Records
Council on Clinical Classifications, sponsored by:

American Academy of Pediatrics
American College of Obstetricians and Gynecologists
American College of Physicians
American College of Surgeons
American Psychiatric Association

Commission on Professional and Hospital Activities
Health Care Financing Administration
WHO Center for Classification of Diseases

The resulting *ICD-9-CM* is a clinical modification of the *World Health Organization's International Classification of Diseases, 9th Revision (ICD-9)*. The term "clinical" is used to emphasize the modifications intent; namely, to serve as a useful tool in the area of classification of morbidity data for indexing of medical records, medical care review, ambulatory and other medical care programs, as well as for basic health statistics.

In use since January 1979, *ICD-9-CM* provides a diagnostic coding system that is more precise than those needed only for statistical groupings and trend analysis. Official addenda (updates) to *ICD-9-CM* were issued in October 1986, 1987 and 1988 by the Health Care Financing Administration. A special addendum was published by the U.S. Public Health Service in January 1988 containing codes for AIDS and AIDS related illnesses.

Use of ICD-9-CM Codes for Professional Billing

Until passage of the Medicare Catastrophic Coverage Act of 1988, health care professionals were not required to report *ICD-9-CM* codes when billing government or private insurance carriers for reimbursement. The exception to this requirement was for those health care professionals who filed insurance claims electronically and those who used "code driven" computer billing services or computer systems.

Most health care professionals simply included the text or description of the injury, illness, sign or symptom that was the reason for the encounter. Insurance carriers who used *ICD-9-CM* coding had to code the diagnostic statements prior to input into their computer systems for reimbursement processing.

A specific requirement of the Medicare Catastrophic Coverage Act of 1988 required health care professionals to include *ICD-9-CM* codes on their Medicare claim forms effective April 1, 1989. A two-month grace period, to June 1, 1989, was allowed at the request of the American Medical Association, to allow health care professionals additional time to develop the knowledge and systems necessary to implement the requirement.

TERMINOLOGY

There are terms used throughout this publication that are important fo.
understanding of *ICD-9-CM*. The following terms are defined specifically as .
used for *ICD-9-CM* with the knowledge that some terms may have other definitions
and meanings.

acute	refers to the condition that is the primary reason for the current encounter.
addenda	official updates to *ICD-9-CM* published continuously since 1986, that become effective on October 1st of each year.
adverse	any response to a drug that is noxious and unintended and occurs with proper dosage.
aftercare	an encounter for something planned in advance, for example, cast removal.
AHFS	American Hospital Formulary Service.
alphabetic	the portion of *ICD-9-CM* that lists definitions and codes in alphabetic order. Also called Volume 2.
category	refers to diagnoses codes listed within a specific three-digit category, for example category 250, Diabetes Mellitus.
cause	that which brings about any condition or produces any effect.
chronic	continuing over a long period of time or recurring frequently.
coding	the process of transferring written or verbal descriptions of diseases, injuries and procedures into numerical designations.
combination	a code that combines a diagnosis with an associated secondary process or complication.
complication	the occurrence of two or more diseases in the same patient at the same time.
concurrent	when a patient is being treated by more than one provider for different care conditions at the same time.
conventions	refers to the use of certain abbreviations, punctuation, symbols, type faces, and other instructions that must be clearly understood in order to use *ICD-9-CM*.
CPT	Current Procedural Terminology. Listing of codes and descriptions for procedures, services and supplies published by the American Medical Association. Used to bill insurance carriers.
diagnosis	a written description of the reason(s) for the procedure, service, supply or encounter.
down coding	the process where insurance carriers reduce the value of a procedure, and the resulting reimbursement, due to either 1) a mismatch of CPT code and description or 2) ICD-9-CM code does not justify the procedure or level of service.
E codes	specific ICD-9-CM codes used to identify the cause of injury, poisoning and other adverse effects.
eponyms	medical procedures or conditions named after a person or a place.
etiology	the cause(s) or origin of a disease.
HCFA	Health Care Financing Administration. The government agency that administers the Medicare and Medicaid programs.

HCFA1500	Uniform Health Insurance Claim Form used for billing services to Medicare and other insurance carriers.
hierarchy	a system that ranks items one above another.
ICD-9-CM	International Classification of Diseases, 9th Revision, Clinical Modification.
ICD-10	International Classification of Diseases, 10th Revision
late effect	a residual effect (condition produced) after the acute phase of an illness or injury has ended.
main term	refers to listings in the Alphabetic Index appearing BOLDFACE type.
manifestation	characteristic signs or symptoms of an illness.
multiple	refers to the need to use more than one ICD-9-CM code to fully identify coding a condition.
primary code	the ICD-9-CM code that defines the main reason for the current encounter.
residual	the long-term condition(s) resulting from a previous acute illness or injury.
rule out	refers to a method used to indicate that a condition is probable, suspected, or questionable but unconfirmed. ICD-9-CM has no provisions for the use of this term.
secondary	code(s) listed after the primary code that further indicate the cause(s) codefor the current encounter or define the need for higher levels of care.
sections	refers to portions of the Tabular List that are organized in groups of three-digit code numbers. For example, Malignant Neoplasm of Lip, Oral Cavity and Pharynx (140-149).
sequencing	the process of listing ICD-9-CM codes in the proper order.
specificity	refers to the requirement to code to the highest number of digits possible, 3, 4 or 5, when choosing an ICD-9-CM code.
sub term	refers to listings appearing in the Alphabetic Index under MAIN TERMS and always indented two spaces to the right.
subcategories	refers to groupings of four-digit codes listed under three-digit categories.
tabular list	the portion of ICD-9-CM that lists codes and definitions in numeric order. Also referred to as Volume 1.
V codes	specific ICD-9-CM codes used to identify encounters for reasons other than illness or injury, for example, immunization.
Volume 1	see TABULAR LIST
Volume 2	see ALPHABETIC INDEX
Volume 3	procedure codes used only for hospital coding. Volume 3 contains both a numeric listing and alphabetic index.

FORMAT OF ICD-9-CM

The *International Classification of Diseases, 9th Revision, Clinical Modification* was originally published as a three volume set (2nd edition). Newer versions of ICD-9-CM, Fifth Edition, are available as two separate books (Volume 1 and Volume 2) and as a single book containing Volume 1 and Volume 2, or Volumes 1, 2 and 3 depending on the publisher. It is also now available on CD-ROM from the U.S. Government.

The Third Edition of ICD-9-CM includes all official addenda from October 1986 through October 1988. The Fourth Edition of ICD-9-CM includes all official addenda from October 1986 through October 1994. The Fifth Edition of ICD-9-CM includes all official addenda from October 1986 through October 1996.

The Tabular List (Volume 1)

The Tabular List (Volume 1) is a <u>numeric</u> listing of diagnosis codes and descriptions consisting of 17 chapters that classify diseases and injuries, two sections containing supplementary codes (V codes and E codes) and six appendices.

Classification of Diseases and Injuries

The Classification of Diseases and Injuries includes the following 17 chapters:

Chapter 1   Infectious and Parasitic Diseases (001-139)

Chapter 2   Neoplasms (140-239)

Chapter 3   Endocrine, Nutritional and Metabolic Diseases, and Immunity Disorders (240-279)

Chapter 4   Diseases of the Blood and Blood-Forming Organs (280-289)

Chapter 5   Mental Disorders (290-319)

Chapter 6   Diseases of the Nervous System and Sense Organs

Chapter 7   Diseases of the Circulatory System (390-459)

Chapter 8   Diseases of the Respiratory System (460-519)

Chapter 9   Diseases of the Digestive System (520-579)

Chapter 10   Diseases of the Genitourinary System (580-629)

Chapter 11   Complications of Pregnancy, Childbirth, and the Puerperium (630-676)

Chapter 12   Diseases of the Skin and Subcutaneous Tissue (680-709)

Chapter 13   Diseases of the Musculoskeletal System and Connective Tissue (710-739)

Chapter 14   Congenital Anomalies (740-759)

Chapter 15   Certain Conditions Originating in the Perinatal Period (760-779)

Chapter 16   Symptoms, Signs and Ill-defined Conditions (780-799)

Chapter 17   Injury and Poisoning (800-999)

Each chapter of the Tabular List (Volume 1) is structured into four components; namely:

Sections: groups of three-digit code numbers

Categories: three-digit code numbers

Subcategories: four-digit code numbers

Fifth-Digit Subclassifications: five-digit code numbers

Supplementary Classifications

There are two supplementary classifications included in the Tabular List (Volume 1). These are:

V Codes Supplementary Classification of Factors Influencing Health Status and Contact with Health Services (V01-V82)

E Codes Supplementary Classification of External Causes of Injury and Poisoning (E800-E999)

Appendices

The Tabular List (Volume 1) includes six appendices. These are:

Appendix 1 Morphology of Neoplasms

Appendix 2 Glossary of Mental Disorders

Appendix 3 Classification of Drugs by American Hospital Formulary Service List Number and their ICD-9-CM Equivalents

Appendix 4 Classification of Industrial Accidents According to Agency

Appendix 5 List of Three-Digit Categories

Appendix 6 Supplementary Classification of External Causes of Injury and Poisoning

Specifications for the Tabular List

1. Three-digit rubrics and their contents are unchanged from *ICD-9*.

2. The sequence of three-digit rubrics is unchanged from *ICD-9*.

3. Three-digit rubrics are not added to the main body of the classification.

4.　Unsubdivided three-digit rubrics are subdivided where necessary to:

　　a) Add clinical detail

　　b) Isolate terms for clinical accuracy

5.　The modification in *ICD-9-CM* is accomplished by the addition of a fifth digit to existing *ICD-9* rubrics, except as noted under #7 below.

6.　Four-digit rubrics are added to subdivided three-digit codes only when there is no other means of achieving desired detail. These codes, unique to *ICD-9-CM* (28 three-digit categories) are marked with the symbol in the Tabular List.

7.　The optional dual classification in *ICD-9* is modified.

　　a) Duplicate rubrics are deleted:

　　　　1) Four-digit manifestation categories duplicating etiology entries.

　　　　2) Manifestation inclusion terms duplicating etiology entries.

　　b) Manifestations of diseases are identified, to the extent possible, by creating five digit codes in the etiology rubrics.

　　c) When the manifestation of a disease cannot be included in the etiology rubrics, provision for its identification is made by retaining the *ICD-9* rubrics used for classifying manifestations of disease.

8.　The format of *ICD-9-CM* is revised from that used in *ICD-9*.

　　a) American spelling of medical terms is used.

　　b) Inclusion terms are indented beneath the titles of codes.

　　c) Codes not to be used for primary tabulation of disease are printed in italics with the notation, "code also underlying disease."

The Alphabetical Index (Volume 2)

The Alphabetic Index (Volume 2) of ICD-9-CM consists of an alphabetic list of terms and codes, two supplementary Sections following the alphabetic listing, plus three special tables found within the alphabetic listing. The Alphabetic Index (Volume 2) is structured as follows:

MAIN TERMS: appear in **BOLDFACE** type

SUBTERMS:　are always indented two spaces to the right under main terms

CARRY-OVER LINES:　are always indented more than two spaces from the level of the preceding line

Punctuation

( )   PARENTHESIS are used to enclose supplementary words that may be present or absent in a statement of disease without effecting the code assignment.

[ ]   SQUARE BRACKETS are used to enclose synonyms, alternate wordings or explanatory phrases.

:   COLONS are used after an incomplete phrase or term that requires one or more of the modifiers indented under it to make it assignable to a given category. EXCEPTION to this rule pertains to the abbreviation NOS.

{ }   BRACES are used to connect a series of terms to a common stem. Each term on the left of the brace is incomplete and must be completed by a term to the right of the brace.

Symbols

□   The LOZENGE symbol appearing in the left margin preceding a four-digit code indicates that the code and description are not the same in *ICD-9-CM* as in *ICD-9*. May be ignored for coding purposes.

•   A filled BLACK CIRCLE preceding a code indicates that the code is new to this revision of *ICD-9-CM*. A symbol key appears on all left-hand pages of the Tabular List, Volume 1.

▲   A filled BLACK TRIANGLE preceding a code indicates that there is a revision to the text or notes of an existing code. A symbol key appears on all left-hand pages of the Tabular List, Volume 1.

④ ⑤   A circle containing the number 4 or the number 5 preceding a code indicates that a fourth or fifth digit is required for coding to the highest level of specificity. Valid digits are in [brackets] under each code. Definitions of valid fifth digits are found under the major category.

Other conventions

Type Face:

BOLD: Bold type face is used for all codes and titles in the Tabular List.

Italics: Italicized type face is used for all exclusion notes and to identify those rubrics that are not to be used for primary tabulations of disease.

Format: *ICD-9-CM* uses an indented format for ease in reference.

Instructional Notations

Instructional terms define what is, or what is not, included in a given subdivision. This is accomplished by using both inclusion and exclusion terms.

INCLUDES: Indicates separate terms, such as, modifying adjectives, sites and conditions, entered under a subdivision, such as a category, to further define or give examples of, the content of the category.

Excludes: Exclusion terms are enclosed in a box and are printed in italics to draw attention to their presence. The importance of this instructional term is its use as a guideline to direct the coder to the proper code assignment. In other words, all terms following the word EXCLUDES: are to be coded elsewhere as indicated in each instance.

NOTES   These are used to define terms and give coding instructions. Often used to list the fifth-digit subclassifications for certain categories.

SEE   Acts as a cross reference and, is an explicit direction to look elsewhere. This instructional term must always be followed. (Cross references provide the user with other possible modifiers for a term, or, its synonyms.)

SEE CATEGORY   A variation of the instructional term SEE. This refers the coder to a specific category. You must *always* follow this instructional term.

SEE ALSO   A direction given to look elsewhere if the main term or subterm(s) are not sufficient to code the information you have.

CODE FIRST   This instructional note is used for those codes not intended to be used as a principal diagnosis, or not to be sequenced before the underlying disease. The note requires that the underlying disease (etiology) be coded first with the code the note is applied to being coded second. This note appears only in the tabular list (Vol. 1).

USE ADDITIONAL CODE   This instruction is placed in the Tabular List in those categories where the coder may wish to add further information, by using an additional code, to give a more complete picture of the diagnosis or procedure.

Related terms

AND   Whenever this term appears in a title, it should be interpreted as "and/or."

WITH   When this term is used in a title it indicates a requirement that both parts of the title must be present in the diagnostic statement.

COLOR CODING

All PMIC versions of *ICD-9-CM* include color-coding to alert the user to special coding situations or conditions that require additional attention. The use of color-coding is found in the Tabular List of Volume 1 and the Tabular List of Volume 3. The color is applied as solid rectangular bars over the codes only so that the descriptions remain clear and legible. The color codes and definitions are printed at the bottom of all right-sided pages of Volume 1 and Volume 3.

Volume 1

�▬ Three digit codes. Coding to fourth or fifth digit specificity is required.

▬ Unspecified code. Descriptions include the term "unspecified". Use only if a more specific diagnosis is not known or available.

▬ Nonspecific code. Descriptions include the term "nonspecific, unspecified, other specified or other". A report *may* be required by insurance carriers.

▬ Manifestation codes. Used only to code the manifestation of an underlying disease. Code the underlying disease first.

▬ Medicare secondary payer (MSP) alert. Diagnoses that may trigger a post-payment review by Medicare. Medicare is usually the secondary payer for these diagnoses.

Volume 3*

▬ Noncovered operating room procedure. An operating room procedure that is not covered by Medicare.

▬ Non-operating room procedure. A procedure that is not performed in the operating room that affects DRG assignment.

▬ Bilateral procedure.

▬ Valid operating room procedure. Prompts a change in DRG assignment.

▬ Nonspecific operating room procedure. Choose a more precise code if possible.

*These colors appear only in the three-volume edition

ICD-9-CM CODING FUNDAMENTALS

Learning and following the basic steps of *ICD-9-CM* coding will increase your chances of better and faster reimbursement from third party payers, as well as establish meaningful profiles for future reimbursement rates. To become a proficient coder, two basic principles must be considered.

- It is imperative that you use both the Alphabetic Index (Volume 2) and the Tabular List (Volume 1) when locating and assigning codes. Coding only from the Alphabetic Index will cause you to miss any additional information provided only in the Tabular List: such as, exclusions, instructions to use additional codes or the need for a fifth-digit.

- The level of specificity is important in all coding situations. So, a three-digit code that has subdivisions indicates you must use the appropriate subdivision code. Also, any time a fifth-digit subclassification is provided, you must use the fifth-digit code.

Nine Steps for Accurate ICD-9-CM Coding

1. Locate the main term within the diagnostic statement.

2. Locate that main term in the Alphabetic Index (Volume 2). Keep in mind that the primary arrangement for main terms is by condition in the Alphabetic Index (Volume 2); main terms can be referred to in outmoded, ill-defined and lay terms as well as proper medical terms; main terms can be expressed in broad or specific terms, as nouns, adjectives or eponyms and can be with or without modifiers. Certain conditions may be listed under more than one main term.

3. Remember to refer to all notes under the main term. Be guided by the instructions in any notes appearing in a box immediately after the main term.

4. Examine any modifiers appearing in parentheses next to the main term. See if any of these modifiers apply to any of the qualifying terms used in the diagnostic statement.

5. Take note of the subterms indented beneath the main term. Subterms differ from main terms in that they provide greater specificity becoming more specific the further they are indented to the right of the main term in 2-space increments and, they provide the anatomical sites affected by the disease or injury.

6. Be sure to follow any cross reference instructions. These instructional terms ("see" or "see also") must be followed to locate the correct code.

7. Confirm the code selection in the Tabular List (Volume 1). make certain you have selected the appropriate classification in accordance with the diagnosis.

8. Follow instructional terms in the Tabular List (Volume 1). Watch for exclusion terms, notes and fifth-digit instructions that apply to the code number you are verifying. It is necessary to search not only the selected code number for

instructions but also, the category, section and chapter in which the code number is collapsible. Many times the instructional information is located one or more pages preceding the actual page you find the code number on.

9. Finally, assign the code number you have determined to be correct. Repeat the above steps until all codes have been assigned.

MEDICARE REQUIREMENTS FOR ICD-9-CM CODING

The Medicare Catastrophic Coverage Act of 1988 (PL 100-330) requires that health care professionals submit an appropriate diagnosis code, using the *International Classification of Diseases, 9th Revision, Clinical Modification (ICD-9-CM)* for each procedure, service, or supply billed under Medicare Part B.

To comply with the regulations, health care professionals must convert the reason(s) for the procedures, services or supplies, performed or issued, from written diagnostic statements that may include specific diagnoses, signs, symptoms and/or complaints, into ICD-9-CM diagnosis codes. The Health Care Financing Administration originally set the implementation date for this requirement as April 1, 1989, however, it was subsequently delayed until June 1, 1989, at the request of the American Medical Association, to give health care providers additional time to prepare for the change.

HCFA Guidelines for Using ICD-9-CM Codes

The Health Care Financing Administration (HCFA) has prepared guidelines for using ICD-9-CM codes and instructions on how to report them on claim forms. In addition, HCFA has directed your medicare intermediary to provide you with a written copy of these instructions. The basic HCFA guidelines are summarized below, however, it is very important that you obtain a copy of the guidelines from your Medicare intermediary as implementation of HCFA requirements varies from one intermediary to another.

1. Indicate on the claim form or itemized statement the appropriate code(s) from the ICD-9-CM code range 001.0 through V82.9 to identify diagnoses, symptoms, conditions, problems, complaints or other reason(s) for the procedure, service or supply provided.

   A. In choosing codes to describe the reason for the encounter, the health care professional will frequently be using codes within the range from 001.0 through 999.9, the section of ICD-9-CM for the classification of diseases and injuries (e.g. infectious and parasitic diseases; neoplasms; signs, symptoms and ill-defined conditions). Codes that describe symptoms as opposed to diagnoses are acceptable if this is the highest level of certainty documented by the physician.

   B. ICD-9-CM also provides codes to deal with visits for circumstances other than a disease or injury, such as an encounter for a laboratory test only. These codes are found in the V-code section and range from V01.0 through V82.9.

2.   The ICD-9-CM code for the diagnosis, condition, problem, or other reason for the encounter documented in the medical record as the main reason for the procedure, service or supply provided should be listed first. Additional ICD-9-CM codes that describe any current coexisting conditions are then listed. Do not include codes for conditions that were previously treated and no longer exist.

3.   ICD-9-CM codes should be used at their highest level of specificity.

   A.   Assign three digit codes only if there are no four digit codes within the coding category.

   B.   Assign four digit codes only if there is no fifth digit subclassification for that category.

   C.   Assign the fifth digit subclassification code for those categories where it exists.

   Claims submitted with three or four digit codes where four and five digit codes are available may be returned to you by the Medicare intermediary for proper coding. It is recognized that a very specific diagnosis may not be known at the time of the initial encounter. However, that is not an acceptable reason to submit a three digit code when four or five digits are available.

   For example, if the patient has chronic bronchitis, ICD-9-CM code 491, and the physician has not yet documented whether the bronchitis is simple, mucopurulent, or obstructive, the code for unspecified chronic bronchitis, ICD-9-CM code 491.9, should be listed.

4.   Diagnoses documented as "probable," "suspected," "questionable," or "rule out" should not be coded as if the diagnosis is confirmed. The condition(s) should be coded to the highest degree of certainty for the encounter, such as describing symptoms, signs, abnormal test results, or other reasons for the encounter.

5.   Chronic disease(s) treated on an ongoing basis may be coded and reported as many times as the patient receives treatment and care for the condition(s).

6.   When patients receive ancillary diagnostic services only during an encounter, the appropriate "V code" for the service should be listed first, and the diagnosis or problem for which the diagnostic procedures are being performed should be listed second.

   A.   V codes will be used frequently by radiologists who perform radiological examinations on referrals. For example, ICD-9-CM code V72.5, Radiological examination, not elsewhere classified, describes the reason for the encounter and should be listed first on the claim form or statement. If the reason for the referral is known, a second ICD-9-CM code that describes the signs or symptoms for which the examination was ordered should be listed.

   B.   Failure to list a second ICD-9-CM code in addition to the V code may result in claim delays or denials. The ICD-9-CM code V72.5, Radio-logical examination, not elsewhere classified, includes referrals for routine chest x-rays that are not covered by the Medicare program. Medicare intermediaries may establish screening programs to verify that the referrals were not for routine chest x-rays.

By supplying a second ICD-9-CM code to describe the reason for the referral, these claims can be clearly identified by the Medicare intermediary as referrals to evaluate symptoms, signs or diagnoses. The mission of a second ICD-9-CM code may lead to requests for additional information from Medicare intermediaries prior to processing the claim.

7.   For patients receiving only ancillary therapeutic services during an encounter, list the appropriate V code first, followed by the ICD-9-CM code for the diagnosis or problem for which the services are being performed. For example, a patient with multiple sclerosis presenting for rehabilitation services would be coded using code V57.1, Other physical therapy, or code V57.89, Other care involving use of rehabilitation procedures, followed by code 340, multiple sclerosis.

8.   For surgical procedures, use the ICD-9-CM code for the diagnosis for which the surgery was performed. If the postoperative diagnosis is known to be different at the time the claim is filed, use the ICD-9-CM code for the post-operative diagnosis.

9.   Code all documented conditions that coexist at the time of the visit that require or affect patient care, treatment or management. Do not code conditions that were previously treated and no longer exist.

Completing the HCFA1500 Claim Form

Health care professionals using the Uniform Health Insurance Claim Form, HCFA1500, to file claims for services provided to Medicare beneficiaries must list a minimum of one ICD-9-CM code and may list up to four total ICD-9-CM codes on the claim form.

The ICD-9-CM code for the diagnosis, condition, problem or other reason for the encounter is listed first, followed by up to three additional codes that describe any coexisting conditions. At times, there may be several conditions that equally resulted in the encounter. In these cases, the health care professional is free to select the one that will be listed first.

The ICD-9-CM codes are listed in Box 23 of the "old" HCFA1500 (10/84) claim form and Box 21 of the "new" HCFA1500 (12/90) claim form (see example). In addition, in Box 24 D of both versions of the form, you must indicate by a number from 1 to 4, or combination of numbers, which diagnoses from Box 23 support the procedure, service or supply listed in Box 24 C.

Due to space limitations on the claim form you may use only up to four ICD-9-CM codes for diagnoses, conditions, or signs and symptoms. Frequently the patient may have more than four conditions present at the time of the encounter, however, you must choose only four codes to be listed on the claim form.

If you strongly believe that additional diagnostic information is needed by the Medicare intermediary for proper claim processing you may attach additional supporting documentation to your manual claim. Keep in mind that in most cases the additional documentation will be ignored by the claims examiners, and, in other cases will result in reimbursement delay while someone reviews your documentation.

Medicare Penalties for Non-compliance

The Medicare Catastrophic Coverage Act of 1988 mandates submission of an appropriate ICD-9-CM diagnosis code or codes for each procedure, service, or supply furnished by the health care professional to Medicare Part B beneficiaries. The Act further specifies that compliance is mandatory and that penalties may be assessed for noncompliance.

The penalties for noncompliance differ depending upon whether or not the health care professional has agreed to accept assignment or not.

1. For health care professionals who accept assignment on a Medicare claim and who fail to include ICD-9-CM codes as required will have their claim(s) returned for proper coding and may be subject to post-payment review by the Medicare intermediary, as well as payment denials.

2. For health care professionals who do not accept assignment, the penalties are more severe.

    A. If the original claim form does not include ICD-9-CM codes as required, and the health care professional refuses to provide the codes promptly on request to the Medicare intermediary, the professional may be subject to a civil monetary penalty in an amount not to exceed $2,000, per claim.

    B. If the health care professional continuously fails to provide ICD-9-CM codes as requested, the professional may be subject to the sanction process described in section 1842 (j) (2) (A), that mandates that the professional may be barred from participation in the Medicare program for a period not to exceed five years.

CODING AND BILLING ISSUES

Diagnosis Codes Must Support Procedure Codes

Each service or procedure performed for a patient should be represented by a diagnosis that would substantiate those particular services or procedures as necessary in the investigation or treatment of their condition based on currently accepted standards of practice by the medical profession.

Place (Location) of Service

The actual setting that the services are rendered in for particular diagnoses plays an important part in reimbursement. Many people became accustomed to using Emergency Rooms for any type of illness or injury. By utilizing highly specialized places of service for conditions that were not true emergencies, third party payer were being billed with CPT codes indicating emergency services were rendered. Since the cost of services rendered on an emergency basis is considerably more expensive than those services in an non-emergency situation, third party payers began watching for those claims with diagnoses that did not indicate that a true emergency existed. Payment then was based on what the cost would have been had the patient been treated in the proper setting.

Level of Service Provided

The patient's condition and the treatment of that condition must be billed according to the criteria, as published by the AMA, for each level of service (i.e., minimal, brief, limited, intermediate, extended, comprehensive). Many practices bill the office visit level that they know will pay better rather than to consider the criteria that must be met to use a particular level of service. Again, the patient's diagnosis enters into this concept as well as it is often the diagnosis that indicates the complexity of the level of service to be used.

Frequency of Services

Many times claims are submitted for a patient with the same diagnosis and the same procedure(s) time after time. When the diagnosis indicates a chronic condition and the claims do not indicate any change in the patient's treatment or, give any indication that the patient's condition has been altered (i.e., exacerbated, other symptomology) the third party payer may deny payment based on the frequency of services for the reported condition.

Down Coding

Down coding is the process of reducing a code from one of a higher value to one of a lower value that results in lowered reimbursement. In the area of procedure coding, this process results in the loss of millions of dollars annually by health care professionals and their patients.

With procedure coding, down coding claims is easily resolved by either providing a procedure description that matches that of Current Procedural Terminology (CPT) exactly, or, even better, by eliminating all procedure descriptions from your claim forms, that forces the insurance carrier to allow full value for your procedure, service, or supply. With diagnosis coding, the issue is not mismatch of description to code, as the description is not required, but that the ICD-9-CM code(s) provide justification for the procedure, service or supply or the level of service provided.

A key point to remember is that if there are any current coexisting conditions that may complicate the treatment for the primary condition, it is very important to include the ICD-9-CM codes for the coexisting conditions that will help to justify the level of service provided.

Concurrent Care

Reimbursement problems often arise when a patient is being treated by different professionals, within the same billing entity (medical group or clinic), for different problems at the same time. This is known as concurrent care. For example, a patient may be hospitalized by a clinic's general surgeon for an operation and may also be seen while hospitalized by the group's cardiologist for an unrelated cardiac condition.

If you submit claims for daily hospital visits by both of the above professionals without explanation, most insurance carriers would reject one daily visit as an apparent "duplication" of service. Prior to publication of the 1992 edition of CPT, the key to obtaining proper reimbursement for concurrent care was first, to use the procedure modifier - 75, Concurrent Care, Services Rendered by More than One Physician, and second, to submit a different *ICD-9-CM* code for the services provided by each physician, that support and justify the need for those services.

Note that modifier -75 was deleted in the 1992 edition of CPT, therefore, when using the new CPT Evaluation and Management codes to bill Medicare, the *ICD-9-CM* code becomes the key factor for proper reimbursement of concurrent care.

ICD-10

Since 1948, the World Health Organization has revised the *International Classification of Diseases* approximately every 10 years, with a modified version appearing in the United States about one to three years following the WHO publication. Based on the regular schedule, *ICD-10* should have been released in 1987. However, due to difficulties in coordinating the international committees, the first volume of *ICD-10*, the Tabular List, was not published until June of 1992.

Implementation of ICD-10 in the United States

Prior to being implemented in the United States, *ICD-10* must be converted to "American" English and pass through a variety of private and government committees, agencies, associations and organizations. As of this printing, the official position of the Health Care Financing Administration (HCFA) is that *ICD-10* will not be mandated for Medicare claims until "at least the year 2,000."

Summary of Changes in ICD-10

1. All codes in the *ICD-10* are alphanumeric, just like the V-codes and E-codes are in the *ICD-9-CM*.

2. Explanatory notes and instructions are greatly expanded.

3. Main categories are increased from about 1,200 to over 2,000.

4. Separate chapters have been added for diseases of the eye and ear.

5. There are new categories for coding post-procedural disorders.

6. There is greater coding precision for drug-induced conditions.

WHERE TO GET ANSWERS TO QUESTIONS ABOUT ICD-9-CM

Questions regarding the use and interpretation of the *International Classification of Diseases, 9th Revision, Clinical Modification* should be directed in writing to any of the organizations listed below.

Coding Advice/Central Office on ICD-9-CM
American Hospital Association
One North Franklin
Chicago, Illinois 60606

World Health Organization Collaborating Center
for Classification of Diseases in North America
National Center for Health Statistics
Department of Health and Human Services
6525 Belcrest Road
Hyattsville, Maryland 20782

Morbidity Classification Branch
National Center for Health Statistics
Department of Health and Human Services
6525 Belcrest Road, Room 1100
Hyattsville, Maryland 20782

Health Care Financing Administration (HCFA)
Division of Prospective Payment
Mail Stop C5-06-27
7500 Security Blvd.
Baltimore, MD   21244-1850

Comments, questions or suggestions regarding the PMIC version of *ICD-9-CM*
should be directed in writing to:

Managing Editor
Practice Management Information Corporation
4727 Wilshire Boulevard, Suite 300
Los Angeles, California 90010

DISEASES: TABULAR LIST
VOLUME 1

1. INFECTIOUS AND PARASITIC DISEASES (001-139)

> Note: Categories for "late effects" of infectious and parasitic diseases are to be found at 137-139.
> Includes: diseases generally recognized as communicable or transmissible as well as a few diseases of unknown but possibly infectious origin.
>
> *Excludes:* *acute respiratory infections (460-466)*
> *carrier or suspected carrier of infectious organism (V02.0-V02.9)*
> *certain localized infections*
> *influenza (487.0-487.8)*

INTESTINAL INFECTIOUS DISEASES (001-009)

> *Excludes:* *helminthiases (120.0-129)*

001 Cholera

001.0 Due to Vibrio cholerae

001.1 Due to Vibrio cholerae el tor

001.9 Cholera, unspecified

002 Typhoid and paratyphoid fevers

002.0 Typhoid fever
Typhoid (fever) (infection) [any site]

002.1 Paratyphoid fever A

002.2 Paratyphoid fever B

002.3 Paratyphoid fever C

002.9 Paratyphoid fever, unspecified

003 Other salmonella infections
Includes: infection or food poisoning by Salmonella [any serotype]

003.0 Salmonella gastroenteritis
Salmonellosis

003.1 Salmonella septicemia

003.2 Localized salmonella infections

    003.20 Localized salmonella infection, unspecified

    003.21 Salmonella meningitis

    003.22 Salmonella pneumonia

    003.23 Salmonella arthritis

    003.24 Salmonella osteomyelitis

    003.29 Other

003.8 Other specified salmonella infections

003.9 Salmonella infection, unspecified

004 Shigellosis
Includes: bacillary dysentery

004.0 Shigella dysenteriae
Infection y group A Shigella (Schmitz) (Shiga)

004.1 Shigella flexneri
Infection by group B Shigella

004.2 Shigella boydii
Infection by group C Shigella

004.3 Shigella sonnei
Infection by group D Shigella

004.8 Other specified shigella infections

004.9 Shigellosis, unspecified

005 Other food poisoning (bacterial)

> *Excludes:* *salmonella infections (003.0-003.9)*
> *toxic effect of:*
> *food contaminants (989.7)*
> *noxious foodstuffs (988.0-988.9)*

005.0 Staphylococcal food poisoning
Staphylococcal toxemia specified as due to food

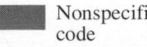

| | Add 4th or 5th digit | | Nonspecific code | | Unspecified code | | Manifestation code |

005.1 Botulism
Food poisoning due to Clostridium botulinum

005.2 Food poisoning due to Clostridium perfringens [C. welchii]
Enteritis necroticans

005.3 Food poisoning due to other Clostridia

005.4 Food poisoning due to Vibrio parahaemolyticus

005.8 Other bacterial food poisoning

Excludes: *salmonella food poisoning (003.0-003.9)*

    005.81   Food poisoning due to Vibrio vulnificus

    005.89   Other bacterial food poisoning
    Food poisoning due to Bacillus cereus

005.9 Food poisoning, unspecified

006 Amebiasis
Includes: infection due to Entamoeba histolytica

Excludes: *amebiasis due to organisms other than Entamoeba histolytica (007.8)*

006.0 Acute amebic dysentery without mention of abscess
Acute amebiasis

006.1 Chronic intestinal amebiasis without mention of abscess
Chronic:
   amebiasis
   amebic dysentery

006.2 Amebic nondysenteric colitis

006.3 Amebic liver abscess
Hepatic amebiasis

006.4 Amebic lung abscess
Amebic abscess of lung (and liver)

006.5 Amebic brain abscess
Amebic abscess of brain (and liver) (and lung)

006.6 Amebic skin ulceration
Cutaneous amebiasis

006.8 Amebic infection of other sites
Amebic: Ameboma
   appendicitis
   balanitis

Excludes: *specific infections by free-living amebae (136.2)*

006.9 Amebiasis, unspecified
Amebiasis NOS

007 Other protozoal intestinal diseases
Includes: protozoal:
         colitis
         diarrhea
         dysentery

007.0 Balantidiasis
Infection by Balantidium coli

007.1 Giardiasis
Infection by Giardia lamblia
Lambliasis

007.2 Coccidiosis
Infection by Isospora belli and Isospora hominis
Isosporiasis

007.3 Intestinal trichomoniasis

007.8 Other specified protozoal intestinal diseases
Amebiasis due to organisms other than Entamoeba histolytica

007.9 Unspecified protozoal intestinal disease
Flagellate diarrhea   Protozoal dysentery NOS

008 Intestinal infections due to other organisms
Includes: any condition classifiable to 009.0-009.3 with mention of the responsible organisms

Excludes: *food poisoning by these organisms (005.0-005.9)*

● Code new   ▲ Revision of   ④ ⑤ Fourth or fifth
   to this edition   existing code   digit required

008.0 Escherichia coli [E. coli]

> **008.00 E. coli, unspecified**
> E. coli enteritis NOS

> **008.01 Enteropathogenic E. coli**

> **008.02 Enterotoxigenic E. coli**

> **008.03 Enteroinvasive E. coli**

> **008.04 Enterohemorrhagic E. coli**

> **008.09 Other intestinal E. coli infections**

008.1 Arizona group of paracolon bacilli

008.2 Aerobacter aerogenes
Enterobacter aerogenes

008.3 Proteus (mirabilis) (morganii)

008.4 Other specified bacteria

> **008.41 Staphylococcus**
> Staphylococcal enterocolitis

> **008.42 Pseudomonas**

> **008.43 Campylobacter**

> **008.44 Yersinia enterocolitica**

> **008.45 Clostridium difficile**
> Pseudomembranous colitis

> **008.46 Other anaerobes**
> Anaerobic enteritis NOS
> Gram-negative anaerobes
> Bacteroides (fragilis)

> **008.47 Other Gram-negative bacteria**
> Gram-negative enteritis NOS

> Excludes: *Gram-negative anaerobes (008.46)*

> **008.49 Other**

008.5 Bacterial enteritis, unspecified

008.6 Enteritis due to specified virus

> **008.61 Rotavirus**

> **008.62 Adenovirus**

> **008.63 Norwalk virus**
> Norwalk-like agent

> **008.64 Other small round viruses [SRV's]**
> Small round virus NOS

> **008.65 Calcivirus**

> **008.66 Astrovirus**

> **008.67 Enterovirus NEC**
> Coxsackie virus
> Echovirus

> Excludes: *poliovirus (045.0-045.9)*

> **008.69 Other viral enteritis**
> Torovirus

008.8 Other organism, not elsewhere classified
Viral:
enteritis NOS
gastroenteritis

> Excludes: *influenza with involvement of gastrointestinal tract (487.8)*

009 Ill-defined intestinal infections

> Excludes: *diarrheal disease or intestinal infection due to specified organism (001.0-008.8)*
> *diarrhea following gastrointestinal surgery (564.4)*
> *intestinal malabsorption (579.0-579.9)*
> *ischemic enteritis (557.0-557.9)*
> *other noninfectious gastroenteritis and colitis (558.1-558.9)*
> *regional enteritis (555.0-555.9)*
> *ulcerative colitis (556)*

	Add 4th or 5th digit		Nonspecific code		Unspecified code		Manifestation code

015.0 Vertebral column
      Pott's disease

Use additional code, if desired, to identify manifestation, as:
          curvature of spine [Pott's] (737.4)
          kyphosis (737.4)
          spondylitis (720.81)

015.1 Hip

015.2 Knee

☐ **015.5 Limb bones**
      Tuberculous dactylitis

☐ **015.6 Mastoid**
      Tuberculous mastoiditis

☐ **015.7 Other specified bone**

015.8 Other specified joint

015.9 Tuberculosis of unspecified bones and joints

⑤ **016 Tuberculosis of genitourinary system**

016.0 Kidney
      Renal tuberculosis

Use additional code, if desired, to identify manifestation, as:
      tuberculous:
          nephropathy (583.81)
          pyelitis (590.81)
          pyelonephritis (590.81)

☐ **016.1 Bladder**

☐ **016.2 Ureter**

☐ **016.3 Other urinary organs**

☐ **016.4 Epididymis**

☐ **016.5 Other male genital organs**

Use additional code, if desired, to identify manifestation, as:
      tuberculosis of:
          prostate (601.4)
          seminal vesicle (608.81)
          testis (608.81)

☐ **016.6 Tuberculous oophoritis and salpingitis**

☐ **016.7 Other female genital organs**
      Tuberculous:
        cervicitis
        endometritis

016.9 Genitourinary tuberculosis, unspecified

⑤ **017 Tuberculosis of other organs**

017.0 Skin and subcutaneous cellular tissue

Lupus:	Tuberculosis:
exedens	colliquativa
vulgaris	cutis
Scrofuloderma	lichenoides
	papulonecrotica
	verrucosa cutis

Excludes: *lupus erythematosus (695.4)*
        disseminated (710.0)
        lupus NOS (710.0)
        nonspecific reaction to tuberculin skin test without active tuberculosis (795.5)
        positive PPD (795.5)
        positive tuberculin skin test without active tuberculosis (795.5)

017.1 Erythema nodosum with hypersensitivity reaction in tuberculosis

Bazin's disease	Tuberculosis indurativa
Erythema:	
induratum	
nodosum, tuberculous	

Excludes: *erythema nodosum NOS (695.2)*

● Code new
  to this edition
▲ Revision of
  existing code
④ ⑤ Fourth or fifth
    digit required

017.2 Peripheral lymph nodes
Scrofula   Tuberculous adenitis
Scrofulous abscess

> *Excludes:* *tuberculosis of lymph nodes:*
> *bronchial and mediastinal (012.1)*
> *mesenteric and retroperitoneal (014.8)*
> *tuberculous tracheobronchial adenopathy (012.1)*

017.3 Eye
Use additional code, if desired, to identify manifestation, as:
  tuberculous:
   chorioretinitis, disseminated (363.13)
   episcleritis (379.09)
   interstitial keratitis (370.59)
   iridocyclitis, chronic (364.11)
   keratoconjunctivitis (phlyctenular) (370.31)

017.4 Ear
  Tuberculosis of ear
  Tuberculous otitis media

> *Excludes:* *tuberculous mastoiditis (015.6)*

017.5 Thyroid gland

017.6 Adrenal glands
  Addison's disease, tuberculous

017.7 Spleen

☐ **017.8 Esophagus**

☐ **017.9 Other specified organs**
Use additional code, if desired, to identify manifestation, as:
  tuberculosis of:
   endocardium [any valve] (424.91)
   myocardium (422.0)
   pericardium (420.0)

⑤ **018 Miliary tuberculosis**
Includes: tuberculosis:
   disseminated
   generalized
   miliary, whether of a single specified site, multiple sites, or unspecified site
   polyserositis

018.0 Acute miliary tuberculosis

018.8 Other specified miliary tuberculosis

018.9 Miliary tuberculosis, unspecified

ZOONOTIC BACTERIAL DISEASES (020-027)

020 Plague
Includes: infection by Yersinia [Pasteurella] pestis

020.0 Bubonic

020.1 Cellulocutaneous

020.2 Septicemic

020.3 Primary pneumonic

020.4 Secondary pneumonic

020.5 Pneumonic, unspecified

020.8 Other specified types of plague
  Abortive plague   Pestis minor
  Ambulatory plague

020.9 Plague, unspecified

021 Tularemia
Includes: deerfly fever
   infection by Francisella [Pasteurella] tularensis
   rabbit fever

021.0 Ulceroglandular tularemia

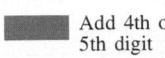 Add 4th or 5th digit   Nonspecific code   Unspecified code 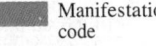 Manifestation code

021.1 Enteric tularemia
Tularemia:
cryptogenic
intestinal
typhoidal

021.2 Pulmonary tularemia
Bronchopneumonic tularemia

021.3 Oculoglandular tularemia

021.8 Other specified tularemia
Tularemia:
generalized or disseminated
glandular

021.9 Unspecified tularemia

022 Anthrax

022.0 Cutaneous anthrax
Malignant pustule

022.1 Pulmonary anthrax
Respiratory anthrax   Wool-sorters' disease

022.2 Gastrointestinal anthrax

022.3 Anthrax septicemia

022.8 Other specified manifestations of anthrax

022.9 Anthrax, unspecified

023 Brucellosis
Includes: fever:
Malta
Mediterranean
undulant

023.0 Brucella melitensis

023.1 Brucella abortus

023.2 Brucella suis

023.3 Brucella canis

023.8 Other brucellosis
Infection by more than one organism

023.9 Brucellosis, unspecified

024 Glanders
Infection by: Farcy
Actinobacillus mallei   Malleus
Malleomyces mallei
Pseudomonas mallei

025 Melioidosis
Infection by:
Malleomyces pseudomallei
Pseudomonas pseudomallei
Whitmore's bacillus
Pseudoglanders

026 Rat-bite fever

026.0 Spirillary fever
Rat-bite fever due to Spirillum minor [S. minus]
Sodoku

026.1 Streptobacillary fever
Epidemic arthritic erythema
Haverhill fever
Rat-bite fever due to Streptobacillus moniliformis

026.9 Unspecified rat-bite fever

027 Other zoonotic bacterial diseases

027.0 Listeriosis
Infection ⎫
Septicemia ⎭ by Listeria monocytogenes

Use additional code, if desired, to identify manifestation, as meningitis (320.7)

Excludes: congenital listeriosis (771.2)

● Code new   ▲ Revision of   ④ ⑤ Fourth or fifth
   to this edition   existing code   digit required

027.1 Erysipelothrix infection
Erysipeloid (of Rosenbach)
Infection ⎫
Septicemia ⎭ by Erysipelothrix insidiosa [E. rhusiopathiae]

027.2 Pasteurellosis
Pasteurella pseudotuberculosis infection
Mesenteric adenitis ⎫
Septic infection (cat bite) (dog bite) ⎭ by Pasteurella multocida [P. septica]

Excludes: infection by:
Francisella [Pasteurella] tularensis (021.0-021.9)
Yersinia [Pasteurella] pestis (020.0-020.9)

027.8 Other specified zoonotic bacterial diseases

027.9 Unspecified zoonotic bacterial disease

OTHER BACTERIAL DISEASES (030-041)

Excludes: bacterial venereal diseases (098.0-099.9)
bartonellosis (088.0)

030 Leprosy
Includes: Hansen's disease
infection by Mycobacterium leprae

030.0 Lepromatous [type L]
Lepromatous leprosy (macular) (diffuse) (infiltrated) (nodular) (neuritic)

030.1 Tuberculoid [type T]
Tuberculoid leprosy (macular) (maculoanesthetic) (major) (minor) (neuritic)

030.2 Indeterminate [group I]
Indeterminate [uncharacteristic] leprosy (macular) (neuritic)

030.3 Borderline [group B]
Borderline or dimorphous leprosy (infiltrated) (neuritic)

030.8 Other specified leprosy

030.9 Leprosy, unspecified

031 Diseases due to other mycobacteria

031.0 Pulmonary
Infection by Mycobacterium:
avium
intracellulare [Battey bacillus]
kansasii
Battey disease

031.1 Cutaneous
Buruli ulcer
Infection by Mycobacterium:
marinum [M. balnei]
ulcerans

031.8 Other specified mycobacterial diseases

031.9 Unspecified diseases due to mycobacteria
Atypical mycobacterium infection NOS

032 Diphtheria
Includes: infection by Corynebacterium diphtheriae

032.0 Faucial diphtheria
Membranous angina, diphtheritic

032.1 Nasopharyngeal diphtheria

032.2 Anterior nasal diphtheria

032.3 Laryngeal diphtheria
Laryngotracheitis, diphtheritic

032.8 Other specified diphtheria

   032.81 Conjunctival diphtheria
Pseudomembranous diphtheritic conjunctivitis

   032.82 Diphtheritic myocarditis

   032.83 Diphtheritic peritonitis

   032.84 Diphtheritic cystitis

   032.85 Cutaneous diphtheria

Add 4th or 5th digit
 Nonspecific code
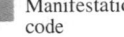 Unspecified code
Manifestation code

040.0 Gas gangrene
    Gas bacillus infection   Malignant edema
      or gangrene   Myonecrosis, clostridial
    Infection by Clostridium: Myositis, clostridial
      histolyticum
      oedematiens
      perfringens [welchii]
      septicum
      sordellii

040.1 Rhinoscleroma

040.2 Whipple's disease
    Intestinal lipodystrophy

040.3 Necrobacillosis

040.8 Other specified bacterial diseases

    040.81 Tropical pyomyositis

    040.89 Other

041 Bacterial infection in conditions classified elsewhere and of unspecified site
Note: This category is provided to be used as an additional code where it is desired to identify the bacterial agent in diseases classified elsewhere. This category will also be used to classify bacterial infections of unspecified nature or site.

    Excludes: bacteremia NOS (790.7)
             septicemia (038.0-038.9)

041.0 Streptococcus

    041.00 Streptococcus, unspecified

    041.01 Group A

    041.02 Group B

    041.03 Group C

    041.04 Group D

    041.05 Group G

    041.09 Other Streptococcus

041.1 Staphylococcus

    041.10 Staphylococcus, unspecified

    041.11 Staphylococcus aureus

    041.19 Other Staphylococcus

041.2 Pneumococcus

041.3 Friedländer's bacillus
    Infection by Klebsiella pneumoniae

041.4 Escherichia coli [E. coli]

041.5 Hemophilus influenzae [H. influenzae]

041.6 Proteus (mirabilis) (morganii)

041.7 Pseudomonas

041.8 Other specified bacterial infections

    041.81 Mycoplasma
        Eaton's agent
        Pleuropneumonia-like organisms [PPLO]

    041.82 Bacillus fragilis

    041.83 Clostridium perfringens

    041.84 Other anaerobes
        Gram-negative anaerobes
        Bacteroides (fragilis)

    Excludes: Helicobacter pylori (041.86)

    041.85 Other Gram-negative organisms
        Aerobacter aerogenes
        Gram-negative bacteria NOS
        Mima polymorpha
        Serratia

    Excludes: Gram-negative anaerobes (041.84)

  ● Code new   ▲ Revision of   ④ ⑤ Fourth or fifth
     to this edition   existing code   digit required

041.86   Helicobacter pylori (H. pylori)

041.89   Other specified bacteria

041.9   Bacterial infection, unspecified

HUMAN IMMUNODEFICIENCY VIRUS (HIV) INFECTION (042)

042 Human immunodeficiency virus [HIV] disease
>   Acquired immune deficiency syndrome
>   Acquired immunodeficiency syndrome
>   AIDS
>   AIDS-like syndrome
>   AIDS-related complex
>   ARC
>   HIV infection, symptomatic

Use additional code(s) to identify all manifestations of HIV

Use additional code, if desired, to identify HIV-2 infection (079.53)

> *Excludes:* asymptomatic HIV infection status (V08)
>
> exposre to HIV virus (V01.7)
>
> nonspecific serologic evidence of HIV (795.71)

POLIOMYELITIS AND OTHER NON-ARTHROPOD-BORNE VIRAL DISEASES OF CENTRAL NERVOUS SYSTEM (045-049)

⑤ 045 Acute poliomyelitis

> *Excludes:* late effects of acute poliomyelitis (138)

The following fifth-digit subclassification is for use with category 045:

   0   poliovirus, unspecified type

   1   poliovirus type I

   2   poliovirus type II

   3   poliovirus type III

045.0 Acute paralytic poliomyelitis specified as bulbar
>   Infantile paralysis (acute)   ⎫
>   Poliomyelitis (acute) (anterior)   ⎬ specified as bulbar
>   Polioencephalitis (acute) (bulbar) ⎭
>   Polioencephalomyelitis (acute) (anterior) (bulbar)

045.1 Acute poliomyelitis with other paralysis
>   Paralysis:
>   acute atrophic, spinal infantile, paralytic
>   Poliomyelitis (acute) ⎫
>   anterior   ⎬ with paralysis except bulbar
>   epidemic   ⎭

045.2 Acute nonparalytic poliomyelitis
>   Poliomyelitis (acute) ⎫
>   anterior   ⎬ specified as nonparalytic
>   epidemic   ⎭

045.9 Acute poliomyelitis, unspecified
>   Infantile paralysis   ⎫
>   Poliomyelitis (acute) ⎬ unspecified whether paralytic or nonparalytic
>   anterior
>   epidemic   ⎭

046 Slow virus infection of central nervous system

046.0 Kuru

046.1 Jakob-Creutzfeldt disease
>   Subacute spongiform encephalopathy

046.2 Subacute sclerosing panencephalitis
>   Dawson's inclusion body encephalitis
>   Van Bogaert's sclerosing leukoencephalitis

046.3 Progressive multifocal leukoencephalopathy
>   Multifocal leukoencephalopathy NOS

046.8   Other specified slow virus infection of central nervous system

046.9   Unspecified slow virus infection of central nervous system

| | Add 4th or 5th digit | | Nonspecific code | | Unspecified code | | Manifestation code |

054.49 Other

054.5 Herpetic septicemia

054.6 Herpetic whitlow
Herpetic felon

054.7 With other specified complications

054.71 Visceral herpes simplex

054.72 Herpes simplex meningitis

054.73 Herpes simplex otitis externa

054.79 Other

054.8 With unspecified complication

054.9 Herpes simplex without mention of complication

055 Measles
Includes: morbilli
rubeola

055.0 Postmeasles encephalitis

055.1 Postmeasles pneumonia

055.2 Postmeasles otitis media

055.7 With other specified complications

055.71 Measles keratoconjunctivitis
Measles keratitis

055.79 Other

055.8 With unspecified complication

055.9 Measles without mention of complication

056 Rubella
Includes: German measles

Excludes: *congenital rubella (771.0)*

056.0 With neurological complications

056.00 With unspecified neurological complication

056.01 Encephalomyelitis due to rubella
Encephalitis
Meningoencephalitis ⎬ due to rubella

056.09 Other

056.7 With other specified complications

056.71 Arthritis due to rubella

056.79 Other

056.8 With unspecified complications

056.9 Rubella without mention of complication

057 Other viral exanthemata

057.0 Erythema infectiosum [fifth disease]

057.8 Other specified viral exanthemata
Dukes (-Filatow) disease   Parascarlatina
Exanthema subitum   Pseudoscarlatina
  [sixth disease]   Roseola infantum
Fourth disease

057.9 Viral exanthem, unspecified

ARTHROPOD-BORNE VIRAL DISEASES (060-066)

Use additional code, if desired, to identify any associated meningitis (321.2)

Excludes: *late effects of viral encephalitis (139.0)*

060 Yellow fever

060.0 Sylvatic
Yellow fever:
  jungle
  sylvan

060.1 Urban

060.9 Yellow fever, unspecified

● Code new
  to this edition

▲ Revision of
  existing code

④ ⑤ Fourth or fifth
  digit required

061 Dengue
Breakbone fever

> *Excludes:* hemorrhagic fever caused by dengue virus (065.4)

062 Mosquito-borne viral encephalitis

062.0 Japanese encephalitis
Japanese B encephalitis

062.1 Western equine encephalitis

062.2 Eastern equine encephalitis

> *Excludes:* Venezuelan equine encephalitis (066.2)

062.3 St. Louis encephalitis

062.4 Australian encephalitis
Australian arboencephalitis
Australian X disease
Murray Valley encephalitis

062.5 California virus encephalitis
Encephalitis: Tahyna fever
California
La Crosse

062.8 Other specified mosquito-borne viral encephalitis
Encephalitis by Ilheus virus

062.9 Mosquito-borne viral encephalitis, unspecified

063 Tick-borne viral encephalitis
Includes: diphasic meningoencephalitis

063.0 Russian spring-summer [taiga] encephalitis

063.1 Louping ill

063.2 Central European encephalitis

063.8 Other specified tick-borne viral encephalitis
Langat encephalitis   Powassan encephalitis

063.9 Tick-borne viral encephalitis, unspecified

064 Viral encephalitis transmitted by other and unspecified arthropods
Arthropod-borne viral encephalitis, vector unknown
Negishi virus encephalitis

> *Excludes:* viral encephalitis NOS (049.9)

065 Arthropod-borne hemorrhagic fever

065.0 Crimean hemorrhagic fever [CHF Congo virus]
Central Asian hemorrhagic fever

065.1 Omsk hemorrhagic fever

065.2 Kyasanur Forest disease

065.3 Other tick-borne hemorrhagic fever

065.4 Mosquito-borne hemorrhagic fever
Chikungunya hemorrhagic fever
Dengue hemorrhagic fever

> *Excludes:* Chikungunya fever (066.3)
> dengue (061)
> yellow fever (060.0-060.9)

065.8 Other specified arthropod-borne hemorrhagic fever
Mite-borne hemorrhagic fever

065.9 Arthropod-borne hemorrhagic fever, unspecified
Arbovirus hemorrhagic fever NOS

066 Other arthropod-borne viral diseases

066.0 Phlebotomus fever
Changuinola fever   Sandfly fever

066.1 Tick-borne fever
Nairobi sheep disease   Tick fever:
Tick fever: Kemerovo
American mountain   Quaranfil
Colorado

Add 4th or 5th digit	Nonspecific code	Unspecified code	Manifestation code

066.2 Venezuelan equine fever
Venezuelan equine encephalitis

066.3 Other mosquito-borne fever

Fever (viral):
Bunyamwera
Bwamba
Chikungunya
GuamaR Mayaro
Mucambo
O'nyong-nyong

Fever (viral):
Oropouche
Pixuna
Rift valley
Ross river
Wesselsbron
West Nile
Zika

Excludes: *dengue (061)*
yellow fever (060.0-060.9)

066.8 Other specified arthropod-borne viral diseases
Chandipura fever   Piry fever

066.9 Arthropod-borne viral disease, unspecified
Arbovirus infection NOS

OTHER DISEASES DUE TO VIRUSES AND CHLAMYDIAE (070-079)

070 Viral hepatitis
Includes: viral hepatitis (acute) (chronic)

Excludes: *cytomegalic inclusion virus hepatitis (078.5)*

The following fifth-digit subclassification is for use with categories 070.2 and 070.3:

0 **acute or unspecified, without mention of hepatitis delta**

1 **acute or unspecified, with hepatitis delta**

2 **chronic, without mention of hepatitis delta**

3 **chronic, with hepatitis delta**

070.0 Viral hepatitis A with hepatic coma

070.1 Viral hepatitis A without mention of hepatic coma
Infectious hepatitis

⑤ **070.2 Viral hepatitis B with hepatic coma**

⑤ **070.3 Viral hepatitis B without mention of hepatic coma**
Serum hepatitis

070.4 Other specified viral hepatitis with hepatic coma

070.41 Acute or unspecified hepatitis C with hepatic coma

070.42 Hepatitis delta without mention of active hepatitis B disease with hepatic coma
Hepatitis delta with hepatitis B carrier state

070.43 Hepatitis E with hepatic coma

070.44 Chronic hepatitis C with hepatic coma

070.49 Other specified viral hepatitis with hepatic coma

070.5 Other specified viral hepatitis without mention of hepatic coma

070.51 Acute or unspecified hepatitis C without mention of hepatic coma

070.52 Hepatitis delta without mention of active hepatitis B disease or hepatic coma

070.53 Hepatitis E without mention of hepatic coma

070.54 Chronic hepatitis C without mention of hepatic coma

070.59 Other specified viral hepatitis without mention of hepatic coma

070.6 Unspecified viral hepatitis with hepatic coma

070.9 Unspecified viral hepatitis without mention of hepatic coma
Viral hepatitis NOS

071 Rabies
Hydrophobia   Lyssa

072 Mumps

072.0 Mumps orchitis

072.1 Mumps meningitis

072.2 Mumps encephalitis
Mumps meningoencephalitis

072.3 Mumps pancreatitis

● Code new
  to this edition

▲ Revision of
  existing code

④ ⑤ Fourth or fifth
     digit required

072.7 Mumps with other specified complications

    072.71 Mumps hepatitis

    072.72 Mumps polyneuropathy

    072.79 Other

072.8 Mumps with unspecified complication

072.9 Mumps without mention of complication
    Epidemic parotitis   Infectious parotitis

073 Ornithosis
    Includes: parrot fever
              psittacosis

073.0 With pneumonia
    Lobular pneumonitis due to ornithosis

073.7 With other specified complications

073.8 With unspecified complication

073.9 Ornithosis, unspecified

074 Specific diseases due to Coxsackie virus

    Excludes: *Coxsackie virus:*
              infection NOS (079.2)
              meningitis (047.0)

074.0 Herpangina
    Vesicular pharyngitis

074.1 Epidemic pleurodynia
    Bornholm disease   Epidemic:
    Devil's grip   myalgia
                        myositis

074.2 Coxsackie carditis

    074.20 Coxsackie carditis, unspecified

    074.21 Coxsackie pericarditis

    074.22 Coxsackie endocarditis

    074.23 Coxsackie myocarditis
        Aseptic myocarditis of newborn

074.3 Hand, foot, and mouth disease
    Vesicular stomatitis and exanthem

074.8 Other specified diseases due to Coxsackie virus
    Acute lymphonodular pharyngitis

075 Infectious mononucleosis
    Glandular fever   Pfeiffer's disease
    Monocytic angina

076 Trachoma

    Excludes: *late effect of trachoma (139.1)*

076.0 Initial stage
    Trachoma dubium

076.1 Active stage
    Granular conjunctivitis (trachomatous)
    Trachomatous:
        follicular conjunctivitis
        pannus

076.9 Trachoma, unspecified
    Trachoma NOS

077 Other diseases of conjunctiva due to viruses and Chlamydiae

    Excludes: *ophthalmic complications of viral diseases classified elsewhere*

077.0 Inclusion conjunctivitis
    Paratrachoma
    Swimming pool conjunctivitis

    Excludes: *inclusion blennorrhea (neonatal) (771.6)*

077.1 Epidemic keratoconjunctivitis
    Shipyard eye

077.2 Pharyngoconjunctival fever

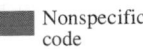 Add 4th or 5th digit   Nonspecific code   Unspecified code   Manifestation code

082.0 Spotted fevers
Rocky mountain spotted fever
São Paulo fever

082.1 Boutonneuse fever
African tick typhus
India tick typhus
Kenya tick typhus

Marseilles fever
Mediterranean tick fever

082.2 North Asian tick fever
Siberian tick typhus

082.3 Queensland tick typhus

082.8 Other specified tick-borne rickettsioses
Lone star fever

082.9 Tick-borne rickettsiosis, unspecified
Tick-borne typhus NOS

083 Other rickettsioses

083.0 Q fever

083.1 Trench fever
Quintan fever
Wolhynian fever

083.2 Rickettsialpox
Vesicular rickettsiosis

083.8 Other specified rickettsioses

083.9 Rickettsiosis, unspecified

084 Malaria

Note: Subcategories 084.0-084.6 exclude the listed conditions with mention of pernicious complications (084.8-084.9).

Excludes: congenital malaria (771.2)

084.0 Falciparum malaria [malignant tertian]
Malaria (fever):
by Plasmodium falciparum
subtertian

084.1 Vivax malaria [benign tertian]
Malaria (fever) by Plasmodium vivax

084.2 Quartan malaria
Malaria (fever) by Plasmodium malariae
Malariae malaria

084.3 Ovale malaria
Malaria (fever) by Plasmodium ovale

084.4 Other malaria
Monkey malaria

084.5 Mixed malaria
Malaria (fever) by more than one parasite

084.6 Malaria, unspecified
Malaria (fever) NOS

084.7 Induced malaria
Therapeutically induced malaria

Excludes: accidental infection from syringe, blood transfusion, etc. (084.0-084.6, above, according to parasite species)
transmission from mother to child during delivery (771.2)

084.8 Blackwater fever
Hemoglobinuric:
fever (bilious)
malaria

Malarial hemoglobinuria

084.9 Other pernicious complications of malaria
Algid malaria
Cerebral malaria

Use additional code, if desired, to identify complication, as:
malarial:
hepatitis (573.2)
nephrosis (581.81)

● Code new
to this edition

▲ Revision of
existing code

④ ⑤ Fourth or fifth
digit required

085 Leishmaniasis

085.0 Visceral [kala-azar]
Dumdum fever
Infection by Leishmania:
donovani
infantum

Leishmaniasis:
dermal, post-kala-azar
Mediterranean
visceral (Indian)

085.1 Cutaneous, urban
Aleppo boil
Baghdad boil
Delhi boil
Infection by Leishmania
tropica (minor)

Leishmaniasis, cutaneous:
dry form
late
recurrent
ulcerating
Oriental sore

085.2 Cutaneous, Asian desert
Infection by Leishmania tropica major
Leishmaniasis, cutaneous:
acute necrotizing
rural
wet form
zoonotic form

085.3 Cutaneous, Ethiopian
Infection by Leishmania ethiopica
Leishmaniasis, cutaneous:
diffuse
lepromatous

085.4 Cutaneous, American
Chiclero ulcer
Infection by Leishmania mexicana
Leishmaniasis tegumentaria diffusa

085.5 Mucocutaneous (American)
Espundia
Infection by Leishmania braziliensis
Uta

085.9 Leishmaniasis, unspecified

086 Trypanosomiasis

Use additional code, if desired, to identify manifestations, as:
trypanosomiasis:
encephalitis (323.2)
meningitis (321.3)

086.0 Chagas' disease with heart involvement
American trypanosomiasis
Infection by Trypanosoma cruzi } with heart involvement
Any condition classifiable to 086.2

086.1 Chagas' disease with other organ involvement
American trypanosomiasis
Infection by Trypanosoma cruzi } with involvement of organ other than heart
Any condition classifiable to 086.2

086.2 Chagas' disease without mention of organ involvement
American trypanosomiasis
Infection by Trypanosoma cruzi

086.3 Gambian trypanosomiasis
Gambian sleeping sickness
Infection by Trypanosoma gambiense

086.4 Rhodesian trypanosomiasis
Infection by Trypanosoma rhodesiense
Rhodesian sleeping sickness

086.5 African trypanosomiasis, unspecified
Sleeping sickness NOS

086.9 Trypanosomiasis, unspecified

087 Relapsing fever
Includes: recurrent fever

087.0 Louse-borne

087.1 Tick-borne

087.9 Relapsing fever, unspecified

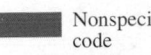 Add 4th or 5th digit

 Nonspecific code

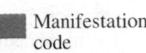 Unspecified code

Manifestation code

088 Other arthropod-borne diseases

088.0 **Bartonellosis**
Carrión's disease   Verruga peruana
Oroya fever

088.8 **Other specified arthropod-borne diseases**

    088.81 **Lyme Disease**
        Erythema chronicum migrans

    088.82 **Babesiosis**
        Babesiasis

    088.89 **Other**

088.9 **Arthropod-borne disease, unspecified**

SYPHILIS AND OTHER VENEREAL DISEASES (090-099)

Excludes: *nonvenereal endemic syphilis (104.0)*
urogenital trichomoniasis (131.0)

090 Congenital syphilis

090.0 **Early congenital syphilis, symptomatic**
Congenital syphilitic: Syphilitic (congenital):
  choroiditis   epiphysitis
  coryza (chronic)   osteochondritis
  hepatomegaly   pemphigus
  mucous patches   Any congenital syphilitic condition specified as early
  periostitis   or manifest less than two years after birth
  splenomegaly

090.1 **Early congenital syphilis, latent**
Congenital syphilis without clinical manifestations, with positive serological reaction
and negative spinal fluid test, less than two years after birth

090.2 **Early congenital syphilis, unspecified**
Congenital syphilis NOS, less than two years after birth

090.3 **Syphilitic interstitial keratitis**
Syphilitic keratitis:
  parenchymatous
  punctata profunda

Excludes: *interstitial keratitis NOS (370.50)*

090.4 **Juvenile neurosyphilis**
Use additional code, if desired, to identify any associated mental disorder

    090.40 **Juvenile neurosyphilis, unspecified**
        Congenital neurosyphilis
        Dementia paralytica juvenilis
        Juvenile:
          general paresis
          tabes
          taboparesis

    090.41 **Congenital syphilitic encephalitis**

    090.42 **Congenital syphilitic meningitis**

    090.49 **Other**

090.5 **Other late congenital syphilis, symptomatic**
Gumma due to congenital syphilis
Hutchinson's teeth
Syphilitic saddle nose
Any congenital syphilitic condition specified as late or manifest two years or more
  after birth

090.6 **Late congenital syphilis, latent**
Congenital syphilis without clinical manifestations, with positive serological reaction
and negative spinal fluid test, two years or more after birth

090.7 **Late congenital syphilis, unspecified**
Congenital syphilis NOS, two years or more after birth

090.9 **Congenital syphilis, unspecified**

091 Early syphilis, symptomatic

Excludes: *early cardiovascular syphilis (093.0-093.9)*
early neurosyphilis (094.0-094.9)

    ● Code new   ▲ Revision of   ④ ⑤ Fourth or fifth
          to this edition   existing code   digit required

091.0 Genital syphilis (primary)
Genital chancre

091.1 Primary anal syphilis

091.2 Other primary syphilis

Primary syphilis of:	Primary syphilis of:
breast	lip
fingers	tonsils

091.3 Secondary syphilis of skin or mucous membranes

Condyloma latum	Secondary syphilis of:
Secondary syphilis of:	skin
anus	tonsils
mouth	vulva
pharynx	

091.4 Adenopathy due to secondary syphilis
Syphilitic adenopathy (secondary)
Syphilitic lymphadenitis (secondary)

091.5 Uveitis due to secondary syphilis

091.50 Syphilitic uveitis, unspecified

091.51 Syphilitic chorioretinitis (secondary)

091.52 Syphilitic iridocyclitis (secondary)

091.6 Secondary syphilis of viscera and bone

091.61 Secondary syphilitic periostitis

091.62 Secondary syphilitic hepatitis
Secondary syphilis of liver

091.69 Other viscera

091.7 Secondary syphilis, relapse
Secondary syphilis, relapse (treated) (untreated)

091.8 Other forms of secondary syphilis

091.81 Acute syphilitic meningitis (secondary)

091.82 Syphilitic alopecia

091.89 Other

091.9 Unspecified secondary syphilis

092 Early syphilis, latent
Includes: syphilis (acquired) without clinical manifestations, with positive serological reaction
and negative spinal fluid test, less than two years after infection

092.0 Early syphilis, latent, serological relapse after treatment

092.9 Early syphilis, latent, unspecified

093 Cardiovascular syphilis

093.0 Aneurysm of aorta, specified as syphilitic
Dilatation of aorta, specified as syphilitic

093.1 Syphilitic aortitis

093.2 Syphilitic endocarditis

093.20 Valve, unspecified
Syphilitic ostial coronary disease

093.21 Mitral valve

093.22 Aortic valve
Syphilitic aortic incompetence or stenosis

093.23 Tricuspid valve

093.24 Pulmonary valve

093.8 Other specified cardiovascular syphilis

093.81 Syphilitic pericarditis

093.82 Syphilitic myocarditis

093.89 Other

093.9 Cardiovascular syphilis, unspecified

094 Neurosyphilis
Use additional code, if desired, to identify any associated mental disorder

 Add 4th or
5th digit

 Nonspecific
code

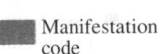 Unspecified
code

Manifestation
code

098.50 Gonococcal arthritis
Gonococcal infection of joint NOS

098.51 Gonococcal synovitis and tenosynovitis

098.52 Gonococcal bursitis

098.53 Gonococcal spondylitis

098.59 Other
Gonococcal rheumatism

098.6 Gonococcal infection of pharynx

098.7 Gonococcal infection of anus and rectum
Gonococcal proctitis

098.8 Gonococcal infection of other specified sites

098.81 Gonococcal keratosis (blennorrhagica)

098.82 Gonococcal meningitis

098.83 Gonococcal pericarditis

098.84 Gonococcal endocarditis

098.85 Other gonococcal heart disease

098.86 Gonococcal peritonitis

098.89 Other
Gonococcemia

099 Other venereal diseases

099.0 Chancroid

Bubo (inguinal):
  chancroidal
  due to Hemophilus ducreyi
	Chancre:
	  Ducrey's
	  simple
	  soft
	Ulcus molle (cutis) (skin)

099.1 Lymphogranuloma venereum

Climatic or tropical bubo (Durand-) Nicolas- Favre disease	Esthiomene Lymphogranuloma inguinale

099.2 Granuloma inguinale

Donovanosis Granuloma pudendi (ulcerating)	Granuloma venereum Pudendal ulcer

099.3 Reiter's disease
Reiter's syndrome

099.4 Other nongonococcal urethritis [NGU]

099.40 Unspecified
Nonspecific urethritis

099.41 Chlamydia trachomatis

099.49 Other specified organism

099.5 Other venereal diseases due to Chlamydia trachomatis

Excludes: *Chlamydia trachomatis infection of conjunctiva (076.0-076.9, 077.0, 077.9)*
Lymphogranuloma venereum (099.1)

099.50 Unspecified site

099.51 Pharynx

099.52 Anus and rectum

099.53 Lower genitourinary sites

Excludes: *urethra (099.41)*

Use additional code, if desired, to specify site of infection, such as:
    bladder (595.4)
    cervix (616.0)
    vagina and vulva (616.11)

099.54 Other genitourinary sites
Use additional code, if desired, to specify site of infection, such as:
    pelvic inflammatory disease NOS (614.9)
    testis and epididymis (604.91)

099.55 Unspecified genitourinary site

● Code new   ▲ Revision of   ④ ⑤ Fourth or fifth
to this edition   existing code   digit required

099.56 **Peritoneum**
Perihepatitis

099.59 **Other specified site**

099.8 **Other specified venereal diseases**

099.9 **Venereal disease, unspecified**

OTHER SPIROCHETAL DISEASES (100-104)

100 **Leptospirosis**

100.0 **Leptospirosis icterohemorrhagica**
Leptospiral or spirochetal jaundice (hemorrhagic)
Weil's disease

100.8 **Other specified leptospiral infections**

100.81 **Leptospiral meningitis (aseptic)**

100.89 **Other**

Fever: Infection by Leptospira:
   Fort Bragg   australis
   pretibial   bataviae
   swamp   pyrogenes

100.9 **Leptospirosis, unspecified**

101 **Vincent's angina**
Acute necrotizing ulcerative: Spirochetal stomatitis
   gingivitis   Trench mouth
   stomatitis   Vincent's:
Fusospirochetal pharyngitis   gingivitis
                                       infection [any site]

102 **Yaws**
Includes: frambesia
            pian

102.0 **Initial lesions**
Chancre of yaws   Initial frambesial ulcer
Frambesia, initial or primary Mother yaw

102.1 **Multiple papillomata and wet crab yaws**
Butter yaws   Planter or palmer papilloma of yaws
Frambesioma
Pianoma

102.2 **Other early skin lesions**
Early yaws (cutaneous) (macular) (papular) (maculopapular) (micropapular)
Frambeside of early yaws
Cutaneous yaws, less than five years after infection

102.3 **Hyperkeratosis**
Ghoul hand
Hyperkeratosis, palmer or plantar (early) (late) due to yaws
Worm-eaten soles

102.4 **Gummata and ulcers**
Nodular late yaws (ulcerated)
Gummatous frambeside

102.5 **Gangosa**
Rhinopharyngitis mutilans

102.6 **Bone and joint lesions**
Goundou
Gumma, bone   } of yaws (late)
Gummatous osteitis or periostitis

Hydrarthrosis
Osteitis   } of yaws (early) (late)
Periostitis (hypertrophic)

102.7 **Other manifestations**
Juxta-articular nodules of yaws
Mucosal yaws

102.8 **Latent yaws**
Yaws without clinical manifestations, with positive serology

102.9 **Yaws, unspecified**

Add 4th or
5th digit
Nonspecific
code
 Unspecified
code
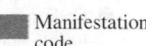 Manifestation
code

103 Pinta

103.0 Primary lesions
Chancre (primary)
Papule (primary) } of pinta [carate]
Pintid

103.1 Intermediate lesions
Erythematous plaques
Hyperchromic lesions } of pinta [carate]
Hyperkeratosis

103.2 Late lesions
Cardiovascular lesions
Skin lesions:
achromic
cicatricial } of pinta [carate]
dyschromic
Vitiligo

103.3 Mixed lesions
Achromic and hyperchromic skin lesions of pinta [carate]

103.9 Pinta, unspecified

104 Other spirochetal infection

104.0 Nonvenereal endemic syphilis
Bejel   Njovera

104.8 Other specified spirochetal infections

Excludes: relapsing fever (087.0-087.9)
syphilis (090.0-097.9)

104.9 Spirochetal infection, unspecified

MYCOSES (110-118)

Use additional code, if desired, to identify manifestation, as:
arthropathy (711.6)
meningitis (321.0-321.1)
otitis externa (380.15)

Excludes: infection by Actinomycetales, such as species of Actinomyces, Actinomadura,
Nocardia, Streptomyces (039.0-039.9)

110 Dermatophytosis
Includes: infection by species of Epidermophyton, Microsporum, and Trichophyton tinea, any
type except those in 111

110.0 Of scalp and beard
Kerion
Sycosis, mycotic
Trichophytic tinea [black dot tinea], scalp

110.1 Of nail
Dermatophytic onychia   Tinea unguium
Onychomycosis

110.2 Of hand
Tinea manuum

110.3 Of groin and perianal area
Dhobie itch   Tinea cruris
Eczema marginatum

110.4 Of foot
Athlete's foot   Tinea pedis

110.5 Of the body
Herpes circinatus
Tinea imbricata [Tokelau]

110.6 Deep seated dermatophytosis
Granuloma trichophyticum
Majocchi's granuloma

110.8 Of other specified sites

110.9 Of unspecified site
Favus NOS   Ringworm NOS
Microsporic tinea NOS

● Code new
to this edition
▲ Revision of
existing code
④ ⑤ Fourth or fifth
digit required

111   Dermatomycosis, other and unspecified

111.0   Pityrlasis versicolor
Infection by Malassezia [Pityrosporum] furfur
Tinea flava
Tinea versicolor

111.1   Tinea nigra
Infection by   Microsporosis nigra
   Cladosporium species   Pityriasis nigra
Keratomycosis nigricans   Tinea palmaris nigra

111.2   Tinea blanca
Infection by Trichosporon (beigelii) cutaneum
White piedra

111.3   Black piedra
Infection by Piedraia hortai

111.8   Other specified dermatomycoses

111.9   Dermatomycosis, unspecified

112   Candidiasis
Includes: infection by Candida species
           moniliasi

Excludes: *neonatal monilial infection (771.7)*

112.0   Of mouth
Thrush (oral)

112.1   Of vulva and vagina
Candidal vulvovaginitis   Monilial vulvovaginitis

112.2   Of other urogenital sites
Candidal balanitis

112.3   Of skin and nails
Candidal intertrigo   Candidal perionyxis [paronychia]
Candidal onychia

112.4   Of lung
Candidal pneumonia

112.5   Disseminated
Systemic candidiasis

112.8   Of other specified sites

    112.81   Candidal endocarditis

    112.82   Candidal otitis externa
        Otomycosis in moniliasis

    112.83   Candidal meningitis

    112.84   Candidal esophagitis

    112.85   Candidal enteritis

    112.89   Other

112.9   Of unspecified site

114   Coccidioidomycosis
Includes: infection by Coccidioides (immitis)
           Posada-Wernicke disease

114.0   Primary coccidioidomycosis (pulmonary)
Acute pulmonary coccidioidomycosis
Coccidioidomycotic pneumonitis
Desert rheumatism
Pulmonary coccidioidomycosis
San Joaquin Valley fever

114.1   Primary extrapulmonary coccidioidomycosis
Chancriform syndrome
Primary cutaneous coccidioidomycosis

114.2   Coccidioidal meningitis

114.3   Other forms of progressive coccidioidomycosis
Coccidioidal granuloma
Disseminated coccidioidomycosis

114.4   Chronic pulmonary coccidioidomycosis

114.5   Pulmonary coccidioidomycosis, unspecified

| | Add 4th or 5th digit | | Nonspecific code | | Unspecified code | | Manifestation code |

136.3 Pneumocystosis
Pneumonia due to Pneumocystis carinii

136.4 Psorospermiasis

136.5 Sarcosporidiosis
Infection by Sarcocystis lindemanni

136.8 Other specified infectious and parasitic diseases
Candiru infestation

136.9 Unspecified infectious and parasitic diseases
Infectious disease NOS
Parasitic disease NOS

LATE EFFECTS OF INFECTIOUS AND PARASITIC DISEASES (137-139)

137 Late effects of tuberculosis

Note: This category is to be used to indicate conditions classifiable to 010-018 as the cause of late effects, which are themselves classified elsewhere. The "late effects" include those specified as such, as sequelae, or as due to old or inactive tuberculosis, without evidence of active disease.

137.0 Late effects of respiratory or unspecified tuberculosis

137.1 Late effects of central nervous system tuberculosis

137.2 Late effects of genitourinary tuberculosis

137.3 Late effects of tuberculosis of bones and joints

137.4 Late effects of tuberculosis of other specified organs

138 Late effects of acute poliomyelitis

Note: This category is to be used to indicate conditions classifiable to 045 as the cause of late effects, which are themselves classified elsewhere. The "late effects" include conditions specified as such, or as sequelae, or as due to old or inactive poliomyelitis, without evidence of active disease.

139 Late effects of other infectious and parasitic diseases

Note: This category is to be used to indicate conditions classifiable to categories 001-009, 020-041, 046-136 as the cause of late effects, which are themselves classified elsewhere. The "late effects" include conditions specified as such; they also include sequela of diseases classifiable to the above categories if there is evidence that the disease itself is no longer present.

139.0 Late effects of viral encephalitis
Late effects of conditions classifiable to 049.8-049.9, 062-064

139.1 Late effects of trachoma
Late effects of conditions classifiable to 076

139.8 Late effects of other and unspecified infectious and parasitic diseases

2. NEOPLASMS (140-239)

Notes:

1. Content
This chapter contains the following broad groups:

140-195	Malignant neoplasms, stated or presumed to be primary, of specified sites, except of lymphatic and hematopoietic tissue
196-198	Malignant neoplasms, stated or presumed to be secondary, of specified sites
199	Malignant neoplasms, without specification of site
200-208	Malignant neoplasms, stated or presumed to be primary, of lymphatic and hematopoietic tissue
210-229	Benign neoplasms
230-234	Carcinoma in situ
235-238	Neoplasms of uncertain behavior [see Note, page 92]
239	Neoplasms of unspecified nature

2. Functional activity
All neoplasms are classified in this chapter, whether or not functionally active. An additional code from Chapter 3 may be used, if desired, to identify such functional activity associated with any neoplasm, e.g.:

catecholamine-producing malignant pheochromocytoma of adrenal:
code 194.0, additional code 255.6
basophil adenoma of pituitary with Cushing's syndrome:
code 227.3, additional code 255.0

3. Morphology [Histology]
For those wishing to identify the histological type of neoplasms, a comprehensive coded nomenclature, which comprises the morphology rubrics of the ICD-Oncology, is given on pages 529-542.

4. Malignant neoplasms overlapping site boundaries
Categories 140-195 are for the classification of primary malignant neoplasms according to their point of origin. A malignant neoplasm that overlaps two or more subcategories within a three-digit rubric and whose point of origin cannot be determined should be classified to the subcategory .8 "Other." For example, "carcinoma involving tip and ventral surface of tongue" should be assigned to 141.8. On the other hand, "carcinoma of tip of tongue, extending to involve the ventral surface" should be coded to 141.2, as the point of origin, the tip, is known. Three subcategories (149.8, 159.8, 165.8) have been provided for malignant neoplasms that overlap the boundaries of three-digit rubrics within certain systems. Overlapping malignant neoplasms that cannot be classified as indicated above should be assigned to the appropriate subdivision of category 195 (Malignant neoplasm of other and ill-defined sites).

MALIGNANT NEOPLASM OF LIP, ORAL CAVITY, AND PHARYNX (140-149)

> *Excludes:* carcinoma in situ (230.0)

140 Malignant neoplasm of lip

> *Excludes:* skin of lip (173.0)

140.0 Upper lip, vermilion border
Upper lip:
NOS
external
lipstick area

140.1 Lower lip, vermilion border
Lower lip:
NOS
external
lipstick area

140.3 Upper lip, inner aspect

Upper lip:	Upper lip:
buccal aspect	mucosa
frenulum	oral aspect

140.4 Lower lip, inner aspect

Lower lip:	Lower lip:
buccal aspect	mucosa
frenulum	oral aspect

▤	Add 4th or 5th digit	▤	Nonspecific code	▤	Unspecified code	▤	Manifestation code

170.0 Bones of skull and face, except mandible

Bone:
ethmoid
frontal
malar
nasal
occipital
orbital
parietal

Bone:
sphenoid
temporal
zygomatic
Maxilla (superior)
Turbinate
Upper jaw bone
Vomer

Excludes: carcinoma, any type except intraosseous or odontogenic:
maxilla, maxillary (sinus) (160.2)
upper jaw bone (143.0)
jaw bone (lower) (170.1)

170.1 Mandible

Inferior maxilla
Jaw bone NOS

Lower jaw bone

Excludes: carcinoma, any type except intraosseous or odontogenic:
jaw bone NOS (143.9)
lower (143.1)
upper jaw bone (170.0)

170.2 Vertebral column, excluding sacrum and coccyx

Spinal column
Spine

Vertebra

Excludes: sacrum and coccyx (170.6)

170.3 Ribs, sternum, and clavicle

Costal cartilage
Costovertebral joint

Xiphoid process

170.4 Scapula and long bones of upper limb

Acromion
Bones NOS of upper limb
Humerus

Radius
Ulna

170.5 Short bones of upper limb

Carpal
Cuneiform, wrist
Metacarpal
Navicular, of hand
Phalanges of hand
Pisiform

Scaphoid (of hand)
Semilunar or lunate
Trapezium
Trapezoid
Unciform

170.6 Pelvic bones, sacrum, and coccyx

Coccygeal vertebra
Ilium
Ischium

Pubic bone
Sacral vertebra

170.7 Long bones of lower limb

Bones NOS of lower limb
Femur

Fibula
Tibia

170.8 Short bones of lower limb

Astragalus [talus]
Calcaneus
Cuboid
Cuneiform, ankle
Metatarsal

Navicular (of ankle)
Patella
Phalanges of foot
Tarsal

170.9 Bone and articular cartilage, site unspecified

● Code new
to this edition

▲ Revision of
existing code

④ ⑤ Fourth or fifth
digit required

171 **Malignant neoplasm of connective and other soft tissue**

    Includes: blood vessel
                bursa
                fascia
                fat
                ligament, except uterine
                muscle
                peripheral, sympathetic, and parasympathetic nerves and ganglia
                synovia
                tendon (sheath)

> *Excludes:* *cartilage (of):*
>   *articular (170.0-170.9)*
>   *larynx (161.3)*
>   *nose (160.0)*
> *connective tissue:*
>   *breast (174.0-175.9)*
>   *internal organs—code to malignant neoplasm of the site [e.g., leiomyosarcoma of*
>   *stomach, 151.9]*
>   *heart (164.1)*
>   *uterine ligament (183.4)*

171.0 Head, face, and neck
    Cartilage of:
      ear
      eyelid

171.2 Upper limb, including shoulder
    Arm   Forearm
    Finger   Hand

171.3 Lower limb, including hip
    Foot   Thigh
    Leg   Toe
    Popliteal space

171.4 Thorax
    Axilla   Great vessels
    Diaphragm

> *Excludes:* *heart (164.1)*
>   *mediastinum (164.2-164.9)*
>   *thymus (164.0)*

171.5 Abdomen
    Abdominal wall   Hypochondrium

> *Excludes:* *peritoneum (158.8)*
>   *retroperitoneum (158.0)*

171.6 Pelvis
    Buttock   Inguinal region
    Groin   Perineum

> *Excludes:* *pelvic peritoneum (158.8)*
>   *retroperitoneum (158.0)*
>   *uterine ligament, any (183.3-183.5)*

171.7 **Trunk, unspecified**
    Back NOS   Flank NOS

171.8 **Other specified sites of connective and other soft tissue**
    Malignant neoplasm of contiguous or overlapping sites of connective tissue whose point
    of origin cannot be determined

171.9 **Connective and other soft tissue, site unspecified**

172 **Malignant melanoma of skin**

    Includes: melanocarcinoma
                melanoma (skin) NOS

> *Excludes:* *skin of genital organs (184.0-184.9, 187.1-187.9)*
>   *sites other than skin—code to malignant neoplasm of the site*

172.0 Lip

> *Excludes:* *vermilion border of lip (140.0-140.1, 140.9)*

172.1 Eyelid, including canthus

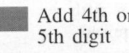 Add 4th or 5th digit   Nonspecific code   Unspecified code   Manifestation code

172.2 Ear and external auditory canal
Auricle (ear)
Auricular canal, external
External [acoustic] meatus
Pinna

172.3 Other and unspecified parts of face

Cheek (external)	Forehead
Chin	Nose, external
Eyebrow	Temple

172.4 Scalp and neck

172.5 Trunk, except scrotum

Axilla	Perianal skin
Breast	Perineum
Buttock	Umbilicus
Groin	

Excludes: *anal canal (154.2)*
anus NOS (154.3)
scrotum (187.7)

172.6 Upper limb, including shoulder

Arm	Forearm
Finger	Hand

172.7 Lower limb, including hip

Ankle	Leg
Foot	Popliteal area
Heel	Thigh
Knee	Toe

172.8 Other specified sites of skin
Malignant melanoma of contiguous or overlapping sites of skin whose point of origin cannot be determined

172.9 Melanoma of skin, site unspecified

173 Other malignant neoplasm of skin
Includes: malignant neoplasm of:
sebaceous glands
sudoriferous, sudoriparous glands
sweat glands

Excludes: *Kaposi's sarcoma (176.0-176.9)*
malignant melanoma of skin (172.0-172.9)
skin of genital organs (184.0-184.9, 187.1-187.9)

173.0 Skin of lip

Excludes: *vermilion border of lip (140.0-140.1, 140.9)*

173.1 Eyelid, including canthus

Excludes: *cartilage of eyelid (171.0)*

173.2 Skin of ear and external auditory canal

Auricle (ear)	External meatus
Auricular canal, external	Pinna

Excludes: *cartilage of ear (171.0)*

173.3 Skin of other and unspecified parts of face

Cheek, external	Forehead
Chin	Nose, external
Eyebrow	Temple

173.4 Scalp and skin of neck

● Code new
to this edition

▲ Revision of
existing code

④ ⑤ Fourth or fifth
digit required

173.5 Skin of trunk, except scrotum
Axillary fold
Perianal skin
Skin of:
  abdominal wall
  anus
  back
  breast

Skin of:
  buttock
  chest wall
  groin
  perineum
Umbilicus

Excludes: anal canal (154.2)
         anus NOS (154.3)
         skin of scrotum (187.7)

173.6 Skin of upper limb, including shoulder
Arm
Finger
Forearm
Hand

173.7 Skin of lower limb, including hip
Ankle
Foot
Heel
Knee

Leg
Popliteal area
Thigh
Toe

173.8 Other specified sites of skin
Malignant neoplasm of contiguous or overlapping sites of skin whose point of origin cannot be determined

173.9 Skin, site unspecified

174 Malignant neoplasm of female breast
Includes:
  breast (female)
  connective tissue
  soft parts

Paget's disease of:
  breast
  nipple

Excludes: skin of breast (172.5, 173.5)

174.0 Nipple and areola

174.1 Central portion

174.2 Upper-inner quadrant

174.3 Lower-inner quadrant

174.4 Upper-outer quadrant

174.5 Lower-outer quadrant

174.6 Axillary tail

174.8 Other specified sites of female breast
Ectopic sites
Inner breast
Lower breast
Malignant neoplasm of
  contiguous or overlapping
  sites of breast whose point of
  origin cannot be determined

Midline of breast
Outer breast
Upper breast

174.9 Breast (female), unspecified

175 Malignant neoplasm of male breast

Excludes: skin of breast (172.5, 173.5)

175.0 Nipple and areola

175.9 Other and unspecified sites of male breast
Ectopic breast tissue, male

176 Kaposi's sarcoma

176.0 Skin

176.1 Soft Tissue
Includes:
  blood vessel
  connective tissue
  fascia

ligament
lymphatic(s) NEC
muscle

Excludes: lymph glands and nodes (176.5)

176.2 Palate

176.3 Gastrointestinal sites

Add 4th or
5th digit

Nonspecific
code

Unspecified
code

Manifestation
code

188.8 Other specified sites of bladder
Malignant neoplasm of contiguous or overlapping sites of bladder whose point of origin cannot be determined

188.9 Bladder, part unspecified
Bladder wall NOS

189 Malignant neoplasm of kidney and other and unspecified urinary organs

189.0 Kidney, except pelvis
Kidney NOS   Kidney parenchyma

189.1 Renal pelvis
Renal calyces   Ureteropelvic junction

189.2 Ureter

Excludes: ureteric orifice of bladder (188.6)

189.3 Urethra

Excludes: urethral orifice of bladder (188.5)

189.4 Paraurethral glands

189.8 Other specified sites of urinary organs
Malignant neoplasm of contiguous or overlapping sites of kidney and other urinary organs whose point of origin cannot be determined

189.9 Urinary organ, site unspecified
Urinary system NOS

MALIGNANT NEOPLASM OF OTHER AND UNSPECIFIED SITES (190-199)

Excludes: carcinoma in situ (234.0-234.9)

190 Malignant neoplasm of eye

Excludes: carcinoma in situ (234.0)
eyelid (skin) (172.1, 173.1)
cartilage (171.0)
optic nerve (192.0)
orbital bone (170.0)

190.0 Eyeball, except conjunctiva, cornea, retina, and choroid
Ciliary body   Sclera
Crystalline lens   Uveal tract
Iris

190.1 Orbit
Connective tissue of orbit
Extraocular muscle
Retrobulbar

Excludes: bone of orbit (170.0)

190.2 Lacrimal gland

190.3 Conjunctiva

190.4 Cornea

190.5 Retina

190.6 Choroid

190.7 Lacrimal duct
Lacrimal sac   Nasolacrimal duct

190.8 Other specified sites of eye
Malignant neoplasm of contiguous or overlapping sites of eye whose point of origin cannot be determined

190.9 Eye, part unspecified

191 Malignant neoplasm of brain

Excludes: cranial nerves (192.0)
retrobulbar area (190.1)

191.0 Cerebrum, except lobes and ventricles
Basal ganglia   Globus pallidus
Cerebral cortex   Hypothalamus
Corpus striatum   Thalamus

191.1 Frontal lobe

● Code new   ▲ Revision of   ④ ⑤ Fourth or fifth
   to this edition   existing code   digit required

191.2 Temporal lobe
Hippocampus   Uncus

191.3 Parietal lobe

191.4 Occipital lobe

191.5 Ventricles
Choroid plexus   Floor of ventricle

191.6 Cerebellum NOS
Cerebellopontine angle

191.7 Brain stem
Cerebral peduncle   Midbrain
Medulla oblongata   Pons

191.8 Other parts of brain
Corpus callosum
Tapetum
Malignant neoplasm of contiguous or overlapping sites of brain whose point of origin cannot be determined

191.9 Brain, unspecified
Cranial fossa NOS

192 Malignant neoplasm of other and unspecified parts of nervous system

Excludes: peripheral, sympathetic, and parasympathetic nerves and ganglia (171.0-171.9)

192.0 Cranial nerves
Olfactory bulb

192.1 Cerebral meninges
Dura (mater)   Meninges NOS
Falx (cerebelli) (cerebri)   Tentorium

192.2 Spinal cord
Cauda equina

192.3 Spinal meninges

192.8 Other specified sites of nervous system
Malignant neoplasm of contiguous or overlapping sites of other parts of nervous system whose point of origin cannot be determined

192.9 Nervous system, part unspecified
Nervous system (central) NOS

Excludes: meninges NOS (192.1)

193 Malignant neoplasm of thyroid gland
Sipple's syndrome   Thyroglossal duct
Use additional code, if desired, to identify any functional activity

194 Malignant neoplasm of other endocrine glands and related structures
Use additional code, if desired, to identify any functional activity

Excludes: islets of Langerhans (157.4)
     ovary (183.0)
     testis (186.0-186.9)
     thymus (164.0)

194.0 Adrenal gland
Adrenal cortex   Suprarenal gland
Adrenal medulla

194.1 Parathyroid gland

194.3 Pituitary gland and craniopharyngeal duct
Craniobuccal pouch   Rathke's pouch
Hypophysis   Sella turcica

194.4 Pineal gland

194.5 Carotid body

194.6 Aortic body and other paraganglia
Coccygeal body   Para-aortic body
Glomus jugulare

194.8 Other
Pluriglandular involvement NOS
Note: If the sites of multiple involvements are known, they should be coded separately.

194.9 Endocrine gland, site unspecified

	Add 4th or 5th digit		Nonspecific code		Unspecified code		Manifestation code

195 **Malignant neoplasm of other and ill-defined sites**

Includes: malignant neoplasms of contiguous sites, not elsewhere classified, whose point of origin cannot be determined

Excludes: *malignant neoplasm:*
lymphatic and hematopoietic tissue (200.0-208.9)
secondary sites (196.0-198.8)
unspecified site (199.0-199.1)

195.0 **Head, face, and neck**
Cheek NOS   Nose NOS
Jaw NOS   Supraclavicular region NOS

195.1 **Thorax**
Axilla   Intrathoracic NOS
Chest (wall) NOS

195.2 **Abdomen**
Intra-abdominal NOS

195.3 **Pelvis**
Groin
Inguinal region NOS
Presacral region
Sacrococcygeal region
Sites overlapping systems within pelvis, as:
rectovaginal (septum)
rectovesical (septum)

195.4 **Upper limb**

195.5 **Lower limb**

195.8 **Other specified sites**
Back NOS   Trunk NOS
Flank NOS

196 **Secondary and unspecified malignant neoplasm of lymph nodes**

Excludes: *any malignant neoplasm of lymph nodes, specified as primary (200.0-202.9)*
Hodgkin's disease (201.0-201.9)
lymphosarcoma (200.1)
reticulosarcoma (200.0)
other forms of lymphoma (202.0-202.9)

196.0 **Lymph nodes of head, face, and neck**
Cervical   Scalene
Cervicofacial   Supraclavicular

196.1 **Intrathoracic lymph nodes**
Bronchopulmonary   Mediastinal
Intercostal   Tracheobronchial

196.2 **Intra-abdominal lymph nodes**
Intestinal   Retroperitoneal
Mesenteric

196.3 **Lymph nodes of axilla and upper limb**
Brachial   Infraclavicular
Epitrochlear   Pectoral

196.5 **Lymph nodes of inguinal region and lower limb**
Femoral   Popliteal
Groin   Tibial

196.6 **Intrapelvic lymph nodes**
Hypogastric   Obturator
Iliac   Parametrial

196.8 **Lymph nodes of multiple sites**

196.9 **Site unspecified**
Lymph nodes NOS

197 **Secondary malignant neoplasm of respiratory and digestive systems**

Excludes: *lymph node metastasis (196.0-196.9)*

197.0 **Lung**
Bronchus

197.1 **Mediastinum**

197.2 **Pleura**

● Code new   ▲ Revision of   ④ ⑤ Fourth or fifth
  to this edition   existing code   digit required

197.3 Other respiratory organs
 Trachea

197.4 Small intestine, including duodenum

197.5 Large intestine and rectum

197.6 Retroperitoneum and peritoneum

197.7 Liver, specified as secondary

197.8 Other digestive organs and spleen

198 Secondary malignant neoplasm of other specified sites

 Excludes: lymph node metastasis (196.0-196.9)

198.0 Kidney

198.1 Other urinary organs

198.2 Skin
 Skin of breast

198.3 Brain and spinal cord

198.4 Other parts of nervous system
 Meninges (cerebral) (spinal)

198.5 Bone and bone marrow

198.6 Ovary

198.7 Adrenal gland
 Suprarenal gland

198.8 Other specified sites

 198.81 Breast

 Excludes: skin of breast (198.2)

 198.82 Genital organs

 198.89 Other

 Excludes: retroperitoneal lymph nodes (196.2)

199 Malignant neoplasm without specification of site

199.0 Disseminated
 Carcinomatosis
 Generalized:
  cancer
  malignancy
 Multiple cancer ⎱ unspecified site (primary) (secondary)

199.1 Other
 Cancer
 Carcinoma ⎱ unspecified site (primary) (secondary)
 Malignancy

MALIGNANT NEOPLASM OF LYMPHATIC AND HEMATOPOIETIC TISSUE (200-208)

 Excludes: secondary neoplasm of:
  bone marrow (198.5)
  spleen (197.8)
  secondary and unspecified neoplasm of lymph nodes (196.0-196.9)

The following fifth-digit subclassification is for use with categories 200-202:

 0 unspecified site, extranodal and solid organ sites

 1 lymph nodes of head, face, and neck

 2 intrathoracic lymph nodes

 3 intra-abdominal lymph nodes

 4 lymph nodes of axilla and upper limb

 5 lymph nodes of inguinal region and lower limb

 6 intrapelvic lymph nodes

 7 spleen

 8 lymph nodes of multiple sites

 Add 4th or
5th digit

 Nonspecific
code

Unspecified
code

Manifestation
code

⑤ 200 **Lymphosarcoma and reticulosarcoma**

200.0 Reticulosarcoma
Lymphoma (malignant):
  histiocytic (diffuse):
    nodular
    pleomorphic cell type
  reticulum cell type
Reticulum cell sarcoma:
  NOS
  pleomorphic cell type

200.1 Lymphosarcoma
Lymphoblastoma (diffuse)   Lymphosarcoma:
Lymphoma (malignant):   NOS
  lymphoblastic (diffuse)   diffuse NOS
  lymphocytic (cell type)   lymphoblastic (diffuse)
    (diffuse)   lymphocytic (diffuse)
  lymphosarcoma type   prolymphocytic

Excludes: *lymphosarcoma:*
> *follicular or nodular (202.0)*
> *mixed cell type (200.8)*
> *lymphosarcoma cell leukemia (207.8)*

200.2 Burkitt's tumor or lymphoma
Malignant lymphoma, Burkitt's type

200.8 Other named variants
Lymphoma (malignant):
  lymphoplasmacytoid type
  mixed lymphocytic-histiocytic (diffuse)
Lymphosarcoma, mixed cell type (diffuse)
Reticulolymphosarcoma (diffuse)

⑤ 201 **Hodgkin's disease**

201.0 Hodgkin's paragranuloma

201.1 Hodgkin's granuloma

201.2 Hodgkin's sarcoma

201.4 Lymphocytic-histiocytic predominance

201.5 Nodular sclerosis
Hodgkin's disease, nodular sclerosis:
  NOS
  cellular phase

201.6 Mixed cellularity

201.7 Lymphocytic depletion
Hodgkin's disease, lymphocytic depletion:
  NOS
  diffuse fibrosis
  reticular type

201.9 Hodgkin's disease, unspecified
Hodgkin's: Malignant:
  disease NOS   lymphogranuloma
  lymphoma NOS   lymphogranulomatosis

⑤ 202 **Other malignant neoplasms of lymphoid and histiocytic tissue**

202.0 Nodular lymphoma
Brill-Symmers disease   Lymphosarcoma:
Lymphoma: follicular (giant)
  follicular (giant)   nodular
  lymphocytic, nodular   Reticulosarcoma, follicular or nodular

202.1 Mycosis fungoides

202.2 Sézary's disease

202.3 Malignant histiocytosis
Histiocytic medullary reticulosis
Malignant:
  reticuloendotheliosis
  reticulosis

202.4 Leukemic reticuloendotheliosis
Hairy-cell leukemia

● Code new   ▲ Revision of   ④ ⑤ Fourth or fifth
  to this edition   existing code   digit required

202.5 Letterer-Siwe disease
Acute:
differentiated progressive histiocytosis
histiocytosis X (progressive)
infantile reticuloendotheliosis
reticulosis of infancy

Excludes: *Hand-Schüller-Christian disease (277.8)*
histiocytosis (acute) (chronic) (277.8)
histiocytosis X (chronic) (277.8)

202.6 Malignant mast cell tumors

Malignant:	Mast cell sarcoma
mastocytoma	Systemic tissue mast cell disease
mastocytosis	

Excludes: *mast cell leukemia (207.8)*

202.8 Other lymphomas
Lymphoma (malignant):
NOS
diffuse

Excludes: *benign lymphoma (229.0)*

202.9 Other and unspecified malignant neoplasms of lymphoid and histiocytic tissue
Malignant neoplasm of bone marrow NOS

⑤ **203 Multiple myeloma and immunoproliferative neoplasms**
The following fifth-digit subclassification is for use with category 203

  0   without mention of remission

  1   in remission

203.0 Multiple myeloma
Kahler's disease   Myelomatosis

Excludes: *solitary myeloma (238.6)*

203.1 Plasma cell leukemia
Plasmacytic leukemia

203.8 Other immunoproliferative neoplasms

⑤ **204 Lymphoid leukemia**
Includes:

leukemia:	leukemia:
lymphatic	lymphocytic
lymphoblastic	lymphogenous

The following fifth-digit subclassification is for use with category 204

  0   without mention of remission

  1   in remission

204.0 Acute

Excludes: *acute exacerbation of chronic lymphoid leukemia (204.1)*

204.1 Chronic

204.2 Subacute

204.8 Other lymphoid leukemia
Aleukemic leukemia:
lymphatic
lymphocytic
lymphoid

204.9 Unspecified lymphoid leukemia

⑤ **205 Myeloid leukemia**
Includes:

leukemia:	leukemia:
granulocytic	myelomonocytic
myeloblastic	myelosclerotic
myelocytic	myelosis
Tmyelogenous	

The following fifth-digit subclassification is for use with category 205

  0   without mention of remission

  1   in remission

Add 4th or 5th digit	Nonspecific code	Unspecified code	Manifestation code

81

205.0 Acute
    Acute promyelocytic leukemia

    Excludes: *acute exacerbation of chronic myeloid leukemia (205.1)*

205.1 Chronic
    Eosinophilic leukemia   Neutrophilic leukemia

205.2 Subacute

205.3 Myeloid sarcoma
    Chloroma
    Granulocytic sarcoma

205.8 Other myeloid leukemia
    Aleukemic leukemia:
      granulocytic
      myelogenous
      myeloid
    Aleukemic myelosis

205.9 Unspecified myeloid leukemia

⑤ **206 Monocytic leukemia**
    Includes: leukemia:
             histiocytic
             monoblastic
             monocytoid

The following fifth-digit subclassification is for use with category 206

    0 without mention of remission

    1 in remission

206.0 Acute

    Excludes: *acute exacerbation of chronic monocytic leukemia (206.1)*

206.1 Chronic

206.2 Subacute

206.8 Other monocytic leukemia
    Aleukemic:
      monocytic leukemia
      monocytoid leukemia

206.9 Unspecified monocytic leukemia

⑤ **207 Other specified leukemia**

    Excludes: *leukemic reticuloendotheliosis (202.4)*
               plasma cell leukemia (203.1)

The following fifth-digit subclassification is for use with category 207

    0 without mention of remission

    1 in remission

207.0 Acute erythremia and erythroleukemia
    Acute erythremic myelosis   Erythremic myelosis
    Di Guglielmo's disease

207.1 Chronic erythremia
    Heilmeyer-Schöner disease

207.2 Megakaryocytic leukemia
    Megakaryocytic myelosis   Thrombocytic leukemia

207.8 Other specified leukemia
    Lymphosarcoma cell leukemia

⑤ **208 Leukemia of unspecified cell type**
The following fifth-digit subclassification is for use with category 208

    0 without mention of remission

    1 in remission

208.0 Acute
    Acute leukemia NOS   Stem cell leukemia
    Blast cell leukemia

    Excludes: *acute exacerbation of chronic unspecified leukemia (208.1)*

208.1 Chronic
    Chronic leukemia NOS

● Code new
  to this edition
    ▲ Revision of
      existing code
    ④ ⑤ Fourth or fifth
        digit required

208.2 Subacute
   Subacute leukemia NOS

208.8 Other leukemia of unspecified cell type

208.9 Unspecified leukemia
   Leukemia NOS

BENIGN NEOPLASMS (210-229)

210 Benign neoplasm of lip, oral cavity, and pharynx

   Excludes: cyst (of):
   > *jaw (526.0-526.2, 526.89)*
   > *oral soft tissue (528.4)*
   > *radicular (522.8)*

210.0 Lip
   Frenulum labii
   Lip (inner aspect) (mucosa) (vermilion border)

   Excludes: labial commissure (210.4)
   > *skin of lip (216.0)*

210.1 Tongue
   Lingual tonsil

210.2 Major salivary glands
   Gland:
   > parotid
   > sublingual
   > submandibular

   Excludes: benign neoplasms of minor salivary glands:
   > *NOS (210.4)*
   > *buccal mucosa (210.4)*
   > *lips (210.0)*
   > *palate (hard) (soft) (210.4)*
   > *tongue (210.1)*
   > *tonsil, palatine (210.5)*

210.3 Floor of mouth

210.4 Other and unspecified parts of mouth
Gingiva	Oral mucosa
Gum (upper) (lower)	Palate (hard) (soft)
Labial commissure	Uvula
Oral cavity NOS	

   Excludes: benign odontogenic neoplasms of bone (213.0-213.1)
   > *developmental odontogenic cysts (526.0)*
   > *mucosa of lips (210.0)*
   > *nasopharyngeal [posterior] [superior] surface of soft palate (210.7)*

210.5 Tonsil
   Tonsil (faucial) (palatine)

   Excludes: lingual tonsil (210.1)
   > *pharyngeal tonsil (210.7)*
   > *tonsillar:*
   > * fossa (210.6)*
   > * pillars (210.6)*

210.6 Other parts of oropharynx
   Branchial cleft or vestiges
   Epiglottis, anterior aspect
   Fauces NOS
   Mesopharynx NOS
   Tonsillar:
   > fossa
   > pillars
   Vallecula

   Excludes: epiglottis:
   > *NOS (212.1)*
   > *suprahyoid portion (212.1)*

210.7 Nasopharynx
Adenoid tissue	Pharyngeal tonsil
Lymphadenoid tissue	Posterior nasal septum

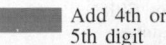 Add 4th or
5th digit

 Nonspecific
code

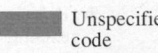 Unspecified
code

Manifestation
code

210.8 Hypopharynx
Arytenoid fold   Postcricoid region
Laryngopharynx   Pyriform fossa

210.9 Pharynx, unspecified
Throat NOS

211 Benign neoplasm of other parts of digestive system

211.0 Esophagus

211.1 Stomach
Body   ⎫
Cardia   ⎬ stomach   Cardiac orifice
Fundus   ⎭   Pylorus

211.2 Duodenum, jejunum, and ileum
Small intestine NOS

Excludes: *ampulla of Vater (211.5)*
              ileocecal valve (211.3)

211.3 Colon
Appendix   Ileocecal valve
Cecum   Large intestine NOS

Excludes: *rectosigmoid junction (211.4)*

211.4 Rectum and anal canal
Anal canal or sphincter   Rectosigmoid junction
Anus NOS

Excludes: *anus:*
                margin (216.5)
                skin (216.5)
                perianal skin (216.5)

211.5 Liver and biliary passages
Ampulla of Vater   Gallbladder
Common bile duct   Hepatic duct
Cystic duct   Sphincter of Oddi

211.6 Pancreas, except islets of Langerhans

211.7 Islets of Langerhans
Islet cell tumor

Use additional code, if desired, to identify any functional activity

211.8 Retroperitoneum and peritoneum
Mesentery   Omentum
Mesocolon   Retroperitoneal tissue

211.9 Other and unspecified site
Alimentary tract NOS   Intestinal tract NOS
Digestive system NOS   Intestine NOS
Gastrointestinal tract NOS Spleen, not elsewhere classified

212 Benign neoplasm of respiratory and intrathoracic organs

212.0 Nasal cavities, middle ear, and accessory sinuses
Cartilage of nose   Sinus:
Eustachian tube   ethmoidal
Nares   frontal
Septum of nose   maxillary
                                             sphenoidal

Excludes: *auditory canal (external) (216.2)*
                bone of:
                  ear (213.0)
                  nose [turbinates] (213.0)
                cartilage of ear (215.0)
                ear (external) (skin) (216.2)
                nose NOS (229.8)
                  skin (216.3)
                olfactory bulb (225.1)
                polyp of:
                  accessory sinus (471.8)
                  ear (385.30-385.35)
                  nasal cavity (471.0)
                posterior margin of septum and choanae (210.7)

● Code new   ▲ Revision of   ④ ⑤ Fourth or fifth
   to this edition   existing code   digit required

212.1 Larynx

Cartilage:	Epiglottis (suprahyoid portion) NOS
arytenoid	Glottis
cricoid	Vocal cords (false) (true)
cuneiform	
thyroid	

> Excludes: epiglottis, anterior aspect (210.6)
> polyp of vocal cord or larynx (478.4)

212.2 Trachea

212.3 Bronchus and lung

Carina   Hilus of lung

212.4 Pleura

212.5 Mediastinum

212.6 Thymus

212.7 Heart

> Excludes: great vessels (215.4)

212.8 Other specified sites

212.9 Site unspecified

Respiratory organ NOS
Upper respiratory tract NOS

> Excludes: intrathoracic NOS (229.8)
> thoracic NOS (229.8)

213 Benign neoplasm of bone and articular cartilage

Includes: cartilage (articular) (joint)
periosteum

> Excludes: cartilage of:
> ear (215.0)
> eyelid (215.0)
> larynx (212.1)
> nose (212.0)
> exostosis NOS (726.91)
> synovia (215.0-215.9)

213.0 Bones of skull and face

> Excludes: lower jaw bone (213.1)

213.1 Lower jaw bone

213.2 Vertebral column, excluding sacrum and coccyx

213.3 Ribs, sternum, and clavicle

213.4 Scapula and long bones of upper limb

213.5 Short bones of upper limb

213.6 Pelvic bones, sacrum, and coccyx

213.7 Long bones of lower limb

213.8 Short bones of lower limb

213.9 Bone and articular cartilage, site unspecified

214 Lipoma

Includes: angiolipoma
fibrolipoma
hibernoma
lipoma (fetal) (infiltrating) (intramuscular)
myelolipoma
myxolipoma

214.0 Skin and subcutaneous tissue of face

214.1 Other skin and subcutaneous tissue

214.2 Intrathoracic organs

214.3 Intra-abdominal organs

214.4 Spermatic cord

214.8 Other specified sites

214.9 Lipoma, unspecified site

	Add 4th or 5th digit		Nonspecific code		Unspecified code		Manifestation code

215 Other benign neoplasm of connective and other soft tissue

Includes:

blood vessel	peripheral, sympathetic, and parasympathetic nerves
bursa	and ganglia
fascia	synovia
ligament	tendon (sheath)
muscle	

Excludes: cartilage:
  articular (213.0-213.9)
  larynx (212.1)
  nose (212.0)
connective tissue of:
  breast (217)
  internal organ, except lipoma and hemangioma — code to benign neoplasm of
    the site
lipoma (214.0-214.9)

215.0 Head, face, and neck

215.2 Upper limb, including shoulder

215.3 Lower limb, including hip

215.4 Thorax

Excludes: heart (212.7)
  mediastinum (212.5)
  thymus (212.6)

215.5 Abdomen

Abdominal wall	Hypochondrium

215.6 Pelvis

Buttock	Inguinal region
Groin	Perineum

Excludes: uterine:
  leiomyoma (218.0-218.9)
  ligament, any (221.0)

215.7 Trunk, unspecified

Back NOS	Flank NOS

215.8 Other specified sites

215.9 Site unspecified

216 Benign neoplasm of skin

Includes:

blue nevus	pigmented nevus
dermatofibroma	syringoadenoma
hydrocystoma	syringoma

Excludes: skin of genital organs (221.0-222.9)

216.0 Skin of lip

Excludes: vermilion border of lip (210.0)

216.1 Eyelid, including canthus

Excludes: cartilage of eyelid (215.0)

216.2 Ear and external auditory canal

Auricle (ear)	External meatus
Auricular canal, external	Pinna

Excludes: cartilage of ear (215.0)

216.3 Skin of other and unspecified parts of face

Cheek, external	Nose, external
Eyebrow	Temple

216.4 Scalp and skin of neck

● Code new	▲ Revision of	④ ⑤ Fourth or fifth
to this edition	existing code	digit required

216.5 Skin of trunk, except scrotum
Axillary fold
Perianal skin
Skin of:
  abdominal wall
  anus
  back
  breast
Skin of:
  buttock
  chest wall
  groin
  perineum
Umbilicus

Excludes: *anal canal (211.4)*
    anus NOS (211.4)
    skin of scrotum (222.4)

216.6 Skin of upper limb, including shoulder

216.7 Skin of lower limb, including hip

216.8 Other specified sites of skin

216.9 Skin, site unspecified

217 Benign neoplasm of breast
Breast (male) (female)
  connective tissue
  glandular tissue
  soft parts

Excludes: *adenofibrosis (610.2)*
    benign cyst of breast (610.0)
    fibrocystic disease (610.1)
    skin of breast (216.5)

218 Uterine leiomyoma
Includes: fibroid (bleeding) (uterine)
    uterine:
      fibromyoma
      myoma

218.0 Submucous leiomyoma of uterus

218.1 Intramural leiomyoma of uterus
Interstitial leiomyoma of uterus

218.2 Subserous leiomyoma of uterus
Subperitoneal leiomyoma of uterus

218.9 Leiomyoma of uterus, unspecified

219 Other benign neoplasm of uterus

219.0 Cervix uteri

219.1 Corpus uteri
Endometrium   Myometrium
Fundus

219.8 Other specified parts of uterus

219.9 Uterus, part unspecified

220 Benign neoplasm of ovary
Use additional code, if desired, to identify any functional activity (256.0-256.1)

Excludes: *cyst:*
    corpus albicans (620.2)
    corpus luteum (620.1)
    endometrial (617.1)
    follicular (atretic) (620.0)
    graafian follicle (620.0)
    ovarian NOS (620.2)
    retention (620.2)

221 Benign neoplasm of other female genital organs
Includes: adenomatous polyp
    benign teratoma

Excludes: *cyst:*
    epoophoron (752.11)
    fimbrial (752.11)
    Gartner's duct (752.11)
    parovarian (752.11)

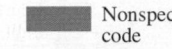 Add 4th or 5th digit   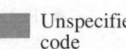 Nonspecific code   Unspecified code   Manifestation code

221.0 Fallopian tube and uterine ligaments
    Oviduct   Uterine ligament (broad) (round) (uterosacral)
    Parametrium   Uterine tube

221.1 Vagina

221.2 Vulva
    Clitoris
    External female genitalia NOS
    Greater vestibular [Bartholin's] gland
    Labia (majora) (minora)
    Pudendum

> Excludes: *Bartholin's (duct) (gland) cyst (616.2)*

221.8 Other specified sites of female genital organs

221.9 Female genital organ, site unspecified
    Female genitourinary tract NOS

222 Benign neoplasm of male genital organs

222.0 Testis

Use additional code, if desired, to identify any functional activity

222.1 Penis
    Corpus cavernosum   Prepuce
    Glans penis

222.2 Prostate

> Excludes: *adenomatous hyperplasia of prostate (600)*
>   *prostatic:*
>   *adenoma (600)*
>   *enlargement (600)*
>   *hypertrophy (600)*

222.3 Epididymis

222.4 Scrotum
    Skin of scrotum

222.8 Other specified sites of male genital organs
    Seminal vesicle   Spermatic cord

222.9 Male genital organ, site unspecified
    Male genitourinary tract NOS

223 Benign neoplasm of kidney and other urinary organs

223.0 Kidney, except pelvis
    Kidney NOS

> Excludes: *renal:*
>   *calyces (223.1)*
>   *pelvis (223.1)*

223.1 Renal pelvis

223.2 Ureter

> Excludes: *ureteric orifice of bladder (223.3)*

223.3 Bladder

223.8 Other specified sites of urinary organs
    223.81 Urethra

> Excludes: *urethral orifice of bladder (223.3)*

    223.89 Other
        Paraurethral glands

223.9 Urinary organ, site unspecified
    Urinary system NOS

224 Benign neoplasm of eye

> Excludes: *cartilage of eyelid (215.0)*
>   *eyelid (skin) (216.1)*
>   *optic nerve (225.1)*
>   *orbital bone (213.0)*

224.0 Eyeball, except conjunctiva, cornea, retina, and choroid
    Ciliary body   Sclera
    Iris   Uveal tract

● Code new   ▲ Revision of   ④ ⑤ Fourth or fifth
  to this edition   existing code   digit required

224.1 Orbit

> *Excludes:* bone of orbit (213.0)

224.2 Lacrimal gland

224.3 Conjunctiva

224.4 Cornea

224.5 Retina

> *Excludes:* hemangioma of retina (228.03)

224.6 Choroid

224.7 Lacrimal duct
    Lacrimal sac   Nasolacrimal duct

224.8 Other specified parts of eye

224.9 Eye, part unspecified

225 Benign neoplasm of brain and other parts of nervous system

> *Excludes:* hemangioma (228.02)
>   neurofibromatosis (237.7)
>   peripheral, sympathetic, and parasympathetic nerves and ganglia (215.0-215.9)
>   retrobulbar (224.1)

225.0 Brain

225.1 Cranial nerves

225.2 Cerebral meninges
    Meninges NOS   Meningioma (cerebral)

225.3 Spinal cord
    Cauda equina

225.4 Spinal meninges
    Spinal meningioma

225.8 Other specified sites of nervous system

225.9 Nervous system, part unspecified
    Nervous system (central) NOS

> *Excludes:* meninges NOS (225.2)

226 Benign neoplasm of thyroid glands
    Use additional code, if desired, to identify any functional activity

227 Benign neoplasm of other endocrine glands and related structures
    Use additional code, if desired, to identify any functional activity

> *Excludes:* ovary (220)
>   pancreas (211.6)
>   testis (222.0)

227.0 Adrenal gland
    Suprarenal gland

227.1 Parathyroid gland

227.3 Pituitary gland and craniopharyngeal duct (pouch)
    Craniobuccal pouch   Rathke's pouch
    Hypophysis   Sella turcica

227.4 Pineal gland
    Pineal body

227.5 Carotid body

227.6 Aortic body and other paraganglia
    Coccygeal body   Para-aortic body
    Glomus jugulare

227.8 Other

227.9 Endocrine gland, site unspecified

| | Add 4th or 5th digit | | Nonspecific code | | Unspecified code | | Manifestation code |

228 **Hemangioma and lymphangioma, any site**
    Includes: angioma (benign) (cavernous) (congenital) NOS
                cavernous nevus
                glomus tumor
                hemangioma (benign) (congenital)

    Excludes: *benign neoplasm of spleen, except hemangioma and lymphangioma (211.9)*
           glomus jugulare (227.6)
           nevus:
              NOS (216.0-216.9)
              blue or pigmented (216.0-216.9)
              vascular (757.32)

   228.0 **Hemangioma, any site**

     228.00 **Of unspecified site**

     228.01 **Of skin and subcutaneous tissue**

     228.02 **Of intracranial structures**

     228.03 **Of retina**

     228.04 **Of intra-abdominal structures**
         Peritoneum   Retroperitoneal tissue

     228.09 **Of other sites**
         Systemic angiomatosis

   228.1 **Lymphangioma, any site**
       Congenital lymphangioma   Lymphatic nevus

229 **Benign neoplasm of other and unspecified sites**

   229.0 **Lymph nodes**

     Excludes: *lymphangioma (228.1)*

   229.8 **Other specified sites**
       Intrathoracic NOS   Thoracic NOS

   229.9 **Site unspecified**

CARCINOMA IN SITU (230-234)

    Includes: Bowen's disease
                erythroplasia
                Queyrat's erythroplasia

    Excludes: *leukoplakia—see Alphabetic Index*

230 **Carcinoma in situ of digestive organs**

   230.0 **Lip, oral cavity, and pharynx**
       Gingiva   Oropharynx
       Hypopharynx   Salivary gland or duct
       Mouth [any part]   Tongue
       Nasopharynx

     Excludes: *aryepiglottic fold or interarytenoid fold, laryngeal aspect (231.0)*
           epiglottis:
              NOS (231.0)
              suprahyoid portion (231.0)
            skin of lip (232.0)

   230.1 **Esophagus**

   230.2 **Stomach**
       Body   Cardiac orifice
       Cardia   } of stomach   Pylorus
       Fundus

   230.3 **Colon**
       Appendix   Ileocecal valve
       Cecum   Large intestine NOS

     Excludes: *rectosigmoid junction (230.4)*

   230.4 **Rectum**
       Rectosigmoid junction

   230.5 **Anal canal**
       Anal sphincter

● Code new   ▲ Revision of   ④ ⑤ Fourth or fifth
  to this edition   existing code   digit required

230.6 Anus, unspecified

Excludes: *anus:*
> *margin (232.5)*
> *skin (232.5)*
> *perianal skin (232.5)*

230.7 Other and unspecified parts of intestine

Duodenum	Jejunum
Ileum	Small intestine NOS

Excludes: *ampulla of Vater (230.8)*

230.8 Liver and biliary system

Ampulla of Vater	Gallbladder
Common bile duct	Hepatic duct
Cystic duct	Sphincter of Oddi

230.9 Other and unspecified digestive organs

Digestive organ NOS	Pancreas
Gastrointestinal tract NOS	Spleen

231 Carcinoma in situ of respiratory system

231.0 Larynx

Cartilage:	Epiglottis:
arytenoid	NOS
cricoid	posterior surface
cuneiform	suprahyoid portion
thyroid	Vocal cords (false) (true)

Excludes: *aryepiglottic fold or interarytenoid fold:*
> *NOS (230.0)*
> *hypopharyngeal aspect (230.0)*
> *marginal zone (230.0)*

231.1 Trachea

231.2 Bronchus and lung

Carina	Hilus of lung

231.8 Other specified parts of respiratory system

Accessory sinuses	Nasal cavities
Middle ear	Pleura

Excludes: *ear (external) (skin) (232.2)*
> *nose NOS (234.8)*
> *skin (232.3)*

231.9 Respiratory system, part unspecified

Respiratory organ NOS

232 Carcinoma in situ of skin

Includes: pigment cells

232.0 Skin of lip

Excludes: *vermilion border of lip (230.0)*

232.1 Eyelid, including canthus

232.2 Ear and external auditory canal

232.3 Skin of other and unspecified parts of face

232.4 Scalp and skin of neck

232.5 Skin of trunk, except scrotum

Anus, margin	Skin of:
Axillary fold	breast
Perianal skin	buttock
Skin of:	chest wall
abdominal wall	groin
anus	perineum
back	Umbilicus

Excludes: *anal canal (230.5)*
> *anus NOS (230.6)*
> *skin of genital organs (233.3, 233.5-233.6)*

232.6 Skin of upper limb, including shoulder

232.7 Skin of lower limb, including hip

232.8 Other specified sites of skin

▮ Add 4th or 5th digit	▮ Nonspecific code	▮ Unspecified code	▮ Manifestation code

243 Congenital hypothyroidism
Congenital thyroid insufficiency
Cretinism (athyrotic) (endemic)
Use additional code to identify associated mental retardation

> Excludes: congenital (dyshormonogenic) goiter (246.1)

244 Acquired hypothyroidism
Includes: athyroidism (acquired)
hypothyroidism (acquired)
myxedema (adult) (juvenile)
thyroid (gland) insufficiency (acquired)

244.0 Postsurgical hypothyroidism

244.1 Other postablative hypothyroidism
Hypothyroidism following therapy, such as irradiation

244.2 Iodine hypothyroidism
Hypothyroidism resulting from administration or ingestion of iodide
Use additional E code to identify drug

244.3 Other iatrogenic hypothyroidism
Hypothyroidism resulting from:
P-aminosalicylic acid [PAS]
Phenylbutazone
Resorcinol
Iatrogenic hypothyroidism NOS
Use additional E code to identify drug

244.8 Other specified acquired hypothyroidism
Secondary hypothyroidism NEC

244.9 Unspecified hypothyroidism
Hypothyroidism
Myxedema } primary or NOS

245 Thyroiditis

245.0 Acute thyroiditis
Abscess of thyroid
Thyroiditis:
nonsuppurative, acute
pyogenic
suppurative
Use additional code to identify organism

245.1 Subacute thyroiditis
Thyroiditis: Thyroiditis:
de Quervain's   granulomatous
giant cell   viral

245.2 Chronic lymphocytic thyroiditis
Hashimoto's disease   Thyroiditis:
Struma lymphomatosa   autoimmune
lymphocytic (chronic)

245.3 Chronic fibrous thyroiditis
Struma fibrosa
Thyroiditis:
invasive (fibrous)
ligneous
Riedel's

245.4 Iatrogenic thyroiditis
Use additional code to identify cause

245.8 Other and unspecified chronic thyroiditis
Chronic thyroiditis:
NOS
nonspecific

245.9 Thyroiditis, unspecified
Thyroiditis NOS

246 Other disorders of thyroid

246.0 Disorders of thyrocalcitonin secretion
Hypersecretion of calcitonin or thyrocalcitonin

● Code new   ▲ Revision of   ④ ⑤ Fourth or fifth
to this edition   existing code   digit required

246.1 Dyshormonogenic goiter
Congenital (dyshormonogenic) goiter
Goiter due to enzyme defect in synthesis of thyroid hormone
Goitrous cretinism (sporadic)

246.2 Cyst of thyroid

Excludes: cystadenoma of thyroid (226)

246.3 Hemorrhage and infarction of thyroid

246.8 Other specified disorders of thyroid
Abnormality of   Hyper-TBG-nemia
   thyroid-binding globulin   Hypo-TBG-nemia
Atrophy of thyroid

246.9 Unspecified disorder of thyroid

DISEASES OF OTHER ENDOCRINE GLANDS (250-259)

⑤ **250 Diabetes mellitus**

Excludes: gestational diabetes (648.8)
hyperglycemia NOS (790.6)
neonatal diabetes mellitus (775.1)
nonclinical diabetes (790.2)

The following fifth-digit subclassification is for use with category 250:

0   **type II [non-insulin dependent type] [NIDDM type] [adult-onset type] or unspecified type, not stated as uncontrolled**

1   **type I [insulin dependent type] [IDDM] [juvenile type], not stated as uncontrolled**

2   **type II [non-insulin dependent type] [NIDDM type] [adult-onset type] or unspecified type, uncontrolled**

3   **type I [insulin dependent type] [IDDM] [juvenile type], uncontrolled**

250.0 Diabetes mellitus without mention of complication
Diabetes mellitus without mention of complication or manifestation classifiable to
250.1-250.9
Diabetes (mellitus) NOS

250.1 Diabetes with ketoacidosis
Diabetic:
  acidosis ⎫
  ketosis   ⎬ without mention of coma

☐ **250.2 Diabetes with hyperosmolarity**
Hyperosmolar (nonketotic) coma

☐ **250.3 Diabetes with other coma**
Diabetic coma (with ketoacidosis)
Diabetic hypoglycemic coma
Insulin coma NOS

Excludes: diabetes with hyperosmolar coma (250.2)

☐ **250.4 Diabetes with renal manifestations**
Use additional code to identify manifestation, as:
  diabetic:
    nephropathy NOS (583.81)
    nephrosis (581.81)
    intercapillary glomerulosclerosis (581.81)
    Kimmelstiel-Wilson syndrome (581.81)

☐ **250.5 Diabetes with ophthalmic manifestations**
Use additional code to identify manifestation, as:
  diabetic:
    blindness (369.00-369.9)
    cataract (366.41)
    glaucoma (365.44)
    retinal edema (362.83)
    retinopathy (362.01-362.02)

| | Add 4th or 5th digit | | Nonspecific code | | Unspecified code | |

253.9 Unspecified
Dyspituitarism

254 Diseases of thymus gland

Excludes: *aplasia or dysplasia with immunodeficiency (279.2)*
hypoplasia with immunodeficiency (279.2)
myasthenia gravis (358.0)

254.0 Persistent hyperplasia of thymus
Hypertrophy of thymus

254.1 Abscess of thymus

254.8 Other specified diseases of thymus gland
Atrophy ⎫
Cyst ⎬ of thymus

Excludes *thymoma (212.6)*

254.9 Unspecified disease of thymus gland

255 Disorders of adrenal glands
Includes: the listed conditions whether the basic disorder is in the adrenals or is pituitary-induced

255.0 Cushing's syndrome
Adrenal hyperplasia due to   Ectopic ACTH syndrome
  excess ACTH   Iatrogenic syndrome of excess cortisol
Cushing's syndrome: Overproduction of cortisol
  NOS
  iatrogenic
  idiopathic
  pituitary-dependent
Use additional E code to identify cause, if drug-induced

Excludes: *congenital adrenal hyperplasia (255.2)*

255.1 Hyperaldosteronism
Aldosteronism (primary)   Bartter's syndrome
(secondary)   Conn's syndrome

255.2 Adrenogenital disorders
Adrenogenital syndromes, virilizing or feminizing, whether acquired or associated with congenital adrenal hyperplasia consequent on inborn enzyme defects in hormone synthesis
Achard-Thiers syndrome
Congenital adrenal hyperplasia
Female adrenal pseudohermaphroditism
Male:
  macrogenitosomia praecox
  sexual precocity with adrenal hyperplasia
Virilization (female) (suprarenal)

Excludes: *adrenal hyperplasia due to excess ACTH (255.0)*
isosexual virilization (256.4)

255.3 Other corticoadrenal overactivity
Acquired benign adrenal androgenic overactivity
Overproduction of ACTH

255.4 Corticoadrenal insufficiency
Addisonian crisis   Adrenal:
Addison's disease NOS   crisis
Adrenal: hemorrhage
  atrophy (autoimmune)   infarction
  calcification   insufficiency NOS

Excludes: *tuberculous Addison's disease (017.6)*

255.5 Other adrenal hypofunction
Adrenal medullary insufficiency

Excludes: *Waterhouse-Friderichsen syndrome (meningococcal) (036.3)*

255.6 Medulloadrenal hyperfunction
Catecholamine secretion by pheochromocytoma

255.8 Other specified disorders of adrenal glands
Abnormality of cortisol-binding globulin

255.9 Unspecified disorder of adrenal glands

● Code new   ▲ Revision of   ④ ⑤ Fourth or fifth
  to this edition   existing code   digit required

256 Ovarian dysfunction

256.0 Hyperestrogenism

256.1 Other ovarian hyperfunction
Hypersecretion of ovarian androgens

256.2 Postablative ovarian failure
Ovarian failure:
iatrogenic
postirradiation
postsurgical

256.3 Other ovarian failure
Premature menopause NOS
Primary ovarian failure

256.4 Polycystic ovaries
Isosexual virilization   Stein-Leventhal syndrome

256.8 Other ovarian dysfunction

256.9 Unspecified ovarian dysfunction

257 Testicular dysfunction

257.0 Testicular hyperfunction
Hypersecretion of testicular hormones

257.1 Postablative testicular hypofunction
Testicular hypofunction:
iatrogenic
postirradiation
postsurgical

257.2 Other testicular hypofunction
Defective biosynthesis of testicular androgen
Eunuchoidism:
NOS
hypogonadotropic
Failure:
Leydig's cell, adult
seminiferous tubule, adult
Testicular hypogonadism

Excludes: azoospermia (606.0)

257.8 Other testicular dysfunction
Goldberg-Maxwell syndrome
Male pseudohermaphroditism with testicular feminization
Testicular feminization

257.9 Unspecified testicular dysfunction

258 Polyglandular dysfunction and related disorders

258.0 Polyglandular activity in multiple endocrine adenomatosis
Wermer's syndrome

258.1 Other combinations of endocrine dysfunction
Lloyd's syndrome   Schmidt's syndrome

258.8 Other specified polyglandular dysfunction

258.9 Polyglandular dysfunction, unspecified

259 Other endocrine disorders

259.0 Delay in sexual development and puberty, not elsewhere classified
Delayed puberty

259.1 Precocious sexual development and puberty, not elsewhere classified
Sexual precocity:
NOS
constitutional
cryptogenic
idiopathic

259.2 Carcinoid syndrome
Hormone secretion by carcinoid tumors

259.3 Ectopic hormone secretion, not elsewhere classified
Ectopic:
antidiuretic hormone secretion [ADH]
hyperparathyroidism

Excludes: ectopic ACTH syndrome (255.0)

103

| | Add 4th or 5th digit | | Nonspecific code | | Unspecified code | | Manifestation code |

259.4 Dwarfism, not elsewhere classified
Dwarfism:
NOS
constitutional

Excludes: dwarfism:

achondroplastic (756.4)
intrauterine (759.7)
nutritional (263.2)
pituitary (253.3)
renal (588.0)
progeria (259.8)

259.8 Other specified endocrine disorders
Pineal gland dysfunction   Werner's syndrome
Progeria

259.9 Unspecified endocrine disorder
Disturbance: Infantilism NOS
endocrine NOS
hormone NOS

NUTRITIONAL DEFICIENCIES (260-269)

Excludes: deficiency anemias (280.0-281.9)

260 Kwashiorkor
Nutritional edema with dyspigmentation of skin and hair

261 Nutritional marasmus
Nutritional atrophy   Severe malnutrition NOS
Severe calorie deficiency

262 Other severe protein-calorie malnutrition
Nutritional edema without mention of dyspigmentation of skin and hair

263 Other and unspecified protein-calorie malnutrition

263.0 Malnutrition of moderate degree

263.1 Malnutrition of mild degree

263.2 Arrested development following protein-calorie malnutrition
Nutritional dwarfism
Physical retardation due to malnutrition

263.8 Other protein-calorie malnutrition

263.9 Unspecified protein-calorie malnutrition
Dystrophy due to malnutrition
Malnutrition (calorie) NOS

Excludes: nutritional deficiency NOS (269.9)

264 Vitamin A deficiency

264.0 With conjunctival xerosis

264.1 With conjunctival xerosis and Bitot's spot
Bitot's spot in the young child

264.2 With corneal xerosis

264.3 With corneal ulceration and xerosis

264.4 With keratomalacia

264.5 With night blindness

264.6 With xerophthalmic scars of cornea

264.7 Other ocular manifestations of vitamin A deficiency
Xerophthalmia due to vitamin A deficiency

264.8 Other manifestations of vitamin A deficiency
Follicular keratosis } due to vitamin A deficiency
Xeroderma

264.9 Unspecified vitamin A deficiency
Hypovitaminosis A NOS

265 Thiamine and niacin deficiency states

265.0 Beriberi

265.1 Other and unspecified manifestations of thiamine deficiency
Other vitamin B_1 deficiency states

● Code new to this edition   ▲ Revision of existing code   ④ ⑤ Fourth or fifth digit required

265.2 Pellagra
Deficiency:
   niacin (-tryptophan)
   nicotinamide
   nicotinic acid
   vitamin PP
Pellagra (alcoholic)

266 Deficiency of B-complex components

266.0 Ariboflavinosis
Riboflavin [vitamin B_2] deficiency

266.1 Vitamin B_6 deficiency
Deficiency: Vitamin B_6 deficiency syndrome
   pyridoxal
   pyridoxamine
   pyridoxine

Excludes: *vitamin B_6-responsive sideroblastic anemia (285.0)*

266.2 Other B-complex deficiencies
Deficiency:
   cyanocobalamin
   folic acid
   vitamin B_{12}

Excludes: *combined system disease with anemia (281.0-281.1)*
         deficiency anemias (281.0-281.9)
         subacute degeneration of spinal cord with anemia (281.0-281.1)

266.9 Unspecified vitamin B deficiency

267 Ascorbic acid deficiency
Deficiency of vitamin C   Scurvy

Excludes: *scorbutic anemia (281.8)*

268 Vitamin D deficiency

Excludes: *vitamin D-resistant:*
         osteomalacia (275.3)
         rickets (275.3)

268.0 Rickets, active

Excludes: *celiac rickets (579.0)*
         renal rickets (588.0)

268.1 Rickets, late effect
Any condition specified as due to rickets and stated to be a late effect or sequela of rickets

Use additional code to identify the nature of late effect

268.2 Osteomalacia, unspecified

268.9 Unspecified vitamin D deficiency
Avitaminosis D

269 Other nutritional deficiencies

269.0 Deficiency of vitamin K

Excludes: *deficiency of coagulation factor due to vitamin K deficiency (286.7)*
         vitamin K deficiency of newborn (776.0)

269.1 Deficiency of other vitamins
Deficiency:
   vitamin E
   vitamin P

269.2 Unspecified vitamin deficiency
Multiple vitamin deficiency NOS

Add 4th or 5th digit   Nonspecific code   Unspecified code   Manifestation code

269.3 Mineral deficiency, not elsewhere classified
Deficiency:
calcium, dietary
iodine

Excludes: *deficiency:*
calcium NOS (275.4)
potassium (276.8)
sodium (276.1)

269.8 Other nutritional deficiency

Excludes: *failure to thrive (783.4)*
feeding problems (783.3)
newborn (779.3)

269.9 Unspecified nutritional deficiency

OTHER METABOLIC AND IMMUNITY DISORDERS (270-279)

Use additional code to identify any associated mental retardation

270 Disorders of amino-acid transport and metabolism

Excludes: *abnormal findings without manifest disease (790.0-796.9)*
disorders of purine and pyrimidine metabolism (277.1-277.2)
gout (274.0-274.9)

270.0 Disturbances of amino-acid transport
Cystinosis
Cystinuria
Fanconi (-de Toni) (-Debré) syndrome
Glycinuria (renal)
Hartnup disease

270.1 Phenylketonuria [PKU]
Hyperphenylalaninemia

270.2 Other disturbances of aromatic amino-acid metabolism

Albinism	Hypertyrosinemia
Alkaptonuria	Indicanuria
Alkaptonuric ochronosis	Kynureninase defects
Disturbances of metabolism	Oasthouse urine disease
of tyrosine and tryptophan	Ochronosis
Homogentisic acid defects	Tyrosinosis
Hydroxykynureninuria	Tyrosinuria
	Waardenburg syndrome

Excludes: *vitamin B6-deficiency syndrome (266.1)*

270.3 Disturbances of branched-chain amino-acid metabolism
Disturbances of metabolism of leucine, isoleucine, and valine
Hypervalinemia
Intermittent branched-chain ketonuria
Leucine-induced hypoglycemia
Leucinosis
Maple syrup urine disease

270.4 Disturbances of sulphur-bearing amino-acid metabolism
Cystathioninemia
Cystathioninuria
Disturbances of metabolism of methionine, homocystine, and cystathionine
Homocystinuria
Hypermethioninemia
Methioninemia

270.5 Disturbances of histidine metabolism

Carnosinemia	Hyperhistidinemia
Histidinemia	Imidazole aminoaciduria

270.6 Disorders of urea cycle metabolism
Argininosuccinic aciduria
Citrullinemia
Disorders of metabolism of ornithine, citrulline, argininosuccinic acid, arginine, and
ammonia
Hyperammonemia
Hyperornithinemia

● Code new
to this edition
▲ Revision of
existing code
④ ⑤ Fourth or fifth
digit required

270.7 Other disturbances of straight-chain amino-acid metabolism

Glucoglycinuria
Glycinemia (with methyl-
  malonic acidemia)
Hyperglycinemia
Hyperlysinemia
Pipecolic acidemia

Saccharopinuria
Other disturbances of metabolism of glycine, threonine,
  serine, glutamine, and lysine

270.8 Other specified disorders of amino-acid metabolism

Alaninemia
Ethanolaminuria
Glycoprolinuria
Hydroxyprolinemia
Hyperprolinemia

Iminoacidopathy
Prolinemia
Prolinuria
Sarcosinemia

270.9 Unspecified disorder of amino-acid metabolism

271 Disorders of carbohydrate transport and metabolism

Excludes: *abnormality of secretion of glucagon (251.4)*
         diabetes mellitus (250.0-250.9)
         hypoglycemia NOS (251.2)
         mucopolysaccharidosis (277.5)

271.0 Glycogenosis

Amylopectinosis
Glucose-6-phosphatase
  deficiency
Glycogen storage disease

McArdle's disease
Pompe's disease
von Gierke's disease

271.1 Galactosemia

Galactose-1-phosphate uridyl transferase deficiency
Galactosuria

271.2 Hereditary fructose intolerance

Essential benign fructosuria
Fructosemia

271.3 Intestinal disaccharidase deficiencies and disaccharide malabsorption

Intolerance or malabsorption (congenital) (of):
  glucose-galactose
  lactose
  sucrose-isomaltose

271.4 Renal glycosuria

Renal diabetes

271.8 Other specified disorders of carbohydrate transport and metabolism

Essential benign pentosuria
Fucosidosis
Glycolic aciduria
Hyperoxaluria (primary)

Mannosidosis
Oxalosis
Xylosuria
Xylulosuria

271.9 Unspecified disorder of carbohydrate transport and metabolism

272 Disorders of lipoid metabolism

Excludes: *localized cerebral lipidoses (330.1)*

272.0 Pure hypercholesterolemia

Familial hypercholesterolemia
Fredrickson Type IIa hyperlipoproteinemia
Hyperbetalipoproteinemia
Hyperlipidemia, Group A
Low-density-lipoid-type [LDL] hyperlipoproteinemia

272.1 Pure hyperglyceridemia

Endogenous hyperglyceridemia
Frederickson Type IV hyperlipoproteinemia
Hyperlipidemia, Group B
Hyperprebetalipoproteinemia
Hypertriglyceridemia, essential
Very-low-density-lipoid-type [VLDL] hyperlipoproteinemia

272.2 Mixed hyperlipidemia

Broad- or floating-betalipoproteinemia
Fredrickson Type IIb or III hyperlipoproteinemia
Hypercholesterolemia with endogenous hyperglyceridemia
Hyperbetalipoproteinemia with prebetalipoproteinemia
Tubo-eruptive xanthoma
Xanthoma tuberosum

| | Add 4th or 5th digit | | Nonspecific code | | Unspecified code | Manifestation code |

272.3 Hyperchylomicronemia
Bürger-Grütz syndrome
Fredrickson type I or V
hyperlipoproteinemia
Hyperlipidemia, Group D
Mixed hyperglyceridemia

272.4 Other and unspecified hyperlipidemia
Alpha-lipoproteinemia
Combined hyperlipidemia
Hyperlipidemia NOS
Hyperlipoproteinemia NOS

272.5 Lipoprotein deficiencies
Abetalipoproteinemia
Bassen-Kornzweig syndrome
High-density lipoid deficiency
Hypoalphalipoproteinemia
Hypobetalipoproteinemia (familial)

272.6 Lipodystrophy
Barraquer-Simons disease
Progressive lipodystrophy

Use additional E code to identify cause, if iatrogenic

Excludes: intestinal lipodystrophy (040.2)

272.7 Lipidoses
Chemically-induced lipidosis
Disease:
  Anderson's
  Fabry's
  Gaucher's
  I cell [mucolipidosis I]
  lipoid storage NOS
  Neimann-Pick
  pseudo-Hurler's or
    mucolipidosis III
Disease:
  triglyceride storage, Type I or II
  Wolman's or triglyceride storage, Type III
Mucolipidosis II
Primary familial xanthomatosis

Excludes: cerebral lipidoses (330.1)
Tay-Sachs disease (330.1)

272.8 Other disorders of lipoid metabolism
Hoffa's disease or liposynovitis prepatellaris
Launois-Bensaude's lipomatosis
Lipoid dermatoarthritis

272.9 Unspecified disorder of lipoid metabolism

273 Disorders of plasma protein metabolism

Excludes: agammaglobulinemia and hypogammaglobulinemia (279.0 -279.2)
coagulation defects (286.0-286.9)
hereditary hemolytic anemias (282.0-282.9)

273.0 Polyclonal hypergammaglobulinemia
Hypergammaglobulinemic purpura:
  benign primary
  Waldenström's

273.1 Monoclonal paraproteinemia
Benign monoclonal hypergammaglobulinemia [BMH]
Monoclonal gammopathy:
  NOS
  associated with lymphoplasmacytic dyscrasias
  benign
Paraproteinemia:
  benign (familial)
  secondary to malignant or inflammatory disease

273.2 Other paraproteinemias
Cryoglobulinemic:
  purpura
  vasculitis
Mixed cryoglobulinemia

273.3 Macroglobulinemia
Macroglobulinemia (idiopathic) (primary)
Waldenström's macroglobulinemia

273.8 Other disorders of plasma protein metabolism
Abnormality of transport protein
Bisalbuminemia

273.9 Unspecified disorder of plasma protein metabolism

● Code new
to this edition
▲ Revision of
existing code
④ ⑤ Fourth or fifth
digit required

274 Gout

Excludes: lead gout (984.0-984.9)

274.0 Gouty arthropathy

274.1 Gouty nephropathy

274.10 Gouty nephropathy, unspecified

274.11 Uric acid nephrolithiasis

274.19 Other

274.8 Gout with other specified manifestations

274.81 Gouty tophi of ear

274.82 Gouty tophi of other sites
Gouty tophi of heart

274.89 Other
Use additional code to identify manifestations, as:
gouty:
iritis (364.11)
neuritis (357.4)

274.9 Gout, unspecified

275 Disorders of mineral metabolism

Excludes: abnormal findings without manifest disease (790.0-796.9)

275.0 Disorders of iron metabolism

Bronzed diabetes	Pigmentary cirrhosis (of liver)
Hemochromatosis	

Excludes: anemia:
iron deficiency (280.0-280.9)
sideroblastic (285.0)

275.1 Disorders of copper metabolism
Hepatolenticular degeneration
Wilson's disease

275.2 Disorders of magnesium metabolism

Hypermagnesemia	Hypomagnesemia

275.3 Disorders of phosphorus metabolism
Familial hypophosphatemia
Hypophosphatasia
Vitamin D-resistant:
osteomalacia
rickets

275.4 Disorders of calcium metabolism

Calcinosis	Nephrocalcinosis
Hypercalcemia	Pseudohypoparathyroidism
Hypercalcinuria	Pseudo-pseudohypoparathyroidism

Excludes: parathyroid disorders (252.0-252.9)
vitamin D deficiency (268.0-268.9)

275.8 Other specified disorders of mineral metabolism

275.9 Unspecified disorder of mineral metabolism

276 Disorders of fluid, electrolyte, and acid-base balance

Excludes: diabetes insipidus (253.5)
familial periodic paralysis (359.3)

276.0 Hyperosmolality and/or hypernatremia

Sodium [Na] excess	Sodium [Na] overload

276.1 Hyposmolality and/or hyponatremia
Sodium [Na] deficiency

276.2 Acidosis
Acidosis:
NOS
lactic
metabolic
respiratory

Excludes: diabetic acidosis (250.1)

	Add 4th or 5th digit		Nonspecific code		Unspecified code		Manifestation code

276.3 Alkalosis
    Alkalosis:
      NOS
      metabolic
      respiratory

276.4 Mixed acid-base balance disorder
    Hypercapnia with mixed acid-base disorder

276.5 Volume depletion
    Dehydration
    Depletion of volume of plasma or extracellular fluid
    Hypovolemia

    Excludes: *hypovolemic shock:*
        postoperative (998.0)
        traumatic (958.4)

276.6 Fluid overload
    Fluid retention

    Excludes: *ascites (789.5)*
        localized edema (782.3)

276.7 Hyperpotassemia
    Hyperkalemia
    Potassium [K]:
      excess
      intoxication
      overload

276.8 Hypopotassemia
    Hypokalemia   Potassium [K] deficiency

276.9 Electrolyte and fluid disorders not elsewhere classified
    Electrolyte imbalance   Hypochloremia
    Hyperchloremia

    Excludes: *electrolyte imbalance:*
        associated with hyperemesis gravidarum (643.1)
        complicating labor and delivery (669.0)
        following abortion and ectopic or molar pregnancy (634-638 with .4, 639.4)

277 Other and unspecified disorders of metabolism

277.0 Cystic fibrosis
    Fibrocystic disease of the pancreas
    Mucoviscidosis

    277.00 Without mention of meconium ileus

    277.01 With meconium ileus
        Meconium:
          ileus (of newborn)
          obstruction of intestine in mucoviscidosis

277.1 Disorders of porphyrin metabolism
    Hematoporphyria   Porphyrinuria
    Hematoporphyrinuria   Protocoproporphyria
    Hereditary coproporphyria   Protoporphyria
    Porphyria   Pyrroloporphyria

277.2 Other disorders of purine and pyrimidine metabolism
    Hypoxanthine-guanine-phosphoribosyltransferase deficiency [HG-PRT deficiency]
    Lesch-Nyhan syndrome
    Xanthinuria

    Excludes: *gout (274.0-274.9)*
        orotic aciduric anemia (281.4)

277.3 Amyloidosis
    Amyloidosis:
      NOS
      inherited systemic
      nephropathic
      neuropathic (Portuguese) (Swiss)
      secondary
    Benign paroxysmal peritonitis
    Familial Mediterranean fever
    Hereditary cardiac amyloidosis

● Code new to this edition   ▲ Revision of existing code   ④ ⑤ Fourth or fifth digit required

277.4 Disorders of bilirubin excretion

Hyperbilirubinemia: Syndrome:
  congenital   Crigler-Najjar
  constitutional   Dubin-Johnson
                      Gilbert's
                      Rotor's

Excludes: hyperbilirubinemias specific to the perinatal period (774.0-774.7)

277.5 Mucopolysaccharidosis

Gargoylism   Morquio-Brailsford disease
Hunter's syndrome   Osteochondrodystrophy
Hurler's syndrome   Sanfilippo's syndrome
Lipochondrodystrophy Scheie's syndrome
Maroteaux-Lamy syndrome

277.6 Other deficiencies of circulating enzymes

Alpha 1-antitrypsin deficiency
Hereditary angioedema

277.8 Other specified disorders of metabolism

Hand-Schüller-Christian disease
Histiocytosis (acute) (chronic)
Histiocytosis X (chronic)

Excludes: histiocytosis:
    acute differentiated progressive (202.5)
    X, acute (progressive) (202.5)

277.9 Unspecified disorder of metabolism

Enzymopathy NOS

278 Obesity and other hyperalimentation

Excludes: hyperalimentation NOS (783.6)
    poisoning by vitamins NOS (963.5)
    polyphagia (783.6)

278.0 Obesity

Excludes: adiposogenital dystrophy (253.8)
    obesity of endocrine origin NOS (259.9)

    278.00 Obesity, unspecified

        Obesity NOS

    278.01 Morbid obesity

278.1 Localized adiposity

Fat pad

278.2 Hypervitaminosis A

278.3 Hypercarotinemia

278.4 Hypervitaminosis D

278.8 Other hyperalimentation

279 Disorders involving the immune mechanism

279.0 Deficiency of humoral immunity

    279.00 Hypogammaglobulinemia, unspecified

        Agammaglobulinemia NOS

    279.01 Selective IgA immunodeficiency

    279.02 Selective IgM immunodeficiency

    279.03 Other selective immunoglobulin deficiencies

        Selective deficiency of IgG

    279.04 Congenital hypogammaglobulinemia

        Agammaglobulinemia:
          Bruton's type
          X-linked

    279.05 Immunodeficiency with increased IgM

        Immunodeficiency with hyper-IgM:
          autosomal recessive
          X-linked

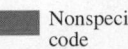 Add 4th or 5th digit   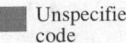 Nonspecific code   Unspecified code   Manifestation code

    279.06 **Common variable immunodeficiency**
Dysgammaglobulinemia (acquired) (congenital) (primary)
Hypogammaglobulinemia:
  acquired primary
  congenital non-sex-linked
  sporadic

    `279.09` **Other**
Transient hypogammaglobulinemia of infancy

279.1 **Deficiency of cell-mediated immunity**

    `279.10` **Immunodeficiency with predominant T-cell defect, unspecified**

    279.11 **DiGeorge's syndrome**
Pharyngeal pouch syndrome
Thymic hypoplasia

    279.12 **Wiskott-Aldrich syndrome**

    279.13 **Nezelof's syndrome**
Cellular immunodeficiency with abnormal immunoglobulin deficiency

    `279.19` **Other**

  Excludes: *ataxia-telangiectasia (334.8)*

279.2 **Combined immunity deficiency**
Agammaglobulinemia:
  autosomal recessive
  Swiss-type
  x-linked recessive
Severe combined immunodeficiency [SCID]
Thymic:
  alymphoplasia
  aplasia or dysplasia with immunodeficiency

  Excludes: *thymic hypoplasia (279.11)*

`279.3` **Unspecified immunity deficiency**

279.4 **Autoimmune disease, not elsewhere classified**
Autoimmune disease NOS

  Excludes: *transplant failure or rejection (996.80-996.89)*

`279.8` **Other specified disorders involving the immune mechanism**
Single complement [C_1-C_9] deficiency or dysfunction

`279.9` **Unspecified disorder of immune mechanism**

   ● Code new
     to this edition   ▲ Revision of
                   existing code   ④ ⑤ Fourth or fifth
                                             digit required

4. **DISEASES OF THE BLOOD AND BLOOD-FORMING ORGANS (280-289)**

Excludes: *anemia complicating pregnancy or the puerperium (648.2)*

280 **Iron deficiency anemias**
Includes: anemia:
  asiderotic
  hypochromic-microcytic
  sideropenic

Excludes: *familial microcytic anemia (282.4)*

280.0 Secondary to blood loss (chronic)
Normocytic anemia due to blood loss

Excludes: *acute posthemorrhagic anemia (285.1)*

280.1 Secondary to inadequate dietary iron intake

280.8 Other specified iron deficiency anemias
Paterson-Kelly syndrome
Plummer-Vinson syndrome
Sideropenic dysphagia

280.9 Iron deficiency anemia, unspecified
Anemia:
  achlorhydric
  chlorotic
  idiopathic hypochromic
  iron [Fe] deficiency NOS

281 **Other deficiency anemias**

281.0 Pernicious anemia
Anemia: Congenital intrinsic factor [Castle's] deficiency
  Addison's
  Biermer's
  congenital pernicious

Excludes: *combined system disease without mention of anemia (266.2)*
  subacute degeneration of spinal cord without mention of anemia (266.2)

281.1 Other vitamin B_{12} deficiency anemia
Anemia:
  vegan's
  vitamin B_{12} deficiency (dietary)
  due to selective vitamin B_{12} malabsorption with proteinuria
Syndrome:
  Imerslund's
  Imerslund-Gräsbeck

Excludes: *combined system disease without mention of anemia (266.2)*
  subacute degeneration of spinal cord without mention of anemia (266.2)

281.2 Folate-deficiency anemia
Congenital folate malabsorption
Folate or folic acid deficiency anemia:
  NOS
  dietary
  drug-induced
Goat's milk anemia
Nutritional megaloblastic anemia (of infancy)
Use additional E code, if desired, to identify drug

281.3 Other specified megaloblastic anemias not elsewhere classified
Combined B_{12} and folate-deficiency anemia
Refractory megaloblastic anemia

281.4 Protein-deficiency anemia
Amino-acid-deficiency anemia

281.8 Anemia associated with other specified nutritional deficiency
Scorbutic anemia

281.9 Unspecified deficiency anemia
Anemia: Anemia:
  dimorphic   nutritional NOS
  macrocytic   simple chronic
  megaloblastic NOS

| | Add 4th or 5th digit | | Nonspecific code | | Unspecified code | | Manifestation code |

282 Hereditary hemolytic anemias

282.0 Hereditary spherocytosis
Acholuric (familial) jaundice
Congenital hemolytic anemia (spherocytic)
Congenital spherocytosis
Minkowski-Chauffard syndrome
Spherocytosis (familial)

Excludes: hemolytic anemia of newborn (773.0-773.5)

282.1 Hereditary elliptocytosis
Elliptocytosis (congenital)
Ovalocytosis (congenital) (hereditary)

282.2 Anemias due to disorders of glutathione metabolism
Anemia:
6-phosphogluconic dehydrogenase deficiency
enzyme deficiency, drug-induced
erythrocytic glutathione deficiency
glucose-6-phosphate dehydrogenase [G-6-PD] deficiency
glutathione-reductase deficiency
hemolytic nonspherocytic (hereditary), type I
Disorder of pentose phosphate pathway
Favism

282.3 Other hemolytic anemias due to enzyme deficiency
Anemia:
hemolytic nonspherocytic (hereditary), type II
hexokinase deficiency
pyruvate kinase [PK] deficiency
triosephosphate isomerase deficiency

282.4 Thalassemias
Cooley's anemia
Hereditary leptocytosis
Mediterranean anemia (with other hemoglobinopathy)
Microdrepanocytosis
Sickle-cell thalassemia
Thalassemia (alpha) (beta) (intermedia) (major) (minima) (minor) (mixed) (trait) (with other hemoglobinopathy)
Thalassemia-Hb-S disease

Excludes: sickle-cell:
anemia (282.60-282.69)
trait (282.5)

282.5 Sickle-cell trait
Hb-AS genotype   Heterozygous:
Hemoglobin S [Hb-S] trait   hemoglobin S
                                   Hb-S

Excludes: that with other hemoglobinopathy (282.60-282.69)
that with thalassemia (282.4)

282.6 Sickle-cell anemia

Excludes: sickle-cell thalassemia (282.4)
sickle-cell trait (282.5)

282.60 Sickle-cell anemia, unspecified

282.61 Hb-S disease without mention of crisis

282.62 Hb-S disease with mention of crisis
Sickle-cell crisis NOS

282.63 Sickle-cell/Hb-C disease
Hb-S/Hb-C disease

282.69 Other
Disease: Disease:
Hb-S/Hb-D   sickle-cell/Hb-D
Hb-S/Hb-E   sickle-cell/Hb-E

● Code new
to this edition
▲ Revision of
existing code
④ ⑤ Fourth or fifth
digit required

282.7 **Other hemoglobinopathies**
Abnormal hemoglobin NOS
Congenital Heinz-body anemia
Disease:
Hb-Bart's
hemoglobin C [Hb-C]
hemoglobin D [Hb-D]
hemoglobin E [Hb-E]
hemoglobin Zurich [Hb-Zurich]
Hemoglobinopathy NOS
Hereditary persistence of fetal hemoglobin [HPFH]
Unstable hemoglobin hemolytic disease

Excludes: *familial polycythemia (289.6)*
hemoglobin M [Hb-M] disease (289.7)
high-oxygen-affinity hemoglobin (289.0)

282.8 **Other specified hereditary hemolytic anemias**
Stomatocytosis

282.9 **Hereditary hemolytic anemia, unspecified**
Hereditary hemolytic anemia NOS

283 Acquired hemolytic anemias

283.0 **Autoimmune hemolytic anemias**
Autoimmune hemolytic anemias (cold type) (warm type)
Chronic cold hemagglutinin disease
Cold agglutinin disease or hemoglobinuria
Hemolytic anemia:
cold type (secondary) (symptomatic)
drug-induced
warm type (secondary) (symptomatic)
Use additional E code, if desired, to identify cause, if drug-induced

Excludes: *Evans' syndrome (287.3)*
hemolytic disease of newborn (773.0-773.5)

283.1 **Non-autoimmune hemolytic anemias**

283.10 **Non-autoimmune hemolytic anemia, unspecified**

283.11 **Hemolytic-uremic syndrome**

283.19 **Other non-autoimmune hemolytic anemias**
Hemolytic anemia:
mechanical
microangiopathic
toxic
Use additional E code, if desired, to identify cause

283.2 **Hemoglobinuria due to hemolysis from external causes**
Acute intravascular hemolysis
Hemoglobinuria:
from exertion
march
paroxysmal (cold) (nocturnal)
due to other hemolysis
Marchiafava-Micheli syndrome
Use additional E code, if desired, to identify cause

283.9 **Acquired hemolytic anemia, unspecified**
Acquired hemolytic anemia NOS
Chronic idiopathic hemolytic anemia

284 Aplastic anemia

284.0 **Constitutional aplastic anemia**
Aplasia, (pure) red cell: Familial hypoplastic anemia
congenital   Fanconi's anemia
of infants   Pancytopenia with malformations
primary
Blackfan-Diamond syndrome

| | Add 4th or 5th digit | | Nonspecific code | | Unspecified code | | Manifestation code |

286.9 **Other and unspecified coagulation defects**
Defective coagulation NOS
Deficiency, coagulation factor NOS
Delay, coagulation
Disorder:
  coagulation
  hemostasis

Excludes: *abnormal coagulation profile (790.92)*
hemorrhagic disease of newborn (776.0)
that complicating:
  abortion (634-638 with .1, 639.1)
  pregnancy or the puerperium (641.3, 666.3)

287 **Purpura and other hemorrhagic conditions**

Excludes: *hemorrhagic thrombocythemia (238.7)*
purpura fulminans (286.6)

287.0 **Allergic purpura**
Peliosis rheumatica
Purpura:
  anaphylactoid
  autoimmune
  Henoch's
Purpura:
  nonthrombocytopenic:
    hemorrhagic
    idiopathic
    rheumatica
    Schönlein-Henoch
    vascular
Vasculitis, allergic

Excludes: *hemorrhagic purpura (287.3)*
purpura annularis telangiectodes (709.1)

287.1 **Qualitative platelet defects**
Thrombasthenia (hemorrhagic) (hereditary)
Thrombocytasthenia
Thrombocytopathy (dystrophic)
Thrombopathy (Bernard-Soulier)

Excludes: *von Willebrand's disease (286.4)*

287.2 **Other nonthrombocytopenic purpuras**
Purpura:
  NOS
  senile
  simplex

287.3 **Primary thrombocytopenia**
Evans' syndrome
Megakaryocytic hypoplasia
Purpura, thrombocytopenic
  congenital
  hereditary
  idiopathic
Thrombocytopenia:
  congenital
  hereditary
  primary
Tidal platelet dysgenesis

Excludes: *thrombotic thrombocytopenic purpura (446.6)*
transient thrombocytopenia of newborn (776.1)

287.4 **Secondary thrombocytopenia**
Posttransfusion purpura
Thrombocytopenia (due to):
  dilutional
  drugs
  extracorporeal circulation of blood
  massive blood transfusion
  platelet alloimmunization
Use additional E code, if desired, to identify cause

Excludes: *transient thrombocytopenia of newborn (776.1)*

287.5 **Thrombocytopenia, unspecified**

287.8 **Other specified hemorrhagic conditions**
Capillary fragility (hereditary)
Vascular pseudohemophilia

287.9 **Unspecified hemorrhagic conditions**
Hemorrhagic diathesis (familial)

● Code new   ▲ Revision of   ④ ⑤ Fourth or fifth
  to this edition   existing code   digit required

288 **Diseases of white blood cells**

> *Excludes:* *leukemia (204.0-208.9)*

288.0 Agranulocytosis

Infantile genetic agranulo-cytosis	Neutropenia:
Kostmann's syndrome	drug-induced
Neutropenia:	immune
NOS	periodic
cyclic	toxic
	Neutropenic splenomegaly

Use additional E code, if desired, to identify drug or other cause

> *Excludes:* *transitory neonatal neutropenia (776.7)*

288.1 Functional disorders of polymorphonuclear neutrophils
Chronic (childhood) granulomatous disease
Congenital dysphagocytosis
Job's syndrome
Lipochrome histiocytosis (familial)
Progressive septic granulomatosis

288.2 Genetic anomalies of leukocytes
Anomaly (granulation) (granulocyte) or syndrome:
  Alder's (-Reilly)
  Chédiak-Steinbrinck (-Higashi)
  Jordan's
  May-Hegglin
  Pelger-Huet
Hereditary:
  hypersegmentation
  hyposegmentation
  leukomelanopathy

288.3 Eosinophilia
Eosinophilia
  allergic
  hereditary
  idiopathic
  secondary
Eosinophilic leukocytosis

> *Excludes:* *Löffler's syndrome (518.3)*
>   *pulmonary eosinophilia (518.3)*

288.8 **Other specified disease of white blood cells**

Leukemoid reaction	Lymphocytosis (symptomatic)
lymphocytic	Lymphopenia
monocytic	Monocytosis (symptomatic)
myelocytic	Plasmacytosis
Leukocytosis	
Lymphocytopenia	

> *Excludes:* *immunity disorders (279.0-279.9)*

288.9 **Unspecified disease of white blood cells**

289 **Other diseases of blood and blood-forming organs**

289.0 Polycythemia, secondary

High-oxygen-affinity hemoglobin	Polycythemia:
Polycythemia:	emotional
acquired	erythropoietin
benign	hypoxemic
due to:	nephrogenous
fall in plasma volume	relative
high altitude	spurious
	stress

> *Excludes:* *polycythemia:*
>   *neonatal (776.4)*
>   *primary (238.4)*
>   *vera (238.4)*

Add 4th or 5th digit	Nonspecific code	Unspecified code	Manifestation code

290.12 Presenile dementia with delusional features
Presenile dementia, paranoid type

290.13 Presenile dementia with depressive features
Presenile dementia, depressed type

290.2 Senile dementia with delusional or depressive features

Excludes: *senile dementia:*
NOS (290.0)
with delirium and/or confusion (290.3)

290.20 Senile dementia with delusional features
Senile dementia, paranoid type
Senile psychosis NOS

290.21 Senile dementia with depressive features

290.3 Senile dementia with delirium
Senile dementia with acute confusional state

Excludes: *senile:*
dementia NOS (290.0)
psychosis NOS (290.20)

290.4 Arteriosclerotic dementia
Multi-infarct dementia or psychosis
Use additional code to identify cerebral atherosclerosis (437.0)

Excludes: *suspected cases with no clear evidence of arteriosclerosis (290.9)*

290.40 Arteriosclerotic dementia, uncomplicated
Arteriosclerotic dementia:
NOS
simple type

290.41 Arteriosclerotic dementia with delirium
Arteriosclerotic dementia with acute confusional state

290.42 Arteriosclerotic dementia with delusional features
Arteriosclerotic dementia, paranoid type

290.43 Arteriosclerotic dementia with depressive features
Arteriosclerotic dementia, depressed type

290.8 Other specified senile psychotic conditions
Presbyophrenic psychosis

290.9 Unspecified senile psychotic condition

291 Alcoholic psychoses

Excludes: *alcoholism without psychosis (303.0-303.9)*

291.0 Alcohol withdrawal delirium
Alcoholic delirium   Delirium tremens

Excludes: *alcohol withdrawal (291.81)*

291.1 Alcohol amnestic syndrome
Alcoholic polyneuritic psychosis
Korsakoff's psychosis, alcoholic
Wernicke-Korsakoff syndrome (alcoholic)

291.2 Other alcoholic dementia
Alcoholic dementia NOS
Alcoholism associated with dementia NOS
Chronic alcoholic brain syndrome

291.3 Alcohol withdrawal hallucinosis
Alcoholic:
hallucinosis (acute)
psychosis with hallucinosis

Excludes: *alcohol withdrawal with delirium (291.0)*
schizophrenia (295.0-295.9) and paranoid states (297.0-297.9) taking the form of chronic hallucinosis with clear consciousness in an alcoholic

● Code new   ▲ Revision of   ④ ⑤ Fourth or fifth
to this edition   existing code   digit required

291.4 Idiosyncratic alcohol intoxication
Pathologic:
   alcohol intoxication
   drunkenness

| Excludes: | acute alcohol intoxication (305.0) |

   in alcoholism (303.0)
   simple drunkenness (305.0)

291.5 Alcoholic jealousy
Alcoholic:
   paranoia
   psychosis, paranoid type

| Excludes: | nonalcoholic paranoid states (297.0-297.9) |

   schizophrenia, paranoid type (295.3)

291.8 Other specified alcoholic psychosis

● **291.81 Alcohol withdrawal**
Alcohol:
   withdrawal syndrome or symptoms
   abstinence syndrome or symptoms

| Excludes: | alcohol withdrawal: |

   delirium (291.0)
   hallucinosis (291.3)
   delirium tremens (291.0)

● **291.89 Other**

291.9 Unspecified alcoholic psychosis
Alcoholic:
   mania NOS
   psychosis NOS
Alcoholism (chronic) with psychosis

292 Drug psychoses
Includes: drug-induced mental disorders
   organic brain syndrome associated with consumption of drugs

Use additional code for any associated drug dependence (304.0-304.9)

Use additional E code, if desired, to identify drug

292.0 Drug withdrawal syndrome
Drug:
   abstinence syndrome or symptoms
   withdrawal syndrome or symptoms

292.1 Paranoid and/or hallucinatory states induced by drugs

292.11 Drug-induced organic delusional syndrome
Paranoid state induced by drugs

292.12 Drug-induced hallucinosis
Hallucinatory state induced by drugs

| Excludes: | states following LSD or other hallucinogens, lasting only a few days or less ["bad trips"] (305.3) |

292.2 Pathological drug intoxication
Drug reaction:
   NOS
   idiosyncratic } resulting in brief psychotic states
   pathologic

| Excludes: | expected brief psychotic reactions to hallucinogens ["bad trips"] (305.3) |

   physiological side-effects of drugs (e.g., dystonias)

292.8 Other specified drug-induced mental disorders

292.81 Drug-induced delirium

292.82 Drug-induced dementia

292.83 Drug-induced amnestic syndrome

292.84 Drug-induced organic affective syndrome
Depressive state induced by drugs

292.89 Other
Drug-induced organic personality syndrome

292.9 Unspecified drug-induced mental disorder
Organic psychosis NOS due to or associated with drugs

| | Add 4th or 5th digit | | Nonspecific code | | Unspecified code | | Manifestation code |

123

293 **Transient organic psychotic conditions**
Includes: transient organic mental disorders not associated with alcohol or drugs
Code first the associated physical or neurological condition

> Excludes: *confusional state or delirium superimposed on senile dementia (290.3)*
> *dementia due to:*
> *alcohol (291.0-291.9)*
> *arteriosclerosis (290.40-290.43)*
> *drugs (292.82)*
> *senility (290.0)*

293.0 Acute delirium
Acute:
confusional state
infective psychosis
organic reaction
posttraumatic organic
psychosis
psycho-organic syndrome

Acute psychosis associated with endocrine, metabolic,
or cerebrovascular disorder
Epileptic:
confusional state
twilight state

293.1 Subacute delirium
Subacute:
confusional state
infective psychosis
organic reaction
posttraumatic organic
psychosis

Subacute:
psycho-organic syndrome
psychosis associated with endocrine or metabolic
disorder

293.8 Other specified transient organic mental disorders

293.81   Organic delusional syndrome
Transient organic psychotic condition, paranoid type

293.82   Organic hallucinosis syndrome
Transient organic psychotic condition, hallucinatory type

293.83   Organic affective syndrome
Transient organic psychotic condition, depressive type

● **293.84   Organic anxiety syndrome**

293.89   Other

293.9 **Unspecified transient organic mental disorder**
Organic psychosis: Psycho-organic syndrome
infective NOS
posttraumatic NOS
transient NOS

294 **Other organic psychotic conditions (chronic)**
Includes: organic psychotic brain syndromes (chronic), not elsewhere classified

294.0 Amnestic syndrome
Korsakoff's psychosis or syndrome (nonalcoholic)

> Excludes: *alcoholic:*
> *amnestic syndrome (291.1)*
> *Korsakoff's psychosis (291.1)*

294.1 Dementia in conditions classified elsewhere
Code first any underlying physical condition, as:
dementia in:
Alzheimer's disease (331.0)
cerebral lipidoses (330.1)
epilepsy (345.0-345.9)
general paresis [syphilis] (094.1)
hepatolenticular degeneration (275.1)
Huntington's chorea (333.4)
Jakob-Creutzfeldt disease (046.1)
multiple sclerosis (340)
Pick's disease of the brain (331.1)
polyarteritis nodosa (446.0)
syphilis (094.1)

> Excludes: *dementia:*
> *arteriosclerotic (290.40-290.43)*
> *presenile (290.10-290.13)*
> *senile (290.0)*
> *epileptic psychosis NOS (294.8)*

● Code new   ▲ Revision of   ④ ⑤ Fourth or fifth
   to this edition   existing code   digit required

294.8 **Other specified organic brain syndromes (chronic)**
    Epileptic psychosis NOS
    Mixed paranoid and affective organic psychotic states
Use additional code for associated epilepsy (345.0-345.9)

    Excludes: *mild memory disturbances, not amounting to dementia (310.1)*

294.9 **Unspecified organic brain syndrome (chronic)**
    Organic psychosis (chronic)

OTHER PSYCHOSES (295-299)

Use additional code to identify any associated physical disease, injury, or condition affecting the brain with psychoses classifiable to 295-298

⑤ **295** **Schizophrenic disorders**
    Includes: schizophrenia of the types described in 295.0-295.9 occurring in children

    Excludes: *childhood type schizophrenia (299.9)*
              infantile autism (299.0)

The following fifth-digit subclassification is for use with category 295:

    0 **unspecified**

    1 **subchronic**

    2 **chronic**

    3 **subchronic with acute exacerbation**

    4 **chronic with acute exacerbation**

    5 **in remission**

295.0 **Simple type**
    Schizophrenia simplex

    Excludes: *latent schizophrenia (295.5)*

295.1 **Disorganized type**
    Hebephrenia
    Hebephrenic type schizophrenia

295.2 **Catatonic type**
    Catatonic (schizophrenia):   Schizophrenic:
      agitation   catalepsy
      excitation   catatonia
      excited type   flexibilitas cerea
      stupor
      withdrawn type

295.3 **Paranoid type**
    Paraphrenic schizophrenia

    Excludes: *involutional paranoid state (297.2)*
              paranoia (297.1)
              paraphrenia (297.2)

295.4 **Acute schizophrenic episode**
    Oneirophrenia
    Schizophreniform:
      attack
      disorder
      psychosis, confusional type

    Excludes: *acute forms of schizophrenia of:*
           catatonic type (295.2)
           hebephrenic type (295.1)
           paranoid type (295.3)
           simple type (295.0)
           undifferentiated type (295.8)

295.5 **Latent schizophrenia**
    Latent schizophrenic reaction   Schizophrenia:
    Schizophrenia: prepsychotic
      borderline   prodromal
      incipient   pseudoneurotic
                          pseudopsychopathic

    Excludes: *schizoid personality (301.20-301.22)*

    Add 4th or   Nonspecific   Unspecified   Manifestation
    5th digit   code   code   code

295.6 Residual schizophrenia
    Chronic undifferentiated schizophrenia
    Restzustand (schizophrenic)
    Schizophrenic residual state

295.7 Schizo-affective type
    Cyclic schizophrenia
    Mixed schizophrenic and affective psychosis
    Schizo-affective psychosis
    Schizophreniform psychosis, affective type

295.8 Other specified types of schizophrenia
    Acute (undifferentiated) schizophrenia
    Atypical schizophrenia
    Cenesthopathic schizophrenia

> Excludes: infantile autism (299.0)

295.9 Unspecified schizophrenia
    Schizophrenia: Schizophrenic reaction NOS
       NOS   Schizophreniform psychosis NOS
       mixed NOS
       undifferentiated NOS

296 Affective psychoses
    Includes: episodic affective disorders

> Excludes: neurotic depression (300.4)
>   reactive depressive psychosis (298.0)
>   reactive excitation (298.1)

The following fifth-digit subclassification is for use with categories 296.0-296.6:

0 unspecified

1 mild

2 moderate

3 severe, without mention of psychotic behavior

4 severe, specified as with psychotic behavior

5 in partial or unspecified remission

6 in full remission

□ ⑤ **296.0 Manic disorder, single episode**
    Hypomania (mild) NOS
    Hypomanic psychosis
    Mania (monopolar) NOS   } single episode or unspecified
    Manic-depressive psychosis or reaction:
      hypomanic
      manic

> Excludes: circular type, if there was a previous attack of depression (296.4)

□ ⑤ **296.1 Manic disorder, recurrent episode**
    Any condition classifiable to 296.0, stated to be recurrent

> Excludes: circular type, if there was a previous attack of depression (296.4)

□ ⑤ **296.2 Major depressive disorder, single episode**
    Depressive psychosis
    Endogenous depression
    Involutional melancholia
    Manic-depressive psychosis or reaction,   } single episode or unspecified
      depressed type
    Monopolar depression
    Psychotic depression

> Excludes: circular type, if previous attack was of manic type (296.5)
>   depression NOS (311)
>   reactive depression (neurotic) (300.4)
>   psychotic (298.0)

● Code new   ▲ Revision of   ④ ⑤ Fourth or fifth
  to this edition   existing code   digit required

☐ ⑤ **296.3 Major depressive disorder, recurrent episode**
Any condition classifiable to 296.2, stated to be recurrent

Excludes: *circular type, if previous attack was of manic type (296.5)*
depression NOS (311)
reactive depression (neurotic) (300.4)
psychotic (298.0)

☐ ⑤ **296.4 Bipolar affective disorder, manic**
Bipolar disorder, now manic
Manic-depressive psychosis, circular type but currently manic

Excludes: *brief compensatory or rebound mood swings (296.99)*

☐ ⑤ **296.5 Bipolar affective disorder, depressed**
Bipolar disorder, now depressed
Manic-depressive psychosis, circular type but currently depressed

Excludes: *brief compensatory or rebound mood swings (296.99)*

☐ ⑤ **296.6 Bipolar affective disorder, mixed**
Manic-depressive psychosis, circular type, mixed

☐ **296.7 Bipolar affective disorder, unspecified**
Atypical bipolar affective disorder NOS
Manic-depressive psychosis, circular type, current condition not specified as either manic or depressive

☐ **296.8 Manic-depressive psychosis, other and unspecified**

296.80 Manic-depressive psychosis, unspecified
Manic-depressive:
reaction NOS
syndrome NOS

296.81 Atypical manic disorder

296.82 Atypical depressive disorder

296.89 Other
Manic-depressive psychosis, mixed type

☐ **296.9 Other and unspecified affective psychoses**

Excludes: *psychogenic affective psychoses (298.0-298.8)*

296.90 Unspecified affective psychosis
Affective psychosis NOS
Melancholia NOS

296.99 Other specified affective psychoses
Mood swings:
brief compensatory
rebound

297 Paranoid states
Includes: paranoid disorders

Excludes: *acute paranoid reaction (298.3)*
alcoholic jealousy or paranoid state (291.5)
paranoid schizophrenia (295.3)

297.0 Paranoid state, simple

297.1 Paranoia
Chronic paranoid psychosis
Sander's disease
Systematized delusions

Excludes: *paranoid personality disorder (301.0)*

297.2 Paraphrenia
Involutional paranoid state
Late paraphrenia
Paraphrenia (involutional)

297.3 Shared paranoid disorder
Folie à deux
Induced psychosis or paranoid disorder

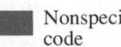 Add 4th or 5th digit

 Nonspecific code

 Unspecified code

Manifestation code

297.8 Other specified paranoid states
    Paranoia querulans
    Sensitiver Beziehungswahn

> *Excludes:* *acute paranoid reaction or state (298.3)*
>   *senile paranoid state (290.20)*

297.9 Unspecified paranoid state

Paranoid:	Paranoid:
disorder NOS	reaction NOS
psychosis	state NOS

298 Other nonorganic psychoses
    Includes: psychotic conditions due to or provoked by:
              emotional stress
              environmental factors as major part of etiology

298.0 Depressive type psychosis
    Psychogenic depressive psychosis
    Psychotic reactive depression
    Reactive depressive psychosis

> *Excludes:* *manic-depressive psychosis, depressed type (296.2-296.3)*
>   *neurotic depression (300.4)*
>   *reactive depression NOS (300.4)*

298.1 Excitative type psychosis
    Acute hysterical psychosis   Reactive excitation
    Psychogenic excitation

> *Excludes:* *manic-depressive psychosis, manic type (296.0-296.1)*

298.2 Reactive confusion
    Psychogenic confusion
    Psychogenic twilight state

> *Excludes:* *acute confusional state (293.0)*

298.3 Acute paranoid reaction
    Acute psychogenic paranoid psychosis
    Bouffée délirante

> *Excludes:* *paranoid states (297.0-297.9)*

298.4 Psychogenic paranoid psychosis
    Protracted reactive paranoid psychosis

298.8 Other and unspecified reactive psychosis
    Brief reactive psychosis NOS
    Hysterical psychosis
    Psychogenic psychosis NOS
    Psychogenic stupor

> *Excludes:* *acute hysterical psychosis (298.1)*

298.9 Unspecified psychosis
    Atypical psychosis   Psychosis NOS

⑤ 299 Psychoses with origin specific to childhood
    Includes: pervasive developmental disorders

> *Excludes:* *adult type psychoses occurring in childhood, as:*
>   *affective disorders (296.0-296.9)*
>   *manic-depressive disorders (296.0-296.9)*
>   *schizophrenia (295.0-295.9)*

The following fifth-digit subclassification is for use with category 299:

    0   current or active state

    1   residual state

299.0 Infantile autism
    Childhood autism   Kanner's syndrome
    Infantile psychosis

> *Excludes:* *disintegrative psychosis (299.1)*
>   *Heller's syndrome (299.1)*
>   *schizophrenic syndrome of childhood (299.9)*

● Code new   ▲ Revision of   ④ ⑤ Fourth or fifth
       to this edition   existing code   digit required

299.1 Disintegrative psychosis
Heller's syndrome
Use additional code to identify any associated neurological disorder

Excludes: *infantile autism (299.0)*
schizophrenic syndrome of childhood (299.9)

299.8 Other specified early childhood psychoses
Atypical childhood psychosis
Borderline psychosis of childhood

Excludes: *simple stereotypies without psychotic disturbance (307.3)*

299.9 Unspecified
Child psychosis NOS
Schizophrenia, childhood type NOS
Schizophrenic syndrome of childhood NOS

Excludes: *schizophrenia of adult type occurring in childhood (295.0-295.9)*

NEUROTIC DISORDERS, PERSONALITY DISORDERS, AND OTHER NONPSYCHOTIC MENTAL DISORDERS (300-316)

300 Neurotic disorders

300.0 Anxiety states

Excludes: *anxiety in:*
acute stress reaction (308.0)
transient adjustment reaction (309.24)
neurasthenia (300.5)
psychophysiological disorders (306.0-306.9)
separation anxiety (309.21)

300.00 Anxiety state, unspecified
Anxiety:
neurosis
reaction
state (neurotic)
Atypical anxiety disorder

300.01 Panic disorder
Panic:
attack
state

300.02 Generalized anxiety disorder

300.09 Other

300.1 Hysteria

Excludes: *adjustment reaction (309.0-309.9)*
anorexia nervosa (307.1)
gross stress reaction (308.0-308.9)
hysterical personality (301.50-301.59)
psychophysiologic disorders (306.0-306.9)

300.10 Hysteria, unspecified

300.11 Conversion disorder
Astasia-abasia, hysterical
Conversion hysteria or reaction
Hysterical:
blindness
deafness
paralysis

300.12 Psychogenic amnesia
Hysterical amnesia

300.13 Psychogenic fugue
Hysterical fugue

300.14 Multiple personality
Dissociative identity disorder

300.15 Dissociative disorder or reaction, unspecified

300.16 Factitious illness with psychological symptoms
Compensation neurosis
Ganser's syndrome, hysterical

300

129

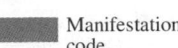

Add 4th or
5th digit

Nonspecific
code

Unspecified
code

Manifestation
code

300.19 Other and unspecified factitious illness
Factitious illness (with physical symptoms) NOS

Excludes: multiple operations or hospital addiction syndrome (301.51)

300.2 Phobic disorders

Excludes: anxiety state not associated with a specific situation or object (300.0-300.09)
obsessional phobias (300.3)

300.20 Phobia, unspecified
Anxiety-hysteria NOS
Phobia NOS

300.21 Agoraphobia with panic attacks
Fear of:
open spaces
streets $\left.\right\}$ with panic attacks
travel

300.22 Agoraphobia without mention of panic attacks
Any condition classifiable to 300.21 without mention of panic attacks

300.23 Social phobia
Fear of:
eating in public
public speaking
washing in public

300.29 Other isolated or simple phobias
Acrophobia   Claustrophobia
Animal phobias   Fear of crowds

300.3 Obsessive-compulsive disorders
Anancastic neurosis   Obsessional phobia [any]
Compulsive neurosis

Excludes: obsessive-compulsive symptoms occurring in:
endogenous depression (296.2-296.3)
organic states (e.g., encephalitis)
schizophrenia (295.0-295.9)

300.4 Neurotic depression
Anxiety depression   Dysthymic disorder
Depression with anxiety   Neurotic depressive state
Depressive reaction   Reactive depression

Excludes: adjustment reaction with depressive symptoms (309.0-309.1)
depression NOS (311)
manic-depressive psychosis, depressed type (296.2-296.3)
reactive depressive psychosis (298.0)

300.5 Neurasthenia
Fatigue neurosis   Psychogenic:
Nervous debility   asthenia
                            general fatigue
Use additional code to identify any associated physical disorder

Excludes: anxiety state (300.00-300.09)
neurotic depression (300.4)
psychophysiological disorders (306.0-306.9)
specific nonpsychotic mental disorders following organic brain damage
(310.0-310.9)

300.6 Depersonalization syndrome
Depersonalization disorder
Derealization (neurotic)
Neurotic state with depersonalization episode

Excludes: depersonalization associated with:
anxiety (300.00-300.09)
depression (300.4)
manic-depressive disorder or psychosis (296.0-296.9)
schizophrenia (295.0-295.9)

● Code new   ▲ Revision of   ④ ⑤ Fourth or fifth
  to this edition   existing code   digit required

300.7 Hypochondriasis
Body dysmorphic disorder

Excludes: *hypochondriasis in:*
 hysteria (300.10-300.19)
 manic-depressive psychosis, depressed type (296.2-296.3)
 neurasthenia (300.5)
 obsessional disorder (300.3)
 schizophrenia (295.0-295.9)

300.8 Other neurotic disorders

300.81 Somatization disorder
Briquet's disorder
Severe somatoform disorder

● 300.82 Undifferentiated somatoform disorder
Atypical somatoform disorder
Somatoform disorder NOS

300.89 Other
Occupational neurosis, including writers' cramp
Psychasthenia
Psychasthenic neurosis

300.9 Unspecified neurotic disorder
Neurosis NOS   Psychoneurosis NOS

301 Personality disorders
Includes: character neurosis

Use additional code to identify any associated neurosis or psychosis, or physical condition

Excludes: *nonpsychotic personality disorder associated with organic brain syndromes*
 (310.0-310.9)

301.0 Paranoid personality disorder
Fanatic personality
Paranoid personality (disorder)
Paranoid traits

Excludes: *acute paranoid reaction (298.3)*
 alcoholic paranoia (291.5)
 paranoid schizophrenia (295.3)
 paranoid states (297.0-297.9)

301.1 Affective personality disorder

Excludes: *affective psychotic disorders (296.0-296.9)*
 neurasthenia (300.5)
 neurotic depression (300.4)

301.10 Affective personality disorder, unspecified

301.11 Chronic hypomanic personality disorder
Chronic hypomanic disorder
Hypomanic personality

301.12 Chronic depressive personality disorder
Chronic depressive disorder
Depressive character or personality

301.13 Cyclothymic disorder
Cycloid personality
Cyclothymia
Cyclothymic personality

301.2 Schizoid personality disorder

Excludes: *schizophrenia (295.0-295.9)*

301.20 Schizoid personality disorder, unspecified

301.21 Introverted personality

301.22 Schizotypal personality

301.3 Explosive personality disorder
Aggressive:	Emotional instability (excessive)
personality	Pathological emotionality
reaction	Quarrelsomeness
Aggressiveness	

Excludes: *dyssocial personality (301.7)*
 hysterical neurosis (300.10-300.19)

131

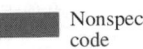 Add 4th or 5th digit   Nonspecific code   Unspecified code   Manifestation code

303.0 Acute alcoholic intoxication
Acute drunkenness in alcoholism

303.9 Other and unspecified alcohol dependence
Chronic alcoholism   Dipsomania

⑤ **304 Drug dependence**

> Excludes: nondependent abuse of drugs (305.1-305.9)

The following fifth-digit subclassification is for use with category 304:

0 unspecified
1 continuous
2 episodic
3 in remission

304.0 Opioid type dependence
Heroin   Opium alkaloids and their derivatives
Meperidine   Synthetics with morphine-like effects
Methadone
Morphine
Opium

304.1 Barbiturate and similarly acting sedative or hypnotic dependence
Barbiturates
Nonbarbiturate sedatives and tranquilizers with a similar effect:
chlordiazepoxide
diazepam
glutethimide
meprobamate
methaqualone

304.2 Cocaine dependence
Coca leaves and derivatives

304.3 Cannabis dependence
Hashish   Marihuana
Hemp

304.4 Amphetamine and other psychostimulant dependence
Methylphenidate   Phenmetrazine

304.5 Hallucinogen dependence
Dimethyltryptamine [DMT]
Lysergic acid diethylamide [LSD] and derivatives
Mescaline
Psilocybin

304.6 Other specified drug dependence
Absinthe addiction   Glue sniffing

> Excludes: tobacco dependence (305.1)

304.7 Combinations of opioid type drug with any other

304.8 Combinations of drug dependence excluding opioid type drug

304.9 Unspecified drug dependence
Drug addiction NOS   Drug dependence NOS

⑤ **305 Nondependent abuse of drugs**

Note: Includes cases where a person, for whom no other diagnosis is possible, has come under medical care because of the maladaptive effect of a drug on which he is not dependent and that he has taken on his own initiative to the detriment of his health or social functioning.

> Excludes: alcohol dependence syndrome (303.0-303.9)
> drug dependence (304.0-304.9)
> drug withdrawal syndrome (292.0)
> poisoning by drugs or medicinal substances (960.0-979.9)

The following fifth-digit subclassification is for use with codes 305.0, 305.2-305.9:

0 unspecified
1 continuous
2 episodic
3 in remission

● Code new   ▲ Revision of   ④ ⑤ Fourth or fifth
                to this edition   existing code   digit required

305.0 Alcohol abuse
    Drunkenness NOS
    Excessive drinking of alcohol NOS
    "Hangover" (alcohol)
    Inebriety NOS

> *Excludes:* *acute alcohol intoxication in alcoholism (303.0)*
> *alcoholic psychoses (291.0-291.9)*
> *physical complications of alcohol, such as:*
>   *cirrhosis of liver (571.2)*
>   *epilepsy (345.00-345.91)*
>   *gastritis (535.3)*

305.1 Tobacco use disorder
    Tobacco dependence

> *Excludes:* *history of tobacco use (V15.82)*

305.2 Cannabis abuse

305.3 Hallucinogen abuse
    Acute intoxication from hallucinogens ["bad trips"]
    LSD reaction

305.4 Barbiturate and similarly acting sedative or hypnotic abuse

305.5 Opioid abuse

305.6 Cocaine abuse

305.7 Amphetamine or related acting sympathomimetic abuse

305.8 Antidepressant type abuse

305.9 Other, mixed, or unspecified drug abuse
    "Laxative habit"
    Misuse of drugs NOS
    Nonprescribed use of drugs or patent medicinals

306 Physiological malfunction arising from mental factors
    Includes: psychogenic:
                physical symptoms
                physiological manifestations   } not involving tissue damage

> *Excludes:* *hysteria (300.11-300.19)*
> *physical symptoms secondary to a psychiatric disorder classified elsewhere*
> *psychic factors associated with physical conditions involving tissue damage*
>   *classified elsewhere (316)*
> *specific nonpsychotic mental disorders following organic brain damage (310.0-310.9)*

306.0 Musculoskeletal
    Psychogenic paralysis   Psychogenic torticollis

> *Excludes:* *Gilles de la Tourette's syndrome (307.23)*
> *paralysis as hysterical or conversion reaction (300.11)*
> *tics (307.20-307.22)*

306.1 Respiratory
    Psychogenic: Psychogenic:
      air hunger   hyperventilation
      cough   yawning
      hiccough

> *Excludes:* *psychogenic asthma (316 and 493.9)*

306.2 Cardiovascular
    Cardiac neurosis
    Cardiovascular neurosis
    Neurocirculatory asthenia
    Psychogenic cardiovascular disorder

> *Excludes:* *psychogenic paroxysmal tachycardia (316 and 427.2)*

306.3 Skin
    Psychogenic pruritus

> *Excludes:* *psychogenic:*
>   *alopecia (316 and 704.00)*
>   *dermatitis (316 and 692.9)*
>   *eczema (316 and 691.8 or 692.9)*
>   *urticaria (316 and 708.0-708.9)*

 Add 4th or 5th digit   Nonspecific code   Unspecified code   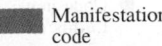 Manifestation code

306.4 Gastrointestinal
Aerophagy
Cyclical vomiting,
psychogenic

Diarrhea, psychogenic
Nervous gastritis
Psychogenic dyspepsia

Excludes: *cyclical vomiting NOS (536.2)*
globus hystericus (300.11)
mucous colitis (316 and 564.1)
psychogenic:
cardiospasm (316 and 530.0)
duodenal ulcer (316 and 532.0-532.9)
gastric ulcer (316 and 531.0-531.9)
peptic ulcer NOS (316 and 533.0-533.9)
vomiting NOS (307.54)

306.5 Genitourinary

Excludes: *enuresis, psychogenic (307.6)*
frigidity (302.72)
impotence (302.72)
psychogenic dyspareunia (302.76)

306.50 Psychogenic genitourinary malfunction, unspecified

306.51 Psychogenic vaginismus
Functional vaginismus

306.52 Psychogenic dysmenorrhea

306.53 Psychogenic dysuria

306.59 Other

306.6 Endocrine

306.7 Organs of special sense

Excludes: *hysterical blindness or deafness (300.11)*
psychophysical visual disturbances (368.16)

306.8 Other specified psychophysiological malfunction
Bruxism   Teeth grinding

306.9 Unspecified psychophysiological malfunction
Psychophysiologic disorder NOS
Psychosomatic disorder NOS

307 Special symptoms or syndromes, not elsewhere classified

Note: This category is intended for use if the psychopathology is manifested by a single specific symptom or group of symptoms which is not part of an organic illness or other mental disorder classifiable elsewhere.

Excludes: *those due to mental disorders classified elsewhere*
those of organic origin

307.0 Stammering and stuttering

Excludes: *dysphasia (784.5)*
lisping or lalling (307.9)
retarded development of speech (315.31-315.39)

307.1 Anorexia nervosa

Excludes: *eating disturbance NOS (307.50)*
feeding problem (783.3)
of nonorganic origin (307.59)
loss of appetite (783.0)
of nonorganic origin (307.59)

307.2 Tics

Excludes: *nail-biting or thumb-sucking (307.9)*
stereotypies occurring in isolation (307.3)
tics of organic origin (333.3)

307.20 Tic disorder, unspecified

307.21 Transient tic disorder of childhood

307.22 Chronic motor tic disorder

307.23 Gilles de la Tourette's disorder
Motor-verbal tic disorder

● Code new
to this edition

▲ Revision of
existing code

④ ⑤ Fourth or fifth
digit required

307.3 Stereotyped repetitive movements

Body-rocking	Spasmus nutans
Head banging	Stereotypies NOS

Excludes: *tics (307.20-307.23)*
> *of organic origin (333.3)*

307.4 Specific disorders of sleep of nonorganic origin

Excludes: *narcolepsy (347)*
> *those of unspecified cause (780.50-780.59)*

307.40 Nonorganic sleep disorder, unspecified

307.41 Transient disorder of initiating or maintaining sleep

Hyposomnia	
Insomnia	associated with acute or intermittent emotional reactions
Sleeplessness	or conflicts

307.42 Persistent disorder of initiating or maintaining sleep
Hyposomnia, insomnia, or sleeplessness associated with:
  anxiety
  conditioned arousal
  depression (major) (minor)
  psychosis

307.43 Transient disorder of initiating or maintaining wakefulness
Hypersomnia associated with acute or intermittent emotional reactions or
  conflicts

307.44 Persistent disorder of initiating or maintaining wakefulness
Hypersomnia associated with depression (major) (minor)

307.45 Phase-shift disruption of 24-hour sleep-wake cycle
Irregular sleep-wake rhythm, nonorganic origin
Jet lag syndrome
Rapid time-zone change
Shifting sleep-work schedule

307.46 Somnambulism or night terrors

307.47 Other dysfunctions of sleep stages or arousal from sleep

Nightmares:	Sleep drunkenness
NOS	
REM-sleep type	

307.48 Repetitive intrusions of sleep
Repetitive intrusion of sleep with:
  atypical polysomnographic features
  environmental disturbances
  repeated REM-sleep interruptions

307.49 Other
"Short-sleeper"
Subjective insomnia complaint

307.5 Other and unspecified disorders of eating

Excludes: *anorexia:*
> *nervosa (307.1)*
> *of unspecified cause (783.0)*
> *overeating, of unspecified cause (783.6)*
> *vomiting:*
> *NOS (787.0)*
> *cyclical (536.2)*
> *psychogenic (306.4)*

307.50 Eating disorder, unspecified

307.51 Bulimia
Overeating of nonorganic origin

307.52 Pica
Perverted appetite of nonorganic origin

307.53 Psychogenic rumination
Regurgitation, of nonorganic origin, of food with reswallowing

Excludes: *obsessional rumination (300.3)*

307.54 Psychogenic vomiting

Add 4th or 5th digit	Nonspecific code	Unspecified code	Manifestation code

307.59 **Other**

Infantile feeding disturbances
Loss of appetite } of nonorganic origin

307.6 **Enuresis**

Enuresis (primary) (secondary) of nonorganic origin

Excludes: *enuresis of unspecified cause (788.3)*

307.7 **Encopresis**

Encopresis (continuous) (discontinuous) of nonorganic origin

Excludes: *encopresis of unspecified cause (787.6)*

307.8 **Psychalgia**

307.80 **Psychogenic pain, site unspecified**

307.81 **Tension headache**

Excludes: *headache:*
NOS (784.0)
migraine (346.0-346.9)

307.89 **Other**

Psychogenic backache

Excludes: *pains not specifically attributable to a psychological cause (in):*
back (724.5)
joint (719.4)
limb (729.5)
lumbago (724.2)
rheumatic (729.0)

307.9 **Other and unspecified special symptoms or syndromes, not elsewhere classified**

Hair plucking   Masturbation
Lalling   Nail-biting
Lisping   Thumb-sucking

308 **Acute reaction to stress**

Includes: catastrophic stress
combat fatigue
gross stress reaction (acute)
transient disorders in response to exceptional physical or mental stress which
usually subside within hours or days

Excludes: *adjustment reaction or disorder (309.0-309.9)*
chronic stress reaction (309.1-309.9)

308.0 **Predominant disturbance of emotions**

Anxiety
Emotional crisis } as acute reaction to exceptional [gross] stress
Panic state

308.1 **Predominant disturbance of consciousness**

Fugues as acute reaction to exceptional [gross] stress

308.2 **Predominant psychomotor disturbance**

Agitation states } as acute reaction to exceptional [gross] stress
Stupor

308.3 **Other acute reactions to stress**

Acute situational disturbance
Brief or acute posttraumatic stress disorder

Excludes: *prolonged posttraumatic emotional disturbance (309.81)*

308.4 **Mixed disorders as reaction to stress**

308.9 **Unspecified acute reaction to stress**

309 **Adjustment reaction**

Includes: adjustment disorders
reaction (adjustment) to chronic stress

Excludes: *acute reaction to major stress (308.0-308.9)*
neurotic disorders (300.0-300.9)

● Code new   ▲ Revision of   ④ ⑤ Fourth or fifth
to this edition   existing code   digit required

309.0 Brief depressive reaction
Adjustment disorder with depressed mood
Grief reaction

Excludes: *affective psychoses (296.0-296.9)*
neurotic depression (300.4)
prolonged depressive reaction (309.1)
psychogenic depressive psychosis (298.0)

309.1 Prolonged depressive reaction

Excludes: *affective psychoses (296.0-296.9)*
brief depressive reaction (309.0)
neurotic depression (300.4)
psychogenic depressive psychosis (298.0)

309.2 With predominant disturbance of other emotions

309.21 Separation anxiety disorder

309.22 Emancipation disorder of adolescence and early adult life

309.23 Specific academic or work inhibition

309.24 Adjustment reaction with anxious mood

309.28 Adjustment reaction with mixed emotional features
Adjustment reaction with anxiety and depression

309.29 Other
Culture shock

309.3 With predominant disturbance of conduct
Conduct disturbance ⎫
Destructiveness ⎭ as adjustment reaction

Excludes: *destructiveness in child (312.9)*
disturbance of conduct NOS (312.9)
dyssocial behavior without manifest psychiatric disorder (V71.01-V71.02)
personality disorder with predominantly sociopathic or asocial manifestations (301.7)

309.4 With mixed disturbance of emotions and conduct

309.8 Other specified adjustment reactions

309.81 Prolonged posttraumatic stress disorder
Chronic posttraumatic stress disorder
Concentration camp syndrome

Excludes: *posttraumatic brain syndrome:*
nonpsychotic (310.2)
psychotic (293.0-293.9)

309.82 Adjustment reaction with physical symptoms

309.83 Adjustment reaction with withdrawal
Elective mutism as adjustment reaction
Hospitalism (in children) NOS

309.89 Other

309.9 Unspecified adjustment reaction
Adaptation reaction NOS   Adjustment reaction NOS

310 Specific nonpsychotic mental disorders due to organic brain damage

Excludes: *neuroses, personality disorders, or other nonpsychotic conditions occurring in a*
form similar to that seen with functional disorders but in association with a
physical condition (300.0-300.9, 301.0-301.9)

310.0 Frontal lobe syndrome
Lobotomy syndrome
Postleucotomy syndrome [state]

Excludes: *postcontusion syndrome (310.2)*

310.1 Organic personality syndrome
Cognitive or personality change of other type, of nonpsychotic severity
Mild memory disturbance
Organic psychosyndrome of nonpsychotic severity
Presbyophrenia NOS
Senility with mental changes of nonpsychotic severity

| | Add 4th or 5th digit | | Nonspecific code | | Unspecified code | | Manifestation code |

310.2 Postconcussion syndrome
  Postcontusion syndrome or encephalopathy
  Posttraumatic brain syndrome, nonpsychotic
  Status postcommotio cerebri

  Excludes: *frontal lobe syndrome (310.0)*
  postencephalitic syndrome (310.8)
  any organic psychotic conditions following head injury (293.0—294.0)

310.8 Other specified nonpsychotic mental disorders following organic brain damage
  Postencephalitic syndrome
  Other focal (partial) organic psychosyndromes

310.9 Unspecified nonpsychotic mental disorder following organic brain damage

311 Depressive disorder, not elsewhere classified
  Depressive disorder NOS
  Depressive state NOS   Depression NOS

  Excludes: *acute reaction to major stress with depressive symptoms (308.0)*
  affective personality disorder (301.10-301.13)
  affective psychoses (296.0-296.9)
  brief depressive reaction (309.0)
  depressive states associated with stressful events (309.0-309.1)
  disturbance of emotions specific to childhood and adolescence, with misery and
  *   unhappiness (313.1)*
  mixed adjustment reaction with depressive symptoms (309.4)
  neurotic depression (300.4)
  prolonged depressive adjustment reaction (309.1)
  psychogenic depressive psychosis (298.0)

312 Disturbance of conduct, not elsewhere classified

  Excludes: *adjustment reaction with disturbance of conduct (309.3)*
  drug dependence (304.0-304.9)
  dyssocial behavior without manifest psychiatric disorder (V71.01-V71.02)
  personality disorder with predominantly sociopathic or asocial manifestations
  *   (301.7)*
  sexual deviations (302.0-302.9)

  The following fifth-digit subclassification is for use with categories 312.0-312.2:

  0 unspecified

  1 mild

  2 moderate

  3 severe

□ ⑤ **312.0 Undersocialized conduct disorder, aggressive type**
  Aggressive outburst   Unsocialized aggressive disorder
  Anger reaction

□ ⑤ **312.1 Undersocialized conduct disorder, unaggressive type**
  Childhood truancy,   Solitary stealing
    unsocialized   Tantrums

□ ⑤ **312.2 Socialized conduct disorder**
  Childhood truancy, socialized
  Group delinquency

  Excludes: *gang activity without manifest psychiatric disorder (V71.01)*

□ **312.3 Disorders of impulse control, not elsewhere classified**
  312.30 Impulse control disorder, unspecified
  312.31 Pathological gambling
  312.32 Kleptomania
  312.33 Pyromania
  312.34 Intermittent explosive disorder
  312.35 Isolated explosive disorder
  312.39 Other

□ **312.4 Mixed disturbance of conduct and emotions**
  Neurotic delinquency

  Excludes: *compulsive conduct disorder (312.3)*

312.8 Other specified disturbances of conduct, not elsewhere classified

---

● Code new   ▲ Revision of   ④ ⑤ Fourth or fifth
     to this edition   existing code   digit required

312.81   **Conduct disorder, childhood onset type**

312.82   **Conduct disorder, adolescent onset type**

312.89   **Other conduct disorder**

312.9 **Unspecified disturbance of conduct**
Delinquency (juvenile)

313 **Disturbance of emotions specific to childhood and adolescence**

> Excludes: adjustment reaction (309.0-309.9)
> emotional disorder of neurotic type (300.0-300.9)
> masturbation, nail-biting, thumb-sucking, and other isolated symptoms (307.0-307.9)

313.0 **Overanxious disorder**
Anxiety and fearfulness } of childhood and adolescence
Overanxious disorder

> Excludes: abnormal separation anxiety (309.21)
> anxiety states (300.00-300.09)
> hospitalism in children (309.83)
> phobic state (300.20-300.29)

313.1 **Misery and unhappiness disorder**

> Excludes: depressive neurosis (300.4)

313.2 **Sensitivity, shyness, and social withdrawal disorder**

> Excludes: infantile autism (299.0)
> schizoid personality (301.20-301.22)
> schizophrenia (295.0-295.9)

313.21   **Shyness disorder of childhood**
Sensitivity reaction of childhood or adolescence

313.22   **Introverted disorder of childhood**
Social withdrawal } of childhood or adolescence
Withdrawal reaction

313.23   **Elective mutism**

> Excludes: elective mutism as adjustment reaction (309.83)

313.3 **Relationship problems**
Sibling jealousy

> Excludes: relationship problems associated with aggression, destruction, or other forms of
> conduct disturbance (312.0-312.9)

313.8 **Other or mixed emotional disturbances of childhood or adolescence**

313.81   **Oppositional disorder**

313.82   **Identity disorder**

313.83   **Academic underachievement disorder**

313.89   **Other**

313.9 **Unspecified emotional disturbance of childhood or adolescence**

314 **Hyperkinetic syndrome of childhood**

> Excludes: hyperkinesis as symptom of underlying disorder—code the underlying disorder

314.0 **Attention deficit disorder**

314.00   **Without mention of hyperactivity**
Predominantly inattentive type

314.01   **With hyperactivity**
Combined type
Overactivity NOS
Predominantly hyperactive/impulsive type
Simple disturbance of attention with overactivity

314.1 **Hyperkinesis with developmental delay**
Developmental disorder of hyperkinesis
Use additional code to identify any associated neurological disorder

314.2 **Hyperkinetic conduct disorder**
Hyperkinetic conduct disorder without developmental delay

> Excludes: hyperkinesis with significant delays in specific skills (314.1)

314.8 **Other specified manifestations of hyperkinetic syndrome**

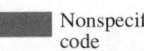 Add 4th or 5th digit   Nonspecific code   Unspecified code   Manifestation code

314.9   Unspecified hyperkinetic syndrome
Hyperkinetic reaction of childhood or adolescence NOS
Hyperkinetic syndrome NOS

315   Specific delays in development

Excludes: *that due to a neurological disorder (320.0-389.9)*

315.0   Specific reading disorder

315.00   Reading disorder, unspecified

315.01   Alexia

315.02   Developmental dyslexia

315.09   Other
Specific spelling difficulty

315.1   Specific arithmetical disorder
Dyscalculia

315.2   Other specific learning difficulties

Excludes: *specific arithmetical disorder (315.1)*
specific reading disorder (315.00-315.09)

315.3   Developmental speech or language disorder

315.31   Developmental language disorder
Developmental aphasia
Expressive language disorder
Word deafness

Excludes: *acquired aphasia (784.3)*
elective mutism (309.83, 313.0, 313.23)

● **315.32   Receptive language disorder (mixed)**
Receptive expressive language disorder

315.39   Other
Developmental articulation disorder
Dyslalia

Excludes: *lisping and lalling (307.9)*
stammering and stuttering (307.0)

315.4   Coordination disorder
Clumsiness syndrome
Dyspraxia syndrome
Specific motor development disorder

315.5   Mixed development disorder

315.8   Other specified delays in development

315.9   Unspecified delay in development
Developmental disorder NOS

316   Psychic factors associated with diseases classified elsewhere
Psychologic factors in physical conditions classified elsewhere
Use additional code to identify the associated physical condition, as:
psychogenic:
asthma (493.9)
dermatitis (692.9)
duodenal ulcer (532.0-532.9)
eczema (691.8, 692.9)
gastric ulcer (531.0-531.9)
mucous colitis (564.1)
paroxysmal tachycardia (427.2)
ulcerative colitis (556)
urticaria (708.0-708.9)
psychosocial dwarfism (259.4)

Excludes: *physical symptoms and physiological malfunctions, not involving tissue damage, of*
mental origin (306.0-306.9)

MENTAL RETARDATION (317-319)

Use additional code(s) to identify any associated psychiatric or physical condition(s)

317   Mild mental retardation
High-grade defect   Mild mental subnormality
IQ 50-70

● Code new   ▲ Revision of   ④ ⑤ Fourth or fifth
to this edition   existing code   digit required

318 **Other specified mental retardation**

    318.0 **Moderate mental retardation**
        IQ 35-49   Moderate mental subnormality

    318.1 **Severe mental retardation**
        IQ 20-34
        Severe mental subnormality

    318.2 **Profound mental retardation**
        IQ under 20   Profound mental subnormality

319 **Unspecified mental retardation**
    Mental deficiency NOS   Mental subnormality NOS

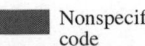 Add 4th or 5th digit   Nonspecific code   Unspecified code   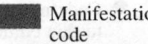 Manifestation code

● Code new
to this edition

▲ Revision of
existing code

④ ⑤ Fourth or fifth
digit required

6. DISEASES OF THE NERVOUS SYSTEM AND SENSE ORGANS (320-389)

INFLAMMATORY DISEASES OF THE CENTRAL NERVOUS SYSTEM (320-326)

320 Bacterial meningitis

Includes:

> arachnoiditis
> leptomeningitis
> meningitis   } bacterial
> meningoencephalitis
> meningomyelitis
> pachymeningitis

320.0 Hemophilus meningitis

Meningitis due to Hemophilus influenzae [H. influenzae]

320.1 Pneumococcal meningitis

320.2 Streptococcal meningitis

320.3 Staphylococcal meningitis

320.7 *Meningitis in other bacterial diseases classified elsewhere*

Code first underlying disease, as:
actinomycosis (039.8)
listeriosis (027.0)
typhoid fever (002.0)
whooping cough (033.0-033.9)

Excludes: *meningitis (in):*

> *epidemic (036.0)*
> *gonococcal (098.82)*
> *meningococcal (036.0)*
> *salmonellosis (003.21)*
> *syphilis:*
>   *NOS (094.2)*
>   *congenital (090.42)*
>   *meningovascular (094.2)*
>   *secondary (091.81)*
> *tuberculous (013.0)*

320.8 Meningitis due to other specified bacteria

320.81 Anaerobic meningitis

Bacteroides (fragilis)
Gram-negative anaerobes

320.82 Meningitis due to Gram-negative bacteria, not elsewhere classified

Aerobacter aerogenes
Escherichia coli [E. coli]
Friedlander bacillus
Klebsiella pneumoniae
Proteus morganii
Pseudomonas

Excludes: *Gram-negative anaerobes (320.81)*

320.89 Meningitis due to other specified bacteria

Bacillus pyocyaneus

320.9 Meningitis due to unspecified bacterium

Meningitis: Meningitis:
bacterial NOS   pyogenic NOS
purulent NOS   suppurative NOS

321 Meningitis due to other organisms

Includes:

> arachnoiditis
> leptomeningitis   } due to organisms other than bacteria
> meningitis
> pachymeningitis

321.0 *Cryptococcal meningitis*

Code first underlying disease (117.5)

321.1 *Meningitis in other fungal diseases*

Code first underlying disease (110.0-118)

Excludes: *meningitis in:*

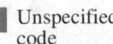 Add 4th or 5th digit   Nonspecific code   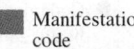 Unspecified code   Manifestation code

145

          candidiasis (112.83)
          coccidioidomycosis (114.2)
          histoplasmosis (115.01, 115.11, 115.91)

`321.2` ***Meningitis due to viruses not elsewhere classified***
    Code first underlying disease, as:
      meningitis due to arbovirus (060.0-066.9)

    | Excludes: | *meningitis (due to):*
          abacterial (047.0-047.9)
          adenovirus (049.1)
          aseptic NOS (047.9)
          Coxsackie (virus) (047.0)
          ECHO virus (047.1)
          enterovirus (047.0-047.9)
          herpes simplex virus (054.72)
          herpes zoster virus (053.0)
          lymphocytic choriomeningitis virus (049.0)
          mumps (072.1)
          viral NOS (047.9)
          meningo-eruptive syndrome (047.1)

`321.3` ***Meningitis due to trypanosomiasis***
    Code first underlying disease (086.0-086.9)

`321.4` ***Meningitis in sarcoidosis***
    Code first underlying disease (135)

`321.8` ***Meningitis due to other nonbacterial organisms classified elsewhere***
    Code first underlying disease

    | Excludes: | *leptospiral meningitis (100.81)*

`322` **Meningitis of unspecified cause**
    Includes:
        arachnoiditis
        leptomeningitis
        meningitis   } with no organism specified as cause
        pachymeningitis

  322.0 **Nonpyogenic meningitis**
    Meningitis with clear cerebrospinal fluid

  322.1 **Eosinophilic meningitis**

  322.2 **Chronic meningitis**

  `322.9` **Meningitis, unspecified**

`323` **Encephalitis, myelitis, and encephalomyelitis**
    Includes: acute disseminated encephalomyelitis
              meningoencephalitis, except bacterial
              meningomyelitis, except bacterial
              myelitis (acute):
                  ascending
                  transverse

    | Excludes: | *bacterial:*
          meningoencephalitis (320.0-320.9)
          meningomyelitis (320.0-320.9)

  `323.0` ***Encephalitis in viral diseases classified elsewhere***
    Code first underlying disease, as:
      cat-scratch disease (078.3)
      infectious mononucleosis (075)
      ornithosis (073.7)

    | Excludes: | *encephalitis (in):*
          arthropod-borne viral (062.0-064)
          herpes simplex (054.3)
          mumps (072.2)
          poliomyelitis (045.0-045.9)
          rubella (056.01)
          slow virus infections of central nervous system (046.0-046.9)
          other viral diseases of central nervous system (049.8-049.9)
          viral NOS (049.9)

  `323.1` ***Encephalitis in rickettsial diseases classified elsewhere***
    Code first underlying disease (080-083.9)

  ● Code new
    to this edition   ▲ Revision of
        existing code   ④ ⑤ Fourth or fifth
           digit required

323.2 *Encephalitis in protozoal diseases classified elsewhere*
> *Code first underlying disease, as:*
>> malaria (084.0-084.9)
>> trypanosomiasis (086.0-086.9)

323.4 *Other encephalitis due to infection classified elsewhere*
> *Code first underlying disease*

> Excludes: *encephalitis (in):*
>> *meningococcal (036.1)*
>> *syphilis:*
>>> *NOS (094.81)*
>>> *congenital (090.41)*
>> *toxoplasmosis (130.0)*
>> *tuberculosis (013.6)*
>> *meningoencephalitis due to free-living ameba [Naegleria] (136.2)*

323.5 Encephalitis following immunization procedures
> Encephalitis ⎱
> Encephalomyelitis ⎰ postimmunization or postvaccinal

Use additional E code, if desired, to identify vaccine

323.6 *Postinfectious encephalitis*
> *Code first underlying disease*

> Excludes: *encephalitis:*
>> *postchickenpox (052.0)*
>> *postmeasles (055.0)*

323.7 *Toxic encephalitis*
> *Code first underlying cause, as:*
>> carbon tetrachloride (982.1)
>> hydroxyquinoline derivatives (961.3)
>> lead (984.0-984.9)
>> mercury (985.0)
>> thallium (985.8)

323.8 Other causes of encephalitis

323.9 Unspecified cause of encephalitis

324 Intracranial and intraspinal abscess

324.0 Intracranial abscess
> Abscess (embolic):
>> cerebellar
>> cerebral

> Abscess (embolic) of brain [any part]:
>> epidural
>> extradural
>> otogenic
>> subdural

> Excludes: *tuberculous (013.3)*

324.1 Intraspinal abscess
> Abscess (embolic) of spinal cord [any part]:
>> epidural
>> extradural
>> subdural

> Excludes: *tuberculous (013.5)*

324.9 Of unspecified site
> Extradural or subdural abscess NOS

325 Phlebitis and thrombophlebitis of intracranial venous sinuses
> Embolism
> Endophlebitis
> Phlebitis, septic or suppurative ⎱
> Thrombophlebitis ⎰ of cavernous, lateral, or other intracranial or unspecified
> Thrombosis ⎰ intracranial venous sinus

> Excludes: *that specified as:*
>> *complicating pregnancy, childbirth, or the puerperium (671.5)*
>> *of nonpyogenic origin (437.6)*

	Add 4th or 5th digit		Nonspecific code		Unspecified code		Manifestation code

326 Late effects of intracranial abscess or pyogenic infection

Note: This category is to be used to indicate conditions whose primary classification is to 320-325 [excluding 320.7, 321.0-321.8, 323.0-323.4, 323.6-323.7] as the cause of late effects, themselves classifiable elsewhere. The "late effects" include conditions specified as such, or as sequelae, which may occur at any time after the resolution of the causal condition.

Use additional code, if desired, to identify condition, as:
hydrocephalus (331.4)
paralysis (342.0-342.9, 344.0-344.9)

HEREDITARY AND DEGENERATIVE DISEASES OF THE CENTRAL NERVOUS SYSTEM (330-337)

Excludes: *hepatolenticular degeneration (275.1)*
multiple sclerosis (340)
other demyelinating diseases of central nervous system (341.0-341.9)

330 Cerebral degenerations usually manifest in childhood
Use additional code, if desired, to identify associated mental retardation

330.0 Leukodystrophy

Krabbe's disease
Leukodystrophy:
 NOS
 globoid cell

Leukodystrophy:
 metachromatic
 sudanophilic
Pelizaeus-Merzbacher disease
Sulfatide lipidosis

330.1 Cerebral lipidoses

Amaurotic (familial) idiocy
Disease:
 Batten
 Jansky-Bielschowsky

Disease:
 Kufs'
 Spielmeyer-Vogt
 Tay-Sachs
Gangliosidosis

330.2 *Cerebral degeneration in generalized lipidoses*
Code first underlying disease, as:
Fabry's disease (272.7)
Gaucher's disease (272.7)
Neimann-Pick disease (272.7)
sphingolipidosis (272.7)

330.3 *Cerebral degeneration of childhood in other diseases classified elsewhere*
Code first underlying disease, as:
Hunter's disease (277.5)
mucopolysaccharidosis (277.5)

330.8 Other specified cerebral degenerations in childhood
Alpers' disease or gray-matter degeneration
Infantile necrotizing encephalomyelopathy
Leigh's disease
Subacute necrotizing encephalopathy or encephalomyelopathy

330.9 Unspecified cerebral degeneration in childhood

331 Other cerebral degenerations

331.0 Alzheimer's disease

331.1 Pick's disease

331.2 Senile degeneration of brain

Excludes: *senility NOS (797)*

331.3 Communicating hydrocephalus

Excludes: *congenital hydrocephalus (741.0, 742.3)*

331.4 Obstructive hydrocephalus
Acquired hydrocephalus NOS

Excludes: *congenital hydrocephalus (741.0, 742.3)*

● Code new
to this edition

▲ Revision of
existing code

④ ⑤ Fourth or fifth
digit required

331.7 *Cerebral degeneration in diseases classified elsewhere*
Code first underlying disease, as:
alcoholism (303.0-303.9)
beriberi (265.0)
cerebrovascular disease (430-438)
congenital hydrocephalus (741.0, 742.3)
neoplastic disease (140.0-239.9)
myxedema (244.0-244.9)
vitamin B$_{12}$ deficiency (266.2)

Excludes: *cerebral degeneration in:*
Jakob-Creutzfeldt disease (046.1)
progressive multifocal leukoencephalopathy (046.3)
subacute spongiform encephalopathy (046.1)

331.8 Other cerebral degeneration

    331.81 Reye's syndrome

    331.89 Other
        Cerebral ataxia

331.9 Cerebral degeneration, unspecified

332 Parkinson's disease

332.0 Paralysis agitans
Parkinsonism or Parkinson's disease:
NOS
idiopathic
primary

332.1 Secondary Parkinsonism
Parkinsonism due to drugs
Use additional E code, if desired, to identify drug, if drug-induced

Excludes: *Parkinsonism (in):*
Huntington's disease (333.4)
progressive supranuclear palsy (333.0)
Shy-Drager syndrome (333.0)
syphilitic (094.82)

333 Other extrapyramidal disease and abnormal movement disorders
Includes: other forms of extrapyramidal, basal ganglia, or striatopallidal disease

Excludes: *abnormal movements of head NOS (781.0)*

333.0 Other degenerative diseases of the basal ganglia
Atrophy or degeneration:
olivopontocerebellar [Déjérine-Thomas syndrome]
pigmentary pallidal [Hallervorden-Spatz disease]
striatonigral
Parkinsonian syndrome associated with:
idiopathic orthostatic hypotension
symptomatic orthostatic hypotension
Progressive supranuclear ophthalmoplegia or palsy
Shy-Drager syndrome

333.1 Essential and other specified forms of tremor
Benign essential tremor   Familial tremor
Use additional E code, if desired, to identify drug, if drug-induced

Excludes: *tremor NOS (781.0)*

333.2 Myoclonus
Familial essential myoclonus
Progressive myoclonic epilepsy
Unverricht-Lundborg disease
Use additional E code, if desired, to identify drug, if drug-induced

333.3 Tics of organic origin

Excludes: *Gilles de la Tourette's syndrome (307.23)*
habit spasm (307.22)
tic NOS (307.20)

Use additional E code, if desired, to identify drug, if drug-induced

333.4 Huntington's chorea

149

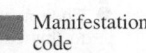

Add 4th or   Nonspecific   Unspecified   Manifestation
5th digit   code   code   code

333.5 **Other choreas**
    Hemiballism(us)
    Paroxysmal choreo-athetosis

    Excludes: *Sydenham's or rheumatic chorea (392.0-392.9)*
Use additional E code, if desired, to identify drug, if drug-induced

333.6 Idiopathic torsion dystonia
    Dystonia:
        deformans progressiva
        musculorum deformans
    (Schwalbe-) Ziehen-Oppenheim disease

333.7 Symptomatic torsion dystonia
    Athetoid cerebral palsy [Vogt's disease]
    Double athetosis (syndrome)
Use additional E code, if desired, to identify drug, if drug-induced

333.8 Fragments of torsion dystonia
Use additional E code, if desired, to identify drug, if drug-induced

    333.81 Blepharospasm

    333.82 Orofacial dyskinesia

    333.83 Spasmodic torticollis

    Excludes: *torticollis:*
        NOS (723.5)
        hysterical (300.11)
        psychogenic (306.0)

    333.84 Organic writers' cramp

    Excludes: *psychogenic (300.89)*

    333.89 Other

333.9 Other and unspecified extrapyramidal diseases and abnormal movement disorders

    333.90 Unspecified extrapyramidal disease and abnormal movement disorder

    333.91 Stiff-man syndrome

    333.92 Neuroleptic malignant syndrome
        Use additional E code to identify drug

    333.93 Benign shuddering attacks

    333.99 Other
        Restless legs

334 Spinocerebellar disease

    Excludes: *olivopontocerebellar degeneration (333.0)*
        peroneal muscular atrophy (356.1)

334.0 Friedreich's ataxia

334.1 Hereditary spastic paraplegia

334.2 Primary cerebellar degeneration
    Cerebellar ataxia:
        Marie's
        Sanger-Brown
    Dyssynergia cerebellaris myoclonica
    Primary cerebellar degeneration:
        NOS
        hereditary
        sporadic

334.3 Other cerebellar ataxia
    Cerebellar ataxia NOS
Use additional E code, if desired, to identify drug, if drug-induced

334.4 Cerebellar ataxia in diseases classified elsewhere
    Code first underlying disease, as:
        alcoholism (303.0-303.9)
        myxedema (244.0-244.9)
        neoplastic disease (140.0-239.9)

334.8 Other spinocerebellar diseases
    Ataxia-telangiectasia [Louis-Bar syndrome]
    Corticostriatal-spinal degeneration

334.9 Spinocerebellar disease, unspecified

● Code new
to this edition
    ▲ Revision of
existing code
    ④ ⑤ Fourth or fifth
digit required

335 Anterior horn cell disease

335.0 Werdnig-Hoffmann disease
Infantile spinal muscular atrophy
Progressive muscular atrophy of infancy

335.1 Spinal muscular atrophy

335.10 Spinal muscular atrophy, unspecified

335.11 Kugelberg-Welander disease
Spinal muscular atrophy:
familial
juvenile

335.19 Other
Adult spinal muscular atrophy

335.2 Motor neuron disease

335.20 Amyotrophic lateral sclerosis
Motor neuron disease (bulbar) (mixed type)

335.21 Progressive muscular atrophy
Duchenne-Aran muscular atrophy
Progressive muscular atrophy (pure)

335.22 Progressive bulbar palsy

335.23 Pseudobulbar palsy

335.24 Primary lateral sclerosis

335.29 Other

335.8 Other anterior horn cell diseases

335.9 Anterior horn cell disease, unspecified

336 Other diseases of spinal cord

336.0 Syringomyelia and syringobulbia

336.1 Vascular myelopathies
Acute infarction of spinal cord (embolic) (nonembolic)
Arterial thrombosis of spinal cord
Edema of spinal cord
Hematomyelia
Subacute necrotic myelopathy

336.2 *Subacute combined degeneration of spinal cord in diseases classified elsewhere*
Code first underlying disease, as:
pernicious anemia (281.0)
other vitamin B_{12} deficiency anemia (281.1)
vitamin B_{12} deficiency (266.2)

336.3 *Myelopathy in other diseases classified elsewhere*
Code first underlying disease, as:
myelopathy in neoplastic disease (140.0-239.9)

Excludes: *myelopathy in:*
intervertebral disc disorder (722.70-722.73)
spondylosis (721.1, 721.41-721.42, 721.91)

336.8 Other myelopathy
Myelopathy:
drug-induced
radiation-induced

Use additional E code, if desired, to identify cause

336.9 Unspecified disease of spinal cord
Cord compression NOS   Myelopathy NOS

Excludes: *myelitis (323.0-323.9)*
spinal (canal) stenosis (723.0, 724.00-724.09)

337 Disorders of the autonomic nervous system
Includes: disorders of peripheral autonomic, sympathetic, parasympathetic, or vegetative system

Excludes: *familial dysautonomia [Riley-Day syndrome] (742.8)*

337.0 Idiopathic peripheral autonomic neuropathy
Carotid sinus syncope or syndrome
Cervical sympathetic dystrophy or paralysis

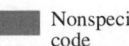 Add 4th or
5th digit

 Nonspecific
code

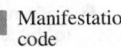 Unspecified
code

Manifestation
code

337.1 *Peripheral autonomic neuropathy in disorders classified elsewhere*
Code first underlying disease, as:
amyloidosis (277.3)
diabetes (250.6)

337.2 Reflex sympathetic dystrophy

337.20 Reflex sympathetic dystrophy, unspecified

337.21 Reflex sympathetic dystrophy of the upper limb

337.22 Reflex sympathetic dystrophy of the lower limb

337.29 Reflex sympathetic dystrophy of other specified site

337.9 Unspecified disorder of autonomic nervous system

OTHER DISORDERS OF THE CENTRAL NERVOUS SYSTEM (340-349)

340 Multiple sclerosis
Disseminated or multiple sclerosis:
NOS
brain stem
cord
generalized

341 **Other demyelinating diseases of central nervous system**

341.0 Neuromyelitis optica

341.1 Schilder's disease
Baló's concentric sclerosis
Encephalitis periaxialis:
concentrica [Baló's]
diffusa [Schilder's]

341.8 **Other demyelinating diseases of central nervous system**
Central demyelination of corpus callosum
Central pontine myelinosis
Marchiafava (-Bignami) disease

341.9 **Demyelinating disease of central nervous system, unspecified**

⑤ **342** **Hemiplegia and hemiparesis**
Note: This category is to be used when hemiplegia (complete) (incomplete) is reported without
further specification, or is stated to be old or long-standing but of unspecified cause. The
category is also for use in multiple coding to identify these types of hemiplegia resulting
from any cause.

The following fifth-digits are for use with codes 342.0-342.9

0 affecting unspecified site

1 affecting dominant site

2 affecting nondominant site

Excludes: *congenital (343.1)*
infantile NOS (343.4)

342.0 Flaccid hemiplegia

342.1 Spastic hemiplegia

342.8 **Other specified hemiplegia**

342.9 **Hemiplegia, unspecified**

343 **Infantile cerebral palsy**
Includes: cerebral:
palsy NOS
spastic infantile paralysis
congenital spastic paralysis (cerebral)
Little's disease
paralysis (spastic) due to birth injury:
intracranial
spinal

Excludes: *hereditary cerebral paralysis, such as:*
hereditary spastic paraplegia (334.1)
Vogt's disease (333.7)
spastic paralysis specified as noncongenital or noninfantile (344.0-344.9)

343.0 Diplegic
Congenital diplegia   Congenital paraplegia

● Code new   ▲ Revision of   ④ ⑤ Fourth or fifth
to this edition   existing code   digit required

343.1 Hemiplegic
Congenital hemiplegia

Excludes: *infantile hemiplegia NOS (343.4)*

343.2 Quadriplegic
Tetraplegic

343.3 Monoplegic

343.4 Infantile hemiplegia
Infantile hemiplegia (postnatal) NOS

343.8 Other specified infantile cerebral palsy

343.9 Infantile cerebral palsy, unspecified
Cerebral palsy NOS

344 Other paralytic syndromes

Note: This category is to be used when the listed conditions are reported without further
specification or are stated to be old or long-standing but of unspecified cause. The category
is also for use in multiple coding to identify these conditions resulting from any cause.
Includes: paralysis (complete) (incomplete), except as classifiable to 342 and 343

Excludes: *congenital or infantile cerebral palsy (343.0-343.9)*
hemiplegia (342.0-342.9)
congenital or infantile (343.1, 343.4)

344.0 Quadriplegia and quadriparesis

344.00 Quadriplegia, unspecified

344.01 C1-C4, complete

344.02 C1-C4, incomplete

344.03 C5-C7, complete

344.04 C5-C7, incomplete

344.09 Other

344.1 Paraplegia
Paralysis of both lower limbs
Paraplegia (lower)

344.2 Diplegia of upper limbs
Diplegia (upper)
Paralysis of both upper limbs

344.3 Monoplegia of lower limb
Paralysis of lower limb

344.30 affecting unspecified side

344.31 affecting dominant side

344.32 affecting nondominant side

344.4 Monoplegia of upper limb
Paralysis of upper limb

344.40 affecting unspecified side

344.41 affecting dominant side

344.42 affecting nondominant side

344.5 Unspecified monoplegia

344.6 Cauda equina syndrome

344.60 Without mention of neurogenic bladder

344.61 With neurogenic bladder
Acontractile bladder
Autonomic hyperreflexia of bladder
Cord bladder
Detrusor hyperreflexia

344.8 Other specified paralytic syndromes

344.81 Locked-in state

344.89 Other specified paralytic syndrome

344.9 Paralysis, unspecified

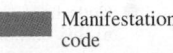

| | Add 4th or 5th digit | | Nonspecific code | | Unspecified code | | Manifestation code |

345 Epilepsy

The following fifth-digit subclassification is for use with categories 345.0, 345.1, 345.4-345.9:

    0 without mention of intractable epilepsy

    1 with intractable epilepsy

Excludes: *progressive myoclonic epilepsy (333.2)*

⑤ **345.0 Generalized nonconvulsive epilepsy**
      Absences:
        atonic
        typical
      Minor epilepsy
      Petit mal
      Pykno-epilepsy
      Seizures:
        akinetic
        atonic

⑤ **345.1 Generalized convulsive epilepsy**
      Epileptic seizures:
        clonic
        myoclonic
        tonic
        tonic-clonic
      Grand mal
      Major epilepsy

Excludes: *convulsions:*
      NOS (780.3)
      infantile (780.3)
      newborn (779.0)
      infantile spasms (345.6)

345.2 Petit mal status
      Epileptic absence status

345.3 Grand mal status
      Status epilepticus NOS

Excludes: *epilepsia partialis continua (345.7)*
      status:
        psychomotor (345.7)
        temporal lobe (345.7)

⑤ **345.4 Partial epilepsy, with impairment of consciousness**
      Epilepsy:
        limbic system
        partial:
          secondarily generalized
          with memory and ideational disturbances
        psychomotor
        psychosensory
        temporal lobe
      Epileptic automatism

⑤ **345.5 Partial epilepsy, without mention of impairment of consciousness**
      Epilepsy:
        Bravais-Jacksonian NOS
        focal (motor) NOS
        Jacksonian NOS
        motor partial
        partial NOS
      Epilepsy:
        sensory-induced
        somatomotor
        somatosensory
        visceral
        visual

⑤ **345.6 Infantile spasms**
      Hypsarrhythmia
      Lightning spasms
      Salaam attacks

Excludes: *salaam tic (781.0)*

⑤ **345.7 Epilepsia partialis continua**
      Kojevnikov's epilepsy

⑤ **345.8 Other forms of epilepsy**
      Epilepsy:
        cursive [running]
        gelastic

⑤ **345.9 Epilepsy, unspecified**
      Epileptic convulsions, fits, or seizures NOS

Excludes: *convulsive seizure or fit NOS (780.3)*

● Code new
  to this edition
    ▲ Revision of
      existing code
    ④ ⑤ Fourth or fifth
      digit required

⑤ **346** **Migraine**

The following fifth-digit subclassification is for use with category 346:

   0   **without mention of intractable migraine**

   1   **with intractable migraine, so stated**

346.0 **Classical migraine**
Migraine preceded or accompanied by transient focal neurological phenomena
Migraine with aura

346.1 **Common migraine**
Atypical migraine   Sick headache

346.2 **Variants of migraine**
Cluster headache   Migraine:
Histamine cephalgia   lower half
Horton's neuralgia   retinal
Migraine: Neuralgia:
   abdominal   ciliary
   basilar   migrainous

346.8 **Other forms of migraine**
Migraine:
   hemiplegic
   ophthalmoplegic

346.9 **Migraine, unspecified**

347 **Cataplexy and narcolepsy**

348 **Other conditions of brain**

348.0 **Cerebral cysts**
Arachnoid cyst   Porencephaly, acquired
Porencephalic cyst   Pseudoporencephaly

   Excludes: *porencephaly (congenital) (742.4)*

348.1 **Anoxic brain damage**

   Excludes: *that occurring in:*
               abortion (634-638 with .7, 639.8)
               ectopic or molar pregnancy (639.8)
               labor or delivery (668.2, 669.4)
               that of newborn (767.0, 768.0-768.9, 772.1-772.2)

Use additional E code, if desired, to identify cause

348.2 **Benign intracranial hypertension**
Pseudotumor cerebri

   Excludes: *hypertensive encephalopathy (437.2)*

348.3 **Encephalopathy, unspecified**

348.4 **Compression of brain**
Compression   ⎫
Herniation   ⎬ brain (stem)
Posterior fossa compression syndrome

348.5 **Cerebral edema**

348.8 **Other conditions of brain**
Cerebral:
   calcification
   fungus

348.9 **Unspecified condition of brain**

349 **Other and unspecified disorders of the nervous system**

349.0 **Reaction to spinal or lumbar puncture**
Headache following lumbar puncture

349.1 **Nervous system complications from surgically implanted device**

   Excludes: *immediate postoperative complications (997.00-997.09)*
               mechanical complications of nervous system device (996.2)

349.2 **Disorders of meninges, not elsewhere classified**
Adhesions, meningeal (cerebral) (spinal)
Cyst, spinal meninges
Meningocele, acquired
Pseudomeningocele, acquired

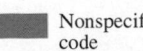 Add 4th or 5th digit

 Nonspecific code

 Unspecified code

Manifestation code

349.8 Other specified disorders of nervous system

349.81 Cerebrospinal fluid rhinorrhea

Excludes: *cerebrospinal fluid otorrhea (388.61)*

349.82 Toxic encephalopathy
Use additional E code, if desired, to identify cause

349.89 Other

349.9 Unspecified disorders of nervous system
Disorder of nervous system (central) NOS

DISORDERS OF THE PERIPHERAL NERVOUS SYSTEM (350-359)

Excludes: *diseases of:*

> *acoustic [8th] nerve (388.5)*
> *oculomotor [3rd, 4th, 6th] nerves (378.0-378.9)*
> *optic [2nd] nerve (377.0-377.9)*
> *peripheral autonomic nerves (337.0-337.9)*
> *neuralgia*
> *neuritis* } *NOS or "rheumatic" (729.2)*
> *radiculitis*
> *peripheral neuritis in pregnancy (646.4)*

350 Trigeminal nerve disorders
Includes: disorders of 5th cranial nerve

350.1 Trigeminal neuralgia
Tic douloureux   Trigeminal neuralgia NOS
Trifacial neuralgia

Excludes: *postherpetic (053.12)*

350.2 Atypical face pain

350.8 Other specified trigeminal nerve disorders

350.9 Trigeminal nerve disorder, unspecified

351 Facial nerve disorders
Includes: disorders of 7th cranial nerve

Excludes: *that in newborn (767.5)*

351.0 Bell's palsy
Facial palsy

351.1 Geniculate ganglionitis
Geniculate ganglionitis NOS

Excludes: *herpetic (053.11)*

351.8 Other facial nerve disorders
Facial myokymia   Melkersson's syndrome

351.9 Facial nerve disorder, unspecified

352 Disorders of other cranial nerves

352.0 Disorders of olfactory [1st] nerve

352.1 Glossopharyngeal neuralgia

352.2 Other disorders of glossopharyngeal [9th] nerve

352.3 Disorders of pneumogastric [10th] nerve
Disorders of vagal nerve

Excludes: *paralysis of vocal cords or larynx (478.30-478.34)*

352.4 Disorders of accessory [11th] nerve

352.5 Disorders of hypoglossal [12th] nerve

352.6 Multiple cranial nerve palsies
Collet-Sicard syndrome   Polyneuritis cranialis

352.9 Unspecified disorder of cranial nerves

353 Nerve root and plexus disorders

Excludes: *conditions due to:*

> *intervertebral disc disorders (722.0-722.9)*
> *spondylosis (720.0-721.9)*
> *vertebrogenic disorders (723.0-724.9)*

● Code new   ▲ Revision of   ④ ⑤ Fourth or fifth
      to this edition   existing code   digit required

353.0 Brachial plexus lesions
Cervical rib syndrome   Thoracic outlet syndrome
Costoclavicular syndrome
Scalenus anticus syndrome

> Excludes: *brachial neuritis or radiculitis NOS (723.4)*
>   *that in newborn (767.6)*

353.1 Lumbosacral plexus lesions

353.2 Cervical root lesions, not elsewhere classified

353.3 Thoracic root lesions, not elsewhere classified

353.4 Lumbosacral root lesions, not elsewhere classified

353.5 Neuralgic amyotrophy
Parsonage-Aldren-Turner syndrome

353.6 Phantom limb (syndrome)

353.8 Other nerve root and plexus disorders

353.9 Unspecified nerve root and plexus disorder

354 Mononeuritis of upper limb and mononeuritis multiplex

354.0 Carpal tunnel syndrome
Median nerve entrapment   Partial thenar atrophy

354.1 Other lesion of median nerve
Median nerve neuritis

354.2 Lesion of ulnar nerve
Cubital tunnel syndrome   Tardy ulnar nerve palsy

354.3 Lesion of radial nerve
Acute radial nerve palsy

354.4 Causalgia of upper limb

> Excludes: *causalgia:*
>   *NOS (355.9)*
>   *lower limb (355.71)*

354.5 Mononeuritis multiplex
Combinations of single conditions classifiable to 354 or 355

354.8 Other mononeuritis of upper limb

354.9 Mononeuritis of upper limb, unspecified

355 Mononeuritis of lower limb and unspecified site

355.0 Lesion of sciatic nerve

> Excludes: *sciatica NOS (724.3)*

355.1 Meralgia paresthetica
Lateral cutaneous femoral nerve of thigh compression or syndrome

355.2 Other lesion of femoral nerve

355.3 Lesion of lateral popliteal nerve
Lesion of common peroneal nerve

355.4 Lesion of medial popliteal nerve

355.5 Tarsal tunnel syndrome

355.6 Lesion of plantar nerve
Morton's metatarsalgia, neuralgia, or neuroma

355.7 Other mononeuritis of lower limb

 355.71 Causalgia of lower limb

> Excludes: *causalgia:*
>   *NOS (355.9)*
>   *upper limb (354.4)*

 355.79 Other mononeuritis of lower limb

355.8 Mononeuritis of lower limb, unspecified

355.9 Mononeuritis of unspecified site
Causalgia NOS

> Excludes: *causalgia:*
>   *lower limb (355.71)*
>   *upper limb (354.4)*

 Add 4th or 5th digit   Nonspecific code   Unspecified code 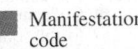 Manifestation code

356 **Hereditary and idiopathic peripheral neuropathy**

356.0 **Hereditary peripheral neuropathy**
Déjérine-Sottas disease

356.1 **Peroneal muscular atrophy**
Charcot-Marie-Tooth disease
Neuropathic muscular atrophy

356.2 **Hereditary sensory neuropathy**

356.3 **Refsum's disease**
Heredopathia atactica polyneuritiformis

356.4 **Idiopathic progressive polyneuropathy**

356.8 **Other specified idiopathic peripheral neuropathy**
Supranuclear paralysis

356.9 **Unspecified**

357 **Inflammatory and toxic neuropathy**

357.0 **Acute infective polyneuritis**
Guillain-Barré syndrome
Postinfectious polyneuritis

357.1 *Polyneuropathy in collagen vascular disease*
Code first underlying disease, as:
disseminated lupus erythematosus (710.0)
polyarteritis nodosa (446.0)
rheumatoid arthritis (714.0)

357.2 *Polyneuropathy in diabetes*
Code first underlying disease (250.6)

357.3 *Polyneuropathy in malignant disease*
Code first underlying disease (140.0-208.9)

357.4 *Polyneuropathy in other diseases classified elsewhere*
Code first underlying disease, as:
amyloidosis (277.3)
beriberi (265.0)
deficiency of B vitamins (266.0-266.9)
diphtheria (032.0-032.9)
hypoglycemia (251.2)
pellagra (265.2)
porphyria (277.1)
sarcoidosis (135)
uremia (585)

Excludes: *polyneuropathy in:*
herpes zoster (053.13)
mumps (072.72)

357.5 **Alcoholic polyneuropathy**

357.6 **Polyneuropathy due to drugs**
Use additional E code, if desired, to identify drug

357.7 **Polyneuropathy due to other toxic agents**
Use additional E code, if desired, to identify toxic agent

357.8 **Other**

357.9 **Unspecified**

358 **Myoneural disorders**

358.0 **Myasthenia gravis**

358.1 *Myasthenic syndromes in diseases classified elsewhere*
Amyotrophy
Eaton-Lambert syndrome } from stated cause classified elsewhere
Code first underlying disease, as:
botulism (005.1)
diabetes mellitus (250.6)
hypothyroidism (244.0-244.9)
malignant neoplasm (140.0-208.9)
pernicious anemia (281.0)
thyrotoxicosis (242.0-242.9)

358.2 **Toxic myoneural disorders**
Use additional E code, if desired, to identify toxic agent

● Code new
to this edition

▲ Revision of
existing code

④ ⑤ Fourth or fifth
digit required

358.8 Other specified myoneural disorders

358.9 Myoneural disorders, unspecified

359 Muscular dystrophies and other myopathies

> *Excludes:* idiopathic polymyositis (710.4)

359.0 Congenital hereditary muscular dystrophy
Benign congenital myopathy
Central core disease
Centronuclear myopathy
Myotubular myopathy
Nemaline body disease

> *Excludes:* arthrogryposis multiplex congenita (754.89)

359.1 Hereditary progressive muscular dystrophy

Muscular dystrophy:
NOS
distal
Duchenne
Erb's
fascioscapulohumeral

Muscular dystrophy:
Gower's
Landouzy-Déjérine
limb-girdle
ocular
oculopharyngeal

359.2 Myotonic disorders

Dystrophia myotonica
Eulenburg's disease
Myotonia congenita

Paramyotonia congenita
Steinert's disease
Thomsen's disease

359.3 Familial periodic paralysis
Hypokalemic familial periodic paralysis

359.4 Toxic myopathy

Use additional E code, if desired, to identify toxic agent

359.5 *Myopathy in endocrine diseases classified elsewhere*
Code first underlying disease, as:
Addison's disease (255.4)
Cushing's syndrome (255.0)
hypopituitarism (253.2)
myxedema (244.0-244.9)
thyrotoxicosis (242.0-242.9)

359.6 *Symptomatic inflammatory myopathy in diseases classified elsewhere*
Code first underlying disease, as:
amyloidosis (277.3)
disseminated lupus erythematosus (710.0)
malignant neoplasm (140.0-208.9)
polyarteritis nodosa (446.0)
rheumatoid arthritis (714.0)
sarcoidosis (135)
scleroderma (710.1)
Sjögren's disease (710.2)

359.8 Other myopathies

359.9 Myopathy, unspecified

DISORDERS OF THE EYE AND ADNEXA (360-379)

360 Disorders of the globe
Includes: disorders affecting multiple structures of eye

360.0 Purulent endophthalmitis

360.00 Purulent endophthalmitis, unspecified

360.01 Acute endophthalmitis

360.02 Panophthalmitis

360.03 Chronic endophthalmitis

360.04 Vitreous abscess

360.1 Other endophthalmitis

360.11 Sympathetic uveitis

360.12 Panuveitis

360.13 Parasitic endophthalmitis NOS

360.14 Ophthalmia nodosa

159

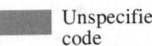 Add 4th or 5th digit   Nonspecific code   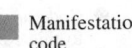 Unspecified code   Manifestation code

360.19 Other
Phacoanaphylactic endophthalmitis

360.2 Degenerative disorders of globe

360.20 Degenerative disorder of globe, unspecified

360.21 Progressive high (degenerative) myopia
Malignant myopia

360.23 Siderosis

360.24 Other metallosis
Chalcosis

360.29 Other

Excludes: xerophthalmia (264.7)

360.3 Hypotony of eye

360.30 Hypotony, unspecified

360.31 Primary hypotony

360.32 Ocular fistula causing hypotony

360.33 Hypotony associated with other ocular disorders

360.34 Flat anterior chamber

360.4 Degenerated conditions of globe

360.40 Degenerated globe or eye, unspecified

360.41 Blind hypotensive eye
Atrophy of globe   Phthisis bulbi

360.42 Blind hypertensive eye
Absolute glaucoma

360.43 Hemophthalmos, except current injury

Excludes: traumatic (871.0-871.9, 921.0-921.9)

360.44 Leucocoria

360.5 Retained (old) intraocular foreign body, magnetic

Excludes: current penetrating injury with magnetic foreign body (871.5)
retained (old) foreign body of orbit (376.6)

360.50 Foreign body, magnetic, intraocular, unspecified

360.51 Foreign body, magnetic, in anterior chamber

360.52 Foreign body, magnetic, in iris or ciliary body

360.53 Foreign body, magnetic, in lens

360.54 Foreign body, magnetic, in vitreous

360.55 Foreign body, magnetic, in posterior wall

360.59 Foreign body, magnetic, in other or multiple sites

360.6 Retained (old) intraocular foreign body, nonmagnetic
Retained (old) foreign body:
NOS
nonmagnetic

Excludes: current penetrating injury with (nonmagnetic) foreign body (871.6)
retained (old) foreign body in orbit (376.6)

360.60 Foreign body, intraocular, unspecified

360.61 Foreign body in anterior chamber

360.62 Foreign body in iris or ciliary body

360.63 Foreign body in lens

360.64 Foreign body in vitreous

360.65 Foreign body in posterior wall

360.69 Foreign body in other or multiple sites

360.8 Other disorders of globe

360.81 Luxation of globe

360.89 Other

360.9 Unspecified disorder of globe

361 Retinal detachments and defects

● Code new   ▲ Revision of   ④ ⑤ Fourth or fifth
to this edition   existing code   digit required

361.0 Retinal detachment with retinal defect
Rhegmatogenous retinal detachment

Excludes: *detachment of retinal pigment epithelium (362.42-362.43)*
retinal detachment (serous) (without defect) (361.2)

361.00 Retinal detachment with retinal defect, unspecified

361.01 Recent detachment, partial, with single defect

361.02 Recent detachment, partial, with multiple defects

361.03 Recent detachment, partial, with giant tear

361.04 Recent detachment, partial, with retinal dialysis
Dialysis (juvenile) of retina (with detachment)

361.05 Recent detachment, total or subtotal

361.06 Old detachment, partial
Delimited old retinal detachment

361.07 Old detachment, total or subtotal

361.1 Retinoschisis and retinal cysts

Excludes: *juvenile retinoschisis (362.73)*
microcystoid degeneration of retina (362.62)
parasitic cyst of retina (360.13)

361.10 Retinoschisis, unspecified

361.11 Flat retinoschisis

361.12 Bullous retinoschisis

361.13 Primary retinal cysts

361.14 Secondary retinal cysts

361.19 Other
Pseudocyst of retina

361.2 Serous retinal detachment
Retinal detachment without retinal defect

Excludes: *central serous retinopathy (362.41)*
retinal pigment epithelium detachment (362.42-362.43)

361.3 Retinal defects without detachment

Excludes: *chorioretinal scars after surgery for detachment (363.30-363.35)*
peripheral retinal degeneration without defect (362.60-362.66)

361.30 Retinal defect, unspecified
Retinal break(s) NOS

361.31 Round hole of retina without detachment

361.32 Horseshoe tear of retina without detachment
Operculum of retina without mention of detachment

361.33 Multiple defects of retina without detachment

361.8 Other forms of retinal detachment

361.81 Traction detachment of retina
Traction detachment with vitreoretinal organization

361.89 Other

361.9 Unspecified retinal detachment

362 Other retinal disorders

Excludes: *chorioretinal scars (363.30-363.35)*
chorioretinitis (363.0-363.2)

362.0 Diabetic retinopathy
Code first diabetes (250.5)

362.01 Background diabetic retinopathy
Diabetic retinal microaneurysms
Diabetic retinopathy NOS

362.02 Proliferative diabetic retinopathy

362.1 Other background retinopathy and retinal vascular changes

362.10 Background retinopathy, unspecified

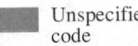

Add 4th or 5th digit	Nonspecific code	Unspecified code	Manifestation code

362.11 Hypertensive retinopathy

362.12 Exudative retinopathy
    Coats' syndrome

362.13 Changes in vascular appearance
    Vascular sheathing of retina
   Use additional code for any associated atherosclerosis (440.8)

362.14 Retinal microaneurysms NOS

362.15 Retinal telangiectasia

362.16 Retinal neovascularization NOS
    Neovascularization:
      choroidal
      subretinal

362.17 Other intraretinal microvascular abnormalities
    Retinal varices

362.18 Retinal vasculitis
    Eales' disease   Retinal:
    Retinal: perivasculitis
      arteritis   phlebitis
      endarteritis

362.2 Other proliferative retinopathy

362.21 Retrolental fibroplasia

362.29 Other nondiabetic proliferative retinopathy

362.3 Retinal vascular occlusion

362.30 Retinal vascular occlusion, unspecified

362.31 Central retinal artery occlusion

362.32 Arterial branch occlusion

362.33 Partial arterial occlusion
    Hollenhorst plaque   Retinal microembolism

362.34 Transient arterial occlusion
    Amaurosis fugax

362.35 Central retinal vein occlusion

362.36 Venous tributary (branch) occlusion

362.37 Venous engorgement
    Occlusion:
      incipient   } of retinal vein
      partial

362.4 Separation of retinal layers

  Excludes: *retinal detachment (serous) (361.2)*
           rhegmatogenous (361.00-361.07)

362.40 Retinal layer separation, unspecified

362.41 Central serous retinopathy

362.42 Serous detachment of retinal pigment epithelium
    Exudative detachment of retinal pigment epithelium

362.43 Hemorrhagic detachment of retinal pigment epithelium

362.5 Degeneration of macula and posterior pole

  Excludes: *degeneration of optic disc (377.21-377.24)*
           hereditary retinal degeneration [dystrophy] (362.70-362.77)

362.50 Macular degeneration (senile), unspecified

362.51 Nonexudative senile macular degeneration
    Senile macular degeneration:
      atrophic
      dry

362.52 Exudative senile macular degeneration
    Kuhnt-Junius degeneration
    Senile macular degeneration:
      disciform
      wet

362.53 Cystoid macular degeneration
    Cystoid macular edema

● Code new
  to this edition
▲ Revision of
  existing code
④ ⑤ Fourth or fifth
     digit required

362.54 **Macular cyst, hole, or pseudohole**

362.55 **Toxic maculopathy**
Use additional E code, if desired, to identify drug, if drug induced

362.56 **Macular puckering**
Preretinal fibrosis

362.57 **Drusen (degenerative)**

362.6 **Peripheral retinal degenerations**

Excludes: *hereditary retinal degeneration [dystrophy] (362.70-362.77)*
retinal degeneration with retinal defect (361.00-361.07)

362.60 **Peripheral retinal degeneration, unspecified**

362.61 **Paving stone degeneration**

362.62 **Microcystoid degeneration**
Blessig's cysts   Iwanoff's cysts

362.63 **Lattice degeneration**
Palisade degeneration of retina

362.64 **Senile reticular degeneration**

362.65 **Secondary pigmentary degeneration**
Pseudoretinitis pigmentosa

362.66 **Secondary vitreoretinal degenerations**

362.7 **Hereditary retinal dystrophies**

362.70 **Hereditary retinal dystrophy, unspecified**

362.71 *Retinal dystrophy in systemic or cerebroretinal lipidoses*
Code first underlying disease, as:
cerebroretinal lipidoses (330.1)
systemic lipidoses (272.7)

362.72 *Retinal dystrophy in other systemic disorders and syndromes*
Code first underlying disease, as:
Bassen-Kornzweig syndrome (272.5)
Refsum's disease (356.3)

362.73 **Vitreoretinal dystrophies**
Juvenile retinoschisis

362.74 **Pigmentary retinal dystrophy**
Retinal dystrophy, albipunctate
Retinitis pigmentosa

362.75 **Other dystrophies primarily involving the sensory retina**
Progressive cone (-rod) dystrophy
Stargardt's disease

362.76 **Dystrophies primarily involving the retinal pigment epithelium**
Fundus flavimaculatus
Vitelliform dystrophy

362.77 **Dystrophies primarily involving Bruch's membrane**
Dystrophy:
hyaline
pseudoinflammatory foveal
Hereditary drusen

362.8 **Other retinal disorders**

Excludes: *chorioretinal inflammations (363.0-363.2)*
chorioretinal scars (363.30-363.35)

362.81 **Retinal hemorrhage**
Hemorrhage:
preretinal
retinal (deep) (superficial)
subretinal

362.82 **Retinal exudates and deposits**

362.83 **Retinal edema**
Retinal:
cotton wool spots
edema (localized) (macular) (peripheral)

362.84 **Retinal ischemia**

362.85 **Retinal nerve fiber bundle defects**

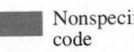 Add 4th or 5th digit

 Nonspecific code

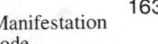 Unspecified code

Manifestation code

362.89	Other retinal disorders
362.9	Unspecified retinal disorder

363 Chorioretinal inflammations, scars, and other disorders of choroid

363.0 Focal chorioretinitis and focal retinochoroiditis

Excludes: *focal chorioretinitis or retinochoroiditis in:*
  histoplasmosis (115.02, 115.12, 115.92)
  toxoplasmosis (130.2)
   congenital infection (771.2)

363.00 **Focal chorioretinitis, unspecified**
  Focal:
   choroiditis or chorioretinitis NOS
   retinitis or retinochoroiditis NOS

363.01 **Focal choroiditis and chorioretinitis, juxtapapillary**

363.03 **Focal choroiditis and chorioretinitis of other posterior pole**

363.04 **Focal choroiditis and chorioretinitis, peripheral**

363.05 **Focal retinitis and retinochoroiditis, juxtapapillary**
  Neuroretinitis

363.06 **Focal retinitis and retinochoroiditis, macular or paramacular**

363.07 **Focal retinitis and retinochoroiditis of other posterior pole**

363.08 **Focal retinitis and retinochoroiditis, peripheral**

363.1 **Disseminated chorioretinitis and disseminated retinochoroiditis**

Excludes: *disseminated choroiditis or chorioretinitis in secondary syphilis (091.51)*
  neurosyphilitic disseminated retinitis or retinochoroiditis (094.83)
  retinal (peri)vasculitis (362.18)

363.10 **Disseminated chorioretinitis, unspecified**
  Disseminated:
   choroiditis or chorioretinitis NOS
   retinitis or retinochoroiditis NOS

363.11 **Disseminated choroiditis and chorioretinitis, posterior pole**

363.12 **Disseminated choroiditis and chorioretinitis, peripheral**

363.13 **Disseminated choroiditis and chorioretinitis, generalized**
  Code first any underlying disease, as:
   tuberculosis (017.3)

363.14 **Disseminated retinitis and retinochoroiditis, metastatic**

363.15 **Disseminated retinitis and retinochoroiditis, pigment epitheliopathy**
  Acute posterior multifocal placoid pigment epitheliopathy

363.2 **Other and unspecified forms of chorioretinitis and retinochoroiditis**

Excludes: *panophthalmitis (360.02)*
  sympathetic uveitis (360.11)
  uveitis NOS (364.3)

363.20 **Chorioretinitis, unspecified**
  Choroiditis NOS
  Retinitis NOS
  Uveitis, posterior NOS

363.21 **Pars planitis**
  Posterior cyclitis

363.22 **Harada's disease**

363.3 **Chorioretinal scars**
  Scar (postinflammatory) (postsurgical) (posttraumatic):
  choroid
  retina

363.30 **Chorioretinal scar, unspecified**

363.31 **Solar retinopathy**

363.32 **Other macular scars**

363.33 **Other scars of posterior pole**

363.34 **Peripheral scars**

363.35 **Disseminated scars**

363.4 **Choroidal degenerations**

● Code new
  to this edition

▲ Revision of
  existing code

④ ⑤ Fourth or fifth
  digit required

363.40 Choroidal degeneration, unspecified
Choroidal sclerosis NOS

363.41 Senile atrophy of choroid

363.42 Diffuse secondary atrophy of choroid

363.43 Angioid streaks of choroid

363.5 Hereditary choroidal dystrophies
Hereditary choroidal atrophy:
partial [choriocapillaris]
total [all vessels]

363.50 Hereditary choroidal dystrophy or atrophy, unspecified

363.51 Circumpapillary dystrophy of choroid, partial

363.52 Circumpapillary dystrophy of choroid, total
Helicoid dystrophy of choroid

363.53 Central dystrophy of choroid, partial
Dystrophy, choroidal:
central areolar
circinate

363.54 Central choroidal atrophy, total
Dystrophy, choroidal:
central gyrate
serpiginous

363.55 Choroideremia

363.56 Other diffuse or generalized dystrophy, partial
Diffuse choroidal sclerosis

363.57 Other diffuse or generalized dystrophy, total
Generalized gyrate atrophy, choroid

363.6 Choroidal hemorrhage and rupture

363.61 Choroidal hemorrhage, unspecified

363.62 Expulsive choroidal hemorrhage

363.63 Choroidal rupture

363.7 Choroidal detachment

363.70 Choroidal detachment, unspecified

363.71 Serous choroidal detachment

363.72 Hemorrhagic choroidal detachment

363.8 Other disorders of choroid

363.9 Unspecified disorder of choroid

364 Disorders of iris and ciliary body

364.0 Acute and subacute iridocyclitis
Anterior uveitis
Cyclitis   } acute
Iridocyclitis   subacute
Iritis

Excludes: *gonococcal (098.41)*
herpes simplex (054.44)
herpes zoster (053.22)

364.00 Acute and subacute iridocyclitis, unspecified

364.01 Primary iridocyclitis

364.02 Recurrent iridocyclitis

364.03 Secondary iridocyclitis, infectious

364.04 Secondary iridocyclitis, noninfectious
Aqueous:
cells
fibrin
flare

364.05 Hypopyon

364.1 Chronic iridocyclitis

Excludes: *posterior cyclitis (363.21)*

364.10 Chronic iridocyclitis, unspecified

165

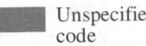
Add 4th or
5th digit

Nonspecific
code

Unspecified
code

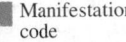
Manifestation
code

364.11 Chronic iridocyclitis in diseases classified elsewhere
Code first underlying disease, as:
  sarcoidosis (135)
  tuberculosis (017.3)
Excludes: syphilitic iridocyclitis (091.52)

364.2 Certain types of iridocyclitis
Excludes: posterior cyclitis (363.21)
  sympathetic uveitis (360.11)

364.21 Fuchs' heterochromic cyclitis

364.22 Glaucomatocyclitic crises

364.23 Lens-induced iridocyclitis

364.24 Vogt-Koyanagi syndrome

364.3 Unspecified iridocyclitis
Uveitis NOS

364.4 Vascular disorders of iris and ciliary body

364.41 Hyphema
Hemorrhage of iris or ciliary body

364.42 Rubeosis iridis
Neovascularization of iris or ciliary body

364.5 Degenerations of iris and ciliary body

364.51 Essential or progressive iris atrophy

364.52 Iridoschisis

364.53 Pigmentary iris degeneration
Acquired heterochromia
Pigment dispersion syndrome } of iris
Translucency

364.54 Degeneration of pupillary margin
Atrophy of sphincter } of iris
Ectropion of pigment epithelium

364.55 Miotic cysts of pupillary margin

364.56 Degenerative changes of chamber angle

364.57 Degenerative changes of ciliary body

364.59 Other iris atrophy
Iris atrophy (generalized) (sector shaped)

364.6 Cysts of iris, ciliary body, and anterior chamber
Excludes: miotic pupillary cyst (364.55)
  parasitic cyst (360.13)

364.60 Idiopathic cysts

364.61 Implantation cysts
Epithelial down-growth, anterior chamber
Implantation cysts (surgical) (traumatic)

364.62 Exudative cysts of iris or anterior chamber

364.63 Primary cyst of pars plana

364.64 Exudative cyst of pars plana

364.7 Adhesions and disruptions of iris and ciliary body
Excludes: flat anterior chamber (360.34)

364.70 Adhesions of iris, unspecified
Synechiae (iris) NOS

364.71 Posterior synechiae

364.72 Anterior synechiae

364.73 Goniosynechiae
Peripheral anterior synechiae

364.74 Pupillary membranes
Iris bombé
Pupillary:
  occlusion
  seclusion

● Code new   ▲ Revision of   ④ ⑤ Fourth or fifth
to this edition   existing code   digit required

364.75 **Pupillary abnormalities**
Deformed pupil   Rupture of sphincter, pupil
Ectopic pupil

364.76 **Iridodialysis**

364.77 **Recession of chamber angle**

364.8 **Other disorders of iris and ciliary body**
Prolapse of iris NOS

Excludes: *prolapse of iris in recent wound (871.1)*

364.9 **Unspecified disorder of iris and ciliary body**

365 Glaucoma

Excludes: *blind hypertensive eye [absolute glaucoma] (360.42)*
congenital glaucoma (743.20-743.22)

365.0 **Borderline glaucoma [glaucoma suspect]**

365.00 **Preglaucoma, unspecified**

365.01 **Open angle with borderline findings**
Open angle with:
borderline intraocular pressure
cupping of optic discs

365.02 **Anatomical narrow angle**

365.03 **Steroid responders**

365.04 **Ocular hypertension**

365.1 **Open-angle glaucoma**

365.10 **Open-angle glaucoma, unspecified**
Wide-angle glaucoma NOS

365.11 **Primary open angle glaucoma**
Chronic simple glaucoma

365.12 **Low tension glaucoma**

365.13 **Pigmentary glaucoma**

365.14 **Glaucoma of childhood**
Infantile or juvenile glaucoma

365.15 **Residual stage of open angle glaucoma**

365.2 **Primary angle-closure glaucoma**

365.20 **Primary angle-closure glaucoma, unspecified**

365.21 **Intermittent angle-closure glaucoma**
Angle-closure glaucoma:
interval
subacute

365.22 **Acute angle-closure glaucoma**

365.23 **Chronic angle-closure glaucoma**

365.24 **Residual stage of angle-closure glaucoma**

365.3 **Corticosteroid-induced glaucoma**

365.31 **Glaucomatous stage**

365.32 **Residual stage**

365.4 **Glaucoma associated with congenital anomalies, dystrophies, and systemic syndromes**

365.41 *Glaucoma associated with chamber angle anomalies*
Code first associated disorder, as:
Axenfeld's anomaly (743.44)
Rieger's anomaly or syndrome (743.44)

365.42 *Glaucoma associated with anomalies of iris*
Code first associated disorder, as:
aniridia (743.45)
essential iris atrophy (364.51)

365.43 *Glaucoma associated with other anterior segment anomalies*
Code first associated disorder, as:
microcornea (743.41)

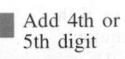 Add 4th or
5th digit

 Nonspecific
code

 Unspecified
code

 Manifestation
code

365.44 *Glaucoma associated with systemic syndromes*
Code first associated disease, as:
neurofibromatosis (237.7)
Sturge-Weber (-Dimitri) syndrome (759.6)

365.5 Glaucoma associated with disorders of the lens

365.51 Phacolytic glaucoma
Use additional code for associated hypermature cataract (366.18)

365.52 Pseudoexfoliation glaucoma
Use additional code for associated pseudoexfoliation of capsule (366.11)

365.59 Glaucoma associated with other lens disorders
Use additional code for associated disorder, as:
dislocation of lens (379.33-379.34)
spherophakia (743.36)

365.6 Glaucoma associated with other ocular disorders

365.60 Glaucoma associated with unspecified ocular disorder

365.61 Glaucoma associated with pupillary block
Use additional code for associated disorder, as:
seclusion of pupil [iris bombé] (364.74)

365.62 Glaucoma associated with ocular inflammations
Use additional code for associated disorder, as:
glaucomatocyclitic crises (364.22)
iridocyclitis (364.0-364.3)

365.63 Glaucoma associated with vascular disorders
Use additional code for associated disorder, as:
central retinal vein occlusion (362.35)
hyphema (364.41)

365.64 Glaucoma associated with tumors or cysts
Use additional code for associated disorder, as:
benign neoplasm (224.0-224.9)
epithelial down-growth (364.61)
malignant neoplasm (190.0-190.9)

365.65 Glaucoma associated with ocular trauma
Use additional code for associated condition, as:
contusion of globe (921.3)
recession of chamber angle (364.77)

365.8 Other specified forms of glaucoma

365.81 Hypersecretion glaucoma

365.82 Glaucoma with increased episcleral venous pressure

365.89 Other specified glaucoma

365.9 Unspecified glaucoma

366 Cataract

Excludes: *congenital cataract (743.30-743.34)*

366.0 Infantile, juvenile, and presenile cataract

366.00 Nonsenile cataract, unspecified

366.01 Anterior subcapsular polar cataract

366.02 Posterior subcapsular polar cataract

366.03 Cortical, lamellar, or zonular cataract

366.04 Nuclear cataract

366.09 Other and combined forms of nonsenile cataract

366.1 Senile cataract

366.10 Senile cataract, unspecified

366.11 Pseudoexfoliation of lens capsule

366.12 Incipient cataract
Cataract: Water clefts
coronary
immature NOS
punctate

366.13 Anterior subcapsular polar senile cataract

366.14 Posterior subcapsular polar senile cataract

● Code new
to this edition

▲ Revision of
existing code

④ ⑤ Fourth or fifth
digit required

366.15 **Cortical senile cataract**

366.16 **Nuclear sclerosis**
Cataracta brunescens
Nuclear cataract

366.17 **Total or mature cataract**

366.18 **Hypermature cataract**
Morgagni cataract

366.19 **Other and combined forms of senile cataract**

366.2 **Traumatic cataract**

366.20 **Traumatic cataract, unspecified**

366.21 **Localized traumatic opacities**
Vossius' ring

366.22 **Total traumatic cataract**

366.23 **Partially resolved traumatic cataract**

366.3 **Cataract secondary to ocular disorders**

366.30 **Cataracts complicata, unspecified**

366.31 **Glaucomatous flecks (subcapsular)**
Code first underlying glaucoma (365.0-365.9)

366.32 **Cataract in inflammatory disorders**
Code first underlying condition, as:
chronic choroiditis (363.0-363.2)

366.33 **Cataract with neovascularization**
Code first underlying condition, as:
chronic iridocyclitis (364.10)

366.34 **Cataract in degenerative disorders**
Sunflower cataract
Code first underlying condition, as:
chalcosis (360.24)
degenerative myopia (360.21)
pigmentary retinal dystrophy (362.74)

366.4 **Cataract associated with other disorders**

366.41 *Diabetic cataract*
Code first diabetes (250.5)

366.42 *Tetanic cataract*
Code first underlying disease, as:
calcinosis (275.4)
hypoparathyroidism (252.1)

366.43 *Myotonic cataract*
Code first underlying disorder (359.2)

366.44 *Cataract associated with other syndromes*
Code first underlying condition, as:
craniofacial dysostosis (756.0)
galactosemia (271.1)

366.45 **Toxic cataract**
Drug-induced cataract
Use additional E code, if desired, to identify drug or other toxic substance

366.46 **Cataract associated with radiation and other physical influences**
Use additional E code, if desired, to identify cause

366.5 **After-cataract**

366.50 **After-cataract, unspecified**
Secondary cataract NOS

366.51 **Soemmering's ring**

366.52 **Other after-cataract, not obscuring vision**

366.53 **After-cataract, obscuring vision**

366.8 **Other cataract**
Calcification of lens

366.9 **Unspecified cataract**

367 **Disorders of refraction and accommodation**

367.0 **Hypermetropia**
Far-sightedness   Hyperopia

169

 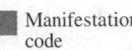

367.1 Myopia
Near-sightedness

367.2 Astigmatism

367.20 Astigmatism, unspecified

367.21 Regular astigmatism

367.22 Irregular astigmatism

367.3 Anisometropia and aniseikonia

367.31 Anisometropia

367.32 Aniseikonia

367.4 Presbyopia

367.5 Disorders of accommodation

367.51 Paresis of accommodation
Cycloplegia

367.52 Total or complete internal ophthalmoplegia

367.53 Spasm of accommodation

367.8 Other disorders of refraction and accommodation

367.81 Transient refractive change

367.89 Other
Drug-induced ⎱
Toxic ⎰ disorders of refraction and accommodation

367.9 Unspecified disorder of refraction and accommodation

368 Visual disturbances

Excludes: electrophysiological disturbances (794.11-794.14)

368.0 Amblyopia ex anopsia

368.00 Amblyopia, unspecified

368.01 Strabismic amblyopia
Suppression amblyopia

368.02 Deprivation amblyopia

368.03 Refractive amblyopia

368.1 Subjective visual disturbances

368.10 Subjective visual disturbance, unspecified

368.11 Sudden visual loss

368.12 Transient visual loss
Concentric fading   Scintillating scotoma

368.13 Visual discomfort
Asthenopia   Photophobia
Eye strain

368.14 Visual distortions of shape and size
Macropsia   Micropsia
Metamorphopsia

368.15 Other visual distortions and entoptic phenomena
Photopsia   Visual halos
Refractive:
diplopia
polyopia

368.16 Psychophysical visual disturbances
Visual:
agnosia
disorientation syndrome
hallucinations

368.2 Diplopia
Double vision

368.3 Other disorders of binocular vision

368.30 Binocular vision disorder, unspecified

368.31 Suppression of binocular vision

368.32 Simultaneous visual perception without fusion

368.33 Fusion with defective stereopsis

● Code new
to this edition

▲ Revision of
existing code

④ ⑤ Fourth or fifth
digit required

368.34 **Abnormal retinal correspondence**

368.4 **Visual field defects**

368.40 **Visual field defect, unspecified**

368.41 **Scotoma involving central area**
Scotoma:
central
centrocecal
paracentral

368.42 **Scotoma of blind spot area**
Enlarged: Paracecal scotoma
angioscotoma
blind spot

368.43 **Sector or arcuate defects**
Scotoma:
arcuate
Bjerrum
Seidel

368.44 **Other localized visual field defect**
Scotoma: Visual field defect:
NOS   nasal step
ring   peripheral

368.45 **Generalized contraction or constriction**

368.46 **Homonymous bilateral field defects**
Hemianopsia (altitudinal) (homonymous)
Quadrant anopia

368.47 **Heteronymous bilateral field defects**
Hemianopsia:
binasal
bitemporal

368.5 **Color vision deficiencies**
Color blindness

368.51 **Protan defect**
Protanomaly   Protanopia

368.52 **Deutan defect**
Deuteranomaly   Deuteranopia

368.53 **Tritan defect**
Tritanomaly   Tritanopia

368.54 **Achromatopsia**
Monochromatism (cone) (rod)

368.55 **Acquired color vision deficiencies**

368.59 **Other color vision deficiencies**

368.6 **Night blindness**
Hemeralopia   Nyctalopia

368.60 **Night blindness, unspecified**

368.61 **Congenital night blindness**
Hereditary night blindness
Oguchi's disease

368.62 **Acquired night blindness**

Excludes: *that due to vitamin A deficiency (264.5)*

368.63 **Abnormal dark adaptation curve**
Abnormal threshold   } of cones or rods
Delayed adaptation

368.69 **Other night blindness**

368.8 **Other specified visual disturbances**
Blurred vision NOS

368.9 **Unspecified visual disturbance**

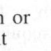 Add 4th or
5th digit

 Nonspecific
code

 Unspecified
code

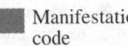 Manifestation
code

369 **Blindness and low vision**

Note: Visual impairment refers to a functional limitation of the eye (e.g., limited visual acuity or visual field). It should be distinguished from visual disability, indicating a limitation of the abilities of the individual (e.g., limited reading skills, vocational skills), and from visual handicap, indicating a limitation of personal and socioeconomic independence (e.g., limited mobility, limited employability.)

The levels of impairment defined in the table on page 174 are based on the recommendations of the WHO Study Group on Prevention of Blindness (Geneva, November 6-10, 1972; WHO Technical Report Series 518), and of the International Council of Ophthalmology (1976).

Note that definitions of blindness vary in different settings.

For international reporting WHO defines blindness as profound impairment. This definition can be applied to blindness of one eye (369.1, 369.6) and to blindness of the individual (369.0).

For determination of benefits in the U.S.A., the definition of legal blindness as severe impairment is often used. This definition applies to blindness of the individual only.

Excludes: *correctable impaired vision due to refractive errors (367.0-367.9)*

369.0 **Profound impairment, both eyes**

369.00 **Impairment level not further specified**
Blindness:
NOS according to WHO definition
both eyes

369.01 **Better eye: total impairment;**
lesser eye: total impairment

369.02 **Better eye: near-total impairment;**
lesser eye: not further specified

369.03 **Better eye: near-total impairment;**
lesser eye: total impairment

369.04 **Better eye: near-total impairment;**
lesser eye: near-total impairment

369.05 **Better eye: profound impairment;**
lesser eye: not further specified

369.06 **Better eye: profound impairment;**
lesser eye: total impairment

369.07 **Better eye: profound impairment;**
lesser eye: near-total impairment

369.08 **Better eye: profound impairment;**
lesser eye: profound impairment

369.1 **Moderate or severe impairment, better eye, profound impairment lesser eye**

369.10 **Impairment level not further specified**
Blindness, one eye, low vision other eye

369.11 **Better eye: severe impairment;**
lesser eye: blind, not further specified

369.12 **Better eye: severe impairment;**
lesser eye: total impairment

369.13 **Better eye: severe impairment;**
lesser eye: near-total impairment

369.14 **Better eye: severe impairment;**
lesser eye: profound impairment

369.15 **Better eye: moderate impairment;**
lesser eye: blind, not further specified

369.16 **Better eye: moderate impairment;**
lesser eye: total impairment

369.17 **Better eye: moderate impairment;**
lesser eye: near-total impairment

369.18 **Better eye: moderate impairment;**
lesser eye: profound impairment

● Code new
to this edition
▲ Revision of
existing code
④ ⑤ Fourth or fifth
digit required

369.2 Moderate or severe impairment, both eyes

369.20 Impairment level not further specified
Low vision, both eyes NOS

369.21 Better eye: severe impairment;
lesser eye: not further specified

369.22 Better eye: severe impairment;
lesser eye: severe impairment

369.23 Better eye: moderate impairment;
lesser eye: not further specified

369.24 Better eye: moderate impairment;
lesser eye: severe impairment

369.25 Better eye: moderate impairment;
lesser eye: moderate impairment

369.3 Unqualified visual loss, both eyes

Excludes: blindness NOS:
legal [U.S.A. definition] (369.4)
WHO definition (369.00)

☐ **369.4 Legal blindness, as defined in U.S.A.**
Blindness NOS according to U.S.A. definition

Excludes: legal blindness with specification of impairment level (369.01-369.08,
369.11-369.14, 369.21-369.22)

369.6 Profound impairment, one eye

369.60 Impairment level not further specified
Blindness, one eye

369.61 One eye: total impairment; other eye: not specified

369.62 One eye: total impairment; other eye: near-normal vision

369.63 One eye: total impairment; other eye: normal vision

369.64 One eye: near-total impairment; other eye: not specified

369.65 One eye: near-total impairment; other eye: near-normal vision

369.66 One eye: near-total impairment; other eye: normal vision

369.67 One eye: profound impairment; other eye: not specified

369.68 One eye: profound impairment; other eye: near-normal vision

369.69 One eye: profound impairment; other eye: normal vision

369.7 Moderate or severe impairment, one eye

369.70 Impairment level not further specified
Low vision, one eye

369.71 One eye: severe impairment; other eye: not specified

369.72 One eye: severe impairment; other eye: near-normal vision

369.73 One eye: severe impairment; other eye: normal vision

369.74 One eye: moderate impairment; other eye: not specified

369.75 One eye: moderate impairment; other eye: near-normal vision

369.76 One eye: moderate impairment; other eye: normal vision

369.8 Unqualified visual loss, one eye

369.9 Unspecified visual loss

370 Keratitis

370.0 Corneal ulcer

Excludes: that due to vitamin A deficiency (264.3)

370.00 Corneal ulcer, unspecified

370.01 Marginal corneal ulcer

370.02 Ring corneal ulcer

370.03 Central corneal ulcer

370.04 Hypopyon ulcer
Serpiginous ulcer

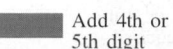 Add 4th or
5th digit

 Nonspecific
code

 Unspecified
code

 Manifestation
code

Classification		LEVELS OF VISUAL IMPAIRMENT					Additional Descriptors which may be encountered
"legal"	WHO	Visual Acuity and/or Visual Field Limitation (*whichever is worse*)					

		RANGE OF NORMAL VISION					
LEGAL BLINDNESS	**(NEAR-) NORMAL VISION**	20/10 2.0	20/13 1.6	20/16 1.25	20/20 1.0	20/25 0.8	
		NEAR-NORMAL VISION					
			20/30 0.7	20/40 0.6	20/50 0.5	20/60 0.4 ... 0.3	
	LOW VISION	MODERATE VISUAL IMPAIRMENT					Moderate low vision
		20/70	20/80 0.25	20/100 0.20	20/125 0.16	20/160 0.12	
		SEVERE VISUAL IMPAIRMENT					Severe low vision, "legal" blindness
			20/200 0.10	20/250 0.08	20/320 0.06	20/400 0.05	
		Visual Field: 20 degrees or less					
	BLINDNESS	PROFOUND VISUAL IMPAIRMENT					Profound low vision, moderate blindness
			20/500 0.04	20/630 0.03	20/800 0.025	20/1000 0.02	
		Count Fingers at: less than 3m (10 ft)					
		Visual Field: 10 degrees or less					
(USA) both eyes	(WHO) one or both eyes	NEAR-TOTAL VISUAL IMPAIRMENT					Severe blindness
		Visual Acuity: less than 0.02 (20/1000)					
		Count Fingers at: 1m (3 ft) or less					
		Hand Movements: 5m (15 ft) or less					Near-total blindness
		Light projection, light perception					
		Visual Field: 5 degrees or less					
		TOTAL VISUAL IMPAIRMENT					Total blindness
		No light perception (NLP)					

Visual acuity refers to best achievable acuity with correction
Non-listed Snellen fractions may be classified by converting to the nearest decimal equivalent, e.g., 10/200=0.05, 6/30=0.20
CF (count fingers) without designation of distance, may be classified to profound impairment.
HM (hand motion) without designation of distance, may be classified to near-total impairment.
Visual field measurements refer to the largest field diameter for a 1/100 white test object.

    370.05   **Mycotic corneal ulcer**

    370.06   **Perforated corneal ulcer**

    370.07   **Mooren's ulcer**

  370.2 **Superficial keratitis without conjunctivitis**

     Excludes: *dendritic [herpes simplex] keratitis (054.42)*

    370.20   **Superficial keratitis, unspecified**

    370.21   **Punctate keratitis**
         Thygeson's superficial punctate keratitis

    370.22   **Macular keratitis**
         Keratitis: Keratitis:
           areolar   stellate
           nummular   striate

    370.23   **Filamentary keratitis**

    370.24   **Photokeratitis**
         Snow blindness   Welders' keratitis

  370.3 **Certain types of keratoconjunctivitis**

    370.31   **Phlyctenular keratoconjunctivitis**
         Phlyctenulosis
     Use additional code for any associated tuberculosis (017.3)

  ● Code new to this edition   ▲ Revision of existing code   ④ ⑤ Fourth or fifth digit required

370.32 Limbar and corneal involvement in vernal conjunctivitis
Use additional code for vernal conjunctivitis (372.13)

370.33 Keratoconjunctivitis sicca, not specified as Sjögren's

Excludes: *Sjögren's syndrome (710.2)*

370.34 Exposure keratoconjunctivitis

370.35 Neurotrophic keratoconjunctivitis

370.4 Other and unspecified keratoconjunctivitis

370.40 Keratoconjunctivitis, unspecified
Superficial keratitis with conjunctivitis NOS

370.44 Keratitis or keratoconjunctivitis in exanthema
Code first underlying condition (050.0-052.9)

Excludes: *herpes simplex (054.43)*
herpes zoster (053.21)
measles (055.71)

370.49 Other

Excludes: *epidemic keratoconjunctivitis (077.1)*

370.5 Interstitial and deep keratitis

370.50 Interstitial keratitis, unspecified

370.52 Diffuse interstitial keratitis
Cogan's syndrome

370.54 Sclerosing keratitis

370.55 Corneal abscess

370.59 Other

Excludes: *disciform herpes simplex keratitis (054.43)*
syphilitic keratitis (090.3)

370.6 Corneal neovascularization

370.60 Corneal neovascularization, unspecified

370.61 Localized vascularization of cornea

370.62 Pannus (corneal)

370.63 Deep vascularization of cornea

370.64 Ghost vessels (corneal)

370.8 Other forms of keratitis

370.9 Unspecified keratitis

371 Corneal opacity and other disorders of cornea

371.0 Corneal scars and opacities

Excludes: *that due to vitamin A deficiency (264.6)*

371.00 Corneal opacity, unspecified
Corneal scar NOS

371.01 Minor opacity of cornea
Corneal nebula

371.02 Peripheral opacity of cornea
Corneal macula not interfering with central vision

371.03 Central opacity of cornea
Corneal: ⎤
  leucoma ⎬ interfering with central vision
  macula ⎦

371.04 Adherent leucoma

371.05 Phthisical cornea
Code first underlying tuberculosis (017.3)

371.1 Corneal pigmentations and deposits

371.10 Corneal deposit, unspecified

371.11 Anterior pigmentations
Stähli's lines

371.12 Stromal pigmentations
Hematocornea

175

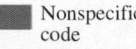 Add 4th or 5th digit   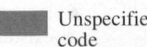 Nonspecific code   Unspecified code   Manifestation code

371.13 **Posterior pigmentations**
Krukenberg spindle

371.14 **Kayser-Fleischer ring**

`371.15` **Other deposits associated with metabolic disorders**

371.16 **Argentous deposits**

371.2 **Corneal edema**

`371.20` **Corneal edema, unspecified**

371.21 **Idiopathic corneal edema**

371.22 **Secondary corneal edema**

371.23 **Bullous keratopathy**

371.24 **Corneal edema due to wearing of contact lenses**

371.3 **Changes of corneal membranes**

`371.30` **Corneal membrane change, unspecified**

371.31 **Folds and rupture of Bowman's membrane**

371.32 **Folds in Descemet's membrane**

371.33 **Rupture in Descemet's membrane**

371.4 **Corneal degenerations**

`371.40` **Corneal degeneration, unspecified**

371.41 **Senile corneal changes**
Arcus senilis   Hassall-Henle bodies

371.42 **Recurrent erosion of cornea**

Excludes: *Mooren's ulcer (370.07)*

371.43 **Band-shaped keratopathy**

`371.44` **Other calcerous degenerations of cornea**

371.45 **Keratomalacia NOS**

Excludes: *that due to vitamin A deficiency (264.4)*

371.46 **Nodular degeneration of cornea**
Salzmann's nodular dystrophy

371.48 **Peripheral degenerations of cornea**
Marginal degeneration of cornea [Terrien's]

`371.49` **Other**
Discrete colliquative keratopathy

371.5 **Hereditary corneal dystrophies**

`371.50` **Corneal dystrophy, unspecified**

371.51 **Juvenile epithelial corneal dystrophy**

`371.52` **Other anterior corneal dystrophies**
Corneal dystrophy:
microscopic cystic
ring-like

371.53 **Granular corneal dystrophy**

371.54 **Lattice corneal dystrophy**

371.55 **Macular corneal dystrophy**

`371.56` **Other stromal corneal dystrophies**
Crystalline corneal dystrophy

371.57 **Endothelial corneal dystrophy**
Combined corneal dystrophy
Cornea guttata
Fuchs' endothelial dystrophy

`371.58` **Other posterior corneal dystrophies**
Polymorphous corneal dystrophy

371.6 **Keratoconus**

`371.60` **Keratoconus, unspecified**

371.61 **Keratoconus, stable condition**

371.62 **Keratoconus, acute hydrops**

● Code new   ▲ Revision of   ④ ⑤ Fourth or fifth
   to this edition   existing code   digit required

371.7 Other corneal deformities

> **371.70** Corneal deformity, unspecified

> **371.71** Corneal ectasia

> **371.72** Descemetocele

> **371.73** Corneal staphyloma

371.8 Other corneal disorders

> **371.81** Corneal anesthesia and hypoesthesia

> **371.82** Corneal disorder due to contact lens

> *Excludes:* *corneal edema due to contact lens (371.24)*

> **371.89** Other

371.9 Unspecified corneal disorder

372 Disorders of conjunctiva

> *Excludes:* *keratoconjunctivitis (370.3-370,4)*

372.0 Acute conjunctivitis

> **372.00** Acute conjunctivitis, unspecified

> **372.01** Serous conjunctivitis, except viral

> *Excludes;* *viral conjunctivitis NOS (077.9)*

> **372.02** Acute follicular conjunctivitis
> Conjunctival folliculosis NOS

> *Excludes:* *conjunctivitis:*
> *adenoviral (acute follicular) (077.3)*
> *epidemic hemorrhagic (077.4)*
> *inclusion (077.0)*
> *Newcastle (077.8)*
> *epidemic keratoconjunctivitis (077.1)*
> *pharyngoconjunctival fever (077.2)*

> **372.03** Other mucopurulent conjunctivitis
> Catarrhal conjunctivitis

> *Excludes:* *blennorrhea neonatorum (gonococcal) (098.40)*
> *neonatal conjunctivitis (771.6)*
> *ophthalmia neonatorum NOS (771.6)*

> **372.04** Pseudomembranous conjunctivitis
> Membranous conjunctivitis

> *Excludes:* *diphtheritic conjunctivitis (032.81)*

> **372.05** Acute atopic conjunctivitis

372.1 Chronic conjunctivitis

> **372.10** Chronic conjunctivitis, unspecified

> **372.11** Simple chronic conjunctivitis

> **372.12** Chronic follicular conjunctivitis

> **372.13** Vernal conjunctivitis

> **372.14** Other chronic allergic conjunctivitis

> **372.15** *Parasitic conjunctivitis*
> Code first underlying disease, as:
> filariasis (125.0-125.9)
> mucocutaneous leishmaniasis (085.5)

372.2 Blepharoconjunctivitis

> **372.20** Blepharoconjunctivitis, unspecified

> **372.21** Angular blepharoconjunctivitis

> **372.22** Contact blepharoconjunctivitis

372.3 Other and unspecified conjunctivitis

> **372.30** Conjunctivitis, unspecified

> **372.31** *Rosacea conjunctivitis*
> Code first underlying rosacea dermatitis (695.3)

Add 4th or 5th digit   Nonspecific code   Unspecified code   Manifestation code

372.33 *Conjunctivitis in mucocutaneous disease*
Code first underlying disease, as:
erythema multiforme (695.1)
Reiter's disease (099.3)

Excludes: ocular pemphigoid (694.61)

372.39 **Other**

372.4 Pterygium

Excludes: pseudopterygium (372.52)

372.40 **Pterygium, unspecified**

372.41 **Peripheral pterygium, stationary**

372.42 **Peripheral pterygium, progressive**

372.43 **Central pterygium**

372.44 **Double pterygium**

372.45 **Recurrent pterygium**

372.5 Conjunctival degenerations and deposits

372.50 **Conjunctival degeneration, unspecified**

372.51 **Pinguecula**

372.52 **Pseudopterygium**

372.53 **Conjunctival xerosis**

Excludes: conjunctival xerosis due to vitamin A deficiency (264.0, 264.1, 264.7)

372.54 **Conjunctival concretions**

372.55 **Conjunctival pigmentations**
Conjunctival argyrosis

372.56 **Conjunctival deposits**

372.6 Conjunctival scars

372.61 **Granuloma of conjunctiva**

372.62 **Localized adhesions and strands of conjunctiva**

372.63 **Symblepharon**
Extensive adhesions of conjunctiva

372.64 **Scarring of conjunctiva**
Contraction of eye socket (after enucleation)

372.7 Conjunctival vascular disorders and cysts

372.71 **Hyperemia of conjunctiva**

372.72 **Conjunctival hemorrhage**
Hyposphagma
Subconjunctival hemorrhage

372.73 **Conjunctival edema**
Chemosis of conjunctiva
Subconjunctival edema

372.74 **Vascular abnormalities of conjunctiva**
Aneurysm(ata) of conjunctiva

372.75 **Conjunctival cysts**

372.8 **Other disorders of conjunctiva**

372.9 **Unspecified disorder of conjunctiva**

373 **Inflammation of eyelids**

373.0 Blepharitis

Excludes: blepharoconjunctivitis (372.20-372.22)

373.00 **Blepharitis, unspecified**

373.01 **Ulcerative blepharitis**

373.02 **Squamous blepharitis**

373.1 Hordeolum and other deep inflammation of eyelid

373.11 **Hordeolum externum**
Hordeolum NOS
Stye

● Code new
to this edition

▲ Revision of
existing code

④ ⑤ Fourth or fifth
digit required

373.12 Hordeolum internum
Infection of meibomian gland

373.13 Abscess of eyelid
Furuncle of eyelid

373.2 Chalazion
Meibomian (gland) cyst

| Excludes: | infected meibomian gland (373.12) |

373.3 Noninfectious dermatoses of eyelid

373.31 Eczematous dermatitis of eyelid

373.32 Contact and allergic dermatitis of eyelid

373.33 Xeroderma of eyelid

373.34 Discoid lupus erythematosus of eyelid

373.4 *Infective dermatitis of eyelid of types resulting in deformity*
Code first underlying disease, as:
leprosy (030.0-030.9)
lupus vulgaris (tuberculous) (017.0)
yaws (102.0-102.9)

373.5 *Other infective dermatitis of eyelid*
Code first underlying disease, as:
actinomycosis (039.3)
impetigo (684)
mycotic dermatitis (110.0-111.9)
vaccinia (051.0)
postvaccination (999.0)

Excludes:	herpes:
	simplex (054.41)
	zoster (053.20)

373.6 *Parasitic infestation of eyelid*
Code first underlying disease, as:
leishmaniasis (085.0-085.9)
loiasis (125.2)
onchocerciasis (125.3)
pediculosis (132.0)

373.8 Other inflammations of eyelids

373.9 Unspecified inflammation of eyelid

374 Other disorders of eyelids

374.0 Entropion and trichiasis of eyelid

374.00 Entropion, unspecified

374.01 Senile entropion

374.02 Mechanical entropion

374.03 Spastic entropion

374.04 Cicatricial entropion

374.05 Trichiasis without entropion

374.1 Ectropion

374.10 Ectropion, unspecified

374.11 Senile ectropion

374.12 Mechanical ectropion

374.13 Spastic ectropion

374.14 Cicatricial ectropion

374.2 Lagophthalmos

374.20 Lagophthalmos, unspecified

374.21 Paralytic lagophthalmos

374.22 Mechanical lagophthalmos

374.23 Cicatricial lagophthalmos

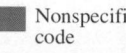 Add 4th or 5th digit   Nonspecific code   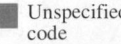 Unspecified code   Manifestation code

374.3 Ptosis of eyelid

> **374.30** **Ptosis of eyelid, unspecified**

> **374.31** **Paralytic ptosis**

> **374.32** **Myogenic ptosis**

> **374.33** **Mechanical ptosis**

> **374.34** **Blepharochalasis**
> Pseudoptosis

374.4 Other disorders affecting eyelid function

> Excludes: *blepharoclonus (333.81)*
> *blepharospasm (333.81)*
> *facial nerve palsy (351.0)*
> *third nerve palsy or paralysis (378.51-378.52)*
> *tic (psychogenic) (307.20-307.23)*
> *organic (333.3)*

> **374.41** **Lid retraction or lag**

> **374.43** **Abnormal innervation syndrome**
> Jaw-blinking
> Paradoxical facial movements

> **374.44** **Sensory disorders**

> **374.45** **Other sensorimotor disorders**
> Deficient blink reflex

> **374.46** **Blepharophimosis**
> Ankyloblepharon

374.5 Degenerative disorders of eyelid and periocular area

> **374.50** **Degenerative disorder of eyelid, unspecified**

> **374.51** *Xanthelasma*
> Xanthoma (planum) (tuberosum) of eyelid
> *Code first underlying condition (272.0-272.9)*

> **374.52** **Hyperpigmentation of eyelid**
> Chloasma   Dyspigmentation

> **374.53** **Hypopigmentation of eyelid**
> Vitiligo of eyelid

> **374.54** **Hypertrichosis of eyelid**

> **374.55** **Hypotrichosis of eyelid**
> Madarosis of eyelid

> **374.56** **Other degenerative disorders of skin affecting eyelid**

374.8 Other disorders of eyelid

> **374.81** **Hemorrhage of eyelid**

> Excludes: *black eye (921.0)*

> **374.82** **Edema of eyelid**
> Hyperemia of eyelid

> **374.83** **Elephantiasis of eyelid**

> **374.84** **Cysts of eyelids**
> Sebaceous cyst of eyelid

> **374.85** **Vascular anomalies of eyelid**

> **374.86** **Retained foreign body of eyelid**

> **374.87** **Dermatochalasis**

> **374.89** **Other disorders of eyelid**

374.9 Unspecified disorder of eyelid

375 Disorders of lacrimal system

375.0 Dacryoadenitis

> **375.00** **Dacryoadenitis, unspecified**

> **375.01** **Acute dacryoadenitis**

> **375.02** **Chronic dacryoadenitis**

> **375.03** **Chronic enlargement of lacrimal gland**

● Code new   ▲ Revision of   ④ ⑤ Fourth or fifth
  to this edition   existing code   digit required

375.1 Other disorders of lacrimal gland

 375.11 Dacryops

 `375.12` **Other lacrimal cysts and cystic degeneration**

 375.13 Primary lacrimal atrophy

 375.14 Secondary lacrimal atrophy

 `375.15` **Tear film insufficiency, unspecified**
  Dry eye syndrome

 375.16 Dislocation of lacrimal gland

375.2 Epiphora

 `375.20` **Epiphora, unspecified as to cause**

 375.21 Epiphora due to excess lacrimation

 375.22 Epiphora due to insufficient drainage

375.3 Acute and unspecified inflammation of lacrimal passages

 Excludes: *neonatal dacryocystitis (771.6)*

 `375.30` **Dacryocystitis, unspecified**

 375.31 Acute canaliculitis, lacrimal

 375.32 Acute dacryocystitis
  Acute peridacryocystitis

 375.33 Phlegmonous dacryocystitis

375.4 Chronic inflammation of lacrimal passages

 375.41 Chronic canaliculitis

 375.42 Chronic dacryocystitis

 375.43 Lacrimal mucocele

375.5 Stenosis and insufficiency of lacrimal passages

 375.51 Eversion of lacrimal punctum

 375.52 Stenosis of lacrimal punctum

 375.53 Stenosis of lacrimal canaliculi

 375.54 Stenosis of lacrimal sac

 375.55 Obstruction of nasolacrimal duct, neonatal

 Excludes: *congenital anomaly of nasolacrimal duct (743.65)*

 375.56 Stenosis of nasolacrimal duct, acquired

 375.57 Dacryolith

375.6 Other changes of lacrimal passages

 375.61 Lacrimal fistula

 `375.69` **Other**

375.8 Other disorders of lacrimal system

 375.81 Granuloma of lacrimal passages

 `375.89` **Other**

`375.9` **Unspecified disorder of lacrimal system**

`376` **Disorders of the orbit**

376.0 Acute inflammation of orbit

 `376.00` **Acute inflammation of orbit, unspecified**

 376.01 Orbital cellulitis
  Abscess of orbit

 376.02 Orbital periostitis

 376.03 Orbital osteomyelitis

 376.04 Tenonitis

376.1 Chronic inflammatory disorders of orbit

 `376.10` **Chronic inflammation of orbit, unspecified**

 376.11 Orbital granuloma
  Pseudotumor (inflammatory) of orbit

 376.12 Orbital myositis

	Add 4th or 5th digit		Nonspecific code		Unspecified code		Manifestation code

376.13 *Parasitic infestation of orbit*
Code first underlying disease, as:
hydatid infestation of orbit (122.3, 122.6, 122.9)
myiasis of orbit (134.0)

376.2 *Endocrine exophthalmos*
Code first underlying thyroid disorder (242.0-242.9)

376.21 *Thyrotoxic exophthalmos*

376.22 *Exophthalmic ophthalmoplegia*

376.3 **Other exophthalmic conditions**

376.30 Exophthalmos, unspecified

376.31 Constant exophthalmos

376.32 Orbital hemorrhage

376.33 Orbital edema or congestion

376.34 Intermittent exophthalmos

376.35 Pulsating exophthalmos

376.36 Lateral displacement of globe

376.4 **Deformity of orbit**

376.40 Deformity of orbit, unspecified

376.41 Hypertelorism of orbit

376.42 Exostosis of orbit

376.43 Local deformities due to bone disease

376.44 Orbital deformities associated with craniofacial deformities

376.45 Atrophy of orbit

376.46 Enlargement of orbit

376.47 Deformity due to trauma or surgery

376.5 **Enophthalmos**

376.50 Enophthalmos, unspecified as to cause

376.51 Enophthalmos due to atrophy of orbital tissue

376.52 Enophthalmos due to trauma or surgery

376.6 **Retained (old) foreign body following penetrating wound of orbit**
Retrobulbar foreign body

376.8 **Other orbital disorders**

376.81 Orbital cysts
Encephalocele of orbit

376.82 Myopathy of extraocular muscles

376.89 Other

376.9 **Unspecified disorder of orbit**

377 **Disorders of optic nerve and visual pathways**

377.0 **Papilledema**

377.00 Papilledema, unspecified

377.01 Papilledema associated with increased intracranial pressure

377.02 Papilledema associated with decreased ocular pressure

377.03 Papilledema associated with retinal disorder

377.04 Foster-Kennedy syndrome

377.1 **Optic atrophy**

377.10 Optic atrophy, unspecified

377.11 Primary optic atrophy

Excludes: neurosyphilitic optic atrophy (094.84)

377.12 Postinflammatory optic atrophy

377.13 Optic atrophy associated with retinal dystrophies

377.14 Glaucomatous atrophy [cupping] of optic disc

377.15 Partial optic atrophy
Temporal pallor of optic disc

● Code new
to this edition

▲ Revision of
existing code

④ ⑤ Fourth or fifth
digit required

377.16 **Hereditary optic atrophy**
Optic atrophy:
dominant hereditary
Leber's

377.2 **Other disorders of optic disc**

377.21 **Drusen of optic disc**

377.22 **Crater-like holes of optic disc**

377.23 **Coloboma of optic disc**

377.24 **Pseudopapilledema**

377.3 **Optic neuritis**

Excludes: *meningococcal optic neuritis (036.81)*

377.30 **Optic neuritis, unspecified**

377.31 **Optic papillitis**

377.32 **Retrobulbar neuritis (acute)**

Excludes: *syphilitic retrobulbar neuritis (094.85)*

377.33 **Nutritional optic neuropathy**

377.34 **Toxic optic neuropathy**
Toxic amblyopia

377.39 **Other**

Excludes: *ischemic optic neuropathy (377.41)*

377.4 **Other disorders of optic nerve**

377.41 **Ischemic optic neuropathy**

377.42 **Hemorrhage in optic nerve sheaths**

377.49 **Other**
Compression of optic nerve

377.5 **Disorders of optic chiasm**

377.51 **Associated with pituitary neoplasms and disorders**

377.52 **Associated with other neoplasms**

377.53 **Associated with vascular disorders**

377.54 **Associated with inflammatory disorders**

377.6 **Disorders of other visual pathways**

377.61 **Associated with neoplasms**

377.62 **Associated with vascular disorders**

377.63 **Associated with inflammatory disorders**

377.7 **Disorders of visual cortex**

Excludes: *visual:*
agnosia (368.16)
hallucinations (368.16)
halos (368.15)

377.71 **Associated with neoplasms**

377.72 **Associated with vascular disorders**

377.73 **Associated with inflammatory disorders**

377.75 **Cortical blindness**

377.9 **Unspecified disorder of optic nerve and visual pathways**

378 **Strabismus and other disorders of binocular eye movements**

Excludes: *nystagmus and other irregular eye movements (379.50-379.59)*

378.0 **Esotropia**
Convergent concomitant strabismus

Excludes: *intermittent esotropia (378.20-378.22)*

378.00 **Esotropia, unspecified**

378.01 **Monocular esotropia**

378.02 **Monocular esotropia with A pattern**

378.03 **Monocular esotropia with V pattern**

| | Add 4th or 5th digit | | Nonspecific code | | Unspecified code | | Manifestation code |

378.04 Monocular esotropia with other noncomitancies
Monocular esotropia with X or Y pattern

378.05 Alternating esotropia

378.06 Alternating esotropia with A pattern

378.07 Alternating esotropia with V pattern

378.08 Alternating esotropia with other noncomitancies
Alternating esotropia with X or Y pattern

378.1 Exotropia
Divergent concomitant strabismus

Excludes: *intermittent exotropia (378.20, 378.23-378.24)*

378.10 Exotropia, unspecified

378.11 Monocular exotropia

378.12 Monocular exotropia with A pattern

378.13 Monocular exotropia with V pattern

378.14 Monocular exotropia with other noncomitancies
Monocular exotropia with X or Y pattern

378.15 Alternating exotropia

378.16 Alternating exotropia with A pattern

378.17 Alternating exotropia with V pattern

378.18 Alternating exotropia with other noncomitancies
Alternating exotropia with X or Y pattern

378.2 Intermittent heterotropia

Excludes: *vertical heterotropia (intermittent) (378.31)*

378.20 Intermittent heterotropia, unspecified
Intermittent:
   esotropia NOS
   exotropia NOS

378.21 Intermittent esotropia, monocular

378.22 Intermittent esotropia, alternating

378.23 Intermittent exotropia, monocular

378.24 Intermittent exotropia, alternating

378.3 Other and unspecified heterotropia

378.30 Heterotropia, unspecified

378.31 Hypertropia
Vertical heterotropia (constant) (intermittent)

378.32 Hypotropia

378.33 Cyclotropia

378.34 Monofixation syndrome
Microtropia

378.35 Accommodative component in esotropia

378.4 Heterophoria

378.40 Heterophoria, unspecified

378.41 Esophoria

378.42 Exophoria

378.43 Vertical heterophoria

378.44 Cyclophoria

378.45 Alternating hyperphoria

378.5 Paralytic strabismus

378.50 Paralytic strabismus, unspecified

378.51 Third or oculomotor nerve palsy, partial

378.52 Third or oculomotor nerve palsy, total

378.53 Fourth or trochlear nerve palsy

378.54 Sixth or abducens nerve palsy

378.55 External ophthalmoplegia

● Code new
  to this edition
    ▲ Revision of
      existing code
    ④ ⑤ Fourth or fifth
        digit required

378.56 Total ophthalmoplegia

378.6 Mechanical strabismus

378.60 Mechanical strabismus, unspecified

378.61 Brown's (tendon) sheath syndrome

378.62 Mechanical strabismus from other musculofascial disorders

378.63 Limited duction associated with other conditions

378.7 Other specified strabismus

378.71 Duane's syndrome

378.72 Progressive external ophthalmoplegia

378.73 Strabismus in other neuromuscular disorders

378.8 Other disorders of binocular eye movements

Excludes: *nystagmus (379.50-379.56)*

378.81 Palsy of conjugate gaze

378.82 Spasm of conjugate gaze

378.83 Convergence insufficiency or palsy

378.84 Convergence excess or spasm

378.85 Anomalies of divergence

378.86 Internuclear ophthalmoplegia

378.87 Other dissociated deviation of eye movements
Skew deviation

378.9 Unspecified disorder of eye movements
Ophthalmoplegia NOS   Strabismus NOS

379 Other disorders of eye

379.0 Scleritis and episcleritis

Excludes: *syphilitic episcleritis (095.0)*

379.00 Scleritis, unspecified
Episcleritis NOS

379.01 Episcleritis periodica fugax

379.02 Nodular episcleritis

379.03 Anterior scleritis

379.04 Scleromalacia perforans

379.05 Scleritis with corneal involvement
Scleroperikeratitis

379.06 Brawny scleritis

379.07 Posterior scleritis
Sclerotenonitis

379.09 Other
Scleral abscess

379.1 Other disorders of sclera

Excludes: *blue sclera (743.47)*

379.11 Scleral ectasia
Scleral staphyloma NOS

379.12 Staphyloma posticum

379.13 Equatorial staphyloma

379.14 Anterior staphyloma, localized

379.15 Ring staphyloma

379.16 Other degenerative disorders of sclera

379.19 Other

379.2 Disorders of vitreous body

379.21 Vitreous degeneration
Vitreous:
cavitation
detachment
liquefaction

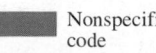 Add 4th or 5th digit

 Nonspecific code

 Unspecified code

Manifestation code

379.22   **Crystalline deposits in vitreous**
   Asteroid hyalitis   Synchysis scintillans

379.23   **Vitreous hemorrhage**

379.24   **Other vitreous opacities**
   Vitreous floaters

379.25   **Vitreous membranes and strands**

379.26   **Vitreous prolapse**

379.29   **Other disorders of vitreous**

Excludes: vitreous abscess (360.04)

379.3 **Aphakia and other disorders of lens**

Excludes: after-cataract (366.50-366.53)

379.31   **Aphakia**

379.32   **Subluxation of lens**

379.33   **Anterior dislocation of lens**

379.34   **Posterior dislocation of lens**

379.39   **Other disorders of lens**

379.4 **Anomalies of pupillary function**

379.40   **Abnormal pupillary function, unspecified**

379.41   **Anisocoria**

379.42   **Miosis (persistent), not due to miotics**

379.43   **Mydriasis (persistent) not due to mydriatics**

379.45   **Argyll Robertson pupil, atypical**
   Argyll Robertson phenomenon or pupil, nonsyphilitic

Excludes: Argyll Robertson pupil (syphilitic) (094.89)

379.46   **Tonic pupillary reaction**
   Adie's pupil or syndrome

379.49   **Other**
   Hippus
   Pupillary paralysis

379.5 **Nystagmus and other irregular eye movements**

379.50   **Nystagmus, unspecified**

379.51   **Congenital nystagmus**

379.52   **Latent nystagmus**

379.53   **Visual deprivation nystagmus**

379.54   **Nystagmus associated with disorders of the vestibular system**

379.55   **Dissociated nystagmus**

379.56   **Other forms of nystagmus**

379.57   **Deficiencies of saccadic eye movements**
   Abnormal optokinetic response

379.58   **Deficiencies of smooth pursuit movements**

379.59   **Other irregularities of eye movements**
   Opsoclonus

379.8 **Other specified disorders of eye and adnexa**

379.9 **Unspecified disorder of eye and adnexa**

379.90   **Disorder of eye, unspecified**

379.91   **Pain in or around eye**

379.92   **Swelling or mass of eye**

379.93   **Redness or discharge of eye**

379.99   **Other ill-defined disorders of eye**

Excludes: blurred vision NOS (368.8)

 ● Code new   ▲ Revision of   ④ ⑤ Fourth or fifth
  to this edition   existing code   digit required

DISEASES OF THE EAR AND MASTOID PROCESS (380-389)

380 Disorders of external ear

    380.0 Perichondritis of pinna
           Perichondritis of auricle

        380.00 Perichondritis of pinna, unspecified

        380.01 Acute perichondritis of pinna

        380.02 Chronic perichondritis of pinna

    380.1 Infective otitis externa

        380.10 Infective otitis externa, unspecified
                Otitis externa (acute):
                    NOS
                    circumscribed
                    diffuse
                    hemorrhagica
                    infective NOS

        380.11 Acute infection of pinna

      Excludes: *furuncular otitis externa (680.0)*

        380.12 Acute swimmers' ear
                Beach ear   Tank ear

        380.13 *Other acute infections of external ear*
                Code first underlying disease, as:
                  erysipelas (035)
                  impetigo (684)
                  seborrheic dermatitis (690.10-690.18)

      Excludes: *herpes simplex (054.73)*
                   herpes zoster (053.71)

        380.14 Malignant otitis externa

        380.15 *Chronic mycotic otitis externa*
                Code first underlying disease, as:
                  aspergillosis (117.3)
                  otomycosis NOS (111.9)

      Excludes: *candidal otitis externa (112.82)*

        380.16 Other chronic infective otitis externa
                 Chronic infective otitis externa NOS

    380.2 Other otitis externa

        380.21 Cholesteatoma of external ear
                Keratosis obturans of external ear (canal)

      Excludes: *cholesteatoma NOS (385.30-385.35)*

                postmastoidectomy (383.32)

        380.22 Other acute otitis externa
                Acute otitis externa:
                  actinic
                  chemical
                  contact
                  eczematoid
                  reactive

        380.23 Other chronic otitis externa
                Chronic otitis externa NOS

    380.3 Noninfectious disorders of pinna

        380.30 Disorder of pinna, unspecified

        380.31 Hematoma of auricle or pinna

        380.32 Acquired deformities of auricle or pinna

      Excludes: *cauliflower ear (738.7)*

        380.39 Other

      Excludes: *gouty tophi of ear (274.81)*

    380.4 Impacted cerumen
           Wax in ear

| Add 4th or 5th digit | Nonspecific code | Unspecified code | Manifestation code |

380.5 Acquired stenosis of external ear canal
Collapse of external ear canal

> **380.50** Acquired stenosis of external ear canal, unspecified as to cause

> **380.51** Secondary to trauma

> **380.52** Secondary to surgery

> **380.53** Secondary to inflammation

380.8 Other disorders of external ear

> **380.81** Exostosis of external ear canal

> **380.89** Other

380.9 Unspecified disorder of external ear

381 Nonsuppurative otitis media and Eustachian tube disorders

381.0 Acute nonsuppurative otitis media
Acute tubotympanic catarrh
Otitis media, acute or subacute:
catarrhal
exudative
transudative
with effusion

> Excludes: otitic barotrauma (993.0)

> **381.00** Acute nonsuppurative otitis media, unspecified

> **381.01** Acute serous otitis media
> Acute or subacute secretory otitis media

> **381.02** Acute mucoid otitis media
> Acute or subacute seromucinous otitis media
> Blue drum syndrome

> **381.03** Acute sanguinous otitis media

> **381.04** Acute allergic serous otitis media

> **381.05** Acute allergic mucoid otitis media

> **381.06** Acute allergic sanguinous otitis media

381.1 Chronic serous otitis media
Chronic tubotympanic catarrh

> **381.10** Chronic serous otitis media, simple or unspecified

> **381.19** Other
> Serosanguinous chronic otitis media

381.2 Chronic mucoid otitis media
Glue ear

> Excludes: adhesive middle ear disease (385.10-385.19)

> **381.20** Chronic mucoid otitis media, simple or unspecified

> **381.29** Other
> Mucosanguinous chronic otitis media

381.3 Other and unspecified chronic nonsuppurative otitis media
Otitis media, chronic: Otitis media, chronic:
allergic   seromucinous
exudative   transudative
secretory   with effusion

381.4 Nonsuppurative otitis media, not specified as acute or chronic
Otitis media: Otitis media:
allergic   secretory
catarrhal   seromucinous
exudative   serous
mucoid   transudative
                     with effusion

381.5 Eustachian salpingitis

> **381.50** Eustachian salpingitis, unspecified

> **381.51** Acute Eustachian salpingitis

> **381.52** Chronic Eustachian salpingitis

● Code new   ▲ Revision of   ④ ⑤ Fourth or fifth
   to this edition   existing code   digit required

381.6 Obstruction of Eustachian tube

Stenosis
Stricture } of Eustachian tube

381.60 Obstruction of Eustachian tube, unspecified

381.61 Osseous obstruction of Eustachian tube
Obstruction of Eustachian tube from cholesteatoma, polyp, or other osseous lesion

381.62 Intrinsic cartilagenous obstruction of Eustachian tube

381.63 Extrinsic cartilagenous obstruction of Eustachian tube
Compression of Eustachian tube

381.7 Patulous Eustachian tube

381.8 Other disorders of Eustachian tube

381.81 Dysfunction of Eustachian tube

381.89 Other

381.9 Unspecified Eustachian tube disorder

382 Suppurative and unspecified otitis media

382.0 Acute suppurative otitis media
Otitis media, acute:
necrotizing NOS
purulent

382.00 Acute suppurative otitis media without spontaneous rupture of ear drum

382.01 Acute suppurative otitis media with spontaneous rupture of ear drum

382.02 *Acute suppurative otitis media in diseases classified elsewhere*
Code first underlying disease, as:
influenza (487.8)
scarlet fever (034.1)

Excludes: postmeasles otitis (055.2)

382.1 Chronic tubotympanic suppurative otitis media
Benign chronic suppurative otitis media
Chronic tubotympanic disease } (with anterior perforation of ear drum)

382.2 Chronic atticoantral suppurative otitis media
Chronic atticoantral disease
Persistent mucosal disease } (with posterior or superior marginal perforation of ear drum)

382.3 Unspecified chronic suppurative otitis media
Chronic purulent otitis media

Excludes: tuberculous otitis media (017.4)

382.4 Unspecified suppurative otitis media
Purulent otitis media NOS

382.9 Unspecified otitis media
Otitis media:
NOS
acute NOS
chronic NOS

383 Mastoiditis and related conditions

383.0 Acute mastoiditis
Abscess of mastoid   Empyema of mastoid

383.00 Acute mastoiditis without complications

383.01 Subperiosteal abscess of mastoid

383.02 Acute mastoiditis with other complications
Gradenigo's syndrome

383.1 Chronic mastoiditis
Caries of mastoid   Fistula of mastoid

Excludes: tuberculous mastoiditis (015.6)

383.2 Petrositis
Coalescing osteitis
Inflammation
Osteomyelitis } of petrous bone

383.20 Petrositis, unspecified

189

Add 4th or
5th digit

 Nonspecific
code

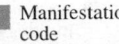 Unspecified
code

Manifestation
code

383.21   Acute petrositis

383.22   Chronic petrositis

383.3 Complications following mastoidectomy

    383.30   Postmastoidectomy complication, unspecified

    383.31   Mucosal cyst of postmastoidectomy cavity

    383.32   Recurrent cholesteatoma of postmastoidectomy cavity

    383.33   Granulations of postmastoidectomy cavity
         Chronic inflammation of postmastoidectomy cavity

383.8 Other disorders of mastoid

    383.81   Postauricular fistula

    383.89   Other

383.9 Unspecified mastoiditis

384 Other disorders of tympanic membrane

384.0 Acute myringitis without mention of otitis media

    384.00   Acute myringitis, unspecified
         Acute tympanitis NOS

    384.01   Bullous myringitis
         Myringitis bullosa hemorrhagica

    384.09   Other

384.1 Chronic myringitis without mention of otitis media
    Chronic tympanitis

384.2 Perforation of tympanic membrane
    Perforation of ear drum:
      NOS
      persistent posttraumatic
      postinflammatory

    Excludes: traumatic perforation [current injury] (872.61)

    384.20   Perforation of tympanic membrane, unspecified

    384.21   Central perforation of tympanic membrane

    384.22   Attic perforation of tympanic membrane
         Pars flaccida

    384.23   Other marginal perforation of tympanic membrane

    384.24   Multiple perforations of tympanic membrane

    384.25   Total perforation of tympanic membrane

384.8 Other specified disorders of tympanic membrane

    384.81   Atrophic flaccid tympanic membrane
         Healed perforation of ear drum

    384.82   Atrophic nonflaccid tympanic membrane

384.9 Unspecified disorder of tympanic membrane

385 Other disorders of middle ear and mastoid

    Excludes: mastoiditis (383.0-383.9)

385.0 Tympanosclerosis

    385.00   Tympanosclerosis, unspecified as to involvement

    385.01   Tympanosclerosis involving tympanic membrane only

    385.02   Tympanosclerosis involving tympanic membrane and ear ossicles

    385.03   Tympanosclerosis involving tympanic membrane, ear ossicles, and middle ear

    385.09   Tympanosclerosis involving other combination of structures

385.1 Adhesive middle ear disease
    Adhesive otitis   Otitis media:
                     chronic adhesive
                     fibrotic

    Excludes: glue ear (381.20-381.29)

    385.10   Adhesive middle ear disease, unspecified as to involvement

    385.11   Adhesions of drum head to incus

● Code new to this edition   ▲ Revision of existing code   ④ ⑤ Fourth or fifth digit required

385.12 **Adhesions of drum head to stapes**

385.13 **Adhesions of drum head to promontorium**

385.19 **Other adhesions and combinations**

385.2 **Other acquired abnormality of ear ossicles**

385.21 **Impaired mobility of malleus**
Ankylosis of malleus

385.22 **Impaired mobility of other ear ossicles**
Ankylosis of ear ossicles, except malleus

385.23 **Discontinuity or dislocation of ear ossicles**

385.24 **Partial loss or necrosis of ear ossicles**

385.3 **Cholesteatoma of middle ear and mastoid**
Cholesterosis ⎫
Epidermosis ⎬ of (middle) ear
Keratosis ⎪
Polyp ⎭

Excludes: *cholesteatoma:*
external ear canal (380.21)
recurrent of postmastoidectomy cavity (383.32)

385.30 **Cholesteatoma, unspecified**

385.31 **Cholesteatoma of attic**

385.32 **Cholesteatoma of middle ear**

385.33 **Cholesteatoma of middle ear and mastoid**

385.35 **Diffuse cholesteatosis**

385.8 **Other disorders of middle ear and mastoid**

385.82 **Cholesterin granuloma**

385.83 **Retained foreign body of middle ear**

385.89 **Other**

385.9 **Unspecified disorder of middle ear and mastoid**

386 **Vertiginous syndromes and other disorders of vestibular system**

Excludes: *vertigo NOS (780.4)*

386.0 **Ménière's disease**
Endolymphatic hydrops   Ménière's syndrome or vertigo
Lermoyez's syndrome

386.00 **Ménière's disease, unspecified**
Ménière's disease (active)

386.01 **Active Ménière's disease, cochleovestibular**

386.02 **Active Ménière's disease, cochlear**

386.03 **Active Ménière's disease, vestibular**

386.04 **Inactive Ménière's disease**
Ménière's disease in remission

386.1 **Other and unspecified peripheral vertigo**

Excludes: *epidemic vertigo (078.81)*

386.10 **Peripheral vertigo, unspecified**

386.11 **Benign paroxysmal positional vertigo**
Benign paroxysmal positional nystagmus

386.12 **Vestibular neuronitis**
Acute (and recurrent) peripheral vestibulopathy

386.19 **Other**
Aural vertigo   Otogenic vertigo

386.2 **Vertigo of central origin**
Central positional nystagmus
Malignant positional vertigo

386.3 **Labyrinthitis**

386.30 **Labyrinthitis, unspecified**

386.31 **Serous labyrinthitis**
Diffuse labyrinthitis

| | Add 4th or 5th digit | | Nonspecific code | | Unspecified code | | Manifestation code |

● Code new
to this edition

▲ Revision of
existing code

④ ⑤ Fourth or fifth
digit required

7. DISEASES OF THE CIRCULATORY SYSTEM (390-459)

ACUTE RHEUMATIC FEVER (390-392)

390 Rheumatic fever without mention of heart involvement
Arthritis, rheumatic, acute or subacute
Rheumatic fever (active) (acute)
Rheumatism, articular, acute or subacute

Excludes: *that with heart involvement (391.0-391.9)*

391 Rheumatic fever with heart involvement

Excludes: *chronic heart diseases of rheumatic origin (393.0-398.9) unless rheumatic fever is also present or there is evidence of recrudescence or activity of the rheumatic process*

391.0 Acute rheumatic pericarditis
Rheumatic:
fever (active) (acute) with pericarditis
pericarditis (acute)
Any condition classifiable to 390 with pericarditis

Excludes: *that not specified as rheumatic (420.0-420.9)*

391.1 Acute rheumatic endocarditis
Rheumatic:
endocarditis, acute
fever (active) (acute) with endocarditis or valvulitis
valvulitis acute
Any condition classifiable to 390 with endocarditis or valvulitis

391.2 Acute rheumatic myocarditis
Rheumatic fever (active) (acute) with myocarditis
Any condition classifiable to 390 with myocarditis

391.8 Other acute rheumatic heart disease
Rheumatic:
fever (active) (acute) with other or multiple types of heart involvement
pancarditis, acute
Any condition classifiable to 390 with other or multiple types of heart involvement

391.9 Acute rheumatic heart disease, unspecified
Rheumatic:
carditis, acute
fever (active) (acute) with unspecified type of heart involvement
heart disease, active or acute
Any condition classifiable to 390 with unspecified type of heart involvement

392 Rheumatic chorea
Includes: Sydenham's chorea

Excludes: *chorea:*
NOS (333.5)
Huntington's (333.4)

392.0 With heart involvement
Rheumatic chorea with heart involvement of any type classifiable to 391

392.9 Without mention of heart involvement

CHRONIC RHEUMATIC HEART DISEASE (393-398)

393 Chronic rheumatic pericarditis
Adherent pericardium, rheumatic
Chronic rheumatic:
mediastinopericarditis
myopericarditis

Excludes: *pericarditis NOS or not specified as rheumatic (423.0-423.9)*

394 Diseases of mitral valve

Excludes: *that with aortic valve involvement (396.0-396.9)*

394.0 Mitral stenosis
Mitral (valve):
obstruction (rheumatic)
stenosis NOS

| | Add 4th or 5th digit | | Nonspecific code | | Unspecified code | | Manifestation code |

394.1 Rheumatic mitral insufficiency
Rheumatic mitral:
  incompetence
  regurgitation

Excludes: *that not specified as rheumatic (424.0)*

394.2 Mitral stenosis with insufficiency
Mitral stenosis with incompetence or regurgitation

394.9 Other and unspecified mitral valve diseases
Mitral (valve):
  disease (chronic)
  failure

395 Diseases of aortic valve

Excludes: *that not specified as rheumatic (424.1)*
        that with mitral valve involvement (396.0-396.9)

395.0 Rheumatic aortic stenosis
Rheumatic aortic (valve) obstruction

395.1 Rheumatic aortic insufficiency
Rheumatic aortic:
  incompetence
  regurgitation

395.2 Rheumatic aortic stenosis with insufficiency
Rheumatic aortic stenosis with incompetence or regurgitation

395.9 Other and unspecified rheumatic aortic diseases
Rheumatic aortic (valve) disease

396 Diseases of mitral and aortic valves
Includes: involvement of both mitral and aortic valves, whether specified as rheumatic or not

396.0 Mitral valve stenosis and aortic valve stenosis
Atypical aortic (valve) stenosis
Mitral and aortic (valve) obstruction (rheumatic)

396.1 Mitral valve stenosis and aortic valve insufficiency

396.2 Mitral valve insufficiency and aortic valve stenosis

396.3 Mitral valve insufficiency and aortic valve insufficiency
Mitral and aortic (valve):
  incompetence
  regurgitation

396.8 Multiple involvement of mitral and aortic valves
Stenosis and insufficiency of mitral or aortic valve with stenosis or insufficiency, or
  both, of the other valve

396.9 Mitral and aortic valve diseases, unspecified

397 Diseases of other endocardial structures

397.0 Diseases of tricuspid valve
Tricuspid (valve) (rheumatic):
  disease
  insufficiency
  obstruction
  regurgitation
  stenosis

397.1 Rheumatic diseases of pulmonary valve

Excludes: *that not specified as rheumatic (424.3)*

397.9 Rheumatic diseases of endocardium, valve unspecified
Rheumatic:
  endocarditis (chronic)
  valvulitis (chronic)

Excludes: *that not specified as rheumatic (424.90-424.99)*

398 Other rheumatic heart disease

398.0 Rheumatic myocarditis
Rheumatic degeneration of myocardium

Excludes: *myocarditis not specified as rheumatic (429.0)*

398.9 Other and unspecified rheumatic heart diseases

● Code new   ▲ Revision of   ④ ⑤ Fourth or fifth
  to this edition   existing code   digit required

398.90 **Rheumatic heart disease, unspecified**
Rheumatic:
carditis
heart disease NOS

Excludes: *carditis not specified as rheumatic (429.89)*
heart disease NOS not specified as rheumatic (429.9)

398.91 **Rheumatic heart failure (congestive)**
Rheumatic left ventricular failure

398.99 **Other**

HYPERTENSIVE DISEASE (401-405)

Excludes: *that complicating pregnancy, childbirth, or the puerperium (642.0-642.9)*
that involving coronary vessels (410.00-414.9)

401 **Essential hypertension**
Includes: high blood pressure
hyperpiesia
hyperpiesis
hypertension (arterial) (essential) (primary) (systemic)
hypertensive vascular:
degeneration
disease

Excludes: *elevated blood pressure without diagnosis of hypertension (796.2)*
pulmonary hypertension (416.0-416.9)
that involving vessels of:
brain (430-438)
eye (362.11)

401.0 **Malignant**

401.1 **Benign**

401.9 **Unspecified**

402 **Hypertensive heart disease**
Includes: hypertensive:
cardiomegaly
cardiopathy
cardiovascular disease
heart (disease) (failure)
any condition classifiable to 428, 429.0-429.3, 429.8, 429.9 due to hypertension

402.0 **Malignant**

402.00 **Without congestive heart failure**

402.01 **With congestive heart failure**

402.1 **Benign**

402.10 **Without congestive heart failure**

402.11 **With congestive heart failure**

402.9 **Unspecified**

402.90 **Without congestive heart failure**

402.91 **With congestive heart failure**

⑤ **403** **Hypertensive renal disease**
The following fifth-digit subclassification is for use with category 403:

0 **without mention of renal failure**

1 **with renal failure**
Includes: arteriolar nephritis
arteriosclerosis of:
kidney
renal arterioles
arteriosclerotic nephritis (chronic) (interstitial)
hypertensive:
nephropathy
renal failure
uremia (chronic)
nephrosclerosis
renal sclerosis with hypertension
any condition classifiable to 585, 586, or 587 with any condition classifiable to 401

Excludes: *acute renal failure (584.5-584.9)*   *continued*

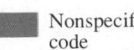

Add 4th or
5th digit

Nonspecific
code

Unspecified
code

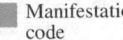

Manifestation
code

renal disease stated as not due to hypertension
renovascular hypertension (405.0-405.9 with fifth-digit 1)

403.0 Malignant

403.1 Benign

403.9 Unspecified

⑤ **404 Hypertensive heart and renal disease**

The following fifth-digit subclassification is for use with category 404:

    0 without mention of congestive heart failure
       or renal failure

    1 with congestive heart failure

    2 with renal failure

    3 with congestive heart failure and renal failure
       Includes: disease:
              cardiorenal
              cardiovascular renal
              any condition classifiable to 402 with any condition classifiable to 403

404.0 Malignant

404.1 Benign

404.9 Unspecified

405 Secondary hypertension

405.0 Malignant

    405.01 Renovascular

    405.09 Other

405.1 Benign

    405.11 Renovascular

    405.19 Other

405.9 Unspecified

    405.91 Renovascular

    405.99 Other

ISCHEMIC HEART DISEASE (410-414)

    Includes: that with mention of hypertension

Use additional code, if desired, to identify presence of hypertension (401.0-405.9)

⑤ **410 Acute myocardial infarction**
      Includes: cardiac infarction
           coronary (artery):
              embolism
              occlusion
              rupture
              thrombosis
           infarction of heart, myocardium, or ventricle
           rupture of heart, myocardium, or ventricle
           any condition classifiable to 414.1-414.9 specified as acute or with a stated
              duration of 8 weeks or less

The following fifth-digit subclassification is for use with category 410:

    0 episode of care unspecified
       Use when the source document does not contain sufficient information for the
       assignment of fifth digit 1 or 2.

    1 initial episode of care
       Use fifth digit 1 to designate the first episode of care (regardless of facility site) for
       a newly diagnosed myocardial infarction. The fifth digit 1 is assigned regardless
       of the number of times a patient may be transferred during the initial episode of
       care

    2 subsequent episode of care
       Use fifth digit 2 to designate an episode of care following the initial episode when
       the patient is admitted for further observation, evaluation, or treatment for a
       myocardial infarction that has received initial treatment, but is still less than 8
       weeks old.

410.0 Of anterolateral wall

   ● Code new
      to this edition
      ▲ Revision of
        existing code
      ④ ⑤ Fourth or fifth
          digit required

410.1 **Of other anterior wall**
Infarction:
anterior (wall) NOS
anteroapical } (with contiguous portion of intraventricular septum)
anteroseptal

410.2 **Of inferolateral wall**

410.3 **Of inferoposterior wall**

410.4 **Of other inferior wall**
Infarction:
diaphragmatic wall
inferior (wall) NOS } (with contiguous portion of intraventricular septum)

410.5 **Of other lateral wall**
Infarction: Infarction:
apical-lateral   high lateral
basal-lateral   posterolateral

410.6 **True posterior wall infarction**
Infarction:
posterobasal
strictly posterior

410.7 **Subendocardial infarction**
Nontransmural infarction

410.8 **Of other specified sites**
Infarction of:
atrium
papillary muscle
septum alone

410.9 **Unspecified site**
Acute myocardial infarction NOS
Coronary occlusion NOS

411 **Other acute and subacute forms of ischemic heart disease**

411.0 **Postmyocardial infarction syndrome**
Dressler's syndrome

411.1 **Intermediate coronary syndrome**
Impending infarction   Preinfarction syndrome
Preinfarction angina   . Unstable angina

     Excludes: *angina (pectoris) (413.9)*
                   decubitus (413.0)

411.8 **Other**

411.81 **Acute coronary occlusion without myocardial infarction**
Coronary (artery):
embolism
occlusion } without or not resulting in myocardial infarction
thrombosis

411.89 **Other**
Coronary insufficiency (acute)
Subendocardial ischemia

412 **Old myocardial infarction**
Healed myocardial infarction
Past myocardial infarction diagnosed on ECG [EKG] or other special investigation, but currently presenting no symptoms

413 **Angina pectoris**

413.0 **Angina decubitus**
Nocturnal angina

413.1 **Prinzmetal angina**
Variant angina pectoris

413.9 **Other and unspecified angina pectoris**
Angina: Anginal syndrome
NOS   Status anginosus
cardiac   Stenocardia
of effort   Syncope anginosa

     Excludes: *preinfarction angina (411.1)*

199

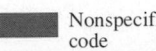

| Add 4th or 5th digit | Nonspecific code | Unspecified code | Manifestation code |

`414` **Other forms of chronic ischemic heart disease**

Excludes: arteriosclerotic cardiovascular disease [ASCVD] (429.2)
cardiovascular:
arteriosclerosis or sclerosis (429.2)
degeneration or disease (429.2)

414.0 Coronary atherosclerosis
Arteriosclerotic heart disease [ASHD]
Atherosclerotic heart disease
Coronary (artery):
arteriosclerosis
arteritis or endarteritis
atheroma
sclerosis
stricture

Excludes: embolism of graft (996.72)
occlusion NOS of graft (996.72)
thrombus of graft (996.72)

▲ `414.00` **Of unspecified type of vessel, native or graft**

`414.01` **Of native coronary artery**

`414.02` **Of autologous vein bypass graft**

`414.03` **Of nonautologous biological bypass graft**

● `414.04` **Of artery bypass graft**
Internal mammary artery

● `414.05` **Of unspecified type of bypass graft**
Bypass graft NOS

414.1 Aneurysm of heart

`414.10` **Of heart (wall)**
Aneurysm (arteriovenous):
mural
ventricular

`414.11` **Of coronary vessels**
Aneurysm (arteriovenous) of coronary vessels

`414.19` **Other**
Arteriovenous fistula, acquired, of heart

`414.8` **Other specified forms of chronic ischemic heart disease**
Chronic coronary insufficiency
Ischemia, myocardial (chronic)
Any condition classifiable to 410 specified as chronic, or presenting with symptoms
after 8 weeks from date of infarction

Excludes: coronary insufficiency (acute) (411.89)

`414.9` **Chronic ischemic heart disease, unspecified**
Ischemic heart disease NOS

DISEASES OF PULMONARY CIRCULATION (415-417)

`415` **Acute pulmonary heart disease**

415.0 Acute cor pulmonale

Excludes: cor pulmonale NOS (416.9)

415.1 Pulmonary embolism and infarction
Pulmonary (artery) (vein):
apoplexy
embolism
infarction (hemorrhagic)
thrombosis

Excludes: that complicating:
abortion (634-638 with .6, 639.6)
ectopic or molar pregnancy (639.6)
pregnancy, childbirth, or the puerperium (673.0-673.8)

`415.11` **Iatrogenic pulmonary embolism and infarction**

`415.19` **Other**

`416` **Chronic pulmonary heart disease**

---

200   ● Code new   ▲ Revision of   ④ ⑤ Fourth or fifth
        to this edition   existing code   digit required

416.0 Primary pulmonary hypertension
Idiopathic pulmonary arteriosclerosis
Pulmonary hypertension (essential) (idiopathic) (primary)

416.1 Kyphoscoliotic heart disease

416.8 Other chronic pulmonary heart diseases
Pulmonary hypertension, secondary

416.9 Chronic pulmonary heart disease, unspecified
Chronic cardiopulmonary disease
Cor pulmonale (chronic) NOS

417 Other diseases of pulmonary circulation

417.0 Arteriovenous fistula of pulmonary vessels

> *Excludes:* *congenital arteriovenous fistula (747.3)*

417.1 Aneurysm of pulmonary artery

> *Excludes:* *congenital aneurysm (747.3)*

417.8 Other specified diseases of pulmonary circulation
Pulmonary:
  arteritis
  endarteritis
  Rupture
  Stricture   } of pulmonary vessel

417.9 Unspecified disease of pulmonary circulation

OTHER FORMS OF HEART DISEASE (420-429)

420 Acute pericarditis
Includes: acute:
        mediastinopericarditis
        myopericarditis
        pericardial effusion
        pleuropericarditis
        pneumopericarditis

> *Excludes:* *acute rheumatic pericarditis (391.0)*
> *postmyocardial infarction syndrome [Dressler's] (411.0)*

420.0 Acute pericarditis in diseases classified elsewhere
Code first underlying disease, as:
  actinomycosis (039.8)
  amebiasis (006.8)
  nocardiosis (039.8)
  tuberculosis (017.9)
  uremia (585)

> *Excludes:* *pericarditis (acute) (in):*
> *Coxsackie (virus) (074.21)*
> *gonococcal (098.83)*
> *histoplasmosis (115.0-115.9 with fifth-digit 3)*
> *meningococcal infection (036.41)*
> *syphilitic (093.81)*

420.9 Other and unspecified acute pericarditis

420.90 Acute pericarditis, unspecified
Pericarditis (acute):
  NOS
  infective NOS
  sicca

420.91 Acute idiopathic pericarditis
Pericarditis, acute:
  benign
  nonspecific
  viral

420.99 Other
Pericarditis (acute):   Pericarditis (acute):
  pneumococcal   streptococcal
  purulent   suppurative
  staphylococcal   Pneumopyopericardium
                  Pyopericardium

> *Excludes:* *pericarditis in diseases classified elsewhere (420.0)*

 Add 4th or 5th digit   Nonspecific code   Unspecified code   Manifestation code

421 Acute and subacute endocarditis

421.0 Acute and subacute bacterial endocarditis

Endocarditis (acute) (chronic) (subacute):
bacterial
infective NOS
lenta
malignant
purulent

Endocarditis (acute) (chronic) (subacute):
septic
ulcerative
vegetative
Infective aneurysm
Subacute bacterial endocarditis [SBE]

Use additional code, if desired, to identify infectious organism [e.g., Streptococcus 041.0, Staphylococcus 041.1]

421.1 *Acute and subacute infective endocarditis in diseases classified elsewhere*
Code first underlying disease, as:
blastomycosis (116.0)
Q fever (083.0)
typhoid (fever) (002.0)

Excludes: *endocarditis (in):*
Coxsackie (virus) (074.22)
gonococcal (098.84)
histoplasmosis (115.0-115.9 with fifth-digit 4)
meningococcal infection (036.42)
monilial (112.81)

421.9 Acute endocarditis, unspecified
Endocarditis
Myoendocarditis } acute or subacute
Periendocarditis

Excludes: *acute rheumatic endocarditis (391.1)*

422 Acute myocarditis

Excludes: *acute rheumatic myocarditis (391.2)*

422.0 *Acute myocarditis in diseases classified elsewhere*
Code first underlying disease, as:
myocarditis (acute):
influenzal (487.8)
tuberculous (017.9)

Excludes: *myocarditis (acute) (due to):*
aseptic, of newborn (074.23)
Coxsackie (virus) (074.23)
diphtheritic (032.82)
meningococcal infection (036.43)
syphilitic (093.82)
toxoplasmosis (130.3)

422.9 Other and unspecified acute myocarditis

422.90 Acute myocarditis, unspecified
Acute or subacute (interstitial) myocarditis

422.91 Idiopathic myocarditis
Myocarditis (acute or subacute):
Fiedler's
giant cell
isolated (diffuse) (granulomatous)
nonspecific granulomatous

422.92 Septic myocarditis
Myocarditis, acute or subacute:
pneumococcal
staphylococcal
Use additional code, if desired, to identify infectious organism [e.g., Staphylococcus 041.1]

Excludes: *myocarditis, acute or subacute:*
in bacterial diseases classified elsewhere (422.0)
streptococcal (391.2)

422.93 Toxic myocarditis

422.99 Other

● Code new
to this edition

▲ Revision of
existing code

④ ⑤ Fourth or fifth
digit required

423 **Other diseases of pericardium**

> *Excludes:* that specified as rheumatic (393)

423.0 **Hemopericardium**

423.1 **Adhesive pericarditis**
Adherent pericardium   Pericarditis:
Fibrosis of pericardium   adhesive
Milk spots   obliterative
          Soldiers' patches

423.2 **Constrictive pericarditis**
Concato's disease
Pick's disease of heart (and liver)

423.8 **Other specified diseases of pericardium**
Calcification ⎫
Fistula   ⎬ of pericardium

423.9 **Unspecified disease of pericardium**

424 **Other diseases of endocardium**

> *Excludes:* bacterial endocarditis (421.0-421.9)
> rheumatic endocarditis (391.1, 394.0-397.9)
> syphilitic endocarditis (093.20-093.24)

424.0 **Mitral valve disorders**
Mitral (valve):
 incompetence ⎫
 insufficiency ⎬ NOS of specified cause, except rheumatic
 regurgitation ⎭

> *Excludes:* mitral (valve):
> disease (394.9)
> failure (394.9)
> stenosis (394.0)
> the listed conditions:
> specified as rheumatic (394.1)
> unspecified as to cause but with mention of:
> diseases of aortic valve (396.0-396.9)
> mitral stenosis or obstruction (394.2)

424.1 **Aortic valve disorders**
Aortic (valve):
 incompetence ⎫
 insufficiency ⎬ NOS of specified cause, except rheumatic
 regurgitation ⎪
 stenosis   ⎭

> *Excludes:* hypertrophic subaortic stenosis (425.1)
> that specified as rheumatic (395.0-395.9)
> that of unspecified cause but with mention of diseases of mitral valve (396.0-396.9)

424.2 **Tricuspid valve disorders, specified as nonrheumatic**
Tricuspid valve:
 incompetence ⎫
 insufficiency ⎬ of specified cause, except rheumatic
 regurgitation ⎪
 stenosis   ⎭

> *Excludes:* rheumatic or of unspecified cause (397.0)

424.3 **Pulmonary valve disorders**
Pulmonic: Pulmonic:
 incompetence NOS   regurgitation NOS
 insufficiency NOS   stenosis NOS

> *Excludes:* that specified as rheumatic (397.1)

424.9 **Endocarditis, valve unspecified**

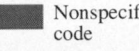 Add 4th or 5th digit   Nonspecific code   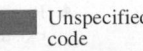 Unspecified code   Manifestation code

424.90 **Endocarditis, valve unspecified, unspecified cause**
Endocarditis (chronic):
NOS
nonbacterial thrombotic
Valvular:
incompetence ⎫
insufficiency ⎪
regurgitation ⎬ of unspecified valve, unspecified
stenosis ⎪ cause
Valvulitis (chronic) ⎭

424.91 *Endocarditis in diseases classified elsewhere*
Code first underlying disease, as:
atypical verrucous endocarditis [Libman-Sacks] (710.0)
disseminated lupus erythematosus (710.0)
tuberculosis (017.9)

Excludes: syphilitic (093.20-093.24)

424.99 **Other**
Any condition classifiable to 424.90 with specified cause, except rheumatic

Excludes: *endocardial fibroelastosis (425.3)*
that specified as rheumatic (397.9)

425 **Cardiomyopathy**
Includes: myocardiopathy

425.0 Endomyocardial fibrosis

425.1 Hypertrophic obstructive cardiomyopathy
Hypertrophic subaortic stenosis (idiopathic)

425.2 Obscure cardiomyopathy of Africa
Becker's disease
Idiopathic mural endomyocardial disease

425.3 Endocardial fibroelastosis
Elastomyofibrosis

425.4 Other primary cardiomyopathies
Cardiomyopathy: Cardiomyopathy:
NOS   idiopathic
congestive   nonobstructive
constrictive   obstructive
familial   restrictive
hypertrophic   Cardiovascular collagenosis

425.5 Alcoholic cardiomyopathy

425.7 *Nutritional and metabolic cardiomyopathy*
Code first underlying disease, as:
amyloidosis (277.3)
beriberi (265.0)
cardiac glycogenosis (271.0)
mucopolysaccharidosis (277.5)
thyrotoxicosis (242.0-242.9)

Excludes: *gouty tophi of heart (274.82)*

425.8 *Cardiomyopathy in other diseases classified elsewhere*
Code first underlying disease, as:
Friedreich's ataxia (334.0)
myotonia atrophica (359.2)
progressive muscular dystrophy (359.1)
sarcoidosis (135)

Excludes: *cardiomyopathy in Chagas' disease (086.0)*

425.9 **Secondary cardiomyopathy, unspecified**

426 **Conduction disorders**

426.0 Atrioventricular block, complete
Third degree atrioventricular block

426.1 Atrioventricular block, other and unspecified

426.10 **Atrioventricular block, unspecified**
Atrioventricular [AV] block (incomplete) (partial)

● Code new   ▲ Revision of   ④ ⑤ Fourth or fifth
to this edition   existing code   digit required

426.11   First degree atrioventricular block
Incomplete atrioventricular block, first degree
Prolonged P-R interval NOS

426.12   Mobitz (type) II atrioventricular block
Incomplete atrioventricular block:
Mobitz (type) II
second degree, Mobitz (type) II

426.13   Other second degree atrioventricular block
Incomplete atrioventricular block:
Mobitz (type) I [Wenckebach's]
second degree:
NOS
Mobitz (type) I
with 2:1 atrioventricular response [block]
Wenckebach's phenomenon

426.2   Left bundle branch hemiblock
Block:
left anterior fascicular
left posterior fascicular

426.3   Other left bundle branch block
Left bundle branch block:
NOS
anterior fascicular with posterior fascicular
complete
main stem

426.4   Right bundle branch block

426.5   Bundle branch block, other and unspecified

426.50   Bundle branch block, unspecified

426.51   Right bundle branch block and left posterior fascicular block

426.52   Right bundle branch block and left anterior fascicular block

426.53   Other bilateral bundle branch block
Bifascicular block NOS
Bilateral bundle branch block NOS
Right bundle branch with left bundle branch block (incomplete) (main stem)

426.54   Trifascicular block

426.6   Other heart block
Intraventricular block: Sinoatrial block
NOS   Sinoauricular block
diffuse
myofibrillar

426.7   Anomalous atrioventricular excitation
Atrioventricular conduction:
accelerated
accessory
pre-excitation
Ventricular pre-excitation
Wolff-Parkinson-White syndrome

426.8   Other specified conduction disorders

426.81   Lown-Ganong-Levine syndrome
Syndrome of short P-R interval, normal QRS complexes, and supraventricular
tachycardias

426.89   Other
Dissociation:
atrioventricular [AV]
interference
isorhythmic
Nonparoxysmal AV nodal tachycardia

426.9   Conduction disorder, unspecified
Heart block NOS   Stokes-Adams syndrome

Add 4th or   Nonspecific   Unspecified   Manifestation
5th digit   code   code   code

427 Cardiac dysrhythmias

> *Excludes:* *that complicating:*
>   *abortion (634-638 with .7, 639.8)*
>   *ectopic or molar pregnancy (639.8)*
>   *labor or delivery (668.1, 669.4)*

427.0 Paroxysmal supraventricular tachycardia
  Paroxysmal tachycardia:
    atrial [PAT]
    atrioventricular [AV]
    junctional
    nodal

427.1 Paroxysmal ventricular tachycardia
  Ventricular tachycardia (paroxysmal)

427.2 Paroxysmal tachycardia, unspecified
  Bouveret-Hoffmann syndrome
  Paroxysmal tachycardia:
    NOS
    essential

427.3 Atrial fibrillation and flutter

  427.31 Atrial fibrillation

  427.32 Atrial flutter

427.4 Ventricular fibrillation and flutter

  427.41 Ventricular fibrillation

  427.42 Ventricular flutter

427.5 Cardiac arrest
  Cardiorespiratory arrest

427.6 Premature beats

  427.60 Premature beats, unspecified
    Ectopic beats
    Extrasystoles
    Extrasystolic arrhythmia
    Premature contractions or systoles NOS

  427.61 Supraventricular premature beats
    Atrial premature beats, contractions, or systoles

  427.69 Other
    Ventricular premature beats, contractions, or systoles

427.8 Other specified cardiac dysrhythmias

  427.81 Sinoatrial node dysfunction
    Sinus bradycardia: Syndrome:
      persistent   sick sinus
      severe   tachycardia-bradycardia

> *Excludes:* *sinus bradycardia NOS (427.89)*

  427.89 Other
    Rhythm disorder: Wandering (atrial) pacemaker
      coronary sinus
      ectopic
      nodal

> *Excludes:* *carotid sinus syncope (337.0)*
>   *reflex bradycardia (337.0)*
>   *tachycardia (785.0)*

427.9 Cardiac dysrhythmia, unspecified
  Arrhythmia (cardiac) NOS

428 Heart failure

> *Excludes:* *following cardiac surgery (429.4)*
>   *rheumatic (398.91)*
>   *that complicating:*
>   *abortion (634-638 with .7, 639.8)*
>   *ectopic or molar pregnancy (639.8)*
>   *labor or delivery (668.1, 669.4)*
>   *that due to hypertension (402.0-402.9 with fifth-digit 1)*

● Code new   ▲ Revision of   ④ ⑤ Fourth or fifth
  to this edition   existing code   digit required

428.0 Congestive heart failure
Congestive heart disease
Right heart failure (secondary to left heart failure)

428.1 Left heart failure
Acute edema of lung
Acute pulmonary edema   } with heart disease NOS or heart failure
Cardiac asthma
Left ventricular failure

428.9 Heart failure, unspecified
Cardiac failure NOS   Myocardial failure NOS
Heart failure NOS   Weak heart

429 Ill-defined descriptions and complications of heart disease

429.0 Myocarditis, unspecified
Myocarditis:
NOS
chronic (interstitial) } (with mention of arteriosclerosis)
fibroid
senile

Use additional code, if desired, to identify presence of arteriosclerosis

Excludes: acute or subacute (422.0-422.9)
rheumatic (398.0)
acute (391.2)
that due to hypertension (402.0-402.9)

429.1 Myocardial degeneration
Degeneration of heart or myocardium:
fatty
mural
muscular   } (with mention of arteriosclerosis)
Myocardial:
degeneration disease

Use additional code, if desired, to identify presence of arteriosclerosis

Excludes: that due to hypertension (402.0-402.9)

429.2 Cardiovascular disease, unspecified
Arteriosclerotic cardiovascular disease [ASCVD]
Cardiovascular arteriosclerosis
Cardiovascular:
degeneration
disease   } (with mention of arteriosclerosis)
sclerosis

Use additional code, if desired, to identify presence of arteriosclerosis

Excludes: that due to hypertension (402.0-402.9)

429.3 Cardiomegaly
Cardiac: Ventricular dilatation
dilatation
hypertrophy

Excludes: that due to hypertension (402.0-402.9)

429.4 Functional disturbances following cardiac surgery
Cardiac insufficiency } following cardiac surgery or due to prosthesis
Heart failure
Postcardiotomy syndrome
Postvalvulotomy syndrome

Excludes: cardiac failure in the immediate postoperative period (997.1)

429.5 Rupture of chordae tendineae

429.6 Rupture of papillary muscle

Add 4th or   Nonspecific   Unspecified   Manifestation
5th digit   code   code   code

429.7 Certain sequelae of myocardial infarction, not elsewhere classified

Use additional code to identify the associated myocardial infarction:
with onset of 8 weeks or less (410.00-410.92)
with onset of more than 8 weeks (414.8)

Excludes: *congenital defects of heart (745, 746)*
coronary aneurysm (414.11)
disorders of papillary muscle (429.6, 429.81)
postmyocardial infarction syndrome (411.0)
rupture of chordae tendineae (429.5)

429.71 Acquired cardiac septal defect

Excludes: *acute septal infarction (410.00-410.92)*

429.79 Other
Mural thrombus (atrial) (ventricular), acquired, following myocardial infarction

429.8 Other ill-defined heart diseases

429.81 Other disorders of papillary muscle
Papillary muscle: Papillary muscle:
atrophy   incompetence
degeneration   incoordination
dysfunction   scarring

429.82 Hyperkinetic heart disease

429.89 Other
Carditis

Excludes: *that due to hypertension (402.0-402.9)*

429.9 Heart disease, unspecified
Heart disease (organic) NOS
Morbus cordis NOS

Excludes: *that due to hypertension (402.0-402.9)*

CEREBROVASCULAR DISEASE (430-438)

Includes: with mention of hypertension (conditions classifiable to 401-405)

Use additional code, if desired, to identify presence of hypertension

Excludes: *any condition classifiable to 430-434, 436, 437 occurring during pregnancy, childbirth, or the puerperium, or specified as puerperal (674.0)*

430 Subarachnoid hemorrhage
Meningeal hemorrhage
Ruptured:
berry aneurysm
(congenital) cerebral aneurysm NOS

Excludes: *syphilitic ruptured cerebral aneurysm (094.87)*

431 Intracerebral hemorrhage
Hemorrhage (of):   Hemorrhage (of):
basilar   intrapontine
bulbar   pontine
cerebellar   subcortical
cerebral   ventricular
cerebromeningeal   Rupture of blood vessel in brain
cortical
internal capsule

432 Other and unspecified intracranial hemorrhage

432.0 Nontraumatic extradural hemorrhage
Nontraumatic epidural hemorrhage

432.1 Subdural hemorrhage
Subdural hematoma, nontraumatic

432.9 Unspecified intracranial hemorrhage
Intracranial hemorrhage NOS

● Code new   ▲ Revision of   ④ ⑤ Fourth or fifth
to this edition   existing code   digit required

⑤ **433** **Occlusion and stenosis of precerebral arteries**

The following fifth-digit subclassification is for use with category 433:

    0 **without mention of cerebral infarction**

    1 **with cerebral infarction**

Includes:

    embolism
    narrowing
    obstruction   } of basilar, carotid, and vertebral arteries
    thrombosis

Excludes: *insufficiency NOS of precerebral arteries (435.0-435.9)*

433.0 **Basilar artery**

433.1 **Carotid artery**

433.2 **Vertebral artery**

433.3 **Multiple and bilateral**

433.8 **Other specified precerebral artery**

433.9 **Unspecified precerebral artery**
    Precerebral artery NOS

⑤ **434** **Occlusion of cerebral arteries**

The following fifth-digit subclassification is for use with category 434:

    0 **without mention of cerebral infarction**

    1 **with cerebral infarction**

434.0 **Cerebral thrombosis**
    Thrombosis of cerebral arteries

434.1 **Cerebral embolism**

434.9 **Cerebral artery occlusion, unspecified**

435 **Transient cerebral ischemia**

Includes: cerebrovascular insufficiency (acute) with transient focal neurological signs and
      symptoms
    insufficiency of basilar, carotid, and vertebral arteries
    spasm of cerebral arteries

Excludes: *acute cerebrovascular insufficiency NOS (437.1)*
        that due to any condition classifiable to 433 (433.0-433.9)

435.0 **Basilar artery syndrome**

435.1 **Vertebral artery syndrome**

435.2 **Subclavian steal syndrome**

435.3 **Vertebrobasilar artery syndrome**

435.8 **Other specified transient cerebral ischemias**

435.9 **Unspecified transient cerebral ischemia**
    Impending cerebrovascular accident
    Intermittent cerebral ischemia
    Transient ischemic attack [TIA]

436 **Acute, but ill-defined, cerebrovascular disease**
    Apoplexy, apoplectic: Cerebral seizure
      NOS   Cerebrovascular accident [CVA] NOS
      attack   Stroke
      cerebral
      seizure

Excludes: *any condition classifiable to categories 430-435*

437 **Other and ill-defined cerebrovascular disease**

437.0 **Cerebral atherosclerosis**
    Atheroma of cerebral arteries
    Cerebral arteriosclerosis

437.1 **Other generalized ischemic cerebrovascular disease**
    Acute cerebrovascular insufficiency NOS
    Cerebral ischemia (chronic)

437.2 **Hypertensive encephalopathy**

Add 4th or   Nonspecific   Unspecified   Manifestation
5th digit   code   code   code

437.3 Cerebral aneurysm, nonruptured
Internal carotid artery, intracranial portion
Internal carotid artery NOS

Excludes: *congenital cerebral aneurysm, nonruptured (747.81)*
internal carotid artery, extracranial portion (442.81)

437.4 Cerebral arteritis

437.5 Moyamoya disease

437.6 Nonpyogenic thrombosis of intracranial venous sinus

Excludes: *pyogenic (325)*

437.7 Transient global amnesia

437.8 Other

437.9 Unspecified
Cerebrovascular disease or lesion NOS

438 Late effects of cerebrovascular disease
Note: This category is to be used to indicate conditions in 430-437 as the cause of late effects, themselves classifiable elsewhere. The "late effects" include conditions specified as such, or as sequelae, which may occur at any time after the onset of the causal condition.
Code first sequelae:
aphasia (784.3)
dysphasia (784.5)
hemiplegia (342.0-342.9)
paralysis (344.0-344.9)

DISEASES OF ARTERIES, ARTERIOLES, AND CAPILLARIES (440-448)

440 Atherosclerosis
Includes: arteriolosclerosis
arteriosclerosis (obliterans) (senile)
arteriosclerotic vascular disease
atheroma
degeneration:
arterial
arteriovascular
vascular
endarteritis deformans or obliterans
senile:
arteritis
endarteritis

Excludes: *atherosclerosis of bypass graft of the extremities (440.30-440.32)*

440.0 Of aorta

440.1 Of renal artery

Excludes: *atherosclerosis of renal arterioles (403.00-403.91)*

440.2 Of native arteries of the extremities

Excludes: *atherosclerosis of bypass graft of the extremities (440.30-440.32)*

440.20 Atherosclerosis of the extremities, unspecified

440.21 Atherosclerosis of the extremities with intermittent claudication

440.22 Atherosclerosis of the extremities with rest pain
Includes: any condition classifiable to 440.21

440.23 Atherosclerosis of the extremities with ulceration
Includes: any condition classifiable to 440.21 and 440.22

440.24 Atherosclerosis of the extremities with gangrene
Includes: any condition classifiable to 440.21, 440.22, and 440.23
with ischemic gangrene 785.4

Excludes: *gas gangrene 040.0*

440.29 Other

440.3 Of bypass graft of the extremities

Excludes: *atherosclerosis of native artery of the extremity (440.21-440.24)*
embolism [occlusion NOS] [thrombus]
of graft (996.74)

440.30 Of unspecified graft

● Code new
 to this edition   ▲ Revision of
 existing code   ④ ⑤ Fourth or fifth
 digit required

440.31   Of autologous vein bypass graft

440.32   Of nonautologous biological bypass graft

440.8   Of other specified arteries

Excludes: basilar (433.0)

carotid (433.1)
cerebral (437.0)
coronary (414.00-414.05)
mesenteric (557.1)
precerebral (433.0-433.9)
pulmonary (416.0)
vertebral (433.2)

440.9   Generalized and unspecified atherosclerosis
Arteriosclerotic vascular disease NOS

Excludes: arteriosclerotic cardiovascular disease [ASCVD] (429.2)

441   Aortic aneurysm and dissection

Excludes: syphilitic aortic aneurysm (093.0)
traumatic aortic aneurysm (901.0, 902.0)

441.0   Dissection of aorta
Dissecting aneurysm of aorta (ruptured)

441.00   Unspecified site

441.01   Thoracic

441.02   Abdominal

441.03   Thoracoabdominal

441.1   Thoracic aneurysm, ruptured

441.2   Thoracic aneurysm without mention of rupture

441.3   Abdominal aneurysm, ruptured

441.4   Abdominal aneurysm without mention of rupture

441.5   Aortic aneurysm of unspecified site, ruptured
Rupture of aorta NOS

441.6   Thoracoabdominal aneurysm, ruptured

441.7   Thoracoabdominal aneurysm, without mention of rupture

☐ **441.9   Aortic aneurysm of unspecified site without mention of rupture**
Aneurysm
Dilatation   } of aorta
Hyaline necrosis

442   Other aneurysm
Includes: aneurysm (ruptured) (cirsoid) (false) (varicose)
aneurysmal varix

Excludes: arteriovenous aneurysm or fistula:
acquired (447.0)
congenital (747.60-747.69)
traumatic (900.0-904.9)

442.0   Of artery of upper extremity

442.1   Of renal artery

442.2   Of iliac artery

442.3   Of artery of lower extremity
Aneurysm:
femoral   } artery
popliteal

442.8   Of other specified artery

442.81   Artery of neck
Aneurysm of carotid artery (common) (external) (internal, extracranial portion)

Excludes: internal carotid artery, intracranial portion (437.3)

442.82   Subclavian artery

442.83   Splenic artery

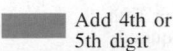 Add 4th or 5th digit   Nonspecific code   Unspecified code   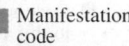 Manifestation code

442.84 **Other visceral artery**
Aneurysm:
celiac
gastroduodenal
gastroepiploic ⎫
Hepatic ⎬ artery
pancreaticoduodenal ⎭
superior mesenteric

442.89 **Other**
Aneurysm:
mediastinal ⎫
spinal ⎬ artery

Excludes: *cerebral (nonruptured) (437.3)*
congenital (747.81)
ruptured (430)
coronary (414.11)
heart (414.10)
pulmonary (417.1)

442.9 **Of unspecified site**

443 **Other peripheral vascular disease**

443.0 **Raynaud's syndrome**
Raynaud's:
disease
phenomenon (secondary)
Use additional code, if desired, to identify gangrene (785.4)

443.1 **Thromboangiitis obliterans [Buerger's disease]**
Presenile gangrene

443.8 **Other specified peripheral vascular diseases**

443.81 *Peripheral angiopathy in diseases classified elsewhere*
Code first underlying disease, as:
diabetes mellitus (250.7)

443.89 **Other**
Acrocyanosis
Acroparesthesia:
simple [Schultze's type]
vasomotor [Nothnagel's type]
Erythrocyanosis
Erythromelalgia

Excludes: *chilblains (991.5)*
frostbite (991.0-991.3)
immersion foot (991.4)

443.9 **Peripheral vascular disease, unspecified**
Intermittent claudication NOS
Peripheral:
angiopathy NOS
vascular disease NOS
Spasm of artery

Excludes: *spasm of cerebral artery (435.0-435.9)*
Atherosclerosis of the arteries of the extremities (440.20-440.22)

444 **Arterial embolism and thrombosis**
Includes: infarction:
embolic
thrombotic
occlusion

Excludes: *that complicating:*
abortion (634-638 with .6, 639.6)
ectopic or molar pregnancy (639.6)
pregnancy, childbirth, or the puerperium (673.0-673.8)

444.0 **Of abdominal aorta**
Aortic bifurcation syndrome   Leriche's syndrome
Aortoiliac obstruction   Saddle embolus

444.1 **Of thoracic aorta**
Embolism or thrombosis of aorta (thoracic)

● Code new   ▲ Revision of   ④ ⑤ Fourth or fifth
to this edition   existing code   digit required

444.2 Of arteries of the extremities

444.21 Upper extremity

444.22 Lower extremity
Arterial embolism or thrombosis:
femoral
peripheral NOS
popliteal

Excludes: *iliofemoral (444.81)*

444.8 Of other specified artery

444.81 Iliac artery

444.89 Other

Excludes: *basilar (433.0)*
carotid (433.1)
cerebral (434.0-434.9)
coronary (410.00-410.92)
mesenteric (557.0)
ophthalmic (362.30-362.34)
precerebral (433.0-433.9)
pulmonary (415.19)
renal (593.81)
retinal (362.30-362.34)
vertebral (433.2)

444.9 Of unspecified artery

446 Polyarteritis nodosa and allied conditions

446.0 Polyarteritis nodosa
Disseminated necrotizing   Panarteritis (nodosa)
periarteritis   Periarteritis (nodosa)
Necrotizing angiitis

446.1 Acute febrile mucocutaneous lymph node syndrome [MCLS]
Kawasaki disease

446.2 Hypersensitivity angiitis

Excludes: *antiglomerular basement membrane disease without pulmonary hemorrhage (583.89)*

446.20 Hypersensitivity angiitis, unspecified

446.21 Goodpasture's syndrome
Antiglomerular basement membrane antibody-mediated nephritis with pulmonary
hemorrhage
Use additional code, if desired, to identify renal disease (583.81)

446.29 Other specified hypersensitivity angiitis

446.3 Lethal midline granuloma
Malignant granuloma of face

446.4 Wegener's granulomatosis
Necrotizing respiratory granulomatosis
Wegener's syndrome

446.5 Giant cell arteritis
Cranial arteritis   Temporal arteritis
Horton's disease

446.6 Thrombotic microangiopathy
Moschcowitz's syndrome
Thrombotic thrombocytopenic purpura

446.7 Takayasu's disease
Aortic arch arteritis   Pulseless disease

447 Other disorders of arteries and arterioles

447.0 Arteriovenous fistula, acquired
Arteriovenous aneurysm, acquired

Excludes: *cerebrovascular (437.3)*
coronary (414.19)
pulmonary (417.0)
surgically created arteriovenous shunt or fistula:
complication (996.1, 996.61-996.62)
status or presence (V45.1)
traumatic (900.0-904.9)

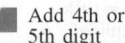 Add 4th or
5th digit

Nonspecific
code

Unspecified
code

 Manifestation
code

447.1 Stricture of artery

447.2 Rupture of artery
Erosion
Fistula, except arteriovenous } of artery
Ulcer

Excludes: *traumatic rupture of artery (900.0-904.9)*

447.3 Hyperplasia of renal artery
Fibromuscular hyperplasia of renal artery

447.4 Celiac artery compression syndrome
Celiac axis syndrome   Marable's syndrome

447.5 Necrosis of artery

447.6 Arteritis, unspecified
Aortitis NOS
Endarteritis NOS

Excludes: *arteritis, endarteritis:*
          aortic arch (446.7)
          cerebral (437.4)
          coronary (414.00-414.05)
          deformans (440.0-440.9)
          obliterans (440.0-440.9)
          pulmonary (417.8)
          senile (440.0-440.9)
      polyarteritis NOS (446.0)
      syphilitic aortitis (093.1)

447.8 Other specified disorders of arteries and arterioles
Fibromuscular hyperplasia of arteries, except renal

447.9 Unspecified disorders of arteries and arterioles

448 Disease of capillaries

448.0 Hereditary hemorrhagic telangiectasia
Rendu-Osler-Weber disease

448.1 Nevus, non-neoplastic
Nevus: Nevus:
  araneus   spider
  senile   stellar

Excludes: *neoplastic (216.0-216.9)*
          port wine (757.32)
          strawberry (757.32)

448.9 Other and unspecified capillary diseases
Capillary:
  hemorrhage
  hyperpermeability
  thrombosis

Excludes: *capillary fragility (hereditary) (287.8)*

DISEASES OF VEINS AND LYMPHATICS, AND OTHER DISEASES OF CIRCULATORY SYSTEM (451-459)

451 Phlebitis and thrombophlebitis
Includes: endophlebitis
           inflammation, vein
           periphlebitis
           suppurative phlebitis
Use additional E Code, if desired, to identify drug, if drug-induced

Excludes: *that complicating:*
          abortion (634-638 with .7, 639.8)
          ectopic or molar pregnancy (639.8)
          pregnancy, childbirth, or the puerperium (671.0-671.9)
          that due to or following:
          implant or catheter device (996.61-996.62)
          infusion, perfusion, or transfusion (999.2)

451.0 Of superficial vessels of lower extremities
Saphenous vein (greater) (lesser)

451.1 Of deep vessels of lower extremities

● Code new   ▲ Revision of   ④ ⑤ Fourth or fifth
   to this edition   existing code   digit required

451.11 Femoral vein (deep) (superficial)

451.19 Other
Femoropopliteal vein
Popliteal vein
Tibial vein

451.2 Of lower extremities, unspecified

451.8 Of other sites

> *Excludes:* intracranial venous sinus (325)
> nonpyogenic (437.6)
> portal (vein) (572.1)

451.81 Iliac vein

451.82 Of superficial veins of upper extremities
Antecubital vein
Basilic vein
Cephalic vein

451.83 Of deep veins of upper extremities
Brachial vein
Radial vein
Ulnar vein

451.84 Of upper extremities, unspecified

451.89 Other
Axillary vein
Jugular vein
Subclavian vein
Thrombophlebitis of breast (Mondor's disease)

451.9 Of unspecified site

452 Portal vein thrombosis
Portal (vein) obstruction

> *Excludes:* hepatic vein thrombosis (453.0)
> phlebitis of portal vein (572.1)

453 Other venous embolism and thrombosis

> *Excludes:* that complicating:
> abortion (634-638 with .7, 639.8)
> ectopic or molar pregnancy (639.8)
> pregnancy, childbirth, or the puerperium (671.0-671.9)
> that with inflammation, phlebitis, and thrombophlebitis (451.0-451.9)

453.0 Budd-Chiari syndrome
Hepatic vein thrombosis

453.1 Thrombophlebitis migrans

453.2 Of vena cava

453.3 Of renal vein

453.8 Of other specified veins

> *Excludes:* cerebral (434.0-434.9)
> coronary (410.00-410.92)
> intracranial venous sinus (325)
> nonpyogenic (437.6)
> mesenteric (557.0)
> portal (452)
> precerebral (433.0-433.9)
> pulmonary (415.19)

453.9 Of unspecified site
Embolism of vein   Thrombosis (vein)

454 Varicose veins of lower extremities

> *Excludes:* that complicating pregnancy, childbirth, or the puerperium (671.0)

454.0 With ulcer
Varicose ulcer (lower extremity, any part)
Varicose veins with ulcer of lower extremity [any part] or of unspecified site
Any condition classifiable to 454.9 with ulcer or specified as ulcerated

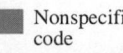 Add 4th or 5th digit   Nonspecific code   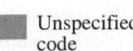 Unspecified code   Manifestation code

454.1 With inflammation
Stasis dermatitis
Varicose veins with inflammation of lower extremity [any part] or of unspecified site
Any condition classifiable to 454.9 with inflammation or specified as inflamed

454.2 With ulcer and inflammation
Varicose veins with ulcer and inflammation of lower extremity [any part] or of unspecified site
Any condition classifiable to 454.9 with ulcer and inflammation

454.9 Without mention of ulcer or inflammation
Phlebectasia
Varicose veins ⎫
Varix   ⎬ of lower extremity [any part] or of unspecified site

455 Hemorrhoids
Includes: hemorrhoids (anus) (rectum)
piles
varicose veins, anus or rectum

Excludes: *that complicating pregnancy, childbirth or the puerperium (671.8)*

455.0 Internal hemorrhoids without mention of complication

455.1 Internal thrombosed hemorrhoids

455.2 Internal hemorrhoids with other complication
Internal hemorrhoids: Internal hemorrhoids:
bleeding   strangulated
prolapsed   ulcerated

455.3 External hemorrhoids without mention of complication

455.4 External thrombosed hemorrhoids

455.5 External hemorrhoids with other complication
External hemorrhoids: External hemorrhoids:
bleeding   strangulated
prolapsed   ulcerated

455.6 Unspecified hemorrhoids without mention of complication
Hemorrhoids NOS

455.7 Unspecified thrombosed hemorrhoids
Thrombosed hemorrhoids, unspecified whether internal or external

455.8 Unspecified hemorrhoids with other complication
Hemorrhoids, unspecified whether internal or external:
bleeding
prolapsed
strangulated
ulcerated

455.9 Residual hemorrhoidal skin tags
Skin tags, anus or rectum

456 Varicose veins of other sites

456.0 Esophageal varices with bleeding

456.1 Esophageal varices without mention of bleeding

456.2 *Esophageal varices in diseases classified elsewhere*
Code first underlying cause, as:
cirrhosis of liver (571.0-571.9)
portal hypertension (572.3)

456.20 *With bleeding*

456.21 *Without mention of bleeding*

456.3 Sublingual varices

456.4 Scrotal varices
Varicocele

456.5 Pelvic varices
Varices of broad ligament

456.6 Vulval varices
Varices of perineum

Excludes: *that complicating pregnancy, childbirth, or the puerperium (671.1)*

456.8 Varices of other sites
Varicose veins of nasal septum (with ulcer)

● Code new   ▲ Revision of   ④ ⑤ Fourth or fifth
to this edition   existing code   digit required

Excludes: *placental varices (656.7)*
retinal varices (362.17)
varicose ulcer of unspecified site (454.0)
varicose veins of unspecified site (454.9)

457 Noninfectious disorders of lymphatic channels

457.0 Postmastectomy lymphedema syndrome
Elephantiasis
Obliteration of lymphatic vessel } due to mastectomy

457.1 Other lymphedema
Elephantiasis (nonfilarial) NOS
Lymphangiectasis
Lymphedema:
  acquired (chronic)
  praecox
  secondary
Obliteration, lymphatic vessel

Excludes: *elephantiasis (nonfilarial):*
congenital (757.0)
eyelid (374.83)
vulva (624.8)

457.2 Lymphangitis
Lymphangitis:
  NOS
  chronic
  subacute

Excludes: *acute lymphangitis (682.0-682.9)*

457.8 Other noninfectious disorders of lymphatic channels
Chylocele (nonfilarial)   Lymph node or vessel:
Chylous: fistula
  ascites   infarction
  cyst   rupture

Excludes: *chylocele:*
filarial (125.0-125.9)
tunica vaginalis (nonfilarial) (608.84)

457.9 Unspecified noninfectious disorder of lymphatic channels

458 Hypotension
Includes: hypopiesis

Excludes: *cardiovascular collapse (785.50)*
maternal hypotension syndrome (669.2)
shock (785.50-785.59)
Shy-Drager syndrome (333.0)

458.0 Orthostatic hypotension
Hypotension:
  orthostatic (chronic)
  postural

458.1 Chronic hypotension
Permanent idiopathic hypotension

458.2 Iatrogenic hypotension
Postoperative hypotension

458.9 Hypotension, unspecified
Hypotension (arterial) NOS

459 Other disorders of circulatory system

459.0 Hemorrhage, unspecified
Rupture of blood vessel NOS
Spontaneous hemorrhage NEC

Excludes: *hemorrhage:*
gastrointestinal NOS (578.9)
in newborn NOS (772.9)
secondary or recurrent following trauma (958.2)
traumatic rupture of blood vessel (900.0-904.9)

459.1 Postphlebitic syndrome

| Add 4th or 5th digit | Nonspecific code | Unspecified code | Manifestation code |

459.2 **Compression of vein**
Stricture of vein
Vena cava syndrome (inferior) (superior)

459.8 **Other specified disorders of circulatory system**

459.81 **Venous (peripheral) insufficiency, unspecified**
Chronic venous insufficiency NOS

Use additional code for any associated ulceration (707.1-707.9)

459.89 **Other**
Collateral circulation (venous), any site
Phlebosclerosis
Venofibrosis

459.9 **Unspecified circulatory system disorder**

● Code new
to this edition

▲ Revision of
existing code

④ ⑤ Fourth or fifth
digit required

8. DISEASES OF THE RESPIRATORY SYSTEM (460-519)

Use additional code, if desired, to identify infectious organism

ACUTE RESPIRATORY INFECTIONS (460-466)

Excludes: *pneumonia and influenza (480.0-487.8)*

460 Acute nasopharyngitis [common cold]

Coryza (acute)	Rhinitis:
Nasal catarrh, acute	acute
Nasopharyngitis:	infective
NOS	
acute	
infective NOS	

Excludes: *nasopharyngitis, chronic (472.2)*
 pharyngitis:
 acute or unspecified (462)
 chronic (472.1)
 rhinitis:
 allergic (477.0-477.9)
 chronic or unspecified (472.0)
 sore throat:
 acute or unspecified (462)
 chronic (472.1)

461 Acute sinusitis

Includes: abscess
 empyema
 infection   } acute, of sinus (accessory) (nasal)
 inflammation
 suppuration

Excludes: *chronic or unspecified sinusitis (473.0-473.9)*

461.0 Maxillary
 Acute antritis

461.1 Frontal

461.2 Ethmoidal

461.3 Sphenoidal

461.8 Other acute sinusitis
 Acute pansinusitis

461.9 Acute sinusitis, unspecified
 Acute sinusitis NOS

462 Acute pharyngitis

Acute sore throat NOS	Pharyngitis (acute):
Pharyngitis (acute):	staphylococcal
NOS	suppurative
gangrenous	ulcerative
infective	Sore throat (viral) NOS
phlegmonous	Viral pharyngitis
pneumococcal	

Excludes: *abscess:*
 peritonsillar [quinsy] (475)
 pharyngeal NOS (478.29)
 retropharyngeal (478.24)
 chronic pharyngitis (472.1)
 infectious mononucleosis (075)
 that specified as (due to):
 Coxsackie (virus) (074.0)
 gonococcus (098.6)
 herpes simplex (054.79)
 influenza (487.1)
 septic (034.0)
 streptococcal (034.0)

Add 4th or 5th digit	Nonspecific code	Unspecified code	Manifestation code

463 Acute tonsillitis

Tonsillitis (acute):
    NOS
    follicular
    gangrenous
    infective
    pneumococcal

Tonsillitis (acute):
    septic
    staphylococcal
    suppurative
    ulcerative
    viral

Excludes: *chronic tonsillitis (474.0)*
    hypertrophy of tonsils (474.1)
    peritonsillar abscess [quinsy] (475)
    sore throat:
      acute or NOS (462)
      septic (034.0)
    streptococcal tonsillitis (034.0)

464 Acute laryngitis and tracheitis

Excludes: *that associated with influenza (487.1)*
    that due to Streptococcus (034.0)

464.0 Acute laryngitis

Laryngitis (acute):
    NOS
    edematous
    Hemophilus influenza
      [H. influenzae]

Laryngitis (acute):
    pneumococcal
    septic
    suppurative
    ulcerative

Excludes: *chronic laryngitis (476.0-476.1)*
    influenzal laryngitis (487.1)

464.1 Acute tracheitis

Tracheitis (acute):
    NOS
    catarrhal
    viral

Excludes: *chronic tracheitis (491.8)*

    464.10 Without mention of obstruction

    464.11 With obstruction

464.2 Acute laryngotracheitis

Laryngotracheitis (acute)
Tracheitis (acute) with laryngitis (acute)

Excludes: *chronic laryngotracheitis (476.1)*

    464.20 Without mention of obstruction

    464.21 With obstruction

464.3 Acute epiglottitis

Viral epiglottitis

Excludes: *epiglottitis, chronic (476.1)*

    464.30 Without mention of obstruction

    464.31 With obstruction

464.4 Croup

Croup syndrome

465 Acute upper respiratory infections of multiple or unspecified sites

Excludes: *upper respiratory infection due to:*
    influenza (487.1)
    Streptococcus (034.0)

465.0 Acute laryngopharyngitis

465.8 Other multiple sites

Multiple URI

465.9 Unspecified site

Acute URI NOS
Upper respiratory infection (acute)

● Code new
  to this edition

▲ Revision of
  existing code

④ ⑤ Fourth or fifth
    digit required

466 **Acute bronchitis and bronchiolitis**
Includes: that with:
bronchospasm
obstruction

466.0 **Acute bronchitis**
Bronchitis, acute or subacute:
fibrinous
membranous
pneumococcal
purulent
septic
viral
with tracheitis
Croupous bronchitis
Tracheobronchitis, acute

466.1 **Acute bronchiolitis**
Bronchiolitis (acute)
Capillary pneumonia

● **466.11** **Acute bronchiolitis due to respiratory syncytial virus (RSV)**

● **466.19** **Acute bronchiolitis due to other infectious organisms**
Use additional code to identify organism

OTHER DISEASES OF THE UPPER RESPIRATORY TRACT (470-478)

470 **Deviated nasal septum**
Deflected septum (nasal) (acquired)

Excludes: *congenital (754.0)*

471 **Nasal polyps**

Excludes: *adenomatous polyps (212.0)*

471.0 **Polyp of nasal cavity**
Polyp:
choanal
nasopharyngeal

471.1 **Polypoid sinus degeneration**
Woakes' syndrome or ethmoiditis

471.8 **Other polyp of sinus**
Polyp of sinus: Polyp of sinus:
accessory   maxillary
ethmoidal   sphenoidal

471.9 **Unspecified nasal polyp**
Nasal polyp NOS

472 **Chronic pharyngitis and nasopharyngitis**

472.0 **Chronic rhinitis**
Ozena   Rhinitis:
Rhinitis: hypertrophic
NOS   obstructive
atrophic   purulent
granulomatous   ulcerative

Excludes: *allergic rhinitis (477.0-477.9)*

472.1 **Chronic pharyngitis**
Chronic sore throat
Pharyngitis:
atrophic
granular (chronic)
hypertrophic

472.2 **Chronic nasopharyngitis**

Excludes: *acute or unspecified nasopharyngitis (460)*

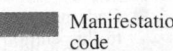
Add 4th or   Nonspecific   Unspecified   Manifestation
5th digit   code   code   code

473 **Chronic sinusitis**
Includes:

abscess
empyema
infection
suppuration
} (chronic) of sinus (accessory) (nasal)

Excludes: acute sinusitis (461.0-461.9)

473.0 **Maxillary**
Antritis (chronic)

473.1 **Frontal**

473.2 **Ethmoidal**

Excludes: Woakes' ethmoiditis (471.1)

473.3 **Sphenoidal**

473.8 **Other chronic sinusitis**
Pansinusitis (chronic)

473.9 **Unspecified sinusitis (chronic)**
Sinusitis (chronic) NOS

474 **Chronic disease of tonsils and adenoids**

474.0 **Chronic tonsillitis**

Excludes: acute or unspecified tonsillitis (463)

474.1 **Hypertrophy of tonsils and adenoids**
Enlargement
Hyperplasia
Hypertrophy
} of tonsils or adenoids

Excludes: that with tonsillitis (474.0)

474.10 **Tonsils with adenoids**

474.11 **Tonsils alone**

474.12 **Adenoids alone**

474.2 **Adenoid vegetations**

474.8 **Other chronic disease of tonsils and adenoids**
Amygdalolith
Calculus, tonsil
Cicatrix of tonsil (and adenoid)
Tonsillar tag
Ulcer, tonsil

474.9 **Unspecified chronic disease of tonsils and adenoids**
Disease (chronic) of tonsils (and adenoids)

475 **Peritonsillar abscess**
Abscess of tonsil   Quinsy
Peritonsillar cellulitis

Excludes: tonsillitis:

acute or NOS (463)
chronic (474.0)

476 **Chronic laryngitis and laryngotracheitis**

476.0 **Chronic laryngitis**
Laryngitis:
catarrhal
hypertrophic
sicca

476.1 **Chronic laryngotracheitis**
Laryngitis, chronic, with tracheitis (chronic)
Tracheitis, chronic, with laryngitis

Excludes: chronic tracheitis (491.8)

laryngitis and tracheitis, acute or unspecified (464.0-464.4)

● Code new
to this edition

▲ Revision of
existing code

④ ⑤ Fourth or fifth
digit required

477 Allergic rhinitis
Includes: allergic rhinitis (nonseasonal) (seasonal)
hay fever
spasmodic rhinorrhea

Excludes: *allergic rhinitis with asthma (bronchial) (493.0)*

477.0 Due to pollen
Pollinosis

477.8 Due to other allergen

477.9 Cause unspecified

478 Other diseases of upper respiratory tract

478.0 Hypertrophy of nasal turbinates

478.1 Other diseases of nasal cavity and sinuses
Abscess
Necrosis } of nose (septum)
Ulcer
Cyst or mucocele of sinus (nasal)
Rhinolith

Excludes: *varicose ulcer of nasal septum (456.8)*

478.2 Other diseases of pharynx, not elsewhere classified

478.20 Unspecified disease of pharynx

478.21 Cellulitis of pharynx or nasopharynx

478.22 Parapharyngeal abscess

478.24 Retropharyngeal abscess

478.25 Edema of pharynx or nasopharynx

478.26 Cyst of pharynx or nasopharynx

478.29 Other
Abscess of pharynx or nasopharynx

Excludes: *ulcerative pharyngitis (462)*

478.3 Paralysis of vocal cords or larynx

478.30 Paralysis, unspecified
Laryngoplegia   Paralysis of glottis

478.31 Unilateral, partial

478.32 Unilateral, complete

478.33 Bilateral, partial

478.34 Bilateral, complete

478.4 Polyp of vocal cord or larynx

Excludes: *adenomatous polyps (212.1)*

478.5 Other diseases of vocal cords
Abscess
Cellulitis } of vocal cords
Granuloma
Leukoplakia
Chorditis (fibrinous) (nodosa) (tuberosa)
Singers' nodes

478.6 Edema of larynx
Edema (of):
glottis
subglottic
supraglottic

478.7 Other diseases of larynx, not elsewhere classified

478.70 Unspecified disease of larynx

478.71 Cellulitis and perichondritis of larynx

478.74 Stenosis of larynx

478.75 Laryngeal spasm
Laryngismus (stridulus)

| Add 4th or 5th digit | Nonspecific code | Unspecified code | Manifestation code |

478.79 **Other**

Abscess
Necrosis
Obstruction } of larynx
Pachyderma
Ulcer

Excludes: ulcerative laryngitis (464.0)

478.8 **Upper respiratory tract hypersensitivity reaction, site unspecified**

Excludes: hypersensitivity reaction of lower respiratory tract, as:
extrinsic allergic alveolitis (495.0-495.9)
pneumoconiosis (500-505)

478.9 **Other and unspecified diseases of upper respiratory tract**

Abscess } of trachea
Cicatrix

PNEUMONIA AND INFLUENZA (480-487)

Excludes: pneumonia:
allergic or eosinophilic (518.3)
aspiration:
NOS (507.0)
newborn (770.1)
solids and liquids (507.0-507.8)
congenital (770.0)
lipoid (507.1)
passive (514)
rheumatic (390)

480 **Viral pneumonia**

480.0 **Pneumonia due to adenovirus**

480.1 **Pneumonia due to respiratory syncytial virus**

480.2 **Pneumonia due to parainfluenza virus**

480.8 **Pneumonia due to other virus not elsewhere classified**

Excludes: congenital rubella pneumonitis (771.0)
influenza with pneumonia, any form (487.0)
pneumonia complicating viral diseases classified elsewhere (484.1-484.8)

480.9 **Viral pneumonia, unspecified**

481 **Pneumococcal pneumonia [Streptococcus pneumoniae pneumonia]**
Lobar pneumonia, organism unspecified

482 **Other bacterial pneumonia**

482.0 **Pneumonia due to Klebsiella pneumoniae**

482.1 **Pneumonia due to Pseudomonas**

482.2 **Pneumonia due to Hemophilus influenzae [H. influenzae]**

482.3 **Pneumonia due to Streptococcus**

Excludes: Streptococcus pneumoniae pneumonia (481)

482.30 **Streptococcus, unspecified**

482.31 **Group A**

482.32 **Group B**

482.39 **Other Streptococcus**

482.4 **Pneumonia due to Staphylococcus**

482.8 **Pneumonia due to other specified bacteria**

Excludes: pneumonia complicating infectious disease classified elsewhere (484.1-484.8)

482.81 **Anaerobes**
Bacteroides (melaninogenicus)
Gram-negative anaerobes

482.82 **Escherichia coli [E. coli]**

● Code new
to this edition
▲ Revision of
existing code
④ ⑤ Fourth or fifth
digit required

482.83 Other Gram-negative bacteria
    Gram-negative pneumonia NOS
    Proteus
    Serratia marcescens

Excludes: *Gram-negative anaerobes (482.81)*

482.89 Other specified bacteria

482.9 Bacterial pneumonia unspecified

483 Pneumonia due to other specified organism

    483.0 Mycoplasma pneumoniae
        Eaton's agent
        Pleuropneumonia-like organism [PPLO]

  ● **483.1 Chlamydia**

    483.8 Other specified organism

484 Pneumonia in infectious diseases classified elsewhere

    Excludes: *influenza with pneumonia, any form (487.0)*

    484.1 *Pneumonia in cytomegalic inclusion disease*
        Code first underlying disease (078.5)

    484.3 *Pneumonia in whooping cough*
        Code first underlying disease (033.0-033.9)

    484.5 *Pneumonia in anthrax*
        Code first underlying disease (022.1)

    484.6 *Pneumonia in aspergillosis*
        Code first underlying disease (117.3)

    484.7 *Pneumonia in other systemic mycoses*
        Code first underlying disease

    Excludes: *pneumonia in:*
          candidiasis (112.4)
          coccidioidomycosis (114.0)
          histoplasmosis (115.0-115.9 with fifth-digit 5)

    484.8 *Pneumonia in other infectious diseases classified elsewhere*
        Code first underlying disease, as:
        Q fever (083.0)
        typhoid fever (002.0)

    Excludes: *pneumonia in:*
          actinomycosis (039.1)
          measles (055.1)
          nocardiosis (039.1)
          ornithosis (073.0)
          Pneumocystis carinii (136.3)
          salmonellosis (003.22)
          toxoplasmosis (130.4)
          tuberculosis (011.6)
          tularemia (021.2)
          varicella (052.1)

485 Bronchopneumonia, organism unspecified

    Bronchopneumonia: Pneumonia:
      hemorrhagic   lobular
      terminal   segmental
    Pleurobronchopneumonia

    Excludes: *bronchiolitis (acute) (466.11-466.19)*
          chronic (491.8)
          lipoid pneumonia (507.1)

486 Pneumonia, organism unspecified

    Excludes: *hypostatic or passive pneumonia (514)*
         influenza with pneumonia, any form (487.0)
         inhalation or aspiration pneumonia due to foreign materials (507.0-507.8)
         pneumonitis due to fumes and vapors (506.0)

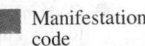

| | Add 4th or 5th digit | | Nonspecific code | | Unspecified code | | Manifestation code |

487 Influenza

> *Excludes:* *Hemophilus influenzae [H. influenzae]:*
> *infection NOS (041.5)*
> *laryngitis (464.0)*
> *meningitis (320.0)*
> *pneumonia (482.2)*

487.0 With pneumonia
Influenza with pneumonia, any form
Influenzal:
  bronchopneumonia
  pneumonia

487.1 With other respiratory manifestations
Influenza NOS
Influenzal:
  laryngitis
  pharyngitis
  respiratory infection (upper) (acute)

487.8 With other manifestations
Encephalopathy due to influenza
Influenza with involvement of gastrointestinal tract

> *Excludes:* *"intestinal flu" [viral gastroenteritis] (008.8)*

CHRONIC OBSTRUCTIVE PULMONARY DISEASE AND ALLIED CONDITIONS (490-496)

490 Bronchitis, not specified as acute or chronic
Bronchitis NOS: Tracheobronchitis NOS
  catarrhal
  with tracheitis NOS

> *Excludes:* *bronchitis:*
> *allergic NOS (493.9)*
> *asthmatic NOS (493.9)*
> *due to fumes and vapors (506.0)*

491 Chronic bronchitis

> *Excludes:* *chronic obstructive asthma (493.2)*

491.0 Simple chronic bronchitis
Catarrhal bronchitis, chronic
Smokers' cough

491.1 Mucopurulent chronic bronchitis
Bronchitis (chronic) (recurrent):
  fetid
  mucopurulent
  purulent

491.2 Obstructive chronic bronchitis
Bronchitis: Bronchitis with:
  asthmatic, chronic   chronic airway obstruction
  emphysematous   emphysema
  obstructive (chronic) (diffuse)

> *Excludes:* *asthmatic bronchitis (acute) NOS (493.9)*
> *chronic obstructive asthma (493.2)*

491.20 Without mention of acute exacerbation
Chronic asthmatic bronchitis
Emphysema with chronic bronchitis

491.21 With acute exacerbation
Acute bronchitis with chronic obstructive pulmonary disease [COPD]
Acute and chronic obstructive bronchitis
Chronic asthmatic bronchitis with acute exacerbation
Emphysema with both acute and chronic bronchitis

491.8 Other chronic bronchitis
Chronic:
  tracheitis
  tracheobronchitis

491.9 Unspecified chronic bronchitis

492 Emphysema

● Code new   ▲ Revision of   ④ ⑤ Fourth or fifth
   to this edition   existing code   digit required

492.0 Emphysematous bleb
Giant bullous emphysema
Ruptured emphysematous bleb
Tension pneumatocele
Vanishing lung

492.8 Other emphysema

Emphysema (lung or
pulmonary):
NOS
centriacinar
centrilobular
obstructive
panacinar

Emphysema (lung or pulmonary):
panlobular
unilateral
vesicular
MacLeod's syndrome
Swyer-James syndrome
Unilateral hyperlucent lung

Excludes: *emphysema:*
compensatory (518.2)
due to fumes and vapors (506.4)
interstitial (518.1)
newborn (770.2)
mediastinal (518.1)
surgical (subcutaneous) (998.81)
traumatic (958.7)
with chronic bronchitis (491.20)
with both acute and chronic bronchitis (491.21)

⑤ **493 Asthma**

The following fifth-digit subclassification is for use with category 493:

0 without mention of status asthmaticus

1 with status asthmaticus

493.0 extrinsic asthma
Asthma:
allergic with stated cause
atopic
childhood
hay
platinum
Hay fever with asthma

Excludes: *asthma:*
allergic NOS (493.9)
detergent (507.8)
miners' (500)
wood (495.8)

493.1 Intrinsic asthma
Late-onset asthma

493.2 Chronic obstructive asthma
Asthma with chronic obstructive pulmonary disease [COPD]

Excludes: *chronic asthmatic bronchitis (491.2)*
chronic obstructive bronchitis (491.2)

493.9 Asthma, unspecified
Asthma (bronchial) (allergic NOS)
Bronchitis:
allergic
asthmatic

494 Bronchiectasis
Bronchiectasis (fusiform) (postinfectious) (recurrent)
Bronchiolectasis

Excludes: *congenital (748.61)*
tuberculous bronchiectasis (current disease) (011.5)

495 Extrinsic allergic alveolitis
Includes: allergic alveolitis and pneumonitis due to inhaled organic dust particles of fungal,
thermophilic actinomycete, or other origin

495.0 Farmers' lung

495.1 Bagassosis

495.2 Bird-fanciers' lung
Budgerigar-fanciers' disease or lung
Pigeon-fanciers' disease or lung

Add 4th or
5th digit

Nonspecific
code

Unspecified
code

Manifestation
code

495.3 Suberosis
Cork-handlers' disease or lung

495.4 Malt workers' lung
Alveolitis due to Aspergillus clavatus

495.5 Mushroom workers' lung

495.6 Maple bark-strippers' lung
Alveolitis due to Cryptostroma corticale

495.7 "Ventilation" pneumonitis
Allergic alveolitis due to fungal, thermophilic actinomycete, and other organisms
growing in ventilation [air conditioning] systems

495.8 Other specified allergic alveolitis and pneumonitis
Cheese-washers' lung   Pituitary snuff-takers' disease
Coffee workers' lung   Sequoiosis or red-cedar asthma
Fish-meal workers' lung   Wood asthma
Furriers' lung
Grain-handlers' disease or lung

495.9 Unspecified allergic alveolitis and pneumonitis
Alveolitis, allergic (extrinsic)
Hypersensitivity pneumonitis

496 Chronic airway obstruction, not elsewhere classified
Note: This code is not to be used with any code from categories 491-493
Chronic:
nonspecific lung disease
obstructive lung disease
obstructive pulmonary disease [COPD] NOS

Excludes: *chronic obstructive lung disease [COPD] specified (as) (with):*
allergic alveolitis (495.0-495.9)
asthma (493.2)
bronchiectasis (494)
bronchitis (491.20-491.21)
with emphysema (491.20-491.21)
emphysema (492.0-492.8)

PNEUMOCONIOSES AND OTHER LUNG DISEASES DUE TO EXTERNAL AGENTS (500-508)

500 Coal workers' pneumoconiosis
Anthracosilicosis   Coal workers' lung
Anthracosis   Miner's asthma
Black lung disease

501 Asbestosis

502 Pneumoconiosis due to other silica or silicates
Pneumoconiosis due to talc
Silicotic fibrosis (massive) of lung
Silicosis (simple) (complicated)

503 Pneumoconiosis due to other inorganic dust
Aluminosis (of lung)   Graphite fibrosis (of lung)
Bauxite fibrosis (of lung)   Siderosis
Berylliosis   Stannosis

504 Pneumonopathy due to inhalation of other dust
Byssinosis   Flax-dressers' disease
Cannabinosis

Excludes: *allergic alveolitis (495.0-495.9)*
asbestosis (501)
bagassosis (495.1)
farmers' lung (495.0)

505 Pneumoconiosis, unspecified

506 Respiratory conditions due to chemical fumes and vapors
Use additional E code, if desired, to identify cause

506.0 Bronchitis and pneumonitis due to fumes and vapors
Chemical bronchitis (acute)

506.1 Acute pulmonary edema due to fumes and vapors
Chemical pulmonary edema (acute)

● Code new   ▲ Revision of   ④ ⑤ Fourth or fifth
to this edition   existing code   digit required

> Excludes: *acute pulmonary edema NOS (518.4)*
> *chronic or unspecified pulmonary edema (514)*

506.2 Upper respiratory inflammation due to fumes and vapors

506.3 Other acute and subacute respiratory conditions due to fumes and vapors

506.4 Chronic respiratory conditions due to fumes and vapors
  Emphysema (diffuse) (chronic)
  Obliterative bronchiolitis (chronic) (subacute)   } due to inhalation of chemical
  Pulmonary fibrosis (chronic)   fumes and vapors

506.9 Unspecified respiratory conditions due to fumes and vapors
  Silo-fillers' disease

507 Pneumonitis due to solids and liquids

> Excludes: *fetal aspiration pneumonitis (770.1)*

507.0 Due to inhalation of food or vomitus
  Aspiration pneumonia (due to):
    NOS
    food (regurgitated)
    gastric secretions
    milk
    saliva
    vomitus

507.1 Due to inhalation of oils and essences
  Lipoid pneumonia (exogenous)

> Excludes: *endogenous lipoid pneumonia (516.8)*

507.8 Due to other solids and liquids
  Detergent asthma

508 Respiratory conditions due to other and unspecified external agents
Use additional E code, if desired, to identify cause

508.0 Acute pulmonary manifestations due to radiation
  Radiation pneumonitis

508.1 Chronic and other pulmonary manifestations due to radiation
  Fibrosis of lung following radiation

508.8 Respiratory conditions due to other specified external agents

508.9 Respiratory conditions due to unspecified external agent

OTHER DISEASES OF RESPIRATORY SYSTEM (510-519)

510 Empyema
Use additional code, if desired, to identify infectious organism (041.0-041.9)

> Excludes: *abscess of lung (513.0)*

510.0 With fistula
  Fistula: Fistula:
    bronchocutaneous   mediastinal
    bronchopleural   pleural
    hepatopleural   thoracic
  Any condition classifiable to 510.9 with fistula

510.9 Without mention of fistula
  Abscess: Pleurisy:
    pleura   purulent
    thorax   septic
  Empyema (chest) (lung)   seropurulent
    (pleura)   suppurative
  Fibrinopurulent pleurisy   Pyopneumothorax
                              Pyothorax

511 Pleurisy

> Excludes: *malignant pleural effusion (197.2)*
> *pleurisy with mention of tuberculosis, current disease (012.0)*

500

| ▓ | Add 4th or 5th digit | ▓ | Nonspecific code | ▓ | Unspecified code | ▓ | Manifestation code |

511.0 Without mention of effusion or current tuberculosis

Adhesion, lung or pleura
Calcification of pleura
Pleurisy (acute) (sterile):
  diaphragmatic
  fibrinous
  interlobar

Pleurisy:
  NOS
  pneumococcal
  staphylococcal
  streptococcal
Thickening of pleura

511.1 With effusion, with mention of a bacterial cause other than tuberculosis

Pleurisy with effusion (exudative) (serous):
  pneumococcal
  staphylococcal
  streptococcal
  other specified nontuberculous bacterial cause

511.8 Other specified forms of effusion, except tuberculous

Encysted pleurisy
Hemopneumothorax
Hemothorax

Hydropneumothorax
Hydrothorax

Excludes: *traumatic (860.2-860.5)*

511.9 Unspecified pleural effusion

Pleural effusion NOS
Pleurisy:
  exudative
  serofibrinous

Pleurisy:
  serous
  with effusion NOS

512 Pneumothorax

512.0 Spontaneous tension pneumothorax

512.1 Iatrogenic pneumothorax

Postoperative pneumothorax

512.8 Other spontaneous pneumothorax

Pneumothorax:
  NOS
  acute
  chronic

Excludes: *pneumothorax:*
    congenital (770.2)
    traumatic (860.0-860.1, 860.4-860.5)
    tuberculous, current disease (011.7)

513 Abscess of lung and mediastinum

513.0 Abscess of lung

Abscess (multiple) of lung
Gangrenous or necrotic pneumonia
Pulmonary gangrene or necrosis

513.1 Abscess of mediastinum

514 Pulmonary congestion and hypostasis

Hypostatic:
  bronchopneumonia
  pneumonia
Passive pneumonia
Pulmonary congestion (chronic) (passive)
Pulmonary edema:
  NOS
  chronic

Excludes: *acute pulmonary edema:*
    NOS (518.4)
    with mention of heart disease or failure (428.1)

515 Postinflammatory pulmonary fibrosis

Cirrhosis of lung
Fibrosis of lung (atrophic)
  (confluent) (massive)
  (perialveolar) (peribronchial)
Induration of lung
} chronic or unspecified

516 Other alveolar and parietoalveolar pneumonopathy

516.0 Pulmonary alveolar proteinosis

● Code new
to this edition

▲ Revision of
existing code

④ ⑤ Fourth or fifth
digit required

516.1 *Idiopathic pulmonary hemosiderosis*
Essential brown induration of lung
Code first underlying disease (275.0)

516.2 Pulmonary alveolar microlithiasis

516.3 Idiopathic fibrosing alveolitis
Alveolar capillary block
Diffuse (idiopathic) (interstitial) pulmonary fibrosis
Hamman-Rich syndrome

516.8 Other specified alveolar and parietoalveolar pneumonopathies
Endogenous lipoid pneumonia
Interstitial pneumonia (desquamative) (lymphoid)

Excludes: *lipoid pneumonia, exogenous or unspecified (507.1)*

516.9 Unspecified alveolar and parietoalveolar pneumonopathy

517 Lung involvement in conditions classified elsewhere

Excludes: *rheumatoid lung (714.81)*

517.1 *Rheumatic pneumonia*
Code first underlying disease (390)

517.2 *Lung involvement in systemic sclerosis*
Code first underlying disease (710.1)

517.8 *Lung involvement in other diseases classified elsewhere*
Code first underlying disease, as:
amyloidosis (277.3)
polymyositis (710.4)
sarcoidosis (135)
Sjögren's disease (710.2)
systemic lupus erythematosus (710.0)

Excludes: *syphilis (095.1)*

518 Other diseases of lung

518.0 Pulmonary collapse
Atelectasis
Collapse of lung
Middle lobe syndrome

Excludes: *atelectasis:*
congenital (partial) (770.5)
primary (770.4)
tuberculous, current disease (011.8)

518.1 Interstitial emphysema
Mediastinal emphysema

Excludes: *surgical (subcutaneous) emphysema (998.81)*
that in fetus or newborn (770.2)
traumatic emphysema (958.7)

518.2 Compensatory emphysema

518.3 Pulmonary eosinophilia
Eosinophilic asthma   Tropical eosinophilia
Löffler's syndrome
Pneumonia:
allergic
eosinophilic

518.4 Acute edema of lung, unspecified
Acute pulmonary edema NOS
Pulmonary edema, postoperative

Excludes: *pulmonary edema:*
acute, with mention of heart disease or failure (428.1)
chronic or unspecified (514)
due to external agents (506.0-508.9)

518.5 Pulmonary insufficiency following trauma and surgery
Adult respiratory distress syndrome
Pulmonary insufficiency following:
shock
surgery
trauma
Shock lung

231

Add 4th or   Nonspecific   Unspecified   Manifestation
5th digit   code   code   code

Excludes: *adult respiratory distress syndrome associated with other conditions (518.82)*
    pneumonia:
      aspiration (507.0)
      hypostatic (514)
    respiratory failure in other conditions (518.81)

518.8 Other diseases of lung

    518.81 Respiratory failure
      Respiratory failure:
        NOS
        acute
        acute and chronic (acute-on-chronic)
        chronic

Excludes: *acute respiratory distress (518.82)*
    respiratory arrest (799.1)
    respiratory failure, newborn (770.8)

    518.82 Other pulmonary insufficiency, not elsewhere classified
      Acute respiratory distress
      Acute respiratory insufficiency
      Adult respiratory distress syndrome NEC

Excludes: *adult respiratory distress syndrome associated with trauma and surgery (518.5)*
    pulmonary insufficiency following trauma and surgery (518.5)
    respiratory distress:
      NOS (786.09)
      newborn (770.8)
      syndrome, newborn (769)
    shock lung (518.5)

    518.89 Other diseases of lung, not elsewhere classified
      Broncholithiasis   Lung disease NOS
      Calcification of lung Pulmolithiasis

519 Other diseases of respiratory system

519.0 Tracheostomy complication
    Hemorrhage from
    Sepsis of   } tracheostomy stoma

    Tracheal stenosis
    Tracheoesophageal fistula } following tracheostomy

    Tracheostomy:
      hemorrhage
      obstruction
      sepsis

519.1 Other diseases of trachea and bronchus, not elsewhere classified
    Calcification
    Stenosis   } of bronchus or trachea
    Ulcer

519.2 Mediastinitis

519.3 Other diseases of mediastinum, not elsewhere classified
    Fibrosis
    Hernia   } of mediastinum
    Retraction

519.4 Disorders of diaphragm
    Diaphragmitis
    Paralysis of diaphragm
    Relaxation of diaphragm

Excludes: *congenital defect of diaphragm (756.6)*
    diaphragmatic hernia (551-553 with .3)
    congenital (756.6)

519.8 Other diseases of respiratory system, not elsewhere classified

519.9 Unspecified disease of respiratory system
    Respiratory disease (chronic) NOS

● Code new   ▲ Revision of   ④ ⑤ Fourth or fifth
  to this edition   existing code   digit required

9. DISEASES OF THE DIGESTIVE SYSTEM (520-579)

DISEASES OF ORAL CAVITY, SALIVARY GLANDS, AND JAWS (520-529)

520 Disorders of tooth development and eruption

520.0 Anodontia
Absence of teeth (complete) (congenital) (partial)
Hypodontia
Oligodontia

Excludes: *acquired absence of teeth (525.1)*

520.1 Supernumerary teeth
Distomolar Paramolar
Fourth molar Supplemental teeth
Mesiodens

Excludes: *supernumerary roots (520.2)*

520.2 Abnormalities of size and form
Concrescence ⎫ Macrodontia
Fusion ⎬ of teeth Microdontia
Gemination ⎭ Peg-shaped [conical] teeth
Dens evaginatus Supernumerary roots
Dens in dente Taurodontism
Dens invaginatus Tuberculum paramolare
Enamel pearls

Excludes: *that due to congenital syphilis (090.5)*
tuberculum Carabelli, which is regarded as a normal variation

520.3 Mottled teeth
Dental fluorosis
Mottling of enamel
Nonfluoride enamel opacities

520.4 Disturbances of tooth formation
Aplasia and hypoplasia of cementum Horner's teeth
Dilaceration of tooth Hypocalcification of teeth
Enamel hypoplasia (neonatal) (postnatal) (prenatal) Regional odontodysplasia
Turner's tooth

Excludes: *Hutchinson's teeth and mulberry molars in congenital syphilis (090.5)*
mottled teeth (520.3)

520.5 Hereditary disturbances in tooth structure, not elsewhere classified
Amelogenesis ⎫
Dentinogenesis ⎬ imperfecta
Odontogenesis ⎭
Dentinal dysplasia
Shell teeth

520.6 Disturbances in tooth eruption
Teeth: Tooth eruption:
embedded late
impacted obstructed
natal premature
neonatal
primary [deciduous]:
persistent
shedding, premature

Excludes: *exfoliation of teeth (attributable to disease of surrounding tissues) (525.0-525.1)*
impacted or embedded teeth with abnormal position of such teeth or adjacent teeth (524.3)

520.7 Teething syndrome

520.8 Other specified disorders of tooth development and eruption
Color changes during tooth formation
Pre-eruptive color changes

Excludes: *posteruptive color changes (521.7)*

520.9 Unspecified disorder of tooth development and eruption

▨ Add 4th or 5th digit	▨ Nonspecific code	▨ Unspecified code	▨ Manifestation code

521 **Diseases of hard tissues of teeth**

521.0 Dental caries
Caries (of):
arrested
cementum
dentin (acute) (chronic)
enamel (acute) (chronic) (incipient)
Infantile melanodontia
Odontoclasia
White spot lesions of teeth

521.1 Excessive attrition
Approximal wear   Occlusal wear

521.2 Abrasion
Abrasion:
dentifrice
habitual
occupational   } of teeth
ritual
traditional
Wedge defect NOS

521.3 Erosion
Erosion of teeth: Erosion of teeth:
NOS   idiopathic
due to: occupational
medicine
persistent vomiting

521.4 Pathological resorption
Internal granuloma of pulp
Resorption of tooth or root (external) (internal)

521.5 Hypercementosis
Cementation hyperplasia

521.6 Ankylosis of teeth

521.7 Posteruptive color changes
Staining [discoloration] of teeth:
NOS
due to:
drugs
metals
pulpal bleeding

Excludes: *accretions [deposits] on teeth (523.6)*
          pre-eruptive color changes (520.8)

521.8 Other specified diseases of hard tissues of teeth
Irradiated enamel   Sensitive dentin

521.9 Unspecified disease of hard tissues of teeth

522 **Diseases of pulp and periapical tissues**

522.0 Pulpitis
Pulpal: Pulpitis:
abscess   acute
polyp   chronic (hyperplastic) (ulcerative)
                           suppurative

522.1 Necrosis of the pulp
Pulp gangrene

522.2 Pulp degeneration
Denticles   Pulp stones
Pulp calcifications

522.3 Abnormal hard tissue formation in pulp
Secondary or irregular dentin

522.4 Acute apical periodontitis of pulpal origin

522.5 Periapical abscess without sinus
Abscess:
dental
dentoalveolar

Excludes: *periapical abscess with sinus (522.7)*

● Code new   ▲ Revision of   ④ ⑤ Fourth or fifth
     to this edition   existing code   digit required

522.6 Chronic apical periodontitis
Apical or periapical granuloma
Apical periodontitis NOS

522.7 Periapical abscess with sinus
Fistula:
alveolar process
dental

522.8 Radicular cyst
Cyst:
apical (periodontal)
periapical
radiculodental
residual radicular

Excludes: lateral developmental or lateral periodontal cyst (526.0)

522.9 Other and unspecified diseases of pulp and periapical tissues

523 Gingival and periodontal diseases

523.0 Acute gingivitis

Excludes: acute necrotizing ulcerative gingivitis (101)
herpetic gingivostomatitis (054.2)

523.1 Chronic gingivitis
Gingivitis (chronic):
NOS
desquamative
hyperplastic

Gingivitis (chronic):
simple marginal
ulcerative
Gingivostomatitis

Excludes: herpetic gingivostomatitis (054.2)

523.2 Gingival recession
Gingival recession (generalized) (localized) (postinfective) (postoperative)

523.3 Acute periodontitis
Acute:
pericementitis
pericoronitis

Paradontal abscess
Periodontal abscess

Excludes: acute apical periodontitis (522.4)
periapical abscess (522.5, 522.7)

523.4 Chronic periodontitis
Alveolar pyorrhea
Chronic pericoronitis
Pericementitis (chronic)

Periodontitis:
NOS
complex
simplex

Excludes: chronic apical periodontitis (522.6)

523.5 Periodontosis

523.6 Accretions on teeth
Dental calculus:
subgingival
supragingival

Deposits on teeth:
betel
materia alba
soft
tartar
tobacco

523.8 Other specified periodontal diseases
Giant cell:
epulis
peripheral granuloma
Gingival:
cysts
enlargement NOS
fibromatosis

Gingival polyp
Periodontal lesions due to traumatic occlusion
Peripheral giant cell granuloma

Excludes: leukoplakia of gingiva (528.6)

523.9 Unspecified gingival and periodontal disease

524 Dentofacial anomalies, including malocclusion

524.0 Major anomalies of jaw size

Excludes: hemifacial atrophy or hypertrophy (754.0)
unilateral condylar hyperplasia or hypoplasia of mandible (526.89)

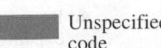

| Add 4th or 5th digit | Nonspecific code | Unspecified code | Manifestation code |

524.00 Unspecified anomaly
524.01 Maxillary hyperplasia
524.02 Mandibular hyperplasia
524.03 Maxillary hypoplasia
524.04 Mandibular hypoplasia
524.05 Macrogenia
524.06 Microgenia
524.09 Other specified anomaly

524.1 Anomalies of relationship of jaw to cranial base

524.10 Unspecified anomaly
  prognathism
  retrognathism

524.11 Maxillary asymmetry
524.12 Other jaw asymmetry
524.19 Other specified anomaly

524.2 Anomalies of dental arch relationship
Crossbite (anterior) (posterior)   Overbite (excessive)
Disto-occlusion   deep
Mesio-occlusion   horizontal
Midline deviation   vertical
Open bite (anterior) (posterior)   Overjet
                                     Posterior lingual occlusion of mandibular teeth
                                     Soft tissue impingement

Excludes: hemifacial atrophy or hypertrophy (754.0)
  unilateral condylar hyperplasia or hypoplasia of mandible (526.89)

524.3 Anomalies of tooth position
Crowding
Diastema
Displacement   } of tooth, teeth
Rotation
Spacing, abnormal
Transposition
Impacted or embedded teeth with abnormal position of such teeth or adjacent teeth

524.4 Malocclusion, unspecified

524.5 Dentofacial functional abnormalities
Abnormal jaw closure
Malocclusion due to:
  abnormal swallowing
  mouth breathing
  tongue, lip, or finger habits

524.6 Temporomandibular joint disorders

Excludes: current temporomandibular joint:
  dislocation (830.0-830.1)
  strain (848.1)

524.60 Temporomandibular joint disorders, unspecified
  Temporomandibular joint-pain-dysfunction syndrome [TMJ]

524.61 Adhesions and ankylosis (bony or fibrous)
524.62 Arthralgia of temporomandibular joint
524.63 Articular disc disorder (reducing or non-reducing)
524.69 Other specified temporomandibular joint disorders

524.7 Dental alveolar anomalies

524.70 Unspecified alveolar anomaly
524.71 Alveolar maxillary hyperplasia
524.72 Alveolar mandibular hyperplasia
524.73 Alveolar maxillary hypoplasia
524.74 Alveolar mandibular hypoplasia
524.79 Other specified alveolar anomaly

524.8 Other specified dentofacial anomalies

● Code new   ▲ Revision of   ④ ⑤ Fourth or fifth
to this edition   existing code   digit required

524.9 Unspecified dentofacial anomalies

525 Other diseases and conditions of the teeth and supporting structures

    525.0 Exfoliation of teeth due to systemic causes

    525.1 Loss of teeth due to accident, extraction, or local periodontal disease
Acquired absence of teeth

    525.2 Atrophy of edentulous alveolar ridge

    525.3 Retained dental root

    525.8 Other specified disorders of the teeth and supporting structures
Enlargement of alveolar ridge NOS
Irregular alveolar process

    525.9 Unspecified disorder of the teeth and supporting structures

526 Diseases of the jaws

    526.0 Developmental odontogenic cysts

Cyst:	Cyst:
dentigerous	lateral periodontal
eruption	primordial
follicular	Keratocyst
lateral developmental	

Excludes: *radicular cyst (522.8)*

    526.1 Fissural cysts of jaw
Cyst:
globulomaxillary
incisor canal
median anterior maxillary
median palatal
nasopalatine
palatine of papilla

Excludes: *cysts of oral soft tissues (528.4)*

    526.2 Other cysts of jaws

Cyst of jaw:	Cyst of jaw:
NOS	hemorrhagic
aneurysmal	traumatic

    526.3 Central giant cell (reparative) granuloma

Excludes: *peripheral giant cell granuloma (523.8)*

    526.4 Inflammatory conditions
Abscess
Osteitis
Osteomyelitis (neonatal) ⎫ of jaw (acute) (chronic) (suppurative)
Periostitis ⎭
Sequestrum of jaw bone

Excludes: *alveolar osteitis (526.5)*

    526.5 Alveolitis of jaw
Alveolar osteitis
Dry socket

    526.8 Other specified diseases of the jaws

        526.81 Exostosis of jaw
Torus mandibularis
Torus palatinus

        526.89 Other
Cherubism
Fibrous dysplasia ⎫ of jaw(s)
Latent bone cyst ⎬
Osteoradionecrosis of jaw(s) ⎭
Unilateral condylar hyperplasia or hypoplasia of mandible

    526.9 Unspecified disease of the jaws

527 Diseases of the salivary glands

    527.0 Atrophy

    527.1 Hypertrophy

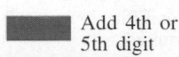 Add 4th or
5th digit

 Nonspecific
code

 Unspecified
code

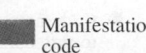 Manifestation
code

527.2 Sialoadenitis
Parotitis:
    NOS
    allergic
    toxic

Sialoangitis
Sialodochitis

> Excludes: *epidemic or infectious parotitis (072.0-072.9)*
>   *uveoparotid fever (135)*

527.3 Abscess

527.4 Fistula

> Excludes: *congenital fistula of salivary glands (750.24)*

527.5 Sialolithiasis
Calculus
Stone } of salivary gland or duct
Sialodocholithiasis

527.6 Mucocele
Mucous:
    extravasation cyst of salivary gland
    retention cyst of salivary gland
Ranula

527.7 Disturbance of salivary secretion
Hyposecretion
Ptyalism

Sialorrhea
Xerostomia

527.8 Other specified diseases of the salivary glands
Benign lymphoepithelial lesion of salivary gland
Sialectasia
Sialosis
Stenosis
Stricture } of salivary duct

527.9 Unspecified disease of the salivary glands

528 Diseases of the oral soft tissues, excluding lesions specific for gingiva and tongue

528.0 Stomatitis
Stomatitis:
    NOS
    ulcerative

Vesicular stomatitis

> Excludes: *stomatitis:*
>   *acute necrotizing ulcerative (101)*
>   *aphthous (528.2)*
>   *gangrenous (528.1)*
>   *herpetic (054.2)*
>   *Vincent's (101)*

528.1 Cancrum oris
Gangrenous stomatitis

Noma

528.2 Oral aphthae
Aphthous stomatitis
Canker sore
Periadenitis mucosa necrotica recurrens

Recurrent aphthous ulcer
Stomatitis herpetiformis

> Excludes: *herpetic stomatitis (054.2)*

528.3 Cellulitis and abscess
Cellulitis of mouth (floor)
Ludwig's angina
Oral fistula

> Excludes: *abscess of tongue (529.0)*
>   *cellulitis or abscess of lip (528.5)*
>   *fistula (of):*
>   *dental (522.7)*
>   *lip (528.5)*
>   *gingivitis (523.0-523.1)*

● Code new
   to this edition

▲ Revision of
   existing code

④ ⑤ Fourth or fifth
     digit required

528.4 Cysts
Dermoid cyst
Epidermoid cyst
Epstein's pearl   } of mouth
Lymphoepithelial cyst
Nasoalveolar cyst
Nasolabial cyst

Excludes: cyst:
    gingiva (523.8)
    tongue (529.8)

528.5 Diseases of lips
Abscess   Cheilitis:
Cellulitis   NOS
Fistula   of lip(s)   angular
Hypertrophy   Cheilodynia
                             Cheilosis

Excludes: actinic cheilitis (692.79)
        congenital fistula of lip (750.25)
        leukoplakia of lips (528.6)

528.6 Leukoplakia of oral mucosa, including tongue
Leukokeratosis of oral mucosa
Leukoplakia of:
    gingiva
    lips
    tongue

Excludes: carcinoma in situ (230.0, 232.0)
        leukokeratosis nicotina palati (528.7)

528.7 Other disturbances of oral epithelium, including tongue
Erythroplakia
Focal epithelial
    hyperplasia
Leukoedema   } of mouth or tongue
Leukokeratosis
    nicotina palati

Excludes: carcinoma in situ (230.0, 232.0)
        leukokeratosis NOS (702)

528.8 Oral submucosal fibrosis, including of tongue

528.9 Other and unspecified diseases of the oral soft tissues
Cheek and lip biting
Denture sore mouth
Denture stomatitis
Melanoplakia
Papillary hyperplasia of palate
Eosinophilic granuloma
Irritative hyperplasia   } of oral mucosa
Pyogenic granuloma
Ulcer (traumatic)

529 Diseases and other conditions of the tongue

529.0 Glossitis
Abscess   } of tongue
Ulceration (traumatic)

Excludes: glossitis:
        benign migratory (529.1)
        Hunter's (529.4)
        median rhomboid (529.2)
        Moeller's (529.4)

529.1 Geographic tongue
Benign migratory glossitis
Glossitis areata exfoliativa

529.2 Median rhomboid glossitis

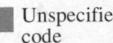

Add 4th or   Nonspecific   Unspecified   Manifestation
5th digit   code   code   code

529.3 Hypertrophy of tongue papillae
Black hairy tongue
Coated tongue
Hypertrophy of foliate papillae
Lingua villosa nigra

529.4 Atrophy of tongue papillae
Bald tongue   Glossodynia exfoliativa
Glazed tongue   Smooth atrophic tongue
Glossitis:
    Hunter's
    Moeller's

529.5 Plicated tongue
Fissured
Furrowed   } tongue
Scrotal

Excludes: *fissure of tongue, congenital (750.13)*

529.6 Glossodynia
Glossopyrosis   Painful tongue

Excludes: *glossodynia exfoliativa (529.4)*

529.8 Other specified conditions of the tongue
Atrophy
Crenated
Enlargement   } (of) tongue
Hypertrophy
Glossocele
Glossoptosis

Excludes: *erythroplasia of tongue (528.7)*
leukoplakia of tongue (528.6)
macroglossia (congenital) (750.15)
microglossia (congenital) (750.16)
oral submucosal fibrosis (528.8)

529.9 Unspecified condition of the tongue

DISEASES OF ESOPHAGUS, STOMACH, AND DUODENUM (530-537)

530 Diseases of esophagus

Excludes: *esophageal varices (456.0-456.2)*

530.0 Achalasia and cardiospasm
Achalasia (of cardia)
Aperistalsis of esophagus
Megaesophagus

Excludes: *congenital cardiospasm (750.7)*

530.1 Esophagitis
Abscess of esophagus   Esophagitis:
Esophagitis: postoperative
    NOS   regurgitant
    chemical
    peptic
Use additional E code, if desired, to identify cause, if induced by chemical

Excludes: *tuberculous esophagitis (017.8)*

    530.10 Esophagitis, unspecified

    530.11 Reflux esophagitis

    530.19 Other esophagitis

530.2 Ulcer of esophagus
Ulcer of esophagus   Ulcer of esophagus due to ingestion of:
    fungal   aspirin
    peptic   chemicals
                                      medicines
Use additional E code, if desired, to identify cause, if induced by chemical or drug

● Code new   ▲ Revision of   ④ ⑤ Fourth or fifth
  to this edition   existing code   digit required

530.3 Stricture and stenosis of esophagus
Compression of esophagus
Obstruction of esophagus

Excludes: congenital stricture of esophagus (750.3)

530.4 Perforation of esophagus
Rupture of esophagus

Excludes: traumatic perforation of esophagus (862.22, 862.32, 874.4-874.5)

530.5 Dyskinesia of esophagus
Corkscrew esophagus   Esophagospasm
Curling esophagus   Spasm of esophagus

Excludes: cardiospasm (530.0)

530.6 Diverticulum of esophagus, acquired
Diverticulum, acquired:
  epiphrenic
  pharyngoesophageal
  pulsion
  subdiaphragmatic
  traction
  Zenker's (hypopharyngeal)
Esophageal pouch, acquired
Esophagocele, acquired

Excludes: congenital diverticulum of esophagus (750.4)

530.7 Gastroesophageal laceration-hemorrhage syndrome
Mallory-Weiss syndrome

530.8 Other specified disorders of esophagus

    530.81 Esophageal reflux
        Gastroesophageal reflux

Excludes: reflux esophagitis (530.11)

    530.82 Esophageal hemorrhage

Excludes: hemorrhage due to esophageal varices (456.0-456.2)

    530.83 Esophageal leukoplakia

    530.84 Tracheoesophageal fistula

Excludes: congenital tracheoesophageal fistula (750.3)

    530.89 Other

Excludes: Paterson-Kelly syndrome (280.8)

530.9 Unspecified disorder of esophagus

⑤ **531 Gastric ulcer**
Includes: ulcer (peptic):
       prepyloric
       pylorus
       stomach
Use additional E code, if desired, to identify drug, if drug-induced

Excludes: peptic ulcer NOS (533.0-533.9)
The following fifth-digit subclassification is for use with category 531:

   0 without mention of obstruction

   1 with obstruction

531.0 Acute with hemorrhage

531.1 Acute with perforation

531.2 Acute with hemorrhage and perforation

531.3 Acute without mention of hemorrhage or perforation

531.4 Chronic or unspecified with hemorrhage

531.5 Chronic or unspecified with perforation

531.6 Chronic or unspecified with hemorrhage and perforation

531.7 Chronic without mention of hemorrhage or perforation

531.9 Unspecified as acute or chronic, without mention of hemorrhage or perforation

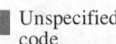 Add 4th or
5th digit

Nonspecific
code

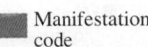 Unspecified
code

Manifestation
code

⑤ **532 Duodenal ulcer**

Includes: erosion (acute) of duodenum
ulcer (peptic):
duodenum
postpyloric

Use additional E code, if desired, to identify drug, if drug-induced

Excludes: peptic ulcer NOS (533.0-533.9)

The following fifth-digit subclassification is for use with category 532:

  0 without mention of obstruction

  1 with obstruction

532.0 Acute with hemorrhage

532.1 Acute with perforation

532.2 Acute with hemorrhage and perforation

532.3 Acute without mention of hemorrhage or perforation

532.4 Chronic or unspecified with hemorrhage

532.5 Chronic or unspecified with perforation

532.6 Chronic or unspecified with hemorrhage and perforation

532.7 Chronic without mention of hemorrhage or perforation

532.9 Unspecified as acute or chronic, without mention of hemorrhage or perforation

⑤ **533 Peptic ulcer, site unspecified**

Includes: gastroduodenal ulcer NOS
peptic ulcer NOS
stress ulcer NOS

Use additional E code, if desired, to identify drug, if drug-induced

Excludes: peptic ulcer:
duodenal (532.0-532.9)
gastric (531.0-531.9)

The following fifth-digit subclassification is for use with category 533:

  0 without mention of obstruction

  1 with obstruction

533.0 Acute with hemorrhage

533.1 Acute with perforation

533.2 Acute with hemorrhage and perforation

533.3 Acute without mention of hemorrhage and perforation

533.4 Chronic or unspecified with hemorrhage

533.5 Chronic or unspecified with perforation

533.6 Chronic or unspecified with hemorrhage and perforation

533.7 Chronic without mention of hemorrhage or perforation

533.9 Unspecified as acute or chronic, without mention of hemorrhage or perforation

⑤ **534 Gastrojejunal ulcer**

Includes: ulcer (peptic) or erosion:
anastomotic
gastrocolic
gastrointestinal
gastrojejunal
jejunal
marginal
stomal

Excludes: primary ulcer of small intestine (569.82)

The following fifth-digit subclassification is for use with category 534:

  0 without mention of obstruction

  1 with obstruction

534.0 Acute with hemorrhage

534.1 Acute with perforation

534.2 Acute with hemorrhage and perforation

534.3 Acute without mention of hemorrhage or perforation

534.4 Chronic or unspecified with hemorrhage

● Code new
to this edition

▲ Revision of
existing code

④ ⑤ Fourth or fifth
digit required

534.5 Chronic or unspecified with perforation

534.6 Chronic or unspecified with hemorrhage and perforation

534.7 Chronic without mention of hemorrhage or perforation

534.9 Unspecified as acute or chronic, without mention of hemorrhage or perforation

⑤ **535 Gastritis and duodenitis**

The following fifth-digit subclassification is for use with category 535

    0 without mention of hemorrhage

    1 with hemorrhage

535.0 Acute gastritis

535.1 Atrophic gastritis
Gastritis:
  atrophic-hyperplastic
  chronic (atrophic)

535.2 Gastric mucosal hypertrophy
Hypertrophic gastritis

535.3 Alcoholic gastritis

535.4 Other specified gastritis
Gastritis: Gastritis:
  allergic   superficial
  bile induced   toxic
  irritant

535.5 Unspecified gastritis and gastroduodenitis

535.6 Duodenitis

536 Disorders of function of stomach

> Excludes: *functional disorders of stomach specified as psychogenic (306.4)*

536.0 Achlorhydria

536.1 Acute dilatation of stomach
Acute distention of stomach

536.2 Persistent vomiting
Habit vomiting
Persistent vomiting [not of pregnancy]
Uncontrollable vomiting

> Excludes: *excessive vomiting in pregnancy (643.0-643.9)*
>   *vomiting NOS (787.0)*

536.3 Gastroparesis

536.8 Dyspepsia and other specified disorders of function of stomach
Achylia gastrica   Hyperchlorhydria
Hourglass contraction of stomach   Hypochlorhydria
Hyperacidity   Indigestion

> Excludes: *achlorhydria (536.0)*
>   *heartburn (787.1)*

536.9 Unspecified functional disorder of stomach
Functional gastrointestinal:
  disorder
  disturbance
  irritation

537 Other disorders of stomach and duodenum

537.0 Acquired hypertrophic pyloric stenosis
Constriction
Obstruction   } of pylorus, acquired or adult
Stricture

> Excludes: *congenital or infantile pyloric stenosis (750.5)*

537.1 Gastric diverticulum

> Excludes: *congenital diverticulum of stomach (750.7)*

537.2 Chronic duodenal ileus

	Add 4th or 5th digit		Nonspecific code		Unspecified code		Manifestation code

537.3 **Other obstruction of duodenum**
Cicatrix
Stenosis ⎤
Stricture ⎬ of duodenum
Volvulus ⎦

Excludes: *congenital obstruction of duodenum (751.1)*

537.4 **Fistula of stomach or duodenum**
Gastrocolic fistula
Gastrojejunocolic fistula

537.5 **Gastroptosis**

537.6 **Hourglass stricture or stenosis of stomach**
Cascade stomach

Excludes: *congenital hourglass stomach (750.7)*
hourglass contraction of stomach (536.8)

537.8 **Other specified disorders of stomach and duodenum**

537.81 **Pylorospasm**

Excludes: *congenital pylorospasm (750.5)*

537.82 **Angiodysplasia of stomach and duodenum without mention of hemorrhage**

537.83 **Angiodysplasia of stomach and duodenum with hemorrhage**

537.89 **Other**
Gastric or duodenal:
prolapse
rupture
Intestinal metaplasia of gastric mucosa
Passive congestion of stomach

Excludes: *diverticula of duodenum (562.00-562.01)*
gastrointestinal hemorrhage (578.0-578.9)

537.9 **Unspecified disorder of stomach and duodenum**

APPENDICITIS (540-543)

540 **Acute appendicitis**

540.0 **With generalized peritonitis**
Appendicitis (acute): ⎤
fulminating
gangrenous ⎬ with: perforation peritonitis (generalized) rupture
obstructive
Cecitis (acute)
Rupture of appendix ⎦

Excludes: *acute appendicitis with peritoneal abscess (540.1)*

540.1 **With peritoneal abscess**
Abscess of appendix
With generalized peritonitis

540.9 **Without mention of peritonitis**
Acute:
appendicitis: ⎤
fulminating
gangrenous ⎬ without mention of perforation, peritonitis, or rupture
inflamed
obstructive
cecitis ⎦

541 **Appendicitis, unqualified**

542 **Other appendicitis**
Appendicitis: Appendicitis:
chronic   relapsing
recurrent   subacute

Excludes: *hyperplasia (lymphoid) of appendix (543.0)*

543 **Other diseases of appendix**

543.0 **Hyperplasia of appendix (lymphoid)**

● Code new   ▲ Revision of   ④ ⑤ Fourth or fifth
   to this edition   existing code   digit required

543.9 Other and unspecified diseases of appendix
Appendicular or appendiceal:
colic
concretion
fistula
Diverticulum ⎫
Fecalith ⎪
Intussusception ⎬ of appendix
Mucocele ⎪
Stercolith ⎭

HERNIA OF ABDOMINAL CAVITY (550-553)

Includes: hernia:
acquired
congenital, except diaphragmatic or hiatal

⑤ **550 Inguinal hernia**
Includes: bubonocele
inguinal hernia (direct) (double) (indirect) (oblique) (sliding)
scrotal hernia

The following fifth-digit subclassification is for use with category 550:

0 unilateral or unspecified (not specified as recurrent)
Unilateral NOS

1 unilateral or unspecified, recurrent

2 bilateral (not specified as recurrent)
Bilateral NOS

3 bilateral, recurrent

550.0 Inguinal hernia, with gangrene
Inguinal hernia with gangrene (and obstruction)

550.1 Inguinal hernia, with obstruction, without mention of gangrene
Inguinal hernia with mention of incarceration, irreducibility, or strangulation

550.9 Inguinal hernia, without mention of obstruction or gangrene
Inguinal hernia NOS

551 Other hernia of abdominal cavity, with gangrene
Includes: that with gangrene (and obstruction)

551.0 Femoral hernia with gangrene

551.00 Unilateral or unspecified (not specified as recurrent)
Femoral hernia NOS with gangrene

551.01 Unilateral or unspecified, recurrent

551.02 Bilateral (not specified as recurrent)

551.03 Bilateral, recurrent

551.1 Umbilical hernia with gangrene
Parumbilical hernia specified as gangrenous

551.2 Ventral hernia with gangrene

551.20 Ventral, unspecified, with gangrene

551.21 Incisional, with gangrene
Hernia: ⎫
postoperative ⎬ specified as gangrenous
recurrent, ventral ⎭

551.29 Other
Epigastric hernia specified as gangrenous

551.3 Diaphragmatic hernia with gangrene
Hernia: ⎫
hiatal (esophageal) (sliding) ⎪
paraesophageal ⎬ specified as gangrenous
Thoracic stomach ⎭

Excludes: *congenital diaphragmatic hernia (756.6)*

551.8 Hernia of other specified sites, with gangrene
Any condition classifiable to 553.8 if specified as gangrenous

551.9 Hernia of unspecified site, with gangrene
Any condition classifiable to 553.9 if specified as gangrenous

| | Add 4th or 5th digit | | Nonspecific code | | Unspecified code | | Manifestation code |

552 **Other hernia of abdominal cavity, with obstruction, but without mention of gangrene**

Excludes: that with mention of gangrene (551.0-551.9)

552.0 **Femoral hernia with obstruction**
Femoral hernia specified as incarcerated, irreducible, strangulated, or causing obstruction

552.00 **Unilateral or unspecified (not specified as recurrent)**

552.01 **Unilateral or unspecified, recurrent**

552.02 **Bilateral (not specified as recurrent)**

552.03 **Bilateral, recurrent**

552.1 **Umbilical hernia with obstruction**
Parumbilical hernia specified as incarcerated, irreducible, strangulated, or causing obstruction

552.2 **Ventral hernia with obstruction**
Ventral hernia specified as incarcerated, irreducible, strangulated, or causing obstruction

552.20 **Ventral, unspecified, with obstruction**

552.21 **Incisional, with obstruction**
Hernia:
postoperative } specified as incarcerated, irreducible, strangulated, or
recurrent, ventral } causing obstruction

552.29 **Other**
Epigastric hernia specified as incarcerated, irreducible, strangulated, or causing obstruction

552.3 **Diaphragmatic hernia with obstruction**
Hernia:
hiatal (esophageal) (sliding) } specified as incarcerated,
paraesophageal } irreducible, strangulated, or
Thoracic stomach } causing obstruction

Excludes: congenital diaphragmatic hernia (756.6)

552.8 **Hernia of other specified sites, with obstruction**
Any condition classifiable to 553.8 if specified as incarcerated, irreducible, strangulated, or causing obstruction

552.9 **Hernia of unspecified site, with obstruction**
Any condition classifiable to 553.9 if specified as incarcerated, irreducible, strangulated, or causing obstruction

553 **Other hernia of abdominal cavity without mention of obstruction or gangrene**

Excludes: the listed conditions with mention of:
gangrene (and obstruction) (551.0-551.9)
obstruction (552.0-552.9)

553.0 **Femoral hernia**

553.00 **Unilateral or unspecified (not specified as recurrent)**
Femoral hernia NOS

553.01 **Unilateral or unspecified, recurrent**

553.02 **Bilateral (not specified as recurrent)**

553.03 **Bilateral, recurrent**

553.1 **Umbilical hernia**
Parumbilical hernia

553.2 **Ventral hernia**

553.20 **Ventral, unspecified**

553.21 **Incisional**
Hernia:
postoperative
recurrent, ventral

553.29 **Other**
Hernia:
epigastric
spigelian

● Code new
to this edition
▲ Revision of
existing code
④ ⑤ Fourth or fifth
digit required

553.3 Diaphragmatic hernia
Hernia:
hiatal (esophageal) (sliding)
paraesophageal
Thoracic stomach

Excludes: congenital:
diaphragmatic hernia (756.6)
hiatal hernia (750.6)
esophagocele (530.6)

553.8 Hernia of other specified sites

Hernia: Hernia:
ischiatic   retroperitoneal
ischiorectal   sciatic
lumbar   Other abdominal hernia of specified site
obturator
pudendal

Excludes: vaginal enterocele (618.6)

553.9 Hernia of unspecified site

Enterocele   Hernia:
Epiplocele   intestinal
Hernia: intra-abdominal
  NOS   Rupture (nontraumatic)
  interstitial   Sarcoepiplocele

NONINFECTIOUS ENTERITIS AND COLITIS (555-558)

555 Regional enteritis
Includes: Crohn's disease
Granulomatous enteritis

Excludes: ulcerative colitis (556)

555.0 Small intestine

Ileitis: Regional enteritis or Crohn's disease of:
regional   duodenum
segmental   ileum
terminal   jejunum

555.1 Large intestine

Colitis: Regional enteritis or Crohn's disease of:
granulomatous   colon
regional   large bowel
transmural   rectum

555.2 Small intestine with large intestine
Regional ileocolitis

555.9 Unspecified site
Crohn's disease NOS
Regional enteritis NOS

556 Ulcerative colitis

556.0 Ulcerative (chronic) enterocolitis

556.1 Ulcerative (chronic) ileocolitis

556.2 Ulcerative (chronic) proctitis

556.3 Ulcerative (chronic) proctosigmoiditis

556.4 Pseudopolyposis of colon

556.5 Left-sided ulcerative (chronic) colitis

556.6 Universal ulcerative (chronic) colitis
Pancolitis

556.8 Other ulcerative colitis

556.9 Ulcerative colitis, unspecified
Ulcerative enteritis NOS

557 Vascular insufficiency of intestine

Excludes: necrotizing enterocolitis of the newborn (777.5)

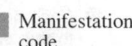

	Add 4th or 5th digit		Nonspecific code		Unspecified code		Manifestation code

247

557.0 Acute vascular insufficiency of intestine
Acute:
hemorrhagic enterocolitis
ischemic colitis, enteritis, or enterocolitis
massive necrosis of intestine
Bowel infarction
Embolism of mesenteric artery
Fulminant enterocolitis
Hemorrhagic necrosis of intestine
Intestinal gangrene
Intestinal infarction (acute) (agnogenic) (hemorrhagic) (nonocclusive)
Mesenteric infarction (embolic) (thrombotic)
Terminal hemorrhagic enteropathy
Thrombosis of mesenteric artery

557.1 Chronic vascular insufficiency of intestine
Angina, abdominal
Chronic ischemic colitis, enteritis, or enterocolitis
Ischemic stricture of intestine
Mesenteric:
angina
artery syndrome (superior)
vascular insufficiency

557.9 Unspecified vascular insufficiency of intestine
Alimentary pain due to vascular insufficiency
Ischemic colitis, enteritis, or enterocolitis NOS

558 Other noninfectious gastroenteritis and colitis

Excludes: *infectious:*

colitis, enteritis, or gastroenteritis (009.0-009.1)
diarrhea (009.2-009.3)

558.1 Gastroenteritis and colitis due to radiation
Radiation enterocolitis

558.2 Toxic gastroenteritis and colitis
Use additional E code, if desired, to identify cause

558.9 Other and unspecified noninfectious gastroenteritis and colitis
Colitis
Enteritis
Gastroenteritis
Ileitis } NOS, allergic, dietetic, or noninfectious
Jejunitis
Sigmoiditis

OTHER DISEASES OF INTESTINES AND PERITONEUM (560-569)

560 Intestinal obstruction without mention of hernia

Excludes: *duodenum (537.2-537.3)*

inguinal hernia with obstruction (550.1)
intestinal obstruction complicating hernia (552.0-552.9)
mesenteric:
embolism (557.0)
infarction (557.0)
thrombosis (557.0)
neonatal intestinal obstruction (277.01, 777.1-777.2, 777.4)

560.0 Intussusception
Intussusception (colon) (intestine) (rectum)
Invagination of intestine or colon

Excludes: *intussusception of appendix (543.9)*

560.1 Paralytic ileus
Adynamic ileus
Ileus (of intestine) (of bowel) (of colon)
Paralysis of intestine or colon

Excludes: *gallstone ileus (560.31)*

● Code new   ▲ Revision of   ④ ⑤ Fourth or fifth
to this edition   existing code   digit required

560.2 Volvulus
Knotting
Strangulation } of intestine, bowel, or colon
Torsion
Twist

560.3 Impaction of intestine

560.30 **Impaction of intestine, unspecified**
Impaction of colon

560.31 **Gallstone ileus**
Obstruction of intestine by gallstone

560.39 **Other**
Concretion of intestine
Enterolith
Fecal impaction

560.8 Other specified intestinal obstruction

560.81 **Intestinal or peritoneal adhesions with obstruction (postoperative) (postinfection)**

Excludes: *adhesions without obstruction (568.0)*

560.89 **Other**
Mural thickening causing obstruction

Excludes: *ischemic stricture of intestine (557.1)*

560.9 Unspecified intestinal obstruction
Enterostenosis
Obstruction
Occlusion } of intestine or colon
Stenosis
Stricture

Excludes: *congenital stricture or stenosis of intestine (751.1-751.2)*

562 Diverticula of intestine
Use additional code, if desired, to identify any associated:
peritonitis (567.0-567.9)

Excludes: *congenital diverticulum of colon (751.5)*
diverticulum of appendix (543.9)
Meckel's diverticulum (751.0)

562.0 Small intestine

562.00 **Diverticulosis of small intestine (without mention of hemorrhage)**
Diverticulosis:
duodenum
ileum } without mention of diverticulitis
jejunum

562.01 **Diverticulitis of small intestine (without mention of hemorrhage)**
Diverticulitis (with diverticulosis):
duodenum
ileum
jejunum
small intestine

562.02 **Diverticulosis of small intestine with hemorrhage**

562.03 **Diverticulitis of small intestine with hemorrhage**

562.1 Colon

562.10 **Diverticulosis of colon (without mention of hemorrhage)**
Diverticulosis:
NOS
intestine (large) } without mention of diverticulitis
Diverticular disease (colon)

562.11 **Diverticulitis of colon (without mention of hemorrhage)**
Diverticulitis (with diverticulosis):
NOS
colon
intestine (large)

562.12 **Diverticulosis of colon with hemorrhage**

562.13 **Diverticulitis of colon with hemorrhage**

Add 4th or 5th digit   Nonspecific code   Unspecified code   Manifestation code

564 **Functional digestive disorders, not elsewhere classified**

> *Excludes:* functional disorders of stomach (536.0-536.9)
> those specified as psychogenic (306.4)

564.0 **Constipation**

564.1 **Irritable colon**

Colitis:
  adaptive
  membranous
  mucous

Enterospasm
Irritable bowel syndrome
Spastic colon

564.2 **Postgastric surgery syndromes**

Dumping syndrome
Jejunal syndrome

Postgastrectomy syndrome
Postvagotomy syndrome

> *Excludes:* malnutrition following gastrointestinal surgery (579.3)
> postgastrojejunostomy ulcer (534.0-534.9)

564.3 **Vomiting following gastrointestinal surgery**

Vomiting (bilious) following gastrointestinal surgery

564.4 **Other postoperative functional disorders**

Diarrhea following gastrointestinal surgery

> *Excludes:* colostomy and enterostomy complications (569.60-569.69)

564.5 **Functional diarrhea**

> *Excludes:* diarrhea:
> NOS (787.91)
> psychogenic (306.4)

564.6 **Anal spasm**

Proctalgia fugax

564.7 **Megacolon, other than Hirschsprung's**

Dilatation of colon

> *Excludes:* megacolon:
> congenital [Hirschsprung's] (751.3)
> toxic (556)

564.8 **Other specified functional disorders of intestine**

Atony of colon

> *Excludes:* malabsorption (579.0-579.9)

564.9 **Unspecified functional disorder of intestine**

565 **Anal fissure and fistula**

565.0 **Anal fissure**

Tear of anus, nontraumatic

> *Excludes:* traumatic (863.89, 863.99)

565.1 **Anal fistula**

Fistula:
  anorectal
  rectal
  rectum to skin

> *Excludes:* fistula of rectum to internal organs—see Alphabetic Index
> ischiorectal fistula (566)
> rectovaginal fistula (619.1)

566 **Abscess of anal and rectal regions**

Abscess:
  ischiorectal
  perianal
  perirectal

Cellulitis:
  anal
  perirectal
  rectal
Ischiorectal fistula

  ● Code new
to this edition
  ▲ Revision of
existing code
  ④ ⑤ Fourth or fifth
digit required

567 Peritonitis

> *Excludes:* peritonitis:
>> benign paroxysmal *(277.3)*
>> pelvic, female *(614.5, 614.7)*
>> periodic familial *(277.3)*
>> puerperal *(670)*
>> with or following:
>>> abortion *(634-638 with .0, 639.0)*
>>> appendicitis *(540.0-540.1)*
>>> ectopic or molar pregnancy *(639.0)*

567.0 Peritonitis in infectious diseases classified elsewhere
> Code first underlying disease

> *Excludes:* peritonitis:
>> gonococcal *(098.86)*
>> syphilitic *(095.2)*
>> tuberculous *(014.0)*

567.1 Pneumococcal peritonitis

567.2 Other suppurative peritonitis

Abscess (of):	Abscess (of):
abdominopelvic	subhepatic
mesenteric	subphrenic
omentum	Peritonitis (acute):
peritoneum	general
retrocecal	pelvic, male
retroperitoneal	subphrenic
subdiaphragmatic	suppurative

567.8 Other specified peritonitis
> Chronic proliferative peritonitis
> Fat necrosis of peritoneum
> Mesenteric saponification
> Peritonitis due to:
>> bile
>> urine

567.9 Unspecified peritonitis
> Peritonitis:
>> NOS
>> of unspecified cause

568 Other disorders of peritoneum

568.0 Peritoneal adhesions (postoperative) (postinfection)

Adhesions (of):	Adhesions (of):
abdominal (wall)	mesenteric
diaphragm	omentum
intestine	stomach
male pelvis	Adhesive bands

> *Excludes:* adhesions:
>> pelvic, female *(614.6)*
>> with obstruction:
>>> duodenum *(537.3)*
>>> intestine *(560.81)*

568.8 Other specified disorders of peritoneum

568.81 Hemoperitoneum (nontraumatic)

568.82 Peritoneal effusion (chronic)

> *Excludes:* ascites NOS *(789.5)*

568.89 Other
> Peritoneal:
>> cyst
>> granuloma

568.9 Unspecified disorder of peritoneum

569 Other disorders of intestine

569.0 Anal and rectal polyp
> Anal and rectal polyp NOS

> *Excludes:* adenomatous anal and rectal polyp *(211.4)*

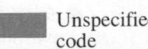 Add 4th or 5th digit   Nonspecific code   Unspecified code   Manifestation code

569.1 Rectal prolapse

Procidentia:
 anus (sphincter)
 rectum (sphincter)
Proctoptosis

Prolapse:
 anal canal
 rectal mucosa

Excludes: prolapsed hemorrhoids (455.2, 455.5)

569.2 Stenosis of rectum and anus
 Stricture of anus (sphincter)

569.3 Hemorrhage of rectum and anus

Excludes: gastrointestinal bleeding NOS (578.9)
 melena (578.1)

569.4 Other specified disorders of rectum and anus

569.41 Ulcer of anus and rectum
 Solitary ulcer ⎱
 Stercoral ulcer ⎰ of anus (sphincter) or rectum (sphincter)

569.42 Anal or rectal pain

569.49 Other
 Granuloma ⎱
 Rupture ⎰ of rectum (sphincter)

 Hypertrophy of anal papillae
 Proctitis NOS

Excludes: fistula of rectum to:
 internal organs—see Alphabetic Index
 skin (565.1)
 hemorrhoids (455.0-455.9)
 incontinence of sphincter ani (787.6)

569.5 Abscess of intestine

Excludes: appendiceal abscess (540.1)

569.6 Colostomy and enterostomy complications

569.60 Unspecified complication

569.61 Infection of colostomy or enterostomy
 Cellulitis or abscess
 Use additional code to identify organism (041.00-041.9)

569.69 Other complication
 Malfunction

569.8 Other specified disorders of intestine

569.81 Fistula of intestine, excluding rectum and anus
 Fistula:
 abdominal wall
 enterocolic

 Fistula:
 enteroenteric
 ileorectal

Excludes: fistula of intestine to internal organs —see Alphabetic Index
 persistent postoperative fistula (998.6)

569.82 Ulceration of intestine
 Primary ulcer of intestine
 Ulceration of colon

Excludes: that with perforation (569.83)

569.83 Perforation of intestine

569.84 Angiodysplasia of intestine (without mention of hemorrhage)

569.85 Angiodysplasia of intestine with hemorrhage

569.89 Other
 Enteroptosis
 Granuloma ⎱
 Prolapse ⎰ of intestine
 Pericolitis
 Perisigmoiditis
 Visceroptosis

Excludes: gangrene of intestine, mesentery, or omentum (557.0)
 hemorrhage of intestine NOS (578.9)
 obstruction of intestine (560.0-560.9)

● Code new
 to this edition

▲ Revision of
 existing code

④ ⑤ Fourth or fifth
 digit required

569.9 Unspecified disorder of intestine

OTHER DISEASES OF DIGESTIVE SYSTEM (570-579)

570 Acute and subacute necrosis of liver
Acute hepatic failure
Acute or subacute hepatitis, not specified as infective
Necrosis of liver (acute) (diffuse) (massive) (subacute)
Parenchymatous degeneration of liver
Yellow atrophy (liver) (acute) (subacute)

Excludes: *icterus gravis of newborn (773.0-773.2)*
serum hepatitis (070.2-070.3)
that with:
abortion (634-638 with .7, 639.8)
ectopic or molar pregnancy (639.8)
pregnancy, childbirth, or the puerperium (646.7)
viral hepatitis (070.0-070.9)

571 Chronic liver disease and cirrhosis

571.0 Alcoholic fatty liver

571.1 Acute alcoholic hepatitis
Acute alcoholic liver disease

571.2 Alcoholic cirrhosis of liver
Florid cirrhosis
Laennec's cirrhosis (alcoholic)

571.3 Alcoholic liver damage, unspecified

571.4 Chronic hepatitis

Excludes: *viral hepatitis (acute) (chronic) (070.0-070.9)*

571.40 Chronic hepatitis, unspecified

571.41 Chronic persistent hepatitis

571.49 Other
Chronic hepatitis:
active
aggressive
Recurrent hepatitis

571.5 Cirrhosis of liver without mention of alcohol
Cirrhosis of liver: Cirrhosis of liver:
NOS   posthepatitic
cryptogenic   postnecrotic
macronodular   Healed yellow atrophy (liver)
micronodular   Portal cirrhosis

571.6 Biliary cirrhosis
Chronic nonsuppurative destructive cholangitis
Cirrhosis:
cholangitic
cholestatic

571.8 Other chronic nonalcoholic liver disease
Chronic yellow atrophy (liver)
Fatty liver, without mention of alcohol

571.9 Unspecified chronic liver disease without mention of alcohol

572 Liver abscess and sequelae of chronic liver disease

572.0 Abscess of liver

Excludes: *amebic liver abscess (006.3)*

572.1 Portal pyemia
Phlebitis of portal vein   Pylephlebitis
Portal thrombophlebitis   Pylethrombophlebitis

572.2 Hepatic coma
Hepatic encephalopathy
Hepatocerebral intoxication
Portal-systemic encephalopathy

572.3 Portal hypertension

572.4 Hepatorenal syndrome

Excludes: *that following delivery (674.8)*

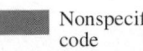 Add 4th or
5th digit   Nonspecific
code   Unspecified
code   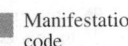 Manifestation
code

572.8 **Other sequelae of chronic liver disease**

573 **Other disorders of liver**

> *Excludes:* *amyloid or lardaceous degeneration of liver (277.3)*
> *congenital cystic disease of liver (751.62)*
> *glycogen infiltration of liver (271.0)*
> *hepatomegaly NOS (789.1)*
> *portal vein obstruction (452)*

573.0 **Chronic passive congestion of liver**

573.1 **Hepatitis in viral diseases classified elsewhere**
Code first underlying disease as:
Coxsackie virus disease (074.8)
cytomegalic inclusion virus disease (078.5)
infectious mononucleosis (075)

> *Excludes:* *hepatitis (in):*
> *mumps (072.71)*
> *viral (070.0-070.9)*
> *yellow fever (060.0-060.9)*

573.2 **Hepatitis in other infectious diseases classified elsewhere**
Code first underlying disease, as:
malaria (084.9)

> *Excludes:* *hepatitis in:*
> *late syphilis (095.3)*
> *secondary syphilis (091.62)*
> *toxoplasmosis (130.5)*

573.3 **Hepatitis, unspecified**
Toxic (noninfectious) hepatitis
Use additional E code, if desired, to identify cause

573.4 **Hepatic infarction**

573.8 **Other specified disorders of liver**
Hepatoptosis

573.9 **Unspecified disorder of liver**

⑤ **574** **Cholelithiasis**

The following fifth-digit subclassification is for use with category 574:

    0 **without mention of obstruction**

    1 **with obstruction**

574.0 **Calculus of gallbladder with acute cholecystitis**
Biliary calculus
Calculus of cystic } with acute cholecystitis
  duct
Cholelithiasis
Any condition classifiable to 574.2 with acute cholecystitis

574.1 **Calculus of gallbladder with other cholecystitis**
Biliary calculus
Calculus of cystic } with cholecystitis
  duct
Cholelithiasis
Cholecystitis with cholelithiasis NOS
Any condition classifiable to 574.2 with cholecystitis (chronic)

574.2 **Calculus of gallbladder without mention of cholecystitis**
Biliary: Cholelithiasis NOS
  calculus NOS   Colic (recurrent) of gallbladder
  colic NOS   Gallstone (impacted)
Calculus of cystic duct

574.3 **Calculus of bile duct with acute cholecystitis**
Calculus of bile
  duct [any] } with acute cholecystitis
Choledocholithiasis
Any condition classifiable to 574.5 with acute cholecystitis

574.4 **Calculus of bile duct with other cholecystitis**
Calculus of bile
  duct [any] } with cholecystitis (chronic)
Choledocholithiasis
Any condition classifiable to 574.5 with cholecystitis (chronic)

● Code new   ▲ Revision of   ④ ⑤ Fourth or fifth
  to this edition   existing code   digit required

574.5 Calculus of bile duct without mention of cholecystitis

Calculus of:
  bile duct [any]
  common duct
  hepatic duct

Choledocholithiasis
Hepatic:
  colic (recurrent)
  lithiasis

● **574.6 Calculus of gallbladder and bile duct with acute cholecystitis**
Any condition classifiable to 574.0 and 574.3

● **574.7 Calculus of gallbladder and bile duct with other cholecystitis**
Any condition classifiable to 574.1 and 574.4

● **574.8 Calculus of gallbladder and bile duct with acute and chronic cholecystitis**
Any condition classifiable to 574.6 and 574.7

● **574.9 Calculus of gallbladder and bile duct without cholecystitis**
Any condition classifiable to 574.2 and 574.5

575 Other disorders of gallbladder

575.0 Acute cholecystitis

Abscess of gallbladder
Angiocholecystitis
Cholecystitis:
  emphysematous (acute)
  gangrenous
  suppurative
Empyema of gallbladder
Gangrene of gallbladder

} without mention of calculus

Excludes: *that with:*
    acute and chronic cholecystitis (575.12)
    choledocholithiasis (574.3)
    choledocholithiasis and cholelithiasis (574.6)
    cholelithiasis (574.0)

575.1 Other cholecystitis

Cholecystitis:
  NOS
  chronic

} without mention of calculus

Excludes: *that with:*
    choledocholithiasis (574.4)
    choledocholithiasis and cholelithiasis (574.8)
    cholelithiasis (574.1)

● **575.10 Cholecystitis, unspecified**
Cholecystitis NOS

● **575.11 Chronic cholecystitis**

● **575.12 Acute and chronic cholecystits**

575.2 Obstruction of gallbladder

Occlusion
Stenosis
Stricture

} of cystic duct or gallbladder without mention of calculus

Excludes: *that with calculus (574.0-574.2 with fifth-digit 1)*

575.3 Hydrops of gallbladder
Mucocele of gallbladder

575.4 Perforation of gallbladder
Rupture of cystic duct or gallbladder

575.5 Fistula of gallbladder
Fistula:
  cholecystoduodenal
  cholecystoenteric

575.6 Cholesterolosis of gallbladder
Strawberry gallbladder

575.8 Other specified disorders of gallbladder

Adhesions
Atrophy
Cyst
Hypertrophy
Nonfunctioning
Ulcer
Biliary dyskinesia

} (of) { cystic duct / gallbladder

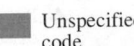

| | Add 4th or 5th digit | | Nonspecific code | | Unspecified code | | Manifestation code |

Excludes: *nonvisualization of gallbladder (793.3)*

575.9 **Unspecified disorder of gallbladder**

576 **Other disorders of biliary tract**

Excludes: *that involving the:*
   cystic duct (575.0-575.9)
   gallbladder (575.0-575.9)

576.0 **Postcholecystectomy syndrome**

576.1 **Cholangitis**

Cholangitis:
   NOS
   acute
   ascending
   chronic
   primary

Cholangitis:
   recurrent
   sclerosing
   secondary
   stenosing
   suppurative

576.2 **Obstruction of bile duct**

Occlusion
Stenosis
Stricture
} of bile duct, except cystic duct, without mention of calculus

Excludes: *congenital (751.61)*
   that with calculus (574.3-574.5 with fifth-digit 1)

576.3 **Perforation of bile duct**

Rupture of bile duct, except cystic duct

576.4 **Fistula of bile duct**

Choledochoduodenal fistula

576.5 **Spasm of sphincter of Oddi**

576.8 **Other specified disorders of biliary tract**

Adhesions
Atrophy
Cyst
Hypertrophy
Stasis
Ulcer
} of bile duct [any]

Excludes: *congenital choledochal cyst (751.69)*

576.9 **Unspecified disorder of biliary tract**

577 **Diseases of pancreas**

577.0 **Acute pancreatitis**

Abscess of pancreas
Necrosis of pancreas:
   acute
   infective

Pancreatitis:
   NOS
   acute (recurrent)
   apoplectic
   hemorrhagic
   subacute
   suppurative

Excludes: *mumps pancreatitis (072.3)*

577.1 **Chronic pancreatitis**

Chronic pancreatitis:
   NOS
   infectious
   interstitial

Pancreatitis:
   painless
   recurrent
   relapsing

577.2 **Cyst and pseudocyst of pancreas**

577.8 **Other specified diseases of pancreas**

Atrophy
Calculus
Cirrhosis
Fibrosis
} of pancreas

Pancreatic:
   infantilism
   necrosis:
      NOS
      aseptic
      fat
Pancreatolithiasis

Excludes: *fibrocystic disease of pancreas (277.00-277.01)*
   islet cell tumor of pancreas (211.7)
   pancreatic steatorrhea (579.4)

● Code new
   to this edition

▲ Revision of
   existing code

④ ⑤ Fourth or fifth
   digit required

577.9 Unspecified disease of pancreas

578 **Gastrointestinal hemorrhage**

Excludes: *that with mention of :*
angiodysplasia of stomach and duodenum (537.83)
angiodysplasia of intestine (569.85)
diverticulitis, intestine:
  large (562.13)
  small (562.03)
diverticulosis, intestine:
  large (562.12)
  small (562.02)
gastritis and duodenitis (535.0-535.6)
ulcer:
  duodenal (532.0-532.9)
  gastric (531.0-531.9)
  gastrojejunal (534.0-534.9)
  peptic (533.0-533.9)

578.0 **Hematemesis**
Vomiting of blood

578.1 **Blood in stool**
Melena

Excludes: *occult blood (792.1)*

578.9 **Hemorrhage of gastrointestinal tract, unspecified**
Gastric hemorrhage   Intestinal hemorrhage

579 **Intestinal malabsorption**

579.0 **Celiac disease**
Celiac: Gee (-Herter) disease
  crisis   Gluten enteropathy
  infantilism   Idiopathic steatorrhea
  rickets   Nontropical sprue

579.1 **Tropical sprue**
Sprue: Tropical steatorrhea
  NOS
  tropical

579.2 **Blind loop syndrome**
Postoperative blind loop syndrome

579.3 **Other and unspecified postsurgical nonabsorption**
Hypoglycemia ⎫
Malnutrition ⎬ following gastrointestinal surgery

579.4 **Pancreatic steatorrhea**

579.8 **Other specified intestinal malabsorption**
Enteropathy: Steatorrhea (chronic)
  exudative
  protein-losing

579.9 **Unspecified intestinal malabsorption**
Malabsorption syndrome NOS

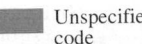 Add 4th or 5th digit   Nonspecific code   Unspecified code   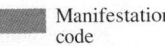 Manifestation code

● Code new
to this edition
▲ Revision of
existing code
④ ⑤ Fourth or fifth
digit required

10. DISEASES OF THE GENITOURINARY SYSTEM (580-629)

NEPHRITIS, NEPHROTIC SYNDROME, AND NEPHROSIS (580-589)

> *Excludes:* hypertensive renal disease (403.00-403.91)

580 Acute glomerulonephritis
Includes: acute nephritis

580.0 With lesion of proliferative glomerulonephritis
Acute (diffuse) proliferative glomerulonephritis
Acute poststreptococcal glomerulonephritis

580.4 With lesion of rapidly progressive glomerulonephritis
Acute nephritis with lesion of necrotizing glomerulitis

580.8 With other specified pathological lesion in kidney

> **580.81 *Acute glomerulonephritis in diseases classified elsewhere***
> Code first underlying disease, as:
> infectious hepatitis (070.0-070.9)
> mumps (072.79)
> subacute bacterial endocarditis (421.0)
> typhoid fever (002.0)

> **580.89 Other**
> Glomerulonephritis, acute, with lesion of:
> exudative nephritis
> interstitial (diffuse) (focal) nephritis

580.9 Acute glomerulonephritis with unspecified pathological lesion in kidney
Glomerulonephritis:
NOS
hemorrhagic   } specified as acute
Nephritis
Nephropathy

581 Nephrotic syndrome

581.0 With lesion of proliferative glomerulonephritis

581.1 With lesion of membranous glomerulonephritis
Epimembranous nephritis
Idiopathic membranous glomerular disease
Nephrotic syndrome with lesion of:
focal glomerulosclerosis
sclerosing membranous glomerulonephritis
segmental hyalinosis

581.2 With lesion of membranoproliferative glomerulonephritis
Nephrotic syndrome with lesion (of):
endothelial
hypocomplementemic persistent
lobular   } glomerulonephritis
mesangiocapillary
mixed membranous and proliferative

581.3 With lesion of minimal change glomerulonephritis
Foot process disease   Minimal change:
Lipoid nephrosis   glomerular disease
                                          glomerulitis
                                          nephrotic syndrome

581.8 With other specified pathological lesion in kidney

> **581.81 *Nephrotic syndrome in diseases classified elsewhere***
> Code first underlying disease, as:
> amyloidosis (277.3)
> diabetes mellitus (250.4)
> malaria (084.9)
> polyarteritis (446.0)
> systemic lupus erythematosus (710.0)

> *Excludes:* nephrosis in epidemic hemorrhagic fever (078.6)

> **581.89 Other**
> Glomerulonephritis with edema and lesion of:
> exudative nephritis
> interstitial (diffuse) (focal) nephritis

259

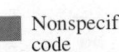 Add 4th or 5th digit   Nonspecific code   Unspecified code   Manifestation code

581.9 **Nephrotic syndrome with unspecified pathological lesion in kidney**
Glomerulonephritis with edema NOS
Nephritis:
nephrotic NOS
with edema NOS
Nephrosis NOS
Renal disease with edema NOS

582 **Chronic glomerulonephritis**
Includes: chronic nephritis

582.0 **With lesion of proliferative glomerulonephritis**
Chronic (diffuse) proliferative glomerulonephritis

582.1 **With lesion of membranous glomerulonephritis**
Chronic glomerulonephritis:
membranous
sclerosing
Focal glomerulosclerosis
Segmental hyalinosis

582.2 **With lesion of membranoproliferative glomerulonephritis**
Chronic glomerulonephritis:
endothelial
hypocomplementemic persistent
lobular
membranoproliferative
mesangiocapillary
mixed membranous and proliferative

582.4 **With lesion of rapidly progressive glomerulonephritis**
Chronic nephritis with lesion of necrotizing glomerulitis

582.8 **With other specified pathological lesion in kidney**

582.81 *Chronic glomerulonephritis in diseases classified elsewhere*
Code first underlying disease, as:
amyloidosis (277.3)
systemic lupus erythematosus (710.0)

582.89 **Other**
Chronic glomerulonephritis with lesion of:
exudative nephritis
interstitial (diffuse) (focal) nephritis

582.9 **Chronic glomerulonephritis with unspecified pathological lesion in kidney**
Glomerulonephritis:
NOS
hemorrhagic ⎫
Nephritis ⎬ specified as chronic
Nephropathy ⎭

583 **Nephritis and nephropathy, not specified as acute or chronic**
Includes: "renal disease" so stated, not specified as acute or chronic but with stated pathology
or cause

583.0 **With lesion of proliferative glomerulonephritis**
Proliferative:
glomerulonephritis (diffuse) NOS
nephritis NOS
nephropathy NOS

583.1 **With lesion of membranous glomerulonephritis**
Membranous: Membranous nephropathy NOS
glomerulonephritis NOS
nephritis NOS

583.2 **With lesion of membranoproliferative glomerulonephritis**
Membranoproliferative:
glomerulonephritis NOS
nephritis NOS
nephropathy NOS
Nephritis NOS, with lesion of:
hypocomplementemic persistent ⎫
lobular ⎬ glomerulonephritis
mesangiocapillary ⎪
mixed membranous and proliferative ⎭

● Code new   ▲ Revision of   ④ ⑤ Fourth or fifth
to this edition   existing code   digit required

583.4 With lesion of rapidly progressive glomerulonephritis
Necrotizing or rapidly progressive:
glomerulitis NOS
glomerulonephritis NOS
nephritis NOS
nephropathy NOS
Nephritis, unspecified, with lesion of necrotizing glomerulitis

583.6 With lesion of renal cortical necrosis
Nephritis NOS   ⎤ with (renal) cortical necrosis
Nephropathy NOS   ⎦
Renal cortical necrosis NOS

583.7 With lesion of renal medullary necrosis
Nephritis NOS   ⎤ with (renal) medullary [papillary] necrosis
Nephropathy NOS   ⎦

583.8 With other specified pathological lesion in kidney

583.81 *Nephritis and nephropathy, not specified as acute or chronic, in diseases classified elsewhere*
Code first underlying disease, as:
amyloidosis (277.3)
diabetes mellitus (250.4)
gonococcal infection (098.19)
Goodpasture's syndrome (446.21)
systemic lupus erythematosus (710.0)
tuberculosis (016.0)

Excludes: *gouty nephropathy (274.10)*
syphilitic nephritis (095.4)

583.89 Other
Glomerulitis   ⎤
Glomerulo-   ⎥ with lesion of:
  nephritis   ⎬ exudative nephritis
Nephritis   ⎥ interstitial nephritis
Nephropathy   ⎥
Renal disease   ⎦

583.9 With unspecified pathological lesion in kidney
Glomerulitis   ⎤
Glomerulonephritis ⎥ NOS
Nephritis   ⎬
Nephropathy   ⎦

Excludes: *nephropathy complicating pregnancy, labor, or the puerperium (642.0-642.9, 646.2)*
renal disease NOS with no stated cause (593.9)

584 Acute renal failure

Excludes: *following labor and delivery (669.3)*
posttraumatic (958.5)
that complicating:
abortion (634-638 with .3, 639.3)
ectopic or molar pregnancy (639.3)

584.5 With lesion of tubular necrosis
Lower nephron nephrosis
Renal failure with (acute) tubular necrosis
Tubular necrosis:
NOS
acute

584.6 With lesion of renal cortical necrosis

584.7 With lesion of renal medullary [papillary] necrosis
Necrotizing renal papillitis

584.8 With other specified pathological lesion in kidney

584.9 Acute renal failure, unspecified

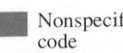 Add 4th or 5th digit   Nonspecific code   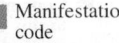 Unspecified code   Manifestation code

585 Chronic renal failure
Chronic uremia

Use additional code, if desired, to identify manifestation as:
uremic:
neuropathy (357.4)
pericarditis (420.0)

Excludes: *that with any condition classifiable to 401 (403.0-403.9 with fifth-digit 1)*

586 Renal failure, unspecified
Uremia NOS

Excludes: *following labor and delivery (669.3)*
posttraumatic renal failure (958.5)
that complicating:
abortion (634-638 with .3, 639.3)
ectopic or molar pregnancy (639.3)
uremia:
extrarenal (788.9)
prerenal (788.9)
with any condition classifiable to 401 (403.0-403.9 with fifth-digit 1)

587 Renal sclerosis, unspecified
Atrophy of kidney   Renal:
Contracted kidney   cirrhosis
                               fibrosis

Excludes: *nephrosclerosis (arteriolar) (arteriosclerotic) (403.00-403.92)*
with hypertension (403.00-403.92)

588 Disorders resulting from impaired renal function

588.0 Renal osteodystrophy
Azotemic osteodystrophy   Renal:
Phosphate-losing tubular   dwarfism
  disorders   infantilism
                                rickets

588.1 Nephrogenic diabetes insipidus

Excludes: *diabetes insipidus NOS (253.5)*

588.8 Other specified disorders resulting from impaired renal function
Hypokalemic nephropathy
Secondary hyperparathyroidism (of renal origin)

Excludes: *secondary hypertension (405.0-405.9)*

588.9 Unspecified disorder resulting from impaired renal function

589 Small kidney of unknown cause

589.0 Unilateral small kidney

589.1 Bilateral small kidneys

589.9 Small kidney, unspecified

OTHER DISEASES OF URINARY SYSTEM (590-599)

590 Infections of kidney

Use additional code, if desired, to identify organism, such as Escherichia coli [E. coli] (041.4)

590.0 Chronic pyelonephritis
Chronic pyelitis   Chronic pyonephrosis
Code first any associated vesicoureteral reflux (593.70-593.73)

590.00 Without lesion of renal medullary necrosis

590.01 With lesion of renal medullary necrosis

590.1 Acute pyelonephritis
Acute pyelitis   Acute pyonephrosis

590.10 Without lesion of renal medullary necrosis

590.11 With lesion of renal medullary necrosis

● Code new   ▲ Revision of   ④ ⑤ Fourth or fifth
  to this edition   existing code   digit required

590.2 Renal and perinephric abscess
Abscess: Carbuncle of kidney
   kidney
   nephritic
   perirenal

590.3 Pyeloureteritis cystica
Infection of renal pelvis and ureter
Ureteritis cystica

590.8 Other pyelonephritis or pyonephrosis, not specified as acute or chronic

590.80 Pyelonephritis, unspecified
Pyelitis NOS   Pyelonephritis NOS

Excludes: calculous pyelonephritis (592.9)

590.81 Pyelitis or pyelonephritis in diseases classified elsewhere
Code first underlying disease, as:
   tuberculosis (016.0)

590.9 Infection of kidney, unspecified

Excludes: urinary tract infection NOS (599.0)

591 Hydronephrosis
Hydrocalycosis   Hydroureteronephrosis
Hydronephrosis

Excludes: congenital hydronephrosis (753.29)
        hydroureter (593.5)

592 Calculus of kidney and ureter

Excludes: nephrocalcinosis (275.4)

592.0 Calculus of kidney
Nephrolithiasis NOS   Staghorn calculus
Renal calculus or stone   Stone in kidney

Excludes: uric acid nephrolithiasis (274.11)

592.1 Calculus of ureter
Ureteric stone   Ureterolithiasis

592.9 Urinary calculus, unspecified
Calculous pyelonephritis

593 Other disorders of kidney and ureter

593.0 Nephroptosis
Floating kidney   Mobile kidney

593.1 Hypertrophy of kidney

593.2 Cyst of kidney, acquired
Cyst (multiple) (solitary) of kidney, not congenital
Peripelvic (lymphatic) cyst

Excludes: calyceal or pyelogenic cyst of kidney (591)
        congenital cyst of kidney (753.1)
        polycystic (disease of) kidney (753.1)

593.3 Stricture or kinking of ureter
Angulation   ⎫
Constriction   ⎬ of ureter (postoperative)
Stricture of pelviureteric junction ⎭

593.4 Other ureteric obstruction
Idiopathic retroperitoneal fibrosis
Occlusion NOS of ureter

Excludes: that due to calculus (592.1)

593.5 Hydroureter

Excludes: congenital hydroureter (753.22)
        hydroureteronephrosis (591)

593.6 Postural proteinuria
Benign postural proteinuria
Orthostatic proteinuria

Excludes: proteinuria NOS (791.0)

263

	Add 4th or 5th digit		Nonspecific code		Unspecified code	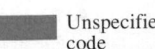	Manifestation code

593.7 Vesicoureteral reflux

Use additional code to identify:
      chronic pyelonephritis (590.00-590.01)
      renal agenesis (753.0)
      renal dysplasia (753.15)

    593.70 Unspecified or without reflux nephropathy

    593.71 With reflux nephropathy, unilateral

    593.72 With reflux nephropathy, bilateral

    593.73 With reflux nephropathy NOS

593.8 Other specified disorders of kidney and ureter

    593.81 Vascular disorders of kidney
        Renal (artery):   Renal infarction
          embolism
          hemorrhage
          thrombosis

    593.82 Ureteral fistula
        Intestinoureteral fistula

    Excludes: *fistula between ureter and female genital tract (619.0)*

    593.89 Other
        Adhesions, kidney or   Polyp of ureter
          ureter   Pyelectasia
        Periureteritis   Ureterocele

    Excludes: *tuberculosis of ureter (016.2)*
          ureteritis cystica (590.3)

593.9 Unspecified disorder of kidney and ureter
    Renal disease NOS
    Salt-losing nephritis or syndrome

    Excludes: *cystic kidney disease (753.1)*
          nephropathy, so stated (583.0-583.9)
          renal disease:
            acute (580.0-580.9)
            arising in pregnancy or the puerperium (642.1-642.2, 642.4-642.7, 646.2)
            chronic (582.0-582.9)
            not specified as acute or chronic, but with stated pathology or cause
             (583.0-583.9)

594 Calculus of lower urinary tract

594.0 Calculus in diverticulum of bladder

594.1 Other calculus in bladder
    Urinary bladder stone

    Excludes: *staghorn calculus (592.0)*

594.2 Calculus in urethra

594.8 Other lower urinary tract calculus

594.9 Calculus of lower urinary tract, unspecified

    Excludes: *calculus of urinary tract NOS (592.9)*

595 Cystitis

    Excludes: *prostatocystitis (601.3)*

Use additional code, if desired, to identify organism, such as Escherichia coli [E. coli] (041.4)

595.0 Acute cystitis

    Excludes: *trigonitis (595.3)*

595.1 Chronic interstitial cystitis
    Hunner's ulcer   Submucous cystitis
    Panmural fibrosis of bladder

595.2 Other chronic cystitis
    Chronic cystitis NOS   Subacute cystitis

    Excludes: *trigonitis (595.3)*

● Code new   ▲ Revision of   ④ ⑤ Fourth or fifth
   to this edition   existing code   digit required

595.3 Trigonitis
>> Follicular cystitis
>> Trigonitis (acute) (chronic)
>> Urethrotrigonitis

595.4 Cystitis in diseases classified elsewhere
>> *Code first underlying disease, as:*
>> actinomycosis (039.8)
>> amebiasis (006.8)
>> bilharziasis (120.0-120.9)
>> Echinococcus infestation (122.3, 122.6)

> Excludes: *cystitis:*
>> *diphtheritic (032.84)*
>> *gonococcal (098.11, 098.31)*
>> *monilial (112.2)*
>> *trichomonal (131.09)*
>> *tuberculous (016.1)*

595.8 Other specified types of cystitis

> **595.81 Cystitis cystica**

> **595.82 Irradiation cystitis**
>> Use additional E code, if desired, to identify cause

> **595.89 Other**
>> Abscess of bladder
>> Cystitis:
>>> bullous
>>> emphysematous
>>> glandularis

595.9 Cystitis, unspecified

596 Other disorders of bladder
Use additional code, if desired, to identify urinary incontinence (625.6, 788.30-788.39)

596.0 Bladder neck obstruction
>> Contracture (acquired)
>> Obstruction (acquired) } of bladder neck or vesicourethral orifice
>> Stenosis (acquired)

> Excludes: *congenital (753.6)*

596.1 Intestinovesical fistula
>> Fistula: Fistula:
>> enterovesical   vesicoenteric
>> vesicocolic   vesicorectal

596.2 Vesical fistula, not elsewhere classified
>> Fistula: Fistula:
>> bladder NOS   vesicocutaneous
>> urethrovesical   vesicoperineal

> Excludes: *fistula between bladder and female genital tract (619.0)*

596.3 Diverticulum of bladder
>> Diverticulitis
>> Diverticulum (acquired) } of bladder
>> (false)

> Excludes: *that with calculus in diverticulum of bladder (594.0)*

596.4 Atony of bladder
>> High compliance bladder
>> Hypotonicity } of bladder
>> Inertia

> Excludes: *neurogenic bladder (596.54)*

596.5 Other functional disorders of bladder

> Excludes: *cauda equina syndrome*
>> *with neurogenic bladder (344.61)*

> **596.51 Hypertonicity of bladder**
>> Hyperactivity

> **596.52 Low bladder compliance**

> **596.53 Paralysis of bladder**

265

| Add 4th or 5th digit | Nonspecific code | Unspecified code | Manifestation code |

596.54 Neurogenic bladder NOS

596.55 Detrusor sphincter dyssynergia

596.59 Other functional disorder of bladder
Detrusor instability

596.6 Rupture of bladder, nontraumatic

596.7 Hemorrhage into bladder wall
Hyperemia of bladder

Excludes: *acute hemorrhagic cystitis (595.0)*

596.8 Other specified disorders of bladder
Bladder: Bladder:
  calcified   hemorrhage
  contracted   hypertrophy

Excludes: *cystocele, female (618.0, 618.2-618.4)*
        hernia or prolapse of bladder, female (618.0, 618.2-618.4)

596.9 Unspecified disorder of bladder

597 Urethritis, not sexually transmitted, and urethral syndrome

Excludes: *nonspecific urethritis, so stated (099.4)*

597.0 Urethral abscess
Abscess of: Abscess:
  bulbourethral gland   periurethral
  Cowper's gland   urethral (gland)
  Littré's gland   Periurethral cellulitis

Excludes: *urethral caruncle (599.3)*

597.8 Other urethritis

597.80 Urethritis, unspecified

597.81 Urethral syndrome NOS

597.89 Other
Adenitis, Skene's   Meatitis, urethral
  glands   Ulcer, urethra (meatus)
Cowperitis   Verumontanitis

Excludes: *trichomonal (131.02)*

598 Urethral stricture
Includes: pinhole meatus
         stricture of urinary meatus

Excludes: *congenital stricture of urethra and urinary meatus (753.6)*
Use additional code to identify urinary incontinence (625.6, 788.30-788.39)

598.0 Urethral stricture due to infection

598.00 Due to unspecified infection

598.01 *Due to infective diseases classified elsewhere*
Code first underlying disease, as:
  gonococcal infection (098.2)
  schistosomiasis (120.0-120.9)
  syphilis (095.8)

598.1 Traumatic urethral stricture
Stricture of urethra:
  late effect of injury
  postobstetric

Excludes: *postoperative following surgery on genitourinary tract (598.2)*

598.2 Postoperative urethral stricture
Postcatheterization stricture of urethra

598.8 Other specified causes of urethral stricture

598.9 Urethral stricture, unspecified

599 Other disorders of urethra and urinary tract

599.0 Urinary tract infection, site not specified
Pyuria

Excludes: *Candidiasis of urinary tract (112.2)*
Use additional code to identify organism, such as Escherichia coli [*E. coli*] (041.4)

  ● Code new   ▲ Revision of   ④ ⑤ Fourth or fifth
        to this edition   existing code   digit required

599.1 Urethral fistula
  Fistula: Urinary fistula NOS
    urethroperineal
    urethrorectal

  Excludes: *fistula:*
            urethroscrotal (608.89)
            urethrovaginal (619.0)
            urethrovesicovaginal (619.0)

599.2 Urethral diverticulum

599.3 Urethral caruncle
  Polyp of urethra

599.4 Urethral false passage

599.5 Prolapsed urethral mucosa
  Prolapse of urethra   Urethrocele

  Excludes: *urethrocele, female (618.0, 618.2-618.4)*

599.6 Urinary obstruction, unspecified
  Obstructive uropathy NOS
  Urinary (tract) obstruction NOS

  Excludes: *obstructive nephropathy NOS (593.89)*
Use additional code, if desired, to identify urinary incontinence (625.6, 788.30-788.39)

599.7 Hematuria
  Hematuria (benign) (essential)

  Excludes: *hemoglobinuria (791.2)*

599.8 Other specified disorders of urethra and urinary tract

  Excludes: *symptoms and other conditions classifiable to 788.0-788.9, 791.0-791.9*
Use additional code, if desired, to identify urinary incontinence (625.6, 788.30-788.39)

  599.81 Urethral hypermobility

  599.82 Intrinsic (urethral) sphincter deficiency [ISD]

  599.83 Urethral instability

  599.84 Other specified disorders of urethra
        Rupture of urethra (nontraumatic)
        Urethral:
          cyst
          granuloma

  599.89 Other specified disorders of urinary tract

599.9 Unspecified disorder of urethra and urinary tract

DISEASES OF MALE GENITAL ORGANS (600-608)

600 Hyperplasia of prostate
  Adenofibromatous hypertrophy ⎫
  Adenoma (benign)   ⎪
  Enlargement (benign)   ⎪
  Fibroadenoma   ⎬ of prostate
  Fibroma   ⎪
  Hypertrophy (benign)   ⎪
  Myoma   ⎪
  Median bar (prostate)   ⎭
  Prostatic obstruction NOS

  Excludes: *benign neoplasms of prostate (222.2)*
Use additional code, if desired, to identify urinary incontinence (788.30-788.39)

601 Inflammatory diseases of prostate
  Use additional code, if desired, to identify organism, such as Staphylococcus (041.1), or
    Streptococcus (041.0)

  601.0 Acute prostatitis

  601.1 Chronic prostatitis

  601.2 Abscess of prostate

  601.3 Prostatocystitis

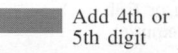 Add 4th or
5th digit

 Nonspecific
code

Unspecified
code

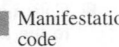 Manifestation
code

601.4 *Prostatitis in diseases classified elsewhere*
    Code first underlying disease, as:
      actinomycosis (039.8)
      blastomycosis (116.0)
      syphilis (095.8)
      tuberculosis (016.5)

   Excludes: *prostatitis:*
      gonococcal (098.12, 098.32)
      monilial (112.2)
      trichomonal (131.03)

601.8 **Other specified inflammatory diseases of prostate**
    Prostatitis:
      cavitary
      diverticular
      granulomatous

601.9 **Prostatitis, unspecified**
    Prostatitis NOS

602 **Other disorders of prostate**

  602.0 **Calculus of prostate**
    Prostatic stone

  602.1 **Congestion or hemorrhage of prostate**

  602.2 **Atrophy of prostate**

602.8 **Other specified disorders of prostate**
    Fistula
    Infarction } of prostate   Periprostatic adhesions
    Stricture

602.9 **Unspecified disorder of prostate**

603 **Hydrocele**
    Includes: hydrocele of spermatic cord, testis, or tunica vaginalis

   Excludes: *congenital (778.6)*

  603.0 **Encysted hydrocele**

  603.1 **Infected hydrocele**
  Use additional code, if desired, to identify organism

603.8 **Other specified types of hydrocele**

603.9 **Hydrocele, unspecified**

604 **Orchitis and epididymitis**
  Use additional code, if desired, to identify organism, such as Escherichia coli [E. coli] (041.4),
    Staphylococcus (041.1), or Streptococcus (041.0)

  604.0 **Orchitis, epididymitis, and epididymo-orchitis, with abscess**
    Abscess of epididymis or testis

  604.9 **Other orchitis, epididymitis, and epididymo-orchitis, without mention of abscess**

    604.90 **Orchitis and epididymitis, unspecified**

    604.91 *Orchitis and epididymitis in diseases classified elsewhere*
      Code first underlying disease, as:
        diphtheria (032.89)
        filariasis (125.0-125.9)
        syphilis (095.8)

   Excludes: *orchitis:*
      gonococcal (098.13, 098.33)
      mumps (072.0)
      tuberculous (016.5)
      tuberculous epididymitis (016.4)

    604.99 **Other**

605 **Redundant prepuce and phimosis**
    Adherent prepuce   Phimosis (congenital)
    Paraphimosis   Tight foreskin

606 Infertility, male

606.0 Azoospermia
    Absolute infertility
    Infertility due to:
      germinal (cell) aplasia
      spermatogenic arrest (complete)

606.1 Oligospermia
    Infertility due to:
      germinal cell desquamation
      hypospermatogenesis
      incomplete spermatogenic arrest

606.8 Infertility due to extratesticular causes
    Infertility due to:
      drug therapy
      infection
      obstruction of efferent ducts
      radiation
      systemic disease

606.9 Male infertility, unspecified

607 Disorders of penis

> *Excludes:* phimosis (605)

607.0 Leukoplakia of penis
    Kraurosis of penis

> *Excludes:* carcinoma in situ of penis (233.5)
>   erythroplasia of Queyrat (233.5)

607.1 Balanoposthitis
    Balanitis

Use additional code, if desired, to identify organism

607.2 Other inflammatory disorders of penis
    Abscess
    Boil
    Carbuncle   } of corpus cavernosum or penis
    Cellulitis
    Cavernitis (penis)

Use additional code, if desired, to identify organism

> *Excludes:* herpetic infection (054.13)

607.3 Priapism
    Painful erection

607.8 Other specified disorders of penis

    607.81 Balanitis xerotica obliterans
        Induratio penis plastica

    607.82 Vascular disorders of penis
        Embolism
        Hematoma
          (nontraumatic) } of corpus cavernosum or penis
        Hemorrhage
        Thrombosis

    607.83 Edema of penis

    607.84 Impotence of organic origin

> *Excludes:* nonorganic or unspecified (302.72)

    607.89 Other
        Atrophy
        Fibrosis   } of corpus cavernosum or penis
        Hypertrophy
        Ulcer (chronic)

607.9 Unspecified disorder of penis

| | Add 4th or 5th digit | | Nonspecific code | | Unspecified code | | Manifestation code |

608 **Other disorders of male genital organs**

608.0 Seminal vesiculitis
Abscess ⎫
Cellulitis ⎬ of seminal vesicle
Vesiculitis (seminal) ⎭
Use additional code, if desired, to identify organism

Excludes: gonococcal infection (098.14, 098.34)

608.1 Spermatocele

608.2 Torsion of testis
Torsion of:
epididymis
spermatic cord
testicle

608.3 Atrophy of testis

608.4 **Other inflammatory disorders of male genital organs**
Abscess ⎫
Boil ⎪
Carbuncle ⎬ of scrotum, spermatic cord, testis [except abscess],
Cellulitis ⎪ tunica vaginalis, or vas deferens
Vasitis ⎭
Use additional code, if desired, to identify organism

Excludes: abscess of testis (604.0)

608.8 Other specified disorders of male genital organs

608.81 *Disorders of male genital organs in diseases classified elsewhere*
Code first underlying disease, as:
filariasis (125.0-125.9)
tuberculosis (016.5)

608.83 Vascular disorders
Hematoma (nontraumatic) ⎫ of seminal vesicle, spermatic
Hemorrhage ⎬ cord, testis, scrotum, tunica
⎭ vaginalis, or vas deferens

Thrombosis
Hematocele NOS, male

608.84 Chylocele of tunica vaginalis

608.85 Stricture
Stricture of:
spermatic cord
tunica vaginalis
vas deferens

608.86 Edema

608.89 **Other**
Atrophy ⎫
Fibrosis ⎬ of seminal vesicle, spermatic cord, testis, scrotum,
Hypertrophy ⎪ tunica vaginalis, or vas deferens
Ulcer ⎭

Excludes: atrophy of testis (608.3)

608.9 **Unspecified disorder of male genital organs**

DISORDERS OF BREAST (610-611)

610 **Benign mammary dysplasias**

610.0 Solitary cyst of breast
Cyst (solitary) of breast

610.1 Diffuse cystic mastopathy
Chronic cystic mastitis   Fibrocystic disease of breast
Cystic breast

610.2 Fibroadenosis of breast
Fibroadenosis of breast: Fibroadenosis of breast:
NOS   diffuse
chronic   periodic
cystic   segmental

610.3 Fibrosclerosis of breast

● Code new   ▲ Revision of   ④ ⑤ Fourth or fifth
to this edition   existing code   digit required

610.4 Mammary duct ectasia
Comedomastitis
Dust ectasia

Mastitis:
    periductal
    plasma cell

610.8 Other specified benign mammary dysplasias
Mazoplasia
Sebaceous cyst of breast

610.9 Benign mammary dysplasia, unspecified

611 Other disorders of breast

Excludes: *that associated with lactation or the puerperium (675.0-676.9)*

611.0 Inflammatory disease of breast
Abscess (acute) (chronic) (nonpuerperal) of:
    areola
    breast
Mammillary fistula
Mastitis (acute) (subacute) (nonpuerperal):
    NOS
    infective
    retromammary
    submammary

Excludes: *carbuncle of breast (680.2)*
        chronic cystic mastitis (610.1)
        neonatal infective mastitis (771.5)
        thrombophlebitis of breast [Mondor's disease] (451.89)

611.1 Hypertrophy of breast
Gynecomastia

Hypertrophy of breast:
    NOS
    massive pubertal

611.2 Fissure of nipple

611.3 Fat necrosis of breast
Fat necrosis (segmental) of breast

611.4 Atrophy of breast

611.5 Galactocele

611.6 Galactorrhea not associated with childbirth

611.7 Signs and symptoms in breast

611.71 Mastodynia
Pain in breast

611.72 Lump or mass in breast

611.79 Other
Induration of breast   Nipple discharge
Inversion of nipple   Retraction of nipple

611.8 Other specified disorders of breast
Hematoma (nontraumatic) ⎫
Infarction   ⎬ of breast
Occlusion of breast duct
Subinvolution of breast (postlactational) (postpartum)

611.9 Unspecified breast disorder

INFLAMMATORY DISEASE OF FEMALE PELVIC ORGANS (614-616)

Use additional code, if desired, to identify organism, such as Staphylococcus (041.1), or
    Streptococcus (041.0)

Excludes: *that associated with pregnancy, abortion, childbirth, or the puerperium (630-676.9)*

614 Inflammatory disease of ovary, fallopian tube, pelvic cellular tissue, and peritoneum

Excludes: *endometritis (615.0-615.9)*
        major infection following delivery (670)
        that complicating:
        abortion (634-638 with .0, 639.0)
        ectopic or molar pregnancy (639.0)
        pregnancy or labor (646.6)

614.0 Acute salpingitis and oophoritis
Any condition classifiable to 614.2, specified as acute or subacute

| | Add 4th or 5th digit | | Nonspecific code | | Unspecified code | | Manifestation code |

614.1 Chronic salpingitis and oophoritis
Hydrosalpinx
Salpingitis:
  follicularis
  isthmica nodosa
Any condition classifiable to 614.2, specified as chronic

614.2 Salpingitis and oophoritis not specified as acute, subacute, or chronic

Abscess (of):   Perisalpingitis
  fallopian tube   Pyosalpinx
  ovary   Salpingitis
  tubo-ovarian   Salpingo-oophoritisRTubo-ovarian inflammatory disease
Oophoritis
Perioophoritis

Excludes: *gonococcal infection (chronic) (098.37)*
        acute (098.17)
        tuberculous (016.6)

614.3 Acute parametritis and pelvic cellulitis
Acute inflammatory pelvic disease
Any condition classifiable to 614.4, specified as acute

614.4 Chronic or unspecified parametritis and pelvic cellulitis
Abscess (of):
  broad ligament
  parametrium   } chronic or NOS
  pelvis, female
  pouch of Douglas
Chronic inflammatory pelvic disease
Pelvic cellulitis, female

Excludes: *tuberculous (016.7)*

614.5 Acute or unspecified pelvic peritonitis, female

614.6 Pelvic peritoneal adhesions, female (postoperative) (postinfection)
Adhesions:
  peritubal
  tubo-ovarian

Use additional code, if desired, to identify any associated infertility (628.2)

614.7 Other chronic pelvic peritonitis, female

Excludes: *tuberculous (016.7)*

614.8 Other specified inflammatory disease of female pelvic organs and tissues

614.9 Unspecified inflammatory disease of female pelvic organs and tissues
Pelvic infection or inflammation, female NOS
Pelvic inflammatory disease [PID]

615 Inflammatory diseases of uterus, except cervix

Excludes: *following delivery (670)*
        hyperplastic endometritis (621.3)
        that complicating:
          abortion (634-638 with .0, 639.0)
          ectopic or molar pregnancy (639.0)
          pregnancy or labor (646.6)

615.0 Acute
Any condition classifiable to 615.9, specified as acute or subacute

615.1 Chronic
Any condition classifiable to 615.9, specified as chronic

615.9 Unspecified inflammatory disease of uterus
Endometritis   Perimetritis
Endomyometritis   Pyometra
Metritis   Uterine abscess
Myometritis

616 Inflammatory disease of cervix, vagina, and vulva

Excludes: *that complicating:*
        abortion (634-638 with .0, 639.0)
        ectopic or molar pregnancy (639.0)
        pregnancy, childbirth, or the puerperium (646.6)

● Code new   ▲ Revision of   ④ ⑤ Fourth or fifth
  to this edition   existing code   digit required

616.0 Cervicitis and endocervicitis

Cervicitis ⎫
Endocervicitis ⎬ with or without mention of erosion or ectropion
Nabothian (gland) cyst or follicle

> Excludes: *erosion or ectropion without mention of cervicitis (622.0)*

616.1 Vaginitis and vulvovaginitis

> **616.10 Vaginitis and vulvovaginitis, unspecified**
> Vaginitis: Vulvitis NOS
>   NOS   Vulvovaginitis NOS
>   postirradiation
> Use additional code, if desired, to identify organism, such as Escherichia coli [E. coli] (041.4), Staphylococcus (041.1), or Streptococcus (041.0)

> Excludes: *noninfective leukorrhea (623.5)*
>
> *postmenopausal or senile vaginitis (627.3)*

> **616.11 Vaginitis and vulvovaginitis in diseases classified elsewhere**
> *Code first underlying disease, as:*
>   *pinworm vaginitis (127.4)*

> Excludes: *herpetic vulvovaginitis (054.11)*
>
> *monilial vulvovaginitis (112.1)*
> *trichomonal vaginitis or vulvovaginitis (131.01)*

616.2 Cyst of Bartholin's gland

Bartholin's duct cyst

616.3 Abscess of Bartholin's gland

Vulvovaginal gland abscess

616.4 Other abscess of vulva

Abscess ⎫
Carbuncle ⎬ of vulva
Furuncle ⎭

616.5 Ulceration of vulva

> **616.50 Ulceration of vulva, unspecified**
> Ulcer NOS of vulva

> **616.51 Ulceration of vulva in diseases classified elsewhere**
> *Code first underlying disease, as:*
>   Behçet's syndrome (136.1)
>   tuberculosis (016.7)

> Excludes: *vulvar ulcer (in):*
>
> *gonococcal (098.0)*
> *herpes simplex (054.12)*
> *syphilitic (091.0)*

616.8 Other specified inflammatory diseases of cervix, vagina, and vulva

Caruncle, vagina or labium
Ulcer, vagina

> Excludes: *noninflammatory disorders of:*
>
> *cervix (622.0-622.9)*
> *vagina (623.0-623.9)*
> *vulva (624.0-624.9)*

616.9 Unspecified inflammatory disease of cervix, vagina, and vulva

OTHER DISORDERS OF FEMALE GENITAL TRACT (617-629)

617 Endometriosis

617.0 Endometriosis of uterus

Adenomyosis   Endometriosis:
                            cervix
                            internal
                            myometrium

> Excludes: *stromal endometriosis (236.0)*

617.1 Endometriosis of ovary

Chocolate cyst of ovary
Endometrial cystoma of ovary

617.2 Endometriosis of fallopian tube

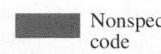 Add 4th or 5th digit   Nonspecific code   Unspecified code   Manifestation code

617.3 Endometriosis of pelvic peritoneum
Endometriosis: Endometriosis:
  broad ligament   parametrium
  cul-de-sac (Douglas')   round ligament

617.4 Endometriosis of rectovaginal septum and vagina

617.5 Endometriosis of intestine
Endometriosis:
  appendix
  colon
  rectum

617.6 Endometriosis in scar of skin

`617.8` Endometriosis of other specified sites
Endometriosis: Endometriosis:
  bladder   umbilicus
  lung   vulva

`617.9` Endometriosis, site unspecified

`618` Genital prolapse

Use additional code, if desired, to identify urinary incontinence (625.6, 788.31, 788.33-788.39)

   Excludes: *that complicating pregnancy, labor, or delivery (654.4)*

618.0 Prolapse of vaginal walls without mention of uterine prolapse
Cystocele
Cystourethrocele
Proctocele, female
Rectocele   } without mention of uterine prolapse
Urethrocele, female
Vaginal prolapse

   Excludes: *that with uterine prolapse (618.2-618.4)*
       enterocele (618.6)
       vaginal vault prolapse following hysterectomy (618.5)

618.1 Uterine prolapse without mention of vaginal wall prolapse
Descensus uteri   Uterine prolapse:
Uterine prolapse: first degree
  NOS   second degree
  complete   third degree

   Excludes: *that with mention of cystocele, urethrocele, or rectocele (618.2-618.4)*

618.2 Uterovaginal prolapse, incomplete

618.3 Uterovaginal prolapse, complete

`618.4` Uterovaginal prolapse, unspecified

618.5 Prolapse of vaginal vault after hysterectomy

618.6 Vaginal enterocele, congenital or acquired
Pelvic enterocele, congenital or acquired

618.7 Old laceration of muscles of pelvic floor

`618.8` Other specified genital prolapse
Incompetence or weakening of pelvic fundus
Relaxation of vaginal outlet or pelvis

`618.9` Unspecified genital prolapse

`619` Fistula involving female genital tract

   Excludes: *vesicorectal and intestinovesical fistula (596.1)*

619.0 Urinary-genital tract fistula, female
Fistula: Fistula:
  cervicovesical   uteroureteric
  ureterovaginal   uterovesical
  urethrovaginal   vesicocervicovaginal
  urethrovesicovaginal vesicovaginal

619.1 Digestive-genital tract fistula, female
Fistula: Fistula:
  intestinouterine   rectovulval
  intestinovaginal   sigmoidovaginal
  rectovaginal   uterorectal

● Code new   ▲ Revision of   ④ ⑤ Fourth or fifth
  to this edition   existing code   digit required

619.2 Genital tract-skin fistula, female
Fistula:
uterus to abdominal wall
vaginoperineal

619.8 Other specified fistulas involving female genital tract
Fistula: Fistula:
cervix   uterus
cul-de-sac (Douglas') vagina

619.9 Unspecified fistula involving female genital tract

620 Noninflammatory disorders of ovary, fallopian tube, and broad ligament

> *Excludes:* hydrosalpinx (614.1)

620.0 Follicular cyst of ovary
Cyst of graafian follicle

620.1 Corpus luteum cyst or hematoma
Corpus luteum hemorrhage or rupture
Lutein cyst

620.2 Other and unspecified ovarian cyst
Cyst:
NOS
corpus albicans ⎫
retention NOS   ⎬ of ovary
serous   ⎪
theca-lutein   ⎭
Simple cystoma of ovary

> *Excludes:* cystadenoma (benign) (serous) (220)
> developmental cysts (752.0)
> neoplastic cysts (220)
> polycystic ovaries (256.4)
> Stein-Leventhal syndrome (256.4)

620.3 Acquired atrophy of ovary and fallopian tube
Senile involution of ovary

620.4 Prolapse or hernia of ovary and fallopian tube
Displacement of ovary and fallopian tube
Salpingocele

620.5 Torsion of ovary, ovarian pedicle, or fallopian tube
Torsion:
accessory tube
hydatid of Morgagni

620.6 Broad ligament laceration syndrome
Masters-Allen syndrome

620.7 Hematoma of broad ligament
Hematocele, broad ligament

620.8 Other noninflammatory disorders of ovary, fallopian tube, and broad ligament
Cyst   ⎫
Polyp   ⎬ of broad ligament or fallopian tube
Infarction ⎫
Rupture   ⎬ of ovary or fallopian tube
Hematosalpinx

> *Excludes:* hematosalpinx in ectopic pregnancy (639.2)
> peritubal adhesions (614.6)
> torsion of ovary, ovarian pedicle, or fallopian tube (620.5)

620.9 Unspecified noninflammatory disorder of ovary, fallopian tube, and broad ligament

621 Disorders of uterus, not elsewhere classified

621.0 Polyp of corpus uteri
Polyp:
endometrium
uterus NOS

> *Excludes:* cervical polyp NOS (622.7)

621.1 Chronic subinvolution of uterus

> *Excludes:* puerperal (674.8)

275

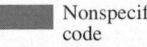 Add 4th or
5th digit

 Nonspecific
code

Unspecified
code

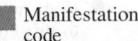 Manifestation
code

621.2 Hypertrophy of uterus
Bulky or enlarged uterus

Excludes: *puerperal (674.8)*

621.3 Endometrial cystic hyperplasia
Hyperplasia (adenomatous) (cystic) (glandular) of endometrium
Hyperplastic endometritis

621.4 Hematometra
Hemometra

Excludes: *that in congenital anomaly (752.2-752.3)*

621.5 Intrauterine synechiae
Adhesions of uterus   Band(s) of uterus

621.6 Malposition of uterus
Anteversion
Retroflexion   } of uterus
Retroversion

Excludes: *malposition complicating pregnancy, labor, or delivery (654.3-654.4)*
prolapse of uterus (618.1-618.4)

621.7 Chronic inversion of uterus

Excludes: *current obstetrical trauma (665.2)*
prolapse of uterus (618.1-618.4)

621.8 Other specified disorders of uterus, not elsewhere classified
Atrophy, acquired
Cyst
Fibrosis NOS   } of uterus
Old laceration (postpartum)
Ulcer

Excludes: *bilharzial fibrosis (120.0-120.9)*
endometriosis (617.0)
fistulas (619.0-619.8)
inflammatory diseases (615.0-615.9)

621.9 Unspecified disorder of uterus

622 Noninflammatory disorders of cervix

Excludes: *abnormality of cervix complicating pregnancy, labor, or delivery (654.5-654.6)*
fistula (619.0-619.8)

622.0 Erosion and ectropion of cervix
Eversion   } of cervix
Ulcer

Excludes: *that in chronic cervicitis (616.0)*

622.1 Dysplasia of cervix (uteri)
Anaplasia of cervix
Cervical atypism

Excludes: *carcinoma in situ of cervix (233.1)*
cervical intraepithelial neoplasia III [CIN III] (233.1)

622.2 Leukoplakia of cervix (uteri)

Excludes: *carcinoma in situ of cervix (233.1)*

622.3 Old laceration of cervix
Adhesions
Band(s)   } of cervix
Cicatrix (postpartum)

Excludes: *current obstetrical trauma (665.3)*

622.4 Stricture and stenosis of cervix
Atresia (acquired)
Contracture   } of cervix
Occlusion
Pinpoint os uteri

Excludes: *congenital (752.49)*
that complicating labor (654.6)

● Code new   ▲ Revision of   ④ ⑤ Fourth or fifth
to this edition   existing code   digit required

622.5 Incompetence of cervix

> Excludes: *complicating pregnancy (654.5)*
> *that affecting fetus or newborn (761.0)*

622.6 Hypertrophic elongation of cervix

622.7 Mucous polyp of cervix
Polyp NOS of cervix

> Excludes: *adenomatous polyp of cervix (219.0)*

622.8 Other specified noninflammatory disorders of cervix
Atrophy (senile)
Cyst
Fibrosis   } of cervix
Hemorrhage

> Excludes: *endometriosis (617.0)*
> *fistula (619.0-619.8)*
> *inflammatory diseases (616.0)*

622.9 Unspecified noninflammatory disorder of cervix

623 Noninflammatory disorders of vagina

> Excludes: *abnormality of vagina complicating pregnancy, labor, or delivery (654.7)*
> *congenital absence of vagina (752.49)*
> *congenital diaphragm or bands (752.49)*
> *fistulas involving vagina (619.0-619.8)*

623.0 Dysplasia of vagina

> Excludes: *carcinoma in situ of vagina (233.3)*

623.1 Leukoplakia of vagina

623.2 Stricture or atresia of vagina
Adhesions (postoperative) (postradiation) of vagina
Occlusion of vagina
Stenosis, vagina

Use additional E code, if desired, to identify any external cause

> Excludes: *congenital atresia or stricture (752.49)*

623.3 Tight hymenal ring
Rigid hymen
Tight hymenal ring } acquired or congenital
Tight introitus

> Excludes: *imperforate hymen (752.42)*

623.4 Old vaginal laceration

> Excludes: *old laceration involving muscles of pelvic floor (618.7)*

623.5 Leukorrhea, not specified as infective
Leukorrhea NOS of vagina   Vaginal discharge NOS

> Excludes: *trichomonal (131.00)*

623.6 Vaginal hematoma

> Excludes: *current obstetrical trauma (665.7)*

623.7 Polyp of vagina

623.8 Other specified noninflammatory disorders of vagina
Cyst
Hemorrhage } of vagina

623.9 Unspecified noninflammatory disorder of vagina

624 Noninflammatory disorders of vulva and perineum

> Excludes: *abnormality of vulva and perineum complicating pregnancy, labor, or delivery*
> *(654.8)*
> *condyloma acuminatum (078.1)*
> *fistulas involving:*
> *perineum—see Alphabetic Index*
> *vulva (619.0-619.8)*
> *vulval varices (456.6)*
> *vulvar involvement in skin conditions (690-709.9)*

	Add 4th or 5th digit		Nonspecific code		Unspecified code		Manifestation code

624.0 Dystrophy of vulva
Kraurosis
Leukoplakia } of vulva

Excludes: carcinoma in situ of vulva (233.3)

624.1 Atrophy of vulva

624.2 Hypertrophy of clitoris

Excludes: that in endocrine disorders (255.2, 256.1)

624.3 Hypertrophy of labia
Hypertrophy of vulva NOS

624.4 Old laceration or scarring of vulva

624.5 Hematoma of vulva

Excludes: that complicating delivery (664.5)

624.6 Polyp of labia and vulva

624.8 Other specified noninflammatory disorders of vulva and perineum
Cyst
Edema } of vulva
Stricture

624.9 Unspecified noninflammatory disorder of vulva and perineum

625 Pain and other symptoms associated with female genital organs

625.0 Dyspareunia

Excludes: psychogenic dyspareunia (302.76)

625.1 Vaginismus
Colpospasm   Vulvismus

Excludes: psychogenic vaginismus (306.51)

625.2 Mittelschmerz
Intermenstrual pain   Ovulation pain

625.3 Dysmenorrhea
Painful menstruation

Excludes: psychogenic dysmenorrhea (306.52)

625.4 Premenstrual tension syndromes
Menstrual: Premenstrual syndrome
  migraine   Premenstrual tension NOS
  molimen

625.5 Pelvic congestion syndrome
Congestion-fibrosis syndrome
Taylor's syndrome

625.6 Stress incontinence, female

Excludes: mixed incontinence (788.33)
        stress incontinence, male (788.32)

625.8 Other specified symptoms associated with female genital organs

625.9 Unspecified symptom associated with female genital organs

626 Disorders of menstruation and other abnormal bleeding from female genital tract

Excludes: menopausal and premenopausal bleeding (627.0)
        pain and other symptoms associated with menstrual cycle (625.2-625.4)
        postmenopausal bleeding (627.1)

626.0 Absence of menstruation
Amenorrhea (primary) (secondary)

626.1 Scanty or infrequent menstruation
Hypomenorrhea   Oligomenorrhea

626.2 Excessive or frequent menstruation
Heavy periods   Menorrhagia
Menometrorrhagia   Polymenorrhea

Excludes: premenopausal (627.0)
        that in puberty (626.3)

● Code new   ▲ Revision of   ④ ⑤ Fourth or fifth
  to this edition   existing code   digit required

626.3 Puberty bleeding
Excessive bleeding associated with onset of menstrual periods
Pubertal menorrhagia

626.4 Irregular menstrual cycle
Irregular:
  bleeding NOS
  menstruation
  periods

626.5 Ovulation bleeding
Regular intermenstrual bleeding

626.6 Metrorrhagia
Bleeding unrelated to menstrual cycle
Irregular intermenstrual bleeding

626.7 Postcoital bleeding

626.8 Other
Dysfunctional or functional uterine hemorrhage NOS
Menstruation:
  retained
  suppression of

626.9 Unspecified

627 Menopausal and postmenopausal disorders

627.0 Premenopausal menorrhagia
Excessive bleeding associated   Menorrhagia:
  with onset of menopause   climacteric
                                       menopausal
                                       preclimacteric

627.1 Postmenopausal bleeding

627.2 Menopausal or female climacteric states
Symptoms, such as flushing, sleeplessness, headache, lack of concentration, associated
with the menopause

627.3 Postmenopausal atrophic vaginitis
Senile (atrophic) vaginitis

627.4 States associated with artificial menopause
Postartificial menopause syndromes
Any condition classifiable to 627.1, 627.2, or 627.3 which follows induced menopause

627.8 Other specified menopausal and postmenopausal disorders

Excludes: premature menopause NOS (256.3)

627.9 Unspecified menopausal and postmenopausal disorder

628 Infertility, female
Includes: primary and secondary sterility

628.0 Associated with anovulation
Anovulatory cycle

Use additional code for any associated Stein-Leventhal syndrome (256.4)

628.1 Of pituitary-hypothalamic origin
Code first underlying cause, as:
  adiposogenital dystrophy (253.8)
  anterior pituitary disorder (253.0-253.4)

628.2 Of tubal origin
Infertility associated with congenital anomaly of tube
Tubal:
  block
  occlusion
  stenosis

Use additional code for any associated peritubal adhesions (614.6)

628.3 Of uterine origin
Infertility associated with congenital anomaly of uterus
Nonimplantation

Use additional code for any associated tuberculous endometritis (016.7)

	Add 4th or 5th digit		Nonspecific code		Unspecified code		Manifestation code

628.4 Of cervical or vaginal origin
Infertility associated with:
  anomaly of cervical mucus
  congenital structural anomaly
  dysmucorrhea

628.8 Of other specified origin

628.9 Of unspecified origin

629 Other disorders of female genital organs

629.0 Hematocele, female, not elsewhere classified

Excludes: *hematocele or hematoma:*
  broad ligament (620.7)
  fallopian tube (620.8)
  that associated with ectopic pregnancy (633.0-633.9)
  uterus (621.4)
  vagina (623.6)
  vulva (624.5)

629.1 Hydrocele, canal of Nuck
Cyst of canal of Nuck (acquired)

Excludes: *congenital (752.41)*

629.8 Other specified disorders of female genital organs

629.9 Unspecified disorder of female genital organs
Habitual aborter without current pregnancy

● Code new
  to this edition
▲ Revision of
  existing code
④ ⑤ Fourth or fifth
    digit required

11. COMPLICATIONS OF PREGNANCY, CHILDBIRTH, AND THE PUERPERIUM (630-677)

ECTOPIC AND MOLAR PREGNANCY (630-633)

Use additional code from category 639 to identify any complications

630 Hydatidiform mole
Trophoblastic disease NOS
Vesicular mole

> Excludes: *chorioadenoma (destruens) (236.1)*
> *chorionepithelioma (181)*
> *malignant hydatidiform mole (236.1)*

631 Other abnormal product of conception

Blighted ovum	Mole:
Mole:	fleshy
NOS	stone
carneous	

632 Missed abortion
Early fetal death before completion of 22 weeks' gestation with retention of dead fetus
Retained products of conception, not following spontaneous or induced abortion or delivery

> Excludes: *failed induced abortion (638.0-638.9)*
> *fetal death (intrauterine) (late) (656.4)*
> *missed delivery (656.4)*
> *that with abnormal product of conception (630, 631)*

633 Ectopic pregnancy
Includes: ruptured ectopic pregnancy

633.0 Abdominal pregnancy
Intraperitoneal pregnancy

633.1 Tubal pregnancy
Fallopian pregnancy
Rupture of (fallopian) tube due to pregnancy
Tubal abortion

633.2 Ovarian pregnancy

633.8 Other ectopic pregnancy

Pregnancy:	Pregnancy:
cervical	intraligamentous
combined	mesometric
cornual	mural

633.9 Unspecified ectopic pregnancy

OTHER PREGNANCY WITH ABORTIVE OUTCOME (634-639)

Note: Use the following fifth-digit subclassification with categories 634-637:

  0 Unspecified

  1 Incomplete

  2 Complete

The following fourth-digit subdivisions are for use with categories 634-638:

.0 Complicated by genital tract and pelvic infection
Endometritis
Salpingo-oophoritis
Sepsis NOS
Septicemia NOS
Any condition classifiable to 639.0, with condition classifiable to 634-638

> Excludes: *urinary tract infection (634-638 with .7)*

.1 Complicated by delayed or excessive hemorrhage
Afibrinogenemia
Defibrination syndrome
Intravascular hemolysis
Any condition classifiable to 639.1, with condition classifiable to 634-638

.2 Complicated by damage to pelvic organs and tissues
Laceration, perforation, or tear of:
  bladder
  uterus
Any condition classifiable to 639.2, with condition classifiable to 634-638

	Add 4th or 5th digit		Nonspecific code		Unspecified code		Manifestation code

    .3 Complicated by renal failure
       Oliguria
       Uremia
       Any condition classifiable to 639.3, with condition classifiable to 634-638

    .4 Complicated by metabolic disorder
       Electrolyte imbalance with conditions classifiable to 634-638

    .5 Complicated by shock
       Circulatory collapse
       Shock (postoperative) (septic)
       Any condition classifiable to 639.5, with condition classifiable to 634-638

    .6 Complicated by embolism
       Embolism:
        NOS
        amniotic fluid
        pulmonary
       Any condition classifiable to 639.6, with condition classifiable to 634-638

    .7 With other specified complications
       Cardiac arrest or failure
       Urinary tract infection
       Any condition classifiable to 639.8, with condition classifiable to 634-638

    .8 With unspecified complication

    .9 Without mention of complication

⑤ **634 Abortion**
      Includes: miscarriage
                spontaneous abortion

    634.0 Complicated by genital tract and pelvic infection

    634.1 Complicated by delayed or excessive hemorrhage

    634.2 Complicated by damage to pelvic organs or tissues

    634.3 Complicated by renal failure

    634.4 Complicated by metabolic disorder

    634.5 Complicated by shock

    634.6 Complicated by embolism

    634.7 With other specified complications

    634.8 With unspecified complication

    634.9 Without mention of complication

⑤ **635 Legally induced abortion**
      Includes: abortion or termination of pregnancy:
                elective
                legal
                therapeutic

    Excludes: *menstrual extraction or regulation (V25.3)*

    635.0 Complicated by genital tract and pelvic infection

    635.1 Complicated by delayed or excessive hemorrhage

    635.2 Complicated by damage to pelvic organs or tissues

    635.3 Complicated by renal failure

    635.4 Complicated by metabolic disorder

    635.5 Complicated by shock

    635.6 Complicated by embolism

    635.7 With other specified complications

    635.8 With unspecified complication

    635.9 Without mention of complication

⑤ **636 Illegally induced abortion**
      Includes: abortion:
                criminal
                illegal
                self-induced

    636.0 Complicated by genital tract and pelvic infection

    636.1 Complicated by delayed or excessive hemorrhage

    636.2 Complicated by damage to pelvic organs or tissues

● Code new   ▲ Revision of   ④ ⑤ Fourth or fifth
  to this edition   existing code   digit required

636.3　Complicated by renal failure

636.4　Complicated by metabolic disorder

636.5　Complicated by shock

636.6　Complicated by embolism

636.7　With other specified complications

636.8　With unspecified complication

636.9　Without mention of complication

⑤ **637**　Unspecified abortion
　　Includes:　abortion NOS
　　　　　　　retained products of conception following abortion, not classifiable elsewhere

637.0　Complicated by genital tract and pelvic infection

637.1　Complicated by delayed or excessive hemorrhage

637.2　Complicated by damage to pelvic organs or tissues

637.3　Complicated by renal failure

637.4　Complicated by metabolic disorder

637.5　Complicated by shock

637.6　Complicated by embolism

637.7　With other specified complications

637.8　With unspecified complication

637.9　Without mention of complication

638　Failed attempted abortion
　　Includes:　failure of attempted induction of (legal) abortion

　　Excludes: *incomplete abortion (634.0-637.9)*

638.0　Complicated by genital tract and pelvic infection

638.1　Complicated by delayed or excessive hemorrhage

638.2　Complicated by damage to pelvic organs or tissues

638.3　Complicated by renal failure

638.4　Complicated by metabolic disorder

638.5　Complicated by shock

638.6　Complicated by embolism

638.7　With other specified complications

638.8　With unspecified complication

638.9　Without mention of complication

639　Complications following abortion and ectopic and molar pregnancies

Note: This category is provided for use when it is required to classify separately the
　　complications classifiable to the fourth-digit level in categories 634-638; for example:
　　　　a)　when the complication itself was responsible for an episode of medical care, the
　　　　　　abortion, ectopic or molar pregnancy itself having been dealt with at a previous
　　　　　　episode
　　　　b)　when these conditions are immediate complications of ectopic or molar pregnancies
　　　　　　classifiable to 630-633 where they cannot be identified at fourth-digit level.

639.0　**Genital tract and pelvic infection**
　　　　Endometritis
　　　　Parametritis
　　　　Pelvic peritonitis
　　　　Salpingitis　　　　　　}　following conditions classifiable to 630-638
　　　　Salpingo-oophoritis
　　　　Sepsis NOS
　　　　Septicemia NOS

　　Excludes: *urinary tract infection (639.8)*

639.1　**Delayed or excessive hemorrhage**
　　　　Afibrinogenemia
　　　　Defibrination syndrome　}　following conditions classifiable to 630-638
　　　　Intravascular hemolysis

	Add 4th or 5th digit		Nonspecific code		Unspecified code		Manifestation code

639.2 **Damage to pelvic organs and tissues**
Laceration, perforation, or tear of:
bladder
bowel
broad ligament } following conditions classifiable
cervix to 630-638
periurethral tissue
uterus
vagina

639.3 **Renal failure**
Oliguria
Renal:
failure (acute) } following conditions classifiable to 630-638
shutdown
tubular necrosis
Uremia

639.4 **Metabolic disorders**
Electrolyte imbalance following conditions classifiable to 630-638

639.5 **Shock**
Circulatory collapse } following conditions classifiable
Shock (postoperative) (septic) to 630-638

639.6 **Embolism**
Embolism:
NOS
air
amniotic fluid
blood-clot
fat } following conditions classifiable to 630-638
pulmonary
pyemic
septic
soap

639.8 **Other specified complications following abortion or ectopic and molar pregnancy**
Acute yellow atrophy or necrosis of liver
Cardiac arrest or failure } following conditions classifiable
Cerebral anoxia to 630-638
Urinary tract infection

639.9 **Unspecified complication following abortion or ectopic and molar pregnancy**
Complication(s) not further specified following conditions classifiable to 630-638

COMPLICATIONS MAINLY RELATED TO PREGNANCY (640-648)

Includes: the listed conditions even if they arose or were present during labor, delivery, or the puerperium

The following fifth-digit subclassification is for use with categories 640-648 to denote the current episode of care:

0 **unspecified as to episode of care or not applicable**

1 **delivered, with or without mention of antepartum condition**
Antepartum condition with delivery
Delivery NOS
Intrapartum obstetric condition } (with mention of antepartum
Pregnancy, delivered complication during current episode of care)

2 **delivered, with mention of postpartum complication**
Delivery with mention of puerperal complication during current episode of care

3 **antepartum condition or complication**
Antepartum obstetric condition, not delivered during the current episode of care

4 **postpartum condition or complication**
Postpartum or puerperal obstetric condition or complication following delivery that occurred:
during previous episode of care
outside hospital, with subsequent admission for observation or care

⑤ **640** **Hemorrhage in early pregnancy**
Includes: hemorrhage before completion of 22 weeks' gestation

640.0 **Threatened abortion**
[0,1,3]

● Code new   ▲ Revision of   ④ ⑤ Fourth or fifth
to this edition   existing code   digit required

640.8 Other specified hemorrhage in early pregnancy
[0,1,3]

640.9 Unspecified hemorrhage in early pregnancy
[0,1,3]

⑤ **641** Antepartum hemorrhage, abruptio placentae, and placenta previa

641.0 Placenta previa without hemorrhage
[0,1,3]   Low implantation of placenta
Placenta previa noted:
  during pregnancy   } without hemorrhage
  before labor (and delivered by cesarean delivery)

641.1 Hemorrhage from placenta previa
[0,1,3]   Low-lying placenta
Placenta previa
  incomplete   } NOS or with hemorrhage (intrapartum)
  marginal
  partial
  total

> Excludes: hemorrhage from vasa previa (663.5)

641.2 Premature separation of placenta
[0,1,3]   Ablatio placentae
Abruptio placentae
Accidental antepartum hemorrhage
Couvelaire uterus
Detachment of placenta (premature)
Premature separation of normally implanted placenta

641.3 Antepartum hemorrhage associated with coagulation defects
[0,1,3]   Antepartum or intrapartum hemorrhage associated with:
  afibrinogenemia
  hyperfibrinolysis
  hypofibrinogenemia

641.8 Other antepartum hemorrhage
[0,1,3]   Antepartum or intrapartum hemorrhage associated with:
  trauma
  uterine leiomyoma

641.9 Unspecified antepartum hemorrhage
[0,1,3]   Hemorrhage:
  antepartum NOS
  intrapartum NOS
  of pregnancy NOS

⑤ **642** Hypertension complicating pregnancy, childbirth, and the puerperium

642.0 Benign essential hypertension complicating pregnancy, childbirth, and the puerperium
[0-4]   Hypertension:
  benign essential
  chronic NOS   } specified as complicating, or as a reason for obstetric
  essential   care during pregnancy, childbirth, or the puerperium
  pre-existing NOS

642.1 Hypertension secondary to renal disease, complicating pregnancy, childbirth, and the puerperium
[0-4]   Hypertension secondary to renal disease, specified as complicating, or as a reason for
  obstetric care during pregnancy, childbirth, or the puerperium

642.2 Other pre-existing hypertension complicating pregnancy, childbirth, and the puerperium
[0-4]   Hypertensive:
  heart and renal disease } specified as complicating, as a reason for obstetric care
  heart disease   during pregnancy, childbirth, or the puerperium
  renal disease
Malignant hypertension

642.3 Transient hypertension of pregnancy
[0-4]   Gestational hypertension
Transient hypertension, so described, in pregnancy, childbirth, or the puerperium

Add 4th or 5th digit   Nonspecific code   Unspecified code   Manifestation code

642.4 Mild or unspecified pre-eclampsia
[0-4] Hypertension in pregnancy, childbirth, or the puerperium, not specified as pre-existing, with either albuminuria or edema, or both; mild or unspecified

Pre-eclampsia: Toxemia (pre-eclamptic):
  NOS   NOS
  mild   mild

> *Excludes:* *albuminuria in pregnancy, without mention of hypertension (646.2)*
> *edema in pregnancy, without mention of hypertension (646.1)*

642.5 Severe pre-eclampsia
[0-4] Hypertension in pregnancy, childbirth, or the puerperium, not specified as pre-existing, with either albuminuria or edema, or both; specified as severe
Pre-eclampsia, severe
Toxemia (pre-eclamptic), severe

642.6 Eclampsia
[0-4] Toxemia:
  eclamptic
  with convulsions

642.7 Pre-eclampsia or eclampsia superimposed on pre-existing hypertension
[0-4] Conditions classifiable to 642.4-642.6, with conditions classifiable to 642.0-642.2

642.9 Unspecified hypertension complicating pregnancy, childbirth, or the puerperium
[0-4] Hypertension NOS, without mention of albuminuria or edema, complicating pregnancy, childbirth, or the puerperium

⑤ **643 Excessive vomiting in pregnancy**
Includes:
hyperemesis
vomiting: } arising during pregnancy
  persistent
  vicious
hyperemesis gravidarum

643.0 Mild hyperemesis gravidarum
[0,1,3] Hyperemesis gravidarum, mild or unspecified, starting before the end of the 22nd week of gestation

643.1 Hyperemesis gravidarum with metabolic disturbance
[0,1,3] Hyperemesis gravidarum, starting before the end of the 22nd week of gestation, with metabolic disturbance, such as:
carbohydrate depletion
dehydration
electrolyte imbalance

643.2 Late vomiting of pregnancy
[0,1,3] Excessive vomiting starting after 22 completed weeks of gestation

643.8 Other vomiting complicating pregnancy
[0,1,3] Vomiting due to organic disease or other cause, specified as complicating pregnancy, or as a reason for obstetric care during pregnancy
Use additional code, if desired, to specify cause

643.9 Unspecified vomiting of pregnancy
[0,1,3] Vomiting as a reason for care during pregnancy, length of gestation unspecified

⑤ **644 Early or threatened labor**

☐ **644.0 Threatened premature labor**
[0,3] Premature labor after 22 weeks, but before 37 completed weeks of gestation without delivery

> *Excludes:* *that occurring before 22 completed weeks of gestation (640.0)*

☐ **644.1 Other threatened labor**
[0,3] False labor:
  NOS
  after 37 completed weeks of gestation   }
Threatened labor NOS   without delivery

☐ **644.2 Early onset of delivery**
[0,1] Onset (spontaneous) of delivery   } before 37 completed weeks of
Premature labor with onset of delivery   gestation

⑤ **645 Prolonged pregnancy**
[0,1,3] Post-term pregnancy
Pregnancy which has advanced beyond 42 weeks of gestation
Use 0 as fourth-digit for this category

● Code new
to this edition

▲ Revision of
existing code

④ ⑤ Fourth or fifth
digit required

⑤ 646 Other complications of pregnancy, not elsewhere classified
Use additional code(s) to further specify complication

646.0 Papyraceous fetus
[0,1,3]

646.1 Edema or excessive weight gain in pregnancy, without mention of hypertension
[0-4]   Gestational edema
        Maternal obesity syndrome

Excludes: that with mention of hypertension (642.0-642.9)

646.2 Unspecified renal disease in pregnancy, without mention of hypertension
[0-4]   Albuminuria ⎫
        Nephropathy NOS ⎪
        Renal disease NOS ⎬ in pregnancy or the puerperium, without mention of hypertension
        Uremia ⎪
        Gestational proteinuria ⎭

Excludes: that with mention of hypertension (642.0-642.9)

646.3 Habitual aborter
[0,1,3]

Excludes: with current abortion (634.0-634.9)
          without current pregnancy (629.9)

646.4 Peripheral neuritis in pregnancy
[0-4]

646.5 Asymptomatic bacteriuria in pregnancy
[0-4]

646.6 Infections of genitourinary tract in pregnancy
[0-4]   Conditions classifiable to 590, 595, 597, 599.0, 616 complicating pregnancy, childbirth,
        or the puerperium
    Conditions classifiable to 614-615 complicating pregnancy or labor

Excludes: major puerperal infection (670)

646.7 Liver disorders in pregnancy
[0,1,3]   Acute yellow atrophy of liver (obstetric) (true) ⎫
       Icterus gravis ⎬ of pregnancy
       Necrosis of liver ⎭

Excludes: hepatorenal syndrome following delivery (674.8)
          viral hepatitis (647.6)

646.8 Other specified complications of pregnancy
[0-4]   Fatigue during pregnancy   Insufficient weight gain of pregnancy
        Herpes gestationis

646.9 Unspecified complication of pregnancy
[0,1,3]

⑤ 647 Infectious and parasitic conditions in the mother classifiable elsewhere, but complicating pregnancy, childbirth, or the puerperium
Includes: the listed conditions when complicating the pregnant state, aggravated by the
         pregnancy, or when a main reason for obstetric care

Excludes: those conditions in the mother known or suspected to have affected the fetus
        (655.0-655.9)

Use additional code(s) to further specify complication

647.0 Syphilis
[0-4]   Conditions classifiable to 090-097

647.1 Gonorrhea
[0-4]   Conditions classifiable to 098

647.2 Other venereal diseases
[0-4]   Conditions classifiable to 099

647.3 Tuberculosis
[0-4]   Conditions classifiable to 010-018

647.4 Malaria
[0-4]   Conditions classifiable to 084

647.5 Rubella
[0-4]   Conditions classifiable to 056

647.6 Other viral diseases
[0-4]   Conditions classifiable to 042 and 050-079, except 056

	Add 4th or 5th digit		Nonspecific code		Unspecified code		Manifestation code

647.8 **Other specified infectious and parasitic diseases**
[0-4]

647.9 **Unspecified infection or infestation**
[0-4]

⑤ **648** **Other current conditions in the mother classifiable elsewhere, but complicating pregnancy, childbirth, or the puerperium**
Includes: the listed conditions when complicating the pregnant state, aggravated by the pregnancy, or when a main reason for obstetric care

Excludes: *those conditions in the mother known or suspected to have affected the fetus (655.0-655.9)*

Use additional code(s) to identify the condition

648.0 **Diabetes mellitus**
[0-4]   Conditions classifiable to 250

Excludes: *gestational diabetes (648.8)*

648.1 **Thyroid dysfunction**
[0-4]   Conditions classifiable to 240-246

648.2 **Anemia**
[0-4]   Conditions classifiable to 280-285

648.3 **Drug dependence**
[0-4]   Conditions classifiable to 304

648.4 **Mental disorders**
[0-4]   Conditions classifiable to 290-303, 305-316, 317-319

648.5 **Congenital cardiovascular disorders**
[0-4]   Conditions classifiable to 745-747

648.6 **Other cardiovascular diseases**
[0-4]   Conditions classifiable to 390-398, 410-429

Excludes: *cerebrovascular disorders in the puerperium (674.0)*
venous complications (671.0-671.9)

648.7 **Bone and joint disorders of back, pelvis, and lower limbs**
[0-4]   Conditions classifiable to 720-724, and those classifiable to 711-719 or 725-738, specified as affecting the lower limbs

648.8 **Abnormal glucose tolerance**
[0-4]   Conditions classifiable to 790.2
Gestational diabetes

648.9 **Other current conditions classifiable elsewhere**
[0-4]   Conditions classifiable to 440-459
Nutritional deficiencies [conditions classifiable to 260-269]

NORMAL DELIVERY, AND OTHER INDICATIONS FOR CARE IN PREGNANCY, LABOR, AND DELIVERY (650-659)

The following fifth-digit subclassification is for use with categories 651-659 to denote the current episode of care:

0 **unspecified as to episode of care or not applicable**

1 **delivered, with or without mention of antepartum condition**

2 **delivered, with mention of postpartum complication**

3 **antepartum condition or complication**

4 **postpartum condition or complication**

650 **Normal delivery**
Delivery requiring minimal or no assistance, with or without episiotomy, without fetal manipulation [e.g., rotation version] or instrumentation [forceps] of spontaneous, cephalic, vaginal, full-term, single, live born infant. This code is for use as a single diagnosis code and is not to be used with any other code in the range 630-676.

Excludes: *breech delivery (assisted) (spontaneous) NOS (652.2)*
delivery by vacuum extractor, forceps, cesarean section, or breech extraction, without specified complication (669.5-669.7)

Use additional code to indicate outcome of delivery (V27.0)

● Code new   ▲ Revision of   ④ ⑤ Fourth or fifth
              to this edition   existing code   digit required

⑤ **651** **Multiple gestation**

651.0 **Twin pregnancy**
[0,1,3]

651.1 **Triplet pregnancy**
[0,1,3]

651.2 **Quadruplet pregnancy**
[0,1,3]

651.3 **Twin pregnancy with fetal loss and retention of one fetus**
[0,1,3]

651.4 **Triplet pregnancy with fetal loss and retention of one or more fetus(es)**
[0,1,3]

651.5 **Quadruplet pregnancy with fetal loss and retention of one or more fetus(es)**
[0,1,3]

651.6 **Other multiple pregnancy with fetal loss and retention of one or more fetus(es)**
[0,1,3]

651.8 **Other specified multiple gestation**
[0,1,3]

651.9 **Unspecified multiple gestation**
[0,1,3]

⑤ **652** **Malposition and malpresentation of fetus**
Code first any associated obstructed labor (660.0)

652.0 **Unstable lie**
[0,1,3]

652.1 **Breech or other malpresentation successfully converted to cephalic presentation**
[0,1,3]   Cephalic version NOS

652.2 **Breech presentation without mention of version**
[0,1,3]   Breech delivery (assisted) (spontaneous) NOS

652.3 **Transverse or oblique presentation**
[0,1,3]   Oblique lie   Transverse lie

> *Excludes:* transverse arrest of fetal head (660.3)

652.4 **Face or brow presentation**
[0,1,3]   Mentum presentation

652.5 **High head at term**
[0,1,3]   Failure of head to enter pelvic brim

652.6 **Multiple gestation with malpresentation of one fetus or more**
[0,1,3]

652.7 **Prolapsed arm**
[0,1,3]

652.8 **Other specified malposition or malpresentation**
[0,1,3]   Compound presentation

652.9 **Unspecified malposition or malpresentation**
[0,1,3]

⑤ **653** **Disproportion**
Code first any associated obstructed labor (660.1)

653.0 **Major abnormality of bony pelvis, not further specified**
[0,1,3]   Pelvic deformity NOS

653.1 **Generally contracted pelvis**
[0,1,3]   Contracted pelvis NOS

653.2 **Inlet contraction of pelvis**
[0,1,3]   Inlet contraction (pelvis)

653.3 **Outlet contraction of pelvis**
[0,1,3]   Outlet contraction (pelvis)

653.4 **Fetopelvic disproportion**
[0,1,3]   Cephalopelvic disproportion NOS
             Disproportion of mixed maternal and fetal origin, with normally formed fetus

	Add 4th or 5th digit		Nonspecific code		Unspecified code		Manifestation code

653.5 Unusually large fetus causing disproportion
[0,1,3]   Disproportion of fetal origin with normally formed fetus
        Fetal disproportion NOS

> Excludes: *that when the reason for medical care was concern for the fetus (656.6)*

653.6 Hydrocephalic fetus causing disproportion
[0,1,3]

> Excludes: *that when the reason for medical care was concern for the fetus (655.0)*

653.7   Other fetal abnormality causing disproportion
[0,1,3]   Conjoined twins   Fetal:
        Fetal: myelomeningocele
          ascites   sacral teratoma
          hydrops   tumor

653.8   Disproportion of other origin
[0,1,3]

> Excludes: *shoulder (girdle) dystocia (660.4)*

653.9   Unspecified disproportion
[0,1,3]

⑤ **654   Abnormality of organs and soft tissues of pelvis**
        Includes: the listed conditions during pregnancy, childbirth, or the puerperium
        Code first any associated obstructed labor (660.2)

654.0 Congenital abnormalities of uterus
[0-4]   Double uterus   Uterus bicornis

654.1 Tumors of body of uterus
[0-4]   Uterine fibroids

654.2 Previous cesarean delivery NOS
[0,1,3] Uterine scar from previous cesarean delivery

654.3 Retroverted and incarcerated gravid uterus
[0-4]

654.4   Other abnormalities in shape or position of gravid uterus and of neighboring structures
[0-4]   Cystocele   Prolapse of gravid uterus
        Pelvic floor repair   Rectocele
        Pendulous abdomen   Rigid pelvic floor

654.5 Cervical incompetence
[0-4]   Presence of Shirodkar suture with or without mention of cervical incompetence

654.6   Other congenital or acquired abnormality of cervix
[0-4]   Cicatricial cervix   Stenosis or stricture of cervix
        Polyp of cervix   Tumor of cervix
        Previous surgery to cervix
        Rigid cervix (uteri)

654.7 Congenital or acquired abnormality of vagina
[0-4]   Previous surgery to vagina   Stricture of vagina
        Septate vagina   Tumor of vagina
        Stenosis of vagina (acquired)
          (congenital)

654.8 Congenital or acquired abnormality of vulva
[0-4]   Fibrosis of perineum
        Persistent hymen
        Previous surgery to perineum or vulva
        Rigid perineum
        Tumor of vulva

> Excludes: *varicose veins of vulva (671.1)*

654.9   Other and unspecified
[0-4]   Uterine scar NEC

● Code new   ▲ Revision of   ④ ⑤ Fourth or fifth
  to this edition   existing code   digit required

⑤ **655 Known or suspected fetal abnormality affecting management of mother**
> Includes: the listed conditions in the fetus as a reason for observation or obstetrical care of the
> mother, or for termination of pregnancy

655.0 Central nervous system malformation in fetus
[0,1,3]
> Fetal or suspected fetal:
>> anencephaly
>> hydrocephalus
>> spina bifida (with myelomeningocele)

655.1 Chromosomal abnormality in fetus
[0,1,3]

655.2 Hereditary disease in family possibly affecting fetus
[0,1,3]

655.3 Suspected damage to fetus from viral disease in the mother
[0,1,3]
> Suspected damage to fetus from maternal rubella

655.4 Suspected damage to fetus from other disease in the mother
[0,1,3]
> Suspected damage to fetus from maternal:
>> alcohol addiction
>> listeriosis
>> toxoplasmosis

655.5 Suspected damage to fetus from drugs
[0,1,3]

> *Excludes:* fetal distress in labor and delivery due to drug administration (656.3)

655.6 Suspected damage to fetus from radiation
[0,1,3]

655.8 Other known or suspected fetal abnormality, not elsewhere classified
[0,1,3]
> Suspected damage to fetus from:
>> environmental toxins
>> intrauterine contraceptive device

655.9 Unspecified
[0,1,3]

⑤ **656 Other fetal and placental problems affecting management of mother**

656.0 Fetal-maternal hemorrhage
[0,1,3]
> Leakage (microscopic) of fetal blood into maternal circulation

656.1 Rhesus isoimmunization
[0,1,3]
> Anti-D [Rh] antibodies
> Rh incompatibility

656.2 Isoimmunization from other and unspecified blood-group incompatibility
[0,1,3]
> ABO isoimmunization

656.3 Fetal distress
[0,1,3]
> Abnormal fetal:
>> acid-base balance
>> heart rate or rhythm
> Fetal:
>> acidemia
>> bradycardia
>> tachycardia
> Meconium in liquor

656.4 Intrauterine death
[0,1,3]
> Fetal death:
>> NOS
>> after completion of 22 weeks' gestation
>> late
> Missed delivery

> *Excludes:* missed abortion (632)

656.5 Poor fetal growth
[0,1,3]
> "Light-for-dates"   "Small-for-dates"
> "Placental insufficiency"

656.6 Excessive fetal growth
[0,1,3]
> "Large-for-dates"

| | Add 4th or 5th digit | | Nonspecific code | | Unspecified code | | Manifestation code |

656.7 **Other placental conditions**
[0,1,3] Abnormal placenta   Placental infarct

> *Excludes:* placental polyp (674.4)
>   placentitis (658.4)

656.8 **Other specified fetal and placental problems**
[0,1,3] Lithopedian

656.9 **Unspecified fetal and placental problem**
[0,1,3]

⑤ **657** **Polyhydramnios**
[0,1,3] Hydramnios
Use 0 as fourth-digit for this category

⑤ **658** **Other problems associated with amniotic cavity and membranes**

> *Excludes:* amniotic fluid embolism (673.1)

658.0 **Oligohydramnios**
[0,1,3] Oligohydramnios without mention of rupture of membranes

658.1 **Premature rupture of membranes**
[0,1,3] Rupture of amniotic sac less than 24 hours prior to the onset of labor

658.2 **Delayed delivery after spontaneous or unspecified rupture of membranes**
[0,1,3] Prolonged rupture of membranes NOS
Rupture of amniotic sac 24 hours or more prior to the onset of labor

658.3 **Delayed delivery after artificial rupture of membranes**
[0,1,3]

658.4 **Infection of amniotic cavity**
[0,1,3] Amnionitis   Membranitis
Chorioamnionitis   Placentitis

658.8 **Other**
[0,1,3] Amnion nodosum
Amniotic cyst

658.9 **Unspecified**
[0,1,3]

⑤ **659** **Other indications for care or intervention related to labor and delivery, not elsewhere classified**

659.0 **Failed mechanical induction**
[0,1,3] Failure of induction of labor by surgical or other instrumental methods

659.1 **Failed medical or unspecified induction**
[0,1,3] Failed induction NOS
Failure of induction of labor by medical methods, such as oxytocic drugs

659.2 **Maternal pyrexia during labor, unspecified**
[0,1,3]

659.3 **Generalized infection during labor**
[0,1,3] Septicemia during labor

659.4 **Grand multiparity**
[0,1,3]

> *Excludes:* supervision only, in pregnancy (V23.3)
>   without current pregnancy (V61.5)

659.5 **Elderly primigravida**
[0,1,3]

> *Excludes:* supervision only, in pregnancy (V23.8)

659.6 **Other advanced maternal age**
[0,1,3]

> *Excludes:* elderly primigravida 659.5

659.8 **Other specified indications for care or intervention related to labor and delivery**
[0,1,3]

659.9 **Unspecified indication for care or intervention related to labor and delivery**
[0,1,3]

● Code new   ▲ Revision of   ④ ⑤ Fourth or fifth
  to this edition   existing code   digit required

COMPLICATIONS OCCURRING MAINLY IN THE COURSE OF LABOR AND DELIVERY (660-669)

The following fifth-digit subclassification is for use with categories 660-669 to denote the current episode of care:

0 unspecified as to episode of care or not applicable

1 delivered, with or without mention of antepartum condition

2 delivered, with mention of postpartum complication

3 antepartum condition or complication

4 postpartum condition or complication

⑤ **660** Obstructed labor

660.0 Obstruction caused by malposition of fetus at onset of labor
[0,1,3]   Any condition classifiable to 652, causing obstruction during labor
Use additional code from 652.0-652.9, if desired, to identify condition

660.1 Obstruction by bony pelvis
[0,1,3]   Any condition classifiable to 653, causing obstruction during labor
Use additional code from 653.0-653.9, if desired, to identify condition

660.2 Obstruction by abnormal pelvic soft tissues
[0,1,3]   Prolapse of anterior lip of cervix
Any condition classifiable to 654, causing obstruction during labor
Use additional code from 654.0-654.9, if desired, to identify condition

660.3 Deep transverse arrest and persistent occipitoposterior position
[0,1,3]

660.4 Shoulder (girdle) dystocia
[0,1,3]   Impacted shoulders

660.5 Locked twins
[0,1,3]

660.6 Failed trial of labor, unspecified
[0,1,3]   Failed trial of labor, without mention of condition or suspected condition

660.7 Failed forceps or vacuum extractor, unspecified
[0,1,3]   Application of ventouse or forceps, without mention of condition

660.8 Other causes of obstructed labor
[0,1,3]

660.9 Unspecified obstructed labor
[0,1,3]   Dystocia:
NOS
fetal NOS
maternal NOS

⑤ **661** Abnormality of forces of labor

661.0 Primary uterine inertia
[0,1,3]   Failure of cervical dilation
Hypotonic uterine dysfunction, primary
Prolonged latent phase of labor

661.1 Secondary uterine inertia
[0,1,3]   Arrested active phase of labor
Hypotonic uterine dysfunction, secondary

661.2 Other and unspecified uterine inertia
[0,1,3]   Atony of uterus   Poor contractions
Desultory labor   Slow slope active phase of labor
Irregular labor

661.3 Precipitate labor
[0,1,3]

661.4 Hypertonic, incoordinate, or prolonged uterine contractions
[0,1,3]   Cervical spasm   Incoordinate uterine action
Contraction ring (dystocia)   Retraction ring (Bandl's) (pathological)
Dyscoordinate labor   Tetanic contractions
Hourglass contraction of   Uterine dystocia NOS
uterus   Uterine spasm
Hypertonic uterine dysfunction

661.9 Unspecified abnormality of labor
[0,1,3]

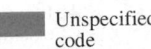 Add 4th or 5th digit   Nonspecific code   Unspecified code   Manifestation code

⑤ **662 Long labor**

> **662.0 Prolonged first stage**
> [0,1,3]

> **662.1 Prolonged labor, unspecified**
> [0,1,3]

> **662.2 Prolonged second stage**
> [0,1,3]

> **662.3 Delayed delivery of second twin, triplet, etc.**
> [0,1,3]

⑤ **663 Umbilical cord complications**

> **663.0 Prolapse of cord**
> [0,1,3]   Presentation of cord

> **663.1 Cord around neck, with compression**
> [0,1,3]   Cord tightly around neck

> **663.2 Other and unspecified cord entanglement, with compression**
> [0,1,3]   Entanglement of cords of twins in mono-amniotic sac
>   Knot in cord (with compression)

> **663.3 Other and unspecified cord entanglement, without mention of compression**
> [0,1,3]

> **663.4 Short cord**
> [0,1,3]

> **663.5 Vasa previa**
> [0,1,3]   Velamentous insertion of umbilical cord

> **663.6 Vascular lesions of cord**
> [0,1,3]   Bruising of cord   Thrombosis of vessels of cord
>   Hematoma of cord

> **663.8 Other umbilical cord complications**
> [0,1,3]

> **663.9 Unspecified umbilical cord complication**
> [0,1,3]

⑤ **664 Trauma to perineum and vulva during delivery**
> Includes: damage from instruments
>   that from extension of episiotomy

> **664.0 First-degree perineal laceration**
> [0,1,4]   Perineal laceration, rupture, or tear involving:
>   fourchette
>   hymen
>   labia
>   skin
>   vagina
>   vulva

> **664.1 Second-degree perineal laceration**
> [0,1,4]   Perineal laceration, rupture, or tear (following episiotomy) involving:
>   pelvic floor
>   perineal muscles
>   vaginal muscles
>
> Excludes: *that involving anal sphincter (664.2)*

> **664.2 Third-degree perineal laceration**
> [0,1,4]   Perineal laceration, rupture, or tear (following episiotomy) involving:
>   anal sphincter
>   rectovaginal septum
>   sphincter NOS
>
> Excludes: *that with anal or rectal mucosal laceration (664.3)*

> **664.3 Fourth-degree perineal laceration**
> [0,1,4]   Perineal laceration, rupture, or tear as classifiable to 664.2 and involving also:
>   anal mucosa
>   rectal mucosa

> **664.4 Unspecified perineal laceration**
> [0,1,4]   Central laceration

> **664.5 Vulval and perineal hematoma**
> [0,1,4]

● Code new
  to this edition

▲ Revision of
  existing code

④ ⑤ Fourth or fifth
   digit required

664.8 Other specified trauma to perineum and vulva
[0,1,4]

664.9 Unspecified trauma to perineum and vulva
[0,1,4]

⑤ **665** Other obstetrical trauma
Includes: damage from instruments

665.0 Rupture of uterus before onset of labor
[0,1,3]

665.1 Rupture of uterus during labor
[0,1] Rupture of uterus NOS

665.2 Inversion of uterus
[0,2,4]

665.3 Laceration of cervix
[0,1,4]

665.4 High vaginal laceration
[0,1,4] Laceration of vaginal wall or sulcus without mention of perineal laceration

665.5 Other injury to pelvic organs
[0,1,4] Injury to:
bladder
urethra

665.6 Damage to pelvic joints and ligaments
[0,1,4] Avulsion of inner symphyseal cartilage
Damage to coccyx
Separation of symphysis (pubis)

665.7 Pelvic hematoma
[0,1,2,4] Hematoma of vagina

665.8 Other specified obstetrical trauma
[0-4]

665.9 Unspecified obstetrical trauma
[0-4]

⑤ **666** Postpartum hemorrhage

666.0 Third-stage hemorrhage
[0,2,4] Hemorrhage associated with retained, trapped, or adherent placenta
Retained placenta NOS

666.1 Other immediate postpartum hemorrhage
[0,2,4] Hemorrhage within the first 24 hours following delivery of placenta
Postpartum hemorrhage (atonic) NOS

666.2 Delayed and secondary postpartum hemorrhage
[0,2,4] Hemorrhage:
after the first 24 hours following delivery
associated with retained portions of placenta or membranes
Postpartum hemorrhage specified as delayed or secondary
Retained products of conception NOS, following delivery

666.3 Postpartum coagulation defects
[0,2,4] Postpartum:
afibrinogenemia
fibrinolysis

⑤ **667** Retained placenta or membranes, without hemorrhage

667.0 Retained placenta without hemorrhage
[0,2,4] Placenta accreta
Retained placenta: ⎱ without hemorrhage
NOS
total

667.1 Retained portions of placenta or membranes, without hemorrhage
[0,2,4] Retained products of conception following delivery, without hemorrhage

⑤ **668** Complications of the administration of anesthetic or other sedation in labor and delivery
Includes: complications arising from the administration of a general or local anesthetic,
analgesic, or other sedation in labor and delivery

Excludes:	reaction to spinal or lumbar puncture (349.0)
	spinal headache (349.0)

Use additional code(s) to further specify complication

295

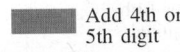 Add 4th or
5th digit

 Nonspecific
code

 Unspecified
code

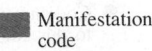 Manifestation
code

668.0 Pulmonary complications
[0-4]   Inhalation [aspiration] of stomach contents or
          secretions   } following anesthesia or other
          Mendelson's syndrome   sedation in labor or delivery
          Pressure collapse of lung

668.1 Cardiac complications
[0-4]   Cardiac arrest or failure following anesthesia or other sedation in labor and delivery

668.2 Central nervous system complications
[0-4]   Cerebral anoxia following anesthesia or other sedation in labor and delivery

668.8 Other complications of anesthesia or other sedation in labor and delivery
[0-4]

668.9 Unspecified complication of anesthesia and other sedation
[0-4]

⑤ **669 Other complications of labor and delivery, not elsewhere classified**

669.0 Maternal distress
[0-4]   Metabolic disturbance in labor and delivery

669.1 Shock during or following labor and delivery
[0-4]   Obstetric shock

669.2 Maternal hypotension syndrome
[0-4]

669.3 Acute renal failure following labor and delivery
[0,2,4]

669.4 Other complications of obstetrical surgery and procedures
[0-4]   Cardiac:
          arrest   } following cesarean or other obstetrical surgery or
          failure   procedure, including delivery NOS
          Cerebral anoxia

   Excludes: complications of obstetrical surgical wounds (674.1-674.3)

669.5 Forceps or vacuum extractor delivery without mention of indication
[0,1]   Delivery by ventouse, without mention of indication

669.6 Breech extraction, without mention of indication
[0,1]

   Excludes: breech delivery NOS (652.2)

669.7 Cesarean delivery, without mention of indication
[0,1]

669.8 Other complications of labor and delivery
[0-4]

669.9 Unspecified complication of labor and delivery
[0-4]

COMPLICATIONS OF THE PUERPERIUM (670-677)

Note: Categories 671 and 673-676 include the listed conditions even if they occur during
      pregnancy or childbirth.

The following fifth-digit subclassification is for use with categories 670-676 to denote the
      current episode of care:

   0 unspecified as to episode of care or not applicable
   1 delivered, with or without mention of antepartum condition
   2 delivered, with mention of postpartum complication
   3 antepartum condition or complication
   4 postpartum condition or complication

● Code new   ▲ Revision of   ④ ⑤ Fourth or fifth
  to this edition   existing code   digit required

⑤ **670 Major puerperal infection**
[0,2,4]   Puerperal: Puerperal:
          endometritis   peritonitis
          fever   pyemia
          pelvic: salpingitis
            cellulitis   septicemia
            sepsis
       Use 0 as fourth-digit for this category

   Excludes: *infection following abortion (639.0)*
              minor genital tract infection following delivery (646.6)
              urinary tract infection following delivery (646.6)

⑤ **671 Venous complications in pregnancy and the puerperium**

   671.0 Varicose veins of legs
   [0-4]   Varicose veins NOS

   671.1 Varicose veins of vulva and perineum
   [0-4]

   671.2 Superficial thrombophlebitis
   [0-4]   Thrombophlebitis (superficial)

   671.3 Deep phlebothrombosis, antepartum
   [0,1,3]   Deep-vein thrombosis, antepartum

   671.4 Deep phlebothrombosis, postpartum
   [0,2,4]   Deep-vein thrombosis, postpartum
             Pelvic thrombophlebitis, postpartum
             Phlegmasia alba dolens (puerperal)

   671.5 Other phlebitis and thrombosis
   [0-4]   Cerebral venous thrombosis
             Thrombosis of intracranial venous sinus

   671.8 Other venous complications
   [0-4]   Hemorrhoids

   671.9 Unspecified venous complication
   [0-4]   Phlebitis NOS
             Thrombosis NOS

⑤ **672 Pyrexia of unknown origin during the puerperium**
   [0,2,4]   Puerperal pyrexia NOS
       Use 0 as fourth-digit for this category

⑤ **673 Obstetrical pulmonary embolism**
       Includes: pulmonary emboli in pregnancy, childbirth, or the puerperium, or specified as
                  puerperal

   Excludes: *embolism following abortion (639.6)*

   673.0 Obstetrical air embolism
   [0-4]

   673.1 Amniotic fluid embolism
   [0-4]

   673.2 Obstetrical blood-clot embolism
   [0-4]   Puerperal pulmonary embolism NOS

   673.3 Obstetrical pyemic and septic embolism
   [0-4]

   673.8 Other pulmonary embolism
   [0-4]   Fat embolism

⑤ **674 Other and unspecified complications of the puerperium, not elsewhere classified**

   674.0 Cerebrovascular disorders in the puerperium
   [0-4]   Any condition classifiable to 430-434, 436-437 occurring during pregnancy, childbirth, or
             the puerperium, or specified as puerperal

   Excludes: *intracranial venous sinus thrombosis (671.5)*

   674.1 Disruption of cesarean wound
   [0,2,4]   Dehiscence or disruption of uterine wound

   674.2 Disruption of perineal wound
   [0,2,4]   Breakdown of perineum   Secondary perineal tear
             Disruption of wound of:
               episiotomy
               perineal laceration

▓	Add 4th or 5th digit	▓	Nonspecific code	▓	Unspecified code	▓	Manifestation code

297

674.3 **Other complications of obstetrical surgical wounds**
[0,2,4]   Hematoma
          Hemorrhage   } of cesarean section or perineal wound
          Infection

Excludes: damage from instruments in delivery (664.0-665.9)

674.4 **Placental polyp**
[0,2,4]

674.8 **Other**
[0,2,4]   Hepatorenal syndrome, following delivery
          Postpartum:
            cardiomyopathy
            subinvolution of uterus
            uterine hypertrophy

674.9 **Unspecified**
[0,2,4]   Sudden death of unknown cause during the puerperium

⑤ **675** **Infections of the breast and nipple associated with childbirth**
       Includes: the listed conditions during pregnancy, childbirth, or the puerperium

675.0 **Infections of nipple**
[0-4]   Abscess of nipple

675.1 **Abscess of breast**
[0-4]   Abscess: Mastitis:
            mammary   purulent
            subareolar   retromammary
            submammary   submammary

675.2 **Nonpurulent mastitis**
[0-4]   Lymphangitis of breast   Mastitis:
                                      NOS
                                      interstitial
                                      parenchymatous

675.8 **Other specified infections of the breast and nipple**
[0-4]

675.9 **Unspecified infection of the breast and nipple**
[0-4]

⑤ **676** **Other disorders of the breast associated with childbirth and disorders of lactation**
       Includes: the listed conditions during pregnancy, the puerperium, or lactation

676.0 **Retracted nipple**
[0-4]

676.1 **Cracked nipple**
[0-4]   Fissure of nipple

676.2 **Engorgement of breasts**
[0-4]

676.3 **Other and unspecified disorder of breast**
[0-4]

676.4 **Failure of lactation**
[0-4]   Agalactia

676.5 **Suppressed lactation**
[0-4]

676.6 **Galactorrhea**
[0-4]

Excludes: galactorrhea not associated with childbirth (611.6)

676.8 **Other disorders of lactation**
[0-4]   Galactocele

676.9 **Unspecified disorder of lactation**
[0-4]

677 **Late effect of complication of pregnancy, childbirth, and the puerperium**
       Note: This category is to be used to indicate conditions in 632-648.9 and 651-676.9 as the cause
           of the late effect, themselves classifiable elsewhere. The "late effects" include conditions
           specified as such, or as sequelae, which may occur at any time after the puerperium.
       Code first any sequelae

● Code new   ▲ Revision of   ④ ⑤ Fourth or fifth
         to this edition   existing code   digit required

12.   DISEASES OF THE SKIN AND SUBCUTANEOUS TISSUE (680-709)

INFECTIONS OF SKIN AND SUBCUTANEOUS TISSUE (680-686)

Excludes: *certain infections of skin classified under "Infectious and Parasitic Diseases," such
as:*
erysipelas (035)
erysipeloid of Rosenbach (027.1)
herpes:
  simplex (054.0-054.9)
  zoster (053.0-053.9)
molluscum contagiosum (078.0)
viral warts (078.1)

680   Carbuncle and furuncle
Includes: boil
            furunculosis

680.0   Face
Ear [any part]
Face [any part, except eye]
Nose (septum)
Temple (region)

Excludes: *eyelid (373.13)*
          lacrimal apparatus (375.31)
          orbit (376.01)

680.1   Neck

680.2   Trunk
Abdominal wall	Flank
Back [any part, except	Groin
buttocks]	Pectoral region
Breast	Perineum
Chest wall	Umbilicus

Excludes: *buttocks (680.5)*
          external genital organs:
          female (616.4)
          male (607.2, 608.4)

680.3   Upper arm and forearm
Arm [any part, except hand]
Axilla
Shoulder

680.4   Hand
Finger [any]   Wrist
Thumb

680.5   Buttock
Anus   Gluteal region

680.6   Leg, except foot
Ankle   Knee
Hip   Thigh

680.7   Foot
Heel   Toe

680.8   Other specified sites
Head [any part, except face]
Scalp

Excludes: *external genital organs:*
          female (616.4)
          male (607.2, 608.4)

680.9   Unspecified site
Boil NOS   Furuncle NOS
Carbuncle NOS

681   Cellulitis and abscess of finger and toe
Includes: that with lymphangitis
Use additional code, if desired, to identify organism, such as Staphylococcus (041.1)

681.0   Finger
681.00   Cellulitis and abscess, unspecified

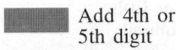 Add 4th or
5th digit

 Nonspecific
code

 Unspecified
code

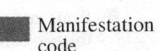 Manifestation
code

681.01 Felon
Pulp abscess   Whitlow

Excludes: *herpetic whitlow (054.6)*

681.02 Onychia and paronychia of finger
Panaritium ⎤
Perionychia ⎦ of finger

681.1 Toe

681.10 Cellulitis and abscess, unspecified

681.11 Onychia and paronychia of toe
Panaritium ⎤
Perionychia ⎦ of toe

681.9 Cellulitis and abscess of unspecified digit
Infection of nail NOS

682 Other cellulitis and abscess
Includes:

abscess (acute) ⎤
cellulitis (diffuse) ⎬ (with lymphangitis) except of finger or toe
lymphangitis, acute ⎦

Use additional code, if desired, to identify organism, such as Staphylococcus (041.1)

Excludes: *lymphangitis (chronic) (subacute) (457.2)*

682.0 Face
Cheek, external   Nose, external
Chin   Submandibular
Forehead   Temple (region)

Excludes: *ear [any part] (380.10-380.16)*
eyelid (373.13)
lacrimal apparatus (375.31)
lip (528.5)
mouth (528.3)
nose (internal) (478.1)
orbit (376.01)

682.1 Neck

682.2 Trunk
Abdominal wall   Groin
Back [any part, except   Pectoral region
   buttock]   Perineum
Chest wall   Umbilicus, except newborn
Flank

Excludes: *anal and rectal regions (566)*
breast:
NOS (611.0)
puerperal (675.1)
external genital organs:
female (616.3-616.4)
male (604.0, 607.2, 608.4)
umbilicus, newborn (771.4)

682.3 Upper arm and forearm
Arm [any part, except hand]
Axilla
Shoulder

Excludes: *hand (682.4)*

682.4 Hand, except fingers and thumb
Wrist

Excludes: *finger and thumb (681.00-681.02)*

682.5 Buttock
Gluteal region

Excludes: *anal and rectal regions (566)*

682.6 Leg, except foot
Ankle   Knee
Hip   Thigh

● Code new   ▲ Revision of   ④ ⑤ Fourth or fifth
   to this edition   existing code   digit required

682.7 Foot, except toes
  Heel

Excludes: *toe (681.10-681.11)*

682.8 Other specified sites
  Head [except face]   Scalp

Excludes: *face (682.0)*

682.9 Unspecified site
  Abscess NOS   Lymphangitis, acute NOS
  Cellulitis NOS

Excludes: *lymphangitis NOS (457.2)*

683 Acute lymphadenitis
  Abscess (acute)
  Adenitis, acute   } lymph gland or node, except mesenteric
  Lymphadenitis, acute

Use additional code, if desired, to identify organism, such as Staphylococcus (041.1)

Excludes: *enlarged glands NOS (785.6)*
          lymphadenitis:
            chronic or subacute, except mesenteric (289.1)
            mesenteric (acute) (chronic) (subacute) (289.2)
            unspecified (289.3)

684 Impetigo
  Impetiginization of other dermatoses
  Impetigo (contagiosa) [any site] [any organism]:
    bullous
    circinate
    neonatorum
    simplex
  Pemphigus neonatorum

Excludes: *impetigo herpetiformis (694.3)*

685 Pilonidal cyst
  Includes:
            fistula   }
            sinus   } coccygeal or pilonidal

685.0 With abscess

685.1 Without mention of abscess

686 Other local infections of skin and subcutaneous tissue
  Use additional code, if desired, to identify any infectious organism (041.0-041.8)

686.0 Pyoderma
  Dermatitis:
    purulent
    septic
    suppurative

686.1 Pyogenic granuloma
  Granuloma:
    septic
    suppurative
    telangiectaticum

Excludes: *pyogenic granuloma of oral mucosa (528.9)*

686.8 Other specified local infections of skin and subcutaneous tissue
  Bacterid (pustular)   Ecthyma
  Dermatitis vegetans   Perlèche

Excludes: *dermatitis infectiosa eczematoides (690.8)*
          panniculitis (729.30-729.39)

686.9 Unspecified local infection of skin and subcutaneous tissue
  Fistula of skin NOS   Skin infection NOS

Excludes: *fistula to skin from internal organs—see Alphabetic Index*

OTHER INFLAMMATORY CONDITIONS OF SKIN AND SUBCUTANEOUS TISSUE (690-698)

Excludes: *panniculitis (729.30-729.39)*

	Add 4th or 5th digit		Nonspecific code		Unspecified code		Manifestation code

690 Erythematosquamous dermatosis

> Excludes: *eczematous dermatitis of eyelid (373.31)*
> *parakeratosis variegata (696.2)*
> *psoriasis (696.0-696.1)*
> *seborrheic keratosis (702)*

690.1 Seborrheic dermatitis

690.10 Seborrheic dermatitis, unspecified
Seborrheic dermatitis NOS

690.11 Seborrhea capitis
Cradle cap

690.12 Seborrheic infantile dermatitis

690.18 Other seborrheic dermatitis

690.8 Other erythematosquamous dermatosis

691 Atopic dermatitis and related conditions

691.0 Diaper or napkin rash
Ammonia dermatitis
Diaper or napkin:
dermatitis
erythema
rash
Psoriasiform napkin eruption

691.8 Other atopic dermatitis and related conditions
Atopic dermatitis   Neurodermatitis:
Besnier's prurigo   atopic
Eczema: diffuse (of Brocq)
atopic
flexural
intrinsic (allergic)

692 Contact dermatitis and other eczema
Includes:

dermatitis: eczema (acute) (chronic):
NOS   NOS
contact   allergic
occupational   erythematous
venenata   occupational

> Excludes: *allergy NOS (995.3)*
> *contact dermatitis of eyelids (373.32)*
> *dermatitis due to substances taken internally (693.0-693.9)*
> *eczema of external ear (380.22)*
> *perioral dermatitis (695.3)*
> *urticarial reactions (708.0-708.9, 995.1)*

692.0 Due to detergents

692.1 Due to oils and greases

692.2 Due to solvents
Dermatitis due to solvents of:
chlorocompound ⎫
cyclohexane   ⎪
ester   ⎬ group
glycol   ⎪
hydrocarbon   ⎪
ketone   ⎭

692.3 Due to drugs and medicines in contact with skin
Dermatitis (allergic) (contact) due to:
arnica
fungicides
iodine
keratolytics
mercurials
neomycin
pediculocides
phenols
scabicides
any drug applied to skin
Dermatitis medicamentosa due to drug applied to skin
Use additional E code, if desired, to identify drug

● Code new   ▲ Revision of   ④ ⑤ Fourth or fifth
  to this edition   existing code   digit required

Excludes: *allergy NOS due to drugs (995.2)*
dermatitis due to ingested drugs (693.0)
dermatitis medicamentosa NOS (693.0)

692.4 Due to other chemical products

Dermatitis due to:
acids
adhesive plaster
alkalis
caustics
dichromate

Dermatitis due to:
insecticide
nylon
plastic
rubber

692.5 Due to food in contact with skin

Dermatitis, contact, due to:
cereals
fish
flour

Dermatitis, contact, due to:
fruit
meat
milk

Excludes: *dermatitis due to:*
dyes (692.89)
ingested foods (693.1)
preservatives (692.89)

692.6 Due to plants [except food]

Dermatitis due to:
lacquer tree [Rhus verniciflua]
poison:
ivy [Rhus toxicodendron]
oak [Rhus diversiloba]
sumac [Rhus venenata]
vine [Rhus radicans]
primrose [Primula]
ragweed [Senecio jacobae]
other plants in contact with the skin

Excludes: *allergy NOS due to pollen (477.0)*
nettle rash (708.8)

692.7 Due to solar radiation

692.70 Unspecified dermatitis due to sun

692.71 Sunburn

692.72 Acute dermatitis due to solar radiation
Berloque dermatitis
Photoallergic response
Phototoxic response
Polymorphus light eruption
Acute solar skin damage NOS

Excludes: *sunburn (692.71)*
Use additional E code, if desired, to identify drug, if drug induced

692.73 Actinic reticuloid and actinic granuloma

692.74 Other chronic dermatitis due to solar radiation
solar elastosis
chronic solar skin damage NOS

Excludes: *actinic [solar] keratosis (702.0)*

692.79 Other dermatitis due to solar radiation
Hydroa aestivale
Photodermatitis ⎫
Photosensitiveness ⎬ (due to sun)
Solar skin damage NOS ⎭

692.8 Due to other specified agents

692.81 Dermatitis due to cosmetics

692.82 Dermatitis due to other radiation
infrared rays
light, except from sun
radiation NOS
ultraviolet rays, except from sun
x-rays

Excludes: *that due to solar radiation (692.70-692.79)*

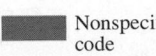 Add 4th or
5th digit

Nonspecific
code

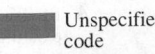 Unspecified
code

Manifestation
code

692.83　Dermatitis due to metals
　　　jewelry

692.89　Other
　　Dermatitis due to:
　　　cold weather
　　　dyes
　　　furs
　　　hot weather
　　　preservatives

> *Excludes:* *allergy NOS due to animal hair, dander (animal), or dust (477.8)*
> 　　　*sunburn (692.71)*

692.9　Unspecified cause
　　Dermatitis:　　　　　　Eczema NOS
　　　NOS
　　　contact NOS
　　　venenata NOS

693　Dermatitis due to substances taken internally

> *Excludes:* *adverse effect NOS of drugs and medicines (995.2)*
> 　　　*allergy NOS (995.3)*
> 　　　*contact dermatitis (692.0-692.9)*
> 　　　*urticarial reactions (708.0-708.9, 995.1)*

693.0　Due to drugs and medicines
　　Dermatitis medicamentosa NOS

Use additional E code, if desired, to identify drug

> *Excludes:* *that due to drugs in contact with skin (692.3)*

693.1　Due to food

693.8　Due to other specified substances taken internally

693.9　Due to unspecified substance taken internally

> *Excludes:* *dermatitis NOS (692.9)*

694　Bullous dermatoses

694.0　Dermatitis herpetiformis
　　Dermatosis herpetiformis
　　Duhring's disease
　　Hydroa herpetiformis

> *Excludes:* *herpes gestationis (646.8)*
> 　　　*dermatitis herpetiformis:*
> 　　　*juvenile (694.2)*
> 　　　*senile (694.5)*

694.1　Subcorneal pustular dermatosis
　　Sneddon-Wilkinson disease or syndrome

694.2　Juvenile dermatitis herpetiformis
　　Juvenile pemphigoid

694.3　Impetigo herpetiformis

694.4　Pemphigus
　　Pemphigus:　　　　　　Pemphigus:
　　　NOS　　　　　　　　malignant
　　　erythematosus　　　vegetans
　　　foliaceus　　　　　vulgaris

> *Excludes:* *pemphigus neonatorum (684)*

694.5　Pemphigoid
　　Benign pemphigus NOS
　　Bullous pemphigoid
　　Herpes circinatus bullosus
　　Senile dermatitis herpetiformis

694.6　Benign mucous membrane pemphigoid
　　Cicatricial pemphigoid
　　Mucosynechial atrophic bullous dermatitis

694.60　Without mention of ocular involvement

694.61　With ocular involvement
　　Ocular pemphigus

304　● Code new　　▲ Revision of　　④ ⑤ Fourth or fifth
　　to this edition　　existing code　　digit required

694.8 **Other specified bullous dermatoses**

Excludes: herpes gestationis (646.8)

694.9 **Unspecified bullous dermatoses**

695 **Erythematous conditions**

695.0 **Toxic erythema**
Erythema venenatum

695.1 **Erythema multiforme**
Erythema iris   Scalded skin syndrome
Herpes iris   Stevens-Johnson syndrome
Lyell's syndrome   Toxic epidermal necrolysis

695.2 **Erythema nodosum**

Excludes: tuberculous erythema nodosum (017.1)

695.3 **Rosacea**
Acne: Perioral dermatitis
  erythematosa   Rhinophyma
  rosacea

695.4 **Lupus erythematosus**
Lupus:
  erythematodes (discoid)
  erythematosus (discoid), not disseminated

Excludes: lupus (vulgaris) NOS (017.0)
         systemic [disseminated] lupus erythematosus (710.0)

695.8 **Other specified erythematous conditions**

    695.81 **Ritter's disease**
        Dermatitis exfoliativa neonatorum

    695.89 **Other**
        Erythema intertrigo
        Intertrigo
        Pityriasis rubra (Hebra)

Excludes: mycotic intertrigo (111.0-111.9)

695.9 **Unspecified erythematous condition**
Erythema NOS   Erythroderma (secondary)

696 **Psoriasis and similar disorders**

696.0 **Psoriatic arthropathy**

696.1 **Other psoriasis**
Acrodermatitis continua
Dermatitis repens
Psoriasis:
  NOS
  any type, except arthropathic

Excludes: psoriatic arthropathy (696.0)

696.2 **Parapsoriasis**
Parakeratosis variegata
Parapsoriasis lichenoides chronica
Pityriasis lichenoides et varioliformis

696.3 **Pityriasis rosea**
Pityriasis circinata (et maculata)

696.4 **Pityriasis rubra pilaris**
Devergie's disease
Lichen ruber acuminatus

Excludes: pityriasis rubra (Hebra) (695.89)

696.5 **Other and unspecified pityriasis**
Pityriasis:
  NOS
  alba
  streptogenes

Excludes: pityriasis simplex (690.18)
         pityriasis versicolor (111.0)

696.8 **Other**

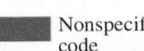 Add 4th or
5th digit

 Nonspecific
code

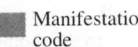 Unspecified
code

Manifestation
code

697 Lichen

Excludes: lichen:
obtusus corneus (698.3)
pilaris (congenital) (757.39)
ruber acuminatus (696.4)
sclerosus et atrophicus (701.0)
scrofulosus (017.0)
simplex chronicus (698.3)
spinulosus (congenital) (757.39)
urticatus (698.2)

697.0 Lichen planus
Lichen:
planopilaris
ruber planus

697.1 Lichen nitidus
Pinkus' disease

697.8 Other lichen, not elsewhere classified
Lichen:
ruber moniliforme
striata

697.9 Lichen, unspecified

698 Pruritus and related conditions

Excludes: pruritus specified as psychogenic (306.3)

698.0 Pruritus ani
Perianal itch

698.1 Pruritus of genital organs

698.2 Prurigo
Lichen urticatus   Urticaria papulosa (Hebra)
Prurigo:
NOS
Hebra's
mitis
simplex

Excludes: prurigo nodularis (698.3)

698.3 Lichenification and lichen simplex chronicus
Hyde's disease
Neurodermatitis (circumscripta) (local)
Prurigo nodularis

Excludes: neurodermatitis, diffuse (of Brocq) (691.8)

698.4 Dermatitis factitia [artefacta]
Dermatitis ficta
Neurotic excoriation
Use additional code, if desired, to identify any associated mental disorder

698.8 Other specified pruritic conditions
Pruritus: Winter itch
hiemalis
senilis

698.9 Unspecified pruritic disorder
Itch NOS   Pruritus NOS

OTHER DISEASES OF SKIN AND SUBCUTANEOUS TISSUE (700-709)

Excludes: conditions confined to eyelids (373.0-374.9)
congenital conditions of skin, hair, and nails (757.0-757.9)

700 Corns and callosities
Callus   Clavus

701 Other hypertrophic and atrophic conditions of skin

Excludes: dermatomyositis (710.3)
hereditary edema of legs (757.0)
scleroderma (generalized) (710.1)

● Code new   ▲ Revision of   ④ ⑤ Fourth or fifth
to this edition   existing code   digit required

701.0 Circumscribed scleroderma
　　Addison's keloid
　　Dermatosclerosis, localized
　　Lichen sclerosus et atrophicus
　　Morphea
　　Scleroderma, circumscribed or localized

701.1 Keratoderma, acquired
　　Acquired:
　　　ichthyosis
　　　keratoderma palmaris et plantaris
　　Elastosis perforans serpiginosa
　　Hyperkeratosis:
　　　NOS
　　　follicularis in cutem penetrans
　　　palmoplantaris climacterica
　　Keratoderma:
　　　climactericum
　　　tylodes, progressive
　　Keratosis (blennorrhagica)

　　Excludes: *Darier's disease [keratosis follicularis] (congenital) (757.39)*
　　　　　　　keratosis:
　　　　　　　　arsenical (692.4)
　　　　　　　　gonococcal (098.81)

701.2 Acquired acanthosis nigricans
　　Keratosis nigricans

701.3 Striae atrophicae
　　Atrophic spots of skin
　　Atrophoderma maculatum
　　Atrophy blanche (of Milian)
　　Degenerative colloid atrophy
　　Senile degenerative atrophy
　　Striae distensae

701.4 Keloid scar
　　Cheloid　　　　　　　　　Keloid
　　Hypertrophic scar

701.5 Other abnormal granulation tissue
　　Excessive granulation

701.8 Other specified hypertrophic and atrophic conditions of skin
　　Acrodermatitis atrophicans chronica
　　Atrophia cutis senilis
　　Atrophoderma neuriticum
　　Confluent and reticulate papillomatosis
　　Cutis laxa senilis
　　Elastosis senilis
　　Folliculitis ulerythematosa reticulata
　　Gougerot-Carteaud syndrome or disease

701.9 Unspecified hypertrophic and atrophic conditions of skin
　　Atrophoderma

702 Other dermatoses

　　Excludes: *carcinoma in situ (232.0-232.9)*

702.0 Actinic keratosis

702.1 Seborrheic keratosis

　　702.11　Inflamed seborrheic keratosis

　　702.19　Other seborrheic keratosis
　　　　Seborrheic keratosis NOS

702.8 Other specified dermatoses

703 Diseases of nail

　　Excludes: *congenital anomalies (757.5)*
　　　　　　onychia and paronychia (681.02, 681.11)

703.0 Ingrowing nail
　　Ingrowing nail with infection
　　Unguis incarnatus

　　Excludes: *infection, nail NOS (681.9)*

700

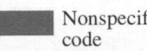

| Add 4th or 5th digit | Nonspecific code | Unspecified code | Manifestation code |

703.8 **Other specified diseases of nail**
Dystrophia unguium
Hypertrophy of nail
Koilonychia
Leukonychia (punctata) (striata)
Onychauxis
Onychogryposis
Onycholysis

703.9 **Unspecified disease of nail**

704 **Diseases of hair and hair follicles**

Excludes: congenital anomalies (757.4)

704.0 **Alopecia**

Excludes: madarosis (374.55)
syphilitic alopecia (091.82)

704.00 **Alopecia, unspecified**
Baldness
Loss of hair

704.01 **Alopecia areata**
Ophiasis

704.02 **Telogen effluvim**

704.09 **Other**
Folliculitis decalvans
Hypotrichosis:
NOS
postinfectional NOS
Pseudopelade

704.1 **Hirsutism**
Hypertrichosis:
NOS
lanuginosa, acquired
Polytrichia

Excludes: hypertrichosis of eyelid (374.54)

704.2 **Abnormalities of the hair**
Atrophic hair
Clastothrix
Fragilitas crinium
Trichiasis:
NOS
cicatrical
Trichorrhexis (nodosa)

Excludes: trichiasis of eyelid (374.05)

704.3 **Variations in hair color**
Canities (premature)
Grayness, hair (premature)
Heterochromia of hair
Poliosis:
NOS
circumscripta, acquired

704.8 **Other specified diseases of hair and hair follicles**
Folliculitis:
NOS
abscedens et suffodiens
pustular
Perifolliculitis:
NOS
capitis abscedens et suffodiens
scalp
Sycosis:
NOS
barbae [not parasitic]
lupoid
vulgaris

704.9 **Unspecified disease of hair and hair follicles**

705 **Disorders of sweat glands**

705.0 **Anhidrosis**
Hypohidrosis
Oligohidrosis

705.1 **Prickly heat**
Heat rash
Miliaria rubra (tropicalis)
Sudamina

705.8 **Other specified disorders of sweat glands**

705.81 **Dyshidrosis**
Cheiropompholyx
Pompholyx

705.82 **Fox-Fordyce disease**

705.83 **Hidradenitis**
Hidradenitis suppurativa

● Code new
to this edition
▲ Revision of
existing code
④ ⑤ Fourth or fifth
digit required

705.89 Other
Bromhidrosis Granulosis rubra nasi
Chromhidrosis Urhidrosis

Excludes: *hidrocystoma (216.0-216.9)*
hyperhidrosis (780.8)

705.9 Unspecified disorder of sweat glands
Disorder of sweat glands NOS

706 Diseases of sebaceous glands

706.0 Acne varioliformis
Acne:
frontalis
necrotica

706.1 Other acne
Acne: Blackhead
NOS Comedo
conglobata
cystic
pustular
vulgaris

Excludes: *acne rosacea (695.3)*

706.2 Sebaceous cyst
Atheroma, skin Wen
Keratin cyst

706.3 Seborrhea

Excludes: *seborrhea:*
capitis (704.8)
sicca (690.18)
seborrheic keratosis (702)

706.8 Other specified diseases of sebaceous glands
Asteatosis (cutis) Xerosis cutis

706.9 Unspecified disease of sebaceous glands

707 Chronic ulcer of skin
Includes: non-infected sinus of skin
non-healing ulcer

Excludes: *specific infections classified under "Infectious and Parasitic Diseases" (001.0-136.9)*
varicose ulcer (454.0, 454.2)

707.0 Decubitus ulcer
Bed sore Plaster ulcer
Decubitus ulcer [any site] Pressure ulcer

707.1 Ulcer of lower limbs, except decubitus
Ulcer, chronic:
neurogenic ⎫
trophic ⎬ of lower limb

Excludes: *that with atherosclerosis of the extremities (440.23)*

707.8 Chronic ulcer of other specified sites
Ulcer, chronic: ⎫
neurogenic ⎬ of other specified sites
trophic ⎭

707.9 Chronic ulcer of unspecified site
Chronic ulcer NOS Tropical ulcer NOS
Trophic ulcer NOS Ulcer of skin NOS

708 Urticaria

Excludes: *edema:*
angioneurotic (995.1)
Quincke's (995.1)
hereditary angioedema (277.6)
urticaria:
giant (995.1)
papulosa (Hebra) (698.2)
pigmentosa (juvenile) (congenital) (757.33)

708.0 Allergic urticaria

Add 4th or Nonspecific Unspecified Manifestation
5th digit code code code

708.1 Idiopathic urticaria

708.2 Urticaria due to cold and heat
Thermal urticaria

708.3 Dermatographic urticaria
Dermatographia   Factitial urticaria

708.4 Vibratory urticaria

708.5 Cholinergic urticaria

708.8 Other specified urticaria
Nettle rash
Urticaria:
    chronic
    recurrent periodic

708.9 Urticaria, unspecified
Hives NOS

709 Other disorders of skin and subcutaneous tissue

709.0 Dyschromia

709.00 Dyschromia, unspecified

709.01 Vitiligo

709.09 Other

Excludes: albinism (270.2)
            pigmented nevus (216.0-216.9)
            that of eyelid (374.52-374.53)

709.1 Vascular disorders of skin
Angioma serpiginosum
Purpura (primary) annularis telangiectodes

709.2 Scar conditions and fibrosis of skin
Adherent scar (skin)
Cicatrix
Disfigurement (due to scar)
Fibrosis, skin NOS
Scar NOS

Excludes: keloid scar (701.4)

709.3 Degenerative skin disorders
Calcinosis: Degeneration, skin
    circumscripta   Deposits, skin
    cutis   Senile dermatosis NOS
Colloid milium   Subcutaneous calcification

709.4 Foreign body granuloma of skin and subcutaneous tissue

Excludes: that of muscle (728.82)

709.8 Other specified disorders of skin
Epithelial hyperplasia   Vesicular eruption
Menstrual dermatosis

709.9 Unspecified disorder of skin and subcutaneous tissue
Dermatosis NOS

● Code new   ▲ Revision of   ④ ⑤ Fourth or fifth
  to this edition   existing code   digit required

13. DISEASES OF THE MUSCULOSKELETAL SYSTEM AND CONNECTIVE TISSUE (710-739)

The following fifth-digit subclassification is for use with categories 711-712, 715-716, 718-719, and 730:

0 site unspecified

1 **shoulder region**
Acromioclavicular
Glenohumeral   } joint(s)
Sternoclavicular
Clavicle
Scapula

2 **upper arm**
Elbow joint   Humerus

3 **forearm**
Radius   Wrist joint
Ulna

4 **hand**
Carpus   Phalanges [fingers]
Metacarpus

5 **pelvic region and thigh**
Buttock   Hip (joint)
Femur

6 **lower leg**
Fibula   Patella
Knee joint   Tibia

7 **ankle and foot**
Ankle joint   Phalanges, foot
Digits [toes]   Tarsus
Metatarsus   Other joints in foot

8 **other specified sites**
Head   Skull
Neck   Trunk
Ribs   Vertebral column

9 **multiple sites**

ARTHROPATHIES AND RELATED DISORDERS (710-719)

> *Excludes:* disorders of spine (720.0-724.9)

710 **Diffuse diseases of connective tissue**
Includes: all collagen diseases whose effects are not mainly confined to a single system

Use additional code, if desired, to identify manifestation, as:
lung involvement (517.8)
myopathy (359.6)

> *Excludes:* those affecting mainly the cardiovascular system, i.e., polyarteritis nodosa and allied conditions (446.0-446.7)

710.0 **Systemic lupus erythematosus**
Disseminated lupus erythematosus
Libman-Sacks disease

Use additional code, if desired, to identify manifestation, as:
endocarditis (424.91)
nephritis (583.81)
chronic (582.81)
nephrotic syndrome (581.81)

> *Excludes:* lupus erythematosus (discoid) NOS (695.4)

710.1 **Systemic sclerosis**
Acrosclerosis
CRST syndrome
Progressive systemic sclerosis
Scleroderma

> *Excludes:* circumscribed scleroderma (701.0)

710.2 **Sicca syndrome**
Keratoconjunctivitis sicca
Sjögren's disease

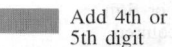 Add 4th or 5th digit   Nonspecific code   Unspecified code   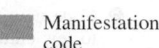 Manifestation code

311

710.3 Dermatomyositis
Poikilodermatomyositis
Polymyositis with skin involvement

710.4 Polymyositis

710.5 Eosinophilia myalgia syndrome
Toxic oil syndrome

Use additional E code, if desired, to identify drug, if drug induced

710.8 Other specified diffuse diseases of connective tissue
Multifocal fibrosclerosis (idiopathic) NEC
Systemic fibrosclerosing syndrome

710.9 Unspecified diffuse connective tissue disease
Collagen disease NOS

⑤ **711 Arthropathy associated with infections**
Includes:

arthritis
arthropathy   } associated with conditions classifiable below
polyarthritis
polyarthropathy

Excludes: *rheumatic fever (390)*

The following fifth-digit subclassification is for use with category 711; valid digits are in
[brackets] under each code. For definitions, see the beginning of this chapter:

0   site unspecified

1   shoulder region

2   upper arm

3   forearm

4   hand

5   pelvic region and thigh

6   lower leg

7   ankle and foot

8   other specified sites

9   multiple sites

711.0 Pyogenic arthritis
[0-9]   Arthritis or polyarthritis (due to):
coliform [Escherichia coli]
Hemophilus influenzae [H. influenzae]
pneumococcal
Pseudomonas
staphylococcal
streptococcal
Pyarthrosis

Use additional code, if desired, to identify infectious organism (041.0-041.8)

711.1 *Arthropathy associated with Reiter's disease and nonspecific urethritis*
[0-9]   *Code first underlying disease, as:*
nonspecific urethritis (099.4)
Reiter's disease (099.3)

711.2 *Arthropathy in Behçet's syndrome*
[0-9]   *Code first underlying disease (136.1)*

711.3 *Postdysenteric arthropathy*
[0-9]   *Code first underlying disease, as:*
dysentery (009.0)
enteritis, infectious (008.0-009.3)
paratyphoid fever (002.1-002.9)
typhoid fever (002.0)

Excludes: *salmonella arthritis (003.23)*

● Code new
to this edition
▲ Revision of
existing code
④ ⑤ Fourth or fifth
digit required

711.4 *Arthropathy associated with other bacterial diseases*
[0-9] *Code first underlying disease, as:*
diseases classifiable to 010-040, 090-099, except as in 711.1, 711.3, and 713.5
leprosy (030.0-030.9)
tuberculosis (015.0-015.9)

Excludes: *gonococcal arthritis (098.50)*
meningococcal arthritis (036.82)

711.5 *Arthropathy associated with other viral diseases*
[0-9] *Code first underlying disease, as:*
diseases classifiable to 045-049, 050-079, 480, 487
O'nyong nyong (066.3)

Excludes: *that due to rubella (056.71)*

711.6 *Arthropathy associated with mycoses*
[0-9] *Code first underlying disease (110.0-118)*

711.7 *Arthropathy associated with helminthiasis*
[0-9] *Code first underlying disease, as:*
filariasis (125.0-125.9)

711.8 *Arthropathy associated with other infectious and parasitic diseases*
[0-9] *Code first underlying disease, as:*
diseases classifiable to 080-088, 100-104, 130-136

Excludes: *arthropathy associated with sarcoidosis (713.7)*

711.9 **Unspecified infective arthritis**
[0-9] Infective arthritis or polyarthritis (acute) (chronic) (subacute) NOS

⑤ **712** **Crystal arthropathies**
Includes: crystal-induced arthritis and synovitis

Excludes: *gouty arthropathy (274.0)*

The following fifth-digit subclassification is for use with category 712; valid digits are in [brackets] under each code. See beginning of this chapter for definitions:

0 **site unspecified**

1 **shoulder region**

2 **upper arm**

3 **forearm**

4 **hand**

5 **pelvic region and thigh**

6 **lower leg**

7 **ankle and foot**

8 **other specified sites**

9 **multiple sites**

712.1 *Chondrocalcinosis due to dicalcium phosphate crystals*
[0-9] Chondrocalcinosis due to dicalcium phosphate crystals (with other crystals)
Code first underlying disease (275.4)

712.2 *Chondrocalcinosis due to pyrophosphate crystals*
[0-9] *Code first underlying disease (275.4)*

712.3 *Chondrocalcinosis, unspecified*
[0-9] *Code first underlying disease (275.4)*

712.8 **Other specified crystal arthropathies**
[0-9]

712.9 **Unspecified crystal arthropathy**
[0-9]

Add 4th or 5th digit   Nonspecific code   Unspecified code   Manifestation code

713 **Arthropathy associated with other disorders classified elsewhere**
Includes:
arthritis
arthropathy
polyarthritis   } associated with conditions classifiable below
polyarthropathy

713.0 *Arthropathy associated with other endocrine and metabolic disorders*
Code first underlying disease, as:
acromegaly (253.0)
hemochromatosis (275.0)
hyperparathyroidism (252.0)
hypogammaglobulinemia (279.00-279.09)
hypothyroidism (243-244.9)
lipoid metabolism disorder (272.0-272.9)
ochronosis (270.2)

Excludes: *arthropathy associated with:*
amyloidosis (713.7)
crystal deposition disorders, except gout (712.1-712.9)
diabetic neuropathy (713.5)
gouty arthropathy (274.0)

713.1 *Arthropathy associated with gastrointestinal conditions other than infections*
Code first underlying disease, as:
regional enteritis (555.0-555.9)
ulcerative colitis (556)

713.2 *Arthropathy associated with hematological disorders*
Code first underlying disease, as:
hemoglobinopathy (282.4-282.7)
hemophilia (286.0-286.2)
leukemia (204.0-208.9)
malignant reticulosis (202.3)
multiple myelomatosis (203.0)

Excludes: *arthropathy associated with Henoch-Schönlein purpura (713.6)*

713.3 *Arthropathy associated with dermatological disorders*
Code first underlying disease, as:
erythema multiforme (695.1)
erythema nodosum (695.2)

Excludes: *psoriatic arthropathy (696.0)*

713.4 *Arthropathy associated with respiratory disorders*
Code first underlying disease, as:
diseases classifiable to 490-519

Excludes: *arthropathy associated with respiratory infections (711.0, 711.4-711.8)*

713.5 *Arthropathy associated with neurological disorders*
Charcot's arthropathy   }
Neuropathic arthritis   } associated with diseases classifiable elsewhere
Code first underlying disease, as:
neuropathic joint disease [Charcot's joints]:
NOS (094.0)
diabetic (250.6)
syringomyelic (336.0)
tabetic [syphilitic] (094.0)

713.6 *Arthropathy associated with hypersensitivity reaction*
Code first underlying disease, as:
Henoch (-Schönlein) purpura (287.0)
serum sickness (999.5)

Excludes: *allergic arthritis NOS (716.2)*

713.7 *Other general diseases with articular involvement*
Code first underlying disease, as:
amyloidosis (277.3)
familial Mediterranean fever (277.3)
sarcoidosis (135)

● Code new   ▲ Revision of   ④ ⑤ Fourth or fifth
to this edition   existing code   digit required

713.8 *Arthropathy associated with other conditions classifiable elsewhere*
Code first underlying disease, as:
conditions classifiable elsewhere except as in 711.1-711.8, 712, and 713.0-713.7

714 Rheumatoid arthritis and other inflammatory polyarthropathies

Excludes: *rheumatic fever (390)*
rheumatoid arthritis of spine NOS (720.0)

714.0 Rheumatoid arthritis
Arthritis or polyarthritis:
atrophic
rheumatic (chronic)
Use additional code, if desired, to identify manifestation, as:
myopathy (359.6)
polyneuropathy (357.1)

Excludes: *juvenile rheumatoid arthritis NOS (714.30)*

714.1 Felty's syndrome
Rheumatoid arthritis with splenoadenomegaly and leukopenia

714.2 Other rheumatoid arthritis with visceral or systemic involvement
Rheumatoid carditis

714.3 Juvenile chronic polyarthritis

714.30 Polyarticular juvenile rheumatoid arthritis, chronic or unspecified
Juvenile rheumatoid arthritis NOS
Still's disease

714.31 Polyarticular juvenile rheumatoid arthritis, acute

714.32 Pauciarticular juvenile rheumatoid arthritis

714.33 Monoarticular juvenile rheumatoid arthritis

714.4 Chronic postrheumatic arthropathy
Chronic rheumatoid nodular fibrositis
Jaccoud's syndrome

714.8 Other specified inflammatory polyarthropathies

714.81 Rheumatoid lung
Caplan's syndrome
Diffuse interstitial rheumatoid disease of lung
Fibrosing alveolitis, rheumatoid

714.89 Other

714.9 Unspecified inflammatory polyarthropathy
Inflammatory polyarthropathy or polyarthritis NOS

Excludes: *polyarthropathy NOS (716.5)*

⑤ 715 Osteoarthrosis and allied disorders
Note: Localized, in the subcategories below, includes bilateral involvement of the same site.
Includes: arthritis or polyarthritis:
degenerative
hypertrophic
degenerative joint disease
osteoarthritis

Excludes: *Marie-Strümpell spondylitis (720.0)*
osteoarthrosis [osteoarthritis] of spine (721.0-721.9)

The following fifth-digit subclassification is for use with category 715; valid digits are in [brackets] under each code. See beginning of this chapter for definitions:

0 site unspecified

1 shoulder region

2 upper arm

3 forearm

4 hand

5 pelvic region and thigh

6 lower leg

7 ankle and foot

8 other specified sites

9 multiple sites

	Add 4th or 5th digit		Nonspecific code		Unspecified code		Manifestation code

715.0 Osteoarthrosis, generalized
[0,4,9]   Degenerative joint disease, involving multiple joints
         Primary generalized hypertrophic osteoarthrosis

715.1 Osteoarthrosis, localized, primary
[0-8]   Localized osteoarthropathy, idiopathic

715.2 Osteoarthrosis, localized, secondary
[0-8]   Coxae malum senilis

715.3 Osteoarthrosis, localized, not specified whether primary or secondary
[0-8]   Otto's pelvis

715.8 Osteoarthrosis involving, or with mention of more than one site, but not specified as generalized

[0,9]

715.9 Osteoarthrosis, unspecified whether generalized or localized
[0-8]

⑤ **716 Other and unspecified arthropathies**

Excludes: cricoarytenoid arthropathy (478.79)

The following fifth-digit subclassification is for use with category 716; valid digits are in [brackets] under each code. See beginning of this chapter for definitions:

0   site unspecified

1   shoulder region

2   upper arm

3   forearm

4   hand

5   pelvic region and thigh

6   lower leg

7   ankle and foot

8   other specified sites

9   multiple sites

716.0 Kaschin-Beck disease
[0-9]   Endemic polyarthritis

716.1 Traumatic arthropathy
[0-9]

716.2 Allergic arthritis
[0-9]

Excludes: arthritis associated with Henoch-Schönlein purpura or serum sickness (713.6)

716.3 Climacteric arthritis
[0-9]   Menopausal arthritis

716.4 Transient arthropathy
[0-9]

Excludes: palindromic rheumatism (719.3)

716.5 Unspecified polyarthropathy or polyarthritis
[0-9]

716.6 Unspecified monoarthritis
[0-8]   Coxitis

716.8 Other specified arthropathy
[0-9]

716.9 Arthropathy, unspecified
[0-9]   Arthritis   ⎫
         Arthropathy   ⎬ (acute) (chronic) (subacute)
         Articular rheumatism (chronic)
         Inflammation of joint NOS

● Code new   ▲ Revision of   ④ ⑤ Fourth or fifth
     to this edition   existing code   digit required

717 Internal derangement of knee

Includes:

degeneration
rupture, old } of articular cartilage or meniscus of knee
tear, old

Excludes: *acute derangement of knee (836.0-836.6)*
ankylosis (718.5)
contracture (718.4)
current injury (836.0-836.6)
deformity (736.4-736.6)
recurrent dislocation (718.3)

717.0 Old bucket handle tear of medial meniscus
Old bucket handle tear of unspecified cartilage

717.1 Derangement of anterior horn of medial meniscus

717.2 Derangement of posterior horn of medial meniscus

717.3 Other and unspecified derangement of medial meniscus
Degeneration of internal semilunar cartilage

717.4 Derangement of lateral meniscus

> **717.40 Derangement of lateral meniscus, unspecified**
>
> **717.41 Bucket handle tear of lateral meniscus**
>
> **717.42 Derangement of anterior horn of lateral meniscus**
>
> **717.43 Derangement of posterior horn of lateral meniscus**
>
> **717.49 Other**

717.5 Derangement of meniscus, not elsewhere classified
Congenital discoid meniscus
Cyst of semilunar cartilage
Derangement of semilunar cartilage NOS

717.6 Loose body in knee
Joint mice, knee
Rice bodies, knee (joint)

717.7 Chondromalacia of patella
Chondromalacia patellae
Degeneration [softening] of articular cartilage of patella

717.8 Other internal derangement of knee

> **717.81 Old disruption of lateral collateral ligament**
>
> **717.82 Old disruption of medial collateral ligament**
>
> **717.83 Old disruption of anterior cruciate ligament**
>
> **717.84 Old disruption of posterior cruciate ligament**
>
> **717.85 Old disruption of other ligaments of knee**
> Capsular ligament of knee
>
> **717.89 Other**
> Old disruption of ligaments of knee NOS

717.9 Unspecified internal derangement of knee
Derangement NOS of knee

⑤ **718 Other derangement of joint**

Excludes: *current injury (830.0-848.9)*
jaw (524.6)

The following fifth-digit subclassification is for use with category 718; valid digits are in [brackets] under each code. See beginning of this chapter for definitions:

0 site unspecified

1 shoulder region

2 upper arm

3 forearm

4 hand

5 pelvic region and thigh

6 lower leg

7 ankle and foot

continued

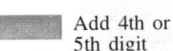 Add 4th or 5th digit   Nonspecific code   Unspecified code   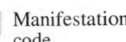 Manifestation code

8 **other specified sites**

9 **multiple sites**

718.0 Articular cartilage disorder
[0-5, 7-9] Meniscus:
    disorder
    rupture, old
    tear, old
    Old rupture of ligament(s) of joint NOS

Excludes: *articular cartilage disorder:*
    in ochronosis (270.2)
    knee (717.0-717.9)
    chondrocalcinosis (275.4)
    metastatic calcification (275.4)

718.1 Loose body in joint
[0-5, 7-9] Joint mice

Excludes: *knee (717.6)*

718.2 Pathological dislocation
[0-9]   Dislocation or displacement of joint, not recurrent and not current injury
    Spontaneous dislocation (joint)

718.3 Recurrent dislocation of joint
[0-9]

718.4 Contracture of joint
[0-9]

718.5 Ankylosis of joint
[0-9]   Ankylosis of joint (fibrous) (osseous)

Excludes: *spine (724.9)*

        stiffness of joint without mention of ankylosis (719.5)

718.6 Unspecified intrapelvic protrusion of acetabulum
[0, 5]   Protrusio acetabuli, unspecified

718.8 Other joint derangement, not elsewhere classified
[0-9]   Flail joint (paralytic)   Instability of joint

Excludes: *deformities classifiable to 736 (736.0-736.9)*

718.9 Unspecified derangement of joint
[0-5, 7-9]

Excludes: *knee (717.9)*

⑤ **719 Other and unspecified disorders of joint**

Excludes: *jaw (524.6)*

The following fifth-digit subclassification is for use with category 719; valid digits are in [brackets] under each code. See beginning of this chapter for definitions:

0 **site unspecified**

1   **shoulder region**

2   **upper arm**

3   **forearm**

4   **hand**

5   **pelvic region and thigh**

6   **lower leg**

7   **ankle and foot**

8 **other specified sites**

9 **multiple sites**

719.0 Effusion of joint
[0-9]   Hydrarthrosis
    Swelling of joint, with or without pain

Excludes: *intermittent hydrarthrosis (719.3)*

● Code new   ▲ Revision of   ④ ⑤ Fourth or fifth
  to this edition   existing code   digit required

719.1 Hemarthrosis
[0-9]

> Excludes: current injury (840.0-848.9)

719.2 Villonodular synovitis
[0-9]

719.3 Palindromic rheumatism
[0-9]   Hench-Rosenberg syndrome
          Intermittent hydrarthrosis

719.4 Pain in joint
[0-9]   Arthralgia

719.5 Stiffness of joint, not elsewhere classified
[0-9]

719.6 Other symptoms referable to joint
[0-9]   Joint crepitus   Snapping hip

719.7 Difficulty in walking
[0, 5-9]

> Excludes: abnormality of gait (781.2)

719.8 Other specified disorders of joint
[0-9]   Calcification of joint   Fistula of joint

> Excludes: temporomandibular joint-pain-dysfunction syndrome [Costen's syndrome] (524.6)

719.9 Unspecified disorder of joint
[0-9]

DORSOPATHIES (720-724)

> Excludes: curvature of spine (737.0-737.9)
>   osteochondrosis of spine (juvenile) (732.0)
>   adult (732.8)

720 Ankylosing spondylitis and other inflammatory spondylopathies

720.0 Ankylosing spondylitis
          Rheumatoid arthritis of spine NOS
          Spondylitis:
            Marie-Strümpell
            rheumatoid

720.1 Spinal enthesopathy
          Disorder of peripheral ligamentous or muscular attachments of spine
          Romanus lesion

720.2 Sacroiliitis, not elsewhere classified
          Inflammation of sacroiliac joint NOS

720.8 Other inflammatory spondylopathies

> **720.81 Inflammatory spondylopathies in diseases classified elsewhere**
>   Code first underlying disease, as:
>   tuberculosis (015.0)

> **720.89 Other**

720.9 Unspecified inflammatory spondylopathy
          Spondylitis NOS

721 Spondylosis and allied disorders

721.0 Cervical spondylosis without myelopathy
          Cervical or cervicodorsal:
            arthritis
            osteoarthritis
            spondylarthritis

721.1 Cervical spondylosis with myelopathy
          Anterior spinal artery compression syndrome
          Spondylogenic compression of cervical spinal cord
          Vertebral artery compression syndrome

| | Add 4th or 5th digit | | Nonspecific code | | Unspecified code | | Manifestation code |

721.2 Thoracic spondylosis without myelopathy
Thoracic:
arthritis
osteoarthritis
spondylarthritis

721.3 Lumbosacral spondylosis without myelopathy
Lumbar or lumbosacral:
arthritis
osteoarthritis
spondylarthritis

721.4 Thoracic or lumbar spondylosis with myelopathy

   721.41 Thoracic region
Spondylogenic compression of thoracic spinal cord

   721.42 Lumbar region
Spondylogenic compression of lumbar spinal cord

721.5 Kissing spine
Baastrup's syndrome

721.6 Ankylosing vertebral hyperostosis

721.7 Traumatic spondylopathy
Kümmell's disease or spondylitis

721.8 Other allied disorders of spine

721.9 Spondylosis of unspecified site

   721.90 Without mention of myelopathy
Spinal:
arthritis (deformans) (degenerative) (hypertrophic)
osteoarthritis NOS
Spondylarthrosis NOS

   721.91 With myelopathy
Spondylogenic compression of spinal cord NOS

722 Intervertebral disc disorders

722.0 Displacement of cervical intervertebral disc without myelopathy
Neuritis (brachial) or radiculitis due to displacement or rupture of cervical intervertebral
disc
Any condition classifiable to 722.2 of the cervical or cervicothoracic intervertebral disc

722.1 Displacement of thoracic or lumbar intervertebral disc without myelopathy

   722.10 Lumbar intervertebral disc without myelopathy
Lumbago or sciatica due to displacement of intervertebral disc
Neuritis or radiculitis due to displacement or rupture of lumbar intervertebral
disc
Any condition classifiable to 722.2 of the lumbar or lumbosacral intervertebral
disc

   722.11 Thoracic intervertebral disc without myelopathy
Any condition classifiable to 722.2 of thoracic intervertebral disc

722.2 Displacement of intervertebral disc, site unspecified, without myelopathy
Discogenic syndrome NOS
Herniation of nucleus pulposus NOS
Intervertebral disc NOS:
extrusion
prolapse
protrusion
rupture
Neuritis or radiculitis due to displacement or rupture of intervertebral disc

722.3 Schmorl's nodes

   722.30 Unspecified region

   722.31 Thoracic region

   722.32 Lumbar region

   722.39 Other

722.4 Degeneration of cervical intervertebral disc
Degeneration of cervicothoracic intervertebral disc

722.5 Degeneration of thoracic or lumbar intervertebral disc

   722.51 Thoracic or thoracolumbar intervertebral disc

   722.52 Lumbar or lumbosacral intervertebral disc

● Code new
to this edition

▲ Revision of
existing code

④ ⑤ Fourth or fifth
digit required

722.6 Degeneration of intervertebral disc, site unspecified
Degenerative disc disease NOS
Narrowing of intervertebral disc or space NOS

722.7 Intervertebral disc disorder with myelopathy

    722.70 Unspecified region

    722.71 Cervical region

    722.72 Thoracic region

    722.73 Lumbar region

722.8 Postlaminectomy syndrome

    722.80 Unspecified region

    722.81 Cervical region

    722.82 Thoracic region

    722.83 Lumbar region

722.9 Other and unspecified disc disorder
Calcification of intervertebral cartilage or disc
Discitis

    722.90 Unspecified region

    722.91 Cervical region

    722.92 Thoracic region

    722.93 Lumbar region

723 Other disorders of cervical region

    Excludes: conditions due to:
        intervertebral disc disorders (722.0-722.9)
        spondylosis (721.0-721.9)

723.0 Spinal stenosis in cervical region

723.1 Cervicalgia
Pain in neck

723.2 Cervicocranial syndrome
Barré-Liéou syndrome
Posterior cervical sympathetic syndrome

723.3 Cervicobrachial syndrome (diffuse)

723.4 Brachial neuritis or radiculitis NOS
Cervical radiculitis
Radicular syndrome of upper limbs

723.5 Torticollis, unspecified
Contracture of neck

    Excludes: congenital (754.1)
        due to birth injury (767.8)
        hysterical (300.11)
        psychogenic (306.0)
        spasmodic (333.83)
        traumatic, current (847.0)

723.6 Panniculitis specified as affecting neck

723.7 Ossification of posterior longitudinal ligament in cervical region

723.8 Other syndromes affecting cervical region
Cervical syndrome NEC   Klippel's disease

723.9 Unspecified musculoskeletal disorders and symptoms referable to neck
Cervical (region) disorder NOS

724 Other and unspecified disorders of back

    Excludes: collapsed vertebra (code to cause, e.g., osteoporosis, 733.00-733.09)
        conditions due to:
        intervertebral disc disorders (722.0-722.9)
        spondylosis (721.0-721.9)

724.0 Spinal stenosis, other than cervical

    724.00 Spinal stenosis, unspecified region

    724.01 Thoracic region

    724.02 Lumbar region

| | Add 4th or 5th digit | | Nonspecific code | 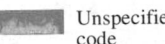 Unspecified code | | Manifestation code |

724.09 Other

724.1 Pain in thoracic spine

724.2 Lumbago
Low back pain   Lumbalgia
Low back syndrome

724.3 Sciatica
Neuralgia or neuritis of sciatic nerve

> Excludes: *specified lesion of sciatic nerve (355.0)*

724.4 Thoracic or lumbosacral neuritis or radiculitis, unspecified
Radicular syndrome of lower limbs

724.5 Backache, unspecified
Vertebrogenic (pain) syndrome NOS

724.6 Disorders of sacrum
Ankylosis
Instability   } lumbosacral or sacroiliac (joint)

724.7 Disorders of coccyx

   724.70 Unspecified disorder of coccyx

   724.71 Hypermobility of coccyx

   724.79 Other
Coccygodynia

724.8 Other symptoms referable to back
Ossification of posterior longitudinal ligament NOS
Panniculitis specified as sacral or affecting back

724.9 Other unspecified back disorders
Ankylosis of spine NOS
Compression of spinal nerve root NEC
Spinal disorder NOS

> Excludes: *sacroiliitis (720.2)*

RHEUMATISM, EXCLUDING THE BACK (725-729)

Includes: disorders of muscles and tendons and their attachments, and of other soft tissues

725 Polymyalgia rheumatica

726 Peripheral enthesopathies and allied syndromes
Note: Enthesopathies are disorders of peripheral ligamentous or muscular attachments.

> Excludes: *spinal enthesopathy (720.1)*

726.0 Adhesive capsulitis of shoulder

726.1 Rotator cuff syndrome of shoulder and allied disorders

   726.10 Disorders of bursae and tendons in shoulder region, unspecified
Rotator cuff syndrome NOS
Supraspinatus syndrome NOS

   726.11 Calcifying tendinitis of shoulder

   726.12 Bicipital tenosynovitis

   726.19 Other specified disorders

> Excludes: *complete rupture of rotator cuff, nontraumatic (727.61)*

726.2 Other affections of shoulder region, not elsewhere classified
Periarthritis of shoulder
Scapulohumeral fibrositis

726.3 Enthesopathy of elbow region

   726.30 Enthesopathy of elbow, unspecified

   726.31 Medial epicondylitis

   726.32 Lateral epicondylitis
Epicondylitis NOS   Tennis elbow
Golfers' elbow

   726.33 Olecranon bursitis
Bursitis of elbow

   726.39 Other

● Code new   ▲ Revision of   ④ ⑤ Fourth or fifth
to this edition   existing code   digit required

726.4 Enthesopathy of wrist and carpus
Bursitis of hand or wrist
Periarthritis of wrist

726.5 Enthesopathy of hip region
Bursitis of hip   Psoas tendinitis
Gluteal tendinitis   Trochanteric tendinitis
Iliac crest spur

726.6 Enthesopathy of knee

726.60 **Enthesopathy of knee, unspecified**
Bursitis of knee NOS

726.61 **Pes anserinus tendinitis or bursitis**

726.62 **Tibial collateral ligament bursitis**
Pellegrini-Stieda syndrome

726.63 **Fibular collateral ligament bursitis**

726.64 **Patellar tendinitis**

726.65 **Prepatellar bursitis**

726.69 **Other**
Bursitis:
infrapatellar
subpatellar

726.7 Enthesopathy of ankle and tarsus

726.70 **Enthesopathy of ankle and tarsus, unspecified**
Metatarsalgia NOS

Excludes: *Morton's metatarsalgia (355.6)*

726.71 **Achilles bursitis or tendinitis**

726.72 **Tibialis tendinitis**
Tibialis (anterior) (posterior) tendinitis

726.73 **Calcaneal spur**

726.79 **Other**
Peroneal tendinitis

726.8 Other peripheral enthesopathies

726.9 Unspecified enthesopathy

726.90 **Enthesopathy of unspecified site**
Capsulitis NOS   Tendinitis NOS
Periarthritis NOS

726.91 **Exostosis of unspecified site**
Bone spur NOS

727 Other disorders of synovium, tendon, and bursa

727.0 Synovitis and tenosynovitis

727.00 **Synovitis and tenosynovitis, unspecified**
Synovitis NOS   Tenosynovitis NOS

727.01 *Synovitis and tenosynovitis in diseases classified elsewhere*
Code first underlying disease, as:
tuberculosis (015.0-015.9)

Excludes: *crystal-induced (275.4)*
gonococcal (098.51)
gouty (274.0)
syphilitic (095.7)

727.02 **Giant cell tumor of tendon sheath**

727.03 **Trigger finger (acquired)**

727.04 **Radial styloid tenosynovitis**
de Quervain's disease

727.05 **Other tenosynovitis of hand and wrist**

727.06 **Tenosynovitis of foot and ankle**

727.09 **Other**

727.1 Bunion

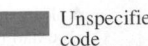

| | Add 4th or 5th digit | | Nonspecific code | | Unspecified code | | Manifestation code |

727.2 Specific bursitides often of occupational origin
Beat: Chronic crepitant synovitis of wrist
   elbow   Miners':
   hand   elbow
   knee   knee

727.3 Other bursitis
Bursitis NOS

Excludes: bursitis:
> gonococcal (098.52)
> subacromial (726.19)
> subcoracoid (726.19)
> subdeltoid (726.19)
> syphilitic (095.7)
> "frozen shoulder" (726.0)

727.4 Ganglion and cyst of synovium, tendon, and bursa

727.40 Synovial cyst, unspecified

Excludes: that of popliteal space (727.51)

727.41 Ganglion of joint

727.42 Ganglion of tendon sheath

727.43 Ganglion, unspecified

727.49 Other
Cyst of bursa

727.5 Rupture of synovium

727.50 Rupture of synovium, unspecified

727.51 Synovial cyst of popliteal space
Baker's cyst (knee)

727.59 Other

727.6 Rupture of tendon, nontraumatic

727.60 Nontraumatic rupture of unspecified tendon

727.61 Complete rupture of rotator cuff

727.62 Tendons of biceps (long head)

727.63 Extensor tendons of hand and wrist

727.64 Flexor tendons of hand and wrist

727.65 Quadriceps tendon

727.66 Patellar tendon

727.67 Achilles tendon

727.68 Other tendons of foot and ankle

727.69 Other

727.8 Other disorders of synovium, tendon, and bursa

727.81 Contracture of tendon (sheath)
Short Achilles tendon (acquired)

727.82 Calcium deposits in tendon and bursa
Calcification of tendon NOS
Calcific tendinitis NOS

Excludes: peripheral ligamentous or muscular attachments (726.0-726.9)

727.89 Other
Abscess of bursa or tendon

Excludes: xanthomatosis localized to tendons (272.7)

727.9 Unspecified disorder of synovium, tendon, and bursa

728 Disorders of muscle, ligament, and fascia

Excludes: enthesopathies (726.0-726.9)
> muscular dystrophies (359.0-359.1)
> myoneural disorders (358.0-358.9)
> myopathies (359.2-359.9)
> old disruption of ligaments of knee (717.81-717.89)

● Code new to this edition   ▲ Revision of existing code   ④ ⑤ Fourth or fifth digit required

728.0 Infective myositis
Myositis:
  purulent
  suppurative

Excludes: myositis:
  epidemic (074.1)
  interstitial (728.81)
  syphilitic (095.6)
  tropical (040.81)

728.1 Muscular calcification and ossification

728.10 Calcification and ossification, unspecified
  Massive calcification (paraplegic)

728.11 Progressive myositis ossificans

728.12 Traumatic myositis ossificans
  Myositis ossificans (circumscripta)

728.13 Postoperative heterotopic calcification

728.19 Other
  Polymyositis ossificans

728.2 Muscular wasting and disuse atrophy, not elsewhere classified
  Amyotrophia NOS   Myofibrosis

Excludes: *neuralgic amyotrophy (353.5)*
  progressive muscular atrophy (335.0-335.9)

728.3 Other specific muscle disorders
  Arthrogryposis
  Immobility syndrome (paraplegic)

Excludes: *arthrogryposis multiplex congenita (754.89)*
  stiff-man syndrome (333.91)

728.4 Laxity of ligament

728.5 Hypermobility syndrome

728.6 Contracture of palmar fascia
  Dupuytren's contracture

728.7 Other fibromatoses

728.71 Plantar fascial fibromatosis
  Contracture of plantar fascia
  Plantar fasciitis (traumatic)

728.79 Other
  Garrod's or knuckle pads
  Nodular fasciitis
  Pseudosarcomatous fibromatosis (proliferative) (subcutaneous)

728.8 Other disorders of muscle, ligament, and fascia

728.81 Interstitial myositis

728.82 Foreign body granuloma of muscle
  Talc granuloma of muscle

728.83 Rupture of muscle, nontraumatic

728.84 Diastasis of muscle
  Diastasis recti (abdomen)

Excludes: *diastasis recti complicating pregnancy, labor, and delivery (665.8)*

728.85 Spasm of muscle

728.86 Necrotizing fasciitis
  Use additional code to identify:
  infectious organism (041.00 - 041.89)
  gangrene (785.4), if applicable

728.89 Other
  Eosinophilic fasciitis
  Use additional E code, if desired, to identify drug, if drug induced

728.9 Unspecified disorder of muscle, ligament, and fascia

| Add 4th or 5th digit | Nonspecific code | Unspecified code | Manifestation code |

729 Other disorders of soft tissues

Excludes: *acroparesthesia (443.89)*
carpal tunnel syndrome (354.0)
disorders of the back (720.0-724.9)
entrapment syndromes (354.0-355.9)
palindromic rheumatism (719.3)
periarthritis (726.0-726.9)
psychogenic rheumatism (306.0)

729.0 Rheumatism, unspecified and fibrositis

729.1 Myalgia and myositis, unspecified
Fibromyositis NOS

729.2 Neuralgia, neuritis, and radiculitis, unspecified

Excludes: *brachial radiculitis (723.4)*
cervical radiculitis (723.4)
lumbosacral radiculitis (724.4)
mononeuritis (354.0-355.9)
radiculitis due to intervertebral disc involvement (722.0-722.2, 722.7)
sciatica (724.3)

729.3 Panniculitis, unspecified

729.30 Panniculitis, unspecified site
Weber-Christian disease

729.31 Hypertrophy of fat pad, knee
Hypertrophy of infrapatellar fat pad

729.39 Other site

Excludes: *panniculitis specified as (affecting):*
back (724.8)
neck (723.6)
sacral (724.8)

729.4 Fasciitis, unspecified

Excludes: *necrotizing fasciitis (728.86)*
nodular fasciitis (728.79)

729.5 Pain in limb

729.6 Residual foreign body in soft tissue

Excludes: *foreign body granuloma:*
muscle (728.82)
skin and subcutaneous tissue (709.4)

729.8 Other musculoskeletal symptoms referable to limbs

729.81 Swelling of limb

729.82 Cramp

729.89 Other

Excludes: *abnormality of gait (781.2)*
tetany (781.7)
transient paralysis of limb (781.4)

729.9 Other and unspecified disorders of soft tissue
Polyalgia

OSTEOPATHIES, CHONDROPATHIES, AND ACQUIRED MUSCULOSKELETAL DEFORMITIES (730-739)

⑤ **730** Osteomyelitis, periostitis, and other infections involving bone

Excludes: *jaw (526.4-526.5)*
petrous bone (383.2)

Use additional code, if desired, to identify organism, such as Staphylococcus (041.1)

The following fifth-digit subclassification is for use with category 730; valid digits are in [brackets] under each code. See beginning of this chapter for definitions:

0 site unspecified

1 shoulder region

2 upper arm

3 forearm

● Code new
to this edition

▲ Revision of
existing code

④ ⑤ Fourth or fifth
digit required

4   **hand**

5   **pelvic region and thigh**

6   **lower leg**

7   **ankle and foot**

8   **other specified sites**

9   **multiple sites**

730.0   Acute osteomyelitis
[0-9]   Abscess of any bone except accessory sinus, jaw, or mastoid
Acute or subacute osteomyelitis, with or without mention of periostitis

730.1   Chronic osteomyelitis
[0-9]   Brodie's abscess
Chronic or old osteomyelitis, with or without mention of periostitis

Necrosis (acute) ⎱
Sequestrum   ⎰ of bone

Sclerosing osteomyelitis of Garré

Excludes: *aseptic necrosis of bone (733.40-733.49)*

730.2   Unspecified osteomyelitis
[0-9]   Osteitis or osteomyelitis NOS, with or without mention of periostitis

730.3   Periostitis without mention of osteomyelitis
[0-9]
Abscess of periosteum ⎱ without mention of osteomyelitis
Periostosis   ⎰

Excludes: *that in secondary syphilis (091.61)*

730.7   *Osteopathy resulting from poliomyelitis*
[0-9]   *Code first underlying disease (045.0-045.9)*

730.8   *Other infections involving bone in diseases classified elsewhere*
[0-9]   *Code first underlying disease, as:*
tuberculosis (015.0-015.9)
typhoid fever (002.0)

Excludes: *syphilis of bone NOS (095.5)*

730.9   Unspecified infection of bone
[0-9]

731   Osteitis deformans and osteopathies associated with other disorders classified elsewhere

731.0   Osteitis deformans without mention of bone tumor
Paget's disease of bone

731.1   *Osteitis deformans in diseases classified elsewhere*
Code first underlying disease, as:
malignant neoplasm of bone (170.0-170.9)

731.2   Hypertrophic pulmonary osteoarthropathy
Bamberger-Marie disease

731.8   *Other bone involvement in diseases classified elsewhere*
Code first underlying disease, as:
diabetes mellitus (250.8)

732   Osteochondropathies

732.0   Juvenile osteochondrosis of spine
Juvenile osteochondrosis (of):
marginal or vertebral epiphysis (of Scheuermann)
spine NOS
Vertebral epiphysitis

Excludes: *adolescent postural kyphosis (737.0)*

732.1   Juvenile osteochondrosis of hip and pelvis
Coxa plana
Ischiopubic synchondrosis (of van Neck)
Osteochondrosis (juvenile) of:
acetabulum
head of femur (of Legg-Calvé-Perthes)
iliac crest (of Buchanan)
symphysis pubis (of Pierson)
Pseudocoxalgia

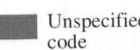 Add 4th or 5th digit   Nonspecific code   Unspecified code   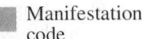 Manifestation code

732.2 Nontraumatic slipped upper femoral epiphysis
Slipped upper femoral epiphysis NOS

732.3 Juvenile osteochondrosis of upper extremity
Osteochondrosis (juvenile) of:
capitulum of humerus (of Panner)
carpal lunate (of Kienbock)
hand NOS
head of humerus (of Haas)
heads of metacarpals (of Mauclaire)
lower ulna (of Burns)
radial head (of Brailsford)
upper extremity NOS

732.4 Juvenile osteochondrosis of lower extremity, excluding foot
Osteochondrosis (juvenile) of:
lower extremity NOS
primary patellar center (of Köhler)
proximal tibia (of Blount)
secondary patellar center (of Sinding-Larsen)
tibial tubercle (of Osgood-Schlatter)
Tibia vara

732.5 Juvenile osteochondrosis of foot
Calcaneal apophysitis
Epiphysitis, os calcis
Osteochondrosis (juvenile) of:
astragalus (of Diaz)
calcaneum (of Sever)
foot NOS
metatarsal
second (of Freiberg)
fifth (of Iselin)
os tibiale externum (Haglund)
tarsal navicular (of Köhler)

732.6 Other juvenile osteochondrosis
Apophysitis
Epiphysitis
Osteochondritis } specified as juvenile, of other site, or site NOS
Osteochondrosis

732.7 Osteochondritis dissecans

732.8 Other specified forms of osteochondropathy
Adult osteochondrosis of spine

732.9 Unspecified osteochondropathy
Apophysitis
Epiphysitis } NOS
Osteochondritis } Not specified as adult or juvenile, of unspecified site
Osteochondrosis

733 Other disorders of bone and cartilage

Excludes: *bone spur (726.91)*

cartilage of, or loose body in, joint (717.0-717.9, 718.0-718.9)
giant cell granuloma of jaw (526.3)
osteitis fibrosa cystica generalisata (252.0)
osteomalacia (268.2)
polyostotic fibrous dysplasia of bone (756.54)
prognathism, retrognathism (524.1)
xanthomatosis localized to bone (272.7)

733.0 Osteoporosis

733.00 Osteoporosis, unspecified
Wedging of vertebra NOS

733.01 Senile osteoporosis
Postmenopausal osteoporosis

733.02 Idiopathic osteoporosis

733.03 Disuse osteoporosis

733.09 Other
Drug-induced osteoporosis
Use additional E code, if desired, to identify drug

● Code new
to this edition

▲ Revision of
existing code

④ ⑤ Fourth or fifth
digit required

733.1 Pathologic fracture
Spontaneous fracture

Excludes: *traumatic fracture (800-829)*

733.10 Pathologic fracture, unspecified site

733.11 Pathologic fracture of humerus

733.12 Pathologic fracture of distal radius and ulna
Wrist NOS

733.13 Pathologic fracture of vertebrae
Collapse of vertebra NOS

733.14 Pathologic fracture of neck of femur
Femur NOS
Hip NOS

733.15 Pathologic fracture of other specified part of femur

733.16 Pathologic fracture of tibia or fibula
Ankle NOS

733.19 Pathologic fracture of other specified site

733.2 Cyst of bone

733.20 Cyst of bone (localized), unspecified

733.21 Solitary bone cyst
Unicameral bone cyst

733.22 Aneurysmal bone cyst

733.29 Other
Fibrous dysplasia (monostotic)

Excludes: *cyst of jaw (526.0-526.2, 526.89)*
osteitis fibrosa cystica (252.0)
polyostotic fibrous dysplasia of bone (756.54)

733.3 Hyperostosis of skull
Hyperostosis interna frontalis
Leontiasis ossium

733.4 Aseptic necrosis of bone

Excludes: *necrosis of bone NOS (730.1)*
osteochondropathies (732.0-732.9)

733.40 Aseptic necrosis of bone, site unspecified

733.41 Head of humerus

733.42 Head and neck of femur
Femur NOS

Excludes: *Legg-Calvé-Perthes disease (732.1)*

733.43 Medial femoral condyle

733.44 Talus

733.49 Other

733.5 Osteitis condensans
Piriform sclerosis of ilium

733.6 Tietze's disease
Costochondral junction syndrome
Costochondritis

733.7 Algoneurodystrophy
Disuse atrophy of bone   Sudeck's atrophy

733.8 Malunion and nonunion of fracture

733.81 Malunion of fracture

733.82 Nonunion of fracture
Pseudoarthrosis (bone)

733.9 Other and unspecified disorders of bone and cartilage

733.90 Disorder of bone and cartilage, unspecified

733.91 Arrest of bone development or growth
Epiphyseal arrest

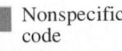	Add 4th or 5th digit		Nonspecific code		Unspecified code	Manifestation code

733.92 Chondromalacia
Chondromalacia:
  NOS
  localized, except patella
  systemic
  tibial plateau

Excludes: *chondromalacia of patella (717.7)*

733.99 Other
Diaphysitis   Relapsing polychondritis
Hypertrophy of bone

734 Flat foot
Pes planus (acquired)
Talipes planus (acquired)

Excludes: *congenital (754.61)*
  rigid flat foot (754.61)
  spastic (everted) flat foot (754.61)

735 Acquired deformities of toe

Excludes: *congenital (754.60-754.69, 755.65-755.66)*

735.0 Hallux valgus (acquired)

735.1 Hallux varus (acquired)

735.2 Hallux rigidus

735.3 Hallux malleus

735.4 Other hammer toe (acquired)

735.5 Claw toe (acquired)

735.8 Other acquired deformities of toe

735.9 Unspecified acquired deformity of toe

736 Other acquired deformities of limbs

Excludes: *congenital (754.3-755.9)*

736.0 Acquired deformities of forearm, excluding fingers

736.00 Unspecified deformity
Deformity of elbow, forearm, hand, or wrist (acquired) NOS

736.01 Cubitus valgus (acquired)

736.02 Cubitus varus (acquired)

736.03 Valgus deformity of wrist (acquired)

736.04 Varus deformity of wrist (acquired)

736.05 Wrist drop (acquired)

736.06 Claw hand (acquired)

736.07 Club hand, acquired

736.09 Other

736.1 Mallet finger

736.2 Other acquired deformities of finger

736.20 Unspecified deformity
Deformity of finger (acquired) NOS

736.21 Boutonniere deformity

736.22 Swan-neck deformity

736.29 Other

Excludes: *trigger finger (727.03)*

736.3 Acquired deformities of hip

736.30 Unspecified deformity
Deformity of hip (acquired) NOS

736.31 Coxa valga (acquired)

736.32 Coxa vara (acquired)

736.39 Other

736.4 Genu valgum or varum (acquired)

736.41 Genu valgum (acquired)

● Code new   ▲ Revision of   ④ ⑤ Fourth or fifth
  to this edition   existing code   digit required

736.42 Genu varum (acquired)

736.5 Genu recurvatum (acquired)

736.6 Other acquired deformities of knee
Deformity of knee (acquired) NOS

736.7 Other acquired deformities of ankle and foot

> *Excludes:* *deformities of toe (acquired) (735.0-735.9)*
> *pes planus (acquired) (734)*

736.70 Unspecified deformity of ankle and foot, acquired

736.71 Acquired equinovarus deformity
Clubfoot, acquired

> *Excludes:* *clubfoot not specified as acquired (754.5-754.7)*

736.72 Equinus deformity of foot, acquired

736.73 Cavus deformity of foot

> *Excludes:* *that with claw foot (736.74)*

736.74 Claw foot, acquired

736.75 Cavovarus deformity of foot, acquired

736.76 Other calcaneus deformity

736.79 Other
Acquired:
pes   ⎫
talipes   ⎬ not elsewhere classified
          ⎭

736.8 Acquired deformities of other parts of limbs

736.81 Unequal leg length (acquired)

736.89 Other
Deformity (acquired):
arm or leg, not elsewhere classified
shoulder

736.9 Acquired deformity of limb, site unspecified

737 Curvature of spine

> *Excludes:* *congenital (754.2)*

737.0 Adolescent postural kyphosis

> *Excludes:* *osteochondrosis of spine (juvenile) (732.0)*
> *adult (732.8)*

737.1 Kyphosis (acquired)

737.10 Kyphosis (acquired) (postural)

737.11 Kyphosis due to radiation

737.12 Kyphosis, postlaminectomy

737.19 Other

> *Excludes:* *that associated with conditions classifiable elsewhere (737.41)*

737.2 Lordosis (acquired)

737.20 Lordosis (acquired) (postural)

737.21 Lordosis, postlaminectomy

737.22 Other postsurgical lordosis

737.29 Other

> *Excludes:* *that associated with conditions classifiable elsewhere (737.42)*

737.3 Kyphoscoliosis and scoliosis

737.30 Scoliosis [and kyphoscoliosis], idiopathic

737.31 Resolving infantile idiopathic scoliosis

737.32 Progressive infantile idiopathic scoliosis

737.33 Scoliosis due to radiation

737.34 Thoracogenic scoliosis

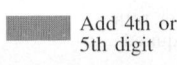 Add 4th or
5th digit

 Nonspecific
code

 Unspecified
code

 Manifestation
code

737.39 Other

Excludes: *that associated with conditions classifiable elsewhere (737.43)*
that in kyphoscoliotic heart disease (416.1)

737.4 Curvature of spine associated with other conditions
Code first associated condition, as:
Charcot-Marie-Tooth disease (356.1)
mucopolysaccharidosis (277.5)
neurofibromatosis (237.7)
osteitis deformans (731.0)
osteitis fibrosa cystica (252.0)
osteoporosis (733.00-733.09)
poliomyelitis (138)
tuberculosis [Pott's curvature] (015.0)

737.40 *Curvature of spine, unspecified*

737.41 *Kyphosis*

737.42 *Lordosis*

737.43 *Scoliosis*

737.8 **Other curvatures of spine**

737.9 **Unspecified curvature of spine**
Curvature of spine (acquired) (idiopathic) NOS
Hunchback, acquired

Excludes: *deformity of spine NOS (738.5)*

738 **Other acquired deformity**

Excludes: *congenital (754.0-756.9, 758.0-759.9)*
dentofacial anomalies (524.0-524.9)

738.0 Acquired deformity of nose
Deformity of nose (acquired)
Overdevelopment of nasal bones

Excludes: *deflected or deviated nasal septum (470)*

738.1 Other acquired deformity of head

738.10 **Unspecified deformity**

738.11 **Zygomatic hyperplasia**

738.12 **Zygomatic hypoplasia**

738.19 **Other specified deformity**

738.2 Acquired deformity of neck

738.3 Acquired deformity of chest and rib

Deformity:	Pectus:
chest (acquired)	carinatum, acquired
rib (acquired)	excavatum, acquired

738.4 Acquired spondylolisthesis
Degenerative spondylolisthesis
Spondylolysis, acquired

Excludes: *congenital (756.12)*

738.5 **Other acquired deformity of back or spine**
Deformity of spine NOS

Excludes: *curvature of spine (737.0-737.9)*

738.6 Acquired deformity of pelvis
Pelvic obliquity

Excludes: *intrapelvic protrusion of acetabulum (718.6)*
that in relation to labor and delivery (653.0-653.4, 653.8-653.9)

738.7 Cauliflower ear

738.8 **Acquired deformity of other specified site**
Deformity of clavicle

738.9 **Acquired deformity of unspecified site**

● Code new
  to this edition

▲ Revision of
  existing code

④ ⑤ Fourth or fifth
  digit required

739 **Nonallopathic lesions, not elsewhere classified**
  Includes: segmental dysfunction
         somatic dysfunction

739.0 Head region
    Occipitocervical region

739.1 Cervical region
    Cervicothoracic region

739.2 Thoracic region
    Thoracolumbar region

739.3 Lumbar region
    Lumbosacral region

739.4 Sacral region
    Sacrococcygeal region   Sacroiliac region

739.5 Pelvic region
    Hip region   Pubic region

739.6 Lower extremities

739.7 Upper extremities
    Acromioclavicular region   Sternoclavicular region

739.8 Rib cage
    Costochondral region   Sternochondral region
    Costovertebral region

739.9 Abdomen and other

 Add 4th or
5th digit

 Nonspecific
code

Unspecified
code

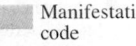 Manifestation
code

● Code new
to this edition

▲ Revision of
existing code

④ ⑤ Fourth or fifth
digit required

14. **CONGENITAL ANOMALIES (740-759)**

740 **Anencephalus and similar anomalies**

740.0 Anencephalus

Acrania
Amyelencephalus

Hemianencephaly
Hemicephaly

740.1 Craniorachischisis

740.2 Iniencephaly

⑤ **741** **Spina bifida**

Excludes: *spina bifida occulta (756.17)*

The following fifth-digit subclassification is for use with category 741:

0 **unspecified region**

1 **cervical region**

2 **dorsal [thoracic] region**

3 **lumbar region**

741.0 With hydrocephalus

Arnold-Chiari syndrome, type II
Any condition classifiable to 741.9 with any condition classifiable to 742.3
Chiari malformation, type II

741.9 Without mention of hydrocephalus

Hydromeningocele (spinal)
Hydromyelocele
Meningocele (spinal)
Meningomyelocele
Myelocele

Myelocystocele
Rachischisis
Spina bifida (aperta)
Syringomyelocele

742 **Other congenital anomalies of nervous system**

742.0 Encephalocele

Encephalocystocele
Encephalomyelocele
Hydroencephalocele
Hydromeningocele, cranial

Meningocele, cerebral
Meningoencephalocele

742.1 Microcephalus

Hydromicrocephaly

Micrencephaly

742.2 Reduction deformities of brain

Absence
Agenesis
Aplasia
Hypoplasia

} of part of brain

Agyria
Arhinencephaly
Holoprosencephaly
Microgyria

742.3 Congenital hydrocephalus

Aqueduct of Sylvius:
anomaly
obstruction, congenital
stenosis
Atresia of foramina of Magendie and Luschka
Hydrocephalus in newborn

Excludes: *hydrocephalus:*
acquired (331.3-331.4)
due to congenital toxoplasmosis (771.2)
with any condition classifiable to 741.9 (741.0)

742.4 **Other specified anomalies of brain**

Congenital cerebral cyst
Macroencephaly
Macrogyria
Megalencephaly

Multiple anomalies of brain NOS
Porencephaly
Ulegyria

742.5 Other specified anomalies of spinal cord

742.51 Diastematomyelia

742.53 Hydromyelia

Hydrorhachis

Add 4th or
5th digit

Nonspecific
code

Unspecified
code

Manifestation
code

742.59 **Other**
Amyelia
Atelomyelia
Congenital anomaly of spinal meninges
Defective development of cauda equina
Hypoplasia of spinal cord
Myelatelia
Myelodysplasia

742.8 **Other specified anomalies of nervous system**
Agenesis of nerve   Jaw-winking syndrome
Displacement of brachial   Marcus-Gunn syndrome
   plexus   Riley-Day syndrome
Familial dysautonomia

Excludes: *neurofibromatosis (237.7)*

742.9 **Unspecified anomaly of brain, spinal cord, and nervous system**
Anomaly
Congenital:
  disease   } of { brain
  lesion   nervous system
Deformity   spinal cord

743 **Congenital anomalies of eye**

743.0 **Anophthalmos**

743.00 **Clinical anophthalmos, unspecified**
Agenesis
Congenital absence   } of eye
Anophthalmos NOS

743.03 **Cystic eyeball, congenital**

743.06 **Cryptophthalmos**

743.1 **Microphthalmos**
Dysplasia
Hypoplasia   } of eye
Rudimentary eye

743.10 **Microphthalmos, unspecified**

743.11 **Simple microphthalmos**

743.12 **Microphthalmos associated with other anomalies of eye and adnexa**

743.2 **Buphthalmos**
Glaucoma: Hydrophthalmos
  congenital
  newborn

Excludes: *glaucoma of childhood (365.14)*
traumatic glaucoma due to birth injury (767.8)

743.20 **Buphthalmos, unspecified**

743.21 **Simple buphthalmos**

743.22 **Buphthalmos associated with other ocular anomalies**
Keratoglobus, congenital
Megalocornea   } associated with buphthalmos

743.3 **Congenital cataract and lens anomalies**

Excludes: *infantile cataract (366.00-366.09)*

743.30 **Congenital cataract, unspecified**

743.31 **Capsular and subcapsular cataract**

743.32 **Cortical and zonular cataract**

743.33 **Nuclear cataract**

743.34 **Total and subtotal cataract, congenital**

743.35 **Congenital aphakia**
Congenital absence of lens

743.36 **Anomalies of lens shape**
Microphakia   Spherophakia

743.37 **Congenital ectopic lens**

743.39 **Other**

● Code new   ▲ Revision of   ④ ⑤ Fourth or fifth
  to this edition   existing code   digit required

743.4　Coloboma and other anomalies of anterior segment

　743.41　Anomalies of corneal size and shape
　　　Microcornea

　Excludes: *that associated with buphthalmos (743.22)*

　743.42　Corneal opacities, interfering with vision, congenital

　743.43　Other corneal opacities, congenital

　743.44　Specified anomalies of anterior chamber, chamber angle, and related structures
　　　Anomaly:
　　　　Axenfeld's
　　　　Peters'
　　　　Rieger's

　743.45　Aniridia

　743.46　Other specified anomalies of iris and ciliary body
　　　Anisocoria, congenital
　　　Atresia of pupil
　　　Coloboma of iris
　　　Corectopia

　743.47　Specified anomalies of sclera

　743.48　Multiple and combined anomalies of anterior segment

　743.49　Other

743.5　Congenital anomalies of posterior segment

　743.51　Vitreous anomalies
　　　Congenital vitreous opacity

　743.52　Fundus coloboma

　743.53　Chorioretinal degeneration, congenital

　743.54　Congenital folds and cysts of posterior segment

　743.55　Congenital macular changes

　743.56　Other retinal changes, congenital

　743.57　Specified anomalies of optic disc
　　　Coloboma of optic disc (congenital)

　743.58　Vascular anomalies
　　　Congenital retinal aneurysm

　743.59　Other

743.6　Congenital anomalies of eyelids, lacrimal system, and orbit

　743.61　Congenital ptosis

　743.62　Congenital deformities of eyelids
　　　Ablepharon　　　　　Congenital:
　　　Absence of eyelid　　　ectropion
　　　Accessory eyelid　　　entropion

　743.63　Other specified congenital anomalies of eyelid
　　　Absence, agenesis, of cilia

　743.64　Specified congenital anomalies of lacrimal gland

　743.65　Specified congenital anomalies of lacrimal passages
　　　Absence, agenesis of:
　　　　lacrimal apparatus
　　　　punctum lacrimale
　　　Accessory lacrimal canal

　743.66　Specified congenital anomalies of orbit

　743.69　Other
　　　Accessory eye muscles

743.8　Other specified anomalies of eye

　Excludes: *congenital nystagmus (379.51)*
　　　　　ocular albinism (270.2)
　　　　　retinitis pigmentosa (362.74)

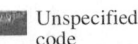 Add 4th or 5th digit　　　Nonspecific code　　　Unspecified code　　　Manifestation code

743.9 **Unspecified anomaly of eye**
Congenital:
anomaly NOS ⎫
deformity NOS ⎬ of eye [any part]

744 **Congenital anomalies of ear, face, and neck**

Excludes: anomaly of:
cervical spine (754.2, 756.10-756.19)
larynx (748.2-748.3)
nose (748.0-748.1)
parathyroid gland (759.2)
thyroid gland (759.2)
cleft lip (749.10-749.25)

744.0 **Anomalies of ear causing impairment of hearing**

Excludes: congenital deafness without mention of cause (389.0-389.9)

744.00 **Unspecified anomaly of ear with impairment of hearing**

744.01 **Absence of external ear**
Absence of:
auditory canal (external)
auricle (ear) (with stenosis or atresia of auditory canal)

744.02 **Other anomalies of external ear with impairment of hearing**
Atresia or stricture of auditory canal (external)

744.03 **Anomaly of middle ear, except ossicles**
Atresia or stricture of osseous meatus (ear)

744.04 **Anomalies of ear ossicles**
Fusion of ear ossicles

744.05 **Anomalies of inner ear**
Congenital anomaly of:
membranous labyrinth
organ of Corti

744.09 **Other**
Absence of ear, congenital

744.1 **Accessory auricle**
Accessory tragus   Supernumerary:
Polyotia   ear
Preauricular appendage   lobule

744.2 **Other specified anomalies of ear**

Excludes: that with impairment of hearing (744.00-744.09)

744.21 **Absence of ear lobe, congenital**

744.22 **Macrotia**

744.23 **Microtia**

744.24 **Specified anomalies of Eustachian tube**
Absence of Eustachian tube

744.29 **Other**
Bat ear   Prominence of auricle
Darwin's tubercle   Ridge ear
Pointed ear

Excludes: preauricular sinus (744.46)

744.3 **Unspecified anomaly of ear**
Congenital:
anomaly NOS ⎫
deformity NOS ⎬ of ear, not elsewhere classified

744.4 **Branchial cleft cyst or fistula; preauricular sinus**

744.41 **Branchial cleft sinus or fistula**
Branchial:
sinus (external) (internal)
vestige

744.42 **Branchial cleft cyst**

744.43 **Cervical auricle**

744.46 **Preauricular sinus or fistula**

744.47 **Preauricular cyst**

● Code new   ▲ Revision of   ④ ⑤ Fourth or fifth
  to this edition   existing code   digit required

744.49 **Other**
>Fistula (of):
>>auricle, congenital
>>cervicoaural

744.5 **Webbing of neck**
>Pterygium colli

744.8 **Other specified anomalies of face and neck**

744.81 **Macrocheilia**
>Hypertrophy of lip, congenital

744.82 **Microcheilia**

744.83 **Macrostomia**

744.84 **Microstomia**

744.89 **Other**

Excludes: *congenital fistula of lip (750.25)*
>*musculoskeletal anomalies (754.0-754.1, 756.0)*

744.9 **Unspecified anomalies of face and neck**
>Congenital:
>>anomaly NOS ⎫
>>deformity NOS ⎬ of face [any part] or neck [any part]

745 **Bulbus cordis anomalies and anomalies of cardiac septal closure**

745.0 **Common truncus**
>Absent septum ⎫
>Communication (abnormal) ⎬ between aorta and pulmonary artery
>Aortic septal defect
>Common aortopulmonary trunk
>Persistent truncus arteriosus

745.1 **Transposition of great vessels**

745.10 **Complete transposition of great vessels**
>Transposition of great vessels:
>>NOS
>>classical

754.11 **Double outlet right ventricle**
>Dextratransposition of aorta
>Incomplete transposition of great vessels
>Origin of both great vessels from right ventricle
>Taussig-Bing syndrome or defect

745.12 **Corrected transposition of great vessels**

745.19 **Other**

745.2 **Tetralogy of Fallot**
>Fallot's pentalogy
>Ventricular septal defect with pulmonary stenosis or atresia, dextraposition of aorta, and hypertrophy of right ventricle

Excludes: *Fallot's triad (746.09)*

745.3 **Common ventricle**
>Cor triloculare biatriatum   Single ventricle

745.4 **Ventricular septal defect**
>Eisenmenger's defect or complex
>Gerbode defect
>Interventricular septal defect
>Left ventricular-right atrial communication
>Roger's disease

Excludes: *common atrioventricular canal type (745.69)*
>*single ventricle (745.3)*

745.5 **Ostium secundum type atrial septal defect**

Defect:	Patent or persistent:
atrium secundum	foramen ovale
fossa ovalis	ostium secundum
Lutembacher's syndrome	

745.6 **Endocardial cushion defects**

745.60 **Endocardial cushion defect, unspecified type**

	Add 4th or 5th digit		Nonspecific code		Unspecified code		Manifestation code

745.61   Ostium primum defect
Persistent ostium primum

745.69   Other
Absence of atrial septum
Atrioventricular canal type ventricular septal defect
Common atrioventricular canal
Common atrium

745.7   Cor biloculare
Absence of atrial and ventricular septa

745.8   Other

745.9   Unspecified defect of septal closure
Septal defect NOS

746   Other congenital anomalies of heart

Excludes: endocardial fibroelastosis (425.3)

746.0   Anomalies of pulmonary valve

Excludes: infundibular or subvalvular pulmonic stenosis (746.83)
tetralogy of Fallot (745.2)

746.00   Pulmonary valve anomaly, unspecified

746.01   Atresia, congenital
Congenital absence of pulmonary valve

746.02   Stenosis, congenital

746.09   Other
Congenital insufficiency of pulmonary valve
Fallot's triad or trilogy

746.1   Tricuspid atresia and stenosis, congenital
Absence of tricuspid valve

746.2   Ebstein's anomaly

746.3   Congenital stenosis of aortic valve
Congenital aortic stenosis

Excludes: congenital:
subaortic stenosis (746.81)
supravalvular aortic stenosis (747.22)

746.4   Congenital insufficiency of aortic valve
Bicuspid aortic valve
Congenital aortic insufficiency

746.5   Congenital mitral stenosis
Fused commissure
Parachute deformity ⎫ of mitral valve
Supernumerary cusps ⎭

746.6   Congenital mitral insufficiency

746.7   Hypoplastic left heart syndrome
Atresia, or marked hypoplasia, of aortic orifice or valve, with hypoplasia of ascending aorta and defective development of left ventricle (with mitral valve atresia)

746.8   Other specified anomalies of heart

746.81   Subaortic stenosis

746.82   Cor triatriatum

746.83   Infundibular pulmonic stenosis
Subvalvular pulmonic stenosis

746.84   Obstructive anomalies of heart, not elsewhere classified
Uhl's disease

746.85   Coronary artery anomaly
Anomalous origin or communication of coronary artery
Arteriovenous malformation of coronary artery
Coronary artery:
absence
arising from aorta or pulmonary trunk
single

746.86   Congenital heart block
Complete or incomplete atrioventricular [AV] block

● Code new
to this edition   ▲ Revision of
existing code   ④ ⑤ Fourth or fifth
digit required

746.87 **Malposition of heart and cardiac apex**
Abdominal heart   Levocardia (isolated)
Dextrocardia   Mesocardia
Ectopia cordis

Excludes: *dextrocardia with complete transposition of viscera (759.3)*

746.89 **Other**
Atresia ⎫
Hypoplasia ⎬ of cardiac vein
Congenital:
    cardiomegaly
    diverticulum, left ventricle
    pericardial defect

746.9 **Unspecified anomaly of heart**
Congenital:
    anomaly of heart NOS
    heart disease NOS

747 **Other congenital anomalies of circulatory system**

747.0 **Patent ductus arteriosus**
Patent ductus Botalli
Persistent ductus arteriosus

747.1 **Coarctation of aorta**

747.10 **Coarctation of aorta (preductal) (postductal)**
Hypoplasia of aortic arch

747.11 **Interruption of aortic arch**

747.2 **Other anomalies of aorta**

747.20 **Anomaly of aorta, unspecified**

747.21 **Anomalies of aortic arch**
Anomalous origin, right subclavian artery
Dextraposition of aorta
Double aortic arch
Kommerell's diverticulum
Overriding aorta
Persistent:
    convolutions, aortic arch
    right aortic arch
Vascular ring

Excludes: *hypoplasia of aortic arch (747.10)*

747.22 **Atresia and stenosis of aorta**
Absence ⎫
Aplasia ⎬ of aorta
Hypoplasia ⎪
Stricture ⎭
Supra (valvular)-aortic stenosis

Excludes: *congenital aortic (valvular) stenosis or stricture, so stated (746.3)*
hypoplasia of aorta in hypoplastic left heart syndrome (746.7)

747.29 **Other**
Aneurysm of sinus of Valsalva
Congenital:
    aneurysm ⎫
    dilation ⎬ of aorta

747.3 **Anomalies of pulmonary artery**
Agenesis ⎫
Anomaly ⎪
Atresia ⎬ of pulmonary artery
Coarctation ⎪
Hypoplasia ⎪
Stenosis ⎭
Pulmonary arteriovenous aneurysm

747.4 **Anomalies of great veins**

747.40 **Anomaly of great veins, unspecified**
Anomaly NOS of:
    pulmonary veins
    vena cava

	Add 4th or 5th digit		Nonspecific code		Unspecified code		Manifestation code

747.41 Total anomalous pulmonary venous connection
Total anomalous pulmonary venous return [TAPVR]:
  subdiaphragmatic
  supradiaphragmatic

747.42 Partial anomalous pulmonary venous connection
Partial anomalous pulmonary venous return

747.49 Other anomalies of great veins
Absence
Congenital stenosis } of vena cava (inferior) (superior)
Persistent:
  left posterior cardinal vein
  left superior vena cava
Scimitar syndrome
Transposition of pulmonary veins NOS

747.5 Absence or hypoplasia of umbilical artery
Single umbilical artery

747.6 Other anomalies of peripheral vascular system
Absence ⎤
Anomaly ⎬ of artery or vein, not elsewhere classified
Atresia ⎦
Arteriovenous aneurysm (peripheral)
Arteriovenous malformation of the peripheral vascular system
Congenital:
  aneurysm (peripheral)
  phlebectasia
  stricture, artery
  varix
Multiple renal arteries

Excludes: anomalies of:
    cerebral vessels (747.81)
    pulmonary artery (747.3)
    congenital retinal aneurysm (743.58)
    hemangioma (228.00-228.09)
    lymphangioma (228.1)

747.60 Anomaly of the peripheral vascular system, unspecified site

747.61 Gastrointestinal vessel anomaly

747.62 Renal vessel anomaly

747.63 Upper limb vessel anomaly

747.64 Lower limb vessel anomaly

747.69 Anomalies of other specified sites of peripheral vascular system

747.8 Other specified anomalies of circulatory system

747.81 Anomalies of cerebrovascular system
Arteriovenous malformation of brain
Cerebral arteriovenous aneurysm, congenital
Congenital anomalies of cerebral vessels

Excludes: ruptured cerebral (arteriovenous) aneurysm (430)

747.82 Spinal vessel anomaly
Arteriovenous malformation of spinal vessel

747.89 Other
Aneurysm, congenital, specified site not elsewhere classified

Excludes: congenital aneurysm:
    coronary (746.85)
    peripheral (747.6)
    pulmonary (747.3)
    retinal (743.58)

747.9 Unspecified anomaly of circulatory system

748 Congenital anomalies of respiratory system

Excludes: congenital defect of diaphragm (756.6)

748.0 Choanal atresia
Atresia ⎤
Congenital stenosis ⎬ of nares (anterior) (posterior)

748.1 **Other anomalies of nose**

Absent nose

Accessory nose

Cleft nose

Deformity of wall of nasal
sinus

Congenital:

deformity of nose

notching of tip of nose

perforation of wall of nasal sinus

Excludes: *congenital deviation of nasal septum (754.0)*

748.2 **Web of larynx**

Web of larynx:

NOS

glottic

subglottic

748.3 **Other anomalies of larynx, trachea, and bronchus**

Absence or agenesis of:

bronchus

larynx

trachea

Anomaly (of):

cricoid cartilage

epiglottis

thyroid cartilage

tracheal cartilage

Atresia (of):

epiglottis

glottis

larynx

trachea

Cleft thyroid, cartilage,
congenital

Congenital:

dilation, trachea

stenosis:

larynx

trachea

tracheocele

Diverticulum:

bronchus

trachea

Fissure of epiglottis

Laryngocele

Posterior cleft of cricoid cartilage (congenital)

Rudimentary tracheal bronchus

Stridor, laryngeal, congenital

748.4 **Congenital cystic lung**

Disease, lung:

cystic, congenital

polycystic, congenital

Honeycomb lung, congenital

Excludes: *acquired or unspecified cystic lung (518.89)*

748.5 **Agenesis, hypoplasia, and dysplasia of lung**

Absence of lung (fissures) (lobe)

Aplasia of lung

Hypoplasia of lung (lobe)

Sequestration of lung

748.6 **Other anomalies of lung**

748.60 **Anomaly of lung, unspecified**

748.61 **Congenital bronchiectasis**

748.69 **Other**

Accessory lung (lobe)

Azygos lobe (fissure), lung

748.8 **Other specified anomalies of respiratory system**

Abnormal communication between pericardial and pleural sacs

Anomaly, pleural folds

Atresia of nasopharynx

Congenital cyst of mediastinum

748.9 **Unspecified anomaly of respiratory system**

Anomaly of respiratory system NOS

749 **Cleft palate and cleft lip**

749.0 **Cleft palate**

749.00 **Cleft palate, unspecified**

749.01 **Unilateral, complete**

749.02 **Unilateral, incomplete**

Cleft uvula

749.03 **Bilateral, complete**

749.04 **Bilateral, incomplete**

749.1 **Cleft lip**

Cheiloschisis

Congenital fissure of lip

Harelip

Labium leporinum

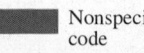 Add 4th or
5th digit

 Nonspecific
code

 Unspecified
code

Manifestation
code

749.10 Cleft lip, unspecified

749.11 Unilateral, complete

749.12 Unilateral, incomplete

749.13 Bilateral, complete

749.14 Bilateral, incomplete

749.2 Cleft palate with cleft lip
Cheilopalatoschisis

749.20 Cleft palate with cleft lip, unspecified

749.21 Unilateral, complete

749.22 Unilateral, incomplete

749.23 Bilateral, complete

749.24 Bilateral, incomplete

749.25 Other combinations

750 **Other congenital anomalies of upper alimentary tract**

Excludes: dentofacial anomalies (524.0-524.9)

750.0 Tongue tie
Ankyloglossia

750.1 Other anomalies of tongue

750.10 Anomaly of tongue, unspecified

750.11 Aglossia

750.12 Congenital adhesions of tongue

750.13 Fissure of tongue
Bifid tongue   Double tongue

750.15 Macroglossia
Congenital hypertrophy of tongue

750.16 Microglossia
Hypoplasia of tongue

750.19 Other

750.2 Other specified anomalies of mouth and pharynx

750.21 Absence of salivary gland

750.22 Accessory salivary gland

750.23 Atresia, salivary duct
Imperforate salivary duct

750.24 Congenital fistula of salivary gland

750.25 Congenital fistula of lip
Congenital (mucus) lip pits

750.26 Other specified anomalies of mouth
Absence of uvula

750.27 Diverticulum of pharynx
Pharyngeal pouch

750.29 Other specified anomalies of pharynx
Imperforate pharynx

750.3 Tracheoesophageal fistula, esophageal atresia and stenosis

Absent esophagus	Congenital fistula:
Atresia of esophagus	esophagobronchial
Congenital:	esophagotracheal
esophageal ring	Imperforate esophagus
stenosis of esophagus	Webbed esophagus
stricture of esophagus	

● Code new
to this edition

▲ Revision of
existing code

④ ⑤ Fourth or fifth
digit required

750.4 Other specified anomalies of esophagus
Dilatation, congenital
Displacement, congenital
Diverticulum
Duplication
Giant
Esophageal pouch
} (of) esophagus

Excludes: *congenital hiatus hernia (750.6)*

750.5 Congenital hypertrophic pyloric stenosis
Congenital or infantile:
constriction
hypertrophy
spasm
stenosis
stricture
} of pylorus

750.6 Congenital hiatus hernia
Displacement of cardia through esophageal hiatus

Excludes: *congenital diaphragmatic hernia (756.6)*

750.7 Other specified anomalies of stomach

Congenital:	Duplication of stomach
cardiospasm	Megalogastria
hourglass stomach	Microgastria
Displacement of stomach	Transposition of stomach
Diverticulum of stomach,	
congenital	

750.8 Other specified anomalies of upper alimentary tract

750.9 Unspecified anomaly of upper alimentary tract
Congenital:
anomaly NOS
deformity NOS
} of upper alimentary tract [any part, except tongue]

751 Other congenital anomalies of digestive system

751.0 Meckel's diverticulum
Meckel's diverticulum (displaced) (hypertrophic)
Persistent:
omphalomesenteric duct
vitelline duct

751.1 Atresia and stenosis of small intestine
Atresia of:
duodenum
ileum
intestine NOS
Congenital:
absence
obstruction
stenosis
stricture
Imperforate jejunum
} of small intestine or intestine NOS

751.2 Atresia and stenosis of large intestine, rectum, and anal canal

Absence:	Congenital or infantile:
anus (congenital)	obstruction of large intestine
appendix, congenital	occlusion of anus
large intestine, congenital	stricture of anus
rectum	Imperforate:
Atresia of:	anus
anus	rectum
colon	Stricture of rectum, congenital
rectum	

751.3 Hirschsprung's disease and other congenital functional disorders of colon

Aganglionosis	Congenital megacolon
Congenital dilation of colon	Macrocolon

345

| | Add 4th or 5th digit | | Nonspecific code | | Unspecified code | | Manifestation code |

751.4 Anomalies of intestinal fixation
Congenital adhesions:
  omental, anomalous
  peritoneal
Jackson's membrane
Malrotation of colon

Rotation of cecum or colon:
  failure of
  incomplete
  insufficient
Universal mesentery

751.5 Other anomalies of intestine
Congenital diverticulum,
  colon
Dolichocolon
Duplication of:
  anus
  appendix
  cecum
  intestine
Ectopic anus

Megaloappendix
Megaloduodenum
Microcolon
Persistent cloaca
Transposition of:
  appendix
  colon
  intestine

751.6 Anomalies of gallbladder, bile ducts, and liver

751.60 Unspecified anomaly of gallbladder, bile ducts, and liver

751.61 Biliary atresia
Congenital:
  absence
  hypoplasia
  obstruction } of bile duct (common) or passage
  stricture

751.62 Congenital cystic disease of liver
Congenital polycystic disease of liver
Fibrocystic disease of liver

751.69 Other anomalies of gallbladder, bile ducts, and liver
Absence of:
  gallbladder, congenital
  liver (lobe)
Accessory:
  hepatic ducts
  liver
Congenital:
  choledochal cyst
  hepatomegaly

Duplication of:
  biliary duct
  cystic duct
  gallbladder
  liver
Floating:
  gallbladder
  liver
Intrahepatic gallbladder

751.7 Anomalies of pancreas
Absence
Agenesis
Hypoplasia } of pancreas
Accessory pancreas

Annular pancreas
Ectopic pancreatic tissue
Pancreatic heterotopia

Excludes: *diabetes mellitus:*
    congenital (250.0-250.9)
    neonatal (775.1)
  fibrocystic disease of pancreas (277.00-277.01)

751.8 Other specified anomalies of digestive system
Absence (complete) (partial) of alimentary tract NOS
Duplication
Malposition, congenital } of digestive organs NOS

Excludes: *congenital diaphragmatic hernia (756.6)*
  congenital hiatus hernia (750.6)

751.9 Unspecified anomaly of digestive system
Congenital:
  anomaly NOS
  deformity NOS } of digestive system NOS

752 Congenital anomalies of genital organs

Excludes: *syndromes associated with anomalies in the number and form of chromosomes*
    (758.0-758.9)
  testicular feminization syndrome (257.8)

● Code new
  to this edition

▲ Revision of
  existing code

④ ⑤ Fourth or fifth
  digit required

752.0 Anomalies of ovaries
Absence, congenital
Accessory
Ectopic } (of) ovary
Streak

752.1 Anomalies of fallopian tubes and broad ligaments

752.10 Unspecified anomaly of fallopian tubes and broad ligaments

752.11 Embryonic cyst of fallopian tubes and broad ligaments
Cyst: Cyst:
  epoophoron   Gartner's duct
  fimbrial   parovarian

752.19 Other
Absence
Accessory } (of) fallopian tube or broad ligament
Atresia

752.2 Doubling of uterus
Didelphic uterus
Doubling of uterus [any degree] (associated with doubling of cervix and vagina)

752.3 Other anomalies of uterus
Absence, congenital
Agenesis } of uterus
Aplasia
Bicornuate uterus
Uterus unicornis
Uterus with only one functioning horn

752.4 Anomalies of cervix, vagina, and external female genitalia

752.40 Unspecified anomaly of cervix, vagina, and external female genitalia

752.41 Embryonic cyst of cervix, vagina, and external female genitalia
Cyst of:
  canal of Nuck, congenital
  vagina, embryonal
  vulva, congenital

752.42 Imperforate hymen

752.49 Other anomalies of cervix, vagina, and external female genitalia
Absence
Agenesis } of cervix, clitoris, vagina, or vulva
Congenital stenosis or stricture of:
  cervical canal
  vagina

Excludes: *double vagina associated with total duplication (752.2)*

▲ **752.5 Undescended and retractile testicle**

● **752.51 Undescended testis**
Cryptorchism
Ectopic testis

● **752.52 Retractile testis**

▲ **752.6 Hypospadias and epispadias and other penile anomalies**

● **752.61 Hypospadias**

● **752.62 Epispadias**
Anaspadias

● **752.63 Congenital chordee**

● **752.64 Micropenis**

● **752.65 Hidden penis**

● **752.69 Other penile anomalies**

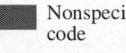 Add 4th or 5th digit   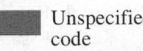 Nonspecific code   Unspecified code   Manifestation code

752.7 Indeterminate sex and pseudohermaphroditism

Gynandrism Pseudohermaphroditism (male) (female)
Hermaphroditism Pure gonadal dysgenesis
Ovotestis

Excludes: *pseudohermaphroditism:*

female, with adrenocortical disorder (255.2)
male, with gonadal disorder (257.8)
with specified chromosomal anomaly (758.0-758.9)
testicular feminization syndrome (257.8)

752.8 Other specified anomalies of genital organs

Absence of: Atresia of:
  prostate   ejaculatory duct
  spermatic cord   vas deferens
  vas deferens Fusion of testes
Anorchism Hypoplasia of testis
Aplasia (congenital) of: Monorchism
  prostate Polyorchism
  round ligament
  testicle

Excludes: *congenital hydrocele (778.6)*

penile anomalies (752.61-752.69)
phimosis or paraphimosis (605)

752.9 Unspecified anomaly of genital organs

Congenital:
  anomaly NOS ⎫
  deformity NOS ⎬ of genital organ, not elsewhere classified

753 Congenital anomalies of urinary system

753.0 Renal agenesis and dysgenesis

Atrophy of kidney: Congenital absence of kidney(s)
  congenital Hypoplasia of kidney(s)
  infantile
Code first any associated vesicoureteral reflux (593.70-593.73)

753.1 Cystic kidney disease

Excludes: *acquired cyst of kidney (593.2)*

753.10 Cystic kidney disease, unspecified

753.11 Congenital single renal cyst

753.12 Polycystic kidney, unspecified type

753.13 Polycystic kidney, autosomal dominant

753.14 Polycystic kidney, autosomal recessive

753.15 Renal dysplasia
Code first any associated vesicoureteral reflux (593.70-593.73)

753.16 Medullary cystic kidney
Nephronopthisis

753.17 Medullary sponge kidney

753.19 Other specified cystic kidney disease
Multicystic kidney

753.2 Obstructive defects of renal pelvis and ureter

● **753.20 Unspecified obstructive defect of renal pelvis and ureter**

● **753.21 Congenital obstruction of ureteropelvic junction**

● **753.22 Congenital obstruction of ureterovesical junction**
Adynamic ureter
Congenital hydroureter

● **753.23 Congenital ureterocele**

● **753.29 Other**

● Code new ▲ Revision of ④ ⑤ Fourth or fifth
  to this edition   existing code   digit required

753.3 **Other specified anomalies of kidney**

Accessory kidney
Congenital:
  calculus of kidney
  displaced kidney
Discoid kidney
Double kidney with double
  pelvis
Ectopic kidney

Fusion of kidneys
Giant kidney
Horseshoe kidney
Hyperplasia of kidney
Lobulation of kidney
Malrotation of kidney
Trifid kidney (pelvis)

753.4 **Other specified anomalies of ureter**

Absent ureter
Accessory ureter
Deviation of ureter
Displaced ureteric orifice

Double ureter
Ectopic ureter
Implantation, anomalous of ureter

753.5 **Exstrophy of urinary bladder**

Ectopia vesicae

Extroversion of bladder

753.6 **Atresia and stenosis of urethra and bladder neck**

Congenital obstruction:
  bladder neck
  urethra
Congenital stricture of:
  urethra (valvular)
  urinary meatus
  vesicourethral orifice

Imperforate urinary meatus
Impervious urethra
Urethral valve formation

753.7 **Anomalies of urachus**

Cyst   ⎫
Fistula ⎬ (of) urachus
Patent ⎭

Persistent umbilical sinus

753.8 **Other specified anomalies of bladder and urethra**

Absence, congenital of:
  bladder
  urethra
Accessory:
  bladder
  urethra
Congenital:
  diverticulum of bladder
  hernia of bladder

Congenital urethrorectal fistula
Congenital prolapse of:
  bladder (mucosa)
  urethra
Double:
  urethra
  urinary meatus

753.9 **Unspecified anomaly of urinary system**

Congenital:
  anomaly NOS ⎫
  deformity NOS ⎬ of urinary system [any part, except urachus]

754 **Certain congenital musculoskeletal deformities**

Includes: nonteratogenic deformities which are considered to be due to intrauterine malposition
and pressure

754.0 **Of skull, face, and jaw**

Asymmetry of face
Compression facies
Depressions in skull
Deviation of nasal
  septum, congenital

Dolichocephaly
Plagiocephaly
Potter's facies
Squashed or bent nose, congenital

Excludes: *dentofacial anomalies (524.0-524.9)*
       syphilitic saddle nose (090.5)

754.1 **Of sternocleidomastoid muscle**

Congenital sternomastoid torticollis
Congenital wryneck
Contracture of sternocleidomastoid (muscle)
Sternomastoid tumor

754.2 **Of spine**

Congenital postural:
  lordosis
  scoliosis

754.3 **Congenital dislocation of hip**

  754.30 **Congenital dislocation of hip, unilateral**
    Congenital dislocation of hip NOS

  754.31 **Congenital dislocation of hip, bilateral**

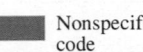 Add 4th or
5th digit

 Nonspecific
code

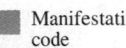 Unspecified
code

Manifestation
code

754.32 Congenital subluxation of hip, unilateral
Congenital flexion deformity, hip or thigh
Predislocation status of hip at birth
Preluxation of hip, congenital

754.33 Congenital subluxation of hip, bilateral

754.35 Congenital dislocation of one hip with subluxation of other hip

754.4 Congenital genu recurvatum and bowing of long bones of leg

754.40 Genu recurvatum

754.41 Congenital dislocation of knee (with genu recurvatum)

754.42 Congenital bowing of femur

754.43 Congenital bowing of tibia and fibula

754.44 Congenital bowing of unspecified long bones of leg

754.5 Varus deformities of feet

Excludes: acquired (736.71, 736.75, 736.79)

754.50 Talipes varus
Congenital varus deformity of foot, unspecified
Pes varus

754.51 Talipes equinovarus
Equinovarus (congenital)

754.52 Metatarsus primus varus

754.53 Metatarsus varus

754.59 Other
Talipes calcaneovarus

754.6 Valgus deformities of feet

Excludes: valgus deformity of foot (acquired) (736.79)

754.60 Talipes valgus
Congenital valgus deformity of foot, unspecified

754.61 Congenital pes planus
Congenital rocker bottom flat foot
Flat foot, congenital

Excludes: pes planus (acquired) (734)

754.62 Talipes calcaneovalgus

754.69 Other
Talipes:
equinovalgus
planovalgus

754.7 Other deformities of feet

Excludes: acquired (736.70-736.79)

754.70 Talipes, unspecified
Congenital deformity of foot NOS

754.71 Talipes cavus
Cavus foot (congenital)

754.79 Other
Asymmetric talipes
Talipes:
calcaneus
equinus

754.8 Other specified nonteratogenic anomalies

754.81 Pectus excavatum
Congenital funnel chest

754.82 Pectus carinatum
Congenital pigeon chest [breast]

754.89 Other
Club hand (congenital)
Congenital:
deformity of chest wall
dislocation of elbow
Generalized flexion contractures of lower limb joints, congenital
Spade-like hand (congenital)

● Code new
to this edition

▲ Revision of
existing code

④ ⑤ Fourth or fifth
digit required

755 **Other congenital anomalies of limbs**

> Excludes: those deformities classifiable to 754.0-754.8

755.0 Polydactyly

755.00 **Polydactyly, unspecified digits**
Supernumerary digits

755.01 **Of fingers**
Accessory fingers

755.02 **Of toes**
Accessory toes

755.1 Syndactyly

Symphalangy   Webbing of digits

755.10 **Of multiple and unspecified sites**

755.11 **Of fingers without fusion of bone**

755.12 **Of fingers with fusion of bone**

755.13 **Of toes without fusion of bone**

755.14 **Of toes with fusion of bone**

755.2 Reduction deformities of upper limb

755.20 **Unspecified reduction deformity of upper limb**
Ectromelia NOS ⎫
Hemimelia NOS ⎬ of upper limb
Shortening of arm, congenital

755.21 **Transverse deficiency of upper limb**
Amelia of upper limb
Congenital absence of:
  fingers, all (complete or partial)
  forearm, including hand and fingers
  upper limb, complete
Congenital amputation of upper limb
Transverse hemimelia of upper limb

755.22 **Longitudinal deficiency of upper limb, not elsewhere classified**
Phocomelia NOS of upper limb
Rudimentary arm

755.23 **Longitudinal deficiency, combined, involving humerus, radius, and ulna (complete or incomplete)**
Congenital absence of arm and forearm (complete or incomplete) with or
  without metacarpal deficiency and/or phalangeal deficiency, incomplete
Phocomelia, complete, of upper limb

755.24 **Longitudinal deficiency, humeral, complete or partial (with or without distal deficiencies, incomplete)**
Congenital absence of humerus (with or without absence of some [but not all]
  distal elements)
Proximal phocomelia of upper limb

755.25 **Longitudinal deficiency, radioulnar, complete or partial (with or without distal deficiencies, incomplete)**
Congenital absence of radius and ulna (with or without absence of some [but
  not all] distal elements)
Distal phocomelia of upper limb

755.26 **Longitudinal deficiency, radial, complete or partial (with or without distal deficiencies, incomplete)**
Agenesis of radius
Congenital absence of radius (with or without absence of some [but not all]
  distal elements)

755.27 **Longitudinal deficiency, ulnar, complete or partial (with or without distal deficiencies, incomplete)**
Agenesis of ulna
Congenital absence of ulna (with or without absence of some [but not all] distal
  elements)

755.28 **Longitudinal deficiency, carpals or metacarpals, complete or partial (with or without incomplete phalangeal deficiency)**

	Add 4th or 5th digit		Nonspecific code		Unspecified code		Manifestation code

755.29 Longitudinal deficiency, phalanges, complete or partial
Absence of finger, congenital
Aphalangia of upper limb, terminal, complete or partial

Excludes: *terminal deficiency of all five digits (755.21)*
transverse deficiency of phalanges (755.21)

755.3 Reduction deformities of lower limb

755.30 Unspecified reduction deformity of lower limb
Ectromelia NOS ⎫
Hemimelia NOS ⎬ of lower limb
Shortening of leg, congenital

755.31 Transverse deficiency of lower limb
Amelia of lower limb
Congenital absence of:
foot
leg, including foot and toes
lower limb, complete
toes, all, complete
Transverse hemimelia of lower limb

755.32 Longitudinal deficiency of lower limb, not elsewhere classified
Phocomelia NOS of lower limb

755.33 Longitudinal deficiency, combined, involving femur, tibia, and fibula (complete or incomplete)
Congenital absence of thigh and (lower) leg (complete or incomplete) with or without metacarpal deficiency and/or phalangeal deficiency, incomplete
Phocomelia, complete, of lower limb

755.34 Longitudinal deficiency, femoral, complete or partial (with or without distal deficiencies, incomplete)
Congenital absence of femur (with or without absence of some [but not all] distal elements)
Proximal phocomelia of lower limb

755.35 Longitudinal deficiency, tibiofibular, complete or partial (with or without distal deficiencies, incomplete)
Congenital absence of tibia and fibula (with or without absence of some [but not all] distal elements)
Distal phocomelia of lower limb

755.36 Longitudinal deficiency, tibia, complete or partial (with or without distal deficiencies, incomplete)
Agenesis of tibia
Congenital absence of tibia (with or without absence of some [but not all] distal elements)

755.37 Longitudinal deficiency, fibular, complete or partial (with or without distal deficiencies, incomplete)
Agenesis of fibula
Congenital absence of fibula (with or without absence of some [but not all] distal elements)

755.38 Longitudinal deficiency, tarsals or metatarsals, complete or partial (with or without incomplete phalangeal deficiency)

755.39 Longitudinal deficiency, phalanges, complete or partial
Absence of toe, congenital
Aphalangia of lower limb, terminal, complete or partial

Excludes: *terminal deficiency of all five digits (755.31)*
transverse deficiency of phalanges (755.31)

755.4 Reduction deformities, unspecified limb
Absence, congenital (complete or partial) of limb NOS
Amelia ⎫
Ectromelia ⎬ of unspecified limb
Hemimelia ⎪
Phocomelia ⎭

755.5 Other anomalies of upper limb, including shoulder girdle

755.50 Unspecified anomaly of upper limb

755.51 Congenital deformity of clavicle

755.52 Congenital elevation of scapula
Sprengel's deformity

755.53 Radioulnar synostosis

● Code new to this edition   ▲ Revision of existing code   ④ ⑤ Fourth or fifth digit required

755.54 **Madelung's deformity**

755.55 **Acrocephalosyndactyly**
Apert's syndrome

755.56 **Accessory carpal bones**

755.57 **Macrodactylia (fingers)**

755.58 **Cleft hand, congenital**
Lobster-claw hand

`755.59` **Other**
Cleidocranial dysostosis
Cubitus:
valgus, congenital
varus, congenital

Excludes: *club hand (congenital) (754.89)*
congenital dislocation of elbow (754.89)

755.6 **Other anomalies of lower limb, including pelvic girdle**

`755.60` **Unspecified anomaly of lower limb**

755.61 **Coxa valga, congenital**

755.62 **Coxa vara, congenital**

`755.63` **Other congenital deformity of hip (joint)**
Congenital anteversion of femur (neck)

Excludes: *congenital dislocation of hip (754.30-754.35)*

755.64 **Congenital deformity of knee (joint)**
Congenital:
absence of patella
genu valgum [knock-knee]
genu varum [bowleg]
Rudimentary patella

755.65 **Macrodactylia of toes**

`755.66` **Other anomalies of toes**
Congenital:
hallux valgus
hallux varus
hammer toe

755.67 **Anomalies of foot, not elsewhere classified**
Astragaloscaphoid synostosis
Calcaneonavicular bar
Coalition of calcaneus
Talonavicular synostosis
Tarsal coalitions

`755.69` **Other**
Congenital:
angulation of tibia
deformity (of):
ankle (joint)
sacroiliac (joint)
fusion of sacroiliac joint

`755.8` **Other specified anomalies of unspecified limb**

`755.9` **Unspecified anomaly of unspecified limb**
Congenital:
anomaly NOS
deformity NOS } of unspecified limb

Excludes: *reduction deformity of unspecified limb (755.4)*

`756` **Other congenital musculoskeletal anomalies**

Excludes: *those deformities classifiable to 754.0-754.8*

| | Add 4th or 5th digit | | Nonspecific code | | Unspecified code | | Manifestation code |

756.0 Anomalies of skull and face bones

Absence of skull bones
Acrocephaly
Congenital deformity of
    forehead
Craniosynostosis
Crouzon's disease
Hypertelorism

Imperfect fusion of skull
Oxycephaly
Platybasia
Premature closure of cranial sutures
Tower skull
Trigonocephaly

Excludes: *acrocephalosyndactyly [Apert's syndrome] (755.55)*
dentofacial anomalies (524.0-524.9)
skull defects associated with brain anomalies, such as:
    anencephalus (740.0)
    encephalocele (742.0)
    hydrocephalus (742.3)
    microcephalus (742.1)

756.1 Anomalies of spine

756.10 Anomaly of spine, unspecified

756.11 Spondylolysis, lumbosacral region
Prespondylolisthesis (lumbosacral)

756.12 Spondylolisthesis

756.13 Absence of vertebra, congenital

756.14 Hemivertebra

756.15 Fusion of spine [vertebra], congenital

756.16 Klippel-Feil syndrome

756.17 Spina bifida occulta

Excludes: *spina bifida (aperta) (741.0-741.9)*

756.19 Other
Platyspondylia
Supernumerary vertebra

756.2 Cervical rib
Supernumerary rib in the cervical region

756.3 Other anomalies of ribs and sternum

Congenital absence of:
    rib
    sternum

Congenital:
    fissure of sternum
    fusion of ribs
    Sternum bifidum

Excludes: *nonteratogenic deformity of chest wall (754.81-754.89)*

756.4 Chondrodystrophy

Achondroplasia
Chondrodystrophia (fetalis)

Dyschondroplasia
Enchondromatosis
Ollier's disease

Excludes: *lipochondrodystrophy [Hurler's syndrome] (277.5)*
Morquio's disease (277.5)

756.5 Osteodystrophies

756.50 Osteodystrophy, unspecified

756.51 Osteogenesis imperfecta
Fragilitas ossium
Osteopsathyrosis

756.52 Osteopetrosis

756.53 Osteopoikilosis

756.54 Polyostotic fibrous dysplasia of bone

756.55 Chondroectodermal dysplasia
Ellis-van Creveld syndrome

756.56 Multiple epiphyseal dysplasia

756.59 Other
Albright (-McCune)-Sternberg syndrome

● Code new
    to this edition

▲ Revision of
    existing code

④ ⑤ Fourth or fifth
        digit required

756.6 Anomalies of diaphragm
Absence of diaphragm   Eventration of diaphragm
Congenital hernia:
  diaphragmatic
  foramen of Morgagni

Excludes: congenital hiatus hernia (750.6)

756.7 Anomalies of abdominal wall
Omphalocele
Exomphalos   Prune belly (syndrome)
Gastroschisis

Excludes: umbilical hernia (551-553 with .1)

756.8 Other specified anomalies of muscle, tendon, fascia, and connective tissue

   756.81 Absence of muscle and tendon
   Absence of muscle (pectoral)

   756.82 Accessory muscle

   756.83 Ehlers-Danlos syndrome

   756.89 Other
   Amyotrophia congenita
   Congenital shortening of tendon

756.9 Other and unspecified anomalies of musculoskeletal system
Congenital:
  anomaly NOS   } of musculoskeletal system, not elsewhere classified
  deformity NOS

757 Congenital anomalies of the integument
Includes: anomalies of skin, subcutaneous tissue, hair, nails, and breast

Excludes: hemangioma (228.00-228.09)
          pigmented nevus (216.0-216.9)

757.0 Hereditary edema of legs
Congenital lymphedema   Milroy's disease
Hereditary trophedema

757.1 Ichthyosis congenita
Congenital ichthyosis
Harlequin fetus
Ichthyosiform erythroderma

757.2 Dermatoglyphic anomalies
Abnormal palmar creases

757.3 Other specified anomalies of skin

   757.31 Congenital ectodermal dysplasia

   757.32 Vascular hamartomas
   Birthmarks
   Port-wine stain
   Strawberry nevus

   757.33 Congenital pigmentary anomalies of skin
   Congenital poikiloderma
   Urticaria pigmentosa
   Xeroderma pigmentosum

   Excludes: albinism (270.2)

   757.39 Other
   Accessory skin tags, congenital
   Congenital scar
   Epidermolysis bullosa
   Keratoderma (congenital)

Excludes: pilonidal cyst (685.0-685.1)

757.4 Specified anomalies of hair
Congenital: Congenital:
  alopecia   hypertrichosis
  atrichosis   monilethrix
  beaded hair   Persistent lanugo

355

757.5 Specified anomalies of nails
Anonychia
Congenital:
  clubnail
  koilonychia
Congenital:
  leukonychia
  onychauxis
  pachyonychia

757.6 Specified anomalies of breast
Absent
Accessory
Supernumerary
Hypoplasia of breast
} breast or nipple

Excludes: *absence of pectoral muscle (756.81)*

757.8 Other specified anomalies of the integument

757.9 Unspecified anomaly of the integument
Congenital:
  anomaly NOS
  deformity NOS
} of integument

758 Chromosomal anomalies
Includes: syndromes associated with anomalies in the number and form of chromosomes

758.0 Down's syndrome
Mongolism
Translocation Down's
  syndrome
Trisomy:
  21 or 22
  G

758.1 Patau's syndrome
Trisomy:
  13
  D_1

758.2 Edwards' syndrome
Trisomy:
  18
  E_3

758.3 Autosomal deletion syndromes
Antimongolism syndrome   Cri-du-chat syndrome

758.4 Balanced autosomal translocation in normal individual

758.5 Other conditions due to autosomal anomalies
Accessory autosomes NEC

758.6 Gonadal dysgenesis
Ovarian dysgenesis
Turner's syndrome
XO syndrome

Excludes: *pure gonadal dysgenesis (752.7)*

758.7 Klinefelter's syndrome
XXY syndrome

▲ **758.8 Other conditions due to chromosome anomalies**
  ● **758.81   Other conditions due to sex chromosome anomalies**
  ● **758.89   Other**

758.9 Conditions due to anomaly of unspecified chromosome

759 Other and unspecified congenital anomalies

759.0 Anomalies of spleen
Aberrant
Absent
Accessory
} spleen
Congenital splenomegaly
Ectopic spleen
Lobulation of spleen

759.1 Anomalies of adrenal gland
Aberrant
Absent
Accessory
} adrenal gland

Excludes: *adrenogenital disorders (255.2)*
          congenital disorders of steroid metabolism (255.2)

● Code new
  to this edition
▲ Revision of
  existing code
④ ⑤ Fourth or fifth
    digit required

759.2 Anomalies of other endocrine glands
Absent parathyroid gland
Accessory thyroid gland
Persistent thyroglossal or thyrolingual duct
Thyroglossal (duct) cyst

Excludes: *congenital:*
goiter (246.1)
hypothyroidism (243)

759.3 Situs inversus
Situs inversus or transversus: Transposition of viscera:
  abdominalis   abdominal
  thoracis   thoracic

Excludes: *dextrocardia without mention of complete transposition (746.87)*

759.4 Conjoined twins
Craniopagus   Thoracopagus
Dicephalus   Xiphopagus
Pygopagus

759.5 Tuberous sclerosis
Bourneville's disease   Epiloia

759.6 Other hamartoses, not elsewhere classified
Syndrome:
Peutz-Jeghers
Sturge-Weber (-Dimitri)
von Hippel-Lindau

Excludes: *neurofibromatosis (237.7)*

759.7 Multiple congenital anomalies, so described
Congenital:
anomaly, multiple NOS
deformity, multiple NOS

759.8 Other specified anomalies

   759.81 Prader-Willi syndrome

   759.82 Marfan syndrome

   759.83 Fragile X syndrome

   759.89 Other
      Congenital malformation syndromes affecting multiple systems, not elsewhere
        classified
      Laurence-Moon-Biedl syndrome

759.9 Congenital anomaly, unspecified

357

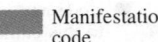

| Add 4th or 5th digit | Nonspecific code | Unspecified code | Manifestation code |

● Code new
to this edition

▲ Revision of
existing code

④ ⑤ Fourth or fifth
digit required

15. CERTAIN CONDITIONS ORIGINATING IN THE PERINATAL PERIOD (760-779)

> Includes: conditions which have their origin in the perinatal period even though death or morbidity occurs later

Use additional code(s) to further specify condition

MATERNAL CAUSES OF PERINATAL MORBIDITY AND MORTALITY (760-763)

760 **Fetus or newborn affected by maternal conditions which may be unrelated to present pregnancy**
Includes: the listed maternal conditions only when specified as a cause of mortality or morbidity of the fetus or newborn

> *Excludes:* *maternal endocrine and metabolic disorders affecting fetus or newborn (775.0-775.9)*

760.0 **Maternal hypertensive disorders**
Fetus or newborn affected by maternal conditions classifiable to 642

760.1 **Maternal renal and urinary tract diseases**
Fetus or newborn affected by maternal conditions classifiable to 580-599

760.2 **Maternal infections**
Fetus or newborn affected by maternal infectious disease classifiable to 001-136 and 487, but fetus or newborn not manifesting that disease

> *Excludes:* *congenital infectious diseases (771.0-771.8)*
> *maternal genital tract and other localized infections (760.8)*

760.3 **Other chronic maternal circulatory and respiratory diseases**
Fetus or newborn affected by chronic maternal conditions classifiable to 390-459, 490-519, 745-748

760.4 **Maternal nutritional disorders**
Fetus or newborn affected by:
maternal disorders classifiable to 260-269
maternal malnutrition NOS

> *Excludes:* *fetal malnutrition (764.10-764.29)*

760.5 **Maternal injury**
Fetus or newborn affected by maternal conditions classifiable to 800-995

760.6 **Surgical operation on mother**

> *Excludes:* *cesarean section for present delivery (763.4)*
> *damage to placenta from amniocentesis, cesarean section, or surgical induction (762.1)*
> *previous surgery to uterus or pelvic organs (763.8)*

760.7 **Noxious influences affecting fetus via placenta or breast milk**
Fetus or newborn affected by noxious substance transmitted via placenta or breast milk

> *Excludes:* *anesthetic and analgesic drugs administered during labor and delivery (763.5)*
> *drug withdrawal syndrome in newborn (779.5)*

760.70 **Unspecified noxious substance**
Fetus or newborn affected by:
Drug NEC

760.71 **Alcohol**
Fetal alcohol syndrome

760.72 **Narcotics**

760.73 **Hallucinogenic agents**

760.74 **Anti-infectives**
Antibiotics

760.75 **Cocaine**

760.76 **Diethylstilbestrol (DES)**

760.79 **Other**
Fetus or newborn affected by:
immune sera transmitted via placenta or breast milk
medicinal agents NEC transmitted via placenta or breast milk
toxic substance NEC transmitted via placenta or breast milk

760.8 **Other specified maternal conditions affecting fetus or newborn**
Maternal genital tract and other localized infection affecting fetus or newborn, but fetus or newborn not manifesting that disease

> *Excludes:* *maternal urinary tract infection affecting fetus or newborn (760.1)*

Add 4th or 5th digit   Nonspecific code   Unspecified code   Manifestation code

760.9 **Unspecified maternal condition affecting fetus or newborn**

761 **Fetus or newborn affected by maternal complications of pregnancy**

Includes: the listed maternal conditions only when specified as a cause of mortality or morbidity of the fetus or newborn

761.0 **Incompetent cervix**

761.1 **Premature rupture of membranes**

761.2 **Oligohydramnios**

Excludes: that due to premature rupture of membranes (761.1)

761.3 **Polyhydramnios**
Hydramnios (acute) (chronic)

761.4 **Ectopic pregnancy**
Pregnancy:
abdominal
intraperitoneal
tubal

761.5 **Multiple pregnancy**
Triplet (pregnancy)   Twin (pregnancy)

761.6 **Maternal death**

761.7 **Malpresentation before labor**
Breech presentation ⎤
External version   ⎥
Oblique lie   ⎬ before labor
Transverse lie   ⎥
Unstable lie   ⎦

761.8 **Other specified maternal complications of pregnancy affecting fetus or newborn**
Spontaneous abortion, fetus

761.9 **Unspecified maternal complication of pregnancy affecting fetus or newborn**

762 **Fetus or newborn affected by complications of placenta, cord, and membranes**

Includes: the listed maternal conditions only when specified as a cause of mortality or morbidity in the fetus or newborn

762.0 **Placenta previa**

762.1 **Other forms of placental separation and hemorrhage**
Abruptio placentae
Antepartum hemorrhage
Damage to placenta from amniocentesis, cesarean section, or surgical induction
Maternal blood loss
Premature separation of placenta
Rupture of marginal sinus

762.2 **Other and unspecified morphological and functional abnormalities of placenta**
Placental:
dysfunction
infarction
insufficiency

762.3 **Placental transfusion syndromes**
Placental and cord abnormality resulting in twin-to-twin or other transplacental transfusion

Use additional code, if desired, to indicate resultant condition in fetus or newborn:
fetal blood loss (772.0)
polycythemia neonatorum (776.4)

762.4 **Prolapsed cord**
Cord presentation

762.5 **Other compression of umbilical cord**
Cord around neck   Knot in cord
Entanglement of cord   Torsion of cord

762.6 **Other and unspecified conditions of umbilical cord**
Short cord   ⎤
Thrombosis   ⎥
Varices   ⎬ of umbilical cord
Velamentous insertion ⎥
Vasa previa   ⎦

Excludes: infection of umbilical cord (771.4)
single umbilical artery (747.5)

● Code new to this edition   ▲ Revision of existing code   ④ ⑤ Fourth or fifth digit required

762.7 Chorioamnionitis
Amnionitis   Placentitis
Membranitis

762.8 Other specified abnormalities of chorion and amnion

762.9 Unspecified abnormality of chorion and amnion

763 Fetus or newborn affected by other complications of labor and delivery
Includes: the listed conditions only when specified as a cause of mortality or morbidity in the
fetus or newborn

763.0 Breech delivery and extraction

763.1 Other malpresentation, malposition, and disproportion during labor and delivery
Fetus or newborn affected by:
abnormality of bony pelvis
contracted pelvis
persistent occipitoposterior position
shoulder presentation
transverse lie
conditions classifiable to 652, 653, and 660

763.2 Forceps delivery
Fetus or newborn affected by forceps extraction

763.3 Delivery by vacuum extractor

763.4 Cesarean delivery

> *Excludes:* *placental separation or hemorrhage from cesarean section (762.1)*

763.5 Maternal anesthesia and analgesia
Reactions and intoxications from maternal opiates and tranquilizers during labor and
delivery

> *Excludes:* *drug withdrawal syndrome in newborn (779.5)*

763.6 Precipitate delivery
Rapid second stage

763.7 Abnormal uterine contractions
Fetus or newborn affected by:
contraction ring
hypertonic labor
hypotonic uterine dysfunction
uterine inertia or dysfunction
conditions classifiable to 661, except 661.3

763.8 Other specified complications of labor and delivery affecting fetus or newborn
Fetus or newborn affected by:
abnormality of maternal soft tissues
destructive operation on live fetus to facilitate delivery
induction of labor (medical)
previous surgery to uterus or pelvic organs
other conditions classifiable to 650-669
other procedures used in labor and delivery

763.9 Unspecified complication of labor and delivery affecting fetus or newborn

OTHER CONDITIONS ORIGINATING IN THE PERINATAL PERIOD (764-779)

The following fifth-digit subclassification is for use with categories 764-765 to denote birthweight:

0   unspecified [weight]

1   less than 500 grams

2   500-749 grams

3   750-999 grams

4   1,000- 1,249 grams

5   1,250-1,499 grams

6   1,500-1,749 grams

7   1,750-1,999 grams

8   2,000-2,499 grams

9   2,500 grams and over

⑤ **764 Slow fetal growth and fetal malnutrition**

> *Excludes:* *low birthweight due to short gestation (765.00-765.19)*

 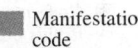

	Add 4th or 5th digit		Nonspecific code		Unspecified code		Manifestation code

361

764.0 **"Light-for-dates" without mention of fetal malnutrition**
Infants underweight for gestational age
"Small-for-dates"

764.1 **"Light-for-dates" with signs of fetal malnutrition**
Infants "light-for-dates" classifiable to 764.0, who in addition show signs of fetal
malnutrition, such as dry peeling skin and loss of subcutaneous tissue

764.2 **Fetal malnutrition without mention of "light-for-dates"**
Infants, not underweight for gestational age, showing signs of fetal malnutrition, such
as dry peeling skin and loss of subcutaneous tissue
Intrauterine malnutrition

764.9 **Fetal growth retardation, unspecified**
Intrauterine growth retardation

⑤ **765** **Disorders relating to short gestation and unspecified low birthweight**
Includes: the listed conditions, without further specification, as causes of mortality, morbidity,
or additional care, in fetus or newborn

Excludes: *low birthweight due to slow fetal growth and fetal malnutrition (764.00-764.99)*

765.0 **Extreme immaturity**
Note: Usually implies a birthweight of less than 1000 grams and/or a gestation of less than 28
completed weeks.

765.1 **Other preterm infants**
Note: Usually implies a birthweight of 1000-2499 grams and/or a gestation of 28-37 completed
weeks.
Prematurity NOS
Prematurity or small size, not classifiable to 765.0 or as "light-for-dates" in 764

766 **Disorders relating to long gestation and high birthweight**
Includes: the listed conditions, without further specification, as causes of mortality, morbidity,
or additional care, in fetus or newborn

766.0 **Exceptionally large baby**
Note: Usually implies a birthweight of 4500 grams or more.

766.1 **Other "heavy-for-dates" infants**
Other fetus or infant "heavy-" or "large-for-dates" regardless of period of gestation

766.2 **Post-term infant, not "heavy-for-dates"**
Fetus or infant with gestation period of 294 days or more [42 or more completed
weeks], not "heavy-" or "large-for-dates"
Postmaturity NOS

767 **Birth trauma**

767.0 **Subdural and cerebral hemorrhage**
Subdural and cerebral hemorrhage, whether described as due to birth trauma or to
intrapartum anoxia or hypoxia
Subdural hematoma (localized)
Tentorial tear
Use additional code, if desired, to identify cause

Excludes: *intraventricular hemorrhage (772.1)*
subarachnoid hemorrhage (772.2)

767.1 **Injuries to scalp**
Caput succedaneum
Cephalhematoma
Chignon (from vacuum extraction)
Massive epicranial subaponeurotic hemorrhage

767.2 **Fracture of clavicle**

767.3 **Other injuries to skeleton**
Fracture of:
long bones
skull

Excludes: *congenital dislocation of hip (754.30-754.35)*
fracture of spine, congenital (767.4)

● Code new
to this edition

▲ Revision of
existing code

④ ⑤ Fourth or fifth
digit required

767.4 Injury to spine and spinal cord
    Dislocation
    Fracture
    Laceration   } of spine or spinal cord due to birth trauma
    Rupture

767.5 Facial nerve injury
    Facial palsy

767.6 Injury to brachial plexus
    Palsy or paralysis:
      brachial
      Erb (-Duchenne)
      Klumpke (-Déjérine)

767.7 Other cranial and peripheral nerve injuries
    Phrenic nerve paralysis

767.8 Other specified birth trauma
    Eye damage   Rupture of:
    Hematoma of: liver
      liver (subcapsular)   spleen
      testes   Scalpel wound
      vulva   Traumatic glaucoma

    Excludes: *hemorrhage classifiable to 772.0-772.9*

767.9 Birth trauma, unspecified
    Birth injury NOS

768 Intrauterine hypoxia and birth asphyxia
Use only when associated with newborn morbidity classifiable elsewhere

    768.0 Fetal death from asphyxia or anoxia before onset of labor or at unspecified time

    768.1 Fetal death from asphyxia or anoxia during labor

    768.2 Fetal distress before onset of labor, in liveborn infant
      Abnormal fetal heart rate or rhythm
      Fetal or intrauterine:
        acidosis   } first noted before onset of labor,
        anoxia or hypoxia   liveborn infant
      Any condition classifiable to 768.4

    768.3 Fetal distress first noted during labor, in liveborn infant
      Abnormal fetal heart rate or rhythm
      Fetal or intrauterine:
        acidosis   } first noted during labor or delivery,
        anoxia or hypoxia   liveborn infant
      Any condition classifiable to 768.4

    768.4 Fetal distress, unspecified, as to time of onset, in liveborn infant
      Abnormal fetal heart rate or rhythm
      Fetal or intrauterine:
        acidosis
        anoxia   } not stated whether first noted
        asphyxia   before or after onset of labor,
        distress   liveborn infant
        hypercapnia
        hypoxia

    768.5 Severe birth asphyxia
      Birth asphyxia with neurologic involvement

    768.6 Mild or moderate birth asphyxia
      Other specified birth asphyxia (without mention of neurologic involvement)

    768.9 Unspecified birth asphyxia in liveborn infant
      Anoxia
      Asphyxia   } NOS, in liveborn infant
      Hypoxia

769 Respiratory distress syndrome
    Cardiorespiratory distress syndrome of newborn
    Hyaline membrane disease (pulmonary)
    Idiopathic respiratory distress syndrome [IRDS or RDS] of newborn
    Pulmonary hypoperfusion syndrome

    Excludes: *transient tachypnea of newborn (770.6)*

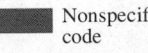 Add 4th or 5th digit   Nonspecific code   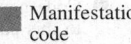 Unspecified code   Manifestation code

770 **Other respiratory conditions of fetus and newborn**

770.0 **Congenital pneumonia**
Infective pneumonia acquired prenatally

Excludes: *pneumonia from infection acquired after birth (480.0-486)*

770.1 **Meconium aspiration syndrome**
Aspiration of contents of birth canal NOS
Meconium aspiration below vocal cords
Pneumonitis:
  fetal aspiration
  meconium

770.2 **Interstitial emphysema and related conditions**
Pneumomediastinum
Pneumopericardium } originating in the perinatal period
Pneumothorax

770.3 **Pulmonary hemorrhage**
Hemorrhage:
  alveolar (lung)
  intra-alveolar (lung) } originating in the perinatal period
  massive pulmonary

770.4 **Primary atelectasis**
Pulmonary immaturity NOS

770.5 **Other and unspecified atelectasis**
Atelectasis:
  NOS
  partial
  secondary } originating in the perinatal period
Pulmonary collapse

770.6 **Transitory tachypnea of newborn**
Idiopathic tachypnea of newborn
Wet lung syndrome

Excludes: *respiratory distress syndrome (769)*

770.7 **Chronic respiratory disease arising in the perinatal period**
Bronchopulmonary dysplasia
Interstitial pulmonary fibrosis of prematurity
Wilson-Mikity syndrome

770.8 **Other respiratory problems after birth**
Apneic spells NOS
Cyanotic attacks NOS
Respiratory distress NOS } originating in the perinatal period
Respiratory failure NOS

770.9 **Unspecified respiratory condition of fetus and newborn**

771 **Infections specific to the perinatal period**
Includes: infections acquired before or during birth or via the umbilicus

Excludes: *congenital pneumonia (770.0)*
congenital syphilis (090.0-090.9)
maternal infectious disease as a cause of mortality or morbidity in fetus or
  newborn, but fetus or newborn not manifesting the disease (760.2)
ophthalmia neonatorum due to gonococcus (098.40)
other infections not specifically classified to this category

771.0 **Congenital rubella**
Congenital rubella pneumonitis

771.1 **Congenital cytomegalovirus infection**
Congenital cytomegalic inclusion disease

771.2 **Other congenital infections**
Congenital: Congenital:
  herpes simplex   toxoplasmosis
  listeriosis   tuberculosis
  malaria

771.3 **Tetanus neonatorum**
Tetanus omphalitis

Excludes: *hypocalcemic tetany (775.4)*

● Code new
  to this edition

▲ Revision of
  existing code

④ ⑤ Fourth or fifth
  digit required

771.4 Omphalitis of the newborn
Infection:
navel cord
umbilical stump

Excludes: tetanus omphalitis (771.3)

771.5 Neonatal infective mastitis

Excludes: noninfective neonatal mastitis (778.7)

771.6 Neonatal conjunctivitis and dacryocystitis
Ophthalmia neonatorum NOS

Excludes: ophthalmia neonatorum due to gonococcus (098.40)

771.7 Neonatal Candida infection
Neonatal moniliasis
Thrush in newborn

771.8 Other infection specific to the perinatal period
Intra-amniotic infection of fetus:
NOS
clostridial
Escherichia coli [E. coli]
Intrauterine sepsis of fetus
Neonatal urinary tract infection
Septicemia [sepsis] of newborn

772 Fetal and neonatal hemorrhage

Excludes: hematological disorders of fetus and newborn (776.0-776.9)

772.0 Fetal blood loss
Fetal blood loss from: Fetal exsanguination
   cut end of co-twin's cord   Fetal hemorrhage into:
   placenta   co-twin
   ruptured cord   mother's circulation
   vasa previa

772.1 Intraventricular hemorrhage
Intraventricular hemorrhage from any perinatal cause

772.2 Subarachnoid hemorrhage
Subarachnoid hemorrhage from any perinatal cause

Excludes: subdural and cerebral hemorrhage (767.0)

772.3 Umbilical hemorrhage after birth
Slipped umbilical ligature

772.4 Gastrointestinal hemorrhage

Excludes: swallowed maternal blood (777.3)

772.5 Adrenal hemorrhage

772.6 Cutaneous hemorrhage
Bruising
Ecchymoses
Petechiae   } in fetus or newborn
Superficial hematoma

772.8 Other specified hemorrhage of fetus or newborn

Excludes: hemorrhagic disease of newborn (776.0)
           pulmonary hemorrhage (770.3)

772.9 Unspecified hemorrhage of newborn

773 Hemolytic disease of fetus or newborn, due to isoimmunization

773.0 Hemolytic disease due to Rh isoimmunization
Anemia   } due to RH:
Erythroblastosis (fetalis)   antibodies
Hemolytic disease (fetus) (newborn)   isoimmunization
Jaundice   maternal/fetal incompatibility
Rh hemolytic disease
Rh isoimmunization

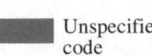 Add 4th or   Nonspecific   Unspecified   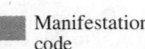 Manifestation
5th digit   code   code   code

773.1 Hemolytic disease due to ABO isoimmunization
ABO hemolytic disease
ABO isoimmunization
Anemia
Erythroblastosis (fetalis)
Hemolytic disease (fetus) (newborn)
Jaundice

due to ABO:
  antibodies
  isoimmunization
  maternal/fetal incompatibility

773.2 Hemolytic disease due to other and unspecified isoimmunization
Erythroblastosis (fetalis) (neonatorum) NOS
Hemolytic disease (fetus) (newborn) NOS
Jaundice or anemia due to other and unspecified blood-group incompatibility

773.3 Hydrops fetalis due to isoimmunization
Use additional code, if desired, to identify type of isoimmunization (773.0-773.2)

773.4 Kernicterus due to isoimmunization
Use additional code, if desired, to identify type of isoimmunization (773.0-773.2)

773.5 Late anemia due to isoimmunization

774 Other perinatal jaundice

774.0 *Perinatal jaundice from hereditary hemolytic anemias*
Code first underlying disease (282.0-282.9)

774.1 Perinatal jaundice from other excessive hemolysis
Fetal or neonatal jaundice from:
  bruising
  drugs or toxins transmitted from mother
  infection
  polycythemia
  swallowed maternal blood
Use additional code, if desired, to identify cause

> Excludes: jaundice due to isoimmunization (773.0-773.2)

774.2 Neonatal jaundice associated with preterm delivery
Hyperbilirubinemia of prematurity
Jaundice due to delayed conjugation associated with preterm delivery

774.3 Neonatal jaundice due to delayed conjugation from other causes

774.30 Neonatal jaundice due to delayed conjugation, cause unspecified

774.31 *Neonatal jaundice due to delayed conjugation in diseases classified elsewhere*
Code first underlying diseases, as:
  congenital hypothyroidism (243)
  Crigler-Najjar syndrome (277.4)
  Gilbert's syndrome (277.4)

774.39 Other
Jaundice due to delayed conjugation from causes, such as:
  breast milk inhibitors
  delayed development of conjugating system

774.4 Perinatal jaundice due to hepatocellular damage
Fetal or neonatal hepatitis
Giant cell hepatitis
Inspissated bile syndrome

774.5 *Perinatal jaundice from other causes*
Code first underlying cause, as:
  congenital obstruction of bile duct (751.61)
  galactosemia (271.1)
  mucoviscidosis (277.00-277.01)

774.6 Unspecified fetal and neonatal jaundice
Icterus neonatorum
Neonatal hyperbilirubinemia (transient)
Physiologic jaundice NOS in newborn

> Excludes: that in preterm infants (774.2)

774.7 Kernicterus not due to isoimmunization
Bilirubin encephalopathy
Kernicterus of newborn NOS

> Excludes: kernicterus due to isoimmunization (773.4)

● Code new
  to this edition
▲ Revision of
  existing code
④ ⑤ Fourth or fifth
  digit required

775 **Endocrine and metabolic disturbances specific to the fetus and newborn**
    Includes: transitory endocrine and metabolic disturbances caused by the infant's response to maternal endocrine and metabolic factors, its removal from them, or its adjustment to extrauterine existence

775.0 **Syndrome of "infant of a diabetic mother"**
    Maternal diabetes mellitus affecting fetus or newborn (with hypoglycemia)

775.1 **Neonatal diabetes mellitus**
    Diabetes mellitus syndrome in newborn infant

775.2 **Neonatal myasthenia gravis**

775.3 **Neonatal thyrotoxicosis**
    Neonatal hyperthyroidism (transient)

775.4 **Hypocalcemia and hypomagnesemia of newborn**
    Cow's milk hypocalcemia
    Hypocalcemic tetany, neonatal
    Neonatal hypoparathyroidism
    Phosphate-loading hypocalcemia

775.5 **Other transitory neonatal electrolyte disturbances**
    Dehydration, neonatal

775.6 **Neonatal hypoglycemia**

> *Excludes:* *infant of mother with diabetes mellitus (775.0)*

775.7 **Late metabolic acidosis of newborn**

775.8 **Other transitory neonatal endocrine and metabolic disturbances**
    Amino-acid metabolic disorders described as transitory

775.9 **Unspecified endocrine and metabolic disturbances specific to the fetus and newborn**

776 **Hematological disorders of fetus and newborn**
    Includes: disorders specific to the fetus or newborn

776.0 **Hemorrhagic disease of newborn**
    Hemorrhagic diathesis of newborn
    Vitamin K deficiency of newborn

> *Excludes:* *fetal or neonatal hemorrhage (772.0-772.9)*

776.1 **Transient neonatal thrombocytopenia**
    Neonatal thrombocytopenia due to:
      exchange transfusion
      idiopathic maternal thrombocytopenia
      isoimmunization

776.2 **Disseminated intravascular coagulation in newborn**

776.3 **Other transient neonatal disorders of coagulation**
    Transient coagulation defect, newborn

776.4 **Polycythemia neonatorum**
    Plethora of newborn
    Polycythemia due to:
      donor twin transfusion
      maternal-fetal transfusion

776.5 **Congenital anemia**
    Anemia following fetal blood loss

> *Excludes:* *anemia due to isoimmunization (773.0-773.2, 773.5)*
>   *hereditary hemolytic anemias (282.0-282.9)*

776.6 **Anemia of prematurity**

776.7 **Transient neonatal neutropenia**
    Isoimmune neutropenia
    Maternal transfer neutropenia

> *Excludes:* *congenital neutropenia (nontransient) (288.0)*

776.8 **Other specified transient hematological disorders**

776.9 **Unspecified hematological disorder specific to fetus or newborn**

777 **Perinatal disorders of digestive system**
    Includes: disorders specific to the fetus and newborn

> *Excludes:* *intestinal obstruction classifiable to 560.0-560.9*

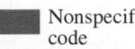 Add 4th or 5th digit   Nonspecific code   Unspecified code   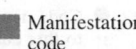 Manifestation code

777.1 Meconium obstruction
Congenital fecaliths
Delayed passage of meconium
Meconium ileus NOS
Meconium plug syndrome

Excludes: *meconium ileus in cystic fibrosis (277.01)*

777.2 Intestinal obstruction due to inspissated milk

777.3 Hematemesis and melena due to swallowed maternal blood
Swallowed blood syndrome in newborn

Excludes: *that not due to swallowed maternal blood (772.4)*

777.4 Transitory ileus of newborn

Excludes: *Hirschsprung's disease (751.3)*

777.5 Necrotizing enterocolitis in fetus or newborn
Pseudomembranous enterocolitis in newborn

777.6 Perinatal intestinal perforation
Meconium peritonitis

777.8 Other specified perinatal disorders of digestive system

777.9 Unspecified perinatal disorder of digestive system

778 Conditions involving the integument and temperature regulation of fetus and newborn

778.0 Hydrops fetalis not due to isoimmunization
Idiopathic hydrops

Excludes: *hydrops fetalis due to isoimmunization (773.3)*

778.1 Sclerema neonatorum
Subcutaneous fat necrosis

778.2 Cold injury syndrome of newborn

778.3 Other hypothermia of newborn

778.4 Other disturbances of temperature regulation of newborn
Dehydration fever in newborn
Environmentally-induced pyrexia
Hyperthermia in newborn
Transitory fever of newborn

778.5 Other and unspecified edema of newborn
Edema neonatorum

778.6 Congenital hydrocele
Congenital hydrocele of tunica vaginalis

778.7 Breast engorgement in newborn
Noninfective mastitis of newborn

Excludes: *infective mastitis of newborn (771.5)*

778.8 Other specified conditions involving the integument of fetus and newborn
Urticaria neonatorum

Excludes: *impetigo neonatorum (684)*
pemphigus neonatorum (684)

778.9 Unspecified condition involving the integument and temperature regulation of fetus and newborn

779 Other and ill-defined conditions originating in the perinatal period

779.0 Convulsions in newborn
Fits ⎫
Seizures ⎬ in newborn

779.1 Other and unspecified cerebral irritability in newborn

779.2 Cerebral depression, coma, and other abnormal cerebral signs
CNS dysfunction in newborn NOS

779.3 Feeding problems in newborn
Regurgitation of food ⎫
Slow feeding ⎬ in newborn
Vomiting ⎭

● Code new
to this edition
▲ Revision of
existing code
④ ⑤ Fourth or fifth
digit required

779.4 Drug reactions and intoxications specific to newborn
Gray syndrome from chloramphenicol administration in newborn

Excludes: *fetal alcohol syndrome (760.71)*

reactions and intoxications from maternal opiates and tranquilizers (763.5)

779.5 Drug withdrawal syndrome in newborn
Drug withdrawal syndrome in infant of dependent mother

Excludes: *fetal alcohol syndrome (760.71)*

779.6 Termination of pregnancy (fetus)
Fetus death due to:
  induced abortion
  termination of pregnancy

Excludes: *spontaneous abortion (fetus) (761.8)*

779.8 Other specified conditions originating in the perinatal period

779.9 Unspecified condition originating in the perinatal period
Congenital debility NOS
Stillbirth NEC

Add 4th or Nonspecific Unspecified Manifestation
5th digit   code   code   code

● Code new
to this edition
▲ Revision of
existing code
④ ⑤ Fourth or fifth
digit required

16. SYMPTOMS, SIGNS, AND ILL-DEFINED CONDITIONS (780-799)

This section includes symptoms, signs, abnormal results of laboratory or other investigative procedures, and ill-defined conditions regarding which no diagnosis classifiable elsewhere is recorded.

Signs and symptoms that point rather definitely to a given diagnosis are assigned to some category in the preceding part of the classification. In general, categories 780-796 include the more ill-defined conditions and symptoms that point with perhaps equal suspicion to two or more diseases or to two or more systems of the body, and without the necessary study of the case to make a final diagnosis. Practically all categories in this group could be designated as "not otherwise specified," or as "unknown etiology," or as "transient." The Alphabetic Index should be consulted to determine which symptoms and signs are to be allocated here and which to more specific sections of the classification; the residual subcategories numbered .9 are provided for other relevant symptoms which cannot be allocated elsewhere in the classification.

The conditions and signs or symptoms included in categories 780-796 consist of: (a) cases for which no more specific diagnosis can be made even after all facts bearing on the case have been investigated; (b) signs or symptoms existing at the time of initial encounter that proved to be transient and whose causes could not be determined; (c) provisional diagnoses in a patient who failed to return for further investigation or care; (d) cases referred elsewhere for investigation or treatment before the diagnosis was made; (e) cases in which a more precise diagnosis was not available for any other reason; (f) certain symptoms which represent important problems in medical care and which it might be desired to classify in addition to a known cause.

SYMPTOMS (780-789)

780 General symptoms

780.0 Alteration of consciousness

> Excludes: coma:
> > diabetic (250.2-250.3)
> > hepatic (572.2)
> > originating in the perinatal period (779.2)

780.01 Coma

780.02 Transient alteration of awareness

780.03 Persistent vegetative state

780.09 Other

Drowsiness	Somnolence
Semicoma	Stupor
Unconsciousness	

780.1 Hallucinations

Hallucinations:	Hallucinations:
NOS	olfactory
auditory	tactile
gustatory	

> Excludes: those associated with mental disorders, as functional psychoses (295.0-298.9)
> > organic brain syndromes (290.0-294.9, 310.0-310.9)
> > visual hallucinations (368.16)

780.2 Syncope and collapse

Blackout	(Near) (Pre) syncope
Fainting	Vasovagal attack

> Excludes: carotid sinus syncope (337.0)
> > heat syncope (992.1)
> > neurocirculatory asthenia (306.2)
> > orthostatic hypotension (458.0)
> > shock NOS (785.50)

780.3 Convulsions

Convulsions:	Convulsive:
NOS	disorder NOS
febrile	seizure NOS
infantile	Fit NOS

> Excludes: convulsions:
> > epileptic (345.10-345.91)
> > in newborn (779.0)

780.4 Dizziness and giddiness

Light-headedness	Vertigo NOS

> Excludes: Ménière's disease and other specified vertiginous syndromes (386.0-386.9)

▰ Add 4th or 5th digit	▰ Nonspecific code	▰ Unspecified code	▰ Manifestation code

780.5 Sleep disturbances

Excludes: *that of nonorganic origin (307.40-307.49)*

  780.50 **Sleep disturbance, unspecified**

  780.51 **Insomnia with sleep apnea**

  780.52 **Other insomnia**
     Insomnia NOS

  780.53 **Hypersomnia with sleep apnea**

  780.54 **Other hypersomnia**
     Hypersomnia NOS

  780.55 **Disruptions of 24-hour sleep-wake cycle**
     Inversion of sleep rhythm
     Irregular sleep-wake rhythm NOS
     Non-24-hour sleep-wake rhythm

  780.56 **Dysfunctions associated with sleep stages or arousal from sleep**

  780.57 **Other and unspecified sleep apnea**

  780.59 **Other**

780.6 Fever
    Chills with fever   Hyperpyrexia NOS
    Fever NOS   Pyrexia NOS
    Fever of unknown origin   Pyrexia of unknown origin
      (FUO)

Excludes: *pyrexia of unknown origin (during):*
    in newborn (778.4)
    labor (659.2)
    the puerperium (672)

780.7 Malaise and fatigue
    Asthenia NOS   Postviral (asthenic) syndrome
    Lethargy   Tiredness

Excludes: *debility, unspecified (799.3)*
    fatigue (during):
      combat (308.0-308.9)
      heat (992.6)
      pregnancy (646.8)
    neurasthenia (300.5)
    senile asthenia (797.5)

780.8 Hyperhidrosis
    Diaphoresis
    Excessive sweating

780.9 Other general symptoms
    Amnesia (retrograde)
    Chill(s) NOS
    Generalized pain
    Hypothermia, not associated with low environmental temperature

Excludes: *hypothermia:*
    NOS (accidental) (991.6)
    due to anesthesia (995.89)
    of newborn (778.2-778.3)
    memory disturbance as part of a pattern of mental disorder

781 Symptoms involving nervous and musculoskeletal systems

Excludes: *depression NOS (311)*
    disorders specifically relating to:
      back (724.0-724.9)
      hearing (388.0-389.9)
      joint (718.0-719.9)
      limb (729.0-729.9)
      neck (723.0-723.9)
      vision (368.0-369.9)
    pain in limb (729.5)

● Code new   ▲ Revision of   ④ ⑤ Fourth or fifth
  to this edition   existing code   digit required

781.0 Abnormal involuntary movements
Abnormal head movements
Fasciculation
Spasms NOS
Tremor NOS

Excludes: abnormal reflex (796.1)
chorea NOS (333.5)
infantile spasms (345.60-345.61)
spastic paralysis (342.1, 343.0-344.9)
specified movement disorders classifiable to 333 (333.0-333.9)
that of nonorganic origin (307.2-307.3)

781.1 Disturbances of sensation of smell and taste
Anosmia   Parosmia
Parageusia

781.2 Abnormality of gait
Gait: Gait:
ataxic   spastic
paralytic   staggering

Excludes: ataxia:
NOS (781.3)
locomotor (progressive) (094.0)
difficulty in walking (719.7)

781.3 Lack of coordination
Ataxia NOS   Muscular incoordination

Excludes: ataxic gait (781.2)
cerebellar ataxia (334.0-334.9)
difficulty in walking (719.7)
vertigo NOS (780.4)

781.4 Transient paralysis of limb
Monoplegia, transient NOS

Excludes: paralysis (342.0-344.9)

781.5 Clubbing of fingers

781.6 Meningismus
Dupré's syndrome
Meningism

781.7 Tetany
Carpopedal spasm

Excludes: tetanus neonatorum (771.3)
tetany:
hysterical (300.11)
newborn (hypocalcemic) (775.4)
parathyroid (252.1)
psychogenic (306.0)

781.8 Neurologic neglect syndrome
Asomatognosia   Left-sided neglect
Hemi-akinesia   Sensory extinction
Hemi-inattention   Sensory neglect
Hemispatial neglect   Visuospatial neglect

781.9 Other symptoms involving nervous and musculoskeletal systems
Abnormal posture

782 Symptoms involving skin and other integumentary tissue

Excludes: symptoms relating to breast (611.71-611.79)

782.0 Disturbance of skin sensation
Anesthesia of skin   Hypoesthesia
Burning or prickling   Numbness
sensation   Paresthesia
Hyperesthesia   Tingling

782.1 Rash and other nonspecific skin eruption
Exanthem

Excludes: vesicular eruption (709.8)

373

| | Add 4th or 5th digit | | Nonspecific code | | Unspecified code | | Manifestation code |

782.2 Localized superficial swelling, mass, or lump
Subcutaneous nodules

Excludes: *localized adiposity (278.1)*

782.3 Edema
Anasarca   Localized edema NOS
Dropsy

Excludes: *ascites (789.5)*
edema of:
newborn NOS (778.5)
pregnancy (642.0-642.9, 646.1)
fluid retention (276.6)
hydrops fetalis (773.3, 778.0)
hydrothorax (511.8)
nutritional edema (260, 262)

782.4 Jaundice, unspecified, not of newborn
Cholemia NOS   Icterus NOS

Excludes: *jaundice in newborn (774.0-774.7)*
due to isoimmunization (773.0-773.2, 773.4)

782.5 Cyanosis

Excludes: *newborn (770.8)*

782.6 Pallor and flushing

782.61 Pallor

782.62 Flushing
Excessive blushing

782.7 Spontaneous ecchymoses
Petechiae

Excludes: *ecchymosis in fetus or newborn (772.6)*
purpura (287.0-287.9)

782.8 Changes in skin texture
Induration }
Thickening } of skin

782.9 Other symptoms involving skin and integumentary tissues

783 Symptoms concerning nutrition, metabolism, and development

783.0 Anorexia
Loss of appetite

Excludes: *anorexia nervosa (307.1)*
loss of appetite of nonorganic origin (307.59)

783.1 Abnormal weight gain

Excludes: *excessive weight gain in pregnancy (646.1)*
obesity (278.00)
morbid (278.01)

783.2 Abnormal loss of weight

783.3 Feeding difficulties and mismanagement
Feeding problem (elderly) (infant)

Excludes: *feeding disturbance or problems:*
in newborn (779.3)
of nonorganic origin (307.50-307.59)

783.4 Lack of expected normal physiological development
Delayed milestone   Lack of growth
Failure to gain weight   Physical retardation
Failure to thrive   Short stature

Excludes: *delay in sexual development and puberty (259.0)*
specific delays in mental development (315.0-315.9)

783.5 Polydipsia
Excessive thirst

● Code new   ▲ Revision of   ④ ⑤ Fourth or fifth
to this edition   existing code   digit required

783.6 Polyphagia
Excessive eating
Hyperalimentation NOS

Excludes: disorders of eating of nonorganic origin (307.50-307.59)

783.9 Other symptoms concerning nutrition, metabolism, and development
Hypometabolism

Excludes: abnormal basal metabolic rate (794.7)
dehydration (276.5)
other disorders of fluid, electrolyte, and acid-base balance (276.0-276.9)

784 Symptoms involving head and neck

Excludes: encephalopathy NOS (348.3)
specific symptoms involving neck classifiable to 723 (723.0-723.9)

784.0 Headache
Facial pain   Pain in head NOS

Excludes: atypical face pain (350.2)
migraine (346.0-346.9)
tension headache (307.81)

784.1 Throat pain

Excludes: dysphagia (787.2)
neck pain (723.1)
sore throat (462)
chronic (472.1)

784.2 Swelling, mass, or lump in head and neck
Space-occupying lesion, intracranial NOS

784.3 Aphasia

Excludes: developmental aphasia (315.31)

784.4 Voice disturbance

   784.40 Voice disturbance, unspecified

   784.41 Aphonia
Loss of voice

   784.49 Other
Change in voice   Hypernasality
Dysphonia   Hyponasality
Hoarseness

784.5 Other speech disturbance
Dysarthria   Slurred speech
Dysphasia

Excludes: stammering and stuttering (307.0)
that of nonorganic origin (307.0, 307.9)

784.6 Other symbolic dysfunction

Excludes: developmental learning delays (315.0-315.9)

   784.60 Symbolic dysfunction, unspecified

   784.61 Alexia and dyslexia
Alexia (with agraphia)

   784.69 Other
Acalculia   Agraphia NOS
Agnosia   Apraxia

784.7 Epistaxis
Hemorrhage from nose   Nosebleed

784.8 Hemorrhage from throat

Excludes: hemoptysis (786.3)

784.9 Other symptoms involving head and neck
Choking sensation   Mouth breathing
Halitosis   Sneezing

785 Symptoms involving cardiovascular system

Excludes: heart failure NOS (428.9)

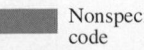 Add 4th or
5th digit

 Nonspecific
code

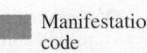 Unspecified
code

Manifestation
code

375

785.0 Tachycardia, unspecified
     Rapid heart beat

  Excludes: *paroxysmal tachycardia (427.0-427.2)*

785.1 Palpitations
     Awareness of heart beat

  Excludes: *specified dysrhythmias (427.0-427.9)*

785.2 Undiagnosed cardiac murmurs
     Heart murmur NOS

785.3 Other abnormal heart sounds
     Cardiac dullness, increased or decreased
     Friction fremitus, cardiac
     Precordial friction

785.4 Gangrene
     Gangrene:
        NOS
        spreading cutaneous
     Phagedena

Code first any associated underlying condition, as:
     diabetes (250.7)
     Raynaud's syndrome (443.0)

  Excludes: *gangrene of certain sites—see Alphabetic Index*
           gangrene with atherosclerosis of the extremities (440.24)
           gas gangrene (040.0)

785.5 Shock without mention of trauma

  785.50 Shock, unspecified
        Failure of peripheral circulation

  785.51 Cardiogenic shock

  785.59 Other
        Shock: Shock:
           endotoxic   hypovolemic
           gram-negative   septic

  Excludes: *shock (due to):*
           anesthetic (995.4)
           anaphylactic (995.0)
            due to serum (999.4)
           electric (994.8)
           following abortion (639.5)
           lightning (994.0)
           obstetrical (669.1)
           postoperative (998.0)
           traumatic (958.4)

785.6 Enlargement of lymph nodes
     Lymphadenopathy   "Swollen glands"

  Excludes: *lymphadenitis (chronic) (289.1-289.3)*
           acute (683)

785.9 Other symptoms involving cardiovascular system
     Bruit (arterial)
     Weak pulse

786 Symptoms involving respiratory system and other chest symptoms

786.0 Dyspnea and respiratory abnormalities

  786.00 Respiratory abnormality, unspecified

  786.01 Hyperventilation

  Excludes: *hyperventilation, psychogenic (306.1)*

  786.02 Orthopnea

● Code new   ▲ Revision of   ④ ⑤ Fourth or fifth
         to this edition   existing code   digit required

786.09 Other

Apnea
Cheyne-Stokes respiration
Respiratory:
   distress
   insufficiency

Shortness of breath
Tachypnea
Wheezing

Excludes: *respiratory distress:*
   following trauma and surgery (518.5)
   newborn (770.8)
   syndrome (newborn) (769)
      adult (518.5)
   respiratory failure (518.81)
      newborn (770.8)
   sleep apnea (780.51, 780.53, 780.57)
   transitory tachypnea of newborn (770.6)

786.1 Stridor

Excludes: *congenital laryngeal stridor (748.3)*

786.2 Cough

Excludes: *cough:*
   psychogenic (306.1)
   smokers' (491.0)
   with hemorrhage (786.3)

786.3 Hemoptysis
Cough with hemorrhage
Pulmonary hemorrhage NOS

Excludes: *pulmonary hemorrhage of newborn (770.3)*

786.4 Abnormal sputum
Abnormal:
   amount
   color   } (of) sputum
   odor
Excessive

786.5 Chest pain

786.50   Chest pain, unspecified

786.51   Precordial pain

786.52   Painful respiration
Pain:
   anterior chest wall
   pleuritic
Pleurodynia

Excludes: *epidemic pleurodynia (074.1)*

786.59   Other
Discomfort
Pressure   } in chest
Tightness

Excludes: *pain in breast (611.71)*

786.6 Swelling, mass, or lump in chest

Excludes: *lump in breast (611.72)*

786.7 Abnormal chest sounds
Abnormal percussion, chest   Rales
Friction sounds, chest   Tympany, chest

Excludes: *wheezing (786.09)*

786.8 Hiccough

Excludes: *psychogenic hiccough (306.1)*

786.9 Other symptoms involving respiratory system and chest
Breath-holding spell

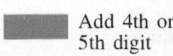 Add 4th or
5th digit

 Nonspecific
code

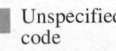 Unspecified
code

Manifestation
code

787 **Symptoms involving digestive system**

> *Excludes:* constipation (564.0)
>   pylorospasm (537.81)
>   congenital (750.5)

787.0 **Nausea and vomiting**
    Emesis

> *Excludes:* hematemesis NOS (578.0)
>   vomiting:
>   bilious, following gastrointestinal surgery (564.3)
>   cyclical (536.2)
>   psychogenic (306.4)
>   excessive, in pregnancy (643.0-643.9)
>   habit (536.2)
>   of newborn (779.3)
>   psychogenic NOS (307.54)

    787.01 **Nausea with vomiting**

    787.02 **Nausea alone**

    787.03 **Vomiting alone**

787.1 **Heartburn**
    Pyrosis
    Waterbrash

> *Excludes:* dyspepsia or indigestion (536.8)

787.2 **Dysphagia**
    Difficulty in swallowing

787.3 **Flatulence, eructation, and gas pain**
    Abdominal distention (gaseous)
    Bloating
    Tympanites (abdominal) (intestinal)

> *Excludes:* aerophagy (306.4)

787.4 **Visible peristalsis**
    Hyperperistalsis

787.5 **Abnormal bowel sounds**
    Absent bowel sounds
    Hyperactive bowel sounds

787.6 **Incontinence of feces**
    Encopresis NOS
    Incontinence of sphincter ani

> *Excludes:* that of nonorganic origin (307.7)

787.7 **Abnormal feces**
    Bulky stools

> *Excludes:* abnormal stool content (792.1)
>   melena:
>   NOS (578.1)
>   newborn (772.4, 777.3)

787.9 **Other symptoms involving digestive system**

> *Excludes:* gastrointestinal hemorrhage (578.0-578.9)
>   intestinal obstruction (560.0-560.9)
>   specific functional digestive disorders:
>   esophagus (530.0-530.9)
>   stomach and duodenum (536.0-536.9)
>   those not elsewhere classified (564.0-564.9)

    787.91 **Diarrhea**
        Diarrhea NOS

    787.99 **Other**
        Change in bowel habits
        Tenesmus (rectal)

● Code new   ▲ Revision of   ④ ⑤ Fourth or fifth
   to this edition   existing code   digit required

788 Symptoms involving urinary system

Excludes: hematuria (599.7)
  nonspecific findings on examination of the urine (791.0-791.9)
  small kidney of unknown cause (589.0-589.9)
  uremia NOS (586)

788.0 Renal colic
Colic (recurrent) of:
  kidney
  ureter

788.1 Dysuria
Painful urination
Strangury

788.2 Retention of urine

788.20 Retention of urine, unspecified

788.21 Incomplete bladder emptying

788.29 Other specified retention of urine

788.3 Incontinence of urine

Excludes: that of nonorganic origin (307.6)
Code first any underlying condition, such as:
  congenital ureterocele (753.23)
  genital prolapse (618.0-618.9)

788.30 Urinary incontinence, unspecified
Enuresis NOS

788.31 Urge incontinence

788.32 Stress incontinence, male

Excludes: stress incontinence (female) (625.6)

788.33 Mixed incontinence (male) (female)
Urge and stress

788.34 Incontinence without sensory awareness

788.35 Post-void dribbling

788.36 Nocturnal enuresis

788.37 Continuous leakage

788.39 Other urinary incontinence

788.4 Frequency of urination and polyuria

788.41 Urinary frequency
Frequency of micturition

788.42 Polyuria

788.43 Nocturia

788.5 Oliguria and anuria
Deficient secretion of urine
Suppression of urinary secretion

Excludes: that complicating:
  abortion (634-638 with .3, 639.3)
  ectopic or molar pregnancy (639.3)
  pregnancy, childbirth, or the puerperium (642.0-642.9, 646.2)

788.6 Other abnormality of urination

788.61 Splitting of urinary stream
Intermittent urinary stream

788.62 Slowing of urinary stream
Weak stream

788.69 Other

788.7 Urethral discharge
Penile discharge   Urethrorrhea

788.8 Extravasation of urine

379

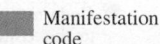

| | Add 4th or 5th digit | | Nonspecific code | | Unspecified code | | Manifestation code |

788.9 **Other symptoms involving urinary system**
Extrarenal uremia
Vesical:
pain
tenesmus

789 **Other symptoms involving abdomen and pelvis**
The following fifth-digit subclassification is to be used for codes 789.0, 789.3, 789.4, 789.6

0 **unspecified site**

1 **right upper quadrant**

2 **left upper quadrant**

3 **right lower quadrant**

4 **left lower quadrant**

5 **periumbilic**

6 **epigastric**

7 **generalized**

9 **other specified site**
multiple sites

Excludes: *symptoms referable to genital organs:*
female (625.0-625.9)
male (607.0-608.9)
psychogenic (302.70-302.79)

789.0 **Abdominal pain**
Colic:
NOS
infantile
Cramps, abdominal

Excludes: *renal colic (788.0)*

789.1 **Hepatomegaly**
Enlargement of liver

789.2 **Splenomegaly**
Enlargement of spleen

789.3 **Abdominal or pelvic swelling, mass, or lump**
Diffuse or generalized swelling or mass:
abdominal NOS
umbilical

Excludes: *abdominal distention (gaseous) (787.3)*
ascites (789.5)

789.4 **Abdominal rigidity**

789.5 **Ascites**
Fluid in peritoneal cavity ·

789.6 **Abdominal tenderness**
Rebound tenderness

789.9 **Other symptoms involving abdomen and pelvis**
Umbilical:
bleeding
discharge

NONSPECIFIC ABNORMAL FINDINGS (790-796)

790 **Nonspecific findings on examination of blood**

Excludes: *abnormality of:*
platelets (287.0-287.9)
thrombocytes (287.0-287.9)
white blood cells (288.0-288.9)

● Code new
to this edition

▲ Revision of
existing code

④ ⑤ Fourth or fifth
digit required

790.0 Abnormality of red blood cells

Abnormal red cell:	Anisocytosis
morphology NOS	Poikilocytosis
volume NOS	

Excludes: *anemia:*
congenital (776.5)
newborn, due to isoimmunization (773.0-773.2, 773.5)
of premature infant (776.6)
other specified types (280.0-285.9)
hemoglobin disorders (282.5-282.7)
polycythemia:
familial (289.6)
neonatorum (776.4)
secondary (289.0)
vera (238.4)

790.1 Elevated sedimentation rate

790.2 Abnormal glucose tolerance test

Excludes: *that complicating pregnancy, childbirth, or the puerperium (648.8)*

790.3 Excessive blood level of alcohol
Elevated blood-alcohol

790.4 Nonspecific elevation of levels of transaminase or lactic acid dehydrogenase [LDH]

790.5 Other nonspecific abnormal serum enzyme levels

Abnormal serum level of:	Abnormal serum level of:
acid phosphatase	amylase
alkaline phosphatase	lipase

Excludes: *deficiency of circulating enzymes (277.6)*

790.6 Other abnormal blood chemistry

Abnormal blood level of:	Abnormal blood level of:
cobalt	magnesium
copper	mineral
iron	zinc
lithium	

Excludes: *abnormality of electrolyte or acid-base balance (276.0-276.9)*
hypoglycemia NOS (251.2)
specific finding indicating abnormality of:
amino-acid transport and metabolism (270.0-270.9)
carbohydrate transport and metabolism (271.0-271.9)
lipid metabolism (272.0-272.9)
uremia NOS (586)

790.7 Bacteremia

Excludes: *septicemia (038)*
Use additional code, if desired, to identify organism (041)

790.8 Viremia, unspecified

790.9 Other nonspecific findings on examination of blood

790.91 Abnormal arterial blood gases

790.92 Abnormal coagulation profile
Abnormal or prolonged:
bleeding time
coagulation time
partial thromboplastin time [PTT]
prothrombin time [PT]

Excludes: *coagulation (hemorrhagic) disorders (286.0-286.9)*

790.93 Elevated prostate specific antigen (PSA)

790.99 Other

791 Nonspecific findings on examination of urine

Excludes: *hematuria NOS (599.7)*
specific findings indicating abnormality of:
amino-acid transport and metabolism (270.0-270.9)
carbohydrate transport and metabolism (271.0-271.9)

Add 4th or 5th digit	Nonspecific code	Unspecified code	Manifestation code

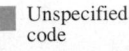

791.0 Proteinuria
  Albuminuria   Bence-Jones proteinuria

  Excludes: postural proteinuria (593.6)
         that arising during pregnancy or the puerperium (642.0-642.9, 646.2)

791.1 Chyluria

  Excludes: filarial (125.0-125.9)

791.2 Hemoglobinuria

791.3 Myoglobinuria

791.4 Biliuria

791.5 Glycosuria

  Excludes: renal glycosuria (271.4)

791.6 Acetonuria
  Ketonuria

791.7 Other cells and casts in urine

791.9 Other nonspecific findings on examination of urine
  Crystalluria
  Elevated urine levels of:
    17-ketosteroids
    catecholamines
    indolacetic acid
    vanillylmandelic acid [VMA]
  Melanuria

792 Nonspecific abnormal findings in other body substances

  Excludes: that in chromosomal analysis (795.2)

792.0 Cerebrospinal fluid

792.1 Stool contents
  Abnormal stool color
  Fat in stool   Occult blood
  Mucus in stool   Pus in stool

  Excludes: blood in stool [melena] (578.1)
          newborn (772.4, 777.3)

792.2 Semen
  Abnormal spermatozoa

  Excludes: azoospermia (606.0)
          oligospermia (606.1)

792.3 Amniotic fluid

792.4 Saliva

  Excludes: that in chromosomal analysis (795.2)

792.9 Other nonspecific abnormal findings in body substances
  Peritoneal fluid   Synovial fluid
  Pleural fluid   Vaginal fluids

793 Nonspecific abnormal findings on radiological and other examination of body structure
  Includes: nonspecific abnormal findings of:
        thermography
        ultrasound examination [echogram]
        x-ray examination

  Excludes: abnormal results of function studies and radioisotope scans (794.0-794.9)

793.0 Skull and head

  Excludes: nonspecific abnormal echoencephalogram (794.01)

793.1 Lung field
  Coin lesion   ⎫
  Shadow   ⎬ (of) lung

793.2 Other intrathoracic organ
  Abnormal: Mediastinal shift
    echocardiogram
    heart shadow
    ultrasound cardiogram

● Code new   ▲ Revision of   ④ ⑤ Fourth or fifth
     to this edition   existing code   digit required

793.3 Biliary tract
Nonvisualization of gallbladder

793.4 Gastrointestinal tract

793.5 Genitourinary organs
Filling defect:
  bladder
  kidney
  ureter

793.6 Abdominal area, including retroperitoneum

793.7 Musculoskeletal system

793.8 Breast
Abnormal mammogram

793.9 Other
Abnormal:
  placental finding by x-ray or ultrasound method
  radiological findings in skin and subcutaneous tissue

Excludes: *abnormal finding by radioisotope localization of placenta (794.9)*

794 Nonspecific abnormal results of function studies
Includes: radioisotope:
      scans
      uptake studies
    scintiphotography

794.0 Brain and central nervous system

794.00 Abnormal function study, unspecified

794.01 Abnormal echoencephalogram

794.02 Abnormal electroencephalogram [EEG]

794.09 Other
Abnormal brain scan

794.1 Peripheral nervous system and special senses

794.10 Abnormal response to nerve stimulation, unspecified

794.11 Abnormal retinal function studies
Abnormal electroretinogram [ERG]

794.12 Abnormal electro-oculogram [EOG]

794.13 Abnormal visually evoked potential

794.14 Abnormal oculomotor studies

794.15 Abnormal auditory function studies

794.16 Abnormal vestibular function studies

794.17 Abnormal electromyogram [EMG]

Excludes: *that of eye (794.14)*

794.19 Other

794.2 Pulmonary
Abnormal lung scan
Reduced:
  ventilatory capacity
  vital capacity

794.3 Cardiovascular

794.30 Abnormal function study, unspecified

794.31 Abnormal electrocardiogram [ECG] [EKG]

794.39 Other
Abnormal:
  ballistocardiogram
  phonocardiogram
  vectorcardiogram

794.4 Kidney
Abnormal renal function test

383

| | Add 4th or 5th digit | | Nonspecific code | | Unspecified code | | Manifestation code |

794.5 Thyroid
  Abnormal thyroid:
    scan
    uptake

794.6 Other endocrine function study

794.7 Basal metabolism
  Abnormal basal metabolic rate [BMR]

794.8 Liver
  Abnormal liver scan

794.9 Other

Bladder	Placenta
Pancreas	Spleen

795 Nonspecific abnormal histological and immunological findings

  Excludes: *nonspecific abnormalities of red blood cells (790.0)*

795.0 Nonspecific abnormal Papanicolaou smear of cervix
  Dyskaryotic cervical smear

795.1 Nonspecific abnormal Papanicolaou smear of other site

795.2 Nonspecific abnormal findings on chromosomal analysis
  Abnormal karyotype

795.3 Nonspecific positive culture findings
  Positive culture findings in:
    nose
    sputum
    throat
    wound

  Excludes: *that of:*
      blood (790.7-790.8)
      urine (599.0)

795.4 Other nonspecific abnormal histological findings

795.5 Nonspecific reaction to tuberculin skin test without active tuberculosis
  Abnormal result of Mantoux test
  PPD positive
  Tuberculin (skin test):
    positive
    reactor

795.6 False positive serological test for syphilis
  False positive Wassermann reaction

795.7 Other nonspecific immunological findings

  Excludes: *isoimmunization, in pregnancy (656.1-656.2)*
        affecting fetus or newborn (773.0-773.2)

  795.71 Nonspecific serologic evidence of human immunodeficiency virus [HIV]
    Inconclusive human immunodeficiency virus [HIV] test (adult) (infant)

Note: This code is ONLY to be used when a test finding is reported as nonspecific.
  Asymptomatic positive findings are coded to V08. If any HIV infection symptom or
  condition is present, see code 042. Negative findings are not coded.

  Excludes: *acquired immunodeficiency syndrome [AIDS] (042)*
      asymptomatic immunodeficiency virus, [HIV] infection status (V08)
      HIV infection, symptomatic (042)
      human immunodeficiency virus [HIV] disease (042)
      positive (status) NOS (V08)

  795.79 Other and unspecified nonspecific immunological findings
    Raised antibody titer
    Raised level of immunoglobulins

796 Other nonspecific abnormal findings

796.0 Nonspecific abnormal toxicological findings
  Abnormal levels of heavy metals or drugs in blood, urine, or other tissue

  Excludes: *excessive blood level of alcohol (790.3)*

796.1 Abnormal reflex

● Code new
  to this edition

▲ Revision of
  existing code

④ ⑤ Fourth or fifth
  digit required

796.2 Elevated blood pressure reading without diagnosis of hypertension

Note: This category is to be used to record an episode of elevated blood pressure in a patient in whom no formal diagnosis of hypertension has been made, or as an incidental finding.

796.3 Nonspecific low blood pressure reading

796.4 Other abnormal clinical findings

796.9 Other

ILL-DEFINED AND UNKNOWN CAUSES OF MORBIDITY AND MORTALITY (797-799)

797 Senility without mention of psychosis

Old age	Senile:
Senescence	debility
Senile asthenia	exhaustion

> *Excludes:* senile psychoses (290.0-290.9)

798 Sudden death, cause unknown

798.0 Sudden infant death syndrome
Cot death
Crib death
Sudden death of nonspecific cause in infancy

798.1 Instantaneous death

798.2 Death occurring in less than 24 hours from onset of symptoms, not otherwise explained
Death known not to be violent or instantaneous, for which no cause could be discovered
Died without sign of disease

798.9 Unattended death
Death in circumstances where the body of the deceased was found and no cause could be discovered
Found dead

799 Other ill-defined and unknown causes of morbidity and mortality

799.0 Asphyxia

> *Excludes:* asphyxia (due to):
> carbon monoxide (986)
> inhalation of food or foreign body (932-934.9)
> newborn (768.0-768.9)
> traumatic (994.7)

799.1 Respiratory arrest
Cardiorespiratory failure

> *Excludes:* cardiac arrest (427.5)
> failure of peripheral circulation (785.50)
> respiratory distress:
> NOS (786.09)
> acute (518.82)
> following trauma and surgery (518.5)
> newborn (770.8)
> syndrome (newborn) (769)
> adult (following trauma and surgery) (518.5)
> other (518.82)
> respiratory failure (518.81)
> newborn (770.8)
> respiratory insufficiency (786.09)
> acute (518.82)

799.2 Nervousness
"Nerves"

799.3 Debility, unspecified

> *Excludes:* asthenia (780.7)
> nervous debility (300.5)
> neurasthenia (300.5)
> senile asthenia (797)

799.4 Cachexia
Wasting disease

> *Excludes:* nutritional marasmus (261)

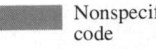 Add 4th or 5th digit

 Nonspecific code

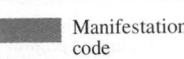 Unspecified code

Manifestation code

799.8 Other ill-defined conditions

799.9 Other unknown and unspecified cause

Undiagnosed disease, not specified as to site or system involved

Unknown cause of morbidity or mortality

● Code new
  to this edition

▲ Revision of
  existing code

④ ⑤ Fourth or fifth
  digit required

17. INJURY AND POISONING (800-999)

Use E code(s) to identify the cause and intent of the injury or poisoning (E800-E999)

Note:

1. The principle of multiple coding of injuries should be followed wherever possible. Combination categories for multiple injuries are provided for use when there is insufficient detail as to the nature of the individual conditions, or for primary tabulation purposes when it is more convenient to record a single code; otherwise, the component injuries should be coded separately.

    Where multiple sites of injury are specified in the titles, the word "with" indicates involvement of both sites, and the word "and" indicates involvement of either or both sites. The word "finger" includes thumb.

2. Categories for "late effect" of injuries are to be found at 905-909.

FRACTURES (800-829)

> Excludes: *malunion (733.81)*
> *nonunion (733.82)*
> *pathologic or spontaneous fracture (733.10-733.19)*

The terms "condyle," "coronoid process," "ramus," and "symphysis" indicate the portion of the bone fractured, not the name of the bone involved.

The descriptions "closed" and "open" used in the fourth-digit subdivisions include the following terms:

closed (with or without delayed healing):

comminuted	impacted
depressed	linear
elevated	march
fissured	simple
fracture NOS	slipped epiphysis
greenstick	spiral

open (with or without delayed healing):

compound	puncture
infected	with foreign body
missile	

A fracture not indicated as closed or open should be classified as closed.

FRACTURE OF SKULL (800-804)

The following fifth-digit subclassification is for use with the appropriate codes in categories 800, 801, 803, and 804:

0 unspecified state of consciousness

1 with no loss of consciousness

2 with brief [less than one hour] loss of consciousness

3 with moderate [1-24 hours] loss of consciousness and return to pre-existing conscious level

4 with prolonged [more than 24 hours] loss of consciousness and return to pre-existing conscious level

5 with prolonged [more than 24 hours] loss of consciousness, without return to pre-existing conscious level
Use fifth-digit 5 to designate when a patient is unconscious and dies before regaining consciousness, regardless of the duration of the loss of consciousness

6 with loss of consciousness of unspecified duration

9 with concussion, unspecified

⑤ **800** **Fracture of vault of skull**
Includes: frontal bone
parietal bone

800.0 Closed without mention of intracranial injury

☐ **800.1** Closed with cerebral laceration and contusion

☐ **800.2** Closed with subarachnoid, subdural, and extradural hemorrhage

☐ **800.3** Closed with other and unspecified intracranial hemorrhage

☐ **800.4** Closed with intracranial injury of other and unspecified nature

☐ **800.5** Open without mention of intracranial injury

☐ **800.6** Open with cerebral laceration and contusion

☐ **800.7** Open with subarachnoid, subdural, and extradural hemorrhage

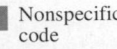

| Add 4th or 5th digit | Nonspecific code | Unspecified code | Medicare secondary payer(MSP) alert |

☐ **800.8** Open with other and unspecified intracranial hemorrhage

☐ **800.9** Open with intracranial injury of other and unspecified nature

⑤ **801** Fracture of base of skull

Includes:

fossa:	sinus:
anterior	ethmoid
middle	frontal
posterior	sphenoid bone
occiput bone	temporal bone
orbital roof	

801.0 Closed without mention of intracranial injury

☐ **801.1** Closed with cerebral laceration and contusion

☐ **801.2** Closed with subarachnoid, subdural, and extradural hemorrhage

☐ **801.3** Closed with other and unspecified intracranial hemorrhage

☐ **801.4** Closed with intracranial injury of other and unspecified nature

☐ **801.5** Open without mention of intracranial injury

☐ **801.6** Open with cerebral laceration and contusion

☐ **801.7** Open with subarachnoid, subdural, and extradural hemorrhage

☐ **801.8** Open with other and unspecified intracranial hemorrhage

☐ **801.9** Open with intracranial injury of other and unspecified nature

802 Fracture of face bones

802.0 Nasal bones, closed

802.1 Nasal bones, open

802.2 Mandible, closed

Inferior maxilla   Lower jaw (bone)

     802.20 Unspecified site

     802.21 Condylar process

     802.22 Subcondylar

     802.23 Coronoid process

     802.24 Ramus, unspecified

     802.25 Angle of jaw

     802.26 Symphysis of body

     802.27 Alveolar border of body

     802.28 Body, other and unspecified

     802.29 Multiple sites

802.3 Mandible, open

     802.30 Unspecified site

     802.31 Condylar process

     802.32 Subcondylar

     802.33 Coronoid process

     802.34 Ramus, unspecified

     802.35 Angle of jaw

     802.36 Symphysis of body

     802.37 Alveolar border of body

     802.38 Body, other and unspecified

     802.39 Multiple sites

802.4 Malar and maxillary bones, closed

Superior maxilla   Zygoma

Upper jaw (bone)   Zygomatic arch

802.5 Malar and maxillary bones, open

802.6 Orbital floor (blow-out), closed

802.7 Orbital floor (blow-out), open

● Code new
to this edition
     ▲ Revision of
existing code
     ④ ⑤ Fourth or fifth
digit required

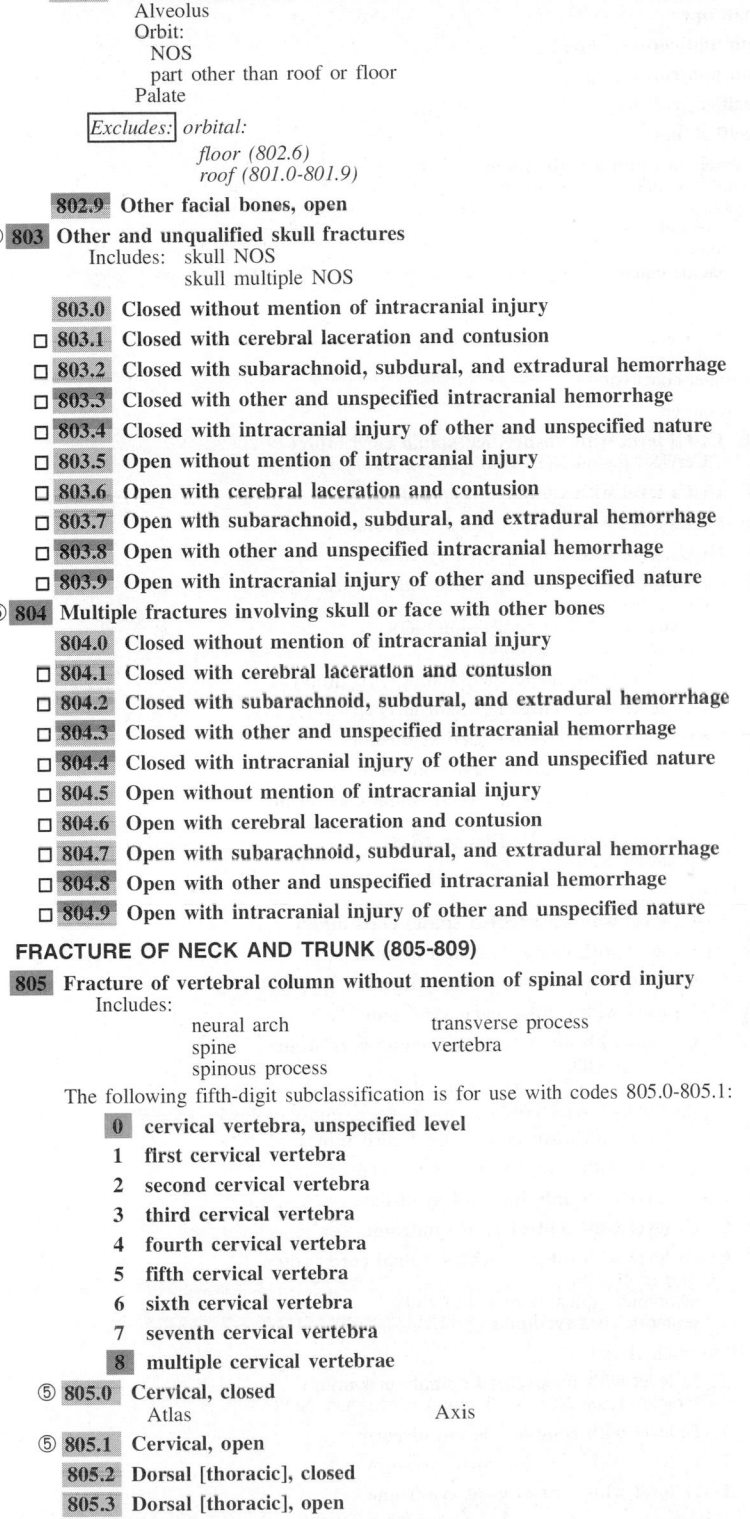

802.8 Other facial bones, closed
   Alveolus
   Orbit:
    NOS
    part other than roof or floor
   Palate

   Excludes: orbital:
          floor (802.6)
          roof (801.0-801.9)

802.9 Other facial bones, open

⑤ **803 Other and unqualified skull fractures**
   Includes: skull NOS
          skull multiple NOS

   803.0 Closed without mention of intracranial injury

☐ **803.1 Closed with cerebral laceration and contusion**

☐ **803.2 Closed with subarachnoid, subdural, and extradural hemorrhage**

☐ **803.3 Closed with other and unspecified intracranial hemorrhage**

☐ **803.4 Closed with intracranial injury of other and unspecified nature**

☐ **803.5 Open without mention of intracranial injury**

☐ **803.6 Open with cerebral laceration and contusion**

☐ **803.7 Open with subarachnoid, subdural, and extradural hemorrhage**

☐ **803.8 Open with other and unspecified intracranial hemorrhage**

☐ **803.9 Open with intracranial injury of other and unspecified nature**

⑤ **804 Multiple fractures involving skull or face with other bones**

   804.0 Closed without mention of intracranial injury

☐ **804.1 Closed with cerebral laceration and contusion**

☐ **804.2 Closed with subarachnoid, subdural, and extradural hemorrhage**

☐ **804.3 Closed with other and unspecified intracranial hemorrhage**

☐ **804.4 Closed with intracranial injury of other and unspecified nature**

☐ **804.5 Open without mention of intracranial injury**

☐ **804.6 Open with cerebral laceration and contusion**

☐ **804.7 Open with subarachnoid, subdural, and extradural hemorrhage**

☐ **804.8 Open with other and unspecified intracranial hemorrhage**

☐ **804.9 Open with intracranial injury of other and unspecified nature**

FRACTURE OF NECK AND TRUNK (805-809)

805 Fracture of vertebral column without mention of spinal cord injury
   Includes:
            neural arch   transverse process
            spine   vertebra
            spinous process

   The following fifth-digit subclassification is for use with codes 805.0-805.1:

   0 cervical vertebra, unspecified level

   1 first cervical vertebra

   2 second cervical vertebra

   3 third cervical vertebra

   4 fourth cervical vertebra

   5 fifth cervical vertebra

   6 sixth cervical vertebra

   7 seventh cervical vertebra

   8 multiple cervical vertebrae

⑤ **805.0 Cervical, closed**
   Atlas   Axis

⑤ **805.1 Cervical, open**

   805.2 Dorsal [thoracic], closed

   805.3 Dorsal [thoracic], open

| ▆ Add 4th or 5th digit | ▆ Nonspecific code | ▆ Unspecified code | ▒ Medicare secondary payer(MSP) alert |

805.4 Lumbar, closed

805.5 Lumbar, open

805.6 Sacrum and coccyx, closed

805.7 Sacrum and coccyx, open

805.8 Unspecified, closed

805.9 Unspecified, open

806 Fracture of vertebral column with spinal cord injury

Includes: any condition classifiable to 805 with:
  complete or incomplete transverse lesion (of cord)
  hematomyelia
  injury to:
    cauda equina
    nerve
  paralysis
  paraplegia
  quadriplegia
  spinal concussion

806.0 Cervical, closed

806.00 C_1-C_4 level with unspecified spinal cord injury
Cervical region NOS with spinal cord injury NOS

806.01 C_1-C_4 level with complete lesion of cord

806.02 C_1-C_4 level with anterior cord syndrome

806.03 C_1-C_4 level with central cord syndrome

806.04 C_1-C_4 level with other specified spinal cord injury
C_1-C_4 level with:
  incomplete spinal cord lesion NOS
  posterior cord syndrome

806.05 C_5-C_7 level with unspecified spinal cord injury

806.06 C_5-C_7 level with complete lesion of cord

806.07 C_5-C_7 level with anterior cord syndrome

806.08 C_5-C_7 level with central cord syndrome

806.09 C_5-C_7 level with other specified spinal cord injury
C_5-C_7 level with:
  incomplete spinal cord lesion NOS
  posterior cord syndrome

806.1 Cervical, open

806.10 C_1-C_4 level with unspecified spinal cord injury

806.11 C_1-C_4 level with complete lesion of cord

806.12 C_1-C_4 level with anterior cord syndrome

806.13 C_1-C_4 level with central cord syndrome

806.14 C_1-C_4 level with other specified spinal cord injury
C_1-C_4 level with:
  incomplete spinal cord lesion NOS
  posterior cord syndrome

806.15 C_5-C_7 level with unspecified spinal cord injury

806.16 C_5-C_7 level with complete lesion of cord

806.17 C_5-C_7 level with anterior cord syndrome

806.18 C_5-C_7 level with central cord syndrome

806.19 C_5-C_7 level with other specified spinal cord injury
C_5-C_7 level with:
  incomplete spinal cord lesion NOS
  posterior cord syndrome

806.2 Dorsal [thoracic], closed

806.20 T_1-T_6 level with unspecified spinal cord injury
Thoracic region NOS with spinal cord injury NOS

806.21 T_1-T_6 level with complete lesion of cord

806.22 T_1-T_6 level with anterior cord syndrome

806.23 T_1-T_6 level with central cord syndrome

● Code new
to this edition

▲ Revision of
existing code

④ ⑤ Fourth or fifth
digit required

806.24 T_1-T_6 level with other specified spinal cord injury
T_1-T_6 level with:
   incomplete spinal cord lesion NOS
   posterior cord syndrome

806.25 T_7-T_{12} level with unspecified spinal cord injury

806.26 T_7-T_{12} level with complete lesion of cord

806.27 T_7-T_{12} level with anterior cord syndrome

806.28 T_7-T_{12} level with central cord syndrome

806.29 T_7-T_{12} level with other specified spinal cord injury
T_7-T_{12} level with:
   incomplete spinal cord lesion NOS
   posterior cord syndrome

806.3 Dorsal [thoracic], open

806.30 T_1-T_6 level with unspecified spinal cord injury

806.31 T_1-T_6 level with complete lesion of cord

806.32 T_1-T_6 level with anterior cord syndrome

806.33 T_1-T_6 level with central cord syndrome

806.34 T_1-T_6 level with other specified spinal cord injury
T_1-T_6 level with:
   incomplete spinal cord lesion NOS
   posterior cord syndrome

806.35 T_7-T_{12} level with unspecified spinal cord injury

806.36 T_7-T_{12} level with complete lesion of cord

806.37 T_7-$T1_2$ level with anterior cord syndrome

806.38 T_7-T_{12} level with central cord syndrome

806.39 T_7-T_{12} level with other specified spinal cord injury
T_7-T_{12} level with:
   incomplete spinal cord lesion NOS
   posterior cord syndrome

806.4 Lumbar, closed

806.5 Lumbar, open

806.6 Sacrum and coccyx, closed

806.60 With unspecified spinal cord injury

806.61 With complete cauda equina lesion

806.62 With other cauda equina injury

806.69 With other spinal cord injury

806.7 Sacrum and coccyx, open

806.70 With unspecified spinal cord injury

806.71 With complete cauda equina lesion

806.72 With other cauda equina injury

806.79 With other spinal cord injury

806.8 Unspecified, closed

806.9 Unspecified, open

807 Fracture of rib(s), sternum, larynx, and trachea
The following fifth-digit subclassification is for use with codes 807.0-807.1:

0 rib(s), unspecified

1 one rib

2 two ribs

3 three ribs

4 four ribs

5 five ribs

6 six ribs

7 seven ribs

8 eight or more ribs

9 multiple ribs, unspecified

	Add 4th or 5th digit		Nonspecific code		Unspecified code		Medicare secondary payer(MSP) alert

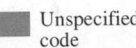

⑤ **807.0** **Rib(s), closed**

⑤ **807.1** **Rib(s), open**

807.2 **Sternum, closed**

807.3 **Sternum, open**

807.4 **Flail chest**

807.5 **Larynx and trachea, closed**
Hyoid bone   Trachea
Thyroid cartilage

807.6 **Larynx and trachea, open**

808 **Fracture of pelvis**

808.0 **Acetabulum, closed**

808.1 **Acetabulum, open**

808.2 **Pubis, closed**

808.3 **Pubis, open**

808.4 **Other specified part, closed**

  808.41 **Ilium**

  808.42 **Ischium**

  808.43 **Multiple pelvic fractures with disruption of pelvic circle**

  808.49 **Other**
  Innominate bone   Pelvic rim

808.5 **Other specified part, open**

  808.51 **Ilium**

  808.52 **Ischium**

  808.53 **Multiple pelvic fractures with disruption of pelvic circle**

  808.59 **Other**

808.8 **Unspecified, closed**

808.9 **Unspecified, open**

809 **Ill-defined fractures of bones of trunk**
Includes: bones of trunk with other bones except those of skull and face
multiple bones of trunk

Excludes: *multiple fractures of:*
pelvic bones alone (808.0-808.9)
ribs alone (807.0-807.1, 807.4)
ribs or sternum with limb bones (819.0-819.1, 828.0-828.1)
skull or face with other bones (804.0-804.9)

809.0 **Fracture of bones of trunk, closed**

809.1 **Fracture of bones of trunk, open**

FRACTURE OF UPPER LIMB (810-819)

⑤ **810** **Fracture of clavicle**
Includes: collar bone
interligamentous part of clavicle

The following fifth-digit subclassification is for use with category 810:

  0 **unspecified part**
  Clavicle NOS

  1 **sternal end of clavicle**

  2 **shaft of clavicle**

  3 **acromial end of clavicle**

810.0 **Closed**

810.1 **Open**

⑤ **811** **Fracture of scapula**
Includes: shoulder blade

The following fifth-digit subclassification is for use with category 811:

  0 **unspecified part**

  1 **acromial process**
  Acromion (process)

continued

● Code new
to this edition

▲ Revision of
existing code

④ ⑤ Fourth or fifth
digit required

    2   **coracoid process**

    3   **glenoid cavity and neck of scapula**

    9   **other**
       Scapula body

811.0 **Closed**

811.1 **Open**

812 **Fracture of humerus**

  812.0 **Upper end, closed**

    812.00 **Upper end, unspecified part**
        Proximal end
        Shoulder

    812.01 **Surgical neck**
        Neck of humerus NOS

    812.02 **Anatomical neck**

    812.03 **Greater tuberosity**

    812.09 **Other**
        Head   Upper epiphysis

  812.1 **Upper end, open**

    812.10 **Upper end, unspecified part**

    812.11 **Surgical neck**

    812.12 **Anatomical neck**

    812.13 **Greater tuberosity**

    812.19 **Other**

  812.2 **Shaft or unspecified part, closed**

    812.20 **Unspecified part of humerus**
        Humerus NOS   Upper arm NOS

    812.21 **Shaft of humerus**

  812.3 **Shaft or unspecified part, open**

    812.30 **Unspecified part of humerus**

    812.31 **Shaft of humerus**

  812.4 **Lower end, closed**
      Distal end of humerus   Elbow

    812.40 **Lower end, unspecified part**

    812.41 **Supracondylar fracture of humerus**

    812.42 **Lateral condyle**
        External condyle

    812.43 **Medial condyle**
        Internal epicondyle

    812.44 **Condyle(s), unspecified**
        Articular process NOS
        Lower epiphysis NOS

    812.49 **Other**
        Multiple fractures of lower end
        Trochlea

  812.5 **Lower end, open**

    812.50 **Lower end, unspecified part**

    812.51 **Supracondylar fracture of humerus**

    812.52 **Lateral condyle**

    812.53 **Medial condyle**

    812.54 **Condyle(s), unspecified**

    812.59 **Other**

813 **Fracture of radius and ulna**

  □ **813.0** **Upper end, closed**
      Proximal end

    813.00 **Upper end of forearm, unspecified**

    813.01 **Olecranon process of ulna**

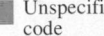 Add 4th or 5th digit   Nonspecific code   Unspecified code   Medicare secondary payer(MSP) alert

813.02   Coronoid process of ulna

813.03   Monteggia's fracture

813.04   **Other and unspecified fractures of proximal end of ulna (alone)**
Multiple fractures of ulna, upper end

813.05   **Head of radius**

813.06   **Neck of radius**

813.07   **Other and unspecified fractures of proximal end of radius (alone)**
Multiple fractures of radius, upper end

813.08   **Radius with ulna, upper end [any part]**

☐ 813.1 **Upper end, open**

813.10   **Upper end of forearm, unspecified**

813.11   **Olecranon process of ulna**

813.12   **Coronoid process of ulna**

813.13   **Monteggia's fracture**

813.14   **Other and unspecified fractures of proximal end of ulna (alone)**

813.15   **Head of radius**

813.16   **Neck of radius**

813.17   **Other and unspecified fractures of proximal end of radius (alone)**

813.18   **Radius with ulna, upper end [any part]**

813.2 **Shaft, closed**

813.20   **Shaft, unspecified**

813.21   **Radius (alone)**

813.22   **Ulna (alone)**

813.23   **Radius with ulna**

813.3 **Shaft, open**

813.30   **Shaft, unspecified**

813.31   **Radius (alone)**

813.32   **Ulna (alone)**

813.33   **Radius with ulna**

813.4 **Lower end, closed**
Distal end

813.40   **Lower end of forearm, unspecified**

813.41   **Colles' fracture**
Smith's fracture

813.42   **Other fractures of distal end of radius (alone)**
Dupuytren's fracture, radius
Radius, lower end

813.43   **Distal end of ulna (alone)**
Ulna: Ulna:
head   lower epiphysis
lower end   styloid process

813.44   **Radius with ulna, lower end**

813.5 **Lower end, open**

813.50   **Lower end of forearm, unspecified**

813.51   **Colles' fracture**

813.52   **Other fractures of distal end of radius (alone)**

813.53   **Distal end of ulna (alone)**

813.54   **Radius with ulna, lower end**

☐ 813.8 **Unspecified part, closed**

813.80   **Forearm, unspecified**

813.81   **Radius (alone)**

813.82   **Ulna (alone)**

813.83   **Radius with ulna**

☐ 813.9 **Unspecified part, open**

813.90   **Forearm, unspecified**

● Code new   ▲ Revision of   ④ ⑤ Fourth or fifth
  to this edition   existing code   digit required

813.91 **Radius (alone)**

813.92 **Ulna (alone)**

813.93 **Radius with ulna**

⑤ **814 Fracture of carpal bone(s)**

The following fifth-digit subclassification is for use with category 814:

0 **carpal bone, unspecified**
Wrist NOS

1 **navicular [scaphoid] of wrist**

2 **lunate [semilunar] bone of wrist**

3 **triquetral [cuneiform] bone of wrist**

4 **pisiform**

5 **trapezium bone [larger multangular]**

6 **trapezoid bone [smaller multangular]**

7 **capitate bone [os magnum]**

8 **hamate [unciform] bone**

9 **other**

814.0 **Closed**

814.1 **Open**

⑤ **815 Fracture of metacarpal bone(s)**
Includes: hand [except finger]
metacarpus

The following fifth-digit subclassification is for use with category 815:

0 **metacarpal bone(s), site unspecified**

1 **base of thumb [first] metacarpal**
Bennett's fracture

2 **base of other metacarpal bone(s)**

3 **shaft of metacarpal bone(s)**

4 **neck of metacarpal bone(s)**

9 **multiple sites of metacarpus**

815.0 **Closed**

815.1 **Open**

⑤ **816 Fracture of one or more phalanges of hand**
Includes: finger(s)
thumb

The following fifth-digit subclassification is for use with category 816:

0 **phalanx or phalanges, unspecified**

1 **middle or proximal phalanx or phalanges**

2 **distal phalanx or phalanges**

3 **multiple sites**

816.0 **Closed**

816.1 **Open**

817 Multiple fractures of hand bones
Includes: metacarpal bone(s) with phalanx or phalanges of same hand

817.0 **Closed**

817.1 **Open**

818 Ill-defined fractures of upper limb
Includes: arm NOS
multiple bones of same upper limb

Excludes: *multiple fractures of:*
metacarpal bone(s) with phalanx or phalanges (817.0-817.1)
phalanges of hand alone (816.0-816.1)
radius with ulna (813.0-813.9)

818.0 **Closed**

818.1 **Open**

	Add 4th or 5th digit		Nonspecific code		Unspecified code		Medicare secondary payer(MSP) alert

819 **Multiple fractures involving both upper limbs, and upper limb with rib(s) and sternum**
　　Includes:　arm(s) with rib(s) or sternum
　　　　　　　both arms [any bones]

　　819.0　Closed
　　819.1　Open

FRACTURE OF LOWER LIMB (820-829)

820　Fracture of neck of femur

　　820.0　Transcervical fracture, closed

　　　　820.00　Intracapsular section, unspecified

　　　　820.01　Epiphysis (separation) (upper)
　　　　　　　　Transepiphyseal

　　　　820.02　Midcervical section
　　　　　　　　Transcervical NOS

　　　　820.03　Base of neck
　　　　　　　　Cervicotrochanteric section

　　　　820.09　Other
　　　　　　　　Head of femur
　　　　　　　　Subcapital

　　820.1　Transcervical fracture, open

　　　　820.10　Intracapsular section, unspecified

　　　　820.11　Epiphysis (separation) (upper)

　　　　820.12　Midcervical section

　　　　820.13　Base of neck

　　　　820.19　Other

　　820.2　Pertrochanteric fracture, closed

　　　　820.20　Trochanteric section, unspecified
　　　　　　　　Trochanter:
　　　　　　　　　NOS
　　　　　　　　　greater
　　　　　　　　　lesser

　　　　820.21　Intertrochanteric section

　　　　820.22　Subtrochanteric section

　　820.3　Pertrochanteric fracture, open

　　　　820.30　Trochanteric section, unspecified

　　　　820.31　Intertrochanteric section

　　　　820.32　Subtrochanteric section

　　820.8　Unspecified part of neck of femur, closed
　　　　Hip NOS　　　　　　　　　Neck of femur NOS

　　820.9　Unspecified part of neck of femur, open

821　Fracture of other and unspecified parts of femur

　　821.0　Shaft or unspecified part, closed

　　　　821.00　Unspecified part of femur
　　　　　　　　Thigh　　　　　　　Upper leg

　　　　Excludes: hip NOS (820.8)

　　　　821.01　Shaft

　　821.1　Shaft or unspecified part, open

　　　　821.10　Unspecified part of femur

　　　　821.11　Shaft

　　821.2　Lower end, closed
　　　　Distal end

　　　　821.20　Lower end, unspecified part

　　　　821.21　Condyle, femoral

　　　　821.22　Epiphysis, lower (separation)

　　　　821.23　Supracondylar fracture of femur

　● Code new　　　　▲ Revision of　　　④ ⑤ Fourth or fifth
　　　to this edition　　　　existing code　　　　digit required

821.29 **Other**
Multiple fractures of lower end

821.3 **Lower end, open**

821.30 **Lower end, unspecified part**

821.31 **Condyle, femoral**

821.32 **Epiphysis, lower (separation)**

821.33 **Supracondylar fracture of femur**

821.39 **Other**

822 **Fracture of patella**

822.0 **Closed**

822.1 **Open**

⑤ 823 **Fracture of tibia and fibula**

> Excludes: *Dupuytren's fracture (824.4-824.5)*
>   *ankle (824.4-824.5)*
>   *radius (813.42, 813.52)*
>   *Pott's fracture (824.4-824.5)*
>   *that involving ankle (824.0-824.9)*

The following fifth-digit subclassification is for use with category 823:

    0   **tibia alone**

    1   **fibula alone**

    2   **fibula with tibia**

☐ 823.0 **Upper end, closed**

Head	Tibia:
Proximal end	condyles
	tuberosity

☐ 823.1 **Upper end, open**

823.2 **Shaft, closed**

823.3 **Shaft, open**

☐ 823.8 **Unspecified part, closed**
Lower leg NOS

☐ 823.9 **Unspecified part, open**

824 **Fracture of ankle**

824.0 **Medial malleolus, closed**
Tibia involving:
   ankle
   malleolus

824.1 **Medial malleolus, open**

824.2 **Lateral malleolus, closed**
Fibula involving:
   ankle
   malleolus

824.3 **Lateral malleolus, open**

824.4 **Bimalleolar, closed**
Dupuytren's fracture, fibula
Pott's fracture

824.5 **Bimalleolar, open**

824.6 **Trimalleolar, closed**
Lateral and medial malleolus with anterior or posterior lip of tibia

824.7 **Trimalleolar, open**

824.8 **Unspecified, closed**
Ankle NOS

824.9 **Unspecified, open**

825 **Fracture of one or more tarsal and metatarsal bones**

825.0 **Fracture of calcaneus, closed**
Heel bone   Os calcis

825.1 **Fracture of calcaneus, open**

825.2 **Fracture of other tarsal and metatarsal bones, closed**

| | Add 4th or 5th digit | | Nonspecific code | | Unspecified code | | Medicare secondary payer(MSP) alert |

825.20 **Unspecified bone(s) of foot [except toes]**
Instep

825.21 **Astragalus**
Talus

825.22 **Navicular [scaphoid], foot**

825.23 **Cuboid**

825.24 **Cuneiform, foot**

825.25 **Metatarsal bone(s)**

825.29 **Other**
Tarsal with metatarsal bone(s) only

Excludes: calcaneus (825.0)

825.3 **Fracture of other tarsal and metatarsal bones, open**

825.30 **Unspecified bone(s) of foot [except toes]**

825.31 **Astragalus**

825.32 **Navicular [scaphoid], foot**

825.33 **Cuboid**

825.34 **Cuneiform, foot**

825.35 **Metatarsal bone(s)**

825.39 **Other**

826 **Fracture of one or more phalanges of foot**
Includes: toe(s)

826.0 **Closed**

826.1 **Open**

827 **Other, multiple, and ill-defined fractures of lower limb**
Includes: leg NOS
multiple bones of same lower limb

Excludes: multiple fractures of:
ankle bones alone (824.4-824.9)
phalanges of foot alone (826.0-826.1)
tarsal with metatarsal bones (825.29, 825.39)
tibia with fibula (823.0-823.9 with fifth-digit 2)

827.0 **Closed**

827.1 **Open**

828 **Multiple fractures involving both lower limbs, lower with upper limb, and lower limb(s) with rib(s) and sternum**
Includes: arm(s) with leg(s) [any bones]
both legs [any bones]
leg(s) with rib(s) or sternum

828.0 **Closed**

828.1 **Open**

829 **Fracture of unspecified bones**

829.0 **Unspecified bone, closed**

829.1 **Unspecified bone, open**

DISLOCATION (830-839)

Includes: displacement
subluxation

Excludes: congenital dislocation (754.0-755.8)
pathological dislocation (718.2)
recurrent dislocation (718.3)

The descriptions "closed" and "open", used in the fourth-digit subdivisions, include the following terms:

closed:	open:
complete	compound
dislocation NOS	infected
partial	with foreign body
simple	
uncomplicated	

A dislocation not indicated as closed or open should be classified as closed.

● Code new
to this edition

▲ Revision of
existing code

④ ⑤ Fourth or fifth
digit required

830 **Dislocation of jaw**
  Includes: jaw (cartilage) (meniscus)
      mandible
      maxilla (inferior)
      temporomandibular (joint)

830.0 Closed dislocation

830.1 Open dislocation

⑤ **831** **Dislocation of shoulder**

  Excludes: *sternoclavicular joint (839.61, 839.71)*
      sternum (839.61, 839.71)

  The following fifth-digit subclassification is for use with category 831:

  0 **shoulder, unspecified**
      Humerus NOS

  1 **anterior dislocation of humerus**

  2 **posterior dislocation of humerus**

  3 **inferior dislocation of humerus**

  4 **acromioclavicular (joint)**
      Clavicle

  9 **other**
      Scapula

831.0 Closed dislocation

831.1 Open dislocation

⑤ **832** **Dislocation of elbow**

  The following fifth-digit subclassification is for use with category 832:

  0 **elbow unspecified**

  1 **anterior dislocation of elbow**

  2 **posterior dislocation of elbow**

  3 **medial dislocation of elbow**

  4 **lateral dislocation of elbow**

  9 **other**

832.0 Closed dislocation

832.1 Open dislocation

⑤ **833** **Dislocation of wrist**

  The following fifth-digit subclassification is for use with category 833:

  0 **wrist, unspecified part**
      Carpal (bone)   Radius, distal end

  1 **radioulnar (joint), distal**

  2 **radiocarpal (joint)**

  3 **midcarpal (joint)**

  4 **carpometacarpal (joint)**

  5 **metacarpal (bone), proximal end**

  9 **other**
      Ulna, distal end

833.0 Closed dislocation

833.1 Open dislocation

⑤ **834** **Dislocation of finger**
  Includes: finger(s)
        phalanx of hand
        thumb

  The following fifth-digit subclassification is for use with category 834:

  0 **finger, unspecified part**

  1 **metacarpophalangeal (joint)**
      Metacarpal (bone), distal end

  2 **interphalangeal (joint), hand**

834.0 Closed dislocation

834.1 Open dislocation

⑤ **835 Dislocation of hip**
The following fifth-digit subclassification is for use with category 835:

0 dislocation of hip, unspecified
1 posterior dislocation
2 obturator dislocation
3 other anterior dislocation

835.0 Closed dislocation
835.1 Open dislocation

836 Dislocation of knee

Excludes: *dislocation of knee:*
old or pathological (718.2)
recurrent (718.3)
internal derangement of knee joint (717.0-717.5, 717.8-717.9)
old tear of cartilage or meniscus of knee (717.0-717.5, 717.8-717.9)

836.0 Tear of medial cartilage or meniscus of knee, current
Bucket handle tear:
NOS ⎫
medial meniscus ⎭ current injury

836.1 Tear of lateral cartilage or meniscus of knee, current

836.2 Other tear of cartilage or meniscus of knee, current
Tear of:
cartilage (semilunar) ⎫ current injury, not specified as medial or lateral
meniscus ⎭

836.3 Dislocation of patella, closed
836.4 Dislocation of patella, open
836.5 Other dislocation of knee, closed

836.50 Dislocation of knee, unspecified
836.51 Anterior dislocation of tibia, proximal end
Posterior dislocation of femur, distal end

836.52 Posterior dislocation of tibia, proximal end
Anterior dislocation of femur, distal end

836.53 Medial dislocation of tibia, proximal end
836.54 Lateral dislocation of tibia, proximal end
836.59 Other

836.6 Other dislocation of knee, open

836.60 Dislocation of knee, unspecified
836.61 Anterior dislocation of tibia, proximal end
836.62 Posterior dislocation of tibia, proximal end
836.63 Medial dislocation of tibia, proximal end
836.64 Lateral dislocation of tibia, proximal end
836.69 Other

837 Dislocation of ankle
Includes:

astragalus   navicular, foot
fibula, distal end   scaphoid, foot
                        tibia, distal end

837.0 Closed dislocation
837.1 Open dislocation

⑤ **838 Dislocation of foot**
The following fifth-digit subclassification is for use with category 838:

0 foot, unspecified
1 tarsal (bone), joint unspecified
2 midtarsal (joint)
3 tarsometatarsal (joint)
4 metatarsal (bone), joint unspecified
5 metatarsophalangeal (joint)

400

● Code new   ▲ Revision of   ④ ⑤ Fourth or fifth
to this edition   existing code   digit required

6 **interphalangeal (joint), foot**

9 **other**
Phalanx of foot   Toe(s)

838.0 Closed dislocation

838.1 Open dislocation

839 **Other, multiple, and ill-defined dislocations**

839.0 Cervical vertebra, closed
Cervical spine   Neck

839.00 **Cervical vertebra, unspecified**

839.01 **First cervical vertebra**

839.02 **Second cervical vertebra**

839.03 **Third cervical vertebra**

839.04 **Fourth cervical vertebra**

839.05 **Fifth cervical vertebra**

839.06 **Sixth cervical vertebra**

839.07 **Seventh cervical vertebra**

839.08 **Multiple cervical vertebrae**

839.1 Cervical vertebra, open

839.10 **Cervical vertebra, unspecified**

839.11 **First cervical vertebra**

839.12 **Second cervical vertebra**

839.13 **Third cervical vertebra**

839.14 **Fourth cervical vertebra**

839.15 **Fifth cervical vertebra**

839.16 **Sixth cervical vertebra**

839.17 **Seventh cervical vertebra**

839.18 **Multiple cervical vertebrae**

839.2 Thoracic and lumbar vertebra, closed

839.20 **Lumbar vertebra**

839.21 **Thoracic vertebra**
Dorsal [thoracic] vertebra

839.3 Thoracic and lumbar vertebra, open

839.30 **Lumbar vertebra**

839.31 **Thoracic vertebra**

839.4 Other vertebra, closed

839.40 **Vertebra, unspecified site**
Spine NOS

839.41 **Coccyx**

839.42 **Sacrum**
Sacroiliac (joint)

839.49 **Other**

839.5 Other vertebra, open

839.50 **Vertebra, unspecified site**

839.51 **Coccyx**

839.52 **Sacrum**

839.59 **Other**

839.6 Other location, closed

839.61 **Sternum**
Sternoclavicular joint

839.69 **Other**
Pelvis

839.7 Other location, open

839.71 **Sternum**

839.79 **Other**

	Add 4th or 5th digit		Nonspecific code		Unspecified code		Medicare secondary payer(MSP) alert

839.8 **Multiple and ill-defined, closed**
Arm
Back
Hand
Multiple locations, except fingers or toes alone
Other ill-defined locations
Unspecified location

839.9 **Multiple and ill-defined, open**

SPRAINS AND STRAINS OF JOINTS AND ADJACENT MUSCLES (840-848)

Includes:

avulsion
hemarthrosis
laceration } of:
rupture
sprain
strain
tear

joint capsule
ligament
muscle
tendon

Excludes: *laceration of tendon in open wounds (880-884 and 890-894 with .2)*

840 **Sprains and strains of shoulder and upper arm**

840.0 **Acromioclavicular (joint) (ligament)**

840.1 **Coracoclavicular (ligament)**

840.2 **Coracohumeral (ligament)**

840.3 **Infraspinatus (muscle) (tendon)**

840.4 **Rotator cuff (capsule)**

840.5 **Subscapularis (muscle)**

840.6 **Supraspinatus (muscle) (tendon)**

840.8 **Other specified sites of shoulder and upper arm**

840.9 **Unspecified site of shoulder and upper arm**
Arm NOS   Shoulder NOS

841 **Sprains and strains of elbow and forearm**

841.0 **Radial collateral ligament**

841.1 **Ulnar collateral ligament**

841.2 **Radiohumeral (joint)**

841.3 **Ulnohumeral (joint)**

841.8 **Other specified sites of elbow and forearm**

841.9 **Unspecified site of elbow and forearm**
Elbow NOS

842 **Sprains and strains of wrist and hand**

842.0 **Wrist**

842.00 **Unspecified site**

842.01 **Carpal (joint)**

842.02 **Radiocarpal (joint) (ligament)**

842.09 **Other**
Radioulnar joint, distal

842.1 **Hand**

842.10 **Unspecified site**

842.11 **Carpometacarpal (joint)**

842.12 **Metacarpophalangeal (joint)**

842.13 **Interphalangeal (joint)**

842.19 **Other**
Midcarpal (joint)

843 **Sprains and strains of hip and thigh**

843.0 **Iliofemoral (ligament)**

843.1 **Ischiocapsular (ligament)**

843.8 **Other specified sites of hip and thigh**

● Code new
to this edition
▲ Revision of
existing code
④ ⑤ Fourth or fifth
digit required

843.9 **Unspecified site of hip and thigh**
Hip NOS   Thigh NOS

844 **Sprains and strains of knee and leg**

844.0 **Lateral collateral ligament of knee**

844.1 **Medial collateral ligament of knee**

844.2 **Cruciate ligament of knee**

844.3 **Tibiofibular (joint) (ligament), superior**

844.8 **Other specified sites of knee and leg**

844.9 **Unspecified site of knee and leg**
Knee NOS   Leg NOS

845 **Sprains and strains of ankle and foot**

845.0 **Ankle**

845.00 **Unspecified site**

845.01 **Deltoid (ligament), ankle**
Internal collateral (ligament), ankle

845.02 **Calcaneofibular (ligament)**

845.03 **Tibiofibular (ligament), distal**

845.09 **Other**
Achilles tendon

845.1 **Foot**

845.10 **Unspecified site**

845.11 **Tarsometatarsal (joint) (ligament)**

845.12 **Metatarsophalangeal (joint)**

845.13 **Interphalangeal (joint), toe**

845.19 **Other**

846 **Sprains and strains of sacroiliac region**

846.0 **Lumbosacral (joint) (ligament)**

846.1 **Sacroiliac ligament**

846.2 **Sacrospinatus (ligament)**

846.3 **Sacrotuberous (ligament)**

846.8 **Other specified sites of sacroiliac region**

846.9 **Unspecified site of sacroiliac region**

847 **Sprains and strains of other and unspecified parts of back**

Excludes: *lumbosacral (846.0)*

847.0 **Neck**
Anterior longitudinal (ligament), cervical
Atlanto-axial (joints)
Atlanto-occipital (joints)
Whiplash injury

Excludes: *neck injury NOS (959.0)*
        thyroid region (848.2)

847.1 **Thoracic**

847.2 **Lumbar**

847.3 **Sacrum**
Sacrococcygeal (ligament)

847.4 **Coccyx**

847.9 **Unspecified site of back**
Back NOS

848 **Other and ill-defined sprains and strains**

848.0 **Septal cartilage of nose**

848.1 **Jaw**
Temporomandibular (joint) (ligament)

848.2 **Thyroid region**
Cricoarytenoid (joint) (ligament)
Cricothyroid (joint) (ligament)
Thyroid cartilage

| | Add 4th or 5th digit | | Nonspecific code | | Unspecified code | | Medicare secondary payer(MSP) alert |

848.3 Ribs
Chondrocostal (joint)
Costal cartilage } without mention of injury to sternum

848.4 Sternum

848.40 Unspecified site

848.41 Sternoclavicular (joint) (ligament)

848.42 Chondrosternal (joint)

848.49 Other
Xiphoid cartilage

848.5 Pelvis
Symphysis pubis

Excludes: *that in childbirth (665.6)*

848.8 Other specified sites of sprains and strains

848.9 Unspecified site of sprain and strain

INTRACRANIAL INJURY, EXCLUDING THOSE WITH SKULL FRACTURE (850-854)

Excludes: *intracranial injury with skull fracture (800-801 and 803-804, except .0 and .5)*
open wound of head without intracranial injury (870.0-873.9)
skull fracture alone (800-801 and 803-804 with .0, .5)

The description "with open intracranial wound," used in the fourth-digit subdivisions, includes those specified as open or with mention of infection or foreign body.

The following fifth-digit subclassification is for use with categories 851-854:

0 unspecified state of consciousness

1 with no loss of consciousness

2 with brief [less than one hour] loss of consciousness

3 with moderate [1-24 hours] loss of consciousness

4 with prolonged [more than 24 hours] loss of consciousness and return to pre-existing conscious level

5 with prolonged [more than 24 hours] loss of consciousness, without return to pre-existing conscious level

Use fifth-digit 5 to designate when a patient is unconscious and dies before regaining consciousness, regardless of the duration of the loss of consciousness

6 with loss of consciousness of unspecified duration

9 with concussion, unspecified

850 Concussion
Includes: commotio cerebri

Excludes: *Concussion with:*
cerebral laceration or contusion (851.0-851.9)
cerebral hemorrhage (852-853)
head injury NOS (854)

850.0 With no loss of consciousness
Concussion with mental confusion or disorientation, without loss of consciousness

850.1 With brief loss of consciousness
Loss of consciousness for less than one hour

850.2 With moderate loss of consciousness
Loss of consciousness for 1-24 hours

850.3 With prolonged loss of consciousness and return to pre-existing conscious level
Loss of consciousness for more than 24 hours with complete recovery

850.4 With prolonged loss of consciousness, without return to pre-existing conscious level

850.5 With loss of consciousness of unspecified duration

850.9 Concussion, unspecified

⑤ **851 Cerebral laceration and contusion**

☐ **851.0 Cortex (cerebral) contusion without mention of open intracranial wound**

☐ **851.1 Cortex (cerebral) contusion with open intracranial wound**

☐ **851.2 Cortex (cerebral) laceration without mention of open intracranial wound**

☐ **851.3 Cortex (cerebral) laceration with open intracranial wound**

☐ **851.4 Cerebellar or brain stem contusion without mention of open intracranial wound**

● Code new
to this edition ▲ Revision of
existing code ④ ⑤ Fourth or fifth
digit required

☐ 851.5 Cerebellar or brain stem contusion with open intracranial wound

☐ 851.6 Cerebellar or brain stem laceration without mention of open intracranial wound

☐ 851.7 Cerebellar or brain stem laceration with open intracranial wound

☐ 851.8 Other and unspecified cerebral laceration and contusion, without mention of open intracranial wound
　　Brain (membrane) NOS

☐ 851.9 Other and unspecified cerebral laceration and contusion, with open intracranial wound

⑤ 852 Subarachnoid, subdural, and extradural hemorrhage, following injury

　　Excludes: Cerebral contusion or laceration (with hemorrhage) (851.0-851.9)

☐ 852.0 Subarachnoid hemorrhage following injury without mention of open intracranial wound
　　Middle meningeal hemorrhage following injury

☐ 852.1 Subarachnoid hemorrhage following injury with open intracranial wound

☐ 852.2 Subdural hemorrhage following injury without mention of open intracranial wound

☐ 852.3 Subdural hemorrhage following injury with open intracranial wound

☐ 852.4 Extradural hemorrhage following injury without mention of open intracranial wound
　　Epidural hematoma following injury

☐ 852.5 Extradural hemorrhage following injury with open intracranial wound

⑤ 853 Other and unspecified intracranial hemorrhage following injury

853.0 Without mention of open intracranial wound
　　Cerebral compression due to injury
　　Intracranial hematoma following injury
　　Traumatic cerebral hemorrhage

853.1 With open intracranial wound

⑤ 854 Intracranial injury of other and unspecified nature
　　Includes:　brain injury NOS
　　　　　　head injury NOS

　　Excludes: any condition classifiable to 850-853

854.0 Without mention of open intracranial wound

854.1 With open intracranial wound

INTERNAL INJURY OF THORAX, ABDOMEN, AND PELVIS (860-869)

　　Includes:

blast injuries	
blunt trauma	
bruise	
concussion injuries (except cerebral)	
crushing	of internal organs
hematoma	
laceration	
puncture	
tear	
traumatic rupture	

　　Excludes: concussion NOS (850.0-850.9)
　　　　flail chest (807.4)
　　　　foreign body entering through orifice (930.0-939.9)
　　　　injury to blood vessels (901.0-902.9)

The description "with open wound," used in the fourth-digit subdivisions, includes those with mention of infection or foreign body.

860 Traumatic pneumothorax and hemothorax

860.0 Pneumothorax without mention of open wound into thorax

860.1 Pneumothorax with open wound into thorax

860.2 Hemothorax without mention of open wound into thorax

860.3 Hemothorax with open wound into thorax

860.4 Pneumohemothorax without mention of open wound into thorax

860.5 Pneumohemothorax with open wound into thorax

| ▉ Add 4th or 5th digit | ▉ Nonspecific code | ▉ Unspecified code | ▒ Medicare secondary payer(MSP) alert |

861 **Injury to heart and lung**

> *Excludes:* *injury to blood vessels of thorax (901.0-901.9)*

861.0 **Heart, without mention of open wound into thorax**

861.00 **Unspecified injury**

861.01 **Contusion**
    Cardiac contusion   Myocardial contusion

861.02 **Laceration without penetration of heart chambers**

861.03 **Laceration with penetration of heart chambers**

861.1 **Heart, with open wound into thorax**

861.10 **Unspecified injury**

861.11 **Contusion**

861.12 **Laceration without penetration of heart chambers**

861.13 **Laceration with penetration of heart chambers**

861.2 **Lung, without mention of open wound into thorax**

861.20 **Unspecified injury**

861.21 **Contusion**

861.22 **Laceration**

861.3 **Lung, with open wound into thorax**

861.30 **Unspecified injury**

861.31 **Contusion**

861.32 **Laceration**

862 **Injury to other and unspecified intrathoracic organs**

> *Excludes:* *injury to blood vessels of thorax (901.0-901.9)*

862.0 **Diaphragm, without mention of open wound into cavity**

862.1 **Diaphragm, with open wound into cavity**

862.2 **Other specified intrathoracic organs, without mention of open wound into cavity**

862.21 **Bronchus**

862.22 **Esophagus**

862.29 **Other**
    Pleura   Thymus gland

862.3 **Other specified intrathoracic organs, with open wound into cavity**

862.31 **Bronchus**

862.32 **Esophagus**

862.39 **Other**

862.8 **Multiple and unspecified intrathoracic organs, without mention of open wound into cavity**
    Crushed chest
    Multiple intrathoracic organs

862.9 **Multiple and unspecified intrathoracic organs, with open wound into cavity**

863 **Injury to gastrointestinal tract**

> *Excludes:* *anal sphincter laceration during delivery (664.2)*
> *bile duct (868.0-868.1 with fifth-digit 2)*
> *gallbladder (868.0-868.1 with fifth-digit 2)*

863.0 **Stomach, without mention of open wound into cavity**

863.1 **Stomach, with open wound into cavity**

863.2 **Small intestine, without mention of open wound into cavity**

863.20 **Small intestine, unspecified site**

863.21 **Duodenum**

863.29 **Other**

863.3 **Small intestine, with open wound into cavity**

863.30 **Small intestine, unspecified site**

863.31 **Duodenum**

863.39 **Other**

● Code new
to this edition

▲ Revision of
existing code

④ ⑤ Fourth or fifth
digit required

863.4 Colon or rectum, without mention of open wound into cavity

863.40 Colon, unspecified site

863.41 Ascending [right] colon

863.42 Transverse colon

863.43 Descending [left] colon

863.44 Sigmoid colon

863.45 Rectum

863.46 Multiple sites in colon and rectum

863.49 Other

863.5 Colon or rectum, with open wound into cavity

863.50 Colon, unspecified site

863.51 Ascending [right] colon

863.52 Transverse colon

863.53 Descending [left] colon

863.54 Sigmoid colon

863.55 Rectum

863.56 Multiple sites in colon and rectum

863.59 Other

863.8 Other and unspecified gastrointestinal sites, without mention of open wound into cavity

863.80 Gastrointestinal tract, unspecified site

863.81 Pancreas, head

863.82 Pancreas, body

863.83 Pancreas, tail

863.84 Pancreas, multiple and unspecified sites

863.85 Appendix

863.89 Other
　　　　Intestine NOS

863.9 Other and unspecified gastrointestinal sites, with open wound into cavity

863.90 Gastrointestinal tract, unspecified site

863.91 Pancreas, head

863.92 Pancreas, body

863.93 Pancreas, tail

863.94 Pancreas, multiple and unspecified sites

863.95 Appendix

863.99 Other

⑤ **864 Injury to liver**

The following fifth-digit subclassification is for use with category 864:

0 unspecified injury

1 hematoma and contusion

2 laceration, minor
　　　Laceration involving capsule only, or without significant involvement of hepatic
　　　　parenchyma [i.e., less than 1 cm deep]

3 laceration, moderate
　　　Laceration involving parenchyma but without major disruption of parenchyma [i.e., less
　　　　than 10 cm long and less than 3 cm deep]

4 laceration, major
　　　Laceration with significant disruption of hepatic parenchyma [i.e., 10 cm long and 3
　　　　cm deep]
　　　Multiple moderate lacerations, with or without hematoma
　　　Stellate lacerations of liver

5 laceration, unspecified

9 other

864.0 Without mention of open wound into cavity

864.1 With open wound into cavity

407

	Add 4th or 5th digit		Nonspecific code		Unspecified code		Medicare secondary payer(MSP) alert

⑤ **865** Injury to spleen

The following fifth-digit subclassification is for use with category 865:

0 unspecified injury

1 hematoma without rupture of capsule

2 capsular tears, without major disruption of parenchyma

3 laceration extending into parenchyma

4 massive parenchymal disruption

9 other

865.0 Without mention of open wound into cavity

865.1 With open wound into cavity

⑤ **866** Injury to kidney

The following fifth-digit subclassification is for use with category 866:

0 unspecified injury

1 hematoma without rupture of capsule

2 laceration

3 complete disruption of kidney parenchyma

866.0 Without mention of open wound into cavity

866.1 With open wound into cavity

867 Injury to pelvic organs

Excludes: injury during delivery (664.0-665.9)

867.0 Bladder and urethra, without mention of open wound into cavity

867.1 Bladder and urethra, with open wound into cavity

867.2 Ureter, without mention of open wound into cavity

867.3 Ureter, with open wound into cavity

867.4 Uterus, without mention of open wound into cavity

867.5 Uterus, with open wound into cavity

867.6 Other specified pelvic organs, without mention of open wound into cavity

Fallopian tube	Seminal vesicle
Ovary	Vas deferens
Prostate	

867.7 Other specified pelvic organs, with open wound into cavity

867.8 Unspecified pelvic organs, without mention of open wound into cavity

867.9 Unspecified pelvic organ, with open wound into cavity

⑤ **868** Injury to other intra-abdominal organs

The following fifth-digit subclassification is for use with category 868:

0 unspecified intra-abdominal organ

1 adrenal gland

2 bile duct and gallbladder

3 peritoneum

4 retroperitoneum

9 other and multiple intra-abdominal organs

868.0 Without mention of open wound into cavity

868.1 With open wound into cavity

869 Internal injury to unspecified or ill-defined organs

Includes: internal injury NOS
multiple internal injury NOS

869.0 Without mention of open wound into cavity

869.1 With open wound into cavity

● Code new
to this edition

▲ Revision of
existing code

④ ⑤ Fourth or fifth
digit required

OPEN WOUND (870-897)

Includes:
animal bite	laceration
avulsion	puncture wound
cut	traumatic amputation

Excludes: *burn (940.0-949.5)*
crushing (925-929.9)
puncture of internal organs (860.0-869.1)
superficial injury (910.0-919.9)
that incidental to:
   dislocation (830.0-839.9)
   fracture (800.0-829.1)
   internal injury (860.0-869.1)
   intracranial injury (851.0-854.1)

The description "complicated" used in the fourth-digit subdivisions includes those with mention of delayed healing, delayed treatment, foreign body, or major infection.

OPEN WOUND OF HEAD, NECK, AND TRUNK (870-879)

870 Open wound of ocular adnexa

   870.0 Laceration of skin of eyelid and periocular area

   870.1 Laceration of eyelid, full-thickness, not involving lacrimal passages

   870.2 Laceration of eyelid involving lacrimal passages

   870.3 Penetrating wound of orbit, without mention of foreign body

   870.4 Penetrating wound of orbit with foreign body

     Excludes: *retained (old) foreign body in orbit (376.6)*

   870.8 Other specified open wounds of ocular adnexa

   870.9 Unspecified open wound of ocular adnexa

871 Open wound of eyeball

     Excludes: *2nd cranial nerve [optic] injury (950.0-950.9)*
       3rd cranial nerve [oculomotor] injury (951.0)

   871.0 Ocular laceration without prolapse of intraocular tissue

   871.1 Ocular laceration with prolapse or exposure of intraocular tissue

   871.2 Rupture of eye with partial loss of intraocular tissue

   871.3 Avulsion of eye
     Traumatic enucleation

   871.4 Unspecified laceration of eye

   871.5 Penetration of eyeball with magnetic foreign body

     Excludes: *retained (old) magnetic foreign body in globe (360.50-360.59)*

   871.6 Penetration of eyeball with (nonmagnetic) foreign body

     Excludes: *retained (old) (nonmagnetic) foreign body in globe (360.60-360.69)*

   871.7 Unspecified ocular penetration

   871.9 Unspecified open wound of eyeball

872 Open wound of ear

   872.0 External ear, without mention of complication

     872.00 External ear, unspecified site

     872.01 Auricle, ear
       Pinna

     872.02 Auditory canal

   872.1 External ear, complicated

     872.10 External ear, unspecified site

     872.11 Auricle, ear

     872.12 Auditory canal

   872.6 Other specified parts of ear, without mention of complication

     872.61 Ear drum
       Drumhead   Tympanic membrane

     872.62 Ossicles

▮ Add 4th or 5th digit	▮ Nonspecific code	▮ Unspecified code	▮ Medicare secondary payer(MSP) alert

872.63   Eustachian tube

872.64   Cochlea

872.69   Other and multiple sites

872.7   **Other specified parts of ear, complicated**

    872.71   **Ear drum**

    872.72   **Ossicles**

    872.73   **Eustachian tube**

    872.74   **Cochlea**

    872.79   Other and multiple sites

872.8   **Ear, part unspecified, without mention of complication**
    Ear NOS

872.9   **Ear, part unspecified, complicated**

873   **Other open wound of head**

> Excludes: *that with mention of intracranial injury (851.0-854.1)*

873.0   **Scalp, without mention of complication**

873.1   **Scalp, complicated**

873.2   **Nose, without mention of complication**

    873.20   Nose, unspecified site

    873.21   **Nasal septum**

    873.22   **Nasal cavity**

    873.23   **Nasal sinus**

    873.29   Multiple sites

873.3   **Nose, complicated**

    873.30   Nose, unspecified site

    873.31   **Nasal septum**

    873.32   **Nasal cavity**

    873.33   **Nasal sinus**

    873.39   Multiple sites

873.4   **Face, without mention of complication**

    873.40   Face, unspecified site

    873.41   **Cheek**

    873.42   **Forehead**
        Eyebrow

    873.43   **Lip**

    873.44   **Jaw**

    873.49   Other and multiple sites

873.5   **Face, complicated**

    873.50   Face, unspecified site

    873.51   **Cheek**

    873.52   **Forehead**

    873.53   **Lip**

    873.54   **Jaw**

    873.59   Other and multiple sites

873.6   **Internal structures of mouth, without mention of complication**

    873.60   Mouth, unspecified site

    873.61   **Buccal mucosa**

    873.62   **Gum (alveolar process)**

    873.63   **Tooth (broken)**

    873.64   **Tongue and floor of mouth**

    873.65   **Palate**

    873.69   Other and multiple sites

873.7   **Internal structures of mouth, complicated**

● Code new
to this edition

▲ Revision of
existing code

④ ⑤ Fourth or fifth
digit required

873.70 Mouth, unspecified site

873.71 Buccal mucosa

873.72 Gum (alveolar process)

873.73 Tooth (broken)

873.74 Tongue and floor of mouth

873.75 Palate

873.79 Other and multiple sites

873.8 Other and unspecified open wound of head without mention of complication
Head NOS

873.9 Other and unspecified open wound of head, complicated

874 Open wound of neck

874.0 Larynx and trachea, without mention of complication

874.00 Larynx with trachea

874.01 Larynx

874.02 Trachea

874.1 Larynx and trachea, complicated

874.10 Larynx with trachea

874.11 Larynx

874.12 Trachea

874.2 Thyroid gland, without mention of complication

874.3 Thyroid gland, complicated

874.4 Pharynx, without mention of complication
Cervical esophagus

874.5 Pharynx, complicated

874.8 Other and unspecified parts, without mention of complication
Nape of neck   Throat NOS
Supraclavicular region

874.9 Other and unspecified parts, complicated

875 Open wound of chest (wall)

> Excludes: open wound into thoracic cavity (860.0-862.9)
>   traumatic pneumothorax and hemothorax (860.1, 860.3, 860.5)

875.0 Without mention of complication

875.1 Complicated

876 Open wound of back
Includes: loin   lumbar region

> Excludes: open wound into thoracic cavity (860.0-862.9)
>   traumatic pneumothorax and hemothorax (860.1, 860.3, 860.5)

876.0 Without mention of complication

876.1 Complicated

877 Open wound of buttock
Includes: sacroiliac region

877.0 Without mention of complication

877.1 Complicated

878 Open wound of genital organs (external), including traumatic amputation

> Excludes: injury during delivery (664.0-665.9)
>   internal genital organs (867.0-867.9)

878.0 Penis, without mention of complication

878.1 Penis, complicated

878.2 Scrotum and testes, without mention of complication

878.3 Scrotum and testes, complicated

878.4 Vulva, without mention of complication
Labium (majus) (minus)

878.5 Vulva, complicated

878.6 Vagina, without mention of complication

 Add 4th or
5th digit

 Nonspecific
code

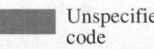 Unspecified
code

Medicare secondary
payer(MSP) alert

878.7 **Vagina, complicated**

`878.8` **Other and unspecified parts, without mention of complication**

`878.9` **Other and unspecified parts, complicated**

`879` **Open wound of other and unspecified sites, except limbs**

879.0 **Breast, without mention of complication**

879.1 **Breast, complicated**

879.2 **Abdominal wall, anterior, without mention of complication**

Abdominal wall NOS	Pubic region
Epigastric region	Umbilical region
Hypogastric region	

879.3 **Abdominal wall, anterior, complicated**

879.4 **Abdominal wall, lateral, without mention of complication**

Flank	Iliac (region)
Groin	Inguinal region
Hypochondrium	

879.5 **Abdominal wall, lateral, complicated**

`879.6` **Other and unspecified parts of trunk, without mention of complication**

Pelvic region	Trunk NOS
Perineum	

`879.7` **Other and unspecified parts of trunk, complicated**

`879.8` **Open wound(s) (multiple) of unspecified site(s) without mention of complication**

Multiple open wounds NOS
Open wound NOS

`879.9` **Open wound(s) (multiple) of unspecified site(s), complicated**

OPEN WOUND OF UPPER LIMB (880-887)

⑤ `880` **Open wound of shoulder and upper arm**

The following fifth-digit subclassification is for use with category 880:

  0 shoulder region

  1 scapular region

  2 axillary region

  3 upper arm

  `9` **multiple sites**

880.0 **Without mention of complication**

880.1 **Complicated**

880.2 **With tendon involvement**

⑤ `881` **Open wound of elbow, forearm, and wrist**

The following fifth-digit subclassification is for use with category 881:

  0 forearm

  1 elbow

  2 wrist

881.0 **Without mention of complication**

881.1 **Complicated**

881.2 **With tendon involvement**

`882` **Open wound of hand except finger(s) alone**

882.0 **Without mention of complication**

882.1 **Complicated**

882.2 **With tendon involvement**

`883` **Open wound of finger(s)**

Includes: fingernail   thumb (nail)

883.0 **Without mention of complication**

883.1 **Complicated**

883.2 **With tendon involvement**

`884` **Multiple and unspecified open wound of upper limb**

Includes: arm NOS
           multiple sites of one upper limb
           upper limb NOS

● Code new   ▲ Revision of   ④ ⑤ Fourth or fifth
     to this edition   existing code   digit required

884.0 Without mention of complication

884.1 Complicated

884.2 With tendon involvement

885 Traumatic amputation of thumb (complete) (partial)
Includes: thumb(s) (with finger(s) of either hand)

885.0 Without mention of complication

885.1 Complicated

886 Traumatic amputation of other finger(s) (complete) (partial)
Includes: finger(s) of one or both hands, without mention of thumb(s)

886.0 Without mention of complication

886.1 Complicated

887 Traumatic amputation of arm and hand (complete) (partial)

887.0 Unilateral, below elbow, without mention of complication

887.1 Unilateral, below elbow, complicated

887.2 Unilateral, at or above elbow, without mention of complication

887.3 Unilateral, at or above elbow, complicated

887.4 Unilateral, level not specified, without mention of complication

887.5 Unilateral, level not specified, complicated

887.6 Bilateral [any level], without mention of complication
One hand and other arm

887.7 Bilateral [any level], complicated

OPEN WOUND OF LOWER LIMB (890-897)

890 Open wound of hip and thigh

890.0 Without mention of complication

890.1 Complicated

890.2 With tendon involvement

891 Open wound of knee, leg [except thigh], and ankle
Includes: leg NOS
multiple sites of leg, except thigh

Excludes: that of thigh (890.0-890.2)
with multiple sites of lower limb (894.0-894.2)

891.0 Without mention of complication

891.1 Complicated

891.2 With tendon involvement

892 Open wound of foot except toe(s) alone
Includes: heel

892.0 Without mention of complication

892.1 Complicated

892.2 With tendon involvement

893 Open wound of toe(s)
Includes: toenail

893.0 Without mention of complication

893.1 Complicated

893.2 With tendon involvement

894 Multiple and unspecified open wound of lower limb
Includes: lower limb NOS
multiple sites of one lower limb, with thigh

894.0 Without mention of complication

894.1 Complicated

894.2 With tendon involvement

895 Traumatic amputation of toe(s) (complete) (partial)
Includes: toe(s) of one or both feet

895.0 Without mention of complication

895.1 Complicated

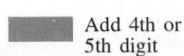 Add 4th or
5th digit

 Nonspecific
code

 Unspecified
code

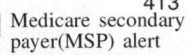 Medicare secondary
payer(MSP) alert

896 Traumatic amputation of foot (complete) (partial)

  896.0 Unilateral, without mention of complication

  896.1 Unilateral, complicated

  896.2 Bilateral, without mention of complication

  > *Excludes:* one foot and other leg (897.6-897.7)

  896.3 Bilateral, complicated

897 Traumatic amputation of leg(s) (complete) (partial)

  897.0 Unilateral, below knee, without mention of complication

  897.1 Unilateral, below knee, complicated

  897.2 Unilateral, at or above knee, without mention of complication

  897.3 Unilateral, at or above knee, complicated

  897.4 Unilateral, level not specified, without mention of complication

  897.5 Unilateral, level not specified, complicated

  897.6 Bilateral [any level], without mention of complication
  One foot and other leg

  897.7 Bilateral [any level], complicated

INJURY TO BLOOD VESSELS (900-904)

Includes:

arterial hematoma	
avulsion	of blood vessel, secondary to
cut	other injuries e.g., fracture or
laceration	open wound
rupture	
traumatic aneurysm or fistula (arteriovenous)	

> *Excludes:* accidental puncture or laceration during medical procedure (998.2)
> intracranial hemorrhage following injury (851.0-854.1)

900 Injury to blood vessels of head and neck

  900.0 Carotid artery

  900.00 Carotid artery, unspecified

  900.01 Common carotid artery

  900.02 External carotid artery

  900.03 Internal carotid artery

  900.1 Internal jugular vein

  900.8 Other specified blood vessels of head and neck

  900.81 External jugular vein
  Jugular vein NOS

  900.82 Multiple blood vessels of head and neck

  900.89 Other

  900.9 Unspecified blood vessel of head and neck

901 Injury to blood vessels of thorax

  > *Excludes:* traumatic hemothorax (860.2-860.5)

  901.0 Thoracic aorta

  901.1 Innominate and subclavian arteries

  901.2 Superior vena cava

  901.3 Innominate and subclavian veins

  901.4 Pulmonary blood vessels

  901.40 Pulmonary vessel(s), unspecified

  901.41 Pulmonary artery

  901.42 Pulmonary vein

  901.8 Other specified blood vessels of thorax

  901.81 Intercostal artery or vein

  901.82 Internal mammary artery or vein

  901.83 Multiple blood vessels of thorax

● Code new to this edition	▲ Revision of existing code	④ ⑤ Fourth or fifth digit required

901.89 Other
Azygos vein   Hemiazygos vein

901.9 Unspecified blood vessel of thorax

902 Injury to blood vessels of abdomen and pelvis

902.0 Abdominal aorta

902.1 Inferior vena cava

902.10 Inferior vena cava, unspecified

902.11 Hepatic veins

902.19 Other

902.2 Celiac and mesenteric arteries

902.20 Celiac and mesenteric arteries, unspecified

902.21 Gastric artery

902.22 Hepatic artery

902.23 Splenic artery

902.24 Other specified branches of celiac axis

902.25 Superior mesenteric artery (trunk)

902.26 Primary branches of superior mesenteric artery
Ileo-colic artery

902.27 Inferior mesenteric artery

902.29 Other

902.3 Portal and splenic veins

902.31 Superior mesenteric vein and primary subdivisions
Ileo-colic vein

902.32 Inferior mesenteric vein

902.33 Portal vein

902.34 Splenic vein

902.39 Other
Cystic vein   Gastric vein

902.4 Renal blood vessels

902.40 Renal vessel(s), unspecified

902.41 Renal artery

902.42 Renal vein

902.49 Other
Suprarenal arteries

902.5 Iliac blood vessels

902.50 Iliac vessel(s), unspecified

902.51 Hypogastric artery

902.52 Hypogastric vein

902.53 Iliac artery

902.54 Iliac vein

902.55 Uterine artery

902.56 Uterine vein

902.59 Other

902.8 Other specified blood vessels of abdomen and pelvis

902.81 Ovarian artery

902.82 Ovarian vein

902.87 Multiple blood vessels of abdomen and pelvis

902.89 Other

902.9 Unspecified blood vessel of abdomen and pelvis

903 Injury to blood vessels of upper extremity

903.0 Axillary blood vessels

903.00 Axillary vessel(s), unspecified

903.01 Axillary artery

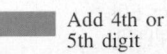 Add 4th or 5th digit   Nonspecific code   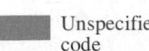 Unspecified code   Medicare secondary payer(MSP) alert

903.02   Axillary vein

903.1   Brachial blood vessels

903.2   Radial blood vessels

903.3   Ulnar blood vessels

903.4   Palmar artery

903.5   Digital blood vessels

`903.8`   Other specified blood vessels of upper extremity
Multiple blood vessels of upper extremity

`903.9`   Unspecified blood vessel of upper extremity

`904`   Injury to blood vessels of lower extremity and unspecified sites

904.0   Common femoral artery
Femoral artery above profunda origin

904.1   Superficial femoral artery

904.2   Femoral veins

904.3   Saphenous veins
Saphenous vein (greater) (lesser)

904.4   Popliteal blood vessels

`904.40`   Popliteal vessel(s), unspecified

904.41   Popliteal artery

904.42   Popliteal vein

904.5   Tibial blood vessels

`904.50`   Tibial vessel(s), unspecified

904.51   Anterior tibial artery

904.52   Anterior tibial vein

904.53   Posterior tibial artery

904.54   Posterior tibial vein

904.6   Deep plantar blood vessels

`904.7`   Other specified blood vessels of lower extremity
Multiple blood vessels of lower extremity

`904.8`   Unspecified blood vessel of lower extremity

`904.9`   Unspecified site
Injury to blood vessel NOS

LATE EFFECTS OF INJURIES, POISONINGS, TOXIC EFFECTS, AND OTHER EXTERNAL CAUSES (905-909)

Note: These categories are to be used to indicate conditions classifiable to 800-999 as the cause of late effects, which are themselves classified elsewhere. The "late effects" include those specified as such, or as sequelae, which may occur at any time after the acute injury.

`905`   Late effects of musculoskeletal and connective tissue injuries

905.0   Late effect of fracture of skull and face bones
Late effect of injury classifiable to 800-804

905.1   Late effect of fracture of spine and trunk without mention of spinal cord lesion
Late effect of injury classifiable to 805, 807-809

905.2   Late effect of fracture of upper extremities
Late effect of injury classifiable to 810-819

905.3   Late effect of fracture of neck of femur
Late effect of injury classifiable to 820

905.4   Late effect of fracture of lower extremities
Late effect of injury classifiable to 821-827

905.5   Late effect of fracture of multiple and unspecified bones
Late effect of injury classifiable to 828-829

905.6   Late effect of dislocation
Late effect of injury classifiable to 830-839

905.7   Late effect of sprain and strain without mention of tendon injury
Late effect of injury classifiable to 840-848, except tendon injury

● Code new
to this edition

▲ Revision of
existing code

④ ⑤ Fourth or fifth
digit required

905.8 Late effect of tendon injury
Late effect of tendon injury due to:
open wound [injury classifiable to 880-884 with .2, 890-894 with .2]
sprain and strain [injury classifiable to 840-848]

905.9 Late effect of traumatic amputation
Late effect of injury classifiable to 885-887, 895-897

Excludes: *late amputation stump complication (997.60-997.69)*

906 Late effects of injuries to skin and subcutaneous tissues

906.0 Late effect of open wound of head, neck, and trunk
Late effect of injury classifiable to 870-879

906.1 Late effect of open wound of extremities without mention of tendon injury
Late effect of injury classifiable to 880-884, 890-894 except .2

906.2 Late effect of superficial injury
Late effect of injury classifiable to 910-919

906.3 Late effect of contusion
Late effect of injury classifiable to 920-924

906.4 Late effect of crushing
Late effect of injury classifiable to 925-929

906.5 Late effect of burn of eye, face, head, and neck
Late effect of injury classifiable to 940-941

906.6 Late effect of burn of wrist and hand
Late effect of injury classifiable to 944

906.7 Late effect of burn of other extremities
Late effect of injury classifiable to 943 or 945

906.8 Late effect of burns of other specified sites
Late effect of injury classifiable to 942, 946-947

906.9 Late effect of burn of unspecified site
Late effect of injury classifiable to 948-949

907 Late effects of injuries to the nervous system

907.0 Late effect of intracranial injury without mention of skull fracture
Late effect of injury classifiable to 850-854

907.1 Late effect of injury to cranial nerve
Late effect of injury classifiable to 950-951

907.2 Late effect of spinal cord injury
Late effect of injury classifiable to 806, 952

907.3 Late effect of injury to nerve root(s), spinal plexus(es), and other nerves of trunk
Late effect of injury classifiable to 953-954

907.4 Late effect of injury to peripheral nerve of shoulder girdle and upper limb
Late effect of injury classifiable to 955

907.5 Late effect of injury to peripheral nerve of pelvic girdle and lower limb
Late effect of injury classifiable to 956

907.9 Late effect of injury to other and unspecified nerve
Late effect of injury classifiable to 957

908 Late effects of other and unspecified injuries

908.0 Late effect of internal injury to chest
Late effect of injury classifiable to 860-862

908.1 Late effect of internal injury to intra-abdominal organs
Late effect of injury classifiable to 863 866, 868

908.2 Late effect of internal injury to other internal organs
Late effect of injury classifiable to 867 or 869

908.3 Late effect of injury to blood vessel of head, neck, and extremities
Late effect of injury classifiable to 900, 903-904

908.4 Late effect of injury to blood vessel of thorax, abdomen, and pelvis
Late effect of injury classifiable to 901-902

908.5 Late effect of foreign body in orifice
Late effect of injury classifiable to 930-939

908.6 Late effect of certain complications of trauma
Late effect of complications classifiable to 958

908.9 Late effect of unspecified injury
Late effect of injury classifiable to 959

| | Add 4th or 5th digit | | Nonspecific code | | Unspecified code | | Medicare secondary payer(MSP) alert |

909 **Late effects of other and unspecified external causes**

909.0 **Late effect of poisoning due to drug, medicinal or biological substance**
Late effect of conditions classifiable to 960-979

Excludes: *late effect of adverse effect of drug, medicinal or biological substance (909.5)*

909.1 **Late effect of toxic effects of nonmedical substances**
Late effect of conditions classifiable to 980-989

909.2 **Late effect of radiation**
Late effect of conditions classifiable to 990

909.3 **Late effect of complications of surgical and medical care**
Late effect of conditions classifiable to 996-999

909.4 **Late effect of certain other external causes**
Late effect of conditions classifiable to 991-994

909.5 **Late effect of adverse effect of drug, medicinal or biological substance**

Excludes: *late effect of poisoning due to drug, medicinal or biological substance (909.0)*

909.9 **Late effect of other and unspecified external causes**
Late effect of conditions classifiable to 995

SUPERFICIAL INJURY (910-919)

Excludes: *burn (blisters) (940.0-949.5)*
contusion (920-924.9)
foreign body:
granuloma (728.82)
inadvertently left in operative wound (998.4)
residual, in soft tissue (729.6)
insect bite, venomous (989.5)
open wound with incidental foreign body (870.0-897.7)

910 **Superficial injury of face, neck, and scalp except eye**
Includes:

cheek	lip
ear	nose
gum	throat

Excludes: *eye and adnexa (918.0-918.9)*

910.0 **Abrasion or friction burn without mention of infection**

910.1 **Abrasion or friction burn, infected**

910.2 **Blister without mention of infection**

910.3 **Blister, infected**

910.4 **Insect bite, nonvenomous, without mention of infection**

910.5 **Insect bite, nonvenomous, infected**

910.6 **Superficial foreign body (splinter) without major open wound and without mention of infection**

910.7 **Superficial foreign body (splinter) without major open wound, infected**

910.8 **Other and unspecified superficial injury of face, neck, and scalp without mention of infection**

910.9 **Other and unspecified superficial injury of face, neck, and scalp, infected**

911 **Superficial injury of trunk**
Includes:

abdominal wall	interscapular region
anus	labium (majus) (minus)
back	penis
breast	perineum
buttock	scrotum
chest wall	testis
flank	vagina
groin	vulva

Excludes: *hip (916.0-916.9)*
scapular region (912.0-912.9)

911.0 **Abrasion or friction burn without mention of infection**

911.1 **Abrasion or friction burn, infected**

911.2 **Blister without mention of infection**

911.3 **Blister, infected**

● Code new
to this edition

▲ Revision of
existing code

④ ⑤ Fourth or fifth
digit required

911.4   Insect bite, nonvenomous, without mention of infection

911.5   Insect bite, nonvenomous, infected

911.6   Superficial foreign body (splinter) without major open wound and without mention of infection

911.7   Superficial foreign body (splinter) without major open wound, infected

911.8   Other and unspecified superficial injury of trunk without mention of infection

911.9   Other and unspecified superficial injury of trunk, infected

912   **Superficial injury of shoulder and upper arm**
    Includes: axilla   scapular region

912.0   Abrasion or friction burn without mention of infection

912.1   Abrasion or friction burn, infected

912.2   Blister without mention of infection

912.3   Blister, infected

912.4   Insect bite, nonvenomous, without mention of infection

912.5   Insect bite, nonvenomous, infected

912.6   Superficial foreign body (splinter) without major open wound and without mention of infection

912.7   Superficial foreign body (splinter) without major open wound, infected

912.8   Other and unspecified superficial injury of shoulder and upper arm without mention of infection

912.9   Other and unspecified superficial injury of shoulder and upper arm, infected

913   **Superficial injury of elbow, forearm, and wrist**

913.0   Abrasion or friction burn without mention of infection

913.1   Abrasion or friction burn, infected

913.2   Blister without mention of infection

913.3   Blister, infected

913.4   Insect bite, nonvenomous, without mention of infection

913.5   Insect bite, nonvenomous, infected

913.6   Superficial foreign body (splinter) without major open wound and without mention of infection

913.7   Superficial foreign body (splinter) without major open wound, infected

913.8   Other and unspecified superficial injury of elbow, forearm, and wrist without mention of infection

913.9   Other and unspecified superficial injury of elbow, forearm, and wrist, infected

914   **Superficial injury of hand(s) except finger(s) alone**

914.0   Abrasion or friction burn without mention of infection

914.1   Abrasion or friction burn, infected

914.2   Blister without mention of infection

914.3   Blister, infected

914.4   Insect bite, nonvenomous, without mention of infection

914.5   Insect bite, nonvenomous, infected

914.6   Superficial foreign body (splinter) without major open wound and without mention of infection

914.7   Superficial foreign body (splinter) without major open wound, infected

914.8   Other and unspecified superficial injury of hand without mention of infection

914.9   Other and unspecified superficial injury of hand, infected

915   **Superficial injury of finger(s)**
    Includes: fingernail   thumb (nail)

915.0   Abrasion or friction burn without mention of infection

915.1   Abrasion or friction burn, infected

915.2   Blister without mention of infection

915.3   Blister, infected

915.4   Insect bite, nonvenomous, without mention of infection

915.5   Insect bite, nonvenomous, infected

| | Add 4th or 5th digit | | Nonspecific code | | Unspecified code | 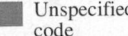 | Medicare secondary payer(MSP) alert |

915.6 Superficial foreign body (splinter) without major open wound and without mention of infection

915.7 Superficial foreign body (splinter) without major open wound, infected

915.8 Other and unspecified superficial injury of fingers without mention of infection

915.9 Other and unspecified superficial injury of fingers, infected

916 Superficial injury of hip, thigh, leg, and ankle

916.0 Abrasion or friction burn without mention of infection

916.1 Abrasion or friction burn, infected

916.2 Blister without mention of infection

916.3 Blister, infected

916.4 Insect bite, nonvenomous, without mention of infection

916.5 Insect bite, nonvenomous, infected

916.6 Superficial foreign body (splinter) without major open wound and without mention of infection

916.7 Superficial foreign body (splinter) without major open wound, infected

916.8 Other and unspecified superficial injury of hip, thigh, leg, and ankle without mention of infection

916.9 Other and unspecified superficial injury of hip, thigh, leg, and ankle, infected

917 Superficial injury of foot and toe(s)

    Includes: heel   toenail

917.0 Abrasion or friction burn without mention of infection

917.1 Abrasion or friction burn, infected

917.2 Blister without mention of infection

917.3 Blister, infected

917.4 Insect bite, nonvenomous, without mention of infection

917.5 Insect bite, nonvenomous, infected

917.6 Superficial foreign body (splinter) without major open wound and without mention of infection

917.7 Superficial foreign body (splinter) without major open wound, infected

917.8 Other and unspecified superficial injury of foot and toes without mention of infection

917.9 Other and unspecified superficial injury of foot and toes, infected

918 Superficial injury of eye and adnexa

    Excludes: burn (940.0-940.9)

               foreign body on external eye (930.0-930.9)

918.0 Eyelids and periocular area

    Abrasion   Superficial foreign body (splinter)

    Insect bite

918.1 Cornea

    Corneal abrasion   Superficial laceration

    Excludes: corneal injury due to contact lens (371.82)

918.2 Conjunctiva

918.9 Other and unspecified superficial injuries of eye

    Eye (ball) NOS

919 Superficial injury of other, multiple, and unspecified sites

    Excludes: multiple sites classifiable to the same three-digit category (910.0-918.9)

919.0 Abrasion or friction burn without mention of infection

919.1 Abrasion or friction burn, infected

919.2 Blister without mention of infection

919.3 Blister, infected

919.4 Insect bite, nonvenomous, without mention of infection

919.5 Insect bite, nonvenomous, infected

919.6 Superficial foreign body (splinter) without major open wound and without mention of infection

919.7 Superficial foreign body (splinter) without major open wound, infected

● Code new   ▲ Revision of   ④ ⑤ Fourth or fifth
  to this edition   existing code   digit required

919.8 Other and unspecified superficial injury without mention of infection

919.9 Other and unspecified superficial injury, infected

CONTUSION WITH INTACT SKIN SURFACE (920-924)

Includes:

bruise
hematoma } without fracture or open wound

Excludes: concussion (850.0-850.9)
hemarthrosis (840.0-848.9)
internal organs (860.0-869.1)
that incidental to:
    crushing injury (925-929.9)
    dislocation (830.0-839.9)
    fracture (800.0-829.1)
    internal injury (860.0-869.1)
    intracranial injury (850.0-854.1)
    nerve injury (950.0-957.9)
    open wound (870.0-897.7)

920 Contusion of face, scalp, and neck except eye(s)

Cheek	Mandibular joint area
Ear (auricle)	Nose
Gum	Throat
Lip	

921 Contusion of eye and adnexa

921.0 Black eye, not otherwise specified

921.1 Contusion of eyelids and periocular area

921.2 Contusion of orbital tissues

921.3 Contusion of eyeball

921.9 Unspecified contusion of eye
Injury of eye NOS

922 Contusion of trunk

922.0 Breast

922.1 Chest wall

922.2 Abdominal wall
Flank   Groin

922.3 Back

Excludes: scapular region (923.01)

● **922.31 Back**

Excludes: interscapular region (922.33)

● **922.32 Buttock**

● **922.33 Interscapular region**

922.4 Genital organs

Labium (majus) (minus)	Testis
Penis	Vagina
Perineum	Vulva
Scrotum	

922.8 Multiple sites of trunk

922.9 Unspecified part
Trunk NOS

923 Contusion of upper limb

923.0 Shoulder and upper arm

923.00 Shoulder region

923.01 Scapular region

923.02 Axillary region

923.03 Upper arm

923.09 Multiple sites

923.1 Elbow and forearm

923.10 Forearm

Add 4th or 5th digit	Nonspecific code	Unspecified code	Medicare secondary payer(MSP) alert

923.11   **Elbow**

923.2   **Wrist and hand(s), except finger(s) alone**

923.20   **Hand(s)**

923.21   **Wrist**

923.3   **Finger**
Fingernail   Thumb (nail)

`923.8`   **Multiple sites of upper limb**

`923.9`   **Unspecified part of upper limb**
Arm NOS

`924`   **Contusion of lower limb and of other and unspecified sites**

924.0   **Hip and thigh**

924.00   **Thigh**

924.01   **Hip**

924.1   **Knee and lower leg**

924.10   **Lower leg**

924.11   **Knee**

924.2   **Ankle and foot, excluding toe(s)**

924.20   **Foot**
Heel

924.21   **Ankle**

924.3   **Toe**
Toenail

`924.4`   **Multiple sites of lower limb**

`924.5`   **Unspecified part of lower limb**
Leg NOS

`924.8`   **Multiple sites, not elsewhere classified**

`924.9`   **Unspecified site**

CRUSHING INJURY (925-929)

Excludes: concussion (850.0-850.9)
fractures (800-829)
internal organs (860.0-869.1)
that incidental to:
internal injury (860.0-869.1)
intracranial injury (850.0-854.1)

`925`   **Crushing injury of face, scalp, and neck**
Cheek   Pharynx
Ear   Throat
Larynx

925.1   **Crushing injury of face and scalp**
Cheek   Ear

925.2   **Crushing injury of neck**
Larynx   Throat
Pharynx

`926`   **Crushing injury of trunk**

Excludes: crush injury of internal organs (860.0-869.1)

926.0   **External genitalia**
Labium (majus) (minus)   Testis
Penis   Vulva
Scrotum

926.1   **Other specified sites**

926.11   **Back**

926.12   **Buttock**

`926.19`   **Other**
Breast

Excludes: crushing of chest (860.0-862.9)

`926.8`   **Multiple sites of trunk**

● Code new   ▲ Revision of   ④ ⑤ Fourth or fifth
to this edition   existing code   digit required

926.9 Unspecified site
Trunk NOS

927 Crushing injury of upper limb

927.0 Shoulder and upper arm

927.00 Shoulder region

927.01 Scapular region

927.02 Axillary region

927.03 Upper arm

927.09 Multiple sites

927.1 Elbow and forearm

927.10 Forearm

927.11 Elbow

927.2 Wrist and hand(s), except finger(s) alone

927.20 Hand(s)

927.21 Wrist

927.3 Finger(s)

927.8 Multiple sites of upper limb

927.9 Unspecified site
Arm NOS

928 Crushing injury of lower limb

928.0 Hip and thigh

928.00 Thigh

928.01 Hip

928.1 Knee and lower leg

928.10 Lower leg

928.11 Knee

928.2 Ankle and foot, excluding toe(s) alone

928.20 Foot
Heel

928.21 Ankle

928.3 Toe(s)

928.8 Multiple sites of lower limb

928.9 Unspecified site
Leg NOS

929 Crushing injury of multiple and unspecified sites

Excludes: *multiple internal injury NOS (869.0-869.1)*

929.0 Multiple sites, not elsewhere classified

929.9 Unspecified site

EFFECTS OF FOREIGN BODY ENTERING THROUGH ORIFICE (930-939)

Excludes: *foreign body:*
granuloma (728.82)
inadvertently left in operative wound (998.4, 998.7)
in open wound (800-839, 851-897)
residual, in soft tissues (729.6)
superficial without major open wound (910-919 with .6 or .7)

930 Foreign body on external eye

Excludes: *foreign body in penetrating wound of:*
eyeball (871.5-871.6)
retained (old) (360.5-360.6)
ocular adnexa (870.4)
retained (old) (376.6)

930.0 Corneal foreign body

930.1 Foreign body in conjunctival sac

930.2 Foreign body in lacrimal punctum

930.8 Other and combined sites

| | Add 4th or 5th digit | | Nonspecific code | | Unspecified code | | Medicare secondary payer(MSP) alert |

930.9 Unspecified site
External eye NOS

931 Foreign body in ear
Auditory canal   Auricle

932 Foreign body in nose
Nasal sinus   Nostril

933 Foreign body in pharynx and larynx

    933.0 Pharynx
Nasopharynx   Throat NOS

    933.1 Larynx
Asphyxia due to   Choking due to:
  foreign body   food (regurgitated)
                         phlegm

934 Foreign body in trachea, bronchus, and lung

    934.0 Trachea

    934.1 Main bronchus

    934.8 Other specified parts
Bronchioles   Lung

    934.9 Respiratory tree, unspecified
Inhalation of liquid or vomitus, lower respiratory tract NOS

935 Foreign body in mouth, esophagus, and stomach

    935.0 Mouth

    935.1 Esophagus

    935.2 Stomach

936 Foreign body in intestine and colon

937 Foreign body in anus and rectum
Rectosigmoid (junction)

938 Foreign body in digestive system, unspecified
Alimentary tract NOS   Swallowed foreign body

939 Foreign body in genitourinary tract

    939.0 Bladder and urethra

    939.1 Uterus, any part

    Excludes: intrauterine contraceptive device:
            complications from (996.32, 996.65)
            presence of (V45.51)

    939.2 Vulva and vagina

    939.3 Penis

    939.9 Unspecified site

BURNS (940-949)

    Includes: burns from:
            electrical heating appliance
            electricity
            flame
            hot object
            lightning
            radiation
        chemical burns (external) (internal)
        scalds

    Excludes: friction burns (910-919 with .0, .1)
            sunburn (692.71)

940 Burn confined to eye and adnexa

    940.0 Chemical burn of eyelids and periocular area

    940.1 Other burns of eyelids and periocular area

    940.2 Alkaline chemical burn of cornea and conjunctival sac

    940.3 Acid chemical burn of cornea and conjunctival sac

    940.4 Other burn of cornea and conjunctival sac

    940.5 Burn with resulting rupture and destruction of eyeball

● Code new   ▲ Revision of   ④ ⑤ Fourth or fifth
to this edition   existing code   digit required

940.9 Unspecified burn of eye and adnexa

⑤ **941** Burn of face, head, and neck

> *Excludes:* mouth (947.0)

The following fifth-digit subclassification is for use with category 941:

0 face and head, unspecified site

1 ear [any part]

2 eye (with other parts of face, head, and neck)

3 lip(s)

4 chin

5 nose (septum)

6 scalp [any part]
Temple (region)

7 forehead and cheek

8 neck

9 multiple sites [except with eye] of face, head, and neck

941.0 Unspecified degree

941.1 Erythema [first degree]

941.2 Blisters, epidermal loss [second degree]

941.3 Full-thickness skin loss [third degree NOS]

□ 941.4 Deep necrosis of underlying tissues [deep third degree] without mention of loss of a body part

□ 941.5 Deep necrosis of underlying tissues [deep third degree] with loss of a body part

⑤ **942** Burn of trunk

> *Excludes:* scapular region (943.0-943.5 with fifth-digit 6)

The following fifth-digit subclassification is for use with category 942:

0 trunk, unspecified site

1 breast

2 chest wall, excluding breast and nipple

3 abdominal wall
Flank   Groin

4 back [any part]
Buttock   Interscapular region

5 genitalia
Labium (majus) (minus)   Scrotum
Penis   Testis
Perineum   Vulva

9 other and multiple sites of trunk

942.0 Unspecified degree

942.1 Erythema [first degree]

942.2 Blisters, epidermal loss [second degree]

942.3 Full-thickness skin loss [third degree NOS]

□ 942.4 Deep necrosis of underlying tissues [deep third degree] without mention of loss of a body part

□ 942.5 Deep necrosis of underlying tissues [deep third degree] with loss of a body part

⑤ **943** Burn of upper limb, except wrist and hand

The following fifth-digit subclassification is for use with category 943:

0 upper limb, unspecified site

1 forearm

2 elbow

3 upper arm

4 axilla

5 shoulder

6 scapular region

9 multiple sites of upper limb, except wrist and hand

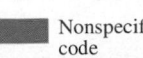 Add 4th or 5th digit   Nonspecific code   Unspecified code   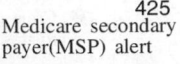 Medicare secondary payer(MSP) alert

943.0 Unspecified degree

943.1 Erythema [first degree]

943.2 Blisters, epidermal loss [second degree]

943.3 Full-thickness skin loss [third degree NOS]

☐ 943.4 Deep necrosis of underlying tissues [deep third degree] without mention of loss of a body part

☐ 943.5 Deep necrosis of underlying tissues [deep third degree] with loss of a body part

⑤ **944** Burn of wrist(s) and hand(s)

The following fifth-digit subclassification is for use with category 944:

0 hand, unspecified site

1 single digit [finger (nail)] other than thumb

2 thumb (nail)

3 two or more digits, not including thumb

4 two or more digits including thumb

5 palm

6 back of hand

7 wrist

8 multiple sites of wrist(s) and hand(s)

944.0 Unspecified degree

944.1 Erythema [first degree]

944.2 Blisters, epidermal loss [second degree]

944.3 Full-thickness skin loss [third degree NOS]

☐ 944.4 Deep necrosis of underlying tissues [deep third degree] without mention of loss of a body part

☐ 944.5 Deep necrosis of underlying tissues [deep third degree] with loss of a body part

⑤ **945** Burn of lower limb(s)

The following fifth-digit subclassification is for use with category 945:

0 lower limb [leg], unspecified site

1 toe(s) (nail)

2 foot

3 ankle

4 lower leg

5 knee

6 thigh [any part]

9 multiple sites of lower limb(s)

945.0 Unspecified degree

945.1 Erythema [first degree]

945.2 Blisters, epidermal loss [second degree]

945.3 Full-thickness skin loss [third degree NOS]

☐ 945.4 Deep necrosis of underlying tissues [deep third degree] without mention of loss of a body part

☐ 945.5 Deep necrosis of underlying tissues [deep third degree] with loss of a body part

946 Burns of multiple specified sites

Includes: burns of sites classifiable to more than one three-digit category in 940-945

Excludes: *multiple burns NOS (949.0-949.5)*

946.0 Unspecified degree

946.1 Erythema [first degree]

946.2 Blisters, epidermal loss [second degree]

946.3 Full-thickness skin loss [third degree NOS]

☐ **946.4** Deep necrosis of underlying tissues [deep third degree] without mention of loss of a body part

☐ **946.5** Deep necrosis of underlying tissues [deep third degree] with loss of a body part

947 Burn of internal organs

Includes: burns from chemical agents (ingested)

● Code new to this edition ▲ Revision of existing code ④ ⑤ Fourth or fifth digit required

947.0 Mouth and pharynx
Gum   Tongue

947.1 Larynx, trachea, and lung

947.2 Esophagus

947.3 Gastrointestinal tract
Colon   Small intestine
Rectum   Stomach

947.4 Vagina and uterus

947.8 Other specified sites

947.9 Unspecified site

⑤ **948 Burns classified according to extent of body surface involved**

Note: This category is to be used when the site of the burn is unspecified, or with categories 940-947 when the site is specified.

The following fifth-digit subclassification is for use with category 948 to indicate the percent of *body surface* with *third degree* burn; valid digits are in [brackets] under each code:

0 less than 10 percent or unspecified

1 10-19%

2 20-29%

3 30-39%

4 40-49%

5 50-59%

6 60-69%

7 70-79%

8 80-89%

9 90% or more of body surface

948.0 Burn [any degree] involving less than 10 percent of body surface
[0]

948.1 10-19 percent of body surface
[0-1]

948.2 20-29 percent of body surface
[0-2]

948.3 30-39 percent of body surface
[0-3]

948.4 40-49 percent of body surface
[0-4]

948.5 50-59 percent of body surface
[0-5]

948.6 60-69 percent of body surface
[0-6]

948.7 70-79 percent of body surface
[0-7]

948.8 80-89 percent of body surface
[0-8]

948.9 90 percent or more of body surface
[0-9]

949 Burn, unspecified
Includes:
burn NOS   multiple burns NOS

Excludes: burn of unspecified site but with statement of the extent of body surface involved (948.0-948.9)

949.0 Unspecified degree

949.1 Erythema [first degree]

949.2 Blisters, epidermal loss [second degree]

949.3 Full-thickness skin loss [third degree NOS]

□ **949.4 Deep necrosis of underlying tissues [deep third degree] without mention of loss of a body part**

□ **949.5 Deep necrosis of underlying tissues [deep third degree] with loss of a body part**

| | Add 4th or 5th digit | | Nonspecific code | | Unspecified code | | Medicare secondary payer(MSP) alert |

INJURY TO NERVES AND SPINAL CORD (950-957)

Includes:
division of nerve
lesion in continuity
traumatic neuroma
traumatic transient paralysis
} (with open wound)

Excludes: *accidental puncture or laceration during medical procedure (998.2)*

950 **Injury to optic nerve and pathways**

950.0 **Optic nerve injury**
Second cranial nerve

950.1 **Injury to optic chiasm**

950.2 **Injury to optic pathways**

950.3 **Injury to visual cortex**

950.9 **Unspecified**
Traumatic blindness NOS

951 **Injury to other cranial nerve(s)**

951.0 **Injury to oculomotor nerve**
Third cranial nerve

951.1 **Injury to trochlear nerve**
Fourth cranial nerve

951.2 **Injury to trigeminal nerve**
Fifth cranial nerve

951.3 **Injury to abducens nerve**
Sixth cranial nerve

951.4 **Injury to facial nerve**
Seventh cranial nerve

951.5 **Injury to acoustic nerve**
Auditory nerve   Traumatic deafness NOS
Eighth cranial nerve

951.6 **Injury to accessory nerve**
Eleventh cranial nerve

951.7 **Injury to hypoglossal nerve**
Twelfth cranial nerve

951.8 **Injury to other specified cranial nerves**
Glossopharyngeal [9th cranial] nerve
Olfactory [1st cranial] nerve
Pneumogastric [10th cranial] nerve
Traumatic anosmia NOS
Vagus [10th cranial] nerve

951.9 **Injury to unspecified cranial nerve**

952 **Spinal cord injury without evidence of spinal bone injury**

952.0 **Cervical**

952.00 C_1-C_4 level with unspecified spinal cord injury
Spinal cord injury, cervical region NOS

952.01 C_1-C_4 level with complete lesion of spinal cord

952.02 C_1-C_4 level with anterior cord syndrome

952.03 C_1-C_4 level with central cord syndrome

952.04 C_1-C_4 level with other specified spinal cord injury
Incomplete spinal cord lesion at C_1-C_4 level:
NOS
with posterior cord syndrome

952.05 C_5-C_7 level with unspecified spinal cord injury

952.06 C_5-C_7 level with complete lesion of spinal cord

952.07 C_5-C_7 level with anterior cord syndrome

952.08 C_5-C_7 level with central cord syndrome

● Code new
to this edition

▲ Revision of
existing code

④ ⑤ Fourth or fifth
digit required

952.09 C_5-C_7 level with other specified spinal cord injury
Incomplete spinal cord lesion at C_5-C_7 level:
NOS
with posterior cord syndrome

952.1 Dorsal [thoracic]

952.10 T_1-T_6 level with unspecified spinal cord injury
Spinal cord injury, thoracic region NOS

952.11 T_1-T_6 level with complete lesion of spinal cord

952.12 T_1-T_6 level with anterior cord syndrome

952.13 T_1-T_6 level with central cord syndrome

952.14 T_1-T_6 level with other specified spinal cord injury
Incomplete spinal cord lesion at T_1-T_6 level:
NOS
with posterior cord syndrome

952.15 T_7-T_{12} level with unspecified spinal cord injury

952.16 T_7-T_{12} level with complete lesion of spinal cord

952.17 T_7-T_{12} level with anterior cord syndrome

952.18 T_7-T_{12} level with central cord syndrome

952.19 T_7-T_{12} level with other specified spinal cord injury
Incomplete spinal cord lesion at T_7-T_{12} level:
NOS
with posterior cord syndrome

952.2 Lumbar

952.3 Sacral

952.4 Cauda equina

952.8 Multiple sites of spinal cord

952.9 Unspecified site of spinal cord

953 Injury to nerve roots and spinal plexus

953.0 Cervical root

953.1 Dorsal root

953.2 Lumbar root

953.3 Sacral root

953.4 Brachial plexus

953.5 Lumbosacral plexus

953.8 Multiple sites

953.9 Unspecified site

954 Injury to other nerve(s) of trunk, excluding shoulder and pelvic girdles

954.0 Cervical sympathetic

954.1 Other sympathetic
Celiac ganglion or plexus   Splanchnic nerve(s)
Inferior mesenteric plexus   Stellate ganglion

954.8 Other specified nerve(s) of trunk

954.9 Unspecified nerve of trunk

955 Injury to peripheral nerve(s) of shoulder girdle and upper limb

955.0 Axillary nerve

955.1 Median nerve

955.2 Ulnar nerve

955.3 Radial nerve

955.4 Musculocutaneous nerve

955.5 Cutaneous sensory nerve, upper limb

955.6 Digital nerve

955.7 Other specified nerve(s) of shoulder girdle and upper limb

955.8 Multiple nerves of shoulder girdle and upper limb

955.9 Unspecified nerve of shoulder girdle and upper limb

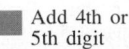 Add 4th or
5th digit

 Nonspecific
code

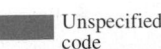 Unspecified
code

Medicare secondary
payer(MSP) alert

956 Injury to peripheral nerve(s) of pelvic girdle and lower limb

    956.0 Sciatic nerve

    956.1 Femoral nerve

    956.2 Posterior tibial nerve

    956.3 Peroneal nerve

    956.4 Cutaneous sensory nerve, lower limb

    956.5 Other specified nerve(s) of pelvic girdle and lower limb

    956.8 Multiple nerves of pelvic girdle and lower limb

    956.9 Unspecified nerve of pelvic girdle and lower limb

957 Injury to other and unspecified nerves

    957.0 Superficial nerves of head and neck

    957.1 Other specified nerve(s)

    957.8 Multiple nerves in several parts
        Multiple nerve injury NOS

    957.9 Unspecified site
        Nerve injury NOS

CERTAIN TRAUMATIC COMPLICATIONS AND UNSPECIFIED INJURIES (958-959)

958 Certain early complications of trauma

    Excludes: *adult respiratory distress syndrome (518.5)*
        flail chest (807.4)
        shock lung (518.5)
        that occurring during or following medical procedures (996.0-999.9)

    958.0 Air embolism
        Pneumathemia

        Excludes: *that complicating:*
            abortion (634-638 with .6, 639.6)
            ectopic or molar pregnancy (639.6)
            pregnancy, childbirth, or the puerperium (673.0)

    958.1 Fat embolism

        Excludes: *that complicating:*
            abortion (634-638 with .6, 639.6)
            pregnancy, childbirth, or the puerperium (673.8)

    958.2 Secondary and recurrent hemorrhage

    958.3 Posttraumatic wound infection, not elsewhere classified

    958.4 Traumatic shock
        Shock (immediate) (delayed) following injury

        Excludes: *shock:*
            anaphylactic (995.0)
             due to serum (999.4)
            anesthetic (995.4)
            electric (994.8)
            following abortion (639.5)
            lightning (994.0)
            nontraumatic NOS (785.50)
            obstetric (669.1)
            postoperative (998.0)

    958.5 Traumatic anuria
        Crush syndrome
        Renal failure following crushing

        Excludes: *that due to a medical procedure (997.5)*

    958.6 Volkmann's ischemic contracture
        Posttraumatic muscle contracture

    958.7 Traumatic subcutaneous emphysema

        Excludes: *subcutaneous emphysema resulting from a procedure (998.81)*

    958.8 Other early complications of trauma

  ● Code new   ▲ Revision of   ④ ⑤ Fourth or fifth
       to this edition   existing code   digit required

959 **Injury, other and unspecified**
Includes: injury NOS

> *Excludes:* *injury NOS of:*
> *blood vessels (900.0-904.9)*
> *eye (921.0-921.9)*
> *head (854.0-854.1)*
> *internal organs (860.0-869.1)*
> *intracranial sites (854.1)*
> *nerves (950.0-951.9, 953.0-957.9)*
> *spinal cord (952.0-952.9)*

959.0 **Face and neck**

Cheek	Mouth
Ear	Nose
Eyebrow	Throat
Lip	

959.1 **Trunk**

Abdominal wall	External genital organs
Back	Flank
Breast	Groin
Buttock	Interscapular region
Chest wall	Perineum

> *Excludes:* *scapular region (959.2)*

959.2 **Shoulder and upper arm**
Axilla   Scapular region

959.3 **Elbow, forearm, and wrist**

959.4 **Hand, except finger**

959.5 **Finger**
Fingernail   Thumb (nail)

959.6 **Hip and thigh**
Upper leg

959.7 **Knee, leg, ankle, and foot**

959.8 **Other specified sites, including multiple**

> *Excludes:* *multiple sites classifiable to the same four-digit category (959.0-959.7)*

959.9 **Unspecified site**

POISONING BY DRUGS, MEDICINAL AND BIOLOGICAL SUBSTANCES (960-979)

> Includes: overdose of these substances
> wrong substances given or taken in error

> *Excludes:* *adverse effects ["hypersensitivity," "reaction," etc.] of correct substance properly*
> *administered. Such cases are to be classified according to the nature of the*
> *adverse effect, such as:*
> *adverse effect NOS (995.2)*
> *allergic lymphadenitis (289.3)*
> *aspirin gastritis (535.4)*
> *blood disorders (280.0-289.9)*
> *dermatitis:*
> *contact (692.0-692.9)*
> *due to ingestion (693.0-693.9)*
> *nephropathy (583.9)*
> *[The drug giving rise to the adverse effect may be identified by use of categories*
> *E930-E949]*
> *drug dependence (304.0-304.9)*
> *drug reaction and poisoning affecting the newborn (760.0-779.9)*
> *nondependent abuse of drugs (305.0-305.9)*
> *pathological drug intoxication (292.2)*

Use additional code to specify the effects of the poisoning

960 **Poisoning by antibiotics**

> *Excludes:* *antibiotics:*
> *ear, nose, and throat (976.6)*
> *eye (976.5)*
> *local (976.0)*

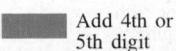 Add 4th or 5th digit

 Nonspecific code

 Unspecified code

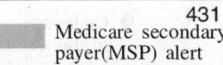 Medicare secondary payer(MSP) alert

960.0 Penicillins
Ampicillin
Carbenicillin

Cloxacillin
Penicillin G

960.1 Antifungal antibiotics
Amphotericin B
Griseofulvin

Nystatin
Trichomycin

Excludes: preparations intended for topical use (976.0-976.9)

960.2 Chloramphenicol group
Chloramphenicol

Thiamphenicol

960.3 Erythromycin and other macrolides
Oleandomycin

Spiramycin

960.4 Tetracycline group
Doxycycline
Minocycline

Oxytetracycline

960.5 Cephalosporin group
Cephalexin
Cephaloglycin

Cephaloridine
Cephalothin

960.6 Antimycobacterial antibiotics
Cycloserine
Kanamycin

Rifampin
Streptomycin

960.7 Antineoplastic antibiotics
Actinomycin such as:
  Cactinomycin
  Dactinomycin

Bleomycin
Daunorubicin
Mitomycin

960.8 Other specified antibiotics

960.9 Unspecified antibiotic

961 Poisoning by other anti-infectives

Excludes: anti-infectives:
  ear, nose, and throat (976.6)
  eye (976.5)
  local (976.0)

961.0 Sulfonamides
Sulfadiazine
Sulfafurazole

Sulfamethoxazole

961.1 Arsenical anti-infectives

961.2 Heavy metal anti-infectives
Compounds of:
  antimony
  bismuth

Compounds of:
  lead
  mercury

Excludes: mercurial diuretics (974.0)

961.3 Quinoline and hydroxyquinoline derivatives
Chiniofon

Diiodohydroxyquin

Excludes: antimalarial drugs (961.4)

961.4 Antimalarials and drugs acting on other blood protozoa
Chloroquine
Cycloguanil
Primaquine

Proguanil [chloroguanide]
Pyrimethamine
Quinine

961.5 Other antiprotozoal drugs
Emetine

961.6 Anthelmintics
Hexylresorcinol
Piperazine

Thiabendazole

961.7 Antiviral drugs
Methisazone

Excludes: amantadine (966.4)
  cytarabine (963.1)
  idoxuridine (976.5)

961.8 Other antimycobacterial drugs
Ethambutol
Ethionamide
Isoniazid

Para-aminosalicylic acid derivatives
Sulfones

● Code new
to this edition

▲ Revision of
existing code

④ ⑤ Fourth or fifth
digit required

961.9 Other and unspecified anti-infectives
Flucytosine   Nitrofuran derivatives

962 Poisoning by hormones and synthetic substitutes

Excludes: oxytocic hormones (975.0)

962.0 Adrenal cortical steroids
Cortisone derivatives
Desoxycorticosterone derivatives
Fluorinated corticosteroids

962.1 Androgens and anabolic congeners
Methandriol   Oxymetholone
Nandrolone   Testosterone

962.2 Ovarian hormones and synthetic substitutes
Contraceptives, oral
Estrogens
Estrogens and progestogens, combined
Progestogens

962.3 Insulins and antidiabetic agents
Acetohexamide   Insulin
Biguanide derivatives, oral   Phenformin
Chlorpropamide   Sulfonylurea derivatives, oral
Glucagon   Tolbutamide

962.4 Anterior pituitary hormones
Corticotropin
Gonadotropin
Somatotropin [growth hormone]

962.5 Posterior pituitary hormones
Vasopressin

Excludes: oxytocic hormones (975.0)

962.6 Parathyroid and parathyroid derivatives

962.7 Thyroid and thyroid derivatives
Dextrothyroxin   Liothyronine
Levothyroxine sodium   Thyroglobulin

962.8 Antithyroid agents
Iodides   Thiourea
Thiouracil

962.9 Other and unspecified hormones and synthetic substitutes

963 Poisoning by primarily systemic agents

963.0 Antiallergic and antiemetic drugs
Antihistamines   Diphenylpyraline
Chlorpheniramine   Thonzylamine
Diphenhydramine   Tripelennamine

Excludes: phenothiazine-based tranquilizers (969.1)

963.1 Antineoplastic and immunosuppressive drugs
Azathioprine   Cytarabine
Busulfan   Fluorouracil
Chlorambucil   Mercaptopurine
Cyclophosphamide   thio-TEPA

Excludes: antineoplastic antibiotics (960.7)

963.2 Acidifying agents

963.3 Alkalizing agents

963.4 Enzymes, not elsewhere classified
Penicillinase

963.5 Vitamins, not elsewhere classified
Vitamin A   Vitamin D

Excludes: nicotinic acid (972.2)
vitamin K (964.3)

963.8 Other specified systemic agents
Heavy metal antagonists

963.9 Unspecified systemic agent

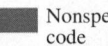 Add 4th or
5th digit

 Nonspecific
code

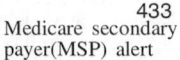 Unspecified
code

Medicare secondary
payer(MSP) alert

964 **Poisoning by agents primarily affecting blood constituents**

964.0 **Iron and its compounds**
Ferric salts
Ferrous sulfate and other ferrous salts

964.1 **Liver preparations and other antianemic agents**
Folic acid

964.2 **Anticoagulants**
Coumarin   Phenindione
Heparin   Warfarin sodium

964.3 **Vitamin K [phytonadione]**

964.4 **Fibrinolysis-affecting drugs**
Aminocaproic acid   Streptokinase
Streptodornase   Urokinase

964.5 **Anticoagulant antagonists and other coagulants**
Hexadimethrine   Protamine sulfate

964.6 **Gamma globulin**

964.7 **Natural blood and blood products**
Blood plasma   Packed red cells
Human fibrinogen   Whole blood

Excludes: transfusion reactions (999.4-999.8)

964.8 **Other specified agents affecting blood constituents**
Macromolecular blood substitutes
Plasma expanders

964.9 **Unspecified agent affecting blood constituents**

965 **Poisoning by analgesics, antipyretics, and antirheumatics**

Excludes: drug dependence (304.0-304.9)
nondependent abuse (305.0-305.9)

965.0 **Opiates and related narcotics**

965.00 **Opium (alkaloids), unspecified**

965.01 **Heroin**
Diacetylmorphine

965.02 **Methadone**

965.09 **Other**
Codeine [methylmorphine]
Meperidine [pethidine]
Morphine

965.1 **Salicylates**
Acetylsalicylic acid [aspirin]
Salicylic acid salts

965.4 **Aromatic analgesics, not elsewhere classified**
Acetanilid
Paracetamol [acetaminophen]
Phenacetin [acetophenetidin]

965.5 **Pyrazole derivatives**
Aminophenazone [aminopyrine]
Phenylbutazone

965.6 **Antirheumatics [antiphlogistics]**
Gold salts   Indomethacin

Excludes: salicylates (965.1)
steroids (962.0-962.9)

965.7 **Other non-narcotic analgesics**
Pyrabital

965.8 **Other specified analgesics and antipyretics**
Pentazocine

965.9 **Unspecified analgesic and antipyretic**

966 **Poisoning by anticonvulsants and anti-Parkinsonism drugs**

966.0 **Oxazolidine derivatives**
Paramethadione   Trimethadione

966.1 **Hydantoin derivatives**
Phenytoin

● Code new to this edition   ▲ Revision of existing code   ④ ⑤ Fourth or fifth digit required

966.2 Succinimides
Ethosuximide   Phensuximide

966.3 Other and unspecified anticonvulsants
Primidone

> Excludes: *barbiturates (967.0)*
> *sulfonamides (961.0)*

966.4 Anti-Parkinsonism drugs
Amantadine
Ethopropazine [profenamine]
Levodopa [L-dopa]

967 Poisoning by sedatives and hypnotics

> Excludes: *drug dependence (304.0-304.9)*
> *nondependent abuse (305.0-305.9)*

967.0 Barbiturates
Amobarbital [amylobarbitone]
Barbital [barbitone]
Butabarbital [butabarbitone]
Pentobarbital [pentobarbitone]
Phenobarbital [phenobarbitone]
Secobarbital [quinalbarbitone]

> Excludes: *thiobarbiturate anesthetics (968.3)*

967.1 Chloral hydrate group

967.2 Paraldehyde

967.3 Bromine compounds
Bromide   Carbromal (derivatives)

967.4 Methaqualone compounds

967.5 Glutethimide group

967.6 Mixed sedatives, not elsewhere classified

967.8 Other sedatives and hypnotics

967.9 Unspecified sedative or hypnotic
Sleeping:
drug
pill ⎫ NOS
tablet ⎭

968 Poisoning by other central nervous system depressants and anesthetics

> Excludes: *drug dependence (304.0-304.9)*
> *nondependent abuse (305.0-305.9)*

968.0 Central nervous system muscle-tone depressants
Chlorphenesin (carbamate)   Methocarbamol
Mephenesin

968.1 Halothane

968.2 Other gaseous anesthetics
Ether
Halogenated hydrocarbon derivatives, except halothane
Nitrous oxide

968.3 Intravenous anesthetics

> Ketamine *Methohexital [methohexitone]*
> *Thiobarbiturates, such as thiopental sodium*

968.4 Other and unspecified general anesthetics

968.5 Surface [topical] and infiltration anesthetics
Cocaine   Procaine
Lidocaine [lignocaine]   Tetracaine

968.6 Peripheral nerve and plexus-blocking anesthetics

968.7 Spinal anesthetics

968.9 Other and unspecified local anesthetics

969 Poisoning by psychotropic agents

> Excludes: *drug dependence (304.0-304.9)*
> *nondependent abuse (305.0-305.9)*

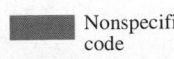 Add 4th or 5th digit

 Nonspecific code

 Unspecified code

Medicare secondary payer(MSP) alert

969.0 Antidepressants
Amitriptyline
Imipramine   Monoamine oxidase [MAO] inhibitors

969.1 Phenothiazine-based tranquilizers
Chlorpromazine   Prochlorperazine
Fluphenazine   Promazine

969.2 Butyrophenone-based tranquilizers
Haloperidol   Trifluperidol
Spiperone

969.3 Other antipsychotics, neuroleptics, and major tranquilizers

969.4 Benzodiazepine-based tranquilizers
Chlordiazepoxide   Lorazepam
Diazepam   Medazepam
Flurazepam   Nitrazepam

969.5 Other tranquilizers
Hydroxyzine   Meprobamate

969.6 Psychodysleptics [hallucinogens]
Cannabis (derivatives)   Mescaline
Lysergide [LSD]   Psilocin
Marihuana (derivatives)   Psilocybin

969.7 Psychostimulants
Amphetamine   Caffeine

Excludes: *central appetite depressants (977.0)*

969.8 Other specified psychotropic agents

969.9 Unspecified psychotropic agent

970 Poisoning by central nervous system stimulants

970.0 Analeptics
Lobeline   Nikethamide

970.1 Opiate antagonists
Levallorphan   Naloxone
Nalorphine

970.8 Other specified central nervous system stimulants

970.9 Unspecified central nervous system stimulant

971 Poisoning by drugs primarily affecting the autonomic nervous system

971.0 Parasympathomimetics [cholinergics]
Acetylcholine   Pilocarpine
Anticholinesterase:
  organophosphorus
  reversible

971.1 Parasympatholytics [anticholinergics and antimuscarinics] and spasmolytics
Atropine   Hyoscine [scopolamine]
Homatropine   Quaternary ammonium derivatives

Excludes: *papaverine (972.5)*

971.2 Sympathomimetics [adrenergics]
Epinephrine [adrenalin]
Levarterenol [noradrenalin]

971.3 Sympatholytics [antiadrenergics]
Phenoxybenzamine   Tolazoline hydrochloride

971.9 Unspecified drug primarily affecting autonomic nervous system

972 Poisoning by agents primarily affecting the cardiovascular system

972.0 Cardiac rhythm regulators
Practolol   Propranolol
Procainamide   Quinidine

Excludes: *lidocaine (968.5)*

972.1 Cardiotonic glycosides and drugs of similar action
Digitalis glycosides   Strophanthins
Digoxin

● Code new   ▲ Revision of   ④ ⑤ Fourth or fifth
to this edition   existing code   digit required

972.2 Antilipemic and antiarteriosclerotic drugs
    Clofibrate
    Nicotinic acid derivatives

972.3 Ganglion-blocking agents
    Pentamethonium bromide

972.4 Coronary vasodilators
    Dipyridamole   Nitrites
    Nitrates [nitroglycerin]

`972.5` Other vasodilators
    Cyclandelate   Papaverine
    Diazoxide

    Excludes: *nicotinic acid (972.2)*

`972.6` Other antihypertensive agents
    Clonidine   Rauwolfia alkaloids
    Guanethidine   Reserpine

972.7 Antivaricose drugs, including sclerosing agents
    Sodium morrhuate   Zinc salts

972.8 Capillary-active drugs
    Adrenochrome derivatives
    Metaraminol

`972.9` Other and unspecified agents primarily affecting the cardiovascular system

`973` Poisoning by agents primarily affecting the gastrointestinal system

973.0 Antacids and antigastric secretion drugs
    Aluminum hydroxide   Magnesium trisilicate

973.1 Irritant cathartics
    Bisacodyl   Phenolphthalein
    Castor oil

973.2 Emollient cathartics
    Dioctyl sulfosuccinates

`973.3` Other cathartics, including intestinal atonia drugs
    Magnesium sulfate

973.4 Digestants
    Pancreatin   Pepsin
    Papain

973.5 Antidiarrheal drugs
    Kaolin   Pectin

    Excludes: *anti-infectives (960.0-961.9)*

973.6 Emetics

`973.8` Other specified agents primarily affecting the gastrointestinal system

`973.9` Unspecified agent primarily affecting the gastrointestinal system

`974` Poisoning by water, mineral, and uric acid metabolism drugs

974.0 Mercurial diuretics
    Chlormerodrin   Mersalyl
    Mercaptomerin

974.1 Purine derivative diuretics
    Theobromine   Theophylline

    Excludes: *aminophylline [theophylline ethylenediamine] (975.7)*
             caffeine (969.7)

974.2 Carbonic acid anhydrase inhibitors
    Acetazolamide

974.3 Saluretics
    Benzothiadiazides   Chlorothiazide group

`974.4` Other diuretics
    Ethacrynic acid   Furosemide

974.5 Electrolytic, caloric, and water-balance agents

`974.6` Other mineral salts, not elsewhere classified

974.7 Uric acid metabolism drugs
    Allopurinol   Probenecid
    Colchicine

	Add 4th or 5th digit		Nonspecific code		Unspecified code		Medicare secondary payer(MSP) alert

975 Poisoning by agents primarily acting on the smooth and skeletal muscles and respiratory system

975.0 **Oxytocic agents**
Ergot alkaloids   Prostaglandins
Oxytocin

975.1 **Smooth muscle relaxants**
Adiphenine
Metaproterenol [orciprenaline]

Excludes: papaverine (972.5)

975.2 **Skeletal muscle relaxants**

975.3 **Other and unspecified drugs acting on muscles**

975.4 **Antitussives**
Dextromethorphan   Pipazethate

975.5 **Expectorants**
Acetylcysteine   Terpin hydrate
Guaifenesin

975.6 **Anti-common cold drugs**

975.7 **Antiasthmatics**
Aminophylline [theophylline ethylenediamine]

975.8 **Other and unspecified respiratory drugs**

976 Poisoning by agents primarily affecting skin and mucous membrane, ophthalmological, otorhinolaryngological, and dental drugs

976.0 **Local anti-infectives and anti-inflammatory drugs**

976.1 **Antipruritics**

976.2 **Local astringents and local detergents**

976.3 **Emollients, demulcents, and protectants**

976.4 **Keratolytics, keratoplastics, other hair treatment drugs and preparations**

976.5 **Eye anti-infectives and other eye drugs**
Idoxuridine

976.6 **Anti-infectives and other drugs and preparations for ear, nose, and throat**

976.7 **Dental drugs topically applied**

Excludes: anti-infectives (976.0)
          local anesthetics (968.5)

976.8 **Other agents primarily affecting skin and mucous membrane**
Spermicides [vaginal contraceptives]

976.9 **Unspecified agent primarily affecting skin and mucous membrane**

977 Poisoning by other and unspecified drugs and medicinal substances

977.0 **Dietetics**
Central appetite depressants

977.1 **Lipotropic drugs**

977.2 **Antidotes and chelating agents, not elsewhere classified**

977.3 **Alcohol deterrents**

977.4 **Pharmaceutical excipients**
Pharmaceutical adjuncts

977.8 **Other specified drugs and medicinal substances**
Contrast media used for diagnostic x-ray procedures
Diagnostic agents and kits

977.9 **Unspecified drug or medicinal substance**

978 Poisoning by bacterial vaccines

978.0 **BCG**

978.1 **Typhoid and paratyphoid**

978.2 **Cholera**

978.3 **Plague**

978.4 **Tetanus**

978.5 **Diphtheria**

978.6 **Pertussis vaccine, including combinations with a pertussis component**

438   ● Code new   ▲ Revision of   ④ ⑤ Fourth or fifth
           to this edition   existing code   digit required

978.8 Other and unspecified bacterial vaccines

978.9 Mixed bacterial vaccines, except combinations with a pertussis component

979 Poisoning by other vaccines and biological substances

> Excludes: *gamma globulin (964.6)*

979.0 Smallpox vaccine

979.1 Rabies vaccine

979.2 Typhus vaccine

979.3 Yellow fever vaccine

979.4 Measles vaccine

979.5 Poliomyelitis vaccine

979.6 Other and unspecified viral and rickettsial vaccines
Mumps vaccine

979.7 Mixed viral-rickettsial and bacterial vaccines, except combinations with a pertussis component

> Excludes: *combinations with a pertussis component (978.6)*

979.9 Other and unspecified vaccines and biological substances

TOXIC EFFECTS OF SUBSTANCES CHIEFLY NONMEDICAL AS TO SOURCE (980-989)

> Excludes: *burns from chemical agents (ingested) (947.0-947.9)*
> *localized toxic effects indexed elsewhere (001.0-799.9)*
> *respiratory conditions due to external agents (506.0-508.9)*

Use additional code to specify the nature of the toxic effect

980 Toxic effect of alcohol

980.0 Ethyl alcohol
Denatured alcohol   Grain alcohol
Ethanol

> Excludes: *acute alcohol intoxication (305.0)*
> *in alcoholism (303.0)*
> *drunkenness (simple) (305.0)*
> *pathological (291.4)*

980.1 Methyl alcohol
Methanol   Wood alcohol

980.2 Isopropyl alcohol
Dimethyl carbinol   Rubbing alcohol
Isopropanol

980.3 Fusel oil
Alcohol:
amyl
butyl
propyl

980.8 Other specified alcohols

980.9 Unspecified alcohol

981 Toxic effect of petroleum products
Benzine   Petroleum:
Gasoline   ether
Kerosene   naphtha
Paraffin wax   spirit

982 Toxic effect of solvents other than petroleum-based

982.0 Benzene and homologues

982.1 Carbon tetrachloride

982.2 Carbon disulfide
Carbon bisulfide

982.3 Other chlorinated hydrocarbon solvents
Tetrachloroethylene   Trichloroethylene

> Excludes: *chlorinated hydrocarbon preparations other than solvents (989.2)*

982.4 Nitroglycol

982.8 Other nonpetroleum-based solvents
Acetone

439

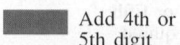 Add 4th or
5th digit

 Nonspecific
code

 Unspecified
code

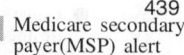 Medicare secondary
payer(MSP) alert

983 **Toxic effect of corrosive aromatics, acids, and caustic alkalis**

983.0 **Corrosive aromatics**
Carbolic acid or phenol   Cresol

983.1 **Acids**
Acid:
hydrochloric
nitric
sulfuric

983.2 **Caustic alkalis**
Lye   Sodium hydroxide
Potassium hydroxide

983.9 **Caustic, unspecified**

984 **Toxic effect of lead and its compounds (including fumes)**
Includes: that from all sources except medicinal substances

984.0 **Inorganic lead compounds**
Lead dioxide   Lead salts

984.1 **Organic lead compounds**
Lead acetate   Tetraethyl lead

984.8 **Other lead compounds**

984.9 **Unspecified lead compound**

985 **Toxic effect of other metals**
Includes: that from all sources except medicinal substances

985.0 **Mercury and its compounds**
Minamata disease

985.1 **Arsenic and its compounds**

985.2 **Manganese and its compounds**

985.3 **Beryllium and its compounds**

985.4 **Antimony and its compounds**

985.5 **Cadmium and its compounds**

985.6 **Chromium**

985.8 **Other specified metals**
Brass fumes   Iron compounds
Copper salts   Nickel compounds

985.9 **Unspecified metal**

986 **Toxic effect of carbon monoxide**
Carbon monoxide from any source

987 **Toxic effect of other gases, fumes, or vapors**

987.0 **Liquefied petroleum gases**
Butane   Propane

987.1 **Other hydrocarbon gas**

987.2 **Nitrogen oxides**
Nitrogen dioxide   Nitrous fumes

987.3 **Sulfur dioxide**

987.4 **Freon**
Dichloromonofluoromethane

987.5 **Lacrimogenic gas**
Bromobenzyl cyanide   Ethyliodoacetate
Chloroacetophenone

987.6 **Chlorine gas**

987.7 **Hydrocyanic acid gas**

987.8 **Other specified gases, fumes, or vapors**
Phosgene   Polyester fumes

987.9 **Unspecified gas, fume, or vapor**

988 **Toxic effect of noxious substances eaten as food**

Excludes: *allergic reaction to food, such as:*
gastroenteritis (558.9)
rash (692.5, 693.1)
food poisoning (bacterial) (005.0-005.9)

continued

● Code new   ▲ Revision of   ④ ⑤ Fourth or fifth
  to this edition   existing code   digit required

toxic effects of food contaminants, such as:
aflatoxin and other mycotoxin (989.7)
mercury (985.0)

988.0 Fish and shellfish

988.1 Mushrooms

988.2 Berries and other plants

988.8 Other specified noxious substances eaten as food

988.9 Unspecified noxious substance eaten as food

989 Toxic effect of other substances, chiefly nonmedicinal as to source

989.0 Hydrocyanic acid and cyanides
Potassium cyanide   Sodium cyanide

Excludes: gas and fumes (987.7)

989.1 Strychnine and salts

989.2 Chlorinated hydrocarbons
Aldrin   DDT
Chlordane   Dieldrin

Excludes: chlorinated hydrocarbon solvents (982.0-982.3)

989.3 Organophosphate and carbamate
Carbaryl   Parathion
Dichlorvos   Phorate
Malathion   Phosdrin

989.4 Other pesticides, not elsewhere classified
Mixtures of insecticides

989.5 Venom
Bites of venomous snakes, lizards, and spiders
Tick paralysis

989.6 Soaps and detergents

989.7 Aflatoxin and other mycotoxin [food contaminants]

989.8 Other substances, chiefly nonmedicinal as to source

    989.81 Asbestos

Excludes: asbestosis (501)
exposure to asbestos (V15.84)

    989.82 Latex

    989.83 Silicone

    989.84 Tobacco

    989.89 Other

989.9 Unspecified substance, chiefly nonmedicinal as to source

OTHER AND UNSPECIFIED EFFECTS OF EXTERNAL CAUSES (990-995)

990 Effects of radiation, unspecified
Complication of: Radiation sickness
phototherapy
radiation therapy

Excludes: specified adverse effects of radiation
Such conditions are to be classified according to the nature of the adverse effect,
as:
burns (940.0-949.5)
dermatitis (692.7-692.8)
leukemia (204.0-208.9)
pneumonia (508.0)
sunburn (692.71)
[The type of radiation giving rise to the adverse effect may be identified by use
of the E codes.]

991 Effects of reduced temperature

991.0 Frostbite of face

991.1 Frostbite of hand

991.2 Frostbite of foot

991.3 Frostbite of other and unspecified sites

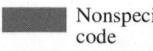

Add 4th or
5th digit

Nonspecific
code

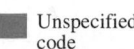

Unspecified
code

Medicare secondary
payer(MSP) alert

991.4 Immersion foot
Trench foot

991.5 Chilblains
Erythema pernio   Perniosis

991.6 Hypothermia
Hypothermia (accidental)

> *Excludes:* *hypothermia following anesthesia (995.89)*
> *hypothermia not associated with low environmental temperature (780.9)*

991.8 Other specified effects of reduced temperature

991.9 Unspecified effect of reduced temperature
Effects of freezing or excessive cold NOS

992 Effects of heat and light

> *Excludes:* *burns (940.0-949.5)*
> *diseases of sweat glands due to heat (705.0-705.9)*
> *malignant hyperpyrexia following anesthesia (995.89)*
> *sunburn (692.71)*

992.0 Heat stroke and sunstroke
Heat apoplexy   Siriasis
Heat pyrexia   Thermoplegia
Ictus solaris

992.1 Heat syncope
Heat collapse

992.2 Heat cramps

992.3 Heat exhaustion, anhydrotic
Heat prostration due to water depletion

> *Excludes:* *that associated with salt depletion (992.4)*

992.4 Heat exhaustion due to salt depletion
Heat prostration due to salt (and water) depletion

992.5 Heat exhaustion, unspecified
Heat prostration NOS

992.6 Heat fatigue, transient

992.7 Heat edema

992.8 Other specified heat effects

992.9 Unspecified

993 Effects of air pressure

993.0 Barotrauma, otitic
Aero-otitis media
Effects of high altitude on ears

993.1 Barotrauma, sinus
Aerosinusitis
Effects of high altitude on sinuses

993.2 Other and unspecified effects of high altitude
Alpine sickness   Hypobaropathy
Andes disease   Mountain sickness
Anoxia due to high altitude

993.3 Caisson disease
Bends   Decompression sickness
Compressed-air disease   Divers' palsy or paralysis

993.4 Effects of air pressure caused by explosion

993.8 Other specified effects of air pressure

993.9 Unspecified effect of air pressure

994 Effects of other external causes

> *Excludes:* *certain adverse effects not elsewhere classified (995.0-995.8)*

994.0 Effects of lightning
Shock from lightning   Struck by lightning NOS

> *Excludes:* *burns (940.0-949.5)*

994.1 Drowning and nonfatal submersion
Bathing cramp   Immersion

● Code new   ▲ Revision of   ④ ⑤ Fourth or fifth
    to this edition   existing code   digit required

994.2 **Effects of hunger**
Deprivation of food   Starvation

994.3 **Effects of thirst**
Deprivation of water

994.4 **Exhaustion due to exposure**

994.5 **Exhaustion due to excessive exertion**
Overexertion

994.6 **Motion sickness**
Air sickness   Travel sickness
Seasickness

994.7 **Asphyxiation and strangulation**
Suffocation (by):   Suffocation (by):
  bedclothes   plastic bag
  cave-in   pressure
  constriction   strangulation
  mechanical

Excludes: *asphyxia from:*
     carbon monoxide (986)
     inhalation of food or foreign body (932-934.9)
     other gases, fumes, and vapors (987.0-987.9)

994.8 **Electrocution and nonfatal effects of electric current**
Shock from electric current

Excludes: *electric burns (940.0-949.5)*

994.9 **Other effects of external causes**
Effects of:
  abnormal gravitational [G] forces or states
  weightlessness

995 **Certain adverse effects not elsewhere classified**

Excludes: *complications of surgical and medical care (996.0-999.9)*

995.0 **Other anaphylactic shock**
Code first any underlying condition such as:
  poisoning by drugs, medicinals and biologic substances (960-979)
  toxic effects of substances chiefly nonmedical as to source (980-989)
Use additional E code, if desired, to identify external cause, such as:
  adverse effects of correct medicinal substance properly administered (E930-E949)

Allergic shock
Anaphylactic reaction   } NOS or due to adverse effect of correct medicinal
Anaphylaxis   substance properly administered

Excludes: *anaphylactic reaction to serum (999.4)*
     anaphylactic shock due to adverse food reaction (995.60-995.69)

995.1 **Angioneurotic edema**
Giant urticaria

Excludes: *Urticaria:*
     due to serum (999.5)
     other specified (698.2, 708.0-708.9, 757.33)

995.2 **Unspecified adverse effect of drug, medicinal and biological substance**
Adverse effect
Allergic reaction
Hypersensitivity   } (due) to correct medicinal substance properly administered
Idiosyncrasy

Drug:
  hypersensitivity NOS
  reaction NOS

Excludes: *pathological drug intoxication (292.2)*

995.3 **Allergy, unspecified**
Allergic reaction NOS   Idiosyncrasy NOS
Hypersensitivity NOS

continued

Add 4th or   Nonspecific   Unspecified   Medicare secondary
5th digit   code   code   payer(MSP) alert

Excludes: *allergic reaction NOS to correct medicinal substance properly administered (995.2)*
specific types of allergic reaction, such as:
allergic diarrhea (558.9)
dermatitis (691.0-693.9)
hay fever (477.0-477.9)

995.4 Shock due to anesthesia
Shock due to anesthesia in which the correct substance was properly administered

Excludes: *complications of anesthesia in labor or delivery (668.0-668.9)*
overdose or wrong substance given (968.0-969.9)
postoperative shock NOS (998.0)
specified adverse effects of anesthesia classified elsewhere, such as:
anoxic brain damage (348.1)
hepatitis (070.0-070.9), etc.
unspecified adverse effect of anesthesia (995.2)

995.5 Child maltreatment syndrome
Use additional code(s) to identify any associated injuries
Use additional E code to identify:
nature of abuse (E960-E968)
perpetrator (E967.0-E967.9)

- ● `995.50` **Child abuse, unspecified**
- ● **995.51** **Child emotional/psychological abuse**
- ● **995.52** **Child neglect (nutritional)**
- ● **995.53** **Child sexual abuse**
- ● **995.54** **Child physical abuse**
Battered baby or child syndrome

Excludes: *Shaken infant syndrome (995.55)*

- ● **995.55** **Shaken infant syndrome**
Use additional code(s) to identify any associated injuries

- ● `995.59` **Other child abuse and neglect**
Multiple forms of abuse

995.6 Anaphylactic shock due to adverse food reaction
Anaphylactic shock due to nonpoisonous foods

- `995.60` **Due to unspecified food**
- **995.61** **Due to peanuts**
- **995.62** **Due to crustaceans**
- **995.63** **Due to fruits and vegetables**
- **995.64** **Due to tree nuts and seeds**
- **995.65** **Due to fish**
- **995.66** **Due to food additives**
- **995.67** **Due to milk products**
- **995.68** **Due to eggs**
- `995.69` **Due to other specified food**

995.8 Other specified adverse effects, not elsewhere classified

- ● `995.80` **Adult maltreatment, unspecified**
Abused person NOS

Use additional code to identify:
any associated injury
perpetrator (E967.0-E967.9)

- ▲ **995.81** **Adult physical abuse**
Battered:
person syndrome NEC
man
spouse
woman

Use additional code to identify:
any associated injury
nature of abuse (E960-E968)
perpetrator (E967.0-E967.9)

- ● **995.82** **Adult emotional/psychological abuse**

● Code new
to this edition

▲ Revision of
existing code

④ ⑤ Fourth or fifth
digit required

Use additional E code to identify perpetrator (E967.0-E967.9)

● **995.83   Adult sexual abuse**

Use additional code to identify:
  any associated injury
  perpetrator (E967.0-E967.9)

● **995.84   Adult neglect (nutritional)**

Use additional code to identify:
  intent of neglect (E904.0, E968.4)
  perpetrator (E967.0-967.9)

● **995.85**   **Other adult abuse and neglect**
  Multiple forms of abuse and neglect

Use additional code to identify:
  any associated injury
  intent of neglect (E904.0, E968.4)
  nature of abuse (E960-E968)
  perpetrator (E967.0-E967.9)

995.89   **Other**
  Malignant hyperpyrexia or hypothermia due to anesthesia

COMPLICATIONS OF SURGICAL AND MEDICAL CARE, NOT ELSEWHERE CLASSIFIED (996-999)

Excludes: *adverse effects of medicinal agents (001.0-799.9, 995.0-995.8)*
 burns from local applications and irradiation (940.0-949.5)
 complications of:
  conditions for which the procedure was performed
  surgical procedures during abortion, labor, and delivery (630-676.9)
 poisoning and toxic effects of drugs and chemicals (960.0-989.9)
 postoperative conditions in which no complications are present, such as:
  artificial opening status (V44.0-V44.9)
  closure of external stoma (V55.0-V55.9)
  fitting of prosthetic device (V52.0-V52.9)
 specified complications classified elsewhere
  anesthetic shock (995.4)
  electrolyte imbalance (276.0-276.9)
  postlaminectomy syndrome (772.80-722.83)
  postmastectomy lymphedema syndrome (457.0)
  postoperative psychosis (293.0-293.9)
  any other condition classified elsewhere in the Alphabetic Index when described
   as due to a procedure

996   **Complications peculiar to certain specified procedures**
 Includes: complications, not elsewhere classified, in the use of artificial substitutes [e.g., Dacron, metal, Silastic, Teflon] or natural sources [e.g., bone] involving:
   anastomosis (internal)
   graft (bypass) (patch)
   implant
   internal device:
    catheter
    electronic
    fixation
    prosthetic
   reimplant
   transplant

Excludes: *accidental puncture or laceration during procedure (998.2)*
 complications of internal anastomosis of:
  gastrointestinal tract (997.4)
  urinary tract (997.5)
 other specified complications classified elsewhere, such as:
  hemolytic anemia (283.1)
  functional cardiac disturbances (429.4)
  serum hepatitis (070.2-070.3)

996.0   **Mechanical complication of cardiac device, implant, and graft**

Breakdown (mechanical)	Obstruction, mechanical
Displacement	Perforation
Leakage	Protrusion

996.00   **Unspecified device, implant, and graft**

996.01   **Due to cardiac pacemaker (electrode)**

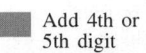 Add 4th or 5th digit   Nonspecific code   Unspecified code   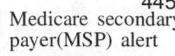 Medicare secondary payer(MSP) alert

996.02   **Due to heart valve prosthesis**

996.03   **Due to coronary bypass graft**

Excludes: *atherosclerosis of graft (414.02, 414.03)*

         embolism [occlusion NOS] [thrombus] of graft (996.72)

996.04   **Due to automatic implantable cardiac defibrillator**

996.09   **Other**

996.1   **Mechanical complication of other vascular device, implant, and graft**

    Mechanical complications involving:
      aortic (bifurcation) graft (replacement)
      arteriovenous:
        fistula   } surgically created
        shunt
      balloon (counterpulsation) device, intra-aortic
      carotid artery bypass graft
      dialysis catheter
      femoral-popliteal bypass graft
      umbrella device, vena cava

Excludes: *atherosclerosis of biological graft (440.30-440.32)*

         embolism [occlusion NOS] [thrombus] of (biological) (synthetic) graft (996.74)

996.2   **Mechanical complication of nervous system device, implant, and graft**

    Mechanical complications involving:
      dorsal column stimulator
      electrodes implanted in brain [brain "pacemaker"]
      peripheral nerve graft
      ventricular (communicating) shunt

996.3   **Mechanical complication of genitourinary device, implant, and graft**

996.30   **Unspecified device, implant, and graft**

996.31   **Due to urethral [indwelling] catheter**

996.32   **Due to intrauterine contraceptive device**

996.39   **Other**

      Cystostomy catheter
      Prosthetic reconstruction of vas deferens
      Repair (graft) of ureter without mention of resection

Excludes: *complications due to:*

        external stoma of urinary tract (997.5)
        internal anastomosis of urinary tract (997.5)

996.4   **Mechanical complication of internal orthopedic device, implant, and graft**

    Mechanical complications involving:
      external (fixation) device utilizing internal screw(s), pin(s) or other methods of fixation
      grafts of bone, cartilage, muscle, or tendon
      internal (fixation) device such as nail, plate, rod, etc.

Excludes: *complications of external orthopedic device, such as:*

        pressure ulcer due to cast (707.0)

996.5   **Mechanical complication of other specified prosthetic device, implant, and graft**

    Mechanical complications involving:
      prosthetic implant in:
        bile duct
        breast
        chin
        orbit of eye
      nonabsorbable surgical material NOS
      other graft, implant, and internal device, not elsewhere classified

996.51   **Due to corneal graft**

996.52   **Due to graft of other tissue, not elsewhere classified**

      Skin graft failure or rejection

Excludes: *sloughing of temporary skin allografts or xenografts (pigskin)—omit code*

996.53   **Due to ocular lens prosthesis**

Excludes: *contact lenses—code to condition*

996.54   **Due to breast prosthesis**

      Breast capsule (prosthesis)
      Mammary implant

  ● Code new   ▲ Revision of   ④ ⑤ Fourth or fifth
     to this edition   existing code   digit required

996.59 **Due to other implant and internal device, not elsewhere classified**
Nonabsorbable surgical material NOS
Prosthetic implant in:
bile duct
chin
orbit of eye

996.6 **Infection and inflammatory reaction due to internal prosthetic device, implant, and graft**

Infection (causing obstruction) $\left.\begin{array}{l}\\\\\end{array}\right\}$ due to (presence of) any device,
Inflammation implant, and graft classifiable to
996.0-996.5

996.60 **Due to unspecified device, implant, and graft**

996.61 **Due to cardiac device, implant, and graft**
Cardiac pacemaker or defibrillator:
electrode(s), lead(s)
pulse generator
subcutaneous pocket
Coronary artery bypass graft
Heart valve prosthesis

996.62 **Due to other vascular device, implant, and graft**
Arterial graft
Arteriovenous fistula or shunt
Infusion pump
Vascular catheter (arterial) (dialysis) (venous)

996.63 **Due to nervous system device, implant, and graft**
Electrodes implanted in brain
Peripheral nerve graft
Spinal canal catheter
Ventricular (communicating) shunt (catheter)

996.64 **Due to indwelling urinary catheter**

996.65 **Due to other genitourinary device, implant, and graft**
Intrauterine contraceptive device

996.66 **Due to internal joint prosthesis**

996.67 **Due to other internal orthopedic device, implant, and graft**
Bone growth stimulator (electrode)
Internal fixation device (pin) (rod) (screw)

996.69 **Due to other internal prosthetic device, implant, and graft**
Breast prosthesis
Ocular lens prosthesis
Prosthetic orbital implant

996.7 **Other complications of internal (biological) (synthetic) prosthetic device, implant, and graft**
Complication NOS $\left.\begin{array}{l}\\\\\\\\\\\\\end{array}\right.$
occlusion NOS
Embolism
Fibrosis due to (presence of) any device, implant, and graft
Hemorrhage classifiable to 996.0-996.5
Pain
Stenosis
Thrombus

Excludes: *transplant rejection (996.8)*

996.70 **Due to unspecified device, implant, and graft**

996.71 **Due to heart valve prosthesis**

996.72 **Due to other cardiac device, implant, and graft**
Cardiac pacemaker or defibrillator:
electrode(s), lead(s)
subcutaneous pocket
Coronary artery bypass (graft)

Excludes: *occlusion due to atherosclerosis (414.02-414.03)*

996.73 **Due to renal dialysis device, implant, and graft**

996.74 **Due to other vascular device, implant, and graft**

Excludes: *occlusion of biological graft due to atherosclerosis (440.30-440.32)*

996.75 **Due to nervous system device, implant, and graft**

Add 4th or 5th digit	Nonspecific code	Unspecified code	Medicare secondary payer(MSP) alert

996.76   **Due to genitourinary device, implant, and graft**

996.77   **Due to internal joint prosthesis**

996.78   **Due to other internal orthopedic device, implant, and graft**

996.79   **Due to other internal prosthetic device, implant, and graft**

996.8 **Complications of transplanted organ**

Use additional code, if desired, to identify nature of complication, such as:
    Cytomegalovirus (CMV) infection (078.5)
    Transplant failure or rejection

996.80   **Transplanted organ, unspecified**

996.81   **Kidney**

996.82   **Liver**

996.83   **Heart**

996.84   **Lung**

996.85   **Bone Marrow**
    Graft-versus-host disease (acute) (chronic)

996.86   **Pancreas**

996.89   **Other specified transplanted organ**
    Intestines

996.9 **Complications of reattached extremity or body part**

996.90   **Unspecified extremity**

996.91   **Forearm**

996.92   **Hand**

996.93   **Finger(s)**

996.94   **Upper extremity, other and unspecified**

996.95   **Foot and toe(s)**

996.96   **Lower extremity, other and unspecified**

996.99   **Other specified body part**

997 Complications affecting specified body systems, not elsewhere classified

Use additional code to identify complication

> *Excludes:* *the listed conditions when specified as:*
>   *causing shock (998.0)*
>   *complications of:*
>   *anesthesia:*
>   *adverse effect (001.0-799.9, 995.0-995.8)*
>   *in labor or delivery (668.0-668.9)*
>   *poisoning (968.0-969.9)*
>   *implanted device or graft (996.0-996.9)*
>   *obstetrical procedures (669.0-669.4)*
>   *reattached extremity (996.90-996.96)*
>   *transplanted organ (996.80-996.89)*

997.0 **Nervous system complications**

997.00   **Nervous system complication, unspecified**

997.01   **Central nervous system complication**
    Anoxic brain damage
    Cerebral hypoxia

> *Excludes:* *cerebrovascular hemorrhage or infarction (997.02)*

997.02   **Iatrogenic cerebrovascular infarction or hemorrhage**
    Postoperative stroke

997.09   **Other nervous system complications**

997.1 **Cardiac complications**
    Cardiac:
      arrest
      insufficiency
    Cardiorespiratory failure   } during or resulting from a procedure
    Heart failure

> *Excludes:* *the listed conditions as long-term effects of cardiac surgery or due to the presence of cardiac prosthetic device (429.4)*

● Code new   ▲ Revision of   ④ ⑤ Fourth or fifth
   to this edition   existing code   digit required

997.2 Peripheral vascular complications

Phlebitis or thrombophlebitis during or resulting from a procedure

Excludes: *the listed conditions due to:*
> *implant or catheter device (996.62)*
> *infusion, perfusion, or transfusion (999.2)*
> *complications affecting internal blood vessels, such as:*
> *mesenteric artery (997.4)*
> *renal artery (997.5)*

997.3 Respiratory complications

Mendelson's syndrome ⎫
Pneumonia (aspiration) ⎬ resulting from a procedure

Excludes: *iatrogenic [postoperative] pneumothorax (512.1)*
> *iatrogenic pulmonary embolism (415.11)*
> *Mendelson's syndrome in labor and delivery (668.0)*
> *specified complications classified elsewhere, such as:*
> *adult respiratory distress syndrome (518.5)*
> *pulmonary edema, postoperative (518.4)*
> *respiratory insufficiency, acute, postoperative (518.5)*
> *shock lung (518.5)*
> *tracheostomy complication (519.0)*

997.4 Digestive system complications

Complications of intestinal (internal) anastomosis and bypass, not elsewhere classified, except that involving urinary tract

Hepatic failure ⎫
Hepatorenal syndrome ⎬ specified as due to a procedure
Intestinal obstruction NOS ⎭

Excludes: *specified gastrointestinal complications classified elsewhere, such as:*
> *blind loop syndrome (579.2)*
> *colostomy or enterostomy complications (569.60-569.69)*
> *gastrojejunal ulcer (534.0-534.9)*
> *infection of external stoma (569.61)*
> *pelvic peritoneal adhesions, female (614.6)*
> *peritoneal adhesions (568.0)*
> *peritoneal adhesions with obstruction (560.81)*
> *postcholecystectomy syndrome (576.0)*
> *postgastric surgery syndromes (564.2)*

997.5 Urinary complications

Complications of:
external stoma of urinary tract
internal anastomosis and bypass of urinary tract, including that involving intestinal tract

Oliguria or anuria ⎫
Renal: ⎪
failure (acute) ⎬ specified as due to procedure
insufficiency (acute) ⎪
Tubular necrosis (acute) ⎭

Excludes: *specified complications classified elsewhere, such as:*
> *postoperative stricture of:*
> *ureter (593.3)*
> *urethra (598.2)*

▲ **997.6 Amputation stump complication**

Excludes: *admission for treatment for a current traumatic amputation; code to complicated traumatic amputation*
> *phantom limb (syndrome) (353.6)*

997.60 Unspecified complication

997.61 Neuroma of amputation stump

997.62 Infection (chronic)

Use additional code to identify the organism

997.69 Other

449

| | Add 4th or 5th digit | | Nonspecific code | | Unspecified code | | Medicare secondary payer(MSP) alert |

997.9 Complications affecting other specified body systems, not elsewhere classified

Excludes: specified complications classified elsewhere, such as:
broad ligament laceration syndrome (620.6)
postartificial menopause syndrome (627.4)
postoperative stricture of vagina (623.2)

997.91 Hypertension

Excludes: essential hypertension (401.0-401.9)

997.99 Other
Vitreous touch syndrome

998 Other complications of procedures, NEC

998.0 Postoperative shock
Collapse NOS
Shock (endotoxic) (hypo-
volemic) (septic) } during or resulting from a surgical procedure

Excludes: shock:
anaphylactic due to serum (999.4)
anesthetic (995.4)
electric (994.8)
following abortion (639.5)
obstetric (669.1)
traumatic (958.4)

▲ **998.1 Hemorrhage or hematoma or seroma complicating a procedure**

Excludes: hemorrhage due to implanted device or graft (996.70-996.79)
hemorrhage, hematoma or seroma complicating cesarean section or puerperal perineal wound (674.3)

● **998.11 Hemorrhage complicating a procedure**
● **998.12 Hematoma complicating a procedure**
● **998.13 Seroma complicating a procedure**

998.2 Accidental puncture or laceration during a procedure
Accidental perforation by catheter or other instrument during a procedure on:
blood vessel
nerve
organ

Excludes: iatrogenic [postoperative] pneumothorax (512.1)
puncture or laceration caused by implanted device intentionally left in operation wound (996.0-996.5)
specified complications classified elsewhere, such as:
broad ligament laceration syndrome (620.6)
trauma from instruments during delivery (664.0-665.9)

998.3 Disruption of operation wound
Dehiscence
Rupture } of operation wound

Excludes: disruption of:
cesarean wound (674.1)
perineal wound, puerperal (674.2)

998.4 Foreign body accidentally left during a procedure
Adhesions
Obstruction
Perforation } due to foreign body accidentally left in operative wound
or body cavity during a procedure

Excludes: obstruction or perforation caused by implanted device intentionally left in body (996.0-996.5)

998.5 Postoperative infection

Excludes: infection due to:
implanted device (996.60-996.69)
infusion, perfusion, or transfusion (999.3)
postoperative obstetrical wound infection (674.3)

● **998.51 Infected postoperative seroma**
Use additional code to identify organism

● Code new to this edition   ▲ Revision of existing code   ④ ⑤ Fourth or fifth digit required

● **998.59 Other postoperative infection**
    Abscess: postoperative
      intra-abdominal postoperative
      stitch postoperative
      subphrenic postoperative
      wound postoperative
    Septicemia postoperative
Use additional code to identify infection

998.6 Persistent postoperative fistula

998.7 Acute reaction to foreign substance accidentally left during a procedure
    Peritonitis:
      aseptic
      chemical

998.8 Other specified complications of procedures, not elsewhere classified

  998.81 Emphysema (subcutaneous) (surgical) resulting from a procedure

  998.82 Cataract fragments in eye following cataract surgery

● **998.83 Non-healing surgical wound**

  998.89 Other specified complications

998.9 Unspecified complication of procedure, not elsewhere classified
    Postoperative complication NOS

    Excludes: complication NOS of obstetrical surgery or procedure (669.4)

999 Complications of medical care, not elsewhere classified
    Includes: complications, not elsewhere classified, of:
          dialysis (hemodialysis) (peritoneal) (renal)
          extracorporeal circulation
          hyperalimentation therapy
          immunization
          infusion
          inhalation therapy
          injection
          inoculation
          perfusion
          transfusion
          vaccination
          ventilation therapy

    Excludes: specified complications classified elsewhere such as:
          complications of implanted device (996.0-996.9)
          contact dermatitis due to drugs (692.3)
          dementia dialysis (294.8)
            transient (293.9)
          dialysis disequilibrium syndrome (276.0-276.9)
          poisoning and toxic effects of drugs and chemicals (960.0-989.9)
          postvaccinal encephalitis (323.5)
          water and electrolyte imbalance (276.0-276.9)

999.0 Generalized vaccinia

999.1 Air embolism
    Air embolism to any site following infusion, perfusion, or transfusion

    Excludes: embolism specified as:
          complicating:
            abortion (634-638 with .6, 639.6)
            ectopic or molar pregnancy (639.6)
            pregnancy, childbirth, or the puerperium (673.0)
          due to implanted device (996.7)
          traumatic (958.0)

999.2 Other vascular complications
    Phlebitis
    Thromboembolism   } following infusion, perfusion, or transfusion
    Thrombophlebitis

    Excludes: the listed conditions when specified as:
          due to implanted device (996.61-996.62, 996.72-996.74)
          postoperative NOS (997.2)

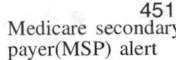

999.3 **Other infection**
Infection
Sepsis } following infusion, injection, transfusion, or vaccination
Septicemia

Excludes: *the listed conditions when specified as:*
due to implanted device (996.60-996.69)
postoperative NOS (998.51-998.59)

999.4 **Anaphylactic shock due to serum**

Excludes: *shock:*
allergic NOS (995.0)
anaphylactic:
NOS (995.0)
due to drugs and chemicals (995.0)

999.5 **Other serum reaction**
Intoxication by serum   Serum sickness
Protein sickness   Urticaria due to serum
Serum rash

Excludes: *serum hepatitis (070.2-070.3)*

999.6 **ABO incompatibility reaction**
Incompatible blood transfusion
Reaction to blood group incompatibility in infusion or transfusion

999.7 **Rh incompatibility reaction**
Reactions due to Rh factor in infusion or transfusion

999.8 **Other transfusion reaction**
Septic shock due to transfusion
Transfusion reaction NOS

Excludes: *postoperative shock (998.0)*

999.9 **Other and unspecified complications of medical care, not elsewhere classified**
Complications, not elsewhere classified, of:
electroshock
inhalation
ultrasound } therapy
ventilation
Unspecified misadventure of medical care

Excludes: *unspecified complication of:*
phototherapy (990)
radiation therapy (990)

● Code new   ▲ Revision of   ④ ⑤ Fourth or fifth
to this edition   existing code   digit required

SUPPLEMENTARY CLASSIFICATION OF FACTORS INFLUENCING HEALTH STATUS AND CONTACT WITH HEALTH SERVICES (V01-V82)

This classification is provided to deal with occasions when circumstances other than a disease or injury classifiable to categories 001-999 (the main part of ICD)are recorded as "diagnoses" or "problems." This can arise mainly in three ways:

a) When a person who is not currently sick encounters the health services for some specific purpose, such as to act as a donor of an organ or tissue, to receive prophylactic vaccination, or to discuss a problem which is in itself not a disease or injury. This will be a fairly rare occurrence among hospital inpatients, but will be relatively more common among hospital outpatients and patients of family practitioners, health clinics, etc.

b) When a person with a known disease or injury, whether it is current or resolving, encounters the health care system for a specific treatment of that disease or injury (e.g., dialysis for renal disease; chemotherapy for malignancy; cast change).

c) When some circumstance or problem is present which influences the person's health status but is not in itself a current illness or injury. Such factors may be elicited during population surveys, when the person may or may not be currently sick, or be recorded as an additional factor to be borne in mind when the person is receiving care for some current illness or injury classifiable to categories 001-999.

In the latter circumstances the V code should be used only as a supplementary code and should not be the one selected for use in primary, single cause tabulations. Examples of these circumstances are a personal history of certain diseases, or a person with an artificial heart valve in situ.

PERSONS WITH POTENTIAL HEALTH HAZARDS RELATED TO COMMUNICABLE DISEASES (V01-V06)

> Excludes: *family history of infectious and parasitic diseases (V18.8)*
> *personal history of infectious and parasitic diseases (V12.0)*

V01 **Contact with or exposure to communicable diseases**

V01.0 **Cholera**
Conditions classifiable to 001

V01.1 **Tuberculosis**
Conditions classifiable to 010-018

V01.2 **Poliomyelitis**
Conditions classifiable to 045

V01.3 **Smallpox**
Conditions classifiable to 050

V01.4 **Rubella**
Conditions classifiable to 056

V01.5 **Rabies**
Conditions classifiable to 071

V01.6 **Venereal diseases**
Conditions classifiable to 090-099

V01.7 **Other viral diseases**
Conditions classifiable to 042-078, except as above

V01.8 **Other communicable diseases**
Conditions classifiable to 001-136, except as above

V01.9 **Unspecified communicable disease**

V02 **Carrier or suspected carrier of infectious diseases**

V02.0 **Cholera**

V02.1 **Typhoid**

V02.2 **Amebiasis**

V02.3 **Other gastrointestinal pathogens**

V02.4 **Diphtheria**

V02.5 **Other specified bacterial diseases**
Bacterial disease:
meningococcal
staphylococcal
streptococcal

V02.6 **Viral hepatitis**
Hepatitis Australian-antigen [HAA] [SH] carrier
Serum hepatitis carrier

V02.7 **Gonorrhea**

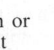 Add 4th or 5th digit   Nonspecific code   Unspecified code   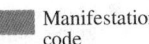 Manifestation code

V02.8 Other venereal diseases

V02.9 Other specified infectious organism

V03 Need for prophylactic vaccination and inoculation against bacterial diseases

Excludes: *vaccination not carried out because of contraindication (V64.0)*
vaccines against combinations of diseases (V06.0-V06.9)

V03.0 Cholera alone

V03.1 Typhoid-paratyphoid alone [TAB]

V03.2 Tuberculosis [BCG]

V03.3 Plague

V03.4 Tularemia

V03.5 Diphtheria alone

V03.6 Pertussis alone

V03.7 Tetanus toxoid alone

V03.8 Other specified vaccinations against single bacterial diseases

    V03.81 Hemophilus influenza, type B [Hib]

    V03.82 Streptococcus pneumoniae [pneumococcus]

    V03.89 Other specified vaccination

V03.9 Unspecified single bacterial disease

V04 Need for prophylactic vaccination and inoculation against certain viral diseases

Excludes: *vaccines against combinations of diseases (V06.0-V06.9)*

V04.0 Poliomyelitis

V04.1 Smallpox

V04.2 Measles alone

V04.3 Rubella alone

V04.4 Yellow fever

V04.5 Rabies

V04.6 Mumps alone

V04.7 Common cold

V04.8 Influenza

V05 Need for other prophylactic vaccination and inoculation against single diseases

Excludes: *vaccines against combinations of diseases (V06.0-V06.9)*

V05.0 Arthropod-borne viral encephalitis

V05.1 Other arthropod-borne viral diseases

V05.2 Leishmaniasis

V05.3 Viral hepatitis

V05.4 Varicella
    Chickenpox

V05.8 Other specified disease

V05.9 Unspecified single disease

V06 Need for prophylactic vaccination and inoculation against combinations of diseases

Note: Use additional single vaccination codes from categories V03-V05 to identify any vaccinations not included in a combination code.

V06.0 Cholera with typhoid-paratyphoid [cholera + TAB]

V06.1 Diphtheria-tetanus-pertussis, combined [DTP]

V06.2 Diphtheria-tetanus-pertussis with typhoid-paratyphoid [DTP + TAB]

V06.3 Diphtheria-tetanus-pertussis with poliomyelitis [DTP + polio]

V06.4 Measles-mumps-rubella [MMR]

V06.5 Tetanus-diphtheria [Td]

V06.6 Streptococcus pneumoniae [pneumococcus] and influenza

V06.8 Other combinations

Excludes: *multiple single vaccination codes (V03.0-V05.9)*

V06.9 Unspecified combined vaccine

● Code new
  to this edition
▲ Revision of
  existing code
④ ⑤ Fourth or fifth
    digit required

PERSONS WITH NEED FOR ISOLATION, OTHER POTENTIAL HEALTH HAZARDS AND PROPHYLACTIC MEASURES (V07-V09)

V07 **Need for isolation and other prophylactic measures**

> Excludes: *prophylactic organ removal (V50.41-V50.49)*

V07.0 **Isolation**
> Admission to protect the individual from his surroundings or for isolation of individual after contact with infectious diseases

V07.1 **Desensitization to allergens**

V07.2 **Prophylactic immunotherapy**
> Administration of:
> antivenin
> immune sera [gamma globulin]
> RhoGAM
> tetanus antitoxin

V07.3 **Other prophylactic chemotherapy**

> **V07.31** **Prophylactic fluoride administration**

> **V07.39** **Other prophylactic chemotherapy**

> Excludes: *maintenance chemotherapy following disease (V58.1)*

V07.4 **Postmenopausal hormone replacement therapy**

V07.8 **Other specified prophylactic measure**

V07.9 **Unspecified prophylactic measure**

V08 **Asymptomatic human immunodeficiency virus [HIV] infection status**
> HIV positive NOS
>
> Note: This code is ONLY to be used when NO HIV infection symptoms or conditions are present. If any HIV infection symptoms or conditions are present, see code 042.

> Excludes: *AIDS (042)*
> *human immunodeficiency virus [HIV] disease (042)*
> *exposure to HIV (V01.7)*
> *nonspecific serologic evidence of HIV (795.71)*
> *symptomatic human immunodeficiency virus [HIV] infection (042)*

V09 **Infection with drug-resistant microorganisms**
> Note: This category is intended for use as an additional code for infectious conditions classified elsewhere to indicate the presence of drug-resistance of the infectious organism.

V09.0 **Infection with microorganisms resistant to penicillins**

V09.1 **Infection with microorganisms resistant to cephalosporins and other B-lactam antibiotics**

V09.2 **Infection with microorganisms resistant to macrolides**

V09.3 **Infection with microorganisms resistant to tetracyclines**

V09.4 **Infection with microorganisms resistant to aminoglycosides**

V09.5 **Infection with microorganisms resistant to quinolones and fluoroquinolones**

> **V09.50** **Without mention of resistance to multiple quinolones and fluoroquinolones**

> **V09.51** **With resistance to multiple quinolones and fluoroquinolones**

V09.6 **Infection with microorganisms resistant to sulfonamides**

V09.7 **Infection with microorganisms resistant to other specified antimycobacterial agents**

> Excludes: *Amikacin (V09.4)*
> *Kanamycin (V09.4)*
> *Streptomycin [SM] (V09.4)*

> **V09.70** **Without mention of resistance to multiple antimycobacterial agents**

> **V09.71** **With resistance to multiple antimycobacterial agents**

V09.8 **Infection with microorganisms resistant to other specified drugs**

> **V09.80** **Without mention of resistance to multiple drugs**

> **V09.81** **With resistance to multiple drugs**

V09.9 **Infection with drug-resistant microorganisms, unspecified**
> Drug resistance NOS

> **V09.90** **Without mention of multiple drug resistance**

> **V09.91** **With multiple drug resistance**
> Multiple drug resistance NOS

455

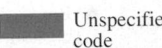

| | Add 4th or 5th digit | | Nonspecific code | | Unspecified code | | Manifestation code |

PERSONS WITH POTENTIAL HEALTH HAZARDS RELATED TO PERSONAL AND FAMILY HISTORY (V10-V19)

Excludes: obstetric patients where the possibility that the fetus might be affected is the reason for observation or management during pregnancy (655.0-655.9)

V10 **Personal history of malignant neoplasm**

V10.0 Gastrointestinal tract
History of conditions classifiable to 140-159

V10.00 Gastrointestinal tract, unspecified

V10.01 Tongue

V10.02 Other and unspecified oral cavity and pharynx

V10.03 Esophagus

V10.04 Stomach

V10.05 Large intestine

V10.06 Rectum, rectosigmoid junction, and anus

V10.07 Liver

V10.09 Other

V10.1 Trachea, bronchus, and lung
History of conditions classifiable to 162

V10.11 Bronchus and lung

V10.12 Trachea

V10.2 Other respiratory and intrathoracic organs
History of conditions classifiable to 160, 161, 163-165

V10.20 Respiratory organ, unspecified

V10.21 Larynx

V10.22 Nasal cavities, middle ear, and accessory sinuses

V10.29 Other

V10.3 Breast
History of conditions classifiable to 174 and 175

V10.4 Genital organs
History of conditions classifiable to 179-187

V10.40 Female genital organ, unspecified

V10.41 Cervix uteri

V10.42 Other parts of uterus

V10.43 Ovary

V10.44 Other female genital organs

V10.45 Male genital organ, unspecified

V10.46 Prostate

V10.47 Testis

V10.49 Other male genital organs

V10.5 Urinary organs
History of conditions classifiable to 188 and 189

V10.50 Urinary organ, unspecified

V10.51 Bladder

V10.52 Kidney

V10.59 Other

V10.6 Leukemia
Conditions classifiable to 204-208

Excludes: leukemia in remission (204-208)

V10.60 Leukemia, unspecified

V10.61 Lymphoid leukemia

V10.62 Myeloid leukemia

V10.63 Monocytic leukemia

V10.69 Other

V10.7 Other lymphatic and hematopoietic neoplasms

● Code new
to this edition

▲ Revision of
existing code

④ ⑤ Fourth or fifth
digit required

Conditions classifiable to 200-203

Excludes: *listed conditions in 200-203 in remission*

    V10.71 **Lymphosarcoma and reticulosarcoma**

    V10.72 **Hodgkin's disease**

    V10.79 **Other**

V10.8 **Personal history of malignant neoplasm of other sites**
History of conditions classifiable to 170-173, 190-195

    V10.81 **Bone**

    V10.82 **Malignant melanoma of skin**

    V10.83 **Other malignant neoplasm of skin**

    V10.84 **Eye**

    V10.85 **Brain**

    V10.86 **Other parts of nervous system**

Excludes: *peripheral, sympathetic, and parasympathetic nerves (V10.89)*

    V10.87 **Thyroid**

    V10.88 **Other endocrine glands and related structures**

    V10.89 **Other**

V10.9 **Unspecified personal history of malignant neoplasm**

V11 **Personal history of mental disorder**

V11.0 **Schizophrenia**

Excludes: *that in remission (295.0-295.9 with fifth-digit 5)*

V11.1 **Affective disorders**
Personal history of manic-depressive psychosis

Excludes: *that in remission (296.0-296.6 with fifth-digit*
    5, 6)

V11.2 **Neurosis**

V11.3 **Alcoholism**

V11.8 **Other mental disorders**

V11.9 **Unspecified mental disorder**

V12 **Personal history of certain other diseases**

V12.0 **Infectious and parasitic diseases**

    V12.00 **Unspecified infectious and parasitic disease**

    V12.01 **Tuberculosis**

    V12.02 **Poliomyelitis**

    V12.03 **Malaria**

    V12.09 **Other**

V12.1 **Nutritional deficiency**

V12.2 **Endocrine, metabolic, and immunity disorders**

Excludes: *history of allergy (V14.0-V14.9, V15.0)*

V12.3 **Diseases of blood and blood-forming organs**

V12.4 **Disorders of nervous system and sense organs**

V12.5 **Diseases of circulatory system**

Excludes: *old myocardial infarction (412)*
    postmyocardial infarction syndrome (411.0)

    V12.50 **Unspecified circulatory disease**

    V12.51 **Venous thrombosis and embolism**
        Pulmonary embolism

    V12.52 **Thrombophlebitis**

    V12.59 **Other**

V12.6 **Diseases of respiratory system**

V12.7 **Diseases of digestive system**

    V12.70 **Unspecified digestive disease**

457

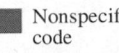 Add 4th or 5th digit

 Nonspecific code

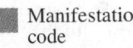 Unspecified code

Manifestation code

V12.71 Peptic ulcer disease

V12.72 Colonic polyps

V12.79 Other

V13 Personal history of other diseases

V13.0 Disorders of urinary system

V13.00 Unspecified urinary disorder

V13.01 Urinary calculi

V13.09 Other

V13.1 Trophoblastic disease

Excludes: *supervision during a current pregnancy (V23.1)*

V13.2 Other genital system and obstetric disorders

Excludes: *supervision during a current pregnancy of a woman with poor obstetric history
(V23.0-V23.9)
habitual aborter (646.3)
without current history (629.9)*

V13.3 Diseases of skin and subcutaneous tissue

V13.4 Arthritis

V13.5 Other musculoskeletal disorders

V13.6 Congenital malformations

V13.7 Perinatal problems

V13.8 Other specified diseases

V13.9 Unspecified disease

V14 Personal history of allergy to medicinal agents

V14.0 Penicillin

V14.1 Other antibiotic agent

V14.2 Sulfonamides

V14.3 Other anti-infective agent

V14.4 Anesthetic agent

V14.5 Narcotic agent

V14.6 Analgesic agent

V14.7 Serum or vaccine

V14.8 Other specified medicinal agents

V14.9 Unspecified medicinal agent

V15 Other personal history presenting hazards to health

V15.0 Allergy, other than to medicinal agents

V15.1 Surgery to heart and great vessels

Excludes: *replacement by transplant or other means (V42.1-V42.2, V43.2-V43.4)*

V15.2 Surgery to other major organs

Excludes: *replacement by transplant or other means (V42.0-V43.8)*

V15.3 Irradiation
Previous exposure to therapeutic or other ionizing radiation

V15.4 Psychological trauma

Excludes: *history of condition classifiable to 290-316 (V11.0-V11.9)*

● V15.41 History of physical abuse
Rape

● V15.42 History of emotional abuse
Neglect

● V15.49 Other

V15.5 Injury

V15.6 Poisoning

● Code new
to this edition
▲ Revision of
existing code
④ ⑤ Fourth or fifth
digit required

V15.7 Contraception

> *Excludes:* *current contraceptive management (V25.0-V25.4)*
> *presence of intrauterine contraceptive device as incidental finding (V45.5)*

V15.8 Other specified personal history presenting hazards to health

    V15.81 Noncompliance with medical treatment

    V15.82 History of tobacco use

> *Excludes:* *tobacco dependence (305.1)*

    V15.84 Exposure to asbestos

    V15.85 Exposure to potentially hazardous body fluids

    V15.86 Exposure to lead

    V15.89 Other

V15.9 Unspecified personal history presenting hazards to health

V16 Family history of malignant neoplasm

V16.0 Gastrointestinal tract
Family history of condition classifiable to 140-159

V16.1 Trachea, bronchus, and lung
Family history of condition classifiable to 162

V16.2 Other respiratory and intrathoracic organs
Family history of condition classifiable to 160-161, 163-165

V16.3 Breast
Family history of condition classifiable to 174

V16.4 Genital organs
Family history of condition classifiable to 179-187

V16.5 Urinary organs
Family history of condition classifiable to 189

V16.6 Leukemia
Family history of condition classifiable to 204-208

V16.7 Other lymphatic and hematopoietic neoplasms
Family history of condition classifiable to 200-203

V16.8 Other specified malignant neoplasm
Family history of other condition classifiable to 140-199

V16.9 Unspecified malignant neoplasm

V17 Family history of certain chronic disabling diseases

V17.0 Psychiatric condition

> *Excludes:* *family history of mental retardation (V18.4)*

V17.1 Stroke (cerebrovascular)

V17.2 Other neurological diseases
Epilepsy   Huntington's chorea

V17.3 Ischemic heart disease

V17.4 Other cardiovascular diseases

V17.5 Asthma

V17.6 Other chronic respiratory conditions

V17.7 Arthritis

V17.8 Other musculoskeletal diseases

V18 Family history of certain other specific conditions

V18.0 Diabetes mellitus

V18.1 Other endocrine and metabolic diseases

V18.2 Anemia

V18.3 Other blood disorders

V18.4 Mental retardation

V18.5 Digestive disorders

V18.6 Kidney diseases

V18.7 Other genitourinary diseases

V18.8 Infectious and parasitic diseases

	Add 4th or 5th digit		Nonspecific code		Unspecified code		Manifestation code

V19 Family history of other conditions

V19.0 Blindness or visual loss

V19.1 Other eye disorders

V19.2 Deafness or hearing loss

V19.3 Other ear disorders

V19.4 Skin conditions

V19.5 Congenital anomalies

V19.6 Allergic disorders

V19.7 Consanguinity

V19.8 Other condition

PERSONS ENCOUNTERING HEALTH SERVICES IN CIRCUMSTANCES RELATED TO REPRODUCTION AND DEVELOPMENT (V20-V29)

V20 Health supervision of infant or child

V20.0 Foundling

V20.1 Other healthy infant or child receiving care
Medical or nursing care supervision of healthy infant in cases of:
maternal illness, physical or psychiatric
socioeconomic adverse condition at home
too many children at home preventing or interfering with normal care

V20.2 Routine infant or child health check
Developmental testing of infant or child
Immunizations appropriate for age
Routine vision and hearing testing

Excludes: special screening for developmental handicaps (V79.3)
Use additional code(s) to identify:
Special screening examination(s) performed (V73.0-V82.9)

V21 Constitutional states in development

V21.0 Period of rapid growth in childhood

V21.1 Puberty

V21.2 Other adolescence

V21.8 Other specified constitutional states in development

V21.9 Unspecified constitutional state in development

V22 Normal pregnancy

Excludes: pregnancy examination or test, pregnancy unconfirmed (V72.4)

V22.0 Supervision of normal first pregnancy

V22.1 Supervision of other normal pregnancy

V22.2 Pregnant state, incidental
Pregnant state NOS

V23 Supervision of high-risk pregnancy

V23.0 Pregnancy with history of infertility

V23.1 Pregnancy with history of trophoblastic disease
Pregnancy with history of:
hydatidiform mole
vesicular mole

Excludes: that without current pregnancy (V13.1)

V23.2 Pregnancy with history of abortion
Pregnancy with history of conditions classifiable to 634-638

Excludes: habitual aborter:
care during pregnancy (646.3)
that without current pregnancy (629.9)

V23.3 Grand multiparity

Excludes: care in relation to labor and delivery (659.4)
that without current pregnancy (V61.5)

V23.4 Pregnancy with other poor obstetric history
Pregnancy with history of other conditions classifiable to 630-676

---

460   ● Code new   ▲ Revision of   ④ ⑤ Fourth or fifth
to this edition   existing code   digit required

V23.5 Pregnancy with other poor reproductive history
Pregnancy with history of stillbirth or neonatal death

V23.7 Insufficient prenatal care
History of little or no prenatal care

V23.8 Other high-risk pregnancy

V23.9 Unspecified high-risk pregnancy

V24 Postpartum care and examination

V24.0 Immediately after delivery
Care and observation in uncomplicated cases

V24.1 Lactating mother
Supervision of lactation

V24.2 Routine postpartum follow-up

V25 Encounter for contraceptive management

V25.0 General counseling and advice

V25.01 Prescription of oral contraceptives

V25.02 Initiation of other contraceptive measures
Fitting of diaphragm
Prescription of foams, creams, or other agents

V25.09 Other
Family planning advice

V25.1 Insertion of intrauterine contraceptive device

V25.2 Sterilization
Admission for interruption of fallopian tubes or vas deferens

V25.3 Menstrual extraction
Menstrual regulation

V25.4 Surveillance of previously prescribed contraceptive methods
Checking, reinsertion, or removal of contraceptive device
Repeat prescription for contraceptive method
Routine examination in connection with contraceptive maintenance

Excludes: *presence of intrauterine contraceptive device as incidental finding (V45.5)*

V25.40 Contraceptive surveillance, unspecified

V25.41 Contraceptive pill

V25.42 Intrauterine contraceptive device
Checking, reinsertion, or removal of intrauterine device

V25.43 Implantable subdermal contraceptive

V25.49 Other contraceptive method

V25.5 Insertion of implantable subdermal contraceptive

V25.8 Other specified contraceptive management
Postvasectomy sperm count

V25.9 Unspecified contraceptive management

V26 Procreative management

V26.0 Tuboplasty or vasoplasty after previous sterilization

V26.1 Artificial insemination

V26.2 Investigation and testing
Fallopian insufflation   Sperm counts

Excludes: *postvasectomy sperm count (V25.8)*

V26.3 Genetic counseling

V26.4 General counseling and advice

V26.8 Other specified procreative management

V26.9 Unspecified procreative management

V27 Outcome of delivery
Note: This category is intended for the coding of the outcome of delivery on the mother's record.

V27.0 Single liveborn

V27.1 Single stillborn

V27.2 Twins, both liveborn

V27.3 Twins, one liveborn and one stillborn

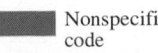 Add 4th or 5th digit   Nonspecific code   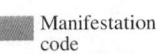 Unspecified code   Manifestation code

V27.4 **Twins, both stillborn**

V27.5 **Other multiple birth, all liveborn**

V27.6 **Other multiple birth, some liveborn**

V27.7 **Other multiple birth, all stillborn**

V27.9 **Unspecified outcome of delivery**
Single birth }
Multiple birth } outcome to infant unspecified

V28 **Antenatal screening**

> *Excludes:* *routine prenatal care (V22.0-V23.9)*

V28.0 **Screening for chromosomal anomalies by amniocentesis**

V28.1 **Screening for raised alpha-fetoprotein levels in amniotic fluid**

V28.2 **Other screening based on amniocentesis**

V28.3 **Screening for malformation using ultrasonics**

V28.4 **Screening for fetal growth retardation using ultrasonics**

V28.5 **Screening for isoimmunization**

V28.8 **Other specified antenatal screening**

V28.9 **Unspecified antenatal screening**

V29 **Observation and evaluation of newborns for suspected condition not found**

> Note: This category is to be used for newborns, within the neonatal period, (the first 28 days of life) who are suspected of having an abnormal condition resulting from exposure from the mother or the birth process, but without signs or symptoms, and, which after examination and observation, is found not to exist.

V29.0 **Observation for suspected infectious condition**

V29.1 **Observation for suspected neurological condition**

V29.2 **Observation for suspected respiratory condition**

V29.8 **Observation for other specified suspected condition**

V29.9 **Observation for unspecified suspected condition**

LIVEBORN INFANTS ACCORDING TO TYPE OF BIRTH (V30-V39)

> Note: These categories are intended for the coding of liveborn infants who are consuming health care [e.g., crib or bassinet occupancy].

The following fourth-digit subdivisions are for use with categories V30-V39:

.0 **Born in hospital**

.1 **Born before admission to hospital**

.2 **Born outside hospital and not hospitalized**

The following two fifth-digits are for use with the fourth-digit .0, Born in hospital:

0 **delivered without mention of cesarean delivery**

1 **delivered by cesarean delivery**

④ **V30** **Single liveborn**

④ **V31** **Twin, mate liveborn**

④ **V32** **Twin, mate stillborn**

④ **V33** **Twin, unspecified**

④ **V34** **Other multiple, mates all liveborn**

④ **V35** **Other multiple, mates all stillborn**

④ **V36** **Other multiple, mates live- and stillborn**

④ **V37** **Other multiple, unspecified**

④ **V39** **Unspecified**

PERSONS WITH A CONDITION INFLUENCING THEIR HEALTH STATUS (V40-V49)

> Note: These categories are intended for use when these conditions are recorded as "diagnoses" or "problems."

V40 **Mental and behavioral problems**

V40.0 **Problems with learning**

V40.1 **Problems with communication [including speech]**

V40.2 **Other mental problems**

● Code new
  to this edition   ▲ Revision of
                              existing code   ④ ⑤ Fourth or fifth
                                                        digit required

V40.3 Other behavioral problems

V40.9 Unspecified mental or behavioral problem

V41 Problems with special senses and other special functions

V41.0 Problems with sight

V41.1 Other eye problems

V41.2 Problems with hearing

V41.3 Other ear problems

V41.4 Problems with voice production

V41.5 Problems with smell and taste

V41.6 Problems with swallowing and mastication

V41.7 Problems with sexual function

> Excludes: *marital problems (V61.10)*
> *psychosexual disorders (302.0-302.9)*

V41.8 Other problems with special functions

V41.9 Unspecified problem with special functions

V42 Organ or tissue replaced by transplant

Includes: homologous or heterologous (animal) (human) transplant organ status

V42.0 Kidney

V42.1 Heart

V42.2 Heart valve

V42.3 Skin

V42.4 Bone

V42.5 Cornea

V42.6 Lung

V42.7 Liver

V42.8 Other specified organ or tissue

Intestine   Pancreas

V42.9 Unspecified organ or tissue

V43 Organ or tissue replaced by other means

Includes: replacement of organ by:
artificial device
mechanical device
prosthesis

> Excludes: *cardiac pacemaker in situ (V45.01)*
> *fitting and adjustment of prosthetic device (V52.0-V52.9)*
> *renal dialysis status (V45.1)*

V43.0 Eye globe

V43.1 Lens

Pseudophakos

V43.2 Heart

V43.3 Heart valve

V43.4 Blood vessel

V43.5 Bladder

V43.6 Joint

V43.60 Unspecified joint

V43.61 Shoulder

V43.62 Elbow

V43.63 Wrist

V43.64 Hip

V43.65 Knee

V43.66 Ankle

V43.69 Other

V43.7 Limb

V43.8 Other organ or tissue

	Add 4th or 5th digit		Nonspecific code		Unspecified code		Manifestation code

V43.81 **Larynx**

V43.82 **Breast**

`V43.89` **Other**

V44 **Artificial opening status**

> *Excludes:* artificial openings requiring attention or management (V55.0-V55.9)

V44.0 **Tracheostomy**

V44.1 **Gastrostomy**

V44.2 **Ileostomy**

V44.3 **Colostomy**

`V44.4` **Other artificial opening of gastrointestinal tract**

V44.5 **Cystostomy**

`V44.6` **Other artificial opening of urinary tract**
  Nephrostomy   Urethrostomy
  Ureterostomy

V44.7 **Artificial vagina**

`V44.8` **Other artificial opening status**

`V44.9` **Unspecified artificial opening status**

V45 **Other postsurgical states**

> *Excludes:* aftercare management (V51-V58.9)
>
> > malfunction or other complication—code to condition

V45.0 **Cardiac device in situ**

`V45.00` **Unspecified cardiac device**

V45.01 **Cardiac pacemaker**

V45.02 **Automatic implantable cardiac defibrillator**

`V45.09` **Other specified cardiac device**
  Carotid sinus pacemaker in situ

V45.1 **Renal dialysis status**
  Patient requiring intermittent renal dialysis
  Presence of arterial-venous shunt (for dialysis)

> *Excludes:* admission for dialysis treatment, or session (V56.0)

V45.2 **Presence of cerebrospinal fluid drainage device**
  Cerebral ventricle (communicating) shunt, valve, or device in situ

> *Excludes:* malfunction (996.2)

V45.3 **Intestinal bypass or anastomosis status**

V45.4 **Arthrodesis status**

V45.5 **Presence of contraceptive device**

> *Excludes:* checking, reinsertion, or removal of device (V25.42)
>
> > complication from device (996.32)
> > insertion of device (V25.1)

V45.51 **Intrauterine contraceptive device**

V45.52 **Subdermal contraceptive implant**

`V45.59` **Other**

V45.6 **States following surgery of eye and adnexa**
  Cataract extraction
  Filtering bleb   } state following eye surgery
  Surgical eyelid adhesion

> *Excludes:* aphakia (379.31)
>
> > artificial:
> > eye globe (V43.0)
> > lens (V43.1)

V45.8 **Other postsurgical status**

V45.81 **Aortocoronary bypass status**

V45.82 **Percutaneous transluminal coronary angioplasty status**

V45.83 **Breast implant removal status**

● Code new   ▲ Revision of   ④ ⑤ Fourth or fifth
    to this edition   existing code   digit required

V45.89 Other
Presence of neuropacemaker or other electronic device

Excludes: *artificial heart valve in situ (V43.3)*
vascular prosthesis in situ (V43.4)

V46 Other dependence on machines

V46.0 Aspirator

V46.1 Respirator
Iron lung

V46.8 Other enabling machines
Hyperbaric chamber
Possum [Patient-Operated-Selector-Mechanism]

Excludes: *cardiac pacemaker (V45.0)*
kidney dialysis machine (V45.1)

V46.9 Unspecified machine dependence

V47 Other problems with internal organs

V47.0 Deficiencies of internal organs

V47.1 Mechanical and motor problems with internal organs

V47.2 Other cardiorespiratory problems
Cardiovascular exercise intolerance with pain (with):
at rest
less than ordinary activity
ordinary activity

V47.3 Other digestive problems

V47.4 Other urinary problems

V47.5 Other genital problems

V47.9 Unspecified

V48 Problems with head, neck, and trunk

V48.0 Deficiencies of head

Excludes: *deficiencies of ears, eyelids, and nose (V48.8)*

V48.1 Deficiencies of neck and trunk

V48.2 Mechanical and motor problems with head

V48.3 Mechanical and motor problems with neck and trunk

V48.4 Sensory problem with head

V48.5 Sensory problem with neck and trunk

V48.6 Disfigurements of head

V48.7 Disfigurements of neck and trunk

V48.8 Other problems with head, neck, and trunk

V48.9 Unspecified problem with head, neck, or trunk

V49 Problems with limbs and other problems

V49.0 Deficiencies of limbs

V49.1 Mechanical problems with limbs

V49.2 Motor problems with limbs

V49.3 Sensory problems with limbs

V49.4 Disfigurements of limbs

V49.5 Other problems of limbs

V49.6 Upper limb amputation status

V49.60 Unspecified level

V49.61 Thumb

V49.62 Other finger(s)

V49.63 Hand

V49.64 Wrist
Disarticulation of wrist

V49.65 Below elbow

V49.66 Above elbow
Disarticulation of elbow

465

| | Add 4th or 5th digit | | Nonspecific code | | Unspecified code | | Manifestation code |

V49.67 **Shoulder**
Disarticulation of shoulder

V49.7 **Lower limb amputation status**

`V49.70` **Unspecified level**

V49.71 **Great toe**

`V49.72` **Other toe(s)**

V49.73 **Foot**

V49.74 **Ankle**
Disarticulation of ankle

V49.75 **Below knee**

V49.76 **Above knee**
Disarticulation of knee

V49.77 **Hip**
Disarticulation of hip

`V49.8` **Other specified problems influencing health status**

`V49.9` **Unspecified**

PERSONS ENCOUNTERING HEALTH SERVICES FOR SPECIFIC PROCEDURES AND AFTERCARE (V50-V59)

Note: Categories V51-V58 are intended for use to indicate a reason for care in patients who may have already been treated for some disease or injury not now present, but who are receiving care to consolidate the treatment, to deal with residual states, or to prevent recurrence.

Excludes: follow-up examination for medical surveillance following treatment (V67.0-V67.9)

`V50` **Elective surgery for purposes other than remedying health states**

V50.0 **Hair transplant**

`V50.1` **Other plastic surgery for unacceptable cosmetic appearance**
Breast augmentation or reduction
Face-lift

Excludes: plastic surgery following healed injury or operation (V51)

V50.2 **Routine or ritual circumcision**
Circumcision in the absence of significant medical indication

V50.3 **Ear piercing**

V50.4 **Prophylactic organ removal**

Excludes: organ donations (V59.0-V59.9)
therapeutic organ removal—code to condition

V50.41 **Breast**

V50.42 **Ovary**

`V50.49` **Other**

`V50.8` **Other**

`V50.9` **Unspecified**

V51 **Aftercare involving the use of plastic surgery**
Plastic surgery following healed injury or operation
Repair of scarred tissue

Excludes: cosmetic plastic surgery (V50.1)
plastic surgery as treatment for current injury—code to condition

`V52` **Fitting and adjustment of prosthetic device and implant**
Includes: removal of device

Excludes: malfunction or complication of prosthetic device (996.0-996.7)
status only, without need for care (V43.0-V43.8)

V52.0 **Artificial arm (complete) (partial)**

V52.1 **Artificial leg (complete) (partial)**

V52.2 **Artificial eye**

V52.3 **Dental prosthetic device**

V52.4 **Breast prosthesis and implant**

Excludes: admission for implant insertion (V50.1)

● Code new
to this edition
▲ Revision of
existing code
④ ⑤ Fourth or fifth
digit required

V52.8 Other specified prosthetic device

V52.9 Unspecified prosthetic device

V53 Fitting and adjustment of other device
   Includes: removal of device
                   replacement of device

   Excludes: *status only, without need for care (V45.0-V45.8)*

V53.0 Devices related to nervous system and special senses
   Auditory substitution device
   Visual substitution device
   Neuropacemaker (brain) (peripheral nerve) (spinal cord)

V53.1 Spectacles and contact lenses

V53.2 Hearing aid

V53.3 Cardiac device
   Reprogramming

   V53.31 Cardiac pacemaker

   Excludes: *mechanical complication of cardiac pacemaker (996.01)*

   V53.32 Automatic implantable cardiac defibrillator

   V53.39 Other cardiac device

V53.4 Orthodontic devices

V53.5 Other intestinal appliance

   Excludes: *colostomy (V55.3)*
                   ileostomy (V55.2)
                   other artificial opening of digestive tract (V55.4)

V53.6 Urinary devices
   Urinary catheter

   Excludes: *cystostomy (V55.5)*
                   nephrostomy (V55.6)
                   ureterostomy (V55.6)
                   urethrostomy (V55.6)

V53.7 Orthopedic devices
   Orthopedic: Orthopedic:
     brace   corset
     cast   shoes

   Excludes: *other orthopedic aftercare (V54)*

V53.8 Wheelchair

V53.9 Other and unspecified device

V54 Other orthopedic aftercare

   Excludes: *fitting and adjustment of orthopedic devices (V53.7)*
                   malfunction of internal orthopedic device (996.4)
                   other complication of nonmechanical nature (996.60-996.79)

V54.0 Aftercare involving removal of fracture plate or other internal fixation device
   Removal of: Removal of:
     pins   rods
     plates   screws

   Excludes: *removal of external fixation device (V54.8)*

V54.8 Other orthopedic aftercare
   Change, checking, or removal of:
     Kirschner wire
     plaster cast
     splint, external
     other external fixation or traction device

V54.9 Unspecified orthopedic aftercare

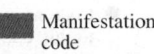

| Add 4th or 5th digit | Nonspecific code | Unspecified code | Manifestation code |

V55 **Attention to artificial openings**
    Includes: adjustment or repositioning of catheter
                closure
                passage of sounds or bougies
                reforming
                removal or replacement of catheter
                toilet or cleansing

    Excludes: *complications of external stoma (519.0, 569.60-569.69, 997.4, 997.5)*
            status only, without need for care (V44.0-V44.9)

    V55.0 Tracheostomy

    V55.1 Gastrostomy

    V55.2 Ileostomy

    V55.3 Colostomy

    V55.4 Other artificial opening of digestive tract

    V55.5 Cystostomy

    V55.6 Other artificial opening of urinary tract
        Nephrostomy   Urethrostomy
        Ureterostomy

    V55.7 Artificial vagina

    V55.8 Other specified artificial opening

    V55.9 Unspecified artificial opening

V56 **Encounter for dialysis and dialysis catheter care**
    Use additional code to identify the associated condition

    Excludes: *dialysis preparation—code to condition*

    V56.0 Extracorporeal dialysis
        Dialysis (renal) NOS

    Excludes: *dialysis status (V45.1)*

    V56.1 Fitting and adjustment of dialysis (extracorporeal) (peritoneal) catheter
        Removal or replacement of catheter
        Toilet or cleansing

    V56.8 Other dialysis
        Peritoneal dialysis

V57 **Care involving use of rehabilitation procedures**
    Use additional code to identify underlying condition

    V57.0 Breathing exercises

    V57.1 Other physical therapy
        Therapeutic and remedial exercises, except breathing

    V57.2 Occupational therapy and vocational rehabilitation

        V57.21 Encounter for occupational therapy

        V57.22 Encounter for vocational therapy

    V57.3 Speech therapy

    V57.4 Orthoptic training

    V57.8 Other specified rehabilitation procedure

        V57.81 Orthotic training
            Gait training in the use of artificial limbs

        V57.89 Other
            Multiple training or therapy

    V57.9 Unspecified rehabilitation procedure

V58 **Encounter for other and unspecified procedures and aftercare**

    Excludes: *convalescence and palliative care (V66)*

    V58.0 Radiotherapy
        Encounter or admission for radiotherapy

    Excludes: *encounter for radioactive implant—code to condition*
            radioactive iodine therapy—code to condition

● Code new   ▲ Revision of   ④ ⑤ Fourth or fifth
       to this edition   existing code   digit required

V58.1 Chemotherapy
Encounter or admission for chemotherapy

Excludes: *prophylactic chemotherapy against disease which has never been present (V03.0-V07.9)*

V58.2 Blood transfusion, without reported diagnosis

V58.3 Attention to surgical dressings and sutures
Change of dressings   Removal of sutures

V58.4 Other aftercare following surgery

Excludes: *attention to artificial openings (V55.0-V55.9)*
orthopedic aftercare (V54.0-V54.9)

V58.41 Encounter for planned postoperative wound closure

Excludes: *disruption of operative wound (998.3)*

V58.49 Other specified aftercare following surgery

V58.5 Orthodontics

Excludes: *fitting and adjustment of orthodontic device (V53.4)*

V58.6 Long-term (current) drug use

V58.61 Long-term (current) use of anticoagulants

V58.69 Long-term (current) use of other medications
High-risk medications

V58.8 Other specified procedures and aftercare

V58.81 Fitting and adjustment of vascular catheter
Removal or replacement of catheter
Toilet or cleansing

Excludes: *complication of renal dialysis catheter (996.73)*
complication of vascular catheter (996.74)
dialysis preparation -- code to condition
encounter for dialysis (V56.0-V56.8)
fitting and adjustment of dialysis catheter (V56.1)

V58.82 Fitting and adjustment of non-vascular catheter NEC
Removal or replacement of catheter
Toilet or cleansing

Excludes: *fitting and adjustment of peritoneal dialysis catheter (V56.1)*
fitting and adjustment of urinary catheter (V53.6)

V58.89 Other specified aftercare

V58.9 Unspecified aftercare

V59 Donors

Excludes: *examination of potential donor (V70.8)*
self-donation of organ or tissue -- code to condition

V59.0 Blood

V59.01 Whole blood

V59.02 Stem cells

V59.09 Other

V59.1 Skin

V59.2 Bone

V59.3 Bone marrow

V59.4 Kidney

V59.5 Cornea

V59.6 Liver

V59.8 Other specified organ or tissue

V59.9 Unspecified organ or tissue

	Add 4th or 5th digit		Nonspecific code		Unspecified code		Manifestation code

PERSONS ENCOUNTERING HEALTH SERVICES IN OTHER CIRCUMSTANCES (V60-V68)

V60 **Housing, household, and economic circumstances**

V60.0 Lack of housing

Hobos	Transients
Social migrants	Vagabonds
Tramps	

V60.1 Inadequate housing
Lack of heating
Restriction of space
Technical defects in home preventing adequate care

V60.2 Inadequate material resources
Economic problem   Poverty NOS

V60.3 Person living alone

V60.4 No other household member able to render care
Person requiring care (has) (is):
family member too handicapped, ill, or otherwise unsuited to render care
partner temporarily away from home
temporarily away from usual place of abode

Excludes: *holiday relief care (V60.5)*

V60.5 Holiday relief care
Provision of health care facilities to a person normally cared for at home, to enable
relatives to take a vacation

V60.6 Person living in residential institution
Boarding school resident

V60.8 **Other specified housing or economic circumstances**

V60.9 **Unspecified housing or economic circumstance**

V61 **Other family circumstances**
Includes: when these circumstances or fear of them, affecting the person directly involved or
others, are mentioned as the reason, justified or not, for seeking or receiving
medical advice or care

V61.0 Family disruption
Divorce   Estrangement

▲ **V61.1 Counseling for marital and partner problems**

Excludes: *problems related to:*
psychosexual disorders (302.0-302.9)
sexual function (V41.7)

● **V61.10** **Counseling for marital and partner problems, unspecified**
Marital conflict
Partner conflict

● **V61.11 Counseling for victim of spousal and partner abuse**

Excludes: *encounter for treatment of current injuries due to abuse (995.80-995.85)*

● **V61.12 Counseling for perpetrator of spousal and partner abuse**

V61.2 Parent-child problems

▲ **V61.20** **Counseling for parent-child problem, unspecified**
Concern about behavior of child
Parent-child conflict

▲ **V61.21 Counseling for victim of child abuse**
Child battering   Child neglect

Excludes: *current injuries due to abuse (995.50-995.59)*

● **V61.22 Counseling for perpetrator of parental child abuse**

Excludes: *counseling for non-parental abuser (V62.83)*

V61.29 **Other**
Problem concerning adopted or foster child

V61.3 Problems with aged parents or in-laws

V61.4 Health problems within family

V61.41 Alcoholism in family

● Code new   ▲ Revision of   ④ ⑤ Fourth or fifth
to this edition   existing code   digit required

V61.49 **Other**
Care of }
Presence of } sick or handicapped person in family or household

V61.5 **Multiparity**

V61.6 **Illegitimacy or illegitimate pregnancy**

V61.7 **Other unwanted pregnancy**

V61.8 **Other specified family circumstances**
Problems with family members NEC

V61.9 **Unspecified family circumstance**

V62 **Other psychosocial circumstances**
Includes: those circumstances or fear of them, affecting the person directly involved or others,
mentioned as the reason, justified or not, for seeking or receiving medical advice or
care

Excludes: *previous psychological trauma (V15.41-V15.49)*

V62.0 **Unemployment**

Excludes: *circumstances when main problem is economic inadequacy or poverty (V60.2)*

V62.1 **Adverse effects of work environment**

V62.2 **Other occupational circumstances or maladjustment**
Career choice problem
Dissatisfaction with employment

V62.3 **Educational circumstances**
Dissatisfaction with school environment
Educational handicap

V62.4 **Social maladjustment**
Cultural deprivation   Social:
Political, religious, or sex   isolation
discrimination   persecution

V62.5 **Legal circumstances**
Imprisonment   Litigation
Legal investigation   Prosecution

V62.6 **Refusal of treatment for reasons of religion or conscience**

V62.8 **Other psychological or physical stress, not elsewhere classified**

V62.81 **Interpersonal problems, not elsewhere classified**

V62.82 **Bereavement, uncomplicated**

Excludes: *bereavement as adjustment reaction (309.0)*

● **V62.83** **Counseling for perpetrator of physical/sexual abuse**

Excludes: *counseling for perpetrator of parental child abuse (V61.22)*
counseling for perpetrator of spousal and partner abuse (V61.12)

V62.89 **Other**
Life circumstance problems
Phase of life problems

V62.9 **Unspecified psychosocial circumstance**

V63 **Unavailability of other medical facilities for care**

V63.0 **Residence remote from hospital or other health care facility**

V63.1 **Medical services in home not available**

Excludes: *no other household member able to render care (V60.4)*

V63.2 **Person awaiting admission to adequate facility elsewhere**

V63.8 **Other specified reasons for unavailability of medical facilities**
Person on waiting list undergoing social agency investigation

V63.9 **Unspecified reason for unavailability of medical facilities**

V64 **Persons encountering health services for specific procedures, not carried out**

V64.0 **Vaccination not carried out because of contraindication**

V64.1 **Surgical or other procedure not carried out because of contraindication**

V64.2 **Surgical or other procedure not carried out because of patient's decision**

V64.3 **Procedure not carried out for other reasons**

V65 **Other persons seeking consultation without complaint or sickness**

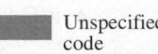 Add 4th or
5th digit

Nonspecific
code

Unspecified
code

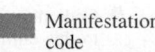 Manifestation
code

V65.0 Healthy person accompanying sick person
Boarder

V65.1 Person consulting on behalf of another person
Advice or treatment for nonattending third party

Excludes: concern (normal) about sick person in family (V61.41-V61.49)

V65.2 Person feigning illness
Malingerer   Peregrinating patient

V65.3 Dietary surveillance and counseling
Dietary surveillance and counseling (in):
NOS
colitis
diabetes mellitus
food allergies or intolerance
gastritis
hypercholesterolemia
hypoglycemia
obesity

V65.4 Other counseling, not elsewhere classified
Health:
advice
education
instruction

Excludes: counseling (for):
contraception (V25.40-V25.49)
genetic (V26.3)
on behalf of third party (V65.1)
procreative management (V26.4)

V65.40 Counseling NOS

V65.41 Exercise counseling

V65.42 Counseling on substance use and abuse

V65.43 Counseling on injury prevention

V65.44 Human immunodeficiency virus [HIV] counseling

V65.45 Counseling on other sexually transmitted diseases

V65.49 Other specified counseling

V65.5 Person with feared complaint in whom no diagnosis was made
Feared condition not demonstrated
Problem was normal state
"Worried well"

V65.8 Other reasons for seeking consultation

Excludes: specified symptoms

V65.9 Unspecified reason for consultation

▲ **V66 Convalescence and palliative care**

V66.0 Following surgery

V66.1 Following radiotherapy

V66.2 Following chemotherapy

V66.3 Following psychotherapy and other treatment for mental disorder

V66.4 Following treatment of fracture

V66.5 Following other treatment

V66.6 Following combined treatment

● **V66.7 Encounter for palliative care**
End-of-life care
Hospice care
Terminal care

Code first underlying disease

V66.9 Unspecified convalescence

V67 Follow-up examination
Includes: surveillance only following completed treatment

Excludes: surveillance of contraception (V25.40-V25.49)

V67.0 Following surgery

● Code new
to this edition
▲ Revision of
existing code
④ ⑤ Fourth or fifth
digit required

V67.1 Following radiotherapy

V67.2 Following chemotherapy
    Cancer chemotherapy follow-up

V67.3 Following psychotherapy and other treatment for mental disorder

▲ **V67.4 Following treatment of healed fracture**

    Excludes: *current (healing) fracture aftercare (V54.0-V54.9)*

V67.5 Following other treatment

    V67.51 Following completed treatment with high-risk medication, NEC

    Excludes: *long-term (current) drug use (V58.61-V58.69)*

    V67.59 Other

V67.6 Following combined treatment

V67.9 Unspecified follow-up examination

V68 Encounters for administrative purposes

V68.0 Issue of medical certificates
    Issue of medical certificate of: cause of death
                                      fitness
                                      incapacity

    Excludes: *encounter for general medical examination (V70.0-V70.9)*

V68.1 Issue of repeat prescriptions
    Issue of repeat prescription for: appliance
                                        glasses
                                      medications

    Excludes: *repeat prescription for contraceptives (V25.41-V25.49)*

V68.2 Request for expert evidence

V68.8 Other specified administrative purpose

    V68.81 Referral of patient without examination or treatment

    V68.89 Other

V68.9 Unspecified administrative purpose

V69 Problems related to lifestyle

V69.0 Lack of physical exercise

V69.1 Inappropriate diet and eating habits

    Excludes: *anorexia nervosa (307.1)*
             bulimia (783.6)
             malnutrition and other nutritional deficiencies (260-269.9)
             other and unspecified eating disorders (307.50-307.59)

V69.2 High-risk sexual behavior

V69.3 Gambling and betting

    Excludes: *pathological gambling (312.31)*

V69.8 Other problems related to lifestyle
    Self-damaging behavior

V69.9 Problem related to lifestyle, unspecified

PERSONS WITHOUT REPORTED DIAGNOSIS ENCOUNTERED DURING EXAMINATION AND INVESTIGATION OF INDIVIDUALS AND POPULATIONS (V70-V82)

    Note: Nonspecific abnormal findings disclosed at the time of these examinations are classifiable to categories 790-796.

V70 General medical examination

    Use additional code(s) to identify any special screening examination(s) performed (V73.0-V82.9)

V70.0 Routine general medical examination at a health care facility
    Health checkup

    Excludes: *health checkup of infant or child (V20.2)*

V70.1 General psychiatric examination, requested by the authority

V70.2 General psychiatric examination, other and unspecified

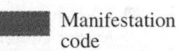

473

| | Add 4th or 5th digit | | Nonspecific code | | Unspecified code | | Manifestation code |

V70.3 Other medical examination for administrative purposes

General medical examination for:

admission to old age home	marriage
adoption	prison
camp	school admission
driving license	sports competition
immigration and naturalization	
insurance certification	

Excludes: *attendance for issue of medical certificates (V68.0)*
pre-employment screening (V70.5)

V70.4 Examination for medicolegal reasons

Blood-alcohol tests   Blood-drug tests

Excludes: *examination and observation following:*
accidents (V71.3, V71.4)
assault (V71.6)
rape (V71.5)

V70.5 Health examination of defined subpopulations

Armed forces personnel	Preschool children
Inhabitants of institutions	Prisoners
Occupational health	Prostitutes
examinations	Refugees
Pre-employment screening	School children
	Students

V70.6 Health examination in population surveys

Excludes: *special screening (V73.0-V82.9)*

V70.7 Examination for normal comparison or control in clinical research

V70.8 Other specified general medical examinations

Examination of potential donor of organ or tissue

V70.9 Unspecified general medical examination

V71 Observation and evaluation for suspected conditions not found

Note: This category is to be used when persons without a diagnosis are suspected of having an
abnormal condition, without signs or symptoms, which requires study, but after
examination and observation, is found not to exist. This category is also for use for
administrative and legal observation status.

V71.0 Observation for suspected mental condition

V71.01 Adult antisocial behavior

Dyssocial behavior or gang activity in adult without manifest psychiatric
disorder

V71.02 Childhood or adolescent antisocial behavior

Dyssocial behavior or gang activity in child or adolescent without manifest
psychiatric disorder

V71.09 Other suspected mental condition

V71.1 Observation for suspected malignant neoplasm

V71.2 Observation for suspected tuberculosis

V71.3 Observation following accident at work

V71.4 Observation following other accident

Examination of individual involved in motor vehicle traffic accident

V71.5 Observation following alleged rape or seduction

Examination of victim or culprit

V71.6 Observation following other inflicted injury

Examination of victim or culprit

V71.7 Observation for suspected cardiovascular disease

V71.8 Observation for other specified suspected conditions

V71.9 Observation for unspecified suspected condition

V72 Special investigations and examinations

Includes: routine examination of specific system

Excludes: *general medical examination (V70.0-V70.4)*
general screening examination of defined population groups (V70.5, V70.6, V70.7)
routine examination of infant or child (V20.2)

Use additional code(s) to identify any special screening examination(s) performed (V73.0-V82.9)

● Code new   ▲ Revision of   ④ ⑤ Fourth or fifth
          to this edition   existing code   digit required

V72.0 Examination of eyes and vision

V72.1 Examination of ears and hearing

V72.2 Dental examination

V72.3 Gynecological examination
Papanicolaou smear as part of general gynecological examination
Pelvic examination (annual) (periodic)

Excludes: *cervical Papanicolaou smear without general gynecological examination (V76.2)*
routine examination in contraceptive management (V25.40-V25.49)

V72.4 Pregnancy examination or test, pregnancy unconfirmed
Possible pregnancy, not (yet) confirmed

Excludes: *pregnancy examination with immediate confirmation (V22.0-V22.1)*

V72.5 Radiological examination, not elsewhere classified
Routine chest x-ray

Excludes: *examination for suspected tuberculosis (V71.2)*

V72.6 Laboratory examination

Excludes: *that for suspected disorder (V71.0-V71.9)*

V72.7 Diagnostic skin and sensitization tests
Allergy tests
Skin tests for hypersensitivity

Excludes: *diagnostic skin tests for bacterial diseases (V74.0-V74.9)*

V72.8 Other specified examinations

V72.81 Pre-operative cardiovascular examination

V72.82 Pre-operative respiratory examination

V72.83 Other specified pre-operative examination

V72.84 Pre-operative examination, unspecified

V72.85 Other specified examination

V72.9 Unspecified examination

V73 Special screening examination for viral and chlamydial diseases

V73.0 Poliomyelitis

V73.1 Smallpox

V73.2 Measles

V73.3 Rubella

V73.4 Yellow fever

V73.5 Other arthropod-borne viral diseases
Dengue fever   Viral encephalitis:
Hemorrhagic fever   mosquito-borne
         tick-borne

V73.6 Trachoma

V73.8 Other specified viral and chlamydial diseases

V73.88 Other specified chlamydial diseases

V73.89 Other specified viral diseases

V73.9 Unspecified viral and chlamydial disease

V73.98 Unspecified chlamydial disease

V73.99 Unspecified viral disease

V74 Special screening examination for bacterial and spirochetal diseases
Includes: diagnostic skin tests for these diseases

V74.0 Cholera

V74.1 Pulmonary tuberculosis

V74.2 Leprosy [Hansen's disease]

V74.3 Diphtheria

V74.4 Bacterial conjunctivitis

V74.5 Venereal disease

V74.6 Yaws

 Add 4th or 5th digit Nonspecific code Unspecified code 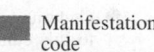 Manifestation code

V74.8 Other specified bacterial and spirochetal diseases
Brucellosis   Tetanus
Leptospirosis   Whooping cough
Plague

V74.9 Unspecified bacterial and spirochetal disease

V75 Special screening examination for other infectious diseases

V75.0 Rickettsial diseases

V75.1 Malaria

V75.2 Leishmaniasis

V75.3 Trypanosomiasis
Chagas' disease   Sleeping sickness

V75.4 Mycotic infections

V75.5 Schistosomiasis

V75.6 Filariasis

V75.7 Intestinal helminthiasis

V75.8 Other specified parasitic infections

V75.9 Unspecified infectious disease

V76 Special screening for malignant neoplasms

V76.0 Respiratory organs

V76.1 Breast

V76.2 Cervix
Routine cervical Papanicolaou smear

Excludes: *that as part of a general gynecological examination (V72.3)*

V76.3 Bladder

V76.4 Other sites

    V76.41 Rectum

    V76.42 Oral cavity

    V76.43 Skin

    V76.49 Other

V76.8 Other neoplasm

V76.9 Unspecified

V77 Special screening for endocrine, nutritional, metabolic, and immunity disorders

V77.0 Thyroid disorders

V77.1 Diabetes mellitus

V77.2 Malnutrition

V77.3 Phenylketonuria [PKU]

V77.4 Galactosemia

V77.5 Gout

V77.6 Cystic fibrosis
Screening for mucoviscidosis

V77.7 Other inborn errors of metabolism

V77.8 Obesity

V77.9 Other and unspecified endocrine, nutritional, metabolic, and immunity disorders

V78 Special screening for disorders of blood and blood-forming organs

V78.0 Iron deficiency anemia

V78.1 Other and unspecified deficiency anemia

V78.2 Sickle-cell disease or trait

V78.3 Other hemoglobinopathies

V78.8 Other disorders of blood and blood-forming organs

V78.9 Unspecified disorder of blood and blood-forming organs

V79 Special screening for mental disorders and developmental handicaps

V79.0 Depression

V79.1 Alcoholism

● Code new   ▲ Revision of   ④ ⑤ Fourth or fifth
to this edition   existing code   digit required

V79.2 **Mental retardation**

V79.3 **Developmental handicaps in early childhood**

V79.8 **Other specified mental disorders and developmental handicaps**

V79.9 **Unspecified mental disorder and developmental handicap**

V80 **Special screening for neurological, eye, and ear diseases**

V80.0 **Neurological conditions**

V80.1 **Glaucoma**

V80.2 **Other eye conditions**
Screening for:
cataract
congenital anomaly of eye
senile macular lesions

Excludes: *general vision examination (V72.0)*

V80.3 **Ear diseases**

Excludes: *general hearing examination (V72.1)*

V81 **Special screening for cardiovascular, respiratory, and genitourinary diseases**

V81.0 **Ischemic heart disease**

V81.1 **Hypertension**

V81.2 **Other and unspecified cardiovascular conditions**

V81.3 **Chronic bronchitis and emphysema**

V81.4 **Other and unspecified respiratory conditions**

Excludes: *screening for:*
lung neoplasm (V76.0)
pulmonary tuberculosis (V74.1)

V81.5 **Nephropathy**
Screening for asymptomatic bacteriuria

V81.6 **Other and unspecified genitourinary conditions**

V82 **Special screening for other conditions**

V82.0 **Skin conditions**

V82.1 **Rheumatoid arthritis**

V82.2 **Other rheumatic disorders**

V82.3 **Congenital dislocation of hip**

V82.4 **Postnatal screening for chromosomal anomalies**

Excludes: *antenatal screening by amniocentesis (V28.0)*

V82.5 **Chemical poisoning and other contamination**
Screening for:
heavy metal poisoning
ingestion of radioactive substance
poisoning from contaminated water supply
radiation exposure

V82.6 **Multiphasic screening**

V82.8 **Other specified conditions**

V82.9 **Unspecified condition**

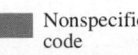 Add 4th or
5th digit

 Nonspecific
code

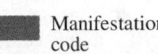 Unspecified
code

Manifestation
code

● Code new
to this edition

▲ Revision of
existing code

④ ⑤ Fourth or fifth
digit required

SUPPLEMENTARY CLASSIFICATION OF EXTERNAL CAUSES OF INJURY AND POISONING (E800-E999)

This section is provided to permit the classification of environmental events, circumstances, and conditions as the cause of injury, poisoning, and other adverse effects. Where a code from this section is applicable, it is intended that it shall be used in addition to a code from one of the main chapters of *ICD-9-CM*, indicating the nature of the condition. Certain other conditions which may be stated to be due to external causes are classified in Chapters 1 to 16 of *ICD-9-CM*. For these, the "E" code classification should be used for more detailed analysis.

Machinery accidents [other than those connected with transport] are classifiable to category E919, in which the fourth-digit allows a broad classification of the type of machinery involved. If a more detailed classification of type of machinery is required, it is suggested that the "Classification of Industrial Accidents according to Agency," prepared by the International Labor Office, be used in addition. This is reproduced on page 571, for optional use.

Categories for "late effects" of accidents and other external causes are to be found at E929, E959, E969, E977, E989, and E999.

Definitions and examples related to transport accidents

(a) A **transport accident** (E800-E848) is any accident involving a device designed primarily for, or being used at the time primarily for, conveying persons or goods from one place to another.

Includes: accidents involving:
aircraft and spacecraft (E840-E845)
watercraft (E830-E838)
motor vehicle (E810-E825)
railway (E800-E807)
other road vehicles (E826-E829)

In classifying accidents which involve more than one kind of transport, the above order of precedence of transport accidents should be used.

Accidents involving agriculture and construction machines, such as tractors, cranes, and bulldozers, are regarded as transport accidents only when these vehicles are under their own power on a highway [otherwise the vehicles are regarded as machinery]. Vehicles which can travel on land or water, such as hovercraft and other amphibious vehicles, are regarded as watercraft when on the water, as motor vehicles when on the highway, and as off-road motor vehicles when on land, but off the highway.

Excludes: *accidents:*
in sports which involve the use of transport but where the transport vehicle itself was not involved in the accident
involving vehicles which are part of industrial equipment used entirely on industrial premises
occurring during transportation but unrelated to the hazards associated with the means of transportation [e.g., injuries received in a fight on board ship; transport vehicle involved in a cataclysm such as an earthquake]
to persons engaged in the maintenance or repair of transport equipment or vehicle not in motion, unless injured by another vehicle in motion

(b) A **railway accident** is a transport accident involving a railway train or other railway vehicle operated on rails, whether in motion or not.

Excludes: *accidents:*
in repair shops
in roundhouse or on turntable
on railway premises but not involving a train or other railway vehicle

(c) A **railway train** or **railway vehicle** is any device with or without cars coupled to it, designed for traffic on a railway.

Includes: interurban:
electric car ⎫ (operated chiefly on its own right-of-way, not open to
streetcar ⎭ other traffic)

railway train, any power [diesel] [electric] [steam]
funicular
monorail or two-rail
subterranean or elevated
other vehicle designed to run on a railway track

Excludes: *interurban electric cars [streetcars] specified to be operating on a right-of-way that forms part of the public street or highway [definition (n)]*

(d) A **railway** or **railroad** is a right-of-way designed for traffic on rails, which is used by carriages or wagons transporting passengers or freight, and by other rolling stock, and which is not open to other public vehicular traffic.

E CODES

479

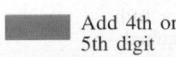 Add 4th or 5th digit

 Nonspecific code

 Unspecified code

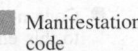 Manifestation code

(e) A **motor vehicle accident** is a transport accident involving a motor vehicle. It is defined as a motor vehicle traffic accident or as a motor vehicle nontraffic accident according to whether the accident occurs on a public highway or elsewhere.

Excludes: *injury or damage due to cataclysm*

injury or damage while a motor vehicle, not under its own power, is being loaded on, or unloaded from, another conveyance

(f) A **motor vehicle traffic accident** is any motor vehicle accident occurring on a public highway [i.e., originating, terminating, or involving a vehicle partially on the highway]. A motor vehicle accident is assumed to have occurred on the highway unless another place is specified, except in the case of accidents involving only off-road motor vehicles which are classified as nontraffic accidents unless the contrary is stated.

(g) A **motor vehicle nontraffic accident** is any motor vehicle accident which occurs entirely in any place other than a public highway.

(h) A **public highway [trafficway]** or **street** is the entire width between property lines [or other boundary lines] of every way or place, of which any part is open to the use of the public for purposes of vehicular traffic as a matter of right or custom. A roadway is that part of the public highway designed, improved, and ordinarily used, for vehicular travel.

Includes: approaches (public) to:
docks
public building
station

Excludes: *driveway (private)*
parking lot
ramp
roads in:
airfield
farm
industrial premises
mine
private grounds
quarry

(i) A **motor vehicle** is any mechanically or electrically powered device, not operated on rails, upon which any person or property may be transported or drawn upon a highway. Any object such as a trailer, coaster, sled, or wagon being towed by a motor vehicle is considered a part of the motor vehicle.

Includes: automobile [any type]
bus
construction machinery, farm and industrial machinery, steam roller, tractor, army tank, highway grader, or similar vehicle on wheels or treads, while in transport under own power
fire engine (motorized)
motorcycle
motorized bicycle [moped] or scooter
trolley bus not operating on rails
truck
van

Excludes: *devices used solely to move persons or materials within the confines of a building and its premises, such as:*
building elevator
coal car in mine
electric baggage or mail truck used solely within a railroad station
electric truck used solely within an industrial plant
moving overhead crane

(j) A **motorcycle** is a two-wheeled motor vehicle having one or two riding saddles and sometimes having a third wheel for the support of a sidecar. The sidecar is considered part of the motorcycle.

Includes: motorized:
bicycle [moped]
scooter
tricycle

(k) An **off-road motor vehicle** is a motor vehicle of special design, to enable it to negotiate rough or soft terrain or snow. Examples of special design are high construction, special wheels and tires, driven by treads, or support on a cushion of air.

Includes: all terrain vehicle [ATV]
army tank
hovercraft, on land or swamp
snowmobile

● Code new
to this edition   ▲ Revision of
existing code   ④ ⑤ Fourth or fifth
digit required

(l) A **driver** of a motor vehicle is the occupant of the motor vehicle operating it or intending to operate it. A **motorcyclist** is the driver of a motorcycle. Other authorized occupants of a motor vehicle are **passengers**.

(m) An **other road vehicle** is any device, except a motor vehicle, in, on, or by which any person or property may be transported on a highway.

    Includes: animal carrying a person or goods
                animal-drawn vehicle
                animal harnessed to conveyance
                bicycle [pedal cycle]
                streetcar
                tricycle (pedal)

> **Excludes:** *pedestrian conveyance [definition (q)]*

(n) A **streetcar** is a device designed and used primarily for transporting persons within a municipality, running on rails, usually subject to normal traffic control signals, and operated principally on a right-of-way that forms part of the traffic way. A trailer being towed by a streetcar is considered a part of the streetcar.

    Includes: interurban or intraurban electric or streetcar, when specified to be operating on a street or public highway
                tram (car)
                trolley (car)

(o) A **pedal cycle** is any road transport vehicle operated solely by pedals.

    Includes: bicycle
                pedal cycle
                tricycle

> **Excludes:** *motorized bicycle [definition (i)]*

(p) A **pedal cyclist** is any person riding on a pedal cycle or in a sidecar attached to such a vehicle.

(q) A **pedestrian conveyance** is any human powered device by which a pedestrian may move other than by walking or by which a walking person may move another pedestrian.

    Includes:

baby carriage	roller skates
coaster wagon	scooter
ice skates	skateboard
perambulator	skis
pushcart	sled
pushchair	wheelchair

(r) A **pedestrian** is any person involved in an accident who was not at the time of the accident riding in or on a motor vehicle, railroad train, streetcar, animal-drawn or other vehicle, or on a bicycle or animal.

    Includes: person:
                  changing tire of vehicle
                  in or operating a pedestrian conveyance
                  making adjustment to motor of vehicle
                  on foot

(s) A **watercraft** is any device for transporting passengers or goods on the water.

(t) A **small boat** is any watercraft propelled by paddle, oars, or small motor, with a passenger capacity of less than ten.

    Includes:

boat NOS	rowboat
canoe	rowing shell
coble	scull
dinghy	skiff
punt	small motorboat
raft	

> **Excludes:** *barge*
> *lifeboat (used after abandoning ship)*
> *raft (anchored) being used as diving platform*
> *yacht*

(u) An **aircraft** is any device for transporting passengers or goods in the air.

    Includes: airplane [any type]
                balloon
                bomber
                dirigible
                glider (hang)
                military aircraft
                parachute

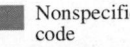 Add 4th or 5th digit   Nonspecific code   Unspecified code   Manifestation code

(v) A **commercial transport aircraft** is any device for collective passenger or freight transportation by air, whether run on commercial lines for profit or by government authorities, with the exception of military craft.

RAILWAY ACCIDENTS (E800-E807)

Note: For definitions of railway accident and related terms see definitions (a) to (d).

Excludes: *accidents involving railway train and:*
> *aircraft (E840.0-E845.9)*
> *motor vehicle (E810.0-E825.9)*
> *watercraft (E830.0-E838.9)*

The following fourth-digit subdivisions are for use with categories E800-E807 to identify the injured person:

.0 Railway employee
> Any person who by virtue of his employment in connection with a railway, whether by the railway company or not, is at increased risk of involvement in a railway accident, such as:
> catering staff of train
> driver
> guard
> porter
> postal staff on train
> railway fireman
> shunter
> sleeping car attendant

.1 Passenger on railway
> Any authorized person traveling on a train, except a railway employee.

Excludes: *intending passenger waiting at station (.8)*
> *unauthorized rider on railway vehicle (.8)*

.2 Pedestrian
> See definition (r)

.3 Pedal cyclist
> See definition (p)

.8 Other specified person
> Intending passenger or bystander waiting at station
> Unauthorized rider on railway vehicle

.9 Unspecified person

④ **E800 Railway accident involving collision with rolling stock**
> Includes: collision between railway trains or railway vehicles, any kind
> collision NOS on railway
> derailment with antecedent collision with rolling stock or NOS

④ **E801 Railway accident involving collision with other object**
> Includes: collision of railway train with:
> buffers
> fallen tree on railway
> gates
> platform
> rock on railway
> streetcar
> other nonmotor vehicle
> other object

Excludes: *collision with:*
> *aircraft (E840.0-E842.9)*
> *motor vehicle (E810.0-E810.9, E820.0-E822.9)*

④ **E802 Railway accident involving derailment without antecedent collision**

④ **E803 Railway accident involving explosion, fire, or burning**

Excludes: *explosion or fire, with antecedent derailment (E802.0-E802.9)*
> *explosion or fire, with mention of antecedent collision (E800.0-E801.9)*

④ **E804 Fall in, on, or from railway train**
> Includes: fall while alighting from or boarding railway train

Excludes: *fall related to collision, derailment, or explosion of railway train (E800.0-E803.9)*

● Code new to this edition   ▲ Revision of existing code   ④ ⑤ Fourth or fifth digit required

④ **E805 Hit by rolling stock**
    Includes:

        crushed
        injured
        killed   } by railway train or part
        knocked down
        run over

    Excludes: *pedestrian hit by object set in motion by railway train (E806.0-E806.9)*

④ **E806 Other specified railway accident**
    Includes: hit by object falling in railway train
               injured by door or window on railway train
               nonmotor road vehicle or pedestrian hit by object set in motion by railway train
               railway train hit by falling:
                   earth NOS
                   rock
                   tree
                   other object

    Excludes: *railway accident due to cataclysm (E908-E909)*

④ **E807 Railway accident of unspecified nature**
    Includes:

        found dead   } on railway right-of-way NOS
        injured
        railway accident NOS

MOTOR VEHICLE TRAFFIC ACCIDENTS (E810-E819)

    Note: For definitions of motor vehicle traffic accident, and related terms, see definitions (e) to (k).

    Excludes: *accidents involving motor vehicle and aircraft (E840.0-E845.9)*

    The following fourth-digit subdivisions are for use with categories E810-E819 to identify the injured person:

    .0 Driver of motor vehicle other than motorcycle
        See definition (l)

    .1 Passenger in motor vehicle other than motorcycle
        See definition (l)

    .2 Motorcyclist
        See definition (l)

    .3 Passenger on motorcycle
        See definition (l)

    .4 Occupant of streetcar

    .5 Rider of animal; occupant of animal-drawn vehicle

    .6 Pedal cyclist
        See definition (p)

    .7 Pedestrian
        See definition (r)

    .8 Other specified person
        Occupant of vehicle other than above
        Person in railway train involved in accident
        Unauthorized rider of motor vehicle

    .9 Unspecified person

④ **E810 Motor vehicle traffic accident involving collision with train**

    Excludes: *motor vehicle collision with object set in motion by railway train (E815.0-E815.9)*
              railway train hit by object set in motion by motor vehicle (E818.0-E818.9)

④ **E811 Motor vehicle traffic accident involving re-entrant collision with another motor vehicle**
    Includes: collision between motor vehicle which accidentally leaves the roadway then re-enters
               the same roadway, or the opposite roadway on a divided highway, and another
               motor vehicle

    Excludes: *collision on the same roadway when none of the motor vehicles involved have left*
               and re-entered the roadway (E812.0-E812.9)

④ **E812 Other motor vehicle traffic accident involving collision with motor vehicle**
    Includes: collision with another motor vehicle parked, stopped, stalled, disabled, or abandoned
               on the highway
               motor vehicle collision NOS

continued

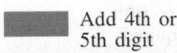 Add 4th or 5th digit   Nonspecific code   Unspecified code   Manifestation code

> *Excludes:* *collision with object set in motion by another motor vehicle (E815.0-E815.9)*
> *re-entrant collision with another motor vehicle (E811.0-E811.9)*

④ **E813** **Motor vehicle traffic accident involving collision with other vehicle**
  Includes: collision between motor vehicle, any kind, and:
      other road (nonmotor transport) vehicle, such as:
        animal carrying a person
        animal-drawn vehicle
        pedal cycle
      streetcar

> *Excludes:* *collision with:*
> *object set in motion by nonmotor road vehicle (E815.0-E815.9)*
> *pedestrian (E814.0-E814.9)*
> *nonmotor road vehicle hit by object set in motion by motor vehicle*
> *(E818.0-E818.9)*

④ **E814** **Motor vehicle traffic accident involving collision with pedestrian**
  Includes: collision between motor vehicle, any kind, and pedestrian
      pedestrian dragged, hit, or run over by motor vehicle, any kind

> *Excludes:* *pedestrian hit by object set in motion by motor vehicle (E818.0-E818.9)*

④ **E815** **Other motor vehicle traffic accident involving collision on the highway**
  Includes: collision (due to loss of control) (on highway) between motor vehicle, any kind, and:
      abutment (bridge) (overpass)
      animal (herded) (unattended)
      fallen stone, traffic sign, tree, utility pole
      guard rail or boundary fence
      interhighway divider
      landslide (not moving)
      object set in motion by railway train or road vehicle (motor) (nonmotor)
      object thrown in front of motor vehicle
      safety island
      temporary traffic sign or marker
      wall of cut made for road
      other object, fixed, movable, or moving

> *Excludes:* *collision with:*
> *any object off the highway (resulting from loss of control) (E816.0-E816.9)*
> *any object which normally would have been off the highway and is not stated to*
> *have been on it (E816.0-E816.9)*
> *motor vehicle parked, stopped, stalled, disabled, or abandoned on highway*
> *(E812.0-E812.9)*
> *moving landslide (E909)*
> *motor vehicle hit by object:*
> *set in motion by railway train or road vehicle (motor) (nonmotor)*
> *(E818.0-E818.9)*
> *thrown into or on vehicle (E818.0-E818.9)*

④ **E816** **Motor vehicle traffic accident due to loss of control, without collision on the highway**
  Includes: motor vehicle:
      failing to make curve ⎫
      going out of control (due to): ⎪
        blowout ⎪   and:
        burst tire ⎬   colliding with object off the
        driver falling asleep ⎪   highway
        driver inattention ⎪   overturning
        excessive speed ⎪   stopping abruptly off the highway
        failure of mechanical part ⎭

> *Excludes:* *collision on highway following loss of control (E810.0-E815.9)*
> *loss of control of motor vehicle following collision on the highway*
> *(E810.0-E815.9)*

④ **E817** **Noncollision motor vehicle traffic accident while boarding or alighting**
  Includes:
      fall down stairs of motor bus ⎫
      fall from car in street ⎪
      injured by moving part of the vehicle ⎬ while boarding or alighting
      trapped by door of motor bus ⎭

● Code new
    to this edition   ▲ Revision of
                             existing code   ④ ⑤ Fourth or fifth
                                                      digit required

④ **E818** **Other noncollision motor vehicle traffic accident**

Includes:

accidental poisoning from exhaust gas generated by ⎫
breakage of any part of
explosion of any part of
fall, jump, or being accidentally pushed from
fire starting in
hit by object thrown into or on ⎬ motor vehicle while in
injured by being thrown against some part of, motion
   or object in
injury from moving part of
object falling in or on
object thrown on ⎭
collision of railway train or road vehicle except motor vehicle, with object set in
   motion by motor vehicle
motor vehicle hit by object set in motion by railway train or road vehicle (motor)
   (nonmotor)
pedestrian, railway train, or road vehicle (motor) (nonmotor) hit by object set in
   motion by motor vehicle

Excludes: *collision between motor vehicle and:*

object set in motion by railway train or road vehicle (motor) (nonmotor)
(E815.0-E815.9)
object thrown towards the motor vehicle (E815.0-E815.9)
person overcome by carbon monoxide generated by stationary motor vehicle off the
roadway with motor running (E868.2)

④ **E819** **Motor vehicle traffic accident of unspecified nature**

Includes: motor vehicle traffic accident NOS
traffic accident NOS

MOTOR VEHICLE NONTRAFFIC ACCIDENTS (E820-E825)

Note: For definitions of motor vehicle nontraffic accident and related terms see definitions (a) to
   (k).

Includes: accidents involving motor vehicles being used in recreational or sporting activities off
    the highway
collision and noncollision motor vehicle accidents occurring entirely off the highway

Excludes: *accidents involving motor vehicle and:*

aircraft (E840.0-E845.9)
watercraft (E830.0-E838.9)
accidents, not on the public highway, involving agricultural and construction
machinery but not involving another motor vehicle (E919.0, E919.2, E919.7)

The following fourth-digit subdivisions are for use with categories E820-E825 to identify the
   injured person:

.0 Driver of motor vehicle other than motorcycle
See definition (l)

.1 Passenger in motor vehicle other than motorcycle
See definition (l)

.2 Motorcyclist
See definition (l)

.3 Passenger on motorcycle
See definition (l)

.4 Occupant of streetcar

.5 Rider of animal; occupant of animal-drawn vehicle

.6 Pedal cyclist
See definition (p)

.7 Pedestrian
See definition (r)

.8 Other specified person
Occupant of vehicle other than above
Person on railway train involved in accident
Unauthorized rider of motor vehicle

.9 Unspecified person

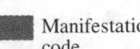

Add 4th or   Nonspecific   Unspecified   Manifestation
5th digit   code   code   code

④ **E820**   **Nontraffic accident involving motor-driven snow vehicle**
      Includes:

breakage of part of fall from hit by overturning of run over or dragged by	motor-driven snow vehicle (not on public highway)

        collision of motor-driven snow vehicle with:
          animal (being ridden) (-drawn vehicle)
          another off-road motor vehicle
          other motor vehicle, not on public highway
          railway train
          other object, fixed or movable
        injury caused by rough landing of motor-driven snow vehicle (after leaving
          ground on rough terrain)

      Excludes: *accident on the public highway involving motor driven snow vehicle*
         (E810.0-E819.9)

④ **E821**   **Nontraffic accident involving other off-road motor vehicle**
      Includes:

breakage of part of fall from hit by overturning of run over or dragged by thrown against some part of or object in	off-road motor vehicle, except snow vehicle (not on public highway)

        collision with:
          animal (being ridden) (-drawn vehicle)
          another off-road motor vehicle, except snow vehicle
          other motor vehicle, not on public highway
          other object, fixed or movable

      Excludes: *accident on public highway involving off-road motor vehicle (E810.0-E819.9)*
         collision between motor driven snow vehicle and other off-road motor vehicle
          (E820.0-E820.9)
         hovercraft accident on water (E830.0-E838.9)

④ **E822**   **Other motor vehicle nontraffic accident involving collision with moving object**
      Includes: collision, not on public highway, between motor vehicle, except off-road motor
          vehicle and:
        animal
        nonmotor vehicle
        other motor vehicle, except off-road motor vehicle
        pedestrian
        railway train
        other moving object

      Excludes: *collision with:*
         motor-driven snow vehicle (E820.0-E820.9)
         other off-road motor vehicle (E821.0-E821.9)

④ **E823**   **Other motor vehicle nontraffic accident involving collision with stationary object**
      Includes: collision, not on public highway, between motor vehicle, except off-road motor
          vehicle, and any object, fixed or movable, but not in motion

④ **E824**   **Other motor vehicle nontraffic accident while boarding and alighting**
      Includes:

fall injury from moving part of motor vehicle trapped by door of motor vehicle	while boarding or alighting from motor vehicle, except off-road motor vehicle, not on public highway

● Code new   ▲ Revision of   ④ ⑤ Fourth or fifth
  to this edition   existing code   digit required

④ **E825** **Other motor vehicle nontraffic accident of other and unspecified nature**
Includes:

accidental poisoning from carbon monoxide
  generated by
breakage of any part of
explosion of any part of
fall, jump, or being accidentally pushed from
fire starting in
hit by object thrown into, towards, or on
injured by being thrown against some part of,
  or object in
injury from moving part of
object falling in or on
motor vehicle nontraffic accident NOS
} motor vehicle while in motion, not on public highway

Excludes: *fall from or in stationary motor vehicle (E884.9, E885)*
overcome by carbon monoxide or exhaust gas generated by stationary motor
  vehicle off the roadway with motor running (E868.2)
struck by falling object from or in stationary motor vehicle (E916)

OTHER ROAD VEHICLE ACCIDENTS (E826-E829)

Note: Other road vehicle accidents are transport accidents involving road vehicles other than motor
  vehicles. For definitions of other road vehicle and related terms see definitions (m) to (o).
Includes: accidents involving other road vehicles being used in recreational or sporting activities

Excludes: *collision of other road vehicle [any] with:*
aircraft (E840.0-E845.9)
motor vehicle (E813.0-E813.9, E820.0-E822.9)
railway train (E801.0-E801.9)

The following fourth-digit subdivisions are for use with categories E826-E829 to identify the
  injured person:

.0 Pedestrian
See definition (r)

.1 Pedal cyclist
See definition (p)

.2 Rider of animal

.3 Occupant of animal-drawn vehicle

.4 Occupant of streetcar

.8 Other specified person

.9 Unspecified person

④ **E826** **Pedal cycle accident**
[0-9]
Includes: breakage of any part of pedal cycle
collision between pedal cycle and:
  animal (being ridden) (herded) (unattended)
  another pedal cycle
  nonmotor road vehicle, any
  pedestrian
  other object, fixed, movable, or moving, not set in motion by motor vehicle,
    railway train, or aircraft
entanglement in wheel of pedal cycle
fall from pedal cycle
hit by object falling or thrown on the pedal cycle
pedal cycle accident NOS
pedal cycle overturned

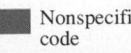 Add 4th or
5th digit

 Nonspecific
code

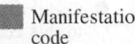 Unspecified
code

Manifestation
code

④ **E827** **Animal-drawn vehicle accident**
[0,2-4,8,9]
    Includes   breakage of any part of vehicle
            collision between animal-drawn vehicle and:
              animal (being ridden) (herded) (unattended)
              nonmotor road vehicle, except pedal cycle
              pedestrian, pedestrian conveyance, or pedestrian vehicle
              other object, fixed, movable, or moving, not set in motion by motor vehicle,
                 railway train, or aircraft

fall from
knocked down by
overturning of   } animal-drawn vehicle
run over by
thrown from

      Excludes: *collision of animal-drawn vehicle with pedal cycle (E826.0-E826.9)*

④ **E828** **Accident involving animal being ridden**
[0,2,4,8,9]
    Includes: collision between animal being ridden and:
              another animal
              nonmotor road vehicle, except pedal cycle, and animal-drawn vehicle
              pedestrian, pedestrian conveyance, or pedestrian vehicle
              other object, fixed, movable, or moving, not set in motion by motor vehicle,
                 railway train, or aircraft

fall from
knocked down by   } animal being ridden
thrown from
trampled by

              ridden animal stumbled and fell

      Excludes: *collision of animal being ridden with:*
            animal-drawn vehicle (E827.0-E827.9)
            pedal cycle (E826.0-E826.9)

④ **E829** **Other road vehicle accidents**
[0,4,8,9]
    Includes:

accident while boarding or alighting from
blow from object in
breakage of any part of
caught in door of   } streetcar nonmotor road vehicle
derailment of   not classifiable to E826-E828
fall in, on, or from
fire in

              collision between streetcar or nonmotor road vehicle, except as in E826-E828, and:
                animal (not being ridden)
                another nonmotor road vehicle not classifiable to E826-E828
                pedestrian
                other object, fixed, movable, or moving, not set in motion by motor vehicle,
                   railway train, or aircraft
               nonmotor road vehicle accident NOS
               streetcar accident NOS

      Excludes: *collision with:*
            animal being ridden (E828.0-E828.9)
            animal-drawn vehicle (E827.0-E827.9)
            pedal cycle (E826.0-E826.9)

WATER TRANSPORT ACCIDENTS (E830-E838)

    Note: For definitions of water transport accident and related terms see definitions (a), (s), and (t).

    Includes: watercraft accidents in the course of recreational activities

    Excludes: *accidents involving both aircraft, including objects set in motion by aircraft, and watercraft (E840.0-E845.9)*

    The following fourth-digit subdivisions are for use with categories E830-E838 to identify the injured person:

    .0 Occupant of small boat, unpowered

    .1 Occupant of small boat, powered
        See definition (t)

continued

● Code new
to this edition

▲ Revision of
existing code

④ ⑤ Fourth or fifth
digit required

Excludes: *water skier (.4)*

.2 Occupant of other watercraft—crew
Persons:
engaged in operation of watercraft
providing passenger services [cabin attendants, ship's physician, catering personnel]
working on ship during voyage in other capacity [musician in band, operators of
shops and beauty parlors]

.3 Occupant of other watercraft—other than crew
Passenger
Occupant of lifeboat, other than crew, after abandoning ship

.4 Water skier

.5 Swimmer

.6 Dockers, stevedores
Longshoreman employed on the dock in loading and unloading ships

.8 Other specified person
Immigration and custom officials on board ship
Person:
accompanying passenger or member of crew
visiting boat
Pilot (guiding ship into port)

.9 Unspecified person

④ **E830 Accident to watercraft causing submersion**
Includes: submersion and drowning due to:
boat overturning
boat submerging
falling or jumping from burning ship
falling or jumping from crushed watercraft
ship sinking
other accident to watercraft

④ **E831 Accident to watercraft causing other injury**
Includes: any injury, except submersion and drowning, as a result of an accident to watercraft
burned while ship on fire
crushed between ships in collision
crushed by lifeboat after abandoning ship
fall due to collision or other accident to watercraft
hit by falling object due to accident to watercraft
injured in watercraft accident involving collision
struck by boat or part thereof after fall or jump from damaged boat

Excludes: *burns from localized fire or explosion on board ship (E837.0-E837.9)*

④ **E832 Other accidental submersion or drowning in water transport accident**
Includes: submersion or drowning as a result of an accident other than accident to the
watercraft, such as:
fall:
from gangplank
from ship
overboard
thrown overboard by motion of ship
washed overboard

Excludes: *submersion or drowning of swimmer or diver who voluntarily jumps from boat not
involved in an accident (E910.0-E910.9)*

④ **E833 Fall on stairs or ladders in water transport**

Excludes: *fall due to accident to watercraft (E831.0-E831.9)*

④ **E834 Other fall from one level to another in water transport**

Excludes: *fall due to accident to watercraft (E831.0-E831.9)*

④ **E835 Other and unspecified fall in water transport**   -

Excludes: *fall due to accident to watercraft (E831.0-E831.9)*

Add 4th or
5th digit

Nonspecific
code

Unspecified
code

Manifestation
code

④ **E836** **Machinery accident in water transport**
      Includes: injuries in water transport caused by:
                deck
                engine room
                galley   } machinery
                laundry
                loading

④ **E837** **Explosion, fire, or burning in watercraft**
      Includes: explosion of boiler on steamship
                  localized fire on ship

        Excludes: *burning ship (due to collision or explosion) resulting in:*
                  submersion or drowning (E830.0-E830.9)
                  other injury (E831.0-E831.9)

④ **E838** **Other and unspecified water transport accident**
      Includes: accidental poisoning by gases or fumes on ship
                  atomic power plant malfunction in watercraft
                  crushed between ship and stationary object [wharf]
                  crushed between ships without accident to watercraft
                  crushed by falling object on ship or while loading or unloading
                  hit by boat while water skiing
                  struck by boat or part thereof (after fall from boat)
                  watercraft accident NOS

AIR AND SPACE TRANSPORT ACCIDENTS (E840-E845)

    Note: For definition of aircraft and related terms see definitions (u) and (v).

    The following fourth-digit subdivisions are for use with categories E840-E845 to identify the injured person:

    .0 **Occupant of spacecraft**

    .1 **Occupant of military aircraft, any**
        Crew
        Passenger (civilian)   } in military aircraft [air force]
                (military)   [army] [national guard] [navy]
        Troops

    Excludes: *occupants of aircraft operated under jurisdiction of police departments (.5)*
             parachutist (.7)

    .2 **Crew of commercial aircraft (powered) in surface to surface transport**

    .3 **Other occupant of commercial aircraft (powered) in surface to surface transport**
        Flight personnel:
          not part of crew
          on familiarization flight
        Passenger on aircraft (powered) NOS

    .4 **Occupant of commercial aircraft (powered) in surface to air transport**
        Occupant [crew] [passenger] of aircraft (powered) engaged in activities, such as:
        aerial spraying (crops) (fire retardants)
        air drops of emergency supplies
        air drops of parachutists, except from military craft
        crop dusting
        lowering of construction material [bridge or telephone pole]
        sky writing

    .5 **Occupant of other powered aircraft**
        Occupant [crew] [passenger] of aircraft [powered] engaged in activities, such as:
        aerobatic flying
        aircraft racing
        rescue operation
        storm surveillance
        traffic surveillance
        Occupant of private plane NOS

    .6 **Occupant of unpowered aircraft, except parachutist**
        Occupant of aircraft classifiable to E842

    .7 **Parachutist (military) (other)**
        Person making voluntary descent

    Excludes: *person making descent after accident to aircraft (.1-.6)*

    ● Code new   ▲ Revision of   ④ ⑤ Fourth or fifth
       to this edition   existing code   digit required

.8 **Ground crew, airline employee**
Persons employed at airfields (civil) (military) or launching pads, not occupants of aircraft

.9 **Other person**

④ **E840 Accident to powered aircraft at takeoff or landing**
Includes:
collision of aircraft with any object, fixed,
    movable, or moving
crash
explosion on aircraft   } while taking off or landing
fire on aircraft
forced landing

④ **E841 Accident to powered aircraft, other and unspecified**
Includes: aircraft accident NOS
aircraft crash or wreck NOS
any accident to powered aircraft while in transit or when not specified whether in
    transit, taking off, or landing
collision of aircraft with another aircraft, bird, or any object, while in transit
explosion on aircraft while in transit
fire on aircraft while in transit

④ **E842 Accident to unpowered aircraft**
[6-9]
Includes: any accident, except collision with powered aircraft, to:
balloon
glider
hang glider
kite carrying a person
hit by object falling from unpowered aircraft

④ **E843 Fall in, on, or from aircraft**
[0-9]
Includes: accident in boarding or alighting from aircraft, any kind
fall in, on, or from aircraft [any kind], while in transit, taking off, or landing,
    except when as a result of an accident to aircraft

④ **E844 Other specified air transport accidents**
[0-9]
Includes:
hit by:
  aircraft
  object falling from aircraft
injury by or from:
  machinery on aircraft
  rotating propeller   } without accident to aircraft
  voluntary parachute descent
poisoning by carbon monoxide from aircraft
  while in transit
sucked into jet
any accident involving other transport vehicle (motor) (nonmotor) due to being hit
    by object set in motion by aircraft (powered)

Excludes: *air sickness (E903)*

effects of:
high altitude (E902.0-E902.1)
pressure change (E902.0-E902.1)
injury in parachute descent due to accident to aircraft (840.0-E842.9)

④ **E845 Accident involving spacecraft**
[0,8,9]
Includes: launching pad accident

Excludes: *effects of weightlessness in spacecraft (E928.0)*

	Add 4th or 5th digit		Nonspecific code		Unspecified code		Manifestation code

VEHICLE ACCIDENTS NOT ELSEWHERE CLASSIFIABLE (E846-E848)

E846 Accidents involving powered vehicles used solely within the buildings and premises of industrial or commercial establishment

Accident to, on, or involving:
  battery powered airport passenger vehicle
  battery powered trucks (baggage) (mail)
  coal car in mine
  logging car
  self propelled truck, industrial
  station baggage truck (powered)
  tram, truck, or tub (powered) in mine or quarry
Breakage of any part of vehicle
Collision with:
  pedestrian
  other vehicle or object within premises
Explosion of ⎫
Fall from   ⎬ powered vehicle, industrial or commercial
Overturning of ⎮
Struck by   ⎭

> Excludes: *accidental poisoning by exhaust gas from vehicle not elsewhere classifiable (E868.2)*
> *injury by crane, lift (fork), or elevator (E919.2)*

E847 Accidents involving cable cars not running on rails

Accident to, on, or involving:
  cable car, not on rails
  ski chair-lift
  ski-lift with gondola
  téléférique
Breakage of cable ⎫
Caught or dragged by ⎮
Fall or jump from   ⎬ cable car, not on rails
Object thrown from or in ⎭

E848 Accidents involving other vehicles, not elsewhere classifiable

Accident to, on, or involving:
  ice yacht
  land yacht
  nonmotor, nonroad vehicle NOS

□ *E849 Place of occurrence*

The following category is for use to denote the place where the injury or poisoning occurred.

□ *E849.0 Home*

Apartment	*Private:*
Boarding house	*driveway*
Farm house	*garage*
Home premises	*garden*
House (residential)	*home*
Noninstitutional place	*walk*
of residence	*Swimming pool in private house or garden*
	Yard of home

> Excludes: *home under construction but not yet occupied (E849.3)*
> *institutional place of residence (E849.7)*

□ *E849.1 Farm*

Farm:
  buildings
  land under cultivation

> Excludes: *farm house and home premises of farm (E849.0)*

E849.2 Mine and quarry

Gravel pit	*Tunnel under construction*
Sand pit	

● Code new to this edition   ▲ Revision of existing code   ④ ⑤ Fourth or fifth digit required

☐ **E849.3 Industrial place and premises**

Building under construction
Dockyard
Dry dock
Factory
  building
  premises
Garage (place of work)

Industrial yard
Loading platform (factory) (store)
Plant, industrial
Railway yard
Shop (place of work)
Warehouse
Workhouse

☐ **E849.4 Place for recreation and sport**

Amusement park
Baseball field
Basketball court
Beach resort
Cricket ground
Fives court
Football field
Golf course
Gymnasium
Hockey field
Holiday camp
Ice palace
Lake resort
Mountain resort
Playground, including
  school playground

Public park
Racecourse
Resort NOS
Riding school
Rifle range
Seashore resort
Skating rink
Sports ground
Sports palace
Stadium
Swimming pool, public
Tennis court
Vacation resort

Excludes: that in private house or garden (E849.0)

☐ **E849.5 Street and highway**

☐ **E849.6 Public building**

Building (including adjacent grounds) used by the general public or by a particular
  group of the public, such as:

airport
bank
café
casino
church
cinema
clubhouse
courthouse
dance hall
garage building (for car
  storage)
hotel
market (grocery or other
  commodity)
movie house
music hall

nightclub
office
office building
opera house
post office
public hall
radio broadcasting station
restaurant
school (state) (public) (private)
shop, commercial
station (bus) (railway)
store
theater

Excludes: home garage (E849.0)
          industrial building or workplace (E849.3)

☐ **E849.7 Residential institution**

Children's home
Dormitory
Hospital
Jail

Old people's home
Orphanage
Prison
Reform school

☐ **E849.8 Other specified places**

Beach NOS
Canal
Caravan site NOS
Derelict house
Desert
Dock
Forest
Harbor
Hill
Lake NOS
Mountain
Parking lot
Parking place

Pond or pool (natural)
Prairie
Public place NOS
Railway line
Reservoir
River
Sea
Seashore NOS
Stream
Swamp
Trailer court
Woods

☐ **E849.9 Unspecified place**

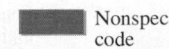 Add 4th or
5th digit

 Nonspecific
code

 Unspecified
code

Manifestation
code

493

ACCIDENTAL POISONING BY DRUGS, MEDICINAL SUBSTANCES, AND BIOLOGICALS (E850-E858)

Includes: accidental overdose of drug, wrong drug given or taken in error, and drug taken inadvertently
accidents in the use of drugs and biologicals in medical and surgical procedures

Excludes: *administration with suicidal or homicidal intent or intent to harm, or in circumstances classifiable to E980-E989 (E950.0-E950.5, E962.0, E980.0-E980.5)*
correct drug properly administered in therapeutic or prophylactic dosage, as the cause of adverse effect (E930.0-E949.9)

See Alphabetic Index for more complete list of specific drugs to be classified under the fourth-digit subdivisions. The American Hospital Formulary numbers can be used to classify new drugs listed by the American Hospital Formulary Service (AHFS). See appendix C.

E850 Accidental poisoning by analgesics, antipyretics, and antirheumatics

☐ **E850.0 Heroin**
Diacetylmorphine

☐ **E850.1 Methadone**

☐ **E850.2 Other opiates and related narcotics**
Codeine [methylmorphine]   Morphine
Meperidine [pethidine]   Opium (alkaloids)

☐ **E850.3 Salicylates**
Acetylsalicylic acid [aspirin]
Amino derivatives of salicylic acid
Salicylic acid salts

☐ **E850.4 Aromatic analgesics, not elsewhere classified**
Acetanilid
Paracetamol [acetaminophen]
Phenacetin [acetophenetidin]

☐ **E850.5 Pyrazole derivatives**
Aminophenazone [amidopyrine]
Phenylbutazone

☐ **E850.6 Antirheumatics [antiphlogistics]**
Gold salts   Indomethacin

Excludes: *salicylates (E850.3)*
steroids (E858.0)

☐ **E850.7 Other non-narcotic analgesics**
Pyrabital

E850.8 Other specified analgesics and antipyretics
Pentazocine

E850.9 Unspecified analgesic or antipyretic

E851 Accidental poisoning by barbiturates
Amobarbital [amylobarbitone]
Barbital [barbitone]
Butabarbital [butabarbitone]
Pentobarbital [pentobarbitone]
Phenobarbital [phenobarbitone]
Secobarbital [quinalbarbitone]

Excludes: *thiobarbiturates (E855.1)*

E852 Accidental poisoning by other sedatives and hypnotics

E852.0 Chloral hydrate group

E852.1 Paraldehyde

E852.2 Bromine compounds
Bromides   Carbromal (derivatives)

E852.3 Methaqualone compounds

E852.4 Glutethimide group

E852.5 Mixed sedatives, not elsewhere classified

E852.8 Other specified sedatives and hypnotics

● Code new
to this edition
▲ Revision of
existing code
④ ⑤ Fourth or fifth
digit required

E852.9 Unspecified sedative or hypnotic

Sleeping:
  drug
  pill ⎫ NOS
  tablet ⎭

E853 Accidental poisoning by tranquilizers

E853.0 Phenothiazine-based tranquilizers

Chlorpromazine	Prochlorperazine
Fluphenazine	Promazine

E853.1 Butyrophenone-based tranquilizers

Haloperidol	Trifluperidol
Spiperone	

E853.2 Benzodiazepine-based tranquilizers

Chlordiazepoxide	Lorazepam
Diazepam	Medazepam
Flurazepam	Nitrazepam

E853.8 Other specified tranquilizers

Hydroxyzine	Meprobamate

E853.9 Unspecified tranquilizer

E854 Accidental poisoning by other psychotropic agents

E854.0 Antidepressants

Amitriptyline	Monoamine oxidase [MAO] inhibitors
Imipramine	

E854.1 Psychodysleptics [hallucinogens]

Cannabis derivatives	Mescaline
Lysergide [LSD]	Psilocin
Marihuana (derivatives)	Psilocybin

E854.2 Psychostimulants

Amphetamine	Caffeine

Excludes: central appetite depressants (E858.8)

E854.3 Central nervous system stimulants

Analeptics	Opiate antagonists

E854.8 Other psychotropic agents

E855 Accidental poisoning by other drugs acting on central and autonomic nervous system

E855.0 Anticonvulsant and anti-Parkinsonism drugs

Amantadine
Hydantoin derivatives
Levodopa [L-dopa]
Oxazolidine derivatives [paramethadione] [trimethadione]
Succinimides

E855.1 Other central nervous system depressants

Ether	Intravenous anesthetics
Gaseous anesthetics	Thiobarbiturates, such as thiopental sodium
Halogenated hydrocarbon derivatives	

E855.2 Local anesthetics

Cocaine	Procaine
Lidocaine [lignocaine]	Tetracaine

E855.3 Parasympathomimetics [cholinergics]

Acetylcholine	Pilocarpine
Anticholinesterase:	
organophosphorus	
reversible	

E855.4 Parasympatholytics [anticholinergics and antimuscarinics] and spasmolytics

Atropine	Hyoscine [scopolamine]
Homatropine	Quaternary ammonium derivatives

E855.5 Sympathomimetics [adrenergics]

Epinephrine [adrenalin]
Levarterenol [noradrenalin]

E855.6 Sympatholytics [antiadrenergics]

Phenoxybenzamine	Tolazoline hydrochloride

E855.8 Other specified drugs acting on central and autonomic nervous systems

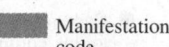

▰ Add 4th or 5th digit	▰ Nonspecific code	▰ Unspecified code	▰ Manifestation code

E855.9 Unspecified drug acting on central and autonomic nervous systems

E856 Accidental poisoning by antibiotics

E857 Accidental poisoning by other anti-infectives

E858 Accidental poisoning by other drugs

E858.0 Hormones and synthetic substitutes

E858.1 Primarily systemic agents

E858.2 Agents primarily affecting blood constituents

E858.3 Agents primarily affecting cardiovascular system

E858.4 Agents primarily affecting gastrointestinal system

E858.5 Water, mineral, and uric acid metabolism drugs

E858.6 Agents primarily acting on the smooth and skeletal muscles and respiratory system

E858.7 Agents primarily affecting skin and mucous membrane, ophthalmological, otorhinolaryngological, and dental drugs

E858.8 Other specified drugs
Central appetite depressants

E858.9 Unspecified drug

ACCIDENTAL POISONING BY OTHER SOLID AND LIQUID SUBSTANCES, GASES, AND VAPORS (E860-E869)

Note: Categories in this section are intended primarily to indicate the external cause of poisoning states classifiable to 980-989. They may also be used to indicate external causes of localized effects classifiable to 001-799.

E860 Accidental poisoning by alcohol, not elsewhere classified

E860.0 Alcoholic beverages
Alcohol in preparations intended for consumption

E860.1 Other and unspecified ethyl alcohol and its products
| Denatured alcohol | Grain alcohol NOS |
| Ethanol NOS | Methylated spirit |

E860.2 Methyl alcohol
Methanol   Wood alcohol

E860.3 Isopropyl alcohol
Dimethyl carbinol   Secondary propyl alcohol
Isopropanol
Rubbing alcohol substitute

E860.4 Fusel oil
Alcohol:
amyl
butyl
propyl

E860.8 Other specified alcohols

E860.9 Unspecified alcohol

E861 Accidental poisoning by cleansing and polishing agents, disinfectants, paints, and varnishes

E861.0 Synthetic detergents and shampoos

E861.1 Soap products

E861.2 Polishes

E861.3 Other cleansing and polishing agents
Scouring powders

E861.4 Disinfectants
Household and other disinfectants not ordinarily used on the person

Excludes: carbolic acid or phenol (E864.0)

E861.5 Lead paints

E861.6 Other paints and varnishes
Lacquers   Paints, other than lead
Oil colors   White washes

E861.9 Unspecified

E862 Accidental poisoning by petroleum products, other solvents and their vapors, not elsewhere classified

E862.0 Petroleum solvents

● Code new
  to this edition

▲ Revision of
  existing code

④ ⑤ Fourth or fifth
    digit required

Petroleum:
  ether
  benzine
  naphtha

E862.1 Petroleum fuels and cleaners
  Antiknock additives to petroleum fuels
  Gas oils
  Gasoline or petrol
  Kerosene

  Excludes: kerosene insecticides (E863.4)

E862.2 Lubricating oils

E862.3 Petroleum solids
  Paraffin wax

E862.4 Other specified solvents
  Benzene

E862.9 Unspecified solvent

E863 Accidental poisoning by agricultural and horticultural chemical and pharmaceutical preparations other than plant foods and fertilizers

  Excludes: plant foods and fertilizers (E866.5)

E863.0 Insecticides of organochlorine compounds
  Benzene hexachloride   Dieldrin
  Chlordane   Endrine
  DDT   Toxaphene

E863.1 Insecticides of organophosphorus compounds
  Demeton   Parathion
  Diazinon   Phenylsulphthion
  Dichlorvos   Phorate
  Malathion   Phosdrin
  Methyl parathion

E863.2 Carbamates
  Aldicarb   Propoxur
  Carbaryl

E863.3 Mixtures of insecticides

E863.4 Other and unspecified insecticides
  Kerosene insecticides

E863.5 Herbicides
  2, 4-Dichlorophenoxyacetic acid [2, 4-D]
  2, 4, 5-Trichlorophenoxyacetic acid [2, 4, 5-T]
  Chlorates
  Diquat
  Mixtures of plant food and fertilizers with herbicides
  Paraquat

E863.6 Fungicides
  Organic mercurials (used in seed dressing)
  Pentachlorophenols

E863.7 Rodenticides
  Fluoroacetates   Warfarin
  Squill and derivatives   Zinc phosphide
  Thallium

E863.8 Fumigants
  Cyanides   Phosphine
  Methyl bromide

E863.9 Other and unspecified

E864 Accidental poisoning by corrosives and caustics, not elsewhere classified

  Excludes: those as components of disinfectants (E861.4)

E864.0 Corrosive aromatics
  Carbolic acid or phenol

E864.1 Acids
  Acid:
    hydrochloric
    nitric
    sulfuric

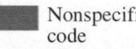 Add 4th or 5th digit   Nonspecific code   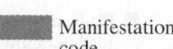 Unspecified code   Manifestation code

E864.2 Caustic alkalis
　　　　Lye

E864.3 Other specified corrosives and caustics

E864.4 Unspecified corrosives and caustics

E865 Accidental poisoning from poisonous foodstuffs and poisonous plants
　　　Includes:　any meat, fish, or shellfish
　　　　　　　　plants, berries, and fungi eaten as, or in mistake for, food, or by a child

　　　Excludes: *anaphylactic shock due to adverse food reaction (995.6)*
　　　　　　　　food poisoning (bacterial) (005.0-005.9)
　　　　　　　　poisoning and toxic reactions to venomous plants (E905.6-E905.7)

E865.0 Meat

E865.1 Shellfish

E865.2 Other fish

E865.3 Berries and seeds

E865.4 Other specified plants

E865.5 Mushrooms and other fungi

E865.8 Other specified foods

E865.9 Unspecified foodstuff or poisonous plant

E866 Accidental poisoning by other and unspecified solid and liquid substances

　　　Excludes: *these substances as a component of:*
　　　　　　　　medicines (E850.0-E858.9)
　　　　　　　　paints (E861.5-E861.6)
　　　　　　　　pesticides (E863.0-E863.9)
　　　　　　　　petroleum fuels (E862.1)

E866.0 Lead and its compounds and fumes

E866.1 Mercury and its compounds and fumes

E866.2 Antimony and its compounds and fumes

E866.3 Arsenic and its compounds and fumes

E866.4 Other metals and their compounds and fumes
　　　　Beryllium (compounds)　　　　Iron (compounds)
　　　　Brass fumes　　　　　　　　　Manganese (compounds)
　　　　Cadmium (compounds)　　　　 Nickel (compounds)
　　　　Copper salts　　　　　　　　　Thallium (compounds)

E866.5 Plant foods and fertilizers

　　　Excludes: *mixtures with herbicides (E863.5)*

E866.6 Glues and adhesives

E866.7 Cosmetics

E866.8 Other specified solid or liquid substances

E866.9 Unspecified solid or liquid substance

E867 Accidental poisoning by gas distributed by pipeline
　　　Carbon monoxide from incomplete combustion of piped gas
　　　Coal gas NOS
　　　Liquefied petroleum gas distributed through pipes (pure or mixed with air)
　　　Piped gas (natural) (manufactured)

E868 Accidental poisoning by other utility gas and other carbon monoxide

E868.0 Liquefied petroleum gas distributed in mobile containers
　　　　Butane　　　　　　　　　　　　⎫ or carbon monoxide from
　　　　Liquefied hydrocarbon gas NOS　⎬　incomplete combustion of
　　　　Propane　　　　　　　　　　　　⎭　these gases

E868.1 Other and unspecified utility gas
　　　　Acetylene　　　　　 ⎫
　　　　Gas NOS used for　　⎪
　　　　　lighting,　　　　　⎬ or carbon monoxide from incomplete combustion of these gases
　　　　　heating, or　　　 ⎪
　　　　　cooking　　　　　⎪
　　　　Water gas　　　　　 ⎭

　　● Code new　　　　▲ Revision of　　　④ ⑤ Fourth or fifth
　　　　to this edition　　　　existing code　　　　digit required

E868.2 Motor vehicle exhaust gas
Exhaust gas from:
farm tractor, not in transit
gas engine
motor pump
motor vehicle, not in transit
any type of combustion engine not in watercraft

Excludes: *poisoning by carbon monoxide from:*
aircraft while in transit (E844.0-E844.9)
motor vehicle while in transit (E818.0-E818.9)
watercraft whether or not in transit (E838.0-E838.9)

E868.3 Carbon monoxide from incomplete combustion of other domestic fuels
Carbon monoxide from incomplete combustion of:
coal
coke
kerosene } in domestic stove or fireplace
wood

Excludes: *carbon monoxide from smoke and fumes due to conflagration (E890.0-E893.9)*

E868.8 Carbon monoxide from other sources
Carbon monoxide from:
blast furnace gas
incomplete combustion of fuels in industrial use
kiln vapor

E868.9 Unspecified carbon monoxide

E869 Accidental poisoning by other gases and vapors

Excludes: *effects of gases used as anesthetics (E855.1, E938.2)*
fumes from heavy metals (E866.0-E866.4)
smoke and fumes due to conflagration or explosion (E890.0-E899)

E869.0 Nitrogen oxides

E869.1 Sulfur dioxide

E869.2 Freon

E869.3 Lacrimogenic gas [tear gas]
Bromobenzyl cyanide   Ethyliodoacetate
Chloroacetophenone

E869.4 Second-hand tobacco smoke

E869.8 Other specified gases and vapors
Chlorine   Hydrocyanic acid gas

E869.9 Unspecified gases and vapors

MISADVENTURES TO PATIENTS DURING SURGICAL AND MEDICAL CARE (E870-E876)

Excludes: *accidental overdose of drug and wrong drug given in error (E850.0-E858.9)*
surgical and medical procedures as the cause of abnormal reaction by the patient,
without mention of misadventure at the time of procedure (E878.0-E879.9)

E870 Accidental cut, puncture, perforation, or hemorrhage during medical care

E870.0 Surgical operation

E870.1 Infusion or transfusion

E870.2 Kidney dialysis or other perfusion

E870.3 Injection or vaccination

E870.4 Endoscopic examination

E870.5 Aspiration of fluid or tissue, puncture, and catheterization
Abdominal paracentesis   Lumbar puncture
Aspirating needle biopsy   Thoracentesis
Blood sampling

Excludes: *heart catheterization (E870.6)*

E870.6 Heart catheterization

E870.7 Administration of enema

E870.8 Other specified medical care

E870.9 Unspecified medical care

E871 Foreign object left in body during procedure

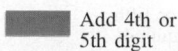 Add 4th or 5th digit   Nonspecific code   Unspecified code   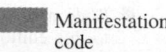 Manifestation code

E871.0 Surgical operation

E871.1 Infusion or transfusion

E871.2 Kidney dialysis or other perfusion

E871.3 Injection or vaccination

E871.4 Endoscopic examination

E871.5 Aspiration of fluid or tissue, puncture, and catheterization

Abdominal paracentesis   Lumbar puncture
Aspiration needle biopsy   Thoracentesis
Blood sampling

Excludes: heart catheterization (E871.6)

E871.6 Heart catheterization

E871.7 Removal of catheter or packing

E871.8 Other specified procedures

E871.9 Unspecified procedure

E872 Failure of sterile precautions during procedure

E872.0 Surgical operation

E872.1 Infusion or transfusion

E872.2 Kidney dialysis and other perfusion

E872.3 Injection or vaccination

E872.4 Endoscopic examination

E872.5 Aspiration of fluid or tissue, puncture, and catheterization

Abdominal paracentesis   Lumbar puncture
Aspirating needle biopsy   Thoracentesis
Blood sampling

Excludes: heart catheterization (E872.6)

E872.6 Heart catheterization

E872.8 Other specified procedures

E872.9 Unspecified procedure

E873 Failure in dosage

Excludes: accidental overdose of drug, medicinal or biological substance (E850.0-E858.9)

E873.0 Excessive amount of blood or other fluid during transfusion or infusion

E873.1 Incorrect dilution of fluid during infusion

E873.2 Overdose of radiation in therapy

E873.3 Inadvertent exposure of patient to radiation during medical care

E873.4 Failure in dosage in electroshock or insulin-shock therapy

E873.5 Inappropriate [too hot or too cold] temperature in local application and packing

E873.6 Nonadministration of necessary drug or medicinal substance

E873.8 Other specified failure in dosage

E873.9 Unspecified failure in dosage

E874 Mechanical failure of instrument or apparatus during procedure

E874.0 Surgical operation

E874.1 Infusion and transfusion

Air in system

E874.2 Kidney dialysis and other perfusion

E874.3 Endoscopic examination

E874.4 Aspiration of fluid or tissue, puncture, and catheterization

Abdominal paracentesis   Lumbar puncture
Aspirating needle biopsy   Thoracentesis
Blood sampling

Excludes: heart catheterization (E874.5)

E874.5 Heart catheterization

E874.8 Other specified procedures

E874.9 Unspecified procedure

● Code new
   to this edition

▲ Revision of
   existing code

④ ⑤ Fourth or fifth
     digit required

E875 Contaminated or infected blood, other fluid, drug, or biological substance

    Includes: presence of:
                bacterial pyrogens
                endotoxin-producing bacteria
                serum hepatitis-producing agent

  E875.0 Contaminated substance transfused or infused

  E875.1 Contaminated substance injected or used for vaccination

  E875.2 Contaminated drug or biological substance administered by other means

  E875.8 Other

  E875.9 Unspecified

E876 Other and unspecified misadventures during medical care

  E876.0 Mismatched blood in transfusion

  E876.1 Wrong fluid in infusion

  E876.2 Failure in suture and ligature during surgical operation

  E876.3 Endotracheal tube wrongly placed during anesthetic procedure

  E876.4 Failure to introduce or to remove other tube or instrument

    Excludes: *foreign object left in body during procedure (E871.0-E871.9)*

  E876.5 Performance of inappropriate operation

  E876.8 Other specified misadventures during medical care
      Performance of inappropriate treatment NEC

  E876.9 Unspecified misadventure during medical care

SURGICAL AND MEDICAL PROCEDURES AS THE CAUSE OF ABNORMAL REACTION OF PATIENT OR LATER COMPLICATION, WITHOUT MENTION OF MISADVENTURE AT THE TIME OF PROCEDURE (E878-E879)

    Includes: procedures as the cause of abnormal reaction, such as:
                displacement or malfunction of prosthetic device
                hepatorenal failure, postoperative
                malfunction of external stoma
                postoperative intestinal obstruction
                rejection of transplanted organ

    Excludes: *anesthetic management properly carried out as the cause of adverse effect*
        (E937.0-E938.9)
        infusion and transfusion, without mention of misadventure in the technique of
        procedure (E930.0-E949.9)

E878 Surgical operation and other surgical procedures as the cause of abnormal reaction of patient, or of later complication, without mention of misadventure at the time of operation

  E878.0 Surgical operation with transplant of whole organ
      Transplantation of:
        heart
        kidney
        liver

  E878.1 Surgical operation with implant of artificial internal device
      Cardiac pacemaker   Heart valve prosthesis
      Electrodes implanted in brain   Internal orthopedic device

  E878.2 Surgical operation with anastomosis, bypass, or graft, with natural or artificial tissues used as implant
      Anastomosis: Graft of blood vessel, tendon, or skin
        arteriovenous
        gastrojejunal

    Excludes: *external stoma (E878.3)*

  E878.3 Surgical operation with formation of external stoma
      Colostomy   Gastrostomy
      Cystostomy   Ureterostomy
      Duodenostomy

  E878.4 Other restorative surgery

  E878.5 Amputation of limb(s)

  E878.6 Removal of other organ (partial) (total)

  E878.8 Other specified surgical operations and procedures

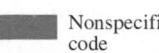 Add 4th or 5th digit   Nonspecific code   Unspecified code   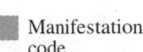 Manifestation code

E878.9 Unspecified surgical operations and procedures

E879 Other procedures, without mention of misadventure at the time of procedure, as the cause of abnormal reaction of patient, or of later complication

E879.0 Cardiac catheterization

E879.1 Kidney dialysis

E879.2 Radiological procedure and radiotherapy

> *Excludes:* radio-opaque dyes for diagnostic x-ray procedures (E947.8)

E879.3 Shock therapy
Electroshock therapy   Insulin-shock therapy

E879.4 Aspiration of fluid
Lumbar puncture   Thoracentesis

E879.5 Insertion of gastric or duodenal sound

E879.6 Urinary catheterization

E879.7 Blood sampling

E879.8 Other specified procedures
Blood transfusion

E879.9 Unspecified procedure

ACCIDENTAL FALLS (E880-E888)

> *Excludes:* falls (in or from):
> burning building (E890.8, E891.8)
> into fire (E890.0-E899)
> into water (with submersion or drowning) (E910.0-E910.9)
> machinery (in operation) (E919.0-E919.9)
> on edged, pointed, or sharp object (E920.0-E920.9)
> transport vehicle (E800.0-E845.9)
> vehicle not elsewhere classifiable (E846-E848)

E880 Fall on or from stairs or steps

E880.0 Escalator

E880.1 Fall on or from sidewalk curb

> *Excludes:* fall from moving sidewalk (E885)

E880.9 Other stairs or steps

E881 Fall on or from ladders or scaffolding

E881.0 Fall from ladder

E881.1 Fall from scaffolding

E882 Fall from or out of building or other structure
Fall from: Fall from:
balcony   turret
bridge   viaduct
building   wall
flagpole   window
tower   Fall through roof

> *Excludes:* collapse of a building or structure (E916)
> fall or jump from burning building (E890.8, E891.8)

E883 Fall into hole or other opening in surface
Includes:
fall into: fall into:
cavity   shaft
dock   swimming pool
hole   tank
pit   well
quarry

> *Excludes:* fall into water NOS (E910.9)
> that resulting in drowning or submersion without mention of injury (E910.0-E910.9)

E883.0 Accident from diving or jumping into water [swimming pool]
Strike or hit:
against bottom when jumping or diving into water
wall or board of swimming pool
water surface

● Code new
to this edition   ▲ Revision of
existing code   ④ ⑤ Fourth or fifth
digit required

Excludes: *diving with insufficient air supply (E913.2)*
effects of air pressure from diving (E902.2)

E883.1 Accidental fall into well

E883.2 Accidental fall into storm drain or manhole

E883.9 Fall into other hole or other opening in surface

E884 Other fall from one level to another

E884.0 Fall from playground equipment

Excludes: *recreational machinery (E919.8)*

E884.1 Fall from cliff

E884.2 Fall from chair

E884.3 Fall from wheelchair

E884.4 Fall from bed

E884.5 Fall from other furniture

E884.6 Fall from commode
Toilet

E884.9 Other fall from one level to another
Fall from: Fall from:
  embankment   stationary vehicle
  haystack   tree

E885 Fall on same level from slipping, tripping, or stumbling
Fall on moving sidewalk

E886 Fall on same level from collision, pushing, or shoving, by or with other person

Excludes: *crushed or pushed by a crowd or human stampede (E917.1)*

E886.0 In sports
Tackles in sports

Excludes: *kicked, stepped on, struck by object, in sports (E917.0)*

E886.9 Other and unspecified
Fall from collision of pedestrian (conveyance) with another pedestrian (conveyance)

E887 Fracture, cause unspecified

E888 Other and unspecified fall
Accidental fall NOS
Fall from bumping against object
Fall on same level NOS

ACCIDENTS CAUSED BY FIRE AND FLAMES (E890-E899)

Includes: asphyxia or poisoning due to conflagration or ignition
burning by fire
secondary fires resulting from explosion

Excludes: *arson (E968.0)*

fire in or on:
* machinery (in operation) (E919.0-E919.9)*
* transport vehicle other than stationary vehicle (E800.0-E845.9)*
* vehicle not elsewhere classifiable (E846-E848)*

E890 Conflagration in private dwelling
Includes: conflagration in:
  apartment
  boarding house
  camping place
  caravan
  farmhouse
  house
  lodging house
  mobile home
  private garage
  rooming house
  tenement
conflagration originating from sources classifiable to E893-E898 in the above
  buildings

E890.0 Explosion caused by conflagration

503

    Add 4th or   Nonspecific   Unspecified   Manifestation
    5th digit   code   code   code

E890.1 **Fumes from combustion of polyvinylchloride [PVC] and similar material in conflagration**

E890.2 **Other smoke and fumes from conflagration**
    Carbon monoxide ⎱
    Fumes NOS   ⎬ from conflagration in private building
    Smoke NOS ⎰

E890.3 **Burning caused by conflagration**

E890.8 **Other accident resulting from conflagration**
    Collapse of ⎱
    Fall from
    Hit by object falling from ⎬ burning private building
    Jump from ⎰

E890.9 **Unspecified accident resulting from conflagration in private dwelling**

E891 **Conflagration in other and unspecified building or structure**

Conflagration in: Conflagration in:
  barn   farm outbuildings
  church   hospital
  convalescent and other   hotel
    residential home   school
  dormitory of educational   store
    institution   theater
  factory

Conflagration originating from sources classifiable to E893-E898, in the above buildings

E891.0 **Explosion caused by conflagration**

E891.1 **Fumes from combustion of polyvinylchloride [PVC] and similar material in conflagration**

E891.2 **Other smoke and fumes from conflagration**
    Carbon monoxide ⎱
    Fumes NOS   ⎬ from conflagration in building or structure
    Smoke NOS ⎰

E891.3 **Burning caused by conflagration**

E891.8 **Other accident resulting from conflagration**
    Collapse of ⎱
    Fall from
    Hit by object falling from ⎬ burning building or structure
    Jump from ⎰

E891.9 **Unspecified accident resulting from conflagration of other and unspecified building or structure**

E892 **Conflagration not in building or structure**
Fire (uncontrolled) (in) (of):
  forest
  grass
  hay
  lumber
  mine
  prairie
  transport vehicle [any], except while in transit
  tunnel

E893 **Accident caused by ignition of clothing**

    ☐Excludes:☐ *ignition of clothing:*
             from highly inflammable material (E894)
             with conflagration (E890.0-E892)

E893.0 **From controlled fire in private dwelling**
    Ignition of clothing from:
      normal fire (charcoal) (coal) (electric) (gas) ⎱
        (wood) in:
        brazier ⎬ in private dwelling (as listed in
        fireplace   E890)
        furnace
        stove ⎰

  ● Code new   ▲ Revision of   ④ ⑤ Fourth or fifth
      to this edition   existing code   digit required

E893.1 From controlled fire in other building or structure

Ignition of clothing from:
normal fire (charcoal) (coal) (electric)
  (gas) (wood) in:
    brazier   }   in other building or structure (as
    fireplace   listed in E891)
    furnace
    stove

E893.2 From controlled fire not in building or structure

Ignition of clothing from:
  bonfire (controlled)
  brazier fire (controlled), not in building or structure
  trash fire (controlled)

Excludes: *conflagration not in building (E892)*
           trash fire out of control (E892)

E893.8 From other specified sources

Ignition of clothing from: Ignition of clothing from:
  blowlamp   cigarette
  blowtorch   lighter
  burning bedspread   matches
  candle   pipe
  cigar   welding torch

E893.9 Unspecified source

Ignition of clothing (from controlled fire NOS) (in building NOS) NOS

E894 Ignition of highly inflammable material

Ignition of:
  benzine
  gasoline
  fat   }   (with ignition of clothing)
  kerosene
  paraffin
  petrol

Excludes: *ignition of highly inflammable material with:*
           conflagration (E890.0-E892)
           explosion (E923.0-E923.9)

E895 Accident caused by controlled fire in private dwelling

Burning by (flame of) normal fire (charcoal) (coal)
  (electric) (gas) (wood) in:
    brazier   }   in private dwelling (as listed in
    fireplace   E890)
    furnace
    stove

Excludes: *burning by hot objects not producing fire or flames (E924.0-E924.9)*
           ignition of clothing from these sources (E893.0)
           poisoning by carbon monoxide from incomplete combustion of fuel (E867-E868.9)
           that with conflagration (E890.0-E890.9)

E896 Accident caused by controlled fire in other and unspecified building or structure

Burning by (flame of) normal fire (charcoal) (coal)
  (electric) (gas) (wood) in:
    brazier   }   in other building or structure (as
    fireplace   listed in E891)
    furnace
    stove

Excludes: *burning by hot objects not producing fire or flames (E924.0-E924.9)*
           ignition of clothing from these sources (E893.1)
           poisoning by carbon monoxide from incomplete combustion of fuel (E867-E868.9)
           that with conflagration (E891.0-E891.9)

E897 Accident caused by controlled fire not in building or structure

Burns from flame of:
  bonfire (controlled)
  brazier fire (controlled), not in building or structure
  trash fire (controlled)

continues

Add 4th or   Nonspecific   Unspecified   Manifestation
5th digit   code   code   code

Excludes: ignition of clothing from these sources (E893.2)
  trash fire out of control (E892)
  that with conflagration (E892)

E898 **Accident caused by other specified fire and flames**

Excludes: conflagration (E890.0-E892)
  that with ignition of:
    clothing (E893.0-E893.9)
    highly inflammable material (E894)

E898.0 **Burning bedclothes**
Bed set on fire NOS

E898.1 **Other**

Burning by:	Burning by:
blowlamp	lamp
blowtorch	lighter
candle	matches
cigar	pipe
cigarette	welding torch
fire in room NOS	

E899 **Accident caused by unspecified fire**
Burning NOS

ACCIDENTS DUE TO NATURAL AND ENVIRONMENTAL FACTORS (E900-E909)

E900 **Excessive heat**

E900.0 **Due to weather conditions**
Excessive heat as the external cause of:
  ictus solaris
  siriasis
  sunstroke

E900.1 **Of man-made origin**

Heat (in):	Heat (in):
boiler room	generated in transport vehicle
drying room	kitchen
factory	
furnace room	

E900.9 **Of unspecified origin**

E901 **Excessive cold**

E901.0 **Due to weather conditions**
Excessive cold as the cause of:
  chilblains NOS
  immersion foot

E901.1 **Of man-made origin**
Contact with or inhalation of:
  dry ice
  liquid air
  liquid hydrogen
  liquid nitrogen
Prolonged exposure in:
  deep freeze unit
  refrigerator

E901.8 **Other specified origin**

E901.9 **Of unspecified origin**

E902 **High and low air pressure and changes in air pressure**

E902.0 **Residence or prolonged visit at high altitude**
Residence or prolonged visit at high altitude as the cause of:
  Acosta syndrome
  Alpine sickness
  altitude sickness
  Andes disease
  anoxia, hypoxia
  barotitis, barodontalgia, barosinusitis, otitic barotrauma
  hypobarism, hypobaropathy
  mountain sickness
  range disease

● Code new
to this edition
▲ Revision of
existing code
④ ⑤ Fourth or fifth
digit required

E902.1 In aircraft
Sudden change in air pressure in aircraft during ascent or descent as the cause of:
aeroneurosis
aviators' disease

E902.2 Due to diving
High air pressure from rapid descent in water } as the cause of:
Reduction in atmospheric pressure while } caisson disease
surfacing from deep water diving } divers' disease
} divers' palsy or paralysis

E902.8 Due to other specified causes
Reduction in atmospheric pressure while surfacing from underground

E902.9 Unspecified cause

E903 Travel and motion

E904 Hunger, thirst, exposure, and neglect

Excludes: any condition resulting from homicidal intent (E968.0-E968.9)

hunger, thirst, and exposure resulting from accidents connected with transport (E800.0-E848)

E904.0 Abandonment or neglect of infants and helpless persons
Exposure to weather }
conditions } resulting from abandonment or neglect
Hunger or thirst }

Desertion of newborn
Inattention at or after birth
Lack of care (helpless person) (infant)

Excludes: criminal [purposeful] neglect (E968.4)

E904.1 Lack of food
Lack of food as the cause of:
inanition
insufficient nourishment
starvation

Excludes: hunger resulting from abandonment or neglect (E904.0)

E904.2 Lack of water
Lack of water as the cause of:
dehydration
inanition

Excludes: dehydration due to acute fluid loss (276.5)

E904.3 Exposure (to weather conditions), not elsewhere classifiable
Exposure NOS   Struck by hailstones
Humidity

Excludes: struck by lightning (E907)

E904.9 Privation, unqualified
Destitution

E905 Venomous animals and plants as the cause of poisoning and toxic reactions
Includes: chemical released by animal
insects
release of venom through fangs, hairs, spines, tentacles, and other venom apparatus

Excludes: eating of poisonous animals or plants (E865.0-E865.9)

E905.0 Venomous snakes and lizards
Cobra   Mamba
Copperhead snake   Rattlesnake
Coral snake   Sea snake
Fer de lance   Snake (venomous)
Gila monster   Viper
Krait   Water moccasin

Excludes: bites of snakes and lizards known to be nonvenomous (E906.2)

E905.1 Venomous spiders
Black widow spider   Tarantula (venomous)
Brown spider

E905.2 Scorpion

E905.3 Hornets, wasps, and bees
Yellow jacket

507

E905.4 Centipede and venomous millipede (tropical)

E905.5 Other venomous arthropods
Sting of:
  ant
  caterpillar

E905.6 Venomous marine animals and plants

Puncture by sea urchin spine   Sting of:
Sting of: nematocysts
  coral   sea anemone
  jelly fish   sea cucumber
                                             other marine animal or plant

> *Excludes:* *bites and other injuries caused by nonvenomous marine animal (E906.2-E906.8)*
> *bite of sea snake (venomous) (E905.0)*

E905.7 Poisoning and toxic reactions caused by other plants
Injection of poisons or toxins into or through skin by plant thorns, spines, or other mechanisms

> *Excludes:* *puncture wound NOS by plant thorns or spines (E920.8)*

E905.8 Other specified

E905.9 Unspecified
Sting NOS   Venomous bite NOS

E906 Other injury caused by animals

> *Excludes:* *poisoning and toxic reactions caused by venomous animals and insects (E905.0-E905.9)*
> *road vehicle accident involving animals (E827.0-E828.9)*
> *tripping or falling over an animal (E885)*

E906.0 Dog bite

E906.1 Rat bite

E906.2 Bite of nonvenomous snakes and lizards

E906.3 Bite of other animal except arthropod
Cats   Rodents, except rats
Moray eel   Shark

E906.4 Bite of nonvenomous arthropod
Insect bite NOS

E906.5 Bite by unspecified animal
Animal bite NOS

E906.8 Other specified injury caused by animal
Butted by animal
Fallen on by horse or other animal, not being ridden
Gored by animal
Implantation of quills of porcupine
Pecked by bird
Run over by animal, not being ridden
Stepped on by animal, not being ridden

> *Excludes:* *injury by animal being ridden (E828.0-E828.9)*

E906.9 Unspecified injury caused by animal

E907 Lightning

> *Excludes:* *injury from:*
> *fall of tree or other object caused by lightning (E916)*
> *fire caused by lightning (E890.0-E892)*

E908 Cataclysmic storms, and floods resulting from storms

> *Excludes:* *collapse of dam or man-made structure causing flood (E909.3)*

E908.0 Hurricane
Storm surge
"Tidal wave" caused by storm action
Typhoon

E908.1 Tornado
Cyclone
Twisters

E908.2 Floods

● Code new   ▲ Revision of   ④ ⑤ Fourth or fifth
  to this edition   existing code   digit required

Torrential rainfall
Flash flood

Excludes: *collapse of dam or man-made structure causing flood (909.3)*

E908.3 Blizzard (snow) (ice)

E908.4 Dust storm

E908.8 Other cataclysmic storms

E908.9 Unspecified cataclysmic storms, and floods resulting from storms
Storm NOS

E909 Cataclysmic earth surface movements and eruptions

Excludes: *"tidal wave" caused by storm action (E908.0)*
transport accident involving collision with avalanche or landslide not in motion (E800.0-E848)

E909.0 Earthquakes

E909.1 Volcanic eruptions
Burns from lava
Ash inhalation

E909.2 Avalanche, landslide, or mudslide

E909.3 Collapse of dam or man-made structure

E909.4 Tidal wave caused by earthquake
Tidal wave NOS
Tsunami

Excludes: *tidal wave caused by tropical storm (E908.0)*

E909.8 Other cataclysmic earth surface movements and eruptions

E909.9 Unspecified cataclysmic earth surface movements and eruptions

ACCIDENTS CAUSED BY SUBMERSION, SUFFOCATION, AND FOREIGN BODIES (E910-E915)

E910 Accidental drowning and submersion
Includes: immersion
swimmers' cramp

Excludes: *diving accident (NOS) (resulting in injury except drowning) (E883.0)*
diving with insufficient air supply (E913.2)
drowning and submersion due to:
cataclysm (E908-E909)
machinery accident (E919.0-E919.9)
transport accident (E800.0-E845.9)
effect of high and low air pressure (E902.2)
injury from striking against objects while in running water (E917.2)

E910.0 While water-skiing
Fall from water skis with submersion or drowning

Excludes: *accident to water-skier involving a watercraft and resulting in submersion or other injury (E830.4, E831.4)*

E910.1 While engaged in other sport or recreational activity with diving equipment
Scuba diving NOS
Skin diving NOS
Underwater spear fishing NOS

E910.2 While engaged in other sport or recreational activity without diving equipment
Fishing or hunting, except from boat or with diving equipment
Ice skating
Playing in water
Surfboarding
Swimming NOS
Voluntarily jumping from boat, not involved in accident, for swim NOS
Wading in water

Excludes: *jumping into water to rescue another person (E910.3)*

E910.3 While swimming or diving for purposes other than recreation or sport
Marine salvage
Pearl diving
Placement of fishing nets } (with diving equipment)
Rescue (attempt) of another person
Underwater construction or repairs

509

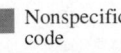 Add 4th or 5th digit   Nonspecific code   Unspecified code   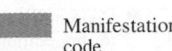 Manifestation code

E910.4 In bathtub

E910.8 Other accidental drowning or submersion
>Drowning in:
>>quenching tank
>>swimming pool

E910.9 Unspecified accidental drowning or submersion
>Accidental fall into water NOS
>Drowning NOS

E911 Inhalation and ingestion of food causing obstruction of respiratory tract or suffocation
>Aspiration and inhalation of food [any] (into respiratory tract) NOS
>Asphyxia by
>Choked on } food [including bone, seed in food, regurgitated food]
>Suffocation by
>
>Compression of trachea
>Interruption of respiration } by food lodged in esophagus
>Obstruction of respiration
>
>Obstruction of pharynx by food (bolus)

>*Excludes:* *injury, except asphyxia and obstruction of respiratory passage, caused by food (E915)*
>>*obstruction of esophagus by food without mention of asphyxia or obstruction of respiratory passage (E915)*

E912 Inhalation and ingestion of other object causing obstruction of respiratory tract or suffocation
>Aspiration and inhalation of foreign body except food (into respiratory tract) NOS
>Foreign object [bean] [marble] in nose
>Obstruction of pharynx by foreign body
>Compression
>Interruption of respiration } by foreign body in esophagus
>Obstruction of respiration

>*Excludes:* *injury, except asphyxia and obstruction of respiratory passage, caused by foreign body (E915)*
>>*obstruction of esophagus by foreign body without mention of asphyxia or obstruction in respiratory passage (E915)*

E913 Accidental mechanical suffocation

>*Excludes:* *mechanical suffocation from or by:*
>>*accidental inhalation or ingestion of:*
>>>*food (E911)*
>>>*foreign object (E912)*
>>*cataclysm (E908-E909)*
>>*explosion (E921.0-E921.9, E923.0-E923.9)*
>>*machinery accident (E919.0-E919.9)*

E913.0 In bed or cradle

>*Excludes:* *suffocation by plastic bag (E913.1)*

E913.1 By plastic bag

E913.2 Due to lack of air (in closed place)
>Accidentally closed up in refrigerator or other airtight enclosed space
>Diving with insufficient air supply

>*Excludes:* *suffocation by plastic bag (E913.1)*

E913.3 By falling earth or other substance
>Cave-in NOS

>*Excludes:* *cave-in caused by cataclysmic earth surface movements and eruptions (E909)*
>>*struck by cave-in without asphyxiation or suffocation (E916)*

E913.8 Other specified means
>Accidental hanging, except in bed or cradle

E913.9 Unspecified means
>Asphyxia, mechanical NOS
>Strangulation NOS
>Suffocation NOS

E914 Foreign body accidentally entering eye and adnexa

>*Excludes:* *corrosive liquid (E924.1)*

● Code new
to this edition ▲ Revision of
existing code ④ ⑤ Fourth or fifth
digit required

E915 **Foreign body accidentally entering other orifice**

> Excludes: *aspiration and inhalation of foreign body, any, (into respiratory tract) NOS (E911-E912)*

OTHER ACCIDENTS (E916-E928)

E916 **Struck accidentally by falling object**
Collapse of building, except on fire
Falling:
  rock
  snowslide NOS
  stone
  tree

Object falling from:
  machine, not in operation
  stationary vehicle

Code first: collapse of building on fire (E890.0-E891.9)
  falling object in:
    cataclysm (E908-E909)
    machinery accidents (E919.0-E919.9)
    transport accidents (E800.0-E845.9)
    vehicle accidents not elsewhere classifiable (E846-E848)
  object set in motion by:
    explosion (E921.0-E921.9, E923.0-E923.9)
    firearm (E922.0-E922.9)
  projected object (E917.0-E917.9)

E917 **Striking against or struck accidentally by objects or persons**
Includes:

bumping into or against colliding with kicking against stepping on struck by	object (moving) (projected) (stationary) pedestrian conveyance person

> Excludes: *fall from:*
> *bumping into or against object (E888)*
> *collision with another person, except when caused by a crowd (E886.0-E886.9)*
> *stumbling over object (E885)*
> *injury caused by:*
> *assault (E960.0-E960.1, E967.0-E967.9)*
> *cutting or piercing instrument (E920.0-E920.9)*
> *explosion (E921.0-E921.9, E923.0-E923.9)*
> *firearm (E922.0-E922.9)*
> *machinery (E919.0-E919.9)*
> *transport vehicle (E800.0-E845.9)*
> *vehicle not elsewhere classifiable (E846-E848)*

E917.0 **In sports**
Kicked or stepped on during game (football) (rugby)
Knocked down while boxing
Struck by hit or thrown ball
Struck by hockey stick or puck

E917.1 **Caused by a crowd, by collective fear or panic**
Crushed
Pushed } by crown or human stampede
Stepped on

E917.2 **In running water**

> Excludes: *drowning or submersion (E910.0-E910.9)*
> *that in sports (E917.0)*

E917.9 **Other**
Accident caused by air rifle [BB gun]

E918 **Caught accidentally in or between objects**
Caught, crushed, jammed, or pinched in or between moving or stationary objects, such as:
escalator
folding object
hand tools, appliances, or implements
sliding door and door frame
under packing crate
washing machine wringer

continued

Add 4th or 5th digit	Nonspecific code	Unspecified code	Manifestation code

Excludes: injury caused by:
> cutting or piercing instrument (E920.0-E920.9)
> machinery (E919.0-E919.9)
> transport vehicle (E800.0-E845.9)
> vehicle not elsewhere classifiable (E846-E848)
> struck accidentally by:
> falling object (E916)
> object (moving) (projected) (E917.0-E917.9)

E919 **Accidents caused by machinery**
Includes:

burned by	
caught in (moving parts of)	
collapse of	
crushed by	
cut or pierced by	
drowning or submersion caused by	
explosion of, on, in	
fall from or into moving part of	
fire starting in or on	machinery (accident)
mechanical suffocation caused by	
object falling from, on, in motion by	
overturning of	
pinned under	
run over by	
struck by	
thrown from	

caught between machinery and other object
machinery accident NOS

Excludes: accidents involving machinery, not in operation (E884.9, E916-E918)
> injury caused by:
> electric current in connection with machinery (E925.0-E925.9)
> escalator (E880.0, E918)
> explosion of pressure vessel in connection with machinery (E921.0-E921.9)
> moving sidewalk (E885)
> powered hand tools, appliances, and implements (E916-E918, E920.0-E921.9,
> E923.0-E926.9)
> transport vehicle accidents involving machinery (E800.0-E848.9)
> poisoning by carbon monoxide generated by machine (E868.8)

E919.0 **Agriculture machines**

Animal-powered	Farm tractor
agricultural machine	Harvester
Combine	Hay mower or rake
Derrick, hay	Reaper
Farm machinery NOS	Thresher

Excludes: that in transport under own power on the highway (E810.0-E819.9)
> that being towed by another vehicle on the highway (E810.0-E819.9,
> E827.0-E827.9, E829.0-E829.9)
> that involved in accident classifiable to E820-E829 (E820.0-E829.9)

E919.1 **Mining and earth-drilling machinery**

Bore or drill (land) (seabed)	Shaft lift
Shaft hoist	Under-cutter

Excludes: coal car, tram, truck, and tub in mine (E846)

E919.2 **Lifting machines and appliances**

Chain hoist	
Crane	
Derrick	
Elevator (building) (grain)	except in agricultural or mining operations
Forklift truck	
Lift	
Pulley block	
Winch	

Excludes: that being towed by another vehicle on the highway (E810.0-E819.9,
> E827.0-E827.9, E829.0-E829.9)
> that in transport under own power on the highway (E810.0-E819.9)
> that involved in accident classifiable to E820-E829 (E820.0-E829.9)

● Code new
to this edition

▲ Revision of
existing code

④ ⑤ Fourth or fifth
digit required

E919.3 Metalworking machines
Abrasive wheel
Forging machine
Lathe
Mechanical shears

Metal:
drilling machine
milling machine
power press
rolling-mill
sawing machine

E919.4 Woodworking and forming machines
Band saw
Bench saw
Circular saw
Molding machine
Overhead plane

Powered saw
Radial saw
Sander

Excludes: *hand saw (E920.1)*

E919.5 Prime movers, except electrical motors
Gas turbine
Internal combustion engine

Steam engine
Water driven turbine

Excludes: *that being towed by other vehicle on the highway (E810.0-E819.9, E827.0-E827.9, E829.0-E829.9)*
that in transport under own power on the highway (E810.0-E819.9)

E919.6 Transmission machinery
Transmission:
  belt
  cable
  chain
  gear

Transmission:
  pinion
  pulley
  shaft

E919.7 Earth moving, scraping, and other excavating machines
Bulldozer
Road scraper

Steam shovel

Excludes: *that being towed by other vehicle on the highway (E810.0-E819.9, E827.0-E827.9, E829.0-E829.9)*
that in transport under own power on the highway (E810.0-E819.9)

E919.8 Other specified machinery
Machines for manufacture of:
  clothing
  foodstuffs and beverages
  paper

Printing machine
Recreational machinery
Spinning, weaving, and textile machines

E919.9 Unspecified machinery

E920 Accidents caused by cutting and piercing instruments or objects
Includes: accidental injury by fall on object:
  edged
  pointed
  sharp

E920.0 Powered lawn mower

E920.1 Other powered hand tools
Any powered hand tool [compressed air] [electric] [explosive cartridge] [hydraulic power], such as:
  drill
  hand saw
  hedge clipper

rivet gun
snow blower
staple gun

Excludes: *band saw (E919.4)*
bench saw (E919.4)

E920.2 Powered household appliances and implements
Blender
Electric:
  beater or mixer
  can opener
  fan

Electric:
  knife
  sewing machine
Garbage disposal appliance

E920.3 Knives, swords, and daggers

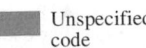

Add 4th or 5th digit   Nonspecific code   Unspecified code   Manifestation code

E920.4 Other hand tools and implements

Axe	Paper cutter
Can opener NOS	Pitchfork
Chisel	Rake
Fork	Scissors
Hand saw	Screwdriver
Hoe	Sewing machine, not powered
Ice pick	Shovel
Needle (sewing)	

E920.5 Hypodermic needle

Contaminated needle
Needle stick

E920.8 Other specified cutting and piercing instruments or objects

Arrow	Nail
Broken glass	Plant thorn
Dart	Splinter
Edge of stiff paper	Tin can lid
Lathe turnings	

Excludes: *animal spines or quills (E906.8)*
flying glass due to explosion (E921.0-E923.9)

E920.9 Unspecified cutting and piercing instrument or object

E921 Accident caused by explosion of pressure vessel

Includes: accidental explosion of pressure vessels, whether or not part of machinery

Excludes: *explosion of pressure vessel on transport vehicle (E800.0-E845.9)*

E921.0 Boilers

E921.1 Gas cylinders

Air tank   Pressure gas tank

E921.8 Other specified pressure vessels

Aerosol can   Pressure cooker
Automobile tire

E921.9 Unspecified pressure vessel

E922 Accident caused by firearm missile

E922.0 Handgun

Pistol   Revolver

Excludes: *Verey pistol (E922.8)*

E922.1 Shotgun (automatic)

E922.2 Hunting rifle

Excludes: *air rifle [BB gun] (E917.9)*

E922.3 Military firearms

Army rifle   Machine gun

E922.8 Other specified firearm missile

Verey pistol [flare]

E922.9 Unspecified firearm missile

Gunshot wound NOS   Shot NOS

E923 Accident caused by explosive material

Includes: flash burns and other injuries resulting from explosion of explosive material
ignition of highly explosive material with explosion

Excludes: *explosion:*

in or on machinery (E919.0-E919.9)
on any transport vehicle, except stationary motor vehicle (E800.0-E848)
with conflagration (E890.0, E891.0, E892)
secondary fires resulting from explosion (E890.0-E899)

E923.0 Fireworks

E923.1 Blasting materials

Blasting cap   Explosive [any] used in blasting operations
Detonator
Dynamite

● Code new
  to this edition

▲ Revision of
  existing code

④ ⑤ Fourth or fifth
    digit required

E923.2 Explosive gases
Acetylene
Butane
Coal gas
Explosion in mine NOS
Fire damp
Gasoline fumes
Methane
Propane

E923.8 Other explosive materials
Bomb
Explosive missile
Grenade
Mine
Shell
Torpedo
Explosion in munitions:
dump
factory

E923.9 Unspecified explosive material
Explosion NOS

E924 Accident caused by hot substance or object, caustic or corrosive material, and steam

Excludes: burning NOS (E899)
chemical burn resulting from swallowing a corrosive substance (E860.0-E864.4)
fire caused by these substances and objects (E890.0-E894)
radiation burns (E926.0-E926.9)
therapeutic misadventures (E870.0-E876.9)

E924.0 Hot liquids and vapors, including steam
Burning or scalding by:
boiling water
hot or boiling liquids not primarily caustic or corrosive
liquid metal
steam
other hot vapor

Excludes: hot (boiling) tap water (E924.2)

E924.1 Caustic and corrosive substances
Burning by:
acid [any kind]
ammonia
caustic oven cleaner or other substance
corrosive substance
lye
vitriol

E924.2 Hot (boiling) tap water

E924.8 Other
Burning by:
heat from electric heating appliance
hot object NOS
light bulb
steam pipe

E924.9 Unspecified

E925 Accident caused by electric current
Includes: electric current from exposed wire, faulty appliance, high voltage cable, live rail, or
open electric socket as the cause of:
burn
cardiac fibrillation
convulsion
electric shock
electrocution
puncture wound
respiratory paralysis

Excludes: burn by heat from electrical appliance (E924.8)
lightning (E907)

E925.0 Domestic wiring and appliances

E925.1 Electric power generating plants, distribution stations, transmission lines
Broken power line

E925.2 Industrial wiring, appliances, and electrical machinery
Conductors
Control apparatus
Electrical equipment and machinery
Transformers

515

E925.8 Other electric current

Wiring and appliances in
or on:
    farm [not farmhouse]
    outdoors
    public building

Wiring and appliances in or on:
    residential institutions
    schools

E925.9 Unspecified electric current

Burns or other injury from electric current NOS
Electric shock NOS
Electrocution NOS

E926 Exposure to radiation

Excludes: abnormal reaction to or complication of treatment without mention of
    misadventure (E879.2)
    atomic power plant malfunction in water transport (E838.0-E838.9)
    misadventure to patient in surgical and medical procedures (E873.2-E873.3)
    use of radiation in war operations (E996-E997.9)

E926.0 Radiofrequency radiation

Overexposure to:
    microwave radiation
    radar radiation
    radiofrequency
    radiofrequency radiation [any]

from:
    high-powered radio and
      television transmitters
    industrial radiofrequency
    induction heaters
    radar installations

E926.1 Infra-red heaters and lamps

Exposure to infra-red radiation from heaters and lamps as the cause of:
    blistering
    burning
    charring
    inflammatory change

Excludes: physical contact with heater or lamp (E924.8)

E926.2 Visible and ultraviolet light sources

Arc lamps
Black light sources
Electrical welding arc

Oxygas welding torch
Sun rays

Excludes: excessive heat from these sources (E900.1-E900.9)

E926.3 X-rays and other electromagnetic ionizing radiation

Gamma rays

X-rays (hard) (soft)

E926.4 Lasers

E926.5 Radioactive isotopes

Radiobiologicals

Radiopharmaceuticals

E926.8 Other specified radiation

Artificially accelerated beams of ionized particles generated by:
    betatrons
    synchrotrons

E926.9 Unspecified radiation

Radiation NOS

E927 Overexertion and strenuous movements

Excessive physical exercise
Overexertion (from):
    lifting
    pulling
    pushing

Strenuous movements in:
    recreational activities
    other activities

E928 Other and unspecified environmental and accidental causes

E928.0 Prolonged stay in weightless environment

Weightlessness in spacecraft (simulator)

E928.1 Exposure to noise

Noise (pollution)
Sound waves

Supersonic waves

E928.2 Vibration

E928.8 Other

E928.9 Unspecified accident

Accident NOS
Blow NOS

● Code new
   to this edition

▲ Revision of
   existing code

④ ⑤ Fourth or fifth
    digit required

Casualty (not due to war)
Decapitation
Injury [any part of body, or unspecified]
Killed
Knocked down
Mangled
Wound

} stated as accidentally inflicted,
but not otherwise specified

Excludes: *fracture, cause unspecified (E887)*
injuries undetermined whether accidentally or purposely inflicted (E980.0-E989)

LATE EFFECTS OF ACCIDENTAL INJURY (E929)

Note: This category is to be used to indicate accidental injury as the cause of death or disability from late effects, which are themselves classifiable elsewhere. The "late effects" include conditions reported as such or as sequelae which may occur at any time after the acute injury.

E929 **Late effects of accidental injury**

Excludes: *late effects of:*
surgical and medical procedures (E870.0-E879.9)
therapeutic use of drugs and medicines (E930.0-E949.9)

E929.0 Late effects of motor vehicle accident
Late effects of accidents classifiable to E810-E825

E929.1 Late effects of other transport accident
Late effects of accidents classifiable to E800-E807, E826-E838, E840-E848

E929.2 Late effects of accidental poisoning
Late effects of accidents classifiable to E850-E858, E860-E869

E929.3 Late effects of accidental fall
Late effects of accidents classifiable to E880-E888

E929.4 Late effects of accident caused by fire
Late effects of accidents classifiable to E890-E899

E929.5 Late effects of accident due to natural and environmental factors
Late effects of accidents classifiable to E900-E909

E929.8 Late effects of other accidents
Late effects of accidents classifiable to E910-E928.8

E929.9 Late effects of unspecified accident
Late effects of accidents classifiable to E928.9

DRUGS, MEDICINAL AND BIOLOGICAL SUBSTANCES CAUSING ADVERSE EFFECTS IN THERAPEUTIC USE (E930-E949)

Includes: correct drug properly administered in therapeutic or prophylactic dosage, as the cause of any adverse effect including allergic or hypersensitivity reactions

Excludes: *accidental overdose of drug and wrong drug given or taken in error*
(E850.0-E858.9)
accidents in the technique of administration of drug or biological substance, such as accidental puncture during injection, or contamination of drug
(E870.0-E876.9)
administration with suicidal or homicidal intent or intent to harm, or in circumstances classifiable to E980-E989 (E950.0-E950.5, E962.0, E980.0-E980.5)

See Alphabetic Index for more complete list of specific drugs to be classified under the fourth-digit subdivisions. The American Hospital Formulary numbers can be used to classify new drugs listed by the American Hospital Formulary Service (AHFS). See appendix C.

E930 **Antibiotics**

Excludes: *that used as eye, ear, nose, and throat [ENT], and local anti-infectives*
(E946.0-E946.9)

E930.0 Penicillins
Natural
Synthetic

Semisynthetic, such as:
ampicillin
cloxacillin
nafcillin
oxacillin

E930.1 Antifungal antibiotics
Amphotericin B
Griseofulvin

Hachimycin [trichomycin]
Nystatin

517

| | Add 4th or 5th digit | | Nonspecific code | | Unspecified code | | Manifestation code |

E930.2 Chloramphenicol group
Chloramphenicol   Thiamphenicol

E930.3 Erythromycin and other macrolides
Oleandomycin   Spiramycin

E930.4 Tetracycline group
Doxycycline   Oxytetracycline
Minocycline

E930.5 Cephalosporin group
Cephalexin   Cephaloridine
Cephaloglycin   Cephalothin

E930.6 Antimycobacterial antibiotics
Cycloserine   Rifampin
Kanamycin   Streptomycin

E930.7 Antineoplastic antibiotics
Actinomycins, such as: Bleomycin
Cactinomycin   Daunorubicin
Dactinomycin   Mitomycin

Excludes: other antineoplastic drugs (E933.1)

E930.8 Other specified antibiotics

E930.9 Unspecified antibiotic

E931 Other anti-infectives

Excludes: ENT, and local anti-infectives (E946.0-E946.9)

E931.0 Sulfonamides
Sulfadiazine   Sulfamethoxazole
Sulfafurazole

E931.1 Arsenical anti-infectives

E931.2 Heavy metal anti-infectives
Compounds of: Compounds of:
antimony   lead
bismuth   mercury

Excludes: mercurial diuretics (E944.0)

E931.3 Quinoline and hydroxyquinoline derivatives
Chiniofon   Diiodohydroxyquin

Excludes: antimalarial drugs (E931.4)

E931.4 Antimalarials and drugs acting on other blood protozoa
Chloroquine phosphate   Proguanil [chloroguanide]
Cycloguanil   Pyrimethamine
Primaquine   Quinine (sulphate)

E931.5 Other antiprotozoal drugs
Emetine

E931.6 Anthelmintics
Hexylresorcinol   Piperazine
Male fern oleoresin   Thiabendazole

E931.7 Antiviral drugs
Methisazone

Excludes: amantadine (E936.4)
cytarabine (E933.1)
idoxuridine (E946.5)

E931.8 Other antimycobacterial drugs
Ethambutol   Para-aminosalicylic acid derivatives
Ethionamide   Sulfones
Isoniazid

E931.9 Other and unspecified anti-infectives
Flucytosine   Nitrofuran derivatives

E932 Hormones and synthetic substitutes

E932.0 Adrenal cortical steroids
Cortisone derivatives
Desoxycorticosterone derivatives
Fluorinated corticosteroids

● Code new   ▲ Revision of   ④ ⑤ Fourth or fifth
to this edition   existing code   digit required

E932.1 Androgens and anabolic congeners
Nandrolone phenpropionate
Oxymetholone
Testosterone and preparations

E932.2 Ovarian hormones and synthetic substitutes
Contraceptives, oral
Estrogens
Estrogens and progestogens combined
Progestogens

E932.3 Insulins and antidiabetic agents
Acetohexamide   Insulin
Biguanide derivatives, oral   Phenformin
Chlorpropamide   Sulfonylurea derivatives, oral
Glucagon   Tolbutamide

Excludes: *adverse effect of insulin administered for shock therapy (E879.3)*

E932.4 Anterior pituitary hormones
Corticotropin   Somatotropin [growth hormone]
Gonadotropin

E932.5 Posterior pituitary hormones
Vasopressin

Excludes: *oxytocic agents (E945.0)*

E932.6 Parathyroid and parathyroid derivatives

E932.7 Thyroid and thyroid derivatives
Dextrothyroxine   Liothyronine
Levothyroxine sodium Thyroglobulin

E932.8 Antithyroid agents
Iodides   Thiourea
Thiouracil

E932.9 Other and unspecified hormones and synthetic substitutes

E933 Primarily systemic agents

E933.0 Antiallergic and antiemetic drugs
Antihistamines   Diphenylpyraline
Chlorpheniramine   Thonzylamine
Diphenhydramine   Tripelennamine

Excludes: *phenothiazine-based tranquilizers (E939.1)*

E933.1 Antineoplastic and immunosuppressive drugs
Azathioprine   Mechlorethamine hydrochloride
Busulfan   Mercaptopurine
Chlorambucil   Triethylenethiophosphoramide [thio-TEPA]
Cyclophosphamide
Cytarabine
Fluorouracil

Excludes: *antineoplastic antibiotics (E930.7)*

E933.2 Acidifying agents

E933.3 Alkalizing agents

E933.4 Enzymes, not elsewhere classified
Penicillinase

E933.5 Vitamins, not elsewhere classified
Vitamin A   Vitamin D

Excludes: *nicotinic acid (E942.2)*
vitamin K (E934.3)

E933.8 Other systemic agents, not elsewhere classified
Heavy metal antagonists

E933.9 Unspecified systemic agent

E934 Agents primarily affecting blood constituents

E934.0 Iron and its compounds
Ferric salts
Ferrous sulphate and other ferrous salts

E934.1 Liver preparations and other antianemic agents
Folic acid

	Add 4th or 5th digit		Nonspecific code		Unspecified code		Manifestation code

E934.2 Anticoagulants
Coumarin
Heparin
Phenindione
Prothrombin synthesis inhibitor
Warfarin sodium

E934.3 Vitamin K [phytonadione]

E934.4 Fibrinolysis-affecting drugs
Aminocaproic acid
Streptodornase
Streptokinase
Urokinase

E934.5 Anticoagulant antagonists and other coagulants
Hexadimethrine bromide
Protamine sulfate

E934.6 Gamma globulin

E934.7 Natural blood and blood products
Blood plasma
Human fibrinogen
Packed red cells
Whole blood

E934.8 Other agents affecting blood constituents
Macromolecular blood substitutes

E934.9 Unspecified agent affecting blood constituents

E935 Analgesics, antipyretics, and antirheumatics

E935.0 Heroin
Diacetylmorphine

☐ **E935.1 Methadone**

☐ **E935.2 Other opiates and related narcotics**
Codeine [methylmorphine]
Morphine
Opium (alkaloids)
Meperidine [pethidine]

☐ **E935.3 Salicylates**
Acetylsalicylic acid [aspirin]
Amino derivatives of salicylic acid
Salicylic acid salts

☐ **E935.4 Aromatic analgesics, not elsewhere classified**
Acetanilid
Paracetamol [acetaminophen]
Phenacetin [acetophenetidin]

☐ **E935.5 Pyrazole derivatives**
Aminophenazone [aminopyrine]
Phenylbutazone

☐ **E935.6 Antirheumatics [antiphlogistics]**
Gold salts
Indomethacin

Excludes: *salicylates (E935.3)*
steroids (E932.0)

☐ **E935.7 Other non-narcotic analgesics**
Pyrabital

E935.8 Other specified analgesics and antipyretics
Pentazocine

E935.9 Unspecified analgesic and antipyretic

E936 Anticonvulsants and anti-Parkinsonism drugs

E936.0 Oxazolidine derivatives
Paramethadione
Trimethadione

E936.1 Hydantoin derivatives
Phenytoin

E936.2 Succinimides
Ethosuximide
Phensuximide

E936.3 Other and unspecified anticonvulsants
Beclamide
Primidone

E936.4 Anti-Parkinsonism drugs
Amantadine
Ethopropazine [profenamine]
Levodopa [L-dopa]

E937 Sedatives and hypnotics

E937.0 Barbiturates
Amobarbital [amylobarbitone]
Barbital [barbitone]

● Code new
to this edition

▲ Revision of
existing code

④ ⑤ Fourth or fifth
digit required

Butabarbital [butabarbitone]
Pentobarbital [pentobarbitone]
Phenobarbital [phenobarbitone]
Secobarbital [quinalbarbitone]

Excludes: *thiobarbiturates (E938.3)*

E937.1 Chloral hydrate group

E937.2 Paraldehyde

E937.3 Bromine compounds
Bromide   Carbromal (derivatives)

E937.4 Methaqualone compounds

E937.5 Glutethimide group

E937.6 Mixed sedatives, not elsewhere classified

E937.8 Other sedatives and hypnotics

E937.9 Unspecified
Sleeping:
  drug
  pill } NOS
  tablet

E938 Other central nervous system depressants and anesthetics

E938.0 Central nervous system muscle-tone depressants
Chlorphenesin (carbamate)   Methocarbamol
Mephenesin

E938.1 Halothane

E938.2 Other gaseous anesthetics
Ether
Halogenated hydrocarbon derivatives, except halothane
Nitrous oxide

E938.3 Intravenous anesthetics
Ketamine   Thiobarbiturates, such as thiopental sodium
Methohexital [methohexitone]

E938.4 Other and unspecified general anesthetics

E938.5 Surface and infiltration anesthetics
Cocaine   Procaine
Lidocaine [lignocaine]   Tetracaine

E938.6 Peripheral nerve- and plexus-blocking anesthetics

E938.7 Spinal anesthetics

E938.9 Other and unspecified local anesthetics

E939 Psychotropic agents

E939.0 Antidepressants
Amitriptyline   Monoamine oxidase [MAO] inhibitors
Imipramine

E939.1 Phenothiazine-based tranquilizers
Chlorpromazine   Prochlorperazine
Fluphenazine   Promazine
Phenothiazine

E939.2 Butyrophenone-based tranquilizers
Haloperidol   Trifluperidol
Spiperone

E939.3 Other antipsychotics, neuroleptics, and major tranquilizers

E939.4 Benzodiazepine-based tranquilizers
Chlordiazepoxide   Lorazepam
Diazepam   Medazepam
Flurazepam   Nitrazepam

E939.5 Other tranquilizers
Hydroxyzine   Meprobamate

E939.6 Psychodysleptics [hallucinogens]
Cannabis (derivatives)   Mescaline
Lysergide [LSD]   Psilocin
Marihuana (derivatives)   Psilocybin

E939.7 Psychostimulants
Amphetamine   Caffeine

521

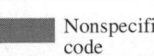 Add 4th or 5th digit

 Nonspecific code

Unspecified code

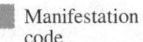 Manifestation code

Excludes: central appetite depressants (E947.0)

E939.8 Other psychotropic agents

E939.9 Unspecified psychotropic agent

E940 Central nervous system stimulants

E940.0 Analeptics
Lobeline   Nikethamide

E940.1 Opiate antagonists
Levallorphan   Naloxone
Nalorphine

E940.8 Other specified central nervous system stimulants

E940.9 Unspecified central nervous system stimulant

E941 Drugs primarily affecting the autonomic nervous system

E941.0 Parasympathomimetics [cholinergics]
Acetylcholine   Pilocarpine
Anticholinesterase:
  organophosphorus
  reversible

E941.1 Parasympatholytics [anticholinergics and antimuscarinics] and spasmolytics
Atropine   Hyoscine [scopolamine]
Homatropine   Quaternary ammonium derivatives

Excludes: papaverine (E942.5)

E941.2 Sympathomimetics [adrenergics]
Epinephrine [adrenalin]
Levarterenol [noradrenalin]

E941.3 Sympatholytics [antiadrenergics]
Phenoxybenzamine   Tolazoline hydrochloride

E941.9 Unspecified drug primarily affecting the autonomic
nervous system

E942 Agents primarily affecting the cardiovascular system

E942.0 Cardiac rhythm regulators
Practolol   Propranolol
Procainamide   Quinidine

E942.1 Cardiotonic glycosides and drugs of similar action
Digitalis glycosides   Strophanthins
Digoxin

E942.2 Antilipemic and antiarteriosclerotic drugs
Cholestyramine   Nicotinic acid derivatives
Clofibrate   Sitosterols

Excludes: dextrothyroxine (E932.7)

E942.3 Ganglion-blocking agents
Pentamethonium bromide

E942.4 Coronary vasodilators
Dipyridamole   Nitrites
Nitrates [nitroglycerin]   Prenylamine

E942.5 Other vasodilators
Cyclandelate   Hydralazine
Diazoxide   Papaverine

E942.6 Other antihypertensive agents
Clonidine   Rauwolfia alkaloids
Guanethidine   Reserpine

E942.7 Antivaricose drugs, including sclerosing agents
Monoethanolamine   Zinc salts

E942.8 Capillary-active drugs
Adrenochrome derivatives   Metaraminol
Bioflavonoids

E942.9 Other and unspecified agents primarily affecting the cardiovascular system

E943 Agents primarily affecting gastrointestinal system

E943.0 Antacids and antigastric secretion drugs
Aluminum hydroxide   Magnesium trisilicate

● Code new   ▲ Revision of   ④ ⑤ Fourth or fifth
   to this edition   existing code   digit required

E943.1 Irritant cathartics
 Bisacodyl   Phenolphthalein
 Castor oil

E943.2 Emollient cathartics
 Sodium dioctyl sulfosuccinate

E943.3 Other cathartics, including intestinal atonia drugs
 Magnesium sulfate

E943.4 Digestants
 Pancreatin   Pepsin
 Papain

E943.5 Antidiarrheal drugs
 Bismuth subcarbonate Pectin
 Kaolin

 Excludes: *anti-infectives (E930.0-E931.9)*

E943.6 Emetics

E943.8 Other specified agents primarily affecting the gastrointestinal system

E943.9 Unspecified agent primarily affecting the gastrointestinal system

E944 Water, mineral, and uric acid metabolism drugs

E944.0 Mercurial diuretics
 Chlormerodrin   Mercurophylline
 Mercaptomerin   Mersalyl

E944.1 Purine derivative diuretics
 Theobromine   Theophylline

 Excludes: *aminophylline [theophylline ethylenediamine] (E945.7)*

E944.2 Carbonic acid anhydrase inhibitors
 Acetazolamide

E944.3 Saluretics
 Benzothiadiazides
 Chlorothiazide group

E944.4 Other diuretics
 Ethacrynic acid   Furosemide

E944.5 Electrolytic, caloric, and water-balance agents

E944.6 Other mineral salts, not elsewhere classified

E944.7 Uric acid metabolism drugs
 Cinchophen and congeners Phenoquin
 Colchicine   Probenecid

E945 Agents primarily acting on the smooth and skeletal muscles and respiratory system

E945.0 Oxytocic agents
 Ergot alkaloids   Prostaglandins

E945.1 Smooth muscle relaxants
 Adiphenine
 Metaproterenol [orciprenaline]

 Excludes: *papaverine (E942.5)*

E945.2 Skeletal muscle relaxants
 Alcuronium chloride Suxamethonium chloride

E945.3 Other and unspecified drugs acting on muscles

E945.4 Antitussives
 Dextromethorphan Pipazethate hydrochloride

E945.5 Expectorants
 Acetylcysteine   Ipecacuanha
 Cocillana   Terpin hydrate
 Guaifenesin [glyceryl guaiacolate]

E945.6 Anti-common cold drugs

E945.7 Antiasthmatics
 Aminophylline [theophylline ethylenediamine]

E945.8 Other and unspecified respiratory drugs

E946 Agents primarily affecting skin and mucous membrane, ophthalmological, otorhinolaryngological, and dental drugs

E946.0 Local anti-infectives and anti-inflammatory drugs

523

 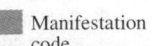

E946.1 **Antipruritics**

E946.2 **Local astringents and local detergents**

E946.3 **Emollients, demulcents, and protectants**

E946.4 **Keratolytics, keratoplastics, other hair treatment drugs and preparations**

E946.5 **Eye anti-infectives and other eye drugs**
Idoxuridine

E946.6 **Anti-infectives and other drugs and preparations for ear, nose, and throat**

E946.7 **Dental drugs topically applied**

E946.8 **Other agents primarily affecting skin and mucous membrane**
Spermicides

E946.9 **Unspecified agent primarily affecting skin and mucous membrane**

E947 **Other and unspecified drugs and medicinal substances**

E947.0 **Dietetics**

E947.1 **Lipotropic drugs**

E947.2 **Antidotes and chelating agents, not elsewhere classified**

E947.3 **Alcohol deterrents**

E947.4 **Pharmaceutical excipients**

E947.8 **Other drugs and medicinal substances**
Contrast media used for diagnostic x-ray procedures
Diagnostic agents and kits

E947.9 **Unspecified drug or medicinal substance**

E948 **Bacterial vaccines**

E948.0 **BCG vaccine**

E948.1 **Typhoid and paratyphoid**

E948.2 **Cholera**

E948.3 **Plague**

E948.4 **Tetanus**

E948.5 **Diphtheria**

E948.6 **Pertussis vaccine, including combinations with a pertussis component**

E948.8 **Other and unspecified bacterial vaccines**

E948.9 **Mixed bacterial vaccines, except combinations with a pertussis component**

E949 **Other vaccines and biological substances**

Excludes: *gamma globulin (E934.6)*

E949.0 **Smallpox vaccine**

E949.1 **Rabies vaccine**

E949.2 **Typhus vaccine**

E949.3 **Yellow fever vaccine**

E949.4 **Measles vaccine**

E949.5 **Poliomyelitis vaccine**

E949.6 **Other and unspecified viral and rickettsial vaccines**
Mumps vaccine

E949.7 **Mixed viral-rickettsial and bacterial vaccines, except combinations with a pertussis component**

Excludes: *combinations with a pertussis component (E948.6)*

E949.9 **Other and unspecified vaccines and biological substances**

SUICIDE AND SELF-INFLICTED INJURY (E950-E959)

Includes: injuries in suicide and attempted suicide
self-inflicted injuries specified as intentional

E950 **Suicide and self-inflicted poisoning by solid or liquid substances**

E950.0 **Analgesics, antipyretics, and antirheumatics**

E950.1 **Barbiturates**

E950.2 **Other sedatives and hypnotics**

E950.3 **Tranquilizers and other psychotropic agents**

● Code new
   to this edition
▲ Revision of
   existing code
④ ⑤ Fourth or fifth
   digit required

E950.4   **Other specified drugs and medicinal substances**

E950.5   **Unspecified drug or medicinal substances**

  E950.6   **Agricultural and horticultural chemical and pharmaceutical preparations other than plant foods and fertilizers**

  E950.7   **Corrosive and caustic substances**
      Suicide and self-inflicted poisoning by substances classifiable to E864

  E950.8   **Arsenic and its compounds**

E950.9   **Other and unspecified solid and liquid substances**

E951   **Suicide and self-inflicted poisoning by gases in domestic use**

  E951.0   **Gas distributed by pipeline**

  E951.1   **Liquefied petroleum gas distributed in mobile containers**

E951.8   **Other utility gas**

E952   **Suicide and self-inflicted poisoning by other gases and vapors**

  E952.0   **Motor vehicle exhaust gas**

E952.1   **Other carbon monoxide**

E952.8   **Other specified gases and vapors**

E952.9   **Unspecified gases and vapors**

E953   **Suicide and self-inflicted injury by hanging, strangulation, and suffocation**

  E953.0   **Hanging**

  E953.1   **Suffocation by plastic bag**

E953.8   **Other specified means**

E953.9   **Unspecified means**

E954   **Suicide and self-inflicted injury by submersion [drowning]**

E955   **Suicide and self-inflicted injury by firearms and explosives**

  E955.0   **Handgun**

  E955.1   **Shotgun**

  E955.2   **Hunting rifle**

  E955.3   **Military firearms**

E955.4   **Other and unspecified firearm**
      Gunshot NOS   Shot NOS

  E955.5   **Explosives**

E955.9   **Unspecified**

E956   **Suicide and self-inflicted injury by cutting and piercing instrument**

E957   **Suicide and self-inflicted injuries by jumping from high place**

  E957.0   **Residential premises**

E957.1   **Other man-made structures**

  E957.2   **Natural sites**

E957.9   **Unspecified**

E958   **Suicide and self-inflicted injury by other and unspecified means**

  E958.0   **Jumping or lying before moving object**

  E958.1   **Burns, fire**

  E958.2   **Scald**

  E958.3   **Extremes of cold**

  E958.4   **Electrocution**

  E958.5   **Crashing of motor vehicle**

  E958.6   **Crashing of aircraft**

  E958.7   **Caustic substances, except poisoning**

      Excludes: *poisoning by caustic substance (E950.7)*

E958.8   **Other specified means**

E958.9   **Unspecified means**

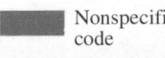 Add 4th or 5th digit   Nonspecific code   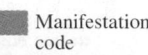 Unspecified code   Manifestation code

E959   Late effects of self-inflicted injury

> Note: This category is to be used to indicate circumstances classifiable to E950-E958 as the cause of death or disability from late effects, which are themselves classifiable elsewhere. The "late effects" include conditions reported as such or as sequelae which may occur at any time after the attempted suicide or self-inflicted injury.

HOMICIDE AND INJURY PURPOSELY INFLICTED BY OTHER PERSONS (E960-E969)

> Includes: injuries inflicted by another person with intent to injure or kill, by any means

> *Excludes:* *injuries due to:*
> > *legal intervention (E970-E978)*
> > *operations of war (E990-E999)*

E960   Fight, brawl, rape

E960.0   Unarmed fight or brawl
> Beatings NOS
> Brawl or fight with hands, fists, feet
> Injured or killed in fight NOS

> *Excludes:* *homicidal:*
> > *injury by weapons (E965.0-E966, E969)*
> > *strangulation (E963)*
> > *submersion (E964)*

E960.1   Rape

E961   Assault by corrosive or caustic substance, except poisoning
> Injury or death purposely caused by corrosive or caustic substance, such as:
> acid [any]
> corrosive substance
> vitriol

> *Excludes:* *burns from hot liquid (E968.3)*
> > *chemical burns from swallowing a corrosive substance (E962.0-E962.9)*

E962   Assault by poisoning

E962.0   Drugs and medicinal substances
> Homicidal poisoning by any drug or medicinal substance

E962.1   Other solid and liquid substances

E962.2   Other gases and vapors

E962.9   Unspecified poisoning

E963   Assault by hanging and strangulation
> Homicidal (attempt):
> garrotting or ligature
> hanging
> strangulation
> suffocation

E964   Assault by submersion [drowning]

E965   Assault by firearms and explosives

E965.0   Handgun
> Pistol   Revolver

E965.1   Shotgun

E965.2   Hunting rifle

E965.3   Military firearms

E965.4   Other and unspecified firearm

E965.5   Antipersonnel bomb

E965.6   Gasoline bomb

E965.7   Letter bomb

E965.8   Other specified explosive
> Bomb NOS (placed in):   Dynamite
> car
> house

E965.9   Unspecified explosive

E966   Assault by cutting and piercing instrument

● Code new
to this edition   ▲ Revision of
existing code   ④ ⑤ Fourth or fifth
digit required

Assassination (attempt), homicide (attempt) by any instrument classifiable under E920

Homicidal:

> cut
> puncture
> stab } any part of body
> Stabbed

▲ **E967** **Child and adult battering and other maltreatment**

▲ E967.0 **By father or stepfather**

E967.1 **By other specified person**

● E967.2 **By mother or stepmother**

● E967.3 **By spouse or partner**
Ex-spouse
Ex-partner

● E967.4 **By child**

● E967.5 **By sibling**

● E967.6 **By grandparent**

● E967.7 **By other relative**

● E967.8 **By non-related caregiver**

E967.9 **By unspecified person**

E968 **Assault by other and unspecified means**

E968.0 **Fire**
Arson   Homicidal burns NOS

Excludes: *burns from hot liquid (E968.3)*

E968.1 **Pushing from a high place**

E968.2 **Striking by blunt or thrown object**

E968.3 **Hot liquid**
Homicidal burns by scalding

E968.4 **Criminal neglect**
Abandonment of child, infant, or other helpless person with intent to injure or kill

E968.5 **Transport vehicle**
Being struck by other vehicle or run down with intent to injure
Pushed in front of, thrown from, or dragged by moving vehicle with intent to injure

E968.8 **Other specified means**
Bite of human being

E968.9 **Unspecified means**
Assassination (attempt) NOS   Manslaughter (nonaccidental)
Homicidal (attempt):   Murder (attempt) NOS
  injury NOS   Violence, non-accidental
  wound NOS

E969 **Late effects of injury purposely inflicted by other person**

Note: This category is to be used to indicate circumstances classifiable to E960-E968 as the cause of death or disability from late effects, which are themselves classifiable elsewhere. The "late effects" include conditions reported as such, or as sequelae which may occur at any time after the acute injury.

LEGAL INTERVENTION (E970-E978)

Includes: injuries inflicted by the police or other law-enforcing agents, including military on duty, in the course of arresting or attempting to arrest lawbreakers, suppressing disturbances, maintaining order, and other legal action
legal execution

Excludes: *injuries caused by civil insurrections (E990.0-E999)*

E970 **Injury due to legal intervention by firearms**
Gunshot wound   Injury by:
Injury by: rifle pellet or rubber bullet
  machine gun   shot NOS
  revolver

527

Add 4th or
5th digit

Nonspecific
code

Unspecified
code

Manifestation
code

E971   Injury due to legal intervention by explosives
Injury by:
dynamite
explosive shell
grenade
mortar bomb

E972   Injury due to legal intervention by gas
Asphyxiation by gas
Injury by tear gas
Poisoning by gas

E973   Injury due to legal intervention by blunt object
Hit, struck by:
baton (nightstick)
blunt object
stave

E974   Injury due to legal intervention by cutting and piercing instrument

Cut	Incised wound
Injured by bayonet	Stab wound

E975   Injury due to legal intervention by other specified means
Blow
Manhandling

E976   Injury due to legal intervention by unspecified means

E977   Late effects of injuries due to legal intervention
Note: This category is to be used to indicate circumstances classifiable to E970-E976 as the cause of death or disability from late effects, which are themselves classifiable elsewhere. The "late effects" include conditions reported as such, or as sequelae which may occur at any time after the acute injury due to legal intervention.

E978   Legal execution
All executions performed at the behest of the judiciary or ruling authority [whether permanent or temporary] as:

asphyxiation by gas	hanging
beheading, decapitation	poisoning
(by guillotine)	shooting
capital punishment	other specified means
electrocution	

INJURY UNDETERMINED WHETHER ACCIDENTALLY OR PURPOSELY INFLICTED (E980-E989)

Note: Categories E980-E989 are for use when it is unspecified or it cannot be determined whether the injuries are accidental (unintentional), suicide (attempted), or assault.

E980   Poisoning by solid or liquid substances, undetermined whether accidentally or purposely inflicted

E980.0   Analgesics, antipyretics, and antirheumatics

E980.1   Barbiturates

E980.2   Other sedatives and hypnotics

E980.3   Tranquilizers and other psychotropic agents

E980.4   Other specified drugs and medicinal substances

E980.5   Unspecified drug or medicinal substance

E980.6   Corrosive and caustic substances
Poisoning, undetermined whether accidental or purposeful, by substances classifiable to E864

E980.7   Agricultural and horticultural chemical and pharmaceutical preparations other than plant foods and fertilizers

E980.8   Arsenic and its compounds

E980.9   Other and unspecified solid and liquid substances

E981   Poisoning by gases in domestic use, undetermined whether accidentally or purposely inflicted

E981.0   Gas distributed by pipeline

E981.1   Liquefied petroleum gas distributed in mobile containers

E981.8   Other utility gas

E982   Poisoning by other gases, undetermined whether accidentally or purposely inflicted

E982.0   Motor vehicle exhaust gas

● Code new
   to this edition

▲ Revision of
   existing code

④ ⑤ Fourth or fifth
   digit required

E982.1 Other carbon monoxide

E982.8 Other specified gases and vapors

E982.9 Unspecified gases and vapors

E983 Hanging, strangulation, or suffocation, undetermined whether accidentally or purposely inflicted

E983.0 Hanging

E983.1 Suffocation by plastic bag

E983.8 Other specified means

E983.9 Unspecified means

E984 Submersion [drowning], undetermined whether accidentally or purposely inflicted

E985 Injury by firearms and explosives, undetermined whether accidentally or purposely inflicted

E985.0 Handgun

E985.1 Shotgun

E985.2 Hunting rifle

E985.3 Military firearms

E985.4 Other and unspecified firearm

E985.5 Explosives

E986 Injury by cutting and piercing instruments, undetermined whether accidentally or purposely inflicted

E987 Falling from high place, undetermined whether accidentally or purposely inflicted

E987.0 Residential premises

E987.1 Other man-made structures

E987.2 Natural sites

E987.9 Unspecified site

E988 Injury by other and unspecified means, undetermined whether accidentally or purposely inflicted

E988.0 Jumping or lying before moving object

E988.1 Burns, fire

E988.2 Scald

E988.3 Extremes of cold

E988.4 Electrocution

E988.5 Crashing of motor vehicle

E988.6 Crashing of aircraft

E988.7 Caustic substances, except poisoning

E988.8 Other specified means

E988.9 Unspecified means

E989 Late effects of injury, undetermined whether accidentally or purposely inflicted

   Note: This category is to be used to indicate circumstances classifiable to E980-E988 as the cause of death or disability from late effects, which are themselves classifiable elsewhere. The "late effects" include conditions reported as such or as sequelae which may occur at any time after the acute injury, undetermined whether accidentally or purposely inflicted.

INJURY RESULTING FROM OPERATIONS OF WAR (E990-E999)

   Includes: injuries to military personnel and civilians caused by war and civil insurrections and occurring during the time of war and insurrection

   Excludes: *accidents during training of military personnel, manufacture of war material and transport, unless attributable to enemy action*

E990 Injury due to war operations by fires and conflagrations

   Includes: asphyxia, burns, or other injury originating from fire caused by a fire-producing device or indirectly by any conventional weapon

E990.0 From gasoline bomb

E990.9 From other and unspecified source

E991 Injury due to war operations by bullets and fragments

E991.0 Rubber bullets (rifle)

E991.1 Pellets (rifle)

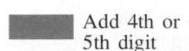 Add 4th or 5th digit

 Nonspecific code

 Unspecified code

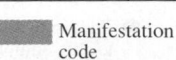 Manifestation code

E991.2 **Other bullets**

Bullet [any, except rubber bullets and pellets]
 carbine
 machine gun
 pistol
 rifle
 shotgun

E991.3 **Antipersonnel bomb (fragments)**

E991.9 **Other and unspecified fragments**

Fragments from:	Fragments from:
artillery shell	land mine
bombs, except antipersonnel	rockets
grenade	shell
guided missile	Shrapnel

E992 **Injury due to war operations by explosion of marine weapons**

Depth charge	Sea-based artillery shell
Marine mines	Torpedo
Mine NOS, at sea or in harbor	Underwater blast

E993 **Injury due to war operations by other explosion**

Accidental explosion of munitions	Explosion of:
being used in war	artillery shell
Accidental explosion of own weapons	breech block
Air blast NOS	cannon block
Blast NOS	mortar bomb
Explosion NOS	Injury by weapon burst

E994 **Injury due to war operations by destruction of aircraft**

Airplane:	Crushed by falling airplane
burned	
exploded	
shot down	

E995 **Injury due to war operations by other and unspecified forms of conventional warfare**

Battle wounds	Drowned in war operations
Bayonet injury	

E996 **Injury due to war operations by nuclear weapons**

Blast effects
Exposure to ionizing radiation from nuclear weapons
Fireball effects
Heat
Other direct and secondary effects of nuclear weapons

E997 **Injury due to war operations by other forms of unconventional warfare**

E997.0 **Lasers**

E997.1 **Biological warfare**

E997.2 **Gases, fumes, and chemicals**

E997.8 **Other specified forms of unconventional warfare**

E997.9 **Unspecified form of unconventional warfare**

E998 **Injury due to war operations but occurring after cessation of hostilities**

Injuries due to operations of war but occurring after cessation of hostilities by any means
 classifiable under E990-E997
Injuries by explosion of bombs or mines placed in the course of operations of war, if the
 explosion occurred after cessation of hostilities

E999 **Late effect of injury due to war operations**

Note: This category is to be used to indicate circumstances classifiable to E990-E998 as the
 cause of death or disability from late effects, which are themselves classifiable elsewhere.
 The "late effects" include conditions reported as such or as sequelae which may occur at
 any time after the acute injury, resulting from operations of war.

● Code new   ▲ Revision of   ④ ⑤ Fourth or fifth
 to this edition   existing code   digit required

MORPHOLOGY OF NEOPLASMS

The World Health Organization has published an adaptation of the International Classification of Diseases for oncology (ICD-O). It contains a coded nomenclature for the morphology of neoplasms, which is reproduced here for those who wish to use it in conjunction with Chapter 2 of the *International Classification of Diseases, 9th Revision, Clinical Modification.*

The morphology code numbers consist of five digits; the first four identify the histological type of the neoplasm and the fifth indicates its behavior. The one-digit behavior code is as follows:

/0 Benign

/1 Uncertain whether benign or malignant
    Borderline malignancy

/2 Carcinoma in situ
    Intraepithelial
    Noninfiltrating
    Noninvasive

/3 Malignant, primary site

/6 Malignant, metastatic site
    Secondary site

/9 Malignant, uncertain whether primary or metastatic site

In the nomenclature below, the morphology code numbers include the behavior code appropriate to the histological type of neoplasm, but this behavior code should be changed if other reported information makes this necessary. For example, "chordoma (M9370/3)" is assumed to be malignant; the term "benign chordoma" should be coded M9370/0. Similarly, "superficial spreading adenocarcinoma (M8143/3)" described as "noninvasive" should be coded M8143/2 and "melanoma (M8720/3)" described as "secondary" should be coded M8720/6.

The following table shows the correspondence between the morphology code and the different sections of Chapter 2:

Morphology code Histology/Behavior			ICD-9-CM Chapter 2
Any	0	210-229	Benign neoplasms
M8000-M8004	1	239	Neoplasms of unspecified nature
M8010+	1	235-238	Neoplasms of uncertain behavior
Any	2	230-234	Carcinoma in situ
Any	3	140-195	Malignant neoplasms, stated or presumed to be primary
		200-208	
Any	6	196-198	Malignant neoplasms, stated or presumed to be secondary

The ICD-O behavior digit /9 is inapplicable in an ICD context, since all malignant neoplasms are presumed to be primary (/3) or secondary (/6) according to other information on the medical record.

Only the first-listed term of the full ICD-O morphology nomenclature appears against each code number in the list below. The ICD-9-CM Alphabetical Index (Volume 2), however, includes all the ICD-O synonyms as well as a number of other morphological names still likely to be encountered on medical records but omitted from ICD-O as outdated or otherwise undesirable.

A coding difficulty sometimes arises where a morphological diagnosis contains two qualifying adjectives that have different code numbers. An example is "transitional cell epidermoid carcinoma." "Transitional cell carcinoma NOS" is M8120/3 and "epidermoid carcinoma NOS" is M8070/3. In such circumstances, the higher number (M8120/3 in this example) should be used, as it is usually more specific.

CODED NOMENCLATURE FOR MORPHOLOGY OF NEOPLASMS

M800   **Neoplasms NOS**
M8000/0   *Neoplasm, benign*
M8000/1   *Neoplasm, uncertain whether benign or malignant*
M8000/3   *Neoplasm, malignant*
M8000/6   *Neoplasm, metastatic*
M8000/9   *Neoplasm, malignant, uncertain whether primary or metastatic*
M8001/0   *Tumor cells, benign*
M8001/1   *Tumor cells, uncertain whether benign or malignant*
M8001/3   *Tumor cells, malignant*
M8002/3   *Malignant tumor, small cell type*
M8003/3   *Malignant tumor, giant cell type*
M8004/3   *Malignant tumor, fusiform cell type*

M801-M804   **Epithelial neoplasms NOS**
M8010/0   *Epithelial tumor, benign*
M8010/2   *Carcinoma in situ NOS*
M8010/3   *Carcinoma NOS*
M8010/6   *Carcinoma, metastatic NOS*
M8010/9   *Carcinomatosis*
M8011/0   *Epithelioma, benign*
M8011/3   *Epithelioma, malignant*
M8012/3   *Large cell carcinoma NOS*
M8020/3   *Carcinoma, undifferentiated type NOS*
M8021/3   *Carcinoma, anaplastic type NOS*
M8022/3   *Pleomorphic carcinoma*
M8030/3   *Giant cell and spindle cell carcinoma*
M8031/3   *Giant cell carcinoma*
M8032/3   *Spindle cell carcinoma*
M8033/3   *Pseudosarcomatous carcinoma*
M8034/3   *Polygonal cell carcinoma*
M8035/3   *Spheroidal cell carcinoma*
M8040/1   *Tumorlet*
M8041/3   *Small cell carcinoma NOS*
M8042/3   *Oat cell carcinoma*
M8043/3   *Small cell carcinoma, fusiform cell type*

M805-M808   **Papillary and squamous cell neoplasms**
M8050/0   *Papilloma NOS (except Papilloma of urinary bladder M8120/1)*
M8050/2   *Papillary carcinoma in situ*
M8050/3   *Papillary carcinoma NOS*
M8051/0   *Verrucous papilloma*
M8051/3   *Verrucous carcinoma NOS*
M8052/0   *Squamous cell papilloma*
M8052/3   *Papillary squamous cell carcinoma*
M8053/0   *Inverted papilloma*
M8060/0   *Papillomatosis NOS*
M8070/2   *Squamous cell carcinoma in situ NOS*
M8070/3   *Squamous cell carcinoma NOS*
M8070/6   *Squamous cell carcinoma, metastatic NOS*
M8071/3   *Squamous cell carcinoma, keratinizing type NOS*
M8072/3   *Squamous cell carcinoma, large cell, nonkeratinizing type*
M8073/3   *Squamous cell carcinoma, small cell, nonkeratinizing type*
M8074/3   *Squamous cell carcinoma, spindle cell type*
M8075/3   *Adenoid squamous cell carcinoma*
M8076/2   *Squamous cell carcinoma in situ with questionable stromal invasion*
M8076/3   *Squamous cell carcinoma, microinvasive*
M8080/2   *Queyrat's erythroplasia*
M8081/2   *Bowen's disease*
M8082/3   *Lymphoepithelial carcinoma*

M809-M811   **Basal cell neoplasms**
M8090/1   *Basal cell tumor*
M8090/3   *Basal cell carcinoma NOS*
M8091/3   *Multicentric basal cell carcinoma*
M8092/3   *Basal cell carcinoma, morphea type*
M8093/3   *Basal cell carcinoma, fibroepithelial type*
M8094/3   *Basosquamous carcinoma*
M8095/3   *Metatypical carcinoma*
M8096/0   *Intraepidermal epithelioma of Jadassohn*
M8100/0   *Trichoepithelioma*
M8101/0   *Trichofolliculoma*

M8102/0	*Tricholemmoma*
M8110/0	*Pilomatrixoma*

M812-M813 Transitional cell papillomas and carcinomas

M8120/0	*Transitional cell papilloma NOS*
M8120/1	*Urothelial papilloma*
M8120/2	*Transitional cell carcinoma in situ*
M8120/3	*Transitional cell carcinoma NOS*
M8121/0	*Schneiderian papilloma*
M8121/1	*Transitional cell papilloma, inverted type*
M8121/3	*Schneiderian carcinoma*
M8122/3	*Transitional cell carcinoma, spindle cell type*
M8123/3	*Basaloid carcinoma*
M8124/3	*Cloacogenic carcinoma*
M8130/3	*Papillary transitional cell carcinoma*

M814-M838 Adenomas and adenocarcinomas

M8140/0	*Adenoma NOS*
M8140/1	*Bronchial adenoma NOS*
M8140/2	*Adenocarcinoma in situ*
M8140/3	*Adenocarcinoma NOS*
M8140/6	*Adenocarcinoma, metastatic NOS*
M8141/3	*Scirrhous adenocarcinoma*
M8142/3	*Linitis plastica*
M8143/3	*Superficial spreading adenocarcinoma*
M8144/3	*Adenocarcinoma, intestinal type*
M8145/3	*Carcinoma, diffuse type*
M8146/0	*Monomorphic adenoma*
M8147/0	*Basal cell adenoma*
M8150/0	*Islet cell adenoma*
M8150/3	*Islet cell carcinoma*
M8151/0	*Insulinoma NOS*
M8151/3	*Insulinoma, malignant*
M8152/0	*Glucagonoma NOS*
M8152/3	*Glucagonoma, malignant*
M8153/1	*Gastrinoma NOS*
M8153/3	*Gastrinoma, malignant*
M8154/3	*Mixed islet cell and exocrine adenocarcinoma*
M8160/0	*Bile duct adenoma*
M8160/3	*Cholangiocarcinoma*
M8161/0	*Bile duct cystadenoma*
M8161/3	*Bile duct cystadenocarcinoma*
M8170/0	*Liver cell adenoma*
M8170/3	*Hepatocellular carcinoma NOS*
M8180/0	*Hepatocholangioma, benign*
M8180/3	*Combined hepatocellular carcinoma and cholangiocarcinoma*
M8190/0	*Trabecular adenoma*
M8190/3	*Trabecular adenocarcinoma*
M8191/0	*Embryonal adenoma*
M8200/0	*Eccrine dermal cylindroma*
M8200/3	*Adenoid cystic carcinoma*
M8201/3	*Cribriform carcinoma*
M8210/0	*Adenomatous polyp NOS*
M8210/3	*Adenocarcinoma in adenomatous polyp*
M8211/0	*Tubular adenoma NOS*
M8211/3	*Tubular adenocarcinoma*
M8220/0	*Adenomatous polyposis coli*
M8220/3	*Adenocarcinoma in adenomatous polyposis coli*
M8221/0	*Multiple adenomatous polyps*
M8230/3	*Solid carcinoma NOS*
M8231/3	*Carcinoma simplex*
M8240/1	*Carcinoid tumor NOS*
M8240/3	*Carcinoid tumor, malignant*
M8241/1	*Carcinoid tumor, argentaffin NOS*
M8241/3	*Carcinoid tumor, argentaffin, malignant*
M8242/1	*Carcinoid tumor, nonargentaffin NOS*
M8242/3	*Carcinoid tumor, nonargentaffin, malignant*
M8243/3	*Mucocarcinoid tumor, malignant*
M8244/3	*Composite carcinoid*
M8250/1	*Pulmonary adenomatosis*
M8250/3	*Bronchiolo-alveolar adenocarcinoma*
M8251/0	*Alveolar adenoma*

M8251/3	*Alveolar adenocarcinoma*
M8260/0	*Papillary adenoma NOS*
M8260/3	*Papillary adenocarcinoma NOS*
M8261/1	*Villous adenoma NOS*
M8261/3	*Adenocarcinoma in villous adenoma*
M8262/3	*Villous adenocarcinoma*
M8263/0	*Tubulovillous adenoma*
M8270/0	*Chromophobe adenoma*
M8270/3	*Chromophobe carcinoma*
M8280/0	*Acidophil adenoma*
M8280/3	*Acidophil carcinoma*
M8281/0	*Mixed acidophil-basophil adenoma*
M8281/3	*Mixed acidophil-basophil carcinoma*
M8290/0	*Oxyphilic adenoma*
M8290/3	*Oxyphilic adenocarcinoma*
M8300/0	*Basophil adenoma*
M8300/3	*Basophil carcinoma*
M8310/0	*Clear cell adenoma*
M8310/3	*Clear cell adenocarcinoma NOS*
M8311/1	*Hypernephroid tumor*
M8312/3	*Renal cell carcinoma*
M8313/0	*Clear cell adenofibroma*
M8320/3	*Granular cell carcinoma*
M8321/0	*Chief cell adenoma*
M8322/0	*Water-clear cell adenoma*
M8322/3	*Water-clear cell adenocarcinoma*
M8323/0	*Mixed cell adenoma*
M8323/3	*Mixed cell adenocarcinoma*
M8324/0	*Lipoadenoma*
M8330/0	*Follicular adenoma*
M8330/3	*Follicular adenocarcinoma NOS*
M8331/3	*Follicular adenocarcinoma, well differentiated type*
M8332/3	*Follicular adenocarcinoma, trabecular type*
M8333/0	*Microfollicular adenoma*
M8334/0	*Macrofollicular adenoma*
M8340/3	*Papillary and follicular adenocarcinoma*
M8350/3	*Nonencapsulated sclerosing carcinoma*
M8360/1	*Multiple endocrine adenomas*
M8361/1	*Juxtaglomerular tumor*
M8370/0	*Adrenal cortical adenoma NOS*
M8370/3	*Adrenal cortical carcinoma*
M8371/0	*Adrenal cortical adenoma, compact cell type*
M8372/0	*Adrenal cortical adenoma, heavily pigmented variant*
M8373/0	*Adrenal cortical adenoma, clear cell type*
M8374/0	*Adrenal cortical adenoma, glomerulosa cell type*
M8375/0	*Adrenal cortical adenoma, mixed cell type*
M8380/0	*Endometrioid adenoma NOS*
M8380/1	*Endometrioid adenoma, borderline malignancy*
M8380/3	*Endometrioid carcinoma*
M8381/0	*Endometrioid adenofibroma NOS*
M8381/1	*Endometrioid adenofibroma, borderline malignancy*
M8381/3	*Endometrioid adenofibroma, malignant*
M839-M842	**Adnexal and skin appendage neoplasms**
M8390/0	*Skin appendage adenoma*
M8390/3	*Skin appendage carcinoma*
M8400/0	*Sweat gland adenoma*
M8400/1	*Sweat gland tumor NOS*
M8400/3	*Sweat gland adenocarcinoma*
M8401/0	*Apocrine adenoma*
M8401/3	*Apocrine adenocarcinoma*
M8402/0	*Eccrine acrospiroma*
M8403/0	*Eccrine spiradenoma*
M8404/0	*Hidrocystoma*
M8405/0	*Papillary hydradenoma*
M8406/0	*Papillary syringadenoma*
M8407/0	*Syringoma NOS*
M8410/0	*Sebaceous adenoma*
M8410/3	*Sebaceous adenocarcinoma*
M8420/0	*Ceruminous adenoma*
M8420/3	*Ceruminous adenocarcinoma*

M843   **Mucoepidermoid neoplasms**
M8430/1   *Mucoepidermoid tumor*
M8430/3   *Mucoepidermoid carcinoma*

M844-M849 **Cystic, mucinous, and serous neoplasms**
M8440/0   *Cystadenoma NOS*
M8440/3   *Cystadenocarcinoma NOS*
M8441/0   *Serous cystadenoma NOS*
M8441/1   *Serous cystadenoma, borderline malignancy*
M8441/3   *Serous cystadenocarcinoma NOS*
M8450/0   *Papillary cystadenoma NOS*
M8450/1   *Papillary cystadenoma, borderline malignancy*
M8450/3   *Papillary cystadenocarcinoma NOS*
M8460/0   *Papillary serous cystadenoma NOS*
M8460/1   *Papillary serous cystadenoma, borderline malignancy*
M8460/3   *Papillary serous cystadenocarcinoma*
M8461/0   *Serous surface papilloma NOS*
M8461/1   *Serous surface papilloma, borderline malignancy*
M8461/3   *Serous surface papillary carcinoma*
M8470/0   *Mucinous cystadenoma NOS*
M8470/1   *Mucinous cystadenoma, borderline malignancy*
M8470/3   *Mucinous cystadenocarcinoma NOS*
M8471/0   *Papillary mucinous cystadenoma NOS*
M8471/1   *Papillary mucinous cystadenoma, borderline malignancy*
M8471/3   *Papillary mucinous cystadenocarcinoma*
M8480/0   *Mucinous adenoma*
M8480/3   *Mucinous adenocarcinoma*
M8480/6   *Pseudomyxoma peritonei*
M8481/3   *Mucin-producing adenocarcinoma*
M8490/3   *Signet ring cell carcinoma*
M8490/6   *Metastatic signet ring cell carcinoma*

M850-M854 **Ductal, lobular, and medullary neoplasms**
M8500/2   *Intraductal carcinoma, noninfiltrating NOS*
M8500/3   *Infiltrating duct carcinoma*
M8501/2   *Comedocarcinoma, noninfiltrating*
M8501/3   *Comedocarcinoma NOS*
M8502/3   *Juvenile carcinoma of the breast*
M8503/0   *Intraductal papilloma*
M8503/2   *Noninfiltrating intraductal papillary adenocarcinoma*
M8504/0   *Intracystic papillary adenoma*
M8504/2   *Noninfiltrating intracystic carcinoma*
M8505/0   *Intraductal papillomatosis NOS*
M8506/0   *Subareolar duct papillomatosis*
M8510/3   *Medullary carcinoma NOS*
M8511/3   *Medullary carcinoma with amyloid stroma*
M8512/3   *Medullary carcinoma with lymphoid stroma*
M8520/2   *Lobular carcinoma in situ*
M8520/3   *Lobular carcinoma NOS*
M8521/3   *Infiltrating ductular carcinoma*
M8530/3   *Inflammatory carcinoma*
M8540/3   *Paget's disease, mammary*
M8541/3   *Paget's disease and infiltrating duct carcinoma of breast*
M8542/3   *Paget's disease, extramammary (except Paget's disease of bone)*

M855   **Acinar cell neoplasms**
M8550/0   *Acinar cell adenoma*
M8550/1   *Acinar cell tumor*
M8550/3   *Acinar cell carcinoma*

M856-M858 **Complex epithelial neoplasms**
M8560/3   *Adenosquamous carcinoma*
M8561/0   *Adenolymphoma*
M8570/3   *Adenocarcinoma with squamous metaplasia*
M8571/3   *Adenocarcinoma with cartilaginous and osseous metaplasia*
M8572/3   *Adenocarcinoma with spindle cell metaplasia*
M8573/3   *Adenocarcinoma with apocrine metaplasia*
M8580/0   *Thymoma, benign*
M8580/3   *Thymoma, malignant*

M859-M867 **Specialized gonadal neoplasms**
M8590/1   *Sex cord-stromal tumor*
M8600/0   *Thecoma NOS*
M8600/3   *Theca cell carcinoma*

M8610/0	*Luteoma NOS*
M8620/1	*Granulosa cell tumor NOS*
M8620/3	*Granulosa cell tumor, malignant*
M8621/1	*Granulosa cell-theca cell tumor*
M8630/0	*Androblastoma, benign*
M8630/1	*Androblastoma NOS*
M8630/3	*Androblastoma, malignant*
M8631/0	*Sertoli-Leydig cell tumor*
M8632/1	*Gynandroblastoma*
M8640/0	*Tubular androblastoma NOS*
M8640/3	*Sertoli cell carcinoma*
M8641/0	*Tubular androblastoma with lipid storage*
M8650/0	*Leydig cell tumor, benign*
M8650/1	*Leydig cell tumor NOS*
M8650/3	*Leydig cell tumor, malignant*
M8660/0	*Hilar cell tumor*
M8670/0	*Lipid cell tumor of ovary*
M8671/0	*Adrenal rest tumor*

M868-M871 Paragangliomas and glomus tumors

M8680/1	*Paraganglioma NOS*
M8680/3	*Paraganglioma, malignant*
M8681/1	*Sympathetic paraganglioma*
M8682/1	*Parasympathetic paraganglioma*
M8690/1	*Glomus jugulare tumor*
M8691/1	*Aortic body tumor*
M8692/1	*Carotid body tumor*
M8693/1	*Extra-adrenal paraganglioma NOS*
M8693/3	*Extra-adrenal paraganglioma, malignant*
M8700/0	*Pheochromocytoma NOS*
M8700/3	*Pheochromocytoma, malignant*
M8710/3	*Glomangiosarcoma*
M8711/0	*Glomus tumor*
M8712/0	*Glomangioma*

M872-M879 Nevi and melanomas

M8720/0	*Pigmented nevus NOS*
M8720/3	*Malignant melanoma NOS*
M8721/3	*Nodular melanoma*
M8722/0	*Balloon cell nevus*
M8722/3	*Balloon cell melanoma*
M8723/0	*Halo nevus*
M8724/0	*Fibrous papule of the nose*
M8725/0	*Neuronevus*
M8726/0	*Magnocellular nevus*
M8730/0	*Nonpigmented nevus*
M8730/3	*Amelanotic melanoma*
M8740/0	*Junctional nevus*
M8740/3	*Malignant melanoma in junctional nevus*
M8741/2	*Precancerous melanosis NOS*
M8741/3	*Malignant melanoma in precancerous melanosis*
M8742/2	*Hutchinson's melanotic freckle*
M8742/3	*Malignant melanoma in Hutchinson's melanotic freckle*
M8743/3	*Superficial spreading melanoma*
M8750/0	*Intradermal nevus*
M8760/0	*Compound nevus*
M8761/1	*Giant pigmented nevus*
M8761/3	*Malignant melanoma in giant pigmented nevus*
M8770/0	*Epithelioid and spindle cell nevus*
M8771/3	*Epithelioid cell melanoma*
M8772/3	*Spindle cell melanoma NOS*
M8773/3	*Spindle cell melanoma, type A*
M8774/3	*Spindle cell melanoma, type B*
M8775/3	*Mixed epithelioid and spindle cell melanoma*
M8780/0	*Blue nevus NOS*
M8780/3	*Blue nevus, malignant*
M8790/0	*Cellular blue nevus*

M880 Soft tissue tumors and sarcomas NOS

M8800/0	*Soft tissue tumor, benign*
M8800/3	*Sarcoma NOS*
M8800/9	*Sarcomatosis NOS*
M8801/3	*Spindle cell sarcoma*

M8802/3	*Giant cell sarcoma (except of bone M9250/3)*
M8803/3	*Small cell sarcoma*
M8804/3	*Epithelioid cell sarcoma*

M881-M883 Fibromatous neoplasms

M8810/0	*Fibroma NOS*
M8810/3	*Fibrosarcoma NOS*
M8811/0	*Fibromyxoma*
M8811/3	*Fibromyxosarcoma*
M8812/0	*Periosteal fibroma*
M8812/3	*Periosteal fibrosarcoma*
M8813/0	*Fascial fibroma*
M8813/3	*Fascial fibrosarcoma*
M8814/3	*Infantile fibrosarcoma*
M8820/0	*Elastofibroma*
M8821/1	*Aggressive fibromatosis*
M8822/1	*Abdominal fibromatosis*
M8823/1	*Desmoplastic fibroma*
M8830/0	*Fibrous histiocytoma NOS*
M8830/1	*Atypical fibrous histiocytoma*
M8830/3	*Fibrous histiocytoma, malignant*
M8831/0	*Fibroxanthoma NOS*
M8831/1	*Atypical fibroxanthoma*
M8831/3	*Fibroxanthoma, malignant*
M8832/0	*Dermatofibroma NOS*
M8832/1	*Dermatofibroma protuberans*
M8832/3	*Dermatofibrosarcoma NOS*

M884   Myxomatous neoplasms

M8840/0	*Myxoma NOS*
M8840/3	*Myxosarcoma*

M885-M888 Lipomatous neoplasms

M8850/0	*Lipoma NOS*
M8850/3	*Liposarcoma NOS*
M8851/0	*Fibrolipoma*
M8851/3	*Liposarcoma, well differentiated type*
M8852/0	*Fibromyxolipoma*
M8852/3	*Myxoid liposarcoma*
M8853/3	*Round cell liposarcoma*
M8854/3	*Pleomorphic liposarcoma*
M8855/3	*Mixed type liposarcoma*
M8856/0	*Intramuscular lipoma*
M8857/0	*Spindle cell lipoma*
M8860/0	*Angiomyolipoma*
M8860/3	*Angiomyoliposarcoma*
M8861/0	*Angiolipoma NOS*
M8861/1	*Angiolipoma, infiltrating*
M8870/0	*Myelolipoma*
M8880/0	*Hibernoma*
M8881/0	*Lipoblastomatosis*

M889-M892 Myomatous neoplasms

M8890/0	*Leiomyoma NOS*
M8890/1	*Intravascular leiomyomatosis*
M8890/3	*Leiomyosarcoma NOS*
M8891/1	*Epithelioid leiomyoma*
M8891/3	*Epithelioid leiomyosarcoma*
M8892/1	*Cellular leiomyoma*
M8893/0	*Bizarre leiomyoma*
M8894/0	*Angiomyoma*
M8894/3	*Angiomyosarcoma*
M8895/0	*Myoma*
M8895/3	*Myosarcoma*
M8900/0	*Rhabdomyoma NOS*
M8900/3	*Rhabdomyosarcoma NOS*
M8901/3	*Pleomorphic rhabdomyosarcoma*
M8902/3	*Mixed type rhabdomyosarcoma*
M8903/0	*Fetal rhabdomyoma*
M8904/0	*Adult rhabdomyoma*
M8910/3	*Embryonal rhabdomyosarcoma*
M8920/3	*Alveolar rhabdomyosarcoma*

M893-M899 Complex mixed and stromal neoplasms

M8930/3	*Endometrial stromal sarcoma*
M8931/1	*Endolymphatic stromal myosis*
M8932/0	*Adenomyoma*
M8940/0	*Pleomorphic adenoma*
M8940/3	*Mixed tumor, malignant NOS*
M8950/3	*Mullerian mixed tumor*
M8951/3	*Mesodermal mixed tumor*
M8960/1	*Mesoblastic nephroma*
M8960/3	*Nephroblastoma NOS*
M8961/3	*Epithelial nephroblastoma*
M8962/3	*Mesenchymal nephroblastoma*
M8970/3	*Hepatoblastoma*
M8980/3	*Carcinosarcoma NOS*
M8981/3	*Carcinosarcoma, embryonal type*
M8982/0	*Myoepithelioma*
M8990/0	*Mesenchymoma, benign*
M8990/1	*Mesenchymoma, NOS*
M8990/3	*Mesenchymoma, malignant*
M8991/3	*Embryonal sarcoma*

M900-M903 Fibroepithelial neoplasms

M9000/0	*Brenner tumor NOS*
M9000/1	*Brenner tumor, borderline malignancy*
M9000/3	*Brenner tumor, malignant*
M9010/0	*Fibroadenoma NOS*
M9011/0	*Intracanalicular fibroadenoma NOS*
M9012/0	*Pericanalicular fibroadenoma*
M9013/0	*Adenofibroma NOS*
M9014/0	*Serous adenofibroma*
M9015/0	*Mucinous adenofibroma*
M9020/0	*Cellular intracanalicular fibroadenoma*
M9020/1	*Cystosarcoma phyllodes NOS*
M9020/3	*Cystosarcoma phyllodes, malignant*
M9030/0	*Juvenile fibroadenoma*

M904 Synovial neoplasms

M9040/0	*Synovioma, benign*
M9040/3	*Synovial sarcoma NOS*
M9041/3	*Synovial sarcoma, spindle cell type*
M9042/3	*Synovial sarcoma, epithelioid cell type*
M9043/3	*Synovial sarcoma, biphasic type*
M9044/3	*Clear cell sarcoma of tendons and aponeuroses*

M905 Mesothelial neoplasms

M9050/0	*Mesothelioma, benign*
M9050/3	*Mesothelioma, malignant*
M9051/0	*Fibrous mesothelioma, benign*
M9051/3	*Fibrous mesothelioma, malignant*
M9052/0	*Epithelioid mesothelioma, benign*
M9052/3	*Epithelioid mesothelioma, malignant*
M9053/0	*Mesothelioma, biphasic type, benign*
M9053/3	*Mesothelioma, biphasic type, malignant*
M9054/0	*Adenomatoid tumor NOS*

M906-M909 Germ cell neoplasms

M9060/3	*Dysgerminoma*
M9061/3	*Seminoma NOS*
M9062/3	*Seminoma, anaplastic type*
M9063/3	*Spermatocytic seminoma*
M9064/3	*Germinoma*
M9070/3	*Embryonal carcinoma NOS*
M9071/3	*Endodermal sinus tumor*
M9072/3	*Polyembryoma*
M9073/1	*Gonadoblastoma*
M9080/0	*Teratoma, benign*
M9080/1	*Teratoma NOS*
M9080/3	*Teratoma, malignant NOS*
M9081/3	*Teratocarcinoma*
M9082/3	*Malignant teratoma, undifferentiated type*
M9083/3	*Malignant teratoma, intermediate type*
M9084/0	*Dermoid cyst*
M9084/3	*Dermoid cyst with malignant transformation*

M9090/0	*Struma ovarii NOS*
M9090/3	*Struma ovarii, malignant*
M9091/1	*Strumal carcinoid*

M910 **Trophoblastic neoplasms**
M9100/0	*Hydatidiform mole NOS*
M9100/1	*Invasive hydatidiform mole*
M9100/3	*Choriocarcinoma*
M9101/3	*Choriocarcinoma combined with teratoma*
M9102/3	*Malignant teratoma, trophoblastic*

M911 **Mesonephromas**
M9110/0	*Mesonephroma, benign*
M9110/1	*Mesonephric tumor*
M9110/3	*Mesonephroma, malignant*
M9111/1	*Endosalpingioma*

M912-M916 Blood vessel tumors
M9120/0	*Hemangioma NOS*
M9120/3	*Hemangiosarcoma*
M9121/0	*Cavernous hemangioma*
M9122/0	*Venous hemangioma*
M9123/0	*Racemose hemangioma*
M9124/3	*Kupffer cell sarcoma*
M9130/0	*Hemangioendothelioma, benign*
M9130/1	*Hemangioendothelioma NOS*
M9130/3	*Hemangioendothelioma, malignant*
M9131/0	*Capillary hemangioma*
M9132/0	*Intramuscular hemangioma*
M9140/3	*Kaposi's sarcoma*
M9141/0	*Angiokeratoma*
M9142/0	*Verrucous keratotic hemangioma*
M9150/0	*Hemangiopericytoma, benign*
M9150/1	*Hemangiopericytoma NOS*
M9150/3	*Hemangiopericytoma, malignant*
M9160/0	*Angiofibroma NOS*
M9161/1	*Hemangioblastoma*

M917 **Lymphatic vessel tumors**
M9170/0	*Lymphangioma NOS*
M9170/3	*Lymphangiosarcoma*
M9171/0	*Capillary lymphangioma*
M9172/0	*Cavernous lymphangioma*
M9173/0	*Cystic lymphangioma*
M9174/0	*Lymphangiomyoma*
M9174/1	*Lymphangiomyomatosis*
M9175/0	*Hemolymphangioma*

M918-M920 Osteomas and osteosarcomas
M9180/0	*Osteoma NOS*
M9180/3	*Osteosarcoma NOS*
M9181/3	*Chondroblastic osteosarcoma*
M9182/3	*Fibroblastic osteosarcoma*
M9183/3	*Telangiectatic osteosarcoma*
M9184/3	*Osteosarcoma in Paget's disease of bone*
M9190/3	*Juxtacortical osteosarcoma*
M9191/0	*Osteoid osteoma NOS*
M9200/0	*Osteoblastoma*

M921-M924 Chondromatous neoplasms
M9210/0	*Osteochondroma*
M9210/1	*Osteochondromatosis NOS*
M9220/0	*Chondroma NOS*
M9220/1	*Chondromatosis NOS*
M9220/3	*Chondrosarcoma NOS*
M9221/0	*Juxtacortical chondroma*
M9221/3	*Juxtacortical chondrosarcoma*
M9230/0	*Chondroblastoma NOS*
M9230/3	*Chondroblastoma, malignant*
M9240/3	*Mesenchymal chondrosarcoma*
M9241/0	*Chondromyxoid fibroma*

M925 **Giant cell tumors**
M9250/1	*Giant cell tumor of bone NOS*
M9250/3	*Giant cell tumor of bone, malignant*

M9251/1	Giant cell tumor of soft parts NOS
M9251/3	Malignant giant cell tumor of soft parts

M926   **Miscellaneous bone tumors**

M9260/3	Ewing's sarcoma
M9261/3	Adamantinoma of long bones
M9262/0	Ossifying fibroma

M927-M934 Odontogenic tumors

M9270/0	Odontogenic tumor, benign
M9270/1	Odontogenic tumor NOS
M9270/3	Odontogenic tumor, malignant
M9271/0	Dentinoma
M9272/0	Cementoma NOS
M9273/0	Cementoblastoma, benign
M9274/0	Cementifying fibroma
M9275/0	Gigantiform cementoma
M9280/0	Odontoma NOS
M9281/0	Compound odontoma
M9282/0	Complex odontoma
M9290/0	Ameloblastic fibro-odontoma
M9290/3	Ameloblastic odontosarcoma
M9300/0	Adenomatoid odontogenic tumor
M9301/0	Calcifying odontogenic cyst
M9310/0	Ameloblastoma NOS
M9310/3	Ameloblastoma, malignant
M9311/0	Odontoameloblastoma
M9312/0	Squamous odontogenic tumor
M9320/0	Odontogenic myxoma
M9321/0	Odontogenic fibroma NOS
M9330/0	Ameloblastic fibroma
M9330/3	Ameloblastic fibrosarcoma
M9340/0	Calcifying epithelial odontogenic tumor

M935-M937 Miscellaneous tumors

M9350/1	Craniopharyngioma
M9360/1	Pinealoma
M9361/1	Pineocytoma
M9362/3	Pineoblastoma
M9363/0	Melanotic neuroectodermal tumor
M9370/3	Chordoma

M938-M948 Gliomas

M9380/3	Glioma, malignant
M9381/3	Gliomatosis cerebri
M9382/3	Mixed glioma
M9383/1	Subependymal glioma
M9384/1	Subependymal giant cell astrocytoma
M9390/0	Choroid plexus papilloma NOS
M9390/3	Choroid plexus papilloma, malignant
M9391/3	Ependymoma NOS
M9392/3	Ependymoma, anaplastic type
M9393/1	Papillary ependymoma
M9394/1	Myxopapillary ependymoma
M9400/3	Astrocytoma NOS
M9401/3	Astrocytoma, anaplastic type
M9410/3	Protoplasmic astrocytoma
M9411/3	Gemistocytic astrocytoma
M9420/3	Fibrillary astrocytoma
M9421/3	Pilocytic astrocytoma
M9422/3	Spongioblastoma NOS
M9423/3	Spongioblastoma polare
M9430/3	Astroblastoma
M9440/3	Glioblastoma NOS
M9441/3	Giant cell glioblastoma
M9442/3	Glioblastoma with sarcomatous component
M9443/3	Primitive polar spongioblastoma
M9450/3	Oligodendroglioma NOS
M9451/3	Oligodendroglioma, anaplastic type
M9460/3	Oligodendroblastoma
M9470/3	Medulloblastoma NOS
M9471/3	Desmoplastic medulloblastoma
M9472/3	Medullomyoblastoma

M9480/3   *Cerebellar sarcoma NOS*
M9481/3   *Monstrocellular sarcoma*

M949-M952   Neuroepitheliomatous neoplasms
M9490/0   *Ganglioneuroma*
M9490/3   *Ganglioneuroblastoma*
M9491/0   *Ganglioneuromatosis*
M9500/3   *Neuroblastoma NOS*
M9501/3   *Medulloepithelioma NOS*
M9502/3   *Teratoid medulloepithelioma*
M9503/3   *Neuroepithelioma NOS*
M9504/3   *Spongioneuroblastoma*
M9505/1   *Ganglioglioma*
M9506/0   *Neurocytoma*
M9507/0   *Pacinian tumor*
M9510/3   *Retinoblastoma NOS*
M9511/3   *Retinoblastoma, differentiated type*
M9512/3   *Retinoblastoma, undifferentiated type*
M9520/3   *Olfactory neurogenic tumor*
M9521/3   *Esthesioneurocytoma*
M9522/3   *Esthesioneuroblastoma*
M9523/3   *Esthesioneuroepithelioma*

M953   Meningiomas
M9530/0   *Meningioma NOS*
M9530/1   *Meningiomatosis NOS*
M9530/3   *Meningioma, malignant*
M9531/0   *Meningotheliomatous meningioma*
M9532/0   *Fibrous meningioma*
M9533/0   *Psammomatous meningioma*
M9534/0   *Angiomatous meningioma*
M9535/0   *Hemangioblastic meningioma*
M9536/0   *Hemangiopericytic meningioma*
M9537/0   *Transitional meningioma*
M9538/1   *Papillary meningioma*
M9539/3   *Meningeal sarcomatosis*

M954-M957   Nerve sheath tumor
M9540/0   *Neurofibroma NOS*
M9540/1   *Neurofibromatosis NOS*
M9540/3   *Neurofibrosarcoma*
M9541/0   *Melanotic neurofibroma*
M9550/0   *Plexiform neurofibroma*
M9560/0   *Neurilemmoma NOS*
M9560/1   *Neurinomatosis*
M9560/3   *Neurilemmoma, malignant*
M9570/0   *Neuroma NOS*

M958   Granular cell tumors and alveolar soft part sarcoma
M9580/0   *Granular cell tumor NOS*
M9580/3   *Granular cell tumor, malignant*
M9581/3   *Alveolar soft part sarcoma*

M959-M963   Lymphomas, NOS or diffuse
M9590/0   *Lymphomatous tumor, benign*
M9590/3   *Malignant lymphoma NOS*
M9591/3   *Malignant lymphoma, non Hodgkin's type*
M9600/3   *Malignant lymphoma, undifferentiated cell type NOS*
M9601/3   *Malignant lymphoma, stem cell type*
M9602/3   *Malignant lymphoma, convoluted cell type NOS*
M9610/3   *Lymphosarcoma NOS*
M9611/3   *Malignant lymphoma, lymphoplasmacytoid type*
M9612/3   *Malignant lymphoma, immunoblastic type*
M9613/3   *Malignant lymphoma, mixed lymphocytic-histiocytic NOS*
M9614/3   *Malignant lymphoma, centroblastic-centrocytic, diffuse*
M9615/3   *Malignant lymphoma, follicular center cell NOS*
M9620/3   *Malignant lymphoma, lymphocytic, well differentiated NOS*
M9621/3   *Malignant lymphoma, lymphocytic, intermediate differentiation NOS*
M9622/3   *Malignant lymphoma, centrocytic*
M9623/3   *Malignant lymphoma, follicular center cell, cleaved NOS*
M9630/3   *Malignant lymphoma, lymphocytic, poorly differentiated NOS*
M9631/3   *Prolymphocytic lymphosarcoma*
M9632/3   *Malignant lymphoma, centroblastic type NOS*
M9633/3   *Malignant lymphoma, follicular center cell, noncleaved NOS*

M964	**Reticulosarcomas**
M9640/3	*Reticulosarcoma NOS*
M9641/3	*Reticulosarcoma, pleomorphic cell type*
M9642/3	*Reticulosarcoma, nodular*

M965-M966	**Hodgkin's disease**
M9650/3	*Hodgkin's disease NOS*
M9651/3	*Hodgkin's disease, lymphocytic predominance*
M9652/3	*Hodgkin's disease, mixed cellularity*
M9653/3	*Hodgkin's disease, lymphocytic depletion NOS*
M9654/3	*Hodgkin's disease, lymphocytic depletion, diffuse fibrosis*
M9655/3	*Hodgkin's disease, lymphocytic depletion, reticular type*
M9656/3	*Hodgkin's disease, nodular sclerosis NOS*
M9657/3	*Hodgkin's disease, nodular sclerosis, cellular phase*
M9660/3	*Hodgkin's paragranuloma*
M9661/3	*Hodgkin's granuloma*
M9662/3	*Hodgkin's sarcoma*

M969	**Lymphomas, nodular or follicular**
M9690/3	*Malignant lymphoma, nodular NOS*
M9691/3	*Malignant lymphoma, mixed lymphocytic-histiocytic, nodular*
M9692/3	*Malignant lymphoma, centroblastic-centrocytic, follicular*
M9693/3	*Malignant lymphoma, lymphocytic, well differentiated, nodular*
M9694/3	*Malignant lymphoma, lymphocytic, intermediate differentiation, nodular*
M9695/3	*Malignant lymphoma, follicular center cell, cleaved, follicular*
M9696/3	*Malignant lymphoma, lymphocytic, poorly differentiated, nodular*
M9697/3	*Malignant lymphoma, centroblastic type, follicular*
M9698/3	*Malignant lymphoma, follicular center cell, noncleaved, follicular*

M970	**Mycosis fungoides**
M9700/3	*Mycosis fungoides*
M9701/3	*Sezary's disease*

M971-M972	**Miscellaneous reticuloendothelial neoplasms**
M9710/3	*Microglioma*
M9720/3	*Malignant histiocytosis*
M9721/3	*Histiocytic medullary reticulosis*
M9722/3	*Letterer-Siwe's disease*

M973	**Plasma cell tumors**
M9730/3	*Plasma cell myeloma*
M9731/0	*Plasma cell tumor, benign*
M9731/1	*Plasmacytoma NOS*
M9731/3	*Plasma cell tumor, malignant*

M974	**Mast cell tumors**
M9740/1	*Mastocytoma NOS*
M9740/3	*Mast cell sarcoma*
M9741/3	*Malignant mastocytosis*

M975	**Burkitt's tumor**
M9750/3	*Burkitt's tumor*

M980-M994	**Leukemias**

M980	**Leukemias NOS**
M9800/3	*Leukemia NOS*
M9801/3	*Acute leukemia NOS*
M9802/3	*Subacute leukemia NOS*
M9803/3	*Chronic leukemia NOS*
M9804/3	*Aleukemic leukemia NOS*

M981	**Compound leukemias**
M9810/3	*Compound leukemia*

M982	**Lymphoid leukemias**
M9820/3	*Lymphoid leukemia NOS*
M9821/3	*Acute lymphoid leukemia*
M9822/3	*Subacute lymphoid leukemia*
M9823/3	*Chronic lymphoid leukemia*
M9824/3	*Aleukemic lymphoid leukemia*
M9825/3	*Prolymphocytic leukemia*

M983	**Plasma cell leukemias**
M9830/3	*Plasma cell leukemia*

M984	**Erythroleukemias**
M9840/3	*Erythroleukemia*
M9841/3	*Acute erythremia*

M9842/3	*Chronic erythremia*
M985	**Lymphosarcoma cell leukemias**
M9850/3	*Lymphosarcoma cell leukemia*
M986	**Myeloid leukemias**
M9860/3	*Myeloid leukemia NOS*
M9861/3	*Acute myeloid leukemia*
M9862/3	*Subacute myeloid leukemia*
M9863/3	*Chronic myeloid leukemia*
M9864/3	*Aleukemic myeloid leukemia*
M9865/3	*Neutrophilic leukemia*
M9866/3	*Acute promyelocytic leukemia*
M987	**Basophilic leukemias**
M9870/3	*Basophilic leukemia*
M988	**Eosinophilic leukemias**
M9880/3	*Eosinophilic leukemia*
M989	**Monocytic leukemias**
M9890/3	*Monocytic leukemia NOS*
M9891/3	*Acute monocytic leukemia*
M9892/3	*Subacute monocytic leukemia*
M9893/3	*Chronic monocytic leukemia*
M9894/3	*Aleukemic monocytic leukemia*
M990-M994	**Miscellaneous leukemias**
M9900/3	*Mast cell leukemia*
M9910/3	*Megakaryocytic leukemia*
M9920/3	*Megakaryocytic myelosis*
M9930/3	*Myeloid sarcoma*
M9940/3	*Hairy cell leukemia*
M995-M997	**Miscellaneous myeloproliferative and lymphoproliferative disorders**
M9950/1	*Polycythemia vera*
M9951/1	*Acute panmyelosis*
M9960/1	*Chronic myeloproliferative disease*
M9961/1	*Myelosclerosis with myeloid metaplasia*
M9962/1	*Idiopathic thrombocythemia*
M9970/1	*Chronic lymphoproliferative disease*

GLOSSARY OF MENTAL DISORDERS

The psychiatric terms which appear in Chapter 5, "Mental Disorders," are listed here in alphabetic sequence. Many of the glossary descriptions originally appeared in the section on Mental Disorders in the *International Classification of Diseases, 9th Revision*,[1] and others are included to define the psychiatric conditions added to *ICD-9-CM*. The additional definitions are based on material furnished by the American Psychiatric Association's Task Force on Nomenclature and Statistics[2] and from *A Psychiatric Glossary*.[3] In a few instances definitions were obtained from *Dorland's Illustrated Medical Dictionary*[4] and from *Stedman's Medical Dictionary, Illustrated*.[5]

1. Manual of the *International Classification of Diseases, Injuries, and Causes of Death*, 9th Revision. World Health Organization, Geneva, Switzerland, 1975.
2. American Psychiatric Association, Task Force on Nomenclature and Statistics, Robert L. Spitzer, Chairman.
3. A *Psychiatric Glossary*, Fourth Edition, American Psychiatric Association, Washington, D.C., 1975.
4. *Dorland's Illustrated Medical Dictionary*, Twenty-fifth Edition, W.B. Saunders Company, Philadelphia, 1974.
5. *Stedman's Medical Dictionary*, Illustrated, Twenty-third Edition, Williams and Wilkins, Baltimore, 1976.

Academic underachievement disorder: Failure to achieve in most school tasks despite adequate intellectual capacity, a supportive and encouraging social environment, and apparent effort. The failure occurs in the absence of a demonstrable specific learning disability and is caused by emotional conflict not clearly associated with any other mental disorder.[2]

Adaptation reaction—*see* Adjustment reaction

Adjustment reaction or disorder: Mild or transient disorders lasting longer than acute stress reactions which occur in individuals of any age without any apparent pre-existing mental disorder. Such disorders are often relatively circumscribed or situation-specific, are generally reversible, and usually last only a few months. They are usually closely related in time and content to stresses such as bereavement, migration, or other experiences. Reactions to major stress that last longer than a few days are also included. In children such disorders are associated with no significant distortion of development.[1]

    conduct disturbance: Mild or transient disorders in which the main disturbance predominantly involves a disturbance of conduct (e.g., an adolescent grief reaction resulting in aggressive or antisocial disorder).[1]

    depressive reaction: States of depression, not specifiable as manic-depressive, psychotic, or neurotic.[1]

        brief: Generally transient, in which the depressive symptoms are usually closely related in time and content to some stressful event.[1]

        prolonged: Generally long-lasting, usually developing in association with prolonged exposure to a stressful situation.[1]

    emotional disturbance: An adjustment disorder in which the main symptoms are emotional in type (e.g., anxiety, fear, worry) but not specifically depressive.[1]

    mixed conduct and emotional disturbance: An adjustment reaction in which both emotional disturbance and disturbance of conduct are prominent features.[1]

Affective psychoses: Mental disorders, usually recurrent, in which there is a severe disturbance of mood (mostly compounded of depression and anxiety but also manifested as elation, and excitement) which is accompanied by one or more of the following: delusions, perplexity, disturbed attitude to self, disorder of perception and behavior; these are all in keeping with the individual's prevailing mood (as are hallucinations when they occur). There is a strong tendency to suicide. For practical reasons, mild disorders of mood may also be included here if the symptoms match closely the descriptions given; this applies particularly to mild hypomania.[1]

    bipolar: A manic-depressive psychosis which has appeared in both the depressive and manic form, either alternating or separated by an interval of normality.[1]

        atypical: An episode of affective psychosis with some, but not all, of the features of the one form of the disorder in individuals who have had a previous episode of the other form of the disorder.[2]

        depressed: A manic-depressive psychosis, circular type, in which the depressive form is currently present.[1]

        manic: A manic-depressive psychosis, circular type, in which the manic form is currently present.[1]

        mixed: A manic-depressive psychosis, circular type, in which both manic and depressive symptoms are present at the same time.[1]

    depressed type: A manic-depressive psychosis in which there is a widespread depressed mood of gloom and wretchedness with some degree of anxiety. There is often reduced activity but there may be restlessness and agitation. There is marked tendency to recurrence; in a few cases this may be at regular intervals.[1]

atypical: An affective depressive disorder that cannot be classified as a manic-depressive psychosis, depressed type, or chronic depressive personality disorder, or as an adjustment disorder.[2]

manic type: A manic-depressive psychosis characterized by states of elation or excitement out of keeping with the individual's circumstances and varying from enhanced liveliness (hypomania) to violent, almost uncontrollable, excitement. Aggression and anger, flight of ideas, distractibility, impaired judgement, and grandiose ideas are common.[1]

mixed type: Manic-depressive psychosis syndromes corresponding to both the manic and depressed types, but which for other reasons cannot be classified more specifically.[1]

Aggressive personality—*see* Personality disorder, explosive type

Agoraphobia—*see* agoraphobia under Phobia

Alcohol dependence syndrome: A state, psychic and usually also physical, resulting from taking alcohol, characterized by behavioral and other responses that always include a compulsion to take alcohol on a continuous or periodic basis in order to experience its psychic effects, and sometimes to avoid the discomfort of its absence; tolerance may or may not be present. A person may be dependent on alcohol and other drugs; if so, also record the diagnosis of drug dependence to identify the agent. If alcohol dependence is associated with alcoholic psychosis or with physical complications, *both* diagnoses should be recorded.[1]

Alcohol intoxication

acute: A psychic and physical state resulting from alcohol ingestion characterized by slurred speech, unsteady gait, poor coordination, flushed facies, nystagmus, sluggish reflexes, fetor alcoholica, loud speech, emotional instability (e.g., jollity followed by lugubriousness), excessive conviviality, loquacity, and poorly inhibited sexual and aggressive behavior.[2]

idiosyncratic: Acute psychotic episodes induced by relatively small amounts of alcohol. These are regarded as individual idiosyncratic reactions to alcohol, not due to excessive consumption and without conspicuous neurological signs of intoxication.[1]

pathological—*see* Alcohol intoxication, idiosyncratic

Alcoholic psychoses: Organic psychotic states due mainly to excessive consumption of alcohol; defects of nutrition are thought to play an important role.[1]

alcohol abstinence syndrome—*see* alcohol withdrawal syndrome below

alcohol amnestic syndrome: A syndrome of prominent and lasting reduction of memory span, including striking loss of recent memory, disordered time appreciation and confabulation, occurring in alcoholics as the sequel to an acute alcoholic psychosis (especially delirium tremens) or, more rarely, in the course of chronic alcoholism. It is usually accompanied by peripheral neuritis and may be associated with Wernicke's encephalopathy.[1]

alcohol withdrawal delirium [delirium tremens]: Acute or subacute organic psychotic states in alcoholics, characterized by clouded consciousness, disorientation, fear, illusions, delusions, hallucinations of any kind, notably visual and tactile, and restlessness, tremor and sometimes fever.[1]

alcohol withdrawal hallucinosis: A psychosis usually of less than six months' duration, with slight or no clouding of consciousness and much anxious restlessness in which auditory hallucinations, mostly of voices uttering insults and threats, predominate.[1]

alcohol withdrawal syndrome: Tremor of hands, tongue, and eyelids following cessation of prolonged heavy drinking of alcohol. Nausea and vomiting, dry mouth, headache, heavy perspiration, fitful sleep, acute anxiety attacks, mood depression, feelings of guilt and remorse, and irritability are associated features.[2]

alcohol delirium—*see* alcohol withdrawal delirium above

alcoholic dementia: Nonhallucinatory dementias occurring in association with alcoholism, but not characterized by the features of either alcohol withdrawal delirium [delirium tremens] or alcohol amnestic syndrome [Korsakoff's alcoholic psychosis].[1]

alcoholic hallucinosis—*see* alcohol withdrawal hallucinosis above

alcoholic jealousy: Chronic paranoid psychosis characterized by delusional jealousy and associated with alcoholism.[1]

alcoholic paranoia—*see* Alcoholic jealousy

alcoholic polyneuritic psychosis—*see* alcohol amnestic syndrome above

Alcoholism

acute—*see* Alcohol intoxication, acute

chronic—*see* Alcohol dependence syndrome

Alexia: Loss of a previously possessed reading facility that cannot be explained by defective visual acuity.[3]

Amnesia, psychogenic: A form of dissociative hysteria in which there is a temporary disturbance in the ability to recall important personal information which has already been registered and stored in memory. The sudden onset of this disturbance in the absence of an underlying organic mental disorder, and the extent of the disturbance being too great to be explained by ordinary forgetfulness, are the essential features.[2]

Amnestic syndrome: A syndrome of prominent and lasting reduction of memory span, including striking loss of recent memory, disordered time appreciation, and confabulation. The commonest causes are chronic alcoholism [alcohol amnestic syndrome; Korsakoff's alcoholic psychosis], chronic barbiturate dependence, and malnutrition. An amnestic syndrome may be the predominating disturbance in the early states of presenile and senile dementia, arteriosclerotic dementia, and in encephalitis and other inflammatory and degenerative diseases in which there is particular bilateral involvement of the temporal lobes, and certain temporal lobe tumors.[2]

alcoholic—*see* alcohol amnestic syndrome under Alcoholic psychoses

Amoral personality—*see* Personality disorder, antisocial type

Anancastic [anankastic] neurosis—*see* Neurotic disorder, obsessive-compulsive

Anancastic [anankastic] personality—*see* Personality disorder, compulsive type

Anorexia nervosa: A disorder in which the main features are persistent active refusal to eat and marked loss of weight. The level of activity and alertness is characteristically high in relation to the degree of emaciation. Typically the disorder begins in teenage girls but it may sometimes begin before puberty and rarely it occurs in males. Amenorrhea is usual and there may be a variety of other physiological changes including slow pulse and respiration, low body temperature, and dependent edema. Unusual eating habits and attitudes toward food are typical and sometimes starvation follows or alternates with periods of overeating. The accompanying psychiatric symptoms are diverse.[1]

Anxiety hysteria—*see* phobia under Neurotic disorders

Anxiety state (neurotic): Apprehension, tension, or uneasiness that stems from the anticipation of danger, the source of which is largely unknown or unrecognized.[3]

atypical: An anxiety disorder that does not fulfill the criteria of generalized or panic attack anxiety. An example might be an individual with a single morbid fear.[2]

generalized: A disorder of at least six months' duration in which the predominant feature is limited to diffuse and persistent anxiety without the specific symptoms that characterize phobic disorders, panic disorder, or obsessive-compulsive disorder.[2]

panic attack: An episodic and often chronic, recurrent disorder in which the predominant features are anxiety attacks and nervousness. The anxiety attacks are manifested by discrete periods of sudden onset of intense apprehension, fearfulness, or terror often associated with feelings of impending doom.[2]

Aphasia, developmental: A delay in the production of spoken language. Rarely, there is also a developmental delay in the comprehension of speech sounds.[1]

Arteriosclerotic dementia: Dementia attributable, because of physical signs (on examination of the central nervous system), to degenerative arterial disease of the brain. Symptoms suggesting a focal lesion in the brain are common. There may be a fluctuating or patchy intellectual defect with insight, and an intermittent course is common. Clinical differentiation from senile or presenile dementia, which may coexist with it, may be very difficult or impossible. The diagnosis of cerebral atherosclerosis should also be recorded.[1]

Asocial personality—*see* Personality disorder, antisocial type

Astasia-abasia, hysterical: A form of conversion hysteria in which the individual is unable to stand or walk although the legs are otherwise under control.[4]

Asthenia, psychogenic—*see* neurasthenia under Neurotic disorders

Asthenic personality—*see* Personality disorder, dependent type

Attention deficit disorder—*see* attention deficit disorder under Hyperkinetic syndrome of childhood.

Autism, infantile: A syndrome present from birth or beginning almost invariably in the first 30 months. Responses to auditory and sometimes to visual stimuli are abnormal, and there are usually severe problems in the understanding of spoken language. Speech is delayed and, if it develops, is characterized by echolalia, the reversal of pronouns, immature grammatical structure, and inability to use abstract terms. There is generally an impairment in the social use of both verbal and gestural language. Problems in social relationships are most severe before the age of five years and include an impairment in the development of eye-to-eye gaze, social attachments, and cooperative play. Ritualistic behavior is usual and may include abnormal routines, resistance to change, attachment to odd objects and stereotyped patterns of play. The capacity for abstract or symbolic thought and for imaginative play is diminished. Intelligence ranges from severely subnormal to normal or above. Performance is usually better on tasks involving rote memory or visuospatial skills than on those requiring symbolic or linguistic skills.[1]

Avoidant personality—*see* Personality disorder, avoidant type

"Bad trips": Acute intoxication from hallucinogen abuse, manifested by hallucinatory states lasting only a few days or less.[1]

Barbiturate abuse: Cases where an individual has taken the drug to the detriment of his health or social functioning, in doses above or for periods beyond those normally regarded as therapeutic.[1]

Bestiality—*see* Zoophilia

Bipolar disorder—*see* Affective psychosis, bipolar

  atypical—*see* Affective psychosis, bipolar, atypical

Body-rocking—*see* Stereotyped repetitive movements

Borderline personality—*see* Personality disorder, borderline type

Borderline psychosis of childhood—*see* Psychosis, atypical childhood

Borderline schizophrenia—*see* Schizophrenia, latent

Bouffée délirante—*see* Paranoid reaction, acute

Briquet's disorder—*see* somatization disorder under Neurotic disorders

Bulimia: An episodic pattern of overeating [binge eating] accompanied by an awareness of the disordered eating pattern with a fear of not being able to stop eating voluntarily. Depressive moods and self-deprecating thoughts follow the episodes of binge eating.[2]

Catalepsy schizophrenia—*see* Schizophrenia, catatonic type

Catastrophic stress—*see* Gross stress reaction

Catatonia (schizophrenic)—*see* Schizophrenia, catatonic type

Character neurosis—*see* Personality disorders

Childhood autism—*see* Autism, infantile

Childhood type schizophrenia—*see* Psychosis, child

Chronic alcoholic brain syndrome—*see* alcoholic dementia under Alcoholic psychoses

Clay-eating—*see* Pica

Clumsiness syndrome—*see* coordination disorder under Developmental delay disorders, specific

Combat fatigue—*see* Posttraumatic disorder, acute

Compensation neurosis—*see* compensation neurosis under Neurotic disorders

Compulsive conduct disorder—*see* impulse control disorders under Conduct disorders

Compulsive neurosis—*see* Neurotic disorder, obsessive-compulsive

Compulsive personality—*see* Personality disorder, compulsive type

Concentration camp syndrome—*see* Posttraumatic stress disorder, prolonged

Conduct disorders: Disorders mainly involving aggressive and destructive behavior and disorders involving delinquency. It should be used for abnormal behavior, in individuals of any age, which gives rise to social disapproval but which is not part of any other psychiatric condition. Minor emotional disturbances may also be present. To be included, the behavior, as judged by its frequency, severity, and type of associations with other symptoms, must be abnormal in its context. Disturbances of conduct are distinguished from an adjustment reaction by a longer duration and by a lack of close relationship in time and content to some stress. They differ from a personality disorder by the absence of deeply ingrained maladaptive patterns of behavior present from adolescence or earlier.[1]

  impulse control disorders: A failure to resist an impulse, drive, or temptation to perform some action which is harmful to the individual or to others. The impulse may or may not be consciously resisted, and the act may or may not be premeditated or planned. Prior to committing the act, there is an increasing sense of tension, and at the time of committing the act, there is an experience of either pleasure, gratification, or release. Immediately following the act, there may or may not be genuine regret, self-reproach, or guilt.[2] *See also* Intermittent explosive disorder, Isolated explosive disorder, Kleptomania, Pathological gambling, and Pyromania.

  mixed disturbance of conduct and emotions: A disorder characterized by features of undersocialized and socialized disturbance of conduct, but in which there is also considerable emotional disturbance as shown, for example, by anxiety, misery, or obsessive manifestations.[1]

  socialized conduct disorder: Conduct disorders in individuals who have acquired the values or behavior of a delinquent peer group to whom they are loyal and with whom they characteristically steal, play truant, and stay out late at night. There may also be sexual promiscuity.[1]

  undersocialized conduct disturbance

    aggressive type: A disorder characterized by a persistent pattern of disrespect for the feelings and well-being of others (bullying, physical aggression, cruel behavior, hostility, verbal abusiveness, impudence, defiance, negativism), aggressive antisocial behavior (destructiveness, stealing, persistent lying, frequent truancy, and vandalism), and failure to develop close and stable relationships with others.[2]

unaggressive type: A disorder in which there is a lack of concern for the rights and feelings of others to a degree which indicates a failure to establish a normal degree of affection, empathy, or bond with others. There are two patterns of behavior found. In one, the child is fearful and timid, lacking self-assertiveness, resorts to self-protective and manipulative lying, indulges in whining demandingness and temper tantrums, feels rejected and unfairly treated, and is mistrustful of others. In the other pattern of the disorder, the child approaches others strictly for his own gains and acts exclusively because of exploitative and extractive goals. The child lies brazenly and steals, appearing to feel no guilt, and forms no social bonds to other individuals.[2]

Confusion, psychogenic—*see* Psychosis, reactive confusion

Confusion, reactive—*see* Psychosis, reactive confusion

Confusional state

acute—*see* Delirium, acute

epileptic—*see* Delirium, acute

subacute—*see* Delirium, subacute

Conversion hysteria—*see* hysteria, conversion type under Neurotic disorders

Coordination disorder—*see* coordination disorder under Developmental delay disorders, specific

Culture shock: A form of stress reaction associated with an individual's assimilation into a new culture which is vastly different from that in which he was raised.[5]

Cyclic schizophrenia—*see* Schizophrenia, schizo-affective type

Cyclothymic personality or disorder—*see* Personality disorder, cyclothymic type

Delirium: Transient organic psychotic conditions with a short course in which there is a rapidly developing onset of disorganization of higher mental processes manifested by some degree of impairment of information processing, impaired or abnormal attention, perception, memory, and thinking. Clouded consciousness, confusion, disorientation, delusions, illusions, and often vivid hallucinations predominate in the clinical picture.[1,2]

acute: short-lived states, lasting hours or days, of the above type.[1]

subacute: states of the above type in which the symptoms, usually less florid, last for several weeks or longer, during which they may show marked fluctuations in intensity.[1]

Delirium tremens—*see* alcohol withdrawal delirium under Alcoholic psychoses

Delusions, systematized—*see* Paranoia

Dementia: A decrement in intellectual functioning of sufficient severity to interfere with occupational or social performance, or both. There is impairment of memory and abstract thinking, the ability to learn new skills, problem solving, and judgment. There is often also personality change or impairment in impulse control. Dementia in organic psychoses may be of a chronic or progressive nature, which if untreated are usually irreversible and terminal.[1,2]

alcoholic—*see* alcoholic dementia under Alcoholic psychoses

arteriosclerotic—*see* Arteriosclerotic dementia

multi-infarct—*see* Arteriosclerotic dementia

presenile—*see* Presenile dementia

repeated infarct—*see* Arteriosclerotic dementia

senile—*see* Senile dementia

Depersonalization syndrome—*see* depersonalization syndrome under Neurotic disorders

Depression: States of depression, usually of moderate but occasionally of marked intensity, which have no specifically manic-depressive or other psychotic depressive features, and which do not appear to be associated with stressful events or other features specified under neurotic depression.[1]

anxiety—*see* depression under Neurotic disorders

endogenous—*see* Affective psychosis, depressed type

monopolar—*see* Affective psychosis, depressed type

neurotic—*see* depression under Neurotic disorders

psychotic—*see* Affective psychosis, depressed type

psychotic reactive—*see* Psychosis, depressive

reactive—*see* depression under Neurotic disorders

reactive psychotic—*see* Psychosis, depressive

Depressive personality or character—*see* Personality disorder, chronic depressive type

Depressive reaction—*see* depressive reaction under Adjustment reaction

Depressive psychosis—*see* Affective psychosis, depressed type

Derealization (neurotic)—*see* depersonalization syndrome under Neurotic disorders

Developmental delay disorders, specific: A group of disorders in which a specific delay in development is the main feature. For many the delay is not explicable in terms of general intellectual retardation or of inadequate schooling. In each case development is related to biological maturation, but it is also influenced by nonbiological factors. A diagnosis of a specific developmental delay carries no etiological implications. A diagnosis of specific delay in development should not be made if it is due to a known neurological disorder.[1]

arithmetical disorder: Disorders in which the main feature is a serious impairment in the development of arithmetical skills.[1]

articulation disorder: A delay in the development of normal word-sound production resulting in defects of articulation. Omissions or substitutions of consonants are most frequent.[1]

coordination disorder: Disorders in which the main feature is a serious impairment in the development of motor coordination which is not explicable in terms of general intellectual retardation. The clumsiness is commonly associated with perceptual difficulties.[1]

mixed development disorder: A delay in the development of one specific skill (e.g., reading, arithmetic, speech, or coordination) is frequently associated with lesser delays in other skills. When this occurs the diagnosis should be made according to the skill most seriously impaired. The mixed category should be used only where the mixture of delayed skills is such that no one skill is preponderantly affected.[1]

motor retardation—*see* coordination disorder above

reading disorder or retardation: Disorders in which the main feature is a serious impairment in the development of reading or spelling skills which is not explicable in terms of general intellectual retardation or of inadequate schooling. Speech or language difficulties, impaired right-left differentiation, perceptuo-motor problems, and coding difficulties are frequently associated. Similar problems are often present in other members of the family. Adverse psychosocial factors may be present.[1]

speech or language disorder: Disorders in which the main feature is a serious impairment in the development of speech or language (syntax or semantic) which is not explicable in terms of general intellectual retardation. Most commonly there is a delay in the development of normal word-sound production resulting in defects of articulation. Omissions or substitutions of consonants are most frequent. There may also be a delay in the production of spoken language. Rarely, there is also a developmental delay in the comprehension of sounds. Includes cases in which delay is largely due to environmental privation.[1]

Dipsomania—*see* Alcohol dependence syndrome

Disorganized schizophrenia—*see* Schizophrenia, disorganized type

Dissociative hysteria—*see* hysteria, dissociative type under Neurotic disorders

Drug abuse: Includes cases where an individual, for whom no other diagnosis is possible, has come under medical care because of the maladaptive effect of a drug on which he is not dependent (*see* Drug dependence) and that he has taken on his own initiative to the detriment of his health or social functioning. When drug abuse is secondary to a psychiatric disorder, record the disorder as an additional diagnosis.[1]

Drug dependence: A state, psychic and sometimes also physical, resulting from taking a drug, characterized by behavioral and other responses that always include a compulsion to take a drug on a continuous or periodic basis in order to experience its psychic effects, and sometimes to avoid the discomfort of its absence. Tolerance may or may not be present. A person may be dependent on more than one drug.[1]

Drug psychoses: Organic mental syndromes which are due to consumption of drugs (notably amphetamines, barbiturates, and opiate and LSD groups) and solvents. Some of the syndromes in this group are not as severe as most conditions labeled "psychotic," but they are included here for practical reasons. The drug should be identified, and also a diagnosis of drug dependence should be recorded, if present.[1]

drug-induced hallucinosis: Hallucinatory states of more than a few days, but not more than a few months' duration, associated with large or prolonged intake of drugs, notably of the amphetamine and LSD groups. Auditory hallucinations usually predominate and there may be anxiety or restlessness. States following LSD or other hallucinogens lasting only a few days or less ["bad trips"] are not included.[1]

drug-induced organic delusional syndrome: Paranoid states of more than a few days, but not more than a few months' duration, associated with large or prolonged intake of drugs, notably of the amphetamine and LSD groups.[1]

drug withdrawal syndrome: States associated with drug withdrawal ranging from severe, as specified for alcohol withdrawal delirium [delirium tremens], to less severe states characterized by one or more symptoms such as convulsions, tremor, anxiety, restlessness, gastrointestinal and muscular complaints, and mild disorientation and memory disturbance.[1]

Drunkenness:

acute—*see* Alcohol intoxication, acute

pathologic—*see* Alcohol intoxication, idiosyncratic

simple: A state of inebriation due to alcohol consumption without conspicuous neurological signs of intoxication.[2]

sleep: An inability to fully arouse from the sleep state characterized by failure to attain full consciousness after arousal.[2]

Dyscalculia—*see* arithmetical disorder under Developmental delay disorders, specific

Dyslalia—*see* articulation disorder under Developmental delay disorders, specific

Dyslexia, developmental: A disorder in which the main feature is a serious impairment of reading skills which is not explicable in terms of general intellectual retardation or of inadequate schooling. Word-blindness and strephosymbolia (tendency to reverse letters and words in reading) are included.[1,3]

Dysmenorrhea, psychogenic: Painful menstruation due to disturbance of psychic control.[4]

Dyspareunia, functional—*see* functional dyspareunia under Psychosexual dysfunctions

Dyspraxia syndrome—*see* coordination disorder under Developmental delay disorders, specific

Dyssocial personality—*see* Personality disorder, antisocial type

Dysuria, psychogenic: Difficulty in passing urine due to psychic factors.[4]

Eating disorders: A group of disorders characterized by a conspicuous disturbance in eating behavior.[2] *See also* Bulimia, Pica, and Rumination, psychogenic.

Eccentric personality—*see* Personality disorder, eccentric type

Elective mutism: A pervasive and persistent refusal to speak in situations not attributable to a mental disorder. In some cases the behavior may manifest a form of withdrawal reaction to a specific stressful situation, or as a predominant feature in children exhibiting shyness or social withdrawal disorders.[2]

Emancipation disorder: An adjustment reaction in adolescents or young adults in which there is symptomatic expression (e.g., difficulty in making independent decisions, increased dependence on parental advice, adoption of values deliberately oppositional to parents) of a conflict over independence following the recent assumption of a status in which the individual is more independent of parental control or supervision.[2]

Emotional disturbances specific to childhood and adolescence: Less well-differentiated emotional disorders characteristic of the childhood period. When the emotional disorder takes the form of a neurosis, the appropriate diagnosis should be made. These disorders differ from adjustment reactions in terms of longer duration and by the lack of close relationship in time and content to some stress.[1] *See also* Academic underachievement disorder, Elective mutism, Identity disorder, Introverted disorder of childhood, Misery and unhappiness disorder, Oppositional disorder, Overanxious disorder, and Shyness disorder of childhood.

Encopresis: A disorder in which the main manifestation is the persistent voluntary or involuntary passage of formed stools of normal or near-normal consistency into places not intended for that purpose in the individual's own sociocultural setting. Sometimes the child has failed to gain bowel control, and sometimes he has gained control but then later again became encopretic. There may be a variety of associated psychiatric symptoms and there may be smearing of feces. The condition would not usually be diagnosed under the age of four years.[1]

Endogenous depression—*see* Affective psychosis, depressed type

Enuresis: A disorder in which the main manifestation is a persistent involuntary voiding of urine by day or night which is considered abnormal for the age of the individual. Sometimes the child will have failed to gain bladder control and in other cases he will have gained control and then lost it. Episodic or fluctuating enuresis should be included. The disorder would not usually be diagnosed under the age of four years.[1]

Epileptic confusional or twilight state—*see* Delirium, acute

Excitation

catatonic—*see* Schizophrenia, catatonic type

psychogenic—*see* Psychosis, excitative type

reactive—*see* Psychosis, excitative type

Exhaustion delirium—*see* Stress reaction, acute

Exhibitionism: Sexual deviation in which the main sexual pleasure and gratification is derived from exposure of the genitals to a person of the opposite sex.[1]

Explosive personality disorder—*see* Personality disorder, explosive type

Factitious illness: A form of hysterical neurosis in which there are physical or psychological symptoms that are not real, genuine, or natural, which are produced by the individual and are under his voluntary control.[2]

physical symptom type: The presentation of physical symptoms that may be total fabrication, self-inflicted, an exaggeration or exacerbation of a pre-existing physical condition, or any combination or variation of these.[2]

psychological symptom type: The voluntary production of symptoms suggestive of a mental disorder. Behavior may mimic psychosis or, rather, the individual's idea of psychosis.[2]

Fanatic personality—*see* Personality disorder, paranoid type

Fatigue neurosis—*see* neurasthenia under Neurotic disorders

Feeble-minded—*see* Mental retardation, mild

Fetishism: A sexual deviation in which nonliving objects are utilized as a preferred or exclusive method of stimulating erotic arousal.[2]

Finger-flicking—*see* Stereotyped repetitive movements

Folie à deux—*see* Shared paranoid disorder

Frigidity: A psychosexual dysfunction in which there is partial or complete failure to attain or maintain the lubrication-swelling response of sexual excitement until completion of the sexual act.[2]

Frontal lobe syndrome: Changes in behavior following damage to the frontal areas of the brain or following interference with the connections of those areas. There is a general diminution of self-control, foresight, creativity, and spontaneity, which may be manifest as increased irritability, selfishness, restlessness and lack of concern for others. Conscientiousness and powers of concentration are often diminished, but measurable deterioration of intellect or memory is not necessarily present. The overall picture is often one of emotional dullness, lack of drive, and slowness; but, particularly in persons previously with energetic, restless, or aggressive characteristics, there may be a change towards impulsiveness, boastfulness, temper outbursts, silly fatuous humor, and the development of unrealistic ambitions; the direction of change usually depends upon the previous personality. A considerable degree of recovery is possible and may continue over the course of several years.[1]

Fugue, psychogenic: A form of dissociative hysteria characterized by an episode of wandering with inability to recall one's prior identity. Both onset and recovery are rapid. Following recovery there is no recollection of events which took place during the fugue state.[2]

Ganser's syndrome (hysterical): A form of factitious illness in which the patient voluntarily produces symptoms suggestive of a mental disorder.[2]

Gender identity disorder—*see* gender identity disorder under Psychosexual identity disorders

Gilles de la Tourette's disorder or syndrome—*see* Gilles de la Tourette's disorder under Tics

Grief reaction—*see* depressive reaction, brief under Adjustment reaction

Gross stress reaction—*see* Stress reaction, acute

Group delinquency—*see* socialized conduct disorder under Conduct disorders

Habit spasm—*see* chronic motor tic disorder under Tics

Hangover (alcohol)—*see* Drunkenness, simple

Head-banging—*see* Stereotyped repetitive movements

Hebephrenia—*see* Schizophrenia, disorganized type

Heller's syndrome—*see* Psychosis, disintegrative

High grade defect—*see* Mental retardation, mild

Homosexuality: Exclusive or predominant sexual attraction for persons of the same sex with or without physical relationship. Record homosexuality as a diagnosis whether or not it is considered as a mental disorder.[1]

Hospital addiction syndrome—*see* Munchausen syndrome

Hospital hoboes—*see* Munchausen syndrome

Hospitalism: A mild or transient adjustment reaction characterized by withdrawal seen in hospitalized patients. In young children this may be manifested by elective mutism.[1]

Hyperkinetic syndrome of childhood: Disorders in which the essential features are short attention-span and distractibility. In early childhood the most striking symptom is disinhibited, poorly organized and poorly regulated extreme overactivity but in adolescence this may be replaced by underactivity. Impulsiveness, marked mood fluctuations, and aggression are also common symptoms. Delays in the development of specific skills are often present and disturbed, poor relationships are common. If the hyperkinesis is symptomatic of an underlying disorder, the diagnosis of the underlying disorder is recorded instead.[1]

attention deficit disorder: Cases of hyperkinetic syndrome in which short attention span, distractibility, and overactivity are the main manifestations without significant disturbance of conduct or delay in specific skills.[1]

hyperkinesis with developmental delay: Cases in which the hyperkinetic syndrome is associated with speech delay, clumsiness, reading difficulties, or other delays of specific skills.[1]

hyperkinetic conduct disorder: Cases in which the hyperkinetic syndrome is associated with marked conduct disturbance but not developmental delay.[1]

Hypersomnia: A disorder of initiating arousal from sleep or maintaining wakefulness.

persistent: Chronic difficulty in initiating arousal from sleep or maintaining wakefulness associated with major or minor depressive mental disorders.[2]

transient: Episodes of difficulty in arousal from sleep or maintaining wakefulness associated with acute or intermittent emotional reactions or conflicts.[2]

Hypochondriasis—*see* hypochondriasis under Neurotic disorders

Hypomania—*see* Affective psychosis, manic type

Hypomanic personality—*see* Personality disorder, chronic hypomanic type

Hyposomnia—*see* Insomnia

Hysteria—*see* hysteria under Neurotic disorders

anxiety—*see* phobia under Neurotic disorders

psychosis—*see* Psychosis, reactive

acute—*see* Psychosis, excitative type

Hysterical personality—*see* Personality disorder, histrionic type

Identity disorder: An emotional disorder caused by distress over the inability to reconcile aspects of the self into a relatively coherent and acceptable sense of self, not secondary to another mental disorder. The disturbance is manifested by intense subjective distress regarding uncertainty about a variety of issues relating to identity, including long-term goals, career choice, friendship patterns, values, and loyalties.[2]

Idiocy—*see* Mental retardation, profound

Imbecile—*see* Mental retardation, moderate

Impotence: A psychosexual dysfunction in which there is partial or complete failure to attain or maintain erection until completion of the sexual act.[2]

Impulse control disorder—*see* impulse control disorders under Conduct disorders

Inadequate personality—*see* Personality disorder, dependent type

Induced paranoid disorder—*see* Shared paranoid disorder

Inebriety—*see* Drunkenness, simple

Infantile autism—*see* Autism, infantile

Insomnia: A disorder of initiating or maintaining sleep.[2]

persistent: A chronic state of sleeplessness associated with chronic anxiety, major or minor depressive disorders, or psychoses.[2]

transient: Episodes of sleeplessness associated with acute or intermittent emotional reactions or conflicts.[2]

Intermittent explosive disorder: Recurrent episodes of sudden and significant loss of control of aggressive impulses, not accounted for by any other mental disorder, which results in serious assault or destruction of property. The magnitude of the behavior during an episode is grossly out of proportion to any psychosocial stressors which may have played a role in eliciting the episode of lack of control. Following each episode there is genuine regret or self-reproach at the consequences of the action and the inability to control the aggressive impulse.[2]

Introverted disorder of childhood: An emotional disturbance in children chiefly manifested by a lack of interest in social relationships and indifference to social praise or criticism.[2]

Introverted personality—*see* Personality disorder, introverted type

Involutional melancholia—*see* Affective psychosis, depressed type

Involutional paranoid state—*see* Paraphrenia

Isolated explosive disorder: A disorder of impulse control in which there is a single discrete episode characterized by failure to resist an impulse which leads to a single, violent externally- directed act, which has a catastrophic impact on others, and for which the available information does not justify the diagnosis of another mental disorder.[2]

Isolated phobia—*see* simple phobia under Phobia

Jet lag syndrome: A phase-shift disruption of the 24-hour sleep-wake cycle due to rapid time-zone changes experienced in long-distance travel.[2]

Kanner's syndrome—*see* Autism, infantile

Kleptomania: A disorder of impulse control characterized by a recurrent failure to resist impulses to steal objects not for immediate use or their monetary value. An increasing sense of tension is experienced prior to committing the act, with an intense experience of gratification at the time of committing the theft.[2]

Korsakoff's psychosis:

    alcoholic—*see* alcohol amnestic syndrome under Alcoholic psychoses

    nonalcoholic—*see* Amnestic syndrome

Latent schizophrenia—*see* Schizophrenia, latent

Lesbianism—*see* Homosexuality

Lobotomy syndrome—*see* Frontal lobe syndrome

LSD reaction: Acute intoxication from hallucinogen abuse, manifested by hallucinatory states lasting only a few days or less.[1]

Major depressive disorder—*see* Affective psychosis, depressed type

Malingering: A clinical picture in which the predominant feature is the presentation of fake or grossly exaggerated physical or psychiatric illness apparently under voluntary control. In contrast to factitious illness, the symptoms produced in malingering are in pursuit of a goal which, when known, is recognizable and obviously understandable in light of knowledge of the individual's circumstances. Examples of understandable goals include, but are not limited to, becoming a "patient" in order to avoid conscription or military duty, avoid work, obtain financial compensation, evade criminal prosecution, and obtain drugs.[2]

Mania (monopolar)—*see* Affective psychosis, manic type

Manic-depressive psychosis

    circular type—*see* Affective psychosis, bipolar

    depressed type—*see* Affective psychosis, depressed type

    manic type—*see* Affective psychosis, manic type

    mixed type—*see* Affective psychosis, mixed type

Manic disorder—*see* Affective psychosis, manic type

    atypical—*see* Affective psychosis, manic type, atypical

Masochistic personality—*see* Personality disorder, masochistic type

Melancholia—*see* Affective psychoses

    involutional—*see* Affective psychosis, depressed type

Mental retardation: A condition of arrested or incomplete development of mind which is especially characterized by subnormality of intelligence. The coding should be made on the individual's *current* level of functioning *without regard to its nature* or causation, such as psychosis, cultural deprivation, Down's syndrome, etc. Where there is a specific cognitive handicap—such as in speech—the diagnosis of mental retardation should be based on assessments of cognition *outside the area of specific handicap*. The assessment of intellectual level should be based on whatever information is available, including clinical evidence, adaptive behavior, and psychometric findings. The IQ levels given are based on a test with a mean of 100 and a standard deviation of 15, such as the Wechsler scales. They are provided only as a guide and should not be applied rigidly. Mental retardation often involves psychiatric disturbances and may often develop as a result of some physical disease or injury. In these cases, an additional diagnosis should be recorded to identify any associated condition, psychiatric or physical.[1]

    mild mental retardation: IQ criteria 50-70. Individuals with this level of retardation are usually educable. During the pre-school period they can develop social and communication skills, have minimal retardation in sensorimotor areas, and often are not distinguished from normal children until a later age. During the school age period they can learn academic skills up to approximately the sixth-grade level. During the adult years, they can usually achieve social and vocational skills adequate for minimum self-support, but may need guidance and assistance when under social or economic stress.[2]

    moderate mental retardation: IQ criteria 35-49. Individuals with this level of retardation are usually trainable. During the pre-school period they can talk or learn to communicate. They have poor social awareness and fair motor development. During the school age period they can profit from training in social and occupational skills, but they are unlikely to progress beyond the second-grade level in academic subjects. During their adult years they may achieve self-maintenance in unskilled or semi-skilled work under sheltered conditions. They need supervision and guidance when under mild social or economic stress.[2]

    severe mental retardation: IQ criteria 20-34. Individuals with this level of retardation evidence poor motor development, minimal speech, and are generally unable to profit from training and self-help during the pre-school period. During the school age period they can talk or learn to communicate, can be trained in elementary health habits, and may profit from systematic habit training. During the adult years they may contribute partially to self-maintenance under complete supervision.[2]

profound mental retardation: IQ criteria under 20. Individuals with this level of retardation evidence minimal capacity for sensorimotor functioning and need nursing care during the pre-school period. During the school age period some further motor development may occur, and they may respond to minimal or limited training in self-help. During the adult years some motor and speech development may occur, and they may achieve very limited self-care and need nursing care.[2]

Merycism—*see* Rumination, psychogenic

Minimal brain dysfunction [MBD]—*see* Hyperkinetic syndrome of childhood

Misery and unhappiness disorder: An emotional disorder characteristic of childhood in which the main symptoms involve misery and unhappiness. There may also be eating and sleep disturbances.[1]

Mood swings (brief compensatory) (rebound): Mild disorders of mood (depression and anxiety or elation and excitement, occurring alternatingly or episodically) seen in affective psychosis.[1]

Motor tic disorders—*see* Tics

Motor-verbal tic disorder—*see* Gilles de la Tourette's disorder under Tics

Multi-infarct dementia or psychosis—*see* Arteriosclerotic dementia

Multiple operations syndrome—*see* Munchausen syndrome

Multiple personality: A form of dissociative hysteria in which there is the domination of the individual at any one time by one of two or more distinct personalities. Each personality is a full-integrated and complex unit with memories, behavior patterns, and social friendships which determine the nature of the individual's acts when uppermost in consciousness.[2]

Munchausen syndrome: A chronic form of factitious illness in which the individual demonstrates a plausible presentation of voluntarily produced physical symptomatology of such a degree that he is able to obtain and sustain multiple hospitalizations.[2]

Narcissistic personality—*see* Personality disorder, narcissistic type

Nervous debility—*see* neurasthenia under Neurotic disorders

Neurasthenia—*see* neurasthenia under Neurotic disorders

Neurotic delinquency—*see* mixed disturbance of conduct and emotions under Conduct disorders

Neurotic disorders: Neurotic disorders are mental disorders without any demonstrable organic basis in which the individual may have considerable insight and has unimpaired reality testing, in that he usually does not confuse his morbid subjective experiences and fantasies with external reality. Behavior may be greatly affected although usually remaining within socially acceptable limits, but personality is not disorganized. The principal manifestations include excessive anxiety, hysterical symptoms, phobias, obsessional and compulsive symptoms, and depression.[1]

anxiety states: Various combinations of physical and mental manifestations of anxiety, not attributable to real danger and occurring either in attacks [*see* Anxiety state, panic attacks] or as a persisting state [*see* Anxiety state, generalized]. The anxiety is usually diffuse and may extend to panic. Other neurotic features such as obsessional or hysterical symptoms may be present but do not dominate the clinical picture.[1]

compensation neurosis: Certain unconscious neurotic reactions in which features of secondary gain, such as a situational or financial advantage, are prominent.[3]

depersonalization: A neurotic disorder with an unpleasant state of disturbed perception in which external objects or parts of one's own body are experienced as changed in their quality, unreal, remote, or automatized. The patient is aware of the subjective nature of the change he experiences. If depersonalization occurs as a feature of anxiety, schizophrenia, or other mental disorder, the condition is classified according to the major psychiatric disorder.[1]

depression: A neurotic disorder characterized by disproportionate depression which has usually recognizably ensued on a distressing experience; it does not include among its features delusions or hallucinations, and there is often preoccupation with the psychic trauma which preceded the illness, e.g., loss of a cherished person or possession. Anxiety is also frequently present and mixed states of anxiety and depression should be included here. The distinction between depressive neurosis and psychosis should be made not only upon the degree of depression but also on the presence or absence of other neurotic and psychotic characteristics, and upon the degree of disturbance of the individual's behavior.[1]

hypochondriasis: A neurotic disorder in which the conspicuous features are excessive concern with one's health in general or the integrity and functioning of some part of one's body, or less frequently, one's mind. It is usually associated with anxiety and depression. It may occur as a feature of some other severe mental disorder (e.g., manic-depressive psychosis, depressed type, schizophrenia, hysteria) and in that case should be classified according to the corresponding major disorder.[1]

hysteria: A neurotic mental disorder in which motives, of which the patient seems unaware, produce either a restriction of the field of consciousness or disturbances of motor or sensory function which may seem to have psychological advantage or symbolic value.[1] There are three subtypes:

conversion type: The chief or only symptoms of the hysterical neurosis consist of psychogenic disturbance of function in some part of the body, e.g., paralysis, tremor, blindness, deafness, seizures.[1]

dissociative type: The most prominent feature of the hysterical neurosis is a narrowing of the field of consciousness which seems to serve an unconscious purpose and is commonly accompanied or followed by a selective amnesia. There may be dramatic but essentially superficial changes of personality [multiple personality], or sometimes the patient enters into a wandering state [fugue].[1]

factitious illness: Physical or psychological symptoms that are not real, genuine, or natural, which are produced by the individual and are under his voluntary control.[2]

neurasthenia: A neurotic disorder characterized by fatigue, irritability, headache, depression, insomnia, difficulty in concentration, and lack of capacity for enjoyment [anhedonia]. It may follow or accompany an infection or exhaustion, or arise from continued emotional stress. If neurasthenia is associated with a physical disorder, the latter should also be recorded as a diagnosis.[1]

obsessive-compulsive: States in which the outstanding symptom is a feeling of subjective compulsion, which must be resisted, to carry out some action, to dwell on an idea, to recall an experience, or to ruminate on an abstract topic. Unwanted thoughts which intrude, the insistency of words or ideas, ruminations or trains of thought are perceived by the individual to be inappropriate or nonsensical. The obsessional urge or idea is recognized as alien to the personality but as coming from within the self. Obsessional actions may be quasi-ritual performances designed to relieve anxiety, e.g., washing the hands to cope with contamination. Attempts to dispel the unwelcome thought or urges may lead to a severe inner struggle, with intense anxiety.[1]

occupational: A neurosis characterized by a functional disorder of a group of muscles used chiefly in one's occupation, marked by the occurrence of spasm, paresis, or incoordination on attempt to repeat the habitual movements (e.g., writers' cramp).[5]

phobic disorders: Neurotic states with abnormally intense dread of certain objects or specific situations which would not normally have that effect. If the anxiety tends to spread from a specified situation or object to a wider range of circumstances, it becomes akin to or identical with anxiety state and should be classified as such.[1] *See also* Phobia.

somatization disorder: A chronic, but fluctuating, neurotic disorder which begins early in life and is characterized by recurrent and multiple somatic complaints for which medical attention is sought but which are not apparently due to any physical illness. Complaints are presented in a dramatic, vague, or exaggerated way, or are part of a complicated medical history in which often many specific diagnoses have allegedly been made by other physicians. Complaints invariably refer to many organ systems (headache, fatigue, palpitations, fainting, nausea and vomiting, abdominal pains, bowel trouble, allergies, menstrual and sexual difficulties), and the individual frequently receives medical care from a number of physicians, sometimes simultaneously.[2]

Neurosis—*see* Neurotic disorders

Nightmares: Anxiety attacks occurring in dreams during REM sleep.[2]

Night terrors: A pathology of arousal from stage 4 sleep in which the individual experiences excessive terror and extreme panic (screaming, verbalizations), symptoms of autonomic activity, confusion, and poor recall for event.[2]

Nymphomania: Abnormal and excessive need or desire in the woman for sexual intercourse.[3]

Obsessional personality—*see* Personality disorder, compulsive type

Occupational neurosis—*see* Neurotic disorder, occupational

Oneirophrenia—*see* Schizophrenia, acute episode

Oppositional disorder of childhood or adolescence: A disorder characterized by pervasive opposition to all in authority regardless of self-interest, a continuous argumentativeness, and an unwillingness to respond to reasonable persuasion, not accounted for by a conduct disorder, adjustment disorder, or a psychosis of childhood. The oppositional behavior in this disorder is evoked by any demand, rule, suggestion, request, or admonishment placed on the individual.[2]

Organic affective syndrome: A clinical picture in which the predominating symptoms closely resemble those seen in either the depressive or manic affective disorders, occurring in the presence of evidence or history of a specific organic factor which is etiologically related to the disturbance, such as head trauma, endocranial tumors, and exocranial tumors secreting neurotoxic diatheses (e.g., pancreatic carcinoma). Excessive use of steroids, Cushing's syndrome, and other endocrine disorders may lead to an organic affective syndrome.[2]

Organic personality syndrome: Chronic, mild states of memory disturbance and intellectual deterioration, of nonpsychotic nature, often accompanied by increased irritability, querulousness, lassitude, and complaints of physical weakness. These states are often associated with old age, and may precede more severe states due to brain damage classifiable under senile or presenile dementia, dementia associated with other chronic organic psychotic brain syndromes, or delirium, delusions, hallucinosis, and depression in transient organic psychotic conditions.[1]

Organic psychosyndrome, focal (partial): A nonpsychotic organic mental disorder resembling the postconcussion syndrome associated with localized diseases of the brain or surrounding tissues.[1]

Organic psychotic conditions: Syndromes in which there is impairment of orientation, memory, comprehension, calculation, learning capacity, and judgment. These are the essential features but there may also be shallowness or lability of affect, or a more persistent disturbance of mood, lowering of ethical standards and exaggeration or emergence of personality traits, and diminished capacity for independent decision.[1] See also Alcohol psychoses, Arteriosclerotic dementia, Drug psychoses, Presenile dementia, and Senile dementia.

    mixed paranoid and affective: Organic psychosis in which depressive and paranoid symptoms are the main features.[1]

    transient: States characterized by clouded consciousness, confusion, disorientation, illusions, and often vivid hallucinations. They are usually due to some intra- or extracerebral toxic, infectious, metabolic or other systemic disturbance and are generally reversible. Depressive and paranoid symptoms may also be present but are not the main feature. The diagnosis of the associated physical or neurological condition should also be recorded.[1]

        acute delirium: Short-lived states, lasting hours or days, of the above type.[1]

        subacute delirium: States of the above type in which the symptoms, usually less florid, last for several weeks or longer during which they may show marked fluctuations in intensity.[1]

Organic reaction—*see* Organic psychotic conditions, transient

Overanxious disorder: An ill-defined emotional disorder characteristic of childhood in which the main symptoms involve anxiety and fearfulness.[1]

Panic disorder—*see* panic attack under Anxiety state

Paranoia: A rare chronic psychosis in which logically constructed systematized delusions have developed gradually without concomitant hallucinations or the schizophrenic type of disordered thinking. The delusions are mostly of grandeur (the paranoiac prophet or inventor), persecution, or somatic abnormality.[1]

    alcoholic—*see* alcoholic jealousy under Alcoholic psychoses

    querulans: A paranoid state which, though in many ways akin to schizophrenic or affective states, differs from other paranoid states and psychogenic paranoid psychosis.[1]

    senile—*see* Paraphrenia

Paranoid personality—*see* Personality disorder, paranoid type

Paranoid reaction, acute: Paranoid states apparently provoked by some emotional stress. The stress is often misconstrued as an attack or threat. Such states are particularly prone to occur in prisoners or as acute reactions to a strange and threatening environment, e.g., in immigrants.[1]

Paranoid schizophrenia—*see* Schizophrenia, paranoid type

Paranoid state

    involutional—*see* Paraphrenia

    senile—*see* Paraphrenia

    simple: A psychosis, acute or chronic, not classifiable as schizophrenia or affective psychosis, in which delusions, especially of being influenced, persecuted, or treated in some special way, are the main symptoms. The delusions are of a fairly fixed, elaborate, and systematized kind.[1]

Paranoid traits—*see* Personality disorder, paranoid type

Paraphilia—*see* Sexual deviations

Paraphrenia: Paranoid psychosis in which there are conspicuous hallucinations, often in several modalities. Affective symptoms and disordered thinking, if present, do not dominate the clinical picture, and the personality is well preserved.[1]

Paraphrenic schizophrenia—*see* Schizophrenia, paranoid type

Passive-aggressive personality — *see* Personality disorder, passive- aggressive type

Passive personality—*see* Personality disorder, dependent type

Pathological

    alcohol intoxication—*see* Alcohol intoxication, idiosyncratic

    drug intoxication: Individual idiosyncratic reactions to comparatively small quantities of a drug, which take the form of acute, brief psychotic states of any type.[1]

    drunkenness—*see* Alcohol intoxication, idiosyncratic

    gambling: A disorder of impulse control characterized by a chronic and progressive preoccupation with gambling and urge to gamble, with subsequent gambling behavior that compromises, disrupts, or damages personal, family, and vocational pursuits.[2]

    personality—*see* Personality disorder

Pedophilia: Sexual deviations in which an adult engages in sexual activity with a child of the same or opposite sex.[1]

Peregrinating patient—*see* Malingering

Personality disorders: Deeply ingrained maladaptive patterns of behavior generally recognizable by the time of adolescence or earlier and continuing throughout most of adult life, although often becoming less obvious in middle or old age. The personality is abnormal either in the balance of its components, their quality and expression, or in its total aspect. Because of this deviation or psychopathy the patient suffers or others have to suffer, and there is an adverse effect upon the individual or on society. It includes what is sometimes called psychopathic personality, but if this is determined primarily by malfunctioning of the brain, it should be classified as one of the nonpsychotic organic brain syndromes. When the patient exhibits an anomaly of personality directly related to his neurosis or psychosis, e.g., schizoid personality and schizophrenia or anancastic personality and obsessive compulsive neurosis, the relevant neurosis or psychosis which is in evidence should be diagnosed in addition.[1]

> **affective type:** A chronic personality disorder characterized by lifelong predominance of a pronounced mood. The illness does not have a clear onset, and there may be intermittent periods of disturbed mood separated by periods of normal mood.[1]

> **anancastic [anankastic] type**—*see* Personality disorder, compulsive type

> **antisocial type:** A personality disorder characterized by disregard for social obligations, lack of feeling for others, and impetuous violence or callous unconcern. There is a gross disparity between behavior and the prevailing social norms. Behavior is not readily modifiable by experience, including punishment. People with this personality are often affectively cold, and may be abnormally aggressive or irresponsible. Their tolerance to frustration is low; they blame others or offer plausible rationalizations for the behavior which brings them into conflict with society.[1]

> **asthenic type**—*see* Personality disorder, dependent type

> **avoidant type:** Individuals with this disorder exhibit excessive social inhibitions and shyness, a tendency to withdraw from opportunities for developing close relationships, and a fearful expectation that they will be belittled and humiliated. Desires for affection and acceptance are strong, but they are unwilling to enter relationships unless given unusually strong guarantees that they will be uncritically accepted. Therefore, they have few close relationships and suffer from feelings of loneliness and isolation.[2]

> **borderline type:** Individuals with this disorder are characterized by instability in a variety of areas, including interpersonal relationships, behavior, mood, and self image. Interpersonal relationships are often intense and unstable with marked shifts of attitude over time. Frequently there is impulsive and unpredictable behavior which is potentially physically self-damaging. There may be problems tolerating being alone, and chronic feelings of emptiness or boredom.[2]

> **chronic depressive type:** An affective personality disorder characterized by lifelong predominance of a chronic nonpsychotic disturbance involving either intermittent or sustained periods of depressed mood (marked by worry, pessimism, low output of energy, and a sense of futility).[2]

> **chronic hypomanic type:** An affective personality disorder characterized by lifelong predominance of a chronic nonpsychotic disturbance involving either intermittent or sustained periods of abnormally elevated mood (unshakable optimism and an enhanced zest for life and activity).[2]

> **compulsive type:** A personality disorder characterized by feelings of personal insecurity, doubt, and incompleteness leading to excessive conscientiousness, checking, stubbornness, and caution. There may be insistent and unwelcome thoughts or impulses which do not attain the severity of an obsessional neurosis. There is perfectionism and meticulous accuracy and a need to check repeatedly in an attempt to ensure this. Rigidity and excessive doubt may be conspicuous.[1]

> **cyclothymic type:** A chronic nonpsychotic disturbance involving depressed and elevated mood, lasting at least two years, separated by periods of normal mood.[2]

> **dependent type:** A personality disorder characterized by passive compliance with the wishes of elders and others and a weak inadequate response to the demands of daily life. Lack of vigor may show itself in the intellectual or emotional spheres; there is little capacity for enjoyment.[1]

> **eccentric type:** A personality disorder characterized by oddities of behavior which do not conform to the clinical syndromes of personality disorders described elsewhere.[2]

> **explosive type:** A personality disorder characterized by instability of mood with liability to intemperate outbursts of anger, hate, violence, or affection. Aggression may be expressed in words or in physical violence. The outbursts cannot readily be controlled by the affected persons, who are not otherwise prone to antisocial behavior.[1]

> **histrionic type:** A personality disorder characterized by shallow, labile affectivity, dependence on others, craving for appreciation and attention, suggestibility, and theatricality. There is often sexual immaturity, e.g., frigidity and over-responsiveness to stimuli. Under stress hysterical symptoms [neurosis] may develop.[1]

> **hysterical type**—*see* Personality disorder, histrionic type

> **inadequate type**—*see* Personality disorder, dependent type

introverted type: A form of schizoid personality in which the essential features are a profound defect in the ability to form social relationships and to respond to the usual forms of social reinforcements. Such patients are characteristically "loners" who do not appear distressed by their social distance and are not interested in greater social involvements.[2]

masochistic type: A personality disorder in which the individual appears to arrange life situations so as to be defeated and humiliated.[2]

narcissistic type: A personality disorder in which interpersonal difficulties are caused by an inflated sense of self-worth, and indifference to the welfare of others. Achievement deficits and social irresponsibilities are justified and sustained by a boastful arrogance, expansive fantasies, facile rationalization, and frank prevarication.[2]

paranoid type: A personality disorder in which there is excessive sensitiveness to setbacks or to what are taken to be humiliations and rebuffs, a tendency to distort experience by misconstruing the neutral or friendly actions of others as hostile or contemptuous, and a combative and tenacious sense of personal rights. There may be a proneness to jealousy or excessive self-importance. Such persons may feel helplessly humiliated and put upon; others, likewise excessively sensitive, are aggressive and insistent. In all cases there is excessive self-reference.[1]

passive-aggressive type: A personality disorder characterized by aggressive behavior manifested in passive ways, such as obstructionism, pouting, procrastination, intentional inefficiency, or stubbornness. The *aggression* often arises from resentment at failing to find gratification in a relationship with an individual or institution upon which the individual is overdependent.[3]

passive type—*see* Personality disorder, dependent type

schizoid type: A personality disorder in which there is withdrawal from affectional, social, and other contacts with autistic preference for fantasy and introspective reserve. Behavior may be slightly eccentric or indicate avoidance of competitive situations. Apparent coolness and detachment may mask an incapacity to express feeling.

schizotypal type: A form of schizoid personality in which individuals with this disorder manifest various oddities of thinking, perception, communication, and behavior. The disturbance in thinking may be expressed as magical thinking, ideas of reference, or paranoid ideation. Perceptual disturbances may include recurrent illusions and derealization [depersonalization]. Frequently, but not invariably, the behavioral manifestations include social isolation and constricted or inappropriate affect which interferes with rapport in face-to-face interaction without any of the frank psychotic features which characterize schizophrenia.[2]

Phobia: Neurotic states with abnormally intense dread of certain objects or specific situations which would not normally have that effect. If the anxiety tends to spread from a specified situation or object to a wider range of circumstances, it becomes akin to or identical with anxiety state, and should be classified as such.[1]

acrophobia: Fear of heights[3]

agoraphobia: fear of leaving the familiar setting of the home, and is almost always preceded by a phase during which there are recurrent panic attacks. Because of the anticipatory fear of helplessness when having a panic attack, the patient is reluctant or refuses to be alone, travel or walk alone, or to be in situations where there is no ready access to help, such as in crowds, closed or open spaces, or crowded stores.[2]

ailurophobia: Fear of cats[3]

algophobia: Fear of pain[3]

claustrophobia: Fear of closed spaces[3]

isolated phobia—*see* simple phobia below

mysophobia: Fear of dirt or germs[3]

obsessional—*see* Neurotic disorder, obsessive-compulsive

panphobia: Fear of everything[3]

simple phobia: Fear of a discrete object or situation which is neither fear of leaving the familiar setting of the home [agoraphobia], or of being observed by others in certain situations [social phobia]. Examples of simple phobia are fear of animals, acrophobia, and claustrophobia.

social phobia: Fear of situations in which the subject is exposed to possible scrutiny by others, and the possibility exists that he may act in a fashion that will be considered shameful. The most common social phobias are fears of public speaking, blushing, eating in public, writing in front of others, or using public lavatories.[2]

xenophobia: Fear of strangers[3]

Pica: Perverted appetite of nonorganic origin in which there is persistent eating of non-nutritional substances. Typically, infants ingest paint, plaster, string, hair, or cloth. Older children may have access to animal droppings, sand, bugs, leaves, or pebbles. In the adult, eating of starch or clay-earth has been observed.[2]

Postconcussion syndrome: States occurring after generalized contusion of the brain, in which the symptom picture may resemble that of the frontal lobe syndrome or that of any of the neurotic disorders, but in which in addition, headache, giddiness, fatigue, insomnia, and a subjective feeling of impaired intellectual ability are usually prominent. Mood may fluctuate, and quite ordinary stress may produce exaggerated fear and apprehension. There may be marked intolerance of mental and physical exertion, undue sensitivity to noise, and hypochondriacal preoccupation. The symptoms are more common in persons who have previously suffered from neurotic or personality disorders, or when there is a possibility of compensation. This syndrome is particularly associated with the closed type of head injury when signs of localized brain damage are slight or absent, but it may also occur in other conditions.[1]

Postcontusion syndrome or encephalopathy—*see* Postconcussion syndrome

Postencephalitic syndrome: A nonpsychotic organic mental disorder resembling the postconcussion syndrome associated with central nervous system infections.[1]

Postleucotomy syndrome—*see* Frontal lobe syndrome

Posttraumatic brain syndrome, nonpsychotic—*see* Postconcussion syndrome

Posttraumatic organic psychosis—*see* Organic psychotic conditions, transient

Posttraumatic stress disorder: The development of characteristic symptoms (re-experiencing the traumatic event, numbing of responsiveness to or involvement with the external world, and a variety of other autonomic, dysphoric, or cognitive symptoms) after experiencing a psychologically traumatic event or events outside the normal range of human experience (e.g., rape or assault, military combat, natural catastrophes such as flood or earthquake, or other disaster, such as airplane crash, fires, bombings).[2]

    acute: Brief, episodic, or recurrent disorders lasting less than six months' duration after the onset of trauma.[2]

    prolonged: Chronic disorders of the above type lasting six months or more following the trauma.[2]

Premature ejaculation—*see* premature ejaculation under Psychosexual dysfunction.

Prepsychotic schizophrenia—*see* Schizophrenia, latent

Presbyophrenia—*see* Organic personality syndrome

Presenile dementia: Dementia occuring usually before the age of 65 in patients with the relatively rare forms of diffuse or lobar cerebral atrophy. The associated neurological condition (e.g., Alzheimer's disease, Pick's disease, Jakob-Creutzfeldt disease) should also be recorded as a diagnosis.[1]

Prodromal schizophrenia—*see* Schizophrenia, latent

Pseudoneurotic schizophrenia—*see* Schizophrenia, latent

Psychalgia: Pains of mental origin, e.g., headache or backache, for which a more precise medical or psychiatric diagnosis cannot be made.[1]

Psychasthenia: A functional neurosis marked by stages of pathological fear or anxiety, obsessions, fixed ideas, tics, feelings of inadequacy, self-accusation, and peculiar feelings of strangeness, unreality, and depersonalization.[4]

Psychic shock: A sudden disturbance of mental equilibrium produced by strong emotion in response to physical or mental stress.[4]

Psychic factors associated with physical diseases: Mental disturbances or psychic factors of any type thought to have played a major part in the etiology of physical conditions, usually involving tissue damage, classified elsewhere. The mental disturbance is usually mild and nonspecific, and the psychic factors (worry, fear, conflict, etc.) may be present without any overt psychiatric disorder. Examples of these conditions are asthma, dermatitis, eczema, duodenal ulcer, ulcerative colitis, and urticaria, specified as due to psychogenic factors.
Use an additional diagnosis to identify the physical condition. In the rare instance that an overt psychiatric disorder is thought to have caused the physical condition, the psychiatric diagnosis should be recorded in addition.[1]

Psychoneurosis—*see* Neurotic disorders

Psycho-organic syndrome—*see* Organic psychotic conditions, transient

Psychopathic constitutional state—*see* Personality disorders

Psychopathic personality—*see* Personality disorders

Psychophysiological disorders: A variety of physical symptoms or types of physiological malfunctions of mental origin, not involving tissue damage, and usually mediated through the autonomic nervous system. The disorders are classified according to the body system involved. If the physical symptom is secondary to a psychiatric disorder classifiable elsewhere, the physical symptom is not classified as a psychophysiological disorder. If tissue damage is involved, then the diagnosis is classified as a *Psychic factor associated with diseases classified elsewhere.*[1]

Psychosexual dysfunctions: A group of disorders in which there is recurrent and persistent dysfunction encountered during sexual activity. The dysfunction may be lifelong or acquired, generalized or situational, and total or partial.[2]

functional dyspareunia: Recurrent and persistent genital pain associated with coitus.[2]

functional vaginismus: A history of recurrent and persistent involuntary spasm of the musculature of the outer one-third of the vagina that interferes with sexual activity.[2]

inhibited female orgasm: Recurrent and persistent inhibition of the female orgasm as manifested by a delay or absence of orgasm following a normal sexual excitement phase during sexual activity.[2]

inhibited male orgasm: Recurrent and persistent inhibition of the male orgasm as manifested by a delay or absence of either the emission or ejaculation phases, or more usually, both following an adequate phase of sexual excitement.[2]

inhibited sexual desire: Persistent inhibition of desire for engaging in a particular form of sexual activity.[2]

inhibited sexual excitement: Recurrent and persistent inhibition of sexual excitement during sexual activity, manifested either by partial or complete failure to attain or maintain erection until completion of the sexual act [impotence], or partial or complete failure to attain or maintain the lubrication-swelling response of sexual excitement until completion of the sexual act [frigidity].[2]

premature ejaculation: Ejaculation occurs before the individual wishes it, because of recurrent and persistent absence of reasonable voluntary control of ejaculation and orgasm during sexual activity.[2]

Psychosexual gender identity disorders: Behavior occurring in preadolescents of immature psychosexuality, or in adults, in which there is an incongruence between the individual's anatomic sex and gender identity.[2]

gender identity disorder: In children or in adults a condition in which the individual would prefer to be of the other sex, and strongly prefers the clothes, toys, activities, and companionship of the other sex. Cross-dressing is intermittent, although it may be frequent. In children the commonest form is feminism in boys.[2]

trans-sexualism: A psychosexual identity disorder centered around fixed beliefs that the overt bodily sex is wrong. The resulting behavior is directed towards either changing the sexual organs by operation, or completely concealing the bodily sex by adopting both the dress and behavior of the opposite sex.[1]

Psychosomatic disorders—*see* Psychophysiological disorders

Psychosis: Mental disorders in which impairment of mental function has developed to a degree that interferes grossly with insight, ability to meet some ordinary demands of life or to maintain adequate contact with reality. It is not an exact or well defined term. Mental retardation is excluded.[1]

affective—*see* Affective psychoses

alcoholic—*see* Alcoholic psychoses

atypical childhood: A variety of atypical infantile psychoses which may show some, but not all, of the features of infantile autism. Symptoms may include stereotyped repetitive movements, hyperkinesis, self-injury, retarded speech development, echolalia, and impaired social relationships. Such disorders may occur in children of any level of intelligence but are particularly common in those with mental retardation.[1]

borderline, of childhood—*see* Psychosis, atypical childhood

child: A group of disorders in children, characterized by distortions in the timing, rate, and sequence of many psychological functions involving language development and social relations in which the severe qualitative abnormalities are not normal for any stage of development.[2] See also Autism, infantile, Psychosis, disintegrative, Psychosis, atypical childhood.

depressive—*see* Affective psychosis, depressed type

depressive type: A depressive psychosis which can be similar in its symptoms to manic-depressive psychosis, depressed type but is apparently provoked by saddening stress such as a bereavement, or a severe disappointment or frustration. There may be less diurnal variation of symptoms than in manic-depressive psychosis, depressed type, and the delusions are more often understandable in the context of the life experiences. There is usually a serious disturbance of behavior, e.g., major suicidal attempt.[1]

disintegrative: A disorder in which normal or near-normal development for the first few years is followed by a loss of social skills and of speech, together with a severe disorder of emotions, behavior, and relationships. Usually this loss of speech and of social competence takes place over a period of a few months and is accompanied by the emergence of overactivity and of stereotypies. In most cases there is intellectual impairment, but this is not a necessary part of the disorder. The condition may follow overt brain disease, such as measles encephalitis, but it may also occur in the absence of any known organic brain disease or damage. Any associated neurological disorder should also be recorded.[1]

epileptic: An organic psychotic condition associated with epilepsy.[1]

excitative type: An affective psychosis similar in its symptoms to manic-depressive psychosis, manic type, but apparently provoked by emotional stress.[1]

hypomanic—*see* Affective psychosis, manic type

hysterical—*see* Psychosis, reactive

    acute—*see* Psychosis, excitative type

induced—*see* Shared paranoid disorder

infantile—*see* Autism, infantile

infective—*see* Organic psychotic conditions, transient

Korsakoff's:

    alcoholic—*see* alcohol amnestic syndrome under Alcoholic psychoses

    nonalcoholic—*see* Amnestic syndrome

manic-depressive—*see* Affective psychoses

multi-infarct—*see* Arteriosclerotic dementia

paranoid

    chronic—*see* Paranoia

    protracted reactive—*see* Psychosis, paranoid, psychogenic

    psychogenic: Psychogenic or reactive paranoid psychosis of any type which is more protracted than the reactions described under paranoid reaction, acute.[1]
        acute—*see* Paranoid reaction, acute

postpartum—*see* Psychosis, puerperal

psychogenic—*see* Psychosis, reactive

    depressive—*see* Psychosis, depressive type

puerperal: Any psychosis occurring within a fixed period (approximately 90 days) after childbirth.[3] The diagnosis should be classified according to the predominant symptoms or characteristics, such as schizophrenia, affective psychosis, paranoid states, or other specified psychosis.

reactive: A psychotic condition which is largely or entirely attributable to a recent life experience. This diagnosis is not used for the wider range of psychoses in which environmental factors play some, but not the *major,* part in etiology.[1]

    brief: A florid psychosis of at least a few hours' duration but lasting no more than two weeks, with sudden onset immediately following a severe environmental stress and eventually terminating in complete recovery to the pre-psychotic state.[2]

    confusion: Mental disorders with clouded consciousness, disorientation (though less marked than in organic confusion), and diminished accessibility often accompanied by excessive activity and apparently provoked by emotional stress.[1]

    depressive—*see* Psychosis, depressive type

schizo-affective—*see* Schizophrenia, schizo-affective type

schizophrenic—*see* Schizophrenia

schizophreniform—*see* Schizophrenia

    affective type—*See* Schizophrenia, schizo-affective type

    confusional type—*see* Schizophrenia, acute episode

senile—*see* Senile dementia, delusional type

Pyromania: A disorder of impulse control characterized by a recurrent failure to resist impulses to set fires without regard for the consequences, or with deliberate destructive intent. Invariably there is intense fascination with the setting of fires, seeing fires burn, and a satisfaction with the resultant destruction.[2]

Relationship problems of childhood: Emotional disorders characteristic of childhood in which the main symptoms involve relationship problems.[1]

Repeated infarct dementia—*see* Arteriosclerotic dementia

Residual schizophrenia—*.see* Schizophrenia, residual type

Restzustand (schizophrenia)—*see* Schizophrenia, residual type

Rumination:

    obsessional: The constant preoccupation with certain thoughts, with inability to dismiss them from the mind.[4] *see* Neurotic disorder, obsessive-compulsive.

    psychogenic: In children the regurgitation of food, with failure to thrive or weight loss developing after a period of normal functioning. Food is brought up without nausea, retching, or disgust. The food is then ejected from the mouth, or chewed and reswallowed.[2]

Sander's disease—*see* Paranoia

Satyriasis: Pathologic or exaggerated sexual desire or excitement in the man.[3]

Schizoid personality disorder—*see* Personality disorder, schizoid type

Schizophrenia: A group of psychoses in which there is a fundamental disturbance of personality, a characteristic distortion of thinking, often a sense of being controlled by alien forces, delusions which may be bizarre, disturbed perception, abnormal affect out of keeping with the real situation, and autism. Nevertheless, clear consciousness and intellectual capacity are usually maintained. The disturbance of personality involves its most basic functions which give the normal person his feeling of individuality, uniqueness, and self-direction. The most intimate thoughts, feelings, and acts are often felt to be known to or shared by others and explanatory delusions may develop, to the effect that natural or supernatural forces are at work to influence the schizophrenic person's thoughts and actions in ways that are often bizarre. He may see himself as the pivot of all that happens. Hallucinations, especially of hearing, are common and may comment on the patient or address him. Perception is frequently disturbed in other ways; there may be perplexity, irrelevant features may become all-important and accompanied by passivity feeling, may lead the patient to believe that everyday objects and situations possess a special, usually sinister, meaning intended for him. In the characteristic schizophrenic disturbance of thinking, peripheral and irrelevant features of a total concept, which are inhibited in normal directed mental activity, are brought to the forefront and utilized in place of the elements relevant and appropriate to the situation. Thus, thinking becomes vague, elliptical and obscure, and its expression in speech sometimes incomprehensible. Breaks and interpolations in the flow of consecutive thought are frequent, and the patient may be convinced that his thoughts are being withdrawn by some outside agency. Mood may be shallow, capricious, or incongruous. Ambivalence and disturbance of volition may appear as inertia, negativism, or stupor. Catatonia may be present. The diagnosis "schizophrenia" should not be made unless there is, or has been evident during the same illness, characteristic disturbance of thought, perception, mood, conduct, or personality—preferably in at least two of these areas. The diagnosis should not be restricted to conditions running a protracted, deteriorating, or chronic course. In addition to making the diagnosis on the criteria just given, effort should be made to specify one of the following subtypes of schizophrenia, according to the predominant symptoms.[1]

acute (undifferentiated): Schizophrenia of florid nature which cannot be classified as simple, catatonic, hebephrenic, paranoid, or any other types.[1]

acute episode: Schizophrenic disorders, other than simple, hebephrenic, catatonic, and paranoid, in which there is a dream-like state with slight clouding of consciousness and perplexity. External things, people, and events may become charged with personal significance for the patient. There may be ideas of reference and emotional turmoil. In many such cases remission occurs within a few weeks or months, even without treatment.[1]

atypical—*see* Schizophrenia, acute (undifferentiated)

borderline—*see* Schizophrenia, latent

catatonic type: Includes as an essential feature prominent psychomotor disturbances often alternating between extremes such as hyperkinesis and stupor, or automatic obedience and negativism. Constrained attitudes may be maintained for long periods: if the patient's limbs are put in some unnatural position they may be held there for some time after the external force has been removed. Severe excitement may be a striking feature of the condition. Depressive or hypomanic concomitants may be present.[1]

cenesthopathic—*see* Schizophrenia, acute (undifferentiated)

childhood type—*see* Psychosis, child

chronic undifferentiated—*see* Schizophrenia, residual

cyclic—*see* Schizophrenia, schizo-affective type

disorganized type: A form of schizophrenia in which affective changes are prominent, delusions and hallucinations fleeting and fragmentary, behavior irresponsible and unpredictable, and mannerisms common. The mood is shallow and inappropriate, accompanied by giggling or self-satisfied, self—absorbed smiling, or by a lofty manner, grimaces, mannerisms, pranks, hypochondriacal complaints, and reiterated phrases. Thought is disorganized. There is a tendency to remain solitary, and behavior seems empty of purpose and feeling. This form of schizophrenia usually starts between the ages of 15 and 25 years.[1]

hebephrenic type:—*see* Schizophrenia, disorganized type

latent: It has not been possible to produce a generally acceptable description for this condition. It is not recommended for general use, but a description is provided for those who believe it to be useful: a condition of eccentric or inconsequent behavior and anomalies of affect which give the impression of schizophrenia though no definite and characteristic schizophrenic anomalies, present or past, have been manifest.[1]

paranoid type: The form of schizophrenia in which relatively stable delusions, which may be accompanied by hallucinations, dominate the clinical picture. The delusions are frequently of persecution, but may take other forms (for example, of jealousy, exalted birth, Messianic mission, or bodily change). Hallucinations and erratic behavior may occur; in some cases conduct is seriously disturbed from the outset, thought disorder may be gross, and affective flattening with fragmentary delusions and hallucinations may develop.[1]

prepsychotic—*see* Schizophrenia, latent

prodromal—*see* Schizophrenia, latent

pseudoneurotic—*see* Schizophrenia, latent

residual: A chronic form of schizophrenia in which the symptoms that persist from the acute phase have mostly lost their sharpness. Emotional response is blunted and thought disorder, even when gross, does not prevent the accomplishment of routine work.[1]

schizo-affective type: A psychosis in which pronounced manic or depressive features are intermingled with schizophrenic features and which tends towards remission without permanent defect, but which is prone to recur. The diagnosis should be made only when both the affective and schizophrenic symptoms are pronounced.[1]

simple type: A psychosis in which there is insidious development of oddities of conduct, inability to meet the demands of society, and decline in total performance. Delusions and hallucinations are not in evidence and the condition is less obviously psychotic than are the hebephrenic, catatonic, and paranoid types of schizophrenia. With increasing social impoverishment vagrancy may ensue and the patient becomes self-absorbed, idle, and aimless. Because the schizophrenic symptoms are not clear-cut, diagnosis of this form should be made sparingly, if at all.[1]

simplex—*see* Schizophrenia, simple type

Schizophrenic syndrome of childhood—*see* Psychosis, child

Schizophreniform

attack—*see* Schizophrenia, acute episode

disorder—*see* Schizophrenia, acute episode

psychosis—*see* Schizophrenia

affective type—*see* Schizophrenia, schizo-affective type

confusional type—*see* Schizophrenia, acute episode

Schizotypal personality—Dementia occurring usually after the age of 65 in which any cerebral pathology other than that of senile atrophic change can be reasonably excluded.[1]

delirium: Senile dementia with a superimposed reversible episode of acute confusional state.[1]

delusional type: A type of senile dementia characterized by development in advanced old age, progressive in nature, in which delusions, varying from simple poorly formed paranoid delusions to highly formed paranoid delusional states, and hallucinations are also present.[1,2]

depressed type: A type of senile dementia characterized by development in advanced old age, progressive in nature, in which depressive features, ranging from mild to severe forms of manic-depressive affective psychosis, are also present. Disturbance of the sleep-waking cycle and preoccupation with dead people are often particularly prominent.[1,2]

paranoid type—*see* Senile dementia, delusional type

simple type—*see* Senile dementia

Sensitiver Beziehungswahn: A paranoid state which, though in many ways akin to schizophrenic or affective states, differs from paranoia, simple paranoid state, shared paranoid disorder, or psychogenic psychosis.[1]

Sensitivity reaction of childhood or adolescence—*see* Shyness disorder of childhood

Separation anxiety disorder: A clinical disorder in children in which the predominant disturbance is exaggerated distress at separation from parents, home, or other familial surroundings. When separation is instituted, the child may experience anxiety to the point of panic. In adults a similar disorder is seen in agoraphobic reactions.[2]

Sexual deviations: Abnormal sexual inclinations or behavior which are part of a referral problem. The limits and features of normal sexual behavior have not been stated absolutely in different societies and cultures, but are broadly such as serve approved social and biological purposes. The sexual activity of affected persons is directed primarily either towards people not of the opposite sex, or towards sexual acts not associated with coitus normally, or towards coitus performed under abnormal circumstances. If the anomalous behavior becomes manifest only during psychosis or other mental illness the condition should be classified under the major illness. It is common for more than one anomaly to occur together in the same individual; in that case the predominant deviation is classified. It is preferable not to diagnose sexual deviation in individuals who perform deviant sexual acts when normal sexual outlets are not available to them.[1] *see also* exhibitionism, Fetishism, Homosexuality, Nymphomania, Pedophilia, Satyriasis, Sexual masochism, Sexual sadism, Transvestism, Voyeurism, and Zoophilia.

Gender identity disorder and trans-sexualism are considered to be psychosexual gender identity disorders and are not included here.

Sexual masochism: A sexual deviation in which sexual arousal and pleasure is produced in an individual by his own physical or psychological suffering, and in which there are insistent and persistent fantasies wherein sexual excitement is produced as a result of suffering.[2]

Sexual sadism: A sexual deviation in which physical or psychological suffering inflicted on another person is utilized as a method of stimulating erotic excitement and orgasm, and in which there are insistent and persistent fantasies wherein sexual excitement is produced as a result of suffering inflicted on the partner.[2]

Shared paranoid disorder: Mainly delusional psychosis, usually chronic and often without florid features, which appears to have developed as a result of a close, if not dependent, relationship with another person who already has an established similar psychosis. The delusions are at least partly shared. The rare cases in which several persons are affected should also be included here.[1]

Shifting sleep-work schedule: A sleep disorder in which the phase- shift disruption of the 24-hour sleep-wake cycle occurs due to rapid changes in the individual's work schedule.[2]

Short sleeper: Individuals who typically need only 4-6 hours of sleep within the 24-hour cycle.[2]

Shyness disorder of childhood: A persistent and excessive shrinking from familiarity or contact with all strangers of sufficient severity as to interfere with peer functioning, yet there are warm and satisfying relationships with family members. A critical feature of this disorder is that the avoidant behavior with strangers persists even after prolonged exposure or contact.[2]

Sibling jealousy or rivalry: An emotional disorder related to competition between siblings for the love of a parent or for other recognition or gain.[3]

Simple phobia—*see* simple phobia under Phobia

Situational disturbance, acute—*see* Stress reaction, acute

Social phobia—*see* social phobia under Phobia

Social withdrawal of childhood—*see* Introverted disorder of childhood

Socialized conduct disorder—*see* socialized conduct disorder under Conduct disorders

Somatization disorder—*see* somatization disorder under Neurotic disorders

Somatoform disorder, atypical—*see* hypochondriasis under Neurotic disorders

Spasmus nutans—*see* Stereotyped repetitive movements

Specific academic or work inhibition: An adjustment reaction in which a specific academic or work inhibition occurs in an individual whose intellectual capacity, skills, and previous academic or work performance have been at least adequate, and in which the inhibition occurs despite apparent effort and is not due to any other mental disorder.[2]

Stammering—*see* Stuttering

Starch-eating—*see* Pica

Status postcommotio cerebri—*see* Postconcussion syndrome

Stereotyped repetitive movements: Disorders in which voluntary repetitive stereotyped movements, which are not due to any psychiatric or neurological condition, constitute the main feature. Includes head-banging, spasmus nutans, rocking, twirling, finger-flicking mannerisms, and eye poking. Such movements are particularly common in cases of mental retardation with sensory impairment or with environmental monotony.[1]

Stereotypies—*see* Stereotyped repetitive movements

Stress reaction

　acute: Acute transient disorders of any severity and nature of emotions, consciousness, and psychomotor states (singly or in combination) which occur in individuals, without any apparent pre-existing mental disorder, in response to exceptional physical or mental stress, such as natural catastrophe or battle, and which usually subside within hours or days.[1]

　chronic—*see* Adjustment reaction

Stupor

　catatonic—*see* Schizophrenia, catatonic type

　psychogenic—*see* Psychosis, reactive

Stuttering: Disorders in the rhythm of speech, in which the individual knows precisely what he wishes to say, but at the time is unable to say it because of an involuntary, repetitive prolongation or cessation of a sound.[1]

Subjective insomnia complaint: a complaint of insomnia made by the individual, which has not been investigated or proven.[2]

Systematized delusions—*see* Paranoia

Tension headache: Headache of mental origin for which a more precise medical or psychiatric diagnosis cannot be made.[1]

Tics: Disorders of no known organic origin in which the outstanding feature consists of quick, involuntary, apparently purposeless, and frequently repeated movements which are not due to any neurological condition. Any part of the body may be involved but the face is most frequently affected. Only one form of tic may be present, or there may be a combination of tics which are carried out simultaneously, alternatively, or consecutively.[1]

　chronic motor tic disorder: A tic disorder starting in childhood and persisting into adult life. The tic is limited to no more than three motor areas, and rarely has a verbal component.[2]

Gilles de la Tourette's disorder [motor-verbal tic disorder]: a rare disorder occurring in individuals of any level of intelligence in which facial tics and tic-like throat noises become more marked and more generalized, and in which later whole words or short sentences (often with obscene content) are ejaculated spasmodically and involuntarily. There is some overlap with other varieties of tic.[1]

transient tic disorder of childhood: Facial or other tics beginning in childhood, but limited to one year in duration.[2]

Tobacco use disorder: Cases in which tobacco is used to the detriment of a person's health or social functioning or in which there is tobacco dependence. Dependence is included here rather than under drug dependence because tobacco differs from other drugs of dependence in its psychotoxic effects.[1]

Tranquilizer abuse: Cases where an individual has taken the drug to the detriment of his health or social functioning, in doses above or for periods beyond those normally regarded as therapeutic.[1]

Transient organic psychotic condition—*see* Organic psychotic conditions, transient

Trans-sexualism—*see* trans-sexualism under Psychosexual identity disorders

Transvestism: Sexual deviation in which there is recurrent and persistent dressing in clothes of the opposite sex, and initially in the early stage of the illness, for the purpose of sexual arousal.[2]

Twilight state

confusional—*see* Delirium, acute

psychogenic—*see* Psychosis, reactive confusion

Undersocialized conduct disorder—*see* undersocialized conduct disorder under Conduct disorders

Unsocialized aggressive disorder—*see* undersocialized conduct disorder, aggressive type under Conduct disorders

Vaginismus, functional—*see* functional vaginismus under Psychosexual dysfunctions

Vorbeireden: The symptom of the approximate answer or talking past the point, seen in the Ganser syndrome, a form of factitious illness.[2]

Voyeurism: A sexual deviation in which the individual repetitively seeks out situations in which he engages in looking at unsuspecting women who are either naked, in the act of disrobing, or engaging in sexual activity. The act of looking is accompanied by sexual excitement, frequently with orgasm. In its severe form, the act of peeping constitutes the preferred or exclusive sexual activity of the individual.[2]

Wernicke-Korsakoff syndrome—*see* alcohol amnestic syndrome under Alcoholic psychoses

Withdrawal reaction of childhood or adolescence—*see* Introverted disorder of childhood

Word-deafness: A developmental delay in the comprehension of speech sounds.[1]

Zoophilia: Sexual or anal intercourse with animals.[1]

1. Manual of the *International Classification of Diseases, Injuries, and Causes of Death.* 9th Revision. World Health Organization, Geneva, Switzerland, 1975.
2. American Psychiatric Association, Task Force on Nomenclature and Statistics, Robert L. Spitzer, Chairman.
3. *A Psychiatric Glossary*, Fourth Edition, American Psychiatric Association, Washington, D.C., 1975.
4. *Dorland's Illustrated Medical Dictionary.* Twenty-fifth Edition, W. B. Saunders Company, Philadelphia, 1974.
5. *Stedman's Medical Dictionary. Illustrated,* Twenty-third Edition, Williams and Wilkins, Baltimore, 1976.

CLASSIFICATION OF DRUGS BY AMERICAN HOSPITAL FORMULARY SERVICE LIST NUMBER AND THEIR ICD-9-CM EQUIVALENTS

The coding of adverse effects of drugs is keyed to the continually revised Hospital Formulary of the American Hospital Formulary Service (AHFS) published under the direction of the American Society of Hospital Pharmacists.

The following section gives the ICD-9-CM diagnosis code for each AHFS list.

	AHFS* LIST	ICD-9-CM Diagnosis Code
4:00	**ANTIHISTAMINE DRUGS**	963.0
8:00	**ANTI-INFECTIVE AGENTS**	
8:04	Amebacides	961.5
	hydroxyquinoline derivatives	961.3
	arsenical anti-infectives	961.1
8:08	Anthelmintics	961.6
	quinoline derivatives	961.3
8:12.04	Antifungal Antibiotics	960.1
	nonantibiotics	961.9
8:12.06	Cephalosporins	960.5
8:12.08	Chloramphenicol	960.2
8:12.12	The Erythromycins	960.3
8:12.16	The Penicillins	960.0
8:12.20	The Streptomycins	960.6
8:12.24	The Tetracyclines	960.4
8:12.28	Other Antibiotics	960.8
	antimycobacterial antibiotics	960.6
	macrolides	960.3
8:16	Antituberculars	961.8
	antibiotics	960.6
8:18	Antivirals	961.7
8:20	Plasmodicides (antimalarials)	961.4
8:24	Sulfonamides	961.0
8:26	The Sulfones	961.8
8:28	Treponemicides	961.2
8:32	Trichomonacides	961.5
	hydroxyquinoline derivatives	961.3
	nitrofuran derivatives	961.9
8:36	Urinary Germicides	961.9
	quinoline derivatives	961.3
8:40	Other Anti-Infectives	961.9
10:00	**ANTINEOPLASTIC AGENTS**	963.1
	antibiotics	960.7
	progestogens	962.2
12:00	**AUTONOMIC DRUGS**	
12:04	Parasympathomimetic (Cholinergic) Agents	971.0
12:08	Parasympatholytic (Cholinergic Blocking) Agents	971.1
12:12	Sympathomimetic (Adrenergic) Agents	971.2
12:16	Sympatholytic (Adrenergic Blocking) Agents	971.3
12:20	Skeletal Muscle Relaxants	975.2
	central nervous system muscle-tone depressants	968.0

AHFS* LIST		ICD-9-CM Diagnosis Code
16:00	**BLOOD DERIVATIVES**	964.7
20:00	**BLOOD FORMATION AND COAGULATION**	
20:04	Antianemia Drugs	964.1
20:04.04	Iron Preparations	964.0
20:04.08	Liver and Stomach Preparations	964.1
20:12.04	Anticoagulants	964.2
20:12.08	Antiheparin agents	964.5
20:12.12	Coagulants	964.5
20:12.16	Hemostatics	964.5
	capillary-active drugs	972.8
	fibrinolysis-affecting agents	964.4
	natural products	964.7
24:00	**CARDIOVASCULAR DRUGS**	
24:04	Cardiac Drugs	972.9
	cardiotonic agents	972.1
	rhythm regulators	972.0
24:06	Antilipemic Agents	972.2
	thyroid derivatives	962.7
24:08	Hypotensive Agents	972.6
	adrenergic blocking agents	971.3
	ganglion-blocking agents	972.3
	vasodilators	972.5
24:12	Vasodilating Agents	972.5
	coronary	972.4
	nicotinic acid derivatives	972.2
24:16	Sclerosing Agents	972.7
28:00	**CENTRAL NERVOUS SYSTEM DRUGS**	
28:04	General Anesthetics	968.4
	gaseous anesthetics	968.2
	halothane	968.1
	intravenous anesthetics	968.3
28:08	Analgesics and Antipyretics	965.9
	antirheumatics	965.6
	aromatic analgesics	965.4
	non-narcotics NEC	965.7
	opium alkaloids	965.00
	heroin	965.01
	methadone	965.02
	specified type NEC	965.09
	pyrazole derivatives	965.5
	salicylates	965.1
	specified type NEC	965.8
28:10	Narcotic Antagonists	970.1
28:12	Anticonvulsants	966.3
	barbiturates	967.0
	benzodiazepine-based tranquilizers	969.4
	bromides	967.3
	hydantoin derivatives	966.1
	oxazolidine derivative	966.0
	succinimides	966.2
28:16.04	Antidepressants	969.0
28:16.08	Tranquilizers	969.5
	benzodiazepine-based	969.4
	butyrophenone-based	969.2
	major NEC	969.3
	phenothiazine-based	969.1

* American Hospital Formulary Service

AHFS* LIST	ICD-9-CM Diagnosis Code
28:16.12 Other Psychotherapeutic Agents	969.8
28:20 Respiratory and Cerebral Stimulants	970.9
analeptics	970.0
anorexigenic agents	977.0
psychostimulants	969.7
specified type NEC	970.8
28:24 Sedatives and Hypnotics	967.9
barbiturates	967.0
benzodiazepine-based tranquilizers	969.4
chloral hydrate group	967.1
glutethamide group	967.5
intravenous anesthetics	968.3
methaqualone	967.4
paraldehyde	967.2
phenothiazine-based tranquilizers	969.1
specified type NEC	967.8
thiobarbiturates	968.3
tranquilizer NEC	969.5
36:00 **DIAGNOSTIC AGENTS**	977.8
40:00 **ELECTROLYTE, CALORIC, AND WATER BALANCE AGENTS NEC**	974.5
40:04 Acidifying Agents	963.2
40:08 Alkalinizing Agents	963.3
40:10 Ammonia Detoxicants	974.5
40:12 Replacement Solutions NEC	974.5
plasma volume expanders	964.8
40:16 Sodium-Removing Resins	974.5
40:18 Potassium-Removing Resins	974.5
40:20 Caloric Agents	974.5
40:24 Salt and Sugar Substitutes	974.5
40:28 Diuretics NEC	974.4
carbonic acid anhydrase inhibitors	974.2
mercurials	974.0
purine derivatives	974.1
saluretics	974.3
40:36 Irrigating Solutions	974.5
40:40 Uricosuric Agents	974.7
44:00 **ENZYMES NEC**	963.4
fibrinolysis-affecting agents	964.4
gastric agents	973.4
48:00 **EXPECTORANTS AND COUGH PREPARATIONS**	
antihistamine agents	963.0
antitussives	975.4
codeine derivatives	965.09
expectorants	975.5
narcotic agents NEC	965.09
52:00 **EYE, EAR, NOSE, AND THROAT PREPARATIONS**	
52:04 Anti-Infectives	
ENT	976.6
ophthalmic	976.5
52:04.04 Antibiotics	
ENT	976.6
ophthalmic	976.5

	AHFS* LIST	ICD-9-CM Diagnosis Code
52:04.06	Antivirals	
	ENT	976.6
	ophthalmic	976.5
52:04.08	Sulfonamides	
	ENT	976.6
	ophthalmic	976.5
52:04.12	Miscellaneous Anti-Infectives	
	ENT	976.6
	ophthalmic	976.5
52:08	Anti-Inflammatory Agents	
	ENT	976.6
	ophthalmic	976.5
52:10	Carbonic Anhydrase Inhibitors	974.2
52:12	Contact Lens Solutions	976.5
52:16	Local Anesthetics	968.5
52:20	Miotics	971.0
52:24	Mydriatics	
	adrenergics	971.2
	anticholinergics	971.1
	antimuscarinics	971.1
	parasympatholytics	971.1
	spasmolytics	971.1
	sympathomimetics	971.2
52:28	Mouth Washes and Gargles	976.6
52:32	Vasoconstrictors	971.2
52:36	Unclassified Agents	
	ENT	976.6
	ophthalmic	976.5
56:00	**GASTROINTESTINAL DRUGS**	
56:04	Antacids and Absorbants	973.0
56:08	Anti-Diarrhea Agents	973.5
56:10	Antiflatulents	973.8
56:12	Cathartics NEC	973.3
	emollients	973.2
	irritants	973.1
56:16	Digestants	973.4
56:20	Emetics and Antiemetics	
	antiemetics	963.0
	emetics	973.6
56:24	Lipotropic Agents	977.1
60:00	**GOLD COMPOUNDS**	965.6
64:00	**HEAVY METAL ANTAGONISTS**	963.8
68:00	**HORMONES AND SYNTHETIC SUBSTITUTES**	
68:04	Adrenals	962.0
68:08	Androgens	962.1
68:12	Contraceptives	962.2
68:16	Estrogens	962.2
68:18	Gonadotropins	962.4
68:20	Insulins and Antidiabetic Agents	962.3
68:20.08	Insulins	962.3
68:24	Parathyroid	962.6

	AHFS* LIST	ICD-9-CM Diagnosis Code
68:28	Pituitary	
	anterior	962.4
	posterior	962.5
68:32	Progestogens	962.2
68:34	Other Corpus Luteum Hormones	962.2
68:36	Thyroid and Antithyroid	
	antithyroid	962.8
	thyroid	962.7
72:00	**LOCAL ANESTHETICS NEC**	968.9
	topical (surface) agents	968.5
	infiltrating agents (intradermal) (subcutaneous)	
	(submucosal)	968.5
	nerve blocking agents (peripheral)	968.6
	(plexus)(regional)	
	spinal	968.7
76:00	**OXYTOCICS**	975.0
78:00	**RADIOACTIVE AGENTS**	990
80:00	**SERUMS, TOXOIDS, AND VACCINES**	
80:04	Serums	979.9
	immune globulin (gamma) (human)	964.6
80:08	Toxoids NEC	978.8
	diphtheria	978.5
	and tetanus	978.9
	with pertussis component	978.6
	tetanus	978.4
	and diphtheria	978.9
	with pertussis component	978.6
80:12	Vaccines NEC	979.9
	bacterial NEC	978.8
	with	
	other bacterial component	978.9
	pertussis component	978.6
	viral and rickettsial component	979.7
	rickettsial NEC	979.6
	with	
	bacterial component	979.7
	pertussis component	978.6
	viral component	979.7
	viral NEC	979.6
	with	
	bacterial component	979.7
	pertussis component	978.6
	rickettsial component	979.7
84:00	**SKIN AND MUCOUS MEMBRANE PREPARATIONS**	
84:04	Anti-Infectives	976.0
84:04.04	Antibiotics	976.0
84:04.08	Fungicides	976.0
84:04.12	Scabicides and Pediculicides	976.0
84:04.16	Miscellaneous Local Anti-Infectives	976.0
84:06	Anti-Inflammatory Agents	976.0
84:08	Antipruritics and Local Anesthetics	
	antipruritics	976.1
	local anesthetics	968.5
84:12	Astringents	976.2
84:16	Cell Stimulants and Proliferants	976.8
84:20	Detergents	976.2

	AHFS* LIST	ICD-9-CM Diagnosis Code
84:24	Emollients, Demulcents, and Protectants	976.3
84:28	Keratolytic Agents	976.4
84:32	Keratoplastic Agents	976.4
84:36	Miscellaneous Agents	976.8
86:00	**SPASMOLYTIC AGENTS**	975.1
	antiasthmatics	975.7
	papaverine	972.5
	theophyllin	974.1
88:00	**VITAMINS**	
88:04	Vitamin A	963.5
88:08	Vitamin B Complex	963.5
	hematopoietic vitamin	964.1
	nicotinic acid derivatives	972.2
88:12	Vitamin C	963.5
88:16	Vitamin D	963.5
88:20	Vitamin E	963.5
88:24	Vitamin K Activity	964.3
88:28	Multivitamin Preparations	963.5
92:00	**UNCLASSIFIED THERAPEUTIC AGENTS**	977.8

* American Hospital Formulary Service

CLASSIFICATION OF INDUSTRIAL ACCIDENTS ACCORDING TO AGENCY

Annex B to the Resolution concerning Statistics of Employment Injuries adopted by the Tenth International Conference of Labor Statisticians on 12 October 1962

1 MACHINES

11 Prime-Movers, except Electrical Motors
111 Steam engines
112 Internal combustion engines
119 Others

12 Transmission Machinery
121 Transmission shafts
122 Transmission belts, cables, pulleys, pinions, chains, gears
129 Others

13 Metalworking Machines
131 Power presses
132 Lathes
133 Milling machines
134 Abrasive wheels
135 Mechanical shears
136 Forging machines
137 Rolling-mills
139 Others

14 Wood and Assimilated Machines
141 Circular saws
142 Other saws
143 Molding machines
144 Overhand planes
149 Others

15 Agricultural Machines
151 Reapers (including combine reapers)
152 Threshers
159 Others

16 Mining Machinery
161 Under-cutters
169 Others

19 Other Machines Not Elsewhere Classified
191 Earth-moving machines, excavating and scraping machines, except means of transport
192 Spinning, weaving and other textile machines
193 Machines for the manufacture of foodstuffs and beverages
194 Machines for the manufacture of paper
195 Printing machines
199 Others

2 MEANS OF TRANSPORT AND LIFTING EQUIPMENT

21 Lifting Machines and Appliances
211 Cranes
212 Lifts and elevators
213 Winches
214 Pulley blocks
219 Others

22 Means of Rail Transport
221 Inter-urban railways
222 Rail transport in mines, tunnels, quarries, industrial establishments, docks, etc.
229 Others

23 Other Wheeled Means of Transport, Excluding Rail Transport
231 Tractors
232 Lorries
233 Trucks
234 Motor vehicles, not elsewhere classified
235 Animal-drawn vehicles

2 MEANS OF TRANSPORT AND LIFTING EQUIPMENT *continued*

236 Hand-drawn vehicles
239 Others

24 Means of Air Transport

25 Means of Water Transport
251 Motorized means of water transport
252 Non-motorized means of water transport

26 Other Means of Transport
261 Cable-cars
262 Mechanical conveyors, except cable-cars
269 Others

3 OTHER EQUIPMENT

31 Pressure Vessels
311 Boilers
312 Pressurized containers
313 Pressurized piping and accessories
314 Gas cylinders
315 Caissons, diving equipment
319 Others

32 Furnaces, Ovens, Kilns
321 Blast furnaces
322 Refining furnaces
323 Other furnaces
324 Kilns
325 Ovens

33 Refrigerating Plants

34 Electrical Installations, Including Electric Motors, but Excluding Electric Hand Tools
341 Rotating machines
342 Conductors
343 Transformers
344 Control apparatus
349 Others

35 Electric Hand Tools

36 Tools, Implements, and Appliances, Except Electric Hand Tools
361 Power-driven hand tools, except electric hand tools
362 Hand tools, not power-driven
369 Others

37 Ladders, Mobile Ramps

38 Scaffolding

39 Other Equipment, Not Elsewhere Classified

4 MATERIALS, SUBSTANCES AND RADIATIONS

41 Explosives

42 Dusts, Gases, Liquids and Chemicals, Excluding Explosives
421 Dusts
422 Gases, vapors, fumes
423 Liquids, not elsewhere classified
424 Chemicals, not elsewhere classified

43 Flying Fragments

44 Radiations
441 Ionizing radiations
449 Others

49 Other Materials and Substances Not Elsewhere Classified

5 WORKING ENVIRONMENT

51 Outdoor
511 Weather

5 WORKING ENVIRONMENT *continued*

    512   Traffic and working surfaces
    513   Water
    519   Others

    52 Indoor
    521   Floors
    522   Confined quarters
    523   Stairs
    524   Other traffic and working surfaces
    525   Floor openings and wall openings
    526   Environmental factors (lighting, ventilation, temperature, noise, etc.)
    529   Others

    53 Underground
    531   Roofs and faces of mine roads and tunnels, etc.
    532   Floors of mine roads and tunnels, etc.
    533   Working-faces of mines, tunnels, etc.
    534   Mine shafts
    535   Fire
    536   Water
    539   Others

6 OTHER AGENCIES, NOT ELSEWHERE CLASSIFIED

    61 Animals
    611   Live animals
    612   Animals products

    69 Other Agencies, Not Elsewhere Classified

7 AGENCIES NOT CLASSIFIED FOR LACK OF SUFFICIENT DATA

LIST OF THREE-DIGIT CATEGORIES

1. INFECTIOUS AND PARASITIC DISEASES

Intestinal infectious diseases (001-009)

- 001 Cholera
- 002 Typhoid and paratyphoid fevers
- 003 Other salmonella infections
- 004 Shigellosis
- 005 Other food poisoning (bacterial)
- 006 Amebiasis
- 007 Other protozoal intestinal diseases
- 008 Intestinal infections due to other organisms
- 009 Ill-defined intestinal infections

Tuberculosis (010-018)

- 010 Primary tuberculous infection
- 011 Pulmonary tuberculosis
- 012 Other respiratory tuberculosis
- 013 Tuberculosis of meninges and central nervous system
- 014 Tuberculosis of intestines, peritoneum, and mesenteric glands
- 015 Tuberculosis of bones and joints
- 016 Tuberculosis of genitourinary system
- 017 Tuberculosis of other organs
- 018 Miliary tuberculosis

Zoonotic bacterial diseases (020-027)

- 020 Plague
- 021 Tularemia
- 022 Anthrax
- 023 Brucellosis
- 024 Glanders
- 025 Melioidosis
- 026 Rat-bite fever
- 027 Other zoonotic bacterial diseases

Other bacterial diseases (030-041)

- 030 Leprosy
- 031 Diseases due to other mycobacteria
- 032 Diphtheria
- 033 Whooping cough
- 034 Streptococcal sore throat and scarlet fever
- 035 Erysipelas
- 036 Meningococcal infection
- 037 Tetanus
- 038 Septicemia
- 039 Actinomycotic infections
- 040 Other bacterial diseases
- 041 Bacterial infection in conditions classified elsewhere and of unspecified site

Human immunodeficiency virus (042)

- 042 Human immunodeficiency virus [HIV] disease

Poliomyelitis and other non-arthropod-borne viral diseases of central nervous system (045-049)

- 045 Acute poliomyelitis
- 046 Slow virus infection of central nervous system
- 047 Meningitis due to enterovirus
- 048 Other enterovirus diseases of central nervous system
- 049 Other non-arthropod-borne viral diseases of central nervous system

Viral diseases accompanied by exanthem (050-057)

- 050 Smallpox
- 051 Cowpox and paravaccinia
- 052 Chickenpox
- 053 Herpes zoster
- 054 Herpes simplex
- 055 Measles
- 056 Rubella
- 057 Other viral exanthemata

1. INFECTIOUS AND PARASITIC DISEASES *continued*

Arthropod-borne viral diseases (060-066)
060   Yellow fever
061   Dengue
062   Mosquito-borne viral encephalitis
063   Tick-borne viral encephalitis
064   Viral encephalitis transmitted by other and unspecified arthropods
065   Arthropod-borne hemorrhagic fever
066   Other arthropod-borne viral diseases

Other diseases due to viruses and Chlamydiae (070-079)
070   Viral hepatitis
071   Rabies
072   Mumps
073   Ornithosis
074   Specific diseases due to Coxsackie virus
075   Infectious mononucleosis
076   Trachoma
077   Other diseases of conjunctiva due to viruses and Chlamydiae
078   Other diseases due to viruses and Chlamydiae
079   Viral and Chlamydial infection in conditions classified elsewhere and of unspecified site

Rickettsioses and other arthropod-borne diseases (080-088)
080   Louse-borne [epidemic] typhus
081   Other typhus
082   Tick-borne rickettsioses
083   Other rickettsioses
084   Malaria
085   Leishmaniasis
086   Trypanosomiasis
087   Relapsing fever
088   Other arthropod-borne diseases

Syphilis and other venereal diseases (090-099)
090   Congenital syphilis
091   Early syphilis, symptomatic
092   Early syphilis, latent
093   Cardiovascular syphilis
094   Neurosyphilis
095   Other forms of late syphilis, with symptoms
096   Late syphilis, latent
097   Other and unspecified syphilis
098   Gonococcal infections
099   Other venereal diseases

Other spirochetal diseases (100-104)
100   Leptospirosis
101   Vincent's angina
102   Yaws
103   Pinta
104   Other spirochetal infection

Mycoses (110-118)
110   Dermatophytosis
111   Dermatomycosis, other and unspecified
112   Candidiasis
114   Coccidioidomycosis
115   Histoplasmosis
116   Blastomycotic infection
117   Other mycoses
118   Opportunistic mycoses

Helminthiases (120-129)
120   Schistosomiasis [bilharziasis]
121   Other trematode infections
122   Echinococcosis
123   Other cestode infection
124   Trichinosis
125   Filarial infection and dracontiasis

1. INFECTIOUS AND PARASITIC DISEASES *continued*

126 Ancylostomiasis and necatoriasis
127 Other intestinal helminthiases
128 Other and unspecified helminthiases
129 Intestinal parasitism, unspecified

Other infectious and parasitic diseases (130-136)

130 Toxoplasmosis
131 Trichomoniasis
132 Pediculosis and phthirus infestation
133 Acariasis
134 Other infestation
135 Sarcoidosis
136 Other and unspecified infectious and parasitic diseases

Late effects of infectious and parasitic diseases (137-139)

137 Late effects of tuberculosis
138 Late effects of acute poliomyelitis
139 Late effects of other infectious and parasitic diseases

2. NEOPLASMS

Malignant neoplasm of lip, oral cavity, and pharynx (140-149)

140 Malignant neoplasm of lip
141 Malignant neoplasm of tongue
142 Malignant neoplasm of major salivary glands
143 Malignant neoplasm of gum
144 Malignant neoplasm of floor of mouth
145 Malignant neoplasm of other and unspecified parts of mouth
146 Malignant neoplasm of oropharynx
147 Malignant neoplasm of nasopharynx
148 Malignant neoplasm of hypopharynx
149 Malignant neoplasm of other and ill-defined sites within the lip, oral cavity, and pharynx

Malignant neoplasm of digestive organs and peritoneum (150-159)

150 Malignant neoplasm of esophagus
151 Malignant neoplasm of stomach
152 Malignant neoplasm of small intestine, including duodenum
153 Malignant neoplasm of colon
154 Malignant neoplasm of rectum, rectosigmoid junction, and anus
155 Malignant neoplasm of liver and intrahepatic bile ducts
156 Malignant neoplasm of gallbladder and extrahepatic bile ducts
157 Malignant neoplasm of pancreas
158 Malignant neoplasm of retroperitoneum and peritoneum
159 Malignant neoplasm of other and ill-defined sites within the digestive organs and peritoneum

Malignant neoplasm of respiratory and intrathoracic organs (160-165)

160 Malignant neoplasm of nasal cavities, middle ear, and accessory sinuses
161 Malignant neoplasm of larynx
162 Malignant neoplasm of trachea, bronchus, and lung
163 Malignant neoplasm of pleura
164 Malignant neoplasm of thymus, heart, and mediastinum
165 Malignant neoplasm of other and ill-defined sites within the respiratory system and intrathoracic organs

Malignant neoplasm of bone, connective tissue, skin, and breast (170-176)

170 Malignant neoplasm of bone and articular cartilage
171 Malignant neoplasm of connective and other soft tissue
172 Malignant melanoma of skin
173 Other malignant neoplasm of skin
174 Malignant neoplasm of female breast
175 Malignant neoplasm of male breast
176 Kaposi's sarcoma

Malignant neoplasm of genitourinary organs (179-189)

179 Malignant neoplasm of uterus, part unspecified
180 Malignant neoplasm of cervix uteri
181 Malignant neoplasm of placenta
182 Malignant neoplasm of body of uterus

2. NEOPLASMS *continued*

183   Malignant neoplasm of ovary and other uterine adnexa
184   Malignant neoplasm of other and unspecified female genital organs
185   Malignant neoplasm of prostate
186   Malignant neoplasm of testis
187   Malignant neoplasm of penis and other male genital organs
188   Malignant neoplasm of bladder
189   Malignant neoplasm of kidney and other and unspecified urinary organs

Malignant neoplasm of other and unspecified sites (190-199)

190   Malignant neoplasm of eye
191   Malignant neoplasm of brain
192   Malignant neoplasm of other and unspecified parts of nervous system
193   Malignant neoplasm of thyroid gland
194   Malignant neoplasm of other endocrine glands and related structures
195   Malignant neoplasm of other and ill-defined sites
196   Secondary and unspecified malignant neoplasm of lymph nodes
197   Secondary malignant neoplasm of respiratory and digestive systems
198   Secondary malignant neoplasm of other specified sites
199   Malignant neoplasm without specification of site

Malignant neoplasm of lymphatic and hematopoietic tissue (200-208)

200   Lymphosarcoma and reticulosarcoma
201   Hodgkin's disease
202   Other malignant neoplasm of lymphoid and histiocytic tissue
203   Multiple myeloma and immunoproliferative neoplasms
204   Lymphoid leukemia
205   Myeloid leukemia
206   Monocytic leukemia
207   Other specified leukemia
208   Leukemia of unspecified cell type

Benign neoplasms (210-229)

210   Benign neoplasm of lip, oral cavity, and pharynx
211   Benign neoplasm of other parts of digestive system
212   Benign neoplasm of respiratory and intrathoracic organs
213   Benign neoplasm of bone and articular cartilage
214   Lipoma
215   Other benign neoplasm of connective and other soft tissue
216   Benign neoplasm of skin
217   Benign neoplasm of breast
218   Uterine leiomyoma
219   Other benign neoplasm of uterus
220   Benign neoplasm of ovary
221   Benign neoplasm of other female genital organs
222   Benign neoplasm of male genital organs
223   Benign neoplasm of kidney and other urinary organs
224   Benign neoplasm of eye
225   Benign neoplasm of brain and other parts of nervous system
226   Benign neoplasm of thyroid gland
227   Benign neoplasm of other endocrine glands and related structures
228   Hemangioma and lymphangioma, any site
229   Benign neoplasm of other and unspecified sites

Carcinoma in situ (230-234)

230   Carcinoma in situ of digestive organs
231   Carcinoma in situ of respiratory system
232   Carcinoma in situ of skin
233   Carcinoma in situ of breast and genitourinary system
234   Carcinoma in situ of other and unspecified sites

Neoplasms of uncertain behavior (235-238)

235   Neoplasm of uncertain behavior of digestive and respiratory systems
236   Neoplasm of uncertain behavior of genitourinary organs
237   Neoplasm of uncertain behavior of endocrine glands and nervous system
238   Neoplasm of uncertain behavior of other and unspecified sites and tissues

Neoplasm of unspecified nature (239)

239   Neoplasm of unspecified nature

3. ENDOCRINE, NUTRITIONAL AND METABOLIC DISEASES, AND IMMUNITY DISORDERS

Disorders of thyroid gland (240-246)

240 Simple and unspecified goiter
241 Nontoxic nodular goiter
242 Thyrotoxicosis with or without goiter
243 Congenital hypothyroidism
244 Acquired hypothyroidism
245 Thyroiditis
246 Other disorders of thyroid

Diseases of other endocrine glands (250-259)

250 Diabetes mellitus
251 Other disorders of pancreatic internal secretion
252 Disorders of parathyroid gland
253 Disorders of the pituitary gland and its hypothalamic control
254 Diseases of thymus gland
255 Disorders of adrenal glands
256 Ovarian dysfunction
257 Testicular dysfunction
258 Polyglandular dysfunction and related disorders
259 Other endocrine disorders

Nutritional deficiencies (260-269)

260 Kwashiorkor
261 Nutritional marasmus
262 Other severe protein-calorie malnutrition
263 Other and unspecified protein-calorie malnutrition
264 Vitamin A deficiency
265 Thiamine and niacin deficiency states
266 Deficiency of B-complex components
267 Ascorbic acid deficiency
268 Vitamin D deficiency
269 Other nutritional deficiencies

Other metabolic disorders and immunity disorders (270-279)

270 Disorders of amino-acid transport and metabolism
271 Disorders of carbohydrate transport and metabolism
272 Disorders of lipoid metabolism
273 Disorders of plasma protein metabolism
274 Gout
275 Disorders of mineral metabolism
276 Disorders of fluid, electrolyte, and acid-base balance
277 Other and unspecified disorders of metabolism
278 Obesity and other hyperalimentation
279 Disorders involving the immune mechanism

4. DISEASES OF THE BLOOD AND BLOOD-FORMING ORGANS

Diseases of blood and blood-forming organs (280-289)

280 Iron deficiency anemias
281 Other deficiency anemias
282 Hereditary hemolytic anemias
283 Acquired hemolytic anemias
284 Aplastic anemia
285 Other and unspecified anemias
286 Coagulation defects
287 Purpura and other hemorrhagic conditions
288 Diseases of white blood cells
289 Other diseases of blood and blood-forming organs

5. MENTAL DISORDERS

Organic psychotic conditions (290-294)

290 Senile and presenile organic psychotic conditions
291 Alcoholic psychoses
292 Drug psychoses
293 Transient organic psychotic conditions
294 Other organic psychotic conditions (chronic)

5. MENTAL DISORDERS *continued*

Other psychoses (295-299)
295 Schizophrenic psychoses
296 Affective psychoses
297 Paranoid states
298 Other nonorganic psychoses
299 Psychoses with origin specific to childhood

Neurotic disorders, personality disorders, and other nonpsychotic mental disorders (300-316)
300 Neurotic disorders
301 Personality disorders
302 Sexual deviations and disorders
303 Alcohol dependence syndrome
304 Drug dependence
305 Nondependent abuse of drugs
306 Physiological malfunction arising from mental factors
307 Special symptoms or syndromes, not elsewhere classified
308 Acute reaction to stress
309 Adjustment reaction
310 Specific nonpsychotic mental disorders due to organic brain damage
311 Depressive disorder, not elsewhere classified
312 Disturbance of conduct, not elsewhere classified
313 Disturbance of emotions specific to childhood and adolescence
314 Hyperkinetic syndrome of childhood
315 Specific delays in development
316 Psychic factors associated with diseases classified elsewhere

Mental retardation (317-319)
317 Mild mental retardation
318 Other specified mental retardation
319 Unspecified mental retardation

6. DISEASES OF THE NERVOUS SYSTEM AND SENSE ORGANS

Inflammatory diseases of the central nervous system (320-326)
320 Bacterial meningitis
321 Meningitis due to other organisms
322 Meningitis of unspecified cause
323 Encephalitis, myelitis, and encephalomyelitis
324 Intracranial and intraspinal abscess
325 Phlebitis and thrombophlebitis of intracranial venous sinuses
326 Late effects of intracranial abscess or pyogenic infection

Hereditary and degenerative diseases of the central nervous system (330-337)
330 Cerebral degenerations usually manifest in childhood
331 Other cerebral degenerations
332 Parkinson's disease
333 Other extrapyramidal disease and abnormal movement disorders
334 Spinocerebellar disease
335 Anterior horn cell disease
336 Other diseases of spinal cord
337 Disorders of the autonomic nervous system

Other disorders of the central nervous system (340-349)
340 Multiple sclerosis
341 Other demyelinating diseases of central nervous system
342 Hemiplegia and hemiparesis
343 Infantile cerebral palsy
344 Other paralytic syndromes
345 Epilepsy
346 Migraine
347 Cataplexy and narcolepsy
348 Other conditions of brain
349 Other and unspecified disorders of the nervous system

Disorders of the peripheral nervous system (350-359)
350 Trigeminal nerve disorders
351 Facial nerve disorders
352 Disorders of other cranial nerves
353 Nerve root and plexus disorders

6. DISEASES OF THE NERVOUS SYSTEM AND SENSE ORGANS *continued*

354 Mononeuritis of upper limb and mononeuritis multiplex
355 Mononeuritis of lower limb and unspecified site
356 Hereditary and idiopathic peripheral neuropathy
357 Inflammatory and toxic neuropathy
358 Myoneural disorders
359 Muscular dystrophies and other myopathies

Disorders of the eye and adnexa (360-379)

360 Disorders of the globe
361 Retinal detachments and defects
362 Other retinal disorders
363 Chorioretinal inflammations and scars and other disorders of choroid
364 Disorders of iris and ciliary body
365 Glaucoma
366 Cataract
367 Disorders of refraction and accommodation
368 Visual disturbances
369 Blindness and low vision
370 Keratitis
371 Corneal opacity and other disorders of cornea
372 Disorders of conjunctiva
373 Inflammation of eyelids
374 Other disorders of eyelids
375 Disorders of lacrimal system
376 Disorders of the orbit
377 Disorders of optic nerve and visual pathways
378 Strabismus and other disorders of binocular eye movements
379 Other disorders of eye

Diseases of the ear and mastoid process (380-389)

380 Disorders of external ear
381 Nonsuppurative otitis media and Eustachian tube disorders
382 Suppurative and unspecified otitis media
383 Mastoiditis and related conditions
384 Other disorders of tympanic membrane
385 Other disorders of middle ear and mastoid
386 Vertiginous syndromes and other disorders of vestibular system
387 Otosclerosis
388 Other disorders of ear
389 Hearing loss

7. DISEASES OF THE CIRCULATORY SYSTEM

Acute rheumatic fever (390-392)

390 Rheumatic fever without mention of heart involvement
391 Rheumatic fever with heart involvement
392 Rheumatic chorea

Chronic rheumatic heart disease (393-398)

393 Chronic rheumatic pericarditis
394 Diseases of mitral valve
395 Diseases of aortic valve
396 Diseases of mitral and aortic valves
397 Diseases of other endocardial structures
398 Other rheumatic heart disease

Hypertensive disease (401-405)

401 Essential hypertension
402 Hypertensive heart disease
403 Hypertensive renal disease
404 Hypertensive heart and renal disease
405 Secondary hypertension

Ischemic heart disease (410-414)

410 Acute myocardial infarction
411 Other acute and subacute form of ischemic heart disease
412 Old myocardial infarction
413 Angina pectoris
414 Other forms of chronic ischemic heart disease

7. DISEASES OF THE CIRCULATORY SYSTEM *continued*

Diseases of pulmonary circulation (415-417)
- 415 Acute pulmonary heart disease
- 416 Chronic pulmonary heart disease
- 417 Other diseases of pulmonary circulation

Other forms of heart disease (420-429)
- 420 Acute pericarditis
- 421 Acute and subacute endocarditis
- 422 Acute myocarditis
- 423 Other diseases of pericardium
- 424 Other diseases of endocardium
- 425 Cardiomyopathy
- 426 Conduction disorders
- 427 Cardiac dysrhythmias
- 428 Heart failure
- 429 Ill-defined descriptions and complications of heart disease

Cerebrovascular disease (430-438)
- 430 Subarachnoid hemorrhage
- 431 Intracerebral hemorrhage
- 432 Other and unspecified intracranial hemorrhage
- 433 Occlusion and stenosis of precerebral arteries
- 434 Occlusion of cerebral arteries
- 435 Transient cerebral ischemia
- 436 Acute but ill-defined cerebrovascular disease
- 437 Other and ill-defined cerebrovascular disease
- 438 Late effects of cerebrovascular disease

Diseases of arteries, arterioles, and capillaries (440-448)
- 440 Atherosclerosis
- 441 Aortic aneurysm and dissection
- 442 Other aneurysm
- 443 Other peripheral vascular disease
- 444 Arterial embolism and thrombosis
- 446 Polyarteritis nodosa and allied conditions
- 447 Other disorders of arteries and arterioles
- 448 Diseases of capillaries

Diseases of veins and lymphatics, and other diseases of circulatory system (451-459)
- 451 Phlebitis and thrombophlebitis
- 452 Portal vein thrombosis
- 453 Other venous embolism and thrombosis
- 454 Varicose veins of lower extremities
- 455 Hemorrhoids
- 456 Varicose veins of other sites
- 457 Noninfective disorders of lymphatic channels
- 458 Hypotension
- 459 Other disorders of circulatory system

8. DISEASES OF THE RESPIRATORY SYSTEM

Acute respiratory infections (460-466)
- 460 Acute nasopharyngitis [common cold]
- 461 Acute sinusitis
- 462 Acute pharyngitis
- 463 Acute tonsillitis
- 464 Acute laryngitis and tracheitis
- 465 Acute upper respiratory infections of multiple or unspecified sites
- 466 Acute bronchitis and bronchiolitis

Other diseases of upper respiratory tract (470-478)
- 470 Deviated nasal septum
- 471 Nasal polyps
- 472 Chronic pharyngitis and nasopharyngitis
- 473 Chronic sinusitis
- 474 Chronic disease of tonsils and adenoids
- 475 Peritonsillar abscess
- 476 Chronic laryngitis and laryngotracheitis
- 477 Allergic rhinitis

8. DISEASES OF THE RESPIRATORY SYSTEM *continued*

478 Other diseases of upper respiratory tract

Pneumonia and influenza (480-487)

480 Viral pneumonia
481 Pneumococcal pneumonia [Streptococcus pneumoniae pneumonia]
482 Other bacterial pneumonia
483 Pneumonia due to other specified organism
484 Pneumonia in infectious diseases classified elsewhere
485 Bronchopneumonia, organism unspecified
486 Pneumonia, organism unspecified
487 Influenza

Chronic obstructive pulmonary disease and allied conditions (490-496)

490 Bronchitis, not specified as acute or chronic
491 Chronic bronchitis
492 Emphysema
493 Asthma
494 Bronchiectasis
495 Extrinsic allergic alveolitis
496 Chronic airways obstruction, not elsewhere classified

Pneumoconioses and other lung diseases due to external agents (500-508)

500 Coalworkers' pneumoconiosis
501 Asbestosis
502 Pneumoconiosis due to other silica or silicates
503 Pneumoconiosis due to other inorganic dust
504 Pneumopathy due to inhalation of other dust
505 Pneumoconiosis, unspecified
506 Respiratory conditions due to chemical fumes and vapors
507 Pneumonitis due to solids and liquids
508 Respiratory conditions due to other and unspecified external agents

Other diseases of respiratory system (510-519)

510 Empyema
511 Pleurisy
512 Pneumothorax
513 Abscess of lung and mediastinum
514 Pulmonary congestion and hypostasis
515 Postinflammatory pulmonary fibrosis
516 Other alveolar and parietoalveolar pneumopathy
517 Lung involvement in conditions classified elsewhere
518 Other diseases of lung
519 Other diseases of respiratory system

9. DISEASES OF THE DIGESTIVE SYSTEM

Diseases of oral cavity, salivary glands, and jaws (520-529)

520 Disorders of tooth development and eruption
521 Diseases of hard tissues of teeth
522 Diseases of pulp and periapical tissues
523 Gingival and periodontal diseases
524 Dentofacial anomalies, including malocclusion
525 Other diseases and conditions of the teeth and supporting structures
526 Diseases of the jaws
527 Diseases of the salivary glands
528 Diseases of the oral soft tissues, excluding lesions specific for gingiva and tongue
529 Diseases and other conditions of the tongue

Diseases of esophagus, stomach, and duodenum (530-537)

530 Diseases of esophagus
531 Gastric ulcer
532 Duodenal ulcer
533 Peptic ulcer, site unspecified
534 Gastrojejunal ulcer
535 Gastritis and duodenitis
536 Disorders of function of stomach
537 Other disorders of stomach and duodenum

9. DISEASES OF THE DIGESTIVE SYSTEM *continued*

Appendicitis (540-543)
- 540 Acute appendicitis
- 541 Appendicitis, unqualified
- 542 Other appendicitis
- 543 Other diseases of appendix

Hernia of abdominal cavity (550-553)
- 550 Inguinal hernia
- 551 Other hernia of abdominal cavity, with gangrene
- 552 Other hernia of abdominal cavity, with obstruction, but without mention of gangrene
- 553 Other hernia of abdominal cavity without mention of obstruction or gangrene

Noninfectious enteritis and colitis (555-558)
- 555 Regional enteritis
- 556 Ulcerative colitis
- 557 Vascular insufficiency of intestine
- 558 Other noninfectious gastroenteritis and colitis

Other diseases of intestines and peritoneum (560-569)
- 560 Intestinal obstruction without mention of hernia
- 562 Diverticula of intestine
- 564 Functional digestive disorders, not elsewhere classified
- 565 Anal fissure and fistula
- 566 Abscess of anal and rectal regions
- 567 Peritonitis
- 568 Other disorders of peritoneum
- 569 Other disorders of intestine

Other diseases of digestive system (570-579)
- 570 Acute and subacute necrosis of liver
- 571 Chronic liver disease and cirrhosis
- 572 Liver abscess and sequelae of chronic liver disease
- 573 Other disorders of liver
- 574 Cholelithiasis
- 575 Other disorders of gallbladder
- 576 Other disorders of biliary tract
- 577 Diseases of pancreas
- 578 Gastrointestinal hemorrhage
- 579 Intestinal malabsorption

10. DISEASES OF THE GENITOURINARY SYSTEM

Nephritis, nephrotic syndrome, and nephrosis (580-589)
- 580 Acute glomerulonephritis
- 581 Nephrotic syndrome
- 582 Chronic glomerulonephritis
- 583 Nephritis and nephropathy, not specified as acute or chronic
- 584 Acute renal failure
- 585 Chronic renal failure
- 586 Renal failure, unspecified
- 587 Renal sclerosis, unspecified
- 588 Disorders resulting from impaired renal function
- 589 Small kidney of unknown cause

Other diseases of urinary system (590-599)
- 590 Infections of kidney
- 591 Hydronephrosis
- 592 Calculus of kidney and ureter
- 593 Other disorders of kidney and ureter
- 594 Calculus of lower urinary tract
- 595 Cystitis
- 596 Other disorders of bladder
- 597 Urethritis, not sexually transmitted, and urethral syndrome
- 598 Urethral stricture
- 599 Other disorders of urethra and urinary tract

Diseases of male genital organs (600-608)
- 600 Hyperplasia of prostate
- 601 Inflammatory diseases of prostate

10. DISEASES OF THE GENITOURINARY SYSTEM *continued*

602 Other disorders of prostate
603 Hydrocele
604 Orchitis and epididymitis
605 Redundant prepuce and phimosis
606 Infertility, male
607 Disorders of penis
608 Other disorders of male genital organs

Disorders of breast (610-611)
610 Benign mammary dysplasias
611 Other disorders of breast

Inflammatory disease of female pelvic organs (614-616)
614 Inflammatory disease of ovary, fallopian tube, pelvic cellular tissue, and peritoneum
615 Inflammatory diseases of uterus, except cervix
616 Inflammatory disease of cervix, vagina, and vulva

Other disorders of female genital tract (617-629)
617 Endometriosis
618 Genital prolapse
619 Fistula involving female genital tract
620 Noninflammatory disorders of ovary, fallopian tube, and broad ligament
621 Disorders of uterus, not elsewhere classified
622 Noninflammatory disorders of cervix
623 Noninflammatory disorders of vagina
624 Noninflammatory disorders of vulva and perineum
625 Pain and other symptoms associated with female genital organs
626 Disorders of menstruation and other abnormal bleeding from female genital tract
627 Menopausal and postmenopausal disorders
628 Infertility, female
629 Other disorders of female genital organs

11. COMPLICATIONS OF PREGNANCY, CHILDBIRTH AND THE PUERPERIUM

Ectopic and molar pregnancy (630-633)
630 Hydatidiform mole
631 Other abnormal product of conception
632 Missed abortion
633 Ectopic pregnancy

Other pregnancy with abortive outcome (634-639)
634 Abortion
635 Legally induced abortion
636 Illegally induced abortion
637 Unspecified abortion
638 Failed attempted abortion
639 Complications following abortion and ectopic and molar pregnancies

Complications mainly related to pregnancy (640-648)
640 Hemorrhage in early pregnancy
641 Antepartum hemorrhage, abruptio placentae, and placenta previa
642 Hypertension complicating pregnancy, childbirth, and the puerperium
643 Excessive vomiting in pregnancy
644 Early or threatened labor
645 Prolonged pregnancy
646 Other complications of pregnancy, not elsewhere classified
647 Infective and parasitic conditions in the mother classifiable elsewhere but complicating pregnancy, childbirth, and the puerperium
648 Other current conditions in the mother classifiable elsewhere but complicating pregnancy, childbirth, and the puerperium

Normal delivery, and other indications for care in pregnancy, labor, and delivery (650-659)
650 Normal delivery
651 Multiple gestation
652 Malposition and malpresentation of fetus
653 Disproportion
654 Abnormality of organs and soft tissues of pelvis
655 Known or suspected fetal abnormality affecting management of mother
656 Other fetal and placental problems affecting management of mother
657 Polyhydramnios

11. COMPLICATIONS OF PREGNANCY, CHILDBIRTH AND THE PUERPERIUM *continued*

658   Other problems associated with amniotic cavity and membranes
659   Other indications for care or intervention related to labor and delivery and not elsewhere classified

Complications occurring mainly in the course of labor and delivery (660-669)

660   Obstructed labor
661   Abnormality of forces of labor
662   Long labor
663   Umbilical cord complications
664   Trauma to perineum and vulva during delivery
665   Other obstetrical trauma
666   Postpartum hemorrhage
667   Retained placenta or membranes, without hemorrhage
668   Complications of the administration of anesthetic or other sedation in labor and delivery
669   Other complications of labor and delivery, not elsewhere classified

Complications of the puerperium (670-677)

670   Major puerperal infection
671   Venous complications in pregnancy and the puerperium
672   Pyrexia of unknown origin during the puerperium
673   Obstetrical pulmonary embolism
674   Other and unspecified complications of the puerperium, not elsewhere classified
675   Infections of the breast and nipple associated with childbirth
676   Other disorders of the breast associated with childbirth, and disorders of lactation
677   Late effect of complication of pregnancy, childbirth, and the puerperium

12. DISEASES OF THE SKIN AND SUBCUTANEOUS TISSUE

Infections of skin and subcutaneous tissue (680-686)

680   Carbuncle and furuncle
681   Cellulitis and abscess of finger and toe
682   Other cellulitis and abscess
683   Acute lymphadenitis
684   Impetigo
685   Pilonidal cyst
686   Other local infections of skin and subcutaneous tissue

Other inflammatory conditions of skin and subcutaneous tissue (690-698)

690   Erythematosquamous dermatosis
691   Atopic dermatitis and related conditions
692   Contact dermatitis and other eczema
693   Dermatitis due to substances taken internally
694   Bullous dermatoses
695   Erythematous conditions
696   Psoriasis and similar disorders
697   Lichen
698   Pruritus and related conditions

Other diseases of skin and subcutaneous tissue (700-709)

700   Corns and callosities
701   Other hypertrophic and atrophic conditions of skin
702   Other dermatoses
703   Diseases of nail
704   Diseases of hair and hair follicles
705   Disorders of sweat glands
706   Diseases of sebaceous glands
707   Chronic ulcer of skin
708   Urticaria
709   Other disorders of skin and subcutaneous tissue

13. DISEASES OF THE MUSCULOSKELETAL SYSTEM AND CONNECTIVE TISSUE

Arthropathies and related disorders (710-719)

710   Diffuse diseases of connective tissue
711   Arthropathy associated with infections
712   Crystal arthropathies
713   Arthropathy associated with other disorders classified elsewhere
714   Rheumatoid arthritis and other inflammatory polyarthropathies
715   Osteoarthrosis and allied disorders

13. DISEASES OF THE MUSCULOSKELETAL SYSTEM AND CONNECTIVE TISSUE
continued

716 Other and unspecified arthropathies
717 Internal derangement of knee
718 Other derangement of joint
719 Other and unspecified disorder of joint

Dorsopathies (720-724)

720 Ankylosing spondylitis and other inflammatory spondylopathies
721 Spondylosis and allied disorders
722 Intervertebral disc disorders
723 Other disorders of cervical region
724 Other and unspecified disorders of back

Rheumatism, excluding the back (725-729)

725 Polymyalgia rheumatica
726 Peripheral enthesopathies and allied syndromes
727 Other disorders of synovium, tendon, and bursa
728 Disorders of muscle, ligament, and fascia
729 Other disorders of soft tissues

Osteopathies, chondropathies, and acquired musculoskeletal deformities (730-739)

730 Osteomyelitis, periostitis, and other infections involving bone
731 Osteitis deformans and osteopathies associated with other disorders classified elsewhere
732 Osteochondropathies
733 Other disorders of bone and cartilage
734 Flat foot
735 Acquired deformities of toe
736 Other acquired deformities of limbs
737 Curvature of spine
738 Other acquired deformity
739 Nonallopathic lesions, not elsewhere classified

14. CONGENITAL ANOMALIES

740 Anencephalus and similar anomalies
741 Spina bifida
742 Other congenital anomalies of nervous system
743 Congenital anomalies of eye
744 Congenital anomalies of ear, face, and neck
745 Bulbus cordis anomalies and anomalies of cardiac septal closure
746 Other congenital anomalies of heart
747 Other congenital anomalies of circulatory system
748 Congenital anomalies of respiratory system
749 Cleft palate and cleft lip
750 Other congenital anomalies of upper alimentary tract
751 Other congenital anomalies of digestive system
752 Congenital anomalies of genital organs
753 Congenital anomalies of urinary system
754 Certain congenital musculoskeletal deformities
755 Other congenital anomalies of limbs
756 Other congenital musculoskeletal anomalies
757 Congenital anomalies of the integument
758 Chromosomal anomalies
759 Other and unspecified congenital anomalies

15. CERTAIN CONDITIONS ORIGINATING IN THE PERINATAL PERIOD

Maternal causes of perinatal morbidity and mortality (760-763)

760 Fetus or newborn affected by maternal conditions which may be unrelated to present pregnancy
761 Fetus or newborn affected by maternal complications of pregnancy
762 Fetus or newborn affected by complications of placenta, cord, and membranes
763 Fetus or newborn affected by other complications of labor and delivery

Other conditions originating in the perinatal period (764-779)

764 Slow fetal growth and fetal malnutrition
765 Disorders relating to short gestation and unspecified low birthweight
766 Disorders relating to long gestation and high birthweight
767 Birth trauma

15. CERTAIN CONDITIONS ORIGINATING IN THE PERINATAL PERIOD *continued*

    768   Intrauterine hypoxia and birth asphyxia
    769   Respiratory distress syndrome
    770   Other respiratory conditions of fetus and newborn
    771   Infections specific to the perinatal period
    772   Fetal and neonatal hemorrhage
    773   Hemolytic disease of fetus or newborn, due to isoimmunization
    774   Other perinatal jaundice
    775   Endocrine and metabolic disturbances specific to the fetus and newborn
    776   Hematological disorders of fetus and newborn
    777   Perinatal disorders of digestive system
    778   Conditions involving the integument and temperature regulation of fetus and newborn
    779   Other and ill-defined conditions originating in the perinatal period

16. SYMPTOMS, SIGNS, AND ILL-DEFINED CONDITIONS

Symptoms (780-789)

    780   General symptoms
    781   Symptoms involving nervous and musculoskeletal systems
    782   Symptoms involving skin and other integumentary tissue
    783   Symptoms concerning nutrition, metabolism, and development
    784   Symptoms involving head and neck
    785   Symptoms involving cardiovascular system
    786   Symptoms involving respiratory system and other chest symptoms
    787   Symptoms involving digestive system
    788   Symptoms involving urinary system
    789   Other symptoms involving abdomen and pelvis

Nonspecific abnormal findings (790-796)

    790   Nonspecific findings on examination of blood
    791   Nonspecific findings on examination of urine
    792   Nonspecific abnormal findings in other body substances
    793   Nonspecific abnormal findings on radiological and other examination of body structure
    794   Nonspecific abnormal results of function studies
    795   Nonspecific abnormal histological and immunological findings
    796   Other nonspecific abnormal findings

Ill-defined and unknown causes of morbidity and mortality (797-799)

    797   Senility without mention of psychosis
    798   Sudden death, cause unknown
    799   Other ill-defined and unknown causes of morbidity and mortality

17. INJURY AND POISONING

Fracture of skull (800-804)

    800   Fracture of vault of skull
    801   Fracture of base of skull
    802   Fracture of face bones
    803   Other and unqualified skull fractures
    804   Multiple fractures involving skull or face with other bones

Fracture of neck and trunk (805-809)

    805   Fracture of vertebral column without mention of spinal cord injury
    806   Fracture of vertebral column with spinal cord injury
    807   Fracture of rib(s), sternum, larynx, and trachea
    808   Fracture of pelvis
    809   Ill-defined fractures of bones of trunk

Fracture of upper limb (810-819)

    810   Fracture of clavicle
    811   Fracture of scapula
    812   Fracture of humerus
    813   Fracture of radius and ulna
    814   Fracture of carpal bone(s)
    815   Fracture of metacarpal bone(s)
    816   Fracture of one or more phalanges of hand
    817   Multiple fractures of hand bones
    818   Ill-defined fractures of upper limb
    819   Multiple fractures involving both upper limbs, and upper limb with rib(s) and sternum

17. INJURY AND POISONING *continued*

Fracture of lower limb (820-829)
820 Fracture of neck of femur
821 Fracture of other and unspecified parts of femur
822 Fracture of patella
823 Fracture of tibia and fibula
824 Fracture of ankle
825 Fracture of one or more tarsal and metatarsal bones
826 Fracture of one or more phalanges of foot
827 Other, multiple, and ill-defined fractures of lower limb
828 Multiple fractures involving both lower limbs, lower with upper limb, and lower
    limb(s) with rib(s) and sternum
829 Fracture of unspecified bones

Dislocation (830-839)
830 Dislocation of jaw
831 Dislocation of shoulder
832 Dislocation of elbow
833 Dislocation of wrist
834 Dislocation of finger
835 Dislocation of hip
836 Dislocation of knee
837 Dislocation of ankle
838 Dislocation of foot
839 Other, multiple, and ill-defined dislocations

Sprains and strains of joints and adjacent muscles (840-848)
840 Sprains and strains of shoulder and upper arm
841 Sprains and strains of elbow and forearm
842 Sprains and strains of wrist and hand
843 Sprains and strains of hip and thigh
844 Sprains and strains of knee and leg
845 Sprains and strains of ankle and foot
846 Sprains and strains of sacroiliac region
847 Sprains and strains of other and unspecified parts of back
848 Other and ill-defined sprains and strains

Intracranial injury, excluding those with skull fracture (850-854)
850 Concussion
851 Cerebral laceration and contusion
852 Subarachnoid, subdural, and extradural hemorrhage, following injury
853 Other and unspecified intracranial hemorrhage following injury
854 Intracranial injury of other and unspecified nature

Internal injury of thorax, abdomen, and pelvis (860-869)
860 Traumatic pneumothorax and hemothorax
861 Injury to heart and lung
862 Injury to other and unspecified intrathoracic organs
863 Injury to gastrointestinal tract
864 Injury to liver
865 Injury to spleen
866 Injury to kidney
867 Injury to pelvic organs
868 Injury to other intra-abdominal organs
869 Internal injury to unspecified or ill-defined organs

Open wound of head, neck, and trunk (870-879)
870 Open wound of ocular adnexa
871 Open wound of eyeball
872 Open wound of ear
873 Other open wound of head
874 Open wound of neck
875 Open wound of chest (wall)
876 Open wound of back
877 Open wound of buttock
878 Open wound of genital organs (external), including traumatic amputation
879 Open wound of other and unspecified sites, except limbs

Open wound of upper limb (880-887)
880 Open wound of shoulder and upper arm

17. INJURY AND POISONING *continued*

881   Open wound of elbow, forearm, and wrist
882   Open wound of hand except finger(s) alone
883   Open wound of finger(s)
884   Multiple and unspecified open wound of upper limb
885   Traumatic amputation of thumb (complete) (partial)
886   Traumatic amputation of other finger(s) (complete) (partial)
887   Traumatic amputation of arm and hand (complete) (partial)

Open wound of lower limb (890-897)

890   Open wound of hip and thigh
891   Open wound of knee, leg [except thigh], and ankle
892   Open wound of foot except toe(s) alone
893   Open wound of toe(s)
894   Multiple and unspecified open wound of lower limb
895   Traumatic amputation of toe(s) (complete) (partial)
896   Traumatic amputation of foot (complete) (partial)
897   Traumatic amputation of leg(s) (complete) (partial)

Injury to blood vessels (900-904)

900   Injury to blood vessels of head and neck
901   Injury to blood vessels of thorax
902   Injury to blood vessels of abdomen and pelvis
903   Injury to blood vessels of upper extremity
904   Injury to blood vessels of lower extremity and unspecified sites

Late effects of injuries, poisonings, toxic effects, and other external causes (905-909)

905   Late effects of musculoskeletal and connective tissue injuries
906   Late effects of injuries to skin and subcutaneous tissues
907   Late effects of injuries to the nervous system
908   Late effects of other and unspecified injuries
909   Late effects of other and unspecified external causes

Superficial injury (910-919)

910   Superficial injury of face, neck, and scalp except eye
911   Superficial injury of trunk
912   Superficial injury of shoulder and upper arm
913   Superficial injury of elbow, forearm, and wrist
914   Superficial injury of hand(s) except finger(s) alone
915   Superficial injury of finger(s)
916   Superficial injury of hip, thigh, leg, and ankle
917   Superficial injury of foot and toe(s)
918   Superficial injury of eye and adnexa
919   Superficial injury of other, multiple, and unspecified sites

Contusion with intact skin surface (920-924)

920   Contusion of face, scalp, and neck except eye(s)
921   Contusion of eye and adnexa
922   Contusion of trunk
923   Contusion of upper limb
924   Contusion of lower limb and of other and unspecified sites

Crushing injury (925-929)

925   Crushing injury of face, scalp, and neck
926   Crushing injury of trunk
927   Crushing injury of upper limb
928   Crushing injury of lower limb
929   Crushing injury of multiple and unspecified sites

Effects of foreign body entering through orifice (930-939)

930   Foreign body on external eye
931   Foreign body in ear
932   Foreign body in nose
933   Foreign body in pharynx and larynx
934   Foreign body in trachea, bronchus, and lung
935   Foreign body in mouth, esophagus, and stomach
936   Foreign body in intestine and colon
937   Foreign body in anus and rectum
938   Foreign body in digestive system, unspecified
939   Foreign body in genitourinary tract

17. INJURY AND POISONING *continued*

Burns (940-949)
- 940 Burn confined to eye and adnexa
- 941 Burn of face, head, and neck
- 942 Burn of trunk
- 943 Burn of upper limb, except wrist and hand
- 944 Burn of wrist(s) and hand(s)
- 945 Burn of lower limb(s)
- 946 Burns of multiple specified sites
- 947 Burn of internal organs
- 948 Burns classified according to extent of body surface involved
- 949 Burn, unspecified

Injury to nerves and spinal cord (950-957)
- 950 Injury to optic nerve and pathways
- 951 Injury to other cranial nerve(s)
- 952 Spinal cord injury without evidence of spinal bone injury
- 953 Injury to nerve roots and spinal plexus
- 954 Injury to other nerve(s) of trunk excluding shoulder and pelvic girdles
- 955 Injury to peripheral nerve(s) of shoulder girdle and upper limb
- 956 Injury to peripheral nerve(s) of pelvic girdle and lower limb
- 957 Injury to other and unspecified nerves

Certain traumatic complications and unspecified injuries (958-959)
- 958 Certain early complications of trauma
- 959 Injury, other and unspecified

Poisoning by drugs, medicinal and biological substances (960-979)
- 960 Poisoning by antibiotics
- 961 Poisoning by other anti-infectives
- 962 Poisoning by hormones and synthetic substitutes
- 963 Poisoning by primarily systemic agents
- 964 Poisoning by agents primarily affecting blood constituents
- 965 Poisoning by analgesics, antipyretics, and antirheumatics
- 966 Poisoning by anticonvulsants and anti-Parkinsonism drugs
- 967 Poisoning by sedatives and hypnotics
- 968 Poisoning by other central nervous system depressants and anesthetics
- 969 Poisoning by psychotropic agents
- 970 Poisoning by central nervous system stimulants
- 971 Poisoning by drugs primarily affecting the autonomic nervous system
- 972 Poisoning by agents primarily affecting the cardiovascular system
- 973 Poisoning by agents primarily affecting the gastrointestinal system
- 974 Poisoning by water, mineral, and uric acid metabolism drugs
- 975 Poisoning by agents primarily acting on the smooth and skeletal muscles and respiratory system
- 976 Poisoning by agents primarily affecting skin and mucous membrane, ophthalmological, otorhinolaryngological, and dental drugs
- 977 Poisoning by other and unspecified drugs and medicinals
- 978 Poisoning by bacterial vaccines
- 979 Poisoning by other vaccines and biological substances

Toxic effects of substances chiefly nonmedicinal as to source (980-989)
- 980 Toxic effect of alcohol
- 981 Toxic effect of petroleum products
- 982 Toxic effect of solvents other than petroleum-based
- 983 Toxic effect of corrosive aromatics, acids, and caustic alkalis
- 984 Toxic effect of lead and its compounds (including fumes)
- 985 Toxic effect of other metals
- 986 Toxic effect of carbon monoxide
- 987 Toxic effect of other gases, fumes, or vapors
- 988 Toxic effect of noxious substances eaten as food
- 989 Toxic effect of other substances, chiefly nonmedicinal as to source

Other and unspecified effects of external causes (990-995)
- 990 Effects of radiation, unspecified
- 991 Effects of reduced temperature
- 992 Effects of heat and light
- 993 Effects of air pressure
- 994 Effects of other external causes

17. INJURY AND POISONING *continued*

    995   Certain adverse effects, not elsewhere classified

Complications of surgical and medical care, not elsewhere classified (996-999)
    996   Complications peculiar to certain specified procedures
    997   Complications affecting specified body systems, not elsewhere classified
    998   Other complications of procedures, not elsewhere classified
    999   Complications of medical care, not elsewhere classified

SUPPLEMENTARY CLASSIFICATION OF FACTORS INFLUENCING HEALTH STATUS AND CONTACT WITH HEALTH SERVICES

Persons with potential health hazards related to communicable diseases (V01-V09)
    V01   Contact with or exposure to communicable diseases
    V02   Carrier or suspected carrier of infectious diseases
    V03   Need for prophylactic vaccination and inoculation against bacterial diseases
    V04   Need for prophylactic vaccination and inoculation against certain viral diseases
    V05   Need for other prophylactic vaccination and inoculation against single diseases
    V06   Need for prophylactic vaccination and inoculation against combinations of diseases
    V07   Need for isolation and other prophylactic measures
    V08   Asymptomatic human immunodeficiency virus (HIV) infection status
    V09   Infection with drug-resistant microorganisms

Persons with potential health hazards related to personal and family history (V10-V19)
    V10   Personal history of malignant neoplasm
    V11   Personal history of mental disorder
    V12   Personal history of certain other diseases
    V13   Personal history of other diseases
    V14   Personal history of allergy to medicinal agents
    V15   Other personal history presenting hazards to health
    V16   Family history of malignant neoplasm
    V17   Family history of certain chronic disabling diseases
    V18   Family history of certain other specific conditions
    V19   Family history of other conditions

Persons encountering health services in circumstances related to reproduction and development (V20-V29)
    V20   Health supervision of infant or child
    V21   Constitutional states in development
    V22   Normal pregnancy
    V23   Supervision of high-risk pregnancy
    V24   Postpartum care and examination
    V25   Encounter for contraceptive management
    V26   Procreative management
    V27   Outcome of delivery
    V28   Antenatal screening
    V29   Observation and evaluation of newborns and infants for suspected condition not found

Liveborn infants according to type of birth (V30-V39)
    V30   Single liveborn
    V31   Twin, mate liveborn
    V32   Twin, mate stillborn
    V33   Twin, unspecified
    V34   Other multiple, mates all liveborn
    V35   Other multiple, mates all stillborn
    V36   Other multiple, mates live- and stillborn
    V37   Other multiple, unspecified
    V39   Unspecified

Persons with a condition influencing their health status (V40-V49)
    V40   Mental and behavioral problems
    V41   Problems with special senses and other special functions
    V42   Organ or tissue replaced by transplant
    V43   Organ or tissue replaced by other means
    V44   Artificial opening status
    V45   Other postsurgical states
    V46   Other dependence on machines
    V47   Other problems with internal organs
    V48   Problems with head, neck, and trunk
    V49   Problems with limbs and other problems

SUPPLEMENTARY CLASSIFICATION...HEALTH STATUS/HEALTH SERVICES *continued*

Persons encountering health services for specific procedures and aftercare (V50-V59)

V50 Elective surgery for purposes other than remedying health states
V51 Aftercare involving the use of plastic surgery
V52 Fitting and adjustment of prosthetic device and implant
V53 Fitting and adjustment of other device
V54 Other orthopedic aftercare
V55 Attention to artificial openings
V56 Encounter for dialysis and dialysis catheter care
V57 Care involving use of rehabilitation procedures
V58 Encounter for other and unspecified procedures and aftercare
V59 Donors

Persons encountering health services in other circumstances (V60-V69)

V60 Housing, household, and economic circumstances
V61 Other family circumstances
V62 Other psychosocial circumstances
V63 Unavailability of other medical facilities for care
V64 Persons encountering health services for specific procedures, not carried out
V65 Other persons seeking consultation without complaint or sickness
V66 Convalescence and palliative care
V67 Follow-up examination
V68 Encounters for administrative purposes
V69 Problems related to lifestyle

Persons without reported diagnosis encountered during examination and investigation of individuals and populations (V70-V82)

V70 General medical examination
V71 Observation and evaluation for suspected conditions not found
V72 Special investigations and examinations
V73 Special screening examination for viral and chlamydial diseases
V74 Special screening examination for bacterial and spirochetal diseases
V75 Special screening examination for other infectious diseases
V76 Special screening for malignant neoplasms
V77 Special screening for endocrine, nutritional, metabolic, and immunity disorders
V78 Special screening for disorders of blood and blood-forming organs
V79 Special screening for mental disorders and developmental handicaps
V80 Special screening for neurological, eye, and ear diseases
V81 Special screening for cardiovascular, respiratory, and genitourinary diseases
V82 Special screening for other conditions

SUPPLEMENTARY CLASSIFICATION OF EXTERNAL CAUSES OF INJURY AND POISONING

Railway accidents (E800-E807)

E800 Railway accident involving collision with rolling stock
E801 Railway accident involving collision with other object
E802 Railway accident involving derailment without antecedent collision
E803 Railway accident involving explosion, fire, or burning
E804 Fall in, on, or from railway train
E805 Hit by rolling stock
E806 Other specified railway accident
E807 Railway accident of unspecified nature

Motor vehicle traffic accidents (E810-E819)

E810 Motor vehicle traffic accident involving collision with train
E811 Motor vehicle traffic accident involving re-entrant collision with another motor vehicle
E812 Other motor vehicle traffic accident involving collision with another motor vehicle
E813 Motor vehicle traffic accident involving collision with other vehicle
E814 Motor vehicle traffic accident involving collision with pedestrian
E815 Other motor vehicle traffic accident involving collision on the highway
E816 Motor vehicle traffic accident due to loss of control, without collision on the highway
E817 Noncollision motor vehicle traffic accident while boarding or alighting
E818 Other noncollision motor vehicle traffic accident
E819 Motor vehicle traffic accident of unspecified nature

Motor vehicle nontraffic accidents (E820-E825)

E820 Nontraffic accident involving motor-driven snow vehicle
E821 Nontraffic accident involving other off-road motor vehicle

SUPPLEMENTARY CLASSIFICATION...INJURY AND POISONING *continued*

    E822 Other motor vehicle nontraffic accident involving collision with moving object
    E823 Other motor vehicle nontraffic accident involving collision with stationary object
    E824 Other motor vehicle nontraffic accident while boarding and alighting
    E825 Other motor vehicle nontraffic accident of other and unspecified nature

Other road vehicle accidents (E826-E829)
    E826 Pedal cycle accident
    E827 Animal-drawn vehicle accident
    E828 Accident involving animal being ridden
    E829 Other road vehicle accidents

Water transport accidents (E830-E838)
    E830 Accident to watercraft causing submersion
    E831 Accident to watercraft causing other injury
    E832 Other accidental submersion or drowning in water transport accident
    E833 Fall on stairs or ladders in water transport
    E834 Other fall from one level to another in water transport
    E835 Other and unspecified fall in water transport
    E836 Machinery accident in water transport
    E837 Explosion, fire, or burning in watercraft
    E838 Other and unspecified water transport accident

Air and space transport accidents (E840-E845)
    E840 Accident to powered aircraft at takeoff or landing
    E841 Accident to powered aircraft, other and unspecified
    E842 Accident to unpowered aircraft
    E843 Fall in, on, or from aircraft
    E844 Other specified air transport accidents
    E845 Accident involving spacecraft

Vehicle accidents, not elsewhere classifiable (E846-E849)
    E846 Accidents involving powered vehicles used solely within the buildings and premises
        of an industrial or commercial establishment
    E847 Accidents involving cable cars not running on rails
    E848 Accidents involving other vehicles, not elsewhere classifiable
    E849 Place of occurrence

Accidental poisoning by drugs, medicinal substances, and biologicals (E850-E858)
    E850 Accidental poisoning by analgesics, antipyretics, and antirheumatics
    E851 Accidental poisoning by barbiturates
    E852 Accidental poisoning by other sedatives and hypnotics
    E853 Accidental poisoning by tranquilizers
    E854 Accidental poisoning by other psychotropic agents
    E855 Accidental poisoning by other drugs acting on central and autonomic nervous systems
    E856 Accidental poisoning by antibiotics
    E857 Accidental poisoning by other anti-infectives
    E858 Accidental poisoning by other drugs

Accidental poisoning by other solid and liquid substances, gases, and vapors (E860-E869)
    E860 Accidental poisoning by alcohol, not elsewhere classified
    E861 Accidental poisoning by cleansing and polishing agents, disinfectants, paints, and
        varnishes
    E862 Accidental poisoning by petroleum products, other solvents and their vapors, not
        elsewhere classified
    E863 Accidental poisoning by agricultural and horticultural chemical and pharmaceutical
        preparations other than plant foods and fertilizers
    E864 Accidental poisoning by corrosives and caustics, not elsewhere classified
    E865 Accidental poisoning from poisonous foodstuffs and poisonous plants
    E866 Accidental poisoning by other and unspecified solid and liquid substances
    E867 Accidental poisoning by gas distributed by pipeline
    E868 Accidental poisoning by other utility gas and other carbon monoxide
    E869 Accidental poisoning by other gases and vapors

Misadventures to patients during surgical and medical care (E870-E876)
    E870 Accidental cut, puncture, perforation, or hemorrhage during medical care
    E871 Foreign object left in body during procedure
    E872 Failure of sterile precautions during procedure
    E873 Failure in dosage
    E874 Mechanical failure of instrument or apparatus during procedure

SUPPLEMENTARY CLASSIFICATION...INJURY AND POISONING *continued*

E875 Contaminated or infected blood, other fluid, drug, or biological substance

E876 Other and unspecified misadventures during medical care

Surgical and medical procedures as the cause of abnormal reaction of patient or later complication, without mention of misadventure at the time of procedure (E878-E879)

E878 Surgical operation and other surgical procedures as the cause of abnormal reaction of patient, or of later complication, without mention of misadventure at the time of operation

E879 Other procedures, without mention of misadventure at the time of procedure, as the cause of abnormal reaction of patient, or of later complication

Accidental falls (E880-E888)

E880 Fall on or from stairs or steps

E881 Fall on or from ladders or scaffolding

E882 Fall from or out of building or other structure

E883 Fall into hole or other opening in surface

E884 Other fall from one level to another

E885 Fall on same level from slipping, tripping, or stumbling

E886 Fall on same level from collision, pushing or shoving, by or with other person

E887 Fracture, cause unspecified

E888 Other and unspecified fall

Accidents caused by fire and flames (E890-E899)

E890 Conflagration in private dwelling

E891 Conflagration in other and unspecified building or structure

E892 Conflagration not in building or structure

E893 Accident caused by ignition of clothing

E894 Ignition of highly inflammable material

E895 Accident caused by controlled fire in private dwelling

E896 Accident caused by controlled fire in other and unspecified building or structure

E897 Accident caused by controlled fire not in building or structure

E898 Accident caused by other specified fire and flames

E899 Accident caused by unspecified fire

Accidents due to natural and environmental factors (E900-E909)

E900 Excessive heat

E901 Excessive cold

E902 High and low air pressure and changes in air pressure

E903 Travel and motion

E904 Hunger, thirst, exposure, and neglect

E905 Venomous animals and plants as the cause of poisoning and toxic reactions

E906 Other injury caused by animals

E907 Lightning

E908 Cataclysmic storms, and floods resulting from storms

E909 Cataclysmic earth surface movements and eruptions

Accidents caused by submersion, suffocation, and foreign bodies (E910-E915)

E910 Accidental drowning and submersion

E911 Inhalation and ingestion of food causing obstruction of respiratory tract or suffocation

E912 Inhalation and ingestion of other object causing obstruction of respiratory tract or suffocation

E913 Accidental mechanical suffocation

E914 Foreign body accidentally entering eye and adnexa

E915 Foreign body accidentally entering other orifice

Other accidents (E916-E928)

E916 Struck accidentally by falling object

E917 Striking against or struck accidentally by objects or persons

E918 Caught accidentally in or between objects

E919 Accidents caused by machinery

E920 Accidents caused by cutting and piercing instruments or objects

E921 Accident caused by explosion of pressure vessel

E922 Accident caused by firearm missile

E923 Accident caused by explosive material

E924 Accident caused by hot substance or object, caustic or corrosive material, and steam

E925 Accident caused by electric current

E926 Exposure to radiation

E927 Overexertion and strenuous movements

E928 Other and unspecified environmental and accidental causes

SUPPLEMENTARY CLASSIFICATION...INJURY AND POISONING *continued*

Late effects of accidental injury (E929)
E929 Late effects of accidental injury

Drugs, medicinal and biological substances causing adverse effects in therapeutic use (E930-E949)
E930 Antibiotics
E931 Other anti-infectives
E932 Hormones and synthetic substitutes
E933 Primarily systemic agents
E934 Agents primarily affecting blood constituents
E935 Analgesics, antipyretics, and antirheumatics
E936 Anticonvulsants and anti-Parkinsonism drugs
E937 Sedatives and hypnotics
E938 Other central nervous system depressants and anesthetics
E939 Psychotropic agents
E940 Central nervous system stimulants
E941 Drugs primarily affecting the autonomic nervous system
E942 Agents primarily affecting the cardiovascular system
E943 Agents primarily affecting gastrointestinal system
E944 Water, mineral, and uric acid metabolism drugs
E945 Agents primarily acting on the smooth and skeletal muscles and respiratory system
E946 Agents primarily affecting skin and mucous membrane, ophthalmological, otorhinolaryngological, and dental drugs
E947 Other and unspecified drugs and medicinal substances
E948 Bacterial vaccines
E949 Other vaccines and biological substances

Suicide and self-inflicted injury (E950-E959)
E950 Suicide and self-inflicted poisoning by solid or liquid substances
E951 Suicide and self-inflicted poisoning by gases in domestic use
E952 Suicide and self-inflicted poisoning by other gases and vapors
E953 Suicide and self inflicted injury by hanging, strangulation, and suffocation
E954 Suicide and self-inflicted injury by submersion [drowning]
E955 Suicide and self-inflicted injury by firearms and explosives
E956 Suicide and self-inflicted injury by cutting and piercing instruments
E957 Suicide and self-inflicted injuries by jumping from high place
E958 Suicide and self-inflicted injury by other and unspecified means
E959 Late effects of self-inflicted injury

Homicide and injury purposely inflicted by other persons (E960-E969)
E960 Fight, brawl, and rape
E961 Assault by corrosive or caustic substance, except poisoning
E962 Assault by poisoning
E963 Assault by hanging and strangulation
E964 Assault by submersion [drowning]
E965 Assault by firearms and explosives
E966 Assault by cutting and piercing instrument
E967 Child and adult battering and other maltreatment
E968 Assault by other and unspecified means
E969 Late effects of injury purposely inflicted by other person

Legal intervention (E970-E978)
E970 Injury due to legal intervention by firearms
E971 Injury due to legal intervention by explosives
E972 Injury due to legal intervention by gas
E973 Injury due to legal intervention by blunt object
E974 Injury due to legal intervention by cutting and piercing instruments
E975 Injury due to legal intervention by other specified means
E976 Injury due to legal intervention by unspecified means
E977 Late effects of injuries due to legal intervention
E978 Legal execution

Injury undetermined whether accidentally or purposely inflicted (E980-E989)
E980 Poisoning by solid or liquid substances, undetermined whether accidentally or purposely inflicted
E981 Poisoning by gases in domestic use, undetermined whether accidentally or purposely inflicted

SUPPLEMENTARY CLASSIFICATION...INJURY AND POISONING *continued*

E982 Poisoning by other gases, undetermined whether accidentally or purposely inflicted

E983 Hanging, strangulation, or suffocation, undetermined whether accidentally or purposely inflicted

E984 Submersion [drowning], undetermined whether accidentally or purposely inflicted

E985 Injury by firearms and explosives, undetermined whether accidentally or purposely inflicted

E986 Injury by cutting and piercing instruments, undetermined whether accidentally or purposely inflicted

E987 Falling from high place, undetermined whether accidentally or purposely inflicted

E988 Injury by other and unspecified means, undetermined whether accidentally or purposely inflicted

E989 Late effects of injury, undetermined whether accidentally or purposely inflicted

Injury resulting from operations of war (E990-E999)

E990 Injury due to war operations by fires and conflagrations

E991 Injury due to war operations by bullets and fragments

E992 Injury due to war operations by explosion of marine weapons

E993 Injury due to war operations by other explosion

E994 Injury due to war operations by destruction of aircraft

E995 Injury due to war operations by other and unspecified forms of conventional warfare

E996 Injury due to war operations by nuclear weapons

E997 Injury due to war operations by other forms of unconventional warfare

E998 Injury due to war operations but occurring after cessation of hostilities

E999 Late effects of injury due to war operations

DISEASES: ALPHABETIC INDEX
VOLUME 2

A

AAV (disease) (illness) (infection)—*see* Human immunodeficiency virus (disease) (illness) (infection)
Abactio —*see* Abortion, induced
Abactus venter —*see* Abortion, induced
Abarognosis 781.9
Abasia (-astasia) 307.9
  atactica 781.3
  choreic 781.3
  hysterical 300.11
  paroxysmal trepidant 781.3
  spastic 781.3
  trembling 781.3
  trepidans 781.3
Abderhalden-Kaufmann-Lignac syndrome (cystinosis) 270.0
Abdomen, abdominal —*see also* condition
  accordion 306.4
  acute 789.0
  angina 557.1
  burst 868.00
  convulsive equivalent (*see also* Epilepsy) 345.5
  heart 746.87
  muscle deficiency syndrome 756.7
  obstipum 756.7
Abdominalgia 789.0
  periodic 277.3
Abduction contracture, hip or other joint —*see* Contraction, joint
Abercrombie's syndrome (amyloid degeneration) 277.3
Aberrant (congenital)—*see also* Malposition, congenital
  adrenal gland 759.1
  blood vessel NEC 747.60
    arteriovenous NEC 747.60
    cerebrovascular 747.81
    gastrointestinal 747.61
    lower limb 747.64
    renal 747.62
    spinal 747.82
    upper limb 747.63
  breast 757.6
  endocrine gland NEC 759.2
  gastrointestinal vessel (peripheral) 747.61
  hepatic duct 751.69
  lower limb vessel (peripheral) 747.64
  pancreas 751.7
  parathyroid gland 759.2
  peripheral vascular vessel NEC 747.60
  pituitary gland (pharyngeal) 759.2
  renal blood vessel 747.62
  sebaceous glands, mucous membrane, mouth 750.26
  spinal vessel 747.82
  spleen 759.0
  testis (descent) 752.51
  thymus gland 759.2
  thyroid gland 759.2
  upper limb vessel (peripheral) 747.63
Aberratio
  lactis 757.6
  testis 752.51
Aberration —*see also* Anomaly
  chromosome—*see* Anomaly, chromosome(s)
  distantial 368.9
  mental (*see also* Disorder, mental, nonpsychotic) 300.9

Abetalipoproteinemia 272.5
Abionarce 780.7
Abiotrophy 799.8
Ablatio
  placentae—*see* Placenta, ablatio
  retinae (*see also* Detachment, retina) 361.9
Ablation
  pituitary (gland) (with hypofunction) 253.7
  placenta—*see* Placenta, ablatio
  uterus 621.8
Ablepharia, ablepharon, ablephary 743.62
Ablepsia —*see* Blindness
Ablepsy —*see* Blindness
Ablutomania 300.3
Abnormal, abnormality, abnormalities —*see also* Anomaly
  acid-base balance 276.4
    fetus or newborn—*see* Distress, fetal
  adaptation curve, dark 368.63
  alveolar ridge 525.9
  amnion 658.9
    affecting fetus or newborn 762.9
  anatomical relationship NEC 759.9
  apertures, congenital, diaphragm 756.6
  auditory perception NEC 388.40
  autosomes NEC 758.5
    13 758.1
    18 758.2
    21 or 22 758.0
    D_1 758.1
    E_3 758.2
    G 758.0
  ballistocardiogram 794.39
  basal metabolic rate (BMR) 794.7
  biosynthesis, testicular androgen 257.2
  blood level (of)
    cobalt 790.6
    copper 790.6
    iron 790.6
    lithium 790.6
    magnesium 790.6
    mineral 790.6
    zinc 790.6
  blood pressure
    elevated (without diagnosis of hypertension) 796.2
    low (*see also* Hypotension) 458.9
      reading (incidental) (isolated) (nonspecific) 796.3
  bowel sounds 787.5
  breathing behavior—*see* Respiration
  caloric test 794.19
  cervix (acquired) NEC 622.9
    congenital 752.40
    in pregnancy or childbirth 654.6
      causing obstructed labor 660.2
        affecting fetus or newborn 763.1
  chemistry, blood NEC 790.6
  chest sounds 786.7
  chorion 658.9
    affecting fetus or newborn 762.9
  chromosomal NEC 758.89
    analysis, nonspecific result 795.2
    autosomes (*see also* Abnormal, autosomes NEC) 758.5
    fetal, (suspected) affecting management of pregnancy 655.1
    sex 758.81

Abnormal, abnormality . . .—*continued*
clinical findings NEC 796.4
communication—*see* Fistula
configuration of pupils 379.49
coronary
    artery 746.85
    vein 746.9
cortisol-binding globulin 255.8
course, Eustachian tube 744.24
dentofacial NEC 524.9
    functional 524.5
    specified type NEC 524.8
development, developmental NEC 759.9
    bone 756.9
    central nervous system 742.9
direction, teeth 524.3
Dynia (see also Defect, coagulation) 286.9
Ebstein 746.2
echocardiogram 793.2
echoencephalogram 794.01
echogram NEC—*see* Findings, abnormal,
    structure
electrocardiogram (ECG) (EKG) 794.31
electroencephalogram (EEG) 794.02
electromyogram (EMG) 794.17
    ocular 794.14
electro-oculogram (EOG) 794.12
electroretinogram (ERG) 794.11
erythrocytes 289.9
    congenital, with perinatal jaundice 282.9
        [774.0]
Eustachian valve 746.9
excitability under minor stress 301.9
fat distribution 782.9
feces 787.7
fetal heart rate—*see* Distress, fetal
fetus NEC
    affecting management of pregnancy—*see*
        Pregnancy, management affected by, fetal
    causing disproportion 653.7
        affecting fetus or newborn 763.1
        causing obstructed labor 660.1
            affecting fetus or newborn 763.1
findings without manifest disease—*see*
    Findings, abnormal
fluid
    amniotic 792.3
    cerebrospinal 792.0
    peritoneal 792.9
    pleural 792.9
    synovial 792.9
    vaginal 792.9
forces of labor NEC 661.9
    affecting fetus or newborn 763.7
form, teeth 520.2
function studies
    auditory 794.15
    bladder 794.9
    brain 794.00
    cardiovascular 794.30
    endocrine NEC 794.6
    kidney 794.4
    liver 794.8
    nervous system
        central 794.00
        peripheral 794.19
    oculomotor 794.14
    pancreas 794.9
    placenta 794.9
    pulmonary 794.2

Abnormal, abnormality . . .—*continued*
    retina 794.11
    special senses 794.19
    spleen 794.9
    thyroid 794.5
    vestibular 794.16
gait 781.2
    hysterical 300.11
gastrin secretion 251.5
globulin
    cortisol-binding 255.8
    thyroid-binding 246.8
glucagon secretion 251.4
glucose tolerance test 790.2
    in pregnancy, childbirth, or puerperium 648.8
        fetus or newborn 775.0
gravitational (G) forces or states 994.9
hair NEC 704.2
hard tissue formation in pulp 522.3
head movement 781.0
heart
    rate, fetus—*see* Distress, fetal
    shadow 793.2
    sounds NEC 785.3
hemoglobin (*see also* Disease, hemoglobin)
    282.7
    trait—*see* Trait, hemoglobin, abnormal
hemorrhage, uterus—*see* Hemorrhage, uterus
histology NEC 795.4
increase
    in
        appetite 783.6
        development 783.9
involuntary movement 781.0
jaw closure 524.5
karyotype 795.2
knee jerk 796.1
labor NEC 661.9
    affecting fetus or newborn 763.7
laboratory findings—*see* Findings, abnormal
length, organ or site, congenital—*see* Distortion
loss of weight 783.2
lung shadow 793.1
mammogram 793.8
Mantoux test 795.5
membranes (fetal)
    affecting fetus or newborn 762.9
    complicating pregnancy 658.8
menstruation—*see* Menstruation
metabolism (*see also* condition) 783.9
movement 781.0
    disorder, NEC 333.90
        specified, NEC 333.99
    head 781.0
    involuntary 781.0
    specified type NEC 333.99
muscle contraction, localized 728.85
myoglobin (Aberdeen) (Annapolis) 289.9
narrowness, eyelid 743.62
optokinetic response 379.57
organs or tissues of pelvis NEC
    in pregnancy or childbirth 654.9
        affecting fetus or newborn 763.8
        causing obstructed labor 660.2
            affecting fetus or newborn 763.1
origin—*see* Malposition, congenital
palmar creases 757.2
Papanicolaou (smear)
    cervix 795.0
    other site 795.1

Abnormal, abnormality . . .—*continued*
parturition
  affecting fetus or newborn 763.9
  mother—*see* Delivery, complicated
pelvis (bony)—*see* Deformity, pelvis
percussion, chest 786.7
periods (grossly) (see also Menstruation) 626.9
phonocardiogram 794.39
placenta—*see* Placenta, abnormal
plantar reflex 796.1
plasma protein—*see* Deficiency, plasma, protein
pleural folds 748.8
position—*see also* Malposition
  gravid uterus 654.4
    causing obstructed labor 660.2
      affecting fetus or newborn 763.1
posture NEC 781.9
presentation (fetus)—*see* Presentation, fetus,
  abnormal
product of conception NEC 631
puberty—*see* Puberty
pulmonary
  artery 747.3
  function, newborn 770.8
  test results 794.2
  ventilation, newborn 770.8
    hyperventilation 786.01
pulsations in neck 785.1
pupil reflexes 379.40
quality of milk 676.8
radiological examination 793.9
  abdomen NEC 793.6
  biliary tract 793.3
  breast 793.8
  gastrointestinal tract 793.4
  genitourinary organs 793.5
  head 793.0
  intrathoracic organ NEC 793.2
  lung (field) 793.1
  musculoskeletal system 793.7
  retroperitoneum 793.6
  skin and subcutaneous tissue 793.9
  skull 793.0
red blood cells 790.0
  morphology 790.0
  volume 790.0
reflex NEC 796.1
renal function test 794.4
respiration signs—*see* Respiration
response to nerve stimulation 794.10
retinal correspondence 368.34
rhythm, heart—*see also* Arrhythmia fetus—*see*
  Distress, fetal
saliva 792.4
scan
  brain 794.09
  kidney 794.4
  liver 794.8
  lung 794.2
  thyroid 794.5
secretion
  gastrin 251.5
  glucagon 251.4
semen 792.2
serum level (of)
  acid phosphatase 790.5
  alkaline phosphatase 790.5
  amylase 790.5
  enzymes NEC 790.5
  lipase 790.5

Abnormal, abnormality . . .—*continued*
shape
  cornea 743.41
  gallbladder 751.69
  gravid uterus 654.4
    affecting fetus or newborn 763.8
    causing obstructed labor 660.2
      affecting fetus or newborn 763.1
  head (see also Anomaly, skull) 756.0
  organ or site, congenital NEC—*see* Distortion
sinus venosus 747.40
size
  fetus, complicating delivery 653.5
    causing obstructed labor 660.1
  gallbladder 751.69
  head (see also Anomaly, skull) 756.0
  organ or site, congenital NEC—*see* Distortion
  teeth 520.2
skin and appendages, congenital NEC **757.9**
soft parts of pelvis—*see* Abnormal, organs or
  tissues of pelvis
spermatozoa 792.2
sputum (amount) (color) (excessive) (odor)
  (purulent) 786.4
stool NEC 787.7
  bloody 578.1
    occult 792.1
  bulky 787.7
  color (dark) (light) 792.1
  content (fat) (mucus) (pus) 792.1
  occult blood 792.1
synchondrosis 756.9
test results without manifest disease—*see*
  Findings, abnormal
thebesian valve 746.9
thermography—*see* Findings, abnormal,
  structure
threshold, cones or rods (eye) 368.63
thyroid-binding globulin 246.8
thyroid product 246.8
toxicology (findings) NEC 796.0
tracheal cartilage (congenital) 748.3
transport protein 273.8
ultrasound results—*see* Findings, abnormal,
  structure
umbilical cord
  affecting fetus or newborn 762.6
  complicating delivery 663.9
  specified NEC 663.8
union
  cricoid cartilage and thyroid cartilage 748.3
  larynx and trachea 748.3
  thyroid cartilage and hyoid bone 748.3
urination NEC 788.69
  psychogenic 306.53
  stream
    intermittent 788.61
    slowing 788.62
    splitting 788.61
    weak 788.62
urine (constituents) NEC 791.9
uterine hemorrhage (see also Hemorrhage,
  uterus) 626.9
  climacteric 627.0
  postmenopausal 627.1
vagina (acquired) (congenital)
  in pregnancy or childbirth 654.7
    affecting fetus or newborn 763.8
    causing obstructed labor 660.2
      affecting fetus or newborn 763.1
vascular sounds 785.9

Abnormal, abnormality . . .—*continued*
vectorcardiogram 794.39
visually evoked potential (VEP) 794.13
vulva (acquired) (congenital)
  in pregnancy or childbirth 654.8
    affecting fetus or newborn 763.8
    causing obstructed labor 660.2
      affecting fetus or newborn 763.1
weight
  gain 783.1
    of pregnancy 646.1
      with hypertension—see Toxemia, of
        pregnancy
  loss 783.2
x-ray examination—*see* Abnormal, radiological
    examination
Abnormally formed uterus —*see* Anomaly,
  uterus
Abnormity (any organ or part)—*see* Anomaly
ABO
hemolytic disease 773.1
incompatibility reaction 999.6
Abocclusion 524.2
Abolition, language 784.69
Aborter, habitual or recurrent NEC
without current pregnancy 629.9
current abortion (*see also* Abortion,
  spontaneous) 634.9
  affecting fetus or newborn 761.8
observation in current pregnancy 646.3
Abortion (complete) (incomplete) (inevitable)
  (with retained products of conception) 637.9

> Note—Use the following fifth-digit
> subclassification with categories 634-637:
>
> 0 *unspecified*
> 1 *incomplete*
> 2 *complete*

with
  complication(s) (any) following previous
    abortion—*see* category 639
  damage to pelvic organ (laceration) (rupture)
    (tear) 637.2
  embolism (air) (amniotic fluid) (blood clot)
    (pulmonary) (pyemic) (septic) (soap) 637.6
  genital tract and pelvic infection 637.0
  hemorrhage, delayed or excessive 637.1
  metabolic disorder 637.4
  renal failure (acute) 637.3
  sepsis (genital tract) (pelvic organ) 637.0
    urinary tract 637.7
  shock (postoperative) (septic) 637.5
  specified complication NEC 637.7
  toxemia 637.3
  unspecified complication(s) 637.8
  urinary tract infection 637.7
accidental—*see* Abortion, spontaneous
artificial—*see* Abortion, induced
attempted (failed)—*see* Abortion, failed
criminal—*see* Abortion, illegal
early—*see* Abortion, spontaneous
elective—*see* Abortion, legal
failed (legal) 638.9
  with
    damage to pelvic organ (laceration)
      (rupture) (tear) 638.2
    embolism (air) (amniotic fluid) (blood clot)
      (pulmonary) (pyemic) (septic) (soap)
      638.6
    genital tract and pelvic infection 638.0

Abortion—*continued*
  hemorrhage, delayed or excessive 638.1
  metabolic disorder 638.4
  renal failure (acute) 638.3
  sepsis (genital tract) (pelvic organ) 638.0
    urinary tract 638.7
  shock (postoperative) (septic) 638.5
  specified complication NEC 638.7
  toxemia 638.3
  unspecified complication(s) 638.8
  urinary tract infection 638.7
fetal indication—*see* Abortion, legal
fetus 779.6
following threatened abortion—*see* Abortion,
  by type
habitual or recurrent (care during pregnancy)
  646.3
  with current abortion (*see also* Abortion,
    spontaneous) 634.9
    affecting fetus or newborn 761.8
  without current pregnancy 629.9
homicidal—*see* Abortion, illegal
illegal 636.9
  with
    damage to pelvic organ (laceration)
      (rupture) (tear) 636.2
    embolism (air) (amniotic fluid) (blood clot)
      (pulmonary) (pyemic) (septic) (soap)
      636.6
    genital tract and pelvic infection 636.0
    hemorrhage, delayed or excessive 636.1
    metabolic disorder 636.4
    renal failure 636.3
    sepsis (genital tract) (pelvic organ) 636.0
      urinary tract 636.7
    shock (postoperative) (septic) 636.5
    specified complication NEC 636.7
    toxemia 636.3
    unspecified complication(s) 636.8
    urinary tract infection 636.7
  fetus 779.6
induced 637.9
  illegal—*see* Abortion, illegal
  legal indications—*see* Abortion, legal
  medical indications—*see* Abortion, legal
  therapeutic—*see* Abortion, legal
late—*see* Abortion, spontaneous
legal (legal indication) (medical indication)
  (under medical supervision) 635.9
  with
    damage to pelvic organ (laceration)
      (rupture) (tear) 635.2
    embolism (air) (amniotic fluid) (blood clot)
      (pulmonary) (pyemic) (septic) (soap)
      635.6
    genital tract and pelvic infection 635.0
    hemorrhage, delayed or excessive 635.1
    metabolic disorder 635.4
    renal failure (acute) 635.3
    sepsis (genital tract) (pelvic organ) 635.0
      urinary tract 635.7
    shock (postoperative) (septic) 635.5
    specified complication NEC 635.7
    toxemia 635.3
    unspecified complication(s) 635.8
    urinary tract infection 635.7
  fetus 779.6
medical indication—*see* Abortion, legal
mental hygiene problem—*see* Abortion, legal
missed 632
operative—*see* Abortion, legal

Abortion—*continued*
  psychiatric indication—*see* Abortion, legal
  recurrent—*see* Abortion, spontaneous
  self-induced—*see* Abortion, illegal
  septic—*see* Abortion, by type, with sepsis
  spontaneous 634.9
    with
      damage to pelvic organ (laceration)
        (rupture) (tear) 634.2
      embolism (air) (amniotic fluid) (blood clot)
        (pulmonary) (pyemic) (septic) (soap)
        634.6
      genital tract and pelvic infection 634.0
      hemorrhage, delayed or excessive 634.1
      metabolic disorder 634.4
      renal failure 634.3
      sepsis (genital tract) (pelvic organ) 634.0
        urinary tract 634.7
      shock (postoperative) (septic) 634.5
      specified complication NEC 634.7
      toxemia 634.3
      unspecified complication(s) 634.8
      urinary tract infection 634.7
    fetus 761.8
    threatened 640.0
      affecting fetus or newborn 762.1
  surgical—*see* Abortion, legal
  therapeutic—*see* Abortion, legal
  threatened 640.0
    affecting fetus or newborn 762.1
  tubal—*see* Pregnancy, tubal
  voluntary—*see* Abortion, legal
Abortus fever 023.9
Aboulomania 301.6
Abrachia 755.20
Abrachiatism 755.20
Abrachiocephalia 759.89
Abrachiocephalus 759.89
Abrami's disease (acquired hemolytic jaundice)
  283.9
Abramov-Fiedler myocarditis (acute isolated
  myocarditis) 422.91
Abrasion —*see also* Injury, superficial, by site
  dental 521.2
  teeth, tooth (dentifrice) (habitual) (hard tissues)
    (occupational) (ritual) (traditional) (wedge
    defect) 521.2
Abrikossov's tumor (M9580/0)—*see also*
  Neoplasm, connective tissue, benign
  malignant (M9580/3)—*see* Neoplasm,
  connective tissue, malignant
Abrism 988.8
Abruption, placenta —*see* Placenta, abruptio
Abruptio placentae —*see* Placenta, abruptio
Abscess (acute) (chronic) (infectional)
  (lymphangitic) (metastatic) (multiple)
  (pyogenic) (septic) (with lymphangitis) (*see
  also* Cellulitis) 682.9
  abdomen, abdominal
    cavity—*see* Abscess, peritoneum
    wall 682.2
  abdominopelvic—*see* Abscess, peritoneum
  accessory sinus (chronic) (*see also* Sinusitis)
    473.9
  adrenal (capsule) (gland) 255.8
  alveolar 522.5
    with sinus 522.7
  amebic 006.3
    bladder 006.8
    brain (with liver or lung abscess) 006.5

Abscess—*continued*
  liver (without mention of brain or lung
    abscess) 006.3
    with
      brain abscess (and lung abscess) 006.5
      lung abscess 006.4
    lung (with liver abscess) 006.4
      with brain abscess 006.5
    seminal vesicle 006.8
    specified site NEC 006.8
    spleen 006.8
  anaerobic 040.0
  ankle 682.6
  anorectal 566
  antecubital space 682.3
  antrum (chronic) (Highmore) (*see also*
    Sinusitis, maxillary) 473.0
  anus 566
  apical (tooth) 522.5
    with sinus (alveolar) 522.7
  appendix 540.1
  areola (acute) (chronic) (nonpuerperal) 611.0
    puerperal, postpartum 675.1
  arm (any part, above wrist) 682.3
  artery (wall) 447.2
  atheromatous 447.2
  auditory canal (external) 380.10
  auricle (ear) (staphylococcal) (streptococcal)
    380.10
  axilla, axillary (region) 682.3
    lymph gland or node 683
  back (any part) 682.2
  Bartholin's gland 616.3
    with
      abortion—*see* Abortion, by type, with sepsis
      ectopic pregnancy (*see also* categories
        633.0-633.9) 639.0
      molar pregnancy (*see also* categories
        630-632) 639.0
    complicating pregnancy or puerperium 646.6
    following
      abortion 639.0
      ectopic or molar pregnancy 639.0
  bartholinian 616.3
  Bezold's 383.01
  bile, biliary, duct or tract (*see also*
    Cholecystitis) 576.8
  bilharziasis 120.1
  bladder (wall) 595.89
    amebic 006.8
  bone (subperiosteal) (*see also* Osteomyelitis)
    730.0
    accessory sinus (chronic) (*see also* Sinusitis)
      473.9
    acute 730.0
    chronic or old 730.1
    jaw (lower) (upper) 526.4
    mastoid—*see* Mastoiditis, acute
    petrous (*see also* Petrositis) 383.20
    spinal (tuberculous) (*see also* Tuberculosis)
      015.0 *[730.88]*
      nontuberculous 730.08
  bowel 569.5
  brain (any part) 324.0
    amebic (with liver or lung abscess) 006.5
    cystic 324.0
    late effect—*see* category 326
    otogenic 324.0
    tuberculous (*see also* Tuberculosis) 013.3
  breast (acute) (chronic) (nonpuerperal) 611.0
    newborn 771.5

Abscess—*continued*
  puerperal, postpartum 675.1
    tuberculous (*see also* Tuberculosis) 017.9
  broad ligament (chronic) (*see also* Disease,
    pelvis, inflammatory) 614.4
    acute 614.3
  Brodie's (chronic) (localized) (*see also*
    Osteomyelitis) 730.1
  bronchus 519.1
  buccal cavity 528.3
  bulbourethral gland 597.0
  bursa 727.89
    pharyngeal 478.29
  buttock 682.5
  canaliculus, breast 611.0
  canthus 372.20
  cartilage 733.99
  cecum 540.1
  cerebellum, cerebellar 324.0
    late effect—*see* category 326
  cerebral (embolic) 324.0
    late effect—*see* category 326
  cervical (neck region) 682.1
    lymph gland or node 683
    stump (*see also* Cervicitis) 616.0
  cervix (stump) (uteri) (*see also* Cervicitis) 616.0
  cheek, external 682.0
    inner 528.3
  chest 510.9
    with fistula 510.0
    wall 682.2
  chin 682.0
  choroid 363.00
  ciliary body 364.3
  circumtonsillar 475
  cold (tuberculous)—*see also* Tuberculosis,
    abscess
    articular—*see* Tuberculosis, joint
  colon (wall) 569.5
  colostomy or enterostomy 569.6
  conjunctiva 372.00
  connective tissue NEC 682.9
  cornea 370.55
    with ulcer 370.00
  corpus
    cavernosum 607.2
    luteum (*see also* Salpingo-oophoritis) 614.2
  Cowper's gland 597.0
  cranium 324.0
  cul-de-sac (Douglas') (posterior) (*see also*
    Disease, pelvis, inflammatory) 614.4
    acute 614.3
  dental 522.5
    with sinus (alveolar) 522.7
  dentoalveolar 522.5
    with sinus (alveolar) 522.7
  diaphragm, diaphragmatic—*see* Abscess,
    peritoneum
  digit NEC 681.9
  Douglas' cul-de-sac or pouch (*see also* Disease,
    pelvis, inflammatory) 614.4
    acute 614.3
  Dubois' 090.5
  ductless gland 259.8
  ear
    acute 382.00
    external 380.10
    inner 386.30
    middle—*see* Otitis media
  elbow 682.3
  endamebic—*see* Abscess, amebic

Abscess—*continued*
  entamebic—*see* Abscess, amebic
  enterostomy 569.6
  epididymis 604.0
  epidural 324.9
    brain 324.0
    late effect—*see* category 326
    spinal cord 324.1
  epiglottis 478.79
  epiploon, epiploic—*see* Abscess, peritoneum
  erysipelatous (*see also* Erysipelas) 035
  esophagus 530.19
  ethmoid (bone) (chronic) (sinus) (*see also*
    Sinusitis, ethmoidal) 473.2
  external auditory canal 380.10
  extradural 324.9
    brain 324.0
    late effect—*see* category 326
    spinal cord 324.1
  extraperitoneal—*see* Abscess, peritoneum
  eye 360.00
  eyelid 373.13
  face (any part, except eye) 682.0
  fallopian tube (*see also* Salpingo-oophoritis)
    614.2
  fascia 728.89
  fauces 478.29
  fecal 569.5
  femoral (region) 682.6
  filaria, filarial (*see also* Infestation, filarial)
    125.9
  finger (any) (intrathecal) (periosteal)
    (subcutaneous) (subcuticular) 681.00
  fistulous NEC 682.9
  flank 682.2
  foot (except toe) 682.7
  forearm 682.3
  forehead 682.0
  frontal (sinus) (chronic) (*see also* Sinusitis,
    frontal) 473.1
  gallbladder (*see also* Cholecystitis, acute) 575.0
  gastric 535.0
  genital organ or tract NEC
    female 616.9
      with
        abortion—*see* Abortion, by type, with
          sepsis
        ectopic pregnancy (*see also* categories
          633.0-633.9) 639.0
        molar pregnancy (*see also* categories
          630-632) 639.0
      following
        abortion 639.0
        ectopic or molar pregnancy 639.0
      puerperal, postpartum, childbirth 670
    male 608.4
  genitourinary system, tuberculous (*see also*
    Tuberculosis) 016.9
  gingival 523.3
  gland, glandular (lymph) (acute) NEC 683
  glottis 478.79
  gluteal (region) 682.5
  gonorrheal NEC (*see also* Gonococcus) 098.0
  groin 682.2
  gum 523.3
  hand (except finger or thumb) 682.4
  head (except face) 682.8
  heart 429.89
  heel 682.7
  helminthic (*see also* Infestation, by specific
    parasite) 128.9

Abscess—*continued*
  hepatic 572.0
    amebic (*see also* Abscess, liver, amebic) 006.3
    duct 576.8
  hip 682.6
    tuberculous (active) (*see also* Tuberculosis)
      015.1
  ileocecal 540.1
  ileostomy (bud) 569.6
  iliac (region) 682.2
    fossa 540.1
  iliopsoas (tuberculous) (*see also* Tuberculosis)
    015.0 *[730.88]*
    nontuberculous 728.89
  infraclavicular (fossa) 682.3
  inguinal (region) 682.2
    lymph gland or node 683
  intersphincteric (anus) 566
  intestine, intestinal 569.5
    rectal 566
  intra-abdominal (*see also* Abscess, peritoneum)
    567.2
    postoperative 998.59
  intracranial 324.0
    late effect—*see* category 326
  intramammary—*see* Abscess, breast
  intramastoid (*see also* Mastoiditis, acute) 383.00
  intraorbital 376.01
  intraperitoneal—*see* Abscess, peritoneum
  intraspinal 324.1
    late effect—*see* category 326
  intratonsillar 475
  iris 364.3
  ischiorectal 566
  jaw (bone) (lower) (upper) 526.4
    skin 682.0
  joint (*see also* Arthritis, pyogenic) 711.0
    vertebral (tuberculous) (*see also* Tuberculosis)
      015.0 *[730.88]*
    nontuberculous 724.8
  kidney 590.2
    with
      abortion—*see* Abortion, by type, with
        urinary tract infection
      calculus 592.0
      ectopic pregnancy (*see also* categories
        633.0-633.9) 639.8
      molar pregnancy (*see also* categories
        630-632) 639.8
    complicating pregnancy or puerperium 646.6
      affecting fetus or newborn 760.1
    following
      abortion 639.8
      ectopic or molar pregnancy 639.8
  knee 682.6
    joint 711.06
    tuberculous (active) (*see also* Tuberculosis)
      015.2
  labium (majus) (minus) 616.4
    complicating pregnancy, childbirth, or
      puerperium 646.6
  lacrimal (passages) (sac) (*see also*
    Dacryocystitis) 375.30
    caruncle 375.30
    gland (*see also* Dacryoadenitis) 375.00
  lacunar 597.0
  larynx 478.79
  lateral (alveolar) 522.5
    with sinus 522.7
  leg, except foot 682.6
  lens 360.00

Abscess—*continued*
  lid 373.13
  lingual 529.0
    tonsil 475
  lip 528.5
  Littre's gland 597.0
  liver 572.0
    amebic 006.3
      with
        brain abscess (and lung abscess) 006.5
        lung abscess 006.4
      due to Entamoeba histolytica 006.3
      dysenteric (*see also* Abscess, liver, amebic)
        006.3
      pyogenic 572.0
      tropical (*see also* Abscess, liver, amebic) 006.3
  loin (region) 682.2
  lumbar (tuberculous) (*see also* Tuberculosis)
    015.0 *[730.88]*
    nontuberculous 682.2
  lung (miliary) (putrid) 513.0
    amebic (with liver abscess) 006.4
      with brain abscess 006.5
  lymph, lymphatic, gland or node (acute) 683
    any site, except mesenteric 683
    mesentery 289.2
  lymphangitic, acute—*see* Cellulitis
  malar 526.4
  mammary gland—*see* Abscess, breast
  marginal (anus) 566
  mastoid (process) (*see also* Mastoiditis, acute)
    383.00
    subperiosteal 383.01
  maxilla, maxillary 526.4
    molar (tooth) 522.5
      with sinus 522.7
    premolar 522.5
    sinus (chronic) (*see also* Sinusitis, maxillary)
      473.0
  mediastinum 513.1
  meibomian gland 373.12
  meninges (*see also* Meningitis) 320.9
  mesentery, mesenteric—*see* Abscess,
    peritoneum
  mesosalpinx (*see also* Salpingo-oophoritis)
    614.2
  milk 675.1
  Monro's (psoriasis) 696.1
  mons pubis 682.2
  mouth (floor) 528.3
  multiple sites NEC 682.9
  mural 682.2
  muscle 728.89
  myocardium 422.92
  nabothian (follicle) (*see also* Cervicitis) 616.0
  nail (chronic) (with lymphangitis) 681.9
    finger 681.02
    toe 681.11
  nasal (fossa) (septum) 478.1
    sinus (chronic) (*see also* Sinusitis) 473.9
  nasopharyngeal 478.29
  nates 682.5
  navel 682.2
    newborn NEC 771.4
  neck (region) 682.1
    lymph gland or node 683
  nephritic (*see also* Abscess, kidney) 590.2
  nipple 611.0
    puerperal, postpartum 675.0
  nose (septum) 478.1
    external 682.0

Abscess—*continued*
puerperal—Puerperal, abscess, by site
pulmonary—*see* Abscess, lung
pulp, pulpal (dental) 522.0
   finger 681.01
   toe 681.10
pyemic—*see* Septicemia
pyloric valve 535.0
rectovaginal septum 569.5
rectovesical 595.89
rectum 566
regional NEC 682.9
renal (*see also* Abscess, kidney) 590.2
retina 363.00
retrobulbar 376.01
retrocecal—*see* Abscess, peritoneum
retrolaryngeal 478.79
retromammary—*see* Abscess, breast
retroperineal 682.2
retroperitoneal—*see* Abscess, peritoneum
retropharyngeal 478.24
   tuberculous (*see also* Tuberculosis) 012.8
retrorectal 566
retrouterine (*see also* Disease, pelvis,
    inflammatory) 614.4
   acute 614.3
retrovesical 595.89
root, tooth 522.5
   with sinus (alveolar) 522.7
round ligament (*see also* Disease, pelvis,
    inflammatory) 614.4
   acute 614.3
rupture (spontaneous) NEC 682.9
sacrum (tuberculous) (*see also* Tuberculosis)
   015.0 *[730.88]*
   nontuberculous 730.08
salivary duct or gland 527.3
scalp (any part) 682.8
scapular 730.01
sclera 379.09
scrofulous (*see also* Tuberculosis) 017.2
scrotum 608.4
seminal vesicle 608.0
   amebic 006.8
septal, dental 522.5
   with sinus (alveolar) 522.7
septum (nasal) 478.1
serous (*see also* Periostitis) 730.3
shoulder 682.3
side 682.2
sigmoid 569.5
sinus (accessory) (chronic) (nasal) (*see also*
    Sinusitis) 473.9
   intracranial venous (any) 324.0
   late effect—*see* category 326
Skene's duct or gland 597.0
skin NEC 682.9
   tuberculous (primary) (*see also* Tuberculosis)
    017.0
sloughing NEC 682.9
specified site NEC 682.8
   amebic 006.8
spermatic cord 608.4
sphenoidal (sinus) (*see also* Sinusitis,
    sphenoidal) 473.3
spinal
   cord (any part) (staphylococcal) 324.1
    tuberculous (*see also* Tuberculosis) 013.5
   epidural 324.1
spine (column) (tuberculous) (*see also*
    Tuberculosis) 015.0 *[730.88]*

Abscess—*continued*
nontuberculous 730.08
spleen 289.59
   amebic 006.8
staphylococcal NEC 682.9
stitch 998.59
stomach (wall) 535.0
strumous (tuberculous) (*see also* Tuberculosis)
   017.2
subarachnoid 324.9
   brain 324.0
   cerebral 324.0
   late effect—*see* category 326
   spinal cord 324.1
subareolar—*see also* Abscess, breast
   puerperal, postpartum 675.1
subcecal 540.1
subcutaneous NEC 682.9
subdiaphragmatic—*see* Abscess, peritoneum
subdorsal 682.2
subdural 324.9
   brain 324.0
   late effect—*see* category 326
   spinal cord 324.1
subgaleal 682.8
subhepatic—*see* Abscess, peritoneum
sublingual 528.3
   gland 527.3
submammary—*see* Abscess, breast
submandibular (region) (space) (triangle) 682.0
   gland 527.3
submaxillary (region) 682.0
   gland 527.3
submental (pyogenic) 682.0
   gland 527.3
subpectoral 682.2
subperiosteal—*see* Abscess, bone
subperitoneal—*see* Abscess, peritoneum
subphrenic—*see also* Abscess, peritoneum
   postoperative 998.59
subscapular 682.2
subungual 681.9
suburethral 597.0
sudoriparous 705.89
suppurative NEC 682.9
supraclavicular (fossa) 682.3
suprahepatic—*see* Abscess, peritoneum
suprapelvic (*see also* Disease, pelvis,
    inflammatory) 614.4
   acute 614.3
suprapubic 682.2
suprarenal (capsule) (gland) 255.8
sweat gland 705.89
syphilitic 095.8
teeth, tooth (root) 522.5
   with sinus (alveolar) 522.7
   supporting structures NEC 523.3
temple 682.0
temporal region 682.0
temporosphenoidal 324.0
   late effect—*see* category 326
tendon (sheath) 727.89
testicle—*see* Orchitis
thecal 728.89
thigh (acquired) 682.6
thorax 510.9
   with fistula 510.0
throat 478.29
thumb (intrathecal) (periosteal) (subcutaneous)
    (subcuticular) 681.00
thymus (gland) 254.1

Abscess—*continued*
thyroid (gland) 245.0
toe (any) (intrathecal) (periosteal)
(subcutaneous) (subcuticular) 681.10
tongue (staphylococcal) 529.0
tonsil(s) (lingual) 475
tonsillopharyngeal 475
tooth, teeth (root) 522.5
with sinus (alveolar) 522.7
supporting structure NEC 523.3
trachea 478.9
trunk 682.2
tubal (*see also* Salpingo-oophoritis) 614.2
tuberculous—*see* Tuberculosis, abscess
tubo-ovarian (*see also* Salpingo-oophoritis)
614.2
tunica vaginalis 608.4
umbilicus NEC 682.2
newborn 771.4
upper arm 682.3
upper respiratory 478.9
urachus 682.2
urethra (gland) 597.0
urinary 597.0
uterus, uterine (wall) (*see also* Endometritis)
615.9
ligament (*see also* Disease, pelvis,
inflammatory) 614.4
acute 614.3
neck (*see also* Cervicitis) 616.0
uvula 528.3
vagina (wall) (*see also* Vaginitis) 616.10
vaginorectal (*see also* Vaginitis) 616.10
vas deferens 608.4
vermiform appendix 540.1
vertebra (column) (tuberculous) (*see also*
Tuberculosis) 015.0 *[730.88]*
nontuberculous 730.0
vesical 595.89
vesicouterine pouch (*see also* Disease, pelvis,
inflammatory) 614.4
vitreous (humor) (pneumococcal) 360.04
vocal cord 478.5
von Bezold's 383.01
vulva 616.4
complicating pregnancy, childbirth, or
puerperium 646.6
vulvovaginal gland (*see also* Vaginitis) 616.3
web-space 682.4
wrist 682.4
Absence (organ or part) (complete or partial)
acoustic nerve 742.8
adrenal (gland) (congenital) 759.1
acquired 255.8
albumin (blood) 273.8
alimentary tract (complete) (congenital) (partial)
751.8
lower 751.5
upper 750.8
alpha-fucosidase 271.8
alveolar process (acquired) 525.8
congenital 750.26
anus, anal (canal) (congenital) 751.2
aorta (congenital) 747.22
aortic valve (congenital) 746.89
appendix, congenital 751.2
arm (acquired) V49.60
above elbow V49.66
below elbow V49.65
congenital (*see also* Deformity, reduction,
upper limb) 755.20

Absence—*continued*
lower—*see* Absence, forearm, congenital
upper (complete) (partial) (with absence of
distal elements, incomplete) 755.24
with
complete absence of distal elements
755.21
forearm (incomplete) 755.23
artery (congenital) (peripheral) NEC (*see also*
Anomaly, peripheral vascular system)
747.60
brain 747.81
cerebral 747.81
coronary 746.85
pulmonary 747.3
umbilical 747.5
atrial septum 745.69
auditory canal (congenital) (external) 744.01
auricle (ear) (with stenosis or atresia of auditory
canal), congenital 744.01
bile, biliary duct (common) or passage
(congenital) 751.61
bladder (acquired) 596.8
congenital 753.8
bone (congenital) NEC 756.9
marrow 284.9
acquired (secondary) 284.8
congenital 284.0
hereditary 284.0
idiopathic 284.9
skull 756.0
bowel sounds 787.5
brain 740.0
specified part 742.2
breast(s) (acquired) 611.8
congenital 757.6
broad ligament (congenital) 752.19
bronchus (congenital) 748.3
calvarium, calvaria (skull) 756.0
canaliculus lacrimalis, congenital 743.65
carpal(s) (congenital) (complete) (partial) (with
absence of distal elements, incomplete) (*see
also* Deformity, reduction, upper limb)
755.28
with complete absence of distal elements
755.21
cartilage 756.9
caudal spine 756.13
cecum (acquired) (postoperative)
(posttraumatic) 569.89
congenital 751.2
cementum 520.4
cerebellum (congenital) (vermis) 742.2
cervix (acquired) (uteri) 622.8
congenital 752.49
chin, congenital 744.89
cilia (congenital) 743.63
acquired 374.89
circulatory system, part NEC 747.89
clavicle 755.51
clitoris (congenital) 752.49
coccyx, congenital 756.13
cold sense (see also Disturbance, sensation)
782.0
colon (acquired) (postoperative) 569.89
congenital 751.2
congenital
lumen—see Atresia
organ or site NEC—*see* Agenesis
septum—*see* Imperfect, closure
corpus callosum (congenital) 742.2

Absence—*continued*
  cricoid cartilage 748.3
  diaphragm (congenital) (with hernia) 756.6
    with obstruction 756.6
  digestive organ(s) or tract, congenital
    (complete) (partial) 751.8
    lower 751.5
    upper 750.8
  ductus arteriosus 747.89
  duodenum (acquired) (postoperative) 564.2
    congenital 751.1
  ear, congenital 744.09
    acquired 388.8
    auricle 744.01
    external 744.01
    inner 744.05
    lobe, lobule 744.21
    middle, except ossicles 744.03
      ossicles 744.04
    ossicles 744.04
  ejaculatory duct (congenital) 752.8
  endocrine gland NEC (congenital) 759.2
  epididymis (congenital) 752.8
    acquired 608.89
  epiglottis, congenital 748.3
  epileptic (atonic) (typical) (*see also* Epilepsy)
    345.0
  erythrocyte 284.9
  erythropoiesis 284.9
    congenital 284.0
  esophagus (congenital) 750.3
  Eustachian tube (congenital) 744.24
  extremity (acquired)
    congenital (*see also* Deformity, reduction)
      755.4
    lower V49.70
    upper V49.60
  extrinsic muscle, eye 743.69
  eye (acquired) 360.89
    adnexa (congenital) 743.69
    congenital 743.00
    muscle (congenital) 743.69
  eyelid (fold), congenital 743.62
    acquired 374.89
  face
    bones NEC 756.0
    specified part NEC 744.89
  fallopian tube(s) (acquired) 620.8
    congenital 752.19
  femur, congenital (complete) (partial) (with
    absence of distal elements, incomplete) (*see
    also* Deformity, reduction, lower limb)
    755.34
    with
      complete absence of distal elements 755.31
      tibia and fibula (incomplete) 755.33
  fibrin 790.92
    fibrinogen (congenital) 286.3
    acquired 286.6
  fibula, congenital (complete) (partial) (with
    absence of distal elements, incomplete) (*see
    also* Deformity, reduction, lower limb)
    755.37
    with
      complete absence of distal elements 755.31
      tibia 755.35
        with
          complete absence of distal elements
            755.31
        femur (incomplete) 755.33

Absence—*continued*
    with complete absence of distal
      elements 755.31
  finger (acquired) V49.62
    congenital (complete) (partial) (*see also*
      Deformity, reduction, upper limb) 755.29
    meaning all fingers (complete) (partial)
      755.21
    transverse 755.21
  fissures of lungs (congenital) 748.5
  foot (acquired) V49.73
    congenital (complete) 755.31
  forearm (acquired) V49.65
    congenital (complete) (partial) (with absence
      of distal elements, incomplete) (*see also*
      Deformity, reduction, upper limb) 755.25
    with
      complete absence of distal elements (hand
        and fingers) 755.21
      humerus (incomplete) 755.23
  fovea centralis 743.55
  fucosidase 271.8
  gallbladder (acquired) V45.89
    congenital 751.69
  gamma globulin (blood) 279.00
  genital organs, congenital
    female 752.8
      external 752.49
      internal NEC 752.8
    male 752.8
      penis 752.69
  genitourinary organs, congenital NEC 752.8
  glottis 748.3
  gonadal, congenital NEC 758.6
  hair (congenital) 757.4
    acquired—*see* Alopecia
  hand (acquired) V49.63
    congenital (complete) (*see also* Deformity,
      reduction, upper limb) 755.21
  heart (congenital) 759.89
    acquired—*see* Status, organ replacement
  heat sense (*see also* Disturbance, sensation)
    782.0
  humerus, congenital (complete) (partial) (with
    absence of distal elements, incomplete) (*see
    also* Deformity, reduction, upper limb)
    755.24
    with
      complete absence of distal elements 755.21
      radius and ulna (incomplete) 755.23
  hymen (congenital) 752.49
  ileum (acquired) (postoperative) (posttraumatic)
    569.89
    congenital 751.1
  immunoglobulin, isolated NEC 279.03
    IgA 279.01
    IgG 279.03
    IgM 279.02
  incus (acquired) 385.24
    congenital 744.04
  internal ear (congenital) 744.05
  intestine (acquired) (small) 569.89
    congenital 751.1
      large 751.2
    large 569.89
      congenital 751.2
  iris (congenital) 743.45
  jaw—*see* Absence, mandible
  jejunum (acquired) 569.89
    congenital 751.1
  joint, congenital NEC 755.8

Absence—*continued*
  kidney(s) (acquired) 593.89
    congenital 753.0
  labium (congenital) (majus) (minus) 752.49
  labyrinth, membranous 744.05
  lacrimal apparatus (congenital) 743.65
  larynx (congenital) 748.3
  leg (acquired) V49.70
    above knee V49.76
    below knee V49.75
    congenital (partial) (unilateral) (*see also*
      Deformity, reduction, lower limb) 755.31
      lower (complete) (partial) (with absence of
        distal elements, incomplete) 755.35
        with
          complete absence of distal elements
            (foot and toes) 755.31
          thigh (incomplete) 755.33
            with complete absence of distal
              elements 755.31
      upper—*see* Absence, femur
  lens (congenital) 743.35
    acquired 379.31
  ligament, broad (congenital) 752.19
  limb (acquired)
    congenital (complete) (partial) (*see also*
      Deformity, reduction) 755.4
      lower 755.30
        complete 755.31
        incomplete 755.32
        longitudinal—*see* Deficiency, lower limb,
          longitudinal
        transverse 755.31
      upper 755.20
        complete 755.21
        incomplete 755.22
        longitudinal—*see* Deficiency, upper limb,
          longitudinal
        transverse 755.21
    lower NEC V49.70
    upper NEC V49.60
  lip 750.26
  liver (congenital) (lobe) 751.69
  lumbar (congenital) (vertebra) 756.13
    isthmus 756.11
    pars articularis 756.11
  lumen—*see* Atresia
  lung (bilateral) (congenital) (fissure) (lobe)
    (unilateral) 748.5
    acquired (any part) 518.89
  mandible (congenital) 524.09
  maxilla (congenital) 524.09
  menstruation 626.0
  metacarpal(s), congenital (complete) (partial)
    (with absence of distal elements,
    incomplete) (*see also* Deformity, reduction,
    upper limb) 755.28
    with all fingers, complete 755.21
  metatarsal(s), congenital (complete) (partial)
    (with absence of distal elements,
    incomplete) (*see also* Deformity, reduction,
    lower limb) 755.38
    with complete absence of distal elements
      755.31
  muscle (congenital) (pectoral) 756.81
    ocular 743.69
  musculoskeletal system (congenital) NEC 756.9
  nail(s) (congenital) 757.5
  neck, part 744.89
  nerve 742.8
  nervous system, part NEC 742.8

Absence—*continued*
  neutrophil 288.0
  nipple (congenital) 757.6
  nose (congenital) 748.1
    acquired 738.0
  nuclear 742.8
  ocular muscle (congenital) 743.69
  organ
    of Corti (congenital) 744.05
    or site, congenital NEC 759.89
  osseous meatus (ear) 744.03
  ovary (acquired) 620.8
    congenital 752.0
  oviduct (acquired) 620.8
    congenital 752.19
  pancreas (congenital) 751.7
    acquired (postoperative) (posttraumatic) 577.8
  parathyroid gland (congenital) 759.2
  parotid gland(s) (congenital) 750.21
  patella, congenital 755.64
  pelvic girdle (congenital) 755.69
  penis (congenital) 752.69
    acquired 607.89
  pericardium (congenital) 746.89
  perineal body (congenital) 756.81
  phalange(s), congenital 755.4
    lower limb (complete) (intercalary) (partial)
      (terminal) (*see also* Deformity, reduction,
      lower limb) 755.39
      meaning all toes (complete) (partial) 755.31
      transverse 755.31
    upper limb (complete) (intercalary) (partial)
      (terminal) (*see also* Deformity, reduction,
      upper limb) 755.29
      meaning all digits (complete) (partial)
        755.21
      transverse 755.21
  pituitary gland (congenital) 759.2
  postoperative—*see* Absence, by site, acquired
  prostate (congenital) 752.8
    acquired 602.8
  pulmonary
    artery 747.3
    trunk 747.3
    valve (congenital) 746.01
    vein 747.49
  punctum lacrimale (congenital) 743.65
  radius, congenital (complete) (partial) (with
    absence of distal elements, incomplete)
    755.26
    with
      complete absence of distal elements 755.21
      ulna 755.25
        with
          complete absence of distal elements
            755.21
          humerus (incomplete) 755.23
  ray, congenital 755.4
    lower limb (complete) (partial) (*see also*
      Deformity, reduction, lower limb) 755.38
    meaning all rays 755.31
    transverse 755.31
    upper limb (complete) (partial) (*see also*
      Deformity, reduction, upper limb) 755.28
    meaning all rays 755.21
    transverse 755.21
  rectum (congenital) 751.2
    acquired 569.49
  red cell 284.9
    acquired (secondary) 284.8
    congenital 284.0

Absence— *continued*
  hereditary 284.0
  idiopathic 284.9
  respiratory organ (congenital) NEC 748.9
  rib (acquired) 738.3
    congenital 756.3
  roof of orbit (congenital) 742.0
  round ligament (congenital) 752.8
  sacrum, congenital 756.13
  salivary gland(s) (congenital) 750.21
  scapula 755.59
  scrotum, congenital 752.8
  seminal tract or duct (congenital) 752.8
    acquired 608.89
  septum (congenital)—*see also* Imperfect,
      closure, septum
    atrial 745.69
      and ventricular 745.7
    between aorta and pulmonary artery 745.0
    ventricular 745.3
      and atrial 745.7
  sex chromosomes 758.81
  shoulder girdle, congenital (complete) (partial)
      755.59
  skin (congenital) 757.39
  skull bone 756.0
    with
      anencephalus 740.0
      encephalocele 742.0
      hydrocephalus 742.3
        with spina bifida (*see also* Spina bifida)
          741.0
      microcephalus 742.1
  spermatic cord (congenital) 752.8
  spinal cord 742.59
  spine, congenital 756.13
  spleen (congenital) 759.0
    acquired 289.59
  sternum, congenital 756.3
  stomach (acquired) (partial) (postoperative)
      V45.89
    congenital 750.7
    with postgastric surgery syndrome 564.2
  submaxillary gland(s) (congenital) 750.21
  superior vena cava (congenital) 747.49
  tarsal(s), congenital (complete) (partial) (with
      absence of distal elements, incomplete) (*see
      also* Deformity, reduction, lower limb)
      755.38
  teeth, tooth (congenital) 520.0
    with abnormal spacing 524.3
    acquired 525.1
      with malocclusion 524.3
  tendon (congenital) 756.81
  testis (congenital) 752.8
    acquired 608.89
  thigh (acquired) 736.89
  thumb (acquired) V49.61
    congenital 755.29
  thymus gland (congenital) 759.2
  thyroid (gland) (surgical) 246.8
    with hypothyroidism 244.0
    cartilage, congenital 748.3
    congenital 243
  tibia, congenital (complete) (partial) (with
      absence of distal elements, incomplete) (*see
      also* Deformity, reduction, lower limb)
      755.36
    with
      complete absence of distal elements 755.31
      fibula 755.35

Absence— *continued*
  with
    complete absence of distal elements
        755.31
    femur (incomplete) 755.33
      with complete absence of distal
          elements 755.31
  toe (acquired) V49.72
    congenital (complete) (partial) 755.39
      meaning all toes 755.31
      transverse 755.31
    great V49.71
  tongue (congenital) 750.11
  tooth, teeth, (congenital) 520.0
    with abnormal spacing 524.3
    acquired 525.1
      with malocclusion 524.3
  trachea (cartilage) (congenital) (rings) 748.3
  transverse aortic arch (congenital) 747.21
  tricuspid valve 746.1
  ulna, congenital (complete) (partial) (with
      absence of distal elements, incomplete) (*see
      also* Deformity, reduction, upper limb)
      755.27
    with
      complete absence of distal elements 755.21
      radius 755.25
        with
          complete absence of distal elements
              755.21
      humerus (incomplete) 755.23
  umbilical artery (congenital) 747.5
  ureter (congenital) 753.4
    acquired 593.89
  urethra, congenital 753.8
  urinary system, part NEC 753.8
  uterus (acquired) 621.8
    congenital 752.3
  uvula (congenital) 750.26
  vagina, congenital 752.49
  vas deferens (congenital) 752.8
    acquired 608.89
  vein (congenital) (peripheral) NEC (*see also*
      Anomaly, peripheral vascular system)
      747.60
    brain 747.81
    great 747.49
    portal 747.49
    pulmonary 747.49
  vena cava (congenital) (inferior) (superior)
      747.49
  ventral horn cell 742.59
  ventricular septum 745.3
  vermis of cerebellum 742.2
  vertebra, congenital 756.13
  vulva, congenital 752.49
Absentia epileptica (*see also* Epilepsy) 345.0
Absinthemia (*see also* Dependence) 304.6
Absinthism (*see also* Dependence) 304.6
Absorbent system disease 459.89
Absorption
  alcohol, through placenta or breast milk 760.71
  antibiotics, through placenta or breast milk
      760.74
  anti-infective, through placenta or breast milk
      760.74
  chemical NEC 989.9
    specified chemical or substance—*see* Table of
      drugs and chemicals
    through placenta or breast milk (fetus or
      newborn) 760.70

Absorption—*continued*
  alcohol 760.71
  anti-infective agents 760.74
  cocaine 760.75
  "crack" 760.75
  diethylstilbestrol [DES] 760.76
  hallucinogenic agents 760.73
  medicinal agents NEC 760.79
  narcotics 760.72
  obstetric anesthetic or analgesic drug 763.5
  specified agent NEC 760.79
  suspected, affecting management of
    pregnancy 655.5
cocaine, through placenta or breast milk 760.75
drug NEC (*see also* Reaction, drug) 995.2
  through placenta or breast milk (fetus or
    newborn) 760.70
  alcohol 760.71
  anti-infective agents 760.74
  cocaine 760.75
  "crack" 760.75
  diethylstilbestrol [DES] 760.76
  hallucinogenic agents 760.73
  medicinal agents NEC 760.79
  narcotics 760.72
  obstetric anesthetic or analgesic drug 763.5
  specified agent NEC 760.79
  suspected, affecting management of
    pregnancy 655.5
fat, disturbance 579.8
hallucinogenic agents, through placenta or
  breast milk 760.73
immune sera, through placenta or breast milk
  760.79
lactose defect 271.3
medicinal agents NEC, through placenta or
  breast milk 760.79
narcotics, through placenta or breast milk 760.72
noxious substance,—*see* Absorption, chemical
protein, disturbance 579.8
pus or septic, general—*see* Septicemia
quinine, through placenta or breast milk 760.74
toxic substance—*see* Absorption, chemical
uremic—*see* Uremia
Abstinence symptoms or syndrome
  alcohol 291.81
  drug 292.0
Abt-Letterer-Siwe syndrome (acute
  histiocytosis X) (M9722/3) 202.5
Abulia 799.8
Abulomania 301.6
Abuse
  adult 995.80
    emotional 995.82
    multiple forms 995.85
    neglect (nutritional) 995.84
    physical 995.81
    psychological 995.82
    sexual 995.83
  alcohol (*see also* Alcoholism) 303.9
    non-dependent 305.0
  child 995.50
    counseling
      perpetrator
        non-parent V62.83
        parent V61.22
      victim V61.21
    emotional 995.51
    multiple forms 995.59
    neglect (nutritional) 995.52

Abuse—*continued*
  physical 995.54
    shaken infant syndrome 995.55
  psychological 995.51
  sexual 995.53
drugs, nondependent 305.9

> Note—Use the following fifth-digit
> subclassification with the following codes:
> 305.0, 305.2-305.9:
>
> 0 unspecified
> 1 continuous
> 2 episodic
> 3 in remission

  amphetamine type 305.7
  antidepressants 305.8
  barbiturates 305.4
  caffeine 305.9
  cannabis 305.2
  cocaine type 305.6
  hallucinogens 305.3
  hashish 305.2
  LSD 305.3
  marijuana 305.2
  mixed 305.9
  morphine type 305.5
  opioid type 305.5
  phencyclidine (PCP) 305.9
  specified NEC 305.9
  tranquilizers 305.4
spouse 995.80
tobacco 305.1
Acalcerosis 275.4
Acalcicosis 275.4
Acalculia 784.69
  developmental 315.1
Acanthocheilonemiasis 125.4
Acanthocytosis 272.5
Acanthokeratodermia 701.1
Acantholysis 701.8
  bullosa 757.39
Acanthoma (benign) (M8070/0)—*see also*
  Neoplasm, by site, benign
  malignant (M8070/3)—*see* Neoplasm, by site,
    malignant
Acanthosis (acquired) (nigricans) 701.2
  adult 701.2
  benign (congenital) 757.39
  congenital 757.39
  glycogenic
    esophagus 530.8
  juvenile 701.2
  tongue 529.8
Acanthrocytosis 272.5
Acapnia 276.3
Acarbia 276.2
Acardia 759.89
Acardiacus amorphus 759.89
Acardiotrophia 429.1
Acardius 759.89
Acariasis 133.9
  sarcoptic 133.0
Acaridiasis 133.9
Acarinosis 133.9
Acariosis 133.9
Acarodermatitis 133.9
  urticarioides 133.9
Acarophobia 300.29
Acatalasemia 277.8
Acatalasia 277.8

Acatamathesia 784.69
Acataphasia 784.5
Acathisia 781.0
  due to drugs 333.99
Acceleration, accelerated
  atrioventricular conduction 426.7
  idioventricular rhythm 427.89
Accessory (congenital)
  adrenal gland 759.1
  anus 751.5
  appendix 751.5
  atrioventricular conduction 426.7
  auditory ossicles 744.04
  auricle (ear) 744.1
  autosome(s) NEC 758.5
    21 or 22 758.0
  biliary duct or passage 751.69
  bladder 753.8
  blood vessels (peripheral) (congenital) NEC
    (see also Anomaly, peripheral vascular
    system) 747.60
    cerebral 747.81
    coronary 746.85
  bone NEC 756.9
    foot 755.67
  breast tissue, axilla 757.6
  carpal bones 755.56
  cecum 751.5
  cervix 752.49
  chromosome(s) NEC 758.5
    13-15 758.1
    16-18 758.2
    21 or 22 758.0
    autosome(s) NEC 758.5
    D_1 758.1
    E_3 758.2
    G 758.0
    sex 758.81
  coronary artery 746.85
  cusp(s), heart valve NEC 746.89
    pulmonary 746.09
  cystic duct 751.69
  digits 755.00
  ear (auricle) (lobe) 744.1
  endocrine gland NEC 759.2
  external os 752.49
  eyelid 743.62
  eye muscle 743.69
  face bone(s) 756.0
  fallopian tube (fimbria) (ostium) 752.19
  fingers 755.01
  foreskin 605
  frontonasal process 756.0
  gallbladder 751.69
  genital organ(s)
    female 752.8
      external 752.49
      internal NEC 752.8
    male NEC 752.8
      penis 752.69
  genitourinary organs NEC 752.8
  heart 746.89
    valve NEC 746.89
      pulmonary 746.09
  hepatic ducts 751.69
  hymen 752.49
  intestine (large) (small) 751.5
  kidney 753.3
  lacrimal canal 743.65
  leaflet, heart valve NEC 746.89
    pulmonary 746.09

Accessory—continued
  ligament, broad 752.19
  liver (duct) 751.69
  lobule (ear) 744.1
  lung (lobe) 748.69
  muscle 756.82
  navicular of carpus 755.56
  nervous system, part NEC 742.8
  nipple 757.6
  nose 748.1
  organ or site NEC—see Anomaly, specified
    type NEC
  ovary 752.0
  oviduct 752.19
  pancreas 751.7
  parathyroid gland 759.2
  parotid gland (and duct) 750.22
  pituitary gland 759.2
  placental lobe—see Placenta, abnormal
  preauricular appendage 744.1
  prepuce 605
  renal arteries (multiple) 747.62
  rib 756.3
    cervical 756.2
  roots (teeth) 520.2
  salivary gland 750.22
  sesamoids 755.8
  sinus—see condition
  skin tags 757.39
  spleen 759.0
  sternum 756.3
  submaxillary gland 750.22
  tarsal bones 755.67
  teeth, tooth 520.1
    causing crowding 524.3
  tendon 756.89
  thumb 755.01
  thymus gland 759.2
  thyroid gland 759.2
  toes 755.02
  tongue 750.13
  tragus 744.1
  ureter 753.4
  urethra 753.8
  urinary organ or tract NEC 753.8
  uterus 752.2
  vagina 752.49
  valve, heart NEC 746.89
    pulmonary 746.09
  vertebra 756.19
  vocal cords 748.3
  vulva 752.49
Accident, accidental —see also condition
  birth NEC 767.9
  cardiovascular (see also Disease,
    cardiovascular) 429.2
  cerebral (see also Disease, cerebrovascular,
    acute) 436
  cerebrovascular (current) (CVA) (see also
    Disease, cerebrovascular, acute) 436
    healed or old—see also category 438
      without residuals V12.5
    impending 435.9
    late effect—see category 438
  coronary (see also Infarct, myocardium) 410.9
  craniovascular (see also Disease,
    cerebrovascular, acute) 436
  during pregnancy, to mother
    affecting fetus or newborn 760.5
  heart, cardiac (see also Infarct, myocardium)
    410.9

Accident, accidental—*continued*
 intrauterine 779.8
 vascular—*see* Disease, cerebrovascular, acute
Accommodation
 disorder of 367.51
  drug-induced 367.89
  toxic 367.89
 insufficiency of 367.4
 paralysis of 367.51
  hysterical 300.11
 spasm of 367.53
Accouchement —*see* Delivery
Accreta placenta (without hemorrhage) 667.0
 with hemorrhage 666.0
Accretio cordis (nonrheumatic) 423.1
Accretions on teeth 523.6
Accumulation secretion, prostate 602.8
Acephalia, acephalism, acephaly 740.0
Acephalic monster 740.0
Acephalobrachia monster 759.89
Acephalocardia 759.89
Acephalocardius 759.89
Acephalochiria 759.89
Acephalochirus monster 759.89
Acephalogaster 759.89
Acephalostomus monster 759.89
Acephalothorax 759.89
Acephalus 740.0
Acetonemia 790.6
 diabetic 250.1
Acetonglycosuria 982.8
Acetonuria 791.6
Achalasia 530.0
 cardia 530.0
 digestive organs congenital NEC 751.8
 esophagus 530.0
 pelvirectal 751.3
 psychogenic 306.4
 pylorus 750.5
 sphincteral NEC 564.8
Achard-Thiers syndrome (adrenogenital) 255.2
Ache (s)—*see* Pain
Acheilia 750.26
Acheiria 755.21
Achillobursitis 726.71
Achillodynia 726.71
Achlorhydria, achlorhydric 536.0
 anemia 280.9
 diarrhea 536.0
 neurogenic 536.0
 postvagotomy 564.2
 psychogenic 306.4
 secondary to vagotomy 564.2
Achloroblepsia 368.52
Achloropsia 368.52
Acholia 575.8
Acholuric jaundice (familial) (splenomegalic)
  (*see also* Spherocytosis) 282.0
 acquired 283.9
Achondroplasia 756.4
Achrestic anemia 281.8
Achroacytosis, lacrimal gland 375.00
 tuberculous (*see also* Tuberculosis) 017.3
Achroma, cutis 709.00
Achromate (congenital) 368.54
Achromatopia 368.54
Achromatopsia (congenital) 368.54
Achromia
 congenital 270.2
 parasitica 111.0
 unguium 703.8

Achylia
 gastrica 536.8
  neurogenic 536.3
  psychogenic 306.4
 pancreatica 577.1
Achylosis 536.8
Acid
 burn—*see also* Burn, by site
  from swallowing acid—*see* Burn, internal
   organs
 deficiency
  amide nicotinic 265.2
  amino 270.9
  ascorbic 267
  folic 266.2
  nicotinic (amide) 265.2
  pantothenic 266.2
 intoxication 276.2
 peptic disease 536.8
 stomach 536.8
  psychogenic 306.4
Acidemia 276.2
 arginosuccinic 270.6
 fetal—*see* Distress, fetal
 pipecolic 270.7
Acidity, gastric (high) (low) 536.8
 psychogenic 306.4
Acidocytopenia 288.0
Acidocytosis 288.3
Acidopenia 288.0
Acidosis 276.2
 diabetic 250.1
 fetal—*see also* Distress, fetal
  affecting management of pregnancy 656.3
 intrauterine—*see* Distress, fetal
 kidney tubular 588.8
 lactic 276.2
 metabolic NEC 276.2
  with respiratory acidosis 276.4
  late, of newborn 775.7
 renal
  hyperchloremic 588.8
  tubular (distal) (proximal) 588.8
 respiratory 276.2
  complicated by
   metabolic acidosis 276.4
   metabolic alkalosis 276.4
Aciduria 791.9
 arginosuccinic 270.6
 beta-aminoisobutyric (BAIB) 277.2
 glycolic 271.8
 organic 270.9
 orotic (congenital) (hereditary) (pyrimidine
  deficiency) 281.4
Acladiosis 111.8
 skin 111.8
Aclasis
 diaphyseal 756.4
 tarsoepiphyseal 756.59
Acleistocardia 745.5
Aclusion 524.4
Acmesthesia 782.0
Acne (pustular) (vulgaris) 706.1
 agminata (*see also* Tuberculosis) 017.0
 artificialis 706.1
 atrophica 706.0
 cachecticorum (Hebra) 706.1
 conglobata 706.1
 conjunctiva 706.1
 cystic 706.1
 decalvans 704.09

Adactylia, adactyly—*continued*
    meaning all digits (complete) (partial) 755.31
    transverse (complete) (partial) 755.31
    upper limb (complete) (intercalary) (partial)
        (terminal) (*see also* Deformity, reduction,
        upper limb) 755.29
    meaning all digits (complete) (partial) 755.21
    transverse (complete) (partial) 755.21
Adair-Dighton syndrome (brittle bones and blue
    sclera, deafness) 756.51
Adamantinoblastoma (M9310/0)—*see*
    Ameloblastoma
Adamantinoma (M9310/0)—*see* Ameloblastoma
Adamantoblastoma (M9310/0)—*see*
    Ameloblastoma
Adams-Stokes (-Morgagni) disease or syndrome
    (syncope with heart block) 426.9
Adaptation reaction (*see also* Reaction,
    adjustment) 309.9
Addiction—*see also* **Dependence**
    absinthe 304.6
    alcoholic (ethyl) (methyl) (wood) 303.9
        complicating pregnancy, childbirth, or
            puerperium 648.4
            affecting fetus or newborn 760.71
        suspected damage to fetus affecting
            management of pregnancy 655.4
    drug (*see also* Dependence) 304.9
    ethyl alcohol 303.9
    heroin 304.0
    hospital 301.51
    methyl alcohol 303.9
    methylated spirit 303.9
    morphine (-like substances) 304.0
    nicotine 305.1
    opium 304.0
    tobacco 305.1
    wine 303.9
Addison's
    anemia (pernicious) 281.0
    disease (bronze) (primary adrenal insufficiency)
        255.4
        tuberculous (*see also* Tuberculosis) 017.6
    keloid (morphea) 701.0
    melanoderma (adrenal cortical hypofunction)
        255.4
Addison-Biermer anemia (pernicious) 281.0
Addison-Gull disease —*see* Xanthoma
Addisonian crisis or melanosis (acute
    adrenocortical insufficiency) 255.4
Additional —*see also* Accessory
    chromosome(s) 758.5
        13-15 758.1
        16-18 758.2
        21 758.0
        autosome(s) NEC 758.5
        sex 758.81
Adduction contracture, hip or other joint
    —*see* Contraction, joint
Adenasthenia gastrica 536.0
Aden fever 061
Adenitis (*see also* Lymphadenitis) 289.3
    acute, unspecified site 683
        epidemic infectious 075
    axillary 289.3
        acute 683
        chronic or subacute 289.1
    Bartholin's gland 616.8
    bulbourethral gland (*see also* Urethritis) 597.89

Adenitis—*continued*
    cervical 289.3
        acute 683
        chronic or subacute 289.1
    chancroid (Ducrey's bacillus) 099.0
    chronic (any lymph node, except mesenteric)
        289.1
        mesenteric 289.2
    Cowper's gland (*see also* Urethritis) 597.89
    epidemic, acute 075
    gangrenous 683
    gonorrheal NEC 098.89
    groin 289.3
        acute 683
        chronic or subacute 289.1
    infectious 075
    inguinal (region) 289.3
        acute 683
        chronic or subacute 289.1
    lymph gland or node, except mesenteric 289.3
        acute 683
        chronic or subacute 289.1
        mesenteric (acute) (chronic) (nonspecific)
            (subacute) 289.2
    mesenteric (acute) (chronic) (nonspecific)
        (subacute) 289.2
    due to Pasteurella multocida (P. septica) 027.2
    parotid gland (suppurative) 527.2
    phlegmonous 683
    salivary duct or gland (any) (recurring)
        (suppurative) 527.2
    scrofulous (*see also* Tuberculosis) 017.2
    septic 289.3
    Skene's duct or gland (*see also* Urethritis)
        597.89
    strumous, tuberculous (*see also* Tuberculosis)
        017.2
    subacute, unspecified site 289.1
    sublingual gland (suppurative) 527.2
    submandibular gland (suppurative) 527.2
    submaxillary gland (suppurative) 527.2
    suppurative 683
    tuberculous—*see* Tuberculosis, lymph gland
    urethral gland (*see also* Urethritis) 597.89
    venereal NEC 099.8
    Wharton's duct (suppurative) 527.2
Adenoacanthoma (M8570/3)—*see* Neoplasm,
    by site, malignant
Adenoameloblastoma (M9300/0) 213.1
    upper jaw (bone) 213.0
Adenocarcinoma (M8140/3)—*see also*
    Neoplasm, by site, malignant

Note—The list of adjectival modifiers below is
not exhaustive. A description of
adenocarcinoma that does not appear in this list
should be coded in the same manner as
carcinoma with that description. Thus, "mixed
acidophil-basophil adenocarcinoma," should be
coded in the same manner as "mixed
acidophil-basophil carcinoma," which appears
in the list under "Carcinoma."

Except where otherwise indicated, the
morphological varieties of adenocarcinoma in
the list below should be coded by site as for
"Neoplasm, malignant."

---

    with
        apocrine metaplasia (M8573/3)
        cartilaginous (and osseous) metaplasia
            (M8571/3)

Adenocarcinoma—*continued*
  osseous (and cartilaginous) metaplasia
      (M8571/3)
    spindle cell metaplasia (M8572/3)
    squamous metaplasia (M8570/3)
  acidophil (M8280/3)
    specified site—*see* Neoplasm, by site,
        malignant
    unspecified site 194.3
  acinar (M8550/3)
  acinic cell (M8550/3)
  adrenal cortical (M8370/3) 194.0
  alveolar (M8251/3)
  and
    epidermoid carcinoma, mixed (M8560/3)
    squamous cell carcinoma, mixed (M8560/3)
  apocrine (M8401/3)
    breast—*see* Neoplasm, breast, malignant
    specified site NEC—*see* Neoplasm, skin,
        malignant
    unspecified site 173.9
  basophil (M8300/3)
    specified site—*see* Neoplasm, by site,
        malignant
    unspecified site 194.3
  bile duct type (M8160/3)
    liver 155.1
    specified site NEC—*see* Neoplasm, by site,
        malignant
    unspecified site 155.1
  bronchiolar (M8250/3)—*see* Neoplasm, lung,
      malignant
  ceruminous (M8420/3) 173.2
  chromophobe (M8270/3)
    specified site—*see* Neoplasm, by site,
        malignant
    unspecified site 194.3
  clear cell (mesonephroid type) (M8310/3)
  colloid (M8480/3)
  cylindroid type (M8200/3)
  diffuse type (M8145/3)
    specified site—*see* Neoplasm, by site,
        malignant
    unspecified site 151.9
  duct (infiltrating) (M8500/3)
    with Paget's disease (M8541/3)—*see*
        Neoplasm, breast, malignant
    specified site—*see* Neoplasm, by site,
        malignant
    unspecified site 174.9
  embryonal (M9070/3)
  endometrioid (M8380/3)—*see* Neoplasm, by
      site, malignant
  eosinophil (M8280/3)
    specified site—*see* Neoplasm, by site,
        malignant
    unspecified site 194.3
  follicular (M8330/3)
    and papillary (M8340/3) 193
    moderately differentiated type (M8332/3) 193
    pure follicle type (M8331/3) 193
    specified site—*see* Neoplasm, by site,
        malignant
    trabecular type (M8332/3) 193
    unspecified type 193
    well differentiated type (M8331/3) 193
  gelatinous (M8480/3)
  granular cell (M8320/3)
  Hürthle cell (M8290/3) 193

Adenocarcinoma—*continued*
  in
    adenomatous
      polyp (M8210/3)
      polyposis coli (M8220/3) 153.9
    polypoid adenoma (M8210/3)
    tubular adenoma (M8210/3)
    villous adenoma (M8261/3)
  infiltrating duct (M8500/3)
    with Paget's disease (M8541/3)—*see*
        Neoplasm, breast, malignant
    specified site—*see* Neoplasm, by site,
        malignant
    unspecified site 174.9
  inflammatory (M8530/3)
    specified site—*see* Neoplasm, by site,
        malignant
    unspecified site 174.9
  in situ (M8140/2)—*see* Neoplasm, by site, in
      situ
  intestinal type (M8144/3)
    specified site—*see* Neoplasm, by site,
        malignant
    unspecified site 151.9
  intraductal (noninfiltrating) (M8500/2)
    papillary (M8503/2)
      specified site—*see* Neoplasm, by site, in situ
      unspecified site 233.0
    specified site—*see* Neoplasm, by site, in situ
    unspecified site 233.0
  islet cell (M8150/3)
    and exocrine, mixed (M8154/3)
      specified site—*see* Neoplasm, by site,
          malignant
      unspecified site 157.9
    pancreas 157.4
    specified site NEC—*see* Neoplasm, by site,
        malignant
    unspecified site 157.4
  lobular (M8520/3)
    specified site—*see* Neoplasm, by site,
        malignant
    unspecified site 174.9
  medullary (M8510/3)
  mesonephric (M9110/3)
  mixed cell (M8323/3)
  mucinous (M8480/3)
  mucin-producing (M8481/3)
  mucoid (M8480/3)—*see also* Neoplasm, by
      site, malignant
    cell (M8300/3)
      specified site—*see* Neoplasm, by site,
          malignant
      unspecified site 194.3
  nonencapsulated sclerosing (M8350/3) 193
  oncocytic (M8290/3)
  oxyphilic (M8290/3)
  papillary (M8260/3)
    and follicular (M8340/3) 193
    intraductal (noninfiltrating) (M8503/2)
      specified site—*see* Neoplasm, by site, in situ
      unspecified site 233.0
    serous (M8460/3)
      specified site—*see* Neoplasm, by site,
          malignant
      unspecified site 183.0
  papillocystic (M8450/3)
    specified site—*see* Neoplasm, by site,
        malignant
    unspecified site 183.0
  pseudomucinous (M8470/3)

Adenocarcinoma—*continued*
  specified site—*see* Neoplasm, by site,
    malignant
    unspecified site 183.0
  renal cell (M8312/3) 189.0
  sebaceous (M8410/3)
  serous (M8441/3)—*see also* Neoplasm, by site,
    malignant
  papillary
    specified site—*see* Neoplasm, by site,
      malignant
    unspecified site 183.0
  signet ring cell (M8490/3)
  superficial spreading (M8143/3)
  sweat gland (M8400/3)—*see* Neoplasm, skin,
    malignant
  trabecular (M8190/3)
  tubular (M8211/3)
  villous (M8262/3)
  water-clear cell (M8322/3) 194.1
Adenofibroma (M9013/0)
  clear cell (M8313/0)—*see* Neoplasm, by site,
    benign
  endometrioid (M8381/0) 220
    borderline malignancy (M8381/1) 236.2
    malignant (M8381/3) 183.0
  mucinous (M9015/0)
    specified site—*see* Neoplasm, by site, benign
    unspecified site 220
  prostate 600
  serous (M9014/0)
    specified site—*see* Neoplasm, by site, benign
    unspecified site 220
  specified site—*see* Neoplasm, by site, benign
  unspecified site 220
Adenofibrosis
  breast 610.2
  endometrioid 617.0
Adenoiditis 474.0
  acute 463
Adenoids (congenital) (of nasal fossa) 474.9
  hypertrophy 474.12
  vegetations 474.2
Adenolipomatosis (symmetrical) 272.8
Adenolymphoma (M8561/0)
  specified site—*see* Neoplasm, by site, benign
  unspecified 210.2
Adenoma (sessile) (M8140/0)—*see also*
  Neoplasm, by site, benign

Note—Except where otherwise indicated, the
morphological varieties of adenoma in the list
below should be coded by site as for
"Neoplasm, benign."

---

  acidophil (M8280/0)
    specified site—*see* Neoplasm, by site, benign
    unspecified site 227.3
  acinar (cell) (M8550/0)
  acinic cell (M8550/0)
  adrenal (cortex) (cortical) (functioning)
    (M8370/0) 227.0
    clear cell type (M8373/0) 227.0
    compact cell type (M8371/0) 227.0
    glomerulosa cell type (M8374/0) 227.0
    heavily pigmented variant (M8372/0) 227.0
    mixed cell type (M8375/0) 227.0
  alpha cell (M8152/0)
    pancreas 211.7
    specified site NEC—*see* Neoplasm, by site,
      benign
    unspecified site 211.7

Adenoma—*continued*
  alveolar (M8251/0)
  apocrine (M8401/0)
    breast 217
    specified site NEC—*see* Neoplasm, skin,
      benign
    unspecified site 216.9
  basal cell (M8147/0)
  basophil (M8300/0)
    specified site—*see* Neoplasm, by site, benign
    unspecified site 227.3
  beta cell (M8151/0)
    pancreas 211.7
    specified site NEC—*see* Neoplasm, by site,
      benign
    unspecified site 211.7
  bile duct (M8160/0) 211.5
  black (M8372/0) 227.0
  bronchial (M8140/1) 235.7
    carcinoid type (M8240/3)—*see* Neoplasm,
      lung, malignant
    cylindroid type (M8200/3)—*see* Neoplasm,
      lung, malignant
  ceruminous (M8420/0) 216.2
  chief cell (M8321/0) 227.1
  chromophobe (M8270/0)
    (specified site—*see* Neoplasm, by site, benign
    unspecified site 227.3
  clear cell (M8310/0)
  colloid (M8334/0)
    specified site—*see* Neoplasm, by site, benign
    unspecified site 226
  cylindroid type, bronchus (M8200/3)—*see*
    Neoplasm, lung, malignant
  duct (M8503/0)
  embryonal (M8191/0)
  endocrine, multiple (M8360/1)
    single specified site—*see* Neoplasm, by site,
      uncertain behavior
    two or more specified sites 237.4
    unspecified site 237.4
  endometrioid (M8380/0)—*see also* Neoplasm,
    by site, benign
    borderline malignancy (M8380/1)—*see*
      Neoplasm, by site, uncertain behavior
  eosinophil (M8280/0)
    specified site—*see* Neoplasm, by site, benign
    unspecified site 227.3
  fetal (M8333/0)
    specified site—*see* Neoplasm, by site, benign
    unspecified site 226
  follicular (M8330/0)
    specified site—*see* Neoplasm, by site, benign
    unspecified site 226
  hepatocellular (M8170/0) 211.5
  Hürthle cell (M8290/0) 226
  intracystic papillary (M8504/0)
  islet cell (functioning) (M8150/0)
    pancreas 211.7
    specified site NEC—*see* Neoplasm, by site,
      benign
    unspecified site 211.7
  liver cell (M8170/0) 211.5
  macrofollicular (M8334/0)
    specified site NEC—*see* Neoplasm, by site,
      benign
    unspecified site 226
  malignant, malignum (M8140/3)—*see*
    Neoplasm, by site, malignant
  mesonephric (M9110/0)

Adenoma—*continued*
microfollicular (M8333/0)
 specified site—*see* Neoplasm, by site, benign
 unspecified site 226
mixed cell (M8323/0)
monomorphic (M8146/0)
mucinous (M8480/0)
mucoid cell (M8300/0)
 specified site—*see* Neoplasm, by site, benign
 unspecified site 227.3
multiple endocrine (M8360/1)
 single specified site—*see* Neoplasm, by site,
  uncertain behavior
 two or more specified sites 237.4
 unspecified site 237.4
nipple (M8506/0) 217
oncocytic (M8290/0)
oxyphilic (M8290/0)
papillary (M8260/0)—*see also* Neoplasm, by
 site, benign
 intracystic (M8504/0)
papillotubular (M8263/0)
Pick's tubular (M8640/0)
 specified site—*see* Neoplasm, by site, benign
 unspecified site
  female 220
  male 222.0
pleomorphic (M8940/0)
polypoid (M8210/0)
prostate (benign) 600
rete cell 222.0
sebaceous, sebaceum (gland) (senile)
 (M8410/0)—*see also* Neoplasm, skin,
 benign
 disseminata 759.5
Sertoli cell (M8640/0)
 specified site—*see* Neoplasm, by site, benign
 unspecified site
  female 220
  male 222.0
skin appendage (M8390/0)—*see* Neoplasm,
 skin, benign
sudoriferous gland (M8400/0)—*see* Neoplasm,
 skin, benign
sweat gland or duct (M8400/0)—*see* Neoplasm,
 skin, benign
testicular (M8640/0)
 specified site—*see* Neoplasm, by site, benign
 unspecified site
  female 220
  male 222.0
thyroid 226
trabecular (M8190/0)
tubular (M8211/0)—*see also* Neoplasm, by site,
 benign
 papillary (M8460/3)
 Pick's (M8640/0)
 specified site—*see* Neoplasm, by site,
  benign
 unspecified site
  female 220
  male 222.0
tubulovillous (M8263/0)
villoglandular (M8263/0)
villous (M8261/1)—*see* Neoplasm, by site,
 uncertain behavior
water-clear cell (M8322/0) 227.1
wolffian duct (M9110/0)

Adenomatosis (M8220/0)
endocrine (multiple) (M8360/1)
 single specified site—*see* Neoplasm, by site,
  uncertain behavior
 two or more specified sites 237.4
 unspecified site 237.4
erosive of nipple (M8506/0) 217
pluriendocrine—*see* Adenomatosis, endocrine
pulmonary (M8250/1) 235.7
 malignant (M8250/3)—*see* Neoplasm, lung,
  malignant
specified site—*see* Neoplasm, by site, benign
unspecified site 211.3
Adenomatous
cyst, thyroid (gland)—*see* Goiter, nodular
goiter (nontoxic) (*see also* Goiter, nodular)
 241.9
toxic or with hyperthyroidism 242.3
Adenomyoma (M8932/0)—*see also* Neoplasm,
 by site, benign
 prostate 600
Adenomyometritis 617.0
Adenomyosis (uterus) (internal) 617.0
Adenopathy (lymph gland) 785.6
inguinal 785.6
mediastinal 785.6
mesentery 785.6
syphilitic (secondary) 091.4
tracheobronchial 785.6
 tuberculous (*see also* Tuberculosis) 012.1
  primary, progressive 010.8
tuberculous (*see also* Tuberculosis, lymph
 gland) 017.2
 tracheobronchial 012.1
  primary, progressive 010.8
Adenopharyngitis 462
Adenophlegmon 683
Adenosalpingitis 614.1
Adenosarcoma (M8960/3) 189.0
Adenosclerosis 289.3
Adenosis
breast (sclerosing) 610.2
vagina, congenital 752.49
Adentia (complete) (partial) (*see also* Absence,
 teeth) 520.0
Adherent
labium (minus) 624.4
pericardium (nonrheumatic) 423.1
 rheumatic 393
placenta 667.0
 with hemorrhage 666.0
prepuce 605
scar (skin) NEC 709.2
tendon in scar 709.2
**Adhesion(s), adhesive (postinfection)(postop-
 erative)**
abdominal (wall) (*see also* Adhesions,
 peritoneum) 568.0
amnion to fetus 658.8
 affecting fetus or newborn 762.8
appendix 543.9
arachnoiditis—*see* Meningitis
auditory tube (Eustachian) 381.89
bands—*see also* Adhesions, peritoneum
 cervix 622.3
 uterus 621.5
bile duct (any) 576.8
bladder (sphincter) 596.8
bowel (*see also* Adhesions, peritoneum) 568.0
cardiac 423.1
 rheumatic 398.99

Adhesion—*continued*
  postoperative (gastrointestinal tract) *(See also*
      Adhesions, peritoneum) 568.0
    eyelid 997.9
      surgically created V45.6
    urethra 598.2
  postpartal, old 624.4
  preputial, prepuce 605
  pulmonary 511.0
  pylorus *(see also* Adhesions, peritoneum) 568.0
  Rosenmüller's fossa 478.29
  sciatic nerve 355.0
  seminal vesicle 608.89
  shoulder (joint) 726.0
  sigmoid flexure *(see also* Adhesions,
      peritoneum) 568.0
  spermatic cord (acquired) 608.89
    congenital 752.8
  spinal canal 349.2
    nerve 355.9
      root 724.9
        cervical NEC 723.4
        lumbar NEC 724.4
        lumbosacral 724.4
        thoracic 724.4
  stomach *(see also* Adhesions, peritoneum) 568.0
  subscapular 726.2
  tendonitis 726.90
    shoulder 726.0
  testicle 608.89
  tongue (congenital) (to gum or roof of mouth)
      750.12
    acquired 529.8
  trachea 519.1
  tubo-ovarian 614.6
  tunica vaginalis 608.89
  ureter 593.89
  uterus 621.5
    to abdominal wall 621.5
      in pregnancy or childbirth 654.4
        affecting fetus or newborn 763.8
  vagina (chronic) (postoperative) (postradiation)
      623.2
  vaginitis (congenital) 752.49
  vesical 596.8
  vitreous 379.29
Adie (-Holmes) syndrome (tonic pupillary
      reaction) 379.46
Adiponecrosis neonatorum 778.1
Adiposa dolorosa 272.8
Adiposalgia 272.8
Adiposis 278.0
  cerebralis 253.8
  dolorosa 272.8
  tuberosa simplex 272.8
Adiposity 278.0
  heart *(see also* Degeneration, myocardial) 429.1
  localized 278.1
Adiposogenital dystrophy 253.8
Adjustment
  prosthesis or other device—*see* Fitting of
  reaction—*see* Reaction, adjustment
Administration, prophylactic
  antibiotics V07.39
  antitoxin, any V07.2
  antivenin V07.2
  chemotherapeutic agent NEC V07.39
  chemotherapy NEC V07.39
  diphtheria antitoxin V07.2
  fluoride V07.31
  gamma globulin V07.2

Administration, prophylactic—*continued*
  immune sera (gamma globulin) V07.2
  passive immunization agent V07.2
  RhoGAM V07.2
Admission (encounter)
  as organ donor—*see* Donor
  by mistake V68.9
  for
    adjustment (of)
      artificial
        arm (complete) (partial) V52.0
        eye V52.2
        leg (complete) (partial) V52.1
      brain neuropacemaker V53.0
      breast
        implant V50.1
        prosthesis V52.4
      cardiac device V53.39
        defibrillator, automatic implantable V53.32
        pacemaker V53.31
          carotid sinus V53.39
      catheter
        non-vascular V58.82
        vascular V58.81
      colostomy belt V53.5
      contact lenses V53.1
      cystostomy device V53.6
      dental prosthesis V52.3
      device NEC V53.9
        abdominal V53.5
        cardiac V53.39
          defibrillator, automatic implantable
              V53.32
          pacemaker V53.31
            carotid sinus V53.39
        intrauterine contraceptive V25.1
        nervous system V53.0
        orthodontic V53.4
        prosthetic V52.9
          breast V52.4
          dental V52.3
          eye V52.2
          specified type NEC V52.8
        special senses V53.0
        substitution
          auditory V53.0
          nervous system V53.0
          visual V53.0
        urinary V53.6
      dialysis catheter (extracorporeal)
          (peritoneal) V56.1
      diaphragm (contraceptive) V25.02
      hearing aid V53.2
      ileostomy device V53.5
      intestinal appliance or device NEC V53.5
      intrauterine contraceptive device V25.1
      neuropacemaker (brain) (peripheral nerve)
          (spinal cord) V53.0
      orthodontic device V53.4
      orthopedic (device) V53.7
        brace V53.7
        cast V53.7
        shoes V53.7
      pacemaker
        brain V53.0
        cardiac V53.31
          carotid sinus V53.39
        peripheral nerve V53.0
        spinal cord V53.0

Admission—*continued*

peritoneal V56.8
renal V56.0
dietary surveillance and counseling V65.3
ear piercing V50.3
elective surgery V50.9
  breast
    augmentation or reduction V50.1
    removal, prophylactic V50.41
  circumcision, ritual or routine (in absence of
    medical indication) V50.2
  cosmetic NEC V50.1
    following healed injury or operation V51
  ear piercing V50.3
  face-lift V50.1
  hair transplant V50.0
  plastic
    cosmetic NEC V50.1
    following healed injury or operation V51
  prophylactic organ removal V50.49
    breast V50.41
    ovary V50.42
  repair of scarred tissue (following healed
    injury or operation) V51
  specified type NEC V50.8
end-of-life care V66.7
examination (*see also* Examination) V70.9
  administrative purpose NEC V70.3
  adoption V70.3
  allergy V72.7
  at health care facility V70.0
  athletic team V70.3
  camp V70.3
  cardiovascular, preoperative V72.81
  clinical research investigation V70.7
  dental V72.2
  developmental testing (child) (infant) V20.2
  donor (potential) V70.8
  driver's license V70.3
  ear V72.1
  employment V70.5
  eye V72.0
  follow-up (routine)—*see* Examination,
    follow-up
  for admission to
    old age home V70.3
    school V70.3
  general V70.9
    specified reason NEC V70.8
  gynecological V72.3
  health supervision (child) (infant) V20.2
  hearing V72.1
  immigration V70.3
  insurance certification V70.3
  laboratory V72.6
  marriage license V70.3
  medical (general) (*see also* Examination,
    medical) V70.9
  medicolegal reasons V70.4
  naturalization V70.3
  pelvic (annual) (periodic) V72.3
  postpartum checkup V24.2
  pregnancy (possible) (unconfirmed) V72.4
  preoperative V72.84
    cardiovascular V72.81
    respiratory V72.82
    specified NEC V72.83
  prison V70.3
  psychiatric (general) V70.2
    requested by authority V70.1
  radiological NEC V72.5

Admission—*continued*

  respiratory, preoperative V72.82
  school V70.3
  screening—*see* Screening
  skin hypersensitivity V72.7
  specified type NEC V72.85
  sport competition V70.3
  vision V72.0
  well baby and child care V20.2
exercise therapy V57.1
face-lift, cosmetic reason V50.1
fitting (of)
  artificial
    arm (complete) (partial) V52.0
    eye V52.2
    leg (complete) (partial) V52.1
  brain neuropacemaker V53.0
  breast V52.4
    implant V50.1
    prosthesis V52.4
  cardiac pacemaker V53.31
  catheter
    non-vascular V58.82
    vascular V58.81
  colostomy belt V53.5
  contact lenses V53.1
  cystostomy device V53.6
  dental prosthesis V52.3
  device NEC V53.9
    abdominal V53.5
    intrauterine contraceptive V25.1
    nervous system V53.0
    orthodontic V53.4
    prosthetic V52.9
      breast V52.4
      dental V52.3
      eye V52.2
    special senses V53.0
    substitution
      auditory V53.0
      nervous system V53.0
      visual V53.0
  diaphragm (contraceptive) V25.02
  hearing aid V53.2
  ileostomy device V53.5
  intestinal appliance or device NEC V53.5
  intrauterine contraceptive device V25.1
  neuropacemaker (brain) (peripheral nerve)
    (spinal cord) V53.0
  orthodontic device V53.4
  orthopedic (device) V53.7
    brace V53.7
    cast V53.7
    shoes V53.7
  pacemaker
    brain V53.0
    cardiac V53.31
    carotid sinus V53.39
    spinal cord V53.0
  prosthesis V52.9
    arm (complete) (partial) V52.0
    breast V52.4
    dental V52.3
    eye V52.2
    leg (complete) (partial) V52.1
    specified type NEC V52.8
  spectacles V53.1
  wheelchair V53.8
follow-up examination (routine) (following)
  V67.9
  cancer chemotherapy V67.2

Admission—*continued*
 chemotherapy V67.2
  high-risk medication NEC V67.51
  injury NEC V67.59
  psychiatric V67.3
  psychotherapy V67.3
  radiotherapy V67.1
  surgery V67.0
  treatment (for) V67.9
   combined V67.6
   fracture V67.4
   involving high-risk medication NEC
    V67.51
   mental disorder V67.3
   specified NEC V67.59
 hair transplant, for cosmetic reason V50.0
 health advice, education, or instruction V65.4
 hospice care V66.7
 insertion (of)
  subdermal implantable contraceptive V25.5
 intrauterine device
  insertion V25.1
  management V25.42
 investigation to determine further disposition
  V63.8
 isolation V07.0
 issue of
  medical certificate NEC V68.0
  repeat prescription NEC V68.1
   contraceptive device NEC V25.49
 kidney dialysis V56.0
 mental health evaluation V70.2
  requested by authority V70.1
 nonmedical reason NEC V68.89
 nursing care evaluation V63.8
 observation (without need for further medical
  care) (*see also* Observation) V71.9
  accident V71.4
  alleged rape or seduction V71.5
  criminal assault V71.6
  following accident V71.4
   at work V71.3
  foreign body ingestion V71.8
  growth and development variations,
   childhood V21.0
  inflicted injury NEC V71.6
  ingestion of deleterious agent or foreign
   body V71.8
  injury V71.6
  malignant neoplasm V71.1
  mental disorder V71.09
  newborn—*see* Observation, suspected
   condition, newborn
  rape V71.5
  specified NEC V71.8
  suspected disorder V71.9
   accident V71.4
    at work V71.3
   benign neoplasm V71.8
   cardiovascular V71.7
   heart V71.7
   inflicted injury NEC V71.6
   malignant neoplasm V71.1
   mental NEC V71.09
   specified condition NEC V71.8
   tuberculosis V71.2
  tuberculosis V71.2
 occupational therapy V57.21
 organ transplant, donor—*see* Donor
 ovary, ovarian removal, prophylactic V50.42
 palliative care V66.7

Admission—*continued*
 Papanicolaou smear, cervix V76.2
  for suspected malignant neoplasm V76.2
  no disease found V71.1
  routine, as part of gynecological
   examination V72.3
 passage of sounds or bougie in artificial
  opening—*see* Attention to, artificial,
  opening
 peritoneal dialysis V56.8
 physical therapy NEC V57.1
 plastic surgery
  cosmetic NEC V50.1
  following healed injury or operation V51
 postmenopausal hormone replacement therapy
  V07.4
 postpartum observation
  immediately after delivery V24.0
  routine follow-up V24.2
 poststerilization (for restoration) V26.0
 procreative management V26.9
  specified type NEC V26.8
 prophylactic
  administration of
   antibiotics V07.39
   antitoxin, any V07.2
   antivenin V07.2
   chemotherapeutic agent NEC V07.39
   chemotherapy NEC V07.39
   diphtheria antitoxin V07.2
   fluoride V07.31
   gamma globulin V07.2
   immune sera (gamma globulin) V07.2
   RhoGAM V07.2
   tetanus antitoxin V07.2
  breathing exercises V57.0
  chemotherapy NEC V07.39
  fluoride V07.31
  measure V07.9
   specified type NEC V07.8
  organ removal V50.49
   breast V50.41
   ovary V50.42
 psychiatric examination (general) V70.2
  requested by authority V70.1
 radiation management V58.0
 radiotherapy V58.0
 reforming of artificial opening—*see* Attention
  to, artificial, opening
 rehabilitation V57.9
  multiple types V57.89
  occupational V57.21
  orthoptic V57.4
  orthotic V57.81
  physical NEC V57.1
  specified type NEC V57.89
  speech V57.3
  vocational V57.22
 removal of
  cardiac pacemaker V53.31
  cast (plaster) V54.8
  catheter from artificial opening—*see*
   Attention to, artificial, opening
  cystostomy catheter V55.5
  device
   fixation
    external V54.8
    internal V54.0
   intrauterine contraceptive V25.42
   traction, external V54.8
  dressing V58.3

Admission—*continued*
  fixation device
    external V54.8
    internal V54.0
  intrauterine contraceptive device V25.42
  Kirschner wire V54.8
  neuropacemaker (brain) (peripheral nerve)
    (spinal cord) V53.0
  orthopedic fixation device
    external V54.8
    internal V54.0
  pacemaker device
    brain V53.0
    cardiac V53.31
    carotid sinus V53.39
    nervous system V53.0
  plaster cast V54.8
  plate (fracture) V54.0
  rod V54.0
  screw (fracture) V54.0
  splint, traction V54.8
  Steinmann pin V54.8
  subdermal implantable contraceptive V25.43
  surgical dressing V58.3
  sutures V58.3
  traction device, external V54.8
  ureteral stent V53.6
  repair of scarred tissue (following healed
    injury or operation) V51
  reprogramming of cardiac pacemaker V53.31
  restoration of organ continuity
    (poststerilization) (tuboplasty)
    (vasoplasty) V26.0
  sensitivity test—*see also* Test, skin
    allergy NEC V72.7
    bacterial disease NEC V74.9
    Dick V74.8
    Kveim V82.8
    Mantoux V74.1
    mycotic infection NEC V75.4
    parasitic disease NEC V75.8
    Schick V74.3
    Schultz-Charlton V74.8
  social service (agency) referral or evaluation
    V63.8
  speech therapy V57.3
  sterilization V25.2
  suspected disorder (ruled out) (without need
    for further care)—*see* Observation
  terminal care V66.7
  tests only—*see* Test
  therapy
    blood transfusion, without reported
      diagnosis V58.2
    breathing exercises V57.0
    chemotherapy V58.1
      prophylactic NEC V07.39
        fluoride V07.31
    dialysis (intermittent) (treatment)
      extracorporeal V56.0
      peritoneal V56.8
      renal V56.0
      specified type NEC V56.8
    exercise (remedial) NEC V57.1
      breathing V57.0
    long-term (current) drug use NEC V58.69
      anticoagulant V58.61
    occupational V57.21
    orthoptic V57.4
    physical NEC V57.1
    radiation V58.0

Admission—*continued*
  speech V57.3
  vocational V57.22
  toilet or cleaning
    of artificial opening — *see* Attention to,
      artificial, opening
    of non-vascular catheter V58.82
    of vascular catheter V58.81
  tubal ligation V25.2
  tuboplasty for previous sterilization V26.0
  vaccination, prophylactic (against)
    arthropod-borne virus, viral NEC V05.1
      disease NEC V05.1
      encephalitis V05.0
    Bacille Calmette Guérin (BCG) V03.2
    BCG V03.2
    chickenpox V05.4
    cholera alone V03.0
      with typhoid-paratyphoid (cholera + TAB)
        V06.0
    common cold V04.7
    dengue V05.1
    diphtheria alone V03.5
    diphtheria-tetanus [Td] without pertussis
      V06.5
    diphtheria-tetanus-pertussis (DTP) V06.1
      with
        poliomyelitis (DTP + polio) V06.3
        typhoid-paratyphoid (DTP + TAB)
          V06.2
    disease (single) NEC V05.9
      bacterial NEC V03.9
        specified type NEC V03.89
      combinations NEC V06.9
        specified type NEC V06.8
      specified type NEC V05.8
    encephalitis, viral, arthropod-borne V05.0
    Hemophilus influenzae, type B [Hib] V03.81
    hepatitis, viral V05.3
    immune sera (gamma globulin) V07.2
    influenza V04.8
      with
        Streptococcus pneumoniae
          [pneumococcus] V06.6
    Leishmaniasis V05.2
    measles alone V04.2
    measles-mumps-rubella (MMR) V06.4
    mumps alone V04.6
      with measles and rubella (MMR) V06.4
    not done because of contraindication V64.0
    pertussis alone V03.6
    plague V03.3
    poliomyelitis V04.0
      with diphtheria-tetanus-pertussis (DTP +
        polio) V06.3
    rabies V04.5
    rubella alone V04.3
      with measles and mumps (MMR) V06.4
    smallpox V04.1
    specified type NEC V05.8
    Streptococcus pneumoniae [pneumococcus]
      V03.82
      with
        influenza V06.6
    tetanus toxoid alone V03.7
      with diphtheria [Td] V06.5
        and pertussis (DTP) V06.1
    tuberculosis (BCG) V03.2
    tularemia V03.4

Admission—*continued*
  typhoid alone V03.1
    with diphtheria-tetanus-pertussis (TAB + DTP) V06.2
  typhoid-paratyphoid alone (TAB) V03.1
  typhus V05.8
  varicella V05.4
  viral encephalitis, arthropod-borne V05.0
  viral hepatitis V05.3
  yellow fever V04.4
  vasectomy V25.2
  vasoplasty for previous sterilization V26.0
  vision examination V72.0
  vocational therapy V57.22
  waiting period for admission to other facility V63.2
    undergoing social agency investigation V63.8
  well baby and child care V20.2
  x-ray of chest
    for suspected tuberculosis V71.2
    routine V72.5
Adnexitis (suppurative) (*see also* Salpingo-oophoritis) 614.2
Adolescence NEC V21.2
Adoption
  agency referral V68.89
  examination V70.3
  held for V68.89
Adrenal gland —*see* condition
Adrenalism 255.9
  tuberculous (*see also* Tuberculosis) 017.6
Adrenalitis, adrenitis 255.8
  meningococcal hemorrhagic 036.3
Adrenarche, precocious 259.1
Adrenocortical syndrome 255.2
Adrenogenital syndrome (acquired) (congenital) 255.2
  iatrogenic, fetus or newborn 760.79
Adventitious bursa —*see* Bursitis
Adynamia (episodica) (hereditary) (periodic) 359.3
Adynamic
  ileus or intestine (see also ileus) 560.1
  ureter 753.22
Aeration lung imperfect, newborn 770.5
Aerobullosis 993.3
Aerocele —*see* Embolism, air
Aerodermectasia
  subcutaneous (traumatic) 958.7
    surgical 998.81
  surgical 998.81
Aerodontalgia 993.2
Aeroembolism 993.3
Aerogenes capsulatus infection (*see also* Gangrene, gas) 040.0
Aero-otitis media 993.0
Aerophagy, aerophagia 306.4
  psychogenic 306.4
Aerosinusitis 993.1
Aerotitis 993.0
Affection, affections —*see also* Disease
  sacroiliac (joint), old 724.6
  shoulder region NEC 726.2
Afibrinogenemia 286.3
  acquired 286.6
  congenital 286.3
  postpartum 666.3

African
  sleeping sickness 086.5
  tick fever 087.1
  trypanosomiasis 086.5
    Gambian 086.3
    Rhodesian 086.4
Aftercare V58.9
  artificial openings—*see* Attention to, artificial, opening
  blood transfusion without reported diagnosis V58.2
  breathing exercise V57.0
  cardiac device V53.39
    defibrillator, automatic implantable V53.32
    pacemaker V53.31
      carotid sinus V53.39
  carotid sinus pacemaker V53.39
  chemotherapy session (adjunctive) (maintenance) V58.1
  defibrillator, automatic implantable cardiac V53.32
  exercise (remedial) (therapeutic) V57.1
    breathing V57.0
  extracorporeal dialysis (intermittent) (treatment) V56.0
  following surgery NEC V58.49
    wound closure, planned V58.41
  fracture V54.9
    removal of
      external fixation device V54.8
      internal fixation device V54.0
    specified care NEC V54.8
  gait training V57.1
    for use of artificial limb(s) V57.81
  involving
    dialysis (intermittent) (treatment)
      extracorporeal V56.0
      peritoneal V56.8
      renal V56.0
    gait training V57.1
      for use of artificial limb(s) V57.81
    orthoptic training V57.4
    orthotic training V57.81
  radiotherapy session V58.0
  removal of
    dressings V58.3
    fixation device
      external V54.8
      internal V54.0
    fracture plate V54.0
    pins V54.0
    plaster cast V54.8
    rods V54.0
    screws V54.0
    surgical dressings V58.3
    sutures V58.3
    traction device, external V54.8
  neuropacemaker (brain) (peripheral nerve) (spinal cord) V53.0
  occupational therapy V57.21
  orthodontic V58.5
  orthopedic V54.9
    change of external fixation or traction device V54.8
    removal of fixation device
      external V54.8
      internal V54.0
    specified care NEC V54.8
  orthoptic training V57.4
  orthotic training V57.81

Aftercare—*continued*
pacemaker
  brain V53.0
  cardiac V53.31
  carotid sinus V53.39
  peripheral nerve V53.0
  spinal cord V53.0
peritoneal dialysis (intermittent) (treatment)
  V56.8
physical therapy NEC V57.1
  breathing exercises V57.0
radiotherapy session V58.0
rehabilitation procedure V57.9
  breathing exercises V57.0
  multiple types V57.89
  occupational V57.21
  orthoptic V57.4
  orthotic V57.81
  physical therapy NEC V57.1
  remedial exercises V57.1
  specified type NEC V57.89
  speech V57.3
  therapeutic exercises V57.1
  vocational V57.22
renal dialysis (intermittent) (treatment) V56.0
specified type NEC V58.89
  removal of non-vascular catheter V58.82
  removal of vascular catheter V58.81
speech therapy V57.3
vocational rehabilitation V57.22
After-cataract 366.50
obscuring vision 366.53
specified type, not obscuring vision 366.52
Agalactia 676.4
Agammaglobulinemia 279.00
with lymphopenia 279.2
acquired (primary) (secondary) 279.06
Bruton's X-linked 279.04
infantile sex-linked (Bruton's) (congenital)
  279.04
Swiss-type 279.2
Aganglionosis (bowel) (colon) 751.3
Age (old) (*see also* Senile) 797
Agenesis —*see also* Absence, by site, congenital
acoustic nerve 742.8
adrenal (gland) 759.1
alimentary tract (complete) (partial) NEC 751.8
  lower 751.2
  upper 750.8
anus, anal (canal) 751.2
aorta 747.22
appendix 751.2
arm (complete) (partial) (*see also* Deformity,
  reduction, upper limb) 755.20
artery (peripheral) NEC (*see also* Anomaly,
  peripheral vascular system) 747.60
  brain 747.81
  coronary 746.85
  pulmonary 747.3
  umbilical 747.5
auditory (canal) (external) 744.01
auricle (ear) 744.01
bile, biliary duct or passage 751.61
bone NEC 756.9
brain 740.0
  specified part 742.2
breast 757.6
bronchus 748.3
canaliculus lacrimalis 743.65
carpus NEC (*see also* Deformity, reduction,
  upper limb) 755.28

Agenesis—*continued*
cartilage 756.9
cecum 751.2
cerebellum 742.2
cervix 752.49
chin 744.89
cilia 743.63
circulatory system, part NEC 747.89
clavicle 755.51
clitoris 752.49
coccyx 756.13
colon 751.2
corpus callosum 742.2
cricoid cartilage 748.3
diaphragm (with hernia) 756.6
digestive organ(s) or tract (complete) (partial)
  NEC 751.8
  lower 751.2
  upper 750.8
ductus arteriosus 747.89
duodenum 751.1
ear NEC 744.09
  auricle 744.01
  lobe 744.21
ejaculatory duct 752.8
endocrine (gland) NEC 759.2
epiglottis 748.3
esophagus 750.3
Eustachian tube 744.24
extrinsic muscle, eye 743.69
eye 743.00
  adnexa 743.69
eyelid (fold) 743.62
face
  bones NEC 756.0
  specified part NEC 744.89
fallopian tube 752.19
femur NEC (*see also* Absence, femur,
  congenital) 755.34
fibula NEC (*see also* Absence, fibula,
  congenital) 755.37
finger NEC (*see also* Absence, finger,
  congenital) 755.29
foot (complete) (*see also* Deformity, reduction,
  lower limb) 755.31
gallbladder 751.69
gastric 750.8
genitalia, genital (organ)
  female 752.8
    external 752.49
    internal NEC 752.8
  male 752.8
    penis 752.69
glottis 748.3
gonadal 758.6
hair 757.4
hand (complete) (*see also* Deformity, reduction,
  upper limb) 755.21
heart 746.89
  valve NEC 746.89
    aortic 746.89
    mitral 746.89
    pulmonary 746.01
hepatic 751.69
humerus NEC (*see also* Absence, humerus,
  congenital) 755.24
hymen 752.49
ileum 751.1
incus 744.04
intestine (small) 751.1
  large 751.2

Agenesis—*continued*
  iris (dilator fibers) 743.45
  jaw 524.09
  jejunum 751.1
  kidney(s) (partial) (unilateral) 753.0
  labium (majus) (minus) 752.49
  labyrinth, membranous 744.05
  lacrimal apparatus (congenital) 743.65
  larynx 748.3
  leg NEC (*see also* Deformity, reduction, lower
      limb) 755.30
  lens 743.35
  limb (complete) (partial) (*see also* Deformity,
      reduction) 755.4
    lower NEC 755.30
    upper 755.20
  lip 750.26
  liver 751.69
  lung (bilateral) (fissures) (lobe) (unilateral)
      748.5
  mandible 524.09
  maxilla 524.09
  metacarpus NEC 755.28
  metatarsus NEC 755.38
  muscle (any) 756.81
  musculoskeletal system NEC 756.9
  nail(s) 757.5
  neck, part 744.89
  nerve 742.8
  nervous system, part NEC 742.8
  nipple 757.6
  nose 748.1
  nuclear 742.8
  organ
    of Corti 744.05
    or site not listed—*see* Anomaly, specified
        type NEC
  osseous meatus (ear) 744.03
  ovary 752.0
  oviduct 752.19
  pancreas 751.7
  parathyroid (gland) 759.2
  patella 755.64
  pelvic girdle (complete) (partial) 755.69
  penis 752.69
  pericardium 746.89
  perineal body 756.81
  pituitary (gland) 759.2
  prostate 752.8
  pulmonary
    artery 747.3
    trunk 747.3
    vein 747.49
  punctum lacrimale 743.65
  radioulnar NEC (*see also* Absence, forearm,
      congenital) 755.25
  radius NEC (*see also* Absence, radius,
      congenital) 755.26
  rectum 751.2
  renal 753.0
  respiratory organ NEC 748.9
  rib 756.3
  roof of orbit 742.0
  round ligament 752.8
  sacrum 756.13
  salivary gland 750.21
  scapula 755.59
  scrotum 752.8
  seminal duct or tract 752.8

Agenesis—*continued*
  septum
    atrial 745.69
    between aorta and pulmonary artery 745.0
    ventricular 745.3
  shoulder girdle (complete) (partial) 755.59
  skull (bone) 756.0
    with
      anencephalus 740.0
      encephalocele 742.0
      hydrocephalus 742.3
        with spina bifida (*see also* Spina bifida)
            741.0
      microcephalus 742.1
  spermatic cord 752.8
  spinal cord 742.59
  spine 756.13
    lumbar 756.13
      isthmus 756.11
      pars articularis 756.11
  spleen 759.0
  sternum 756.3
  stomach 750.7
  tarsus NEC 755.38
  tendon 756.81
  testicular 752.8
  testis 752.8
  thymus (gland) 759.2
  thyroid (gland) 243
    cartilage 748.3
  tibia NEC (*see also* Absence, tibia, congenital)
      755.36
  tibiofibular NEC 755.35
  toe (complete) (partial) (*see also* Absence, toe,
      congenital) 755.39
  tongue 750.11
  trachea (cartilage) 748.3
  ulna NEC (*see also* Absence, ulna, congenital)
      755.27
  ureter 753.4
  urethra 753.8
  urinary tract NEC 753.8
  uterus 752.3
  uvula 750.26
  vagina 752.49
  vas deferens 752.8
  vein(s) (peripheral) NEC (*see also* Anomaly,
      peripheral vascular system) 747.60
    brain 747.81
    great 747.49
    portal 747.49
    pulmonary 747.49
  vena cava (inferior) (superior) 747.49
  vermis of cerebellum 742.2
  vertebra 756.13
    lumbar 756.13
      isthmus 756.11
      pars articularis 756.11
  vulva 752.49
Ageusia (*see also* Disturbance, sensation) 781.1
Aggressiveness 301.3
Aggressive outburst (*see also* Disturbance,
      conduct) 312.0
  in children and adolescents 313.9
Aging skin 701.8
Agitated —*see* condition
Agitation 307.9
  catatonic (*see also* Schizophrenia) 295.2
Aglossia (congenital) 750.11
Aglycogenosis 271.0
Agnail (finger) (with lymphangitis) 681.02

Agnosia (body image) (tactile) 784.69
  verbal 784.69
    auditory 784.69
      secondary to organic lesion 784.69
    developmental 315.8
    secondary to organic lesion 784.69
    visual 784.69
      developmental 315.8
      secondary to organic lesion 784.69
  visual 368.16
    developmental 315.31
Agoraphobia 300.22
  with panic attacks 300.21
Agrammatism 784.69
Agranulocytopenia 288.0
Agranulocytosis (angina) (chronic) (cyclical)
  (genetic) (infantile) (periodic) (pernicious)
  288.0
Agraphia (absolute) 784.69
  with alexia 784.61
  developmental 315.39
Agrypnia (*see also* Insomnia) 780.52
Ague (*see also* Malaria) 084.6
  brass-founders' 985.8
  dumb 084.6
  tertian 084.1
Agyria 742.2
Ahumada-del Castillo syndrome (nonpuerperal
  galactorrhea and amenorrhea) 253.1
AIDS 042
AIDS-associated retrovirus (disease) (illness)
  042
  infection—*see* Human immunodeficiency virus,
    infection
AIDS-associated virus (disease) (illness) 042
  infection—*see* Human immunodeficiency virus,
    infection
AIDS-like disease (illness) (syndrome) 042
AIDS-related complex 042
AIDS-related conditions 042
AIDS-related virus (disease) (illness) 042
  infection—*see* Human immunodeficiency virus,
    infection
AIDS virus (disease) (illness) 042
  infection—*see* Human immunodeficiency virus,
    infection
Ailment, heart —*see* Disease, heart
Ailurophobia 300.29
Ainhum (disease) 136.0
Air
  anterior mediastinum 518.1
  compressed, disease 993.3
  embolism (any site) (artery) (cerebral) 958.0
  with
    abortion—*see* Abortion, by type, with
      embolism
    ectopic pregnancy (*see also* categories
      633.0-633.9) 639.6
    molar pregnancy (*see also* categories
      630-632) 639.6
    due to implanted device—*see* Complications,
      due to (presence of) any device, implant,
      or graft classified to 996.0-996.5 NEC
    following
      abortion 639.6
      ectopic or molar pregnancy 639.6
      infusion, perfusion, or transfusion 999.1
    in pregnancy, childbirth, or puerperium 673.0
    traumatic 958.0
  hunger 786.09
    psychogenic 306.1

Air —*continued*
  leak (lung) (pulmonary) (thorax) 512.8
    iatrogenic 512.1
    postoperative 512.1
  rarefied, effects of—*see* Effect, adverse, high
    altitude
  sickness 994.6
Airplane sickness 994.6
Akathisia, acathisia 781.0
  due to drugs 333.99
Akinesia algera 352.6
Akiyami 100.89
Akureyri disease (epidemic neuromyasthenia)
  049.8
Alacrima (congenital) 743.65
Alactasia (hereditary) 271.3
Alalia 784.3
  developmental 315.31
    receptive-expressive 315.32
  secondary to organic lesion 784.3
Alaninemia 270.8
Alastrim 050.1
Albarrán's disease (colibacilluria) 599.0
Albers-Schönberg's disease (marble bones)
  756.52
Albert's disease 726.71
Albinism, albino (choroid) (cutaneous) (eye)
  (generalized) (isolated) (ocular)
  (oculocutaneous) (partial) 270.2
Albinismus 270.2
Albright (-Martin) (-Bantam) disease
  (pseudohypoparathyroidism) 275.4
Albright (-McCune) (-Sternberg) syndrome
  (osteitis fibrosa disseminata) 756.59
Albuminous —*see* condition
Albuminuria, albuminuric (acute) (chronic)
  (subacute) 791.0
  Bence-Jones 791.0
  cardiac 785.9
  complicating pregnancy, childbirth, or
    puerperium 646.2
    with hypertension—*see* Toxemia, of
      pregnancy
    affecting fetus or newborn 760.1
  cyclic 593.6
  gestational 646.2
  gravidarum 646.2
    with hypertension—*see* Toxemia, of
      pregnancy
    affecting fetus or newborn 760.1
  heart 785.9
  idiopathic 593.6
  orthostatic 593.6
  postural 593.6
  pre-eclamptic (mild) 642.4
    affecting fetus or newborn 760.0
    severe 642.5
      affecting fetus or newborn 760.0
  recurrent physiologic 593.6
  scarlatinal 034.1
Albumosuria 791.0
  Bence-Jones 791.0
  myelopathic (M9730/3) 203.0
Alcaptonuria 270.2

Alcohol, alcoholic
abstinance 291.81
acute intoxication 305.0
  with dependence 303.0
addiction (*see also* Alcoholism) 303.9
  maternal
    with suspected fetal damage affecting
      management of pregnancy 655.4
    affecting fetus or newborn 760.71
amnestic disorder, persisting 291.1
anxiety 291.89
brain syndrome, chronic 291.2
cardiopathy 425.5
chronic (*see also* Alcoholism) 303.9
cirrhosis (liver) 571.2
delirium 291.0
  acute 291.0
  chronic 291.1
  tremens 291.0
  withdrawal 291.0
dementia NEC 291.2
deterioration 291.2
drunkenness (simple) 305.0
hallucinosis (acute) 291.3
insanity 291.9
intoxication (acute) 305.0
  with dependence 303.0
  pathological 291.4
jealousy 291.5
Korsakoff's, Korsakov's, Korsakow's 291.1
liver NEC 571.3
  acute 571.1
  chronic 571.2
mania (acute) (chronic) 291.9
mood 291.89
paranoia 291.5
paranoid (type) psychosis 291.5
pellagra 265.2
poisoning, accidental (acute) NEC 980.9
  specified type of alcohol—*see* Table of drugs
    and chemicals
psychosis (*see also* Psychosis, alcoholic) 291.9
  Korsakoff's, Korsakov's, Korsakow's 291.1
  polyneuritic 291.1
  with
    delusions 291.5
    hallucinations 291.3
withdrawal symptoms, syndrome NEC 291.81
  delirium 291.0
  hallucinosis 291.3
Alcoholism 303.9

Note—Use the following fifth-digit
subclassification with category 303:

0 *unspecified*
1 *continuous*
2 *episodic*
3 *in remission*

with psychosis (*see also* Psychosis, alcoholic)
  291.9
acute 303.0
chronic 303.9
  with psychosis 291.9
complicating pregnancy, childbirth, or
  puerperium 648.4
  affecting fetus or newborn 760.71
history V11.3
Korsakoff's, Korsakov's, Korsakow's 291.1
suspected damage to fetus affecting
  management of pregnancy 655.4

Alder's anomaly or syndrome (leukocyte
  granulation anomaly) 288.2
Alder-Reilly anomaly (leukocyte granulation)
  288.2
Aldosteronism (primary) (secondary) 255.1
  congenital 255.1
Aldosteronoma (M8370/1) 237.2
Aldrich (-Wiskott) syndrome
  (eczema-thrombocytopenia) 279.12
Aleppo boil 085.1
Aleukemic —*see* condition
Aleukia
  congenital 288.0
  hemorrhagica 284.9
    acquired (secondary) 284.8
    congenital 284.0
    idiopathic 284.9
  splenica 289.4
Alexia (congenital) (developmental) 315.01
  secondary to organic lesion 784.61
Algoneurodystrophy 733.7
Algophobia 300.29
Alibert's disease (mycosis fungoides) (M9700/3)
  202.1
Alibert-Bazin disease (M9700/3) 202.1
Alice in Wonderland syndrome 293.89
Alienation, mental (*see also* Psychosis) 298.9
Alkalemia 276.3
Alkalosis 276.3
  metabolic 276.3
    with respiratory acidosis 276.4
  respiratory 276.3
Alkaptonuria 270.2
Allen-Masters syndrome 620.6
Allergy, allergic (reaction) 995.3
  air-borne substance (*see also* Fever, hay) 477.9
    specified allergen NEC 477.8
  alveolitis (extrinsic) 495.9
    due to
      Aspergillus clavatus 495.4
      cryptostroma corticale 495.6
      organisms (fungal, thermophilic
        actinomycete, other) growing in
        ventilation (air conditioning systems)
        495.7
    specified type NEC 495.8
  anaphylactic shock 999.4
    due to
      food—*see* Anaphylactic shock, due to, food
  angioneurotic edema 995.1
  animal (dander) (epidermal) (hair) 477.8
  arthritis (*see also* Arthritis, allergic) 716.2
  asthma—*see* Asthma
  bee sting (anaphylactic shock) 989.5
  biological—*see* Allergy, drug
  bronchial asthma—*see* Asthma
  conjunctivitis (eczematous) 372.14
  dander (animal) 477.8
  dandruff 477.8
  dermatitis (venenata)—*see* Dermatitis
  diathesis V15.0
  drug, medicinal substance, and biological (any)
    (correct medicinal substance properly
    administered) (external) (internal) 995.2
    wrong substance given or taken NEC 977.9
      specified drug or substance—*see* Table of
        drugs and chemicals
  dust (house) (stock) 477.8
  eczema—*see* Eczema
  endophthalmitis 360.19
  epidermal (animal) 477.8

Allergy, allergic—*continued*
feathers 477.8
food (any) (ingested) 693.1
  atopic 691.8
  in contact with skin 692.5
gastritis 535.4
gastroenteritis 558.9
gastrointestinal 558.9
grain 477.0
grass (pollen) 477.0
  asthma (*see also* Asthma) 493.0
  hay fever 477.0
hair (animal) 477.8
hay fever (grass) (pollen) (ragweed) (tree) (*see also* Fever, hay) 477.9
history (of) V15.0
horse serum—*see* Allergy, serum
inhalant 477.9
  dust 477.8
  pollen 477.0
  specified allergen other than pollen 477.8
kapok 477.8
medicine—*see* Allergy, drug
migraine 346.2
pannus 370.62
pneumonia 518.3
pollen (any) (hay fever) 477.0
  asthma (*see also* Asthma) 493.0
primrose 477.0
primula 477.0
purpura 287.0
ragweed (pollen) (Senecio jacobae) 477.0
  asthma (*see also* Asthma) 493.0
  hay fever 477.0
respiratory (*see also* Allergy, inhalant) 477.9
  due to
    drug—*see* Allergy, drug
    food—*see* Allergy, food
rhinitis (*see also* Fever, hay) 477.9
rose 477.0
Senecio jacobae 477.0
serum (prophylactic) (therapeutic) 999.5
  anaphylactic shock 999.4
shock (anaphylactic)
  due to
    adverse effect of correct medicinal
      substance properly administered 995.0
    food—*see* Anaphylactic shock, due to, food
    from serum or immunization 999.5
    anaphylactic 999.4
sinusitis (*see also* Fever, hay) 477.9
skin reaction 692.9
  specified substance—*see* Dermatitis, due to
tree (any) (hay fever) (pollen) 477.0
  asthma (*see also* Asthma) 493.0
upper respiratory (*see also* Fever, hay) 477.9
urethritis 597.89
urticaria 708.0
vaccine—*see* Allergy, serum
Allescheriosis 117.6
Alligator skin disease (ichthyosis congenita) 757.1
  acquired 701.1
Allocheiria, allochiria (*see also* Disturbance, sensation) 782.0
Almeida's disease (Brazilian blastomycosis) 116.1
Alopecia (atrophicans) (pregnancy) (premature) (senile) 704.00
adnata 757.4
areata 704.01

Alopecia—*continued*
(celsi 704.01
cicatrisata 704.09
circumscripta 704.01
congenital, congenitalis 757.4
disseminata 704.01
effluvium (telogen) 704.02
febrile 704.09
generalisata 704.09
hereditaria 704.09
marginalis 704.01
mucinosa 704.09
postinfectional 704.09
seborrheica 704.09
specific 091.82
syphilitic (secondary) 091.82
telogen effluvium 704.02
totalis 704.09
toxica 704.09
universalis 704.09
x-ray 704.09
Alper's disease 330.8
Alpha-lipoproteinemia 272.4
Alpha thalassemia 282.4
Alphos 696.1
Alpine sickness 993.2
Alport's syndrome (hereditary hematuria-nephropathy-deafness) 759.89
Alteration (of) altered
awareness 780.09
  transient 780.02
consciousness 780.09
  persistent vegetative state 780.03
  transient 780.02
mental status 780.9
Alternaria (infection) 118
Alternating —*see* condition
Altitude, high (effects)—*see* Effect, adverse, high altitude
Aluminosis (of lung) 503
Alvarez syndrome (transient cerebral ischemia) 435.9
Alveolar capillary block syndrome 516.3
Alveolitis
allergic (extrinsic) 495.9
  due to organisms (fungal, thermophilic actinomycete, other) growing in ventilation (air conditioning systems) 495.7
  specified type NEC 495.8
due to
  Aspergillus clavatus 495.4
  Cryptostroma corticale 495.6
fibrosing (chronic) (cryptogenic) (lung) 516.3
  idiopathic 516.3
  rheumatoid 714.81
jaw 526.5
sicca dolorosa 526.5
Alveolus, alveolar —*see* condition
Alymphocytosis (pure) 279.2
Alymphoplasia, thymic 279.2
Alzheimer's
dementia (senile) 331.0 *[294.1]*
disease or sclerosis 331.0
  with dementia—*see* Alzheimer's, dementia
Amastia (*see also* Absence, breast) 611.8
Amaurosis (acquired) (congenital) (*see also* Blindness) 369.00
fugax 362.34
hysterical 300.11

Amaurosis—*continued*
Leber's (congenital) 362.76
tobacco 377.34
uremic—*see* Uremia
Amaurotic familial idiocy (infantile) (juvenile) (late) 330.1
Ambisexual 752.7
Amblyopia (acquired) (congenital) (partial) 368.00
color 368.59
acquired 368.55
deprivation 368.02
ex anopsia 368.00
hysterical 300.11
nocturnal 368.60
vitamin A deficiency 264.5
refractive 368.03
strabismic 368.01
suppression 368.01
tobacco 377.34
toxic NEC 377.34
uremic—*see* Uremia
Ameba, amebic (histolytica)–*see also* Amebiasis
abscess 006.3
bladder 006.8
brain (with liver and lung abscess) 006.5
liver 006.3
with
brain abscess (and lung abscess) 006.5
lung abscess 006.4
lung (with liver abscess) 006.4
with brain abscess 006.5
seminal vesicle 006.8
spleen 006.8
carrier (suspected of) V02.2
meningoencephalitis
due to Naegleria (gruberi) 136.2
primary 136.2
Amebiasis NEC 006.9
with
brain abscess (with liver or lung abscess) 006.5
liver abscess (without mention of brain or lung abscess) 006.3
lung abscess (with liver abscess) 006.4
with brain abscess 006.5
acute 006.0
bladder 006.8
chronic 006.1
cutaneous 006.6
cutis 006.6
due to organism other than Entamoeba histolytica 007.8
hepatic (*see also* Abscess, liver, amebic) 006.3
nondysenteric 006.2
seminal vesicle 006.8
specified
organism NEC 007.8
site NEC 006.8
Ameboma 006.8
Amelia 755.4
lower limb 755.31
upper limb 755.21
Ameloblastoma (M9310/0) 213.1
jaw (bone) (lower) 213.1
upper 213.0
long bones (M9261/3)—*see* Neoplasm, bone, malignant
malignant (M9310/3) 170.1
jaw (bone) (lower) 170.1
upper 170.0

Ameloblastoma—*continued*
mandible 213.1
tibial (M9261/3) 170.7
Amelogenesis imperfecta 520.5
nonhereditaria (segmentalis) 520.4
Amenorrhea (primary) (secondary) 626.0
due to ovarian dysfunction 256.8
hyperhormonal 256.8
Amentia (*see also* Retardation, mental) 319
Meynert's (nonalcoholic) 294.0
alcoholic 291.1
nevoid 759.6
American
leishmaniasis 085.5
mountain tick fever 066.1
trypanosomiasis—*see* Trypanosomiasis, American
Ametropia (*see also* Disorder, accommodation) 367.9
Amianthosis 501
Amimia 784.69
Amino acid
deficiency 270.9
anemia 281.4
metabolic disorder (*see also* Disorder, amino acid) 270.9
Aminoaciduria 270.9
imidazole 270.5
Amnesia (retrograde) 780.9
auditory 784.69
developmental 315.31
secondary to organic lesion 784.69
hysterical or dissociative type 300.12
psychogenic 300.12
transient global 437.7
Amnestic (confabulatory) syndrome 294.0
alcohol-induced 291.1
drug-induced 292.83
posttraumatic 294.0
Amniocentesis screening (for) V28.2
alpha-fetoprotein level, raised V28.1
chromosomal anomalies V28.0
Amnion, amniotic —*see also* condition
nodosum 658.8
Amnionitis (complicating pregnancy) 658.4
affecting fetus or newborn 762.7
Amoral trends 301.7
Amotio retinae (*see also* Detachment, retina) 361.9
Ampulla
lower esophagus 530.89
phrenic 530.89
Amputation
any part of fetus, to facilitate delivery 763.8
cervix (supravaginal) (uteri) 622.8
in pregnancy or childbirth 654.6
affecting fetus or newborn 763.8
clitoris—*see* Wound, open, clitoris
congenital
lower limb 755.31
upper limb 755.21
neuroma (traumatic)—*see also* Injury, nerve, by site
surgical complications (late) 997.61
penis—*see* Amputation, traumatic, penis
status (without complication)—*see* Absence, by site, acquired
stump (surgical)(posttraumatic)
abnormal, painful, or with complication (late) 997.60

Amputation—*continued*
  healed or old NEC —*see also* Absence, by
    site, acquired
      lower V49.70
      upper V49.60
  traumatic (complete) (partial)

Note—"Complicated" includes traumatic
amputation with delayed healing, delayed
treatment, foreign body, or major infection.

---

    arm 887.4
      at or above elbow 887.2
        complicated 887.3
      below elbow 887.0
        complicated 887.1
      both (bilateral) (any level(s)) 887.6
        complicated 887.7
      complicated 887.5
    finger(s) (one or both hands) 886.0
      with thumb(s) 885.0
        complicated 885.1
      complicated 886.1
    foot (except toe(s) only) 896.0
      and other leg 897.6
        complicated 897.7
      both (bilateral) 896.2
        complicated 896.3
      complicated 896.1
      toe(s) only (one or both feet) 895.0
        complicated 895.1
    genital organ(s) (external) NEC 878.8
      complicated 878.9
    hand (except finger(s) only) 887.0
      and other arm 887.6
        complicated 887.7
      both (bilateral) 887.6
        complicated 887.7
      complicated 887.1
      finger(s) (one or both hands) 886.0
        with thumb(s) 885.0
          complicated 885.1
        complicated 886.1
      thumb(s) (with fingers of either hand) 885.0
        complicated 885.1
    head 874.9
    late effect—*see* Late, effects (of), amputation
    leg 897.4
      and other foot 897.6
        complicated 897.7
      at or above knee 897.2
        complicated 897.3
      below knee 897.0
        complicated 897.1
      both (bilateral) 897.6
        complicated 897.7
      complicated 897.5
    lower limb(s) except toe(s)—*see* Amputation,
      traumatic, leg
    nose—*see* Wound, open, nose
    penis 878.0
      complicated 878.1
    sites other than limbs—*see* Wound, open, by
      site
    thumb(s) (with finger(s) of either hand) 885.0
      complicated 885.1
    toe(s) (one or both feet) 895.0
      complicated 895.1
    upper limb(s)—*see* Amputation, traumatic,
      arm
Amputee (bilateral) (old) —*see* Absence, by site,
  acquired

Amusia 784.69
  developmental 315.39
  secondary to organic lesion 784.69
Amyelencephalus 740.0
Amyelia 742.59
Amygdalitis— *see* Tonsillitis
Amygdalolith 474.8
Amyloid disease or degeneration 277.3
  heart 277.3 *[425.7]*
Amyloidosis (familial) (general) (generalized)
    (genetic) (primary) (secondary) 277.3
  with lung involvement 277.3 *[517.8]*
  heart 277.3 *[425.7]*
  nephropathic 277.3 *[583.81]*
  neuropathic (Portuguese) (Swiss) 277.3 *[357.4]*
  pulmonary 277.3 *[517.8]*
  systemic, inherited 277.3
Amylopectinosis (brancher enzyme deficiency)
    271.0
Amylophagia 307.52
Amyoplasia, congenita 756.89
Amyotonia 728.2
  congenita 358.8
Amyotrophia, amyotrophy, amyotrophic 728.2
  congenita 756.89
  diabetic 250.6 *[358.1]*
  lateral sclerosis (syndrome) 335.20
  neuralgic 353.5
  sclerosis (lateral) 335.20
  spinal progressive 335.21
Anacidity
  gastric 536.0
  psychogenic 306.4
Anaerosis of newborn 770.8
Analbuminemia 273.8
Analgesia (*see also* Anesthesia) 782.0
Analphalipoproteinemia 272.5
Anaphylactic shock or reaction (correct
    substance properly administered) 995.0
  due to
    food 995.60
      additives 995.66
      crustaceans 995.62
      eggs 995.68
      fish 995.65
      fruits 995.63
      milk products 995.67
      nuts (tree) 995.64
      peanuts 995.61
      seeds 995.64
      specified NEC 995.69
      tree nuts 995.64
      vegetables 995.63
    immunization 999.4
    overdose or wrong substance given or taken
      977.9
      specified drug—*see* Table of drugs and
        chemicals
    serum 999.4
  following sting(s) 989.5
  purpura 287.0
  serum 999.4
Anaphylactoid shock or reaction —*see*
  Anaphylactic shock
Anaphylaxis —*see* Anaphylactic shock
Anaplasia, cervix 622.1
Anarthria 784.5
Anarthritic rheumatoid disease 446.5

Anasarca 782.3
    cardiac (*see also* Failure, heart, congestive)
        428.0
    fetus or newborn 778.0
    lung 514
    nutritional 262
    pulmonary 514
    renal (*see also* Nephrosis) 581.9
Anaspadias 752.62
Anastomosis
    aneurysmal—*see* Aneurysm
    arteriovenous, congenital NEC (*see also*
        Anomaly, arteriovenous) 747.60
        ruptured, of brain (*see also* Hemorrhage,
            subarachnoid) 430
    intestinal 569.89
        complicated NEC 997.4
            involving urinary tract 997.5
    retinal and choroidal vessels 743.58
        acquired 362.17
Anatomical narrow angle (glaucoma) 365.02
Ancylostoma (infection) (infestation) 126.9
    americanus 126.1
    braziliense 126.2
    caninum 126.8
    ceylanicum 126.3
    duodenale 126.0
    Necator americanus 126.1
Ancylostomiasis (intestinal) 126.9
    Ancylostoma
        americanus 126.1
        caninum 126.8
        ceylanicum 126.3
        duodenale 126.0
    braziliense 126.2
    Necator americanus 126.1
Anders' disease or syndrome (adiposis tuberosa
    simplex) 272.8
Andersen's glycogen storage disease 271.0
Anderson's disease 272.7
Andes disease 993.2
Andrews' disease (bacterid) 686.8
Androblastoma (M8630/1)
    benign (M8630/0)
        specified site—*see* Neoplasm, by site, benign
        unspecified site
            female 220
            male 222.0
    malignant (M8630/3)
        specified site—*see* Neoplasm, by site,
            malignant
        unspecified site
            female 183.0
            male 186.9
    specified site—*see* Neoplasm, by site, uncertain
        behavior
    tubular (M8640/0)
        with lipid storage (M8641/0)
            specified site—*see* Neoplasm, by site,
                benign
            unspecified site
                female 220
                male 222.0
        specified site—*see* Neoplasm, by site, benign
        unspecified site
            female 220
            male 222.0
    unspecified site
        female 236.2
        male 236.4

Android pelvis 755.69
    with disproportion (fetopelvic) 653.3
        affecting fetus or newborn 763.1
        causing obstructed labor 660.1
            affecting fetus or newborn 763.1
Anectasis, pulmonary (newborn or fetus) 770.5
Anemia 285.9
    with
        disorder of
            anaerobic glycolysis 282.3
            pentose phosphate pathway 282.2
        koilonychia 280.9
        6-phosphogluconic dehydrogenase deficiency
            282.2
    achlorhydric 280.9
    achrestic 281.8
    Addison's (pernicious) 281.0
    Addison-Biermer (pernicious) 281.0
    agranulocytic 288.0
    amino acid deficiency 281.4
    aplastic 284.9
        acquired (secondary) 284.8
        congenital 284.0
        constitutional 284.0
        due to
            chronic systemic disease 284.8
            drugs 284.8
            infection 284.8
            radiation 284.8
        idiopathic 284.9
        myxedema 244.9
        of or complicating pregnancy 648.2
        red cell (acquired) (adult) (pure) (with
            thymoma) 284.8
            congenital 284.0
        specified type NEC 284.8
        toxic (paralytic) 284.8
    aregenerative 284.9
        congenital 284.0
    asiderotic 280.9
    atypical (primary) 285.9—
    autohemolysis of Selwyn and Dacie (type I)
        282.2
    autoimmune hemolytic 283.0
    Baghdad Spring 282.2
    Balantidium coli 007.0
    Biermer's (pernicious) 281.0
    blood loss (chronic) 280.0
        acute 285.1
    bothriocephalus 123.4
    brickmakers' (*see also* Ancylostomiasis) 126.9
    cerebral 437.8
    childhood 285.9
    chlorotic 280.9
    chronica congenita aregenerativa 284.0
    chronic simple 281.9
    combined system disease NEC 281.0 *[336.2]*
        due to dietary deficiency 281.1 *[336.2]*
    complicating pregnancy or childbirth 648.2
    congenital (following fetal blood loss) 776.5
        aplastic 284.0
        due to isoimmunization NEC 773.2
        Heinz-body 282.7
        hereditary hemolytic NEC 282.9
        nonspherocytic
            Type I 282.2
            Type II 282.3
        pernicious 281.0
        spherocytic (*see also* Spherocytosis) 282.0
    Cooley's (erythroblastic) 282.4
    crescent—*see* Disease, sickle-cell

Anemia—*continued*
  cytogenic 281.0
  Dacie's (nonspherocytic)
    Type I 282.2
    Type II 282.3
  Davidson's (refractory) 284.9
  deficiency 281.9
    2, 3 diphosphoglycurate mutase 282.3
    2, 3 PG 282.3
    6-PGD 282.2
    6-phosphogluronic dehydrogenase 282.2
    amino acid 281.4
    combined B_{12} and folate 281.3
    enzyme, drug-induced (hemolytic) 282.2
    erythrocytic glutathione 282.2
    folate 281.2
      dietary 281.2
      drug-induced 281.2
    folic acid 281.2
      dietary 281.2
      drug-induced 281.2
    G-6-PD 282.2
    GGS-R 282.2
    glucose-6-phosphate dehydrogenase (G-6-PD) 282.2
    glucose-phosphate isomerase 282.3
    glutathione peroxidase 282.2
    glutathione reductase 282.2
    glyceraldehyde phosphate dehydrogenase 282.3
    GPI 282.3
    G SH 282.2
    hexokinase 282.3
    iron (Fe) 280.9
      specified NEC 280.8
    nutritional 281.9
      with
        poor iron absorption 280.9
          specified deficiency NEC 281.8
        due to inadequate dietary iron intake 280.1
        specified type NEC 281.8
    of or complicating pregnancy 648.2
    pentose phosphate pathway 282.2
    PFK 282.3
    phosphofructo-aldolase 282.3
    phosphofructokinase 282.3
    phosphoglycerate kinase 282.3
    PK 282.3
    protein 281.4
    pyruvate kinase (PK) 282.3
    TPI 282.3
    triosephosphate isomerase 282.3
    vitamin B_{12} NEC 281.1
      dietary 281.1
      pernicious 281.0
  Diamond-Blackfan (congenital hypoplastic) 284.0
  dibothriocephalus 123.4
  dimorphic 281.9
  diphasic 281.8
  diphtheritic 032.89
  Diphyllobothrium 123.4
  drepanocytic (*see also* Disease, sickle-cell) 282.60
  due to
    blood loss (chronic) 280.0
      acute 285.1
    defect of Embden-Meyerhof pathway glycolysis 282.3
    disorder of glutathione metabolism 282.2
    fetal blood loss 776.5

Anemia—*continued*
  fish tapeworm (D. latum) infestation 123.4
  glutathione metabolism disorder 282.2
  hemorrhage (chronic) 280.0
    acute 285.1
  hexose monophosphate (HMP) shunt deficiency 282.2
  impaired absorption 280.9
  loss of blood (chronic) 280.0
    acute 285.1
  myxedema 244.9
  Necator americanus 126.1
  prematurity 776.6
  selective vitamin B_{12} malabsorption with proteinuria 281.1
  Dyke-Young type (secondary) (symptomatic) 283.9
  dyserythropoietic (congenital) (types I, II, III) 285.8
  dyshemopoietic (congenital) 285.8
  Egypt (*see also* Ancylostomiasis) 126.9
  elliptocytosis (*see also* Elliptocytosis) 282.1
  enzyme deficiency, drug-induced 282.2
  epidemic (*see also* Ancylostomiasis) 126.9
  erythroblastic
    familial 282.4
    fetus or newborn (*see also* Disease, hemolytic) 773.2
    late 773.5
  erythrocytic glutathione deficiency 282.2
  essential 285.9
  Faber's (achlorhydric anemia) 280.9
  factitious (self-induced blood letting) 280.0
  familial erythroblastic (microcytic) 282.4
  Fanconi's (congenital pancytopenia) 284.0
  favism 282.2
  fetal, following blood loss 776.5
  fetus or newborn
    due to
      ABO
        antibodies 773.1
        incompatibility, maternal/fetal 773.1
        isoimmunization 773.1
      Rh
        antibodies 773.0
        incompatibility, maternal/fetal 773.0
        isoimmunization 773.0
      following fetal blood loss 776.5
  fish tapeworm (D. latum) infestation 123.4
  folate (folic acid) deficiency 281.2
    dietary 281.2
    drug-induced 281.2
  folate malabsorption, congenital 281.2
  folic acid deficiency 281.2
    dietary 281.2
    drug-induced 281.2
  G-6-PD 282.2
  general 285.9
  glucose-6-phosphate dehydrogenase deficiency 282.2
  glutathione-reductase deficiency 282.2
  goat's milk 281.2
  granulocytic 288.0
  Heinz-body, congenital 282.7
  hemoglobin deficiency 285.9
  hemolytic 282.9
    acquired 283.9
      with hemoglobinuria NEC 283.2
      autoimmune (cold type) (idiopathic) (primary) (secondary) (symptomatic) (warm type) 283.0

Anemia—*continued*
  late, due to isoimmunization 773.5
    posthemorrhagic 776.5
  nonregenerative 284.9
  nonspherocytic hemolytic—*see* Anemia,
    hemolytic, nonspherocytic
  normocytic (infectional) (not due to blood loss)
    285.9
    due to blood loss (chronic) 280.0
      acute 285.1
    myelophthisic 284.8
  nutritional (deficiency) 281.9
    with
      poor iron absorption 280.9
      specified deficiency NEC 281.8
    due to inadequate dietary iron intake 280.1
    megaloblastic (of infancy) 281.2
  of childhood (*see also* Thalassemia) 282.4
  of or complicating pregnancy 648.2
    affecting fetus or newborn 760.8
  of prematurity 776.6
  orotic aciduric (congenital) (hereditary) 281.4
  osteosclerotic 289.8
  ovalocytosis (hereditary) (*see also*
    Elliptocytosis) 282.1
  paludal (*see also* Malaria) 084.6
  pentose phosphate pathway deficiency 282.2
  pernicious (combined system disease)
        (congenital) (dorsolateral spinal
        degeneration) (juvenile) (myelopathy)
        (neuropathy) (posterior sclerosis) (primary)
        (progressive) (spleen) 281.0
    of or complicating pregnancy 648.2
  pleochromic 285.9
    of sprue 281.8
  portal 285.8
  posthemorrhagic (chronic) 280.0
    acute 285.1
    newborn 776.5
  pressure 285.9
  primary 285.9
  profound 285.9
  progressive 285.9
    malignant 281.0
    pernicious 281.0
  protein-deficiency 281.4
  pseudoleukemica infantum 285.8
  puerperal 648.2
  pure red cell 284.8
    congenital 284.0
  pyridoxine-responsive (hypochromic) 285.0
  pyruvate kinase (PK) deficiency 282.3
  refractoria sideroblastica 285.0
  refractory (primary) 284.9
    with hemochromatosis 285.0
    megaloblastic 281.3
    sideroblastic 285.0
    sideropenic 280.9
  Rietti-Greppi-Micheli (thalassemia minor) 282.4
  scorbutic 281.8
  secondary (to) 285.9
    blood loss (chronic) 280.0
      acute 285.1
    hemorrhage 280.0
      acute 285.1
    inadequate dietary iron intake 280.1
  semiplastic 284.9
  septic 285.9
  sickle-cell (*see also* Disease, sickle-cell) 282.60
  sideroachrestic 285.0

Anemia—*continued*
  sideroblastic (acquired) (any type) (congenital)
        (drug-induced) (due to disease) (hereditary)
        (primary) (refractory) (secondary)
        (sex-linked hypochromic) (vitamin B$_6$
        responsive) 285.0
  sideropenic (refractory) 280.9
    due to blood loss (chronic) 280.0
      acute 285.1
  simple chronic 281.9
  specified type NEC 285.8
  spherocytic (hereditary) (*see also*
    Spherocytosis) 282.0
  splenic 285.8
    familial (Gaucher's) 272.7
  splenomegalic 285.8
  stomatocytosis 282.8
  syphilitic 095.8
  target cell (oval) 282.4
  thalassemia 282.4
  thrombocytopenic (*see also* Thrombocytopenia)
    287.5
  toxic 284.8
  triosephosphate isomerase deficiency 282.3
  tropical, macrocytic 281.2
  tuberculous (*see also* Tuberculosis) 017.9
  vegan's 281.1
  vitamin
    B$_6$-responsive 285.0
    B$_{12}$ deficiency (dietary) 281.1
      pernicious 281.0
  von Jaksch's (pseudoleukemia infantum) 285.8
  Witts' (achlorhydric anemia) 280.9
  Zuelzer (-Ogden) (nutritional megaloblastic
    anemia) 281.2
Anencephalus, anencephaly 740.0
  fetal, affecting management of pregnancy 655.0
Anergasia (*see also* Psychosis, organic) 294.9
  senile 290.0
Anesthesia, anesthetic 782.0
  complication or reaction NEC 995.2
    due to
      correct substance properly administered
        995.2
      overdose or wrong substance given 968.4
        specified anesthetic—*see* Table of drugs
          and chemicals
  cornea 371.81
  death from
    correct substance properly administered 995.4
    during delivery 668.9
    overdose or wrong substance given 968.4
      specified anesthetic—*see* Table of drugs
        and chemicals
  eye 371.81
  functional 300.11
  hyperesthetic, thalamic 348.8
  hysterical 300.11
  local skin lesion 782.0
  olfactory 781.1
  sexual (psychogenic) 302.72
  shock
    due to
      correct substance properly administered
        995.4
      overdose or wrong substance given 968.4
        specified anesthetic—*see* Table of drugs
          and chemicals
  skin 782.0
  tactile 782.0
  testicular 608.9
  thermal 782.0

Anetoderma (maculosum) 701.3
Aneuploidy NEC 758.5
Aneurin deficiency 265.1
Aneurysm (anastomotic) (artery) (cirsoid)
      (diffuse) (false) (fusiform) (multiple)
      (ruptured) (saccular) (varicose) 442.9
   abdominal (aorta) 441.4
      ruptured 441.3
      syphilitic 093.0
   aorta, aortic (nonsyphilitic) 441.9
      abdominal 441.4
         dissecting 441.02
         ruptured 441.3
         syphilitic 093.0
      arch 441.2
         ruptured 441.1
      arteriosclerotic NEC 441.9
         ruptured 441.5
      ascending 441.2
         ruptured 441.1
      congenital 747.29
      descending 441.9
         abdominal 441.4
            ruptured 441.3
         ruptured 441.5
         thoracic 441.2
            ruptured 441.1
      dissecting 441.00
         abdominal 441.02
         thoracic 441.01
         thoracoabdominal 441.03
      due to coarctation (aorta) 747.10
      ruptured 441.5
      sinus, right 747.29
      syphilitic 093.0
      thoracoabdominal 441.7
         ruptured 441.6
      thorax, thoracic (arch) (nonsyphilitic) 441.2
         dissecting 441.01
         ruptured 441.1
         syphilitic 093.0
      transverse 441.2
         ruptured 441.1
      valve (heart) (*see also* Endocarditis, aortic)
         424.1
   arteriosclerotic NEC 442.9
      cerebral 437.3
         ruptured (*see also* Hemorrhage,
            subarachnoid) 430
   arteriovenous (congenital) (peripheral) NEC
         (*see also* Anomaly, arteriovenous) 747.60
      acquired NEC 447.0
         brain 437.3
            ruptured (*see also* Hemorrhage,
               subarachnoid) 430
         coronary 414.11
         pulmonary 417.0
      brain (cerebral) 747.81
         ruptured (*see also* Hemorrhage,
            subarachnoid) 430
      coronary 746.85
      pulmonary 747.3
      retina 743.58
      specified site NEC 747.89
         acquired 447.0
      traumatic (*see also* Injury, blood vessel, by
         site) 904.9
   basal—*see* Aneurysm, brain
   berry (congenital) (ruptured) (*see also*
      Hemorrhage, subarachnoid) 430
   brain 437.3
      arteriosclerotic 437.3

Aneurysm—*continued*
      ruptured (*see also* Hemorrhage,
         subarachnoid) 430
      arteriovenous 747.81
         acquired 437.3
            ruptured (*see also* Hemorrhage,
               subarachnoid) 430
            ruptured (*see also* Hemorrhage,
               subarachnoid) 430
         berry (congenital) (ruptured) (*see also*
            Hemorrhage, subarachnoid) 430
         congenital 747.81
            ruptured (*see also* Hemorrhage,
               subarachnoid) 430
         meninges 437.3
            ruptured (*see also* Hemorrhage,
               subarachnoid) 430
         miliary (congenital) (ruptured) (*see also*
            Hemorrhage, subarachnoid) 430
         mycotic 421.0
            ruptured (*see also* Hemorrhage,
               subarachnoid) 430
         nonruptured 437.3
         ruptured (*see also* Hemorrhage, subarachnoid)
            430
         syphilitic 094.87
      syphilitic (hemorrhage) 094.87
      traumatic—*see* Injury, intracranial
   cardiac (false) (*see also* Aneurysm, heart)
         414.10
   carotid artery (common) (external) 442.81
      internal (intracranial portion) 437.3
         extracranial portion 442.81
         ruptured into brain (*see also* Hemorrhage,
            subarachnoid) 430
         syphilitic 093.89
      intracranial 094.87
   cavernous sinus (*see also* Aneurysm, brain)
         437.3
      arteriovenous 747.81
         ruptured (*see also* Hemorrhage,
            subarachnoid) 430
      congenital 747.81
         ruptured (*see also* Hemorrhage,
            subarachnoid) 430
   celiac 442.84
   central nervous system, syphilitic 094.89
   cerebral—*see* Aneurysm, brain
   chest—*see* Aneurysm, thorax
   circle of Willis (*see also* Aneurysm, brain) 437.3
      congenital 747.81
         ruptured (*see also* Hemorrhage,
            subarachnoid) 430
         ruptured (*see also* Hemorrhage, subarachnoid)
            430
   common iliac artery 442.2
   congenital (peripheral) NEC 747.60
      brain 747.81
         ruptured (*see also* Hemorrhage,
            subarachnoid) 430
      cerebral—*see* Aneurysm, brain, congenital
      coronary 746.85
      gastrointestinal 747.61
      lower limb 747.64
      pulmonary 747.3
      renal 747.62
      retina 743.58
      specified site NEC 747.89
      spinal 747.82
      upper limb 747.63
   conjunctiva 372.74

Aneurysm—*continued*
 conus arteriosus (*see also* Aneurysm, heart)
  414.10
 coronary (arteriosclerotic) (artery) (vein) (*see
  also* Aneurysm, heart) 414.11
  arteriovenous 746.85
  congenital 746.85
  syphilitic 093.89
 cylindrical 441.9
  ruptured 441.5
  syphilitic 093.9
 dissecting 442.9
  aorta 441.00
   abdominal 441.02
   thoracic 441.01
   thoracoabdominal 441.03
  syphilitic 093.9
 ductus arteriosus 747.0
 embolic—*see* Embolism, artery
 endocardial, infective (any valve) 421.0
 femoral 442.3
 gastroduodenal 442.84
 gastroepiploic 442.84
 heart (chronic or with a stated duration of over 8
  weeks) (infectional) (wall) 414.10
  acute or with a stated duration of 8 weeks or
   less (*see also* Infarct, myocardium) 410.9
  congenital 746.89
  valve—*see* Endocarditis
 hepatic 442.84
 iliac (common) 442.2
 infective (any valve) 421.0
 innominate (nonsyphilitic) 442.89
  syphilitic 093.89
 interauricular septum (*see also* Aneurysm,
  heart) 414.10
 interventricular septum (*see also* Aneurysm,
  heart) 414.10
 intracranial—*see* Aneurysm, brain
 intrathoracic (nonsyphilitic) 441.2
  ruptured 441.1
  syphilitic 093.0
 jugular vein 453.8
 lower extremity 442.3
 lung (pulmonary artery) 417.1
 malignant 093.9
 mediastinal (nonsyphilitic) 442.89
  syphilitic 093.89
 miliary (congenital) (ruptured) (*see also*
  Hemorrhage, subarachnoid) 430
 mitral (heart) (valve) 424.0
 mural (arteriovenous) (heart) (*see also*
  Aneurysm, heart) 414.10
 mycotic, any site 421.0
  ruptured, brain (*see also* Hemorrhage,
   subarachnoid) 430
 myocardium (*see also* Aneurysm, heart) 414.10
 neck 442.81
 pancreaticoduodenal 442.84
 patent ductus arteriosus 747.0
 peripheral NEC 442.89
  congenital NEC (*see also* Aneurysm,
   congenital) 747.60
 popliteal 442.3
 pulmonary 417.1
  arteriovenous 747.3
   acquired 417.0
  syphilitic 093.89
  valve (heart) (*see also* Endocarditis,
   pulmonary) 424.3

Aneurysm—*continued*
 racemose 442.9
  congenital (peripheral) NEC 747.60
 radial 442.0
 Rasmussen's (*see also* Tuberculosis) 011.2
 renal 442.1
 retinal (acquired) 362.17
  congenital 743.58
  diabetic 250.5 *[362.01]*
 sinus, aortic (of Valsalva) 747.29
 specified site NEC 442.89
 spinal (cord) 442.89
  congenital 747.82
  syphilitic (hemorrhage) 094.89
 spleen, splenic 442.83
 subclavian 442.82
  syphilitic 093.89
 superior mesenteric 442.84
 syphilitic 093.9
  aorta 093.0
  central nervous system 094.89
  congenital 090.5
  spine, spinal 094.89
 thoracoabdominal 441.7
  ruptured 441.6
 thorax, thoracic (arch) (nonsyphilitic) 441.2
  dissecting 441.01
  ruptured 441.1
  syphilitic 093.0
 traumatic (complication) (early)—*see* Injury,
  blood vessel, by site
 tricuspid (heart) (valve)—*see* Endocarditis,
  tricuspid
 ulnar 442.0
 upper extremity 442.0
 valve, valvular—*see* Endocarditis
 venous 456.8
  congenital NEC (*see also* Aneurysm,
   congenital) 747.60
 ventricle (arteriovenous) (*see also* Aneurysm,
  heart) 414.10
 visceral artery NEC 442.84
Angiectasis 459.89
Angiectopia 459.9
Angiitis 447.6
 allergic granulomatous 446.4
 hypersensitivity 446.20
  Goodpasture's syndrome 446.21
  specified NEC 446.29
 necrotizing 446.0
 Wegener's (necrotizing respiratory
  granulomatosis) 446.4
Angina (attack) (cardiac) (chest) (effort) (heart)
  (pectoris) (syndrome) (vasomotor) 413.9
 abdominal 557.1
 agranulocytic 288.0
 aphthous 074.0
 catarrhal 462
 crescendo 411.1
 croupous 464.4
 cruris 443.9
  due to atherosclerosis NEC (*see also*
   Arteriosclerosis, extremities) 440.20
 decubitus 413.0
 diphtheritic (membranous) 032.0
 erysipelatous 034.0
 erythematous 462
 exudative, chronic 476.0
 faucium 478.29
 gangrenous 462
  diphtheritic 032.0

Angina—*continued*
infectious 462
initial 411.1
intestinal 557.1
ludovici 528.3
Ludwig's 528.3
malignant 462
diphtheritic 032.0
membranous 464.4
diphtheritic 032.0
mesenteric 557.1
monocytic 075
nocturnal 413.0
phlegmonous 475
diphtheritic 032.0
preinfarctional 411.1
Prinzmetal's 413.1
progressive 411.1
pseudomembranous 101
psychogenic 306.2
pultaceous, diphtheritic 032.0
scarlatinal 034.1
septic 034.0
simple 462
stable NEC 413.9
staphylococcal 462
streptococcal 034.0
stridulous, diphtheritic 032.3
syphilitic 093.9
congenital 090.5
tonsil 475
trachealis 464.4
unstable 411.1
variant 413.1
Vincent's 101
Angioblastoma (M9161/1)—*see* Neoplasm, connective tissue, uncertain behavior
Angiocholecystitis (*see also* Cholecystitis, acute) 575.0
Angiocholitis (*see also* Cholecystitis, acute) 576.1
Angiodysgensis spinalis 336.1
Angiodysplasia (intestinalis) (intestine) 569.84
with hemorrhage 569.85
duodenum 537.82
with hemorrhage 537.83
stomach 537.82
with hemorrhage 537.83
Angioedema (allergic) (any site) (with urticaria) 995.1
hereditary 277.6
Angioendothelioma (M9130/1)—*see also* Neoplasm, by site, uncertain behavior
benign (M9130/0) (*see also* Hemangioma, by site) 228.00
bone (M9260/3)—*see* Neoplasm, bone, malignant
Ewing's (M9260/3)—*see* Neoplasm, bone, malignant
nervous system (M9130/0) 228.09
Angiofibroma (M9160/0)—*see also* Neoplasm, by site, benign
juvenile (M9160/0) 210.7
specified site—*see* Neoplasm, by site, benign
unspecified site 210.7
Angiohemophilia (A) (B) 286.4
Angioid streaks (choroid) (retina) 363.43
Angiokeratoma (M9141/0)—*see also* Neoplasm, skin, benign
corporis diffusum 272.7
Angiokeratosis
diffuse 272.7

Angioleiomyoma (M8894/0)—*see* Neoplasm, connective tissue, benign
Angioleucitis 683
Angiolipoma (M8861/0) (*see also* Lipoma, by site) 214.9
infiltrating (M8861/1)—*see* Neoplasm, connective tissue, uncertain behavior
Angioma (M9120/0) (*see also* Hemangioma, by site) 228.00
capillary 448.1
hemorrhagicum hereditaria 448.0
malignant (M9120/3)—*see* Neoplasm, connective tissue, malignant
pigmentosum et atrophicum 757.33
placenta—*see* Placenta, abnormal
plexiform (M9131/0)—*see* Hemangioma, by site
senile 448.1
serpiginosum 709.1
spider 448.1
stellate 448.1
Angiomatosis 757.32
bacillary 083.8
corporis diffusum universale 272.7
cutaneocerebral 759.6
encephalocutaneous 759.6
encephalofacial 759.6
encephalotrigeminal 759.6
hemorrhagic familial 448.0
hereditary familial 448.0
heredofamilial 448.0
meningo-oculofacial 759.6
multiple sites 228.09
neuro-oculocutaneous 759.6
retina (Hippel's disease) 759.6
retinocerebellosa 759.6
retinocerebral 759.6
systemic 228.09
Angiomyolipoma (M8860/0)
specified site—*see* Neoplasm, connective tissue, benign
unspecified site 223.0
Angiomyoliposarcoma (M8860/3)—*see* Neoplasm, connective tissue, malignant
Angiomyoma (M8894/0)—*see* Neoplasm, connective tissue, benign
Angiomyosarcoma (M8894/3)—*see* Neoplasm, connective tissue, malignant
Angioneurosis 306.2
Angioneurotic edema (allergic) (any site) (with urticaria) 995.1
hereditary 277.6
Angiopathia, angiopathy 459.9
diabetic (peripheral) 250.7 *[443.81]*
peripheral 443.9
diabetic 250.7 *[443.81]*
specified type NEC 443.89
retinae syphilitica 093.89
retinalis (juvenilis) 362.18
background 362.10
diabetic 250.5 *[362.01]*
proliferative 362.29
tuberculous (*see also* Tuberculosis) 017.3 *[362.18]*
Angiosarcoma (M9120/3)—*see* Neoplasm, connective tissue, malignant
Angiosclerosis —*see* Arteriosclerosis
Angioscotoma, enlarged 368.42
Angiospasm 443.9
brachial plexus 353.0
cerebral 435.9
cervical plexus 353.2

Angiospasm—*continued*
nerve
  arm 354.9
    axillary 353.0
    median 354.1
    ulnar 354.2
  autonomic (*see also* Neuropathy, peripheral,
    autonomic) 337.9
  axillary 353.0
  leg 355.8
    plantar 355.6
  lower extremity—*see* Angiospasm, nerve, leg
  median 354.1
  peripheral NEC 355.9
  spinal NEC 355.9
  sympathetic (*see also* Neuropathy, peripheral,
    autonomic) 337.9
  ulnar 354.2
  upper extremity—*see* Angiospasm, nerve, arm
peripheral NEC 443.9
traumatic 443.9
  foot 443.9
  leg 443.9
vessel 443.9
Angiospastic disease or edema 443.9
Anguillulosis 127.2
Angulation
cecum (*see also* Obstruction, intestine) 560.9
coccyx (acquired) 738.6
  congenital 756.19
femur (acquired) 736.39
  congenital 755.69
intestine (large) (small) (*see also* Obstruction,
  intestine) 560.9
sacrum (acquired) 738.5
  congenital 756.19
sigmoid (flexure) (*see also* Obstruction,
  intestine) 560.9
spine (*see also* Curvature, spine) 737.9
tibia (acquired) 736.89
  congenital 755.69
ureter 593.3
wrist (acquired) 736.09
  congenital 755.59
Angulus infectiosus 686.8
Anhedonia 302.72
Anhidrosis (lid) (neurogenic) (thermogenic)
  705.0
Anhydration 276.5
with
  hypernatremia 276.0
  hyponatremia 276.1
Anhydremia 276.5
with
  hypernatremia 276.0
  hyponatremia 276.1
Anidrosis 705.0
Aniridia (congenital) 743.45
Anisakiasis (infection) (infestation) 127.1
Anisakis larva infestation 127.1
Aniseikonia 367.32
Anisocoria (pupil) 379.41
  congenital 743.46
Anisocytosis 790.0
Anisometropia (congenital) 367.31
Ankle —*see* condition
Ankyloblepharon (acquired) (eyelid) 374.46
filiforme (adnatum) (congenital) 743.62
total 743.62
Ankylodactly (*see also* Syndactylism) 755.10
Ankyloglossia 750.0

Ankylosis (fibrous) (osseous) 718.50
ankle 718.57
any joint, produced by surgical fusion V45.4
cricoarytenoid (cartilage) (joint) (larynx) 478.79
dental 521.6
ear ossicle NEC 385.22
  malleus 385.21
elbow 718.52
finger 718.54
hip 718.55
incostapedial joint (infectional) 385.22
joint, produced by surgical fusion NEC V45.4
knee 718.56
lumbosacral (joint) 724.6
malleus 385.21
multiple sites 718.59
postoperative (status) V45.4
sacroiliac (joint) 724.6
shoulder 718.51
specified site NEC 718.58
spine NEC 724.9
surgical V45.4
teeth, tooth (hard tissues) 521.6
temporomandibular joint 524.61
wrist 718.53
Ankylostoma— *see* Ancylostoma
Ankylostomiasis (intestinal)—*see*
  Ancylostomiasis
Ankylurethria (*see also* Stricture, urethra) 598.9
Annular —*see also* condition
detachment, cervix 622.8
organ or site, congenital NEC—*see* Distortion
pancreas (congenital) 751.7
Anodontia (complete) (partial) (vera) 520.0
with abnormal spacing 524.3
acquired 525.1
  causing malocclusion 524.3
Anomaly, anomalous (congenital) (unspecified
  type) 759.9
abdomen 759.9
abdominal wall 756.7
acoustic nerve 742.9
adrenal (gland) 759.1
Alder (-Reilly) (leukocyte granulation) 288.2
alimentary tract 751.9
  lower 751.5
  specified type NEC 751.8
  upper (any part, except tongue) 750.9
    tongue 750.10
      specified type NEC 750.19
alveolar ridge (process) 525.8
ankle (joint) 755.69
anus, anal (canal) 751.5
aorta, aortic 747.20
  arch 747.21
  coarctation (postductal) (preductal) 747.10
  cusp or valve NEC 746.9
  septum 745.0
  specified type NEC 747.29
aorticopulmonary septum 745.0
apertures, diaphragm 756.6
appendix 751.5
aqueduct of Sylvius 742.3
  with spina bifida (*see also* Spina bifida) 741.0
arm 755.50
  reduction (*see also* Deformity, reduction,
    upper limb) 755.20
arteriovenous (congenital) (peripheral) NEC
  747.60
  brain 747.81
  cerebral 747.81

Anomaly, anomalous—*continued*
   coronary 746.85
   gastrointestinal 747.61
   lower limb 747.64
   renal 747.62
   specified site NEC 747.69
   spinal 747.82
   upper limb 747.63
  artery (*see also* Anomaly, peripheral vascular
    system) NEC 747.60
   brain 747.81
   cerebral 747.81
   coronary 746.85
   eye 743.9
   pulmonary 747.3
   renal 747.62
   retina 743.9
   umbilical 747.5
  arytenoepiglottic folds 748.3
  atrial
   bands 746.9
   folds 746.9
   septa 745.5
  atrioventricular
   canal 745.69
   common 745.69
   conduction 426.7
   excitation 426.7
   septum 745.4
  atrium—*see* Anomaly, atrial
  auditory canal 744.3
   specified type NEC 744.29
    with hearing impairment 744.02
  auricle
   ear 744.3
    causing impairment of hearing 744.02
   heart 746.9
    septum 745.5
  autosomes, autosomal NEC 758.5
  Axenfeld's 743.44
  back 759.9
  band
   atrial 746.9
   heart 746.9
   ventricular 746.9
  Bartholin's duct 750.9
  biliary duct or passage 751.60
   atresia 751.61
  bladder (neck) (sphincter) (trigone) 753.9
   specified type NEC 753.8
  blood vessel 747.9
   artery—*see* Anomaly, artery
   peripheral vascular—*see* Anomaly, peripheral
    vascular system
   vein—*see* Anomaly, vein
  bone NEC 756.9
   ankle 755.69
   arm 755.50
   chest 756.3
   cranium 756.0
   face 756.0
   finger 755.50
   foot 755.67
   forearm 755.50
   frontal 756.0
   head 756.0
   hip 755.63
   leg 755.60
   lumbosacral 756.10
   nose 748.1
   pelvic girdle 755.60

Anomaly, anomalous—*continued*
   rachitic 756.4
   rib 756.3
   shoulder girdle 755.50
   skull 756.0
    with
     anencephalus 740.0
     encephalocele 742.0
     hydrocephalus 742.3
      with spina bifida (*see also* Spina bifida)
       741.0
     microcephalus 742.1
   toe 755.66
  brain 742.9
   multiple 742.4
   reduction 742.2
   specified type NEC 742.4
   vessel 747.81
  branchial cleft NEC 744.49
   cyst 744.42
   fistula 744.41
   persistent 744.41
   sinus (external) (internal) 744.41
  breast 757.9
  broad ligament 752.10
   specified type NEC 752.19
  bronchus 748.3
  bulbar septum 745.0
  bulbus cordis 745.9
   persistent (in left ventricle) 745.8
  bursa 756.9
  canal of Nuck 752.9
  canthus 743.9
  capillary NEC (*see also* Anomaly, peripheral
    vascular system) 747.60
  cardiac 746.9
   septal closure 745.9
    acquired 429.71
   valve NEC 746.9
    pulmonary 746.00
    specified type NEC 746.89
  cardiovascular system 746.9
   complicating pregnancy, childbirth, or
    puerperium 648.5
  carpus 755.50
  cartilage, trachea 748.3
  cartilaginous 756.9
  caruncle, lacrimal, lachrymal 743.9
  cascade stomach 750.7
  cauda equina 742.59
  cecum 751.5
  cerebral—*see also* Anomaly, brain
   vessels 747.81
  cerebrovascular system 747.81
  cervix (uterus) 752.40
   with doubling of vagina and uterus 752.2
   in pregnancy or childbirth 654.6
    affecting fetus or newborn 763.8
    causing obstructed labor 660.2
     affecting fetus or newborn 763.1
  Chédiak-Higashi (-Steinbrinck) (congenital
    gigantism of peroxidase granules) 288.2
  cheek 744.9
  chest (wall) 756.3
  chin 744.9
   specified type NEC 744.89
  chordae tendineae 746.9
  choroid 743.9
   plexus 742.9

Anomaly, anomalous—*continued*
  chromosomes, chromosomal 758.9
    13 (13-15) 758.1
    18 (16-18) 758.2
    21 or 22 758.0
    autosomes NEC (*see also* Abnormality,
        autosomes) 758.5
      deletion 758.3
    Christchurch 758.3
    D₁ 758.1
    E₃ 758.2
    G 758.0
    mitochondrial 758.9
    mosaics 758.89
    sex 758.81
      complement, XO 758.6
      complement, XXX 758.81
      complement, XYY 758.81
      gonadal dysgenesis 758.6
      Klinefelter's 758.7
      Turner's 758.6
    trisomy 21 758.0
  cilia 743.9
  circulatory system 747.9
    specified type NEC 747.89
  clavicle 755.51
  clitoris 752.40
  coccyx 756.10
  colon 751.5
  common duct 751.60
  communication
    coronary artery 746.85
    left ventricle with right atrium 745.4
  concha (ear) 744.3
  connection
    renal vessels with kidney 747.62
    total pulmonary venous 747.41
  connective tissue 756.9
    specified type NEC 756.89
  cornea 743.9
    shape 743.41
    size 743.41
    specified type NEC 743.49
  coronary
    artery 746.85
    vein 746.89
  cranium—*see* Anomaly, skull
  cricoid cartilage 748.3
  cushion, endocardial 745.60
    specified type NEC 745.69
  cystic duct 751.60
  dental arch relationship 524.2
  dentition 520.6
  dentofacial NEC 524.9
    functional 524.5
    specified type NEC 524.8
  dermatoglyphic 757.2
  Descemet's membrane 743.9
    specified type NEC 743.49
  development
    cervix 752.40
    vagina 752.40
    vulva 752.40
  diaphragm, diaphragmatic (apertures) NEC
      756.6
  digestive organ(s) or system 751.9
    lower 751.5
    specified type NEC 751.8
    upper 750.9
  distribution, coronary artery 746.85

Anomaly, anomalous—*continued*
  ductus
    arteriosus 747.0
    Botalli 747.0
  duodenum 751.5
  dura 742.9
    brain 742.4
    spinal cord 742.59
  ear 744.3
    causing impairment of hearing 744.00
      specified type NEC 744.09
    external 744.3
      causing impairment of hearing 744.02
      specified type NEC 744.29
    inner (causing impairment of hearing) 744.05
    middle, except ossicles (causing impairment
        of hearing) 744.03
      ossicles 744.04
    ossicles 744.04
    prominent auricle 744.29
    specified type NEC 744.29
      with hearing impairment 744.09
  Ebstein's (heart) 746.2
    tricuspid valve 746.2
  ectodermal 757.9
  Eisenmenger's (ventricular septal defect) 745.4
  ejaculatory duct 752.9
    specified type NEC 752.8
  elbow (joint) 755.50
  endocardial cushion 745.60
    specified type NEC 745.69
  endocrine gland NEC 759.2
  epididymis 752.9
  epiglottis 748.3
  esophagus 750.9
    specified type NEC 750.4
  Eustachian tube 744.3
    specified type NEC 744.24
  eye (any part) 743.9
    adnexa 743.9
      specified type NEC 743.69
    anophthalmos 743.00
    anterior
      chamber and related structures 743.9
        angle 743.9
          specified type NEC 743.44
        specified type NEC 743.44
      segment 743.9
        combined 743.48
        multiple 743.48
        specified type NEC 743.49
    cataract (*see also* Cataract) 743.30
    glaucoma (*see also* Buphthalmia) 743.20
    lid 743.9
      specified type NEC 743.63
    microphthalmos (*see also* Microphthalmos)
        743.10
    posterior segment 743.9
      specified type NEC 743.59
      vascular 743.58
      vitreous 743.9
        specified type NEC 743.51
    ptosis (eyelid) 743.61
    retina 743.9
      specified type NEC 743.59
    sclera 743.9
      specified type NEC 743.47
    specified type NEC 743.8
  eyebrow 744.89
  eyelid 743.9
    specified type NEC 743.63

Anomaly, anomalous—*continued*
  face (any part) 744.9
    bone(s) 756.0
    specified type NEC 744.89
  fallopian tube 752.10
    specified type NEC 752.19
  fascia 756.9
    specified type NEC 756.89
  femur 755.60
  fibula 755.60
  finger 755.50
    supernumerary 755.01
    webbed (*see also* Syndactylism, fingers)
      755.11
  fixation, intestine 751.4
  flexion (joint) 755.9
    hip or thigh (*see also* Dislocation, hip,
      congenital) 754.30
  folds, heart 746.9
  foot 755.67
  foramen
    Botalli 745.5
    ovale 745.5
  forearm 755.50
  forehead (*see also* Anomaly, skull) 756.0
  form, teeth 520.2
  fovea centralis 743.9
  frontal bone (*see also* Anomaly, skull) 756.0
  gallbladder 751.60
  Gartner's duct 752.11
  gastrointestinal tract 751.9
    specified type NEC 751.8
    vessel 747.61
  genitalia, genital organ(s) or system
    female 752.9
      external 752.40
        specified type NEC 752.49
      internal NEC 752.9
    male (external and internal) 752.9
      epispadias 752.62
      hidden penis 752.65
      hydrocele, congenital 778.6
      hypospadias 752.61
      micropenis 752.64
      testis, undescended 752.51
        retractile 752.52
    specified type NEC 752.8
  genitourinary NEC 752.9
  Gerbode 745.4
  globe (eye) 743.9
  glottis 748.3
  granulation or granulocyte, genetic 288.2
    constitutional 288.2
    leukocyte 288.2
  gum 750.9
  gyri 742.9
  hair 757.9
    specified type NEC 757.4
  hand 755.50
  hard tissue formation in pulp 522.3
  head (*see also* Anomaly, skull) 756.0
  heart 746.9
    auricle 746.9
    bands 746.9
    fibroelastosis cordis 425.3
    folds 746.9
    malposition 746.87
    maternal, affecting fetus or newborn 760.3
    obstructive NEC 746.84
    patent ductus arteriosus (Botalli) 747.0

  septum 745.9
    acquired 429.71
    aortic 745.0
    aorticopulmonary 745.0
    atrial 745.5
    auricular 745.5
    between aorta and pulmonary artery 745.0
    endocardial cushion type 745.60
      specified type NEC 745.69
    interatrial 745.5
    interventricular 745.4
      with pulmonary stenosis or atresia,
        dextraposition of aorta, and
        hypertrophy of right ventricle 745.2
      acquired 429.71
    specified type NEC 745.8
    ventricular 745.4
      with pulmonary stenosis or atresia,
        dextraposition of aorta, and
        hypertrophy of right ventricle 745.2
      acquired 429.71
  specified type NEC 746.89
  tetralogy of Fallot 745.2
  valve NEC 746.9
    aortic 746.9
      atresia 746.89
      bicuspid valve 746.4
      insufficiency 746.4
      specified type NEC 746.89
      stenosis 746.3
        subaortic 746.81
        supravalvular 747.22
    mitral 746.9
      atresia 746.89
      insufficiency 746.6
      specified type NEC 746.89
      stenosis 746.5
    pulmonary 746.00
      atresia 746.01
      insufficiency 746.09
      stenosis 746.02
        infundibular 746.83
        subvalvular 746.83
    tricuspid 746.9
      atresia 746.1
      stenosis 746.1
    ventricle 746.9
  heel 755.67
  Hegglin's 288.2
  hemianencephaly 740.0
  hemicephaly 740.0
  hemicrania 740.0
  hepatic duct 751.60
  hip (joint) 755.63
  hourglass
    bladder 753.8
    gallbladder 751.69
    stomach 750.7
  humerus 755.50
  hymen 752.40
  hypersegmentation of neutrophils, hereditary
    288.2
  hypophyseal 759.2
  ileocecal (coil) (valve) 751.5
  ileum (intestine) 751.5
  ilium 755.60
  integument 757.9
    specified type NEC 757.8
  intervertebral cartilage or disc 756.10

Anomaly, anomalous—*continued*
  intestine (large) (small) 751.5
    fixational type 751.4
  iris 743.9
    specified type NEC 743.46
  ischium 755.60
  jaw NEC 524.9
    closure 524.5
    size NEC 524.00
    specified type NEC 524.8
  jaw-cranial base relationship 524.10
    specified NEC 524.19
  jejunum 751.5
  joint 755.9
    hip
      dislocation (*see also* Dislocation, hip,
        congenital) 754.30
      predislocation (*see also* Subluxation,
        congenital, hip) 754.32
      preluxation (*see also* Subluxation,
        congenital, hip) 754.32
      subluxation (*see also* Subluxation,
        congenital, hip) 754.32
    lumbosacral 756.10
      spondylolisthesis 756.12
      spondylosis 756.11
    multiple arthrogryposis 754.89
    sacroiliac 755.69
  Jordan's 288.2
  kidney(s) (calyx) (pelvis) 753.9
    vessel 747.62
  Klippel-Feil (brevicollis) 756.16
  knee (joint) 755.64
  labium (majus) (minus) 752.40
  labyrinth, membranous (causing impairment of
    hearing) 744.05
  lacrimal
    apparatus, duct or passage 743.9
      specified type NEC 743.65
    gland 743.9
      specified type NEC 743.64
  Langdon Down (mongolism) 758.0
  larynx, laryngeal (muscle) 748.3
    web, webbed 748.2
  leg (lower) (upper) 755.60
    reduction NEC (*see also* Deformity,
      reduction, lower limb) 755.30
  lens 743.9
    shape 743.36
    specified type NEC 743.39
  leukocytes, genetic 288.2
    granulation (constitutional) 288.2
  lid (fold) 743.9
  ligament 756.9
    broad 752.10
    round 752.9
  limb, except reduction deformity 755.9
    lower 755.60
      reduction deformity (*see also* Deformity,
        reduction, lower limb) 755.30
      specified type NEC 755.69
    upper 755.50
      reduction deformity (*see also* Deformity,
        reduction, upper limb) 755.20
      specified type NEC 755.59
  lip 750.9
    harelip (*see also* Cleft, lip) 749.10
    specified type NEC 750.26
  liver (duct) 751.60
    atresia 751.69

Anomaly, anomalous—*continued*
  lower extremity 755.60
    vessel 747.64
  lumbosacral (joint) (region) 756.10
  lung (fissure) (lobe) NEC 748.60
    agenesis 748.5
    specified type NEC 748.69
  lymphatic system 759.9
  Madelung's (radius) 755.54
  mandible 524.9
    size NEC 524.00
  maxilla 524.9
    size NEC 524.00
  May (-Hegglin) 288.2
  meatus urinarius 753.9
    specified type NEC 753.8
  meningeal bands or folds, constriction of 742.8
  meninges 742.9
    brain 742.4
    spinal 742.59
  meningocele (*see also* Spina bifida) 741.9
  mesentery 751.9
  metacarpus 755.50
  metatarsus 755.67
  middle ear, except ossicles (causing impairment
    of hearing) 744.03
    ossicles 744.04
  mitral (leaflets) (valve) 746.9
    atresia 746.89
    insufficiency 746.6
    specified type NEC 746.89
    stenosis 746.5
  mouth 750.9
    specified type NEC 750.26
  multiple NEC 759.7
    specified type NEC 759.89
  muscle 756.9
    eye 743.9
      specified type NEC 743.69
    specified type NEC 756.89
  musculoskeletal system, except limbs 756.9
    specified type NEC 756.9
  nail 757.9
    specified type NEC 757.5
  narrowness, eyelid 743.62
  nasal sinus or septum 748.1
  neck (any part) 744.9
    specified type NEC 744.89
  nerve 742.9
    acoustic 742.9
      specified type NEC 742.8
    optic 742.9
      specified type NEC 742.8
    specified type NEC 742.8
  nervous system NEC 742.9
    brain 742.9
      specified type NEC 742.4
    specified type NEC 742.8
  neurological 742.9
  nipple 757.9
  nonteratogenic NEC 754.89
  nose, nasal (bone) (cartilage) (septum) (sinus)
    748.1
  ocular muscle 743.9
  omphalomesenteric duct 751.0
  opening, pulmonary veins 747.49
  optic
    disc 743.9
      specified type NEC 743.57
    nerve 742.9
  opticociliary vessels 743.9

Anomaly, anomalous—*continued*
   orbit (eye) 743.9
      specified type NEC 743.66
   organ
      of Corti (causing impairment of hearing)
         744.05
      or site 759.9
         specified type NEC 759.89
   origin
      both great arteries from same ventricle 745.11
      coronary artery 746.85
      innominate artery 747.69
      left coronary artery from pulmonary artery
         746.85
      pulmonary artery 747.3
      renal vessels 747.62
      subclavian artery (left) (right) 747.21
   osseous meatus (ear) 744.03
   ovary 752.0
   oviduct 752.10
   palate (hard) (soft) 750.9
      cleft (*see also* Cleft, palate) 749.00
   pancreas (duct) 751.7
   papillary muscles 746.9
   parathyroid gland 759.2
   paraurethral ducts 753.9
   parotid (gland) 750.9
   patella 755.64
   Pelger-Huët (hereditary hyposegmentation)
      288.2
   pelvic girdle 755.60
      specified type NEC 755.69
   pelvis (bony) 755.60
      complicating delivery 653.0
      rachitic 268.1
         fetal 756.4
   penis (glans) 752.69
   pericardium 746.89
   peripheral vascular system NEC 747.60
      gastrointestinal 747.61
      lower limb 747.64
      renal 747.62
      specified site NEC 747.69
      spinal 747.82
      upper limb 747.63
   Peter's 743.44
   pharynx 750.9
      branchial cleft 744.41
      specified type NEC 750.29
   Pierre Robin 756.0
   pigmentation NEC 709.00
      congenital 757.33
   pituitary (gland) 759.2
   pleural folds 748.8
   portal vein 747.40
   position tooth, teeth 524.3
   preauricular sinus 744.46
   prepuce 752.9
   prostate 752.9
   pulmonary 748.60
      artery 747.3
      circulation 747.3
      specified type NEC 748.69
      valve 746.00
         atresia 746.01
         insufficiency 746.09
         specified type NEC 746.09
         stenosis 746.02
            infundibular 746.83
            subvalvular 746.83
      vein 747.40

Anomaly, anomalous—*continued*
   venous
      connection 747.49
         partial 747.42
         total 747.41
      return 747.49
         partial 747.42
         total (TAPVR) (complete)
            (subdiaphragmatic)
            (supradiaphragmatic) 747.41
   pupil 743.9
   pylorus 750.9
      hypertrophy 750.5
      stenosis 750.5
   rachitic, fetal 756.4
   radius 755.50
   rectovaginal (septum) 752.40
   rectum 751.5
   refraction 367.9
   renal 753.9
      vessel 747.62
   respiratory system 748.9
      specified type NEC 748.8
   rib 756.3
      cervical 756.2
   Rieger's 743.44
   rings, trachea 748.3
   rotation—*see also* Malrotation
      hip or thigh (*see also* Subluxation, congenital,
         hip) 754.32
   round ligament 752.9
   sacroiliac (joint) 755.69
   sacrum 756.10
   saddle
      back 754.2
      nose 754.0
         syphilitic 090.5
   salivary gland or duct 750.9
      specified type NEC 750.26
   scapula 755.50
   sclera 743.9
      specified type NEC 743.47
   scrotum 752.9
   sebaceous gland 757.9
   seminal duct or tract 752.9
   sense organs 742.9
      specified type NEC 742.8
   septum
      heart—*see* Anomaly, heart, septum
      nasal 748.1
   sex chromosomes NEC (*see also* Anomaly,
      chromosomes) 758.81
   shoulder (girdle) (joint) 755.50
      specified type NEC 755.59
   sigmoid (flexure) 751.5
   sinus of Valsalva 747.29
   site NEC 759.9
   skeleton generalized NEC 756.50
   skin (appendage) 757.9
      specified type NEC 757.39
   skull (bone) 756.0
      with
         anencephalus 740.0
         encephalocele 742.0
         hydrocephalus 742.3
            with spina bifida (*see also* Spina bifida)
               741.0
         microcephalus 742.1

Anomaly, anomalous—*continued*
  specified type NEC
    adrenal (gland) 759.1
    alimentary tract (complete) (partial) 751.8
      lower 751.5
      upper 750.8
    ankle 755.69
    anus, anal (canal) 751.5
    aorta, aortic 747.29
      arch 747.21
    appendix 751.5
    arm 755.59
    artery (peripheral) NEC (*see also* Anomaly,
        peripheral vascular system) 747.60
      brain 747.81
      coronary 746.85
      eye 743.58
      pulmonary 747.3
      retinal 743.58
      umbilical 747.5
    auditory canal 744.29
      causing impairment of hearing 744.02
    bile duct or passage 751.69
    bladder 753.8
      neck 753.8
    bone(s) 756.9
      arm 755.59
      face 756.0
      leg 755.69
      pelvic girdle 755.69
      shoulder girdle 755.59
      skull 756.0
        with
          anencephalus 740.0
          encephalocele 742.0
          hydrocephalus 742.3
            with spina bifida (*see also* Spina
                bifida) 741.0
          microcephalus 742.1
    brain 742.4
    breast 757.6
    broad ligament 752.19
    bronchus 748.3
    canal of Nuck 752.8
    cardiac septal closure 745.8
    carpus 755.59
    cartilaginous 756.9
    cecum 751.5
    cervix 752.49
    chest (wall) 756.3
    chin 744.89
    ciliary body 743.46
    circulatory system 747.89
    clavicle 755.51
    clitoris 752.49
    coccyx 756.19
    colon 751.5
    common duct 751.69
    connective tissue 756.89
    cricoid cartilage 748.3
    cystic duct 751.69
    diaphragm 756.6
    digestive organ(s) or tract 751.8
      lower 751.5
      upper 750.8
    duodenum 751.5
    ear 744.29
      auricle 744.29
        causing impairment of hearing 744.02
      causing impairment of hearing 744.09

Anomaly, anomalous—*continued*
    inner (causing impairment of hearing)
        744.05
    middle, except ossicles 744.03
      ossicles 744.04
    ejaculatory duct 752.8
    endocrine 759.2
    epiglottis 748.3
    esophagus 750.4
    Eustachian tube 744.24
    eye 743.8
      lid 743.63
      muscle 743.69
    face 744.89
      bone(s) 756.0
    fallopian tube 752.19
    fascia 756.89
    femur 755.69
    fibula 755.69
    finger 755.59
    foot 755.67
    fovea centralis 743.55
    gallbladder 751.69
    Gartner's duct 752.8
    gastrointestinal tract 751.8
    genitalia, genital organ(s)
      female 752.8
        external 752.49
        internal NEC 752.8
      male 752.8
        penis 752.69
    genitourinary tract NEC 752.8
    glottis 748.3
    hair 757.4
    hand 755.59
    heart 746.89
      valve NEC 746.89
        pulmonary 746.09
    hepatic duct 751.69
    hydatid of Morgagni 752.8
    hymen 752.49
    integument 757.8
    intestine (large) (small) 751.5
      fixational type 751.4
    iris 743.46
    jejunum 751.5
    joint 755.8
    kidney 753.3
    knee 755.64
    labium (majus) (minus) 752.49
    labyrinth, membranous 744.05
    larynx 748.3
    leg 755.69
    lens 743.39
    limb, except reduction deformity 755.8
      lower 755.69
        reduction deformity (*see also* Deformity,
            reduction, lower limb) 755.30
      upper 755.59
        reduction deformity (*see also* Deformity,
            reduction, upper limb) 755.20
    lip 750.26
    liver 751.69
    lung (fissure) (lobe) 748.69
    meatus urinarius 753.8
    metacarpus 755.59
    mouth 750.26
    muscle 756.89
      eye 743.69
    musculoskeletal system, except limbs 756.9
    nail 757.5

Anomaly, anomalous—*continued*
  neck 744.89
  nerve 742.8
    acoustic 742.8
    optic 742.8
  nervous system 742.8
  nipple 757.6
  nose 748.1
  organ NEC 759.89
    of Corti 744.05
  osseous meatus (ear) 744.03
  ovary 752.0
  oviduct 752.19
  pancreas 751.7
  parathyroid 759.2
  patella 755.64
  pelvic girdle 755.69
  penis 752.69
  pericardium 746.89
  peripheral vascular system NEC (*see also*
    Anomaly, peripheral vascular system)
    747.60
  pharynx 750.29
  pituitary 759.2
  prostate 752.8
  radius 755.59
  rectum 751.5
  respiratory system 748.8
  rib 756.3
  round ligament 752.8
  sacrum 756.19
  salivary duct or gland 750.26
  scapula 755.59
  sclera 743.47
  scrotum 752.8
  seminal duct or tract 752.8
  shoulder girdle 755.59
  site NEC 759.89
  skin 757.39
  skull (bone(s)) 756.0
    with
      anencephalus 740.0
      encephalocele 742.0
      hydrocephalus 742.3
        with spina bifida (*see also* Spina bifida)
        741.0
      microcephalus 742.1
  specified organ or site NEC 759.89
  spermatic cord 752.8
  spinal cord 742.59
  spine 756.19
  spleen 759.0
  sternum 756.3
  stomach 750.7
  tarsus 755.67
  tendon 756.89
  testis 752.8
  thorax (wall) 756.3
  thymus 759.2
  thyroid (gland) 759.2
    cartilage 748.3
  tibia 755.69
  toe 755.66
  tongue 750.19
  trachea (cartilage) 748.3
  ulna 755.59
  urachus 753.7
  ureter 753.4
    obstructive 753.29
  urethra 753.8
    obstructive 753.6

Anomaly, anomalous—*continued*
  urinary tract 753.8
  uterus 752.3
  uvula 750.26
  vagina 752.49
  vascular NEC (*see also* Anomaly, peripheral
    vascular system) 747.60
    brain 747.81
  vas deferens 752.8
  vein(s) (peripheral) NEC (*see also* Anomaly,
    peripheral vascular system) 747.60
    brain 747.81
    great 747.49
    portal 747.49
    pulmonary 747.49
  vena cava (inferior) (superior) 747.49
  vertebra 756.19
  vulva 752.49
  spermatic cord 752.9
  spine, spinal 756.10
    column 756.10
    cord 742.9
      meningocele (*see also* Spina bifida) 741.9
      specified type NEC 742.59
      spina bifida (*see also* Spina bifida) 741.9
      vessel 747.82
    meninges 742.59
    nerve root 742.9
  spleen 759.0
  Sprengel's 755.52
  sternum 756.3
  stomach 750.9
    specified type NEC 750.7
  submaxillary gland 750.9
  superior vena cava 747.40
  talipes—*see* Talipes
  tarsus 755.67
    with complete absence of distal elements
    755.31
  teeth, tooth NEC 520.9
    position 524.3
    spacing 524.3
  tendon 756.9
    specified type NEC 756.89
  termination
    coronary artery 746.85
  testis 752.9
  thebesian valve 746.9
  thigh 755.60
    flexion (*see also* Subluxation, congenital, hip)
    754.32
  thorax (wall) 756.3
  throat 750.9
  thumb 755.50
    supernumerary 755.01
  thymus gland 759.2
  thyroid (gland) 759.2
    cartilage 748.3
  tibia 755.60
    saber 090.5
  toe 755.66
    supernumerary 755.02
    webbed (*see also* Syndactylism, toes) 755.13
  tongue 750.10
    specified type NEC 750.19
  trachea, tracheal 748.3
    cartilage 748.3
    rings 748.3
  tragus 744.3
  transverse aortic arch 747.21
  trichromata 368.59

Anomaly, anomalous—*continued*
  trichromatopsia 368.59
  tricuspid (leaflet) (valve) 746.9
    atresia 746.1
    Ebstein's 746.2
    specified type NEC 746.89
    stenosis 746.1
  trunk 759.9
  Uhl's (hypoplasia of myocardium, right
    ventricle) 746.84
  ulna 755.50
  umbilicus 759.9
    artery 747.5
  union, trachea with larynx 748.3
  unspecified site 759.9
  upper extremity 755.50
    vessel 747.63
  urachus 753.7
    specified type NEC 753.7
  ureter 753.9
    obstructive 753.20
    specified type NEC 753.4
      obstructive 753.29
  urethra (valve) 753.9
    obstructive 753.6
    specified type NEC 753.8
  urinary tract or system (any part, except
    urachus) 753.9
    specified type NEC 753.8
    urachus 753.7
  uterus 752.3
    with only one functioning horn 752.3
    in pregnancy or childbirth 654.0
      affecting fetus or newborn 763.8
      causing obstructed labor 660.2
        affecting fetus or newborn 763.1
  uvula 750.9
  vagina 752.40
  valleculae 748.3
  valve (heart) NEC 746.9
    formation, ureter 753.29
    pulmonary 746.00
    specified type NEC 746.89
  vascular NEC (*see also* Anomaly, peripheral
    vascular system) 747.60
    ring 747.21
  vas deferens 752.9
  vein(s) (peripheral) NEC (*see also* Anomaly,
    peripheral vascular system) 747.60
    brain 747.81
    cerebral 747.81
    coronary 746.89
    great 747.40
      specified type NEC 747.49
    portal 747.40
    pulmonary 747.40
    retina 743.9
  vena cava (inferior) (superior) 747.40
  venous return (pulmonary) 747.49
    partial 747.42
    total 747.41
  ventricle, ventricular (heart) 746.9
    bands 746.9
    folds 746.9
    septa 745.4
  vertebra 756.10
  vesicourethral orifice 753.9
  vessels NEC (*see also* Anomaly, peripheral
    vascular system) 747.60
    optic papilla 743.9
  vitelline duct 751.0

Anomaly, anomalous—*continued*
  vitreous humor 743.9
    specified type NEC 743.51
  vulva 752.40
  wrist (joint) 755.50
Anomia 784.69
Anonychia 757.5
  acquired 703.8
Anophthalmos, anophthalmus (clinical)
  (congenital) (globe) 743.00
  acquired 360.89
Anopsia (altitudinal) (quadrant) 368.46
Anorchia 752.8
Anorchism, anorchidism 752.8
Anorexia 783.0
  hysterical 300.11
  nervosa 307.1
Anosmia (*see also* Disturbance, sensation) 781.1
  hysterical 300.11
  postinfectional 478.9
  psychogenic 306.7
  traumatic 951.8
Anosognosia 780.9
Anosphrasia 781.1
Anosteoplasia 756.50
Anotia 744.09
Anovulatory cycle 628.0
Anoxemia 799.0
  newborn 770.8
Anoxia 799.0
  altitude 993.2
  cerebral 348.1
    with
      abortion—*see* Abortion, by type,
        with specified complication NEC
      ectopic pregnancy (*see also* categories
        633.0-633.9) 639.8
      molar pregnancy (*see also* categories
        630-632) 639.8
    complicating
      delivery (cesarean) (instrumental) 669.4
      ectopic or molar pregnancy 639.8
      obstetric anesthesia or sedation 668.2
    during or resulting from a procedure 997.01
    following
      abortion 639.8
      ectopic or molar pregnancy 639.8
    newborn (*see also* Distress, fetal, liveborn
      infant) 768.9
  due to drowning 994.1
  heart—*see* Insufficiency, coronary
  high altitude 993.2
  intrauterine
    fetal death (before onset of labor) 768.0
      during labor 768.1
    liveborn infant—*see* Distress, fetal, liveborn
      infant
  myocardial—*see* Insufficiency, coronary
  newborn 768.9
    mild or moderate 768.6
    severe 768.5
  pathological 799.0
Anteflexion —*see* Anteversion
Antenatal
  care, normal pregnancy V22.1
    first V22.0
  screening (for) V28.9
    based on amniocentesis NEC V28.2
      chromosomal anomalies V28.0
      raised alphafetoprotein levels V28.1
    chromosomal anomalies V28.0

Antenatal—*continued*
  fetal growth retardation using ultrasonics
    V28.4
  isoimmunization V28.5
  malformations using ultrasonics V28.3
  raised alphafetoprotein levels in amniotic fluid
    V28.1
  specified condition NEC V28.8
Antepartum —*see* condition
Anterior —*see also* condition
  spinal artery compression syndrome 721.1
Antero-occlusion 524.2
Anteversion
  cervix (*see also* Anteversion, uterus) 621.6
  femur (neck), congenital 755.63
  uterus, uterine (cervix) (postinfectional)
    (postpartal, old) 621.6
    congenital 752.3
    in pregnancy or childbirth 654.4
      affecting fetus or newborn 763.8
      causing obstructed labor 660.2
        affecting fetus or newborn 763.1
Anthracosilicosis (occupational) 500
Anthracosis (lung) (occupational) 500
  lingua 529.3
Anthrax 022.9
  with pneumonia 022.1 *[484.5]*
  colitis 022.2
  cutaneous 022.0
  gastrointestinal 022.2
  intestinal 022.2
  pulmonary 022.1
  respiratory 022.1
  septicemia 022.3—
  specified manifestation NEC 022.8
Anthropoid pelvis 755.69
  with disproportion (fetopelvic) 653.2
    affecting fetus or newborn 763.1
    causing obstructed labor 660.1
      affecting fetus or newborn 763.1
Anthropophobia 300.29
Antibioma, breast 611.0
Antibodies
  maternal (blood group) (*see also*
    Incompatibility) 656.2
  anti-D, cord blood 656.1
    fetus or newborn 773.0
Antibody deficiency syndrome
  agammaglobulinemic 279.00
  congenital 279.04
  hypogammaglobulinemic 279.00
Anticoagulant, circulating (*see also* Circulating
  anticoagulants) 286.5
Antimongolism syndrome 758.3
Antimonial cholera 985.4
Antisocial personality 301.7
Antithrombinemia (*see also* Circulating
  anticoagulants) 286.5
Antithromboplastinemia (*see also* Circulating
  anticoagulants) 286.5
Antithromboplastinogenemia (*see also*
  Circulating anticoagulants) 286.5
Antitoxin complication or reaction —*see*
  Complications, vaccination
Anton (-Babinski) syndrome
  (hemiasomatognosia) 307.9
Antritis (chronic) 473.0
  acute 461.0
Antrum, antral —*see* condition

Anuria 788.5
  with
    abortion—*see* Abortion, by type, with renal
      failure
    ectopic pregnancy (*see also* categories
      633.0-633.9) 639.3
    molar pregnancy (*see also* categories
      630-632) 639.3
  calculus (impacted) (recurrent) 592.9
    kidney 592.0
    ureter 592.1
  congenital 753.3
  due to a procedure 997.5
  following
    abortion 639.3
    ectopic or molar pregnancy 639.3
  newborn 753.3
  postrenal 593.4
  puerperal, postpartum, childbirth 669.3
  specified as due to a procedure 997.5
  sulfonamide
    correct substance properly administered 788.5
    overdose or wrong substance given or taken
      961.0
  traumatic (following crushing) 958.5
Anus, anal —*see* condition
Anusitis 569.49
Anxiety (neurosis) (reaction) (state) 300.00
  alcohol-induced 291.89
  depression 300.4
  drug-induced 292.89
  generalized 300.02
  hysteria 300.20
  in
    acute stress reaction 308.0
    transient adjustment reaction 309.24
  panic type 300.01
  separation, abnormal 309.21
  syndrome (organic) (transient) 293.84
Aorta, aortic —*see* condition
Aortectasia 441.9
Aortitis (nonsyphilitic) 447.6
  arteriosclerotic 440.0
  calcific 447.6
  Döhle-Heller 093.1
  luetic 093.1
  rheumatic (*see also* Endocarditis, acute,
    rheumatic) 391.1
  rheumatoid—*see* Arthritis, rheumatoid
  specific 093.1
  syphilitic 093.1
    congenital 090.5
Apathetic thyroid storm (*see also*
  Thyrotoxicosis) 242.9
Apepsia 536.8
  achlorhydric 536.0
  psychogenic 306.4
Aperistalsis, esophagus 530.0
Apert's syndrome (acrocephalosyndactyly)
  755.55
Apert-Gallais syndrome (adrenogenital) 255.2
Apertognathia 524.2
Aphagia 783.0
  psychogenic 307.1
Aphakia (acquired) (bilateral) (postoperative)
  (unilateral) 379.31
  congenital 743.35
Aphalangia (congenital) 755.4
  lower limb (complete) (intercalary) (partial)
    (terminal) 755.39

Aphalangia—*continued*
  meaning all digits (complete) (partial) 755.31
    transverse 755.31
  upper limb (complete) (intercalary) (partial)
    (terminal) 755.29
  meaning all digits (complete) (partial) 755.21
    transverse 755.21
Aphasia (amnestic) (ataxic) (auditory) (Broca's)
  (choreatic) (classic) (expressive) (global)
  (ideational) (ideokinetic) (ideomotor) (jargon)
  (motor) (nominal) (receptive) (semantic)
  (sensory) (syntactic) (verbal) (visual)
  (Wernicke's) 784.3
  developmental 315.31
  syphilis, tertiary 094.89
  uremic—*see* Uremia
Aphemia 784.3
  uremic—*see* Uremia
Aphonia 784.41
  clericorum 784.49
  hysterical 300.11
  organic 784.41
  psychogenic 306.1
Aphthae, aphthous —*see also* condition
  Bednar's 528.2
  cachectic 529.0
  epizootic 078.4
  fever 078.4
  oral 528.2
  stomatitis 528.2
  thrush 112.0
  ulcer (oral) (recurrent) 528.2
    genital organ(s) NEC
      female 629.8
      male 608.89
    larynx 478.79
Apical —*see* condition
Aplasia —*see also* Agenesis
  alveolar process (acquired) 525.8
    congenital 750.26
  aorta (congenital) 747.22
  aortic valve (congenital) 746.89
  axialis extracorticalis (congenital) 330.0
  bone marrow (myeloid) 284.9
    acquired (secondary) 284.8
    congenital 284.0
    idiopathic 284.9
  brain 740.0
    specified part 742.2
  breast 757.6
  bronchus 748.3
  cementum 520.4
  cerebellar 742.2
  congenital pure red cell 284.0
  corpus callosum 742.2
  erythrocyte 284.8
    congenital 284.0
  extracortical axial 330.0
  eye (congenital) 743.00
  fovea centralis (congenital) 743.55
  germinal (cell) 606.0
  iris 743.45
  labyrinth, membranous 744.05
  limb (congenital) 755.4
    lower NEC 755.30
    upper NEC 755.20
  lung (bilateral) (congenital) (unilateral) 748.5
  nervous system NEC 742.8
  nuclear 742.8
  ovary 752.0
  Pelizaeus-Merzbacher 330.0

Aplasia—*continued*
  prostate (congenital) 752.8
  red cell (pure) (with thymoma) 284.8
    acquired (adult) (secondary) 284.8
    congenital 284.0
    hereditary 284.0
    of infants 284.0
    primary 284.0
  round ligament (congenital) 752.8
  salivary gland 750.21
  skin (congenital) 757.39
  spinal cord 742.59
  spleen 759.0
  testis (congenital) 752.8
  thymic, with immunodeficiency 279.2
  thyroid 243
  uterus 752.3
  ventral horn cell 742.59
Apleuria 756.3
Apnea, apneic (spells) 786.09
  newborn, neonatorum 770.8
  psychogenic 306.1
  sleep NEC 780.57
    with
      hypersomnia 780.53
      hyposomnia 780.51
      insomnia 780.51
      sleep disturbance NEC 780.57
Apneumatosis newborn 770.4
Apodia 755.31
Apophysitis (bone) (*see also* Osteochondrosis)
  732.9
  calcaneus 732.5
  juvenile 732.6
Apoplectiform convulsions (*see also* Disease,
  cerebrovascular, acute) 436
Apoplexia, apoplexy, apoplectic (*see also*
  Disease, cerebrovascular, acute) 436
  abdominal 569.89
  adrenal 036.3
  attack 436
  basilar (*see also* Disease, cerebrovascular,
    acute) 436
  brain (*see also* Disease, cerebrovascular, acute)
    436
  bulbar (*see also* Disease, cerebrovascular,
    acute) 436
  capillary (*see also* Disease, cerebrovascular,
    acute) 436
  cardiac (*see also* Infarct, myocardium) 410.9
  cerebral (*see also* Disease, cerebrovascular,
    acute) 436
  chorea (*see also* Disease, cerebrovascular,
    acute) 436
  congestive (*see also* Disease, cerebrovascular,
    acute) 436
    newborn 767.4
  embolic (*see also* Embolism, brain) 434.1
  fetus 767.0
  fit (*see also* Disease, cerebrovascular, acute) 436
  healed or old—*see also* category 438
    without residuals V12.59
  heart (auricle) (ventricle) (*see also* Infarct,
    myocardium) 410.9
  heat 992.0
  hemiplegia (*see also* Disease, cerebrovascular,
    acute) 436
  hemorrhagic (stroke) (*see also* Hemorrhage,
    brain) 432.9
  ingravescent (*see also* Disease, cerebrovascular,
    acute) 436

Apoplexia, apoplexy, apoplectic—*continued*
  late effect—*see* category 438
  lung—*see* Embolism, pulmonary
  meninges, hemorrhagic (*see also* Hemorrhage,
    subarachnoid) 430
  neonatorum 767.0
  newborn 767.0
  pancreatitis 577.0
  placenta 641.2
  progressive (*see also* Disease, cerebrovascular,
    acute) 436
  pulmonary (artery) (vein)—*see* Embolism,
    pulmonary
  sanguineous (*see also* Disease, cerebrovascular,
    acute) 436
  seizure (*see also* Disease, cerebrovascular,
    acute) 436
  serous (*see also* Disease, cerebrovascular,
    acute) 436
  spleen 289.59
  stroke (*see also* Disease, cerebrovascular, acute)
    436
  thrombotic (*see also* Thrombosis, brain) 434.0
  uremic—*see* Uremia
  uteroplacental 641.2
Appendage
  fallopian tube (cyst of Morgagni) 752.11
  intestine (epiploic) 751.5
  preauricular 744.1
  testicular (organ of Morgagni) 752.8
Appendicitis 541
  with
    perforation, peritonitis (generalized), or
      rupture 540.0
      with peritoneal abscess 540.1
    peritoneal abscess 540.1
  acute (catarrhal) (fulminating) (gangrenous)
    (inflammatory) (obstructive) (retrocecal)
    (suppurative) 540.9
    with
      perforation, peritonitis, or rupture 540.0
        with peritoneal abscess 540.1
      peritoneal abscess 540.1
  amebic 006.8
  chronic (recurrent) 542
  exacerbation—*see* Appendicitis, acute
  fulminating—*see* Appendicitis, acute
  gangrenous—*see* Appendicitis, acute
  healed (obliterative) 542
  interval 542
  neurogenic 542
  obstructive 542
  pneumococcal 541
  recurrent 542
  relapsing 542
  retrocecal 541
  subacute (adhesive) 542
  subsiding 542
  suppurative—*see* Appendicitis, acute
  tuberculous (*see also* Tuberculosis) 014.8
Appendiclausis 543.9
Appendicolithiasis 543.9
Appendicopathia oxyurica 127.4
Appendix, appendicular —*see also* condition
  Morgagni (male) 752.8
  fallopian tube 752.11
Appetite
  depraved 307.52
  excessive 783.6
    psychogenic 307.51

Appetite—*continued*
  lack or loss (*see also* Anorexia) 783.0
    nonorganic origin 307.59
  perverted 307.52
    hysterical 300.11
Apprehension, apprehensiveness (abnormal)
  (state) 300.00
  specified type NEC 300.09
Approximal wear 521.1
Apraxia (classic) (ideational) (ideokinetic)
  (ideomotor) (motor) 784.69
  oculomotor, congenital 379.51
  verbal 784.69
Aptyalism 527.7
Arabicum elephantiasis (*see also* Infestation,
  filarial) 125.9
Arachnidism 989.5
Arachnitis —*see* Meningitis
Arachnodactyly 759.82
Arachnoidism 989.5
Arachnoiditis (acute) (adhesive) (basic) (brain)
  (cerebrospinal) (chiasmal) (chronic) (spinal)
  (*see also* Meningitis) 322.9
  meningococcal (chronic) 036.0
  syphilitic 094.2
  tuberculous (*see also* Tuberculosis, meninges)
    013.0
Araneism 989.5
Arboencephalitis, Australian 062.4
Arborization block (heart) 426.6
Arbor virus, arbovirus (infection) NEC 066.9
ARC 042
Arches —*see* condition
Arcuatus uterus 752.3
Arcus (cornea)
  juvenilis 743.43
    interfering with vision 743.42
  senilis 371.41
Arc-welders' lung 503
Arc-welders' syndrome (photokeratitis) 370.24
Areflexia 796.1
Areola —*see* condition
Argentaffinoma (M8241/1)—*see also*
  Neoplasm, by site, uncertain behavior
  benign (M8241/0)—*see* Neoplasm, by site,
    benign
  malignant (M8241/3)—*see* Neoplasm, by site,
    malignant
  syndrome 259.2
Argentinian hemorrhagic fever 078.7
Arginosuccinicaciduria 270.6
Argonz-Del Castillo syndrome (nonpuerperal
  galactorrhea and amenorrhea) 253.1
**Argyll-Robertson phenomenon pupil, or
  syndrome** (syphilitic) 094.89
  atypical 379.45
  nonluetic 379.45
  nonsyphilitic 379.45
  reversed 379.45
Argyria, argyriasis NEC 985.8
  conjunctiva 372.55
  cornea 371.16
  from drug or medicinal agent
    correct substance properly administered
      709.09
    overdose or wrong substance given or taken
      961.2
Arhinencephaly 742.2
Arias-Stella phenomenon 621.3
Ariboflavinosis 266.0
Arizona enteritis 008.1

Arm —*see* condition
Armenian disease 277.3
Arnold-Chiari obstruction or syndrome (*see also* Spina bifida) 741.0
  type I 348.4
  type II (*see also* Spina bifida) 741.0
  type III 742.0
  type IV 742.2
Arrest, arrested
  active phase of labor 661.1
    affecting fetus or newborn 763.7
  any plane in pelvis
    complicating delivery 660.1
      affecting fetus or newborn 763.1
  bone marrow (*see also* Anemia, aplastic) 284.9
  cardiac 427.5
    with
      abortion—*see* Abortion, by type, with specified complication NEC
      ectopic pregnancy (*see also* categories 633.0-633.9) 639.8
      molar pregnancy (*see also* categories 630-632) 639.8
  complicating
    anesthesia
      correct substance properly administered 427.5
      obstetric 668.1
      overdose or wrong substance given 968.4
        specified anesthetic—*see* Table of drugs and chemicals
    delivery (cesarean) (instrumental) 669.4
    ectopic or molar pregnancy 639.8
    surgery (nontherapeutic) (therapeutic) 997.1
  fetus or newborn 779.8
  following
    abortion 639.8
    ectopic or molar pregnancy 639.8
    postoperative (immediate) 997.1
      long-term effect of cardiac surgery 429.4
  cardiorespiratory (*see also* Arrest, cardiac) 427.5
  deep transverse 660.3
    affecting fetus or newborn 763.1
  development or growth
    bone 733.91
    child 783.4
    fetus 764.9
      affecting management of pregnancy 656.5
    tracheal rings 748.3
  epiphyseal 733.91
  granulopoiesis 288.0
  heart—*see* Arrest, cardiac
  respiratory 799.1
    newborn 770.8
  sinus 426.6
  transverse (deep) 660.3
    affecting fetus or newborn 763.1
Arrhenoblastoma (M8630.1)
  benign (M8630/0)
    specified site—*see* Neoplasm, by site, benign
    unspecified site
      female 220
      male 222.0
  malignant (M8630/3)
    specified site— *see* Neoplasm, by site, malignant
    unspecified site
      female 183.0
      male 186.9
  specified site—*see* Neoplasm, by site, uncertain behavior

Arrhenoblastoma—*continued*
  unspecified site
    female 236.2
    male 236.4
Arrhinencephaly 742.2
  due to
    trisomy 13 (13-15) 758.1
    trisomy 18 (16-l8) 758.2
Arrhythmia (auricle) (cardiac) (cordis) (gallop rhythm) (juvenile) (nodal) (reflex) (sinus) (supraventricular) (transitory) (ventricle) 427.9
  bigeminal rhythm 427.89
  block 426.9
  bradycardia 427.89
  contractions, premature 427.60
  coronary sinus 427.89
  ectopic 427.89
  extrasystolic 427.60
  postoperative 997.1
  psychogenic 306.2
  vagal 780.2
Arrillaga-Ayerza syndrome (pulmonary artery sclerosis with pulmonary hypertension) 416.0
Arsenical
  dermatitis 692.4
  keratosis 692.4
  pigmentation 985.1
    from drug or medicinal agent
      correct substance properly administered 709.09
      overdose or wrong substance given or taken 961.1
Arsenism 985.1
  from drug or medicinal agent
    correct substance properly administered 692.4
    overdose or wrong substance given or taken 961.1
Arterial —*see* condition
Arteriectasis 447.8
Arteriofibrosis —*see* Arteriosclerosis
Arteriolar sclerosis —*see* Arteriosclerosis
Arteriolith —*see* Arteriosclerosis
Arteriolitis 447.6
  necrotizing, kidney 447.5
  renal—*see* Hypertension, kidney
Arteriolosclerosis —*see* Arteriosclerosis
Arterionephrosclerosis (*see also* Hypertension, kidney) 403.90
Arteriopathy 447.9
Arteriosclerosis, arteriosclerotic (artery) (deformans) (diffuse) (disease) (endarteritis) (general) (obliterans) (obliterative) (occlusive) (senile) (with calcification) 440.9
  with
    gangrene 440.24
    psychosis (*see also* Psychosis, arteriosclerotic) 290.40
  aorta 440.0
  arteries of extremities NEC — *see* Arteriosclerosis, extremities
  basilar (artery) (*see also* Occlusion, artcry, basilar) 433.0
  brain 437.0
  bypass graft
    coronary artery 414.05
      autologous artery (gastroepiploic) (internal mammary) 414.04
      autologous vein 414.02
      nonautologous biological 414.03

NOTE—Use the following fifth-digit
subclassification with categories 711-712,
715-716:

0 *site unspecified*
1 *shoulder region*
2 *upper arm*
3 *forearm*
4 *hand*
5 *pelvic region and thigh*
6 *lower leg*
7 *ankle and foot*
8 *other specified sites*
9 *multiple sites*

Arthropathy (*see also* Arthritis) 716.9

NOTE—Use the following fifth-digit
subclassification with categories 711-712, 716:

0 *site unspecified*
1 *shoulder region*
2 *upper arm*
3 *forearm*
4 *hand*
5 *pelvic region and thigh*
6 *lower leg*
7 *ankle and foot*
8 *other specified sites*
9 *multiple sites*

  Behçet's 136.1 *[711.2]*
  Charcot's 094.0 *[713.5]*
    diabetic 250.6 *[713.5]*
    syringomyelic 336.0 *[713.5]*
    tabetic 094.0 *[713.5]*
  crystal (-induced)—*see* Arthritis, due to crystals
  gouty 274.0
  neurogenic, neuropathic (Charcot's) (tabetic)
    094.0 *[713.5]*
    diabetic 250.6 *[713.5]*
    nonsyphilitic NEC 349.9 *[713.5]*
    syringomyelic 336.0 *[713.5]*
  postdysenteric NEC 009.0 *[711.3]*
  postrheumatic, chronic (Jaccoud's) 714.4
  psoriatic 696.0
  pulmonary 731.2
  specified NEC 716.8
  syringomyelia 336.0 *[713.5]*
  tabes dorsalis 094.0 *[713.5]*
  tabetic 094.0 *[713.5]*
  transient 716.4
  traumatic 716.1
  uric acid 274.0
Arthrophyte (*see also* Loose, body, joint) 718.1
Arthrophytis 719.80
  ankle 719.87
  elbow 719.82
  foot 719.87
  hand 719.84
  hip 719.85
  knee 719.86
  multiple sites 719.89
  pelvic region 719.85
  shoulder (region) 719.81
  specified site NEC 719.88
  wrist 719.83
Arthropyosis (*see also* Arthritis, pyogenic) 711.0
Arthrosis (deformans) (degenerative) (*see also*
  Osteoarthrosis) 715.9
  Charcot's 094.0 *[713.5]*
  polyarticular 715.09
  spine (*see also* Spondylosis) 721.90
Arthus' phenomenon 995.2
  due to
    correct substance properly administered 995.2
    overdose or wrong substance given or taken
      977.9
      specified drug—*see* Table of drugs and
        chemicals
    serum 999.5
Articular —*see also* condition
  disc disorder (reducing or non-reducing) 524.63
  spondylolisthesis 756.12

Artificial
  device (prosthetic)—*see* Fitting, device
  insemination V26.1
  menopause (states) (symptoms) (syndrome)
    627.4
  opening status (functioning) (without
    complication) V55.9
    anus (colostomy) V44.3
    colostomy V44.3
    cystostomy V44.5
    enterostomy V44.4
    gastrostomy V44.1
    ileostomy V44.2
    intestinal tract NEC V44.4
    jejunostomy V44.4
    nephrostomy V44.6
    specified site NEC V44.8
    tracheostomy V44.0
    ureterostomy V44.6
    urethrostomy V44.6
    urinary tract NEC V44.6
    vagina V44.7
  vagina status V44.7
ARV (disease) (illness) (infection)—*see* Human
  immunodeficiency virus (disease) (illness)
  (infection)
Arytenoid —*see* condition
Asbestosis (occupational) 501
Asboe-Hansen's disease (incontinentia
  pigmenti) 757.33
Ascariasis (intestinal) (lung) 127.0
Ascaridiasis 127.0
Ascaridosis 127.0
Ascaris 127.0
  lumbricoides (infestation) 127.0
  pneumonia 127.0
Ascending —*see* condition
Aschoff's bodies (*see also* Myocarditis,
  rheumatic) 398.0
Ascites 789.5
  abdominal NEC 789.5
  cancerous (M8000/6) 197.6
  cardiac 428.0
  chylous (nonfilarial) 457.8
    filarial (*see also* Infestation, filarial) 125.9
  congenital 778.0
  due to S. japonicum 120.2
  fetal, causing fetopelvic disproportion 653.7
  heart 428.0
  joint (*see also* Effusion, joint) 719.0
  malignant (M8000/6) 197.6
  pseudochylous 789.5
  syphilitic 095.2
  tuberculous (*see also* Tuberculosis) 014.0
Ascorbic acid (vitamin C) deficiency (scurvy)
  267
ASCVD (arteriosclerotic cardiovascular disease)
  429.2
Aseptic —*see* condition
Asherman's syndrome 621.5
Asialia 527.7
Asiatic cholera (*see also* Cholera) 001.9
Asocial personality or trends 301.7
Asomatognosia 781.8
Aspergillosis 117.3
  with pneumonia 117.3 *[484.6]*
  nonsyphilitic NEC 117.3
Aspergillus (flavus) (fumigatus) (infection)
  (terreus) 117.3
Aspermatogenesis 606.0
Aspermia (testis) 606.0

Asphyxia, asphyxiation (by) 799.0
  antenatal—*see* Distress, fetal
  bedclothes 994.7
  birth (*see also* Asphyxia, newborn) 768.9
  bunny bag 994.7
  carbon monoxide 986
  caul (*see also* Asphyxia, newborn) 768.9
  cave-in 994.7
    crushing—*see* Injury, internal, intrathoracic
      organs
  constriction 994.7
  crushing—*see* Injury, internal, intrathoracic
      organs
  drowning 994.1
  fetal—*see* Asphyxia, intrauterine
  food or foreign body (in larynx) 933.1
    bronchioles 934.8
    bronchus (main) 934.1
    lung 934.8
    nasopharynx 933.0
    nose, nasal passages 932
    pharynx 933.0
    respiratory tract 934.9
      specified part NEC 934.8
    throat 933.0
    trachea 934.0
  gas, fumes, or vapor NEC 987.9
    specified—*see* Table of drugs and chemicals
  gravitational changes 994.7
  hanging 994.7
  inhalation—*see* Inhalation
  intrauterine
    fetal death (before onset of labor) 768.0
      during labor 768.1
    liveborn infant—*see* Distress, fetal, liveborn
      infant
  local 443.0
  mechanical 994.7
    during birth (*see also* Distress, fetal) 768.4
  mucus 933.1
    bronchus (main) 934.1
    larynx 933.1
    lung 934.8
    nasal passages 932
    newborn 770.1
    pharynx 933.0
    respiratory tract 934.9
      specified part NEC 934.8
    throat 933.0
    trachea 934.0
    vaginal (fetus or newborn) 770.1
  newborn 768.9
    blue 768.6
    livida 768.6
    mild or moderate 768.6
    pallida 768.5
    severe 768.5
    white 768.5
    with neurologic involvement 768.5
  pathological 799.0
  plastic bag 994.7
  postnatal (*see also* Asphyxia, newborn) 768.9
    mechanical 994.7
  pressure 994.7
  reticularis 782.61
  strangulation 994.7
  submersion 994.1
  traumatic NEC—*see* Injury, internal,
      intrathoracic organs
  vomiting, vomitus—*see* Asphyxia, food or
      foreign body

Aspiration
  acid pulmonary (syndrome) 997.3
    obstetric 668.0
  amniotic fluid 770.1
  bronchitis 507.0
  contents of birth canal 770.1
  fetal pneumonitis 770.1
  food, foreign body, or gasoline (with
      asphyxiation)—*see* Asphyxia, food or
      foreign body
  meconium 770.1
  mucus 933.1
    into
      bronchus (main) 934.1
      lung 934.8
      respiratory tract 934.9
        specified part NEC 934.8
      trachea 934.0
    newborn 770.1
    vaginal (fetus or newborn) 770.1
  newborn 770.1
  pneumonia 507.0
  pneumonitis 507.0
    fetus or newborn 770.1
    obstetric 668.0
  syndrome of newborn (massive) (meconium)
      770.1
  vernix caseosa 770.1
Asplenia 759.0
  with mesocardia 746.87
Assam fever 085.0
Assimilation, pelvis
  with disproportion 653.2
    affecting fetus or newborn 763.1
    causing obstructed labor 660.1
      affecting fetus or newborn 763.1
Assmann's focus (*see also* Tuberculosis) 011.0
Astasia (-abasia) 307.9
  hysterical 300.11
Asteatosis 706.8
  cutis 706.8
Astereognosis 780.9
Asterixis 781.3
  in liver disease 572.8
Asteroid hyalitis 379.22
Asthenia, asthenic 780.7
  cardiac (*see also* Failure, heart) 428.9
    psychogenic 306.2
  cardiovascular (*see also* Failure, heart) 428.9
    psychogenic 306.2
  heart (*see also* Failure, heart) 428.9
    psychogenic 306.2
  hysterical 300.11
  myocardial (*see also* Failure, heart) 428.9
    psychogenic 306.2
  nervous 300.5
  neurocirculatory 306.2
  neurotic 300.5
  psychogenic 300.5
  psychoneurotic 300.5
  psychophysiologic 300.5
  reaction, psychoneurotic 300.5
  senile 797
  Stiller's 780.7
  tropical anhidrotic 705.1
Asthenopia 368.13
  accommodative 367.4
  hysterical (muscular) 300.11
  psychogenic 306.7
Asthenospermia 792.2

Asthma, asthmatic (bronchial) (catarrh) (spasmodic) 493.9

NOTE—Use the following fifth-digit subclassification with category 493:

0 *without mention of status asthmaticus*
1 *with status asthmaticus*

with
  chronic obstructive pulmonary disease (COPD) 493.2
  hay fever 493.0
  rhinitis, allergic 493.0
allergic 493.9
  stated cause (external allergen) 493.0
atopic 493.0
cardiac (*see also* Failure, ventricular, left) 428.1
cardiobronchial (*see also* Failure, ventricular, left) 428.1
cardiorenal (*see also* Hypertension, cardiorenal) 404.90
childhood 493.0
colliers' 500
croup 493.9
detergent 507.8
due to
  detergent 507.8
  inhalation of fumes 506.3
  internal immunological process 493.0
endogenous (intrinsic) 493.1
eosinophilic 518.3
exogenous (cosmetics) (dander or dust) (drugs) (dust) (feathers) (food) (hay) (platinum) (pollen) 493.0
extrinsic 493.0
grinders' 502
hay 493.0
heart (*see also* Failure, ventricular, left) 428.1
IgE 493.0
infective 493.1
intrinsic 493.1
Kopp's 254.8
late-onset 493.1
meat-wrappers' 506.9
Millar's (laryngismus stridulus) 478.75
millstone makers' 502
miners' 500
Monday morning 504
New Orleans (epidemic) 493.0
platinum 493.0
pneumoconiotic (occupational) NEC 505
potters' 502
psychogenic 316 *[493.9]*
pulmonary eosinophilic 518.3
red cedar 495.8
Rostan's (*see also* Failure, ventricular, left) 428.1
sandblasters' 502
sequoiosis 495.8
stonemasons' 502
thymic 254.8
tuberculous (*see also* Tuberculosis, pulmonary) 011.9
Wichmann's (laryngismus stridulus) 478.75
wood 495.8
Astigmatism (compound) (congenital) 367.20
irregular 367.22
regular 367.21

Astroblastoma (M9430/3)
nose 748.1
specified site—*see* Neoplasm, by site, malignant
unspecified site 191.9
Astrocytoma (cystic) (M9400/3)
anaplastic type (M9401/3)
  specified site—*see* Neoplasm, by site, malignant
  unspecified site 191.9
fibrillary (M9420/3)
  specified site—*see* Neoplasm, by site, malignant
  unspecified site 191.9
fibrous (M9420/3)
  specified site—*see* Neoplasm, by site, malignant
  unspecified site 191.9
gemistocytic (M9411/3)
  specified site—*see* Neoplasm, by site, malignant
  unspecified site 191.9
juvenile (M9421/3)
  specified site—*see* Neoplasm, by site, malignant
  unspecified site 191.9
nose 748.1
pilocytic (M9421/3)
  specified site—*see* Neoplasm, by site, malignant
  unspecified site 191.9
piloid (M9421/3)
  specified site—*see* Neoplasm, by site, malignant
  unspecified site 191.9
protoplasmic (M9410/3)
  specified site—*see* Neoplasm, by site, malignant
  unspecified site 191.9
specified site—*see* Neoplasm, by site, malignant
subependymal (M9383/1) 237.5
  giant cell (M9384/1) 237.5
unspecified site 191.9
Astroglioma (M9400/3)
nose 748.1
specified site—*see* Neoplasm, by site, malignant
unspecified site 191.9
Asymbolia 784.60
Asymmetrical breathing 786.09
Asymmetry —*see also* Distortion
chest 786.9
face 754.0
jaw NEC 524.12
  maxillary 524.11
pelvis with disproportion 653.0
  affecting fetus or newborn 763.1
  causing obstructed labor 660.1
    affecting fetus or newborn 763.1
Asynergia 781.3
Asynergy 781.3
ventricular 429.89
Asystole (heart) (*see also* Arrest, cardiac) 427.5
Ataxia, ataxy, ataxic 781.3
acute 781.3
brain 331.89
cerebellar 334.3
  hereditary (Marie's) 334.2
  in
    alcoholism 303.9 *[334.4]*
    myxedema (*see also* Myxedema) 244.9 *[334.4]*
    neoplastic disease NEC 239.9 *[334.4]*

Ataxia, ataxy, ataxic—*continued*
　cerebral 331.89
　family, familial 334.2
　　cerebral (Marie's) 334.2
　　spinal (Friedreich's) 334.0
　Friedreich's (heredofamilial) (spinal) 334.0
　frontal lobe 781.3
　gait 781.2
　　hysterical 300.11
　general 781.3
　hereditary NEC 334.2
　　cerebellar 334.2
　　spastic 334.1
　　spinal 334.0
　heredofamilial (Marie's) 334.2
　hysterical 300.11
　locomotor (progressive) 094.0
　　diabetic 250.6 *[337.1]*
　Marie's (cerebellar) (heredofamilial) 334.2
　nonorganic origin 307.9
　partial 094.0
　postchickenpox 052.7
　progressive 094.0
　psychogenic 307.9
　Sanger-Brown's 334.2
　spastic 094.0
　　hereditary 334.1
　　syphilitic 094.0
　spinal
　　hereditary 334.0
　　progressive 094.0
　telangiectasia 334.8
Ataxia-telangiectasia 334.8
Atelectasis (absorption collapse) (complete)
　　(compression) (massive) (partial)
　　(postinfective) (pressure collapse)
　　(pulmonary) (relaxation) 518.0
　newborn (congenital) (partial) 770.5
　　primary 770.4
　primary 770.4
　tuberculous (*see also* Tuberculosis, pulmonary)
　　011.9
Ateleiosis, ateliosis 253.3
Atelia —*see* Distortion
Ateliosis 253.3
Atelocardia 746.9
Atelomyelia 742.59
Athelia 757.6
Atheroembolism *see* Atherosclerosis
Atheroma, atheromatous (*see also*
　　Arteriosclerosis) 440.9
　aorta, aortic 440.0
　　valve (*see also* Endocarditis, aortic) 424.1
　artery—*see* Arteriosclerosis
　basilar, (artery) (*see also* Occlusion, artery,
　　basilar) 433.0
　carotid (artery) (common) (internal) (*see also*
　　Occlusion, artery, carotid) 433.1
　cerebral (arteries) 437.0
　coronary (artery)—*see* Arteriosclerosis,
　　coronary
　degeneration—*see* Arteriosclerosis
　heart, cardiac —*see* Arteriosclerosis, coronary
　mitral (valve) 424.0
　myocardium, myocardial —*see* Arteriosclerosis,
　　coronary
　pulmonary valve (heart) (*see also* Endocarditis,
　　pulmonary) 424.3
　skin 706.2
　tricuspid (heart) (valve) 424.2

Atheroma, atheromatous—*continued*
　valve, valvular—*see* Endocarditis
　vertebral (artery) (*see also* Occlusion, artery,
　　vertebral) 433.2
Atheromatosis —*see also* Arteriosclerosis
　arterial, congenital 272.8
Atherosclerosis —*see* Arteriosclerosis
Athetosis (acquired) 781.0
　bilateral 333.7
　congenital (bilateral) 333.7
　double 333.7
　unilateral 781.0
Athlete's
　foot 110.4
　heart 429.3
Athletic team examination V70.3
Athrepsia 261
Athyrea (acquired) (*see also* Hypothyroidism)
　　244.9
　congenital 243
Athyreosis (congenital) 243
　acquired—*see* Hypothyroidism
Athyroidism (acquired) (*see also*
　　Hypothyroidism) 244.9
　congenital 243
Atmospheric pyrexia 992.0
Atonia, atony, atonic
　abdominal wall 728.2
　bladder (sphincter) 596.4
　　neurogenic NEC 596.54
　　　with cauda equina syndrome 344.61
　capillary 448.9
　cecum 564.8
　　psychogenic 306.4
　colon 564.8
　　psychogenic 306.4
　congenital 779.8
　dyspepsia 536.3
　　psychogenic 306.4
　intestine 564.8
　　psychogenic 306.4
　stomach 536.3
　　neurotic or psychogenic 306.4
　　psychogenic 306.4
　uterus 661.2
　　affecting fetus or newborn 763.7
　vesical 596.4
Atopy NEC V15.0
Atransferrinemia, congenital 273.8
Atresia, atretic (congenital) 759.89
　alimentary organ or tract NEC 751.8
　　lower 751.2
　　upper 750.8
　ani, anus, anal (canal) 751.2
　aorta 747.22
　　with hypoplasia of ascending aorta and
　　　defective development of left ventricle
　　　(with mitral valve atresia) 746.7
　　arch 747.11
　　ring 747.21
　aortic (orifice) (valve) 746.89
　　arch 747.11
　aqueduct of Sylvius 742.3
　　with spina bifida (*see also* Spina bifida) 741.0
　artery NEC (*see also* Atresia, blood vessel)
　　　747.60
　　cerebral 747.81
　　coronary 746.85
　　eye 743.58
　　pulmonary 747.3
　　umbilical 747.5

Atresia, atretic—*continued*
  auditory canal (external) 744.02
  bile, biliary duct (common) or passage 751.61
    acquired (*see also* Obstruction, biliary) 576.2
  bladder (neck) 753.6
  blood vessel (peripheral) NEC 747.60
    cerebral 747.81
    gastrointestinal 747.61
    lower limb 747.64
    pulmonary artery 747.3
    renal 747.62
    spinal 747.82
    upper limb 747.63
  bronchus 748.3
  canal, ear 744.02
  cardiac
    valve 746.89
      aortic 746.89
      mitral 746.89
      pulmonary 746.01
      tricuspid 746.1
  cecum 751.2
  cervix (acquired) 622.4
    congenital 752.49
    in pregnancy or childbirth 654.6
      affecting fetus or newborn 763.8
      causing obstructed labor 660.2
        affecting fetus or newborn 763.1
  choana 748.0
  colon 751.2
  cystic duct 751.61
    acquired 575.8
      with obstruction (*see also* Obstruction, gallbladder) 575.2
  digestive organs NEC 751.8
  duodenum 751.1
  ear canal 744.02
  ejaculatory duct 752.8
  epiglottis 748.3
  esophagus 750.3
  Eustachian tube 744.24
  fallopian tube (acquired) 628.2
    congenital 752.19
  follicular cyst 620.0
  foramen of
    Luschka 742.3
      with spina bifida (*see also* Spina bifida) 741.0
    Magendie 742.3
      with spina bifida (*see also* Spina bifida) 741.0
  gallbladder 751.69
  genital organ
    external
      female 752.49
      male NEC 752.8
        penis 752.69
    internal
      female 752.8
      male 752.8
  glottis 748.3
  gullet 750.3
  heart
    valve NEC 746.89
      aortic 746.89
      mitral 746.89
      pulmonary 746.01
      tricuspid 746.1
  hymen 752.42
    acquired 623.3
    postinfective 623.3

Atresia, atretic—*continued*
  ileum 751.1
  intestine (small) 751.1
    large 751.2
  iris, filtration angle (*see also* Buphthalmia) 743.20
  jejunum 751.1
  kidney 753.3
  lacrimal, apparatus 743.65
    acquired—*see* Stenosis, lacrimal
  larynx 748.3
  ligament, broad 752.19
  lung 748.5
  meatus urinarius 753.6
  mitral valve 746.89
    with atresia or hypoplasia of aortic orifice or valve, with hypoplasia of ascending aorta and defective development of left ventricle 746.7
  nares (anterior) (posterior) 748.0
  nasolacrimal duct 743.65
  nasopharynx 748.8
  nose, nostril 748.0
    acquired 738.0
  organ or site NEC—*see* Anomaly, specified type NEC
  osseous meatus (ear) 744.03
  oviduct (acquired) 628.2
    congenital 752.19
  parotid duct 750.23
    acquired 527.8
  pulmonary (artery) 747.3
    valve 746.01
    vein 747.49
  pulmonic 746.01
  pupil 743.46
  rectum 751.2
  salivary duct or gland 750.23
    acquired 527.8
  sublingual duct 750.23
    acquired 527.8
  submaxillary duct or gland 750.23
    acquired 527.8
  trachea 748.3
  tricuspid valve 746.1
  ureter 753.29
  ureteropelvic junction 753.21
  ureterovesical orifice 753.22
  urethra (valvular) 753.6
  urinary tract NEC 753.29
  uterus 752.3
    acquired 621.8
  vagina (acquired) 623.2
    congenital 752.49
    postgonococcal (old) 098.2
    postinfectional 623.2
    senile 623.2
  vascular NEC (*see also* Atresia, blood vessel) 747.60
    cerebral 747.81
  vas deferens 752.8
  vein NEC (*see also* Atresia, blood vessel) 747.60
    cardiac 746.89
    great 747.49
    portal 747.49
    pulmonary 747.49
    vena cava (inferior) (superior) 747.49
  vesicourethral orifice 753.6
  vulva 752.49
    acquired 624.8

Atrichia, atrichosis 704.00
  congenital (universal) 757.4
Atrioventricularis commune 745.69
Atrophia —*see also* Atrophy
  alba 709.09
  cutis 701.8
    idiopathica progressiva 701.8
    senilis 701.8
  dermatological, diffuse (idiopathic) 701.8
  flava hepatis (acuta) (subacuta) (*see also*
      Necrosis, liver) 570
  gyrata of choroid and retina (central) 363.54
    generalized 363.57
  senilis 797
    dermatological 701.8
  unguium 703.8
    congenita 757.5
Atrophoderma, atrophodermia 701.9
  diffusum (idiopathic) 701.8
  maculatum 701.3
    et striatum 701.3
      due to syphilis 095.8
    syphilitic 091.3
  neuriticum 701.8
  pigmentosum 757.33
  reticulatum symmetricum faciei 701.8
  senile 701.8
  symmetrical 701.8
  vermiculata 701.8
Atrophy, atrophic
  adrenal (autoimmune) (capsule) (cortex) (gland)
      255.4
    with hypofunction 255.4
  alveolar process or ridge (edentulous) 525.2
  appendix 543.9
  Aran-Duchenne muscular 335.21
  arm 728.2
  arteriosclerotic—*see* Arteriosclerosis
  arthritis 714.0
    spine 720.9
  bile duct (any) 576.8
  bladder 596.8
  blanche (of Milian) 701.3
  bone (senile) 733.99
    due to
      disuse 733.7
      infection 733.99
      tabes dorsalis (neurogenic) 094.0
    posttraumatic 733.99
  brain (cortex) (progressive) 331.9
    with dementia 290.10
      Alzheimer's 331.0
      with dementia—*see* Alzheimer's dementia
    circumscribed (Pick's) 331.1
      with dementia 331.1 *[294.1]*
    congenital 742.4
    hereditary 331.9
    senile 331.2
  breast 611.4
    puerperal, postpartum 676.3
  buccal cavity 528.9
  cardiac (brown) (senile) (*see also* Degeneration,
      myocardial) 429.1
  cartilage (infectional) (joint) 733.99
  cast, plaster of Paris 728.2
  cerebellar—*see* Atrophy, brain
  cerebral—*see* Atrophy, brain
  cervix (endometrium) (mucosa) (myometrium)
      (senile) (uteri) 622.8
    menopausal 627.8
  Charcot-Marie-Tooth 356.1

Atrophy, atrophic—*continued*
  choroid 363.40
    diffuse secondary 363.42
    hereditary (*see also* Dystrophy, choroid)
        363.50
    gyrate
      central 363.54
      diffuse 363.57
      generalized 363.57
    senile 363.41
  ciliary body 364.57
  colloid, degenerative 701.3
  conjunctiva (senile) 372.8
  corpus cavernosum 607.89
  cortical (*see also* Atrophy, brain) 331.9
  Cruveilhier's 335.21
  cystic duct 576.8
  dacryosialadenopathy 710.2
  degenerative
    colloid 701.3
    senile 701.3
  Déjérine-Thomas 333.0
  diffuse idiopathic, dermatological 701.8
  disuse
    bone 733.7
    muscle 728.2
  Duchenne-Aran 335.21
  ear 388.9
  edentulous alveolar ridge 525.2
  emphysema, lung 492.8
  endometrium (senile) 621.8
    cervix 622.8
  enteric 569.89
  epididymis 608.3
  eyeball, cause unknown 360.41
  eyelid (senile) 374.50
  facial (skin) 701.9
  facioscapulohumeral (Landouzy-Déjérine) 359.1
  fallopian tube (senile), acquired 620.3
  fatty, thymus (gland) 254.8
  gallbladder 575.8
  gastric 537.89
  gastritis (chronic) 535.1
  gastrointestinal 569.89
  genital organ, male 608.89
  glandular 289.3
  globe (phthisis bulbi) 360.41
  gum 523.2
  hair 704.2
  heart (brown) (senile) (*see also* Degeneration,
      myocardial) 429.1
  hemifacial 754.0
    Romberg 349.89
  hydronephrosis 591
  infantile 261
    paralysis, acute (*see also* Poliomyelitis, with
        paralysis) 045.1
  intestine 569.89
  iris (generalized) (postinfectional) (sector
      shaped) 364.59
    essential 364.51
    progressive 364.51
    sphincter 364.54
  kidney (senile) (*see also* Sclerosis, renal) 587
    with hypertension (*see also* Hypertension,
        kidney) 403.90
    congenital 753.0
    hydronephrotic 591
    infantile 753.0
  lacrimal apparatus (primary) 375.13
    secondary 375.14

Atrophy, atrophic—*continued*
  Landouzy-Déjérine 359.1
  laryngitis, infection 476.0
  larynx 478.79
  Leber's optic 377.16
  lip 528.5
  liver (acute) (subacute) (*see also* Necrosis,
      liver) 570
    chronic (yellow) 571.8
    yellow (congenital) 570
      with
        abortion—*see* Abortion, by type, with
            specified complication NEC
        ectopic pregnancy (*see also* categories
            633.0-633.9) 639.8
        molar pregnancy (*see also* categories
            630-632) 639.8
      chronic 571.8
      complicating pregnancy 646.7
      following
        abortion 639.8
        ectopic or molar pregnancy 639.8
      from injection, inoculation or transfusion
          (onset within 8 months after
          administration)—*see* Hepatitis, viral
      healed 571.5
      obstetric 646.7
      postabortal 639.8
      postimmunization—*see* Hepatitis, viral
      posttransfusion—*see* Hepatitis, viral
      puerperal, postpartum 674.8
  lung (senile) 518.89
    congenital 748.69
  macular (dermatological) 701.3
    syphilitic, skin 091.3
      striated 095.8
  muscle, muscular 728.2
    disuse 728.2
    Duchenne-Aran 335.21
    extremity (lower) (upper) 728.2
    familial spinal 335.11
    general 728.2
    idiopathic 728.2
    infantile spinal 335.0
    myelopathic (progressive) 335.10
    myotonic 359.2
    neuritic 356.1
    neuropathic (peroneal) (progressive) 356.1
    peroneal 356.1
    primary (idiopathic) 728.2
    progressive (familial) (hereditary) (pure)
        335.21
      adult (spinal) 335.19
      infantile (spinal) 335.0
      juvenile (spinal) 335.11
      spinal 335.10
        adult 335.19
        hereditary or familial 335.11
        infantile 335.0
    pseudohypertrophic 359.1
    spinal (progressive) 335.10
      adult 335.19
      Aran-Duchenne 335.10
      familial 335.11
      hereditary 335.11
      infantile 335.0
      juvenile 335.11
    syphilitic 095.6
  myocardium (*see also* Degeneration,
      myocardial) 429.1

Atrophy, atrophic—*continued*
  myometrium (senile) 621.8
    cervix 622.8
  myotatic 728.2
  myotonia 359.2
  nail 703.8
    congenital 757.5
  nasopharynx 472.2
  nerve—*see also* Disorder, nerve
    abducens 378.54
    accessory 352.4
    acoustic or auditory 388.5
    cranial 352.9
      first (olfactory) 352.0
      second (optic) (*see also* Atrophy, optic
          nerve) 377.10
      third (oculomotor) (partial) 378.51
        total 378.52
      fourth (trochlear) 378.53
      fifth (trigeminal) 350.8
      sixth (abducens) 378.54
      seventh (facial) 351.8
      eighth (auditory) 388.5
      ninth (glossopharyngeal) 352.2
      tenth (pneumogastric) (vagus) 352.3
      eleventh (accessory) 352.4
      twelfth (hypoglossal) 352.5
    facial 351.8
    glossopharyngeal 352.2
    hypoglossal 352.5
    oculomotor (partial) 378.51
      total 378.52
    olfactory 352.0
    peripheral 355.9
    pneumogastric 352.3
    trigeminal 350.8
    trochlear 378.53
    vagus (pneumogastric) 352.3
  nervous system, congenital 742.8
  neuritic (*see also* Disorder, nerve) 355.9
  neurogenic NEC 355.9
    bone
      tabetic 094.0
  nutritional 261
  old age 797
  olivopontocerebellar 333.0
  optic nerve (ascending) (descending)
      (infectional) (nonfamilial) (papillomacular
      bundle) (postretinal) (secondary NEC)
      (simple) 377.10
    associated with retinal dystrophy 377.13
    dominant hereditary 377.16
    glaucomatous 377.14
    hereditary (dominant) (Leber's) 377.16
    Leber's (hereditary) 377.16
    partial 377.15
    postinflammatory 377.12
    primary 377.11
    syphilitic 094.84
      congenital 090.49
      tabes dorsalis 094.0
  orbit 376.45
  ovary (senile), acquired 620.3
  oviduct (senile), acquired 620.3
  palsy, diffuse 335.20
  pancreas (duct) (senile) 577.8
  papillary muscle 429.81
  paralysis 355.9
  parotid gland 527.0
  patches skin 701.3
    senile 701.8

Atrophy, atrophic—*continued*
  penis 607.89
  pharyngitis 472.1
  pharynx 478.29
  pluriglandular 258.8
  polyarthritis 714.0
  prostate 602.2
  pseudohypertrophic 359.1
  renal (*see also* Sclerosis, renal) 587
  reticulata 701.8
  retina (*see also* Degeneration, retina) 362.60
    hereditary (*see also* Dystrophy, retina) 362.70
  rhinitis 472.0
  salivary duct or gland 527.0
  scar NEC 709.2
  sclerosis, lobar (of brain) 331.0
    with dementia 331.0 *[294.1]*
  scrotum 608.89
  seminal vesicle 608.89
  senile 797
    degenerative, of skin 701.3
  skin (patches) (senile) 701.8
  spermatic cord 608.89
  spinal (cord) 336.8
    acute 336.8
    muscular (chronic) 335.10
      adult 335.19
      familial 335.11
      juvenile 335.10
    paralysis 335.10
      acute (*see also* Poliomyelitis, with paralysis)
        045.1
  spine (column) 733.99
  spleen (senile) 289.59
  spots (skin) 701.3
    senile 701.8
  stomach 537.89
  striate and macular 701.3
    syphilitic 095.8
  subcutaneous 701.9
    due to injection 999.9
  sublingual gland 527.0
  submaxillary gland 527.0
  Sudeck's 733.7
  suprarenal (autoimmune) (capsule) (gland) 255.4
    with hypofunction 255.4
  tarso-orbital fascia, congenital 743.66
  testis 608.3
  thenar, partial 354.0
  throat 478.29
  thymus (fat) 254.8
  thyroid (gland) 246.8
    with
      cretinism 243
      myxedema 244.9
    congenital 243
  tongue (senile) 529.8
    papillae 529.4
    smooth 529.4
  trachea 519.1
  tunica vaginalis 608.89
  turbinate 733.99
  tympanic membrane (nonflaccid) 384.82
    flaccid 384.81
  ulcer (*see also* Ulcer, skin) 707.9
  upper respiratory tract 478.9
  uterus, uterine (acquired) (senile) 621.8
    cervix 622.8
    due to radiation (intended effect) 621.8
  vagina (senile) 627.3
  vascular 459.89

Atrophy, atrophic—*continued*
  vas deferens 608.89
  vertebra (senile) 733.99
  vulva (primary) (senile) 624.1
  Werdnig-Hoffmann 335.0
  yellow (acute) (congenital) (liver) (subacute)
    (*see also* Necrosis, liver) 570
    chronic 571.8
    resulting from administration of blood,
      plasma, serum, or other biological
      substance (within 8 months of
      administration)—*see* Hepatitis, viral
Attack
  akinetic (*see also* Epilepsy) 345.0
  angina—*see* Angina
  apoplectic (*see also* Disease, cerebrovascular,
    acute) 436
  benign shuddering 333.93
  bilious—*see* Vomiting
  cataleptic 300.11
  cerebral (*see also* Disease, cerebrovascular,
    acute) 436
  coronary (*see also* Infarct, myocardium) 410.9
  cyanotic, newborn 770.8
  epileptic (*see also* Epilepsy) 345.9
  epileptiform 780.3
  heart (*see also* Infarct, myocardium) 410.9
  hemiplegia (*see also* Disease, cerebrovascular,
    acute) 436
  hysterical 300.11
  jacksonian (*see also* Epilepsy) 345.5
  myocardium, myocardial (*see also* Infarct,
    myocardium) 410.9
  myoclonic (*see also* Epilepsy) 345.1
  panic 300.01
  paralysis (*see also* Disease, cerebrovascular,
    acute) 436
  paroxysmal 780.3
  psychomotor (*see also* Epilepsy) 345.4
  salaam (*see also* Epilepsy) 345.6
  schizophreniform (*see also* Schizophrenia) 295.4
  sensory and motor 780.3
  syncope 780.2
  toxic, cerebral 780.3
  transient ischemic (TIA) 435.9
  unconsciousness 780.2
    hysterical 300.11
  vasomotor 780.2
  vasovagal (idiopathic) (paroxysmal) 780.2
Attention to
  artificial
    opening (of) V55.9
      digestive tract NEC V55.4
      specified site NEC V55.8
      urinary tract NEC V55.6
      vagina V55.7
    colostomy V55.3
    cystostomy V55.5
    gastrostomy V55.1
    ileostomy V55.2
    jejunostomy V55.4
    nephrostomy V55.6
    surgical dressings V58.3
    sutures V58.3
    tracheostomy V55.0
    ureterostomy V55.6
    urethrostomy V55.6
Attrition
  gum 523.2
  teeth (excessive) (hard tissues) 521.1

B

Baader's syndrome (erythema multiforme exudativum) 695.1
Baastrup's syndrome 721.5
Babesiasis 088.82
Babesiosis 088.82
Babington's disease (familial hemorrhagic telangiectasia) 448.0
Babinski's syndrome (cardiovascular syphilis) 093.89
Babinski-Fröhlich syndrome (adiposogenital dystrophy) 253.8
Babinski-Nageotte syndrome 344.89
Bacillary —*see* condition
Bacilluria 599.0
  asymptomatic, in pregnancy or puerperium 646.5
  tuberculous (*see also* Tuberculosis) 016.9
Bacillus—*see also* **Infection, bacillus**
  abortus infection 023.1
  anthracis infection 022.9
  coli
    infection 041.4
      generalized 038.42
      intestinal 008.00
      pyemia 038.42
      septicemia 038.42
  Flexner's 004.1
  fusiformis infestation 101
  mallei infection 024
  Shiga's 004.0
  suipestifer infection (*see also* Infection, Salmonella) 003.9
Back —*see* condition
Backache (postural) 724.5
  psychogenic 307.89
  sacroiliac 724.6
Backflow (pyelovenous) (*see also* Disease, renal) 593.9
Backknee (*see also* Genu, recurvatum) 736.5
Bacteremia (*see also* Infection, bacillus) 790.7
  with
    sepsis—*see* Septicemia
  during
    labor 659.3
    pregnancy 647.8
  newborn 771.8
Bacteria
  in blood (*see also* Bacteremia) 790.7
  in urine (*see also* Bacteriuria) 599.0
Bacterial —*see* condition
Bactericholia (*see also* Cholecystitis, acute) 575.0
Bacterid, bacteride (Andrews' pustular) 686.8
Bacteriuria, bacteruria 791.9
  with
    urinary tract infection 599.0
  asymptomatic 791.9
    in pregnancy or puerperium 646.5
      affecting fetus or newborn 760.1
Bad
  breath 784.9
  heart—*see* Disease, heart
  trip (*see also* Abuse, drugs, nondependent) 305.3
Baehr-Schiffrin disease (thrombotic thrombocytopenic purpura) 446.6
Baelz's disease (cheilitis glandularis apostematosa) 528.5
Baerensprung's disease (eczema marginatum) 110.3

Bagassosis (occupational) 495.1
Baghdad boil 085.1
Bagratuni's syndrome (temporal arteritis) 446.5
Baker's
  cyst (knee) 727.51
    tuberculous (*see also* Tuberculosis) 015.2
  itch 692.89
Bakwin-Krida syndrome (craniometaphyseal dysplasia) 756.89
Balanitis (circinata) (gangraenosa) (infectious) (vulgaris) 607.1
  amebic 006.8
  candidal 112.2
  chlamydial 099.53
  due to Ducrey's bacillus 099.0
  erosiva circinata et gangraenosa 607.1
  gangrenous 607.1
  gonococcal (acute) 098.0
    chronic or duration of 2 months or over 098.2
  nongonococcal 607.1
  phagedenic 607.1
  venereal NEC 099.8
  xerotica obliterans 607.81
Balanoposthitis 607.1
  chlamydial 099.53
  gonococcal (acute) 098.0
    chronic or duration of 2 months or over 098.2
  ulcerative NEC 099.8
Balanorrhagia —*see* Balanitis
Balantidiasis 007.0
Balantidiosis 007.0
Balbuties, balbutio 307.0
Bald
  patches on scalp 704.00
  tongue 529.4
Baldness (*see also* Alopecia) 704.00
Balfour's disease (chloroma) 205.3
Balint's syndrome (psychic paralysis of visual fixation) 368.16
Balkan grippe 083.0
Ball
  food 938
  hair 938
Ballantyne (-Runge) syndrome (postmaturity) 766.2
Balloon disease (*see also* Effect, adverse, high altitude) 993.2
Ballooning posterior leaflet syndrome 424.0
Baló's disease or concentric sclerosis 341.1
Bamberger's disease (hypertrophic pulmonary osteoarthropathy) 731.2
Bamberger-Marie disease (hypertrophic pulmonary osteoarthropathy) 731.2
Bamboo spine 720.0
Bancroft's filariasis 125.0
Band(s)
  adhesive (*see also* Adhesions, peritoneum) 568.0
  amniotic 658.8
    affecting fetus or newborn 762.8
  anomalous or congenital—*see also* Anomaly, specified type NEC
    atrial 746.9
    heart 746.9
    intestine 751.4
    omentum 751.4
    ventricular 746.9
  cervix 622.3
  gallbladder (congenital) 751.69

Band(s)—*continued*
  intestinal (adhesive) (*see also* Adhesions,
    peritoneum) 568.0
    congenital 751.4
  obstructive (*see also* Obstruction, intestine)
    560.81
  periappendiceal (congenital) 751.4
  peritoneal (adhesive) (*see also* Adhesions,
    peritoneum) 568.0
    with intestinal obstruction 560.81
    congenital 751.4
  uterus 621.5
  vagina 623.2
Bandl's ring (contraction)
  complicating delivery 661.4
    affecting fetus or newborn 763.7
Bang's disease (Brucella abortus) 023.1
Bangkok hemorrhagic fever 065.4
Bannister's disease 995.1
Bantam-Albright-Martin disease
  (pseudohypoparathyroidism) 275.4
Banti's disease or syndrome (with cirrhosis)
  (with portal hypertension)—*see* Cirrhosis,
  liver
Bar
  calcaneocuboid 755.67
  calcaneonavicular 755.67
  cubonavicular 755.67
  prostate 600
  talocalcaneal 755.67
Baragnosis 780.9
Barasheh, barashek 266.2
Barcoo disease or rot (*see also* Ulcer, skin) 707.9
Bard-Pic syndrome (carcinoma, head of
  pancreas) 157.0
Bärensprung's disease (eczema marginatum)
  110.3
Baritosis 503
Barium lung disease 503
Barlow's syndrome (meaning mitral valve
  prolapse) 424.0
Barlow (-Möller) disease or syndrome (meaning
  infantile scurvy) 267
Barodontalgia 993.2
Baron Münchausen syndrome 301.51
Barosinusitis 993.1
Barotitis 993.0
Barotrauma 993.2
  odontalgia 993.2
  otitic 993.0
  sinus 993.1
Barraquer's disease or syndrome (progressive
  lipodystrophy) 272.6
Barré-Guillain syndrome 357.0
Barré-Liéou syndrome (posterior cervical
  sympathetic) 723.2
Barrel chest 738.3
Barrett's syndrome or ulcer (chronic peptic
  ulcer of esophagus) 530.2
Bársony-Polgár syndrome (corkscrew
  esophagus) 530.5
Bársony-Teschendorf syndrome (corkscrew
  esophagus) 530.5
Bartholin's
  adenitis (*see also* Bartholinitis) 616.8
  gland—*see* condition
Bartholinitis (suppurating) 616.8
  gonococcal (acute) 098.0
    chronic or duration of 2 months or over 098.2
Bartonellosis 088.0

Bartter's syndrome (secondary
  hyperaldosteronism with juxtaglomerular
  hyperplasia) 255.1
Basal—*see* **condition**
Basan's (hidrotic) ectodermal dysplasia 757.31
Baseball finger 842.13
Basedow's disease or syndrome (exophthalmic
  goiter) 242.0
Basic —*see* condition
Basilar —*see* condition
Bason's (hidrotic) ectodermal dysplasia 757.31
Basopenia 288.0
Basophilia 288.8
Basophilism (corticoadrenal) (Cushing's)
  (pituitary) (thymic) 255.0
Bassen-Kornzweig syndrome
  (abetalipoproteinemia) 272.5
Bat ear 744.29
Bateman's
  disease 078.0
  purpura (senile) 287.2
Bathing cramp 994.1
Bathophobia 300.23
Batten's disease, retina 330.1 *[362.71]*
Batten-Mayou disease 330.1 *[362.71]*
Batten-Steinert syndrome 359.2
Battered
  adult (syndrome) 995.81
  baby or child (syndrome) 995.54
  spouse (syndrome) 995.81
Battey mycobacterium infection 031.0
Battledore placenta —*see* Placenta, abnormal
Battle exhaustion (*see also* Reaction, stress,
  acute) 308.9
Baumgarten-Cruveilhier (cirrhosis) disease, or
  syndrome 571.5
Bauxite
  fibrosis (of lung) 503
  workers' disease 503
Bayle's disease (dementia paralytica) 094.1
Bazin's disease (primary) (*see also* Tuberculosis)
  017.1
Beach ear 380.12
Beaded hair (congenital) 757.4
Beard's disease (neurasthenia) 300.5
Bearn-Kunkel (-Slater) syndrome (lupoid
  hepatitis) 571.49
Beat
  elbow 727.2
  hand 727.2
  knee 727.2
Beats
  ectopic 427.60
  escaped, heart 427.60
    postoperative 997.1
  premature (nodal) 427.60
    atrial 427.61
    auricular 427.61
    postoperative 997.1
    specified type NEC 427.69
    supraventricular 427.61
    ventricular 427.69
Beau's
  disease or syndrome (*see also* Degeneration,
    myocardial) 429.1
  lines (transverse furrows on fingernails) 703.8
Bechterew's disease (ankylosing spondylitis)
  720.0
Bechterew-Strümpell-Marie syndrome
  (ankylosing spondylitis) 720.0

Beck's syndrome (anterior spinal artery
    occlusion) 433.8
Becker's
    disease (idiopathic mural endomyocardial
        disease) 425.2
    dystrophy 359.1
Beckwith (-Wiedemann) syndrome 759.89
Bedclothes, asphyxiation or suffocation by
    994.7
Bednar's aphthae 528.2
Bedsore 707.0
    with gangrene 707.0 [785.4]
Bedwetting (see also Enuresis) 788.36
Beer-drinkers' heart (disease) 425.5
Bee sting (with allergic or anaphylactic shock)
    989.5
Begbie's disease (exophthalmic goiter) 242.0
Behavior disorder, disturbance —see also
    Disturbance, conduct
    antisocial, without manifest psychiatric disorder
        adolescent V71.02
        adult V71.01
        child V71.02
    dyssocial, without manifest psychiatric disorder
        adolescent V71.02
        adult V71.01
        child V71.02
    high-risk—see Problem
Behçet's syndrome 136.1
Behr's disease 362.50
Beigel's disease or morbus (white piedra) 111.2
Bejel 104.0
Bekhterev's disease (ankylosing spondylitis)
    720.0
Bekhterev-Strümpell-Marie syndrome
    (ankylosing spondylitis) 720.0
Belching (see also Eructation) 787.3
Bell's
    disease (see also Psychosis, affective) 296.0
    mania (see also Psychosis, affective) 296.0
    palsy, paralysis 351.0
        infant 767.5
        newborn 767.5
        syphilitic 094.89
    spasm 351.0
Bence-Jones albuminuria, albuminosuria, or
    proteinuria 791.0
Bends 993.3
Benedikt's syndrome (paralysis) 344.89
Benign —see also condition
    prostate
        hyperplasia 600
        neoplasm 222.2
Bennett's
    disease (leukemia) 208.9
    fracture (closed) 815.01
        open 815.11
Benson's disease 379.22
Bent
    back (hysterical) 300.11
    nose 738.0
        congenital 754.0
Bereavement V62.82
    as adjustment reaction 309.0
Berger's paresthesia (lower limb) 782.0
Bergeron's disease (hysteroepilepsy) 300.11
Beriberi (acute) (atrophic) (chronic) (dry)
    (subacute) (wet) 265.0
    with polyneuropathy 265.0 [357.4]
    heart (disease) 265.0 [425.7]
    leprosy 030.1
    neuritis 265.0 [357.4]

Berlin's disease or edema (traumatic) 921.3
Berloque dermatitis 692.72
Bernard-Horner syndrome (see also
    Neuropathy, peripheral, autonomic) 337.9
Bernard-Sergent syndrome (acute
    adrenocortical insufficiency) 255.4
Bernard-Soulier disease or thrombopathy
    287.1
Bernhardt's disease or paresthesia 355.1
Bernhardt-Roth disease or syndrome
    (paresthesia) 355.1
Bernheim's syndrome (see also Failure, heart,
    congestive) 428.0
Bertielliasis 123.8
Bertolotti's syndrome (sacralization of fifth
    lumbar vertebra) 756.15
Berylliosis (acute) (chronic) (lung)
    (occupational) 503
Besnier's
    lupus pernio 135
    prurigo (atopic dermatitis) (infantile eczema)
        691.8
Besnier-Boeck disease or sarcoid 135
Besnier-Boeck-Schaumann disease
    (sarcoidosis) 135
Best's disease 362.76
Bestiality 302.1
Beta-adrenergic hyperdynamic circulatory
    state 429.82
Beta-aminoisobutyric aciduria 277.2
Beta-mercaptolactate-cysteine disulfiduria
    270.0
Beta thalassemia (major) (minor) (mixed) 282.4
Beurmann's disease (sporotrichosis) 117.1
Bezoar 938
    intestine 936
    stomach 935.2
Bezold's abscess (see also Mastoiditis) 383.01
Bianchi's syndrome (aphasia-apraxia-alexia)
    784.69
Bicornuate or bicornis uterus 752.3
    in pregnancy or childbirth 654.0
        with obstructed labor 660.2
            affecting fetus or newborn 763.1
        affecting fetus or newborn 763.8
Bicuspid aortic valve 746.4
Biedl-Bardet syndrome 759.89
Bielschowsky's disease 330.1
Bielschowsky-Jansky
    amaurotic familial idiocy 330.1
    disease 330.1
Biemond's syndrome (obesity, polydactyly, and
    mental retardation) 759.89
Biermer's anemia or disease (pernicious
    anemia) 281.0
Biett's disease 695.4
Bifid (congenital)—see also Imperfect, closure
    apex, heart 746.89
    clitoris 752.49
    epiglottis 748.3
    kidney 753.3
    nose 748.1
    patella 755.64
    scrotum 752.8
    toe 755.66
    tongue 750.13
    ureter 753.4
    uterus 752.3
    uvula 749.02
        with cleft lip (see also Cleft, palate, with cleft
            lip) 749.20

Biforis uterus (suprasimplex) 752.3
Bifurcation (congenital)—*see also* Imperfect,
　closure
　gallbladder 751.69
　kidney pelvis 753.3
　renal pelvis 753.3
　rib 756.3
　tongue 750.13
　trachea 748.3
　ureter 753.4
　urethra 753.8
　uvula 749.02
　　with cleft lip (*see also* Cleft, palate, with cleft
　　　lip) 749.20
　vertebra 756.19
Bigeminal pulse 427.89
Bigeminy 427.89
Big spleen syndrome 289.4
Bilateral —*see* condition
Bile duct —*see* condition
Bile pigments in urine 791.4
Bilharziasis (*see also* Schistosomiasis) 120.9
　chyluria 120.0
　cutaneous 120.3
　galacturia 120.0
　hematochyluria 120.0
　intestinal 120.1
　lipemia 120.9
　lipuria 120.0
　Oriental 120.2
　piarhemia 120.9
　pulmonary 120.2
　tropical hematuria 120.0
　vesical 120.0
Biliary —*see* condition
Bilious (attack)—*see also* Vomiting
　fever, hemoglobinuric 084.8
Bilirubinuria 791.4
Biliuria 791.4
Billroth's disease
　meningocele (*see also* Spina bifida) 741.9
Bilobate placenta —*see* Placenta, abnormal
Bilocular
　heart 745.7
　stomach 536.8
Bing-Horton syndrome (histamine cephalgia)
　346.2
Binswanger's disease or dementia 290.12
Biörck (-Thorson) syndrome (malignant
　carcinoid) 259.2
Biparta, bipartite —*see also* Imperfect, closure
　carpal scaphoid 755.59
　patella 755.64
　placenta—*see* Placenta, abnormal
　vagina 752.49
Bird
　face 756.0
　fanciers' lung or disease 495.2
Bird's disease (oxaluria) 271.8
Birth
　abnormal fetus or newborn 763.9
　accident, fetus or newborn—*see* Birth, injury
　complications in mother—*see* Delivery,
　　complicated
　compression during NEC 767.9
　defect—*see* Anomaly
　delayed, fetus 763.9
　difficult NEC, affecting fetus or newborn 763.9
　dry, affecting fetus or newborn 761.1
　forced, NEC, affecting fetus or newborn 763.8
　forceps, affecting fetus or newborn 763.2

Birth— *continued*
　hematoma of sternomastoid 767.8
　immature 765.1
　　extremely 765.0
　inattention, after or at 995.52
　induced, affecting fetus or newborn 763.8
　infant—*see* Newborn
　injury NEC 767.9
　　adrenal gland 767.8
　　basal ganglia 767.0
　　brachial plexus (paralysis) 767.6
　　brain (compression) (pressure) 767.0
　　cerebellum 767.0
　　cerebral hemorrhage 767.0
　　conjunctiva 767.8
　　eye 767.8
　　fracture
　　　bone, any except clavicle or spine 767.3
　　　clavicle 767.2
　　　femur 767.3
　　　humerus 767.3
　　　long bone 767.3
　　　radius and ulna 767.3
　　　skeleton NEC 767.3
　　　skull 767.3
　　　spine 767.4
　　　tibia and fibula 767.3
　　hematoma 767.8
　　　liver (subcapsular) 767.8
　　　mastoid 767.8
　　　skull 767.1
　　　sternomastoid 767.8
　　　testes 767.8
　　　vulva 767.8
　　intracranial (edema) 767.0
　　laceration
　　　brain 767.0
　　　by scalpel 767.8
　　　peripheral nerve 767.7
　　liver 767.8
　　meninges
　　　brain 767.0
　　　spinal cord 767.4
　　nerves (cranial, peripheral) 767.7
　　　brachial plexus 767.6
　　　facial 767.5
　　paralysis 767.7
　　　brachial plexus 767.6
　　　Erb (-Duchenne) 767.6
　　　facial nerve 767.5
　　　Klumpke (-Déjérine) 767.6
　　　radial nerve 767.6
　　　spinal (cord) (hemorrhage) (laceration)
　　　　(rupture) 767.4
　　rupture
　　　intracranial 767.0
　　　liver 767.8
　　　spinal cord 767.4
　　　spleen 767.8
　　　viscera 767.8
　　scalp 767.1
　　scalpel wound 767.8
　　skeleton NEC 767.3
　　specified NEC 767.8
　　spinal cord 767.4
　　spleen 767.8
　　subdural hemorrhage 767.0
　　tentorial, tear 767.0
　　testes 767.8
　　vulva 767.8

Birth—*continued*
  instrumental, NEC, affecting fetus or newborn
    763.2
  lack of care, after or at 995.52
  multiple
    affected by maternal complications of
      pregnancy 761.5
    healthy liveborn—*see* Newborn, multiple
  neglect, after or at 995.52
  newborn—*see* Newborn
  palsy or paralysis NEC 767.7
  precipitate, fetus or newborn 763.6
  premature (infant) 765.1
  prolonged, affecting fetus or newborn 763.9
  retarded, fetus or newborn 763.9
  shock, newborn 779.8
  strangulation or suffocation
    due to aspiration of amniotic fluid 770.1
    mechanical 767.8
  trauma NEC 767.9
  triplet
    affected by maternal complications of
      pregnancy 761.5
    healthy liveborn—*see* Newborn, multiple
  twin
    affected by maternal complications of
      pregnancy 761.5
    healthy liveborn—*see* Newborn, twin
  ventouse, affecting fetus or newborn 763.3
Birthmark 757.32
Bisalbuminemia 273.8
Biskra button 085.1
Bite (s)
  with intact skin surface—*see* Contusion
  animal—*see* Wound, open, by site
    intact skin surface—*see* Contusion
  centipede 989.5
  chigger 133.8
  fire ant 989.5
  flea—*see* Injury, superficial, by site
  human (open wound)—*see also* Wound, open,
    by site
    intact skin surface—*see* Contusion
  insect
    nonvenomous—*see* Injury, superficial, by site
    venomous 989.5
  mad dog (death from) 071
  poisonous 989.5
  red bug 133.8
  reptile 989.5
    nonvenomous—*see* Wound, open, by site
  snake 989.5
    nonvenomous—*see* Wound, open, by site
  spider (venomous) 989.5
    nonvenomous—*see* Injury, superficial, by site
  venomous 989.5
Biting
  cheek or lip 528.9
  nail 307.9
Black
  death 020.9
  eye NEC 921.0
  hairy tongue 529.3
  lung disease 500
Blackfan-Diamond anemia or syndrome
  (congenital hypoplastic anemia) 284.0
Blackhead 706.1
Blackout 780.2
Blackwater fever 084.8
Bladder —*see* Condition

Blast
  blindness 921.3
  concussion—*see* Blast, injury
  injury 869.0
    with open wound into cavity 869.1
    abdomen or thorax—*see* Injury, internal, by
      site
    brain (*see also* Concussion, brain) 850.9
      with skull fracture—*see* Fracture, skull
    ear (acoustic nerve trauma) 951.5
      with perforation, tympanic membrane—*see*
        Wound, open, ear, drum
    lung (*see also* Injury, internal, lung) 861.20
    otitic (explosive) 388.11
Blastomycosis, blastomycotic (chronic)
  (cutaneous) (disseminated) (lung)
  (pulmonary) (systemic) 116.0
  Brazilian 116.1
  European 117.5
  keloidal 116.2
  North American 116.0
  primary pulmonary 116.0
  South American 116.1
Bleb(s) 709.8
  emphysematous (bullous) (diffuse) (lung)
    (ruptured) (solitary) 492.0
  filtering, eye (postglaucoma) (status) V45.6
    with complication 997.99
    postcataract extraction (complication) 997.99
  lung (ruptured) 492.0
    congenital 770.5
  subpleural (emphysematous) 492.0
Bleeder (familial) (hereditary) (*see also* Defect,
  coagulation) 286.9
  nonfamilial 286.9
Bleeding (*see also* Hemorrhage) 459.0
  anal 569.3
  anovulatory 628.0
  atonic, following delivery 666.1
  capillary 448.9
  due to subinvolution 621.1
    puerperal 666.2
  ear 388.69
  excessive, associated with menopausal onset
    627.0
  familial (*see also* Defect, coagulation) 286.9
  following intercourse 626.7
  gastrointestinal 578.9
  gums 523.8
  hemorrhoids—*see* Hemorrhoids, bleeding
  intermenstrual
    irregular 626.6
    regular 626.5
  intraoperative 998.11
  irregular NEC 626.4
  menopausal 627.0
  mouth 528.9
  nipple 611.79
  nose 784.7
  ovulation 626.5
  postclimacteric 627.1
  postcoital 626.7
  postmenopausal 627.1
    following induced menopause 627.4
  postoperative 998.11
  preclimacteric 627.0
  puberty 626.3
    excessive, with onset of menstrual periods
      626.3
  rectum, rectal 569.3
  tendencies (*see also* Defect, coagulation) 286.9

Bleeding—*continued*
  throat 784.8
  umbilical stump 772.3
  umbilicus 789.9
  unrelated to menstrual cycle 626.6
  uterus, uterine 626.9
    climacteric 627.0
    dysfunctional 626.8
    functional 626.8
    unrelated to menstrual cycle 626.6
    vagina, vaginal 623.8
      functional 626.8
    vicarious 625.8
Blennorrhagia, blennorrhagic —*see*
  Blennorrhea
Blennorrhea (acute) 098.0
  adultorum 098.40
  alveolaris 523.4
  chronic or duration of 2 months or over 098.2
  gonococcal (neonatorum) 098.40
  inclusion (neonatal) (newborn) 771.6
  neonatorum 098.40
Blepharelosis (*see also* Entropion) 374.00
Blepharitis (eyelid) 373.00
  angularis 373.01
  ciliaris 373.00
    with ulcer 373.01
  marginal 373.00
    with ulcer 373.01
  scrofulous (*see also* Tuberculosis) 017.3
    [373.00]
  squamous 373.02
  ulcerative 373.01
Blepharochalasis 374.34
  congenital 743.62
Blepharoclonus 333.81
Blepharoconjunctivitis (*see also* Conjunctivitis)
    372.20
  angular 372.21
  contact 372.22
Blepharophimosis (eyelid) 374.46
  congenital 743.62
Blepharoplegia 374.89
Blepharoptosis 374.30
  congenital 743.61
Blepharopyorrhea 098.49
Blepharospasm 333.81
Blessig's cyst 362.62
Blighted ovum 631
Blind
  bronchus (congenital) 748.3
  eye—*see also* Blindness
    hypertensive 360.42
    hypotensive 360.41
  loop syndrome (postoperative) 579.2
  sac, fallopian tube (congenital) 752.19
  spot, enlarged 368.42
  tract or tube (congenital) NEC—*see* Atresia
Blindness (acquired) (congenital) (both eyes)
    369.00
  blast 921.3
    with nerve injury—*see* Injury, nerve, optic
  Bright's—*see* Uremia
  color (congenital) 368.59
    acquired 368.55
    blue 368.53
    green 368.52
    red 368.51
    total 368.54
  concussion 950.9
  cortical 377.75

Blindness— *continued*
  day 368.60
    acquired 368.62
    congenital 368.61
    hereditary 368.61
    specified type NEC 368.69
  due to
    injury NEC 950.9
    refractive error—*see* Error, refractive
  eclipse (total) 363.31
  emotional 300.11
  hysterical 300.11
  legal (both eyes) (USA definition) 369.4
    with impairment of better (less impaired) eye
      near-total 369.02
        with
          lesser eye impairment 369.02
            near-total 369.04
            total 369.03
      profound 369.05
        with
          lesser eye impairment 369.05
            near-total 369.07
            profound 369.08
            total 369.06
      severe 369.21
        with
          lesser eye impairment 369.21
            blind 369.11
            near-total 369.13
            profound 369.14
            severe 369.22
            total 369.12
      total
        with lesser eye impairment total 369.01
  mind 784.69
  moderate
    both eyes 369.25
      with impairment of lesser eye (specified as)
        blind, not further specified 369.15
        low vision, not further specified 369.23
        near-total 369.17
        profound 369.18
        severe 369.24
        total 369.16
    one eye 369.74
      with vision of other eye (specified as)
        near-normal 369.75
        normal 369.76
  near-total
    both eyes 369.04
      with impairment of lesser eye (specified as)
        blind, not further specified 369.02
        total 369.03
    one eye 369.64
      with vision of other eye (specified as)
        near-normal 369.65
        normal 369.66
  night 368.60
    acquired 368.62
    congenital (Japanese) 368.61
    hereditary 368.61
    specified type NEC 368.69
    vitamin A deficiency 264.5
  nocturnal—*see* Blindness, night
  one eye 369.60
    with low vision of other eye 369.10
  profound
    both eyes 369.08
      with impairment of lesser eye (specified as)
        blind, not further specified 369.05

Block—*continued*
  portal (vein) 452
  sinoatrial 426.6
  sinoauricular 426.6
  spinal cord 336.9
  trifascicular 426.54
  tubal 628.2
  vein NEC 453.9
Blocq's disease or syndrome (astasia-abasia) 307.9
Blood
  constituents, abnormal NEC 790.6
  disease 289.9
    specified NEC 289.8
  donor V59.01
    other blood components V59.09
    stem cells V59.02
    whole blood V59.01
  dyscrasia 289.9
    with
      abortion—*see* Abortion, by type, with hemorrhage, delayed or excessive
      ectopic pregnancy (*see also* categories 633.0-633.9) 639.1
      molar pregnancy (*see also* categories 630-632) 639.1
    fetus or newborn NEC 776.9
    following
      abortion 639.1
      ectopic or molar pregnancy 639.1
    puerperal, postpartum 666.3
  flukes NEC (*see also* Infestation, Schistosoma) 120.9
  in
    feces (*see also* Melena) 578.1
      occult 792.1
    urine (*see also* Hematuria) 599.7
  mole 631
  occult 792.1
  poisoning (*see also* Septicemia) 038.9
  pressure
    decreased, due to shock following injury 958.4
    fluctuating 796.4
    high (*see also* Hypertension) 401.9
      incidental reading (isolated) (nonspecific), without diagnosis of hypertension 796.2
    low (*see also* Hypotension) 458.9
      incidental reading (isolated) (nonspecific), without diagnosis of hypotension 796.3
  spitting (*see also* Hemoptysis) 786.3
  staining cornea 371.12
  transfusion
    without reported diagnosis V58.2
    donor V59.01
      stem cells V59.02
    reaction or complication—*see* Complications, transfusion
  tumor—*see* Hematoma
  vessel rupture—*see* Hemorrhage
  vomiting (*see also* Hematemesis) 578.0
Blood-forming organ disease 289.9
Bloodgood's disease 610.1
Bloodshot eye 379.93
Bloom (-Machacek) (-Torre) syndrome 757.39
Blotch, palpebral 372.55
Blount's disease (tibia vara) 732.4
Blount-Barber syndrome (tibia vara) 732.4
Blue
  baby 746.9
  bloater 491.20
    with acute bronchitis or exacerbation 491.21

Blue —*continued*
  diaper syndrome 270.0
  disease 746.9
  dome cyst 610.0
  drum syndrome 381.02
  sclera 743.47
    with fragility of bone and deafness 756.51
  toe syndrome—*see* Atherosclerosi*s*
Blueness (*see also* Cyanosis) 782.5
Blurring, visual 368.8
Blushing (abnormal) (excessive) 782.62
Boarder, hospital V65.0
  infant V65.0
Bockhart's impetigo (superficial folliculitis) 704.8
Bodechtel-Guttmann disease (subacute sclerosing panencephalitis) 046.2
Boder-Sedgwick syndrome (ataxia-telangiectasia) 334.8
Body, bodies
  Aschoff (*see also* Myocarditis, rheumatic) 398.0
  asteroid, vitreous 379.22
  choroid, colloid (degenerative) 362.57
    hereditary 362.77
  cytoid (retina) 362.82
  drusen (retina) (*see also* Drusen) 362.57
    optic disc 377.21
  fibrin, pleura 511.0
  foreign—*see* Foreign body
  Hassall-Henle 371.41
  loose
    joint (*see also* Loose, body, joint) 718.1
      knee 717.6
    knee 717.6
    sheath, tendon 727.82
  Mallory's 034.1
  Mooser 081.0
  Negri 071
  rice (joint) (*see also* Loose, body, joint) 718.1
    knee 717.6
  rocking 307.3
Boeck's
  disease (sarcoidosis) 135
  lupoid (miliary) 135
  sarcoid 135
Boerhaave's syndrome (spontaneous esophageal rupture) 530.4
Boggy
  cervix 622.8
  uterus 621.8
Boil (*see also* Carbuncle) 680.9
  abdominal wall 680.2
  Aleppo 085.1
  ankle 680.6
  anus 680.5
  arm (any part, above wrist) 680.3
  auditory canal, external 680.0
  axilla 680.3
  back (any part) 680.2
  Baghdad 085.1
  breast 680.2
  buttock 680.5
  chest wall 680.2
  corpus cavernosum 607.2
  Delhi 085.1
  ear (any part) 680.0
  eyelid 373.13
  face (any part, except eye) 680.0
  finger (any) 680.4
  flank 680.2
  foot (any part) 680.7

Boil —*continued*
  forearm 680.3
  Gafsa 085.1
  genital organ, male 608.4
  gluteal (region) 680.5
  groin 680.2
  hand (any part) 680.4
  head (any part, except face) 680.8
  heel 680.7
  hip 680.6
  knee 680.6
  labia 616.4
  lacrimal (*see also* Dacryocystitis) 375.30
    gland (*see also* Dacryoadenitis) 375.00
    passages (duct) (sac) (*see also* Dacryocystitis) 375.30
  leg, any part except foot 680.6
  multiple sites 680.9
  Natal 085.1
  neck 680.1
  nose (external) (septum) 680.0
  orbit, orbital 376.01
  partes posteriores 680.5
  pectoral region 680.2
  penis 607.2
  perineum 680.2
  pinna 680.0
  scalp (any part) 680.8
  scrotum 608.4
  seminal vesicle 608.0
  shoulder 680.3
  skin NEC 680.9
  specified site NEC 680.8
  spermatic cord 608.4
  temple (region) 680.0
  testis 608.4
  thigh 680.6
  thumb 680.4
  toe (any) 680.7
  tropical 085.1
  trunk 680.2
  tunica vaginalis 608.4
  umbilicus 680.2
  upper arm 680.3
  vas deferens 608.4
  vulva 616.4
  wrist 680.4
Bold hives (*see also* Urticaria) 708.9
Bolivian hemorrhagic fever 078.7
Bombé, iris 364.74
Bomford-Rhoads anemia (refractory) 284.9
Bone —*see* condition
Bonnevie-Ullrich syndrome 758.6
Bonnier's syndrome 386.19
Bonvale Dam fever 780.7
Bony block of joint 718.80
  ankle 718.87
  elbow 718.82
  foot 718.87
  hand 718.84
  hip 718.85
  knee 718.86
  multiple sites 718.89
  pelvic region 718.85
  shoulder (region) 718.81
  specified site NEC 718.88
  wrist 718.83
Borderline
  intellectual functioning V62.89
  pelvis 653.1
    with obstruction during labor 660.1

Borderline—*continued*
  affecting fetus or newborn 763.1
  psychosis (*see also* Schizophrenia) 295.5
    of childhood (*see also* Psychosis, childhood) 299.8
  schizophrenia (*see also* Schizophrenia) 295.5
Borna disease 062.9
Bornholm disease (epidemic pleurodynia) 074.1
Borrelia vincentii (mouth) (pharynx) (tonsils) 101
Bostock's catarrh (*see also* Fever, hay) 477.9
Boston exanthem 048
Botalli, ductus (patent) (persistent) 747.0
Bothriocephalus latus infestation 123.4
Botulism 005.1
Bouba (*see also* Yaws) 102.9
Bouffée délirante 298.3
Bouillaud's disease or syndrome (rheumatic heart disease) 391.9
Bourneville's disease (tuberous sclerosis) 759.5
Boutonneuse fever 082.1
Boutonniere
  deformity (finger) 736.21
  hand (intrinsic) 736.21
Bouveret (-Hoffmann) disease or syndrome (paroxysmal tachycardia) 427.2
Bovine heart —*see* Hypertrophy, cardiac
Bowel —*see* condition
Bowen's
  dermatosis (precancerous) (M8081/2)—*see* Neoplasm, skin, in situ
  disease (M8081/2)—*see* Neoplasm, skin, in situ
  epithelioma (M8081/2)—*see* Neoplasm, skin, in situ
  type
    epidermoid carcinoma in situ (M8081/2)—*see* Neoplasm, skin, in situ
    intraepidermal squamous cell carcinoma (M8081/2)–*see* Neoplasm, skin, in situ
Bowing
  femur 736.89
    congenital 754.42
  fibula 736.89
    congenital 754.43
  forearm 736.09
    away from midline (cubitus valgus) 736.01
    toward midline (cubitus varus) 736.02
  leg(s), long bones, congenital 754.44
  radius 736.09
    away from midline (cubitus valgus) 736.01
    toward midline (cubitus varus) 736.02
  tibia 736.89
    congenital 754.43
Bowleg (s) 736.42
  congenital 754.44
  rachitic 268.1
Boyd's dysentery 004.2
Brachial —*see* condition
Brachman-de Lange syndrome (Amsterdam dwarf, mental retardation, and brachycephaly) 759.89
Brachycardia 427.89
Brachycephaly 756.0
Brachymorphism and ectopia lentis 759.89
Bradley's disease (epidemic vomiting) 078.82
Bradycardia 427.89
  chronic (sinus) 427.81
  newborn 770.8
  nodal 427.89
  postoperative 997.1
  reflex 337.0

Bradycardia— *continued*
  sinoatrial 427.89
    with paroxysmal tachyarrhythmia or
      tachycardia 427.81
    chronic 427.81
  sinus 427.89
    with paroxysmal tachyarrhythmia or
      tachycardia 427.81
    chronic 427.81
    persistent 427.81
    severe 427.81
  tachycardia syndrome 427.81
  vagal 427.89
Bradypnea 786.09
Brailsford's disease 732.3
  radial head 732.3
  tarsal scaphoid 732.5
Brailsford-Morquio disease or syndrome
  (mucopolysaccharidosis IV) 277.5
Brain —*see also* condition
  death 348.8
  syndrome (acute) (chronic) (nonpsychotic)
    (organic) (with neurotic reaction) (with
    behavioral reaction) (*see also* Syndrome,
    brain) 310.9
    with
      presenile brain disease 290.10
      psychosis, psychotic reaction (*see also*
        Psychosis, organic) 294.9
    congenital (*see also* Retardation, mental) 319
Branched-chain amino-acid disease 270.3
Branchial —*see* condition
Brandt's syndrome (acrodermatitis
  enteropathica) 686.8
Brash (water) 787.1
Brass-founders' ague 985.8
Bravais-Jacksonian epilepsy (*see also* Epilepsy)
  345.5
Braxton Hicks contractions 644.1
Braziers' disease 985.8
Brazilian
  blastomycosis 116.1
  leishmaniasis 085.5
Break
  cardiorenal—*see* Hypertension, cardiorenal
  retina (*see also* Defect, retina) 361.30
Breakbone fever 061
Breakdown
  device, implant, or graft—*see* Complications,
    mechanical
  nervous (*see also* Disorder, mental,
    nonpsychotic) 300.9
  perineum 674.2
Breast —*see* condition
Breath
  foul 784.9
  holder, child 312.81
  holding spells 786.9
  shortness 786.09
Breathing
  asymmetrical 786.09
  bronchial 786.09
  exercises V57.0
  labored 786.09
  mouth 784.9
  periodic 786.09
  tic 307.20
Breathlessness 786.09
Breda's disease (*see also* Yaws) 102.9

Breech
  delivery, affecting fetus or newborn 763.0
  extraction, affecting fetus or newborn 763.0
  presentation 652.2
    with successful version 652.1
    before labor, affecting fetus or newborn 761.7
    causing obstructed labor 660.0
    during labor, affecting fetus or newborn 763.0
Breisky's disease (kraurosis vulvae) 624.0
Brennemann's syndrome (acute mesenteric
  lymphadenitis) 289.2
Brenner's
  tumor (benign) (M9000/0) 220
    borderline malignancy (M9000/1) 236.2
    malignant (M9000/3) 183.0
    proliferating (M9000/1) 236.2
Bretonneau's disease (diphtheritic malignant
  angina) 032.0
Breus' mole 631
Brevicollis 756.16
Bricklayers' itch 692.89
Brickmakers' anemia 126.9
Bridge
  myocardial 746.85
Bright's
  blindness—*see* Uremia
  disease (*see also* Nephritis) 583.9
    arteriosclerotic (*see also* Hypertension,
      kidney) 403.90
Brill's disease (recrudescent typhus) 081.1
  flea-borne 081.0
  louse-borne 081.1
Brill-Symmers disease (follicular lymphoma)
  (M9690/3) 202.0
Brill-Zinsser disease (recrudescent typhus) 081.1
Brinton's disease (linitis plastica) (M8142/3)
  151.9
Brion-Kayser disease (*see also* Fever,
  paratyphoid) 002.9
Briquet's disorder or syndrome 300.81
Brissaud's
  infantilism (infantile myxedema) 244.9
  motor-verbal tic 307.23
Brissaud-Meige syndrome (infantile
  myxedema) 244.9
Brittle
  bones (congenital) 756.51
  nails 703.8
    congenital 757.5
Broad —*see also* condition
  beta disease 272.2
  ligament laceration syndrome 620.6
Brock's syndrome (atelectasis due to enlarged
  lymph nodes) 518.0
Brocq's disease 691.8
  atopic (diffuse) neurodermatitis 691.8
  lichen simplex chronicus 698.3
  parakeratosis psoriasiformis 696.2
  parapsoriasis 696.2
Brocq-Duhring disease (dermatitis
  herpetiformis) 694.0
Brodie's
  abscess (localized) (chronic) (*see also*
    Osteomyelitis) 730.1
  disease (joint) (*see also* Osteomyelitis) 730.1
Broken
  arches 734
    congenital 755.67
  back—*see* Fracture, vertebra, by site
  bone—*see* Fracture, by site
  compensation—*see* Disease, heart

Broken—*continued*
  implant or internal device—*see* listing under
    Complications, mechanical
  neck—*see* Fracture, vertebra, cervical
  nose 802.0
    open 802.1
  tooth, teeth 873.63
    complicated 873.73
Bromhidrosis 705.89
Bromidism, bromism
  acute 967.3
    correct substance properly administered
      349.82
    overdose or wrong substance given or taken
      967.3
  chronic (*see also* Dependence) 304.1
Bromidrosiphobia 300.23
Bromidrosis 705.89
Bronchi, bronchial —*see* condition
Bronchiectasis (cylindrical) (diffuse) (fusiform)
    (localized) (moniliform) (postinfectious)
    (recurrent) (saccular) 494
  congenital 748.61
  tuberculosis (*see also* Tuberculosis) 011.5
Bronchiolectasis —*see* Bronchiectasis
Bronchiolitis (acute) (infectious) (subacute)
    466.19
  with
    bronchospasm or obstruction 466.19
    influenza, flu, or grippe 487.1
  catarrhal (acute) (subacute) 466.19
  chemical 506.0
    chronic 506.4
  chronic (obliterative) 491.8
  due to external agent—*see* Bronchitis, acute,
    due to
  fibrosa obliterans 491.8
  influenzal 487.1
  obliterans 491.8
    status post lung transplant 996.84
    with organizing pneumonia (B.O.O.P.) 516.8
  obliterative (chronic) (diffuse) (subacute) 491.8
    due to fumes or vapors 506.4
  respiratory syncytial virus 466.11
  vesicular—*see* Pneumonia, broncho-
Bronchitis (diffuse) (hypostatic) (infectious)
    (inflammatory) (simple) 490
  with
    emphysema—*see* Emphysema
    influenza, flu, or grippe 487.1
    obstruction airway, chronic 491.20
      with acute exacerbation 491.21
    tracheitis 490
      acute or subacute 466.0
        with bronchospasm or obstruction 466.0
      chronic 491.8
  acute or subacute 466.0
    with
      bronchospasm 466.0
      chronic
        bronchitis (obstructive) 491.21
        obstructive pulmonary disease (COPD)
          491.21
      obstruction 466.0
      tracheitis 466.0
    chemical (due to fumes or vapors) 506.0
    due to
      fumes or vapors 506.0
      radiation 508.8
  allergic (acute) (*see also* Asthma) 493.9
  arachidic 934.1

Bronchitis—*continued*
  aspiration 507.0
    due to fumes or vapors 506.0
  asthmatic (acute) (*see also* Asthma) 493.9
    chronic 491.20
      with acute bronchitis or acute exacerbation
        491.21
  capillary 466.19
    with bronchospasm or obstruction 466.19
    chronic 491.8
  caseous (*see also* Tuberculosis) 011.3
  Castellani's 104.8
  catarrhal 490
    acute—*see* Bronchitis, acute
    chronic 491.0
  chemical (acute) (subacute) 506.0
    chronic 506.4
    due to fumes or vapors (acute) (subacute)
      506.0
      chronic 506.4
  chronic 491.9
    with
      tracheitis (chronic) 491.8
    asthmatic 491.20
      with acute bronchitis or acute exacerbation
        491.21
    catarrhal 491.0
    chemical (due to fumes and vapors) 506.4
    due to
      fumes or vapors (chemical) (inhalation)
        506.4
      radiation 508.8
      tobacco smoking 491.0
    mucopurulent 491.1
    obstructive 491.20
      with acute bronchitis or acute exacerbation
        491.21
    purulent 491.1
    simple 491.0
    specified type NEC 491.8
  croupous 466.0
    with bronchospasm or obstruction 466.0
    due to fumes or vapors 506.0
  emphysematous 491.20
    with
      acute bronchitis or acute exacerbation 491.21
  exudative 466.0
  fetid (chronic) (recurrent) 491.1
  fibrinous, acute or subacute 466.0
    with bronchospasm or obstruction 466.0
  grippal 487.1
  influenzal 487.1
  membranous, acute or subacute 466.0
    with bronchospasm or obstruction 466.0
  moulders' 502
  mucopurulent (chronic) (recurrent) 491.1
    acute or subacute 466.0
  non-obstructive 491.0
  obliterans 491.8
  obstructive (chronic) 491.20
    with
      acute bronchitis or acute exacerbation 491.21
    acute 466.0
  pituitous 491.1
  plastic (inflammatory) 466.0
  pneumococcal, acute or subacute 466.0
    with bronchospasm or obstruction 466.0
  pseudomembranous 466.0
  purulent (chronic) (recurrent) 491.1
    acute or subacute 466.0
      with bronchospasm or obstruction 466.0

Bronchitis—*continued*
putrid 491.1
scrofulous (*see also* Tuberculosis) 011.3
senile 491.9
septic, acute or subacute 466.0
  with bronchospasm or obstruction 466.0
smokers' 491.0
spirochetal 104.8
suffocative, acute or subacute 466.0
summer (*see also* Asthma) 493.9
suppurative (chronic) 491.1
  acute or subacute 466.0
tuberculous (*see also* Tuberculosis) 011.3
ulcerative 491.8
  Vincent's 101
Vincent's 101
viral, acute or subacute 466.0
  with bronchospasm or obstruction 466.0
Bronchoalveolitis 485
Bronchoaspergillosis 117.3
Bronchocele
meaning
  dilatation of bronchus 519.1
  goiter 240.9
Bronchogenic carcinoma 162.9
Bronchohemisporosis 117.9
Broncholithiasis 518.89
tuberculous (*see also* Tuberculosis) 011.3
Bronchomoniliasis 112.89
Bronchomycosis 112.89
Bronchonocardiosis 039.1
Bronchopleuropneumonia —*see* Pneumonia,
  broncho-
Bronchopneumonia —*see* Pneumonia, broncho-
Bronchopneumonitis —*see* Pneumonia,
  broncho-
Bronchopulmonary —*see* condition
Bronchopulmonitis —*see* Pneumonia, broncho-
Bronchorrhagia 786.3
newborn 770.3
tuberculous (*see also* Tuberculosis) 011.3
Bronchorrhea (chronic) (purulent) 491.0
acute 466.0
Bronchospasm 519.1
with
  asthma—*see* Asthma
  bronchiolitis, acute 466.19
    due to respiratory syncytial virus 466.11
  bronchitis—*see* Bronchitis
  COPD 496
  emphysema—*see* Emphysema
due to external agent—*see* Condition,
  respiratory, acute, due to
Bronchospirochetosis 104.8
Bronchostenosis 519.1
Bronchus —*see* condition
Bronze, bronzed
diabetes 275.0
disease (Addison's) (skin) 255.4
  tuberculous (*see also* Tuberculosis) 017.6
Brooke's disease or tumor (M8100/0)—*see*
  Neoplasm, skin, benign
Brown's tendon sheath syndrome 378.61
Brown enamel of teeth (hereditary) 520.5
Brown-Séquard's paralysis (syndrome) 344.89
Brow presentation complicating delivery 652.4
causing obstructed labor 660.0
Brucella, brucellosis (infection) 023.9
abortus 023.1
canis 023.3
dermatitis, skin 023.9

Brucella, brucellosis—*continued*
melitensis 023.0
mixed 023.8
suis 023.2
Bruck's disease 733.99
Bruck-de Lange disease or syndrome
  (Amsterdam dwarf, mental retardation, and
  brachycephaly) 759.89
Brug's filariasis 125.1
Brugsch's syndrome (acropachyderma) 757.39
Bruhl's disease (splenic anemia with fever) 285.8
Bruise (skin surface intact)—*see also* Contusion
with
  fracture—*see* Fracture, by site
  open wound—*see* Wound, open, by site
internal organ (abdomen, chest, or pelvis)—*see*
  Injury, internal, by site
umbilical cord 663.6
  affecting fetus or newborn 762.6
Bruit 785.9
arterial (abdominal) (carotid) 785.9
supraclavicular 785.9
Brushburn —*see* Injury, superficial, by site
Bruton's X-linked agammaglobulinemia 279.04
Bruxism 306.8
Bubbly lung syndrome 770.7
Bubo 289.3
blennorrhagic 098.89
chancroidal 099.0
climatic 099.1
due to Hemophilus ducreyi 099.0
gonococcal 098.89
indolent NEC 099.8
inguinal NEC 099.8
  chancroidal 099.0
  climatic 099.1
  due to H. ducreyi 099.0
scrofulous (*see also* Tuberculosis) 017.2
soft chancre 099.0
suppurating 683
syphilitic 091.0
  congenital 090.0
tropical 099.1
venereal NEC 099.8
virulent 099.0
Bubonic plague 020.0
Bubonocele —*see* Hernia, inguinal
Buccal —*see* condition
Buchanan's disease (juvenile osteochondrosis of
  iliac crest) 732.1
Buchem's syndrome (hyperostosis corticalis)
  733.3
Buchman's disease (osteochondrosis, juvenile)
  732.1
Bucket handle fracture (semilunar cartilage)
  (*see also* Tear, meniscus) 836.2
Budd-Chiari syndrome (hepatic vein
  thrombosis) 453.0
Budgerigar-fanciers' disease or lung 495.2
Büdinger-Ludloff-Läwen disease 717.89
Buerger's disease (thromboangiitis obliterans)
  443.1
Bulbar —*see* condition
Bulbus cordis 745.9
persistent (in left ventricle) 745.8
Bulging fontanels (congenital) 756.0
Bulimia 783.6
nonorganic origin 307.51
Bulky uterus 621.2
Bulla(e) 709.8
lung (emphysematous) (solitary) 492.0

Bullet wound —*see also* Wound, open, by site
  fracture—*see* Fracture, by site, open
  internal organ (abdomen, chest, or pelvis)—*see*
    Injury, internal, by site, with open wound
  intracranial—*see* Laceration, brain, with open
    wound
Bullis fever 082.8
Bullying (*see also* Disturbance, conduct) 312.0
Bundle
  branch block (complete) (false) (incomplete)
    426.50
    bilateral 426.53
    left (*see also* Block, bundle branch, left) 426.3
      hemiblock 426.2
    right (*see also* Block, bundle branch, right)
      426.4
  of His—*see* condition
  of Kent syndrome (anomalous atrioventricular
    excitation) 426.7
Bungpagga 040.81
Bunion 727.1
Bunionette 727.1
Bunyamwera fever 066.3
Buphthalmia, buphthalmos (congenital) 743.20
  associated with
    keratoglobus, congenital 743.22
    megalocornea 743.22
    ocular anomalies NEC 743.22
  isolated 743.21
  simple 743.21
Bürger-Grütz disease or syndrome (essential
  familial hyperlipemia) 272.3
Buried roots 525.3
Burke's syndrome 577.8
Burkitt's
  tumor (M9750/3) 200.2
  type malignant, lymphoma, lymphoblastic, or
    undifferentiated (M9750/3) 200.2
Burn (acid) (cathode ray) (caustic) (chemical)
  (electric heating appliance) (electricity) (fire)
  (flame) (hot liquid or object) (irradiation)
  (lime) (radiation) (steam) (thermal) (x-ray)
  949.0

Note—Use the following fifth-digit
subclassification with category 948 to indicate
the percent of body surface with third degree
burn:

0 *less than 10% or unspecified*
1 *10-19%*
2 *20-29%*
3 *30-39%*
4 *40-49%*
5 *50-59%*
6 *60-69%*
7 *70-79%*
8 *80-89%*
9 *90% or more of body surface*

---

  with
    blisters—*see* Burn, by site, second degree
    erythema—*see* Burn, by site, first degree
    skin loss (epidermal)—*see also* Burn, by site,
      second degree
      full thickness—*see also* Burn, by site, third
        degree
        with necrosis of underlying tissues—*see*
          Burn, by site, third degree, deep
    first degree—*see* Burn, by site, first degree
    second degree—*see* Burn, by site, second degree

Burn—*continued*
  third degree—*see also* Burn, by site, third
    degree
    deep—*see* Burn, by site, third degree, deep
  abdomen, abdominal (muscle) (wall) 942.03
    with
      other site(s), except trunk—*see* Burn,
        multiple, specified sites
      trunk—*see* Burn, trunk, multiple sites
    first degree 942.13
    second degree 942.23
    third degree 942.33
      deep 942.43
        with loss of body part 942.53
  ankle 945.03
    with
      lower limb(s)–*see* Burn, leg, multiple sites
      other site(s), except lower limb(s)—*see*
        Burn, multiple, specified sites
    first degree 945.13
    second degree 945.23
    third degree 945.33
      deep 945.43
        with loss of body part 945.53
  anus—*see* Burn, trunk, specified site NEC
  arm(s) 943.00
    with other site(s) (classifiable to more than
      one category in 940-945)—*see* Burn,
      multiple, specified sites
    first degree 943.10
    second degree 943.20
    third degree 943.30
      deep 943.40
        with loss of body part 943.50
    lower—*see* Burn, forearm(s)
    multiple sites, except hand(s) or wrist(s)
      943.09
      first degree 943.19
      second degree 943.29
      third degree 943.39
        deep 943.49
          with loss of body part 943.59
    upper 943.03
      with other site(s) of upper limb(s), except
        hand(s) or wrist(s)—*see* Burn, arm(s),
        multiple sites
      first degree 943.13
      second degree 943.23
      third degree 943.33
        deep 943.43
          with loss of body part 943.53
  auditory canal (external)—*see* Burn, ear
  auricle (ear)—*see* Burn, ear
  axilla 943.04
    with
      hand(s) and wrist(s)—*see* Burn, multiple,
        specified sites
      other site(s), except upper limb(s)—*see*
        Burn, multiple, specified sites
      upper limb(s) except hand(s) or
        wrist(s)—*see* Burn, arm(s), multiple sites
    first degree 943.14
    second degree 943.24
    third degree 943.34
      deep 943.44
        with loss of body part 943.54
  back 942.04
    with
      other site(s), except trunk—*see* Burn,
        multiple, specified sites
      trunk—*see* Burn, trunk, multiple sites

Burn—*continued*

first degree 942.14
second degree 942.24
third degree 942.34
deep 942.44—
with loss of body part 942.54
biceps
brachii—*see* Burn, arm(s), upper
femoris—*see* Burn, thigh
breast(s) 942.01
with
other site(s), except trunk—*see* Burn,
multiple, specified sites
trunk—*see* Burn, trunk, multiple sites
first degree 942.11
second degree 942.21
third degree 942.31
deep 942.41
with loss of body part 942.51
brow—*see* Burn, forehead
buttock(s)—*see* Burn, back
canthus (eye) 940.1
chemical 940.0
cervix (uteri) 947.4
cheek (cutaneous) 941.07
with
face or head—*see* Burn, head, multiple sites
other site(s), except face or head—*see* Burn,
multiple, specified sites
first degree 941.17
second degree 941.27
third degree 941.37
deep 941.47
with loss of body part 941.57
chest wall (anterior) 942.02
with
other site(s), except trunk—*see* Burn,
multiple, specified sites
trunk—*see* Burn, trunk, multiple sites
first degree 942.12
second degree 942.22
third degree 942.32
deep 942.42
with loss of body part 942.52
chin 941.04
with
face or head—*see* Burn, head, multiple sites
other site(s), except face or head—*see* Burn,
multiple, specified sites
first degree 941.14
second degree 941.24
third degree 941.34
deep 941.44
with loss of body part 941.54
clitoris—*see* Burn, genitourinary organs,
external
colon 947.3
conjunctiva (and cornea) 940.4
chemical
acid 940.3
alkaline 940.2
cornea (and conjunctiva) 940.4
chemical
acid 940.3
alkaline 940.2
costal region—*see* Burn, chest wall
due to ingested chemical agent—*see* Burn,
internal organs
ear (auricle) (canal) (drum) (external) 941.01
with
face or head—*see* Burn, head, multiple sites

Burn—*continued*

other site(s), except face or head—*see* Burn,
multiple, specified sites
first degree 941.11
second degree 941.21
third degree 941.31
deep 941.41
with loss of a body part 941.51
elbow 943.02
with
hand(s) and wrist(s)—*see* Burn, multiple
specified sites
other site(s), except upper limb(s)—*see*
Burn, multiple, specified sites
upper limb(s) except hand(s) or
wrist(s)—*see also* Burn, arm(s),
multiple sites
first degree 943.12
second degree 943.22
third degree 943.32
deep 943.42
with loss of body part 943.52
electricity, electric current—*see* Burn, by site
entire body—*see* Burn, multiple, specified sites
epididymis—*see* Burn, genitourinary organs,
external
epigastric region—*see* Burn, abdomen
epiglottis 947.1
esophagus 947.2
extent (percent of body surface)
less than 10 percent 948.0
10-19 percent 948.1
20-29 percent 948.2
30-39 percent 948.3
40-49 percent 948.4
50-59 percent 948.5
60-69 percent 948.6
70-79 percent 948.7
80-89 percent 948.8
90 percent or more 948.9
extremity
lower—*see* Burn, leg
upper—*see* Burn, arm(s)
eye(s) (and adnexa) (only) 940.9
with
face, head, or neck 941.02
first degree 941.12
second degree 941.22
third degree 941.32
deep 941.42
with loss of body part 941.52
other sites (classifiable to more than one
category in 940-945)—*see* Burn,
multiple, specified sites
resulting rupture and destruction of eyeball
940.5
specified part—*see* Burn, by site
eyeball—*see also* Burn, eye
with resulting rupture and destruction of
eyeball 940.5
eyelid(s) 940.1
chemical 940.0
face—*see* Burn, head
finger (nail) (subungual) 944.01
with
hand(s)—*see* Burn, hand(s), multiple sites
other sites—*see* Burn, multiple, specified
sites
thumb 944.04
first degree 944.14

Burn—*continued*

      second degree 944.24
      third degree 944.34
        deep 944.44
          with loss of body part 944.54
    first degree 944.11
    second degree 944.21
    third degree 944.31
      deep 944.41
        with loss of body part 944.51
    multiplc (digits) 944.03
      with thumb—*see* Burn, finger, with thumb
    first degree 944.13
    second degree 944.23
    third degree 944.33
      deep 944.43
        with loss of body part 944.53
flank—*see* Burn, abdomen
foot 945.02
  with
    lower limb(s)—*see* Burn, leg, multiple sites
    other site(s), except lower limb(s)—*see*
      Burn, multiple, specified sites
  first degree 945.12
  second degree 945.22
  third degree 945.32
    deep 945.42
      with loss of body part 945.52
forearm(s) 943.01
  with
    hand(s) and wrist(s)—*see* Burn, multiple,
      specified sites
    other site(s), except upper limb(s)—*see*
      Burn, multiple, specified sites
    upper limb(s) except hand(s) or
      wrist(s)—*see* Burn, arm(s), multiple sites
  first degree 943.11
  second degree 943.21
  third degree 943.31
    deep 943.41
      with loss of body part 943.51
forehead 941.07
  with
    face or head—*see* Burn, head, multiple sites
    other site(s), except face or head—*see* Burn,
      multiple, specified sites
  first degree 941.17
  second degree 941.27
  third degree 941.37
    deep 941.47
      with loss of body part 941.57
fourth degree—*see* Burn, by site, third degree,
  deep
friction—*see* Injury, superficial, by site
from swallowing caustic or corrosive substance
  NEC—*see* Burn, internal organs
full thickness—*see* Burn, by site, third degree
gastrointestinal tract 947.3
genitourinary organs
  external 942.05
    with
      other site(s), except trunk—*see* Burn
        multiple, specified sites
      trunk—*see* Burn, trunk, multiple sites
    first degree 942.15
    second degree 942.25
    third degree 942.35
      deep 942.45
        with loss of body part 942.55
  internal 947.8
globe (eye)—*see* Burn, eyeball

Burn—*continued*

groin—*see* Burn, abdomen
gum 947.0
hand(s) (phalanges) (and wrist) 944.00
  with other site(s) (classifiable to more than
    category in 940-945)—*see* Burn, multiple,
    specified sites
  first degree 944.10
  second degree 944.20
  third degree 944.30
    deep 944.40
      with loss of body part 944.50
  back (dorsal surface) 944.06
    first degree 944.16
    second degree 944.26
    third degree 944.36
      deep 944.46
        with loss of body part 944.56
  multiple sites 944.08
    first degree 944.18
    second degree 944.28
    third degree 944.38
      deep 944.48
        with loss of body part 944.58
head (and face) 941.00
  with other site(s) except face or neck—*see*
    Burn, multiple, specified sites
  eye(s) only 940.9
  specified part—*see* Burn, by site
  first degree 941.10
  second degree 941.20
  third degree 941.30
    deep 941.40
      with loss of body part 941.50
  multiple sites 941.09
    with eyes—*see* Burn, eyes, with face, head,
      or neck
    first degree 941.19
    second degree 941.29
    third degree 941.39
      deep 941.49
        with loss of body part 941.59
heel—*see* Burn, foot
hip—*see* Burn, trunk, specified site NEC
iliac region—*see* Burn, trunk, specified site NEC
infected 958.3
inhalation (*see also* Burn, internal organs) 947.9
internal organs 947.9
  from caustic or corrosive substance
    (swallowing) NEC 947.9
  specified NEC (*see also* Burn, by site) 947.8
interscapular region—*see* Burn, back
intestine (large) (small) 947.3
iris—*see* Burn, eyeball
knee 945.05
  with
    lower limb(s)—*see* Burn, leg, multiple sites
    other site(s), except lower limb(s)—*see*
      Burn, multiple, specified sites
  first degree 945.15
  second degree 945.25
  third degree 945.35
    deep 945.45
      with loss of body part 945.55
labium (majus) (minus)—*see* Burn,
  genitourinary organs, external
lacrimal apparatus, duct, gland, or sac 940.1
  chemical 940.0
larynx 947.1
late effect—*see* Late, effects (of), burn
leg 945.00

Burn—*continued*
  with other site(s) (classifiable to more than
      category in 940-945)—*see* Burn, multiple,
      specified sites
  first degree 945.10
  second degree 945.20
  third degree 945.30
      deep 945.40
          with loss of body part 945.50
  lower 945.04
      with other part(s) of lower limb(s)—*see*
          Burn, leg, multiple sites
      first degree 945.14
      second degree 945.24
      third degree 945.34
          deep 945.44
              with loss of body part 945.54
  multiple sites 945.09
      first degree 945.19
      second degree 945.29
      third degree 945.39
          deep 945.49
              with loss of body part 945.59
  upper—*see* Burn, thigh
  lightning—*see* Burn, by site
  limb(s)
      lower (including foot or toe(s))—*see* Burn, leg
      upper (except wrist and hand)—*see* Burn,
          arm(s)
  lip(s) 941.03
      with
          face or head—*see* Burn, head, multiple sites
          other site(s)—*see* Burn,
              multiple, specified sites
      first degree 941.13
      second degree 941.23
      third degree 941.33
          deep 941.43
              with loss of body part 941.53
  lumbar region—*see* Burn, back
  lung 947.1
  malar region—*see* Burn, cheek
  mastoid region—*see* Burn, scalp
  membrane, tympanic—*see* Burn, ear
  midthoracic region—*see* Burn, chest wall
  mouth 947.0
  multiple (*see also* Burn, unspecified) 949.0
      specified sites (classifiable to more than one
          category in 940-945) 946.0
      first degree 946.1
      second degree 946.2
      third degree 946.3
          deep 946.4
              with loss of body part 946.5
  muscle, abdominal—*see* Burn, abdomen
  nasal (septum)—*see* Burn, nose
  neck 941.08
      with
          face or head—*see* Burn, head, multiple sites
          other site(s), except face or head—*see* Burn,
              multiple, specified sites
      first degree 941.18
      second degree 941.28
      third degree 941.38
          deep 941.48
              with loss of body part 941.58
  nose (septum) 941.05
      with
          face or head—*see* Burn, head, multiple sites
          other site(s), except face or head—*see* Burn,
              multiple, specified sites

Burn—*continued*
  first degree 941.15
  second degree 941.25
  third degree 941.35
      deep 941.45
          with loss of body part 941.55
  occipital region—*see* Burn, scalp
  orbit region 940.1
      chemical 940.0
  oronasopharynx 947.0
  palate 947.0
  palm(s) 944.05
      with
          hand(s) and wrist(s)—*see* Burn, hand(s),
              multiple sites
          other site(s), except hand(s) or wrist(s)—*see*
              Burn, multiple, specified sites
      first degree 944.15
      second degree 944.25
      third degree 944.35
          deep 944.45
              with loss of a body part 944.55
  parietal region—*see* Burn, scalp
  penis—*see* Burn, genitourinary organs, external
  perineum—*see* Burn, genitourinary organs,
      external
  periocular area 940.1
      chemical 940.0
  pharynx 947.0
  pleura 947.1
  popliteal space—*see* Burn, knee
  prepuce—*see* Burn, genitourinary organs,
      external
  pubic region—*see* Burn, genitourinary organs,
      external
  pudenda—*see* Burn, genitourinary organs,
      external
  rectum 947.3
  sac, lacrimal 940.1
      chemical 940.0
  sacral region—*see* Burn, back
  salivary (ducts) (glands) 947.0
  scalp 941.06
      with
          face or neck—*see* Burn, head, multiple sites
          other site(s), except face or neck—*see* Burn,
              multiple, specified sites
      first degree 941.16
      second degree 941.26
      third degree 941.36
          deep 941.46
              with loss of body part 941.56
  scapular region 943.06
      with
          other site(s), except upper limb(s)—*see*
              Burn, multiple, specified sites
          upper limb(s), except hand(s) or
              wrist(s)—*see* Burn, arm(s), multiple sites
      first degree 943.16
      second degree 943.26
      third degree 943.36
          deep 943.46
              with loss of body part 943.56
  sclera—*see* Burn, eyeball
  scrotum—*see* Burn, genitourinary organs,
      external
  septum, nasal—*see* Burn, nose
  shoulder(s) 943.05
      with
          hand(s) and wrist(s)—*see* Burn, multiple,
              specified sites

Burn—*continued*

other site(s), except upper limb(s)—*see* Burn, multiple, specified sites

upper limb(s), except hand(s) or wrist(s)—*see* Burn, arm(s), multiple sites

first degree 943.15

second degree 943.25

third degree 943.35

deep 943.45

with loss of body part 943.55

skin NEC (*see also* Burn, unspecified) 949.0

skull—*see* Burn, head

small intestine 947.3

sternal region—*see* Burn, chest wall

stomach 947.3

subconjunctival—*see* Burn, conjunctiva

subcutaneous—*see* Burn, by site, third degree

submaxillary region—*see* Burn, head

submental region—*see* Burn, chin

supraclavicular fossa—*see* Burn, neck

supraorbital—*see* Burn, forehead

temple—*see* Burn, scalp

temporal region—*see* Burn, scalp

testicle—*see* Burn, genitourinary organs, external

testis—*see* Burn, genitourinary organs, external

thigh 945.06

with

lower limb(s)–*see* Burn, leg, multiple sites

other site(s), except lower limb(s)—*see* Burn, multiple, specified sites

first degree 945.16

second degree 945.26

third degree 945.36

deep 945.46

with loss of body part 945.56

thorax (external)—*see* Burn, chest wall

throat 947.0

thumb(s) (nail) (subungual) 944.02

with

finger(s)—*see* Burn, finger, with other sites, thumb

hand(s) and wrist(s)—*see* Burn, hand(s), multiple sites

other site(s), except hand(s) or wrist(s)—*see* Burn, multiple, specified sites

first degree 944.12

second degree 944.22

third degree 944.32

deep 944.42

with loss of body part 944.52

toe (nail) (subungual) 945.01

with

lower limb(s)—*see* Burn, leg, multiple sites

other site(s), except lower limb(s)—*see* Burn, multiple, specified sites

first degree 945.11

second degree 945.21

third degree 945.31

deep 945.41

with loss of body part 945.51

tongue 947.0

tonsil 947.0

trachea 947.1

trunk 942.00

with other site(s) (classifiable to more than one category in 940-945)—*see* Burn, multiple, specified sites

first degree 942.10

second degree 942.20

Burn—*continued*

third degree 942.30

deep 942.40

with loss of body part 942.50

multiple sites 942.09

first degree 942.19

second degree 942.29

third degree 942.39

deep 942.49

with loss of body part 942.59

specified site NEC 942.09

first degree 942.19

second degree 942.29

third degree 942.39

deep 942.49

with loss of body part 942.59

tunica vaginalis—*see* Burn, genitourinary organs, external

tympanic membrane—*see* Burn, ear

tympanum—*see* Burn, ear

unspecified site (multiple) 949.0

with extent of body surface involved specified

less than 10 percent 948.0

10-19 percent 948.1

20-29 percent 948.2

30-39 percent 948.3

40-49 percent 948.4

50-59 percent 948.5

60-69 percent 948.6

70-79 percent 948.7

80-89 percent 948.8

90 percent or more 948.9

first degree 949.1

second degree 949.2

third degree 949.3

deep 949.4

with loss of body part 949.5

uterus 947.4

uvula 947.0

vagina 947.4

vulva—*see* Burn, genitourinary organs, external

wrist(s) 944.07

with

hand(s)—*see* Burn, hand(s), multiple sites

other site(s), except hand(s)—*see* Burn, multiple, specified sites

first degree 944.17

second degree 944.27

third degree 944.37

deep 944.47

with loss of body part 944.57

Burnett's syndrome (milk-alkali) 999.9

Burnier's syndrome (hypophyseal dwarfism) 253.3

Burning

feet syndrome 266.2

sensation (*see also* Disturbance, sensation) 782.0

tongue 529.6

Burns' disease (osteochondrosis, lower ulna) 732.3

Bursa —*see also* condition

pharynx 478.29

Bursitis NEC 727.3

Achilles tendon 726.71

adhesive 726.90

shoulder 726.0

ankle 726.79

buttock 726.5

calcaneal 726.79

C

Cacergasia 300.9
Cachexia 799.4
  cancerous (M8000/3) 199.1
  cardiac—*see* Disease, heart
  dehydration 276.5
    with
      hypernatremia 276.0
      hyponatremia 276.1
  due to malnutrition 261
  exophthalmic 242.0
  heart—*see* Disease, heart
  hypophyseal 253.2
  hypopituitary 253.2
  lead 984.9
    specified type of lead—*see* Table of drugs and
      chemicals
  malaria 084.9
  malignant (M8000/3) 199.1
  marsh 084.9
  nervous 300.5
  old age 797
  pachydermic—*see* Hypothyroidism
  paludal 084.9
  pituitary (postpartum) 253.2
  renal (*see also* Disease, renal) 593.9
  saturnine 984.9
    specified type of lead—*see* Table of drugs and
      chemicals
  senile 797
  Simmonds' (pituitary cachexia) 253.2
  splenica 289.59
  strumipriva (*see also* Hypothyroidism) 244.9
  tuberculous NEC (*see also* Tuberculosis) 011.9
café au lait spots 709.09
Caffey's disease or syndrome (infantile cortical
  hyperostosis) 756.59
Caisson disease 993.3
Caked breast (puerperal, postpartum) 676.2
Cake kidney 753.3
Calabar swelling 125.2
Calcaneal spur 726.73
Calcaneoapophysitis 732.5
Calcaneonavicular bar 755.67
Calcareous —*see* condition
Calcicosis (occupational) 502
Calciferol (vitamin D) deficiency 268.9
  with
    osteomalacia 268.2
    rickets (*see also* Rickets) 268.0
Calcification
  adrenal (capsule) (gland) 255.4
    tuberculous (*see also* Tuberculosis) 017.6
  aorta 440.0
  artery (annular)—*see* Arteriosclerosis
  auricle (ear) 380.89
  bladder 596.8
    due to S. hematobium 120.0
  brain (cortex)—*see* Calcification, cerebral
  bronchus 519.1
  bursa 727.82
  cardiac (*see also* Degeneration, myocardial)
    429.1
  cartilage (postinfectional) 733.99
  cerebral (cortex) 348.8
    artery 437.0
  cervix (uteri) 622.8
  choroid plexus 349.2
  conjunctiva 372.54

Calcification—*continued*
  corpora cavernosa (penis) 607.89
  cortex (brain)—*see* Calcification, cerebral
  dental pulp (nodular) 522.2
  dentinal papilla 520.4
  disc, intervertebral 722.90
    cervical, cervicothoracic 722.91
    lumbar, lumbosacral 722.93
    thoracic, thoracolumbar 722.92
  fallopian tube 620.8
  falx cerebri—*see* Calcification, cerebral
  fascia 728.89
  gallbladder 575.8
  general 275.4
  heart (*see also* Degeneration, myocardial) 429.1
    valve—*see* Endocarditis
  intervertebral cartilage or disc (postinfectional)
    722.90
    cervical, cervicothoracic 722.91
    lumbar, lumbosacral 722.93
    thoracic, thoracolumbar 722.92
  intracranial—*see* Calcification, cerebral
  intraspinal ligament 728.89
  joint 719.80
    ankle 719.87
    elbow 719.82
    foot 719.87
    hand 719.84
    hip 719.85
    knee 719.86
    multiple sites 719.89
    pelvic region 719.85
    shoulder (region) 719.81
    specified site NEC 719.88
    wrist 719.83
  kidney 593.89
    tuberculous (*see also* Tuberculosis) 016.0
  larynx (senile) 478.79
  lens 366.8
  ligament 728.89
    intraspinal 728.89
    knee (medial collateral) 717.89
  lung 518.89
    active 518.89
    postinfectional 518.89
    tuberculous (*see also* Tuberculosis,
      pulmonary) 011.9
  lymph gland or node (postinfectional) 289.3
    tuberculous (*see also* Tuberculosis, lymph
      gland) 017.2
  massive (paraplegic) 728.10
  medial NEC (*see also* Arteriosclerosis,
    extremities) 440.20
  meninges (cerebral) 349.2
  metastatic 275.4
  Mönckeberg's—*see* Arteriosclerosis
  muscle 728.10
    heterotopic, postoperative 728.13
  myocardium, myocardial (*see also*
    Degeneration, myocardial) 429.1
  ovary 620.8
  pancreas 577.8
  penis 607.99
  periarticular 728.89
  pericardium (*see also* Pericarditis) 423.8
  pineal gland 259.8
  pleura 511.0
    postinfectional 518.89

Calcification—*continued*
tuberculous (*see also* Tuberculosis, pleura)
012.0
pulp (dental) (nodular) 522.2
renal 593.89
rider's bone 733.99
sclera 379.16
semilunar cartilage 717.89
spleen 289.59
subcutaneous 709.3
suprarenal (capsule) (gland) 255.4
tendon (sheath) 727.82
with bursitis, synovitis or tenosynovitis 727.82
trachea 519.1
ureter 593.89
uterus 621.8
vitreous 379.29
Calcified —*see also* Calcification
hematoma NEC 959.9
Calcinosis (generalized) (interstitial) (tumoral)
(universalis) 275.4
circumscripta 709.3
cutis 709.3
intervertebralis 275.4 (722.90)
Raynaud's
phenomenonsclerodactylytelangiectasis
(CRST) 710.1
Calcium
blood
high (*see also* Hypercalcemia) 275.4
low (*see also* Hypocalcemia) 275.4
deposits—*see also* Calcification, by site
in bursa 727.82
in tendon (sheath) 727.82
with bursitis, synovitis or tenosynovitis
727.82
salts or soaps in vitreous 379.22
Calciuria 791.9
Calculi —*see* Calculus
Calculosis, intrahepatic —*see*
Choledocholithiasis
Calculus, calculi, calculous 592.9
ampulla of Vater—*see* Choledocholithiasis
anuria (impacted) (recurrent) 592.0
appendix 543.9
bile duct (any)—*see* Choledocholithiasis
biliary—*see* Cholelithiasis
bilirubin, multiple—*see* Cholelithiasis
bladder (encysted) (impacted) (urinary) 594.1
diverticulum 594.0
bronchus 518.89
calyx (kidney) (renal) 592.0
congenital 753.3
cholesterol (pure) (solitary)—*see* Cholelithiasis
common duct (bile)—*see* Choledocholithiasis
conjunctiva 372.54
cystic 594.1
duct—*see* Cholelithiasis
dental 523.6
subgingival 523.6
supragingival 523.6
epididymis 608.89
gallbladder—*see also* Cholelithiasis
congenital 751.69
hepatic (duct)—*see* Choledocholithiasis
intestine (impaction) (obstruction) 560.39
kidney (impacted) (multiple) (pelvis) (recurrent)
(staghorn) 592.0
congenital 753.3
lacrimal (passages) 375.57
liver (impacted)—*see* Choledocholithiasis

Calculus, calculi, calculous— *continued*
lung 518.89
nephritic (impacted) (recurrent) 592.0
nose 478.1
pancreas (duct) 577.8
parotid gland 527.5
pelvis, encysted 592.0
prostate 602.0
pulmonary 518.89
pyelitis (impacted) (recurrent) 592.9
pyelonephritis (impacted) (recurrent) 592.9
pyonephrosis (impacted) (recurrent) 592.9
renal (impacted) (recurrent) 592.0
congenital 753.3
salivary (duct) (gland) 527.5
seminal vesicle 608.89
staghorn 592.0
Stensen's duct 527.5
sublingual duct or gland 527.5
congenital 750.26
submaxillary duct, gland, or region 527.5
suburethral 594.8
tonsil 474.8
tooth, teeth 523.6
tunica vaginalis 608.89
ureter (impacted) (recurrent) 592.1
urethra (impacted) 594.2
urinary (duct) (impacted) (passage) (tract) 592.9
lower tract NEC 594.9
specified site 594.8
vagina 623.8
vesical (impacted) 594.1
Wharton's duct 527.5
Caliectasis 593.89
California
disease 114.0
encephalitis 062.5
Caligo cornea 371.03
Callositas, callosity (infected) 700
Callus (infected) 700
bone 726.91
excessive, following fracture—*see also* Late,
effect (of), fracture
Calvé (-Perthes) disease (osteochondrosis,
femoral capital) 732.1
Calvities (*see also* Alopecia) 704.00
Cameroon fever (*see also* Malaria) 084.6
Camptocormia 300.11
Camptodactyly (congenital) 755.59
Camurati-Engelmann disease (diaphyseal
sclerosis) 756.59
Canal— *see* condition
Canaliculitis (lacrimal) (acute) 375.31
Actinomyces 039.8
chronic 375.41
Canavan's disease 330.0
Cancer (M8000/3)—*see also* Neoplasm, by site,
malignant

---

*Note—The term "cancer" when modified by an
adjective or adjectival phrase indicating a
morphological type should be coded in the same
manner as "carcinoma" with that adjective or
phrase. Thus, "squamous-cell cancer" should
be coded in the same manner as
"squamous-cell carcinoma," which appears in
the list under "Carcinoma."*

---

bile duct type (M8160/3), liver 155.1
hepatocellular (M8170/3) 155.0
Cancerous (M8000/3)—*see* Neoplasm, by site,
malignant
Cancerphobia 300.29

Cancrum oris 528.1
Candidiasis, candidal 112.9
  with pneumonia 112.4
  balanitis 112.2
  congenital 771.7
  disseminated 112.5
  endocarditis 112.81
  esophagus 112.84
  intertrigo 112.3
  intestine 112.85
  lung 112.4
  meningitis 112.83
  mouth 112.0
  nails 112.3
  neonatal 771.7
  onychia 112.3
  otitis externa 112.82
  otomycosis 112.82
  paronychia 112.3
  perionyxis 112.3
  pneumonia 112.4
  pneumonitis 112.4
  skin 112.3
  specified site NEC 112.89
  systemic 112.5
  urogenital site NEC 112.2
  vagina 112.1
  vulva 112.1
  vulvovaginitis 112.1
Candidiosis —*see* Candidiasis
Candiru infection or infestation 136.8
Canities (premature) 704.3
  congenital 757.4
Canker (mouth) (sore) 528.2
  rash 034.1
Cannabinosis 504
Canton fever 081.9
Cap
  cradle 690.11
Capillariasis 127.5
Capillary —*see* condition
Caplan's syndrome 714.81
Caplan-Colinet syndrome 714.81
Capsule —*see* condition
Capsulitis (joint) 726.90
  adhesive (shoulder) 726.0
  labyrinthine 387.8
  thyroid 245.9
Caput
  crepitus 756.0
  medusae 456.8
  succedaneum 767.1
Carapata disease 087.1
Carate —*see* Pinta
Carboxyhemoglobinemia 986
Carbuncle 680.9
  abdominal wall 680.2
  ankle 680.6
  anus 680.5
  arm (any part, above wrist) 680.3
  auditory canal, external 680.0
  axilla 680.3
  back (any part) 680.2
  breast 680.2
  buttock 680.5
  chest wall 680.2
  corpus cavernosum 607.2
  ear (any part) (external) 680.0
  eyelid 373.13
  face (any part, except eye) 680.0
  finger (any) 680.4

Carbuncle— *continued*
  flank 680.2
  foot (any part) 680.7
  forearm 680.3
  genital organ (male) 608.4
  gluteal (region) 680.5
  groin 680.2
  hand (any part) 680.4
  head (any part, except face) 680.8
  heel 680.7
  hip 680.6
  kidney (*see also* Abscess, kidney) 590.2
  knee 680.6
  labia 616.4
  lacrimal
    gland (*see also* Dacryoadenitis) 375.00
    passages (duct) (sac) (*see also* Dacryocystitis) 375.30
  leg, any part except foot 680.6
  lower extremity, any part except foot 680.6
  malignant 022.0
  multiple sites 680.9
  neck 680.1
  nose (external) (septum) 680.0
  orbit, orbital 376.01
  partes posteriores 680.5
  pectoral region 680.2
  penis 607.2
  perineum 680.2
  pinna 680.0
  scalp (any part) 680.8
  scrotum 608.4
  seminal vesicle 608.0
  shoulder 680.3
  skin NEC 680.9
  specified site NEC 680.8
  spermatic cord 608.4
  temple (region) 680.0
  testis 608.4
  thigh 680.6
  thumb 680.4
  toe (any) 680.7
  trunk 680.2
  tunica vaginalis 608.4
  umbilicus 680.2
  upper arm 680.3
  urethra 597.0
  vas deferens 608.4
  vulva 616.4
  wrist 680.4
Carbunculus (*see also* Carbuncle) 680.9
Carcinoid (tumor) (M8240/1)—*see also* Neoplasm, by site, uncertain behavior
  and struma ovarii (M9091/1) 236.2
  argentaffin (M8241/1)—*see* Neoplasm, by site uncertain behavior
    malignant (M8241/3)—*see* Neoplasm, by site, malignant
  benign (M9091/0) 220
  composite (M8244/3)—*see* Neoplasm, by site, malignant
  goblet cell (M8243/3)—*see* Neoplasm, by site, malignant
  malignant (M8240/3)—*see* Neoplasm, by site, malignant
  nonargentaffin (M8242/1)—*see also* Neoplasm, by site, uncertain behavior
    malignant (M8242/3)—*see* Neoplasm, by site, malignant

Carcinoid—*continued*
  strumal (M9091/1) 236.2
  syndrome (intestinal) (metastatic) 259.2
  type bronchial adenoma (M8240/3)—*see*
    Neoplasm, lung, malignant
Carcinoidosis 259.2
Carcinoma (M8010/3)—*see also* Neoplasm, by
  site, malignant

Note—*Except where otherwise indicated, the morphological varieties of carcinoma in the list below should be coded by site as for "Neoplasm, malignant."*

---

  with
    apocrine metaplasia (M8573/3)
    cartilaginous (and osseous) metaplasia
      (M8571/3)
    osseous (and cartilaginous) metaplasia
      (M8571/3)
    productive fibrosis (M8141/3)
    spindle cell metaplasia (M8572/3)
    squamous metaplasia (M8570/3)
  acidophil (M8280/3)
    specified site—*see* Neoplasm, by site,
      malignant
    unspecified site 194.3
  acidophil-basophil, mixed (M8281/3)
    specified site—*see* Neoplasm, by site,
      malignant
    unspecified site 194.3
  acinar (cell) (M8550/3)
  acinic cell (M8550/3)
  adenocystic (M8200/3)
  adenoid
    cystic (M8200/3)
    squamous cell (M8075/3)
  adenosquamous (M8560/3)
  adnexal (skin) (M8390/3)—*see* Neoplasm, skin,
    malignant
  adrenal cortical (M8370/3) 194.0
  alveolar (M8251/3)
    cell (M8250/3)—*see* Neoplasm, lung,
      malignant
  anaplastic type (M8021/3)
  apocrine (M8401/3)
    breast—*see* Neoplasm, breast, malignant
    specified site NEC—*see* Neoplasm, skin,
      malignant
    unspecified site 173.9
  basal cell (pigmented) (M8090/3)—*see also*
    Neoplasm, skin, malignant
    fibro-epithelial type (M8093/3)—*see*
      Neoplasm, skin, malignant
    morphea type (M8092/3)—*see* Neoplasm,
      skin, malignant
    multicentric (M8091/3)—*see* Neoplasm, skin,
      malignant
  basaloid (M8123/3)
  basal-squamous cell, mixed (M8094/3)—*see*
    Neoplasm, skin, malignant
  basophil (M8300/3)
    specified site—*see* Neoplasm, by site,
      malignant
    unspecified site 194.3
  basophil-acidophil, mixed (M8281/3)
    specified site—*see* Neoplasm, by site,
      malignant
    unspecified site 194.3
  basosquamous (M8094/3)—*see* Neoplasm,
    skin, malignant

Carcinoma—*continued*
  bile duct type (M8160/3)
    and hepatocellular, mixed (M8180/3) 155.0
    liver 155.1
    specified site NEC—*see* Neoplasm, by site,
      malignant
    unspecified site 155.1
  branchial or branchiogenic 146.8
  bronchial or bronchogenic—*see* Neoplasm,
    lung, malignant
  bronchiolar (terminal) (M8250/3)—*see*
    Neoplasm, lung, malignant
  bronchiolo-alveolar (M8250/3)—*see* Neoplasm,
    lung, malignant
  bronchogenic (epidermoid) 162.9
  C cell (M8510/3)
    specified site—*see* Neoplasm, by site,
      malignant
    unspecified site 193
  ceruminous (M8420/3) 173.2
  chorionic (M9100/3)
    specified site—*see* Neoplasm, by site,
      malignant
    unspecified site
      female 181
      male 186.9
  chromophobe (M8270/3)
    specified site—*see* Neoplasm, by site,
      malignant
    unspecified site 194.3
  clear cell (mesonephroid type) (M8310/3)
  cloacogenic (M8124/3)
    specified site—*see* Neoplasm, by site,
      malignant
    unspecified site 154.8
  colloid (M8480/3)
  cribriform (M8201/3)
  cylindroid type (M8200/3)
  diffuse type (M8145/3)
    specified site—*see* Neoplasm, by site,
      malignant
    unspecified site 151.9
  duct (cell) (M8500/3)
    with Paget's disease (M8541/3)—*see*
      Neoplasm, breast, malignant
    infiltrating (M8500/3)
      specified site—*see* Neoplasm, by site,
        malignant
      unspecified site 174.9
  ductal (M8500/3)
  ductular, infiltrating (M8521/3)
  embryonal (M9070/3)
    and teratoma, mixed (M9081/3)
    combined with choriocarcinoma
      (M9101/3)—*see* Neoplasm, by site,
      malignant
    infantile type (M9071/3)
    liver 155.0
    polyembryonal type (M9072/3)
  endometrioid (M8380/3)
  eosinophil (M8280/3)
    specified site—*see* Neoplasm, by site,
      malignant
    unspecified site 194.3
  epidermoid (M8070/3)—*see also* Carcinoma,
    squamous cell
    and adenocarcinoma, mixed (M8560/3)
    in situ, Bowen's type (M8081/2)—*see*
      Neoplasm, skin, in situ
  intradermal—*see* Neoplasm, skin, in situ

Carcinoma—*continued*
  fibroepithelial type basal cell (M8093/3)—*see*
    Neoplasm, skin, malignant
  follicular (M8330/3)
    and papillary (mixed) (M8340/3) 193
    moderately differentiated type (M8332/3) 193
    pure follicle type (M8331/3) 193
    specified site—*see* Neoplasm, by site,
      malignant
    trabecular type (M8332/3) 193
    unspecified site 193
    well differentiated type (M8331/3) 193
  gelatinous (M8480/3)
  giant cell (M8031/3)
    and spindle cell (M8030/3)
  granular cell (M8320/3)
  granulosa cell (M8620/3) 183.0
  hepatic cell (M8170/3) 155.0
  hepatocellular (M8170/3) 155.0
    and bile duct, mixed (M8180/3)
      155.0
  hepatocholangiolitic (M8180/3) 155.0
  Hurthle cell (thyroid) 193
  hypernephroid (M8311/3)
  in
    adenomatous
      polyp (M8210/3)
      polyposis coli (M8220/3) 153.9
    pleomorphic adenoma (M8940/3)
    polypoid adenoma (M8210/3)
    situ (M8010/3)—*see* Carcinoma,
      in situ
    tubular adenoma (M8210/3)
    villous adenoma (M8261/3)
  infiltrating duct (M8500/3)
    with Paget's disease (M8541/3)—*see*
      Neoplasm, breast, malignant
    specified site—*see* Neoplasm, by site,
      malignant
    unspecified site 174.9
  inflammatory (M8530/3)
    specified site—*see* Neoplasm, by site,
      malignant
    unspecified site 174.9
  in situ (M8010/2)—*see also* Neoplasm, by site,
    in situ
    epidermoid (M8070/2)—*see also* Neoplasm,
      by site, in situ
      with questionable stromal invasion
        (M8076/2)
        specified site—*see* Neoplasm, by site, in
          situ
        unspecified site 233.1
      Bowen's type (M8081/2)—*see* Neoplasm,
        skin, in situ
    intraductal (M8500/2)
      specified site—*see* Neoplasm, by site, in situ
      unspecified site 233.0
    lobular (M8520/2)
      specified site—*see* Neoplasm, by site, in situ
      unspecified site 233.0
    papillary (M8050/2)—*see* Neoplasm, by site,
      in situ
    squamous cell (M8070/2)—*see also*
      Neoplasm, by site, in situ
    with questionable stromal invasion (M8076/2)
      specified site—*see* Neoplasm, by site, in
        situ
      unspecified site 233.1
    transitional cell (M8120/2)—*see* Neoplasm,
      by site, in situ

Carcinoma—*continued*
  intestinal type (M8144/3)
    specified site—*see* Neoplasm, by site,
      malignant
    unspecified site 151.9
  intraductal (noninfiltrating) (M8500/2)
    papillary (M8503/2)
      specified site—*see* Neoplasm, by site, in situ
      unspecified site 233.0
    specified site—*see* Neoplasm, by site, in situ
    unspecified site 233.0
  intraepidermal (M8070/2)—*see also* Neoplasm,
    skin, in situ
    squamous cell, Bowen's type (M8081/2)—*see*
      Neoplasm, skin, in situ
  intraepithelial (M8010/2)—*see also* Neoplasm,
    by site, in situ
    squamous cell (M8072/2)—*see* Neoplasm, by
      site, in situ
  intraosseous (M9270/3) 170.1
    upper jaw (bone) 170.0
  islet cell (M8150/3)
    and exocrine, mixed (M8154/3)
      specified site—*see* Neoplasm, by site,
        malignant
      unspecified site 157.9
    pancreas 157.4
    specified site NEC—*see* Neoplasm, by site,
      malignant
    unspecified site 157.4
  juvenile, breast (M8502/3)—*see* Neoplasm,
    breast, malignant
  Kulchitsky's cell (carcinoid tumor of intestine)
    259.2
  large cell (M8012/3)
    squamous cell, nonkeratinizing type
      (M8072/3)
  Leydig cell (testis) (M8650/3)
    specified site—*see* Neoplasm, by site,
      malignant
    unspecified site 186.9
      female 183.0
      male 186.9
  liver cell (M8170/3) 155.0
  lobular (infiltrating) (M8520/3)
    non-infiltrating (M8520/3)
      specified site—*see* Neoplasm, by site, in situ
      unspecified site 233.0
    specified site—*see* Neoplasm, by site,
      malignant
    unspecified site 174.9
  lymphoepithelial (M8082/3)
  medullary (M8510/3)
    with
      amyloid stroma (M8511/3)
        specified site—*see* Neoplasm, by site,
          malignant
        unspecified site 193
      lymphoid stroma (M8512/3)
        specified site—*see* Neoplasm, by site,
          malignant
        unspecified site 174.9
  mesometanephric (M9110/3)
  mesonephric (M9110/3)
  metastatic (M8010/6)—*see* Metastasis, cancer
  metatypical (M8095/3)—*see* Neoplasm, skin,
    malignant
  morphea type basal cell (M8092/3)—*see*
    Neoplasm, skin, malignant
  mucinous (M8480/3)
  mucin-producing (M8481/3)

Carcinoma— *continued*
  mucin-secreting (M8481/3)
  mucoepidermoid (M8430/3)
  mucoid (M8480/3)
    cell (M8300/3)
      specified site—*see* Neoplasm, by site,
        malignant
      unspecified site 194.3
  mucous (M8480/3)
  nonencapsulated sclerosing (M8350/3) 193
  noninfiltrating
    intracystic (M8504/2)—*see* Neoplasm, by
      site, in situ
    intraductal (M8500/2)
      papillary (M8503/2)
        specified site—*see* Neoplasm, by site, in
          situ
        unspecified site 233.0
      specified site—*see* Neoplasm, by site, in situ
      unspecified site 233.0
    lobular (M8520/2)
      specified site—*see* Neoplasm, by site, in situ
      unspecified site 233.0
  oat cell (M8042/3)
    specified site—*see* Neoplasm, by site,
      malignant
    unspecified site 162.9
  odontogenic (M9270/3) 170.1
    upper jaw (bone) 170.0
  onocytic (M8290/3)
  oxyphilic (M8290/3)
  papillary (M8050/3)
    and follicular (mixed) (M8340/3) 193
    epidermoid (M8052/3)
    intraductal (noninfiltrating) (M8503/2)
      specified site—*see* Neoplasm, by site, in situ
      unspecified site 233.0
    serous (M8460/3)
      specified site—*see* Neoplasm, by site,
        malignant
      surface (M8461/3)
        specified site—*see* Neoplasm, by site,
          malignant
        unspecified site 183.0
      unspecified site 183.0
    squamous cell (M8052/3)
    transitional cell (M8130/3)
  papillocystic (M8450/3)
    specified site—*see* Neoplasm, by site,
      malignant
    unspecified site 183.0
  parafollicular cell (M8510/3)
    specified site—*see* Neoplasm, by site,
      malignant
    unspecified site 193
  pleomorphic (M8022/3)
  polygonal cell (M8034/3)
  prickle cell (M8070/3)
  pseudoglandular, squamous cell (M8075/3)
  pseudomucinous (M8470/3)
    specified site—*see* Neoplasm, by site,
      malignant
    unspecified site 183.0
  pseudosarcomatous (M8033/3)
  regaud type (M8082/3)—*see* Neoplasm,
    nasopharynx, malignant
  renal cell (M8312/3) 189.0
  reserve cell (M8041/3)
  round cell (M8041/3)
  Schmincke (M8082/3)—*see* Neoplasm,
    nasopharynx, malignant

Carcinoma— *continued*
  Schneiderian (M8121/3)
    specified site—*see* Neoplasm, by site,
      malignant
    unspecified site 160.0
  scirrhous (M8141/3)
  sebaceous (M8410/3)—*see* Neoplasm, skin,
    malignant
  secondary (M8010/6)—*see* Neoplasm, by site,
    malignant, secondary
  secretory, breast (M8502/3)—*see* Neoplasm,
    breast, malignant
  serous (M8441/3)
    papillary (M8460/3)
      specified site—*see* Neoplasm, by site,
        malignant
      unspecified site 183.0
    surface, papillary (M8461/3)
      specified site—*see* Neoplasm, by site,
        malignant
      unspecified site 183.0
  Sertoli cell (M8640/3)
    specified site—*see* Neoplasm, by site,
      malignant
    unspecified site 186.9
  signet ring cell (M8490/3)
    metastatic (M8490/6)—*see* Neoplasm, by site,
      secondary
  simplex (M8231/3)
  skin appendage (M8390/3)—*see* Neoplasm,
    skin, malignant
  small cell (M8041/3)
    fusiform cell type (M8043/3)
    squamous cell, non-keratinizing type
      (M8073/3)
  solid (M8230/3)
    with amyloid stroma (M8511/3)
      specified site—*see* Neoplasm, by site,
        malignant
      unspecified site 193
  spheroidal cell (M8035/3)
  spindle cell (M8032/3)
    and giant cell (M8030/3)
  spinous cell (M8070/3)
  squamous (cell) (M8070/3)
    adenoid type (M8075/3)
    and adenocarcinoma, mixed (M8560/3)
    intraepidermal, Bowen's type—*see*
      Neoplasm, skin, in situ
    keratinizing type (large cell) (M8071/3)
    large cell, non-keratinizing type (M8072/3)
    microinvasive (M8076/3)
      specified site—*see* Neoplasm, by site,
        malignant
      unspecified site 180.9
    non-keratinizing type (M8072/3)
    papillary (M8052/3)
    pseudoglandular (M8075/3)
    small cell, non-keratinizing type (M8073/3)
    spindle cell type (M8074/3)
    verrucous (M8051/3)
  superficial spreading (M8143/3)
  sweat gland (M8400/3)—*see* Neoplasm, skin,
    malignant
  theca cell (M8600/3) 183.0
  thymic (M8580/3) 164.0
  trabecular (M8190/3)
  transitional (cell) (M8120/3)
    papillary (M8130/3)
    spindle cell type (M8122/3)

Carcinoma—*continued*
  tubular (M8211/3)
  undifferentiated type (M8020/3)
  urothelial (M8120/3)
  ventriculi 151.9
  verrucous (epidermoid) (squamous cell)
    (M8051/3)
  villous (M8262/3)
  water-clear cell (M8322/3) 194.1
  wolffian duct (M9110/3)
Carcinomaphobia 300.29
Carcinomatosis
  peritonei (M8010/6) 197.6
  specified site NEC (M8010/3)—*see* Neoplasm,
    by site, malignant
  unspecified site (M8010/6) 199.0
Carcinosarcoma (M8980/3)—*see also*
    Neoplasm, by site, malignant
  embryonal type (M8981/3)—*see* Neoplasm, by
    site, malignant
Cardia, cardial —*see* condition
Cardiac —*see also* condition
  death—*see* Disease, heart
  device
    defibrillator, automatic implantable V45.02
    in situ NEC V45.00
    pacemaker
      cardiac
        fitting or adjustment V53.3
        in situ V45.01
      carotid sinus
        fitting or adjustment V53.3
        in situ V45.09
  pacemaker—*see* Cardiac, device, pacemaker
  tamponade 423.9
Cardialgia (*see also* Pain, precordial) 786.51
Cardiectasis —*see* Hypertrophy, cardiac
Cardiochalasia 530.81
Cardiomalacia (*see also* Degeneration,
    myocardial) 429.1
Cardiomegalia glycogenica diffusa 271.0
Cardiomegaly (*see also* Hypertrophy, cardiac)
    429.3
  congenital 746.89
  glycogen 271.0
  hypertensive (*see also* Hypertension, heart)
    402.90
  idiopathic 429.3
Cardiomyoliposis (*see also* Degeneration,
    myocardial) 429.1
Cardiomyopathy (congestive) (constrictive)
    (familial) (infiltrative) (obstructive)
    (restrictive) (sporadic) 425.4
  alcoholic 425.5
  amyloid 277.3 *[425.7]*
  beriberi 265.0 *[425.7]*
  cobalt-beer 425.5
  congenital 425.3
  due to
    amyloidosis 277.3 *[425.7]*
    beriberi 265.0 *[425.7]*
    cardiac glycogenesis 271.0 *[425.7]*
    Chagas' disease 086.0
    Friedreich's ataxia 334.0 *[425.8]*
    hypertension —*see* Hypertension, with, heart
      involvement
    mucopolysaccharidosis 277.5 *[425.7]*
    myotonia atrophica 359.2 *[425.8]*
    progressive muscular dystrophy 359.1 *[425.8]*
    sarcoidosis 135 *[425.8]*

Cardiomyopathy—*continued*
  glycogen storage 271.0 *[425.7]*
  hypertensive—*see* Hypertension, with, heart
    involvement
  hypertrophic
    nonobstructive 425.4
    obstructive 425.1
      congenital 746.84
  idiopathic (concentric) 425.4
  in
    Chagas' disease 086.0
    sarcoidosis 135 *[425.8]*
  ischemic 414.8
  metabolic NEC 277.9 *[425.7]*
    amyloid 277.3 *[425.7]*
    thyrotoxic (*see also* Thyrotoxicosis) 242.9
      [425.7]
    thyrotoxicosis (*see also* Thyrotoxicosis) 242.9
      [425.7]
  nutritional 269.9 *[425.7]*
    beriberi 265.0 *[425.7]*
  obscure of Africa 425.2
  postpartum 674.8
  primary 425.4
  secondary 425.9
  thyrotoxic (*see also* Thyrotoxicosis) 242.9
    [425.7]
  toxic NEC 425.9
  tuberculous (*see also* Tuberculosis) 017.9
    [425.8]
Cardionephritis —*see* Hypertension, cardiorenal
Cardionephropathy —*see* Hypertension,
    cardiorenal
Cardionephrosis —*see* Hypertension,
    cardiorenal
Cardioneurosis 306.2
Cardiopathia nigra 416.0
Cardiopathy (*see also* Disease, heart) 429.9
  hypertensive (*see also* Hypertension, heart)
    402.90
  idiopathic 425.4
  mucopolysaccharidosis 277.5 *[425.7]*
Cardiopericarditis (*see also* Pericarditis) 423.9
Cardiophobia 300.29
Cardioptosis 746.87
Cardiorenal —*see* condition
Cardiorrhexis (*see also* Infarct, myocardium)
    410.9
Cardiosclerosis —*see* Arteriosclerosis, coronary
Cardiosis —*see* Disease, heart
Cardiospasm (esophagus) (reflex) (stomach)
    530.0
  congenital 750.7
Cardiostenosis —*see* Disease, heart
Cardiosymphysis 423.1
Cardiothyrotoxicosis —*see* Hyperthyroidism
Cardiovascular —*see* condition
Carditis (acute) (bacterial) (chronic) (subacute)
    429.89
  Coxsackie 074.20
  hypertensive (*see also* Hypertension, heart)
    402.90
  meningococcal 036.40
  rheumatic—*see* Disease, heart, rheumatic
  rheumatoid 714.2
Care (of)
  child (routine) V20.1
  convalescent following V66.9
    chemotherapy V66.2
    medical NEC V66.5
    psychotherapy V66.3

Care—*continued*
  radiotherapy V66.1
  surgery V66.0
  surgical NEC V66.0
  treatment (for) V66.5
    combined V66.6
    fracture V66.4
    mental disorder NEC V66.3
    specified type NEC V66.5
  end-of-life care V66.7
  family member (handicapped) (sick)
    creating problem for family V61.49
    provided away from home for holiday relief
      V60.5
    unavailable, due to
      absence (person rendering care) (sufferer)
        V60.4
      inability (any reason) of person rendering
        care V60.4
  holiday relief V60.5
  hospice V66.7
  lack of (at or after birth) (infant) (child) 995.52
    adult 995.84
  lactation of mother V24.1
  palliative V66.7
  postpartum
    immediately after delivery V24.0
    routine follow-up V24.2
  prenatal V22.1
    first pregnancy V22.0
    high risk pregnancy V23.9
      specified problem NEC V23.8
  terminal V66.7
  unavailable, due to
    absence of person rendering care V60.4
    inability (any reason) of person rendering care
      V60.4
  well baby V20.1
Caries (bone) (*see also* Tuberculosis, bone)
    015.9 *[730.8]*
  arrested 521.0
  cementum 521.0
  cerebrospinal (tuberculous) 015.0 *[730.88]*
  dental (acute) (chronic) (incipient) (infected)
    (with pulp exposure) 521.0
  dentin (acute) (chronic) 521.0
  enamel (acute) (chronic) (incipient) 521.0
  external meatus 380.89
  hip (*see also* Tuberculosis) 015.1 *[730.85]*
  knee 015.2 *[730.86]*
  labyrinth 386.8
  limb NEC 015.7 *[730.88]*
  mastoid (chronic) (process) 383.1
  middle ear 385.89
  nose 015.7 *[730.88]*
  orbit 015.7 *[730.88]*
  ossicle 385.24
  petrous bone 383.20
  sacrum (tuberculous) 015.0 *[730.88]*
  spine, spinal (column) (tuberculous) 015.0
    [730.88]
  syphilitic 095.5
    congenital 090.0 *[730.8]*
  teeth (internal) 521.0
  vertebra (column) (tuberculous) 015.0 *[730.88]*
Carini's syndrome (ichthyosis congenita) 757.1
Carious teeth 521.0
Carneous mole 631
Carnosinemia 270.5
Carotid body or sinus syndrome 337.0
Carotidynia 337.0

Carotinemia (dietary) 278.3
Carotinosis (cutis) (skin) 278.3
Carpal tunnel syndrome 354.0
Carpenter's syndrome 759.89
Carpopedal spasm (*see also* Tetany) 781.7
Carpoptosis 736.05
Carrier (suspected) of
  amebiasis V02.2
  bacterial disease (meningococcal,
    staphylococcal, streptococcal) NEC V02.5
  cholera V02.0
  defective gene V19.8
  diphtheria V02.4
  dysentery (bacillary) V02.3
    amebic V02.2
  Endamoeba histolytica V02.2
  gastrointestinal pathogens NEC V02.3
  genetic defect V19.8
  gonorrhea V02.7
  HAA (hepatitis Australian-antigen) V02.6
  hepatitis V02.6
    Australian-antigen (HAA) V02.6
    serum V02.6
    viral V02.6
  infective organism NEC V02.9
  malaria V02.9
  paratyphoid V02.3
  Salmonella V02.3
    typhosa V02.1
  serum hepatitis V02.6
  Shigella V02.3
  staphylococcus NEC V02.5
  typhoid V02.1
  venereal disease NEC V02.8
Carrión's disease (Bartonellosis) 088.0
Car sickness 994.6
Carter's
  relapsing fever (Asiatic) 087.0
Cartilage —*see* condition
Caruncle (inflamed)
  abscess, lacrimal (*see also* Dacryocystitis)
    375.30
  conjunctiva 372.00
    acute 372.00
  eyelid 373.00
  labium (majus) (minus) 616.8
  lacrimal 375.30
  urethra (benign) 599.3
  vagina (wall) 616.8
Cascade stomach 537.6
Caseation lymphatic gland (*see also*
    Tuberculosis) 017.2
Caseous
  bronchitis—*see* Tuberculosis, pulmonary
  meningitis 013.0
  pneumonia—*see* Tuberculosis, pulmonary
Cassidy (-Scholte) syndrome (malignant
    carcinoid) 259.2
Castellani's bronchitis 104.8
Castleman's tumor or lymphoma (mediastinal
    lymph node hyperplasia) 785.6
Castration, traumatic 878.2
  complicated 878.3
Casts in urine 791.7
Cat's ear 744.29
Catalepsy 300.11
  catatonic (acute) (*see also* Schizophrenia) 295.2
  hysterical 300.11
  schizophrenic (*see also* Schizophrenia) 295.2
Cataphasia 307.0
Cataplexy (idiopathic) 347

Cataract (anterior cortical) (anterior polar)
    (black) (capsular) (central) (cortical)
    (hypermature) (immature) (incipient) (mature)
    (nuclear) 366.9
  anterior
    and posterior axial embryonal 743.33
    pyramidal 743.31
    subcapsular polar
      infantile, juvenile, or presenile 366.01
      senile 366.13
  associated with
    calcinosis 275.4 *[366.42]*
    craniofacial dysostosis 756.0 *[366.44]*
    galactosemia 271.1 *[366.44]*
    hypoparathyroidism 252.1 *[366.42]*
    myotonic disorders 359.2 *[366.43]*
    neovascularization 366.33
  blue dot 743.39
  cerulean 743.39
  complicated NEC 366.30
  congenital 743.30
    capsular or subcapsular 743.31
    cortical 743.32
    nuclear 743.33
    specified type NEC 743.39
    total or subtotal 743.34
    zonular 743.32
  coronary (congenital) 743.39
    acquired 366.12
  cupuliform 366.14
  diabetic 250.5 *[366.41]*
  drug-induced 366.45
  due to
    chalcosis 360.24 *[366.34]*
    chronic choroiditis (*see also* Choroiditis)
      363.20 *[366.32]*
    degenerative myopia 360.21 *[366.34]*
    glaucoma (*see also* Glaucoma) 365.9 *[366.31]*
    infection, intraocular NEC 366.32
    inflammatory ocular disorder NEC 366.32
    iridocyclitis, chronic 364.10 *[366.33]*
    pigmentary retinal dystrophy 362.74 *[366.34]*
    radiation 366.46
  electric 366.46
  glassblowers' 366.46
  heat ray 366.46
  heterochromic 366.33
  in eye disease NEC 366.30
  infantile (*see also* Cataract, juvenile) 366.00
  intumescent 366.12
  irradiational 366.46
  juvenile 366.00
    anterior subcapsular polar 366.01
    combined forms 366.09
    cortical 366.03
    lamellar 366.03
    nuclear 366.04
    posterior subcapsular polar 366.02
    specified NEC 366.09
    zonular 366.03
  lamellar 743.32
    infantile, juvenile, or presenile 366.03
  morgagnian 366.18
  myotonic 359.2 *[366.43]*
  myxedema 244.9 *[366.44]*
  posterior, polar (capsular) 743.31
    infantile, juvenile, or presenile 366.02
    senile 366.14
  presenile (*see also* Cataract, juvenile) 366.00
  punctate
    acquired 366.12

Cataract—*continued*
  congenital 743.39
  secondary (membrane) 366.50
    obscuring vision 366.53
    specified type, not obscuring vision 366.52
  senile 366.10
    anterior subcapsular polar 366.13
    combined forms 366.19
    cortical 366.15
    hypermature 366.18
    immature 366.12
    incipient 366.12
    mature 366.17
    nuclear 366.16
    posterior subcapsular polar 366.14
    specified NEC 366.19
    total or subtotal 366.17
  snowflake 250.5 *[366.41]*
  specified NEC 366.8
  subtotal (senile) 366.17
    congenital 743.34
  sunflower 360.24 *[366.34]*
  tetanic NEC 252.1 *[366.42]*
  total (mature) (senile) 366.17
    congenital 743.34
    localized 366.21
    traumatic 366.22
  toxic 366.45
  traumatic 366.20
    partially resolved 366.23
    total 366.22
  zonular (perinuclear) 743.32
    infantile, juvenile, or presenile 366.03
Cataracta 366.10
  brunescens 366.16
  cerulea 743.39
  complicata 366.30
  congenita 743.30
  coralliformis 743.39
  coronaria (congenital) 743.39
    acquired 366.12
  diabetic 250.5 *[366.41]*
  floriformis 360.24 *[366.34]*
  membranacea
    accreta 366.50
    congenita 743.39
  nigra 366.16
Catarrh, catarrhal (inflammation) (*see also*
    condition) 460
  acute 460
  asthma, asthmatic (*see also* Asthma) 493.9
  Bostock's (*see also* Fever, hay) 477.9
  bowel—*see* Enteritis
  bronchial 490
    acute 466.0
    chronic 491.0
    subacute 466.0
  cervix, cervical (canal) (uteri)—*see* Cervicitis
  chest (*see also* Bronchitis) 490
  chronic 472.0
  congestion 472.0
  conjunctivitis 372.03
  due to syphilis 095.9
    congenital 090.0
  enteric—*see* Enteritis
  epidemic 487.1
  Eustachian 381.50
  eye (acute) (vernal) 372.03
  fauces (*see also* Pharyngitis) 462
  febrile 460
  fibrinous acute 466.0

Catarrh, catarrhal—*continued*
gastroenteric—*see* Enteritis
gastrointestinal—*see* Enteritis
gingivitis 523.0
hay (*see also* Fever, hay) 477.9
infectious 460
intestinal—*see* Enteritis
larynx (*see also* Laryngitis, chronic) 476.0
liver 070.1
   with hepatic coma 070.0
lung (*see also* Bronchitis) 490
   acute 466.0
   chronic 491.0
middle ear (chronic)—*see* Otitis media, chronic
mouth 528.0
nasal (chronic) (*see also* Rhinitis) 472.0
   acute 460
nasobronchial 472.2
nasopharyngeal (chronic) 472.2
   acute 460
nose—*see* Catarrh, nasal
ophthalmia 372.03
pneumococcal, acute 466.0
pulmonary (*see also* Bronchitis) 490
   acute 466.0
   chronic 491.0
spring (eye) 372.13
suffocating (*see also* Asthma) 493.9
summer (hay) (*see also* Fever, hay) 477.9
throat 472.1
tracheitis 464.10
   with obstruction 464.11
tubotympanal 381.4
   acute (*see also* Otitis media, acute,
      nonsuppurative) 381.00
   chronic 381.10
vasomotor (*see also* Fever, hay) 477.9
vesical (bladder)—*see* Cystitis
Catarrhus aestivus (*see also* Fever, hay) 477.9
Catastrophe, cerebral (*see also* Disease,
   cerebrovascular, acute) 436
Catatonia, catatonic (acute) 781.9
agitation 295.2
dementia (praecox) 295.2
excitation 295.2
excited type 295.2
schizophrenia 295.2
stupor 295.2
with
   affective psychosis —*see* Psychosis, affective)
Cat-scratch —*see also* Injury, superficial
   disease or fever 078.3
Cauda equina —*see also* condition syndrome
   344.60
Cauliflower ear 738.7
Caul over face 768.9
Causalgia 355.9
lower limb 355.71
upper limb 354.4
Cause
external, general effects NEC 994.9
not stated 799.9
unknown 799.9
Caustic burn —*see also* Burn, by site
from swallowing caustic or corrosive
   substance—*see* Burn, internal organs
Cavare's disease (familial periodic paralysis)
   359.3
Cave-in, injury
crushing (severe) (*see also* Crush, by site) 869.1
suffocation 994.7

Cavernitis (penis) 607.2
lymph vessel—*see* Lymphangioma
Cavernositis 607.2
Cavernous —*see* condition
Cavitation of lung (*see also* Tuberculosis) 011.2
nontuberculous 518.89
primary, progressive 010.8
Cavity
lung—*see* Cavitation of lung
optic papilla 743.57
pulmonary—*see* Cavitation of lung
teeth 521.0
vitreous (humor) 379.21
Cavovarus foot, congenital 754.59
Cavus foot (congenital) 754.71
acquired 736.73
Cazenave's
disease (pemphigus) NEC 694.4
lupus (erythematosus) 695.4
Cecitis —*see* Appendicitis
Cecocele —*see* Hernia
Cecum —*see* condition
Celiac
artery compression syndrome 447.4
disease 579.0
infantilism 579.0
Cell, cellular —*see also* condition
anterior chamber (eye) (positive aqueous ray)
   364.04
Cellulitis (diffuse) (with lymphangitis) (*see also*
   Abscess) 682.9
abdominal wall 682.2
anaerobic (*see also* Gas gangrene) 040.0
ankle 682.6
anus 566
areola 611.0
arm (any part, above wrist) 682.3
artificial opening (external) 569.61
auditory canal (external) 380.10
axilla 682.3
back (any part) 682.2
breast 611.0
   postpartum 675.1
broad ligament (*see also* Disease, pelvis,
   inflammatory) 614.4
   acute 614.3
buttock 682.5
cervical (neck region) 682.1
cervix (uteri) (*see also* Cervicitis) 616.0
cheek, external 682.0
   internal 528.3
chest wall 682.2
chronic NEC 682.9
colostomy 569.61
corpus cavernosum 607.2
digit 681.9
Douglas' cul-de-sac or pouch (chronic) (*see*
   also Disease, pelvis, inflammatory) 614.4
   acute 614.3
drainage site (following operation) 998.59
ear, external 380.10
enterostomy 569.61
erysipelar (*see also* Erysipelas) 035
eyelid 373.13
face (any part, except eye) 682.0
finger (intrathecal) (periosteal) (subcutaneous)
   (subcuticular) 681.00
flank 682.2
foot (except toe) 682.7
forearm 682.3
gangrenous (*see also* Gangrene) 785.4

Cellulitis—*continued*
genital organ NEC
  female—*see* Abscess, genital organ, female
  male 608.4
glottis 478.71
gluteal (region) 682.5
gonococcal NEC 098.0
groin 682.2
hand (except finger or thumb) 682.4
head (except face) NEC 682.8
heel 682.7
hip 682.6
jaw (region) 682.0
knee 682.6
labium (majus) (minus) (*see also* Vulvitis)
  616.10
larynx 478.71
leg, except foot 682.6
lip 528.5
mammary gland 611.0
mouth (floor) 528.3
multiple sites NEC 682.9
nasopharynx 478.21
navel 682.2
  newborn NEC 771.4
neck (region) 682.1
nipple 611.0
nose 478.1
  external 682.0
orbit, orbital 376.01
palate (soft) 528.3
pectoral (region) 682.2
pelvis, pelvic
  with
    abortion—*see* Abortion, by type, with sepsis
    ectopic pregnancy (*see also* categories
      633.0-633.9) 639.0
    molar pregnancy (*see also* categories
      630-632) 639.0
  female (*see also* Disease, pelvis,
    inflammatory) 614.4
    acute 614.3
  following
    abortion 639.0
    ectopic or molar pregnancy 639.0
  male (*see also* Abscess, peritoneum) 567.2
  puerperal, postpartum, childbirth 670
penis 607.2
perineal, perineum 682.2
perirectal 566
peritonsillar 475
periurethral 597.0
periuterine (*see also* Disease, pelvis,
  inflammatory) 614.4
  acute 614.3
pharynx 478.21
phlegmonous NEC 682.9
rectum 566
retromammary 611.0
retroperitoneal (*see also* Peritonitis) 567.2
round ligament (*see also* Disease, pelvis,
  inflammatory) 614.4
  acute 614.3
scalp (any part) 682.8
  dissecting 704.8
scrotum 608.4
septic NEC 682.9
shoulder 682.3
specified sites NEC 682.8
spermatic cord 608.4

Cellulitis—*continued*
submandibular (region) (space) (triangle) 682.0
  gland 527.3
submaxillary 528.3
  gland 527.3
submental (pyogenic) 682.0
  gland 527.3
suppurative NEC 682.9
testis 608.4
thigh 682.6
thumb (intrathecal) (periosteal) (subcutaneous)
  (subcuticular) 681.00
toe (intrathecal) (periosteal) (subcutaneous)
  (subcuticular) 681.10
tonsil 475
trunk 682.2
tuberculous (primary) (*see also* Tuberculosis)
  017.0
tunica vaginalis 608.4
umbilical 682.2
  newborn NEC 771.4
vaccinal 999.3
vagina—*see* Vaginitis
vas deferens 608.4
vocal cords 478.5
vulva (*see also* Vulvitis) 616.10
wrist 682.4
Cementoblastoma, benign (M9273/0) 213.1
upper jaw (bone) 213.0
Cementoma (M9273/0) 213.1
gigantiform (M9276/0) 213.1
  upper jaw (bone) 213.0
upper jaw (bone) 213.0
Cementoperiostitis 523.4
Cephalgia, cephalalgia (*see also* Headache)
  784.0
histamine 346.2
nonorganic origin 307.81
psychogenic 307.81
tension 307.81
Cephalhematocele, cephalematocele
due to birth injury 767.1
fetus or newborn 767.1
traumatic (*see also* Contusion, head) 920
Cephalhematoma, cephalematoma (calcified)
due to birth injury 767.1
fetus or newborn 767.1
traumatic (*see also* Contusion, head) 920
Cephalic —*see* condition
Cephalitis —*see* Encephalitis
Cephalocele 742.0
Cephaloma —*see* Neoplasm, by site,
  malignant
Cephalomenia 625.8
Cephalopelvic —*see* condition
Cercomoniasis 007.3
Cerebellitis —*see* Encephalitis
Cerebellum (cerebellar)—*see* condition
Cerebral —*see* condition
Cerebritis —*see* Encephalitis
Cerebrohepatorenal syndrome 759.89
Cerebromacular degeneration 330.1
Cerebromalacia (*see also* Softening, brain) 434.9
Cerebrosidosis 272.7
Cerebrospasticity —*see* Palsy, cerebral
Cerebrospinal —*see* condition
Cerebrum —*see* condition
Ceroid storage disease 272.7
Cerumen (accumulation) (impacted) 380.4
Cervical —*see also* condition
auricle 744.43—
rib 756.2

Cervicalgia 723.1
Cervicitis (acute) (chronic) (nonvenereal)
  (subacute) (with erosion or ectropion) 616.0
  with
    abortion—*see* Abortion, by type, with sepsis
    ectopic pregnancy (*see also* categories
      633.0-633.9) 639.0
    molar pregnancy (*see also* categories
      630-632) 639.0
    ulceration 616.0
  chlamydial 099.53
  complicating pregnancy or puerperium 646.6
    affecting fetus or newborn 760.8
  following
    abortion 639.0
    ectopic or molar pregnancy 639.0
  gonococcal (acute) 098.15
    chronic or duration of 2 months or more
      098.35
  senile (atrophic) 616.0
  syphilitic 095.8
  trichomonal 131.09
  tuberculous (*see also* Tuberculosis) 016.7
Cervicoaural fistula 744.49
Cervicocolpitis (emphysematosa) (*see also*
  Cervicitis) 616.0
Cervix —*see* condition
Cesarean delivery, operation or section NEC
  669.7
  affecting fetus or newborn 763.4
  post mortem, affecting fetus or newborn 761.6
  previous, affecting management of pregnancy
    654.2
Céstan's syndrome 344.89
Céstan-Chenais paralysis 344.89
Céstan-Raymond syndrome 433.8
Cestode infestation NEC 123.9
  specified type NEC 123.8
Cestodiasis 123.9
Chaberts' disease 022.9
Chacaleh 266.2
Chafing 709.8
Chagas' disease (*see also* Trypanosomiasis,
  American) 086.2
  with heart involvement 086.0
Chagres fever 084.0
Chalasia (cardiac sphincter) 530.81
Chalazion 373.2
Chalazoderma 757.39
Chalcosis 360.24
  cornea 371.15
  crystalline lens 360.24 [366.34]
  retina 360.24.
Chalicosis (occupational) (pulmonum) 502
Chancre (any genital site) (hard) (indurated)
  (infecting) (primary) (recurrent) 091.0
  congenital 090.0
  conjunctiva 091.2
  Ducrey's 099.0
  extragenital 091.2
  eyelid 091.2
  Hunterian 091.0
  lip (syphilis) 091.2
  mixed 099.8
  nipple 091.2
  Nisbet's 099.0
  of
    carate 103.0
    pinta 103.0
    yaws 102.0

Chancre—*continued*
  palate, soft 091.2
  phagedenic 099.0
  Ricord's 091.0
  Rollet's (syphilitic) 091.0
  seronegative 091.0
  seropositive 091.0
  simple 099.0
  soft 099.0
    bubo 099.0
  urethra 091.0
  yaws 102.0
Chancriform syndrome 114.1
Chancroid 099.0
  anus 099.0
  penis (Ducrey's bacillus) 099.0
  perineum 099.0
  rectum 099.0
  scrotum 099.0
  urethra 099.0
  vulva 099.0
Chandipura fever 066.8
Chandler's disease (osteochondritis dissecans,
  hip) 732.7
Change (s) (of)—*see also* Removal of
  arteriosclerotic—*see* Arteriosclerosis
  battery
    cardiac pacemaker V53.31
  bone 733.90
    diabetic 250.8 [731.8]
    in disease, unknown cause 733.90
  bowel habits 787.99
  cardiorenal (vascular) (*see also* Hypertension,
    cardiorenal) 404.90
  cardiovascular—*see* Disease, cardiovascular
  circulatory 459.9
  cognitive or personality change of other type,
    nonpsychotic 310.1
  color, teeth, tooth
    during formation 520.8
    posteruptive 521.7
  contraceptive device V25.42
  cornea, corneal
    degenerative NEC 371.40
    membrane NEC 371.30
    senile 371.41
  coronary (*see also* Ischemia, heart) 414.9
  degenerative
    chamber angle (anterior) (iris) 364.56
    ciliary body 364.57
    spine or vertebra (*see also* Spondylosis)
      721.90
  dental pulp, regressive 522.2
  dressing V58.3
  fixation device V54.8
    external V54.8
    internal V54.0
  heart—*see also* Disease, heart
  hip joint 718.95
  hyperplastic larynx 478.79
  hypertrophic
    nasal sinus (*see also* Sinusitis) 473.9
    turbinate, nasal 478.0
    upper respiratory tract 478.9
  inflammatory—*see* Inflammation
  joint (*see also* Derangement, joint) 718.90
    sacroiliac 724.6
  Kirschner wire V54.8
  knee 717.9
  macular, congenital 743.55

Change(s) (of)—*continued*
  malignant (M——/3)—*see also* Neoplasm, by
    site, malignant

> *Note—for malignant change occurring in a*
> *neoplasm, use the appropriate M code with*
> *behavior digit /3 e.g., malignant change in*
> *uterine fibroid—M8890/3. For malignant*
> *change occurring in a nonneoplastic condition*
> *(e.g., gastric ulcer) use the M code M8000/3.*

  mental (status) NEC 780.9
    due to or associated with physical
        condition—*see* Syndrome, brain
  myocardium, myocardial—*see* Degeneration,
    myocardial
  of life (*see also* Menopause) 627.2
  pacemaker battery (cardiac) V53.31
  peripheral nerve 355.9
  personality (nonpsychotic) NEC 310.1
  plaster cast V54.8
  refractive, transient 367.81
  regressive, dental pulp 522.2
  retina 362.9
    myopic (degenerative) (malignant) 360.21
    vascular appearance 362.13
  sacroiliac joint 724.6
  scleral 379.19
    degenerative 379.16
  senile (*see also* Senility) 797
  sensory (*see also* Disturbance, sensation) 782.0
  skin texture 782.8
  spinal cord 336.9
  splint, external V54.8
  subdermal implantable contraceptive V25.5
  suture V58.3
  traction device V54.8
  trophic 355.9
    arm NEC 354.9
    leg NEC 355.8
    lower extremity NEC 355.8
    upper extremity NEC 354.9
  vascular 459.9
  vasomotor 443.9
  voice 784.49
    psychogenic 306.1
Changing sleep-work schedule, affecting sleep
  307.45
Changuinola fever 066.0
Chapping skin 709.8
Character
  depressive 301.12
Charcot's
  arthropathy 094.0 *[713.5]*
  cirrhosis—*see* Cirrhosis, biliary
  disease 094.0
    spinal cord 094.0
  fever (biliary) (hepatic) (intermittent)—*see*
    Choledocholithiasis
  joint (disease) 094.0 *[713.5]*
    diabetic 250.6 *[713.5]*
    syringomyelic 336.0 *[713.5]*
  syndrome (intermittent claudication) 443.9
    due to atherosclerosis 440.21
Charcot-Marie-Tooth disease, paralysis, or syn-
  drome 356.1
Charleyhorse (quadriceps) 843.8
  muscle, except quadriceps—*see* Sprain, by site
Charlouis' disease (*see also* Yaws) 102.9
Chauffeur's fracture —*see* Fracture, ulna,
  lower end

Cheadle (-Möller) (-Barlow) disease or
  syndrome (infantile scurvy) 267
Checking (of)
  contraceptive device (intrauterine) V25.42
  device
    fixation V54.8
      external V54.8
      internal V54.0
    traction V54.8
  Kirschner wire V54.8
  plaster cast V54.8
  splint, external V54.8
Checkup
  following treatment—*see* Examination
  health V70.0
  infant (not sick) V20.2
  pregnancy (normal) V22.1
    first V22.0
    high risk pregnancy V23.9
      specified problem NEC V23.8
Chédiak-Higashi (-Steinbrinck) anomaly,
  disease, or syndrome (congenital gigantism of
  peroxidase granules) 288.2
Cheek —*see also* condition
  biting 528.9
Cheese itch 133.8
Cheese washers' lung 495.8
Cheilitis 528.5
  actinic (due to sun) 692.72
    chronic NEC 692.74
      due to radiation, except from sun 692.82
    due to radiation, except from sun 692.82
  acute 528.5
  angular 528.5
  catarrhal 528.5
  chronic 528.5
  exfoliative 528.5
  gangrenous 528.5
  glandularis apostematosa 528.5
  granulomatosa 351.8
  infectional 528.5
  membranous 528.5
  Miescher's 351.8
  suppurative 528.5
  ulcerative 528.5
  vesicular 528.5
Cheilodynia 528.5
Cheilopalatoschisis (*see also* Cleft, palate, with
  cleft lip) 749.20
Cheilophagia 528.9
Cheiloschisis (*see also* Cleft, lip) 749.10
Cheilosis 528.5
  with pellagra 265.2
  angular 528.5
  due to
    dietary deficiency 266.0
    vitamin deficiency 266.0
Cheiromegaly 729.89
Cheiropompholyx 705.81
Cheloid (*see also* Keloid) 701.4
Chemical burn —*see also* Burn, by site
  from swallowing chemical—*see* Burn, internal
    organs
Chemodectoma (M8693/1)—*see*
  Paraganglioma, nonchromaffin
Chemoprophylaxis NEC V07.39
Chemosis, conjunctiva 372.73
Chemotherapy
  convalescence V66.2
  encounter (for) V58.1
  maintenance V58.1

Cholelithiasis (impacted) (multiple) 574.2

> *Note—Use the following fifth-digit*
> *subclassification with category 574:*
>
> 0   without mention of obstruction
> 1   with obstruction

  with
    cholecystitis 574.1
      acute 574.0
      chronic 574.1
    choledocholithiasis 574.9
      with
        cholecystitis 574.7
          acute 574.6
            and chronic 574.8
        chronic cholecystitis 574.7
Cholemia (*see also* Jaundice) 782.4
  familial 277.4
  Gilbert's (familial nonhemolytic) 277.4
Cholemic gallstone —*see* Cholelithiasis
Choleperitoneum, choleperitonitis (*see also*
  Disease, gallbladder) 567.8
Cholera (algid) (Asiatic) (asphyctic) (epidemic)
  (gravis) (Indian) (malignant) (morbus)
  (pestilential) (spasmodic) 001.9
  antimonial 985.4
  carrier (suspected) of V02.0
  classical 001.0
  contact V01.0
  due to
    Vibrio
      cholerae (Inaba, Ogawa, Hikojima
        serotypes) 001.0
        El Tor 001.1
  El Tor 001.1
  exposure to V01.0
  vaccination, prophylactic (against) V03.0
Cholerine (*see also* Cholera) 001.9
Cholestasis 576.8
Cholesteatoma (ear) 385.30
  attic (primary) 385.31
  diffuse 385.35
  external ear (canal) 380.21
  marginal (middle ear) 385.32
    with involvement of mastoid cavity 385.33
    secondary (with middle ear involvement)
      385.33
  mastoid cavity 385.30
  middle ear (secondary) 385.32
    with involvement of mastoid cavity 385.33
  postmastoidectomy cavity (recurrent) 383.32
  primary 385.31
  recurrent, postmastoidectomy cavity 383.32
  secondary (middle ear) 385.32
    with involvement of mastoid cavity 385.33
Cholesteatosis (middle ear) (*see also*
  Cholesteatoma) 385.30
  diffuse 385.35
Cholesteremia 272.0
Cholesterin
  granuloma, middle ear 385.82
  in vitreous 379.22
Cholesterol
  deposit
    retina 362.82
    vitreous 379.22
  imbibition of gallbladder (*see also* Disease,
    gallbladder) 575.6

Cholesterolemia 272.0
  essential 272.0
  familial 272.0
  hereditary 272.0
Cholesterosis, cholesterolosis (gallbladder) 575.6
  middle ear (*see also* Cholesteatoma) 385.30
  with
    cholecystitis—*see* Cholecystitis
    cholelithiasis—*see* Cholelithiasis
Cholocolic fistula (*see also* Fistula, gallbladder)
  575.5
Choluria 791.4
Chondritis (purulent) 733.99
  costal 733.6
    Tietze's 733.6
  patella, posttraumatic 717.7
  posttraumatica patellae 717.7
  tuberculous (active) (*see also* Tuberculosis)
    015.9
    intervertebral 015.0 *[730.88]*
Chondroangiopathia calcarea seu punctate
  756.59
Chondroblastoma (M9230/0)—*see also*
  Neoplasm, bone, benlgn
  malignant (M9230/3)—*see* Neoplasm, bone,
    malignant
Chondrocalcinosis (articular) (crystal
  deposition) (dihydrate) (*see also* Arthritis, due
  to, crystals) 275.4 *[712.3]*
  due to
    calcium pyrophosphate 275.4 *[712.2]*
    dicalcium phosphate crystals 275.4 *[712.1]*
    pyrophosphate crystals 275.4 *[712.2]*
Chondrodermatitis nodularis helicis 380.00
Chondrodysplasia 756.4
  angiomatose 756.4
  calcificans congenita 756.59
  epiphysialis punctata 756.59
  hereditary deforming 756.4
Chondrodystrophia (fetalis) 756.4
  calcarea 756.4
  calcificans congenita 756.59
  fetalis hypoplastica 756.59
  hypoplastica calcinosa 756.59
  punctata 756.59
  tarda 277.5
Chondrodystrophy (familial) (hypoplastic) 756.4
Chondroectodermal dysplasia 756.55
Chondrolysis 733.99
Chondroma (M9220/0)—*see also* Neoplasm
  cartilage, benign
  juxtacortical (M9221/0)—*see* Neoplasm, bone,
    benign
  periosteal (M9221/0)—*see* Neoplasm, bone,
    benign
Chondromalacia 733.92
  epiglottis (congenital) 748.3
  generalized 733.92
  knee 717.7
  larynx (congenital) 748.3
  localized, except patella 733.92
  patella, patellae 717.7
  systemic 733.92
  tibial plateau 733.92
  trachea (congenital) 748.3
Chondromatosis (M9220/1)—*see* Neoplasm,
  cartilage, uncertain behavior
Chondromyxosarcoma (M9220/3)—*see*
  Neoplasm, cartilage, malignant
Chondro-osteodysplasia (Morquio-Brailsford
  type) 277.5

Chondro-osteodystrophy 277.5
Chondro-osteodystrophy 277.5
Chondro-osteoma (M9210/0)—*see* Neoplasm,
    bone, benign
Chondropathia tuberosa 733.6
Chondrosarcoma (M9220/3)—*see also*
    Neoplasm, cartilage, malignant
    juxtacortical (M9221/3)—*see* Neoplasm, bone,
        malignant
    mesenchymal (M9240/3)—*see* Neoplasm,
        connective tissue, malignant
Chordae tendineae rupture (chronic) 429.5
Chordee (nonvenereal) 607.89
    congenital 752.63
    gonococcal 098.2
Chorditis (fibrinous) (nodosa) (tuberosa) 478.5
Chordoma (M9370/3)—*see* Neoplasm, by site,
    malignant
Chorea (gravis) (minor) (spasmodic) 333.5
    with
        heart involvement—*see* Chorea with
            rheumatic heart disease
        rheumatic heart disease (chronic, inactive, or
            quiescent) (conditions classifiable to
            393-398)—*see also* Rheumatic heart
            condition involved
            active or acute (conditions classifiable to
                391) 392.0
    acute—*see* Chorea, Sydenham's
    apoplectic (*see also* Disease, cerebrovascular,
        acute) 436
    chronic 333.4
    electric 049.8
    gravidarum—*see* Eclampsia, pregnancy
    habit 307.22
    hereditary 333.4
    Huntington's 333.4
    posthemiplegic 344.89
    pregnancy—*see* Eclampsia, pregnancy
    progressive 333.4
        chronic 333.4
        hereditary 333.4
    rheumatic (chronic) 392.9
        with heart disease or involvement—*see*
            Chorea, with rheumatic heart disease
    senile 333.5
    Sydenham's 392.9
        with heart involvement—*see* Chorea, with
            rheumatic heart disease
        nonrheumatic 333.5
    variabilis 307.23
Choreoathetosis (paroxysmal) 333.5
Chorioadenoma (destruens) (M9100/1) 236.1
Chorioamnionitis 658.4
    affecting fetus or newborn 762.7
Chorioangioma (M9120/0) 219.8
Choriocarcinoma (M9100/3)
    combined with
        embryonal carcinoma (M9101/3)—*see*
            Neoplasm, by site, malignant
        teratoma (M9101/3)—*see* Neoplasm, by site,
            malignant
    specified site—*see* Neoplasm, by site, malignant
    unspecified site
        female 181
        male 186.9
Chorioencephalitis, lymphocytic (acute)
    (serous) 049.0
Chorioepithelioma (M9100/3)—*see*
    Choriocarcinoma
Choriomeningitis (acute) (benign) (lymphocytic)
    (serous) 049.0

Chorionepithelioma (M9100/3)—*see*
    Choriocarcinoma
Chorionitis (*see also* Scleroderma) 710.1
Chorioretinitis 363.20
    disseminated 363.10
        generalized 363.13
        in
            neurosyphilis 094.83
            secondary syphilis 091.51
        peripheral 363.12
        posterior pole 363.11
        tuberculous (*see also* Tuberculosis) 017.3
            [363.13]
    due to
        histoplasmosis (*see also* Histoplasmosis)
            115.92
        toxoplasmosis (acquired) 130.2
            congenital (active) 771.2
    focal 363.00
        juxtapapillary 363.01
        peripheral 363.04
        posterior pole NEC 363.03
    juxtapapillaris, juxtapapillary 363.01
    progressive myopia (degeneration) 360.21
    syphilitic (secondary) 091.51
        congenital (early) 090.0 [363.13]
            late 090.5 [363.13]
        late 095.8 [363.13]
    tuberculous (*see also* Tuberculosis) 017.3
        [363.13]
Choristoma —*see* Neoplasm, by site, benign
Choroid —*see* condition
Choroideremia, choroidermia (initial stage)
    (late stage) (partial or total atrophy) 363.55
Choroiditis (*see also* Chorioretinitis) 363.20
    leprous 030.9 [363.13]
    senile guttate 363.41
    sympathetic 360.11
    syphilitic (secondary) 091.51
        congenital (early) 090.0 [363.13]
            late 090.5 [363.13]
        late 095.8 [363.13]
    Tay's 363.41
    tuberculous (*see also* Tuberculosis) 017.3
        [363.13]
Choroidopathy NEC 363.9
    degenerative (*see also* Degeneration, choroid)
        363.40
    hereditary (*see also* Dystrophy, choroid) 363.50
    specified type NEC 363.8
Choroidoretinitis —*see* Chorioretinitis
Choroidosis, central serous 362.41
Choroidretinopathy, serous 362.41
Christian's syndrome (chronic histiocytosis X)
    277.8
Christian-Weber disease (nodular
    nonsuppurative panniculitis) 729.30
Christmas disease 286.1
Chromaffinoma (M8700/0)—*see also*
    Neoplasm, by site, benign
    malignant (M8700/3)—*see* Neoplasm, by site,
        malignant
Chromatopsia 368.59
Chromhidrosis, chromidrosis 705.89
Chromoblastomycosis 117.2
Chromomycosis 117.2
Chromophytosis 111.0
Chromotrichomycosis 111.8
Chronic —*see* condition
Chyle cyst, mesentery 457.8

Chylocele (nonfilarial) 457.8
  filarial (*see also* Infestation, filarial) 125.9
  tunica vaginalis (nonfilarial) 608.84
    filarial (*see also* Infestation, filarial) 125.9
Chylomicronemia (fasting) (with
    hyperprebetalipoproteinemia) 272.3
Chylopericardium (acute) 420.90
Chylothorax (nonfilarial) 457.8
  filarial (*see also* Infestation, filarial) 125.9
Chylous
  ascites 457.8
  cyst of peritoneum 457.8
  hydrocele 603.9
  hydrothorax (nonfilarial) 457.8
    filarial (*see also* Infestation, filarial) 125.9
Chyluria 791.1
  bilharziasis 120.0
  due to
    Brugia (malayi) 125.1
    Wuchereria (bancrofti) 125.0
      malayi 125.1
  filarial (*see also* Infestation, filarial) 125.9
  filariasis (*see also* Infestation, filarial) 125.9
  nonfilarial 791.1
Cicatricial (deformity)—*see* Cicatrix
Cicatrix (adherent) (contracted) (painful)
    (vicious) 709.2
  adenoid 474.8
  alveolar process 525.8
  anus 569.49
  auricle 380.89
  bile duct (*see also* Disease, biliary) 576.8
  bladder 596.8
  bone 733.99
  brain 348.8
  cervix (postoperative) (postpartal) 622.3
    in pregnancy or childbirth 654.6
      causing obstructed labor 660.2
  chorioretinal 363.30
    disseminated 363.35
    macular 363.32
    peripheral 363.34
    posterior pole NEC 363.33
  choroid—*see* Cicatrix, chorioretinal
  common duct (*see also* Disease, biliary) 576.8
  congenital 757.39
  conjunctiva 372.64
  cornea 371.00
    tuberculous (*see also* Tuberculosis) 017.3
      [371.05]
  duodenum (bulb) 537.3
  esophagus 530.3
  eyelid 374.46
    with
      ectropion—*see* Ectropion
      entropion—*see* Entropion
  hypopharynx 478.29
  knee, semilunar cartilage 717.5
  lacrimal
    canaliculi 375.53
    duct
      acquired 375.56
      neonatal 375.55
    punctum 375.52
    sac 375.54
  larynx 478.79
  limbus (cystoid) 372.64
  lung 518.89
  macular 363.32
    disseminated 363.35
    peripheral 363.34

Cicatrix—*continued*
  middle ear 385.89
  mouth 528.9
  muscle 728.89
  nasolacrimal duct
    acquired 375.56
    neonatal 375.55
  nasopharynx 478.29
  palate (soft) 528.9
  penis 607.89
  prostate 602.8
  rectum 569.49
  retina 363.30
    disseminated 363.35
    macular 363.32
    peripheral 363.34
    posterior pole NEC 363.33
  semilunar cartilage—*see* Derangement,
    meniscus
  seminal vesicle 608.89
  skin 709.2
    infected 686.8
    postinfectional 709.2
    tuberculous (*see also* Tuberculosis) 017.0
  specified site NEC 709.2
  throat 478.29
  tongue 529.8
  tonsil (and adenoid) 474.8
  trachea 478.9
  tuberculous NEC (*see also* Tuberculosis) 011.9
  ureter 593.89
  urethra 599.84
  uterus 621.8
  vagina 623.4
    in pregnancy or childbirth 654.7
      causing obstructed labor 660.2
  vocal cord 478.5
  wrist, constricting (annular) 709.2
Cinchonism
  correct substance properly administered 386.9
  overdose or wrong substance given or taken
    961.4
Circine herpes 110.5
Circle of Willis —*see* condition
Circular —*see also* condition
  hymen 752.49
Circulating anticoagulants 286.5
  following childbirth 666.3
  postpartum 666.3
Circulation
  collateral (venous), any site 459.89
  defective 459.9
    congenital 747.9
    lower extremity 459.89
  embryonic 747.9
  failure 799.8
    fetus or newborn 779.8
    peripheral 785.59
  fetal, persistent 747.89
  heart, incomplete 747.9
Circulatory system —*see* condition
Circulus senilis 371.41
Circumcision
  in absence of medical indication V50.2
  ritual V50.2
  routine V50.2
Circumscribed —*see* condition
Circumvallata placenta —*see* Placenta,
  abnormal

Claudication, intermittent 443.9
  cerebral (artery) (*see also* Ischemia, cerebral,
    transient) 435.9
  due to atherosclerosis 440.21
  spinal cord (arteriosclerotic) 435.1
    syphilitic 094.89
  spinalis 435.1
  venous (axillary) 453.8
Claudicatio venosa intermittens 453.8
Claustrophobia 300.29
Clavus (infected) 700
Claw foot (congenital) 754.71
  acquired 736.74
Claw hand (acquired) 736.06
  congenital 755.59
Clawtoe (congenital) 754.71
  acquired 735.5
Clay eating 307.52
Clay shovelers' fracture —*see* Fracture,
  vertebra, cervical
Cleansing of artificial opening (*see also*
  Attention to artificial opening) V55.9
Cleft (congenital)—*see also* Imperfect, closure
  alveolar process 525.8
  branchial (persistent) 744.41
    cyst 744.42
  clitoris 752.49
  cricoid cartilage, posterior 748.3
  facial (*see also* Cleft, lip) 749.10
  lip 749.10
    with cleft palate 749.20
      bilateral (lip and palate) 749.24
        with unilateral lip or palate 749.25
        complete 749.23
        incomplete 749.24
      unilateral (lip and palate) 749.22
        with bilateral lip or palate 749.25
        complete 749.21
        incomplete 749.22
    bilateral 749.14
      with cleft palate, unilateral 749.25
      complete 749.13
      incomplete 749.14
    unilateral 749.12
      with cleft palate, bilateral 749.25
      complete 749.11
      incomplete 749.12
  nose 748.1
  palate 749.00
    with cleft lip 749.20
      bilateral (lip and palate) 749.24
        with unilateral lip or palate 749.25
        complete 749.23
        incomplete 749.24
      unilateral (lip and palate) 749.22
        with bilateral lip or palate 749.25
        complete 749.21
        incomplete 749.22
    bilateral 749.04
      with cleft lip, unilateral 749.25
      complete 749.03
      incomplete 749.04
    unilateral 749.02
      with cleft lip, bilateral 749.25
      complete 749.01
      incomplete 749.02
  penis 752.69
  posterior, cricoid cartilage 748.3
  scrotum 752.8
  sternum (congenital) 756.3
  thyroid cartilage (congenital) 748.3

Cleft—*continued*
  tongue 750.13
  uvula 749.02
    with cleft lip (*see also* Cleft, lip, with cleft
      palate) 749.20
  water 366.12
Cleft hand (congenital) 755.58
Cleidocranial dysostosis 755.59
Cleidotomy, fetal 763.8
Cleptomania 312.32
Clérambault's syndrome 297.8
  erotomania 302.89
Clergyman's sore throat 784.49
Click, clicking
  systolic syndrome 785.2
Clifford's syndrome (postmaturity) 766.2
Climacteric (*see also* Menopause) 627.2
  arthritis NEC (*see also* Arthritis, climacteric)
    716.3
  depression (*see also* Psychosis, affective) 296.2
  disease 627.2
    recurrent episode 296.3
    single episode 296.2
  female (symptoms) 627.2
  male (symptoms) (syndrome) 608.89
  melancholia (*see also* Psychosis, affective)
    296.2
    recurrent episode 296.3
    single episode 296.2
  paranoid state 297.2
  paraphrenia 297.2
  polyarthritis NEC 716.39
    male 608.89
  symptoms (female) 627.2
Clinical research investigation V70.7
Clinodactyly 755.59
Clitoris —*see* condition
Cloaca, persistent 751.5
Clonorchiasis 121.1
Clonorchiosis 121.1
Clonorchis infection, liver 121.1
Clonus 781.0
Closed bite 524.2
Closure
  artificial opening (*see also* Attention to artificial
    opening) V55.9
  congenital, nose 748.0
  cranial sutures, premature 756.0
  defective or imperfect NEC—*see* Imperfect,
    closure
  fistula, delayed—*see* Fistula
  fontanelle, delayed 756.0
  foramen ovale, imperfect 745.5
  hymen 623.3
  interauricular septum, defective 745.5
  interventricular septum, defective 745.4
  lacrimal duct 375.56
    congenital 743.65
    neonatal 375.55
  nose (congenital) 748.0
    acquired 738.0
  vagina 623.2
  valve—*see* Endocarditis
  vulva 624.8
Clot (blood)
  artery (obstruction) (occlusion) (*see also*
    Embolism) 444.9
  bladder 596.7
  brain (extradural or intradural) (*see also*
    Thrombosis, brain) 434.0
    late effects—*see* category 438

Clot —*continued*
  circulation 444.9
  heart (*see also* Infarct, myocardium) 410.9
  vein (*see also* Thrombosis) 453.9
Clotting defect NEC (*see also* Defect,
    coagulation) 286.9
Clouded state 780.09
  epileptic (*see also* Epilepsy) 345.9
  paroxysmal (idiopathic) (*see also* Epilepsy)
    345.9
Clouding
  corneal graft 996.51
Cloudy antrum, antra 473.0
Clouston's (hidrotic) ectodermal dysplasia 757.31
Clubbing of fingers 781.5
Clubfinger 736.29
  acquired 736.29
  congenital 754.89
Clubfoot (congenital) 754.70
  acquired 736.71
  equinovarus 754.51
  paralytic 736.71
Club hand (congenital) 754.89
  acquired 736.07
Clubnail (acquired) 703.8
  congenital 757.5
Clump kidney 753.3
Clumsiness 781.3
  syndrome 315.4
Cluttering 307.0
Clutton's joints 090.5
Coagulation, intravascular (diffuse)
    (disseminated) (*see also* Fibrinolysis) 286.6
  newborn 776.2
Coagulopathy (*see also* Defect, coagulation)
    286.9
  consumption 286.6
  intravascular (disseminated) NEC 286.6
  newborn 776.2
Coalition
  calcaneoscaphoid 755.67
  calcaneus 755.67
  tarsal 755.67
Coal miners'
  elbow 727.2
  lung 500
Coal workers' lung or pneumoconiosis 500
Coarctation
  aorta (postductal) (preductal) 747.10
  pulmonary artery 747.3
Coated tongue 529.3
Coats' disease 362.12
Cocainism (*see also* Dependence) 304.2
Coccidioidal granuloma 114.3
Coccidioidomycosis 114.9
  with pneumonia 114.0
  cutaneous (primary) 114.1
  disseminated 114.3
  extrapulmonary (primary) 114.1
  lung 114.5
    acute 114.0
    chronic 114.4
    primary 114.0
  meninges 114.2
  primary (pulmonary) 114.0
    acute 114.0
  prostate 114.3
  pulmonary 114.5
    acute 114.0
    chronic 114.4
    primary 114.0

Coccidioidomycosis— *continued*
  specified site NEC 114.3
Coccidioidosis 114.9
  lung 114.5
    acute 114.0
    chronic 114.4
    primary 114.0
  meninges 114.2
Coccidiosis (colitis) (diarrhea) (dysentery) 007.2
Cocciuria 599.0
Coccus in urine 599.0
Coccydynia 724.79
Coccygodynia 724.79
Coccyx —*see* condition
Cochin-China
  diarrhea 579.1
    anguilluliasis 127.2
  ulcer 085.1
Cock's peculiar tumor 706.2
Cockayne's disease or syndrome (microcephaly
    and dwarfism) 759.89
Cockayne-Weber syndrome (epidermolysis
    bullosa) 757.39
Cocked-up toe 735.2
Codman's tumor (benign chondroblastoma)
    (M9230/0)—*see* Neoplasm, bone, benign
Coenurosis 123.8
Coffee workers' lung 495.8
Cogan's syndrome 370.52
  congenital oculomotor apraxia 379.51
  nonsyphilitic interstitial keratitis 370.52
Coiling, umbilical cord —*see* Complications,
    umbilical cord
Coitus, painful (female) 625.0
  male 608.89
  psychogenic 302.76
Cold 460
  with influenza, flu, or grippe 487.1
  abscess—*see also* Tuberculosis, abscess
    articular—*see* Tuberculosis, joint
  agglutinin
    disease (chronic) or syndrome 283.0
    hemoglobinuria 283.0
      paroxysmal (cold) (nocturnal) 283.2
  allergic (*see also* Fever, hay) 477.9
  bronchus or chest—*see* Bronchitis
    with grippe or influenza 487.1
  common (head) 460
    vaccination, prophylactic (against) V04.7
  deep 464.10
  effects of 991.9
    specified effect NEC 991.8
  excessive 991.9
    specified effect NEC 991.8
  exhaustion from 991.8
  exposure to 991.9
    specified effect NEC 991.8
  grippy 487.1
  head 460
  injury syndrome (newborn) 778.2
  intolerance 780.9
  on lung—*see* Bronchitis
  rose 477.0
  sensitivity, autoimmune 283.0
  virus 460
Coldsore (*see also* Herpes, simplex) 054.9
Colibacillosis 041.4
  generalized 038.42
Colibacilluria 599.0

Colic (recurrent) 789.0
abdomen 789.0
(recurrent)psychogenic 307.89
appendicular 543.9
appendix 543.9
bile duct—*see* Choledocholithiasis
biliary—*see* Cholelithiasis
bilious—*see* Cholelithiasis
common duct—*see* Choledocholithiasis
Devonshire NEC 984.9
specified type of lead—*see* Table of drugs and chemicals
flatulent 787.3
gallbladder or gallstone—*see* Cholelithiasis
gastric 536.8
hepatic (duct)—*see* Choledocholithiasis
hysterical 300.11
infantile 789.0
intestinal 789.0
kidney 788.0
lead NEC 984.9
specified type of lead—*see* Table of drugs and chemicals
liver (duct)—*see* Choledocholithiasis
mucous 564.1
psychogenic 316 *[564.1]*
nephritic 788.0
painter's NEC 984.9
pancreas 577.8
psychogenic 306.4
renal 788.0
saturnine NEC 984.9
specified type of lead—*see* Table of drugs and chemicals
spasmodic 789.0
ureter 788.0
urethral 599.84
due to calculus 594.2
uterus 625.8
menstrual 625.3
vermicular 543.9
virus 460
worm NEC 128.9
Colicystitis (*see also* Cystitis) 595.9
Colitis (acute) (catarrhal) (croupous) (cystica superficialis) (exudative) (hemorrhagic) (noninfectious) (phlegmonous) (presumed noninfectious) 558.9
adaptive 564.1
allergic 558.9
amebic (*see also* Amebiasis) 006.9
nondysenteric 006.2
anthrax 022.2
bacillary (*see also* Infection, Shigella) 004.9
balantidial 007.0
chronic 558.9
ulcerative (*see also* Colitis, ulcerative) 556.9
coccidial 007.2
dietetic 558.9
due to radiation 558.1
functional 558.9
gangrenous 009.0
giardial 007.1
granulomatous 555.1
gravis (*see also* Colitis, ulcerative) 556.9
infectious (*see also* Enteritis, due to, specific organism) 009.0
presumed 009.1
ischemic 557.9
acute 557.0
chronic 557.1

Colitis—*continued*
due to mesenteric artery insufficiency 557.1
membranous 564.1
psychogenic 316 *[564.1]*
mucous 564.1
psychogenic 316 *[564.1]*
necrotic 009.0
polyposa (*see also* Colitis, ulcerative) 556.9
protozoal NEC 007.9
pseudomembranous 008.45
pseudomucinous 564.1
regional 555.1
segmental 555.1
septic (*see also* Enteritis, due to, specific organism) 009.0
spastic 564.1
psychogenic 316 *[564.1]*
staphylococcus 008.41
food 005.0
thromboulcerative 557.0
toxic 558.2
transmural 555.1
trichomonal 007.3
tuberculous (ulcerative) 014.8
ulcerative (chronic) (idiopathic) (nonspecific) 556.9
entero- 556.0
fulminant 557.0
ileo- 556.1
left-sided 556.5
procto- 556.2
proctosigmoid 556.3
psychogenic 316 *[556]*
specified NEC 556.8
universal 556.6
Collagen disease NEC 710.9
nonvascular 710.9
vascular (allergic) (*see also* Angiitis, hypersensitivity) 446.20
Collagenosis (*see also* Collagen disease) 710.9
cardiovascular 425.4
mediastinal 519.3
Collapse 780.2
adrenal 255.8
cardiorenal (*see also* Hypertension, cardiorenal) 404.90
cardiorespiratory 785.51
fetus or newborn 779.8
cardiovascular (*see also* Disease, heart) 785.51
fetus or newborn 779.8
circulatory (peripheral) 785.59
with
abortion—*see* Abortion, by type, with shock
ectopic pregnancy (*see also* categories 633.0-633.9) 639.5
molar pregnancy (*see also* categories 630-632) 639.5
during or after labor and delivery 669.1
fetus or newborn 779.8
following
abortion 639.5
ectopic or molar pregnancy 639.5
during or after labor and delivery 669.1
fetus or newborn 779.8
external ear canal 380.50
secondary to
inflammation 380.53
surgery 380.52
trauma 380.51
general 780.2
heart—*see* Disease, heart

Collapse—*continued*
heat 992.1
hysterical 300.11
labyrinth, membranous (congenital) 744.05
lung (massive) (*see also* Atelectasis) 518.0
pressure, during labor 668.0
myocardial—*see* Disease, heart
nervous (*see also* Disorder, mental,
nonpsychotic) 300.9
neurocirculatory 306.2
nose 738.0
postoperative (cardiovascular) 998.0
pulmonary (*see also* Atelectasis) 518.0
fetus or newborn 770.5
partial 770.5
primary 770.4
thorax 512.8
iatrogenic 512.1
postoperative 512.1
trachea 519.1
valvular—*see* Endocarditis
vascular (peripheral) 785.59
with
abortion—*see* Abortion, by type, with shock
ectopic pregnancy (*see also* categories
633.0-633.9) 639.5
molar pregnancy (*see also* categories
630-632) 639.5
cerebral (*see also* Disease, cerebrovascular,
acute) 436
during or after labor and delivery 669.1
fetus or newborn 779.8
following
abortion 639.5
ectopic or molar pregnancy 639.5
vasomotor 785.59
vertebra 733.13
Collateral —*see also* condition
circulation (venous) 459.89
dilation, veins 459.89
Colles' fracture (closed) (reversed) (separation)
813.41
open 813.51
Collet's syndrome 352.6
Collet-Sicard syndrome 352.6
Colliculitis urethralis (*see also* Urethritis) 597.89
Colliers'
asthma 500
lung 500
phthisis (*see also* Tuberculosis) 011.4
Collodion baby (ichthyosis congenita) 757.1
Colloid milium 709.3
Coloboma NEC 743.49
choroid 743.59
fundus 743.52
iris 743.46
lens 743.36
lids 743.62
optic disc (congenital) 743.57
acquired 377.23
retina 743.56
sclera 743.47
Coloenteritis —*see* Enteritis
Colon —*see* condition
Coloptosis 569.89
Color
amblyopia NEC 368.59
acquired 368.55
blindness NEC (congenital) 368.59
acquired 368.55

Colostomy
attention to V55.3
fitting or adjustment V53.5
malfunctioning 569.69
status V44.3
Colpitis (*see also* Vaginitis) 616.10
Colpocele 618.6
Colpocystitis (*see also* Vaginitis) 616.10
Colporrhexis 665.4
Colpospasm 625.1
Column, spinal, vertebral —*see* condition
Coma 780.01
apoplectic (*see also* Disease, cerebrovascular,
acute) 436
diabetic (with ketoacidosis) 250.3
hyperosmolar 250.2
eclamptic (*see also* Eclampsia) 780.3
epileptic 345.3
hepatic 572.2
hyperglycemic 250.2
hyperosmolar (diabetic) (nonketotic) 250.2
hypoglycemic 251.0
diabetic 250.3
insulin 250.3
hyperosmolar 250.2
non-diabetic 251.0
organic hyperinsulinism 251.0
Kussmaul's (diabetic) 250.3
liver 572.2
newborn 779.2
prediabetic 250.2
uremic—*see* Uremia
Combat fatigue (*see also* Reaction, stress, acute)
308.9
Combined —*see* condition
Comedo 706.1
Comedocarcinoma (M8501/3)—*see also*
Neoplasm, breast, malignant
noninfiltrating (M8501/2)
specified site—*see* Neoplasm, by site, in situ
unspecified site 233.0
Comedomastitis 610.4
Comedones 706.1
lanugo 757.4
Comma bacillus, carrier (suspected) of V02.3
Comminuted fracture —*see* Fracture, by site
Common
aortopulmonary trunk 745.0
atrioventricular canal (defect) 745.69
atrium 745.69
cold (head) 460
vaccination, prophylactic (against) V04.7
truncus (arteriosus) 745.0
ventricle 745.3
Commotio (current)
cerebri (*see also* Concussion, brain) 850.9
with skull fracture—*see* Fracture, skull, by site
retinae 921.3
spinalis—*see* Injury, spinal, by site
Commotion (current)
brain (without skull fracture) (*see also*
Concussion, brain) 850.9
with skull fracture—*see* Fracture, skull, by site
spinal cord—*see* Injury, spinal, by site
Communication
abnormal—*see also* Fistula
between
base of aorta and pulmonary artery 745.0
left ventricle and right atrium 745.4
pericardial sac and pleural sac 748.8
pulmonary artery and pulmonary vein 747.3

Communication— *continued*
   congenital, between uterus and anterior
      abdominal wall 752.3
      bladder 752.3
      intestine 752.3
      rectum 752.3
   left ventricular-right atrial 745.4
   pulmonary artery-pulmonary vein 747.3
Compensation
   broken—*see* Failure, heart, congestive
   failure—*see* Failure, heart, congestive
   neurosis, psychoneurosis 300.11
Complaint —*see also* Disease
   bowel, functional 564.9
      psychogenic 306.4
   intestine, functional 564.9
      psychogenic 306.4
   kidney (*see also* Disease, renal) 593.9
   liver 573.9
   miners' 500
Complete —*see* condition
Complex
   cardiorenal (*see also* Hypertension, cardiorenal)
      404.90
   castration 300.9
   Costen's 524.60
   ego-dystonic homosexuality 302.0
   Eisenmenger's (ventricular septal defect) 745.4
   homosexual, ego-dystonic 302.0
   hypersexual 302.89
   inferiority 301.9
   jumped process
      spine—*see* Dislocation, vertebra
   primary, tuberculosis (*see also* Tuberculosis)
      010.0
   Taussig-Bing (transposition, aorta and
      overriding pulmonary artery) 745.11
Complications
   abortion NEC—*see* categories 634-639
   accidental puncture or laceration during a
      procedure 998.2
   amputation stump (late) (surgical) 997.60
      traumatic—*see* Amputation, traumatic
   anastomosis (and bypass)—*see also*
      Complications, due to (presence of) any
      device, implant, or graft classified to
      996.0-996.5 NEC
      hemorrhage NEC 998.11
      intestinal (internal) NEC 997.4
         involving urinary tract 997.5
      mechanical—*see* Complications, mechanical,
         graft
      urinary tract (involving intestinal tract) 997.5
   anesthesia, anesthetic NEC (*see also*
      Anesthesia, complication) 995.2
      in labor and delivery 668.9
         affecting fetus or newborn 763.5
         cardiac 668.1
         central nervous system 668.2
         pulmonary 668.0
         specified type NEC 668.8
   aortocoronary (bypass) graft 996.03
      atherosclerosis —*see* Arteriosclerosis,
         coronary
      embolism 996.72
      occlusion NEC 996.72
      thrombus 996.72
   arthroplasty 996.4
   artificial opening
      cecostomy 569.60
      colostomy 569.6

Complications— *continued*
      cystostomy 997.5
      enterostomy 569.60
      gastrostomy 997.4
      ileostomy 569.60
      jejunostomy 569.60
      nephrostomy 997.5
      tracheostomy 519.0
      ureterostomy 997.5
      urethrostomy 997.5
   bile duct implant (prosthetic) NEC 996.79
      infection or inflammation 996.69
      mechanical 996.59
   bleeding (intraoperative) (postoperative) 998.11
   blood vessel graft 996.1
      aortocoronary 996.03
         atherosclerosis —*see* Arteriosclerosis,
            coronary
         embolism 996.72
         occlusion NEC 996.72
         thrombus 996.72
      atherosclerosis —*see* Arteriosclerosis,
         extremities
      embolism 996.74
      occlusion NEC 996.74
      thrombus 996.74
   bone growth stimulator NEC 996.78
      infection or inflammation 996.67
   bone marrow transplant 996.85
   breast implant (prosthetic) NEC 996.79
      infection or inflammation 996.69
      mechanical 996.54
   bypass—*see also* Complications, anastomosis
      aortocoronary 996.03
         atherosclerosis —*see* Arteriosclerosis,
            coronary
         embolism 996.72
         occlusion NEC 996.72
         thrombus 996.72
      carotid artery 996.1
         atherosclerosis —*see* Arteriosclerosis,
            extremities
         embolism 996.74
         occlusion NEC 996.74
         thrombus 996.74
   cardiac (*see also* Disease, heart) 429.9
      device, implant, or graft NEC 996.72
         infection or inflammation 996.61
         long-term effect 429.4
         mechanical (*see also* Complications,
            mechanical, by type) 996.00
         valve prosthesis 996.71
            infection or inflammation 996.61
      postoperative NEC 997.1
         long-term effect 429.4
   cardiorenal (*see also* Hypertension, cardiorenal)
      404.90
   carotid artery bypass graft 996.1
      atherosclerosis —*see* Arteriosclerosis,
         extremities
      embolism 996.74
      occlusion NEC 996.74
      thrombus 996.74
   cataract fragments in eye 998.82
   catheter device—*see also* Complications, due to
      (presence of) any device, implant, or graft
      classified to 996.0-996.5 NEC
      mechanical—*see* Complications, mechanical,
         catheter
   cecostomy 569.60
   cesarean section wound 674.3

Complications—*continued*
  chin implant (prosthetic) NEC 996.79
    infection or inflammation 996.69
    mechanical 996.59
  colostomy (enterostomy) 569.60
  contraceptive device, intrauterine NEC 996.76
    infection 996.65
    inflammation 996.65
    mechanical 996.32
  cord (umbilical)—*see* Complications, umbilical
    cord
  cornea
    due to
      contact lens 371.82
  coronary (artery) bypass (graft) NEC 996.03
    atherosclerosis —*see* Arteriosclerosis,
      coronary
    embolism 996.72
    infection or inflammation 996.61
    mechanical 996.03
    occlusion NEC 996.72
    specified type NEC 996.72
    thrombus 996.72
  cystostomy 997.5
  delivery 669.9
    procedure (instrumental) (manual) (surgical)
      669.4
    specified type NEC 669.8
  dialysis (hemodialysis) (peritoneal) (renal) NEC
    999.9
    catheter—*see also* Complications, due to
      (presence of) any device, implant or graft
      classified to 996.0-996.5 NEC
    infection or inflammation 996.62
      peritoneal 996.69
    mechanical 996.1
      peritoneal 996.59
  due to (presence of) any device, implant, or
    graft classified to 996.0-996.5
    with infection or inflammation—*see*
      Complications, infection or inflammation,
      due to (presence of) any device, implant,
      or graft classified to 996.0-996.5 NEC
    arterial NEC 996.74
      coronary NEC 996.03
        atherosclerosis —*see* Arteriosclerosis,
          coronary
        embolism 996.72
        occlusion NEC 996.72
        specified type NEC 996.72
        thrombus 996.72
      renal dialysis 996.73
    arteriovenous fistula or shunt NEC 996.74
    bone growth stimulator 996.78
    breast NEC 996.79
    cardiac NEC 996.72
      defibrillator 996.72
      pacemaker 996.72
      valve prosthesis 996.71
    catheter NEC 996.79
      spinal 996.75
      urinary, indwelling 996.76
      vascular NEC 996.74
        renal dialysis 996.73
      ventricular shunt 996.75
    coronary (artery) bypass (graft) NEC 996.03
      atherosclerosis —*see* Arteriosclerosis,
        coronary
      embolism 996.72
      occlusion NEC 996.72
      thrombus 996.72

Complications—*continued*
  electrodes
    brain 996.75
    heart 996.72
  gastrointestinal NEC 996.79
  genitourinary NEC 996.76
  heart valve prosthesis NEC 996.71
  infusion pump 996.74
  internal
    joint prosthesis 996.77
      orthopedic NEC 996.78
      specified type NEC 996.79
  intrauterine contraceptive device NEC 996.76
  joint prosthesis, internal NEC 996.77
  mechanical—*see* Complications, mechanical
  nervous system NEC 996.75
  ocular lens NEC 996.79
  orbital NEC 996.79
  orthopedic NEC 996.78
    joint, internal 996.77
  renal dialysis 996.73
  specified type NEC 996.79
  urinary catheter, indwelling 996.76
  vascular NEC 996.74
  ventricular shunt 996.75
  during dialysis NEC 999.9
  ectopic or molar pregnancy NEC 639.9
  electroshock therapy NEC 999.9
  enterostomy 569.60
  external (fixation) device with internal
    component(s) NEC 996.78
    infection or inflammation 996.67
    mechanical 996.4
  extracorporeal circulation NEC 999.9
  eye implant (prosthetic) NEC 996.79
    infection or inflammation 996.69
    mechanical
      ocular lens 996.53
      orbital globe 996.59
  gastrointestinal, postoperative NEC (*see also*
    Complications, surgical procedures) 997.4
  gastrostomy 997.4
  genitourinary device, implant or graft NEC
    996.76
    infection or inflammation 996.65
    urinary catheter, indwelling 996.64
    mechanical (*see also* Complications,
      mechanical, by type) 996.30
    specified NEC 996.39
  graft (bypass) (patch)—*see also* Complications,
    due to (presence of) any device, implant, or
    graft classified to 996.0-996.5 NEC
    bone marrow 996.85
    corneal NEC 996.79
      infection or inflammation 996.69
      rejection or reaction 996.51
    mechanical—*see* Complications, mechanical,
      graft
    organ (immune or nonimmune cause) (partial)
      (total) 996.80
      bone marrow 996.85
      heart 996.83
      intestines 996.89
      kidney 996.81
      liver 996.82
      lung 996.84
      pancreas 996.86
      specified NEC 996.89
    skin NEC 996.79
      infection or inflammation 996.69
      rejection 996.52

Complications—*continued*
heart—*see also* Disease, heart
  transplant (immune or nonimmune cause)
    996.83
hematoma (intraoperative) (postoperative)
  998.12
hemorrhage (intraoperative) (postoperative)
  998.11
hyperalimentation therapy NEC 999.9
immunization (procedure)—*see* Complications,
  vaccination
implant—*see also* Complications, due to
  (presence of) any device, implant, or graft
  classified to 996.0-996.5 NEC
  mechanical—*see* Complications, mechanical,
    implant
infection and inflammation
  due to (presence of) any device, implant, or
    graft classified to 996.0-996.5 NEC 996.60
    arterial NEC 996.62
      coronary 996.61
      renal dialysis 996.62
    arteriovenous fistula or shunt 996.62
    bone growth stimulator 996.67
    breast 996.69
    cardiac 996.61
    catheter NEC 996.69
      peritoneal 996.69
      spinal 996.63
      urinary, indwelling 996.64
      vascular NEC 996.62
      ventricular shunt 996.63
    coronary artery bypass 996.61
    electrodes
      brain 996.63
      heart 996.61
    gastrointestinal NEC 996.69
    genitourinary NEC 996.65
      indwelling urinary catheter 996.64
    heart valve 996.61
    infusion pump 996.62
    intrauterine contraceptive device 996.65
    joint prosthesis, internal 996.66
    ocular lens 996.69
    orbital (implant) 996.69
    orthopedic NEC 996.67
      joint, internal 996.66
    specified type NEC 996.69
    urinary catheter, indwelling 996.64
    ventricular shunt 996.63
infusion (procedure) 999.9
  blood—*see* Complications, transfusion
  infection NEC 999.3
  sepsis NEC 999.3
inhalation therapy NEC 999.9
injection (procedure) 999.9
  drug reaction (*see also* Reaction, drug) 995.2
  infection NEC 999.3
  sepsis NEC 999.3
  serum (prophylactic) (therapeutic)—*see*
    Complications, vaccination
  vaccine (any)—*see* Complications, vaccination
inoculation (any)—*see* Complications,
  vaccination
internal device (catheter) (electronic) (fixation)
  (prosthetic) NEC—*see also* Complications,
  due to (presence of) any device, implant, or
  graft classified to 996.0-996.5 NEC
  mechanical—*see* Complications, mechanical
intestinal transplant (immune or nonimmune
  cause) 996.89

Complications—*continued*
intraoperative bleeding or hemorrhage 998.11
intrauterine contraceptive device (*see also*
  Complications, contraceptive device) 996.76
  infection or inflammation 996.65
  with fetal damage affecting management of
    pregnancy 655.8
jejunostomy 569.60
kidney transplant (immune or nonimmune
  cause) 996.81
labor 669.9
  specified condition NEC 669.8
liver transplant (immune or nonimmune cause)
  996.82
lumbar puncture 349.0
mechanical
  anastomosis—*see* Complications, mechanical,
    graft
  bypass—*see* Complications, mechanical, graft
  catheter NEC 996.59
    cardiac 996.09
    cystostomy 996.39
    dialysis 996.1
    during a procedure 998.2
    urethral, indwelling 996.31
  device NEC 996.59
    balloon (counterpulsation), intra-aortic 996.1
    cardiac 996.00
      long-term effect 429.4
      specified NEC 996.09
    contraceptive, intrauterine 996.32
    counterpulsation, intra-aortic 996.1
    fixation, external, with internal components
      996.4
    fixation, internal (nail, rod, plate) 996.4
    genitourinary 996.30
      specified NEC 996.39
    nervous system 996.2
    orthopedic, internal 996.4
    prosthetic NEC 996.59
    umbrella, vena cava 996.1
    vascular 996.1
  dorsal column stimulator 996.2
  electrode NEC 996.59
    brain 996.2
    cardiac 996.01
    spinal column 996.2
  fistula, arteriovenous, surgically created 996.1
  graft NEC 996.52
    aortic (bifurcation) 996.1
    aortocoronary bypass 996.03
    blood vessel NEC 996.1
    bone 996.4
    cardiac 996.00
    carotid artery bypass 996.1
    cartilage 996.4
    corneal 996.51
    coronary bypass 996.03
    genitourinary 996.30
      specified NEC 996.39
    muscle 996.4
    nervous system 996.2
    organ (immune or nonimmune cause) 996.80
      heart 996.83
      intestines 996.89
      kidney 996.81
      liver 996.82
      lung 996.84
      pancreas 996.86
      specified NEC 996.89
    orthopedic, internal 996.4

Complications—*continued*

    peripheral nerve 996.2
    prosthetic NEC 996.59
    skin 996.52
    specified NEC 996.59
   • tendon 996.4
    tissue NEC 996.52
    tooth 996.59
    ureter, without mention of resection 996.39
    vascular 996.1
  heart valve prosthesis 996.02
    long-term effect 429.4
  implant NEC 996.59
    cardiac 996.00
      long-term effect 429.4
      specified NEC 996.09
    electrode NEC 996.59
      brain 996.2
      cardiac 996.01
      spinal column 996.2
    genitourinary 996.30
    nervous system 996.2
    orthopedic, internal 996.4
    prosthetic NEC 996.59
      in
        bile duct 996.59
        breast 996.54
        chin 996.59
        eye
          ocular lens 996.53
          orbital globe 996.59
      vascular 996.1
  nonabsorbable surgical material 996.59
  pacemaker NEC 996.59
    brain 996.2
    cardiac 996.01
    nerve (phrenic) 996.2
  patch—*see* Complications, mechanical, graft
  prosthesis NEC 996.59
    bile duct 996.59
    breast 996.54
    chin 996.59
    ocular lens 996.53
    reconstruction, vas deferens 996.39
  reimplant NEC 996.59
    extremity (*see also* Complications,
      reattached, extremity) 996.90
    organ (*see also* Complications, transplant,
      organ, by site) 996.80
  repair—*see* Complications, mechanical, graft
  shunt NEC 996.59
    arteriovenous, surgically created 996.1
    ventricular (communicating) 996.2
  stent NEC 996.59
  vas deferens reconstruction 996.39
  medical care NEC 999.9
    cardiac NEC 997.1
    gastrointestinal NEC 997.4
    nervous system NEC 997.00
    peripheral vascular NEC 997.2
    respiratory NEC 997.3
    urinary NEC 997.5
  nephrostomy 997.5
  nervous system
    device, implant, or graft NEC 349.1
      mechanical 996.2
    postoperative NEC 997.00
  obstetric 669.9
    procedure (instrumental) (manual) (surgical)
      669.4
    specified NEC 669.8

Complications—*continued*

  surgical wound 674.3
  ocular lens implant NEC 996.79
    infection or inflammation 996.69
    mechanical 996.53
  organ transplant—*see* Complications,
    transplant, organ, by site
  orthopedic device, implant, or graft
    internal (fixation) (nail) (plate) (rod) NEC
      996.78
    infection or inflammation 996.67
    joint prosthesis 996.77
      infection or inflammation 996.66
    mechanical 996.4
  pacemaker (cardiac) 996.72
    infection or inflammation 996.61
    mechanical 996.01
  pancreas transplant (immune or nonimmune
    cause) 996.86
  perfusion NEC 999.9
  perineal repair (obstetrical) 674.3
    disruption 674.2
  pessary (uterus) (vagina)—*see* Complications,
    contraceptive device
  phototherapy 990
  postcystoscopic 997.5
  postmastoidectomy NEC 383.30
  postoperative—*see* Complications, surgical
    procedures
  pregnancy NEC 646.9
    affecting fetus or newborn 761.9
  prosthetic device, internal—*see also*
    Complications, due to (presence of) any
    device, implant, or graft classified to
    996.0-996.5 NEC
    mechanical NEC (*see also* Complications,
      mechanical) 996.59
  puerperium NEC (*see also* Puerperal) 674.9
  puncture, spinal 349.0
  pyelogram 997.5
  radiation 990
  radiotherapy 990
  reattached
    body part, except extremity 996.99
    extremity (infection) (rejection) 996.90
      arm(s) 996.94
      digit(s) (hand) 996.93
        foot 996.95
      finger(s) 996.93
      foot 996.95
      forearm 996.91
      hand 996.92
      leg 996.96
      lower NEC 996.96
      toe(s) 996.95
      upper NEC 996.94
  reimplant—*see also* Complications, due to
    (presence of) any device, implant, or graft
    classified to 996.0-996.5 NEC
    bone marrow 996.85
    extremity (*see also* Complications, reattached,
      extremity) 996.90
    due to infection 996.90
    mechanical—*see* Complications, mechanical,
      reimplant
    organ (immune or nonimmune cause) (partial)
      (total) (*see also* Complications, transplant,
      organ, by site) 996.80
  renal allograft 996.81
  renal dialysis—*see* Complications, dialysis
  respiratory 519.9

Complications—*continued*
  device, implant or graft NEC 996.79
    infection or inflammation 996.69
    mechanical 996.59
  distress syndrome, adult, following trauma or
    surgery 518.5
  insufficiency, acute, postoperative 518.5
  postoperative NEC 997.3
  therapy NEC 999.9
  sedation during labor and delivery 668.9
    affecting fetus or newborn 763.5
    cardiac 668.1
    central nervous system 668.2
    pulmonary 668.0
    specified type NEC 668.8
  seroma (intraoperative) (postoperative)
    (noninfected) 998.13
    infected 998.51
  shunt—*see also* Complications, due to
    (presence of) any device, implant, or graft
    classified to 996.0-996.5 NEC
    mechanical—*see* Complications, mechanical,
      shunt
  specified body system NEC
    device, implant, or graft—*see* Complications,
      due to (presence of) any device, implant,
      or graft classified to 996.0-996.5 NEC
    postoperative NEC 997.99
  spinal puncture or tap 349.0
  stoma, external
    gastrointestinal tract NEC 997.4
    urinary tract 997.5
  surgical procedures 998.9
    accidental puncture or laceration 998.2
    amputation stump (late) 997.60
    anastomosis—*see* Complications, anastomosis
    burst stitches or sutures 998.3
    cardiac 997.1
      long-term effect following cardiac surgery
        429.4
    cataract fragments in eye 998.82
    catheter device—*see* Complications, catheter
      device
    cecostomy malfunction 569.69
    colostomy malfunction 569.69
    cystostomy malfunction 997.5
    dehiscence (of incision) 998.3
    dialysis NEC (*see also* Complications,
      dialysis) 999.9
    disruption
      anastomosis (internal)—*see* Complications,
        mechanical, graft
      internal suture (line) 998.3
      wound 998.3
    dumping syndrome (postgastrectomy) 564.2
    elephantiasis or lymphedema 997.99
      postmastectomy 457.0
    emphysema (surgical) 998.81
    enterostomy malfunction 569.69
    evisceration 998.3
    fistula (persistent postoperative) 998.6
    foreign body inadvertently left in wound
      (sponge) (suture) (swab) 998.4
    from nonabsorbable surgical material
      (Dacron) (mesh) (permanent suture)
      (reinforcing) (Teflon)—*see*
      Complications, due to (presence of) any
      device, implant, or graft classified to
      996.0-996.5 NEC
    gastrointestinal NEC 997.4
    gastrostomy malfunction 997.4

Complications—*continued*
  hematoma 998.12
  hemorrhage 998.11
  ileostomy malfunction 569.69
  internal prosthetic device NEC (*see also*
    Complications, internal device) 996.70
    hemolytic anemia 283.19
    infection or inflammation 996.60
    malfunction—*see* Complications,
      mechanical
    mechanical complication—*see*
      Complications, mechanical
    thrombus 996.70
  jejunostomy malfunction 569.69
  malfunction of colostomy or enterostomy
    569.69
  nervous system NEC 997.00
  obstruction, internal anastomosis—*see*
    Complications, mechanical, graft
  other body system NEC 997.99
  peripheral vascular NEC 997.2
  postcardiotomy syndrome 429.4
  postcholecystectomy syndrome 576.0
  postcommissurotomy syndrome 429.4
  postgastrectomy dumping syndrome 564.2
  postmastectomy lymphedema syndrome 457.0
  postmastoidectomy 383.30
    cholesteatoma, recurrent 383.32
    cyst, mucosal 383.31
    granulation 383.33
    inflammation, chronic 383.33
  postvagotomy syndrome 564.2
  postvalvulotomy syndrome 429.4
  reattached extremity (infection) (rejection)
    (*see also* Complications, reattached,
    extremity) 996.90
  respiratory NEC 997.3
  seroma 998.13
  shock (endotoxic) (hypovolemic) (septic)
    998.0
  shunt, prosthetic (thrombus)—*see also*
    Complications, due to (presence of) any
    device, implant, or graft classified to
    996.0-996.5 NEC
    hemolytic anemia 283.19
  specified complication NEC 998.89
  stitch abscess 998.59
  transplant—*see* Complications, graft
  ureterostomy malfunction 997.5
  urethrostomy malfunction 997.5
  urinary NEC 997.5
  wound infection 998.59
  therapeutic misadventure NEC 999.9
  surgical treatment 998.9
  tracheostomy 519.0
  transfusion (blood) (lymphocytes) (plasma)
    NEC 999.8
  atrophy, liver, yellow, subacute (within 8
    months of administration)—*see* Hepatitis,
    viral
  bone marrow 996.85
  embolism
    air 999.1
    thrombus 999.2
  hemolysis NEC 999.8
    bone marrow 996.85
  hepatitis (serum) (type B) (within 8 months
    after administration) *see* Hepatitis, viral
  incompatibility reaction (ABO) (blood group)
    999.6
    Rh (factor) 999.7

Complications—*continued*
   infection 999.3
   jaundice (serum) (within 8 months after
      administration) *see* Hepatitis, viral
   sepsis 999.3
   shock or reaction NEC 999.8
      bone marrow 996.85
   subacute yellow atrophy of liver (within 8
      months after administration) *see* Hepatitis,
      viral
   thromboembolism 999.2
   transplant—*see also* Complications, due to
      (presence of) any device, implant, or graft
      classified to 996.0-996.5 NEC
   bone marrow 996.85
   organ (immune or nonimmune cause) (partial)
      (total) 996.80
      bone marrow 996.85
      heart 996.83
      intestines 996.89
      kidney 996.81
      liver 996.82
      lung 996.84
      pancreas 996.86
      specified NEC 996.89
   trauma NEC (early) 958.8
   ultrasound therapy NEC 999.9
   umbilical cord
      affecting fetus or newborn 762.6
      complicating delivery 663.9
         affecting fetus or newborn 762.6
         specified type NEC 663.8
   urethral catheter NEC 996.76
      infection or inflammation 996.64
      mechanical 996.31
   urinary, postoperative NEC 997.5
   vaccination 999.9
      anaphylaxis NEC 999.4
      cellulitis 999.3
      encephalitis or encephalomyelitis 323.5
      hepatitis (serum) (type B) (within 8 months
         after administration) *see* Hepatitis, viral
      infection (general) (local) NEC 999.3
      jaundice (serum) (within 8 months after
         administration) *see* Hepatitis, viral
      meningitis 997.09 *[321.8]*
      myelitis 323.5
      protein sickness 999.5
      reaction (allergic) 999.5
         Herxheimer's 995.0
         serum 999.5
      sepsis 999.3
      serum intoxication, sickness, rash, or other
         serum reaction NEC 999.5
      shock (allergic) (anaphylactic) 999.4
      subacute yellow atrophy of liver (within 8
         months after administration) *see* Hepatitis,
         viral
      vaccinia (generalized) 999.0
         localized 999.3
   vascular
      device, implant, or graft NEC 996.74
         infection or inflammation 996.62
         mechanical NEC 996.1
            cardiac (*see also* Complications,
               mechanical, by type) 996.00
      following infusion, perfusion, or transfusion
         999.2
      postoperative NEC 997.2
   ventilation therapy NEC 999.9

Compound presentation complicating delivery
   652.8
   causing obstructed labor 660.0
Compressed air disease 993.3
Compression
   with injury—*see* specific injury
   arm NEC 354.9
   artery 447.1
      celiac, syndrome 447.4
   brachial plexus 353.0
   brain (stem) 348.4
      due to
         contusion, brain—*see* Contusion, brain
         injury NEC—*see also* Hemorrhage, brain,
            traumatic
         birth—*see* Birth, injury, brain
         laceration, brain—*see* Laceration, brain
      osteopathic 739.0
   bronchus 519.1
   by cicatrix—*see* Cicatrix
   cardiac 423.9
   cauda equina 344.60
      with neurogenic bladder 344.61
   celiac (artery) (axis) 447.4
   cerebral—*see* Compression, brain
   cervical plexus 353.2
   cord (umbilical)—*see* Compression, umbilical
      cord
   cranial nerve 352.9
      second 377.49
      third (partial) 378.51
         total 378.52
      fourth 378.53
      fifth 350.8
      sixth 378.54
      seventh 351.8
   divers' squeeze 993.3
   duodenum (external) (*see also* Obstruction,
      duodenum) 537.3
   during birth 767.9
   esophagus 530.3
      congenital, external 750.3
   Eustachian tube 381.63
   facies (congenital) 754.0
   fracture—*see* Fracture, by site
   heart—*see* Disease, heart
   intestine (*see also* Obstruction, intestine) 560.9
      with hernia—*see* Hernia, by site, with
         obstruction
   laryngeal nerve, recurrent 478.79
   leg NEC 355.8
   lower extremity NEC 355.8
   lumbosacral plexus 353.1
   lung 518.89
   lymphatic vessel 457.1
   medulla—*see* Compression, brain
   nerve NEC—*see also* Disorder, nerve
      arm NEC 354.9
      autonomic nervous system (*see also*
         Neuropathy, peripheral, autonomic) 337.9
      axillary 353.0
      cranial NEC 352.9
      due to displacement of intervertebral disc
         722.2
         with myelopathy 722.70
      cervical 722.0
         with myelopathy 722.71
      lumbar, lumbosacral 722.10
         with myelopathy 722.73
      thoracic, thoracolumbar 722.11
         with myelopathy 722.72

Compression—*continued*
  iliohypogastric 355.79
  ilioinguinal 355.79
  leg NEC 355.8
  lower extremity NEC 355.8
  median (in carpal tunnel) 354.0
  obturator 355.79
  optic 377.49
  plantar 355.6
  posterior tibial (in tarsal tunnel) 355.5
  root (by scar tissue) NEC 724.9
    cervical NEC 723.4
    lumbar NEC 724.4
    lumbosacral 724.4
    thoracic 724.4
  saphenous 355.79
  sciatic (acute) 355.0
  sympathetic 337.9
  traumatic—*see* Injury, nerve
  ulnar 354.2
  upper extremity NEC 354.9
  peripheral—*see* Compression, nerve
  spinal (cord) (old or nontraumatic) 336.9
    by displacement of intervertebral disc—*see*
        Displacement, intervertebral disc
    nerve
      root NEC 724.9
        postoperative 722.80
          cervical region 722.81
          lumbar region 722.83
          thoracic region 722.82
        traumatic—*see* Injury, nerve, spinal
        traumatic—*see* Injury, nerve, spinal
    spondylogenic 721.91
      cervical 721.1
      lumbar, lumbosacral 721.42
      thoracic 721.41
    traumatic—*see also* Injury, spinal, by site
      with fracture, vertebra—*see* Fracture,
          vertebra, by site, with spinal cord injury
    spondylogenic—*see* Compression, spinal cord,
        spondylogenic
  subcostal nerve (syndrome) 354.8
  sympathetic nerve NEC 337.9
  syndrome 958.5
  thorax 512.8
    iatrogenic 512.1
    postoperative 512.1
  trachea 519.1
    congenital 748.3
  ulnar nerve (by scar tissue) 354.2
  umbilical cord
    affecting fetus or newborn 762.5
      cord prolapsed 762.4
    complicating delivery 663.2
      cord around neck 663.1
      cord prolapsed 663.0
  upper extremity NEC 354.9
  ureter 593.3
  urethra—*see* Stricture, urethra
  vein 459.2
  vena cava (inferior) (superior) 459.2
  vertebral NEC—*see* Compression, spinal (cord)
Compulsion, compulsive
  eating 307.51
  neurosis (obsessive) 300.3
  personality 301.4
  states (mixed) 300.3
  swearing 300.3
    in Gilles de la Tourette's syndrome 307.23
  tics and spasms 307.22

Compulsion, compulsive—*continued*
  water drinking NEC (syndrome) 307.9
Concato's disease (pericardial polyserositis)
    423.2
  peritoneal 568.82
  pleural—*see* Pleurisy
Concavity, chest wall 738.3
Concealed
  hemorrhage NEC 459.0
  penis 752.65
Concentric fading 368.12
Concern (normal) about sick person in family
    V61.49
Concrescence (teeth) 520.2
Concretio cordis 423.1
  rheumatic 393
Concretion —*see also* Calculus
  appendicular 543.9
  canaliculus 375.57
  clitoris 624.8
  conjunctiva 372.54
  eyelid 374.56
  intestine (impaction) (obstruction) 560.39
  lacrimal (passages) 375.57
  prepuce (male) 605
    female (clitoris) 624.8
  salivary gland (any) 527.5
  seminal vesicle 608.89
  stomach 537.89
  tonsil 474.8
Concussion (current) 850.9
  with
    loss of consciousness 850.5
      brief (less than one hour) 850.1
      moderate (1-24 hours) 850.2
      prolonged (more than 24 hours) (with
          complete recovery) (with return to
          pre-existing conscious level) 850.3
        without return to pre-existing conscious
            level 850.4
    mental confusion or disorientation (without
        loss of consciousness) 850.0
      with loss of consciousness—*see*
          Concussion, with, loss of consciousness
    without loss of consciousness 850.0
  blast (air) (hydraulic) (immersion) (underwater)
      869.0
    with open wound into cavity 869.1
    abdomen or thorax—*see* Injury, internal, by
        site
    brain—*see* Concussion, brain
    ear (acoustic nerve trauma) 951.5
      with perforation, tympanic membrane—*see*
          Wound, open, ear drum
    thorax—*see* Injury, internal, intrathoracic
        organs NEC
  brain or cerebral (without skull fracture) 850.9
    with
      loss of consciousness 850.5
        brief (less than one hour) 850.1
        moderate (1-24 hours) 850.2
        prolonged (more than 24 hours) (with
            complete recovery) (with return to
            pre-existing conscious level) 850.3
          without return to pre-existing conscious
              level 850.4
      mental confusion or disorientation (without
          loss of consciousness) 850.0
        with loss of consciousness—*see*
            Concussion, brain, with, loss of
            consciousness

Concussion—*continued*
    skull fracture—*see* Fracture, skull, by site
      without loss of consciousness 850.0
  cauda equina 952.4
  cerebral—*see* Concussion, brain
  conus medullaris (spine) 952.4
  hydraulic—*see* Concussion, blast
  internal organs—*see* Injury, internal, by site
  labyrinth—*see* Injury, intracranial
  ocular 921.3
  osseous labyrinth—*see* Injury, intracranial
  spinal (cord)—*see also* Injury, spinal, by site
    due to
      broken
        back—*see* Fracture, vertebra, by site, with
          spinal cord injury
        neck—*see* Fracture, vertebra, cervical,
          with spinal cord injury
      fracture, fracture dislocation, or
        compression fracture of spine or
        vertebra—*see* Fracture, vertebra, by site,
        with spinal cord injury
  syndrome 310.2
  underwater blast—*see* Concussion, blast
Condition —*see also* Disease
  psychiatric 298.9
  respiratory NEC 519.9
    acute or subacute NEC 519.9
      due to
        external agent 508.9
          specified type NEC 508.8
          fumes or vapors (chemical) (inhalation)
            506.3
          radiation 508.0
    chronic NEC 519.9
      due to
        external agent 508.9
          specified type NEC 508.8
          fumes or vapors (chemical) (inhalation)
            506.4
          radiation 508.1
    due to
      external agent 508.9
        specified type NEC 508.8
        fumes or vapors (chemical) (inhalation)
          506.9
Conduct disturbance (*see also* Disturbance,
  conduct) 312.9
  adjustment reaction 309.3
  hyperkinetic 314.2
Condyloma NEC 078.10
  acuminatum 078.11
  gonorrheal 098.0
  latum 091.3
  syphilitic 091.3
    congenital 090.0
  venereal, syphilitic 091.3
Confinement —*see* Delivery
Conflagration —*see also* Burn, by site
  asphyxia (by inhalation of smoke, gases, fumes,
    or vapors) 987.9
    specified agent—*see* Table of drugs and
      chemicals
Conflict
  family V61.9
    specified circumstance NEC V61.8
  interpersonal NEC V62.81
  marital V61.10
    involving divorce or estrangement V61.0
  parent-child V61.20
  partner V61.10

Confluent —*see* condition
Confusion, confused (mental) (state) (*see also*
  State, confusional) 298.9
  acute 293.0
  epileptic 293.0
  postoperative 293.9
  psychogenic 298.2
  reactive (from emotional stress, psychological
    trauma) 298.2
  subacute 293.1
Congelation 991.9
Congenital —*see also* condition
  aortic septum 747.29
  intrinsic factor deficiency 281.0
  malformation—*see* Anomaly
Congestion, congestive (chronic) (passive)
  asphyxia, newborn 768.9
  bladder 596.8
  bowel 569.89
  brain (*see also* Disease, cerebrovascular NEC)
    437.8
    malarial 084.9
  breast 611.79
  bronchi 519.1
  bronchial tube 519.1
  catarrhal 472.0
  cerebral—*see* Congestion, brain
  cerebrospinal—*see* Congestion, brain
  chest 514
  chill 780.9
    malarial (*see also* Malaria) 084.6
  circulatory NEC 459.9
  conjunctiva 372.71
  due to disturbance of circulation 459.9
  duodenum 537.3
  enteritis—*see* Enteritis
  eye 372.71
  fibrosis syndrome (pelvic) 625.5
  gastroenteritis—*see* Enteritis
  general 799.8
  glottis 476.0
  heart (*see also* Failure, heart, congestive) 428.0
  hepatic 573.0
  hypostatic (lung) 514
  intestine 569.89
  intracranial—*see* Congestion, brain
  kidney 593.89
  labyrinth 386.50
  larynx 476.0
  liver 573.0
  lung 514
    active or acute (*see also* Pneumonia) 486
      congenital 770.0
    chronic 514
    hypostatic 514
    idiopathic, acute 518.5
    passive 514
  malaria, malarial (brain) (fever) (*see also*
    Malaria) 084.6
  medulla—*see* Congestion, brain
  nasal 478.1
  orbit, orbital 376.33
    inflammatory (chronic) 376.10
      acute 376.00
  ovary 620.8
  pancreas 577.8
  pelvic, female 625.5
  pleural 511.0
  prostate (active) 602.1
  pulmonary—*see* Congestion, lung
  renal 593.89

Congestion, congestive—*continued*
  retina 362.89
  seminal vesicle 608.89
  spinal cord 336.1
  spleen 289.51
    chronic 289.51
  stomach 537.89
  trachea 464.11
  urethra 599.84
  uterus 625.5
    with subinvolution 621.1
  viscera 799.8
Congestive —*see* Congestion
Conical
  cervix 622.6
  cornea 371.60
  teeth 520.2
Conjoined twins 759.4
  causing disproportion (fetopelvic) 653.7
Conjugal maladjustment V61.10
  involving divorce or estrangement V61.0
Conjunctiva —*see* condition
Conjunctivitis (exposure) (infectious)
  (nondiphtheritic) (pneumococcal) (pustular)
  (staphylococcal) (streptococcal) NEC 372.30
  actinic 370.24
  acute 372.00
    atopic 372.05
    contagious 372.03
    follicular 372.02
    hemorrhagic (viral) 077.4
  adenoviral (acute) 077.3
  allergic (chronic) 372.14
    with hay fever 372.05
  anaphylactic 372.05
  angular 372.03
  Apollo (viral) 077.4
  atopic 372.05
  blennorrhagic (neonatorum) 098.40
  catarrhal 372.03
  chemical 372.05
  chlamydial 077.98
    due to
      Chlamydial trachomatis—*see* Trachoma
      paratrachoma 077.0
  chronic 372.10
    allergic 372.14
    follicular 372.12
    simple 372.11
    specified type NEC 372.14
    vernal 372.13
  diphtheritic 032.81
  due to
    dust 372.05
    enterovirus type 70 077.4
    erythema multiforme 695.1 *[372.33]*
    filariasis (*see also* Filariasis) 125.9 *[372.15]*
    mucocutaneous
      disease NEC 372.33
      leishmaniasis 085.5 *[372.15]*
    Reiter's disease 099.3 *[372.33]*
    syphilis 095.8 *[372.10]*
    toxoplasmosis (acquired) 130.1
      congenital (active) 771.2
    trachoma—*see* Trachoma
  dust 372.05
  eczematous 370.31
  epidemic 077.1
    hemorrhagic 077.4
  follicular (acute) 372.02
    adenoviral (acute) 077.3

Conjunctivitis—*continued*
  chronic 372.12
  glare 370.24
  gonococcal (neonatorum) 098.40
  granular (trachomatous) 076.1
    late effect 139.1
  hemorrhagic (acute) (epidemic) 077.4
  herpetic (simplex) 054.43
    zoster 053.21
  inclusion 077.0
  infantile 771.6
  influenzal 372.03
  Koch-Weeks 372.03
  light 372.05
  medicamentosa 372.05
  membranous 372.04
  meningococcic 036.89
  Morax-Axenfeld 372.02
  mucopurulent NEC 372.03
  neonatal 771.6
    gonococcal 098.40
  Newcastle's 077.8
  nodosa 360.14
  of Beal 077.3
  parasitic 372.15
    filariasis (*see also* Filariasis) 125.9 *[372.15]*
    mucocutaneous leishmaniasis 085.5 *[372.15]*
  Parinaud's 372.02
  petrificans 372.39
  phlyctenular 370.31
  pseudomembranous 372.04
    diphtheritic 032.81
  purulent 372.03
  Reiter's 099.3 *[372.33]*
  rosacea 695.3 *[372.31]*
  serous 372.01
    viral 077.99
  simple chronic 372.11
  specified NEC 372.39
  sunlamp 372.04
  swimming pool 077.0
  trachomatous (follicular) 076.1
    acute 076.0
    late effect 139.1
  traumatic NEC 372.39
  tuberculous (*see also* Tuberculosis) 017.3
    [370.31]
  tularemic 021.3
  tularensis 021.3
  vernal 372.13
    limbar 372.13 *[370.32]*
  viral 077.99
    acute hemorrhagic 077.4
    specified NEC 077.8
Conjunctoblepharitis —*see* Conjunctivitis
Conn (-Louis) syndrome (primary aldosteronism)
  255.1
Connective tissue —*see* condition
Conradi (-Hünermann) syndrome or disease
  (chondrodysplasia calcificans congenita)
  756.59
Consanguinity V19.7
Consecutive —*see* condition
Consolidated lung (base)—*see* Pneumonia, lobar
Constipation (atonic) (neurogenic) (simple)
  (spastic) 564.0
  drug induced
    correct substance properly administered 564.0
    overdose or wrong substance given or taken
      977.9

Constipation—*continued*
  specified drug—*see* Table of drugs and
    chemicals
  neurogenic 564.0
  psychogenic 306.4
Constitutional —*see also* condition
  arterial hypotension (*see also* Hypotension)
    458.9
  obesity 278.00
    morbid 278.01
  psychopathic state 301.9
  short stature 783.4
  state, developmental V21.9
    specified development NEC V21.8
  substandard 301.6
Constitutionally substandard 301.6
Constriction
  anomalous, meningeal bands or folds 742.8
  aortic arch (congenital) 747.10
  asphyxiation or suffocation by 994.7
  bronchus 519.1
  canal, ear (*see also* Stricture, ear canal,
    acquired) 380.50
  duodenum 537.3
  gallbladder (*see also* Obstruction, gallbladder)
    575.2
    congenital 751.69
  intestine (*see also* Obstruction, intestine) 560.9
  larynx 478.74
    congenital 748.3
  meningeal bands or folds, anomalous 742.8
  organ or site, congenital NEC—*see* Atresia
  prepuce (congenital) 605
  pylorus 537.0
    adult hypertrophic 537.0
    congenital or infantile 750.5
    newborn 750.5
  ring (uterus) 661.4
    affecting fetus or newborn 763.7
  spastic—*see also* Spasm
    ureter 593.3
    urethra—*see* Stricture, urethra
  stomach 537.89
  ureter 593.3
  urethra—*see* Stricture, urethra
  visual field (functional) (peripheral) 368.45
Constrictive —*see* condition
Consultation V65.9
  medical—*see also* Counseling, medical
  specified reason NEC V65.8
  without complaint or sickness V65.9
    feared complaint unfounded V65.5
    specified reason NEC V65.8
Consumption —*see* Tuberculosis
Contact
  with
    AIDS virus V01.7
    cholera V01.0
    communicable disease V01.9
      specified type NEC V01.8
      viral NEC V01.7
    German measles V01.4
    gonorrhea V01.6
    HIV V01.7
    human immunodeficiency virus V01.7
    parasitic disease NEC V01.8
    poliomyelitis V01.2
    rabies V01.5
    rubella V01.4
    smallpox V01.3
    syphilis V01.6

Contact—*continued*
    tuberculosis V01.1
    venereal disease V01.6
    viral disease NEC V01.7
  dermatitis—*see* Dermatitis
Contamination, food (*see also* Poisoning, food)
  005.9
Contraception, contraceptive
  advice NEC V25.09
    family planning V25.09
    fitting of diaphragm V25.02
    prescribing or use of
      oral contraceptive agent V25.01
      specified agent NEC V25.02
  counseling NEC V25.09
    family planning V25.09
    fitting of diaphragm V25.02
    prescribing or use of
      oral contraceptive agent V25.01
      specified agent NEC V25.02
  device (in situ) V45.59
    causing menorrhagia 996.76
    checking V25.42
    complications 996.32
    insertion V25.1
      intrauterine V45.51
    reinsertion V25.42
    removal V25.42
    subdermal V45.52
  fitting of diaphragm V25.02
  insertion
    intrauterine contraceptive device V25.1
    subdermal implantable V25.5
  maintenance V25.40
    examination V25.40
      intrauterine device V25.42
      oral contraceptive V25.41
      specified method NEC V25.49
      subdermal implantable V25.43
    intrauterine device V25.42
    oral contraceptive V25.41
    specified method NEC V25.49
    subdermal implantable V25.43
  management NEC V25.49
  prescription
    oral contraceptive agent V25.01
      repeat V25.41
    specified agent NEC V25.02
      repeat V25.49
  sterilization V25.2
  surveillance V25.40
    intrauterine device V25.42
    oral contraceptive agent V25.41
    specified method NEC V25.49
    subdermal implantable V25.43
Contraction, contracture, contracted
  Achilles tendon (*see also* Short, tendon,
    Achilles) 727.81
  anus 564.8
  axilla 729.9
  bile duct (*see also* Disease, biliary) 576.8
  bladder 596.8
    neck or sphincter 596.0
  bowel (*see also* Obstruction, intestine) 560.9
  Braxton Hicks 644.1
  bronchus 519.1
  burn (old)—*see* Cicatrix
  cecum (*see also* Obstruction, intestine) 560.9
  cervix (*see also* Stricture, cervix) 622.4
    congenital 752.49
  cicatricial—*see* Cicatrix

Contraction . . .—*continued*
  colon (*see also* Obstruction, intestine) 560.9
  conjunctiva trachomatous, active 076.1
    late effect 139.1
  Dupuytren's 728.6
  eyelid 374.41
  eye socket (after enucleation) 372.64
  face 729.9
  fascia (lata) (postural) 728.89
    Dupuytren's 728.6
    palmar 728.6
    plantar 728.71
  finger NEC 736.29
    congenital 755.59
    joint (*see also* Contraction, joint) 718.44
  flaccid, paralytic
    joint (*see also* Contraction, joint) 718.4
    muscle 728.85
      ocular 378.50
  gallbladder (*see also* Obstruction, gallbladder)
      575.2
  hamstring 728.89
    tendon 727.81
  heart valve—*see* Endocarditis
  Hicks' 644.1
  hip (*see also* Contraction, joint) 718.4
  hourglass
    bladder 596.8
      congenital 753.8
    gallbladder (*see also* Obstruction, gallbladder)
        575.2
      congenital 751.69
    stomach 536.8
      congenital 750.7
      psychogenic 306.4
    uterus 661.4
      affecting fetus or newborn 763.7
  hysterical 300.11
  infantile (*see also* Epilepsy) 345.6
  internal os (*see also* Stricture, cervix) 622.4
  intestine (*see also* Obstruction, intestine) 560.9
  joint (abduction) (acquired) (adduction)
      (flexion) (rotation) 718.40
    ankle 718.47
    congenital NEC 755.8
      generalized or multiple 754.89
        lower limb joints 754.89
      hip (*see also* Subluxation, congenital, hip)
          754.32
      lower limb (including pelvic girdle) not
          involving hip 754.89
      upper limb (including shoulder girdle) 755.59
    elbow 718.42
    foot 718.47
    hand 718.44
    hip 718.45
    hysterical 300.11
    knee 718.46
    multiple sites 718.49
    pelvic region 718.45
    shoulder (region) 718.41
    specified site NEC 718.48
    wrist 718.43
  kidney (granular) (secondary) (*see also*
      Sclerosis, renal) 587
    congenital 753.3
    hydronephritic 591
    pyelonephritic (*see also* Pyelitis, chronic)
        590.00
    tuberculous (*see also* Tuberculosis) 016.0

Contraction . . .—*continued*
  ligament 728.89
    congenital 756.89
  liver—*see* Cirrhosis, liver
  muscle (postinfectional) (postural) NEC 728.85
    congenital 756.89
      sternocleidomastoid 754.1
    extraocular 378.60
    eye (extrinsic) (*see also* Strabismus) 378.9
      paralytic (*see also* Strabismus, paralytic)
          378.50
    flaccid 728.85
    hysterical 300.11
    ischemic (Volkmann's) 958.6
    paralytic 728.85
    posttraumatic 958.6
    psychogenic 306.0
      specified as conversion reaction 300.11
  myotonic 728.85
  neck (*see also* Torticollis) 723.5
    congenital 754.1
    psychogenic 306.0
  ocular muscle (*see also* Strabismus) 378.9
    paralytic (*see also* Strabismus, paralytic)
        378.50
  organ or site, congenital NEC—*see* Atresia
  outlet (pelvis)—*see* Contraction, pelvis
  palmar fascia 728.6
  paralytic
    joint (*see also* Contraction, joint) 718.4
    muscle 728.85
    ocular (*see also* Strabismus, paralytic)
        378.50
  pelvis (acquired) (general) 738.6
    affecting fetus or newborn 763.1
    complicating delivery 653.1
      causing obstructed labor 660.1
    generally contracted 653.1
      causing obstructed labor 660.1
    inlet 653.2
      causing obstructed labor 660.1
    midpelvic 653.8
      causing obstructed labor 660.1
    midplane 653.8
      causing obstructed labor 660.1
    outlet 653.3
      causing obstructed labor 660.1
  plantar fascia 728.71
  premature
    atrial 427.61
    auricular 427.61
    auriculoventricular 427.61
    heart (junctional) (nodal) 427.60
    supraventricular 427.61
    ventricular 427.69
  prostate 602.8
  pylorus (*see also* Pylorospasm) 537.81
  rectosigmoid (*see also* Obstruction, intestine)
      560.9
  rectum, rectal (sphincter) 564.8
    psychogenic 306.4
  ring (Bandl's) 661.4
    affecting fetus or newborn 763.7
  scar—*see* Cicatrix
  sigmoid (*see also* Obstruction, intestine) 560.9
  socket, eye 372.64
  spine (*see also* Curvature, spine) 737.9

Contraction . . .—*continued*
  stomach 536.8
    hourglass 536.8
      congenital 750.7
      psychogenic 306.4
    psychogenic 306.4
  tendon (sheath) (*see also* Short, tendon) 727.81
  toe 735.8
  ureterovesical orifice (postinfectional) 593.3
  urethra 599.84
  uterus 621.8
    abnormal 661.9
      affecting fetus or newborn 763.7
    clonic, hourglass or tetanic 661.4
      affecting fetus or newborn 763.7
    dyscoordinate 661.4
      affecting fetus or newborn 763.7
    hourglass 661.4
      affecting fetus or newborn 763.7
    hypotonic NEC 661.2
      affecting fetus or newborn 763.7
    incoordinate 661.4
      affecting fetus or newborn 763.7
    inefficient or poor 661.2
      affecting fetus or newborn 763.7
    irregular 661.2
      affecting fetus or newborn 763.7
    tetanic 661.4
      affecting fetus or newborn 763.7
  vagina (outlet) 623.2
  vesical 596.8
    neck or urethral orifice 596.0
  visual field, generalized 368.45
  Volkmann's (ischemic) 958.6
Contusion (skin surface intact) 924.9
  with
    crush injury—*see* Crush
    dislocation—*see* Dislocation, by site
    fracture—*see* Fracture, by site
    internal injury—*see also* Injury, internal, by
      site
      heart—*see* Contusion, cardiac
      kidney—*see* Contusion, kidney
      liver—*see* Contusion, liver
      lung—*see* Contusion, lung
      spleen—*see* Contusion, spleen
    intracranial injury—*see* Injury, intracranial
    nerve injury—*see* Injury, nerve
    open wound—*see* Wound, open, by site
  abdomen, abdominal (muscle) (wall) 922.2
    organ(s) NEC 868.00
  adnexa, eye NEC 921.9
  ankle 924.21
    with other parts of foot 924.20
  arm 923.9
    lower (with elbow) 923.10
    upper 923.03
      with shoulder or axillary region 923.09
  auditory canal (external) (meatus) (and other
    part(s) of neck, scalp, or face, except eye)
    920
  auricle, ear (and other part(s) of neck, scalp, or
    face except eye) 920
  axilla 923.02
    with shoulder or upper arm 923.09
  back 922.31
  bone NEC 924.9

Contusion—*continued*
  brain (cerebral) (membrane) (with hemorrhage)
    851.8

Note—Use the following fifth-digit
subclassification with categories 851-854:

0 *unspecified state of consciousness*
1 *with no loss of consciousness*
2 *with brief [less than one hour] loss*
    of consciousness
3 *with moderate [1-24 hours] loss of*
    consciousness
4 *with prolonged [more than 24 hours] loss of*
    consciousness and return to pre-existing
    conscious level
5 *with prolonged [more than 24 hours] loss of*
    consciousness, without return to pre-existing
    conscious level
Use fifth-digit 5 to designate when a patient is
unconscious and dies before regaining
conciousness, regardless of the duration of the
loss of conciousness
6 *with loss of consciousness of unspecified*
    duration
9 *with concussion, unspecified*

---

    with
      open intracranial wound 851.9
      skull fracture—*see* Fracture, skull, by site
    cerebellum 851.4
      with open intracranial wound 851.5
    cortex 851.0
      with open intracranial wound 851.1
    occipital lobe 851.4
      with open intracranial wound 851.5
    stem 851.4
      with open intracranial wound 851.5
  breast 922.0
  brow (and other part(s) of neck, scalp, or face,
    except eye) 920
  buttock 922.32
  canthus 921.1
  cardiac 861.01
    with open wound into thorax 861.11
  cauda equina (spine) 952.4
  cerebellum—*see* Contusion, brain, cerebellum
  cerebral—*see* Contusion, brain
  cheek(s) (and other part(s) of neck, scalp, or
    face, except eye) 920
  chest (wall) 922.1
  chin (and other part(s) of neck, scalp, or face,
    except eye) 920
  clitoris 922.4
  conjunctiva 921.1
  conus medullaris (spine) 952.4
  cornea 921.3
  corpus cavernosum 922.4
  cortex (brain) (cerebral)—*see* Contusion, brain,
    cortex
  costal region 922.1
  ear (and other part(s) of neck, scalp, or face
    except eye) 920
  elbow 923.11
    with forearm 923.10
  epididymis 922.4
  epigastric region 922.2
  eye NEC 921.9
  eyeball 921.3
  eyelid(s) (and periocular area) 921.1
  face (and neck, or scalp any part, except eye)
    920

Contusion—*continued*

femoral triangle 922.2
fetus or newborn 772.6
finger(s) (nail) (subungual) 923.3
flank 922.2
foot (with ankle) (excluding toe(s)) 924.20
forearm (and elbow) 923.10
forehead (and other part(s) of neck, scalp, or face, except eye) 920
genital organs, external 922.4
globe (eye) 921.3
groin 922.2
gum(s) (and other part(s) of neck, scalp, or face, except eye) 920
hand(s) (except fingers alone) 923.20
head (any part, except eye) (and face) (and neck) 920
heart—*see* Contusion, cardiac
heel 924.20
hip 924.01
    with thigh 924.00
iliac region 922.2
inguinal region 922.2
internal organs (abdomen, chest, or pelvis) NEC—*see* Injury, internal, by site
interscapular region 922.33
iris (eye) 921.3
kidney 866.01
    with open wound into cavity 866.11
knee 924.11
    with lower leg 924.10
labium (majus) (minus) 922.4
lacrimal apparatus, gland, or sac 921.1
larynx (and other part(s) of neck, scalp, or face, except eye) 920
late effect—*see* Late, effects (of), contusion
leg 924.5
    lower (with knee) 924.10
lens 921.3
lingual (and other part(s) of neck, scalp, or face, except eye) 920
lip(s) (and other part(s) of neck, scalp, or face, except eye) 920
liver 864.01
    with
        laceration—*see* Laceration, liver
        open wound into cavity 864.11
lower extremity 924.5
    multiple sites 924.4
lumbar region 922.31
lung 861.21
    with open wound into thorax 861.31
malar region (and other part(s) of neck, scalp, or face, except eye) 920
mandibular joint (and other part(s) of neck, scalp, or face, except eye) 920
mastoid region (and other part(s) of neck, scalp, or face, except eye) 920
membrane, brain—*see* Contusion, brain
midthoracic region 922.1
mouth (and other part(s) of neck, scalp, or face, except eye) 920
multiple sites (not classifiable to same three-digit category) 924.8
    lower limb 924.4
    trunk 922.8
    upper limb 923.8
muscle NEC 924.9
myocardium—*see* Contusion, cardiac
nasal (septum) (and other part(s) of neck, scalp, or face, except eye) 920

Contusion—*continued*

neck (and scalp, or face any part, except eye) 920
nerve—*see* Injury, nerve, by site
continued nose (and other part(s) of neck, scalp, or face, except eye) 920
occipital region (scalp) (and neck or face, except eye) 920
    lobe—*see* Contusion, brain, occipital lobe
orbit (region) (tissues) 921.2
palate (soft) (and other part(s) of neck, scalp, or face, except eye) 920
parietal region (scalp) (and neck, or face, except eye) 920
    lobe—*see* Contusion, brain
penis 922.4
pericardium—*see* Contusion, cardiac
perineum 922.4
periocular area 921.1
pharynx (and other part(s) of neck, scalp, or face, except eye) 920
popliteal space (*see also* Contusion, knee) 924.11
prepuce 922.4
pubic region 922.4
pudenda 922.4
pulmonary—*see* Contusion, lung
quadriceps femoralis 924.00
rib cage 922.1
sacral region 922.32
salivary ducts or glands (and other part(s) of neck, scalp, or face, except eye) 920
scalp (and neck, or face any part, except eye) 920
scapular region 923.01
    with shoulder or upper arm 923.09
sclera (eye) 921.3
scrotum 922.4
shoulder 923.00
    with upper arm or axillar regions 923.09
skin NEC 924.9
skull 920
spermatic cord 922.4
spinal cord—*see also* Injury, spinal, by site
    cauda equina 952.4
    conus medullaris 952.4
spleen 865.01
    with open wound into cavity 865.11
sternal region 922.1
stomach—*see* Injury, internal, stomach
subconjunctival 921.1
subcutaneous NEC 924.9
submaxillary region (and other part(s) of neck, scalp, or face, except eye) 920
submental region (and other part(s) of neck, scalp, or face, except eye) 920
subperiosteal NEC 924.9
supraclavicular fossa (and other part(s) of neck, scalp, or face, except eye) 920
supraorbital (and other part(s) of neck, scalp, or face, except eye) 920
temple (region) (and other part(s) of neck, scalp, or face, except eye) 920
testis 922.4
thigh (and hip) 924.00
thorax 922.1
    organ—*see* Injury, internal, intrathoracic
throat (and other part(s) of neck, scalp, or face, except eye) 920
thumb(s) (nail) (subungual) 923.3
toe(s) (nail) (subungual) 924.3

Contusion—*continued*
tongue (and other part(s) of neck, scalp, or face, except eye) 920
trunk 922.9
multiple sites 922.8
specified site—*see* Contusion, by site
tunica vaginalis 922.4
tympanum (membrane) (and other part(s) of neck, scalp, or face, except eye) 920
upper extremity 923.9
multiple sites 923.8
uvula (and other part(s) of neck, scalp, or face, except eye) 920
vagina 922.4
vocal cord(s) (and other part(s) of neck, scalp, or face, except eye) 920
vulva 922.4
wrist 923.21
with hand(s), except finger(s) alone 923.20
Conus (any type) (congenital) 743.57
acquired 371.60
medullaris syndrome 336.8
Convalescence (following) V66.9
chemotherapy V66.2
medical NEC V66.5
psychotherapy V66.3
radiotherapy V66.1
surgery NEC V66.0
treatment (for) NEC V66.5
combined V66.6
fracture V66.4
mental disorder NEC V66.3
specified disorder NEC V66.5
Conversion
hysteria, hysterical, any type 300.11
neurosis, any 300.11
reaction, any 300.11
Converter, tuberculosis (test reaction) 795.5
Convulsions (idiopathic) 780.3
apoplectiform (*see also* Disease, cerebrovascular, acute) 436
brain 780.3
cerebral 780.3
cerebrospinal 780.3
due to trauma NEC—*see* Injury, intracranial
eclamptic (*see also* Eclampsia) 780.3
epileptic (*see also* Epilepsy) 345.9
epileptiform (*see also* Seizure, epileptiform) 780.3
epileptoid (*see also* Seizure, epileptiform) 780.3
ether
anesthetic
correct substance properly administered 780.3
overdose or wrong substance given 968.2
other specified type—*see* Table of drugs and chemicals
febrile 780.3
generalized 780.3
hysterical 300.11
infantile 780.3
epilepsy—*see* Epilepsy
internal 780.3
jacksonian (*see also* Epilepsy) 345.5
myoclonic 333.2
newborn 779.0
paretic 094.1
pregnancy (nephritic) (uremic)—*see* Eclampsia, pregnancy
psychomotor (*see also* Epilepsy) 345.4

Convulsions—*continued*
puerperal, postpartum—*see* Eclampsia, pregnancy
recurrent 780.3
epileptic—*see* Epilepsy
reflex 781.0
repetitive 780.3
epileptic—*see* Epilepsy
salaam (*see also* Epilepsy) 345.6
scarlatinal 034.1
spasmodic 780.3
tetanus, tetanic (*see also* Tetanus) 037
thymic 254.8
uncinate 780.3
uremic 586
Convulsive —*see also* Convulsions
disorder or state 780.3
epileptic—*see* Epilepsy
equivalent, abdominal (*see also* Epilepsy) 345.5
Cooke-Apert-Gallais syndrome (adrenogenital) 255.2
Cooley's anemia (erythroblastic) 282.4
Coolie itch 126.9
Cooper's
disease 610.1
hernia—*see* Hernia, Cooper's
Coordination disturbance 781.3
Copper wire arteries, retina 362.13
Copra itch 133.8
Coprolith 560.39
Coprophilia 302.89
Coproporphyria, hereditary 277.1
Coprostasis 560.39
with hernia—*see also* Hernia, by site, with obstruction
gangrenous—*see* Hernia, by site, with gangrene
Cor
biloculare 745.7
bovinum—*see* Hypertrophy, cardiac
bovis—*see also* Hypertrophy, cardiac
pulmonale (chronic) 416.9
acute 415.0
triatriatum, triatrium 746.82
triloculare 745.8
biatriatum 745.3
biventriculare 745.69
Corbus' disease 607.1
Cord— *see also* condition
around neck (tightly) (with compression)
affecting fetus or newborn 762.5
complicating delivery 663.1
without compression 663.3
affecting fetus or newborn 762.6
bladder NEC 344.61
tabetic 094.0
prolapse
affecting fetus or newborn 762.4
complicating delivery 663.0
Cord's angiopathy (*see also* Tuberculosis) 017.3 *[362.18]*
Cordis ectopia 746.87
Corditis (spermatic) 608.4
Corectopia 743.46
Cori type glycogen storage disease —*see* Disease, glycogen storage
Cork-handlers' disease or lung 495.3
Corkscrew esophagus 530.5
Corlett's pyosis (impetigo) 684
Corn (infected) 700

Cornea—*see also* condition
  donor V59.5
  guttata (dystrophy) 371.57
  plana 743.41
Cornelia de Lange's syndrome (Amsterdam
    dwarf, mental retardation, and brachycephaly)
    759.89
Cornual gestation or pregnancy —*see*
    Pregnancy, cornual
Cornu cutaneum 702.8
Coronary (artery)—*see also* condition
  arising from aorta or pulmonary trunk 746.85
Corpora —*see also* condition
  amylacea (prostate) 602.8
  cavernosa—*see* condition
Corpulence (*see also* Obesity) 278.0
Corpus —*see* condition
Corrigan's disease —*see* Insufficiency, aortic
Corrosive burn —*see* Burn, by site
Corsican fever (*see also* Malaria) 084.6
Cortical —*see also* condition
  blindness 377.75
  necrosis, kidney (bilateral) 583.6
Corticoadrenal —*see* condition
Corticosexual syndrome 255.2
Coryza (acute) 460
  with grippe or influenza 487.1
  syphilitic 095.8
    congenital (chronic) 090.0
Costen's syndrome or complex 524.60
Costiveness (*see also* Constipation) 564.0
Costochondritis 733.6
Cotard's syndrome (paranoia) 297.1
Cot death 798.0
Cotungo's disease 724.3
Cough 786.2
  with hemorrhage (*see also* Hemoptysis) 786.3
  affected 786.2
  bronchial 786.2
    with grippe or influenza 487.1
  chronic 786.2
  epidemic 786.2
  functional 306.1
  hemorrhagic 786.3
  hysterical 300.11
  laryngeal, spasmodic 786.2
  nervous 786.2
  psychogenic 306.1
  smokers' 491.0
  tea tasters' 112.89
Counseling NEC V65.40
  abuse victim
    child V61.21
    partner V61.11
    spouse V61.11
  child abuse, maltreatment, or neglect V61.21
  contraceptive NEC V25.09
    device (intrauterine) V25.02
    maintenance V25.40
      intrauterine contraceptive device V25.42
      oral contraceptive (pill) V25.41
      specified type NEC V25.49
      subdermal implantable V25.43
    management NEC V25.9
    oral contraceptive (pill) V25.01
    prescription NEC V25.02
      oral contraceptive (pill) V25.01
        repeat prescription V25.41
      repeat prescription V25.40
    subdermal implantable V25.43
    surveillance V25.40

Counseling—*continued*
  dietary V65.3
  exercise V65.41
  explanation of
    investigation finding NEC V65.49
    medication NEC V65.49
  family planning V25.09
  for nonattending third party V65.1
  genetic V26.3
  gonorrhea V65.45
  health (advice) (education) (instruction) NEC
      V65.49
  HIV V65.44
  human immunodeficiency virus V65.44
  injury prevention V65.43
  marital V61.10
  medical (for) V65.9
    boarding school resident V60.6
    condition not demonstrated V65.5
    feared complaint and no disease found V65.5
    institutional resident V60.1
    on behalf of another V65.1
    person living alone V60.3
  parent-child conflict V61.20
    specified problem NEC V61.29
  partner abuse
    perpetrator V61.12
    victim V61.11
  perpetrator of
    child abuse V62.83
      parental V61.22
    partner abuse V61.12
    spouse abuse V61.12
  procreative V65.49
  sex NEC V65.49
    transmitted disease NEC V65.45
      HIV V65.44
  specified reason NEC V65.49
  spousal abuse
    perpetrator V61.12
    victim V61.11
  substance use and abuse V65.42
  syphilis V65.45
  victim (of)
    child abuse V61.21
    partner abuse V61.11
    spousal abuse V61.11
  without complaint or sickness V65.49
Coupled rhythm 427.89
Couvelaire uterus (complicating delivery)—*see*
    Placenta, separation
Cowper's gland —*see* condition
Cowperitis (*see also* Urethritis) 597.89
  gonorrheal (acute) 098.0
    chronic or duration of 2 months or over 098.2
Cowpox (abortive) 051.0
  due to vaccination 999.0
  eyelid 051.0 *[373.5]*
    postvaccination 999.0 *[373.5]*
Coxa
  plana 732.1
  valga (acquired) 736.31
    congenital 755.61
    late effect of rickets 268.1
  vara (acquired) 736.32
    congenital 755.62
    late effect of rickets 268.1
Coxae malum senilis 715.25
Coxalgia (nontuberculous) 719.45
  tuberculous (*see also* Tuberculosis) 015.1
    [730.85]

Coxalgic pelvis 736.30
Coxitis 716.65
Coxsackie (infection) (virus) 079.2
  central nervous system NEC 048
  endocarditis 074.22
  enteritis 008.67
  meningitis (aseptic) 047.0
  myocarditis 074.23
  pericarditis 074.21
  pharyngitis 074.0
  pleurodynia 074.1
  specific disease NEC 074.8
Crabs, meaning pubic lice 132.2
Crack baby 760.75
Cracked nipple 611.2
  puerperal, postpartum 676.1
Cradle cap 690.11
Craft neurosis 300.89
Craigiasis 007.8
Cramp (s) 729.82
  abdominal 789.0
  bathing 994.1
  colic 789.0
    psychogenic 306.4
  due to immersion 994.1
  extremity (lower) (upper) NEC 729.82
  fireman 992.2
  heat 992.2
  hysterical 300.11
  immersion 994.1
  intestinal 789.0
    psychogenic 306.4
  linotypist's 300.89
    organic 333.84
  muscle (extremity) (general) 729.82
    due to immersion 994.1
    hysterical 300.11
  occupational (hand) 300.89
    organic 333.84
  psychogenic 307.89
  salt depletion 276.1
  stoker 992.2
  stomach 789.0
  telegraphers' 308.9
    organic 333.84
  typists' 300.89
    organic 333.84
  uterus 625.8
    menstrual 625.3
  writers' 300.89
    organic 333.84
Cranial —*see* condition
Cranioclasis, fetal 763.8
Craniocleidodysostosis 755.59
Craniofenestria (skull) 756.0
Craniolacunia (skull) 756.0
Craniopagus 759.4
Craniopathy, metabolic 733.3
Craniopharyngeal —*see* condition
Craniopharyngioma (M9350/1) 237.0
Craniorachischisis (totalis) 740.1
Cranioschisis 756.0
Craniostenosis 756.0
Craniosynostosis 756.0
Craniotabes (cause unknown) 733.3
  rachitic 268.1
  syphilitic 090.5
Craniotomy, fetal 763.8
Cranium —*see* condition
Craw-craw 125.3

Creaking joint 719.60
  ankle 719.67
  elbow 719.62
  foot 719.67
  hand 719.64
  hip 719.65
  knee 719.66
  multiple sites 719.69
  pelvic region 719.65
  shoulder (region) 719.61
  specified site NEC 719.68
  wrist 719.63
Creeping
  eruption 126.9
  palsy 335.21
  paralysis 335.21
Crenated tongue 529.8
Creotoxism 005.9
Crepitus
  caput 756.0
  joint 719.60
    ankle 719.67
    elbow 719.62
    foot 719.67
    hand 719.64
    hip 719.65
    knee 719.66
    multiple sites 719.69
    pelvic region 719.65
    shoulder (region) 719.61
    specified site NEC 719.68
    wrist 719.63
Crescent or conus choroid, congenital 743.57
Cretin, cretinism (athyrotic) (congenital)
    (endemic) (metabolic) (nongoitrous)
    (sporadic) 243
  goitrous (sporadic) 246.1
  pelvis (dwarf type) (male type) 243
    with disproportion (fetopelvic) 653.1
      affecting fetus or newborn 763.1
      causing obstructed labor 660.1
        affecting fetus or newborn 763.1
  pituitary 253.3
Cretinoid degeneration 243
Creutzfeldt-Jakob disease (syndrome) 046.1
  with dementia 046.1 *[294.1]*
Crib death 798.0
Cribriform hymen 752.49
Cri-du-chat syndrome 758.3
Crigler-Najjar disease or syndrome (congenital
    hyperbilirubinemia) 277.4
Crimean hemorrhagic fever 065.0
Criminalism 301.7
Crisis
  abdomen 789.0
  addisonian (acute adrenocortical insufficiency)
    255.4
  adrenal (cortical) 255.4
  asthmatic—*see* Asthma
  brain, cerebral (*see also* Disease,
    cerebrovascular, acute) 436
  celiac 579.0
  Dietl's 593.4
  emotional NEC 309.29
    acute reaction to stress 308.0
    adjustment reaction 309.9
    specific to childhood and adolescence 313.9
  gastric (tabetic) 094.0
  glaucomatocyclitic 364.22
  heart (*see also* Failure, heart) 428.9
  hypertensive—*see* Hypertension

Crisis—*continued*
  nitritoid
    correct substance properly administered 458.2
    overdose or wrong substance given or taken
      961.1
  oculogyric 378.87
    psychogenic 306.7
  Pel's 094.0
  psychosexual identity 302.6
  rectum 094.0
  renal 593.81
  sickle cell 282.62
  stomach (tabetic) 094.0
  tabetic 094.0
  thyroid (*see also* Thyrotoxicosis) 242.9
  thyrotoxic (*see also* Thyrotoxicosis) 242.9
  vascular—*see* Disease, cerebrovascular, acute
Crocq's disease (acrocyanosis) 443.89
Crohn's disease (*see also* Enteritis, regional)
  555.9
Cronkhite-Canada syndrome 211.3
Crooked septum, nasal 470
Cross
  birth (of fetus) complicating delivery 652.3
    with successful version 652.1
    causing obstructed labor 660.0
  bite, anterior or posterior 524.2
  eye (*see also* Esotropia) 378.00
Crossed ectopia of kidney 753.3
Crossfoot 754.50
Croup, croupus (acute) (angina) (catarrhal)
    (infective) (inflammatory) (laryngeal)
    (membranous) (nondiphtheritic)
    (pseudomembranous) 464.4
  asthmatic (*see also* Asthma) 493.9
  bronchial 466.0
  diphtheritic (membranous) 032.3
  false 478.75
  spasmodic 478.75
    diphtheritic 032.3
  stridulous 478.75
    diphtheritic 032.3
Crouzon's disease (craniofacial dysostosis) 756.0
Crowding, teeth 524.3
CRST syndrome (cutaneous systemic sclerosis)
  710.1
Cruchet's disease (encephalitis lethargica) 049.8
Cruelty in children (*see also* Disturbance,
  conduct) 312.9
Crural ulcer (*see also* Ulcer, lower extremity)
  707.1
Crush, crushed, crushing (injury) 929.9
  with
    fracture—*see* Fracture, by site
  abdomen 926.19
    internal—*see* Injury, internal, abdomen
  ankle 928.21
    with other parts of foot 928.20
  arm 927.9
    lower (and elbow) 927.10
    upper 927.03
      with shoulder or axillary region 927.09
  axilla 927.02
    with shoulder or upper arm 927.09
  back 926.11
  breast 926.19
  buttock 926.12
  cheek 925.1
  chest—*see* Injury, internal, chest
  ear 925.1

Crush, crushed, crushing—*continued*
  elbow 927.11
    with forearm 927.10
  face 925.1
  finger(s) 927.3
    with hand(s) 927.20
      and wrist(s) 927.21
  flank 926.19
  foot, excluding toe(s) alone (with ankle) 928.20
  forearm (and elbow) 927.10
  genitalia, external (female) (male) 926.0
    internal—*see* Injury, internal, genital organ
      NEC
  hand, except finger(s) alone (and wrist) 927.20
  head—*see* Fracture, skull, by site
  heel 928.20
  hip 928.01
    with thigh 928.00
  internal organ (abdomen, chest, or pelvis)—*see*
    Injury, internal, by site
  knee 928.11
    with leg, lower 928.10
  labium (majus) (minus) 926.0
  larynx 925.2
  late effect—*see* Late, effects (of), crushing
  leg 928.9
    lower 928.10
      and knee 928.11
    upper 928.00
  limb
    lower 928.9
      multiple sites 928.8
    upper 927.9
      multiple sites 927.8
  multiple sites NEC 929.0
  neck 925.2
  nerve—*see* Injury, nerve, by site
  nose 802.0
    open 802.1
  penis 926.0
  pharynx 925.2
  scalp 925.2
  scapular region 927.01
    with shoulder or upper arm 927.09
  scrotum 926.0
  shoulder 927.00
    with upper arm or axillary region 927.09
  skull or cranium—*see* Fracture, skull, by site
  spinal cord—*see* Injury, spinal, by site
  syndrome (complication of trauma) 958.5
  testis 926.0
  thigh (with hip) 928.00
  throat 925.2
  thumb(s) (and fingers) 927.3
  toe(s) 928.3
    with foot 928.20
      and ankle 928.21
  tonsil 925.2
  trunk 926.9
    chest—*see* Injury, internal, intrathoracic
      organs NEC
    internal organ—*see* Injury, internal, by site
    multiple sites 926.8
    specified site NEC 926.19
  vulva 926.0
  wrist 927.21
    with hand(s), except fingers alone 927.20
Crusta lactea 690.11
Crusts 782.8
Crutch paralysis 953.4
Cruveilhier's disease 335.21

Cruveilhier-Baumgarten cirrhosis, disease, or syndrome 571.5
Cruz-Chagas disease (*see also* Trypanosomiasis) 086.2
Cryoglobulinemia (mixed) 273.2
Crypt (anal) (rectal) 569.49
Cryptitis (anal) (rectal) 569.49
Cryptococcosis (European) (pulmonary) (systemic) 117.5
Cryptococcus 117.5
  epidermicus 117.5
  neoformans, infection by 117.5
Cryptopapillitis (anus) 569.49
Cryptophthalmos (eyelid) 743.06
Cryptorchid, cryptorchism, cryptorchidism 752.51
Cryptosporidiosis 007.8
Cryptotia 744.29
Crystallopathy
  calcium pyrophosphate (*see also* Arthritis) 275.4 *[712.2]*
  dicalcium phosphate (*see also* Arthritis) 275.4 *[712.1]*
  gouty 274.0
  pyrophosphate NEC (*see also* Arthritis) 275.4 *[712.2]*
  uric acid 274.0
Crystalluria 791.9
Csillag's disease (lichen sclerosus et atrophicus) 701.0
Cuban itch 050.1
Cubitus
  valgus (acquired) 736.01
    congenital 755.59
    late effect of rickets 268.1
  varus (acquired) 736.02
    congenital 755.59
    late effect of rickets 268.1
Cultural deprivation V62.4
Cupping of optic disc 377.14
Curling's ulcer —*see* Ulcer, duodenum
Curling esophagus 530.5
Curschmann (-Batten) (-Steinert) disease or syndrome 359.2
Curvature
  organ or site, congenital NEC—*see* Distortion
  penis (lateral) 752.69
  Pott's (spinal) (*see also* Tuberculosis) 015.0 *[737.43]*
  radius, idiopathic, progressive (congenital) 755.54
  spine (acquired) (angular) (idiopathic) (incorrect) (postural) 737.9
    congenital 754.2
    due to or associated with
      Charcot-Marie-Tooth disease 356.1 *[737.40]*
      mucopolysaccharidosis 277.5 *[737.40]*
      neurofibromatosis 237.71 *[737.40]*
      osteitis
        deformans 731.0 *[737.40]*
        fibrosa cystica 252.0 *[737.40]*
      osteoporosis (*see also* Osteoporosis) 733.00 *[737.40]*
      poliomyelitis (*see also* Poliomyelitis) 138 *[737.40]*
      tuberculosis (Pott's curvature) (*see also* Tuberculosis) 015.0 *[737.43]*
    kyphoscoliotic (*see also* Kyphoscoliosis) 737.30
    kyphotic (*see also* Kyphosis) 737.10
    late effect of rickets 268.1 *[737.40]*

Curvature—*continued*
  Pott's 015.0 *[737.40]*
  scoliotic (*see also* Scoliosis) 737.30
  specified NEC 737.8
  tuberculous 015.0 *[737.40]*
Cushing's
  basophilism, disease, or syndrome (iatrogenic) (idiopathic) (pituitary basophilism) (pituitary dependent) 255.0
  ulcer—*see* Ulcer, peptic
Cushingoid due to steroid therapy
  correct substance properly administered 255.0
  overdose or wrong substance given or taken 962.0
Cut (external)—*see* Wound, open, by site
Cutaneous —*see also* condition
  hemorrhage 782.7
  horn (cheek) (eyelid) (mouth) 702.8
  larva migrans 126.9
Cutis —*see also* condition
  hyperelastic 756.83
    acquired 701.8
  laxa 756.83
    senilis 701.8
  marmorata 782.61
  osteosis 709.3
  pendula 756.83
    acquired 701.8
  rhomboidalis nuchae 701.8
  verticis gyrata 757.39
    acquired 701.8
Cyanopathy, newborn 770.8
Cyanosis 782.5
  autotoxic 289.7
  common atrioventricular canal 745.69
  congenital 770.8
  conjunctiva 372.71
  due to
    endocardial cushion defect 745.60
    nonclosure, foramen botalli 745.5
    patent foramen botalli 745.5
    persistent foramen ovale 745.5
  enterogenous 289.7
  fetus or newborn 770.8
  ostium primum defect 745.61
  paroxysmal digital 443.0
  retina, retinal 362.10
Cycle
  anovulatory 628.0
  menstrual, irregular 626.4
Cyclencephaly 759.89
Cyclical vomiting 536.2
  psychogenic 306.4
Cyclitic membrane 364.74
Cyclitis (*see also* Iridocyclitis) 364.3
  acute 364.00
    primary 364.01
    recurrent 364.02
  chronic 364.10
    in
      sarcoidosis 135 *[364.11]*
      tuberculosis (*see also* Tuberculosis) 017.3 *[364.11]*
  Fuchs' heterochromic 364.21
  granulomatous 364.10
  lens induced 364.23
  nongranulomatous 364.00
  posterior 363.21
  primary 364.01
  recurrent 364.02

Cyclitis—*continued*
secondary (noninfectious) 364.04
infectious 364.03
subacute 364.00
primary 364.01
recurrent 364.02
Cyclokeratitis —*see* Keratitis
Cyclophoria 378.44
Cyclopia, cyclops 759.89
Cycloplegia 367.51
Cyclospasm 367.53
Cyclothymia 301.13
Cyclothymic personality 301.13
Cyclotropia 378.33
Cyesis —*see* Pregnancy
Cylindroma (M8200/3)—*see also* Neoplasm, by
site, malignant
eccrine dermal (M8200/0)—*see* Neoplasm,
skin, benign
skin (M8200/0)—*see* Neoplasm, skin, benign
Cylindruria 791.7
Cyllosoma 759.89
Cynanche
diphtheritic 032.3
tonsillaris 475
Cynorexia 783.6
Cyphosis —*see* Kyphosis
Cyprus fever (*see also* Brucellosis) 023.9
Cyriax's syndrome (slipping rib) 733.99
Cyst (mucus) (retention) (serous) (simple)

---

*Note—In general, cysts are not neoplastic and
are classified to the appropriate category for
disease of the specified anatomical site. This
generalization does not apply to certain types of
cysts which are neoplastic in nature, for
example, dermoid, nor does it apply to cysts of
certain structures, for example, branchial cleft,
which are classified as developmental
anomalies. The following listing includes some
of the most frequently reported sites of cysts as
well as qualifiers which indicate the type of
cyst. The latter qualifiers usually are not
repeated under the anatomical sites. Since the
code assignment for a given site may vary
depending upon the type of cyst, the coder
should refer to the listings under the specified
type of cyst before consideration is given to the
site.*

---

accessory, fallopian tube 752.11
adenoid (infected) 474.8
adrenal gland 255.8
congenital 759.1
air, lung 518.89
allantoic 753.7
alveolar process (jaw bone) 526.2
amnion, amniotic 658.8
anterior chamber (eye) 364.60
exudative 364.62
implantation (surgical) (traumatic) 364.61
parasitic 360.13
anterior nasopalatine 526.1
antrum 478.1
anus 569.49
apical (periodontal) (tooth) 522.8
appendix 543.9
arachnoid, brain 348.0
arytenoid 478.79
auricle 706.2
Baker's (knee) 727.51
tuberculous (*see also* Tuberculosis) 015.2

Cyst —*continued*
Bartholin's gland or duct 616.2
bile duct (*see also* Disease, biliary) 576.8
bladder (multiple) (trigone) 596.8
Blessig's 362.62
blood, endocardial (*see also* Endocarditis)
424.90
blue dome 610.0
bone (local) 733.20
aneurysmal 733.22
jaw 526.2
developmental (odontogenic) 526.0
fissural 526.1
latent 526.89
solitary 733.21
unicameral 733.21
brain 348.0
congenital 742.4
hydatid (*see also* Echinococcus) 122.9
third ventricle (colloid) 742.4
branchial (cleft) 744.42
branchiogenic 744.42
breast (benign) (blue dome) (pedunculated)
(solitary) (traumatic) 610.0
involution 610.4
sebaceous 610.8
broad ligament (benign) 620.8
embryonic 752.11
bronchogenic (mediastinal) (sequestration)
518.89
congenital 748.4
buccal 528.4
bulbourethral gland (Cowper's) 599.89
bursa, bursal 727.49
pharyngeal 478.26
calcifying odontogenic (M9301/0) 213.1
upper jaw (bone) 213.0
canal of Nuck (acquired) (serous) 629.1
congenital 752.41
canthus 372.75
carcinomatous (M8010/3)—*see* Neoplasm, by
site, malignant
cartilage (joint)—*see* Derangement, joint
cauda equina 336.8
cavum septi pellucidi NEC 348.0
celomic (pericardium) 746.89
cerebellopontine (angle)—*see* Cyst, brain
cerebellum—*see* Cyst, brain
cerebral—*see* Cyst, brain
cervical lateral 744.42
cervix 622.8
embryonal 752.41
nabothian (gland) 616.0
chamber, anterior (eye) 364.60
exudative 364.62
implantation (surgical) (traumatic) 364.61
parasitic 360.13
chiasmal, optic NEC (*see also* Lesion,
chiasmal) 377.54
chocolate (ovary) 617.1
choledochal (congenital) 751.69
acquired 576.8
choledochus 751.69
chorion 658.8
choroid plexus 348.0
chyle, mesentery 457.8
ciliary body 364.60
exudative 364.64
implantation 364.61
primary 364.63
clitoris 624.8

Cyst —*continued*
  coccyx (*see also* Cyst, bone) 733.20
  colloid
    third ventricle (brain) 742.4
    thyroid gland—*see* Goiter
  colon 569.89
  common (bile) duct (*see also* Disease, biliary) 576.8
  congenital NEC 759.89
    adrenal glands 759.1
    epiglottis 748.3
    esophagus 750.4
    fallopian tube 752.11
    kidney 753.10
      multiple 753.19
      single 753.11
    larynx 748.3
    liver 751.62
    lung 748.4
    mediastinum 748.8
    ovary 752.0
    oviduct 752.11
    pancreas 751.7
    periurethral (tissue) 753.8
    prepuce NEC 752.69
      penis 752.69
    sublingual 750.26
    submaxillary gland 750.26
    thymus (gland) 759.2
    tongue 750.19
    ureterovesical orifice 753.4
    vulva 752.41
  conjunctiva 372.75
  cornea 371.23
  corpora quadrigemina 348.0
  corpus
    albicans (ovary) 620.2
    luteum (ruptured) 620.1
  Cowper's gland (benign) (infected) 599.89
  cranial meninges 348.0
  craniobuccal pouch 253.8
  craniopharyngeal pouch 253.8
  cystic duct (*see also* Disease, gallbladder) 575.8
  Cysticercus (any site) 123.1
  Dandy-Walker 742.3
    with spina bifida (*see also* Spina bifida) 741.0
  dental 522.8
    developmental 526.0
    eruption 526.0
    lateral periodontal 526.0
    primordial (keratocyst) 526.0
    root 522.8
  dentigerous 526.0
    mandible 526.0
    maxilla 526.0
  dermoid (M9084/0)—*see also* Neoplasm, by site, benign
    with malignant transformation (M9084/3) 183.0
    implantation
      external area or site (skin) NEC 709.8
      iris 364.61
      skin 709.8
      vagina 623.8
      vulva 624.8
    mouth 528.4
    oral soft tissue 528.4
    sacrococcygeal 685.1
      with abscess 685.0
  developmental of ovary, ovarian 752.0

Cyst —*continued*
  dura (cerebral) 348.0
    spinal 349.2
  ear (external) 706.2
  echinococcal (*see also* Echinococcus) 122.9
  embryonal
    cervix uteri 752.41
    genitalia, female external 752.41
    uterus 752.3
    vagina 752.41
  endometrial 621.8
    ectopic 617.9
  endometrium (uterus) 621.8
    ectopic—*see* Endometriosis
  enteric 751.5
  enterogenous 751.5
  epidermal (inclusion) (*see also* Cyst, skin) 706.2
  epidermoid (inclusion) (*see also* Cyst, skin) 706.2
    mouth 528.4
    not of skin—*see* Cyst, by site
    oral soft tissue 528.4
  epididymis 608.89
  epiglottis 478.79
  epiphysis cerebri 259.8
  epithelial (inclusion) (*see also* Cyst, skin) 706.2
  epoophoron 752.11
  eruption 526.0
  esophagus 530.89
  ethmoid sinus 478.1
  eye (retention) 379.8
    congenital 743.03
    posterior segment, congenital 743.54
  eyebrow 706.2
  eyelid (sebaceous) 374.84
    infected 373.13
    sweat glands or ducts 374.84
  falciform ligament (inflammatory) 573.8
  fallopian tube 620.8
  female genital organs NEC 629.8
  fimbrial (congenital) 752.11
  fissural (oral region) 526.1
  follicle (atretic) (graafian) (ovarian) 620.0
    nabothian (gland) 616.0
  follicular (atretic) (ovarian) 620.0
    dentigerous 526.0
  frontal sinus 478.1
  gallbladder or duct 575.8
  ganglion 727.43
  Gartner's duct 752.11
  gas, of mesentery 568.89
  gingiva 523.8
  gland of moll 374.84
  globulomaxillary 526.1
  graafian follicle 620.0
  granulosal lutein 620.2
  hemangiomatous (M9121/0) (*see also* Hemangioma) 228.00
  hydatid (*see also* Echinococcus) 122.9
    fallopian tube (Morgagni) 752.11
    liver NEC 122.8
    lung NEC 122.9
    Morgagni 752.8
      fallopian tube 752.11
    specified site NEC 122.9
  hymen 623.8
    embryonal 752.41
  hypopharynx 478.26
  hypophysis, hypophyseal (duct) (recurrent) 253.8
    cerebri 253.8

Cyst —*continued*
  implantation (dermoid)
    anterior chamber (eye) 364.61
    external area or site (skin) NEC 709.8
    iris 364.61
    vagina 623.8
    vulva 624.8
  incisor, incisive canal 526.1
  inclusion (epidermal) (epithelial) (epidermoid)
    (mucous) (squamous) (*see also* Cyst, skin)
    706.2
    not of skin—*see* Neoplasm, by site, benign
  intestine (large) (small) 569.89
  intracranial—*see* Cyst, brain
  intraligamentous 728.89
    knee 717.89
  intrasellar 253.8
  iris (idiopathic) 364.60
    exudative 364.62
    implantation (surgical) (traumatic) 364.61
    miotic pupillary 364.55
    parasitic 360.13
  Iwanoff's 362.62
  jaw (bone) (aneurysmal) (extravasation)
    (hemorrhagic) (traumatic) 526.2
    developmental (odontogenic) 526.0
    fissural 526.1
  keratin 706.2
  kidney (congenital) 753.10
    acquired 593.2
    calyceal (*see also* Hydronephrosis) 591
    multiple 753.19
    pyelogenic (*see also* Hydronephrosis) 591
    simple 593.2
    single 753.11
    solitary (not congenital) 593.2
  labium (majus) (minus) 624.8
    sebaceous 624.8
  lacrimal
    apparatus 375.43
    gland or sac 375.12
  larynx 478.79
  lens 379.39
    congenital 743.39
  lip (gland) 528.5
  liver 573.8
    congenital 751.62
    hydatid (*see also* Echinococcus) 122.8
      granulosis 122.0
      multilocularis 122.5
  lung 518.89
    congenital 748.4
    giant bullous 492.0
  lutein 620.1
  lymphangiomatous (M9173/0) 228.1
  lymphoepithelial
    mouth 528.4
    oral soft tissue 528.4
  macula 362.54
  malignant (M8000/3)—*see* Neoplasm, by site,
    malignant
  mammary gland (sweat gland) (*see also* Cyst,
    breast) 610.0
  mandible 526.2
    dentigerous 526.0
    radicular 522.8
  maxilla 526.2
    dentigerous 526.0
    radicular 522.8
  median
    anterior maxillary 526.1
    palatal 526.1

Cyst —*continued*
  mediastinum (congenital) 748.8
  meibomian (gland) (retention) 373.2
    infected 373.12
  membrane, brain 348.0
  meninges (cerebral) 348.0
    spinal 349.2
  meniscus knee 717.5
  mesentery, mesenteric (gas) 568.89
    chyle 457.8
    gas 568.89
  mesonephric duct 752.8
  mesothelial
    peritoneum 568.89
    pleura (peritoneal) 568.89
  milk 611.5
  miotic pupillary (iris) 364.55
  Morgagni (hydatid) 752.8
    fallopian tube 752.11
  mouth 528.4
  mullerian duct 752.8
  multilocular (ovary) (M8000/1) 239.5
  myometrium 621.8
  nabothian (follicle) (ruptured) 616.0
  nasal sinus 478.1
  nasoalveolar 528.4
  nasolabial 528.4
  nasopalatine (duct) 526.1
    anterior 526.1
  nasopharynx 478.26
  neoplastic (M8000/1)—*see also* Neoplasm, by
    site, unspecified nature
    benign (M8000/0)—*see* Neoplasm, by site,
      benign
    uterus 621.8
  nervous system—*see* Cyst, brain
  neuroenteric 742.59
  neuroepithelial ventricle 348.0
  nipple 610.0
  nose 478.1
    skin of 706.2
  odontogenic, developmental 526.0
  omentum (lesser) 568.89
    congenital 751.8
  oral soft tissue (dermoid) (epidermoid)
    (lymphoepithelial) 528.4
  ora serrata 361.19
  orbit 376.81
  ovary, ovarian (twisted) 620.2
    adherent 620.2
    chocolate 617.1
    corpus
      albicans 620.2
      luteum 620.1
    dermoid (M9084/0) 220
    developmental 752.0
    due to failure of involution NEC 620.2
    endometrial 617.1
    follicular (atretic) (graafian) (hemorrhagic)
      620.0
    hemorrhagic 620.2
    in pregnancy or childbirth 654.4
      affecting fetus or newborn 763.8
      causing obstructed labor 660.2
        affecting fetus or newborn 763.1
    multilocular (M8000/1) 239.5
    pseudomucinous (M8470/0) 220
    retention 620.2
    serous 620.2
    theca lutein 620.2
    tuberculous (*see also* Tuberculosis) 016.6

Cyst —*continued*
  unspecified 620.2
  oviduct 620.8
  palatal papilla (jaw) 526.1
  palate 526.1
    fissural 526.1
    median (fissural) 526.1
  palatine, of papilla 526.1
  pancreas, pancreatic 577.2
    congenital 751.7
    false 577.2
    hemorrhagic 577.2
    true 577.2
  paranephric 593.2
  para ovarian 752.11
  paraphysis, cerebri 742.4
  parasitic NEC 136.9
  parathyroid (gland) 252.8
  paratubal (fallopian) 620.8
  paraurethral duct 599.89
  paroophoron 752.11
  parotid gland 527.6
    mucous extravasation or retention 527.6
  parovarian 752.11
  pars planus 364.60
    exudative 364.64
    primary 364.63
  pelvis, female
    in pregnancy or childbirth 654.4
      affecting fetus or newborn 763.8
      causing obstructed labor 660.2
        affecting fetus or newborn 763.1
  penis (sebaceous) 607.89
  periapical 522.8
  pericardial (congenital) 746.89
    acquired (secondary) 423.8
  pericoronal 526.0
  perineural (Tarlov's) 355.9
  periodontal 522.8
    lateral 526.0
  peripancreatic 577.2
  peripelvic (lymphatic) 593.2
  peritoneum 568.89
    chylous 457.8
  pharynx (wall) 478.26
  pilonidal (infected) (rectum) 685.1
    with abscess 685.0
    malignant (M9084/3) 173.5
  pituitary (duct) (gland) 253.8
  placenta (amniotic)—*see* Placenta, abnormal
  pleura 519.8
  popliteal 727.51
  porencephalic 742.4
    acquired 348.0
  postanal (infected) 685.1
    with abscess 685.0
  posterior segment of eye, congenital 743.54
  postmastoidectomy cavity 383.31
  preauricular 744.47
  prepuce 607.89
    congenital 752.69
  primordial (jaw) 526.0
  prostate 600
  pseudomucinous (ovary) (M8470/0) 220
  pudenda (sweat glands) 624.8
  pupillary, miotic 364.55
    sebaceous 624.8
  radicular (residual) 522.8
  radiculodental 522.8
  ranular 527.6
  Rathke's pouch 253.8

Cyst —*continued*
  rectum (epithelium) (mucous) 569.49
  renal—*see* Cyst, kidney
  residual (radicular) 522.8
  retention (ovary) 620.2
  retina 361.19
    macular 362.54
    parasitic 360.13
    primary 361.13
    secondary 361.14
  retroperitoneal 568.89
  sacrococcygeal (dermoid) 685.1
    with abscess 685.0
  salivary gland or duct 527.6
    mucous extravasation or retention 527.6
  Sampson's 617.1
  sclera 379.19
  scrotum (sebaceous) 706.2
    sweat glands 706.2
  sebaceous (duct) (gland) 706.2
    breast 610.8
    eyelid 374.84
    genital organ NEC
      female 629.8
      male 608.89
    scrotum 706.2
  semilunar cartilage (knee) (multiple) 717.5
  seminal vesicle 608.89
  serous (ovary) 620.2
  sinus (antral) (ethmoidal) (frontal) (maxillary)
    (nasal) (sphenoidal) 478.1
  Skene's gland 599.89
  skin (epidermal) (epidermoid, inclusion)
    (epithelial) (inclusion) (retention)
    (sebaceous) 706.2
    breast 610.8
    eyelid 374.84
    genital organ NEC
      female 629.8
      male 608.89
    neoplastic 216.3
    scrotum 706.2
    sweat gland or duct 705.89
  solitary
    bone 733.21
    kidney 593.2
  spermatic cord 608.89
  sphenoid sinus 478.1
  spinal meninges 349.2
  spine (*see also* Cyst, bone) 733.20
  spleen NEC 289.59
    congenital 759.0
    hydatid (*see also* Echinococcus) 122.9
  spring water (pericardium) 746.89
  subarachnoid 348.0
    intrasellar 793.0
  subdural (cerebral) 348.0
    spinal cord 349.2
  sublingual gland 527.6
    mucous extravasation or retention 527.6
  submaxillary gland 527.6
    mucous extravasation or retention 527.6
  suburethral 599.89
  suprarenal gland 255.8
  suprasellar—*see* Cyst, brain
  sweat gland or duct 705.89
  sympathetic nervous system 337.9
  synovial 727.40
    popliteal space 727.51
  Tarlov's 355.9
  tarsal 373.2

Cyst —*continued*
tendon (sheath) 727.42
testis 608.89
theca-lutein (ovary) 620.2
Thornwaldt's, Tornwaldt's 478.26
thymus (gland) 254.8
thyroglossal (duct) (infected) (persistent) 759.2
thyroid (gland) 246.2
  adenomatous—*see* Goiter, nodular
  colloid (*see also* Goiter) 240.9
thyrolingual duct (infected) (persistent) 759.2
tongue (mucous) 529.8
tonsil 474.8
tooth (dental root) 522.8
tubo-ovarian 620.8
  inflammatory 614.1
tunica vaginalis 608.89
turbinate (nose) (*see also* Cyst, bone) 733.20
Tyson's gland (benign) (infected) 607.89
umbilicus 759.89
urachus 753.7
ureter 593.89
ureterovesical orifice 593.89
  congenital 753.4
urethra 599.84
urethral gland (Cowper's) 599.89
uterine
  ligament 620.8
    embryonic 752.11
  tube 620.8
uterus (body) (corpus) (recurrent) 621.8
  embryonal 752.3
utricle (ear) 386.8
  prostatic 599.89
utriculus masculinus 599.89
vagina, vaginal (squamous cell) (wall) 623.8
  embryonal 752.41
  implantation 623.8
  inclusion 623.8
vallecula, vallecular 478.79
ventricle, neuroepithelial 348.0
verumontanum 599.89
vesical (orifice) 596.8
vitreous humor 379.29
vulva (sweat glands) 624.8
  congenital 752.41
  implantation 624.8
  inclusion 624.8
  sebaceous gland 624.8
vulvovaginal gland 624.8
wolffian 752.8
Cystadenocarcinoma (M8440/3)—*see also*
  Neoplasm, by site, malignant
bile duct type (M8161/3) 155.1
endometrioid (M8380/3)—*see* Neoplasm, by
  site, malignant
mucinous (M8470/3)
  papillary (M8471/3)
    specified site—*see* Neoplasm, by site,
      malignant
    unspecified site 183.0
  specified site—*see* Neoplasm, by site,
    malignant
  unspecified site 183.0
papillary (M8450/3)
  mucinous (M8471/3)
    specified site—*see* Neoplasm, by site,
      malignant
    unspecified site 183.0

Cystadenocarcinoma— *continued*
  pseudomucinous (M8471/3)
    specified site—*see* Neoplasm, by site,
      malignant
    unspecified site 183.0
  serous (M8460/3)
    specified site—*see* Neoplasm, by site,
      malignant
    unspecified site 183.0
  specified site—*see* Neoplasm, by site,
    malignant
  unspecified 183.0
pseudomucinous (M8470/3)
  papillary (M8471/3)
    specified site—*see* Neoplasm, by site,
      malignant
    unspecified site 183.0
  specified site—*see* Neoplasm, by site,
    malignant
  unspecified site 183.0
serous (M8441/3)
  papillary (M8460/3)
    specified site—*see* Neoplasm, by site,
      malignant
    unspecified site 183.0
  specified site—*see* Neoplasm, by site,
    malignant
  unspecified site 183.0
Cystadenofibroma (M9013/0)
clear cell (M8313/0)—*see* Neoplasm, by site,
  benign
endometrioid (M8381/0) 220
  borderline malignancy (M8381/1) 236.2
  malignant (M8381/3) 183.0
mucinous (M9015/0)
  specified site—*see* Neoplasm, by site, benign
  unspecified site 220
serous (M9014/0)
  specified site—*see* Neoplasm, by site, benign
  unspecified site 220
specified site—*see* Neoplasm, by site, benign
unspecified site 220
Cystadenoma (M8440/0)—*see also* Neoplasm,
  by site, benign
bile duct (M8161/0) 211.5
endometrioid (M8380/0)—*see also* Neoplasm,
  by site, benign
  borderline malignancy (M8380/1)—*see*
    Neoplasm, by site, uncertain behavior
  malignant (M8440/3)—*see* Neoplasm, by site,
    malignant
mucinous (M8470/0)
  borderline malignancy (M8470/1)
    specified site—*see* Neoplasm, uncertain
      behavior
    unspecified site 236.2
  papillary (M8471/0)
    borderline malignancy (M8471/1)
      specified site—*see* Neoplasm, by site,
        uncertain behavior
      unspecified site 236.2
    specified site—*see* Neoplasm, by site,
      benign
    unspecified site 220
  specified site—*see* Neoplasm, by site, benign
  unspecified site 220
papillary (M8450/0)
  borderline malignancy (M8450/1)
    specified site—*see* Neoplasm, by site,
      uncertain behavior
    unspecified site 236.2

Cystadenoma—*continued*
  lymphomatosum (M8561/0) 210.2
  mucinous (M8471/0)
    borderline malignancy (M8471/1)
      specified site—*see* Neoplasm, by site,
        uncertain behavior
      unspecified site 236.2
    specified site—*see* Neoplasm, by site,
      benign
    unspecified site 220
  pseudomucinous (M8471/0)
    borderline malignancy (M8471/1)
      specified site—*see* Neoplasm, by site,
        uncertain behavior
      unspecified site 236.2
    specified site—*see* Neoplasm, by site,
      benign
    unspecified site 220
  serous (M8460/0)
    borderline malignancy (M8460/1)
      specified site—*see* Neoplasm, by site,
        uncertain behavior
      unspecified site 236.2
    specified site—*see* Neoplasm, by site,
      benign
    unspecified site 220
  specified site—*see* Neoplasm, by site, benign
  unspecified site 220
  pseudomucinous (M8470/0)
    borderline malignancy (M8470/1)
      specified site—*see* Neoplasm, by site,
        uncertain behavior
      unspecified site 236.2
    papillary (M8471/0)
      borderline malignancy (M8471/1)
        specified site—*see* Neoplasm, by site,
          uncertain behavior
        unspecified site 236.2
      specified site—*see* Neoplasm, by site,
        benign
      unspecified site 220
    specified site—*see* Neoplasm, by site, benign
    unspecified site 220
  serous (M8441/0)
    borderline malignancy (M8441/1)
      specified site—*see* Neoplasm, by site,
        uncertain behavior
      unspecified site 236.2
    papillary (M8460/0)
      borderline malignancy (M8460/1)
        specified site—*see* Neoplasm, by site,
          uncertain behavior
        unspecified site 236.2
      specified site—*see* Neoplasm, by site,
        benign
      unspecified site 220
    specified site—*see* Neoplasm, by site, benign
    unspecified site 220
  thyroid 226
Cystathioninemia 270.4
Cystathioninuria 270.4
Cystic —*see also* condition
  breast, chronic 610.1
  corpora lutea 620.1
  degeneration, congenital
    brain 742.4
  kidney (*see also* Cystic, disease, kidney)
    753.10

Cystic—*continued*
  disease
    breast, chronic 610.1
    kidney, congenital 753.10
      medullary 753.16
      multiple 753.19
      polycystic—*see* Polycystic, kidney
      single 753.11
      specified NEC 753.19
    liver, congenital 751.62
    lung 518.89
      congenital 748.4
    pancreas, congenital 751.7
    semilunar cartilage 717.5
  duct—*see* condition
  eyeball, congenital 743.03
  fibrosis (pancreas) 277.00
  hygroma (M9173/0) 228.1
  kidney, congenital 753.10
    medullary 753.16
    multiple 753.19
    polycystic—*see* Polycystic, kidney
    single 753.11
    specified NEC 753.19
  liver, congenital 751.62
  lung 518.89
    congenital 748.4
  mass—*see* Cyst
  mastitis, chronic 610.1
  ovary 620.2
  pancreas, congenital 751.7
Cysticerciasis 123.1
Cysticercosis (mammary) (subretinal) 123.1
Cysticercus 123.1
  cellulosae infestation 123.1
Cystinosis (malignant) 270.0
Cystinuria 270.0
Cystitis (bacillary) (colli) (diffuse) (exudative)
    (hemorrhagic) (purulent) (recurrent) (septic)
    (suppurative) (ulcerative) 595.9
  with
    abortion—*see* Abortion, by type, with urinary
      tract infection
    ectopic pregnancy (*see also* categories
      633.0-633.9) 639.8
    fibrosis 595.1
    leukoplakia 595.1
    malakoplakia 595.1
    metaplasia 595.1
    molar pregnancy (*see also* categories
      630-632) 639.8
  actinomycotic 039.8 *[595.4]*
  acute 595.0
    of trigone 595.3
  allergic 595.89
  amebic 006.8 *[595.4]*
  bilharzial 120.9 *[595.4]*
  blennorrhagic (acute) 098.11
    chronic or duration of 2 months or more
      098.31
  bullous 595.89
  calculous 594.1
  chlamydial 099.53
  chronic 595.2
    interstitial 595.1
    of trigone 595.3
  complicating pregnancy, childbirth, or
    puerperium 646.6
    affecting fetus or newborn 760.1
  cystic(a) 595.81
  diphtheritic 032.84

Cystitis—*continued*
  echinococcal
    granulosus 122.3 *[595.4]*
    multilocularis 122.6 *[595.4]*
  emphysematous 595.89
  encysted 595.81
  follicular 595.3
  following
    abortion 639.8
    ectopic or molar pregnancy 639.8
  gangrenous 595.89
  glandularis 595.89
  gonococcal (acute) 098.11
    chronic or duration of 2 months or more
      098.31
  incrusted 595.89
  interstitial 595.1
  irradiation 595.82
  irritation 595.89
  malignant 595.89
  monilial 112.2
  of trigone 595.3
  panmural 595.1
  polyposa 595.89
  prostatic 601.3
  radiation 595.82
  Reiter's (abacterial) 099.3
  specified NEC 595.89
  subacute 595.2
  submucous 595.1
  syphilitic 095.8
  trichomoniasis 131.09
  tuberculous (*see also* Tuberculosis) 016.1
  ulcerative 595.1
Cystocele (-rectocele)
  female (without uterine prolapse) 618.0
    with uterine prolapse 618.4
      complete 618.3
      incomplete 618.2
  in pregnancy or childbirth 654.4
    affecting fetus or newborn 763.8
    causing obstructed labor 660.2
      affecting fetus or newborn 763.1
  male 596.8
Cystoid
  cicatrix limbus 372.64
  degeneration macula 362.53
Cystolithiasis 594.1
Cystoma (M8440/0)—*see also* Neoplasm, by
  site, benign
  endometrial, ovary 617.1
  mucinous (M8470/0)
    specified site—*see* Neoplasm, by site, benign
    unspecified site 220
  serous (M8441/0)
    specified site—*see* Neoplasm, by site, benign
    unspecified site 220
  simple (ovary) 620.2
Cystoplegia 596.53
Cystoptosis 596.8
Cystopyelitis (*see also* Pyelitis) 590.80
Cystorrhagia 596.8
Cystosarcoma phyllodes (M9020/1) 238.3
  benign (M9020/0) 217
  malignant (M9020/3)—*see* Neoplasm, breast,
    malignant
Cystostomy status V44.5
  with complication 997.5
Cystourethritis (*see also* Urethritis) 597.89

Cystourethrocele (*see also* Cystocele)
  female (without uterine prolapse) 618.0
    with uterine prolapse 618.4
      complete 618.3
      incomplete 618.2
  male 596.8
Cytomegalic inclusion disease 078.5
  congenital 771.1
Cytomycosis, reticuloendothelial (*see also*
  Histoplasmosis, American) 115.00
Czerny's disease (periodic hydrarthrosis of the
  knee) 719.06

D

Daae (-Finsen) disease (epidemic pleurodynia) 074.1
Dabney's grip 074.1
Da Costa's syndrome (neurocirculatory asthenia) 306.2
Dacryoadenitis, dacryadenitis 375.00
  acute 375.01
  chronic 375.02
Dacryocystitis 375.30
  acute 375.32
  chronic 375.42
  neonatal 771.6
  phlegmonous 375.33
  syphilitic 095.8
    congenital 090.0
  trachomatous, active 076.1
    late effect 139.1
  tuberculous (*see also* Tuberculosis) 017.3
Dacryocystoblennorrhea 375.42
Dacryocystocele 375.43
Dacryolith, dacryolithiasis 375.57
Dacryoma 375.43
Dacryopericystitis (acute) (subacute) 375.32
  chronic 375.42
Dacryops 375.11
Dacryosialadenopathy, atrophic 710.2
Dacryostenosis 375.56
  congenital 743.65
Dactylitis 686.9
  bone (*see also* Osteomyelitis) 730.2
  sickle-cell 282.61
  syphilitic 095.5
  tuberculous (*see also* Tuberculosis) 015.5
Dactylolysis spontanea 136.0
Dactylosymphysis (*see also* Syndactylism) 755.10
Damage
  arteriosclerotic—*see* Arteriosclerosis
  brain 348.9
    anoxic, hypoxic 348.1
      during or resulting from a procedure 997.01
    child NEC 343.9
    due to birth injury 767.0
    minimal (child) (*see also* Hyperkinesia) 314.9
    newborn 767.0
  cardiac—*see also* Disease, heart
  cardiorenal (vascular) (*see also* Hypertension, cardiorenal) 404.90
  central nervous system—*see* Damage, brain
  cerebral NEC—*see* Damage, brain
  coccyx, complicating delivery 665.6
  coronary (*see also* Ischemia, heart) 414.9
  eye, birth injury 767.8
  heart—*see also* Disease, heart
    valve—*see* Endocarditis
  hypothalamus NEC 348.9
  liver 571.9
    alcoholic 571.3
  myocardium (*see also* Degeneration, myocardial) 429.1
  pelvic
    joint or ligament, during delivery 665.6
    organ NEC
      with
        abortion—*see* Abortion, by type, with damage to pelvic organs
        ectopic pregnancy (*see also* categories 633.0-633.9) 639.2

Damage—*continued*
      molar pregnancy (*see also* categories 630-632) 639.2
      during delivery 665.5
      following
        abortion 639.2
        ectopic or molar pregnancy 639.2
  renal (*see also* Disease, renal) 593.9
  skin, solar 692.79
    acute 692.72
    chronic 692.74
  subendocardium, subendocardial (*see also* Degeneration, myocardial) 429.1
  vascular 459.9
Dameshek's syndrome (erythroblastic anemia) 282.4
Dana-Putnam syndrome (subacute combined sclerosis with pernicious anemia) 281.0 [336.2]
Danbolt (-Closs) syndrome (acrodermatitis enteropathica) 686.8
Dandruff 690.18
Dandy fever 061
Dandy-Walker deformity or syndrome (atresia, foramen of Magendie) 742.3
  with spina bifida (*see also* Spina bifida) 741.0
Dangle foot 736.79
Danielssen's disease (anesthetic leprosy) 030.1
Danlos' syndrome 756.83
Darier's disease (congenital) (keratosis follicularis) 757.39
  due to vitamin A deficiency 264.8
  meaning erythema annulare centrifugum 695.0
Darier-Roussy sarcoid 135
Darling's
  disease (*see also* Histoplasmosis, American) 115.00
  histoplasmosis (*see also* Histoplasmosis, American) 115.00
Dartre 054.9
Darwin's tubercle 744.29
Davidson's anemia (refractory) 284.9
Davies' disease 425.0
Davies-Colley syndrome (slipping rib) 733.99
Dawson's encephalitis 046.2
Day blindness (*see also* Blindness, day) 368.60
Dead
  fetus
    retained (in utero) 656.4
      early pregnancy (death before 22 completed weeks gestation) 632
      late (death after 22 completed weeks gestation) 656.4
    syndrome 641.3
  labyrinth 386.50
  ovum, retained 631
Deaf and dumb NEC 389.7
Deaf mutism (acquired) (congenital) NEC 389.7
  endemic 243
  hysterical 300.11
  syphilitic, congenital 090.0

DEF

Deafness (acquired) (bilateral) (both ears)
  (complete) (congenital) (hereditary) (middle
  ear) (partial) (unilateral) 389.9
  with blue sclera and fragility of bone 756.51
  auditory fatigue 389.9
  aviation 993.0
    nerve injury 951.5
  boilermakers' 951.5
  central 389.14
    with conductive hearing loss 389.2
  conductive (air) 389.00
    with sensorineural hearing loss 389.2
    combined types 389.08
    external ear 389.01
    inner ear 389.04
    middle ear 389.03
    multiple types 389.08
    tympanic membrane 389.02
  emotional (complete) 300.11
  functional (complete) 300.11
  high frequency 389.8
  hysterical (complete) 300.11
  injury 951.5
  low frequency 389.8
  mental 784.69
  mixed conductive and sensorineural 389.2
  nerve 389.12
    with conductive hearing loss 389.2
  neural 389.12
    with conductive hearing loss 389.2
  noise-induced 388.12
    nerve injury 951.5
  nonspeaking 389.7
  perceptive 389.10
    with conductive hearing loss 389.2
    central 389.14
    combined types 389.18
    multiple types 389.18
    neural 389.12
    sensory 389.11
  psychogenic (complete) 306.7
  sensorineural (*see also* Deafness, perceptive)
    389.10
  sensory 389.11
    with conductive hearing loss 389.2
  specified type NEC 389.8
  sudden NEC 388.2
  syphilitic 094.89
  transient ischemic 388.02
  transmission—*see* Deafness, conductive
  traumatic 951.5
  word (secondary to organic lesion) 784.69
    developmental 315.31
Death
  after delivery (cause not stated) (sudden) 674.9
  anesthetic
    due to
      correct substance properly administered
        995.4
      overdose or wrong substance given 968.4
        specified anesthetic—*see* Table of drugs
          and chemicals
    during delivery 668.9
  brain 348.8
  cardiac—*see* Disease, heart
  cause unknown 798.2
  cot (infant) 798.0
  crib (infant) 798.0

Death—*continued*
  fetus, fetal (cause not stated) (intrauterine) 779.9
    early, with retention (before 22 completed
      weeks gestation) 632
    from asphyxia or anoxia (before labor) 768.0
      during labor 768.1
    late, affecting management of pregnancy
      (after 22 completed weeks gestation) 656.4
  from pregnancy NEC 646.9
  instantaneous 798.1
  intrauterine (*see also* Death, fetus) 779.9
    complicating pregnancy 656.4
  maternal, affecting fetus or newborn 761.6
  neonatal NEC 779.9
  sudden (cause unknown) 798.1
    during delivery 669.9
      under anesthesia NEC 668.9
    infant, syndrome (SIDS) 798.0
    puerperal, during puerperium 674.9
  unattended (cause unknown) 798.9
  under anesthesia NEC
    due to
      correct substance properly administered
        995.4
      overdose or wrong substance given 968.4
        specified anesthetic—*see* Table of drugs
          and chemicals
    during delivery 668.9
  violent 798.1
de Beurmann-Gougerot disease (sporotrichosis)
  117.1
Debility (general) (infantile) (postinfectional)
  799.3
  with nutritional difficulty 269.9
  congenital or neonatal NEC 779.9
  nervous 300.5
  old age 797
  senile 797
Débove's disease (splenomegaly) 789.2
Decalcification
  bone (*see also* Osteoporosis) 733.00
  teeth 521.8
Decapitation 874.9
  fetal (to facilitate delivery) 763.8
Decapsulation, kidney 593.89
Decay
  dental 521.0
  senile 797
  tooth, teeth 521.0
Decensus, uterus —*see* Prolapse, uterus
Deciduitis (acute)
  with
    abortion—*see* Abortion, by type, with sepsis
    ectopic pregnancy (*see also* categories
      633.0-633.9) 639.0
    molar pregnancy (*see also* categories
      630-632) 639.0
  affecting fetus or newborn 760.8
  following
    abortion 639.0
    ectopic or molar pregnancy 639.0
  in pregnancy 646.6
  puerperal, postpartum 670
Deciduoma malignum (M9100/3) 181
Deciduous tooth (retained) 520.6
Decline (general) (*see also* Debility) 799.3

Decompensation
cardiac (acute) (chronic) (*see also* Disease,
    heart) 429.9
  failure—*see* Failure, heart, congestive
cardiorenal (*see also* Hypertension, cardiorenal)
    404.90
cardiovascular (*see also* Disease,
    cardiovascular) 429.2
heart (*see also* Disease, heart) 429.9
  failure—*see* Failure, heart, congestive
hepatic 572.2
myocardial (acute) (chronic) (*see also* Disease,
    heart) 429.9
  failure—*see* Failure, heart, congestive
respiratory 519.9
Decompression sickness 993.3
Decrease, decreased
blood
  platelets (*see also* Thrombocytopenia) 287.5
  pressure 796.3
    due to shock following
      injury 958.4
      operation 998.0
cardiac reserve—*see* Disease, heart
estrogen 256.3
  postablative 256.2
fragility of erythrocytes 289.8
function
  adrenal (cortex) 255.4
    medulla 255.5
  ovary in hypopituitarism 253.4
  parenchyma of pancreas 577.8
  pituitary (gland) (lobe) (anterior) 253.2
    posterior (lobe) 253.8
functional activity 780.9
glucose 790.2
haptoglobin (serum) NEC 273.8
platelets (*see also* Thrombocytopenia) 287.5
pulse pressure 785.9
respiration due to shock following injury 958.4
tear secretion NEC 375.15
tolerance
  fat 579.8
  glucose 790.2
  salt and water 276.9
vision NEC 369.9
Decubital gangrene 707.0 *[785.4]*
Decubiti (*see also* Decubitus) 707.0
Decubitus (ulcer) 707.0
  with gangrene 707.0 *[785.4]*
Deepening acetabulum 718.85
Defect, defective 759.9
3-beta-hydroxysteroid dehydrogenase 255.2
11-hydroxylase 255.2
21-hydroxylase 255.2
abdominal wall, congenital 756.7
aorticopulmonary septum 745.0
aortic septal 745.0
atrial septal (ostium secundum type) 745.5
  acquired 429.71
  ostium primum type 745.61
atrioventricular
  canal 745.69
  septum 745.4
    acquired 429.71
atrium secundum 745.5
  acquired 429.71
auricular septal 745.5
  acquired 429.71

Defect, defective—*continued*
bilirubin excretion 277.4
biosynthesis, testicular androgen 257.2
bulbar septum 745.0
butanol-insoluble iodide 246.1
chromosome—*see* Anomaly, chromosome
circulation (acquired) 459.9
  congenital 747.9
  newborn 747.9
clotting NEC (*see also* Defect, coagulation)
  286.9
coagulation (factor) (*see also* Deficiency,
  coagulation factor) 286.9
  with
    abortion—*see* Abortion, by type, with
      hemorrhage
    ectopic pregnancy (*see also* categories
      634-638) 639.1
    molar pregnancy (*see also* categories
      630-632) 639.1
  acquired (any) 286.7
  antepartum or intrapartum 641.3
    affecting fetus or newborn 762.1
  causing hemorrhage of pregnancy or delivery
    641.3
  due to
    liver disease 286.7
    vitamin K deficiency 286.7
  newborn, transient 776.3
  postpartum 666.3
  specified type NEC 286.3
conduction (heart) 426.9
  bone (*see also* Deafness, conductive) 389.00
congenital, organ or site NEC—*see also*
  Anomaly
  circulation 747.9
  Descemet's membrane 743.9
    specified type NEC 743.49
  diaphragm 756.6
  ectodermal 757.9
  esophagus 750.9
  pulmonic cusps—*see* Anomaly, heart valve
  respiratory system 748.9
    specified type NEC 748.8
cushion endocardial 745.60
dentin (hereditary) 520.5
Descemet's membrane (congenital) 743.9
  acquired 371.30
  specific type NEC 743.49
deutan 368.52
developmental—*see also* Anomaly, by site
  cauda equina 742.59
  left ventricle 746.9
    with atresia or hypoplasia of aortic orifice or
      valve, with hypoplasia of ascending
      aorta 746.7
    in hypoplastic left heart syndrome 746.7
  testis 752.9
  vessel 747.9
diaphragm
  with elevation, eventration, or hernia—*see*
    Hernia, diaphragm
  congenital 756.6
    with elevation, eventration, or hernia 756.6
    gross (with elevation, eventration, or hernia)
      756.6
ectodermal, congenital 757.9
Eisenmenger's (ventricular septal defect) 745.4
endocardial cushion 745.60
  specified type NEC 745.69

Defect, defective—*continued*
  esophagus, congenital 750.9
  extensor retinaculum 728.9
  fibrin polymerization (*see also* Defect,
      coagulation) 286.3
  filling
    biliary tract 793.3
    bladder 793.5
    gallbladder 793.3
    kidney 793.5
    stomach 793.4
    ureter 793.5
  fossa ovalis 745.5
  gene, carrier (suspected) of V19.8
  Gerbode 745.4
  glaucomatous, without elevated tension 365.89
  Hageman (factor) (*see also* Defect, coagulation)
      286.3
  hearing (*see also* Deafness) 389.9
  high grade 317
  homogentisic acid 270.2
  interatrial septal 745.5
    acquired 429.71
  interauricular septal 745.5
    acquired 429.71
  interventricular septal 745.4
    with pulmonary stenosis or atresia,
        dextroposition of aorta, and hypertrophy
        of right ventricle 745.2
    acquired 429.71
    in tetralogy of Fallot 745.2
  iodide trapping 246.1
  iodotyrosine dehalogenase 246.1
  kynureninase 270.2
  learning, specific 315.2
  mental (*see also* Retardation, mental) 319
  osteochondral NEC 738.8
  ostium
    primum 745.61
    secundum 745.5
  pericardium 746.89
  peroxidase-binding 246.1
  placental blood supply—*see* Placenta,
      insufficiency
  platelet (qualitative) 287.1
    constitutional 286.4
  postural, spine 737.9
  protan 368.51
  pulmonic cusps, congenital 746.00
  renal pelvis 753.9
    obstructive 753.29
    specified type NEC 753.3
  respiratory system, congenital 748.9
    specified type NEC 748.8
  retina, retinal 361.30
    with detachment (*see also* Detachment, retina,
        with retinal defect) 361.00
    multiple 361.33
      with detachment 361.02
    nerve fiber bundle 362.85
    single 361.30
      with detachment 361.01
  septal (closure) (heart) NEC 745.9
    acquired 429.71
    atrial 745.5
    specified type NEC 745.8
  speech NEC 784.5
    developmental 315.39
    secondary to organic lesion 784.5
  Taussig-Bing (transposition, aorta and
      overriding pulmonary artery) 745.11

Defect, defective—*continued*
  teeth, wedge 521.2
  thyroid hormone synthesis 246.1
  tritan 368.53
  ureter 753.9
    obstructive 753.29
  vascular (acquired) (local) 459.9
    congenital (peripheral) NEC 747.60
      gastrointestinal 747.61
      lower limb 747.64
      renal 747.62
      specified NEC 747.69
      spinal 747.82
      upper limb 747.63
  ventricular septal 745.4
    with pulmonary stenosis or atresia,
        dextraposition of aorta, and hypertrophy
        of right ventricle 745.2
    acquired 429.71
    atrioventricular canal type 745.69
    between infundibulum and anterior portion
        745.4
    in tetralogy of Fallot 745.2
    isolated anterior 745.4
  vision NEC 369.9
  visual field 368.40
    arcuate 368.43
    heteronymous, bilateral 368.47
    homonymous, bilateral 368.46
    localized NEC 368.44
    nasal step 368.44
    peripheral 368.44
    sector 368.43
  voice 784.40
  wedge, teeth (abrasion) 521.2
Defeminization syndrome 255.2
Deferentitis 608.4
  gonorrheal (acute) 098.14
    chronic or duration of 2 months or over 098.34
Defibrination syndrome (*see also* Fibrinolysis)
      286.6
Deficiency, deficient
  3-beta-hydroxysteroid dehydrogenase 255.2
  6-phosphogluconic dehydrogenase (anemia)
      282.2
  11-beta-hydroxylase 255.2
  17-alpha-hydroxylase 255.2
  18-hydroxysteroid dehydrogenase 255.2
  20-alpha-hydroxylase 255.2
  21-hydroxylase 255.2
  abdominal muscle syndrome 756.7
  accelerator globulin (Ac G) (blood) (*see also*
      Defect, coagulation) 286.3
  AC globulin (congenital) (*see also* Defect,
      coagulation) 286.3
    acquired 286.7
  activating factor (blood) (*see also* Defect,
      coagulation) 286.3
  adenohypophyseal 253.2
  adenosine deaminase 277.2
  aldolase (hereditary) 271.2
  alpha-1-antitrypsin 277.6
  alpha-1-trypsin inhibitor 277.6
  alpha-fucosidase 271.8
  alpha-lipoprotein 272.5
  alpha-mannosidase 271.8
  amino acid 270.9
  anemia—*see* Anemia, deficiency
  aneurin 265.1
    with beriberi 265.0

Deficiency, deficient—*continued*
antibody NEC 279.00
antidiuretic hormone 253.5
antihemophilic
  factor (A) 286.0
    B 286.1
    C 286.2
  globulin (AHG) NEC 286.0
antitrypsin 277.6
argininosuccinate synthetase or lyase 270.6
ascorbic acid (with scurvy) 267
autoprothrombin
  I (*see also* Defect, coagulation) 286.3
  II 286.1
  C (*see also* Defect, coagulation) 286.3
bile salt 579.8
biotin 266.2
biotindtdase 277.6
bradykinase-1 277.6
brancher enzyme (amylopectinosis) 271.0
calciferol 268.9
  with
    osteomalacia 268.2
    rickets (*see also* Rickets) 268.0
calcium 275.4
  dietary 269.3
calorie, severe 261
carbamyl phosphate synthetase 270.6
cardiac (*see also* Insufficiency, myocardial)
  428.0
carnitine palmityl transferase 791.3
carotene 264.9
Carr factor (*see also* Defect, coagulation) 286.9
central nervous system 349.9
ceruloplasmin 275.1
cevitamic acid (with scurvy) 267
choline 266.2
Christmas factor 286.1
chromium 269.3
citrin 269.1
clotting (blood) (*see also* Defect, coagulation)
  286.9
coagulation factor NEC 286.9
  with
    abortion—*see* Abortion, by type, with
      hemorrhage
    ectopic pregnancy (*see also* categories
      634-638) 639.1
    molar pregnancy (*see also* categories
      630-632) 639.1
  acquired (any) 286.7
  antepartum or intrapartum 641.3
    affecting fetus or newborn 762.1
  due to
    liver disease 286.7
    vitamin K deficiency 286.7
  newborn, transient 776.3
  postpartum 666.3
  specified type NEC 286.3
color vision (congenital) 368.59
  acquired 368.55
combined, two or more coagulation factors (*see
  also* Defect, coagulation) 286.9
complement factor NEC 279.8
contact factor (*see also* Defect, coagulation)
  286.3
copper NEC 275.1
corticoadrenal 255.4
craniofacial axis 756.0
cyanocobalamin (vitamin B₁₂) 266.2

Deficiency, deficient—*continued*
debrancher enzyme (limit dextrinosis) 271.0
desmolase 255.2
diet 269.9
dihydrofolate reductase 281.2
dihydropteridine reductase 270.1
disaccharidase (intestinal) 271.3
disease NEC 269.9
ear(s) V48.8
edema 262
endocrine 259.9
enzymes, circulating NEC (*see also* Deficiency,
  by specific enzyme) 277.6
ergosterol 268.9
  with
    osteomalacia 268.2
    rickets (*see also* Rickets) 268.0
erythrocytic glutathione (anemia) 282.2
eyelid(s) V48.8
factor (*see also* Defect, coagulation) 286.9
  I (congenital) (fibrinogen) 286.3
    antepartum or intrapartum 641.3
      affecting fetus or newborn 762.1
    newborn, transient 776.3
    postpartum 666.3
  II (congenital) (prothrombin) 286.3
  V (congenital) (labile) 286.3
  VII (congenital) (stable) 286.3
  VIII (congenital) (functional) 286.0
    with
      functional defect 286.0
      vascular defect 286.4
  IX (Christmas) (congenital) (functional) 286.1
  X (congenital) (Stuart-Prower) 286.3
  XI (congenital) (plasma thromboplastin
    antecedent) 286.2
  XII (congenital) (Hageman) 286.3
  XIII (congenital) (fibrin stabilizing) 286.3
  Hageman 286.3
  multiple (congenital) 286.9
    acquired 286.7
fibrinase (*see also* Defect, coagulation) 286.3
fibrinogen (congenital) (*see also* Defect,
  coagulation) 286.3
  acquired 286.6
fibrin stabilizing factor (congenital) (*see also*
  Defect, coagulation) 286.3
  acquired 286.7
finger—*see* Absence, finger
Fletcher factor (*see also* Defect, coagulation)
  286.9
fluorine 269.3
folate, anemia 281.2
folic acid (vitamin Bc) 266.2
  anemia 281.2
follicle-stimulating hormone (FSH) 253.4
fructokinase 271.2
fructose-1, 6-diphosphate 271.2
fructose-1-phosphate aldolase 271.2
FSH (follicle-stimulating hormone) 253.4
fucosidase 271.8
galactokinase 271.1
galactose-1-phosphate uridyl transferase 271.1
gamma globulin in blood 279.00
glass factor (*see also* Defect, coagulation) 286.3
glucocorticoid 255.4
glucose-6-phosphatase 271.0
glucose-6-phosphate dehydrogenase anemia
  282.2
glucuronyl transferase 277.4
glutathione-reductase (anemia) 282.2

Deficiency, deficient—*continued*
glycogen synthetase 271.0
growth hormone 253.3
Hageman factor (congenital) (*see also* Defect,
    coagulation) 286.3
head V48.0
hemoglobin (*see also* Anemia) 285.9
hepatophosphorylase 271.0
hexose monophosphate (HMP) shunt 282.2
HGH (human growth hormone) 253.3
HG-PRT 277.2
homogentisic acid oxidase 270.2
hormone—*see also* Deficiency, by specific
    hormone
    anterior pituitary (isolated) (partial) NEC
        253.4
        growth (human) 253.3
    follicle-stimulating 253.4
    growth (human) (isolated) 253.3
    human growth 253.3
    interstitial cell-stimulating 253.4
    luteinizing 253.4
    melanocyte-stimulating 253.4
    testicular 257.2
human growth hormone 253.3
humoral 279.00
    with
        hyper-IgM 279.05
            autosomal recessive 279.05
            X-linked 279.05
        increased IgM 279.05
    congenital hypogammaglobulinemia 279.04
    non-sex-linked 279.06
    selective immunoglobulin NEC 279.03
        IgA 279.01
        IgG 279.03
        IgM 279.02
            increased 279.05
    specified NEC 279.09
hydroxylase 255.2
hypoxanthine-guanine
    phosphoribosyltransferase (HG-PRT) 277.2
ICSH (interstitial cell-stimulating hormone)
    253.4
immunity NEC 279.3
    cell-mediated 279.10
        with
            hyperimmunoglobulinemia 279.2
            thrombocytopenia and eczema 279.12
        specified NEC 279.19
    combined (severe) 279.2
        syndrome 279.2
    common variable 279.06
    humoral NEC 279.00
    IgA (secretory) 279.01
    IgG 279.03
    IgM 279.02
immunoglobulin, selective NEC 279.03
    IgA 279.01
    IgG 279.03
    IgM 279.02
inositol (B complex) 266.2
interferon 279.4
internal organ V47.0
interstitial cell-stimulating hormone (ICSH)
    253.4
intrinsic (urethral) sphincter (ISD) 599.82
intrinsic factor (Castle's) (congenital) 281.0
invertase 271.3
iodine 269.3
iron, anemia 280.9

Deficiency, deficient—*continued*
labile factor (congenital) (*see also* Defect,
    coagulation) 286.3
    acquired 286.7
lacrimal fluid (acquired) 375.15
    congenital 743.64
lactase 271.3
Laki-Lorand factor (*see also* Defect,
    coagulation) 286.3
lecithin-cholesterol acyltranferase 272.5
LH (luteinizing hormone) 253.4
limb V49.0
    lower V49.0
        congenital (*see also* Deficiency, lower limb,
            congenital) 755.30
    upper V49.0
        congenital (*see also* Deficiency, upper limb,
            congenital) 755.20
lipocaic 577.8
lipoid (high-density) 272.5
lipoprotein (familial) (high density) 272.5
liver phosphorylase 271.0
lower limb V49.0
    congenital 755.30
        with complete absence of distal elements
            755.31
        longitudinal (complete) (partial) (with distal
            deficiencies, incomplete) 755.32
            with complete absence of distal elements
                755.31
            combined femoral, tibial, fibular
                (incomplete) 755.33
            femoral 755.34
            fibular 755.37
            metatarsal(s) 755.38
            phalange(s) 755.39
                meaning all digits 755.31
            tarsal(s) 755.38
            tibia 755.36
            tibiofibular 755.35
            transverse 755.31
luteinizing hormone (LH) 253.4
lysosomal alpha-1, 4 glucosidase 271.0
magnesium 275.2
mannosidase 271.8
melanocyte-stimulating hormone (MSH) 253.4
menadione (vitamin K) 269.0
    newborn 776.0
mental (familial) (hereditary) (*see also*
    Retardation, mental) 319
mineral NEC 269.3
molybdenum 269.3
moral 301.7
multiple, syndrome 260
myocardial (*see also* Insufficiency myocardial)
    428.0
myophosphorylase 271.0
NADH (DPNH) -methemoglobin-reductase
    (congenital) 289.7
NADH diaphorase or reductase (congenital)
    289.7
neck V48.1
niacin (amide) (-tryptophan) 265.2
nicotinamide 265.2
nicotinic acid (amide) 265.2
nose V48.8
number of teeth (*see also* Anodontia) 520.0
nutrition, nutritional 269.9
    specified NEC 269.8

Deficiency, deficient—*continued*
ornithine transcarbamylase 270.6
ovarian 256.3
oxygen (*see also* Anoxia) 799.0
pantothenic acid 266.2
parathyroid (gland) 252.1
phenylalanine hydroxylase 270.1
phosphofructokinase 271.2
phosphoglucomutase 271.0
phosphohexosisomerase 271.0
phosphorylase kinase, liver 271.0
pituitary (anterior) 253.2
  posterior 253.5
placenta—*see* Placenta, insufficiency
plasma
  cell 279.00
  protein (paraproteinemia) (pyroglobulinemia)
    273.8
    gamma globulin 279.00
  thromboplastin
    antecedent (PTA) 286.2
    component (PTC) 286.1
platelet NEC 287.1
  constitutional 286.4
polyglandular 258.9
potassium (K) 276.8
proaccelerin (congenital) (*see also* Defect,
  congenital) 286.3
  acquired 286.7
proconvertin factor (congenital) (*see also*
  Defect, coagulation) 286.3
  acquired 286.7
prolactin 253.4
protein 260
  anemia 281.4
  plasma—*see* Deficiency, plasma, protein
prothrombin (congenital) (*see also* Defect,
  coagulation) 286.3
  acquired 286.7
Prower factor (*see also* Defect, coagulation)
  286.3
PRT 277.2
pseudocholinesterase 289.8
psychobiological 301.6
PTA 286.2
PTC 286.1
purine nucleoside phosphorylase 277.2
pyracin (alpha) (beta) 266.1
pyridoxal 266.1
pyridoxamine 266.1
pyridoxine (derivatives) 266.1
pyruvate kinase (PK) 282.3
riboflavin (vitamin B_2) 266.0
saccadic eye movements 379.57
salivation 527.7
salt 276.1
secretion
  ovary 256.3
  salivary gland (any) 527.7
  urine 788.5
selenium 269.3
serum
  antitrypsin, familial 277.6
  protein (congenital) 273.8
smooth pursuit movements (eye) 379.58
sodium (Na) 276.1
SPCA (*see also* Defect, coagulation) 286.3
specified NEC 269.8
stable factor (congenital) (*see also* Defect,
  coagulation) 286.3
acquired 286.7

Deficiency, deficient—*continued*
Stuart (-Prower) factor (*see also* Defect,
  coagulation) 286.3
sucrase 271.3
sucrase-isomaltase 271.3
sulfite oxidase 270.0
syndrome, multiple 260
thiamine, thiaminic (chloride) 265.1
thrombokinase (*see also* Defect, coagulation)
  286.3
  newborn 776.0
thrombopoieten 287.3
thymolymphatic 279.2
thyroid (gland) 244.9
tocopherol 269.1
toe—*see* Absence, toe
tooth bud (*see also* Anodontia) 520.0
trunk V48
UDPG-glycogen transferase 271.0
upper limb V49.0
  congenital 755.20
    with complete absence of distal elements
      755.21
    longitudinal (complete) (partial) (with distal
      deficiencies, incomplete) 755.22
      carpal(s) 755.28
      combined humeral, radial, ulnar
        (incomplete) 755.23
      humeral 755.24
      metacarpal(s) 755.28
      phalange(s) 755.29
        meaning all digits 755.21
      radial 755.26
      radioulnar 755.25
      ulnar 755.27
    transverse (complete) (partial) 755.21
vascular 459.9
vasopressin 253.5
viosterol (*see also* Deficiency, calciferol) 268.9
vitamin (multiple) NEC 269.2
  A 264.9
    with
      Bitôt's spot 264.1
        corneal 264.2
          with corneal ulceration 264.3
      keratomalacia 264.4
      keratosis, follicular 264.8
      night blindness 264.5
      scar of cornea, xerophthalmic 264.6
      specified manifestation NEC 264.8
        ocular 264.7
      xeroderma 264.8
      xerophthalmia 264.7
      xerosis
        conjunctival 264.0
          with Bitôt's spot 264.1
        corneal 264.2
          with corneal ulceration 264.3
  B (complex) NEC 266.9
    with
      beriberi 265.0
      pellagra 265.2
    specified type NEC 266.2
  B_1 NEC 265.1
    beriberi 265.0
  B_2 266.0
  B_6 266.1
  B_{12} 266.2
  B_c (folic acid) 266.2

Deficiency, deficient—*continued*
C (ascorbic acid) (with scurvy) 267
D (calciferol) (ergosterol) 268.9
with
osteomalacia 268.2
rickets (*see also* Rickets) 268.0
E 269.1
folic acid 266.2
G 266.0
H 266.2
K 269.0
of newborn 776.0
nicotinic acid 265.2
P 269.1
PP 265.2
specified NEC 269.1
zinc 269.3
Deficient —*see also* Deficiency
blink reflex 374.45
craniofacial axis 756.0
number of teeth (*see also* Anodontia) 520.0
secretion of urine 788.5
Deficit
neurologic NEC 781.9
due to
cerebrovascular lesion (*see also* Disease,
cerebrovascular, acute) 436
late effect—*see* category 438
transient ischemic attack 435.9
oxygen 799.0
Deflection
radius 736.09
septum (acquired) (nasal) (nose) 470
spine—*see* Curvature, spine
turbinate (nose) 470
Defluvium
capillorum (*see also* Alopecia) 704.00
ciliorum 374.55
unguium 703.8
Deformity 759.9
abdomen, congenital 759.9
abdominal wall
acquired 738.8
congenital 756.7
muscle deficiency syndrome 756.7
acquired (unspecified site) 738.9
specified site NEC 738.8
adrenal gland (congenital) 759.1
alimentary tract, congenital 751.9
lower 751.5
specified type NEC 751.8
upper (any part, except tongue) 750.9
specified type NEC 750.8
tongue 750.10
specified type NEC 750.19
ankle (joint) (acquired) 736.70
abduction 718.47
congenital 755.69
contraction 718.47
anus (congenital) 751.5
acquired 569.49
aorta (congenital) 747.20
acquired 447.8
arch 747.21
acquired 447.8
coarctation 747.10

Deformity—*continued*
aortic
arch 747.21
acquired 447.8
cusp or valve (congenital) 746.9
acquired (*see also* Endocarditis, aortic) 424.1
ring 747.21
appendix 751.5
arm (acquired) 736.89
congenital 755.50
arteriovenous (congenital) (peripheral) NEC
747.60
gastrointestinal 747.61
lower limb 747.64
renal 747.62
specified NEC 747.69
spinal 747.82
upper limb 747.63
artery (congenital) (peripheral) NEC (*see also*
Deformity, vascular) 747.60
acquired 447.8
cerebral 747.81
coronary (congenital) 746.85
acquired (*see also* Ischemia, heart) 414.9
retinal 743.9
umbilical 747.5
atrial septal (congenital) (heart) 745.5
auditory canal (congenital) (external) (*see also*
Deformity, ear) 744.3
acquired 380.50
auricle
ear (congenital) (*see also* Deformity, ear)
744.3
acquired 380.32
heart (congenital) 746.9
back (acquired)—*see* Deformity, spine
Bartholin's duct (congenital) 750.9
bile duct (congenital) 751.60
acquired 576.8
with calculus, choledocholithiasis, or
stones—*see* Choledocholithiasis
biliary duct or passage (congenital) 751.60
acquired 576.8
with calculus, choledocholithiasis, or
stones—*see* Choledocholithiasis
bladder (neck) (sphincter) (trigone) (acquired)
596.8
congenital 753.9
bone (acquired) NEC 738.9
congenital 756.9
turbinate 738.0
boutonniere (finger) 736.21
brain (congenital) 742.9
acquired 348.8
multiple 742.4
reduction 742.2
vessel (congenital) 747.81
breast (acquired) 611.8
congenital 757.9
bronchus (congenital) 748.3
acquired 519.1
bursa, congenital 756.9
canal of Nuck 752.9
canthus (congenital) 743.9
acquired 374.89
capillary (acquired) 448.9
congenital NEC (*see also* Deformity,
vascular) 747.60
cardiac—*see* Deformity, heart
cardiovascular system (congenital) 746.9

Deformity—*continued*

caruncle, lacrimal (congenital) 743.9
  acquired 375.69
cascade, stomach 537.6
cecum (congenital) 751.5
  acquired 569.89
cerebral (congenital) 742.9
  acquired 348.8
cervix (acquired) (uterus) 622.8
  congenital 752.40
cheek (acquired) 738.19
  congenital 744.9
chest (wall) (acquired) 738.3
  congenital 754.89
  late effect of rickets 268.1
chin (acquired) 738.19
  congenital 744.9
choroid (congenital) 743.9
  acquired 363.8
  plexus (congenital) 742.9
    acquired 349.2
cicatricial—*see* Cicatrix
cilia (congenital) 743.9
  acquired 374.89
circulatory system (congenital) 747.9
clavicle (acquired) 738.8
  congenital 755.51
clitoris (congenital) 752.40
  acquired 624.8
clubfoot—*see* Clubfoot
coccyx (acquired) 738.6
  congenital 756.10
colon (congenital) 751.5
  acquired 569.89
concha (ear) (congenital) (*see also* Deformity,
  ear) 744.3
  acquired 380.32
congenital, organ or site not listed (*see also*
  Anomaly) 759.9
cornea (congenital) 743.9
  acquired 371.70
coronary artery (congenital) 746.85
  acquired (*see also* Ischemia, heart) 414.9
cranium (acquired) 738.19
  congenital (*see also* Deformity, skull,
    congenital) 756.0
cricoid cartilage (congenital) 748.3
  acquired 478.79
cystic duct (congenital) 751.60
  acquired 575.8
Dandy-Walker 742.3
  with spina bifida (*see also* Spina bifida) 741.0
diaphragm (congenital) 756.6
  acquired 738.8
digestive organ(s) or system (congenital) NEC
  751.9
  specified type NEC 751.8
ductus arteriosus 747.0
duodenal bulb 537.89
duodenum (congenital) 751.5
  acquired 537.89
dura (congenital) 742.9
  brain 742.4
    acquired 349.2
  spinal 742.59
    acquired 349.2

Deformity—*continued*

ear (congenital) 744.3
  acquired 380.32
  auricle 744.3
    causing impairment of hearing 744.02
  causing impairment of hearing 744.00
  external 744.3
    causing impairment of hearing 744.02
  internal 744.05
  lobule 744.3
  middle 744.03
    ossicles 744.04
  ossicles 744.04
ectodermal (congenital) NEC 757.9
  specified type NEC 757.8
ejaculatory duct (congenital) 752.9
  acquired 608.89
elbow (joint) (acquired) 736.00
  congenital 755.50
  contraction 718.42
endocrine gland NEC 759.2
epididymis (congenital) 752.9
  acquired 608.89
  torsion 608.2
epiglottis (congenital) 748.3
  acquired 478.79
esophagus (congenital) 750.9
  acquired 530.89
Eustachian tube (congenital) NEC 744.3
  specified type NEC 744.24
extremity (acquired) 736.9
  congenital, except reduction deformity 755.9
    lower 755.60
    upper 755.50
  reduction—*see* Deformity, reduction
eye (congenital) 743.9
  acquired 379.8
  muscle 743.9
eyebrow (congenital) 744.89
eyelid (congenital) 743.9
  acquired 374.89
  specified type NEC 743.62
face (acquired) 738.19
  congenital (any part) 744.9
    due to intrauterine malposition and pressure
      754.0
fallopian tube (congenital) 752.10
  acquired 620.8
femur (acquired) 736.89
  congenital 755.60
fetal
  with fetopelvic disproportion 653.7
    affecting fetus or newborn 763.1
  causing obstructed labor 660.1
    affecting fetus or newborn 763.1
  known or suspected, affecting management of
    pregnancy 655.9
finger (acquired) 736.20
  boutonniere type 736.21
  congenital 755.50
  flexion contracture 718.44
  swan neck 736.22
flexion (joint) (acquired) 736.9
  congenital NEC 755.9
  hip or thigh (acquired) 736.39
    congenital (*see also* Subluxation,
      congenital, hip) 754.32

Deformity—*continued*
  liver (congenital) 751.60
    acquired 573.8
    duct (congenital) 751.60
      acquired 576.8
        with calculus, choledocholithiasis, or
          stones—*see* Choledocholithiasis
  lower extremity—*see* Deformity, leg
  lumbosacral (joint) (region) (congenital) 756.10
    acquired 738.5
  lung (congenital) 748.60
    acquired 518.89
    specified type NEC 748.69
  lymphatic system, congenital 759.9
  Madelung's (radius) 755.54
  maxilla (acquired) (congenital) 524.9
  meninges or membrane (congenital) 742.9
    brain 742.4
      acquired 349.2
    spinal (cord) 742.59
      acquired 349.2
  mesentery (congenital) 751.9
    acquired 568.89
  metacarpus (acquired) 736.00
    congenital 755.50
  metatarsus (acquired) 736.70
    congenital 754.70
  middle ear, except ossicles (congenital) 744.03
    ossicles 744.04
  mitral (leaflets) (valve) (congenital) 746.9
    acquired—*see* Endocarditis, mitral
    Ebstein's 746.89
    parachute 746.5
    specified type NEC 746.89
    stenosis, congenital 746.5
  mouth (acquired) 528.9
    congenital NEC 750.9
      specified type NEC 750.26
  multiple, congenital NEC 759.7
    specified type NEC 759.89
  muscle (acquired) 728.9
    congenital 756.9
      specified type NEC 756.89
      sternocleidomastoid (due to intrauterine
        malposition and pressure) 754.1
  musculoskeletal system, congenital NEC 756.9
    specified type NEC 756.9
  nail (acquired) 703.9
    congenital 757.9
  nasal—*see* Deformity, nose
  neck (acquired) NEC 738.2
    congenital (any part) 744.9
      sternocleidomastoid 754.1
  nervous system (congenital) 742.9
  nipple (congenital) 757.9
    acquired 611.8
  nose, nasal (cartilage) (acquired) 738.0
    bone (turbinate) 738.0
    congenital 748.1
      bent 754.0
      squashed 754.0
    saddle 738.0
      syphilitic 090.5
    septum 470
      congenital 748.1
    sinus (wall) (congenital) 748.1
      acquired 738.0
    syphilitic (congenital) 090.5
      late 095.8
  ocular muscle (congenital) 743.9
    acquired 378.60

Deformity—*continued*
  opticociliary vessels (congenital) 743.9
  orbit (congenital) (eye) 743.9
    acquired NEC 376.40
      associated with craniofacial deformities
        376.44
      due to
        bone disease 376.43
        surgery 376.47
        trauma 376.47
  organ of Corti (congenital) 744.05
  ovary (congenital) 752.0
    acquired 620.8
  oviduct (congenital) 752.10
    acquired 620.8
  palate (congenital) 750.9
    acquired 526.89
    cleft (congenital) (*see also* Cleft, palate)
      749.00
    hard, acquired 526.89
    soft, acquired 528.9
  pancreas (congenital) 751.7
    acquired 577.8
  parachute, mitral valve 746.5
  parathyroid (gland) 759.2
  parotid (gland) (congenital) 750.9
    acquired 527.8
  patella (acquired) 736.6
    congenital 755.64
  pelvis, pelvic (acquired) (bony) 738.6
    with disproportion (fetopelvic) 653.0
      affecting fetus or newborn 763.1
      causing obstructed labor 660.1
        affecting fetus or newborn 763.1
    congenital 755.60
    rachitic (late effect) 268.1
  penis (glans) (congenital) 752.9
    acquired 607.89
  pericardium (congenital) 746.9
    acquired—*see* Pericarditis
  pharynx (congenital) 750.9
    acquired 478.29
  Pierre Robin (congenital) 756.0
  pinna (acquired) 380.32
    congenital 744.3
  pituitary (congenital) 759.2
  pleural folds (congenital) 748.8
  portal vein (congenital) 747.40
  posture—*see* Curvature, spine
  prepuce (congenital) 752.9
    acquired 607.89
  prostate (congenital) 752.9
    acquired 602.8
  pulmonary valve—*see* Endocarditis, pulmonary
  pupil (congenital) 743.9
    acquired 364.75
  pylorus (congenital) 750.9
    acquired 537.89
  rachitic (acquired), healed or old 268.1
  radius (acquired) 736.00
    congenital 755.50
    reduction—*see* Deformity, reduction, upper
      limb
  rectovaginal septum (congenital) 752.40
    acquired 623.8
  rectum (congenital) 751.5
    acquired 569.49

Deformity—*continued*
  thumb (acquired) 736.20
    congenital 755.50
  thymus (tissue) (congenital) 759.2
  thyroid (gland) (congenital) 759.2
    cartilage 748.3
      acquired 478.79
  tibia (acquired) 736.89
    congenital 755.60
    saber 090.5
  toe (acquired) 735.9
    congenital 755.66
    specified NEC 735.8
  tongue (congenital) 750.10
    acquired 529.8
  tooth, teeth NEC 520.9
  trachea (rings) (congenital) 748.3
    acquired 519.1
  transverse aortic arch (congenital) 747.21
  tricuspid (leaflets) (valve) (congenital) 746.9
    acquired—*see* Endocarditis, tricuspid
    atresia or stenosis 746.1
    specified type NEC 746.89
  trunk (acquired) 738.3
    congenital 759.9
  ulna (acquired) 736.00
    congenital 755.50
  upper extremity—*see* Deformity, arm
  urachus (congenital) 753.7
  ureter (opening) (congenital) 753.9
    acquired 593.89
  urethra (valve) (congenital) 753.9
    acquired 599.84
  urinary tract or system (congenital) 753.9
    urachus 753.7
  uterus (congenital) 752.3
    acquired 621.8
  uvula (congenital) 750.9
    acquired 528.9
  vagina (congenital) 752.40
    acquired 623.8
  valve, valvular (heart) (congenital) 746.9
    acquired—*see* Endocarditis
    pulmonary 746.00
    specified type NEC 746.89
  vascular (peripheral) NEC 747.60
    acquired 459.9
    gastrointestinal 747.61
    lower limb 747.64
    renal 747.62
    specified site NEC 747.69
    spinal 747.82
    upper limb 747.63
  vas deferens (congenital) 752.9
    acquired 608.89
  vein (congenital) NEC (*see also* Deformity,
      vascular) 747.60
    brain 747.81
    coronary 746.9
    great 747.40
  vena cava (inferior) (superior) (congenital)
      747.40
  vertebra—*see* Deformity, spine
  vesicourethral orifice (acquired) 596.8
    congenital NEC 753.9
      specified type NEC 753.8
  vessels of optic papilla (congenital) 743.9
  visual field (contraction) 368.45
  vitreous humor (congenital) 743.9
    acquired 379.29

Deformity—*continued*
  vulva (congenital) 752.40
    acquired 624.8
  wrist (joint) (acquired) 736.00
    congenital 755.50
    contraction 718.43
    valgus 736.03
      congenital 755.59
    varus 736.04
      congenital 755.59

Degeneration, degenerative
  adrenal (capsule) (gland) 255.8
    with hypofunction 255.4
    fatty 255.8
    hyaline 255.8
    infectional 255.8
    lardaceous 277.3
  amyloid (any site) (general) 277.3
  anterior cornua, spinal cord 336.8
  aorta, aortic 440.0
    fatty 447.8
    valve (heart) (*see also* Endocarditis, aortic)
        424.1
  arteriovascular—*see* Arteriosclerosis
  artery, arterial (atheromatous) (calcareous)—*see*
      also Arteriosclerosis
    amyloid 277.3
    lardaceous 277.3
    medial NEC (*see also* Arteriosclerosis,
        extremities) 440.20
  articular cartilage NEC (*see also* Disorder,
      cartilage, articular) 718.0
    elbow 718.02
    knee 717.5
    patella 717.7
    shoulder 718.01
    spine (*see also* Spondylosis) 721.90
  atheromatous—*see* Arteriosclerosis
  bacony (any site) 277.3
  basal nuclei or ganglia NEC 333.0
  bone 733.90
  brachial plexus 353.0
  brain (cortical) (progressive) 331.9
    arteriosclerotic 437.0
    childhood 330.9
      specified type NEC 330.8
    congenital 742.4
    cystic 348.0
      congenital 742.4
    familial NEC 331.89
    grey matter 330.8
    heredofamilial NEC 331.89
    in
      alcoholism 303.9 *[331.7]*
      beriberi 265.0 *[331.7]*
      cerebrovascular disease 437.9 *[331.7]*
      congenital hydrocephalus 742.3 *[331.7]*
        with spina bifida (*see also* Spina bifida)
            741.0 *[331.7]*
      Fabry's disease 272.7 *[330.2]*
      Gaucher's disease 272.7 *[330.2]*
      Hunter's disease or syndrome 277.5 *[330.3]*
      lipidosis
        cerebral 330.1
        generalized 272.7 *[330.2]*
      mucopolysaccharidosis 277.5 *[330.3]*
      myxedema (*see also* Myxedema) 244.9
          [331.7]
      neoplastic disease NEC (M8000/1) 239.9
          [331.7]
      Niemann-Pick disease 272.7 *[330.2]*

Degeneration, degenerative— *continued*
  sphingolipidosis 272.7 *[330.2]*
    vitamin B₁₂ deficiency 266.2 *[331.7]*
  motor centers 331.89
  senile 331.2
  specified type NEC 331.89
  breast—*see* Disease, breast
  Bruch's membrane 363.40
  bundle of His 426.50
    left 426.3
    right 426.4
  calcareous NEC 275.4
  capillaries 448.9
    amyloid 277.3
    fatty 448.9
    lardaceous 277.3
  cardiac (brown) (calcareous) (fatty) (fibrous)
      (hyaline) (mural) (muscular) (pigmentary)
      (senile) (with arteriosclerosis) (*see also*
      Degeneration, myocardial) 429.1
    valve, valvular—*see* Endocarditis
  cardiorenal (*see also* Hypertension, cardiorenal)
      404.90
  cardiovascular (*see also* Disease,
      cardiovascular) 429.2
    renal (*see also* Hypertension, cardiorenal)
      404.90
  cartilage (joint)—*see* Derangement, joint
  cerebellar NEC 334.9
    primary (hereditary) (sporadic) 334.2
  cerebral—*see* Degeneration, brain
  cerebromacular 330.1
  cerebrovascular 437.1
    due to hypertension 437.2
    late effect—*see* category 438
  cervical plexus 353.2
  cervix 622.8
    due to radiation (intended effect) 622.8
      adverse effect or misadventure 622.8
  changes, spine or vertebra (*see also*
      Spondylosis) 721.90
  chitinous 277.3
  chorioretinal 363.40
    congenital 743.53
    hereditary 363.50
  choroid (colloid) (drusen) 363.40
    hereditary 363.50
    senile 363.41
      diffuse secondary 363.42
  cochlear 386.8
  collateral ligament (knee) (medial) 717.82
    lateral 717.81
  combined (spinal cord) (subacute) 266.2 *[336.2]*
    with anemia (pernicious) 281.0 *[336.2]*
      due to dietary deficiency 281.1 *[336.2]*
    due to vitamin B₁₂ deficiency anemia (dietary)
      281.1 *[336.2]*
  conjunctiva 372.50
    amyloid 277.3 *[372.50]*
  cornea 371.40
    calcerous 371.44
    familial (hereditary) (*see also* Dystrophy,
        cornea) 371.50
      macular 371.55
      reticular 371.54
    hyaline (of old scars) 371.41
    marginal (Terrien's) 371.48
    mosaic (shagreen) 371.41
    nodular 371.46
    peripheral 371.48
    senile 371.41

Degeneration, degenerative— *continued*
  cortical (cerebellar) (parenchymatous) 334.2
    alcoholic 303.9 *[334.4]*
    diffuse, due to arteriopathy 437.0
  corticostriatal-spinal 334.8
  cretinoid 243
  cruciate ligament (knee) (posterior) 717.84
    anterior 717.83
  cutis 709.3
    amyloid 277.3
  dental pulp 522.2
  disc disease—*see* Degeneration, intervertebral
      disc
  dorsolateral (spinal cord)—*see* Degeneration,
      combined
  endocardial 424.90
  extrapyramidal NEC 333.90
  eye NEC 360.40
    macular (*see also* Degeneration, macula)
        362.50
      congenital 362.75
      hereditary 362.76
  fatty (diffuse) (general) 272.8
    liver 571.8
      alcoholic 571.0
    localized site—*see* Degeneration, by site, fatty
    placenta—*see* Placenta, abnormal
  globe (eye) NEC 360.40
    macular—*see* Degeneration, macula
  grey matter 330.8
  heart (brown) (calcareous) (fatty) (fibrous)
      (hyaline) (mural) (muscular) (pigmentary)
      (senile) (with arteriosclerosis) (*see also*
      Degeneration, myocardial) 429.1
    amyloid 277.3 *[425.7]*
    atheromatous —*see* Arteriosclerosis, coronary
    gouty 274.82
    hypertensive (*see also* Hypertension, heart)
        402.90
    ischemic 414.9
    valve, valvular—*see* Endocarditis
  hepatolenticular (Wilson's) 275.1
  hepatorenal 572.4
  heredofamilial
    brain NEC 331.89
    spinal cord NEC 336.8
  hyaline (diffuse) (generalized) 728.9
    localized—*see also* Degeneration, by site
      cornea 371.41
      keratitis 371.41
  hypertensive vascular—*see* Hypertension
  infrapatellar fat pad 729.31
  internal semilunar cartilage 717.3
  intervertebral disc 722.6
    with myelopathy 722.70
    cervical, cervicothoracic 722.4
      with myelopathy 722.71
    lumbar, lumbosacral 722.52
      with myelopathy 722.73
    thoracic, thoracolumbar 722.51
      with myelopathy 722.72
  intestine 569.89
    amyloid 277.3
    lardaceous 277.3
  iris (generalized) (*see also* Atrophy, iris) 364.59
    pigmentary 364.53
    pupillary margin 364.54
  ischemic—*see* Ischemia
  joint disease (*see also* Osteoarthrosis) 715.9
    multiple sites 715.09
    spine (*see also* Spondylosis) 721.90

Degeneration, degenerative— *continued*
  kidney (*see also* Sclerosis, renal) 587
    amyloid 277.3 *[583.81]*
    cyst, cystic (multiple) (solitary) 593.2
      congenital (*see also* Cystic, disease, kidney) 753.10
    fatty 593.89
    fibrocystic (congenital) 753.19
    lardaceous 277.3 *[583.81]*
    polycystic (congenital) 753.12
      adult type (APKD) 753.13
      autosomal dominant 753.13
      autosomal recessive 753.14
      childhood type (CPKD) 753.14
      infantile type 753.14
    waxy 277.3 *[583.81]*
  Kuhnt-Junius (retina) 362.52
  labyrinth, osseous 386.8
  lacrimal passages, cystic 375.12
  lardaceous (any site) 277.3
  lateral column (posterior), spinal cord (*see also* Degeneration, combined) 266.2 *[336.2]*
  lattice 362.63
  lens 366.9
    infantile, juvenile, or presenile 366.00
    senile 366.10
  lenticular (familial) (progressive) (Wilson's) (with cirrhosis of liver) 275.1
    striate artery 437.0
  lethal ball, prosthetic heart valve 996.02
  ligament
    collateral (knee) (medial) 717.82
      lateral 717.81
    cruciate (knee) (posterior) 717.84
      anterior 717.83
  liver (diffuse) 572.8
    amyloid 277.3
    congenital (cystic) 751.62
    cystic 572.8
      congenital 751.62
    fatty 571.8
      alcoholic 571.0
    hypertrophic 572.8
    lardaceous 277.3
    parenchymatous, acute or subacute (*see also* Necrosis, liver) 570
    pigmentary 572.8
    toxic (acute) 573.8
    waxy 277.3
  lung 518.8
  lymph gland 289.3
    hyaline 289.3
    lardaceous 277.3
  macula (acquired) (senile) 362.50
    atrophic 362.51
    Best's 362.76
    congenital 362.75
    cystic 362.54
    cystoid 362.53
    disciform 362.52
    dry 362.51
    exudative 362.52
    familial pseudoinflammatory 362.77
    hereditary 362.76
    hole 362.54
    juvenile (Stargardt's) 362.75
    nonexudative 362.51
    pseudohole 362.54
    wet 362.52

Degeneration, degenerative— *continued*
  medullary—*see* Degeneration, brain
  membranous labyrinth, congenital (causing impairment of hearing) 744.05
  meniscus—*see* Derangement, joint
  microcystoid 362.62
  mitral—*see* Insufficiency, mitral
  Mönckeberg's (*see also* Arteriosclerosis, extremities) 440.20
  moral 301.7
  motor centers, senile 331.2
  mural (*see also* Degeneration, myocardial) 429.1
    heart, cardiac (*see also* Degeneration, myocardial) 429.1
    myocardium, myocardial (*see also* Degeneration, myocardial) 429.1
  muscle 728.9
    fatty 728.9
    fibrous 728.9
    heart (*see also* Degeneration, myocardial) 429.1
    hyaline 728.9
  muscular progressive 728.2
  myelin, central nervous system NEC 341.9
  myocardium, myocardial (brown) (calcareous) (fatty) (fibrous) (hyaline) (mural) (muscular) (pigmentary) (senile) (with arteriosclerosis) 429.1
    with rheumatic fever (conditions classifiable to 390) 398.0
      active, acute, or subacute 391.2
        with chorea 392.0
      inactive or quiescent (with chorea) 398.0
    amyloid 277.3 *[425.7]*
    congenital 746.89
    fetus or newborn 779.8
    gouty 274.82
    hypertensive (*see also* Hypertension, heart) 402.90
    ischemic 414.8
    rheumatic (*see also* Degeneration, myocardium, with rheumatic fever) 398.0
    syphilitic 093.82
  nasal sinus (mucosa) (*see also* Sinusitis) 473.9
    frontal 473.1
    maxillary 473.0
  nerve—*see* Disorder, nerve
  nervous system 349.89
    amyloid 277.3 *[357.4]*
    autonomic (*see also* Neuropathy, peripheral, autonomic) 337.9
    fatty 349.89
    peripheral autonomic NEC (*see also* Neuropathy, peripheral, autonomic) 337.9
  nipple 611.9
  nose 478.1
  oculoacousticocerebral, congenital (progressive) 743.8
  olivopontocerebellar (familial) (hereditary) 333.0
  osseous labyrinth 386.8
  ovary 620.8
    cystic 620.2
    microcystic 620.2
  pallidal, pigmentary (progressive) 333.0
  pancreas 577.8
    tuberculous (*see also* Tuberculosis) 017.9
  papillary muscle 429.81
  paving stone 362.61
  penis 607.89
  peritoneum 568.89

Degeneration, degenerative— *continued*
pigmentary (diffuse) (general)
  localized—*see* Degeneration, by site
  pallidal (progressive) 333.0
  secondary 362.65
pineal gland 259.8
pituitary (gland) 253.8
placenta (fatty) (fibrinoid) (fibroid)—*see*
  Placenta, abnormal
popliteal fat pad 729.31
posterolateral (spinal cord) (*see also*
  Degeneration, combined) 266.2 *[336.2]*
pulmonary valve (heart) (*see also* Endocarditis,
  pulmonary) 424.3
pulp (tooth) 522.2
pupillary margin 364.54
renal (*see also* Sclerosis, renal) 587
  fibrocystic 753.19
  polycystic 753.12
    adult type (APKD) 753.13
    autosomal dominant 753.13
    autosomal recessive 753.14
    childhood type (CPKD) 753.14
    infantile type 753.14
reticuloendothelial system 289.8
retina (peripheral) 362.60
  with retinal defect (*see also* Detachment,
    retina, with retinal defect) 361.00
  cystic (senile) 362.50
  cystoid 362.53
  hereditary (*see also* Dystrophy, retina) 362.70
    cerebroretinal 362.71
    congenital 362.75
    juvenile (Stargardt's) 362.75
    macula 362.76
    Kuhnt-Junius 362.52
    lattice 362.63
  macular (*see also* Degeneration, macula)
    362.50
  microcystoid 362.62
  palisade 362.63
  paving stone 362.61
  pigmentary (primary) 362.74
    secondary 362.65
  posterior pole (*see also* Degeneration, macula)
    362.50
  secondary 362.66
  senile 362.60
    cystic 362.53
    reticular 362.64
saccule, congenital (causing impairment of
  hearing) 744.05
sacculocochlear 386.8
senile 797
  brain 331.2
  cardiac, heart, or myocardium (*see also*
    Degeneration, myocardial) 429.1
  motor centers 331.2
  reticule 362.64
  retina, cystic 362.50
  vascular—*see* Arteriosclerosis
silicone rubber poppet (prosthetic valve) 996.02
sinus (cystic) (*see also* Sinusitis) 473.9
  polypoid 471.1
skin 709.3
  amyloid 277.3
  colloid 709.3

Degeneration, degenerative— *continued*
spinal (cord) 336.8
  amyloid 277.3
  column 733.90
  combined (subacute) (*see also* Degeneration,
    combined) 266.2 *[336.2]*
    with anemia (pernicious) 281.0 *[336.2]*
  dorsolateral (*see also* Degeneration,
    combined) 266.2 *[336.2]*
  familial NEC 336.8
  fatty 336.8
  funicular (*see also* Degeneration, combined)
    266.2 *[336.2]*
  heredofamilial NEC 336.8
  posterolateral (*see also* Degeneration,
    combined) 266.2 *[336.2]*
  subacute combined—*see* Degeneration,
    combined
  tuberculous (*see also* Tuberculosis) 013.8
spine 733.90
spleen 289.59
  amyloid 277.3
  lardaceous 277.3
stomach 537.89
  lardaceous 277.3
strionigral 333.0
sudoriparous (cystic) 705.89
suprarenal (capsule) (gland) 255.8
  with hypofunction 255.4
sweat gland 705.89
synovial membrane (pulpy) 727.9
tapetoretinal 362.74
  adult or presenile form 362.50
testis (postinfectional) 608.89
thymus (gland) 254.8
  fatty 254.8
  lardaceous 277.3
thyroid (gland) 246.8
tricuspid (heart) (valve)—*see* Endocarditis,
  tricuspid
tuberculous NEC (*see also* Tuberculosis) 011.9
turbinate 733.90
uterus 621.8
  cystic 621.8
vascular (senile)—*see also* Arteriosclerosis
  hypertensive—*see* Hypertension
vitreoretinal (primary) 362.73
  secondary 362.66
vitreous humor (with infiltration) 379.21
wallerian NEC—*see* Disorder, nerve
waxy (any site) 277.3
Wilson's hepatolenticular 275.1
Deglutition
paralysis 784.9
  hysterical 300.11
pneumonia 507.0
Degos' disease or syndrome 447.8
**Degradation disorder, branched-chain
  amino-acid** 270.3
Dehiscence
anastomosis—*see* Complications, anastomosis
cesarean wound 674.1
episiotomy 674.2
operation wound 998.3
perineal wound (postpartum) 674.2
postoperative 998.3
  abdomen 998.3
uterine wound 674.1

Dehydration (cachexia) 276.5
  hypertonic 276.0
  hypotonic 276.1
  newborn 775.5
Deiters' nucleus syndrome 386.19
Déjérine's disease 356.0
Déjérine-Klumpke paralysis 767.6
Déjérine-Roussy syndrome 348.8
Déjérine-Sottas disease or neuropathy
    (hypertrophic) 356.0
Déjérine-Thomas atrophy or syndrome 333.0
de Lange's syndrome (Amsterdam dwarf,
    mental retardation, and brachycephaly) 759.89
Delay, delayed
  adaptation, cones or rods 368.63
  any plane in pelvis
    affecting fetus or newborn 763.1
    complicating delivery 660.1
  birth or delivery NEC 662.1
    affecting fetus or newborn 763.8
    second twin, triplet, or multiple mate 662.3
  closure—*see also* Fistula
    cranial suture 756.0
    fontanel 756.0
  coagulation NEC 790.92
  conduction (cardiac) (ventricular) 426.9
  delivery NEC 662.1
    second twin, triplet, etc. 662.3
      affecting fetus or newborn 763.8
  development 783.4
    intellectual NEC 315.9
    learning NEC 315.2
    physiological 783.4
    reading 315.00
    sexual 259.0
    speech 315.39
      associated with hyperkinesis 314.1
    spelling 315.09
  gastric emptying 536.8
  menarche 256.3
    due to pituitary hypofunction 253.4
  menstruation (cause unknown) 626.8
  milestone 783.4
  motility—*see* Hypomotility
  passage of meconium (newborn) 777.1
  primary respiration 768.9
  puberty 259.0
  sexual maturation, female 259.0
Del Castillo's syndrome (germinal aplasia) 606.0
Deleage's disease 359.8
Delhi (boil) (button) (sore) 085.1
Delinquency (juvenile) 312.9
  group (*see also* Disturbance, conduct) 312.2
  neurotic 312.4
Delirium, delirious 780.09
  acute (psychotic) 293.0
  alcoholic 291.0
    acute 291.0
    chronic 291.1
  alcoholicum 291.0
  chronic (*see also* Psychosis) 293.89
    due to or associated with physical
      condition—*see* Psychosis, organic
  drug-induced 292.81
  eclamptic (*see also* Eclampsia) 780.3
  exhaustion (*see also* Reaction, stress, acute)
    308.9
  hysterical 300.11

Delirium, delirious—*continued*
  in
    presenile dementia 290.11
    senile dementia 290.3
  induced by drug 292.81
  manic, maniacal (acute) (*see also* Psychosis,
    affective) 296.0
    recurrent episode 296.1
    single episode 296.0
  puerperal 293.9
  senile 290.3
  subacute (psychotic) 293.1
  thyroid (*see also* Thyrotoxicosis) 242.9
  traumatic—*see also* Injury, intracranial
    with
      lesion, spinal cord—*see* Injury, spinal, by
        site
      shock, spinal—*see* Injury, spinal, by site
  tremens (impending) 291.0
  uremic—*see* Uremia
  withdrawal
    alcoholic (acute) 291.0
      chronic 291.1
    drug 292.0
Delivery

Note—Use the following fifth-digit
subclassification with categories 640-648,
651-676:

0 *unspecified as to episode of care*
1 *delivered, with or without mention of*
2 *delivered, with mention of*
    postpartum complication
3 *antepartum condition or complication*
4 *postpartum condition or*
    complication

  breech (assisted) (spontaneous) 652.2
    affecting fetus or newborn 763.0
    extraction NEC 669.6
  cesarean (for) 669.7
    abnormal
      cervix 654.6
      pelvic organs or tissues 654.9
      pelvis (bony) (major) NEC 653.0
      presentation or position 652.9
        in multiple gestation 652.6
      size, fetus 653.5
      soft parts (of pelvis) 654.9
      uterus, congenital 654.0
      vagina 654.7
      vulva 654.8
    abruptio placentae 641.2
    acromion presentation 652.8
    affecting fetus or newborn 763.4
    anteversion, cervix or uterus 654.4
    atony, uterus 661.2
    bicornis or bicornuate uterus 654.0
    breech presentation 652.2
    brow presentation 652.4
    cephalopelvic disproportion (normally formed
      fetus) 653.4
    chin presentation 652.4
    cicatrix of cervix 654.6
    contracted pelvis (general) 653.1
      inlet 653.2
      outlet 653.3
    cord presentation or prolapse 663.0
    cystocele 654.4

Delivery—*continued*

deformity (acquired) (congenital)
  pelvic organs or tissues NEC 654.9
  pelvis (bony) NEC 653.0
displacement, uterus NEC 654.4
disproportion NEC 653.9
distress
  fetal 656.3
  maternal 669.0
eclampsia 642.6
face presentation 652.4
failed
  forceps 660.7
  trial of labor NEC 660.6
  vacuum extraction 660.7
  ventouse 660.7
fetal deformity 653.7
fetal-maternal hemorrhage 656.0
fetus, fetal
  distress 656.3
  prematurity 656.8
fibroid (tumor) (uterus) 654.1
hemorrhage (antepartum) (intrapartum) NEC 641.9
hydrocephalic fetus 653.6
incarceration of uterus 654.3
incoordinate uterine action 661.4
inertia, uterus 661.2
  primary 661.0
  secondary 661.1
lateroversion, uterus or cervix 654.4
mal lie 652.9
malposition
  fetus 652.9
    in multiple gestation 652.6
  pelvic organs or tissues NEC 654.9
  uterus NEC or cervix 654.4
malpresentation NEC 652.9
  in multiple gestation 652.6
maternal
  diabetes mellitus 648.0
  heart disease NEC 648.6
meconium in liquor 656.3
  without mention of fetal distress—omit code
  staining only 792.3
oblique presentation 652.3
oversize fetus 653.5
pelvic tumor NEC 654.9
placental insufficiency 656.5
placenta previa 641.0
  with hemorrhage 641.1
poor dilation, cervix 661.0
pre-eclampsia 642.4
  severe 642.5
previous
  cesarean delivery 654.2
  surgery (to)
    cervix 654.6
    gynecological NEC 654.9
    uterus NEC 654.9
      from previous cesarean delivery 654.2
    vagina 654.7
prolapse
  arm or hand 652.7
  uterus 654.4
prolonged labor 662.1
rectocele 654.4
retroversion, uterus or cervix 654.3
rigid
  cervix 654.6
  pelvic floor 654.4

Delivery—*continued*

  perineum 654.8
  vagina 654.7
  vulva 654.8
sacculation, pregnant uterus 654.4
scar(s)
  cervix 654.6
  cesarean delivery 654.2
  uterus NEC 654.9
    due to previous cesarean delivery 654.2
Shirodkar suture in situ 654.5
shoulder presentation 652.8
stenosis or stricture, cervix 654.6
transverse presentation or lie 652.3
tumor, pelvic organs or tissues NEC 654.4
umbilical cord presentation or prolapse 663.0
completely normal case—*see category* 650
complicated (by) NEC 669.9
  abdominal tumor, fetal 653.7
    causing obstructed labor 660.1
  abnormal, abnormality of
    cervix 654.6
      causing obstructed labor 660.2
    forces of labor 661.9
    formation of uterus 654.0
    pelvic organs or tissues 654.9
      causing obstructed labor 660.2
    pelvis (bony) (major) NEC 653.0
      causing obstructed labor 660.1
    presentation or position NEC 652.9
      causing obstructed labor 660.0
    size, fetus 653.5
      causing obstructed labor 660.1
    soft parts (of pelvis) 654.9
      causing obstructed labor 660.2
    uterine contractions NEC 661.9
    uterus (formation) 654.0
      causing obstructed labor 660.2
    vagina 654.7
      causing obstructed labor 660.2
  abnormally formed uterus (any type)
    (congenital) 654.0
    causing obstructed labor 660.2
  acromion presentation 652.8
    causing obstructed labor 660.0
  adherent placenta 667.0
    with hemorrhage 666.0
  adhesions, uterus (to abdominal wall) 654.4
  advanced maternal age NEC 659.6
    primigravida 659.5
  air embolism 673.0
  amnionitis 658.4
  amniotic fluid embolism 673.1
  anesthetic death 668.9
  annular detachment, cervix 665.3
  antepartum hemorrhage—*see* Delivery,
    complicated, hemorrhage
  anteversion, cervix or uterus 654.4
    causing obstructed labor 660.2
  apoplexy 674.0
    placenta 641.2
  arrested active phase 661.1
  asymmetrical pelvis bone 653.0
    causing obstructed labor 660.1
  atony, uterus (hypotonic) (inertia) 661.2
    hypertonic 661.4
  Bandl's ring 661.4
  battledore placenta—*see* Placenta, abnormal
  bicornis or bicornuate uterus 654.0
    causing obstructed labor 660.2

Delivery—*continued*

birth injury to mother NEC 665.9

bleeding (*see also* Delivery, complicated, hemorrhage) 641.9

breech presentation (assisted) (spontaneous) 652.2

with successful version 652.1

causing obstructed labor 660.0

brow presentation 652.4

causing obstructed labor 660.0

cephalopelvic disproportion (normally formed fetus) 653.4

causing obstructed labor 660.1

cerebral hemorrhage 674.0

cervical dystocia 661.0

chin presentation 652.4

causing obstructed labor 660.0

cicatrix

cervix 654.6

causing obstructed labor 660.2

vagina 654.7

causing obstructed labor 660.2

colporrhexis 665.4

with perineal laceration 664.0

compound presentation 652.8

causing obstructed labor 660.0

compression of cord (umbilical) 663.2

around neck 663.1

cord prolapsed 663.0

contraction, contracted pelvis 653.1

causing obstructed labor 660.1

general 653.1

causing obstructed labor 660.1

inlet 653.2

causing obstructed labor 660.1

midpelvic 653.8

causing obstructed labor 660.1

midplane 653.8

causing obstructed labor 660.1

outlet 653.3

causing obstructed labor 660.1

contraction ring 661.4

cord (umbilical) 663.9

around neck, tightly or with compression 663.1

without compression 663.3

bruising 663.6

complication NEC 663.9

specified type NEC 663.8

compression NEC 663.2

entanglement NEC 663.3

with compression 663.2

forelying 663.0

hematoma 663.6

marginal attachment 663.8

presentation 663.0

prolapse (complete) (occult) (partial) 663.0

short 663.4

specified complication NEC 663.8

thrombosis (vessels) 663.6

vascular lesion 663.6

velamentous insertion 663.5

Couvelaire uterus 641.2

cretin pelvis (dwarf type) (male type) 653.1

causing obstructed labor 660.1

crossbirth 652.3

with successful version 652.1

causing obstructed labor 660.0

cyst (Gartner's duct) 654.7

cystocele 654.4

causing obstructed labor 660.2

Delivery—*continued*

death of fetus (near term) 656.4

early (before 22 completed weeks' gestation) 632

deformity (acquired) (congenital)

fetus 653.7

causing obstructed labor 660.1

pelvic organs or tissues NEC 654.9

causing obstructed labor 660.2

pelvis (bony) NEC 653.0

causing obstructed labor 660.1

delay, delayed

delivery in multiple pregnancy 662.3

due to locked mates 660.5

following rupture of membranes (spontaneous) 658.2

artificial 658.3

depressed fetal heart tones 656.3

diastasis recti 665.8

dilatation

bladder 654.4

causing obstructed labor 660.2

cervix, incomplete, poor or slow 661.0

diseased placenta 656.7

displacement uterus NEC 654.4

causing obstructed labor 660.2

disproportion NEC 653.9

causing obstructed labor 660.1

disruptio uteri—*see* Delivery, complicated, rupture, uterus

distress

fetal 656.3

maternal 669.0

double uterus (congenital) 654.0

causing obstructed labor 660.2

dropsy amnion 657

dysfunction, uterus 661.9

hypertonic 661.4

hypotonic 661.2

primary 661.0

secondary 661.1

incoordinate 661.4

dystocia

cervical 661.0

fetal—*see* Delivery, complicated, abnormal, presentation

maternal—*see* Delivery, complicated, prolonged labor

pelvic—*see* Delivery, complicated, contraction pelvis

positional 652.8

shoulder girdle 660.4

eclampsia 642.6

ectopic kidney 654.4

causing obstructed labor 660.2

edema, cervix 654.6

causing obstructed labor 660.2

effusion, amniotic fluid 658.1

elderly primigravida 659.5

embolism (pulmonary) 673.2

air 673.0

amniotic fluid 673.1

blood-clot 673.2

cerebral 674.0

fat 673.8

pyemic 673.3

septic 673.3

entanglement, umbilical cord 663.3

with compression 663.2

around neck (with compression) 663.1

eversion, cervix or uterus 665.2

Delivery—*continued*
　　excessive
　　　　fetal growth 653.5
　　　　　　causing obstructed labor 660.1
　　　　size of fetus 653.5
　　　　　　causing obstructed labor 660.1
　　face presentation 652.4
　　　　causing obstructed labor 660.0
　　　　to pubes 660.3
　　failure, fetal head to enter pelvic brim 652.5
　　　　causing obstructed labor 660.0
　　fetal
　　　　acid-base balance 656.3
　　　　death (near term) NEC 656.4
　　　　　　early (before 22 completed weeks'
　　　　　　　　gestation) 632
　　　　deformity 653.7
　　　　　　causing obstructed labor 660.1
　　　　distress 656.3
　　　　heart-rate or rhythm 656.3
　　fetopelvic disproportion 653.4
　　　　causing obstructed labor 660.1
　　fever during labor 659.2
　　fibroid (tumor) (uterus) 654.1
　　　　causing obstructed labor 660.2
　　fibromyomata 654.1
　　　　causing obstructed labor 660.2
　　forelying umbilical cord 663.0
　　fracture of coccyx 665.6
　　hematoma 664.5
　　　　broad ligament 665.7
　　　　ischial spine 665.7
　　　　pelvic 665.7
　　　　perineum 664.5
　　　　soft tissues 665.7
　　　　subdural 674.0
　　　　umbilical cord 663.6
　　　　vagina 665.7
　　　　vulva or perineum 664.5
　　hemorrhage (uterine) (antepartum)
　　　　(intrapartum) (pregnancy) 641.9
　　　　accidental 641.2
　　　　associated with
　　　　　　afibrinogenemia 641.3
　　　　　　coagulation defect 641.3
　　　　　　　　hyperfibrinolysis 641.3
　　　　　　　　hypofibrinogenemia 641.3
　　　　cerebral 674.0
　　　　due to
　　　　　　low-lying placenta 641.1
　　　　　　placenta previa 641.1
　　　　　　premature separation of placenta
　　　　　　　　(normally implanted) 641.2
　　　　　　retained placenta 666.0
　　　　　　trauma 641.8
　　　　　　uterine leiomyoma 641.8
　　　　marginal sinus rupture 641.2
　　　　placenta NEC 641.9
　　　　postpartum (atonic) (immediate) (within 24
　　　　　　hours) 666.1
　　　　　　with retained or trapped placenta 666.0
　　　　　　third stage 666.0
　　　　　　delayed 666.2
　　　　　　secondary 666.2
　　hourglass contraction, uterus 661.4
　　hydramnios 657
　　hydrocephalic fetus 653.6
　　　　causing obstructed labor 660.1
　　hydrops fetalis 653.7
　　　　causing obstructed labor 660.1

Delivery—*continued*
　　hypertension—*see* Hypertension,
　　　　complicating pregnancy
　　hypertonic uterine dysfunction 661.4
　　hypotonic uterine dysfunction 661.2
　　impacted shoulders 660.4
　　incarceration, uterus 654.3
　　　　causing obstructed labor 660.2
　　incomplete dilation (cervix) 661.0
　　incoordinate uterus 661.4
　　indication NEC 659.9
　　　　specified type NEC 659.8
　　inertia, uterus 661.2
　　　　hypertonic 661.4
　　　　hypotonic 661.2
　　　　primary 661.0
　　　　secondary 661.1
　　infantile
　　　　genitalia 654.4
　　　　　　causing obstructed labor 660.2
　　　　uterus (os) 654.4
　　　　　　causing obstructed labor 660.2
　　injury (to mother) NEC 665.9
　　intrauterine fetal death (near term) NEC 656.4
　　　　early (before 22 completed weeks'
　　　　　　gestation) 632
　　inversion, uterus 665.2
　　kidney, ectopic 654.4
　　　　causing obstructed labor 660.2
　　knot (true), umbilical cord 663.2
　　labor, premature (before 37 completed weeks
　　　　gestation) 644.2
　　laceration 664.9
　　　　anus (sphincter) 664.2
　　　　　　with mucosa 664.3
　　　　bladder (urinary) 665.5
　　　　bowel 665.5
　　　　central 664.4
　　　　cervix (uteri) 665.3
　　　　fourchette 664.0
　　　　hymen 664.0
　　　　labia (majora) (minora) 664.0
　　　　pelvic
　　　　　　floor 664.1
　　　　　　organ NEC 665.5
　　　　perineum, perineal 664.4
　　　　　　first degree 664.0
　　　　　　second degree 664.1
　　　　　　third degree 664.2
　　　　　　fourth degree 664.3
　　　　　　central 664.4
　　　　　　extensive NEC 664.4
　　　　　　muscles 664.1
　　　　　　skin 664.0
　　　　　　slight 664.0
　　　　peritoneum 665.5
　　　　periurethral tissue 665.5
　　　　rectovaginal (septum) (without perineal
　　　　　　laceration) 665.4
　　　　　　with perineum 664.2
　　　　　　　　with anal or rectal mucosa 664.3
　　　　skin (perineum) 664.0
　　　　specified site or type NEC 664.8
　　　　sphincter ani 664.2
　　　　　　with mucosa 664.3
　　　　urethra 665.5
　　　　uterus 665.1
　　　　　　before labor 665.0
　　　　vagina, vaginal (deep) (high) (sulcus) (wall)
　　　　　　(without perineal laceration) 665.4
　　　　　　with perineum 664.0

Delivery—*continued*
    muscles, with perineum 664.1
        vulva 664.0
    lateroversion, uterus or cervix 654.4
        causing obstructed labor 660.2
    locked mates 660.5
    low implantation of placenta—*see* Delivery,
        complicated, placenta, previa
    mal lie 652.9
        causing obstructed labor 660.0
    malposition
        fetus NEC 652.9
            causing obstructed labor 660.0
        pelvic organs or tissues NEC 654.9
            causing obstructed labor 660.2
        placenta 641.1
            without hemorrhage 641.0
        uterus NEC or cervix 654.4
            causing obstructed labor 660.2
    malpresentation 652.9
        causing obstructed labor 660.0
    marginal sinus (bleeding) (rupture) 641.2
    maternal hypotension syndrome 669.2
    meconium in liquor 656.3
    membranes, retained—*see* Delivery,
        complicated, placenta, retained
    mentum presentation 652.4
        causing obstructed labor 660.0
    metrorrhagia (myopathia)—*see* Delivery,
        complicated, hemorrhage
    metrorrhexis—*see* Delivery, complicated,
        rupture, uterus
    multiparity (grand) 659.4
    myelomeningocele, fetus 653.7
        causing obstructed labor 660.1
    Nägele's pelvis 653.0
        causing obstructed labor 660.1
    nonengagement, fetal head 652.5
        causing obstructed labor 660.0
    oblique presentation 652.3
        causing obstructed labor 660.0
    obstetric
        shock 669.1
        trauma NEC 665.9
    obstructed labor 660.9
        due to
            abnormality pelvic organs or tissues
                (conditions classifiable to
                654.0-654.9) 660.2
            deep transverse arrest 660.3
            impacted shoulders 660.4
            locked twins 660.5
            malposition and malpresentation of fetus
                (conditions classifiable to
                652.0-652.9) 660.0
            persistent occipitoposterior 660.3
            shoulder dystocia 660.4
    occult prolapse of umbilical cord 663.0
    oversize fetus 653.5
        causing obstructed labor 660.1
    pathological retraction ring, uterus 661.4
    pelvic
        arrest (deep) (high) (of fetal head)
            (transverse) 660.3
        deformity (bone)—*see also* Deformity,
            pelvis, with disproportion
        soft tissue 654.9
            causing obstructed labor 660.2
        tumor NEC 654.9

Delivery—*continued*
    causing obstructed labor 660.2
    penetration, pregnant uterus by instrument
        665.1
    perforation—*see* Delivery, complicated,
        laceration
    persistent
        hymen 654.8
            causing obstructed labor 660.2
        occipitoposterior 660.3
    placenta, placental
        ablatio 641.2
        abnormality 656.7
            with hemorrhage 641.2
        abruptio 641.2
        accreta 667.0
            with hemorrhage 666.0
        adherent (without hemorrhage) 667.0
            with hemorrhage 666.0
        apoplexy 641.2
        battledore 663.8
        detachment (premature) 641.2
        disease 656.7
        hemorrhage NEC 641.9
        increta (without hemorrhage) 667.0
            with hemorrhage 666.0
        low (implantation) 641.1
            without hemorrhage 641.0
        malformation 656.7
            with hemorrhage 641.2
        malposition 641.1
            without hemorrhage 641.0
        marginal sinus rupture 641.2
        percreta 667.0
            with hemorrhage 666.0
        premature separation 641.2
        previa (central) (lateral) (marginal) (partial)
            641.1
            without hemorrhage 641.0
        retained (with hemorrhage) 666.0
            without hemorrhage 667.0
        rupture of marginal sinus 641.2
        separation (premature) 641.2
        trapped 666.0
            without hemorrhage 667.0
        vicious insertion 641.1
    polyhydramnios 657
    polyp, cervix 654.6
        causing obstructed labor 660.2
    precipitate labor 661.3
    premature
        labor (before 37 completed weeks gestation)
            644.2
        rupture, membranes 658.1
            delayed delivery following 658.2
    presenting umbilical cord 663.0
    previous
        cesarean delivery 654.2
        surgery
            cervix 654.6
                causing obstructed labor 660.2
            gynecological NEC 654.9
                causing obstructed labor 660.2
            perineum 654.3
            uterus NEC 654.9
                due to previous cesarean delivery 654.2
            vagina 654.7
                causing obstructed labor 660.2
            vulva 654.8
    primary uterine inertia 661.0
    primipara, elderly or old 659.5

Delivery—*continued*
  prolapse
    arm or hand 652.7
      causing obstructed labor 660.0
    cord (umbilical) 663.0
    fetal extremity 652.8
    foot or leg 652.8
      causing obstructed labor 660.0
    umbilical cord (complete) (occult) (partial)
      663.0
    uterus 654.4
      causing obstructed labor 660.2
  prolonged labor 662.1
    first stage 662.0
    second stage 662.2
    active phase 661.2
    due to
      cervical dystocia 661.0
      contraction ring 661.4
      tetanic uterus 661.4
      uterine inertia 661.2
        primary 661.0
        secondary 661.1
    latent phase 661.0
  pyrexia during labor 659.2
  rachitic pelvis 653.2
    causing obstructed labor 660.1
  rectocele 654.4
    causing obstructed labor 660.2
  retained membranes or portions of placenta
    666.2
    without hemorrhage 667.1
  retarded (prolonged) birth 662.1
  retention secundines (with hemorrhage) 666.2
    without hemorrhage 667.1
  retroversion, uterus or cervix 654.3
    causing obstructed labor 660.2
  rigid
    cervix 654.6
      causing obstructed labor 660.2
    pelvic floor 654.4
      causing obstructed labor 660.2
    perineum or vulva 654.8
      causing obstructed labor 660.2
    vagina 654.7
      causing obstructed labor 660.2
  Robert's pelvis 653.0
    causing obstructed labor 660.1
  rupture—*see also* Delivery, complicated,
    laceration
    bladder (urinary) 665.5
    cervix 665.3
    marginal sinus 641.2
    membranes, premature 658.1
    pelvic organ NEC 665.5
    perineum (without mention of other
      laceration)—*see* Delivery, complicated,
      laceration, perineum
    peritoneum 665.5
    urethra 665.5
    uterus (during labor) 665.1
      before labor 665.0
  sacculation, pregnant uterus 654.4
  sacral teratomas, fetal 653.7
    causing obstructed labor 660.1
  scar(s)
    cervix 654.6
      causing obstructed labor 660.2
    cesarean delivery 654.2
      causing obstructed labor 660.2

Delivery—*continued*
    perineum 654.8
      causing obstructed labor 660.2
    uterus NEC 654.9
      causing obstructed labor 660.2
      due to previous cesarean delivery 654.2
    vagina 654.7
      causing obstructed labor 660.2
    vulva 654.8
      causing obstructed labor 660.2
  scoliotic pelvis 653.0
    causing obstructed labor 660.1
  secondary uterine inertia 661.1
  secundines, retained—*see* Delivery,
    complicated, placenta, retained
  separation
    placenta (premature) 641.2
    pubic bone 665.6
    symphysis pubis 665.6
  septate vagina 654.7
    causing obstructed labor 660.2
  shock (birth) (obstetric) (puerperal) 669.1
  short cord syndrome 663.4
  shoulder
    girdle dystocia 660.4
    presentation 652.8
      causing obstructed labor 660.0
  Siamese twins 653.7
    causing obstructed labor 660.1
  slow slope active phase 661.2
  spasm
    cervix 661.4
    uterus 661.4
  spondylolisthesis, pelvis 653.3
    causing obstructed labor 660.1
  spondylolysis (lumbosacral) 653.3
    causing obstructed labor 660.1
  spondylosis 653.0
    causing obstructed labor 660.1
  stenosis or stricture
    cervix 654.6
      causing obstructed labor 660.2
    vagina 654.7
      causing obstructed labor 660.2
  sudden death, unknown cause 669.9
  tear (pelvic organ) (*see also* Delivery,
    complicated, laceration) 664.9
  teratomas, sacral, fetal 653.7
    causing obstructed labor 660.1
  tetanic uterus 661.4
  tipping pelvis 653.0
    causing obstructed labor 660.1
  transverse
    arrest (deep) 660.3
    presentation or lie 652.3
      with successful version 652.1
      causing obstructed labor 660.0
  trauma (obstetrical) NEC 665.9
  tumor
    abdominal, fetal 653.7
      causing obstructed labor 660.1
    pelvic organs or tissues NEC 654.9
      causing obstructed labor 660.2
  umbilical cord (*see also* Delivery,
    complicated, cord) 663.9
    around neck tightly, or with compression
      663.1
    entanglement NEC 663.3
      with compression 663.2
    prolapse (complete) (occult) (partial) 663.0

Delivery—*continued*
  unstable lie 652.0
    causing obstructed labor 660.0
  uterine
    inertia (*see also* Delivery, complicated,
      inertia, uterus) 661.2
    spasm 661.4
    vasa previa 663.5
    velamentous insertion of cord 663.5
  delayed NEC 662.1
    following rupture of membranes
      (spontaneous) 658.2
      artificial 658.3
    second twin, triplet, etc. 662.3
  difficult NEC 669.9
    previous, affecting management of pregnancy
      or childbirth V23.4
    specified type NEC 669.8
  early onset (spontaneous) 644.2
  forceps NEC 669.5
    affecting fetus or newborn 763.2
  missed (at or near term) 656.4
  multiple gestation NEC 651.9
    with fetal loss and retention of one or more
      fetus(es) 651.6
    specified type NEC 651.8
      with fetal loss and retention of one or more
        fetus(es) 651.6
  nonviable infant 656.4
  normal—*see* category 650
  precipitate 661.3
    affecting fetus or newborn 763.6
  premature NEC (before 37 completed weeks
    gestation) 644.2
    previous, affecting management of pregnancy
      V23.4
  quadruplet NEC 651.2
    with fetal loss and retention of one or more
      fetus(es) 651.5
  quintuplet NEC 651.8
    with fetal loss and retention of one or more
      fetus(es) 651.6
  sextuplet NEC 651.8
    with fetal loss and retention of one or more
      fetus(es) 651.6
  specified complication NEC 669.8
  stillbirth (near term) NEC 656.4
    early (before 22 completed weeks' gestation)
      632
  term pregnancy (live birth) NEC—*see* category
    650
    stillbirth NEC 656.4
  threatened premature 644.2
  triplets NEC 651.1
    with fetal loss and retention of one or more
      fetus(es) 651.4
    delayed delivery (one or more mates) 662.3
    locked mates 660.5
  twins NEC 651.0
    with fetal loss and retention of one or more
      fetus(es) 651.3
    delayed delivery (one or more mates) 662.3
    locked mates 660.5
  uncomplicated—*see* category 650
  vacuum extractor NEC 669.5
    affecting fetus or newborn 763.3
  ventouse NEC 669.5
    affecting fetus or newborn 763.3
Dellen, cornea 371.41

Delusions (paranoid) 297.9
  grandiose 297.1
  parasitosis 300.29
  systematized 297.1
Dementia 294.8
  alcoholic (*see also* Psychosis, alcoholic) 291.2
  Alzheimer's—*see* Alzheimer's dementia
  arteriosclerotic (simple type) (uncomplicated)
    290.40
    with
      acute confusional state 290.41
      delirium 290.41
      delusional features 290.42
      depressive features 290.43
      depressed type 290.43
      paranoid type 290.42
  Binswanger's 290.12
  catatonic (acute) (*see also* Schizophrenia) 295.2
  congenital (*see also* Retardation, mental) 319
  degenerative 290.9
    presenile-onset—*see* Dementia, presenile
    senile-onset—*see* Dementia, senile
  developmental (*see also* Schizophrenia) 295.9
  dialysis 294.8
    transient 293.9
  due to or associated with condition(s) classified
    elsewhere 294.1
    multiple sclerosis 294.1
    polyarteritis nodosa 294.1
  hebephrenic (acute) 295.1
  Heller's (infantile psychosis) (*see also*
    Psychosis, childhood) 299.1
  idiopathic 290.9
    presenile-onset—*see* Dementia, presenile
    senile-onset—*see* Dementia, senile
  in
    Alzheimer's disease—*see* Alzheimer's
      dementia
    arteriosclerotic brain disease 290.40
    cerebral lipidoses 294.1
    epilepsy 294.1
    general paralysis of the insane 294.1
    hepatolenticular degeneration 294.1
    Huntington's chorea 294.1
    Jakob-Creutzfeldt disease 046.1 *[294.1]*
    multiple sclerosis 294.1
    neurosyphilis 294.1
    Pelizaeus-Merzbacher disease 294.1
    Pick's disease 331.1 *[294.1]*
    polyarteritis nodosa 294.1
    senility 290.0
    Wilson's disease 294.1
  induced by drug 292.82
  infantile, infantilia (*see also* Psychosis,
    childhood) 299.0
  multi-infarct (cerebrovascular) (*see also*
    Dementia, arteriosclerotic) 290.40
  old age 290.0
  paralytica, paralytic 094.1
    juvenilis 090.40
    syphilitic 094.1
      congenital 090.40
    tabetic form 094.1
  paranoid (*see also* Schizophrenia) 295.3
  paraphrenic (*see also* Schizophrenia) 295.3
  paretic 094.1
  praecox (*see also* Schizophrenia) 295.9

Dementia—*continued*
  presenile 290.10
    with
      acute confusional state 290.11
      delirium 290.11
      delusional features 290.12
      depressive features 290.13
      depressed type 290.13
      paranoid type 290.12
      simple type 290.10
      uncomplicated 290.10
    primary (acute) (*see also* Schizophrenia) 295.0
    progressive, syphilitic 094.1
    puerperal—*see* Psychosis, puerperal
    schizophrenic (*see also* Schizophrenia) 295.9
    senile 290.0
      with
        acute confusional state 290.3
        delirium 290.3
        delusional features 290.20
        depressive features 290.21
        depressed type 290.21
        exhaustion 290.0
        paranoid type 290.20
      simple type (acute) (*see also* Schizophrenia)
        295.0
      simplex (acute) (*see also* Schizophrenia) 295.0
      syphilitic 094.1
      uremic—*see* Uremia
Demerol dependence (*see also* Dependence)
  304.0
Demineralization, ankle (*see also* Osteoporosis)
  733.00
Demodex folliculorum (infestation) 133.8
de Morgan's spots (senile angiomas) 448.1
Demyelination, demyelinization
  central nervous system 341.9
    specified NEC 341.8
  corpus callosum (central) 341.8
  global 340
Dengue (fever) 061
  sandfly 061
  vaccination, prophylactic (against) V05.1
  virus hemorrhagic fever 065.4
Dens
  evaginatus 520.2
  in dente 520.2
  invaginatus 520.2
Density
  increased, bone (disseminated) (generalized)
    (spotted) 733.99
  lung (nodular) 518.89
Dental —*see also* condition
  examination only V72.2
Dentia praecox 520.6
Denticles (in pulp) 522.2
Dentigerous cyst 526.0
Dentin
  irregular (in pulp) 522.3
  opalescent 520.5
  secondary (in pulp) 522.3
  sensitive 521.8
Dentinogenesis imperfecta 520.5
Dentinoma (M9271/0) 213.1
  upper jaw (bone) 213.0

Dentition 520.7
  abnormal 520.6
  anomaly 520.6
  delayed 520.6
  difficult 520.7
  disorder of 520.6
  precocious 520.6
  retarded 520.6
Denture sore (mouth) 528.9
Dependence

> Note—Use the following fifth-digit
> subclassification with category 304:
>
> 0 *unspecified*
> 1 *continuous*
> 2 *episodic*
> 3 *in remission*

  with
    withdrawal symptoms
      alcohol 291.81
      drug 292.0
  14-hydroxy-dihydromorphinone 304.0
  absinthe 304.6
  acemorphan 304.0
  acetanilid(e) 304.6
  acetophenetidin 304.6
  acetorphine 304.0
  acetyldihydrocodeine 304.0
  acetyldihydrocodeinone 304.0
  Adalin 304.1
  Afghanistan black 304.3
  agrypnal 304.1
  alcohol, alcoholic (ethyl) (methyl) (wood) 303.9
    maternal, with suspected fetal damage
      affecting management of pregnancy 655.4
  allobarbitone 304.1
  allonal 304.1
  allylisopropylacetylurea 304.1
  alphaprodine (hydrochloride) 304.0
  Alurate 304.1
  Alvodine 304.0
  amethocaine 304.6
  amidone 304.0
  amidopyrine 304.6
  aminopyrine 304.6
  amobarbital 304.1
  amphetamine(s) (type) (drugs classifiable to
    969.7) 304.4
  amylene hydrate 304.6
  amylobarbitone 304.1
  amylocaine 304.6
  Amytal (sodium) 304.1
  analgesic (drug) NEC 304.6
    synthetic with morphine-like effect 304.0
  anesthetic (agent) (drug) (gas) (general) (local)
    NEC 304.6
  Angel dust 304.6
  anileridine 304.0
  antipyrine 304.6
  aprobarbital 304.1
  aprobarbitone 304.1
  atropine 304.6
  Avertin (bromide) 304.6
  barbenyl 304.1
  barbital(s) 304.1
  barbitone 304.1
  barbiturate(s) (compounds) (drugs classifiable
    to 967.0) 304.1
  barbituric acid (and compounds) 304.1
  benzedrine 304.4

Dependence—*continued*
- benzylmorphine 304.0
- Beta-chlor 304.1
- bhang 304.3
- blue velvet 304.0
- Brevital 304.1
- bromal (hydrate) 304.1
- bromide(s) NEC 304.1
- bromine compounds NEC 304.1
- bromisovalum 304.1
- bromoform 304.1
- Bromo-seltzer 304.1
- bromural 304.1
- butabarbital (sodium) 304.1
- butabarpal 304.1
- butallylonal 304.1
- butethal 304.1
- buthalitone (sodium) 304.1
- Butisol 304.1
- butobarbitone 304.1
- butyl chloral (hydrate) 304.1
- caffeine 304.4
- cannabis (indica) (sativa) (resin) (derivatives) (type) 304.3
- carbamazepine 304.6
- Carbrital 304.1
- carbromal 304.1
- carisoprodol 304.6
- Catha (edulis) 304.4
- chloral (betaine) (hydrate) 304.1
- chloralamide 304.1
- chloralformamide 304.1
- chloralose 304.1
- chlordiazepoxide 304.1
- Chloretone 304.1
- chlorobutanol 304.1
- chlorodyne 304.1
- chloroform 304.6
- Cliradon 304.0
- coca (leaf) and derivatives 304.2
- cocaine 304.2
  - hydrochloride 304.2
  - salt (any) 304.2
- codeine 304.0
- combination of drugs (excluding morphine or opioid type drug) NEC 304.8
  - morphine or opioid type drug with any other drug 304.7
- croton-chloral 304.1
- cyclobarbital 304.1
- cyclobarbitone 304.1
- dagga 304.3
- Delvinal 304.1
- Demerol 304.0
- desocodeine 304.0
- desomorphine 304.0
- desoxyephedrine 304.4
- DET 304.5
- dexamphetamine 304.4
- dexedrine 304.4
- dextromethorphan 304.0
- dextromoramide 304.0
- dextronorpseudoephedrine 304.4
- dextrorphan 304.0
- diacetylmorphine 304.0
- Dial 304.1
- diallylbarbituric acid 304.1
- diamorphine 304.0
- diazepam 304.1
- dibucaine 304.6

Dependence—*continued*
- dichloroethane 304.6
- diethyl barbituric acid 304.1
- diethylsulfone-diethylmethane 304.1
- difencloxazine 304.0
- dihydrocodeine 304.0
- dihydrocodeinone 304.0
- dihydrohydroxycodeinone 304.0
- dihydroisocodeine 304.0
- dihydromorphine 304.0
- dihydromorphinone 304.0
- dihydroxcodeinone 304.0
- Dilaudid 304.0
- dimenhydrinate 304.6
- dimethylmeperidine 304.0
- dimethyltriptamine 304.5
- Dionin 304.0
- diphenoxylate 304.6
- dipipanone 304.0
- d-lysergic acid diethylamide 304.5
- DMT 304.5
- Dolophine 304.0
- DOM 304.2
- Doriden 304.1
- dormiral 304.1
- Dormison 304.1
- Dromoran 304.0
- drug NEC 304.9
  - analgesic NEC 304.6
  - combination (excluding morphine or opioid type drug) NEC 304.8
    - morphine or opioid type drug with any other drug 304.7
  - complicating pregnancy, childbirth, or puerperium 648.3
    - affecting fetus or newborn 779.5
  - hallucinogenic 304.5
  - hypnotic NEC 304.1
  - narcotic NEC 304.9
  - psychostimulant NEC 304.4
  - sedative 304.1
  - soporific NEC 304.1
  - specified type NEC 304.6
  - suspected damage to fetus affecting management of pregnancy 655.5
  - synthetic, with morphine-like effect 304.0
  - tranquilizing 304.1
- duboisine 304.6
- ectylurea 304.1
- Endocaine 304.6
- Equanil 304.1
- Eskabarb 304.1
- ethchlorvynol 304.1
- ether (ethyl) (liquid) (vapor) (vinyl) 304.6
- ethidene 304.6
- ethinamate 304.1
- ethoheptazine 304.6
- ethyl
  - alcohol 303.9
  - bromide 304.6
  - carbamate 304.6
  - chloride 304.6
  - morphine 304.0
- ethylene (gas) 304.6
  - dichloride 304.6
- ethylidene chloride 304.6
- etilfen 304.1
- etorphine 304.0
- etoval 304.1
- eucodal 304.0

Dependence—*continued*
  opioid type drug 304.0
    with any other drug 304.7
  opium (alkaloids) (derivatives) (tincture) 304.0
  ortal 304.1
  Oxazepam 304.1
  oxycodone 304.0
  oxymorphone 304.0
  Palfium 304.0
  Panadol 304.6
  pantopium 304.0
  pantopon 304.0
  papaverine 304.0
  paracetamol 304.6
  paracodin 304.0
  paraldehyde 304.1
  paregoric 304.0
  Parzone 304.0
  PCP (phencyclidine) 304.6
  Pearly Gates 304.5
  pentazocine 304.0
  pentobarbital 304.1
  pentobarbitone (sodium) 304.1
  Pentothal 304.1
  Percaine 304.6
  Percodan 304.0
  Perichlor 304.1
  Pernocton 304.1
  Pernoston 304.1
  peronine 304.0
  pethidine (hydrochloride) 304.0
  petrichloral 304.1
  peyote 304.5
  Phanodorn 304.1
  phenacetin 304.6
  phenadoxone 304.0
  phenaglycodol 304.1
  phenazocine 304.0
  phencyclidine 304.6
  phenmetrazine 304.4
  phenobal 304.1
  phenobarbital 304.1
  phenobarbitone 304.1
  phenomorphan 304.0
  phenonyl 304.1
  phenoperidine 304.0
  pholcodine 304.0
  piminodine 304.0
  Pipadone 304.0
  Pitkin's solution 304.6
  Placidyl 304.1
  polysubstance 304.8
  Pontocaine 304.6
  pot 304.3
  potassium bromide 304.1
  Preludin 304.4
  Prinadol 304.0
  probarbital 304.1
  procaine 304.6
  propanal 304.1
  propoxyphene 304.6
  psilocibin 304.5
  psilocin 304.5
  psilocybin 304.5
  psilocyline 304.5
  psilocyn 304.5
  psychedelic agents 304.5
  psychostimulant NEC 304.4
  psychotomimetic agents 304.5
  pyrahexyl 304.3
  Pyramidon 304.6

Dependence—*continued*
  quinalbarbitone 304.1
  racemoramide 304.0
  racemorphan 304.0
  Rela 304.6
  scopolamine 304.6
  secobarbital 304.1
  Seconal 304.1
  sedative NEC 304.1
    nonbarbiturate with barbiturate effect 304.1
  Sedormid 304.1
  sernyl 304.1
  sodium bromide 304.1
  Soma 304.6
  Somnal 304.1
  Somnos 304.1
  Soneryl 304.1
  soporific (drug) NEC 304.1
  specified drug NEC 304.6
  speed 304.4
  spinocaine 304.6
  Stovaine 304.6
  STP 304.5
  stramonium 304.6
  Sulfonal 304.1
  sulfonethylmethane 304.1
  sulfonmethane 304.1
  Surital 304.1
  synthetic drug with morphine-like effect 304.0
  talbutal 304.1
  tetracaine 304.6
  tetrahydrocannabinol 304.3
  tetronal 304.1
  THC 304.3
  thebacon 304.0
  thebaine 304.0
  thiamil 304.1
  thiamylal 304.1
  thiopental 304.1
  tobacco 305.1
  toluene, toluol 304.6
  tranquilizer NEC 304.1
    nonbarbiturate with barbiturate effect 304.1
  tribromacetaldehyde 304.6
  tribromethanol 304.6
  tribromomethane 304.6
  trichloroethanol 304.6
  trichoroethyl phosphate 304.1
  triclofos 304.1
  Trional 304.1
  Tuinal 304.1
  Turkish Green 304.3
  urethan(e) 304.6
  Valium 304.1
  Valmid 304.1
  veganin 304.0
  veramon 304.1
  Veronal 304.1
  versidyne 304.6
  vinbarbital 304.1
  vinbarbitone 304.1
  vinyl bitone 304.1
  vitamin B$_6$ 266.1
  wine 303.9
  Zactane 304.6
Dependency
  passive 301.6
  reactions 301.6
Depersonalization (episode, in neurotic state)
  (neurotic) (syndrome) 300.6

Depletion
carbohydrates 271.9
complement factor 279.8
extracellular fluid 276.5
plasma 276.5
potassium 276.8
nephropathy 588.8
salt or sodium 276.1
causing heat exhaustion or prostration 992.4
nephropathy 593.9
volume 276.5
extracellular fluid 276.5
plasma 276.5
Deposit
argentous, cornea 371.16
bone, in Boeck's sarcoid 135
calcareous, calcium—*see* Calcification
cholesterol
retina 362.82
skin 709.3
vitreous (humor) 379.22
conjunctival 372.56
cornea, corneal NEC 371.10
argentous 371.16
in
cystinosis 270.0 *[371.15]*
mucopolysaccharidosis 277.5 *[371.15]*
crystalline, vitreous (humor) 379.22
hemosiderin, in old scars of cornea 371.11
metallic, in lens 366.45
skin 709.3
teeth, tooth (betel) (black) (green) (materia alba)
(orange) (soft) (tobacco) 523.6
urate, in kidney (*see also* Disease, renal) 593.9
Depraved appetite 307.52
Depression 311
acute (*see also* Psychosis, affective) 296.2
recurrent episode 296.3
single episode 296.2
agitated (*see also* Psychosis, affective) 296.2
recurrent episode 296.3
single episode 296.2
anaclitic 309.21
anxiety 300.4
arches 734
congenital 754.61
autogenous (*see also* Psychosis, affective) 296.2
recurrent episode 296.3
single episode 296.2
basal metabolic rate (BMR) 794.7
bone marrow 289.9
central nervous system 799.1
newborn 779.2
cerebral 331.9
newborn 779.2
cerebrovascular 437.8
newborn 779.2
chest wall 738.3
endogenous (*see also* Psychosis, affective) 296.2
recurrent episode 296.3
single episode 296.2
functional activity 780.9
hysterical 300.11
involutional, climacteric, or menopausal (*see
also* Psychosis, affective) 296.2
recurrent episode 296.3
single episode 296.2
manic (*see also* Psychosis, affective) 296.80
medullary 348.8
newborn 779.2

Depression—*continued*
mental 300.4
metatarsal heads—*see* Depression, arches
metatarsus—*see* Depression, arches
monopolar (*see also* Psychosis, affective) 296.2
recurrent episode 296.3
single episode 296.2
nervous 300.4
neurotic 300.4
nose 738.0
postpartum 648.4
psychogenic 300.4
reactive 298.0
psychoneurotic 300.4
psychotic (*see also* Psychosis, affective) 296.2
reactive 298.0
recurrent episode 296.3
single episode 296.2
reactive 300.4
neurotic 300.4
psychogenic 298.0
psychoneurotic 300.4
psychotic 298.0
recurrent 296.3
respiratory center 348.8
newborn 770.8
scapula 736.89
senile 290.21
situational (acute) (brief) 309.0
prolonged 309.1
skull 754.0
sternum 738.3
visual field 368.40
Depressive reaction —*see also* Reaction,
depressive
acute (transient) 309.0
with anxiety 309.28
prolonged 309.1
situational (acute) 309.0
prolonged 309.1
Deprivation
cultural V62.4
emotional V62.89
affecting
adult 995.82
infant or child 995.51
food 994.2
specific substance NEC 269.8
protein (familial) (kwashiorkor) 260
social V62.4
affecting
adult 995.82
infant or child 995.51
symptoms, syndrome
alcohol 291.81
drug 292.0
vitamins (*see also* Deficiency, vitamin) 269.2
water 994.3
de Quervain's
disease (tendon sheath) 727.04
thyroiditis (subacute granulomatous thyroiditis)
245.1
Derangement
ankle (internal) 718.97
current injury (*see also* Dislocation, ankle)
837.0
recurrent 718.37
cartilage (articular) NEC (*see also* Disorder,
cartilage, articular) 718.0

Derangement—*continued*
  knee 717.9
    recurrent 718.36
  recurrent 718.3
  collateral ligament (knee) (medial) (tibial)
    717.82
    current injury 844.1
      lateral (fibular) 844.0
    lateral (fibular) 717.81
      current injury 844.0
  cruciate ligament (knee) (posterior) 717.84
    anterior 717.83
      current injury 844.2
    current injury 844.2
  elbow (internal) 718.92
    current injury (*see also* Dislocation, elbow)
      832.00
    recurrent 718.32
  gastrointestinal 536.9
  heart—*see* Disease, heart
  hip (joint) (internal) (old) 718.95
    current injury (*see also* Dislocation, hip)
      835.00
    recurrent 718.35
  intervertebral disc—*see* Displacement,
    intervertebral disc
  joint (internal) 718.90
    ankle 718.97
    current injury—*see also* Dislocation, by site
      knee, meniscus or cartilage (*see also* Tear,
        meniscus) 836.2
    elbow 718.92
    foot 718.97
    hand 718.94
    hip 718.95
    knee 717.9
    multiple sites 718.99
    pelvic region 718.95
    recurrent 718.30
      ankle 718.37
      elbow 718.32
      foot 718.37
      hand 718.34
      hip 718.35
      knee 718.36
      multiple sites 718.39
      pelvic region 718.35
      shoulder (region) 718.31
      specified site NEC 718.38
      temporomandibular (old) 524.69
      wrist 718.33
    shoulder (region) 718.91
    specified site NEC 718.98
    spine NEC 724.9
    temporomandibular 524.69
    wrist 718.93
  knee (cartilage) (internal) 717.9
    current injury (*see also* Tear, meniscus) 836.2
    ligament 717.89
      capsular 717.85
      collateral—*see* Derangement, collateral
        ligament
      cruciate—*see* Derangement, cruciate
        ligament
      specified NEC 717.85
    recurrent 718.36
  low back NEC 724.9
  meniscus NEC (knee) 717.5
    current injury (*see also* Tear, meniscus) 836.2

Derangement—*continued*
  lateral 717.40
    anterior horn 717.42
    posterior horn 717.43
    specified NEC 717.49
  medial 717.3
    anterior horn 717.1
    posterior horn 717.2
  recurrent 718.3
  site other than knee—*see* Disorder, cartilage,
    articular
  mental (*see also* Psychosis) 298.9
  rotator cuff (recurrent) (tear) 726.10
    current 840.4
  sacroiliac (old) 724.6
    current—*see* Dislocation, sacroiliac
  semilunar cartilage (knee) 717.5
    current injury 836.2
      lateral 836.1
      medial 836.0
    recurrent 718.3
  shoulder (internal) 718.91
    current injury (*see also* Dislocation, shoulder)
      831.00
    recurrent 718.31
  spine (recurrent) NEC 724.9
    current—*see* Dislocation, spine
  temporomandibular (internal) (joint) (old)
    524.69
    current—*see* Dislocation, jaw
Dercum's disease or syndrome (adiposis
    dolorosa) 272.8
Derealization (neurotic) 300.6
Dermal —*see* condition
Dermaphytid —*see* Dermatophytosis
Dermatergosis —*see* Dermatitis
Dermatitis (allergic) (contact) (occupational)
    (venenata) 692.9
  ab igne 692.82
  acneiform 692.9
  actinic (due to sun) 692.70
    acute 692.72
    chronic NEC 692.74
    other than from sun NEC 692.82
  ambustionis
    due to
      burn or scald—*see* Burn, by site
      sunburn 692.71
  amebic 006.6
  ammonia 691.0
  anaphylactoid NEC 692.9
  arsenical 692.4
  artefacta 698.4
    psychogenic 316 *[698.4]*
  asthmatic 691.8
  atopic (allergic) (intrinsic) 691.8
    psychogenic 316 *[691.8]*
  atrophicans 701.8
    diffusa 701.8
    maculosa 701.3
  berlock, berloque 692.72
  blastomycetic 116.0
  blister beetle 692.89
  Brucella NEC 023.9
  bullosa 694.9
    striata pratensis 692.6
  bullous 694.9
    mucosynechial, atrophic 694.60
      with ocular involvement 694.61
    seasonal 694.8

Dermatitis—*continued*
calorica
due to
burn or scald—*see* Burn, by site
cold 692.89
sunburn 692.71
caterpillar 692.89
cercarial 120.3
combustionis
due to
burn or scald—*see* Burn, by site
sunburn 692.71
congelationis 991.5
contusiformis 695.2
diabetic 250.8
diaper 691.0
diphtheritica 032.85
due to
acetone 692.2
acids 692.4
adhesive plaster 692.4
alcohol (skin contact) (substances classifiable
to 980.0-980.9) 692.4
taken internally 693.8
alkalis 692.4
allergy NEC 692.9
ammonia (household) (liquid) 692.4
arnica 692.3
arsenic 692.4
taken internally 693.8
blister beetle 692.89
cantharides 692.3
carbon disulphide 692.2
caterpillar 692.89
caustics 692.4
cereal (ingested) 693.1
contact with skin 692.5
chemical(s) NEC 692.4
internal 693.8
irritant NEC 692.4
taken internally 693.8
chlorocompounds 692.2
coffee (ingested) 693.1
contact with skin 692.5
cold weather 692.89
cosmetics 692.81
cyclohexanes 692.2
deodorant 692.81
detergents 692.0
dichromate 692.4
drugs and medicinals (correct substance
properly administered) (internal use) 693.0
external (in contact with skin) 692.3
wrong substance given or taken 976.9
specified substance—*see* Table of drugs
and chemicals
wrong substance given or taken 977.9
specified substance—*see* Table of drugs
and chemicals
dyes 692.89
hair 692.89
epidermophytosis—*see* Dermatophytosis
esters 692.2
external irritant NEC 692.9
specified agent NEC 692.89
eye shadow 692.81
fish (ingested) 693.1
contact with skin 692.5
flour (ingested) 693.1
contact with skin 692.5

Dermatitis—*continued*
food (ingested) 693.1
in contact with skin 692.5
fruit (ingested) 693.1
contact with skin 692.5
fungicides 692.3
furs 692.89
glycols 692.2
greases NEC 692.1
hair dyes 692.89
hot
objects and materials—*see* Burn, by site
weather or places 692.89
hydrocarbons 692.2
infrared rays, except from sun 692.82
solar NEC (*see* also Dermatitis, due to, sun)
692.70
ingested substance 693.9
drugs and medicinals (*see also* Dermatitis,
due to, drugs and medicinals) 693.0
food 693.1
specified substance NEC 693.8
ingestion or injection of
chemical 693.8
drug (correct substance properly
administered) 693.0
wrong substance given or taken 977.9
specified substance—*see* Table of drugs
and chemicals
insecticides 692.4
internal agent 693.9
drugs and medicinals (*see also* Dermatitis,
due to, drugs and medicinals) 693.0
food (ingested) 693.1
in contact with skin 692.5
specified agent NEC 693.8
iodine 692.3
iodoform 692.3
irradiation 692.82
jewelry 692.83
keratolytics 692.3
ketones 692.2
lacquer tree (Rhus verniciflua) 692.6
light (sun) NEC (*see also* Dermatitis, due to,
sun) 692.70
other 692.82
low temperature 692.89
mascara 692.81
meat (ingested) 693.1
contact with skin 692.5
mercury, mercurials 692.3
metals 692.83
milk (ingested) 693.1
contact with skin 692.5
Neomycin 692.3
nylon 692.4
oils NEC 692.1
paint solvent 692.2
pediculocides 692.3
petroleum products (substances classifiable to
981) 692.4
phenol 692.3
photosensitiveness, photosensitivity (sun)
692.72
other light 692.82
plants NEC 692.6
plasters, medicated (any) 692.3
plastic 692.4

Dermatitis—*continued*
  poison
    ivy (Rhus toxicodendron) 692.6
    oak (Rhus diversiloba) 692.6
    plant or vine 692.6
    sumac (Rhus venenata) 692.6
    vine (Rhus radicans) 692.6
  preservatives 692.89
  primrose (primula) 692.6
  primula 692.6
  radiation 692.82
    sun NEC (*see also* Dermatitis, due to, sun)
      692.70
  radioactive substance 692.82
  radium 692.82
  ragweed (Senecio jacobae) 692.6
  Rhus (diversiloba) (radicans) (toxicodendron)
    (venenata) (verniciflua) 692.6
  rubber 692.4
  scabicides 692.3
  Senecio jacobae 692.6
  solar radiation—*see* Dermatitis, due to, sun
  solvents (any) (substances classifiable to
    982.0-982.8) 692.2
    chlorocompound group 692.2
    cyclohexane group 692.2
    ester group 692.2
    glycol group 692.2
    hydrocarbon group 692.2
    ketone group 692.2
    paint 692.2
  specified agent NEC 692.89
  sun 692.70
    acute 692.72
    chronic NEC 692.74
    specified NEC 692.79
  sunburn 692.71
  sunshine NEC (*see also* Dermatitis, due to,
    sun) 692.70
  tetrachlorethylene 692.2
  toluene 692.2
  topical medications 692.3
  turpentine 692.2
  ultraviolet rays, except from sun 692.82
    sun NEC (*see also* Dermatitis, due to, sun)
      692.70
  vaccine or vaccination (correct substance
    properly administered) 693.0
    wrong substance given or taken
      bacterial vaccine 978.8
        specified—*see* Table of drugs and
          chemicals
      other vaccines NEC 979.9
        specified—*see* Table of drugs and
          chemicals
  varicose veins (*see also* Varicose, vein,
    inflamed or infected) 454.1
  x-rays 692.82
  dyshydrotic 705.81
  dysmenorrheica 625.8
  eczematoid NEC 692.9
    infectious 690.8
  eczematous NEC 692.9
  epidemica 695.89
  erysipelatosa 695.81
  escharotica—*see* Burn, by site
  exfoliativa, exfoliative 695.89
    generalized 695.89
    infantum 695.81
    neonatorum 695.81

Dermatitis—*continued*
  eyelid 373.31
    allergic 373.32
    contact 373.32
    eczematous 373.31
    herpes (zoster) 053.20
      simplex 054.41
    infective 373.5
      due to
        actinomycosis 039.3 *[373.5]*
        herpes
          simplex 054.41
          zoster 053.20
        impetigo 684 *[373.5]*
        leprosy (*see also* Leprosy) 030.0 *[373.4]*
        lupus vulgaris (tuberculous) (*see also*
          Tuberculosis) 017.0 *[373.4]*
        mycotic dermatitis (*see also*
          Dermatomycosis) 111.9 *[373.5]*
        vaccinia 051.0 *[373.5]*
          postvaccination 999.0 *[373.5]*
        yaws (*see also* Yaws) 102.9 *[373.4]*
  facta, factitia 698.4
    psychogenic 316 *[698.4]*
  ficta 698.4
    psychogenic 316 *[698.4]*
  flexural 691.8
  follicularis 704.8
  friction 709.8
  fungus 111.9
    specified type NEC 111.8
  gangrenosa, gangrenous (infantum) (*see also*
    Gangrene) 785.4
  gestationis 646.8
  gonococcal 098.89
  gouty 274.89
  harvest mite 133.8
  heat 692.89
  herpetiformis (bullous) (erythematous)
    (pustular) (vesicular) 694.0
    juvenile 694.2
    senile 694.5
  hiemalis 692.89
  hypostatic, hypostatica 454.1
    with ulcer 454.2
  impetiginous 684
  infantile (acute) (chronic) (intertriginous)
    (intrinsic) (seborrheic) 690.12
  infectiosa eczematoides 690.8
  infectious (staphylococcal) (streptococcal) 686.9
    eczematoid 690.8
  infective eczematoid 690.8
  Jacquet's (diaper dermatitis) 691.0
  leptus 133.8
  lichenified NEC 692.9
  lichenoid, chronic 701.0
  lichenoides purpurica pigmentosa 709.1
  meadow 692.6
  medicamentosa (correct substance properly
    administered) (internal use) (*see also*
    Dermatitis, due to, drugs or medicinals)
    693.0
    due to contact with skin 692.3
  mite 133.8
  multiformis 694.0
    juvenile 694.2
    senile 694.5
  napkin 691.0
  neuro 698.3
  neurotica 694.0
  nummular NEC 692.9

Dermatitis—*continued*
  osteatosis, osteatotic 706.8
  papillaris capillitii 706.1
  pellagrous 265.2
  perioral 695.3
  perstans 696.1
  photosensitivity (sun) 692.72
    other light 692.82
  pigmented purpuric lichenoid 709.1
  polymorpha dolorosa 694.0
  primary irritant 692.9
  pruriginosa 694.0
  pruritic NEC 692.9
  psoriasiform nodularis 696.2
  psychogenic 316
  purulent 686.0
  pustular contagious 051.2
  pyococcal 686.0
  pyocyaneus 686.0
  pyogenica 686.0
  radiation 692.82
  repens 696.1
  Ritter's (exfoliativa) 695.81
  Schamberg's (progressive pigmentary
    dermatosis) 709.09
  schistosome 120.3
  seasonal bullous 694.8
  seborrheic 690.10
    infantile 690.12
  sensitization NEC 692.9
  septic 686.0
    gonococcal 098.89
  solar, solare NEC (*see also* Dermatitis, due to,
    sun) 692.70
  stasis 459.81
    due to
      postphlebitic syndrome 459.1
      varicose veins—*see* Varicose
    ulcerated or with ulcer (varicose) 454.2
  sunburn 692.71
  suppurative 686.0
  traumatic NEC 709.8
  trophoneurotica 694.0
  ultraviolet, except from sun 692.82
    due to sun NEC (*see also* Dermatitis, due to,
      sun) 692.70
  varicose 454.1
    with ulcer 454.2
  vegetans 686.8
  verrucosa 117.2
  xerotic 706.8
Dermatoarthritis, lipoid 272.8 *[713.0]*
Dermatochalasia, dermatochalasis 374.87
Dermatofibroma (lenticulare) (M8832/0)—*see
  also* Neoplasm, skin, benign
  protuberans (M8832/1)—*see* Neoplasm, skin,
    uncertain behavior
Dermatofibrosarcoma (protuberans) (M8832/3)
  see Neoplasm, skin, malignant
Dermatographia 708.3
Dermatolysis (congenital) (exfoliativa) 757.39
  acquired 701.8
  eyelids 374.34
  palpebrarum 374.34
  senile 701.8
Dermatomegaly NEC 701.8
Dermatomucomyositis 710.3
Dermatomycosis 111.9
  furfuracea 111.0
  specified type NEC 111.8
Dermatomyositis (acute) (chronic) 710.3
Dermatoneuritis of children 985.0

Dermatophiliasis 134.1
Dermatophytide —*see* Dermatophytosis
Dermatophytosis (Epidermophyton) (infection)
  (microsporum) (tinea) (Trichophyton) 110.9
  beard 110.0
  body 110.5
  deep seated 110.6
  fingernails 110.1
  foot 110.4
  groin 110.3
  hand 110.2
  nail 110.1
  perianal (area) 110.3
  scalp 110.0
  scrotal 110.8
  specified site NEC 110.8
  toenails 110.1
  vulva 110.8
Dermatopolyneuritis 985.0
Dermatorrhexis 756.83
  acquired 701.8
Dermatosclerosis (*see also* Scleroderma) 710.1
  localized 701.0
Dermatosis 709.9
  Andrews' 686.8
  atopic 691.8
  Bowen's (M8081/2)—*see* Neoplasm, skin, in
    situ
  bullous 694.9
    specified type NEC 694.8
  erythematosquamous 690.8
  exfoliativa 695.89
  factitial 698.4
  gonococcal 098.89
  herpetiformis 694.0
    juvenile 694.2
    senile 694.5
  hysterical 300.11
  menstrual NEC 709.8
  neutrophilic, acute febrile 695.89
  occupational (*see also* Dermatitis) 692.9
  papulosa nigra 709.8
  pigmentary NEC 709.00
    progressive 709.09
    Schamberg's 709.09
    Siemens-Bloch 757.33
  progressive pigmentary 709.09
  psychogenic 316
  pustular subcorneal 694.1
  Schamberg's (progressive pigmentary) 709.09
  senile NEC 709.3
  Unna's (seborrheic dermatitis) 690.10
Dermographia 708.3
Dermographism 708.3
Dermoid (cyst) (M9084/0)—*see also* Neoplasm,
  by site, benign
  with malignant transformation (M9084/3) 183.0
Dermopathy
  infiltrative, with thyrotoxicosis 242.0
  senile NEC 709.3
Dermophytosis —*see* Dermatophytosis
Descemet's membrane —*see* condition
Descemetocele 371.72
Descending —*see* condition
Descensus uteri (complete) (incomplete)
  (partial) (without vaginal wall prolapse) 618.1
  with mention of vaginal wall prolapse—*see*
    Prolapse, uterovaginal
Desensitization to allergens V07.1

Desert
rheumatism 114.0
sore (see also Ulcer, skin) 707.9
Desertion (child) (newborn) 995.52
adult 995.84
Desmoid (extra-abdominal) (tumor)
(M8821/1)—see also Neoplasm, connective
tissue, uncertain behavior
abdominal (M8822/1)—see Neoplasm,
connective tissue, uncertain behavior
Despondency 300.4
Desquamative dermatitis NEC 695.89
Destruction
articular facet (see also Derangement, joint)
718.9
vertebra 724.9
bone 733.90
syphilitic 095.5
joint (see also Derangement, joint) 718.9
sacroiliac 724.6
kidney 593.89
live fetus to facilitate birth NEC 763.8
ossicles (ear) 385.24
rectal sphincter 569.49
septum (nasal) 478.1
tuberculous NEC (see also Tuberculosis) 011.9
tympanic membrane 384.82
tympanum 385.89
vertebral disc—see Degeneration, intervertebral
disc
Destructiveness (see also Disturbance, conduct)
312.9
adjustment reaction 309.3
Detachment
cartilage—see also Sprain, by site
knee—see Tear, meniscus
cervix, annular 622.8
complicating delivery 665.3
choroid (old) (postinfectional) (simple)
(spontaneous) 363.70
hemorrhagic 363.72
serous 363.71
knee, medial meniscus (old) 717.3
current injury 836.0
ligament—see Sprain, by site
placenta (premature)—see Placenta, separation
retina (recent) 361.9
with retinal defect (rhegmatogenous) 361.00
giant tear 361.03
multiple 361.02
partial
with
giant tear 361.03
multiple defects 361.02
retinal dialysis (juvenile) 361.04
single defect 361.01
retinal dialysis (juvenile) 361.04
single 361.01
subtotal 361.05
total 361.05
delimited (old) (partial) 361.06
old
delimited 361.06
partial 361.06
total or subtotal 361.07
pigment epithelium (RPE) (serous) 362.42
exudative 362.42
hemorrhagic 362.43
rhegmatogenous (see also Detachment, retina,
with retinal defect) 361.00
serous (without retinal defect) 361.2

Detachment—continued
specified type NEC 361.89
traction (with vitreoretinal organization)
361.81
vitreous humor 379.21
Detergent asthma 507.8
Deterioration
epileptic 294.1
heart, cardiac (see also Degeneration,
myocardial) 429.1
mental (see also Psychosis) 298.9
myocardium, myocardial (see also
Degeneration, myocardial) 429.1
senile (simple) 797
transplanted organ—see Complications,
transplant, organ, by site
de Toni-Fanconi syndrome (cystinosis) 270.0
Deuteranomaly 368.52
Deuteranopia (anomalous trichromat)
(complete) (incomplete) 368.52
Deutschländer's disease —see Fracture, foot
Development
abnormal, bone 756.9
arrested 783.4
bone 733.91
child 783.4
due to malnutrition (protein-calorie) 263.2
fetus or newborn 764.9
tracheal rings (congenital) 748.3
defective, congenital—see also Anomaly
cauda equina 742.59
left ventricle 746.9
with atresia or hypoplasia of aortic orifice or
valve with hypoplasia of ascending aorta
746.7
in hypoplastic left heart syndrome 746.7
delayed (see also Delay, development) 783.4
arithmetical skills 315.1
language (skills) 315.31
expressive 315.31
mixed receptive-expressive 315.32
learning skill, specified NEC 315.2
mixed skills 315.5
motor coordination 315.4
reading 315.00
specified
learning skill NEC 315.2
type NEC, except learning 315.8
speech 315.39
associated with hyperkinesia 314.1
phonological 315.39
spelling 315.09
written expression 315.2
imperfect, congenital—see also Anomaly
heart 746.9
lungs 748.60
improper (fetus or newborn) 764.9
incomplete (fetus or newborn) 764.9
affecting management of pregnancy 656.5
bronchial tree 748.3
organ or site not listed—see Hypoplasia
respiratory system 748.9
sexual, precocious NEC 259.1
tardy, mental (see also Retardation, mental) 319
Developmental —see condition
Devergie's disease (pityriasis rubra pilaris) 696.4

Deviation
  conjugate (eye) 378.87
    palsy 378.81
    spasm, spastic 378.82
  esophagus 530.89
  eye, skew 378.87
  midline (jaw) (teeth) 524.2
  specified site NEC—*see* Malposition
  organ or site, congenital NEC—*see*
    Malposition, congenital
  septum (acquired) (nasal) 470
    congenital 754.0
  sexual 302.9
    bestiality 302.1
    coprophilia 302.89
    ego-dystonic
      homosexuality 302.0
      lesbianism 302.0
    erotomania 302.89
      Clérambault's 297.8
    exhibitionism (sexual) 302.4
    fetishism 302.81
      transvestic 302.3
    frotteurism 302.89
    homosexuality, ego-dystonic 302.0
      pedophilic 302.2
    lesbianism, ego-dystonic 302.0
    masochism 302.83
    narcissism 302.89
    necrophilia 302.89
    nymphomania 302.89
    pederosis 302.2
    pedophilia 302.2
    sadism 302.84
    sadomasochism 302.84
    satyriasis 302.89
    specified type NEC 302.89
    transvestic fetishism 302.3
    transvestism 302.3
    voyeurism 302.82
    zoophilia (erotica) 302.1
  teeth, midline 524.2
  trachea 519.1
  ureter (congenital) 753.4
Devic's disease 341.0
Device
  cerebral ventricle (communicating) in situ V45.2
  contraceptive—*see* Contraceptive, device
  drainage, cerebrospinal fluid V45.2
Devil's
  grip 074.1
  pinches (purpura simplex) 287.2
Devitalized tooth 522.9
Devonshire colic 984.9
  specified type of lead—*see* Table of drugs and
    chemicals
Dextraposition, aorta 747.21
  with ventricular septal defect, pulmonary
    stenosis or atresia, and hypertrophy of right
    ventricle 745.2
  in tetralogy of Fallot 745.2
Dextratransposition, aorta 745.11
Dextrinosis, limit (debrancher enzyme
  deficiency) 271.0
Dextrocardia (corrected) (false) (isolated)
  (secondary) (true) 746.87
  with
  complete transposition of viscera 759.3
  situs inversus 759.3
Dextroversion, kidney (left) 753.3
Dhobie itch 110.3

Diabetes, diabetic (brittle) (congenital) (familial)
  (mellitus) (severe) (slight) (without
  complication) 250.0

Note—Use the following fifth-digit
subclassification with category 250:

0 type II [non-insulin dependent type]
  [NIDDM type] [adult-onset type] or
  unspecified type, not stated as uncontrolled
1 type I [insulin dependent type]
  [IDDM] [juvenile type], not stated as uncon-
  trolled
2 type II [non-insulin dependent type] [NIDDM
  type] [adult-onset type] or unspecified type,
  uncontrolled
3 type I [insulin dependent type] [IDDM]
  [juvenile type], uncontrolled

---

  with
    coma (with ketoacidosis) 250.3
      hyperosmolar (nonketotic) 250.2
    complication NEC 250.9
      specified NEC 250.8
    gangrene 250.7 *[785.4]*
    hyperosmolarity 250.2
    ketosis, ketoacidosis 250.1
    osteomyelitis 250.8 *[731.8]*
    specified manifestations NEC 250.8
  acetonemia 250.1
  acidosis 250.1
  amyotrophy 250.6 *[358.1]*
  angiopathy, peripheral 250.7 *[443.81]*
  asymptomatic 790.2
  autonomic neuropathy (peripheral) 250.6
    [337.1]
  bone change 250.8 *[731.8]*
  bronze, bronzed 275.0
  cataract 250.5 *[366.41]*
  chemical 790.2
    complicating pregnancy, childbirth, or
      puerperium 648.8
  coma (with ketoacidosis) 250.3
    hyperglycemic 250.3
    hyperosmolar (nonketotic) 250.2
    hypoglycemic 250.3
    insulin 250.3
  complicating pregnancy, childbirth, or
    puerperium (maternal) 648.0
    affecting fetus or newborn 775.0
  complication NEC 250.9
    specified NEC 250.8
  dorsal sclerosis 250.6 *[340]*
  dwarfism-obesity syndrome 258.1
  gangrene 250.7 *[785.4]*
  gastroparesis 250.6 *[536.3]*
  gestational 648.8
    complicating pregnancy, childbirth, or
      puerperium 648.8
  glaucoma 240.5 *[365.44]*
  glomerulosclerosis (intercapillary) 250.4
    [581.81]
  glycogenosis, secondary 250.8 *[259.8]*
  hemochromatosis 275.0
  hyperosmolar coma 250.2
  hyperosmolarity 250.2
  hypertension-nephrosis syndrome 250.4
    [581.81]
  hypoglycemia 250.8
  hypoglycemic shock 250.8

Diabetes, diabetic—*continued*
  insipidus 253.5
    nephrogenic 588.1
    pituitary 253.5
    vasopressin-resistant 588.1
  intercapillary glomerulosclerosis 250.4 *[581.81]*
  iritis 250.5 *[364.42]*
  ketosis, ketoacidosis 250.1
  Kimmelstiel (-Wilson) disease or syndrome
      (intercapillary glomerulosclerosis) 250.4
      [581.81]
  Lancereaux's (diabetes mellitus with marked
      emaciation) 250.8 *[261]*
  latent (chemical) 790.2
    complicating pregnancy, childbirth, or
        puerperium 648.8
  lipoidosis 250.8 *[272.7]*
  macular edema 250.5 *[362.83]*
  maternal
    with manifest disease in the infant 775.1
    affecting fetus or newborn 775.0
  microaneurysms, retinal 250.5 *[362.01]*
  mononeuropathy 250.6 *[355.9]*
  neonatal, transient 775.1
  nephropathy 250.4 *[583.81]*
  nephrosis (syndrome) 250.4 *[581.81]*
  neuralgia 250.6 *[357.2]*
  neuritis 250.6 *[357.2]*
  neurogenic arthropathy 250.6 *[713.5]*
  neuropathy 250.6 *[357.2]*
  nonclinical 790.2
  osteomyelitis 250.8 *[731.8]*
  peripheral autonomic neuropathy 250.6 *[337.1]*
  phosphate 275.3
  polyneuropathy 250.6 *[357.2]*
  renal (true) 271.4
  retinal
    edema 250.5 *[362.83]*
    hemorrhage 250.5 *[362.01]*
    microaneurysms 250.5 *[362.01]*
  retinitis 250.5 *[362.01]*
  retinopathy 250.5 *[362.01]*
    background 250.5 *[362.01]*
    proliferative 250.5 *[362.02]*
  steroid induced
    correct substance properly administered 251.8
    overdose or wrong substance given or taken
        962.0
  stress 790.2
  subclinical 790.2
  subliminal 790.2
  sugar 250.0
  ulcer (skin) 250.8 *[707.9]*
    lower extremity 250.8 *[707.1]*
    specified site NEC 250.8 *[707.8]*
  xanthoma 250.8 *[272.2]*
Diacyclothrombopathia 287.1
Diagnosis deferred 799.9
Dialysis (intermittent) (treatment)
  anterior retinal (juvenile) (with detachment)
      361.04
  extracorporeal V56.0
  peritoneal V56.8
  renal V56.0
    status only V45.1
  specified type NEC V56.8
Diamond-Blackfan anemia or syndrome
      (congenital hypoplastic anemia) 284.0
Diamond-Gardener syndrome (autoerythrocyte
      sensitization) 287.2
Diaper rash 691.0

Diaphoresis (excessive) NEC 780.8
Diaphragm —*see* condition
Diaphragmalgia 786.52
Diaphragmitis 519.4
Diaphyseal aclasis 756.4
Diaphysitis 733.99
Diarrhea, diarrheal (acute) (autumn) (bilious)
      (bloody) (catarrhal) (choleraic) (chronic)
      (gravis) (green) (infantile) (lienteric)
      (noninfectious) (presumed noninfectious)
      (putrefactive) (secondary) (sporadic)
      (summer) (symptomatic) (thermic) 787.91
  achlorhydric 536.0
  allergic 558.9
  amebic (*see also* Amebiasis) 006.9
    with abscess—*see* Abscess, amebic
    acute 006.0
    chronic 006.1
    nondysenteric 006.2
  bacillary—*see* Dysentery, bacillary
  bacterial NEC 008.5
  balantidial 007.0
  bile salt-induced 579.8
  cachectic NEC 558.9
  chilomastix 007.8
  choleriformis 001.1
  coccidial 007.2
  Cochin-China 579.1
    anguilluliasis 127.2
    psilosis 579.1
  Dientamoeba 007.8
  dietetic 558.9
  due to
    achylia gastrica 536.8
    Aerobacter aerogenes 008.2
    Bacillus coli—*see* Enteritis, E. coli
    bacteria NEC 008.5
    bile salts 579.8
    Capillaria
      hepatica 128.8
      philippinensis 127.5
    Clostridium perfringens (C) (F) 008.46
    Enterobacter aerogenes 008.2
    enterococci 008.49
    Escherichia coli—*see* Enteritis, E. coli
    Giardia lamblia 007.1
    Heterophyes heterophyes 121.6
    irritating foods 558.9
    Metagonimus yokogawai 121.5
    Necator americanus 126.1
    Paracolobactrum arizonae 008.1
    Paracolon bacillus NEC 008.47
      Arizona 008.1
    Proteus (bacillus) (mirabilis) (Morganii) 008.3
    Pseudomonas aeruginosa 008.42
    S. japonicum 120.2
    specified organism NEC 008.8
      bacterial 008.49
      viral NEC 008.69
    Staphylococcus 008.41
    Streptococcus 008.49
      anaerobic 008.46
    Strongyloides stercoralis 127.2
    Trichuris trichiuria 127.3
    virus NEC (*see also* Enteritis, viral) 008.69
  dysenteric 009.2
    due to specified organism NEC 008.8
  dyspeptic 558.9
  endemic 009.3
  epidemic 009.3
  fermentative 558.9

Diarrhea, diarrheal—*continued*
  flagellate 007.9
  Flexner's (ulcerative) 004.1
  functional 564.5
    following gastrointestinal surgery 564.4
    psychogenic 306.4
  giardial 007.1
  Giardia lamblia 007.1
  hill 579.1
  hyperperistalsis (nervous) 306.4
  infectious 009.2
    presumed 009.3
  inflammatory 558.9
    due to specified organism NEC 008.8
  malarial (*see also* Malaria) 084.6
  mite 133.8
  mycotic 117.9
  nervous 306.4
  neurogenic 564.5
  parenteral NEC 009.2
  postgastrectomy 564.4
  postvagotomy 564.4
  prostaglandin induced 579.8
  protozoal NEC 007.9
  psychogenic 306.4
  septic 009.2
    due to specified organism NEC 008.8
  specified organism NEC 008.8
    bacterial 008.49
    viral NEC 008.69
  Staphylococcus 008.41
  Streptococcus 008.49
    anaerobic 088.46
  toxic 558.2
  travelers' 009.2
    due to specified organism NEC 008.8
  trichomonal 007.3
  tropical 579.1
  tuberculous 014.8
  ulcerative (chronic) (*see also* Colitis, ulcerative)
    556.9
  viral (*see also* Enteritis, viral) 008.8
  zymotic NEC 009.2
Diastasis
  cranial bones 733.99
    congenital 756.0
  joint (traumatic)—*see* Dislocation, by site
  muscle 728.84
    congenital 756.89
  recti (abdomen) 728.84
    complicating delivery 665.8
    congenital 756.7
Diastema, teeth, tooth 524.3
Diastematomyelia 742.51
Diataxia, cerebral, infantile 343.0
Diathesis
  allergic V15.0
  bleeding (familial) 287.9
  cystine (familial) 270.0
  gouty 274.9
  hemorrhagic (familial) 287.9
    newborn NEC 776.0
  oxalic 271.8
  scrofulous (*see also* Tuberculosis) 017.2
  spasmophilic (*see also* Tetany) 781.7
  ulcer 536.9
  uric acid 274.9
Diaz's disease or osteochondrosis 732.5
Dibothriocephaliasis 123.4
  larval 123.5

Dibothriocephalus (infection) (infestation)
    (latus) 123.4
  larval 123.5
Dicephalus 759.4
Dichotomy, teeth 520.2
Dichromat, dichromata (congenital) 368.59
Dichromatopsia (congenital) 368.59
Dichuchwa 104.0
Dicroceliasis 121.8
Didelphys, didelphic (*see also* Double uterus)
    752.2
Didymitis (*see also* Epididymitis) 604.90
Died —*see also* Death
  without
    medical attention (cause unknown) 798.9
    sign of disease 798.2
Dientamoeba diarrhea 007.8
Dietary
  inadequacy or deficiency 269.9
  surveillance and counseling V65.3
Dietl's crisis 593.4
Dieulafoy's ulcer —*see* Ulcer, stomach
Difficult
  birth, affecting fetus or newborn 763.9
  delivery NEC 669.9
Difficulty
  feeding 783.3
    newborn 779.3
    nonorganic (infant) NEC 307.59
  mechanical, gastroduodenal stoma 537.89
  reading 315.00
  specific, spelling 315.09
  swallowing (*see also* Dysphagia) 787.2
  walking 719.7
Diffuse —*see* condition
Diffused ganglion 727.42
DiGeorge's syndrome (thymic hypoplasia)
    279.11
Digestive —*see* condition
Di Guglielmo's disease or syndrome (M9841/3)
    207.0
Diktyoma (M9051/3)—*see* Neoplasm, by site,
    malignant
Dilaceration, tooth 520.4
Dilatation
  anus 564.8
    venule—*see* Hemorrhoids
  aorta (focal) (general) (*see also* Aneurysm,
      aorta) 441.9
    congenital 747.29
    infectional 093.0
    ruptured 441.5
    syphilitic 093.0
  appendix (cystic) 543.9
  artery 447.8
  bile duct (common) (cystic) (congenital) 751.69
    acquired 576.8
  bladder (sphincter) 596.8
    congenital 753.8
    in pregnancy or childbirth 654.4
      causing obstructed labor 660.2
        affecting fetus or newborn 763.1
  blood vessel 459.89
  bronchus, bronchi 494
  calyx (due to obstruction) 593.89
  capillaries 448.9
  cardiac (acute) (chronic) (*see also* Hypertrophy,
      cardiac) 429.3
    congenital 746.89
      valve NEC 746.89
        pulmonary 746.09

Dilatation—*continued*
  hypertensive (*see also* Hypertension, heart)
    402.90
  cavum septi pellucidi 742.4
  cecum 564.8
    psychogenic 306.4
  cervix (uteri)—*see also* Incompetency, cervix
    incomplete, poor, slow
      affecting fetus or newborn 763.7
      complicating delivery 661.0
        affecting fetus or newborn 763.7
  colon 564.7
    congenital 751.3
    due to mechanical obstruction 560.89
    psychogenic 306.4
  common bile duct (congenital) 751.69
    acquired 576.8
      with calculus, choledocholithiasis, or
        stones—*see* Choledocholithiasis
  cystic duct 751.69
    acquired (any bile duct) 575.8
  duct, mammary 610.4
  duodenum 564.8
  esophagus 530.89
    congenital 750.4
    due to
      achalasia 530.0
      cardiospasm 530.0
  Eustachian tube, congenital 744.24
  fontanel 756.0
  gallbladder 575.8
    congenital 751.69
  gastric 536.8
    acute 536.1
    psychogenic 306.4
  heart (acute) (chronic) (*see also* Hypertrophy,
      cardiac) 429.3
    congenital 746.89
    hypertensive (*see also* Hypertension, heart)
      402.90
    valve—*see also* Endocarditis
      congenital 746.89
  ileum 564.8
    psychogenic 306.4
  inguinal rings—*see* Hernia, inguinal
  jejunum 564.8
    psychogenic 306.4
  kidney (calyx) (collecting structures) (cystic)
      (parenchyma) (pelvis) 593.89
  lacrimal passages 375.69
  lymphatic vessel 457.1
  mammary duct 610.4
  Meckel's diverticulum (congenital) 751.0
  meningeal vessels, congenital 742.8
  myocardium (acute) (chronic) (*see also*
      Hypertrophy, cardiac) 429.3
  organ or site, congenital NEC—*see* Distortion
  pancreatic duct 577.8
  pelvis, kidney 593.89
  pericardium—*see* Pericarditis
  pharynx 478.29
  prostate 602.8
  pulmonary
    artery (idiopathic) 417.8
      congenital 747.3
    valve, congenital 746.09
  pupil 379.43
  rectum 564.8
  renal 593.89
  saccule vestibularis, congenital 744.05
  salivary gland (duct) 527.8

Dilatation—*continued*
  sphincter ani 564.8
  stomach 536.8
    acute 536.1
    psychogenic 306.4
  submaxillary duct 527.8
  trachea, congenital 748.3
  ureter (idiopathic) 593.89
    congenital 753.20
    due to obstruction 593.5
  urethra (acquired) 599.84
  vasomotor 443.9
  vein 459.89
  ventricular, ventricle (acute) (chronic) (*see also*
      Hypertrophy, cardiac) 429.3
    cerebral, congenital 742.4
    hypertensive (*see also* Hypertension, heart)
      402.90
  venule 459.89
    anus—*see* Hemorrhoids
  vesical orifice 596.8
Dilated, dilation —*see* Dilatation
Diminished
  hearing (acuity) (*see also* Deafness) 389.9
  pulse pressure 785.9
  vision NEC 369.9
  vital capacity 794.2
Diminuta taenia 123.6
Diminution, sense or sensation (cold) (heat)
    (tactile) (vibratory) (*see also* Disturbance,
    sensation) 782.0
Dimitri-Sturge-Weber disease
    (encephalocutaneous angiomatosis) 759.6
Dimple
  parasacral 685.1
    with abscess 685.0
  pilonidal 685.1
    with abscess 685.0
  postanal 685.1
    with abscess 685.0
Dioctophyma renale (infection) (infestation)
    128.8
Dipetalonemiasis 125.4
Diphallus 752.69
Diphtheria, diphtheritic (gangrenous)
    (hemorrhagic) 032.9
  carrier (suspected) of V02.4
  cutaneous 032.85
  cystitis 032.84
  faucial 032.0
  infection of wound 032.85
  inoculation (anti) (not sick) V03.5
  laryngeal 032.3
  myocarditis 032.82
  nasal anterior 032.2
  nasopharyngeal 032.1
  neurological complication 032.89
  peritonitis 032.83
  specified site NEC 032.89
Diphyllobothriasis (intestine) 123.4
  larval 123.5
Diplacusis 388.41
Diplegia (upper limbs) 344.2
  brain or cerebral 437.8
    congenital 343.0
  facial 351.0
    congenital 352.6
  infantile or congenital (cerebral) (spastic)
      (spinal) 343.0
  lower limbs 344.1
  syphilitic, congenital 090.49

Diplococcus, diplococcal —*see* condition
Diplomyelia 742.59
Diplopia 368.2
  refractive 368.15
Dipsomania (*see also* Alcoholism) 303.9
  with psychosis (*see also* Psychosis, alcoholic)
    291.9
Dipylidiasis 123.8
  intestine 123.8
Direction, teeth, abnormal 524.3
Dirt-eating child 307.52
Disability
  heart—*see* Disease, heart
  learning NEC 315.2
  special spelling 315.09
Disarticulation (*see also* Derangement, joint)
  718.9
  meaning
    amputation
      status—*see* Absence, by site
      traumatic —*see* Amputation, traumatic
    dislocation, traumatic or congenital—*see*
      Dislocation
Disaster, cerebrovascular (*see also* Disease,
  cerebrovascular, acute) 436
Discharge
  anal NEC 787.99
  breast (female) (male) 611.79
  conjunctiva 372.8
  continued locomotor idiopathic (*see also*
    Epilepsy) 345.5
  diencephalic autonomic idiopathic (*see also*
    Epilepsy) 345.5
  ear 388.60
    blood 388.69
    cerebrospinal fluid 388.61
  excessive urine 788.42
  eye 379.93
  nasal 478.1
  nipple 611.79
  patterned motor idiopathic (*see also* Epilepsy)
    345.5
  penile 788.7
  postnasal—*see* Sinusitis
  sinus, from mediastinum 510.0
  umbilicus 789.9
  urethral 788.7
    bloody 599.84
  vaginal 623.5
Discitis 722.90
  cervical, cervicothoracic 722.91
  lumbar, lumbosacral 722.93
  thoracic, thoracolumbar 722.92
Discogenic syndrome —*see* Displacement,
  intervertebral disc
Discoid
  kidney 753.3
  meniscus, congenital 717.5
  semilunar cartilage 717.5
Discoloration
  mouth 528.9
  nails 703.8
  teeth 521.7
    due to
      drugs 521.7
      metals (copper) (silver) 521.7
      pulpal bleeding 521.7
    during formation 520.8
    posteruptive 521.7
Discomfort
  chest 786.59
  visual 368.13

Discomycosis —*see* Actinomycosis
Discontinuity, ossicles, ossicular chain 385.23
Discrepancy, leg length (acquired) 736.81
  congenital 755.30
Discrimination
  political V62.4
  racial V62.4
  religious V62.4
  sex V62.4
Disease, diseased —*see also* Syndrome
  Abrami's (acquired hemolytic jaundice) 283.9
  absorbent system 459.89
  accumulation—*see* Thesaurismosis
  acid-peptic 536.8
  Acosta's 993.2
  Adams-Stokes (-Morgagni) (syncope with heart
    block) 426.9
  Addison's (bronze) (primary adrenal
    insufficiency) 255.4
    anemia (pernicious) 281.0
    tuberculous (*see also* Tuberculosis) 017.6
  Addison-Gull—*see* Xanthoma
  adenoids (and tonsils) (chronic) 474.9
  adrenal (gland) (capsule) (cortex) 255.9
    hyperfunction 255.3
    hypofunction 255.4
    specified type NEC 255.8
  ainhum (dactylolysis spontanea) 136.0
  akamushi (scrub typhus) 081.2
  Akureyri (epidemic neuromyasthenia) 049.8
  Albarrán's (colibacilluria) 599.0
  Albers-Schönberg's (marble bones) 756.52
  Albert's 726.71
  Albright (-Martin) (-Bantam) 275.4
  Alibert's (mycosis fungoides) (M9700/3) 202.1
  Alibert-Bazin (M9700/3) 202.1
  alimentary canal 569.9
  alligator skin (ichthyosis congenital) 757.1
    acquired 701.1
  Almeida's (Brazilian blastomycosis) 116.1
  Alpers' 330.8
  alpine 993.2
  altitude 993.2
  alveoli, teeth 525.9
  Alzheimer's—*see* Alzheimer's
  amyloid (any site) 277.3
  anarthritic rheumatoid 446.5
  Anders' (adiposis tuberosa simplex) 272.8
  Andersen's (glycogenosis IV) 271.0
  Anderson's (angiokeratoma corporis diffusum)
    272.7
  Andes 993.2
  Andrews' (bacterid) 686.8
  angiospastic, angiospasmodic 443.9
    cerebral 435.9
      with transient neurologic deficit 435.9
    vein 459.89
  anterior
    chamber 364.9
    horn cell 335.9
      specified type NEC 335.8
  antral (chronic) 473.0
    acute 461.0
  anus NEC 569.49
  aorta (nonsyphilitic) 447.9
    syphilitic NEC 093.89
  aortic (heart) (valve) (*see also* Endocarditis,
    aortic) 424.1
  apollo 077.4
  aponeurosis 726.90
  appendix 543.9

Disease, diseased—*continued*
aqueous (chamber) 364.9
arc-welders' lung 503
Armenian 277.3
Arnold-Chiari (*see also* Spina bifida) 741.0
arterial 447.9
  occlusive (*see also* Occlusion, by site) 444.22
    with embolus or thrombus—*see* Occlusion,
      by site
  due to stricture or stenosis 447.1
  specified type NEC 447.8
arteriocardiorenal (*see also* Hypertension,
    cardiorenal) 404.90
arteriolar (generalized) (obliterative) 447.9
  specified type NEC 447.8
arteriorenal—*see* Hypertension, kidney
arteriosclerotic—*see also* Arteriosclerosis
  cardiovascular 429.2
  coronary —*see* Arteriosclerosis, coronary
  heart —*see* Arteriosclerosis, coronary
  vascular—*see* Arteriosclerosis
artery 447.9
  cerebral 437.9
  coronary —*see* Arteriosclerosis, coronary
  specified type NEC 447.8
arthropod-borne NEC 088.9
  specified type NEC 088.89
Asboe-Hansen's (incontinentia pigmenti) 757.33
atticoantral, chronic (with posterior or superior
    marginal perforation of ear drum) 382.2
auditory canal, ear 380.9
Aujeszky's 078.89
auricle, ear NEC 380.30
Australian X 062.4
autoimmune NEC 279.4
  hemolytic (cold type) (warm type) 283.0
  parathyroid 252.1
  thyroid 245.2
aviators' (*see also* Effect, adverse, high altitude)
    993.2
ax(e)-grinders' 502
Ayala's 756.89
Ayerza's (pulmonary artery sclerosis with
    pulmonary hypertension) 416.0
Babington's (familial hemorrhagic
    telangiectasia) 448.0
back bone NEC 733.90
bacterial NEC 040.89
  zoonotic NEC 027.9
  specified type NEC 027.8
Baehr-Schiffrin (thrombotic thrombocytopenic
    purpura) 446.6
Baelz's (cheilitis glandularis apostematosa)
    528.5
Baerensprung's (eczema marginatum) 110.3
Balfour's (chloroma) 205.3
balloon (*see also* Effect, adverse, high altitude)
    993.2
Baló's 341.1
Bamberger (-Marie) (hypertrophic pulmonary
    osteoarthropathy) 731.2
Bang's (Brucella abortus) 023.1
Bannister's 995.1
Banti's (with cirrhosis) (with portal
    hypertension)—*see* Cirrhosis, liver
Barcoo (*see also* Ulcer, skin) 707.9
barium lung 503
Barlow (-Möller) (infantile scurvy) 267
barometer makers' 985.0
Barraquer (-Simons) (progressive
    lipodystrophy) 272.6

Disease, diseased—*continued*
basal ganglia 333.90
  degenerative NEC 333.0
  specified NEC 333.89
Basedow's (exophthalmic goiter) 242.0
basement membrane NEC 583.89
  with
    pulmonary hemorrhage (Goodpasture's
      syndrome) 446.21 *[583.81]*
Bateman's 078.0
  purpura (senile) 287.2
Batten's 330.1 *[362.71]*
Batten-Mayou (retina) 330.1 *[362.71]*
Batten-Steinert 359.2
Battey 031.0
Baumgarten-Cruveilhier (cirrhosis of liver)
    571.5
bauxite-workers' 503
Bayle's (dementia paralytica) 094.1
Bazin's (primary) (*see also* Tuberculosis) 017.1
Beard's (neurasthenia) 300.5
Beau's (*see also* Degeneration, myocardial)
    429.1
Bechterew's (ankylosing spondylitis) 720.0
Becker's (idiopathic mural endomyocardial
    disease) 425.2
Begbie's (exophthalmic goiter) 242.0
Behr's 362.50
Beigel's (white piedra) 111.2
Bekhterev's (ankylosing spondylitis) 720.0
Bell's (*see also* Psychosis, affective) 296.0
Bennett's (leukemia) 208.9
Benson's 379.22
Bergeron's (hysteroepilepsy) 300.11
Berlin's 921.3
Bernard-Soulier (thrombopathy) 287.1
Bernhardt (-Roth) 355.1
beryllium 503
Besnier-Boeck (-Schaumann) (sarcoidosis) 135
Best's 362.76
Beurmann's (sporotrichosis) 117.1
Bielschowsky (-Jansky) 330.1
Biermer's (pernicious anemia) 281.0
Biett's (discoid lupus erythematosus) 695.4
bile duct (*see also* Disease, biliary) 576.9
biliary (duct) (tract) 576.9
  with calculus, choledocholithiasis, or
    stones—*see* Choledocholithiasis
Billroth's (meningocele) (*see also* Spina bifida)
    741.9
Binswanger's 290.12
Bird's (oxaluria) 271.8
bird fanciers' 495.2
black lung 500
bladder 596.9
  specified NEC 596.8
bleeder's 286.0
Bloch-Sulzberger (incontinentia pigmenti)
    757.33
Blocq's (astasia-abasia) 307.9
blood (-forming organs) 289.9
  specified NEC 289.8
  vessel 459.9
Bloodgood's 610.1
Blount's (tibia vara) 732.4
blue 746.9
Bodechtel-Guttmann (subacute sclerosing
    panencephalitis) 046.2
Boeck's (sarcoidosis) 135

Disease, diseased—*continued*
bone 733.90
  fibrocystic NEC 733.29
    jaw 526.2
  marrow 289.9
  Paget's (osteitis deformans) 731.0
  specified type NEC 733.99
  von Recklinghausen's (osteitis fibrosa cystica)
    252.0
Bonfils'—*see* Disease, Hodgkin's
Borna 062.9
Bornholm (epidemic pleurodynia) 074.1
Bostock's (*see also* Fever, hay) 477.9
Bouchard's (myopathic dilatation of the
  stomach) 536.1
Bouillaud's (rheumatic heart disease) 391.9
Bourneville (-Brissaud) (tuberous sclerosis)
  759.5
Bouveret (-Hoffmann) (paroxysmal
  tachycardia) 427.2
bowel 569.9
  functional 564.9
  psychogenic 306.4
Bowen's (M8081/2)—*see* Neoplasm, skin, in
  situ
Bozzolo's (multiple myeloma) (M9730/3) 203.0
Bradley's (epidemic vomiting) 078.82
Brailsford's 732.3
  radius, head 732.3
  tarsal, scaphoid 732.5
Brailsford-Morquio (mucopolysaccharidosis
  IV) 277.5
brain 348.9
  Alzheimer's 331.0
    with dementia—*see* Alzheimer's, dementia
  arterial, artery 437.9
  arteriosclerotic 437.0
  congenital 742.9
  degenerative—*see* Degeneration, brain
  inflammatory—*see also* Encephalitis
  late effect—*see* category 326
  organic 348.9
    arteriosclerotic 437.0
  parasitic NEC 123.9
  Pick's 331.1
    with dementia 331.1 *[294.1]*
  senile 331.2
braziers' 985.8
breast 611.9
  cystic (chronic) 610.1
  fibrocystic 610.1
  inflammatory 611.0
  Paget's (M8540/3) 174.0
  puerperal, postpartum NEC 676.3
  specified NEC 611.8
Breda's (*see also* Yaws) 102.9
Breisky's (kraurosis vulvae) 624.0
Bretonneau's (diphtheritic malignant angina)
  032.0
Bright's (*see also* Nephritis) 583.9
  arteriosclerotic (*see also* Hypertension,
    kidney) 403.90
Brill's (recrudescent typhus) 081.1
  flea-borne 081.0
  louse-borne 081.1
Brill-Symmers (follicular lymphoma)
  (M9690/3) 202.0
Brill-Zinsser (recrudescent typhus) 081.1
Brinton's (leather bottle stomach) (M8142/3)
  151.9

Disease, diseased—*continued*
Brion-Kayser (*see also* Fever, paratyphoid)
  002.9
broad
  beta 272.2
  ligament, noninflammatory 620.9
    specified NEC 620.8
Brocq's 691.8
  meaning
    atopic (diffuse) neurodermatitis 691.8
    dermatitis herpetiformis 694.0
    lichen simplex chronicus 698.3
    parapsoriasis 696.2
    prurigo 698.2
Brocq-Duhring (dermatitis herpetiformis) 694.0
Brodie's (joint) (*see also* Osteomyelitis) 730.1
bronchi 519.1
bronchopulmonary 519.1
bronze (Addison's) 255.4
  tuberculous (*see also* Tuberculosis) 017.6
Brown-Séquard 344.89
Bruck's 733.99
Bruck-de Lange (Amsterdam dwarf, mental
  retardation, and brachycephaly) 759.89
Bruhl's (splenic anemia with fever) 285.8
Bruton's (X-linked agammaglobulinemia)
  279.04
buccal cavity 528.9
Buchanan's (juvenile osteochondrosis, iliac
  crest) 732.1
Buchman's (osteochondrosis juvenile) 732.1
Budgerigar-fanciers' 495.2
Büdinger-Ludloff-Läwen 717.89
Buerger's (thromboangiitis obliterans) 443.1
Bürger-Grütz (essential familial hyperlipemia)
  272.3
Burns' (lower ulna) 732.3
bursa 727.9
Bury's (erythema elevatum diutinum) 695.89
Buschke's 710.1
Busquet's (*see also* Osteomyelitis) 730.1
Busse-Buschke (cryptococcosis) 117.5
C$_2$ (*see also* Alcoholism) 303.9
Caffey's (infantile cortical hyperostosis) 756.59
caisson 993.3
calculous 592.9
California 114.0
Calvé (-Perthes) (osteochondrosis, femoral
  capital) 732.1
Camurati-Engelmann (diaphyseal sclerosis)
  756.59
Canavan's 330.0
capillaries 448.9
Carapata 087.1
cardiac-*see* Disease, heart
cardiopulmonary, chronic 416.9
cardiorenal (arteriosclerotic) (hepatic)
  (hypertensive) (vascular) (*see also*
  Hypertension, cardiorenal) 404.90
cardiovascular (arteriosclerotic) 429.2
  congenital 746.9
  hypertensive (*see also* Hypertension, heart)
    402.90
    benign 402.10
    malignant 402.00
  renal (*see also* Hypertension, cardiorenal)
    404.90
  syphilitic (asymptomatic) 093.9
carotid gland 259.8
Carrión's (Bartonellosis) 088.0

Disease, diseased—*continued*
  cartilage NEC 733.90
    specified NEC 733.99
  Castellani's 104.8
  cat-scratch 078.3
  Cavare's (familial periodic paralysis) 359.3
  Cazenave's (pemphigus) 694.4
  cecum 569.9
  celiac (adult) 579.0
    infantile 579.0
  cellular tissue NEC 709.9
  central core 359.0
  cerebellar, cerebellum—*see* Disease, brain
  cerebral (*see also* Disease, brain) 348.9
    arterial, artery 437.9
    degenerative—*see* Degeneration, brain
  cerebrospinal 349.9
  cerebrovascular NEC 437.9
    acute 436
      embolic—*see* Embolism, brain
      late effect—*see* category 438
      puerperal, postpartum, childbirth 674.0
      thrombotic—*see* Thrombosis, brain
    arteriosclerotic 437.0
      embolic—*see* Embolism, brain
      ischemic, generalized NEC 437.1
      late effect or sequela—*see* category 438
      occlusive 437.1
      puerperal, postpartum, childbirth 674.0
      specified type NEC 437.8
      thrombotic—*see* Thrombosis, brain
  ceroid storage 272.7
  cervix (uteri)
    inflammatory 616.9
      specified NEC 616.8
    noninflammatory 622.9
      specified NEC 622.8
  Chabert's 022.9
  Chagas' (*see also* Trypanosomiasis, American)
    086.2
  Chandler's (osteochondritis dissecans, hip)
    732.7
  Charcot's (joint) 094.0 *[713.5]*
    spinal cord 094.0
  Charcot-Marie-Tooth 356.1
  Charlouis' (*see also* Yaws) 102.9
  Cheadle (-Möller) (-Barlow) (infantile scurvy)
    267
  Chédiak-Steinbrinck (-Higashi) (congenital
    gigantism of peroxidase granules) 288.2
  cheek, inner 528.9
  chest 519.9
  Chiari's (hepatic vein thrombosis) 453.0
  Chicago (North American blastomycosis) 116.0
  chignon (white piedra) 111.2
  chigoe, chigo (jigger) 134.1
  childhood granulomatous 288.1
  Chinese liver fluke 121.1
  chlamydial NEC 078.88
  cholecystic (*see also* Disease, gallbladder) 575.9
  choroid 363.9
    degenerative (*see also* Degeneration, choroid)
      363.40
    hereditary (*see also* Dystrophy, choroid)
      363.50
    specified type NEC 363.8

Disease, diseased—*continued*
  Christian's (chronic histiocytosis X) 277.8
  Christian-Weber (nodular nonsuppurative
    panniculitis) 729.30
  Christmas 286.1
  ciliary body 364.9
  circulatory (system) NEC 459.9
    chronic, maternal, affecting fetus or newborn
      760.3
    specified NEC 459.89
    syphilitic 093.9
      congenital 090.5
  Civatte's (poikiloderma) 709.09
  climacteric 627.2
    male 608.89
  coagulation factor deficiency (congenital) (*see
    also* Defect, coagulation) 286.9
  Coats' 362.12
  coccidioidal pulmonary 114.5
    acute 114.0
    chronic 114.4
    primary 114.0
    residual 114.4
  Cockayne's (microcephaly and dwarfism)
    759.89
  Cogan's 370.52
  cold
    agglutinin 283.0
      or hemoglobinuria 283.0
      paroxysmal (cold) (nocturnal) 283.2
    hemagglutinin (chronic) 283.0
  collagen NEC 710.9
    nonvascular 710.9
    specified NEC 710.8
    vascular (allergic) (*see also* Angiitis,
      hypersensitivity) 446.20
  colon 569.9
    functional 564.9
      congenital 751.3
    ischemic 557.0
  combined system (of spinal cord) 266.2 *[336.2]*
    with anemia (pernicious) 281.0 *[336.2]*
  compressed air 993.3
  Concato's (pericardial polyserositis) 423.2
    peritoneal 568.82
    pleural—*see* Pleurisy
  congenital NEC 799.8
  conjunctiva 372.9
    chlamydial 077.98
      specified NEC 077.8
    specified type NEC 372.8
    viral 077.99
      specified NEC 077.8
  connective tissue, diffuse (*see also* Disease,
    collagen) 710.9
  Conor and Bruch's (boutonneuse fever) 082.1
  Conradi (-Hünermann) 756.59
  Cooley's (erythroblastic anemia) 282.4
  Cooper's 610.1
  Corbus' 607.1
  cork-handlers' 495.3
  cornea (*see also* Keratopathy) 371.9
  coronary (*see also* Ischemia, heart) 414.9
    congenital 746.85
    ostial, syphilitic 093.20
      aortic 093.22
      mitral 093.21
      pulmonary 093.24
      tricuspid 093.23

Disease, diseased—*continued*
  Corrigan's—*see* Insufficiency, aortic
  Cotugno's 724.3
  Coxsackie (virus) NEC 074.8
  cranial nerve NEC 352.9
  Creutzfeldt-Jakob 046.1
    with dementia 046.1 *[294.1]*
  Crigler-Najjar (congenital hyperbilirubinemia)
    277.4
  Crocq's (acrocyanosis) 443.89
  Crohn's (intestine) (*see also* Enteritis, regional)
    555.9
  Crouzon's (craniofacial dysostosis) 756.0
  Cruchet's (encephalitis lethargica) 049.8
  Cruveilhier's 335.21
  Cruz-Chagas (*see also* Trypanosomiasis,
    American) 086.2
  crystal deposition (*see also* Arthritis, due to,
    crystals) 712.9
  Csillag's (lichen sclerosus et atrophicus) 701.0
  Curschmann's 359.2
  Cushing's (pituitary basophilism) 255.0
  cystic
    breast (chronic) 610.1
    kidney, congenital (*see also* Cystic, disease,
      kidney) 753.10
    liver, congenital 751.62
    lung 518.89
      congenital 748.4
    pancreas 577.2
      congenital 751.7
    renal, congenital (*see also* Cystic, disease,
      kidney) 753.10
    semilunar cartilage 717.5
  cysticercus 123.1
  cystine storage (with renal sclerosis) 270.0
  cytomegalic inclusion (generalized) 078.5
    with
      pneumonia 078.5 *[484.1]*
    congenital 771.1
  Czerny's (periodic hydrarthrosis of the knee)
    719.06
  Daae (-Finsen) (epidemic pleurodynia) 074.1
  dancing 297.8
  Danielssen's (anesthetic leprosy) 030.1
  Darier's (congenital) (keratosis follicularis)
    757.39
    erythema annulare centrifugum 695.0
    vitamin A deficiency 264.8
  Darling's (histoplasmosis) (*see also*
    Histoplasmosis, American) 115.00
  Davies' 425.0
  de Beurmann-Gougerot (sporotrichosis) 117.1
  Débove's (splenomegaly) 789.2
  deer fly (*see also* Tularemia) 021.9
  deficiency 269.9
  degenerative—*see also* Degeneration
    disc—*see* Degeneration, intervertebral disc
  Degos' 447.8
  Déjérine (-Sottas) 356.0
  Deleage's 359.8
  demyelinating, demyelinizating (brain stem)
    (central nervous system) 341.9
    multiple sclerosis 340
    specified NEC 341.8
  de Quervain's (tendon sheath) 727.04
    thyroid (subacute granulomatous thyroiditis)
      245.1

Disease, diseased—*continued*
  Dercum's (adiposis dolorosa) 272.8
  Deutschländer's—*see* Fracture, foot
  Devergie's (pityriasis rubra pilaris) 696.4
  Devic's 341.0
  diaphorase deficiency 289.7
  diaphragm 519.4
  diarrheal, infectious 009.2
  diatomaceous earth 502
  Diaz's (osteochondrosis astragalus) 732.5
  digestive system 569.9
  Di Guglielmo's (erythemic myelosis)
    (M9841/3) 207.0
  Dimitri-Sturge-Weber (encephalocutaneous
    angiomatosis) 759.6
  disc, degenerative—*see* Degeneration,
    intervertebral disc
  discogenic (*see also* Disease, intervertebral
    disc) 722.90
  diverticular—*see* Diverticula
  Down's (mongolism) 758.0
  Dubini's (electric chorea) 049.8
  Dubois' (thymus gland) 090.5
  Duchenne's 094.0
    locomotor ataxia 094.0
    muscular dystrophy 359.1
    paralysis 335.22
    pseudohypertrophy, muscles 359.1
  Duchenne-Griesinger 359.1
  ductless glands 259.9
  Duhring's (dermatitis herpetiformis) 694.0
  Dukes (-Filatov) 057.8
  duodenum NEC 537.9
    specified NEC 537.89
  Duplay's 726.2
  Dupré's (meningism) 781.6
  Dupuytren's (muscle contracture) 728.6
  Durand-Nicolas-Favre (climatic bubo) 099.1
  Duroziez's (congenital mitral stenosis) 746.5
  Dutton's (trypanosomiasis) 086.9
  Eales' 362.18
  ear (chronic) (inner) NEC 388.9
    middle 385.9
      adhesive (*see also* Adhesions, middle ear)
        385.10
      specified NEC 385.89
  Eberth's (typhoid fever) 002.0
  Ebstein's
    heart 746.2
    meaning diabetes 250.4 *[581.81]*
  Echinococcus (*see also* Echinococcus) 122.9
  ECHO virus NEC 078.89
  Economo's (encephalitis lethargica) 049.8
  Eddowes' (brittle bones and blue sclera) 756.51
  Edsall's 992.2
  Eichstedt's (pityriasis versicolor) 111.0
  Ellis-van Creveld (chondroectodermal
    dysplasia) 756.55
  endocardium—*see* Endocarditis
  endocrine glands or system NEC 259.9
    specified NEC 259.8
  endomyocardial, idiopathic mural 425.2
  Engel-von Recklinghausen (osteitis fibrosa
    cystica) 252.0
  Engelmann's (diaphyseal sclerosis) 756.59
  English (rickets) 268.0
  Engman's (infectious eczematoid dermatitis)
    690.8
  enteroviral, enterovirus NEC 078.89
    central nervous system NEC 048

Disease, diseased—*continued*
  epidemic NEC 136.9
  epididymis 608.9
  epigastric, functional 536.9
    psychogenic 306.4
  Erb (-Landouzy) 359.1
  Erb-Goldflam 358.0
  Erichsen's (railway spine) 300.16
  esophagus 530.9
    functional 530.5
    psychogenic 306.4
  Eulenburg's (congenital paramyotonia) 359.2
  Eustachian tube 381.9
  Evans' (thrombocytopenic purpura) 287.3
  external auditory canal 380.9
  extrapyramidal NEC 333.90
  eye 379.90
    anterior chamber 364.9
    inflammatory NEC 364.3
    muscle 378.9
  eyeball 360.9
  eyelid 374.9
  eyeworm of Africa 125.2
  Fabry's (angiokeratoma corporis diffusum) 272.7
  facial nerve (seventh) 351.9
    newborn 767.5
  Fahr-Volhard (malignant nephrosclerosis) 403.00
  fallopian tube, noninflammatory 620.9
    specified NEC 620.8
  familial periodic 277.3
    paralysis 359.3
  Fanconi's (congenital pancytopenia) 284.0
  Farber's (disseminated lipogranulomatosis) 272.8
  fascia 728.9
    inflammatory 728.9
  Fauchard's (periodontitis) 523.4
  Favre-Durand-Nicolas (climatic bubo) 099.1
  Favre-Racouchot (elastoidosis cutanea nodularis) 701.8
  Fede's 529.0
  Feer's 985.0
  Felix's (juvenile osteochondrosis, hip) 732.1
  Fenwick's (gastric atrophy) 537.89
  Fernels' (aortic aneurysm) 441.9
  fibrocaseous, of lung (*see also* Tuberculosis, pulmonary) 011.9
  fibrocystic—*see also* Fibrocystic, disease
    newborn 277.01
  Fiedler's (leptospiral jaundice) 100.0
  fifth 057.0
  Filatoff's (infectious mononucleosis) 075
  Filatov's (infectious mononucleosis) 075
  file-cutters' 984.9
    specified type of lead—*see* Table of drugs and chemicals
  filterable virus NEC 078.89
  fish skin 757.1
    acquired 701.1
  Flajani (-Basedow) (exophthalmic goiter) 242.0
  Flatau-Schilder 341.1
  flax-dressers' 504
  Fleischner's 732.3
  flint 502
  fluke—*see* Infestation, fluke
  Følling's (phenylketonuria) 270.1
  foot and mouth 078.4
  foot process 581.3

Disease, diseased—*continued*
  Forbes' (glycogenosis III) 271.0
  Fordyce's (ectopic sebaceous glands) (mouth) 750.26
  Fordyce-Fox (apocrine miliaria) 705.82
  Fothergill's
    meaning scarlatina anginosa 034.1
    neuralgia (*see also* Neuralgia, trigeminal) 350.1
  Fournier's 608.83
  fourth 057.8
  Fox (-Fordyce) (apocrine miliaria) 705.82
  Francis' (*see also* Tularemia) 021.9
  Franklin's (heavy chain) 273.2
  Frei's (climatic bubo) 099.1
  Freiberg's (flattening metatarsal) 732.5
  Friedländer's (endarteritis obliterans)—*see* Arteriosclerosis
  Friedreich's
    combined systemic or ataxia 334.0
    facial hemihypertrophy 756.0
    myoclonia 333.2
  Fröhlich's (adiposogenital dystrophy) 253.8
  Frommel's 676.6
  frontal sinus (chronic) 473.1
    acute 461.1
  Fuller's earth 502
  fungus, fungous NEC 117.9
  Gaisböck's (polycythemia hypertonica) 289.0
  gallbladder 575.9
    congenital 751.60
  Gamna's (siderotic splenomegaly) 289.51
  Gamstorp's (adynamia episodica hereditaria) 359.3
  Gandy-Nanta (siderotic splenomegaly) 289.51
  gannister (occupational) 502
  Garré's (*see also* Osteomyelitis) 730.1
  gastric (*see also* Disease, stomach) 537.9
  gastrointestinal (tract) 569.9
    amyloid 277.3
    functional 536.9
    psychogenic 306.4
  Gaucher's (adult) (cerebroside lipidosis) (infantile) 272.7
  Gayet's (superior hemorrhagic polioencephalitis) 265.1
  Gee (-Herter) (-Heubner) (-Thaysen) (nontropical sprue) 579.0
  generalized neoplastic (M8000/6) 199.0
  genital organs NEC
    female 629.9
      specified NEC 629.8
    male 608.9
  Gerhardt's (erythromelalgia) 443.89
  Gerlier's (epidemic vertigo) 078.81
  Gibert's (pityriasis rosea) 696.3
  Gibney's (perispondylitis) 720.9
  Gierke's (glycogenosis I) 271.0
  Gilbert's (familial nonhemolytic jaundice) 277.4
  Gilchrist's (North American blastomycosis) 116.0
  Gilford (-Hutchinson) (progeria) 259.8
  Gilles de la Tourette's (motor-verbal tic) 307.23
  Giovannini's 117.9
  gland (lymph) 289.9
  Glanzmann's (hereditary hemorrhagic thrombasthenia) 287.1
  glassblowers' 527.1
  Glénard's (enteroptosis) 569.89
  Glisson's (*see also* Rickets) 268.0

Disease, diseased—*continued*
glomerular
  membranous, idiopathic 581.1
  minimal change 581.3
glycogen storage (Andersen's) (Cori types 1-7)
    (Forbes') (McArdle-Schmid-Pearson)
    (Pompe's) (types I-VII) 271.0
  cardiac 271.0 *[425.7]*
  generalized 271.0
  glucose-6-phosphatase deficiency 271.0
  heart 271.0 *[425.7]*
  hepatorenal 271.0
  liver and kidneys 271.0
  myocardium 271.0 *[425.7]*
  von Gierke's (glycogenosis I) 271.0
Goldflam-Erb 358.0
Goldscheider's (epidermolysis bullosa) 757.39
Goldstein's (familial hemorrhagic
    telangiectasia) 448.0
gonococcal NEC 098.0
Goodall's (epidemic vomiting) 078.82
Gordon's (exudative enteropathy) 579.8
Gougerot's (trisymptomatic) 709.1
Gougerot-Carteaud (confluent reticulate
    papillomatosis) 701.8
Gougerot-Hailey-Hailey (benign familial
    chronic pemphigus) 757.39
graft-versus-host (bone marrow) 996.85
  due to organ transplant NEC—*see*
      Complications, transplant, organ
grain-handlers' 495.8
Grancher's (splenopneumonia)—*see* Pneumonia
granulomatous (childhood) (chronic) 288.1
graphite lung 503
Graves' (exophthalmic goiter) 242.0
Greenfield's 330.0
green monkey 078.89
Griesinger's (*see also* Ancylostomiasis) 126.9
grinders' 502
Grisel's 723.5
Gruby's (tinea tonsurans) 110.0
Guertin's (electric chorea) 049.8
Guillain-Barré 357.0
Guinon's (motor-verbal tic) 307.23
Gull's (thyroid atrophy with myxedema) 244.8
Gull and Sutton's—*see* Hypertension, kidney
gum NEC 523.9
Günther's (congenital erythropoietic porphyria)
    277.1
gynecological 629.9
  specified NEC 629.8
H 270.0
Haas' 732.3
Habermann's (acute parapsoriasis varioliformis)
    696.2
Haff 985.1
Hageman (congenital factor XII deficiency) (*see
    also* Defect, congenital) 286.3
Haglund's (osteochondrosis os tibiale
    externum) 732.5
Hagner's (hypertrophic pulmonary
    osteoarthropathy) 731.2
Hailey-Hailey (benign familial chronic
    pemphigus) 757.39
hair (follicles) NEC 704.9
  specified type NEC 704.8
Hallervorden-Spatz 333.0

Disease, diseased—*continued*
Hallopeau's (lichen sclerosus et atrophicus)
    701.0
Hamman's (spontaneous mediastinal
    emphysema) 518.1
hand, foot, and mouth 074.3
Hand-Schüller-Christian (chronic histiocytosis
    X) 277.8
Hanot's—*see* Cirrhosis, biliary
Hansen's (leprosy) 030.9
  benign form 030.1
  malignant form 030.0
Harada's 363.22
Harley's (intermittent hemoglobinuria) 283.2
Hart's (pellagra-cerebellar ataxia renal
    aminoaciduria) 270.0
Hartnup (pellagra-cerebellar ataxia-renal
    aminoaciduria) 270.0
Hashimoto's (struma lymphomatosa) 245.2
Hb—*see* Disease, hemoglobin
heart (organic) 429.9
  with
    acute pulmonary edema (*see also* Failure,
        ventricular, left) 428.1
    hypertensive 402.91
      with renal failure 404.92
      benign 402.11
        with renal failure 404.12
      malignant 402.01
        with renal failure 404.02
    kidney disease—*see* Hypertension,
        cardiorenal
    rheumatic fever (conditions classifiable to
        390)
      active 391.9
        with chorea 392.0
      inactive or quiescent (with chorea) 398.90
  amyloid 277.3 *[425.7]*
  aortic (valve) (*see also* Endocarditis, aortic)
      424.1
  arteriosclerotic or sclerotic (minimal)
      (senile)—*see* Arteriosclerosis, coronary
  artery, arterial —*see* Arteriosclerosis, coronary
  atherosclerotic —*see* Arteriosclerosis,
      coronary
  beer drinkers' 425.5
  beriberi 265.0 *[425.7]*
  black 416.0
  congenital NEC 746.9
    cyanotic 746.9
    maternal, affecting fetus or newborn 760.3
    specified type NEC 746.89
  congestive (*see also* Failure, heart,
      congestive) 428.0
  coronary 414.9
  cryptogenic 429.9
  due to
    amyloidosis 277.3 *[425.7]*
    beriberi 265.0 *[425.7]*
    cardiac glycogenosis 271.0 *[425.7]*
    Friedreich's ataxia 334.0 *[425.8]*
    gout 274.82
    mucopolysaccharidosis 277.5 *[425.7]*
    myotonia atrophica 359.2 *[425.8]*
    progressive muscular dystrophy 359.1
        [425.8]
    sarcoidosis 135 *[425.8]*
  fetal 746.9
    inflammatory 746.89
  fibroid (*see also* Myocarditis) 429.0

Disease, diseased—*continued*
functional 427.9
postoperative 997.1
psychogenic 306.2
glycogen storage 271.0 *[425.7]*
gonococcal NEC 098.85
gouty 274.82
hypertensive (*see also* Hypertension, heart)
402.90
benign 402.10
malignant 402.00
hyperthyroid (*see also* Hyperthyroidism)
242.9 *[425.7]*
incompletely diagnosed—*see* Disease, heart
ischemic (chronic) (*see also* Ischemia, heart)
414.9
acute (*see also* Infarct, myocardium) 410.9
without myocardial infarction 411.89
with coronary (artery) occlusion 411.81
asymptomatic 412
diagnosed on ECG or other special
investigation but currently presenting no
symptoms 412
kyphoscoliotic 416.1
mitral (*see also* Endocarditis, mitral) 394.9
muscular (*see also* Degeneration, myocardial)
429.1
postpartum 674.8
psychogenic (functional) 306.2
pulmonary (chronic) 416.9
acute 415.0
specified NEC 416.8
rheumatic (chronic) (inactive) (old)
(quiescent) (with chorea) 398.90
active or acute 391.9
with chorea (active) (rheumatic)
(Sydenham's) 392.0
specified type NEC 391.8
maternal, affecting fetus or newborn 760.3
rheumatoid—*see* Arthritis, rheumatoid
sclerotic —*see* Arteriosclerosis, coronary
senile (*see also* Myocarditis) 429.0
specified type NEC 429.89
syphilitic 093.89
aortic 093.1
aneurysm 093.0
asymptomatic 093.89
congenital 090.5
thyroid (gland) (*see also* Hyperthyroidism)
242.9 *[425.7]*
thyrotoxic (*see also* Thyrotoxicosis) 242.9
[425.7]
tuberculous (*see also* Tuberculosis) 017.9
[425.8]
valve, valvular (obstructive)
(regurgitant)—*see also* Endocarditis
congenital NEC (*see also* Anomaly, heart,
valve) 746.9
pulmonary 746.00
specified type NEC 746.89
vascular—*see* Disease, cardiovascular
heavy-chain (gamma G) 273.2
Heberden's 715.04
Hebra's
dermatitis exfoliativa 695.89
erythema multiforme exudativum 695.1
pityriasis
maculata et circinata 696.3
rubra 695.89
pilaris 696.4
prurigo 698.2

Disease, diseased—*continued*
Heerfordt's (uveoparotitis) 135
Heidenhain's 290.10
with dementia 290.10
Heilmeyer-Schöner (M9842/3) 207.1
Heine-Medin (*see also* Poliomyelitis) 045.9
Heller's (*see also* Psychosis, childhood) 299.1
Heller-Döhle (syphilitic aortitis) 093.1
hematopoietic organs 289.9
hemoglobin (Hb) 282.7
with thalassemia 282.4
abnormal (mixed) NEC 282.7
with thalassemia 282.4
AS genotype 282.5
Bart's 282.7
C (Hb-C) 282.7
with other abnormal hemoglobin NEC 282.7
elliptocytosis 282.7
Hb-S 282.63
sickle-cell 282.63
thalassemia 282.4
constant spring 282.7
D (Hb-D) 282.7
with other abnormal hemoglobin NEC 282.7
Hb-S 282.69
sickle-cell 282.69
thalassemia 282.4
E (Hb-E) 282.7
with other abnormal hemoglobin NEC 282.7
Hb-S 282.69
sickle-cell 282.69
thalassemia 282.4
elliptocytosis 282.7
F (Hb-F) 282.7
G (Hb-G) 282.7
H (Hb-H) 282.4
hereditary persistence, fetal (HPFH) ("Swiss
variety") 282.7
high fetal gene 282.7
I thalassemia 282.4
M 289.7
S—*see* Disease, sickle-cell, Hb-S
spherocytosis 282.7
unstable, hemolytic 282.7
Zurich (Hb-Zurich) 282.7
hemolytic (fetus) (newborn) 773.2
autoimmune (cold type) (warm type) 283.0
due to or with
incompatibility
ABO (blood group) 773.1
blood (group) (Duffy) (Kell) (Kidd)
(Lewis) (M) NEC 773.2
Rh (blood group) (factor) 773.0
Rh negative mother 773.0
unstable hemoglobin 282.7
hemorrhagic 287.9
newborn 776.0
Henoch (-Schönlein) (purpura nervosa) 287.0
hepatic—*see* Disease, liver
hepatolenticular 275.1
heredodegenerative NEC
brain 331.89
spinal cord 336.8
Hers' (glycogenosis VI) 271.0
Herter (-Gee) (-Heubner) (nontropical sprue)
579.0
Herxheimer's (diffuse idiopathic cutaneous
atrophy) 701.8
Heubner's 094.89
Heubner-Herter (nontropical sprue) 579.0

Disease, diseased—*continued*
  high fetal gene or hemoglobin thalassemia 282.4
  Hildenbrand's (typhus) 081.9
  hip (joint) NEC 719.95
    congenital 755.63
    suppurative 711.05
    tuberculous (*see also* Tuberculosis) 015.1
      [730.85]
  Hippel's (retinocerebral angiomatosis) 759.6
  Hirschfeld's (acute diabetes mellitus) (*see also* Diabetes) 250.0
  Hirschsprung's (congenital megacolon) 751.3
  His (-Werner) (trench fever) 083.1
  HIV 042
  Hodgkin's (M9650/3) 201.9

Note—Use the following fifth-digit subclassification with categories 201:

0 *unspecified site*
1 *lymph nodes of head, face, and neck*
2 *intrathoracic lymph nodes*
3 *intra-abdominal lymph nodes*
4 *lymph nodes of axilla and upper limb*
5 *lymph nodes of inguinal region and lower limb*
6 *intrapelvic lymph nodes*
7 *spleen*
8 *lymph nodes of multiple sites*

---

    lymphocytic
      depletion (M9653/3) 201.7
        diffuse fibrosis (M9654/3) 201.7
        reticular type (M9655/3) 201.7
      predominance (M9651/3) 201.4
    lymphocytic-histiocytic predominance (M9651/3) 201.4
    mixed cellularity (M9652/3) 201.6
    nodular sclerosis (M9656/3) 201.5
      cellular phase (M9657/3) 201.5
  Hodgson's 441.9
    ruptured 441.5
  Hoffa (-Kastert) (liposynovitis prepatellaris) 272.8
  Holla (*see also* Spherocytosis) 282.0
  homozygous-Hb-S 282.61
  hoof and mouth 078.4
  hookworm (*see also* Ancylostomiasis) 126.9
  Horton's (temporal arteritis) 446.5
  host-versus-graft (immune or nonimmune cause) 996.80
    bone marrow 996.85
    heart 996.83
    intestines 996.89
    kidney 996.81
    liver 996.82
    lung 996.84
    pancreas 996.86
    specified NEC 996.89
  HPFH (hereditary persistence of fetal hemoglobin) ("Swiss variety") 282.7
  Huchard's (continued arterial hypertension) 401.9
  Huguier's (uterine fibroma) 218.9
  human immunodeficiency (virus) 042
  hunger 251.1
  Hunt's
    dyssynergia cerebellaris myoclonica 334.2
    herpetic geniculate ganglionitis 053.11
  Huntington's 333.4
  Huppert's (multiple myeloma) (M9730/3) 203.0

Disease, diseased—*continued*
  Hurler's (mucopolysaccharidosis I) 277.5
  Hutchinson's, meaning
    angioma serpiginosum 709.1
    cheiropompholyx 705.81
    prurigo estivalis 692.72
  Hutchinson-Boeck (sarcoidosis) 135
  Hutchinson-Gilford (progeria) 259.8
  hyaline (diffuse) (generalized) 728.9
    membrane (lung) (newborn) 769
  hydatid (*see also* Echinococcus) 122.9
  Hyde's (prurigo nodularis) 698.3
  hyperkinetic (*see also* Hyperkinesia) 314.9
    heart 429.82
  hypertensive (*see also* Hypertension) 401.9
  hypophysis 253.9
    hyperfunction 253.1
    hypofunction 253.2
  Iceland (epidemic neuromyasthenia) 049.8
  I cell 272.7
  ill-defined 799.8
  immunologic NEC 279.9
  immunoproliferative 203.8
  inclusion 078.5
    salivary gland 078.5
  infancy, early NEC 779.9
  infective NEC 136.9
  inguinal gland 289.9
  internal semilunar cartilage, cystic 717.5
  intervertebral disc 722.90
    with myelopathy 722.70
    cervical, cervicothoracic 722.91
      with myelopathy 722.71
    lumbar, lumbosacral 722.93
      with myelopathy 722.73
    thoracic, thoracolumbar 722.92
      with myelopathy 722.72
  intestine 569.9
    functional 564.9
      congenital 751.3
      psychogenic 306.4
    lardaceous 277.3
    organic 569.9
    protozoal NEC 007.9
  iris 364.9
  iron
    metabolism 275.0
    storage 275.0
  Isambert's (*see also* Tuberculosis, larynx) 012.3
  Iselin's (osteochondrosis, fifth metatarsal) 732.5
  Island (scrub typhus) 081.2
  itai-itai 985.5
  Jadassohn's (maculopapular erythroderma) 696.2
  Jadassohn-Pellizari's (anetoderma) 701.3
  Jakob-Creutzfeldt 046.1
    with dementia 046.1 *[294.1]*
  Jaksch (-Luzet) (pseudoleukemia infantum) 285.8
  Janet's 300.89
  Jansky-Bielschowsky 330.1
  jaw NEC 526.9
    fibrocystic 526.2
  Jensen's 363.05
  Jeune's (asphyxiating thoracic dystrophy) 756.4
  jigger 134.1
  Johnson-Stevens (erythema multiforme exudativum) 695.1

Disease, diseased—*continued*
  joint NEC 719.9
    ankle 719.97
    Charcot 094.0 *[713.5]*
    degenerative (*see also* Osteoarthrosis) 715.9
      multiple 715.09
      spine (*see also* Spondylosis) 721.90
    elbow 719.92
    foot 719.97
    hand 719.94
    hip 719.95
    hypertrophic (chronic) (degenerative) (*see also* Osteoarthrosis) 715.9
      spine (*see also* Spondylosis) 721.90
    knee 719.96
    Luschka 721.90
    multiple sites 719.99
    pelvic region 719.95
    sacroiliac 724.6
    shoulder (region) 719.91
    specified site NEC 719.98
    spine NEC 724.9
      pseudarthrosis following fusion 733.82
      sacroiliac 724.6
    wrist 719.93
  Jourdain's (acute gingivitis) 523.0
  Jüngling's (sarcoidosis) 135
  Kahler (-Bozzolo) (multiple myeloma) (M9730/3) 203.0
  Kalischer's 759.6
  Kaposi's 757.33
    lichen ruber 697.8
      acuminatus 696.4
      moniliformis 697.8
    xeroderma pigmentosum 757.33
  Kaschin-Beck (endemic polyarthritis) 716.00
    ankle 716.07
    arm 716.02
      lower (and wrist) 716.03
      upper (and elbow) 716.02
    foot (and ankle) 716.07
    forearm (and wrist) 716.03
    hand 716.04
    leg 716.06
      lower 716.06
      upper 716.05
    multiple sites 716.09
    pelvic region (hip) (thigh) 716.05
    shoulder region 716.01
    specified site NEC 716.08
  Katayama 120.2
  Kawasaki 446.1
  Kedani (scrub typhus) 081.2
  kidney (functional) (pelvis) (*see also* Disease, renal) 593.9
    cystic (congenital) 753.10
      multiple 753.19
      single 753.11
      specified NEC 753.19
    fibrocystic (congenital) 753.19
    in gout 274.10
    polycystic (congenital) 753.12
      adult type (APKD) 753.13
      autosomal dominant 753.13
      autosomal recessive 753.14
      childhood type (CPKD) 753.14
      infantile type 753.14

Disease, diseased—*continued*
  Kienböck's (carpal lunate) (wrist) 732.3
  Kimmelstiel (-Wilson) (intercapillary glomerulosclerosis) 250.4 *[581.81]*
  Kinnier Wilson's (hepatolenticular degeneration) 275.1
  kissing 075
  Kleb's (*see also* Nephritis) 583.9
  Klinger's 446.4
  Klippel's 723.8
  Klippel-Feil (brevicollis) 756.16
  knight's 911.1
  Köbner's (epidermolysis bullosa) 757.39
  Koenig-Wichmann (pemphigus) 694.4
  Köhler's
    first (osteoarthrosis juvenilis) 732.5
    second (Freiberg's infraction, metatarsal head) 732.5
    patellar 732.4
    tarsal navicular (bone) (osteoarthrosis juvenilis) 732.5
  Köhler-Freiberg (infraction, metatarsal head) 732.5
  Köhler-Mouchet (osteoarthrosis juvenilis) 732.5
  Köhler-Pellegrini-Stieda (calcification, knee joint) 726.62
  König's (osteochondritis dissecans) 732.7
  Korsakoff's (nonalcoholic) 294.0
    alcoholic 291.1
  Kostmann's (infantile genetic agranulocytosis) 288.0
  Krabbe's 330.0
  Kraepelin-Morel (*see also* Schizophrenia) 295.9
  Kraft-Weber-Dimitri 759.6
  Kufs' 330.1
  Kugelberg-Welander 335.11
  Kuhnt-Junius 362.52
  Kümmell's (-Verneuil) (spondylitis) 721.7
  Kundrat's (lymphosarcoma) 200.1
  kuru 046.0
  Kussmaul (-Meier) (polyarteritis nodosa) 446.0
  Kyasanur Forest 065.2
  Kyrle's (hyperkeratosis follicularis in cutem penetrans) 701.1
  labia
    inflammatory 616.9
      specified NEC 616.8
    noninflammatory 624.9
      specified NEC 624.8
  labyrinth, ear 386.8
  lacrimal system (apparatus) (passages) 375.9
    gland 375.00
    specified NEC 375.89
  Lafora's 333.2
  Lagleyze-von Hippel (retinocerebral angiomatosis) 759.6
  Lancereaux-Mathieu (leptospiral jaundice) 100.0
  Landry's 357.0
  Lane's 569.89
  lardaceous (any site) 277.3
  Larrey-Weil (leptospiral jaundice) 100.0
  Larsen (-Johansson) (juvenile osteopathia patellae) 732.4
  larynx 478.70
  Lasègue's (persecution mania) 297.9
  Leber's 377.16
  Lederer's (acquired infectious hemolytic anemia) 283.19
  Legg's (capital femoral osteochondrosis) 732.1

Disease, diseased—*continued*
  Legg-Calvé-Perthes (capital femoral
      osteochondrosis) 732.1
  Legg-Calvé-Waldenström (femoral capital
      osteochondrosis) 732.1
  Legg-Perthes (femoral capital osteochondrosis)
      732.1
  Legionnaire's 482.83
  Leigh's 330.8
  Leiner's (exfoliative dermatitis) 695.89
  Leloir's (lupus erythematosus) 695.4
  Lenegre's 426.0
  lens (eye) 379.39
  Leriche's (osteoporosis, posttraumatic) 733.7
  Letterer-Siwe (acute histiocytosis X) (M9722/3)
      202.5
  Lev's (acquired complete heart block) 426.0
  Lewandowski's (*see also* Tuberculosis) 017.0
  Lewandowski-Lutz (epidermodysplasia
      verruciformis) 078.19
  Leyden's (periodic vomiting) 536.2
  Libman-Sacks (verrucous endocarditis) 710.0
      [424.91]
  Lichtheim's (subacute combined sclerosis with
      pernicious anemia) 281.0 *[336.2]*
  ligament 728.9
  light chain 203.0
  Lightwood's (renal tubular acidosis) 588.8
  Lignac's (cystinosis) 270.0
  Lindau's (retinocerebral angiomatosis) 759.6
  Lindau-von Hippel (angiomatosis
      retinocerebellosa) 759.6
  lip NEC 528.5
  lipidosis 272.7
  lipoid storage NEC 272.7
  Lipschütz's 616.50
  Little's—*see* Palsy, cerebral
  liver 573.9
    alcoholic 571.3
      acute 571.1
      chronic 571.3
    chronic 571.9
      alcoholic 571.3
    cystic, congenital 751.62
    drug-induced 573.3
    due to
      chemicals 573.3
      fluorinated agents 573.3
      hypersensitivity drugs 573.3
      isoniazids 573.3
    fibrocystic (congenital) 751.62
    glycogen storage 271.0
    organic 573.9
    polycystic (congenital) 751.62
  Lobo's (keloid blastomycosis) 116.2
  Lobstein's (brittle bones and blue sclera) 756.61
  locomotor system 334.9
  Lorain's (pituitary dwarfism) 253.3
  Lucas-Championnière (fibrinous bronchitis)
      466.0
  Ludwig's (submaxillary cellulitis) 528.3
  luetic—*see* Syphilis
  lumbosacral region 724.6
  lung NEC 518.89
    black 500
    congenital 748.60
    cystic 518.89
      congenital 748.4
    fibroid (chronic) (*see also* Fibrosis, lung) 515

Disease, diseased—*continued*
  fluke 121.2
    Oriental 121.2
  in
    amyloidosis 277.3 *[517.8]*
    polymyositis 710.4 *[517.8]*
    sarcoidosis 135 *[517.8]*
    Sjögren's syndrome 710.2 *[517.8]*
    syphilis 095.1
    systemic lupus erythematosus 710.0 *[517.8]*
    systemic sclerosis 710.1 *[517.2]*
  interstitial (chronic) 515
    acute 136.3
  nonspecific, chronic 496
  obstructive (chronic) (COPD) 496
    with
      acute exacerbation NEC 491.21
      alveolitis, allergic (*see also* Alveolitis,
          allergic) 495.9
      asthma (chronic) (obstructive) 493.2
      bronchiectasis 494
      bronchitis (chronic) 491.20
        with acute exacerbation 491.21
      emphysema NEC 492.8
    diffuse (with fibrosis) 496
  polycystic 518.89
    asthma (chronic) (obstructive) 493.2
    congenital 748.4
    purulent (cavitary) 513.0
  restrictive 518.89
  rheumatoid 714.81
    diffuse interstitial 714.81
  specified NEC 518.89
  Lutembacher's (atrial septal defect with mitral
      stenosis) 745.5
  Lutz-Miescher (elastosis perforans serpiginosa)
      701.1
  Lutz-Splendore-de Almeida (Brazilian
      blastomycosis) 116.1
  Lyell's (toxic epidermal necrolysis) 695.1
    due to drug
      correct substance properly administered
          695.1
      overdose or wrong substance given or taken
          977.9
      specific drug—*see* Table of drugs and
          chemicals
  Lyme 088.81
  lymphatic (gland) (system) 289.9
    channel (noninfective) 457.9
    vessel (noninfective) 457.9
      specified NEC 457.8
  lymphoproliferative (chronic) (M9970/1) 238.7
  Madelung's (lipomatosis) 272.8
  Madura (actinomycotic) 039.9
    mycotic 117.4
  Magitot's 526.4
  Majocchi's (purpura annularis telangiectodes)
      709.1
  malarial (*see also* Malaria) 084.6
  Malassez's (cystic) 608.89
  Malibu 919.8
    infected 919.9
  malignant (M8000/3)—*see also* Neoplasm, by
      site, malignant
    previous, affecting management of pregnancy
        V23.8
  Manson's 120.1
  maple bark 495.6
  maple syrup (urine) 270.3
  Marburg (virus) 078.89
  Marchiafava (-Bignami) 341.8

Disease, diseased—*continued*
  Marfan's 090.49
    congenital syphilis 090.49
    meaning Marfan's syndrome 759.82
  Marie-Bamberger (hypertrophic pulmonary
      osteoarthropathy) (secondary) 731.2
    primary or idiopathic (acropachyderma)
      757.39
    pulmonary (hypertrophic osteoarthropathy)
      731.2
  Marie-Strümpell (ankylosing spondylitis) 720.0
  Marion's (bladder neck obstruction) 596.0
  Marsh's (exophthalmic goiter) 242.0
  Martin's 715.27
  mast cell 757.33
    systemic (M9741/3) 202.6
  mastoid (*see also* Mastoiditis) 383.9
    process 385.9
  maternal, unrelated to pregnancy NEC,
      affecting fetus or newborn 760.9
  Mathieu's (leptospiral jaundice) 100.0
  Mauclaire's 732.3
  Mauriac's (erythema nodosum syphiliticum)
      091.3
  Maxcy's 081.0
  McArdle (-Schmid-Pearson) (glycogenosis V)
      271.0
  mediastinum NEC 519.3
  Medin's (*see also* Poliomyelitis) 045.9
  Mediterranean (with hemoglobinopathy) 282.4
  medullary center (idiopathic) (respiratory) 348.8
  Meige's (chronic hereditary edema) 757.0
  Meleda 757.39
  Ménétrier's (hypertrophic gastritis) 535.2
  Ménière's (active) 386.00
    cochlear 386.02
    cochleovestibular 386.01
    inactive 386.04
    in remission 386.04
    vestibular 386.03
  meningeal—*see* Meningitis
  mental (*see also* Psychosis) 298.9
  Merzbacher-Pelizaeus 330.0
  mesenchymal 710.9
  mesenteric embolic 557.0
  metabolic NEC 277.9
  metal polishers' 502
  metastatic—*see* Metastasis
  Mibelli's 757.39
  microdrepanocytic 282.4
  Miescher's 709.3
  Mikulicz's (dryness of mouth, absent or
      decreased lacrimation) 527.1
  Milkman (-Looser) (osteomalacia with
      pseudofractures) 268.2
  Miller's (osteomalacia) 268.2
  Mills' 335.29
  Milroy's (chronic hereditary edema) 757.0
  Minamata 985.0
  Minor's 336.1
  Minot's (hemorrhagic disease, newborn) 776.0
  Minot-von Willebrand-Jürgens
      (angiohemophilia) 286.4
  Mitchell's (erythromelalgia) 443.89
  mitral—*see* Endocarditis, mitral
  Mljet (mal de Meleda) 757.39
  Möbius', Moebius' 346.8
  Moeller's 267
  Möller (-Barlow) (infantile scurvy) 267

Disease, diseased—*continued*
  Mönckeberg's (*see also* arteriosclerosis,
      extremities) 440.20
  Mondor's (thrombophlebitis of breast) 451.89
  Monge's 993.2
  Morel-Kraepelin (*see also* Schizophrenia) 295.9
  Morgagni's (syndrome) (hyperostosis frontalis
      interna) 733.3
  Morgagni-Adams-Stokes (syncope with heart
      block) 426.9
  Morquio (-Brailsford) (-Ullrich)
      (mucopolysaccharidosis IV) 277.5
  Morton's (with metatarsalgia) 355.6
  Morvan's 336.0
  motor neuron (bulbar) (mixed type) 335.20
  Mouchet's (juvenile osteochondrosis, foot)
      732.5
  mouth 528.9
  Moyamoya 437.5
  Mucha's (acute parapsoriasis varioliformis)
      696.2
  mu-chain 273.2
  mucolipidosis (I) (II) (III) 272.7
  Münchmeyer's (exostosis luxurians) 728.11
  Murri's (intermittent hemoglobinuria) 283.2
  muscle 359.9
    inflammatory 728.9
    ocular 378.9
    musculoskeletal system 729.9
  mushroom workers' 495.5
  Myà's (congenital dilation, colon) 751.3
  mycotic 117.9
  myeloproliferative (chronic) (M9960/1) 238.7
  myocardium, myocardial (*see also*
      Degeneration, myocardial) 429.1
    hypertensive (*see also* Hypertension, heart)
      402.90
    primary (idiopathic) 425.4
  myoneural 358.9
  Naegeli's 287.1
  nail 703.9
    specified type NEC 703.8
  Nairobi sheep 066.1
  nasal 478.1
    cavity NEC 478.1
    sinus (chronic)—*see* Sinusitis
  navel (newborn) NEC 779.8
  nemaline body 359.0
  neoplastic, generalized (M8000/6) 199.0
  nerve—*see* Disorder, nerve
  nervous system (central) 349.9
    autonomic, peripheral (*see also* Neuropathy,
      peripheral, autonomic) 337.9
    congenital 742.9
    inflammatory—*see* Encephalitis
    parasympathetic (*see also* Neuropathy,
      peripheral, autonomic) 337.9
    peripheral NEC 355.9
    specified NEC 349.89
    sympathetic (*see also* Neuropathy, peripheral,
      autonomic) 337.9
    vegetative (*see also* Neuropathy, peripheral,
      autonomic) 337.9
  Nettleship's (urticaria pigmentosa) 757.33
  Neumann's (pemphigus vegetans) 694.4
  neurologic (central) NEC (*see also* Disease,
      nervous system) 349.9
    peripheral NEC 355.9

Disease, diseased—*continued*
  neuromuscular system NEC 358.9
  Newcastle 077.8
  Nicolas (-Durand) -Favre (climatic bubo) 099.1
  Niemann-Pick (lipid histiocytosis) 272.7
  nipple 611.9
    Paget's (M8540/3) 174.0
  Nishimoto (-Takeuchi) 437.5
  nonarthropod-borne NEC 078.89
    central nervous system NEC 049.9
    enterovirus NEC 078.89
  non-autoimmune hemolytic NEC 283.10
  Nonne-Milroy-Meige (chronic hereditary
    edema) 757.0
  Norrie's (congenital progressive
    oculoacousticocerebral degeneration) 743.8
  nose 478.1
  nucleus pulposus—*see* Disease, intervertebral
    disc
  nutritional 269.9
    maternal, affecting fetus or newborn 760.4
  oasthouse, urine 270.2
  obliterative vascular 447.1
  Odelberg's (juvenile osteochondrosis) 732.1
  Oguchi's (retina) 368.61
  Ohara's (*see also* Tularemia) 021.9
  Ollier's (chondrodysplasia) 756.4
  Opitz's (congestive splenomegaly) 289.51
  Oppenheim's 358.8
  Oppenheim-Urbach (necrobiosis lipoidica
    diabeticorum) 250.8 *[709.3]*
  optic nerve NEC 377.49
  orbit 376.9
    specified NEC 376.89
  Oriental liver fluke 121.1
  Oriental lung fluke 121.2
  Ormond's 593.4
  Osgood's tibia (tubercle) 732.4
  Osgood-Schlatter 732.4
  Osler (-Vaquez) (polycythemia vera) (M9950/1)
    238.4
  Osler-Rendu (familial hemorrhagic
    telangiectasia) 448.0
  osteofibrocystic 252.0
  Otto's 715.35
  outer ear 380.9
  ovary (noninflammatory) NEC 620.9
    cystic 620.2
    polycystic 256.4
    specified NEC 620.8
  Owren's (congenital) (*see also* Defect,
    coagulation) 286.3
  Paas' 756.59
  Paget's (osteitis deformans) 731.0
    with infiltrating duct carcinoma of the breast
      (M8541/3)—*see* Neoplasm, breast,
      malignant
    bone 731.0
      osteosarcoma in (M9184/3)—*see*
        Neoplasm, bone, malignant
    breast (M8540/3) 174.0
    extramammary (M8542/3)—*see also*
      Neoplasm, skin, malignant
      anus 154.3
      skin 173.5
    malignant (M8540/3)
      breast 174.0
      specified site NEC (M8542/3)—*see*
        Neoplasm, skin, malignant
      unspecified site 174.0

Disease, diseased—*continued*
    mammary (M8540/3) 174.0
    nipple (M8540/3) 174.0
  palate (soft) 528.9
  Paltauf-Sternberg 201.9
  pancreas 577.9
    cystic 577.2
      congenital 751.7
    fibrocystic 277.00
  Panner's 732.3
    capitellum humeri 732.3
    head of humerus 732.3
    tarsal navicular (bone) (osteochondrosis) 732.5
  panvalvular—*see* Endocarditis, mitral
  parametrium 629.9
  parasitic NEC 136.9
    cerebral NEC 123.9
    intestinal NEC 129
    mouth 112.0
    skin NEC 134.9
    specified type—*see* Infestation
    tongue 112.0
  parathyroid (gland) 252.9
    specified NEC 252.8
  Parkinson's 332.0
  parodontal 523.9
  Parrot's (syphilitic osteochondritis) 090.0
  Parry's (exophthalmic goiter) 242.0
  Parson's (exophthalmic goiter) 242.0
  Pavy's 593.6
  Paxton's (white piedra) 111.2
  Payr's (splenic flexure syndrome) 569.89
  pearl-workers' (chronic osteomyelitis) (*see also*
    Osteomyelitis) 730.1
  Pel-Ebstein—*see* Disease, Hodgkin's
  Pelizaeus-Merzbacher 330.0
    with dementia 294.1
  Pellegrini-Stieda (calcification, knee joint)
    726.62
  pelvis, pelvic
    female NEC 629.9
      specified NEC 629.8
    gonococcal (acute) 098.19
      chronic or duration of 2 months or over
        098.39
    infection (*see also* Disease, pelvis,
      inflammatory) 614.9
    inflammatory (female) (PID) 614.9
      with
        abortion—*see* Abortion, by type, with
          sepsis
        ectopic pregnancy (*see also* categories
          633.0-633.9) 639.0
        molar pregnancy (*see also* categories
          630-632) 639.0
      acute 614.3
      chronic 614.4
      complicating pregnancy 646.6
        affecting fetus or newborn 760.8
      following
        abortion 639.0
        ectopic or molar pregnancy 639.0
      peritonitis (acute) 614.5
        chronic NEC 614.7
      puerperal, postpartum, childbirth 670
      specified NEC 614.8
    organ, female NEC 629.9
      specified NEC 629.8
    peritoneum, female NEC 629.9
      specified NEC 629.8

Disease, diseased—*continued*
  penis 607.9
    inflammatory 607.2
  peptic NEC 536.9
    acid 536.8
  periapical tissues NEC 522.9
  pericardium 423.9
    specified type NEC 423.8
  perineum
    female
      inflammatory 616.9
        specified NEC 616.8
      noninflammatory 624.9
        specified NEC 624.8
    male (inflammatory) 682.2
  periodic (familial) (Reimann's) NEC 277.3
    paralysis 359.3
  periodontal NEC 523.9
    specified NEC 523.8
  periosteum 733.90
  peripheral
    arterial 443.9
    autonomic nervous system (*see also*
      Neuropathy, autonomic) 337.9
    nerve NEC (*see also* Neuropathy) 356.9
      multiple—*see* Polyneuropathy
    vascular 443.9
      specified type NEC 443.89
  peritoneum 568.9
    pelvic, female 629.9
      specified NEC 629.8
  Perrin-Ferraton (snapping hip) 719.65
  persistent mucosal (middle ear) (with posterior
    or superior marginal perforation of ear
    drum) 382.2
  Perthes' (capital femoral osteochondrosis) 732.1
  Petit's (*see also* Hernia, lumbar) 553.8
  Peutz-Jeghers 759.6
  Peyronie's 607.89
  Pfeiffer's (infectious mononucleosis) 075
  pharynx 478.20
  Phocas' 610.1
  photochromogenic (acid-fast bacilli)
    (pulmonary) 031.0
    nonpulmonary 031.9
  Pick's
    brain 331.1
      with dementia 331.1 *[294.1]*
    cerebral atrophy 331.1
      with dementia 331.1 *[294.1]*
    lipid histiocytosis 272.7
    liver (pericardial pseudocirrhosis of liver)
      423.2
    pericardium (pericardial pseudocirrhosis of
      liver) 423.2
    polyserositis (pericardial pseudocirrhosis of
      liver) 423.2
  Pierson's (osteochondrosis) 732.1
  pigeon fancier's or breeders' 495.2
  pineal gland 259.8
  pink 985.0
  Pinkus' (lichen nitidus) 697.1
  pinworm 127.4
  pituitary (gland) 253.9
    hyperfunction 253.1
    hypofunction 253.2
  pituitary snuff-takers' 495.8

Disease, diseased—*continued*
  placenta
    affecting fetus or newborn 762.2
    complicating pregnancy or childbirth 656.7
  pleura (cavity) (*see also* Pleurisy) 511.0
  Plummer's (toxic nodular goiter) 242.3
  pneumatic
    drill 994.9
    hammer 994.9
  policeman's 729.2
  Pollitzer's (hidradenitis suppurativa) 705.83
  polycystic (congenital) 759.89
    kidney or renal 753.12
      adult type (APKD) 753.13
      autosomal dominant 753.13
      autosomal recessive 753.14
      childhood type (CPKD) 753.14
      infantile type 753.14
    liver or hepatic 751.62
    lung or pulmonary 518.89
      congenital 748.4
    ovary, ovaries 256.4
    spleen 759.0
  Pompe's (glycogenosis II) 271.0
  Poncet's (tuberculous rheumatism) (*see also*
    Tuberculosis) 015.9
  Posada-Wernicke 114.9
  Potain's (pulmonary edema) 514
  Pott's (*see also* Tuberculosis) 015.0 *[730.88]*
    osteomyelitis 015.0 *[730.88]*
    paraplegia 015.0 *[730.88]*
    spinal curvature 015.0 *[737.43]*
    spondylitis 015.0 *[720.81]*
  Potter's 753.0
  Poulet's 714.2
  pregnancy NEC (*see also* Pregnancy) 646.9
  Preiser's (osteoporosis) 733.09
  Pringle's (tuberous sclerosis) 759.5
  Profichet's 729.9
  prostate 602.9
    specified type NEC 602.8
  protozoal NEC 136.8
    intestine, intestinal NEC 007.9
  pseudo-Hurler's (mucolipidosis III) 272.7
  psychiatric (*see also* Psychosis) 298.9
  psychotic (*see also* Psychosis) 298.9
  Puente's (simple glandular cheilitis) 528.5
  puerperal NEC (*see also* Puerperal) 674.9
  pulmonary—*see also* Disease, lung
    amyloid 277.3 *[517.8]*
    artery 417.9
    circulation, circulatory 417.9
      specified NEC 417.8
    diffuse obstructive (chronic) 496
      with
        acute exacerbation NEC 491.21
        asthma (chronic) (obstructive) 493.2
        bronchitis (chronic) 491.20
          with acute exacerbation 491.21
    heart (chronic) 416.9
      specified NEC 416.8
    hypertensive (vascular) 416.0
      cardiovascular 416.0
    obstructive diffuse (chronic) 496
      with
        acute exacerbation NEC 491.21
        asthma (chronic) (obstructive) 493.2
    valve (*see also* Endocarditis, pulmonary) 424.3

Disease, diseased—*continued*
pulp (dental) NEC 522.9
pulseless 446.7
Putnam's (subacute combined sclerosis with pernicious anemia) 281.0 *[336.2]*
Pyle (-Cohn) (craniometaphyseal dysplasia) 756.89
pyramidal tract 333.90
Quervain's
 tendon sheath 727.04
 thyroid (subacute granulomatous thyroiditis) 245.1
Quincke's—*see* Edema, angioneurotic
Quinquaud (acne decalvans) 704.09
rag sorters' 022.1
Raynaud's (Paroxysmal digital cyanosis) 443.0
reactive airway—*see* Asthma
Recklinghausen's (M9540/1) 237.71
 bone (osteitis fibrosa cystica) 252.0
Recklinghausen-Applebaum (hemochromatosis) 275.0
Reclus' (cystic) 610.1
rectum NEC 569.49
Refsum's (heredopathia atactica polyneuritiformis) 356.3
Reichmann's (gastrosuccorrhea) 536.8
Reimann's (periodic) 277.3
Reiter's 099.3
renal (functional) (pelvis) 593.9
 with
  edema (*see also* Nephrosis) 581.9
  exudative nephritis 583.89
  lesion of interstitial nephritis 583.89
  stated generalized cause—*see* Nephritis
 acute—*see* Nephritis, acute
 basement membrane NEC 583.89
  with
   pulmonary hemorrhage (Goodpasture's syndrome) 446.21 *[583.81]*
 chronic—*see* Nephritis, chronic
 complicating pregnancy or puerperium NEC 646.2
  with hypertension—*see* Toxemia, of pregnancy
  affecting fetus or newborn 760.1
 cystic, congenital (*see also* Cystic, disease, kidney) 753.10
 diabetic 250.4 *[583.81]*
 due to
  amyloidosis 277.3 *[583.81]*
  diabetes mellitus 250.4 *[583.81]*
  systemic lupus erythematosis 710.0 *[583.81]*
 end-stage 585
 exudative 583.89
 fibrocystic (congenital) 753.19
 gonococcal 098.19 *[583.81]*
 gouty 274.10
 hypertensive (*see also* Hypertension, kidney) 403.90
 immune complex NEC 583.89
 interstitial (diffuse) (focal) 583.89
 lupus 710.0 *[583.81]*
 maternal, affecting fetus or newborn 760.1
  hypertensive 760.0
 phosphate-losing (tubular) 588.0
 polycystic (congenital) 753.12
  adult type (APKD) 753.13
  autosomal dominant 753.13
  autosomal recessive 753.14
  childhood type (CPKD) 753.14
  infantile type 753.14

Disease, diseased—*continued*
 specified lesion or cause NEC (*see also* Glomerulonephritis) 583.89
 subacute 581.9
 syphilitic 095.4
 tuberculous (*see also* Tuberculosis) 016.0 *[583.81]*
 tubular (*see also* Nephrosis, tubular) 584.5
Rendu-Olser-Weber (familial hemorrhagic telangiectasia) 448.0
renovascular (arteriosclerotic) (*see also* Hypertension, kidney) 403.90
respiratory (tract) 519.9
 acute or subacute (upper) NEC 465.9
  due to fumes or vapors 506.3
  multiple sites NEC 465.8
  noninfectious 478.9
  streptococcal 034.0
 chronic 519.9
  arising in the perinatal period 770.7
  due to fumes or vapors 506.4
 due to
  aspiration of liquids or solids 508.9
  external agents NEC 508.9
   specified NEC 508.8
  fumes or vapors 506.9
   acute or subacute NEC 506.3
   chronic 506.4
 fetus or newborn NEC 770.9
 obstructive 496
 specified type NEC 519.8
 upper (acute) (infectious) NEC 465.9
  multiple sites NEC 465.8
  noninfectious NEC 478.9
  streptococcal 034.0
retina, retinal NEC 362.9
 Batten's or Batten-Mayou 330.1 *[362.71]*
 degeneration 362.89
 vascular lesion 362.17
rheumatic (*see also* Arthritis) 716.8
 heart—*see* Disease, heart, rheumatic
rheumatoid (heart)—*see* Arthritis, rheumatoid
rickettsial NEC 083.9
 specified type NEC 083.8
Riedel's (ligneous thyroiditis) 245.3
Riga (-Fede) (cachectic aphthae) 529.0
Riggs' (compound periodontitis) 523.4
Ritter's 695.81
Rivalta's (cervicofacial actinomycosis) 039.3
Robles' (onchocerciasis) 125.3 *[360.13]*
Roger's (congenital interventricular septal defect) 745.4
Rokitansky's (*see also* Necrosis, liver) 570
Romberg's 349.89
Rosenthal's (factor XI deficiency) 286.2
Rossbach's (hyperchlorhydria) 536.8
 psychogenic 306.4
Roth (-Bernhardt) 355.1
Runeberg's (progressive pernicious anemia) 281.0
Rust's (tuberculous spondylitis) (*see also* Tuberculosis) 015.0 *[720.81]*
Rustitskii's (multiple myeloma) (M9730/3) 203.0
Ruysch's (Hirschsprung's disease) 751.3
Sachs (-Tay) 330.1
sacroiliac NEC 724.6
salivary gland or duct NEC 527.9
 inclusion 078.5
  streptococcal 034.0
 virus 078.5

Disease, diseased—*continued*
Stuttgart 100.89
Sudeck's 733.7
supporting structures of teeth NEC 525.9
suprarenal (gland) (capsule) 255.9
  hyperfunction 255.3
  hypofunction 255.4
Sutton's 709.09
Sutton and Gull's—*see* Hypertension, kidney
sweat glands NEC 705.9
  specified type NEC 705.89
sweating 078.2
Sweeley-Klionsky 272.4
Swift (-Feer) 985.0
swimming pool (bacillus) 031.1
swineherd's 100.89
Sylvest's (epidemic pleurodynia) 074.1
Symmers (follicular lymphoma) (M9690/3)
  202.0
sympathetic nervous system (*see also*
  Neuropathy, peripheral, autonomic) 337.9
synovium 727.9
syphilitic—*see* Syphilis
systemic tissue mast cell (M9741/3) 202.6
Taenzer's 757.4
Takayasu's (pulseless) 446.7
Talma's 728.85
Tangier (familial high-density lipoprotein
  deficiency) 272.5
Tarral-Besnier (pityriasis rubra pilaris) 696.4
Tay-Sachs 330.1
Taylor's 701.8
tear duct 375.69
teeth, tooth 525.9
  hard tissues NEC 521.9
  pulp NEC 522.9
tendon 727.9
  inflammatory NEC 727.9
terminal vessel 443.9
testis 608.9
Thaysen-Gee (nontropical sprue) 579.0
Thomsen's 359.2
Thomson's (congenital poikiloderma) 757.33
Thornwaldt's, Tornwaldt's (pharyngeal bursitis)
  478.29
throat 478.20
  septic 034.0
thromboembolic (*see also* Embolism) 444.9
thymus (gland) 254.9
  specified NEC 254.8
thyroid (gland) NEC 246.9
  heart (*see also* Hyperthyroidism) 242.9 *[425.7]*
  lardaceous 277.3
  specified NEC 246.8
Tietze's 733.6
Tommaselli's
  correct substance properly administered 599.7
  overdose or wrong substance given or taken
    961.4
tongue 529.9
tonsils, tonsillar (and adenoids) (chronic) 474.9
  specified NEC 474.8
tooth, teeth 525.9
  hard tissues NEC 521.9
  pulp NEC 522.9
Tornwaldt's (pharyngeal bursitis) 478.29

Disease, diseased—*continued*
Tourette's 307.23
trachea 519.1
tricuspid—*see* Endocarditis, tricuspid
triglyceride-storage, type I, II, III 272.7
triple vessel (coronary arteries) —*see*
  Arteriosclerosis, coronary
trisymptomatic, Gougerot's 709.1
trophoblastic (*see also* Hydatidiform mole) 630
  previous, affecting management of pregnancy
    V23.1
tsutsugamushi (scrub typhus) 081.2
tube (fallopian), noninflammatory 620.9
  specified NEC 620.8
tuberculous NEC (*see also* Tuberculosis) 011.9
tubo-ovarian
  inflammatory (*see also* Salpingo-oophoritis)
    614.2
  noninflammatory 620.9
  specified NEC 620.8
tubotympanic, chronic (with anterior perforation
  of ear drum) 382.1
tympanum 385.9
Uhl's 746.84
umbilicus (newborn) NEC 779.8
Underwood's (sclerema neonatorum) 778.1
undiagnosed 799.9
Unna's (seborrheic dermatitis) 690.18
unstable hemoglobin hemolytic 282.7
Unverricht (-Lundborg) 333.2
Urbach-Oppenheim (necrobiosis lipoidica
  diabeticorum) 250.8 *[709.3]*
Urbach-Wiethe (lipoid proteinosis) 272.8
ureter 593.9
urethra 599.9
  specified type NEC 599.84
urinary (tract) 599.9
  bladder 596.9
    specified NEC 596.8
  maternal, affecting fetus or newborn 760.1
Usher-Senear (pemphigus erythematosus) 694.4
uterus (organic) 621.9
  infective (*see also* Endometritis) 615.9
  inflammatory (*see also* Endometritis) 615.9
  noninflammatory 621.9
    specified type NEC 621.8
uveal tract
  anterior 364.9
  posterior 363.9
vagabonds' 132.1
vagina, vaginal
  inflammatory 616.9
    specified NEC 616.8
  noninflammatory 623.9
    specified NEC 623.8
Valsuani's (progressive pernicious anemia,
  puerperal) 648.2
  complicating pregnancy or puerperium 648.2
valve, valvular—*see* Endocarditis
van Bogaert-Nijssen (-Peiffer) 330.0
van Creveld-von Gierke (glycogenosis I) 271.0
van den Bergh's (enterogenous cyanosis) 289.7
van Neck's (juvenile osteochondrosis) 732.1
Vaquez (-Osler) (polycythemia vera) (M9950/1)
  238.4

Disease, diseased—*continued*
  Willis' (diabetes mellitus) (*see also* Diabetes)
    250.0
  Wilson's (hepatolenticular degeneration) 275.1
  Wilson-Brocq (dermatitis exfoliativa) 695.89
  winter vomiting 078.82
  Wise's 696.2
  Wohlfart-Kugelberg-Welander 335.11
  Woillez's (acute idiopathic pulmonary
    congestion) 518.5
  Wolman's (primary familial xanthomatosis)
    272.7
  wool-sorters' 022.1
  Zagari's (xerostomia) 527.7
  Zahorsky's (exanthem subitum) 057.8
  Ziehen-Oppenheim 333.6
  zoonotic, bacterial NEC 027.9
    specified type NEC 027.8
Disfigurement (due to scar) 709.2
  head V48.6
  limb V49.4
  neck V48.7
  trunk V48.7
Disgerminoma —*see* Dysgerminoma
Disinsertion, retina 361.04
Disintegration, complete, of the body 799.8
  traumatic 869.1
Disk kidney 753.3
Dislocatable hip, congenita l (*see also*
    Dislocation, hip, congenital) 754.30
Dislocation (articulation) (closed) (displacement)
    (simple) (subluxation) 839.8

Note—"Closed" includes simple, complete,
partial, uncomplicated, and unspecified
dislocation. "Open" includes dislocation
specified as infected or compound and
dislocation with foreign body. "Chronic,"
"habitual," "old," or "recurrent" dislocations
should be coded as indicated under the entry
"Dislocation, recurrent"; and "pathological" as
indicated under the entry "Dislocation,
pathological." For late effect of dislocation see
Late, effect, dislocation.

---

  with fracture—*see* Fracture, by site
  acromioclavicular (joint) (closed) 831.04
    open 831.14
  anatomical site (closed)
    specified NEC 839.69
      open 839.79
    unspecified or ill-defined 839.8
      open 839.9
  ankle (scaphoid bone) (closed) 837.0
    open 837.1
  arm (closed) 839.8
    open 839.9
  astragalus (closed) 837.0
    open 837.1
  atlanto-axial (closed) 839.01
    open 839.11
  atlas (closed) 839.01
    open 839.11
  axis (closed) 839.02
    open 839.12
  back (closed) 839.8
    open 839.9
  Bell-Daly 723.8

Dislocation—*continued*
  breast bone (closed) 839.61
    open 839.71
  capsule, joint—*see* Dislocation, by site
  carpal (bone)—*see* Dislocation, wrist
  carpometacarpal (joint) (closed) 833.04
    open 833.14
  cartilage (joint)—*see also* Dislocation, by site
    knee—*see* Tear, meniscus
  cervical, cervicodorsal, or cervicothoracic
    (spine) (vertebra)—*see* Dislocation,
    vertebra, cervical
  chiropractic (*see also* Lesion, nonallopathic)
    739.9
  chondrocostal—*see* Dislocation, costochondral
  chronic—*see* Dislocation, recurrent
  clavicle (closed) 831.04
    open 831.14
  coccyx (closed) 839.41
    open 839.51
  collar bone (closed) 831.04
    open 831.14
  compound (open) NEC 839.9
  congenital NEC 755.8
    hip (*see also* Dislocation, hip, congenital)
      754.30
    lens 743.37
    rib 756.3
    sacroiliac 755.69
    spine NEC 756.19
    vertebra 756.19
  coracoid (closed) 831.09
    open 831.19
  costal cartilage (closed) 839.69
    open 839.79
  costochondral (closed) 839.69
    open 839.79
  cricoarytenoid articulation (closed) 839.69
    open 839.79
  cricothyroid (cartilage) articulation (closed)
    839.69
    open 839.79
  dorsal vertebrae (closed) 839.21
    open 839.31
  ear ossicle 385.23
  elbow (closed) 832.00
    anterior (closed) 832.01
      open 832.11
    congenital 754.89
    divergent (closed) 832.09
      open 832.19
    lateral (closed) 832.04
      open 832.14
    medial (closed) 832.03
      open 832.13
    open 832.10
    posterior (closed) 832.02
      open 832.12
    recurrent 718.32
    specified type NEC 832.09
      open 832.19
  eye 360.81
    lateral 376.36
  eyeball 360.81
    lateral 376.36

Dislocation—*continued*
femur
  distal end (closed) 836.50
    anterior 836.52
      open 836.62
    lateral 836.53
      open 836.63
    medial 836.54
      open 836.64
    open 836.60
    posterior 836.51
      open 836.61
  proximal end (closed) 835.00
    anterior (pubic) 835.03
      open 835.13
    obturator 835.02
      open 835.12
    open 835.10
    posterior 835.01
      open 835.11
fibula
  distal end (closed) 837.0
    open 837.1
  proximal end (closed) 836.59
    open 836.69
finger(s) (phalanx) (thumb) (closed) 834.00
  interphalangeal (joint) 834.02
    open 834.12
  metacarpal (bone), distal end 834.01
    open 834.11
  metacarpophalangeal (joint) 834.01
    open 834.11
  open 834.10
  recurrent 718.34
foot (closed) 838.00
  open 838.10
  recurrent 718.37
forearm (closed) 839.8
  open 839.9
fracture—*see* Fracture, by site
glenoid (closed) 831.09
  open 831.19
habitual—*see* Dislocation, recurrent
hand (closed) 839.8
  open 839.9
hip (closed) 835.00
  anterior 835.03
    obturator 835.02
      open 835.12
    open 835.13
  congenital (unilateral) 754.30
    with subluxation of other hip 754.35
    bilateral 754.31
  open 835.10
  posterior 835.01
    open 835.11
  recurrent 718.35
humerus (closed) 831.00
  distal end (*see also* Dislocation, elbow) 832.00
  open 831.10
  proximal end (closed) 831.00
    anterior (subclavicular) (subcoracoid)
      (subglenoid) (closed) 831.01
      open 831.11
    inferior (closed) 831.03
      open 831.13
    open 831.10
    posterior (closed) 831.02
      open 831.12

Dislocation—*continued*
implant—*see* Complications, mechanical
incus 385.23
infracoracoid (closed) 831.01
  open 831.11
innominate (pubic junction) (sacral junction)
    (closed) 839.69
  acetabulum (*see also* Dislocation, hip) 835.00
  open 839.79
interphalangeal (joint)
  finger or hand (closed) 834.02
    open 834.12
  foot or toe (closed) 838.06
    open 838.16
jaw (cartilage) (meniscus) (closed) 830.0
  open 830.1
  recurrent 524.69
joint NEC (closed) 839.8
  open 839.9
  pathological—*see* Dislocation, pathological
  recurrent—*see* Dislocation, recurrent
knee (closed) 836.50
  anterior 836.51
    open 836.61
  congenital (with genu recurvatum) 754.41
  habitual 718.36
  lateral 836.54
    open 836.64
  medial 836.53
    open 836.63
  old 718.36
  open 836.60
  posterior 836.52
    open 836.62
  recurrent 718.36
  rotatory 836.59
    open 836.69
lacrimal gland 375.16
leg (closed) 839.8
  open 839.9
lens (crystalline) (complete) (partial) 379.32
  anterior 379.33
  congenital 743.37
  ocular implant 996.53
  posterior 379.34
  traumatic 921.3
ligament—*see* Dislocation, by site
lumbar (vertebrae) (closed) 839.20
  open 839.30
lumbosacral (vertebrae) (closed) 839.20
  congenital 756.19
  open 839.30
mandible (closed) 830.0
  open 830.1
maxilla (inferior) (closed) 830.0
  open 830.1
meniscus (knee)—*see also* Tear, meniscus
  other sites—*see* Dislocation, by site
metacarpal (bone)
  distal end (closed) 834.01
    open 834.11
  proximal end (closed) 833.05
    open 833.15
metacarpophalangeal (joint) (closed) 834.01
  open 834.11
metatarsal (bone) (closed) 838.04
  open 838.14
metatarsophalangeal (joint) (closed) 838.05
  open 838.15

Dislocation—*continued*
  midcarpal (joint) (closed) 833.03
    open 833.13
  midtarsal (joint) (closed) 838.02
    open 838.12
  Monteggia's—*see* Dislocation, hip
  multiple locations (except fingers only or toes
    only) (closed) 839.8
    open 839.9
  navicular (bone) foot (closed) 837.0
    open 837.1
  neck (*see also* Dislocation, vertebra, cervical)
    839.00
  Nélaton's—*see* Dislocation, ankle
  nontraumatic (joint)—*see* Dislocation,
    pathological
  nose (closed) 839.69
    open 839.79
  not recurrent, not current injury—*see*
    Dislocation, pathological
  occiput from atlas (closed) 839.01
    open 839.11
  old—*see* Dislocation, recurrent
  open (compound) NEC 839.9
  ossicle, ear 385.23
  paralytic (flaccid) (spastic)—*see* Dislocation,
    pathological
  patella (closed) 836.3
    congenital 755.64
    open 836.4
  pathological NEC 718.20
    ankle 718.27
    elbow 718.22
    foot 718.27
    hand 718.24
    hip 718.25
    knee 718.26
    lumbosacral joint 724.6
    multiple sites 718.29
    pelvic region 718.25
    sacroiliac 724.6
    shoulder (region) 718.21
    specified site NEC 718.28
    spine 724.8
      sacroiliac 724.6
    wrist 718.23
  pelvis (closed) 839.69
    acetabulum (*see also* Dislocation, hip) 835.00
    open 839.79
  phalanx
    foot or toe (closed) 838.09
      open 838.19
    hand or finger (*see also* Dislocation, finger)
      834.00
  postpoliomyelitic—*see* Dislocation, pathological
  prosthesis, internal—*see* Complications,
    mechanical
  radiocarpal (joint) (closed) 833.02
    open 833.12
  radioulnar (joint)
    distal end (closed) 833.01
      open 833.11
    proximal end (*see also* Dislocation, elbow)
      832.00

Dislocation—*continued*
  radius
    distal end (closed) 833.00
      open 833.10
    proximal end (closed) 832.01
      open 832.11
  recurrent (*see also* Derangement, joint,
    recurrent) 718.3
    elbow 718.32
    hip 718.35
    joint NEC 718.38
    knee 718.36
    lumbosacral (joint) 724.6
    patella 718.36
    sacroiliac 724.6
    shoulder 718.31
    temporomandibular 524.69
  rib (cartilage) (closed) 839.69
    congenital 756.3
    open 839.79
  sacrococcygeal (closed) 839.42
    open 839.52
  sacroiliac (joint) (ligament) (closed) 839.42
    congenital 755.69
    open 839.52
    recurrent 724.6
  sacrum (closed) 839.42
    open 839.52
  scaphoid (bone)
    ankle or foot (closed) 837.0
      open 837.1
    wrist (closed) (*see also* Dislocation, wrist)
      833.00
      open 833.10
  scapula (closed) 831.09
    open 831.19
  semilunar cartilage, knee—*see* Tear, meniscus
  septal cartilage (nose) (closed) 839.69
    open 839.79
  septum (nasal) (old) 470
  sesamoid bone—*see* Dislocation, by site
  shoulder (blade) (ligament) (closed) 831.00
    anterior (subclavicular) (subcoracoid)
      (subglenoid) (closed) 831.01
      open 831.11
    chronic 718.31
    inferior 831.03
      open 831.13
    open 831.10
    posterior (closed) 831.02
      open 831.12
    recurrent 718.31
  skull—*see* Injury, intracranial
  Smith's—*see* Dislocation, foot
  spine (articular process) (*see also* Dislocation,
    vertebra) (closed) 839.40
    atlanto-axial (closed) 839.01
      open 839.11
      recurrent 723.8
    cervical, cervicodorsal, cervicothoracic
      (closed) (*see also* Dislocation, vertebrae,
      cervical) 839.00
      open 839.10
      recurrent 723.8
    coccyx 839.41
      open 839.51
    congenital 756.19
    due to birth trauma 767.4
    open 839.50

Dislocation—*continued*
  recurrent 724.9
  sacroiliac 839.42
    recurrent 724.6
  sacrum (sacrococcygeal) (sacroiliac) 839.42
    open 839.52
  spontaneous—*see* Dislocation, pathological
  sternoclavicular (joint) (closed) 839.61
    open 839.71
  sternum (closed) 839.61
    open 839.71
  subastragalar—*see* Dislocation, foot
  subglenoid (closed) 831.01
    open 831.11
  symphysis
    jaw (closed) 830.0
      open 830.1
    mandibular (closed) 830.0
      open 830.1
    pubis (closed) 839.69
      open 839.79
  tarsal (bone) (joint) 838.01
    open 838.11
  tarsometatarsal (joint) 838.03
    open 838.13
  temporomandibular (joint) (closed) 830.0
    open 830.1
    recurrent 524.69
  thigh
    distal end (*see also* Dislocation, femur, distal
      end) 836.50
    proximal end (*see also* Dislocation, hip)
      835.00
  thoracic (vertebrae) (closed) 839.21
    open 839.31
  thumb(s) (*see also* Dislocation, finger) 834.00
  thyroid cartilage (closed) 839.69
    open 839.79
  tibia
    distal end (closed) 837.0
      open 837.1
    proximal end (closed) 836.50
      anterior 836.51
        open 836.61
      lateral 836.54
        open 836.64
      medial 836.53
        open 836.63
      open 836.60
      posterior 836.52
        open 836.62
      rotatory 836.59
        open 836.69
  tibiofibular
    distal (closed) 837.0
      open 837.1
    superior (closed) 836.59
      open 836.69
  toe(s) (closed) 838.09
    open 838.19
  trachea (closed) 839.69
    open 839.79
  ulna
    distal end (closed) 833.09
      open 833.19
    proximal end—*see* Dislocation, elbow

Dislocation—*continued*
  vertebra (articular process) (body) (closed)
    839.40
    cervical, cervicodorsal or cervicothoracic
      (closed) 839.00
      first (atlas) 839.01
        open 839.11
      second (axis) 839.02
        open 839.12
      third 839.03
        open 839.13
      fourth 839.04
        open 839.14
      fifth 839.05
        open 839.15
      sixth 839.06
        open 839.16
      seventh 839.07
        open 839.17
      congenital 756.19
      multiple sites 839.08
        open 839.18
      open 839.10
    congenital 756.19
    dorsal 839.21
      open 839.31
      recurrent 724.9
    lumbar, lumbosacral 839.20
      open 839.30
    open NEC 839.50
    recurrent 724.9
    specified region NEC 839.49
      open 839.59
    thoracic 839.21
      open 839.31
  wrist (carpal bone) (scaphoid) (semilunar)
    (closed) 833.00
    carpometacarpal (joint) 833.04
      open 833.14
    metacarpal bone, proximal end 833.05
      open 833.15
    midcarpal (joint) 833.03
      open 833.13
    open 833.10
    radiocarpal (joint) 833.02
      open 833.12
    radioulnar (joint) 833.01
      open 833.11
    recurrent 718.33
    specified site NEC 833.09
      open 833.19
  xiphoid cartilage (closed) 839.61
    open 839.71
Disobedience, hostile (covert) (overt) (*see also*
    Disturbance, conduct) 312.0
Disorder —*see also* Disease
  academic underachievement, childhood and
    adolescence 313.83
  accommodation 367.51
    drug-induced 367.89
    toxic 367.89
  adjustment (*see also* Reaction, adjustment) 309.9
  adrenal (capsule) (cortex) (gland) 255.9
    specified type NEC 255.8
  adrenogenital 255.2
  affective (*see also* Psychosis, affective) 296.90
    atypical 296.81
  aggressive, unsocialized (*see also* Disturbance,
    conduct) 312.0

Disorder—*continued*
  alcohol, alcoholic (*see also* Alcohol) 291.9
  allergic—*see* Allergy
  amino acid (metabolic) (*see also* Disturbance,
      metabolism, amino acid) 270.9
    albinism 270.2
    alkaptonuria 270.2
    argininosuccinicaciduria 270.6
    beta-amino-isobutyricaciduria 277.2
    cystathioninuria 270.4
    cystinosis 270.0
    cystinuria 270.0
    glycinuria 270.0
    homocystinuria 270.4
    imidazole 270.5
    maple syrup (urine) disease 270.3
    neonatal, transitory 775.8
    oasthouse urine disease 270.2
    ochronosis 270.2
    phenylketonuria 270.1
    phenylpyruvic oligophrenia 270.1
    purine NEC 277.2
    pyrimidine NEC 277.2
    renal transport NEC 270.0
    specified type NEC 270.8
    transport NEC 270.0
      renal 270.0
    xanthinuria 277.2
  amnestic (*see also* Amnestic syndrome) 294.0
  anaerobic glycolysis with anemia 282.3
  anxiety (*see also* Anxiety) 300.00
  arteriole 447.9
    specified type NEC 447.8
  artery 447.9
    specified type NEC 447.8
  articulation—*see* Disorder, joint
  Asperger's 299.8
  attachment of infancy 313.89
  attention deficit 314.00
    with hyperactivity 314.01
    predominantly
      combined hyperactive/inattentive 314.01
      hyperactive/impulsive 314.01
      inattentive 314.00
    residual type 314.8
  autistic 299.0
  autoimmune NEC 279.4
    hemolytic (cold type) (warm type) 283.0
    parathyroid 252.1
    thyroid 245.2
  avoidant, childhood or adolescence 313.21
  balance
    acid-base 276.9
      mixed (with hypercapnia) 276.4
    electrolyte 276.9
    fluid 276.9
  behavior NEC (*see also* Disturbance, conduct)
      312.9
  bilirubin excretion 277.4
  bipolar (affective) (alternating) (Type I) (*see
      also* Psychosis, affective) 296.7
    atypical 296.7
    currently
      depressed 296.5
      hypomanic 296.4
      manic 296.4
    mixed 296.6
    Type II (recurrent major depressive episodes
        with hypomania) 296.89

Disorder—*continued*
  bladder 596.9
    functional NEC 596.59
    specified NEC 596.8
  bone NEC 733.90
    specified NEC 733.99
  brachial plexus 353.0
  branched-chain amino-acid degradation 270.3
  breast 611.9
    puerperal, postpartum 676.3
    specified NEC 611.8
  Briquet's 300.81
  bursa 727.9
    shoulder region 726.10
  carbohydrate metabolism, congenital 271.9
  cardiac, functional 427.9
    postoperative 997.1
    psychogenic 306.2
  cardiovascular, psychogenic 306.2
  cartilage NEC 733.90
    articular 718.00
      ankle 718.07
      elbow 718.02
      foot 718.07
      hand 718.04
      hip 718.05
      knee 717.9
      multiple sites 718.09
      pelvic region 718.05
      shoulder region 718.01
      specified
        site NEC 718.08
        type NEC 733.99
      wrist 718.03
  cervical region NEC 723.9
  cervical root (nerve) NEC 353.2
  character NEC (*see also* Disorder, personality)
      301.9
  coagulation (factor) (*see also* Defect,
      coagulation) 286.9
    factor VIII (congenital) (functional) 286.0
    factor IX (congenital) (functional) 286.1
    neonatal, transitory 776.3
  coccyx 724.70
    specified NEC 724.79
  cognitive 294.9
  colon 569.9
    functional 564.9
      congenital 751.3
  conduct (*see also* Disturbance, conduct) 312.9
    adjustment reaction 309.3
    adolescent onset type 312.82
    childhood onset type 312.81
    compulsive 312.30
      specified type NEC 312.39
    hyperkinetic 314.2
    socialized (type) 312.20
      aggressive 312.23
      unaggressive 312.21
    specified NEC 312.89
  conduction, heart 426.9
    specified NEC 426.89
  convulsive (secondary) (*see also* Convulsions)
      780.3
    due to injury at birth 767.0
    idiopathic 780.3
  coordination 781.3
  cornea NEC 371.89
    due to contact lens 371.82
  corticosteroid metabolism NEC 255.2
  cranial nerve—*see* Disorder, nerve, cranial

Disorder—*continued*
  cyclothymic 301.13
  degradation, branched-chain amino acid 270.3
  dentition 520.6
  depressive NEC 311
    atypical 296.82
    major (*see also* Psychosis, affective) 296.2
      recurrent episode 296.3
      single episode 296.2
  development, specific 315.9
    associated with hyperkinesia 314.1
    language 315.31
    learning 315.2
      arithmetical 315.1
      reading 315.00
    mixed 315.5
    motor coordination 315.4
    specified type NEC 315.8
    speech 315.39
  diaphragm 519.4
  digestive 536.9
    fetus or newborn 777.9
      specified NEC 777.8
    psychogenic 306.4
  disintegrative (childhood) 299.1
  dissociative 300.14
    identity 300.14
  dysmorphic body 300.7
  dysthymic 300.4
  ear 388.9
    degenerative NEC 388.00
    external 380.9
      specified 380.89
    pinna 380.30
    specified type NEC 388.8
    vascular NEC 388.00
  eating NEC 307.50
  electrolyte NEC 276.9
    with
      abortion—*see* Abortion, by type, with
        metabolic disorder
      ectopic pregnancy (*see also* categories
        633.0-633.9) 639.4
      molar pregnancy (*see also* categories
        630-632) 639.4
    acidosis 276.2
      metabolic 276.2
      respiratory 276.2
    alkalosis 276.3
      metabolic 276.3
      respiratory 276.3
    following
      abortion 639.4
      ectopic or molar pregnancy 639.4
    neonatal, transitory NEC 775.5
  emancipation as adjustment reaction 309.22
  emotional (*see also* Disorder, mental,
    nonpsychotic) V40.9
  endocrine 259.9
    specified type NEC 259.8
  esophagus 530.9
    functional 530.5
    psychogenic 306.4
  explosive
    intermittent 312.34
    isolated 312.35
  expressive language 315.31
  eye 379.90
    globe—*see* Disorder, globe
    ill-defined NEC 379.99
    limited duction NEC 378.63

Disorder—*continued*
    specified NEC 379.8
  eyelid 374.9
    degenerative 374.50
    sensory 374.44
    specified type NEC 374.89
    vascular 374.85
  factitious —*see* Illness, factitious
  factor, coagulation (*see also* Defect,
    coagulation) 286.9
    VIII (congenital) (functional) 286.0
    IX (congenital) (functional) 286.1
  fascia 728.9
  feeding —*see* Feeding
  female sexual arousal 302.72
  fluid NEC 276.9
  gastric (functional) 536.9
    motility 536.8
    psychogenic 306.4
    secretion 536.8
  gastrointestinal (functional) NEC 536.9
    newborn (neonatal) 777.9
      specified NEC 777.8
    psychogenic 306.4
  gender (child) 302.6
    adult 302.85
  gender identity (childhood) 302.6
    adult-life 302.85
  genitourinary system, psychogenic 306.50
  globe 360.9
    degenerative 360.20
      specified NEC 360.29
    specified type NEC 360.89
  hearing—*see also* Deafness
    conductive type (air) (*see also* Deafness,
      conductive) 389.00
    mixed conductive and sensorineural 389.2
    nerve 389.12
    perceptive (*see also* Deafness, perceptive)
      389.10
    sensorineural type NEC (*see also* Deafness,
      perceptive) 389.10
  heart action 427.9
    postoperative 997.1
  hematological, transient neonatal 776.9
    specified type NEC 776.8
  hematopoietic organs 289.9
  hemorrhagic NEC 287.9
    due to circulating anticoagulants 286.5
    specified type NEC 287.8
  hemostasis (*see also* Defect, coagulation) 286.9
  homosexual conflict 302.0
  hypomanic (chronic) 301.11
  identity
    childhood and adolescence 313.82
      gender 302.6
    gender 302.6
  immune mechanism (immunity) 279.9
    single complement (C_1-C_9) 279.8
    specified type NEC 279.8
  impulse control (*see also* Disturbance, conduct,
    compulsive) 312.30
  integument, fetus or newborn 778.9
    specified type NEC 778.8
  interactional psychotic (childhood) (*see also*
    Psychosis, childhood) 299.1
  intermittent explosive 312.34
  intervertebral disc 722.90
    cervical, cervicothoracic 722.91
    lumbar, lumbosacral 722.93
    thoracic, thoracolumbar 722.92

Disorder—*continued*
  intestinal 569.9
    functional NEC 564.9
      congenital 751.3
      postoperative 564.4
    psychogenic 306.4
  introverted, of childhood and adolescence
      313.22
  iron, metabolism 275.0
  isolated explosive 312.35
  joint NEC 719.90
    ankle 719.97
    elbow 719.92
    foot 719.97
    hand 719.94
    hip 719.95
    knee 719.96
    multiple sites 719.99
    pelvic region 719.95
    psychogenic 306.0
    shoulder (region) 719.91
    specified site NEC 719.98
    temporomandibular 524.60
      specified NEC 524.69
    wrist 719.93
  kidney 593.9
    functional 588.9
      specified NEC 588.8
  labyrinth, labyrinthine 386.9
    specified type NEC 386.8
  lactation 676.9
  language (developmental) (expressive) 315.31
    mixed (receptive) (receptive-expressive)
        315.32
  ligament 728.9
  ligamentous attachments, peripheral—*see also*
      Enthesopathy
    spine 720.1
  limb NEC 729.9
    psychogenic 306.0
  lipid
    metabolism, congenital 272.9
    storage 272.7
  lipoprotein deficiency (familial) 272.5
  low back NEC 724.9
    psychogenic 306.0
  lumbosacral
    plexus 353.1
    root (nerve) NEC 353.4
  lymphoproliferative (chronic) NEC (M9970/1)
      238.7
  major depressive (*see also* Psychosis, affective)
      296.2
    recurrent episode 296.3
    single episode 296.2
  male erectile 302.72
    organic origin 607.84
  manic (*see also* Psychosis, affective) 296.0
    atypical 296.81
  meniscus NEC (*see also* Disorder, cartilage,
      articular) 718.0
  menopausal 627.9
    specified NEC 627.8
  menstrual 626.9
    psychogenic 306.52
    specified NEC 626.8

Disorder—*continued*
  mental (nonpsychotic) 300.9
    affecting management of pregnancy,
        childbirth, or puerperium 648.4
    drug-induced 292.9
      hallucinogen persistent perception 292.89
      specified type NEC 292.89
    due to or associated with
      alcoholism 291.9
      drug consumption NEC 292.9
        specified type NEC 292.89
    induced by drug 292.9
      specified type NEC 292.89
    neurotic (*see also* Neurosis) 300.9
    presenile 310.1
      psychotic NEC 290.10
    previous, affecting management of pregnancy
        V23.8
    psychoneurotic (*see also* Neurosis) 300.9
    psychotic (*see also* Psychosis) 298.9
      senile 290.20
    specific, following organic brain damage 310.9
      cognitive or personality change of other
          type 310.1
      frontal lobe syndrome 310.0
      postconcussional syndrome 310.2
      specified type NEC 310.8
  metabolism NEC 277.9
    with
      abortion—*see* Abortion, by type, with
          metabolic disorder
      ectopic pregnancy (*see also* categories
          633.0-633.9) 639.4
      molar pregnancy (*see also* categories
          630-632) 639.4
    alkaptonuria 270.2
    amino acid (*see also* Disorder, amino acid)
        270.9
      specified type NEC 270.8
    ammonia 270.6
    arginine 270.6
    argininosuccinic acid 270.6
    basal 794.7
    bilirubin 277.4
    calcium 275.4
    carbohydrate 271.9
      specified type NEC 271.8
    cholesterol 272.9
    citrulline 270.6
    copper 275.1
    corticosteroid 255.2
    cystine storage 270.0
    cystinuria 270.0
    fat 272.9
    following
      abortion 639.4
      ectopic or molar pregnancy 639.4
    fructosemia 271.2
    fructosuria 271.2
    fucosidosis 271.8
    galactose-1-phosphate uridyl transferase 271.1
    glutamine 270.7
    glycine 270.7
    glycogen storage NEC 271.0
      hepatorenal 271.0
    hemochromatosis 275.0
    in labor and delivery 669.0
    iron 275.0
    lactose 271.3

Disorder—*continued*
  lipid 272.9
    specified type NEC 272.8
    storage 272.7
  lipoprotein—*see also* Hyperlipemia
    deficiency (familial) 272.5
  lysine 270.7
  magnesium 275.2
  mannosidosis 271.8
  mineral 275.9
    specified type NEC 275.8
  mucopolysaccharide 277.5
  nitrogen 270.9
  ornithine 270.6
  oxalosis 271.8
  pentosuria 271.8
  phenylketonuria 270.1
  phosphate 275.3
  phosphorus 275.3
  plasma protein 273.9
    specified type NEC 273.8
  porphyrin 277.1
  purine 277.2
  pyrimidine 277.2
  serine 270.7
  sodium 276.9
  specified type NEC 277.8
  steroid 255.2
  threonine 270.7
  urea cycle 270.6
  xylose 271.8
  micturition NEC 788.69
    psychogenic 306.53
  misery and unhappiness, of childhood and
    adolescence 313.1
  motor tic 307.20
    chronic 307.22
    transient, childhood 307.21
  movement NEC 333.90
    hysterical 300.11
    specified type NEC 333.99
    stereotypic 307.3
  mucopolysaccharide 277.5
  muscle 728.9
    psychogenic 306.0
    specified type NEC 728.3
  muscular attachments, peripheral—*see also*
    Enthesopathy
    spine 720.1
  musculoskeletal system NEC 729.9
    psychogenic 306.0
  myeloproliferative (chronic) NEC (M9960/1)
    238.7
  myoneural 358.9
    due to lead 358.2
    specified type NEC 358.8
    toxic 358.2
  myotonic 359.2
  neck region NEC 723.9
  nerve 349.9
    abducens NEC 378.54
    accessory 352.4
    acoustic 388.5
    auditory 388.5
    auriculotemporal 350.8
    axillary 353.0
    cerebral—*see* Disorder, nerve, cranial
    cranial 352.9
      first 352.0
      second 377.49

Disorder—*continued*
    third
      partial 378.51
      total 378.52
    fourth 378.53
    fifth 350.9
    sixth 378.54
    seventh NEC 351.9
    eighth 388.5
    ninth 352.2
    tenth 352.3
    eleventh 352.4
    twelfth 352.5
    multiple 352.6
    entrapment—*see* Neuropathy, entrapment
    facial 351.9
      specified NEC 351.8
    femoral 355.2
    glossopharyngeal NEC 352.2
    hypoglossal 352.5
    iliohypogastric 355.79
    ilioinguinal 355.79
    intercostal 353.8
    lateral
      cutaneous of thigh 355.1
      popliteal 355.3
    lower limb NEC 355.8
    medial, popliteal 355.4
    median NEC 354.1
    obturator 355.79
    oculomotor
      partial 378.51
      total 378.52
    olfactory 352.0
    optic 377.49
      ischemic 377.41
      nutritional 377.33
      toxic 377.34
    peroneal 355.3
    phrenic 354.8
    plantar 355.6
    pneumogastric 352.3
    posterior tibial 355.5
    radial 354.3
    recurrent laryngeal 352.3
    root 353.9
      specified NEC 353.8
    saphenous 355.79
    sciatic NEC 355.0
    specified NEC 355.9
      lower limb 355.79
      upper limb 354.8
    spinal 355.9
    sympathetic NEC 337.9
    trigeminal 350.9
      specified NEC 350.8
    trochlear 378.53
    ulnar 354.2
    upper limb NEC 354.9
    vagus 352.3
  nervous system NEC 349.9
    autonomic (peripheral) (*see also* Neuropathy,
      peripheral, autonomic) 337.9
    cranial 352.9
    parasympathetic (*see also* Neuropathy,
      peripheral, autonomic) 337.9
    specified type NEC 349.89
    sympathetic (*see also* Neuropathy, peripheral,
      autonomic) 337.9
    vegetative (*see also* Neuropathy, peripheral,
      autonomic) 337.9

Disorder—*continued*
  neurohypophysis NEC 253.6
  neurological NEC 781.9
    peripheral NEC 355.9
  neuromuscular NEC 358.9
    hereditary NEC 359.1
    specified NEC 358.8
    toxic 358.2
  neurotic 300.9
    specified type NEC 300.89
  neutrophil, polymorphonuclear (functional)
    288.1
  obsessive-compulsive 300.3
  oppositional, childhood and adolescence 313.81
  optic
    chiasm 377.54
      associated with
        inflammatory disorders 377.54
        neoplasm NEC 377.52
          pituitary 377.51
        pituitary disorders 377.51
        vascular disorders 377.53
    nerve 377.49
    radiations 377.63
    tracts 377.63
  orbit 376.9
    specified NEC 376.89
  overanxious, of childhood and adolescence
    313.0
  pancreas, internal secretion (other than diabetes
    mellitus) 251.9
    specified type NEC 251.8
  panic 300.01
    with agoraphobia 300.21
  papillary muscle NEC 429.81
  paranoid 297.9
    induced 297.3
    shared 297.3
  parathyroid 252.9
    specified type NEC 252.8
  paroxysmal, mixed 780.3
  pentose phosphate pathway with anemia 282.2
  personality 301.9
    affective 301.10
    aggressive 301.3
    amoral 301.7
    anancastic, anankastic 301.4
    antisocial 301.7
    asocial 301.7
    asthenic 301.6
    borderline 301.83
    compulsive 301.4
    cyclothymic 301.13
    dependent-passive 301.6
    dyssocial 301.7
    emotional instability 301.59
    epileptoid 301.3
    explosive 301.3
    following organic brain damage 310.1
    histrionic 301.50
    hyperthymic 301.11
    hypomanic (chronic) 301.11
    hypothymic 301.12
    hysterical 301.50
    immature 301.89
    inadequate 301.6
    introverted 301.21
    labile 301.59
    moral deficiency 301.7
    obsessional 301.4
    obsessive (-compulsive) 301.4

Disorder—*continued*
    overconscientious 301.4
    paranoid 301.0
    passive (-dependent) 301.6
    passive-aggressive 301.84
    pathological NEC 301.9
    pseudosocial 301.7
    psychopathic 301.9
    schizoid 301.20
      introverted 301.21
      schizotypal 301.22
    schizotypal 301.22
    seductive 301.59
    type A 301.4
    unstable 301.59
  pervasive developmental, childhood-onset 299.8
  pigmentation, choroid (congenital) 743.53
  pinna 380.30
    specified type NEC 380.39
  pituitary, thalamic 253.9
    anterior NEC 253.4
    iatrogenic 253.7
    postablative 253.7
    specified NEC 253.8
  pityriasis-like NEC 696.8
  platelets (blood) 287.1
  polymorphonuclear neutrophils (functional)
    288.1
  porphyrin metabolism 277.1
  postmenopausal 627.9
    specified type NEC 627.8
  posttraumatic stress 309.81
    acute 308.3
    brief 308.3
    chronic 309.81
  psoriatic-like NEC 696.8
  psychic, with diseases classified elsewhere 316
  psychogenic NEC (*see also* condition) 300.9
    allergic NEC
      respiratory 306.1
    anxiety 300.00
      atypical 300.00
      generalized 300.02
    appetite 307.50
    articulation, joint 306.0
    asthenic 300.5
    blood 306.8
    cardiovascular (system) 306.2
    compulsive 300.3
    cutaneous 306.3
    depressive 300.4
    digestive (system) 306.4
    dysmenorrheic 306.52
    dyspneic 306.1
    eczematous 306.3
    endocrine (system) 306.6
    eye 306.7
    feeding 307.59
    functional NEC 306.9
    gastric 306.4
    gastrointestinal (system) 306.4
    genitourinary (system) 306.50
    heart (function) (rhythm) 306.2
    hemic 306.8
    hyperventilatory 306.1
    hypochondriacal 300.7
    hysterical 300.10
    intestinal 306.4
    joint 306.0
    learning 315.2
    limb 306.0

Disorder—*continued*
  lymphatic (system) 306.8
  menstrual 306.52
  micturition 306.53
  monoplegic NEC 306.0
  motor 307.9
  muscle 306.0
  musculoskeletal 306.0
  neurocirculatory 306.2
  obsessive 300.3
  occupational 300.89
  organ or part of body NEC 306.9
  organs of special sense 306.7
  paralytic NEC 306.0
  phobic 300.20
  physical NEC 306.9
  pruritic 306.3
  rectal 306.4
  respiratory (system) 306.1
  rheumatic 306.0
  sexual (function) 302.70
    specified type NEC 302.79
  skin (allergic) (eczematous) (pruritic) 306.3
  sleep 307.40
    initiation or maintenance 307.41
      persistent 307.42
      transient 307.41
    specified type NEC 307.49
  specified part of body NEC 306.8
  stomach 306.4
  psychomotor NEC 307.9
    hysterical 300.11
  psychoneurotic (*see also* Neurosis) 300.9
    mixed NEC 300.89
  psychophysiologic (*see also* Disorder,
    psychosomatic) 306.9
  psychosexual identity (childhood) 302.6
    adult-life 302.85
  psychosomatic NEC 306.9
    allergic NEC
      respiratory 306.1
    articulation, joint 306.0
    cardiovascular (system) 306.2
    cutaneous 306.3
    digestive (system) 306.4
    dysmenorrheic 306.52
    dyspneic 306.1
    endocrine (system) 306.6
    eye 306.7
    gastric 306.4
    gastrointestinal (system) 306.4
    genitourinary (system) 306.50
    heart (functional) (rhythm) 306.2
    hyperventilatory 306.1
    intestinal 306.4
    joint 306.0
    limb 306.0
    lymphatic (system) 306.8
    menstrual 306.52
    micturition 306.53
    monoplegic NEC 306.0
    muscle 306.0
    musculoskeletal 306.0
    neurocirculatory 306.2
    organs of special sense 306.7
    paralytic NEC 306.0
    pruritic 306.3
    rectal 306.4
    respiratory (system) 306.1
    rheumatic 306.0

Disorder—*continued*
  sexual (function) 302.70
    specified type NEC 302.79
  skin 306.3
  specified part of body NEC 306.8
  stomach 306.4
  purine metabolism NEC 277.2
  pyrimidine metabolism NEC 277.2
  reactive attachment (of infancy or early
    childhood) 313.89
  reading, developmental 315.00
  reflex 796.1
  renal function, impaired 588.9
    specified type NEC 588.8
  renal transport NEC 588.8
  respiration, respiratory NEC 519.9
    due to
      aspiration of liquids or solids 508.9
      inhalation of fumes or vapors 506.9
    psychogenic 306.1
  retina 362.9
    specified type NEC 362.89
  sacroiliac joint NEC 724.6
  sacrum 724.6
  schizo-affective (*see also* Schizophrenia) 295.7
  schizoid, childhood or adolescence 313.22
  schizophreniform 295.4
  schizotypal personality 301.22
  secretion, thyrocalcitonin 246.0
  seizure 780.3
    recurrent 780.3
      epileptic—*see* Epilepsy
  sense of smell 781.1
    psychogenic 306.7
  separation anxiety 309.21
  sexual (*see also* Deviation, sexual) 302.9
    function, psychogenic 302.70
  shyness, of childhood and adolescence 313.21
  single complement (C_1-C_9) 279.8
  skin NEC 709.9
    fetus or newborn 778.9
      specified type 778.8
    psychogenic (allergic) (eczematous) (pruritic)
      306.3
    specified type NEC 709.8
    vascular 709.1
  sleep 780.50
    circadian rhythm 307.45
    initiation or maintenance (*see also* Insomnia)
      780.52
      nonorganic origin (transient) 307.41
        persistent 307.42
    nonorganic origin 307.40
      specified type NEC 307.49
    specified NEC 780.59
    with apnea—*see* Apnea, sleep
  social, of childhood and adolescence 313.22
    specified NEC 780.59
  soft tissue 729.9
  somatization 300.81
  somatoform (atypical) (undifferentiated) 300.82
    severe 300.81
  speech NEC 784.5
    nonorganic origin 307.9
  spine NEC 724.9
    ligamentous or muscular attachments,
      peripheral 720.1
  steroid metabolism NEC 255.2

Disorder—*continued*
stomach (functional) (*see also* Disorder, gastric)
  536.9
  psychogenic 306.4
storage, iron 275.0
stress (*see also* Reaction, stress, acute) 308.9
  posttraumatic
    acute 308.3
    brief 308.3
    chronic 309.81
substitution 300.11
suspected—*see* Observation
synovium 727.9
temperature regulation, fetus or newborn 778.4
temporomandibular joint NEC 524.60
  specified NEC 524.69
tendon 727.9
  shoulder region 726.10
thoracic root (nerve) NEC 353.3
thyrocalcitonin secretion 246.0
thyroid (gland) NEC 246.9
  specified type NEC 246.8
tic 307.20
  chronic (motor or vocal) 307.22
  motor-verbal 307.23
  organic origin 333.1
  transient of childhood 307.21
tooth NEC 525.9
  development NEC 520.9
    specified type NEC 520.8
  eruption 520.6
    with abnormal position 524.3
  specified type NEC 525.8
transport, carbohydrate 271.9
  specified type NEC 271.8
tubular, phosphate-losing 588.0
tympanic membrane 384.9
unaggressive, unsocialized (*see also*
  Disturbance, conduct) 312.1
undersocialized, unsocialized—*see also*
  Disturbance, conduct
  aggressive (type) 312.0
  unaggressive (type) 312.1
vision, visual NEC 368.9
  binocular NEC 368.30
  cortex 377.73
    associated with
      inflammatory disorders 377.73
      neoplasms 377.71
      vascular disorders 377.72
  pathway NEC 377.63
    associated with
      inflammatory disorders 377.63
      neoplasms 377.61
      vascular disorders 377.62
wakefulness (*see also* Hypersomnia) 780.54
  nonorganic origin (transient) 307.43
  persistent 307.44
Disorganized globe 360.29
Displacement, displaced

> Note—For acquired displacement of
> bones, cartilage, joints, tendons, due to injury,
> see also Dislocation. Displacements at ages
> under one year should be considered
> congenital, provided there is no indication the
> condition was acquired after birth.

acquired traumatic of bond, cartilage, joint,
  tendon NEC (without fracture) (*see also*
  Dislocation) 839.8
  with fracture—*see* Fracture, by site

Displacement, displaced—*continued*
adrenal gland (congenital) 759.1
appendix, retrocecal (congenital) 751.5
auricle (congenital) 744.29
bladder (acquired) 596.8
  congenital 753.8
brachial plexus (congenital) 742.8
brain stem, caudal 742.4
canaliculus lacrimalis 743.65
cardia, through esophageal hiatus 750.6
cerebellum, caudal 742.4
cervix (*see also* Malposition, uterus) 621.6
colon (congenital) 751.4
device, implant, or graft—*see* Complications,
  mechanical
epithelium
  columnar of cervix 622.1
  cuboidal, beyond limits of external os (uterus)
    752.49
esophageal mucosa into cardia of stomach,
  congenital 750.4
esophagus (acquired) 530.89
  congenital 750.4
eyeball (acquired) (old) 376.36
  congenital 743.8
  current injury 871.3
  lateral 376.36
fallopian tube (acquired) 620.4
  congenital 752.19
  opening (congenital) 752.19
gallbladder (congenital) 751.69
gastric mucosa 750.7
  into
    duodenum 750.7
    esophagus 750.7
    Meckel's diverticulum, congenital 750.7
globe (acquired) (lateral) (old) 376.36
  current injury 871.3
heart (congenital) 746.87
  acquired 429.89
hymen (congenital) (upward) 752.49
internal prosthesis NEC—*see* Complications,
  mechanical
intervertebral disc (with neuritis, radiculitis,
  sciatica, or other pain) 722.2
  with myelopathy 722.70
  cervical, cervicodorsal, cervicothoracic 722.0
    with myelopathy 722.71
    due to major trauma—*see* Dislocation,
      vertebra, cervical
  due to major trauma—*see* Dislocation,
    vertebra
  lumbar, lumbosacral 722.10
    with myelopathy 722.73
    due to major trauma—*see* Dislocation,
      vertebra, lumbar
  thoracic, thoracolumbar 722.11
    with myelopathy 722.72
    due to major trauma—*see* Dislocation,
      vertebra, thoracic
intrauterine device 996.32
kidney (acquired) 593.0
  congenital 753.3
lacrimal apparatus or duct (congenital) 743.65
macula (congenital) 743.55
Meckel's diverticulum (congenital) 751.0
nail (congenital) 757.5
  acquired 703.8
opening of Wharton's duct in mouth 750.26
organ or site, congenital NEC—*see*
  Malposition, congenital

Displacement, displaced—*continued*
  ovary (acquired) 620.4
    congenital 752.0
    free in peritoneal cavity (congenital) 752.0
    into hernial sac 620.4
  oviduct (acquired) 620.4
    congenital 752.19
  parathyroid (gland) 252.8
  parotid gland (congenital) 750.26
  punctum lacrimale (congenital) 743.65
  sacroiliac (congenital) (joint) 755.69
    current injury—*see* Dislocation, sacroiliac
    old 724.6
  spine (congenital) 756.19
  spleen, congenital 759.0
  stomach (congenital) 750.7
    acquired 537.89
  subglenoid (closed) 831.01
  sublingual duct (congenital) 750.26
  teeth, tooth 524.3
  tongue (congenital) (downward) 750.19
  trachea (congenital) 748.3
  ureter or ureteric opening or orifice (congenital) 753.4
  uterine opening of oviducts or fallopian tubes 752.19
  uterus, uterine (*see also* Malposition, uterus) 621.6
    congenital 752.3
  ventricular septum 746.89
    with rudimentary ventricle 746.89
  xyphoid bone (process) 738.3
Disproportion 653.9
  affecting fetus or newborn 763.1
  caused by
    conjoined twins 653.7
    contraction, pelvis (general) 653.1
      inlet 653.2
      midpelvic 653.8
      midplane 653.8
      outlet 653.3
    fetal
      ascites 653.7
      hydrocephalus 653.6
      hydrops 653.7
      meningomyelocele 653.7
      sacral teratoma 653.7
      tumor 653.7
    hydrocephalic fetus 653.6
    pelvis, pelvic, abnormality (bony) NEC 653.0
    unusually large fetus 653.5
  causing obstructed labor 660.1
  cephalopelvic, normally formed fetus 653.4
    causing obstructed labor 660.1
  fetal NEC 653.5
    causing obstructed labor 660.1
  fetopelvic, normally formed fetus 653.4
    causing obstructed labor 660.1
  mixed maternal and fetal origin, normally formed fetus 653.4
  pelvis, pelvic (bony) NEC 653.1
    causing obstructed labor 660.1
  specified type NEC 653.8
Disruption
  cesarean wound 674.1
  family V61.0
  gastrointestinal anastomosis 997.4

Disruption—*continued*
  ligament(s)—*see also* Sprain
    knee
      current injury—*see* Dislocation, knee
      old 717.89
        capsular 717.85
        collateral (medial) 717.82
          lateral 717.81
        cruciate (posterior) 717.84
          anterior 717.83
        specified site NEC 717.85
  marital V61.10
    involving divorce or estrangement V61.0
  operation wound 998.3
  organ transplant, anastomosis site—*see* Complications, transplant, organ, by site
  ossicles, ossicular chain 385.23
    traumatic—*see* Fracture, skull, base
  parenchyma
    liver (hepatic)—*see* Laceration, liver, major
    spleen—*see* Laceration, spleen, parenchyma, massive
  phase-shift, of 24-hour sleep-wake cycle 780.55
    nonorganic origin 307.45
  sleep-wake cycle (24-hour) 780.55
    circadian rhythm 307.45
    nonorganic origin 307.45
  suture line (external) 998.3
    internal 998.3
  wound
    cesarean operation 674.1
    episiotomy 674.2
    operation 998.3
      cesarean 674.1
    perineal (obstetric) 674.2
    uterine 674.1
Disruptio uteri —*see also* Rupture, uterus
  complicating delivery—*see* Delivery, complicated, rupture, uterus
Dissatisfaction with
  employment V62.2
  school environment V62.3
Dissecting —*see* condition
Dissection
  aorta 441.00
    abdominal 441.02
    thoracic 441.01
    thoracoabdominal 441.03
  vascular 459.9
  wound—*see* Wound, open, by site
Disseminated —*see* condition
Dissociated personality NEC 300.15
Dissociation
  auriculoventricular or atrioventricular (any degree) (AV) 426.89
    with heart block 426.0
  interference 426.89
  isorhythmic 426.89
  rhythm
    atrioventricular (AV) 426.89
    interference 426.89
Dissociative
  identity disorder 300.14
  reaction NEC 300.15
Dissolution, vertebra (*see also* Osteoporosis) 733.00
Distention
  abdomen (gaseous) 787.3
  bladder 596.8
  cecum 569.89
  colon 569.89

Distention—*continued*
  gallbladder 575.8
  gaseous (abdomen) 787.3
  intestine 569.89
  kidney 593.89
  liver 573.9
  seminal vesicle 608.89
  stomach 536.8
    acute 536.1
    psychogenic 306.4
  ureter 593.5
  uterus 621.8
Distichia, distichiasis (eyelid) 743.63
Distoma hepaticum infestation 121.3
Distomiasis 121.9
  bile passages 121.3
    due to Clonorchis sinensis 121.1
  hemic 120.9
  hepatic (liver) 121.3
    due to Clonorchis sinensis (clonorchiasis)
      121.1
  intestinal 121.4
  liver 121.3
    due to Clonorchis sinensis 121.1
  lung 121.2
  pulmonary 121.2
Distomolar (fourth molar) 520.1
  causing crowding 524.3
Disto-occlusion 524.2
Distortion (congenital)
  adrenal (gland) 759.1
  ankle (joint) 755.69
  anus 751.5
  aorta 747.29
  appendix 751.5
  arm 755.59
  artery (peripheral) NEC (*see also* Distortion,
      peripheral vascular system) 747.60
    cerebral 747.81
    coronary 746.85
    pulmonary 747.3
    retinal 743.58
    umbilical 747.5
  auditory canal 744.29
    causing impairment of hearing 744.02
  bile duct or passage 751.69
  bladder 753.8
  brain 742.4
  bronchus 748.3
  cecum 751.5
  cervix (uteri) 752.49
  chest (wall) 756.3
  clavicle 755.51
  clitoris 752.49
  coccyx 756.19
  colon 751.5
  common duct 751.69
  cornea 743.41
  cricoid cartilage 748.3
  cystic duct 751.69
  duodenum 751.5
  ear 744.29
    auricle 744.29
      causing impairment of hearing 744.02
    causing impairment of hearing 744.09
    external 744.29
      causing impairment of hearing 744.02
    inner 744.05
    middle, except ossicles 744.03
      ossicles 744.04
    ossicles 744.04

Distortion—*continued*
  endocrine (gland) NEC 759.2
  epiglottis 748.3
  Eustachian tube 744.24
  eye 743.8
    adnexa 743.69
  face bone(s) 756.0
  fallopian tube 752.19
  femur 755.69
  fibula 755.69
  finger(s) 755.59
  foot 755.67
  gallbladder 751.69
  genitalia, genital organ(s)
    female 752.8
      external 752.49
      internal NEC 752.8
    male 752.8
      penis 752.69
  glottis 748.3
  gyri 742.4
  hand bone(s) 755.59
  heart (auricle) (ventricle) 746.89
    valve (cusp) 746.89
  hepatic duct 751.69
  humerus 755.59
  hymen 752.49
  ileum 751.5
  intestine (large) (small) 751.5
    with anomalous adhesions, fixation or
      malrotation 751.4
  jaw NEC 524.8
  jejunum 751.5
  kidney 753.3
  knee (joint) 755.64
  labium (majus) (minus) 752.49
  larynx 748.3
  leg 755.69
  lens 743.36
  liver 751.69
  lumbar spine 756.19
    with disproportion (fetopelvic) 653.0
      affecting fetus or newborn 763.1
      causing obstructed labor 660.1
  lumbosacral (joint) (region) 756.19
  lung (fissures) (lobe) 748.69
  nerve 742.8
  nose 748.1
  organ
    of Corti 744.05
    or site not listed—*see* Anomaly, specified
      type NEC
  ossicles, ear 744.04
  ovary 752.0
  oviduct 752.19
  pancreas 751.7
  parathyroid (gland) 759.2
  patella 755.64
  peripheral vascular system NEC 747.60
    gastrointestinal 747.61
    lower limb 747.64
    renal 747.62
    spinal 747.82
    upper limb 747.63
  pituitary (gland) 759.2
  radius 755.59
  rectum 751.5
  rib 756.3
  sacroiliac joint 755.69
  sacrum 756.19
  scapula 755.59

Distortion— *continued*
  shoulder girdle 755.59
  site not listed—*see* Anomaly, specified type
    NEC
  skull bone(s) 756.0
    with
      anencephalus 740.0
      encephalocele 742.0
      hydrocephalus 742.3
        with spina bifida (*see also* Spina bifida)
          741.0
      microcephalus 742.1
  spinal cord 742.59
  spine 756.19
  spleen 759.0
  sternum 756.3
  thorax (wall) 756.3
  thymus (gland) 759.2
  thyroid (gland) 759.2
    cartilage 748.3
  tibia 755.69
  toe(s) 755.66
  tongue 750.19
  trachea (cartilage) 748.3
  ulna 755.59
  ureter 753.4
    causing obstruction 753.20
  urethra 753.8
    causing obstruction 753.6
  uterus 752.3
  vagina 752.49
  vein (peripheral) NEC (*see also* Distortion,
    peripheral vascular system) 747.60
    great 747.49
    portal 747.49
    pulmonary 747.49
  vena cava (inferior) (superior) 747.49
  vertebra 756.19
  visual NEC 368.15
    shape or size 368.14
  vulva 752.49
  wrist (bones) (joint) 755.59
Distress
  abdomen 789.0
  colon 789.0
  emotional V40.9
  epigastric 789.0
  fetal (syndrome) 768.4
    affecting management of pregnancy or
      childbirth 656.3
    liveborn infant 768.4
      first noted
        before onset of labor 768.2
        during labor or delivery 768.3
      stillborn infant (death before onset of labor)
        768.0
        death during labor 768.1
  gastrointestinal (functional) 536.9
    psychogenic 306.4
  intestinal (functional) NEC 564.9
    psychogenic 306.4
  intrauterine (*see also* Distress, fetal) 768.4
  leg 729.5
  maternal 669.0
  mental V40.9
  respiratory 786.09
    acute (adult) 518.82
    adult syndrome (following shock, surgery, or
      trauma) 518.5
    specified NEC 518.82

Distress— *continued*
    fetus or newborn 770.8
    syndrome (idiopathic) (newborn) 769
  stomach 536.9
    psychogenic 306.4
Distribution vessel, atypical NEC 747.60
  coronary artery 746.85
  spinal 747.82
Districhiasis 704.2
Disturbance —*see also* Disease
  absorption NEC 579.9
    calcium 269.3
    carbohydrate 579.8
    fat 579.8
    protein 579.8
    specified type NEC 579.8
    vitamin (*see also* Deficiency, vitamin) 269.2
  acid-base equilibrium 276.9
  activity and attention, simple, with hyperkinesis
    314.01
  amino acid (metabolic) (*see also* Disorder,
    amino acid) 270.9
    imidazole 270.5
    maple syrup (urine) disease 270.3
    transport 270.0
  assimilation, food 579.9
  attention, simple 314.00
    with hyperactivity 314.01
  auditory, nerve, except deafness 388.5
  behavior (*see also* Disturbance, conduct) 312.9
  blood clotting (hypoproteinemia) (mechanism)
    (*see also* Defect, coagulation) 286.9
  central nervous system NEC 349.9
  cerebral nerve NEC 352.9
  circulatory 459.9
  conduct 312.9

Note—Use the following fifth-digit
subclassification with categories 312.0-312.2:

0 unspecified
1 mild
2 moderate
3 severe

---

    adjustment reaction 309.3
    adolescent onset type 312.82
    childhood onset type 312.81
    compulsive 312.30
      intermittent explosive disorder 312.34
      isolated explosive disorder 312.35
      kleptomania 312.32
      pathological gambling 312.31
      pyromania 312.33
    hyperkinetic 314.2
    intermittent explosive 312.34
    isolated explosive 312.35
    mixed with emotions 312.4
    socialized (type) 312.20
      aggressive 312.23
      unaggressive 312.21
    specified type NEC 312.89
    undersocialized, unsocialized
      aggressive (type) 312.0
      unaggressive (type) 312.1
  coordination 781.3
  cranial nerve NEC 352.9
  deep sensibility—*see* Disturbance, sensation
  digestive 536.9
    psychogenic 306.4
  electrolyte—*see* Imbalance, electrolyte

Disturbance—*continued*
  emotions specific to childhood and adolescence 313.9
    with
      academic underachievement 313.83
      anxiety and fearfulness 313.0
      elective mutism 313.23
      identity disorder 313.82
      jealousy 313.3
      misery and unhappiness 313.1
      oppositional disorder 313.81
      overanxiousness 313.0
      sensitivity 313.21
      shyness 313.21
      social withdrawal 313.22
      withdrawal reaction 313.22
    involving relationship problems 313.3
    mixed 313.89
    specified type NEC 313.89
  endocrine (gland) 259.9
    neonatal, transitory 775.9
    specified NEC 775.8
  equilibrium 780.4
  feeding (elderly) (infant) 783.3
    newborn 779.3
    nonorganic origin NEC 307.59
    psychogenic NEC 307.59
  fructose metabolism 271.2
  gait 781.2
    hysterical 300.11
  gastric (functional) 536.9
    motility 536.8
    psychogenic 306.4
    secretion 536.8
  gastrointestinal (functional) 536.9
    psychogenic 306.4
  habit, child 307.9
  hearing, except deafness 388.40
  heart, functional (conditions classifiable to 426, 427, 428)
    due to presence of (cardiac) prosthesis 429.4
    postoperative (immediate) 997.1
      long-term effect of cardiac surgery 429.4
    psychogenic 306.2
  hormone 259.9
  innervation uterus, sympathetic, parasympathetic 621.8
  keratinization NEC
    gingiva 523.1
    lip 528.5
    oral (mucosa) (soft tissue) 528.7
    tongue 528.7
  labyrinth, labyrinthine (vestibule) 386.9
  learning, specific NEC 315.2
  memory (*see also* Amnesia) 780.9
    mild, following organic brain damage 310.1
  mental (*see also* Disorder, mental) 300.9
    associated with diseases classified elsewhere 316
  metabolism (acquired) (congenital) (*see also* Disorder, metabolism) 277.9
    with
      abortion—*see* Abortion, by type, with metabolic disorder
      ectopic pregnancy (*see also* categories 633.0-633.9) 639.4
      molar pregnancy (*see also* categories 630-632) 639.4

Disturbance—*continued*
  amino acid (*see also* Disorder, amino acid) 270.9
    aromatic NEC 270.2
    branched-chain 270.3
    specified type NEC 270.8
    straight-chain NEC 270.7
    sulfur-bearing 270.4
    transport 270.0
  ammonia 270.6
  arginine 270.6
  argininosuccinic acid 270.6
  carbohydrate NEC 271.9
  cholesterol 272.9
  citrulline 270.6
  cystathionine 270.4
  fat 272.9
  following
    abortion 639.4
    ectopic or molar pregnancy 639.4
  general 277.9
    carbohydrate 271.9
    iron 275.0
    phosphate 275.3
    sodium 276.9
  glutamine 270.7
  glycine 270.7
  histidine 270.5
  homocystine 270.4
  in labor or delivery 669.0
  iron 275.0
  isoleucine 270.3
  leucine 270.3
  lipoid 272.9
    specified type NEC 272.8
  lysine 270.7
  methionine 270.4
  neonatal, transitory 775.9
    specified type NEC 775.8
  nitrogen 788.9
  ornithine 270.6
  phosphate 275.3
  phosphatides 272.7
  serine 270.7
  sodium NEC 276.9
  threonine 270.7
  tryptophan 270.2
  tyrosine 270.2
  urea cycle 270.6
  valine 270.3
  motor 796.1
  nervous functional 799.2
  neuromuscular mechanism (eye) due to syphilis 094.84
  nutritional 269.9
    nail 703.8
  ocular motion 378.87
    psychogenic 306.7
  oculogyric 378.87
    psychogenic 306.7
  oculomotor NEC 378.87
    psychogenic 306.7
  olfactory nerve 781.1
  optic nerve NEC 377.49
  oral epithelium, including tongue 528.7
  personality (pattern) (trait) (*see also* Disorder, personality) 301.9
    following organic brain damage 310.1
  polyglandular 258.9
  psychomotor 307.9

Disturbance—*continued*
pupillary 379.49
reflex 796.1
rhythm, heart 427.9
  postoperative (immediate) 997.1
    long-term effect of cardiac surgery 429.4
  psychogenic 306.2
salivary secretion 527.7
sensation (cold) (heat) (localization) (tactile
  discrimination localization) (texture)
  (vibratory) NEC 782.0
  hysterical 300.11
  skin 782.0
  smell 781.1
  taste 781.1
sensory (*see also* Disturbance, sensation) 782.0
  innervation 782.0
situational (transient) (*see also* Reaction,
  adjustment) 309.9
  acute 308.3
sleep 780.50
  initiation or maintenance (*see also* Insomnia)
    780.52
    nonorganic origin 307.41
  nonorganic origin 307.40
    specified type NEC 307.49
  specified NEC 780.59
    nonorganic origin 307.49
  wakefulness (*see also* Hypersomnia) 780.54
    nonorganic origin 307.43
  with apnea—*see* Apnea, sleep
sociopathic 301.7
speech NEC 784.5
  developmental 315.39
    associated with hyperkinesis 314.1
  secondary to organic lesion 784.5
stomach (functional) (*see also* Disturbance,
  gastric) 536.9
sympathetic (nerve) (*see also* Neuropathy,
  peripheral, autonomic) 337.9
temperature sense 782.0
  hysterical 300.11
tooth
  eruption 520.6
  formation 520.4
  structure, hereditary NEC 520.5
touch (*see also* Disturbance, sensation) 782.0
vascular 459.9
  arteriosclerotic—*see* Arteriosclerosis
vasomotor 443.9
vasospastic 443.9
vestibular labyrinth 386.9
vision, visual NEC 368.9
  psychophysical 368.16
  specified NEC 368.8
  subjective 368.10
voice 784.40
wakefulness (initiation or maintenance) (*see
  also* Hypersomnia) 780.54
  nonorganic origin 307.43
Disulfiduria, beta-mercaptolactate-cysteine 270.0
Disuse atrophy, bone 733.7
Ditthomska syndrome 307.81
Diuresis 788.42
Divers'
  palsy or paralysis 993.3
  squeeze 993.3

Diverticula, diverticulosis, diverticulum (acute)
  (multiple) (perforated) (ruptured) 562.10
with diverticulitis 562.11
aorta (Kommerell's) 747.21
appendix (noninflammatory) 543.9
bladder (acquired) (sphincter) 596.3
  congenital 753.8
broad ligament 620.8
bronchus (congenital) 748.3
  acquired 494
calyx, calyceal (kidney) 593.89
cardia (stomach) 537.1
cecum 562.10
  with
    diverticulitis 562.11
      with hemorrhage 562.13
    hemorrhage 562.12
  congenital 751.5
colon (acquired) 562.10
  with
    diverticulitis 562.11
      with hemorrhage 562.13
    hemorrhage 562.12
  congenital 751.5
duodenum 562.00
  with
    diverticulitis 562.01
      with hemorrhage 562.03
    hemorrhage 562.02
  congenital 751.5
epiphrenic (esophagus) 530.6
esophagus (congenital) 750.4
  acquired 530.6
  epiphrenic 530.6
  pulsion 530.6
  traction 530.6
  Zenker's 530.6
Eustachian tube 381.89
fallopian tube 620.8
gallbladder (congenital) 751.69
gastric 537.1
heart (congenital) 746.89
ileum 562.00
  with
    diverticulitis 562.01
      with hemorrhage 562.03
    hemorrhage 562.02
intestine (large) 562.10
  with
    diverticulitis 562.11
      with hemorrhage 562.13
    hemorrhage 562.12
  congenital 751.5
  small 562.00
    with
      diverticulitis 562.01
        with hemorrhage 562.03
      hemorrhage 562.02
    congenital 751.5
jejunum 562.00
  with
    diverticulitis 562.01
      with hemorrhage 562.03
    hemorrhage 562.02
kidney (calyx) (pelvis) 593.89
  with calculus 592.0
Kommerell's 747.21
laryngeal ventricle (congenital) 748.3
Meckel's (displaced) (hypertrophic) 751.0
midthoracic 530.6

Diverticula, diverticulosis . . .—*continued*
organ or site, congenital NEC—*see* Distortion
pericardium (congenital) (cyst) 746.89
    acquired (true) 423.8
pharyngoesophageal (pulsion) 530.6
pharynx (congenital) 750.27
pulsion (esophagus) 530.6
rectosigmoid 562.10
    with
        diverticulitis 562.11
            with hemorrhage 562.13
        hemorrhage 562.12
    congenital 751.5
rectum 562.10
    with
        diverticulitis 562.11
            with hemorrhage 562.13
        hemorrhage 562.12
renal (calyces) (pelvis) 593.89
    with calculus 592.0
Rokitansky's 530.6
seminal vesicle 608.0
sigmoid 562.10
    with
        diverticulitis 562.11
            with hemorrhage 562.13
        hemorrhage 562.12
    congenital 751.5
small intestine 562.00
    with
        diverticulitis 562.01
            with hemorrhage 562.03
        hemorrhage 562.02
stomach (cardia) (juxtacardia) (juxtapyloric)
        (acquired) 537.1
    congenital 750.7
subdiaphragmatic 530.6
trachea (congenital) 748.3
    acquired 519.1
traction (esophagus) 530.6
ureter (acquired) 593.89
    congenital 753.4
ureterovesical orifice 593.89
urethra (acquired) 599.2
    congenital 753.8
ventricle, left (congenital) 746.89
vesical (urinary) 596.3
    congenital 753.8
Zenker's (esophagus) 530.6
Diverticulitis (acute) (*see also* Diverticula)
    562.11
with hemorrhage 562.13
bladder (urinary) 596.3
cecum (perforated) 562.11
    with hemorrhage 562.13
colon (perforated) 562.11
    with hemorrhage 562.13
duodenum 562.01
    with hemorrhage 562.03
esophagus 530.6
ileum (perforated) 562.01
    with hemorrhage 562.03
intestine (large) (perforated) 562.11
    with hemorrhage 562.13
    small 562.01
        with hemorrhage 562.03
jejunum (perforated) 562.01
    with hemorrhage 562.03
Meckel's (perforated) 751.0
pharyngoesophageal 530.6

Diverticulitis—*continued*
rectosigmoid (perforated) 562.11
    with hemorrhage 562.13
rectum 562.11
    with hemorrhage 562.13
sigmoid (old) (perforated) 562.11
    with hemorrhage 562.13
small intestine (perforated) 562.01
    with hemorrhage 562.03
vesical (urinary) 596.3
Diverticulosis —*see* Diverticula
Division
cervix uteri 622.8
    external os into two openings by frenum
        752.49
    external (cervical) into two openings by frenum
        752.49
glans penis 752.69
hymen 752.49
labia minora (congenital) 752.49
ligament (partial or complete) (current)—*see
        also* Sprain, by site
    with open wound—*see* Wound, open, by site
muscle (partial or complete) (current)—*see also*
        Sprain, by site
    with open wound—*see* Wound, open, by site
nerve—*see* Injury, nerve, by site
penis glans 752.69
spinal cord—*see* Injury, spinal, by site
vein 459.9
traumatic—*see* Injury, vascular, by site
Divorce V61.0
Dix-Hallpike neurolabyrinthitis 386.12
Dizziness 780.4
hysterical 300.11
psychogenic 306.9
Doan-Wiseman syndrome (primary splenic
        neutropenia) 288.0
Dog bite —*see* Wound, open, by site
Döhle-Heller aortitis 093.1
Döhle body-panmyelopathic syndrome 288.2
Dolichocephaly, dolichocephalus 754.0
Dolichocolon 751.5
Dolichostenomelia 759.82
Donohue's syndrome (leprechaunism) 259.8
Donor
blood V59.01
    other blood components V59.09
    stem cells V59.02
    whole blood V59.01
bone V59.2
    marrow V59.3
cornea V59.5
heart V59.8
kidney V59.4
liver V59.6
lung V59.8
lymphocyte V59.8
organ V59.9
    specified NEC V59.8
potential, examination of V70.8
skin V59.1
specified organ or tissue NEC V59.8
stem cells V59.02
tissue V59.9
    specified type NEC V59.8
Donovanosis (granuloma venereum) 099.2
DOPS (diffuse obstructive pulmonary syndrome)
    496

Double
  albumin 273.8
  aortic arch 747.21
  auditory canal 744.29
  auricle (heart) 746.82
  bladder 753.8
  external (cervical) os 752.49
  kidney with double pelvis (renal) 753.3
  larynx 748.3
  meatus urinarius 753.8
  organ or site NEC—*see* Accessory
  orifice
    heart valve NEC 746.89
      pulmonary 746.09
  outlet, right ventricle 745.11
  pelvis (renal) with double ureter 753.4
  penis 752.69
  tongue 750.13
  ureter (one or both sides) 753.4
    with double pelvis (renal) 753.4
  urethra 753.8
  urinary meatus 753.8
  uterus (any degree) 752.2
    with doubling of cervix and vagina 752.2
    in pregnancy or childbirth 654.0
      affecting fetus or newborn 763.8
  vagina 752.49
    with doubling of cervix and uterus 752.2
  vision 368.2
  vocal cords 748.3
  vulva 752.49
  whammy (syndrome) 360.81
Douglas' pouch, cul-de-sac —*see* condition
Down's disease or syndrome (mongolism) 758.0
Down-growth, epithelial (anterior chamber)
  364.61
Dracontiasis 125.7
Dracunculiasis 125.7
Dracunculosis 125.7
Drainage
  abscess (spontaneous)—*see* Abscess
  anomalous pulmonary veins to hepatic veins or
    right atrium 747.41
  stump (amputation) (surgical) 997.62
  suprapubic, bladder 596.8
Dream state, hysterical 300.13
Drepanocytic anemia (*see also* Disease, sickle
  cell) 282.60
Dresbach's syndrome (elliptocytosis) 282.1
Dreschlera (infection) 118
  hawaiiensis 117.8
Dressler's syndrome (postmyocardial infarction)
  411.0
Dribbling (post-void) 788.35
Drift, ulnar 736.09
Drinking (alcohol)—*see also* Alcoholism
  excessive, to excess NEC (*see also* Abuse,
    drugs, nondependent) 305.0
  bouts, periodic 305.0
  continual 303.9
  episodic 305.0
  habitual 303.9
  periodic 305.0
Drip, postnasal (chronic)—*see* Sinusitis
Drivers' license examination V70.3
Droop, Cooper's 611.8
Drop
  finger 736.29
  foot 736.79
  toe 735.8
  wrist 736.05

Dropped
  dead 798.1
  heart beats 426.6
Dropsy, dropsical (*see also* Edema) 782.3
  abdomen 789.5
  amnion (*see also* Hydramnios) 657
  brain—*see* Hydrocephalus
  cardiac (*see also* Failure, heart, congestive)
    428.0
  cardiorenal (*see also* Hypertension, cardiorenal)
    404.90
  chest 511.9
  fetus or newborn 778.0
    due to isoimmunization 773.3
  gangrenous (*see also* Gangrene) 785.4
  heart (*see also* Failure, heart, congestive) 428.0
  hepatic—*see* Cirrhosis, liver
  infantile—*see* Hydrops, fetalis
  kidney (*see also* Nephrosis) 581.9
  liver—*see* Cirrhosis, liver
  lung 514
  malarial (*see also* Malaria) 084.9
  neonatorum—*see* Hydrops, fetalis
  nephritic 581.9
  newborn—*see* Hydrops, fetalis
  nutritional 269.9
  ovary 620.8
  pericardium (*see also* Pericarditis) 423.9
  renal (*see also* Nephrosis) 581.9
  uremic—*see* Uremia
Drowned, drowning 994.1
  lung 518.5
Drowsiness 780.09
Drug —*see also* condition
  addiction (*see also* listing under Dependence)
    304.9
  adverse effect NEC, correct substance properly
    administered 995.2
  dependence (*see also* listing under Dependence)
    304.9
  habit (*see also* listing under Dependence) 304.9
  overdose—*see* Table of drugs and chemicals
  poisoning—*see* Table of drugs and chemicals
  therapy (maintenance) status NEC V58.1
    long-term (current) use V58.69
      anticoagulant V58.61
  wrong substance given or taken in error—*see*
    Table of drugs and chemicals
Drunkenness (*see also* Abuse, drugs,
  nondependent) 305.0
  acute in alcoholism (*see also* Alcoholism) 303.0
  chronic (*see also* Alcoholism) 303.9
  pathologic 291.4
  simple (acute) 305.0
    in alcoholism 303.0
  sleep 307.47
Drusen
  optic disc or papilla 377.21
  retina (colloid) (hyaloid degeneration) 362.57
    hereditary 362.77
Drusenfieber 075
Dry, dryness —*see also* condition
  eye 375.15
    syndrome 375.15
  larynx 478.79
  mouth 527.7
  nose 478.1
  skin syndrome 701.1
  socket (teeth) 526.5
  throat 478.29
Duane's retraction syndrome 378.71

Duane-Stilling-Turk syndrome (ocular
    retraction syndrome) 378.71
Dubin-Johnson disease or syndrome 277.4
Dubini's disease (electric chorea) 049.8
Dubois' abscess or disease 090.5
Duchenne's
    disease 094.0
        locomotor ataxia 094.0
        muscular dystrophy 359.1
        pseudohypertrophy, muscles 359.1
    paralysis 335.22
    syndrome 335.22
Duchenne-Aran myelopathic muscular atrophy
    (nonprogressive) (progressive) 335.21
Duchenne-Griesinger disease 359.1
Ducrey's
    bacillus 099.0
    chancre 099.0
    disease (chancroid) 099.0
Duct, ductus —*see* condition
Duengero 061
Duhring's disease (dermatitis herpetiformis)
    694.0
Dukes (-Filatov) disease 057.8
Dullness
    cardiac (decreased) (increased) 785.3
Dumb ague (*see also* Malaria) 084.6
Dumbness (*see also* Aphasia) 784.3
Dumdum fever 085.0
Dumping syndrome (postgastrectomy) 564.2
    nonsurgical 536.8
Duodenitis (nonspecific) (peptic) 535.60
    due to
        Strongyloides stercoralis 127.2
    with hemorrhage 535.61
Duodenocholangitis 575.8
Duodenum, duodenal —*see* condition
Duplay's disease, periarthritis, or syndrome 726.2
Duplex —*see also* Accessory
    kidney 753.3
    placenta—*see* Placenta, abnormal
    uterus 752.2
Duplication —*see also* Accessory
    anus 751.5
    aortic arch 747.21
    appendix 751.5
    biliary duct (any) 751.69
    bladder 753.8
    cecum 751.5
        and appendix 751.5
    clitoris 752.49
    cystic duct 751.69
    digestive organs 751.8
    duodenum 751.5
    esophagus 750.4
    fallopian tube 752.19
    frontonasal process 756.0
    gallbladder 751.69
    ileum 751.5
    intestine (large) (small) 751.5
    jejunum 751.5
    kidney 753.3
    liver 751.69
    nose 748.1
    pancreas 751.7
    penis 752.69
    respiratory organs NEC 748.9
    salivary duct 750.22
    spinal cord (incomplete) 742.51
    stomach 750.7
    ureter 753.4

Duplication—*continued*
    vagina 752.49
    vas deferens 752.8
    vocal cords 748.3
Dupré's disease or syndrome (meningism) 781.6
Dupuytren's
    contraction 728.6
    disease (muscle contracture) 728.6
    fracture (closed) 824.4
        ankle (closed) 824.4
            open 824.5
        fibula (closed) 824.4
            open 824.5
        open 824.5
        radius (closed) 813.42
            open 813.52
    muscle contracture 728.6
Durand-Nicolas-Favre disease (climatic bubo)
    099.1
Duroziez's disease (congenital mitral stenosis)
    746.5
Dust
    conjunctivitis 372.05
    reticulation (occupational) 504
Dutton's
    disease (trypanosomiasis) 086.9
    relapsing fever (West African) 087.1
Dwarf, dwarfism 259.4
    with infantilism (hypophyseal) 253.3
    achondroplastic 756.4
    Amsterdam 759.89
    bird-headed 759.89
    congenital 259.4
    constitutional 259.4
    hypophyseal 253.3
    infantile 259.4
    Levi type 253.3
    Lorain-Levi (pituitary) 253.3
    Lorain type (pituitary) 253.3
    metatropic 756.4
    nephrotic-glycosuric, with hypophosphatemic
        rickets 270.0
    nutritional 263.2
    ovarian 758.6
    pancreatic 577.8
    pituitary 253.3
    polydystrophic 277.5
    primordial 253.3
    psychosocial 259.4
    renal 588.0
        with hypertension—*see* Hypertension, kidney
    Russell's (uterine dwarfism and craniofacial
        dysostosis) 759.89
Dyke-Young anemia or syndrome (acquired
    macrocytic hemolytic anemia) (secondary)
    (symptomatic) 283.9
Dynia abnormality (*see also* Defect,
    coagulation) 286.9
Dysacousis 388.40
Dysadrenocortism 255.9
    hyperfunction 255.3
    hypofunction 255.4
Dysarthria 784.5
Dysautonomia (*see also* Neuropathy, peripheral,
    autonomic) 337.9
    familial 742.8
Dysbarism 993.3
Dysbasia 719.7
    angiosclerotica intermittens 443.9
        due to atherosclerosis 440.21
    hysterical 300.11

Dysbasia—*continued*
  lordotica (progressiva) 333.6
  nonorganic origin 307.9
  psychogenic 307.9
Dysbetalipoproteinemia (familial) 272.2
Dyscalculia 315.1
Dyschezia (*see also* Constipation) 564.0
Dyschondroplasia (with hemangiomata) 756.4
  Voorhoeve's 756.4
Dyschondrosteosis 756.59
Dyschromia 709.00
Dyscollagenosis 710.9
Dyscoria 743.41
Dyscraniopyophalangy 759.89
Dyscrasia
  blood 289.9
    with antepartum hemorrhage 641.3
    fetus or newborn NEC 776.9
    hemorrhage, subungual 287.8
    puerperal, postpartum 666.3
  ovary 256.8
  plasma cell 273.9
  pluriglandular 258.9
  polyglandular 258.9
Dysdiadochokinesia 781.3
Dysectasia, vesical neck 596.8
Dysendocrinism 259.9
Dysentery, dysenteric (bilious) (catarrhal)
    (diarrhea) (epidemic) (gangrenous)
    (hemorrhagic) (infectious) (sporadic)
    (tropical) (ulcerative) 009.0
  abscess, liver (*see also* Abscess, amebic) 006.3
  amebic (*see also* Amebiasis) 006.9
    with abscess—*see* Abscess, amebic
    acute 006.0
    carrier (suspected) of V02.2
    chronic 006.1
  arthritis (*see also* Arthritis, due to, dysentery)
    009.0 *[711.3]*
    bacillary 004.9 *[711.3]*
  asylum 004.9
  bacillary 004.9
    arthritis 004.9 *[711.3]*
    Boyd 004.2
    Flexner 004.1
    Schmitz (-Stutzer) 004.0
    Shiga 004.0
    Shigella 004.9
      group A 004.0
      group B 004.1
      group C 004.2
      group D 004.3
      specified type NEC 004.8
    Sonne 004.3
    specified type NEC 004.8
  bacterium 004.9
  balantidial 007.0
  Balantidium coli 007.0
  Boyd's 004.2
  Chilomastix 007.8
  Chinese 004.9
  choleriform 001.1
  coccidial 007.2
  Dientamoeba fragilis 007.8
  due to specified organism NEC—*see* Enteritis,
    due to, by organism
  Embadomonas 007.8
  Endolimax nana—*see* Dysentery, amebic
  Entamoeba, entamebic—*see* Dysentery, amebic
  Flexner's 004.1
  Flexner-Boyd 004.2

Dysentery, dysenteric—*continued*
  giardial 007.1
  Giardia lamblia 007.1
  Hiss-Russell 004.1
  lamblia 007.1
  leishmanial 085.0
  malarial (*see also* Malaria) 084.6
  metazoal 127.9
  Monilia 112.89
  protozoal NEC 007.9
  Russell's 004.8
  salmonella 003.0
  schistosomal 120.1
  Schmitz (-Stutzer) 004.0
  Shiga 004.0
  Shigella NEC (*see also* Dysentery, bacillary)
    004.9
    boydii 004.2
    dysenteriae 004.0
      Schmitz 004.0
      Shiga 004.0
    flexneri 004.1
    Group A 004.0
    Group B 004.1
    Group C 004.2
    Group D 004.3
    Schmitz 004.0
    Shiga 004.0
    Sonnei 004.3
  Sonne 004.3
  strongyloidiasis 127.2
  trichomonal 007.3
  tuberculous (*see also* Tuberculosis) 014.8
  viral (*see also* Enteritis, viral) 008.8
Dysequilibrium 780.4
Dysesthesia 782.0
  hysterical 300.11
Dysfibrinogenemia (congenital) (*see also*
    Defect, coagulation) 286.3
Dysfunction
  adrenal (cortical) 255.9
    hyperfunction 255.3
    hypofunction 255.4
  associated with sleep stages or arousal from
    sleep 780.56
    nonorganic origin 307.47
  bladder NEC 596.59
  bleeding, uterus 626.8
  brain, minimal (*see also* Hyperkinesia) 314.9
  cerebral 348.3
  colon 564.9
    psychogenic 306.4
  colostomy or enterostomy 569.69
  cystic duct 575.8
  diastolic 429.9
    with heart failure—*see* Failure, heart
    due to
      cardiomyopathy—*see* Cardiomyopathy
      hypertension—*see* Hypertension, heart
  endocrine NEC 259.9
  endometrium 621.8
  enteric stoma 569.69
  enterostomy 569.69
  Eustachian tube 381.81
  gallbladder 575.8
  gastrointestinal 536.9
  gland, glandular NEC 259.9
  heart 427.9
    postoperative (immediate) 997.1
      long-term effect of cardiac surgery 429.4
  hemoglobin 288.8

Dysfunction—*continued*
  hepatic 573.9
  hepatocellular NEC 573.9
  hypophysis 253.9
    hyperfunction 253.1
    hypofunction 253.2
    posterior lobe 253.6
      hypofunction 253.5
  kidney (*see also* Disease, renal) 593.9
  labyrinthine 386.50
    specified NEC 386.58
  liver 573.9
    constitutional 277.4
  minimal brain (child) (*see also* Hyperkinesia)
      314.9
  ovary, ovarian 256.9
    hyperfunction 256.1
      estrogen 256.0
    hypofunction 256.3
      postablative 256.2
    postablative 256.2
    specified NEC 256.8
  papillary muscle 429.81
    with myocardial infarction 410.8
  parathyroid 252.8
    hyperfunction 252.0
    hypofunction 252.1
  pineal gland 259.8
  pituitary (gland) 253.9
    hyperfunction 253.1
    hypofunction 253.2
    posterior 253.6
      hypofunction 253.5
  placental—*see* Placenta, insufficiency
  platelets (blood) 287.1
  polyglandular 258.9
    specified NEC 258.8
  psychosexual 302.70
    with
      dyspareunia (functional) (psychogenic)
          302.76
      frigidity 302.72
      impotence 302.72
      inhibition
        orgasm
          female 302.73
          male 302.74
        sexual
          desire 302.71
          excitement 302.72
      premature ejaculation 302.75
      sexual aversion 302.79
      specified disorder NEC 302.79
      vaginismus 306.51
  pylorus 537.9
  rectum 564.9
    psychogenic 306.4
  segmental (*see also* Dysfunction, somatic) 739.9
  senile 797
  sinoatrial node 427.81
  somatic 739.9
    abdomen 739.9
    acromioclavicular 739.7
    cervical 739.1
    cervicothoracic 739.1
    costochondral 739.8
    costovertebral 739.8
    extremities
      lower 739.6
      upper 739.7
    head 739.0

Dysfunction—*continued*
  hip 739.5
  umbar, lumbosacral 739.3
  occipitocervical 739.0
  pelvic 739.5
  pubic 739.5
  rib cage 739.8
  sacral 739.4
  sacrococcygeal 739.4
  sacroiliac 739.4
  specified site NEC 739.9
  sternochondral 739.8
  sternoclavicular 739.7
  temporomandibular 739.0
  thoracic, thoracolumbar 739.2
  stomach 536.9
    psychogenic 306.4
  suprarenal 255.9
    hyperfunction 255.3
    hypofunction 255.4
  symbolic NEC 784.60
    specified type NEC 784.69
  temporomandibular (joint)
      (joint-pain-syndrome) NEC 524.60
    specified NEC 524.69
  testicular 257.9
    hyperfunction 257.0
    hypofunction 257.2
    specified type NEC 257.8
  thymus 254.9
  thyroid 246.9
    complicating pregnancy, childbirth, or
        puerperium 648.1
    hyperfunction—*see* Hyperthyroidism
    hypofunction—*see* Hypothyroidism
  uterus, complicating delivery 661.9
    affecting fetus or newborn 763.7
    hypertonic 661.4
    hypotonic 661.2
      primary 661.0
      secondary 661.1
  velopharyngeal (acquired) 528.9
    congenital 750.29
  ventricular 429.9
    with congestive heart failure (*see also* Failure,
        heart, congestive) 428.0
    due to
      cardiomyopathy—*see* Cardiomyopathy
      hypertension—*see* Hypertension, heart
  vesicourethral NEC 596.59
  vestibular 386.50
    specified type NEC 386.58
Dysgammaglobulinemia 279.06
Dysgenesis
  gonadal (due to chromosomal anomaly) 758.6
    pure 752.7
  kidney(s) 753.0
  ovarian 758.6
  renal 753.0
  reticular 279.2
  seminiferous tubules 758.6
  tidal platelet 287.3
Dysgerminoma (M9060/3)
  specified site—*see* Neoplasm, by site, malignant
  unspecified site
    female 183.0
    male 186.9
Dysgeusia 781.1
Dysgraphia 781.3
Dyshidrosis 705.81
Dysidrosis 705.81

Dysinsulinism 251.8
Dyskaryotic cervical smear 795.0
Dyskeratosis (*see also* Keratosis) 701.1
  bullosa hereditaria 757.39
  cervix 622.1
  congenital 757.39
  follicularis 757.39
    vitamin A deficiency 264.8
  gingiva 523.8
  oral soft tissue NEC 528.7
  tongue 528.7
  uterus NEC 621.8
Dyskinesia 781.3
  biliary 575.8
  esophagus 530.5
  hysterical 300.11
  intestinal 564.8
  nonorganic origin 307.9
  orofacial 333.82
  psychogenic 307.9
  tardive (oral) 333.82
Dyslalia 784.5
  developmental 315.39
Dyslexia 784.61
  developmental 315.02
  secondary to organic lesion 784.61
Dysmaturity (*see also* Immaturity) 765.1
  lung 770.4
  pulmonary 770.4
Dysmenorrhea (essential) (exfoliative)
    (functional) (intrinsic) (membranous)
    (primary) (secondary) 625.3
  psychogenic 306.52
Dysmetria 781.3
Dysmorodystrophia mesodermalis congenita
    759.82
Dysnomia 784.3
Dysorexia 783.0
  hysterical 300.11
Dysostosis
  cleidocranial, cleidocranialis 755.59
  craniofacial 756.0
  Fairbank's (idiopathic familial generalized
    osteophytosis) 756.50
  mandibularis 756.0
  mandibulofacial, incomplete 756.0
  multiplex 277.5
  orodigitofacial 759.89
Dyspareunia (female) 625.0
  male 608.89
  psychogenic 302.76
Dyspepsia (allergic) (congenital) (fermentative)
    (flatulent) (functional) (gastric)
    (gastrointestinal) (neurogenic) (occupational)
    (reflex) 536.8
  acid 536.8
  atonic 536.3
    psychogenic 306.4
  diarrhea 558.9
    psychogenic 306.4
  intestinal 564.8
    psychogenic 306.4
  nervous 306.4
  neurotic 306.4
  psychogenic 306.4
Dysphagia 787.2
  functional 300.11
  hysterical 300.11
  nervous 300.11
  psychogenic 306.4
  sideropenic 280.8
  spastica 530.5

Dysphagocytosis, congenital 288.1
Dysphasia 784.5
Dysphonia 784.49
  clericorum 784.49
  functional 300.11
  hysterical 300.11
  psychogenic 306.1
  spastica 478.79
Dyspigmentation —*see also* Pigmentation
  eyelid (acquired) 374.52
Dyspituitarism 253.9
  hyperfunction 253.1
  hypofunction 253.2
  posterior lobe 253.6
Dysplasia —*see also* Anomaly
  artery
    fibromuscular NEC 447.8
      carotid 447.8
      renal 447.3
  bladder 596.8
  bone (fibrous) NEC 733.29
    diaphyseal, progressive 756.59
    jaw 526.89
    monostotic 733.29
    polyostotic 756.54
    solitary 733.29
  brain 742.9
  bronchopulmonary, fetus or newborn 770.7
  cervix (uteri) 622.1
    cervical intraepithelial neoplasia III [CIN III]
      233.1
  CIN III 233.1
  chondroectodermal 756.55
  chondromatose 756.4
  craniocarpotarsal 759.89
  craniometaphyseal 756.89
  dentinal 520.5
  diaphyseal, progressive 756.59
  ectodermal (anhidrotic) (Bason) (Clouston's)
      (congenital) (Feinmesser) (hereditary)
      (hidrotic) (Marshall) (Robinson's) 757.31
  epiphysealis 756.9
    multiplex 756.56
    punctata 756.59
  epiphysis 756.9
    multiple 756.56
  epithelial
    epiglottis 478.79
    uterine cervix 622.1
  erythroid NEC 289.8
  eye (*see also* Microphthalmos) 743.10
  familial metaphyseal 756.89
  fibromuscular, artery NEC 447.8
    carotid 447.8
    renal 447.3
  fibrous
    bone NEC 733.29
    diaphyseal, progressive 756.59
    jaw 526.89
    monostotic 733.29
    polyostotic 756.54
    solitary 733.29
  hip (congenital) 755.63
    with dislocation (*see also* Dislocation, hip,
      congenital) 754.30
  hypohidrotic ectodermal 757.31
  joint 755.8
  kidney 753.15
  leg 755.69
  linguofacialis 759.89
  lung 748.5

Dysplasia—*continued*
  macular 743.55
  mammary (benign) (gland) 610.9
    cystic 610.1
    specified type NEC 610.8
  metaphyseal 756.9
    familial 756.89
  monostotic fibrous 733.29
  muscle 756.89
  myeloid NEC 289.8
  nervous system (general) 742.9
  neuroectodermal 759.6
  oculoauriculovertebral 756.0
  oculodentodigital 759.89
  olfactogenital 253.4
  osteo-onycho-arthro (hereditary) 756.89
  periosteum 733.99
  polyostotic fibrous 756.54
  progressive diaphyseal 756.59
  renal 753.15
  renofacialis 753.0
  retinal NEC 743.56
  retrolental 362.21
  spinal cord 742.9
  thymic, with immunodeficiency 279.2
  vagina 623.0
  vocal cord 478.5
  vulva 624.8
    VIN III 233.3
Dyspnea (nocturnal) (paroxysmal) 786.09
  asthmatic (bronchial) (*see also* Asthma) 493.9
    with bronchitis (*see also* Asthma) 493.9
      chronic 491.20
        with acute exacerbation 491.21
    cardiac (*see also* Failure, ventricular, left)
      428.1
  cardiac (*see also* Failure, ventricular, left) 428.1
  functional 300.11
  hyperventilation 786.01
  hysterical 300.11
  Monday morning 504
  newborn 770.8
  psychogenic 306.1
  uremic—*see* Uremia
Dyspraxia 781.3
  syndrome 315.4
Dysproteinemia 273.8
  transient with copper deficiency 281.4
Dysprothrombinemia (constitutional) (*see also*
    Defect, coagulation) 286.3
Dysrhythmia
  cardiac 427.9
    postoperative (immediate) 997.1
      long-term effect of cardiac surgery 429.4
    specified type NEC 427.89
  cerebral or cortical 348.3
Dyssecretosis, mucoserous 710.2
Dyssocial reaction **without manifest**
    psychiatric disorder
  adolescent V71.02
  adult V71.01
  child V71.02
Dyssomnia NEC 780.56
  nonorganic origin 307.47
Dyssplenism 289.4
Dyssynergia
  biliary (*see also* Disease, biliary) 576.8
  cerebellaris myoclonica 334.2
  detrusor sphincter (bladder) 596.55
  ventricular 429.89
Dystasia, hereditary areflexic 334.3
Dysthymia 300.4

Dysthymic disorder 300.4
Dysthyroidism 246.9
Dystocia 660.9
  affecting fetus or newborn 763.1
  cervical 661.0
    affecting fetus or newborn 763.7
  contraction ring 661.4
    affecting fetus or newborn 763.7
  fetal 660.9
    abnormal size 653.5
      affecting fetus or newborn 763.1
    deformity 653.7
  maternal 660.9
    affecting fetus or newborn 763.1
  positional 660.0
    affecting fetus or newborn 763.1
  shoulder (girdle) 660.4
    affecting fetus or newborn 763.1
  uterine NEC 661.4
    affecting fetus or newborn 763.7
Dystonia
  deformans progressiva 333.6
  due to drugs 333.7
  lenticularis 333.6
  musculorum deformans 333.6
  torsion (idiopathic) 333.6
    fragments (of) 333.89
    symptomatic 333.7
Dystonic
  movements 781.0
Dystopia kidney 753.3
Dystrophy, dystrophia 783.9
  adiposogenital 253.8
  asphyxiating thoracic 756.4
  Becker's type 359.1
  brevicollis 756.16
  Bruch's membrane 362.77
  cervical (sympathetic) NEC 337.0
  chondro-osseus with punctate epiphyseal
    dysplasia 756.59
  choroid (hereditary) 363.50
    central (areolar) (partial) 363.53
      total (gyrate) 363.54
    circinate 363.53
    circumpapillary (partial) 363.51
      total 363.52
    diffuse
      partial 363.56
      total 363.57
    generalized
      partial 363.56
      total 363.57
    gyrate
      central 363.54
      generalized 363.57
    helicoid 363.52
    peripapillary—*see* Dystrophy, choroid,
      circumpapillary
    serpiginous 363.54
  cornea (hereditary) 371.50
    anterior NEC 371.52
    Cogan's 371.52
    combined 371.57
    crystalline 371.56
    endothelial (Fuchs') 371.57
    epithelial 371.50
      juvenile 371.51
      microscopic cystic 371.52
    granular 371.53
    lattice 371.54
    macular 371.55

Dystrophy, dystrophia—*continued*
  marginal (Terrien's) 371.48
  Meesman's 371.51
  microscopic cystic (epithelial) 371.52
  nodular, Salzmann's 371.46
  polymorphous 371.58
  posterior NEC 371.58
  ring-like 371.52
  Salzmann's nodular 371.46
  stromal NEC 371.56
  dermatochondrocorneal 371.50
  Duchenne's 359.1
  due to malnutrition 263.9
  Erb's 359.1
  familial
    hyperplastic periosteal 756.59
    osseous 277.5
  foveal 362.77
  Fuchs', cornea 371.57
  Gowers' muscular 359.1
  hair 704.2
  hereditary, progressive muscular 359.1
  hypogenital, with diabetic tendency 759.81
  Landouzy-Déjérine 359.1
  Leyden-Möbius 359.1
  mesodermalis congenita 759.82
  muscular 359.1
    congenital (hereditary) 359.0
      myotonic 359.2
    distal 359.1
    Duchenne's 359.1
    Erb's 359.1
    fascioscapulohumeral 359.1
    Gowers' 359.1
    hereditary (progressive) 359.1
    Landouzy-Déjérine 359.1
    limb-girdle 359.1
    myotonic 359.2
    progressive (hereditary) 359.1
      Charcot-Marie-Tooth 356.1
    pseudohypertrophic (infantile) 359.1
  myocardium, myocardial (*see also*
    Degeneration, myocardial) 429.1
  myotonic 359.2
  myotonica 359.2
  nail 703.8
    congenital 757.5
  neurovascular (traumatic) (*see also* Neuropathy,
    peripheral, autonomic) 337.9
  nutritional 263.9
  ocular 359.1
  oculocerebrorenal 270.8
  oculopharyngeal 359.1
  ovarian 620.8
  papillary (and pigmentary) 701.1
  pelvicrural atrophic 359.1
  pigmentary (*see also* Acanthosis) 701.2
  pituitary (gland) 253.8
  polyglandular 258.8
  posttraumatic sympathetic—*see* Dystrophy,
    sympathetic
  progressive ophthalmoplegic 359.1
  retina, retinal (hereditary) 362.70
    albipunctate 362.74
    Bruch's membrane 362.77
    cone, progressive 362.75
    hyaline 362.77
    in
      Bassen-Kornzweig syndrome 272.5 *[362.72]*
      cerebroretinal lipidosis 330.1 *[362.71]*
      Refsum's disease 356.3 *[362.72]*
      systemic lipidosis 272.7 *[362.71]*

Dystrophy, dystrophia—*continued*
  juvenile (Stargardt's) 362.75
  pigmentary 362.74
  pigment epithelium 362.76
  progressive cone (-rod) 362.75
  pseudoinflammatory foveal 362.77
  rod, progressive 362.75
  sensory 362.75
  vitelliform 362.76
  Salzmann's nodular 371.46
  scapuloperoneal 359.1
  skin NEC 709.9
  sympathetic (posttraumatic) (reflex) 337.20
    lower limb 337.22
    specified NEC 337.29
    upper limb 337.21
  tapetoretinal NEC 362.74
  thoracic asphyxiating 756.4
  unguium 703.8
    congenital 757.5
  vitreoretinal (primary) 362.73
    secondary 362.66
  vulva 624.0
Dysuria 788.1
  psychogenic 306.53

E

Eales' disease (syndrome) 362.18
Ear —*see also* condition
  ache 388.70
    otogenic 388.71
    referred 388.72
  lop 744.29
  piercing V50.3
  swimmers' acute 380.12
  tank 380.12
  tropical 111.8 *[380.15]*
  wax 380.4
Earache 388.70
  otogenic 388.71
  referred 388.72
Eaton-Lambert syndrome (*see also* Neoplasm,
  by site, malignant) 199.1 *[358.1]*
Eberth's disease (typhoid fever) 002.0
Ebstein's
  anomaly or syndrome (downward displacement,
    tricuspid valve into right ventricle) 746.2
  disease (diabetes) 250.4 *[581.81]*
Eccentro-osteochondrodysplasla 277.5
Ecchondroma (M9210/0)—*see* Neoplasm, bone,
  benign
Ecchondrosis (M9210/1) 238.0
Ecchordosis physaliphora 756.0
Ecchymosis (multiple) 459.89
  conjunctiva 372.72
  eye (traumatic) 921.0
  eyelids (traumatic) 921.1
  newborn 772.6
  spontaneous 782.7
  traumatic—*see* Contusion
Echinococciasis —*see* Echinococcus
Echinococcosis —*see* Echinococcus
Echinococcus (infection) 122.9
  granulosus 122.4
    liver 122.0
    lung 122.1
    orbit 122.3 *[376.13]*
    specified site NEC 122.3
    thyroid 122.2
  liver NEC 122.8
    granulosus 122.0
    multilocularis 122.5
  lung NEC 122.9
    granulosus 122.1
    multilocularis 122.6
  multilocularis 122.7
    liver 122.5
    specified site NEC 122.6
  orbit 122.9 *[376.13]*
    granulosus 122.3 *[376.13]*
    multilocularis 122.6 *[376.13]*
  specified site NEC 122.9
    granulosus 122.3
    multilocularis 122.6 *[376.13]*
  thyroid NEC 122.9
    granulosus 122.2
    multilocularis 122.6
Echinorhynchiasis 127.7
Echinostomiasis 121.8
Echolalia 784.69
ECHO virus infection NEC 079.1

Eclampsia, eclamptic (coma) (convulsions)
  (delirium) 780.3
  female, child-bearing age NEC—*see* Eclampsia,
    pregnancy
  gravidarum—*see* Eclampsia, pregnancy
  male 780.3
  not associated with pregnancy or childbirth
    780.3
  pregnancy, childbirth or puerperium 642.6
    with pre-existing hypertension 642.7
    affecting fetus or newborn 760.0
  uremic 586
Eclipse blindness (total) 363.31
Economic circumstance affecting care V60.9
  specified type NEC V60.8
Economo's disease (encephalitis lethargica)
  049.8
Ectasia, ectasis
  aorta (*see also* Aneurysm, aorta) 441.9
    ruptured 441.5
  breast 610.4
  capillary 448.9
  cornea (marginal) (postinfectional) 371.71
  duct (mammary) 610.4
  kidney 593.89
  mammary duct (gland) 610.4
  papillary 448.9
  renal 593.89
  salivary gland (duct) 527.8
  scar, cornea 371.71
  sclera 379.11
Ecthyma 686.8
  contagiosum 051.2
  gangrenosum 686.0
  infectiosum 051.2
Ectocardia 746.87
Ectodermal dysplasia, congenital 757.31
Ectodermosis erosiva pluriorificialis 695.1
Ectopic, ectopia (congenital) 759.89
  abdominal viscera 751.8
    due to defect in anterior abdominal wall 756.7
  ACTH syndrome 255.0
  adrenal gland 759.1
  anus 751.5
  auricular beats 427.61
  beats 427.60
  bladder 753.5
  bone and cartilage in lung 748.69
  brain 742.4
  breast tissue 757.6
  cardiac 746.87
  cerebral 742.4
  cordis 746.87
  endometrium 617.9
  gallbladder 751.69
  gastric mucosa 750.7
  gestation—*see* Pregnancy, ectopic
  heart 746.87
  hormone secretion NEC 259.3
  hyperparathyroidism 259.3
  kidney (crossed) (intrathoracic) (pelvis) 753.3
    in pregnancy or childbirth 654.4
      causing obstructed labor 660.2
  lens 743.37
  lentis 743.37
  mole—*see* Pregnancy, ectopic

Ectopic, ectopia—*continued*
  organ or site NEC—*see* Malposition, congenital
  ovary 752.0
  pancreas, pancreatic tissue 751.7
  pregnancy—*see* Pregnancy, ectopic
  pupil 364.75
  renal 753.3
  sebaceous glands of mouth 750.26
  secretion
    ACTH 255.0
    adrenal hormone 259.3
    adrenalin 259.3
    adrenocorticotropin 255.0
    antidiuretic hormone (ADH) 259.3
    epinephrine 259.3
    hormone NEC 259.3
    norepinephrine 259.3
    pituitary (posterior) 259.3
  spleen 759.0
  testis 752.51
  thyroid 759.2
  ureter 753.4
  ventricular beats 427.69
  vesicae 753.5
Ectrodactyly 755.4
  finger (*see also* Absence, finger, congenital)
    755.29
  toe (*see also* Absence, toe, congenital) 755.39
Ectromelia 755.4
  lower limb 755.30
  upper limb 755.20
Ectropion 374.10
  anus 569.49
  cervix 622.0
    with mention of cervicitis 616.0
  cicatricial 374.14
  congenital 743.62
  eyelid 374.10
    cicatricial 374.14
    congenital 743.62
    mechanical 374.12
    paralytic 374.12
    senile 374.11
    spastic 374.13
  iris (pigment epithelium) 364.54
  lip (congenital) 750.26
    acquired 528.5
  mechanical 374.12
  paralytic 374.12
  rectum 569.49
  senile 374.11
  spastic 374.13
  urethra 599.84
  uvea 364.54
Eczema (acute) (allergic) (chronic)
    (erythematous) (fissum) (occupational)
    (rubrum) (squamous) 692.9
  asteatotic 706.8
  atopic 691.8
  contact NEC 692.9
  dermatitis NEC 692.9
  due to specified cause—*see* Dermatitis, due to
  dyshidrotic 705.81
  external ear 380.22
  flexural 691.8
  gouty 274.89
  herpeticum 054.0
  hypertrophicum 701.8
  hypostatic—*see* Varicose, vein

Eczema—*continued*
  impetiginous 684
  infantile (acute) (chronic) (due to any
    substance) (intertriginous) (seborrheic)
    690.12
  intertriginous NEC 692.9
    infantile 690.12
  intrinsic 691.8
  lichenified NEC 692.9
  marginatum 110.3
  nummular 692.9
  pustular 686.8
  seborrheic 690.18
    infantile 690.12
  solare 692.72
  stasis (lower extremity) 454.1
    ulcerated 454.2
  vaccination, vaccinatum 999.0
  varicose (lower extremity)—*see* Varicose, vein
  verrucosum callosum 698.3
Eczematoid, exudative 691.8
Eddowes' syndrome (brittle bones and blue
    sclera) 756.51
Edema, edematous 782.3
  with nephritis (*see also* Nephrosis) 581.9
  allergic 995.1
  angioneurotic (allergic) (any site) (with
    urticaria) 995.1
    hereditary 277.6
  angiospastic 443.9
  Berlin's (traumatic) 921.3
  brain 348.5
    due to birth injury 767.8
    fetus or newborn 767.8
  cardiac (*see also* Failure, heart, congestive)
    428.0
  cardiovascular (*see also* Failure, heart,
    congestive) 428.0
  cerebral—*see* Edema, brain
  cerebrospinal vessel—*see* Edema, brain
  cervix (acute) (uteri) 622.8
    puerperal, postpartum 674.8
  chronic hereditary 757.0
  circumscribed, acute 995.1
    hereditary 277.6
  complicating pregnancy (gestational) 646.1
    with hypertension—*see* Toxemia, of
      pregnancy
  conjunctiva 372.73
  connective tissue 782.3
  cornea 371.20
    due to contact lenses 371.24
    idiopathic 371.21
    secondary 371.22
  due to
    lymphatic obstruction—*see* Edema, lymphatic
    salt retention 276.0
  epiglottis—*see* Edema, glottis
  essential, acute 995.1
    hereditary 277.6
  extremities, lower—*see* Edema, legs
  eyelid NEC 374.82
  familial, hereditary (legs) 757.0
  famine 262
  fetus or newborn 778.5
  genital organs
    female 629.8
    male 608.86

Edema, edematous—*continued*
gestational 646.1
  with hypertension—*see* Toxemia, of
    pregnancy
glottis, glottic, glottides (obstructive) (passive)
  478.6
  allergic 995.1
    hereditary 277.6
  due to external agent—*see* Condition,
    respiratory, acute, due to specified agent
heart (*see also* Failure, heart, congestive) 428.0
  newborn 779.8
heat 992.7
hereditary (legs) 757.0
inanition 262
infectious 782.3
intracranial 348.5
  due to injury at birth 767.8
iris 364.8
joint (*see also* Effusion, joint) 719.0
larynx (*see also* Edema, glottis) 478.6
legs 782.3
  due to venous obstruction 459.2
  hereditary 757.0
localized 782.3
  due to venous obstruction 459.2
    lower extremity 459.2
lower extremities—*see* Edema, legs
lungs 514
  acute 518.4
    with heart disease or failure (*see also*
      Failure, ventricular, left) 428.1
      congestive 428.0
    chemical (due to fumes or vapors) 506.1
    due to
      external agent(s) NEC 508.9
        specified NEC 508.8
      fumes and vapors (chemical) (inhalation)
        506.1
      radiation 508.0
  chemical (acute) 506.1
    chronic 506.4
  chronic 514
    chemical (due to fumes or vapors) 506.4
    due to
      external agent(s) NEC 508.9
        specified NEC 508.8
      fumes or vapors (chemical) (inhalation)
        506.4
      radiation 508.1
  due to
    external agent 508.9
      specified NEC 508.8
    high altitude 993.2
    near drowning 994.1
  postoperative 518.4
  terminal 514
lymphatic 457.1
  due to mastectomy operation 457.0
macula 362.83
  cystoid 362.53
  diabetic 250.5 *[362.83]*
malignant (*see also* Gangrene, gas) 040.0
Milroy's 757.0
nasopharynx 478.25
neonatorum 778.5
nutritional (newborn) 262
  with dyspigmentation, skin and hair 260
optic disc or nerve—*see* Papilledema

Edema, edematous—*continued*
orbit 376.33
  circulatory 459.89
palate (soft) (hard) 528.9
pancreas 577.8
penis 607.83
periodic 995.1
  hereditary 277.6
pharynx 478.25
pitting 782.3
pulmonary—*see* Edema, lung
Quincke's 995.1
  hereditary 277.6
renal (*see also* Nephrosis) 581.9
retina (localized) (macular) (peripheral) 362.83
  cystoid 362.53
  diabetic 250.5 *[362.83]*
salt 276.0
scrotum 608.86
seminal vesicle 608.86
spermatic cord 608.86
spinal cord 336.1
starvation 262
subconjunctival 372.73
subglottic (*see also* Edema, glottis) 478.6
supraglottic (*see also* Edema, glottis) 478.6
testis 608.86
toxic NEC 782.3
traumatic NEC 782.3
tunica vaginalis 608.86
vas deferens 608.86
vocal cord—*see* Edema, glottis
vulva (acute) 624.8
Edentia (complete) (partial) (*see also* Absence,
  tooth) 520.0
causing malocclusion 524.3
congenital (deficiency of tooth buds) 520.0
due to accident, extraction, or local periodontal
  disease 525.1
Edsall's disease 992.2
Educational handicap V62.3
Edwards' syndrome 758.2
Effect, adverse NEC
abnormal gravitational (G) forces or states 994.9
air pressure—*see* Effect, adverse, atmospheric
  pressure
altitude (high)—*see* Effect, adverse, high
  altitude
anesthetic
  in labor and delivery NEC 668.9
    affecting fetus or newborn 763.5
antitoxin—*see* Complications, vaccination
atmospheric pressure 993.9
  due to explosion 993.4
  high 993.3
  low—*see* Effect, adverse, high altitude
  specified effect NEC 993.8
biological, correct substance properly
  administered (*see also* Effect, adverse, drug)
  995.2
blood (derivatives) (serum) (transfusion)—*see*
  Complications, transfusion
chemical substance NEC 989.9
  specified—*see* Table of drugs and chemicals
cobalt, radioactive (*see also* Effect, adverse,
  radioactive substance) 990
cold (temperature) (weather) 991.9
  chilblains 991.5
  frostbite—*see* Frostbite
  specified effect NEC 991.8

Effect, adverse—*continued*
drugs and medicinals NEC 995.2
  correct substance properly administered 995.2
  overdose or wrong substance given or taken
    977.9
    specified drug—*see* Table of drugs and
      chemicals
electric current (shock) 994.8
  burn—*see* Burn, by site
electricity (electrocution) (shock) 994.8
  burn—*see* Burn, by site
exertion (excessive) 994.5
exposure 994.9
  exhaustion 994.4
external cause NEC 994.9
fallout (radioactive) NEC 990
fluoroscopy NEC 990
foodstuffs
  allergic reaction (*see also* Allergy, food) 693.1
    anaphylactic shock due to food NEC 995.60
  noxious 988.9
    specified type NEC (*see also* Poisoning, by
      name of noxious foodstuff) 988.8
gases, fumes, or vapors—*see* Table of drugs
  and chemicals
glue (airplane) sniffing 304.6
heat—*see* Heat
high altitude NEC 993.2
  anoxia 993.2
  on
    fears 993.0
    sinuses 993.1
  polycythemia 289.0
hot weather—*see* Heat
hunger 994.2
immersion, foot 991.4
immunization—*see* Complications, vaccination
immunological agents—*see* Complications,
  vaccination
implantation (removable) of isotope or radium
  NEC 990
infrared (radiation) (rays) NEC 990
  burn—*see* Burn, by site
  dermatitis or eczema 692.82
infusion—*see* Complications, infusion
ingestion or injection of isotope (therapeutic)
  NEC 990
irradiation NEC (*see also* Effect, adverse,
  radiation) 990
isotope (radioactive) NEC 990
lack of care (child) (infant) (newborn) 995.52
  adult 995.84
lightning 994.0
  burn—*see* Burn, by site
Lirugin—*see* Complications, vaccination
medicinal substance, correct, properly
  administered (*see also* Effect, adverse,
  drugs) 995.2
mesothorium NEC 990
motion 994.6
noise, inner ear 388.10
overheated places—*see* Heat
polonium NEC 990
psychosocial, of work environment V62.1

Effect, adverse—*continued*
radiation (diagnostic) (fallout) (infrared)
  (natural source) (therapeutic) (tracer)
  (ultraviolet) (x-ray) NEC 990
  with pulmonary manifestations
    acute 508.0
    chronic 508.1
  dermatitis or eczema 692.82
    due to sun NEC (*see also* Dermatitis, due to,
      sun) 692.70
  fibrosis of lungs 508.1
  maternal with suspected damage to fetus
    affecting management of pregnancy 655.6
  pneumonitis 508.0
radioactive substance NEC 990
  dermatitis or eczema 692.82
radioactivity NEC 990
radiotherapy NEC 990
  dermatitis or eczema 692.82
radium NEC 990
reduced temperature 991.9
  frostbite—*see* Frostbite
  immersion, foot (hand) 991.4
  specified effect NEC 991.8
roentgenography NEC 990
roentgenoscopy NEC 990
roentgen rays NEC 990
serum (prophylactic) (therapeutic) NEC 999.5
specified NEC 995.89
  external cause NEC 994.9
strangulation 994.7
submersion 994.1
teletherapy NEC 990
thirst 994.3
transfusion—*see* Complications, transfusion
ultraviolet (radiation) (rays) NEC 990
  burn—*see also* Burn, by site
    from sun 692.71
  dermatitis or eczema 692.82
    due to sun NEC (*see also* Dermatitis, due to,
      sun) 692.70
uranium NEC 990
vaccine (any)—*see* Complications, vaccination
weightlessness 994.9
whole blood—*see also* Complications,
  transfusion
  overdose or wrong substance given (*see also*
    Table of drugs and chemicals) 964.7
working environment V62.1
x-rays NEC 990
  dermatitis or eczema 692.82
Effect, remote
of cancer, —*see* condition
Effects, late —*see* Late, effect (of)
Effluvium, telogen 704.02
Effort
intolerance 306.2
syndrome (aviators) (psychogenic) 306.2
Effusion
Amniotic fluid (*see also* Rupture, membranes,
  premature) 658.1
brain (serous) 348.5
bronchial (*see also* Bronchitis) 490
cerebral 348.5
cerebrospinal (*see also* Meningitis) 322.9
  vessel 348.5
chest—*see* Effusion, pleura
intracranial 348.5

Effusion—*continued*
  joint 719.00
    ankle 719.07
    elbow 719.02
    foot 719.07
    hand 719.04
    hip 719.05
    knee 719.06
    multiple sites 719.09
    pelvic region 719.05
    shoulder (region) 719.01
    specified site NEC 719.08
    wrist 719.03
  meninges (*see also* Meningitis) 322.9
  pericardium, pericardial (*see also* Pericarditis)
    423.9
    acute 420.90
  peritoneal (chronic) 568.82
  pleura, pleurisy, pleuritic, pleuropericardial
    511.9
    bacterial, nontuberculous 511.1
    fetus or newborn 511.9
    malignant 197.2
    nontuberculous 511.9
      bacterial 511.1
    pneumococcal 511.1
    staphylococcal 511.1
    streptococcal 511.1
    tuberculous (*see also* Tuberculosis, pleura)
      012.0
      primary progressive 010.1
  pulmonary—*see* Effusion, pleura
  spinal (*see also* Meningitis) 322.9
  thorax, thoracic—*see* Effusion, pleura
Eggshell nails 703.8
  congenital 757.5
Ego-dystonic
  homosexuality 302.0
  lesbianism 302.0
Egyptian splenomegaly 120.1
Ehlers-Danlos syndrome 756.83
Eichstedt's disease (pityriasis versicolor) 111.0
Eisenmenger's complex or syndrome
  (ventricular septal defect) 745.4
Ejaculation, semen
  painful 608.89
    psychogenic 306.59
  premature 302.75
Ekbom syndrome (restless legs) 333.99
Ekman's syndrome (brittle bones and blue
  sclera) 756.51
Elastic skin 756.83
  acquired 701.8
Elastofibroma (M8820/0)—*see* Neoplasm,
  connective tissue, benign
Elastoidosis
  cutanea nodularis 701.8
  cutis cystica et comedonica 701.8
Elastoma 757.39
  juvenile 757.39
  Miescher's (elastosis perforans serpiginosa)
    701.1
Elastomyofibrosis 425.3
Elastosis 701.8
  atrophicans 701.8
  perforans serpiginosa 701.1
  reactive perforating 701.1
  senilis 701.8
  solar (actinic) 692.74
Elbow —*see* condition

Electric
  current, electricity, effects (concussion) (fatal)
    (nonfatal) (shock) 994.8
  burn—*see* Burn, by site
  feet (foot) syndrome 266.2
Electrocution 994.8
Electrolyte imbalance 276.9
  with
    abortion—*see* Abortion, by type, with
      metabolic disorder
    ectopic pregnancy (*see also* categories
      633.0-633.9) 639.4
    hyperemesis gravidarum (before 22 completed
      weeks gestation) 643.1
    molar pregnancy (*see also* categories
      630-632) 639.4
  following
    abortion 639.4
    ectopic or molar pregnancy 639.4
Elephantiasis (nonfilarial) 457.1
  arabicum (*see also* Infestation, filarial) 125.9
  congenita hereditaria 757.0
  congenital (any site) 757.0
  due to
    Brugia (malayi) 125.1
    mastectomy operation 457.0
    Wuchereria (bancrofti) 125.0
      malayi 125.1
  eyelid 374.83
  filarial (*see also* Infestation, filarial) 125.9
  filariensis (*see also* Infestation, filarial) 125.9
  gingival 523.8
  glandular 457.1
  graecorum 030.9
  lymphangiectatic 457.1
  lymphatic vessel 457.1
    due to mastectomy operation 457.0
  neuromatosa 237.71
  postmastectomy 457.0
  scrotum 457.1
  streptococcal 457.1
  surgical 997.99
    postmastectomy 457.0
  telangiectodes 457.1
  vulva (nonfilarial) 624.8
Elevated —*see* Elevation
Elevation
  17-ketosteroids 791.9
  acid phosphatase 790.5
  alkaline phosphatase 790.5
  amylase 790.5
  antibody titers 795.79
  basal metabolic rate (BMR) 794.7
  blood pressure (*see also* Hypertension) 401.9
    reading (incidental) (isolated) (nonspecific),
      no diagnosis of hypertension 796.2
  body temperature (of unknown origin) (*see also*
    Pyrexia) 780.6
  conjugate, eye 378.81
  diaphragm, congenital 756.6
  immunoglobulin level 795.79
  indolacetic acid 791.9
  lactic acid dehydrogenase (LDH) level 790.4
  lipase 790.5
  prostate specific antigen (PSA) 790.93
  renin 790.99
    in hypertension (*see also* Hypertension,
      renovascular) 405.91
  Rh titer 999.7

Elevation—*continued*
  scapula, congenital 755.52
  sedimentation rate 790.1
  SGOT 790.4
  SGPT 790.4
  transaminase 790.4
  vanillylmandelic acid 791.9
  venous pressure 459.89
  VMA 791.9
Elliptocytosis (congenital) (hereditary) 282.1
  Hb-C (disease) 282.7
  hemoglobin disease 282.7
  sickle-cell (disease) 282.60
    trait 282.5
Ellis-van Creveld disease or syndrome
    (chondroectodermal dysplasia) 756.55
Ellison-Zollinger syndrome (gastric
    hypersecretion with pancreatic islet cell
    tumor) 251.5
Elongation, elongated (congenital)—*see also*
    Distortion
  bone 756.9
  cervix (uteri) 752.49
    acquired 622.6
    hypertrophic 622.6
  colon 751.5
  common bile duct 751.69
  cystic duct 751.69
  frenulum, penis 752.69
  labia minora, acquired 624.8
  ligamentum patellae 756.89
  petiolus (epiglottidis) 748.3
  styloid bone (process) 733.99
  tooth, teeth 520.2
  uvula 750.26
    acquired 528.9
Elschnig bodies or pearls 366.51
El Tor cholera 001.1
Emaciation (due to malnutrition) 261
Emancipation disorder 309.22
Embadomoniasis 007.8
Embarrassment heart, cardiac —*see* Disease,
    heart
Embedded tooth, teeth 520.6
  with abnormal position (same or adjacent tooth)
    524.3
  root only 525.3
Embolic —*see* condition
Embolism (septic) 444.9
  with
    abortion—*see* Abortion, by type, with
      embolism
    ectopic pregnancy (*see also* categories
      633.0-633.9) 639.6
    molar pregnancy (*see also* categories
      630-632) 639.6
  air (any site) 958.0
    with
      abortion—*see* Abortion, by type, with
        embolism
      ectopic pregnancy (*see also* categories
        633.0-633.9) 639.6
      molar pregnancy (*see also* categories
        630-632) 639.6
    due to implanted device—*see* Complications,
      due to (presence of) any device, implant,
      or graft classified to 996.0-996.5 NEC

Embolism—*continued*
  following
    abortion 639.6
    ectopic or molar pregnancy 639.6
    infusion, perfusion, or transfusion 999.1
  in pregnancy, childbirth, or puerperium 673.0
  traumatic 958.0
  amniotic fluid (pulmonary) 673.1
    with
      abortion—*see* Abortion, by type, with
        embolism
      ectopic pregnancy (*see also* categories
        633.0-633.9) 639.6
      molar pregnancy (*see also* categories
        630-632) 639.6
    following
      abortion 639.6
      ectopic or molar pregnancy 639.6
  aorta, aortic 444.1
    abdominal 444.0
    bifurcation 444.0
    saddle 444.0
    thoracic 444.1
  artery 444.9
    auditory, internal 433.8
    basilar (*see also* Occlusion, artery, basilar)
      433.0
    bladder 444.89
    carotid (common) (internal) (*see also*
      Occlusion, artery, carotid) 433.1
    cerebellar (anterior inferior) (posterior
      inferior) (superior) 433.8
    cerebral (*see also* Embolism, brain) 434.1
    choroidal (anterior) 433.8
    communicating posterior 433.8
    coronary (*see also* Infarct, myocardium) 410.9
      without myocardial infarction 411.81
    extremity 444.22
      lower 444.22
      upper 444.21
    hypophyseal 433.8
    mesenteric (with gangrene) 557.0
    ophthalmic (*see also* Occlusion, retina) 362.30
    peripheral 444.22
    pontine 433.8
    precerebral NEC—*see* Occlusion, artery,
      precerebral
    pulmonary—*see* Embolism, pulmonary
    renal 593.81
    retinal (*see also* Occlusion, retina) 362.30
    specified site NEC 444.89
    vertebral (*see also* Occlusion, artery,
      vertebral) 433.2
  auditory, internal 433.8
  basilar (artery) (*see also* Occlusion, artery,
    basilar) 433.0
  birth, mother—*see* Embolism, obstetrical
  blood-clot
    with
      abortion—*see* Abortion, by type, with
        embolism
      ectopic pregnancy (*see also* categories
        633.0-633.9) 639.6
      molar pregnancy (*see also* categories
        630-632) 639.6
    following
      abortion 639.6
      ectopic or molar pregnancy 639.6
    in pregnancy, childbirth, or puerperium 673.2

Embolism—*continued*
  brain 434.1
    with
      abortion—*see* Abortion, by type, with
        embolism
      ectopic pregnancy (*see also* categories
        633.0-633.9) 639.6
      molar pregnancy (*see also* categories
        630-632) 639.6
    following
      abortion 639.6
      ectopic or molar pregnancy 639.6
    late effect—*see* category 438
    puerperal, postpartum, childbirth 674.0
  capillary 448.9
  cardiac (*see also* Infarct, myocardium) 410.9
  carotid (artery) (common) (internal) (*see also*
    Occlusion, artery, carotid) 433.1
  cavernous sinus (venous)—*see* Embolism,
    intracranial venous sinus
  cerebral (*see also* Embolism, brain) 434.1
  choroidal (anterior) (artery) 433.8
  coronary (artery or vein) (systemic) (*see also*
    Infarct, myocardium) 410.9
    without myocardial infarction 411.81
  due to (presence of) any device, implant, or
    graft classifiable to 996.0-996.5 —*see*
    Complications, due to (presence of) any
    device, implant, or graft classified to
    996.0-996.5 NEC
  encephalomalacia (*see also* Embolism, brain)
    434.1
  extremities 444.22
    lower 444.22
    upper 444.21
  eye 362.30
  fat (cerebral) (pulmonary) (systemic) 958.1
    with
      abortion—*see* Abortion, by type, with
        embolism
      ectopic pregnancy (*see also* categories
        633.0-633.9) 639.6
      molar pregnancy (*see also* categories
        630-632) 639.6
    complicating delivery or puerperium 673.8
    following
      abortion 639.6
      ectopic or molar pregnancy 639.6
    in pregnancy, childbirth, or the puerperium
      673.8
  femoral (artery) 444.22
    vein 453.8
  following
    abortion 639.6
    ectopic or molar pregnancy 639.6
    infusion, perfusion, or transfusion
      air 999.1
      thrombus 999.2
  heart (fatty) (*see also* Infarct, myocardium)
    410.9
  hepatic (vein) 453.0
  iliac (artery) 444.81
  iliofemoral 444.81
  in pregnancy, childbirth, or puerperium
    (pulmonary)—*see* Embolism, obstetrical
  intestine (artery) (vein) (with gangrene) 557.0
  intracranial (*see also* Embolism, brain) 434.1
    venous sinus (any) 325
      late effect—*see* category 326
      nonpyogenic 437.6
        in pregnancy or puerperium 671.5

Embolism—*continued*
  kidney (artery) 593.81
  lateral sinus (venous)—*see* Embolism,
    intracranial venous sinus
  longitudinal sinus (venous)—*see* Embolism,
    intracranial venous sinus
  lower extremity 444.22
  lung (massive)—*see* Embolism, pulmonary
  meninges (*see also* Embolism, brain) 434.1
  mesenteric (artery) (with gangrene) 557.0
  multiple NEC 444.9
  obstetrical (pulmonary) 673.2
    air 673.0
    amniotic fluid (pulmonary) 673.1
    blood-clot 673.2
    cardiac 674.8
    fat 673.8
    heart 674.8
    pyemic 673.3
    septic 673.3
    specified NEC 674.8
  ophthalmic (*see also* Occlusion, retina) 362.30
  paradoxical NEC 444.9
  penis 607.82
  peripheral arteries NEC 444.22
    lower 444.22
    upper 444.21
  pituitary 253.8
  popliteal (artery) 444.22
  portal (vein) 452
  postoperative NEC 997.2
    cerebral 997.02
    peripheral vascular 997.2
    pulmonary 415.11
  precerebral artery (*see also* Occlusion, artery,
    precerebral) 433.9
  puerperal—*see* Embolism, obstetrical
  pulmonary (artery) (vein) 415.1
    with
      abortion—*see* Abortion, by type, with
        embolism
      ectopic pregnancy (*see also* categories
        633.0-633.9) 639.6
      molar pregnancy (*see also* categories
        630-632) 639.6
    following
      abortion 639.6
      ectopic or molar pregnancy 639.6
    iatrogenic 415.11
    in pregnancy, childbirth, or puerperium—*see*
      Embolism, obstetrical
    postoperative 415.11
  pyemic (multiple) 038.9
    with
      abortion—*see* Abortion, by type, with
        embolism
      ectopic pregnancy (*see also* categories
        633.0-633.9) 639.6
      molar pregnancy (*see also* categories
        630-632) 639.6
    Aerobacter aerogenes 038.49
    enteric gram-negative bacilli 038.40
    Enterobacter aerogenes 038.49
    Escherichia coli 038.42
    following
      abortion 639.6
      ectopic or molar pregnancy 639.6
    Hemophilus influenzae 038.41
    pneumococcal 038.2
    Proteus vulgaris 038.49
    Pseudomonas (aeruginosa) 038.43

Embolism—*continued*
  puerperal, postpartum, childbirth (any
     organism) 673.3
    Serratia 038.44
    specified organism NEC 038.8
    staphylococcal 038.1
    streptococcal 038.0
  renal (artery) 593.81
    vein 453.3
  retina, retinal (*see also* Occlusion, retina) 362.30
  saddle (aorta) 444.0
  septicemic—*see* Embolism, pyemic
  sinus—*see* Embolism, intracranial venous sinus
  soap
    with
      abortion—*see* Abortion, by type, with
        embolism
      ectopic pregnancy (*see also* categories
        633.0-633.9) 639.6
      molar pregnancy (*see also* categories
        630-632) 639.6
    following
      abortion 639.6
      ectopic or molar pregnancy 639.6
  spinal cord (nonpyogenic) 336.1
    in pregnancy or puerperium 671.5
    pyogenic origin 324.1
    late effect—*see* category 326
  spleen, splenic (artery) 444.89
  thrombus (thromboembolism) following
    infusion, perfusion, or transfusion 999.2
  upper extremity 444.21
  vein 453.9
    with inflammation or phlebitis—*see*
      Thrombophlebitis
    cerebral (*see also* Embolism, brain) 434.1
    coronary (*see also* Infarct, myocardium) 410.9
      without myocardial infarction 411.81
    hepatic 453.0
    mesenteric (with gangrene) 557.0
    portal 452
    pulmonary—*see* Embolism, pulmonary
    renal 453.3
    specified NEC 453.8
      with inflammation or phlebitis—*see*
        Thrombophlebitis
  vena cava (inferior) (superior) 453.2
  vessels of brain (*see also* Embolism, brain)
    434.1
Embolization —*see* Embolism
Embolus —*see* Embolism
Embryoma (M9080/1)—*see also* Neoplasm, by
  site, uncertain behavior
  benign (M9080/0)—*see* Neoplasm, by site,
    benign
  kidney (M8960/3) 189.0
  liver (M8970/3) 155.0
  malignant (M9080/3)—*see also* Neoplasm, by
    site, malignant
    kidney (M8960/3) 189.0
    liver (M8970/3) 155.0
    testis (M9070/3) 186.9
      undescended 186.0
  testis (M9070/3) 186.9
    undescended 186.0
Embryonic
  circulation 747.9
  heart 747.9
  vas deferens 752.8

Embryopathia NEC 759.9
Embryotomy, fetal 763.8
Embryotoxon 743.43
  interfering with vision 743.42
Emesis —*see* also Vomiting
  gravidarum—*see* Hyperemesis, gravidarum
Emissions, nocturnal (semen) 608.89
Emotional
  crisis—*see* Crisis, emotional
  disorder (*see also* Disorder, mental) 300.9
  instability (excessive) 301.3
  overlay—*see* Reaction, adjustment
  upset 300.9
Emotionality, pathological 301.3
Emotogenic disease (*see also* Disorder,
  psychogenic) 306.9
Emphysema (atrophic) (centriacinar)
    (centrilobular) (chronic) (diffuse) (essential)
    (hypertrophic) (interlobular) (lung)
    (obstructive) (panlobular) (paracicatricial)
    (paracinar) (postural) (pulmonary) (senile)
    (subpleural) (traction) (unilateral) (unilobular)
    (vesicular) 492.8
  with
    bronchitis
      acute and chronic 491.21
      chronic 491.20
        with acute bronchitis or acute
          exacerbation 491.21
  bullous (giant) 492.0
  cellular tissue 958.7
    surgical 998.81
  compensatory 518.2
  congenital 770.2
  conjunctiva 372.8
  connective tissue 958.7
    surgical 998.81
  due to fumes or vapors 506.4
  eye 376.89
  eyelid 374.85
    surgical 998.81
    traumatic 958.7
  fetus or newborn (interstitial) (mediastinal)
    (unilobular) 770.2
  heart 416.9
  interstitial 518.1
    congenital 770.2
    fetus or newborn 770.2
  laminated tissue 958.7
    surgical 998.81
  mediastinal 518.1
    fetus or newborn 770.2
  newborn (interstitial) (mediastinal) (unilobular)
    770.2
  obstructive diffuse with fibrosis 492.8
  orbit 376.89
  subcutaneous 958.7
    due to trauma 958.7
    nontraumatic 518.1
    surgical 998.81
  surgical 998.81
  thymus (gland) (congenital) 254.8
  traumatic 958.7
  tuberculous (*see also* Tuberculosis, pulmonary)
    011.9
Employment examination (certification) V70.5
Empty sella (turcica) syndrome 253.8

Empyema (chest) (diaphragmatic) (double)
(encapsulated) (general) (interlobar) (lung)
(medial) (necessitatis) (perforating chest wall)
(pleura) (pneumococcal) (residual)
(sacculated) (streptococcal)
(supradiaphragmatic) 510.9
with fistula 510.0
accessory sinus (chronic) (*see also* Sinusitis)
473.9
acute 510.9
with fistula 510.0
antrum (chronic) (*see also* Sinusitis, maxillary)
473.0
brain (any part) (*see also* Abscess, brain) 324.0
ethmoidal (sinus) (chronic) (*see also* Sinusitis,
ethmoidal) 473.2
extradural (*see also* Abscess, extradural) 324.9
frontal (sinus) (chronic) (*see also* Sinusitis,
frontal) 473.1
gallbladder (*see also* Cholecystitis, acute) 575.0
mastoid (process) (acute) (*see also* Mastoiditis,
acute) 383.00
maxilla, maxillary 526.4
sinus (chronic) (*see also* Sinusitis, maxillary)
473.0
nasal sinus (chronic) (*see also* Sinusitis) 473.9
sinus (accessory) (nasal) (*see also* Sinusitis)
473.9
sphenoidal (chronic) (sinus) (*see also* Sinusitis,
sphenoidal) 473.3
subarachnoid (*see also* Abscess, extradural)
324.9
subdural (*see also* Abscess, extradural) 324.9
tuberculous (*see also* Tuberculosis, pleura)
012.0
ureter (*see also* Ureteritis) 593.89
ventricular (*see also* Abscess, brain) 324.0
Enameloma 520.2
Encephalitis (bacterial) (chronic) (hemorrhagic)
(idiopathic) (nonepidemic) (spurious)
(subacute) 323.9
acute—*see also* Encephalitis, viral
disseminated (postinfectious) NEC 136.9
[323.6]
postimmunization or postvaccination 323.5
inclusional 049.8
inclusion body 049.8
necrotizing 049.8
arboviral, arbovirus NEC 064
arthropod-borne (*see also* Encephalitis, viral,
arthropod-borne) 064
Australian X 062.4
Bwamba fever 066.3
California (virus) 062.5
Central European 063.2
Czechoslovakian 063.2
Dawson's (inclusion body) 046.2
diffuse sclerosing 046.2
due to
actinomycosis 039.8 *[323.4]*
cat-scratch disease 078.3 *[323.0]*
infectious mononucleosis 075 *[323.0]*
malaria (*see also* Malaria) 084.6 *[323.2]*
Negishi virus 064
ornithosis 073.7 *[323.0]*
prophylactic inoculation against smallpox
323.5
rickettsiosis (*see also* Rickettsiosis) 083.9
[323.1]

Encephalitis—*continued*
rubella 056.01
toxoplasmosis (acquired) 130.0
congenital (active) 771.2 *[323.4]*
typhus (fever) (*see also* Typhus) 081.9 *[323.1]*
vaccination (smallpox) 323.5
Eastern equine 062.2
endemic 049.8
epidemic 049.8
equine (acute) (infectious) (viral) 062.9
Eastern 062.2
Venezuelan 066.2
Western 062.1
Far Eastern 063.0
following vaccination or other immunization
procedure 323.5
herpes 054.3
Ilheus (virus) 062.8
inclusion body 046.2
infectious (acute) (virus) NEC 049.8
influenzal 487.8 *[323.4]*
lethargic 049.8
Japanese (B type) 062.0
La Crosse 062.5
Langat 063.8
late effect—*see* Late, effect, encephalitis
lead 984.9 *[323.7]*
lethargic (acute) (infectious) (influenzal) 049.8
lethargica 049.8
louping ill 063.1
lupus 710.0
lymphatica 049.0
Mengo 049.8
meningococcal 036.1
mumps 072.2
Murray Valley 062.4
myoclonic 049.8
Negishi virus 064
otitic NEC 382.4 *[323.4]*
parasitic NEC 123.9 *[323.4]*
periaxialis (concentrica) (diffusa) 341.1
postchickenpox 052.0
postexanthematous NEC 057.9 *[323.6]*
postimmunization 323.5
postinfectious NEC 136.9 *[323.6]*
postmeasles 055.0
posttraumatic 323.8
postvaccinal (smallpox) 323.5
postvaricella 052.0
postviral NEC 079.99 *[323.6]*
postexanthematous 057.9 *[323.6]*
specified NEC 057.8 *[323.6]*
Powassan 063.8
progressive subcortical (Binswanger's) 290.12
Rio Bravo 049.8
rubella 056.01
Russian
autumnal 062.0
spring-summer type (taiga) 063.0
saturnine 984.9 *[323.7]*
Semliki Forest 062.8
serous 048
slow-acting virus NEC 046.8
specified cause NEC 323.8
St. Louis type 062.3
subacute sclerosing 046.2
subcorticalis chronica 290.12
summer 062.0
suppurative 324.0

Encephalitis—*continued*
syphilitic 094.81
  congenital 090.41
tick-borne 063.9
torula, torular 117.5 *[323.4]*
toxic NEC 989.9 *[323.7]*
toxoplasmic (acquired) 130.0
  congenital (active) 771.2 *[323.4]*
trichinosis 124 *[323.4]*
Trypanosomiasis (*see also* Trypanosomiasis)
  086.9 *[323.2]*
tuberculous (*see also* Tuberculosis) 013.6
type B (Japanese) 062.0
type C 062.3
van Bogaert's 046.2
Venezuelan 066.2
Vienna type 049.8
viral, virus 049.9
  arthropod-borne NEC 064
    mosquito-borne 062.9
      Australian X disease 062.4
      California virus 062.5
      Eastern equine 062.2
      Ilheus virus 062.8
      Japanese (B type) 062.0
      Murray Valley 062.4
      specified type NEC 062.8
      St. Louis 062.3
      type B 062.0
      type C 062.3
      Western equine 062.1
    tick-borne 063.9
      biundulant 063.2
      Central European 063.2
      Czechoslovakian 063.2
      diphasic meningoencephalitis 063.2
      Far Eastern 063.0
      Langat 063.8
      louping ill 063.1
      Powassan 063.8
      Russian spring-summer (taiga) 063.0
      specified type NEC 063.8
    vector unknown 064
  slow acting NEC 046.8
  specified type NEC 049.8
  vaccination, prophylactic (against) V05.0
von Economo's 049.8
Western equine 062.1
West Nile type 066.3
Encephalocele 742.0
  orbit 376.81
Encephalocystocele 742.0
Encephalomalacia (brain) (cerebellar) (cerebral)
  (cerebrospinal) (*see also* Softening, brain)
  434.9
  due to
    hemorrhage (*see also* Hemorrhage, brain) 431
    recurrent spasm of artery 435.9
  embolic (cerebral) (*see also* Embolism, brain)
    434.1
  subcorticalis chronicus arteriosclerotica 290.12
  thrombotic (*see also* Thrombosis, brain) 434.0
Encephalomeningitis —*see* Meningoencephalitis
Encephalomeningocele 742.0
Encephalomeningomyelitis —*see*
  Meningoencephalitis
Encephalomeningopathy (*see also*
  Meningoencephalitis) 349.9

Encephalomyelitis (chronic) (granulomatous)
  (hemorrhagic necrotizing, acute) (myalgic,
  benign) (*see also* Encephalitis) 323.9
  abortive disseminated 049.8
  acute disseminated (postinfectious) 136.9
    [323.6]
    postimmunization 323.5
  due to or resulting from vaccination (any) 323.5
  equine (acute) (infectious) 062.9
    Eastern 062.2
    Venezuelan 066.2
    Western 062.1
  funicularis infectiosa 049.8
  late effect—*see* Late, effect, encephalitis
  Munch-Peterson's 049.8
  postchickenpox 052.0
  postimmunization 323.5
  postmeasles 055.0
  postvaccinal (smallpox) 323.5
  rubella 056.01
  specified cause NEC 323.8
  syphilitic 094.81
Encephalomyelocele 742.0
Encephalomyelomeningitis —*see*
  Meningoencephalitis
Encephalomyeloneuropathy 349.9
Encephalomyelopathy 349.9
  subacute necrotizing (infantile) 330.8
Encephalomyeloradiculitis (acute) 357.0
Encephalomyeloradiculoneuritis (acute) 357.0
Encephalomyeloradiculopathy 349.9
Encephalomyocarditis 074.23
Encephalopathia hyperbilirubinemica
  newborn 774.7
  due to isoimmunization (conditions classifiable
    to 773.0-773.2) 773.4
Encephalopathy (acute) 348.3
  alcoholic 291.2
  anoxic—*see* Damage, brain, anoxic
  arteriosclerotic 437.0
    late effect—*see* category 438
  bilirubin, newborn 774.7
    due to isoimmunization 773.4
  congenital 742.9
  demyelinating (callosal) 341.8
  due to
    birth injury (intracranial) 767.8
    dialysis 294.8
      transient 293.9
    hyperinsulinism—*see* Hyperinsulinism
    influenza (virus) 487.8
    lack of vitamin (*see also* Deficiency, vitamin)
      269.2
    nicotinic acid deficiency 291.2
    serum (nontherapeutic) (therapeutic) 999.5
    syphilis 094.81
    trauma (postconcussional) 310.2
      current (*see also* Concussion, brain) 850.9
        with skull fracture—*see* Fracture, skull, by
          site, with intracranial injury
    vaccination 323.5
  hepatic 572.2
  hyperbilirubinemic, newborn 774.7
    due to isoimmunization (conditions
      classifiable to 773.0-773.2) 773.4
  hypertensive 437.2
  hypoglycemic 251.2
  hypoxic—*see* Damage, brain, anoxic
  infantile cystic necrotizing (congenital) 341.8

Encephalopathy—*continued*
  lead 984.9 *[323.7]*
  leukopolio 330.0
  metabolic (toxic)—*see* Delirium
  necrotizing, subacute 330.8
  pellagrous 265.2
  portal-systemic 572.2
  postcontusional 310.2
  posttraumatic 310.2
  saturnine 984.9 *[323.7]*
  spongioform, subacute (viral) 046.1
  subacute
    necrotizing 330.8
    spongioform 046.1
    viral, spongioform 046.1
  subcortical progressive (Schilder) 341.1
    chronic (Binswanger's) 290.12
  toxic 349.82
    metabolic—*see* Delirium
  traumatic (postconcussional) 310.2
    current (*see also* Concussion, brain) 850.9
      with skull fracture—*see* Fracture, skull, by
        site, with intracranial injury
  vitamin B deficiency NEC 266.9
  Wernicke's (superior hemorrhagic
    polioencephalitis) 265.1
Enchephalorrhagia (*see also* Hemorrhage,
  brain) 432.9
  healed or old—*see also* category 438
    without residuals V12.59
  late effect—*see* category 438
Encephalosis, posttraumatic 310.2
Enchondroma (M9220/0)—*see also* Neoplasm,
  bone, benign
  multiple, congenital 756.4
Enchondromatosis (cartilaginous) (congenital)
  (multiple) 756.4
Enchondroses, multiple (cartilaginous)
  (congenital) 756.4
Encopresis (*see also* Incontinence, feces) 787.6
  nonorganic origin 307.7
Encounter for —*see also* Admission for
  administrative purpose only V68.9
    referral of patient without examination or
      treatment V68.81
    specified purpose NEC V68.89
  chemotherapy V58.1
  end-of-life care V66.7
  hospice care V66.7
  palliative care V66.7
  radiotherapy V58.0
  terminal care V66.7
Encystment —*see* Cyst
End-of-life care V66.7
Endamebiasis —*see* Amebiasis
Endamoeba —*see* Amebiasis
Endarteritis (bacterial, subacute) (infective)
  (septic) 447.6
  brain, cerebral or cerebrospinal 437.4
    late effect—*see* category 438
  coronary (artery) —*see* Arteriosclerosis,
    coronary
  deformans—*see* Arteriosclerosis
  embolic (*see also* Embolism) 444.9
  obliterans—*see also* Arteriosclerosis
    pulmonary 417.8
  pulmonary 417.8
  retina 362.18
  senile—*see* Arteriosclerosis
  syphilitic 093.89
    brain or cerebral 094.89

Endarteritis—*continued*
  congenital 090.5
  spinal 094.89
  tuberculous (*see also* Tuberculosis) 017.9
Endemic —*see* condition
Endocarditis (chronic) (indeterminate)
  (interstitial) (marantis) (nonbacterial
  thrombotic) (residual) (sclerotic) (sclerous)
  (senile) (valvular) 424.90
  with
    rheumatic fever (conditions classifiable to 390)
      active—*see* Endocarditis, acute, rheumatic
      inactive or quiescent (with chorea) 397.9
  acute or subacute 421.9
    rheumatic (aortic) (mitral) (pulmonary)
      (tricuspid) 391.1
      with chorea (acute) (rheumatic)
        (Sydenham's) 392.0
  aortic (heart) (nonrheumatic) (valve) 424.1
    with
      mitral (valve) disease 396.9
        active or acute 391.1
          with chorea (acute) (rheumatic)
            (Sydenham's) 392.0
      rheumatic fever (conditions classifiable to
        390)
        active—*see* Endocarditis, acute, rheumatic
        inactive or quiescent (with chorea) 395.9
        with mitral disease 396.9
    acute or subacute 421.9
    arteriosclerotic 424.1
    congenital 746.89
    hypertensive 424.1
    rheumatic (chronic) (inactive) 395.9
      with mitral (valve) disease 396.9
        active or acute 391.1
          with chorea (acute) (rheumatic)
            (Sydenham's) 392.0
      active or acute 391.1
        with chorea (acute) (rheumatic)
          (Sydenham's) 392.0
    specified cause, except rheumatic 424.1
    syphilitic 093.22
  arteriosclerotic or due to arteriosclerosis 424.99
  atypical verrucous (Libman-Sacks) 710.0
    [424.91]
  bacterial (acute) (any valve) (chronic)
    (subacute) 421.0
  blastomycotic 116.0 *[421.1]*
  candidal 112.81
  congenital 425.3
  constrictive 421.0
  Coxsackie 074.22
  due to
    blastomycosis 116.0 *[421.1]*
    candidiasis 112.81
    Coxsackie (virus) 074.22
    disseminated lupus erythematosus 710.0
      [424.91]
    histoplasmosis (*see also* Histoplasmosis)
      115.94
    hypertension (benign) 424.99
    moniliasis 112.81
    prosthetic cardiac valve 996.61
    Q fever 083.0 *[421.1]*
    serratia marcescens 421.0
    typhoid (fever) 002.0 *[421.1]*
  fetal 425.3
  gonococcal 098.84
  hypertensive 424.99

Endocarditis—*continued*
  infectious or infective (acute) (any valve)
      (chronic) (subacute) 421.0
  lenta (acute) (any valve) (chronic) (subacute)
      421.0
  Libman-Sacks 710.0 *[424.91]*
  Loeffler's (parietal fibroplastic) 421.0
  malignant (acute) (any valve) (chronic)
      (subacute) 421.0
  meningococcal 036.42
  mitral (chronic) (double) (fibroid) (heart)
      (inactive) (valve) (with chorea) 394.9
    with
      aortic (valve) disease 396.9
        active or acute 391.1
          with chorea (acute) (rheumatic)
              (Sydenham's) 392.0
        rheumatic fever (conditions classifiable to
            390)
          active—*see* Endocarditis, acute, rheumatic
          inactive or quiescent (with chorea) 394.9
            with aortic valve disease 396.9
      active or acute 391.1
        bacterial 421.0
        with chorea (acute) (rheumatic)
            (Sydenham's) 392.0
      arteriosclerotic 424.0
      congenital 746.89
      hypertensive 424.0
      nonrheumatic 424.0
        acute or subacute 421.9
      syphilitic 093.21
  monilial 112.81
  mycotic (acute) (any valve) (chronic) (subacute)
      421.0
  pneumococcic (acute) (any valve) (chronic)
      (subacute) 421.0
  pulmonary (chronic) (heart) (valve) 424.3
    with
      rheumatic fever (conditions classifiable to
          390)
        active—*see* Endocarditis, acute, rheumatic
        inactive or quiescent (with chorea) 397.1
      acute or subacute 421.9
        rheumatic 391.1
          with chorea (acute) (rheumatic)
              (Sydenham's) 392.0
      arteriosclerotic or due to arteriosclerosis 424.3
      congenital 746.09
      hypertensive or due to hypertension (benign)
          424.3
      rheumatic (chronic) (inactive) (with chorea)
          397.1
        active or acute 391.1
          with chorea (acute) (rheumatic)
              (Sydenham's) 392.0
      syphilitic 093.24
  purulent (acute) (any valve) (chronic)
      (subacute) 421.0
  rheumatic (chronic) (inactive) (with chorea)
      397.9
    active or acute (aortic) (mitral) (pulmonary)
        (tricuspid) 391.1
      with chorea (acute) (rheumatic)
          (Sydenham's) 392.0
  septic (acute) (any valve) (chronic) (subacute)
      421.0
  specified cause, except rheumatic 424.99
  streptococcal (acute) (any valve) (chronic)
      (subacute) 421.0
  subacute—*see* Endocarditis, acute

Endocarditis—*continued*
  suppurative (any valve) (acute) (chronic)
      (subacute) 421.0
  syphilitic NEC 093.20
  toxic (*see also* Endocarditis, acute) 421.9
  tricuspid (chronic) (heart) (inactive) (rheumatic)
      (valve) (with chorea) 397.0
    with
      rheumatic fever (conditions classifiable to
          390)
        active—*see* Endocarditis, acute, rheumatic
        inactive or quiescent (with chorea) 397.0
      active or acute 391.1
        with chorea (acute) (rheumatic)
            (Sydenham's) 392.0
      arteriosclerotic 424.2
      congenital 746.89
      hypertensive 424.2
      nonrheumatic 424.2
        acute or subacute 421.9
      specified cause, except rheumatic 424.2
      syphilitic 093.23
  tuberculous (*see also* Tuberculosis) 017.9
      [424.91]
  typhoid 002.0 *[421.1]*
  ulcerative (acute) (any valve) (chronic)
      (subacute) 421.0
  vegetative (acute) (any valve) (chronic)
      (subacute) 421.0
  verrucous (acute) (any valve) (chronic)
      (subacute) NEC 710.0 *[424.91]*
    nonbacterial 710.0 *[424.91]*
    nonrheumatic 710.0 *[424.91]*
Endocardium, endocardial —*see also* condition
  cushion defect 745.60
    specified type NEC 745.69
Endocervicitis (*see also* Cervicitis) 616.0
  due to
    intrauterine (contraceptive) device 996.65
  gonorrheal (acute) 098.15
    chronic or duration of 2 months or over 098.35
  hyperplastic 616.0
  syphilitic 095.8
  trichomonal 131.09
  tuberculous (*see also* Tuberculosis) 016.7
Endocrine —*see* condition
Endocrinopathy, pluriglandular 258.9
Endodontitis 522.0
Endomastoiditis (*see also* Mastoiditis) 383.9
Endometrioma 617.9
Endometriosis 617.9
  appendix 617.5
  bladder 617.8
  bowel 617.5
  broad ligament 617.3
  cervix 617.0
  colon 617.5
  cul-de-sac (Douglas') 617.3
  exocervix 617.0
  fallopian tube 617.2
  female genital organ NEC 617.8
  gallbladder 617.8
  in scar of skin 617.6
  internal 617.0
  intestine 617.5
  lung 617.8
  myometrium 617.0
  ovary 617.1
  parametrium 617.3

Endometriosis—*continued*
pelvic peritoneum 617.3
peritoneal (pelvic) 617.3
rectovaginal septum 617.4
rectum 617.5
round ligament 617.3
skin 617.6
specified site NEC 617.8
stromal (M8931/1) 236.0
umbilicus 617.8
uterus 617.0
  internal 617.0
vagina 617.4
vulva 617.8
Endometritis (nonspecific) (purulent) (septic)
  (suppurative) 615.9
with
  abortion—*see* Abortion, by type, with sepsis
  ectopic pregnancy (*see also* categories
    633.0-633.9) 639.0
  molar pregnancy (*see also* categories
    630-632) 639.0
acute 615.0
blennorrhagic 098.16
  acute 098.16
  chronic or duration of 2 months or over 098.36
cervix, cervical (*see also* Cervicitis) 616.0
  hyperplastic 616.0
chronic 615.1
complicating pregnancy 646.6
  affecting fetus or newborn 760.8
decidual 615.9
following
  abortion 639.0
  ectopic or molar pregnancy 639.0
gonorrheal (acute) 098.16
  chronic or duration of 2 months or over 098.36
hyperplastic 621.3
  cervix 616.0
polypoid—*see* Endometritis, hyperplastic
puerperal, postpartum, childbirth 670
senile (atrophic) 615.9
subacute 615.0
tuberculous (*see also* Tuberculosis) 016.7
Endometrium —*see* condition
Endomyocardiopathy, South African 425.2
Endomyocarditis —*see* Endocarditis
Endomyofibrosis 425.0
Endomyometritis (*see also* Endometritis) 615.9
Endopericarditis —*see* Endocarditis
Endoperineuritis —*see* Disorder, nerve
Endophlebitis (*see also* Phlebitis) 451.9
leg 451.2
  deep (vessels) 451.19
  superficial (vessels) 451.0
portal (vein) 572.1
retina 362.18
specified site NEC 451.89
syphilitic 093.89
Endophthalmia (*see also* Endophthalmitis)
  360.00
gonorrheal 098.42
Endophthalmitis (globe) (infective) (metastatic)
  (purulent) (subacute) 360.00
acute 360.01
chronic 360.03
parasitic 360.13
phacoanaphylactic 360.19
specified type NEC 360.19
sympathetic 360.11

Endosalpingioma (M9111/1) 236.2
Endosteitis —*see* Osteomyelitis
Endothelioma, bone (M9260/3)—*see* Neoplasm,
  bone, malignant
Endotheliosis 287.8
  hemorrhagic infectional 287.8
Endotoxic shock 785.59
Endotrachelitis (*see also* Cervicitis) 616.0
Enema rash 692.89
Engel-von Recklinghausen disease or syndrome
  (osteitis fibrosa cystica) 252.0
Engelmann's disease (diaphyseal sclerosis)
  756.59
English disease (*see also* Rickets) 268.0
Engman's disease (infectious eczematoid
  dermatitis) 690.8
Engorgement
breast 611.79
  newborn 778.7
  puerperal, postpartum 676.2
liver 573.9
lung 514
pulmonary 514
retina, venous 362.37
stomach 536.8
venous, retina 362.37
Enlargement, enlarged —*see also* Hypertrophy
abdomen 789.3
adenoids 474.12
  and tonsils 474.10
alveolar process or ridge 525.8
apertures of diaphragm (congenital) 756.6
blind spot, visual field 368.42
gingival 523.8
heart, cardiac (*see also* Hypertrophy, cardiac)
  429.3
lacrimal gland, chronic 375.03
liver (*see also* Hypertrophy, liver) 789.1
lymph gland or node 785.6
orbit 376.46
organ or site, congenital NEC—*see* Anomaly,
  specified type NEC
parathyroid (gland) 252.0
pituitary fossa 793.0
prostate, simple 600
sella turcica 793.0
spleen (*see also* Splenomegaly) 789.2
  congenital 759.0
thymus (congenital) (gland) 254.0
thyroid (gland) (*see also* Goiter) 240.9
tongue 529.8
tonsils 474.11
  and adenoids 474.10
uterus 621.2
Enophthalmos 376.50
due to
  atrophy of orbital tissue 376.51
  surgery 376.52
  trauma 376.52
Enostosis 526.89
Entamebiasis —*see* Amebiasis
Entamebic —*see* Amebiasis
Entanglement, umbilical cord (s) 663.3
with compression 663.2
  affecting fetus or newborn 762.5
around neck with compression 663.1
twins in monoamniotic sac 663.2
Enteralgia 789.0
Enteric —*see* condition

Enteritis (acute) (catarrhal) (choleraic) (chronic)
(congestive) (diarrheal) (exudative)
(follicular) (hemorrhagic) (infantile)
(lienteric) (noninfectious) (perforative)
(phlegmonous) (presumed noninfectious)
(pseudomembranous) 558.9
  adaptive 564.1
  aertrycke infection 003.0
  allergic 558.9
  amebic (*see also* Amebiasis) 006.9
    with abscess—*see* Abscess, amebic
    acute 006.0
      with abscess—*see* Abscess, amebic
      nondysenteric 006.2
    chronic 006.1
      with abscess—*see* Abscess, amebic
      nondysenteric 006.2
    nondysenteric 006.2
  anaerobic (cocci) (gram-negative)
    (gram-positive) (mixed) NEC 008.46
  bacillary NEC 004.9
  bacterial NEC 008.5
    specified NEC 008.49
  Bacteroides (fragilis) (melaninogeniscus)
    (oralis) 008.46
  Butyrivibrio (fibriosolvens) 008.46
  Campylobacter 008.43
  Candida 112.85
  Chilomastix 007.8
  choleriformis 001.1
  chronic 558.9
    ulcerative (*see also* Colitis, ulcerative) 556.9
  cicatrizing (chronic) 555.0
  Clostridium
    botulinum 005.1
    difficile 008.45
    haemolyticum 008.46
    novyi 008.46
    perfringens (C) (F) 008.46
    specified type NEC 008.46
  coccidial 007.2
  dietetic 558.9
  due to
    achylia gastrica 536.8
    adenovirus 008.62
    Aerobacter aerogenes 008.2
    anaerobes—*see* Enteritis, anaerobic 008.46
    Arizona (bacillus) 008.1
    astrovirus 008.66
    Bacillus coli—*see* Enteritis, E. coli 008.0
    bacteria NEC 008.5
      specified NEC 008.49
    Bacteroides 008.46
    Butyrivibrio (fibriosolvens) 008.46
    Calcivirus 008.65
    Campylobacter 008.43
    Clostridium—*see* Enteritis, Clostridium
    Cockle agent 008.64
    Coxsackie (virus) 008.67
    Ditchling agent 008.64
    ECHO virus 008.67
    Enterobacter aerogenes 008.2
    enterococci 008.49
    enterovirus NEC 008.67
    Escherichia coli—*see* Enteritis, E. coli
    Eubacterium 008.46
    Fusobacterium (nucleatum) 008.46
    gram-negative bacteria NEC 008.47
      anaerobic NEC 008.46

Enteritis—*continued*
    Hawaii agent 008.63
    irritating foods 558.9
    Klebsiella aerogenes 008.47
    Marin County agent 008.66
    Montgomery County agent 008.63
    Norwalk-like agent 008.63
    Norwalk virus 008.63
    Otofuke agent 008.63
    Paracolobactrum arizonae 008.1
    paracolon bacillus NEC 008.47
      Arizona 008.1
    Paramatta agent 008.64
    Peptococcus 008.46
    Peptostreptococcus 008.46
    Propionibacterium 008.46
    Proteus (bacillus) (mirabilis) (morganii) 008.3
    Pseudomonas aeruginosa 008.42
    Rotavirus 008.61
    Sapporo agent 008.63
    small round virus (SRV) NEC 008.64
      featureless NEC 008.63
      structured NEC 008.63
    Snow Mountain (SM) agent 008.63
    specified
      bacteria NEC 008.49
      organism, nonbacterial NEC 008.8
      virus NEC 008.69
    Staphylococcus 008.41
    Streptococcus 008.49
      anaerobic 008.46
    Taunton agent 008.63
    Torovirus 008.69
    Treponema 008.46
    Veillonella 008.46
    virus 008.8
      specified type NEC 008.69
    Wollan (W) agent 008.64
    Yersinia enterocolitica 008.44
  dysentery—*see* Dysentery
  E. coli 008.00
    enterohemorrhagic 008.04
    enteroinvasive 008.03
    enteropathogenic 008.01
    enterotoxigenic 008.02
    specified type NEC 008.09
  el tor 001.1
  embadomonial 007.8
  epidemic 009.0
  Eubacterium 008.46
  fermentative 558.9
  fulminant 557.0
  Fusobacterium (nucleatum) 008.46
  gangrenous (*see also* Enteritis, due to, by
    organism) 009.0
  giardial 007.1
  gram-negative bacteria NEC 008.47
    anaerobic NEC 008.46
  infectious NEC (*see also* Enteritis, due to, by
    organism) 009.0
    presumed 009.1
  influenzal 487.8
  ischemic 557.9
    acute 557.0
    chronic 557.1
    due to mesenteric artery insufficiency 557.1
  membranous 564.1
  mucous 564.1
  myxomembranous 564.1

Enteritis—*continued*
necrotic (*see also* Enteritis, due to, by organism) 009.0
necroticans 005.2
necrotizing of fetus or newborn 777.5
neurogenic 564.1
newborn 777.8
  necrotizing 777.5
parasitic NEC 129
paratyphoid (fever) (*see also* Fever, paratyphoid) 002.9
Peptococcus 008.46
Peptostreptococcus 008.46
Propionibacterium 008.46
protozoal NEC 007.9
regional (of) 555.9
  intestine
    large (bowel, colon, or rectum) 555.1
      with small intestine 555.2
    small (duodenum, ileum, or jejunum) 555.0
      with large intestine 555.2
Salmonella infection 003.0
salmonellosis 003.0
segmental (*see also* Enteritis, regional) 555.9
septic (*see also* Enteritis, due to, by organism) 009.0
Shigella 004.9
simple 558.9
spasmodic 564.1
spastic 564.1
staphylococcal 008.41
  due to food 005.0
streptococcal 008.49
  anaerobic 008.46
toxic 558.2
Treponema (denticola) (macrodentium) 008.46
trichomonal 007.3
tuberculous (*see also* Tuberculosis) 014.8
typhosa 002.0
ulcerative (chronic) (*see also* Colitis, ulcerative) 556.9
Veillonella 008.46
viral 008.8
  adenovirus 008.62
  enterovirus 008.67
  specified virus NEC 008.69
Yersinia enterocolitica 008.44
zymotic 009.0
Enteroarticular syndrome 099.3
Enterobiasis 127.4
Enterobius vermicularis 127.4
Enterocele (*see also* Hernia) 553.9
pelvis, pelvic (acquired) (congenital) 618.6
vagina, vaginal (acquired) (congenital) 618.6
Enterocolitis   *see also* Enteritis
fetus or newborn 777.8
  necrotizing 777.5
fulminant 557.0
granulomatous 555.2
hemorrhagic (acute) 557.0
  chronic 557.1
necrotizing (acute) (membranous) 557.0
primary necrotizing 777.5
pseudomembranous 008.45
radiation 558.1
  newborn 777.5
ulcerative 556.0
Enterocystoma 751.5
Enterogastritis —*see* Enteritis
Enterogenous cyanosis 289.7

Enterolith, enterolithiasis (impaction) 560.39
with hernia—*see also* Hernia, by site, with obstruction
  gangrenous—*see* Hernia, by site, with gangrene
Enteropathy 569.9
exudative (of Gordon) 579.8
gluten 579.0
hemorrhagic, terminal 557.0
protein-losing 579.8
Enteroperitonitis (*see also* Peritonitis) 567.9
Enteroptosis 569.89
Enterorrhagia 578.9
Enterospasm 564.1
psychogenic 306.4
Enterostenosis (*see also* Obstruction, intestine) 560.9
Enterostomy status V44.4
with complication 569.60
Enthesopathy 726.39
ankle and tarsus 726.70
elbow region 726.30
  specified NEC 726.39
hip 726.5
knee 726.60
peripheral NEC 726.8
shoulder region 726.10
  adhesive 726.0
spinal 720.1
wrist and carpus 726.4
Entrance, air into vein —*see* Embolism, air
Entrapment, nerve —*see* Neuropathy, entrapment
Entropion (eyelid) 374.00
cicatricial 374.04
congenital 743.62
late effect of trachoma (healed) 139.1
mechanical 374.02
paralytic 374.02
senile 374.01
spastic 374.03
Enucleation of eye (current) (traumatic) 871.3
Enuresis 788.30
habit disturbance 307.6
nocturnal 788.36
  psychogenic 307.6
nonorganic origin 307.6
psychogenic 307.6
Enzymopathy 277.9
Eosinopenia 288.0
Eosinophilia 288.3
allergic 288.3
hereditary 288.3
idiopathic 288.3
infiltrative 518.3
Loeffler's 518.3
myalgia syndrome 710.5
pulmonary (tropical) 518.3
secondary 288.3
tropical 518.3
Eosinophilic —*see also* condition
fasciitis 728.89
granuloma (bone) 277.8
infiltration lung 518.3
Ependymitis (acute) (cerebral) (chronic) (granular) (*see also* Meningitis) 322.9
Ependymoblastoma (M9392/3)
specified site—*see* Neoplasm, by site, malignant
unspecified site 191.9

Ependymoma (epithelial) (malignant) (M9391/3)
  anaplastic type (M9392/3)
    specified site—*see* Neoplasm, by site,
      malignant
    unspecified site 191.9
  benign (M9391/0)
    specified site—*see* Neoplasm, by site, benign
    unspecified site 225.0
  myxopapillary (M9394/1) 237.5
  papillary (M9393/1) 237.5
  specified site—*see* Neoplasm, by site, malignant
  unspecified site 191.9
Ependymopathy 349.2
  spinal cord 349.2
Ephelides, ephelis 709.09
Ephemeral fever (*see also* Pyrexia) 780.6
Epiblepharon (congenital) 743.62
Epicanthus, epicanthic fold (congenital)
  (eyelid) 743.63
Epicondylitis (elbow) (lateral) 726.32
  medial 726.31
Epicystitis (*see also* Cystitis) 595.9
Epidemic —*see* condition
Epidermidalization, cervix —*see* condition
Epidermidization, cervix *see* condition
Epidermis, epidermal —*see* condition
Epidermization, cervix —*see* condition
Epidermodysplasia verruciformis 078.19
Epidermoid
  cholesteatoma—*see* Cholesteatoma
  inclusion (*see also* Cyst, skin) 706.2
Epidermolysis
  acuta (combustiformis) (toxica) 695.1
  bullosa 757.39
  necroticans combustiformis 695.1
    due to drug
      correct substance properly administered
        695.1
      overdose or wrong substance given or taken
        977.9
        specified drug—*see* Table of drugs and
          chemicals
Epidermophytid —*see* Dermatophytosis
Epidermophytosis (infected)—*see*
  Dermatophytosis
Epidermosis, ear (middle) (*see also*
  Cholesteatoma) 385.30
Epididymis —*see* condition
Epididymitis (nonvenereal) 604.90
  with abscess 604.0
  acute 604.99
  blennorrhagic (acute) 098.0
    chronic or duration of 2 months or over 098.2
  caseous (*see also* Tuberculosis) 016.4
  chlamydial 099.54
  diphtheritic 032.89 *[604.91]*
  filarial 125.9 *[604.91]*
  gonococcal (acute) 098.0
    chronic or duration of 2 months or over 098.2
  recurrent 604.99
  residual 604.99
  syphilitic 095.8 *[604.91]*
  tuberculous (*see also* Tuberculosis) 016.4
Epididymo-orchitis (*see also* Epididymitis)
  604.90
  with abscess 604.0
  chlamydial 099.54
  gonococcal (acute) 098.13
    chronic or duration of 2 months or over 098.33
Epidural —*see* condition
Epigastritis (*see also* Gastritis) 535.5

Epigastrium, epigastric —*see* condition
Epigastrocele (*see also* Hernia, epigastric) 553.29
Epiglottiditis (acute) 464.30
  with obstruction 464.31
  chronic 476.1
  viral 464.30
    with obstruction 464.31
Epiglottis —*see* condition
Epiglottitis (acute) 464.30
  with obstruction 464.31
  chronic 476.1
  viral 464.30
    with obstruction 464.31
Epignathus 759.4
Epilepsia
  partialis continua (*see also* Epilepsy) 345.7
  procursiva (*see also* Epilepsy) 345.8
Epilepsy, epileptic (idiopathic) 345.9

Note—use the following fifth-digit
subclassification with categories 345.0, 345.1,
345.4-345.9

0 without mention of intractable epilepsy
1 with intractable epilepsy

---

  abdominal 345.5
  absence (attack) 345.0
  akinetic 345.0
    psychomotor 345.4
  automatism 345.4
  autonomic diencephalic 345.5
  brain 345.9
  Bravais-Jacksonian 345.5
  cerebral 345.9
  climacteric 345.9
  clonic 345.1
  clouded state 345.9
  coma 345.3
  communicating 345.4
  congenital 345.9
  convulsions 345.9
  cortical (focal) (motor) 345.5
  cursive (running) 345.8
  cysticercosis 123.1
  deterioration 294.1
  due to syphilis 094.89
  equivalent 345.5
  fit 345.9
  focal (motor) 345.5
  gelastic 345.8
  generalized 345.9
    convulsive 345.1
    flexion 345.1
    nonconvulsive 345.0
  grand mal (idiopathic) 345.1
  Jacksonian (motor) (sensory) 345.5
  Kojevnikoff's, Kojevnikov's, Kojewnikoff's
    345.7
  laryngeal 786.2
  limbic system 345.4
  major (motor) 345.1
  minor 345.0
  mixed (type) 345.9
  motor partial 345.5
  musicogenic 345.1
  myoclonus, myoclonic 345.1
    progressive (familial) 333.2
  nonconvulsive, generalized 345.0

Epilepsy, epileptic—*continued*
parasitic NEC 123.9
partial (focalized) 345.5
with
impairment of consciousness 345.4
memory and ideational disturbances 345.4
abdominal type 345.5
motor type 345.5
psychomotor type 345.4
psychosensory type 345.4
secondarily generalized 345.4
sensory type 345.5
somatomotor type 345.5
somatosensory type 345.5
temporal lobe type 345.4
visceral type 345.5
visual type 345.5
peripheral 345.9
petit mal 345.0
photokinetic 345.8
progressive myoclonic (familial) 333.2
psychic equivalent 345.5
psychomotor 345.4
psychosensory 345.4
reflex 345.1
seizure 345.9
senile 345.9
sensory-induced 345.5
sleep 347
somatomotor type 345.5
somatosensory 345.5
specified type NEC 345.8
status (grand mal) 345.3
focal motor 345.7
petit mal 345.2
psychomotor 345.7
temporal lobe 345.7
symptomatic 345.9
temporal lobe 345.4
tonic (-clonic) 345.1
traumatic (injury unspecified) 907.0
injury specified—*see* Late, effect (of)
specified injury
twilight 293.0
uncinate (gyrus) 345.4
Unverricht (-Lundborg) (familial myoclonic)
333.2
visceral 345.5
visual 345.5
Epileptiform
convulsions 780.3
seizure 780.3
Epiloia 759.5
Epimenorrhea 626.2
Epipharyngitis (*see also* Nasopharyngitis) 460
Epiphora 375.20
due to
excess lacrimation 375.21
insufficient drainage 375.22
Epiphyseal arrest 733.91
femoral head 732.2
Epiphyseolysis, epiphysiolysis (*see also*
Osteochondrosis) 732.9
Epiphysitis (*see also* Osteochondrosis) 732.9
juvenile 732.6
marginal (Scheuermann's) 732.0
os calcis 732.5
syphilitic (congenital) 090.0
vertebral (Scheuermann's) 732.0
Epiplocele (*see also* Hernia) 553.9
Epiploitis (*see also* Peritonitis) 567.9

Epiplosarcomphalocele (*see also* Hernia,
umbilicus) 553.1
Episcleritis 379.00
gouty 274.89 *[379.09]*
nodular 379.02
periodica fugax 379.01
angioneurotic—*see* Edema, angioneurotic
specified NEC 379.09
staphylococcal 379.00
suppurative 379.00
syphilitic 095.0
tuberculous (*see also* Tuberculosis) 017.3
[379.09]
Episode
brain (*see also* Disease, cerebrovascular, acute)
436
cerebral (*see also* Disease, cerebrovascular,
acute) 436
depersonalization (in neurotic state) 300.6
psychotic (*see also* Psychosis) 298.9
organic, transient 293.9
schizophrenic (acute) NEC (*see also*
Schizophrenia) 295.4
Epispadias
female 753.8
male 752.62
Episplenitis 289.59
Epistaxis (multiple) 784.7
hereditary 448.0
vicarious menstruation 625.8
Epithelioma (malignant) (M8011/3)—*see also*
Neoplasm, by site, malignant
adenoides cysticum (M8100/0)—*see* Neoplasm,
skin, benign
basal cell (M8090/3)—*see* Neoplasm, skin,
malignant
benign (M8011/0)—*see* Neoplasm, by site,
benign
Bowen's (M8081/2)—*see* Neoplasm, skin, in
situ
calcifying (benign) (Malherbe's)
(M8110/0)—*see* Neoplasm, skin, benign
external site—*see* Neoplasm, skin, malignant
intraepidermal, Jadassohn (M8096/0)—*see*
Neoplasm, skin, benign
squamous cell (M8070/3)—*see* Neoplasm, by
site, malignant
Epitheliopathy
pigment, retina 363.15
posterior multifocal placoid (acute) 363.15
Epithelium, epithelial —*see* condition
Epituberculosis (allergic) (with atelectasis) (*see
also* Tuberculosis) 010.8
Eponychia 757.5
Epstein's
nephrosis or syndrome (*see also* Nephrosis)
581.9
pearl (mouth) 528.4
Epstein-Barr infection (viral) 075
Epulis (giant cell) (gingiva) 523.8
Equinia 024
Equinovarus (congenital) 754.51
acquired 736.71
Equivalent
convulsive (abdominal) (*see also* Epilepsy)
345.5
epileptic (psychic) (*see also* Epilepsy) 345.5

Erythema, erythematous—*continued*
elevatum diutinum 695.89
endemic 265.2
epidemic, arthritic 026.1
figuratum perstans 695.0
gluteal 691.0
gyratum (perstans) (repens) 695.1
heat—*see* Burn, by site, first degree
ichthyosiforme congenitum 757.1
induratum (primary) (scrofulosorum) (*see also*
    Tuberculosis) 017.1
  nontuberculous 695.2
infantum febrile 057.8
infectional NEC 695.9
infectiosum 057.0
inflammation NEC 695.9
intertrigo 695.89
iris 695.1
lupus (discoid) (localized) (*see also* Lupus,
    erythematosus) 695.4
marginatum 695.0
  rheumaticum—*see* Fever, rheumatic
medicamentosum—*see* Dermatitis, due to, drug
migrans 529.1
multiforme 695.1
  bullosum 695.1
  conjunctiva 695.1
  exudativum (Hebra) 695.1
  pemphigoides 694.5
napkin 691.0
neonatorum 778.8
nodosum 695.2
  tuberculous (*see also* Tuberculosis) 017.1
nummular, nummulare 695.1
palmar 695.0
palmaris hereditarium 695.0
pernio 991.5
perstans solare 692.72
rash, newborn 778.8
scarlatiniform (exfoliative) (recurrent) 695.0
simplex marginatum 057.8
solare 692.71
streptogenes 696.5
toxic, toxicum NEC 695.0
  newborn 778.8
tuberculous (primary) (*see also* Tuberculosis)
    017.0
venenatum 695.0
Erythematosus —*see* condition
Erythematous —*see* condition
Erythermalgia (primary) 443.89
Erythralgia 443.89
Erythrasma 039.0
Erythredema 985.0
polyneuritica 985.0
polyneuropathy 985.0
Erythremia (acute) (M9841/3) 207.0
chronic (M9842/3) 207.1
secondary 289.0
Erythroblastopenia (acquired) 284.8
congenital 284.0
Erythroblastophthisis 284.0
Erythroblastosis (fetalis) (newborn) 773.2
due to
  ABO
    antibodies 773.1
    incompatibility, maternal/fetal 773.1
    isoimmunization 773.1
  Rh
    antibodies 773.0
    incompatibility, maternal/fetal 773.0
    isoimmunization 773.0

Erythrocyanosis (crurum) 443.89
Erythrocythemia —*see* Erythremia
Erythrocytosis (megalosplenic)
familial 289.6
oval, hereditary (*see also* Elliptocytosis) 282.1
secondary 289.0
stress 289.0
Erythroderma (*see also* Erythema) 695.9
desquamativa (in infants) 695.89
exfoliative 695.89
ichthyosiform, congenital 757.1
infantum 695.89
maculopapular 696.2
neonatorum 778.8
psoriaticum 696.1
secondary 695.9
Erythrogenesis imperfecta 284.0
Erythroleukemia (M9840/3) 207.0
Erythromelalgia 443.89
Erythromelia 701.8
Erythrophagocytosis 289.9
Erythrophobia 300.23
Erythroplakia
oral mucosa 528.7
tongue 528.7
Erythroplasia (Queyrat) (M8080/2)
specified site—*see* Neoplasm, skin, in situ
unspecified site 233.5
Erythropoiesis, idiopathic ineffective 285.0
Escaped beats, heart 427.60
postoperative 997.1
Esoenteritis —*see* Enteritis
Esophagalgia 530.89
Esophagectasis 530.89
due to cardiospasm 530.0
Esophagismus 530.5
Esophagitis (acute) (alkaline) (chemical)
    (chronic) (infectional) (necrotic) (peptic)
    (postoperative) (regurgitant) 530.10
candidal 112.84
reflux 530.11
specified NEC 530.19
tuberculous (*see also* Tuberculosis) 017.8
Esophagocele 530.6
Esophagodynia 530.89
Esophagomalacia 530.89
Esophagoptosis 530.89
Esophagospasm 530.5
Esophagostenosis 530.3
Esophagostomiasis 127.7
Esophagotracheal —*see* condition
Esophagus —*see* condition
Esophoria 378.41
convergence, excess 378.84
divergence, insufficiency 378.85
Esotropia (nonaccommodative) 378.00
accommodative 378.35
alternating 378.05
  with
    A pattern 378.06
    specified noncomitancy NEC 378.08
    V pattern 378.07
    X pattern 378.08
    Y pattern 378.08
  intermittent 378.22
intermittent 378.20
  alternating 378.22
  monocular 378.21

Esotropia—*continued*
monocular 378.01
  with
   A pattern 378.02
   specified noncomitancy NEC 378.04
   V pattern 378.03
   X pattern 378.04
   Y pattern 378.04
  intermittent 378.21
Espundia 085.5
Essential —*see* condition
Esterapenia 289.8
Esthesioneuroblastoma (M9522/3) 160.0
Esthesioneurocytoma (M9521/3) 160.0
Esthesioneuroepithelioma (M9523/3) 160.0
Esthiomene 099.1
Estivo-autumnal
  fever 084.0
  malaria 084.0
Estrangement V61.0
Estriasis 134.0
Ethanolaminuria 270.8
Ethanolism (*see also* Alcoholism) 303.9
Ether dependence, dependency (*see also*
  Dependence) 304.6
Etherism (*see also* Dependence) 304.6
Ethmoid, ethmoidal —*see* condition
Ethmoiditis (chronic) (nonpurulent) (purulent)
  (*see also* Sinusitis, ethmoidal) 473.2
  influenzal 487.1
  Woakes' 471.1
Ethylism (*see also* Alcoholism) 303.9
Eulenburg's disease (congenital paramyotonia)
  359.2
Eunuchism 257.2
Eunuchoidism 257.2
  hypogonadotropic 257.2
European blastomycosis 117.5
Eustachian —*see* condition
Euthyroidism 244.9
Evaluation
  for suspected condition (*see also* Observation)
   V71.9
  newborn—*see* Observation, suspected,
   condition, newborn
  specified condition NEC V71.8
  mental health V70.2
   requested by authority V70.1
  nursing care V63.8
  social service V63.8
Evan's syndrome (thrombocytopenic purpura)
  287.3
Eventration
  colon into chest—*see* Hernia, diaphragm
  diaphragm (congenital) 756.6
Eversion
  bladder 596.8
  cervix (uteri) 622.0
   with mention of cervicitis 616.0
  foot NEC 736.79
   congenital 755.67
  lacrimal punctum 375.51
  punctum lacrimale (postinfectional) (senile)
   375.51
  ureter (meatus) 593.89
  urethra (meatus) 599.84
  uterus 618.1
   complicating delivery 665.2
    affecting fetus or newborn 763.8
   puerperal, postpartum 674.8

Evisceration
  birth injury 767.8
  bowel (congenital)—*see* Hernia, ventral
  congenital (*see also* Hernia, ventral) 553.29
  operative wound 998.3
  traumatic NEC 869.1
   eye 871.3
Evulsion —*see* Avulsion
Ewing's
  angioendothelioma (M9260/3)—*see* Neoplasm,
   bone, malignant
  sarcoma (M9260/3)—*see* Neoplasm, bone,
   malignant
  tumor (M9260/3)—*see* Neoplasm, bone,
   malignant
Exaggerated lumbosacral angle (with
  impinging spine) 756.12
Examination (general) (routine) (of) (for) V70.9
  allergy V72.7
  annual V70.0
  cardiovascular preoperative V72.81
  cervical Papanicolaou smear V76.2
   as a part of routine gynecological examination
    V72.3
  child care (routine) V20.2
  clinical research investigation (normal control
   patient) V70.7
  dental V72.2
  developmental testing (child) (infant) V20.2
  donor (potential) V70.8
  ear V72.1
  eye V72.0
  following
   accident (motor vehicle) V71.4
   alleged rape or seduction (victim or culprit)
    V71.5
   inflicted injury (victim or culprit) NEC V71.6
   rape or seduction, alleged (victim or culprit)
    V71.5
   treatment (for) V67.9
    combined V67.6
    fracture V67.4
    involving high-risk medication NEC V67.51
    mental disorder V67.3
    specified condition NEC V67.59
  follow-up (routine) (following) V67.9
   cancer chemotherapy V67.2
   chemotherapy V67.2
   disease NEC V67.59
   high-risk medication NEC V67.51
   injury NEC V67.59
   population survey V70.6
   postpartum V24.2
   psychiatric V67.3
   psychotherapy V67.3
   radiotherapy V67.1
   surgery V67.0
  gynecological V72.3
   for contraceptive maintenance V25.40
    intrauterine device V25.42
    pill V25.41
    specified method NEC V25.49
  health (of)
   armed forces personnel V70.5
   checkup V70.0
   child, routine V20.2
   defined subpopulation NEC V70.5
   inhabitants of institutions V70.5
   occupational V70.5
   pre-employment screening V70.5

Examination—*continued*
  preschool children V70.5
    for admission to school V70.3
  prisoners V70.5
    for entrance into prison V70.3
  prostitutes V70.5
  refugees V70.5
  school children V70.5
  students V70.5
 hearing V72.1
 infant V20.2
 laboratory V72.6
 lactating mother V24.1
 medical (for) (of) V70.9
  administrative purpose NEC V70.3
  admission to
    old age home V70.3
    prison V70.3
    school V70.3
  adoption V70.3
  armed forces personnel V70.5
  at health care facility V70.0
  camp V70.3
  child, routine V20.2
  clinical research, normal comparison in V70.7
  control subject in clinical research V70.7
  defined subpopulation NEC V70.5
  donor (potential) V70.8
  driving license V70.3
  general V70.9
    routine V70.0
    specified reason NEC V70.8
  immigration V70.3
  inhabitants of institutions V70.5
  insurance certification V70.3
  marriage V70.3
  medicolegal reasons V70.4
  naturalization V70.3
  occupational V70.5
  population survey V70.6
  pre-employment V70.5
  preschool children V70.5
    for admission to school V70.3
  prison V70.3
  prisoners V70.5
    for entrance into prison V70.3
  prostitutes V70.5
  refugees V70.5
  school children V70.5
  specified reason NEC V70.8
  sport competition V70.3
  students V70.5
 medicolegal reason V70.4
 pelvic (annual) (periodic) V72.3
 periodic (annual) (routine) V70.0
 postpartum
  immediately after delivery V24.0
  routine follow-up V24.2
 pregnancy (unconfirmed) (possible) V72.4
 prenatal V22.1
  first pregnancy V22.0
  high-risk pregnancy V23.9
    specified problem NEC V23.8
 preoperative V72.84
  cardiovascular V72.81
  respiratory V72.82
  specified NEC V72.83
 psychiatric V70.2
  follow-up not needing further care V67.3
  requested by authority V70.1

Examination—*continued*
 radiological NEC V72.5
 respiratory preoperative V72.82
 screening—*see* Screening
 sensitization V72.7
 skin V72.7
  hypersensitivity V72.7
 special V72.9
 specified type or reason NEC V72.85
  preoperative V72.83
    specified NEC V72.83
 teeth V72.2
 victim or culprit following
  alleged rape or seduction V71.5
  inflicted injury NEC V71.6
 vision V72.0
 well baby V20.2
Exanthem, exanthema *(see also* Rash) 782.1
 Boston 048
 epidemic, with meningitis 048
 lichenoid psoriasiform 696.2
 subitum 057.8
 viral, virus NEC 057.9
  specified type NEC 057.8
Excess, excessive, excessively
 alcohol level in blood 790.3
 carbohydrate tissue, localized 278.1
 carotene (dietary) 278.3
 cold 991.9
  specified effect NEC 991.8
 convergence 378.84
 development, breast 611.1
 diaphoresis 780.8
 divergence 378.85
 drinking (alcohol) NEC *(see also* Abuse, drugs,
    nondependent) 305.0
  continual *(see also* Alcoholism) 303.9
  habitual *(see also* Alcoholism) 303.9
 eating 783.6
 eyelid fold (congenital) 743.62
 fat 278.00
  in heart *(see also* Degeneration, myocardial)
    429.1
  tissue, localized 278.1
 foreskin 605
 gas 787.3
 gastrin 251.5
 glucagon 251.4
 heat *(see also* Heat) 992.9
 large
  colon 564.7
    congenital 751.3
  fetus or infant 766.0
    with obstructed labor 660.1
    affecting management of pregnancy 656.6
    causing disproportion 653.5
  newborn (weight of 4500 grams or more)
    766.0
  organ or site, congenital NEC—*see* Anomaly,
    specified type NEC
 lid fold (congenital) 743.62
 long
  colon 751.5
  organ or site, congenital NEC—*see* Anomaly,
    specified type NEC
  umbilical cord (entangled)
    affecting fetus or newborn 762.5
    in pregnancy or childbirth 663.3
    with compression 663.2

Excess, excessive, excessively—*continued*
- menstruation 626.2
- number of teeth 520.1
  - causing crowding 524.3
- nutrients (dietary) NEC 783.6
- potassium (K) 276.7
- salivation (*see also* Ptyalism) 527.7
- secretion—*see also* Hypersecretion
  - milk 676.6
  - sputum 786.4
  - sweat 780.8
- short
  - organ or site, congenital NEC—*see* Anomaly, specified type NEC
  - umbilical cord
    - affecting fetus or newborn 762.6
    - in pregnancy or childbirth 663.4
- skin NEC 701.9
  - eyelid 743.62
    - acquired 374.30
- sodium (Na) 276.0
- sputum 786.4
- sweating 780.8
- tearing (ducts) (eye) (*see also* Epiphora) 375.20
- thirst 783.5
  - due to deprivation of water 994.3
- vitamin
  - A (dietary) 278.2
    - administered as drug (chronic) (prolonged excessive intake) 278.2
    - reaction to sudden overdose 963.5
  - D (dietary) 278.4
    - administered as drug (chronic) (prolonged excessive intake) 278.4
    - reaction to sudden overdose 963.5
- weight 278.00
  - gain 783.1
    - of pregnancy 646.1
  - loss 783.2

Excitability, abnormal , under minor stress 309.29

Excitation
- catatonic (*see also* Schizophrenia) 295.2
- psychogenic 298.1
- reactive (from emotional stress, psychological trauma) 298.1

Excitement
- manic (*see also* Psychosis, affective) 296.0
  - recurrent episode 296.1
  - single episode 296.0
- mental, reactive (from emotional stress, psychological trauma) 298.1
- state, reactive (from emotional stress, psychological trauma) 298.1

Excluded pupils 364.76

Excoriation (traumatic) (*see also* Injury, superficial, by site) 919.8
- neurotic 698.4

Excyclophoria 378.44

Excyclotropia 378.33

Exencephalus, exencephaly 742.0

Exercise
- breathing V57.0
- remedial NEC V57.1
- therapeutic NEC V57.1

Exfoliation, teeth due to systemic causes 525.0

Exfoliative —*see also* condition
- dermatitis 695.89

Exhaustion, exhaustive (physical NEC) 780.7
- battle (*see also* Reaction, stress, acute) 308.9
- cardiac (*see also* Failure, heart) 428.9
- delirium (*see also* Reaction, stress, acute) 308.9
- due to
  - cold 991.8
  - excessive exertion 994.5
  - exposure 994.4
- fetus or newborn 779.8
- heart (*see also* Failure, heart) 428.9
- heat 992.5
  - due to
    - salt depletion 992.4
    - water depletion 992.3
- manic (*see also* Psychosis, affective) 296.0
  - recurrent episode 296.1
  - single episode 296.0
- maternal, complicating delivery 669.8
  - affecting fetus or newborn 763.8
- mental 300.5
- myocardium, myocardial (*see also* Failure, heart) 428.9
- nervous 300.5
- old age 797
- postinfectional NEC 780.7
- psychogenic 300.5
- psychosis (*see also* Reaction, stress, acute) 308.9
- senile 797
  - dementia 290.0

Exhibitionism (sexual) 302.4

Exomphalos 756.7

Exophoria 378.42
- convergence, insufficiency 378.83
- divergence, excess 378.85

Exophthalmic
- cachexia 242.0
- goiter 242.0
- ophthalmoplegia 242.0 *[376.22]*

Exophthalmos 376.30
- congenital 743.66
- constant 376.31
- endocrine NEC 259.9 *[376.22]*
- hyperthyroidism 242.0 *[376.21]*
- intermittent NEC 376.34
- malignant 242.0 *[376.21]*
- pulsating 376.35
  - endocrine NEC 259.9 *[376.22]*
- thyrotoxic 242.0 *[376.21]*

Exostosis 726.91
- cartilaginous (M9210/0)—*see* Neoplasm, bone, benign
- congenital 756.4
- ear canal, external 380.81
- gonococcal 098.89
- hip 726.5
- intracranial 733.3
- jaw (bone) 526.81
- luxurians 728.11
- multiple (cancellous) (congenital) (hereditary) 756.4
- nasal bones 726.91
- orbit, orbital 376.42
- osteocartilaginous (M9210/0)—*see* Neoplasm, bone, benign
- spine 721.8
  - with spondylosis—*see* Spondylosis
- syphilitic 095.5
- wrist 726.4

Exotropia 378.10
  alternating 378.15
    with
      A pattern 378.16
      specified noncomitancy 378.18
      V pattern 378.17
      X pattern 378.18
      Y pattern 378.18
    intermittent 378.24
  intermittent 378.20
    alternating 378.24
    monocular 378.23
  monocular 378.11
    with
      A pattern 378.12
      specified noncomitancy NEC 378.14
      V pattern 378.13
      X pattern 378.14
      Y pattern 378.14
    intermittent 378.23
Explanation of
  investigation finding V65.4
  medication V65.4
Exposure 994.9
  cold 991.9
    specified effect NEC 991.8
  effects of 994.9
  exhaustion due to 994.4
  to
    AIDS virus V01.7
    asbestos V15.84
    body fluids (hazardous) V15.85
    cholera V01.0
    communicable disease V01.9
      specified type NEC V01.8
    German measles V01.4
    gonorrhea V01.6
    hazardous body fluids V15.85
    HIV V01.7
    human immunodeficiency virus V01.7
    lead V15.86
    parasitic disease V01.8
    poliomyelitis V01.2
    potentially hazardous body fluids V15.85
    rabies V01.5
    rubella V01.4
    smallpox V01.3
    syphilis V01.6
    tuberculosis V01.1
    venereal disease V01.6
    viral disease NEC V01.7
Exsanguination, fetal 772.0
Exstrophy
  abdominal content 751.8
  bladder (urinary) 753.5
Extensive —*see* condition
Extra —*see also* Accessory
  rib 756.3
    cervical 756.2
Extraction
  with hook 763.8
  breech NEC 669.6
    affecting fetus or newborn 763.0
  cataract postsurgical V45.6
  manual NEC 669.8
    affecting fetus or newborn 763.8
Extrasystole 427.60
  atrial 427.61
  postoperative 997.1
  ventricular 427.69
Extrauterine gestation or pregnancy —*see*
  Pregnancy, ectopic

Extravasation
  blood 459.0
    lower extremity 459.0
  chyle into mesentery 457.8
  pelvicalyceal 593.4
  pyelosinus 593.4
  urine 788.8
    from ureter 788.8
Extremity —*see* condition
Extrophy —*see* Exstrophy
Extroversion
  bladder 753.5
  uterus 618.1
    complicating delivery 665.2
      affecting fetus or newborn 763.8
    postpartal (old) 618.1
Extrusion
  breast implant (prosthetic) 996.54
  device, implant, or graft—*see* Complications,
    mechanical
  eye implant (ball) (globe) 996.59
  intervertebral disc—*see* Displacement,
    intervertebral disc
  lacrimal gland 375.43
  mesh (reinforcing) 996.59
  ocular lens implant 996.53
  prosthetic device NEC—*see* Complications,
    mechanical
  vitreous 379.26
Exudate, pleura —*see* Effusion, pleura
Exudates, retina 362.82
Exudative —*see* condition
Eye, eyeball, eyelid —*see* condition
Eyestrain 368.13
Eyeworm disease of Africa 125.2

F

Faber's anemia or syndrome (achlorhydric anemia) 280.9
Fabry's disease (angiokeratoma corporis diffusum) 272.7
Face, facial —*see* condition
Facet of cornea 371.44
Faciocephalalgia, autonomic (*see also* Neuropathy, peripheral, autonomic) 337.9
Facioscapulohumeral myopathy 359.1
Factitious disorder, illness —*see* Illness, factitious
Factor
  deficiency—*see* Deficiency, factor
  psychic, associated with diseases classified elsewhere 316
  risk—*see* Problem
Fahr-Volhard disease (malignant nephrosclerosis) 403.00
Failure, failed
  adenohypophyseal 253.2
  attempted abortion (legal) (*see also* Abortion, failed) 638.9
  bone marrow (anemia) 284.9
    acquired (secondary) 284.8
    congenital 284.0
    idiopathic 284.9
  cardiac (*see also* Failure, heart) 428.9
    newborn 779.8
  cardiorenal (chronic) 428.9
    hypertensive (*see also* Hypertension, cardiorenal) 404.93
  cardiorespiratory 799.1
    specified during or due to a procedure 997.1
      long-term effect of cardiac surgery 429.4
  cardiovascular (chronic) 428.9
  cerebrovascular 437.8
  cervical dilatation in labor 661.0
    affecting fetus or newborn 763.7
  circulation, circulatory 799.8
    fetus or newborn 779.8
    peripheral 785.50
  compensation—*see* Disease, heart
  congestive (*see also* Failure, heart, congestive) 428.0
  coronary (*see also* Insufficiency, coronary) 411.89
  descent of head (at term) 652.5
    affecting fetus or newborn 763.1
    in labor 660.0
      affecting fetus or newborn 763.1
  device, implant, or graft—*see* Complications, mechanical
  engagement of head NEC 652.5
    in labor 660.0
  extrarenal 788.9
  fetal head to enter pelvic brim 652.5
    affecting fetus or newborn 763.1
    in labor 660.0
      affecting fetus or newborn 763.1
  forceps NEC 660.7
    affecting fetus or newborn 763.1
  fusion (joint) (spinal) 996.4
  growth 783.4
  heart (acute) (sudden) 428.9
    with
      abortion—*see* Abortion, by type, with specified complication NEC

Failure, failed—*continued*
  acute pulmonary edema (*see also* Failure, ventricular, left) 428.1
    with congestion 428.0
  decompensation (*see also* Failure, heart, congestive) 428.0
  dilation—*see* Disease, heart
  ectopic pregnancy (*see also* categories 633.0-633.9) 639.8
  molar pregnancy (*see also* categories 630-632) 639.8
  arteriosclerotic 440.9
  combined left-right sided 428.0
  compensated (*see also* Failure, heart, congestive) 428.0
  complicating
    abortion—*see* Abortion, by type, with specified complication NEC
    delivery (cesarean) (instrumental) 669.4
    ectopic pregnancy (*see also* categories 633.0-633.9) 639.8
    molar pregnancy (*see also* categories 630-632) 639.8
    obstetric anesthesia or sedation 668.1
    surgery 997.1
  congestive (compensated) (decompensated) 428.0
    with rheumatic fever (conditions classifiable to 390)
      active 391.8
      inactive or quiescent (with chorea) 398.91
    fetus or newborn 779.8
    hypertensive (*see also* Hypertension, heart) 402.91
      with renal disease (*see also* Hypertension, cardiorenal) 404.91
        with renal failure 404.93
      benign 402.11
      malignant 402.01
    rheumatic (chronic) (inactive) (with chorea) 398.91
      active or acute 391.8
        with chorea (Sydenham's) 392.0
  decompensated (*see also* Failure, heart, congestive) 428.0
  degenerative (*see also* Degeneration, myocardial) 429.1
  due to presence of (cardiac) prosthesis 429.4
  fetus or newborn 779.8
  following
    abortion 639.8
    cardiac surgery 429.4
    ectopic or molar pregnancy 639.8
  high output NEC 428.9
  hypertensive (*see also* Hypertension, heart) 402.91
    with renal disease (*see also* Hypertension, cardiorenal) 404.91
      with renal failure 404.93
    benign 402.11
    malignant 402.01
  left (ventricular) (*see also* Failure, ventricular, left) 428.1
    with right-sided failure 428.0
  low output (syndrome) NEC 428.9

Failure, failed—*continued*
  organic—*see* Disease, heart
  postoperative (immediate) 997.1
    long term effect of cardiac surgery 429.4
  rheumatic (chronic) (congestive) (inactive)
    398.91
  right (secondary to left heart failure,
    conditions classifiable to 428.1)
    (ventricular) (*see also* Failure, heart,
    congestive) 428.0
  senile 797
  specified during or due to a procedure 997.1
    long-term effect of cardiac surgery 429.4
  thyrotoxic (*see also* Thyrotoxicosis) 242.9
    [425.7]
  valvular—*see* Endocarditis
 hepatic 572.8
  acute 570
  due to a procedure 997.4
 hepatorenal 572.4
 hypertensive heart (*see also* Hypertension,
  heart) 402.91
  benign 402.11
  malignant 402.01
 induction (of labor) 659.1
  abortion (legal) (*see also* Abortion, failed)
    638.9
  affecting fetus or newborn 763.8
  by oxytocic drugs 659.1
  instrumental 659.0
  mechanical 659.0
  medical 659.1
  surgical 659.0
 initial alveolar expansion, newborn 770.4
 involution, thymus (gland) 254.8
 kidney—*see* Failure, renal
 lactation 676.4
 Leydig's cell, adult 257.2
 liver 572.8
  acute 570
 medullary 799.8
 mitral—*see* Endocarditis, mitral
 myocardium, myocardial (*see also* Failure,
  heart) 428.9
  chronic (*see also* Failure, heart, congestive)
    428.0
  congestive (*see also* Failure, heart,
    congestive) 428.0
 ovarian (primary) 256.3
  iatrogenic 256.2
  postablative 256.2
  postirradiation 256.2
  postsurgical 256.2
 ovulation 628.0
 prerenal 788.9
 renal 586
  with
    abortion—*see* Abortion, by type, with renal
      failure
    ectopic pregnancy (*see also* categories
      633.0-633.9) 639.3
    edema (*see also* Nephrosis) 581.9
    hypertension (*see also* Hypertension,
      kidney) 403.91
    hypertensive heart disease (conditions
      classifiable to 402) 404.92
      with heart failure 404.93
      benign 404.12
        with heart failure 404.13

Failure, failed—*continued*
  malignant 404.02
    with heart failure 404.03
  molar pregnancy (*see also* categories
    630-632) 639.3
  tubular necrosis (acute) 584.5
  acute 584.9
    with lesion of
      necrosis
        cortical (renal) 584.6
        medullary (renal) (papillary) 584.7
        tubular 584.5
      specified pathology NEC 584.8
  chronic 585
    hypertensive or with hypertension (*see also*
      Hypertension, kidney) 403.91
  due to a procedure 997.5
  following
    abortion 639.3
    crushing 958.5
    ectopic or molar pregnancy 639.3
    labor and delivery (acute) 669.3
  hypertensive (*see also* Hypertension, kidney)
    403.91
  puerperal, postpartum 669.3
 respiration, respiratory 518.81
  acute (acute-on-chronic) 518.81
  center 348.8
    newborn 770.8
  chronic 518.81
  due to trauma, surgery or shock 518.5
  newborn 770.8
 rotation
  cecum 751.4
  colon 751.4
  intestine 751.4
  kidney 753.3
 segmentation—*see also* Fusion
  fingers (*see also* Syndactylism, fingers) 755.11
  toes (*see also* Syndactylism, toes) 755.13
 seminiferous tubule, adult 257.2
 senile (general) 797
  with psychosis 290.20
 testis, primary (seminal) 257.2
 to thrive 783.4
 transplant 996.80
  bone marrow 996.85
  organ (immune or nonimmune cause) 996.80
    bone marrow 996.85
    heart 996.83
    intestines 996.89
    kidney 996.81
    liver 996.82
    lung 996.84
    pancreas 996.86
    specified NEC 996.89
  skin 996.52
    temporary allograft or pigskin graft—*omit
      code*
 trial of labor NEC 660.6
  affecting fetus or newborn 763.1
 urinary 586
 vacuum extraction
  abortion—*see* Abortion, failed
  delivery NEC 660.7
    affecting fetus or newborn 763.1
 ventouse NEC 660.7
  affecting fetus or newborn 763.1

Failure, failed—*continued*
ventricular (*see also* Failure, heart) 428.9
  left 428.1
    with rheumatic fever (conditions classifiable
      to 390)
      active 391.8
        with chorea 392.0
      inactive or quiescent (with chorea) 398.91
    hypertensive (*see also* Hypertension, heart)
      402.91
      benign 402.11
      malignant 402.01
    rheumatic (chronic) (inactive) (with chorea)
      398.91
      active or acute 391.8
        with chorea 392.0
  right (*see also* Failure, heart, congestive) 428.0
  vital centers, fetus or newborn 779.8
  weight gain 783.4
Fainting (fit) (spell) 780.2
Falciform hymen 752.49
Fall, maternal, affecting fetus or newborn
  760.5
Fallen arches 734
Falling, any organ or part —*see* Prolapse
Fallopian
  insufflation V26.2
  tube—*see* condition
Fallot's
  pentalogy 745.2
  tetrad or tetralogy 745.2
  triad or trilogy 746.09
Fallout, radioactive (adverse effect) NEC 990
False —*see also* condition
  bundle branch block 426.50
  bursa 727.89
  croup 478.75
  joint 733.82
  labor (pains) 644.1
  opening, urinary, male 752.69
  passage, urethra (prostatic) 599.4
  positive
    serological test for syphilis 795.6
    Wassermann reaction 795.6
  pregnancy 300.11
Family, familial —*see also* condition
  disruption V61.0
  planning advice V25.09
  problem V61.9
    specified circumstance NEC V61.8
Famine 994.2
  edema 262
Fanconi's anemia (congenital pancytopenia)
  284.0
Fanconi (-de Toni) (-Debré) syndrome
  (cystinosis) 270.0
Farber (-Uzman) syndrome or disease
  (disseminated lipogranulomatosis) 272.8
Farcin 024
Farcy 024
Farmers '
  lung 495.0
  skin 692.74
Farsightedness 367.0
Fascia —*see* condition
Fasciculation 781.0
Fasciculitis optica 377.32

Fasciitis 729.4
  eosinophilic 728.89
  necrotizing 728.86
  nodular 728.79
  perirenal 593.4
  plantar 728.71
  pseudosarcomatous 728.79
  traumatic (old) NEC 728.79
  current—*see* Sprain, by site
Fasciola hepatica infestation 121.3
Fascioliasis 121.3
Fasciolopsiasis (small intestine) 121.4
Fasciolopsis (small intestine) 121.4
Fast pulse 785.0
Fat
  embolism (cerebral) (pulmonary) (systemic)
    958.1
    with
      abortion—*see* Abortion, by type, with
        embolism
      ectopic pregnancy (*see also* categories
        633.0-633.9) 639.6
      molar pregnancy (*see also* categories
        630-632) 639.6
    complicating delivery or puerperium 673.8
    following
      abortion 639.6
      ectopic or molar pregnancy 639.6
    in pregnancy, childbirth, or the puerperium
      673.8
  excessive 278.00
    in heart (*see also* Degeneration, myocardial)
      429.1
  general 278.00
  hernia, herniation 729.30
    eyelid 374.34
    knee 729.31
    orbit 374.34
    retro-orbital 374.34
    retropatellar 729.31
    specified site NEC 729.39
  indigestion 579.8
  in stool 792.1
  localized (pad) 278.1
    heart (*see also* Degeneration, myocardial)
      429.1
    knee 729.31
    retropatellar 729.31
  necrosis—*see also* Fatty, degeneration
    breast (aseptic) (segmental) 611.3
    mesentery 567.8
    omentum 567.8
  pad 278.1
Fatal syncope 798.1
Fatigue 780.7
  auditory deafness (*see also* Deafness) 389.9
  chronic, syndrome 780.7
  combat (*see also* Reaction, stress, acute) 308.9
  during pregnancy 646.8
  general 780.7
    psychogenic 300.5
  heat (transient) 992.6
  muscle 729.89
  myocardium (*see also* Failure, heart) 428.9
  nervous 300.5
  neurosis 300.5
  operational 300.89
  postural 729.89
  posture 729.89
  psychogenic (general) 300.5

Fatigue—*continued*
  senile 797
  syndrome NEC 300.5
    chronic 780.7
  undue 780.7
  voice 784.49
Fatness 278.00
Fatty —*see also* condition
  apron 278.1
  degeneration (diffuse) (general) NEC 272.8
    localized—*see* Degeneration, by site, fatty
    placenta—*see* Placenta, abnormal
    heart (enlarged) (*see also* Degeneration,
      myocardial) 429.1
  infiltration (diffuse) (general) (*see also*
    Degeneration, by site, fatty) 272.8
    heart (enlarged) (*see also* Degeneration,
      myocardial) 429.1
  liver 571.8
    alcoholic 571.0
  necrosis—*see* Degeneration, fatty
  phanerosis 272.8
Fauces —*see* condition
Fauchard's disease (periodontitis) 523.4
Faucitis 478.29
Faulty —*see also* condition
  position of teeth 524.3
Favism (anemia) 282.2
Favre-Racouchot disease (elastoidosis cutanea
  nodularis) 701.8
Favus 110.9
  beard 110.0
  capitis 110.0
  corporis 110.5
  eyelid 110.8
  foot 110.4
  hand 110.2
  scalp 110.0
  specified site NEC 110.8
Fear, fearfulness (complex) (reaction) 300.20
  child 313.0
  of
    animals 300.29
    closed spaces 300.29
    crowds 300.29
    eating in public 300.23
    heights 300.29
    open spaces 300.22
      with panic attacks 300.21
    public speaking 300.23
    streets 300.22
      with panic attacks 300.21
    travel 300.22
      with panic attacks 300.21
    washing in public 300.23
  transient 308.0
Feared complaint unfounded V65.5
Febricula (continued) (simple) (*see also* Pyrexia)
  780.6
Febrile (*see also* Pyrexia) 780.6
Febris (*see also* Fever) 780.6
  aestiva (*see also* Fever, hay) 477.9
  flava (*see also* Fever, yellow) 060.9
  melitensis 023.0
  pestis (*see also* Plague) 020.9
  puerperalis 670
  recurrens (*see also* Fever, relapsing) 087.9
    pediculo vestimenti 087.0
  rubra 034.1
  typhoidea 002.0
  typhosa 002.0

Fecal —*see* condition
Fecalith (impaction) 560.39
  with hernia—*see also* Hernia, by site, with
    obstruction
    gangrenous—*see* Hernia, by site, with
      gangrene
  appendix 543.9
  congenital 777.1
Fede's disease 529.0
Feeble-minded 317
Feeble rapid pulse due to shock following
  injury 958.4
Feeding
  faulty (elderly) (infant) 783.3
    newborn 779.3
  formula check V20.2
  improper (elderly) (infant) 783.3
    newborn 779.3
  problem (elderly) (infant) 783.3
    newborn 779.3
  nonorganic origin 307.59
Feer's disease 985.0
Feet —*see* condition
Feigned illness V65.2
Feil-Klippel syndrome (brevicollis) 756.16
Feinmesser's (hidrotic) ectodermal dysplasia
  757.31
Felix's disease (juvenile osteochondrosis, hip)
  732.1
Felon (any digit) (with lymphangitis) 681.01
  herpetic 054.6
Felty's syndrome (rheumatoid arthritis with
  splenomegaly and leukopenia) 714.1
Feminism in boys 302.6
Feminization, testicular 257.8
  with pseudohermaphroditism, male 257.8
Femoral hernia —*see* Hernia, femoral
Femora vara 736.32
Femur, femoral —*see* condition
Fenestrata placenta —*see* Placenta, abnormal
Fenestration, fenestrated —*see also* Imperfect,
  closure
  aorta-pulmonary 745.0
  aorticopulmonary 745.0
  aortopulmonary 745.0
  cusps, heart valve NEC 746.89
    pulmonary 746.09
  hymen 752.49
  pulmonic cusps 746.09
Fenwick's disease 537.89
Fermentation (gastric) (gastrointestinal)
  (stomach) 536.8
  intestine 564.8
    psychogenic 306.4
  psychogenic 306.4
Fernell's disease (aortic aneurysm) 441.9
Fertile eunuch syndrome 257.2
Fertility, meaning multiparity—*see* Multiparity
Fetal alcohol syndrome 760.71
Fetalis uterus 752.3
Fetid
  breath 784.9
  sweat 705.89
Fetishism 302.81
  transvestic 302.3
Fetomaternal hemorrhage
  affecting management of pregnancy 656.0
  fetus or newborn 772.0
Fetus, fetal —*see also* condition
  papyraceous 779.8
  type lung tissue 770.4

Fever 780.6
with chills 780.6
in malarial regions (*see also* Malaria) 084.6
abortus NEC 023.9
Aden 061
African tick-borne 087.1
American
mountain tick 066.1
spotted 082.0
and ague (*see also* Malaria) 084.6
aphthous 078.4
arbovirus hemorrhagic 065.9
Assam 085.0
Australian A or Q 083.0
Bangkok hemorrhagic 065.4
biliary, Charcot's intermittent—*see*
Choledocholithiasis
bilious, hemoglobinuric 084.8
blackwater 084.8
blister 054.9
Bonvale Dam 780.7
boutonneuse 082.1
brain 323.9
late effect—*see* category 326
breakbone 061
Bullis 082.8
Bunyamwera 066.3
Burdwan 085.0
Bwamba (encephalitis) 066.3
Cameroon (*see also* Malaria) 084.6
Canton 081.9
catarrhal (acute) 460
chronic 472.0
cat-scratch 078.3
cerebral 323.9
late effect—*see* category 326
cerebrospinal (meningococcal) (*see also*
Meningitis, cerebrospinal) 036.0
Chagres 084.0
Chandipura 066.8
changuinola 066.0
Charcot's (biliary) (hepatic) (intermittent)—*see*
Choledocholithiasis
Chikungunya (viral) 066.3
hemorrhagic 065.4
childbed 670
Chitral 066.0
Colombo (*see also* Fever, paratyphoid) 002.9
Colorado tick (virus) 066.1
congestive
malarial (*see also* Malaria) 084.6
remittent (*see also* Malaria) 084.6
Congo virus 065.0
continued 780.6
malarial 084.0
Corsican (*see also* Malaria) 084.6
Crimean hemorrhagic 065.0
Cyprus (*see also* Brucellosis) 023.9
dandy 061
deer fly (*see also* Tularemia) 021.9
dehydration, newborn 778.4
dengue (virus) 061
hemorrhagic 065.4
desert 114.0
due to heat 992.0
Dumdum 085.0
enteric 002.0
ephemeral (of unknown origin) (*see also*
Pyrexia) 780.6
epidemic, hemorrhagic of the Far East 065.0

Fever—*continued*
erysipelatous (*see also* Erysipelas) 035
estivo-autumnal (malarial) 084.0
etiocholanolone 277.3
famine—*see also* Fever, relapsing
meaning typhus—*see* Typhus
Far Eastern hemorrhagic 065.0
five day 083.1
Fort Bragg 100.89
gastroenteric 002.0
gastromalarial (*see also* Malaria) 084.6
Gibraltar (*see also* Brucellosis) 023.9
glandular 075
Guama (viral) 066.3
Haverhill 026.1
hay (allergic) (with rhinitis) 477.9
with
asthma (bronchial) (*see also* Asthma) 493.0
due to
dander 477.8
dust 477.8
fowl 477.8
pollen, any plant or tree 477.0
specified allergen other than pollen 477.8
heat (effects) 992.0
hematuric, bilious 084.8
hemoglobinuric (malarial) 084.8
bilious 084.8
hemorrhagic (arthropod-borne) NEC 065.9
with renal syndrome 078.6
arenaviral 078.7
Argentine 078.7
Bangkok 065.4
Bolivian 078.7
Central Asian 065.0
chikungunya 065.4
Crimean 065.0
dengue (virus) 065.4
epidemic 078.6
of Far East 065.0
Far Eastern 065.0
Junin virus 078.7
Korean 078.6
Kyasanur forest 065.2
Machupo virus 078.7
mite-borne NEC 065.8
mosquito-borne 065.4
Omsk 065.1
Philippine 065.4
Russian (Yaroslav) 078.6
Singapore 065.4
Southeast Asia 065.4
Thailand 065.4
tick-borne NEC 065.3
hepatic (*see also* Cholecystitis) 575.8
intermittent (Charcot's)—*see*
Choledocholithiasis
herpetic (*see also* Herpes) 054.9
Hyalomma tick 065.0
icterohemorrhagic 100.0
inanition 780.6
newborn 778.4
infective NEC 136.9
intermittent (bilious) (*see also* Malaria) 084.6
hepatic (Charcot)—*see* Choledocholithiasis
of unknown origin (*see also* Pyrexia) 780.6
pernicious 084.0
iodide
correct substance properly administe
overdose or wrong substance give
975.5

Fever—*continued*
rose 477.0
Ross river (viral) 066.3
Russian hemorrhagic 078.6
sandfly 066.0
San Joaquin (valley) 114.0
São Paulo 082.0
scarlet 034.1
septic—*see* Septicemia
seven-day 061
  Japan 100.89
  Queensland 100.89
shin bone 083.1
Singapore hemorrhagic 065.4
solar 061
sore 054.9
South African tick-bite 087.1
Southeast Asia hemorrhagic 065.4
spinal—*see* Meningitis
spirillary 026.0
splenic (*see also* Anthrax) 022.9
spotted (Rocky Mountain) 082.0
  American 082.0
  Brazilian 082.0
  Colombian 082.0
  meaning
    cerebrospinal meningitis 036.0
    typhus 082.9
spring 309.23
steroid
  correct substance properly administered 780.6
  overdose or wrong substance given or taken
    962.0
streptobacillary 026.1
subtertian 084.0
Sumatran mite 081.2
sun 061
swamp 100.89
sweating 078.2
swine 003.8
sylvatic yellow 060.0
Tahyna 062.5
tertian—*see* Malaria, tertian
Thailand hemorrhagic 065.4
thermic 992.0
three day 066.0
  with Coxsackie exanthem 074.8
tick
  American mountain 066.1
  Colorado 066.1
  Kemerovo 066.1
  Mediterranean 082.1
  mountain 066.1
  nonexanthematous 066.1
  Quaranfil 066.1
tick-bite NEC 066.1
tick-borne NEC 066.1
  hemorrhagic NEC 065.3
transitory of newborn 778.4
trench 083.1
tsutsugamushi 081.2
typhogastric 002.0
typhoid (abortive) (ambulant) (any site)
    (hemorrhagic) (infection) (intermittent)
    (malignant) (rheumatic) 002.0
typhomalarial (*see also* Malaria) 084.6
typhus—*see* Typhus
undulant (*see also* Brucellosis) 023.9
unknown origin (*see also* Pyrexia) 780.6
uremic—*see* Uremia

Fever—*continued*
uveoparotid 135
valley (Coccidioidomycosis) 114.0
Venezuelan equine 066.2
Volhynian 083.1
Wesselsbron (viral) 066.3
West
  African 084.8
  Nile (viral) 066.3
Whitmore's 025
Wolhynian 083.1
worm 128.9
Yaroslav hemorrhagic 078.6
yellow 060.9
  jungle 060.0
  sylvatic 060.0
  urban 060.1
  vaccination, prophylactic (against) V04.4
Zika (viral) 066.3
Fibrillation
atrial (established) (paroxysmal) 427.31
auricular (atrial) (established) 427.31
cardiac (ventricular) 427.41
coronary (*see also* Infarct, myocardium) 410.9
heart (ventricular) 427.41
muscular 728.9
postoperative 997.1
ventricular 427.41
Fibrin
ball or bodies, pleural (sac) 511.0
chamber, anterior (eye) (gelatinous exudate)
    364.04
Fibrinogenolysis (hemorrhagic)—*see*
  Fibrinolysis
Fibrinogenopenia (congenital) (hereditary) (*see*
    also Defect, coagulation) 286.3
acquired 286.6
Fibrinolysis (acquired) (hemorrhagic)
    (pathologic) 286.6
with
  abortion—*see* Abortion, by type, with
      hemorrhage, delayed or excessive
  ectopic pregnancy (*see also* categories
      633.0-633.9) 639.1
  molar pregnancy (*see also* categories
      630-632) 639.1
antepartum or intrapartum 641.3
  affecting fetus or newborn 762.1
following
  abortion 639.1
  ectopic or molar pregnancy 639.1
newborn, transient 776.2
postpartum 666.3
Fibrinopenia (hereditary) (*see also* Defect,
    coagulation) 286.3
acquired 286.6
Fibrinopurulent —*see* condition
Fibrinous —*see* condition
Fibroadenoma (M9010/0)
cellular intracanalicular (M9020/0) 217
giant (intracanalicular) (M9020/0) 217
intracanalicular (M9011/0)
  cellular (M9020/0) 217
  giant (M9020/0) 217
  specified site—*see* Neoplasm, by site, benign
  unspecified site 217
juvenile (M9030/0) 217
pericanalicular (M9012/0)
  specified site—*see* Neoplasm, by site, benign
  unspecified site 217

Fibroadenoma—*continued*
  phyllodes (M9020/0) 217
  prostate 600
  specified site—*see* Neoplasm, by site, benign
  unspecified site 217
Fibroadenosis, breast (chronic) (cystic) (diffuse)
  (periodic) (segmental) 610.2
Fibroangioma (M9160/0)—*see also* Neoplasm,
  by site, benign
  juvenile (M9160/0)
    specified site—*see* Neoplasm, by site, benign
    unspecified site 210.7
Fibrocellulitis progressiva ossificans 728.11
Fibrochondrosarcoma (M9220/3)—*see*
  Neoplasm, cartilage, malignant
Fibrocystic
  disease 277.00
    bone NEC 733.29
    breast 610.1
    jaw 526.2
    kidney (congenital) 753.19
    liver 751.62
    lung 518.89
      congenital 748.4
    pancreas 277.00
  kidney (congenital) 753.19
Fibrodysplasia ossificans multiplex
  (progressiva) 728.11
Fibroelastosis (cordis) (endocardial)
  (endomyocardial) 425.3
Fibroid (tumor) (M8890/0)—*see also* Neoplasm,
  connective tissue, benign
  disease, lung (chronic) (*see also* Fibrosis, lung)
    515
  heart (disease) (*see also* Myocarditis) 429.0
  induration, lung (chronic) (*see also* Fibrosis,
    lung) 515
  in pregnancy or childbirth 654.1
    affecting fetus or newborn 763.8
    causing obstructed labor 660.2
      affecting fetus or newborn 763.1
  liver—*see* Cirrhosis, liver
  lung (*see also* Fibrosis, lung) 515
  pneumonia (chronic) (*see also* Fibrosis, lung)
    515
  uterus (M8890/0) (*see also* Leiomyoma, uterus)
    218.9
Fibrolipoma (M8851/0) (*see also* Lipoma, by
  site) 214.9
Fibroliposarcoma (M8850/3)—*see* Neoplasm,
  connective tissue, malignant
Fibroma (M8810/0)—*see also* Neoplasm,
  connective tissue, benign
  ameloblastic (M9330/0) 213.1
    upper jaw (bone) 213.0
  bone (nonossifying) 733.99
    ossifying (M9262/0)—*see* Neoplasm, bone,
      benign
  cementifying (M9274/0)—*see* Neoplasm, bone,
    benign
  chondromyxoid (M9241/0)—*see* Neoplasm,
    bone, benign
  desmoplastic (M8823/1)—*see* Neoplasm,
    connective tissue, uncertain behavior
  facial (M8813/0)—*see* Neoplasm, connective
    tissue, benign
  invasive (M8821/1)—*see* Neoplasm, connective
    tissue, uncertain behavior

Fibroma—*continued*
  molle (M8851/0) (*see also* Lipoma, by site)
    214.9
  myxoid (M8811/0)—*see* Neoplasm, connective
    tissue, benign
  nasopharynx, nasopharyngeal (juvenile)
    (M9160/0) 210.7
  nonosteogenic (nonossifying)—*see* Dysplasia,
    fibrous
  odontogenic (M9321/0) 213.1
    upper jaw (bone) 213.0
  ossifying (M9262/0)—*see* Neoplasm, bone,
    benign
  periosteal (M8812/0)—*see* Neoplasm, bone,
    benign
  prostate 600
  soft (M8851/0) (*see also* Lipoma, by site) 214.9
Fibromatosis
  abdominal (M8822/1)—*see* Neoplasm,
    connective tissue, uncertain behavior
  aggressive (M8821/1)—*see* Neoplasm,
    connective tissue, uncertain behavior
  Dupuytren's 728.6
  gingival 523.8
  plantar fascia 728.71
  proliferative 728.79
  pseudosarcomatous (proliferative)
    (subcutaneous) 728.79
  subcutaneous pseudosarcomatous (proliferative)
    728.79
Fibromyalgia 729.1
Fibromyoma (M8890/0)—*see also* Neoplasm,
  connective tissue, benign
  uterus (corpus) (*see also* Leiomyoma, uterus)
    218.9
    in pregnancy or childbirth 654.1
      affecting fetus or newborn 763.8
      causing obstructed labor 660.2
        affecting fetus or newborn 763.1
Fibromyositis (*see also* Myositis) 729.1
  scapulohumeral 726.2
Fibromyxolipoma (M8852/0) (*see also* Lipoma,
  by site) 214.9
Fibromyxoma (M8811/0)—*see* Neoplasm,
  connective tissue, benign
Fibromyxosarcoma (M8811/3)—*see* Neoplasm,
  connective tissue, malignant
Fibro-odontoma, ameloblastic (M9290/0) 213.1
  upper jaw (bone) 213.0
Fibro-osteoma (M9262/0)—*see* Neoplasm,
  bone, benign
Fibroplasia, retrolental 362.21
Fibropurulent —*see* condition
Fibrosarcoma (M8810/3)—*see also* Neoplasm,
  connective tissue, malignant
  ameloblastic (M9330/3) 170.1
    upper jaw (bone) 170.0
  congenital (M8814/3)—*see* Neoplasm,
    connective tissue, malignant
  fascial (M8813/3)—*see* Neoplasm, connective
    tissue, malignant
  infantile (M8814/3)—*see* Neoplasm, connective
    tissue, malignant
  odontogenic (M9330/3) 170.1
    upper jaw (bone) 170.0
  periosteal (M8812/3)—*see* Neoplasm, bone,
    malignant

Fibrosclerosis
breast 610.3
corpora cavernosa (penis) 607.89
familial multifocal NEC 710.8
multifocal (idiopathic) NEC 710.8
penis (corpora cavernosa) 607.89
Fibrosis, fibrotic
adrenal (gland) 255.8
alveolar (diffuse) 516.3
amnion 658.8
anal papillae 569.49
anus 569.49
appendix, appendiceal, noninflammatory 543.9
arteriocapillary—see Arteriosclerosis
bauxite (of lung) 503
biliary 576.8
due to Clonorchis sinensis 121.1
bladder 596.8
interstitial 595.1
localized submucosal 595.1
panmural 595.1
bone, diffuse 756.59
breast 610.3
capillary—see also Arteriosclerosis
lung (chronic) (see also Fibrosis, lung) 515
cardiac (see also Myocarditis) 429.0
cervix 622.8
chorion 658.8
corpus cavernosum 607.89
cystic (of pancreas) 277.00
due to (presence of) any device, implant, or
graft—see Complications, due to (presence
of) any device, implant, or graft classified to
996.0-996.5 NEC
ejaculatory duct 608.89
endocardium (see also Endocarditis) 424.90
endomyocardial (African) 425.0
epididymis 608.89
eye muscle 378.62
graphite (of lung) 503
heart (see also Myocarditis) 429.0
hepatic—see also Cirrhosis, liver
due to Clonorchis sinensis 121.1
hepatolienal—see Cirrhosis, liver
hepatosplenic—see Cirrhosis, liver
infrapatellar fat pad 729.31
interstitial pulmonary, newborn 770.7
intrascrotal 608.89
kidney (see also Sclerosis, renal) 587
liver—see Cirrhosis, liver
lung (atrophic) (capillary) (chronic) (confluent)
(massive) (perialveolar) (peribronchial) 515
with
anthracosilicosis (occupational) 500
anthracosis (occupational) 500
asbestosis (occupational) 501
bagassosis (occupational) 495.1
bauxite 503
berylliosis (occupational) 503
byssinosis (occupational) 504
calcicosis (occupational) 502
chalicosis (occupational) 502
dust reticulation (occupational) 504
farmers' lung 495.0
gannister disease (occupational) 502
graphite 503
pneumonoconiosis (occupational) 505
pneumosiderosis (occupational) 503
siderosis (occupational) 503
silicosis (occupational) 502
tuberculosis (see also Tuberculosis) 011.4

Fibrosis, fibrotic—continued
diffuse (idiopathic) (interstitial) 516.3
due to
bauxite 503
fumes or vapors (chemical) (inhalation)
506.4
graphite 503
following radiation 508.1
postinflammatory 515
silicotic (massive) (occupational) 502
tuberculous (see also Tuberculosis) 011.4
lymphatic gland 289.3
median bar 600
mediastinum (idiopathic) 519.3
meninges 349.2
muscle NEC 728.2
iatrogenic (from injection) 999.9
myocardium, myocardial (see also Myocarditis)
429.0
oral submucous 528.8
ovary 620.8
oviduct 620.8
pancreas 577.8
cystic 277.00
penis 607.89
periappendiceal 543.9
periarticular (see also Ankylosis) 718.5
pericardium 423.1
perineum, in pregnancy or childbirth 654.8
affecting fetus or newborn 763.8
causing obstructed labor 660.2
affecting fetus or newborn 763.1
perineural NEC 355.9
foot 355.6
periureteral 593.89
placenta—see Placenta, abnormal
pleura 511.0
popliteal fat pad 729.31
preretinal 362.56
prostate (chronic) 600
pulmonary (chronic) (see also Fibrosis, lung)
515
alveolar capillary block 516.3
interstitial
diffuse (idiopathic) 516.3
newborn 770.7
radiation—see Effect, adverse, radiation
rectal sphincter 569.49
retroperitoneal, idiopathic 593.4
scrotum 608.89
seminal vesicle 608.89
senile 797
skin NEC 709.2
spermatic cord 608.89
spleen 289.59
bilharzial (see also Schistosomiasis) 120.9
subepidermal nodular (M8832/0)—see
Neoplasm, skin, benign
submucous NEC 709.2
oral 528.8
tongue 528.8
syncytium—see Placenta, abnormal
testis 608.89
chronic, due to syphilis 095.8
thymus (gland) 254.8
tunica vaginalis 608.89
ureter 593.89
urethra 599.84
uterus (nonneoplastic) 621.8
bilharzial (see also Schistosomiasis) 120.9
neoplastic (see also Leiomyoma, uterus) 218.9

Fibrosis, fibrotic—*continued*
vagina 623.8
valve, heart (*see also* Endocarditis) 424.90
vas deferens 608.89
vein 459.89
lower extremities 459.89
vesical 595.1
Fibrositis (periarticular) (rheumatoid) 729.0
humeroscapular region 726.2
nodular, chronic
Jaccoud's 714.4
rheumatoid 714.4
ossificans 728.11
scapulohumeral 726.2
Fibrothorax 511.0
Fibrotic —*see* Fibrosis
Fibrous —*see* condition
Fibroxanthoma (M8831/0)—*see also* Neoplasm,
connective tissue, benign
atypical (M8831/1)—*see* Neoplasm, connective
tissue, uncertain behavior
malignant (M8831/3)—*see* Neoplasm,
connective tissue, malignant
Fibroxanthosarcoma (M8831/3)—*see*
Neoplasm, connective tissue, malignant
Fiedler's
disease (leptospiral jaundice) 100.0
myocarditis or syndrome (acute isolated
myocarditis) 422.91
Fiessinger-Leroy (-Reiter) syndrome 099.3
Fiessinger-Rendu syndrome (erythema
muliforme exudativum) 695.1
Fifth disease (eruptive) 057.0
venereal 099.1
Filaria, filarial —*see* Infestation, filarial
Filariasis (*see also* Infestation, filarial) 125.9
bancroftian 125.0
Brug's 125.1
due to
bancrofti 125.0
Brugia (Wuchereria) (malayi) 125.1
Loa loa 125.2
malayi 125.1
organism NEC 125.6
Wuchereria (bancrofti) 125.0
malayi 125.1
Malayan 125.1
ozzardi 125.5
specified type NEC 125.6
Filatoff's, Filatov's, Filatow's disease
(infectious mononucleosis) 075
File-cutters' disease 984.9
specified type of lead—*see* Table of drugs and
chemicals
Filling defect
biliary tract 793.3
bladder 793.5
duodenum 793.4
gallbladder 793.3
gastrointestinal tract 793.4
intestine 793.4
kidney 793.5
stomach 793.4
ureter 793.5
Filtering bleb, eye (postglaucoma) (status) V45.6
with complication or rupture 997.99
postcataract extraction (complication) 997.99
Fimbrial cyst (congenital) 752.11
Fimbriated hymen 752.49
Financial problem affecting care V60.2

Findings, abnormal, without diagnosis
(examination) (laboratory test) 796.4
17-ketosteroids, elevated 791.9
acetonuria 791.6
acid phosphatase 790.5
albumin-globulin ratio 790.99
albuminuria 791.0
alcohol in blood 790.3
alkaline phosphatase 790.5
amniotic fluid 792.3
amylase 790.5
anisocytosis 790.0
antibody titers, elevated 795.79
antigen-antibody reaction 795.79
bacteriuria 791.9
ballistocardiogram 794.39
bicarbonate 276.9
bile in urine 791.4
bilirubin 277.4
bleeding time (prolonged) 790.92
blood culture, positive 790.7
blood gas level 790.91
blood sugar level 790.2
high 790.2
low 251.2
calcium 275.4
carbonate 276.9
casts, urine 791.7
catecholamines 791.9
cells, urine 791.7
cerebrospinal fluid (color) (content) (pressure)
792.0
chloride 276.9
cholesterol 272.9
chromosome analysis 795.2
chyluria 791.1
circulation time 794.39
cloudy urine 791.9
coagulation study 790.92
cobalt, blood 790.6
color of urine (unusual) NEC 791.9
copper, blood 790.6
crystals, urine 791.9
culture, positive NEC 795.3
blood 790.7
HIV V08
human immunodeficiency virus V08
nose 795.3
skin lesion NEC 795.3
spinal fluid 792.0
sputum 795.3
stool 792.1
throat 795.3
urine 791.9
viral
human immunodeficiency V08
wound 795.3
echocardiogram 793.2
echoencephalogram 794.01
echogram NEC—*see* Findings, abnormal,
structure
electrocardiogram (ECG) (EKG) 794.31
electroencephalogram (EEG) 794.02
electrolyte level, urinary 791.9
electromyogram (EMG) 794.17
ocular 794.14
electro-oculogram (EOG) 794.12
electroretinogram (ERG) 794.11
enzymes, serum NEC 790.5
fibrinogen titer coagulation study 790.92

Findings, abnormal without diagnosis—*cont.*
  filling defect—*see* Filling defect
  function study NEC 794.9
    auditory 794.15
    bladder 794.9
    brain 794.00
    cardiac 794.30
    endocrine NEC 794.6
      thyroid 794.5
    kidney 794.4
    liver 794.8
    nervous system
      central 794.00
      peripheral 794.19
    oculomotor 794.14
    pancreas 794.9
    placenta 794.9
    pulmonary 794.2
    retina 794.11
    special senses 794.19
    spleen 794.9
    vestibular 794.16
  gallbladder, nonvisualization 793.3
  glucose 790.2
    tolerance test 790.2
  glycosuria 791.5
  heart
    shadow 793.2
    sounds 785.3
  hematinuria 791.2
  hematocrit
    elevated 282.7
    low 285.9
  hematologic NEC 790.99
  hematuria 599.7
  hemoglobin
    elevated 282.7
    low 285.9
  hemoglobinuria 791.2
  histological NEC 795.4
  hormones 259.9
  immunoglobulins, elevated 795.79
  indolacetic acid, elevated 791.9
  iron 790.6
  karyotype 795.2
  ketonuria 791.6
  lactic acid dehydrogenase (LDH) 790.4
  lipase 790.5
  lipids NEC 272.9
  lithium, blood 790.6
  lung field (coin lesion) (shadow) 793.1
  magnesium, blood 790.6
  mammogram 793.8
  mediastinal shift 793.2
  melanin, urine 791.9
  microbiologic NEC 795.3
  mineral, blood NEC 790.6
  myoglobinuria 791.3
  nitrogen derivatives, blood 790.6
  nonvisualization of gallbladder 793.3
  nose culture, positive 795.3
  odor of urine (unusual) NEC 791.9
  oxygen saturation 790.91
  Papanicolaou (smear) 795.1
    cervix (dyskaryotic) 795.0
    other site 795.1
  peritoneal fluid 792.9
  phonocardiogram 794.39
  phosphorus 275.3
  pleural fluid 792.9
  pneumoencephalogram 793.0

Findings, abnormal without diagnosis—*cont.*
  PO_2-oxygen ratio 790.91
  poikilocytosis 790.0
  potassium
    deficiency 276.8
    excess 276.7
  PPD 795.5
  prostate specific antigen (PSA) 790.93
  protein, serum NEC 790.99
  proteinuria 791.0
  prothrombin time (partial) (prolonged) (PT)
    (PTT) 790.92
  pyuria 599.0
  radiologic (x-ray) 793.9
    abdomen 793.6
    biliary tract 793.3
    breast 793.8
    gastrointestinal tract 793.4
    genitourinary organs 793.5
    head 793.0
    intrathoracic organs NEC 793.2
    lung 793.1
    musculoskeletal 793.7
    placenta 793.9
    retroperitoneum 793.6
    skin 793.9
    skull 793.0
    subcutaneous tissue 793.9
  red blood cell 790.0
    count 790.0
    morphology 790.0
    sickling 790.0
    volume 790.0
  saliva 792.4
  scan NEC 794.9
    bladder 794.9
    bone 794.9
    brain 794.09
    kidney 794.4
    liver 794.8
    lung 794.2
    pancreas 794.9
    placental 794.9
    spleen 794.9
    thyroid 794.5
  sedimentation rate, elevated 790.1
  semen 792.2
  serological (for)
    human immunodeficiency virus (HIV)
      inconclusive 795.71
      positive V08
    syphilis—*see* Findings, serology for syphilis
  serology for syphilis
    false positive 795.6
    positive 097.1
      false 795.6
      follow-up of latent syphilis—*see* Syphilis,
        latent
      only finding—*see* Syphilis, latent
  serum 790.99
    blood NEC 790.99
    enzymes NEC 790.5
    proteins 790.99
  SGOT 790.4
  SGPT 790.4
  sickling of red blood cells 790.0
  skin test, positive 795.79
    tuberculin (without active tuberculosis) 795.5

Findings, abnormal without diagnosis—*cont.*
  sodium 790.6
    deficiency 276.1
    excess 276.0
  spermatozoa 792.2
  spinal fluid 792.0
    culture, positive 792.0
  sputum culture, positive 795.3
    for acid-fast bacilli 795.3
  stool NEC 792.1
    bloody 578.1
      occult 792.1
    color 792.1
    culture, positive 792.1
    occult blood 792.1
  structure, body (echogram) (thermogram)
      (ultrasound) (x-ray) NEC 793.9
    abdomen 793.6
    breast 793.8
    gastrointestinal tract 793.4
    genitourinary organs 793.5
    head 793.0
      echogram (ultrasound) 794.01
    intrathoracic organs NEC 793.2
    lung 793.1
    musculoskeletal 793.7
    placenta 793.9
    retroperitoneum 793.6
    skin 793.9
    subcutaneous tissue NEC 793.9
  synovial fluid 792.9
  thermogram—*see* Finding, abnormal, structure
  throat culture, positive 795.3
  thyroid (function) 794.5
    metabolism (rate) 794.5
    scan 794.5
    uptake 794.5
  total proteins 790.99
  toxicology (drugs) (heavy metals) 796.0
  transaminase (level) 790.4
  triglycerides 272.9
  tuberculin skin test (without active tuberculosis)
      795.5
  ultrasound—*see also* Finding, abnormal,
      structure
    cardiogram 793.2
  uric acid, blood 790.6
  urine, urinary constituents 791.9
    acetone 791.6
    albumin 791.0
    bacteria 791.9
    bile 791.4
    blood 599.7
    casts or cells 791.7
    chyle 791.1
    culture, positive 791.9
    glucose 791.5
    hemoglobin 791.2
    ketone 791.6
    protein 791.0
    pus 599.0
    sugar 791.5
  vaginal fluid 792.9
  vanillylmandelic acid, elevated 791.9
  vectorcardiogram (VCG) 793.2
  ventriculogram (cerebral) 793.0
  VMA, elevated 791.9

Findings, abnormal without diagnosis—*cont.*
  Wassermann reaction
    false positive 795.6
    positive 097.1
      follow-up of latent syphilis—*see* Syphilis,
        latent
      only finding—*see* Syphilis, latent
  white blood cell 288.9
    count 288.9
      elevated 288.8
      low 288.0
    differential 288.9
    morphology 288.9
  wound culture 795.3
  xerography 793.8
  zinc, blood 790.6
Finger —*see* condition
Fire, St. Anthony's (*see also* Erysipelas) 035
Fish
  hook stomach 537.89
  meal workers' lung 495.8
Fisher's syndrome 357.0
Fissure, fissured
  abdominal wall (congenital) 756.7
  anus, anal 565.0
    congenital 751.5
  buccal cavity 528.9
  clitoris (congenital) 752.49
  ear, lobule (congenital) 744.29
  epiglottis (congenital) 748.3
  larynx 478.79
    congenital 748.3
  lip 528.5
    congenital (*see also* Cleft, lip) 749.10
  nipple 611.2
    puerperal, postpartum 676.1
  palate (congenital) (*see also* Cleft, palate)
      749.00
  postanal 565.0
  rectum 565.0
  skin 709.8
    streptococcal 686.9
  spine (congenital) (*see also* Spina bifida) 741.9
  sternum (congenital) 756.3
  tongue (acquired) 529.5
    congenital 750.13
Fistula (sinus) 686.9
  abdomen (wall) 569.81
    bladder 596.2
    intestine 569.81
    ureter 593.82
    uterus 619.2
  abdominorectal 569.81
  abdominosigmoidal 569.81
  abdominothoracic 510.0
  abdominouterine 619.2
    congenital 752.3
  abdominovesical 596.2
  accessory sinuses (*see also* Sinusitis) 473.9
  actinomycotic—*see* Actinomycosis
  alveolar
    antrum (*see also* Sinusitis, maxillary) 473.0
    process 522.7
  anorectal 565.1
  antrobuccal (*see also* Sinusitis, maxillary) 473.0
  antrum (*see also* Sinusitis, maxillary) 473.0
  anus, anal (infectional) (recurrent) 565.1
    congenital 751.5
    tuberculous (*see also* Tuberculosis) 014.8
  aortic sinus 747.29
  aortoduodenal 447.2

Fistula—*continued*
  appendix, appendicular 543.9
  arteriovenous (acquired) 447.0
    brain 437.3
      congenital 747.81
        ruptured (*see also* Hemorrhage,
          subarachnoid) 430
      ruptured (*see also* Hemorrhage,
        subarachnoid) 430
    cerebral 437.3
      congenital 747.81
    congenital (peripheral) 747.60
      brain—*see* Fistula, arteriovenous, brain,
        congenital
      coronary 746.85
      gastrointestinal 747.61
      lower limb 747.64
      pulmonary 747.3
      renal 747.62
      specified NEC 747.69
      upper limb 747.63
    coronary 414.19
      congenital 746.85
    heart 414.19
    pulmonary (vessels) 417.0
      congenital 747.3
    surgically created (for dialysis) V45.1
      complication NEC 996.73
        atherosclerosis —*see* Arteriosclerosis,
          extremities
        embolism 996.74
        infection or inflammation 996.62
        mechanical 996.1
        occlusion NEC 996.74
        thrombus 996.74
    traumatic—*see* Injury, blood vessel, by site
  artery 447.2
  aural 383.81
    congenital 744.49
  auricle 383.81
    congenital 744.49
  Bartholin's gland 619.8
  bile duct (*see also* Fistula, biliary) 576.4
  biliary (duct) (tract) 576.4
    congenital 751.69
  bladder (neck) (sphincter) 596.2
    into seminal vesicle 596.2
  bone 733.99
  brain 348.8
    arteriovenous—*see* Fistula, arteriovenous,
      brain
  branchial (cleft) 744.41
  branchiogenous 744.41
  breast 611.0
    puerperal, postpartum 675.1
  bronchial 510.0
  bronchocutaneous, bronchomediastinal,
    bronchopleural, bronchopleuromediastinal
    (infective) 510.0
    tuberculous (*see also* Tuberculosis) 011.3
  bronchoesophageal 530.89
    congenital 750.3
  buccal cavity (infective) 528.3
  canal, ear 380.89
  carotid-cavernous
    congenital 747.81
      with hemorrhage 430
    traumatic 900.82
      with hemorrhage (see also Hemorrhage,
        brain, traumatic) 853.0
      late effect 908.3

Fistula—*continued*
  cecosigmoidal 569.81
  cecum 569.81
  cerebrospinal (fluid) 349.81
  cervical, lateral (congenital) 744.41
  cervicoaural (congenital) 744.49
  cervicosigmoidal 619.1
  cervicovesical 619.0
  cervix 619.8
  chest (wall) 510.0
  cholecystocolic (*see also* Fistula, gallbladder)
    575.5
  cholecystocolonic (*see also* Fistula, gallbladder)
    575.5
  cholecystoduodenal (*see also* Fistula,
    gallbladder) 575.5
  cholecystoenteric (*see also* Fistula, gallbladder)
    575.5
  cholecystogastric (*see also* Fistula, gallbladder)
    575.5
  cholecystointestinal (*see also* Fistula,
    gallbladder) 575.5
  choledochoduodenal 576.4
  cholocolic (*see also* Fistula, gallbladder) 575.5
  coccyx 685.1
    with abscess 685.0
  colon 569.81
  colostomy 569.69
  colovaginal (acquired) 619.1
  common duct (bile duct) 576.4
  congenital, NEC—*see* Anomaly, specified type
    NEC
  cornea, causing hypotony 360.32
  coronary, arteriovenous 414.19
    congenital 746.85
  costal region 510.0
  cul-de-sac, Douglas' 619.8
  cutaneous 686.9
  cystic duct (*see also* Fistula, gallbladder) 575.5
    congenital 751.69
  dental 522.7
  diaphragm 510.0
    bronchovisceral 510.0
    pleuroperitoneal 510.0
    pulmonoperitoneal 510.0
  duodenum 537.4
  ear (canal) (external) 380.89
  enterocolic 569.81
  enterocutaneous 569.81
  enteroenteric 569.81
  entero-uterine 619.1
    congenital 752.3
  enterovaginal 619.1
    congenital 752.49
  enterovesical 596.1
  epididymis 608.89
    tuberculous (*see also* Tuberculosis) 016.4
  esophagobronchial 530.89
    congenital 750.3
  esophagocutaneous 530.89
  esophagopleurocutaneous 530.89
  esophagotracheal 530.84
    congenital 750.3
  esophagus 530.89
    congenital 750.4
  ethmoid (*see also* Sinusitis, ethmoidal) 473.2
  eyeball (cornea) (sclera) 360.32
  eyelid 373.11
  fallopian tube (external) 619.2
  fecal 569.81
    congenital 751.5

Fistula—*continued*
from periapical lesion 522.7
frontal sinus (*see also* Sinusitis, frontal) 473.1
gallbladder 575.5
  with calculus, cholelithiasis, stones (*see also*
    Cholelithiasis) 574.2
  congenital 751.69
gastric 537.4
gastrocolic 537.4
  congenital 750.7
  tuberculous (*see also* Tuberculosis) 014.8
gastroenterocolic 537.4
gastroesophageal 537.4
gastrojejunal 537.4
gastrojejunocolic 537.4
genital
  organs
    female 619.9
      specified site NEC 619.8
    male 608.89
  tract-skin (female) 619.2
hepatopleural 510.0
hepatopulmonary 510.0
horseshoe 565.1
ileorectal 569.81
ileosigmoidal 569.81
ileostomy 569.69
ileovesical 596.1
ileum 569.81
in ano 565.1
  tuberculous (*see also* Tuberculosis) 014.8
inner ear (*see also* Fistula, labyrinth) 386.40
intestine 569.81
intestinocolonic (abdominal) 569.81
intestinoureteral 593.82
intestinouterine 619.1
intestinovaginal 619.1
  congenital 752.49
intestinovesical 596.1
involving female genital tract 619.9
  digestive-genital 619.1
  genital tract-skin 619.2
  specified site NEC 619.8
  urinary-genital 619.0
ischiorectal (fossa) 566
jejunostomy 569.69
jejunum 569.81
joint 719.80
  ankle 719.87
  elbow 719.82
  foot 719.87
  hand 719.84
  hip 719.85
  knee 719.86
  multiple sites 719.89
  pelvic region 719.85
  shoulder (region) 719.81
  specified site NEC 719.88
  tuberculous—*see* Tuberculosis, joint
  wrist 719.83
kidney 593.89
labium (majus) (minus) 619.8
labyrinth, labyrinthine NEC 386.40
  combined sites 386.48
  multiple sites 386.48
  oval window 386.42
  round window 386.41
  semicircular canal 386.43
lacrimal, lachrymal (duct) (gland) (sac) 375.61
lacrimonasal duct 375.61
laryngotracheal 748.3

Fistula—*continued*
larynx 478.79
lip 528.5
  congenital 750.25
lumbar, tuberculous (*see also* Tuberculosis)
  015.0 *[730.8]*
lung 510.0
lymphatic (node) (vessel) 457.8
mamillary 611.0
mammary (gland) 611.0
  puerperal, postpartum 675.1
mastoid (process) (region) 383.1
maxillary (*see also* Sinusitis, maxillary) 473.0
mediastinal 510.0
mediastinobronchial 510.0
mediastinocutaneous 510.0
middle ear 385.89
mouth 528.3
nasal 478.1
  sinus (*see also* Sinusitis) 473.9
nasopharynx 478.29
nipple—*see* Fistula, breast
nose 478.1
oral (cutaneous) 528.3
  maxillary (*see also* Sinusitis, maxillary) 473.0
  nasal (with cleft palate) (*see also* Cleft, palate)
    749.00
orbit, orbital 376.10
oro-antral (*see also* Sinusitis, maxillary) 473.0
oval window (internal ear) 386.42
oviduct (external) 619.2
palate (hard) 526.89
  soft 528.9
pancreatic 577.8
pancreaticoduodenal 577.8
parotid (gland) 527.4
  region 528.3
pelvoabdominointestinal 569.81
penis 607.89
perianal 565.1
pericardium (pleura) (sac) (*see also* Pericarditis)
  423.8
pericecal 569.81
perineal—*see* Fistula, perineum
perineorectal 569.81
perineosigmoidal 569.81
perineo-urethroscrotal 608.89
perineum, perineal (with urethral involvement)
  NEC 599.1
  tuberculous (*see also* Tuberculosis) 017.9
  ureter 593.82
perirectal 565.1
  tuberculous (*see also* Tuberculosis) 014.8
peritoneum (*see also* Peritonitis) 567.2
periurethral 599.1
pharyngo-esophageal 478.29
pharynx 478.29
  branchial cleft (congenital) 744.41
pilonidal (infected) (rectum) 685.1
  with abscess 685.0
pleura, pleural, pleurocutaneous,
  pleuroperitoneal 510.0
  stomach 510.0
  tuberculous (*see also* Tuberculosis) 012.0
pleuropericardial 423.8
postauricular 383.81
postoperative, persistent 998.6
preauricular (congenital) 744.46
prostate 602.8

Fistula—*continued*
  pulmonary 510.0
    arteriovenous 417.0
      congenital 747.3
    tuberculous (*see also* Tuberculosis,
        pulmonary) 011.9
  pulmonoperitoneal 510.0
  rectolabial 619.1
  rectosigmoid (intercommunicating) 569.81
  rectoureteral 593.82
  rectourethral 599.1
    congenital 753.8
  rectouterine 619.1
    congenital 752.3
  rectovaginal 619.1
    congenital 752.49
    old, postpartal 619.1
    tuberculous (*see also* Tuberculosis) 014.8
  rectovesical 596.1
    congenital 753.8
  rectovesicovaginal 619.1
  rectovulvar 619.1
    congenital 752.49
  rectum (to skin) 565.1
    tuberculous (*see also* Tuberculosis) 014.8
  renal 593.89
  retroauricular 383.81
  round window (internal ear) 386.41
  salivary duct or gland 527.4
    congenital 750.24
  sclera 360.32
  scrotum (urinary) 608.89
    tuberculous (*see also* Tuberculosis) 016.5
  semicircular canals (internal ear) 386.43
  sigmoid 569.81
    vesicoabdominal 596.1
  sigmoidovaginal 619.1
    congenital 752.49
  skin 686.9
    ureter 593.82
    vagina 619.2
  sphenoidal sinus (*see also* Sinusitis, sphenoidal)
      473.3
  splenocolic 289.59
  stercoral 569.81
  stomach 537.4
  sublingual gland 527.4
    congenital 750.24
  submaxillary
    gland 527.4
      congenital 750.24
    region 528.3
  thoracic 510.0
    duct 457.8
  thoracicoabdominal 510.0
  thoracicogastric 510.0
  thoracicointestinal 510.0
  thoracoabdominal 510.0
  thoracogastric 510.0
  thorax 510.0
  thyroglossal duct 759.2
  thyroid 246.8
  trachea (congenital) (external) (internal) 748.3
  tracheoesophageal 530.84
    congenital 750.3
    following tracheostomy 519.0
  traumatic
    arteriovenous (*see also* Injury, blood vessel,
        by site) 904.9
    brain—*see* Injury, intracranial

Fistula—*continued*
  tuberculous—*see* Tuberculosis, by site
  typhoid 002.0
  umbilical 759.89
  umbilico-urinary 753.8
  urachal, urachus 753.7
  ureter (persistent) 593.82
  ureteroabdominal 593.82
  ureterocervical 593.82
  ureterorectal 593.82
  ureterosigmoido-abdominal 593.82
  ureterovaginal 619.0
  ureterovesical 596.2
  urethra 599.1
    congenital 753.8
    tuberculous (*see also* Tuberculosis) 016.3
  urethroperineal 599.1
  urethroperineovesical 596.2
  urethrorectal 599.1
    congenital 753.8
  urethroscrotal 608.89
  urethrovaginal 619.0
  urethrovesical 596.2
  urethrovesicovaginal 619.0
  urinary (persistent) (recurrent) 599.1
  uteroabdominal (anterior wall) 619.2
    congenital 752.3
  uteroenteric 619.1
  uterofecal 619.1
  uterointestinal 619.1
    congenital 752.3
  uterorectal 619.1
    congenital 752.3
  uteroureteric 619.0
  uterovaginal 619.8
  uterovesical 619.0
    congenital 752.3
  uterus 619.8
  vagina (wall) 619.8
    postpartal, old 619.8
  vaginocutaneous (postpartal) 619.2
  vaginoileal (acquired) 619.1
  vaginoperineal 619.2
  vesical NEC 596.2
  vesicoabdominal 596.2
  vesicocervicovaginal 619.0
  vesicocolic 596.1
  vesicocutaneous 596.2
  vesicoenteric 596.1
  vesicointestinal 596.1
  vesicometrorectal 619.1
  vesicoperineal 596.2
  vesicorectal 596.1
    congenital 753.8
  vesicosigmoidal 596.1
  vesicosigmoidovaginal 619.1
  vesicoureteral 596.2
  vesicoureterovaginal 619.0
  vesicourethral 596.2
  vesicourethrorectal 596.1
  vesicouterine 619.0
    congenital 752.3
  vesicovaginal 619.0
  vulvorectal 619.1
    congenital 752.49
Fit 780.3
  apoplectic (*see also* Disease, cerebrovascular,
      acute) 436
    late effect—*see* category 438
  epileptic (*see also* Epilepsy) 345.9

Fit —*continued*
  fainting 780.2
  hysterical 300.11
  newborn 779.0
Fitting (of)
  artificial
    arm (complete) (partial) V52.0
    breast V52.4
    eye(s) V52.2
    leg(s) (complete) (partial) V52.1
  brain neuropacemaker V53.0
  cardiac pacemaker V53.31
  carotid sinus pacemaker V53.39
  colostomy belt V53.5
  contact lenses V53.1
  cystostomy device V53.6
  defibrillator, automatic implantable V53.32
  dentures V52.3
  device NEC V53.9
    abdominal V53.5
    cardiac
      defibrillator, automatic implantable V53.32
      pacemaker V53.31
      specified NEC V53.39
    intrauterine contraceptive V25.1
    nervous system V53.0
    orthodontic V53.4
    orthoptic V53.1
    prosthetic V52.9
      breast V52.4
      dental V52.3
      eye V52.2
      specified type NEC V52.8
    special senses V53.0
    substitution
      auditory V53.0
      nervous system V53.0
      visual V53.0
    urinary V53.6
  diaphragm (contraceptive) V25.02
  glasses (reading) V53.1
  hearing aid V53.2
  ileostomy device V53.5
  intestinal appliance or device NEC V53.5
  intrauterine contraceptive device V25.1
  neuropacemaker (brain) (peripheral nerve)
    (spinal cord) V53.0
  orthodontic device V53.4
  orthopedic (device) V53.7
    brace V53.7
    cast V53.7
    corset V53.7
    shoes V53.7
  pacemaker (cardiac) V53.31
    brain V53.0
    carotid sinus V53.39
    peripheral nerve V53.0
    spinal cord V53.0
  prosthesis V52.9
    arm (complete) (partial) V52.0
    breast V52.4
    dental V52.3
    eye V52.2
    leg (complete) (partial) V52.1
    specified type NEC V52.8
  spectacles V53.1
  wheelchair V53.8
Fitz's syndrome (acute hemorrhagic
  pancreatitis) 577.0
Fitz-Hugh and Curtis syndrome (gonococcal
  peritonitis) 098.86

Fixation
  joint—*see* Ankylosis
  larynx 478.79
  pupil 364.76
  stapes 385.22
    deafness (*see also* Deafness, conductive)
      389.04
  uterus (acquired)—*see* Malposition, uterus
  vocal cord 478.5
Flaccid —*see* condition
  foot 736.79
  forearm 736.09
  palate, congenital 750.26
Flail
  chest 807.4
    newborn 767.3
  joint (paralytic) 718.80
    ankle 718.87
    elbow 718.82
    foot 718.87
    hand 718.84
    hip 718.85
    knee 718.86
    multiple sites 718.89
    pelvic region 718.85
    shoulder (region) 718.81
    specified site NEC 718.88
    wrist 718.83
Flajani (-Basedow) syndrome or disease
  (exophthalmic goiter) 242.0
Flap, liver 572.8
Flare, anterior chamber (aqueous) (eye) 364.04
Flashback phenomena (drug) (hallucinogenic)
  292.89
Flat
  chamber (anterior) (eye) 360.34
  chest, congenital 754.89
  electroencephalogram (EEG) 348.8
  foot (acquired) (fixed type) (painful) (postural)
    (spastic) 734
    congenital 754.61
      rocker bottom 754.61
      vertical talus 754.61
    rachitic 268.1
    rocker bottom (congenital) 754.61
    vertical talus, congenital 754.61
  organ or site, congenital NEC—*see* Anomaly,
    specified type NEC
  pelvis 738.6
    with disproportion (fetopelvic) 653.2
      affecting fetus or newborn 763.1
      causing obstructed labor 660.1
        affecting fetus or newborn 763.1
    congenital 755.69
Flatau-Schilder disease 341.1
Flattening
  head, femur 736.39
  hip 736.39
  lip (congenital) 744.89
  nose (congenital) 754.0
    acquired 738.0
Flatulence 787.3
Flatus 787.3
  vaginalis 629.8
Flax dressers' disease 504
Flea bite —*see* Injury, superficial, by site
Fleischer (-Kayser) ring (corneal pigmentation)
  275.1 *[371.14]*
Fleischner's disease 732.3
Fleshy mole 631
Flexibilitas cerea (*see also* Catalepsy) 300.11

Flexion
  cervix (*see also* Malposition, uterus) 621.6
  contracture, joint (*see also* Contraction, joint)
    718.4
  deformity, joint (*see also* Contraction, joint)
    718.4
    hip, congenital (*see also* Subluxation,
      congenital, hip) 754.32
  uterus (*see also* Malposition, uterus) 621.6
Flexner's
  bacillus 004.1
  diarrhea (ulcerative) 004.1
  dysentery 004.1
Flexner-Boyd dysentery 004.2
Flexure —*see* condition
Floater, vitreous 379.24
Floating
  cartilage (joint) (*see also* Disorder, cartilage,
    articular) 718.0
    knee 717.6
  gallbladder (congenital) 751.69
  kidney 593.0
    congenital 753.3
  liver (congenital) 751.69
  rib 756.3
  spleen 289.59
Flooding 626.2
Floor —*see* condition
Floppy
  infant NEC 781.9
  valve syndrome (mitral) 424.0
Flu —*see also* Influenza
  gastric NEC 008.8
Fluctuating blood pressure 796.4
Fluid
  abdomen 789.5
  chest (*see also* Pleurisy, with effusion) 511.9
  heart (*see also* Failure, heart, congestive) 428.0
  joint (*see also* Effusion, joint) 719.0
  loss (acute) 276.5
    with
      hypernatremia 276.0
      hyponatremia 276.1
  lung—*see also* Edema, lung
    encysted 511.8
  peritoneal cavity 789.5
  pleural cavity (*see also* Pleurisy, with effusion)
    511.9
  retention 276.6
Flukes NEC (*see also* Infestation, fluke) 121.9
  blood NEC (*see also* Infestation, Schistosoma)
    120.9
  liver 121.3
Fluor (albus) (vaginalis) 623.5
  trichomonal (Trichomonas vaginalis) 131.00
Fluorosis (dental) (chronic) 520.3
Flushing 782.62
  menopausal 627.2
Flush syndrome 259.2
Flutter
  atrial or auricular 427.32
  heart (ventricular) 427.42
    atrial 427.32
  impure 427.32
  postoperative 997.1
  ventricular 427.42
Flux (bloody) (serosanguineous) 009.0
Focal —*see* condition
Fochier's abscess —*see* Abscess, by site
Focus, Assmann's (*see also* Tuberculosis) 011.0
Fogo selvagem 694.4
Foix-Alajouanine syndrome 336.1

Folds, anomalous —*see also* Anomaly, specified
    type NEC
  Bowman's membrane 371.31
  Descemet's membrane 371.32
  epicanthic 743.63
  heart 746.89
  posterior segment of eye, congenital 743.54
Folie à deux 297.3
Follicle
  cervix (nabothian) (ruptured) 616.0
  graafian, ruptured, with hemorrhage 620.0
  nabothian 616.0
Folliclis (primary) (*see also* Tuberculosis) 017.0
Follicular —*see also* condition
  cyst (atretic) 620.0
Folliculitis 704.8
  abscedens et suffodiens 704.8
  decalvans 704.09
  gonorrheal (acute) 098.0
    chronic or duration of 2 months or more 098.2
  keloid, keloidalis 706.1
  pustular 704.8
  ulerythematosa reticulata 701.8
Folliculosis, conjunctival 372.02
Folling's disease (phenylketonuria) 270.1
Follow-up (examination) (routine) (following)
    V67.9
  cancer chemotherapy V67.2
  chemotherapy V67.2
  fracture V67.4
  high-risk medication V67.51
  injury NEC V67.59
  postpartum
    immediately after delivery V24.0
    routine V24.2
  psychiatric V67.3
  psychotherapy V67.3
  radiotherapy V67.1
  specified condition NEC V67.59
  surgery V67.0
  treatment V67.9
    combined NEC V67.6
    fracture V67.4
    involving high-risk medication NEC V67.51
    mental disorder V67.3
    specified NEC V67.59
Fong's syndrome (hereditary
    osteoonychodysplasia) 756.89
Food
  allergy 693.1
  anaphylactic shock—*see* Anaphylactic shock,
    due to, food
  asphyxia (from aspiration or inhalation) (*see*
    also Asphyxia, food) 933.1
  choked on (*see also* Asphyxia, food) 933.1
  deprivation 994.2
    specified kind of food NEC 269.8
  intoxication (*see also* Poisoning, food) 005.9
  lack of 994.2
  poisoning (*see also* Poisoning, food) 005.9
  refusal or rejection NEC 307.59
  strangulation or suffocation (*see also* Asphyxia,
    food) 933.1
  toxemia (*see also* Poisoning, food) 005.9
Foot —*see also* condition
  and mouth disease 078.4
  process disease 581.3
Foramen ovale (nonclosure) (patent) (persistent)
    745.5
Forbes' (glycogen storage) disease 271.0

Forbes-Albright syndrome (nonpuerperal amenorrhea and lactation associated with pituitary tumor) 253.1
Forced birth or delivery NEC 669.8
affecting fetus or newborn NEC 763.8
Forceps
delivery NEC 669.5
affecting fetus or newborn 763.2
Fordyce's disease (ectopic sebaceous glands) (mouth) 750.26
Fordyce-Fox disease (apocrine miliaria) 705.82
Forearm —*see* condition
Foreign body

Note—For foreign body with open wound or other injury, see Wound, open, or the type of injury specified.

---

accidentally left during a procedure 998.4
anterior chamber (eye) 871.6
  magnetic 871.5
    retained or old 360.51
  retained or old 360.61
ciliary body (eye) 871.6
  magnetic 871.5
    retained or old 360.52
  retained or old 360.62
entering through orifice (current) (old)
  accessory sinus 932
  air passage (upper) 933.0
    lower 934.8
  alimentary canal 938
  alveolar process 935.0
  antrum (Highmore) 932
  anus 937
  appendix 936
  asphyxia due to (*see also* Asphyxia, food) 933.1
  auditory canal 931
  auricle 931
  bladder 939.0
  bronchioles 934.8
  bronchus (main) 934.1
  buccal cavity 935.0
  canthus (inner) 930.1
  cecum 936
  cervix (canal) uterine 939.1
  coil, ileocecal 936
  colon 936
  conjunctiva 930.1
  conjunctival sac 930.1
  cornea 930.0
  digestive organ or tract NEC 938
  duodenum 936
  ear (external) 931
  esophagus 935.1
  eye (external) 930.9
    combined sites 930.8
    intraocular—*see* Foreign body, by site
    specified site NEC 930.8
  eyeball 930.8
    intraocular—*see* Foreign body, intraocular
  eyelid 930.1
    retained or old 374.86
  frontal sinus 932
  gastrointestinal tract 938
  genitourinary tract 939.9
  globe 930.8
    penetrating 871.6
      magnetic 871.5
        retained or old 360.50
      retained or old 360.60

Foreign body—*continued*
  gum 935.0
  Highmore's antrum 932
  hypopharynx 933.0
  ileocecal coil 936
  ileum 936
  inspiration (of) 933.1
  intestine (large) (small) 936
  lacrimal apparatus, duct, gland, or sac 930.2
  larynx 933.1
  lung 934.8
  maxillary sinus 932
  mouth 935.0
  nasal sinus 932
  nasopharynx 933.0
  nose (passage) 932
  nostril 932
  oral cavity 935.0
  palate 935.0
  penis 939.3
  pharynx 933.0
  pyriform sinus 933.0
  rectosigmoid 937
    junction 937
  rectum 937
  respiratory tract 934.9
    specified part NEC 934.8
  sclera 930.1
  sinus 932
    accessory 932
    frontal 932
    maxillary 932
    nasal 932
    pyriform 933.0
  small intestine 936
  stomach (hairball) 935.2
  suffocation by (*see also* Asphyxia, food) 933.1
  swallowed 938
    tongue 933.0
  tear ducts or glands 930.2
  throat 933.0
  tongue 935.0
    swallowed 933.0
  tonsil, tonsillar 933.0
    fossa 933.0
  trachea 934.0
  ureter 939.0
  urethra 939.0
  uterus (any part) 939.1
  vagina 939.2
  vulva 939.2
  wind pipe 934.0
granuloma (old) 728.82
  bone 733.99
  in operative wound (inadvertently left) 998.4
    due to surgical material intentionally
      left—*see* Complications, due to
      (presence of) any device, implant, or
      graft classified to 996.0-996.5 NEC
  muscle 728.82
  skin 709.4
  soft tissue NEC 728.82
  subcutaneous tissue 709.4
in
  bone (residual) 733.99
  open wound—*see* Wound, open, by site
    complicated
  soft tissue (residual) 729.6
inadvertently left in operation wound (causing
  adhesions, obstruction, or perforation) 998.4

Foreign body—*continued*
  ingestion, ingested NEC 938
  inhalation or inspiration (*see also* Asphyxia,
    food) 933.1
  internal organ, not entering through an
    orifice—*see* Injury, internal, by site, with
    open wound
  intraocular (nonmagnetic) 871.6
    combined sites 871.6
      magnetic 871.5
        retained or old 360.59
      retained or old 360.69
    magnetic 871.5
      retained or old 360.50
    retained or old 360.60
    specified site NEC 871.6
      magnetic 871.5
        retained or old 360.59
      retained or old 360.69
  iris (nonmagnetic) 871.6
    magnetic 871.5
      retained or old 360.52
    retained or old 360.62
  lens (nonmagnetic) 871.6
    magnetic 871.5
      retained or old 360.53
    retained or old 360.63
  lid, eye 930.1
  ocular muscle 870.4
    retained or old 376.6
  old or residual
    bone 733.99
    eyelid 374.86
    middle ear 385.83
    muscle 729.6
      ocular 376.6
    retrobulbar 376.6
    skin 709.4
    soft tissue 729.6
    subcutaneous tissue 709.4
  operation wound, left accidentally 998.4
  orbit 870.4
    retained or old 376.6
  posterior wall, eye 871.6
    magnetic 871.5
      retained or old 360.55
    retained or old 360.65
  respiratory tree 934.9
    specified site NEC 934.8
  retained (old) (nonmagnetic) (in)
    anterior chamber (eye) 360.61
      magnetic 360.51
    ciliary body 360.62
      magnetic 360.52
    eyelid 374.86
    globe 360.60
      magnetic 360.50
    intraocular 360.60
      magnetic 360.50
      specified site NEC 360.69
        magnetic 360.59
    iris 360.62
      magnetic 360.52
    lens 360.63
      magnetic 360.53
    muscle 729.6
    orbit 376.6
    posterior wall of globe 360.65
      magnetic 360.55
    retina 360.65
      magnetic 360.55

Foreign body—*continued*
  retrobulbar 376.6
  soft tissue 729.6
  vitreous 360.64
    magnetic 360.54
  retina 871.6
    magnetic 871.5
      retained or old 360.55
    retained or old 360.65
  superficial, without major open wound (*see also*
    Injury, superficial, by site) 919.6
  swallowed NEC 938
  vitreous (humor) 871.6
    magnetic 871.5
      retained or old 360.54
    retained or old 360.64
Forking, aqueduct of Sylvius 742.3
  with spina bifida (*see also* Spina bifida) 741.0
Formation
  bone in scar tissue (skin) 709.3
  connective tissue in vitreous 379.25
  Elschnig pearls (postcataract extraction) 366.51
  hyaline in cornea 371.49
  sequestrum in bone (due to infection) (*see also*
    Osteomyelitis) 730.1
  valve
    colon, congenital 751.5
    ureter (congenital) 753.29
Formication 782.0
Fort Bragg fever 100.89
Fossa —*see also* condition
  pyriform—*see* condition
Foster-Kennedy syndrome 377.04
Fothergill's
  disease, meaning scarlatina anginosa 034.1
  neuralgia (*see also* Neuralgia, trigeminal) 350.1
Foul breath 784.9
Found dead (cause unknown) 798.9
Foundling V20.0
Fournier's disease (idiopathic gangrene) 608.83
Fourth
  cranial nerve—*see* condition
  disease 057.8
  molar 520.1
Foville's syndrome 344.89
Fox's
  disease (apocrine miliaria) 705.82
  impetigo (contagiosa) 684
Fox-Fordyce disease (apocrine miliaria) 705.82

Fracture (abduction) (adduction) (avulsion) (compression) (crush) (dislocation) (oblique) (separation) (closed) 829.0

Note—For fracture of any of the following sites with fracture of other bones—see Fracture, multiple.

"Closed" includes the following descriptions of fractures, with or without delayed healing, unless they are specified as open or compound:

> *comminuted*
> *depressed*
> *elevated*
> *fissured*
> *greenstick*
> *impacted*
> *linear*
> *march*
> *simple*
> *slipped epiphysis*
> *spiral*
> *unspecified*

"Open" includes the following descriptions of fractures, with or without delayed healing:

> *compound*
> *infected*
> *missile*
> *puncture*
> *with foreign body*

For late effect of fracture, see Late, effect, fracture, by site.

with
  internal injuries in same region (conditions classifiable to 860-869)—*see also* Injury, internal, by site
  pelvic region—*see* Fracture, pelvis
acetabulum (with visceral injury) (closed) 808.0
  open 808.1
acromion (process) (closed) 811.01
  open 811.11
alveolus (closed) 802.8
  open 802.9
ankle (malleolus) (closed) 824.8
  bimalleolar (Dupuytren's) (Pott's) 824.4
    open 824.5
  bone 825.21
    open 825.31
  lateral malleolus only (fibular) 824.2
    open 824.3
  medial malleolus only (tibial) 824.0
    open 824.1
  open 824.9
  pathologic 733.16
  talus 825.21
    open 825.31
  trimalleolar 824.6
    open 824.7
antrum—*see* Fracture, skull, base
arm (closed) 818.0
  and leg(s) (any bones) 828.0
    open 828.1
  both (any bones) (with rib(s)) (with sternum) 819.0
    open 819.1
  lower 813.80
    open 813.90

Fracture—*continued*
  open 818.1
  upper—*see* Fracture, humerus
astragalus (closed) 825.21
  open 825.31
atlas—*see* Fracture, vertebra, cervical, first
axis—*see* Fracture, vertebra, cervical, second
back—*see* Fracture, vertebra, by site
Barton's—*see* Fracture, radius, lower end
basal (skull)—*see* Fracture, skull, base
Bennett's (closed) 815.01
  open 815.11
bimalleolar (closed) 824.4
  open 824.5
bone (closed) NEC 829.0
  birth injury NEC 767.3
  open 829.1
  pathologic NEC (*see also* Fracture, pathologic) 733.10
boot top—*see* Fracture, fibula
boxers'—*see* Fracture, metacarpal bone(s)
breast bone—*see* Fracture, sternum
bucket handle (semilunar cartilage)—*see* Tear, meniscus
bursting—*see* Fracture, phalanx, hand, distal
calcaneus (closed) 825.0
  open 825.1
capitate (bone) (closed) 814.07
  open 814.17
capitellum (humerus) (closed) 812.49
  open 812.59
carpal bone(s) (wrist NEC) (closed) 814.00
  open 814.10
  specified site NEC 814.09
    open 814.19
cartilage, knee (semilunar)—*see* Tear, meniscus
cervical—*see* Fracture, vertebra, cervical
chauffeur's—*see* Fracture, ulna, lower end
chisel—*see* Fracture, radius, upper end
clavicle (interligamentous part) (closed) 810.00
  acromial end 810.03
    open 810.13
  due to birth trauma 767.2
  open 810.10
  shaft (middle third) 810.02
    open 810.12
  sternal end 810.01
    open 810.11
clayshovelers'—*see* Fracture, vertebra, cervical
coccyx—*see also* Fracture, vertebra, coccyx
  complicating delivery 665.6
collar bone—*see* Fracture, clavicle
Colles' (reversed) (closed) 813.41
  open 813.51
comminuted—*see* Fracture, by site
compression—*see also* Fracture, by site
  nontraumatic—*see* Fracture, pathologic
congenital 756.9
coracoid process (closed) 811.02
  open 811.12
coronoid process (ulna) (closed) 813.02
  mandible (closed) 802.23
    open 802.33
  open 813.12
costochondral junction—*see* Fracture, rib
costosternal junction—*see* Fracture, rib
cranium—*see* Fracture, skull, by site
cricoid cartilage (closed) 807.5
  open 807.6
cuboid (ankle) (closed) 825.23
  open 825.33

Fracture—*continued*
  cuneiform
    foot (closed) 825.24
      open 825.34
    wrist (closed) 814.03
      open 814.13
  due to
    birth injury—*see* Birth injury, fracture
    gunshot—*see* Fracture, by site, open
    neoplasm—*see* Fracture, pathologic
    osteoporosis—*see* Fracture, pathologic
  Dupuytren's (ankle) (fibula) (closed) 824.4
    open 824.5
    radius 813.42
      open 813.52
  Duverney's—*see* Fracture, ilium
  elbow—*see also* Fracture, humerus, lower end
    olecranon (process) (closed) 813.01
      open 813.11
    supracondylar (closed) 812.41
      open 812.51
  ethmoid (bone) (sinus)—*see* Fracture, skull,
    base
  face bone(s) (closed) NEC 802.8
    with
      other bone(s)—*see also* Fracture, multiple,
        skull
      skull—*see also* Fracture, skull
        involving other bones—*see* Fracture,
          multiple, skull
    open 802.9
  fatigue—*see* Fracture, march
  femur, femoral (closed) 821.00
    cervicotrochanteric 820.03
      open 820.13
    condyles, epicondyles 821.21
      open 821.31
    distal end—*see* Fracture, femur, lower end
    epiphysis (separation)
      capital 820.01
        open 820.11
      head 820.01
        open 820.11
      lower 821.22
        open 821.32
      trochanteric 820.01
        open 820.11
      upper 820.01
        open 820.11
    head 820.09
      open 820.19
    lower end or extremity (distal end) (closed)
      821.20
      condyles, epicondyles 821.21
        open 821.31
      epiphysis (separation) 821.22
        open 821.32
      multiple sites 821.29
        open 821.39
      open 821.30
      specified site NEC 821.29
        open 821.39
      supracondylar 821.23
        open 821.33
      T-shaped 821.21
        open 821.31
    neck (closed) 820.8
      base (cervicotrochanteric) 820.03
        open 820.13
      extracapsular 820.20
        open 820.30

Fracture—*continued*
    intertrochanteric (section) 820.21
      open 820.31
    intracapsular 820.00
      open 820.10
    intratrochanteric 820.21
      open 821.31
    midcervical 820.02
      open 820.12
    open 820.9
    pathologic 733.14
      specified part NEC 733.15
    specified site NEC 820.09
      open 820.19
    transcervical 820.02
      open 820.12
    transtrochanteric 820.20
      open 820.30
    open 821.10
    pathologic 733.14
      specified part NEC 733.15
    peritrochanteric (section) 820.20
      open 820.30
    shaft (lower third) (middle third) (upper third)
      821.01
      open 821.11
    subcapital 820.09
      open 820.19
    subtrochanteric (region) (section) 820.22
      open 820.32
    supracondylar 821.23
      open 821.33
    transepiphyseal 820.01
      open 820.11
    trochanter (greater) (lesser) (*see also* Fracture,
      femur, neck, by site) 820.20
      open 820.30
    T-shaped, into knee joint 821.21
      open 821.31
    upper end 820.8
      open 820.9
  fibula (closed) 823.81
    with tibia 823.82
      open 823.92
    distal end 824.8
      open 824.9
    epiphysis
      lower 824.8
        open 824.9
      upper—*see* Fracture, fibula, upper end
    head—*see* Fracture, fibula, upper end
    involving ankle 824.2
      open 824.3
    lower end or extremity 824.8
      open 824.9
    malleolus (external) (lateral) 824.2
      open 824.3
    open NEC 823.91
    pathologic 733.16
    proximal end—*see* Fracture, fibula, upper end
    shaft 823.21
      with tibia 823.22
        open 823.32
      open 823.31
    upper end or extremity (epiphysis) (head)
      (proximal end) (styloid) 823.01
      with tibia 823.02
        open 823.12
      open 823.11

Fracture—*continued*
  finger(s), of one hand (closed) (*see also*
    Fracture, phalanx, hand) 816.00
    with
      metacarpal bone(s), of same hand 817.0
        open 817.1
      thumb of same hand 816.03
        open 816.13
    open 816.10
  foot, except toe(s) alone (closed) 825.20
    open 825.30
  forearm (closed) NEC 813.80
    lower end (distal end) (lower epiphysis)
      813.40
      open 813.50
      open 813.90
    shaft 813.20
      open 813.30
    upper end (proximal end) (upper epiphysis)
      813.00
      open 813.10
  fossa, anterior, middle, or posterior—*see*
    Fracture, skull, base
  frontal (bone)—*see also* Fracture, skull, vault
    sinus—*see* Fracture, skull base
  Galeazzi's—*see* Fracture, radius, lower end
  glenoid (cavity) (fossa) (scapula) (closed)
    811.03
    open 811.13
  Gosselin's—*see* Fracture, ankle
  greenstick—*see* Fracture, by site
  grenade-throwers'—*see* Fracture, humerus, shaft
  gutter—*see* Fracture, skull, vault
  hamate (closed) 814.08
    open 814.18
  hand, one (closed) 815.00
    carpals 814.00
      open 814.10
      specified site NEC 814.09
        open 814.19
    metacarpals 815.00
      open 815.10
    multiple, bones of one hand 817.0
      open 817.1
      open 815.10
    phalanges (*see also* Fracture, phalanx, hand)
      816.00
      open 816.10
  healing or old
    aftercare or convalescence V54.9
    change of cast V54.8
    complications—*see* condition
    removal of
      cast V54.8
      fixation device
        external V54.8
        internal V54.0
  heel bone (closed) 825.0
    open 825.1
  hip (closed) (*see also* Fracture, femur, neck)
    820.8
    open 820.9
    pathologic 733.14
  humerus (closed) 812.20
    anatomical neck 812.02
      open 812.12
    articular process (*see also* Fracture, humerus,
      condyle(s) 812.44
      open 812.54

Fracture—*continued*
  capitellum 812.49
    open 812.59
  condyle(s) 812.44
    lateral (external) 812.42
      open 812.52
    medial (internal epicondyle) 812.43
      open 812.53
      open 812.54
  distal end—*see* Fracture, humerus, lower end
  epiphysis
    lower (*see also* Fracture, humerus,
      condyle(s)) 812.44
      open 812.54
    upper 812.09
      open 812.19
  external condyle 812.42
    open 812.52
  great tuberosity 812.03
    open 812.13
  head 812.09
    open 812.19
  internal epicondyle 812.43
    open 812.53
  lesser tuberosity 812.09
    open 812.19
  lower end or extremity (distal end) (*see also*
    Fracture, humerus, by site) 812.40
    multiple sites NEC 812.49
      open 812.59
    open 812.50
    specified site NEC 812.49
      open 812.59
  neck 812.01
    open 812.11
    open 812.30
  pathologic 733.11
  proximal end—*see* Fracture, humerus, upper
    end
  shaft 812.21
    open 812.31
  supracondylar 812.41
    open 812.51
  surgical neck 812.01
    open 812.11
  trochlea 812.49
    open 812.59
  T-shaped 812.44
    open 812.54
  tuberosity—*see* Fracture, humerus, upper end
  upper end or extremity (proximal end) (*see
    also* Fracture, humerus, by site) 812.00
    open 812.10
    specified site NEC 812.09
      open 812.19
  hyoid bone (closed) 807.5
    open 807.6
  hyperextension—*see* Fracture, radius, lower end
  ilium (with visceral injury) (closed) 808.41
    open 808.51
  impaction, impacted—*see* Fracture, by site
  incus—*see* Fracture, skull, base
  innominate bone (with visceral injury) (closed)
    808.49
    open 808.59
  instep, of one foot (closed) 825.20
    with toe(s) of same foot 827.0
      open 827.1
    open 825.30

Fracture—*continued*

internal
  ear—*see* Fracture, skull, base
  semilunar cartilage, knee—*see* Tear, meniscus, medial
intertrochanteric—*see* Fracture, femur, neck, intertrochanteric
ischium (with visceral injury) (closed) 808.42
  open 808.52
jaw (bone) (lower) (closed) (*see also* Fracture, mandible) 802.20
  angle 802.25
    open 802.35
  open 802.30
  upper—*see* Fracture, maxilla
knee
  cap (closed) 822.0
    open 822.1
  cartilage (semilunar)—*see* Tear, meniscus
labyrinth (osseous)—*see* Fracture, skull, base
larynx (closed) 807.5
  open 807.6
late effect—*see* Late, effects (of), fracture
Le Fort's—*see* Fracture, maxilla
leg (closed) 827.0
  with rib(s) or sternum 828.0
    open 828.1
  both (any bones) 828.0
    open 828.1
  lower—*see* Fracture, tibia
    open 827.1
  upper—*see* Fracture, femur
limb
  lower (multiple) (closed) NEC 827.0
    open 827.1
  upper (multiple) (closed) NEC 818.0
    open 818.1
long bones, due to birth trauma—*see* Birth injury, fracture
lumbar—*see* Fracture, vertebra, lumbar
lunate bone (closed) 814.02
  open 814.12
malar bone (closed) 802.4
  open 802.5
Malgaigne's (closed) 808.43
  open 808.53
malleolus (closed)0 824.8
  bimalleolar 824.4
    open 824.5
  lateral 824.2
    and medial—*see also* Fracture, malleolus, bimalleolar
      with lip of tibia—*see* Fracture, malleolus, trimalleolar
    open 824.3
  medial (closed) 824.0
    and lateral—*see also* Fracture, malleolus, bimalleolar
      with lip of tibia—*see* Fracture, malleolus, trimalleolar
    open 824.1
  open 824.9
  trimalleolar (closed) 824.6
    open 824.7
malleus—*see* Fracture, skull, base
malunion 733.81

Fracture—*continued*

mandible (closed) 802.20
  angle 802.25
    open 802.35
  body 802.28
    alveolar border 802.27
      open 802.37
    open 802.38
    symphysis 802.26
      open 802.36
  condylar process 802.21
    open 802.31
  coronoid process 802.23
    open 802.33
  multiple sites 802.29
    open 802.39
  open 802.30
  ramus NEC 802.24
    open 802.34
  subcondylar 802.22
    open 802.32
manubrium—*see* Fracture, sternum
march (closed) 825.20
  open 825.30
maxilla, maxillary (superior) (upper jaw) (closed) 802.4
  inferior—*see* Fracture, mandible
  open 802.5
meniscus, knee—*see* Tear, meniscus
metacarpus, metacarpal (bone(s)), of one hand (closed) 815.00
  with phalanx, phalanges, hand (finger(s)) (thumb) of same hand 817.0
    open 817.1
  base 815.02
    first metacarpal 815.01
      open 815.11
    open 815.12
    thumb 815.01
      open 815.11
  multiple sites 815.09
    open 815.19
  neck 815.04
    open 815.14
  open 815.10
  shaft 815.03
    open 815.13
metatarsus, metatarsal (bone(s)), of one foot (closed) 825.25
  with tarsal bone(s) 825.29
    open 825.39
  open 825.35
Monteggia's (closed) 813.03
  open 813.13
Moore's—*see* Fracture, radius, lower end
multangular bone (closed)
  larger 814.05
    open 814.15
  smaller 814.06
    open 814.16
multiple (closed) 829.0

Fracture—*continued*

Note—Multiple fractures of sites classifiable to the same three- or four-digit category are coded to that category, except for sites classifiable to 810-818 or 820-827 in different limbs.

Multiple fractures of sites classifiable to different fourth-digit subdivisions within the same three- digit category should be dealt with according to coding rules.

Multiple fractures of sites classifiable to different three-digit categories (identifiable from the listing under "Fracture"), and of sites classifiable to 810-818 or 820-827 in different limbs should be coded according to the following list, which should be referred to in the following priority order: skull or face bones, pelvis or vertebral column, legs, arms.

arm (multiple bones in same arm except in hand alone) (sites classifiable to 810-817 with sites classifiable to a different three-digit category in 810-817 in same arm) (closed) 818.0
  open 818.1
arms, both or arm(s) with rib(s) or sternum (sites classifiable to 810-818 with sites classifiable to same range of categories in other limb or to 807) (closed) 819.0
  open 819.1
bones of trunk NEC (closed) 809.0
  open 809.1
hand, metacarpal bone(s) with phalanx or phalanges of same hand (sites classifiable to 815 with sites classifiable to 816 in same hand) (closed) 817.0
  open 817.1
leg (multiple bones in same leg) (sites classifiable to 820-826 with sites classifiable to a different three-digit category in that range in same leg) (closed) 827.0
  open 827.1
legs, both or leg(s) with arm(s), rib(s), or sternum (sites classifiable to 820-827 with sites classifiable to same range of categories in other leg or to 807 or 810-819) (closed) 828.0
  open 828.1
open 829.1
pelvis with other bones except skull or face bones (sites classifiable to 808 with sites classifiable to 805-807 or 810-829) (closed) 809.0
  open 809.1
skull, specified or unspecified bones, or face bone(s) with any other bone(s) (sites classifiable to 800-803 with sites classifiable to 805-829) (closed) 804.0

Fracture—*continued*

Note—Use the following fifth-digit subclassification with categories 800, 801, 803, and 804:

0 unspecified state of consciousness
1 with no loss of consciousness
2 with brief [less than one hour] loss of consciousness
3 with moderate [1-24 hours] loss of consciousness
4 with prolonged [more than 24 hours] loss of consciousness and return to pre-existing conscious level
5 with prolonged [more than 24 hours] loss of consciousness, without return to pre-existing conscious level
Use fifth-digit 5 to designate when a patient is unconcious and dies before regaining conciousness, regardless of the duration of the loss of conciousness
6 with loss of consciousness of unspecified duration
9 with concussion, unspecified

with
  contusion, cerebral 804.1
  epidural hemorrhage 804.2
  extradural hemorrhage 804.2
  hemorrhage (intracranial) NEC 804.3
  intracranial injury NEC 804.4
  laceration, cerebral 804.1
  subarachnoid hemorrhage 804.2
  subdural hemorrhage 804.2
  open 804.5
  with
    contusion, cerebral 804.6
    epidural hemorrhage 804.7
    extradural hemorrhage 804.7
    hemorrhage (intracranial) NEC 804.8
    intracranial injury NEC 804.9
    laceration, cerebral 804.6
    subarachnoid hemorrhage 804.7
    subdural hemorrhage 804.7
  vertebral column with other bones, except skull or face bones (sites classifiable to 805 or 806 with sites classifiable to 807-808 or 810-829) (closed) 809.0
    open 809.1
nasal (bone(s)) (closed) 802.0
  open 802.1
  sinus—Fracture, skull, base
navicular
  carpal (wrist) (closed) 814.01
    open 814.11
  tarsal (ankle) (closed) 825.22
    open 825.32
neck—*see* Fracture, vertebra, cervical
neural arch—*see* Fracture, vertebra, by site
nonunion 733.82
nose, nasal, (bone) (septum) (closed) 802.0
  open 802.1
occiput—*see* Fracture, skull, base
odontoid process—*see* Fracture, vertebra, cervical
olecranon (process) (ulna) (closed) 813.01
  open 813.11
open 829.1
orbit, orbital (bone) (region) (closed) 802.8
  floor (blow-out) 802.6
    open 802.7

Fracture—*continued*
  open 802.9
  roof—*see* Fracture, skull, base
  specified part NEC 802.8
    open 802.9
  os
    calcis (closed) 825.0
      open 825.1
    magnum (closed) 814.07
      open 814.17
    pubis (with visceral injury) (closed) 808.2
      open 808.3
    triquetrum (closed) 814.03
      open 814.13
  osseous
    auditory meatus—*see* Fracture, skull, base
    labyrinth—*see* Fracture, skull, base
  ossicles, auditory (incus) (malleus)
      (stapes)—*see* Fracture, skull, base
  osteoporotic—*see* Fracture, pathologic
  palate (closed) 802.8
    open 802.9
  paratrooper—*see* Fracture, tibia, lower end
  parietal bone—*see* Fracture, skull, vault
  parry—*see* Fracture, Monteggia's
  patella (closed) 822.0
    open 822.1
  pathologic (cause unknown) 733.10
    ankle 733.16
    femur (neck) 733.14
      specified NEC 733.15
    fibula 733.16
    hip 733.14
    humerus 733.11
    radius 733.12
    specified site NEC 733.19
    tibia 733.16
    ulna 733.12
    vertebrae (collapse) 733.13
    wrist 733.12
  pedicle (of vertebral arch)—*see* Fracture,
      vertebra, by site
  pelvis, pelvic (bone(s)) (with visceral injury)
      (closed) 808.8
    multiple (with disruption of pelvic circle)
      808.43
      open 808.53
    open 808.9
    rim (closed) 808.49
      open 808.59
  peritrochanteric (closed) 820.20
    open 820.30
  phalanx, phalanges, of one
    foot (closed) 826.0
      with bone(s) of same lower limb 827.0
        open 827.1
      open 826.1
    hand (closed) 816.00
      with metacarpal bone(s) of same hand 817.0
        open 817.1
      distal 816.02
        open 816.12
      middle 816.01
        open 816.11
      multiple sites NEC 816.03
        open 816.13
      open 816.10
      proximal 816.01
        open 816.11
  pisiform (closed) 814.04
    open 814.14

Fracture—*continued*
  pond—Fracture, skull, vault
  Pott's (closed) 824.4
    open 824.5
  prosthetic device, internal—*see* Complications,
      mechanical
  pubis (with visceral injury) (closed) 808.2
    open 808.3
  Quervain's (closed) 814.01
    open 814.11
  radius (alone) (closed) 813.81
    with ulna NEC 813.83
      open 813.93
    distal end—*see* Fracture, radius, lower end
    epiphysis
      lower—*see* Fracture, radius, lower end
      upper—*see* Fracture, radius, upper end
    head—*see* Fracture, radius, upper end
    lower end or extremity (distal end) (lower
        epiphysis) 813.42
      with ulna (lower end) 813.44
        open 813.54
      open 813.52
    neck—*see* Fracture, radius, upper end
    open NEC 813.91
    pathologic 733.12
    proximal end—*see* Fracture, radius, upper end
    shaft (closed) 813.21
      with ulna (shaft) 813.23
        open 813.33
      open 813.31
    upper end 813.07
      with ulna (upper end) 813.08
        open 813.18
      epiphysis 813.05
        open 813.15
      head 813.05
        open 813.15
      multiple sites 813.07
        open 813.17
      neck 813.06
        open 813.16
      open 813.17
      specified site NEC 813.07
        open 813.17
  ramus
    inferior or superior (with visceral injury)
        (closed) 808.2
      open 808.3
    ischium—*see* Fracture, ischium
    mandible 802.24
      open 802.34
  rib(s) (closed) 807.0

Note—Use the following fifth-digit
subclassification with categories 807.0-807.1:

0 rib(s), unspecified
1 one rib
2 two ribs
3 three ribs
4 four ribs
5 five ribs
6 six ribs
7 seven ribs
8 eight or more ribs
9 multiple ribs, unspecified

    with flail chest (open) 807.4
    open 807.1
  root, tooth 873.63
    complicated 873.73

Fracture—*continued*
  sacrum—*see* Fracture, vertebra, sacrum
  scaphoid
    ankle (closed) 825.22
      open 825.32
    wrist (closed) 814.01
      open 814.11
  scapula (closed) 811.00
    acromial, acromion (process) 811.01
      open 811.11
    body 811.09
      open 811.19
    coracoid process 811.02
      open 811.12
    glenoid (cavity) (fossa) 811.03
      open 811.13
    neck 811.03
      open 811.13
    open 811.10
  semilunar
    bone, wrist (closed) 814.02
      open 814.12
    cartilage (interior) (knee)—*see* Tear, meniscus
  sesamoid bone—*see* Fracture, by site
  Shepherd's (closed) 825.21
    open 825.31
  shoulder—*see also* Fracture, humerus, upper end
    blade—*see* Fracture, scapula
  silverfork—*see* Fracture, radius, lower end
  sinus (ethmoid) (frontal) (maxillary) (nasal)
    (sphenoidal)—*see* Fracture, skull, base
    maxillary—*see* Fracture, maxilla
  Skillern's—*see* Fracture, radius, shaft
  skull (multiple NEC) (with face bones) (closed)
    803.0

> Note—Use the following fifth-digit
> subclassification with categories 800, 801, 803,
> and 804:
>
> *0 unspecified state of consciousness*
> *1 with no loss of consciousness*
> *2 with brief [less than one hour] loss of*
> *   consciousness*
> *3 with moderate [1-24 hours] loss of*
> *   consciousness*
> *4 with prolonged [more than 24 hours] loss of*
> *   consciousness and return to pre-existing*
> *   conscious level*
> *5 with prolonged [more than 24 hours] loss of*
> *   consciousness, without return to pre-existing*
> *   conscious level*
> *Use fifth-digit 5 to designate when a patient is*
> *unconscious and dies before regaining*
> *consciousness, regardless of the duration of the*
> *loss of consciousness*
> *6 with loss of consciousness of unspecified*
> *   duration*
> *9 with concussion, unspecified*

    with
      contusion, cerebral 803.1
      epidural hemorrhage 803.2
      extradural hemorrhage 803.2
      hemorrhage (intracranial) NEC 803.3
      intracranial injury NEC 803.4
      laceration, cerebral 803.1
      other bones—*see* Fracture, multiple, skull
      subarachnoid hemorrhage 803.2
      subdural hemorrhage 803.2

Fracture—*continued*
  base (antrum) (ethmoid bone) (fossa) (internal
    ear) (nasal sinus) (occiput) (sphenoid)
    (temporal bone) (closed) 801.0
    with
      contusion, cerebral 801.1
      epidural hemorrhage 801.2
      extradural hemorrhage 801.2
      hemorrhage (intracranial) NEC 801.3
      intracranial injury NEC 801.4
      laceration, cerebral 801.1
      subarachnoid hemorrhage 801.2
      subdural hemorrhage 801.2
    open 801.5
      with
        contusion, cerebral 801.6
        epidural hemorrhage 801.7
        extradural hemorrhage 801.7
        hemorrhage (intracranial) NEC 801.8
        intracranial injury NEC 801.9
        laceration, cerebral 801.6
        subarachnoid hemorrhage 801.7
        subdural hemorrhage 801.7
  birth injury 767.3
  face bones—*see* Fracture, face bones
  open 803.5
    with
      contusion, cerebral 803.6
      epidural hemorrhage 803.7
      extradural hemorrhage 803.7
      hemorrhage (intracranial) NEC 803.8
      intracranial injury NEC 803.9
      laceration, cerebral 803.6
      subarachnoid hemorrhage 803.7
      subdural hemorrhage 803.7
  vault (frontal bone) (parietal bone) (vertex)
    (closed) 800.0
    with
      contusion, cerebral 800.1
      epidural hemorrhage 800.2
      extradural hemorrhage 800.2
      hemorrhage (intracranial) NEC 800.3
      intracranial injury NEC 800.4
      laceration, cerebral 800.1
      subarachnoid hemorrhage 800.2
      subdural hemorrhage 800.2
    open 800.5
      with
        contusion, cerebral 800.6
        epidural hemorrhage 800.7
        extradural hemorrhage 800.7
        hemorrhage (intracranial) NEC 800.8
        intracranial injury NEC 800.9
        laceration, cerebral 800.6
        subarachnoid hemorrhage 800.7
        subdural hemorrhage 800.7
  Smith's 813.41
    open 813.51
  sphenoid (bone) (sinus)—*see* Fracture, skull,
    base
  spine—*see also* Fracture, vertebra, by site
    due to birth trauma 767.4
  spinous process—*see* Fracture, vertebra, by site
  spontaneous—*see* Fracture, pathologic
  sprinters'—*see* Fracture, ilium
  stapes—*see* Fracture, skull, base
  stave—*see also* Fracture, metacarpus,
    metacarpal bone(s)
    spine—*see* Fracture, tibia, upper end
  sternum (closed) 807.2
    with flail chest (open) 807.4

Fracture—*continued*
  open 807.3
  Stieda's—*see* Fracture, femur, lower end
  stress—*see* Fracture, pathologic
  styloid process
    metacarpal (closed) 815.02
      open 815.12
    radius—*see* Fracture, radius, lower end
    temporal bone—*see* Fracture, skull, base
    ulna—*see* Fracture, ulna, lower end
  supracondylar, elbow 812.41
    open 812.51
  symphysis pubis (with visceral injury) (closed)
    808.2
    open 808.3
  talus (ankle bone) (closed) 825.21
    open 825.31
  tarsus, tarsal bone(s) (with metatarsus) of one
    foot (closed) NEC 825.29
    open 825.39
  temporal bone (styloid)—*see* Fracture, skull,
    base
  tendon—*see* Sprain, by site
  thigh—*see* Fracture, femur, shaft
  thumb (and finger(s)) of one hand (closed) (*see*
    also Fracture, phalanx, hand) 816.00
    with metacarpal bone(s) of same hand 817.0
      open 817.1
    metacarpal(s)—*see* Fracture, metacarpus
    open 816.10
  thyroid cartilage (closed) 807.5
    open 807.6
  tibia (closed) 823.80
    with fibula 823.82
      open 823.92
    condyles—*see* Fracture, tibia, upper end
    distal end 824.8
      open 824.9
    epiphysis
      lower 824.8
        open 824.9
      upper—*see* Fracture, tibia, upper end
    head (involving knee joint)—*see* Fracture,
      tibia, upper end
    intercondyloid eminence—*see* Fracture, tibia,
      upper end
    involving ankle 824.0
      open 824.1
    lower end or extremity (anterior lip) (posterior
      lip) 824.8
      open 824.9
    malleolus (internal) (medial) 824.0
      open 824.1
    open NEC 823.90
    pathologic 733.16
    proximal end—*see* Fracture, tibia, upper end
    shaft 823.20
      with fibula 823.22
        open 823.32
      open 823.30
    spine—*see* Fracture, tibia, upper end
    tuberosity—*see* Fracture, tibia, upper end
    upper end or extremity (condyle) (epiphysis)
      (head) (spine) (proximal end) (tuberosity)
      823.00
      with fibula 823.02
        open 823.12
      open 823.10
  toe(s), of one foot (closed) 826.0
    with bone(s) of same lower limb 827.0
      open 827.1

Fracture—*continued*
  open 826.1
  tooth (root) 873.63
    complicated 873.73
  trachea (closed) 807.5
    open 807.6
  transverse process—*see* Fracture, vertebra, by
    site
  trapezium (closed) 814.05
    open 814.15
  trapezoid bone (closed) 814.06
    open 814.16
  trimalleolar (closed) 824.6
    open 824.7
  triquetral (bone) (closed) 814.03
    open 814.13
  trochanter (greater) (lesser) (closed) (*see also*
    Fracture, femur, neck, by site) 820.20
    open 820.30
  trunk (bones) (closed) 809.0
    open 809.1
  tuberosity (external)—*see* Fracture, by site
  ulna (alone) (closed) 813.82
    with radius NEC 813.83
      open 813.93
    coronoid process (closed) 813.02
      open 813.12
    distal end—*see* Fracture, ulna, lower end
    epiphysis
      lower—*see* Fracture, ulna, lower end
      upper—*see* Fracture, ulna, upper, end
    head—*see* Fracture, ulna, lower end
    lower end (distal end) (head) (lower
      epiphysis) (styloid process) 813.43
      with radius (lower end) 813.44
        open 813.54
      open 813.53
    olecranon process (closed) 813.01
      open 813.11
    open NEC 813.92
    pathologic 733.12
    proximal end—*see* Fracture, ulna, upper end
    shaft 813.22
      with radius (shaft) 813.23
        open 813.33
      open 813.32
    styloid process—*see* Fracture, ulna, lower end
    transverse—*see* Fracture, ulna, by site
    upper end (epiphysis) 813.04
      with radius (upper end) 813.08
        open 813.18
      multiple sites 813.04
        open 813.14
      open 813.14
      specified site NEC 813.04
        open 813.14
  unciform (closed) 814.08
    open 814.18
  vertebra, vertebral (back) (body) (column)
    (neural arch) (pedicle) (spine) (spinous
    process) (transverse process) (closed) 805.8
    with
      hematomyelia—*see* Fracture, vertebra, by
        site, with spinal cord injury
      injury to
        cauda equina—*see* Fracture, vertebra,
          sacrum, with spinal cord injury
        nerve—*see* Fracture, vertebra, by site,
          with spinal cord injury
        paralysis—*see* Fracture, vertebra, by site,
          with spinal cord injury

Fracture—*continued*

paraplegia—*see* Fracture, vertebra, by site, with spinal cord injury

quadriplegia—*see* Fracture, vertebra, by site, with spinal cord injury

spinal concussion—*see* Fracture, vertebra, by site, with spinal cord injury

spinal cord injury (closed) NEC 806.8

Note—Use the following fifth-digit subclassification with categories 806.0-806.3:

C_1-C_4 *or unspecified level and* D_1-D_6 *(T_1-T_6) or unspecified level with:*

0 *unspecified spinal cord injury*
1 *complete lesion of cord*
2 *anterior cord syndrome*
3 *central cord syndrome*
4 *specified injury NEC*

C_5-C_7 *level and* D_7-D_{12} *level with:*

5 *unspecified spinal cord injury*
6 *complete lesion of cord*
7 *anterior cord syndrome*
8 *central cord syndrome*
9 *specified injury NEC*

cervical 806.0
open 806.1
dorsal, dorsolumbar 806.2
open 806.3
thoracic, thoracolumbar 806.2
open 806.3
atlanto-axial—*see* Fracture, vertebra, cervical
cervical (hangman) (teardrop) (closed) 805.00
with spinal cord injury—*see* Fracture, vertebra, with spinal cord injury, cervical
first (atlas) 805.01
open 805.11
second (axis) 805.02
open 805.12
third 805.03
open 805.13
fourth 805.04
open 805.14
fifth 805.05
open 805.15
sixth 805.06
open 805.16
seventh 805.07
open 805.17
multiple sites 805.08
open 805.18
open 805.10
coccyx (closed) 805.6
with spinal cord injury (closed) 806.60
cauda equina injury 806.62
complete lesion 806.61
open 806.71
open 806.72
open 806.70
specified type NEC 806.69
open 806.79
open 805.7
collapsed 733.13
compression, not due to trauma 733.13
dorsal (closed) 805.2
with spinal cord injury—*see* Fracture, vertebra, with spinal cord injury, dorsal

Fracture—*continued*

open 805.3
dorsolumbar (closed) 805.2
with spinal cord injury—*see* Fracture, vertebra, with spinal cord injury, dorsal
open 805.3
due to osteoporosis 733.13
fetus or newborn 767.4
lumbar (closed) 805.4
with spinal cord injury (closed) 806.4
open 806.5
open 805.5
nontraumatic 733.13
open NEC 805.9
pathologic 733.13
sacrum (closed) 805.6
with spinal cord injury 806.60
cauda equina injury 806.62
complete lesion 806.61
open 806.71
open 806.72
open 806.70
specified type NEC 806.69
open 806.79
open 805.7
site unspecified (closed) 805.8
with spinal cord injury (closed) 806.8
open 806.9
open 805.9
thoracic (closed) 805.2
with spinal cord injury—*see* Fracture, vertebra, with spinal cord injury, thoracic
open 805.3
vertex—*see* Fracture, skull, vault
vomer (bone) 802.0
open 802.1
Wagstaffe's—*see* Fracture, ankle
wrist (closed) 814.00
open 814.10
pathologic 733.12
xiphoid (process)—*see* Fracture, sternum
zygoma (zygomatic arch) (closed) 802.4
open 802.5
Fragile X syndrome 759.83
Fragilitas
crinium 704.2
hair 704.2
ossium 756.51
with blue sclera 756.51
unguium 703.8
congenital 757.5
Fragility
bone 756.51
with deafness and blue sclera 756.51
capillary (hereditary) 287.8
hair 704.2
nails 703.8
Fragmentation —*see* Fracture, by site
Frambesia, frambesial (tropica) (*see also* Yaws) 102.9
initial lesion or ulcer 102.0
primary 102.0
Frambeside
gummatous 102.4
of early yaws 102.2
Frambesioma 102.1
Franceschetti's syndrome (mandibulofacial dysostosis) 756.0
Francis' disease (*see also* Tularemia) 021.9
Frank's essential thrombocytopenia (*see also* Purpura, thrombocytopenic) 287.3

Franklin's disease (heavy chain) 273.2
Fraser's syndrome 759.89
Freckle 709.09
  malignant melanoma in (M8742/3)—*see*
    Melanoma
  melanotic (of Hutchinson) (M8742/2)—*see*
    Neoplasm, skin, in situ
Freeman-Sheldon syndrome 759.89
Freezing 991.9
  specified effect NEC 991.8
Frei's disease (climatic bubo) 099.1
Freiberg's
  disease (osteochondrosis, second metatarsal)
    732.5
  infraction of metatarsal head 732.5
  osteochondrosis 732.5
Fremitus, friction, cardiac 785.3
Frenulum lingua 750.0
Frenum
  external os 752.49
  tongue 750.0
Frequency (urinary) NEC 788.41
  micturition 788.41
  nocturnal 788.43
  psychogenic 306.53
Frey's syndrome (auriculotemporal syndrome)
  350.8
Friction
  burn (*see also* Injury, superficial, by site) 919.0
  fremitus, cardiac 785.3
  precordial 785.3
  sounds, chest 786.7
Friderichsen-Waterhouse syndrome or disease
  036.3
Friedländer's
  B (bacillus) NEC (*see also* condition) 041.3
    sepsis or septicemia 038.49
  disease (endarteritis obliterans)—*see*
    Arteriosclerosis
Friedreich's
  ataxia 334.0
  combined systemic disease 334.0
  disease 333.2
    combined systemic 334.0
  myoclonia 333.2
  sclerosis (spinal cord) 334.0
Friedrich-Erb-Arnold syndrome
  (acropachyderma) 757.39
Frigidity 302.72
  psychic or psychogenic 302.72
Fröhlich's disease or syndrome (adiposogenital
  dystrophy) 253.8
Froin's syndrome 336.8
Frommel's disease 676.6
Frommel-Chiari syndrome 676.6
Frontal —*see also* condition
  lobe syndrome 310.0
Frostbite 991.3
  face 991.0
  foot 991.2
  hand 991.1
  specified site NEC 991.3
Frotteurism 302.89
Frozen 991.9
  pelvis 620.8
  shoulder 726.0
Fructosemia 271.2
Fructosuria (benign) (essential) 271.2

Fuchs'
  black spot (myopic) 360.21
  corneal dystrophy (endothelial) 371.57
  heterochromic cyclitis 364.21
Fucosidosis 271.8
Fugue 780.9
  hysterical (dissociative) 300.13
  reaction to exceptional stress (transient) 308.1
Fuller Albright's syndrome (osteitis fibrosa
  disseminata) 756.59
Fuller's earth disease 502
Fulminant, fulminating —*see* condition
Functional —*see* condition
Fundus —*see also* condition
  flavimaculatus 362.76
Fungemia 117.9
Fungus, fungous
  cerebral 348.8
  disease NEC 117.9
  infection—*see* Infection, fungus
  testis (*see also* Tuberculosis) 016.5 *[608.81]*
Funiculitis (acute) 608.4
  chronic 608.4
  endemic 608.4
  gonococcal (acute) 098.14
    chronic or duration of 2 months or over 098.34
  tuberculous (*see also* Tuberculosis) 016.5
F.U.O. (*see also* Pyrexia) 780.6
Funnel
  breast (acquired) 738.3
    congenital 754.81
    late effect of rickets 268.1
  chest (acquired) 738.3
    congenital 754.81
    late effect of rickets 268.1
  pelvis (acquired) 738.6
    with disproportion (fetopelvic) 653.3
      affecting fetus or newborn 763.1
      causing obstructed labor 660.1
        affecting fetus or newborn 763.1
    congenital 755.69
    tuberculous (*see also* Tuberculosis) 016.9
Furfur 690.18
  microsporon 111.0
Furor, paroxysmal (idiopathic) (*see also*
  Epilepsy) 345.8
Furriers' lung 495.8
Furrowed tongue 529.5
  congenital 750.13
Furrowing nail (s) (transverse) 703.8
  congenital 757.5
Furuncle 680.9
  abdominal wall 680.2
  ankle 680.6
  anus 680.5
  arm (any part, above wrist) 680.3
  auditory canal, external 680.0
  axilla 680.3
  back (any part) 680.2
  breast 680.2
  buttock 680.5
  chest wall 680.2
  corpus cavernosum 607.2
  ear (any part) 680.0
  eyelid 373.13
  face (any part, except eye) 680.0
  finger (any) 680.4
  flank 680.2
  foot (any part) 680.7
  forearm 680.3
  gluteal (region) 680.5

Furuncle—*continued*
  groin 680.2
  hand (any part) 680.4
  head (any part, except face) 680.8
  heel 680.7
  hip 680.6
  kidney (*see also* Abscess, kidney) 590.2
  knee 680.6
  labium (majus) (minus) 616.4
  lacrimal
    gland (*see also* Dacryoadenitis) 375.00
    passages (duct) (sac) (see *also* Dacryocystitis)
      375.30
  leg, any part except foot 680.6
  malignant 022.0
  multiple sites 680.9
  neck 680.1
  nose (external) (septum) 680.0
  orbit 376.01
  partes posteriores 680.5
  pectoral region 680.2
  penis 607.2
  perineum 680.2
  pinna 680.0
  scalp (any part) 680.8
  scrotum 608.4
  seminal vesicle 608.0
  shoulder 680.3
  skin NEC 680.9
  specified site NEC 680.8
  spermatic cord 608.4
  temple (region) 680.0
  testis 604.90
  thigh 680.6
  thumb 680.4
  toe (any) 680.7
  trunk 680.2
  tunica vaginalis 608.4
  umbilicus 680.2
  upper arm 680.3
  vas deferens 608.4
  vulva 616.4
  wrist 680.4
Furunculosis (*see also* Furuncle) 680.9
  external auditory meatus 680.0 *[380.13]*
Fusarium (infection) 118
Fusion, fused (congenital)
  anal (with urogenital canal) 751.5
  aorta and pulmonary artery 745.0
  astragaloscaphoid 755.67
  atria 745.5
  atrium and ventricle 745.69
  auditory canal 744.02
  auricles, heart 745.5
  binocular, with defective stereopsis 368.33
  bone 756.9
  cervical spine—*see* Fusion, spine
  choanal 748.0
  commissure, mitral valve 746.5
  cranial sutures, premature 756.0
  cusps, heart valve NEC 746.89
    mitral 746.5
    tricuspid 746.89
  ear ossicles 744.04
  fingers (*see also* Syndactylism, fingers) 755.11
  hymen 752.42
  hymeno-urethral 599.89
    causing obstructed labor 660.1
      affecting fetus or newborn 763.1
  joint (acquired)—*see also* Ankylosis
    congenital 755.8

Fusion, fused—*continued*
  kidneys (incomplete) 753.3
  labium (majus) (minus) 752.49
  larynx and trachea 748.3
  limb 755.8
    lower 755.69
    upper 755.59
  lobe, lung 748.5
  lumbosacral (acquired) 724.6
    congenital 756.15
    surgical V45.4
  nares (anterior) (posterior) 748.0
  nose, nasal 748.0
  nostril(s) 748.0
  organ or site NEC—*see* Anomaly, specified
    type NEC
  ossicles 756.9
    auditory 744.04
  pulmonary valve segment 746.02
  pulmonic cusps 746.02
  ribs 756.3
  sacroiliac (acquired) (joint) 724.6
    congenital 755.69
    surgical V45.4
  skull, imperfect 756.0
  spine (acquired) 724.9
    arthrodesis status V45.4
    congenital (vertebra) 756.15
    postoperative status V45.4
  sublingual duct with submaxillary duct at
    opening in mouth 750.26
  talonavicular (bar) 755.67
  teeth, tooth 520.2
  testes 752.8
  toes (*see also* Syndactylism, toes) 755.13
  trachea and esophagus 750.3
  twins 759.4
  urethral-hymenal 599.89
  vagina 752.49
  valve cusps—*see* Fusion, cusps, heart valve
  ventricles, heart 745.4
  vertebra (arch)—*see* Fusion, spine
  vulva 752.49
Fusospirillosis (mouth) (tongue) (tonsil) 101

G

Gafsa boil 085.1
Gain, weight (abnormal) (excessive) (*see also*
    Weight, gain) 783.1
Gaisböck's disease or syndrome (polycythemia
    hypertonica) 289.0
Gait
    abnormality 781.2
        hysterical 300.11
    ataxic 781.2
        hysterical 300.11
    disturbance 781.2
        hysterical 300.11
    paralytic 781.2
    scissor 781.2
    spastic 781.2
    staggering 781.2
        hysterical 300.11
Galactocele (breast) (infected) 611.5
    puerperal, postpartum 676.8
Galactophoritis 611.0
    puerperal, postpartum 675.2
Galactorrhea 676.6
    not associated with childbirth 611.6
Galactosemia (classic) (congenital) 271.1
Galactosuria 271.1
Galacturia 791.1
    bilharziasis 120.0
Galen's vein —*see* condition
Gallbladder —*see also* condition
    acute (*see also* Disease, gallbladder) 575.0
Gall duct —*see* condition
Gallop rhythm 427.89
Gallstone (cholemic) (colic) (impacted)—*see*
    also Cholelithiasis
    causing intestinal obstruction 560.31
Gambling, pathological 312.31
Gammaloidosis 277.3
Gammopathy 273.9
    macroglobulinemia 273.3
    monoclonal (benign) (essential) (idiopathic)
        (with lymphoplasmacytic dyscrasia) 273.1
Gamna's disease (siderotic splenomegaly)
    289.51
Gampsodactylia (congenital) 754.71
Gamstorp's disease (adynamia episodica
    hereditaria) 359.3
Gandy-Nanta disease (siderotic splenomegaly)
    289.51
Gang activity without manifest psychiatric
    disorder V71.09
    adolescent V71.02
    adult V71.01
    child V71.02
Gangliocytoma (M9490/0)—*see* Neoplasm,
    connective tissue, benign
Ganglioglioma (M9505/1)—*see* Neoplasm, by
    site, uncertain behavior
Ganglion 727.43
    joint 727.41
    of yaws (early) (late) 102.6
    periosteal (*see also* Periostitis) 730.3
    tendon sheath (compound) (diffuse) 727.42
    tuberculous (*see also* Tuberculosis) 015.9
Ganglioneuroblastoma (M9490/3)—*see*
    Neoplasm, connective tissue, malignant

Ganglioneuroma (M9490/0)—*see also*
    Neoplasm, connective tissue, benign
    malignant (M9490/3)—*see* Neoplasm,
    connective tissue, malignant
Ganglioneuromatosis (M9491/0)—*see*
    Neoplasm, connective tissue, benign
Ganglionitis
    fifth nerve (*see also* Neuralgia, trigeminal) 350.1
    gasserian 350.1
    geniculate 351.1
        herpetic 053.11
        newborn 767.5
    herpes zoster 053.11
    herpetic geniculate (Hunt's syndrome) 053.11
Gangliosidosis 330.1
Gangosa 102.5
Gangrene, gangrenous (anemia) (artery)
    (cellulitis) (dermatitis) (dry) (infective)
    (moist) (pemphigus) (septic) (skin) (stasis)
    (ulcer) 785.4
    with
        arteriosclerosis (native artery) 440.24
            bypass graft 440.30
                autologous vein 440.31
                nonautologous biological 440.32
        diabetes (mellitus) 250.7 *[785.4]*
    abdomen (wall) 785.4
    arteriosclerotic 440.29 *[785.4]*
    adenitis 683
    alveolar 526.5
    angina 462
        diphtheritic 032.0
    anus 569.49
    appendices epiploicae—*see* Gangrene,
        mesentery
    appendix—*see* Appendicitis, acute
    arteriosclerotic —*see* Arteriosclerosis, with,
        gangrene
    auricle 785.4
    Bacillus welchii (*see also* Gangrene, gas) 040.0
    bile duct (*see also* Cholangitis) 576.8
    bladder 595.89
    bowel—*see* Gangrene, intestine
    cecum—*see* Gangrene, intestine
    Clostridium perfringens or welchii (*see also*
        Gangrene, gas) 040.0
    colon—*see* Gangrene, intestine
    connective tissue 785.4
    cornea 371.40
    corpora cavernosa (infective) 607.2
        noninfective 607.89
    cutaneous, spreading 785.4
    decubital 707.0 *[785.4]*
    diabetic (any site) 250.7 *[785.4]*
    dropsical 785.4
    emphysematous (*see also* Gangrene, gas) 040.0
    epidemic (ergotized grain) 988.2
    epididymis (infectional) (*see also* Epididymitis)
        604.99
    erysipelas (*see also* Erysipelas) 035
    extremity (lower) (upper) 785.4
    gallbladder or duct (*see also* Cholecystitis,
        acute) 575.0

GHI

Gangrene, gangrenous—*continued*
  gas (bacillus) 040.0
    with
      abortion—*see* Abortion, by type, with sepsis
      ectopic pregnancy (*see also* categories
        633.0-633.9) 639.0
      molar pregnancy (*see also* categories
        630-632) 639.0
    following
      abortion 639.0
      ectopic or molar pregnancy 639.0
    puerperal, postpartum, childbirth 670
  glossitis 529.0
  gum 523.8
  hernia—*see* Hernia, by site, with gangrene
  hospital noma 528.1
  intestine, intestinal (acute) (hemorrhagic)
    (massive) 557.0
    with
      hernia—*see* Hernia, by site, with gangrene
      mesenteric embolism or infarction 557.0
      obstruction (*see also* Obstruction, intestine)
        560.9
  laryngitis 464.0
  liver 573.8
  lung 513.0
    spirochetal 104.8
  lymphangitis 457.2
  Meleney's (cutaneous) 686.0
  mesentery 557.0
    with
      embolism or infarction 557.0
      intestinal obstruction (*see also* Obstruction,
        intestine) 560.9
  mouth 528.1
  noma 528.1
  orchitis 604.90
  ovary (*see also* Salpingo-oophoritis) 614.2
  pancreas 577.0
  penis (infectional) 607.2
    noninfective 607.89
  perineum 785.4
  pharynx 462
    septic 034.0
  pneumonia 513.0
  Pott's 440.24
  presenile 443.1
  pulmonary 513.0
  pulp, tooth 522.1
  quinsy 475
  Raynaud's (symmetric gangrene) 443.0 *[785.4]*
  rectum 569.49
  retropharyngeal 478.24
  rupture—*see* Hernia, by site, with gangrene
  scrotum 608.4
    noninfective 608.83
  senile 440.24
  sore throat 462
  spermatic cord 608.4
    noninfective 608.89
  spine 785.4
  spirochetal NEC 104.8
  spreading cutaneous 785.4
  stomach 537.89
  stomatitis 528.1
  symmetrical 443.0 *[785.4]*
  testis (infectional) (*see also* Orchitis) 604.99
    noninfective 608.89
  throat 462
    diphtheritic 032.0
  thyroid (gland) 246.8

Gangrene, gangrenous—*continued*
  tonsillitis (acute) 463
  tooth (pulp) 522.1
  tuberculous NEC (*see also* Tuberculosis) 011.9
  tunica vaginalis 608.4
    noninfective 608.89
  umbilicus 785.4
  uterus (*see also* Endometritis) 615.9
  uvulitis 528.3
  vas deferens 608.4
    noninfective 608.89
  vulva (*see also* Vulvitis) 616.10
Gannister disease (occupational) 502
  with tuberculosis—*see* Tuberculosis, pulmonary
Ganser's syndrome, hysterical 300.16
Gardner-Diamond syndrome (autoerythrocyte
  sensitization) 287.2
Gargoylism 277.5
Garré's
  disease (*see also* Osteomyelitis) 730.1
  osteitis (sclerosing) (*see also* Osteomyelitis)
    730.1
  osteomyelitis (*see also* Osteomyelitis) 730.1
Garrod's pads, knuckle 728.79
Gartner's duct
  cyst 752.11
  persistent 752.11
Gas
  asphyxia, asphyxiation, inhalation, poisoning,
    suffocation NEC 987.9
    specified gas—*see* Table of drugs and
      chemicals
  bacillus gangrene or infection—*see* Gas,
    gangrene
  cyst, mesentery 568.89
  excessive 787.3
  gangrene 040.0
    with
      abortion—*see* Abortion, by type, with sepsis
      ectopic pregnancy (*see also* categories
        633.0-633.9) 639.0
      molar pregnancy (*see also* categories
        630-632) 639.0
    following
      abortion 639.0
      ectopic or molar pregnancy 639.0
    puerperal, postpartum, childbirth 670
  on stomach 787.3
  pains 787.3
Gastradenitis 535.0
Gastralgia 536.8
  psychogenic 307.89
Gastrectasis, gastrectasia 536.1
  psychogenic 306.4
Gastric —*see* condition
Gastrinoma (M8153/1)
  malignant (M8153/3)
    pancreas 157.4
    specified site NEC—*see* Neoplasm, by site,
      malignant
    unspecified site 157.4
  specified site—*see* Neoplasm, by site,
    uncertain behavior
  unspecified site 235.5

Gastritis 535.5

> Note—Use the following fifth-digit subclassification for category 535:
>
> 0 *without mention of hemorrhage*
> 1 *with hemorrhage*

acute 535.0
alcoholic 535.3
allergic 535.4
antral 535.4
atrophic 535.1
atrophic-hyperplastic 535.1
bile-induced 535.4
catarrhal 535.0
chronic (atrophic) 535.1
cirrhotic 535.4
corrosive (acute) 535.4
dietetic 535.4
due to diet deficiency 269.9 *[535.4]*
eosinophilic 535.4
erosive 535.4
follicular 535.4
　chronic 535.1
giant hypertrophic 535.2
glandular 535.4
　chronic 535.1
hypertrophic (mucosa) 535.2
　chronic giant 211.1
irritant 535.4
nervous 306.4
phlegmonous 535.0
psychogenic 306.4
sclerotic 535.4
spastic 536.8
subacute 535.0
superficial 535.4
suppurative 535.0
toxic 535.4
tuberculous (*see also* Tuberculosis) 017.9
Gastrocarcinoma (M8010/3) 151.9
Gastrocolic —*see* condition
Gastrocolitis —*see* Enteritis
Gastrodisciasis 121.8
Gastroduodenitis (*see also* Gastritis) 535.5
catarrhal 535.0
infectional 535.0
virus, viral 008.8
　specified type NEC 008.69
Gastrodynia 536.8
Gastroenteritis (acute) (catarrhal) (chronic)
　(congestive) (hemorrhagic) (noninfectious)
　(*see also* Enteritis) 558.9
aertrycke infection 003.0
allergic 558.9
chronic 558.9
　ulcerative (*see also* Colitis, ulcerative) 556.9
dietetic 558.9
due to
　food poisoning (*see also* Poisoning, food)
　　005.9
　radiation 558.1
epidemic 009.0
functional 558.9
infectious (*see also* Enteritis, due to, by
　organism) 009.0
　presumed 009.1
salmonella 003.0
septic (*see also* Enteritis, due to, by organism)
　009.0
toxic 558.2

Gastroenteritis—*continued*
tuberculous (*see also* Tuberculosis) 014.8
ulcerative (*see also* Colitis, ulcerative) 556.9
viral NEC 008.8
　specified type NEC 008.69
zymotic 009.0
Gastroenterocolitis —*see* Enteritis
Gastroenteropathy, protein-losing 579.8
Gastroenteroptosis 569.89
Gastroesophageal laceration-hemorrhage
　syndrome 530.7
Gastroesophagitis 530.19
Gastrohepatitis (*see also* Gastritis) 535.5
Gastrointestinal —*see* condition
Gastrojejunal —*see* condition
Gastrojejunitis (*see also* Gastritis) 535.5
Gastrojejunocolic —*see* condition
Gastroliths 537.89
Gastromalacia 537.89
Gastroparalysis 536.8
　diabetic 250.6 *[337.1]*
Gastroparesis 536.3
　diabetic 250.6 *[536.3]*
Gastropathy, exudative 579.8
Gastroptosis 537.5
Gastrorrhagia 578.0
Gastrorrhea 536.8
　psychogenic 306.4
Gastroschisis (congenital) 756.7
　acquired 569.89
Gastrospasm (neurogenic) (reflex) 536.8
　neurotic 306.4
　psychogenic 306.4
Gastrostaxis 578.0
Gastrostenosis 537.89
Gastrostomy status V44.1
　with complication 997.4
Gastrosuccorrhea (continuous) (intermittent)
　536.8
　neurotic 306.4
　psychogenic 306.4
Gaucher's
disease (adult) (cerebroside lipidosis) (infantile)
　272.7
hepatomegaly 272.7
splenomegaly (cerebroside lipidosis) 272.7
Gayet's disease (superior hemorrhagic
　polioencephalitis) 265.1
Gayet-Wernicke's syndrome (superior
　hemorrhagic polioencephalitis) 265.1
Gee (-Herter) (-Heubner) (-Thaysen) disease or
　syndrome (nontropical sprue) 579.0
Gélineau's syndrome 347
Gemination, teeth 520.2
Gemistocytoma (M9411/3)
specified site—*see* Neoplasm, by site, malignant
unspecified site 191.9
General, generalized —*see* condition
Genital —*see* condition
Genito-anorectal syndrome 099.1
Genitourinary system —*see* condition
Genu
congenital 755.64
extrorsum (acquired) 736.42
　congenital 755.64
　late effects of rickets 268.1
introrsum (acquired) 736.41
　congenital 755.64
　late effects of rickets 268.1
rachitic (old) 268.1

Genu—*continued*
recurvatum (acquired) 736.5
  congenital 754.40
    with dislocation of knee 754.41
  late effects of rickets 268.1
valgum (acquired) (knock-knee) 736.41
  congenital 755.64
  late effects of rickets 268.1
varum (acquired) (bowleg) 736.42
  congenital 755.64
  late effects of rickets 268.1
Geographic tongue 529.1
Geophagia 307.52
Geotrichosis 117.9
intestine 117.9
lung 117.9
mouth 117.9
Gephyrophobia 300.29
Gerbode defect 745.4
Gerhardt's
disease (erythromelalgia) 443.89
syndrome (vocal cord paralysis) 478.30
Gerlier's disease (epidemic vertigo) 078.81
German measles 056.9
exposure to V01.4
Germinoblastoma (diffuse) (M9614/3) 202.8
follicular (M9692/3) 202.0
Germinoma (M9064/3)—*see* Neoplasm, by site, malignant
Gerontoxon 371.41
Gerstmann's syndrome (finger agnosia) 784.69
Gestation (period)—*see also* Pregnancy
ectopic NEC (*see also* Pregnancy, ectopic) 633.9
Gestational proteinuria 646.2
with hypertension—*see* Toxemia, of pregnancy
Ghon tubercle primary infection (*see also* Tuberculosis) 010.0
Ghost
teeth 520.4
vessels, cornea 370.64
Ghoul hand 102.3
Giant
cell
  epulis 523.8
  peripheral (gingiva) 523.8
  tumor, tendon sheath 727.02
colon (congenital) 751.3
esophagus (congenital) 750.4
kidney 753.3
urticaria 995.1
  hereditary 277.6
Giardia lamblia infestation 007.1
Giardiasis 007.1
Gibert's disease (pityriasis rosea) 696.3
Gibraltar fever —*see* Brucellosis
Giddiness 780.4
hysterical 300.11
psychogenic 306.9
Gierke's disease (glycogenosis I) 271.0
Gigantism (cerebral) (hypophyseal) (pituitary) 253.0
Gilbert's disease or cholemia (familial nonhemolytic jaundice) 277.4
Gilchrist's disease (North American blastomycosis) 116.0
Gilford (-Hutchinson) disease or syndrome (progeria) 259.8
Gilles de la Tourette's disease (motor-verbal tic) 307.23
Gillespie's syndrome (dysplasia oculodentodigitalis) 759.89

Gingivitis 523.1
acute 523.0
  necrotizing 101
catarrhal 523.0
chronic 523.1
desquamative 523.1
expulsiva 523.4
hyperplastic 523.1
marginal, simple 523.1
necrotizing, acute 101
pellagrous 265.2
ulcerative 523.1
  acute necrotizing 101
Vincent's 101
Gingivoglossitis 529.0
Gingivopericementitis 523.4
Gingivosis 523.1
Gingivostomatitis 523.1
herpetic 054.2
Giovannini's disease 117.9
Gland, glandular —*see* condition
Glanders 024
Glanzmann (-Naegeli) disease or thrombasthenia 287.1
Glassblowers' disease 527.1
Glaucoma (capsular) (inflammatory) (noninflammatory) (primary) 365.9
with increased episcleral venous pressure 365.82
absolute 360.42
acute 365.22
  narrow angle 365.22
  secondary 365.60
angle closure 365.20
  acute 365.22
  chronic 365.23
  intermittent 365.21
  interval 365.21
  residual stage 365.24
  subacute 365.21
border line 365.00
chronic 365.11
  noncongestive 365.11
  open angle 365.11
  simple 365.11
closed angle—*see* Glaucoma, angle closure
congenital 743.20
  associated with other eye anomalies 743.22
  simple 743.21
congestive—*see* Glaucoma, narrow angle
corticosteroid-induced (glaucomatous stage) 365.31
  residual stage 365.32
hemorrhagic 365.60
hypersecretion 365.81
in or with
  aniridia 743.45 *[365.42]*
  Axenfeld's anomaly 743.44 *[365.41]*
  concussion of globe 921.3 *[365.65]*
  congenital syndromes NEC 759.89 *[365.44]*
  dislocation of lens
    anterior 379.33 *[365.59]*
    posterior 379.34 *[365.59]*
  disorder of lens NEC 365.59
  epithelial down-growth 364.61 *[365.64]*
  glaucomatocyclitic crisis 364.22 *[365.62]*
  hypermature cataract 366.18 *[365.51]*
  hyphema 364.41 *[365.63]*
  inflammation, ocular 365.62
  iridocyclitis 364.3 *[365.62]*

Glaucoma—*continued*
  iris
    anomalies NEC 743.46 *[365.42]*
    atrophy, essential 364.51 *[365.42]*
    bombé 364.74 *[365.61]*
    rubeosis 364.42 *[365.63]*
  microcornea 743.41 *[365.43]*
  neurofibromatosis 237.71 *[365.44]*
  ocular
    cysts NEC 365.64
    disorders NEC 365.60
    trauma 365.65
    tumors NEC 365.64
  postdislocation of lens
    anterior 379.33 *[365.59]*
    posterior 379.34 *[365.59]*
  pseudoexfoliation of capsule 366.11 *[365.52]*
  pupillary block or seclusion 364.74 *[365.61]*
  recession of chamber angle 364.77 *[365.65]*
  retinal vein occlusion 362.35 *[365.63]*
  Rieger's anomaly or syndrome 743.44
    [365.41]
  rubeosis of iris 364.42 *[365.63]*
  seclusion of pupil 364.74 *[365.61]*
  spherophakia 743.36 *[365.59]*
  Sturge-Weber (-Dimitri) syndrome 759.6
    [365.44]
  systemic syndrome NEC 365.44
  tumor of globe 365.64
  vascular disorders NEC 365.63
  infantile 365.14
    congenital 743.20
      associated with other eye anomalies 743.22
      simple 743.21
  juvenile 365.14
  low tension 365.12
  malignant 365.20
  narrow angle (primary) 365.20
    acute 365.22
    chronic 365.23
    intermittent 365.21
    interval 365.21
    residual stage 365.24
    subacute 365.21
  newborn 743.20
    associated with other eye anomalies 743.22
    simple 743.21
  noncongestive (chronic) 365.11
  nonobstructive (chronic) 365.11
  obstructive 365.60
    due to lens changes 365.59
  open angle 365.10
    with
      borderline intraocular pressure 365.01
      cupping of optic discs 365.01
    primary 365.11
    residual stage 365.15
  phacolytic 365.51
    with hypermature cataract 366.18 *[365.51]*
  pigmentary 365.13
  postinfectious 365.60
  pseudoexfoliation 365.52
    with pseudoexfoliation of capsule 366.11
      [365.52]
  secondary NEC 365.60
  simple (chronic) 365.11
  simplex 365.11
  steroid responders 365.03
  suspect 365.00
  syphilitic 095.8

Glaucoma—*continued*
  traumatic NEC 365.65
    newborn 767.8
  tuberculous (*see also* Tuberculosis) 017.3
    [365.62]
  wide angle (*see also* Glaucoma, open angle)
    365.10
Glaucomatous flecks (subcapsular) 366.31
Glazed tongue 529.4
Gleet 098.2
Glénard's disease or syndrome (enteroptosis)
  569.89
Glinski-Simmonds syndrome (pituitary
  cachexia) 253.2
Glioblastoma (multiforme) (M9440/3)
  with sarcomatous component (M9442/3)
    specified site—*see* Neoplasm, by site,
      malignant
    unspecified site 191.9
  giant cell (M9441/3)
    specified site—*see* Neoplasm, by site,
      malignant
    unspecified site 191.9
  specified site—*see* Neoplasm, by site, malignant
  unspecified site 191.9
Glioma (malignant) (M9380/3)
  astrocytic (M9400/3)
    specified site—*see* Neoplasm, by site,
      malignant
    unspecified site 191.9
  mixed (M9382/3)
    specified site—*see* Neoplasm, by site,
      malignant
    unspecified site 191.9
  nose 748.1
  specified site NEC—*see* Neoplasm, by site,
    malignant
  subependymal (M9383/1) 237.5
  unspecified site 191.9
Gliomatosis cerebri (M9381/3) 191.0
Glioneuroma (M9505/1)—*see* Neoplasm, by
  site, uncertain behavior
Gliosarcoma (M9380/3)
  specified site—*see* Neoplasm, by site, malignant
  unspecified site 191.9
Gliosis (cerebral) 349.89
  spinal 336.0
Glisson's
  cirrhosis—*see* Cirrhosis, portal
  disease (*see also* Rickets) 268.0
Glissonitis 573.3
Globinuria 791.2
Globus 306.4
  hystericus 300.11
Glomangioma (M8712/0) (*see also*
  Hemangioma) 228.00
Glomangiosarcoma (M8710/3)—*see* Neoplasm,
  connective tissue, malignant
Glomerular nephritis (*see also* Nephritis) 583.9
Glomerulitis (*see also* Nephritis) 583.9
Glomerulonephritis (*see also* Nephritis) 583.9
  with
    edema (*see also* Nephrosis) 581.9
    lesion of
      exudative nephritis 583.89
      interstitial nephritis (diffuse) (focal) 583.89
      necrotizing glomerulitis 583.4
        acute 580.4
        chronic 582.4

Glomerulonephritis—*continued*
   septic (*see also* Pyelitis) 590.80
   specified pathology or lesion NEC 583.89
      with nephrotic syndrome 581.89
      acute 580.89
      chronic 582.89
   suppurative (acute) (disseminated) (*see also*
      Pyelitis) 590.80
   toxic—*see* Nephritis, acute
   tubal, tubular—*see* Nephrosis, tubular
   type II (Ellis)—*see* Nephrosis
   vascular—*see* Hypertension, kidney
Glomerulosclerosis (*see also* Sclerosis, renal)
      587
   focal 582.1
      with nephrotic syndrome 581.1
   intercapillary (nodular) (with diabetes) 250.4
      [581.81]
Glossagra 529.6
Glossalgia 529.6
Glossitis 529.0
   areata exfoliativa 529.1
   atrophic 529.4
   benign migratory 529.1
   gangrenous 529.0
   Hunter's 529.4
   median rhomboid 529.2
   Moeller's 529.4
   pellagrous 265.2
Glossocele 529.8
Glossodynia 529.6
   exfoliativa 529.4
Glossoncus 529.8
Glossophytia 529.3
Glossoplegia 529.8
Glossoptosis 529.8
Glossopyrosis 529.6
Glossotrichia 529.3
Glossy skin 701.9
Glottis —*see* condition
Glottitis —*see* Glossitis
Glucagonoma (M8152/0)
   malignant (M8152/3)
      pancreas 157.4
      specified site NEC—*see* Neoplasm, by site,
         malignant
      unspecified site 157.4
   pancreas 211.7
   specified site NEC—*see* Neoplasm, by site,
      benign
   unspecified site 211.7
Glucoglycinuria 270.7
Glue ear syndrome 381.20
Glue sniffing (airplane glue) (*see also*
      Dependence) 304.6
Glycinemia (with methylmalonic acidemia) 270.7
Glycinuria (renal) (with ketosis) 270.0
Glycogen
   infiltration (*see also* Disease, glycogen storage)
      271.0
   storage disease (*see also* Disease, glycogen
      storage) 271.0
Glycogenosis (*see also* Disease, glycogen
      storage) 271.0
   cardiac 271.0 *[425.7]*
   Cori, types I-VII 271.0
   diabetic, secondary 250.8 *[259.8]*
   diffuse (with hepatic cirrhosis) 271.0
   generalized 271.0
   glucose-6-phosphatase deficiency 271.0
   hepatophosphorylase deficiency 271.0

Glycogenosis—*continued*
   hepatorenal 271.0
   myophosphorylase deficiency 271.0
Glycopenia 251.2
Glycoprolinuria 270.8
Glycosuria 791.5
   renal 271.4
Gnathostoma (spinigerum) (infection)
      (infestation) 128.1
   wandering swellings from 128.1
Gnathostomiasis 128.1
Goiter (adolescent) (colloid) (diffuse) (dipping)
      (due to iodine deficiency) (endemic)
      (euthyroid) (heart) (hyperplastic) (internal)
      (intrathoracic) (juvenile) (mixed type)
      (nonendemic) (parenchymatous) (plunging)
      (sporadic) (subclavicular) (substernal) 240.9
   with
      hyperthyroidism (recurrent) (*see also* Goiter,
         toxic) 242.0
      . thyrotoxicosis (*see also* Goiter, toxic) 242.0
   adenomatous (*see also* Goiter, nodular) 241.9
   cancerous (M8000/3) 193
   complicating pregnancy, childbirth, or
      puerperium 648.1
   congenital 246.1
   cystic (*see also* Goiter, nodular) 241.9
   due to enzyme defect in synthesis of thyroid
      hormone (butane-insoluble iodine)
      (coupling) (deiodinase) (iodide trapping or
      organification) (iodotyrosine dehalogenase)
      (peroxidase) 246.1
   dyshormonogenic 246.1
   exophthalmic (*see also* Goiter, toxic) 242.0
   familial (with deaf-mutism) 243
   fibrous 245.3
   lingual 759.2
   lymphadenoid 245.2
   malignant (M8000/3) 193
   multinodular (nontoxic) 241.1
      toxic or with hyperthyroidism (*see also*
         Goiter, toxic) 242.2
   nodular (nontoxic) 241.9
      with
         hyperthyroidism (*see also* Goiter, toxic)
            242.3
         thyrotoxicosis (*see also* Goiter, toxic) 242.3
      endemic 241.9
      exophthalmic (diffuse) (*see also* Goiter, toxic)
         242.0
      multinodular (nontoxic) 241.1
      sporadic 241.9
      toxic (*see also* Goiter, toxic) 242.3
      uninodular (nontoxic) 241.0
   nontoxic (nodular) 241.9
      multinodular 241.1
      uninodular 241.0
   pulsating (*see also* Goiter, toxic) 242.0
   simple 240.0
   toxic 242.0

Note—Use the following fifth-digit
subclassification with category 242:

0   without mention of thyrotoxic crisis
    or storm
1   with mention of thyrotoxic crisis or storm

      adenomatous 242.3
         multinodular 242.2
         uninodular 242.1
      multinodular 242.2

Goiter—*continued*
  nodular 242.3
    multinodular 242.2
    uninodular 242.1
  uninodular 242.1
  uninodular (nontoxic) 241.0
  toxic or with hyperthyroidism (*see also*
    Goiter, toxic) 242.1
Goldberg (-Maxwell) (-Morris) syndrome
  (testicular feminization) 257.8
Goldblatt's
  hypertension 440.1
  kidney 440.1
Goldenhar's syndrome (oculoauriculovertebral
  dysplasia) 756.0
Goldflam-Erb disease or syndrome 358.0
Goldscheider's disease (epidermolysis bullosa)
  757.39
Goldstein's disease (familial hemorrhagic
  telangiectasia) 448.0
Golfer's elbow 726.32
Goltz-Gorlin syndrome (dermal hypoplasia)
  757.39
Gonadoblastoma (M9073/1)
  specified site—*see* Neoplasm, by site uncertain
    behavior
  unspecified site
    female 236.2
    male 236.4
Gonecystitis (*see also* Vesiculitis) 608.0
Gongylonemiasis 125.6
  mouth 125.6
Goniosynechiae 364.73
Gonococcemia 098.89
Gonococcus, gonococcal (disease) (infection)
  (*see also* condition) 098.0
  anus 098.7
  bursa 098.52
  chronic NEC 098.2
  complicating pregnancy, childbirth, or
    puerperium 647.1
    affecting fetus or newborn 760.2
  conjunctiva, conjunctivitis (neonatorum) 098.40
  dermatosis 098.89
  endocardium 098.84
  epididymo-orchitis 098.13
    chronic or duration of 2 months or over 098.33
  eye (newborn) 098.40
  fallopian tube (chronic) 098.37
    acute 098.17
  genitourinary (acute) (organ) (system) (tract)
    (*see also* Gonorrhea) 098.0
    lower 098.0
      chronic 098.2
    upper 098.10
      chronic 098.30
  heart NEC 098.85
  joint 098.50
  keratoderma 098.81
  keratosis (blennorrhagica) 098.81
  lymphatic (gland) (node) 098.89
  meninges 098.82
  orchitis (acute) 098.13
    chronic or duration of 2 months or over 098.33
  pelvis (acute) 098.19
    chronic or duration of 2 months or over 098.39
  pericarditis 098.83
  peritonitis 098.86
  pharyngitis 098.6
  pharynx 098.6

Gonococcus, gonococcal— *continued*
  proctitis 098.7
  pyosalpinx (chronic) 098.37
    acute 098.17
  rectum 098.7
  septicemia 098.89
  skin 098.89
  specified site NEC 098.89
  synovitis 098.51
  tendon sheath 098.51
  throat 098.6
  urethra (acute) 098.0
    chronic of duration of 2 months or over 098.2
  vulva (acute) 098.0
    chronic or duration of 2 months or over 098.2
Gonocytoma (M9073/1)
  specified site—*see* Neoplasm, by site, uncertain
    behavior
  unspecified site
    female 236.2
    male 236.4
Gonorrhea 098.0
  acute 098.0
  Bartholin's gland (acute) 098.0
    chronic or duration of 2 months or over 098.2
  bladder (acute) 098.11
    chronic or duration of 2 months or over 098.31
  carrier (suspected of) V02.7
  cervix (acute) 098.15
    chronic or duration of 2 months or over 098.35
  chronic 098.2
  complicating pregnancy, childbirth, or
    puerperium 647.1
    affecting fetus or newborn 760.2
  conjunctiva, conjunctivitis (neonatorum) 098.40
  contact V01.6
  Cowper's gland (acute) 098.0
    chronic or duration of 2 months or over 098.2
  duration of two months or over 098.2
  exposure to V01.6
  fallopian tube (chronic) 098.37
    acute 098.17
  genitourinary (acute) (organ) (system) (tract)
    098.0
    chronic 098.2
    duration of two months or over 098.2
  kidney (acute) 098.19
    chronic or duration of 2 months or over 098.39
  ovary (acute) 098.19
    chronic or duration of 2 months or over 098.39
  pelvis (acute) 098.19
    chronic or duration of 2 months or over 098.39
  penis (acute) 098.0
    chronic or duration of 2 months or over 098.2
  prostate (acute) 098.12
    chronic or duration of 2 months or over 098.32
  seminal vesicle (acute) 098.14
    chronic or duration of 2 months or over 098.34
  specified site NEC—*see* Gonococcus
  spermatic cord (acute) 098.14
    chronic or duration of 2 months or over 098.34
  urethra (acute) 098.0
    chronic or duration of 2 months or over 098.2
  vagina (acute) 098.0
    chronic or duration of 2 months or over 098.2
  vas deferens (acute) 098.14
    chronic or duration of 2 months or over 098.34
  vulva (acute) 098.0
    chronic or duration of 2 months or over 098.2
Goodpasture's syndrome (pneumorenal) 446.21

Gopalan's syndrome (burning feet) 266.2
Gordon's disease (exudative enteropathy) 579.8
Gorlin-Chaudhry-Moss syndrome 759.89
Gougerot's syndrome (trisymptomatic) 709.1
Gougerot-Blum syndrome (pigmented purpuric
lichenoid dermatitis) 709.1
Gougerot-Carteaud disease or syndrome
(confluent reticulate papillomatosis) 701.8
Gougerot-Hailey-Hailey disease (benign
familial chronic pemphigus) 757.39
Gougerot (-Houwer) -Sjögren syndrome
(keratoconjunctivitis sicca) 710.2
Gouley's syndrome (constrictive pericarditis)
423.2
Goundou 102.6
Gout, gouty 274.9
with specified manifestations NEC 274.89
arthritis (acute) 274.0
arthropathy 274.0
degeneration, heart 274.82
diathesis 274.9
eczema 274.89
episcleritis 274.89 [379.09]
external ear (tophus) 274.81
glomerulonephritis 274.10
iritis 274.89 [364.11]
joint 274.0
kidney 274.10
lead 984.9
specified type of lead—see Table of drugs and
chemicals
nephritis 274.10
neuritis 274.89 [357.4]
phlebitis 274.89 [451.9]
rheumatic 714.0
saturnine 984.9
specified type of lead—see Table of drugs and
chemicals
spondylitis 274.0
synovitis 274.0
syphilitic 095.8
tophi 274.0
ear 274.81
heart 274.82
specified site NEC 274.82
Gowers'
muscular dystrophy 359.1
syndrome (vasovagal attack) 780.2
Gowers-Paton-Kennedy syndrome 377.04
Gradenigo's syndrome 383.02
Graft-versus-host disease (bone marrow) 996.85
due to organ transplant NEC—see
Complications, transplant, organ
Graham Steell's murmur (pulmonic
regurgitation) (see also Endocarditis,
pulmonary) 424.3
Grain-handlers' disease or lung 495.8
Grain mite (itch) 133.8
Grand
mal (idiopathic) (see also Epilepsy) 345.1
hysteria of Charcot 300.11
nonrecurrent or isolated 780.3
multipara
affecting management of labor and delivery
659.4
status only (not pregnant) V61.5
Granite workers' lung 502

Granular —see also condition
inflammation, pharynx 472.1
kidney (contracting) (see also Sclerosis, renal)
587
liver—see Cirrhosis, liver
nephritis—see Nephritis
Granulation tissue, abnormal —see also
Granuloma
abnormal or excessive 701.5
postmastoidectomy cavity 383.33
postoperative 701.5
skin 701.5
Granulocytopenia, granulocytopenic (primary)
288.0
malignant 288.0
Granuloma NEC 686.1
abdomen (wall) 568.89
skin (pyogenicum) 686.1
from residual foreign body 709.4
annulare 695.89
anus 569.49
apical 522.6
appendix 543.9
aural 380.23
beryllium (skin) 709.4
lung 503
bone (see also Osteomyelitis) 730.1
eosinophilic 277.8
from residual foreign body 733.99
canaliculus lacrimalis 375.81
cerebral 348.8
cholesterin, middle ear 385.82
coccidioidal (progressive) 114.3
lung 114.4
meninges 114.2
primary (lung) 114.0
colon 569.89
conjunctiva 372.61
dental 522.6
ear, middle (cholesterin) 385.82
with otitis media—see Otitis media
eosinophilic 277.8
bone 277.8
lung 277.8
oral mucosa 528.9
exuberant 701.5
eyelid 374.89
facial
lethal midline 446.3
malignant 446.3
fissuratum (gum) 523.8
foot NEC 686.1
foreign body (in soft tissue) NEC 728.82
bone 733.99
in operative wound 998.4
muscle 728.82
skin 709.4
subcutaneous tissue 709.4
fungoides 202.1
gangraenescens 446.3
giant cell (central) (jaw) (reparative) 526.3
gingiva 523.8
peripheral (gingiva) 523.8
gland (lymph) 289.3
Hodgkin's (M9661/3) 201.1
ileum 569.89
infectious NEC 136.9
inguinale (Donovan) 099.2
venereal 099.2
intestine 569.89

Granuloma—*continued*
iridocyclitis 364.10
jaw (bone) 526.3
reparative giant cell 526.3
kidney (*see also* Infection, kidney) 590.9
lacrimal sac 375.81
larynx 478.79
lethal midline 446.3
lipid 277.8
lipoid 277.8
liver 572.8
lung (infectious) (*see also* Fibrosis, lung) 515
coccidioidal 114.4
eosinophilic 277.8
lymph gland 289.3
Majocchi's 110.6
malignant, face 446.3
mandible 526.3
mediastinum 519.3
midline 446.3
monilial 112.3
muscle 728.82
from residual foreign body 728.82
nasal sinus (*see also* Sinusitis) 473.9
operation wound 998.59
foreign body 998.4
stitch (external) 998.89
internal wound 996.7
talc 998.7
oral mucosa, eosinophilic or pyogenic 528.9
orbit, orbital 376.11
paracoccidioidal 116.1
penis, venereal 099.2
periapical 522.6
peritoneum 568.89
due to ova of helminths NEC (*see also*
Helminthiasis) 128.9
postmastoidectomy cavity 383.33
postoperative–*see* Granuloma, operation wound
prostate 601.8
pudendi (ulcerating) 099.2
pudendorum (ulcerative) 099.2
pulp, internal (tooth) 521.4
pyogenic, pyogenicum (skin) 686.1
maxillary alveolar ridge 522.6
oral mucosa 528.9
rectum 569.49
reticulohistiocytic 277.8
rubrum nasi 705.89
sarcoid 135
Schistosoma 120.9
septic (skin) 686.1
silica (skin) 709.4
sinus (accessory) (infectional) (nasal) (*see also*
Sinusitis) 473.9
skin (pyogenicum) 686.1
from foreign body or material 709.4
sperm 608.89
spine
syphilitic (epidural) 094.89
tuberculous (*see also* Tuberculosis) 015.0
[730.88]
stitch (postoperative) 998.89
internal wound 996.7
suppurative (skin) 686.1
suture (postoperative) 998.89
internal wound 996.7
swimming pool 031.1
talc 728.82
in operation wound 998.7

Granuloma—*continued*
telangiectaticum (skin) 686.1
trichophyticum 110.6
tropicum 102.4
umbilicus 686.1
newborn 771.4
urethra 599.84
uveitis 364.10
vagina 099.2
venereum 099.2
vocal cords 478.5
Wegener's (necrotizing respiratory
granulomatosis) 446.4
Granulomatosis NEC 686.1
disciformis chronica et progressiva 709.3
infantiseptica 771.2
lipoid 277.8
lipophagic, intestinal 040.2
miliary 027.0
necrotizing, respiratory 446.4
progressive, septic 288.1
Wegener's (necrotizing respiratory) 446.4
Granulomatous tissue —*see* Granuloma
Granulosis rubra nasi 705.89
Graphite fibrosis (of lung) 503
Graphospasm 300.89
organic 333.84
Grating scapula 733.99
Gravel (urinary) (*see also* Calculus) 592.9
Graves' disease (exophthalmic goiter) (*see also*
Goiter, toxic) 242.0
Gravis —*see* condition
Grawitz's tumor (hypernephroma) (M8312/3)
189.0
Grayness, hair (premature) 704.3
congenital 757.4
Gray or grey syndrome (chloramphenicol)
(newborn) 779.4
Greenfield's disease 330.0
Green sickness 280.9
Greenstick fracture —*see* Fracture, by site
Greig's syndrome (hypertelorism) 756.0
Griesinger's disease (*see also* Ancylostomiasis)
126.9
Grinder's
asthma 502
lung 502
phthisis (*see also* Tuberculosis) 011.4
Grinding, teeth 306.8
Grip
Dabney's 074.1
devil's 074.1
Grippe, grippal —*see also* Influenza
Balkan 083.0
intestinal 487.8
summer 074.8
Grippy cold 487.1
Grisel's disease 723.5
Groin —*see* condition
Grooved
nails (transverse) 703.8
tongue 529.5
congenital 750.13
Ground itch 126.9
Growing pains, children 781.9

Growth (fungoid) (neoplastic) (new)
  (M8000/1)—*see also* Neoplasm, by site,
    unspecified nature
  adenoid (vegetative) 474.12
  benign (M8000/0)—*see* Neoplasm, by site,
    benign
  fetal, poor 764.9
    affecting management of pregnancy 656.5
  malignant (M8000/3)—*see* Neoplasm, by site
    malignant
  rapid, childhood V21.0
  secondary (M8000/6)—*see* Neoplasm, by site,
    malignant, secondary
Gruber's hernia —*see* Hernia, Gruber's
Gruby's disease (tinea tonsurans) 110.0
G-trisomy 758.0
Guama fever 066.3
Gubler (-Millard) paralysis or syndrome 344.89
Guérin-Stern syndrome (arthrogryposis
    multiplex congenita) 754.89
Guertin's disease (electric chorea) 049.8
Guillain-Barré disease or syndrome 357.0
Guinea worms (infection) (infestation) 125.7
Guinon's disease (motor-verbal tic) 307.23
Gull's disease (thyroid atrophy with myxedema)
    244.8
Gull and Sutton's disease —*see* Hypertension,
    kidney
Gum —*see* condition
Gumboil 522.7
Gumma (syphilitic) 095.9
  artery 093.89
    cerebral or spinal 094.89
  bone 095.5
    of yaws (late) 102.6
  brain 094.89
  cauda equina 094.89
  central nervous system NEC 094.9
  ciliary body 095.8 *[364.11]*
  congenital 090.5
    testis 090.5
  eyelid 095.8 *[373.5]*
  heart 093.89
  intracranial 094.89
  iris 095.8 *[364.11]*
  kidney 095.4
  larynx 095.8
  leptomeninges 094.2
  liver 095.3
  meninges 094.2
  myocardium 093.82
  nasopharynx 095.8
  neurosyphilitic 094.9
  nose 095.8
  orbit 095.8
  palate (soft) 095.8
  penis 095.8
  pericardium 093.81
  pharynx 095.8
  pituitary 095.8
  scrofulous (*see also* Tuberculosis) 017.0
  skin 095.8
  specified site NEC 095.8
  spinal cord 094.89
  tongue 095.8
  tonsil 095.8
  trachea 095.8
  tuberculous (*see also* Tuberculosis) 017.0

Gumma— *continued*
  ulcerative due to yaws 102.4
  ureter 095.8
  yaws 102.4
    bone 102.6
Gunn's syndrome (jaw-winking syndrome)
    742.8
Gunshot wound —*see also* Wound, open, by site
  fracture—*see* Fracture, by site, open
  internal organs (abdomen, chest, or pelvis)—*see*
    Injury, internal, by site, with open wound
  intracranial—*see* Laceration, brain, with open
    intracranial wound
Günther's disease or syndrome (congenital
    erythropoietic porphyria) 277.1
Gustatory hallucination 780.1
Gynandrism 752.7
Gynandroblastoma (M8632/1)
  specified site—*see* Neoplasm, by site, uncertain
    behavior
  unspecified site
    female 236.2
    male 236.4
Gynandromorphism 752.7
Gynatresia (congenital) 752.49
Gynecoid pelvis, male 738.6
Gynecological examination V72.3
  for contraceptive maintenance V25.40
Gynecomastia 611.1
Gynephobia 300.29
Gyrate scalp 757.39

H

Haas' disease (osteochondrosis head of humerus) 732.3
Habermann's disease (acute parapsoriasis varioliformis) 696.2
Habit, habituation
  chorea 307.22
  disturbance, child 307.9
  drug (*see also* Dependence) 304.9
  laxative (*see also* Abuse, drugs, nondependent) 305.9
  spasm 307.20
    chronic 307.22
    transient of childhood 307.21
  tic 307.20
    chronic 307.22
    transient of childhood 307.21
  use of
    nonprescribed drugs (*see also* Abuse, drugs, nondependent) 305.9
    patent medicines (*see also* Abuse, drugs, nondependent) 305.9
  vomiting 536.2
Hadfield-Clarke syndrome (pancreatic infantilism) 577.8
Haff disease 985.1
Hageman factor defect, deficiency, or disease (*see also* Defect, coagulation) 286.3
Haglund's disease (osteochondrosis os tibiale externum) 732.5
Haglund-Läwen-Fründ syndrome 717.89
Hagner's disease (hypertrophic pulmonary osteoarthropathy) 731.2
Hag teeth, tooth 524.3
Hailey-Hailey disease (benign familial chronic pemphigus) 757.39
Hair —*see also* condition
  plucking 307.9
Hairball in stomach 935.2
Hairy black tongue 529.3
Half vertebra 756.14
Halitosis 784.9
Hallermann-Streiff syndrome 756.0
Hallervorden-Spatz disease or syndrome 333.0
Hallopeau's
  acrodermatitis (continua) 696.1
  disease (lichen sclerosis et atrophicus) 701.0
Hallucination (auditory) (gustatory) (olfactory) (tactile) 780.1
  alcoholic 291.3
  drug-induced 292.12
  visual 368.16
Hallucinosis 298.9
  alcoholic (acute) 291.3
  drug-induced 292.12
Hallus —*see* Hallux
Hallux 735.9
  malleus (acquired) 735.3
  rigidus (acquired) 735.2
    congenital 755.66
    late effects of rickets 268.1
  valgus (acquired) 735.0
    congenital 755.66
  varus (acquired) 735.1
    congenital 755.66
Halo, visual 368.15
Hamartoblastoma 759.6

Hamartoma 759.6
  epithelial (gingival), odontogenic, central, or peripheral (M9321/0) 213.1
  upper jaw (bone) 213.0
  vascular 757.32
Hamartosis, hamartoses NEC 759.6
Hamman's disease or syndrome (spontaneous mediastinal emphysema) 518.1
Hamman-Rich syndrome (diffuse interstitial pulmonary fibrosis) 516.3
Hammer toe (acquired) 735.4
  congenital 755.66
  late effects of rickets 268.1
Hand —*see* condition
Hand-Schüller-Christian disease or syndrome (chronic histiocytosis x) 277.8
Hand-foot syndrome 282.61
Hanging (asphyxia) (strangulation) (suffocation) 994.7
Hangnail (finger) (with lymphangitis) 681.02
Hangover (alcohol) (*see also* Abuse, drugs, nondependent) 305.0
Hanot's cirrhosis or disease —*see* Cirrhosis, biliary
Hanot-Chauffard (-Troisier) syndrome (bronze diabetes) 275.0
Hansen's disease (leprosy) 030.9
  benign form 030.1
  malignant form 030.0
Harada's disease or syndrome 363.22
Hard chancre 091.0
Hardening
  artery—*see* Arteriosclerosis
  brain 348.8
  liver 571.8
Hare's syndrome (M8010/3) (carcinoma, pulmonary apex) 162.3
Harelip (*see also* Cleft, lip) 749.10
Harkavy's syndrome 446.0
Harlequin (fetus) 757.1
  color change syndrome 779.8
Harley's disease (intermittent hemoglobinuria) 283.2
Harris'
  lines 733.91
  syndrome (organic hyperinsulinism) 251.1
Hart's disease or syndrome (pellagra-cerebellar ataxia-renal aminoaciduria) 270.0
Hartmann's pouch (abnormal sacculation of gallbladder neck) 575.8
Hartnup disease (pellagra-cerebellar ataxia-renal aminoaciduria) 270.0
Harvester lung 495.0
Hashimoto's disease or struma (struma lymphomatosa) 245.2
Hassall-Henle bodies (corneal warts) 371.41
Haut mal (*see also* Epilepsy) 345.1
Haverhill fever 026.1
Hawaiian wood rose dependence 304.5
Hawkins' keloid 701.4
Hay
  asthma (*see also* Asthma) 493.0
  fever (allergic) (with rhinitis) 477.9
    with asthma (bronchial) (*see also* Asthma) 493.0

Hay —*continued*
allergic, due to grass, pollen, ragweed, or tree 477.0
conjunctivitis 372.05
due to
dander 477.8
dust 477.8
fowl 477.8
pollen 477.0
specified allergen other than pollen 477.8
Hayem-Faber syndrome (achlorhydric anemia) 280.9
Hayem-Widal syndrome (acquired hemolytic jaundice) 283.9
Haygarth's nodosities 715.04
Hazard-Crile tumor (M8350/3) 193
Hb (abnormal)
disease—*see* Disease, hemoglobin
trait—*see* Trait
H disease 270.0
Head —*see also* condition
banging 307.3
Headache 784.0
allergic 346.2
cluster 346.2
due to
loss, spinal fluid 349.0
lumbar puncture 349.0
saddle block 349.0
emotional 307.81
histamine 346.2
lumbar puncture 349.0
menopausal 627.2
migraine 346.9
nonorganic origin 307.81
postspinal 349.0
psychogenic 307.81
psychophysiologic 307.81
sick 346.1
spinal fluid loss 349.0
tension 307.81
vascular 784.0
migraine type 346.9
vasomotor 346.9
Health
advice V65.4
audit V70.0
checkup V70.0
education V65.4
hazard (*see also* History of) V15.9
specified cause NEC V15.89
instruction V65.4
services provided because of (of)
boarding school residence V60.6
holiday relief for person providing home care V60.5
inadequate
housing V60.1
resources V60.2
lack of housing V60.0
no care available in home V60.4
person living alone V60.3
poverty V60.3
residence in institution V60.6
specified cause NEC V60.8
vacation relief for person providing home care V60.5

Healthy
donor (*see also* Donor) V59.9
infant or child
accompanying sick mother V65.0
receiving care V20.1
person
accompanying sick relative V65.0
admitted for sterilization V25.2
receiving prophylactic inoculation or vaccination (*see also* Vaccination, prophylactic) V05.9
Hearing examination V72.1
Heart —*see* condition
Heartburn 787.1
psychogenic 306.4
Heat (effects) 992.9
apoplexy 992.0
burn—*see also* Burn, by site
from sun 692.71
collapse 992.1
cramps 992.2
dermatitis or eczema 692.89
edema 992.7
erythema—*see* Burn, by site
excessive 992.9
specified effect NEC 992.8
exhaustion 992.5
anhydrotic 992.3
due to
salt (and water) depletion 992.4
water depletion 992.3
fatigue (transient) 992.6
fever 992.0
hyperpyrexia 992.0
prickly 705.1
prostration—*see* Heat, exhaustion
pyrexia 992.0
rash 705.1
specified effect NEC 992.8
stroke 992.0
sunburn 692.71
syncope 992.1
Heavy-chain disease 273.2
Heavy-for-dates (fetus or infant) 766.1
4500 grams or more 766.0
exceptionally 766.0
Hebephrenia, hebephrenic (acute) (*see also* Schizophrenia) 295.1
dementia (praecox) (*see also* Schizophrenia) 295.1
schizophrenia (*see also* Schizophrenia) 295.1
Heberden's
disease or nodes 715.04
syndrome (angina pectoris) 413.9
Hebra's disease
dermatitis exfoliativa 695.89
erythema multiforme exudativum 695.1
pityriasis 695.89
maculata et circinata 696.3
rubra 695.89
pilaris 696.4
prurigo 698.2
Hebra, nose 040.1
Hedinger's syndrome (malignant carcinoid) 259.2
Heel —*see* condition
Heerfordt's disease or syndrome (uveoparotitis) 135

Hegglin's anomaly or syndrome 288.2
Heidenhain's disease 290.10
  with dementia 290.10
Heilmeyer-Schöner disease (M9842/3) 207.1
Heine-Medin disease (*see also* Poliomyelitis)
  045.9
Heinz-body anemia, congenital 282.7
Heller's disease or syndrome (infantile
  psychosis) (*see also* Psychosis, childhood)
  299.1
H.E.L.L.P. 642.5
Helminthiasis (*see also* Infestation, by specific
  parasite) 128.9
  Ancylostoma (*see also* Ancylostoma) 126.9
  intestinal 127.9
    mixed types (types classifiable to more than
      one of the titles 120.0-127.7) 127.8
    specified type 127.7
  mixed types (intestinal) (types classifiable to
    more than one of the titles 120.0-127.7)
    127.8
  Necator americanus 126.1
  specified type NEC 128.8
  Trichinella 124
Heloma 700
Hemangioblastoma (M9161/1)—*see also*
  Neoplasm, connective tissue, uncertain
  behavior
  malignant (M9161//3)—*see* Neoplasm,
    connective tissue, malignant
Hemangioblastomatosis, cerebelloretinal 759.6
Hemangloendothelioma (M9130/1)—*see also*
  Neoplasm, by site, uncertain behavior
  benign (M9130/0) 228.00
  bone (diffuse) (M9130/3)—*see* Neoplasm,
    bone, malignant
  malignant (M9130/3)—*see* Neoplasm,
    connective tissue, malignant
  nervous system (M9130/0) 228.09
Hemangioendotheliosarcoma (M9130/3)—*see*
  Neoplasm, connective tissue, malignant
Hemangiofibroma (M9160/0)—*see* Neoplasm,
  by site, benign
Hemangiolipoma (M8861/0)—*see* Lipoma
Hemangioma (M9120/0) 228.00
  arteriovenous (M9123/0)—*see* Hemangioma,
    by site
  brain 228.02
  capillary (M9131/0)—*see* Hemangioma, by site
  cavernous (M9121/0)—*see* Hemangioma, by
    site
  central nervous system NEC 228.09
  choroid 228.09
  heart 228.09
  infantile (M9131/0)—*see* Hemangioma, by site
  intra-abdominal structures 228.04
  intracranial structures 228.02
  intramuscular (M9132/0)—*see* Hemangioma,
    by site
  iris 228.09
  juvenile (M9131/0)—*see* Hemangioma, by site
  malignant (M9120/3)—*see* Neoplasm,
    connective tissue, malignant
  meninges 228.09
    brain 228.02
    spinal cord 228.09
  peritoneum 228.04
  placenta—*see* Placenta, abnormal
  plexiform (M9131/0)—*see* Hemangioma, by site
  racemose (M9123/0)—*see* Hemangioma, by site
  retina 228.03
  retroperitoneal tissue 228.04

Hemangioma—*continued*
  sclerosing (M8832/0)—*see* Neoplasm, skin,
    benign
  simplex (M9131/0)—*see* Hemangioma, by site
  skin and subcutaneous tissue 228.01
  specified site NEC 228.09
  spinal cord 228.09
  venous (M9122/0)—*see* Hemangioma, by site
  verrucous keratotic (M9142/0)—*see*
    Hemangioma, by site
Hemangiomatosis (systemic) 757.32
  involving single site—*see* Hemangioma
Hemangiopericytoma (M9150/1)—*see also*
  Neoplasm, connective tissue, uncertain
  behavior
  benign (M9150/0)—*see* Neoplasm, connective
    tissue, benign
  malignant (M9150/3)—*see* Neoplasm,
    connective tissue, malignant
Hemangiosarcoma (M9120/3)—*see* Neoplasm,
  connective tissue, malignant
Hemarthrosis (nontraumatic) 719.0
  ankle 719.17
  elbow 719.12
  foot 719.17
  hand 719.14
  hip 719.15
  knee 719.16
  multiple sites 719.19
  pelvic region 719.15
  shoulder (region) 719.11
  specified site NEC 719.18
  traumatic—*see* Sprain, by site
  wrist 719.13
Hematemesis 578.0
  with ulcer—*see* Ulcer, by site, with hemorrhage
  due to S. japonicum 120.2
  Goldstein's (familial hemorrhagic
    telangiectasia) 448.0
  newborn 772.4
    due to swallowed maternal blood 777.3
Hematidrosis 705.89
Hematinuria (*see also* Hemoglobinuria) 791.2
  malarial 084.8
  paroxysmal 283.2
Hematite miners' lung 503
Hematobilia 576.8
Hematocele (congenital) (diffuse) (idiopathic)
  608.83
  broad ligament 620.7
  canal of Nuck 629.0
  cord, male 608.83
  fallopian tube 620.8
  female NEC 629.0
  ischiorectal 569.89
  male NEC 608.83
  ovary 629.0
  pelvis, pelvic
    female 629.0
      with ectopic pregnancy (*see also* Pregnancy,
        ectopic) 633.9
    male 608.83
  periuterine 629.0
  retrouterine 629.0
  scrotum 608.83
  spermatic cord (diffuse) 608.83
  testis 608.84
  traumatic—*see* Injury, internal, pelvis
  tunica vaginalis 608.83
  uterine ligament 629.0
  uterus 621.4

Hematocele—*continued*
 vagina 623.6
 vulva 624.5
Hematocephalus 742.4
Hematochezia (*see also* Melena) 578.1
Hematochyluria (*see also* Infestation, filarial)
 125.9
Hematocolpos 626.8
Hematocornea 371.12
Hematogenous —*see* condition
Hematoma (skin surface intact) (traumatic)—*see*
 also Contusion

Note—Hematomas are coded according to
origin and the nature and site of the hematoma
or the accompanying injury. Hematomas of
unspecified origin are coded as injuries of the
sites involved, except:
(a) hematomas of genital organs which are
 coded as diseases of the organ involved
 unless they complicate pregnancy or delivery
(b) hematomas of the eye which are coded as
 diseases of the eye.

For late effect of hematoma classifiable to
920-924 see Late, effect, contusion

---

 with
 crush injury—*see* Crush
 fracture—*see* Fracture, by site
 injury of internal organs—*see also* Injury,
 internal, by site
 kidney—*see* Hematoma, kidney, traumatic
 liver—*see* Hematoma, liver, traumatic
 spleen—*see* Hematoma, spleen
 nerve injury—*see* Injury, nerve
 open wound—*see* Wound, open, by site
 skin surface intact—*see* Contusion
 abdomen (wall)—*see* Contusion, abdomen
 amnion 658.8
 aorta, dissecting 441.00
 abdominal 441.02
 thoracic 441.01
 thoracoabdominal 441.03
 arterial (complicating trauma) 904.9
 specified site—*see* Injury, blood vessel, by site
 auricle (ear) 380.31
 birth injury 767.8
 skull 767.1
 brain (traumatic) 853.0

Note—Use the following fifth-digit
subclassification with categories 851-854:

0 unspecified state of consciousness
1 with no loss of consciousness
2 with brief [less than one hour] loss of
 consciousness
3 with moderate [1-24 hours] loss of
 consciousness
4 with prolonged [more than 24 hours] loss of
 consciousness and return to pre-existing
 conscious level
5 with prolonged [more than 24 hours] loss of
 consciousness, without return to pre-existing
 conscious level
Use fifth-digit 5 to designate when a patient is
unconscious and dies before regaining
consciousness, regardless of the duration of the
loss of consciousness
6 with loss of consciousness of unspecified
 duration
9 with concussion, unspecified

Hematoma— *continued*
 with
 cerebral
 contusion—*see* Contusion, brain
 laceration—*see* Laceration, brain
 open intracranial wound 853.1
 skull fracture—*see* Fracture, skull, by site
 extradural or epidural 852.4
 with open intracranial wound 852.5
 fetus or newborn 767.0
 nontraumatic 432.0
 fetus or newborn NEC 767.0
 nontraumatic (*see also* Hemorrhage, brain)
 431
 epidural or extradural 432.0
 newborn NEC 772.8
 subarachnoid, arachnoid, or meningeal (*see*
 also Hemorrhage, subarachnoid) 430
 subdural (*see also* Hemorrhage, subdural)
 432.1
 subarachnoid, arachnoid, or meningeal 852.0
 with open intracranial wound 852.1
 fetus or newborn 772.2
 nontraumatic (*see also* Hemorrhage,
 subarachnoid) 430
 subdural 852.2
 with open intracranial wound 852.3
 fetus or newborn (localized) 767.0
 nontraumatic (*see also* Hemorrhage,
 subdural) 432.1
 breast (nontraumatic) 611.8
 broad ligament (nontraumatic) 620.7
 complicating delivery 665.7
 traumatic—*see* Injury, internal, broad ligament
 calcified NEC 959.9
 capitis 920
 due to birth injury 767.1
 newborn 767.1
 cerebral—*see* Hematoma, brain
 cesarean section wound 674.3
 chorion—*see* Placenta, abnormal
 complicating delivery (perineum) (vulva) 664.5
 pelvic 665.7
 vagina 665.7
 corpus
 cavernosum (nontraumatic) 607.82
 luteum (nontraumatic) (ruptured) 620.1
 dura (mater)—*see* Hematoma, brain, subdural
 epididymis (nontraumatic) 608.83
 epidural (traumatic)—*see also* Hematoma,
 brain, extradural
 spinal—*see* Injury, spinal, by site
 episiotomy 674.3
 external ear 380.31
 extradural—*see also* Hematoma, brain,
 extradural
 fetus or newborn 767.0
 nontraumatic 432.0
 fetus or newborn 767.0
 fallopian tube 620.8
 genital organ (nontraumatic)
 female NEC 629.8
 male NEC 608.83
 traumatic (external site) 922.4
 internal—*see* Injury, internal, genital organ
 graafian follicle (ruptured) 620.0
 internal organs (abdomen, chest, or pelvis)—*see*
 also Injury, internal, by site
 kidney—*see* Hematoma, kidney, traumatic
 liver—*see* Hematoma, liver, traumatic
 spleen—*see* Hematoma, spleen

Hematoma—*continued*
intracranial—*see* Hematoma, brain
kidney, cystic 593.81
  traumatic 866.01
    with open wound into cavity 866.11
labia (nontraumatic) 624.5
lingual (and other parts of neck, scalp, or face, except eye) 920
liver (subcapsular) 573.8
  birth injury 767.8
  fetus or newborn 767.8
  traumatic NEC 864.01
    with
        laceration—*see* Laceration, liver
        open wound into cavity 864.11
mediastinum—*see* Injury, internal, mediastinum
meninges, meningeal (brain)—*see also*
      Hematoma, brain, subarachnoid
  spinal—*see* Injury, spinal, by site
mesosalpinx (nontraumatic) 620.8
  traumatic—*see* Injury, internal, pelvis
muscle (traumatic)—*see* Contusion, by site
nasal (septum) (and other part(s) of neck, scalp, or face, except eye) 920
obstetrical surgical wound 674.3
orbit, orbital (nontraumatic) 376.32
  traumatic 921.2
ovary (corpus luteum) (nontraumatic) 620.1
  traumatic—*see* Injury, internal, ovary
pelvis (female) (nontraumatic) 629.8
  complicating delivery 665.7
  male 608.83
  traumatic—*see also* Injury, internal, pelvis
    specified organ NEC (*see also* Injury, internal, pelvis) 867.6
penis (nontraumatic) 607.82
pericranial (and neck, or face any part, except eye) 920
  due to injury at birth 767.1
perineal wound (obstetrical) 674.3
  complicating delivery 664.5
perirenal, cystic 593.81
pinna 380.31
placenta—*see* Placenta, abnormal
postoperative 998.12
retroperitoneal (nontraumatic) 568.81
  traumatic—*see* Injury, internal, retroperitoneum
retropubic, male 568.81
scalp (and neck, or face any part, except eye) 920
  fetus or newborn 767.1
scrotum (nontraumatic) 608.83
  traumatic 922.4
seminal vesicle (nontraumatic) 608.83
  traumatic—*see* Injury, internal, seminal vesicle
spermatic cord—*see also* Injury, internal, spermatic cord
  nontraumatic 608.83
spinal (cord) (meninges)—*see also* Injury, spinal, by site
  fetus or newborn 767.4
  nontraumatic 336.1
spleen 865.01
  with
        laceration—*see* Laceration, spleen
        open wound into cavity 865.11
sternocleidomastoid, birth injury 767.8

Hematoma—*continued*
sternomastoid, birth injury 767.8
subarachnoid—*see also* Hematoma, brain, subarachnoid
  fetus or newborn 772.2
  nontraumatic (*see also* Hemorrhage, subarachnoid) 430
  newborn 772.2
subdural—*see also* Hematoma, brain, subdural
  fetus or newborn (localized) 767.0
  nontraumatic (*see also* Hemorrhage, subdural) 432.1
subperiosteal (syndrome) 267
  traumatic—*see* Hematoma, by site
superficial, fetus or newborn 772.6
syncytium—*see* Placenta, abnormal
testis (nontraumatic) 608.83
  birth injury 767.8
  traumatic 922.4
tunica vaginalis (nontraumatic) 608.83
umbilical cord 663.6
  affecting fetus or newborn 762.6
uterine ligament (nontraumatic) 620.7
  traumatic—*see* Injury, internal, pelvis
uterus 621.4
  traumatic—*see* Injury, internal, pelvis
vagina (nontraumatic) (ruptured) 623.6
  complicating delivery 665.7
  traumatic 922.4
vas deferens (nontraumatic) 608.83
  traumatic—*see* Injury, internal, vas deferens
vitreous 379.23
vocal cord 920
vulva (nontraumatic) 624.5
  complicating delivery 664.5
  fetus or newborn 767.8
  traumatic 922.4
Hematometra 621.4
Hematomyelia 336.1
  with fracture of vertebra (*see also* Fracture, vertebra, by site, with spinal cord injury) 806.8
  fetus or newborn 767.4
Hematomyelitis 323.9
  late effect—*see* category 326
Hematoperitoneum (*see also* Hemoperitoneum) 568.81
Hematopneumothorax (*see also* Hemothorax) 511.8
Hematoporphyria (acquired) (congenital) 277.1
Hematoporphyrinuria (acquired) (congenital) 277.1
Hematorachis, hematorrhachis 336.1
  fetus or newborn 767.4
Hematosalpinx 620.8
  with
      ectopic pregnancy (*see also* categories 633.0-633.9) 639.2
      molar pregnancy (*see also* categories 630-632) 639.2
  infectional (*see also* Salpingo-oophoritis) 614.2
Hematospermia 608.83
Hematothorax (*see also* Hemothorax) 511.8
Hematotympanum 381.03
Hematuria (benign) (essential) (idiopathic) 599.7
  due to S. hematobium 120.0
  endemic 120.0
  intermittent 599.7
  malarial 084.8
  paroxysmal 599.7

Hematuria—*continued*
  sulfonamide
    correct substance properly administered 599.7
    overdose or wrong substance given or taken
      961.0
  tropical (bilharziasis) 120.0
  tuberculous (*see also* Tuberculosis) 016.9
Hematuric bilious fever 084.8
Hemeralopia 368.60
  meaning day blindness 368.10
  vitamin A deficiency 264.5
Hemiabiotrophy 799.8
Hemi-akinesia 781.8
Hemianalgesia (*see also* Disturbance, sensation)
  782.0
Hemianencephaly 740.0
Hemianesthesia (*see also* Disturbance,
  sensation) 782.0
Hemianopia, hemianopsia (altitudinal)
    (homonymous) 368.46
  binasal 368.47
  bitemporal 368.47
  heteronymous 368.47
  syphilitic 095.8
Hemiasomatognosia 307.9
Hemiathetosis 781.0
Hemiatrophy 799.8
  cerebellar 334.8
  face 349.89
    progressive 349.89
  fascia 728.9
  leg 728.2
  tongue 529.8
Hemiballism (us) 333.5
Hemiblock (cardiac) (heart) (left) 426.2
Hemicardia 746.89
Hemicephalus, hemicephaly 740.0
Hemichorea 333.5
Hemicrania 346.9
  congenital malformation 740.0
Hemidystrophy —*see* Hemiatrophy
Hemiectromelia 755.4
Hemihypalgesia (*see also* Disturbance,
  sensation) 782.0
Hemihypertrophy (congenital) 759.89
  cranial 756.0
Hemihypesthesia (*see also* Disturbance,
  sensation) 782.0
Hemi-inattention 781.8
Hemimelia 755.4
  lower limb 755.30
    paraxial (complete) (incomplete) (intercalary)
      (terminal) 755.32
      fibula 755.37
      tibia 755.36
    transverse (complete) (partial) 755.31
  upper limb 755.20
    paraxial (complete) (incomplete) (intercalary)
      (terminal) 755.22
      radial 755.26
      ulnar 755.27
    transverse (complete) (partial) 755.21
Hemiparalysis (*see also* Hemiplegia) 342.9
Hemiparesis (*see also* Hemiplegia) 342.9
Hemiparesthesia (*see also* Disturbance,
  sensation) 782.0

Hemiplegia 342.9
  acute (*see also* Disease, cerebrovascular, acute)
    436
  alternans facialis 344.89
  apoplectic (*see also* Disease, cerebrovascular,
    acute) 436
    late effect or residual—*see* category 438
  arteriosclerotic 437.0
    late effect or residual—*see* category 438
  ascending (spinal) NEC 344.89
  attack (*see also* Disease, cerebrovascular, acute)
    436
  brain, cerebral (current episode) 437.8
    congenital 343.1
  cerebral—*see* Hemiplegia, brain
  congenital (cerebral) (spastic) (spinal) 343.1
  conversion neurosis (hysterical) 300.11
  cortical—*see* Hemiplegia, brain
  due to
    arteriosclerosis 437.0
      late effect or residual—*see* category 438
    cerebrovascular lesion (*see also* Disease,
      cerebrovascular, acute) 436
      late effect—*see* category 438
  embolic (current) (*see also* Embolism, brain)
    434.1
    late effect—*see* category 438
  flaccid 342.0
  hypertensive (current episode) 437.8
  infantile (postnatal) 343.4
  late effect
    birth injury, intracranial or spinal 343.4
    cerebrovascular lesion—*see* category 438
    viral encephalitis 139.0
  middle alternating NEC 344.89
  newborn NEC 767.0
  seizure (current episode) (*see also* Disease,
    cerebrovascular, acute) 436
  spastic 342.1
    congenital or infantile 343.1
  specified NEC 342.8
  thrombotic (current) (*see also* Thrombosis,
    brain) 434.0
    late effect—*see* category 438
Hemisection, spinal cord —*see* Fracture,
  vertebra, by site, with spinal cord injury
Hemispasm 781.0
  facial 781.0
Hemispatial neglect 781.8
Hemisporosis 117.9
Hemitremor 781.0
Hemivertebra 756.14
Hemobilia 576.8
Hemocholecyst 575.8
Hemochromatosis (acquired) (diabetic)
    (hereditary) (liver) (myocardium) (primary
    idiopathic) (secondary) 275.0
  with refractory anemia 285.0
Hemodialysis V56.0
Hemoglobin —*see also* condition
  abnormal (disease)—*see* Disease, hemoglobin
  AS genotype 282.5
  fetal, hereditary persistence 282.7
  high-oxygen-affinity 289.0
  low NEC 285.9
  S (Hb-S), heterozygous 282.5
Hemoglobinemia 283.2
  due to blood transfusion NEC 999.8
    bone marrow 996.85
  paroxysmal 283.2

Hemoglobinopathy (mixed) (*see also* Disease, hemoglobin) 282.7
  with thalassemia 282.4
  sickle-cell 282.60
    with thalassemia 282.4
Hemoglobinuria, hemoglobinuric 791.2
  with anemia, hemolytic, acquired (chronic) NEC 283.2
  cold (agglutinin) (paroxysmal) (with Raynaud's syndrome) 283.2
  due to
    exertion 283.2
    hemolysis (from external causes) NEC 283.2
  exercise 283.2
  fever (malaria) 084.8
  infantile 791.2
  intermittent 283.2
  malarial 084.8
  march 283.2
  nocturnal (paroxysmal) 283.2
  paroxysmal (cold) (nocturnal) 283.2
Hemolymphangioma (M9175/0) 228.1
Hemolysis
  fetal—*see* Jaundice, fetus or newborn
  intravascular (disseminated) NEC 286.6
    with
      abortion—*see* Abortion, by type, with hemorrhage, delayed or excessive
      ectopic pregnancy (*see also* categories 633.0-633.9) 639.1
      hemorrhage of pregnancy 641.3
        affecting fetus or newborn 762.1
      molar pregnancy (*see also* categories 630-632) 639.1
    acute 283.2
    following
      abortion 639.1
      ectopic or molar pregnancy 639.1
  neonatal—*see* Jaundice, fetus or newborn
  transfusion NEC 999.8
    bone marrow 996.85
Hemolytic —*see also* condition
  anemia—*see* Anemia, hemolytic
  uremic syndrome 283.11
Hemometra 621.4
Hemopericardium (with effusion) 423.0
  newborn 772.8
  traumatic (*see also* Hemothorax, traumatic) 860.2
    with open wound into thorax 860.3
Hemoperitoneum 568.81
  infectional (*see also* Peritonitis) 567.2
  traumatic—*see* Injury, internal, peritoneum
Hemophilia (familial) (hereditary) 286.0
  A 286.0
  B (Leyden) 286.1
  B$_m$ 286.1
  C 286.2
  calcipriva (*see also* Fibrinolysis) 286.7
  classical 286.0
  nonfamilial 286.7
  vascular 286.4
Hemophilus influenzae NEC 041.5
  arachnoiditis (basic) (brain) (spinal) 320.0
    late effect—*see* category 326
  bronchopneumonia 482.2
  cerebral ventriculitis 320.0
    late effect—*see* category 326
  cerebrospinal inflammation 320.0
    late effect—*see* category 326

Hemophilus influenzae—*continued*
  infection NEC 041.5
  leptomeningitis 320.0
    late effect—*see* category 326
  meningitis (cerebral) (cerebrospinal) (spinal) 320.0
    late effect—*see* category 326
  meningomyelitis 320.0
    late effect—*see* category 326
  pachymeningitis (adhesive) (fibrous) (hemorrhagic) (hypertrophic) (spinal) 320.0
    late effect—*see* category 326
  pneumonia (broncho-) 482.2
Hemophthalmos 360.43
Hemopneumothorax (*see also* Hemothorax) 511.8
  traumatic 860.4
    with open wound into thorax 860.5
Hemoptysis 786.3
  due to Paragonimus (westermani) 121.2
  newborn 770.3
  tuberculous (*see also* Tuberculosis, pulmonary) 011.9
Hemorrhage, hemorrhagic (nontraumatic) 459.0
  abdomen 459.0
  accidental (antepartum) 641.2
    affecting fetus or newborn 762.1
  adenoid 474.8
  adrenal (capsule) (gland) (medulla) 255.4
    newborn 772.5
  after labor—*see* Hemorrhage, postpartum
  alveolar
    lung, newborn 770.3
    process 525.8
  alveolus 525.8
  amputation stump (surgical) 998.1
    secondary, delayed 997.69
  anemia (chronic) 280.0
    acute 285.1
  antepartum—*see* Hemorrhage, pregnancy
  anus (sphincter) 569.3
  apoplexy (stroke) 432.9
  arachnoid—*see* Hemorrhage, subarachnoid
  artery NEC 459.0
    brain (*see also* Hemorrhage, brain) 431
    middle meningeal—*see* Hemorrhage, subarachnoid
  basilar (ganglion) (*see also* Hemorrhage, brain) 431
  bladder 596.8
  blood dyscrasia 289.9
  bowel 578.9
    newborn 772.4
  brain (miliary) (nontraumatic) 431
    with
      birth injury 767.0
      arachnoid—*see* Hemorrhage, subarachnoid
    due to
      birth injury 767.0
      rupture of aneurysm (congenital) (*see also* Hemorrhage, subarachnoid) 430
        mycotic 431
      syphilis 094.89
    epidural or extradural—*see* Hemorrhage, extradural
    fetus or newborn (anoxic) (hypoxic) (due to birth trauma) (nontraumatic) 767.0
    iatrogenic 997.02
    postoperative 997.02
    puerperal, postpartum, childbirth 674.0
    stem 431

Hemorrhage, hemorrhagic— *continued*
    subarachnoid, arachnoid or meningeal—*see*
        Hemorrhage, subarachnoid
    subdural—*see* Hemorrhage, subdural
        traumatic NEC 853.0

Note—Use the following fifth-digit
subclassification with categories 851-854:

0 *unspecified state of consciousness*
1 *with no loss of consciousness*
2 *with brief [less than one hour] loss of
consciousness*
3 *with moderate [1-24 hours] loss of
consciousness*
4 *with prolonged [more than 24 hours] loss of
consciousness and return to pre-existing
conscious level*
5 *with prolonged [more than 24 hours] loss of
consciousness, without return to pre-existing
conscious level*
*Use fifth-digit 5 to designate when a patient is
unconscious and dies before regaining
consciousness, regardless of the duration of the
loss of consciousness*
6 *with loss of consciousness of unspecified
duration*
9 *with concussion, unspecified*

---

    with
      cerebral
        contusion—*see* Contusion, brain
        laceration—*see* Laceration, brain
      open intracranial wound 853.1
      skull fracture—*see* Fracture, skull, by site
    extradural or epidural 852.4
      with open intracranial wound 852.5
    subarachnoid 852.0
      with open intracranial wound 852.1
    subdural 852.2
      with open intracranial wound 852.3
    breast 611.79
    bronchial tube—*see* Hemorrhage, lung
    bronchopulmonary—*see* Hemorrhage, lung
    bronchus (cause unknown) (*see also*
      Hemorrhage, lung) 786.3
    bulbar (*see also* Hemorrhage, brain) 431
    bursa 727.89
    capillary 448.9
      primary 287.8
    capsular—*see* Hemorrhage, brain
    cardiovascular 429.89
    cecum 578.9
    cephalic (*see also* Hemorrhage, brain) 431
    cerebellar (*see also* Hemorrhage, brain) 431
    cerebellum (*see also* Hemorrhage, brain) 431
    cerebral (*see also* Hemorrhage, brain) 431
      fetus or newborn (anoxic) (traumatic) 767.0
    cerebromeningeal (*see also* Hemorrhage, brain)
      431
    cerebrospinal (*see also* Hemorrhage, brain) 431
    cerebrum (*see also* Hemorrhage, brain) 431
    cervix (stump) (uteri) 622.8
    cesarean section wound 674.3
    chamber, anterior (eye) 364.41
    childbirth—*see* Hemorrhage, complicating,
      delivery
    choroid 363.61
      expulsive 363.62
    ciliary body 364.41
    cochlea 386.8
    colon—*see* Hemorrhage, intestine

  complicating
    delivery 641.9
      affecting fetus or newborn 762.1
      associated with
        afibrinogenemia 641.3
          affecting fetus or newborn 763.8
        coagulation defect 641.3
          affecting fetus or newborn 763.8
        hyperfibrinolysis 641.3
          affecting fetus or newborn 763.8
        hypofibrinogenemia 641.3
          affecting fetus or newborn 763.8
      due to
        low-lying placenta 641.1
          affecting fetus or newborn 762.0
        placenta previa 641.1
          affecting fetus or newborn 762.0
        premature separation of placenta 641.2
          affecting fetus or newborn 762.1
        retained
          placenta 666.0
          secundines 666.2
        trauma 641.8
          affecting fetus or newborn 763.8
        uterine leiomyoma 641.8
          affecting fetus or newborn 763.8
    surgical procedure 998.11
  concealed NEC 459.0
  congenital 772.9
  conjunctiva 372.72
    newborn 772.8
  cord, newborn 772.0
    slipped ligature 772.3
    stump 772.3
  corpus luteum (ruptured) 620.1
  cortical (*see also* Hemorrhage, brain) 431
  cranial 432.9
  cutaneous 782.7
    newborn 772.6
  cyst, pancreas 577.2
  cystitis—*see* Cystitis
  delayed
    with
      abortion—*see* Abortion, by type, with
        hemorrhage, delayed or excessive
      ectopic pregnancy (*see also* categories
        633.0-633.9) 639.1
      molar pregnancy (*see also* categories
        630-632) 639.1
    following
      abortion 639.1
      ectopic or molar pregnancy 639.1
    postpartum 666.2
  diathesis (familial) 287.9
    newborn 776.0
  disease 287.9
    newborn 776.0
    specified type NEC 287.8
  disorder 287.9
    due to circulating anticoagulants 286.5
    specified type NEC 287.8
  due to
    any device, implant, or graft (presence of)
      classifiable to 996.0-996.5—*see*
      Complications, due to (presence of) any
      device, implant, or graft classified to
      996.0—996.5 NEC
    circulating anticoagulant 286.5
  duodenum, duodenal 537.89
    ulcer—*see* Ulcer, duodenum, with hemorrhage

Hemorrhage, hemorrhagic— *continued*
dura mater—*see* Hemorrhage, subdural
endotracheal—*see* Hemorrhage, lung
epidural—*see* Hemorrhage, extradural
episiotomy 674.3
esophagus 530.82
  varix (*see also* Varix, esophagus, bleeding)
    456.0
excessive
  with
    abortion—*see* Abortion, by type, with
      hemorrhage, delayed or excessive
    ectopic pregnancy (*see also* categories
      633.0-633.9) 639.1
    molar pregnancy (*see also* categories
      630-632) 639.1
  following
    abortion 639.1
    ectopic or molar pregnancy 639.1
external 459.0
extradural (traumatic)—*see also* Hemorrhage,
  brain, traumatic, extradural
  birth injury 767.0
  fetus or newborn (anoxic) (traumatic) 767.0
  nontraumatic 432.0
eye 360.43
  chamber (anterior) (aqueous) 364.41
  fundus 362.81
eyelid 374.81
fallopian tube 620.8
fetomaternal 772.0
  affecting management of pregnancy or
    puerperium 656.0
fetus, fetal 772.0
  from
    cut end of co-twin's cord 772.0
    placenta 772.0
    ruptured cord 772.0
    vasa previa 772.0
  into
    co-twin 772.0
    mother's circulation 772.0
      affecting management of pregnancy or
        puerperium 656.0
fever (*see also* Fever, hemorrhagic) 065.9
  with renal syndrome 078.6
  arthropod-borne NEC 065.9
  Bangkok 065.4
  Crimean 065.0
  dengue virus 065.4
  epidemic 078.6
  Junin virus 078.7
  Korean 078.6
  Machupo virus 078.7
  mite-borne 065.8
  mosquito-borne 065.4
  Philippine 065.4
  Russian (Yaroslav) 078.6
  Singapore 065.4
  southeast Asia 065.4
  Thailand 065.4
  tick-borne NEC 065.3
fibrinogenolysis (*see also* Fibrinolysis) 286.6
fibrinolytic (acquired) (*see also* Fibrinolysis)
  286.6
fontanel 767.1
from tracheostomy stoma 519.0
fundus, eye 362.81
funis
  affecting fetus or newborn 772.0
  complicating delivery 663.8

Hemorrhage, hemorrhagic— *continued*
gastric (*see also* Hemorrhage, stomach) 578.9
gastroenteric 578.9
  newborn 772.4
gastrointestinal (tract) 578.9
  newborn 772.4
genitourinary (tract) NEC 599.89
gingiva 523.8
globe 360.43
gravidarum—*see* Hemorrhage, pregnancy
gum 523.8
heart 429.89
hypopharyngeal (throat) 784.8
intermenstrual 626.8
  irregular 626.6
  regular 626.5
internal (organs) 459.0
  capsule (*see also* Hemorrhage brain) 431
  ear 386.8
  newborn 772.8
intestine 578.9
  congenital 772.4
  newborn 772.4
into
  bladder wall 596.7
  bursa 727.89
  corpus luysii (*see also* Hemorrhage, brain) 431
intra-abdominal 459.0
  during or following surgery 998.11
intra-alveolar, newborn (lung) 770.3
intracerebral (*see also* Hemorrhage, brain) 431
intracranial NEC 432.9
  puerperal, postpartum, childbirth 674.0
  traumatic—*see* Hemorrhage, brain, traumatic
intramedullary NEC 336.1
intraocular 360.43
intraoperative 998.11
intrapartum—*see* Hemorrhage, complicating,
  delivery
intrapelvic
  female 629.8
  male 459.0
intraperitoneal 459.0
intrapontine (*see also* Hemorrhage, brain) 431
intrauterine 621.4
  complicating delivery—*see* Hemorrhage,
    complicating, delivery
  in pregnancy or childbirth—*see* Hemorrhage,
    pregnancy
  postpartum (*see also* Hemorrhage,
    postpartum) 666.1
intraventricular (*see also* Hemorrhage, brain)
  431
  fetus or newborn (anoxic) (traumatic) 772.1
intravesical 596.7
iris (postinfectional) (postinflammatory) (toxic)
  364.41
joint (nontraumatic) 719.10
  ankle 719.17
  elbow 719.12
  foot 719.17
  forearm 719.13
  hand 719.14
  hip 719.15
  knee 719.16
  lower leg 719.16
  multiple sites 719.19
  pelvic region 719.15
  shoulder (region) 719.11
  specified site NEC 719.18

Hemorrhage, hemorrhagic—*continued*
  thigh 719.15
  upper arm 719.12
  wrist 719.13
  kidney 593.81
  knee (joint) 719.16
  labyrinth 386.8
  leg NEC 459.0
  lenticular striate artery (*see also* Hemorrhage,
    brain) 431
  ligature, vessel 998.11
  liver 573.8
  lower extremity NEC 459.0
  lung 786.3
    newborn 770.3
    tuberculous (*see also* Tuberculosis,
      pulmonary) 011.9
  malaria 084.8
  marginal sinus 641.2
  massive subaponeurotic, birth injury 767.1
  maternal, affecting fetus or newborn 762.1
  mediastinum 786.3
  medulla (*see also* Hemorrhage, brain) 431
  membrane (brain) (*see also* Hemorrhage,
    subarachnoid) 430
    spinal cord—*see* Hemorrhage, spinal cord
  meninges, meningeal (brain) (middle) (*see also*
    Hemorrhage, subarachnoid) 430
    spinal cord—*see* Hemorrhage, spinal cord
  mesentery 568.81
  metritis 626.8
  midbrain (*see also* Hemorrhage, brain) 431
  mole 631
  mouth 528.9
  mucous membrane NEC 459.0
    newborn 772.8
  muscle 728.89
  nail (subungual) 703.8
  nasal turbinate 784.7
    newborn 772.8
  nasopharynx 478.29
  navel, newborn 772.3
  newborn 772.9
    adrenal 772.5
    alveolar (lung) 770.3
    brain (anoxic) (hypoxic) (due to birth trauma)
      767.0
    cerebral (anoxic) (hypoxic) (due to birth
      trauma) 767.0
    conjunctiva 772.8
    cutaneous 772.6
    diathesis 776.0
    due to vitamin K deficiency 776.0
    gastrointestinal 772.4
    internal (organs) 772.8
    intestines 772.4
    intra-alveolar (lung) 770.3
    intracranial (from any perinatal cause) 767.0
    intraventricular (from any perinatal cause)
      772.1
    lung 770.3
    pulmonary (massive) 770.3
    spinal cord, traumatic 767.4
    stomach 772.4
    subaponeurotic (massive) 767.1
    subarachnoid (from any perinatal cause) 772.2
    subconjunctival 772.8
    umbilicus 772.0
      slipped ligature 772.3
      vasa previa 772.0

Hemorrhage, hemorrhagic—*continued*
  nipple 611.79
  nose 784.7
    newborn 772.8
  obstetrical surgical wound 674.3
  omentum 568.89
    newborn 772.4
  optic nerve (sheath) 377.42
  orbit 376.32
  ovary 620.1
  oviduct 620.8
  pancreas 577.8
  parathyroid (gland) (spontaneous) 252.8
  parturition—*see* Hemorrhage, complicating,
    delivery
  penis 607.82
  pericardium, pericarditis 423.0
  perineal wound (obstetrical) 674.3
  peritoneum, peritoneal 459.0
  peritonsillar tissue 474.8
    after operation on tonsils 998.11
    due to infection 475
  petechial 782.7
  pituitary (gland) 253.8
  placenta NEC 641.9
    affecting fetus or newborn 762.1
    from surgical or instrumental damage 641.8
      affecting fetus or newborn 762.1
    previa 641.1
      affecting fetus or newborn 762.0
  pleura—*see* Hemorrhage, lung
  polioencephalitis, superior 265.1
  polymyositis—*see* Polymyositis
  pons (*see also* Hemorrhage, brain) 431
  pontine (*see also* Hemorrhage, brain) 431
  popliteal 459.0
  postcoital 626.7
  postextraction (dental) 998.11
  postmenopausal 627.1
  postnasal 784.7
  postoperative 998.11
  postpartum (atonic) (following delivery of
    placenta) 666.1
    delayed or secondary (after 24 hours) 666.2
    retained placenta 666.0
    third stage 666.0
  pregnancy (concealed) 641.9
    accidental 641.2
      affecting fetus or newborn 762.1
    affecting fetus or newborn 762.1
    before 22 completed weeks gestation 640.9
      affecting fetus or newborn 762.1
    due to
      abruptio placenta 641.2
        affecting fetus or newborn 762.1
      afibrinogenemia or other coagulation defect
        (conditions classifiable to 286.0-286.9)
        641.3
        affecting fetus or newborn 762.1
      coagulation defect 641.3
        affecting fetus or newborn 762.1
      hyperfibrinolysis 641.3
        affecting fetus or newborn 762.1
      hypofibrinogenemia 641.3
        affecting fetus or newborn 762.1
      leiomyoma, uterus 641.8
        affecting fetus or newborn 762.1
      low-lying placenta 641.1
        affecting fetus or newborn 762.1
      marginal sinus (rupture) 641.2
        affecting fetus or newborn 762.1

Hemorrhage, hemorrhagic—*continued*
 placenta previa 641.1
  affecting fetus or newborn 762.0
 premature separation of placenta (normally
  implanted) 641.2
  affecting fetus or newborn 762.1
 threatened abortion 640.0
  affecting fetus or newborn 762.1
 trauma 641.8
  affecting fetus or newborn 762.1
 early (before 22 completed weeks gestation)
  640.9
  affecting fetus or newborn 762.1
 previous, affecting management of pregnancy
  or childbirth V23.4
 unavoidable—*see* Hemorrhage, pregnancy,
  due to placenta previa
 prepartum (mother)—*see* Hemorrhage,
  pregnancy
 preretinal, cause unspecified 362.81
 prostate 602.1
 puerperal (*see also* Hemorrhage, postpartum)
  666.1
 pulmonary—*see also* Hemorrhage, lung
  newborn (massive) 770.3
  renal syndrome 446.21
 purpura (primary) (*see also* Purpura,
  thrombocytopenic) 287.3
 rectum (sphincter) 569.3
 recurring, following initial hemorrhage at time
  of injury 958.2
 renal 593.81
  pulmonary syndrome 446.21
 respiratory tract (*see also* Hemorrhage, lung)
  786.3
 retina, retinal (deep) (superficial) (vessels)
  362.81
  diabetic 250.5 *[362.01]*
  due to birth injury 772.8
 retrobulbar 376.89
 retroperitoneal 459.0
 retroplacental (*see also* Placenta, separation)
  641.2
 scalp 459.0
  due to injury at birth 767.1
 scrotum 608.83
 secondary (nontraumatic) 459.0
  following initial hemorrhage at time of injury
  958.2
 seminal vesicle 608.83
 skin 782.7
  newborn 772.6
 spermatic cord 608.83
 spinal (cord) 336.1
  aneurysm (ruptured) 336.1
   syphilitic 094.89
  due to birth injury 767.4
  fetus or newborn 767.4
 spleen 289.59
 spontaneous NEC 459.0
  petechial 782.7
 stomach 578.9
  newborn 772.4
  ulcer—*see* Ulcer, stomach, with hemorrhage
 subaponeurotic, newborn 767.1
  massive (birth injury) 767.1
 subarachnoid (nontraumatic) 430
  fetus or newborn (anoxic) (traumatic) 772.2
  puerperal, postpartum, childbirth 674.0
  traumatic—*see* Hemorrhage, brain, traumatic,
   subarachnoid

Hemorrhage, hemorrhagic—*continued*
 subconjunctival 372.72
  due to birth injury 772.8
  newborn 772.8
 subcortical (*see also* Hemorrhage, brain) 431
 subcutaneous 782.7
 subdiaphragmatic 459.0
 subdural (nontraumatic) 432.1
  due to birth injury 767.0
  fetus or newborn (anoxic) (hypoxic) (due to
   birth trauma) 767.0
  puerperal, postpartum, childbirth 674.0
  spinal 336.1
  traumatic—*see* Hemorrhage, brain, traumatic,
   subdural
 subhyaloid 362.81
 subperiosteal 733.99
 subretinal 362.81
 subtentorial (*see also* Hemorrhage, subdural)
  432.1
 subungual 703.8
  due to blood dyscrasia 287.8
 suprarenal (capsule) (gland) 255.4
  fetus or newborn 772.5
 tentorium (traumatic)—*see also* Hemorrhage,
  brain, traumatic
  fetus or newborn 767.0
  nontraumatic—*see* Hemorrhage, subdural
 testis 608.83
 thigh 459.0
 third stage 666.0
 thorax—*see* Hemorrhage, lung
 throat 784.8
 thrombocythemia 238.7
 thymus (gland) 254.8
 thyroid (gland) 246.3
  cyst 246.3
 tongue 529.8
 tonsil 474.8
  postoperative 998.11
 tooth socket (postextraction) 998.11
 trachea—*see* Hemorrhage, lung
 traumatic—*see also* nature of injury
  brain—*see* Hemorrhage, brain, traumatic
  recurring or secondary (following initial
   hemorrhage at time of injury) 958.2
 tuberculous NEC (*see also* Tuberculosis,
  pulmonary) 011.9
 tunica vaginalis 608.83
 ulcer—*see* Ulcer, by site, with hemorrhage
 umbilicus, umbilical cord 772.0
  after birth, newborn 772.3
  complicating delivery 663.8
   affecting fetus or newborn 772.0
  slipped ligature 772.3
  stump 772.3
 unavoidable (due to placenta previa) 641.1
  affecting fetus or newborn 762.0
 upper extremity 459.0
 urethra (idiopathic) 599.84
 uterus, uterine (abnormal) 626.9
  climacteric 627.0
  complicating delivery—*see* Hemorrhage,
   complicating, delivery
  due to
   intrauterine contraceptive device 996.76
    perforating uterus 996.32
  functional or dysfunctional 626.8
  in pregnancy—*see* Hemorrhage, pregnancy

Hemorrhage, hemorrhagic— *continued*
  intermenstrual 626.8
    irregular 626.6
    regular 626.5
  postmenopausal 627.1
  postpartum (*see also* Hemorrhage,
    postpartum) 666.1
  prepubertal 626.8
  pubertal 626.3
  puerperal (immediate) 666.1
  vagina 623.8
  vasa previa 663.5
    affecting fetus or newborn 772.0
  vas deferens 608.83
  ventricular (*see also* Hemorrhage, brain) 431
  vesical 596.8
  viscera 459.0
    newborn 772.8
  vitreous (humor) (intraocular) 379.23
  vocal cord 478.5
  vulva 624.8
Hemorrhoids (anus) (rectum) (without
  complication) 455.6
  bleeding, prolapsed, strangulated, or ulcerated
    NEC 455.8
  external 455.5
  internal 455.2
  complicated NEC 455.8
  complicating pregnancy and puerperium 671.8
  external 455.3
    with complication NEC 455.5
    bleeding, prolapsed, strangulated, or ulcerated
      455.5
    thrombosed 455.4
  internal 455.0
    with complication NEC 455.2
    bleeding, prolapsed, strangulated, or ulcerated
      455.2
    thrombosed 455.1
  residual skin tag 455.9
  sentinel pile 455.9
  thrombosed NEC 455.7
    external 455.4
    internal 455.1
Hemosalpinx 620.8
Hemosiderosis 275.0
  dietary 275.0
  pulmonary (idiopathic) 275.0 *[516.1]*
  transfusion NEC 999.8
    bone marrow 996.85
Hemospermia 608.83
Hemothorax 511.8
  bacterial, nontuberculous 511.1
  newborn 772.8
  nontuberculous 511.8
    bacterial 511.1
  pneumococcal 511.1
  staphylococcal 511.1
  streptococcal 511.1
  traumatic 860.2
    with
      open wound into thorax 860.3
      pneumothorax 860.4
        with open wound into thorax 860.5
  tuberculous (*see also* Tuberculosis, pleura)
    012.0
Hemotympanum 385.89
Hench-Rosenberg syndrome (palindromic
  arthritis) (*see also* Rheumatism, palindromic)
  719.3
Henle's warts 371.41

Henoch (-Schönlein)
  disease or syndrome (allergic purpura) 287.0
  purpura (allergic) 287.0
Henpue, henpuye 102.6
Heparitinuria 277.5
Hepar lobatum 095.3
Hepatalgia 573.8
Hepatic —*see also* condition
  flexure syndrome 569.89
Hepatitis 573.3
  acute (*see also* Necrosis, liver) 570
    alcoholic 571.1
    infective 070.1
      with hepatic coma 070.0
  alcoholic 571.1
  amebic—*see* Abscess, liver, amebic
  anicteric (acute)—*see* Hepatitis, viral
  antigen-associated (HAA) *see* Hepatitis, viral,
    type B
  Australian antigen (positive) *see* Hepatitis, viral,
    type B
  catarrhal (acute) 070.1
    with hepatic coma 070.0
    chronic 571.40
    newborn 070.1
      with hepatic coma 070.0
  chemical 573.3
  cholangiolitic 573.8
  cholestatic 573.8
  chronic 571.40
    active 571.49
      viral—*see* Hepatitis, viral
    aggressive 571.49
    persistent 571.41
    viral—*see* Hepatitis, viral
  cytomegalic inclusion virus 078.5 *[573.1]*
  diffuse 573.3
  "dirty needle"—*see* Hepatitis, viral
    with hepatic coma 070.2
  drug-induced 573.3
  due to
    Coxsackie 074.8 *[573.1]*
    cytomegalic inclusion virus 078.5 *[573.1]*
    infectious mononucleosis 075 *[573.1]*
    malaria 084.9 *[573.2]*
    mumps 072.71
    secondary syphilis 091.62
    toxoplasmosis (acquired) 130.5
      congenital (active) 771.2
  epidemic—*see* Hepatitis, viral, type A
  fetus or newborn 774.4
  fibrous (chronic) 571.49
    acute 570
  from injection, inoculation, or transfusion
    (blood) (other substance) (plasma) (serum)
    (onset within 8 months after administration)
    see Hepatitis, viral
  fulminant (viral) (*see also* Hepatitis, viral) 070.9
    with hepatic coma 070.6
    type A 070.1
      with hepatic coma 070.0
    type B—*see* Hepatitis, viral, Type B
  giant cell (neonatal) 774.4
  hemorrhagic 573.8
  homologous serum—*see* Hepatitis, viral
  hypertrophic (chronic) 571.49
    acute 570
  infectious, infective (acute) (chronic) (subacute)
    070.1
    with hepatic coma 070.0

Hepatitis—*continued*
  inoculation—*see* Hepatitis, viral
  interstitial (chronic) 571.49
    acute 570
  lupoid 571.49
  malarial 084.9 *[573.2]*
  malignant (*see also* Necrosis, liver) 570
  neonatal (toxic) 774.4
  newborn 774.4
  parenchymatous (acute) (*see also* Necrosis,
    liver) 570
  peliosis 573.3
  persistent, chronic 571.41
  plasma cell 571.49
  postimmunization—*see* Hepatitis, viral
  postnecrotic 571.49
  posttransfusion—*see* Hepatitis, viral
  recurrent 571.49
  septic 573.3
  serum—*see* Hepatitis, viral
    carrier (suspected) of V02.6
  subacute (*see also* Necrosis, liver) 570
  suppurative (diffuse) 572.0
  syphilitic (late) 095.3
    congenital (early) 090.0 *[573.2]*
      late 090.5 *[573.2]*
    secondary 091.62
  toxic (noninfectious) 573.3
    fetus or newborn 774.4
  tuberculous (*see also* Tuberculosis) 017.9
  viral (acute) (anicteric) (cholangiolitic)
    (cholestatic) (chronic) (subacute) 070.9
    with hepatic coma 070.6
    AU-SH type virus—*see* Hepatitis, viral, type B
    Australian antigen—*see* Hepatitis, viral, type
      B
    B-antigen—*see* Hepatitis, viral, type B
    Coxsackie 074.8 *[573.1]*
    cytomegalic inclusion 078.5 *[573.1]*
    IH (virus)—*see* Hepatitis, viral, type A
    infectious hepatitis virus—*see* Hepatitis, viral,
      type A
    serum hepatitis virus—*see* Hepatitis, viral,
      type B
    SH—*see* Hepatitis, viral, type B
    specified type NEC 070.59
      with hepatic coma 070.49
    type A 070.1
      with hepatic coma 070.0
    type B (acute) 070.30
      with
        hepatic coma 070.20
          with hepatitis delta 070.21
        hepatitis delta 070.31
          with hepatic coma 070.21
      chronic 070.32
        with
          hepatic coma 070.22
            with hepatitis delta 070.23
          hepatitis delta 070.33
            with hepatic coma 070.23
    type C (acute) 070.51
      with hepatic coma 070.41
      chronic 070.54
        with hepatic coma 070.44
    type delta (with hepatitis B carrier state)
      070.52
      with
        active hepatitis B disease—*see* Hepatitis,
          viral, type B
        hepatic coma 070.42

Hepatitis—*continued*
  type E 070.53
    with hepatic coma 070.43
  vaccination and inoculation (prophylactic)
    V05.3
  Waldenström's (lupoid hepatitis) 571.49
Hepatization, lung (acute)—*see also*
  Pneumonia, lobar
  chronic (*see also* Fibrosis, lung) 515
Hepatoblastoma (M8970/3) 155.0
Hepatocarcinoma (M8170/3) 155.0
Hepatocholangiocarcinoma (M8180/3) 155.0
Hepatocholangioma, benign (M8180/0) 211.5
Hepatocholangitis 573.8
Hepatocystitis (*see also* Cholecystitis) 575.10
Hepatodystrophy 570
Hepatolenticular degeneration 275.1
Hepatolithiasis —*see* Choledocholithiasis
Hepatoma (malignant) (M8170/3) 155.0
  benign (M8170/0) 211.5
  congenital (M8970/3) 155.0
  embryonal (M8970/3) 155.0
Hepatomegalia glycogenica diffusa 271.0
Hepatomegaly (*see also* Hypertrophy, liver)
  789.1
  congenital 751.69
    syphilitic 090.0
  due to Clonorchis sinensis 121.1
  Gaucher's 272.7
  syphilitic (congenital) 090.0
Hepatoptosis 573.8
Hepatorrhexis 573.8
Hepatosis, toxic 573.8
Hepatosplenomegaly 571.8
  due to S. japonicum 120.2
  hyperlipemic (Burger-Grutz type) 272.3
Herald patch 696.3
Hereditary —*see* condition
Heredodegeneration 330.9
  macular 362.70
Heredopathia atactica polyneuritiformis 356.3
Heredosyphilis (*see also* Syphilis, congenital)
  090.9
Hermaphroditism (true) 752.7
  with specified chromosomal anomaly—*see*
    Anomaly, chromosomes, sex
Hernia, hernial (acquired) (recurrent) 553.9
  with
    gangrene (obstructed) NEC 551.9
    obstruction NEC 552.9
      and gangrene 551.9
  abdomen (wall)—*see* Hernia, ventral
  abdominal, specified site NEC 553.8
    with
      gangrene (obstructed) 551.8
      obstruction 552.8
        and gangrene 551.8
  appendix 553.8
    with
      gangrene (obstructed) 551.8
      obstruction 552.8
        and gangrene 551.8
  bilateral (inguinal)—*see* Hernia, inguinal
  bladder (sphincter)
    congenital (female) (male) 753.8
    female 618.0
    male 596.8
  brain 348.4
    congenital 742.0

Hernia, hernial—*continued*
broad ligament 553.8
cartilage, vertebral—*see* Displacement,
   intervertebral disc
cerebral 348.4
   congenital 742.0
   endaural 742.0
ciliary body 364.8
   traumatic 871.1
colic 553.9
   with
      gangrene (obstructed) 551.9
      obstruction 552.9
         and gangrene 551.9
colon 553.9
   with
      gangrene (obstructed) 551.9
      obstruction 552.9
         and gangrene 551.9
colostomy (stoma) 569.69
Cooper's (retroperitoneal) 553.8
   with
      gangrene (obstructed) 551.8
      obstruction 552.8
         and gangrene 551.8
crural—*see* Hernia, femoral
diaphragm, diaphragmatic 553.3
   with
      gangrene (obstructed) 551.3
      obstruction 552.3
         and gangrene 551.3
   congenital 756.6
   due to gross defect of diaphragm 756.6
   traumatic 862.0
      with open wound into cavity 862.1
direct (inguinal)—*see* Hernia, inguinal
disc, intervertebral—*see* Displacement,
   intervertebral disc
diverticulum, intestine 553.9
   with
      gangrene (obstructed) 551.9
      obstruction 552.9
         and gangrene 551.9
double (inguinal)—*see* Hernia, inguinal
duodenojejunal 553.8
   with
      gangrene (obstructed) 551.8
      obstruction 552.8
         and gangrene 551.8
en glissade—*see* Hernia, inguinal
enterostomy (stoma) 569.69
epigastric 553.29
   with
      gangrene (obstruction) 551.29
      obstruction 552.29
         and gangrene 551.29
   recurrent 553.21
      with
         gangrene (obstructed) 551.21
         obstruction 552.21
            and gangrene 551.21
esophageal hiatus (sliding) 553.3
   with
      gangrene (obstructed) 551.3
      obstruction 552.3
         and gangrene 551.3
   congenital 750.6
external (inguinal)—*see* Hernia, inguinal
fallopian tube 620.4

Hernia, hernial—*continued*
fascia 728.89
fat 729.30
   eyelid 374.34
   orbital 374.34
   pad 729.30
      eye, eyelid 374.34
      knee 729.31
      orbit 374.34
      popliteal (space) 729.31
      specified site NEC 729.39
femoral (unilateral) 553.00
   with
      gangrene (obstructed) 551.00
      obstruction 552.00
         with gangrene 551.00
   bilateral 553.02
      gangrenous (obstructed) 551.02
      obstructed 552.02
         with gangrene 551.02
      recurrent 553.03
         gangrenous (obstructed) 551.03
         obstructed 552.03
            with gangrene 551.03
   recurrent (unilateral) 553.01
      bilateral 553.03
         gangrenous (obstructed) 551.03
         obstructed 552.03
            with gangrene 551.03
      gangrenous (obstructed) 551.01
      obstructed 552.01
         with gangrene 551.01
foramen
   Bochdalek 553.3
      with
         gangrene (obstructed) 551.3
         obstruction 552.3
            and gangrene 551.3
      congenital 756.6
   magnum 348.4
   Morgagni, morgagnian 553.3
      with
         gangrene 551.3
         obstruction 552.3
            and gangrene 551.3
      congenital 756.6
funicular (umbilical) 553.1
   with
      gangrene (obstructed) 551.1
      obstruction 552.1
         and gangrene 551.1
   spermatic cord—*see* Hernia, inguinal
gangrenous—*see* Hernia, by site, with gangrene
gastrointestinal tract 553.9
   with
      gangrene (obstructed) 551.9
      obstruction 552.9
         and gangrene 551.9
gluteal—*see* Hernia, femoral
Gruber's (internal mesogastric) 553.8
   with
      gangrene (obstructed) 551.8
      obstruction 552.8
         and gangrene 551.8
Hesselbach's 553.8
   with
      gangrene (obstructed) 551.8
      obstruction 552.8
         and gangrene 551.8

Hernia, hernial—*continued*
  hiatal (esophageal) (sliding) 553.3
    with
      gangrene (obstructed) 551.3
      obstruction 552.3
        and gangrene 551.3
    congenital 750.6
  incarcerated (*see also* Hernia, by site, with
      obstruction) 552.9
    gangrenous (*see also* Hernia, by site, with
        gangrene) 551.9
  incisional 553.21
    with
      gangrene (obstructed) 551.21
      obstruction 552.21
        and gangrene 551.21
  lumbar—*see* Hernia, lumbar
  recurrent 553.21
    with
      gangrene (obstructed) 551.21
      obstruction 552.21
        and gangrene 551.21
  indirect (inguinal)—*see* Hernia, inguinal
  infantile—*see* Hernia, inguinal
  infrapatellar fat pad 729.31
  inguinal (direct) (double) (encysted) (external)
      (funicular) (indirect) (infantile) (internal)
      (interstitial) (oblique) (scrotal) (sliding)
      550.9

  Note—Use the following fifth-digit
  subclassification with category 550:

  0 *unilateral or unspecified (not specified as
     recurrent)*
  1 *unilateral or unspecified, recurrent*
  2 *bilateral (not specified as recurrent)*
  3 *bilateral, recurrent*

    with
      gangrene (obstructed) 550.0
      obstruction 550.1
        and gangrene 550.0
  internal 553.8
    with
      gangrene (obstructed) 551.8
      obstruction 552.8
        and gangrene 551.8
    inguinal—*see* Hernia, inguinal
  interstitial 553.9
    with
      gangrene (obstructed) 551.9
      obstruction 552.9
        and gangrene 551.9
    inguinal—*see* Hernia, inguinal
  intervertebral cartilage or disc—*see*
      Displacement, intervertebral disc
  intestine, intestinal 553.9
    with
      gangrene (obstructed) 551.9
      obstruction 552.9
        and gangrene 551.9
  intra-abdominal 553.9
    with
      gangrene (obstructed) 551.9
      obstruction 552.9
        and gangrene 551.9
  intraparietal 553.9
    with
      gangrene (obstructed) 551.9
      obstruction 552.9
        and gangrene 551.9

Hernia, hernial—*continued*
  iris 364.8
    traumatic 871.1
  irreducible (*see also* Hernia, by site, with
      obstruction) 552.9
    gangrenous (with obstruction) (*see also*
        Hernia, by site, with gangrene) 551.9
  ischiatic 553.8
    with
      gangrene (obstructed) 551.8
      obstruction 552.8
        and gangrene 551.8
  ischiorectal 553.8
    with
      gangrene (obstructed) 551.8
      obstruction 552.8
        and gangrene 551.8
  lens 379.32
    traumatic 871.1
  linea
    alba—*see* Hernia, epigastric
    semilunaris—*see* Hernia, spigelian
  Littre's (diverticular) 553.9
    with
      gangrene (obstructed) 551.9
      obstruction 552.9
        and gangrene 551.9
  lumbar 553.8
    with
      gangrene (obstructed) 551.8
      obstruction 552.8
        and gangrene 551.8
    intervertebral disc 722.10
  lung (subcutaneous) 518.89
    congenital 748.69
  mediastinum 519.3
  mesenteric (internal) 553.8
    with
      gangrene (obstructed) 551.8
      obstruction 552.8
        and gangrene 551.8
  mesocolon 553.8
    with
      gangrene (obstructed) 551.8
      obstruction 552.8
        and gangrene 551.8
  muscle (sheath) 728.89
  nucleus pulposus—*see* Displacement,
      intervertebral disc
  oblique (inguinal)—*see* Hernia, inguinal
  obstructive (*see also* Hernia, by site, with
      obstruction) 552.9
    gangrenous (with obstruction) (*see also*
        Hernia, by site, with gangrene) 551.9
  obturator 553.8
    with
      gangrene (obstructed) 551.8
      obstruction 552.8
        and gangrene 551.8
  omental 553.8
    with
      gangrene (obstructed) 551.8
      obstruction 552.8
        and gangrene 551.8
  orbital fat (pad) 374.34
  ovary 620.4
  oviduct 620.4
  paracolostomy (stoma) 569.69

Hernia, hernial—*continued*
  paraduodenal 553.8
    with
      gangrene (obstructed) 551.8
      obstruction 552.8
      and gangrene 551.8
  paraesophageal 553.3
    with
      gangrene (obstructed) 551.3
      obstruction 552.3
      and gangrene 551.3
    congenital 750.6
  parahiatal 553.3
    with
      gangrene (obstructed) 551.3
      obstruction 552.3
      and gangrene 551.3
  paraumbilical 553.1
    with
      gangrene (obstructed) 551.1
      obstruction 552.1
      and gangrene 551.1
  parietal 553.9
    with
      gangrene (obstructed) 551.9
      obstruction 552.9
      and gangrene 551.9
  perineal 553.8
    with
      gangrene (obstructed) 551.8
      obstruction 552.8
      and gangrene 551.8
  peritoneal sac, lesser 553.8
    with
      gangrene (obstructed) 551.8
      obstruction 552.8
      and gangrene 551.8
  popliteal fat pad 729.31
  postoperative 553.21
    with
      gangrene (obstructed) 551.21
      obstruction 552.21
      and gangrene 551.21
  pregnant uterus 654.4
  prevesical 596.8
  properitoneal 553.8
    with
      gangrene (obstructed) 551.8
      obstruction 552.8
      and gangrene 551.8
  pudendal 553.8
    with
      gangrene (obstructed) 551.8
      obstruction 552.8
      and gangrene 551.8
  rectovaginal 618.6
  retroperitoneal 553.8
    with
      gangrene (obstructed) 551.8
      obstruction 552.8
      and gangrene 551.8
  Richter's (parietal) 553.9
    with
      gangrene (obstructed) 551.9
      obstruction 552.9
      and gangrene 551.9
  Rieux's, Riex's (retrocecal) 553.8
    with
      gangrene (obstructed) 551.8
      obstruction 552.8
      and gangrene 551.8

Hernia, hernial—*continued*
  sciatic 553.8
    with
      gangrene (obstructed) 551.8
      obstruction 552.8
      and gangrene 551.8
  scrotum, scrotal—*see* Hernia, inguinal
  sliding (inguinal)—*see also* Hernia, inguinal
    hiatus—*see* Hernia, hiatal
  spigelian 553.29
    with
      gangrene (obstructed) 551.29
      obstruction 552.29
      and gangrene 551.29
  spinal (*see also* Spina bifida) 741.9
    with hydrocephalus 741.0
  strangulated (*see also* Hernia, by site, with
    obstruction) 552.9
    gangrenous (with obstruction) (*see also*
      Hernia, by site, with gangrene) 551.9
  supraumbilicus (linea alba)—*see* Hernia,
    epigastric
  tendon 727.9
  testis (nontraumatic) 095.8
  Treitz's (fossa) 553.8
    with
      gangrene (obstructed) 551.8
      obstruction 552.8
      and gangrene 551.8
  tunica
    albuginea 608.89
    vaginalis 752.8
  umbilicus, umbilical 553.1
    with
      gangrene (obstructed) 551.1
      obstruction 552.1
      and gangrene 551.1
  ureter 593.89
    with obstruction 593.4
  uterus 621.8
    pregnant 654.4
  vaginal (posterior) 618.6
  Velpeau's (femoral) (*see also* Hernia, femoral)
    553.00
  ventral 553.20
    with
      gangrene (obstructed) 551.20
      obstruction 552.20
      and gangrene 551.20
    recurrent 553.21
      with
        gangrene (obstructed) 551.21
        obstruction 552.21
        and gangrene 551.21
  vesical
    congenital (female) (male) 753.8
    female 618.0
    male 596.8
  vitreous (into anterior chamber) 379.21
    traumatic 871.1
Herniation —*see also* Hernia
  brain (stem) 348.4
  cerebral 348.4
  gastric mucosa (into duodenal bulb) 537.89
  mediastinum 519.3
  nucleus pulposus—*see* Displacement,
    intervertebral disc
Herpangina 074.0

Hidradenoma (nodular) (M8400/0)—*see also*
  Neoplasm, skin, benign
  clear cell (M8402/0)—*see* Neoplasm, skin,
    benign
  papillary (M8405/0)—*see* Neoplasm, skin,
    benign
Hidrocystoma (M8404/0)—*see* Neoplasm, skin,
  benign
High
  A$_2$ anemia 282.4
  altitude effects 993.2
    anoxia 993.2
    on
      ears 993.0
      sinuses 993.1
    polycythemia 289.0
  arch
    foot 755.67
    palate 750.26
  artery (arterial) tension (*see also* Hypertension)
    401.9
    without diagnosis of hypertension 796.2
  basal metabolic rate (BMR) 794.7
  blood pressure (*see also* Hypertension) 401.9
    incidental reading (isolated) (nonspecific), no
      diagnosis of hypertension 796.2
  compliance bladder 596.4
  diaphragm (congenital) 756.6
  frequency deafness (congenital) (regional) 389.8
  head at term 652.5
    affecting fetus or newborn 763.1
    causing obstructed labor 660.0
      affecting fetus or newborn 763.1
  output failure (cardiac) (*see also* Failure, heart)
    428.9
  oxygen-affinity hemoglobin 289.0
  palate 750.26
  risk
    behavior —*see* Problem
    family situation V61.9
      specified circumstance NEC V61.8
    individual NEC V62.89
    infant NEC V20.1
    patient taking drugs (prescribed) V67.51
      nonprescribed (*see also* Abuse, drugs,
        nondependent) 305.9
    pregnancy V23.9
      inadequate prenatal care V23.7
      specified problem NEC V23.8
  temperature (of unknown origin) (*see also*
    Pyrexia) 780.6
  thoracic rib 756.3
Hildenbrand's disease (typhus) 081.9
Hilger's syndrome 337.0
Hill diarrhea 579.1
Hilliard's lupus (*see also* Tuberculosis) 017.0
Hilum —*see* condition
Hip —*see* condition
Hippel's disease (retinocerebral angiomatosis)
  759.6
Hippus 379.49
Hirschfeld's disease (acute diabetes mellitus)
  (*see also* Diabetes) 250.0
Hirschsprung's disease or megacolon
  (congenital) 751.3
Hirsuties (*see also* Hypertrichosis) 704.1
Hirsutism (*see also* Hypertrichosis) 704.1
Hirudiniasis (external) (internal) 134.2
His-Werner disease (trench fever) 083.1
Hiss-Russell dysentery 004.1
Histamine cephalgia 346.2
Histidinemia 270.5

Histidinuria 270.5
Histiocytoma (M8832/0)—*see also* Neoplasm,
  skin, benign
  fibrous (M8830/0)—*see also* Neoplasm, skin,
    benign
    atypical (M8830/1)—*see* Neoplasm,
      connective tissue, uncertain behavior
    malignant (M8830/0)—*see* Neoplasm,
      connective tissue, malignant
Histiocytosis (acute) (chronic) (subacute) 277.8
  acute differentiated progressive (M9722/3) 202.5
  cholesterol 277.8
  essential 277.8
  lipid, lipoid (essential) 272.7
  lipochrome (familial) 288.1
  malignant (M9720/3) 202.3
  X (chronic) 277.8
    acute (progressive) (M9722/3) 202.5
Histoplasmosis 115.90
  with
    endocarditis 115.94
    meningitis 115.91
    pericarditis 115.93
    pneumonia 115.95
    retinitis 115.92
    specified manifestation NEC 115.99
  African (due to Histoplasma duboisii) 115.10
    with
      endocarditis 115.14
      meningitis 115.11
      pericarditis 115.13
      pneumonia 115.15
      retinitis 115.12
      specified manifestation NEC 115.19
  American (due to Histoplasma capsulatum)
    115.00
    with
      endocarditis 115.04
      meningitis 115.01
      pericarditis 115.03
      pneumonia 115.05
      retinitis 115.02
      specified manifestation NEC 115.09
  Darling's—*see* Histoplasmosis, American
  large form (*see also* Histoplasmosis, African)
    115.10
  lung 115.05
  small form (*see also* Histoplasmosis, American)
    115.00
History (personal) of
  abuse
    emotional V15.42
    neglect V15.42
    physical V15.41
  affective psychosis V11.1
  alcoholism V11.3
    specified as drinking problem (*see also*
      Abuse, drugs, nondependent) 305.0
  allergy to
    analgesic agent NEC V14.6
    anesthetic NEC V14.4
    antibiotic agent NEC V14.1
      penicillin V14.0
    anti-infective agent NEC V14.3
    diathesis V15.0
    drug V14.9
      specified type NEC V14.8
    medicinal agents V14.9
      specified type NEC V14.8
    narcotic agent NEC V14.5
    penicillin V14.0

History—*continued*
- bone V16.8
- brain V16.8
- breast V16.3
  - male V16.8
- bronchus V16.1
- cecum V16.0
- cervix V16.4
- colon V16.0
- duodenum V16.0
- esophagus V16.0
- eye V16.8
- gallbladder V16.0
- gastrointestinal tract V16.0
- genital organs V16.4
- hemopoietic NEC V16.7
- ileum V16.0
- ilium V16.8
- intestine V16.0
- intrathoracic organs NEC V16.2
- kidney V16.5
- larynx V16.2
- liver V16.0
- lung V16.1
- lymphatic NEC V16.7
- ovary V16.4
- oviduct V16.4
- pancreas V16.0
- penis V16.4
- prostate V16.4
- rectum V16.0
- respiratory organs NEC V16.2
- skin V16.8
- specified site NEC V16.8
- stomach V16.0
- testis V16.4
- trachea V16.1
- ureter V16.5
- urethra V16.5
- urinary organs V16.5
- uterus V16.4
- vagina V16.4
- vulva V16.4
- mental retardation V18.4
- metabolic disease NEC V18.1
- mongolism V19.5
- multiple myeloma V16.7
- musculoskeletal disease NEC V17.8
- nephritis V18.6
- nephrosis V18.6
- parasitic disease V18.8
- psychiatric disorder V17.0
- psychosis V17.0
- retardation, mental V18.4
- retinitis pigmentosa V19.1
- schizophrenia V17.0
- skin conditions V19.4
- specified condition NEC V19.8
- stroke (cerebrovascular) V17.1
- visual loss V19.0
- genital system disorder V13.2
- health hazard V15.9
  - specified cause NEC V15.89
- Hodgkin's disease V10.72
- immunity disorder V12.2
- infectious disease V12.00
  - malaria V12.03
  - poliomyelitis V12.02
  - specified NEC V12.09
  - tuberculosis V12.01
- injury NEC V15.5

History—*continued*
- insufficient prenatal care V23.7
- irradiation V15.3
- leukemia V10.60
  - lymphoid V10.61
  - monocytic V10.63
  - myeloid V10.62
  - specified type NEC V10.69
- little or no prenatal care V23.7
- lymphosarcoma V10.71
- malaria V12.03
- malignant neoplasm (of) V10.9
  - accessory sinus V10.22
  - adrenal V10.88
  - anus V10.06
  - bile duct V10.09
  - bladder V10.51
  - bone V10.81
  - brain V10.85
  - breast V10.3
  - bronchus V10.11
  - cervix uteri V10.41
  - colon V10.05
  - connective tissue NEC V10.89
  - corpus uteri V10.42
  - digestive system V10.00
    - specified part NEC V10.09
  - duodenum V10.09
  - endocrine gland NEC V10.88
  - esophagus V10.03
  - eye V10.84
  - fallopian tube V10.44
  - female genital organ V10.40
    - specified site NEC V10.44
  - gallbladder V10.09
  - gastrointestinal tract V10.00
  - gum V10.02
  - hematopoietic NEC V10.79
  - hypopharynx V10.02
  - ileum V10.09
  - intrathoracic organs NEC V10.20
  - jejunum V10.09
  - kidney V10.52
  - large intestine V10.05
  - larynx V10.21
  - lip V10.02
  - liver V10.07
  - lung V10.11
  - lymphatic NEC V10.79
  - lymph glands or nodes NEC V10.79
  - male genital organ V10.45
    - specified site NEC V10.49
  - mediastinum V10.29
  - melanoma (of skin) V10.82
  - middle ear V10.22
  - mouth V10.02
    - specified part NEC V10.02
  - nasal cavities V10.22
  - nasopharynx V10.02
  - nervous system NEC V10.86
  - nose V10.22
  - oropharynx V10.02
  - ovary V10.43
  - pancreas V10.09
  - parathyroid V10.88
  - penis V10.49
  - pharynx V10.02
  - pineal V10.88
  - pituitary V10.88
  - placenta V10.44
  - pleura V10.29

History—*continued*
  prostate V10.46
  rectosigmoid junction V10.06
  rectum V10.06
  respiratory organs NEC V10.20
  salivary gland V10.02
  skin V10.83
    melanoma V10.82
  small intestine NEC V10.09
  soft tissue NEC V10.89
  specified site NEC V10.89
  stomach V10.04
  testis V10.47
  thymus V10.29
  thyroid V10.87
  tongue V10.01
  trachea V10.12
  ureter V10.59
  urethra V10.59
  urinary organ V10.50
  uterine adnexa V10.44
  uterus V10.42
  vagina V10.44
  vulva V10.44
  manic-depressive psychosis V11.1
  mental disorder V11.9
    affective type V11.1
    manic-depressive V11.1
    neurosis V11.2
    schizophrenia V11.0
    specified type NEC V11.8
  metabolic disorder V12.2
  musculoskeletal disorder NEC V13.5
  myocardial infarction 412
  neglect (emotional) V15.42
  nervous system disorder V12.4
  neurosis V11.2
  noncompliance with medical treatment V15.81
  nutritional deficiency V12.1
  obstetric disorder V13.2
    affecting management of current pregnancy V23.4
  parasitic disease V12.00
    specified NEC V12.09
  perinatal problems V13.7
  physical abuse V15.41
  poisoning V15.6
  poliomyelitis V12.02
  polyps, colonic V12.72
  poor obstetric V23.4
  psychiatric disorder V11.9
    affective type V11.1
    manic-depressive V11.1
    neurosis V11.2
    schizophrenia V11.0
    specified type NEC V11.8
  psychological trauma V15.49
    emotional abuse V15.42
    neglect V15.42
    physical abuse V15.41
    rape V15.41
  psychoneurosis V11.2
  radiation therapy V15.3
  rape V15.41
  respiratory system disease V12.6
  reticulosarcoma V10.71
  schizophrenia V11.0
  skin disease V13.3
  smoking (tobacco) V15.82
  subcutaneous tissue disease V13.3

History—*continued*
  surgery (major) to
    great vessels V15.1
    heart V15.1
    major organs NEC V15.2
  thrombophlebitis V12.52
  thrombosis V12.51
  tobacco use V15.82
  trophoblastic disease V13.1
    affecting management of pregnancy V23.1
  tuberculosis V12.01
  ulcer, peptic V12.71
  urinary system disorder V13.00
    calculi V13.01
    specified NEC V13.09
HIV infection (disease) (illness)—*see* Human immunodeficiency virus (disease) (illness) (infection)
Hives (bold) (*see also* Urticaria) 708.9
Hoarseness 784.49
Hobnail liver —*see* Cirrhosis, portal
Hobo, hoboism V60.0
Hodgkin's
  disease (M9650/3) 201.9
    lymphocytic
      depletion (M9653/3) 201.7
        diffuse fibrosis (M9654/3) 201.7
        reticular type (M9655/3) 201.7
      predominance (M9651/3) 201.4
    lymphocytic-histiocytic predominance (M9651/3) 201.4
    mixed cellularity (M9652/3) 201.6
    nodular sclerosis (M9656/3) 201.5
      cellular phase (M9657/3) 201.5
  granuloma (M9661/3) 201.1
  lymphogranulomatosis (M9650/3) 201.9
  lymphoma (M9650/3) 201.9
  lymphosarcoma (M9650/3) 201.9
  paragranuloma (M9660/3) 201.0
  sarcoma (M9662/3) 201.2
Hodgson's disease (aneurysmal dilatation of aorta) 441.9
  ruptured 441.5
Hodi-potsy 111.0
Hoffa -(Kastert) disease or syndrome (liposynovitis prepatellaris) 272.8
Hoffmann's syndrome 244.9 *[359.5]*
Hoffmann-Bouveret syndrome (paroxysmal tachycardia) 427.2
Hole
  macula 362.54
  optic disc, crater-like 377.22
  retina (macula) 362.54
  round 361.31
    with detachment 361.01
Holla disease (*see also* Spherocytosis) 282.0
Holländer-Simons syndrome (progressive lipodystrophy) 272.6
Hollow foot (congenital) 754.71
  acquired 736.73
Holmes' syndrome (visual disorientation) 368.16
Holoprosencephaly 742.2
  due to
    trisomy 13 758.1
    trisomy 18 758.2
Holthouse's hernia —*see* Hernia, inguinal
Homesickness 309.89
Homocystinemia 270.4
Homocystinuria 270.4
Homologous serum jaundice (prophylactic) (therapeutic)—*see* Hepatitis, viral

Homosexuality —*omit code*
  ego-dystonic 302.0
  pedophilic 302.2
  problems with 302.0
Homozygous Hb-S disease 282.61
Honeycomb lung 518.89
  congenital 748.4
Hong Kong ear 117.3
HOOD (hereditary osteo-onychodysplasia)
  756.89
Hooded
  clitoris 752.49
  penis 752.69
Hookworm (anemia) (disease) (infestation)—*see*
  Ancylostomiasis
Hoppe-Goldflam syndrome 358.0
Hordeolum (external) (eyelid) 373.11
  internal 373.12
Horn
  cutaneous 702.8
    cheek 702.8
    eyelid 702.8
    penis 702.8
  iliac 756.89
  nail 703.8
    congenital 757.5
  papillary 700
Horner's
  syndrome (*see also* Neuropathy, peripheral,
    autonomic) 337.9
    traumatic 954.0
  teeth 520.4
Horseshoe kidney (congenital) 753.3
Horton's
  disease (temporal arteritis) 446.5
  headache or neuralgia 346.2
Hospice care V66.7
Hospitalism (in children) NEC 309.83
Hourglass contraction, contracture
  bladder 596.8
  gallbladder 575.2
    congenital 751.69
  stomach 536.8
    congenital 750.7
    psychogenic 306.4
  uterus 661.4
    affecting fetus or newborn 763.7
Household circumstance affecting care V60.9
  specified type NEC V60.8
Housemaid's knee 727.2
Housing circumstance affecting care V60.9
  specified type NEC V60.8
Huchard's disease (continued arterial
  hypertension) 401.9
Hudson-Stähli lines 371.11
Huguier's disease (uterine fibroma) 218.9
Hum, venous —*omit code*
Human bite (open wound)—*see also* Wound,
  open, by site
  intact skin surface—*see* Contusion
Human immunovirus (disease) (illness)
  (infection)—*see* Human immunodeficiency
  virus (disease) (illness) (infection)
Human immunodeficiency virus (disease)
  (illness) 042
  infection V08
    with symptoms, symptomatic 042
Human immunodeficiency virus-2 infection
  079.53
Human T-cell lymphotrophic virus I infection
  079.51

Human T-cell lymphotrophic virus II infection
  079.52
Human T-cell lymphotropic virus-III (disease)
  (illness) (infection)—*see* Human
  immunodeficiency virus (disease) (illness)
  (infection)
HTLV-I infection 079.51
HTLV-II infection 079.52
HTLV-III (disease) (illness) (infection)—*see*
  Human immunodeficiency virus (disease)
  (illness) (infection)
HTLV-III/LAV
  (disease) (illness) (infection)—*see* Human
  immunodeficiency virus (disease) (illness)
  (infection)
Humpback (acquired) 737.9
  congenital 756.19
Hunchback (acquired) 737.9
  congenital 756.19
Hunger 994.2
  air, psychogenic 306.1
  disease 251.1
Hunner's ulcer (*see also* **Cystitis**) **595.1**
Hunt's
  neuralgia 053.11
  syndrome (herpetic geniculate ganglionitis)
    053.11
  dyssynergia cerebellaris myoclonica 334.2
Hunter's glossitis 529.4
Hunter (-Hurler) syndrome
  (mucopolysaccharidosis II) 277.5
Hunterian chancre 091.0
Huntington's
  chorea 333.4
  disease 333.4
Huppert's disease (multiple myeloma)
  (M9730/3) 203.0
Hurler (-Hunter) disease or syndrome
  (mucopolysaccharidosis II) 277.5
Hürthle cell
  adenocarcinoma (M8290/3) 193
  adenoma (M8290/0) 226
  carcinoma (M8290/3) 193
  tumor (M8290/0) 226
Hutchinson's
  disease meaning
    angioma serpiginosum 709.1
    cheiropompholyx 705.81
    prurigo estivalis 692.72
    summer eruption, or summer prurigo 692.72
  incisors 090.5
  melanotic freckle (M8742/2)—*see also*
    Neoplasm, skin, in situ
    malignant melanoma in (M8742/3)—*see*
      Melanoma
  teeth or incisors (congenital syphilis) 090.5
Hutchinson-Boeck disease or syndrome
  (sarcoidosis) 135
Hutchinson-Gilford disease or syndrome
  (progeria) 259.8
Hyaline
  degeneration (diffuse) (generalized) 728.9
    localized—*see* Degeneration, by site
  membrane (disease) (lung) (newborn) 769
Hyalinosis cutis et mucosae 272.8
Hyalin plaque, sclera, senile 379.16
Hyalitis (asteroid) 379.22
  syphilitic 095.8
Hydatid
  cyst or tumor—*see also* Echinococcus
    fallopian tube 752.11

Hydatid—*continued*
　mole—*see* Hydatidiform mole
　Morgagni (congenital) 752.8
　　fallopian tube 752.11
Hydatidiform mole (benign) (complicating
　pregnancy) (delivered) (undelivered) 630
　invasive (M9100/1) 236.1
　malignant (M9100/1) 236.1
　previous, affecting management of pregnancy
　　V23.1
Hydatidosis —*see* Echinococcus
Hyde's disease (prurigo nodularis) 698.3
Hydradenitis 705.83
Hydradenoma (M8400/0)—*see* Hidradenoma
Hydralazine lupus or syndrome
　correct substance properly administered 695.4
　overdose or wrong substance given or taken
　　972.6
Hydramnios 657
　affecting fetus or newborn 761.3
Hydrancephaly 742.3
　with spina bifida (*see also* Spina bifida) 741.0
Hydranencephaly 742.3
　with spina bifida (*see also* Spina bifida) 741.0
Hydrargyrism NEC 985.0
Hydrarthrosis (*see also* Effusion, joint) 719.0
　gonococcal 098.50
　intermittent (*see also* Rheumatism, palindromic)
　　719.3
　of yaws (early) (late) 102.6
　syphilitic 095.8
　　congenital 090.5
Hydremia 285.9
Hydrencephalocele (congenital) 742.0
Hydrencephalomeningocele (congenital) 742.0
Hydroa 694.0
　aestivale 692.72
　gestationis 646.8
　herpetiformis 694.0
　pruriginosa 694.0
　vacciniforme 692.72
Hydroadenitis 705.83
Hydrocalycosis (*see also* Hydronephrosis) 591
　congenital 753.29
Hydrocalyx (*see also* Hydronephrosis) 591
Hydrocele (calcified) (chylous) (idiopathic)
　(infantile) (inguinal canal) (recurrent) (senile)
　(spermatic cord) (testis) (tunica vaginalis)
　603.9
　canal of Nuck (female) 629.1
　　male 603.9
　congenital 778.6
　encysted 603.0
　　congenital 778.6
　female NEC 629.8
　infected 603.1
　round ligament 629.8
　specified type NEC 603.8
　　congenital 778.6
　spinalis (*see also* Spina bifida) 741.9
　vulva 624.8
Hydrocephalic fetus
　affecting management of pregnancy 655.0
　causing disproportion 653.6
　　with obstructed labor 660.1
　　　affecting fetus or newborn 763.1
Hydrocephalus (acquired) (external) (internal)
　(malignant) (noncommunicating) (obstructive)
　(recurrent) 331.4
　aqueduct of Sylvius stricture 742.3
　　with spina bifida (*see also* Spina bifida) 741.0

Hydrocephalus—*continued*
　chronic 742.3
　　with spina bifida (*see also* Spina bifida) 741.0
　communicating 331.3
　congenital (external) (internal) 742.3
　　with spina bifida (*see also* Spina bifida) 741.0
　due to
　　stricture of aqueduct of Sylvius 742.3
　　　with spina bifida (*see also* Spina bifida)
　　　　741.0
　　toxoplasmosis (congenital) 771.2
　fetal affecting management of pregnancy 655.0
　foramen Magendie block (acquired) 331.3
　　congenital 742.3
　　　with spina bifida (*see also* Spina bifida)
　　　　741.0
　newborn 742.3
　　with spina bifida (*see also* Spina bifida) 741.0
　otitic 331.4
　syphilitic, congenital 090.49
　tuberculous (*see also* Tuberculosis) 013.8
Hydrocolpos (congenital) 623.8
Hydrocystoma (M8404/0)—*see* Neoplasm, skin,
　benign
Hydroencephalocele (congenital) 742.0
Hydroencephalomeningocele (congenital) 742.0
Hydrohematopneumothorax (*see also*
　Hemothorax) 511.8
Hydromeningitis —*see* Meningitis
Hydromeningocele (spinal) (*see also* Spina
　bifida) 741.9
　cranial 742.0
Hydrometra 621.8
Hydrometrocolpos 623.8
Hydromicrocephaly 742.1
Hydromphalus (congenital) (since birth) 757.39
Hydromyelia 742.53
Hydromyelocele (*see also* Spina bifida) 741.9
Hydronephrosis 591
　atrophic 591
　congenital 753.29
　due to S. hematobium 120.0
　early 591
　functionless (infected) 591
　infected 591
　intermittent 591
　primary 591
　secondary 591
　tuberculous (*see also* Tuberculosis) 016.0
Hydropericarditis (*see also* Pericarditis) 423.9
Hydropericardium (*see also* Pericarditis) 423.9
Hydroperitoneum 789.5
Hydrophobia 071
Hydrophthalmos (*see also* Buphthalmia) 743.20
Hydropneumohemothorax (*see also*
　Hemothorax) 511.8
Hydropneumopericarditis (*see also*
　Pericarditis) 423.9
Hydropneumopericardium (*see also*
　Pericarditis) 423.9
Hydropneumothorax 511.8
　nontuberculous 511.8
　　bacterial 511.1
　pneumococcal 511.1
　staphylococcal 511.1
　streptococcal 511.1
　traumatic 860.0
　　with open wound into thorax 860.1
　tuberculous (*see also* Tuberculosis, pleural)
　　012.0

Hypercholesterinemia —*see*
Hypercholesterolemia
Hypercholesterolemia 272.0
with hyperglyceridemia, endogenous 272.2
essential 272.0
familial 272.0
hereditary 272.0
primary 272.0
pure 272.0
Hypercholesterolosis 272.0
Hyperchylia gastricsa 536.8
psychogenic 306.4
Hyperchylomicronemia (familial) (with
hyperbetalipoproteinemia) 272.3
Hypercoagulation syndrome 289.8
Hypercorticosteronism
correct substance properly administered 255.3
overdose or wrong substance given or taken
962.0
Hypercortisonism
correct substance properly administered 255.3
overdose or wrong substance given or taken
962.0
**Hyperdynamic beta-adrenergic state or syn-
drome** (circulatory) 429.82
Hyperelectrolytemia 276.9
Hyperemesis 536.2
arising during pregnancy—*see* Hyperemesis,
gravidarum
gravidarum (mild) (before 22 completed weeks
gestation) 643.0
with
carbohydrate depletion 643.1
dehydration 643.1
electrolyte imbalance 643.1
metabolic disturbance 643.1
affecting fetus or newborn 761.8
severe (with metabolic disturbance) 643.1
psychogenic 306.4
Hyperemia (acute) 780.9
anal mucosa 569.49
bladder 596.7
cerebral 437.8
conjunctiva 372.71
ear, internal, acute 386.30
enteric 564.8
eye 372.71
eyelid (active) (passive) 374.82
intestine 564.8
iris 364.41
kidney 593.81
labyrinth 386.30
liver (active) (passive) 573.8
lung 514
ovary 620.8
passive 780.9
pulmonary 514
renal 593.81
retina 362.89
spleen 289.59
stomach 537.89
Hyperesthesia (body surface) (*see also*
Disturbance, sensation) 782.0
larynx (reflex) 478.79
hysterical 300.11
pharynx (reflex) 478.29
Hyperestrinism 256.0
Hyperestrogenism 256.0
Hyperestrogenosis 256.0

Hyperextension, joint 718.80
ankle 718.87
elbow 718.82
foot 718.87
hand 718.84
hip 718.85
knee 718.86
multiple sites 718.89
pelvic region 718.85
shoulder (region) 718.81
specified site NEC 718.88
wrist 718.83
Hyperfibrinolysis —*see* Fibrinolysis
Hyperfolliculinism 256.0
Hyperfructosemia 271.2
Hyperfunction
adrenal (cortex) 255.3
androgenic, acquired benign 255.3
medulla 255.6
virilism 255.2
corticoadrenal NEC 255.3
labyrinth—*see* Hyperactive, labyrinth
medulloadrenal 255.6
ovary 256.1
estrogen 256.0
pancreas 577.8
parathyroid (gland) 252.0
pituitary (anterior) (gland) (lobe) 253.1
testicular 257.0
Hypergammaglobulinemia 289.8
monoclonal, benign (BMH) 273.1
polyclonal 273.0
Waldenström's 273.0
Hyperglobulinemia 273.8
Hyperglycemia 790.6
maternal
affecting fetus or newborn 775.0
manifest diabetes in infant 775.1
postpancreatectomy (complete) (partial) 251.3
Hyperglyceridemia 272.1
endogenous 272.1
essential 272.1
familial 272.1
hereditary 272.1
mixed 272.3
pure 272.1
Hyperglycinemia 270.7
Hypergonadism
ovarian 256.1
testicular (infantile) (primary) 257.0
Hyperheparinemia (*see also* Circulating
anticoagulants) 286.5
Hyperhidrosis, hyperidrosis 780.8
psychogenic 306.3
Hyperhistldinemia 270.5
Hyperinsulinism (ectopic) (functional) (organic)
NEC 251.1
iatrogenic 251.0
reactive 251.2
spontaneous 251.2
therapeutic misadventure (from administration
of insulin) 962.3
Hyperiodemia 276.9
Hyperirritability (cerebral), in newborn 779.1
Hyperkalemia 276.7
Hyperkeratosis (*see also* Keratosis) 701.1
cervix 622.1
congenital 757.39
cornea 371.89
due to yaws (early) (late) (palmar or plantar)
102.3

Hyperkeratosis—*continued*
  eccentrica 757.39
  figurata centrifuga atrophica 757.39
  follicularis 757.39
    in cutem penetrans 701.1
  limbic (cornea) 371.89
  palmoplantaris climacterica 701.1
  pinta (carate) 103.1
  senile (with pruritus) 702.0
  tongue 528.7
  universalis congenita 757.1
  vagina 623.1
  vocal cord 478.5
  vulva 624.0
Hyperkinesia, hyperkinetic (disease) (reaction)
  (syndrome) 314.9
  with
    attention deficit —*see* Disorder, attention
      deficit
    conduct disorder 314.2
    developmental delay 314.1
    simple disturbance of activity and attention
      314.01
    specified manifestation NEC 314.8
  heart (disease) 429.82
  of childhood or adolescence NEC 314.9
Hyperlacrimation (*see also* Epiphora) 375.20
Hyperlipemia (*see also* Hyperlipidemia) 272.4
Hyperlipidemia 272.4
  carbohydrate-induced 272.1
  combined 272.4
  endogenous 272.1
  exogenous 272.3
  fat-induced 272.3
  group
    A 272.0
    B 272.1
    C 272.2
    D 272.3
  mixed 272.2
  specified type NEC 272.4
Hyperlipidosis 272.7
  hereditary 272.7
Hyperlipoproteinemia (acquired) (essential)
  (familial) (hereditary) (primary) (secondary)
  272.4
  Fredrickson type
    I 272.3
    IIa 272.0
    IIb 272.2
    III 272.2
    IV 272.1
    V 272.3
  low-density-lipoid-type (LDL) 272.0
  very-low-density-lipoid-type [VLDL] 272.1
Hyperlucent lung, unilateral 492.8
Hyperluteinization 256.1
Hyperlysinemia 270.7
Hypermagnesemia 275.2
  neonatal 775.5
Hypermaturity (fetus or newborn) 766.2
Hypermenorrhea 626.2
Hypermetabolism 794.7
Hypermethioninemia 270.4
Hypermetropia (congenital) 367.0
Hypermobility
  cecum 564.1
  coccyx 724.71
  colon 564.1
    psychogenic 306.4
  ileum 564.8

Hypermobility—*continued*
  joint (acquired) 718.80
    ankle 718.87
    elbow 718.82
    foot 718.87
    hand 718.84
    hip 718.85
    knee 718.86
    multiple sites 718.89
    pelvic region 718.85
    shoulder (region) 718.81
    specified site NEC 718.88
    wrist 718.83
  kidney, congenital 753.3
  meniscus (knee) 717.5
  scapula 718.81
  stomach 536.8
    psychogenic 306.4
  syndrome 728.5
  testis, congenital 752.52
  urethral 599.81
Hypermotility
  gastrointestinal 536.8
  intestine 564.1
    psychogenic 306.4
  stomach 536.8
Hypernasality 784.49
Hypernatremia 276.0
  with water depletion 276.0
Hypernephroma (M8312/3) 189.0
Hyperopia 367.0
Hyperorexia 783.6
Hyperornithinemia 270.6
Hyperosmia (*see also* Disturbance, sensation)
  781.1
Hyperosmolality 276.0
Hyperosteogenesis 733.99
Hyperostosis 733.99
  calvarial 733.3
  cortical 733.3
    infantile 756.59
  frontal, internal of skull 733.3
  interna frontalis 733.3
  monomelic 733.99
  skull 733.3
    congenital 756.0
  vertebral 721.8
    with spondylosis—*see* Spondylosis
    ankylosing 721.6
Hyperovarianism 256.1
Hyperovarism, hyperovaria 256.1
Hyperoxaluria (primary) 271.8
Hyperoxia 987.8
Hyperparathyroidism 252.0
  ectopic 259.3
  secondary, of renal origin 588.8
Hyperpathia (*see also* Disturbance, sensation)
  782.0
  psychogenic 307.80
Hyperperistalsis 787.4
  psychogenic 306.4
Hyperpermeability, capillary 448.9
Hyperphagia 783.6
Hyperphenylalaninemia 270.1
Hyperphoria 378.40
  alternating 378.45
Hyperphosphatemia 275.3
Hyperpiesia (*see also* Hypertension) 401.9
Hyperpiesis (*see also* Hypertension) 401.9
Hyperpigmentation —*see* Pigmentation
Hyperpinealism 259.8

Hyperpipecolatemia 270.7
Hyperpituitarism 253.1
Hyperplasia, hyperplastic
  adenoids (lymphoid tissue) 474.12
    and tonsils 474.10
  adrenal (capsule) (cortex) (gland) 255.8
    with
      sexual precocity (male) 255.2
      virilism, adrenal 255.2
      virilization (female) 255.2
    congenital 255.2
    due to excess ACTH (ectopic) (pituitary) 255.0
    medulla 255.8
  alpha cells (pancreatic)
    with
      gastrin excess 251.5
      glucagon excess 251.4
  appendix (lymphoid) 543.0
  artery, fibromuscular NEC 447.8
    carotid 447.8
    renal 447.3
  bone 733.99
    marrow 289.9
  breast (see also Hypertrophy, breast) 611.1
  carotid artery 447.8
  cementation, cementum (teeth) (tooth) 521.5
  cervical gland 785.6
  cervix (uteri) 622.1
    basal cell 622.1
    congenital 752.49
    endometrium 622.1
    polypoid 622.1
  chin 524.05
  clitoris, congenital 752.49
  dentin 521.5
  endocervicitis 616.0
  endometrium, endometrial (adenomatous)
      (atypical) (cystic) (glandular) (polypoid)
      (uterus) 621.3
    cervix 622.1
  epithelial 709.8
    focal, oral, including tongue 528.7
    mouth (focal) 528.7
    nipple 611.8
    skin 709.8
    tongue (focal) 528.7
    vaginal wall 623.0
  erythroid 289.9
  fascialis ossificans (progressiva) 728.11
  fibromuscular, artery NEC 447.8
    carotid 447.8
    renal 447.3
  genital
    female 629.8
    male 608.89
  gingiva 523.8
  glandularis
    cystica uteri 621.3
    endometrium (uterus) 621.3
    interstitialis uteri 621.3
  granulocytic 288.8
  gum 523.8
  hymen, congenital 752.49
  islands of Langerhans 251.1
  islet cell (pancreatic) 251.9
    alpha cells
      with excess
        gastrin 251.5
        glucagon 251.4
    beta cells 251.1
  juxtaglomerular (complex) (kidney) 593.89

Hyperplasia, hyperplastic—continued
  kidney (congenital) 753.3
  liver (congenital) 751.69
  lymph node (gland) 785.6
  lymphoid (diffuse) (nodular) 785.6
    appendix 543.0
    intestine 569.89
  mandibular 524.02
    alveolar 524.72
    unilateral condylar 526.89
  Marchand multiple nodular (liver)—see
      Cirrhosis, postnecrotic
  maxillary 524.01
    alveolar 524.71
  medulla, adrenal 255.8
  myometrium, myometrial 621.2
  nose (lymphoid) (polypoid) 478.1
  oral soft tissue (inflammatory) (irritative)
      (mucosa) NEC 528.9
    gingiva 523.8
    tongue 529.8
  organ or site, congenital NEC—see Anomaly,
      specified type NEC
  ovary 620.8
  palate, papillary 528.9
  pancreatic islet cells 251.9
    alpha
      with excess
        gastrin 251.5
        glucagon 251.4
    beta 251.1
  parathyroid (gland) 252.0
  persistent, vitreous (primary) 743.51
  pharynx (lymphoid) 478.29
  prostate (adenofibromatous) (nodular) 600
  renal artery (fibromuscular) 447.3
  reticuloendothelial (cell) 289.9
  salivary gland (any) 527.1
  Schimmelbusch's 610.1
  suprarenal (capsule) (gland) 255.8
  thymus (gland) (persistent) 254.0
  thyroid (see also Goiter) 240.9
    primary 242.0
    secondary 242.2
  tonsil (lymphoid tissue) 474.11
    and adenoids 474.10
  urethrovaginal 599.89
  uterus, uterine (myometrium) 621.2
    endometrium 621.3
  vitreous (humor), primary persistent 743.51
  vulva 624.3
  zygoma 738.11
Hyperpnea (see also Hyperventilation) 786.01
Hyperpotassemia 276.7
Hyperprebetalipoproteinemia 272.1
  with chylomicronemia 272.3
  familial 272.1
Hyperprolactinemia 253.1
Hyperprolinemia 270.8
Hyperproteinemia 273.8
Hyperprothrombinemia 289.8
Hyperpselaphesia 782.0
Hyperpyrexia 780.6
  heat (effects of) 992.0
  malarial (see also Malaria) 084.6
  malignant, due to anesthetic 995.89
  rheumatic—see Fever, rheumatic
  unknown origin (see also Pyrexia) 780.6
Hyperreactor, vascular 780.2
Hyperreflexia 796.1
  bladder, autonomic 596.54

Hyperreflexia—*continued*
 with cauda equina 344.61
 detrusor 344.61
Hypersalivation (*see also* Ptyalism) 527.7
Hypersarcosinemia 270.8
Hypersecretion
 ACTH 255.3
 androgens (ovarian) 256.1
 calcitonin 246.0
 corticoadrenal 255.3
 cortisol 255.0
 estrogen 256.0
 gastric 536.8
 psychogenic 306.4
 gastrin 251.5
 glucagon 251.4
 hormone
  ACTH 255.3
  anterior pituitary 253.1
  growth NEC 253.0
  ovarian androgen 256.1
  testicular 257.0
  thyroid stimulating 242.8
 insulin—*see* Hyperinsulinism
 lacrimal glands (*see also* Epiphora) 375.20
 medulloadrenal 255.6
 milk 676.6
 ovarian androgens 256.1
 pituitary (anterior) 253.1
 salivary gland (any) 527.7
 testicular hormones 257.0
 thyrocalcitonin 246.0
 upper respiratory 478.9
Hypersegmentation, hereditary 288.2
 eosinophils 288.2
 neutrophil nuclei 288.2
Hypersensitive, hypersensitiveness
 hypersensitivity —*see also* Allergy
 angiitis 446.20
  specified NEC 446.29
 carotid sinus 337.0
 colon 564.1
  psychogenic 306.4
 DNA (deoxyribonucleic acid) NEC 287.2
 drug (*see also* Allergy, drug) 995.2
 esophagus 530.89
 insect bites—*see* Injury, superficial, by site
 labyrinth 386.58
 pain (*see also* Disturbance, sensation) 782.0
 pneumonitis NEC 495.9
 reaction (*see also* Allergy) 995.3
  upper respiratory tract NEC 478.8
 stomach (allergic) (nonallergic) 536.8
  psychogenic 306.4
Hypersomatotropism (classic) 253.0
Hypersomnia 780.54
 with sleep apnea 780.53
 nonorganic origin 307.43
  persistent (primary) 307.44
  transient 307.43
Hypersplenia 289.4
Hypersplenism 289.4
Hypersteatosis 706.3
Hypersuprarenalism 255.3
Hypersusceptibility —*see* Allergy
Hyper-TBG-nemia 246.8
Hypertelorism 756.0
 orbit, orbital 376.41

*"H" listing resumes after
Hypertension table...*

Hypertension, hypertensive

[handwritten notes: "Blood pressure not level controlled (life treating)" and "Don't know how patient's pressure is going to before"]

	Malignant	Benign	Unspecified
(arterial) (arteriolar) (crisis) (degeneration) (disease) (essential) (fluctuating) (idiopathic) (intermittent) (labile) (low renin) (orthostatic) (paroxysmal) (primary) (systemic) (uncontrolled) (vascular)	401.0	401.1	401.9
with			
heart involvement (conditions classifiable to 425.8, 428, 429.0-429.3, 429.8, 429.9 due to hypertension) (*see also* Hypertension, heart)	402.00	402.10	402.90
with kidney involvement—*see* Hypertension, cardiorenal			
renal involvement (only conditions classifiable to 585, 586, 587) (excludes conditions classifiable to 584) (*see also* Hypertension, kidney)	403.00	403.10	403.90
with heart involvement—*see* Hypertension, cardiorenal			
failure (and sclerosis) (*see also* Hypertension, kidney) .	403.01	403.11	403.91
sclerosis without failure (*see also* Hypertension, kidney) .	403.00	403.10	403.90
accelerated (*see also* Hypertension, by type, malignant) . .	401.0	—	—
antepartum—*see* Hypertension complicating pregnancy, childbirth, or the puerperium			
cardiorenal (disease)	404.00	404.10	404.90
with			
heart failure (congestive)	404.01	404.11	404.91
and renal failure	404.03	404.13	404.93
renal failure	404.02	404.12	404.92
and heart failure (congestive)	404.03	404.13	404.93
cardiovascular disease (arteriosclerotic) (sclerotic)	402.00	402.10	402.90
with			
heart failure (congestive)	402.01	402.11	402.91
renal involvement (conditions classifiable to 403) (*see also* Hypertension, cardiorenal)	404.00	404.10	404.90
cardiovascular renal (disease) (sclerosis) (*see also* Hypertension cardiorenal)	404.00	404.10	404.90
cerebrovascular disease NEC	437.2	437.2	437.2
complicating pregnancy, childbirth, or the puerperium . . .	642.2	642.0	642.9
with			
albuminuria (and edema) (mild)	—	—	642.4
severe	—	—	642.5
edema (mild)	—	—	642.4
severe	—	—	642.5
heart disease	642.2	642.2	642.2
and renal disease	642.2	642.2	642.2
renal disease	642.2	642.2	642.2
and heart disease	642.2	642.2	642.2
chronic	642.2	642.0	642.0
with pre-eclampsia or eclampsia	642.7	642.7	642.7
fetus or newborn	760.0	760.0	760.0
essential	—	642.0	642.0
with pre-eclampsia or eclampsia	—	642.7	642.7
fetus or newborn	760.0	760.0	760.0
fetus or newborn	760.0	760.0	760.0
gestational	—	—	642.3
pre-existing	642.2	642.0	642.0
with pre-eclampsia or eclampsia	642.7	642.7	642.7
fetus or newborn	760.0	760.0	760.0
secondary to renal disease	642.1	642.1	642.1
with pre-eclampsia or eclampsia	642.7	642.7	642.7
fetus or newborn	760.0	760.0	760.0
transient	—	—	642.3
due to			
aldosteronism,primary	405.09	405.19	405.99
brain tumor	405.09	405.19	405.99
bulbar poliomyelitis	405.09	405.19	405.99
calculus			
kidney	405.09	405.19	405.99
ureter	405.09	405.19	405.99
coarctation, aorta	405.09	405.19	405.99
Cushing's disease	405.09	405.19	405.99
glomerulosclerosis (*see also* Hypertension, kidney) . . .	403.00	403.10	403.90
periarteritis nodosa	405.09	405.19	405.99
pheochromocytoma	405.09	405.19	405.99
polycystic kidney(s)	405.09	405.19	405.99
polycythemia	405.09	405.19	405.99
porphyria	405.09	405.19	405.99
pyelonephritis	405.09	405.19	405.99

	Malignant	Benign	Unspecified
renal (artery)			
aneurysm	405.01	405.11	405.91
anomaly	405.01	405.11	405.91
embolism	405.01	405.11	405.91
fibromuscular hyperplasia	405.01	405.11	405.91
occlusion	405.01	405.11	405.91
stenosis	405.01	405.11	405.91
thrombosis	405.01	405.11	405.91
encephalopathy	437.2	437.2	437.2
gestational (transient) NEC	—	—	642.3
Goldblatt's	440.1	440.1	440.1
heart (disease) (conditions classifiable to 425.8, 428, 429.0-429.3, 429.8, 429.9 due to hypertension)	402.00	402.10	402.90
with			
heart failure	402.01	402.11	402.91
congestive	402.01	402.11	402.91
hypertensive kidney disease (conditions classifiable to 403)			
(*see also* Hypertension, cardiorenal)	404.00	404.10	404.90
renal sclerosis (*see also* Hypertension, cardiorenal)	404.00	404.10	404.90
intracranial, benign	—	348.2	
intraocular	—	—	365.04
kidney	403.00	403.10	403.90
with			
heart involvement (conditions classifiable to 425.8, 428, 429.0-429.3, 429.8, 429.9 due to hypertension) (*see also* Hypertension cardiorenal)	404.00	404.10	404.90
hypertensive heart (disease) (conditions classifiable to 402)			
(*see also* Hypertension, cardiorenal)	404.00	404.10	404.90
lesser circulation	—	—	416.0
necrotizing	401.0	—	—
ocular	—	—	365.04
portal (due to chronic liver disease)	—	—	572.3
postoperative 997.91			
psychogenic	—	—	306.2
puerperal, postpartum—*see* Hypertension, complicating pregnancy, childbirth, or the puerperium			
pulmonary (artery) (idiopathic) (primary) (solitary)	—	—	416.0
with cor pulmonale (chronic)	—	—	416.8
acute	—	—	415.0
secondary	—	—	416.8
renal (disease) (*see also* Hypertension, kidney)	403.00	403.10	403.90
renovascular NEC	405.01	405.11	405.91
secondary NEC	405.09	405.19	405.99
due to			
aldosteronism, primary	405.09	405.19	405.99
brain tumor	405.09	405.19	405.99
bulbar poliomyelitis	405.09	405.19	405.99
calculus			
kidney	405.09	405.19	405.99
ureter	405.09	405.19	405.99
coarctation, aorta	405.09	405.19	405.99
Cushing's disease	405.09	405.19	405.99
glomerulosclerosis (*see also* Hypertension, kidney)	403.00	403.10	403.90
periarteritis nodosa	405.09	405.19	405.99
pheochromocytoma	405.09	405.19	405.99
polycystic kidney(s)	405.09	405.19	405.99
polycythemia	405.09	405.19	405.99
porphyria	405.09	405.19	405.99
pyelonephritis	405.09	405.19	405.99
renal (artery)			
aneurysm	405.01	405.11	405.91
anomaly	405.01	405.11	405.91
embolism	405.01	405.11	405.91
fibromuscular hyperplasia	405.01	405.11	405.91
occlusion	405.01	405.11	405.91
stenosis	405.01	405.11	405.91
thrombosis	405.01	405.11	405.91
transient	—	—	796.2
of pregnancy	—	—	642.3

Hyperthecosis, ovary 256.8
Hyperthermia (of unknown origin) (*see also* Pyrexia) 780.6
  malignant (due to anesthesia) 995.89
  newborn 778.4
Hyperthymergasia (*see also* Psychosis, affective) 296.0
  reactive (from emotional stress, psychological trauma) 298.1
  recurrent episode 296.1
  single episode 296.0
Hyperthymism 254.8
Hyperthyroid (recurrent)—*see* Hyperthyroidism
Hyperthyroidism (latent) (preadult) (recurrent) (without goiter) 242.9

Note—Use the following fifth-digit subclassification with category 242:

0 without mention of thyrotoxic crisis or storm
1 with mention of thyrotoxic crisis or storm

---

  with
    goiter (diffuse) 242.0
      adenomatous 242.3
        multinodular 242.2
        uninodular 242.1
      nodular 242.3
        multinodular 242.2
        uninodular 242.1
    thyroid nodule 242.1
  complicating pregnancy, childbirth, or puerperium 648.1
  neonatal (transient) 775.3
Hypertonia —Hypertonicity
Hypertonicity
  bladder 596.51
  fetus or newborn 779.8
  gastrointestinal (tract) 536.8
  infancy 779.8
    due to electrolyte imbalance 779.8
  muscle 728.85
  stomach 536.8
    psychogenic 306.4
  uterus, uterine (contractions) 661.4
    affecting fetus or newborn 763.7
Hypertony —*see* Hypertonicity
Hypertransaminemia 790.4
Hypertrichosis 704.1
  congenital 757.4
  eyelid 374.54
  lanuginosa 757.4
    acquired 704.1
Hypertriglyceridemia, essential 272.1
Hypertrophy, hypertrophic
  adenoids (infectional) 474.12
    and tonsils (faucial) (infective) (lingual) (lymphoid) 474.10
  adrenal 255.8
  alveolar process or ridge 525.8
  anal papillae 569.49
  apocrine gland 705.82
  artery NEC 447.8
    carotid 447.8
    congenital (peripheral) NEC 747.60
    gastrointestinal 747.61
    lower limb 747.64
    renal 747.62
    specified NEC 747.69
    spinal 747.82
    upper limb 747.63

Hypertrophy, hypertrophic—*continued*
  arthritis (chronic) (*see also* Osteoarthrosis) 715.9
    spine (*see also* Spondylosis) 721.90
  arytenoid 478.79
  asymmetrical (heart) 429.9
  auricular—*see* Hypertrophy, cardiac
  Bartholin's gland 624.8
  bile duct 576.8
  bladder (sphincter) (trigone) 596.8
  blind spot, visual field 368.42
  bone 733.99
  brain 348.8
  breast 611.1
    cystic 610.1
    fetus or newborn 778.7
    fibrocystic 610.1
    massive pubertal 611.1
    puerperal, postpartum 676.3
    senile (parenchymatous) 611.1
  cardiac (chronic) (idiopathic) 429.3
    with
      rheumatic fever (conditions classifiable to 390)
        active 391.8
          with chorea 392.0
        inactive or quiescent (with chorea) 398.99
    congenital NEC 746.89
    fatty (*see also* Degeneration, myocardial) 429.1
    hypertensive (*see also* Hypertension, heart) 402.90
    rheumatic (with chorea) 398.99
      active or acute 391.8
        with chorea 392.0
    valve (*see also* Endocarditis) 424.90
      congenital NEC 746.89
  cartilage 733.99
  cecum 569.89
  cervix (uteri) 622.6
    congenital 752.49
    elongation 622.6
  clitoris (cirrhotic) 624.2
    congenital 752.49
  colon 569.89
    congenital 751.3
  conjunctiva, lymphoid 372.73
  cornea 371.89
  corpora cavernosa 607.89
  duodenum 537.89
  endometrium (uterus) 621.3
    cervix 622.6
  epididymis 608.89
  esophageal hiatus (congenital) 756.6
    with hernia—*see* Hernia, diaphragm
  eyelid 374.30
  falx, skull 733.99
  fat pad 729.30
    infrapatellar 729.31
    knee 729.31
    orbital 374.34
    popliteal 729.31
    prepatellar 729.31
    retropatellar 729.31
    specified site NEC 729.39
  foot (congenital) 755.67
  frenum, frenulum (tongue) 529.8
    linguae 529.8
    lip 528.5
  gallbladder or cystic duct 575.8
  gastric mucosa 535.2
  gingiva 523.8

Hypertrophy, hypertrophic—*continued*
gland, glandular (general) NEC 785.6
gum (mucous membrane) 523.8
heart (idiopathic)—*see also* Hypertrophy,
  cardiac
  valve—*see also* Endocarditis
  congenital NEC 746.89
hemifacial 754.0
hepatic—*see* Hypertrophy, liver
hiatus (esophageal) 756.6
hilus gland 785.6
hymen, congenital 752.49
ileum 569.89
infrapatellar fat pad 729.31
intestine 569.89
jejunum 569.89
kidney (compensatory) 593.1
  congenital 753.3
labial frenulum 528.5
labium (majus) (minus) 624.3
lacrimal gland, chronic 375.03
ligament 728.9
  spinal 724.8
linguae frenulum 529.8
lingual tonsil (infectional) 474.11
lip (frenum) 528.5
  congenital 744.81
liver 789.1
  acute 573.8
  cirrhotic—*see* Cirrhosis, liver
  congenital 751.69
  fatty—*see* Fatty, liver
lymph gland 785.6
  tuberculous—*see* Tuberculosis, lymph gland
mammary gland—*see* Hypertrophy, breast
maxillary frenulum 528.5
Meckel's diverticulum (congenital) 751.0
medial meniscus, acquired 717.3
median bar 600
mediastinum 519.3
meibomian gland 373.2
meniscus, knee, congenital 755.64
metatarsal head 733.99
metatarsus 733.99
mouth 528.9
mucous membrane
  alveolar process 523.8
  nose 478.1
  turbinate (nasal) 478.0
muscle 728.9
muscular coat, artery NEC 447.8
  carotid 447.8
  renal 447.3
myocardium (*see also* Hypertrophy, cardiac)
  429.3
  idiopathic 425.4
myometrium 621.2
nail 703.8
  congenital 757.5
nasal 478.1
  alae 478.1
  bone 738.0
  cartilage 478.1
  mucous membrane (septum) 478.1
  sinus (*see also* Sinusitis) 473.9
  turbinate 478.0
nasopharynx, lymphoid (infectional) (tissue)
  (wall) 478.29
neck, uterus 622.6
nipple 611.1
normal aperture diaphragm (congenital) 756.6

Hypertrophy, hypertrophic—*continued*
nose (*see also* Hypertrophy, nasal) 478.1
orbit 376.46
organ or site, congenital NEC—*see* Anomaly,
  specified type NEC
osteoarthropathy (pulmonary) 731.2
ovary 620.8
palate (hard) 526.89
  soft 528.9
pancreas (congenital) 751.7
papillae
  anal 569.49
  tongue 529.3
parathyroid (gland) 252.0
parotid gland 527.1
penis 607.89
phallus 607.89
  female (clitoris) 624.2
pharyngeal tonsil 474.12
pharyngitis 472.1
pharynx 478.29
  lymphoid (infectional) (tissue) (wall) 478.29
pituitary (fossa) (gland) 253.8
popliteal fat pad 729.31
preauricular (lymph) gland (Hampstead) 785.6
prepuce (congenital) 605
  female 624.2
prostate (adenofibromatous) (asymptomatic)
    (benign) (early) (recurrent) 600
  congenital 752.8
psuedoedematous hypodermal 757.0
pseudomuscular 359.1
pylorus (muscle) (sphincter) 537.0
  congenital 750.5
  infantile 750.5
rectal sphincter 569.49
rectum 569.49
renal 593.1
rhinitis (turbinate) 472.0
salivary duct or gland 527.1
  congenital 750.26
scaphoid (tarsal) 733.99
scar 701.4
scrotum 608.89
sella turcica 253.8
seminal vesicle 608.89
sigmoid 569.89
skin condition NEC 701.9
spermatic cord 608.89
spinal ligament 728.9
spleen—*see* Splenomegaly
spondylitis (spine) (*see also* Spondylosis) 721.90
stomach 537.89
subaortic stenosis (idiopathic) 425.1
sublingual gland 527.1
  congenital 750.26
submaxillary gland 527.1
suprarenal (gland) 255.8
tendon 727.9
testis 608.89
  congenital 752.8
thymic, thymus (congenital) (gland) 254.0
thyroid (gland) (*see also* Goiter) 240.9
  primary 242.0
  secondary 242.2
toe (congenital) 755.65
  acquired 735.8
tongue 529.8
  congenital 750.15
  frenum 529.8
  papillae (foliate) 529.3

Hypertrophy, hypertrophic—*continued*
tonsil (faucial) (infective) (lingual) (lymphoid) 474.11
  and adenoids 474.10
  with tonsillitis 474.0
tunica vaginalis 608.89
turbinate (mucous membrane) 478.0
ureter 593.89
urethra 599.84
uterus 621.2
  puerperal, postpartum 674.8
uvula 528.9
vagina 623.8
vas deferens 608.89
vein 459.89
ventricle, ventricular (heart) (left) (right)—*see also* Hypertrophy, cardiac
  congenital 746.89
  due to hypertension (left) (right) (*see also* Hypertension, heart) 402.90
    benign 402.10
    malignant 402.00
  right with ventricular septal defect, pulmonary stenosis or atresia, and dextraposition of aorta 745.2
verumontanum 599.89
vesical 596.8
vocal cord 478.5
vulva 624.3
  stasis (nonfilarial) 624.3
Hypertropia (intermittent) (periodic) 378.31
Hypertyrosinemia 270.2
Hyperuricemia 790.6
Hypervalinemia 270.3
Hyperventilation (tetany) 786.01
hysterical 300.11
psychogenic 306.1
syndrome 306.1
Hyperviscidosis 277.00
Hyperviscosity (of serum) (syndrome) NEC 273.3
polycythemic 289.0
sclerocythemic 282.8
Hypervitaminosis (dietary) NEC 278.8
A (dietary) 278.2
D (dietary) 278.4
from excessive administration or use of vitamin preparations (chronic) 278.8
  reaction to sudden overdose 963.5
vitamin A 278.2
  reaction to sudden overdose 963.5
vitamin D 278.4
  reaction to sudden overdose 963.5
vitamin K
  correct substance properly administered 278.8
  overdose or wrong substance given or taken 964.3
Hypervolemia 276.6
Hypesthesia (*see also* Disturbance, sensation) 782.0
cornea 371.81
Hyphema (anterior chamber) (ciliary body) (iris) 364.41
traumatic 921.3
Hyphemia —*see* Hyphema
Hypoacidity, gastric 536.8
psychogenic 306.4
Hypoactive labyrinth (function)—*see* Hypofunction, labyrinth

Hypoadrenalism 255.4
tuberculous (*see also* Tuberculosis) 017.6
Hypoadrenocorticism 255.4
pituitary 253.4
Hypoalbuminemia 273.8
Hypoalphalipoproteinemia 272.5
Hypobarism 993.2
Hypobaropathy 993.2
Hypobetalipoproteinemia (familial) 272.5
Hypocalcemia 275.4
cow's milk 775.4
dietary 269.3
neonatal 775.4
phosphate-loading 775.4
Hypocalcification, teeth 520.4
Hypochloremia 276.9
Hypochlorhydria 536.8
neurotic 306.4
psychogenic 306.4
Hypocholesteremia 272.5
Hypochondria (reaction) 300.7
Hypochondriac 300.7
Hypochondriasis 300.7
Hypochromasia blood cells 280.9
Hypochromic anemia 280.9
due to blood loss (chronic) 280.0
  acute 285.1
microcytic 280.9
Hypocoagulability (*see also* Defect, coagulation) 286.9
Hypocomplementemia 279.8
Hypocythemia (progressive) 284.9
Hypodontia (*see also* Anodontia) 520.0
Hypoeosinophilia 288.8
Hypoesthesia (*see also* Disturbance, sensation) 782.0
cornea 371.81
tactile 782.0
Hypoestrinism 256.3
Hypoestrogenism 256.3
Hypoferremia 280.9
due to blood loss (chronic) 280.0
Hypofertility
female 628.9
male 606.1
Hypofibrinogenemia) 286.3
acquired 286.6
congenital 286.3
Hypofunction
adrenal (gland) 255.4
  cortex 255.4
  medulla 255.5
  specified NEC 255.5
cerebral 331.9
corticoadrenal NEC 255.4
intestinal 564.8
labyrinth (unilateral) 386.53
  with loss of labyrinthine reactivity 386.55
  bilateral 386.54
    with loss of labyrinthine reactivity 386.56
Leydig cell 257.2
ovary 256.3
  postablative 256.2
pituitary (anterior) (gland) (lobe) 253.2
  posterior 253.5
testicular 257.2
  iatrogenic 257.1
  postablative 257.1
  postirradiation 257.1
  postsurgical 257.1

Hypogammaglobulinemia 279.00
acquired primary 279.06
non-sex-linked, congenital 279.06
sporadic 279.06
transient of infancy 279.09
Hypogenitalism (congenital) (female) (male)
752.8
penis 752.69
Hypoglycemia (spontaneous) 251.2
coma 251.0
diabetic 250.3
diabetic 250.8
due to insulin 251.0
therapeutic misadventure 962.3
familial (idiopathic) 251.2
following gastrointestinal surgery 579.3
infantile (idiopathic) 251.2
in infant of diabetic mother 775.0
leucine-induced 270.3
neonatal 775.6
reactive 251.2
specified NEC 251.1
Hypoglycemic shock 251.0
diabetic 250.8
due to insulin 251.0
functional (syndrome) 251.1
Hypogonadism
female 256.3
gonadotrophic (isolated) 253.4
hypogonadotropic (isolated) (with anosmia)
253.4
isolated 253.4
male 257.2
ovarian (primary) 256.3
pituitary (secondary) 253.4
testicular (primary) (secondary) 257.2
Hypohidrosis 705.0
Hypohidrotic ectodermal dysplasia 757.31
Hypoidrosis 705.0
Hypoinsulinemia, postsurgical 251.3
postpancreatectomy (complete) (partial) 251.3
Hypokalemia 276.8
Hypokinesia 780.9
Hypoleukia splenica 289.4
Hypoleukocytosis 288.8
Hypolipidemia 272.5
Hypolipoproteinemia 272.5
Hypomagnesemia 275.2
neonatal 775.4
Hypomania, hypomanic reaction (*see also*
Psychosis, affective) 296.0
recurrent episode 296.1
single episode 296.0
Hypomastia (congenital) 757.6
Hypomenorrhea 626.1
Hypometabolism 783.9
Hypomotility
gastrointestinal tract 536.8
psychogenic 306.4
intestine 564.8
psychogenic 306.4
stomach 536.8
psychogenic 306.4
Hyponasality 784.49
Hyponatremia 276.1
with water depletion 276.1
Hypo-ovarianism 256.3
Hypo-ovarism 256.3
Hypoparathyroidism (idiopathic) (surgically
induced) 252.1
neonatal 775.4

Hypopharyngitis 462
Hypophoria 378.40
Hypophosphatasia 275.3
Hypophosphatemia (acquired) (congenital)
(familial) 275.3
renal 275.3
Hypophyseal, hypophysis —*see also* condition
dwarfism 253.3
gigantism 253.0
syndrome 253.8
Hypophyseothalamic syndrome 253.8
Hypopiesis —*see* Hypotension
Hypopigmentation 709.00
eyelid 374.53
Hypopinealism 259.8
Hypopituitarism (juvenile) (syndrome) 253.2
due to
hormone therapy 253.7
hypophysectomy 253.7
radiotherapy 253.7
postablative 253.7
postpartum hemorrhage 253.2
Hypoplasia, hypoplasis 759.89
adrenal (gland) 759.1
alimentary tract 751.8
lower 751.2
upper 750.8
anus, anal (canal) 751.2
aorta 747.22
aortic
arch (tubular) 747.10
orifice or valve with hypoplasia of ascending
aorta and defective development of left
ventricle (with mitral valve atresia) 746.7
appendix 751.2
areola 757.6
arm (*see also* Absence, arm, congenital) 755.20
artery (congenital) (peripheral) NEC 747.60
brain 747.81
cerebral 747.81
coronary 746.85
gastrointestinal 747.61
lower limb 747.64
pulmonary 747.3
renal 747.62
retinal 743.58
specified NEC 747.69
spinal 747.82
umbilical 747.5
upper limb 747.63
auditory canal 744.29
causing impairment of hearing 744.02
biliary duct (common) or passage 751.61
bladder 753.8
bone NEC 756.9
face 756.0
malar 756.0
mandible 524.04
alveolar 524.74
marrow 284.9
acquired (secondary) 284.8
congenital 284.0
idiopathic 284.9
maxilla 524.03
alveolar 524.73
skull (*see also* Hypoplasia, skull) 756.0
brain 742.1
gyri 742.2
specified part 742.2
breast (areola) 757.6
bronchus (tree) 748.3

Hypoplasia, hypoplasis—*continued*
  cardiac 746.89
    valve—*see* Hypoplasia, heart, valve
    vein 746.89
  carpus (*see also* Absence, carpal, congenital) 755.28
  cartilaginous 756.9
  cecum 751.2
  cementum 520.4
    hereditary 520.5
  cephalic 742.1
  cerebellum 742.2
  cervix (uteri) 752.49
  chin 524.06
  clavicle 755.51
  coccyx 756.19
  colon 751.2
  corpus callosum 742.2
  cricoid cartilage 748.3
  dermal, focal (Goltz) 757.39
  digestive organ(s) or tract NEC 751.8
    lower 751.2
    upper 750.8
  ear 744.29
    auricle 744.23
    lobe 744.29
    middle, except ossicles 744.03
      ossicles 744.04
    ossicles 744.04
  enamel of teeth (neonatal) (postnatal) (prenatal) 520.4
    hereditary 520.5
  endocrine (gland) NEC 759.2
  endometrium 621.8
  epididymis 752.8
  epiglottis 748.3
  erythroid, congenital 284.0
  erythropoietic, chronic acquired 284.8
  esophagus 750.3
  Eustachian tube 744.24
  eye (*see also* Microphthalmos) 743.10
    lid 743.62
  face 744.89
    bone(s) 756.0
  fallopian tube 752.19
  femur (*see also* Absence, femur, congenital) 755.34
  fibula (*see also* Absence, fibula, congenital) 755.37
  finger (*see also* Absence, finger, congenital) 755.29
  focal dermal 757.39
  foot 755.31
  gallbladder 751.69
  genitalia, genital organ(s)
    female 752.8
      external 752.49
      internal NEC 752.8
    in adiposogenital dystrophy 253.8
    male 752.8
      penis 752.69
  glottis 748.3
  hair 757.4
  hand 755.21
  heart 746.89
    left (complex) (syndrome) 746.7
    valve NEC 746.89
    pulmonary 746.01
  humerus (*see also* Absence, humerus, congenital) 755.24
  hymen 752.49

Hypoplasia, hypoplasis—*continued*
  intestine (small) 751.1
    large 751.2
  iris 743.46
  jaw 524.09
  kidney(s) 753.0
  labium (majus) (minus) 752.49
  labyrinth, membranous 744.05
  lacrimal duct (apparatus) 743.65
  larynx 748.3
  leg (*see also* Absence, limb, congenital, lower) 755.30
  limb 755.4
    lower (*see also* Absence, limb, congenital, lower) 755.30
    upper (*see also* Absence, limb, congenital, upper) 755.20
  liver 751.69
  lung (lobe) 748.5
  mammary (areolar) 757.6
  mandibular 524.04
    alveolar 524.74
    unilateral condylar 526.89
  maxillary 524.03
    alveolar 524.73
  medullary 284.9
  megakaryocytic 287.3
  metacarpus (*see also* Absence, metacarpal, congenital) 755.28
  metatarsus (*see also* Absence, metatarsal, congenital) 755.38
  muscle 756.89
    eye 743.69
  myocardium (congenital) (Uhl's anomaly) 746.84
  nail(s) 757.5
  nasolacrimal duct 743.65
  nervous system NEC 742.8
  neural 742.8
  nose, nasal 748.1
  ophthalmic (*see also* Microphthalmos) 743.10
  organ
    of Corti 744.05
    or site NEC—*see* Anomaly, by site
  osseous meatus (ear) 744.03
  ovary 752.0
  oviduct 752.19
  pancreas 751.7
  parathyroid (gland) 759.2
  parotid gland 750.26
  patella 755.64
  pelvis, pelvic girdle 755.69
  penis 752.69
  peripheral vascular system (congenital) NEC 747.60
    gastrointestinal 747.61
    lower limb 747.64
    renal 747.62
    specified NEC 747.69
    spinal 747.82
    upper limb 747.63
  pituitary (gland) 759.2
  pulmonary 748.5
    arteriovenous 747.3
    artery 747.3
    valve 746.01
  punctum lacrimale 743.65
  radioulnar (*see also* Absence, radius, congenital, with ulna) 755.25
  radius (*see also* Absence, radius, congenital) 755.26

Hypoplasia, hypoplasis—*continued*
  rectum 751.2
  respiratory system NEC 748.9
  rib 756.3
  sacrum 756.19
  scapula 755.59
  shoulder girdle 755.59
  skin 757.39
  skull (bone) 756.0
    with
      anencephalus 740.0
      encephalocele 742.0
      hydrocephalus 742.3
        with spina bifida (*see also* Spina bifida)
          741.0
      microcephalus 742.1
  spinal (cord) (ventral horn cell) 742.59
    vessel 747.82
  spine 756.19
  spleen 759.0
  sternum 756.3
  tarsus (*see also* Absence, tarsal, congenital)
    755.38
  testis, testicle 752.8
  thymus (gland) 279.11
  thyroid (gland) 243
    cartilage 748.3
  tibiofibular (*see also* Absence, tibia, congenital,
    with fibula) 755.35
  toe (*see also* Absence, toe, congenital) 755.39
  tongue 750.16
  trachea (cartilage) (rings) 748.3
  Turner's (tooth) 520.4
  ulna (*see also* Absence, ulna, congenital) 755.27
  umbilical artery 747.5
  ureter 753.29
  uterus 752.3
  vagina 752.49
  vascular (peripheral) NEC (*see also* Hypoplasia,
    peripheral vascular system) 747.60
    brain 747.81
  vein(s) (peripheral) NEC (*see also* Hypoplasia,
    peripheral vascular system) 747.60
    brain 747.81
    cardiac 746.89
    great 747.49
    portal 747.49
    pulmonary 747.49
  vena cava (inferior) (superior) 747.49
  vertebra 756.19
  vulva 752.49
  zonule (ciliary) 743.39
  zygoma 738.12
Hypopotassemia 276.8
Hypoproaccelerinemia (*see also* Defect,
    coagulation) 286.3
Hypoproconvertinemia (congenital) (*see also*
    Defect, coagulation) 286.3
Hypoproteinemia (essential) (hypermetabolic)
    (idiopathic) 273.8
Hypoproteinosis 260
Hypoprothrombinemia (congenital) (hereditary)
    (idiopathic) (*see also* Defect, coagulation)
    286.3
  acquired 286.7
  newborn 776.3
Hypopselaphesia 782.0
Hypopyon (anterior chamber) (eye) 364.05
  iritis 364.05
  ulcer (cornea) 370.04
Hypopyrexia 780.9

Hyporeflex 796.1
Hyporeninemia, extreme 790.99
  in primary aldosteronism 255.1
Hyposecretion
  ACTH 253.4
    ovary 256.3
    postablative 256.2
  salivary gland (any) 527.7
Hyposegmentation of neutrophils, hereditary
    288.2
Hyposiderinemia 280.9
Hyposmolality 276.1
  syndrome 276.1
Hyposomatotropism 253.3
Hyposomnia (*see also* Insomnia) 780.52
Hypospadias (male) 752.61
  female 753.8
Hypospermatogenesis 606.1
Hyposphagma 372.72
Hyposplenism 289.59
Hypostasis, pulmonary 514
Hypostatic —*see* condition
Hyposthenuria 593.89
Hyposuprarenalism 255.4
Hypo-TBG-nemia 246.8
Hypotension (arterial) (constitutional) 458.9
  chronic 458.1
  iatrogenic 458.2
  maternal, syndrome (following labor and
    delivery) 669.2
  orthostatic (chronic) 458.0
    dysautonomic-dyskinetic syndrome 333.0
  permanent idiopathic 458.1
  postoperative 458.2
  postural 458.0
  transient 796.3
Hypothermia (accidental) 991.6
  anesthetic 995.89
  newborn NEC 778.3
  not associated with low environmental
    temperature 780.9
Hypothymergasia (*see also* Psychosis, affective)
    296.2
  recurrent episode 296.3
  single episode 296.2
Hypothyroidism (acquired) 244.9
  complicating pregnancy, childbirth, or
    puerperium 648.1
  congenital 243
  due to
    ablation 244.1
      radioactive iodine 244.1
      surgical 244.0
    iodine (administration) (ingestion) 244.2
      radioactive 244.1
    irradiation therapy 244.1
    p-aminosalicylic acid (PAS) 244.3
    phenylbutazone 244.3
    resorcinol 244.3
    specified cause NEC 244.8
    surgery 244.0
  goitrous (sporadic) 246.1
  iatrogenic NEC 244.3
  iodine 244.2
  pituitary 244.8
  postablative NEC 244.1
  postsurgical 244.0
  primary 244.9
  secondary NEC 244.8
  specified cause NEC 244.8
  sporadic goitrous 246.1

Hypotonia, hypotonicity, hypotony 781.3
  benign congenital 358.8
  bladder 596.4
  congenital 779.8
    benign 358.8
  eye 360.30
    due to
      fistula 360.32
      ocular disorder NEC 360.33
    following loss of aqueous or vitreous 360.33
    primary 360.31
  infantile muscular (benign) 359.0
  muscle 728.9
  uterus, uterine (contractions)—*see* Inertia, uterus
Hypotrichosis 704.09
  congenital 757.4
  lid (congenital) 757.4
    acquired 374.55
  postinfectional NEC 704.09
Hypotropia 378.32
Hypoventilation 786.09
Hypovitaminosis (*see also* Deficiency, vitamin)
  269.2
Hypovolemia 276.5
  surgical shock 998.0
  traumatic (shock) 958.4
Hypoxemia (*see also* Anoxia) 799.0
Hypoxia (*see also* Anoxia) 799.0
  cerebral 348.1
    during or resulting from a procedure 997.01
    newborn 768.9
      mild or moderate 768.6
      severe 768.5
  fetal—*see* Distress, fetal
  intrauterine—*see* Distress, fetal
  myocardial (*see also* Insufficiency, coronary)
    411.89
    arteriosclerotic —*see* Arteriosclerosis,
      coronary
  newborn—*see* Asphyxia, newborn
Hypsarrhythmia (*see also* Epilepsy) 345.6
Hysteralgia, pregnant uterus 646.8
Hysteria, hysterical 300.10
  anxiety 300.20
  Charcot's gland 300.11
  conversion (any manifestation) 300.11
  dissociative type NEC 300.15
  psychosis, acute 298.1
Hysteroepilepsy 300.11
Hysterotomy, affecting fetus or newborn 763.8

I

Iatrogenic syndrome of excess cortisol 255.0
Iceland disease (epidemic neuromyasthenia) 049.8
Ichthyosis (congenita) 757.1
  acquired 701.1
  fetalis gravior 757.1
  follicularis 757.1
  hystrix 757.39
  lamellar 757.1
  lingual 528.6
  palmaris and plantaris 757.39
  simplex 757.1
  vera 757.1
  vulgaris 757.1
Ichthyotoxism 988.0
  bacterial (*see also* Poisoning, food) 005.9
Icteroanemia, hemolytic (acquired) 283.9
  congenital (*see also* Spherocytosis) 282.0
Icterus (*see also* Jaundice) 782.4
  catarrhal—*see* Icterus, infectious
  conjunctiva 782.4
    newborn 774.6
  epidemic—*see* Icterus, infectious
  febrilis—*see* Icterus, infectious
  fetus or newborn—*see* Jaundice, fetus or newborn
  gravis (*see also* Necrosis, liver) 570
    complicating pregnancy 646.7
      affecting fetus or newborn 760.8
    fetus or newborn NEC 773.0
    obstetrical 646.7
      affecting fetus or newborn 760.8
  hematogenous (acquired) 283.9
  hemolytic (acquired) 283.9
    congenital (*see also* Spherocytosis) 282.0
  hemorrhagic (acute) 100.0
    leptospiral 100.0
    newborn 776.0
    spirochetal 100.0
  infectious 070.1
    with hepatic coma 070.0
    leptospiral 100.0
    spirochetal 100.0
  intermittens juvenilis 277.4
  malignant (*see also* Necrosis, liver) 570
  neonatorum (*see also* Jaundice, fetus or newborn) 774.6
  pernicious (*see also* Necrosis, liver) 570
  spirochetal 100.0
Ictus solaris, solis 992.0
Identity disorder 313.82
  dissociative 300.14
  gender role (child) 302.6
    adult 302.85
  psychosexual (child) 302.6
    adult 302.85
Idioglossia 307.9
Idiopathic — *see* condition
Idiosyncrasy (*see also* Allergy) 995.3
  drug, medicinal substance, and biological—*see* Allergy, drug
Idiot, idiocy (congenital) 318.2
  amaurotic (Bielschowsky) (-Jansky) (family) (infantile (late)) (juvenile (late)) (Vogt-Spielmeyer) 330.1
  microcephalic 742.1
  Mongolian 758.0
  oxycephalic 756.0
Id reaction (due to bacteria) 692.89

IgE asthma 493.0
Ileitis (chronic) (*see also* Enteritis) 558.9
  infectious 009.0
  noninfectious 558.9
  regional (ulcerative) 555.0
    with large intestine 555.2
  segmental 555.0
    with large intestine 555.2
  terminal (ulcerative) 555.0
    with large intestine 555.2
Ileocolitis (*see also* Enteritis) 558.9
  infectious 009.0
  regional 555.2
  ulcerative 556.1
Ileostomy status V44.2
  with complication 569.60
Ileotyphus 002.0
Ileum —*see* condition
Ileus (adynamic) (bowel) (colon) (inhibitory) (intestine) (neurogenic) (paralytic) 560.1
  arteriomesenteric duodenal 537.2
  due to gallstone (in intestine) 560.31
  duodenal, chronic 537.2
  following gastrointestinal surgery 997.4
  gallstone 560.31
  mechanical (*see also* Obstruction, intestine) 560.9
  meconium 777.1
    due to cystic fibrosis 277.01
  myxedema 564.8
  postoperative 997.4
  transitory, newborn 777.4
Iliac —*see* condition
Ill, louping 063.1
Illegitimacy V61.6
Illness —*see also* Disease
  factitious (with physical symptoms) 300.19
    with psychological symptoms 300.16
  chronic (with physical symptoms) 301.51
  heart—*see* Disease, heart
  manic-depressive (*see also* Psychosis, affective) 296.80
  mental (*see also* Disorder, mental) 300.9
Imbalance 781.2
  autonomic (*see also* Neuropathy, peripheral, autonomic) 337.9
  electrolyte 276.9
    with
      abortion—*see* Abortion, by type, with metabolic disorder
      ectopic pregnancy (*see also* categories 633.0 633.9) 639.4
      hyperemesis gravidarum (before 22 completed weeks gestation) 643.1
      molar pregnancy (*see also* categories 630-632) 639.4
    following
      abortion 639.4
      ectopic or molar pregnancy 639.4
    neonatal, transitory NEC 775.5
  endocrine 259.9
  eye muscle NEC 378.9
    heterophoria—*see* Heterophoria
  glomerulotubular NEC 593.89
  hormone 259.9
  hysterical (*see also* Hysteria) 300.10

Imbalance—*continued*
  labyrinth NEC 386.50
  posture 729.9
  sympathetic (*see also* Neuropathy, peripheral,
    autonomic) 337.9
Imbecile, imbecility 318.0
  moral 301.7
  old age 290.9
  senile 290.9
  specified IQ—*see* IQ
  unspecified IQ 318.0
Imbedding, intrauterine device 996.32
Imbibition, cholesterol (gallbladder) 575.6
Imerslund (-Gräsbeck) syndrome (anemia due to
  familial selective vitamin B_{12} malabsorption)
  281.1
Iminoacidopathy 270.8
Iminoglycinuria, familial 270.8
Immature —*see also* Immaturity
  personality 301.89
Immaturity 765.1
  extreme 765.0
  fetus or infant light-for-dates—*see*
    Light-for-dates
  lung, fetus or newborn 770.4
  organ or site NEC—*see* Hypoplasia
  pulmonary, fetus or newborn 770.4
  reaction 301.89
  sexual (female) (male) 259.0
Immersion 994.1
  foot 991.4
  hand 991.4
Immobile, immobility
  intestine 564.8
  joint—*see* Ankylosis
  syndrome (paraplegic) 728.3
Immunization
  ABO
    affecting management of pregnancy 656.2
      fetus or newborn 773.1
  complication—*see* Complications, vaccination
  Rh factor
    affecting management of pregnancy 656.1
      fetus or newborn 773.0
    from transfusion 999.7
Immunodeficiency 279.3
  with
    adenosine-deaminase deficiency 279.2
    defect, predominant
      B-cell 279.00
      T-cell 279.10
    hyperimmunoglobulinemia 279.2
    lymphopenia, hereditary 279.2
    thrombocytopenia and eczema 279.12
    thymic
      aplasia 279.2
      dysplasia 279.2
  autosomal recessive, Swiss-type 279.2
  common variable 279.06
  severe combined (SCID) 279.2
  to Rh factor
    affecting management of pregnancy 656.1
      fetus or newborn 773.0
  X-linked, with increased IgM 279.05
Immunotherapy, prophylactic V07.2
Impaction, impacted
  bowel, colon, rectum 560.30
    with hernia—*see also* Hernia, by site, with
      obstruction
      gangrenous—*see* Hernia, by site, with
        gangrene

Impaction, impacted—*continued*
  by
    calculus 560.39
    gallstone 560.31
    fecal 560.39
    specified type NEC 560.39
  calculus—*see* Calculus
  cerumen (ear) (external) 380.4
  cuspid 520.6
    with abnormal position (same or adjacent
      tooth) 524.3
  dental 520.6
    with abnormal position (same or adjacent
      tooth) 524.3
  fecal, feces 560.39
    with hernia—*see also* Hernia, by site, with
      obstruction
    gangrenous—*see* Hernia, by site, with
      gangrene
  fracture—*see* Fracture, by site
  gallbladder—*see* Cholelithiasis
  gallstone(s)—*see* Cholelithiasis
    in intestine (any part) 560.31
  intestine(s) 560.30
    with hernia—*see also* Hernia, by site, with
      obstruction
    gangrenous—*see* Hernia, by site, with
      gangrene
  by
    calculus 560.39
    gallstone 560.31
    fecal 560.39
    specified type NEC 560.39
  intrauterine device (IUD) 996.32
  molar 520.6
    with abnormal position (same or adjacent
      tooth) 524.3
  shoulder 660.4
    affecting fetus or newborn 763.1
  tooth, teeth 520.6
    with abnormal position (same or adjacent
      tooth) 524.3
  turbinate 733.99
Impaired, impairment (function)
  arm V49.1
    movement, involving
      musculoskeletal system V49.1
      nervous system V49.2
  auditory discrimination 388.43
  back V48.3
  body (entire) V49.8
  hearing (*see also* Deafness) 389.9
  heart—*see* Disease, heart
  kidney (*see also* Disease, renal) 593.9
    disorder resulting from 588.9
      specified NEC 588.8
  leg V49.1
    movement, involving
      musculoskeletal system V49.1
      nervous system V49.2
  limb V49.1
    movement, involving
      musculoskeletal system V49.1
      nervous system V49.2
  liver 573.8
  mastication 524.9
  mobility
    ear ossicles NEC 385.22
    incostapedial joint 385.22
    malleus 385.21

Impaired, impairment—*continued*
  myocardium, myocardial (*see also*
    Insufficiency, myocardial) 428.0
  neuromusculoskeletal NEC V49.8
    back V48.3
    head V48.2
    limb V49.2
    neck V48.3
    spine V48.3
    trunk V48.3
  rectal sphincter 787.99
  renal (*see also* Disease, renal) 593.9
    disorder resulting from 588.9
      specified NEC 588.8
  spine V48.3
  vision NEC 369.9
    both eyes NEC 369.3
    moderate 369.74
      both eyes 369.25
        with impairment of lesser eye (specified
          as)
          blind, not further specified 369.15
          low vision, not further specified 369.23
          near-total 369.17
          profound 369.18
          severe 369.24
          total 369.16
      one eye 369.74
        with vision of other eye (specified as)
          near-normal 369.75
          normal 369.76
    near-total 369.64
      both eyes 369.04
        with impairment of lesser eye (specified
          as)
          blind, not further specified 369.02
          total 369.03
      one eye 369.64
        with vision of other eye (specified as)
          near-normal 369.65
          normal 369.66
    one eye 369.60
      with low vision of other eye 369.10
    profound 369.67
      both eyes 369.08
        with impairment of lesser eye (specified
          as)
          blind, not further specified 369.05
          near-total 369.07
          total 369.06
      one eye 369.67
        with vision of other eye (specified as)
          near-normal 369.68
          normal 369.69
    severe 369.71
      both eyes 369.22
        with impairment of lesser eye (specified
          as)
          blind, not further specified 369.11
          low vision, not further specified 369.21
          near-total 369.13
          profound 369.14
          total 369.12
      one eye 369.71
        with vision of other eye (specified as)
          near-normal 369.72
          normal 369.73
    total
      both eyes 369.01

Impaired, impairment—*continued*
  one eye 369.61
    with vision of other eye (specified as)
      near-normal 369.62
      normal 369.63
Impaludism —*see* Malaria
Impediment, speech NEC 784.5
  psychogenic 307.9
  secondary to organic lesion 784.5
Impending
  cerebrovascular accident or attack 435.9
  coronary syndrome 411.1
  delirium tremens 291.0
  myocardial infarction 411.1
Imperception, auditory (acquired) (congenital)
  389.9
Imperfect
  aeration, lung (newborn) 770.5
  closure (congenital)
    alimentary tract NEC 751.8
      lower 751.5
      upper 750.8
    atrioventricular ostium 745.69
    atrium (secundum) 745.5
      primum 745.61
    branchial cleft or sinus 744.41
    choroid 743.59
    cricoid cartilage 748.3
    cusps, heart valve NEC 746.89
      pulmonary 746.09
    ductus
      arteriosus 747.0
      Botalli 747.0
    ear drum 744.29
      causing impairment of hearing 744.03
    endocardial cushion 745.60
    epiglottis 748.3
    esophagus with communication to bronchus
      or trachea 750.3
    Eustachian valve 746.89
    eyelid 743.62
    face, facial (*see also* Cleft, lip) 749.10
    foramen
      Botalli 745.5
      ovale 745.5
    genitalia, genital organ(s) or system
      female 752.8
        external 752.49
        internal NEC 752.8
        uterus 752.3
      male 752.8
        penis 752.69
    glottis 748.3
    heart valve (cusps) NEC 746.89
    interatrial ostium or septum 745.5
    interauricular ostium or septum 745.5
    interventricular ostium or septum 745.4
    iris 743.46
    kidney 753.3
    larynx 748.3
    lens 743.36
    lip (*see also* Cleft, lip) 749.10
    nasal septum or sinus 748.1
    nose 748.1
    omphalomesenteric duct 751.0
    optic nerve entry 743.57
    organ or site NEC—*see* Anomaly, specified
      type, by site
    ostium
      interatrial 745.5
      interauricular 745.5

Imperfect—*continued*
   interventricular 745.4
   palate (*see also* Cleft, palate) 749.00
   preauricular sinus 744.46
   retina 743.56
   roof of orbit 742.0
   sclera 743.47
   septum
     aortic 745.0
     aorticopulmonary 745.0
     atrial (secundum) 745.5
       primum 745.61
     between aorta and pulmonary artery 745.0
     heart 745.9
     interatrial (secundum) 745.5
       primum 745.61
     interauricular (secundum) 745.5
       primum 745.61
     interventricular 745.4
       with pulmonary stenosis or atresia,
         dextraposition of aorta, and
         hypertrophy of right ventricle 745.2
       in tetralogy of Fallot 745.2
     nasal 748.1
     ventricular 745.4
       with pulmonary stenosis or atresia,
         dextraposition of aorta, and
         hypertrophy of right ventricle 745.2
       in tetralogy of Fallot 745.2
   skull 756.0
     with
       anencephalus 740.0
       encephalocele 742.0
       hydrocephalus 742.3
         with spina bifida (*see also* Spina bifida)
          741.0
       microcephalus 742.1
   spine (with meningocele) (*see also* Spina
     bifida) 741.90
   thyroid cartilage 748.3
   trachea 748.3
   tympanic membrane 744.29
     causing impairment of hearing 744.03
   uterus (with communication to bladder,
     intestine, or rectum) 752.3
   uvula 749.02
     with cleft lip (*see also* Cleft, palate, with
       cleft lip) 749.20
   vitelline duct 751.0
   development—*see* Anomaly, by site
   erection 607.84
   fusion—*see* Imperfect, closure
   inflation lung (newborn) 770.5
   intestinal canal 751.5
   poise 729.9
   rotation—*see* Malrotation
   septum, ventricular 745.4
Imperfectly descended testis 752.51
Imperforate (congenital)—*see also* Atresia
   anus 751.2
   bile duct 751.61
   cervix (uteri) 752.49
   esophagus 750.3
   hymen 752.42
   intestine (small) 751.1
     large 751.2
   jejunum 751.1
   pharynx 750.29
   rectum 751.2
   salivary duct 750.23

Imperforate— *continued*
   urethra 753.6
   urinary meatus 753.6
   vagina 752.49
Impervious (congenital)—*see also* Atresia
   anus 751.2
   bile duct 751.61
   esophagus 750.3
   intestine (small) 751.1
     large 751.5
   rectum 751.2
   urethra 753.6
Impetiginization of other dermatoses 684
Impetigo (any organism) (any site) (bullous)
   (circinate) (contagiosa) (neonatorum)
   (simplex) 684
   Bockhart's (superficial folliculitis) 704.8
   external ear 684 *[380.13]*
   eyelid 684 *[373.5]*
   Fox's (contagiosa) 684
   furfuracea 696.5
   herpetiformis 694.3
     nonobstetrical 694.3
   staphylococcal infection 684
   ulcerative 686.8
   vulgaris 684
Impingement, soft tissue between teeth 524.2
Implant, endometrial 617.9
Implantation
   anomalous—*see also* Anomaly, specified type,
     by site
     ureter 753.4
   cyst
     external area or site (skin) NEC 709.8
     iris 364.61
     vagina 623.8
     vulva 624.8
   dermoid (cyst)
     external area or site (skin) NEC 709.8
     iris 364.61
     vagina 623.8
     vulva 624.8
   placenta, low or marginal—*see* Placenta previa
Impotence (sexual) (psychogenic) 302.72
   organic origin NEC 607.84
Impoverished blood 285.9
Impression, basilar 756.0
Imprisonment V62.5
Improper
   development, infant 764.9
Improperly tied umbilical cord (causing
   hemorrhage) 772.3
Impulses, obsessional 300.3
Impulsive neurosis 300.3
Inaction, kidney (*see also* Disease, renal) 593.9
Inactive —*see* condition
Inadequate, inadequacy
   biologic 301.6
   cardiac and renal—*see* Hypertension,
     cardiorenal
   constitutional 301.6
   development
     child 783.4
     fetus 764.9
       affecting management of pregnancy 656.5
     genitalia
       after puberty NEC 259.0
       congenital—*see* Hypoplasia, genitalia
     lungs 748.5
     organ or site NEC—*see* Hypoplasia, by site
   dietary 269.9

Inadequate, inadequacy—*continued*
education V62.3
environment
  economic problem V60.2
  household condition NEC V60.1
  poverty V60.2
  unemployment V62.0
functional 301.6
household care, due to
  family member
    handicapped or ill V60.4
    temporarily away from home V60.4
      on vacation V60.5
  technical defects in home V60.1
  temporary absence from home of person
    rendering care V60.4
housing (heating) (space) V60.1
material resources V60.2
mental (*see also* Retardation, mental) 319
nervous system 799.2
personality 301.6
prenatal care in current pregnancy V23.7
pulmonary
  function 786.09
    newborn 770.8
  ventilation, newborn 770.8
respiration 786.09
  newborn 770.8
social 301.6
Inanition 263.9
with edema 262
due to
  deprivation of food 994.2
  malnutrition 263.9
fever 780.6
Inappropriate secretion
ACTH 255.0
antidiuretic hormone (ADH) (excessive) 253.6
  deficiency 253.5
ectopic hormone NEC 259.3
pituitary (posterior) 253.6
Inattention after or at birth 995.52
Inborn errors of metabolism —*see* Disorder,
  metabolism
Incarceration, incarcerated
bubonocele—*see also* Hernia, inguinal, with
  obstruction
  gangrenous—*see* Hernia, inguinal, with
    gangrene
colon (by hernia)—*see also* Hernia, by site,
  with obstruction
  gangrenous—*see* Hernia, by site, with
    gangrene
enterocele 552.9
  gangrenous 551.9
epigastrocele 552.29
  gangrenous 551.29
epiplocele 552.9
  gangrenous 551.9
exomphalos 552.1
  gangrenous 551.1
fallopian tube 620.8
hernia—*see also* Hernia, by site, with
  obstruction

Incarceration, incarcerated—*continued*
gangrenous—*see* Hernia, by site, with
  gangrene
iris, in wound 871.1
lens, in wound 871.1
merocele (*see also* Hernia, femoral, with
  obstruction) 552.00
Omentum (by hernia)—*see also* Hernia, by site,
  with obstruction
  gangrenous—*see* Hernia, by site, with
    gangrene
omphalocele 756.7
rupture (meaning hernia) (*see also* Hernia, by
  site, with obstruction) 552.9
  gangrenous (*see also* Hernia, by site, with
    gangrene) 551.9
sarcoepiplocele 552.9
  gangrenous 551.9
sarcoepiplomphalocele 552.1
  with gangrene 551.1
uterus 621.8
  gravid 654.3
    causing obstructed labor 660.2
      affecting fetus or newborn 763.1
Incident, cerebrovascular (*see also* Disease,
  cerebrovascular, acute) 436
Incineration (entire body) (from fire,
  conflagration, electricity, or lightning)—*see*
  Burn, multiple, specified sites
Incised wound
external—*see* Wound, open, by site
internal organs (abdomen, chest, or pelvis)—*see*
  Injury, internal, by site, with open wound
Incision, incisional
hernia—*see* Hernia, incisional
surgical, complication—*see* Complications,
  surgical procedures
traumatic
  external—*see* Wound, open, by site
  internal organs (abdomen, chest or
    pelvis)—*see* Injury, internal, by site, with
    open wound
Inclusion
azurophilic leukocytic 288.2
blennorrhea (neonatal) (newborn) 771.6
cyst—*see* Cyst, skin
gallbladder in liver (congenital) 751.69
Incompatibility
ABO
  affecting management of pregnancy 656.2
  fetus or newborn 773.1
  infusion or transfusion reaction 999.6
blood (group) (Duffy) (E) (K(ell)) (Kidd)
  (Lewis) (M) (N) (P) (S) NEC
  affecting management of pregnancy 656.2
  fetus or newborn 773.2
  infusion or transfusion reaction 999.6
marital V61.10
  involving divorce or estrangement V61.0
Rh (blood group) (factor)
  affecting management of pregnancy 656.1
  fetus or newborn 773.0
  infusion or transfusion reaction 999.7
Rhesus—*see* Incompatibility, Rh
Incompetency, incompetence, incompetent
annular
  aortic (valve) (*see also* Insufficiency, aortic)
    424.1
    mitral (valve)—(*see also* Insufficiency,
      mitral) 424.0

Incompetency, Incompetence . . .—*continued*
  pulmonary valve (heart) (*see also*
    Endocarditis, pulmonary) 424.3
  aortic (valve) (*see also* Insufficiency, aortic)
    424.1
    syphilitic 093.22
  cardiac (orifice) 530.0
    valve—*see* Endocarditis
  cervix, cervical (os) 622.5
    in pregnancy 654.5
      affecting fetus or newborn 761.0
  esophagogastric (junction) (sphincter) 530.0
  heart valve, congenital 746.89
  mitral (valve)—*see* Insufficiency, mitral
  papillary muscle (heart) 429.81
  pelvic fundus 618.8
  pulmonary valve (heart) (*see also* Endocarditis,
    pulmonary) 424.3
    congenital 746.09
  tricuspid (annular) (rheumatic) (valve) (*see also*
    Endocarditis, tricuspid) 397.0
  valvular—*see* Endocarditis
  vein, venous (saphenous) (varicose) (*see also*
    Varicose, vein) 454.9
  velopharyngeal (closure)
    acquired 528.9
    congenital 750.29
Incomplete —*see also* condition
  bladder emptying 788.21
  expansion lungs (newborn) 770.5
  gestation (liveborn)—*see* Immaturity
  rotation—*see* Malrotation
Incontinence 788.30
  without sensory awareness 788.34
  anal sphincter 787.6
  continuous leakage 788.37
  feces 787.6
    due to hysteria 300.11
    nonorganic origin 307.7
  hysterical 300.11
  mixed (male) (female) (urge and stress) 788.33
  overflow 788.39
  paradoxical 788.39
  rectal 787.6
  specified NEC 788.39
  stress (female) 625.6
    male NEC 788.32
  urethral sphincter 599.84
  urge 788.31
    and stress (male) (female) 788.33
  urine 788.30
    active 788.30
    male 788.30
      stress 788.32
        and urge 788.33
    neurogenic 788.39
    nonorganic origin 307.6
    stress (female) 625.6
      male NEC 788.32
    urge 788.31
      and stress 788.33
Incontinentia pigmenti 757.33
Incoordinate
  uterus (action) (contractions) 661.4
    affecting fetus or newborn 763.7
Incoordination
  esophageal-pharyngeal (newborn) 787.2
  muscular 781.3
  papillary muscle 429.81

Increase, increased
  abnormal, in development 783.9
  androgens (ovarian) 256.1
  anticoagulants (antithrombin) (anti-VIIIa)
    (anti-IXa) (anti-Xa) (anti-XIa) 286.5
    postpartum 666.3
  cold sense (*see also* Disturbance, sensation)
    782.0
  estrogen 256.0
  function
    adrenal (cortex) 255.3
      medulla 255.6
    pituitary (anterior) (gland) (lobe) 253.1
      posterior 253.6
  heat sense (*see also* Disturbance, sensation)
    782.0
  intracranial pressure 348.2
    injury at birth 767.8
  light reflex of retina 362.13
  permeability, capillary 448.9
  pressure
    intracranial 348.2
      injury at birth 767.8
    intraocular 365.00
  pulsations 785.9
  pulse pressure 785.9
  sphericity, lens 743.36
  splenic activity 289.4
  venous pressure 459.89
    portal 572.3
Incrustation, cornea, lead or zinc 930.0
Incyclophoria 378.44
Incyclotropia 378.33
Indeterminate sex 752.7
India rubber skin 756.83
Indicanuria 270.2
Indigestion (bilious) (functional) 536.8
  acid 536.8
  catarrhal 536.8
  due to decomposed food NEC 005.9
  fat 579.8
  nervous 306.4
  psychogenic 306.4
Indirect —*see* condition
Indolent bubo NEC 099.8
Induced
  abortion—*see* Abortion, induced
  birth, affecting fetus or newborn 763.8
  delivery—*see* Delivery
  labor—*see* Delivery
Induration, indurated
  brain 348.8
  breast (fibrous) 611.79
    puerperal, postpartum 676.3
  broad ligament 620.8
  chancre 091.0
    anus 091.1
    congenital 090.0
    extragenital NEC 091.2
  corpora cavernosa (penis) (plastic) 607.89
  liver (chronic) 573.8
    acute 573.8
  lung (black) (brown) (chronic) (fibroid) (*see*
    also Fibrosis, lung) 515
    essential brown 275.0 [516.1]
  penile 607.89
  phlebitic—*see* Phlebitis
  skin 782.8
  stomach 537.89
Induratio penis plastica 607.89
Industrial —*see* condition

Inebriety (*see also* Abuse, drugs, nondependent) 305.0
Inefficiency
 kidney (*see also* Disease, renal) 593.9
 thyroid (acquired) (gland) 244.9
Inelasticity, skin 782.8
Inequality, leg (acquired) (length) 736.81
 congenital 755.30
Inertia
 bladder 596.4
  neurogenic 596.54
   with cauda equina syndrome 344.61
 stomach 536.8
  psychogenic 306.4
 uterus, uterine 661.2
  affecting fetus or newborn 763.7
  primary 661.0
  secondary 661.1
 vesical 596.4
  neurogenic 596.54
   with cauda equina 344.61
Infant —*see also* condition
 held for adoption V68.89
 newborn—*see* Newborn
 syndrome of diabetic mother 775.0
"Infant Hercules" syndrome 255.2
Infantile —*see also* condition
 genitalia, genitals 259.0
  in pregnancy or childbirth NEC 654.4
   affecting fetus or newborn 763.8
   causing obstructed labor 660.2
    affecting fetus or newborn 763.1
 heart 746.9
 kidney 753.3
 lack of care 995.52
 macula degeneration 362.75
 melanodontia 521.0
 os, uterus (*see also* Infantile, genitalia) 259.0
 pelvis 738.6
  with disproportion (fetopelvic) 653.1
   affecting fetus or newborn 763.1
  causing obstructed labor 660.1
   affecting fetus or newborn 763.1
 penis 259.0
 testis 257.2
 uterus (*see also* Infantile, genitalia) 259.0
 vulva 752.49
Infantilism 259.9
 with dwarfism (hypophyseal) 253.3
 Brissaud's (infantile myxedema) 244.9
 celiac 579.0
 Herter's (nontropical sprue) 579.0
 hypophyseal 253.3
 hypothalamic (with obesity) 253.8
 idiopathic 259.9
 intestinal 579.0
 pancreatic 577.8
 pituitary 253.3
 renal 588.0
 sexual (with obesity) 259.0
Infants, healthy liveborn —*see* Newborn
Infarct, infarction
 adrenal (capsule) (gland) 255.4
 amnion 658.8
 anterior (with contiguous portion of
  intraventricular septum) NEC (*see also*
  Infarct, myocardium) 410.1
 appendices epiploicae 557.0
 bowel 557.0

Infarct, infarction—*continued*
 brain (stem) 434.91
  embolic (*see also* Embolism, brain) 434.11
  healed or old—*see also* category 438
   without residuals V12.59
   iatrogenic 997.02
   postoperative 997.02
  late effect—*see* category 438
  puerperal, postpartum, childbirth 674.0
  thrombotic (*see also* Thrombosis, brain)
   434.01
 breast 611.8
 Brewer's (kidney) 593.81
 cardiac (*see also* Infarct, myocardium) 410.9
 cerebellar (*see also* Infarct, brain) 434.91
  embolic (*see also* Embolism, brain) 434.11
 cerebral (*see also* Infarct, brain) 434.91
  embolic (*see also* Embolism, brain) 434.11
 chorion 658.8
 colon (acute) (agnogenic) (embolic)
   (hemorrhagic) (nonocclusive)
   (nonthrombotic) (occlusive) (segmental)
   (thrombotic) (with gangrene) 557.0
 coronary artery (*see also* Infarct, myocardium)
   410.9
 embolic (*see also* Embolism) 444.9
 fallopian tube 620.8
 gallbladder 575.8
 heart (*see also* Infarct, myocardium) 410.9
 hepatic 573.4
 hypophysis (anterior lobe) 253.8
 impending (myocardium) 411.1
 intestine (acute) (agnogenic) (embolic)
   (hemorrhagic) (nonocclusive)
   (nonthrombotic) (occlusive) (thrombotic)
   (with gangrene) 557.0
 kidney 593.81
 liver 573.4
 lung (embolic) (thrombotic) 415.19
  with
   abortion—*see* Abortion, by type, with,
    embolism
   ectopic pregnancy (*see also* categories
    633.0-633.9) 639.6
   molar pregnancy (*see also* categories
    630-632) 639.6
  following
   abortion 639.6
   ectopic or molar pregnancy 639.6
  iatrogenic 415.11
  in pregnancy, childbirth, or puerperium—*see*
   Embolism, obstetrical
  postoperative 415.11
 lymph node or vessel 457.8
 medullary (brain)—*see* Infarct, brain
 meibomian gland (eyelid) 374.85
 mesentery, mesenteric (embolic) (thrombotic)
   (with gangrene) 557.0
 midbrain—*see* Infarct, brain
 myocardium, myocardial (acute or with a stated
   duration of 8 weeks or less) (with
   hypertension) 410.9

> Note—use the following fifth-digit
> subclassification with category 410
>
> 0 *episode unspecified*
> 1 *initial episode*
> 2 *subsequent episode without recurrence*

Infarct, infarction—*continued*
   with symptoms after 8 weeks from date of
      infarction 414.8
   anterior (wall) (with contiguous portion of
      intraventricular septum) NEC 410.1
   anteroapical (with contiguous portion of
      intraventricular septum) 410.1
   anterolateral (wall) 410.0
   anteroseptal (with contiguous portion of
      intraventricular septum) 410.1
   apical-lateral 410.5
   atrial 410.8
   basal-lateral 410.5
   chronic (with symptoms after 8 weeks from
      date of infarction) 414.8
   diagnosed on ECG, but presenting no
      symptoms 412
   diaphragmatic wall (with contiguous portion
      of intraventricular septum) 410.4
   healed or old, currently presenting no
      symptoms 412
   high lateral 410.5
   impending 411.1
   inferior (wall) (with contiguous portion of
      intraventricular septum) 410.4
   inferolateral (wall) 410.2
   inferoposterior wall 410.3
   lateral wall 410.5
   nontransmural 410.7
   papillary muscle 410.8
   past (diagnosed on ECG or other special
      investigation, but correctly presenting no
      symptoms) 412
      with symptoms NEC 414.8
   posterior (strictly) (true) (wall) 410.6
   posterobasal 410.6
   posteroinferior 410.3
   posterolateral 410.5
   previous, currently presenting no symptoms
      412
   septal 410.8
   specified site NEC 410.8
   subendocardial 410.7
   syphilitic 093.82
   nontransmural 410.7
   omentum 557.0
   ovary 620.8
   pancreas 577.8
   papillary muscle (*see also* Infarct, myocardium)
      410.8
   parathyroid gland 252.8
   pituitary (gland) 253.8
   placenta (complicating pregnancy) 656.7
      affecting fetus or newborn 762.2
   pontine—*see* Infarct, brain
   posterior NEC (*see also* Infarct, myocardium)
      410.6
   prostate 602.8
   pulmonary (artery) (hemorrhagic) (vein) 415.19
      with
         abortion—*see* Abortion, by type, with
            embolism
         ectopic pregnancy (*see also* categories
            633.0-633.9) 639.6
         molar pregnancy (*see also* categories
            630-632) 639.6
      following
         abortion 639.6
         ectopic or molar pregnancy 639.6
      iatrogenic 415.11

Infarct, infarction—*continued*
   in pregnancy, childbirth, or puerperium—*see*
      Embolism, obstetrical
   postoperative 415.11
   renal 593.81
      embolic or thrombotic 593.81
   retina, retinal 362.84
      with occlusion—*see* Occlusion, retina
   spinal (acute) (cord) (embolic) (nonembolic)
      336.1
   spleen 289.59
      embolic or thrombotic 444.89
   subchorionic—*see* Infarct, placenta
   subendocardial (*see also* Infarct, myocardium)
      410.7
   suprarenal (capsule) (gland) 255.4
   syncytium—*see* Infarct, placenta
   testis 608.83
   thrombotic (*see also* Thrombosis) 453.9
      artery, arterial—*see* Embolism
   thyroid (gland) 246.3
   ventricle (heart) (*see also* Infarct, myocardium)
      410.9
Infecting —*see* condition
Infection, infected, infective (opportunistic)
      136.9
   with lymphangitis—*see* Lymphangitis
   abortion—*see* Abortion, by type, with sepsis
   abscess (skin)—*see* Abscess, by site
   Absidia 117.7
   Acanthocheilonema (perstans) 125.4
      streptocerca 125.6
   accessory sinus (chronic) (*see also* Sinusitis)
      473.9
   Achorion—*see* Dermatophytosis
   Acremonium falciforme 117.4
   acromioclavicular (joint) 711.91
   actinobacillus
      lignieresii 027.8
      mallei 024
      muris 026.1
   actinomadura—*see* Actinomycosis
   Actinomyces (israelii)—*see also* Actinomycosis
      muris-ratti 026.1
   Actinomycetales (actinomadura) (Actinomyces)
      (Nocardia) (Streptomyces)—*see*
      Actinomycosis
   actinomycotic NEC (*see also* Actinomycosis)
      039.9
   adenoid (chronic) 474.0
      acute 463
      and tonsil (chronic) 474.0
         acute or subacute 463
   adenovirus NEC 079.0
      in diseases classified elsewhere—*see* category
         079
      unspecified nature or site 079.0
   Aerobacter aerogenes NEC 041.85
      enteritis 008.2
   aerogenes capsulatus (*see also* Gangrene, gas)
      040.0
   aertrycke (*see also* Infection, Salmonella) 003.9
   ajellomyces dermatitidis 116.0
   alimentary canal NEC (*see also* Enteritis, due
      to, by organism) 009.0
   Allescheria boydii 117.6
   Alternaria 118
   alveolus, alveolar (process) (pulpal origin) 522.4
   ameba, amebic (histolytica) (*see also*
      Amebiasis) 006.9
      acute 006.0

Infection, infected, infective—*continued*
- chronic 006.1
  - free-living 136.2
  - hartmanni 007.8
  - specified
    - site NEC 006.8
    - type NEC 007.8
- amniotic fluid or cavity 658.4
  - affecting fetus or newborn 762.7
- anaerobes (cocci) (gram-negative) (gram positive) (mixed) NEC 041.84
- anal canal 569.49
- Ancylostoma braziliense 126.2
- Angiostrongylus cantonensis 128.8
- anisakiasis 127.1
- Anisakis larva 127.1
- anthrax (*see also* Anthrax) 022.9
- antrum (chronic) (*see also* Sinusitis, maxillary) 473.0
- anus (papillae) (sphincter) 569.49
- arbor virus NEC 066.9
- arbovirus NEC 066.9
- argentophil-rod 027.0
- Ascaris lumbricoides 127.0
- ascomycetes 117.4
- Aspergillus (flavus) (fumigatus) (terreus) 117.3
- atypical
  - acid-fast (bacilli) (*see also* Mycobacterium, atypical) 031.9
  - mycobacteria (*see also* Mycobacterium, atypical) 031.9
- auditory meatus (circumscribed) (diffuse) (external) (*see also* Otitis, externa) 380.10
- auricle (ear) (*see also* Otitis, externa) 380.10
- axillary gland 683
- Babesiasis 088.82
- Babesiosis 088.82
- Bacillus NEC 041.89
  - abortus 023.1
  - anthracis (*see also* Anthrax) 022.9
  - cereus (food poisoning) 005.89
  - coli—*see* Infection, Escherichia coli
  - coliform NEC 041.85
  - Ducrey's (any location) 099.0
  - Flexner's 004.1
  - fragilis NEC 041.82
  - Friedländer's NEC 041.3
  - fusiformis 101
  - gas (gangrene) (*see also* Gangrene, gas) 040.0
  - mallei 024
  - melitensis 023.0
  - paratyphoid, paratyphosus 002.9
    - A 002.1
    - B 002.2
    - C 002.3
  - Schmorl's 040.3
  - Shiga 004.0
  - suipestifer (*see also* Infection, Salmonella) 003.9
  - swimming pool 031.1
  - typhosa 002.0
  - welchii (*see also* Gangrene, gas) 040.0
  - Whitmore's 025
- bacterial NEC 041.9
  - specified NEC 041.89
    - anaerobic NEC 041.84
    - gram-negative NEC 041.85
      - anaerobic NEC 041.84
- Bacterium
  - paratyphosum 002.9
    - A 002.1

Infection, infected, infective—*continued*
- B 002.2
- C 002.3
- typhosum 002.0
- Bacteroides (fragilis) (melaninogenicus) (oralis) NEC 041.84
- balantidium coli 007.0
- Bartholin's gland 616.8
- Basidiobolus 117.7
- Bedsonia 079.98
  - specified NEC 079.88
- bile duct 576.1
- bladder (*see also* Cystitis) 595.9
- Blastomyces, blastomycotic 116.0
  - brasiliensis 116.1
  - dermatitidis 116.0
  - European 117.5
  - Loboi 116.2
  - North American 116.0
  - South American 116.1
- blood stream—*see* Septicemia
- bone 730.9
  - specified—*see* Osteomyelitis
- Bordetella 033.9
  - bronchiseptica 033.8
  - parapertussis 033.1
  - pertussis 033.0
- Borrelia
  - bergdorfi 088.81
  - vincentii (mouth) (pharynx) (tonsil) 101
- brain (*see also* Encephalitis) 323.9
  - late effect—*see* category 326
  - membranes—(*see also* Meningitis) 322.9
  - septic 324.0
    - late effect—*see* category 326
  - meninges (*see also* Meningitis) 320.9
- branchial cyst 744.42
- breast 611.0
  - puerperal, postpartum 675.2
    - with nipple 675.9
      - specified type NEC 675.8
    - nonpurulent 675.2
    - purulent 675.1
- bronchus (*see also* Bronchitis) 490
  - fungus NEC 117.9
- Brucella 023.9
  - abortus 023.1
  - canis 023.3
  - melitensis 023.0
  - mixed 023.8
  - suis 023.2
- Brugia (Wuchereria) malayi 125.1
- bursa—*see* Bursitis
- buttocks (skin) 686.9
- Candida (albicans) (tropicalis) (*see also* Candidiasis) 112.9
  - congenital 771.7
- Candiru 136.8
- Capillaria
  - hepatica 128.8
  - philippinensis 127.5
- cartilage 733.99
- cat liver fluke 121.0
- cellulitis—*see* Cellulitis, by site
- Cephalosporum falciforme 117.4
- Cercomonas hominis (intestinal) 007.3
- cerebrospinal (*see also* Meningitis) 322.9
  - late effect—*see* category 326
- cervical gland 683
- cervix (*see also* Cervicitis) 616.0
- cesarean section wound 674.3

Infection, infected, infective—*continued*
Chilomastix (intestinal) 007.8
Chlamydia 079.98
  specified NEC 079.88
Cholera (*see also* Cholera) 001.9
chorionic plate 658.8
Cladosporium
  bantianum 117.8
  carrionii 117.2
  mansoni 111.1
  trichoides 117.8
  wernecki 111.1
Clonorchis (sinensis) (liver) 121.1
Clostridium (haemolyticum) (novyi) NEC
    041.84
  botulinum 005.1
  congenital 771.8
  histolyticum (*see also* Gangrene, gas) 040.0
  oedematiens (*see also* Gangrene, gas) 040.0
  perfringens 041.83
    due to food 005.2
  septicum (*see also* Gangrene, gas) 040.0
  sordelii (*see also* Gangrene, gas) 040.0
  welchii (*see also* Gangrene, gas) 040.0
    due to food 005.2
Coccidioides (immitis) (*see also*
    Coccidioidomycosis) 114.9
coccus NEC 041.89
colon (*see also* Enteritis, due to, by organism)
    009.0
  bacillus—*see* Infection, Escherichia coli
colostomy or enterostomy 569.61
common duct 576.1
complicating pregnancy, childbirth, or
    puerperium NEC 647.9
  affecting fetus or newborn 760.2
Condiobolus 117.7
congenital NEC 771.8
  Candida albicans 771.7
  chronic 771.2
  clostridial 771.8
  Cytomegalovirus 771.1
  Escherichia coli 771.8
  hepatitis, viral 771.2
  Herpes simplex 771.2
  listeriosis 771.2
  malaria 771.2
  poliomyelitis 771.2
  rubella 771.0
  Salmonella 771.8
  streptococcal 771.8
  toxoplasmosis 771.2
  tuberculosis 771.2
  urinary (tract) 771.8
  vaccinia 771.2
corpus luteum (*see also* Salpingo-oophoritis)
    614.2
Corynebacterium diphtheriae—*see* Diphtheria
Coxsackie (*see also* Coxsackie) 079.2
  endocardium 074.22
  heart NEC 074.20
  in diseases classified elsewhere—*see* category
    079
  meninges 047.0
  myocardium 074.23
  pericardium 074.21
  pharynx 074.0
  specified disease NEC 074.8
  unspecified nature or site 079.2
Cryptococcus neoformans 117.5
Cryptosporidia 007.8

Infection, infected, infective—*continued*
Cunninghamella 117.7
cyst—*see* Cyst
Cysticercus cellulosae 123.1
cytomegalovirus 078.5
  congenital 771.1
dental (pulpal origin) 522.4
deuteromycetes 117.4
Dicrocoelium dendriticum 121.8
Dipetalonema (perstans) 125.4
  streptocerca 125.6
diphtherial—*see* Diphtheria
Diphyllobothrium (adult) (latum) (pacificum)
    123.4
  larval 123.5
Diplogonoporus (grandis) 123.8
Dipylidium (caninum) 123.8
Dirofilaria 125.6
dog tapeworm 123.8
Dracunculus medinensis 125.7
Dreschlera 118
  hawaiiensis 117.8
Ducrey's bacillus (any site) 099.0
due to or resulting from
  device, implant, or graft (any) (presence
    of)—*see* Complications, infection and
    inflammation, due to (presence of) any
    device, implant, or graft classified to
    996.0-996.5 NEC
  injection, inoculation, infusion, transfusion, or
    vaccination (prophylactic) (therapeutic)
    999.3
  injury NEC—*see* Wound, open, by site,
    complicated
  surgery 998.59
duodenum 535.6
ear—*see also* Otitis
  external (*see also* Otitis, externa) 380.10
  inner (*see also* Labyrinthitis) 386.30
  middle —*see* Otitis, media
Eaton's agent NEC 041.81
Eberthella typhosa 002.0
echinococcosis 122.9
Echinococcus (*see also* Echinococcus) 122.9
Echinostoma 121.8
ECHO virus 079.1
  in diseases classified elsewhere—*see* category
    079
  unspecified nature or site 079.1
Endamoeba—*see* Infection, ameba
endocardium (*see also* Endocarditis) 421.0
endocervix (*see also* Cervicitis) 616.0
Entamoeba—*see* Infection, ameba
enteric (*see also* Enteritis, due to, by organism)
    009.0
Enterobacter aerogenes NEC 041.85
Enterobius vermicularis 127.4
Enterococcus NEC 041.00
enterovirus NEC 079.89
  central nervous system NEC 048
  enteritis 008.67
  meningitis 047.9
Entomophthora 117.7
Epidermophyton—*see* Dermatophytosis
epidermophytosis—*see* Dermatophytosis
episiotomy 674.3
Epstein-Barr virus 075
erysipeloid 027.1
Erysipelothrix (insidiosa) (rhusiopathiae) 027.1
erythema infectiosum 057.0
Escherichia coli NEC 041.4

Infection, infected, infective—*continued*
  congenital 771.8
  enteritis—*see* Enteritis, E. coli
  generalized 038.42
  intestinal—*see* Enteritis, E. coli
  ethmoidal (chronic) (sinus) (*see also* Sinusitis,
    ethmoidal) 473.2
  Eubacterium 041.84
  Eustachian tube (ear) 381.50
    acute 381.51
    chronic 381.52
  exanthema subitum 057.8
  external auditory canal (meatus) (*see also* Otitis,
    externa) 380.10
  eye NEC 360.00
  eyelid 373.9
    specified NEC 373.8
  fallopian tube (*see also* Salpingo-oophoritis)
    614.2
  fascia 728.89
  Fasciola
    gigantica 121.3
    hepatica 121.3
  Fasciolopsis (buski) 121.4
  fetus (intra-amniotic)—*see* Infection, congenital
  filarial—*see* Infestation, filarial
  finger (skin) 686.9
    abscess (with lymphangitis) 681.00
      pulp 681.01
    cellulitis (with lymphangitis) 681.00
    distal closed space (with lymphangitis) 681.00
    nail 681.02
      fungus 110.1
  fish tapeworm 123.4
    larval 123.5
  flagellate, intestinal 007.9
  fluke—*see* Infestation, fluke
  focal
    teeth (pulpal origin) 522.4
    tonsils 474.0
  Fonsecaea
    compactum 117.2
    pedrosoi 117.2
  food (*see also* Poisoning, food) 005.9
  foot (skin) 686.9
    fungus 110.4
  Francisella tularensis (*see also* Tularemia) 021.9
  frontal sinus (chronic) (*see also* Sinusitis,
    frontal) 473.1
  fungus NEC 117.9
    beard 110.0
    body 110.5
    dermatiacious NEC 117.8
    foot 110.4
    groin 110.3
    hand 110.2
    nail 110.1
    pathogenic to compromised host only 118
    perianal (area) 110.3
    scalp 110.0
    scrotum 110.8
    skin 111.9
      foot 110.4
      hand 110.2
    toenails 110.1
    trachea 117.9
  Fusarium 118
  Fusobacterium 041.84
  gallbladder (*see also* Cholecystitis, acute) 575.0
  gas bacillus (*see also* Gas, gangrene) 040.0
  gastric (*see also* Gastritis) 535.5

Infection, infected, infective—*continued*
  Gastrodiscoides hominis 121.8
  gastroenteric (*see also* Enteritis, due to, by
    organism) 009.0
  gastrointestinal (*see also* Enteritis, due to, by
    organism) 009.0
  generalized NEC (*see also* Septicemia) 038.9
  genital organ or tract NEC
    female 614.9
      with
        abortion—*see* Abortion, by type, with
          sepsis
        ectopic pregnancy (*see also* categories
          633.0-633.9) 639.0
        molar pregnancy (*see also* categories
          630-632) 639.0
      complicating pregnancy 646.6
        affecting fetus or newborn 760.8
      following
        abortion 639.0
        ectopic or molar pregnancy 639.0
      puerperal, postpartum, childbirth 670
      minor or localized 646.6
        affecting fetus or newborn 760.8
    male 608.4
  genitourinary tract NEC 599.0
  Ghon tubercle, primary (*see also* Tuberculosis)
    010.0
  Giardia lamblia 007.1
  gingival (chronic) 523.1
    acute 523.0
    Vincent's 101
  glanders 024
  Glenosporopsis amazonica 116.2
  Gnathostoma spinigerum 128.1
  Gongylonema 125.6
  gonococcal NEC (*see also* Gonococcus) 098.0
  gram-negative bacilli NEC 041.85
    anaerobic 041.84
  guinea worm 125.7
  gum (*see also* Infection, gingival) 523.1
  Hantavirus 079.81
  heart 429.89
  Helicobacter pylori (H. pylori) 041.86
  helminths NEC 128.9
    intestinal 127.9
      mixed (types classifiable to more than one
        category in 120.0-127.7) 127.8
      specified type NEC 127.7
    specified type NEC 128.8
  Hemophilus influenzae NEC 041.5
    generalized 038.41
  Herpes (simplex) (*see also* Herpes, simplex)
    054.9
    congenital 771.2
    zoster (*see also* Herpes, zoster) 053.9
      eye NEC 053.29
  Heterophyes heterophyes 121.6
  Histoplasma (*see also* Histoplasmosis) 115.90
    capsulatum (*see also* Histoplasmosis,
      American) 115.00
    duboisii (*see also* Histoplasmosis, African)
      115.10
  HIV V08
    with symptoms, symptomatic 042
  hookworm (*see also* Ancylostomiasis) 126.9
  human immunodeficiency virus V08
    with symptoms, symptomatic 042
  human papilloma virus 079.4
  hydrocele 603.1
  hydronephrosis 591

Infection, infected, infective—*continued*
  Hymenolepis 123.6
  hypopharynx 478.29
  inguinal glands 683
    due to soft chancre 099.0
  intestine, intestinal (*see also* Enteritis, due to, by organism) 009.0
  intrauterine (*see also* Endometritis) 615.9
    complicating delivery 646.6
  isospora belli or hominis 007.2
  Japanese B encephalitis 062.0
  jaw (bone) (acute) (chronic) (lower) (subacute) (upper) 526.4
  joint—*see* Arthritis, infectious or infective
  kidney (cortex) (hematogenous) 590.9
    with
      abortion—*see* Abortion, by type, with urinary tract infection
      calculus 592.0
      ectopic pregnancy (*see also* categories 633.0-633.9) 639.8
      molar pregnancy (*see also* categories 630-632) 639.8
    complicating pregnancy or puerperium 646.6
      affecting fetus or newborn 760.1
    following
      abortion 639.8
      ectopic or molar pregnancy 639.8
    pelvis and ureter 590.3
  Klebsiella pneumoniae NEC 041.3
  knee (skin) NEC 686.9
    joint—*see* Arthritis, infectious
  Koch's (*see also* Tuberculosis, pulmonary) 011.9
  labia (majora) (minora) (*see also* Vulvitis) 616.10
  lacrimal
    gland (*see also* Dacryoadenitis) 375.00
    passages (duct) (sac) (*see also* Dacryocystitis) 375.30
  larynx NEC 478.79
  leg (skin) NEC 686.9
  Leishmania (*see also* Leishmaniasis) 085.9
    braziliensis 085.5
    donovani 085.0
    Ethiopica 085.3
    furunculosa 085.1
    infantum 085.0
    mexicana 085.4
    tropica (minor) 085.1
      major 085.2
  Leptosphaeria senegalensis 117.4
  leptospira (*see also* Leptospirosis) 100.9
    Australis 100.89
    Bataviae 100.89
    pyrogenes 100.89
    specified type NEC 100.89
  leptospirochetal NEC (*see also* Leptospirosis) 100.9
  Leptothrix—*see* Actinomycosis
  Listeria monocytogenes (listeriosis) 027.0
    congenital 771.2
  liver fluke—*see* Infestation, fluke, liver
  Loa loa 125.2
    eyelid 125.2 [373.6]
  Loboa loboi 116.2
  local, skin (staphylococcal) (streptococcal) NEC 686.9
    abscess—*see* Abscess, by site

Infection, infected, infective—*continued*
  cellulitis—*see* Cellulitis, by site
  ulcer (*see also* Ulcer, skin) 707.9
  Loefflerella
    mallei 024
    whitmori 025
  lung 518.89
    atypical Mycobacterium 031.0
      tuberculous (*see also* Tuberculosis, pulmonary) 011.9
    basilar 518.89
    chronic 518.89
    fungus NEC 117.9
    spirochetal 104.8
    virus—*see* Pneumonia, virus
  lymph gland (axillary) (cervical) (inguinal) 683
    mesenteric 289.2
  lymphoid tissue, base of tongue or posterior pharynx, NEC 474.0
  madurella
    grisea 117.4
    mycetomii 117.4
  major
    with
      abortion—*see* Abortion, by type, with sepsis
      ectopic pregnancy (*see also* categories 633.0-633.9) 639.0
      molar pregnancy (*see also* categories 630-632) 639.0
    following
      abortion 639.0
      ectopic or molar pregnancy 639.0
    puerperal, postpartum, childbirth 670
  malarial—*see* Malaria
  Malassezia furfur 111.0
  Malleomyces
    mallei 024
    pseudomallei 025
  mammary gland 611.0
    puerperal, postpartum 675.2
  Mansonella (ozzardi) 125.5
  mastoid (suppurative)—*see* Mastoiditis
  maxilla, maxillary 526.4
    sinus (chronic) (*see also* Sinusitis, maxillary) 473.0
  mediastinum 519.2
  medina 125.7
  meibomian
    cyst 373.12
    gland 373.12
  melioidosis 025
  meninges (*see also* Meningitis) 320.9
  meningococcal (*see also* condition) 036.9
    brain 036.1
    cerebrospinal 036.0
    endocardium 036.42
    generalized 036.2
    meninges 036.0
    meningococcemia 036.2
    specified site NEC 036.89
  mesenteric lymph nodes or glands NEC 289.2
  Metagonimus 121.5
  metatarsophalangeal 711.97
  microorganism resistant to drugs—*see* Resistance (to), drugs by microorganisms
  Microsporidia 136.8
  microsporum, microsporic—*see* Dermatophytosis
  Mima polymorpha NEC 041.85
  mixed flora NEC 041.89
  Monilia (*see also* Candidiasis) 112.9

Infection, infected, infective—*continued*
  neonatal 771.7
  Monosporium apiospermum 117.6
  mouth (focus) NEC 528.9
    parasitic 112.0
  Mucor 117.7
  muscle NEC 728.89
  mycelium NEC 117.9
  mycetoma
    actinomycotic NEC (*see also* Actinomycosis)
      039.9
    mycotic NEC 117.4
  Mycobacterium, mycobacterial (*see also*
    Mycobacterium) 031.9
  mycoplasma NEC 041.81
  mycotic NEC 117.9
    pathogenic to compromised host only 118
    skin NEC 111.9
    systemic 117.9
  myocardium NEC 422.90
  nail (chronic) (with lymphangitis) 681.9
    finger 681.02
      fungus 110.1
    ingrowing 703.0
    toe 681.11
      fungus 110.1
  nasal sinus (chronic) (*see also* Sinusitis) 473.9
  nasopharynx (chronic) 478.29
    acute 460
  navel 686.9
    newborn 771.4
  Neisserian—*see* Gonococcus
  Neotestudina rosatii 117.4
  newborn, generalized 771.8
  nipple 611.0
    puerperal, postpartum 675.0
      with breast 675.9
        specified type NEC 675.8
  Nocardia—*see* Actinomycosis
  nose 478.1
  nostril 478.1
  obstetrical surgical wound 674.3
  Oesophagostomum (apiostomum) 127.7
  Oestrus ovis 134.0
  Oidium albicans (*see also* Candidiasis) 112.9
  Onchocerca (volvulus) 125.3
    eye 125.3 *[360.13]*
    eyelid 125.3 *[373.6]*
  operation wound 998.59
  Opisthorchis (felineus) (tenuicollis) (viverrini)
    121.0
  orbit 376.00
    chronic 376.10
  ovary (*see also* Salpingo-oophoritis) 614.2
  Oxyuris vermicularis 127.4
  pancreas 577.0
  Paracoccidioides brasiliensis 116.1
  Paragonimus (westermani) 121.2
  parainfluenza virus 079.89
  parameningococcus NEC 036.9
    with meningitis 036.0
  parasitic NEC 136.9
  paratyphoid 002.9
    Type A 002.1
    Type B 002.2
    Type C 002.3
  paraurethral ducts 597.89
  parotid gland 527.2

Infection, infected, infective—*continued*
  Pasteurella NEC 027.2
    multocida (cat-bite) (dog-bite) 027.2
    pestis (*see also* Plague) 020.9
    pseudotuberculosis 027.2
    septica (cat-bite) (dog-bite) 027.2
    tularensis (*see also* Tularemia) 021.9
  pelvic, female (*see also* Disease, pelvis,
    inflammatory) 614.9
  penis (glans) (retention) NEC 607.2
    herpetic 054.13
  Peptococcus 041.84
  Peptostreptococcus 041.84
  periapical (pulpal origin) 522.4
  peridental 523.3
  perineal wound (obstetrical) 674.3
  periodontal 523.3
  periorbital 376.00
    chronic 376.10
  perirectal 569.49
  perirenal (*see also* Infection, kidney) 590.9
  peritoneal (*see also* Peritonitis) 567.9
  periureteral 593.89
  periurethral 597.89
  Petriellidium boydii 117.6
  pharynx 478.29
    Coxsackie virus 074.0
    phlegmonous 462
    posterior, lymphoid 474.0
  Phialophora
    gougerotii 117.8
    jeanselmei 117.8
    verrucosa 117.2
  Piedraia hortai 111.3
  pinna, acute 380.11
  pinta 103.9
    intermediate 103.1
    late 103.2
    mixed 103.3
    primary 103.0
  pinworm 127.4
  pityrosporum furfur 111.0
  pleuropneumonia-like organisms NEC (PPLO)
    041.81
  pneumococcal NEC 041.2
    generalized (purulent) 038.2
  Pneumococcus NEC 041.2
  postoperative wound 998.59
  posttraumatic NEC 958.3
  postvaccinal 999.3
  prepuce NEC 607.1
  Propionibacterium 041.84
  prostate (capsule) (*see also* Prostatitis) 601.9
  Proteus (mirabilis) (morganii) (vulgaris) NEC
    041.6
    enteritis 008.3
  protozoal NEC 136.8
    intestinal NEC 007.9
  Pseudomonas NEC 041.7
    mallei 024
    pneumonia 482.1
    pseudomallei 025
  psittacosis 073.9
  puerperal, postpartum (major) 670
    minor 646.6
  pulmonary—*see* Infection, lung
  purulent—*see* Abscess
  putrid, generalized—*see* Septicemia
  pyemic—*see* Septicemia
  Pyrenochaeta romeroi 117.4

Infection, infected, infective—*continued*
  Q fever 083.0
  rabies 071
  rectum (sphincter) 569.49
  renal (*see also* Infection, kidney) 590.9
    pelvis and ureter 590.3
  resistant to drugs—*see* Resistance (to), drugs by
      microorganisms
  respiratory 519.8
    chronic 519.8
    influenzal (acute) (upper) 487.1
    lung 518.89
    rhinovirus 460
    syncytial virus 079.6
    upper (acute) (infectious) NEC 465.9
      with flu, grippe, or influenza 487.1
      influenzal 487.1
      multiple sites NEC 465.8
      streptococcal 034.0
      viral NEC 465.9
  respiratory syncytial virus (RSV) 079.6
  resulting from presence of shunt or other
      internal prosthetic device—*see*
      Complications, infection and inflammation,
      due to (presence of) any device, implant, or
      graft classified to 996.0-996.5 NEC
  retrovirus 079.50
    human immunodeficiency virus type 2
        [HIV-2] 079.53
    human T-cell lymphotrophic virus type I
        [HTLV-I] 079.51
    human T-cell lymphotrophic virus type II
        [HTLV-II] 079.52
    specified NEC 079.59
  Rhinocladium 117.1
  Rhinosporidium (seeberi) 117.0
  rhinovirus
    in diseases classified elsewhere—*see* category
        079
    unspecified nature or site 079.3
  Rhizopus 117.7
  rickettsial 083.9
  rickettsialpox 083.2
  rubella (*see also* Rubella) 056.9
    congenital 771.0
  Saccharomyces (*see also* Candidiasis) 112.9
  Saksenaea 117.7
  salivary duct or gland (any) 527.2
  Salmonella (aertrycke) (callinarum)
      (choleraesuis) (enteritidis) (suipestifer)
      (typhimurium) 003.9
    with
      arthritis 003.23
      gastroenteritis 003.0
      localized infection 003.20
        specified type NEC 003.29
      meningitis 003.21
      osteomyelitis 003.24
      pneumonia 003.22
      septicemia 003.1
      specified manifestation NEC 003.8
    congenital 771.8
    due to food (poisoning) (any serotype) (*see
        also* Poisoning, food, due to, Salmonella)
    hirschfeldii 002.3
    localized 003.20
      specified type NEC 003.29
    paratyphi 002.9
      A 002.1
      B 002.2
      C 002.3

Infection, infected, infective—*continued*
    schottmuelleri 002.2
    specified type NEC 003.8
    typhi 002.0
    typhosa 002.0
  saprophytic 136.8
  Sarcocystis, lindemanni 136.5
  scabies 133.0
  Schistosoma—*see* Infestation, Schistosoma
  Schmorl's bacillus 040.3
  scratch or other superficial injury—*see* Injury,
      superficial, by site
  scrotum (acute) NEC 608.4
  secondary, burn or open wound (dislocation)
      (fracture) 958.3
  seminal vesicle (*see also* Vesiculitis) 608.0
  septic
    generalized—*see* Septicemia
    localized, skin (*see also* Abscess) 682.9
  septicemic—*see* Septicemia
  seroma 998.51
  Serratia (marcescens) 041.85
    generalized 038.44
  sheep liver fluke 121.3
  Shigella 004.9
    boydii 004.2
    dysenteriae 004.0
    Flexneri 004.1
    group
      A 004.0
      B 004.1
      C 004.2
      D 004.3
    Schmitz (-Stutzer) 004.0
    Schmitzii 004.0
    Shiga 004.0
    Sonnei 004.3
    specified type NEC 004.8
  sinus (*see also* Sinusitis) 473.9
    pilonidal 685.1
      with abscess 685.0
    skin NEC 686.9
  Skene's duct or gland (*see also* Urethritis)
      597.89
  skin (local) (staphylococcal) (streptococcal)
      NEC 686.9
    abscess—*see* Abscess, by site
    cellulitis—*see* Cellulitis, by site
    due to fungus 111.9
      specified type NEC 111.8
    mycotic 111.9
      specified type NEC 111.8
    ulcer (*see also* Ulcer, skin) 707.9
  slow virus 046.9
    specified condition NEC 046.8
  Sparganum (mansoni) (proliferum) 123.5
  specific (*see also* Syphilis) 097.9
  spermatic cord NEC 608.4
  sphenoidal (chronic) (sinus) (*see also* Sinusitis,
      sphenoidal) 473.3
  Spherophorus necrophorus 040.3
  spinal cord NEC (*see also* Encephalitis) 323.9
    abscess 324.1
      late effect—*see* category 326
    late effect—*see* category 326
    meninges—*see* Meningitis
    streptococcal 320.2
  Spirillum
    minus or minor 026.0
    morsus muris 026.0
    obermeieri 087.0

Infertility—*continued*
    pituitary-hypothalamus NEC 253.8 *[628.1]*
      anterior pituitary NEC 253.4 *[628.1]*
        hyperfunction NEC 253.1 *[628.1]*
      dwarfism 253.3 *[628.1]*
      panhypopituitarism 253.2 *[628.1]*
    specified NEC 628.8
    tubal (block) (occlusion) (stenosis) 628.2
      adhesions 614.6 *[628.2]*
    uterine 628.3
    vaginal 628.4
    previous, requiring supervision of pregnancy V23.0
  male 606.9
    absolute 606.0
    due to
      azoospermia 606.0
      drug therapy 606.8
      extratesticular cause NEC 606.8
      germinal cell
        aplasia 606.0
        desquamation 606.1
      hypospermatogenesis 606.1
      infection 606.8
      obstruction, afferent ducts 606.8
      oligospermia 606.1
      radiation 606.8
      spermatogenic arrest (complete) 606.0
        incomplete 606.1
      systemic disease 606.8
Infestation 134.9
  Acanthocheilonema (perstans) 125.4
    streptocerca 125.6
  Acariasis 133.9
    demodex folliculorum 133.8
    Sarcoptes scabiei 133.0
    trombiculae 133.8
  Agamofilaria streptocerca 125.6
  Ancylostoma, Ankylostoma 126.9
    americanum 126.1
    braziliense 126.2
    canium 126.8
    ceylanicum 126.3
    duodenale 126.0
    new world 126.1
    old world 126.0
  Angiostrongylus cantonensis 128.8
  anisakiasis 127.1
  Anisakis larva 127.1
  arthropod NEC 134.1
  Ascaris lumbricoides 127.0
  Bacillus fusiformis 101
  Balantidium coli 007.0
  beef tapeworm 123.2
  Bothriocephalus (latus) 123.4
    larval 123.5
  broad tapeworm 123.4
    larval 123.5
  Brugia malayi 125.1
  Candiru 136.8
  Capillaria
    hepatica 128.8
    philippinensis 127.5
  cat liver fluke 121.0
  Cercomonas hominis (intestinal) 007.3
  cestodes 123.9
    specified type NEC 123.8
  chigger 133.8
  chigoe 134.1
  Chilomastix 007.8

Infestation—*continued*
  Clonorchis (sinensis) (liver) 121.1
  coccidia 007.2
  complicating pregnancy, childbirth, or puerperium 647.9
    affecting fetus or newborn 760.8
  Cysticercus cellulosae 123.1
  Demodex folliculorum 133.8
  Dermatobia (hominis) 134.0
  Dibothriocephalus (latus) 123.4
    larval 123.5
  Dicrocoelium dendriticum 121.8
  Diphyllobothrium (adult) (intestinal) (latum) (pacificum) 123.4
    larval 123.5
  Diplogonoporus (grandis) 123.8
  Dipylidium (caninum) 123.8
  Distoma hepaticum 121.3
  dog tapeworm 123.8
  Dracunculus medinensis 125.7
  dragon worm 125.7
  dwarf tapeworm 123.6
  Echinococcus (*see also* Echinococcus) 122.9
  Echinostoma ilocanum 121.8
  Embadomonas 007.8
  Endamoeba (histolytica)—*see* Infection, ameba
  Entamoeba (histolytica)—*see* Infection, ameba
  Enterobius vermicularis 127.4
  Epidermophyton—*see* Dermatophytosis
  eyeworm 125.2
  Fasciola
    gigantica 121.3
    hepatica 121.3
  Fasciolopsis (buski) (small intestine) 121.4
  filarial 125.9
    due to
      Acanthocheilonema (perstans) 125.4
        streptocerca 125.6
      Brugia (Wuchereria) malayi 125.1
      Dracunculus medinensis 125.7
      guinea worms 125.7
      Mansonella (ozzardi) 125.5
      Onchocerca volvulus 125.3
        eye 125.3 *[360.13]*
        eyelid 125.3 *[373.6]*
      Wuchereria (bancrofti) 125.0
        malayi 125.1
    specified type NEC 125.6
  fish tapeworm 123.4
    larval 123.5
  fluke 121.9
    blood NEC (*see also* Schistosomiasis) 120.9
    cat liver 121.0
    intestinal (giant) 121.4
    liver (sheep) 121.3
      cat 121.0
      Chinese 121.1
      clonorchiasis 121.1
      fascioliasis 121.3
      Oriental 121.1
    lung (oriental) 121.2
    sheep liver 121.3
  fly larva 134.0
  Gasterophilus (intestinalis) 134.0
  Gastrodiscoides hominis 121.8
  Giardia lamblia 007.1
  Gnathostoma (spinigerum) 128.1
  Gongylonema 125.6
  guinea worm 125.7

Infestation—*continued*
  helminth NEC 128.9
    intestinal 127.9
      mixed (types classifiable to more than one
        category in 120.0-127.7) 127.8
      specified type NEC 127.7
    specified type NEC 128.8
  Heterophyes heterophyes (small intestine) 121.6
  hookworm (*see also* Infestation, ancylostoma)
    126.9
  Hymenolepis (diminuta) (nana) 123.6
    intestinal NEC 129
  leeches (aquatic) (land) 134.2
  Leishmania—*see* Leishmaniasis
  lice (*see also* infestation, pediculus) 132.9
  Linguatulidae, linguatula (pentastoma) (serrata)
    134.1
  Loa loa 125.2
    eyelid 125.2 *[373.6]*
  louse (*see also* Infestation, pediculus) 132.9
    body 132.1
    head 132.0
    pubic 132.2
  maggots 134.0
  Mansonella (ozzardi) 125.5
  medina 125.7
  Metagonimus yokogawai (small intestine) 121.5
  Microfilaria streptocerca 125.3
    eye 125.3 *[360.13]*
    eyelid 125.3 *[373.6]*
  Microsporon furfur 111.0
  microsporum—*see* Dermatophytosis
  mites 133.9
    scabic 133.0
    specified type NEC 133.8
  Monilia (albicans) (*see also* Candidiasis) 112.9
    vagina 112.1
    vulva 112.1
    mouth 112.0
  Necator americanus 126.1
  nematode (intestinal) 127.9
    Ancylostoma (*see also* Ancylostoma) 126.9
    Ascaris lumbricoides 127.0
    conjunctiva NEC 128.9
    Dioctophyma 128.8
    Enterobius vermicularis 127.4
    Gnathostoma spinigerum 128.1
    Oesophagostomum (apiostomum) 127.7
    Physaloptera 127.4
    specified type NEC 127.7
    Strongyloides stercoralis 127.2
    Ternidens diminutus 127.7
    Trichinella spiralis 124
    Trichostrongylus 127.6
    Trichuris (trichiuria) 127.3
  Oesophagostomum (apiostomum) 127.7
  Oestrus ovis 134.0
  Onchocerca (volvulus) 125.3
    eye 125.3 *[360.13]*
    eyelid 125.3 *[373.6]*
  Opisthorchis (felineus) (tenuicollis) (viverrini)
    121.0
  Oxyuris vermicularis 127.4
  Paragonimus (westermani) 121.2
  parasite, parasitic NEC 136.9
    eyelid 134.9 *[373.6]*
    intestinal 129
    mouth 112.0
    orbit 376.13
    skin 134.9
    tongue 112.0

Infestation—*continued*
  pediculus 132.9
    capitis (humanus) (any site) 132.0
    corporis (humanus) (any site) 132.1
    eyelid 132.0 *[373.6]*
    mixed (classifiable to more than one category
      in 132.0-132.2) 132.3
    pubis (any site) 132.2
  phthirus (pubis) (any site) 132.2
    with any infestation classifiable to 132.0 and
      132.1 132.3
  pinworm 127.4
  pork tapeworm (adult) 123.0
  protozoal NEC 136.8
  pubic louse 132.2
  rat tapeworm 123.6
  red bug 133.8
  roundworm (large) NEC 127.0
  sand flea 134.1
  saprophytic NEC 136.8
  Sarcoptes scabiei 133.0
  scabies 133.0
  Schistosoma 120.9
    bovis 120.8
    cercariae 120.3
    hematobium 120.0
    intercalatum 120.8
    japonicum 120.2
    mansoni 120.1
    mattheii 120.8
    specified
      site—*see* Schistosomiasis
      type NEC 120.8
    spindale 120.8
  screw worms 134.0
  skin NEC 134.9
  Sparganum (mansoni) (proliferum) 123.5
    larval 123.5
  specified type NEC 134.8
  Spirometra larvae 123.5
  Sporozoa NEC 136.8
  Stellantchasmus falcatus 121.6
  Strongyloides 127.2
  Strongylus (gibsoni) 127.7
  Taenia 123.3
    diminuta 123.6
    Echinococcus (*see also* Echinococcus) 122.9
    mediocanellata 123.2
    nana 123.6
    saginata (mediocanellata) 123.2
    solium (intestinal form) 123.0
      larval form 123.1
  Taeniarhynchus saginatus 123.2
  tapeworm 123.9
    beef 123.2
    broad 123.4
      larval 123.5
    dog 123.8
    dwarf 123.6
    fish 123.4
      larval 123.5
    pork 123.0
    rat 123.6
  Ternidens diminutus 127.7
  Tetranychus molestissimus 133.8
  threadworm 127.4
  tongue 112.0
  Toxocara (cani) (cati) (felis) 128.0
  trematode(s) NEC 121.9
  Trichina spiralis 124

Infestation—*continued*
  Trichinella spiralis 124
  Trichocephalus 127.3
  Trichomonas 131.9
    bladder 131.09
    cervix 131.09
    intestine 007.3
    prostate 131.03
    specified site NEC 131.8
    urethra (female) (male) 131.02
    urogenital 131.00
    vagina 131.01
    vulva 131.01
  Trichophyton—*see* Dermatophytosis
  Trichostrongylus instabilis 127.6
  Trichuris (trichiuria) 127.3
  Trombicula (irritans) 133.8
  Trypanosoma—*see* Trypanosomiasis
  Tunga penetrans 134.1
  Uncinaria americana 126.1
  whipworm 127.3
  worms NEC 128.9
    intestinal 127.9
  Wuchereria 125.0
    bancrofti 125.0
    malayi 125.1

Infiltrate, infiltration
  with an iron compound 275.0
  amyloid (any site) (generalized) 277.3
  calcareous (muscle) NEC 275.4
    localized—*see* Degeneration, by site
  calcium salt (muscle) 275.4
  corneal (*see also* Edema, cornea) 371.20
  eyelid 373.9
  fatty (diffuse) (generalized) 272.8
    localized—*see* Degeneration, by site, fatty
  glycogen, glycogenic (*see also* Disease,
    glycogen storage) 271.10
  heart, cardiac
    fatty (*see also* Degeneration, myocardial)
      429.1
    glycogenic 271.0 [425.7]
  inflammatory in vitreous 379.29
  kidney (*see also* Disease, renal) 593.9
  leukemic (M9800/3)—*see* Leukemia
  liver 573.8
    fatty—*see* Fatty, liver
    glycogen (*see also* Disease, glycogen storage)
      271.0
  lung (*see also* Infiltrate, pulmonary) 518.3
    eosinophilic 518.3
    x-ray finding only 793.1
  lymphatic (*see also* Leukemia, lymphatic) 204.9
    gland, pigmentary 289.3
  muscle, fatty 728.9
  myelogenous (*see also* Leukemia, myeloid)
    205.9
  myocardium, myocardial
    fatty (*see also* Degeneration, myocardial)
      429.1
    glycogenic 271.0 [425.7]
  pulmonary 518.3
    with
      eosinophilia 518.3
      pneumonia—*see* Pneumonia, by type
    x-ray finding only 793.1
  Ranke's primary (*see also* Tuberculosis) 010.0
  skin, lymphocyctic (benign) 709.8
  thymus (gland) (fatty) 254.8
  urine 788.8
  vitreous humor 379.29

Infirmity 799.8
  senile 797
Inflammation, inflamed, inflammatory (with
  exudation)
  abducens (nerve) 378.54
  accessory sinus (chronic) (*see also* Sinusitis)
    473.9
  adrenal (gland) 255.8
  alimentary canal—*see* Enteritis
  alveoli (teeth) 526.5
    scorbutic 267
  amnion—*see* Amnionitis
  anal canal 569.49
  antrum (chronic) (*see also* Sinusitis, maxillary)
    473.0
  anus 569.49
  appendix (*see also* Appendicitis) 541
  arachnoid—*see* Meningitis
  areola 611.0
    puerperal, postpartum 675.0
  areolar tissue NEC 686.9
  artery—*see* Arteritis
  auditory meatus (external) (*see also* Otitis,
    externa) 380.10
  Bartholin's gland 616.8
  bile duct or passage 576.1
  bladder (*see also* Cystitis) 595.9
  bone—*see* Osteomyelitis
  bowel (*see also* Enteritis) 558.9
  brain (*see also* Encephalitis) 323.9
    late effect—*see* category 326
    membrane—*see* Meningitis
  breast 611.0
    puerperal, postpartum 675.2
  broad ligament (*see also* Disease, pelvis,
    inflammatory) 614.4
    acute 614.3
  bronchus—*see* Bronchitis
  bursa—*see* Bursitis
  capsule
    liver 573.3
    spleen 289.59
  catarrhal (*see also* Catarrh) 460
    vagina 616.10
  cecum (*see also* Appendicitis) 541
  cerebral (*see also* Encephalitis) 323.9
    late effect—*see* category 326
    membrane—*see* Meningitis
  cerebrospinal (*see also* Meningitis) 322.9
    late effect—*see* category 326
    meningococcal 036.0
    tuberculous (*see also* Tuberculosis) 013.6
  cervix (uteri) (*see also* Cervicitis) 616.0
  chest 519.9
  choroid NEC (*see also* Choroiditis) 363.20
  cicatrix (tissue)—*see* Cicatrix
  colon (*see also* Enteritis) 558.9
    granulomatous 555.1
    newborn 558.9
  connective tissue (diffuse) NEC 728.9
  cornea (*see also* Keratitis) 370.9
    with ulcer (*see also* Ulcer, cornea) 370.00
  corpora cavernosa (penis) 607.2
  cranial nerve—*see* Disorder, nerve, cranial
  diarrhea—*see* Diarrhea
  disc (intervertebral) (space) 722.90
    cervical, cervicothoracic 722.91
    lumbar, lumbosacral 722.93
    thoracic, thoracolumbar 722.93

Inflammation, inflamed, inflammatory—*cont.*
  Douglas' cul-de-sac or pouch (chronic) (*see*
    also Disease, pelvis, inflammatory) 614.4
    acute 614.3
  due to (presence of) any device, implant, or
    graft classifiable to 996.0-996.5—*see*
    Complications, infection and inflammation,
    due to (presence of) any device, implant, or
    graft classified to 996.0-996.5 NEC
  duodenum 535.6
  dura mater—*see* Meningitis
  ear—*see also* Otitis
    external (*see also* Otitis, externa) 380.10
    inner (*see also* Labyrinthitis) 386.30
    middle—*see* Otitis media
  esophagus 530.10
  ethmoidal (chronic) (sinus) (*see also* Sinusitis,
    ethmoidal) 473.2
  Eustachian tube (catarrhal) 381.50
    acute 381.51
    chronic 381.52
  extrarectal 569.49
  eye 379.99
  eyelid 373.9
    specified NEC 373.8
  fallopian tube (*see also* Salpingo-oophoritis)
    614.2
  fascia 728.9
  fetal membranes (acute) 658.4
    affecting fetus or newborn 762.7
  follicular, pharynx 472.1
  frontal (chronic) (sinus) (*see also* Sinusitis,
    frontal) 473.1
  gallbladder (*see also* Cholecystitis, acute) 575.0
  gall duct (*see also* Cholecystitis) 575.10
  gastrointestinal (*see also* Enteritis) 558.9
  genital organ (diffuse) (internal)
    female 614.9
      with
        abortion—*see* Abortion, by type, with
          sepsis
        ectopic pregnancy (*see also* categories
          633.0-633.9) 639.0
        molar pregnancy (*see also* categories
          630-632) 639.0
      complicating pregnancy, childbirth, or
        puerperium 646.6
        affecting fetus or newborn 760.8
      following
        abortion 639.0
        ectopic or molar pregnancy 639.0
    male 608.4
  gland (lymph) (*see also* Lymphadenitis) 289.3
  glottis (*see also* Laryngitis) 464.0
  granular, pharynx 472.1
  gum 523.1
  heart (*see also* Carditis) 429.89
  hepatic duct 576.8
  hernial sac—*see* Hernia, by site
  ileum (*see also* Enteritis) 558.9
    terminal or regional 555.0
      with large intestine 555.2
  intervertebral disc 722.90
    cervical, cervicothoracic 722.91
    lumbar, lumbosacral 722.93
    thoracic, thoracolumbar 722.92
  intestine (*see also* Enteritis) 558.9
  jaw (acute) (bone) (chronic) (lower)
    (suppurative) (upper) 526.4
  jejunum—*see* Enteritis

Inflammation, inflamed, inflammatory—*cont.*
  joint NEC (*see also* Arthritis) 716.9
    sacroiliac 720.2
  kidney (*see also* Nephritis) 583.9
  knee (joint) 716.66
    tuberculous (active) (*see also* Tuberculosis)
      015.2
  labium (majus) (minus) (*see also* Vulvitis)
    616.10
  lacrimal
    gland (*see also* Dacryoadenitis) 375.00
    passages (duct) (sac) (*see also* Dacryocystitis)
      375.30
  larynx (*see also* Laryngitis) 464.0
    diphtheritic 032.3
  leg NEC 686.9
  lip 528.5
  liver (capsule) (*see also* Hepatitis) 573.3
    acute 570
    chronic 571.40
    suppurative 572.0
  lung (acute) (*see also* Pneumonia) 486
    chronic (interstitial) 518.89
  lymphatic vessel (*see also* Lymphangitis) 457.2
  lymph node or gland (*see also* Lymphadenitis)
    289.3
  mammary gland 611.0
    puerperal, postpartum 675.2
  maxilla, maxillary 526.4
    sinus (chronic) (*see also* Sinusitis, maxillary)
      473.0
  membranes of brain or spinal cord—*see*
    Meningitis
  meninges—*see* Meningitis
  mouth 528.0
  muscle 728.9
  myocardium (*see also* Myocarditis) 429.0
  nasal sinus (chronic) (*see also* Sinusitis) 473.9
  nasopharynx—*see* Nasopharyngitis
  navel 686.9
    newborn NEC 771.4
  nerve NEC 729.2
  nipple 611.0
    puerperal, postpartum 675.0
  nose 478.1
    suppurative 472.0
  oculomotor nerve 378.51
  optic nerve 377.30
  orbit (chronic) 376.10
    acute 376.00
    chronic 376.10
  ovary (*see also* Salpingo-oophoritis) 614.2
  oviduct (*see also* Salpingo-oophoritis) 614.2
  pancreas—*see* Pancreatitis
  parametrium (chronic) (*see also* Disease, pelvis,
    inflammatory) 614.4
    acute 614.3
  parotid region 686.9
    gland 527.2
  pelvis, female (*see also* Disease, pelvis,
    inflammatory) 614.9
  penis (corpora cavernosa) 607.2
  perianal 569.49
  pericardium (*see also* Pericarditis) 423.9
  perineum (female) (male) 686.9
  perirectal 569.49
  peritoneum (*see also* Peritonitis) 567.9
  periuterine (*see also* Disease, pelvis,
    inflammatory) 614.9
  perivesical (*see also* Cystitis) 595.9
  petrous bone (*see also* Petrositis) 383.20

Inflammation, inflamed, inflammatory—*cont.*
  pharynx (*see also* Pharyngitis) 462
    follicular 472.1
    granular 472.1
  pia mater—*see* Meningitis
  pleura—*see* Pleurisy
  postmastoidectomy cavity 383.30
    chronic 383.33
  prostate (*see also* Prostatitis) 601.9
  rectosigmoid—*see* Rectosigmoiditis
  rectum (*see also* Proctitis) 569.49
  respiratory, upper (*see also* Infection,
      respiratory, upper) 465.9
    chronic, due to external agent—*see* Condition,
        respiratory, chronic, due to, external agent
    due to
      fumes or vapors (chemical) (inhalation)
          506.2
      radiation 508.1
  retina (*see also* Retinitis) 363.20
  retrocecal (*see also* Appendicitis) 541
  retroperitoneal (*see also* Peritonitis) 567.9
  salivary duct or gland (any) (suppurative) 527.2
  scorbutic, alveoli, teeth 267
  scrotum 608.4
  sigmoid—*see* Enteritis
  sinus (*see also* Sinusitis) 473.9
  Skene's duct or gland (*see also* Urethritis)
      597.89
  skin 686.9
  spermatic cord 608.4
  sphenoidal (sinus) (*see also* Sinusitis,
      sphenoidal) 473.3
  spinal
    cord (*see also* Encephalitis) 323.9
      late effect—*see* category 326
    membrane—*see* Meningitis
    nerve—*see* Disorder, nerve
  spine (*see also* Spondylitis) 720.9
  spleen (capsule) 289.59
  stomach—*see* Gastritis
  stricture, rectum 569.49
  subcutaneous tissue NEC 686.9
  suprarenal (gland) 255.8
  synovial (fringe) (membrane)—*see* Bursitis
  tendon (sheath) NEC 726.90
  testis (*see also* Orchitis) 604.90
  thigh 686.9
  throat (*see also* Sore throat) 462
  thymus (gland) 254.8
  thyroid (gland) (*see also* Thyroiditis) 245.9
  tongue 529.0
  tonsil—*see* Tonsillitis
  trachea—*see* Tracheitis
  trochlear nerve 378.53
  tubal (*see also* Salpingo-oophoritis) 614.2
  tuberculous NEC (*see also* Tuberculosis) 011.9
  tubo-ovarian (*see also* Salpingo-oophoritis)
      614.2
  tunica vaginalis 608.4
  tympanic membrane—*see* Myringitis
  umbilicus, umbilical 686.9
    newborn NEC 771.4
  uterine ligament (*see also* Disease, pelvis,
      inflammatory) 614.4
    acute 614.3
  uterus (catarrhal) (*see also* Endometritis) 615.9
  uveal tract (anterior) (*see also* Iridocyclitis)
      364.3
    posterior—*see* Chorioretinitis
    sympathetic 360.11

Inflammation, inflamed, inflammatory—*cont.*
  vagina (*see also* Vaginitis) 616.10
  vas deferens 608.4
  vein (*see also* Phlebitis) 451.9
    thrombotic 451.9
      cerebral (*see also* Thrombosis, brain) 434.0
    leg 451.2
      deep (vessels) NEC 451.19
      superficial (vessels) 451.0
    lower extremity 451.2
      deep (vessels) NEC 451.19
      superficial (vessels) 451.0
  vocal cord 478.5
  vulva (*see also* Vulvitis) 616.10
Inflation, lung imperfect (newborn) 770.5
Influenza, influenzal 487.1
  with
    bronchitis 487.1
    bronchopneumonia 487.0
    cold (any type) 487.1
    digestive manifestations 487.8
    hemoptysis 487.1
    involvement of
      gastrointestinal tract 487.8
      nervous system 487.8
    laryngitis 487.1
    manifestations NEC 487.8
      respiratory 487.1
        pneumonia 487.0
    pharyngitis 487.1
    pneumonia (any form classifiable to 480-483,
        485-486) 487.0
    respiratory manifestations NEC 487.1
    sinusitis 487.1
    sore throat 487.1
    tonsillitis 487.1
    tracheitis 487.1
    upper respiratory infection (acute) 487.1
  abdominal 487.8
  Asian 487.1
  bronchial 487.1
  bronchopneumonia 487.0
  catarrhal 487.1
  epidemic 487.1
  gastric 487.8
  intestinal 487.8
  laryngitis 487.1
  maternal affecting fetus or newborn 760.2
    manifest influenza in infant 771.2
  pharyngitis 487.1
  pneumonia (any form) 487.0
  respiratory (upper) 487.1
  stomach 487.8
  vaccination, prophylactic (against) V04.8
Influenza-like disease 487.1
Infraction, Freiberg's (metatarsal head) 732.5
**Infusion complication, misadventure or
  reaction** —*see* Complication, infusion
Ingestion
  chemical—*see* Table of drugs and chemicals
  drug or medicinal substance
    correct substance properly administered 995.2
    overdose or wrong substance given or taken
        977.9
      specified drug—*see* Table of drugs and
          chemicals
  foreign body NEC (*see also* Foreign body) 938
Ingrowing
  hair 704.8
  nail (finger) (toe) (infected) 703.0

Inguinal —*see also* condition
  testis 752.51
Inhalation
  carbon monoxide 986
  flame (asphyxia) (*see also* Burn, by site) 949.0
  food or foreign body (*see also* Asphyxia, food
      or foreign body) 933.1
  gas, fumes, or vapor (noxious) 987.9
    specified agent—*see* Table of drugs and
        chemicals
  liquid or vomitus (*see also* Asphyxia, food or
      foreign body) 933.1
    lower respiratory tract NEC 934.9
  meconium (fetus or newborn) 770.1
  mucus (*see also* Asphyxia, mucus) 933.1
  oil (causing suffocation) (*see also* Asphyxia,
      food or foreign body) 933.1
  pneumonia—*see* Pneumonia, aspiration
  smoke 987.9
  steam 987.9
  stomach contents or secretions (*see also*
      Asphyxia, food or foreign body) 933.1
    in labor and deliver 668.0
Inhibition, inhibited
  academic as adjustment reaction 309.23
  orgasm
    female 302.73
    male 302.74
  sexual
    desire 302.71
    excitement 302.72
  work as adjustment reaction 309.23
Inhibitor, systemic lupus erythematosus
    (presence of) 286.5
Iniencephalus, iniencephaly 740.2
Injected eye 372.74
Injury 959.9

Note—For abrasion, insect bite (nonvenomous),
blister, or scratch, *see* Injury, superficial. For
laceration, traumatic rupture, tear, or
penetrating wound of internal organs, such as
heart, lung, liver, kidney, pelvic organs, whether
or not accompanied by open wound in the same
region, *see* Injury, internal. For nerve injury, see
Injury, nerve. For late effect of injuries
classifiable to 850-854, 860-869, 900-919,
950-959, *see* Late, effect, injury, by type.

  abdomen, abdominal (viscera)—*see also* Injury,
      internal, abdomen
    muscle or wall 959.1
  acoustic, resulting in deafness 951.5
  adenoid 959.0
  adrenal (gland)—*see* Injury, internal, adrenal
  alveolar (process) 959.0
  ankle (and foot) (and knee) (and leg, except
      thigh) 959.7
  anterior chamber, eye 921.3
  anus 959.1
  aorta (thoracic) 901.0
    abdominal 902.0
  appendix—*see* Injury, internal, appendix
  arm, upper (and shoulder) 959.2
  artery (complicating trauma) (*see also* Injury,
      blood vessel, by site) 904.9
    cerebral or meningeal (*see also* Hemorrhage,
        brain, traumatic, subarachnoid) 852.0
  auditory canal (external) (meatus) 959.0
  auricle, auris, ear 959.0
  axilla 959.2

Injury—*continued*
  back 959.1
  bile duct—*see* Injury, internal, bile duct
  birth—*see also* Birth, injury
    canal NEC, complicating delivery 665.9
  bladder (sphincter)—*see* Injury, internal, bladder
  blast (air) (hydraulic) (immersion) (underwater)
      NEC 869.0
    with open wound into cavity NEC 869.1
    abdomen or thorax—*see* Injury, internal, by
        site
    brain—*see* Concussion, brain
    ear (acoustic nerve trauma) 951.5
      with perforation of tympanic
          membrane—*see* Wound, open, ear, drum
  blood vessel NEC 904.9
    abdomen 902.9
      multiple 902.87
      specified NEC 902.89
    aorta (thoracic) 901.0
      abdominal 902.0
    arm NEC 903.9
    axillary 903.00
      artery 903.01
      vein 903.02
    azygos vein 901.89
    basilic vein 903.1
    brachial (artery) (vein) 903.1
    bronchial 901.89
    carotid artery 900.00
      common 900.01
      external 900.02
      internal 900.03
    celiac artery 902.20
      specified branch NEC 902.24
    cephalic vein (arm) 903.1
    colica dextra 902.26
    cystic
      artery 902.24
      vein 902.39
    deep plantar 904.6
    digital (artery) (vein) 903.5
    due to accidental puncture or laceration during
        procedure 998.2
    extremity
      lower 904.8
        multiple 904.7
        specified NEC 904.7
      upper 903.9
        multiple 903.8
        specified NEC 903.8
    femoral
      artery (superficial) 904.1
        above profunda origin 904.0
        common 904.0
      vein 904.2
    gastric
      artery 902.21
      vein 902.39
    head 900.9
      intracranial—*see* Injury, intracranial
      multiple 900.82
      specified NEC 900.89
    hemiazygos vein 901.89
    hepatic
      artery 902.22
      vein 902.11
    hypogastric 902.59
      artery 902.51
      vein 902.52

Injury—*continued*
  ileocolic
    artery 902.26
    vein 902.31
  iliac 902.50
    artery 902.53
    specified branch NEC 902.59
    vein 902.54
  innominate
    artery 901.1
    vein 901.3
  intercostal (artery) (vein) 901.81
  jugular vein (external) 900.81
    internal 900.1
  leg NEC 904.8
  mammary (artery) (vein) 901.82
  mesenteric
    artery 902.20
      inferior 902.27
      specified branch NEC 902.29
      superior (trunk) 902.25
        branches, primary 902.26
    vein 902.39
      inferior 902.32
      superior (and primary subdivisions) 902.31
  neck 900.9
    multiple 900.82
    specified NEC 900.89
  ovarian 902.89
    artery 902.81
    vein 902.82
  palmar artery 903.4
  pelvis 902.9
    multiple 902.87
    specified NEC 902.89
  plantar (deep) (artery) (vein) 904.6
  popliteal 904.40
    artery 904.41
    vein 904.42
  portal 902.33
  pulmonary 901.40
    artery 901.41
    vein 901.42
  radial (artery) (vein) 903.2
  renal 902.40
    artery 902.41
    specified NEC 902.49
    vein 902.42
  saphenous
    artery 904.7
    vein (greater) (lesser) 904.3
  splenic
    artery 902.23
    vein 902.34
  subclavian
    artery 901.1
    vein 901.3
  suprarenal 902.49
  thoracic 901.9
    multiple 901.83
    specified NEC 901.89
  tibial 904.50
    artery 904.50
      anterior 904.51
      posterior 904.53
    vein 904.50
      anterior 904.52
      posterior 904.54
  ulnar (artery) (vein) 903.3

Injury—*continued*
  uterine 902.59
    artery 902.55
    vein 902.56
  vena cava
    inferior 902.10
      specified branches NEC 902.19
    superior 901.2
  brachial plexus 953.4
    newborn 767.6
  brain NEC (*see also* Injury, intracranial) 854.0
  breast 959.1
  broad ligament—*see* Injury, internal, broad
    ligament
  bronchus, bronchi—*see* Injury, internal,
    bronchus
  brow 959.0
  buttock 959.1
  canthus, eye 921.1
  cathode ray 990
  cauda equina 952.4
    with fracture, vertebra—*see* Fracture,
      vertebra, sacrum
  cavernous sinus (*see also* Injury, intracranial)
    854.0
  cecum—*see* Injury, internal, cecum
  celiac ganglion or plexus 954.1
  cerebellum (*see also* Injury, intracranial) 854.0
  cervix (uteri)—*see* Injury, internal, cervix
  cheek 959.0
  chest—*see also* Injury, internal, chest wall 959.1
  childbirth—*see also* Birth, injury
    maternal NEC 665.9
  chin 959.0
  choroid (eye) 921.3
  clitoris 959.1
  coccyx 959.1
    complicating delivery 665.6
  colon—*see* Injury, internal, colon
  common duct—*see* Injury, internal, common
    duct
  conjunctiva 921.1
    superficial 918.2
  cord
    spermatic—*see* Injury, internal, spermatic cord
    spinal—*see* Injury, spinal, by site
  cornea 921.3
    abrasion 918.1
    due to contact lens 371.82
    penetrating—*see* Injury, eyeball, penetrating
    superficial 918.1
      due to contact lens 371.82
  cortex (cerebral) (*see also* Injury, intracranial)
    854.0
    visual 950.3
  costal region 959.1
  costochondral 959.1
  cranial
    bones—*see* Fracture, skull, by site
    cavity (*see also* Injury, intracranial) 854.0
    nerve—*see* Injury, nerve, cranial
  crushing—*see* Crush
  cutaneous sensory nerve
    lower limb 956.4
    upper limb 955.5
  delivery—*see also* Birth, injury
    maternal NEC 665.9
  Descemet's membrane—*see* Injury, eyeball,
    penetrating

Injury—*continued*
  diaphragm—*see* Injury, internal, diaphragm
  duodenum—*see* Injury, internal, duodenum
  ear (auricle) (canal) (drum) (external) 959.0
  elbow (and forearm) (and wrist) 959.3
  epididymis 959.1
  epigastric region 959.1
  epiglottis 959.0
  epiphyseal, current—*see* Fracture, by site
  esophagus—*see* Injury, internal, esophagus
  Eustachian tube 959.0
  extremity (lower) (upper) NEC 959.8
  eye 921.9
    penetrating eyeball—*see* Injury, eyeball,
      penetrating
    superficial 918.9
  eyeball 921.3
    penetrating 871.7
      with
        partial loss (of intraocular tissue) 871.12
        prolapse or exposure (of intraocular
          tissue) 871.1
      without prolapse 871.0
      foreign body (nonmagnetic) 871.6
        magnetic 871.5
    superficial 918.9
  eyebrow 959.0
  eyelid(s) 921.1
    laceration—*see* Laceration, eyelid
    superficial 918.0
  face (and neck) 959.0
  fallopian tube—*see* Injury, internal, fallopian
    tube
  finger(s) (nail) 959.5
  flank 959.1
  foot (and ankle) (and knee) (and leg except
    thigh) 959.7
  forceps NEC 767.9
    scalp 767.1
  forearm (and elbow) (and wrist) 959.3
  forehead 959.0
  gallbladder—*see* Injury, internal, gallbladder
  gasserian ganglion 951.2
  gastrointestinal tract—*see* Injury, internal,
    gastrointestinal tract
  genital organ(s)
    with
      abortion—*see* Abortion, by type, with,
        damage to pelvic organs
      ectopic pregnancy (*see also* categories
        633.0-633.9) 639.2
      molar pregnancy (*see also* categories
        630-632) 639.2
    external 959.1
    following
      abortion 639.2
      ectopic or molar pregnancy 639.2
    internal—*see* Injury, internal, genital organs
    obstetrical trauma NEC 665.9
      affecting fetus or newborn 763.8
  gland
    lacrimal 921.1
      laceration 870.8
    parathyroid 959.0
    salivary 959.0
    thyroid 959.0
  globe (eye) (*see also* Injury, eyeball) 921.3
  grease gun—*see* Wound, open, by site,
    complicated
  groin 959.1

Injury—*continued*
  gum 959.0
  hand(s) (except fingers) 959.4
  head NEC (*see also* Injury, intracranial) 854.0
    with
      skull fracture—*see* Fracture, skull, by site
  heart—*see* Injury, internal, heart
  heel 959.7
  hip (and thigh) 959.6
  hymen 959.1
  hyperextension (cervical) (vertebra) 847.0
  ileum—*see* Injury, internal, ileum
  iliac region 959.1
  infrared rays NEC 990
  instrumental (during surgery) 998.2
    birth injury—*see* Birth, injury
    nonsurgical (*see also* Injury, by site) 959.9
    obstetrical 665.9
      affecting fetus or newborn 763.8
      bladder 665.5
      cervix 665.3
      high vaginal 665.4
      perineal NEC 664.9
      urethra 665.5
      uterus 665.5
  internal 869.0

  ┌───┐
  │ Note—For injury of internal organ(s) by foreign │
  │ body entering through a natural orifice (e.g., │
  │ inhaled, ingested, or swallowed)—*see* Foreign │
  │ body, entering through orifice.   │
  │   │
  │ For internal injury of any of the following sites│
  │ with internal injury of any other of the sites— │
  │ *see* Injury, internal, multiple.   │
  └───┘

    with
      fracture
        pelvis—*see* Fracture, pelvis
        specified site, except pelvis—*see* Injury,
          internal, by site
      open wound into cavity 869.1
    abdomen, abdominal (viscera) NEC 868.00
      with
        fracture, pelvis—*see* Fracture, pelvis
        open wound into cavity 868.10
      specified site NEC 868.09
        with open wound into cavity 868.19
    adrenal (gland) 868.01
      with open wound into cavity 868.11
    aorta (thoracic) 901.0
      abdominal 902.0
    appendix 863.85
      with open wound into cavity 863.95
    bile duct 868.02
      with open wound into cavity 868.12
    bladder (sphincter) 867.0
      with
        abortion—*see* Abortion, by type, with,
          damage to pelvic organs
        ectopic pregnancy (*see also* categories
          633.0-633.9) 639.2
        molar pregnancy (*see also* categories
          630-632) 639.2
        open wound into cavity 867.1
      following
        abortion 639.2
        ectopic or molar pregnancy 639.2
      obstetrical trauma 665.5
        affecting fetus or newborn 763.8
    blood vessel—*see* Injury, blood vessel, by site

Injury—*continued*
  broad ligament 867.6
    with open wound into cavity 867.7
  bronchus, bronchi 862.21
    with open wound into cavity 862.31
  cecum 863.89
    with open wound into cavity 863.99
  cervix (uteri) 867.4
    with
      abortion—*see* Abortion, by type, with
        damage to pelvic organs
      ectopic pregnancy (*see also* categories
        633.0-633.9) 639.2
      molar pregnancy (*see also* categories
        630-632) 639.2
      open wound into cavity 867.5
    following
      abortion 639.2
      ectopic or molar pregnancy 639.2
    obstetrical trauma 665.3
      affecting fetus or newborn 763.8
  chest (*see also* Injury, internal, intrathoracic
    organs) 862.8
    with open wound into cavity 862.9
  colon 863.40
    with
      open wound into cavity 863.50
      rectum 863.46
        with open wound into cavity 863.56
    ascending (right) 863.41
      with open wound into cavity 863.51
    descending (left) 863.43
      with open wound into cavity 863.53
    multiple sites 863.46
      with open wound into cavity 863.56
    sigmoid 863.44
      with open wound into cavity 863.54
    specified site NEC 863.49
      with open wound into cavity 863.59
    transverse 863.42
      with open wound into cavity 863.52
  common duct 868.02
    with open wound into cavity 868.12
  complicating delivery 665.9
    affecting fetus or newborn 763.8
  diaphragm 862.0
    with open wound into cavity 862.1
  duodenum 863.21
    with open wound into cavity 863.31
  esophagus (intrathoracic) 862.22
    with open wound into cavity 862.32
    cervical region 874.4
      complicated 874.5
  fallopian tube 867.6
    with open wound into cavity 867.7
  gallbladder 868.02
    with open wound into cavity 868.12
  gastrointestinal tract NEC 863.80
    with open wound into cavity 863.90
  genital organ NEC 867.6
    with open wound into cavity 867.7
  heart 861.00
    with open wound into thorax 861.10
  ileum 863.29
    with open wound into cavity 863.39
  intestine NEC 863.89
    with open wound into cavity 863.99
    large NEC 863.40
      with open wound into cavity 863.50
    small NEC 863.20
      with open wound into cavity 863.30

Injury—*continued*
  intra-abdominal (organ) 868.00
    with open wound into cavity 868.10
    multiple sites 868.09
      with open wound into cavity 868.19
    specified site NEC 868.09
      with open wound into cavity 868.19
  intrathoracic organs (multiple) 862.8
    with open wound into cavity 862.9
    diaphragm (only)—*see* Injury, internal,
      diaphragm
    heart (only)—*see* Injury, internal, heart
    lung (only)—*see* Injury, internal, lung
    specified site NEC 862.29
      with open wound into cavity 862.39
  intrauterine (*see also* Injury, internal, uterus)
    867.4
    with open wound into cavity 867.5
  jejunum 863.29
    with open wound into cavity 863.39
  kidney (subcapsular) 866.00
    with
      disruption of parenchyma (complete)
        866.03
        with open wound into cavity 866.13
      hematoma (without rupture of capsule)
        866.01
        with open wound into cavity 866.11
      laceration 866.02
        with open wound into cavity 866.12
      open wound into cavity 866.10
  liver 864.00
    with
      contusion 864.01
        with open wound into cavity 864.11
      hematoma 864.01
        with open wound into cavity 864.11
      laceration 864.05
        with open wound into cavity 864.15
      major (disruption of hepatic
        parenchyma) 864.04
        with open wound into cavity 864.14
      minor (capsule only) 864.02
        with open wound into cavity 864.12
      moderate (involving parenchyma) 864.03
        with open wound into cavity 864.13
      multiple 864.04
      stellate 864.04
        with open wound in cavity 864.14
    open wound into cavity 864.10
  lung 861.20
    with open wound into thorax 861.30
    hemopneumothorax—*see*
      Hemopneumothorax, traumatic
    hemothorax—*see* Hemothorax, traumatic
    pneumohemothorax—*see*
      Pneumohemothorax, traumatic
    pneumothorax—*see* Pneumothorax,
      traumatic
  mediastinum 862.29
    with open wound into cavity 862.39
  mesentery 863.89
    with open wound into cavity 863.99
  mesosalpinx 867.6
    with open wound into cavity 867.7

Injury—*continued*
  multiple 869.0

> Note—Multiple internal injuries of sites classifiable to the same three- or four- digit category should be classified to that category. Multiple injuries classifiable to different fourth-digit subdivisions of 861 (heart and lung injuries) should be dealt with according to coding rules.

      with open wound into cavity 869.1
      intra-abdominal organ (sites classifiable to 863-868)
        with
          intrathoracic organ(s) (sites classifiable to 861-862) 869.0
            with open wound into cavity 869.1
          other intra-abdominal organ(s) (sites classifiable to 863-868, except where classifiable to the same three-digit category) 868.09
            with open wound into cavity 868.19
      intrathoracic organ (sites classifiable to 861-862)
        with
          intra-abdominal organ(s) (sites classifiable to 863-868) 869.0
            with open wound into cavity 869.1
          other intrathoracic organ(s) (sites classifiable to 861-862, except where classifiable to the same three-digit category) 862.8
            with open wound into cavity 862.9
  myocardium—*see* Injury, internal, heart
  ovary 867.6
    with open wound into cavity 867.7
  pancreas (multiple sites) 863.84
    with open wound into cavity 863.94
    body 863.82
      with open wound into cavity 863.92
    head 863.81
      with open wound into cavity 863.91
    tail 863.83
      with open wound into cavity 863.93
  pelvis, pelvic (organs) (viscera) 867.8
    with
      fracture, pelvis—*see* Fracture, pelvis
      open wound into cavity 867.9
    specified site NEC 867.6
      with open wound into cavity 867.7
  peritoneum 868.03
    with open wound into cavity 868.13
  pleura 862.29
    with open wound into cavity 862.39
  prostate 867.6
  with open wound into cavity 867.7
  rectum 863.45
    with
      colon 863.46
        with open wound into cavity 863.56
      open wound into cavity 863.55
  retroperitoneum 868.04
    with open wound into cavity 868.14
  round ligament 867.6
    with open wound into cavity 867.7
  seminal vesicle 867.6
    with open wound into cavity 867.7
  spermatic cord 867.6
    with open wound into cavity 867.7
    scrotal—*see* Wound, open, spermatic cord

Injury—*continued*
  spleen 865.00
    with
      disruption of parenchyma (massive) 865.04
        with open wound into cavity 865.14
      hematoma (without rupture of capsule) 865.01
        with open wound into cavity 865.11
      open wound into cavity 865.10
      tear, capsular 865.02
        with open wound into cavity 865.12
        extending into parenchyma 865.03
          with open wound into cavity 865.13
  stomach 863.0
    with open wound into cavity 863.1
  suprarenal gland (multiple) 868.01
    with open wound into cavity 868.11
  thorax, thoracic (cavity) (organs) (multiple) (*see also* Injury, internal, intrathoracic organs) 862.8
    with open wound into cavity 862.9
  thymus (gland) 862.29
    with open wound into cavity 862.39
  trachea (intrathoracic) 862.29
    with open wound into cavity 862.39
    cervical region (*see also* Wound, open, trachea) 874.02
  ureter 867.2
    with open wound into cavity 867.3
  urethra (sphincter) 867.0
    with
      abortion—*see* Abortion, by type, with, damage to pelvic organs
      ectopic pregnancy (*see also* categories 633.0-633.9) 639.2
      molar pregnancy (*see also* categories 630-632) 639.2
      open wound into cavity 867.1
    following
      abortion 639.2
      ectopic or molar pregnancy 639.2
    obstetrical trauma 665.5
      affecting fetus or newborn 763.8
  uterus 867.4
    with
      abortion—*see* Abortion, by type, with, damage to pelvic organs
      ectopic pregnancy (*see also* categories 633.0-633.9) 639.2
      molar pregnancy (*see also* categories 630-632) 639.2
      open wound into cavity 867.5
    following
      abortion 639.2
      ectopic or molar pregnancy 639.2
    obstetrical trauma NEC 665.5
      affecting fetus or newborn 763.8
  vas deferens 867.6
    with open wound into cavity 867.7
  vesical (sphincter) 867.0
    with open wound into cavity 867.1
  viscera (abdominal) (*see also* Injury, internal, multiple) 868.00
    with
      fracture, pelvis—*see* Fracture, pelvis
      open wound into cavity 868.10
    thoracic NEC (*see also* Injury, internal, intrathoracic organs) 862.8
      with open wound into cavity 862.9

Injury—*continued*
  interscapular region 959.1
  intervertebral disc 959.1
  intestine—*see* Injury, internal, intestine
  intra-abdominal (organs) NEC—*see* Injury, internal, intra-abdominal
  intracranial 854.0

Note—Use the following fifth-digit subclassification with categories 851-854:

0 *unspecified state of consciousness*
1 *with no loss of consciousness*
2 *with brief [less than one hour] loss of consciousness*
3 *with moderate [1-24 hours] loss of consciousness*
4 *with prolonged [more than 24 hours] loss of consciousness and return to pre-existing conscious level*
5 *with prolonged [more than 24 hours] loss of consciousness, without return to pre-existing conscious level*
Use fifth-digit 5 to designate when a patient is unconscious and dies before regaining consciousness, regardless of the duration of the loss of consciousness
6 *with loss of consciousness of unspecified duration*
9 *with concussion, unspecified*

---

    with
      open intracranial wound 854.1
      skull fracture—*see* Fracture, skull, by site
    contusion 851.8
      with open intracranial wound 851.9
      brain stem 851.4
        with open intracranial wound 851.5
      cerebellum 851.4
        with open intracranial wound 851.5
      cortex (cerebral) 851.0
        with open intracranial wound 851.2
    hematoma—*see* Injury, intracranial, hemorrhage
    hemorrhage 853.0
      with
        laceration—*see* Injury, intracranial, laceration
        open intracranial wound 853.1
      extradural 852.4
        with open intracranial wound 852.5
      subarachnoid 852.0
        with open intracranial wound 852.1
      subdural 852.2
        with open intracranial wound 852.3
    laceration 851.8
      with open intracranial wound 851.9
      brain stem 851.6
        with open intracranial wound 851.7
      cerebellum 851.6
        with open intracranial wound 851.7
      cortex (cerebral) 851.2
        with open intracranial wound 851.3
  intraocular—*see* Injury, eyeball, penetrating
  intrathoracic organs (multiple)—*see* Injury, internal, intrathoracic organs
  intrauterine—*see* Injury, internal, intrauterine
  iris 921.3
    penetrating—*see* Injury, eyeball, penetrating
  jaw 959.0
  jejunum—*see* Injury, internal, jejunum

Injury— *continued*
  joint NEC 959.9
    old or residual 718.80
      ankle 718.87
      elbow 718.82
      foot 718.87
      hand 718.84
      hip 718.85
      knee 718.86
      multiple sites 718.89
      pelvic region 718.85
      shoulder (region) 718.81
      specified site NEC 718.88
      wrist 718.83
  kidney—*see* Injury, internal, kidney
  knee (and ankle) (and foot) (and leg, except thigh) 959.7
  labium (majus) (minus) 959.1
  labyrinth, ear 959.0
  lacrimal apparatus, gland, or sac 921.1
    laceration 870.8
  larynx 959.0
  late effect—*see* Late, effects (of), injury
  leg except thigh (and ankle) (and foot) (and knee) 959.7
    upper or thigh 959.6
  lens, eye 921.3
    penetrating—*see* Injury, eyeball, penetrating
  lid, eye—*see* Injury, eyelid
  lip 959.0
  liver—*see* Injury, internal, liver
  lobe, parietal—*see* Injury, intracranial
  lumbar (region) 959.1
    plexus 953.5
  lumbosacral (region) 959.1
    plexus 953.5
  lung—*see* Injury, internal, lung
  malar region 959.0
  mastoid region 959.0
  maternal, during pregnancy, affecting fetus or newborn 760.5
  maxilla 959.0
  mediastinum—*see* Injury, internal, mediastinum
  membrane
    brain (*see also* Injury, intracranial) 854.0
    tympanic 959.0
  meningeal artery—*see* Hemorrhage, brain, traumatic, subarachnoid
  meninges (cerebral)—*see* Injury, intracranial
  mesenteric
    artery—*see* Injury, blood vessel, mesenteric, artery
    plexus, inferior 954.1
    vein—*see* Injury, blood vessel, mesenteric, vein
  mesentery—*see* Injury, internal, mesentery
  mesosalpinx—*see* Injury, internal, mesosalpinx
  middle ear 959.0
  midthoracic region 959.1
  mouth 959.0
  multiple (sites not classifiable to the same four-digit category in 959.0-959.7) 959.8
    internal 869.0
      with open wound into cavity 869.1
  musculocutaneous nerve 955.4
  nail
    finger 959.5
    toe 959.7
  nasal (septum) (sinus) 959.0
  nasopharynx 959.0

Injury—*continued*
  neck (and face) 959.0
  nerve 957.9
    abducens 951.3
    abducent 951.3
    accessory 951.6
    acoustic 951.5
    ankle and foot 956.9
    anterior crural, femoral 956.1
    arm (*see also* Injury, nerve, upper limb) 955.9
    auditory 951.5
    axillary 955.0
    brachial plexus 953.4
    cervical sympathetic 954.0
    cranial 951.9
      first or olfactory 951.8
      second or optic 950.0
      third or oculomotor 951.0
      fourth or trochlear 951.1
      fifth or trigeminal 951.2
      sixth or abducens 951.3
      seventh or facial 951.4
      eighth, acoustic, or auditory 951.5
      ninth or glossopharyngeal 951.8
      tenth, pneumogastric, or vagus 951.8
      eleventh or accessory 951.6
      twelfth or hypoglossal 951.7
      newborn 767.7
    cutaneous sensory
      lower limb 956.4
      upper limb 955.5
    digital (finger) 955.6
      toe 956.5
    facial 951.4
      newborn 767.5
    femoral 956.1
    finger 955.9
    foot and ankle 956.9
    forearm 955.9
    glossopharyngeal 951.8
    hand and wrist 955.9
    head and neck, superficial 957.0
    hypoglossal 951.7
    involving several parts of body 957.8
    leg (*see also* Injury, nerve, lower limb) 956.9
    lower limb 956.9
      multiple 956.8
      specified site NEC 956.5
    lumbar plexus 953.5
    lumbosacral plexus 953.5
    median 955.1
      forearm 955.1
      wrist and hand 955.1
    multiple (in several parts of body) (sites not
      classifiable to the same three-digit
      category) 957.8
    musculocutaneous 955.4
    musculospiral 955.3
      upper arm 955.3
    oculomotor 951.0
    olfactory 951.8
    optic 950.0
    pelvic girdle 956.9
      multiple sites 956.8
      specified site NEC 956.5
    peripheral 957.9
      multiple (in several regions) (sites not
      classifiable to the same three-digit
      category) 957.8
      specified site NEC 957.1

Injury—*continued*
    peroneal 956.3
      ankle and foot 956.3
      lower leg 956.3
    plantar 956.5
    plexus 957.9
      celiac 954.1
      mesenteric, inferior 954.1
      spinal 953.9
        brachial 953.4
        lumbosacral 953.5
        multiple sites 953.8
      sympathetic NEC 954.1
    pneumogastric 951.8
    radial 955.3
      wrist and hand 955.3
    sacral plexus 953.5
    sciatic 956.0
      thigh 956.0
    shoulder girdle 955.9
      multiple 955.8
      specified site NEC 955.7
    specified site NEC 957.1
    spinal 953.9
      plexus—*see* Injury, nerve, plexus, spinal
      root 953.9
        cervical 953.0
        dorsal 953.1
        lumbar 953.2
        multiple sites 953.8
        sacral 953.3
    splanchnic 954.1
    sympathetic NEC 954.1
      cervical 954.0
    thigh 956.9
    tibial 956.5
      ankle and foot 956.2
      lower leg 956.5
      posterior 956.2
    toe 956.9
    trigeminal 951.2
    trochlear 951.1
    trunk, excluding shoulder and pelvic girdles
      954.9
      specified site NEC 954.8
      sympathetic NEC 954.1
    ulnar 955.2
      forearm 955.2
      wrist (and hand) 955.2
    upper limb 955.9
      multiple 955.8
      specified site NEC 955.7
    vagus 951.8
    wrist and hand 955.9
  nervous system, diffuse 957.8
  nose (septum) 959.0
  obstetrical NEC 665.9
    affecting fetus or newborn 763.8
  occipital (region) (scalp) 959.0
    lobe (*see also* Injury, intracranial) 854.0
  optic 950.9
    chiasm 950.1
    cortex 950.3
    nerve 950.0
    pathways 950.2
  orbit, orbital (region) 921.2
    penetrating 870.3
      with foreign body 870.4
  ovary—*see* Injury, internal, ovary

Injury— *continued*
  paint-gun—*see* Wound, open, by site,
    complicated
  palate (soft) 959.0
  pancreas—*see* Injury, internal, pancreas
  parathyroid (gland) 959.0
  parietal (region) (scalp) 959.0
    lobe—*see* Injury, intracranial
  pelvic
    floor 959.1
      complicating delivery 664.1
        affecting fetus or newborn 763.8
    joint or ligament, complicating delivery 665.6
      affecting fetus or newborn 763.8
    organs—*see also* Injury, internal, pelvis
      with
        abortion—*see* Abortion, by type, with
          damage to pelvic organs
        ectopic pregnancy (*see also* categories
          633.0-633.9) 639.2
        molar pregnancy (*see also* categories
          633.0-633.9) 639.2
      following
        abortion 639.2
        ectopic or molar pregnancy 639.2
      obstetrical trauma 665.5
        affecting fetus or newborn 763.8
  pelvis 959.1
  penis 959.1
  perineum 959.1
  peritoneum—*see* Injury, internal, peritoneum
  periurethral tissue
    with
      abortion—*see* Abortion, by type, with
        damage to pelvic organs
      ectopic pregnancy (*see also* categories
        633.0-633.9) 639.2
      molar pregnancy (*see also* categories
        630-632) 639.2
    complicating delivery 665.5
      affecting fetus or newborn 763.8
    following
      abortion 639.2
      ectopic or molar pregnancy 639.2
  phalanges
    foot 959.7
    hand 959.5
  pharynx 959.0
  pleura—*see* Injury, internal, pleura
  popliteal space 959.7
  prepuce 959.1
  prostate—*see* Injury, internal, prostate
  pubic region 959.1
  pudenda 959.1
  radiation NEC 990
  radioactive substance or radium NEC 990
  rectovaginal septum 959.1
  rectum—*see* Injury, internal, rectum
  retina 921.3
    penetrating—*see* Injury, eyeball, penetrating
  retroperitoneal—*see* Injury, internal,
    retroperitoneum
  roentgen rays NEC 990
  round ligament—*see* Injury, internal, round
    ligament
  sacral (region) 959.1
    plexus 953.5
  sacroiliac ligament NEC 959.1
  sacrum 959.1

Injury— *continued*
  salivary ducts or glands 959.0
  scalp 959.0
    due to birth trauma 767.1
    fetus or newborn 767.1
  scapular region 959.2
  sclera 921.3
    penetrating—*see* Injury, eyeball, penetrating
    superficial 918.2
  scrotum 959.1
  seminal vesicle—*see* Injury, internal, seminal
    vesicle
  shoulder (and upper arm) 959.2
  sinus
    cavernous (*see also* Injury, intracranial) 854.0
    nasal 959.0
  skeleton NEC, birth injury 767.3
  skin NEC 959.9
  skull—*see* Fracture, skull, by site
  soft tissue (of external sites) (severe)—*see*
    Wound, open, by site
  specified site NEC 959.8
  spermatic cord—*see* Injury, internal, spermatic
    cord
  spinal (cord) 952.9
    with fracture, vertebra—*see* Fracture,
      vertebra, by site, with spinal cord injury
    cervical (C_1-C_4) 952.00
      with
        anterior cord syndrome 952.02
        central cord syndrome 952.03
        complete lesion of cord 952.01
        incomplete lesion NEC 952.04
        posterior cord syndrome 952.04
    C_5-C_7 level 952.05
      with
        anterior cord syndrome 952.07
        central cord syndrome 952.08
        complete lesion of cord 952.06
        incomplete lesion NEC 952.09
        posterior cord syndrome 952.09
      specified type NEC 952.09
    specified type NEC 952.04
    dorsal (D_1-D_6) (T_1-T_6) (thoracic) 952.10
      with
        anterior cord syndrome 952.12
        central cord syndrome 952.13
        complete lesion of cord 952.11
        incomplete lesion NEC 952.14
        posterior cord syndrome 952.14
    D_7-D_{12} level (T_7-T_{12}) 952.15
      with
        anterior cord syndrome 952.17
        central cord syndrome 952.18
        complete lesion of cord 952.16
        incomplete lesion NEC 952.19
        posterior cord syndrome 952.19
      specified type NEC 952.19
    specified type NEC 952.14
    lumbar 952.2
    multiple sites 952.8
    nerve (root) NEC—*see* Injury, nerve, spinal,
      root
    plexus 953.9
      brachial 953.4
      lumbosacral 953.5
      multiple sites 953.8
    sacral 952.3
    thoracic (*see also* Injury, spinal, dorsal) 952.10

Injury—*continued*

spleen—*see* Injury, internal, spleen
stellate ganglion 954.1
sternal region 959.1
stomach—*see* Injury, internal, stomach
subconjunctival 921.1
subcutaneous 959.9
subdural—*see* Injury, intracranial
submaxillary region 959.0
submental region 959.0
subungual
   fingers 959.5
   toes 959.7
superficial 919

Note—Use the following fourth-digit
subdivisions with categories 910-919:

.0 *Abrasion or friction burn without mention of
   infection*
.1 *Abrasion or friction burn, infected*
.2 *Blister without mention of infection*
.3 *Blister, infected*
.4 *Insect bite, nonvenomous, without mention
   of infection*
.5 *Insect bite, nonvenomous, infected*
.6 *Superficial foreign body (splinter) without
   major open wound and without mention of
   infection*
.7 *Superficial foreign body (splinter) without
   major open wound, infected*
.8 *Other and unspecified superficial injury
   without mention of infection*
.9 *Other and unspecified superficial injury,
   infected*

For late effects of superficial injury, *see*
category 906.2.

---

abdomen, abdominal (muscle) (wall) (and
   other part(s) of trunk) 911
ankle (and hip, knee, leg, or thigh) 916
anus (and other part(s) of trunk) 911
arm 913
   upper (and shoulder) 912
auditory canal (external) (meatus) (and other
   part(s) of face, neck, or scalp, except eye)
   910
axilla (and upper arm) 912
back (and other part(s) of trunk) 911
breast (and other part(s) of trunk) 911
brow (and other part(s) of face, neck or scalp,
   except eye) 910
buttock (and other part(s) of trunk) 911
canthus, eye 918.0
cheek(s) (and other part(s) of face, neck, or
   scalp, except eye) 910
chest wall (and other part(s) of trunk) 911
chin (and other part(s) of face, neck, or scalp,
   except eye) 910
clitoris (and other part(s) of trunk) 911
conjunctiva 918.2
cornea 918.1
   due to contact lens 371.82
costal region (and other part(s) of trunk) 911
ear(s) (auricle) (canal) (drum) (external) (and
   other part(s) of face, neck, or scalp, except
   eye) 910
elbow (and forearm) (and wrist) 913
epididymis (and other part(s) of trunk) 911

Injury—*continued*

epigastric region (and other part(s) of trunk)
   911
epiglottis (and other part(s) of face, neck, or
   scalp, except eye) 910
eye(s) (and adnexa) NEC 918.9
eyelid(s) (and periocular area) 918.0
face (any part(s), except eye) (and neck or
   scalp) 910
finger(s) (nail) (any) 915
flank (and other part(s) of trunk) 911
foot (phalanges) (and toe(s)) 917
forearm (and elbow) (and wrist) 913
forehead (and other part(s) of face, neck, or
   scalp, except eye) 910
globe (eye) 918.9
groin (and other part(s) of trunk) 911
gum(s) (and other part(s) of face, neck, or
   scalp, except eye) 910
hand(s) (except fingers alone) 914
head (and other part(s) of face, neck, or scalp,
   except eye) 910
heel (and foot or toe) 917
hip (and ankle, knee, leg, or thigh) 916
iliac region (and other part(s) of trunk) 911
interscapular region (and other part(s) of
   trunk) 911
iris 918.9
knee (and ankle, hip, leg, or thigh) 916
labium (majus) (minus) (and other part(s) of
   trunk) 911
lacrimal (apparatus) (gland) (sac) 918.0
leg (lower) (upper) (and ankle, hip, knee, or
   thigh) 916
lip(s) (and other part(s) of face, neck, or scalp,
   except eye) 910
lower extremity (except foot) 916
lumbar region (and other part(s) of trunk) 911
malar region (and other part(s) of face, neck,
   or scalp, except eye) 910
mastoid region (and other part(s) of face,
   neck, or scalp, except eye) 910
midthoracic region (and other part(s) of trunk)
   911
mouth (and other part(s) of face, neck, or
   scalp, except eye) 910
multiple sites (not classifiable to the same
   three-digit category) 919
nasal (septum) (and other part(s) of face,
   neck, or scalp, except eye) 910
neck (and face or scalp, any part(s), except
   eye) 910
nose (septum) (and other part(s) of face, neck,
   or scalp, except eye) 910
occipital region (and other part(s) of face,
   neck, or scalp, except eye) 910
orbital region 918.0
palate (soft) (and other part(s) of face, neck,
   or scalp, except eye) 910
parietal region (and other part(s) of face, neck,
   or scalp, except eye) 910
penis (and other part(s) of trunk) 911
perineum (and other part(s) of trunk) 911
periocular area 918.0
pharynx (and other part(s) of face, neck, or
   scalp, except eye) 910
popliteal space (and ankle, hip, leg, or thigh)
   916
prepuce (and other part(s) of trunk) 911
pubic region (and other part(s) of trunk) 911

Injury—*continued*

  pudenda (and other part(s) of trunk) 911

  sacral region (and other part(s) of trunk) 911

  salivary (ducts) (glands) (and other part(s) of face, neck, or scalp, except eye) 910

  scalp (and other part(s) of face or neck, except eye) 910

  scapular region (and upper arm) 912

  sclera 918.2

  scrotum (and other part(s) of trunk) 911

  shoulder (and upper arm) 912

  skin NEC 919

  specified site(s) NEC 919

  sternal region (and other part(s) of trunk) 911

  subconjunctival 918.2

  subcutaneous NEC 919

  submaxillary region (and other part(s) of face, neck, or scalp, except eye) 910

  submental region (and other part(s) of face, neck, or scalp, except eye) 910

  supraclavicular fossa (and other part(s) of face, neck or scalp, except eye) 910

  supraorbital 918.0

  temple (and other part(s) of face, neck, or scalp, except eye) 910

  temporal region (and other part(s) of face, neck, or scalp, except eye) 910

  testis (and other part(s) of trunk) 911

  thigh (and ankle, hip, knee, or leg) 916

  thorax, thoracic (external) (and other part(s) of trunk) 911

  throat (and other part(s) of face, neck, or scalp, except eye) 910

  thumb(s) (nail) 915

  toe(s) (nail) (subungual) (and foot) 917

  tongue (and other part(s) of face, neck, or scalp, except eye) 910

  tooth, teeth 521.2

  trunk (any part(s)) 911

  tunica vaginalis (and other part(s) of trunk) 911

  tympanum, tympanic membrane (and other part(s) of face, neck, or scalp, except eye) 910

  upper extremity NEC 913

  uvula (and other part(s) of face, neck, or scalp, except eye) 910

  vagina (and other part(s) of trunk) 911

  vulva (and other part(s) of trunk) 911

  wrist (and elbow) (and forearm) 913

  supraclavicular fossa 959.1

  supraorbital 959.0

  surgical complication (external or internal site) 998.2

  symphysis pubis 959.1

  complicating delivery 665.6

    affecting fetus or newborn 763.8

  temple 959.0

  temporal region 959.0

  testis 959.1

  thigh (and hip) 959.6

  thorax, thoracic (external) 959.1

  cavity—*see* Injury, internal, thorax

  internal—*see* Injury, internal, intrathoracic organs

  throat 959.0

  thumb(s) (nail) 959.5

  thymus—*see* Injury, internal, thymus

  thyroid (gland) 959.0

  toe (nail) (any) 959.7

Injury—*continued*

  tongue 959.0

  tonsil 959.0

  tooth NEC 873.63

    complicated 873.73

  trachea—*see* Injury, internal, trachea

  trunk 959.1

  tunica vaginalis 959.1

  tympanum, tympanic membrane 959.0

  ultraviolet rays NEC 990

  ureter—*see* Injury, internal, ureter

  urethra (sphincter)—*see* Injury, internal, urethra

  uterus—*see* Injury, internal, uterus

  uvula 959.0

  vagina 959.1

  vascular—*see* Injury, blood vessel

  vas deferens—*see* Injury, internal, vas deferens

  vein (*see also* Injury, blood vessel, by site) 904.9

  vena cava

    inferior 902.10

    superior 901.2

  vesical (sphincter)—*see* Injury, internal, vesical

  viscera (abdominal)—*see* Injury, internal, viscera

    with fracture, pelvis—*see* Fracture, pelvis

  visual 950.9

    cortex 950.3

  vitreous (humor) 871.2

  vulva 959.1

  whiplash (cervical spine) 847.0

  wringer—*see* Crush, by site

  wrist (and elbow) (and forearm) 959.3

  x-ray NEC 990

Inoculation —*see also* Vaccination

  complication or reaction—*see* Complication, vaccination

Insanity, insane (*see also* Psychosis) 298.9

  adolescent (*see also* Schizophrenia) 295.9

  alternating (*see also* Psychosis, affective, circular) 296.7

  confusional 298.9

    acute 293.0

    subacute 293.1

  delusional 298.9

  paralysis, general 094.1

    progressive 094.1

  paresis, general 094.1

  senile 290.20

Insect

  bite—*see* Injury, superficial, by site

  venomous, poisoning by 989.5

Insemination, artificial V26.1

Insertion

  cord (umbilical) lateral or velamentous 663.5

    affecting fetus or newborn 762.6

  intrauterine contraceptive device V25.1

  placenta, vicious—*see* Placenta, previa

  subdermal implantable contraceptive V25.5

  velamentous, umbilical cord 663.5

    affecting fetus or newborn 762.6

Insolation 992.0

  meaning sunstroke 992.0

Insomnia 780.52

  with sleep apnea 780.51

  nonorganic origin 307.41

    persistent 307.42

    transient 307.41

  subjective complaint 307.49

Inspiration
  food or foreign body (*see also* Asphyxia, food
    or foreign body) 933.1
  mucus (*see also* Asphyxia, mucus) 933.1
Inspissated bile syndrome, newborn 774.4
Instability
  detrusor 596.59
  emotional (excessive) 301.3
  joint (posttraumatic) 718.80
    ankle 718.87
    elbow 718.82
    foot 718.87
    hand 718.84
    hip 718.85
    knee 718.86
    lumbosacral 724.6
    multiple sites 718.89
    pelvic region 718.85
    sacroiliac 724.6
    shoulder (region) 718.81
    specified site NEC 718.88
    wrist 718.83
  lumbosacral 724.6
  nervous 301.89
  personality (emotional) 301.59
  thyroid, paroxysmal 242.9
  urethral 599.83
  vasomotor 780.2
Insufficiency, insufficient
  accommodation 367.4
  adrenal (gland) (acute) (chronic) 255.4
    medulla 255.5
    primary 255.4
    specified NEC 255.5
  adrenocortical 255.4
  anus 569.49
  aortic (valve) 424.1
    with
      mitral (valve) disease 396.1
        insufficiency, incompetence, or
          regurgitation 396.3
        stenosis or obstruction 396.1
      stenosis or obstruction 424.1
        with mitral (valve) disease 396.8
    congenital 746.4
    rheumatic 395.1
      with
        mitral (valve) disease 396.1
          insufficiency, incompetence, or
          regurgitation 396.3
        stenosis or obstruction 396.1
      stenosis or obstruction 395.2
        with mitral (valve) disease 396.8
    specified cause NEC 424.1
    syphilitic 093.22
  arterial 447.1
    basilar artery 435.0
    carotid artery 435.8
    cerebral 437.1
    coronary (acute or subacute) 411.89
    mesenteric 557.1
    peripheral 443.9
    precerebral 435.9
    vertebral artery 435.1
    vertibrobasilar 435.3
  arteriovenous 459.9
  basilar artery 435.0
  biliary 575.8

Insufficiency, insufficient—*continued*
  cardiac (*see also* Insufficiency, myocardial)
    428.0
    complicating surgery 997.1
    due to presence of (cardiac) prosthesis 429.4
    postoperative 997.1
      long-term effect of cardiac surgery 429.4
    specified during or due to a procedure 997.1
      long-term effect of cardiac surgery 429.4
  cardiorenal (*see also* Hypertension, cardiorenal)
    404.90
  cardiovascular (*see also* Disease,
    cardiovascular) 429.2
    renal (*see also* Hypertension, cardiorenal)
      404.90
  carotid artery 435.8
  cerebral (vascular) 437.9
  cerebrovascular 437.9
    with transient focal neurological signs and
      symptoms 435.9
    acute 437.1
      with transient focal neurological signs and
        symptoms 435.9
  circulatory NEC 459.9
    fetus or newborn 779.8
  convergence 378.83
  coronary (acute or subacute) 411.89
    chronic or with a stated duration of over 8
      weeks 414.8
  corticoadrenal 255.4
  dietary 269.9
  divergence 378.85
  food 994.2
  gastroesophageal 530.89
  gonadal
    ovary 256.3
    testis 257.2
  gonadotropic hormone secretion 253.4
  heart—*see also* Insufficiency, myocardial
    fetus or newborn 779.8
    valve (*see also* Endocarditis) 424.90
      congenital NEC 746.89
  hepatic 573.8
  idiopathic autonomic 333.0
  kidney (*see also* Disease, renal) 593.9
  labyrinth, labyrinthine (function) 386.53
    bilateral 386.54
    unilateral 386.53
  lacrimal 375.15
  liver 573.8
  lung (acute) (*see also* Insufficiency, pulmonary)
    518.82
    following trauma, surgery, or shock 518.5
    newborn 770.8
  mental (congenital) (*see also* Retardation,
    mental) 319
  mesenteric 557.1
  mitral (valve) 424.0
    with
      aortic (valve) disease 396.3
        insufficiency, incompetence, or
          regurgitation 396.3
        stenosis or obstruction 396.2
      obstruction or stenosis 394.2
        with aortic valve disease 396.8
    congenital 746.6

Insufficiency, insufficient—*continued*
rheumatic 394.1
  with
    aortic (valve) disease 396.3
      insufficiency, incompetence, or
        regurgitation 396.3
      stenosis or obstruction 396.2
    obstruction or stenosis 394.2
      with aortic valve disease 396.8
    active or acute 391.1
      with chorea, rheumatic (Sydenham's)
        392.0
  specified cause, except rheumatic 424.0
muscle
  heart—*see* Insufficiency, myocardial
  ocular (*see also* Strabismus) 378.9
myocardial, myocardium (with arteriosclerosis)
  428.0
  with rheumatic fever (conditions classifiable
    to 390)
    active, acute, or subacute 391.2
      with chorea 392.0
    inactive or quiescent (with chorea) 398.0
  congenital 746.89
  due to presence of (cardiac) prosthesis 429.4
  fetus or newborn 779.8
  following cardiac surgery 429.4
  hypertensive (*see also* Hypertension, heart)
    402.91
    benign 402.11
    malignant 402.01
  postoperative 997.1
    long-term effect of cardiac surgery 429.4
  rheumatic 398.0
    active, acute, or subacute 391.2
      with chorea (Sydenham's) 392.0
  syphilitic 093.82
nourishment 994.2
organic 799.8
ovary 256.3
  postablative 256.2
pancreatic 577.8
parathyroid (gland) 252.1
peripheral vascular (arterial) 443.9
pituitary (anterior) 253.2
  posterior 253.5
placental—*see* Placenta, insufficiency
platelets 287.5
prenatal care in current pregnancy V23.7
progressive pluriglandular 258.9
pseudocholinesterase 289.8
pulmonary (acute) 518.82
  following
    shock 518.5
    surgery 518.5
    trauma 518.5
  newborn 770.8
  valve (*see also* Endocarditis, pulmonary) 424.3
    congenital 746.09
pyloric 537.0
renal 593.9
  due to a procedure 997.5
respiratory 786.09
  acute 518.82
    following shock, surgery, or trauma 518.5
  newborn 770.8
rotation—*see* Malrotation

Insufficiency, insufficient—*continued*
suprarenal 255.4
  medulla 255.5
tarso-orbital fascia, congenital 743.66
tear film 375.15
testis 257.2
thyroid (gland) (acquired)—*see also*
  Hypothyroidism
  congenital 243
tricuspid (*see also* Endocarditis, tricuspid) 397.0
  congenital 746.89
  syphilitic 093.23
urethral sphincter 599.84
valve, valvular (heart) (*see also* Endocarditis)
  424.90
vascular 459.9
  intestine NEC 557.9
  mesenteric 557.1
  peripheral 443.9
  renal (*see also* Hypertension, kidney) 403.90
velopharyngeal
  acquired 528.9
  congenital 750.29
venous (peripheral) 459.81
ventricular—*see* Insufficiency, myocardial
vertebral artery 435.1
vertibrobasilar artery 435.3
weight gain during pregnancy 646.8
zinc 269.3
Insufflation
fallopian V26.2
meconium 770.1
Insular —*see* condition
Insulinoma (M8151/0)
malignant (M8151/3)
  pancreas 157.4
  specified site—*see* Neoplasm, by site,
    malignant
  unspecified site 157.4
pancreas 211.7
specified site—*see* Neoplasm, by site, benign
unspecified site 211.7
Insuloma —*see* Insulinoma
Insult
brain 437.9
  acute 436
cerebral 437.9
  acute 436
cerebrovascular 437.9
  acute 436
vascular NEC 437.9
  acute 436
Insurance examination (certification) V70.3
Intemperance (*see also* Alcoholism) 303.9
Interception of pregnancy (menstrual
  extraction) V25.3
Intermenstrual
bleeding 626.4
  irregular 626.6
  regular 626.5
hemorrhage 626.4
  irregular 626.6
  regular 626.5
pain(s) 625.2
Intermittent— *see* condition
Internal —*see* condition
Interproximal wear 521.1
Interruption
aortic arch 747.11
bundle of His 426.50
fallopian tube (for sterilization) V25.2

Interruption—*continued*
  phase-shift, sleep cycle 307.45
  repeated REM-sleep 307.48
  sleep
    due to perceived environmental disturbances
      307.48
    phase-shift, of 24-hour sleep-wake cycle
      307.45
    repeated REM-sleep type 307.48
    vas deferens (for sterilization) V25.2
Intersexuality 752.7
Interstitial —*see* condition
Intertrigo 695.89
  labialis 528.5
Intervertebral disc —*see* condition
Intestine, intestinal —*see also* condition
  flu 487.8
Intolerance
  carbohydrate NEC 579.8
  cardiovascular exercise, with pain (at rest) (with
    less than ordinary activity) (with ordinary
    activity) V47.2
  cold 780.9
  disaccharide (hereditary) 271.3
  drug
    correct substance properly administered 995.2
    wrong substance given or taken in error 977.9
    specified drug—*see* Table of drugs and
      chemicals
  effort 306.2
  fat NEC 579.8
  foods NEC 579.8
  fructose (hereditary) 271.2
  glucose (-galactose) (congenital) 271.3
  gluten 579.0
  lactose (hereditary) (infantile) 271.3
  lysine (congenital) 270.7
  milk NEC 579.8
  protein (familial) 270.7
  starch NEC 579.8
  sucrose (-isomaltose) (congenital) 271.3
Intoxicated NEC (*see also* Alcoholism) 305.0
Intoxication
  acid 276.2
  acute
    alcoholic 305.0
      with alcoholism 303.0
      hangover effects 305.0
    caffeine 305.9
    hallucinogenic (*see also* Abuse, drugs,
      nondependent) 305.3
  alcohol (acute) 305.0
    with alcoholism 303.0
    hangover effects 305.0
    idiosyncratic 291.4
    pathological 291.4
  alimentary canal 558.2
  ammonia (hepatic) 572.2
  chemical—*see also* Table of drugs and
    chemicals
  via placenta or breast milk 760.70
    alcohol 760.71
    anti-infective agents 760.74
    cocaine 760.75
    "crack" 760.75
    hallucinogenic agents NEC 760.73
    medicinal agents NEC 760.79
    narcotics 760.72
    obstetric anesthetic or analgesic drug 763.5
    specified agent NEC 760.79

Intoxication—*continued*
  suspected, affecting management of
    pregnancy 655.5
  cocaine, through placenta or breast milk 760.75
  drug
    correct substance properly administered (*see
      also* Allergy, drug) 995.2
    newborn 779.4
    obstetric anesthetic or sedation 668.9
      affecting fetus or newborn 763.5
    overdose or wrong substance given or
      taken—*see* Table of drugs and chemicals
    pathologic 292.2
    specific to newborn 779.4
    via placenta or breast milk 760.70
      alcohol 760.71
      anti-infective agents 760.74
      cocaine 760.75
      "crack" 760.75
      hallucinogenic agents 760.73
      medicinal agents NEC 760.79
      narcotics 760.72
      obstetric anesthetic or analgesic drug 763.5
      specified agent NEC 760.79
    suspected, affecting management of
      pregnancy 655.5
  enteric—*see* Intoxication, intestinal
  fetus or newborn, via placenta or breast milk
    760.70
    alcohol 760.71
    anti-infective agents 760.74
    cocaine 760.75
    "crack" 760.75
    hallucinogenic agents 760.73
    medicinal agents NEC 760.79
    narcotics 760.72
    obstetric anesthetic or analgesic drug 763.5
    specified agent NEC 760.79
    suspected, affecting management of
      pregnancy 655.5
  food—*see* Poisoning, food
  gastrointestinal 558.2
  hallucinogenic (acute) 305.3
  hepatocerebral 572.2
  idiosyncratic alcohol 291.4
  intestinal 569.89
    due to putrefaction of food 005.9
  methyl alcohol (*see also* Alcoholism) 305.0
    with alcoholism 303.0
  pathologic 291.4
    drug 292.2
  potassium (K) 276.7
  septic
    with
      abortion—*see* Abortion, by type, with sepsis
      ectopic pregnancy (*see also* categories
        633.0-633.9) 639.0
      molar pregnancy (*see also* categories
        630-632) 639.0
    during labor 659.3
    following
      abortion 639.0
      ectopic or molar pregnancy 639.0
    generalized—*see* Septicemia
    puerperal, postpartum, childbirth 670
  serum (prophylactic) (therapeutic) 999.5
  uremic—*see* Uremia
  water 276.6
Intracranial —*see* condition
Intrahepatic gallbladder 751.69

Intraligamentous —*see also* condition
   pregnancy—*see* Pregnancy, cornual
Intraocular —*see also* condition
   sepsis 360.00
Intrathoracic —*see also* condition
   kidney 753.3
   stomach—*see* Hernia, diaphragm
Intrauterine contraceptive device
   checking V25.42
   insertion V25.1
   in situ V45.51
   management V25.42
   prescription V25.02
      repeat V25.42
   reinsertion V25.42
   removal V25.42
Intraventricular —*see* condition
Intrinsic deformity —*see* Deformity
Intrusion, repetitive, of sleep (due to
      environmental disturbances) (with atypical
      polysomnographic features) 307.48
Intumescent, lens (eye) NEC 366.9
   senile 366.12
Intussusception (colon) (enteric) (intestine)
      (rectum) 560.0
   appendix 543.9
   congenital 751.5
   fallopian tube 620.8
   ileocecal 560.0
   ileocolic 560.0
   ureter (with obstruction) 593.4
Invagination
   basilar 756.0
   colon or intestine 560.0
Invalid (since birth) 799.8
Invalidism (chronic) 799.8
Inversion
   albumin-globulin (A-G) ratio 273.8
   bladder 596.8
   cecum (*see also* Intussusception) 560.0
   cervix 622.8
   nipple 611.79
      congenital 757.6
      puerperal, postpartum 676.3
   optic papilla 743.57
   organ or site, congenital NEC—*see* Anomaly,
      specified type NEC
   sleep rhythm 780.55
      nonorganic origin 307.45
   testis (congenital) 752.51
   uterus (postinfectional) (postpartal, old) 621.7
      chronic 621.7
      complicating delivery 665.2
         affecting fetus or newborn 763.8
   vagina—*see* Prolapse, vagina
Investigation
   allergens V72.7
   clinical research V70.7
Inviability —*see* Immaturity
Involuntary movement, abnormal 781.0
Involution, involutional —*see also* condition
   breast, cystic or fibrocystic 610.1
   depression (*see also* Psychosis, affective) 296.2
      recurrent episode 296.3
      single episode 296.2
   melancholia (*see also* Psychosis, affective)
      296.2
      recurrent episode 296.3
      single episode 296.2
   ovary, senile 620.3
   paranoid state (reaction) 297.2

Involution, involutional—*continued*
   paraphrenia (climacteric) (menopause) 297.2
   psychosis 298.8
   thymus failure 254.8
IQ
   under 20 318.2
   20-34 318.1
   35-49 318.0
   50-70 317
IRDS 769
Irideremia 743.45
Iridis rubeosis 364.42
   diabetic 250.5 [364.42]
Iridochoroiditis (panuveitis) 360.12
Iridocyclitis NEC 364.3
   acute 364.00
      primary 364.01
      recurrent 364.02
   chronic 364.10
      in
         lepromatous leprosy 030.0 [364.11]
         sarcoidosis 135 [364.11]
         tuberculosis (*see also* Tuberculosis) 017.3
            [364.11]
   due to allergy 364.04
   endogenous 364.01
   gonococcal 098.41
   granulomatous 364.10
   herpetic (simplex) 054.44
      zoster 053.22
   hypopyon 364.05
   lens induced 364.23
   nongranulomatous 364.00
   primary 364.01
   recurrent 364.02
   rheumatic 364.10
   secondary 364.04
      infectious 364.03
      noninfectious 364.04
   subacute 364.00
      primary 364.01
      recurrent 364.02
   sympathetic 360.11
   syphilitic (secondary) 091.52
   tuberculous (chronic) (*see also* Tuberculosis)
      017.3 [364.11]
Iridocyclochoroiditis (panuveitis) 360.12
Iridodialysis 364.76
Iridodonesis 364.8
Iridoplegia (complete) (partial) (reflex) 379.49
Iridoschisis 364.52
Iris —*see* condition
Iritis 364.3
   acute 364.00
      primary 364.01
      recurrent 364.02
   chronic 364.10
      in
         sarcoidosis 135 [364.11]
         tuberculosis (*see also* Tuberculosis) 017.3
            [364.11]
   diabetic 250.5 [364.42]
   due to
      allergy 364.04
      herpes simplex 054.44
      leprosy 030.0 [364.11]
   endogenous 364.01
   gonococcal 098.41
   gouty 274.89 [364.11]
   granulomatous 364.10
   hypopyon 364.05

Iritis —*continued*
  lens induced 364.23
  nongranulomatous 364.00
  papulosa 095.8 *[364.11]*
  primary 364.01
  recurrent 364.02
  rheumatic 364.10
  secondary 364.04
    infectious 364.03
    noninfectious 364.04
  subacute 364.00
    primary 364.01
    recurrent 364.02
  sympathetic 360.11
  syphilitic (secondary) 091.52
    congenital 090.0 *[364.11]*
    late 095.8 *[364.11]*
  tuberculous (*see also* Tuberculosis) 017.3
    [364.11]
  uratic 274.89 *[364.11]*
Iron
  deficiency anemia 280.9
  metabolism disease 275.0
  storage disease 275.0
Iron-miners' lung 503
Irradiated enamel (tooth, teeth) 521.8
Irradiation
  burn—*see* Burn, by site
  effects, adverse 990
Irreducible, irreducibility —*see* condition
Irregular, irregularity
  action, heart 427.9
  alveolar process 525.8
  bleeding NEC 626.4
  breathing 786.09
  colon 569.89
  contour of cornea 743.41
    acquired 371.70
  dentin in pulp 522.3
  eye movements NEC 379.59
  menstruation (cause unknown) 626.4
  periods 626.4
  prostate 602.9
  pupil 364.75
  respiratory 786.09
  septum (nasal) 470
  shape, organ or site, congenital NEC—*see*
    Distortion
  sleep-wake rhythm (non-24-hour) 780.55
    nonorganic origin 307.45
  vertebra 733.99
Irritability (nervous) 799.2
  bladder 596.8
    neurogenic 596.54
      with cauda equina syndrome 344.61
  bowel (syndrome) 564.1
  bronchial (*see also* Bronchitis) 490
  cerebral, newborn 779.1
  colon 564.1
    psychogenic 306.4
  duodenum 564.8
  heart (psychogenic) 306.2
  ileum 564.8
  jejunum 564.8
  myocardium 306.2
  rectum 564.8
  stomach 536.9
    psychogenic 306.4
  sympathetic (nervous system) (*see also*
    Neuropathy, peripheral, autonomic) 337.9
  urethra 599.84
  ventricular (heart) (psychogenic) 306.2

Irritable— *see* Irritability
Irritation
  anus 569.49
  axillary nerve 353.0
  bladder 596.8
  brachial plexus 353.0
  brain (traumatic) (*see also* Injury, intracranial)
    854.0
    nontraumatic—*see* Encephalitis
  bronchial (*see also* Bronchitis) 490
  cerebral (traumatic) (*see also* Injury,
    intracranial) 854.0
    nontraumatic—*see* Encephalitis
  cervical plexus 353.2
  cervix (*see also* Cervicitis) 616.0
  choroid, sympathetic 360.11
  cranial nerve—*see* Disorder, nerve, cranial
  digestive tract 536.9
    psychogenic 306.4
  gastric 536.9
    psychogenic 306.4
  gastrointestinal (tract) 536.9
    functional 536.9
    psychogenic 306.4
  globe, sympathetic 360.11
  intestinal (bowel) 564.1
  labyrinth 386.50
  lumbosacral plexus 353.1
  meninges (traumatic) (*see also* Injury,
    intracranial) 854.0
    nontraumatic—*see* Meningitis
  myocardium 306.2
  nerve—*see* Disorder, nerve
  nervous 799.2
  nose 478.1
  penis 607.89
  perineum 709.9
  peripheral
    autonomic nervous system (*see also*
      Neuropathy, peripheral, autonomic) 337.9
    nerve—*see* Disorder, nerve
  peritoneum (*see also* Peritonitis) 567.9
  pharynx 478.29
  plantar nerve 355.6
  spinal (cord) (traumatic)—*see also* Injury,
    spinal, by site
    nerve—*see also* Disorder, nerve
      root NEC 724.9
      traumatic—*see* Injury, nerve, spinal
    nontraumatic—*see* Myelitis
  stomach 536.9
    psychogenic 306.4
  sympathetic nerve NEC (*see also* Neuropathy,
    peripheral, autonomic) 337.9
  ulnar nerve 354.2
  vagina 623.9
Isambert's disease 012.3
Ischemia, ischemic 459.9
  basilar artery (with transient neurologic deficit)
    435.0
  bone NEC 733.40
  bowel (transient) 557.9
    acute 557.0
    chronic 557.1
    due to mesenteric artery insufficiency 557.1
  brain—*see also* Ischemia, cerebral
    recurrent focal 435.9
  cardiac (*see also* Ischemia, heart) 414.9
  cardiomyopathy 414.8
  carotid artery (with transient neurologic deficit)
    435.8

Ischemia, ischemic—*continued*
  cerebral (chronic) (generalized) 437.1
    arteriosclerotic 437.0
    intermittent (with transient neurologic deficit)
      435.9
    puerperal, postpartum, childbirth 674.0
    recurrent focal (with transient neurologic
      deficit) 435.9
    transient (with transient neurologic deficit)
      435.9
  colon 557.9
    acute 557.0
    chronic 557.1
    due to mesenteric artery insufficiency 557.1
  coronary (chronic) (*see also* Ischemia, heart)
    414.9
  heart (chronic or with a stated duration of over 8
    weeks) 414.9
    acute or with a stated duration of 8 weeks or
      less (*see also* Infarct, myocardium) 410.9
      without myocardial infarction 411.89
        with coronary (artery) occlusion 411.81
    subacute 411.89
  intestine (transient) 557.9
    acute 557.0
    chronic 557.1
    due to mesenteric artery insufficiency 557.1
  kidney 593.81
  labyrinth 386.50
  muscles, leg 728.89
  myocardium, myocardial (chronic or with a
    stated duration of over 8 weeks) 414.8
    acute (*see also* Infarct, myocardium) 410.9
      without myocardial infarction 411.89
        with coronary (artery) occlusion 411.81
  renal 593.81
  retina, retinal 362.84
  small bowel 557.9
    acute 557.0
    chronic 557.1
    due to mesenteric artery insufficiency 557.1
  spinal cord 336.1
  subendocardial (*see also* Insufficiency,
    coronary) 411.89
  vertebral artery (with transient neurologic
    deficit) 435.1
Ischialgia (*see also* Sciatica) 724.3
Ischiopagus 759.4
Ischium, ischial —*see* condition
Ischomenia 626.8
Ischuria 788.5
Iselin's disease or osteochondrosis 732.5
Islands of
  parotid tissue in
    lymph nodes 750.26
    neck structures 750.26
  submaxillary glands in
    fascia 750.26
    lymph nodes 750.26
    neck muscles 750.26
Islet cell tumor, pancreas (M8150/0) 211.7
Isoimmunization NEC (*see also* Incompatibility)
    656.2
  fetus or newborn 773.2
    ABO blood groups 773.1
    Rhesus (Rh) factor 773.0
Isolation V07.0
  social V62.4
Isosporosis 007.2

Issue
  medical certificate NEC V68.0
    cause of death V68.0
    fitness V68.0
    incapacity V68.0
  repeat prescription NEC V68.1
    appliance V68.1
    contraceptive V25.40
      device NEC V25.49
        intrauterine V25.42
        specified type NEC V25.49
      pill V25.41
    glasses V68.1
    medicinal substance V68.1
Itch (*see also* Pruritus) 698.9
  bakers' 692.89
  barbers' 110.0
  bricklayers' 692.89
  cheese 133.8
  clam diggers' 120.3
  coolie 126.9
  copra 133.8
  Cuban 050.1
  dew 126.9
  dhobie 110.3
  eye 379.99
  filarial (*see also* Infestation, filarial) 125.9
  grain 133.8
  grocers' 133.8
  ground 126.9
  harvest 133.8
  jock 110.3
  Malabar 110.9
    beard 110.0
    foot 110.4
    scalp 110.0
  meaning scabies 133.0
  Norwegian 133.0
  perianal 698.0
  poultrymen's 133.8
  sarcoptic 133.0
  scrub 134.1
  seven year V61.10
    meaning scabies 133.0
  straw 133.8
  swimmers' 120.3
  washerwoman's 692.4
  water 120.3
  winter 698.8
Itsenko-Cushing syndrome (pituitary
    basophilism) 255.0
Ivemark's syndrome (asplenia with congenital
    heart disease) 759.0
Ivory bones 756.52
Ixodes 134.8
Ixodiasis 134.8

J

Jaccoud's nodular fibrositis, chronic
  (Jaccoud's syndrome) 714.4
Jackson's
  membrane 751.4
  paralysis or syndrome 344.89
  veil 751.4
Jacksonian
  epilepsy (*see also* Epilepsy) 345.5
  seizures (focal) (*see also* Epilepsy) 345.5
Jacob's ulcer (M8090/3)—*see* Neoplasm, skin,
    malignant, by site
Jacquet's dermatitis (diaper dermatitis) 691.0
Jadassohn's
  blue nevus (M8780/0)—*see* Neoplasm, skin,
    benign
  disease (maculopapular erythroderma) 696.2
  intraepidermal epithelioma (M8096/0)—*see*
    Neoplasm, skin, benign
Jadassohn-Lewandowski syndrome
  (pachyonychia congenita) 757.5
Jadassohn-Pellizari's disease (anetoderma)
  701.3
Jadassohn-Tièche nevus (M8780/0)—*see*
  Neoplasm, skin, benign
Jaffe-Lichtenstein (-Uehlinger) syndrome 252.0
Jahnke's syndrome (encephalocutaneous
  angiomatosis) 759.6
Jakob-Creutzfeldt disease or syndrome 046.1
  with dementia 046.1 *[294.1]*
Jaksch (-Luzet) disease or syndrome
  (pseudoleukemia infantum) 285.8
Jamaican
  neuropathy 349.82
  paraplegic tropical ataxic-spastic syndrome
    349.82
Janet's disease (psychasthenia) 300.89
Janiceps 759.4
Jansky-Bielschowsky amaurotic familial idiocy
  330.1
Japanese
  B type encephalitis 062.0
  river fever 081.2
  seven-day fever 100.89
Jaundice (yellow) 782.4
  acholuric (familial) (splenomegalic) (*see also*
    Spherocytosis) 282.0
    acquired 283.9
  breast milk 774.39
  catarrhal (acute) 070.1
    with hepatic coma 070.0
    chronic 571.9
    epidemic—*see* Jaundice, epidemic
  cholestatic (benign) 782.4
  chronic idiopathic 277.4
  epidemic (catarrhal) 070.1
    with hepatic coma 070.0
    leptospiral 100.0
    spirochetal 100.0
  febrile (acute) 070.1
    with hepatic coma 070.0
    leptospiral 100.0
    spirochetal 100.0

Jaundice—*continued*
  fetus or newborn 774.6
    due to or associated with
      ABO
        antibodies 773.1
        incompatibility, maternal/fetal 773.1
        isoimmunization 773.1
      absence or deficiency of enzyme system for
        bilirubin conjugation (congenital) 774.39
      blood group incompatibility NEC 773.2
      breast milk inhibitors to conjugation 774.39
        associated with preterm delivery 774.2
      bruising 774.1
      Crigler-Najjar syndrome 277.4 *[774.31]*
      delayed conjugation 774.30
        associated with preterm delivery 774.2
        development 774.39
      drugs or toxins transmitted from mother
        774.1
      G-6-PD deficiency 282.2 *[774.0]*
      galactosemia 271.1 *[774.5]*
      Gilbert's syndrome 277.4 *[774.31]*
      hepatocellular damage 774.4
      hereditary hemolytic anemia (*see also*
        Anemia, hemolytic) 282.9 *[774.0]*
      hypothyroidism, congenital 243 *[774.31]*
      incompatibility, maternal/fetal NEC 773.2
      infection 774.1
      inspissated bile syndrome 774.4
      isoimmunization NEC 773.2
      mucoviscidosis 277.01 *[774.5]*
      obliteration of bile duct, congenital 751.61
        [774.5]
      polycythemia 774.1
      preterm delivery 774.2
      red cell defect 282.9 *[774.0]*
      Rh
        antibodies 773.0
        incompatibility, maternal/fetal 773.0
        isoimmunization 773.0
      spherocytosis (congenital) 282.0 *[774.0]*
      swallowed maternal blood 774.1
    physiological NEC 774.6
  from injection, inoculation, infusion, or
    transfusion (blood) (plasma) (serum) (other
    substance) (onset within 8 months after
    administration)—*see* Hepatitis, viral
  Gilbert's (familial nonhemolytic) 277.4
  hematogenous 283.9
  hemolytic (acquired) 283.9
    congenital (*see also* Spherocytosis) 282.0
  hemorrhagic (acute) 100.0
    leptospiral 100.0
    newborn 776.0
    spirochetal 100.0
  hepatocellular 573.8
  homologous (serum)—*see* Hepatitis, viral
  idiopathic, chronic 277.4
  infectious (acute) (subacute) 070.1
    with hepatic coma 070.0
    leptospiral 100.0
    spirochetal 100.0
  leptospiral 100.0
  malignant (*see also* Necrosis, liver) 570
  newborn (physiological) (*see also* Jaundice,
    fetus or newborn) 774.6

Jaundice—*continued*
  nonhemolytic, congenital familial (Gilbert's)
      277.4
  nuclear, newborn (*see also* Kernicterus of
      newborn) 774.7
  obstructive NEC (*see also* Obstruction, biliary)
      576.8
  postimmunization—*see* Hepatitis, viral
  posttransfusion—*see* Hepatitis, viral
  regurgitation (*see also* Obstruction, biliary)
      576.8
  serum (homologous) (prophylactic)
      (therapeutic)—*see* Hepatitis, viral
  spirochetal (hemorrhagic) 100.0
  symptomatic 782.4
    newborn 774.6
Jaw —*see* condition
Jaw-blinking 374.43
  congenital 742.8
Jaw-winking phenomenon or syndrome 742.8
Jealousy
  alcoholic 291.5
  childhood 313.3
  sibling 313.3
Jejunitis (*see also* Enteritis) 558.9
Jejunostomy status V44.4
Jejunum, jejunal —*see* condition
Jensen's disease 363.05
Jericho boil 085.1
Jerks, myoclonic 333.2
Jeune's disease or syndrome (asphyxiating
    thoracic dystrophy) 756.4
Jigger disease 134.1
Job's syndrome (chronic granulomatous disease)
    288.1
Jod-Basedow phenomenon 242.8
Johnson-Stevens disease (erythema multiforme
    exudativum) 695.1
Joint —*see also* condition
  Charcot's 094.0 *[713.5]*
  false 733.82
  flail—*see* Flail, joint
  mice—*see* Loose, body, joint, by site
  sinus to bone 730.9
  von Gies' 095.8
Jordan's anomaly or syndrome 288.2
Josephs-Diamond-Blackfan anemia (congenital
    hypoplastic) 284.0
Jumpers' knee 727.2
Jungle yellow fever 060.0
Jüngling's disease (sarcoidosis) 135
Junin virus hemorrhagic fever 078.7
Juvenile —*see also* condition
  delinquent 312.9
    group (*see also* Disturbance, conduct) 312.2
    neurotic 312.4

K

Kahler (-Bozzolo) disease (multiple myeloma)
(M9730/3) 203.0
Kakergasia 300.9
Kakke 265.0
Kala-azar (Indian) (infantile) (Mediterranean)
(Sudanese) 085.0
Kalischer's syndrome (encephalocutaneous
angiomatosis) 759.6
Kallmann's syndrome (hypogonadotropic
hypogonadism with anosmia) 253.4
Kanner's syndrome (autism) (*see also*
Psychosis, childhood) 299.0
Kaolinosis 502
Kaposi's
disease 757.33
lichen ruber 696.4
acuminatus 696.4
moniliformis 697.8
xeroderma pigmentosum 757.33
sarcoma (M9140/3) 176.9
adipose tissue 176.1
aponeurosis 176.1
artery 176.1
blood vessel 176.1
bursa 176.1
connective tissue 176.1
external genitalia 176.8
fascia 176.1
fatty tissue 176.1
fibrous tissue 176.1
gastrointestinal tract NEC 176.3
ligament 176.1
lung 176.4
lymph
gland(s) 176.5
node(s) 176.5
lymphatic(s) NEC 176.1
muscle (skeletal) 176.1
oral cavity NEC 176.8
palate 176.2
scrotum 176.8
skin 176.0
soft tissue 176.1
specified site NEC 176.8
subcutaneous tissue 176.1
synovia 176.1
tendon (sheath) 176.1
vein 176.1
vessel 176.1
viscera NEC 176.9
vulva 176.8
varicelliform eruption 054.0
vaccinia 999.0
Kartagener's syndrome or triad (sinusitis,
bronchiectasis, situs inversus) 759.3
Kasabach-Merritt syndrome (capillary
hemangioma associated with
thrombocytopenic purpura) 287.3
Kaschin-Beck disease (endemic
polyarthritis)—*see* Disease, Kaschin-Beck
Kast's syndrome (dyschondroplasia with
hemangiomas) 756.4
Katatonia (*see also* Schizophrenia) 295.2
Katayama disease or fever 120.2
Kathisophobia 781.0
Kawasaki disease 446.1
Kayser-Fleischer ring (cornea)
(pseudosclerosis) 275.1 *[371.14]*

Kaznelson's syndrome (congenital hypoplastic
anemia) 284.0
Kedani fever 081.2
Kelis 701.4
Kelly (-Patterson) syndrome (sideropenic
dysphagia) 280.8
Keloid, cheloid 701.4
Addison's (morphea) 701.0
cornea 371.00
Hawkins' 701.4
scar 701.4
Keloma 701.4
Kenya fever 082.1
Keratectasia 371.71
congenital 743.41
Keratitis (nodular) (nonulcerative) (simple)
(zonular) NEC 370.9
with ulceration (*see also* Ulcer, cornea) 370.00
actinic 370.24
arborescens 054.42
areolar 370.22
bullosa 370.8
deep—*see* Keratitis, interstitial
dendritic(a) 054.42
desiccation 370.34
diffuse interstitial 370.52
disciform(is) 054.43
varicella 052.7 *[370.44]*
epithelialis vernalis 372.13 *[370.32]*
exposure 370.34
filamentary 370.23
gonococcal (congenital) (prenatal) 098.43
herpes, herpetic (simplex) NEC 054.43
zoster 053.21
hypopyon 370.04
in
chickenpox 052.7 *[370.44]*
exanthema (*see also* Exanthem) 057.9
[370.44]
paravaccinia (*see also* Paravaccinia) 051.9
[370.44]
smallpox (*see also* Smallpox) 050.9 *[370.44]*
vernal conjunctivitis 372.13 *[370.32]*
interstitial (nonsyphilitic) 370.50
with ulcer (*see also* Ulcer, cornea) 370.00
diffuse 370.52
herpes, herpetic (simplex) 054.43
zoster 053.21
syphilitic (congenital) (hereditary) 090.3
tuberculous (*see also* Tuberculosis) 017.3
[370.59]
lagophthalmic 370.34
macular 370.22
neuroparalytic 370.35
neurotrophic 370.35
nummular 370.22
oyster-shuckers' 370.8
parenchymatous—*see* Keratitis, interstitial
petrificans 370.8
phlyctenular 370.31
postmeasles 055.71
punctata, punctate 370.21
leprosa 030.0 *[370.21]*
profunda 090.3
superficial (Thygeson's) 370.21
purulent 370.8
pustuliformis profunda 090.3

Keratitis—*continued*
  rosacea 695.3 *[370.49]*
  sclerosing 370.54
  specified type NEC 370.8
  stellate 370.22
  striate 370.22
  superficial 370.20
    with conjunctivitis (*see also*
        Keratoconjunctivitis) 370.40
    punctate (Thygeson's) 370.21
  suppurative 370.8
  syphilitic (congenital) (prenatal) 090.3
  trachomatous 076.1
    late effect 139.1
  tuberculous (phlyctenular) (*see also*
        Tuberculosis) 017.3 *[370.31]*
  ulcerated (*see also* Ulcer, cornea) 370.00
  vesicular 370.8
  welders' 370.24
  xerotic (*see also* Keratomalacia) 371.45
    vitamin A deficiency 264.4
Keratoacanthoma 238.2
Keratocele 371.72
Keratoconjunctivitis (*see also* Keratitis) 370.40
  adenovirus type 8 077.1
  epidemic 077.1
  exposure 370.34
  gonococcal 098.43
  herpetic (simplex) 054.43
    zoster 053.21
  in
    chickenpox 052.7 *[370.44]*
    exanthema (*see also* Exanthem) 057.9
        [370.44]
    paravaccinia (*see also* Paravaccinia) 051.9
        [370.44]
    smallpox (*see also* Smallpox) 050.9 *[370.44]*
  infectious 077.1
  neurotrophic 370.35
  phlyctenular 370.31
  postmeasles 055.71
  shipyard 077.1
  sicca (Sjögren's syndrome) 710.2
    not in Sjögren's syndrome 370.33
  specified type NEC 370.49
  tuberculous (phlyctenular) (*see also*
        Tuberculosis) 017.3 *[370.31]*
Keratoconus 371.60
  acute hydrops 371.62
  congenital 743.41
  stable 371.61
Keratocyst (dental) 526.0
Keratoderma, keratodermia (congenital)
    (palmaris et plantaris) (symmetrical) 757.39
  acquired 701.1
  blennorrhagica 701.1
    gonococcal 098.81
  climacterium 701.1
  eccentrica 757.39
  gonorrheal 098.81
  punctata 701.1
  tylodes, progressive 701.1
Keratodermatocele 371.72
Keratoglobus 371.70
  congenital 743.41
    associated with buphthalmos 743.22
Keratohemia 371.12
Keratoiritis (*see also* Iridocyclitis) 364.3
  syphilitic 090.3
  tuberculous (*see also* Tuberculosis) 017.3
    [364.11]

Keratolysis exfoliativa (congenital) 757.39
  acquired 695.89
  neonatorum 757.39
Keratoma 701.1
  congenital 757.39
  malignum congenitale 757.1
  palmaris et plantaris hereditarium 757.39
  senile 702.0
Keratomalacia 371.45
  vitamin A deficiency 264.4
Keratomegaly 743.41
Keratomycosis 111.1
  nigricans (palmaris) 111.1
Keratopathy 371.40
  band (*see also* Keratitis) 371.43
  bullous (*see also* Keratitis) 371.23
  degenerative (*see also* Degeneration, cornea)
        371.40
    hereditary (*see also* Dystrophy, cornea) 371.50
  discrete colliquative 371.49
Keratoscleritis, tuberculous (*see also*
    Tuberculosis) 017.3 *[370.31]*
Keratosis 701.1
  actinic 702.0
  arsenical 692.4
  blennorrhagica 701.1
    gonococcal 098.81
  congenital (any type) 757.39
  ear (middle) (*see also* Cholesteatoma) 385.30
  female genital (external) 629.8
  follicular, vitamin A deficiency 264.8
  follicularis 757.39
    acquired 701.1
    congenital (acneiformis) (Siemens') 757.39
    spinulosa (decalvans) 757.39
    vitamin A deficiency 264.8
  gonococcal 098.81
  larynx, laryngeal 478.79
  male genital (external) 608.89
  middle ear (*see also* Cholesteatoma) 385.30
  nigricans 701.2
    congenital 757.39
  obturans 380.21
  palmaris et plantaris (symmetrical) 757.39
  penile 607.89
  pharyngeus 478.29
  pilaris 757.39
    acquired 701.1
  punctata (palmaris et plantaris) 701.1
  scrotal 608.89
  seborrheic 702.19
    inflamed 702.11
  senilis 702.0
  solar 702.0
  suprafollicularis 757.39
  tonsillaris 478.29
  vagina 623.1
  vegetans 757.39
  vitamin A deficiency 264.8
Kerato-uveitis (*see also* Iridocyclitis) 364.3
Keraunoparalysis 994.0
Kerion (celsi) 110.0
Kernicterus of newborn (not due to
    isoimmunization) 774.7
  due to isoimmunization (conditions classifiable
    to 773.0-773.2) 773.4
Ketoacidosis 276.2
  diabetic 250.1
Ketonuria 791.6
  branched-chain, intermittent 270.3
Ketosis 276.2
  diabetic 250.1

Kidney —*see* condition
Kienböck's
  disease 732.3
  adult 732.8
  osteochondrosis 732.3
Kimmelstiel (-Wilson) disease or syndrome
    (intercapillary glomerulosclerosis) 250.4
    [581.81]
Kink, kinking
  appendix 543.9
  artery 447.1
  cystic duct, congenital 751.61
  hair (acquired) 704.2
  ileum or intestine (*see also* Obstruction,
    intestine) 560.9
  Lane's (*see also* Obstruction, intestine) 560.9
  organ or site, congenital NEC—*see* Anomaly,
    specified type NEC, by site
  ureter (pelvic junction) 593.3
    congenital 753.20
  vein(s) 459.2
    caval 459.2
    peripheral 459.2
Kinnier Wilson's disease (hepatolenticular
    degeneration) 275.1
Kissing
  osteophytes 721.5
  spine 721.5
  vertebra 721.5
Klauder's syndrome (erythema multiforme
    exudativum) 695.1
Kleb's disease (*see also* Nephritis) 583.9
Klein-Waardenburg syndrome
    (ptosisepicanthus) 270.2
Kleine-Levin syndrome 349.89
Kleptomania 312.32
Klinefelter's syndrome 758.7
Klinger's disease 446.4
Klippel's disease 723.8
Klippel-Feil disease or syndrome (brevicollis)
    756.16
Klippel-Trenaunay syndrome 759.89
Klumpke (-Déjérine) palsy, paralysis (birth)
    (newborn) 767.6
Klüver-Bucy (-Terzian) syndrome 310.0
Knee —*see* condition
Knifegrinders' rot (*see also* Tuberculosis) 011.4
Knock-knee (acquired) 736.41
  congenital 755.64
Knot
  intestinal, syndrome (volvulus) 560.2
  umbilical cord (true) 663.2
    affecting fetus or newborn 762.5
Knots, surfer 919.8
  infected 919.9
Knotting (of)
  hair 704.2
  intestine 560.2
Knuckle pads (Garrod's) 728.79
Köbner's disease (epidermolysis bullosa) 757.39
Koch's
  infection (*see also* Tuberculosis, pulmonary)
    011.9
  relapsing fever 087.9
Koch-Weeks conjunctivitis 372.03
Koenig-Wichman disease (pemphigus) 694.4

Köhler's disease (osteochondrosis) 732.5
  first (osteochondrosis juvenilis) 732.5
  second (Freiburg's infarction, metatarsal head)
    732.5
  patellar 732.4
  tarsal navicular (bone) (osteoarthosis juvenilis)
    732.5
Köhler-Mouchet disease (osteoarthrosis
    juvenilis) 732.5
Köhler-Pellegrini-Stieda disease or syndrome
    (calcification, knee joint) 726.62
Koilonychia 703.8
  congenital 757.5
Kojevnikov's, Kojewnikoff's epilepsy (*see also*
    Epilepsy) 345.7
König's
  disease (osteochondritis dissecans) 732.7
  syndrome 564.8
Koniophthisis (*see also* Tuberculosis) 011.4
Koplik's spots 055.9
Kopp's asthma 254.8
Korean hemorrhagic fever 078.6
Korsakoff (-Wernicke) disease, psychosis, or
    syndrome (nonalcoholic) 294.0
  alcoholic 291.1
Korsakov's disease —*see* Korsakoff's disease
Korsakow's disease —*see* Korsakoff's disease
Kostmann's disease or syndrome (infantile
    genetic agranulocytosis) 288.0
Krabbe's
  disease (leukodystrophy) 330.0
  syndrome
    congenital muscle hypoplasia 756.89
    cutaneocerebral angioma 759.6
Kraepelin-Morel disease (*see also*
    Schizophrenia) 295.9
Kraft-Weber-Dimitri disease 759.6
Kraurosis
  ani 569.49
  penis 607.0
  vagina 623.8
  vulva 624.0
Kreotoxism 005.9
Krukenberg's
  spindle 371.13
  tumor (M8490/6) 198.6
Kufs' disease 330.1
Kugelberg-Welander disease 335.11
Kuhnt-Junius degeneration or disease 362.52
Kulchitsky's cell carcinoma (carcinoid tumor of
    intestine) 259.2
Kümmell's disease or spondylitis 721.7
Kundrat's disease (lymphosarcoma) 200.1
Kunekune —*see* Dermatophytosis
Kunkel syndrome (lupoid hepatitis) 571.49
Kupffer cell sarcoma (M9124/3) 155.0
Kuru 046.0
Kussmaul's
  coma (diabetic) 250.3
  disease (polyarteritis nodosa) 446.0
  respiration (air hunger) 786.09
Kwashiorkor (marasmus type) 260
Kyasanur Forest disease 065.2
Kyphoscoliosis, kyphoscoliotic (acquired) (*see
    also* Scoliosis) 737.30
  congenital 756.19
  due to radiation 737.33
  heart (disease) 416.1

Kyphoscoliosis, kyphoscoliotic—*continued*
  idiopathic 737.30
    infantile
      progressive 737.32
      resolving 737.31
  late effect of rickets 268.1 *[737.43]*
  specified NEC 737.39
  thoracogenic 737.34
  tuberculous (*see also* Tuberculosis) 015.0
    [737.43]
Kyphosis, kyphotic (acquired) (postural) 737.10
  adolescent postural 737.0
  congenital 756.19
  dorsalis juvenilis 732.0
  due to or associated with
    Charcot-Marie-Tooth disease 356.1 *[737.41]*
    mucopolysaccharidosis 277.5 *[737.41]*
    neurofibromatosis 237.71 *[737.41]*
    osteitis
      deformans 731.0 *[737.41]*
      fibrosa cystica 252.0 *[737.41]*
    osteoporosis (*see also* Osteoporosis) 733.0
      [737.41]
    poliomyelitis (*see also* Poliomyelitis) 138
      [737.41]
    radiation 737.11
    tuberculosis (*see also* Tuberculosis) 015.0
      [737.41]
  Kümmell's 721.7
  late effect of rickets 268.1 *[737.41]*
  Morquio-Brailsford type (spinal) 277.5 *[737.41]*
  pelvis 738.6
  postlaminectomy 737.12
  specified cause NEC 737.19
  syphilitic, congenital 090.5 *[737.41]*
  tuberculous (*see also* Tuberculosis) 015.0
    [737.41]
Kyrle's disease (hyperkeratosis follicularis in
  cutem penetrans) 701.1

L

Labia, labium —*see* condition
Labiated hymen 752.49
Labile
 blood pressure 796.4
 emotions, emotionality 301.3
 vasomotor system 443.9
Labioglossal paralysis 335.22
Labium leporinum (*see also* Cleft, lip) 749.10
Labor (*see also* Delivery)
 with complications—*see* Delivery, complicated
 abnormal NEC 661.9
  affecting fetus or newborn 763.7
 arrested active phase 661.1
  affecting fetus or newborn 763.7
 desultory 661.2
  affecting fetus or newborn 763.7
 dyscoordinate 661.4
  affecting fetus or newborn 763.7
 early onset (22-36 weeks gestation) 644.2
 failed
  induction 659.1
   mechanical 659.0
   medical 659.1
   surgical 659.0
  trial (vaginal delivery) 660.6
 false 644.1
 forced or induced, affecting fetus or newborn
   763.8
 hypertonic 661.4
  affecting fetus or newborn 763.7
 hypotonic 661.2
  affecting fetus or newborn 763.7
  primary 661.0
   affecting fetus or newborn 763.7
  secondary 661.1
   affecting fetus or newborn 763.7
 incoordinate 661.4
  affecting fetus or newborn 763.7
 irregular 661.2
  affecting fetus or newborn 763.7
 long—*see* Labor, prolonged
 missed (at or near term) 656.4
 obstructed NEC 660.9
  affecting fetus or newborn 763.1
  specified cause NEC 660.8
   affecting fetus or newborn 763.1
 pains, spurious 644.1
 precipitate 661.3
  affecting fetus or newborn 763.6
 premature 644.2
  threatened 644.0
 prolonged or protracted 662.1
  first stage 662.0
   affecting fetus or newborn 763.8
  second stage 662.2
   affecting fetus or newborn 763.8
  affecting fetus or newborn 763.8
 threatened NEC 644.1
 undelivered 644.1

Labored breathing (*see also* Hyperventilation)
  786.09
Labyrinthitis (inner ear) (destructive) (latent)
  386.30
 circumscribed 386.32
 diffuse 386.31
 focal 386.32
 purulent 386.33
 serous 386.31
 suppurative 386.33
 syphilitic 095.8
 toxic 386.34
 viral 386.35
Laceration —*see also* Wound, open, by site
 accidental, complicating surgery 998.2
 Achilles tendon 845.09
  with open wound 892.2
 anus (sphincter) 863.89
  with
   abortion—*see* Abortion, by type, with
    damage to pelvic organs
   ectopic pregnancy (*see also* categories
    633.0-633.9) 639.2
   molar pregnancy (*see also* categories
    630-632) 639.2
  complicating delivery 664.2
   with laceration of anal or rectal mucosa
    664.3
  following
   abortion 639.2
   ectopic or molar pregnancy 639.2
  nontraumatic, nonpuerperal 565.0
 bladder (urinary)
  with
   abortion—*see* Abortion, by type, with
    damage to pelvic organs
   ectopic pregnancy (*see also* categories
    633.0-633.9) 639.2
   molar pregnancy (*see also* categories
    630-632) 639.2
  following
   abortion 639.2
   ectopic or molar pregnancy 639.2
  obstetrical trauma 665.5
 blood vessel—*see* Injury, blood vessel, by site
 bowel
  with
   abortion—*see* Abortion, by type, with
    damage to pelvic organs
   ectopic pregnancy (*see also* categories
    633.0-633.9) 639.2
   molar pregnancy (*see also* categories
    630-632) 639.2
  following
   abortion 639.2
   ectopic or molar pregnancy 639.2
  obstetrical trauma 665.5

Laceration—*continued*
 brain (with hemorrhage) (cerebral) (membrane)
  851.8

Note—Use the following fifth-digit
subclassification with categories 851-854:

0 *unspecified state of consciousness*
1 *with no loss of consciousness*
2 *with brief [less than one hour] loss of
   consciousness*
3 *with moderate [1-24 hours] loss of
   consciousness*
4 *with prolonged [more than 24 hours] loss of
   consciousness and return to pre-existing
   conscious level*
5 *with prolonged [more than 24 hours] loss of
   consciousness, without return to pre-existing
   conscious level*
*Use fifth-digit 5 to designate when a patient is
unconscious and dies before regaining
consciousness, regardless of the duration of the
loss of consciousness*
6 *with loss of consciousness of unspecified
   duration*
9 *with concussion, unspecified*

 with
  open intracranial wound 851.9
  skull fracture—see Fracture, skull, by site
 cerebellum 851.6
  with open intracranial wound 851.7
 cortex 851.2
  with open intracranial wound 851.3
 during birth 767.0
 stem 851.6
  with open intracranial wound 851.7
 broad ligament
  with
   abortion—*see* Abortion, by type, with
    damage to pelvic organs
   ectopic pregnancy (*see also* categories
    633.0-633.9) 639.2
   molar pregnancy (*see also* categories
    630-632) 639.2
  following
   abortion 639.2
   ectopic or molar pregnancy 639.2
  nontraumatic 620.6
  obstetrical trauma 665.6
  syndrome (nontraumatic) 620.6
 capsule, joint—*see* Sprain, by site
 cardiac—*see* Laceration, heart
 causing eversion of cervix uteri (old) 622.0
 central, complicating delivery 664.4
 cerebellum—*see* Laceration, brain, cerebellum
 cerebral—*see also* Laceration, brain
  during birth 767.0
 cervix (uteri)
  with
   abortion—*see* Abortion, by type, with
    damage to pelvic organs
   ectopic pregnancy (*see also* categories
    633.0-633.9) 639.2
   molar pregnancy (*see also* categories
    630-632) 639.2
  following
   abortion 639.2
   ectopic or molar pregnancy 639.2
  nonpuerperal, nontraumatic 622.3
  obstetrical trauma (current) 665.3
  old (postpartal) 622.3

Laceration—*continued*
 traumatic—*see* Injury, internal, cervix
 chordae heart 429.5
 complicated 879.9
 cornea—*see* Laceration, eyeball
 cortex (cerebral)—*see* Laceration, brain, cortex
 esophagus 530.89
 eye(s)—*see* Laceration, ocular
 eyeball NEC 871.4
  with prolapse or exposure of intraocular tissue
   871.1
  penetrating—*see* Penetrating wound, eyeball
  specified as without prolapse of intraocular
   tissue 871.0
 eyelid NEC 870.8
  full thickness 870.1
   involving lacrimal passages 870.2
  skin (and periocular area) 870.0
  penetrating—*see* Penetrating wound, orbit
 fourchette
  with
   abortion—*see* Abortion, by type, with
    damage to pelvic organs
   ectopic pregnancy (*see also* categories
    633.0-633.9) 639.2
   molar pregnancy (*see also* categories
    630-632) 639.2
  complicating delivery 664.0
  following
   abortion 639.2
   ectopic or molar pregnancy 639.2
 heart (without penetration of heart chambers)
  861.02
  with
   open wound into thorax 861.12
   penetration of heart chambers 861.03
    with open wound into thorax 861.13
 hernial sac—*see* Hernia, by site
 internal organ (abdomen) (chest) (pelvis)
  NEC—*see* Injury, internal, by site
 kidney (parenchyma) 866.02
  with
   complete disruption of parenchyma
    (rupture) 866.03
    with open wound into cavity 866.13
   open wound into cavity 866.12
 labia
  complicating delivery 664.0
 ligament—*see also* Sprain, by site
  with open wound—*see* Wound, open, by site
 liver 864.05
  with open wound into cavity 864.15
  major (disruption of hepatic parenchyma)
   864.04
   with open wound into cavity 864.14
  minor (capsule only) 864.02
   with open wound into cavity 864.12
  moderate (involving parenchyma without
   major disruption) 864.03
   with open wound into cavity 864.13
  multiple 864.04
   with open wound into cavity 864.14
  stellate 864.04
   with open wound into cavity 864.14
 lung 861.22
  with open wound into thorax 861.32
 meninges—*see* Laceration, brain
 meniscus (knee) (*see also* Tear, meniscus) 836.2
  old 717.5
  site other than knee—*see also* Sprain, by site

Laceration— *continued*
   old NEC (*see also* Disorder, cartilage,
     articular) 718.0
  muscle—*see also* Sprain, by site
   with open wound—*see* Wound, open, by site
  myocardium—*see* Laceration, heart
  nerve—*see* Injury, nerve, by site
  ocular NEC (*see also* Laceration, eyeball) 871.4
   adnexa NEC 870.8
    penetrating 870.3
     with foreign body 870.4
  orbit (eye) 870.8
   penetrating 870.3
    with foreign body 870.4
  pelvic
   floor (muscles)
    with
     abortion—*see* Abortion, by type, with
      damage to pelvic organs
     ectopic pregnancy (*see also* categories
      633.0-633.9) 639.2
     molar pregnancy (*see also* categories
      630-632) 639.2
    complicating delivery 664.1
    following
     abortion 639.2
     ectopic or molar pregnancy 639.2
    nonpuerperal 618.7
    old (postpartal) 618.7
   organ NEC
    with
     abortion—*see* Abortion, by type, with
      damage to pelvic organs
     ectopic pregnancy (*see also* categories
      633.0-633.9) 639.2
     molar pregnancy (*see also* categories
      630-632) 639.2
    complicating delivery 665.5
     affecting fetus or newborn 763.8
    following
     abortion 639.2
     ectopic or molar pregnancy 639.2
    obstetrical trauma 665.5
  perineum, perineal (old) (postpartal) 618.7
   with
    abortion—*see* Abortion, by type, with
     damage to pelvic floor
    ectopic pregnancy (*see also* categories
     633.0-633.9) 639.2
    molar pregnancy (*see also* categories
     630-632) 639.2
   complicating delivery 664.4
    first degree 664.0
    second degree 664.1
    third degree 664.2
    fourth degree 664.3
    central 664.4
    involving
     anal sphincter 664.2
     fourchette 664.0
     hymen 664.0
     labia 664.0
     pelvic floor 664.1
     perineal muscles 664.1
     rectovaginal septum 664.2
      with anal mucosa 664.3
     skin 664.0
     sphincter (anal) 664.2
      with anal mucosa 664.3
     vagina 664.0
     vaginal muscles 664.1

Laceration— *continued*
   vulva 664.0
    secondary 674.2
   following
    abortion 639.2
    ectopic or molar pregnancy 639.2
   male 879.6
    complicated 879.7
   muscles, complicating delivery 664.1
   nonpuerperal, current injury 879.6
    complicated 879.7
   secondary (postpartal) 674.2
  peritoneum
   with
    abortion—*see* Abortion, by type, with
     damage to pelvic organs
    ectopic pregnancy (*see also* categories
     633.0-633.9) 639.2
    molar pregnancy (*see also* categories
     630-632) 639.2
   following
    abortion 639.2
    ectopic or molar pregnancy 639.2
   obstetrical trauma 665.5
  periurethral tissue
   with
    abortion—*see* Abortion, by type, with
     damage to pelvic organs
    ectopic pregnancy (*see also* categories
     633.0-633.9) 639.2
    molar pregnancy (*see also* categories
     630-632) 639.2
   following
    abortion 639.2
    ectopic or molar pregnancy 639.2
   obstetrical trauma 665.5
  rectovaginal (septum)
   with
    abortion—*see* Abortion, by type, with
     damage to pelvic organs
    ectopic pregnancy (*see also* categories
     633.0-633.9) 639.2
    molar pregnancy (*see also* categories
     630-632) 639.2
   complicating delivery 665.4
    with perineum 664.2
     involving anal or rectal mucosa 664.3
   following
    abortion 639.2
    ectopic or molar pregnancy 639.2
   nonpuerperal 623.4
   old (postpartal) 623.4
  spinal cord (meninges)—*see also* Injury, spinal,
   by site
   due to injury at birth 767.4
   fetus or newborn 767.4
  spleen 865.09
   with
    disruption of parenchyma (massive) 865.04
     with open wound into cavity 865.14
    open wound into cavity 865.19
   capsule (without disruption of parenchyma)
    865.02
    with open wound into cavity 865.12
   parenchyma 865.03
    with open wound into cavity 865.13
    massive disruption (rupture) 865.04
     with open wound into cavity 865.14

Laceration—*continued*
 tendon 848.9
  with open wound–*see* Wound, open, by site
  Achilles 845.09
   with open wound 892.2
  lower limb NEC 844.9
   with open wound NEC 894.2
  upper limb NEC 840.9
   with open wound NEC 884.2
 tentorium cerebelli—*see* Laceration, brain,
   cerebellum
 urethra
  with
   abortion—*see* Abortion, by type, with
     damage to pelvic organs
   ectopic pregnancy (*see also* categories
     633.0- 633.9) 639.2
   molar pregnancy (*see also* categories
     630-632) 639.2
  following
   abortion 639.2
   ectopic or molar pregnancy 639.2
  nonpuerperal, nontraumatic 599.84
  obstetrical trauma 665.5
 uterus
  with
   abortion—*see* Abortion, by type, with
     damage to pelvic organs
   ectopic pregnancy (*see also* categories
     633.0-633.9) 639.2
   molar pregnancy (*see also* categories
     630-632) 639.2
  following
   abortion 639.2
   ectopic or molar pregnancy 639.2
  nonpuerperal, nontraumatic 621.8
  obstetrical trauma NEC 665.1
  old (postpartal) 621.8
 vagina
  with
   abortion—*see* Abortion, by type, with
     damage to pelvic organs
   ectopic pregnancy (*see also* categories
     633.0-633.9) 639.2
   molar pregnancy (*see also* categories
     630-632) 639.2
   perineal involvement, complicating delivery
     664.0
  complicating delivery 665.4
   first degree 664.0
   second degree 664.1
   third degree 664.2
   fourth degree 664.3
   high 665.4
   muscles 664.1
   sulcus 665.4
   wall 665.4
  following
   abortion 639.2
   ectopic or molar pregnancy 639.2
  nonpuerperal, nontraumatic 623.4
  old (postpartal) 623.4
 valve, heart—*see* Endocarditis
 vulva
  with
   abortion—*see* Abortion, by type, with
     damage to pelvic organs
   ectopic pregnancy (*see also* categories
     633.0-633.9) 639.2
   molar pregnancy (*see also* categories
     630-632) 639.2

Laceration— *continued*
 complicating delivery 664.0
 following
  abortion 639.2
  ectopic or molar pregnancy 639.2
 nonpuerperal, nontraumatic 624.4
 old (postpartal) 624.4
Lachrymal —*see* condition
Lachrymonasal duct —*see* condition
Lack of
 appetite (*see also* Anorexia) 783.0
 care
  in home V60.4
  of adult 995.84
  of infant (at or after birth) 995.52
 coordination 781.3
 development—*see also* Hypoplasia
  physiological 783.4
 education V62.3
 energy 780.7
 financial resources V60.2
 food 994.2
  in environment V60.8
 growth 783.4
 heating V60.1
 housing (permanent) (temporary) V60.0
  adequate V60.1
 material resources V60.2
 medical attention 799.8
 memory (*see also* Amnesia) 780.9
  mild, following organic brain damage 310.1
 ovulation 628.0
 person able to render necessary care V60.4
 physical exercise V69.0
 physiologic development 783.4
 prenatal care in current pregnancy V23.7
 shelter V60.0
 water 994.3
Lacrimal —*see* condition
Lacrimation, abnormal (*see also* Epiphora)
  375.20
Lacrimonasal duct —*see* condition
Lactation, lactating (breast) (puerperal)
  (postpartum)
 defective 676.4
 disorder 676.9
  specified type NEC 676.8
 excessive 676.6
 failed 676.4
 mastitis NEC 675.2
 mother (care and/or examination) V24.1
 nonpuerperal 611.6
 suppressed 676.5
Lacticemia 271.3
 excessive 276.2
Lactosuria 271.3
Lacunar skull 756.0
Laennec's cirrhosis (alcoholic) 571.2
 nonalcoholic 571.5
Lafora's disease 333.2
Lag, lid (nervous) 374.41
Lagleyze-von Hippel disease (retinocerebral
  angiomatosis) 759.6
Lagophthalmos (eyelid) (nervous) 374.20
 cicatricial 374.23
 keratitis (*see also* Keratitis) 370.34
 mechanical 374.22
 paralytic 374.21

La grippe —*see* Influenza
Lahore sore 085.1
Lakes, venous (cerebral) 437.8
Laki-Lorand factor deficiency (*see also* Defect, coagulation) 286.3
Lalling 307.9
Lambliasis 007.1
Lame back 724.5
Lancereaux's diabetes (diabetes mellitus with marked emaciation) 250.8 *[261]*
Landouzy-Déjérine dystrophy (fascioscapulohumeral atrophy) 359.1
Landry's disease or paralysis 357.0
Landry-Guillain-Barré syndrome 357.0
Lane's
    band 751.4
    disease 569.89
    kink (*see also* Obstruction, intestine) 560.9
Langdon Down's syndrome (mongolism) 758.0
Language abolition 784.69
Lanugo (persistent) 757.4
Lardaceous
    degeneration (any site) 277.3
    disease 277.3
    kidney 277.3 *[583.81]*
    liver 277.3
Large
    baby (regardless of gestational age) 766.1
        exceptionally (weight of 4500 grams or more) 766.0
        of diabetic mother 775.0
    ear 744.22
    fetus—*see also* Oversize, fetus
        causing disproportion 653.5
            with obstructed labor 660.1
    for dates
        fetus or newborn (regardless of gestational age) 766.1
        affecting management of pregnancy 656.6
        exceptionally (weight of 4500 grams or more) 766.0
    physiological cup 743.57
    waxy liver 277.3
    white kidney—*see* Nephrosis
Larsen's syndrome (flattened facies and multiple congenital dislocations) 755.8
Larsen-Johansson disease (juvenile osteopathia patellae) 732.4
Larva migrans
    cutaneous NEC 126.9
        ancylostoma 126.9
    of Diptera in vitreous 128.0
    visceral NEC 128.0
Laryngeal —*see also* condition
    syncope 786.2
Laryngismus (acute) (infectious) (stridulous) 478.75
    congenital 748.3
    diphtheritic 032.3
Laryngitis (acute) (edematous) (fibrinous) (gangrenous) (infective) (infiltrative) (malignant) (membranous) (phlegmonous) (pneumococcal) (pseudomembranous) (septic) (subglottic) (suppurative) (ulcerative) (viral) 464.0
    with
        influenza, flu, or grippe 487.1
        tracheitis (*see also* Laryngotracheitis) 464.20
            with obstruction 464.21

Laryngitis—*continued*
    acute 464.20
        with obstruction 464.21
    chronic 476.1
    atrophic 476.0
    Borrelia vincentii 101
    catarrhal 476.0
    chronic 476.0
        with tracheitis (chronic) 476.1
        due to external agent—*see* Condition, respiratory, chronic, due to
    diphtheritic (membranous) 032.3
    due to external agent—*see* Inflammation, respiratory, upper, due to
    H. influenzae 464.0
    Hemophilus influenzae 464.0
    hypertrophic 476.0
    influenzal 487.1
    pachydermic 478.79
    sicca 476.0
    spasmodic 478.75
        acute 464.0
    streptococcal 034.0
    stridulous 478.75
    syphilitic 095.8
        congenital 090.5
    tuberculous (*see also* Tuberculosis, larynx) 012.3
    Vincent's 101
Laryngocele (congenital) (ventricular) 748.3
Laryngofissure 478.79
    congenital 748.3
Laryngomalacia (congenital) 748.3
Laryngopharyngitis (acute) 465.0
    chronic 478.9
        due to external agent—*see* Condition, respiratory, chronic, due to
        due to external agent—*see* Inflammation, respiratory, upper, due to
    septic 034.0
Laryngoplegia (*see also* Paralysis, vocal cord) 478.30
Laryngoptosis 478.79
Laryngospasm 478.75
    due to external agent—*see* Condition, respiratory, acute, due to
Laryngostenosis 478.74
    congenital 748.3
Laryngotracheitis (acute) (infectional) (viral) (*see also* Laryngitis) 464.20
    with obstruction 464.21
    atrophic 476.1
    Borrelia vincentii 101
    catarrhal 476.1
    chronic 476.1
        due to external agent—*see* Condition, respiratory, chronic, due to
    diphtheritic (membranous) 032.3
    due to external agent—*see* Inflammation, respiratory, upper, due to
    H. influenzae 464.20
        with obstruction 464.21
    hypertrophic 476.1
    influenzal 487.1
    pachydermic 478.75
    sicca 476.1
    spasmodic 478.75
        acute 464.20
            with obstruction 464.21

Laryngotracheitis—*continued*
  streptococcal 034.0
  stridulous 478.75
  syphilitic 095.8
    congenital 090.5
  tuberculous (*see also* Tuberculosis, larynx)
    012.3
  Vincent's 101
Laryngotracheobronchitis (*see also* Bronchitis)
  490
  acute 466.0
  chronic 491.8
  viral 466.0
Laryngotracheobronchopneumonitis —*see*
  Pneumonia, broncho-
Larynx, laryngeal —*see* condition
Lasègue's disease (persecution mania) 297.9
Lassa fever 078.89
Lassitude (*see also* Weakness) 780.7
Late —*see also* condition
  effect(s) (of)—*see also* condition
    abscess
      intracranial or intraspinal (conditions
        classifiable to 324)–*see* category 326
    adverse effect of drug, medicinal or biological
      substance 909.5
    allergic reaction 909.9
    amputation
      postoperative (late) 997.60
      traumatic (injury classifiable to 885-887 and
        895-897) 905.9
    burn (injury classifiable to 948-949) 906.9
      extremities NEC (injury classifiable to 943
        or 945) 906.7
        hand or wrist (injury classifiable to 944)
          906.6
      eye (injury classifiable to 940) 906.5
      face, head, and neck (injury classifiable to
        941) 906.5
      specified site NEC (injury classifiable to
        942 and 946-947) 906.8
    cerebrovascular disease (conditions
      classifiable to 430-437)—*see* category 438
    childbirth complication(s) 677
    complication(s) of
      childbirth 677
      delivery 677
      pregnancy 677
      puerperium 677
      surgical and medical care (conditions
        classifiable to 996-999) 909.3
      trauma (conditions classifiable to 958) 908.6
    contusion (injury classifiable to 920-924)
      906.3
    crushing (injury classifiable to 925-929) 906.4
    delivery complication(s) 677
    dislocation (injury classifiable to 830-839)
      905.6
    encephalitis or encephalomyelitis (conditions
      classifiable to 323)—*see* category 326
      in infectious diseases 139.8
      viral (conditions classifiable to 049.8,
        049.9, 062-064) 139.0
    external cause NEC (conditions classifiable to
      995) 909.9
      certain conditions classifiable to categories
        991-994 909.4
    foreign body in orifice (injury classifiable to
      930-939) 908.5

Late —*continued*
  fracture (multiple) (injury classifiable to
    828-829) 905.5
    extremity
      lower (injury classifiable to 821-827)
        905.4
      neck of femur (injury classifiable to
        820) 905.3
      upper (injury classifiable to 810-819)
        905.2
    face and skull (injury classifiable to
      800-804) 905.0
    skull and face (injury classifiable to
      800-804) 905.0
    spine and trunk (injury classifiable to 805
      and 807-809) 905.1
      with spinal cord lesion (injury classifiable
        to 806) 907.2
  infection
    pyogenic, intracranial—*see* category 326
  infectious diseases (conditions classifiable to
    001-136) NEC 139.8
  injury (injury classifiable to 959) 908.9
    blood vessel 908.3
      abdomen and pelvis (injury classifiable to
        902) 908.4
      extremity (injury classifiable to 903-904)
        908.3
      head and neck (injury classifiable to 900)
        908.3
      intracranial (injury classifiable to
        850-854) 907.0
        with skull fracture 905.0
      thorax (injury classifiable to 901) 908.4
    internal organ NEC (injury classifiable to
      867 and 869) 908.2
      abdomen (injury classifiable to 863-866
        and 868) 908.1
      thorax (injury classifiable to 860-862)
        908.0
    intracranial (injury classifiable to 850-854)
      907.0
      with skull fracture (injury classifiable to
        800-801 and 803-804) 905.0
    nerve NEC (injury classifiable to 957) 907.9
      cranial (injury classifiable to 950-951)
        907.1
      peripheral NEC (injury classifiable to 957)
        907.9
        lower limb and pelvic girdle (injury
          classifiable to 956) 907.5
        upper limb and shoulder girdle (injury
          classifiable to 955) 907.4
      roots and plexus(es), spinal (injury
        classifiable to 953) 907.3
      trunk (injury classifiable to 954) 907.3
    pregnancy complication(s) 677
    puerperal complication(s) 677
    spinal
      cord (injury classifiable to 806 and 952)
        907.2
      nerve root(s) and plexus(es) (injury
        classifiable to 953) 907.3
    superficial (injury classifiable to 910-919)
      906.2
    tendon (tendon injury classifiable to
      840-848, 880-884 with .2, and 890-894
      with .2) 905.8

Late —*continued*
  meningitis
    bacterial (conditions classifiable to
      320)—*see* category 326
    unspecified cause (conditions classifiable to
      322)—*see* category 326
    myelitis (*see also* Late, effect(s) (of),
      encephalitis)—*see* category 326
    parasitic diseases (conditions classifiable to
      001-136 NEC) 139.8
    phlebitis or thrombophlebitis of intracranial
      venous sinuses (conditions classifiable to
      325)—*see* category 326
    poisoning due to drug, medicinal or biological
      substance (conditions classifiable to
      960-979) 909.0
    poliomyelitis, acute (conditions classifiable to
      045) 138
    radiation (conditions classifiable to 990) 909.2
    rickets 268.1
    sprain and strain without mention of tendon
      injury (injury classifiable to 840-848,
      except tendon injury) 905.7
      tendon involvement 905.8
    toxic effect of
      drug, medicinal or biological substance
        (conditions classifiable to 960-979)
        909.0
      nonmedical substance (conditions
        classifiable to 980-989) 909.1
    trachoma (conditions classifiable to 076) 139.1
    tuberculosis 137.0
      bones and joints (conditions classifiable to
        015) 137.3
      central nervous system (conditions
        classifiable to 013) 137.1
      genitourinary (conditions classifiable to
        016) 137.2
      pulmonary (conditions classifiable to
        010-012) 137.0
      specified organs NEC (conditions
        classifiable to 014, 017-018) 137.4
      viral encephalitis (conditions classifiable to
        049.8, 049.9, 062-064) 139.0
    wound, open
      extremity (injury classifiable to 880-884 and
        890-894, except .2) 906.1
      tendon (injury classifiable to 880-884 with
        .2 and 890-894 with .2) 905.8
      head, neck, and trunk (injury classifiable to
        870-879) 906.0
Latent —*see* condition
Lateral —*see* condition
Laterocession —*see* Lateroversion
Lateroflexion —*see* Lateroversion
Lateroversion
  cervix—*see* Lateroversion, uterus
  uterus, uterine (cervix) (postinfectional)
    (postpartal, old) 621.6
  congenital 752.3
  in pregnancy or childbirth 654.4
    affecting fetus or newborn 763.8
Lathyrism 988.2
Launois' syndrome (pituitary gigantism) 253.0
Launois-Bensaude's lipomatosis 272.8
Launois-Cléret syndrome (adiposogenital
  dystrophy) 253.8
Laurence-Moon-Biedl syndrome (obesity,
  polydactyly, and mental retardation) 759.89

LAV (disease) (illness) (infection)—*see* Human
  immunodeficiency virus (disease) (illness)
  (infection)
LAV/HTLV-III (disease) (illness)
  (infection)—*see* Human immunodeficiency
  virus (disease) (illness) (infection)
Lawford's syndrome (encephalocutaneous
  angiomatosis) 759.6
Lax, laxity —*see also* Relaxation
  ligament 728.4
  skin (acquired) 701.8
    congenital 756.83
Laxative habit (*see also* Abuse, drugs,
  nondependent) 305.9
Lazy leukocyte syndrome 288.0
Lead —*see also* condition
  exposure to V15.86
  incrustation of cornea 371.15
  poisoning 984.9
    specified type of lead—*see* Table of drugs and
      chemicals
Lead miner's lung 503
Leakage
  amniotic fluid 658.1
    with delayed delivery 658.2
    affecting fetus or newborn 761.1
  bile from drainage tube (T tube) 997.4
  blood (microscopic), fetal, into maternal
    circulation 656.0
    affecting management of pregnancy or
      puerperium 656.0
  device, implant, or graft—*see* Complications,
    mechanical
  spinal fluid at lumbar puncture site 997.09
  urine, continuous 788.37
Leaky heart —*see* Endocarditis
Learning defect, specific NEC
  (strephosymbolia) 315.2
Leather bottle stomach (M8142/3) 151.9
Leber's
  congenital amaurosis 362.76
  optic atrophy (hereditary) 377.16
Lederer's anemia or disease (acquired
  infectious hemolytic anemia) 283.19
Lederer-Brill syndrome (acquired infectious
  hemolytic anemia) 283.19
Leeches (aquatic) (land) 134.2
Left-sided neglect 781.8
Leg —*see* condition
Legal investigation V62.5
Legg (-Calvé) -Perthes disease or syndrome
  (osteochondrosis, femoral capital) 732.1
Legionnaires' disease 482.83
Leigh's disease 330.8
Leiner's disease (exfoliative dermatitis) 695.89
Leiofibromyoma (M8890/0)—*see also*
  Leiomyoma
  uterus (cervix) (corpus) (*see also* Leiomyoma,
    uterus) 218.9
Leiomyoblastoma (M8891/1)—*see* Neoplasm,
  connective tissue, uncertain behavior
Leiomyofibroma (M8890/0)—*see also*
  Neoplasm, connective tissue, benign
  uterus (cervix) (corpus) (*see also* Leiomyoma,
    uterus) 218.9
Leiomyoma (M8890/0)—*see* Neoplasm,
  connective tissue, benign
  bizarre (M8893/0)—*see* Neoplasm, connective
    tissue, benign

Leiomyoma—*continued*
cellular (M8892/1)—*see* Neoplasm, connective
    tissue, uncertain behavior
epithelioid (M8891/1)—*see* Neoplasm,
    connective tissue, uncertain behavior
prostate (polypoid) 600
uterus (cervix) (corpus) 218.9
    interstitial 218.1
    intramural 218.1
    submucous 218.0
    subperitoneal 218.2
    subserous 218.2
    vascular (M8894/0)—*see* Neoplasm,
        connective tissue, benign
Leiomyomatosis (intravascular) (M8890/1)—*see*
    Neoplasm, connective tissue, uncertain
    behavior
Leiomyosarcoma (M8890/3)—*see also*
    Neoplasm, connective tissue, malignant
epithelioid (M8891/3)—*see* Neoplasm,
    connective tissue, malignant
Leishmaniasis 085.9
American 085.5
    cutaneous 085.4
    mucocutaneous 085.5
Asian desert 085.2
Brazilian 085.5
cutaneous 085.9
    acute necrotizing 085.2
    American 085.4
    Asian desert 085.2
    diffuse 085.3
    dry form 085.1
    Ethiopian 085.3
    eyelid 085.5 [373.6]
    late 085.1
    lepromatous 085.3
    recurrent 085.1
    rural 085.2
    ulcerating 085.1
    urban 085.1
    wet form 085.2
    zoonotic form 085.2
dermal—*see also* Leishmaniasis, cutaneous
    post kala-azar 085.0
eyelid 085.5 [373.6]
infantile 085.0
Mediterranean 085.0
mucocutaneous (American) 085.5
naso-oral 085.5
nasopharyngeal 085.5
Old World 085.1
tegumentaria diffusa 085.4
vaccination, prophylactic (against) V05.2
visceral (Indian) 085.0
Leishmanoid, dermal —*see also* Leishmaniasis,
    cutaneous
post kala-azar 085.0
Leloir's disease 695.4
Lenegre's disease 426.0
Lengthening, leg 736.81
Lennox's syndrome (*see also* Epilepsy) 345.0
Lens —*see* condition
Lenticonus (anterior) (posterior) (congenital)
    743.36
Lenticular degeneration, progressive 275.1
Lentiglobus (posterior) (congenital) 743.36
Lentigo (congenital) 709.09
juvenile 709.09
Maligna (M8742/2)—*see also* Neoplasm, skin,
    in situ

Lentigo—*continued*
melanoma (M8742/3)—*see* Melanoma
senile 709.09
Leonine leprosy 030.0
Leontiasis
ossium 733.3
syphilitic 095.8
    congenital 090.5
Léopold-Lévi's syndrome (paroxysmal thyroid
    instability) 242.9
Lepore hemoglobin syndrome 282.4
Lepothrix 039.0
Lepra 030.9
Willan's 696.1
Leprechaunism 259.8
Lepromatous leprosy 030.0
Leprosy 030.9
anesthetic 030.1
beriberi 030.1
borderline (group B) (infiltrated) (neuritic) 030.3
cornea (*see also* Leprosy, by type) 030.9
    [371.89]
dimorphous (group B) (infiltrated)
    (lepromatous) (neuritic) (tuberculoid) 030.3
eyelid 030.0 [373.4]
indeterminate (group I) (macular) (neuritic)
    (uncharacteristic) 030.2
leonine 030.0
lepromatous (diffuse) (infiltrated) (macular)
    (neuritic) (nodular) (type L) 030.0
macular (early) (neuritic) (simple) 030.2
maculoanesthetic 030.1
mixed 030.0
neuro 030.1
nodular 030.0
primary neuritic 030.3
specified type or group NEC 030.8
tubercular 030.1
tuberculoid (macular) (maculoanesthetic)
    (major) (minor) (neuritic) (type T) 030.1
Leptocytosis, hereditary 282.4
Leptomeningitis (chronic) (circumscribed)
    (hemorrhagic) (nonsuppurative) (*see also*
    Meningitis) 322.9
aseptic 047.9
    adenovirus 049.1
    Coxsackie virus 047.0
    ECHO virus 047.1
    enterovirus 047.9
    lymphocytic choriomeningitis 049.0
epidemic 036.0
late effect—*see* category 326
meningococcal 036.0
pneumococcal 320.1
syphilitic 094.2
tuberculous (*see also* Tuberculosis, meninges)
    013.0
Leptomeningopathy (*see also* Meningitis) 322.9
Leptospiral —*see* condition
Leptospirochetal —*see* condition
Leptospirosis 100.9
autumnalis 100.89
canicula 100.89
grippotyphosa 100.89
hebdomidis 100.89
icterohemorrhagica 100.0
nanukayami 100.89
pomona 100.89
Weil's disease 100.0
Leptothricosis —*see* Actinomycosis
Leptothrix infestation —*see* Actinomycosis
Leptotricosis —*see* Actinomycosis

Leptus dermatitis 133.8
Léri's pleonosteosis 756.89
Léri-Weill syndrome 756.59
Leriche syndrome (aortic bifurcation occlusion) 444.0
Lermoyez's syndrome (*see also* Disease, Ménière's) 386.00
Lesbianism —*omit code*
  egodystonic 302.0
  problems with 302.0
Lesch-Nyhan syndrome (hypoxanthine-guanine-phosphoribosyltransferase deficiency) 277.2
Lesion
  abducens nerve 378.54
  alveolar process 525.8
  anorectal 569.49
  aortic (valve)—*see* Endocarditis, aortic
  auditory nerve 388.5
  basal ganglion 333.90
  bile duct (*see also* Disease, biliary) 576.8
  bladder 596.9
  bone 733.90
  brachial plexus 353.0
  brain 348.8
    congenital 742.9
    vascular (*see also* Lesion, cerebrovascular) 437.9
      degenerative 437.1
      healed or old—*see also* category 438
        without residuals V12.59
      hypertensive 437.2
      late effect—*see* category 438
  buccal 528.9
  calcified—*see* Calcification
  canthus 373.9
  carate—*see* Pinta, lesions
  cardia 537.89
  cardiac—*see also* Disease, heart congenital 746.9
    valvular—*see* Endocarditis
  cauda equina 344.60
    with neurogenic bladder 344.61
  cecum 569.89
  cerebral—*see* Lesion, brain
  cerebrovascular (*see also* Disease, cerebrovascular NEC) 437.9
    degenerative 437.1
    healed or old—*see also* category 438
      without residuals V12.59
    hypertensive 437.2
    late effect—*see* category 438
    specified type NEC 437.8
  cervical root (nerve) NEC 353.2
  chiasmal 377.54
    associated with
      inflammatory disorders 377.54
      neoplasm NEC 377.52
      pituitary 377.51
      pituitary disorders 377.51
      vascular disorders 377.53
  chorda tympani 351.8
  coin, lung 793.1
  colon 569.89
  congenital—*see* Anomaly
  conjunctiva 372.9
  coronary artery (*see also* Ischemia, heart) 414.9
  cranial nerve 352.9
    first 352.0
    second 377.49
    third
      partial 378.51

Lesion—*continued*
  total 378.52
  fourth 378.53
  fifth 350.9
  sixth 378.54
  seventh 351.9
  eighth 388.5
  ninth 352.2
  tenth 352.3
  eleventh 352.4
  twelfth 352.5
  cystic—*see* Cyst
  degenerative—*see* Degeneration
  dermal (skin) 709.9
  duodenum 537.89
    with obstruction 537.3
  eyelid 373.9
  gasserian ganglion 350.8
  gastric 537.89
  gastroduodenal 537.89
  gastrointestinal 569.89
  glossopharyngeal nerve 352.2
  heart (organic)—*see also* Disease, heart
    vascular—*see* Disease, cardiovascular
  helix (ear) 709.9
  hyperchromic, due to pinta (carate) 103.1
  hyperkeratotic (*see also* Hyperkeratosis) 701.1
  hypoglossal nerve 352.5
  hypopharynx 478.29
  hypothalamic 253.9
  ileocecal coil 569.89
  ileum 569.89
  iliohypogastric nerve 355.79
  ilioinguinal nerve 355.79
  in continuity—*see* Injury, nerve, by site
  inflammatory—*see* Inflammation
  intestine 569.89
  intracerebral—*see* Lesion, brain
  intrachiasmal (optic) (*see also* Lesion, chiasmal) 377.54
  intracranial, space-occupying NEC 784.2
  joint 719.90
    ankle 719.97
    elbow 719.92
    foot 719.97
    hand 719.94
    hip 719.95
    knee 719.96
    multiple sites 719.99
    pelvic region 719.95
    sacroiliac (old) 724.6
    shoulder (region) 719.91
    specified site NEC 719.98
    wrist 719.93
  keratotic (*see also* Keratosis) 701.1
  kidney (*see also* Disease, renal) 593.9
  laryngeal nerve (recurrent) 352.3
  leonine 030.0
  lip 528.5
  liver 573.8
  lumbosacral
    plexus 353.1
    root (nerve) NEC 353.4
  lung 518.89
    coin 793.1
  maxillary sinus 473.0
  mitral—*see* Endocarditis, mitral
  motor cortex 348.8
  nerve (*see also* Disorder, nerve) 355.9
  nervous system 349.9
    congenital 742.9

Lesion—*continued*
  nonallopathic NEC 739.9
    in region (of)
      abdomen 739.9
      acromioclavicular 739.7
      cervical, cervicothoracic 739.1
      costochondral 739.8
      costovertebral 739.8
      extremity
        lower 739.6
        upper 739.7
      head 739.0
      hip 739.5
      lower extremity 739.6
      lumbar, lumbosacral 739.3
      occipitocervical 739.0
      pelvic 739.5
      pubic 739.5
      rib cage 739.8
      sacral, sacrococcygeal, sacroiliac 739.4
      sternochondral 739.8
      sternoclavicular 739.7
      thoracic, thoracolumbar 739.2
      upper extremity 739.7
  nose (internal) 478.1
  obstructive—*see* Obstruction
  obturator nerve 355.79
  occlusive
    artery—*see* Embolism, artery
  organ or site NEC—*see* Disease, by site
  osteolytic 733.90
  paramacular, of retina 363.32
  peptic 537.89
  periodontal, due to traumatic occlusion 523.8
  perirectal 569.49
  peritoneum (granulomatous) 568.89
  pigmented (skin) 709.00
  pinta—*see* Pinta, lesions
  polypoid—*see* Polyp
  prechiasmal (optic) (*see also* Lesion, chiasmal)
    377.54
  primary—*see also* Syphilis, primary
    carate 103.0
    pinta 103.0
    yaws 102.0
  pulmonary 518.89
    valve (*see also* Endocarditis, pulmonary) 424.3
  pylorus 537.89
  radiation NEC 990
  radium NEC 990
  rectosigmoid 569.89
  retina, retinal—*see also* Retinopathy
    vascular 362.17
  retroperitoneal 568.89
  romanus 720.1
  sacroiliac (joint) 724.6
  salivary gland 527.8
    benign lymphoepithelial 527.8
  saphenous nerve 355.79
  secondary—*see* Syphilis, secondary
  sigmoid 569.89
  sinus (accessory) (nasal) (*see also* Sinusitis)
    473.9
  skin 709.9
    suppurative 686.0
  space-occupying, intracranial NEC 784.2
  spinal cord 336.9
    congenital 742.9
    traumatic (complete) (incomplete)
      (transverse)—*see also* Injury, spinal, by
      site

Lesion—*continued*
  with
    broken
      back—*see* Fracture, vertebra, by site,
        with spinal cord injury
      neck—*see* Fracture, vertebra, cervical,
        with spinal cord injury
    fracture, vertebra—*see* Fracture, vertebra,
      by site, with spinal cord injury
  spleen 289.50
  stomach 537.89
  syphilitic—*see* Syphilis
  tertiary—*see* Syphilis, tertiary
  thoracic root (nerve) 353.3
  tonsillar fossa 474.9
  tooth, teeth 525.8
    white spot 521.0
  traumatic NEC (*see also* nature and site of
    injury) 959.9
  tricuspid (valve)—*see* Endocarditis, tricuspid
  trigeminal nerve 350.9
  ulcerated or ulcerative—*see* Ulcer
  uterus NEC 621.9
  vagus nerve 352.3
  valvular—*see* Endocarditis
  vascular 459.9
    affecting central nervous system (*see also*
      Lesion, cerebrovascular) 437.9
    following trauma (*see also* Injury, blood
      vessel, by site) 904.9
    retina 362.17
    traumatic—*see* Injury, blood vessel, by site
    umbilical cord 663.6
      affecting fetus or newborn 762.6
  visual
    cortex NEC (*see also* Disorder, visual, cortex)
      377.73
    pathway NEC (*see also* Disorder, visual,
      pathway) 377.63
  warty—*see* Verruca
  white spot, on teeth 521.0
  x-ray NEC 990
Lethargic —*see* condition
Lethargy 780.7
Letterer-Siwe disease (acute histiocytosis X)
  (M9722/3) 202.5
Leucinosis 270.3
Leucocoria 360.44
Leucosarcoma (M9850/3) 207.8
Leukasmus 270.2
Leukemia, leukemic (congenital) (M9800/3)
  208.9

> Note—Use the following fifth-digit
> subclassification for categories 203-208:
>
> *0 without mention of remission*
> *1 with remission*

  acute NEC (M9801/3) 208.0
  aleukemic NEC (M9804/3) 208.8
    granulocytic (M9864/3) 205.8
  basophilic (M9870/3) 205.1
  blast (cell) (M9801/3) 208.0
  blastic (M9801/3) 208.0
    granulocytic (M9861/3) 205.0
  chronic NEC (M9803/3) 208.1
  compound (M9810/3) 207.8
  eosinophilic (M9880/3) 205.1
  giant cell (M9910/3) 207.2
  granulocytic (M9860/3) 205.9
    acute (M9861/3) 205.0

Leukemia, leukemic— *continued*
  aleukemic (M9864/3) 205.8
  blastic (M9861/3) 205.0
  chronic (M9863/3) 205.1
  subacute (M9862/3) 205.2
  subleukemic (M9864/3) 205.8
  hairy cell (M9940/3) 202.4
  hemoblastic (M9801/3) 208.0
  histiocytic (M9890/3) 206.9
  lymphatic (M9820/3) 204.9
    acute (M9821/3) 204.0
    aleukemic (M9824/3) 204.8
    chronic (M9823/3) 204.1
    subacute (M9822/3) 204.2
    subleukemic (M9824/3) 204.8
  lymphoblastic (M9821/3) 204.0
  lymphocytic (M9820/3) 204.9
    acute (M9821/3) 204.0
    aleukemic (M9824/3) 204.8
    chronic (M9823/3) 204.1
    subacute (M9822/3) 204.2
    subleukemic (M9824/3) 204.8
  lymphogenous (M9820/3)—*see* Leukemia,
    lymphoid
  lymphoid (M9820/3) 204.9
    acute (M9821/3) 204.0
    aleukemic (M9824/3) 204.8
    blastic (M9821/3) 204.0
    chronic (M9823/3) 204.1
    subacute (M9822/3) 204.2
    subleukemic (M9824/3) 204.8
  lymphosarcoma cell (M9850/3) 207.8
  mast cell (M9900/3) 207.8
  megakaryocytic (M9910/3) 207.2
  megakaryocytoid (M9910/3) 207.2
  mixed (cell) (M9810/3) 207.8
  monoblastic (M9891/3) 206.0
  monocytic (Schilling-type) (M9890/3) 206.9
    acute (M9891/3) 206.0
    aleukemic (M9894/3) 206.8
    chronic (M9893/3) 206.1
    Naegeli-type (M9863/3) 205.1
    subacute (M9892/3) 206.2
    subleukemic (M9894/3) 206.8
  monocytoid (M9890/3) 206.9
    acute (M9891/3) 206.0
    aleukemic (M9894/3) 206.8
    chronic (M9893/3) 206.1
    myelogenous (M9863/3) 205.1
    subacute (M9892/3) 206.2
    subleukemic (M9894/3) 206.8
  monomyelocytic (M9860/3)—*see* Leukemia,
    myelomonocytic
  myeloblastic (M9861/3) 205.0
  myelocytic (M9863/3) 205.1
    acute (M9861/3) 205.0
  myelogenous (M9860/3) 205.9
    acute (M9861/3) 205.0
    aleukemic (M9864/3) 205.8
    chronic (M9863/3) 205.1
    monocytoid (M9863/3) 205.1
    subacute (M9862/3) 205.2
    subleukemic (M9864) 205.8
  myeloid (M9860/3) 205.9
    acute (M9861/3) 205.0
    aleukemic (M9864/3) 205.8
    chronic (M9863/3) 205.1
    subacute (M9862/3) 205.2
    subleukemic (M9864/3) 205.8
  myelomonocytic (M9860/3) 205.9
    acute (M9861/3) 205.0

Leukemia, leukemic— *continued*
  chronic (M9863/3) 205.1
  Naegeli-type monocytic (M9863/3) 205.1
  neutrophilic (M9865/3) 205.1
  plasma cell (M9830/3) 203.1
  plasmacytic (M9830/3) 203.1
  prolymphocytic (M9825/3)—*see* Leukemia,
    lymphoid
  promyelocytic, acute (M9866/3) 205.0
  Schilling-type monocytic (M9890/3)—*see*
    Leukemia, monocytic
  stem cell (M9801/3) 208.0
  subacute NEC (M9802/3) 208.2
  subleukemic NEC (M9804/3) 208.8
  thrombocytic (M9910/3) 207.2
  undifferentiated (M9801/3) 208.0
Leukemoid reaction (lymphocytic) (monocytic)
  (myelocytic) 288.8
Leukocoria 360.44
Leukocythemia —*see* Leukemia
Leukocytosis 288.8
  basophilic 288.8
  eosinophilic 288.3
  lymphocytic 288.8
  monocytic 288.8
  neutrophilic 288.8
Leukoderma 709.09
  syphilitic 091.3
    late 095.8
Leukodermia (*see also* Leukoderma) 709.09
Leukodystrophy (cerebral) (globoid cell)
  (metachromatic) (progressive) (sudanophilic)
  330.0
Leukoedema, mouth or tongue 528.7
Leukoencephalitis
  acute hemorrhagic (postinfectious) NEC 136.9
    [323.6]
    postimmunization or postvaccinal 323.5
  subacute sclerosing 046.2
    van Bogaert's 046.2
  van Bogaert's (sclerosing) 046.2
Leukoencephalopathy (*see also* Encephalitis)
  323.9
  acute necrotizing hemorrhagic (postinfectious)
    136.9 *[323.6]*
    postimmunization or postvaccinal 323.5
  metachromatic 330.0
  multifocal (progressive) 046.3
  progressive multifocal 046.3
Leukoerythroblastosis 289.0
Leukoerythrosis 289.0
Leukokeratosis (*see also* Leukoplakia) 702.8
  mouth 528.6
  nicotina palati 528.7
  tongue 528.6
Leukokoria 360.44
Leukokoraurosis vulva, vulvae 624.0
Leukolymphosarcoma (M9850/3) 207.8
Leukoma (cornea) (interfering with central
  vision) 371.03
  adherent 371.04
Leukomelanopathy, hereditary 288.2
Leukonychia (punctata) (striata) 703.8
  congenital 757.5
Leukopathia
  unguium 703.8
    congenital 757.5
Leukopenia 288.0
  cyclic 288.0
  familial 288.0
  malignant 288.0

Leukopenia—*continued*
  periodic 288.0
  transitory neonatal 776.7
Leukopenic —*see* condition
Leukoplakia 702.8
  anus 569.49
  bladder (postinfectional) 596.8
  buccal 528.6
  cervix (uteri) 622.2
  esophagus 530.83
  gingiva 528.6
  kidney (pelvis) 593.89
  larynx 478.79
  lip 528.6
  mouth 528.6
  oral soft tissue (including tongue) (mucosa)
    528.6
  palate 528.6
  pelvis (kidney) 593.89
  penis (infectional) 607.0
  rectum 569.49
  syphilitic 095.8
  tongue 528.6
  tonsil 478.29
  ureter (postinfectional) 593.89
  urethra (postinfectional) 599.84
  uterus 621.8
  vagina 623.1
  vesical 596.8
  vocal cords 478.5
  vulva 624.0
Leukopolioencephalopathy 330.0
Leukorrhea (vagina) 623.5
  due to trichomonas (vaginalis) 131.00
  trichomonal (Trichomonas vaginalis) 131.00
Leukosarcoma (M9850/3) 207.8
Leukosis (M9800/3)—*see* Leukemia
Lev's disease or syndrome (acquired complete
  heart block) 426.0
Levi's syndrome (pituitary dwarfism) 253.3
Levocardia (isolated) 746.87
  with situs inversus 759.3
Levulosuria 271.2
Lewandowski's disease (primary) (*see also*
  Tuberculosis) 017.0
Lewandowski-Lutz disease (epidermodysplasia
  verruciformis) 078.19
Leyden's disease (periodic vomiting) 536.2
Leyden's-Möbius dystrophy 359.1
Leydig cell
  carcinoma (M8650/3)
    specified site—*see* Neoplasm, by site,
      malignant
    unspecified site
      female 183.0
      male 186.9
  tumor (M8650/1)
    benign (M8650/0)
      specified site—*see* Neoplasm, by site,
        benign
      unspecified site
        female 220
        male 222.0
    malignant (M8650/3)
      specified site—*see* Neoplasm, by site,
        malignant
      unspecified site
        female 183.0
        male 186.9
    specified site—*see* Neoplasm, by site,
      uncertain behavior

Leydig cell—*continued*
  unspecified site
    female 236.2
    male 236.4
Leydig-Sertoli cell tumor (M8631/0)
  specified site—*see* Neoplasm, by site, benign
  unspecified site
    female 220
    male 222.0
Liar, pathologic 301.7
Libman-Sacks disease or syndrome 710.0
  [424.91]
Lice (infestation) 132.9
  body (pediculus corporis) 132.1
  crab 132.2
  head (pediculus capitis) 132.0
  mixed (classifiable to more than one of the
    categories 132.0-132.2) 132.3
  pubic (pediculus pubis) 132.2
Lichen 697.9
  albus 701.0
  annularis 695.89
  atrophicus 701.0
  corneus obtusus 698.3
  myxedematous 701.8
  nitidus 697.1
  pilaris 757.39
    acquired 701.1
  planopilaris 697.0
  planus (acute) (chronicus) (hypertrophic)
    (verrucous) 697.0
    morphoeicus 701.0
    sclerosus (et atrophicus) 701.0
  ruber 696.4
    acuminatus 696.4
    moniliformis 697.8
    obtusus corneus 698.3
    of Wilson 697.0
    planus 697.0
  sclerosus (et atrophicus) 701.0
  scrofulosus (primary) (*see also* Tuberculosis)
    017.0
  simplex (Vidal's) 698.3
    chronicus 698.3
    circumscriptus 698.3
  spinulosus 757.39
    mycotic 117.9
  striata 697.8
  urticatus 698.2
Lichenification 698.3
  nodular 698.3
Lichenoides tuberculosis (primary) (*see also*
  Tuberculosis) 017.0
Lichtheim's disease or syndrome (subacute
  combined sclerosis with pernicious anemia)
  281.0 *[336.2]*
Lien migrans 289.59
Lientery (*see also* Diarrhea) 558.9
  infectious 009.2
Life circumstance problem NEC V62.89
Ligament —*see* condition
Light-for-dates (infant) 764.0
  with signs of fetal malnutrition 764.1
  affecting management of pregnancy 656.5
Light-headedness 780.4
Lightning (effects) (shock) (stroke) (struck by)
  994.0
  burn—*see* Burn, by site
  foot 266.2
Lightwood's disease or syndrome (renal tubular
  acidosis) 588.8
Lignac's disease (cystinosis) 270.0

Lignac (-de Toni) (-Fanconi) (-Debré) syndrome (cystinosis) 270.0
Lignac (-Fanconi) syndrome (cystinosis) 270.0
Ligneous thyroiditis 245.3
Likoff's syndrome (angina in menopausal women) 413.9
Limb —*see* condition
Limitation of joint motion (*see also* Stiffness, joint) 719.5
  sacroiliac 724.6
Limit dextrinosis 271.0
Limited
  cardiac reserve—*see* Disease, heart
  duction, eye NEC 378.63
Lindau's disease (retinocerebral angiomatosis) 759.6
Lindau (-von Hippel) disease (angiomatosis retinocerebellosa) 759.6
Linea corneae senilis 371.41
Lines
  Beau's (transverse furrows on fingernails) 703.8
  Harris' 733.91
  Hudson-Stähli 371.11
  Stähli's 371.11
Lingua
  geographical 529.1
  nigra (villosa) 529.3
  plicata 529.5
    congenital 750.13
  tylosis 528.6
Lingual (tongue)—*see also* condition
  thyroid 759.2
Linitis (gastric) 535.4
  plastica (M8142/3) 151.9
Lioderma essentialis (cum melanosis et telangiectasia) 757.33
Lip —*see also* condition
  biting 528.9
Lipalgia 272.8
Lipedema —*see* Edema
Lipemia (*see also* Hyperlipidemia) 272.4
  retina, retinalis 272.3
Lipidosis 272.7
  cephalin 272.7
  cerebral (infantile) (juvenile) (late) 330.1
  cerebroretinal 330.1 *[362.71]*
  cerebroside 272.7
  cerebrospinal 272.7
  chemically-induced 272.7
  cholesterol 272.7
  diabetic 250.8 *[272.7]*
  dystopic (hereditary) 272.7
  glycolipid 272.7
  hepatosplenomegalic 272.3
  hereditary, dystopic 272.7
  sulfatide 330.0
Lipoadenoma (M8324/0)—*see* Neoplasm, by site, benign
Lipoblastoma (M8881/0)—*see* Lipoma, by site
Lipoblastomatosis (M8881/0)—*see* Lipoma, by site
Llpochondrodystrophy 277.5
Lipochrome histiocytosis (familial) 288.1
Lipodystrophia progressiva 272.6
Lipodystrophy (progressive) 272.6
  insulin 272.6
  intestinal 040.2
Lipofibroma (M8851/0)—*see* Lipoma, by site
Lipoglycoproteinosis 272.8
Lipogranuloma, sclerosing 709.8
Lipogranulomatosis (disseminated) 272.8
  kidney 272.8

Lipoid —*see* condition
  histiocytosis 272.7
  essential 272.7
  nephrosis (*see also* Nephrosis) 581.3
  proteinosis of Urbach 272.8
Lipoidemia (*see also* Hyperlipidemia) 272.4
Lipoidosis (*see also* Lipidosis) 272.7
Lipoma (M8850/0) 214.9
  breast (skin) 214.1
  face 214.0
  fetal (M8881/0)—*see also* Lipoma, by site
    fat cell (M8880/0)—*see* Lipoma, by site
  infiltrating (M8856/0)—*see* Lipoma, by site
  intra-abdominal 214.3
  intramuscular (M8856/0)—*see* Lipoma, by site
  intrathoracic 214.2
  kidney 214.3
  mediastinum 214.2
  muscle 214.8
  peritoneum 214.3
  retroperitoneum 214.3
  skin 214.1
    face 214.0
  spermatic cord 214.4
  spindle cell (M8857/0)—*see* Lipoma, by site
  stomach 214.3
  subcutaneous tissue 214.1
    face 214.0
  thymus 214.2
  thyroid gland 214.2
Lipomatosis (dolorosa) 272.8
  fetal (M8881/0)—*see* Lipoma, by site
  Launois-Bensaude's 272.8
Lipomyohemangioma (M8860/0)
  specified site—*see* Neoplasm, connective tissue, benign
  unspecified site 223.0
Lipomyoma (M8860/0)
  specified site—*see* Neoplasm, connective tissue, benign
  unspecified site 223.0
Lipomyxoma (M8852/0)—*see* Lipoma, by site
Lipomyxosarcoma (M8852/3)—*see* Neoplasm, connective tissue, malignant
Lipophagocytosis 289.8
Lipoproteinemia (alpha) 272.4
  broad-beta 272.2
  floating-beta 272.2
  hyper-pre-beta 272.1
Lipoproteinosis (Rössle-Urbach-Wiethe) 272.8
Liposarcoma (M8850/3)—*see also* Neoplasm, connective tissue, malignant
  differentiated type (M8851/3)—*see* Neoplasm, connective tissue, malignant
  embryonal (M8852/3)—*see* Neoplasm, connective tissue, malignant
  mixed type (M8855/3)—*see* Neoplasm, connective tissue, malignant
  myxoid (M8852/3)—*see* Neoplasm, connective tissue, malignant
  pleomorphic (M8854/3)—*see* Neoplasm, connective tissue, malignant
  round cell (M8853/3)—*see* Neoplasm, connective tissue, malignant
  well differentiated type (M8851/3)—*see* Neoplasm, connective tissue, malignant
Liposynovitis prepatellaris 272.8
Lipping
  cervix 622.0
  spine (*see also* Spondylosis) 721.90
  vertebra (*see also* Spondylosis) 721.90
Lip pits (mucus), congenital 750.25

Lordosis—*continued*
　postlaminectomy 737.21
　postsurgical NEC 737.22
　rachitic 268.1 *[737.42]*
　specified NEC 737.29
　tuberculous (*see also* Tuberculosis) 015.0
　　[737.42]
Loss
　appetite 783.0
　　hysterical 300.11
　　nonorganic origin 307.59
　　psychogenic 307.59
　blood—*see* Hemorrhage
　central vision 368.41
　consciousness 780.09
　　transient 780.2
　control, sphincter, rectum 787.6
　　nonorganic origin 307.7
　ear ossicle, partial 385.24
　elasticity, skin 782.8
　extremity or member, traumatic, current—*see*
　　Amputation, traumatic
　fluid (acute) 276.5
　　with
　　　hypernatremia 276.0
　　　hyponatremia 276.1
　　fetus or newborn 775.5
　hair 704.00
　hearing—*see also* Deafness
　　central 389.14
　　conductive (air) 389.00
　　　with sensorineural hearing loss 389.2
　　　combined types 389.08
　　　external ear 389.01
　　　inner ear 389.04
　　　middle ear 389.03
　　　multiple types 389.08
　　　tympanic membrane 389.02
　　mixed type 389.2
　　nerve 389.12
　　neural 389.12
　　noise-induced 388.12
　　perceptive NEC (*see also* Loss, hearing,
　　　sensorineural) 389.10
　　sensorineural 389.10
　　　with conductive hearing loss 389.2
　　　central 389.14
　　　combined types 389.18
　　　multiple types 389.18
　　　neural 389.12
　　　sensory 389.11
　　sensory 389.11
　　specified type NEC 389.8
　　sudden NEC 388.2
　labyrinthine reactivity (unilateral) 386.55
　　bilateral 386.56
　memory (*see also* Amnesia) 780.9
　　mild, following organic brain damage 310.1
　mind (*see also* Psychosis) 298.9
　organ or part—*see* Absence, by site, acquired
　sensation 782.0
　sense of
　　smell (*see also* Disturbance, sensation) 781.1
　　taste (*see also* Disturbance, sensation) 781.1
　　touch (*see also* Disturbance, sensation) 781.1
　sight (acquired) (complete) (congenital)—*see*
　　Blindness
　spinal fluid
　　headache 349.0
　substance of
　　bone (*see also* Osteoporosis) 733.00

Loss —*continued*
　cartilage 733.99
　ear 380.32
　vitreous (humor) 379.26
　tooth, teeth, due to accident, extraction, or local
　　periodontal disease 525.1
　vision, visual (*see also* Blindness) 369.9
　　both eyes (*see also* Blindness, both eyes) 369.3
　　complete (*see also* Blindness, both eyes)
　　　369.00
　　one eye 369.8
　　sudden 368.11
　　transient 368.12
　vitreous 379.26
　voice (*see also* Aphonia) 784.41
　weight (cause unknown) 783.2
Louis-Bar syndrome (ataxia-telangiectasia)
　334.8
Louping ill 063.1
Lousiness —*see* Lice
Low
　back syndrome 724.2
　basal metabolic rate (BMR) 794.7
　birthweight 765.1
　　extreme (less than 1000 grams) 765.0
　　for gestational age 764.0
　bladder compliance 596.52
　blood pressure (*see also* Hypotension) 458.9
　　reading (incidental) (isolated) (nonspecific)
　　　796.3
　cardiac reserve—*see* Disease, heart
　compliance bladder 596.52
　frequency deafness—*see* Disorder, hearing
　function—*see also* Hypofunction
　　kidney (*see also* Disease, renal) 593.9
　　liver 573.9
　hemoglobin 285.9
　implantation, placenta—*see* Placenta, previa
　insertion, placenta—*see* Placenta, previa
　lying
　　kidney 593.0
　　organ or site, congenital—*see* Malposition,
　　　congenital
　　placenta—*see* Placenta, previa
　output syndrome (cardiac) (*see also* Failure,
　　heart) 428.9
　platelets (blood) (*see also* Thrombocytopenia)
　　287.5
　reserve, kidney (*see also* Disease, renal) 593.9
　salt syndrome 593.9
　tension glaucoma 365.12
　vision 369.9
　　both eyes 369.20
　　one eye 369.70
Lowe (-Terrey-MacLachlan) syndrome
　(oculocerebrorenal dystrophy) 270.8
Lower extremity —*see* condition
Lown (-Ganong)-Levine syndrome (short P-R
　interval, normal QRS complex, and
　paroxysmal supraventricular tachycardia)
　426.81
LSD reaction (*see also* Abuse, drugs,
　nondependent) 305.3
L-shaped kidney 753.3
Lucas-Championnière disease (fibrinous
　bronchitis) 466.0
Lucey-Driscoll syndrome (jaundice due to
　delayed conjugation) 774.30
Ludwig's
　angina 528.3
　disease (submaxillary cellulitis) 528.3
Lues (venerea), luetic—*see* Syphilis

Luetscher's syndrome (dehydration) 276.5
Lumbago 724.2
  due to displacement, intervertebral disc 722.10
Lumbalgia 724.2
  due to displacement, intervertebral disc 722.10
Lumbar —*see* condition
Lumbarization, vertebra 756.15
Lumbermen's itch 133.8
Lump —*see also* Mass
  abdominal 789.3
  breast 611.72
  chest 786.6
  epigastric 789.3
  head 784.2
  kidney 753.3
  liver 789.1
  lung 786.6
  mediastinal 786.6
  neck 784.2
  nose or sinus 784.2
  pelvic 789.3
  skin 782.2
  substernal 786.6
  throat 784.2
  umbilicus 789.3
Lunacy (*see also* Psychosis) 298.9
Lunatomalacia 732.3
Lung —*see also* condition
  donor V59.8
  drug addict's 417.8
  mainliners' 417.8
  vanishing 492.0
Lupoid (miliary) of Boeck 135
Lupus 710.0
  Cazenave's (erythematosus) 695.4
  discoid (local) 695.4
  disseminated 710.0
  erythematodes (discoid) (local) 695.4
  erythematosus (discoid) (local) 695.4
    disseminated 710.0
    eyelid 373.34
    systemic 710.0
      with lung involvement 710.0 *[517.8]*
      inhibitor (presence of) 286.5
  exedens 017.0
  eyelid (*see also* Tuberculosis) 017.0 *[373.4]*
  Hilliard's 017.0
  hydralazine
    correct substance properly administered 695.4
    overdose or wrong substance given or taken
      972.6
  miliaris disseminatus faciei 017.0
  nephritis 710.0 *[583.81]*
    acute 710.0 *[580.81]*
    chronic 710.0 *[582.81]*
  nontuberculous, not disseminated 695.4
  pernio (Besnier) 135
  tuberculous (*see also* Tuberculosis) 017.0
    eyelid (*see also* Tuberculosis) 017.0 *[373.4]*
  vulgaris 017.0
Luschka's joint disease 721.90
Luteinoma (M8610/0) 220
Lutembacher's disease or syndrome (atrial
  septal defect with mitral stenosis) 745.5
Luteoma (M8610/0) 220
Lutz-Miescher disease (elastosis perforans
  serpiginosa) 701.1
Lutz-Splendore-de Almeida disease (Brazilian
  blastomycosis) 116.1
Luxatio
  bulbi due to birth injury 767.8

Luxatio—*continued*
  coxae congenita (*see also* Dislocation, hip,
    congenital) 754.30
  erecta—*see* Dislocation, shoulder
  imperfecta—*see* Sprain, by site
  perinealis—*see* Dislocation, hip
Luxation —*see also* Dislocation, by site
  eyeball 360.81
    due to birth injury 767.8
    lateral 376.36
  genital organs (external) NEC—*see* Wound,
    open, genital organs
  globe (eye) 360.81
    lateral 376.36
  lacrimal gland (postinfectional) 375.16
  lens (old) (partial) 379.32
    congenital 743.37
      syphilitic 090.49 *[379.32]*
    Marfan's disease 090.49
    spontaneous 379.32
  penis—*see* Wound, open, penis
  scrotum—*see* Wound, open, scrotum
  testis—*see* Wound, open, testis
L-xyloketosuria 271.8
Lycanthropy (*see also* Psychosis) 298.9
Lyell's disease or syndrome (toxic epidermal
  necrolysis) 695.1
  due to drug
    correct substance properly administered 695.1
    overdose or wrong substance given or taken
      977.9
    specified drug—*see* Table of drugs and
      chemicals
Lyme disease 088.81
Lymph
  gland or node—*see* condition
  scrotum (*see also* Infestation, filarial) 125.9
Lymphadenitis 289.3
  with
    abortion—*see* Abortion, by type, with sepsis
    ectopic pregnancy (*see also* categories
      633.0-633.9) 639.0
    molar pregnancy (*see also* categories
      630-632) 639.0
  acute 683
    mesenteric 289.2
  any site, except mesenteric 289.3
    acute 683
    chronic 289.1
    mesenteric (acute) (chronic) (nonspecific)
      (subacute) 289.2
    subacute 289.1
      mesenteric 289.2
  breast, puerperal, postpartum 675.2
  chancroidal (congenital) 099.0
  chronic 289.1
    mesenteric 289.2
  dermatopathic 695.89
  due to
    anthracosis (occupational) 500
    Brugia (Wuchereria) malayi 125.1
    diphtheria (toxin) 032.89
    lymphogranuloma venereum 099.1
    Wuchereria bancrofti 125.0
  following
    abortion 639.0
    ectopic or molar pregnancy 639.0
  generalized 289.3
  gonorrheal 098.89
  granulomatous 289.1
  infectional 683

Lymphadenitis—*continued*
mesenteric (acute) (chronic) (nonspecific)
(subacute) 289.2
due to Bacillus typhi 002.0
tuberculous (*see also* Tuberculosis) 014.8
mycobacterial 031.8
purulent 683
pyogenic 683
regional 078.3
septic 683
streptococcal 683
subacute, unspecified site 289.1
suppurative 683
syphilitic (early) (secondary) 091.4
late 095.8
tuberculous—*see* Tuberculosis, lymph gland
venereal 099.1
Lymphadenoid goiter 245.2
Lymphadenopathy (general) 785.6
due to toxoplasmosis (acquired) 130.7
congenital (active) 771.2
Lymphadenopathy-associated virus (disease)
(illness) (infection)—*see* Human
Immunodeficiency virus (disease) (illness)
(infection)
Lymphadenosis 785.6
acute 075
Lymphangiectasis 457.1
conjunctiva 372.8
postinfectional 457.1
scrotum 457.1
Lymphangiectatic elephantiasis, nonfilarial
457.1
Lymphangioendothelioma (M9170/0) 228.1
malignant (M9170/3)—*see* Neoplasm,
connective tissue, malignant
Lymphangioma (M9170/0) 228.1
capillary (M9171/0) 228.1
cavernous (M9172/0) 228.1
cystic (M9173/0) 228.1
malignant (M9170/3)—*see* Neoplasm,
connective tissue, malignant
Lymphangiomyoma (M9174/0) 228.1
Lymphangiomyomatosis (M9174/1)—*see*
Neoplasm, connective tissue, uncertain
behavior
Lymphangiosarcoma (M9170/3)—*see*
Neoplasm, connective tissue, malignant
Lymphangitis 457.2
with
abortion—*see* Abortion, by type, with sepsis
abscess—*see* Abscess, by site
cellulitis—*see* Abscess, by site
ectopic pregnancy (*see also* categories
633.0-633.9) 639.0
molar pregnancy (*see also* categories
630-632) 639.0
acute (with abscess or cellulitis) 682.9
specified site—*see* Abscess, by site
breast, puerperal, postpartum 675.2
chancroidal 099.0
chronic (any site) 457.2
due to
Brugia (Wuchereria) malayi 125.1
Wuchereria bancrofti 125.0
following
abortion 639.0
ectopic or molar pregnancy 639.0
gangrenous 457.2
penis
acute 607.2

Lymphangitis—*continued*
gonococcal (acute) 098.0
chronic or duration of 2 months or more
098.2
puerperal, postpartum, childbirth 670
strumous, tuberculous (*see also* Tuberculosis)
017.2
subacute (any site) 457.2
tuberculous—*see* Tuberculosis, lymph gland
Lymphatic (vessel)—*see* condition
Lymphatism 254.8
scrofulous (*see also* Tuberculosis) 017.2
Lymphectasia 457.1
Lymphedema (*see also* Elephantiasis) 457.1
acquired (chronic) 457.1
chronic hereditary 757.0
congenital 757.0
idiopathic hereditary 757.0
praecox 457.1
secondary 457.1
surgical NEC 997.99
postmastectomy (syndrome) 457.0
Lymph-hemangioma (M9120/0)—*see*
Hemangioma, by site
Lymphoblastic —*see* condition
Lymphoblastoma (diffuse) (M9630/3) 200.1
giant follicular (M9690/3) 202.0
macrofollicular (M9690/3) 202.0
Lymphoblastosis, acute benign 075
Lymphocele 457.8
Lymphocythemia 288.8
Lymphocytic —*see also* condition
chorioencephalitis (acute) (serous) 049.0
choriomeningitis (acute) (serous) 049.0
Lymphocytoma (diffuse) (malignant) (M9620/3)
200.1
Lymphocytomatosis (M9620/3) 200.1
Lymphocytopenia 288.8
Lymphocytosis (symptomatic) 288.8
infectious (acute) 078.89
Lymphoepithelioma (M8082/3)—*see*
Neoplasm, by site, malignant
Lymphogranuloma (malignant) (M9650/3) 201.9
inguinale 099.1
venereal (any site) 099.1
with stricture of rectum 099.1
venereum 099.1
Lymphogranulomatosis (malignant) (M9650/3)
201.9
benign (Boeck's sarcoid) (Schaumann's) 135
Hodgkin's (M9650/3) 201.9
Lymphoid —*see* condition
Lympholeukoblastoma (M9850/3) 207.8
Lympholeukosarcoma (M9850/3) 207.8
Lymphoma (malignant) (M9590/3) 202.8

Note—Use the following fifth-digit
subclassification with categories 200-202:

0 *unspecified site*
1 *lymph nodes of head, face and neck*
2 *intrathoracic lymph nodes*
3 *intra-abdominal lymph nodes*
4 *lymph nodes of axilla and upper limb*
5 *lymph nodes of inguinal region and
lower limb*
6 *intrapelvic lymph nodes*
7 *spleen*
8 *lymph nodes of multiple sites*

benign (M9590/0)—*see* Neoplasm, by site,
benign

Lymphoma—*continued*
　Burkitt's type (lymphoblastic) (undifferentiated)
　　(M9750/3) 200.2
　Castleman's (mediastinal lymph node
　　hyperplasia) 785.6
　centroblastic-centrocytic
　　diffuse (M9614/3) 202.8
　　follicular (M9692/3) 202.0
　centroblastic type (diffuse) (M9632/3) 202.8
　　follicular (M9697/3) 202.0
　centrocytic (M9622/3) 202.8
　compound (M9613/3) 200.8
　convoluted cell type (lymphoblastic) (M9602/3)
　　202.8
　diffuse NEC (M9590/3) 202.8
　follicular (giant) (M9690/3) 202.0
　　center cell (diffuse) (M9615/3) 202.8
　　　cleaved (diffuse) (M9623/3) 202.8
　　　　follicular (M9695/3) 202.0
　　　non-cleaved (diffuse) (M9633/3) 202.8
　　　　follicular (M9698/3) 202.0
　　centroblastic-centrocytic (M9692/3) 202.0
　　centroblastic type (M9697/3) 202.0
　　lymphocytic
　　　intermediate differentiation (M9694/3) 202.0
　　　poorly differentiated (M9696/3) 202.0
　　　mixed (cell type) (lymphocytic-histiocytic)
　　　　(small cell and large cell) (M9691/3) 202.0
　germinocytic (M9622/3) 202.8
　giant, follicular or follicle (M9690/3) 202.0
　histiocytic (diffuse) (M9640/3) 200.0
　　nodular (M9642/3) 200.0
　　pleomorphic cell type (M9641/3) 200.0
　Hodgkin's (M9650/3) (*see also* Disease,
　　Hodgkin's) 201.9
　immunoblastic (type) (M9612/3) 200.8
　large cell (M9640/3) 200.0
　　nodular (M9642/3) 200.0
　　pleomorphic cell type (M9641/3) 200.0
　lymphoblastic (diffuse) (M9630/3) 200.1
　　Burkitt's type (M9750/3) 200.2
　　convoluted cell type (M9602/3) 202.8
　lymphocytic (cell type) (diffuse) (M9620/3)
　　200.1
　　with plasmacytoid differentiation, diffuse
　　　(M9611/3) 200.8
　　intermediate differentiation (diffuse)
　　　(M9621/3) 200.1
　　　follicular (M9694/3) 202.0
　　　nodular (M9694/3) 202.0
　　nodular (M9690/3) 202.0
　　poorly differentiated (diffuse) (M9630/3)
　　　200.1
　　　follicular (M9696/3) 202.0
　　　nodular (M9696/3) 202.0
　　well differentiated (diffuse) (M9620/3) 200.1
　　　follicular (M9693/3) 202.0
　　　nodular (M9693/3) 202.0
　lymphocytic-histiocytic, mixed (diffuse)
　　(M9613/3) 200.8
　　follicular (M9691/3) 202.0
　　nodular (M9691/3) 202.0
　lymphoplasmacytoid type (M9611/3) 200.8
　lymphosarcoma type (M9610/3) 200.1
　macrofollicular (M9690/3) 202.0
　mixed cell type (diffuse) (M9613/3) 200.8
　　follicular (M9691/3) 202.0
　　nodular (M9691/3) 202.0

Lymphoma—*continued*
　nodular (M9690/3) 202.0
　　histiocytic (M9642/3) 200.0
　　lymphocytic (M9690.3) 202.0
　　　intermediate differentiation (M9694/3) 202.0
　　　poorly differentiated (M9696/3) 202.0
　　mixed (cell type) (lymphocytic-histiocytic)
　　　(small cell and large cell) (M9691/3) 202.0
　non-Hodgkin's type NEC (M9591/3) 202.8
　reticulum cell (type) (M9640/3) 200.0
　small cell and large cell, mixed (diffuse)
　　(M9613/3) 200.8
　　follicular (M9691/3) 202.0
　　nodular (9691/3) 202.0
　stem cell (type) (M9601/3) 202.8
　undifferentiated (cell type) (non-Burkitt's)
　　(M9600/3) 202.8
　　Burkitt's type (M9750/3) 200.2
Lymphomatosis (M9590/3)—*see also*
　Lymphoma
　granulomatous 099.1
Lymphopathia
　venereum 099.1
　veneris 099.1
Lymphopenia 288.8
　familial 279.2
Lymphoreticulosis, benign (of inoculation)
　078.3
Lymphorrhea 457.8
Lymphosarcoma (M9610/3) 200.1
　diffuse (M9610/3) 200.1
　　with plasmacytoid differentiation (M9611/3)
　　　200.8
　　lymphoplasmacytic (M9611/3) 200.8
　follicular (giant) (M9690/3) 202.0
　　lymphoblastic (M9696/3) 202.0
　　lymphocytic, intermediate differentiation
　　　(M9694/3) 202.0
　　mixed cell type (M9691/3) 202.0
　giant follicular (M9690/3) 202.0
　Hodgkin's (M9650/3) 201.9
　immunoblastic (M9612/3) 200.8
　lymphoblastic (diffuse) (M9630/3) 200.1
　　follicular (M9696/3) 202.0
　　nodular (M9696/3) 202.0
　lymphocytic (diffuse) (M9620/3) 200.1
　　intermediate differentiation (diffuse)
　　　(M9621/3) 200.1
　　　follicular (M9694/3) 202.0
　　　nodular (M9694/3) 202.0
　mixed cell type (diffuse) (M9613/3) 200.8
　　follicular (M9691/3) 202.0
　　nodular (M9691/3) 202.0
　nodular (M9690/3) 202.0
　　lymphoblastic (M9696/3) 202.0
　　lymphocytic, intermediate differentiation
　　　(M9694/3) 202.0
　　mixed cell type (M9691/3) 202.0
　prolymphocytic (M9631/3) 200.1
　reticulum cell (M9640/3) 200.0
Lymphostasis 457.8
Lypemania (*see also* Melancholia) 296.2
Lyssa 071

M

Macacus ear 744.29
Maceration
  fetus (cause not stated) 779.9
  wet feet, tropical (syndrome) 991.4
Machupo virus hemorrhagic fever 078.7
Macleod's syndrome (abnormal transradiancy, one lung) 492.8
Macrocephalia, macrocephaly 756.0
Macrocheilia (congenital) 744.81
Macrochilia (congenital) 744.81
Macrocolon (congenital) 751.3
Macrocornea 743.41
  associated with buphthalmos 743.22
Macrocytic —*see* condition
Macrocytosis 289.8
Macrodactylia, macrodactylism (fingers) (thumbs) 755.57
  toes 755.65
Macrodontia 520.2
Macroencephaly 742.4
Macrogenia 524.05
Macrogenitosomia (female) (male) (praecox) 255.2
Macrogingivae 523.8
Macroglobulinemia (essential) (idiopathic) (monoclonal) (primary) (syndrome) (Waldenström's) 273.3
Macroglossia (congenital) 750.15
  acquired 529.8
Macrognathia, macrognathism (congenital) 524.00
  mandibular 524.02
    alveolar 524.72
  maxillary 524.01
    alveolar 524.71
Macrogyria (congenital) 742.4
Macrohydrocephalus (*see also* Hydrocephalus) 331.4
Macromastia (*see also* Hypertrophy, breast) 611.1
Macropsia 368.14
Macrosigmoid 564.7
  congenital 751.3
Macrospondylitis, acromegalic 253.0
Macrostomia (congenital) 744.83
Macrotia (external ear) (congenital) 744.22
Macula
  cornea, corneal
    congenital 743.43
      interfering with vision 743.42
    interfering with central vision 371.03
    not interfering with central vision 371.02
  degeneration (*see also* Degeneration, macula) 362.50
    hereditary (*see also* Dystrophy, retina) 362.70
  edema, cystoid 362.53
Maculae ceruleae 132.1
Macules and papules 709.8
Maculopathy, toxic 362.55
Madarosis 374.55
Madelung's
  deformity (radius) 755.54
  disease (lipomatosis) 272.8
  lipomatosis 272.8
Madness (*see also* Psychosis) 298.9
  myxedema (acute) 293.0
    subacute 293.1

Madura
  disease (actinomycotic) 039.9
    mycotic 117.4
  foot (actinomycotic) 039.4
    mycotic 117.4
Maduromycosis (actinomycotic) 039.9
  mycotic 117.4
Maffucci's syndrome (dyschondroplasia with hemangiomas) 756.4
Magenblase syndrome 306.4
Main en griffe (acquired) 736.06
  congenital 755.59
Maintenance
  chemotherapy regimen or treatment V58.1
  dialysis regimen or treatment
    extracorporeal (renal) V56.0
    peritoneal V56.8
    renal V56.0
  drug therapy or regimen V58.1
  external fixation NEC V54.8
  radiotherapy V58.0
  traction NEC V54.8
Majocchi's
  disease (purpura annularis telangiectodes) 709.1
  granuloma 110.6
Major —*see* condition
Mal
  cerebral (idiopathic) (*see also* Epilepsy) 345.9
  comital (*see also* Epilepsy) 345.9
  de los pintos (*see also* Pinta) 103.9
  de Meleda 757.39
  de mer 994.6
  lie—*see* Presentation, fetal
  perforant (*see also* Ulcer, lower extremity) 707.1
Malabar itch 110.9
  beard 110.0
  foot 110.4
  scalp 110.0
Malabsorption 579.9
  calcium 579.8
  carbohydrate 579.8
  disaccharide 271.3
  drug-induced 579.8
  due to bacterial overgrowth 579.8
  fat 579.8
  folate, congenital 281.2
  galactose 271.1
  glucose-galactose (congenital) 271.3
  intestinal 579.9
  isomaltose 271.3
  lactose (hereditary) 271.3
  methionine 270.4
  monosaccharide 271.8
  postgastrectomy 579.3
  postsurgical 579.3
  protein 579.8
  sucrose (-isomaltose) (congenital) 271.3
  syndrome 579.9
    postgastrectomy 579.3
    postsurgical 579.3
Malacia, bone 268.2
  juvenile (*see also* Rickets) 268.0
  Kienböck's (juvenile) (lunate) (wrist) 732.3
    adult 732.8

MNO

Malacoplakia
  bladder 596.8
  colon 569.89
  pelvis (kidney) 593.89
  ureter 593.89
  urethra 599.84
Malacosteon 268.2
  juvenile (*see also* Rickets) 268.0
Maladaptation —*see* Maladjustment
Maladie de Roger 745.4
Maladjustment
  conjugal V61.10
    involving divorce or estrangement V61.0
  educational V62.3
  family V61.9
    specified circumstance NEC V61.8
  marital V61.10
    involving divorce or estrangement V61.0
  occupational V62.2
  simple, adult (*see also* Reaction, adjustment)
    309.9
  situational acute (*see also* Reaction, adjustment)
    309.9
  social V62.4
Malaise 780.7
Malakoplakia —*see* Malacoplakia
Malaria, malarial (fever) 084.6
  algid 084.9
  any type, with
    algid malaria 084.9
    blackwater fever 084.8
    fever
      blackwater 084.8
      hemoglobinuric (bilious) 084.8
    hemoglobinuria, malarial 084.8
    hepatitis 084.9 [573.2]
    nephrosis 084.9 [581.81]
    pernicious complication NEC 084.9
      cardiac 084.9
      cerebral 084.9
  cardiac 084.9
  carrier (suspected) of V02.9
  cerebral 084.9
  complicating pregnancy, childbirth, or
    puerperium 647.4
  congenital 771.2
  congestion, congestive 084.6
    brain 084.9
  continued 084.0
  estivo-autumnal 084.0
  falciparum (malignant tertian) 084.0
  hematinuria 084.8
  hematuria 084.8
  hemoglobinuria 084.8
  hemorrhagic 084.6
  induced (therapeutically) 084.7
    accidental—*see* Malaria, by type
  liver 084.9 [573.2]
  malariae (quartan) 084.2
  malignant (tertian) 084.0
  mixed infections 084.5
  monkey 084.4
  ovale 084.3
  pernicious, acute 084.0
  Plasmodium, P.
    falciparum 084.0
    malariae 084.2
    ovale 084.3
    vivax 084.1

Malaria, malarial—*continued*
  quartan 084.2
  quotidian 084.0
  recurrent 084.6
    induced (therapeutically) 084.7
      accidental—*see* Malaria, by type
  remittent 084.6
  specified types NEC 084.4
  spleen 084.6
  subtertian 084.0
  tertian (benign) 084.1
    malignant 084.0
  tropical 084.0
  typhoid 084.6
  vivax (benign tertian) 084.1
Malassez's disease (testicular cyst) 608.89
Malassimilation 579.9
Maldescent, testis 752.51
Maldevelopment —*see also* Anomaly, by site
  brain 742.9
  colon 751.5
  hip (joint) 755.63
    congenital dislocation (*see also* Dislocation,
      hip, congenital) 754.30
  mastoid process 756.0
  middle ear, except ossicles 744.03
    ossicles 744.04
  newborn (not malformation) 764.9
  ossicles, ear 744.04
  spine 756.10
  toe 755.66
Male type pelvis 755.69
  with disproportion (fetopelvic) 653.2
    affecting fetus or newborn 763.1
    causing obstructed labor 660.1
      affecting fetus or newborn 763.1
Malformation (congenital)—*see also* Anomaly
  bone 756.9
  bursa 756.9
  Chiari
    type I 348.4
    type II (*see also* Spina bifida) 741.0
    type III 742.0
    type IV 742.2
  circulatory system NEC 747.9
    specified type NEC 747.89
  cochlea 744.05
  digestive system NEC 751.9
    lower 751.5
    specified type NEC 751.8
    upper 750.9
  eye 743.9
  gum 750.9
  heart NEC 746.9
    specified type NEC 746.89
    valve 746.9
  internal ear 744.05
  joint NEC 755.9
    specified type NEC 755.8
  Mondini's (congenital) (malformation, cochlea)
    744.05
  muscle 756.9
  nervous system (central) 742.9
  pelvic organs or tissues
    in pregnancy or childbirth 654.9
      affecting fetus or newborn 763.8
      causing obstructed labor 660.2
        affecting fetus or newborn 763.1
  placenta (*see also* Placenta, abnormal) 656.7

Malformation—*continued*
respiratory organs 748.9
  specified type NEC 748.8
Rieger's 743.44
sense organs NEC 742.9
  specified type NEC 742.8
skin 757.9
  specified type NEC 757.8
spinal cord 742.9
teeth, tooth NEC 520.9
tendon 756.9
throat 750.9
umbilical cord (complicating delivery) 663.9
  affecting fetus or newborn 762.6
umbilicus 759.9
urinary system NEC 753.9
  specified type NEC 753.8
Malfunction —*see also* Dysfunction
arterial graft 996.1
cardiac pacemaker 996.01
catheter device—*see* Complications,
  mechanical, catheter
colostomy 569.69
cystostomy 997.5
device, implant, or graft NEC—*see*
  Complications, mechanical
enteric stoma 569.69
enterostomy 569.69
gastroenteric 536.8
nephrostomy 997.5
pacemaker—*see* Complications, mechanical,
  pacemaker
prosthetic device, internal—*see* Complications,
  mechanical
tracheostomy 519.0
vascular graft or shunt 996.1
Malgaigne's fracture (closed) 808.43
open 808.53
Malherbe's
calcifying epithelioma (M8110/0)—*see*
  Neoplasm, skin, benign
tumor (M8110/0)—*see* Neoplasm, skin, benign
Malibu disease 919.8
infected 919.9
Malignancy (M8000/3)—*see* Neoplasm, by site,
  malignant
Malignant —*see* condition
Malingerer, malingering V65.2
Mallet, finger (acquired) 736.1
congenital 755.59
late effect of rickets 268.1
Malleus 024
Mallory's bodies 034.1
Mallory-Weiss syndrome 530.7
Malnutrition (calorie) 263.9
complicating pregnancy 648.9
degree
  first 263.1
  second 263.0
  third 262
  mild 263.1
  moderate 263.0
  severe 261
    protein-calorie 262
fetus 764.2
  "light-for-dates" 764.1
following gastrointestinal surgery 579.3
intrauterine or fetal 764.2
  fetus or infant "light-for-dates" 764.1

Malnutrition—*continued*
lack of care, or neglect (child) (infant) 995.52
  adult 995.84
malignant 260
mild 263.1
moderate 263.0
protein 260
protein-calorie 263.9
  severe 262
  specified type NEC 263.8
severe 261
  protein-calorie NEC 262
Malocclusion (teeth) 524.4
due to
  abnormal swallowing 524.5
  accessory teeth (causing crowding) 524.3
  dentofacial abnormality NEC 524.8
  impacted teeth (causing crowding) 524.3
  missing teeth 524.3
  mouth breathing 524.5
  supernumerary teeth (causing crowding) 524.3
  thumb sucking 524.5
  tongue, lip, or finger habits 524.5
temporomandibular (joint) 524.69
Malposition
cardiac apex (congenital) 746.87
cervix—*see* Malposition, uterus
congenital
  adrenal (gland) 759.1
  alimentary tract 751.8
    lower 751.5
    upper 750.8
  aorta 747.21
  appendix 751.5
  arterial trunk 747.29
  artery (peripheral) NEC (*see also* Malposition,
    congenital, peripheral vascular system)
    747.60
    coronary 746.85
    pulmonary 747.3
  auditory canal 744.29
    causing impairment of hearing 744.02
  auricle (ear) 744.29
    causing impairment of hearing 744.02
    cervical 744.43
  biliary duct or passage 751.69
  bladder (mucosa) 753.8
    exteriorized or extroverted 753.5
  brachial plexus 742.8
  brain tissue 742.4
  breast 757.6
  bronchus 748.3
  cardiac apex 746.87
  cecum 751.5
  clavicle 755.51
  colon 751.5
  digestive organ or tract NEC 751.8
    lower 751.5
    upper 750.8
  ear (auricle) (external) 744.29
    ossicles 744.04
  endocrine (gland) NEC 759.2
  epiglottis 748.3
  Eustachian tube 744.24
  eye 743.8
  facial features 744.89
  fallopian tube 752.19
  finger(s) 755.59
    supernumerary 755.01

Malposition—*continued*
    foot 755.67
    gallbladder 751.69
    gastrointestinal tract 751.8
    genitalia, genital organ(s) or tract
        female 752.8
            external 752.49
            internal NEC 752.8
        male 752.8
            penis 752.69
    glottis 748.3
    hand 755.59
    heart 746.87
        dextrocardia 746.87
            with complete transposition of viscera
                759.3
    hepatic duct 751.69
    hip (joint) (*see also* Dislocation, hip,
        congenital) 754.30
    intestine (large) (small) 751.5
        with anomalous adhesions, fixation, or
            malrotation 751.4
    joint NEC 755.8
    kidney 753.3
    larynx 748.3
    limb 755.8
        lower 755.69
        upper 755.59
    liver 751.69
    lung (lobe) 748.69
    nail(s) 757.5
    nerve 742.8
    nervous system NEC 742.8
    nose, nasal (septum) 748.1
    organ or site NEC—*see* Anomaly, specified
        type NEC, by site
    ovary 752.0
    pancreas 751.7
    parathyroid (gland) 759.2
    patella 755.64
    peripheral vascular system 747.60
        gastrointestinal 747.61
        lower limb 747.64
        renal 747.62
        specified NEC 747.69
        spinal 747.82
        upper limb 747.63
    pituitary (gland) 759.2
    respiratory organ or system NEC 748.9
    rib (cage) 756.3
        supernumerary in cervical region 756.2
    scapula 755.59
    shoulder 755.59
    spinal cord 742.59
    spine 756.19
    spleen 759.0
    sternum 756.3
    stomach 750.7
    symphysis pubis 755.69
    testis (undescended) 752.51
    thymus (gland) 759.2
    thyroid (gland) (tissue) 759.2
        cartilage 748.3
    toe(s) 755.66
        supernumerary 755.02
    tongue 750.19
    trachea 748.3
    uterus 752.3

Malposition—*continued*
    vein(s) (peripheral) NEC (*see also*
        Malposition, congenital, peripheral
        vascular system) 747.60
        great 747.49
        portal 747.49
        pulmonary 747.49
        vena cava (inferior) (superior) 747.49
    device, implant, or graft—*see* Complications,
        mechanical
    fetus NEC (*see also* Presentation, fetal) 652.9
        with successful version 652.1
        affecting fetus or newborn 763.1
        before labor, affecting fetus or newborn 761.7
        causing obstructed labor 660.0
        in multiple gestation (one fetus or more) 652.6
            with locking 660.5
            causing obstructed labor 660.0
    gallbladder (*see also* Disease, gallbladder) 575.8
    gastrointestinal tract 569.89
        congenital 751.8
    heart (*see also* Malposition, congenital, heart)
        746.87
    intestine 569.89
        congenital 751.5
    pelvic organs or tissues
        in pregnancy or childbirth 654.4
            affecting fetus or newborn 763.8
            causing obstructed labor 660.2
                affecting fetus or newborn 763.1
    placenta—*see* Placenta, previa
    stomach 537.89
        congenital 750.7
    tooth, teeth (with impaction) 524.3
    uterus or cervix (acquired) (acute) (adherent)
        (any degree) (asymptomatic)
        (postinfectional) (postpartal, old) 621.6
        anteflexion or anteversion (*see also*
            Anteversion, uterus) 621.6
        congenital 752.3
        flexion 621.6
            lateral (*see also* Lateroversion, uterus) 621.6
        in pregnancy or childbirth 654.4
            affecting fetus or newborn 763.8
            causing obstructed labor 660.2
                affecting fetus or newborn 763.1
        inversion 621.6
        lateral (flexion) (version) (*see also*
            Lateroversion, uterus) 621.6
        lateroflexion (*see also* Lateroversion, uterus)
            621.6
        lateroversion (*see also* Lateroversion, uterus)
            621.6
        retroflexion or retroversion (*see also*
            Retroversion, uterus) 621.6
Malposture 729.9
Malpresentation, fetus (*see also* Presentation,
    fetal) 652.9
Malrotation
    cecum 751.4
    colon 751.4
    intestine 751.4
    kidney 753.3
Malta fever (*see also* Brucellosis) 023.9
Maltosuria 271.3
Maltreatment (of)
    adult 995.80
        emotional 995.82
        multiple forms 995.85
        neglect (nutritional) 995.84
        physical 995.81

Maltreatment—*continued*
 psychological 995.82
 sexual 995.83
 child 995.50
  emotional 995.51
  multiple forms 995.59
  neglect (nutritional) 995.52
  psychological 995.51
  physical 995.54
   shaken infant syndrome 995.55
  sexual 995.53
 spouse 995.80—*(see also* Maltreatment, adult)
Malt workers' lung 495.4
Malum coxae senilis 715.25
Malunion, fracture 733.81
Mammillitis *(see also* Mastitis) 611.0
 puerperal, postpartum 675.2
Mammitis *(see also* Mastitis) 611.0
 puerperal, postpartum 675.2
Mammoplasia 611.1
Management
 contraceptive V25.9
  specified type NEC V25.8
 procreative V26.9
  specified type NEC V26.8
Mangled NEC *(see also* nature and site of injury) 959.9
Mania (monopolar) *(see also* Psychosis, affective) 296.0
 alcoholic (acute) (chronic) 291.9
 Bell's—*see* Mania, chronic
 chronic 296.0
  recurrent episode 296.1
  single episode 296.0
 compulsive 300.3
 delirious (acute) 296.0
  recurrent episode 296.1
  single episode 296.0
 epileptic *(see also* Epilepsy) 345.4
 hysterical 300.10
 inhibited 296.89
 puerperal (after delivery) 296.0
  recurrent episode 296.1
  single episode 296.0
 recurrent episode 296.1
 senile 290.8
 single episode 296.0
 stupor 296.89
 stuporous 296.89
 unproductive 296.89
Manic-depressive insanity, psychosis reaction, or syndrome *(see also* Psychosis, affective) 296.80
 circular (alternating) 296.7
  currently
   depressed 296.5
   episode unspecified 296.7
   hypomanic, previously depressed 296.4
   manic 296.4
   mixed 296.6
 depressed (type), depressive 296.2
  atypical 296.82
  recurrent episode 296.3
  single episode 296.2
 hypomanic 296.0
  recurrent episode 296.1
  single episode 296.0
 manic 296.0
  atypical 296.81
  recurrent episode 296.1
  single episode 296.0

Manic-depressive...— *continued*
 mixed NEC 296.89
 perplexed 296.89
 stuporous 296.89
Manifestations, rheumatoid
 lungs 714.81
 pannus—*see* Arthritis, rheumatoid
 subcutaneous nodules—*see* Arthritis, rheumatoid
Mankowsky's syndrome (familial dysplastic osteopathy) 731.2
Mannoheptulosuria 271.8
Mannosidosis 271.8
Manson's
 disease (schistosomiasis) 120.1
 pyosis (pemphigus contagiosus) 684
 schistosomiasis 120.1
Mansonellosis 125.5
Manual —*see* condition
Maple bark disease 495.6
Maple bark-strippers' lung 495.6
Maple syrup (urine) disease or syndrome 270.3
Marable's syndrome (celiac artery compression) 447.4
Marasmus 261
 brain 331.9
 due to malnutrition 261
 intestinal 569.89
 nutritional 261
 senile 797
 tuberculous NEC *(see also* Tuberculosis) 011.9
Marble
 bones 756.52
 skin 782.61
Marburg disease (virus) 078.89
March
 foot (closed) 825.20
  open 825.30
 hemoglobinuria 283.2
Marchand multiple nodular hyperplasia (liver) 571.5
Marchesani (-Weill) syndrome (brachymorphism and ectopia lentis) 759.89
Marchiafava (-Bignami) disease or syndrome 341.8
Marchiafava-Micheli syndrome (paroxysmal nocturnal hemoglobinuria) 283.2
Marcus Gunn's syndrome (jaw-winking syndrome) 742.8
Marfan's
 congenital syphilis 090.49
 disease 090.49
 syndrome (arachnodactyly) 759.82
  meaning congenital syphilis 090.49
  with luxation of lens 090.49 *[379.32]*
Marginal
 implantation, placenta—*see* Placenta, previa
 placenta—*see* Placenta, previa
 sinus (hemorrhage) (rupture) 641.2
  affecting fetus or newborn 762.1
Marie's
 cerebellar ataxia 334.2
 syndrome (acromegaly) 253.0
Marie-Bamberger disease or syndrome (hypertrophic) (pulmonary) (secondary) 731.2
 idiopathic (acropachyderma) 757.39
 primary (acropachyderma) 757.39
Marie-Charcot-Tooth neuropathic atrophy, muscle 356.1
Marie-Strümpell arthritis or disease (ankylosing spondylitis) 720.0

Marihuana, marijuana
  abuse (*see also* Abuse, drugs, nondependent)
       305.2
  dependence (*see also* Dependence) 304.3
Marion's disease (bladder neck obstruction)
       596.0
Marital conflict V61.10
Mark
  port wine 757.32
  raspberry 757.32
  strawberry 757.32
  stretch 701.3
  tattoo 709.09
Maroteaux-Lamy syndrome
       (mucopolysaccharidosis VI) 277.5
Marriage license examination V70.3
Marrow (bone)
  arrest 284.9
  megakaryocytic 287.3
  poor function 289.9
Marseilles fever 082.1
Marsh's disease (exophthalmic goiter) 242.0
Marshall's (hidrotic) ectodermal dysplasia 757.31
Marsh fever (*see also* Malaria) 084.6
Martin's disease 715.27
Martin-Albright syndrome
       (pseudohypoparathyroidism) 275.4
Martorell-Fabre syndrome (pulseless disease)
       446.7
**Masculinization, female with adrenal
       hyperplasia** 255.2
Masculinovoblastoma (M8670/0) 220
Masochism 302.83
Masons' lung 502
Mass
  abdominal 789.3
  anus 787.99
  bone 733.90
  breast 611.72
  check 784.2
  chest 786.6
  cystic—*see* Cyst
  ear 388.8
  epigastric 789.3
  eye 379.92
  female genital organ 625.8
  gum 784.2
  head 784.2
  intracranial 784.2
  joint 719.60
    ankle 719.67
    elbow 719.62
    foot 719.67
    hand 719.64
    hip 719.65
    knee 719.66
    multiple sites 719.69
    pelvic region 719.65
    shoulder (region) 719.61
    specified site NEC 719.68
    wrist 719.63
  kidney (*see also* Disease, kidney) 593.9
  lung 786.6
  lymph node 785.6
  malignant (M8000/3)—*see* Neoplasm, by site,
       malignant
  mediastinal 786.6
  mouth 784.2
  muscle (limb) 729.89
  neck 784.2
  nose or sinus 784.2

Mass—*continued*
  palate 784.2
  pelvis, pelvic 789.3
  penis 607.89
  perineum 625.8
  rectum 787.99
  scrotum 608.89
  skin 782.2
  specified organ NEC—*see* Disease of specified
       organ or site
  splenic 789.2
  substernal 786.6
    thyroid (*see also* Goiter) 240.9
  superficial (localized) 782.2
  testes 608.89
  throat 784.2
  tongue 784.2
  umbilicus 789.3
  uterus 625.8
  vagina 625.8
  vulva 625.8
Massive —*see* condition
Mastalgia 611.71
  psychogenic 307.89
Mast cell
  disease 757.33
    systemic (M9741/3) 202.6
  leukemia (M9900/3) 207.8
  sarcoma (M9742/3) 202.6
  tumor (M9740/1) 238.5
    malignant (M9740/3) 202.6
Masters-Allen syndrome 620.6
Mastitis (acute) (adolescent) (diffuse)
       (interstitial) (lobular) (nonpuerperal)
       (nonsuppurative) (parenchymatous)
       (phlegmonous) (simple) (subacute)
       (suppurative) 611.0
  chronic (cystic) (fibrocystic) 610.1
  cystic 610.1
    Schimmelbusch's type 610.1
  fibrocystic 610.1
  infective 611.0
  lactational 675.2
  lymphangitis 611.0
  neonatal (noninfective) 778.7
    infective 771.5
  periductal 610.4
  plasma cell 610.4
  puerperal, postpartum, (interstitial)
       (nonpurulent) (parenchymatous) 675.2
    purulent 675.1
    stagnation 676.2
  puerperalis 675.2
  retromammary 611.0
    puerperal, postpartum 675.1
  submammary 611.0
    puerperal, postpartum 675.1
Mastocytoma (M9740/1) 238.5
  malignant (M9740/3) 202.6
Mastocytosis 757.33
  malignant (M9741/3) 202.6
  systemic (M9741/3) 202.6
Mastodynia 611.71
  psychogenic 307.89
Mastoid —*see* condition
Mastoidalgia (*see also* Otalgia) 388.70
Mastoiditis (coalescent) (hemorrhagic)
       (pneumococcal) (streptococcal) (suppurative)
       383.9
  acute or subacute 383.00

Mastoiditis—*continued*
  with
    Gradenigo's syndrome 383.02
    petrositis 383.02
    specified complication NEC 383.02
    subperiosteal abscess 383.01
  chronic (necrotic) (recurrent) 383.1
  tuberculous (*see also* Tuberculosis) 015.6
Mastopathy, mastopathia 611.9
  chronica cystica 610.1
  diffuse cystic 610.1
  estrogenic 611.8
  ovarian origin 611.8
Mastoplasia 611.1
Masturbation 307.9
Maternal condition, affecting fetus or newborn
  acute yellow atrophy of liver 760.8
  albuminuria 760.1
  anesthesia or analgesia 763.5
  blood loss 762.1
  chorioamnionitis 762.7
  circulatory disease, chronic (conditions
      classifiable to 390-459, 745-747) 760.3
  congenital heart disease (conditions classifiable
      to 745-746) 760.3
  cortical necrosis of kidney 760.1
  death 761.6
  diabetes mellitus 775.0
    manifest diabetes in the infant 775.1
  disease NEC 760.9
    circulatory system, chronic (conditions
        classifiable to 390-459, 745-747) 760.3
    genitourinary system (conditions classifiable
        to 580-599) 760.1
    respiratory (conditions classifiable to 490-519,
        748) 760.3
  eclampsia 760.0
  hemorrhage NEC 762.1
  hepatitis acute, malignant, or subacute 760.8
  hyperemesis (gravidarum) 761.8
  hypertension (arising during pregnancy)
      (conditions classifiable to 642) 760.0
  infection
    disease classifiable to 001-136 760.2
    genital tract NEC 760.8
    urinary tract 760.1
  influenza 760.2
    manifest influenza in the infant 771.2
  injury (conditions classifiable to 800-996) 760.5
  malaria 760.2
    manifest malaria in infant or fetus 771.2
  malnutrition 760.4
  necrosis of liver 760.8
  nephritis (conditions classifiable to 580-583)
      760.1
  nephrosis (conditions classifiable to 581) 760.1
  noxious substance transmitted via breast milk or
      placenta 760.70
    alcohol 760.71
    anti-infective agents 760.74
    cocaine 760.75
    "crack" 760.75
    diethylstilbestrol [DES] 760.76
    hallucinogenic agents 760.73
    medicinal agents NEC 760.79
    narcotics 760.72
    obstetric anesthetic or analgesic drug 760.72
    specified agent NEC 760.79
  nutritional disorder (conditions classifiable to
      260-269) 760.4
  operation unrelated to current delivery 760.6

Maternal condition, affecting fetus. . .—*cont.*
  pre-eclampsia 760.0
  pyelitis or pyelonephritis, arising during
      pregnancy (conditions classifiable to 590)
      760.1
  renal disease or failure 760.1
  respiratory disease, chronic (conditions
      classifiable to 490-519, 748) 760.3
  rheumatic heart disease (chronic) (conditions
      classifiable to 393-398) 760.3
  rubella (conditions classifiable to 056) 760.2
    manifest rubella in the infant or fetus 771.0
  surgery unrelated to current delivery 760.6
    to uterus or pelvic organs 763.8
  syphilis (conditions classifiable to 090-097)
      760.2
    manifest syphilis in the infant or fetus 090.0
  thrombophlebitis 760.3
  toxemia (of pregnancy) 760.0
    pre-eclamptic 760.0
  toxoplasmosis (conditions classifiable to 130)
      760.2
    manifest toxoplasmosis in the infant or fetus
        771.2
  transmission of chemical substance through the
      placenta 760.70
    alcohol 760.71
    anti-infective 760.74
    cocaine 760.75
    "crack" 760.75
    diethylstilbestrol [DES] 760.76
    hallucinogenic agents 760.73
    narcotics 760.72
    specified substance NEC 760.79
  uremia 760.1
  urinary tract conditions (conditions classifiable
      to 580-599) 760.1
  vomiting (pernicious) (persistent) (vicious)
      761.8
Maternity —*see* Delivery
Matheiu's disease (leptospiral jaundice) 100.0
Mauclaire's disease or osteochondrosis 732.3
Maxcy's disease 081.0
Maxilla, maxillary —*see* condition
May (-Hegglin) anomaly or syndrome 288.2
Mayaro fever 066.3
Mazoplasia 610.8
MBD (minimal brain dysfunction), child (*see
    also* Hyperkinesia) 314.9
McArdle (-Schmid-Pearson) disease or
    syndrome (glycogenosis V) 271.0
McCune-Albright syndrome (osteitis fibrosa
    disseminata) 756.59
MCLS (mucocutaneous lymph node syndrome)
    446.1
McQuarrie's syndrome (idiopathic familial
    hypoglycemia) 251.2
Measles (black) (hemorrhagic) (suppressed) 055.9
  with
    encephalitis 055.0
    keratitis 055.71
    keratoconjunctivitis 055.71
    otitis media 055.2
    pneumonia 055.1
  complication 055.8
    specified type NEC 055.79
  encephalitis 055.0
  French 056.9
  German 056.9
  keratitis 055.71
  keratoconjunctivitis 055.71

Measles—*continued*
  liberty 056.9
  otitis media 055.2
  pneumonia 055.1
  specified complications NEC 055.79
  vaccination, prophylactic (against) V04.2
Meatitis, urethral (*see also* Urethritis) 597.89
Meat poisoning —*see* Poisoning, food
Meatus, meatal —*see* condition
Meat-wrappers' asthma 506.9
Meckel's
  diverticulitis 751.0
  diverticulum (displaced) (hypertrophic) 751.0
Meconium
  aspiration 770.1
  delayed passage in newborn 777.1
  ileus 777.1
    due to cystic fibrosis 277.01
  in liquor 792.3
    noted during delivery—*omit code*
  insufflation 770.1
  obstruction
    fetus or newborn 777.1
      in mucoviscidosis 277.01
  passage of 792.3
    noted during delivery—*omit code*
  peritonitis 777.6
  plug syndrome (newborn) NEC 777.1
Median —*see also* condition
  arcuate ligament syndrome 447.4
  bar (prostate) 600
    vesical orifice 600
  rhomboid glossitis 529.2
Mediastinal shift 793.2
Mediastinitis (acute) (chronic) 519.2
  actinomycotic 039.8
  syphilitic 095.8
  tuberculous (*see also* Tuberculosis) 012.8
Mediastinopericarditis (*see also* Pericarditis)
  423.9
  acute 420.90
  chronic 423.8
    rheumatic 393
    rheumatic, chronic 393
Mediastinum, mediastinal —*see* condition
Medical services provided for —*see* Health,
  services provided because (of)
Medicine poisoning (by overdose) (wrong
  substance given or taken in error) 977.9
  specified drug or substance—*see* Table of drugs
    and chemicals
Medin's disease (poliomyelitis) 045.9
Mediterranean
  anemia (with other hemoglobinopathy) 282.4
  disease or syndrome (hemipathic) 282.4
  fever (*see also* Brucellosis) 023.9
    familial 277.3
  kala-azar 085.0
  leishmaniasis 085.0
  tick fever 082.1
Medulla —*see* condition
Medullary
  cystic kidney 753.16
  sponge kidney 753.17
Medullated fibers
  optic (nerve) 743.57
  retina 362.85
Medulloblastoma (M9470/3)
  desmoplastic (M9471/3) 191.6
  specified site—*see* Neoplasm, by site, malignant
  unspecified site 191.6

Medulloepithelioma (M9501/3)—*see also*
  Neoplasm, by site, malignant
  teratoid (M9502/3)—*see* Neoplasm, by site,
    malignant
Medullomyoblastoma (M9472/3)
  specified site—*see* Neoplasm, by site, malignant
  unspecified site 191.6
Meekeren-Ehlers-Danlos syndrome 756.83
Megacaryocytic —*see* condition
Megacolon (acquired) (functional) (not
  Hirschsprung's disease) 564.7
  aganglionic 751.3
  congenital, congenitum 751.3
  Hirschsprung's (disease) 751.3
  psychogenic 306.4
  toxic (*see also* Colitis, ulcerative) 556.9
Megaduodenum 537.3
Megaesophagus (functional) 530.0
  congenital 750.4
Megakaryocytic —*see* condition
Megalencephaly 742.4
Megalerythema (epidermicum) (infectiosum)
  057.0
Megalia, cutis et ossium 757.39
Megaloappendix 751.5
Megalocephalus, megalocephaly NEC 756.0
Megalocornea 743.41
  associated with buphthalmos 743.22
Megalocytic anemia 281.9
Megalodactylia (fingers) (thumbs) 755.57
  toes 755.65
Megaloduodenum 751.5
Megaloesophagus (functional) 530.0
  congenital 750.4
Megalogastria (congenital) 750.7
Megalomania 307.9
Megalophthalmos 743.8
Megalopsia 368.14
Megalosplenia (*see also* Splenomegaly) 789.2
Megaloureter 593.89
  congenital 753.22
Megarectum 569.49
Megasigmoid 564.7
  congenital 751.3
Megaureter 593.89
  congenital 753.22
Megrim 346.9
Meibomian
  cyst 373.2
    infected 373.12
  gland—*see* condition
  infarct (eyelid) 374.85
  stye 373.11
Meibomitis 373.12
Meige
  -Milroy disease (chronic hereditary edema)
    757.0
  syndrome (blepharospasm-oromandibular
    dystonia) 333.82
Melalgia, nutritional 266.2
Melancholia (*see also* Psychosis, affective)
  296.90
  climacteric 296.2
    recurrent episode 296.3
    single episode 296.2
  hypochondriac 300.7
  intermittent 296.2
    recurrent episode 296.3
    single episode 296.2
  involutional 296.2
    recurrent episode 296.3

Melancholia— *continued*
  single episode 296.2
  menopausal 296.2
    recurrent episode 296.3
    single episode 296.2
  puerperal 296.2
  reactive (from emotional stress, psychological
    trauma) 298.0
  recurrent 296.3
  senile 290.21
  stuporous 296.2
    recurrent episode 296.3
    single episode 296.2
Melanemia 275.0
Melanoameloblastoma (M9363/0)—*see*
  Neoplasm, bone, benign
Melanoblastoma (M8720/3)—*see* Melanoma
Melanoblastosis
  Block-Sulzberger 757.33
  cutis linearis sive systematisata 757.33
Melanocarcinoma (M8720/3)—*see* Melanoma
Melanocytoma, eyeball (M8726/0) 224.0
Melanoderma, melanodermia 709.09
  Addison's (primary adrenal insufficiency) 255.4
Melanodontia, infantile 521.0
Melanoepithelioma (M8720/3)—*see* Melanoma
Melanoma (malignant) (M8720/3) 172.9

> Note—Except where otherwise indicated, the
> morphological varieties of melanoma in the list
> below should be coded by site as for
> "Melanoma (malignant)." Internal sites should
> be coded to malignant neoplasm of those sites.

  abdominal wall 172.5
  ala nasi 172.3
  amelanotic (M8730/3)—*see* Melanoma, by site
  ankle 172.7
  anus, anal 154.3
    canal 154.2
  arm 172.6
  auditory canal (external) 172.2
  auricle (ear) 172.2
  auricular canal (external) 172.2
  axilla 172.5
  axillary fold 172.5
  back 172.5
  balloon cell (M8722/3)—*see* Melanoma, by site
  benign (M8720/0)—*see* Neoplasm, skin, benign
  breast (female) (male) 172.5
  brow 172.3
  buttock 172.5
  canthus (eye) 172.1
  cheek (external) 172.3
  chest wall 172.5
  chin 172.3
  choroid 190.6
  conjunctiva 190.3
  ear (external) 172.2
  epithelioid cell (M8771/3)—*see also*
    Melanoma, by site
    and spindle cell, mixed (M8775/3)—*see*
      Melanoma, by site
  external meatus (ear) 172.2
  eye 190.9
  eyebrow 172.3
  eyelid (lower) (upper) 172.1
  face NEC 172.3
  female genital organ (external) NEC 184.4
  finger 172.6
  flank 172.5
  foot 172.7

Melanoma— *continued*
  forearm 172.6
  forehead 172.3
  foreskin 187.1
  gluteal region 172.5
  groin 172.5
  hand 172.6
  heel 172.7
  helix 172.2
  hip 172.7
  in
    giant pigmented nevus (M8761/3)—*see*
      Melanoma, by site
    Hutchinson's melanotic freckle
      (M8742/3)—*see* Melanoma, by site
    junctional nevus (M8740/3)—*see* Melanoma,
      by site
    precancerous melanosis (M8741/3)—*see*
      Melanoma, by site
  interscapular region 172.5
  iris 190.0
  jaw 172.3
  juvenile (M8770/0)—*see* Neoplasm, skin,
    benign
  knee 172.7
  labium
    majus 184.1
    minus 184.2
  lacrimal gland 190.2
  leg 172.7
  lip (lower) (upper) 172.0
  liver 197.7
  lower limb NEC 172.7
  male genital organ (external) NEC 187.9
  meatus, acoustic (external) 172.2
  meibomian gland 172.1
  metastatic
    of or from specified site—*see* Melanoma, by
      site
    site not of skin—*see* Neoplasm, by site,
      malignant, secondary
    to specified site—*see* Neoplasm, by site,
      malignant, secondary
    unspecified site 172.9
  nail 172.9
    finger 172.6
    toe 172.7
  neck 172.4
  nodular (M8721/3)—*see* Melanoma, by site
  nose, external 172.3
  orbit 190.1
  penis 187.4
  perianal skin 172.5
  perineum 172.5
  pinna 172.2
  popliteal (fossa) (space) 172.7
  prepuce 187.1
  pubes 172.5
  pudendum 184.4
  retina 190.5
  scalp 172.4
  scrotum 187.7
  septum nasal (skin) 172.3
  shoulder 172.6
  skin NEC 172.8
  spindle cell (M8772/3)—*see also* Melanoma, by
    site
    type A (M8773/3) 190.0
    type B (M8774/3) 190.0
  submammary fold 172.5

Melanoma—*continued*
  superficial spreading (M8743/3)—*see*
    Melanoma, by site
  temple 172.3
  thigh 172.7
  toe 172.7
  trunk NEC 172.5
  umbilicus 172.5
  upper limb NEC 172.6
  vagina vault 184.0
  vulva 184.4
Melanoplakia 528.9
Melanosarcoma (M8720/3)—*see also* Melanoma
  epithelioid cell (M8771/3)—*see* Melanoma
Melanosis 709.09
  addisonian (primary adrenal insufficiency) 255.4
    tuberculous (*see also* Tuberculosis) 017.6
  adrenal 255.4
  colon 569.89
  conjunctiva 372.55
    congenital 743.49
  corii degenerativa 757.33
  cornea (presenile) (senile) 371.12
    congenital 743.43
      interfering with vision 743.42
    prenatal 743.43
      interfering with vision 743.42
  eye 372.55
    congenital 743.49
  jute spinners' 709.09
  lenticularis progressiva 757.33
  liver 573.8
  precancerous (M8741/2)—*see also* Neoplasm,
    skin, in situ
    malignant melanoma in (M8741/3)—*see*
      Melanoma
  Riehl's 709.09
  sclera 379.19
    congenital 743.47
  suprarenal 255.4
  tar 709.09
  toxic 709.09
Melanuria 791.9
MELAS 758.89
Melasma 709.09
  adrenal (gland) 255.4
  suprarenal (gland) 255.4
Melena 578.1
  due to
    swallowed maternal blood 777.3
    ulcer—*see* Ulcer, by site, with hemorrhage
  newborn 772.4
    due to swallowed maternal blood 777.3
Meleney's
  gangrene (cutaneous) 686.0
  ulcer (chronic undermining) 686.0
Melioidosis 025
Melitensis, febris 023.0
Melitococcosis 023.0
Melkersson (-Rosenthal) syndrome 351.8
Mellitus, diabetes —*see* Diabetes
Melorheostosis (bone) (leri) 733.99
Meloschisis 744.83
Melotia 744.29
Membrana
  capsularis lentis posterior 743.39
  epipapillaris 743.57
Membranacea placenta —*see* Placenta,
  abnormal
Membranaceous uterus 621.8

Membrane, membranous —*see also* condition
  folds, congenital—*see* Web
  Jackson's 751.4
  over face (causing asphyxia), fetus or newborn
    768.9
  premature rupture—*see* Rupture, membranes,
    premature
  pupillary 364.74
    persistent 743.46
  retained (complicating delivery) (with
    hemorrhage) 666.2
    without hemorrhage 667.1
  secondary (eye) 366.50
  unruptured (causing asphyxia) 768.9
  vitreous humor 379.25
Membranitis, fetal 658.4
  affecting fetus or newborn 762.7
Memory disturbance, loss or lack (*see also*
  Amnesia) 780.9
  mild, following organic brain damage 310.1
Menadione (vitamin K) deficiency 269.0
Menarche, precocious 259.1
Mendacity, pathologic 301.7
Mende's syndrome (ptosis-epicanthus) 270.2
Mendelson's syndrome (resulting from a
  procedure) 997.3
  obstetric 668.0
Ménétrier's disease or syndrome (hypertrophic
  gastritis) 535.2
Ménière's disease, syndrome, or vertigo 386.00
  cochlear 386.02
  cochleovestibular 386.01
  inactive 386.04
  in remission 386.04
  vestibular 386.03
Meninges, meningeal —*see* condition
Meningioma (M9530/0)—*see also* Neoplasm,
  meninges, benign
  angioblastic (M9535/0)—*see* Neoplasm,
    meninges, benign
  angiomatous (M9534/0)—*see* Neoplasm,
    meninges, benign
  endotheliomatous (M9531/0)—*see* Neoplasm,
    meninges, benign
  fibroblastic (M9532/0)—*see* Neoplasm,
    meninges, benign
  fibrous (M9532/0)—*see* Neoplasm, meninges,
    benign
  hemangioblastic (M9535/0)—*see* Neoplasm,
    meninges, benign
  hemangiopericytic (M9536/0)—*see* Neoplasm,
    meninges, benign
  malignant (M9530/3)—*see* Neoplasm,
    meninges, malignant
  meningiothelial (M9531/0)—*see* Neoplasm,
    meninges, benign
  meningotheliomatous (M9531/0)—*see*
    Neoplasm, meninges, benign
  mixed (M9537/0)—*see* Neoplasm, meninges,
    benign
  multiple (M9530/1) 237.6
  papillary (M9538/1) 237.6
  psammomatous (M9533/0)—*see* Neoplasm,
    meninges, benign
  syncytial (M9531/0)—*see* Neoplasm, meninges,
    benign
  transitional (M9537/0)—*see* Neoplasm,
    meninges, benign
Meningiomatosis (diffuse) (M9530/1) 237.6
Meningism (*see also* Meningismus) 781.6

Meningismus (infectional) (pneumococcal) 781.6
  due to serum or vaccine 997.09 *[321.8]*
  influenzal NEC 487.8
Meningitis (basal) (basic) (basilar) (brain)
  (cerebral) (cervical) (congestive) (diffuse)
  (hemorrhagic) (infantile) (membranous)
  (metastatic) (nonspecific) (pontine)
  (progressive) (simple) (spinal) (subacute)
  (sympathetica) (toxic) 322.9
  abacterial NEC (*see also* Meningitis, aseptic)
    047.9
  actinomycotic 039.8 *[320.7]*
  adenoviral 049.1
  Aerobacter aerogenes 320.82
  anaerobes (cocci) (gram-negative)
    (gram-positive) (mixed) (NEC) 320.81
  arbovirus NEC 066.9 *[321.2]*
    specified type NEC 066.8 *[321.2]*
  aseptic (acute) NEC 047.9
    adenovirus 049.1
    Coxsackie virus 047.0
    due to
      adenovirus 049.1
      Coxsackie virus 047.0
      ECHO virus 047.1
      enterovirus 047.9
      mumps 072.1
      poliovirus (*see also* Poliomyelitis) 045.2
        [321.2]
    ECHO virus 047.1
    herpes (simplex) virus 054.72
      zoster 053.0
    leptospiral 100.81
    lymphocytic choriomeningitis 049.0
    noninfective 322.0
  Bacillus pyocyaneus 320.89
  bacterial NEC 320.9
    anaerobic 320.81
    gram-negative 320.82
      anaerobic 320.81
  Bacteroides (fragilis) (oralis) (melaninogenicus)
    320.81
  cancerous (M8000/6) 198.4
  candidal 112.83
  carcinomatous (M8010/6) 198.4
  caseous (*see also* Tuberculosis, meninges) 013.0
  cerebrospinal (acute) (chronic) (diplococcal)
    (endemic) (epidemic) (fulminant)
    (infectious) (malignant) (meningococcal)
    (sporadic) 036.0
    carrier (suspected) of V02.5
  chronic NEC 322.2
  clear cerebrospinal fluid NEC 322.0
  Clostridium (haemolyticum) (novyi) NEC
    320.81
  coccidioidomycosis 114.2
  Coxsackie virus 047.0
  cryptococcal 117.5 *[321.0]*
  diplococcal 036.0
    gram-negative 036.0
    gram-positive 320.1
  Diplococcus pneumoniae 320.1
  due to
    actinomycosis 039.8 *[320.7]*
    adenovirus 049.1
    coccidiomycosis 114.2
    enterovirus 047.9
      specified NEC 047.8
    histoplasmosis (*see also* Histoplasmosis)
      115.91
    Listerosis 027.0 *[320.7]*

Meningitis—*continued*
  Lyme disease 088.81 *[320.7]*
  moniliasis 112.83
  mumps 072.1
  neurosyphilis 094.2
  nonbacterial organisms NEC 321.8
  oidiomycosis 112.83
  poliovirus (*see also* Poliomyelitis) 045.2
    [321.2]
  preventive immunization, inoculation, or
    vaccination 997.09 *[321.8]*
  sarcoidosis 135 *[321.4]*
  sporotrichosis 117.1 *[321.1]*
  syphilis 094.2
    acute 091.81
    congenital 090.42
    secondary 091.81
  trypanosomiasis (*see also* Trypanosomiasis)
    086.9 *[321.3]*
  whooping cough 033.9 *[320.7]*
  E. coli 320.82
  ECHO virus 047.1
  endothelial-leukocytic, benign, recurrent 047.9
  Enterobacter aerogenes 320.82
  enteroviral 047.9
    specified type NEC 047.8
  enterovirus 047.9
    specified NEC 047.8
  eosinophilic 322.1
  epidemic NEC 036.0
  Escherichia coli (E. coli) 320.82
  Eubacterium 320.81
  fibrinopurulent NEC 320.9
    specified type NEC 320.89
  Friedländer (bacillus) 320.82
  fungal NEC 117.9 *[321.1]*
  Fusobacterium 320.81
  gonococcal 098.82
  gram-negative bacteria NEC 320.82
    anaerobic 320.81
    cocci 036.0
      specified NEC 320.82
  gram-negative cocci NEC 036.0
    specified NEC 320.82
  gram-positive cocci NEC 320.9
  H. influenzae 320.0
  herpes (simplex) virus 054.72
    zoster 053.0
  infectious NEC 320.9
  influenzal 320.0
  Klebsiella pneumoniae 320.82
  late effect—*see* Late, effect, meningitis
  leptospiral (aseptic) 100.81
  Listerella (monocytogenes) 027.0 *[320.7]*
  Listeria monocytogenes 027.0 *[320.7]*
  lymphocytic (acute) (benign) (serous) 049.0
    choriomeningitis virus 049.0
  meningococcal (chronic) 036.0
  Mima polymorpha 320.82
  Mollaret's 047.9
  monilial 112.83
  mumps (virus) 072.1
  mycotic NEC 117.9 *[321.1]*
  Neisseria 036.0
  neurosyphilis 094.2
  nonbacterial NEC (*see also* Meningitis, aseptic)
    047.9
  nonpyogenic NEC 322.0
  oidiomycosis 112.83
  ossificans 349.2
  Peptococcus 320.81

Meningitis—*continued*
- Peptostreptococcus 320.81
- pneumococcal 320.1
- poliovirus (*see also* Poliomyelitis) 045.2 *[321.2]*
- Proprionibacterium 320.81
- Proteus morganii 320.82
- Pseudomonas (aeruginosa) (pyocyaneus) 320.82
- purulent NEC 320.9
  - specified organism NEC 320.89
- pyogenic NEC 320.9
  - specified organism NEC 320.89
- Salmonella 003.21
- septic NEC 320.9
  - specified organism NEC 320.89
- serosa circumscripta NEC 322.0
- serous NEC (*see also* Meningitis, aseptic) 047.9
  - lymphocytic 049.0—
  - syndrome 348.2
- Serratia (marcescens) 320.82
- specified organism NEC 320.89
- sporadic cerebrospinal 036.0
- sporotrichosis 117.1 *[321.1]*
- staphylococcal 320.3
- sterile 997.09
- streptococcal (acute) 320.2
- suppurative 320.9
  - specified organism NEC 320.89
- syphilitic 094.2
  - acute 091.81
  - congenital 090.42
  - secondary 091.81
- torula 117.5 *[321.0]*
- traumatic (complication of injury) 958.8
- Treponema (denticola) (macrodenticum) 320.81
- trypanosomiasis 086.1 *[321.3]*
- tuberculous (*see also* Tuberculosis, meninges) 013.0
- typhoid 002.0 *[320.7]*
- Veillonella 320.81
- Vibrio vulnificus 320.82
- viral, virus NEC (*see also* Meningitis, aseptic) 047.9
- Wallgren's (*see also* Meningitis, aseptic) 047.9

Meningocele (congenital) (spinal) (*see also* Spina bifida) 741.9
- acquired (traumatic) 349.2
- cerebral 742.0
- cranial 742.0

Meningocerebritis —*see* Meningoencephalitis
Meningococcemia (acute) (chronic) 036.2
Meningococcus, meningococcal (*see also* condition) 036.9
- adrenalitis, hemorrhagic 036.3
- carditis 036.40
- carrier (suspected) of V02.5
- cerebrospinal fever 036.0
- encephalitis 036.1
- endocarditis 036.42
- infection NEC 036.9
- meningitis (cerebrospinal) 036.0
- myocarditis 036.43
- optic neuritis 036.81
- pericarditis 036.41
- septicemia (chronic) 036.2

Meningoencephalitis (*see also* Encephalitis) 323.9
- acute NEC 048
- bacterial, purulent, pyogenic, or septic—*see* Meningitis
- chronic NEC 094.1
- diffuse NEC 094.1

Meningoencephalitis—*continued*
- diphasic 063.2
- due to
  - actinomycosis 039.8 *[320.7]*
  - blastomycosis NEC (*see also* Blastomycosis) 116.0 *[323.4]*
  - free-living amebae 136.2
  - Listeria monocytogenes 027.0 *[320.7]*
  - Lyme disease 088.81 *[320.7]*
  - mumps 072.2
  - Naegleria (amebae) (gruberi) (organisms) 136.2
  - rubella 056.01
  - sporotrichosis 117.1 *[321.1]*
  - toxoplasmosis (acquired) 130.0
    - congenital (active) 771.2 *[323.4]*
  - Trypanosoma 086.1 *[323.2]*
- epidemic 036.0
- herpes 054.3
- herpetic 054.3
- H. influenzae 320.0
- infectious (acute) 048
- influenzal 320.0
- late effect—*see* category 326
- Listeria monocytogenes 027.0 *[320.7]*
- lymphocytic (serous) 049.0
- mumps 072.2
- parasitic NEC 123.9 *[323.4]*
- pneumococcal 320.1
- primary amebic 136.2
- rubella 056.01
- serous 048
  - lymphocytic 049.0
- specific 094.2
- staphylococcal 320.3
- streptococcal 320.2
- syphilitic 094.2
- toxic NEC 989.9 *[323.7]*
  - due to
    - carbon tetrachloride 987.8 *[323.7]*
    - hydroxyquinoline derivatives poisoning 961.3 *[323.7]*
    - lead 984.9 *[323.7]*
    - mercury 985.0 *[323.7]*
    - thallium 985.8 *[323.7]*
- toxoplasmosis (acquired) 130.0
- trypanosomic 086.1 *[323.2]*
- tuberculous (*see also* Tuberculosis, meninges) 013.0
- virus NEC 048

Meningoencephalocele 742.0
- syphilitic 094.89
  - congenital 090.49

Meningoencephalomyelitis (*see also* Meningoencephalitis) 323.9
- acute NEC 048
  - disseminated (postinfectious) 136.9 *[323.6]*
    - postimmunization or postvaccination 323.5
- due to
  - actinomycosis 039.8 *[320.7]*
  - torula 117.5 *[323.4]*
  - toxoplasma or toxoplasmosis (acquired) 130.0
    - congenital (active) 771.2 *[323.4]*
- late effect—*see* category 326

Meningoencephalomyelopathy (*see also* Meningoencephalomyelitis) 349.9
Meningoencephalopathy (*see also* Meningoencephalitis) 348.3
Meningoencephalopoliomyelitis (*see also* Poliomyelitis, bulbar) 045.0
- late effect 138

Meningomyelitis (*see also* Meningoencephalitis)
323.9
blastomycotic NEC (*see also* Blastomycosis)
116.0 *[323.4]*
due to
actinomycosis 039.8 *[320.7]*
blastomycosis (*see also* Blastomycosis) 116.0
[323.4]
Meningococcus 036.0
sporotrichosis 117.1 *[323.4]*
torula 117.5 *[323.4]*
late effect—*see* category 326
lethargic 049.8
meningococcal 036.0
syphilitic 094.2
tuberculous (*see also* Tuberculosis, meninges)
013.0
Meningomyelocele (*see also* Spina bifida) 741.9
syphilitic 094.89
Meningomyeloneuritis —*see*
Meningoencephalitis
Meningoradiculitis —*see* Meningitis
Meningovascular —*see* condition
Meniscocytosis 282.60
Menkes' syndrome —*see* Syndrome, Menkes'
Menolipsis 626.0
Menometrorrhagia 626.2
Menopause, menopausal (symptoms)
(syndrome) 627.2
arthritis (any site) NEC 716.3
artificial 627.4
bleeding 627.0
crisis 627.2
depression (*see also* Psychosis, affective) 296.2
agitated 296.2
recurrent episode 296.3
single episode 296.2
psychotic 296.2
recurrent episode 296.3
single episode 296.2
recurrent episode 296.3
single episode 296.2
melancholia (*see also* Psychosis, affective)
296.2
recurrent episode 296.3
single episode 296.2
paranoid state 297.2
paraphrenia 297.2
postsurgical 627.4
premature 256.3
postirradiation 256.2
postsurgical 256.2
psychoneurosis 627.2
psychosis NEC 298.8
surgical 627.4
toxic polyarthritis NEC 716.39
Menorrhagia (primary) 626.2
climacteric 627.0
menopausal 627.0
postclimacteric 627.1
postmenopausal 627.1
preclimacteric 627.0
premenopausal 627.0
puberty (menses retained) 626.3
Menorrhalgia 625.3
Menoschesis 626.8
Menostaxis 626.2
Menses, retention 626.8
Menstrual —*see* Menstruation
cycle, irregular 626.4
disorders NEC 626.9

Menstrual—*continued*
extraction V25.3
fluid, retained 626.8
molimen 625.4
period, normal V65.5
regulation V25.3
Menstruation
absent 626.0
anovulatory 628.0
delayed 626.8
difficult 625.3
disorder 626.9
psychogenic 306.52
specified NEC 626.8
during pregnancy 640.8
excessive 626.2
frequent 626.2
infrequent 626.1
irregular 626.4
latent 626.8
membranous 626.8
painful (primary) (secondary) 625.3
psychogenic 306.52
passage of clots 626.2
precocious 626.8
protracted 626.8
retained 626.8
retrograde 626.8
scanty 626.1
suppression 626.8
vicarious (nasal) 625.8
Mentagra (*see also* Sycosis) 704.8
Mental —*see also* condition
deficiency (*see also* Retardation, mental) 319
deterioration (*see also* Psychosis) 298.9
disorder (*see also* Disorder, mental) 300.9
exhaustion 300.5
insufficiency (congenital) (*see also* Retardation,
mental) 319
observation without need for further medical
care NEC V71.09
retardation (*see also* Retardation, mental) 319
subnormality (*see also* Retardation, mental) 319
mild 317
moderate 318.0
profound 318.2
severe 318.1
upset (*see also* Disorder, mental) 300.9
Meralgia paresthetica 355.1
Mercurial —*see* condition
Mercurialism NEC 985.0
Merergasia 300.9
MERFF 758.89
Merocele (*see also* Hernia, femoral) 553.00
Meromelia 755.4
lower limb 755.30
intercalary 755.32
femur 755.34
tibiofibular (complete) (incomplete) 755.33
fibula 755.37
metatarsal(s) 755.38
tarsal(s) 755.38
tibia 755.36
tibiofibular 755.35
terminal (complete) (partial) (transverse)
755.31
longitudinal 755.32
metatarsal(s) 755.38
phalange(s) 755.39
tarsal(s) 755.38
transverse 755.31

Meromelia—*continued*
upper limb 755.20
  intercalary 755.22
    carpal(s) 755.28
    humeral 755.24
      radioulnar (complete) (incomplete) 755.23
    metacarpal(s) 755.28
    phalange(s) 755.29
    radial 755.26
    radioulnar 755.25
    ulnar 755.27
  terminal (complete) (partial) (transverse)
    755.21
    longitudinal 755.22
      carpal(s) 755.28
      metacarpal(s) 755.28
      phalange(s) 755.29
    transverse 755.21
Merosmia 781.1
Merycism (*see also* Rumination)—*see also*
  Vomiting
  psychogenic 307.53
Merzbacher-Pelizaeus disease 330.0
Mesaortitis —*see* Aortitis
Mesarteritis —*see* Arteritis
Mesencephalitis (*see also* Encephalitis) 323.9
  late effect—*see* category 326
Mesenchymoma (M8990/1)—*see also*
  Neoplasm, connective tissue, uncertain
  behavior
  benign (M8990/0)—*see* Neoplasm, connective
    tissue, benign
  malignant (M8990/3)—*see* Neoplasm,
    connective tissue, malignant
Mesentery, mesenteric —*see* condition
Mesiodens, mesiodentes 520.1
  causing crowding 524.3
Mesio-occlusion 524.2
Mesocardia (with asplenia) 746.87
Mesocolon —*see* condition
Mesonephroma (malignant) (M9110/3)—*see*
  also Neoplasm, by site, malignant
  benign (M9110/0)—*see* Neoplasm, by site,
    benign
Mesophlebitis —*see* Phlebitis
Mesostromal dysgenesis 743.51
Mesothelioma (malignant) (M9050/3)—*see also*
  Neoplasm, by site, malignant
  benign (M9050/0)—*see* Neoplasm, by site,
    benign
  biphasic type (M9053/3)—*see also* Neoplasm,
    by site, malignant
  benign (M9053/0)—*see* Neoplasm, by site,
    benign
  epithelioid (M9052/3)—*see also* Neoplasm, by
    site, malignant
  benign (M9052/0)—*see* Neoplasm, by site,
    benign
  fibrous (M9051/3)—*see also* Neoplasm, by site,
    malignant
  benign (M9051/0)—*see* Neoplasm, by site,
    benign
Metabolism disorder 277.9
  specified type NEC 277.8
Metagonimiasis 121.5
Metagonimus infestation (small intestine) 121.5
Metal
  pigmentation (skin) 709.00
  polishers' disease 502
Metalliferous miners' lung 503
Metamorphopsia 368.14

Metaplasia
  bone, in skin 709.3
  breast 611.8
  cervix—*omit code*
  endometrium (squamous) 621.8
  intestinal, of gastric mucosa 537.89
  kidney (pelvis) (squamous) (*see also* Disease,
    renal) 593.89
  myelogenous 289.8
  myeloid (agnogenic) (megakaryocytic) 289.8
  spleen 289.59
  squamous cell
    amnion 658.8
    bladder 596.8
    cervix—*see* condition
    trachea 519.1
    tracheobronchial tree 519.1
    uterus 621.8
    cervix—*see* condition
Metastasis, metastatic
  abscess—*see* Abscess
  calcification 275.4
  cancer, neoplasm, or disease
    from specified site (M8000/3)—*see*
      Neoplasm, by site, malignant
    to specified site (M8000/6)—*see* Neoplasm,
      by site, secondary
  deposits (in) (M8000/6)—*see* Neoplasm, by
    site, secondary
  pneumonia 038.8 *[484.8]*
  spread (to) (M8000/6)—*see* Neoplasm, by site,
    secondary
Metatarsalgia 726.70
  anterior 355.6
  due to Freiberg's disease 732.5
  Morton's 355.6
Metatarsus, metatarsal —*see also* condition
  abductus varus (congenital) 754.53
  adductus valgus (congenital) 754.60
  primus varus 754.52
  valgus (adductus) (congenital) 754.60
  varus (abductus) (congenital) 754.53
  primus 754.52
Methemoglobinemia 289.7
  acquired (with sulfhemoglobinemia) 289.7
  congenital 289.7
  enzymatic 289.7
  Hb-M disease 289.7
  hereditary 289.7
  toxic 289.7
Methemoglobinuria (*see also* Hemoglobinuria)
  791.2
Methioninemia 270.4
Metritis (catarrhal) (septic) (suppurative) (*see*
  also Endometritis) 615.9
  blennorrhagic 098.16
    chronic or duration of 2 months or over 098.36
  cervical (*see also* Cervicitis) 616.0
  gonococcal 098.16
    chronic or duration of 2 months or over 098.36
  hemorrhagic 626.8
  puerperal, postpartum, childbirth 670
  tuberculous (*see also* Tuberculosis) 016.7
Metropathia hemorrhagica 626.8
Metroperitonitis (*see also* Peritonitis, pelvic,
  female) 614.5
Metrorrhagia 626.6
  arising during pregnancy—*see* Hemorrhage,
    pregnancy
  postpartum NEC 666.2
  primary 626.6

Milkers' nodes 051.1
Milk-leg (deep vessels) 671.4
  complicating pregnancy 671.3
  nonpuerperal 451.19
  puerperal, postpartum, childbirth 671.4
Milkman (-Looser) disease or syndrome
    (osteomalacia with pseudofractures) 268.2
Milky urine (*see also* Chyluria) 791.1
Millar's asthma (laryngismus stridulus) 478.75
Millard-Gubler paralysis or syndrome 344.89
Millard-Gubler-Foville paralysis 344.89
Miller's disease (osteomalacia) 268.2
Miller Fisher's syndrome 357.0
Milles' syndrome (encephalocutaneous
    angiomatosis) 759.6
Mills' disease 335.29
Millstone makers' asthma or lung 502
Milroy's disease (chronic hereditary edema)
    757.0
Miners' —*see also* condition
  asthma 500
  elbow 727.2
  knee 727.2
  lung 500
  nystagmus 300.89
  phthisis (*see also* Tuberculosis) 011.4
  tuberculosis (*see also* Tuberculosis) 011.4
Minkowski-Chauffard syndrome (*see also*
    Spherocytosis) 282.0
Minor —*see* condition
Minor's disease 336.1
Minot's disease (hemorrhagic disease, newborn)
    776.0
Minot-von Willebrand (-Jürgens) disease or
    syndrome (angiohemophilia) 286.4
Minus (and plus) hand (intrinsic) 736.09
Miosis (persistent) (pupil) 379.42
Mirizzi's syndrome (hepatic duct stenosis) (*see
    also* Obstruction, biliary) 576.2
  with calculus, cholelithiasis, or stones—*see*
    Choledocholithiasis
Mirror writing 315.09
  secondary to organic lesion 784.69
Misadventure (prophylactic) (therapeutic) (*see
    also* Complications) 999.9
  administration of insulin 962.3
  infusion—*see* Complications, infusion
  local applications (of fomentations, plasters,
    etc.) 999.9
  burn or scald—*see* Burn, by site
  medical care (early) (late) NEC 999.9
    adverse effect of drugs or chemicals—*see*
      Table of drugs and chemicals
    burn or scald—*see* Burn, by site
  radiation NEC 990
  radiotherapy NEC 990
  surgical procedure (early) (late)—*see*
    Complications, surgical procedure
  transfusion—*see* Complications, transfusion
  vaccination or other immunological
    procedure—*see* Complications, vaccination
Misanthropy 301.7
Miscarriage —*see* Abortion, spontaneous
Mischief, malicious, child (*see also* Disturbance,
    conduct) 312.0
Mismanagement, feeding 783.3
Misplaced, misplacement
  kidney (*see also* Disease, renal) 593.0
    congenital 753.3
  organ or site, congenital NEC—*see*
    Malposition, congenital

Missed
  abortion 632
  delivery (at or near term) 656.4
  labor (at or near term) 656.4
Missing —*see also* Absence
  teeth (acquired) 525.1
    congenital (*see also* Anodontia) 520.0
  vertebrae (congenital) 756.13
Misuse of drugs NEC (*see also* Abuse, drug,
    nondependent) 305.9
Mitchell's disease (erythromelalgia) 443.89
Mite (s)
  diarrhea 133.8
  grain (itch) 133.8
  hair follicle (itch) 133.8
  in sputum 133.8
Mitral —*see* condition
Mittelschmerz 625.2
Mixed —*see* condition
Mljet disease (mal de Meleda) 757.39
Mobile, mobility
  cecum 751.4
  coccyx 733.99
  excessive—*see* Hypermobility
  gallbladder 751.69
  kidney 593.0
    congenital 753.3
  organ or site, congenital NEC—*see*
    Malposition, congenital
  spleen 289.59
Mobitz heart block (atrioventricular) 426.10
  type I (Wenckebach's) 426.13
  type II 426.12
Möbius'
  disease 346.8
  syndrome
    congenital oculofacial paralysis 352.6
    ophthalmoplegic migraine 346.8
Moeller (-Barlow) disease (infantile scurvy) 267
  glossitis 529.4
Mohr's syndrome (Types I and II) 759.89
Mola destruens (M9100/1) 236.1
Molarization, premolars 520.2
Molar pregnancy 631
  hydatidiform (delivered) (undelivered) 630
Mold (s) in vitreous 117.9
Molding, head (during birth) 767.3
Mole (pigmented) (M8720/0)—*see also*
    Neoplasm, skin, benign
  blood 631
  Breus' 631
  cancerous (M8720/3)—*see* Melanoma
  carneous 631
  destructive (M9100/1) 236.1
  ectopic—*see* Pregnancy, ectopic
  fleshy 631
  hemorrhagic 631
  hydatid, hydatidiform (benign) (complicating
      pregnancy) (delivered) (undelivered) (*see
      also* Hydatidiform mole) 630
    invasive (M9100/1) 236.1
    malignant (M9100/1) 236.1
    previous, affecting management of pregnancy
      V23.1
  invasive (hydatidiform) (M9100/1) 236.1
  malignant
    meaning
      malignant hydatidiform mole (M9100/1)
        236.1
      melanoma (M8720/3)—*see* Melanoma

Mole—*continued*
nonpigmented (M8730/0)—*see* Neoplasm, skin, benign
pregnancy NEC 631
skin (M8720/0)—*see* Neoplasm, skin, benign
tubal—*see* Pregnancy, tubal
vesicular (*see also* Hydatidiform mole) 630
Molimen, molimina (menstrual) 625.4
Mollaret's meningitis 047.9
Mollities (cerebellar) (cerebral) 437.8
ossium 268.2
Molluscum
contagiosum 078.0
epitheliale 078.0
fibrosum (M8851/0)—*see* Lipoma, by site
pendulum (M8851/0)—*see* Lipoma, by site
Mönckeberg's arteriosclerosis, degeneration disease, or sclerosis (*see also* Arteriosclerosis, extremities) 440.20
Monday fever 504
Monday morning dyspnea or asthma 504
Mondini's malformation (cochlea) 744.05
Mondor's disease (thrombophlebitis of breast) 451.89
Mongolian, mongolianism, mongolism mongoloid 758.0
spot 757.33
Monilethrix (congenital) 757.4
Monilia infestation —*see* Candidiasis
Moniliasis —*see also* Candidiasis
neonatal 771.7
vulvovaginitis 112.1
Monoarthritis 716.60
ankle 716.67
arm 716.62
lower (and wrist) 716.63
upper (and elbow) 716.62
foot (and ankle) 716.67
forearm (and wrist) 716.63
hand 716.64
leg 716.66
lower 716.66
upper 716.65
pelvic region (hip) (thigh) 716.65
shoulder (region) 716.61
specified site NEC 716.68
Monoblastic —*see* condition
Monochromatism (cone) (rod) 368.54
Monocytic —*see* condition
Monocytosis (symptomatic) 288.8
Monofixation syndrome 378.34
Monomania (*see also* Psychosis) 298.9
Mononeuritis 355.9
cranial nerve—*see* Disorder, nerve, cranial
femoral nerve 355.2
lateral
cutaneous nerve of thigh 355.1
popliteal nerve 355.3
lower limb 355.8
specified nerve NEC 355.79
medial popliteal nerve 355.4
median nerve 354.1
multiplex 354.5
plantar nerve 355.6
posterior tibial nerve 355.5
radial nerve 354.3
sciatic nerve 355.0
ulnar nerve 354.2
upper limb 354.9
specified nerve NEC 354.8
vestibular 388.5

Mononeuropathy (*see also* Mononeuritis) 355.9
diabetic NEC 250.6 *[355.9]*
lower limb 250.6 *[355.8]*
upper limb 250.6 *[354.9]*
iliohypogastric nerve 355.79
ilioinguinal nerve 355.79
obturator nerve 355.79
saphenous nerve 355.79
Mononucleosis, infectious 075
with hepatitis 075 *[573.1]*
Monoplegia 344.5
brain (current episode) (*see also* Paralysis, brain) 437.8
fetus or newborn 767.8
cerebral (current episode) (*see also* Paralysis, brain) 437.8
congenital or infantile (cerebral) (spastic) (spinal) 343.3
embolic (current) (*see also* Embolism, brain) 434.1
late effect—*see* category 438
infantile (cerebral) (spastic) (spinal) 343.3
lower limb 344.30
affecting
dominant side 344.31
nondominant side 344.32
newborn 767.8
psychogenic 306.0
specified as conversion reaction 300.11
thrombotic (current) (*see also* Thrombosis, brain) 434.0
late effect—*see* category 438
transient 781.4
upper limb 344.40
affecting
dominant side 344.41
nondominant side 344.42
Monorchism, monorchidism 752.8
Monteggia's fracture (closed) 813.03
open 813.13
Mood swings
brief compensatory 296.99
rebound 296.99
Moore's syndrome (*see also* Epilepsy) 345.5
Mooren's ulcer (cornea) 370.07
Mooser-Neill reaction 081.0
Mooser bodies 081.0
Moral
deficiency 301.7
imbecility 301.7
Morax-Axenfeld conjunctivitis 372.03
Morbilli (*see also* Measles) 055.9
Morbus
anglicus, anglorum 268.0
Beigel 111.2
caducus (*see also* Epilepsy) 345.9
caeruleus 746.89
celiacus 579.0
comitialis (*see also* Epilepsy) 345.9
cordis—*see also* Disease, heart
valvulorum—*see* Endocarditis
coxae 719.95
tuberculous (*see also* Tuberculosis) 015.1
hemorrhagicus neonatorum 776.0
maculosus neonatorum 772.6
renum 593.0
senilis (*see also* Osteoarthrosis) 715.9
Morel-Kraepelin disease (*see also* Schizophrenia) 295.9

Morel-Moore syndrome (hyperostosis frontalis interna) 733.3
Morel-Morgagni syndrome (hyperostosis frontalis interna) 733.3
Morgagni
cyst, organ, hydatid, or appendage 752.8
fallopian tube 752.11
disease or syndrome (hyperostosis frontalis interna) 733.3
Morgagni-Adams-Stokes syndrome (syncope with heart block) 426.9
Morgagni-Stewart-Morel syndrome (hyperostosis frontalis interna) 733.3
Moria (*see also* Psychosis) 298.9
Morning sickness 643.0
Moron 317
Morphea (guttate) (linear) 701.0
Morphine dependence (*see also* Dependence) 304.0
Morphinism (*see also* Dependence) 304.0
Morphinomania (*see also* Dependence) 304.0
Morphoea 701.0
Morquio (-Brailsford) (-Ullrich) disease or syndrome (mucopolysaccharidosis IV) 277.5
kyphosis 277.5
Morris syndrome (testicular feminization) 257.8
Morsus humanus (open wound)—*see also*
Wound, open, by site
skin surface intact—*see* Contusion
Mortification (dry) (moist) (*see also* Gangrene) 785.4
Morton's
disease 355.6
foot 355.6
metatarsalgia (syndrome) 355.6
neuralgia 355.6
neuroma 355.6
syndrome (metatarsalgia) (neuralgia) 355.6
toe 355.6
Morvan's disease 336.0
Mosaicism, mosaic (chromosomal) 758.9
autosomal 758.5
sex 758.81
Moschcowitz's syndrome (thrombotic thrombocytopenic purpura) 446.6
Mother yaw 102.0
Motion sickness (from travel, any vehicle) (from roundabouts or swings) 994.6
Mottled teeth (enamel) (endemic) (nonendemic) 520.3
Mottling enamel (endemic) (nonendemic) (teeth) 520.3
Mouchet's disease 732.5
Mould (s) (in vitreous) 117.9
Moulders'
bronchitis 502
tuberculosis (*see also* Tuberculosis) 011.4
Mounier-Kuhn syndrome 494
Mountain
fever—*see* Fever, mountain
sickness 993.2
with polycythemia, acquired 289.0
acute 289.0
tick fever 066.1
Mouse, joint (*see also* Loose, body, joint) 718.1
knee 717.6
Mouth —*see* condition
Movable
coccyx 724.71
kidney (*see also* Disease, renal) 593.0
congenital 753.3

Movable—*continued*
organ or site, congenital NEC—*see*
Malposition, congenital
spleen 289.59
Movement, abnormal (dystonic) (involuntary) 781.0
paradoxical facial 374.43
Moya Moya disease 437.5
Mozart's ear 744.29
Mucha's disease (acute parapsoriasis varioliformis) 696.2
Mucha-Haberman syndrome (acute parapsoriasis varioliformis) 696.2
Mu-chain disease 273.2
Mucinosis (cutaneous) (papular) 701.8
Mucocele
appendix 543.9
buccal cavity 528.9
gallbladder (*see also* Disease, gallbladder) 575.3
lacrimal sac 375.43
orbit (eye) 376.81
salivary gland (any) 527.6
sinus (accessory) (nasal) 478.1
turbinate (bone) (middle) (nasal) 478.1
uterus 621.8
Mucocutaneous lymph node syndrome (acute) (febrile) (infantile) 446.1
Mucoenteritis 564.1
Mucolipidosis I, II, III 272.7
Mucopolysaccharidosis (types 1-6) 277.5
cardiopathy 277.5 [425.7]
Mucormycosis (lung) 117.7
Mucositis —*see also* Inflammation by site
necroticans agranulocytica 288.0
Mucous —*see also* condition
patches (syphilitic) 091.3
congenital 090.0
Mucoviscidosis 277.00
with meconium obstruction 277.01
Mucus
asphyxia or suffocation (*see also* Asphyxia, mucus) 933.1
newborn 770.1
in stool 792.1
plug (*see also* Asphyxia, mucus) 933.1
aspiration, of newborn 770.1
tracheobronchial 519.1
newborn 770.1
Muguet 112.0
Mulberry molars 090.5
Mullerian mixed tumor (M8950/3)—*see*
Neoplasm, by site, malignant
Multicystic kidney 753.19
Multilobed placenta —*see* Placenta, abnormal
Multiparity V61.5
affecting
fetus or newborn 763.8
management of
labor and delivery 659.4
pregnancy V23.3
requiring contraceptive management (*see also* Contraception) V25.9
Multipartita placenta —*see* Placenta, abnormal
Multiple, multiplex —*see also* condition
birth
affecting fetus or newborn 761.5
healthy liveborn—*see* Newborn, multiple
digits (congenital) 755.00
fingers 755.01
toes 755.02

Multiple, multiplex—*continued*
  organ or site NEC—*see* Accessory
  personality 300.14
  renal arteries 747.62
Mumps 072.9
  with complication 072.8
    specified type NEC 072.79
  encephalitis 072.2
  hepatitis 072.71
  meningitis (aseptic) 072.1
  meningoencephalitis 072.2
  oophoritis 072.79
  orchitis 072.0
  pancreatitis 072.3
  polyneuropathy 072.72
  vaccination, prophylactic (against) V04.6
Mumu (*see also* Infestation, filarial) 125.9
Münchausen syndrome 301.51
Münchmeyer's disease or syndrome (exostosis
  luxurians) 728.11
Mural —*see* condition
Murmur (cardiac) (heart) (nonorganic) (organic)
  785.2
  abdominal 787.5
  aortic (valve) (*see also* Endocarditis, aortic)
    424.1
  benign—*omit code*
  cardiorespiratory 785.2
  diastolic—*see* condition
  Flint (*see also* Endocarditis, aortic) 424.1
  functional—*omit code*
  Graham Steell (pulmonic regurgitation) (*see*
    also Endocarditis, pulmonary) 424.3
  innocent—*omit code*
  insignificant—*omit code*
  midsystolic 785.2
  mitral (valve)—*see* stenosis, mitral
  physiologic—*see* condition
  presystolic, mitral—*see* Insufficiency, mitral
  pulmonic (valve) (*see also* Endocarditis,
    pulmonary) 424.3
  Still's (vibratory)—*omit code*
  systolic (valvular)—*see* condition
  tricuspid (valve)—*see* Endocarditis, tricuspid
  valvular—*see* condition
  vibratory—*omit code*
  undiagnosed 785.2
Murri's disease (intermittent hemoglobinuria)
  283.2
Muscae volitantes 379.24
Muscle, muscular —*see* condition
Musculoneuralgia 729.1
Mushrooming hip 718.95
Mushroom workers' (pickers') lung 495.5
Mutism (*see also* Aphasia) 784.3
  akinetic 784.3
  deaf (acquired) (congenital) 389.7
  elective (selective) 313.23
    adjustment reaction 309.83
  hysterical 300.11
Myà's disease (congenital dilation, colon) 751.3
Myalgia (intercostal) 729.1
  eosinophilia syndrome 710.5
  epidemic 074.1
    cervical 078.89
  psychogenic 307.89
  traumatic NEC 959.9
Myasthenia, myasthenic 358.0
  cordis—*see* Failure, heart
  gravis 358.0
    neonatal 775.2

Myasthenia, myasthenic— *continued*
  pseudoparalytica 358.0
  stomach 536.8
    psychogenic 306.4
  syndrome
    in
      botulism 005.1 *[358.1]*
      diabetes mellitus 250.6 *[358.1]*
      hypothyroidism (*see also* Hypothyroidism)
        244.9 *[358.1]*
      malignant neoplasm NEC 199.1 *[358.1]*
      pernicious anemia 281.0 *[358.1]*
      thyrotoxicosis (*see also* Thyrotoxicosis)
        242.9 *[358.1]*
Mycelium infection NEC 117.9
Mycetismus 988.1
Mycetoma (actinomycotic) 039.9
  bone 039.8
    mycotic 117.4
  foot 039.4
    mycotic 117.4
  madurae 039.9
    mycotic 117.4
  maduromycotic 039.9
    mycotic 117.4
  mycotic 117.4
  nocardial 039.9
Mycobacteriosis —*see* Mycobacterium
Mycobacterium, mycobacterial (infection)
  031.9
  acid-fast (bacilli) 031.9
  anonymous (*see also* Mycobacterium, atypical)
    031.9
  atypical (acid-fast bacilli) 031.9
    cutaneous 031.1
    pulmonary 031.0
      tuberculous (*see also* Tuberculosis,
        pulmonary) 011.9
    specified site NEC 031.8
  avium 031.0
  balnei 031.1
  Battey 031.0
  cutaneous 031.1
  fortuitum 031.0
  intracellulare (battey bacillus) 031.0
  kakerifu 031.8
  kansasii 031.0
  kasongo 031.8
  leprae—*see* Leprosy
  luciflavum 031.0
  marinum 031.1
  pulmonary 031.0
    tuberculous (*see also* Tuberculosis,
      pulmonary) 011.9
  scrofulaceum 031.1
  tuberculosis (human, bovine)—*see also*
    Tuberculosis
    avian type 031.0
  ulcerans 031.1
  xenopi 031.0
Mycosis, mycotic 117.9
  cutaneous NEC 111.9
  ear 111.8 *[380.15]*
  fungoides (M9700/3) 202.1
  mouth 112.0
  pharynx 117.9
  skin NEC 111.9
  stomatitis 112.0
  systemic NEC 117.9
  tonsil 117.9
  vagina, vaginitis 112.1

Mydriasis (persistent) (pupil) 379.43
Myelatelia 742.59
Myelinoclasis, perivascular, acute
  (postinfectious) NEC 136.9 *[323.6]*
  postimmunization or postvaccinal 323.5
Myelinosis, central pontine 341.8
Myelitis (acute) (ascending) (cerebellar)
  (childhood) (chronic) (descending) (diffuse)
  (disseminated) (pressure) (progressive) (spinal
  cord) (subacute) (transverse) (*see also*
  Encephalitis) 323.9
  late effect—*see* category 326
  optic neuritis in 341.0
  postchickenpox 052.7
  postvaccinal 323.5
  syphilitic (transverse) 094.89
  tuberculous (*see also* Tuberculosis) 013.6
  virus 049.9
Myeloblastic —*see* condition
Myelocele (*see also* Spina bifida) 741.9
  with hydrocephalus 741.0
Myelocystocele (*see also* Spina bifida) 741.9
Myelocytic —*see* condition
Myelocytoma 205.1
Myelodysplasia (spinal cord) 742.59
  meaning myelodysplastic syndrome—*see*
    Syndrome, myelodysplastic
Myeloencephalitis —*see* Encephalitis
Myelofibrosis (osteosclerosis) 289.8
Myelogenous —*see* condition
Myeloid —*see* condition
Myelokathexis 288.0
Myeloleukodystrophy 330.0
Myelolipoma (M8870/0)—*see* Neoplasm, by
  site, benign
Myeloma (multiple) (plasma cell) (plasmacytic)
  (M9730/3) 203.0
  monostotic (M9731/1) 238.6
  solitary (M9731/1) 238.6
Myelomalacia 336.8
Myelomata, multiple (M9730/3) 203.0
Myelomatosis (M9730/3) 203.0
Myelomeningitis —*see* Meningoencephalitis
Myelomeningocele (spinal cord) (*see also* Spina
  bifida) 741.9
  fetal, causing fetopelvic disproportion 653.7
Myelo-osteo-musculodysplasia hereditaria
  756.89
Myelopathic —*see* condition
Myelopathy (spinal cord) 336.9
  cervical 721.1
  diabetic 250.6 *[336.3]*
  drug-induced 336.8
  due to or with
    carbon tetrachloride 987.8 *[323.7]*
    degeneration or displacement, intervertebral
      disc 722.70
      cervical, cervicothoracic 722.71
      lumbar, lumbosacral 722.73
      thoracic, thoracolumbar 722.72
    hydroxyquinoline derivatives 961.3 *[323.7]*
    infection—*see* Encephalitis
    intervertebral disc disorder 722.70
      cervical, cervicothoracic 722.71
      lumbar, lumbosacral 722.73
      thoracic, thoracolumbar 722.72
    lead 984.9 *[323.7]*
    mercury 985.0 *[323.7]*
    neoplastic disease (*see also* Neoplasm, by
      site) 239.9 *[336.3]*
    pernicious anemia 281.0 *[336.3]*

Myelopathy—*continued*
  spondylosis 721.91
    cervical 721.1
    lumbar, lumbosacral 721.42
    thoracic 721.41
    thallium 985.8 *[323.7]*
  lumbar, lumbosacral 721.42
  necrotic (subacute) 336.1
  radiation-induced 336.8
  spondylogenic NEC 721.91
    cervical 721.1
    lumbar, lumbosacral 721.42
    thoracic 721.41
  thoracic 721.41
  toxic NEC 989.9 *[323.7]*
  transverse (*see also* Encephalitis) 323.9
  vascular 336.1
Myeloproliferative disease (M9960/1) 238.7
Myeloradiculitis (*see also* Polyneuropathy) 357.0
Myeloradiculodysplasia (spinal) 742.59
Myelosarcoma (M9930/3) 205.3
Myelosclerosis 289.8
  with myeloid metaplasia (M9961/1) 238.7
  disseminated, of nervous system 340
  megakaryocytic (M9961/1) 238.7
Myelosis (M9860/3) (*see also* Leukemia,
  myeloid) 205.9
  acute (M9861/3) 205.0
  aleukemic (M9864/3) 205.8
  chronic (M9863/3) 205.1
  erythremic (M9840/3) 207.0
    acute (M9841/3) 207.0
  megakaryocytic (M9920/3) 207.2
  nonleukemic (chronic) 288.8
  subacute (M9862/3) 205.2
Myesthenia —*see* Myasthenia
Myiasis (cavernous) 134.0
  orbit 134.0 *[376.13]*
Myoadenoma, prostate 600
Myoblastoma
  granular cell (M9580/0)—*see also* Neoplasm,
    connective tissue, benign
    malignant (M9580/3)—*see* Neoplasm,
      connective tissue, malignant
  tongue (M9580/0) 210.1
Myocardial —*see* condition
Myocardiopathy (congestive) (constrictive)
  (familial) (hypertrophic nonobstructive)
  (idiopathic) (infiltrative) (obstructive)
  (primary) (restrictive) (sporadic) 425.4
  alcoholic 425.5
  amyloid 277.3 *[425.7]*
  beriberi 265.0 *[425.7]*
  cobalt-beer 425.5
  due to
    amyloidosis 277.3 *[425.7]*
    beriberi 265.0 *[425.7]*
    cardiac glycogenosis 271.0 *[425.7]*
    Chagas' disease 086.0
    Friedreich's ataxia 334.0 *[425.8]*
    influenza 487.8 *[425.8]*
    mucopolysaccharidosis 277.5 *[425.7]*
   •   myotonia atrophica 359.2 *[425.8]*
    progressive muscular dystrophy 359.1 *[425.8]*
    sarcoidosis 135 *[425.8]*
  glycogen storage 271.0 *[425.7]*
  hypertrophic obstructive 425.1
  metabolic NEC 277.9 *[425.7]*
  nutritional 269.9 *[425.7]*
  obscure (African) 425.2
  postpartum 674.8

Myocardiopathy— *continued*
  secondary 425.9
  thyrotoxic (*see also* Thyrotoxicosis) 242.9
    [425.7]
  toxic NEC 425.9
Myocarditis (fibroid) (interstitial) (old)
    (progressive) (senile) (with arteriosclerosis)
    429.0
  with
    rheumatic fever (conditions classifiable to
      390) 398.0
      active (*see also* Myocarditis, acute,
        rheumatic) 391.2
      inactive or quiescent (with chorea) 398.0
  active (nonrheumatic) 422.90
    rheumatic 391.2
      with chorea (acute) (rheumatic)
        (Sydenham's) 392.0
  acute or subacute (interstitial) 422.90
    due to Streptococcus (beta-hemolytic) 391.2
    idiopathic 422.91
    rheumatic 391.2
      with chorea (acute) (rheumatic)
        (Sydenham's) 392.0
    specified type NEC 422.99
  aseptic of newborn 074.23
  bacterial (acute) 422.92
  chagasic 086.0
  chronic (interstitial) 429.0
  congenital 746.89
  constrictive 425.4
  Coxsackie (virus) 074.23
  diphtheritic 032.82
  due to or in
    Coxsackie (virus) 074.23
    diphtheria 032.82
    epidemic louse-borne typhus 080 *[422.0]*
    influenza 487.8 *[422.0]*
    Lyme disease 088.81 *[422.0]*
    scarlet fever 034.1 *[422.0]*
    toxoplasmosis (acquired) 130.3
    tuberculosis (*see also* Tuberculosis) 017.9
      [422.0]
    typhoid 002.0 *[422.0]*
    typhus NEC 081.9 *[422.0]*
  eosinophilic 422.91
  epidemic of newborn 074.23
  Fiedler's (acute) (isolated) (subacute) 422.91
  giant cell (acute) (subacute) 422.91
  gonococcal 098.85
  granulomatous (idiopathic) (isolated)
    (nonspecific) 422.91
  hypertensive (*see also* Hypertension, heart)
    402.90
  idiopathic 422.91
    granulomatous 422.91
  infective 422.92
  influenzal 487.8 *[422.0]*
  isolated (diffuse) (granulomatous) 422.91
  malignant 422.99
  meningococcal 036.43
  nonrheumatic, active 422.90
  parenchymatous 422.90
  pneumococcal (acute) (subacute) 422.92
  rheumatic (chronic) (inactive) (with chorea)
    398.0
    active or acute 391.2
      with chorea (acute) (rheumatic)
        (Sydenham's) 392.0
  septic 422.92
  specific (giant cell) (productive) 422.91

Myocarditis— *continued*
  staphylococcal (acute) (subacute) 422.92
  suppurative 422.92
  syphilitic (chronic) 093.82
  toxic 422.93
    rheumatic (*see also* Myocarditis, acute
      rheumatic) 391.2
  tuberculous (*see also* Tuberculosis) 017.9
    [422.0]
  typhoid 002.0 *[422.0]*
  valvular—*see* Endocarditis
  viral, except Coxsackie 422.91
    Coxsackie 074.23
    of newborn (Coxsackie) 074.23
Myocardium, myocardial —*see* condition
Myocardosis (*see also* Cardiomyopathy) 425.4
Myoclonia (essential) 333.2
  epileptica 333.2
  Friedrich's 333.2
  massive 333.2
Myoclonic
  epilepsy, familial (progressive) 333.2
  jerks 333.2
Myoclonus (familial essential) (multifocal)
    (simplex) 333.2
  facial 351.8
  massive (infantile) 333.2
  pharyngeal 478.29
Myodiastasis 728.84
Myoendocarditis —*see also* Endocarditis
  acute or subacute 421.9
Myoepithelioma (M8982/0)—*see* Neoplasm, by
    site, benign
Myofascitis (acute) 729.1
  low back 724.2
Myofibroma (M8890/0)—*see also* Neoplasm,
    connective tissue, benign
  uterus (cervix) (corpus) (*see also* Leiomyoma)
    218.9
Myofibrosis 728.2
  heart (*see also* Myocarditis) 429.0
  humeroscapular region 726.2
  scapulohumeral 726.2
Myofibrositis (*see also* Myositis) 729.1
  scapulohumeral 726.2
Myogelosis (occupational) 728.89
Myoglobinuria 791.3
Myoglobulinuria, primary 791.3
Myokymia —*see also* Myoclonus
  facial 351.8
Myolipoma (M8860/0)
  specified site—*see* Neoplasm, connective
    tissue, benign
  unspecified site 223.0
Myoma (M8895/0)—*see also* Neoplasm,
    connective tissue, benign
  cervix (stump) (uterus) (*see also* Leiomyoma)
    218.9
  malignant (M8895/3)—*see* Neoplasm,
    connective tissue, malignant
  prostate 600
  uterus (cervix) (corpus) (*see also* Leiomyoma)
    218.9
    in pregnancy or childbirth 654.1
      affecting fetus or newborn 763.8
      causing obstructed labor 660.2
        affecting fetus or newborn 763.1
Myomalacia 728.9
  cordis, heart (*see also* Degeneration,
    myocardial) 429.1
Myometritis (*see also* Endometritis) 615.9

Myometrium —*see* condition
Myonecrosis, clostridial 040.0
Myopathy 359.9
  alcoholic 359.4
  amyloid 277.3 *[359.6]*
  benign congenital 359.0
  central core 359.0
  centronuclear 359.0
  congenital (benign) 359.0
  distal 359.1
  due to drugs 359.4
  endocrine 259.9 *[359.5]*
    specified type NEC 259.8 *[359.5]*
  extraocular muscles 376.82
  facioscapulohumeral 359.1
  in
    Addison's disease 255.4 *[359.5]*
    amyloidosis 277.3 *[359.6]*
    cretinism 243 *[359.5]*
    Cushing's syndrome 255.0 *[359.5]*
    disseminated lupus erythematosus 710.0
      [359.6]
    giant cell arteritis 446.5 *[359.6]*
    hyperadrenocorticism NEC 255.3 *[359.5]*
    hyperparathyroidism 252.0 *[359.5]*
    hypopituitarism 253.2 *[359.5]*
    hypothyroidism (*see also* Hypothyroidism)
      244.9 *[359.5]*
    malignant neoplasm NEC (M8000/3) 199.1
      [359.6]
    myxedema (*see also* Myxedema) 244.9
      [359.5]
    polyarteritis nodosa 446.0 *[359.6]*
    rheumatoid arthritis 714.0 *[359.6]*
    sarcoidosis 135 *[359.6]*
    scleroderma 710.1 *[359.6]*
    Sjögren's disease 710.2 *[359.6]*
    thyrotoxicosis (*see also* Thyrotoxicosis) 242.9
      [359.5]
  inflammatory 359.8
  limb-girdle 359.1
  myotubular 359.0
  nemaline 359.0
  ocular 359.1
  oculopharyngeal 359.1
  primary 359.8
  progressive NEC 359.8
  rod body 359.0
  scapulohumeral 359.1
  specified type NEC 359.8
  toxic 359.4
Myopericarditis (*see also* Pericarditis) 423.9
Myopia (axial) (congenital) (increased curvature
  or refraction, nucleus of lens) 367.1
  degenerative, malignant 360.21
  malignant 360.21
  progressive high (degenerative) 360.21
Myosarcoma (M8895/3)—*see* Neoplasm,
  connective tissue, malignant
Myosis (persistent) 379.42
  stromal (endolymphatic) (M8931/1) 236.0
Myositis 729.1
  clostridial 040.0
  due to posture 729.1
  epidemic 074.1
  fibrosa or fibrous (chronic) 728.2
    Volkmann's (complicating trauma) 958.6
  infective 728.0
  interstitial 728.81
  multiple—*see* Polymyositis
  occupational 729.1

Myositis-— *continued*
  orbital, chronic 376.12
  ossificans 728.12
    circumscribed 728.12
    progressive 728.11
    traumatic 728.12
  progressive fibrosing 728.11
  purulent 728.0
  rheumatic 729.1
  rheumatoid 729.1
  suppurative 728.0
  syphilitic 095.6
  traumatic (old) 729.1
Myospasia impulsiva 307.23
Myotonia (acquisita) (intermittens) 728.85
  atrophica 359.2
  congenita 359.2
  dystrophica 359.2
Myotonic pupil 379.46
Myriapodiasis 134.1
Myringitis
  with otitis media—*see* Otitis media
  acute 384.00
    specified type NEC 384.09
  bullosa hemorrhagica 384.01
  bullous 384.01
  chronic 384.1
Mysophobia 300.29
Mytilotoxism 988.0
Myxadenitis labialis 528.5
Myxedema (adult) (idiocy) (infantile) (juvenile)
  (thyroid gland) (*see also* Hypothyroidism)
  244.9
  circumscribed 242.9
  congenital 243
  cutis 701.8
  localized (pretibial) 242.9
  madness (acute) 293.0
    subacute 293.1
  papular 701.8
  pituitary 244.8
  postpartum 674.8
  pretibial 242.9
  primary 244.9
Myxochondrosarcoma (M9220/3)—*see*
  Neoplasm, cartilage, malignant
Myxofibroma (M8811/0)—*see also* Neoplasm,
  connective tissue, benign
  odontogenic (M9320/0) 213.1
    upper jaw (bone) 213.0
Myxofibrosarcoma (M8811/3)—*see* Neoplasm,
  connective tissue, malignant
Myxolipoma (M8852/0) (*see also* Lipoma, by
  site) 214.9
Myxoliposarcoma (M8852/3)—*see* Neoplasm,
  connective tissue, malignant
Myxoma (M8840/0)—*see also* Neoplasm,
  connective tissue, benign
  odontogenic (M9320/0) 213.1
    upper jaw (bone) 213.0
Myxosarcoma (M8840/3)—*see* Neoplasm,
  connective tissue, malignant

N

Naegeli's
disease (hereditary hemorrhagic
thrombasthenia) 287.1
leukemia, monocytic (M9863/3) 205.1
syndrome (incontinentia pigmenti) 757.33
Naffziger's syndrome 353.0
Naga sore (*see also* Ulcer, skin) 707.9
Nägele's pelvis 738.6
with disproportion (fetopelvic) 653.0
affecting fetus or newborn 763.1
causing obstructed labor 660.1
affecting fetus or newborn 763.1
Nager-de Reynier syndrome (dysostosis
mandibularis) 756.0
Nail —*see also* condition
biting 307.9
patella syndrome (hereditary
osteo-onychodysplasia) 756.89
Nanism, nanosomia (*see also* Dwarfism) 259.4
hypophyseal 253.3
pituitary 253.3
renis, renalis 588.0
Nanukayami 100.89
Napkin rash 691.0
Narcissism 301.81
Narcolepsy 347
Narcosis
carbon dioxide (respiratory) 786.09
due to drug
correct substance properly administered
780.09
overdose or wrong substance given or taken
977.9
specified drug—*see* Table of drugs and
chemicals
Narcotism (chronic) (*see also* listing under
Dependence) 304.9
acute
correct substance properly administered
349.82
overdose or wrong substance given or taken
967.8
specified drug—*see* Table of drugs and
chemicals
Narrow
anterior chamber angle 365.02
pelvis (inlet) (outlet)—*see* Contraction, pelvis
Narrowing
artery NEC 447.1
auditory, internal 433.8
basilar 433.0
with other precerebral artery 433.3
bilateral 433.3
carotid 433.1
with other precerebral artery 433.3
bilateral 433.3
cerebellar 433.8
choroidal 433.8
communicating posterior 433.8
coronary —*see also* Arteriosclerosis, coronary
congenital 746.85
due to syphilis 090.5
hypophyseal 433.8
pontine 433.8
precerebral NEC 433.9
multiple or bilateral 433.3
specified NEC 433.8

Narrowing—*continued*
vertebral 433.2
with other precerebral artery 433.3
bilateral 433.3
auditory canal (external) (*see also* Stricture, ear
canal, acquired) 380.50
cerebral arteries 437.0
cicatricial—*see* Cicatrix
congenital—*see* Anomaly, congenital
coronary artery—*see* Narrowing, artery,
coronary
ear, middle 385.22
Eustachian tube (*see also* Obstruction,
Eustachian tube) 381.60
eyelid 374.46
congenital 743.62
intervertebral disc or space NEC—*see*
Degeneration, intervertebral disc
joint space, hip 719.85
larynx 478.74
lids 374.46
congenital 743.62
mesenteric artery (with gangrene) 557.0
palate 524.8
palpebral fissure 374.46
retinal artery 362.13
ureter 593.3
urethra (*see also* Stricture, urethra) 598.9
Narrowness, abnormal, eyelid 743.62
Nasal —*see* condition
Nasolacrimal —*see* condition
Nasopharyngeal —*see also* condition
bursa 478.29
pituitary gland 759.2
torticollis 723.5
Nasopharyngitis (acute) (infective) (subacute)
460
chronic 472.2
due to external agent—*see* Condition,
respiratory, chronic, due to
due to external agent—*see* Condition,
respiratory, due to
septic 034.0
streptococcal 034.0
suppurative (chronic) 472.2
ulcerative (chronic) 472.2
Nasopharynx, nasopharyngeal —*see* condition
Natal tooth, teeth 520.6
Nausea (*see also* Vomiting) 787.02
epidemic 078.82
gravidarum—*see* Hyperemesis, gravidarum
marina 994.6
with vomiting 787.01
Naval —*see* condition
Neapolitan fever (*see also* Brucellosis) 023.9
Nearsightedness 367.1
Near-syncope 780.2
Nebécourt's syndrome 253.3
Nebula, cornea (eye) 371.01
congenital 743.43
interfering with vision 743.42
Necator americanus infestation 126.1
Necatoriasis 126.1
Neck —*see* condition
Necrencephalus (*see also* Softening, brain) 437.8
Necrobacillosis 040.3

Necrobiosis 799.8
  brain or cerebral (*see also* Softening, brain)
    437.8
  lipoidica 709.3
    diabeticorum 250.8 *[709.3]*
Necrodermolysis 695.1
Necrolysis, toxic epidermal 695.1
  due to drug
    correct substance properly administered 695.1
    overdose or wrong substance given or taken
      977.9
    specified drug—*see* Table of drugs and
      chemicals
Necrophilia 302.89
Necrosis, necrotic
  adrenal (capsule) (gland) 255.8
  antrum, nasal sinus 478.1
  aorta (hyaline) (*see also* Aneurysm, aorta) 441.9
    cystic medial 441.00
      abdominal 441.02
      thoracic 441.01
      thoracoabdominal 441.03
    ruptured 441.5
  arteritis 446.0
  artery 447.5
  aseptic, bone 733.40
    femur (head) (neck) 733.42
      medial condyle 733.43
    humoral head 733.41
    medial femoral condyle 733.43
    specified site NEC 733.49
    talus 733.44
  avascular, bone NEC (*see also* Necrosis,
    aseptic, bone) 733.40
  bladder (aseptic) (sphincter) 596.8
  bone (*see also* Osteomyelitis) 730.1
    acute 730.0
    aseptic or avascular 733.40
      femur (head) (neck) 733.42
        medial condyle 733.43
      humoral head 733.41
      medial femoral condyle 733.43
      specified site NEC 733.49
      talus 733.44
    ethmoid 478.1
    ischemic 733.40
    jaw 526.4
    marrow 289.8
    Paget's (osteitis deformans) 731.0
    tuberculous—*see* Tuberculosis, bone
  brain (softening) (*see also* Softening, brain)
    437.8
  breast (aseptic) (fat) (segmental) 611.3
  bronchus, bronchi 519.1
  central nervous system NEC (*see also*
    Softening, brain) 437.8
  cerebellar (*see also* Softening, brain) 437.8
  cerebral (softening) (*see also* Softening, brain)
    437.8
  cerebrospinal (softening) (*see also* Softening,
    brain) 437.8
  cornea (*see also* Keratitis) 371.40
  cortical, kidney 583.6
  cystic medial (aorta) 441.00
    abdominal 441.02
    thoracic 441.01
    thoracoabdominal 441.03
  dental 521.0
    pulp 522.1

Necrosis, necrotic—*continued*
  due to swallowing corrosive substance—*see*
    Burn, by site
  ear (ossicle) 385.24
  esophagus 530.89
  ethmoid (bone) 478.1
  eyelid 374.50
  fat, fatty (generalized) (*see also* Degeneration,
    fatty) 272.8
    breast (aseptic) (segmental) 611.3
    intestine 569.89
    localized—*see* Degeneration, by site, fatty
    mesentery 567.8
    omentum 567.8
    pancreas 577.8
    peritoneum 567.8
    skin (subcutaneous) 709.3
      newborn 778.1
  femur (aseptic) (avascular) 733.42
    head 733.42
    medial condyle 733.43
    neck 733.42
  gallbladder (*see also* Cholecystitis, acute) 575.0
  gangrenous 785.4
  gastric 537.89
  glottis 478.79
  heart (myocardium)—*see* Infarct, myocardium
  hepatic (*see also* Necrosis, liver) 570
  hip (aseptic) (avascular) 733.42
  intestine (acute) (hemorrhagic) (massive) 557.0
  ischemic 785.4
  jaw 526.4
  kidney (bilateral) 583.9
    acute 584.9
    cortical 583.6
      acute 584.6
      with
        abortion—*see* Abortion, by type, with
          renal failure
        ectopic pregnancy (*see also* categories
          633.0-633.9) 639.3
        molar pregnancy (*see also* categories
          630-632) 639.3
      complicating pregnancy 646.2
        affecting fetus or newborn 760.1
      following labor and delivery 669.3
    medullary (papillary) (*see also* Pyelitis) 590.80
    in
      acute renal failure 584.7
      nephritis, nephropathy 583.7
    papillary (*see also* Pyelitis) 590.80
    in
      acute renal failure 584.7
      nephritis, nephropathy 583.7
    tubular 584.5
    with
      abortion—*see* Abortion, by type, with
        renal failure
      ectopic pregnancy (*see also* categories
        633.0-633.9) 639.3
      molar pregnancy (*see also* categories
        630-632) 639.3
      complicating
        abortion 639.3
        ectopic or molar pregnancy 639.3
        pregnancy 646.2
          affecting fetus or newborn 760.1
      following labor and delivery 669.3
      traumatic 958.5
  larynx 478.79

Necrosis, necrotic—*continued*
  liver (acute) (congenital) (diffuse) (massive)
    (subacute) 570
    with
      abortion—*see* Abortion, by type, with
        specified complication NEC
      ectopic pregnancy (*see also* categories
        633.0-633.9) 639.8
      molar pregnancy (*see also* categories
        630-632) 639.8
    complicating pregnancy 646.7
      affecting fetus or newborn 760.8
    following
      abortion 639.8
      ectopic or molar pregnancy 639.8
    obstetrical 646.7
    postabortal 639.8
    puerperal, postpartum 674.8
    toxic 573.3
  lung 513.0
  lymphatic gland 683
  mammary gland 611.3
  mastoid (chronic) 383.1
  mesentery 557.0
    fat 567.8
  mitral valve—*see* Insufficiency, mitral
  myocardium, myocardial—*see* Infarct,
    myocardium
  nose (septum) 478.1
  omentum 557.0
    with mesenteric infarction 557.0
    fat 567.8
  orbit, orbital 376.10
  ossicles, ear (aseptic) 385.24
  ovary (*see also* Salpingo-oophoritis) 614.2
  pancreas (aseptic) (duct) (fat) 577.8
    acute 577.0
    infective 577.0
  papillary, kidney (*see also* Pyelitis) 590.80
  peritoneum 557.0
    with mesenteric infarction 557.0
    fat 567.8
  pharynx 462
    in granulocytopenia 288.0
  phosphorus 983.9
  pituitary (gland) (postpartum) (Sheehan) 253.2
  placenta (*see also* Placenta, abnormal) 656.7
  pneumonia 513.0
  pulmonary 513.0
  pulp (dental) 522.1
  pylorus 537.89
  radiation—*see* Necrosis, by site
  radium—*see* Necrosis, by site
  renal—*see* Necrosis, kidney
  sclera 379.19
  scrotum 608.89
  skin or subcutaneous tissue 709.8
    due to burn—*see* Burn, by site
    gangrenous 785.4
  spine, spinal (column) 730.18
    acute 730.18
    cord 336.1
  spleen 289.59
  stomach 537.89
  stomatitis 528.1
  subcutaneous fat 709.3
    fetus or newborn 778.1
  subendocardial—*see* Infarct, myocardium
  suprarenal (capsule) (gland) 255.8

Necrosis, necrotic— *continued*
  teeth, tooth 521.0
  testis 608.89
  thymus (gland) 254.8
  tonsil 474.8
  trachea 519.1
  tuberculous NEC—*see* Tuberculosis
  tubular (acute) (anoxic) (toxic) 584.5
    due to a procedure 997.5
  umbilical cord, affecting fetus or newborn 762.6
  vagina 623.8
  vertebra (lumbar) 730.18
    acute 730.18
    tuberculous (*see also* Tuberculosis) 015.0
      [730.8]
  vesical (aseptic) (bladder) 596.8
  x-ray—*see* Necrosis, by site
Necrospermia 606.0
Necrotizing angiitis 446.0
Negativism 301.7
Neglect (child) (newborn) NEC 995.52
  adult 995.84
  after or at birth 995.52
  hemispatial 781.8
  left-sided 781.8
  sensory 781.8
  visuospatial 781.8
Negri bodies 071
Neill-Dingwall syndrome (microcephaly and
  dwarfism) 759.89
Neisserian infection NEC—*see* Gonococcus
Nematodiasis NEC (*see also* Infestation,
  Nematode) 127.9
  ancylostoma (*see also* Ancylostomiasis) 126.9
Neoformans cryptococcus infection 117.5
Neonatal —*see also* condition
  teeth, tooth 520.6
Neonatorum —*see* condition

          "N" listing resumes after
          "Neoplasm, neoplastic" table...

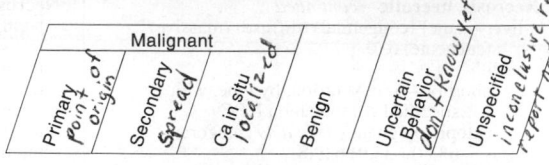

| | Malignant | | | | | |
	Primary Point of origin	Secondary Spread	Ca in situ localized	Benign	Uncertain Behavior don't know yet	Unspecified inconclusive report not back yet
Neoplasm, neoplastic	**199.1**	**199.1**	**234.9**	**229.9**	**238.9**	**239.9**

> Note—1. The list below gives the code numbers for neoplasms by anatomical site. For each site there are six possible code numbers according to whether the neoplasm in question is malignant, benign, in situ, of uncertain behavior, or of unspecified nature. The description of the neoplasm will often indicate which of the six columns is appropriate; e.g., malignant melanoma of skin, benign fibroadenoma of breast, carcinoma in situ of cervix uteri.
>
> Where such descriptors are not present, the remainder of the Index should be consulted where guidance is given to the appropriate column for each morphological (histological) variety listed; e.g., Mesonephroma—see Neoplasm, malignant; Embryoma—see also Neoplasm, uncertain behavior; Disease, Bowen's—see Neoplasm, skin, in situ. However, the guidance in the Index can be overridden if one of the descriptors mentioned above is present; e.g., malignant adenoma of colon is coded to 153.9 and not to 211.3 as the adjective "malignant" overrides the Index entry "Adenoma—see also Neoplasm, benign."
>
> Note—2. Sites marked with the sign * (e.g., face NEC*) should be classified to malignant neoplasm of skin of these sites if the variety of neoplasm is a squamous cell carcinoma or an epidermoid carcinoma and to benign neoplasm of skin of these sites if the variety of neoplasm is a papilloma (any type).

abdomen, abdominal	195.2	198.89	234.8	229.8	238.8	239.8
cavity	195.2	198.89	234.8	229.8	238.8	239.8
organ	195.2	198.89	234.8	229.8	238.8	239.8
viscera	195.2	198.89	234.8	229.8	238.8	239.8
wall	173.5	198.2	232.5	216.5	238.2	239.2
connective tissue	171.5	198.89	—	215.5	238.1	239.2
abdominopelvic	195.8	198.89	234.8	229.8	238.8	239.8
accessory sinus—see Neoplasm, sinus						
acoustic nerve	192.0	198.4	—	225.1	237.9	239.7
acromion (process)	170.4	198.5	—	213.4	238.0	239.2
adenoid (pharynx) (tissue)	147.1	198.89	230.0	210.7	235.1	239.0
adipose tissue *(see also* Neoplasm,						
connective tissue)	171.9	198.89	—	215.9	238.1	239.2
adnexa (uterine)	183.9	198.82	233.3	221.8	236.3	239.5
adrenal (cortex) (gland) (medulla)	194.0	198.7	234.8	227.0	237.2	239.7
ala nasi (external)	173.3	198.2	232.3	216.3	238.2	239.2
alimentary canal or tract NEC	159.9	197.8	230.9	211.9	235.5	239.0
alveolar	143.9	198.89	230.0	210.4	235.1	239.0
mucosa	143.9	198.89	230.0	210.4	235.1	239.0
lower	143.1	198.89	230.0	210.4	235.1	239.0
upper	143.0	198.89	230.0	210.4	235.1	239.0
ridge or process	170.1	198.5	—	213.1	238.0	239.2
carcinoma	143.9	—	—	—	—	—
lower	143.1	—	—	—	—	—
upper	143.0	—	—	—	—	—
lower	170.1	198.5	—	213.1	238.0	239.2
mucosa	143.9	198.89	230.0	210.4	235.1	239.0
lower	143.1	198.89	230.0	210.4	235.1	239.0
upper	143.0	198.89	230.0	210.4	235.1	239.0
upper	170.0	198.5	—	213.0	238.0	239.2
sulcus	145.1	198.89	230.0	210.4	235.1	239.0
alveolus	143.9	198.89	230.0	210.4	235.1	239.0
lower	143.1	198.89	230.0	210.4	235.1	239.0
upper	143.0	198.89	230.0	210.4	235.1	239.0
ampulla of Vater	156.2	197.8	230.8	211.5	235.3	239.0
ankle NEC*	195.5	198.89	232.7	229.8	238.8	239.8
anorectum, anorectal (junction)	154.8	197.5	230.7	211.4	235.2	239.0
antecubital fossa or space*	195.4	198.89	232.6	229.8	238.8	239.8
antrum (Highmore) (maxillary)	160.2	197.3	231.8	212.0	235.9	239.1
pyloric	151.2	197.8	230.2	211.1	235.2	239.0
tympanicum	160.1	197.3	231.8	212.0	235.9	239.1
anus, anal	154.3	197.5	230.6	211.4	235.5	239.0
canal	154.2	197.5	230.5	211.4	235.5	239.0

	Malignant					
	Primary	Secondary	Ca in situ	Benign	Uncertain Behavior	Unspecified
anus, anal—*continued*						
contiguous sites with rectosigmoid junction or rectum	154.8	—	—	—	—	—
margin	173.5	198.2	232.5	216.5	238.2	239.2
skin	173.5	198.2	232.5	216.5	238.2	239.2
sphincter	154.2	197.5	230.5	211.4	235.5	239.0
aorta (thoracic)	171.4	198.89	—	215.4	238.1	239.2
abdominal	171.5	198.89	—	215.5	238.1	239.2
aortic body	194.6	198.89	—	227.6	237.3	239.7
aponeurosis	171.9	198.89	—	215.9	238.1	239.2
palmar	171.2	198.89	—	215.2	238.1	239.2
plantar	171.3	198.89	—	215.3	238.1	239.2
appendix	153.5	197.5	230.3	211.3	235.2	239.0
arachnoid (cerebral)	192.1	198.4	—	225.2	237.6	239.7
spinal	192.3	198.4	—	225.4	237.6	239.7
areola (female)	174.0	198.81	233.0	217	238.3	239.3
male	175.0	198.81	233.0	217	238.3	239.3
arm NEC*	195.4	198.89	232.6	229.8	238.8	239.8
artery—*see* Neoplasm, connective tissue						
aryepiglottic fold	148.2	198.89	230.0	210.8	235.1	239.0
hypopharyngeal aspect	148.2	198.89	230.0	210.8	235.1	239.0
laryngeal aspect	161.1	197.3	231.0	212.1	235.6	239.1
marginal zone	148.2	198.89	230.0	210.8	235.1	239.0
arytenoid (cartilage)	161.3	197.3	231.0	212.1	235.6	239.1
fold—*see* Neoplasm, aryepiglottic						
atlas	170.2	198.5	—	213.2	238.0	239.2
atrium, cardiac	164.1	198.89	—	212.7	238.8	239.8
auditory						
canal (external) (skin)	173.2	198.2	232.2	216.2	238.2	239.2
internal	160.1	197.3	231.8	212.0	235.9	239.1
nerve	192.0	198.4	—	225.1	237.9	239.7
tube	160.1	197.3	231.8	212.0	235.9	239.1
opening	147.2	198.89	230.0	210.7	235.1	239.0
auricle, ear	173.2	198.2	232.2	216.2	238.2	239.2
cartilage	171.0	198.89	—	215.0	238.1	239.2
auricular canal (external)	173.2	198.2	232.2	216.2	238.2	239.2
internal	160.1	197.3	231.8	212.0	235.9	239.1
autonomic nerve or nervous system NEC	171.9	198.89	—	215.9	238.1	239.2
axilla, axillary	195.1	198.89	234.8	229.8	238.8	239.8
fold	173.5	198.2	232.5	216.5	238.2	239.2
back NEC*	195.8	198.89	232.5	229.8	238.8	239.8
Bartholin's gland	184.1	198.82	233.3	221.2	236.3	239.5
basal ganglia	191.0	198.3	—	225.0	237.5	239.6
basis pedunculi	191.7	198.3	—	225.0	237.5	239.6
bile or biliary (tract)	156.9	197.8	230.8	211.5	235.3	239.0
canaliculi (biliferi) (intrahepatic)	155.1	197.8	230.8	211.5	235.3	239.0
canals, interlobular	155.1	197.8	230.8	211.5	235.3	239.0
contiguous sites	156.8	—	—	—	—	—
duct or passage (common) (cyst) (extrahepatic)	156.1	197.8	230.8	211.5	235.3	239.0
contiguous sites with gallbladder	156.8	—	—	—	—	—
interlobular	155.1	197.8	230.8	211.5	235.3	239.0
intrahepatic	155.1	197.8	230.8	211.5	235.3	239.0
and extrahepatic	156.9	197.8	230.8	211.5	235.3	239.0
bladder (urinary)	188.9	198.1	233.7	223.3	236.7	239.4
contiguous sites	188.8	—	—	—	—	—
dome	188.1	198.1	233.7	223.3	236.7	239.4
neck	188.5	198.1	233.7	223.3	236.7	239.4
orifice	188.9	198.1	233.7	223.3	236.7	239.4
ureteric	188.6	198.1	233.7	223.3	236.7	239.4
urethral	188.5	198.1	233.7	223.3	236.7	239.4
sphincter	188.8	198.1	233.7	223.3	236.7	239.4
trigone	188.0	198.1	233.7	223.3	236.7	239.4

	Malignant					
	Primary	Secondary	Ca in situ	Benign	Uncertain Behavior	Unspecified
urachus	188.7	—	233.7	223.3	236.7	239.4
wall	188.9	198.1	233.7	223.3	236.7	239.4
anterior	188.3	198.1	233.7	223.3	236.7	239.4
lateral	188.2	198.1	233.7	223.3	236.7	239.4
posterior	188.4	198.1	233.7	223.3	236.7	239.4
blood vessel—*see* Neoplasm, connective tissue						

> Note—Carcinomas and adenocarcinomas, of any type other than intraosseous or odontogenic, of the sites listed under "Neoplasm, bone" should be considered as constituting metastatic spread from an unspecified primary site and coded to 198.5 for morbidity coding and to 199.1 for underlying cause of death coding.

	Primary	Secondary	Ca in situ	Benign	Uncertain Behavior	Unspecified
bone (periosteum)	170.9	198.5	—	213.9	238.0	239.2
acetabulum	170.6	198.5	—	213.6	238.0	239.2
acromion (process)	170.4	198.5	—	213.4	238.0	239.2
ankle	170.8	198.5	—	213.8	238.0	239.2
arm NEC	170.4	198.5	—	213.4	238.0	239.2
astragalus	170.8	198.5	—	213.8	238.0	239.2
atlas	170.2	198.5	—	213.2	238.0	239.2
axis	170.2	198.5	—	213.2	238.0	239.2
back NEC	170.2	198.5	—	213.2	238.0	239.2
calcaneus	170.8	198.5	—	213.8	238.0	239.2
calvarium	170.0	198.5	—	213.0	238.0	239.2
carpus (any)	170.5	198.5	—	213.5	238.0	239.2
cartilage NEC	170.9	198.5	—	213.9	238.0	239.2
clavicle	170.3	198.5	—	213.3	238.0	239.2
clivus	170.0	198.5	—	213.0	238.0	239.2
coccygeal vertebra	170.6	198.5	—	213.6	238.0	239.2
coccyx	170.6	198.5	—	213.6	238.0	239.2
costal cartilage	170.3	198.5	—	213.3	238.0	239.2
costovertebral joint	170.3	198.5	—	213.3	238.0	239.2
cranial	170.0	198.5	—	213.0	238.0	239.2
cuboid	170.8	198.5	—	213.8	238.0	239.2
cuneiform	170.9	198.5	—	213.9	238.0	239.2
ankle	170.8	198.5	—	213.8	238.0	239.2
wrist	170.5	198.5	—	213.5	238.0	239.2
digital	170.9	198.5	—	213.9	238.0	239.2
finger	170.5	198.5	—	213.5	238.0	239.2
toe	170.8	198.5	—	213.8	238.0	239.2
elbow	170.4	198.5	—	213.4	238.0	239.2
ethmoid (labyrinth)	170.0	198.5	—	213.0	238.0	239.2
face	170.0	198.5	—	213.0	238.0	239.2
lower jaw	170.1	198.5	—	213.1	238.0	239.2
femur (any part)	170.7	198.5	—	213.7	238.0	239.2
fibula (any part)	170.7	198.5	—	213.7	238.0	239.2
finger (any)	170.5	198.5	—	213.5	238.0	239.2
foot	170.8	198.5	—	213.8	238.0	239.2
forearm	170.4	198.5	—	213.4	238.0	239.2
frontal	170.0	198.5	—	213.0	238.0	239.2
hand	170.5	198.5	—	213.5	238.0	239.2
heel	170.8	198.5	—	213.8	238.0	239.2
hip	170.6	198.5	—	213.6	238.0	239.2
humerus (any part)	170.4	198.5	—	213.4	238.0	239.2
hyoid	170.0	198.5	—	213.0	238.0	239.2
ilium	170.6	198.5	—	213.6	238.0	239.2
innominate	170.6	198.5	—	213.6	238.0	239.2
intervertebral cartilage or disc	170.2	198.5	—	213.2	238.0	239.2
ischium	170.6	198.5	—	213.6	238.0	239.2
jaw (lower)	170.1	198.5	—	213.1	238.0	239.2
upper	170.0	198.5	—	213.0	238.0	239.2
knee	170.7	198.5	—	213.7	238.0	239.2
leg NEC	170.7	198.5	—	213.7	238.0	239.2
limb NEC	170.9	198.5	—	213.9	238.0	239.2
lower (long bones)	170.7	198.5	—	213.7	238.0	239.2

| | Malignant | | | | | |
	Primary	Secondary	Ca in situ	Benign	Uncertain Behavior	Unspecified
bone—*continued*						
short bones	170.8	198.5	—	213.8	238.0	239.2
upper (long bones)	170.4	198.5	—	213.4	238.0	239.2
short bones	170.5	198.5	—	213.5	238.0	239.2
long	170.9	198.5	—	213.9	238.0	239.2
lower limbs NEC	170.7	198.5	—	213.7	238.0	239.2
upper limbs NEC	170.4	198.5	—	213.4	238.0	239.2
malar	170.0	198.5	—	213.0	238.0	239.2
mandible	170.1	198.5	—	213.1	238.0	239.2
marrow NEC	202.9	198.5	—	—	—	238.7
mastoid	170.0	198.5	—	213.0	238.0	239.2
maxilla, maxillary (superior)	170.0	198.5	—	213.0	238.0	239.2
inferior	170.1	198.5	—	213.1	238.0	239.2
metacarpus (any)	170.5	198.5	—	213.5	238.0	239.2
metatarsus (any)	170.8	198.5	—	213.8	238.0	239.2
navicular (ankle)	170.8	198.5	—	213.8	238.0	239.2
hand	170.5	198.5	—	213.5	238.0	239.2
nose, nasal	170.0	198.5	—	213.0	238.0	239.2
occipital	170.0	198.5	—	213.0	238.0	239.2
orbit	170.0	198.5	—	213.0	238.0	239.2
parietal	170.0	198.5	—	213.0	238.0	239.2
patella	170.8	198.5	—	213.8	238.0	239.2
pelvic	170.6	198.5	—	213.6	238.0	239.2
phalanges	170.9	198.5	—	213.9	238.0	239.2
foot	170.8	198.5	—	213.8	238.0	239.2
hand	170.5	198.5	—	213.5	238.0	239.2
pubic	170.6	198.5	—	213.6	238.0	239.2
radius (any part)	170.4	198.5	—	213.4	238.0	239.2
rib	170.3	198.5	—	213.3	238.0	239.2
sacral vertebra	170.6	198.5	—	213.6	238.0	239.2
sacrum	170.6	198.5	—	213.6	238.0	239.2
scaphoid (of hand)	170.5	198.5	—	213.5	238.0	239.2
of ankle	170.8	198.5	—	213.8	238.0	239.2
scapula (any part)	170.4	198.5	—	213.4	238.0	239.2
sella turcica	170.0	198.5	—	213.0	238.0	239.2
short	170.9	198.5	—	213.9	238.0	239.2
lower limb	170.8	198.5	—	213.8	238.0	239.2
upper limb	170.5	198.5	—	213.5	238.0	239.2
shoulder	170.4	198.5	—	213.4	238.0	239.2
skeleton, skeletal NEC	170.9	198.5	—	213.9	238.0	239.2
skull	170.0	198.5	—	213.0	238.0	239.2
sphenoid	170.0	198.5	—	213.0	238.0	239.2
spine, spinal (column)	170.2	198.5	—	213.2	238.0	239.2
coccyx	170.6	198.5	—	213.6	238.0	239.2
sacrum	170.6	198.5	—	213.6	238.0	239.2
sternum	170.3	198.5	—	213.3	238.0	239.2
tarsus (any)	170.8	198.5	—	213.8	238.0	239.2
temporal	170.0	198.5	—	213.0	238.0	239.2
thumb	170.5	198.5	—	213.5	238.0	239.2
tibia (any part)	170.7	198.5	—	213.7	238.0	239.2
toe (any)	170.8	198.5	—	213.8	238.0	239.2
trapezium	170.5	198.5	—	213.5	238.0	239.2
trapezoid	170.5	198.5	—	213.5	238.0	239.2
turbinate	170.0	198.5	—	213.0	238.0	239.2
ulna (any part)	170.4	198.5	—	213.4	238.0	239.2
unciform	170.5	198.5	—	213.5	238.0	239.2
vertebra (column)	170.2	198.5	—	213.2	238.0	239.2
coccyx	170.6	198.5	—	213.6	238.0	239.2
sacrum	170.6	198.5	—	213.6	238.0	239.2
vomer	170.0	198.5	—	213.0	238.0	239.2
wrist	170.5	198.5	—	213.5	238.0	239.2
xiphoid process	170.3	198.5	—	213.3	238.0	239.2
zygomatic	170.0	198.5	—	213.0	238.0	239.2

	Malignant					
	Primary	Secondary	Ca in situ	Benign	Uncertain Behavior	Unspecified
book-leaf (mouth)	145.8	198.89	230.0	210.4	235.1	239.0
bowel—*see* Neoplasm, intestine						
brachial plexus	171.2	198.89	—	215.2	238.1	239.2
brain NEC	191.9	198.3	—	225.0	237.5	239.6
basal ganglia	191.0	198.3	—	225.0	237.5	239.6
cerebellopontine angle	191.6	198.3	—	225.0	237.5	239.6
cerebellum NOS	191.6	198.3	—	225.0	237.5	239.6
cerebrum	191.0	198.3	—	225.0	237.5	239.6
choroid plexus	191.5	198.3	—	225.0	237.5	239.6
contiguous sites	191.8	—	—	—	—	—
corpus callosum	191.8	198.3	—	225.0	237.5	239.6
corpus striatum	191.0	198.3	—	225.0	237.5	239.6
cortex (cerebral)	191.0	198.3	—	225.0	237.5	239.6
frontal lobe	191.1	198.3	—	225.0	237.5	239.6
globus pallidus	191.0	198.3	—	225.0	237.5	239.6
hippocampus	191.2	198.3	—	225.0	237.5	239.6
hypothalamus	191.0	198.3	—	225.0	237.5	239.6
internal capsule	191.0	198.3	—	225.0	237.5	239.6
medulla oblongata	191.7	198.3	—	225.0	237.5	239.6
meninges	192.1	198.4	—	225.2	237.6	239.7
midbrain	191.7	198.3	—	225.0	237.5	239.6
occipital lobe	191.4	198.3	—	225.0	237.5	239.6
parietal lobe	191.3	198.3	—	225.0	237.5	239.6
peduncle	191.7	198.3	—	225.0	237.5	239.6
pons	191.7	198.3	—	225.0	237.5	239.6
stem	191.7	198.3	—	225.0	237.5	239.6
tapetum	191.8	198.3	—	225.0	237.5	239.6
temporal lobe	191.2	198.3	—	225.0	237.5	239.6
thalamus	191.0	198.3	—	225.0	237.5	239.6
uncus	191.2	198.3	—	225.0	237.5	239.6
ventricle (floor)	191.5	198.3	—	225.0	237.5	239.6
branchial (cleft) (vestiges)	146.8	198.89	230.0	210.6	235.1	239.0
breast (connective tissue) (female)						
(glandular tissue) (soft parts)	174.9	198.81	233.0	217	238.3	239.3
areola	174.0	198.81	233.0	217	238.3	239.3
male	175.0	198.81	233.0	217	238.3	239.3
axillary tail	174.6	198.81	233.0	217	238.3	239.3
central portion	174.1	198.81	233.0	217	238.3	239.3
contiguous sites	174.8	—	—	—	—	—
ectopic sites	174.8	198.81	233.0	217	238.3	239.3
inner	174.8	198.81	233.0	217	238.3	239.3
lower	174.8	198.81	233.0	217	238.3	239.3
lower-inner quadrant	174.3	198.81	233.0	217	238.3	239.3
lower-outer quadrant	174.5	198.81	233.0	217	238.3	239.3
male	175.9	198.81	233.0	217	238.3	239.3
areola	175.0	198.81	233.0	217	238.3	239.3
ectopic tissue	175.9	198.81	233.0	217	238.3	239.3
nipple	175.0	198.81	233.0	217	238.3	239.3
mastectomy site (skin)	173.5	198.2	—	—	—	—
specified as breast tissue	174.8	198.81	—	—	—	—
midline	174.8	198.81	233.0	217	238.3	239.3
nipple	174.0	198.81	233.0	217	238.3	239.3
male	175.0	198.81	233.0	217	238.3	239.3
outer	174.8	198.81	233.0	217	238.3	239.3
skin	173.5	198.2	232.5	216.5	238.2	239.2
tail (axillary)	174.6	198.81	233.0	217	238.3	239.3
upper	174.8	198.81	233.0	217	238.3	239.3
upper-inner quadrant	174.2	198.81	233.0	217	238.3	239.3
upper-outer quadrant	174.4	198.81	233.0	217	238.3	239.3
broad ligament	183.3	198.82	233.3	221.0	236.3	239.5
bronchiogenic, bronchogenic (lung) . . .	162.9	197.0	231.2	212.3	235.7	239.1
bronchiole	162.9	197.0	231.2	212.3	235.7	239.1

	Malignant					
	Primary	Secondary	Ca in situ	Benign	Uncertain Behavior	Unspecified
bronchus	162.9	197.0	231.2	212.3	235.7	239.1
carina	162.2	197.0	231.2	212.3	235.7	239.1
contiguous sites with lung or trachea .	162.8	—	—	—	—	—
lower lobe of lung	162.5	197.0	231.2	212.3	235.7	239.1
main	162.2	197.0	231.2	212.3	235.7	239.1
middle lobe of lung	162.4	197.0	231.2	212.3	235.7	239.1
upper lobe of lung	162.3	197.0	231.2	212.3	235.7	239.1
brow.	173.3	198.2	232.3	216.3	238.2	239.2
buccal (cavity)	145.9	198.89	230.0	210.4	235.1	239.0
commissure	145.0	198.89	230.0	210.4	235.1	239.0
groove (lower) (upper)	145.1	198.89	230.0	210.4	235.1	239.0
mucosa	145.0	198.89	230.0	210.4	235.1	239.0
sulcus (lower) (upper)	145.1	198.89	230.0	210.4	235.1	239.0
bulbourethral gland	189.3	198.1	233.9	223.81	236.99	239.5
bursa—*see* Neoplasm, connective tissue						
buttock NEC*	195.3	198.89	232.5	229.8	238.8	239.8
calf*	195.5	198.89	232.7	229.8	238.8	239.8
calvarium	170.0	198.5	—	213.0	238.0	239.2
calyx, renal	189.1	198.0	233.9	223.1	236.91	239.5
canal						
anal	154.2	197.5	230.5	211.4	235.5	239.0
auditory (external)	173.2	198.2	232.2	216.2	238.2	239.2
auricular (external)	173.2	198.2	232.2	216.2	238.2	239.2
canaliculi, biliary (biliferi) (intrahepatic)	155.1	197.8	230.8	211.5	235.3	239.0
canthus (eye) (inner) (outer)	173.1	198.2	232.1	216.1	238.2	239.2
capillary—*see* Neoplasm, connective tissue						
caput coli	153.4	197.5	230.3	211.3	235.2	239.0
cardia (gastric)	151.0	197.8	230.2	211.1	235.2	239.0
cardiac orifice (stomach)	151.0	197.8	230.2	211.1	235.2	239.0
cardio-esophageal junction	151.0	197.8	230.2	211.1	235.2	239.0
cardio-esophagus	151.0	197.8	230.2	211.1	235.2	239.0
carina (bronchus)	162.2	197.0	231.2	212.3	235.7	239.1
carotid (artery)	171.0	198.89	—	215.0	238.1	239.2
body.	194.5	198.89	—	227.5	237.3	239.7
carpus (any bone)	170.5	198.5	—	213.5	238.0	239.2
cartilage (articular) (joint) NEC—*see also*						
Neoplasm, bone	170.9	198.5	—	213.9	238.0	239.2
arytenoid	161.3	197.3	231.0	212.1	235.6	239.1
auricular.	171.0	198.89	—	215.0	238.1	239.2
bronchi	162.2	197.3	—	212.3	235.7	239.1
connective tissue—*see* Neoplasm,						
connective tissue						
costal	170.3	198.5	—	213.3	238.0	239.2
cricoid.	161.3	197.3	231.0	212.1	235.6	239.1
cuneiform	161.3	197.3	231.0	212.1	235.6	239.1
ear (external)	171.0	198.89	—	215.0	238.1	239.2
ensiform	170.3	198.5	—	213.3	238.0	239.2
epiglottis	161.1	197.3	231.0	212.1	235.6	239.1
anterior surface	146.4	198.89	230.0	210.6	235.1	239.0
eyelid	171.0	198.89	—	215.0	238.1	239.2
intervertebral	170.2	198.5	—	213.2	238.0	239.2
larynx, laryngeal	161.3	197.3	231.0	212.1	235.6	239.1
nose, nasal	160.0	197.3	231.8	212.0	235.9	239.1
pinna	171.0	198.89	—	215.0	238.1	239.2
rib	170.3	198.5	—	213.3	238.0	239.2
semilunar (knee)	170.7	198.5	—	213.7	238.0	239.2
thyroid	161.3	197.3	231.0	212.1	235.6	239.1
trachea	162.0	197.3	231.1	212.2	235.7	239.1
cauda equina	192.2	198.3	—	225.3	237.5	239.7
cavity						
buccal	145.9	198.89	230.0	210.4	235.1	239.0
nasal	160.0	197.3	231.8	212.0	235.9	239.1
oral	145.9	198.89	230.0	210.4	235.1	239.0

	Malignant					
	Primary	Secondary	Ca in situ	Benign	Uncertain Behavior	Unspecified
cavity—*continued*						
peritoneal	158.9	197.6	—	211.8	235.4	239.0
tympanic	160.1	197.3	231.8	212.0	235.9	239.1
cecum	153.4	197.5	230.3	211.3	235.2	239.0
central						
nervous system—*see* Neoplasm,						
nervous system						
white matter	191.0	198.3	—	225.0	237.5	239.6
cerebellopontine (angle)	191.6	198.3	—	225.0	237.5	239.6
cerebellum, cerebellar	191.6	198.3	—	225.0	237.5	239.6
cerebrum, cerebral (cortex) (hemisphere)						
(white matter)	191.0	198.3	—	225.0	237.5	239.6
meninges	192.1	198.4	—	225.2	237.6	239.7
peduncle	191.7	198.3	—	225.0	237.5	239.6
ventricle (any)	191.5	198.3	—	225.0	237.5	239.6
cervical region	195.0	198.89	234.8	229.8	238.8	239.8
cervix (cervical) (uteri) (uterus)	180.9	198.82	233.1	219.0	236.0	239.5
canal	180.0	198.82	233.1	219.0	236.0	239.5
contiguous sites	180.8	—	—	—	—	—
endocervix (canal) (gland)	180.0	198.82	233.1	219.0	236.0	239.5
exocervix	180.1	198.82	233.1	219.0	236.0	239.5
external os	180.1	198.82	233.1	219.0	236.0	239.5
internal os	180.0	198.82	233.1	219.0	236.0	239.5
nabothian gland	180.0	198.82	233.1	219.0	236.0	239.5
squamocolumnar junction	180.8	198.82	233.1	219.0	236.0	239.5
stump	180.8	198.82	233.1	219.0	236.0	239.5
cheek	195.0	198.89	234.8	229.8	238.8	239.8
external	173.3	198.2	232.3	216.3	238.2	239.2
inner aspect	145.0	198.89	230.0	210.4	235.1	239.0
internal	145.0	198.89	230.0	210.4	235.1	239.0
mucosa	145.0	198.89	230.0	210.4	235.1	239.0
chest (wall) NEC	195.1	198.89	234.8	229.8	238.8	239.8
chiasma opticum	192.0	198.4	—	225.1	237.9	239.7
chin	173.3	198.2	232.3	216.3	238.2	239.2
choana	147.3	198.89	230.0	210.7	235.1	239.0
cholangiole	155.1	197.8	230.8	211.5	235.3	239.0
choledochal duct	156.1	197.8	230.8	211.5	235.3	239.0
choroid	190.6	198.4	234.0	224.6	238.8	239.8
plexus	191.5	198.3	—	225.0	237.5	239.6
ciliary body	190.0	198.4	234.0	224.0	238.8	239.8
clavicle	170.3	198.5	—	213.3	238.0	239.2
clitoris	184.3	198.82	233.3	221.2	236.3	239.5
clivus	170.0	198.5	—	213.0	238.0	239.2
cloacogenic zone	154.8	197.5	230.7	211.4	235.5	239.0
coccygeal						
body or glomus	194.6	198.89	—	227.6	237.3	239.7
vertebra	170.6	198.5	—	213.6	238.0	239.2
coccyx	170.6	198.5	—	213.6	238.0	239.2
colon—*see also* Neoplasm, intestine, large						
and rectum	154.0	197.5	230.4	211.4	235.2	239.0
column, spinal—*see* Neoplasm, spine						
columnella	173.3	198.2	232.3	216.3	238.2	239.2
commissure						
labial, lip	140.6	198.89	230.0	210.4	235.1	239.0
laryngeal	161.0	197.3	231.0	212.1	235.6	239.1
common (bile) duct	156.1	197.8	230.8	211.5	235.3	239.0
concha	173.2	198.2	232.2	216.2	238.2	239.2
nose	160.0	197.3	231.8	212.0	235.9	239.1
conjunctiva	190.3	198.4	234.0	224.3	238.8	239.8

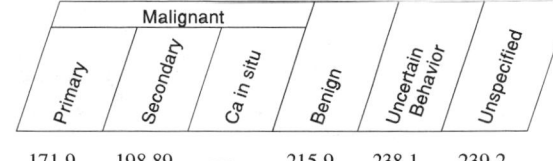

	Malignant					
	Primary	Secondary	Ca in situ	Benign	Uncertain Behavior	Unspecified
connective tissue NEC	171.9	198.89	—	215.9	238.1	239.2

> Note—For neoplasms of connective tissue (blood vessel, bursa, fasica, ligament, muscle, peripheral nerves, sympathetic and parasympathetic nerves, and ganglia, synovia, tendon, etc.) or of morphological types that indicate connective tissue, code according to the list under "Neoplasm, connective tissue;" for sites that do not appear in this list, code to neoplasm of that site; e.g.: liposarcoma, shoulder 171.2; leiomyosarcoma, stomach 151.9; neurofibroma, chest wall 215.4.
>
> Morphological types that indicate connective tissue appear in their proper place in the alphabetic index with the instruction "see Neoplasm, connective tissue..."

	Primary	Secondary	Ca in situ	Benign	Uncertain Behavior	Unspecified
abdomen	171.5	198.89	—	215.5	238.1	239.2
abdominal wall	171.5	198.89	—	215.5	238.1	239.2
ankle	171.3	198.89	—	215.3	238.1	239.2
antecubital fossa or space	171.2	198.89	—	215.2	238.1	239.2
arm	171.2	198.89	—	215.2	238.1	239.2
auricle (ear)	171.0	198.89	—	215.0	238.1	239.2
axilla	171.4	198.89	—	215.4	238.1	239.2
back	171.7	198.89	—	215.7	238.1	239.2
breast (female) *(see also* Neoplasm,						
breast)	174.9	198.81	233.0	217	238.3	239.3
male	175.9	198.81	233.0	217	238.3	239.3
buttock	171.6	198.89	—	215.6	238.1	239.2
calf	171.3	198.89	—	215.3	238.1	239.2
cervical region	171.0	198.89	—	215.0	238.1	239.2
cheek	171.0	198.89	—	215.0	238.1	239.2
chest (wall)	171.4	198.89	—	215.4	238.1	239.2
chin	171.0	198.89	—	215.0	238.1	239.2
contiguous sites	171.8	—	—	—	—	—
diaphragm	171.4	198.89	—	215.4	238.1	239.2
ear (external)	171.0	198.89	—	215.0	238.1	239.2
elbow	171.2	198.89	—	215.2	238.1	239.2
extrarectal	171.6	198.89	—	215.6	238.1	239.2
extremity	171.8	198.89	—	215.8	238.1	239.2
lower	171.3	198.89	—	215.3	238.1	239.2
upper	171.2	198.89	—	215.2	238.1	239.2
eyelid	171.0	198.89	—	215.0	238.1	239.2
face	171.0	198.89	—	215.0	238.1	239.2
finger	171.2	198.89	—	215.2	238.1	239.2
flank	171.7	198.89	—	215.7	238.1	239.2
foot	171.3	198.89	—	215.3	238.1	239.2
forearm	171.2	198.89	—	215.2	238.1	239.2
forehead	171.0	198.89	—	215.0	238.1	239.2
gluteal region	171.6	198.89	—	215.6	238.1	239.2
great vessels NEC	171.4	198.89	—	215.4	238.1	239.2
groin	171.6	198.89	—	215.6	238.1	239.2
hand	171.2	198.89	—	215.2	238.1	239.2
head	171.0	198.89	—	215.0	238.1	239.2
heel	171.3	198.89	—	215.3	238.1	239.2
hip	171.3	198.89	—	215.3	238.1	239.2
hypochondrium	171.5	198.89	—	215.5	238.1	239.2
iliopsoas muscle	171.6	198.89	—	215.5	238.1	239.2
infraclavicular region	171.4	198.89	—	215.4	238.1	239.2
inguinal (canal) (region)	171.6	198.89	—	215.6	238.1	239.2
intrathoracic	171.4	198.89	—	215.4	238.1	239.2
ischorectal fossa	171.6	198.89	—	215.6	238.1	239.2
jaw	143.9	198.89	230.0	210.4	235.1	239.0
knee	171.3	198.89	—	215.3	238.1	239.2
leg	171.3	198.89	—	215.3	238.1	239.2

	Malignant					
	Primary	Secondary	Ca in situ	Benign	Uncertain Behavior	Unspecified
connective tissue—*continued*						
limb NEC	171.9	198.89	—	215.8	238.1	239.2
lower	171.3	198.89	—	215.3	238.1	239.2
upper	171.2	198.89	—	215.2	238.1	239.2
nates	171.6	198.89	—	215.6	238.1	239.2
neck	171.0	198.89	—	215.0	238.1	239.2
orbit	190.1	198.4	234.0	224.1	238.8	239.8
pararectal	171.6	198.89	—	215.6	238.1	239.2
para-urethral	171.6	198.89	—	215.6	238.1	239.2
paravaginal	171.6	198.89	—	215.6	238.1	239.2
pelvis (floor)	171.6	198.89	—	215.6	238.1	239.2
pelvo-abdominal	171.8	198.89	—	215.8	238.1	239.2
perineum	171.6	198.89	—	215.6	238.1	239.2
perirectal (tissue)	171.6	198.89	—	215.6	238.1	239.2
periurethral (tissue)	171.6	198.89	—	215.6	238.1	239.2
popliteal fossa or space	171.3	198.89	—	215.3	238.1	239.2
presacral	171.6	198.89	—	215.6	238.1	239.2
psoas muscle	171.5	198.89	—	215.5	238.1	239.2
pterygoid fossa	171.0	198.89	—	215.0	238.1	239.2
rectovaginal septum or wall	171.6	198.89	—	215.6	238.1	239.2
rectovesical	171.6	198.89	—	215.6	238.1	239.2
retroperitoneum	158.0	197.6	—	211.8	235.4	239.0
sacrococcygeal region	171.6	198.89	—	215.6	238.1	239.2
scalp	171.0	198.89	—	215.0	238.1	239.2
scapular region	171.4	198.89	—	215.4	238.1	239.2
shoulder	171.2	198.89	—	215.2	238.1	239.2
skin (dermis) NEC	173.9	198.2	232.9	216.9	238.2	239.2
submental	171.0	198.89	—	215.0	238.1	239.2
supraclavicular region	171.0	198.89	—	215.0	238.1	239.2
temple	171.0	198.89	—	215.0	238.1	239.2
temporal region	171.0	198.89	—	215.0	238.1	239.2
thigh	171.3	198.89	—	215.3	238.1	239.2
thoracic (duct) (wall)	171.4	198.89	—	215.4	238.1	239.2
thorax	171.4	198.89	—	215.4	238.1	239.2
thumb	171.2	198.89	—	215.2	238.1	239.2
toe	171.3	198.89	—	215.3	238.1	239.2
trunk	171.7	198.89	—	215.7	238.1	239.2
umbilicus	171.5	198.89	—	215.5	238.1	239.2
vesicorectal	171.6	198.89	—	215.6	238.1	239.2
wrist	171.2	198.89	—	215.2	238.1	239.2
conus medullaris	192.2	198.3	—	225.3	237.5	239.7
cord (true) (vocal)	161.0	197.3	231.0	212.1	235.6	239.1
false	161.1	197.3	231.0	212.1	235.6	239.1
spermatic	187.6	198.82	233.6	222.8	236.6	239.5
spinal (cervical) (lumbar) (thoracic) . .	192.2	198.3	—	225.3	237.5	239.7
cornea (limbus)	190.4	198.4	234.0	224.4	238.8	239.8
corpus						
albicans	183.0	198.6	233.3	220	236.2	239.5
callosum, brain	191.8	198.3	—	225.0	237.5	239.6
cavernosum	187.3	198.82	233.5	222.1	236.6	239.5
gastric	151.4	197.8	230.2	211.1	235.2	239.0
penis	187.3	198.82	233.5	222.1	236.6	239.5
striatum, cerebrum	191.0	198.3	—	225.0	237.5	239.6
uteri	182.0	198.82	233.2	219.1	236.0	239.5
isthmus	182.1	198.82	233.2	219.1	236.0	239.5
cortex						
adrenal	194.0	198.7	234.8	227.0	237.2	239.7
cerebral	191.0	198.3	—	225.0	237.5	239.6
costal cartilage	170.3	198.5	—	213.3	238.0	239.2
costovertebral joint	170.3	198.5	—	213.3	238.0	239.2

	Malignant					
	Primary	Secondary	Ca in situ	Benign	Uncertain Behavior	Unspecified
Cowper's gland	189.3	198.1	233.9	223.81	236.99	239.5
cranial (fossa, any)	191.9	198.3	—	225.0	237.5	239.6
meninges	192.1	198.4	—	225.2	237.6	239.7
nerve (any)	192.0	198.4	—	225.1	237.9	239.7
craniobuccal pouch	194.3	198.89	234.8	227.3	237.0	239.7
craniopharyngeal (duct) (pouch)	194.3	198.89	234.8	227.3	237.0	239.7
cricoid	148.0	198.89	230.0	210.8	235.1	239.0
cartilage	161.3	197.3	231.0	212.1	235.6	239.1
cricopharynx	148.0	198.89	230.0	210.8	235.1	239.0
crypt of Morgagni	154.8	197.5	230.7	211.4	235.2	239.0
crystalline lens	190.0	198.4	234.0	224.0	238.8	239.8
cul-de-sac (Douglas')	158.8	197.6	—	211.8	235.4	239.0
cuneiform cartilage	161.3	197.3	231.0	212.1	235.6	239.1
cutaneous—*see* Neoplasm, skin						
cutis—*see* Neoplasm, skin						
cystic (bile) duct (common)	156.1	197.8	230.8	211.5	235.3	239.0
dermis—*see* Neoplasm, skin						
diaphragm	171.4	198.89	—	215.4	238.1	239.2
digestive organs, system, tube, tract NEC	159.9	197.8	230.9	211.9	235.5	239.0
contiguous sites with peritoneum	159.8	—	—	—	—	—
disc, intervertebral	170.2	198.5	—	213.2	238.0	239.2
disease, generalized	199.0	199.0	234.9	229.9	238.9	199.0
disseminated	199.0	199.0	234.9	229.9	238.9	199.0
Douglas' cul-de-sac or pouch	158.8	197.6	—	211.8	235.4	239.0
duodenojejunal junction	152.8	197.4	230.7	211.2	235.2	239.0
duodenum	152.0	197.4	230.7	211.2	235.2	239.0
dura (cranial) (mater)	192.1	198.4	—	225.2	237.6	239.7
cerebral	192.1	198.4	—	225.2	237.6	239.7
spinal	192.3	198.4	—	225.4	237.6	239.7
ear (external)	173.2	198.2	232.2	216.2	238.2	239.2
auricle or auris	173.2	198.2	232.2	216.2	238.2	239.2
canal, external	173.2	198.2	232.2	216.2	238.2	239.2
cartilage	171.0	198.89	—	215.0	238.1	239.2
external meatus	173.2	198.2	232.2	216.2	238.2	239.2
inner	160.1	197.3	231.8	212.0	235.9	239.1
lobule	173.2	198.2	232.2	216.2	238.2	239.2
middle	160.1	197.3	231.8	212.0	235.9	239.1
contiguous sites with accessory sinuses or nasal cavities	160.8	—	—	—	—	—
skin	173.2	198.2	232.2	216.2	238.2	239.2
earlobe	173.2	198.2	232.2	216.2	238.2	239.2
ejaculatory duct	187.8	198.82	233.6	222.8	236.6	239.5
elbow NEC*	195.4	198.89	232.6	229.8	238.8	239.8
endocardium	164.1	198.89	—	212.7	238.8	239.8
endocervix (canal) (gland)	180.0	198.82	233.1	219.0	236.0	239.5
endocrine gland NEC	194.9	198.89	—	227.9	237.4	239.7
pluriglandular NEC	194.8	198.89	234.8	227.8	237.4	239.7
endometrium (gland) (stroma)	182.0	198.82	233.2	219.1	236.0	239.5
ensiform cartilage	170.3	198.5	—	213.3	238.0	239.2
enteric—*see* Neoplasm, intestine						
ependyma (brain)	191.5	198.3	—	225.0	237.5	239.6
epicardium	164.1	198.89	—	212.7	238.8	239.8
epididymis	187.5	198.82	233.6	222.3	236.6	239.5
epidural	192.9	198.4	—	225.9	237.9	239.7
epiglottis	161.1	197.3	231.0	212.1	235.6	239.1
anterior aspect or surface	146.4	198.89	230.0	210.6	235.1	239.0
cartilage	161.3	197.3	231.0	212.1	235.6	239.1
free border (margin)	146.4	198.89	230.0	210.6	235.1	239.0
junctional region	146.5	198.89	230.0	210.6	235.1	239.0
posterior (laryngeal) surface	161.1	197.3	231.0	212.1	235.6	239.1
suprahyoid portion	161.1	197.3	231.0	212.1	235.6	239.1

	Malignant					
	Primary	Secondary	Ca in situ	Benign	Uncertain Behavior	Unspecified
esophagogastric junction	151.0	197.8	230.2	211.1	235.2	239.0
esophagus	150.9	197.8	230.1	211.0	235.5	239.0
abdominal	150.2	197.8	230.1	211.0	235.5	239.0
cervical	150.0	197.8	230.1	211.0	235.5	239.0
contiguous sites	150.8	—	—	—	—	—
distal (third)	150.5	197.8	230.1	211.0	235.5	239.0
lower (third)	150.5	197.8	230.1	211.0	235.5	239.0
middle (third)	150.4	197.8	230.1	211.0	235.5	239.0
proximal (third)	150.3	197.8	230.1	211.0	235.5	239.0
specified part NEC	150.8	197.8	230.1	211.0	235.5	239.0
thoracic	150.1	197.8	230.1	211.0	235.5	239.0
upper (third)	150.3	197.8	230.1	211.0	235.5	239.0
ethmoid (sinus)	160.3	197.3	231.8	212.0	235.9	239.1
bone or labyrinth	170.0	198.5	—	213.0	238.0	239.2
Eustachian tube	160.1	197.3	231.8	212.0	235.9	239.1
exocervix	180.1	198.82	233.1	219.0	236.0	239.5
external						
meatus (ear)	173.2	198.2	232.2	216.2	238.2	239.2
os, cervix uteri	180.1	198.82	233.1	219.0	236.0	239.5
extradural	192.9	198.4	—	225.9	237.9	239.7
extrahepatic (bile) duct	156.1	197.8	230.8	211.5	235.3	239.0
contiguous sites with gallbladder . . .	156.8	—	—	—	—	—
extraocular muscle	190.1	198.4	234.0	224.1	238.8	239.8
extrarectal	195.3	198.89	234.8	229.8	238.8	239.8
extremity*	195.8	198.89	232.8	229.8	238.8	239.8
lower*	195.5	198.89	232.7	229.8	238.8	239.8
upper*	195.4	198.89	232.6	229.8	238.8	239.8
eye NEC	190.9	198.4	234.0	224.9	238.8	239.8
contiguous sites	190.8	—	—	—	—	—
specified sites NEC	190.8	198.4	234.0	224.8	238.8	239.8
eyeball	190.0	198.4	234.0	224.0	238.8	239.8
eyebrow	173.3	198.2	232.3	216.3	238.2	239.2
eyelid (lower) (skin) (upper)	173.1	198.2	232.1	216.1	238.2	239.2
cartilage	171.0	198.89	—	215.0	238.1	239.2
face NEC*	195.0	198.89	232.3	229.8	238.8	239.8
fallopian tube (accessory)	183.2	198.82	233.3	221.0	236.3	239.5
falx (cerebelli) (cerebri)	192.1	198.4	—	225.2	237.6	239.7
fascia—*see also* Neoplasm, connective						
tissue						
palmar	171.2	198.89	—	215.2	238.1	239.2
plantar	171.3	198.89	—	215.3	238.1	239.2
fatty tissue—*see* Neoplasm, connective						
tissue						
fauces, faucial NEC	146.9	198.89	230.0	210.6	235.1	239.0
pillars	146.2	198.89	230.0	210.6	235.1	239.0
tonsil	146.0	198.89	230.0	210.5	235.1	239.0
femur (any part)	170.7	198.5	—	213.7	238.0	239.2
fetal membrane	181	198.82	233.2	219.8	236.1	239.5
fibrous tissue—*see* Neoplasm, connective						
tissue						
fibula (any part)	170.7	198.5	—	213.7	238.0	239.2
filum terminale	192.2	198.3	—	225.3	237.5	239.7
finger NEC*	195.4	198.89	232.6	229.8	238.8	239.8
flank NEC*	195.8	198.89	232.5	229.8	238.8	239.8
follicle, nabothian	180.0	198.82	233.1	219.0	236.0	239.5
foot NEC*	195.5	198.89	232.7	229.8	238.8	239.8
forearm NEC*	195.4	198.89	232.6	229.8	238.8	239.8
forehead (skin)	173.3	198.2	232.3	216.3	238.2	239.2
foreskin	187.1	198.82	233.5	222.1	236.6	239.5

	Malignant					
	Primary	Secondary	Ca in situ	Benign	Uncertain Behavior	Unspecified
fornix						
pharyngeal	147.3	198.89	230.0	210.7	235.1	239.0
vagina	184.0	198.82	233.3	221.1	236.3	239.5
fossa (of)						
anterior (cranial)	191.9	198.3	—	225.0	237.5	239.6
cranial	191.9	198.3	—	225.0	237.5	239.6
ischiorectal	195.3	198.89	234.8	229.8	238.8	239.8
middle (cranial)	191.9	198.3	—	225.0	237.5	239.6
pituitary	194.3	198.89	234.8	227.3	237.0	239.7
posterior (cranial)	191.9	198.3	—	225.0	237.5	239.6
pterygoid	171.0	198.89	—	215.0	238.1	239.2
pyriform	148.1	198.89	230.0	210.8	235.1	239.0
Rosenmüller	147.2	198.89	230.0	210.7	235.1	239.0
tonsillar	146.1	198.89	230.0	210.6	235.1	239.0
fourchette	184.4	198.82	233.3	221.2	236.3	239.5
frenulum						
labii—*see* Neoplasm, lip, internal						
linguae	141.3	198.89	230.0	210.1	235.1	239.0
frontal						
bone	170.0	198.5	—	213.0	238.0	239.2
lobe, brain	191.1	198.3	—	225.0	237.5	239.6
meninges	192.1	198.4	—	225.2	237.6	239.7
pole	191.1	198.3	—	225.0	237.5	239.6
sinus	160.4	197.3	231.8	212.0	235.9	239.1
fundus						
stomach	151.3	197.8	230.2	211.1	235.2	239.0
uterus	182.0	198.82	233.2	219.1	236.0	239.5
gall duct (extrahepatic)	156.1	197.8	230.8	211.5	235.3	239.0
intrahepatic	155.1	197.8	230.8	211.5	235.3	239.0
gallbladder	156.0	197.8	230.8	211.5	235.3	239.0
contiguous sites with extrahepatic						
bile ducts	156.8	—	—	—	—	—
ganglia (*see also* Neoplasm, connective						
tissue)	171.9	198.89	—	215.9	238.1	239.2
basal	191.0	198.3	—	225.0	237.5	239.6
ganglion (*see also* Neoplasm, connective						
tissue)	171.9	198.89	—	215.9	238.1	239.2
cranial nerve	192.0	198.4	—	225.1	237.9	239.7
Gartner's duct	184.0	198.82	233.3	221.1	236.3	239.5
gastric—*see* Neoplasm, stomach						
gastrocolic	159.8	197.8	230.9	211.9	235.5	239.0
gastroesophageal junction	151.0	197.8	230.2	211.1	235.2	239.0
gastrointestinal (tract) NEC	159.9	197.8	230.9	211.9	235.5	239.0
generalized	199.0	199.0	234.9	229.9	238.9	199.0
genital organ or tract						
female NEC	184.9	198.82	233.3	221.9	236.3	239.5
contiguous sites	184.8	—	—	—	—	—
specified site NEC	184.8	198.82	233.3	221.8	236.3	239.5
male NEC	187.9	198.82	233.6	222.9	236.6	239.5
contiguous sites	187.8	—	—	—	—	—
specified site NEC	187.8	198.82	233.6	222.8	236.6	239.5
genitourinary tract						
female	184.9	198.82	233.3	221.9	236.3	239.5
male	187.9	198.82	233.6	222.9	236.6	239.5
gingiva (alveolar) (marginal)	143.9	198.89	230.0	210.4	235.1	239.0
lower	143.1	198.89	230.0	210.4	235.1	239.0
mandibular	143.1	198.89	230.0	210.4	235.1	239.0
maxillary	143.0	198.89	230.0	210.4	235.1	239.0
upper	143.0	198.89	230.0	210.4	235.1	239.0

| | Malignant | | | | | |
	Primary	Secondary	Ca in situ	Benign	Uncertain Behavior	Unspecified
gland, glandular (lymphatic) (system)— *see also* Neoplasm, lymph gland						
endocrine NEC	194.9	198.89	—	227.9	237.4	239.7
salivary—*see* Neoplasm, salivary, gland						
glans penis	187.2	198.82	233.5	222.1	236.6	239.5
globus pallidus	191.0	198.3	—	225.0	237.5	239.6
glomus						
coccygeal	194.6	198.89	—	227.6	237.3	239.7
jugularis	194.6	198.89	—	227.6	237.3	239.7
glosso-epiglottic fold(s)	146.4	198.89	230.0	210.6	235.1	239.0
glossopalatine fold	146.2	198.89	230.0	210.6	235.1	239.0
glossopharyngeal sulcus	146.1	198.89	230.0	210.6	235.1	239.0
glottis	161.0	197.3	231.0	212.1	235.6	239.1
gluteal region*	195.3	198.89	232.5	229.8	238.8	239.8
great vessels NEC	171.4	198.89	—	215.4	238.1	239.2
groin NEC*	195.3	198.89	232.5	229.8	238.8	239.8
gum	143.9	198.89	230.0	210.4	235.1	239.0
contiguous sites	143.8	—	—	—	—	—
lower	143.1	198.89	230.0	210.4	235.1	239.0
upper	143.0	198.89	230.0	210.4	235.1	239.0
hand NEC*	195.4	198.89	232.6	229.8	238.8	239.8
head NEC*	195.0	198.89	232.4	229.8	238.8	239.8
heart	164.1	198.89	—	212.7	238.8	239.8
contiguous sites with mediastinum or thymus	164.8	—	—	—	—	—
heel NEC*	195.5	198.89	232.7	229.8	238.8	239.8
helix	173.2	198.2	232.2	216.2	238.2	239.2
hematopoietic, hemopoietic tissue NEC	202.8	198.89	—	—	—	238.7
hemisphere, cerebral	191.0	198.3	—	225.0	237.5	239.6
hemorrhoidal zone	154.2	197.5	230.5	211.4	235.5	239.0
hepatic	155.2	197.7	230.8	211.5	235.3	239.0
duct (bile)	156.1	197.8	230.8	211.5	235.3	239.0
flexure (colon)	153.0	197.5	230.3	211.3	235.2	239.0
primary	155.0	—	—	—	—	—
hilus of lung	162.2	197.0	231.2	212.3	235.7	239.1
hip NEC*	195.5	198.89	232.7	229.8	238.8	239.8
hippocampus, brain	191.2	198.3	—	225.0	237.5	239.6
humerus (any part)	170.4	198.5	—	213.4	238.0	239.2
hymen	184.0	198.82	233.3	221.1	236.3	239.5
hypopharynx, hypopharyngeal NEC	148.9	198.89	230.0	210.8	235.1	239.0
contiguous sites	148.8	—	—	—	—	—
postcricoid region	148.0	198.89	230.0	210.8	235.1	239.0
posterior wall	148.3	198.89	230.0	210.8	235.1	239.0
pyriform fossa (sinus)	148.1	198.89	230.0	210.8	235.1	239.0
specified site NEC	148.8	198.89	230.0	210.8	235.1	239.0
wall	148.9	198.89	230.0	210.8	235.1	239.0
posterior	148.3	198.89	230.0	210.8	235.1	239.0
hypophysis	194.3	198.89	234.8	227.3	237.0	239.7
hypothalamus	191.0	198.3	—	225.0	237.5	239.6
ileocecum, ileocecal (coil, junction, valve)	153.4	197.5	230.3	211.3	235.2	239.0
ileum	152.2	197.4	230.7	211.2	235.2	239.0
ilium	170.6	198.5	—	213.6	238.0	239.2
immunoproliferative NEC	203.8	—	—	—	—	—
infraclavicular (region)*	195.1	198.89	232.5	229.8	238.8	239.8
inguinal (region)*	195.3	198.89	232.5	229.8	238.8	239.8
insula	191.0	198.3	—	225.0	237.5	239.6
insular tissue (pancreas)	157.4	197.8	230.9	211.7	235.5	239.0
brain	191.0	198.3	—	225.0	237.5	239.6

| | Malignant | | | | | |
	Primary	Secondary	Ca in situ	Benign	Uncertain Behavior	Unspecified
interarytenoid fold	148.2	198.89	230.0	210.8	235.1	239.0
hypopharyngeal aspect	148.2	198.89	230.0	210.8	235.1	239.0
laryngeal aspect	161.1	197.3	231.0	212.1	235.6	239.1
marginal zone	148.2	198.89	230.0	210.8	235.1	239.0
interdental papillae	143.9	198.89	230.0	210.4	235.1	239.0
lower	143.1	198.89	230.0	210.4	235.1	239.0
upper	143.0	198.89	230.0	210.4	235.1	239.0
internal						
capsule	191.0	198.3	—	225.0	237.5	239.6
os (cervix)	180.0	198.82	233.1	219.0	236.0	239.5
intervertebral cartilage or disc	170.2	198.5	—	213.2	238.0	239.2
intestine, intestinal	159.0	197.8	230.7	211.9	235.2	239.0
large	153.9	197.5	230.3	211.3	235.2	239.0
appendix	153.5	197.5	230.3	211.3	235.2	239.0
caput coli	153.4	197.5	230.3	211.3	235.2	239.0
cecum	153.4	197.5	230.3	211.3	235.2	239.0
colon	153.9	197.5	230.3	211.3	235.2	239.0
and rectum	154.0	197.5	230.4	211.4	235.2	239.0
ascending	153.6	197.5	230.3	211.3	235.2	239.0
caput	153.4	197.5	230.3	211.3	235.2	239.0
contiguous sites	153.8	—	—	—	—	—
descending	153.2	197.5	230.3	211.3	235.2	239.0
distal	153.2	197.5	230.3	211.3	235.2	239.0
left	153.2	197.5	230.3	211.3	235.2	239.0
pelvic	153.3	197.5	230.3	211.3	235.2	239.0
right	153.6	197.5	230.3	211.3	235.2	239.0
sigmoid (flexure)	153.3	197.5	230.3	211.3	235.2	239.0
transverse	153.1	197.5	230.3	211.3	235.2	239.0
contiguous sites	153.8	—	—	—	—	—
hepatic flexure	153.0	197.5	230.3	211.3	235.2	239.0
ileocecum,ileocecal (coil, valve)	153.4	197.5	230.3	211.3	235.2	239.0
sigmoid flexure (lower) (upper)	153.3	197.5	230.3	211.3	235.2	239.0
splenic flexure	153.7	197.5	230.3	211.3	235.2	239.0
small	152.9	197.4	230.7	211.2	235.2	239.0
contiguous sites	152.8	—	—	—	—	—
duodenum	152.0	197.4	230.7	211.2	235.2	239.0
ileum	152.2	197.4	230.7	211.2	235.2	239.0
jejunum	152.1	197.4	230.7	211.2	235.2	239.0
tract NEC	159.0	197.8	230.7	211.9	235.2	239.0
intra-abdominal	195.2	198.89	234.8	229.8	238.8	239.8
intracranial NEC	191.9	198.3	—	225.0	237.5	239.6
intrahepatic (bile) duct	155.1	197.8	230.8	211.5	235.3	239.0
intraocular	190.0	198.4	234.0	224.0	238.8	239.8
intraorbital	190.1	198.4	234.0	224.1	238.8	239.8
intrasellar	194.3	198.89	234.8	227.3	237.0	239.7
intrathoracic (cavity) (organs NEC)	195.1	198.89	234.8	229.8	238.8	239.8
contiguous sites with respiratory						
organs	165.8	—	—	—	—	—
iris	190.0	198.4	234.0	224.0	238.8	239.8
ischiorectal (fossa)	195.3	198.89	234.8	229.8	238.8	239.8
ischium	170.6	198.5	—	213.6	238.0	239.2
island of Reil	191.0	198.3	—	225.0	237.5	239.6
islands or islets of Langerhans	157.4	197.8	230.9	211.7	235.5	239.0
isthmus uteri	182.1	198.82	233.2	219.1	236.0	239.5
jaw	195.0	198.89	234.8	229.8	238.8	239.8
bone	170.1	198.5	—	213.1	238.0	239.2
carcinoma	143.9	—	—	—	—	—
lower	143.1	—	—	—	—	—
upper	143.0	—	—	—	—	—
lower	170.1	198.5	—	213.1	238.0	239.2
upper	170.0	198.5	—	213.0	238.0	239.2

| | Malignant | | | | | |
	Primary	Secondary	Ca in situ	Benign	Uncertain Behavior	Unspecified
jaw—*continued*						
carcinoma (any type) (lower) (upper)	195.0	—	—	—	—	—
skin	173.3	198.2	232.3	216.3	238.2	239.2
soft tissues	143.9	198.89	230.0	210.4	235.1	239.0
lower	143.1	198.89	230.0	210.4	235.1	239.0
upper	143.0	198.89	230.0	210.4	235.1	239.0
jejunum	152.1	197.4	230.7	211.2	235.2	239.0
joint NEC *(see also* Neoplasm, bone)	170.9	198.5	—	213.9	238.0	239.2
acromioclavicular	170.4	198.5	—	213.4	238.0	239.2
bursa or synovial membrane—*see* Neoplasm, connective tissue						
costovertebral	170.3	198.5	—	213.3	238.0	239.2
sternocostal	170.3	198.5	—	213.3	238.0	239.2
temporomandibular	170.1	198.5	—	213.1	238.0	239.2
junction						
anorectal	154.8	197.5	230.7	211.4	235.5	239.0
cardioesophageal	151.0	197.8	230.2	211.1	235.2	239.0
esophagogastric	151.0	197.8	230.2	211.1	235.2	239.0
gastroesophageal	151.0	197.8	230.2	211.1	235.2	239.0
hard and soft palate	145.5	198.89	230.0	210.4	235.1	239.0
ileocecal	153.4	197.5	230.3	211.3	235.2	239.0
pelvirectal	154.0	197.5	230.4	211.4	235.2	239.0
pelviureteric	189.1	198.0	233.9	223.1	236.91	239.5
rectosigmoid	154.0	197.5	230.4	211.4	235.2	239.0
squamocolumnar, of cervix	180.8	198.82	233.1	219.0	236.0	239.5
kidney (parenchyma)	189.0	198.0	233.9	223.0	236.91	239.5
calyx	189.1	198.0	233.9	223.1	236.91	239.5
hilus	189.1	198.0	233.9	223.1	236.91	239.5
pelvis	189.1	198.0	233.9	223.1	236.91	239.5
knee NEC*	195.5	198.89	232.7	229.8	238.8	239.8
labia (skin)	184.4	198.82	233.3	221.2	236.3	239.5
majora	184.1	198.82	233.3	221.2	236.3	239.5
minora	184.2	198.82	233.3	221.2	236.3	239.5
labial—*see also* Neoplasm, lip						
sulcus (lower) (upper)	145.1	198.89	230.0	210.4	235.1	239.0
labium (skin)	184.4	198.82	233.3	221.2	236.3	239.5
majus	184.1	198.82	233.3	221.2	236.3	239.5
minus	184.2	198.82	233.3	221.2	236.3	239.5
lacrimal						
canaliculi	190.7	198.4	234.0	224.7	238.8	239.8
duct (nasal)	190.7	198.4	234.0	224.7	238.8	239.8
gland	190.2	198.4	234.0	224.2	238.8	239.8
punctum	190.7	198.4	234.0	224.7	238.8	239.8
sac	190.7	198.4	234.0	224.7	238.8	239.8
Langerhans, islands or islets	157.4	197.8	230.9	211.7	235.5	239.0
laryngopharynx	148.9	198.89	230.0	210.8	235.1	239.0
larynx, laryngeal NEC	161.9	197.3	231.0	212.1	235.6	239.1
aryepiglottic fold	161.1	197.3	231.0	212.1	235.6	239.1
cartilage (arytenoid) (cricoid) (cuneiform) (thyroid)	161.3	197.3	231.0	212.1	235.6	239.1
commissure (anterior) (posterior)	161.0	197.3	231.0	212.1	235.6	239.1
contiguous sites	161.8	—	—	—	—	—
extrinsic NEC	161.1	197.3	231.0	212.1	235.6	239.1
meaning hypopharynx	148.9	198.89	230.0	210.8	235.1	239.0
interarytenoid fold	161.1	197.3	231.0	212.1	235.6	239.1
intrinsic	161.0	197.3	231.0	212.1	235.6	239.1
ventricular band	161.1	197.3	231.0	212.1	235.6	239.1
leg NEC*	195.5	198.89	232.7	229.8	238.8	239.8
lens, crystalline	190.0	198.4	234.0	224.0	238.8	239.8

	Malignant					
	Primary	Secondary	Ca in situ	Benign	Uncertain Behavior	Unspecified
lid (lower) (upper)	173.1	198.2	232.1	216.1	238.2	239.2
ligament—*see also* Neoplasm, connective tissue						
broad	183.3	198.82	233.3	221.0	236.3	239.5
Mackenrodt's	183.8	198.82	233.3	221.8	236.3	239.5
non-uterine—*see* Neoplasm, connective tissue						
round	183.5	198.82	—	221.0	236.3	239.5
sacro-uterine	183.4	198.82	—	221.0	236.3	239.5
uterine	183.4	198.82	—	221.0	236.3	239.5
utero-ovarian	183.8	198.82	233.3	221.8	236.3	239.5
uterosacral	183.4	198.82	—	221.0	236.3	239.5
limb*	195.8	198.89	232.8	229.8	238.8	239.8
lower*	195.5	198.89	232.7	229.8	238.8	239.8
upper*	195.4	198.89	232.6	229.8	238.8	239.8
limbus of cornea	190.4	198.4	234.0	224.4	238.8	239.8
lingual NEC *(see also* Neoplasm, tongue)	141.9	198.89	230.0	210.1	235.1	239.0
lingula, lung	162.3	197.0	231.2	212.3	235.7	239.1
lip (external) (lipstick area) (vermillion border)	140.9	198.89	230.0	210.0	235.1	239.0
buccal aspect—*see* Neoplasm, lip, internal						
commissure	140.6	198.89	230.0	210.4	235.1	239.0
contiguous sites	140.8	—	—	—	—	—
with oral cavity or pharynx	149.8	—	—	—	—	—
frenulum—*see* Neoplasm, lip, internal						
inner aspect—*see* Neoplasm, lip, internal						
internal (buccal) (frenulum) (mucosa) (oral)	140.5	198.89	230.0	210.0	235.1	239.0
lower	140.4	198.89	230.0	210.0	235.1	239.0
upper	140.3	198.89	230.0	210.0	235.1	239.0
lower	140.1	198.89	230.0	210.0	235.1	239.0
internal (buccal) (frenulum) (mucosa) (oral)	140.4	198.89	230.0	210.0	235.1	239.0
mucosa—*see* Neoplasm, lip, internal						
oral aspect—*see* Neoplasm, lip, internal						
skin (commissure) (lower) (upper) . .	173.0	198.2	232.0	216.0	238.2	239.2
upper	140.0	198.89	230.0	210.0	235.1	239.0
internal (buccal) (frenulum) (mucosa) (oral)	140.3	198.89	230.0	210.0	235.1	239.0
liver	155.2	197.7	230.8	211.5	235.3	239.0
primary	155.0	—	—	—	—	—
lobe						
azygos	162.3	197.0	231.2	212.3	235.7	239.1
frontal	191.1	198.3	—	225.0	237.5	239.6
lower	162.5	197.0	231.2	212.3	235.7	239.1
middle	162.4	197.0	231.2	212.3	235.7	239.1
occipital	191.4	198.3	—	225.0	237.5	239.6
parietal	191.3	198.3	—	225.0	237.5	239.6
temporal	191.2	198.3	—	225.0	237.5	239.6
upper	162.3	197.0	231.2	212.3	235.7	239.1
lumbosacral plexus	171.6	198.4	—	215.6	238.1	239.2
lung	162.9	197.0	231.2	212.3	235.7	239.1
azygos lobe	162.3	197.0	231.2	212.3	235.7	239.1
carina	162.2	197.0	231.2	212.3	235.7	239.1
contiguous sites with bronchus or trachea	162.8	—	—	—	—	—
hilus	162.2	197.0	231.2	212.3	235.7	239.1

| | Malignant | | | | | |
	Primary	Secondary	Ca in situ	Benign	Uncertain Behavior	Unspecified
lung—*continued*						
lingula	162.3	197.0	231.2	212.3	235.7	239.1
lobe NEC	162.9	197.0	231.2	212.3	235.7	239.1
lower lobe	162.5	197.0	231.2	212.3	235.7	239.1
main bronchus	162.2	197.0	231.2	212.3	235.7	239.1
middle lobe	162.4	197.0	231.2	212.3	235.7	239.1
upper lobe	162.3	197.0	231.2	212.3	235.7	239.1
lymph, lymphatic						
channel NEC *(see also* Neoplasm,						
connective tissue)	171.9	198.89	—	215.9	238.1	239.2
gland (secondary)	—	196.9	—	229.0	238.8	239.8
abdominal	—	196.2	—	229.0	238.8	239.8
aortic	—	196.2	—	229.0	238.8	239.8
arm	—	196.3	—	229.0	238.8	239.8
auricular (anterior) (posterior)	—	196.0	—	229.0	238.8	239.8
axilla, axillary	—	196.3	—	229.0	238.8	239.8
brachial	—	196.3	—	229.0	238.8	239.8
bronchial	—	196.1	—	229.0	238.8	239.8
bronchopulmonary	—	196.1	—	229.0	238.8	239.8
celiac	—	196.2	—	229.0	238.8	239.8
cervical	—	196.0	—	229.0	238.8	239.8
cervicofacial	—	196.0	—	229.0	238.8	239.8
Cloquet	—	196.5	—	229.0	238.8	239.8
colic	—	196.2	—	229.0	238.8	239.8
common duct	—	196.2	—	229.0	238.8	239.8
cubital	—	196.3	—	229.0	238.8	239.8
diaphragmatic	—	196.1	—	229.0	238.8	239.8
epigastric, inferior	—	196.6	—	229.0	238.8	239.8
epitrochlear	—	196.3	—	229.0	238.8	239.8
esophageal	—	196.1	—	229.0	238.8	239.8
face	—	196.0	—	229.0	238.8	239.8
femoral	—	196.5	—	229.0	238.8	239.8
gastric	—	196.2	—	229.0	238.8	239.8
groin	—	196.5	—	229.0	238.8	239.8
head	—	196.0	—	229.0	238.8	239.8
hepatic	—	196.2	—	229.0	238.8	239.8
hilar (pulmonary)	—	196.1	—	229.0	238.8	239.8
splenic	—	196.2	—	229.0	238.8	239.8
hypogastric	—	196.6	—	229.0	238.8	239.8
ileocolic	—	196.2	—	229.0	238.8	239.8
iliac	—	196.6	—	229.0	238.8	239.8
infraclavicular	—	196.3	—	229.0	238.8	239.8
inguina, inguinal	—	196.5	—	229.0	238.8	239.8
innominate	—	196.1	—	229.0	238.8	239.8
intercostal	—	196.1	—	229.0	238.8	239.8
intestinal	—	196.2	—	229.0	238.8	239.8
intrabdominal	—	196.2	—	229.0	238.8	239.8
intrapelvic	—	196.6	—	229.0	238.8	239.8
intrathoracic	—	196.1	—	229.0	238.8	239.9
jugular	—	196.0	—	229.0	238.8	239.8
leg	—	196.5	—	229.0	238.8	239.8
limb						
lower	—	196.5	—	229.0	238.8	239.8
upper	—	196.3	—	229.0	238.8	239.8
lower limb	—	196.5	—	229.0	238.8	238.9
lumbar	—	196.2	—	229.0	238.8	239.8
mandibular	—	196.0	—	229.0	238.8	239.8
mediastinal	—	196.1	—	229.0	238.8	239.8
mesenteric (inferior) (superior)	—	196.2	—	229.0	238.8	239.8
midcolic	—	196.2	—	229.0	238.8	239.8

	Malignant			Benign	Uncertain Behavior	Unspecified
	Primary	Secondary	Ca in situ			
lymph, lymphatic—*continued*						
multiple sites in categories						
196.0-196.6	—	196.8	—	229.0	238.8	239.8
neck	—	196.0	—	229.0	238.8	239.8
obturator	—	196.6	—	229.0	238.8	239.8
occipital	—	196.0	—	229.0	238.8	239.8
pancreatic	—	196.2	—	229.0	238.8	239.8
para-aortic	—	196.2	—	229.0	238.8	239.8
paracervical	—	196.6	—	229.0	238.8	239.8
parametrial	—	196.6	—	229.0	238.8	239.8
parasternal	—	196.1	—	229.0	238.8	239.8
parotid	—	196.0	—	229.0	238.8	239.8
pectoral	—	196.3	—	229.0	238.8	239.8
pelvic	—	196.6	—	229.0	238.8	239.8
peri-aortic	—	196.2	—	229.0	238.8	239.8
peripancreatic	—	196.2	—	229.0	238.8	239.8
popliteal	—	196.5	—	229.0	238.8	239.8
porta hepatis	—	196.2	—	229.0	238.8	239.8
portal	—	196.2	—	229.0	238.8	239.8
preauricular	—	196.0	—	229.0	238.8	239.8
prelaryngeal	—	196.0	—	229.0	238.8	239.8
presymphysial	—	196.6	—	229.0	238.8	239.8
pretracheal	—	196.0	—	229.0	238.8	239.8
primary (any site) NEC	202.9	—	—	—	—	—
pulmonary (hiler)	—	196.1	—	229.0	238.8	239.8
pyloric	—	196.2	—	229.0	238.8	239.8
retroperitoneal	—	196.2	—	229.0	238.8	239.8
retropharyngeal	—	196.0	—	229.0	238.8	239.8
Rosenmüller's	—	196.5	—	229.0	238.8	239.8
sacral	—	196.6	—	229.0	238.8	239.8
scalene	—	196.0	—	229.0	238.8	239.8
site NEC	—	196.9	—	229.0	238.8	239.8
splenic (hilar)	—	196.2	—	229.0	238.8	239.8
subclavicular	—	196.3	—	229.0	238.8	239.8
subinguinal	—	196.5	—	229.0	238.8	239.8
sublingual	—	196.0	—	229.0	238.8	239.8
submandibular	—	196.0	—	229.0	238.8	239.8
submaxillary	—	196.0	—	229.0	238.8	239.8
submental	—	196.0	—	229.0	238.8	239.8
subscapular	—	196.3	—	229.0	238.8	239.8
supraclavicular	—	196.0	—	229.0	238.8	239.8
thoracic	—	196.1	—	229.0	238.8	239.8
tibial	—	196.5	—	229.0	238.8	239.8
tracheal	—	196.1	—	229.0	238.8	239.8
tracheobronchial	—	196.1	—	229.0	238.8	239.8
upper limb	—	196.3	—	229.0	238.8	239.8
Virchow's		196.0	—	229.0	238.8	239.8
node—*see also* Neoplasm, lymph gland						
primary NEC	202.9	—	—	—	—	—
vessel (*see also* Neoplasm, connective						
tissue)	171.9	198.89	—	215.9	238.1	239.2
Mackenrodt's ligament	183.8	198.82	233.3	221.8	236.3	239.5
malar	170.0	198.5	—	213.0	238.0	239.2
region—*see* Neoplasm, cheek						
mammary gland—*see* Neoplasm, breast						
mandible	170.1	198.5	—	213.1	238.0	239.2
alveolar						
mucose	143.1	198.89	230.0	210.4	235.1	239.0
ridge or process	170.1	198.5	—	213.1	238.0	239.2
carcinoma	143.1	—	—	—	—	—
carcinoma	143.1	—	—	—	—	—

| | Malignant | | | | | |
---	Primary	Secondary	Ca in situ	Benign	Uncertain Behavior	Unspecified
marrow (bone) NEC	202.9	198.5	—	—	—	238.7
mastectomy site (skin)	173.5	198.2	—	—	—	—
specified as breast tissue	174.8	198.81	—	—	—	—
mastoid (air cells) (antrum) (cavity)	160.1	197.3	231.8	212.0	235.9	239.1
bone or process	170.0	198.5	—	213.0	238.0	239.2
maxilla, maxillary (superior)	170.0	198.5	—	213.0	238.0	239.2
alveolar						
mucosa	143.0	198.89	230.0	210.4	235.1	239.0
ridge or process	170.0	198.5	—	213.0	238.0	239.2
carcinoma	143.0	—	—	—	—	—
antrum	160.2	197.3	231.8	212.0	235.9	239.1
carcinoma	143.0	—	—	—	—	—
inferior—see Neoplasm, mandible						
sinus	160.2	197.3	231.8	212.0	235.9	239.1
meatus						
external (ear)	173.2	198.2	232.2	216.2	238.2	239.2
Meckel's diverticulum	152.3	197.4	230.7	211.2	235.2	239.0
mediastinum, mediastinal	164.9	197.1	—	212.5	235.8	239.8
anterior	164.2	197.1	—	212.5	235.8	239.8
contiguous sites with heart and						
thymus	164.8	—	—	—	—	—
posterior	164.3	197.1	—	212.5	235.8	239.8
medulla						
adrenal	194.0	198.7	234.8	227.0	237.2	239.7
oblongata	191.7	198.3	—	225.0	237.5	239.6
meibomian gland	173.1	198.2	232.1	216.1	238.2	239.2
melanoma —see Melanoma						
meninges (brain) (cerebral) (cranial)						
(intracranial)	192.1	198.4	—	225.2	237.6	239.7
spinal (cord)	192.3	198.4	—	225.4	237.6	239.7
meniscus, knee joint (lateral) (medial)	170.7	198.5	—	213.7	238.0	239.2
mesentery, mesenteric	158.8	197.6	—	211.8	235.4	239.0
mesoappendix	158.8	197.6	—	211.8	235.4	239.0
mesocolon	158.8	197.6	—	211.8	235.4	239.0
mesopharynx—see Neoplasm, oropharynx						
mesosalpinx	183.3	198.82	233.3	221.0	236.3	239.5
mesovarium	183.3	198.82	233.3	221.0	236.3	239.5
metacarpus (any bone)	170.5	198.5	—	213.5	238.0	239.2
metastatic NEC—see also Neoplasm,						
by site, secondary	—	199.1	—	—	—	—
metatarsus (any bone)	170.8	198.5	—	213.8	238.0	239.2
midbrain	191.7	198.3	—	225.0	237.5	239.6
milk duct—see Neoplasm, breast						
mons						
pubis	184.4	198.82	233.3	221.2	236.3	239.5
veneris	184.4	198.82	233.3	221.2	236.3	239.5
motor tract	192.9	198.4	—	225.9	237.9	239.7
brain	191.9	198.3	—	225.0	237.5	239.6
spinal	192.2	198.3	—	225.3	237.5	239.7
mouth	145.9	198.89	230.0	210.4	235.1	239.0
contiguous sites	145.8	—	—	—	—	—
floor	144.9	198.89	230.0	210.3	235.1	239.0
anterior portion	144.0	198.89	230.0	210.3	235.1	239.0
contiguous sites	144.8	—	—	—	—	—
lateral portion	144.1	198.89	230.0	210.3	235.1	239.0
roof	145.5	198.89	230.0	210.4	235.1	239.0
specified part NEC	145.8	198.89	230.0	210.4	235.1	239.0
vestibule	145.1	198.89	230.0	210.4	235.1	239.0
mucosa						
alveolar (ridge or process)	143.9	198.89	230.0	210.4	235.1	239.0
lower	143.1	198.89	230.0	210.4	235.1	239.0
upper	143.0	198.89	230.0	210.4	235.1	239.0

	Malignant					
	Primary	Secondary	Ca in situ	Benign	Uncertain Behavior	Unspecified
mucosa—*continued*						
buccal	145.0	198.89	230.0	210.4	235.1	239.0
cheek	145.0	198.89	230.0	210.4	235.1	239.0
lip—*see* Neoplasm, lip, internal						
nasal	160.0	197.3	231.8	212.0	235.9	239.1
oral	145.0	198.89	230.0	210.4	235.1	239.0
Müllerian duct						
female	184.8	198.82	233.3	221.8	236.3	239.5
male	187.8	198.82	233.6	222.8	236.6	239.5
multiple sites NEC	199.0	199.0	234.9	229.9	238.9	199.0
muscle—*see also* Neoplasm, connective tissue						
extraocular	190.1	198.4	234.0	224.1	238.8	239.8
myocardium	164.1	198.89	—	212.7	238.8	239.8
myometrium	182.0	198.82	233.2	219.1	236.0	239.5
myopericardium	164.1	198.89	—	212.7	238.8	239.8
nabothian gland (follicle)	180.0	198.82	233.1	219.0	236.0	239.5
nail	173.9	198.2	232.9	216.9	238.2	239.2
finger	173.6	198.2	232.6	216.6	238.2	239.2
toe	173.7	198.2	232.7	216.7	238.2	239.2
nares, naris (anterior) (posterior)	160.0	197.3	231.8	212.0	235.9	239.1
nasal—*see* Neoplasm, nose						
nasolabial groove	173.3	198.2	232.3	216.3	238.2	239.2
nasolacrimal duct	190.7	198.4	234.0	224.7	238.8	239.8
nasopharynx, nasopharyngeal	147.9	198.89	230.0	210.7	235.1	239.0
contiguous sites	147.8	—	—	—	—	—
floor	147.3	198.89	230.0	210.7	235.1	239.0
roof	147.0	198.89	230.0	210.7	235.1	239.0
specified site NEC	147.8	198.89	230.0	210.7	235.1	239.0
wall	147.9	198.89	230.0	210.7	235.1	239.0
anterior	147.3	198.89	230.0	210.7	235.1	239.0
lateral	147.2	198.89	230.0	210.7	235.1	239.0
posterior	147.1	198.89	230.0	210.7	235.1	239.0
superior	147.0	198.89	230.0	210.7	235.1	239.0
nates	173.5	198.2	232.5	216.5	238.2	239.2
neck NEC*	195.0	198.89	234.8	229.8	238.8	239.8
nerve (autonomic) (ganglion) (parasympathetic) (peripheral) (sympathetic)— *see also* Neoplasm, connective tissue						
abducens	192.0	198.4	—	225.1	237.9	239.7
accessory (spinal)	192.0	198.4	—	225.1	237.9	239.7
acoustic	192.0	198.4	—	225.1	237.9	239.7
auditory	192.0	198.4	—	225.1	237.9	239.7
brachial	171.2	198.89	—	215.2	238.1	239.2
cranial (any)	192.0	198.4	—	225.1	237.9	239.7
facial	192.0	198.4	—	225.1	237.9	239.7
femoral	171.3	198.89	—	215.3	238.1	239.2
glossopharyngeal	192.0	198.4	—	225.1	237.9	239.7
hypoglossal	192.0	198.4	—	225.1	237.9	239.7
intercostal	171.4	198.89	—	215.4	238.1	239.2
lumbar	171.7	198.89	—	215.7	238.1	239.2
median	171.2	198.89	—	215.2	238.1	239.2
obturator	171.3	198.89	—	215.3	238.1	239.2
oculomotor	192.0	198.4	—	225.1	237.9	239.7
olfactory	192.0	198.4	—	225.1	237.9	239.7
optic	192.0	198.4	—	225.1	237.9	239.7
peripheral NEC	171.9	198.89	—	215.9	238.1	239.2
radial	171.2	198.89	—	215.2	238.1	239.2
sacral	171.6	198.89	—	215.6	238.1	239.2
sciatic	171.3	198.89	—	215.3	238.1	239.2
spinal NEC	171.9	198.89	—	215.9	238.1	239.2

	Malignant					
	Primary	Secondary	Ca in situ	Benign	Uncertain Behavior	Unspecified
nerve—*continued*						
trigeminal	192.0	198.4	—	225.1	237.9	239.7
trochlear	192.0	198.4	—	225.1	237.9	239.7
ulnar	171.2	198.89	—	215.2	238.1	239.2
vagus	192.0	198.4	—	225.1	237.9	239.7
nervous system (central) NEC	192.9	198.4	—	225.9	237.9	239.7
autonomic NEC	171.9	198.89	—	215.9	238.1	239.2
brain—*see also* Neoplasm, brain						
membrane or meninges	192.1	198.4	—	225.2	237.6	239.7
contiguous sites	192.8	—	—	—	—	—
parasympathetic NEC	171.9	198.89	—	215.9	238.1	239.2
sympathetic NEC	171.9	198.89	—	215.9	238.1	239.2
nipple (female)	174.0	198.81	233.0	217	238.3	239.3
male	175.0	198.81	233.0	217	238.3	239.3
nose, nasal	195.0	198.89	234.8	229.8	238.8	239.8
ala (external)	173.3	198.2	232.3	216.3	238.2	239.2
bone	170.0	198.5	—	213.0	238.0	239.2
cartilage	160.0	197.3	231.8	212.0	235.9	239.1
cavity	160.0	197.3	231.8	212.0	235.9	239.1
contiguous sites with accessory sinuses or middle ear	160.8	—	—	—	—	—
choana	147.3	198.89	230.0	210.7	235.1	239.0
external (skin)	173.3	198.2	232.3	216.3	238.2	239.2
fossa	160.0	197.3	231.8	212.0	235.9	239.1
internal	160.0	197.3	231.8	212.0	235.9	239.1
mucosa	160.0	197.3	231.8	212.0	235.9	239.1
septum	160.0	197.3	231.8	212.0	235.9	239.1
posterior margin	147.3	198.89	230.0	210.7	235.1	239.0
sinus—*see* Neoplasm, sinus						
skin	173.3	198.2	232.3	216.3	238.2	239.2
turbinate (mucosa)	160.0	197.3	231.8	212.0	235.9	239.1
bone	170.0	198.5	—	213.0	238.0	239.2
vestibule	160.0	197.3	231.8	212.0	235.9	239.1
nostril	160.0	197.3	231.8	212.0	235.9	239.1
nucleus pulposus	170.2	198.5	—	213.2	238.0	239.2
occipital						
bone	170.0	198.5	—	213.0	238.0	239.2
lobe or pole, brain	191.4	198.3	—	225.0	237.5	239.6
odontogenic—*see* Neoplasm, jaw bone						
oesophagus—*see* Neoplasm, esophagus						
olfactory nerve or bulb	192.0	198.4	—	225.1	237.9	239.7
olive (brain)	191.7	198.3	—	225.0	237.5	239.6
omentum	158.8	197.6	—	211.8	235.4	239.0
operculum (brain)	191.0	198.3	—	225.0	237.5	239.6
optic nerve, chiasm, or tract	192.0	198.4	—	225.1	237.9	239.7
oral (cavity)	145.9	198.89	230.0	210.4	235.1	239.0
contiguous sites with lip or pharynx	149.8	—	—	—	—	—
ill-defined	149.9	198.89	230.0	210.4	235.1	239.0
mucosa	145.9	198.89	230.0	210.4	235.1	239.0
orbit	190.1	198.4	234.0	224.1	238.8	239.8
bone	170.0	198.5	—	213.0	238.0	239.2
eye	190.1	198.4	234.0	224.1	238.8	239.8
soft parts	190.1	198.4	234.0	224.1	238.8	239.8
organ of Zuckerkandl	194.6	198.89	—	227.6	237.3	239.7
oropharynx	146.9	198.89	230.0	210.6	235.1	239.0
branchial cleft (vestige)	146.8	198.89	230.0	210.6	235.1	239.0
contiguous sites	146.8	—	—	—	—	—
junctional region	146.5	198.89	230.0	210.6	235.1	239.0
lateral wall	146.6	198.89	230.0	210.6	235.1	239.0
pillars of fauces	146.2	198.89	230.0	210.6	235.1	239.0

	Malignant					
	Primary	Secondary	Ca in situ	Benign	Uncertain Behavior	Unspecified
oropharynx—*continued*						
posterior wall	146.7	198.89	230.0	210.6	235.1	239.0
specified part NEC	146.8	198.89	230.0	210.6	235.1	239.0
vallecula	146.3	198.89	230.0	210.6	235.1	239.0
os						
external	180.1	198.82	233.1	219.0	236.0	239.5
internal	180.0	198.82	233.1	219.0	236.0	239.5
ovary	183.0	198.6	233.3	220	236.2	239.5
oviduct	183.2	198.82	233.3	221.0	236.3	239.5
palate	145.5	198.89	230.0	210.4	235.1	239.0
hard	145.2	198.89	230.0	210.4	235.1	239.0
junction of hard and soft palate	145.5	198.89	230.0	210.4	235.1	239.0
soft	145.3	198.89	230.0	210.4	235.1	239.0
nasopharyngeal surface	147.3	198.89	230.0	210.7	235.1	239.0
posterior surface	147.3	198.89	230.0	210.7	235.1	239.0
superior surface	147.3	198.89	230.0	210.7	235.1	239.0
palatoglossal arch	146.2	198.89	230.0	210.6	235.1	239.0
palatopharyngeal arch	146.2	198.89	230.0	210.6	235.1	239.0
pallium	191.0	198.3	—	225.0	237.5	239.6
palpebra	173.1	198.2	232.1	216.1	238.2	239.2
pancreas	157.9	197.8	230.9	211.6	235.5	239.0
body	157.1	197.8	230.9	211.6	235.5	239.0
contiguous sites	157.8	—	—	—	—	—
duct (of Santorini) (of Wirsung)	157.3	197.8	230.9	211.6	235.5	239.0
ectopic tissue	157.8	197.8	230.9	211.6	235.5	239.0
head	157.0	197.8	230.9	211.6	235.5	239.0
islet cells	157.4	197.8	230.9	211.7	235.5	239.0
neck	157.8	197.8	230.9	211.6	235.5	239.0
tail	157.2	197.8	230.9	211.6	235.5	239.0
para-aortic body	194.6	198.89	—	227.6	237.3	239.7
paraganglion NEC	194.6	198.89	—	227.6	237.3	239.7
parametrium	183.4	198.82	—	221.0	236.3	239.5
paranephric	158.0	197.6	—	211.8	235.4	239.0
pararectal	195.3	198.89	—	229.8	238.8	239.8
parasagittal (region)	195.0	198.89	234.8	229.8	238.8	239.8
parasellar	192.9	198.4	—	225.9	237.9	239.7
parathyroid (gland)	194.1	198.89	234.8	227.1	237.4	239.7
paraurethral	195.3	198.89	—	229.8	238.8	239.8
gland	189.4	198.1	233.9	223.89	236.99	239.5
paravaginal	195.3	198.89	—	229.8	238.8	239.8
parenchyma, kidney	189.0	198.0	233.9	223.0	236.91	239.5
parietal						
bone	170.0	198.5	—	213.0	238.0	239.2
lobe, brain	191.3	198.3	—	225.0	237.5	239.6
paroophoron	183.3	198.82	233.3	221.0	236.3	239.5
parotid (duct) (gland)	142.0	198.89	230.0	210.2	235.0	239.0
parovarium	183.3	198.82	233.3	221.0	236.3	239.5
patella	170.8	198.5	—	213.8	238.0	239.2
peduncle, cerebral	191.7	198.3	—	225.0	237.5	239.6
pelvirectal junction	154.0	197.5	230.4	211.4	235.2	239.0
pelvis, pelvic	195.3	198.89	234.8	229.8	238.8	239.8
bone	170.6	198.5	—	213.6	238.0	239.2
floor	195.3	198.89	234.8	229.8	238.8	239.8
renal	189.1	198.0	233.9	223.1	236.91	239.5
viscera	195.3	198.89	234.8	229.8	238.8	239.8
wall	195.3	198.89	234.8	229.8	238.8	239.8
pelvo-abdominal	195.8	198.89	234.8	229.8	238.8	239.8
penis	187.4	198.82	233.5	222.1	236.6	239.5
body	187.3	198.82	233.5	222.1	236.6	239.5
corpus (cavernosum)	187.3	198.82	233.5	222.1	236.6	239.5
glans	187.2	198.82	233.5	222.1	236.6	239.5
skin NEC	187.4	198.82	233.5	222.1	236.6	239.5

	Malignant					
	Primary	Secondary	Ca in situ	Benign	Uncertain Behavior	Unspecified
periadrenal (tissue)	158.0	197.6	—	211.8	235.4	239.0
perianal (skin)	173.5	198.2	232.5	216.5	238.2	239.2
pericardium	164.1	198.89	—	212.7	238.8	239.8
perinephric	158.0	197.6	—	211.8	235.4	239.0
perineum	195.3	198.89	234.8	229.8	238.8	239.8
periodontal tissue NEC	143.9	198.89	230.0	210.4	235.1	239.0
periosteum—see Neoplasm, bone						
peripancreatic	158.0	197.6	—	211.8	235.4	239.0
peripheral nerve NEC	171.9	198.89	—	215.9	238.1	239.2
perirectal (tissue)	195.3	198.89	—	229.8	238.8	239.8
perirenal (tissue)	158.0	197.6	—	211.8	235.4	239.0
peritoneum, peritoneal (cavity)	158.9	197.6	—	211.8	235.4	239.0
contiguous sites	158.8	—	—	—	—	—
with digestive organs	159.8	—	—	—	—	—
parietal	158.8	197.6	—	211.8	235.4	239.0
pelvic	158.8	197.6	—	211.8	235.4	239.0
specified part NEC	158.8	197.6	—	211.8	235.4	239.0
peritonsillar (tissue)	195.0	198.89	234.8	229.8	238.8	239.8
periurethral tissue	195.3	198.89	—	229.8	238.8	239.8
phalanges	170.9	198.5	—	213.9	238.0	239.2
foot	170.8	198.5	—	213.8	238.0	239.2
hand	170.5	198.5	—	213.5	238.0	239.2
pharynx, pharyngeal	149.0	198.89	230.0	210.9	235.1	239.0
bursa	147.1	198.89	230.0	210.7	235.1	239.0
fornix	147.3	198.89	230.0	210.7	235.1	239.0
recess	147.2	198.89	230.0	210.7	235.1	239.0
region	149.0	198.89	230.0	210.9	235.1	239.0
tonsil	147.1	198.89	230.0	210.7	235.1	239.0
wall (lateral) (posterior)	149.0	198.89	230.0	210.9	235.1	239.0
pia mater (cerebral) (cranial)	192.1	198.4	—	225.2	237.6	239.7
spinal	192.3	198.4	—	225.4	237.6	239.7
pillars of fauces	146.2	198.89	230.0	210.6	235.1	239.0
pineal (body) (gland)	194.4	198.89	234.8	227.4	237.1	239.7
pinna (ear) NEC	173.2	198.2	232.2	216.2	238.2	239.2
cartilage	171.0	198.89	—	215.0	238.1	239.2
piriform fossa or sinus	148.1	198.89	230.0	210.8	235.1	239.0
pituitary (body) (fossa) (gland) (lobe) . .	194.3	198.89	234.8	227.3	237.0	239.7
placenta	181	198.82	233.2	219.8	236.1	239.5
pleura, pleural (cavity)	163.9	197.2	—	212.4	235.8	239.1
contiguous sites	163.8	—	—	—	—	—
parietal	163.0	197.2	—	212.4	235.8	239.1
visceral	163.1	197.2	—	212.4	235.8	239.1
plexus						
brachial	171.2	198.89	—	215.2	238.1	239.2
cervical	171.0	198.89	—	215.0	238.1	239.2
choroid	191.5	198.3	—	225.0	237.5	239.6
lumbosacral	171.6	198.89	—	215.6	238.1	239.2
sacral	171.6	198.89	—	215.6	238.1	239.2
pluri-endocrine	194.8	198.89	234.8	227.8	237.4	239.7
pole						
frontal	191.1	198.3	—	225.0	237.5	239.6
occipital	191.4	198.3	—	225.0	237.5	239.6
pons (varolii)	191.7	198.3	—	225.0	237.5	239.6
popliteal fossa or space*	195.5	198.89	234.8	229.8	238.8	239.8
postcricoid (region)	148.0	198.89	230.0	210.8	235.1	239.0
posterior fossa (cranial)	191.6	198.3	—	225.0	237.5	239.6
postnasal space	147.9	198.89	230.0	210.7	235.1	239.0
prepuce	187.1	198.82	233.5	222.1	236.6	239.5
prepylorus	151.1	197.8	230.2	211.1	235.2	239.0
presacral (region)	195.3	198.89	—	229.8	238.8	239.8

	Malignant					
	Primary	Secondary	Ca in situ	Benign	Uncertain Behavior	Unspecified
prostate (gland)	185	198.82	233.4	222.2	236.5	239.5
utricle	189.3	198.1	233.9	223.81	236.99	239.5
pterygoid fossa	171.0	198.89	—	215.0	238.1	239.2
pubic bone	170.6	198.5	—	213.6	238.0	239.2
pudenda, pudendum (female)	184.4	198.82	233.3	221.2	236.3	239.5
pulmonary	162.9	197.0	231.2	212.3	235.7	239.1
putamen	191.0	198.3	—	225.0	237.5	239.6
pyloric						
antrum	151.2	197.8	230.2	211.1	235.2	239.0
canal	151.1	197.8	230.2	211.1	235.2	239.0
pylorus	151.1	197.8	230.2	211.1	235.2	239.0
pyramid (brain)	191.7	198.3	—	225.0	237.5	239.6
pyriform fossa or sinus	148.1	198.89	230.0	210.8	235.1	239.0
radius (any part)	170.4	198.5	—	213.4	238.0	239.2
Rathke's pouch	194.3	198.89	234.8	227.3	237.0	239.7
rectosigmoid (colon) (junction)	154.0	197.5	230.4	211.4	235.2	239.0
contiguous sites with anus or rectum .	154.8	—	—	—	—	—
rectouterine pouch	158.8	197.6	—	211.8	235.4	239.0
rectovaginal septum or wall	195.3	198.89	234.8	229.8	238.8	239.8
rectovesical septum	195.3	198.89	234.8	229.8	238.8	239.8
rectum (ampulla)	154.1	197.5	230.4	211.4	235.2	239.0
and colon	154.0	197.5	230.4	211.4	235.2	239.0
contiguous sites with anus or						
rectosigmoid junction	154.8	—	—	—	—	—
renal	189.0	198.0	233.9	223.0	236.91	239.5
calyx	189.1	198.0	233.9	223.1	236.91	239.5
hilus	189.1	198.0	233.9	223.1	236.91	239.5
parenchyma	189.0	198.0	233.9	223.0	236.91	239.5
pelvis	189.1	198.0	233.9	223.1	236.91	239.5
respiratory						
organs or system NEC	165.9	197.3	231.9	212.9	235.9	239.1
contiguous sites with intrathoracic						
organs	165.8	—	—	—	—	—
specified sites NEC	165.8	197.3	231.8	212.8	235.9	239.1
tract NEC	165.9	197.3	231.9	212.9	235.9	239.1
upper	165.0	197.3	231.9	212.9	235.9	239.1
retina	190.5	198.4	234.0	224.5	238.8	239.8
retrobulbar	190.1	198.4	—	224.1	238.8	239.8
retrocecal	158.0	197.6	—	211.8	235.4	239.0
retromolar (area) (triangle) (trigone) . .	145.6	198.89	230.0	210.4	235.1	239.0
retro-orbital	195.0	198.89	234.8	229.8	238.8	239.8
retroperitoneal (space) (tissue)	158.0	197.6	—	211.8	235.4	239.0
contiguous sites	158.8	—	—	—	—	—
retroperitoneum	158.0	197.6	—	211.8	235.4	239.0
contiguous sites	158.8	—	—	—	—	—
retropharyngeal	149.0	198.89	230.0	210.9	235.1	239.0
retrovesical (septum)	195.3	198.89	234.8	229.8	238.8	239.8
rhinencephalon	191.0	198.3	—	225.0	237.5	239.6
rib	170.3	198.5	—	213.3	238.0	239.2
Rosenmüller's fossa	147.2	198.89	230.0	210.7	235.1	239.0
round ligament	183.5	198.82	—	221.0	236.3	239.5
sacrococcyx, sacrococcygeal	170.6	198.5	—	213.6	238.0	239.2
region	195.3	198.89	234.8	229.8	238.8	239.8
sacrouterine ligament	183.4	198.82	—	221.0	236.3	239.5
sacrum, sacral (vertebra)	170.6	198.5	—	213.6	238.0	239.2
salivary gland or duct (major)	142.9	198.89	230.0	210.2	235.0	239.0
contiguous sites	142.8	—	—	—	—	—
minor NEC	145.9	198.89	230.0	210.4	235.1	239.0
parotid	142.0	198.89	230.0	210.2	235.0	239.0
pluriglandular	142.8	198.89	230.0	210.2	235.0	239.0

	Malignant					
	Primary	Secondary	Ca in situ	Benign	Uncertain Behavior	Unspecified
salivary gland or duct (major)—*continued*						
sublingual	142.2	198.89	230.0	210.2	235.0	239.0
submandibular	142.1	198.89	230.0	210.2	235.0	239.0
submaxillary	142.1	198.89	230.0	210.2	235.0	239.0
salpinx (uterine)	183.2	198.82	233.3	221.0	236.3	239.5
Santorini's duct	157.3	197.8	230.9	211.6	235.5	239.0
scalp	173.4	198.2	232.4	216.4	238.2	239.2
scapula (any part)	170.4	198.5	—	213.4	238.0	239.2
scapular region	195.1	198.89	234.8	229.8	238.8	239.8
scar NEC (*see also* Neoplasm, skin)	173.9	198.2	232.9	216.9	238.2	239.2
sciatic nerve	171.3	198.89	—	215.3	238.1	239.2
sclera	190.0	198.4	234.0	224.0	238.8	239.8
scrotum (skin)	187.7	198.82	233.6	222.4	236.6	239.5
sebaceous gland—*see* Neoplasm, skin						
sella turcica	194.3	198.89	234.8	227.3	237.0	239.7
bone	170.0	198.5	—	213.0	238.0	239.2
semilunar cartilage (knee)	170.7	198.5	—	213.7	238.0	239.2
seminal vesicle	187.8	198.82	233.6	222.8	236.6	239.5
septum						
nasal	160.0	197.3	231.8	212.0	235.9	239.1
posterior margin	147.3	198.89	230.0	210.7	235.1	239.0
rectovaginal	195.3	198.89	234.8	229.8	238.8	239.8
rectovesical	195.3	198.89	234.8	229.8	238.8	239.8
urethrovaginal	184.9	198.82	233.3	221.9	236.3	239.5
vesicovaginal	184.9	198.82	233.3	221.9	236.3	239.5
shoulder NEC*	195.4	198.89	232.6	229.8	238.8	239.8
sigmoid flexure (lower) (upper)	153.3	197.5	230.3	211.3	235.2	239.0
sinus (accessory)	160.9	197.3	231.8	212.0	235.9	239.1
bone (any)	170.0	198.5	—	213.0	238.0	239.2
contiguous sites with middle ear or nasal cavities	160.8	—	—	—	—	—
ethmoidal	160.3	197.3	231.8	212.0	235.9	239.1
frontal	160.4	197.3	231.8	212.0	235.9	239.1
maxillary	160.2	197.3	231.8	212.0	235.9	239.1
nasal, paranasal NEC	160.9	197.3	231.8	212.0	235.9	239.1
pyriform	148.1	198.89	230.0	210.8	235.1	239.0
sphenoidal	160.5	197.3	231.8	212.0	235.9	239.1
skeleton, skeletal NEC	170.9	198.5	—	213.9	238.0	239.2
Skene's gland	189.4	198.1	233.9	223.89	236.99	239.5
skin NEC	173.9	198.2	232.9	216.9	238.2	239.2
abdominal wall	173.5	198.2	232.5	216.5	238.2	239.2
ala nasi	173.3	198.2	232.3	216.3	238.2	239.2
ankle	173.7	198.2	232.7	216.7	238.2	239.2
antecubital space	173.6	198.2	232.6	216.6	238.2	239.2
anus	173.5	198.2	232.5	216.5	238.2	239.2
arm	173.6	198.2	232.6	216.6	238.2	239.2
auditory canal (external)	173.2	198.2	232.2	216.2	238.2	239.2
auricle (ear)	173.2	198.2	232.2	216.2	238.2	239.2
auricular canal (external)	173.2	198.2	232.2	216.2	238.2	239.2
axilla, axillary fold	173.5	198.2	232.5	216.5	238.2	239.2
back	173.5	198.2	232.5	216.5	238.2	239.2
breast	173.5	198.2	232.5	216.5	238.2	239.2
brow	173.3	198.2	232.3	216.3	238.2	239.2
buttock	173.5	198.2	232.5	216.5	238.2	239.2
calf	173.7	198.2	232.7	216.7	238.2	239.2
canthus (eye) (inner) (outer)	173.1	198.2	232.1	216.1	238.2	239.2
cervical region	173.4	198.2	232.4	216.4	238.2	239.2
cheek (external)	173.3	198.2	232.3	216.3	238.2	239.2
chest (wall)	173.5	198.2	232.5	216.5	238.2	239.2
chin	173.3	198.2	232.3	216.3	238.2	239.2

	Malignant				
	Primary	Secondary	Ca in situ	Benign	Uncertain Behavior	Unspecified

skin NEC—*continued*

	Primary	Secondary	Ca in situ	Benign	Uncertain Behavior	Unspecified
clavicular area	173.5	198.2	232.5	216.5	238.2	239.2
clitoris	184.3	198.82	233.3	221.2	236.3	239.5
columnella	173.3	198.2	232.3	216.3	238.2	239.2
concha	173.2	198.2	232.2	216.2	238.2	239.2
contiguous sites	173.8	—	—	—	—	—
ear (external)	173.2	198.2	232.2	216.2	238.2	239.2
elbow	173.6	198.2	232.6	216.6	238.2	239.2
eyebrow	173.3	198.2	232.3	216.3	238.2	239.2
eyelid	173.1	198.2	232.1	216.1	238.2	239.2
face NEC	173.3	198.2	232.3	216.3	238.2	239.2
female genital organs (external)	184.4	198.82	233.3	221.2	236.3	239.5
clitoris	184.3	198.82	233.3	221.2	236.3	239.5
labium NEC	184.4	198.82	233.3	221.2	236.3	239.5
majus	184.1	198.82	233.3	221.2	236.3	239.5
minus	184.2	198.82	233.3	221.2	236.3	239.5
pudendum	184.4	198.82	233.3	221.2	236.3	239.5
vulva	184.4	198.82	233.3	221.2	236.3	239.5
finger	173.6	198.2	232.6	216.6	238.2	239.2
flank	173.5	198.2	232.5	216.5	238.2	239.2
foot	173.7	198.2	232.7	216.7	238.2	239.2
forearm	173.6	198.2	232.6	216.6	238.2	239.2
forehead	173.3	198.2	232.3	216.3	238.2	239.2
glabella	173.3	198.2	232.3	216.3	238.2	239.2
gluteal region	173.5	198.2	232.5	216.5	238.2	239.2
groin	173.5	198.2	232.5	216.5	238.2	239.2
hand	173.6	198.2	232.6	216.6	238.2	239.2
head NEC	173.4	198.2	232.4	216.4	238.2	239.2
heel	173.7	198.2	232.7	216.7	238.2	239.2
helix	173.2	198.2	232.2	216.2	238.2	239.2
hip	173.7	198.2	232.7	216.7	238.2	239.2
infraclavicular region	173.5	198.2	232.5	216.5	238.2	239.2
inguinal region	173.5	198.2	232.5	216.5	238.2	239.2
jaw	173.3	198.2	232.3	216.3	238.2	239.2
knee	173.7	198.2	232.7	216.7	238.2	239.2
labia						
majora	184.1	198.82	233.3	221.2	236.3	239.5
minora	184.2	198.82	233.3	221.2	236.3	239.5
leg	173.7	198.2	232.7	216.7	238.2	239.2
lid (lower) (upper)	173.1	198.2	232.1	216.1	238.2	239.2
limb NEC	173.9	198.2	232.9	216.9	238.2	239.5
lower	173.7	198.2	232.7	216.7	238.2	239.2
upper	173.6	198.2	232.6	216.6	238.2	239.2
lip (lower) (upper)	173.0	198.2	232.0	216.0	238.2	239.2
male genital organs	187.9	198.82	233.6	222.9	236.6	239.5
penis	187.4	198.82	233.5	222.1	236.6	239.5
prepuce	187.1	198.82	233.5	222.1	236.6	239.5
scrotum	187.7	198.82	233.6	222.4	236.6	239.5
mastectomy site	173.5	198.2	—	—	—	—
specified as breast tissue	174.8	198.81	—	—	—	—
meatus, acoustic (external)	173.2	198.2	232.2	216.2	238.2	239.2
melanoma —*see* Melanoma						
nates	173.5	198.2	232.5	216.5	238.2	239.2
neck	173.4	198.2	232.4	216.4	238.2	239.2
nose (external)	173.3	198.2	232.3	216.3	238.2	239.2
palm	173.6	198.2	232.6	216.6	238.2	239.2
palpebra	173.1	198.2	232.1	216.1	238.2	239.2
penis NEC	187.4	198.82	233.5	222.1	236.6	239.5
perianal	173.5	198.2	232.5	216.5	238.2	239.2
perineum	173.5	198.2	232.5	216.5	238.2	239.2

	Malignant					
	Primary	Secondary	Ca in situ	Benign	Uncertain Behavior	Unspecified
skin NEC—*continued*						
pinna	173.2	198.2	232.2	216.2	238.2	239.2
plantar	173.7	198.2	232.7	216.7	238.2	239.2
popliteal fossa or space	173.7	198.2	232.7	216.7	238.2	239.2
prepuce	187.1	198.82	233.5	222.1	236.6	239.5
pubes	173.5	198.2	232.5	216.5	238.2	239.2
sacrococcygeal region	173.5	198.2	232.5	216.5	238.2	239.2
scalp	173.4	198.2	232.4	216.4	238.2	239.2
scapular region	173.5	198.2	232.5	216.5	238.2	239.2
scrotum	187.7	198.82	233.6	222.4	236.6	239.5
shoulder	173.6	198.2	232.6	216.6	238.2	239.2
sole (foot)	173.7	198.2	232.7	216.7	238.2	239.2
specified sites NEC	173.8	198.2	232.8	216.8	232.8	239.2
submammary fold	173.5	198.2	232.5	216.5	238.2	239.2
supraclavicular region	173.4	198.2	232.4	216.4	238.2	239.2
temple	173.3	198.2	232.3	216.3	238.2	239.2
thigh	173.7	198.2	232.7	216.7	238.2	239.2
thoracic wall	173.5	198.2	232.5	216.5	238.2	239.2
thumb	173.6	198.2	232.6	216.6	238.2	239.2
toe	173.7	198.2	232.7	216.7	238.2	239.2
tragus	173.2	198.2	232.2	216.2	238.2	239.2
trunk	173.5	198.2	232.5	216.5	238.2	239.2
umbilicus	173.5	198.2	232.5	216.5	238.2	239.2
vulva	184.4	198.82	233.3	221.2	236.3	239.5
wrist	173.6	198.2	232.6	216.6	238.2	239.2
skull	170.0	198.5	—	213.0	238.0	239.2
soft parts or tissues—*see* Neoplasm, connective tissue						
specified site NEC	195.8	198.89	234.8	229.8	238.8	239.8
spermatic cord	187.6	198.82	233.6	222.8	236.6	239.5
sphenoid	160.5	197.3	231.8	212.0	235.9	239.1
bone	170.0	198.5	—	213.0	238.0	239.2
sinus	160.5	197.3	231.8	212.0	235.9	239.1
sphincter						
anal	154.2	197.5	230.5	211.4	235.5	239.0
of Oddi	156.1	197.8	230.8	211.5	235.3	239.0
spine, spinal (column)	170.2	198.5	—	213.2	238.0	239.2
bulb	191.7	198.3	—	225.0	237.5	239.6
coccyx	170.6	198.5	—	213.6	238.0	239.2
cord (cervical) (lumbar) (sacral) (thoracic)	192.2	198.3	—	225.3	237.5	239.7
dura mater	192.3	198.4	—	225.4	237.6	239.7
lumbosacral	170.2	198.5	—	213.2	238.0	239.2
membrane	192.3	198.4	—	225.4	237.6	239.7
meninges	192.3	198.4	—	225.4	237.6	239.7
nerve (root)	171.9	198.89	—	215.9	238.1	239.2
pia mater	192.3	198.4	—	225.4	237.6	239.7
root	171.9	198.89	—	215.9	238.1	239.2
sacrum	170.6	198.5	—	213.6	238.0	239.2
spleen, splenic NEC	159.1	197.8	230.9	211.9	235.5	239.0
flexure (colon)	153.7	197.5	230.3	211.3	235.2	239.0
stem, brain	191.7	198.3	—	225.0	237.5	239.6
Stensen's duct	142.0	198.89	230.0	210.2	235.0	239.0
sternum	170.3	198.5	—	213.3	238.0	239.2
stomach	151.9	197.8	230.2	211.1	235.2	239.0
antrum (pyloric)	151.2	197.8	230.2	211.1	235.2	239.0
body	151.4	197.8	230.2	211.1	235.2	239.0
cardia	151.0	197.8	230.2	211.1	235.2	239.0
cardiac orifice	151.0	197.8	230.2	211.1	235.2	239.0
contiguous sites	151.8	—	—	—	—	—
corpus	151.4	197.8	230.2	211.1	235.2	239.0

	Malignant					
	Primary	Secondary	Ca in situ	Benign	Uncertain Behavior	Unspecified
stomach—*continued*						
fundus	151.3	197.8	230.2	211.1	235.2	239.0
greater curvature NEC	151.6	197.8	230.2	211.1	235.2	239.0
lesser curvature NEC	151.5	197.8	230.2	211.1	235.2	239.0
prepylorus	151.1	197.8	230.2	211.1	235.2	239.0
pylorus	151.1	197.8	230.2	211.1	235.2	239.0
wall NEC	151.9	197.8	230.2	211.1	235.2	239.0
anterior NEC	151.8	197.8	230.2	211.1	235.2	239.0
posterior NEC	151.8	197.8	230.2	211.1	235.2	239.0
stroma, endometrial	182.0	198.82	233.2	219.1	236.0	239.5
stump, cervical	180.8	198.82	233.1	219.0	236.0	239.5
subcutaneous (nodule) (tissue) NEC—*see* Neoplasm, connective tissue						
subdural	192.1	198.4	—	225.2	237.6	239.7
subglottis, subglottic	161.2	197.3	231.0	212.1	235.6	239.1
sublingual	144.9	198.89	230.0	210.3	235.1	239.0
gland or duct	142.2	198.89	230.0	210.2	235.0	239.0
submandibular gland	142.1	198.89	230.0	210.2	235.0	239.0
submaxillary gland or duct	142.1	198.89	230.0	210.2	235.0	239.0
submental	195.0	198.89	234.8	229.8	238.8	239.8
subpleural	162.9	197.0	—	212.3	235.7	239.1
substernal	164.2	197.1	—	212.5	235.8	239.8
sudoriferous, sudoriparous gland, site unspecified	173.9	198.2	232.9	216.9	238.2	239.2
specified site—*see* Neoplasm, skin						
supraclavicular region	195.0	198.89	234.8	229.8	238.8	239.8
supraglottis	161.1	197.3	231.0	212.1	235.6	239.1
suprarenal (capsule) (cortex) (gland) (medulla)	194.0	198.7	234.8	227.0	237.2	239.7
suprasellar (region)	191.9	198.3	—	225.0	237.5	239.6
sweat gland (apocrine) (eccrine), site unspecified	173.9	198.2	232.9	216.9	238.2	239.2
specified site—*see* Neoplasm, skin						
sympathetic nerve or nervous system NEC	171.9	198.89	—	215.9	238.1	239.2
symphysis pubis	170.6	198.5	—	213.6	238.0	239.2
synovial membrane—*see* Neoplasm, connective tissue						
tapetum, brain	191.8	198.3	—	225.0	237.5	239.6
tarsus (any bone)	170.8	198.5	—	213.8	238.0	239.2
temple (skin)	173.3	198.2	232.3	216.3	238.2	239.2
temporal						
bone	170.0	198.5	—	213.0	238.0	239.2
lobe or pole	191.2	198.3	—	225.0	237.5	239.6
region	195.0	198.89	234.8	229.8	238.8	239.8
skin	173.3	198.2	232.3	216.3	238.2	239.2
tendon (sheath)—*see* Neoplasm, connective tissue						
tentorium (cerebelli)	192.1	198.4	—	225.2	237.6	239.7
testis, testes (descended) (scrotal)	186.9	198.82	233.6	222.0	236.4	239.5
ectopic	186.0	198.82	233.6	222.0	236.4	239.5
retained	186.0	198.82	233.6	222.0	236.4	239.5
undescended	186.0	198.82	233.6	222.0	236.4	239.5
thalamus	191.0	198.3	—	225.0	237.5	239.6
thigh NEC*	195.5	198.89	234.8	229.8	238.8	239.8
thorax, thoracic (cavity) (organs NEC)	195.1	198.89	234.8	229.8	238.8	239.8
duct	171.4	198.89	—	215.4	238.1	239.2
wall NEC	195.1	198.89	234.8	229.8	238.8	239.8
throat	149.0	198.89	230.0	210.9	235.1	239.0
thumb NEC*	195.4	198.89	232.6	229.8	238.8	239.8

	Malignant					
	Primary	Secondary	Ca in situ	Benign	Uncertain Behavior	Unspecified
thymus (gland)	164.0	198.89	—	212.6	235.8	239.8
contiguous sites with heart and						
mediastinum	164.8	—	—	—	—	—
thyroglossal duct	193	198.89	234.8	226	237.4	239.7
thyroid (gland)	193	198.89	234.8	226	237.4	239.7
cartilage	161.3	197.3	231.0	212.1	235.6	239.1
tibia (any part)	170.7	198.5	—	213.7	238.0	239.2
toe NEC*	195.5	198.89	232.7	229.8	238.8	239.8
tongue	141.9	198.89	230.0	210.1	235.1	239.0
anterior (two-thirds) NEC	141.4	198.89	230.0	210.1	235.1	239.0
dorsal surface	141.1	198.89	230.0	210.1	235.1	239.0
ventral surface	141.3	198.89	230.0	210.1	235.1	239.0
base (dorsal surface)	141.0	198.89	230.0	210.1	235.1	239.0
border (lateral)	141.2	198.89	230.0	210.1	235.1	239.0
contiguous sites	141.8	—	—	—	—	—
dorsal surface NEC	141.1	198.89	230.0	210.1	235.1	239.0
fixed part NEC	141.0	198.89	230.0	210.1	235.1	239.0
foramen cecum	141.1	198.89	230.0	210.1	235.1	239.0
frenulum linguae	141.3	198.89	230.0	210.1	235.1	239.0
junctional zone	141.5	198.89	230.0	210.1	235.1	239.0
margin (lateral)	141.2	198.89	230.0	210.1	235.1	239.0
midline NEC	141.1	198.89	230.0	210.1	235.1	239.0
mobile part NEC	141.4	198.89	230.0	210.1	235.1	239.0
posterior (third)	141.0	198.89	230.0	210.1	235.1	239.0
root	141.0	198.89	230.0	210.1	235.1	239.0
surface (dorsal)	141.1	198.89	230.0	210.1	235.1	239.0
base	141.0	198.89	230.0	210.1	235.1	239.0
ventral	141.3	198.89	230.0	210.1	235.1	239.0
tip	141.2	198.89	230.0	210.1	235.1	239.0
tonsil	141.6	198.89	230.0	210.1	235.1	239.0
tonsil	146.0	198.89	230.0	210.5	235.1	239.0
fauces, faucial	146.0	198.89	230.0	210.5	235.1	239.0
lingual	141.6	198.89	230.0	210.1	235.1	239.0
palatine	146.0	198.89	230.0	210.5	235.1	239.0
pharyngeal	147.1	198.89	230.0	210.7	235.1	239.0
pillar (anterior) (posterior)	146.2	198.89	230.0	210.6	235.1	239.0
tonsillar fossa	146.1	198.89	230.0	210.6	235.1	239.0
tooth socket NEC	143.9	198.89	230.0	210.4	235.1	239.0
trachea (cartilage) (mucosa)	162.0	197.3	231.1	212.2	235.7	239.1
contiguous sites with bronchus or lung	162.8	—	—	—	—	—
tracheobronchial	162.8	197.3	231.1	212.2	235.7	239.1
contiguous sites with lung	162.8	—	—	—	—	—
tragus	173.2	198.2	232.2	216.2	238.2	239.2
trunk NEC*	195.8	198.89	232.5	229.8	238.8	239.8
tubo-ovarian	183.8	198.82	233.3	221.8	236.3	239.5
tunica vaginalis	187.8	198.82	233.6	222.8	236.6	239.5
turbinate (bone)	170.0	198.5	—	213.0	238.0	239.2
nasal	160.0	197.3	231.8	212.0	235.9	239.1
tympanic cavity	160.1	197.3	231.8	212.0	235.9	239.1
ulna (any part)	170.4	198.5	—	213.4	238.0	239.2
umbilicus, umbilical	173.5	198.2	232.5	216.5	238.2	239.2
uncus, brain	191.2	198.3	—	225.0	237.5	239.6
unknown site or unspecified	199.1	199.1	234.9	229.9	238.9	239.9
urachus	188.7	198.1	233.7	223.3	236.7	239.4
ureter, ureteral	189.2	198.1	233.9	223.2	236.91	239.5
orifice (bladder)	188.6	198.1	233.7	223.3	236.7	239.4
ureter-bladder (junction)	188.6	198.1	233.7	223.3	236.7	239.4
urethra, urethral (gland)	189.3	198.1	233.9	223.81	236.99	239.5
orifice, internal	188.5	198.1	233.7	223.3	236.7	239.4
urethrovaginal (septum)	184.9	198.82	233.3	221.9	236.3	239.5

	Malignant					
	Primary	Secondary	Ca in situ	Benign	Uncertain Behavior	Unspecified
urinary organ or system NEC	189.9	198.1	233.9	223.9	236.99	239.5
bladder—*see* Neoplasm, bladder						
contiguous sites	189.8	—	—	—	—	—
specified sites NEC	189.8	198.1	233.9	223.89	236.99	239.5
utero-ovarian	183.8	198.82	233.3	221.8	236.3	239.5
ligament	183.3	198.82	—	221.0	236.3	239.5
uterosacral ligament	183.4	198.82	—	221.0	236.3	239.5
uterus, uteri, uterine	179	198.82	233.2	219.9	236.0	239.5
adnexa NEC	183.9	198.82	233.3	221.8	236.3	239.5
contiguous sites	183.8	—	—	—	—	—
body	182.0	198.82	233.2	219.1	236.0	239.5
contiguous sites	182.8	—	—	—	—	—
cervix	180.9	198.82	233.1	219.0	236.0	239.5
cornu	182.0	198.82	233.2	219.1	236.0	239.5
corpus	182.0	198.82	233.2	219.1	236.0	239.5
endocervix (canal) (gland)	180.0	198.82	233.1	219.0	236.0	239.5
endometrium	182.0	198.82	233.2	219.1	236.0	239.5
exocervix	180.1	198.82	233.1	219.0	236.0	239.5
external os	180.1	198.82	233.1	219.0	236.0	239.5
fundus	182.0	198.82	233.2	219.1	236.0	239.5
internal os	180.0	198.82	233.1	219.0	236.0	239.5
isthmus	182.1	198.82	233.2	219.1	236.0	239.5
ligament	183.4	198.82	—	221.0	236.3	239.5
broad	183.3	198.82	233.3	221.0	236.3	239.5
round	183.5	198.82	—	221.0	236.3	239.5
lower segment	182.1	198.82	233.2	219.1	236.0	239.5
myometrium	182.0	198.82	233.2	219.1	236.0	239.5
squamocolumnar junction	180.8	198.82	233.1	219.0	236.0	239.5
tube	183.2	198.82	233.3	221.0	236.3	239.5
utricle, prostatic	189.3	198.1	233.9	223.81	236.99	239.5
uveal tract	190.0	198.4	234.0	224.0	238.8	239.8
uvula	145.4	198.89	230.0	210.4	235.1	239.0
vagina, vaginal (fornix) (vault) (wall)	184.0	198.82	233.3	221.1	236.3	239.5
vaginovesical	184.9	198.82	233.3	221.9	236.3	239.5
septum	194.9	198.82	233.3	221.9	236.3	239.5
vallecula (epiglottis)	146.3	198.89	230.0	210.6	235.1	239.0
vascular—*see* Neoplasm, connective tissue						
vas deferens	187.6	198.82	233.6	222.8	236.6	239.5
Vater's ampulla	156.2	197.8	230.8	211.5	235.3	239.0
vein, venous—*see* Neoplasm, connective tissue						
vena cava (abdominal) (inferior)	171.5	198.89	—	215.5	238.1	239.2
superior	171.4	198.89	—	215.4	238.1	239.2
ventricle (cerebral) (floor) (fourth) (lateral)						
(third)	191.5	198.3	—	225.0	237.5	239.6
cardiac (left) (right)	164.1	198.89	—	212.7	238.8	239.8
ventricular band of larynx	161.1	197.3	231.0	212.1	235.6	239.1
ventriculus—*see* Neoplasm, stomach						
vermillion border—*see* Neoplasm, lip						
vermis, cerebellum	191.6	198.3	—	225.0	237.5	239.6
vertebra (column)	170.2	198.5	—	213.2	238.0	239.2
coccyx	170.6	198.5	—	213.6	238.0	239.2
sacrum	170.6	198.5	—	213.6	238.0	239.2
vesical—*see* Neoplasm, bladder						
vesicle, seminal	187.8	198.82	233.6	222.8	236.6	239.5
vesicocervical tissue	184.9	198.82	233.3	221.9	236.3	239.5
vesicorectal	195.3	198.89	234.8	229.8	238.8	239.8
vesicovaginal	184.9	198.82	233.3	221.9	236.3	239.5
septum	184.9	198.82	233.3	221.9	236.3	239.5
vessel (blood)—*see* Neoplasm, connective tissue						

	Malignant					
	Primary	Secondary	Ca in situ	Benign	Uncertain Behavior	Unspecified
vestibular gland, greater	184.1	198.82	233.3	221.2	236.3	239.5
vestibule						
mouth	145.1	198.89	230.0	210.4	235.1	239.0
nose	160.0	197.3	231.8	212.0	235.9	239.1
Virchow's gland	—	196.0	—	229.0	238.8	239.8
viscera NEC	195.8	198.89	234.8	229.8	238.8	239.8
vocal cords (true)	161.0	197.3	231.0	212.1	235.6	239.1
false	161.1	197.3	231.0	212.1	235.6	239.1
vomer	170.0	198.5	—	213.0	238.0	239.2
vulva	184.4	198.82	233.3	221.2	236.3	239.5
vulvovaginal gland	184.4	198.82	233.3	221.2	236.3	239.5
Waldeyer's ring	149.1	198.89	230.0	210.9	235.1	239.0
Wharton's duct	142.1	198.89	230.0	210.2	235.0	239.0
white matter (central) (cerebral)	191.0	198.3	—	225.0	237.5	239.6
windpipe	162.0	197.3	231.1	212.2	235.7	239.1
Wirsung's duct	157.3	197.8	230.9	211.6	235.5	239.0
wolffian (body) (duct)						
female	184.8	198.82	233.3	221.8	236.3	239.5
male	187.8	198.82	233.6	222.8	236.6	239.5
womb—*see* Neoplasm, uterus						
wrist NEC*	195.4	198.89	232.6	229.8	238.8	239.8
xiphoid process	170.3	198.5	—	213.3	238.0	239.2
Zuckerkandl's organ	194.6	198.89	—	227.6	237.3	239.7

Neovascularization
  choroid 362.16
  ciliary body 364.42
  cornea 370.60
    deep 370.63
    localized 370.61
  iris 364.42
  retina 362.16
  subretinal 362.16
Nephralgia 788.0
Nephritis, nephritic (albuminuric) (azotemic)
    (congenital) (degenerative) (diffuse)
    (disseminated) (epithelial) (familial) (focal)
    (granulomatous) (hemorrhagic) (infantile)
    (nonsuppurative, excretory) (uremic) 583.9
  with
    edema—see Nephrosis
    lesion of
      glomerulonephritis
        hypocomplementemic persistent 583.2
          with nephrotic syndrome 581.2
          chronic 582.2
        lobular 583.2
          with nephrotic syndrome 581.2
          chronic 582.2
        membranoproliferative 583.2
          with nephrotic syndrome 581.2
          chronic 582.2
        membranous 583.1
          with nephrotic syndrome 581.1
          chronic 582.1
        mesangiocapillary 583.2
          with nephrotic syndrome 581.2
          chronic 582.2
        mixed membranous and proliferative 583.2
          with nephrotic syndrome 581.2
          chronic 582.2
        proliferative (diffuse) 583.0
          with nephrotic syndrome 581.0
          acute 580.0
          chronic 582.0
        rapidly progressive 583.4
          acute 580.4
          chronic 582.4
      interstitial nephritis (diffuse) (focal) 583.89
        with nephrotic syndrome 581.89
        acute 580.89
        chronic 582.89
      necrotizing glomerulitis 583.4
        acute 580.4
        chronic 582.4
      renal necrosis 583.9
        cortical 583.6
        medullary 583.7
      specified pathology NEC 583.89
        with nephrotic syndrome 581.89
        acute 580.89
        chronic 582.89
    necrosis, renal 583.9
      cortical 583.6
      medullary (papillary) 583.7
    nephrotic syndrome (see also Nephrosis) 581.9
    papillary necrosis 583.7
    specified pathology NEC 583.89
  acute 580.9
    extracapillary with epithelial crescents 580.4
    hypertensive (see also Hypertension, kidney)
        403.90
    necrotizing 580.4
    poststreptococcal 580.0
    proliferative (diffuse) 580.0

Nephritis, nephritic—continued
  rapidly progressive 580.4
  specified pathology NEC 580.89
  amyloid 277.3 [583.81]
    chronic 277.3 [582.81]
  arteriolar (see also Hypertension, kidney) 403.90
  arteriosclerotic (see also Hypertension, kidney)
      403.90
  ascending (see also Pyelitis) 590.80
  atrophic 582.9
  basement membrane NEC 583.89
    with
      pulmonary hemorrhage (Goodpasture's
          syndrome) 446.21 [583.81]
  calculous, calculus 592.0
  cardiac (see also Hypertension, kidney) 403.90
  cardiovascular (see also Hypertension, kidney)
      403.90
  chronic 582.9
    arteriosclerotic (see also Hypertension,
        kidney) 403.90
    hypertensive (see also Hypertension, kidney)
        403.90
  cirrhotic (see also Sclerosis, renal) 587
  complicating pregnancy, childbirth, or
      puerperium 646.2
    with hypertension 642.1
      affecting fetus or newborn 760.0
    affecting fetus or newborn 760.1
  croupous 580.9
  desquamative—see Nephrosis
  due to
    amyloidosis 277.3 [583.81]
      chronic 277.3 [582.81]
    arteriosclerosis (see also Hypertension,
        kidney) 403.90
    diabetes mellitus 250.4 [583.81]
      with nephrotic syndrome 250.4 [581.81]
    diphtheria 032.89 [580.81]
    gonococcal infection (acute) 098.19 [583.81]
      chronic or duration of 2 months or over
          098.39 [583.81]
    gout 274.10
    infectious hepatitis 070.9 [580.81]
    mumps 072.79 [580.81]
    specified kidney pathology NEC 583.89
      acute 580.89
      chronic 582.89
    streptotrichosis 039.8 [583.81]
    subacute bacterial endocarditis 421.0 [580.81]
    systemic lupus erythematosus 710.0 [583.81]
      chronic 710.0 [582.81]
    typhoid fever 002.0 [580.81]
  endothelial 582.2
  end stage (chronic) (terminal) NEC 585
  epimembranous 581.1
  exudative 583.89
    with nephrotic syndrome 581.89
    acute 580.89
    chronic 582.89
  gonococcal (acute) 098.19 [583.81]
    chronic or duration of 2 months or over
        098.39 [583.81]
  gouty 274.10
  hereditary (Alport's syndrome) 759.89
  hydremic—see Nephrosis
  hypertensive (see also Hypertension, kidney)
      403.90
  hypocomplementemic persistent 583.2
    with nephrotic syndrome 581.2
    chronic 582.2

Nephritis, nephritic—*continued*
immune complex NEC 583.89
infective (*see also* Pyelitis) 590.80
interstitial (diffuse) (focal) 583.89
  with nephrotic syndrome 581.89
  acute 580.89
  chronic 582.89
latent or quiescent—*see* Nephritis, chronic
lead 984.9
  specified type of lead—*see* Table of drugs and
    chemicals
lobular 583.2
  with nephrotic syndrome 581.2
  chronic 582.2
lupus 710.0 *[583.81]*
  acute 710.0 *[580.81]*
  chronic 710.0 *[582.81]*
membranoproliferative 583.2
  with nephrotic syndrome 581.2
  chronic 582.2
membranous 583.1
  with nephrotic syndrome 581.1
  chronic 582.1
mesangiocapillary 583.2
  with nephrotic syndrome 581.2
  chronic 582.2
minimal change 581.3
mixed membranous and proliferative 583.2
  with nephrotic syndrome 581.2
  chronic 582.2
necrotic, necrotizing 583.4
  acute 580.4
  chronic 582.4
nephrotic—*see* Nephrosis
old—*see* Nephritis, chronic
parenchymatous 581.89
polycystic 753.12
  adult type (APKD) 753.13
  autosomal dominant 753.13
  autosomal recessive 753.14
  childhood type (CPKD) 753.14
  infantile type 753.14
poststreptococcal 580.0
pregnancy—*see* Nephritis, complicating
    pregnancy
proliferative 583.0
  with nephrotic syndrome 581.0
  acute 580.0
  chronic 582.0
purulent (*see also* Pyelitis) 590.80
rapidly progressive 583.4
  acute 580.4
  chronic 582.4
salt-losing or salt-wasting (*see also* Disease,
    renal) 593.9
saturnine 984.9
  specified type of lead—*see* Table of drugs and
    chemicals
septic (*see also* Pyelitis) 590.80
specified pathology NEC 583.89
  acute 580.89
  chronic 582.89
staphylococcal (*see also* Pyelitis) 590.80
streptotrichosis 039.8 *[583.81]*
subacute (*see also* Nephrosis) 581.9
suppurative (*see also* Pyelitis) 590.80
syphilitic (late) 095.4
  congenital 090.5 *[583.81]*
  early 091.69 *[583.81]*
terminal (chronic) (end-stage) NEC 585
toxic—*see* Nephritis, acute

Nephritis, nephritic—*continued*
tubal, tubular—*see* Nephrosis, tubular
tuberculous (*see also* Tuberculosis) 016.0
    [583.81]
type II (Ellis)—*see* Nephrosis
vascular—*see* Hypertension, kidney
war 580.9
Nephroblastoma (M8960/3) 189.0
epithelial (M8961/3) 189.0
mesenchymal (M8962/3) 189.0
Nephrocalcinosis 275.4
Nephrocystitis, pustular (*see also* Pyelitis)
    590.80
Nephrolithiasis (congenital) (pelvis) (recurrent)
    592.0
uric acid 274.11
Nephroma (M8960/3) 189.0
mesoblastic (M8960/1) 236.9
Nephronephritis (*see also* Nephrosis) 581.9
Nephronopthisis 753.16
Nephropathy (*see also* Nephritis) 583.9
with
    exudative nephritis 583.89
    interstitial nephritis (diffuse) (focal) 583.89
    medullary necrosis 583.7
    necrosis 583.9
      cortical 583.6
      medullary or papillary 583.7
    papillary necrosis 583.7
    specified lesion or cause NEC 583.89
analgesic 583.89
  with medullary necrosis, acute 584.7
arteriolar (*see also* Hypertension, kidney) 403.90
arteriosclerotic (*see also* Hypertension, kidney)
    403.90
complicating pregnancy 646.2
diabetic 250.4 *[583.81]*
gouty 274.10
  specified type NEC 274.19
hypercalcemic 588.8
hypertensive (*see also* Hypertension, kidney)
    403.90
hypokalemic (vacuolar) 588.8
obstructive 593.89
  congenital 753.20
phenacetin 584.7
phosphate-losing 588.0
potassium depletion 588.8
proliferative (*see also* Nephritis, proliferative)
    583.0
protein-losing 588.8
salt-losing or salt-wasting (*see also* Disease,
    renal) 593.9
sickle-cell (*see also* Disease, sickle-cell) 282.60
    [583.81]
toxic 584.5
vasomotor 584.5
water-losing 588.8
Nephroptosis (*see also* Disease, renal) 593.0
congenital (displaced) 753.3
Nephropyosis (*see also* Abscess, kidney) 590.2
Nephrorrhagia 593.81
Nephrosclerosis (arteriolar) (arteriosclerotic)
    (chronic) (hyaline) (*see also* Hypertension,
    kidney) 403.90
gouty 274.10
hyperplastic (arteriolar) (*see also* Hypertension,
    kidney) 403.90
senile (*see also* Sclerosis, renal) 587

Nephrosis, nephrotic (Epstein's) (syndrome) 581.9
with
  lesion of
    focal glomerulosclerosis 581.1
    glomerulonephritis
      endothelial 581.2
      hypocomplementemic persistent 581.2
      lobular 581.2
      membranoproliferative 581.2
      membranous 581.1
      mesangiocapillary 581.2
      minimal change 581.3
      mixed membranous and proliferative 581.2
      proliferative 581.0
    segmental hyalinosis 581.1
    specified pathology NEC 581.89
acute—*see* Nephrosis, tubular
anoxic—*see* Nephrosis, tubular
arteriosclerotic (*see also* Hypertension, kidney) 403.90
chemical—*see* Nephrosis, tubular
cholemic 572.4
complicating pregnancy, childbirth, or puerperium—*see* Nephritis, complicating pregnancy
diabetic 250.4 *[581.81]*
hemoglobinuric—*see* Nephrosis, tubular
in
  amyloidosis 277.3 *[581.81]*
  diabetes mellitus 250.4 *[581.81]*
  epidemic hemorrhagic fever 078.6
  malaria 084.9 *[581.81]*
  polyarteritis 446.0 *[581.81]*
  systemic lupus erythematosus 710.0 *[581.81]*
ischemic—*see* Nephrosis, tubular
lipoid 581.3
lower nephron—*see* Nephrosis, tubular
lupoid 710.0 *[581.81]*
lupus 710.0 *[581.81]*
malarial 084.9 *[581.81]*
minimal change 581.3
necrotizing—*see* Nephrosis, tubular
osmotic (sucrose) 588.8
polyarteritic 446.0 *[581.81]*
radiation 581.9
specified lesion or cause NEC 581.89
syphilitic 095.4
toxic—*see* Nephrosis, tubular
tubular (acute) 584.5
  due to a procedure 997.5
  radiation 581.9
Nephrosonephritis hemorrhagic (endemic) 078.6
Nephrostomy status V44.6
with complication 997.5
Nerve —*see* condition
Nerves 799.2
Nervous (*see also* condition) 799.2
breakdown 300.9
heart 306.2
stomach 306.4
tension 799.2
Nervousness 799.2
Nesidioblastoma (M8150/0)
pancreas 211.7
specified site NEC—*see* Neoplasm, by site, benign
unspecified site 211.7
Netherton's syndrome (ichthyosiform erythroderma) 757.1
Nettle rash 708.8

Nettleship's disease (urticaria pigmentosa) 757.33
Neumann's disease (pemphigus vegetans) 694.4
Neuralgia, neuralgic (acute) (*see also* Neuritis) 729.2
accessory (nerve) 352.4
acoustic (nerve) 388.5
ankle 355.8
anterior crural 355.8
anus 787.99
arm 723.4
auditory (nerve) 388.5
axilla 353.0
bladder 788.1
brachial 723.4
brain—*see* Disorder, nerve, cranial
broad ligament 625.9
cerebral—*see* Disorder, nerve, cranial
ciliary 346.2
cranial nerve—*see also* Disorder, nerve, cranial
  fifth or trigeminal (*see also* Neuralgia, trigeminal) 350.1
ear 388.71
  middle 352.1
facial 351.8
finger 354.9
flank 355.8
foot 355.8
forearm 354.9
Fothergill's (*see also* Neuralgia, trigeminal) 350.1
  postherpetic 053.12
glossopharyngeal (nerve) 352.1
groin 355.8
hand 354.9
heel 355.8
Horton's 346.2
Hunt's 053.11
hypoglossal (nerve) 352.5
iliac region 355.8
infraorbital (*see also* Neuralgia, trigeminal) 350.1
inguinal 355.8
intercostal (nerve) 353.8
  postherpetic 053.19
jaw 352.1
kidney 788.0
knee 355.8
loin 355.8
malarial (*see also* Malaria) 084.6
mastoid 385.89
maxilla 352.1
median thenar 354.1
metatarsal 355.6
middle ear 352.1
migrainous 346.2
Morton's 355.6
nerve, cranial—*see* Disorder, nerve, cranial
nose 352.0
olfactory (nerve) 352.0
ophthalmic 377.30
  postherpetic 053.19
optic (nerve) 377.30
penis 607.9
perineum 355.8
pleura 511.0
postherpetic NEC 053.19
  geniculate ganglion 053.11
  ophthalmic 053.19
  trifacial 053.12
  trigeminal 053.12

Neuralgia, neuralgic—*continued*
  pubic region 355.8
  radial (nerve) 723.4
  rectum 787.99
  sacroiliac joint 724.3
  sciatic (nerve) 724.3
  scrotum 608.9
  seminal vesicle 608.9
  shoulder 354.9
  Sluder's 337.0
  specified nerve NEC—*see* Disorder, nerve
  spermatic cord 608.9
  sphenopalatine (ganglion) 337.0
  subscapular (nerve) 723.4
  suprascapular (nerve) 723.4
  testis 608.89
  thenar (median) 354.1
  thigh 355.8
  tongue 352.5
  trifacial (nerve) (*see also* Neuralgia, trigeminal)
      350.1
  trigeminal (nerve) 350.1
      postherpetic 053.12
  tympanic plexus 388.71
  ulnar (nerve) 723.4
  vagus (nerve) 352.3
  wrist 354.9
  writers' 300.89
      organic 333.84
Neurapraxia —*see* Injury, nerve
Neurasthenia 300.5
  cardiac 306.2
  gastric 306.4
  heart 306.2
  postfebrile 780.7
  postviral 780.7
Neurilemmoma (M9560/0)—*see also* Neoplasm,
      connective tissue, benign
  acoustic (nerve) 225.1
  malignant (M9560/3)—*see also* Neoplasm,
      connective tissue, malignant
      acoustic (nerve) 192.0
Neurilemmosarcoma (M9560/3)—*see*
      Neoplasm, connective tissue, malignant
Neurilemoma —*see* Neurilemmoma
Neurinoma (M9560/0)—*see* Neurilemmoma
Neurinomatosis (M9560/1)—*see also*
      Neoplasm, connective tissue, uncertain
      behavior
  centralis 759.5
Neuritis (*see also* Neuralgia) 729.2
  abducens (nerve) 378.54
  accessory (nerve) 352.4
  acoustic (nerve) 388.5
      syphilitic 094.86
  alcoholic 357.5
      with psychosis 291.1
  amyloid, any site 277.3 *[357.4]*
  anterior crural 355.8
  arising during pregnancy 646.4
  arm 723.4
  ascending 355.2
  auditory (nerve) 388.5
  brachial (nerve) NEC 723.4
      due to displacement, intervertebral disc 722.0
  cervical 723.4
  chest (wall) 353.8
  costal region 353.8

Neuritis—*continued*
  cranial nerve—*see also* Disorder, nerve, cranial
      first or olfactory 352.0
      second or optic 377.30
      third or oculomotor 378.52
      fourth or trochlear 378.53
      fifth or trigeminal (*see also* Neuralgia,
          trigeminal) 350.1
      sixth or abducens 378.54
      seventh or facial 351.8
          newborn 767.5
      eighth or acoustic 388.5
      ninth or glossopharyngeal 352.1
      tenth or vagus 352.3
      eleventh or accessory 352.4
      twelfth or hypoglossal 352.5
  Déjérine-Sottas 356.0
  diabetic 250.6 *[357.2]*
  diphtheritic 032.89 *[357.4]*
  due to
      beriberi 265.0 *[357.4]*
      displacement, prolapse, protrusion, or rupture
          of intervertebral disc 722.2
          cervical 722.0
          lumbar, lumbosacral 722.10
          thoracic, thoracolumbar 722.11
      herniation, nucleus pulposus 722.2
          cervical 722.0
          lumbar, lumbosacral 722.10
          thoracic, thoracolumbar 722.11
  endemic 265.0 *[357.4]*
  facial (nerve) 351.8
      newborn 767.5
  general—*see* Polyneuropathy
  geniculate ganglion 351.1
      due to herpes 053.11
  glossopharyngeal (nerve) 352.1
  gouty 274.89 *[357.4]*
  hypoglossal (nerve) 352.5
  ilioinguinal (nerve) 355.8
  in diseases classified elsewhere—*see*
      Polyneuropathy, in
  infectious (multiple) 357.0
  intercostal (nerve) 353.8
  interstitial hypertrophic progressive NEC 356.9
  leg 355.8
  lumbosacral NEC 724.4
  median (nerve) 354.1
      thenar 354.1
  multiple (acute) (infective) 356.9
      endemic 265.0 *[357.4]*
  multiplex endemica 265.0 *[357.4]*
  nerve root (*see also* Radiculitis) 729.2
  oculomotor (nerve) 378.52
  olfactory (nerve) 352.0
  optic (nerve) 377.30
      in myelitis 341.0
      meningococcal 036.81
  pelvic 355.8
  peripheral (nerve)—*see also* Neuropathy,
      peripheral
      complicating pregnancy or puerperium 646.4
      specified nerve NEC—*see* Mononeuritis
  pneumogastric (nerve) 352.3
  postchickenpox 052.7
  postherpetic 053.19
  progressive hypertrophic interstitial NEC 356.9
  puerperal, postpartum 646.4
  radial (nerve) 723.4
  retrobulbar 377.32
      syphilitic 094.85

Neuritis—*continued*
  rheumatic (chronic) 729.2
  sacral region 355.8
  sciatic (nerve) 724.3
    due to displacement of intervertebral disc
      722.10
  serum 999.5
  specified nerve NEC—*see* Disorder, nerve
  spinal (nerve) 355.9
    root (*see also* Radiculitis) 729.2
  subscapular (nerve) 723.4
  suprascapular (nerve) 723.4
  syphilitic 095.8
  thenar (median) 354.1
  thoracic NEC 724.4
  toxic NEC 357.7
  trochlear (nerve) 378.53
  ulnar (nerve) 723.4
  vagus (nerve) 352.3
Neuroangiomatosis, encephalofacial 759.6
Neuroastrocytoma (M9505/1)—*see* Neoplasm,
  by site, uncertain behavior
Neuro-avitaminosis 269.2
Neuroblastoma (M9500/3)
  olfactory (M9522/3) 160.0
  specified site—*see* Neoplasm, by site, malignant
  unspecified site 194.0
Neurochorioretinitis (*see also* Chorioretinitis)
  363.20
Neurocirculatory asthenia 306.2
Neurocytoma (M9506/0)—*see* Neoplasm, by
  site, benign
Neurodermatitis (circumscribed) (circumscripta)
  (local) 698.3
  atopic 691.8
  diffuse (Brocq) 691.8
  disseminated 691.8
  nodulosa 698.3
Neuroencephalomyelopathy, optic 341.0
Neuroepithelioma (M9503/3)—*see also*
  Neoplasm, by site, malignant
  olfactory (M9521/3) 160.0
Neurofibroma (M9540/0)—*see also* Neoplasm,
  connective tissue, benign
  melanotic (M9541/0)—*see* Neoplasm,
    connective tissue, benign
  multiple (M9540/1) 237.70
    Type 1 237.71
    Type 2 237.72
  plexiform (M9550/0)—*see* Neoplasm,
    connective tissue, benign
Neurofibromatosis (multiple) (M9540/1) 237.70
  acoustic 237.72
  malignant (M9540/3)—*see* Neoplasm,
    connective tissue, malignant
  Type 1 237.71
  Type 2 237.72
  von Recklinghausen's 237.71
Neurofibrosarcoma (M9540/3)—*see* Neoplasm,
  connective tissue, malignant
Neurogenic —*see also* condition
  bladder (atonic) (automatic) (autonomic)
    (flaccid) (hypertonic) (hypotonic) (inertia)
    (infranuclear) (irritable) (motor) (nonreflex)
    (nuclear) (paralysis) (reflex) (sensory)
    (spastic) (supranuclear) (uninhibited) 596.54
    with cauda equina syndrome 344.61
  heart 306.2
Neuroglioma (M9505/1)—*see* Neoplasm, by
  site, uncertain behavior
Neurolabyrinthitis (of Dix and Hallpike) 386.12
Neurolathyrism 988.2

Neuroleprosy 030.1
Neuroleptic malignant syndrome 333.92
Neurolipomatosis 272.8
Neuroma (M9570/0)—*see also* Neoplasm,
  connective tissue, benign
  acoustic (nerve) (M9560/0) 225.1
  amputation (traumatic)—*see also* Injury, nerve,
    by site
    surgical complication (late) 997.61
  appendix 211.3
  auditory nerve 225.1
  digital 355.6
    toe 355.6
  interdigital (toe) 355.6
  intermetatarsal 355.6
  Morton's 355.6
  multiple 237.70
    Type 1 237.71
    Type 2 237.72
  nonneoplastic 355.9
    arm NEC 354.9
    leg NEC 355.8
    lower extremity NEC 355.8
    specified site NEC—*see* Mononeuritis, by site
    upper extremity NEC 354.9
  optic (nerve) 225.1
  plantar 355.6
  plexiform (M9550/0)—*see* Neoplasm,
    connective tissue, benign
  surgical (nonneoplastic) 355.9
    arm NEC 354.9
    leg NEC 355.8
    lower extremity NEC 355.8
    upper extremity NEC 354.9
  traumatic—*see also* Injury, nerve, by site
    old—*see* Neuroma, nonneoplastic
Neuromyalgia 729.1
Neuromyasthenia (epidemic) 049.8
Neuromyelitis 341.8
  ascending 357.0
  optica 341.0
Neuromyopathy NEC 358.9
Neuromyositis 729.1
Neuronevus (M8725/0)—*see* Neoplasm, skin,
  benign
Neuronitis 357.0
  ascending (acute) 355.2
  vestibular 386.12
Neuroparalytic —*see* condition
Neuropathy, neuropathic (*see also* Disorder,
  nerve) 355.9
  alcoholic 357.5
    with psychosis 291.1
  arm NEC 354.9
  autonomic (peripheral)—*see* Neuropathy,
    peripheral, autonomic
  axillary nerve 353.0
  brachial plexus 353.0
  cervical plexus 353.2
  chronic
    progressive segmentally demyelinating 357.8
    relapsing demyelinating 357.8
  congenital sensory 356.2
  Déjérine-Sottas 356.0
  diabetic 250.6 [357.2]
  entrapment 355.9
    iliohypogastric nerve 355.79
    ilioinguinal nerve 355.79
    lateral cutaneous nerve of thigh 355.1
    median nerve 354.0
    obturator nerve 355.79

Neuropathy, neuropathic—*continued*
  peroneal nerve 355.3
  posterior tibial nerve 355.5
  saphenous nerve 355.79
  ulnar nerve 354.2
  facial nerve 351.9
  hereditary 356.9
    peripheral 356.0
    sensory (radicular) 356.2
  hypertrophic
    Charcot-Marie-Tooth 356.1
    Déjérine-Sottas 356.0
    interstitial 356.9
    Refsum 356.3
  intercostal nerve 354.8
  ischemic—*see* Disorder, nerve
  Jamaican (ginger) 357.7
  leg NEC 355.8
  lower extremity NEC 355.8
  lumbar plexus 353.1
  median nerve 354.1
  multiple (acute) (chronic) (*see also*
    Polyneuropathy) 356.9
  optic 377.39
    ischemic 377.41
    nutritional 377.33
    toxic 377.34
  peripheral (nerve) (*see also* Polyneuropathy)
    356.9
    arm NEC 354.9
    autonomic 337.9
      amyloid 277.3 *[337.1]*
      idiopathic 337.0
      in
        amyloidosis 277.3 *[337.1]*
        diabetes (mellitus) 250.6 *[337.1]*
        diseases classified elsewhere 337.1
        gout 274.89 *[337.1]*
        hyperthyroidism 242.9 *[337.1]*
    due to
      antitetanus serum 357.6
      arsenic 357.7
      drugs 357.6
      lead 357.7
      organophosphate compounds 357.7
      toxic agent NEC 357.7
    hereditary 356.0
    idiopathic 356.9
      progressive 356.4
      specified type NEC 356.8
    in diseases classified elsewhere—*see*
      Polyneuropathy, in
    leg NEC 355.8
    lower extremity NEC 355.8
    upper extremity NEC 354.9
  plantar nerves 355.6
  progressive hypertrophic interstitial 356.9
  radicular NEC 729.2
    brachial 723.4
    cervical NEC 723.4
    hereditary sensory 356.2
    lumbar 724.4
    lumbosacral 724.4
    thoracic NEC 724.4
  sacral plexus 353.1
  sciatic 355.0
  spinal nerve NEC 355.9
    root (*see also* Radiculitis) 729.2
  toxic 357.7
  trigeminal sensory 350.8
  ulnar nerve 354.2

Neuropathy, neuropathic—*continued*
  upper extremity NEC 354.9
  uremic 585 *[357.4]*
  vitamin B$_{12}$ 266.2 *[357.4]*
    with anemia (pernicious) 281.0 *[357.4]*
    due to dietary deficiency 281.1 *[357.4]*
Neurophthisis —*see also* Disorder, nerve
  peripheral 356.9
  diabetic 250.6 *[357.2]*
Neuropraxia —*see* Injury,nerve
Neuroretinitis 363.05
  syphilitic 094.85
Neurosarcoma (M9540/3)—*see* Neoplasm,
  connective tissue, malignant
Neurosclerosis —*see* Disorder, nerve
Neurosis, neurotic 300.9
  accident 300.16
  anancastic, anankastic 300.3
  anxiety (state) 300.00
    generalized 300.02
    panic type 300.01
  asthenic 300.5
  bladder 306.53
  cardiac (reflex) 306.2
  cardiovascular 306.2
  climacteric, unspecified type 627.2
  colon 306.4
  compensation 300.16
  compulsive, compulsion 300.3
  conversion 300.11
  craft 300.89
  cutaneous 306.3
  depersonalization 300.6
  depressive (reaction) (type) 300.4
  endocrine 306.6
  environmental 300.89
  fatigue 300.5
  functional (*see also* Disorder, psychosomatic)
    306.9
  gastric 306.4
  gastrointestinal 306.4
  genitourinary 306.50
  heart 306.2
  hypochondriacal 300.7
  hysterical 300.10
    conversion type 300.11
    dissociative type 300.15
  impulsive 300.3
  incoordination 306.0
    larynx 306.1
    vocal cord 306.1
  intestine 306.4
  larynx 306.1
    hysterical 300.11
    sensory 306.1
  menopause, unspecified type 627.2
  mixed NEC 300.89
  musculoskeletal 306.0
  obsessional 300.3
    phobia 300.3
  obsessive-compulsive 300.3
  occupational 300.89
  ocular 306.7
  oral 307.0
  organ (*see also* Disorder, psychosomatic) 306.9
  pharynx 306.1
  phobic 300.20
  posttraumatic (acute) (situational) 308.3
    chronic 309.81
  psychasthenic (type) 300.89

Neurosis, neurotic—*continued*
  railroad 300.16
  rectum 306.4
  respiratory 306.1
  rumination 306.4
  senile 300.89
  sexual 302.70
  situational 300.89
  specified type NEC 300.89
  state 300.9
    with depersonalization episode 300.6
  stomach 306.4
  vasomotor 306.2
  visceral 306.4
  war 300.16
Neurospongioblastosis diffusa 759.5
Neurosyphilis (arrested) (early) (inactive) (late)
    (latent) (recurrent) 094.9
  with ataxia (cerebellar) (locomotor) (spastic)
    (spinal) 094.0
  acute meningitis 094.2
  aneurysm 094.89
  arachnoid (adhesive) 094.2
  arteritis (any artery) 094.89
  asymptomatic 094.3
  congenital 090.40
  dura (mater) 094.89
  general paresis 094.1
  gumma 094.9
  hemorrhagic 094.9
  juvenile (asymptomatic) (meningeal) 090.40
  leptomeninges (aseptic) 094.2
  meningeal 094.2
  meninges (adhesive) 094.2
  meningovascular (diffuse) 094.2
  optic atrophy 094.84
  parenchymatous (degenerative) 094.1
  paresis (*see also* Paresis, general) 094.1
  paretic (*see also* Paresis, general) 094.1
  relapse 094.9
  remission in (sustained) 094.9
  serological 094.3
  specified nature or site NEC 094.89
  tabes (dorsalis) 094.0
    juvenile 090.40
  tabetic 094.0
    juvenile 090.40
  taboparesis 094.1
    juvenile 090.40
  thrombosis 094.89
  vascular 094.89
Neurotic (*see also* Neurosis) 300.9
  excoriation 698.4
  psychogenic 306.3
Neurotmesis —*see* Injury, nerve, by site
Neurotoxemia   *see* Toxemia
Neutroclusion 524.2
Neutropenia, neutropenic (chronic) (cyclic)
    (drug-induced) (genetic) (idiopathic)
    (immune) (infantile) (malignant) (periodic)
    (pernicious) (primary) (splenic)
    (splenomegaly) (toxic) 288.0
  chronic hypoplastic 288.0
  congenital (nontransient) 288.0
  neonatal, transitory (isoimmune) (maternal
    transfer) 776.7
Neutrophilia, hereditary giant 288.2
Nevocarcinoma (M8720/3)—*see* Melanoma

Nevus (M8720/0)—*see also* Neoplasm, skin,
  benign

Note—Except where otherwise indicated, the
varieties of nevus in the list below that are
followed by a morphology code number (M——
-/0) should be coded by site as for "Neoplasm,
skin, benign."

---

  acanthotic 702.8
  achromic (M8730/0)
  amelanotic (M8730/0)
  anemic, anemicus 709.09
  angiomatous (M9120/0) (*see also*
    Hemangioma) 228.00
  araneus 448.1
  avasculosus 709.09
  balloon cell (M8722/0)
  bathing trunk (M8761/1) 238.2
  blue (M8780/0)
    cellular (M8790/0)
    giant (M8790/0)
    Jadassohn's (M8780/0)
    malignant (M8780/3)—*see* Melanoma
  capillary (M9131/0) (*see also* Hemangioma)
    228.00
  cavernous (M9121/0) (*see also* Hemangioma)
    228.00
  cellular (M8720/0)
    blue (M8790/0)
  comedonicus 757.33
  compound (M8760/0)
  conjunctiva (M8720/0) 224.3
  dermal (M8750/0)
    and epidermal (M8760/0)
  epithelioid cell (and spindle cell) (M8770/0)
  flammeus 757.32
    osteohypertrophic 759.89
  hairy (M8720/0)
  halo (M8723/0)
  hemangiomatous (M9120/0) (*see also*
    Hemangioma) 228.00
  intradermal (M8750/0)
  intraepidermal (M8740/0)
  involuting (M8724/0)
  Jadassohn's (blue) (M8780/0)
  junction, junctional (M8740/0)
    malignant melanoma in (M8740/3)—*see*
      Melanoma
  juvenile (M8770/0)
  lymphatic (M9170/0) 228.1
  magnocellular (M8726/0)
    specified site—*see* Neoplasm, by site, benign
    unspecified site 224.0
  malignant (M8720/3)—*see* Melanoma
  meaning hemangioma (M9120/0) (*see also*
    Hemangioma) 228.00
  melanotic (pigmented) (M8720/0)
  multiplex 759.5
  nonneoplastic 448.1
  nonpigmented (M8730/0)
  nonvascular (M8720/0)
  oral mucosa, white sponge 750.26
  osteohypertrophic, flammeus 759.89
  papillaris (M8720/0)
  papillomatosus (M8720/0)
  pigmented (M8720/0)
    giant (M8761/1)—*see also* Neoplasm, skin,
      uncertain behavior
    malignant melanoma in (M8761/3)—*see*
      Melanoma
  systematicus 757.33

Nevus—*continued*
  pilosus (M8720/0)
  port wine 757.32
  sanguineous 757.32
  sebaceous (senile) 702.8
  senile 448.1
  spider 448.1
  spindle cell (and epithelioid cell) (M8770/0)
  stellar 448.1
  strawberry 757.32
  syringocystadenomatous papilliferous
    (M8406/0)
  unius lateris 757.33
  Unna's 757.32
  vascular 757.32
  verrucous 757.33
  white sponge (oral mucosa) 750.26
Newborn (infant) (liveborn)
  multiple NEC
    born in hospital (without mention of cesarean
      delivery or section) V37.00
      with cesarean delivery or section V37.01
    born outside hospital
      hospitalized V37.1
      not hospitalized V37.2
    mates all liveborn
      born in hospital (without mention of
        cesarean delivery or section) V34.00
        with cesarean delivery or section V34.01
      born outside hospital
        hospitalized V34.1
        not hospitalized V34.2
    mates all stillborn
      born in hospital (without mention of
        cesarean delivery or section) V35.00
        with cesarean delivery or section V35.01
      born outside hospital
        hospitalized V35.1·
        not hospitalized V35.2
    mates liveborn and stillborn
      born in hospital (without mention of
        cesarean delivery or section) V36.00
        with cesarean delivery or section V36.01
      born outside hospital
        hospitalized V36.1
        not hospitalized V36.2
  single
    born in hospital (without mention of cesarean
      delivery or section) V30.00
      with cesarean delivery or section V30.01
    born outside hospital
      hospitalized V30.1
      not hospitalized V30.2
  twin NEC
    born in hospital (without mention of cesarean
      delivery or section) V33.00
      with cesarean delivery or section V33.01
    born outside hospital
      hospitalized V33.1
      not hospitalized V33.2
    mate liveborn
      born in hospital V31.0
      born outside hospital
        hospitalized V31.1
        not hospitalized V31.2
    mate stillborn
      born in hospital V32.0
      born outside hospital
        hospitalized V32.1
        not hospitalized V32.2

Newborn—*continued*
  unspecified as to single or multiple birth
    born in hospital (without mention of cesarean
      delivery or section) V39.00
      with cesarean delivery or section V39.01
    born outside hospital
      hospitalized V39.1
      not hospitalized V39.2
Newcastle's conjunctivitis or disease 077.8
Nezelof's syndrome (pure alymphocytosis)
  279.13
Niacin (amide) deficiency 265.2
Nicolas-Durand-Favre disease (climatic bubo)
  099.1
Nicolas-Favre disease (climatic bubo) 099.1
Nicotinic acid (amide) deficiency 265.2
Niemann-Pick disease (lipid histiocytosis)
  (splenomegaly) 272.7
Night
  blindness (*see also* Blindness, night) 368.60
    congenital 368.61
    vitamin A deficiency 264.5
  cramps 729.82
  sweats 780.8
  terrors, child 307.46
Nightmare 307.47
  REM-sleep type 307.47
Nipple —*see* condition
Nisbet's chancre 099.0
Nishimoto (-Takeuchi) disease 437.5
Nitritoid crisis or reaction —*see* Crisis, nitritoid
Nitrogen retention, extrarenal 788.9
Nitrosohemoglobinemia 289.8
Njovera 104.0
No
  diagnosis 799.9
  disease (found) V71.9
  room at the inn V65.0
Nocardiasis —*see* Nocardiosis
Nocardiosis 039.9
  with pneumonia 039.1
  lung 039.1
  specified type NEC 039.8
Nocturia 788.43
  psychogenic 306.53
Nocturnal —*see also* condition
  dyspnea (paroxysmal) 786.09
  emissions 608.89
  enuresis 788.36
    psychogenic 307.6
  frequency (micturition) 788.43
    psychogenic 306.53
Nodal rhythm disorder 427.89
Nodding of head 781.0
Node (s)—*see also* Nodule
  Heberden's 715.04
  larynx 478.79
  lymph—*see* condition
  milkers' 051.1
  Osler's 421.0
  rheumatic 729.89
  Schmorl's 722.30
    lumbar, lumbosacral 722.32
    specified region NEC 722.39
    thoracic, thoracolumbar 722.31
  singers' 478.5
  skin NEC 782.2
  tuberculous—*see* Tuberculosis, lymph gland
  vocal cords 478.5
Nodosities, Haygarth's 715.04

Nodule (s), nodular
  actinomycotic (*see also* Actinomycosis) 039.9
  arthritic—*see* Arthritis, nodosa
  cutaneous 782.2
  Haygarth's 715.04
  inflammatory—*see* Inflammation
  juxta-articular 102.7
    syphilitic 095.7
    yaws 102.7
  larynx 478.79
  lung, solitary 518.89
    emphysematous 492.8
  milkers' 051.1
  prostate 600
  rheumatic 729.89
  rheumatoid—*see* Arthritis rheumatoid
  scrotum (inflammatory) 608.4
  singers' 478.5
  skin NEC 782.2
  solitary, lung 518.89
    emphysematous 492.8
  subcutaneous 782.2
  thyroid (gland) (nontoxic) (uninodular) 241.0
    with
      hyperthyroidism 242.1
      thyrotoxicosis 242.1
    toxic or with hyperthyroidism 242.1
  vocal cords 478.5
Noma (gangrenous) (hospital) (infective) 528.1
  auricle (*see also* Gangrene) 785.4
  mouth 528.1
  pudendi (*see also* Vulvitis) 616.10
  vulvae (*see also* Vulvitis) 616.10
Nomadism V60.0
Non-autoimmune hemolytic anemia NEC
  283.10
Nonclosure —*see also* Imperfect, closure
  ductus
    arteriosus 747.0
    Botalli 747.0
  Eustachian valve 746.89
  foramen
    Botalli 745.5
    ovale 745.5
Nondescent (congenital)—*see also* Malposition,
  congenital
  cecum 751.4
  colon 751.4
  testis 752.51
Nondevelopment
  brain 742.1
    specified part 742.2
  heart 746.89
  organ or site, congenital NEC—*see* Hypoplasia
Nonengagement
  head NEC 652.5
    in labor 660.1
      affecting fetus or newborn 763.1
Nonexanthematous tick fever 066.1
Nonexpansion, lung (newborn) NEC 770.4
Nonfunctioning
  cystic duct (*see also* Disease, gallbladder) 575.8
  gallbladder (*see also* Disease, gallbladder) 575.8
  kidney (*see also* Disease, renal) 593.9
  labyrinth 386.58
Nonhealing
  stump (surgical) 997.60
  wound, surgical 998.83
Nonimplantation of ovum, causing infertility
  628.3
Noninsufflation, fallopian tube 628.2

Nonne-Milroy-Meige syndrome (chronic
  hereditary edema) 757.0
Nonovulation 628.0
Nonpatent fallopian tube 628.2
Nonpneumatization, lung NEC 770.4
Nonreflex bladder 596.54
  with cauda equina 344.61
Nonretention of food —*see also* Vomiting
Nonrotation —*see* Malrotation
Nonsecretion, urine (*see also* Anuria) 788.5
  newborn 753.3
Nonunion
  fracture 733.82
  organ or site, congenital NEC—*see* Imperfect,
    closure
  symphysis pubis, congenital 755.69
  top sacrum, congenital 756.19
Nonviability 765.0
Nonvisualization, gallbladder 793.3
Nonvitalized tooth 522.9
Normal
  delivery—*see* category 650
  menses V65.5
  state (feared complaint unfounded) V65.5
Normoblastosis 289.8
Normocytic anemia (infectional) 285.9
  due to blood loss (chronic) 280.0
    acute 285.1
Norrie's disease (congenital) (progressive
  oculoacousticocerebral degeneration) 743.8
North American blastomycosis 116.0
Norwegian itch 133.0
Nose, nasal —*see* condition
Nosebleed 784.7
Nosomania 298.9
Nosophobia 300.29
Nostalgia 309.89
Notch of iris 743.46
Notched lip, congenital (*see also* Cleft, lip)
  749.10
Notching nose, congenital (tip) 748.1
Nothnagel's
  syndrome 378.52
  vasomotor acroparesthesia 443.89
Novy's relapsing fever (American) 087.1
Noxious
  foodstuffs, poisoning by
    fish 988.0
    fungi 988.1
    mushrooms 988.1
    plants (food) 988.2
    shellfish 988.0
    specified type NEC 988.8
    toadstool 988.1
  substances transmitted through placenta or
    breast milk 760.70
    alcohol 760.71
    anti-infective agents 760.74
    cocaine 760.75
    "crack" 760.75
    diethylstilbestrol (DES) 760.76
    hallucinogenic agents NEC 760.73
    medicinal agents NEC 760.79
    narcotics 760.72
    obstetric anesthetic or analgesic 763.5
    specified agent NEC 760.79
    suspected, affecting management of
      pregnancy 655.5
Nuchal hitch (arm) 652.8
Nucleus pulposus —*see* condition
Numbness 782.0

Nuns' knee 727.2
Nursemaid's
  elbow 832.0
  shoulder 831.0
Nutmeg liver 573.8
Nutrition, deficient or insufficient (particular
   kind of food) 269.9
  due to
   insufficient food 994.2
   lack of
    care (child) (infant) 995.52
     adult 995.84
    food 994.2
Nyctalopia (*see also* Blindness, night) 368.60
  vitamin A deficiency 264.5
Nycturia 788.43
  psychogenic 306.53
Nymphomania 302.89
Nystagmus 379.50
  associated with vestibular system disorders
   379.54
  benign paroxysmal positional 386.11
  central positional 386.2
  congenital 379.51
  deprivation 379.53
  dissociated 379.55
  latent 379.52
  miners' 300.89
  positional
   benign paroxysmal 386.11
   central 386.2
  specified NEC 379.56
  vestibular 379.54
  visual deprivation 379.53

O

Oasthouse urine disease 270.2
Obermeyer's relapsing fever (European) 087.0
Obesity (constitutional) (exogenous) (familial) (nutritional) (simple) 278.00
  adrenal 255.8
  due to hyperalimentation 278.00
  endocrine NEC 259.9
  endogenous 259.9
  Fröhlich's (adiposogenital dystrophy) 253.8
  glandular NEC 259.9
  hypothyroid (*see also* Hypothyroidism) 244.9
  morbid 278.01
  of pregnancy 646.1
  pituitary 253.8
  thyroid (*see also* Hypothyroidism) 244.9
Oblique —*see also* condition
  lie before labor, affecting fetus or newborn 761.7
Obliquity, pelvis 738.6
Obliteration
  abdominal aorta 446.7
  appendix (lumen) 543.9
  artery 447.1
  ascending aorta 446.7
  bile ducts 576.8
    with calculus, choledocholithiasis, or stones—*see* Choledocholithiasis
    congenital 751.61
      jaundice from 751.61 *[774.5]*
  common duct 576.8
    with calculus, choledocholithiasis, or stones—*see* Choledocholithiasis
    congenital 751.61
  cystic duct 575.8
    with calculus, choledocholithiasis, or stones—*see* Choledocholithiasis
  disease, arteriolar 447.1
  endometrium 621.8
  eye, anterior chamber 360.34
  fallopian tube 628.2
  lymphatic vessel 457.1
    postmastectomy 457.0
  organ or site, congenital NEC—*see* Atresia
  placental blood vessels—*see* Placenta, abnormal
  supra-aortic branches 446.7
  ureter 593.89
  urethra 599.84
  vein 459.9
  vestibule (oral) 525.8
Observation (for) V71.9
  without need for further medical care V71.9
  accident NEC V71.4
    at work V71.3
  criminal assault V71.6
  deleterious agent ingestion V71.8
  disease V71.9
    cardiovascular V71.7
    heart V71.7
    mental V71.09
    specified condition NEC V71.8
  foreign body ingestion V71.8
  growth and development variations V21.8
  injuries (accidental) V71.4
    inflicted NEC V71.6
      during alleged rape or seduction V71.5
  malignant neoplasm, suspected V71.1
  postpartum
    immediately after delivery V24.0
    routine follow-up V24.2

Observation—*continued*
  pregnancy
    high-risk V23.9
      specified problem NEC V23.8
    normal (without complication) V22.1
      with nonobstetric complication V22.2
      first V22.0
  rape or seduction, alleged V71.5
    injury during V71.5
  suicide attempt, alleged V71.8
  suspected (undiagnosed) (unproven)
    cardiovascular disease V71.7
    child or wife battering victim V71.6
    concussion (cerebral) V71.6
    condition NEC V71.8
      infant—*see* Observation, suspected, condition, newborn
      newborn V29.9
        cardiovascular disease V29.8
        congenital anomaly V29.8
        infectious V29.0
        ingestion foreign object V29.8
        injury V29.8
        neoplasm V29.8
        neurological V29.1
        poison, poisoning V29.8
        respiratory V29.2
        specified NEC V29.8
    infectious disease not requiring isolation V71.8
    malignant neoplasm V71.1
    mental disorder V71.09
    neoplasm
      benign V71.8
      malignant V71.1
    specified condition NEC V71.8
    tuberculosis V71.2
  tuberculosis, suspected V71.2
Obsession, obsessional 300.3
  ideas and mental images 300.3
  impulses 300.3
  neurosis 300.3
  phobia 300.3
  psychasthenia 300.3
  ruminations 300.3
  state 300.3
  syndrome 300.3
Obsessive-compulsive 300.3
  neurosis 300.3
  reaction 300.3
Obstetrical trauma NEC (complicating delivery) 665.9
  with
    abortion—*see* Abortion, by type, with damage to pelvic organs
    ectopic pregnancy (*see also* categories 633.0-633.9) 639.2
    molar pregnancy (*see also* categories 630-632) 639.2
  affecting fetus or newborn 763.8
  following
    abortion 639.2
    ectopic or molar pregnancy 639.2
Obstipation (*see also* Constipation) 564.0
  psychogenic 306.4

Obstruction, obstructed, obstructive
  airway NEC 519.8
    with
      allergic alveolitis NEC 495.9
      asthma NEC (*see also* Asthma) 493.9
      bronchiectasis 494
      bronchitis (*see also* Bronchitis, with,
        obstruction) 491.20
      emphysema NEC 492.8
    chronic 496
      with
        allergic alveolitis NEC 495.5
        asthma NEC (*see also* Asthma) 493.9
        bronchiectasis 494
        bronchitis (*see also* Bronchitis, chronic,
          obstructive) 491.20
        emphysema NEC 492.8
    due to
      bronchospasm 519.1
      foreign body 934.9
      inhalation of fumes or vapors 506.9
      laryngospasm 478.75
  alimentary canal (*see also* Obstruction,
    intestine) 560.9
  ampulla of Vater 576.2
    with calculus, cholelithiasis, or stones—*see*
      Choledocholithiasis
  aortic (heart) (valve) (*see also* Stenosis, aortic)
    424.1
    rheumatic (*see also* Stenosis, aortic,
      rheumatic) 395.0
  aortoiliac 444.0
  aqueduct of Sylvius 331.4
    congenital 742.3
      with spina bifida (*see also* Spina bifida)
        741.0
    Arnold-Chiari (*see also* Spina bifida) 741.0
  artery (*see also* Embolism, artery) 444.9
    basilar (complete) (partial) (*see also*
      Occlusion, artery, basilar) 433.0
    carotid (complete) (partial) (*see also*
      Occlusion, artery, carotid) 433.1
    precerebral—*see* Occlusion, artery,
      precerebral NEC
    retinal (central) (*see also* Occlusion, retina)
      362.30
    vertebral (complete) (partial) (*see also*
      Occlusion, artery, vertebral) 433.2
  asthma (chronic) (with obstructive pulmonary
    disease) 493.2
  band (intestinal) 560.81
  bile duct or passage (*see also* Obstruction,
    biliary) 576.2
    congenital 751.61
      jaundice from 751.61 *[774.5]*
  biliary (duct) (tract) 576.2
    with calculus 574.51
      with cholecystitis (chronic) 574.41
        acute 574.31
    congenital 751.61
      jaundice from 751.61 *[774.5]*
    gallbladder 575.2
      with calculus 574.21
        with cholecystitis (chronic) 574.11
          acute 574.01
  bladder neck (acquired) 596.0
    congenital 753.6
  bowel (*see also* Obstruction, intestine) 560.9
  bronchus 519.1
  canal, ear (*see also* Stricture, ear canal,
    acquired) 380.50

Obstruction, . . . obstructive—*continued*
  cardia 537.89
  caval veins (inferior) (superior) 459.2
  cecum (*see also* Obstruction, intestine) 560.9
  circulatory 459.9
  colon (*see also* Obstruction, intestine) 560.9
    sympathicotonic 560.89
  common duct (*see also* Obstruction, biliary)
    576.2
    congenital 751.61
  coronary —*see* Arteriosclerosis, coronary
  cystic duct (*see also* Obstruction, gallbladder)
    575.2
    congenital 751.61
  device, implant, or graft—*see* Complications,
    due to (presence of) any device, implant, or
    graft classified to 996.0-996.5 NEC
  due to foreign body accidentally left in
    operation wound 998.4
  duodenum 537.3
    congenital 751.1
    due to
      compression NEC 537.3
      cyst 537.3
      intrinsic lesion or disease NEC 537.3
      scarring 537.3
      torsion 537.3
      ulcer 532.91
      volvulus 537.3
  ejaculatory duct 608.89
  endocardium 424.90
    arteriosclerotic 424.99
    specified cause, except rheumatic 424.99
  esophagus 530.3
  Eustachian tube (complete) (partial) 381.60
    cartilaginous
      extrinsic 381.63
      intrinsic 381.62
    due to
      cholesteatoma 381.61
      osseous lesion NEC 381.61
      polyp 381.61
    osseous 381.61
  fallopian tube (bilateral) 628.2
  fecal 560.39
    with hernia—*see also* Hernia, by site, with
      obstruction
    gangrenous—*see* Hernia, by site, with
      gangrene
  foramen of Monro (congenital) 742.3
    with spina bifida (*see also* Spina bifida) 741.0
  foreign body—*see* Foreign body
  gallbladder 575.2
    with calculus, cholelithiasis, or stones 574.21
      with cholecystitis (chronic) 574.11
        acute 574.01
    congenital 751.69
      jaundice from 751.69 *[774.5]*
  gastric outlet 537.0
  gastrointestinal (*see also* Obstruction, intestine)
    560.9
  glottis 478.79
  hepatic 573.8
    duct (*see also* Obstruction, biliary) 576.2
      congenital 751.61
  icterus (*see also* Obstruction, biliary) 576.8
    congenital 751.61
  ileocecal coil (*see also* Obstruction, intestine)
    560.9
  ileum (*see also* Obstruction, intestine) 560.9
  iliofemoral (artery) 444.81

Obstruction, . . . obstructive—*continued*

internal anastomosis—*see* Complications,
  mechanical, graft
intestine (mechanical) (neurogenic)
  (paroxysmal) (postinfectional) (reflex) 560.9
  with
    adhesions (intestinal) (peritoneal) 560.81
    hernia—*see also* Hernia, by site, with
      obstruction
      gangrenous—*see* Hernia, by site, with
        gangrene
  adynamic (*see also* Ileus) 560.1
  by gallstone 560.31
  congenital or infantile (small) 751.1
    large 751.2
  due to
    Ascaris lumbricoides 127.0
    mural thickening 560.89
    procedure 997.4
      involving urinary tract 997.5
  impaction 560.39
  infantile—*see* Obstruction, intestine,
    congenital
  newborn
    due to
      fecaliths 777.1
      inspissated milk 777.2
      meconium (plug) 777.1
        in mucoviscidosis 277.01
      transitory 777.4
  specified cause NEC 560.89
  transitory, newborn 777.4
  volvulus 560.2
intracardiac ball valve prosthesis 996.02
jaundice (*see also* Obstruction, biliary) 576.8
  congenital 751.61
jejunum (*see also* Obstruction, intestine) 560.9
kidney 593.89
labor 660.9
  affecting fetus or newborn 763.1
  by
    bony pelvis (conditions classifiable to
      653.0-653.9) 660.1
    deep transverse arrest 660.3
    impacted shoulder 660.4
    locked twins 660.5
    malposition (fetus) (conditions classifiable
      to 652.0-652.9) 660.0
      head during labor 660.3
    persistent occipitoposterior position 660.3
    soft tissue, pelvic (conditions classifiable to
      654.0-654.9) 660.2
lacrimal
  canaliculi 375.53
  congenital 743.65
  punctum 375.52
  sac 375.54
lacrimonasal duct 375.56
  congenital 743.65
  neonatal 375.55
lacteal, with steatorrhea 579.2
laryngitis (*see also* Laryngitis) 464.0
larynx 478.79
  congenital 748.3
liver 573.8
  cirrhotic (*see also* Cirrhosis, liver) 571.5
lung 518.89
  with
    asthma—*see* Asthma
    bronchitis (chronic) 491.2
    emphysema NEC 492.8

Obstruction, . . . obstructive—*continued*

airway, chronic 496
chronic NEC 496
  with
    asthma (chronic) (obstructive) 493.2
  disease, chronic 496
    with
      asthma (chronic) (obstructive) 493.2
    emphysematous 492.8
lymphatic 457.1
meconium
  fetus or newborn 777.1
    in mucoviscidosis 277.01
  newborn due to fecaliths 777.1
mediastinum 519.3
mitral (rheumatic)—*see* Stenosis, mitral
nasal 478.1
  duct 375.56
    neonatal 375.55
  sinus—*see* Sinusitis
nasolacrimal duct 375.56
  congenital 743.65
  neonatal 375.55
nasopharynx 478.29
nose 478.1
organ or site, congenital NEC—*see* Atresia
pancreatic duct 577.8
parotid gland 527.8
pelviureteral junction (*see also* Obstruction,
  ureter) 593.4
pharynx 478.29
portal (circulation) (vein) 452
prostate 600
  valve (urinary) 596.0
pulmonary
  valve (heart) (*see also* Endocarditis,
    pulmonary) 424.3
  vein, isolated 747.49
pyemic—*see* Septicemia
pylorus (acquired) 537.0
  congenital 750.5
  infantile 750.5
rectosigmoid (*see also* Obstruction, intestine)
  560.9
rectum 569.49
renal 593.89
respiratory 519.8
  chronic 496
retinal (artery) (vein) (central) (*see also*
  Occlusion, retina) 362.30
salivary duct (any) 527.8
  with calculus 527.5
sigmoid (*see also* Obstruction, intestine) 560.9
sinus (accessory) (nasal) (*see also* Sinusitis)
  473.9
Stensen's duct 527.8
stomach 537.89
  acute 536.1
  congenital 750.7
submaxillary gland 527.8
  with calculus 527.5
thoracic duct 457.1
thrombotic—*see* Thrombosis
tooth eruption 520.6
trachea 519.1
tracheostomy airway 519.0
tricuspid—*see* Endocarditis, tricuspid
upper respiratory, congenital 748.8
ureter (functional) 593.4
  congenital 753.20
  due to calculus 592.1

Obstruction, . . . obstructive—*continued*
ureteropelvic junction, congenital 753.21
uretcrovesical junction, congenital 753.22
urethra 599.6
  congenital 753.6
urinary (moderate) 599.6
  organ or tract (lower) 599.6
  prostatic valve 596.0
uropathy 599.6
uterus 621.8
vagina 623.2
valvular—*see* Endocarditis
vascular graft or shunt 996.1
  atherosclerosis —*see* Arteriosclerosis,
    coronary
  embolism 996.74
  occlusion NEC 996.74
  thrombus 996.74
vein, venous 459.2
  caval (inferior) (superior) 459.2
  thrombotic—*see* Thrombosis
vena cava (inferior) (superior) 459.2
ventricular shunt 996.2
vesical 596.0
vesicourethral orifice 596.0
vessel NEC 459.9
Obturator —*see* condition
Occlusal wear, teeth 521.1
Occlusion
anus 569.49
  congenital 751.2
  infantile 751.2
aortoiliac (chronic) 444.0
aqueduct of Sylvius 331.4
  congenital 742.3
    with spina bifida (*see also* Spina bifida)
      741.0
arteries of extremities, lower 444.22
  without thrombus or embolus (*see also*
    Arteriosclerosis, extremities) 440.20
  due to stricture or stenosis 447.1
  upper 444.21
    without thrombus or embolus (*see also*
      Arteriosclerosis, extremities) 440.20
    due to stricture or stenosis 447.1
artery NEC (*see also* Embolism, artery) 444.9
  auditory, internal 433.8
  basilar 433.0
    with other precerebral artery 433.3
    bilateral 433.3
  brain or cerebral (*see also* Infarct, brain) 434.9
  carotid 433.1
    with other precerebral artery 433.3
    bilateral 433.3
  cerebellar (anterior inferior) (posterior
    inferior) (superior) 433.8
  cerebral (*see also* Infarct, brain) 434.9
  choroidal (anterior) 433.8
  communicating posterior 433.8
  coronary (acute) (thrombotic) (*see also*
    Infarct, myocardium) 410.9
    healed or old 412
    without myocardial infarction 411.81
  hypophyseal 433.8
  iliac 444.81
  mesenteric (embolic) (thrombotic) (with
    gangrene) 557.0
  pontine 433.8
  precerebral NEC 433.9
    late effect—*see* category 438
    multiple or bilateral 433.3

Occlusion—*continued*
  puerperal, postpartum, childbirth 674.0
  specified NEC 433.8
renal 593.81
retinal—*see* Occlusion, retina, artery
spinal 433.8
vertebral 433.2
  with other precerebral artery 433.3
  bilateral 433.3
basilar (artery)—*see* Occlusion, artery, basilar
bile duct (any) (*see also* Obstruction, biliary)
  576.2
bowel (*see also* Obstruction, intestine) 560.9
brain (artery) (vascular) (*see also* Infarct, brain)
  434.9
breast (duct) 611.8
carotid (artery) (common) (internal)—*see*
  Occlusion, artery, carotid
cerebellar (anterior inferior) (artery) (posterior
  inferior) (superior) 433.8
cerebral (artery) (*see also* Infarct, brain) 434.9
cerebrovascular (*see also* Infarct, brain) 434.9
  diffuse 437.0
cervical canal (*see also* Stricture, cervix) 622.4
  by falciparum malaria 084.0
cervix (uteri) (*see also* Stricture, cervix) 622.4
choanal 748.0
choroidal (artery) 433.8
colon (*see also* Obstruction, intestine) 560.9
communicating posterior artery 433.8
coronary (acute) (artery) (thrombotic) (*see also*
  Infarct, myocardium) 410.9
  healed or old 412
  without myocardial infarction 411.81
cystic duct (*see also* Obstruction, gallbladder)
  575.2
  congenital 751.69
embolic—*see* Embolism
fallopian tube 628.2
  congenital 752.19
gallbladder (*see also* Obstruction, gallbladder)
  575.2
  congenital 751.69
    jaundice from 751.69 *[774.5]*
gingiva, traumatic 523.8
hymen 623.3
  congenital 752.41
hypophyseal (artery) 433.8
iliac artery 444.81
intestine (*see also* Obstruction, intestine) 560.9
kidney 593.89
lacrimal apparatus—*see* Stenosis, lacrimal
lung 518.89
lymph or lymphatic channel 457.1
mammary duct 611.8
mesenteric artery (embolic) (thrombotic) (with
  gangrene) 557.0
nose 478.1
  congenital 748.0
organ or site, congenital NEC—*see* Atresia
oviduct 628.2
  congenital 752.19
periodontal, traumatic 523.8
peripheral arteries (lower extremity) 444.22
  without thrombus or embolus (*see also*
    Arteriosclerosis, extremities) 440.20
  due to stricture or stenosis 447.1
  upper extremity 444.21
    without thrombus or embolus (*see also*
      Arteriosclerosis, extremities) 440.20
    due to stricture or stenosis 447.1

Occlusion—*continued*
pontine (artery) 433.8
posterior lingual, of mandibular teeth 524.2
precerebral artery—*see* Occlusion, artery,
 precerebral NEC
puncta lacrimalia 375.52
pupil 364.74
pylorus (*see also* Stricture, pylorus) 537.0
renal artery 593.81
retina, retinal (vascular) 362.30
 artery, arterial 362.30
 branch 362.32
 central (total) 362.31
 partial 362.33
 transient 362.34
 tributary 362.32
 vein 362.30
 branch 362.36
 central (total) 362.35
 incipient 362.37
 partial 362.37
 tributary 362.36
spinal artery 433.8
teeth (mandibular) (posterior lingual) 524.2
thoracic duct 457.1
tubal 628.2
ureter (complete) (partial) 593.4
 congenital 753.29
urethra (*see also* Stricture, urethra) 598.9
 congenital 753.6
uterus 621.8
vagina 623.2
vascular NEC 459.9
vein—*see* Thrombosis
vena cava (inferior) (superior) 453.2
ventricle (brain) NEC 331.4
vertebral (artery)—*see* Occlusion, artery,
 vertebral
vessel (blood) NEC 459.9
vulva 624.8
Occlusio pupillae 364.74
Occupational
problems NEC V62.2
therapy V57.21
Ochlophobia 300.29
Ochronosis (alkaptonuric) (congenital)
 (endogenous) 270.2
with chloasma of eyelid 270.2
Ocular muscle —*see also* condition
myopathy 359.1
Oculoauriculovertebral dysplasia 756.0
Oculogyric
crisis or disturbance 378.87
psychogenic 306.7
Oculomotor syndrome 378.81
Oddi's sphincter spasm 576.5
Odelberg's disease (juvenile osteochondrosis)
 732.1
Odontalgia 525.9
Odontoameloblastoma (M9311/0) 213.1
upper jaw (bone) 213.0
Odontoclasia 521.0
Odontoclasis 873.63
complicated 873.73
Odontodysplasia, regional 520.4
Odontogenesis imperfecta 520.5
Odontoma (M9280/0) 213.1
ameloblastic (M9311/0) 213.1
 upper jaw (bone) 213.0
calcified (M9280/0) 213.1
 upper jaw (bone) 213.0

Odontoma—*continued*
complex (M9282/0) 213.1
 upper jaw (bone) 213.0
compound (M9281/0) 213.1
 upper jaw (bone) 213.0
fibroameloblastic (M9290/0) 213.1
 upper jaw (bone) 213.0
follicular 526.0
 upper jaw (bone) 213.0
Odontomyelitis (closed) (open) 522.0
Odontonecrosis 521.0
Odontorrhagia 525.8
Odontosarcoma, ameloblastic (M9290/3) 170.1
upper jaw (bone) 170.0
Odynophagia 787.2
Oesophagostomiasis 127.7
Oesophagostomum infestation 127.7
Oestriasis 134.0
Ogilvie's syndrome (sympathicotonic colon
 obstruction) 560.89
Oguchi's disease (retina) 368.61
Ohara's disease (*see also* Tularemia) 021.9
Oidiomycosis (*see also* Candidiasis) 112.9
Oidiomycotic meningitis 112.83
Oidium albicans infection (*see also* Candidiasis)
 112.9
Old age 797
dementia (of) 290.0
Olfactory —*see* condition
Oligemia 285.9
Oligergasia (*see also* Retardation, mental) 319
Oligoamnios 658.0
affecting fetus or newborn 761.2
Oligoastrocytoma, mixed (M9382/3)
specified site—*see* Neoplasm, by site, malignant
unspecified site 191.9
Oligocythemia 285.9
Oligodendroblastoma (M9460/3)
specified site—*see* Neoplasm, by site, malignant
unspecified site 191.9
Oligodendroglioma (M9450/3)
anaplastic type (M9451/3)
 specified site—*see* Neoplasm, by site,
 malignant
 unspecified site 191.9
specified site—*see* Neoplasm, by site, malignant
unspecified site 191.9
Oligodendroma —*see* Oligodendroglioma
Oligodontia (*see also* Anodontia) 520.0
Oligoencephalon 742.1
Oligohydramnios 658.0
affecting fetus or newborn 761.2
due to premature rupture of membranes 658.1
 affecting fetus or newborn 761.2
Oligohydrosis 705.0
Oligomenorrhea 626.1
Oligophrenia (*see also* Retardation, mental) 319
phenylpyruvic 270.1
Oligospermia 606.1
Oligotrichia 704.09
congenita 757.4
Oliguria 788.5
with
 abortion—*see* Abortion, by type, with renal
 failure
 ectopic pregnancy (*see also* categories
 633.0-633.9) 639.3
 molar pregnancy (*see also* categories
 630-632) 639.3
complicating
 abortion 639.3

Oliguria—*continued*
  ectopic or molar pregnancy 639.3
  pregnancy 646.2
    with hypertension—*see* Toxemia, of
      pregnancy
  due to a procedure 997.5
  following labor and delivery 669.3
  heart or cardiac—*see* Failure, heart, congestive
  puerperal, postpartum 669.3
  specified due to a procedure 997.5
Ollier's disease (chondrodysplasia) 756.4
Omentitis (*see also* Peritonitis) 567.9
Omentocele (*see also* Hernia, omental) 553.8
Omentum, omental —*see* condition
Omphalitis (congenital) (newborn) 771.4
  not of newborn 686.9
  tetanus 771.3
Omphalocele 756.7
Omphalomesenteric duct, persistent 751.0
Omphalorrhagia, newborn 772.3
Omsk hemorrhagic fever 065.1
Onanism 307.9
Onchocerciasis 125.3
  eye 125.3 *[360.13]*
Onchocercosis 125.3
Oncocytoma (M8290/0)—*see* Neoplasm, by site,
  benign
Ondine's curse 348.8
Oneirophrenia (*see also* Schizophrenia) 295.4
Onychauxis 703.8
  congenital 757.5
Onychia (with lymphangitis) 681.9
  dermatophytic 110.1
  finger 681.02
  toe 681.11
Onychitis (with lymphangitis) 681.9
  finger 681.02
  toe 681.11
Onychocryptosis 703.0
Onychodystrophy 703.8
  congenital 757.5
Onychogryphosis 703.8
Onychogryposis 703.8
Onycholysis 703.8
Onychomadesis 703.8
Onychomalacia 703.8
Onychomycosis 110.1
  finger 110.1
  toe 110.1
Onycho-osteodysplasia 756.89
Onychophagy 307.9
Onychoptosis 703.8
Onychorrhexis 703.8
  congenital 757.5
Onychoschizia 703.8
Onychotrophia (*see also* Atrophy, nail) 703.8
O'nyong-nyong fever 066.3
Onyxis (finger) (toe) 703.0
Onyxitis (with lymphangitis) 681.9
  finger 681.02
  toe 681.11
Oophoritis (cystic) (infectional) (interstitial) (*see*
  also Salpingo-oophoritis) 614.2
  complicating pregnancy 646.6
  fetal (acute) 752.0
  gonococcal (acute) 098.19
    chronic or duration of 2 months or over 098.39
  tuberculous (*see also* Tuberculosis) 016.6
Opacity, opacities
  cornea 371.00
    central 371.03

Opacity, opacities—*continued*
  congenital 743.43
    interfering with vision 743.42
  degenerative (*see also* Degeneration, cornea)
    371.40
  hereditary (*see also* Dystrophy, cornea) 371.50
  inflammatory (*see also* Keratitis) 370.9
  late effect of trachoma (healed) 139.1
  minor 371.01
  peripheral 371.02
  enamel (fluoride) (nonfluoride) (teeth) 520.3
  lens (*see also* Cataract) 366.9
  snowball 379.22
  vitreous (humor) 379.24
    congenital 743.51
Opalescent dentin (hereditary) 520.5
Open, opening
  abnormal, organ or site, congenital—*see*
    Imperfect, closure
  angle with
    borderline intraocular pressure 365.01
    cupping of discs 365.01
  bite (anterior) (posterior) 524.2
  false—*see* Imperfect, closure
  wound—*see* Wound, open, by site
Operation
  causing mutilation of fetus 763.8
  destructive, on live fetus, to facilitate birth 763.8
  for delivery, fetus or newborn 763.8
  maternal, unrelated to current delivery, affecting
    fetus or newborn 760.6
Operational fatigue 300.89
Operative —*see* condition
Operculitis (chronic) 523.4
  acute 523.3
Operculum, retina 361.32
  with detachment 361.01
Ophiasis 704.01
Ophthalmia (*see also* Conjunctivitis) 372.30
  actinic rays 370.24
  allergic (acute) 372.05
    chronic 372.14
  blennorrhagic (neonatorum) 098.40
  catarrhal 372.03
  diphtheritic 032.81
  Egyptian 076.1
  electric, electrica 370.24
  gonococcal (neonatorum) 098.40
  metastatic 360.11
  migraine 346.8
  neonatorum, newborn 771.6
    gonococcal 098.40
  nodosa 360.14
  phlyctenular 370.31
    with ulcer (*see also* Ulcer, cornea) 370.00
  sympathetic 360.11
Ophthalmitis —*see* Ophthalmia
Ophthalmocele (congenital) 743.66
Ophthalmoneuromyelitis 341.0
Ophthalmopathy, infiltrative with
  thyrotoxicosis 242.0
Ophthalmoplegia (*see also* Strabismus) 378.9
  anterior internuclear 378.86
  ataxia-areflexia syndrome 357.0
  bilateral 378.9
  diabetic 250.5 *[378.86]*
  exophthalmic 242.0 *[376.22]*
  external 378.55
    progressive 378.72
    total 378.56

Ophthalmoplegia—*continued*
  interna(l) (complete) (total) 367.52
  internuclear 378.86
  migraine 346.8
  painful 378.55
  Parinaud's 378.81
  progressive external 378.72
  supranuclear, progressive 333.0
  total (external) 378.56
    internal 367.52
  unilateral 378.9
Opisthognathism 524.00
Opisthorchiasis (felineus) (tenuicollis)
    (viverrini) 121.0
Opisthotonos, opisthotonus 781.0
Opitz's disease (congestive splenomegaly)
    289.51
Opiumism (*see also* Dependence) 304.0
Oppenheim's disease 358.8
Oppenheim-Urbach disease or syndrome
    (necrobiosis lipoidica diabeticorum) 250.8
    [709.3]
Opsoclonia 379.59
Optic nerve —*see* condition
Orbit —*see* condition
Orchioblastoma (M9071/3) 186.9
Orchitis (nonspecific) (septic) 604.90
  with abscess 604.0
  blennorrhagic (acute) 098.13
    chronic or duration of 2 months or over 098.33
  diphtheritic 032.89 *[604.91]*
  filarial 125.9 *[604.91]*
  gangrenous 604.99
  gonococcal (acute) 098.13
    chronic or duration of 2 months or over 098.33
  mumps 072.0
  parotidea 072.0
  suppurative 604.99
  syphilitic 095.8 *[604.91]*
  tuberculous (*see also* Tuberculosis) 016.5
    [608.81]
Orf 051.2
Organic —*see also* condition
  heart—*see* Disease, heart
  insufficiency 799.8
Oriental
  bilharziasis 120.2
  schistosomiasis 120.2
  sore 085.1
Orifice —*see* condition
Origin, both great vessels from right ventricle
    745.11
Ormond's disease or syndrome 593.4
Ornithosis 073.9
  with
    complication 073.8
      specified NEC 073.7
    pneumonia 073.0
    pneumonitis (lobular) 073.0
Orodigitofacial dysostosis 759.89
Oropouche fever 066.3
Orotaciduria, oroticaciduria (congenital)
    (hereditary) (pyrimidine deficiency) 281.4
Oroya fever 088.0
Orthodontics V58.5
  adjustment V53.4
  aftercare V58.5
  fitting V53.4
Orthopnea 786.02
Orthoptic training V57.4
Os, uterus —*see* condition

Osgood-Schlatter
  disease 732.4
  osteochondrosis 732.4
Osler's
  disease (M9950/1) (polycythemia vera) 238.4
  nodes 421.0
Osler-Rendu disease (familial hemorrhagic
    telangiectasia) 448.0
Osler-Vaquez disease (M9950/1) (polycythemia
    vera) 238.4
Osler-Weber-Rendu syndrome (familial
    hemorrhagic telangiectasia) 448.0
Osmidrosis 705.89
Osseous —*see* condition
Ossification
  artery—*see* Arteriosclerosis
  auricle (ear) 380.39
  bronchus 519.1
  cardiac (*see also* Degeneration, myocardial)
    429.1
  cartilage (senile) 733.99
  coronary —*see* Arteriosclerosis, coronary
  diaphragm 728.10
  ear 380.39
    middle (*see also* Otosclerosis) 387.9
  falx cerebri 349.2
  fascia 728.10
  fontanel
    defective or delayed 756.0
    premature 756.0
  heart (*see also* Degeneration, myocardial) 429.1
    valve—*see* Endocarditis
  larynx 478.79
  ligament
    posterior longitudinal 724.8
      cervical 723.7
  meninges (cerebral) 349.2
    spinal 336.8
  multiple, eccentric centers 733.99
  muscle 728.10
    heterotopic, postoperative 728.13
  myocardium, myocardial (*see also*
    Degeneration, myocardial) 429.1
  penis 607.81
  periarticular 728.89
  sclera 379.16
  tendon 727.82
  trachea 519.1
  tympanic membrane (*see also*
    Tympanosclerosis) 385.00
  vitreous (humor) 360.44
Osteitis (*see also* Osteomyelitis) 730.2
  acute 730.0
  alveolar 526.5
  chronic 730.1
  condensans (ilii) 733.5
  deformans (Paget's) 731.0
    due to or associated with malignant neoplasm
      (*see also* Neoplasm, bone, malignant)
      170.9 *[731.1]*
  due to yaws 102.6
  fibrosa NEC 733.29
    cystica (generalisata) 252.0
    disseminata 756.59
    osteoplastica 252.0
  fragilitans 756.51
  Garré's (sclerosing) 730.1
  infectious (acute) (subacute) 730.0
    chronic or old 730.1
  jaw (acute) (chronic) (lower) (neonatal)
    (suppurative) (upper) 526.4

Osteitis—*continued*
parathyroid 252.0
petrous bone (*see also* Petrositis) 383.20
pubis 733.5
sclerotic, nonsuppurative 730.1
syphilitic 095.5
tuberculosa
cystica (of Jüngling) 135
multiplex cystoides 135
Osteoarthritica spondylitis (spine) (*see also*
Spondylosis) 721.90
Osteoarthritis (*see also* Osteoarthrosis) 715.9
distal interphalangeal 715.9
hyperplastic 731.2
interspinalis (*see also* Spondylosis) 721.90
spine, spinal NEC (*see also* Spondylosis) 721.90
Osteoarthropathy (*see also* Osteoarthrosis)
715.9
chronic idiopathic hypertrophic 757.39
familial idiopathic 757.39
hypertrophic pulmonary 731.2
secondary 731.2
idiopathic hypertrophic 757.39
primary hypertrophic 731.2
pulmonary hypertrophic 731.2
secondary hypertrophic 731.2
Osteoarthrosis (degenerative) (hypertrophic)
(rheumatoid) 715.9

Note—Use the following fifth-digit
subclassification with category 715:

0 site unspecified
1 shoulder region
2 upper arm
3 forearm
4 hand
5 pelvic region and thigh
6 lower leg
7 ankle and foot
8 other specified sites except spine
9 multiple sites

---

deformans alkaptonurica 270.2
generalized 715.09
juvenilis (Köhler's) 732.5
localized 715.3
idiopathic 715.1
primary 715.1
secondary 715.2
multiple sites, not specified as generalized
715.89
polyarticular 715.09
spine (*see also* Spondylosis) 721.90
temperomandibular joint 524.69
Osteoblastoma (M9200/0)—*see* Neoplasm,
bone, benign
Osteochondritis (*see also* Osteochondrosis)
732.9
dissecans 732.7
hip 732.7
ischiopubica 732.1
multiple 756.59
syphilitic (congenital) 090.0
Osteochondrodermodysplasia 756.59
Osteochondrodystrophy 277.5
deformans 277.5
familial 277.5
fetalis 756.4
Osteochondrolysis 732.7

Osteochondroma (M9210/0)—*see also*
Neoplasm, bone, benign
multiple, congenital 756.4
Osteochondromatosis (M9210/1) 238.0
synovial 727.82
Osteochondromyxosarcoma (M9180/3)—*see*
Neoplasm, bone, malignant
Osteochondropathy NEC 732.9
Osteochondrosarcoma (M9180/3)—*see*
Neoplasm, bone, malignant
Osteochondrosis 732.9
acetabulum 732.1
adult spine 732.8
astragalus 732.5
Blount's 732.4
Buchanan's (juvenile osteochondrosis of iliac
crest) 732.1
Buchman's (juvenile osteochondrosis) 732.1
Burns' 732.3
calcaneus 732.5
capitular epiphysis (femur) 732.1
carpal
lunate (wrist) 732.3
scaphoid 732.3
coxae juvenilis 732.1
deformans juvenilis (coxae) (hip) 732.1
Scheuermann's 732.0
spine 732.0
tibia 732.4
vertebra 732.0
Diaz's (astragalus) 732.5
dissecans (knee) (shoulder) 732.7
femoral capital epiphysis 732.1
femur (head) (juvenile) 732.1
foot (juvenile) 732.5
Freiberg's (disease) (second metatarsal) 732.5
Haas' 732.3
Haglund's (os tibiale externum) 732.5
hand (juvenile) 732.3
head of
femur 732.1
humerus (juvenile) 732.3
hip (juvenile) 732.1
humerus (juvenile) 732.3
iliac crest (juvenile) 732.1
ilium (juvenile) 732.1
ischiopubic synchondrosis 732.1
Iselin's (osteochondrosis fifth metatarsal) 732.5
juvenile, juvenilis 732.6
arm 732.3
capital femoral epiphysis 732.1
capitellum humeri 732.3
capitular epiphysis 732.1
carpal scaphoid 732.3
clavicle, sternal epiphysis 732.6
coxae 732.1
deformans 732.1
foot 732.5
hand 732.3
hip and pelvis 732.1
lower extremity, except foot 732.4
lunate, wrist 732.3
medial cuneiform bone 732.5
metatarsal (head) 732.5
metatarsophalangeal 732.5
navicular, ankle 732.5
patella 732.4
primary patellar center (of Köhler) 732.4
specified site NEC 732.6
spine 732.0
tarsal scaphoid 732.5

Osteochondrosis—*continued*
  tibia (epiphysis) (tuberosity) 732.4
  upper extremity 732.3
  vertebra (body) (Calvé) 732.0
    epiphyseal plates (of Scheuermann) 732.0
  Kienböck's (disease) 732.3
  Köhler's (disease) (navicular, ankle) 732.5
    patellar 732.4
    tarsal navicular 732.5
  Legg-Calvé-Perthes (disease) 732.1
  lower extremity (juvenile) 732.4
  lunate bone 732.3
  Mauclaire's 732.3
  metacarpal heads (of Mauclaire) 732.3
  metatarsal (fifth) (head) (second) 732.5
  navicular, ankle 732.5
  os calcis 732.5
  Osgood-Schlatter 732.4
  os tibiale externum 732.5
  Panner's 732.3
  patella (juvenile) 732.4
  patellar center
    primary (of Köhler) 732.4
    secondary (of Sinding-Larsen) 732.4
  pelvis (juvenile) 732.1
  Pierson's 732.1
  radial head (juvenile) 732.3
  Scheuermann's 732.0
  Sever's (calcaneum) 732.5
  Sinding-Larsen (secondary patellar center) 732.4
  spine (juvenile) 732.0
    adult 732.8
  symphysis pubis (of Pierson) (juvenile) 732.1
  syphilitic (congenital) 090.0
  tarsal (navicular) (scaphoid) 732.5
  tibia (proximal) (tubercle) 732.4
  tuberculous—*see* Tuberculosis, bone
  ulna 732.3
  upper extremity (juvenile) 732.3
  van Neck's (juvenile osteochondrosis) 732.1
  vertebral (juvenile) 732.0
    adult 732.8
Osteoclastoma (M9250/1) 238.0
  malignant (M9250/3)—*see* Neoplasm, bone, malignant
Osteocopic pain 733.90
Osteodynia 733.90
Osteodystrophy
  azotemic 588.0
  chronica deformans hypertrophica 731.0
  congenital 756.50
    specified type NEC 756.59
  deformans 731.0
  fibrosa localisata 731.0
  parathyroid 252.0
  renal 588.0
Osteofibroma (M9262/0)—*see* Neoplasm, bone, benign
Osteofibrosarcoma (M9182/3)—*see* Neoplasm, bone, malignant
Osteogenesis imperfecta 756.51
Osteogenic —*see* condition
Osteoma (M9180/0)—*see also* Neoplasm, bone, benign
  osteoid (M9191/0)—*see also* Neoplasm, bone, benign
  giant (M9200/0)—*see* Neoplasm, bone, benign

Osteomalacia 268.2
  chronica deformans hypertrophica 731.0
  due to vitamin D deficiency 268.2
  infantile (*see also* Rickets) 268.0
  juvenile (*see also* Rickets) 268.0
  pelvis 268.2
  vitamin D-resistant 275.3
Osteomalacic bone 268.2
Osteomalacosis 268.2
Osteomyelitis (general) (infective) (localized) (neonatal) (purulent) (pyogenic) (septic) (staphylococcal) (streptococcal) (suppurative) (with periostitis) 730.2

Note—Use the following fifth-digit subclassification with category 730:

0 site unspecified
1 shoulder region
2 upper arm
3 forearm
4 hand
5 pelvic region and thigh
6 lower leg
7 ankle and foot
8 other specified sites
9 multiple sites

  acute or subacute 730.0
  chronic or old 730.1
  due to or associated with
    diabetes mellitus 250.8 *[731.8]*
    tuberculosis (*see also* Tuberculosis, bone) 015.9 *[730.8]*
      limb bones 015.5 *[730.8]*
      specified bones NEC 015.7 *[730.8]*
      spine 015.0 *[730.8]*
    typhoid 002.0 *[730.8]*
  Garré's 730.1
  jaw (acute) (chronic) (lower) (neonatal) (suppurative) (upper) 526.4
  nonsuppurating 730.1
  orbital 376.03
  petrous bone (*see also* Petrositis) 383.20
  Salmonella 003.24
  sclerosing, nonsuppurative 730.1
  sicca 730.1
  syphilitic 095.5
    congenital 090.0 *[730.8]*
  tuberculous—*see* Tuberculosis, bone
  typhoid 002.0 *[730.8]*
Osteomyelofibrosis 289.8
Osteomyelosclerosis 289.8
Osteonecrosis (*see also* Osteomyelitis) 730.1
Osteo-onycho-arthro dysplasia 756.89
Osteo-onychodysplasia, hereditary 756.89
Osteopathia
  condensans disseminata 756.53
  hyperostotica multiplex infantilis 756.59
  hypertrophica toxica 731.2
  striata 756.4
Osteopathy resulting from poliomyelitis (*see also* Poliomyelitis) 045.9 *[730.7]*
  familial dysplastic 731.2
Osteopecilia 756.53
Osteopenia 733.90
Osteoperiostitis (*see also* Osteomyelitis) 730.2
  ossificans toxica 731.2
  toxica ossificans 731.2
Osteopetrosis (familial) 756.52
Osteophyte —*see* Exostosis
Osteophytosis —*see* Exostosis

Otitis—*continued*
  catarrhal 381.4
    acute 381.00
    chronic (simple) 381.10
  chronic 382.9
    with effusion 381.3
    adhesive (*see also* Adhesions, middle ear)
      385.10
    allergic 381.3
    atticoantral, suppurative (with posterior or
      superior marginal perforation of ear
      drum) 382.2
    benign suppurative (with anterior
      perforation of ear drum) 382.1
    catarrhal 381.10
    exudative 381.3
    mucinous 381.20
    mucoid, mucous (simple) 381.20
    mucosanguineous 381.29
    nonsuppurative 381.3
    purulent 382.3
    secretory 381.3
    seromucinous 381.3
    serosanguineous 381.19
    serous (simple) 381.10
    suppurative 382.3
      atticoantral (with posterior or superior
        marginal perforation of ear drum)
        382.2
      benign (with anterior perforation of ear
        drum) 382.1
      tuberculous (*see also* Tuberculosis) 017.4
      tubotympanic 382.1
    transudative 381.3
  exudative 381.4
    acute 381.00
    chronic 381.3
  fibrotic (*see also* Adhesions, middle ear)
    385.10
  mucoid, mucous 381.4
    acute 381.02
    chronic (simple) 381.20
  mucosanguineous, chronic 381.29
  nonsuppurative 381.4
    acute 381.00
    chronic 381.3
  postmeasles 055.2
  purulent 382.4
    acute 382.00
      with spontaneous rupture of ear drum
        382.01
    chronic 382.3
  sanguineous, acute 381.03
    allergic 381.06
  secretory 381.4
    acute or subacute 381.01
    chronic 381.3
  seromucinous 381.4
    acute or subacute 381.02
    chronic 381.3
  serosanguineous, chronic 381.19
  serous 381.4
    acute or subacute 381.01
    chronic (simple) 381.10
  subacute—*see* Otitis, media, acute
  suppurative 382.4
    acute 382.00
      with spontaneous rupture of ear drum
        382.01

Otitis—*continued*
  chronic 382.3
    atticoantral 382.2
    benign 382.1
    tuberculous (*see also* Tuberculosis) 017.4
    tubotympanic 382.1
  transudative 381.4
    acute 381.00
    chronic 381.3
  tuberculous (*see also* Tuberculosis) 017.4
  postmeasles 055.2
Otoconia 386.8
Otolith syndrome 386.19
Otomycosis 111.8 *[380.15]*
  in
    aspergillosis 117.3 *[380.15]*
    moniliasis 112.82
Otopathy 388.9
Otoporosis (*see also* Otosclerosis) 387.9
Otorrhagia 388.69
  traumatic—*see* nature of injury
Otorrhea 388.60
  blood 388.69
  cerebrospinal (fluid) 388.61
Otosclerosis (general) 387.9
  cochlear (endosteal) 387.2
  involving
    otic capsule 387.2
    oval window
      nonobliterative 387.0
      obliterative 387.1
    round window 387.2
  nonobliterative 387.0
  obliterative 387.1
  specified type NEC 387.8
Otospongiosis (*see also* Otosclerosis) 387.9
Otto's disease or pelvis 715.35
Outburst, aggressive (*see also* Disturbance,
  conduct) 312.0
  in children and adolescents 313.9
Outcome of delivery
  multiple birth NEC V27.9
    all liveborn V27.5
    all stillborn V27.7
    some liveborn V27.6
    unspecified V27.9
  single V27.9
    liveborn V27.0
    stillborn V27.1
  twins V27.9
    both liveborn V27.2
    both stillborn V27.4
    one liveborn, one stillborn V27.3
Outlet —*see also* condition
  syndrome (thoracic) 353.0
Outstanding ears (bilateral) 744.29
Ovalocytosis (congenital) (hereditary) (*see also*
  Elliptocytosis) 282.1
Ovarian —*see also* condition
  pregnancy—*see* Pregnancy, ovarian
  vein syndrome 593.4
Ovaritis (cystic) (*see also* Salpingo-oophoritis)
  614.2
Ovary, ovarian —*see* condition
Overactive —*see also* Hyperfunction
  eye muscle (*see also* Strabismus) 378.9
  hypothalamus 253.8
  thyroid (*see also* Thyrotoxicosis) 242.9
Overactivity, child 314.01
Overbite (deep) (excessive) (horizontal)
  (vertical) 524.2

Overbreathing (*see also* Hyperventilation)
  786.01
Overconscientious personality 301.4
Overdevelopment —*see also* Hypertrophy
  breast (female) (male) 611.1
  nasal bones 738.0
  prostate, congenital 752.8
Overdistention —*see* Distention
Overdose overdosage (drug) 977.9
  specified drug or substance—*see* Table of drugs
    and chemicals
Overeating 783.6
  with obesity 278.0
  nonorganic origin 307.51
Overexertion (effects) (exhaustion) 994.5
Overexposure (effects) 994.9
  exhaustion 994.4
Overfeeding (*see also* Overeating) 783.6
Overgrowth, bone NEC 733.99
Overheated (effects) (places)—*see* Heat
Overinhibited child 313.0
Overjet 524.2
Overlaid, overlying (suffocation) 994.7
Overlapping toe (acquired) 735.8
  congenital (fifth toe) 755.66
Overload
  fluid 276.6
  potassium (K) 276.7
  sodium (Na) 276.0
Overnutrition (*see also* Hyperalimentation)
  783.6
Overproduction —*see also* Hypersecretion
  ACTH 255.3
  cortisol 255.0
  growth hormone 253.0
  thyroid-stimulating hormone (TSH) 242.8
Overriding
  aorta 747.21
  finger (acquired) 736.29
    congenital 755.59
  toe (acquired) 735.8
    congenital 755.66
Oversize
  fetus (weight of 4500 grams or more) 766.0
    affecting management of pregnancy 656.6
    causing disproportion 653.5
      with obstructed labor 660.1
      affecting fetus or newborn 763.1
Overstrained 780.7
  heart—*see* Hypertrophy, cardiac
Overweight (*see also* Obesity) 278.00
Overwork 780.7
Oviduct —*see* condition
Ovotestis 752.7
Ovulation (cycle)
  failure or lack of 628.0
  pain 625.2
Ovum
  blighted 631
  dropsical 631
  pathologic 631
Owren's disease or syndrome (parahemophilia)
  (*see also* Defect, coagulation) 286.3
Oxalosis 271.8
Oxaluria 271.8
Ox heart —*see* Hypertrophy, cardiac
OX syndrome 758.6
Oxycephaly, oxycephalic 756.0
  syphilitic, congenital 090.0
Oxyuriasis 127.4
Oxyuris vermicularis (infestation) 127.4
Ozena 472.0

P

Pacemaker syndrome 429.4
Pachyderma, pachydermia 701.8
  laryngis 478.5
  laryngitis 478.79
  larynx (verrucosa) 478.79
Pachydermatitis 701.8
Pachydermatocele (congenital) 757.39
  acquired 701.8
Pachydermatosis 701.8
Pachydermoperiostitis
  secondary 731.2
Pachydermoperiostosis
  primary idiopathic 757.39
  secondary 731.2
Pachymeningitis (adhesive) (basal) (brain)
    (cerebral) (cervical) (chronic) (circumscribed)
    (external) (fibrous) (hemorrhagic)
    (hypertrophic) (internal) (purulent) (spinal)
    (suppurative) (*see also* Meningitis) 322.9
  gonococcal 098.82
Pachyonychia (congenital) 757.5
  acquired 703.8
Pachyperiosteodermia
  primary or idiopathic 757.39
  secondary 731.2
Pachyperiostosis
  primary or idiopathic 757.39
  secondary 731.2
Pacinian tumor (M9507/0)—*see* Neoplasm,
    skin, benign
Pads, knuckle or Garrod's 728.79
Paget's disease (osteitis deformans) 731.0
  with infiltrating duct carcinoma of the breast
      (M8541/3)—*see* Neoplasm, breast,
      malignant
  bone 731.0
    osteosarcoma in (M9184/3)—*see* Neoplasm,
        bone, malignant
  breast (M8540/3) 174.0
  extramammary (M8542/3)—*see also* Neoplasm,
      skin, malignant
    anus 154.3
      skin 173.5
  malignant (M8540/3)
    breast 174.0
    specified site NEC (M8542/3)—*see*
        Neoplasm, skin, malignant
    unspecified site 174.0
  mammary (M8540/3) 174.0
  necrosis of bone 731.0
  nipple (M8540/3) 174.0
  osteitis deformans 731.0
Paget-Schroetter syndrome (intermittent venous
    claudication) 453.8
Pain (s)
  abdominal 789.0
  adnexa (uteri) 625.9
  alimentary, due to vascular insufficiency 557.9
  anginoid (*see also* Pain, precordial) 786.51
  anus 569.42
  arch 729.5
  arm 729.5
  back (postural) 724.5
    low 724.2
    psychogenic 307.89
  bile duct 576.9
  bladder 788.9

Pain —*continued*
  bone 733.90
  breast 611.71
    psychogenic 307.89
  broad ligament 625.9
  cartilage NEC 733.90
  cecum 789.0
  cervicobrachial 723.3
  chest (central) 786.50
    wall (anterior) 786.52
  coccyx 724.79
  colon 789.0
  common duct 576.9
  coronary—*see* Angina
  costochondral 786.52
  diaphragm 786.52
  due to (presence of) any device, implant, or
      graft classifiable to 996.0-996.5—*see*
      Complications, due to (presence of) any
      device, implant, or graft classified to
      996.0-996.5 NEC
  ear (*see also* Otalgia) 388.70
  epigastric, epigastrium 789.0
  extremity (lower) (upper) 729.5
  eye 379.91
  face, facial 784.0
    atypical 350.2
    nerve 351.8
  false (labor) 644.1
  female genital organ NEC 625.9
    psychogenic 307.89
  finger 729.5
  flank 789.0
  foot 729.5
  gallbladder 575.9
  gas (intestinal) 787.3
  gastric 536.8
  generalized 780.9
  genital organ
    female 625.9
    male 608.9
    psychogenic 307.89
  groin 789.0
  growing 781.9
  hand 729.5
  head (*see also* Headache) 784.0
  heart (*see also* Pain, precordial) 786.51
  infraorbital (*see also* Neuralgia, trigeminal)
      350.1
  intermenstrual 625.2
  jaw 526.9
  joint 719.40
    ankle 719.47
    elbow 719.42
    foot 719.47
    hand 719.44
    hip 719.45
    knee 719.46
    multiple sites 719.49
    pelvic region 719.45
    psychogenic 307.89
    shoulder (region) 719.41
    specified site NEC 719.48
    wrist 719.43
  kidney 788.0
  labor, false or spurious 644.1
  laryngeal 784.1

Pain —*continued*
  leg 729.5
  limb 729.5
  low back 724.2
  lumbar region 724.2
  mastoid (*see also* Otalgia) 388.70
  maxilla 526.9
  metacarpophalangeal (joint) 719.44
  metatarsophalangeal (joint) 719.47
  mouth 528.9
  muscle 729.1
    intercostal 786.52
  nasal 478.1
  nasopharynx 478.29
  neck NEC 723.1
    psychogenic 307.89
  nerve NEC 729.2
  neuromuscular 729.1
  nose 478.1
  ocular 379.91
  ophthalmic 379.91
  orbital region 379.91
  osteocopic 733.90
  ovary 625.9
    psychogenic 307.89
  over heart (*see also* Pain, precordial) 786.51
  ovulation 625.2
  pelvic (female) 625.9
    male NEC 789.0
      psychogenic 307.89
    psychogenic 307.89
  penis 607.9
    psychogenic 307.89
  pericardial (*see also* Pain, precordial) 786.51
  perineum
    female 625.9
    male 608.9
  pharynx 478.29
  pleura, pleural, pleuritic 786.52
  post-operative —*see* Pain, by site
  preauricular 388.70
  precordial (region) 786.51
    psychogenic 307.89
  psychogenic 307.80
    cardiovascular system 307.89
    gastrointestinal system 307.89
    genitourinary system 307.89
    heart 307.89
    musculoskeletal system 307.89
    respiratory system 307.89
    skin 306.3
  radicular (spinal) (*see also* Radiculitis) 729.2
  rectum 569.42
  respiration 786.52
  retrosternal 786.51
  rheumatic NEC 729.0
    muscular 729.1
  rib 786.50
  root (spinal) (*see also* Radiculitis) 729.2
  round ligament (stretch) 625.9
  sacroiliac 724.6
  sciatic 724.3
  scrotum 608.9
    psychogenic 307.89
  seminal vesicle 608.9
  sinus 478.1
  skin 782.0
  spermatic cord 608.9
  spinal root (*see also* Radiculitis) 729.2

Pain —*continued*
  stomach 536.8
    psychogenic 307.89
  substernal 786.51
  temporomandibular (joint) 524.62
  temporomaxillary joint 524.62
  testis 608.9
    psychogenic 307.89
  thoracic spine 724.1
    with radicular and visceral pain 724.4
  throat 784.1
  tibia 733.90
  toe 729.5
  tongue 529.6
  tooth 525.9
  trigeminal (*see also* Neuralgia, trigeminal) 350.1
  umbilicus 789.0
  ureter 788.0
  urinary (organ) (system) 788.0
  uterus 625.9
    psychogenic 307.89
  vagina 625.9
  vertebrogenic (syndrome) 724.5
  vesical 788.9
  vulva 625.9
  xiphoid 733.90
Painful —*see also* Pain
  arc syndrome 726.19
  coitus
    female 625.0
    male 608.89
      psychogenic 302.76
  ejaculation (semen) 608.89
      psychogenic 302.79
  erection 607.3
  feet syndrome 266.2
  menstruation 625.3
      psychogenic 306.52
  micturition 788.1
  ophthalmoplegia 378.55
  respiration 786.52
  scar NEC 709.2
  urination 788.1
  wire sutures 998.89
Painters' colic 984.9
  specified type of lead—*see* Table of drugs and chemicals
Palate —*see* condition
Palatoplegia 528.9
Palatoschisis (*see also* Cleft, palate) 749.00
Palilalia 784.69
Palindromic arthritis (*see also* Rheumatism, palindromic) 719.3
Palliative care V66.7
Pallor 782.61
  temporal, optic disc 377.15
Palmar —*see also* condition
  fascia—*see* condition
Palpable
  cecum 569.89
  kidney 593.89
  liver 573.9
  lymph nodes 785.6
  ovary 620.8
  prostate 602.9
  spleen (*see also* Splenomegaly) 789.2
  uterus 625.8
Palpitation (heart) 785.1
  psychogenic 306.2

Palsy (*see also* Paralysis) 344.9
  atrophic diffuse 335.20
  Bell's 351.0
    newborn 767.5
  birth 767.7
  brachial plexus 353.0
    fetus or newborn 767.6
  brain—*see also* Palsy, cerebral
    noncongenital or noninfantile 344.89
      due to vascular lesion—*see* category 438
    syphilitic 094.89
      congenital 090.49
  bulbar (chronic) (progressive) 335.22
    pseudo NEC 335.23
    supranuclear NEC 344.89
  cerebral (congenital) (infantile) (spastic) 343.9
    athetoid 333.7
    diplegic 343.0
      due to previous vascular lesion—*see* category 438
    hemiplegic 343.1
    monoplegic 343.3
    noncongenital or noninfantile 437.8
      due to previous vascular lesion—*see* category 438
    paraplegic 343.0
    quadriplegic 343.2
    spastic, not congenital or infantile 344.89
    syphilitic 094.89
      congenital 090.49
    tetraplegic 343.2
  cranial nerve—*see also* Disorder, nerve, cranial
    multiple 352.6
  creeping 335.21
  divers' 993.3
  Erb's (birth injury) 767.6
  facial 351.0
    newborn 767.5
  glossopharyngeal 352.2
  Klumpke (-Déjérine) 767.6
  lead 984.9
    specified type of lead—*see* Table of drugs and chemicals
  median nerve (tardy) 354.0
  peroneal nerve (acute) (tardy) 355.3
  pseudobulbar NEC 335.23
  radial nerve (acute) 354.3
  seventh nerve 351.0
    newborn 767.5
  shaking (*see also* Parkinsonism) 332.0
  spastic (cerebral) (spinal) 343.9
    hemiplegic 343.1
  specified nerve NEC—*see* Disorder, nerve
  supranuclear NEC 356.8
  ulnar nerve (tardy) 354.2
  wasting 335.21
Paltauf-Sternberg disease 201.9
Paludism —*see* Malaria
Panama fever 084.0
Panaris (with lymphangitis) 681.9
  finger 681.02
  toe 681.11
Panaritium (with lymphangitis) 681.9
  finger 681.02
  toe 681.11
Panarteritis (nodosa) 446.0
  brain or cerebral 437.4
Pancake heart 793.2
  with cor pulmonale (chronic) 416.9

Pancarditis (acute) (chronic) 429.89
  with
    rheumatic
      fever (active) (acute) (chronic) (subacute) 391.8
      inactive or quiescent 398.99
  rheumatic, acute 391.8
    chronic or inactive 398.99
Pancoast's syndrome or tumor (carcinoma, pulmonary apex) (M8010/3) 162.3
Pancoast-Tobias syndrome (M8010/3) (carcinoma, pulmonary apex) 162.3
Pancolitis 556.6
Pancreas, pancreatic —*see* condition
Pancreatitis 577.0
  acute (edematous) (hemorrhagic) (recurrent) 577.0
  annular 577.0
  apoplectic 577.0
  calcereous 577.0
  chronic (infectious) 577.1
    recurrent 577.1
  cystic 577.2
  fibrous 577.8
  gangrenous 577.0
  hemorrhagic (acute) 577.0
  interstitial (chronic) 577.1
    acute 577.0
  malignant 577.0
  mumps 072.3
  painless 577.1
  recurrent 577.1
  relapsing 577.1
  subacute 577.0
  suppurative 577.0
  syphilitic 095.8
Pancreatolithiasis 577.8
Pancytolysis 289.9
Pancytopenia (acquired) 284.8
  with malformations 284.0
  congenital 284.0
Panencephalitis —*see also* Encephalitis
  subacute, sclerosing 046.2
Panhematopenia 284.8
  congenital 284.0
  constitutional 284.0
  splenic, primary 289.4
Panhemocytopenia 284.8
  congenital 284.0
  constitutional 284.0
Panhypogonadism 257.2
Panhypopituitarism 253.2
  prepubertal 253.3
Panic (attack) (state) 300.01
  reaction to exceptional stress (transient) 308.0
Panmyelopathy, familial constitutional 284.0
Panmyelophthisis 284.9
  acquired (secondary) 284.8
  congenital 284.0
  idiopathic 284.9
Panmyelosis (acute) (M9951/1) 238.7
Panner's disease 732.3
  capitellum humeri 732.3
  head of humerus 732.3
  tarsal navicular (bone) (osteochondrosis) 732.5
Panneuritis endemica 265.0 *[357.4]*

Panniculitis 729.30
  back 724.8
  knee 729.31
  neck 723.6
  nodular, nonsuppurative 729.30
  sacral 724.8
  specified site NEC 729.39
Panniculus adiposus (abdominal) 278.1
Pannus 370.62
  allergic eczematous 370.62
  degenerativus 370.62
  keratic 370.62
  rheumatoid—*see* Arthritis, rheumatoid
  trachomatosus, trachomatous (active) 076.1
    [370.62]
    late effect 139.1
Panophthalmitis 360.02
Panotitis —*see* Otitis media
Pansinusitis (chronic) (hyperplastic)
    (nonpurulent) (purulent) 473.8
  acute 461.8
  due to fungus NEC 117.9
  tuberculous (*see also* Tuberculosis) 012.8
Panuveitis 360.12
  sympathetic 360.11
Panvalvular disease —*see* Endocarditis, mitral
Papageienkrankheit 073.9
Papanicolaou smear
  cervix (screening test) V76.2
    as part of gynecological examination V72.3
    for suspected malignant neoplasm V76.2
    no disease found V71.1
    nonspecific abnormal finding 795.0
  specified site, except cervix—*see also*
      Screening, malignant neoplasm
    for suspected malignant neoplasm—*see also*
      Screening, malignant neoplasm
    no disease found V71.1
    nonspecific abnormal finding 795.1
Papilledema 377.00
  associated with
    decreased ocular pressure 377.02
    increased intracranial pressure 377.01
    retinal disorder 377.03
  choked disc 377.00
  infectional 377.00
Papillitis 377.31
  anus 569.49
  chronic lingual 529.4
  necrotizing, kidney 584.7
  optic 377.31
  rectum 569.49
  renal, necrotizing 584.7
  tongue 529.0
Papilloma (M8050/0)—*see also* Neoplasm, by
    site, benign

Note—Except where otherwise indicated, the
morphological varieties of papilloma in the list
below should be coded by site as for
"Neoplasm, benign."

  acuminatum (female) (male) 078.11
  bladder (urinary) (transitional cell) (M8120/1)
    236.7
    benign (M8120/0) 223.3
  choroid plexus (M9390/0) 225.0
    anaplastic type (M9390/3) 191.5
    malignant (M9390/3) 191.5
  ductal (M8503/0)
  dyskeratotic (M8052/0)

Papilloma—*continued*
  epidermoid (M8052/0)
  hyperkeratotic (M8052/0)
  intracystic (M8504/0)
  intraductal (M8503/0)
  inverted (M8053/0)
  keratotic (M8052/0)
  parakeratotic (M8052/0)
  pinta (primary) 103.0
  renal pelvis (transitional cell) (M8120/1) 236.99
    benign (M8120/0) 223.1
  Schneiderian (M8121/0)
    specified site—*see* Neoplasm, by site, benign
    unspecified site 212.0
  serous surface (M8461/0)
    borderline malignancy (M8461/1)
      specified site—*see* Neoplasm, by site,
        uncertain behavior
      unspecified site 236.2
    specified site—*see* Neoplasm, by site, benign
    unspecified site 220
  squamous (cell) (M8052/0)
  transitional (cell) (M8120/0)
    bladder (urinary) (M8120/1) 236.7
    inverted type (M8121/1)—*see* Neoplasm, by
      site, uncertain behavior
    renal pelvis (M8120/1) 236.91
    ureter (M8120/1) 236.91
  ureter (transitional cell) (M8120/1) 236.91
    benign (M8120/0) 223.2
  urothelial (M8120/1)—*see* Neoplasm, by site,
    uncertain behavior
  verrucous (M8051/0)
  villous (M8261/1)—*see* Neoplasm, by site,
    uncertain behavior
  yaws, plantar or palmar 102.1
Papillomata, multiple, of yaws 102.1
Papillomatosis (M8060/0)—*see also* Neoplasm,
    by site, benign
  confluent and reticulate 701.8
  cutaneous 701.8
  ductal, breast 610.1
  Gougerot-Carteaud (confluent reticulate) 701.8
  intraductal (diffuse) (M8505/0)—*see* Neoplasm,
    by site, benign
  subareolar duct (M8506/0) 217
Papillon-Léage and Psaume syndrome
    (orodigitofacial dysostosis) 759.89
Papule 709.8
  carate (primary) 103.0
  fibrous, of nose (M8724/0) 216.3
  pinta (primary) 103.0
Papulosis, malignant 447.8
Papyraceous fetus 779.8
  complicating pregnancy 646.0
Paracephalus 759.7
Parachute mitral valve 746.5
Paracoccidioidomycosis 116.1
  mucocutaneous-lymphangitic 116.1
  pulmonary 116.1
  visceral 116.1
Paracoccidiomycosis —*see*
    Paracoccidioidomycosis
Paracusis 388.40
Paradentosis 523.5
Paradoxical facial movements 374.43
Paraffinoma 999.9

Paraganglioma (M8680/1)
  adrenal (M8700/0) 227.0
    malignant (M8700/3) 194.0
  aortic body (M8691/1) 237.3
    malignant (M8691/3) 194.6
  carotid body (M8692/1) 237.3
    malignant (M8692/3) 194.5
  chromaffin (M8700/0)—*see also* Neoplasm, by
    site, benign
    malignant (M8700/3)—*see* Neoplasm, by site,
      malignant
  extra-adrenal (M8693/1)
    malignant (M8693/3)
      specified site—*see* Neoplasm, by site,
        malignant
      unspecified site 194.6
    specified site—*see* Neoplasm, by site,
      uncertain behavior
    unspecified site 237.3
  glomus jugulare (M8690/1) 237.3
    malignant (M8690/3) 194.6
  jugular (M8690/1) 237.3
    malignant (M8680/3)
      specified site—*see* Neoplasm, by site,
        malignant
      unspecified site 194.6
  nonchromaffin (M8693/1)
    malignant (M8693/3)
      specified site—*see* Neoplasm, by site,
        malignant
      unspecified site 194.6
    specified site—*see* Neoplasm, by site,
      uncertain behavior
    unspecified site 237.3
  parasympathetic (M8682/1)
    specified site—*see* Neoplasm, by site,
      uncertain behavior
    unspecified site 237.3
  specified site—*see* Neoplasm, by site, uncertain
    behavior
  sympathetic (M8681/1)
    specified site—*see* Neoplasm, by site,
      uncertain behavior
    unspecified site 237.3
  unspecified site 237.3
Parageusia 781.1
  psychogenic 306.7
Paragonimiasis 121.2
Paragranuloma, Hodgkin's (M9660/3) 201.0
Parahemophilia (*see also* Defect, coagulation)
  286.3
Parakeratosis 690.8
  psoriasiformis 696.2
  variegata 696.2
Paralysis, paralytic (complete) (incomplete)
  344.9
  with
    broken
      back—*see* Fracture, vertebra, by site, with
        spinal cord injury
      neck—*see* Fracture, vertebra, cervical, with
        spinal cord injury
    fracture, vertebra—*see* Fracture, vertebra, by
      site, with spinal cord injury
    syphilis 094.89
  abdomen and back muscles 355.9
  abdominal muscles 355.9
  abducens (nerve) 378.54
  abductor 355.9
    lower extremity 355.8
    upper extremity 354.9

Paralysis, paralytic—*continued*
  accessory nerve 352.4
  accommodation 367.51
    hysterical 300.11
  acoustic nerve 388.5
  agitans 332.0
    arteriosclerotic 332.0
  alternating 344.89
    oculomotor 344.89
  amyotrophic 335.20
  ankle 355.8
  anterior serratus 355.9
  anus (sphincter) 569.49
  apoplectic (current episode) (*see also* Disease,
    cerebrovascular, acute) 436
    late effect—*see* category 438
  arm 344.40
    affecting
      dominant side 344.41
      nondominant side 344.42
    both 344.2
    due to old CVA—*see* category 438
    hysterical 300.11
    psychogenic 306.0
    transient 781.4
      traumatic NEC (*see also* Injury, nerve,
        upper limb) 955.9
  arteriosclerotic (current episode) 437.0
    late effect—*see* category 438
  ascending (spinal), acute 357.0
  associated, nuclear 344.89
  asthenic bulbar 358.0
  ataxic NEC 334.9
    general 094.1
  athetoid 333.7
  atrophic 356.9
    infantile, acute (*see also* Poliomyelitis, with
      paralysis) 045.1
    muscle NEC 355.9
    progressive 335.21
    spinal (acute) (*see also* Poliomyelitis, with
      paralysis) 045.1
  attack (*see also* Disease, cerebrovascular, acute)
    436
  axillary 353.0
  Babinski-Nageotte's 344.89
  Bell's 351.0
    newborn 767.5
  Benedikt's 344.89
  birth (injury) 767.7
    brain 767.0
    intracranial 767.0
    spinal cord 767.4
  bladder (sphincter) 596.53
    neurogenic 596.54
      with cauda equina syndrome 344.61
    puerperal, postpartum, childbirth 665.5
    sensory 596.54
      with cauda equina 344.61
    spastic 596.54
      with cauda equina 344.61
  bowel, colon, or intestine (*see also* Ileus) 560.1
  brachial plexus 353.0
    due to birth injury 767.6
    newborn 767.6
  brain
    congenital—*see* Palsy, cerebral
    current episode 437.8
    diplegia 344.2

Paralysis, paralytic—*continued*
  due to previous vascular lesion—*see* category 438
  hemiplegia 342.9
    due to previous vascular lesion—*see* category 438
    infantile—*see* Palsy, cerebral
    monoplegia—*see also* Monoplegia
    due to previous vascular lesion—*see* category 438
    paraplegia 344.1
    quadriplegia —*see* Quadriplegia
    syphilitic, congenital 090.49
    triplegia 344.89
  bronchi 519.1
  Brown-Séquard's 344.89
  bulbar (chronic) (progressive) 335.22
    infantile (*see also* Poliomyelitis, bulbar) 045.0
    poliomyelitic (*see also* Poliomyelitis, bulbar) 045.0
    pseudo 335.23
    supranuclear 344.89
  bulbospinal 358.0
  cardiac (*see also* Failure, heart) 428.9
  cerebral
    current episode 437.8
    spastic, infantile—*see* Palsy, cerebral
  cerebrocerebellar 437.8
    diplegic infantile 343.0
  cervical
    plexus 353.2
    sympathetic NEC 337.0
  Céstan-Chenais 344.89
  Charcot-Marie-Tooth type 356.1
  childhood—*see* Palsy, cerebral
  Clark's 343.9
  colon (*see also* Ileus) 560.1
  compressed air 993.3
  compression
    arm NEC 354.9
    cerebral—*see* Paralysis, brain
    leg NEC 355.8
    lower extremity NEC 355.8
    upper extremity NEC 354.9
  congenital (cerebral) (spastic) (spinal)—*see* Palsy, cerebral
  conjugate movement (of eye) 378.81
    cortical (nuclear) (supranuclear) 378.81
  convergence 378.83
  cordis (*see also* Failure, heart) 428.9
  cortical (*see also* Paralysis, brain) 437.8
  cranial or cerebral nerve (*see also* Disorder, nerve, cranial) 352.9
  creeping 335.21
  crossed leg 344.89
  crutch 953.4
  deglutition 784.9
    hysterical 300.11
  dementia 094.1
  descending (spinal) NEC 335.9
  diaphragm (flaccid) 519.4
    due to accidental section of phrenic nerve during procedure 998.2
  digestive organs NEC 564.8
  diplegic—*see* Diplegia
  divergence (nuclear) 378.85
  divers' 993.3
  Duchenne's 335.22
  due to intracranial or spinal birth injury—*see* Palsy, cerebral

Paralysis, paralytic—*continued*
  embolic (current episode) (*see also* Embolism, brain) 434.1
    late effect or old—*see* category 438
  enteric (*see also* Ileus) 560.1
    with hernia—*see* Hernia, by site, with obstruction
  Erb's syphilitic spastic spinal 094.89
  Erb (-Duchenne) (birth) (newborn) 767.6
  esophagus 530.89
  essential, infancy (*see also* Poliomyelitis) 045.9
  extremity
    lower —*see* Paralysis, leg
    spastic (hereditary) 343.3
      noncongenital or noninfantile 344.1
    transient (cause unknown) 781.4
    upper —*see* Paralysis, arm
  eye muscle (extrinsic) 378.55
    intrinsic 367.51
  facial (nerve) 351.0
    birth injury 767.5
    congenital 767.5
    following operation NEC 998.2
    newborn 767.5
  familial 359.3
    periodic 359.3
    spastic 334.1
  fauces 478.29
  finger NEC 354.9
  foot NEC 355.8
  gait 781.2
  gastric nerve 352.3
  gaze 378.81
  general 094.1
    ataxic 094.1
    insane 094.1
    juvenile 090.40
    progressive 094.1
    tabetic 094.1
  glossopharyngeal (nerve) 352.2
  glottis (*see also* Paralysis, vocal cord) 478.30
  gluteal 353.4
  Gubler (-Millard) 344.89
  hand 354.9
    hysterical 300.11
    psychogenic 306.0
  heart (*see also* Failure, heart) 428.9
  hemifacial, progressive 349.89
  hemiplegic—*see* Hemiplegia
  hyperkalemic periodic (familial) 359.3
  hypertensive (current episode) 437.8
  hypoglossal (nerve) 352.5
  hypokalemic periodic 359.3
  Hyrtl's sphincter (rectum) 569.49
  hysterical 300.11
  ileus (*see also* Ileus) 560.1
  infantile (*see also* Poliomyelitis) 045.9
    atrophic acute 045.1
    bulbar 045.0
    cerebral—*see* Palsy, cerebral
    paralytic 045.1
    progressive acute 045.9
    spastic—*see* Palsy, cerebral
    spinal 045.9
  infective (*see also* Poliomyelitis) 045.9
  inferior nuclear 344.9
  insane, general or progressive 094.1
  internuclear 378.86
  interosseous 355.9
  intestine (*see also* Ileus) 560.1

Paralysis, paralytic—*continued*
  intracranial (current episode) (*see also*
       Paralysis, brain) 437.8
     due to birth injury 767.0
  iris 379.49
     due to diphtheria (toxin) 032.81 *[379.49]*
  ischemic, Volkmann's (complicating trauma)
       958.6
  Jackson's 344.89
  jake 357.7
  Jamaica ginger (jake) 357.7
  juvenile general 090.40
  Klumpke (-Déjérine) (birth) (newborn) 767.6
  labioglossal (laryngeal) (pharyngeal) 335.22
  Landry's 357.0
  laryngeal nerve (recurrent) (superior) (*see also*
       Paralysis, vocal cord) 478.30
  larynx (*see also* Paralysis, vocal cord) 478.30
     due to diphtheria (toxin) 032.3
  late effect
     due to
        birth injury, brain or spinal (cord)—*see*
             Palsy, cerebral
        edema, brain or cerebral—*see* Paralysis,
             brain
        lesion
           cerebrovascular—*see* category 438
           spinal (cord)—*see* Paralysis, spinal
  lateral 335.24
  lead 984.9
     specified type of lead—*see* Table of drugs and
          chemicals
  left side—*see* Hemiplegia
  leg 344.30
     affecting
        dominant side 344.31
        nondominant side 344.32
     both (*see also* Paraplegia) 344.1
     crossed 344.89
     hysterical 300.11
     psychogenic 306.0
     transient or transitory 781.4
        traumatic NEC (*see also* Injury, nerve,
             lower limb) 956.9
  levator palpebrae superioris 374.31
  limb NEC 344.5
     all four—*see* Quadriplegia
     quadriplegia—*see* Quadriplegia
  lip 528.5
  Lissauer's 094.1
  local 355.9
  lower limb—*see also* Paralysis, leg
     both (*see also* Paraplegia) 344.1
  lung 518.89
     newborn 770.8
  median nerve 354.1
  medullary (tegmental) 344.89
  mesencephalic NEC 344.89
     tegmental 344.89
  middle alternating 344.89
  Millard-Gubler-Foville 344.89
  monoplegic—*see* Monoplegia
  motor NEC 344.9
     cerebral—*see* Paralysis, brain
     spinal—*see* Paralysis, spinal
  multiple
     cerebral—*see* Paralysis, brain
     spinal—*see* Paralysis, spinal

Paralysis, paralytic—*continued*
  muscle (flaccid) 359.9
     due to nerve lesion NEC 355.9
     eye (extrinsic) 378.55
        intrinsic 367.51
        oblique 378.51
     iris sphincter 364.8
     ischemic (complicating trauma) (Volkmann's)
          958.6
     pseudohypertrophic 359.1
  muscular (atrophic) 359.9
     progressive 335.21
  musculocutaneous nerve 354.9
  musculospiral 354.9
  nerve—*see also* Disorder, nerve
     third or oculomotor (partial) 378.51
        total 378.52
     fourth or trochlear 378.53
     sixth or abducens 378.54
     seventh or facial 351.0
        birth injury 767.5
        due to
           injection NEC 999.9
           operation NEC 997.09
        newborn 767.5
     accessory 352.4
     auditory 388.5
     birth injury 767.7
     cranial or cerebral (*see also* Disorder, nerve,
          cranial) 352.9
     facial 351.0
        birth injury 767.5
        newborn 767.5
     laryngeal (*see also* Paralysis, vocal cord)
          478.30
     newborn 767.7
     phrenic 354.8
        newborn 767.7
     radial 354.3
        birth injury 767.6
        newborn 767.6
     syphilitic 094.89
     traumatic NEC (*see also* Injury, nerve, by
          site) 957.9
     trigeminal 350.9
     ulnar 354.2
  newborn NEC 767.0
  normokalemic periodic 359.3
  obstetrical, newborn 767.7
  ocular 378.9
  oculofacial, congenital 352.6
  oculomotor (nerve) (partial) 378.51
     alternating 344.89
     external bilateral 378.55
     total 378.52
  olfactory nerve 352.0
  palate 528.9
  palatopharyngolaryngeal 352.6
  paratrigeminal 350.9
  periodic (familial) (hyperkalemic)
       (hypokalemic) (normokalemic) (secondary)
       359.3
  peripheral
     autonomic nervous system—*see* Neuropathy,
          peripheral, autonomic
     nerve NEC 355.9
  peroneal (nerve) 355.3
  pharynx 478.29
  phrenic nerve 354.8
  plantar nerves 355.6
  pneumogastric nerve 352.3

Paralysis, paralytic—*continued*
poliomyelitis (current) (*see also* Poliomyelitis,
   with paralysis) 045.1
  bulbar 045.0
popliteal nerve 355.3
pressure (*see also* Neuropathy, entrapment)
   355.9
progressive 335.21
  atrophic 335.21
  bulbar 335.22
  general 094.1
  hemifacial 349.89
  infantile, acute (*see also* Poliomyelitis) 045.9
  multiple 335.20
pseudobulbar 335.23
pseudohypertrophic 359.1
  muscle 359.1
psychogenic 306.0
pupil, pupillary 379.49
quadriceps 355.8
quadriplegic (*see also* Quadriplegia) 344.0
radial nerve 354.3
  birth injury 767.6
rectum (sphincter) 569.49
rectus muscle (eye) 378.55
recurrent laryngeal nerve (*see also* Paralysis,
   vocal cord) 478.30
respiratory (muscle) (system) (tract) 786.09
  center NEC 344.89
   fetus or newborn 770.8
  congenital 768.9
  newborn 768.9
right side—*see* Hemiplegia
Saturday night 354.3
saturnine 984.9
  specified type of lead—*see* Table of drugs and
   chemicals
sciatic nerve 355.0
secondary—*see* Paralysis, late effect
seizure (cerebral) (current episode) (*see also*
   Disease, cerebrovascular, acute) 436
  late effect—*see* category 438
senile NEC 344.9
serratus magnus 355.9
shaking (*see also* Parkinsonism) 332.0
shock (*see also* Disease, cerebrovascular, acute)
   436
  late effect—*see* category 438
shoulder 354.9
soft palate 528.9
spasmodic—*see* Paralysis, spastic
spastic 344.9
  cerebral infantile—*see* Palsy, cerebral
  congenital (cerebral)—*see* Palsy, cerebral
  familial 334.1
  hereditary 334.1
  infantile 343.9
  noncongenital or noninfantile, cerebral 344.9
  syphilitic 094.0
   spinal 094.89
sphincter, bladder (*see also* Paralysis, bladder)
   596.53
spinal (cord) NEC 344.1
  accessory nerve 352.4
  acute (*see also* Poliomyelitis) 045.9
  ascending acute 357.0
  atrophic (acute) (*see also* Poliomyelitis, with
   paralysis) 045.1
   spastic, syphilitic 094.89
  congenital NEC 343.9

Paralysis, paralytic—*continued*
hemiplegic —*see* Hemiplegia
  hereditary 336.8
infantile (*see also* Poliomyelitis) 045.9
late effect NEC 344.89
monoplegic—*see* Monoplegia
nerve 355.9
progressive 335.10
quadriplegic —*see* Quadriplegia
spastic NEC 343.9
traumatic—*see* Injury, spinal, by site
sternomastoid 352.4
stomach 536.3
  nerve 352.3
stroke (current episode) (*see also* Disease,
   cerebrovascular, acute) 436
  late effect—*see* category 438
subscapularis 354.8
superior nuclear NEC 334.9
supranuclear 356.8
sympathetic
  cervical NEC 337.0
  nerve NEC (*see also* Neuropathy, peripheral,
   autonomic) 337.9
  nervous system—*see* Neuropathy, peripheral,
   autonomic
syndrome 344.9
  specified NEC 344.89
syphilitic spastic spinal (Erb's) 094.89
tabetic general 094.1
thigh 355.8
throat 478.29
  diphtheritic 032.0
  muscle 478.29
thrombotic (current episode) (*see also*
   Thrombosis, brain) 434.0
  old—*see* category 438
thumb NEC 354.9
tick (-bite) 989.5
Todd's (postepileptic transitory paralysis)
   344.89
toe 355.6
tongue 529.8
transient
  arm or leg NEC 781.4
  traumatic NEC (*see also* Injury, nerve, by
   site) 957.9
trapezius 352.4
traumatic, transient NEC (*see also* Injury, nerve,
   by site) 957.9
trembling (*see also* Parkinsonism) 332.0
triceps brachii 354.9
trigeminal nerve 350.9
trochlear nerve 378.53
ulnar nerve 354.2
upper limb —*see also* Paralysis, arm
  both (*see also* Diplegia) 344.2
uremic—*see* Uremia
uveoparotitic 135
uvula 528.9
  hysterical 300.11
  postdiphtheritic 032.0
vagus nerve 352.3
vasomotor NEC 337.9
velum palati 528.9
vesical (*see also* Paralysis, bladder) 596.53
vestibular nerve 388.5
visual field, psychic 368.16

Paralysis, paralytic—*continued*
  vocal cord 478.30
    bilateral (partial) 478.33
      complete 478.34
    complete (bilateral) 478.34
    unilateral (partial) 478.31
      complete 478.32
  Volkmann's (complicating trauma) 958.6
  wasting 335.21
  Weber's 344.89
  wrist NEC 354.9
Paramedial orifice, urethrovesical 753.8
Paramenia 626.9
Parametritis (chronic) (*see also* Disease, pelvis,
    inflammatory) 614.4
  acute 614.3
  puerperal, postpartum, childbirth 670
Parametrium, parametric —*see* condition
Paramnesia (*see also* Amnesia) 780.9
Paramolar 520.1
  causing crowding 524.3
Paramyloidosis 277.3
Paramyoclonus multiplex 333.2
Paramyotonia 359.2
  congenita 359.2
Paraneoplastic syndrome —*see* condition
Parangi (*see also* Yaws) 102.9
Paranoia 297.1
  alcoholic 291.5
  querulans 297.8
  senile 290.20
Paranoid
  dementia (*see also* Schizophrenia) 295.3
    praecox (acute) 295.3
    senile 290.20
  personality 301.0
  psychosis 297.9
    alcoholic 291.5
    climacteric 297.2
    drug-induced 292.11
    involutional 297.2
    menopausal 297.2
    protracted reactive 298.4
    psychogenic 298.4
      acute 298.3
    senile 290.20
  reaction (chronic) 297.9
    acute 298.3
  schizophrenia (acute) (*see also* Schizophrenia)
    295.3
  state 297.9
    alcohol-induced 291.5
    climacteric 297.2
    drug-induced 292.11
    due to or associated with
      arteriosclerosis (cerebrovascular) 290.42
      presenile brain disease 290.12
      senile brain disease 290.20
    involutional 297.2
    menopausal 297.2
    senile 290.20
    simple 297.0
    specified type NEC 297.8
  tendencies 301.0
  traits 301.0
  trends 301.0
  type, psychopathic personality 301.0
Paraparesis (*see also* Paralysis) 344.9
Paraphasia 784.3
Paraphilia (*see also* Deviation, sexual) 302.9
Paraphimosis (congenital) 605
  chancroidal 099.0

Paraphrenia, paraphrenic (late) 297.2
  climacteric 297.2
  dementia (*see also* Schizophrenia) 295.3
  involutional 297.2
  menopausal 297.2
  schizophrenia (acute) (*see also* Schizophrenia)
    295.3
Paraplegia 344.1
  with
    broken back—*see* Fracture, vertebra, by site,
      with spinal cord injury
    fracture, vertebra—*see* Fracture, vertebra, by
      site, with spinal cord injury
  ataxic—*see* Degeneration, combined, spinal cord
  brain (current episode) (*see also* Paralysis,
    brain) 437.8
  cerebral (current episode) (*see also* Paralysis,
    brain) 437.8
  congenital or infantile (cerebral) (spastic)
    (spinal) 343.0
  cortical—*see* Paralysis, brain
  familial spastic 334.1
  functional (hysterical) 300.11
  hysterical 300.11
  infantile 343.0
  late effect 344.1
  Pott's (*see also* Tuberculosis) 015.0 *[730.88]*
  psychogenic 306.0
  spastic
    Erb's spinal 094.89
    hereditary 334.1
    not infantile or congenital 344.1
  spinal (cord)
    traumatic NEC—*see* Injury, spinal, by site
  syphilitic (spastic) 094.89
  traumatic NEC—*see* Injury, spinal, by site
Paraproteinemia 273.2
  benign (familial) 273.1
  monoclonal 273.1
  secondary to malignant or inflammatory disease
    273.1
Parapsoriasis 696.2
  en plaques 696.2
  guttata 696.2
  lichenoides chronica 696.2
  retiformis 696.2
  varioliformis (acuta) 696.2
Parascarlatina 057.8
Parasitic —*see also* condition
  disease NEC (*see also* Infestation, parasitic)
    136.9
    contact V01.8
    exposure to V01.8
    intestinal NEC 129
    skin NEC 134.9
  stomatitis 112.0
  sycosis 110.0
    beard 110.0
    scalp 110.0
  twin 759.4
Parasitism NEC 136.9
  intestinal NEC 129
  skin NEC 134.9
  specified—*see* Infestation
Parasitophobia 300.29
Parasomnia 780.59
  nonorganic origin 307.47
Paraspadias 752.69
Paraspasm facialis 351.8
Parathyroid gland —*see* condition
Parathyroiditis (autoimmune) 252.1
Parathyroprival tetany 252.1

Paratrachoma 077.0
Paratyphilitis (*see also* Appendicitis) 541
Paratyphoid (fever)—*see* Fever, paratyphoid
Paratyphus —*see* Fever, paratyphoid
Paraurethral duct 753.8
Para-urethritis 597.89
  gonococcal (acute) 098.0
  chronic or duration of 2 months or over 098.2
Paravaccinia NEC 051.9
  milkers' node 051.1
Paravaginitis (*see also* Vaginitis) 616.10
Parencephalitis (*see also* Encephalitis) 323.9
  late effect—*see* category 326
Parergasia 298.9
Paresis (*see also* Paralysis) 344.9
  accommodation 367.51
  bladder (spastic) (sphincter) (*see also* Paralysis,
    bladder) 596.53
    tabetic 094.0
  bowel, colon, or intestine (*see also* Ileus) 560.1
  brain or cerebral—*see* Paralysis, brain
  extrinsic muscle, eye 378.55
  general 094.1
    arrested 094.1
    brain 094.1
    cerebral 094.1
    insane 094.1
    juvenile 090.40
      remission 090.49
    progressive 094.1
    remission (sustained) 094.1
    tabetic 094.1
  heart (*see also* Failure, heart) 428.9
  infantile (*see also* Poliomyelitis) 045.9
  insane 094.1
  juvenile 090.40
  late effect—*see* Paralysis, late effect
  luetic (general) 094.1
  peripheral progressive 356.9
  pseudohypertrophic 359.1
  senile NEC 344.9
  stomach 536.3
  syphilitic (general) 094.1
    congenital 090.40
  transient, limb 781.4
  vesical (sphincter) NEC 596.53
Paresthesia (*see also* Disturbance, sensation)
    782.0
  Berger's (paresthesia of lower limb) 782.0
  Bernhardt 355.1
  Magnan's 782.0
Paretic —*see* condition
Parinaud's
  conjunctivitis 372.02
  oculoglandular syndrome 372.02
  ophthalmoplegia 378.81
  syndrome (paralysis of conjugate upward gaze)
    378.81
Parkes Weber and Dimitri syndrome
    (encephalocutaneous angiomatosis) 759.6
Parkinson's disease, syndrome, or tremor
    —*see* Parkinsonism
Parkinsonism (arteriosclerotic) (idiopathic)
    (primary) 332.0
  associated with orthostatic hypotension
    (idiopathic) (symptomatic) 333.0
  due to drugs 332.1
  secondary 332.1
  syphilitic 094.82
Parodontitis 523.4
Parodontosis 523.5

Paronychia (with lymphangitis) 681.9
  candidal (chronic) 112.3
  chronic 681.9
    candidal 112.3
  finger 681.02
  toe 681.11
  finger 681.02
  toe 681.11
  tuberculous (primary) (*see also* Tuberculosis)
    017.0
Parorexia NEC 307.52
  hysterical 300.11
Parosmia 781.1
  psychogenic 306.7
Parotid gland —*see* condition
Parotiditis (*see also* Parotitis) 527.2
  epidemic 072.9
  infectious 072.9
Parotitis 527.2
  allergic 527.2
  chronic 527.2
  epidemic (*see also* Mumps) 072.9
  infectious (*see also* Mumps) 072.9
  noninfectious 527.2
  nonspecific toxic 527.2
  not mumps 527.2
  postoperative 527.2
  purulent 527.2
  septic 527.2
  suppurative (acute) 527.2
  surgical 527.2
  toxic 527.2
Paroxysmal —*see also* condition
  dyspnea (nocturnal) 786.09
Parrot's disease (syphilitic osteochondritis) 090.0
Parrot fever 073.9
Parry's disease or syndrome (exophthalmic
    goiter) 242.0
Parry-Romberg syndrome 349.89
Parson's disease (exophthalmic goiter) 242.0
Parsonage-Aldren-Turner syndrome 353.5
Parsonage-Turner syndrome 353.5
Pars planitis 363.21
Particolored infant 757.39
Parturition —*see* Delivery
Passage
  false, urethra 599.4
  of sounds or bougies (*see also* Attention to
    artificial opening) V55.9
Passive —*see* condition
Pasteurella septica 027.2
Pasteurellosis (*see also* Infection, Pasteurella)
    027.2
PAT (paroxysmal atrial tachycardia) 427.0
Patau's syndrome (trisomy D₁) 758.1
Patch
  herald 696.3
Patches
  mucous (syphilitic) 091.3
    congenital 090.0
  smokers' (mouth) 528.6
Patellar —*see* condition
Patent —*see also* Imperfect closure
  atrioventricular ostium 745.69
  canal of Nuck 752.41
  cervix 622.5
    complicating pregnancy 654.5
      affecting fetus or newborn 761.0
  ductus arteriosus or Botalli 747.0

Patent—*continued*
Eustachian
  tube 381.7
  valve 746.89
foramen
  Botalli 745.5
  ovale 745.5
interauricular septum 745.5
interventricular septum 745.4
omphalomesenteric duct 751.0
os (uteri)—*see* Patent, cervix
ostium secundum 745.5
urachus 753.7
vitelline duct 751.0
Paterson's syndrome (sideropenic dysphagia) 280.8
Paterson (-Brown) (-Kelly) syndrome (sideropenic dysphagia) 280.8
Paterson-Kelly syndrome or web (sideropenic dysphagia) 280.8
Pathologic, pathological —*see also* condition
asphyxia 799.0
drunkenness 291.4
emotionality 301.3
liar 301.7
personality 301.9
resorption, tooth 521.4
sexuality (*see also* Deviation, sexual) 302.9
Pathology (of)—*see* Disease
Patterned motor discharges, idiopathic (*see also* Epilepsy) 345.5
Patulous —*see also* Patent
anus 569.49
Eustachian tube 381.7
Pause, sinoatrial 427.81
Pavor nocturnus 307.46
Pavy's disease 593.6
Paxton's disease (white piedra) 111.2
Payr's disease or syndrome (splenic flexure syndrome) 569.89
Pearls
Elschnig 366.51
enamel 520.2
Pearl-workers' disease (chronic osteomyelitis) (*see also* Osteomyelitis) 730.1
Pectenitis 569.49
Pectenosis 569.49
Pectoral —*see* condition
Pectus
carinatum (congenital) 754.82
  acquired 738.3
  rachitic (*see also* Rickets) 268.0
excavatum (congenital) 754.81
  acquired 738.3
  rachitic (*see also* Rickets) 268.0
recurvatum (congenital) 754.81
  acquired 738.3
Pedatrophia 261
Pederosis 302.2
Pediculosis (infestation) 132.9
capitis (head louse) (any site) 132.0
corporis (body louse) (any site) 132.1
eyelid 132.0 *[373.6]*
mixed (classifiable to more than one category in 132.0-132.2) 132.3
pubis (pubic louse) (any site) 132.2
vestimenti 132.1
vulvae 132.2
Pediculus (infestation)—*see* Pediculosis
Pedophilia 302.2
Peg-shaped teeth 520.2
Pel's crisis 094.0

Pel-Ebstein disease —*see* Disease, Hodgkin's
Pelade 704.01
Pelger-Huët anomaly or syndrome (hereditary hyposegmentation) 288.2
Peliosis (rheumatica) 287.0
Pelizaeus-Merzbacher
disease 330.0
sclerosis, diffuse cerebral 330.0
Pellagra (alcoholic or with alcoholism) 265.2
with polyneuropathy 265.2 *[357.4]*
Pellagra-cerebellar-ataxia-renal aminoaciduria syndrome 270.0
Pellegrini's disease (calcification, knee joint) 726.62
Pellegrini (-Stieda) disease or syndrome (calcification, knee joint) 726.62
Pellizzi's syndrome (pineal) 259.8
Pelvic —*see also* condition
congestion-fibrosis syndrome 625.5
kidney 753.3
Pelvioectasis 591
Pelviolithiasis 592.0
Pelviperitonitis
female (*see also* Peritonitis, pelvic, female) 614.5
male (*see also* Peritonitis) 567.2
Pelvis, pelvic —*see also* condition or type
infantile 738.6
Nägele's 738.6
obliquity 738.6
Robert's 755.69
Pemphigoid 694.5
benign, mucous membrane 694.60
  with ocular involvement 694.61
bullous 694.5
cicatricial 694.60
  with ocular involvement 694.61
juvenile 694.2
Pemphigus 694.4
benign 694.5
  chronic familial 757.39
Brazilian 694.4
circinatus 694.0
congenital, traumatic 757.39
conjunctiva 694.61
contagiosus 684
erythematodes 694.4
erythematosus 694.4
foliaceus 694.4
frambesiodes 694.4
gangrenous (*see also* Gangrene) 785.4
malignant 694.4
neonatorum, newborn 684
ocular 694.61
papillaris 694.4
seborrheic 694.4
South American 694.4
syphilitic (congenital) 090.0
vegetans 694.4
vulgaris 694.4
wildfire 694.4
Pendred's syndrome (familial goiter with deaf-mutism) 243
Pendulous
abdomen 701.9
  in pregnancy or childbirth 654.4
    affecting fetus or newborn 763.8
breast 611.8

Penetrating wound —*see also* Wound, open, by
site
with internal injury—*see* Injury, internal, by
site, with open wound
eyeball 871.7
with foreign body (nonmagnetic) 871.6
magnetic 871.5
ocular (*see also* Penetrating wound, eyeball)
871.7
adnexa 870.3
with foreign body 870.4
orbit 870.3
with foreign body 870.4
Penetration, pregnant uterus by instrument
with
abortion—*see* Abortion, by type, with damage
to pelvic organs
ectopic pregnancy (*see also* categories
633.0-633.9) 639.2
molar pregnancy (*see also* categories
630-632) 639.2
complication of delivery 665.1
affecting fetus or newborn 763.8
following
abortion 639.2
ectopic or molar pregnancy 639.2
Penfield's syndrome (*see also* Epilepsy) 345.5
Penicilliosis of lung 117.3
Penis —*see* condition
Penitis 607.2
Penta X syndrome 758.81
Pentalogy (of Fallot) 745.2
Pentosuria (benign) (essential) 271.8
Peptic acid disease 536.8
Peregrinating patient V65.2
Perforated —*see* Perforation
Perforation, perforative (nontraumatic)
antrum (*see also* Sinusitis, maxillary) 473.0
appendix 540.0
with peritoneal abscess 540.1
atrial septum, multiple 745.5
attic, ear 384.22
healed 384.81
bile duct, except cystic (*see also* Disease,
biliary) 576.3
cystic 575.4
bladder (urinary) 596.6
with
abortion—*see* Abortion, by type, with
damage to pelvic organs
ectopic pregnancy (*see also* categories
633.0-633.9) 639.2
molar pregnancy (*see also* categories
630-632) 639.2
following
abortion 639.2
ectopic or molar pregnancy 639.2
obstetrical trauma 665.5
bowel 569.83
with
abortion—*see* Abortion, by type, with
damage to pelvic organs
ectopic pregnancy (*see also* categories
633.0-633.9) 639.2
molar pregnancy (*see also* categories
630-632) 639.2
fetus or newborn 777.6
following
abortion 639.2
ectopic or molar pregnancy 639.2

Perforation, perforative—*continued*
obstetrical trauma 665.5
broad ligament
with
abortion—*see* Abortion, by type, with
damage to pelvic organs
ectopic pregnancy (*see also* categories
633.0-633.9) 639.2
molar pregnancy (*see also* categories
630-632) 639.2
following
abortion 639.2
ectopic or molar pregnancy 639.2
obstetrical trauma 665.6
by
device, implant, or graft—*see* Complications,
mechanical
foreign body left accidentally in operation
wound 998.4
instrument (any) during a procedure,
accidental 998.2
cecum 540.0
with peritoneal abscess 540.1
cervix (uteri)—*see also* Injury, internal, cervix
with
abortion—*see* Abortion, by type, with
damage to pelvic organs
ectopic pregnancy (*see also* categories
633.0-633.9) 639.2
molar pregnancy (*see also* categories
630-632) 639.2
following
abortion 639.2
ectopic or molar pregnancy 639.2
obstetrical trauma 665.3
colon 569.83
common duct (bile) 576.3
cornea (*see also* Ulcer, cornea) 370.00
due to ulceration 370.06
cystic duct 575.4
diverticulum (*see also* Diverticula) 562.10
small intestine 562.00
duodenum, duodenal (ulcer)—*see* Ulcer,
duodenum, with perforation
ear drum—*see* Perforation, tympanum
enteritis—*see* Enteritis
esophagus 530.4
ethmoidal sinus (*see also* Sinusitis, ethmoidal)
473.2
foreign body (external site)—*see also* Wound,
open, by site, complicated
internal site, by ingested object—*see* Foreign
body
frontal sinus (*see also* Sinusitis, frontal) 473.1
gallbladder or duct (*see also* Disease,
gallbladder) 575.4
gastric (ulcer)—*see* Ulcer, stomach, with
perforation
heart valve—*see* Endocarditis
ileum (*see also* Perforation, intestine) 569.83
instrumental
external—*see* Wound, open, by site
pregnant uterus, complicating delivery 665.9
surgical (accidental) (blood vessel) (nerve)
(organ) 998.2
intestine 569.83
with
abortion—*see* Abortion, by type, with
damage to pelvic organs
ectopic pregnancy (*see also* categories
633.0-633.9) 639.2

Perforation, perforative—*continued*
  molar pregnancy (*see also* categories
    630-632) 639.2
  fetus or newborn 777.6
  obstetrical trauma 665.5
  ulcerative NEC 569.83
jejunum, jejunal 569.83
  ulcer—*see* Ulcer, gastrojejunal, with
    perforation
mastoid (antrum) (cell) 383.89
maxillary sinus (*see also* Sinusitis, maxillary)
    473.0
membrana tympani—*see* Perforation, tympanum
nasal
  septum 478.1
    congenital 748.1
    syphilitic 095.8
  sinus (*see also* Sinusitis) 473.9
    congenital 748.1
palate (hard) 526.89
  soft 528.9
    syphilitic 095.8
  syphilitic 095.8
palatine vault 526.89
  syphilitic 095.8
  congenital 090.5
pelvic
  floor
    with
      abortion—*see* Abortion, by type, with
        damage to pelvic organs
      ectopic pregnancy (*see also* categories
        633.0-633.9) 639.2
      molar pregnancy (*see also* categories
        630-632) 639.2
    obstetrical trauma 664.1
  organ
    with
      abortion—*see* Abortion, by type, with
        damage to pelvic organs
      ectopic pregnancy (*see also* categories
        633.0-633.9) 639.2
      molar pregnancy (*see also* categories
        630-632) 639.2
    following
      abortion 639.2
      ectopic or molar pregnancy 639.2
    obstetrical trauma 665.5
perineum—*see* Laceration, perineum
periurethral tissue
  with
    abortion—*see* Abortion, by type, with
      damage to pelvic organs
    ectopic pregnancy (*see also* categories
      630-632) 639.2
    molar pregnancy (*see also* categories
      630-632) 639.2
pharynx 478.29
pylorus, pyloric (ulcer)—*see* Ulcer, stomach,
    with perforation
rectum 569.49
sigmoid 569.83
sinus (accessory) (chronic) (nasal) (*see also*
    Sinusitis) 473.9
sphenoidal sinus (*see also* Sinusitis, sphenoidal)
    473.3
stomach (due to ulcer)—*see* Ulcer, stomach,
    with perforation
surgical (accidental) (by instrument) (blood
    vessel) (nerve) (organ) 998.2

Perforation, perforative—*continued*
  traumatic
    external—*see* Wound, open, by site
    eye (*see also* Penetrating wound, ocular) 871.7
    internal organ—*see* Injury, internal, by site
  tympanum (membrane) (persistent
      posttraumatic) (postinflammatory) 384.20
    attic 384.22
    central 384.21
    healed 384.81
    marginal NEC 384.23
    multiple 384.24
    pars flaccida 384.22
    total 384.25
    traumatic—*see* Wound, open, ear, drum
  typhoid, gastrointestinal 002.0
  ulcer—*see* Ulcer, by site, with perforation
  ureter 593.89
  urethra
    with
      abortion—*see* Abortion, by type, with
        damage to pelvic organs
      ectopic pregnancy (*see also* categories
        633.0-633.9) 639.2
      molar pregnancy (*see also* categories
        630-632) 639.2
    following
      abortion 639.2
      ectopic or molar pregnancy 639.2
    obstetrical trauma 665.5
  uterus—*see also* Injury, internal, uterus
    with
      abortion—*see* Abortion, by type, with
        damage to pelvic organs
      ectopic pregnancy (*see also* categories
        633.0-633.9) 639.2
      molar pregnancy (*see also* categories
        630-632) 639.2
    by intrauterine contraceptive device 996.32
    following
      abortion 639.2
      ectopic or molar pregnancy 639.2
    obstetrical trauma—*see* Injury, internal,
      uterus, obstetrical trauma
  uvula 528.9
    syphilitic 095.8
  vagina—*see* Laceration, vagina
  viscus NEC 799.8
    traumatic 868.00
    with open wound into cavity 868.10
Periadenitis mucosa necrotica recurrens 528.2
Periangiitis 446.0
Periantritis 535.4
Periappendicitis (acute) (*see also* Appendicitis)
    541
Periarteritis (disseminated) (infectious)
    (necrotizing) (nodosa) 446.0
Periarthritis (joint) 726.90
  Duplay's 726.2
  gonococcal 098.50
  humeroscapularis 726.2
  scapulohumeral 726.2
  shoulder 726.2
  wrist 726.4
Periarthrosis (angioneural)—*see* Periarthritis
Peribronchitis 491.9
  tuberculous (*see also* Tuberculosis) 011.3
Pericapsulitis, adhesive (shoulder) 726.0

Pericarditis (granular) (with decompensation)
   (with effusion) 423.9
   with
      rheumatic fever (conditions classifiable to 390)
         active (*see also* Pericarditis, rheumatic)
            391.0
         inactive or quiescent 393
   actinomycotic 039.8 *[420.0]*
   acute (nonrheumatic) 420.90
      with chorea (acute) (rheumatic) (Sydenham's)
         392.0
      bacterial 420.99
      benign 420.91
      hemorrhagic 420.90
      idiopathic 420.91
      infective 420.90
      nonspecific 420.91
      rheumatic 391.0
         with chorea (acute) (rheumatic)
            (Sydenham's) 392.0
      sicca 420.90
      viral 420.91
   adhesive or adherent (external) (internal) 423.1
      acute—*see* Pericarditis, acute
      rheumatic (external) (internal) 393
   amebic 006.8 *[420.0]*
   bacterial (acute) (subacute) (with serous or
      seropurulent effusion) 420.99
   calcareous 423.2
   cholesterol (chronic) 423.8
      acute 420.90
   chronic (nonrheumatic) 423.8
      rheumatic 393
   constrictive 423.2
   Coxsackie 074.21
   due to
      actinomycosis 039.8 *[420.0]*
      amebiasis 006.8 *[420.0]*
      Coxsackie (virus) 074.21
      histoplasmosis (*see also* Histoplasmosis)
         115.93
      nocardiosis 039.8 *[420.0]*
      tuberculosis (*see also* Tuberculosis) 017.9
         [420.0]
   fibrinocaseous (*see also* Tuberculosis) 017.9
      [420.0]
   fibrinopurulent 420.99
   fibrinous—*see* Pericarditis, rheumatic
   fibropurulent 420.99
   fibrous 423.1
   gonococcal 098.83
   hemorrhagic 423.0
   idiopathic (acute) 420.91
   infective (acute) 420.90
   meningococcal 036.41
   neoplastic (chronic) 423.8
      acute 420.90
   nonspecific 420.91
   obliterans, obliterating 423.1
   plastic 423.1
   pneumococcal (acute) 420.99
   postinfarction 411.0
   purulent (acute) 420.99
   rheumatic (active) (acute) (with effusion) (with
      pneumonia) 391.0
      with chorea (acute) (rheumatic) (Sydenham's)
         392.0
      chronic or inactive (with chorea) 393
   septic (acute) 420.99
   serofibrinous—*see* Pericarditis, rheumatic
   staphylococcal (acute) 420.99

Pericarditis—*continued*
   streptococcal (acute) 420.99
   suppurative (acute) 420.99
   syphilitic 093.81
   tuberculous (acute) (chronic) (*see also*
      Tuberculosis) 017.9 *[420.0]*
   uremic 585 *[420.0]*
   viral (acute) 420.91
Pericardium, pericardial —*see* condition
Pericellulitis (*see also* Cellulitis) 682.9
Pericementitis 523.4
   acute 523.3
   chronic (suppurative) 523.4
Pericholecystitis (*see also* Cholecystitis) 575.10
Perichondritis
   auricle 380.00
      acute 380.01
      chronic 380.02
   bronchus 491.9
   ear (external) 380.00
      acute 380.01
      chronic 380.02
   larynx 478.71
      syphilitic 095.8
      typhoid 002.0 *[478.71]*
   nose 478.1
   pinna 380.00
      acute 380.01
      chronic 380.02
   trachea 478.9
Periclasia 523.5
Pericolitis 569.89
Pericoronitis (chronic) 523.4
   acute 523.3
Pericystitis (*see also* Cystitis) 595.9
Pericytoma (M9150/1)—*see also* Neoplasm,
      connective tissue, uncertain behavior
   benign (M9150/0)—*see* Neoplasm, connective
      tissue, benign
   malignant (M9150/3)—*see* Neoplasm,
      connective tissue, malignant
Peridacryocystitis, acute 375.32
Peridiverticulitis (*see also* Diverticulitis) 562.11
Periduodenitis 535.6
Periendocarditis (*see also* Endocarditis) 424.90
   acute or subacute 421.9
Periepididymitis (*see also* Epididymitis) 604.90
Perifolliculitis (abscedens) 704.8
   capitis, abscedens et suffodiens 704.8
   dissecting, scalp 704.8
   scalp 704.8
   superficial pustular 704.8
Perigastritis (acute) 535.0
Perigastrojejunitis (acute) 535.0
Perihepatitis (acute) 573.3
   chlamydial 099.56
   gonococcal 098.86
Peri-ileitis (subacute) 569.89
Perilabyrinthitis (acute)—*see* Labyrinthitis
Perimeningitis —*see* Meningitis
Perimetritis (*see also* Endometritis) 615.9
Perimetrosalpingitis (*see also*
      Salpingo-oophoritis) 614.2
Perinephric —*see* condition
Perinephritic —*see* condition
Perinephritis (*see also* Infection, kidney) 590.9
   purulent (*see also* Abscess, kidney) 590.2
Perineum, perineal —*see* condition
Perineuritis NEC 729.2

Periodic —*see also* condition
  disease (familial) 277.3
  edema 995.1
    hereditary 277.6
  fever 277.3
  paralysis (familial) 359.3
  peritonitis 277.3
  polyserositis 277.3
  somnolence 347
Periodontal
  cyst 522.8
  pocket 523.8
Periodontitis (chronic) (complex) (compound)
    (local) (simplex) 523.4
  acute 523.3
  apical 522.6
    acute (pulpal origin) 522.4
Periodontoclasia 523.5
Periodontosis 523.5
Periods —*see also* Menstruation
  heavy 626.2
  irregular 626.4
Perionychia (with lymphangitis) 681.9
  finger 681.02
  toe 681.11
Perioophoritis (*see also* Salpingo-oophoritis)
    614.2
Periorchitis (*see also* Orchitis) 604.90
Periosteum, periosteal —*see* condition
Periostitis (circumscribed) (diffuse) (infective)
    730.3

Note—Use the following fifth-digit
subclassification with category 730:

0 *site unspecified*
1 *shoulder region*
2 *upper arm*
3 *forearm*
4 *hand*
5 *pelvic region and thigh*
6 *lower leg*
7 *ankle and foot*
8 *other specified sites*
9 *multiple sites*

---

  with osteomyelitis (*see also* Osteomyelitis)
    730.2
    acute or subacute 730.0
    chronic or old 730.1
  albuminosa, albuminosus 730.3
  alveolar 526.5
  alveolodental 526.5
  dental 526.5
  gonorrheal 098.89
  hyperplastica, generalized 731.2
  jaw (lower) (upper) 526.4
  monomelic 733.99
  orbital 376.02
  syphilitic 095.5
    congenital 090.0 *[730.8]*
    secondary 091.61
  tuberculous (*see also* Tuberculosis, bone) 015.9
    [730.8]
  yaws (early) (hypertrophic) (late) 102.6
Periostosis (*see also* Periostitis) 730.3
  with osteomyelitis (*see also* Osteomyelitis)
    730.2
    acute or subacute 730.0
    chronic or old 730.1
  hyperplastic 756.59

Periphlebitis (*see also* Phlebitis) 451.9
  lower extremity 451.2
    deep (vessels) 451.19
    superficial (vessels) 451.0
  portal 572.1
  retina 362.18
  superficial (vessels) 451.0
  tuberculous (*see also* Tuberculosis) 017.9
    retina 017.3 *[362.18]*
Peripneumonia —*see* Pneumonia
Periproctitis 569.49
Periprostatitis (*see also* Prostatitis) 601.9
Perirectal —*see* condition
Perirenal —*see* condition
Perisalpingitis (*see also* Salpingo-oophoritis)
    614.2
Perisigmoiditis 569.89
Perisplenitis (infectional) 289.59
Perispondylitis —*see* Spondylitis
Peristalsis reversed or visible 787.4
Peritendinitis (*see also* Tenosynovitis) 726.90
  adhesive (shoulder) 726.0
Perithelioma (M9150/1)—*see* Pericytoma
Peritoneum, peritoneal —*see* condition
Peritonitis (acute) (adhesive) (fibrinous)
    (hemorrhagic) (idiopathic) (localized)
    (perforative) (primary) (with adhesions) (with
    effusion) 567.9
  with or following
    abortion—*see* Abortion, by type, with sepsis
    abscess 567.2
    appendicitis 540.0
      with peritoneal abscess 540.1
    ectopic pregnancy (*see also* categories
      633.0-633.9) 639.0
    molar pregnancy (*see also* categories
      630-632) 639.0
  aseptic 998.7
  bacterial 567.2
  bile, biliary 567.8
  chemical 998.7
  chlamydial 099.56
  chronic proliferative 567.8
  congenital NEC 777.6
  diaphragmatic 567.2
  diffuse NEC 567.2
  diphtheritic 032.83
  disseminated NEC 567.2
  due to
    bile 567.8
    foreign
      body or object accidentally left during a
        procedure (instrument) (sponge) (swab)
        998.4
      substance accidentally left during a
        procedure (chemical) (powder) (talc)
        998.7
    talc 998.7
    urine 567.8
  fibrinopurulent 567.2
  fibrinous 567.2
  fibrocaseous (*see also* Tuberculosis) 014.0
  fibropurulent 567.2
  general, generalized (acute) 567.2
  gonococcal 098.86
  in infective disease NEC 136.9 *[567.0]*
  meconium (newborn) 777.6
  pancreatic 577.8
  paroxysmal, benign 277.3

Peritonitis—*continued*
pelvic
female (acute) 614.5
chronic NEC 614.7
with adhesions 614.6
puerperal, postpartum, childbirth 670
male (acute) 567.2
periodic (familial) 277.3
phlegmonous 567.2
pneumococcal 567.1
postabortal 639.0
proliferative, chronic 567.8
puerperal, postpartum, childbirth 670
purulent 567.2
septic 567.2
staphylococcal 567.2
streptococcal 567.2
subdiaphragmatic 567.2
subphrenic 567.2
suppurative 567.2
syphilitic 095.2
congenital 090.0 *[567.0]*
talc 998.7
tuberculous (*see also* Tuberculosis) 014.0
urine 567.8
Peritonsillar —*see* condition
Peritonsillitis 475
Perityphlitis (*see also* Appendicitis) 541
Periureteritis 593.89
Periurethral —*see* condition
Periurethritis (gangrenous) 597.89
Periuterine —*see* condition
Perivaginitis (*see also* Vaginitis) 616.10
Perivasculitis, retinal 362.18
Perivasitis (chronic) 608.4
Perivesiculitis (seminal) (*see also* Vesiculitis) 608.0
Perlèche 686.8
due to
moniliasis 112.0
riboflavin deficiency 266.0
Pernicious —*see* condition
Pernio, perniosis 991.5
Persecution
delusion 297.9
social V62.4
Perseveration (tonic) 784.69
Persistence, persistent (congenital) 759.89
anal membrane 751.2
arteria stapedia 744.04
atrioventricular canal 745.69
bloody ejaculate 792.2
branchial cleft 744.41
bulbus cordis in left ventricle 745.8
canal of Cloquet 743.51
capsule (opaque) 743.51
cilioretinal artery or vein 743.51
cloaca 751.5
communication—*see* Fistula, congenital
convolutions
aortic arch 747.21
fallopian tube 752.19
oviduct 752.19
uterine tube 752.19
double aortic arch 747.21
ductus
arteriosus 747.0
Botalli 747.0

Persistence, persistent—*continued*
fetal
circulation 747.89
form of cervix (uteri) 752.49
hemoglobin (hereditary) ("Swiss variety") 282.7
pulmonary hypertension 747.89
foramen
Botalli 745.5
ovale 745.5
Gartner's duct 752.11
hemoglobin, fetal (hereditary) (HPFH) 282.7
hyaloid
artery (generally incomplete) 743.51
system 743.51
hymen (tag)
in pregnancy or childbirth 654.8
causing obstructed labor 660.2
lanugo 757.4
left
posterior cardinal vein 747.49
root with right arch of aorta 747.21
superior vena cava 747.49
Meckel's diverticulum 751.0
mesonephric duct 752.8
fallopian tube 752.11
mucosal disease (middle ear) (with posterior or superior marginal perforation of ear drum) 382.2
nail(s), anomalous 757.5
occiput, anterior or posterior 660.3
fetus or newborn 763.1
omphalomesenteric duct 751.0
organ or site NEC—*see* Anomaly, specified type NEC
ostium
atrioventriculare commune 745.69
primum 745.61
secundum 745.5
ovarian rests in fallopian tube 752.19
pancreatic tissue in intestinal tract 751.5
primary (deciduous)
teeth 520.6
vitreous hyperplasia 743.51
pulmonary hypertension 747.89
pupillary membrane 743.46
iris 743.46
Rhesus (Rh) titer 999.7
right aortic arch 747.21
sinus
urogenitalis 752.8
venosus with imperfect incorporation in right auricle 747.49
thymus (gland) 254.8
hyperplasia 254.0
thyroglossal duct 759.2
thyrolingual duct 759.2
truncus arteriosus or communis 745.0
tunica vasculosa lentis 743.39
umbilical sinus 753.7
urachus 753.7
vegetative state 780.03
vitelline duct 751.0
wolffian duct 752.8
Person (with)
admitted for clinical research, as control subject V70.7
awaiting admission to adequate facility elsewhere V63.2
undergoing social agency investigation V63.8

Person—*continued*
concern (normal) about sick person in family
V61.49
consulting on behalf of another V65.1
feared
complaint in whom no diagnosis was made
V65.5
condition not demonstrated V65.5
feigning illness V65.2
healthy, accompanying sick person V65.0
living (in)
alone V60.3
boarding school V60.6
residence remote from hospital or medical
care facility V63.0
residential institution V60.6
without
adequate
financial resources V60.2
housing (heating) (space) V60.1
housing (permanent) (temporary) V60.0
material resources V60.2
person able to render necessary care V60.4
shelter V60.0
medical services in home not available V63.1
on waiting list V63.2
undergoing social agency investigation V63.8
sick or handicapped in family V61.49
"worried well" V65.5
Personality
affective 301.10
aggressive 301.3
amoral 301.7
anancastic, anankastic 301.4
antisocial 301.7
asocial 301.7
asthenic 301.6
avoidant 301.82
borderline 301.83
change 310.1
compulsive 301.4
cycloid 301.13
cyclothymic 301.13
dependent 301.6
depressive (chronic) 301.12
disorder, disturbance NEC 301.9
with
antisocial disturbance 301.7
pattern disturbance NEC 301.9
sociopathic disturbance 301.7
trait disturbance 301.9
dual 300.14
dyssocial 301.7
eccentric 301.89
"haltlose" type 301.89
emotionally unstable 301.59
epileptoid 301.3
explosive 301.3
fanatic 301.0
histrionic 301.50
hyperthymic 301.11
hypomanic 301.11
hypothymic 301.12
hysterical 301.50
immature 301.89
inadequate 301.6
labile 301.59
masochistic 301.89
morally defective 301.7
multiple 300.14
narcissistic 301.81

Personality—*continued*
obsessional 301.4
obsessive (-compulsive) 301.4
overconscientious 301.4
paranoid 301.0
passive (-dependent) 301.6
passive-aggressive 301.84
pathologic NEC 301.9
pattern defect or disturbance 301.9
pseudosocial 301.7
psychoinfantile 301.59
psychoneurotic NEC 301.89
psychopathic 301.9
with
amoral trend 301.7
antisocial trend 301.7
asocial trend 301.7
pathologic sexuality (*see also* Deviation,
sexual) 302.9
mixed types 301.9
schizoid 301.20
introverted 301.21
schizotypal 301.22
with sexual deviation (*see also* Deviation,
sexual) 302.9
antisocial 301.7
dyssocial 301.7
type A 301.4
unstable (emotional) 301.59
Perthes' disease (capital femoral
osteochondrosis) 732.1
Pertussis (*see also* Whooping cough) 033.9
vaccination, prophylactic (against) V03.6
Peruvian wart 088.0
Perversion, perverted
appetite 307.52
hysterical 300.11
function
pineal gland 259.8
pituitary gland 253.9
anterior lobe
deficient 253.2
excessive 253.1
posterior lobe 253.6
placenta—*see* Placenta, abnormal
sense of smell or taste 781.1
psychogenic 306.7
sexual (*see also* Deviation, sexual) 302.9
Pervious, congenital —*see also* Imperfect,
closure
ductus arteriosus 747.0
Pes (congenital) (*see also* Talipes) 754.70
abductus (congenital) 754.60
acquired 736.79
acquired NEC 736.79
planus 734
adductus (congenital) 754.79
acquired 736.79
cavus 754.71
acquired 736.73
planovalgus (congenital) 754.69
acquired 736.79
planus (acquired) (any degree) 734
congenital 754.61
rachitic 268.1
valgus (congenital) 754.61
acquired 736.79
varus (congenital) 754.50
acquired 736.79
Pest (*see also* Plague) 020.9

Pestis (*see also* Plague) 020.9
  bubonica 020.0
  fulminans 020.0
  minor 020.8
  pneumonica—*see* Plague, pneumonic
Petechia, petechiae 782.7
  fetus or newborn 772.6
Petechial
  fever 036.0
  typhus 081.9
Petges-Cléjat or Petges-Clégat syndrome
  (poikilodermatomyositis) 710.3
Petit's
  disease (*see also* Hernia, lumbar) 553.8
Petit mal (idiopathic) (*see also* Epilepsy) 345.0
  status 345.2
Petrellidosis 117.6
Petrositis 383.20
  acute 383.21
  chronic 383.22
Peutz-Jeghers disease or syndrome 759.6
Peyronie's disease 607.89
Pfeiffer's disease 075
Phacentocele 379.32
  traumatic 921.3
Phacoanaphylaxis 360.19
Phacocele (old) 379.32
  traumatic 921.3
Phaehyphomycosis 117.8
Phagedena (dry) (moist) (*see also* Gangrene)
  785.4
  arteriosclerotic 440.24
  geometric 686.0
  penis 607.89
  senile 440.24
  sloughing 785.4
  tropical (*see also* Ulcer, skin) 707.9
  vulva 616.50
Phagedenic —*see also* condition
  abscess—*see also* Abscess
    chancroid 099.0
  bubo NEC 099.8
  chancre 099.0
  ulcer (tropical) (*see also* Ulcer, skin) 707.9
Phagomania 307.52
Phakoma 362.89
Phantom limb (syndrome) 353.6
Pharyngeal —*see also* condition
  arch remnant 744.41
  pouch syndrome 279.11
Pharyngitis (acute) (catarrhal) (gangrenous)
  (infective) (malignant) (membranous)
  (phlegmonous) (pneumococcal)
  (pseudomembranous) (simple)
  (staphylococcal) (subacute) (suppurative)
  (ulcerative) (viral) 462
  with influenza, flu, or grippe 487.1
  aphthous 074.0
  atrophic 472.1
  chlamydial 099.51
  chronic 472.1
  Coxsackie virus 074.0
  diphtheritic (membranous) 032.0
  follicular 472.1
  fusospirochetal 101
  gonococcal 098.6
  granular (chronic) 472.1
  herpetic 054.79
  hypertrophic 472.1
  infectional, chronic 472.1
  influenzal 487.1

Pharyngitis—*continued*
  lymphonodular, acute 074.8
  septic 034.0
  streptococcal 034.0
  tuberculous (*see also* Tuberculosis) 012.8
  vesicular 074.0
Pharyngoconjunctival fever 077.2
Pharyngoconjunctivitis, viral 077.2
Pharyngolaryngitis (acute) 465.0
  chronic 478.9
  septic 034.0
Pharyngoplegia 478.29
Pharyngotonsillitis 465.8
  tuberculous 012.8
Pharyngotracheitis (acute) 465.8
  chronic 478.9
Pharynx, pharyngeal —*see* condition
Phase of life problem NEC V62.89
Phenomenon
  Arthus'—*see* Arthus' phenomenon
  flashback (drug) 292.89
  jaw-winking 742.8
  Jod-Basedow 242.8
  L. E. cell 710.0
  lupus erythematosus cell 710.0
  Pelger-Huët (hereditary hyposegmentation)
    288.2
  Raynaud's (paroxysmal digital cyanosis)
    (secondary) 443.0
  Reilly's (*see also* Neuropathy, peripheral,
    autonomic) 337.9
  vasomotor 780.2
  vasospastic 443.9
  vasovagal 780.2
  Wenckebach's, heart block (second degree)
    426.13
Phenylketonuria (PKU) 270.1
Phenylpyruvicaciduria 270.1
Pheochromoblastoma (M8700/3)
  specified site—*see* Neoplasm, by site, malignant
  unspecified site 194.0
Pheochromocytoma (M8700/0)
  malignant (M8700/3)
    specified site—*see* Neoplasm, by site,
      malignant
    unspecified site 194.0
  specified site—*see* Neoplasm, by site, benign
  unspecified site 227.0
Phimosis (congenital) 605
  chancroidal 099.0
  due to infection 605
Phlebectasia (*see also* Varicose, vein) 454.9
  congenital NEC 747.60
  esophagus (*see also* Varix, esophagus) 456.1
    with hemorrhage (*see also* Varix, esophagus,
      bleeding) 456.0
Phlebitis (infective) (pyemic) (septic)
  (suppurative) 451.9
  antecubital vein 451.82
  arm NEC 451.84
    axillary vein 451.89
    basilic vein 451.82
    deep 451.83
    superficial 451.82
  basilic vein 451.82
  blue 451.19
  brachial vein 451.83
  breast, superficial 451.89
  cavernous (venous) sinus—*see* Phlebitis,
    intracranial sinus
  cephalic vein 451.82

Phlebitis—*continued*
  cerebral (venous) sinus—*see* Phlebitis,
      intracranial sinus
  chest wall, superficial 451.89
  complicating pregnancy or puerperium 671.9
      affecting fetus or newborn 760.3
  cranial (venous) sinus—*see* Phlebitis,
      intracranial sinus
  deep (vessels) 451.19
      femoral vein 451.11
      specified vessel NEC 451.19
  due to implanted device—*see* Complications,
      due to (presence of) any device, implant, or
      graft classified to 996.0-996.5 NEC
  during or resulting from a procedure 997.2
  femoral vein (deep) (superficial) 451.11
  femoropopliteal 451.19
  following infusion, perfusion, or transfusion
      999.2
  gouty 274.89 *[451.9]*
  hepatic veins 451.89
  iliac vein 451.81
  iliofemoral 451.11
  intracranial sinus (any) (venous) 325
      late effect—*see* category 326
      nonpyogenic 437.6
          in pregnancy or puerperium 671.5
  jugular vein 451.89
  lateral (venous) sinus—*see* Phlebitis,
      intracranial sinus
  leg 451.2
      deep (vessels) 451.19
          femoral vein 451.11
          specified vessel NEC 451.19
      superficial (vessels) 451.0
          femoral vein 451.11
  longitudinal sinus—*see* Phlebitis, intracranial
      sinus
  lower extremity 451.2
      deep (vessels) 451.19
          femoral vein 451.11
          specified vessel NEC 451.19
      superficial (vessels) 451.0
          femoral vein 451.11
  migrans, migrating (superficial) 453.1
  pelvic
      with
          abortion—*see* Abortion, by type, with sepsis
          ectopic pregnancy (*see also* categories
              633.0-633.9) 639.0
          molar pregnancy (*see also* categories
              630-632) 639.0
      following
          abortion 639.0
          ectopic or molar pregnancy 639.0
      puerperal, postpartum 671.4
  popliteal vein 451.19
  portal (vein) 572.1
  postoperative 997.2
  pregnancy 671.9
      deep 671.3
      specified type NEC 671.5
      superficial 671.2
  puerperal, postpartum, childbirth 671.9
      deep 671.4
      lower extremities 671.2
      pelvis 671.4
      specified site NEC 671.5
      superficial 671.2
  radial vein 451.83
  retina 362.18

Phlebitis—*continued*
  saphenous (great) (long) 451.0
      accessory or small 451.0
  sinus (meninges)—*see* Phlebitis, intracranial
      sinus
  specified site NEC 451.89
  subclavian vein 451.89
  syphilitic 093.89
  tibial vein 451.19
  ulcer, ulcerative 451.9
      leg 451.2
          deep (vessels) 451.19
              femoral vein 451.11
              specified vessel NEC 451.19
          superficial (vessels) 451.0
              femoral vein 451.11
      lower extremity 451.2
          deep (vessels) 451.19
              femoral vein 451.11
              specified vessel NEC 451.19
          superficial (vessels) 451.0
  ulnar vein 451.83
  umbilicus 451.89
  upper extremity—*see* Phlebitis, arm
  uterus (septic) (*see also* Endometritis) 615.9
  varicose (leg) (lower extremity) (*see also*
      Varicose, vein) 454.1
Phlebofibrosis 459.89
Phleboliths 459.89
Phlebosclerosis 459.89
Phlebothrombosis —*see* Thrombosis
Phlebotomus fever 066.0
Phlegm, choked on 933.1
Phlegmasia
  alba dolens (deep vessels) 451.19
      complicating pregnancy 671.3
      nonpuerperal 451.19
      puerperal, postpartum, childbirth 671.4
  cerulea dolens 451.19
Phlegmon (*see also* Abscess) 682.9
  erysipelatous (*see also* Erysipelas) 035
  iliac 682.2
      fossa 540.1
  throat 478.29
Phlegmonous —*see* condition
Phlyctenulosis (allergic) (keratoconjunctivitis)
      (nontuberculous) 370.31
  cornea 370.31
      with ulcer (*see also* Ulcer, cornea) 370.00
  tuberculous (*see also* Tuberculosis) 017.3
      [370.31]
Phobia, phobic (reaction) 300.20
  animal 300.29
  isolated NEC 300.29
  obsessional 300.3
  simple NEC 300.29
  social 300.23
  specified NEC 300.29
  state 300.20
Phocas' disease 610.1
Phocomelia 755.4
  lower limb 755.32
      complete 755.33
      distal 755.35
      proximal 755.34
  upper limb 755.22
      complete 755.23
      distal 755.25
      proximal 755.24
Phoria (*see also* Heterophoria) 378.40
Phosphate-losing tubular disorder 588.0

Phosphatemia 275.3
Phosphaturia 275.3
Photoallergic response **692.72**
Photocoproporphyria 277.1
Photodermatitis (sun) 692.72
　light other than sun 692.82
Photokeratitis 370.24
Photo-ophthalmia 370.24
Photophobia 368.13
Photopsia 368.15
Photoretinitis 363.31
Photoretinopathy 363.31
Photosensitiveness (sun) 692.72
　light other than sun 692.82
Photosensitization (sun) skin 692.72
　light other than sun 692.82
Phototoxic response **692.72**
Phrenitis 323.9
Phrynoderma 264.8
Phthiriasis (pubis) (any site) 132.2
　with any infestation classifiable to 132.0
　　and 132.1 132.3
Phthirus infestation —*see* Phthiriasis
Phthisis (*see also* Tuberculosis) 011.9
　bulbi (infectional) 360.41
　colliers' 011.4
　cornea 371.05
　eyeball (due to infection) 360.41
　millstone makers' 011.4
　miners' 011.4
　potters' 011.4
　sandblasters' 011.4
　stonemasons' 011.4
Phycomycosis 117.7
Physalopteriasis 127.7
Physical therapy NEC V57.1
　breathing exercises V57.0
Physiological cup, optic papilla
　borderline, glaucoma suspect 365.00
　enlarged 377.14
　glaucomatous 377.14
Phytobezoar 938
　intestine 936
　stomach 935.2
Pian (*see also* Yaws) 102.9
Pianoma 102.1
Piarhemia, piarrhemia (*see also* Hyperlipemia)
　272.4
　bilharziasis 120.9
Pica 307.52
　hysterical 300.11
Pick's
　cerebral atrophy 331.1
　　with dementia 331.1 *[294.1]*
　disease
　　brain 331.1
　　　dementia in 331.1 *[294.1]*
　　lipid histiocytosis 272.7
　　liver (pericardial pseudocirrhosis of liver)
　　　423.2
　　pericardium (pericardial pseudocirrhosis of
　　　liver) 423.2
　　polyserositis (pericardial pseudocirrhosis of
　　　liver) 423.2
　syndrome
　　heart (pericardial pseudocirrhosis of liver)
　　　423.2
　　liver (pericardial pseudocirrhosis of liver)
　　　423.2
　tubular adenoma (M8640/0)
　　specified site—*see* Neoplasm, by site, benign

Pick's—*continued*
　unspecified site
　　female 220
　　male 222.0
Pick-Herxheimer syndrome (diffuse idiopathic
　cutaneous atrophy) 701.8
Pick-Niemann disease (lipid histiocytosis) 272.7
Pickwickian syndrome (cardiopulmonary
　obesity) 278.8
Piebaldism, classic 709.09
Piedra 111.2
　beard 111.2
　　black 111.3
　　white 111.2
　black 111.3
　scalp 111.3
　　black 111.3
　　white 111.2
　white 111.2
Pierre Marie's syndrome (pulmonary
　hypertrophic osteoarthropathy) 731.2
Pierre Marie-Bamberger syndrome
　(hypertrophic pulmonary osteoarthropathy)
　731.2
Pierre Mauriac's syndrome
　(diabetes-dwarfism-obesity) 258.1
Pierre Robin deformity or syndrome
　(congenital) 756.0
Pierson's disease or osteochondrosis 732.1
Pigeon
　breast or chest (acquired) 738.3
　　congenital 754.82
　　rachitic (*see also* Rickets) 268.0
　breeders' disease or lung 495.2
　fanciers' disease or lung 495.2
　toe 735.8
Pigmentation (abnormal) 709.00
　anomaly 709.00
　　congenital 757.33
　　specified NEC 709.09
　conjunctiva 372.55
　cornea 371.10
　　anterior 371.11
　　posterior 371.13
　　stromal 371.12
　lids (congenital) 757.33
　　acquired 374.52
　limbus corneae 371.10
　metals 709.00
　optic papilla, congenital 743.57
　retina (congenital) (grouped) (nevoid) 743.53
　　acquired 362.74
　scrotum, congenital 757.33
Piles —*see* Hemorrhoids
Pili
　annulati or torti (congenital) 757.4
　incarnati 704.8
Pill roller hand (intrinsic) 736.09
Pilomatrixoma (M8110/0)—*see* Neoplasm, skin,
　benign
Pilonidal —*see* condition
Pimple 709.8
Pinched nerve —*see* Neuropathy, entrapment
Pineal body or gland —*see* condition
Pinealoblastoma (M9362/3) 194.4
Pinealoma (M9360/1) 237.1
　malignant (M9360/3) 194.4
Pineoblastoma (M9362/3) 194.4
Pineocytoma (M9361/1) 237.1
Pinguecula 372.51
Pinhole meatus (*see also* Stricture, urethra) 598.9

Pink
 disease 985.0
 eye 372.03
 puffer 492.8
Pinkus' disease (lichen nitidus) 697.1
Pinpoint
 meatus (*see also* Stricture, urethra) 598.9
 os (uteri) (*see also* Stricture, cervix) 622.4
Pinselhaare (congenital) 757.4
Pinta 103.9
 cardiovascular lesions 103.2
 chancre (primary) 103.0
 erythematous plaques 103.1
 hyperchromic lesions 103.1
 hyperkeratosis 103.1
 lesions 103.9
  cardiovascular 103.2
  hyperchromic 103.1
  intermediate 103.1
  late 103.2
  mixed 103.3
  primary 103.0
  skin (achromic) (cicatricial) (dyschromic)
   103.2
   hyperchromic 103.1
   mixed (achromic and hyperchromic) 103.3
 papule (primary) 103.0
 skin lesions (achromic) (cicatricial)
  (dyschromic) 103.2
  hyperchromic 103.1
  mixed (achromic and hyperchromic) 103.3
 vitiligo 103.2
Pintid 103.0
Pinworms (disease) (infection) (infestation) 127.4
Piry fever 066.8
Pistol wound —*see* Gunshot wound
Pit, lip (mucus), congenital 750.25
Pitchers' elbow 718.82
Pithecoid pelvis 755.69
 with disproportion (fetopelvic) 653.2
  affecting fetus or newborn 763.1
  causing obstructed labor 660.1
Pithiatism 300.11
Pitted —*see also* Pitting
 teeth 520.4
Pitting (edema) (*see also* Edema) 782.3
 lip 782.3
 nail 703.8
  congenital 757.5
Pituitary gland —*see* condition
Pituitary snuff-takers' disease 495.8
Pityriasis 696.5
 alba 696.5
 capitis 690.11
 circinata (et maculata) 696.3
 Hebra's (exfoliative dermatitis) 695.89
 lichenoides et varioliformis 696.2
 maculata (et circinata) 696.3
 nigra 111.1
 pilaris 757.39
  acquired 701.1
  Hebra's 696.4
 rosea 696.3
 rotunda 696.3
 rubra (Hebra) 695.89
  pilaris 696.4
 sicca 690.18
 simplex 690.18
 specified type NEC 696.5
 streptogenes 696.5
 versicolor 111.0
  scrotal 111.0

Placenta, placental
 ablatio 641.2
  affecting fetus or newborn 762.1
 abnormal, abnormality 656.7
  with hemorrhage 641.8
   affecting fetus or newborn 762.1
  affecting fetus or newborn 762.2
 abruptio 641.2
  affecting fetus or newborn 762.1
 accessory lobe—*see* Placenta, abnormal
 accreta (without hemorrhage) 667.0
  with hemorrhage 666.0
 adherent (without hemorrhage) 667.0
  with hemorrhage 666.0
 apoplexy—*see* Placenta, separation
 battledore—*see* Placenta, abnormal
 bilobate—*see* Placenta, abnormal
 bipartita—*see* Placenta, abnormal
 carneous mole 631
 centralis—*see* Placenta, previa
 circumvallata—*see* Placenta, abnormal
 cyst (amniotic)—*see* Placenta, abnormal
 deficiency—*see* Placenta insufficiency
 degeneration—*see* Placenta, insufficiency
 detachment (partial) (premature) (with
   hemorrhage) 641.2
  affecting fetus or newborn 762.1
 dimidiata—*see* Placenta, abnormal
 disease 656.7
  affecting fetus or newborn 762.2
 duplex—*see* Placenta, abnormal
 dysfunction—*see* Placenta, insufficiency
 fenestrata—*see* Placenta, abnormal
 fibrosis—*see* Placenta, abnormal
 fleshy mole 631
 hematoma—*see* Placenta, abnormal
 hemorrhage NEC—*see* Placenta, separation
 hormone disturbance or malfunction—*see*
   Placenta, abnormal
 hyperplasia—*see* Placenta, abnormal
 increta (without hemorrhage) 667.0
  with hemorrhage 666.0
 infarction 656.7
  affecting fetus or newborn 762.2
 insertion, vicious—*see* Placenta, previa
 insufficiency
  affecting
   fetus or newborn 762.2
   management of pregnancy 656.5
 lateral—*see* Placenta, previa
 low implantation or insertion—*see* Placenta,
   previa
 low-lying—*see* Placenta, previa
 malformation—*see* Placenta, abnormal
 malposition—*see* Placenta, previa
 marginalis, marginata—*see* Placenta, previa
 marginal sinus (hemorrhage) (rupture) 641.2
  affecting fetus or newborn 762.1
 membranacea—*see* Placenta, abnormal
 multilobed—*see* Placenta, abnormal
 multipartita—*see* Placenta, abnormal
 necrosis—*see* Placenta, abnormal
 percreta (without hemorrhage) 667.0
  with hemorrhage 666.0
 polyp 674.4
 previa (central) (centralis) (complete) (lateral)
   (marginal) (marginalis) (partial) (partialis)
   (total) (with hemorrhage) 641.1
  affecting fetus or newborn 762.0
  noted

Placenta, placental—*continued*
   before labor, without hemorrhage (with
      cesarean delivery) 641.0
   during pregnancy (without hemorrhage)
      641.0
   without hemorrhage (before labor and
      delivery) (during pregnancy) 641.0
   retention (with hemorrhage) 666.0
   fragments, complicating puerperium (delayed
      hemorrhage) 666.2
   without hemorrhage 667.1
   postpartum, puerperal 666.2
   without hemorrhage 667.0
   separation (normally implanted) (partial)
      (premature) (with hemorrhage) 641.2
   affecting fetus or newborn 762.1
   septuplex—*see* Placenta, abnormal
   small—*see* Placenta, insufficiency
   softening (premature)—*see* Placenta, abnormal
   spuria—*see* Placenta, abnormal
   succenturiata—*see* Placenta, abnormal
   syphilitic 095.8
   transfusion syndromes 762.3
   transmission of chemical substance—*see*
      Absorption, chemical, through placenta
   trapped (with hemorrhage) 666.0
   without hemorrhage 667.0
   trilobate—*see* Placenta, abnormal
   tripartita—*see* Placenta, abnormal
   triplex—*see* Placenta, abnormal
   varicose vessel—*see* Placenta, abnormal
   vicious insertion—*see* Placenta, previa
Placentitis
   affecting fetus or newborn 762.7
   complicating pregnancy 658.4
Plagiocephaly (skull) 754.0
Plague 020.9
   abortive 020.8
   ambulatory 020.8
   bubonic 020.0
   cellulocutaneous 020.1
   lymphatic gland 020.0
   pneumonic 020.5
     primary 020.3
     secondary 020.4
   pulmonary—*see* Plague, pneumonic
   pulmonic—*see* Plague, pneumonic
   septicemic 020.2
   tonsillar 020.9
     septicemic 020.2
   vaccination, prophylactic (against) V03.3
Planning, family V25.09
   contraception V25.9
   procreation V26.4
Plaque
   artery, arterial—*see* Arteriosclerosis
   calcareous—*see* Calcification
   Hollenhorst's (retinal) 362.33
   tongue 528.6
Plasma cell myeloma 203.0
Plasmacytoma, plasmocytoma (solitary)
   (M9731/1) 238.6
   benign (M9731/0)—*see* Neoplasm, by site,
      benign
   malignant (M9731/3) 203.8
Plasmacytosis 288.8
Plaster ulcer (*see also* Decubitus) 707.0
Platybasia 756.0
Platyonychia (congenital) 757.5
   acquired 703.8

Platypelloid pelvis 738.6
   with disproportion (fetopelvic) 653.2
     affecting fetus or newborn 763.1
     causing obstructed labor 660.1
       affecting fetus or newborn 763.1
   congenital 755.69
Platyspondylia 756.19
Plethora 782.62
   newborn 776.4
Pleura, pleural —*see* condition
Pleuralgia 786.52
Pleurisy (acute) (adhesive) (chronic) (costal)
     (diaphragmatic) (double) (dry) (fetid)
     (fibrinous) (fibrous) (interlobar) (latent) (lung)
     (old) (plastic) (primary) (residual) (sicca)
     (sterile) (subacute) (unresolved) (with
     adherent pleura) 511.0
   with
     effusion (without mention of cause) 511.9
       bacterial, nontuberculous 511.1
       nontuberculous NEC 511.9
         bacterial 511.1
       pneumococcal 511.1
       specified type NEC 511.8
       staphylococcal 511.1
       streptococcal 511.1
       tuberculous (*see also* Tuberculosis, pleura)
         012.0
         primary, progressive 010.1
     influenza, flu, or grippe 487.1
     tuberculosis—*see* Pleurisy, tuberculous
   encysted 511.8
   exudative (*see also* Pleurisy, with effusion)
     511.9
     bacterial, nontuberculous 511.1
   fibrinopurulent 510.9
     with fistula 510.0
   fibropurulent 510.9
     with fistula 510.0
   hemorrhagic 511.8
   influenzal 487.1
   pneumococcal 511.0
     with effusion 511.1
   purulent 510.9
     with fistula 510.0
   septic 510.9
     with fistula 510.0
   serofibrinous (*see also* Pleurisy, with effusion)
     511.9
     bacterial, nontuberculous 511.1
   seropurulent 510.9
     with fistula 510.0
   serous (*see also* Pleurisy, with effusion) 511.9
     bacterial, nontuberculous 511.1
   staphylococcal 511.0
     with effusion 511.1
   streptococcal 511.0
     with effusion 511.1
   suppurative 510.9
     with fistula 510.0
   traumatic (post) (current) 862.29
     with open wound into cavity 862.39
   tuberculous (with effusion) (*see also*
     Tuberculosis, pleura) 012.0
     primary, progressive 010.1
Pleuritis sicca —*see* Pleurisy
Pleurobronchopneumonia (*see also* Pneumonia,
   broncho-) 485
Pleurodynia 786.52
   epidemic 074.1
   viral 074.1

Pleurohepatitis 573.8
Pleuropericarditis (*see also* Pericarditis) 423.9
  acute 420.90
Pleuropneumonia (acute) (bilateral) (double)
  (septic) (*see also* Pneumonia) 486
  chronic (*see also* Fibrosis, lung) 515
Pleurorrhea (*see also* Hydrothorax) 511.8
Plexitis, brachial 353.0
Plica
  polonica 132.0
  tonsil 474.8
Plicae dysphonia ventricularis 784.49
Plicated tongue 529.5
  congenital 750.13
Plug
  bronchus NEC 519.1
  meconium (newborn) NEC 777.1
  mucus—*see* Mucus, plug
Plumbism 984.9
  specified type of lead—*see* Table of drugs and
    chemicals
Plummer's disease (toxic nodular goiter) 242.3
Plummer-Vinson syndrome (sideropenic
  dysphagia) 280.8
Pluricarential syndrome of infancy 260
Plurideficiency syndrome of infancy 260
Plus (and minus) hand (intrinsic) 736.09
PMS 625.4
Pneumathemia —*see* Air, embolism, by type
Pneumatic drill or hammer disease 994.9
Pneumatocele (lung) 518.89
  intracranial 348.8
  tension 492.0
Pneumatosis
  cystoides intestinalis 569.89
  peritonei 568.89
  pulmonum 492.8
Pneumaturia 599.84
Pneumoblastoma (M8981/3)—*see* Neoplasm,
  lung, malignant
Pneumocephalus 348.8
Pneumococcemia 038.2
Pneumococcus, pneumococcal —*see* condition
Pneumoconiosis (due to) (inhalation of) 505
  aluminum 503
  asbestos 501
  bagasse 495.1
  bauxite 503
  beryllium 503
  carbon electrode makers' 503
  coal
    miners' (simple) 500
    workers' (simple) 500
  cotton dust 504
  diatomite fibrosis 502
  dust NEC 504
    inorganic 503
    lime 502
    marble 502
    organic NEC 504
  fumes or vapors (from silo) 506.9
  graphite 503
  hard metal 503
  mica 502
  moldy hay 495.0
  rheumatoid 714.81
  silica NEC 502
    and carbon 500
  silicate NEC 502
  talc 502
Pneumocystis carinii pneumonia 136.3

Pneumocystosis 136.3
  with pneumonia 136.3
Pneumoenteritis 025
Pneumohemopericardium (*see also*
  Pericarditis) 423.9
Pneumohemothorax (*see also* Hemothorax)
  511.8
  traumatic 860.4
  with open wound into thorax 860.5
Pneumohydropericardium (*see also*
  Pericarditis) 423.9
Pneumohydrothorax (*see also* Hydrothorax)
  511.8
Pneumomediastinum 518.1
  congenital 770.2
  fetus or newborn 770.2
Pneumomycosis 117.9
Pneumonia (acute) (Alpenstich) (benign)
  (bilateral) (brain) (cerebral) (circumscribed)
  (congestive) (creeping) (delayed resolution)
  (double) (epidemic) (fever) (flash) (fulminant)
  (fungoid) (granulomatous) (hemorrhagic)
  (incipient) (infantile) (infectious) (infiltration)
  (insular) (intermittent) (latent) (lobe)
  (migratory) (newborn) (organized)
  (overwhelming) (primary) (progressive)
  (pseudolobar) (purulent) (resolved)
  (secondary) (senile) (septic) (suppurative)
  (terminal) (true) (unresolved) (vesicular) 486
  with influenza, flu, or grippe 487.0
  adenoviral 480.0
  adynamic 514
  alba 090.0
  allergic 518.3
  alveolar—*see* Pneumonia, lobar
  anaerobes 482.81
  anthrax 022.1 *[484.5]*
  apex, apical—*see* Pneumonia, lobar
  ascaris 127.0 *[484.8]*
  aspiration 507.0
    due to
      aspiration of microorganisms
        bacterial 482.9
          specified type NEC 482.89
        specified organism NEC 483.8
          bacterial NEC 482.89
        viral 480.9
          specified type NEC 480.8
      food (regurgitated) 507.0
      gastric secretions 507.0
      milk 507.0
      oils, essences 507.1
      solids, liquids NEC 507.8
      vomitus 507.0
    newborn 770.1
  asthenic 514
  atypical (disseminated, focal) (primary) 486
    with influenza 487.0
  bacillus 482.9
    specified type NEC 482.89
  bacterial 482.9
    specified type NEC 482.89
  Bacteroides (fragilis) (oralis) (melaninogenicus)
    482.81
  basal, basic, basilar—*see* Pneumonia, lobar
  broncho-, bronchial (confluent) (croupous)
    (diffuse) (disseminated) (hemorrhagic)
    (involving lobes) (lobar) (terminal) 485
    with influenza 487.0
    allergic 518.3

Pneumonia—*continued*
  aspiration (*see also* Pneumonia, aspiration) 507.0
  bacterial 482.9
    specified type NEC 482.89
  capillary 466.19
    with bronchospasm or obstruction 466.19
  chronic (*see also* Fibrosis, lung) 515
  congenital (infective) 770.0
  diplococcal 481
  Eaton's agent 483.0
  Escherichia coli (E. coli) 482.82
  Friedländer's bacillus 482.0
  Hemophilus influenzae 482.2
  hiberno-vernal 083.0 *[484.8]*
  hypostatic 514
  influenzal 487.0
  inhalation (*see also* Pneumonia, aspiration) 507.0
    due to fumes or vapors (chemical) 506.0
  Klebsiella 482.0
  lipid 507.1
    endogenous 516.8
  Mycoplasma (pneumoniae) 483.0
  ornithosis 073.0
  pleuropneumonia-like organisms (PPLO) 483.0
  pneumococcal 481
  Proteus 482.83
  pseudomonas 482.1
  specified organism NEC 483.8
    bacterial NEC 482.89
  staphylococcal 482.4
  streptococcal—*see* Pneumonia, streptococcal
  typhoid 002.0 *[484.8]*
  viral, virus (*see also* Pneumonia, viral) 480.9
  Butyrivibrio (fibriosolvens) 482.81
  Candida 112.4
  capillary 466.19
    with bronchospasm or obstruction 466.19
  caseous (*see also* Tuberculosis) 011.6
  catarrhal—*see* Pneumonia, broncho-
  central—*see* Pneumonia, lobar
  Chlamydia, chlamydial 483.1
    pneumoniae 483.1
    psittaci 073.0
    specified type NEC 483.1
    trachomatis 483.1
  cholesterol 516.8
  chronic (*see also* Fibrosis, lung) 515
  cirrhotic (chronic) (*see also* Fibrosis, lung) 515
  Clostridium (haemolyticum) (novyi) NEC 482.81
  confluent—*see* Pneumonia, broncho-
  congenital (infective) 770.0
    aspiration 770.1
  croupous—*see* Pneumonia, lobar
  cytomegalic inclusion 078.5 *[484.1]*
  deglutition (*see also* Pneumonia, aspiration) 507.0
  desquamative interstitial 516.8
  diffuse—*see* Pneumonia, broncho-
  diplococcal, diplococcus (broncho-) (lobar) 481
  disseminated (focal)—*see* Pneumonia, broncho-
  due to
    adenovirus 480.0
    Bacterium anitratum 482.83
    Chlamydia, chlamydial 483.1
      pneumoniae 483.1
      psittaci 073.0
      specified type NEC 483.1
      trachomatis 483.1

Pneumonia—*continued*
  coccidioidomycosis 114.0
  Diplococcus (pneumoniae) 481
  Eaton's agent 483.0
  Escherichia coli (E. coli) 482.82
  Friedländer's bacillus 482.0
  fumes or vapors (chemical) (inhalation) 506.0
  fungus NEC 117.9 *[484.7]*
    coccidioidomycosis 114.0
  Hemophilus influenzae (H. influenzae) 482.2
  Herellea 482.83
  influenza 487.0
  Klebsiella pneumoniae 482.0
  Mycoplasma (pneumoniae) 483.0
  parainfluenza virus 480.2
  pleuropneumonia-like organism (PPLO) 483.0
  Pneumococcus 481
  Pneumocystis carinii 136.3
  Proteus 482.83
  pseudomonas 482.1
  respiratory syncytial virus 480.1
  rickettsia 083.9 *[484.8]*
  specified
    bacteria NEC 482.89
    organism NEC 483.8
    virus NEC 480.8
  Staphylococcus 482.4
  Streptococcus—*see also* Pneumonia, streptococcal
    pneumoniae 481
  virus (*see also* Pneumonia, viral) 480.9
  Eaton's agent 483.0
  embolic, embolism (*see also* Embolism, pulmonary) 415.1
  eosinophilic 518.3
  Escherichia coli (E. coli) 482.82
  Eubacterium 482.81
  fibrinous—*see* Pneumonia, lobar
  fibroid (chronic) (*see also* Fibrosis, lung) 515
  fibrous (*see also* Fibrosis, lung) 515
  Friedländer's bacillus 482.0
  Fusobacterium (nucleatum) 482.81
  gangrenous 513.0
  giant cell (*see also* Pneumonia, viral) 480.9
  gram-negative bacteria NEC 482.83
    anaerobic 482.81
  grippal 487.0
  Hemophilus influenzae (bronchial) (lobar) 482.2
  hypostatic (broncho-) (lobar) 514
  in
    actinomycosis 039.1
    anthrax 022.1 *[484.5]*
    aspergillosis 117.3 *[484.6]*
    candidiasis 112.4
    coccidioidomycosis 114.0
    cytomegalic inclusion disease 078.5 *[484.1]*
    histoplasmosis (*see also* Histoplasmosis) 115.95
    infectious disease NEC 136.9 *[484.8]*
    measles 055.1
    mycosis, systemic NEC 117.9 *[484.7]*
    nocardiasis, nocardiosis 039.1
    ornithosis 073.0
    pneumocystosis 136.3
    psittacosis 073.0
    Q fever 083.0 *[484.8]*
    salmonellosis 003.22
    toxoplasmosis 130.4
    tularemia 021.2
    typhoid (fever) 002.0 *[484.8]*

Pneumonia—*continued*
  varicella 052.1
  whooping cough (*see also* Whooping cough)
    033.9 *[484.3]*
  infective, acquired prenatally 770.0
  influenzal (broncho) (lobar) (virus) 487.0
  inhalation (*see also* Pneumonia, aspiration)
    507.0
    fumes or vapors (chemical) 506.0
  interstitial 516.8
    with influenzal 487.0
    acute 136.3
    chronic (*see also* Fibrosis, lung) 515
    desquamative 516.8
    hypostatic 514
    lipoid 507.1
    lymphoid 516.8
    plasma cell 136.3
    pseudomonas 482.1
  intrauterine (infective) 770.0
    aspiration 770.1
  Klebsiella pneumoniae 482.0
  lipid, lipoid (exogenous) (interstitial) 507.1
    endogenous 516.8
  lobar (diplococcal) (disseminated) (double)
    (interstitial) (pneumococcal, any type) 481
    with influenza 487.0
    bacterial 482.9
      specified type NEC 482.89
    chronic (*see also* Fibrosis, lung) 515
    Escherichia coli (E. coli) 482.82
    Friedländer's bacillus 482.0
    Hemophilus influenzae (H. influenzae) 482.2
    hypostatic 514
    influenzal 487.0
    Klebsiella 482.0
    ornithosis 073.0
    Proteus 482.83
    pseudomonas 482.1
    psittacosis 073.0
    specified organism NEC 483.8
      bacterial NEC 482.89
    staphylococcal 482.4
    streptococcal—*see* Pneumonia, streptococcal
    viral, virus (*see also* Pneumonia, viral) 480.9
  lobular (confluent)—*see* Pneumonia, broncho-
  Löffler's 518.3
  massive—*see* Pneumonia, lobar
  meconium 770.1
  metastatic NEC 038.8 *[484.8]*
  Mycoplasma (pneumoniae) 483.0
  necrotic 513.0
  nitrogen dioxide 506.9
  orthostatic 514
  parainfluenza virus 480.2
  parenchymatous (*see also* Fibrosis, lung) 515
  passive 514
  patchy—*see* Pneumonia, broncho
  Peptococcus 482.81
  Peptostreptococcus 482.81
  plasma cell 136.3
  pleurolobar—*see* Pneumonia, lobar
  pleuropneumonia-like organism (PPLO) 483.0
  pneumococcal (broncho) (lobar) 481
  Pneumocystis (carinii) 136.3
  postinfectional NEC 136.9 *[484.8]*
  postmeasles 055.1
  postoperative 997.3
  primary atypical 486
  Proprionibacterium 482.81
  Proteus 482.83

Pneumonia—*continued*
  pseudomonas 482.1
  psittacosis 073.0
  radiation 508.0
  respiratory syncytial virus 480.1
  resulting from a procedure 997.3
  rheumatic 390 *[517.1]*
  Salmonella 003.22
  segmented, segmental—*see* Pneumonia,
    broncho-
  Serratia (marcescens) 482.83
  specified
    bacteria NEC 482.89
    organism NEC 483.8
    virus NEC 480.8
  spirochetal 104.8 *[484.8]*
  staphylococcal (broncho) (lobar) 482.4
  static, stasis 514
  streptococcal (broncho) (lobar) NEC 482.30
    Group
      A 482.31
      B 482.32
      specified NEC 482.39
    pneumoniae 481
    specified type NEC 482.39
  Streptococcus pneumoniae 481
  traumatic (complication) (early) (secondary)
    958.8
  tuberculous (any) (*see also* Tuberculosis) 011.6
  tularemic 021.2
  TWAR agent 483.1
  varicella 052.1
  Veillonella 482.81
  viral, virus (broncho) (interstitial) (lobar) 480.9
    with influenza, flu, or grippe 487.0
    adenoviral 480.0
    parainfluenza 480.2
    respiratory syncytial 480.1
    specified type NEC 480.8
  white (congenital) 090.0
Pneumonic —*see* condition
Pneumonitis (acute) (primary) (*see also*
    Pneumonia) 486
  allergic 495.9
    specified type NEC 495.8
  aspiration 507.0
    due to fumes or gases 506.0
    newborn 770.1
    obstetric 668.0
  chemical 506.0
    due to fumes or gases 506.0
  cholesterol 516.8
  chronic (*see also* Fibrosis, lung) 515
  congenital rubella 771.0
  due to
    fumes or vapors 506.0
    inhalation
      food (regurgitated), milk, vomitus 507.0
      oils, essences 507.1
      saliva 507.0
      solids, liquids NEC 507.8
    toxoplasmosis (acquired) 130.4
      congenital (active) 771.2 *[484.8]*
  eosinophilic 518.3
  fetal aspiration 770.1
  hypersensitivity 495.9
  interstitial (chronic) (*see also* Fibrosis, lung) 515
    lymphoid 516.8
  lymphoid, interstitial 516.8
  meconium 770.1
  postanesthetic

Pneumonitis—*continued*
   correct substance properly administered 507.0
     obstetric 668.0
     overdose or wrong substance given 968.4
       specified anesthetic—*see* Table of drugs
         and chemicals
   postoperative 997.3
     obstetric 668.0
   radiation 508.0
   rubella, congenital 771.0
   "ventilation" 495.7
   wood-dust 495.8
Pneumonoconiosis —*see* Pneumoconiosis
Pneumoparotid 527.8
Pneumopathy NEC 518.89
   alveolar 516.9
     specified NEC 516.8
   due to dust NEC 504
   parietoalveolar 516.9
     specified condition NEC 516.8
Pneumopericarditis (*see also* Pericarditis) 423.9
   acute 420.90
Pneumopericardium —*see also* Pericarditis
   congenital 770.2
   fetus or newborn 770.2
   traumatic (post) (*see also* Pneumothorax,
     traumatic) 860.0
     with open wound into thorax 860.1
Pneumoperitoneum 568.89
   fetus or newborn 770.2
Pneumophagia (psychogenic) 306.4
Pneumopleurisy, pneumopleuritis (*see also*
   Pneumonia) 486
Pneumopyopericardium 420.99
Pneumopyothorax (*see also* Pyopneumothorax)
   510.9
   with fistula 510.0
Pneumorrhagia 786.3
   newborn 770.3
   tuberculous (*see also* Tuberculosis, pulmonary)
     011.9
Pneumosiderosis (occupational) 503
Pneumothorax (acute) (chronic) 512.8
   congenital 770.2
   due to operative injury of chest wall or lung
     512.1
     accidental puncture or laceration 512.1
   fetus or newborn 770.2
   iatrogenic 512.1
   postoperative 512.1
   spontaneous 512.8
     fetus or newborn 770.2
     tension 512.0
   sucking 512.8
     iatrogenic 512.1
     postoperative 512.1
   tense valvular, infectional 512.0
   tension 512.0
     iatrogenic 512.1
     postoperative 512.1
     spontaneous 512.0
   traumatic 860.0
     with
       hemothorax 860.4
         with open wound into thorax 860.5
       open wound into thorax 860.1
   tuberculous (*see also* Tuberculosis) 011.7
Pocket (s)
   endocardial (*see also* Endocarditis) 424.90
   periodontal 523.8
Podagra 274.9

Podencephalus 759.89
Poikilocytosis 790.0
Poikiloderma 709.09
   Civatte's 709.09
   congenital 757.33
   vasculare atrophicans 696.2
Poikilodermatomyositis 710.3
Pointed ear 744.29
Poise imperfect 729.9
Poisoned —*see* Poisoning
Poisoning (acute)—*see also* Table of drugs and
   chemicals
   Bacillus, B.
     aertrycke (*see also* Infection, Salmonella)
       003.9
     botulinus 005.1
     cholerae (suis) (*see also* Infection,
       Salmonella) 003.9
     paratyphosus (*see also* Infection, Salmonella)
       003.9
     suipestifer (*see also* Infection, Salmonella)
       003.9
   bacterial toxins NEC 005.9
   berries, noxious 988.2
   blood (general)—*see* Septicemia
   botulism 005.1
   bread, moldy, mouldy—*see* Poisoning, food
   damaged meat—*see* Poisoning, food
   death-cap (Amanita phalloides) (Amanita
     verna) 988.1
   decomposed food—*see* Poisoning, food
   diseased food—*see* Poisoning, food
   drug—*see* Table of drugs and chemicals
   epidemic, fish, meat, or other food—*see*
     Poisoning, food
   fava bean 282.2
   fish (bacterial)—*see also* Poisoning, food
     noxious 988.0
   food (acute) (bacterial) (diseased) (infected)
     NEC 005.9
     due to
       Bacillus
         aertrycke (*see also* Poisoning, food, due to
           Salmonella) 003.9
         botulinus 005.1
         cereus 005.89
         choleraesuis (*see also* Poisoning, food,
           due to Salmonella) 003.9
         paratyphosus (*see also* Poisoning, food,
           due to Salmonella) 003.9
         suipestifer (*see also* Poisoning, food, due
           to Salmonella) 003.9
       Clostridium 005.3
         botulinum 005.1
         perfringens 005.2
         welchii 005.2
       Salmonella (aertrycke) (callinarum)
         (choleraesuis) (enteritidis) (paratyphi)
         (suipestifer) 003.9
         with
           gastroenteritis 003.0
           localized infection(s) (*see also* Infection,
             Salmonella) 003.20
           septicemia 003.1
           specified manifestation NEC 003.8
       specified bacterium NEC 005.89
       Staphylococcus 005.0
       Streptococcus 005.8
       Vibrio parahaemolyticus 005.4
       Vibrio vulnificus 005.81

Poisoning—*continued*
 noxious or naturally toxic 988.0
  berries 988.2
  fish 988.0
  mushroom 988.1
  plants NEC 988.2
 ice cream—*see* Poisoning, food
 ichthyotoxism (bacterial) 005.9
 kreotoxism, food 005.9
 malarial—*see* Malaria
 meat—*see* Poisoning, food
 mushroom (noxious) 988.1
 mussel—*see also* Poisoning, food
  noxious 988.0
 noxious foodstuffs (*see also* Poisoning, food,
  noxious) 988.9
  specified type NEC 988.8
 plants, noxious 988.2
 pork—*see also* Poisoning, food
  specified NEC 988.8
  Trichinosis 124
 ptomaine—*see* Poisoning, food
 putrefaction, food—*see* Poisoning, food
 radiation 508.0
 Salmonella (*see also* Infection, Salmonella)
  003.9
 sausage—*see also* Poisoning, food
  Trichinosis 124
 saxitoxin 988.0
 shellfish—*see also* Poisoning, food
  noxious 988.0
 Staphylococcus, food 005.0
 toxic, from disease NEC 799.8
 truffles—*see* Poisoning, food
 uremic—*see* Uremia
 uric acid 274.9
**Poison ivy, oak, sumac or other plant
 dermatitis** 692.6
Poker spine 720.0
Policeman's disease 729.2
Polioencephalitis (acute) (bulbar) (*see also*
 Poliomyelitis, bulbar) 045.0
 inferior 335.22
 influenzal 487.8
 superior hemorrhagic (acute) (Wernicke's) 265.1
 Wernicke's (superior hemorrhagic) 265.1
Polioencephalomyelitis (acute) (anterior)
 (bulbar) (*see also* Polioencephalitis) 045.0
Polioencephalopathy, superior hemorrhagic
 265.1
 with
  beriberi 265.0
  pellagra 265.2
Poliomeningoencephalitis —*see*
 Meningoencephalitis
Poliomyelitis (acute) (anterior) (epidemic) 045.9

Note—Use the following fifth-digit
subclassification with category 045:

0 poliovirus, unspecified type
1 poliovirus, type I
2 poliovirus, type II
3 poliovirus, type III

 with
  paralysis 045.1
   bulbar 045.0
  abortive 045.2
  ascending 045.9
   progressive 045.9
  bulbar 045.0

Poliomyelitis— *continued*
 cerebral 045.0
 chronic 335.21
 congenital 771.2
 contact V01.2
 deformities 138
 exposure to V01.2
 late effect 138
 nonepidemic 045.9
 nonparalytic 045.2
 old with deformity 138
 posterior, acute 053.19
 residual 138
 sequelae 138
 spinal, acute 045.9
 syphilitic (chronic) 094.89
 vaccination, prophylactic (against) V04.0
Poliosis (eyebrow) (eyelashes) 704.3
 circumscripta (congenital) 757.4
  acquired 704.3
 congenital 757.4
Pollakiuria 788.41
 psychogenic 306.53
Pollinosis 477.0
Pollitzer's disease (hidradenitis suppurativa)
 705.83
Polyadenitis (*see also* Adenitis) 289.3
 malignant 020.0
Polyalgia 729.9
Polyangiitis (essential) 446.0
Polyarteritis (nodosa) (renal) 446.0
Polyarthralgia 719.49
 psychogenic 306.0
Polyarthritis, polyarthropathy NEC 716.59
 due to or associated with other specified
  conditions—*see* Arthritis, due to or
  associated with
 endemic (*see also* Disease, Kaschin-Beck) 716.0
 inflammatory 714.9
  specified type NEC 714.89
 juvenile (chronic) 714.30
  acute 714.31
 migratory—*see* Fever, rheumatic
 rheumatic 714.0
  fever (acute)—*see* Fever, rheumatic
Polycarential syndrome of infancy 260
Polychondritis (atrophic) (chronic) (relapsing)
 733.99
Polycoria 743.46
Polycystic (congenital) (disease) 759.89
 degeneration, kidney—*see* Polycystic, kidney
 kidney (congenital) 753.12
  adult type (APKD) 753.13
  autosomal dominant 753.13
  autosomal recessive 753.14
  childhood type (CPKD) 753.14
  infantile type 753.14
 liver 751.62
 lung 518.89
  congenital 748.4
 ovary, ovaries 256.4
 spleen 759.0
Polycythemia (primary) (rubra) (vera)
 (M9950/1) 238.4
 acquired 289.0
 benign 289.0
  familial 289.6
 due to
  donor twin 776.4
  fall in plasma volume 289.0
  high altitude 289.0

Polycythemia—*continued*
  maternal-fetal transfusion 776.4
  stress 289.0
  emotional 289.0
  erythropoietin 289.0
  familial (benign) 289.6
  Gaisböck's (hypertonica) 289.0
  high altitude 289.0
  hypertonica 289.0
  hypoxemic 289.0
  neonatorum 776.4
  nephrogenous 289.0
  relative 289.0
  secondary 289.0
  spurious 289.0
  stress 289.0
Polycytosis cryptogenica 289.0
Polydactylism, polydactyly 755.00
  fingers 755.01
  toes 755.02
Polydipsia 783.5
Polydystrophic oligophrenia 277.5
Polyembryoma (M9072/3)—*see* Neoplasm, by
  site, malignant
Polygalactia 676.6
Polyglandular
  deficiency 258.9
  dyscrasia 258.9
  dysfunction 258.9
  syndrome 258.8
Polyhydramnios (*see also* Hydramnios) 657
Polymastia 757.6
Polymenorrhea 626.2
Polymicrogyria 742.2
Polymyalgia 725
  arteritica 446.5
  rheumatica 725
Polymyositis (acute) (chronic) (hemorrhagic)
  710.4
  with involvement of
    lung 710.4 *[517.8]*
    skin 710.3
  ossificans (generalisata) (progressiva) 728.19
  Wagner's (dermatomyositis) 710.3
Polyneuritis, polyneuritic (*see also*
  Polyneuropathy) 356.9
  alcoholic 357.5
    with psychosis 291.1
  cranialis 352.6
  diabetic 250.6 *[357.2]*
  due to lack of vitamin NEC 269.2 *[357.4]*
  endemic 265.0 *[357.4]*
  erythredema 985.0
  febrile 357.0
  hereditary ataxic 356.3
  idiopathic, acute 357.0
  infective (acute) 357.0
  nutritional 269.9 *[357.4]*
  postinfectious 357.0
Polyneuropathy (peripheral) 356.9
  alcoholic 357.5
  amyloid 277.3 *[357.4]*
  arsenical 357.7
  diabetic 250.6 *[357.2]*
  due to
    antitetanus serum 357.6
    arsenic 357.7
    drug or medicinal substance 357.6
      correct substance properly administered
        357.6
      overdose or wrong substance given or taken
        977.9

Polyneuropathy—*continued*
    specified drug—*see* Table of drugs and
      chemicals
  lack of vitamin NEC 269.2 *[357.4]*
  lead 357.7
  organophosphate compounds 357.7
  pellagra 265.2 *[357.4]*
  porphyria 277.1 *[357.4]*
  serum 357.6
  toxic agent NEC 357.7
  hereditary 356.0
  idiopathic 356.9
    progressive 356.4
  in
    amyloidosis 277.3 *[357.4]*
    avitaminosis 269.2 *[357.4]*
      specified NEC 269.1 *[357.4]*
    beriberi 265.0 *[357.4]*
    collagen vascular disease NEC 710.9 *[357.1]*
    deficiency
      B-complex NEC 266.2 *[357.4]*
      vitamin B 266.9 *[357.4]*
      vitamin B_6 266.1 *[357.4]*
    diabetes 250.6 *[357.2]*
    diphtheria (*see also* Diphtheria) 032.89
      [357.4]
    disseminated lupus erythematosus 710.0
      [357.1]
    herpes zoster 053.13
    hypoglycemia 251.2 *[357.4]*
    malignant neoplasm (M8000/3) NEC 199.1
      [357.3]
    mumps 072.72
    pellagra 265.2 *[357.4]*
    polyarteritis nodosa 446.0 *[357.1]*
    porphyria 277.1 *[357.4]*
    rheumatoid arthritis 714.0 *[357.1]*
    sarcoidosis 135 *[357.4]*
    uremia 585 *[357.4]*
  lead 357.7
  nutritional 269.9 *[357.4]*
    specified NEC 269.8 *[357.4]*
  postherpetic 053.13
  progressive 356.4
  sensory (hereditary) 356.2
Polyonychia 757.5
Polyopia 368.2
  refractive 368.15
Polyorchism, polyorchidism (three testes) 752.8
Polyorrhymenitis (peritoneal) (*see also*
  Polyserositis) 568.82
  pericardial 423.2
Polyostotic fibrous dysplasia 756.54
Polyotia 744.1
Polyp, polypus

Note—Polyps of organs or sites that do not
appear in the list below should be coded to the
residual category for diseases of the organ or
site concerned.

  accessory sinus 471.8
  adenoid tissue 471.0
  adenomatous (M8210/0)—*see also* Neoplasm,
    by site, benign
      adenocarcinoma in (M8210/3)—*see*
        Neoplasm, by site, malignant
      carcinoma in (M8210/3)—*see* Neoplasm, by
        site, malignant
      multiple (M8221/0)—*see* Neoplasm, by site,
        benign
  antrum 471.8

Polyp, polypus—*continued*
anus, anal (canal) (nonadenomatous) 569.0
  adenomatous 211.4
Bartholin's gland 624.6
bladder (M8120/1) 236.7
broad ligament 620.8—
cervix (uteri) 622.7
  adenomatous 219.0
  in pregnancy or childbirth 654.6
    affecting fetus or newborn 763.8
    causing obstructed labor 660.2
  mucous 622.7
  nonneoplastic 622.7
choanal 471.0
cholesterol 575.6
clitoris 624.6
colon (M8210/0) (*see also* Polyp, adenomatous) 211.3
corpus uteri 621.0
dental 522.0
ear (middle) 385.30
endometrium 621.0
ethmoidal (sinus) 471.8
fallopian tube 620.8
female genital organs NEC 624.8
frontal (sinus) 471.8
gallbladder 575.6
gingiva 523.8
gum 523.8
labia 624.6
larynx (mucous) 478.4
malignant (M8000/3)—*see* Neoplasm, by site, malignant
maxillary (sinus) 471.8
middle ear 385.30
myometrium 621.0
nares
  anterior 471.9
  posterior 471.0
nasal (mucous) 471.9
  cavity 471.0
  septum 471.9
nasopharyngeal 471.0
neoplastic (M8210/0)—*see* Neoplasm, by site, benign
nose (mucous) 471.9
oviduct 620.8
paratubal 620.8
pharynx 478.29
  congenital 750.29
placenta, placental 674.4
prostate 600
pudenda 624.6
pulp (dental) 522.0
rectosigmoid 211.4
rectum (nonadenomatous) 569.0
  adenomatous 211.4
septum (nasal) 471.9
sinus (accessory) (ethmoidal) (frontal) (maxillary) (sphenoidal) 471.8
sphenoidal (sinus) 471.8
stomach (M8210/0) 211.1
tube, fallopian 620.8
turbinate, mucous membrane 471.8
ureter 593.89
urethra 599.3
uterine
  ligament 620.8
  tube 620.8
uterus (body) (corpus) (mucous) 621.0
  in pregnancy or childbirth 654.1

Polyp, polypus—*continued*
  affecting fetus or newborn 763.8
  causing obstructed labor 660.2
vagina 623.7—
vocal cord (mucous) 478.4
vulva 624.6
Polyphagia 783.6
Polypoid —*see* condition
Polyposis —*see also* Polyp
coli (adenomatous) (M8220/0) 211.3
  adenocarcinoma in (M8220/3) 153.9
  carcinoma in (M8220/3) 153.9
familial (M8220/0) 211.3
intestinal (adenomatous) (M8220/0) 211.3
multiple (M8221/0)—*see* Neoplasm, by site, benign
Polyradiculitis (acute) 357.0
Polyradiculoneuropathy (acute) (segmentally demyelinating) 357.0
Polysarcia 278.00
Polyserositis (peritoneal) 568.82
due to pericarditis 423.2
paroxysmal (familial) 277.3
pericardial 423.2
periodic 277.3
pleural—*see* Pleurisy
recurrent 277.3
tuberculous (*see also* Tuberculosis, polyserositis) 018.9
Polysialia 527.7
Polysplenia syndrome 759.0
Polythelia 757.6
Polytrichia (*see also* Hypertrichosis) 704.1
Polyunguia (congenital) 757.5
acquired 703.8
Polyuria 788.42
Pompe's disease (glycogenosis II) 271.0
Pompholyx 705.81
Poncet's disease (tuberculous rheumatism) (*see also* Tuberculosis) 015.9
Pond fracture —*see* Fracture, skull, vault
Ponos 085.0
Pons, pontine —*see* condition
Poor
contractions, labor 661.2
  affecting fetus or newborn 763.7
fetal growth NEC 764.9
  affecting management of pregnancy 656.5
obstetrical history V23.4
sucking reflex (newborn) 796.1
vision NEC 369.9
Poradenitis, nostras 099.1
Porencephaly (congenital) (development) (true) 742.4
acquired 348.0
nondevelopmental 348.0
traumatic (post) 310.2
Porocephaliasis 134.1
Porokeratosis 757.39
Poroma, eccrine (M8402/0)—*see* Neoplasm, skin, benign
Porphyria (acute) (congenital) (constitutional) (erythropoietic) (familial) (hepatica) (idiopathic) (idiosyncratic) (intermittent) (latent) (mixed hepatic) (photosensitive) (South African genetic) (Swedish) 277.1
acquired 277.1
cutaneatarda
  hereditaria 277.1
  symptomatica 277.1
due to drugs

Porphyria—*continued*
  correct substance properly administered 277.1
  overdose or wrong substance given or taken
    977.9
    specified drug—*see* Table of drugs and
      chemicals
  secondary 277.1
  toxic NEC 277.1
  variegata 277.1
Porphyrinuria (acquired) (congenital)
  (secondary) 277.1
Porphyruria (acquired) (congenital) 277.1
Portal —*see* condition
Port wine nevus or mark 757.32
Posadas-Wernicke disease 114.9
Position
  fetus, abnormal (*see also* Presentation, fetal)
    652.9
  teeth, faulty 524.3
Positive
  culture (nonspecific) 795.3
    AIDS virus V08
    blood 790.7
    HIV V08
    human immunodeficiency virus V08
    nose 795.3
    skin lesion NEC 795.3
    spinal fluid 792.0
    sputum 795.3
    stool 792.1
    throat 795.3
    urine 599.0
    wound 795.3
  HIV V08
  human immunodeficiency virus (HIV) V08
  PPD 795.5
  serology
    AIDS virus V08
      inconclusive 795.71
    HIV V08
      inconclusive 795.71
    human immunodeficiency virus V08
      inconclusive 795.71
    syphilis 097.1
      with signs or symptoms—*see* Syphilis, by
        site and stage
      false 795.6
  skin test 795.7
    tuberculin (without active tuberculosis) 795.5
  VDRL 097.1
    with signs or symptoms—*see* Syphilis, by site
      and stage
    false 795.6
  Wassermann reaction 097.1
    false 795.6
Postcardiotomy syndrome 429.4
Postcaval ureter 753.4
Postcholecystectomy syndrome 576.0
Postclimacteric bleeding 627.1
Postcommissurotomy syndrome 429.4
Postconcussional syndrome 310.2
Postcontusional syndrome 310.2
Postcricoid region —*see* condition
Post-dates (pregnancy) 645
Postencephalitic —*see also* condition syndrome
  310.8
Posterior —*see* condition
Posterolateral sclerosis (spinal cord)—*see*
  Degeneration, combined
Postexanthematous —*see* condition
Postfebrile —*see* condition
Postgastrectomy dumping syndrome 564.2

Posthemiplegic chorea 344.89
Posthemorrhagic anemia (chronic) 280.0
  acute 285.1
  newborn 776.5
Posthepatitis syndrome 780.7
Postherpetic neuralgia (intercostal) (syndrome)
  (zoster) 053.19
  geniculate ganglion 053.11
  ophthalmica 053.19
  trigeminal 053.12
Posthitis 607.1
Postimmunization complication or reaction
  —*see* Complications, vaccination
Postinfectious —*see* condition
Postinfluenzal syndrome 780.7
Postlaminectomy syndrome 722.80
  cervical, cervicothoracic 722.81
  kyphosis 737.12
  lumbar, lumbosacral 722.83
  thoracic, thoracolumbar 722.82
Postleukotomy syndrome 310.0
Postlobectomy syndrome 310.0
Postmastectomy lymphedema (syndrome) 457.0
Postmaturity, postmature (fetus or newborn)
  766.2
  affecting management of pregnancy 645
  syndrome 766.2
Postmeasles —*see also* condition
  complication 055.8
    specified NEC 055.79
Postmenopausal
  endometrium (atrophic) 627.8
    suppurative (*see also* Endometritis) 615.9
  hormone replacement V07.4
Postnasal drip —*see* Sinusitis
Postnatal —*see* condition
Postoperative —*see also* condition
  confusion state 293.9
  psychosis 293.9
  status NEC (*see also* Status (post)) V45.89
Postpancreatectomy hyperglycemia 251.3
Postpartum —*see also* condition
  observation
    immediately after delivery V24.0
    routine follow-up V24.2
Postperfusion syndrome NEC 999.8
  bone marrow 996.85
Postpoliomyelitic —*see* condition
Postsurgery status NEC (*see also* Status (post))
  V45.89
Post-term (pregnancy) 645
  infant (294 days or more gestation) 766.2
Posttraumatic —*see* condition
Posttraumatic brain syndrome, nonpsychotic
  310.2
Post-typhoid abscess 002.0
Postures, hysterical 300.11
Postvaccinal reaction or complication —*see*
  Complications, vaccination
Postvagotomy syndrome 564.2
Postvalvulotomy syndrome 429.4
Postvasectomy sperm count V25.8
Potain's disease (pulmonary edema) 514
Potain's syndrome (gastrectasis with dyspepsia)
  536.1
Pott's
  curvature (spinal) (*see also* Tuberculosis) 015.0
    [737.43]
  disease or paraplegia (*see also* Tuberculosis)
    015.0 [730.88]

Pott's—*continued*
  fracture (closed) 824.4
    open 824.5
  gangrene 440.24
  osteomyelitis (*see also* Tuberculosis) 015.0
    [730.88]
  spinal curvature (*see also* Tuberculosis) 015.0
    [737.43]
  tumor, puffy (*see also* Osteomyelitis) 730.2
Potter's
  asthma 502
  disease 753.0
  facies 754.0
  lung 502
  syndrome (with renal agenesis) 753.0
Pouch
  bronchus 748.3
  Douglas'—*see* condition
  esophagus, esophageal (congenital) 750.4
    acquired 530.6
  gastric 537.1
  Hartmann's (abnormal sacculation of
    gallbladder neck) 575.8
  pharynx, pharyngeal (congenital) 750.27
Poulet's disease 714.2
Poultrymen's itch 133.8
Poverty V60.2
Prader-Labhart-Willi-Fanconi syndrome
    (hypogenital dystrophy with diabetic
    tendency) 759.81
Prader-Willi syndrome (hypogenital dystrophy
    with diabetic tendency) 759.81
Preachers' voice 784.49
Pre-AIDS —*see* Human immunodeficiency virus
    (disease) (illness) (infection)
Preauricular appendage 744.1
Prebetalipoproteinemia (acquired) (essential)
    (familial) (hereditary) (primary) (secondary)
    272.1
  with chylomicronemia 272.3
Precipitate labor 661.3
  affecting fetus or newborn 763.6
Preclimacteric bleeding 627.0
  menorrhagia 627.0
Precocious
  adrenarche 259.1
  menarche 259.1
  menstruation 626.8
  pubarche 259.1
  puberty NEC 259.1
  sexual development NEC 259.1
  thelarche 259.1
Precocity, sexual (constitutional) (cryptogenic)
    (female) (idiopathic) (male) NEC 259.1
  with adrenal hyperplasia 255.2
Precordial pain 786.51
  psychogenic 307.89
Predeciduous teeth 520.2
Prediabetes, prediabetic 790.2
  complicating pregnancy, childbirth, or
    puerperium 648.8
  fetus or newborn 775.8
Predislocation status of hip, at birth (*see also*
    Subluxation, congenital, hip) 754.32
Pre-eclampsia (mild) 642.4
  with pre-existing hypertension 642.7
  affecting fetus or newborn 760.0
  severe 642.5
  superimposed on pre-existing hypertensive
    disease 642.7
Preeruptive color change, teeth, tooth 520.8

Preexcitation 426.7
  atrioventricular conduction 426.7
  ventricular 426.7
Preglaucoma 365.00
Pregnancy (single) (uterine) (without sickness)
    V22.2

> Note—Use the following fifth-digit
> subclassification with categories 640-648,
> 651-676:
>
> 0 *unspecified as to episode of care*
> 1 *delivered, with or without mention of*
>   *antepartum condition*
> 2 *delivered, with mention of postpartum*
>   *complication*
> 3 *antepartum condition or complication*
> 4 *postpartum condition or complication*

  abdominal (ectopic) 633.0
    affecting fetus or newborn 761.4
  abnormal NEC 646.9
  ampullar—*see* Pregnancy, tubal
  broad ligament—*see* Pregnancy, cornual
  cervical—*see* Pregnancy, cornual
  combined (extrauterine and intrauterine)—*see*
    Pregnancy, cornual
  complicated (by) 646.9
    abnormal, abnormality NEC 646.9
      cervix 654.6
      cord (umbilical) 663.9
      glucose tolerance (conditions classifiable to
        790.2) 648.8
      pelvic organs or tissues NEC 654.9
      pelvis (bony) 653.0
      perineum or vulva 654.8
      placenta, placental (vessel) 656.7
      position
        cervix 654.4
        placenta 641.1
          without hemorrhage 641.0
        uterus 654.4
      size, fetus 653.5
      uterus (congenital) 654.0
    abscess or cellulitis
      bladder 646.6
      genitourinary tract (conditions classifiable to
        590, 595, 597, 599.0, 614-616) 646.6
      kidney 646.6
      urinary tract NEC 646.6
    air embolism 673.0
    albuminuria 646.2
      with hypertension—*see* Toxemia, of
        pregnancy
    amnionitis 658.4
    amniotic fluid embolism 673.1
    anemia (conditions classifiable to 280-285)
      648.2
    atrophy, yellow (acute) (liver) (subacute)
      646.7
    bacilluria, asymptomatic 646.5
    bacteriuria, asymptomatic 646.5
    bicornis or bicornuate uterus 654.0
    bone and joint disorders (conditions
      classifiable to 720-724 or conditions
      affecting lower limbs classifiable to
      711-719, 725-738) 648.7
    breech presentation 652.2
      with successful version 652.1

Pregnancy—*continued*

  incarceration, uterus 654.3
  incompetent cervix (os) 654.5
  infection 647.9
    amniotic fluid 658.4
    bladder 646.6
    genital organ (conditions classifiable to
      614-616) 646.6
    kidney (conditions classifiable to
      590.0-590.9) 646.6
    urinary (tract) 646.6
      asymptomatic 646.5
  infective and parasitic diseases NEC 647.8
  inflammation
    bladder 646.6
    genital organ (conditions classifiable to
      614-616) 646.6
    urinary tract NEC 646.6
  injury 648.9
    obstetrical NEC 665.9
  insufficient weight gain 646.8
  intrauterine fetal death (near term) NEC 656.4
    early (before 22 completed weeks'
      gestation) 632
  malaria (conditions classifiable to 084) 647.4
  malformation, uterus (congenital) 654.0
  malnutrition (conditions classifiable to
      260-269) 648.9
  malposition
    fetus—*see* Pregnancy, complicated,
      malpresentation
    uterus or cervix 654.4
  malpresentation 652.9
    with successful version 652.1
    in multiple gestation 652.6
    specified type NEC 652.8
  marginal sinus hemorrhage or rupture 641.2
  maternal obesity syndrome 646.1
  menstruation 640.8
  mental disorders (conditions classifiable to
      290-303, 305-316, 317-319) 648.4
  mentum presentation 652.4
  missed
    abortion 632
    delivery (at or near term) 656.4
    labor (at or near term) 656.4
  necrosis
    genital organ or tract (conditions classifiable
      to 614-616) 646.6
    liver (conditions classifiable to 570) 646.7
    renal, cortical 646.2
  nephritis or nephrosis (conditions classifiable
      to 580-589) 646.2
    with hypertension 642.1
  nephropathy NEC 646.2
  neuritis (peripheral) 646.4
  nutritional deficiency (conditions classifiable
      to 260-269) 648.9
  oblique lie or presentation 652.3
    with successful version 652.1
  obstetrical trauma NEC 665.9
  oligohydramnios NEC 658.0
  onset of contractions before 37 weeks 644.0
  oversize fetus 653.5
  papyraceous fetus 646.0
  patent cervix 654.5
  pelvic inflammatory disease (conditions
      classifiable to 614-616) 646.6

Pregnancy—*continued*

  placenta, placental
    abnormality 656.7
    abruptio or ablatio 641.2
    detachment 641.2
    disease 656.7
    infarct 656.7
    low implantation 641.1
      without hemorrhage 641.0
    malformation 656.7
    malposition 641.1
      without hemorrhage 641.0
    marginal sinus hemorrhage 641.2
    previa 641.1
      without hemorrhage 641.0
    separation (premature) (undelivered) 641.2
  placentitis 658.4
  polyhydramnios 657
  postmaturity 645
  prediabetes 648.8
  pre-eclampsia (mild) 642.4
    severe 642.5
    superimposed on pre-existing hypertensive
      disease 642.7
  premature rupture of membranes 658.1
    with delayed delivery 658.2
  previous
    infertility V23.0
    nonobstetric condition V23.8
    poor obstetrical history V23.4
    premature delivery V23.4
    trophoblastic disease (conditions classifiable
      to 630) V23.1
  prolapse, uterus 654.4
  proteinuria (gestational) 646.2
    with hypertension—*see* Toxemia, of
      pregnancy
  pruritus (neurogenic) 646.8
  psychosis or psychoneurosis 648.4
  ptyalism 646.8
  pyelitis (conditions classifiable to
      590.0-590.9) 646.6
  renal disease or failure NEC 646.2
    with secondary hypertension 642.1
    hypertensive 642.2
  retention, retained dead ovum 631
  retroversion, uterus 654.3
  Rh immunization, incompatibility, or
      sensitization 656.1
  rubella (conditions classifiable to 056) 647.5
  rupture
    amnion (premature) 658.1
      with delayed delivery 658.2
    marginal sinus (hemorrhage) 641.2
    membranes (premature) 658.1
      with delayed delivery 658.2
    uterus (before onset of labor) 665.0
  salivation (excessive) 646.8
  salpingo-oophoritis (conditions classifiable to
      614.0-614.2) 646.6
  septicemia (conditions classifiable to
      038.0-038.9) 647.8
  spasms, uterus (abnormal) 646.8
  specified condition NEC 646.8
  spurious labor pains 644.1
  superfecundation 651.9
  superfetation 651.9
  syphilis (conditions classifiable to 090-097)
      647.0

Pregnancy—*continued*
  threatened
    abortion 640.0
    premature delivery 644.2
    premature labor 644.0
  thrombophlebitis (superficial) 671.2
    deep 671.3
  thrombosis 671.9
    venous (superficial) 671.2
      deep 671.3
  thyroid dysfunction (conditions classifiable to
    240-246) 648.1
  thyroiditis 648.1
  thyrotoxicosis 648.1
  torsion of uterus 654.4
  toxemia—*see* Toxemia, of pregnancy
  transverse lie or presentation 652.3
    with successful version 652.1
  trauma 648.9
    obstetrical 665.9
  tuberculosis (conditions classifiable to
    010-018) 647.3
  tumor
    cervix 654.6
    ovary 654.4
    pelvic organs or tissue NEC 654.4
    uterus (body) 654.1
      cervix 654.6
    vagina 654.7
    vulva 654.8
  unstable lie 652.0
  uremia—*see* Pregnancy, complicated, renal
    disease
  urethritis 646.6
  vaginitis or vulvitis (conditions classifiable to
    616.1) 646.6
  varicose
    placental vessels 656.7
    veins (legs) 671.0
      perineum 671.1
      vulva 671.1
  varicosity, labia or vulva 671.1
  venereal disease NEC (conditions classifiable
    to 099) 647.2
  viral disease NEC (conditions classifiable to
    042, 050-055, 057-079) 647.6
  vomiting (incoercible) (pernicious)
    (persistent) (uncontrollable) (vicious)
    643.9
    due to organic disease or other cause 643.8
    early—*see* Hyperemesis, gravidarum
    late (after 22 completed weeks gestation)
      643.2
  complications NEC 646.9
  cornual 633.8
    affecting fetus or newborn 761.4
  death, maternal NEC 646.9
  delivered—*see* Delivery
  ectopic (ruptured) NEC 633.9
    abdominal—*see* Pregnancy, abdominal
    affecting fetus or newborn 761.4
    combined (extrauterine and intrauterine)—*see*
      Pregnancy, cornual
    ovarian—*see* Pregnancy, ovarian
    specified type NEC 633.8
      affecting fetus or newborn 761.4
    tubal—*see* Pregnancy, tubal
  examination, pregnancy not confirmed V72.4
  extrauterine—*see* Pregnancy, ectopic
  fallopian—*see* Pregnancy, tubal

Pregnancy—*continued*
  false 300.11
    labor (pains) 644.1
  fatigue 646.8
  illegitimate V61.6
  incidental finding V22.2
  in double uterus 654.0
  interstitial—*see* Pregnancy, cornual
  intraligamentous—*see* Pregnancy, cornual
  intramural—*see* Pregnancy, cornual
  intraperitoneal—*see* Pregnancy, abdominal
  isthmian—*see* Pregnancy, tubal
  management affected by
    abnormal, abnormality
      fetus (suspected) 655.9
        specified NEC 655.8
      placenta 656.7
    advanced maternal age NEC 659.6
      primigravida 659.5
    antibodies (maternal)
      anti-c 656.1
      anti-d 656.1
      anti-e 656.1
      blood group (ABO) 656.2
        Rh(esus) 656.1
    elderly primigravida 659.5
    fetal (suspected)
      abnormality 655.9
        acid-base balance 656.3
        heart rate or rhythm 656.3
        specified NEC 655.8
      acidemia 656.3
      anencephaly 655.0
      bradycardia 656.3
      central nervous system malformation 655.0
      chromosomal abnormalities (conditions
        classifiable to 758.0-758.9) 655.1
      damage from
        drugs 655.5
          obstetric, anesthetic, or sedative 655.5
        environmental toxins 655.8
        intrauterine contraceptive device 655.8
        maternal
          alcohol addiction 655.4
          disease NEC 655.4
          drug use 655.5
          listeriosis 655.4
          rubella 655.3
          toxoplasmosis 655.4
          viral infection 655.3
        radiation 655.6
      death (near term) 656.4
        early (before 22 completed weeks
          gestation) 632
      distress 656.3
      excessive growth 656.6
      growth retardation 656.5
      hereditary disease 655.2
      hydrocephalus 655.0
      intrauterine death 656.4
      poor growth 656.5
      spina bifida (with myelomeningocele) 655.0
    fetal-maternal hemorrhage 656.0
    hereditary disease in family (possibly)
      affecting fetus 655.2
    incompatibility, blood groups (ABO) 656.2
      rh(esus) 656.1
    insufficient prenatal care V23.7
    intrauterine death 656.4
    isoimmunization (ABO) 656.2
      rh(esus) 656.1

Pregnancy—*continued*
  large-for-dates fetus 656.6
  light-for-dates fetus 656.5
  meconium in liquor 656.3
  mental disorder (conditions classifiable to
    290-303, 305-316, 317-319) 648.4
  multiparity (grand) 659.4
  poor obstetric history V23.4
  postmaturity 645
  previous
    abortion V23.2
      habitual 646.3
    cesarean delivery 654.2
    difficult delivery V23.4
    forceps delivery V23.4
    habitual abortions 646.3
    hemorrhage, antepartum or postpartum
      V23.4
    hydatidiform mole V23.1
    infertility V23.0
    malignancy NEC V23.8
    nonobstetrical conditions V23.8
    premature delivery V23.4
    trophoblastic disease (conditions in 630)
      V23.1
    vesicular mole V23.1
    prolonged pregnancy 645
    small-for-dates fetus 656.5
  maternal death NEC 646.9
  mesometric (mural)—*see* Pregnancy, cornual
  molar 631
    hydatidiform (*see also* Hydatidiform mole)
      630
    previous, affecting management of
      pregnancy V23.1
    previous, affecting management of pregnancy
      V23.4
  multiple NEC 651.9
    with fetal loss and retention of one or more
      fetus(es) 651.6
    affecting fetus or newborn 761.5
    specified type NEC 651.8
      with fetal loss and retention of one or more
        fetus(es) 651.6
  mural—*see* Pregnancy, cornual
  observation NEC V22.1
    first pregnancy V22.0
    high-risk V23.9
      specified problem NEC V23.8
  ovarian 633.2
    affecting fetus or newborn 761.4
  postmature 645
  post-term 645
  prenatal care only V22.1
    first pregnancy V22.0
    high-risk V23.9
      specified problem NEC V23.8
  prolonged 645
  quadruplet NEC 651.2
    with fetal loss and retention of one or more
      fetus(es) 651.5
    affecting fetus or newborn 761.5
  quintuplet NEC 651.8
    with fetal loss and retention of one or more
      fetus(es) 651.6
    affecting fetus or newborn 761.5
  sextuplet NEC 651.8
    with fetal loss and retention of one or more
      fetus(es) 651.6
    affecting fetus or newborn 761.5
  spurious 300.11

Pregnancy—*continued*
  superfecundation NEC 651.9
    with fetal loss and retention of one or more
      fetus(es) 651.6
  superfetation NEC 651.9
    with fetal loss and retention of one or more
      fetus(es) 651.6
  supervision (of) (for)—*see also* Pregnancy,
    management affected by
    high-risk V23.9
      insufficient prenatal care V23.7
      specified problem NEC V23.8
    multiparity V23.3
    normal NEC V22.1
      first V22.0
    poor
      obstetric history V23.4
      reproductive history V23.5
    previous
      abortion V23.2
      hydatidiform mole V23.1
      infertility V23.0
      neonatal death V23.5
      stillbirth V23.5
      trophoblastic disease V23.1
      vesicular mole V23.1
    specified problem NEC V23.8
  triplet NEC 651.1
    with fetal loss and retention of one or more
      fetus(es) 651.4
    affecting fetus or newborn 761.5
  tubal (with rupture) 633.1
    affecting fetus or newborn 761.4
  twin NEC 651.0
    with fetal loss and retention of one or more
      fetus(es) 651.3
    affecting fetus or newborn 761.5
  unconfirmed V72.4
  undelivered (no other diagnosis) V22.2
    with false labor 644.1
    high-risk V23.9
      specified problem NEC V23.8
  unwanted NEC V61.7
Pregnant uterus —*see* condition
Preiser's disease (osteoporosis) 733.09
Prekwashiorkor 260
Preleukemia 238.7
Preluxation of hip, congenital (*see also*
  Subluxation, congenital, hip) 754.32
Premature —*see also* condition
  beats (nodal) 427.60
    atrial 427.61
    auricular 427.61
    postoperative 997.1
    specified type NEC 427.69
    supraventricular 427.61
    ventricular 427.69
  birth NEC 765.1
  closure
    cranial suture 756.0
    fontanel 756.0
    foramen ovale 745.8
  contractions 427.60
    atrial 427.61
    auricular 427.61
    auriculoventricular 427.61
    heart (extrasystole) 427.60
    junctional 427.60
    nodal 427.60
    postoperative 997.1
    ventricular 427.69

Premature—*continued*
ejaculation 302.75
infant NEC 765.1
   excessive 765.0
   light-for-dates—*see* Light-for-dates
labor 644.2
   threatened 644.0
lungs 770.4
menopause 256.3
puberty 259.1
rupture of membranes or amnion 658.1
   affecting fetus or newborn 761.1
   delayed delivery following 658.2
senility (syndrome) 259.8
separation, placenta (partial)—*see* Placenta,
   separation
ventricular systole 427.69
Prematurity NEC 765.1
extreme 765.0
Premenstrual syndrome 625.4
Premenstrual tension 625.4
Premolarization, cuspids 520.2
Premyeloma 273.1
Prenatal
care, normal pregnancy V22.1
   first V22.0
death, cause unknown—*see* Death, fetus
screening—*see* Antenatal, screening
Prepartum —*see* condition
Preponderance, left or right ventricular 429.3
Prepuce —*see* condition
Presbycardia 797
hypertensive (*see also* Hypertension, heart)
   402.90
Presbycusis 388.01
Presbyesophagus 530.89
Presbyophrenia 310.1
Presbyopia 367.4
Prescription of contraceptives NEC V25.02
diaphragm V25.02
oral (pill) V25.01
   repeat V25.41
repeat V25.40
   oral (pill) V25.41
Presenile —*see also* condition
aging 259.8
dementia (*see also* Dementia, presenile) 290.10
Presenility 259.8
Presentation, fetal
abnormal 652.9
   with successful version 652.1
   before labor, affecting fetus or newborn 761.7
   causing obstructed labor 660.0
      affecting fetus or newborn, any, except
         breech 763.1
   in multiple gestation (one or more) 652.6
   specified NEC 652.8
arm 652.7
   causing obstructed labor 660.0
breech 652.2
   with successful version 652.1
      before labor, affecting fetus or newborn
         761.7
   before labor, affecting fetus or newborn 761.7
   causing obstructed labor 660.0
      affecting fetus or newborn 763.0
brow 652.4
   causing obstructed labor 660.0
chin 652.4
   causing obstructed labor 660.0

Presentation, fetal—*continued*
compound 652.8
   causing obstructed labor 660.0
cord 663.0
extended head 652.4
   causing obstructed labor 660.0
face 652.4
   causing obstructed labor 660.0
   to pubes 652.8
      causing obstructed labor 660.3
hand, leg, or foot NEC 652.8
   causing obstructed labor 660.0
mentum 652.4
   causing obstructed labor 660.0
multiple gestation (one fetus or more) 652.6
oblique 652.3
   with successful version 652.1
   causing obstructed labor 660.0
shoulder 652.8
   affecting fetus or newborn 763.1
   causing obstructed labor 660.0
transverse 652.3
   with successful version 652.1
   causing obstructed labor 660.0
umbilical cord 663.0
unstable 652.0
Prespondylolisthesis (congenital) (lumbosacral)
   756.11
Pressure
area, skin ulcer (*see also* Decubitus) 707.0
atrophy, spine 733.99
birth, fetus or newborn NEC 767.9
brachial plexus 353.0
brain 348.4
   injury at birth 767.0
cerebral—*see* Pressure, brain
chest 786.59
cone, tentorial 348.4
   injury at birth 767.0
funis—*see* Compression, umbilical cord
hyposystolic (*see also* Hypotension) 458.9
increased
   intracranial 348.2
      injury at birth 767.8
   intraocular 365.00
lumbosacral plexus 353.1
mediastinum 519.3
necrosis (chronic) (skin) (*see also* Decubitus)
   707.0
nerve—*see* Compression, nerve
paralysis (*see also* Neuropathy, entrapment)
   355.9
sore (chronic) (*see also* Decubitus) 707.0
spinal cord 336.9
ulcer (chronic) (*see also* Decubitus) 707.0
umbilical cord—*see* Compression, umbilical
   cord
venous, increased 459.89
Pre-syncope 780.2
Preterm infant NEC 765.1
extreme 765.0
Priapism (penis) 607.3
Prickling sensation (*see also* Disturbance,
   sensation) 782.0
Prickly heat 705.1
Primary —*see* condition
Primigravida, elderly
affecting
   fetus or newborn 763.8
   management of pregnancy, labor, and delivery
      659.5

Primipara, old
　affecting
　　fetus or newborn 763.8
　　management of pregnancy, labor, and delivery 659.5
Primula dermatitis 692.6
Primus varus (bilateral) (metatarsus) 754.52
P.R.I.N.D. 436
Pringle's disease (tuberous sclerosis) 759.5
Prinzmetal's angina 413.1
Prinzmetal-Massumi syndrome (anterior chest wall) 786.52
Prizefighter ear 738.7
Problem (with) V49.9
　academic V62.3
　acculturation V62.4
　adopted child V61.29
　aged
　　in-law V61.3
　　parent V61.3
　　person NEC V61.8
　alcoholism in family V61.41
　anger reaction (see also Disturbance, conduct) 312.0
　behavior, child 312.9
　behavioral V40.9
　　specified NEC V40.3
　betting V69.3
　cardiorespiratory NEC V47.2
　care of sick or handicapped person in family or household V61.49
　career choice V62.2
　communication V40.1
　conscience regarding medical care V62.6
　delinquency (juvenile) 312.9
　diet, inappropriate V69.1
　digestive NEC V47.3
　ear NEC V41.3
　eating habits, inappropriate V69.1
　economic V60.2
　　affecting care V60.9
　　　specified type NEC V60.8
　educational V62.3
　enuresis, child 307.6
　exercise, lack of V69.0
　eye NEC V41.1
　family V61.9
　　specified circumstance NEC V61.8
　fear reaction, child 313.0
　feeding (elderly) (infant) 783.3
　　newborn 779.3
　　nonorganic 307.50
　fetal, affecting management of pregnancy 656.9
　　specified type NEC 656.8
　financial V60.2
　foster child V61.29
　　specified NEC V41.8
　functional V41.9
　　specified type NEC V41.8
　gambling V69.3
　genital NEC V47.5
　head V48.9
　　deficiency V48.0
　　disfigurement V48.6
　　mechanical V48.2
　　motor V48.2
　　movement of V48.2
　　sensory V48.4
　　specified condition NEC V48.8
　hearing V41.2
　high-risk sexual behavior V69.2

Problem—*continued*
　influencing health status NEC V49.8
　internal organ NEC V47.9
　　deficiency V47.0
　　mechanical or motor V47.1
　interpersonal NEC V62.81
　jealousy, child 313.3
　learning V40.0
　legal V62.5
　life circumstance NEC V62.89
　lifestyle V69.9
　　specified NEC V69.8
　limb V49.9
　　deficiency V49.0
　　disfigurement V49.4
　　mechanical V49.1
　　motor V49.2
　　movement, involving
　　　musculoskeletal system V49.1
　　　nervous system V49.2
　　sensory V49.3
　　specified condition NEC V49.5
　litigation V62.5
　living alone V60.3
　loneliness NEC V62.89
　marital V61.10
　　involving
　　　divorce V61.0
　　　estrangement V61.0
　　　psychosexual disorder 302.9
　　　sexual function V41.7
　mastication V41.6
　medical care, within family V61.49
　mental V40.9
　　specified NEC V40.2
　mental hygiene, adult V40.9
　multiparity V61.5
　nail biting, child 307.9
　neck V48.9
　　deficiency V48.1
　　disfigurement V48.7
　　mechanical V48.3
　　motor V48.3
　　movement V48.3
　　sensory V48.5
　　specified condition NEC V48.8
　neurological NEC 781.9
　none (feared complaint unfounded) V65.5
　occupational V62.2
　parent-child V61.20
　partner V61.10
　personal NEC V62.89
　　interpersonal conflict NEC V62.81
　personality (see also Disorder, personality) 301.9
　phase of life V62.89
　placenta, affecting management of pregnancy 656.9
　　specified type NEC 656.8
　poverty V60.2
　presence of sick or handicapped person in family or household V61.49
　psychiatric 300.9
　psychosocial V62.9
　　specified type NEC V62.89
　relational NEC V62.81
　relationship, childhood 313.3
　religious or spiritual belief
　　other than medical care V62.89
　　regarding medical care V62.6

Problem—*continued*
  self-damaging behavior V69.8
  sexual
    behavior, high-risk V69.2
    function NEC V41.7
  sibling, relational V61.8
  sight V41.0
  sleep disorder, child 307.40
  smell V41.5
  speech V40.1
  spite reaction, child (*see also* Disturbance,
    conduct) 312.0
  spoiled child reaction (*see also* Disturbance,
    conduct) 312.1
  swallowing V41.6
  tantrum, child (*see also* Disturbance, conduct)
    312.1
  taste V41.5
  thumb sucking, child 307.9
  tic, child 307.21
  trunk V48.9
    deficiency V48.1
    disfigurement V48.7
    mechanical V48.3
    motor V48.3
    movement V48.3
    sensory V48.5
    specified condition NEC V48.8
  unemployment V62.0
  urinary NEC V47.4
  voice production V41.4
Procedure (surgical) not done NEC V64.3
  because of
    contraindication V64.1
    patient's decision V64.2
    for reasons of conscience or religion V62.6
    specified reason NEC V64.3
Procidentia
  anus (sphincter) 569.1
  rectum (sphincter) 569.1
  stomach 537.89
  uteri 618.1
Proctalgia 569.42
  fugax 564.6
  spasmodic 564.6
    psychogenic 307.89
Proctitis 569.49
  amebic 006.8
  chlamydial 099.52
  gonococcal 098.7
  granulomatous 555.1
  idiopathic 556.2
    with ulcerative sigmoiditis 556.3
  tuberculous (*see also* Tuberculosis) 014.8
  ulcerative (chronic) (nonspecific) 556.2
    with ulcerative sigmoiditis 556.3
Proctocele
  female (without uterine prolapse) 618.0
    with uterine prolapse 618.4
      complete 618.3
      incomplete 618.2
  male 569.49
Proctocolitis, idiopathic 556.2
  with ulcerative sigmoiditis 556.3
Proctoptosis 569.1
Proctosigmoiditis 569.89
  ulcerative (chronic) 556.3
Proctospasm 564.6
  psychogenic 306.4
Prodromal-AIDS —*see* Human
  immunodeficiency virus (disease) (illness)
  (infection)

Profichet's disease or syndrome 729.9
Progeria (adultorum) (syndrome) 259.8
Prognathism (mandibular) (maxillary) 524.00
Progonoma (melanotic) (M9363/0)—*see*
  Neoplasm, by site, benign
Progressive —*see* condition
Prolapse, prolapsed
  anus, anal (canal) (sphincter) 569.1
  arm or hand, complicating delivery 652.7
    causing obstructed labor 660.0
      affecting fetus or newborn 763.1
    fetus or newborn 763.1
  bladder (acquired) (mucosa) (sphincter)
    congenital (female) (male) 753.8
    female 618.0
    male 596.8
  breast implant (prosthetic) 996.54
  cecostomy 569.69
  cecum 569.89
  cervix, cervical (stump) (hypertrophied) 618.1
    anterior lip, obstructing labor 660.2
      affecting fetus or newborn 763.1
    congenital 752.49
    postpartal (old) 618.1
  ciliary body 871.1
  colon (pedunculated) 569.89
  colostomy 569.69
  conjunctiva 372.73
  cord—*see* Prolapse, umbilical cord
  disc (intervertebral)—*see* Displacement,
    intervertebral disc
  duodenum 537.89
  eye implant (orbital) 996.59
    lens (ocular) 996.53
  fallopian tube 620.4
  fetal extremity, complicating delivery 652.8
    causing obstructed labor 660.0
    fetus or newborn 763.1
  funis—*see* Prolapse, umbilical cord
  gastric (mucosa) 537.89
  genital, female 618.9
    specified NEC 618.8
  globe 360 81
  ileostomy bud 569.69
  intervertebral disc—*see* Displacement,
    intervertebral disc
  intestine (small) 569.89
  iris 364.8
    traumatic 871.1
  kidney (*see also* Disease, renal) 593.0
    congenital 753.3
  laryngeal muscles or ventricle 478.79
  leg, complicating delivery 652.8
    causing obstructed labor 660.0
    fetus or newborn 763.1
  liver 573.8
  meatus urinarius 599.5
  mitral valve 424.0
  ocular lens implant 996.53
  organ or site, congenital NEC—*see*
    Malposition, congenital
  ovary 620.4
  pelvic (floor), female 618.8
  perineum, female 618.8
  pregnant uterus 654.4
  rectum (mucosa) (sphincter) 569.1
    due to Trichuris trichiura 127.3
  spleen 289.59
  stomach 537.89

Prolapse, prolapsed—*continued*
umbilical cord
affecting fetus or newborn 762.4
complicating delivery 663.0
ureter 593.89
with obstruction 593.4
ureterovesical orifice 593.89
urethra (acquired) (infected) (mucosa) 599.5
congenital 753.8
uterovaginal 618.4
complete 618.3
incomplete 618.2
specified NEC 618.8
uterus (first degree) (second degree) (third
degree) (complete) (without vaginal wall
prolapse) 618.1
with mention of vaginal wall prolapse—*see*
Prolapse, uterovaginal
congenital 752.3
in pregnancy or childbirth 654.4
affecting fetus or newborn 763.1
causing obstructed labor 660.2
affecting fetus or newborn 763.1
postpartal (old) 618.1
uveal 871.1
vagina (anterior) (posterior) (vault) (wall)
(without uterine prolapse) 618.0
with uterine prolapse 618.4
complete 618.3
incomplete 618.2
posthysterectomy 618.5
vitreous (humor) 379.26
traumatic 871.1
womb—*see* Prolapse, uterus
Prolapsus, female 618.9
Proliferative —*see* condition
Prolinemia 270.8
Prolinuria 270.8
Prolonged, prolongation
bleeding time (*see also* Defect, coagulation)
790.92
"idiopathic" (in von Willebrand's disease)
286.4
coagulation time (*see also* Defect, coagulation)
790.92
gestation syndrome 766.2
labor 662.1
first stage 662.0
second stage 662.2
affecting fetus or newborn 763.8
PR interval 426.11
prothrombin time (*see also* Defect, coagulation)
790.92
rupture of membranes (24 hours or more prior
to onset of labor) 658.2
uterine contractions in labor 661.4
affecting fetus or newborn 763.7
Prominauris 744.29
Prominence
auricle (ear) (congenital) 744.29
acquired 380.32
ischial spine or sacral promontory
with disproportion (fetopelvic) 653.3
affecting fetus or newborn 763.1
causing obstructed labor 660.1
affecting fetus or newborn 763.1
nose (congenital) 748.1
acquired 738.0

Pronation
ankle 736.79
foot 736.79
congenital 755.67
Prophylactic
administration of
antibiotics V07.39
antitoxin, any V07.2
antivenin V07.2
chemotherapeutic agent NEC V07.39
fluoride V07.31
diphtheria antitoxin V07.2
gamma globulin V07.2
immune sera (gamma globulin) V07.2
RhoGAM V07.2
tetanus antitoxin V07.2
chemotherapy NEC V07.39
fluoride V07.31
immunotherapy V07.2
measure V07.9
specified type NEC V07.8
postmenopausal hormone replacement V07.4
sterilization V25.2
Proptosis (ocular) (*see also* Exophthalmos)
376.30
thyroid 242.0
Propulsion
eyeball 360.81
Prosecution, anxiety concerning V62.5
Prostate, prostatic —*see* condition
Prostatism 600
Prostatitis (congestive) (suppurative) 601.9
acute 601.0
cavitary 601.8
chlamydial 099.54
chronic 601.1
diverticular 601.8
due to Trichomonas (vaginalis) 131.03
fibrous 600
gonococcal (acute) 098.12
chronic or duration of 2 months or over 098.32
granulomatous 601.8
hypertrophic 600
specified type NEC 601.8
subacute 601.1
trichomonal 131.03
tuberculous (*see also* Tuberculosis) 016.5
[601.4]
Prostatocystitis 601.3
Prostatorrhea 602.8
Prostatoseminovesiculitis, trichomonal 131.03
Prostration 780.7
heat 992.5
anhydrotic 992.3
due to
salt (and water) depletion 992.4
water depletion 992.3
nervous 300.5
newborn 779.8
senile 797
Protanomaly 368.51
Protanopia (anomalous trichromat) (complete)
(incomplete) 368.51
Protein
deficiency 260
malnutrition 260
sickness (prophylactic) (therapeutic) 999.5
Proteinemia 790.99

Proteinosis
  alveolar, lung or pulmonary 516.0
    lipid 272.8
Proteinosis
  lipoid (of Urbach) 272.8
Proteinuria (*see also* Albuminuria) 791.0
  Bence-Jones NEC 791.0
  gestational 646.2
    with hypertension—*see* Toxemia, of
      pregnancy
  orthostatic 593.6
  postural 593.6
Proteolysis, pathologic 286.6
Protocoproporphyria 277.1
Protoporphyria (erythrohepatic) (erythropoietic)
    277.1
Protrusio acetabuli 718.65
Protrusion
  acetabulum (into pelvis) 718.65
  device, implant, or graft—*see* Complications,
    mechanical
  ear, congenital 744.29
  intervertebral disc—*see* Displacement,
    intervertebral disc
  nucleus pulposus—*see* Displacement,
    intervertebral disc
Proud flesh 701.5
Prune belly (syndrome) 756.7
Prurigo (ferox) (gravis) (Hebra's) (hebrae)
    (mitis) (simplex) 698.2
  agria 698.3
  asthma syndrome 691.8
  Besnier's (atopic dermatitis) (infantile eczema)
    691.8
  eczematodes allergicum 691.8
  estivalis (Hutchinson's) 692.72
  Hutchinson's 692.72
  nodularis 698.3
  psychogenic 306.3
Pruritus, pruritic 698.9
  ani 698.0
    psychogenic 306.3
  conditions NEC 698.9
    psychogenic 306.3
  due to Onchocerca volvulus 125.3
  ear 698.9
  essential 698.9
  genital organ(s) 698.1
    psychogenic 306.3
  gravidarum 646.8
  hiemalis 698.8
  neurogenic (any site) 306.3
  perianal 698.0
  psychogenic (any site) 306.3
  scrotum 698.1
    psychogenic 306.3
  senile, senilis 698.8
  Trichomonas 131.9
  vulva, vulvae 698.1
    psychogenic 306.3
Psammocarcinoma (M8140/3)—*see* Neoplasm,
    by site, malignant
Pseudarthrosis, pseudoarthrosis (bone) 733.82
  joint following fusion V45.4
Pseudoacanthosis
  nigricans 701.8
Pseudoaneurysm —*see* Aneurysm
Pseudoangina (pectoris)—*see* Angina
Pseudoangioma 452
Pseudo-Argyll-Robertson pupil 379.45
Pseudoarteriosus 747.89

Pseudoarthrosis —*see* Pseudarthrosis
Pseudoataxia 799.8
Pseudobursa 727.89
Pseudocholera 025
Pseudochromidrosis 705.89
Pseudocirrhosis, liver, pericardial 423.2
Pseudocoarctation 747.21
Pseudocowpox 051.1
Pseudocoxalgia 732.1
Pseudocroup 478.75
Pseudocyesis 300.11
Pseudocyst
  lung 518.89
  pancreas 577.2
  retina 361.19
Pseudodementia 300.16
Pseudoelephantiasis neuroarthritica 757.0
Pseudoemphysema 518.89
Pseudoencephalitis
  superior (acute) hemorrhagic 265.1
Pseudoerosion cervix, congenital 752.49
Pseudoexfoliation, lens capsule 366.11
Pseudofracture (idiopathic) (multiple)
    (spontaneous) (symmetrical) 268.2
Pseudoglanders 025
Pseudoglioma 360.44
Pseudogout —*see* Chondrocalcinosis
Pseudohallucination 780.1
Pseudohemianesthesia 782.0
Pseudohemophilia (Bernuth's) (hereditary) (type
    B) 286.4
  type A 287.8
  vascular 287.8
Pseudohermaphroditism 752.7
  with chromosomal anomaly—*see* Anomaly,
    chromosomal
    adrenal 255.2
  female (without adrenocortical disorder) 752.7
    with adrenocortical disorder 255.2
      adrenal 255.2
  male (without gonadal disorder) 752.7
    with
      adrenocortical disorder 255.2
      cleft scrotum 752.7
      feminizing testis 257.8
      gonadal disorder 257.9
        adrenal 255.2
Pseudohole, macula 362.54
Pseudo-Hurler's disease (mucolipidosis III)
    272.7
Pseudohydrocephalus 348.2
Pseudohypertrophic muscular dystrophy
    (Erb's) 359.1
Pseudohypertrophy, muscle 359.1
Pseudohypoparathyroidism 275.4
Pseudoinfluenza 487.1
Pseudoinsomnia 307.49
Pseudoleukemia 288.8
  infantile 285.8
Pseudomembranous —*see* condition
Pseudomeningocele (cerebral) (infective)
    (surgical) 349.2
  spinal 349.2
Pseudomenstruation 626.8
Pseudomucinous
  cyst (ovary) (M8470/0) 220
  peritoneum 568.89
Pseudomyeloma 273.1
Pseudomyxoma peritonei (M8480/6) 197.6
Pseudoneuritis optic (nerve) 377.24
  papilla 377.24
    congenital 743.57

Pseudoneuroma —*see* Injury, nerve, by site
Pseudo-obstruction
  intestine 564.8
Pseudopapilledema 377.24
Pseudoparalysis
  arm or leg 781.4
  atonic, congenital 358.8
Pseudopelade 704.09
Pseudophakia V43.1
Pseudopolycythemia 289.0
Pseudopolyposis, colon 556.4
Pseudoporencephaly 348.0
Pseudopseudohypoparathyroidism 275.4
Pseudopsychosis 300.16
Pseudopterygium 372.52
Pseudoptosis (eyelid) 374.34
Pseudorabies 078.89
Pseudoretinitis, pigmentosa 362.65
Pseudorickets 588.0
  senile (Pozzi's) 731.0
Pseudorubella 057.8
Pseudoscarlatina 057.8
Pseudosclerema 778.1
Pseudosclerosis (brain)
  Jakob's 046.1
  of Westphal (-Strümpell) (hepatolenticular
    degeneration) 275.1
  spastic 046.1
    with dementia 046.1 *[294.1]*
Pseudotabes 799.8
  diabetic 250.6 *[337.1]*
Pseudotetanus (*see also* Convulsions) 780.3
Pseudotetany 781.7
  hysterical 300.11
Pseudothalassemia 285.0
Pseudotrichinosis 710.3
Pseudotruncus arteriosus 747.29
Pseudotuberculosis, pasteurella (infection)
  027.2
Pseudotumor
  cerebri 348.2
  orbit (inflammatory) 376.11
Pseudo-Turner's syndrome 759.89
Pseudoxanthoma elasticum 757.39
Psilosis (sprue) (tropical) 579.1
  Monilia 112.89
  nontropical 579.0
  not sprue 704.00
Psittacosis 073.9
Psoitis 728.89
Psora NEC 696.1
Psoriasis 696.1
  any type, except arthropathic 696.1
  arthritic, arthropathic 696.0
  buccal 528.6
  flexural 696.1
  follicularis 696.1
  guttate 696.1
  inverse 696.1
  mouth 528.6
  nummularis 696.1
  psychogenic 316 *[696.1]*
  punctata 696.1
  pustular 696.1
  rupioides 696.1
  vulgaris 696.1
Psorospermiasis 136.4
Psorospermosis 136.4
  follicularis (vegetans) 757.39
Psychalgia 307.80

Psychasthenia 300.89
  compulsive 300.3
  mixed compulsive states 300.3
  obsession 300.3
Psychiatric disorder or problem NEC 300.9
Psychogenic —*see also* condition
  factors associated with physical conditions 316
Psychoneurosis, psychoneurotic (*see also*
    Neurosis) 300.9
  anxiety (state) 300.00
  climacteric 627.2
  compensation 300.16
  compulsion 300.3
  conversion hysteria 300.11
  depersonalization 300.6
  depressive type 300.4
  dissociative hysteria 300.15
  hypochondriacal 300.7
  hysteria 300.10
    conversion type 300.11
    dissociative type 300.15
  mixed NEC 300.89
  neurasthenic 300.5
  obsessional 300.3
  obsessive-compulsive 300.3
  occupational 300.89
  personality NEC 301.89
  phobia 300.20
  senile NEC 300.89
Psychopathic —*see also* condition
  constitution, posttraumatic 310.2
    with psychosis 293.9
  personality 301.9
    amoral trends 301.7
    antisocial trends 301.7
    asocial trends 301.7
    mixed types 301.7
  state 301.9
Psychopathy, sexual (*see also* Deviation, sexual)
  302.9
Psychophysiologic, psychophysiological
    condition—*see* Reaction, psychophysiologic
Psychose passionelle 297.8
Psychosexual identity disorder 302.6
  adult-life 302.85
  childhood 302.6
Psychosis 298.9
  acute hysterical 298.1
  affecting management of pregnancy, childbirth,
    or puerperium 648.4
  affective NEC 296.90

Note—Use the following fifth-digit
subclassification with categories 296.0-296.6:

0 *unspecified*
1 *mild*
2 *moderate*
3 *severe, without mention of psychotic
   behavior*
4 *severe, specified as with psychotic behavior*
5 *in partial or unspecified remission*
6 *in full remission*

  involutional 296.2
    recurrent episode 296.3
    single episode 296.2
  manic-depressive 296.80
    circular (alternating) 296.7
      currently depressed 296.5
      currently manic 296.4
    depressed type 296.2

Psychosis—*continued*
  atypical 296.82
    recurrent episode 296.3
    single episode 296.2
  manic 296.0
    atypical 296.81
    recurrent episode 296.1
    single episode 296.0
  mixed type NEC 296.89
  specified type NEC 296.89
  senile 290.21
  specified type NEC 296.99
alcoholic 291.9
  with
    anxiety 291.89
    delirium tremens 291.0
    delusions 291.5
    dementia 291.2
    hallucinosis 291.3
    jealousy 291.5
    mood disturbance 291.89
    paranoia 291.5
    persisting amnesia 291.1
    sexual dysfunction 291.89
    sleep disturbance 291.89
  amnestic confabulatory 291.1
  delirium tremens 291.0
  hallucinosis 291.3
  Korsakoff's, Korsakov's, Korsakow's 291.1
  paranoid type 291.5
  pathological intoxication 291.4
  polyneuritic 291.1
  specified type NEC 291.89
alternating (*see also* Psychosis,
  manic-depressive, circular) 296.7
anergastic (*see also* Psychosis, organic) 294.9
arteriosclerotic 290.40
  with
    acute confusional state 290.41
    delirium 290.41
    delusional features 290.42
    depressive features 290.43
  depressed type 290.43
  paranoid type 290.42
  simple type 290.40
  uncomplicated 290.40
atypical 298.9
  depressive 296.82
  manic 296.81
borderline (schizophrenia) (*see also*
  Schizophrenia) 295.5
  of childhood (*see also* Psychosis, childhood)
    299.8
  prepubertal 299.8
brief reactive 298.8
childhood, with origin specific to 299.9

> Note—Use the following fifth-digit
> subclassification with category 299:
>
> 0 *current or active state*
> 1 *residual state*

  atypical 299.8
  specified type NEC 299.8
circular (*see also* Psychosis, manic-depressive,
  circular) 296.7
climacteric (*see also* Psychosis, involutional)
  298.8
confusional 298.9
  acute 293.0
  reactive 298.2

Psychosis—*continued*
  subacute 293.1
  depressive (*see also* Psychosis, affective) 296.2
    atypical 296.82
    involutional 296.2
      recurrent episode 296.3
      single episode 296.2
    psychogenic 298.0
    reactive (emotional stress) (psychological
      trauma) 298.0
    recurrent episode 296.3
      with hypomania (bipolar II) 296.89
    single episode 296.2
  disintegrative (childhood) (*see also* Psychosis,
    childhood) 299.1
  drug 292.9
    with
      affective syndrome 292.84
      amnestic syndrome 292.83
      anxiety 292.89
      delirium 292.81
        withdrawal 292.0
      delusional syndrome 292.11
      dementia 292.82
      depressive state 292.84
      hallucinosis 292.12
      mood disturbance 292.84
      organic personality syndrome NEC 292.89
      sexual dysfunction 292.89
      sleep disturbance 292.89
      withdrawal syndrome (and delirium) 292.0
    affective syndrome 292.84
    delusional state 292.11
    hallucinatory state 292.12
    hallucinosis 292.12
    paranoid state 292.11
    specified type NEC 292.89
    withdrawal syndrome (and delirium) 292.0
  due to or associated with physical condition (*see*
    also Psychosis, organic) 294.9
  epileptic NEC 294.8
  excitation (psychogenic) (reactive) 298.1
  exhaustive (*see also* Reaction, stress, acute)
    308.9
  hypomanic (*see also* Psychosis, affective) 296.0
    recurrent episode 296.1
    single episode 296.0
  hysterical 298.8
    acute 298.1
  incipient 298.8
    schizophrenic (*see also* Schizophrenia) 295.5
  induced 297.3
  infantile (*see also* Psychosis, childhood) 299.0
  infective 293.9
    acute 293.0
    subacute 293.1
  in pregnancy, childbirth, or puerperium 648.4
  interactional (childhood) (*see also* Psychosis,
    childhood) 299.1
  involutional 298.8
    depressive (*see also* Psychosis, affective)
      296.2
      recurrent episode 296.3
      single episode 296.2
    melancholic 296.2
      recurrent episode 296.3
      single episode 296.2
    paranoid state 297.2
    paraphrenia 297.2

Psychosis—*continued*
  Korsakoff's, Korakov's, Korsakow's
    (nonalcoholic) 294.0
  alcoholic 291.1
  mania (phase) (*see also* Psychosis, affective)
    296.0
    recurrent episode 296.1
    single episode 296.0
  manic (*see also* Psychosis, affective) 296.0
    atypical 296.81
    recurrent episode 296.1
    single episode 296.0
  manic-depressive 296.80
    circular 296.7
      currently
        depressed 296.5
        manic 296.4
        mixed 296.6
    depressive 296.2
      recurrent episode 296.3
        with hypomania (bipolar II) 296.89
      single episode 296.2
    hypomanic 296.0
      recurrent episode 296.1
      single episode 296.0
    manic 296.0
      atypical 296.81
      recurrent episode 296.1
      single episode 296.0
    mixed NEC 296.89
    perplexed 296.89
    stuporous 296.89
  menopausal (*see also* Psychosis, involutional)
    298.8
  mixed schizophrenic and affective (*see also*
    Schizophrenia) 295.7
  multi-infarct (cerebrovascular) (*see also*
    Psychosis, arteriosclerotic) 290.40
  organic NEC 294.9
    due to or associated with
      addiction
        alcohol (*see also* Psychosis, alcoholic)
          291.9
        drug (*see also* Psychosis, drug) 292.9
      alcohol intoxication, acute (*see also*
        Psychosis, alcoholic) 291.9
      alcoholism (*see also* Psychosis, alcoholic)
        291.9
      arteriosclerosis (cerebral) (*see also*
        Psychosis, arteriosclerotic) 290.40
      cerebrovascular disease
        acute (psychosis) 293.0
        arteriosclerotic (*see also* Psychosis,
          arteriosclerotic) 290.40
      childbirth—*see* Psychosis, puerperal
      conditions classified elsewhere 294.1
      dependence
        alcohol (*see also* Psychosis, alcoholic)
          291.9
        drug 292.9
      disease
        alcoholic liver (*see also* Psychosis,
          alcoholic) 291.9
        brain
          arteriosclerotic (*see also* Psychosis,
            arteriosclerotic) 290.40
        cerebrovascular
          acute (psychosis) 293.0
          arteriosclerotic (*see also* Psychosis,
            arteriosclerotic) 290.40

Psychosis—*continued*
        endocrine or metabolic 293.9
          acute (psychosis) 293.0
          subacute (psychosis) 293.1
        Jakob-Creutzfeldt 046.1 *[294.1]*
        liver, alcoholic (*see also* Psychosis,
          alcoholic) 291.9
      disorder
        cerebrovascular
          acute (psychosis) 293.0
        endocrine or metabolic 293.9
          acute (psychosis) 293.0
          subacute (psychosis) 293.1
      epilepsy 294.1
        transient (acute) 293.0
      Huntington's chorea 294.1
      infection
        brain 293.9
          acute (psychosis) 293.0
          chronic 294.8
          subacute (psychosis) 293.1
        intracranial NEC 293.9
          acute (psychosis) 293.0
          chronic 294.8
          subacute (psychosis) 293.1
      intoxication
        alcoholic (acute) (*see also* Psychosis,
          alcoholic) 291.9
          pathological 291.4
        drug (*see also* Psychosis, drug) 292.9
      ischemia
        cerebrovascular (generalized) (*see also*
          Psychosis, arteriosclerotic) 290.40
      Jakob-Creutzfeldt disease or syndrome
        046.1 *[294.1]*
      multiple sclerosis 294.1
      physical condition NEC 294.9
      presenility 290.10
      puerperium—*see* Psychosis, puerperal
      sclerosis, multiple 294.1
      senility 290.20
      status epilepticus 294.1
      trauma
        brain (birth) (from electrical current)
          (surgical) 293.9
          acute (psychosis) 293.0
          chronic 294.8
          subacute (psychosis) 293.1
      unspecified physical condition 294.9
    infective 293.9
      acute (psychosis) 293.0
      subacute 293.1
    posttraumatic 293.9
      acute 293.0
      subacute 293.1
    specified type NEC 294.8
    transient 293.9
      with
        anxiety 293.84
        delusions 293.81
        depression 293.83
        hallucinations 293.82
      depressive type 293.83
      hallucinatory type 293.82
      paranoid type 293.81
      specified type NEC 293.89
  paranoic 297.1

Psychosis—*continued*
  paranoid (chronic) 297.9
    alcoholic 291.5
    chronic 297.1
    climacteric 297.2
    involutional 297.2
    menopausal 297.2
    protracted reactive 298.4
    psychogenic 298.4
      acute 298.3
    schizophrenic (*see also* Schizophrenia) 295.3
    senile 290.20
  paroxysmal 298.9
    senile 290.20
  polyneuritic, alcoholic 291.1
  postoperative 293.9
  postpartum—*see* Psychosis, puerperal
  prepsychotic (*see also* Schizophrenia) 295.5
  presbyophrenic (type) 290.8
  presenile (*see also* Dementia, presenile) 290.10
  prison 300.16
  psychogenic 298.8
    depressive 298.0
    paranoid 298.4
      acute 298.3
  puerperal
    specified type—*see* categories 295-298
    unspecified type 293.89
      acute 293.0
      chronic 293.89
      subacute 293.1
  reactive (emotional stress) (psychological
      trauma) 298.8
    brief 298.8
    confusion 298.2
    depressive 298.0
    excitation 298.1
  schizo-affective (depressed) (excited) (*see also*
      Schizophrenia) 295.7
  schizophrenia, schizophrenic (*see also*
      Schizophrenia) 295.9
    borderline type 295.5
      of childhood (*see also* Psychosis, childhood)
          299.8
    catatonic (excited) (withdrawn) 295.2
    childhood type (*see also* Psychosis,
        childhood) 299.9
    hebephrenic 295.1
    incipient 295.5
    latent 295.5
    paranoid 295.3
    prepsychotic 295.5
    prodromal 295.5
    pseudoneurotic 295.5
    pseudopsychopathic 295.5
    schizophreniform 295.4
    simple 295.0
  schizophreniform 295.4
  senile NEC 290.20
    with
      delusional features 290.20
      depressive features 290.21
    depressed type 290.21
    paranoid type 290.20
    simple deterioration 290.20
    specified type—*see* categories 295-298
  shared 297.3
  situational (reactive) 298.8
  symbiotic (childhood) (*see also* Psychosis,
      childhood) 299.1
  toxic (acute) 293.9

Psychotic (*see also* condition) 298.9
  episode 298.9
    due to or associated with physical conditions
        (*see also* Psychosis, organic) 294.9
Pterygium (eye) 372.40
  central 372.43
  colli 744.5
  double 372.44
  peripheral (stationary) 372.41
    progressive 372.42
  recurrent 372.45
Ptilosis 374.55
Ptomaine (poisoning) (*see also* Poisoning, food)
    005.9
Ptosis (adiposa) 374.30
  breast 611.8
  cecum 569.89
  colon 569.89
  congenital (eyelid) 743.61
    specified site NEC—*see* Anomaly, specified
        type NEC
  epicanthus syndrome 270.2
  eyelid 374.30
    congenital 743.61
    mechanical 374.33
    myogenic 374.32
    paralytic 374.31
  gastric 537.5
  intestine 569.89
  kidney (*see also* Disease, renal) 593.0
    congenital 753.3
  liver 573.8
  renal (*see also* Disease, renal) 593.0
    congenital 753.3
  splanchnic 569.89
  spleen 289.59
  stomach 537.5
  viscera 569.89
Ptyalism 527.7
  hysterical 300.11
  periodic 527.2
  pregnancy 646.8
  psychogenic 306.4
Ptyalolithiasis 527.5
Pubarche, precocious 259.1
Pubertas praecox 259.1
Puberty V21.1
  abnormal 259.9
  bleeding 626.3
  delayed 259.0
  precocious (constitutional) (cryptogenic)
      (idiopathic) NEC 259.1
    due to
      adrenal
        cortical hyperfunction 255.2
        hyperplasia 255.2
      cortical hyperfunction 255.2
      ovarian hyperfunction 256.1
        estrogen 256.0
      pineal tumor 259.8
      testicular hyperfunction 257.0
    premature 259.1
      due to
        adrenal cortical hyperfunction 255.2
        pineal tumor 259.8
        pituitary (anterior) hyperfunction 253.1
Puckering, macula 362.56
Pudenda, pudendum —*see* condition
Puente's disease (simple glandular cheilitis)
    528.5

Puerperal
abscess
  areola 675.1
  Bartholin's gland 646.6
  breast 675.1
  cervix (uteri) 670
  fallopian tube 670
  genital organ 670
  kidney 646.6
  mammary 675.1
  mesosalpinx 670
  nabothian 646.6
  nipple 675.0
  ovary, ovarian 670
  oviduct 670
  parametric 670
  para-uterine 670
  pelvic 670
  perimetric 670
  periuterine 670
  retro-uterine 670
  subareolar 675.1
  suprapelvic 670
  tubal (ruptured) 670
  tubo-ovarian 670
  urinary tract NEC 646.6
  uterine, uterus 670
  vagina (wall) 646.6
  vaginorectal 646.6
  vulvovaginal gland 646.6
accident 674.9
adnexitis 670
afibrinogenemia, or other coagulation defect
  666.3
albuminuria (acute) (subacute) 646.2
  pre-eclamptic 642.4
anemia (conditions classifiable to 280-285)
  648.2
anuria 669.3
apoplexy 674.0
asymptomatic bacteriuria 646.5
atrophy, breast 676.3
bacteremia 670
blood dyscrasia 666.3
caked breast 676.2
cardiomyopathy 674.8
cellulitis—*see* Puerperal, abscess
cerebrovascular disorder (conditions classifiable
  to 430-434, 436-437) 674.0
cervicitis (conditions classifiable to 616.0) 646.6
coagulopathy (any) 666.3
complications 674.9
  specified type NEC 674.8
convulsions (eclamptic) (uremic) 642.6
  with pre-existing hypertension 642.7
cracked nipple 676.1
cystitis 646.6
cystopyelitis 646.6
deciduitis (acute) 670
delirium NEC 293.9
diabetes (mellitus) (conditions classifiable to
  250) 648.0
disease 674.9
  breast NEC 676.3
  cerebrovascular (acute) 674.0
  nonobstetric NEC (*see also* Pregnancy,
    complicated, current disease or condition)
    648.9
  pelvis inflammatory 670
  renal NEC 646.2
  tubo-ovarian 670

Puerperal—*continued*
  Valsuani's (progressive pernicious anemia)
    648.2
disorder
  lactation 676.9
    specified type NEC 676.8
  nonobstetric NEC (*see also* Pregnancy,
    complicated, current disease or condition)
    648.9
disruption
  cesarean wound 674.1
  episiotomy wound 674.2
  perineal laceration wound 674.2
drug dependence (conditions classifiable to 304)
  648.3
eclampsia 642.6
  with pre-existing hypertension 642.7
embolism (pulmonary) 673.2
  air 673.0
  amniotic fluid 673.1
  blood-clot 673.2
  brain or cerebral 674.0
  cardiac 674.8
  fat 673.8
  intracranial sinus (venous) 671.5
  pyemic 673.3
  septic 673.3
  spinal cord 671.5
endometritis (conditions classifiable to
  615.0-615.9) 670
endophlebitis—*see* Puerperal, phlebitis
endotrachelitis 646.6
engorgement, breasts 676.2
erysipelas 670
failure
  lactation 676.4
  renal, acute 669.3
fever (meaning sepsis) 670
  meaning pyrexia (of unknown origin) 672
fissure, nipple 676.1
fistula
  breast 675.1
  mammary gland 675.1
  nipple 675.0
galactophoritis 675.2
galactorrhea 676.6
gangrene
  gas 670
  uterus 670
gonorrhea (conditions classifiable to 098) 647.1
hematoma, subdural 674.0
hematosalpinx, infectional 670
hemiplegia, cerebral 674.0
hemorrhage 666.1
  brain 674.0
  bulbar 674.0
  cerebellar 674.0
  cerebral 674.0
  cortical 674.0
  delayed (after 24 hours) (uterine) 666.2
  extradural 674.0
  internal capsule 674.0
  intracranial 674.0
  intrapontine 674.0
  meningeal 674.0
  pontine 674.0
  subarachnoid 674.0
  subcortical 674.0
  subdural 674.0
  uterine, delayed 666.2
  ventricular 674.0

Puerperal—*continued*
  hemorrhoids 671.8
  hepatorenal syndrome 674.8
  hypertrophy
    breast 676.3
    mammary gland 676.3
  induration breast (fibrous) 676.3
  infarction
    lung—*see* Puerperal, embolism
    pulmonary—*see* Puerperal, embolism
  infection
    Bartholin's gland 646.6
    breast 675.2
      with nipple 675.9
        specified type NEC 675.8
    cervix 646.6
    endocervix 646.6
    fallopian tube 670
    generalized 670
    genital tract (major) 670
      minor or localized 646.6
    kidney (bacillus coli) 646.6
    mammary gland 675.2
      with nipple 675.9
        specified type NEC 675.8
    nipple 675.0
      with breast 675.9
        specified type NEC 675.8
    ovary 670
    pelvic 670
    peritoneum 670
    renal 646.6
    tubo-ovarian 670
    urinary (tract) NEC 646.6
      asymptomatic 646.5
    uterus, uterine 670
    vagina 646.6
  inflammation—*see also* Puerperal, infection
    areola 675.1
    Bartholin's gland 646.6
    breast 675.2
    broad ligament 670
    cervix (uteri) 646.6
    fallopian tube 670
    genital organs 670
      localized 646.6
    mammary gland 675.2
    nipple 675.0
    ovary 670
    oviduct 670
    pelvis 670
    periuterine 670
    tubal 670
    vagina 646.6
    vein—*see* Puerperal, phlebitis
  inversion, nipple 676.3
  ischemia, cerebral 674.0
  lymphangitis 670
    breast 675.2
  malaria (conditions classifiable to 084) 647.4
  malnutrition 648.9
  mammillitis 675.0
  mammitis 675.2
  mania 296.0
    recurrent episode 296.1
    single episode 296.0
  mastitis 675.2
    purulent 675.1
    retromammary 675.1
    submammary 675.1

Puerperal—*continued*
  melancholia 296.2
    recurrent episode 296.3
    single episode 296.2
  mental disorder (conditions classifiable to
      290-303, 305-316, 317-319) 648.4
  metritis (septic) (suppurative) 670
  metroperitonitis 670
  metrorrhagia 666.2
  metrosalpingitis 670
  metrovaginitis 670
  milk leg 671.4
  monoplegia, cerebral 674.0
  necrosis
    kidney, tubular 669.3
    liver (acute) (subacute) (conditions
        classifiable to 570) 674.8
    ovary 670
    renal cortex 669.3
  nephritis or nephrosis (conditions classifiable to
      580-589) 646.2
    with hypertension 642.1
  nutritional deficiency (conditions classifiable to
      260-269) 648.9
  occlusion, precerebral artery 674.0
  oliguria 669.3
  oophoritis 670
  ovaritis 670
  paralysis
    bladder (sphincter) 665.5
    cerebral 674.0
  paralytic stroke 674.0
  parametritis 670
  paravaginitis 646.6
  pelviperitonitis 670
  perimetritis 670
  perimetrosalpingitis 670
  perinephritis 646.6
  perioophoritis 670
  periphlebitis—*see* Puerperal, phlebitis
  perisalpingitis 670
  peritoneal infection 670
  peritonitis (pelvic) 670
  perivaginitis 646.6
  phlebitis 671.9
    deep 671.4
    intracranial sinus (venous) 671.5
    pelvic 671.4
    specified site NEC 671.5
    superficial 671.2
  phlegmasia alba dolens 671.4
  placental polyp 674.4
  pneumonia, embolic—*see* Puerperal, embolism
  prediabetes 648.8
  pre-eclampsia (mild) 642.4
    with pre-existing hypertension 642.7
    severe 642.5
  psychosis, unspecified (*see also* Psychosis,
      puerperal) 293.89
  pyelitis 646.6
  pyelocystitis 646.6
  pyelohydronephrosis 646.6
  pyelonephritis 646.6
  pyelonephrosis 646.6
  pyemia 670
  pyocystitis 646.6
  pyohemia 670
  pyometra 670
  pyonephritis 646.6
  pyonephrosis 646.6

Puerperal—*continued*
  pyo-oophoritis 670
  pyosalpingitis 670
  pyosalpinx 670
  pyrexia (of unknown origin) 672
  renal
    disease NEC 646.2
    failure, acute 669.3
  retention
    decidua (fragments) (with delayed
      hemorrhage) 666.2
      without hemorrhage 667.1
    placenta (fragments) (with delayed
      hemorrhage) 666.2
      without hemorrhage 667.1
    secundines (fragments) (with delayed
      hemorrhage) 666.2
      without hemorrhage 667.1
  retracted nipple 676.0
  rubella (conditions classifiable to 056) 647.5
  salpingitis 670
  salpingo-oophoritis 670
  salpingo-ovaritis 670
  salpingoperitonitis 670
  sapremia 670
  secondary perineal tear 674.2
  sepsis (pelvic) 670
  septicemia 670
  subinvolution (uterus) 674.8
  sudden death (cause unknown) 674.9
  suppuration—*see* Puerperal, abscess
  syphilis (conditions classifiable to 090-097)
    647.0
  tetanus 670
  thelitis 675.0
  thrombocytopenia 666.3
  thrombophlebitis (superficial) 671.2
    deep 671.4
    pelvic 671.4
    specified site NEC 671.5
  thrombosis (venous)—*see* Thrombosis,
    puerperal
  thyroid dysfunction (conditions classifiable to
    240-246) 648.1
  toxemia (*see also* Toxemia, of pregnancy) 642.4
    eclamptic 642.6
      with pre-existing hypertension 642.7
    pre-eclamptic (mild) 642.4
      with
        convulsions 642.6
        pre-existing hypertension 642.7
      severe 642.5
  tuberculosis (conditions classifiable to 010-018)
    647.3
  uremia 669.3
  vaginitis (conditions classifiable to 616.1) 646.6
  varicose veins (legs) 671.0
    vulva or perineum 671.1
  vulvitis (conditions classifiable to 616.1) 646.6
  vulvovaginitis (conditions classifiable to 616.1)
    646.6
  white leg 671.4
Pulled muscle —*see* Sprain, by site
Pulmolithiasis 518.89
Pulmonary —*see* condition
Pulmonitis (unknown etiology) 486
Pulpitis (acute) (anachoretic) (chronic)
  (hyperplastic) (putrescent) (suppurative)
  (ulcerative) 522.0
Pulpless tooth 522.9

Pulse
  alternating 427.89
    psychogenic 306.2
  bigeminal 427.89
  fast 785.0
  feeble, rapid, due to shock following injury
    958.4
  rapid 785.0
  slow 427.89
  strong 785.9
  trigeminal 427.89
  water-hammer (*see also* Insufficiency, aortic)
    424.1
  weak 785.9
Pulseless disease 446.7
Pulsus
  alternans or trigeminy 427.89
  psychogenic 306.2
Punch drunk 310.2
Puncta lacrimalia occlusion 375.52
Punctiform hymen 752.49
Puncture (traumatic)—*see also* Wound, open, by
  site
  accidental, complicating surgery 998.2
  bladder, nontraumatic 596.6
  by
    device, implant, or graft—*see* Complications,
      mechanical
    foreign body
      internal organs—*see also* Injury, internal, by
        site
        by ingested object—*see* Foreign body
      left accidentally in operation wound 998.4
  instrument (any) during a procedure,
    accidental 998.2
  internal organs, abdomen, chest, or pelvis—*see*
    Injury, internal, by site
  kidney, nontraumatic 593.89
Pupil —*see* condition
Pupillary membrane 364.74
  persistent 743.46
Pupillotonia 379.46
  pseudotabetic 379.46
Purpura 287.2
  abdominal 287.0
  allergic 287.0
  anaphylactoid 287.0
  annularis telangiectodes 709.1
  arthritic 287.0
  autoerythrocyte sensitization 287.2
  autoimmune 287.0
  bacterial 287.0
  Bateman's (senile) 287.2
  capillary fragility (hereditary) (idiopathic) 287.8
  cryoglobulinemic 273.2
  devil's pinches 287.2
  fibrinolytic (*see also* Fibrinolysis) 286.6
  fulminans, fulminous 286.6
  gangrenous 287.0
  hemorrhagic (*see also* Purpura,
    thrombocytopenic) 287.3
    nodular 272.7
    nonthrombocytopenic 287.0
    thrombocytopenic 287.3
  Henoch's (purpura nervosa) 287.0
  Henoch-Schönlein (allergic) 287.0
  hypergammaglobulinemic (benign primary)
    (Waldenström's) 273.0

Purpura—*continued*
  idiopathic 287.3
    nonthrombocytopenic 287.0
    thrombocytopenic 287.3
  infectious 287.0
  malignant 287.0
  neonatorum 772.6
  nervosa 287.0
  newborn NEC 772.6
  nonthrombocytopenic 287.2
    hemorrhagic 287.0
    idiopathic 287.0
  nonthrombopenic 287.2
  peliosis rheumatica 287.0
  pigmentaria, progressiva 709.09
  posttransfusion 287.4
  primary 287.0
  primitive 287.0
  red cell membrane sensitivity 287.2
  rheumatica 287.0
  Schönlein (-Henoch) (allergic) 287.0
  scorbutic 267
  senile 287.2
  simplex 287.2
  symptomatica 287.0
  telangiectasia annularis 709.1
  thrombocytopenic (congenital) (essential)
    (hereditary) (idiopathic) (primary) (*see also*
    Thrombocytopenia) 287.3
    neonatal, transitory (*see also*
      Thrombocytopenia, neonatal transitory)
      776.1
    puerperal, postpartum 666.3
    thrombotic 446.6
  thrombohemolytic (*see also* Fibrinolysis) 286.6
  thrombopenic (congenital) (essential) (*see also*
    Thrombocytopenia) 287.3
  thrombotic 446.6
    thrombocytic 446.6
    thrombocytopenic 446.6
  toxic 287.0
  variolosa 050.0
  vascular 287.0
  visceral symptoms 287.0
  Werlhof's (*see also* Purpura, thrombocytopenic)
    287.3
Purpuric spots 782.7
Purulent —*see* condition
Pus
  absorption, general—*see* Septicemia
  in
    stool 792.1
    urine 599.0
  tube (rupture) (*see also* Salpingo-oophoritis)
    614.2
Pustular rash 782.1
Pustule 686.9
  malignant 022.0
  nonmalignant 686.9
Putnam's disease (subacute combined sclerosis
  with pernicious anemia) 281.0 *[336.2]*
Putnam-Dana syndrome (subacute combined
  sclerosis with pernicious anemia) 281.0
  [336.2]
Putrefaction, intestinal 569.89
Putrescent pulp (dental) 522.1
Pyarthritis —*see* Pyarthrosis
Pyarthrosis (*see also* Arthritis, pyogenic) 711.0
  tuberculous—*see* Tuberculosis, joint
Pycnoepilepsy, pycnolepsy (idiopathic) (*see also*
  Epilepsy) 345.0

Pyelectasia 593.89
Pyelectasis 593.89
Pyelitis (congenital) (uremic) 590.80
  with
    abortion—*see* Abortion, by type, with
      specified complication NEC
    calculus or stones 592.9
    contracted kidney 590.00
    ectopic pregnancy (*see also* categories
      633.0-633.9) 639.8
    molar pregnancy (*see also* categories
      630-632) 639.8
  acute 590.10
    with renal medullary necrosis 590.11
  chronic 590.00
    with
      calculus 592.9
      renal medullary necrosis 590.01
  complicating pregnancy, childbirth, or
    puerperium 646.6
    affecting fetus or newborn 760.1
  cystica 590.3
  following
    abortion 639.8
    ectopic or molar pregnancy 639.8
  gonococcal 098.19
    chronic or duration of 2 months or over 098.39
  tuberculous (*see also* Tuberculosis) 016.0
    [590.81]
Pyelocaliectasis 593.89
Pyelocystitis (*see also* Pyelitis) 590.80
Pyelohydronephrosis 591
Pyelonephritis (*see also* Pyelitis) 590.80
  acute 590.10
    with renal medullary necrosis 590.11
  calculous 592.9
  chronic 590.00
  syphilitic (late) 095.4
  tuberculous (*see also* Tuberculosis) 016.0
    [590.81]
Pyelonephrosis (*see also* Pyelitis) 590.80
  chronic 590.00
Pyelophlebitis 451.89
Pyelo-ureteritis cystica 590.3
Pyemia, pyemic (purulent) (*see also* Septicemia)
  038.9
  abscess—*see* Abscess
  arthritis (*see also* Arthritis, pyogenic) 711.0
  Bacillus coli 038.42
  embolism—*see* Embolism, pyemic
  fever 038.9
  infection 038.9
  joint (*see also* Arthritis, pyogenic) 711.0
  liver 572.1
  meningococcal 036.2
  newborn 771.8
  phlebitis—*see* Phlebitis
  pneumococcal 038.2
  portal 572.1
  postvaccinal 999.3
  specified organism NEC 038.8
  staphylococcal 038.1
  streptococcal 038.0
  tuberculous—*see* Tuberculosis, miliary
Pygopagus 759.4
Pykno-epilepsy, pyknolepsy (idiopathic) (*see
  also* Epilepsy) 345.0
Pyle (-Cohn) disease (craniometaphyseal
  dysplasia) 756.89
Pylephlebitis (suppurative) 572.1
Pylethrombophlebitis 572.1

Pylethrombosis 572.1
Pyloritis (*see also* Gastritis) 535.5
Pylorospasm (reflex) 537.81
  congenital or infantile 750.5
  neurotic 306.4
  newborn 750.5
  psychogenic 306.4
Pylorus, pyloric —*see* condition
Pyoarthrosis —*see* Pyarthrosis
Pyocele
  mastoid 383.00
  sinus (accessory) (nasal) (*see also* Sinusitis)
    473.9
  turbinate (bone) 473.9
  urethra (*see also* Urethritis) 597.0
Pyococcal dermatitis 686.0
Pyococcide, skin 686.0
Pyocolpos (*see also* Vaginitis) 616.10
Pyocyaneus dermatitis 686.0
Pyocystitis (*see also* Cystitis) 595.9
Pyoderma, pyodermia NEC 686.0
  gangrenosum 686.0
  vegetans 686.8
Pyodermatitis 686.0
  vegetans 686.8
Pyogenic —*see* condition
Pyohemia —*see* Septicemia
Pyohydronephrosis (*see also* Pyelitis) 590.80
Pyometra 615.9
Pyometritis (*see also* Endometritis) 615.9
Pyometrium (*see also* Endometritis) 615.9
Pyomyositis 728.0
  ossificans 728.19
  tropical (bungpagga) 040.81
Pyonephritis (*see also* Pyelitis) 590.80
  chronic 590.00
Pyonephrosis (congenital) (*see also* Pyelitis)
  590.80
  acute 590.10
  -oophoritis (*see also* Salpingo-oophoritis)
    14.2
  arium (*see also* Salpingo-oophoritis)
    2
  arditis 420.99
  dium 420.99
  —*see* Phlebitis
  ricardium 420.99
  rax (infectional) 510.9
  0.0
  ic (*see also* Peritonitis) 567.2
  lso Peritonitis) 567.2
  lso Tuberculosis, pleura)

  alveolaris) 523.4

    Salpingo-oophoritis)

    ingo-oophoritis) 614.2
    cemia

    iosus) 684

    sis, pleura)

    016.2
    2.0

Pyrexia (of unknown origin) (P.U.O.) 780.6
  atmospheric 992.0
  during labor 659.2
  environmentally-induced
    newborn 778.4
  heat 992.0
  newborn, environmentally-induced 778.4
  puerperal 672
Pyroglobulinemia 273.8
Pyromania 312.33
Pyrosis 787.1
Pyrroloporphyria 277.1
Pyuria (bacterial) 599.0

Q

Q fever 083.0
  with pneumonia 083.0 *[484.8]*
Quadricuspid aortic valve 746.89
Quadrilateral fever 083.0
Quadriparesis —*see* Quadriplegia
Quadriplegia 344.00
  with fracture, vertebra (process)—*see* Fracture,
    vertebra, cervical, with spinal cord injury
  brain (current episode) 437.8
  cerebral (current episode) 437.8
  C1-C4
    complete 344.01
    incomplete 344.02
  C5-C7
    complete 344.03
    incomplete 344.04
  congenital or infantile (cerebral) (spastic)
    (spinal) 343.2
  cortical 437.8
  embolic (current episode) (*see also* Embolism,
    brain) 434.1
  infantile (cerebral) (spastic) (spinal) 343.2
  newborn NEC 767.0
  specified NEC 344.09
  thrombotic (current episode) (*see also*
    Thrombosis, brain) 434.0
  traumatic—*see* Injury, spinal, cervical
Quadruplet
  affected by maternal complications of
    pregnancy 761.5
  healthy liveborn—*see* Newborn, multiple
  pregnancy (complicating delivery) NEC 651.8
    with fetal loss and retention of one or more
      fetus(es) 651.5
Quarrelsomeness 301.3
Quartan
  fever 084.2
  malaria (fever) 084.2
Queensland fever 083.0
  coastal 083.0
  seven-day 100.89
Quervain's disease 727.04
  thyroid (subacute granulomatous thyroiditis)
    245.1
Queyrat's erythroplasia (M8080/2)
  specified site—*see* Neoplasm, skin, in situ
  unspecified site 233.5
Quincke's disease or edema —*see* Edema,
  angioneurotic
Quinquaud's disease (acne decalvans) 704.09
Quinsy (gangrenous) 475
Quintan fever 083.1
Quintuplet
  affected by maternal complications of
    pregnancy 761.5
  healthy liveborn—*see* Newborn, multiple
  pregnancy (complicating delivery) NEC 651.2
    with fetal loss and retention of one or more
      fetus(es) 651.6
Quotidian
  fever 084.0
  malaria (fever) 084.0

R

Rabbia 071
Rabbit fever (*see also* Tularemia) 021.9
Rabies 071
  contact V01.5
  exposure to V01.5
  inoculation V04.5
    reaction—*see* Complications, vaccination
  vaccination, prophylactic (against) V04.5
Rachischisis (*see also* Spina bifida) 741.9
Rachitic —*see also* condition
  deformities of spine 268.1
  pelvis 268.1
    with disproportion (fetopelvic) 653.2
      affecting fetus or newborn 763.1
      causing obstructed labor 660.1
        affecting fetus or newborn 763.1
Rachitis, rachitism —*see also* Rickets
  acute 268.0
  fetalis 756.4
  renalis 588.0
  tarda 268.0
Racket nail 757.5
Radial nerve —*see* condition
Radiation effects or sickness —*see also* Effect,
  adverse, radiation
  cataract 366.46
  dermatitis 692.82
  sunburn 692.71
Radiculitis (pressure) (vertebrogenic) 729.2
  accessory nerve 723.4
  anterior crural 724.4
  arm 723.4
  brachial 723.4
  cervical NEC 723.4
  due to displacement of intervertebral disc—*see*
    Neuritis, due to, displacement intervertebral
    disc
  leg 724.4
  lumbar NEC 724.4
  lumbosacral 724.4
  rheumatic 729.2
  syphilitic 094.89
  thoracic (with visceral pain) 724.4
Radiculomyelitis 357.0
  toxic, due to
    Clostridium tetani 037
    Corynebacterium diphtheriae 032.89
Radiculopathy (*see also* Radiculitis) 729.2
Radioactive substances, adverse effect —*see*
  Effect, adverse, radioactive substance
Radiodermal burns (acute) (chronic)
  (occupational)—*see* Burn, by site
Radiodermatitis 692.82
Radionecrosis —*see* Effect, adverse, radiation
Radiotherapy session V58.0
Radium, adverse effect —*see* Effect, adverse,
  radioactive substance
Raeder-Harbitz syndrome (pulseless disease)
  446.7
Rage (*see also* Disturbance, conduct) 312.0
  meaning rabies 071
Rag sorters' disease 022.1
Raillietiniasis 123.8
Railroad neurosis 300.16
Railway spine 300.16
Raised —*see* Elevation
Raiva 071
Rake teeth, tooth 524.3

Rales 786.7
Ramifying renal pelvis 753.3
Ramsay Hunt syndrome (herpetic geniculate
    ganglionitis) 053.11
    meaning dyssynergia cerebellaris myoclonica
        334.2
Ranke's primary infiltration (*see also*
    Tuberculosis) 010.0
Ranula 527.6
    congenital 750.26
Rape (*see* Injury, by site)
    alleged, observation or examination V71.5
Rapid
    feeble pulse, due to shock, following injury
        958.4
    heart (beat) 785.0
        psychogenic 306.2
    respiration 786.09
        psychogenic 306.1
    second stage (delivery) 661.3
        affecting fetus or newborn 763.6
    time-zone change syndrome 307.45
Rarefaction, bone 733.99
Rash 782.1
    canker 034.1
    diaper 691.0
    drug (internal use) 693.0
        contact 692.3
    ECHO 9 virus 078.89
    enema 692.89
    food (*see also* Allergy, food) 693.1
    heat 705.1
    napkin 691.0
    nettle 708.8
    pustular 782.1
    rose 782.1
        epidemic 056.9
        of infants 057.8
    scarlet 034.1
    serum (prophylactic) (therapeutic) 999.5
    toxic 782.1
    wandering tongue 529.1
Rasmussen's aneurysm (*see also* Tuberculosis)
    011.2
Rat-bite fever 026.9
    due to Streptobacillus moniliformis 026.1
    spirochetal (morsus muris) 026.0
Rathke's pouch tumor (M9350/1) 237.0
Raymond (-Céstan) syndrome 433.8
Raynaud's
    disease or syndrome (paroxysmal digital
        cyanosis) 443.0
    gangrene (symmetric) 443.0 *[785.4]*
    phenomenon (paroxysmal digital cyanosis)
        (secondary) 443.0
RDS 769
Reaction
    acute situational maladjustment (*see also*
        Reaction, adjustment) 309.9
    adaptation (*see also* Reaction, adjustment) 309.9
    adjustment 309.9
        with
            anxious mood 309.24
                with depressed mood 309.28
            conduct disturbance 309.3
                combined with disturbance of emotions
                    309.4
            depressed mood 309.0
                brief 309.0
                    with anxious mood 309.28
                prolonged 309.1

Reaction—*continued*
    elective mutism 309.83
    mixed emotions and conduct 309.4
    mutism, elective 309.83
    physical symptoms 309.82
    predominant disturbance (of)
        conduct 309.3
        emotions NEC 309.29
            mixed 309.28
        mixed, emotions and conduct 309.4
        specified type NEC 309.89
    specific academic or work inhibition 309.23
    withdrawal 309.83
    depressive 309.0
        with conduct disturbance 309.4
        brief 309.0
        prolonged 309.1
        specified type NEC 309.89
    affective (*see also* Psychosis, affective) 296.90
        specified type NEC 296.99
    aggressive 301.3
        unsocialized (*see also* Disturbance, conduct)
            312.0
    allergic (*see also* Allergy) 995.3
        drug, medicinal substance, and
            biological—*see* Allergy, drug
        food—*see* Allergy, food
        serum 999.5
    anaphylactic—*see* Shock, anaphylactic
    anesthesia—*see* Anesthesia, complication
    anger 312.0
    antisocial 301.7
    antitoxin (prophylactic) (therapeutic)—*see*
        Complications, vaccination
    anxiety 300.00
    asthenic 300.5
    compulsive 300.3
    conversion (anesthetic) (autonomic)
        (hyperkinetic) (mixed paralytic)
        (paresthetic) 300.11
    deoxyribonuclease (DNA) (DNase)
        hypersensitivity NEC 287.2
    depressive 300.4
        acute 309.0
        affective (*see also* Psychosis, affective) 296.2
            recurrent episode 296.3
            single episode 296.2
        brief 309.0
        manic (*see also* Psychosis, affective) 296.80
        neurotic 300.4
        psychoneurotic 300.4
        psychotic 298.0
    dissociative 300.15
    drug NEC (*see also* Table of drugs and
        chemicals) 995.2
        allergic—*see* Allergy, drug
        correct substance properly administered 995.2
        obstetric anesthetic or analgesic NEC 668.9
            affecting fetus or newborn 763.5
            specified drug—*see* Table of drugs and
                chemicals
        overdose or poisoning 977.9
            specified drug—*see* Table of drugs and
                chemicals
        specific to newborn 779.4
        transmitted via placenta or breast milk—*see*
            Absorption, drug, through placenta
        withdrawal NEC 292.0
            infant of dependent mother 779.5

Reaction—*continued*
    wrong substance given or taken in error 977.9
        specified drug—*see* Table of drugs and
            chemicals
    dyssocial 301.7
    erysipeloid 027.1
    fear 300.20
        child 313.0
    fluid loss, cerebrospinal 349.0
    food—*see also* Allergy, food
        anaphylactic shock—*see* Anaphylactic shock,
            due to food
    foreign
        body NEC 728.82
            in operative wound (inadvertently left) 998.4
            due to surgical material intentionally
                left—*see* Complications, due to
                (presence of) any device, implant, or
                graft classified to 996.0-996.5 NEC
        substance accidentally left during a procedure
            (chemical) (powder) (talc) 998.7
            body or object (instrument) (sponge) (swab)
                998.4
    graft-versus-host (GVH) 996.85
    grief (acute) (brief) 309.0
        prolonged 309.1
    gross stress (*see also* Reaction, stress, acute)
        308.9
    group delinquent (*see also* Disturbance,
        conduct) 312.2
    Herxheimer's 995.0
    hyperkinetic (*see also* Hyperkinesia) 314.9
    hypochondriacal 300.7
    hypoglycemia, due to insulin 251.0
        therapeutic misadventure 962.3
    hypomanic (*see also* Psychosis, affective) 296.0
        recurrent episode 296.1
        single episode 296.0
    hysterical 300.10
        conversion type 300.11
        dissociative 300.15
    id (bacterial cause) 692.89
    immaturity NEC 301.89
        aggressive 301.3
        emotional instability 301.59
    immunization—*see* Complications, vaccination
    incompatibility
        blood group (ABO) (infusion) (transfusion)
            999.6
        Rh (factor) (infusion) (transfusion) 999.7
    inflammatory—*see* Infection
    infusion—*see* Complications, infusion
    inoculation (immune serum)—*see*
        Complications, vaccination
    insulin 995.2
    involutional
        paranoid 297.2
        psychotic (*see also* Psychosis, affective,
            depressive) 296.2
    leukemoid (lymphocytic) (monocytic)
        (myelocytic) 288.8
    LSD (*see also* Abuse, drugs, nondependent)
        305.3
    lumbar puncture 349.0
    manic-depressive (*see also* Psychosis, affective)
        296.80
        depressed 296.2
            recurrent episode 296.3
            single episode 296.2
        hypomanic 296.0
    neurasthenic 300.5

Reaction—*continued*
    neurogenic (*see also* Neurosis) 300.9
    neurotic NEC 300.9
    neurotic-depressive 300.4
    nitritoid—*see* Crisis, nitritoid
    obsessive (-compulsive) 300.3
    organic 293.9
        acute 293.0
        subacute 293.1
    overanxious, child or adolescent 313.0
    paranoid (chronic) 297.9
        acute 298.3
        climacteric 297.2
        involutional 297.2
        menopausal 297.2
        senile 290.20
        simple 297.0
    passive
        aggressive 301.84
        dependency 301.6
    personality (*see also* Disorder, personality)
        301.9
    phobic 300.20
    postradiation—*see* Effect, adverse, radiation
    psychogenic NEC 300.9
    psychoneurotic (*see also* Neurosis) 300.9
        anxiety 300.00
        compulsive 300.3
        conversion 300.11
        depersonalization 300.6
        depressive 300.4
        dissociative 300.15
        hypochondriacal 300.7
        hysterical 300.10
            conversion type 300.11
            dissociative type 300.15
        neurasthenic 300.5
        obsessive 300.3
        obsessive-compulsive 300.3
        phobic 300.20
        tension state 300.9
    psychophysiologic NEC (*see also* Disorder,
        psychosomatic) 306.9
        cardiovascular 306.2
        digestive 306.4
        endocrine 306.6
        gastrointestinal 306.4
        genitourinary 306.50
        heart 306.2
        hemic 306.8
        intestinal (large) (small) 306.4
        laryngeal 306.1
        lymphatic 306.8
        musculoskeletal 306.0
        pharyngeal 306.1
        respiratory 306.1
        skin 306.3
        special sense organs 306.7
    psychosomatic (*see also* Disorder,
        psychosomatic) 306.9
    psychotic (*see also* Psychosis) 298.9
        depressive 298.0
        due to or associated with physical condition
            (*see also* Psychosis, organic) 294.9
        involutional (*see also* Psychosis, affective)
            296.2
            recurrent episode 296.3
            single episode 296.2
    pupillary (myotonic) (tonic) 379.46
    radiation—*see* Effect, adverse, radiation

Reaction—*continued*
 runaway—*see also* Disturbance, conduct
  socialized 312.2
  undersocialized, unsocialized 312.1
 scarlet fever toxin—*see* Complications,
  vaccination
 schizophrenic (*see also* Schizophrenia) 295.9
  latent 295.5
 serological for syphilis—*see* Serology for
  syphilis
 serum (prophylactic) (therapeutic) 999.5
  immediate 999.4
 situational (*see also* Reaction, adjustment) 309.9
  acute, to stress 308.3
 adjustment (*see also* Reaction, adjustment)
  309.9
 somatization (*see also* Disorder, psychosomatic)
  306.9
 spinal puncture 349.0
 spite, child (*see also* Disturbance, conduct)
  312.0
 stress, acute 308.9
  with predominant disturbance (of)
   consciousness 308.1
   emotions 308.0
   mixed 308.4
   psychomotor 308.2
   specified type NEC 308.3
 surgical procedure—*see* Complications,
  surgical procedure
 tetanus antitoxin—*see* Complications,
  vaccination
 toxin-antitoxin—*see* Complications, vaccination
 transfusion (blood) (bone marrow)
  (lymphocytes) (allergic)—*see*
  Complications, transfusion
 tuberculin skin test, nonspecific (without active
  tuberculosis) 795.5
  positive (without active tuberculosis) 795.5
 ultraviolet—*see* Effect, adverse, ultraviolet
 undersocialized, unsocialized—*see also*
  Disturbance, conduct
  aggressive (type) 312.0
  unaggressive (type) 312.1
 vaccination (any)—*see* Complications,
  vaccination
 white graft (skin) 996.52
 withdrawing, child or adolescent 313.22
 x-ray—*see* Effect, adverse, x-rays
Reactive depression (*see also* Reaction,
 depressive) 300.4
 neurotic 300.4
 psychoneurotic 300.4
 psychotic 298.0
Rebound tenderness 789.6
Recalcitrant patient V15.81
Recanalization, thrombus —*see* Thrombosis
Recession, receding
 chamber angle (eye) 364.77
 chin 524.06
 gingival (generalized) (localized) (postinfective)
  (postoperative) 523.2
Recklinghausen's disease (M9540/1) 237.71
 bones (osteitis fibrosa cystica) 252.0
Recklinghausen-Applebaum disease
 (hemochromatosis) 275.0
Reclus' disease (cystic) 610.1
Recrudescent typhus (fever) 081.1
Recruitment, auditory 388.44
Rectalgia 569.42
Rectitis 569.49

Rectocele
 female (without uterine prolapse) 618.0
  with uterine prolapse 618.4
   complete 618.3
   incomplete 618.2
 in pregnancy or childbirth 654.4
  causing obstructed labor 660.2
   affecting fetus or newborn 763.1
 male 569.49
 vagina, vaginal (outlet) 618.0
Rectosigmoiditis 569.89
 ulcerative (chronic) 556.3
Rectosigmoid junction —*see* condition
Rectourethral —*see* condition
Rectovaginal —*see* condition
Rectovesical —*see* condition
Rectum, rectal —*see* condition
Recurrent —*see* condition
Red bugs 133.8
Red cedar asthma 495.8
Redness
 conjunctiva 379.93
 eye 379.93
 nose 478.1
Reduced ventilatory or vital capacity 794.2
Reduction
 function
  kidney (*see also* Disease, renal) 593.9
  liver 573.8
 ventilatory capacity 794.2
 vital capacity 794.2
Redundant, redundancy
 abdomen 701.9
 anus 751.5
 cardia 537.89
 clitoris 624.2
 colon (congenital) 751.5
 foreskin (congenital) 605
 intestine 751.5
 labia 624.3
 organ or site, congenital NEC—*see* Accessory
 panniculus (abdominal) 278.1
 prepuce (congenital) 605
 pylorus 537.89
 rectum 751.5
 scrotum 608.89
 sigmoid 751.5
 skin (of face) 701.9
  eyelids 374.30
 stomach 537.89
 uvula 528.9
 vagina 623.8
Reduplication —*see* Duplication
Referral
 adoption (agency) V68.89
 nursing care V63.8
 patient without examination or treatment V68.81
 social services V63.8
Reflex —*see also* condition
 blink, deficient 374.45
 hyperactive gag 478.29
 neurogenic bladder NEC 596.54
  atonic 596.54
   with cauda equina syndrome 344.61
 vasoconstriction 443.9
 vasovagal 780.2
Reflux
 esophageal 530.81
 esophagitis 530.11
 gastroesophageal 530.81
 mitral—*see* Insufficiency, mitral

Reflux—*continued*
ureteral —*see* Reflux, vesicoureteral
vesicoureteral 593.70
with
reflux nephropathy 593.73
bilateral 593.72
unilateral 593.71
Reformed gallbladder 576.0
Reforming, artificial openings (*see also*
Attention to, artificial, opening) V55.9
Refractive error (*see also* Error, refractive) 367.9
Refsum's disease or syndrome (heredopathia
atactica polyneuritiformis) 356.3
Refusal of
food 307.59
hysterical 300.11
treatment because of, due to
patient's decision NEC V64.2
reason of conscience or religion V62.6
Regaud
tumor (M8082/3)—*see* Neoplasm,
nasopharynx, malignant
type carcinoma (M8082/3)—*see* Neoplasm,
nasopharynx, malignant
Regional —*see* condition
Regulation feeding (elderly) (infant) 783.3
newborn 779.3
Regurgitated
food, choked on 933.1
stomach contents, choked on 933.1
Regurgitation
aortic (valve) (*see also* Insufficiency, aortic)
424.1
congenital 746.4
syphilitic 093.22
food—*see also* Vomiting
with reswallowing—*see* Rumination
newborn 779.3
gastric contents—*see* Vomiting
heart—*see* Endocarditis
mitral (valve)—*see also* Insufficiency, mitral
congenital 746.6
myocardial—*see* Endocarditis
pulmonary (heart) (valve) (*see also*
Endocarditis, pulmonary) 424.3
stomach—*see* Vomiting
tricuspid—*see* Endocarditis, tricuspid
valve, valvular—*see* Endocarditis
vesicoureteral —*see* Reflux, vesicoureteral
Rehabilitation V57.9
multiple types V57.89
occupational V57.21
specified type NEC V57.89
speech V57.3
vocational V57.22
Reichmann's disease or syndrome
(gastrosuccorrhea) 536.8
Reifenstein's syndrome (hereditary familial
hypogonadism, male) 257.2
Reilly's syndrome or phenomenon (*see also*
Neuropathy, peripheral, autonomic) 337.9
Reimann's periodic disease 277.3
Reinsertion, contraceptive device V25.42
Reiter's disease, syndrome, or urethritis 099.3
Rejection
food, hysterical 300.11
transplant 996.80
bone marrow 996.85
corneal 996.51

Rejection—*continued*
organ (immune or nonimmune cause) 996.80
bone marrow 996.85
heart 996.83
intestines 996.89
kidney 996.81
liver 996.82
lung 996.84
pancreas 996.86
specified NEC 996.89
skin 996.52
Relapsing fever 087.9
Carter's (Asiatic) 087.0
Dutton's (West African) 087.1
Koch's 087.9
louse-borne (epidemic) 087.0
Novy's (American) 087.1
Obermeyer's (European) 087.0
Spirillum 087.9
tick-borne (endemic) 087.1
Relaxation
anus (sphincter) 569.49
due to hysteria 300.11
arch (foot) 734
congenital 754.61
back ligaments 728.4
bladder (sphincter) 596.59
cardio-esophageal 530.89
cervix (*see also* Incompetency, cervix) 622.5
diaphragm 519.4
inguinal rings—*see* Hernia, inguinal
joint (capsule) (ligament) (paralytic) (*see also*
Derangement, joint) 718.90
congenital 755.8
lumbosacral joint 724.6
pelvic floor 618.8
pelvis 618.8
perineum 618.8
posture 729.9
rectum (sphincter) 569.49
sacroiliac (joint) 724.6
scrotum 608.89
urethra (sphincter) 599.84
uterus (outlet) 618.8
vagina (outlet) 618.8
vesical 596.59
Remains
canal of Cloquet 743.51
capsule (opaque) 743.51
Remittent fever (malarial) 084.6
Remnant
canal of Cloquet 743.51
capsule (opaque) 743.51
cervix, cervical stump (acquired)
(postoperative) 622.8
cystic duct, postcholecystectomy 576.0
fingernail 703.8
congenital 757.5
meniscus, knee 717.5
thyroglossal duct 759.2
tonsil 474.8
infected 474.0
urachus 753.7
Remote effect of cancer —*see* Condition
Removal (of)
catheter (urinary) (indwelling) V53.6
from artificial opening—*see* Attention to,
artificial, opening
non-vascular V58.82
vascular V58.81

Removal (of)—*continued*
  device—*see also* Fitting (of)
    contraceptive V25.42
    fixation
      external V54.8
      internal V54.0
      traction V54.8
    dressing V58.3
    ileostomy V55.2
    Kirschner wire V54.8
    non-vascular catheter V58.82
    pin V54.0
    plaster cast V54.8
    plate (fracture) V54.0
    rod V54.0
    screw V54.0
    splint, external V54.8
    subdermal implantable contraceptive V25.43
    suture V58.3
    traction device, external V54.8
    vascular catheter V58.81
Ren
  arcuatus 753.3
  mobile, mobilis (*see also* Disease, renal) 593.0
    congenital 753.3
  unguliformis 753.3
Renal —*see also* condition
  glomerulohyalinosis-diabetic syndrome 250.4
    [581.81]
Rendu-Osler-Weber disease or syndrome
  (familial hemorrhagic telangiectasia) 448.0
Reninoma (M8361/1) 236.91
Rénon-Delille syndrome 253.8
Repair
  pelvic floor, previous, in pregnancy or
    childbirth 654.4
    affecting fetus or newborn 763.8
  scarred tissue V51
Replacement by artificial or mechanical device
  or prosthesis of (*see also* Fitting (of))
  bladder V43.5
  blood vessel V43.4
  breast V43.82
  eye globe V43.0
  heart V43.2
    valve V43.3
  intestine V43.89
  joint V43.60
    ankle 43.66
    elbow V43.62
    finger V43.69
    hip (partial) (total) V43.64
    knee V43.65
    shoulder V43.61
    specified NEC V43.69
    wrist V43.63
  kidney V43.89
  larynx V43.81
  lens V43.1
  limb(s) V43.7
  liver V43.89
  lung V43.89
  organ NEC V43.89
  pancreas V43.89
  tissue NEC V43.89
Reprogramming
  cardiac pacemaker V53.31
Request for expert evidence V68.2
Reserve, decreased or low
  cardiac—*see* Disease, heart
  kidney (*see also* Disease, renal) 593.9

Residual —*see also* condition
  bladder 596.8
  foreign body—*see* Retention, foreign body
  state, schizophrenic (*see also* Schizophrenia)
    295.6
  urine 788.69
Resistance, resistant (to)

> Note—Use the following subclassification for
> categories V09.5, V09.7, V09.8, V09.9.:
>
> 0 *without mention of resistance to multiple*
>   *drugs*
> 1 *with resistance to multiple drugs*
>
> V09.5   *quinolones and fluoroquinolones*
> V09.7   *antimycobacterial agents*
> V09.8   *specified drugs NEC*
> V09.9   *unspecified drugs*
>
> 9 *multiple sites*

  drugs by microorganisms V09.9
    Amikacin V09.4
    aminoglycosides V09.4
    Amodiaquine V09.5
    Amoxicillin V09.0
    Ampicillin V09.0
    antimycobacterial agents V09.7
    Azithromycin V09.2
    Azlocillin V09.0
    Aztreonam V09.1
    B-lactam antibiotics V09.1
    Bacampicillin V09.0
    Bacitracin V09.8
    Benznidazole V09.8
    Capreomycin V09.7
    Carbenicillin V09.0
    Cefaclor V09.1
    Cefadroxil V09.1
    Cefamandole V09.1
    Cefatetan V09.1
    Cefazolin V09.1
    Cefixime V09.1
    Cefonicid V09.1
    Cefoperazone V09.1
    Ceforanide V09.1
    Cefotaxime V09.1
    Cefoxitin V09.1
    Ceftazidine V09.1
    Ceftizoxime V09.1
    Ceftriaxone V09.1
    Cefuroxime V09.1
    Cephalexin V09.1
    Cephaloglycin V09.1
    Cephaloridine V09.1
    cephalosporins V09.1
    Cephalothin V09.1
    Cephapirin V09.1
    Cephradine V09.1
    Chloramphenicol V09.8
    Chloraquine V09.5
    Chlorguanide V09.8
    Chlorproguanil V09.8
    Chlortetracycline V09.3
    Cinoxacin V09.5
    Ciprofloxacin V09.5
    Clarithromycin V09.2
    Clindamycin V09.8
    Clioquinol V09.5
    Clofazimine V09.7
    Cloxacillin V09.0

Resistance, resistant (to)—*continued*
  Cyclacillin V09.0
  Cycloserine V09.7
  Dapsone [DZ] V09.7
  Demeclocycline V09.3
  Dicloxacillin V09.0
  Doxycycline V09.3
  Enoxacin V09.5
  Erythromycin V09.2
  Ethambutol [EMB] V09.7
  Ethionamide [ETA] V09.7
  fluoroquinolones NEC V09.5
  Gentamicin V09.4
  Halofantrine V09.8
  Imipenem V09.1
  Iodoquinol V09.5
  Isoniazid [INH] V09.7
  Kanamycin V09.4
  macrolides V09.2
  Mafenide V09.6
  Mefloquine V09.8
  Melassoprol V09.8
  Methacillin V09.0
  Methacycline V09.3
  Methenamine V09.8
  Metronidazole V09.8
  Mezlocillin V09.0
  Minocycline V09.3
  Nafcillin V09.0
  Nalidixic Acid V09.5
  Natamycin V09.2
  Neomycin V09.4
  Netilmicin V09.4
  Nimorazole V09.8
  Nitrofurantoin V09.8
  Nitrofurtimox V09.8
  Norfloxacin V09.5
  Nystatin V09.2
  Ofloxacin V09.5
  Oleandomycin V09.2
  Oxacillin V09.0
  Oxytetracycline V09.3
  Para-amino salicylic acid [PAS] V09.7
  Paromomycin V09.4
  Penicillin (G)(V)(VK) V09.0
  penicillins V09.0
  Pentamidine V09.8
  Piperacillin V09.0
  Primaquine V09.5
  Proguanil V09.8
  Pyrazinamide [PZA] V09.7
  Pyrimethamine/Sulfalene V09.8
  Pyrimethamine/Sulfodoxine V09.8
  Quinacrine V09.5
  Quinidine V09.8
  Quinine V09.8
  quinolones V09.5
  Rifabutin V09.7
  Rifampin [RIF] V09.7
  Rifamycin V09.7
  Rolitetracycline V09.3
  specified drugs NEC V09.8
  Spectinomycin V09.8
  Spiramycin V09.2
  Streptomycin [SM] V09.4
  Sulfacetamide V09.6
  Sulfacytine V90.6
  Sulfadiazine V09.6
  Sulfadoxine V09.6
  Sulfamethoxazole V09.6
  Sulfapyridine V09.6

Resistance, resistant (to)—*continued*
  Sulfasalizine V09.6
  Sulfasoxazole V09.6
  sulfonamides V09.6
  Sulfoxone V09.7
  Tetracycline V09.3
  tetracyclines V09.3
  Thiamphenicol V09.8
  Ticarcillin V09.0
  Tinidazole V09.8
  Tobramycin V09.4
  Triamphenicol V09.8
  Trimethoprim V09.8
  Vancomycin V09.8
Resorption
  biliary 576.8
    purulent or putrid (*see also* Cholecystitis) 576.8
  dental (roots) 521.4
    alveoli 525.8
  septic—*see* Septicemia
  teeth (external) (internal) (pathological) (roots) 521.4
Respiration
  asymmetrical 786.09
  bronchial 786.09
  Cheyne-Stokes (periodic respiration) 786.09
  decreased, due to shock following injury 958.4
  disorder of 786.00
    psychogenic 306.1
    specified NEC 786.09
  failure 518.81
    newborn 770.8
  insufficiency 786.09
    acute 518.82
    newborn NEC 770.8
  Kussmaul (air hunger) 786.09
  painful 786.52
  periodic 786.09
  poor 786.09
    newborn NEC 770.8
  sighing 786.7
    psychogenic 306.1
  wheezing 786.09
Respiratory —*see also* condition
  distress 786.09
    acute 518.82
    fetus or newborn NEC 770.8
    syndrome (newborn) 769
      adult (following shock, surgery, or trauma) 518.5
      specified NEC 518.82
  failure (acute) (chronic) 518.81
Respiratory syncytial virus (RSV) 079.6
  bronchiolitis 466.11
  pneumonia 480.1
Response
  photoallergic 692.72
  phototoxic 692.72
Rest, rests
  mesonephric duct 752.8
    fallopian tube 752.11
  ovarian, in fallopian tubes 752.19
  wolffian duct 752.8
Restless leg (syndrome) 333.99
Restlessness 799.2
Restoration of organ continuity from previous sterilization (tuboplasty) (vasoplasty) V26.0
Restriction of housing space V60.1
Restzustand, schizophrenic (*see also* Schizophrenia) 295.6

Retained —*see* Retention
Retardation
development, developmental, specific (*see also* Disorder, development, specific) 315.9
learning, specific 315.2
arithmetical 315.1
language (skills) 315.31
expressive 315.31
mixed receptive-expressive 315.32
mathematics 315.1
reading 315.00
phonological 315.39
written expression 315.2
motor 315.4
endochondral bone growth 733.91
growth (physical) 783.4
due to malnutrition 263.2
fetal (intrauterine) 764.9
affecting management of pregnancy 656.5
intrauterine growth 764.9
affecting management of pregnancy 656.5
mental 319
borderline V62.89
mild, IQ 50-70 317
moderate, IQ 35-49 318.0
profound, IQ under 20 318.2
severe, IQ 20-34 318.1
motor, specific 315.4
physical 783.4
child 783.4
due to malnutrition 263.2
fetus (intrauterine) 764.9
affecting management of pregnancy 656.5
psychomotor NEC 307.9
reading 315.00
Retching —*see* Vomiting
Retention, retained
bladder NEC (*see also* Retention, urine) 788.20
psychogenic 306.53
carbon dioxide 276.2
cyst—*see* Cyst
dead
fetus (after 22 completed weeks gestation) 656.4
early fetal death (before 22 completed weeks gestation) 632
ovum 631
decidua (following delivery) (fragments) (with hemorrhage) 666.2
without hemorrhage 667.1
deciduous tooth 520.6
dental root 525.3
fecal (*see also* Constipation) 564.0
fluid 276.6
foreign body—*see also* Foreign body, retained
bone 733.99
current trauma—*see* Foreign body, by site or type
middle ear 385.83
muscle 729.6
soft tissue NEC 729.6
gastric 536.8
membranes (following delivery) (with hemorrhage) 666.2
with abortion—*see* Abortion, by type
without hemorrhage 667.1
menses 626.8
milk (puerperal) 676.2
nitrogen, extrarenal 788.9

Retention, retained—*continued*
placenta (total) (with hemorrhage) 666.0
with abortion—*see* Abortion, by type
portions or fragments 666.2
without hemorrhage 667.1
without hemorrhage 667.0
products of conception
early pregnancy (fetal death before 22 completed weeks gestation) 632
following
abortion—*see* Abortion, by type
delivery 666.2
with hemorrhage 666.2
without hemorrhage 667.1
secundines (following delivery) (with hemorrhage) 666.2
with abortion—*see* Abortion, by type
complicating puerperium (delayed hemorrhage) 666.2
without hemorrhage 667.1
smegma, clitoris 624.8
urine NEC 788.20
bladder, incomplete emptying 788.21
psychogenic 306.53
specified NEC 788.29
water (in tissue) (*see also* Edema) 782.3
Reticulation, dust (occupational) 504
Reticulocytosis NEC 790.99
Reticuloendotheliosis
acute infantile (M9722/3) 202.5
leukemic (M9940/3) 202.4
malignant (M9720/3) 202.3
nonlipid (M9722/3) 202.5
Reticulohistiocytoma (giant cell) 277.8
Reticulohistiocytosis, multicentric 272.8
Reticulolymphosarcoma (diffuse) (M9613/3) 200.8
follicular (M9691/3) 202.0
nodular (M9691/3) 202.0
Reticulosarcoma (M9640/3) 200.0
odular (M9642/3) 200.0
pleomorphic cell type (M9641/3) 200.0
Reticulosis (skin)
acute of infancy (M9722/3) 202.5
histiocytic medullary (M9721/3) 202.3
lipomelanotic 695.89
malignant (M9720/3) 202.3
Sézary's (M9701/3) 202.2
Retina, retinal —*see* condition
Retinitis (*see also* Chorioretinitis) 363.20
albuminurica 585 *[363.10]*
arteriosclerotic 440.8 *[362.13]*
central angiospastic 362.41
Coat's 362.12
diabetic 250.5 *[362.01]*
disciformis 362.52
disseminated 363.10
metastatic 363.14
neurosyphilitic 094.83
pigment epitheliopathy 363.15
exudative 362.12
focal 363.00
in histoplasmosis 115.92
capsulatum 115.02
duboisii 115.12
juxtapapillary 363.05
macular 363.06
paramacular 363.06
peripheral 363.08
posterior pole NEC 363.07
gravidarum 646.8

Retinitis—*continued*
  hemorrhagica externa 362.12
  juxtapapillary (Jensen's) 363.05
  luetic—*see* Retinitis, syphilitic
  metastatic 363.14
  pigmentosa 362.74
  proliferans 362.29
  proliferating 362.29
  punctata albescens 362.76
  renal 585 *[363.13]*
  syphilitic (secondary) 091.51
    congenital 090.0 *[363.13]*
    early 091.51
    late 095.8 *[363.13]*
  syphilitica, central, recurrent 095.8 *[363.13]*
  tuberculous (*see also* Tuberculous) 017.3
    [363.13]
Retinoblastoma (M9510/3) 190.5
  differentiated type (M9511/3) 190.5
  undifferentiated type (M9512/3) 190.5
Retinochoroiditis (*see also* Chorioretinitis)
    363.20
  central angiospastic 362.41
  disseminated 363.10
    metastatic 363.14
    neurosyphilitic 094.83
    pigment epitheliopathy 363.15
    syphilitic 094.83
  due to toxoplasmosis (acquired) (focal) 130.2
  focal 363.00
    in histoplasmosis 115.92
      capsulatum 115.02
      duboisii 115.12
    juxtapapillary (Jensen's) 363.05
    macular 363.06
    paramacular 363.06
    peripheral 363.08
    posterior pole NEC 363.07
  juxtapapillaris 363.05
  syphilitic (disseminated) 094.83
Retinopathy (background) 362.10
  arteriosclerotic 440.8 *[362.13]*
  atherosclerotic 440.8 *[362.13]*
  central serous 362.41
  circinate 362.10
  Coat's 362.12
  diabetic 250.5 *[362.01]*
    proliferative 250.5 *[362.02]*
  exudative 362.12
  hypertensive 362.11
  of prematurity 362.21
  pigmentary, congenital 362.74
  proliferative 362.29
    diabetic 250.5 *[362.02]*
    sickle-cell 282.60 *[362.29]*
  solar 363.31
Retinoschisis 361.10
  bullous 361.12
  congenital 743.56
  flat 361.11
  juvenile 362.73
Retractile testis 752.52
Retraction
  cervix (*see also* Retroversion, uterus) 621.6
  drum (membrane) 384.82
  eyelid 374.41
  finger 736.29
  head 781.0
  lid 374.41
  lung 518.89
  mediastinum 519.3

Retraction—*continued*
  nipple 611.79
    congenital 757.6
    puerperal, postpartum 676.0
  palmar fascia 728.6
  pleura (*see also* Pleurisy) 511.0
  ring, uterus (Bandl's) (pathological) 661.4
    affecting fetus or newborn 763.7
  sternum (congenital) 756.3
    acquired 738.3
    during respiration 786.9
  substernal 738.3
  supraclavicular 738.8
  syndrome (Duane's) 378.71
  uterus (*see also* Retroversion, uterus) 621.6
  valve (heart)—*see* Endocarditis
Retrobulbar —*see* condition
Retrocaval ureter 753.4
Retrocecal —*see also* condition
  appendix (congenital) 751.5
Retrocession —*see* Retroversion
Retrodisplacement —*see* Retroversion
Retroflection, retroflexion —*see* Retroversion
Retrognathia, retrognathism (mandibular)
    (maxillary) 524.06
Retrograde menstruation 626.8
Retroiliac ureter 753.4
Retroperineal —*see* condition
Retroperitoneal —*see* condition
Retroperitonitis (*see also* Peritonitis) 567.9
Retropharyngeal —*see* condition
Retroplacental —*see* condition
Retroposition —*see* Retroversion
Retrosternal thyroid (congenital) 759.2
Retroversion, retroverted
  cervix (*see also* Retroversion, uterus) 621.6
  female NEC (*see also* Retroversion, uterus)
    621.6
  iris 364.70
  testis (congenital) 752.51
  uterus, uterine (acquired) (acute) (adherent)
    (any degree) (asymptomatic) (cervix)
    (postinfectional) (postpartal, old) 621.6
    congenital 752.3
    in pregnancy or childbirth 654.3
      affecting fetus or newborn 763.8
      causing obstructed labor 660.2
        affecting fetus or newborn 763.1
Retrusion, premaxilla (developmental) 524.04
Rett's syndrome 330.8
Reverse, reversed
  peristalsis 787.4
Reye's syndrome 331.81
Reye-Sheehan syndrome (postpartum pituitary
    necrosis) 253.2
Rh (factor)
  hemolytic disease 773.0
  incompatibility, immunization, or sensitization
    affecting management of pregnancy 656.1
    fetus or newborn 773.0
    transfusion reaction 999.7
  negative mother, affecting fetus or newborn
    773.0
  titer elevated 999.7
  transfusion reaction 999.7
Rhabdomyolysis (idiopathic) 728.89
Rhabdomyoma (M8900/0)—*see also* Neoplasm,
    connective tissue, benign
  adult (M8904/0)—*see* Neoplasm, connective
    tissue, benign

Rhabdomyoma—*continued*
  fetal (M8903/0)—*see* Neoplasm, connective
    tissue, benign
  glycogenic (M8904/0)—*see* Neoplasm,
    connective tissue, benign
Rhabdomyosarcoma (M8900/3)—*see also*
  Neoplasm connective tissue, malignant
  alveolar (M8920/3)—*see* Neoplasm, connective
    tissue, malignant
  embryonal (M8910/3)—*see* Neoplasm,
    connective tissue malignant
  mixed type (M8902/3)—*see* Neoplasm,
    connective tissue, malignant
  pleomorphic (M8901/3)—*see* Neoplasm,
    connective tissue, malignant
Rhabdosarcoma (M8900/3)—*see*
  Rhabdomyosarcoma
Rhesus (factor) (Rh) incompatibility—*see* Rh,
  incompatibility
Rheumaticosis —*see* Rheumatism
Rheumatism, rheumatic (acute NEC) 729.0
  adherent pericardium 393
  arthritis
    acute or subacute—*see* Fever, rheumatic
    chronic 714.0
    spine 720.0
  articular (chronic) NEC (*see also* Arthritis)
    716.9
    acute or subacute—*see* Fever, rheumatic
  back 724.9
  blennorrhagic 098.59
  carditis—*see* Disease, heart, rheumatic
  cerebral—*see* Fever, rheumatic
  chorea (acute)—*see* Chorea, rheumatic
  chronic NEC 729.0
  coronary arteritis 391.9
    chronic 398.99
  degeneration, myocardium (*see also*
    Degeneration, myocardium, with rheumatic
    fever) 398.0
  desert 114.0
  febrile—*see* Fever, rheumatic
  fever—*see* Fever, rheumatic
  gonococcal 098.59
  gout 274.0
  heart
    disease (*see also* Disease, heart, rheumatic)
      398.90
    failure (chronic) (congestive) (inactive) 398.91
  hemopericardium—*see* Rheumatic, pericarditis
  hydropericardium—*see* Rheumatic, pericarditis
  inflammatory (acute) (chronic) (subacute)—*see*
    Fever, rheumatic
  intercostal 729.0
    meaning Tietze's disease 733.6
  joint (chronic) NEC (*see also* Arthritis) 716.9
    acute—*see* Fever, rheumatic
  mediastinopericarditis—*see* Rheumatic,
    pericarditis
  muscular 729.0
  myocardial degeneration (*see also*
    Degeneration, myocardium, with rheumatic
    fever) 398.0
  myocarditis (chronic) (inactive) (with chorea)
    398.0
    active or acute 391.2
      with chorea (acute) (rheumatic)
        (Sydenham's) 392.0
  myositis 729.1
  neck 724.9
  neuralgic 729.0

Rheumatism, rheumatic—*continued*
  neuritis (acute) (chronic) 729.2
  neuromuscular 729.0
  nodose—*see* Arthritis, nodosa
  nonarticular 729.0
  palindromic 719.30
    ankle 719.37
    elbow 719.32
    foot 719.37
    hand 719.34
    hip 719.35
    knee 719.36
    multiple sites 719.39
    pelvic region 719.35
    shoulder (region) 719.31
    specified site NEC 719.38
    wrist 719.33
  pancarditis, acute 391.8
    with chorea (acute) (rheumatic) (Sydenham's)
      392.0
    chronic or inactive 398.99
  pericarditis (active) (acute) (with effusion) (with
    pneumonia) 391.0
    with chorea (acute) (rheumatic) (Sydenham's)
      392.0
    chronic or inactive 393
  pericardium—*see* Rheumatic, pericarditis
  pleuropericarditis—*see* Rheumatic, pericarditis
  pneumonia 390 *[517.1]*
  pneumonitis 390 *[517.1]*
  pneumopericarditis—*see* Rheumatic, pericarditis
  polyarthritis
    acute or subacute—*see* Fever, rheumatic
    chronic 714.0
  polyarticular NEC (*see also* Arthritis) 716.9
  psychogenic 306.0
  radiculitis 729.2
  sciatic 724.3
  septic—*see* Fever, rheumatic
  spine 724.9
  subacute NEC 729.0
  torticollis 723.5
  tuberculous NEC (*see also* Tuberculosis) 015.9
  typhoid fever 002.0
Rheumatoid —*see also* condition
  lungs 714.81
Rhinitis (atrophic) (catarrhal) (chronic)
  (croupous) (fibrinous) (hyperplastic)
  (hypertrophic) (membranous) (purulent)
  (suppurative) (ulcerative) 472.0
  with
    hay fever (*see also* Fever, hay) 477.9
      with asthma (bronchial) 493.0
    sore throat—*see* Nasopharyngitis
  acute 460
  allergic (nonseasonal) (seasonal) (*see also*
    Fever, hay) 477.9
    with asthma (*see also* Asthma) 493.0
  granulomatous 472.0
  infective 460
  obstructive 472.0
  pneumococcal 460
  syphilitic 095.8
    congenital 090.0
  tuberculous (*see also* Tuberculosis) 012.8
  vasomotor (*see also* Fever, hay) 477.9
Rhinoantritis (chronic) 473.0
  acute 461.0
Rhinodacryolith 375.57
Rhinolalia (aperta) (clausa) (open) 784.49

Rhinolith 478.1
  nasal sinus (*see also* Sinusitis) 473.9
Rhinomegaly 478.1
Rhinopharyngitis (acute) (subacute) (*see also*
    Nasopharyngitis) 460
  chronic 472.2
  destructive ulcerating 102.5
  mutilans 102.5
Rhinophyma 695.3
Rhinorrhea 478.1
  cerebrospinal (fluid) 349.81
  paroxysmal (*see also* Fever, hay) 477.9
  spasmodic (*see also* Fever, hay) 477.9
Rhinosalpingitis 381.50
  acute 381.51
  chronic 381.52
Rhinoscleroma 040.1
Rhinosporidiosis 117.0
Rhinovirus infection 079.3
Rhizomelique, pseudopolyarthritic 446.5
Rhoads and Bomford anemia (refractory) 284.9
Rhus
  diversiloba dermatitis 692.6
  radioans dermatitis 692.6
  toxicodendron dermatitis 692.6
  venenata dermatitis 692.6
  verniciflua dermatitis 692.6
Rhythm
  atrioventricular nodal 427.89
  disorder 427.9
    coronary sinus 427.89
    ectopic 427.89
    nodal 427.89
  escape 427.89
  heart, abnormal 427.9
  idioventricular 426.89
    accelerated 427.89
    nodal 427.89
  sleep, inversion 780.55
    nonorganic origin 307.45
Rhytidosis facialis 701.8
Rib —*see also* condition
  cervical 756.2
Riboflavin deficiency 266.0
Rice bodies (*see also* Loose, body, joint) 718.1
  knee 717.6
Richter's hernia —*see* Hernia, Richter's
Ricinism 988.2
Rickets (active) (acute) (adolescent) (adult)
    (chest wall) (congenital) (current) (infantile)
    (intestinal) 268.0
  celiac 579.0
  fetal 756.4
  hemorrhagic 267
  hypophosphatemic with nephrotic-glycosuric
    dwarfism 270.0
  kidney 588.0
  late effect 268.1
  renal 588.0
  scurvy 267
  vitamin D-resistant 275.3
Rickettsial disease 083.9
  specified type NEC 083.8
Rickettsialpox 083.2
Rickettsiosis NEC 083.9
  specified type NEC 083.8
  tick-borne 082.9
    specified type NEC 082.8
  vesicular 083.2
Ricord's chancre 091.0
Riddoch's syndrome (visual disorientation)
    368.16

Rider's
  bone 733.99
  chancre 091.0
Ridge, alveolus —*see also* condition
  flabby 525.2
Ridged ear 744.29
Riedel's
  disease (ligneous thyroiditis) 245.3
  lobe, liver 751.69
  struma (ligneous thyroiditis) 245.3
  thyroiditis (ligneous) 245.3
Rieger's anomaly or syndrome (mesodermal
    dysgenesis, anterior ocular segment) 743.44
Riehl's melanosis 709.09
Rietti-Greppi-Micheli anemia or syndrome
    282.4
Rieux's hernia —*see* Hernia, Rieux's
Rift Valley fever 066.3
Riga's disease (cachectic aphthae) 529.0
Riga-Fede disease (cachectic aphthae) 529.0
Riggs' disease (compound periodontitis) 523.4
Right middle lobe syndrome 518.0
Rigid, rigidity —*see also* condition
  abdominal 789.4
  articular, multiple congenital 754.89
  back 724.8
  cervix uteri
    in pregnancy or childbirth 654.6
      affecting fetus or newborn 763.8
      causing obstructed labor 660.2
        affecting fetus or newborn 763.1
  hymen (acquired) (congenital) 623.3
  nuchal 781.6
  pelvic floor
    in pregnancy or childbirth 654.4
      affecting fetus or newborn 763.8
      causing obstructed labor 660.2
        affecting fetus or newborn 763.1
  perineum or vulva
    in pregnancy or childbirth 654.8
      affecting fetus or newborn 763.8
      causing obstructed labor 660.2
        affecting fetus or newborn 763.1
  spine 724.8
  vagina
    in pregnancy or childbirth 654.7
      affecting fetus or newborn 763.8
      causing obstructed labor 660.2
        affecting fetus or newborn 763.1
Rigors 780.9
Riley-Day syndrome (familial dysautonomia)
    742.8
Ring (s)
  aorta 747.21
  Bandl's, complicating delivery 661.4
    affecting fetus or newborn 763.7
  contraction, complicating delivery 661.4
    affecting fetus or newborn 763.7
  esophageal (congenital) 750.3
  Fleischer (-Kayser) (cornea) 275.1 *[371.14]*
  hymenal, tight (acquired) (congenital) 623.3
  Kayser-Fleischer (cornea) 275.1 *[371.14]*
  retraction, uterus, pathological 661.4
    affecting fetus or newborn 763.7
  Schatzki's (esophagus) (congenital) (lower)
    750.3
    acquired 530.3
  Soemmering's 366.51
  trachea, abnormal 748.3
  vascular (congenital) 747.21
  Vossius' 921.3
    late effect 366.21

Ringed hair (congenital) 757.4
Ringing in the ear (*see also* Tinnitus) 388.30
Ringworm 110.9
  beard 110.0
  body 110.5
  Burmese 110.9
  corporeal 110.5
  foot 110.4
  groin 110.3
  hand 110.2
  honeycomb 110.0
  nails 110.1
  perianal (area) 110.3
  scalp 110.0
  specified site NEC 110.8
  Tokelau 110.5
Rise, venous pressure 459.89
Risk
  factor —*see* Problem
  suicidal 300.9
Ritter's disease (dermatitis exfoliativa
  neonatorum) 695.81
Rivalry, sibling 313.3
Rivalta's disease (cervicofacial actinomycosis)
  039.3
River blindness 125.3 *[360.13]*
Robert's pelvis 755.69
  with disproportion (fetopelvic) 653.0
    affecting fetus or newborn 763.1
    causing obstructed labor 660.1
      affecting fetus or newborn 763.1
Robin's syndrome 756.0
Robinson's (hidrotic) ectodermal dysplasia
  757.31
Robles' disease (onchocerciasis) 125.3 *[360.13]*
Rochalimea —*see* Rickettsial disease
Rocky Mountain fever (spotted) 082.0
Rodent ulcer (M8090/3)—*see also* Neoplasm,
  skin, malignant
  cornea 370.07
Roentgen ray, adverse effect —*see* Effect,
  adverse, x-ray
Roetheln 056.9
Roger's disease (congenital interventricular
  septal defect) 745.4
Rokitansky's
  disease (*see also* Necrosis, liver) 570
  tumor 620.2
Rokitansky-Aschoff sinuses (mucosal
  outpouching of gallbladder) (*see also* Disease,
  gallbladder) 575.8
Rokitansky-Kuster-Hauser syndrome
  (congenital absence vagina) 752.49
Rollet's chancre (syphilitic) 091.0
Rolling of head 781.0
Romano-Ward syndrome (prolonged Q-T
  interval) 794.31
Romanus lesion 720.1
Romberg's disease or syndrome 349.89
Roof, mouth —*see* condition
Rosacea 695.3
  acne 695.3
  keratitis 695.3 *[370.49]*
Rosary, rachitic 268.0
Rose
  cold 477.0
  fever 477.0
  rash 782.1
    epidemic 056.9
    of infants 057.8
Rosen-Castleman-Liebow syndrome
  (pulmonary proteinosis) 516.0

Rosenbach's erysipelatoid or erysipeloid 027.1
Rosenthal's disease (factor XI deficiency) 286.2
Roseola 057.8
  infantum, infantilis 057.8
Rossbach's disease (hyperchlorhydria) 536.8
  psychogenic 306.4
Rössle-Urbach-Wiethe lipoproteinosis 272.8
Ross river fever 066.3
Rostan's asthma (cardiac) (*see also* Failure,
  ventricular, left) 428.1
Rot
  Barcoo (*see also* Ulcer, skin) 707.9
  knife-grinders' (*see also* Tuberculosis) 011.4
Rot-Bernhardt disease 355.1
Rotation
  anomalous, incomplete or insufficient—*see*
    Malrotation
  cecum (congenital) 751.4
  colon (congenital) 751.4
  manual, affecting fetus or newborn 763.8
  spine, incomplete or insufficient 737.8
  tooth, teeth 524.3
  vertebra, incomplete or insufficient 737.8
Röteln 056.9
Roth's disease or meralgia 355.1
Roth-Bernhardt disease or syndrome 355.1
Rothmund (-Thomson) syndrome 757.33
Rotor's disease or syndrome (idiopathic
  hyperbilirubinemia) 277.4
Rotundum ulcus —*see* Ulcer, stomach
Round
  back (with wedging of vertebrae) 737.10
    late effect of rickets 268.1
  hole, retina 361.31
    with detachment 361.01
  ulcer (stomach)—*see* Ulcer, stomach
  worms (infestation) (large) NEC 127.0
Roussy-Lévy syndrome 334.3
Routine postpartum follow-up V24.2
Roy (-Jutras) syndrome (acropachyderma) 757.39
Rubella (German measles) 056.9
  complicating pregnancy, childbirth, or
    puerperium 647.5
  complication 056.8
    neurological 056.00
      encephalomyelitis 056.01
      specified type NEC 056.09
    specified type NEC 056.79
  congenital 771.0
  contact V01.4
  exposure to V01.4
  maternal
    with suspected fetal damage affecting
      management of pregnancy 655.3
    affecting fetus or newborn 760.2
      manifest rubella in infant 771.0
  specified complications NEC 056.79
  vaccination, prophylactic (against) V04.3
Rubeola (measles) (*see also* Measles) 055.9
  complicated 055.8
  meaning rubella (*see also* Rubella) 056.9
  scarlatinosis 057.8
Rubeosis iridis 364.42
  diabetica 250.5 *[364.42]*
Rubinstein-Taybi's syndrome (brachydactylia,
  short stature and mental retardation) 759.89
Rud's syndrome (mental deficiency, epilepsy,
  and infantilism) 759.89

Rudimentary (congenital)—*see also* Agenesis
  arm 755.22
  bone 756.9
  cervix uteri 752.49
  eye (*see also* Microphthalmos) 743.10
  fallopian tube 752.19
  leg 755.32
  lobule of ear 744.21
  patella 755.64
  respiratory organs in thoracopagus 759.4
  tracheal bronchus 748.3
  uterine horn 752.3
  uterus 752.3
    in male 752.7
    solid or with cavity 752.3
  vagina 752.49
Ruiter-Pompen (-Wyers) syndrome
  (angiokeratoma corporis diffusum) 272.7
Ruled out condition (*see also* Observation,
  suspected) V71.9
Rumination —*see also* Vomiting
  neurotic 300.3
  obsessional 300.3
  psychogenic 307.53
Runaway reaction —*see also* Disturbance,
  conduct
  socialized 312.2
  undersocialized, unsocialized 312.1
Runeberg's disease (progressive pernicious
  anemia) 281.0
Runge's syndrome (postmaturity) 766.2
Rupia 091.3
  congenital 090.0
  tertiary 095.9
Rupture, ruptured 553.9
  abdominal viscera NEC 799.8
    obstetrical trauma 665.5
  abscess (spontaneous)—*see* Abscess, by site
  amnion—*see* Rupture, membranes
  aneurysm—*see* Aneurysm
  anus (sphincter)—*see* Laceration, anus
  aorta, aortic 441.5
    abdominal 441.3
    arch 441.1
    ascending 441.1
    descending 441.5
      abdominal 441.3
      thoracic 441.1
    syphilitic 093.0
    thoracoabdominal 441.6
    thorax, thoracic 441.1
    transverse 441.1
    traumatic (thoracic) 901.0
      abdominal 902.0
    valve or cusp (*see also* Endocarditis, aortic)
      424.1
  appendix (with peritonitis) 540.0
    traumatic—*see* Injury, internal,
      gastrointestinal tract
    with peritoneal abscess 540.1
  arteriovenous fistula, brain (congenital) 430
  artery 447.2
    brain (*see also* Hemorrhage, brain) 431
    coronary (*see also* Infarct, myocardium) 410.9
    heart (*see also* Infarct, myocardium) 410.9
    pulmonary 417.8
    traumatic (complication) (*see also* Injury,
      blood vessel, by site) 904.9

Rupture, ruptured—*continued*
  bile duct, except cystic (*see also* Disease,
    biliary) 576.3
    cystic 575.4
    traumatic—*see* Injury, internal,
      intra-abdominal
  bladder (sphincter) 596.6
    with
      abortion—*see* Abortion, by type, with
        damage to pelvic organs
      ectopic pregnancy (*see also* categories
        633.0-633.9) 639.2
      molar pregnancy (*see also* categories
        630-632) 639.2
    following
      abortion 639.2
      ectopic or molar pregnancy 639.2
    nontraumatic 596.6
    obstetrical trauma 665.5
    spontaneous 596.6
    traumatic—*see* Injury, internal, bladder
  blood vessel (*see also* Hemorrhage) 459.0
    brain (*see also* Hemorrhage, brain) 431
    heart (*see also* Infarct, myocardium) 410.9
    traumatic (complication) (*see also* Injury,
      blood vessel, by site) 904.9
  bone—*see* Fracture, by site
  bowel 569.89
    traumatic—*see* Injury, internal, intestine
  Bowman's membrane 371.31
  brain
    aneurysm (congenital) (*see also* Hemorrhage,
      subarachnoid) 430
      late effect—*see* category 438
      syphilitic 094.87
    hemorrhagic (*see also* Hemorrhage, brain) 431
    injury at birth 767.0
    syphilitic 094.89
  capillaries 448.9
  cardiac (*see also* Infarct, myocardium) 410.9
  cartilage (articular) (current)—*see also* Sprain,
    by site
    knee—*see* Tear, meniscus
    semilunar—*see* Tear, meniscus
  cecum (with peritonitis) 540.0
    traumatic 863.89
      with open wound into cavity 863.99
    with peritoneal abscess 540.1
  cerebral aneurysm (congenital) (*see also*
    Hemorrhage, subarachnoid) 430
    late effect—*see* category 438
  cervix (uteri)
    with
      abortion—*see* Abortion, by type, with
        damage to pelvic organs
      ectopic pregnancy (*see also* categories
        633.0-633.9) 639.2
      molar pregnancy (*see also* categories
        630-632) 639.2
    following
      abortion 639.2
      ectopic or molar pregnancy 639.2
    obstetrical trauma 665.3
    traumatic—*see* Injury, internal, cervix
  chordae tendineae 429.5
  choroid (direct) (indirect) (traumatic) 363.63
  circle of Willis (*see also* Hemorrhage,
    subarachnoid) 430
    late effect—*see* category 438
  colon 569.89
    traumatic—*see* Injury, internal, colon

Rupture, ruptured—*continued*
  cornea (traumatic)—*see also* Rupture, eye
    due to ulcer 370.00
  coronary (artery) (thrombotic) (*see also* Infarct,
    myocardium) 410.9
  corpus luteum (infected) (ovary) 620.1
  cyst—*see* Cyst
  cystic duct (*see also* Disease, gallbladder) 575.4
  Descemet's membrane 371.33
    traumatic—*see* Rupture, eye
  diaphragm—*see also* Hernia, diaphragm
    traumatic—*see* Injury, internal, diaphragm
  diverticulum
    bladder 596.3
    intestine (large) (*see also* Diverticula) 562.10
      small 562.00
  duodenal stump 537.89
  duodenum (ulcer)—*see* Ulcer, duodenum, with
    perforation
  ear drum (*see also* Perforation, tympanum)
    384.20
    with otitis media—*see* Otitis media
    traumatic—*see* Wound, open, ear
  esophagus 530.4
    traumatic 862.22
      with open wound into cavity 862.32
      cervical region—*see* Wound, open,
        esophagus
  eye (without prolapse of intraocular tissue) 871.0
    with
      exposure of intraocular tissue 871.1
      partial loss of intraocular tissue 871.2
      prolapse of intraocular tissue 871.1
    due to burn 940.5
  fallopian tube 620.8
    due to pregnancy—*see* Pregnancy, tubal
    traumatic—*see* Injury, internal, fallopian tube
  fontanel 767.3
  free wall (ventricle) (*see also* Infarct,
    myocardium) 410.9
  gallbladder or duct (*see also* Disease,
    gallbladder) 575.4
    traumatic—*see* Injury, internal, gallbladder
  gastric (*see also* Rupture, stomach) 537.89
    vessel 459.0
  globe (eye) (traumatic)—*see* Rupture, eye
  graafian follicle (hematoma) 620.0
  heart (auricle) (ventricle) (*see also* Infarct,
    myocardium) 410.9
    infectional 422.90
    traumatic—*see* Rupture, myocardium,
      traumatic
  hymen 623.8
  internal
    organ, traumatic—*see also* Injury, internal, by
      site
      heart—*see* Rupture, myocardium, traumatic
      kidney—*see* Rupture, kidney
      liver—*see* Rupture, liver
      spleen—*see* Rupture, spleen, traumatic
    semilunar cartilage—*see* Tear, meniscus
  intervertebral disc—*see* Displacement,
    intervertebral disc
    traumatic (current)—*see* Dislocation, vertebra
  intestine 569.89
    traumatic—*see* Injury, internal, intestine
  intracranial, birth injury 767.0
  iris 364.76
    traumatic—*see* Rupture, eye
  joint capsule—*see* Sprain, by site

Rupture, ruptured—*continued*
  kidney (traumatic) 866.03
    with open wound into cavity 866.13
    due to birth injury 767.8
    nontraumatic 593.89
  lacrimal apparatus (traumatic) 870.2
  lens (traumatic) 366.20
  ligament—*see also* Sprain, by site
    with open wound—*see* Wound, open, by site
    old (*see also* Disorder, cartilage, articular)
      718.0
  liver (traumatic) 864.04
    with open wound into cavity 864.14
    due to birth injury 767.8
    nontraumatic 573.8
  lymphatic (node) (vessel) 457.8
  marginal sinus (placental) (with hemorrhage)
    641.2
    affecting fetus or newborn 762.1
  meaning hernia—*see* Hernia
  membrana tympani (*see also* Perforation,
    tympanum) 384.20
    with otitis media—*see* Otitis media
    traumatic—*see* Wound, open, ear
  membranes (spontaneous)
    artificial
      delayed delivery following 658.3
        affecting fetus or newborn 761.1
      fetus or newborn 761.1
    delayed delivery following 658.2
      affecting fetus or newborn 761.1
    premature (less than 24 hours prior to onset of
      labor) 658.1
      affecting fetus or newborn 761.1
      delayed delivery following 658.2
        affecting fetus or newborn 761.1
  meningeal artery (*see also* Hemorrhage,
    subarachnoid) 430
    late effect—*see* category 438
  meniscus (knee)—*see also* Tear, meniscus
    old (*see also* Derangement, meniscus) 717.5
    site other than knee—*see* Disorder,
      cartilage, articular
    site other than knee—*see* Sprain, by site
  mesentery 568.89
    traumatic—*see* Injury, internal, mesentery
  mitral—*see* Insufficiency, mitral
  muscle (traumatic) NEC—*see also* Sprain, by
    site
    with open wound—*see* Wound, open, by site
    nontraumatic 728.83
  musculotendinous cuff (nontraumatic)
    (shoulder) 840.4
  mycotic aneurysm, causing cerebral hemorrhage
    (*see also* Hemorrhage, subarachnoid) 430
    late effect—*see* category 438
  myocardium, myocardial (*see also* Infarct,
    myocardium) 410.9
    traumatic 861.03
      with open wound into thorax 861.13
  nontraumatic (meaning hernia) (*see also* Hernia,
    by site) 553.9
  obstructed (*see also* Hernia, by site, with
    obstruction) 552.9
    gangrenous (*see also* Hernia, by site, with
      gangrene) 551.9
  operation wound 998.3
  ovary, ovarian 620.8
    corpus luteum 620.1
    follicle (graafian) 620.0

Rupture, ruptured—*continued*
  oviduct 620.8
    due to pregnancy—*see* Pregnancy, tubal
  pancreas 577.8
    traumatic—*see* Injury, internal, pancreas
  papillary muscle (ventricular) 429.6
  pelvic
    floor, complicating delivery 664.1
    organ NEC—*see* Injury, pelvic, organs
  penis (traumatic)—*see* Wound, open, penis
  perineum 624.8
    during delivery (*see also* Laceration,
      perineum, complicating delivery) 664.4
  pharynx (nontraumatic) (spontaneous) 478.29
  pregnant uterus (before onset of labor) 665.0
  prostate (traumatic)—*see* Injury, internal,
    prostate
  pulmonary
    artery 417.8
    valve (heart) (*see also* Endocarditis,
      pulmonary) 424.3
    vein 417.8
    vessel 417.8
  pupil, sphincter 364.75
  pus tube (*see also* Salpingo-oophoritis) 614.2
  pyosalpinx (*see also* Salpingo-oophoritis) 614.2
  rectum 569.49
    traumatic—*see* Injury, internal, rectum
  retina, retinal (traumatic) (without detachment)
    361.30
    with detachment (*see also* Detachment, retina,
      with retinal defect) 361.00
  rotator cuff (capsule) (traumatic) 840.4
    nontraumatic, complete 727.61
  sclera 871.0
  semilunar cartilage, knee (*see also* Tear,
    meniscus) 836.2
    old (*see also* Derangement, meniscus) 717.5
  septum (cardiac) 410.8
  sigmoid 569.89
    traumatic—*see* Injury, internal, colon, sigmoid
  sinus of Valsalva 747.29
  spinal cord—*see also* Injury, spinal, by site
    due to injury at birth 767.4
    fetus or newborn 767.4
    syphilitic 094.89
    traumatic—*see also* Injury, spinal, by site
      with fracture—*see* Fracture, vertebra, by
      site, with spinal cord injury
  spleen 289.59
    congenital 767.8
    due to injury at birth 767.8
    malarial 084.9
    nontraumatic 289.59
    spontaneous 289.59
    traumatic 865.04
      with open wound into cavity 865.14
  splenic vein 459.0
  stomach 537.89
    due to injury at birth 767.8
    traumatic—*see* Injury, internal, stomach
    ulcer—*see* Ulcer, stomach, with perforation
  synovium 727.50
    specified site NEC 727.59
  tendon (traumatic)—*see also* Sprain, by site
    with open wound—*see* Wound, open, by site
    Achilles 845.09
      nontraumatic 727.67
    ankle 845.09
      nontraumatic 727.68

Rupture, ruptured—*continued*
  biceps (long head) 840.8
    nontraumatic 727.62
  foot 845.10
    interphalangeal (joint) 845.13
    metatarsophalangeal (joint) 845.12
    nontraumatic 727.68
    specified site NEC 845.19
    tarsometatarsal (joint) 845.11
  hand 842.10
    carpometacarpal (joint) 842.11
    interphalangeal (joint) 842.13
    metacarpophalangeal (joint) 842.12
    nontraumatic 727.63
      extensors 727.63
      flexors 727.64
    specified site NEC 842.19
  nontraumatic 727.60
    specified site NEC 727.69
  patellar 844.8
    nontraumatic 727.66
  quadriceps 844.8
    nontraumatic 727.65
  rotator cuff (capsule) 840.4
    nontraumatic, complete 727.61
  wrist 842.00
    carpal (joint) 842.01
    nontraumatic 727.63
      extensors 727.63
      flexors 727.64
    radiocarpal (joint) (ligament) 842.02
    radioulnar (joint), distal 842.09
    specified site NEC 842.09
  testis (traumatic) 878.2
    complicated 878.3
    due to syphilis 095.8
  thoracic duct 457.8
  tonsil 474.8
  traumatic
    with open wound—*see* Wound, open, by site
    aorta—*see* Rupture, aorta, traumatic
    ear drum—*see* Wound, open, ear, drum
    external site—*see* Wound, open, by site
    eye 871.2
    globe (eye)—*see* Wound, open, eyeball
    internal organ (abdomen, chest, or
      pelvis)—*see also* Injury, internal, by site
    heart—*see* Rupture, myocardium, traumatic
    kidney—*see* Rupture, kidney
    liver—*see* Rupture, liver
    spleen—*see* Rupture, spleen, traumatic
    ligament, muscle, or tendon—*see also* Sprain,
      by site
      with open wound—*see* Wound, open, by site
    meaning hernia—*see* Hernia
  tricuspid (heart) (valve)—*see* Endocarditis,
    tricuspid
  tube, tubal 620.8
    abscess (*see also* Salpingo-oophoritis) 614.2
    due to pregnancy—*see* Pregnancy, tubal
  tympanum, tympanic (membrane) (*see also*
    Perforation, tympanum) 384.20
    with otitis media—*see* Otitis media
    traumatic—*see* Wound, open, ear, drum
  umbilical cord 663.8
    fetus or newborn 772.0
  ureter (traumatic) (*see also* Injury, internal,
    ureter) 867.2
    nontraumatic 593.89

Rupture, ruptured—*continued*
  urethra 599.84
    with
      abortion—*see* Abortion, by type, with
          damage to pelvic organs
      ectopic pregnancy (*see also* categories
          633.0-633.9) 639.2
      molar pregnancy (*see also* categories
          630-632) 639.2
    following
      abortion 639.2
      ectopic or molar pregnancy 639.2
    obstetrical trauma 665.5
    traumatic—*see* Injury, internal urethra
  uterosacral ligament 620.8
  uterus (traumatic)—*see also* Injury, internal
      uterus
    affecting fetus or newborn 763.8
    during labor 665.1
    nonpuerperal, nontraumatic 621.8
    nontraumatic 621.8
    pregnant (during labor) 665.1
      before labor 665.0
  vaginal 878.6
    complicated 878.7
    complicating delivery—*see* Laceration,
        vagina, complicating delivery
  valve, valvular (heart)—*see* Endocarditis
  varicose vein—*see* Varicose, vein
  varix—*see* Varix
  vena cava 459.0
  ventricle (free wall) (left) (*see also* Infarct,
      myocardium) 410.9
  vesical (urinary) 596.6
    traumatic—*see* Injury, internal, bladder
  vessel (blood) 459.0
    pulmonary 417.8
  viscus 799.8
  vulva 878.4
    complicated 878.5
    complicating delivery 664.9
Russell's dwarf (uterine dwarfism and
    craniofacial dysostosis) 759.89
Russell's dysentery 004.8
Russell (-Silver) syndrome (congenital
    hemihypertrophy and short stature) 759.89
Russian spring-summer type encephalitis 063.0
Rust's disease (tuberculous spondylitis) 015.0
    [720.81]
Rustitskii's disease (multiple myeloma)
    (M9730/3) 203.0
Ruysch's disease (Hirschsprung's disease) 751.3
Rytand-Lipsitch syndrome (complete
    atrioventricular block) 426.0

S

Saber
  shin 090.5
  tibia 090.5
Sac, lacrimal —*see* condition
Saccharomyces infection (*see also* Candidiasis)
  112.9
Saccharopinuria 270.7
Saccular —*see* condition
Sacculation
  aorta (nonsyphilitic) (*see also* Aneurysm, aorta)
    441.9
    ruptured 441.5
    syphilitic 093.0
  bladder 596.3
  colon 569.89
  intralaryngeal (congenital) (ventricular) 748.3
  larynx (congenital) (ventricular) 748.3
  organ or site, congenital—*see* Distortion
  pregnant uterus, complicating delivery 654.4
    affecting fetus or newborn 763.1
      causing obstructed labor 660.2
        affecting fetus or newborn 763.1
  rectosigmoid 569.89
  sigmoid 569.89
  ureter 593.89
  urethra 599.2
  vesical 596.3
Sachs (-Tay) disease (amaurotic familial idiocy)
  330.1
Sacks-Libman disease 710.0 *[424.91]*
Sacralgia 724.6
Sacralization
  fifth lumbar vertebra 756.15
  incomplete (vertebra) 756.15
Sacrodynia 724.6
Sacroiliac joint —*see* condition
Sacroiliitis NEC 720.2
Sacrum —*see* condition
Saddle
  back 737.8
  embolus, aorta 444.0
  nose 738.0
    congenital 754.0
    due to syphilis 090.5
Sadism (sexual) 302.84
Saemisch's ulcer 370.04
Saenger's syndrome 379.46
Sago spleen 277.3
Sailors' skin 692.74
Saint
  Anthony's fire (*see also* Erysipelas) 035
  Guy's dance—*see* Chorea
  Louis-type encephalitis 062.3
  triad (*see also* Hernia, diaphragm) 553.3
  Vitus' dance—*see* Chorea
Salicylism
  correct substance properly administered 535.4
  overdose or wrong substance given or taken
    965.1
Salivary duct or gland —*see also* condition
  virus disease 078.5
Salivation (excessive) (*see also* Ptyalism) 527.7
Salmonella (aertrycke) (choleraesuis)
    (enteritidis) (gallinarum) (suipestifer)
    (typhimurium) (*see also* Infection,
    Salmonella) 003.9
  arthritis 003.23
  carrier (suspected) of V02.3

Salmonella—*continued*
  meningitis 003.21
  osteomyelitis 003.24
  pneumonia 003.22
  septicemia 003.1
  typhosa 002.0
    carrier (suspected) of V02.1
Salmonellosis 003.0
  with pneumonia 003.22
Salpingitis (catarrhal) (fallopian tube) (nodular)
    (pseudofollicular) (purulent) (septic) (*see also*
    Salpingo-oophoritis) 614.2
  ear 381.50
    acute 381.51
    chronic 381.52
  Eustachian (tube) 381.50
    acute 381.51
    chronic 381.52
  follicularis 614.1
  gonococcal (chronic) 098.37
    acute 098.17
  interstitial, chronic 614.1
  isthmica nodosa 614.1
  old—*see* Salpingo-oophoritis, chronic
  puerperal, postpartum, childbirth 670
  specific (chronic) 098.37
    acute 098.17
  tuberculous (acute) (chronic) (*see also*
    Tuberculosis) 016.6
  venereal (chronic) 098.37
    acute 098.17
Salpingocele 620.4
Salpingo-oophoritis (catarrhal) (purulent)
    (ruptured) (septic) (suppurative) 614.2
  acute 614.0
    with
      abortion—*see* Abortion, by type, with sepsis
      ectopic pregnancy (*see also* categories
        633.0-633.9) 639.0
      molar pregnancy (*see also* categories
        630-632) 639.0
    following
      abortion 639.0
      ectopic or molar pregnancy 639.0
    gonococcal 098.17
    puerperal, postpartum, childbirth 670
    tuberculous (*see also* Tuberculosis) 016.6
  chronic 614.1
    gonococcal 098.37
    tuberculous (*see also* Tuberculosis) 016.6
  complicating pregnancy 646.6
    affecting fetus or newborn 760.8
  gonococcal (chronic) 098.37
    acute 098.17
  old—*see* Salpingo-oophoritis, chronic
  puerperal 670
  specific—*see* Salpingo-oophoritis, gonococcal
  subacute (*see also* Salpingo-oophoritis, acute)
    614.0
  tuberculous (acute) (chronic) (*see also*
    Tuberculosis) 016.6
  venereal—*see* Salpingo-oophoritis, gonococcal
Salpingo-ovaritis (*see also* Salpingo-oophoritis)
  614.2
Salpingoperitonitis (*see also*
    Salpingo-oophoritis) 614.2

Sarcomatosis
  meningeal (M9539/3)—*see* Neoplasm,
    meninges, malignant
  specified site NEC (M8800/3)—*see* Neoplasm,
    connective tissue, malignant
  unspecified site (M8800/6) 171.9
Sarcosinemia 270.8
Sarcosporidiosis 136.5
Saturnine —*see* condition
Saturnism 984.9
  specified type of lead—*see* Table of drugs and
    chemicals
Satyriasis 302.89
Sauriasis —*see* Ichthyosis
Sauriderma 757.39
Sauriosis —*see* Ichthyosis
Savill's disease (epidemic exfoliative dermatitis)
  695.89
SBE (subacute bacterial endocarditis) 421.0
Scabies (any site) 133.0
Scabs 782.8
Scaglietti-Dagnini syndrome (acromegalic
  macrospondylitis) 253.0
Scald, scalded —*see also* Burn, by site
  skin syndrome 695.1
Scalenus anticus (anterior) syndrome 353.0
Scales 782.8
Scalp —*see* condition
Scaphocephaly 756.0
Scaphoiditis, tarsal 732.5
Scapulalgia 733.90
Scapulohumeral myopathy 359.1
Scar, scarring (*see also* Cicatrix) 709.2
  adherent 709.2
  atrophic 709.2
  cervix
    in pregnancy or childbirth 654.6
      affecting fetus or newborn 763.8
      causing obstructed labor 660.2
        affecting fetus or newborn 763.1
  cheloid 701.4
  chorioretinal 363.30
    disseminated 363.35
    macular 363.32
    peripheral 363.34
    posterior pole NEC 363.33
  choroid (*see also* Scar, chorioretinal) 363.30
  compression, pericardial 423.9
  congenital 757.39
  conjunctiva 372.64
  cornea 371.00
    xerophthalmic 264.6
  due to previous cesarean delivery, complicating
    pregnancy or childbirth 654.2
    affecting fetus or newborn 763.8
  duodenal (bulb) (cap) 537.3
  hypertrophic 701.4
  keloid 701.4
  labia 624.4
  lung (base) 518.89
  macula 363.32
    disseminated 363.35
    peripheral 363.34
  muscle 728.89
  myocardium, myocardial 412
  painful 709.2
  papillary muscle 429.81
  posterior pole NEC 363.33
    macular—*see* Scar, macula
  postnecrotic (hepatic) (liver) 571.9

Scar, scarring—*continued*
  psychic V15.49
  retina (*see also* Scar, chorioretinal) 363.30
  trachea 478.9
  uterus 621.8
    in pregnancy or childbirth NEC 654.9
      affecting fetus or newborn 763.8
      due to previous cesarean delivery 654.2
  vulva 624.4
Scarabiasis 134.1
Scarlatina 034.1
  anginosa 034.1
  maligna 034.1
  myocarditis, acute 034.1 *[422.0]*
  old (*see also* Myocarditis) 429.0
  otitis media 034.1 *[382.02]*
  ulcerosa 034.1
Scarlatinella 057.8
Scarlet fever (albuminuria) (angina)
  (convulsions) (lesions of lid) (rash) 034.1
Schamberg's disease, dermatitis, or dermatosis
  (progressive pigmentary dermatosis) 709.09
Schatzki's ring (esophagus) (lower) (congenital)
  750.3
  acquired 530.3
Schaufenster krankheit 413.9
Schaumann's
  benign lymphogranulomatosis 135
  disease (sarcoidosis) 135
  syndrome (sarcoidosis) 135
Scheie's syndrome (mucopolysaccharidosis IS)
  277.5
Schenck's disease (sporotrichosis) 117.1
Scheuermann's disease or osteochondrosis
  732.0
Scheuthauer-Marie-Sainton syndrome
  (cleidocranialis dysostosis) 755.59
Schilder (-Flatau) disease 341.1
Schilling-type monocytic leukemia (M9890/3)
  206.9
Schimmelbusch's disease, cystic mastitis, or hy-
  perplasia 610.1
Schirmer's syndrome (encephalocutaneous
  angiomatosis) 759.6
Schistocelia 756.7
Schistoglossia 750.13
Schistosoma infestation —*see* Infestation,
  Schistosoma
Schistosomiasis 120.9
  Asiatic 120.2
  bladder 120.0
  chestermani 120.8
  colon 120.1
  cutaneous 120.3
  due to
    S. hematobium 120.0
    S. japonicum 120.2
    S. mansoni 120.1
    S. mattheii 120.8
  eastern 120.2
  genitourinary tract 120.0
  intestinal 120.1
  lung 120.2
  Manson's (intestinal) 120.1
  Oriental 120.2
  pulmonary 120.2
  specified type NEC 120.8
  vesical 120.0
Schizencephaly 742.4
Schizo-affective psychosis (*see also*
  Schizophrenia) 295.7
Schizodontia 520.2

Schizoid personality 301.20
  introverted 301.21
  schizotypal 301.22
Schizophrenia, schizophrenic (reaction) 295.9

> Note—Use the following fifth-digit
> subclassification with category 295:
>
> 0 *unspecified*
> 1 *subchronic*
> 2 *chronic*
> 3 *subchronic with acute exacerbation*
> 4 *chronic with acute exacerbation*
> 5 *in remission*

  acute (attack) NEC 295.8
    episode 295.4
  atypical form 295.8
  borderline 295.5
  catalepsy 295.2
  catatonic (type) (acute) (excited) (withdrawn)
    295.2
  childhood (type) (*see also* Psychosis,
    childhood) 299.9
  chronic NEC 295.6
  coenesthesiopathic 295.8
  cyclic (type) 295.7
  disorganized (type) 295.1
  flexibilitas cerea 295.2
  hebephrenic (type) (acute) 295.1
  incipient 295.5
  latent 295.5
  paranoid (type) (acute) 295.3
  paraphrenic (acute) 295.3
  prepsychotic 295.5
  primary (acute) 295.0
  prodromal 295.5
  pseudoneurotic 295.5
  pseudopsychopathic 295.5
  reaction 295.9
  residual (state) (type) 295.6
  restzustand 295.6
  schizo-affective (type) (depressed) (excited)
    295.7
  schizophreniform type 295.4
  simple (type) (acute) 295.0
  simplex (acute) 295.0
  specified type NEC 295.8
  syndrome of childhood NEC (*see also*
    Psychosis, childhood) 299.9
  undifferentiated 295.9
    acute 295.8
    chronic 295.6
Schizothymia 301.20
  introverted 301.21
  schizotypal 301.22
Schlafkrankheit 086.5
Schlatter's tibia (osteochondrosis) 732.4
Schlatter-Osgood disease (osteochondrosis,
  tibial tubercle) 732.4
Schloffer's tumor (*see also* Peritonitis) 567.2
Schmidt's syndrome
  sphallo-pharyngo-laryngeal hemiplegia 352.6
  thyroid-adrenocortical insufficiency 258.1
  vagoaccessory 352.6
Schmincke
  carcinoma (M8082/3)—*see* Neoplasm,
    nasopharynx, malignant
  tumor (M8082/3)—*see* Neoplasm,
    nasopharynx, malignant
Schmitz (-Stutzer) dysentery 004.0

Schmorl's disease or nodes 722.30
  lumbar, lumbosacral 722.32
  specified region NEC 722.39
  thoracic, thoracolumbar 722.31
Schneider's syndrome 047.9
Schneiderian
  carcinoma (M8121/3)
    specified site—*see* Neoplasm, by site,
      malignant
    unspecified site 160.0
  papilloma (M8121/0)
    specified site—*see* Neoplasm, by site, benign
    unspecified site 212.0
Schoffer's tumor (*see also* Peritonitis) 567.2
Scholte's syndrome (malignant carcinoid) 259.2
Scholz's disease 330.0
Scholz (-Bielschowsky-Henneberg) syndrome
  330.0
Schönlein (-Henoch) disease (primary) (purpura)
  (rheumatic) 287.0
School examination V70.3
Schottmüller's disease (*see also* Fever,
  paratyphoid) 002.9
Schroeder's syndrome (endocrine-hypertensive)
  255.3
Schüller-Christian disease or syndrome
  (chronic histiocytosis X) 277.8
Schultz's disease or syndrome (agranulocytosis)
  288.0
Schultze's acroparesthesia, simple 443.89
Schwalbe-Ziehen-Oppenheimer disease 333.6
Schwannoma (M9560/0)—*see also* Neoplasm,
  connective tissue, benign
  malignant (M9560/3)—*see* Neoplasm,
    connective tissue, malignant
Schwartz (-Jampel) syndrome 756.89
Schwartz-Bartter syndrome (inappropriate
  secretion of antidiuretic hormone) 253.6
Schweninger-Buzzi disease (macular atrophy)
  701.3
Sciatic —*see* condition
Sciatica (infectional) 724.3
  due to
    displacement of intervertebral disc 722.10
    herniation, nucleus pulposus 722.10
Scimitar syndrome (anomalous venous
  drainage, right lung to inferior vena cava)
  747.49
Sclera —*see* condition
Sclerectasia 379.11
Scleredema
  adultorum 710.1
  Buschke's 710.1
  newborn 778.1
Sclerema
  adiposum (newborn) 778.1
  adultorum 710.1
  edematosum (newborn) 778.1
  neonatorum 778.1
  newborn 778.1
Scleriasis —*see* Scleroderma
Scleritis 379.00
  with corneal involvement 379.05
  anterior (annular) (localized) 379.03
  brawny 379.06
  granulomatous 379.09
  posterior 379.07
  specified NEC 379.09
  suppurative 379.09
  syphilitic 095.0
  tuberculous (nodular) (*see also* Tuberculosis)
    017.3 *[379.09]*

Sclerochoroiditis (*see also* Scleritis) 379.00
Scleroconjunctivitis (*see also* Scleritis) 379.00
Sclerocystic ovary (syndrome) 256.4
Sclerodactylia 701.0
Scleroderma, sclerodermia (acrosclerotic)
    (diffuse) (generalized) (progressive)
    (pulmonary) 710.1
  circumscribed 701.0
  linear 701.0
  localized (linear) 701.0
  newborn 778.1
Sclerokeratitis 379.05
  meaning sclerosing keratitis 370.54
  tuberculous (*see also* Tuberculosis) 017.3
    [379.09]
Scleroma, trachea 040.1
Scleromalacia
  multiple 731.0
  perforans 379.04
Scleromyxedema 701.8
Scleroperikeratitis 379.05
Sclerose en plaques 340
Sclerosis, sclerotic
  adrenal (gland) 255.8
  Alzheimer's 331.0
    with dementia—*see* Alzheimer's, demential
  amyotrophic (lateral) 335.20
  annularis fibrosi
    aortic 424.1
    mitral 424.0
  aorta, aortic 440.0
    valve (*see also* Endocarditis, aortic) 424.1
  artery, arterial, arteriolar, arteriovascular—*see*
    Arteriosclerosis
  ascending multiple 340
  Baló's (concentric) 341.1
  basilar—*see* Sclerosis, brain
  bone (localized) NEC 733.99
  brain (general) (lobular) 341.9
    Alzheimer's—*see* Alzheimer's dementia
    artery, arterial 437.0
    atrophic lobar 331.0
      with dementia 331.0 *[294.1]*
    diffuse 341.1
      familial (chronic) (infantile) 330.0
      infantile (chronic) (familial) 330.0
      Pelizaeus-Merzbacher type 330.0
    disseminated 340
    hereditary 334.2
    infantile, (degenerative) (diffuse) 330.0
    insular 340
    Krabbe's 330.0
    miliary 340
    multiple 340
    Pelizaeus-Merzbacher 330.0
    progressive familial 330.0
    senile 437.0
    tuberous 759.5
  bulbar, progressive 340
  bundle of His 426.50
    left 426.3
    right 426.4
  cardiac—*see* Arteriosclerosis, coronary
  cardiorenal (*see also* Hypertension, cardiorenal)
    404.90
  cardiovascular (*see also* Disease,
    cardiovascular) 429.2
    renal (*see also* Hypertension, cardiorenal)
      404.90

Sclerosis, sclerotic—*continued*
  centrolobar, familial 330.0
  cerebellar—*see* Sclerosis, brain
  cerebral—*see* Sclerosis, brain
  cerebrospinal 340
    disseminated 340
    multiple 340
  cerebrovascular 437.0
  choroid 363.40
    diffuse 363.56
  combined (spinal cord)—*see also* Degeneration,
    combined
    multiple 340
  concentric, Baló's 341.1
  cornea 370.54
  coronary (artery) —*see* Arteriosclerosis,
    coronary
  corpus cavernosum
    female 624.8
    male 607.89
  Dewitzky's
    aortic 424.1
    mitral 424.0
  diffuse NEC 341.1
  disease, heart —*see* Arteriosclerosis, coronary
  disseminated 340
  dorsal 340
  dorsolateral (spinal cord)—*see* Degeneration,
    combined
  endometrium 621.8
  extrapyramidal 333.90
  eye, nuclear (senile) 366.16
  Friedreich's (spinal cord) 334.0
  funicular (spermatic cord) 608.89
  gastritis 535.4
  general (vascular)—*see* Arteriosclerosis
  gland (lymphatic) 457.8
  hepatic 571.9
  hereditary
    cerebellar 334.2
    spinal 334.0
  idiopathic cortical (Garré's) (*see also*
    Osteomyelitis) 730.1
  ilium, piriform 733.5
  insular 340
    pancreas 251.8
  Islands of Langerhans 251.8
  kidney—*see* Sclerosis, renal
  larynx 478.79
  lateral 335.24
    amyotrophic 335.20
    descending 335.24
    primary 335.24
    spinal 335.24
  liver 571.9
  lobar, atrophic (of brain) 331.0
    with dementia 331.0 *[294.1]*
  lung (*see also* Fibrosis, lung) 515
  mastoid 383.1
  mitral—*see* Endocarditis, mitral
  Mönckeberg's (medial) (*see also*
    Arteriosclerosis, extremities) 440.20
  multiple (brain stem) (cerebral) (generalized)
    (spinal cord) 340
  myocardium, myocardial —*see*
    Arteriosclerosis, coronary
  nuclear (senile), eye 366.16
  ovary 620.8
  pancreas 577.8
  penis 607.89

Sclerosis, sclerotic—*continued*
  peripheral arteries NEC (*see also*
    Arteriosclerosis, extremities) 440.20
  plaques 340
  pluriglandular 258.8
  polyglandular 258.8
  posterior (spinal cord) (syphilitic) 094.0
  posterolateral (spinal cord)—*see* Degeneration,
    combined
  prepuce 607.89
  primary lateral 335.24
  progressive systemic 710.1
  pulmonary (*see also* Fibrosis, lung) 515
    artery 416.0
    valve (heart) (*see also* Endocarditis,
      pulmonary) 424.3
  renal 587
    with
      cystine storage disease 270.0
      hypertension (*see also* Hypertension,
        kidney) 403.90
      hypertensive heart disease (conditions
        classifiable to 402) (*see also*
        Hypertension, cardiorenal) 404.90
    arteriolar (hyaline) (*see also* Hypertension,
      kidney) 403.90
    hyperplastic (*see also* Hypertension, kidney)
      403.90
  retina (senile) (vascular) 362.17
  rheumatic
    aortic valve 395.9
    mitral valve 394.9
  Schilder's 341.1
  senile—*see* Arteriosclerosis
  spinal (cord) (general) (progressive)
    (transverse) 336.8
    ascending 357.0
    combined—*see also* Degeneration, combined
      multiple 340
      syphilitic 094.89
    disseminated 340
    dorsolateral—*see* Degeneration, combined
    hereditary (Friedreich's) (mixed form) 334.0
    lateral (amyotrophic) 335.24
    multiple 340
    posterior (syphilitic) 094.0
  stomach 537.89
  subendocardial, congenital 425.3
  systemic (progressive) 710.1
    with lung involvement 710.1 *[517.2]*
  tricuspid (heart) (valve)—*see* Endocarditis,
    tricuspid
  tuberous (brain) 759.5
  tympanic membrane (*see also*
    Tympanosclerosis) 385.00
  valve, valvular (heart)—*see* Endocarditis
  vascular—*see* Arteriosclerosis
  vein 459.89
Sclerotenonitis 379.07
Sclerotitis (*see also* Scleritis) 379.00
  syphilitic 095.0
  tuberculous (*see also* Tuberculosis) 017.3
    [379.09]
Scoliosis (acquired) (postural) 737.30
  congenital 754.2
  due to or associated with
    Charcot-Marie-Tooth disease 356.1 *[737.43]*
    mucopolysaccharidosis 277.5 *[737.43]*
    neurofibromatosis 237.71 *[737.43]*
    osteitis
      deformans 731.0 *[737.43]*

Scoliosis— *continued*
    fibrosa cystica 252.0 *[737.43]*
    osteoporosis (*see also* Osteoporosis) 733.00
      [737.43]
    poliomyelitis 138 *[737.43]*
    radiation 737.33
    tuberculosis (*see also* Tuberculosis) 015.0
      [737.43]
  idiopathic 737.30
  infantile
    progressive 737.32
    resolving 737.31
  paralytic 737.39
  rachitic 268.1
  sciatic 724.3
  specified NEC 737.39
  thoracogenic 737.34
  tuberculous (*see also* Tuberculosis) 015.0
    [737.43]
Scoliotic pelvis 738.6
  with disproportion (fetopelvic) 653.0
    affecting fetus or newborn 763.1
    causing obstructed labor 660.1
      affecting fetus or newborn 763.1
Scorbutus, scorbutic 267
  anemia 281.8
Scotoma (ring) 368.44
  arcuate 368.43
  Bjerrum 368.43
  blind spot area 368.42
  central 368.41
  centrocecal 368.41
  paracecal 368.42
  paracentral 368.41
  scintillating 368.12
  Seidel 368.43
Scratch —*see* Injury, superficial, by site
Screening (for) V82.9
  alcoholism V79.1
  anemia, deficiency NEC V78.1
    iron V78.0
  anomaly, congenital V82.8
  antenatal V28.9
    alphafetoprotein levels, raised V28.1
    based on amniocentesis V28.2
      chromosomal anomalies V28.0
      raised alpha-fetalprotein levels V28.1
    fetal growth retardation using ultrasonics
      V28.4
    isoimmunization V28.5
    malformations using ultrasonics V28.3
    raised alphafetoprotein levels V28.1
    specified condition NEC V28.8
  arterial hypertension V81.1
  arthropod-borne viral disease NEC V73.5
  asymptomatic bacteriuria V81.5
  bacterial
    conjunctivitis V74.4
    disease V74.9
      specified condition NEC V74.8
  bacteriuria, asymptomatic V81.5
  blood disorder NEC V78.9
    specified type NEC V78.8
  bronchitis, chronic V81.3
  brucellosis V74.8
  cancer—*see* Screening, malignant neoplasm
  cardiovascular disease NEC V81.2
  cataract V80.2
  Chagas' disease V75.3
  chemical poisoning V82.5
  cholera V74.0

Screening (for)—*continued*
  chromosomal
    anomalies
      by amniocentesis, antenatal V28.0
      postnatal V82.4
    athletes V70.3
  condition
    cardiovascular NEC V81.2
    eye NEC V80.2
    genitourinary NEC V81.6
    neurological V80.0
    respiratory NEC V81.4
    skin V82.0
    specified NEC V82.8
  congenital
    anomaly V82.8
      eye V80.2
    dislocation of hip V82.3
    eye condition or disease V80.2
  conjunctivitis, bacterial V74.4
  contamination NEC (*see also* Poisoning) V82.5
  coronary artery disease V81.0
  cystic fibrosis V77.6
  deficiency anemia NEC V78.1
    iron V78.0
  dengue fever V73.5
  depression V79.0
  developmental handicap V79.9
    in early childhood V79.3
    specified type NEC V79.8
  diabetes mellitus V77.1
  diphtheria V74.3
  disease or disorder V82.9
    bacterial V74.9
      specified NEC V74.8
    blood V78.9
      specified type NEC V78.8
    blood-forming organ V78.9
      specified type NEC V78.8
    cardiovascular NEC V81.2
      hypertensive V81.1
      ischemic V81.0
    Chagas' V75.3
    chlamydial V73.98
      specified NEC V73.88
    ear NEC V80.3
    endocrine NEC V77.9
    eye NEC V80.2
    genitourinary NEC V81.6
    heart NEC V81.2
      hypertensive V81.1
      ischemic V81.0
    immunity NEC V77.9
    infectious NEC V75.9
    mental V79.9
      specified type NEC V79.8
    metabolic NEC V77.9
      inborn NEC V77.7
    neurological V80.0
    nutritional NEC V77.9
    rheumatic NEC V82.2
    rickettsial V75.0
    sickle-cell V78.2
      trait V78.2
    specified type NEC V82.8
    thyroid V77.0

Screening (for)—*continued*
  vascular NEC V81.2
    ischemic V81.0
  venereal V74.5
  viral V73.99
    arthropod-borne NEC V73.5
    specified type NEC V73.89
  dislocation of hip, congenital V82.3
  drugs in athletes V70.3
  emphysema (chronic) V81.3
  encephalitis, viral (mosquito or tick borne)
      V73.5
  endocrine disorder NEC V77.9
  eye disorder NEC V80.2
    congenital V80.2
  fever
    dengue V73.5
    hemorrhagic V73.5
    yellow V73.4
  filariasis V75.6
  galactosemia V77.4
  genitourinary condition NEC V81.6
  glaucoma V80.1
  gonorrhea V74.5
  gout V77.5
  Hansen's disease V74.2
  heart disease NEC V81.2
    hypertensive V81.1
    ischemic V81.0
  heavy metal poisoning V82.5
  helminthiasis, intestinal V75.7
  hematopoietic malignancy V76.8
  hemoglobinopathies NEC V78.3
  hemorrhagic fever V73.5
  Hodgkin's disease V76.8
  hormones in athletes V70.3
  hypertension V81.1
  immunity disorder NEC V77.9
  inborn errors of metabolism NEC V77.7
  infection
    bacterial V74.9
      specified type NEC V74.8
    mycotic V75.4
    parasitic NEC V75.8
  infectious disease V75.9
    specified type NEC V75.8
  ingestion of radioactive substance V82.5
  intestinal helminthiasis V75.7
  iron deficiency anemia V78.0
  ischemic heart disease V81.0
  lead poisoning V82.5
  leishmaniasis V75.2
  leprosy V74.2
  leptospirosis V74.8
  leukemia V76.8
  lymphoma V76.8
  malaria V75.1
  malignant neoplasm (of) V76.9
    bladder V76.3
    blood V76.8
    breast V76.1
    cervix V76.2
    hematopoietic system V76.8
    lung V76.0
    lymph (glands) V76.8
    oral cavity V76.42
    rectum V76.41
    respiratory organs V76.0

Screening (for)—*continued*
  skin V76.43
  specified sites NEC V76.49
  malnutrition V77.2
  measles V73.2
  mental
    disorder V79.9
      specified type NEC V79.8
    retardation V79.2
  metabolic errors, inborn V77.7
  mucoviscidosis V77.6
  multiphasic V82.6
  mycosis V75.4
  mycotic infection V75.4
  nephropathy V81.5
  neurological condition V80.0
  nutritional disorder V77.9
  obesity V77.8
  parasitic infection NEC V75.8
  phenylketonuria V77.3
  plague V74.8
  poisoning
    chemical NEC V82.5
    contaminated water supply V82.5
    heavy metal V82.5
  poliomyelitis V73.0
  postnatal chromosomal anomalies V82.4
  prenatal—*see* Screening, antenatal
  pulmonary tuberculosis V74.1
  radiation exposure V82.5
  renal disease V81.5
  respiratory condition NEC V81.4
  rheumatic disorder NEC V82.2
  rheumatoid arthritis V82.1
  rickettsial disease V75.0
  rubella V73.3
  schistosomiasis V75.5
  senile macular lesions of eye V80.2
  sickle-cell anemia, disease, or trait V78.2
  skin condition V82.0
  sleeping sickness V75.3
  smallpox V73.1
  special V82.9
    specified condition NEC V82.8
  specified type NEC V82.8
  spirochetal disease V74.9
    specified type NEC V74.8
  stimulants in athletes V70.3
  syphilis V74.5
  tetanus V74.8
  thyroid disorder V77.0
  trachoma V73.6
  trypanosomiasis V75.3
  tuberculosis, pulmonary V74.1
  venereal disease V74.5
  viral encephalitis
    mosquito-borne V73.5
    tick-borne V73.5
  whooping cough V74.8
  worms, intestinal V75.7
  yaws V74.6
  yellow fever V73.4
Scrofula (*see also* Tuberculosis) 017.2
Scrofulide (primary) (*see also* Tuberculosis) 017.0
Scrofuloderma, scrofulodermia (any site) (primary) (*see also* Tuberculosis) 017.0
Scrofulosis (universal) (*see also* Tuberculosis) 017.2
Scrofulosis lichen (primary) (*see also* Tuberculosis) 017.0
Scrofulous —*see* condition

Scrotal tongue 529.5
  congenital 750.13
Scrotum —*see* condition
Scurvy (gum) (infantile) (rickets) (scorbutic) 267
Sea-blue histiocyte syndrome 272.7
Seabright-Bantam syndrome (pseudohypoparathyroidism) 275.4
Seasickness 994.6
Seatworm 127.4
Sebaceous
  cyst (*see also* Cyst, sebaceous) 706.2
  gland disease NEC 706.9
Sebocystomatosis 706.2
Seborrhea, seborrheic 706.3
  adiposa 706.3
  capitis 690.11
  congestiva 695.4
  corporis 706.3
  dermatitis 690.10
    infantile 690.12
  diathesis in infants 695.89
  eczema 690.18
    infantile 690.12
  keratosis 702.19
    inflamed 702.11
  nigricans 705.89
  sicca 690.18
  wart 702.19
    inflamed 702.11
Seckel's syndrome 759.89
Seclusion pupil 364.74
Seclusiveness, child 313.22
Secondary —*see also* condition
  neoplasm—*see* Neoplasm, by site, malignant, secondary
Secretan's disease or syndrome (posttraumatic edema) 782.3
Secretion
  antidiuretic hormone, inappropriate (syndrome) 253.6
  catecholamine, by pheochromocytoma 255.6
  hormone
    antidiuretic, inappropriate (syndrome) 253.6
    by
      carcinoid tumor 259.2
      pheochromocytoma 255.6
    ectopic NEC 259.3
  urinary
    excessive 788.42
    suppression 788.5
Section
  cesarean
    affecting fetus or newborn 763.4
    post mortem, affecting fetus or newborn 761.6
    previous, in pregnancy or childbirth 654.2
      affecting fetus or newborn 763.8
  nerve, traumatic—*see* Injury, nerve, by site
Seeligmann's syndrome (ichthyosis congenita) 757.1
Segmentation, incomplete (congenital)—*see also* Fusion
  bone NEC 756.9
  lumbosacral (joint) 756.15
  vertebra 756.15
    lumbosacral 756.15
Seizure 780.3
  akinetic (idiopathic) (*see also* Epilepsy) 345.0
    psychomotor 345.4
  apoplexy, apoplectic (*see also* Disease, cerebrovascular, acute) 436

Seizure—*continued*
 atonic (*see also* Epilepsy) 345.0
 autonomic 300.11
 brain or cerebral (*see also* Disease,
  cerebrovascular, acute) 436
 convulsive (*see also* Convulsions) 780.3
 cortical (focal) (motor) (*see also* Epilepsy) 345.5
 epilepsy, epileptic (cryptogenic) (*see also*
  Epilepsy) 345.9
 epileptiform, epileptoid 780.3
  focal (*see also* Epilepsy) 345.5
 febrile 780.3
 heart—*see* Disease, heart
 hysterical 300.11
 Jacksonian (focal) (*see also* Epilepsy) 345.5
  motor type 345.5
  sensory type 345.5
 newborn 779.0
 paralysis (*see also* Disease, cerebrovascular,
  acute) 436
 recurrent 780.3
  epileptic—*see* Epilepsy
 repetitive 780.3
  epileptic—*see* Epilepsy
 salaam (*see also* Epilepsy) 345.6
 uncinate (*see also* Epilepsy) 345.4
Self-mutilation 300.9
Semicoma 780.09
Semiconsciousness 780.09
Seminal
 vesicle—*see* condition
 vesiculitis (*see also* Vesiculitis) 608.0
Seminoma (M9061/3)
 anaplastic type (M9062/3)
  specified site—*see* Neoplasm, by site,
   malignant
  unspecified site 186.9
 specified site—*see* Neoplasm, by site, malignant
 spermatocytic (M9063/3)
  specified site—*see* Neoplasm, by site,
   malignant
  unspecified site 186.9
 unspecified site 186.9
Semliki Forest encephalitis 062.8
Senear-Usher disease or syndrome (pemphigus
 erythematosus) 694.4
Senecio jacobae dermatitis 692.6
Senectus 797
Senescence 797
Senile (*see also* condition) 797
 cervix (atrophic) 622.8
 degenerative atrophy, skin 701.3
 endometrium (atrophic) 621.8
 fallopian tube (atrophic) 620.3
 heart (failure) 797
 lung 492.8
 ovary (atrophic) 620.3
 syndrome 259.8
 vagina, vaginitis (atrophic) 627.3
 wart 702.0
Senility 797
 with
  acute confusional state 290.3
  delirium 290.3
  mental changes 290.9
  psychosis NEC (*see also* Psychosis, senile)
   290.20
 premature (syndrome) 259.8

Sensation
 burning (*see also* Disturbance, sensation) 782.0
  tongue 529.6
 choking 784.9
 loss of (*see also* Disturbance, sensation) 782.0
 prickling (*see also* Disturbance, sensation) 782.0
 tingling (*see also* Disturbance, sensation) 782.0
Sense loss (touch) (*see also* Disturbance,
  sensation) 782.0
 smell 781.1
 taste 781.1
Sensibility disturbance NEC (cortical) (deep)
 (vibratory) (*see also* Disturbance, sensation)
 782.0
Sensitive dentine 521.8
Sensitiver Beziehungswahn 297.8
Sensitivity, sensitization —*see also* Allergy
 autoerythrocyte 287.2
 carotid sinus 337.0
 child (excessive) 313.21
 cold, autoimmune 283.0
 methemoglobin 289.7
 suxamethonium 289.8
 tuberculin, without clinical or radiological
  symptoms 795.5
Sensory
 extinction 781.8
 neglect 781.8
Separation
 acromioclavicular—*see* Dislocation, shoulder
 anxiety, abnormal 309.21
 apophysis, traumatic—*see* Fracture, by site
 choroid 363.70
  hemorrhagic 363.72
  serous 363.71
 costochondral (simple) (traumatic)—*see*
  Dislocation, costochondral
 epiphysis, epiphyseal
  nontraumatic 732.9
   upper femoral 732.2
  traumatic—*see* Fracture, by site
 fracture—*see* Fracture, by site
 infundibulum cardiac from right ventricle by a
  partition 746.83
 joint (current) (traumatic)—*see* Dislocation, by
  site
 placenta (normally implanted)—*see* Placenta,
  separation
 pubic bone, obstetrical trauma 665.6
 retina, retinal (*see also* Detachment, retina)
  361.9
  layers 362.40
  sensory (*see also* Retinoschisis) 361.10
  pigment epithelium (exudative) 362.42
   hemorrhagic 362.43
 sternoclavicular (traumatic)—*see* Dislocation,
  sternoclavicular
 symphysis pubis, obstetrical trauma 665.6
 tracheal ring, incomplete (congenital) 748.3
Sepsis (generalized) (*see also* Septicemia) 038.9
 with
  abortion—*see* Abortion, by type, with sepsis
  ectopic pregnancy (*see also* categories
   633.0-633.9) 639.0
  molar pregnancy (*see also* categories
   630-632) 639.0
 buccal 528.3
 complicating labor 659.3
 dental (pulpal origin) 522.4
 female genital organ NEC 614.9

Sepsis—*continued*
  fetus (intrauterine) 771.8
  following
    abortion 639.0
    ectopic or molar pregnancy 639.0
    infusion, perfusion, or transfusion 999.3
  Friedländer's 038.49
  intraocular 360.00
  localized
    in operation wound 998.59
    skin (*see also* Abscess) 682.9
  malleus 024
  newborn (umbilical) (organism unspecified)
    NEC 771.8
  of tracheostomy stoma 519.0
  oral 528.3
  puerperal, postpartum, childbirth (pelvic) 670
  resulting from infusion, injection, transfusion,
    or vaccination 999.3
  skin, localized (*see also* Abscess) 682.9
  umbilical (newborn) (organism unspecified)
    771.8
  tetanus 771.3
  urinary 599.0
Septate —*see also* Septum
Septic —*see also* condition
  arm (with lymphangitis) 682.3
  embolus—*see* Embolism
  finger (with lymphangitis) 681.00
  foot (with lymphangitis) 682.7
  gallbladder (*see also* Cholecystitis) 575.8
  hand (with lymphangitis) 682.4
  joint (*see also* Arthritis, septic) 711.0
  kidney (*see also* Infection, kidney) 590.9
  leg (with lymphangitis) 682.6
  mouth 528.3
  nail 681.9
    finger 681.02
    toe 681.11
  shock (endotoxic) 785.59
  sore (*see also* Abscess) 682.9
    throat 034.0
      milk-borne 034.0
      streptococcal 034.0
  spleen (acute) 289.59
  teeth (pulpal origin) 522.4
  throat 034.0
  thrombus—*see* Thrombosis
  toe (with lymphangitis) 681.10
  tonsils 474.0
  umbilical cord (newborn) (organism
    unspecified) 771.8
  uterus (*see also* Endometritis) 615.9
Septicemia, septicemic (generalized)
    (suppurative) 038.9
  with
    abortion—*see* Abortion, by type, with sepsis
    ectopic pregnancy (*see also* categories
      633.0-633.9) 639.0
    molar pregnancy (*see also* categories
      630-632) 639.0
  Aerobacter aerogenes 038.49
  anaerobic 038.3
  anthrax 022.3
  Bacillus coli 038.42
  Bacteroides 038.3
  Clostridium 038.3
  complicating labor 659.3
  cryptogenic 038.9
  enteric gram-negative bacilli 038.40

Septicemia, septicemic—*continued*
  Enterobacter aerogenes 038.49
  Erysipelothrix (insidiosa) (rhusiopathiae) 027.1
  Escherichia coli 038.42
  following
    abortion 639.0
    ectopic or molar pregnancy 639.0
    infusion, injection, transfusion, or vaccination
      999.3
  Friedländer's (bacillus) 038.49
  gangrenous 038.9
  gonococcal 098.89
  gram-negative (organism) 038.40
    anaerobic 038.3
  Hemophilus influenzae 038.41
  herpes (simplex) 054.5
  herpetic 054.5
  Listeria monocytogenes 027.0
  meningeal—*see* Meningitis
  meningococcal (chronic) (fulminating) 036.2
  navel, newborn (organism unspecified) 771.8
  newborn (umbilical) (organism unspecified)
    771.8
  plague 020.2
  pneumococcal 038.2
  postabortal 639.0
  postoperative 998.59
  Proteus vulgaris 038.49
  Pseudomonas (aeruginosa) 038.43
  puerperal, postpartum 670
  Salmonella (aertrycke) (callinarum)
    (choleraesuis) (enteritidis) (suipestifer) 003.1
  Serratia 038.44
  Shigella (*see also* Dysentery, bacillary) 004.9
  specified organism NEC 038.8
  staphylococcal 038.1
  streptococcal (anaerobic) 038.0
  suipestifer 003.1
  umbilicus, newborn (organism unspecified)
    771.8
  viral 079.99
  Yersinia enterocolitica 038.49
Septum, septate (congenital)—*see also*
    Anomaly, specified type NEC
  anal 751.2
  aqueduct of Sylvius 742.3
    with spina bifida (*see also* Spina bifida) 741.0
  hymen 752.49
  uterus (*see also* Double, uterus) 752.2
  vagina 752.49
    in pregnancy or childbirth 654.7
      affecting fetus or newborn 763.8
      causing obstructed labor 660.2
        affecting fetus or newborn 763.1
Sequestration
  lung (congenital) (extralobar) (intralobar) 748.5
  orbit 376.10
  pulmonary artery (congenital) 747.3
Sequestrum
  bone (*see also* Osteomyelitis) 730.1
    jaw 526.4
  dental 525.8
  jaw bone 526.4
  sinus (accessory) (nasal) (*see also* Sinusitis)
    473.9
    maxillary 473.0
Sequoiosis asthma 495.8

Serology for syphilis
doubtful
with signs or symptoms—*see* Syphilis, by site
and stage
follow-up of latent syphilis—*see* Syphilis,
latent
false positive 795.6
negative, with signs or symptoms—*see*
Syphilis, by site and stage
positive 097.1
with signs or symptoms—*see* Syphilis, by site
and stage
false 795.6
follow-up of latent syphilis—*see* Syphilis,
latent
only finding—*see* Syphilis, latent
reactivated 097.1
Seroma (postoperative) (non-infected) 998.13
infected 998.51
Seropurulent —*see* condition
Serositis, multiple 569.89
pericardial 423.2
peritoneal 568.82
pleural—*see* Pleurisy
Serotonin syndrome 333.99
Serous —*see* condition
Sertoli cell
adenoma (M8640/0)
specified site—*see* Neoplasm, by site, benign
unspecified site
female 220
male 222.0
carcinoma (M8640/3)
specified site—*see* Neoplasm, by site,
malignant
unspecified site 186.9
syndrome (germinal aplasia) 606.0
tumor (M8640/0)
with lipid storage (M8641/0)
specified site—*see* Neoplasm, by site,
benign
unspecified site
female 220
male 222.0
specified site—*see* Neoplasm, by site, benign
unspecified site
female 220
male 222.0
Sertoli-Leydig cell tumor (M8631/0)
specified site—*see* Neoplasm, by site, benign
unspecified site
female 220
male 222.0
Serum
allergy, allergic reaction 999.5
shock 999.4
arthritis 999.5 *[713.6]*
complication or reaction NEC 999.5
disease NEC 999.5
hepatitis—*see* Hepatitis, viral
carrier (suspected) of V02.6
intoxication 999.5
jaundice (homologous) *see* Hepatitis, viral
neuritis 999.5
poisoning NEC 999.5
rash NEC 999.5
reaction NEC 999.5
sickness NEC 999.5
Sesamoiditis 733.99

Seven-day fever 061
of
Japan 100.89
Queensland 100.89
Sever's disease or osteochondrosis (calcaneum)
732.5
Sex chromosome mosaics 758.81
Sextuplet
affected by maternal complications of
pregnancy 761.5
healthy liveborn—*see* Newborn, multiple
pregnancy (complicating delivery) NEC 651.8
with fetal loss and retention of one or more
fetus(es) 651.6
Sexual
anesthesia 302.72
deviation (*see also* Deviation, sexual) 302.9
disorder (*see also* Deviation, sexual) 302.9
frigidity (female) 302.72
function, disorder of (psychogenic) 302.70
specified type NEC 302.79
immaturity (female) (male) 259.0
impotence (psychogenic) 302.72
organic origin NEC 607.84
precoclty (constitutional) (cryptogenic) (female)
(idiopathic) (male) NEC 259.1
with adrenal hyperplasia 255.2
sadism 302.84
Sexuality, pathological (*see also* Deviation,
sexual) 302.9
Sézary's disease, reticulosis, or syndrome
(M9701/3) 202.2
Shadow, lung 793.1
Shaken infant syndrome 995.55
Shaking
head (tremor) 781.0
palsy or paralysis (*see also* Parkinsonism) 332.0
Shallowness, acetabulum 736.39
Shaver's disease or syndrome (bauxite
pneumoconiosis) 503
Sheath (tendon)—*see* condition
Shedding
nail 703.8
teeth, premature, primary (deciduous) 520.6
Sheehan's disease or syndrome (postpartum
pituitary necrosis) 253.2
Shelf, rectal 569.49
Shell
shock (current) (*see also* Reaction, stress, acute)
308.9
lasting state 300.16
teeth 520.5
Shield kidney 753.3
Shift, mediastinal 793.2
Shifting
pacemaker 427.89
sleep-work schedule (affecting sleep) 307.45
Shiga's
bacillus 004.0
dysentery 004.0
Shigella (dysentery) (*see also* Dysentery,
bacillary) 004.9
carrier (suspected) of V02.3
Shigellosis (*see also* Dysentery, bacillary) 004.9
Shingles (*see also* Herpes, zoster) 053.9
eye NEC 053.29
Shin splints 844.9
Shipyard eye or disease 077.1
Shirodkar suture, in pregnancy 654.5

Shock 785.50
  with
    abortion—*see* Abortion, by type, with shock
    ectopic pregnancy (*see also* categories
      633.0-633.9) 639.5
    molar pregnancy (*see also* categories
      630-632) 639.5
  allergic—*see* Shock, anaphylactic
  anaclitic 309.21
  anaphylactic 995.0
    chemical—*see* Table of drugs and chemicals
    correct medicinal substance properly
      administered 995.0
    drug or medicinal substance
      correct substance properly administered
        995.0
      overdose or wrong substance given or taken
        977.9
        specified drug—*see* Table of drugs and
          chemicals
    food—*see* Anaphylactic shock, due to, food
    following sting(s) 989.5
    immunization 999.4
    serum 999.4
  anaphylactoid—*see* Shock, anaphylactic
  anesthetic
    correct substance properly administered 995.4
    overdose or wrong substance given 968.4
      specified anesthetic—*see* Table of drugs
        and chemicals
  birth, fetus or newborn NEC 779.8
  cardiogenic 785.51
  chemical substance—*see* Table of drugs and
    chemicals
  circulatory 785.59
  complicating
    abortion—*see* Abortion, by type, with shock
    ectopic pregnancy (*see also* categories
      633.0-633.9) 639.5
    labor and delivery 669.1
    molar pregnancy (*see also* categories
      630-632) 639.5
  culture 309.29
  due to
    drug 995.0
      correct substance properly administered
        995.0
      overdose or wrong substance given or taken
        977.9
        specified drug—*see* Table of drugs and
          chemicals
    food—*see* Anaphylactic shock, due to, food
  during labor and delivery 669.1
  electric 994.8
  endotoxic 785.59
    due to surgical procedure 998.0
  following
    abortion 639.5
    ectopic or molar pregnancy 639.5
    injury (immediate) (delayed) 958.4
    labor and delivery 669.1
  gram-negative 785.59
  hematogenic 785.59
  hemorrhagic
    due to
      disease 785.59
      surgery (intraoperative) (postoperative)
        998.0
      trauma 958.4
  hypovolemic NEC 785.59
    surgical 998.0

Shock—*continued*
  traumatic 958.4
  insulin 251.0
    therapeutic misadventure 962.3
  kidney 584.5
    traumatic (following crushing) 958.5
  lightning 994.0
  lung 518.5
  nervous (*see also* Reaction, stress, acute) 308.9
  obstetric 669.1
    with
      abortion—*see* Abortion, by type, with shock
      ectopic pregnancy (*see also* categories
        633.0-633.9) 639.5
      molar pregnancy (*see also* categories
        630-632) 639.5
    following
      abortion 639.5
      ectopic or molar pregnancy 639.5
  paralysis, paralytic (*see also* Disease,
    cerebrovascular, acute) 436
    late effect—*see* category 438
  pleural (surgical) 998.0
    due to trauma 958.4
  postoperative 998.0
    with
      abortion—*see* Abortion, by type, with shock
      ectopic pregnancy (*see also* categories
        633.0-633.9) 639.5
      molar pregnancy (*see also* categories
        630-632) 639.5
    following
      abortion 639.5
      ectopic or molar pregnancy 639.5
  psychic (*see also* Reaction, stress, acute) 308.9
    past history (of) V15.49
  psychogenic (*see also* Reaction, stress, acute)
    308.9
  septic 785.59
    with
      abortion—*see* Abortion, by type, with shock
      ectopic pregnancy (*see also* categories
        633.0-633.9) 639.5
      molar pregnancy (*see also* categories
        630-632) 639.5
    due to
      surgical procedure 998.0
      transfusion NEC 999.8
        bone marrow 996.85
    following
      abortion 639.5
      ectopic or molar pregnancy 639.5
      surgical procedure 998.0
      transfusion NEC 999.8
        bone marrow 996.85
  spinal—*see also* Injury, spinal, by site
    with spinal bone injury—*see* Fracture,
      vertebra, by site, with spinal cord injury
  surgical 998.0
  therapeutic misadventure NEC (*see also*
    Complications) 998.89
  thyroxin 962.7
  toxic 040.89
  transfusion—*see* Complications, transfusion
  traumatic (immediate) (delayed) 958.4
Shoemakers' chest 738.3
Short, shortening, shortness
  Achilles tendon (acquired) 727.81
  arm 736.89
    congenital 755.20
  back 737.9

Short, shortening, shortness—*continued*
  bowel syndrome 579.3
  breath 786.09
  common bile duct, congenital 751.69
  cord (umbilical) 663.4
    affecting fetus or newborn 762.6
  cystic duct, congenital 751.69
  esophagus (congenital) 750.4
  femur (acquired) 736.81
    congenital 755.34
  frenulum linguae 750.0
  frenum, lingual 750.0
  hamstrings 727.81
  hip (acquired) 736.39
    congenital 755.63
  leg (acquired) 736.81
    congenital 755.30
  metatarsus (congenital) 754.79
    acquired 736.79
  organ or site, congenital NEC—*see* Distortion
  palate (congenital) 750.26
  P-R interval syndrome 426.81
  radius (acquired) 736.09
    congenital 755.26
  round ligament 629.8
  sleeper 307.49
  stature, constitutional (hereditary) 783.4
  tendon 727.81
    Achilles (acquired) 727.81
      congenital 754.79
    congenital 756.89
  thigh (acquired) 736.81
    congenital 755.34
  tibialis anticus 727.81
  umbilical cord 663.4
    affecting fetus or newborn 762.6
  urethra 599.84
  uvula (congenital) 750.26
  vagina 623.8
Shortsightedness 367.1
Shoshin (acute fulminating beriberi) 265.0
Shoulder —*see* condition
Shovel-shaped incisors 520.2
Shower, thromboembolic —*see* Embolism
Shunt (status)
  aortocoronary bypass V45.81
  arterial-venous (dialysis) V45.1
  arteriovenous, pulmonary (acquired) 417.0
    congenital 747.3
    traumatic (complication) 901.40
  cerebral ventricle (communicating) in situ V45.2
  coronary artery bypass V45.81
  surgical, prosthetic, with complications—*see*
    Complications, shunt
  vascular NEC V45.89
Shutdown
  renal 586
    with
      abortion—*see* Abortion, by type, with renal
        failure
      ectopic pregnancy (*see also* categories
        633.0-633.9) 639.3
      molar pregnancy (*see also* categories
        630-632) 639.3
    complicating
      abortion 639.3
      ectopic or molar pregnancy 639.3
    following labor and delivery 669.3
Shwachman's syndrome 288.0
Shy-Drager syndrome (orthostatic hypotension
  with multisystem degeneration) 333.0

Sialadenitis (any gland) (chronic) (suppurative)
  527.2
  epidemic—*see* Mumps
Sialadenosis, periodic 527.2
Sialaporia 527.7
Sialectasia 527.8
Sialitis 527.2
Sialoadenitis (*see also* Sialadenitis) 527.2
Sialoangitis 527.2
Sialodochitis (fibrinosa) 527.2
Sialodocholithiasis 527.5
Sialolithiasis 527.5
Sialorrhea (*see also* Ptyalism) 527.7
  periodic 527.2
Sialosis 527.8
  rheumatic 710.2
Siamese twin 759.4
Sicard's syndrome 352.6
Sicca syndrome (keratoconjunctivitis) 710.2
Sick 799.9
  cilia syndrome 759.89
  or handicapped person in family V61.49
Sickle-cell
  anemia (*see also* Disease, sickle-cell) 282.60
  disease (*see also* Disease, sickle-cell) 282.60
  hemoglobin
    C disease 282.63
    D disease 282.69
    E disease 282.69
  thalassemia 282.4
  trait 282.5
Sicklemia (*see also* Disease, sickle-cell) 282.60
  trait 282.5
Sickness
  air (travel) 994.6
  airplane 994.6
  alpine 993.2
  altitude 993.2
  Andes 993.2
  aviators' 993.2
  balloon 993.2
  car 994.6
  compressed air 993.3
  decompression 993.3
  green 280.9
  harvest 100.89
  milk 988.8
  morning 643.0
  motion 994.6
  mountain 993.2
    acute 289.0
  protein (*see also* Complications, vaccination)
    999.5
  radiation NEC 990
  roundabout (motion) 994.6
  sea 994.6
  serum NEC 999.5
  sleeping (African) 086.5
    by Trypanosoma 086.5
      gambiense 086.3
      rhodesiense 086.4
    Gambian 086.3
    late effect 139.8
    Rhodesian 086.4
  sweating 078.2
  swing (motion) 994.6
  train (railway) (travel) 994.6
  travel (any vehicle) 994.6
Sick sinus syndrome 427.81
Sideropenia (*see also* Anemia, iron deficiency)
  280.9

Siderosis (lung) (occupational) 503
 cornea 371.15
 eye (bulbi) (vitreous) 360.23
 lens 360.23
Siegal-Cattan-Mamou disease (periodic) 277.3
Siemens' syndrome
 ectodermal dysplasia 757.31
 keratosis follicularis spinulosa (decalvans)
  757.39
Sighing respiration 786.7
Sigmoid
 flexure—*see* condition
 kidney 753.3
Sigmoiditis —*see* Enteritis
Silfverskiöld's syndrome 756.50
Silicosis, sillicotic (complicated) (occupational)
  (simple) 502
 fibrosis, lung (confluent) (massive)
  (occupational) 502
 non-nodular 503
 pulmonum 502
Silicotuberculosis (*see also* Tuberculosis) 011.4
Silo fillers' disease 506.9
Silver's syndrome (congenital hemihypertrophy
  and short stature) 759.89
Silver wire arteries, retina 362.13
Silvestroni-Bianco syndrome (thalassemia
  minima) 282.4
Simian crease 757.2
Simmonds' cachexia or disease (pituitary
  cachexia) 253.2
Simons' disease or syndrome (progressive
  lipodystrophy) 272.6
Simple, simplex —*see* condition
Sinding-Larsen disease (juvenile osteopathia
  patellae) 732.4
Singapore hemorrhagic fever 065.4
Singers' node or nodule 478.5
Single
 atrium 745.69
 coronary artery 746.85
 umbilical artery 747.5
 ventricle 745.3
Singultus 786.8
 epidemicus 078.89
Sinus —*see also* Fistula
 abdominal 569.81
 arrest 426.6
 arrhythmia 427.89
 bradycardia 427.89
 chronic 427.81
 branchial cleft (external) (internal) 744.41
 coccygeal (infected) 685.1
  with abscess 685.0
 dental 522.7
 dermal (congenital) 685.1
  with abscess 685.0
 draining—*see* Fistula
 infected, skin NEC 686.9
 marginal, ruptured or bleeding 641.2
  affecting fetus or newborn 762.1
 pause 426.6
 pericranii 742.0
 pilonidal (infected) (rectum) 685.1
  with abscess 685.0
 preauricular 744.46
 rectovaginal 619.1
 sacrococcygeal (dermoid) (infected) 685.1
  with abscess 685.0

Sinus—*continued*
 skin
  infected NEC 686.9
  noninfected—*see* Ulcer, skin
 tachycardia 427.89
 tarsi syndrome 355.5
 testis 608.89
 tract (postinfectional)—*see* Fistula
 urachus 753.7
Sinuses, Rokitansky-Aschoff (*see also* Disease,
  gallbladder) 575.8
Sinusitis (accessory) (nasal) (hyperplastic)
  (nonpurulent) (purulent) (chronic) 473.9
 with influenza, flu, or grippe 487.1
 acute 461.9
  ethmoidal 461.2
  frontal 461.1
  maxillary 461.0
  specified type NEC 461.8
  sphenoidal 461.3
 allergic (*see also* Fever, hay) 477.9
 antrum—*see* Sinusitis, maxillary
 due to
  fungus, any sinus 117.9
  high altitude 993.1
 ethmoidal 473.2
  acute 461.2
 frontal 473.1
  acute 461.1
 influenzal 478.1
 maxillary 473.0
  acute 461.0
 specified site NEC 473.8
 sphenoidal 473.3
  acute 461.3
 syphilitic, any sinus 095.8
 tuberculous, any sinus (*see also* Tuberculosis)
  012.8
Sinusitis-bronchiectasis-situs inversus
  (syndrome) (triad) 759.3
Sipple's syndrome (medullary thyroid
  carcinoma-pheochromocytoma) 193
Sirenomelia 759.89
Siriasis 992.0
Sirkari's disease 085.0
Siti 104.0
Sitophobia 300.29
Situation, psychiatric 300.9
Situational
 disturbance (transient) (*see also* Reaction,
  adjustment) 309.9
  acute 308.3
 maladjustment, acute (*see also* Reaction,
  adjustment) 309.9
 reaction (*see also* Reaction, adjustment) 309.9
  acute 308.3
Situs inversus or transversus 759.3
 abdominalis 759.3
 thoracis 759.3
Sixth disease 057.8
Sjögren (-Gougerot) syndrome or disease
  (keratoconjunctivitis sicca) 710.2
 with lung involvement 710.2 *[517.8]*
Sjögren-Larsson syndrome (ichthyosis
  congenita) 757.1
Skeletal —*see* condition
Skene's gland —*see* condition
Skenitis (*see also* Urethritis) 597.89
 gonorrheal (acute) 098.0
  chronic or duration of 2 months or over 098.2
Skerljevo 104.0

Skevas-Zerfus disease 989.5
Skin —*see also* condition
   donor V59.1
   hidebound 710.9
Slate-dressers' lung 502
Slate-miners' lung 502
Sleep
   disorder 780.50
      with apnea—*see* Apnea, sleep
      child 307.40
      nonorganic origin 307.40
         specified type NEC 307.49
   disturbance 780.50
      with apnea—*see* Apnea, sleep
      nonorganic origin 307.40
         specified type NEC 307.49
   drunkenness 307.47
   paroxysmal 347
   rhythm inversion 780.55
      nonorganic origin 307.45
   walking 307.46
      hysterical 300.13
Sleeping sickness 086.5
   late effect 139.8
Sleeplessness (*see also* Insomnia) 780.52
   menopausal 627.2
   nonorganic origin 307.41
Slipped, slipping
   epiphysis (postinfectional) 732.9
      traumatic (old) 732.9
         current—*see* Fracture, by site
      upper femoral (nontraumatic) 732.2
   intervertebral disc—*see* Displacement,
      intervertebral disc
   ligature, umbilical 772.3
   patella 717.89
   rib 733.99
   sacroiliac joint 724.6
   tendon 727.9
   ulnar nerve, nontraumatic 354.2
   vertebra NEC (*see also* Spondylolisthesis)
      756.12
Slocumb's syndrome 255.3
Sloughing (multiple) (skin) 686.9
   abscess—*see* Abscess, by site
   appendix 543.9
   bladder 596.8
   fascia 728.9
   graft—*see* Complications, graft
   phagedena (*see also* Gangrene) 785.4
   reattached extremity (*see also* Complications,
      reattached extremity) 996.90
   rectum 569.49
   scrotum 608.89
   tendon 727.9
   transplanted organ (*see also* Rejection,
      transplant, organ, by site) 996.80
   ulcer (*see also* Ulcer, skin) 707.9
Slow
   feeding newborn 779.3
   fetal, growth NEC 764.9
      affecting management of pregnancy 656.5
Slowing
   heart 427.89
   urinary stream 788.62
Sluder's neuralgia or syndrome 337.0
Slurred, slurring, speech 784.5
Small, smallness
   cardiac reserve—*see* Disease, heart
   for dates
      fetus or newborn 764.0

Small, smallness—*continued*
      with malnutrition 764.1
      affecting management of pregnancy 656.5
   infant, term 764.0
      with malnutrition 764.1
      affecting management of pregnancy 656.5
   introitus, vagina 623.3
   kidney, unknown cause 589.9
      bilateral 589.1
      unilateral 589.0
   ovary 620.8
   pelvis
      with disproportion (fetopelvic) 653.1
         affecting fetus or newborn 763.1
      causing obstructed labor 660.1
         affecting fetus or newborn 763.1
   placenta—*see* Placenta, insufficiency
   uterus 621.8
   white kidney 582.9
Small-for-dates (*see also* Light-for-dates) 764.0
   affecting management of pregnancy 656.5
Smallpox 050.9
   contact V01.3
   exposure to V01.3
   hemorrhagic (pustular) 050.0
   malignant 050.0
   modified 050.2
   vaccination
      complications—*see* Complications,
         vaccination
      prophylactic (against) V04.1
Smith's fracture (separation) (closed) 813.41
   open 813.51
Smith-Lemli-Opitz syndrome
   (cerebrohepatorenal syndrome) 759.89
Smith-Strang disease (oasthouse urine) 270.2
Smokers'
   bronchitis 491.0
   cough 491.0
   syndrome (*see also* Abuse, drugs,
      nondependent) 305.1
   throat 472.1
   tongue 528.6
Smothering spells 786.09
Snaggle teeth, tooth 524.3
Snapping
   finger 727.05
   hip 719.65
   jaw 524.69
   knee 717.9
   thumb 727.05
Sneddon-Wilkinson disease or syndrome
   (subcorneal pustular dermatosis) 694.1
Sneezing 784.9
   intractable 478.1
Sniffing
   cocaine (*see also* Dependence) 304.2
   ether (*see also* Dependence) 304.6
   glue (airplane) (*see also* Dependence) 304.6
Snoring 786.09
Snow blindness 370.24
Snuffles (nonsyphilitic) 460
   syphilitic (infant) 090.0
Social migrant V60.0
Sodoku 026.0
Soemmering's ring 366.51
Soft —*see also* condition
   nails 703.8
Softening
   bone 268.2
   brain (necrotic) (progressive) 434.9
      arteriosclerotic 437.0

Softening—*continued*
   congenital 742.4
   embolic (*see also* Embolism, brain) 434.1
   hemorrhagic (*see also* Hemorrhage, brain) 431
   occlusive 434.9
   thrombotic (*see also* Thrombosis, brain) 434.0
   cartilage 733.92
   cerebellar—*see* Softening, brain
   cerebral—*see* Softening, brain
   cerebrospinal—*see* Softening, brain
   myocardial, heart (*see also* Degeneration,
      myocardial) 429.1
   nails 703.8
   spinal cord 336.8
   stomach 537.89
Solar fever 061
Soldier's
   heart 306.2
   patches 423.1
Solitary
   cyst
      bone 733.21
      kidney 593.2
   kidney (congenital) 753.0
   tubercle, brain (*see also* Tuberculosis, brain)
      013.2
   ulcer, bladder 596.8
Somatization reaction, somatic reaction (*see*
   also Disorder, psychosomatic) 306.9
   disorder 300.81
Somatoform disorder 300.82
   atypical 300.82
   severe 300.81
   undifferentiated 300.82
Somnambulism 307.46
   hysterical 300.13
Somnolence 780.09
   nonorganic origin 307.43
   periodic 349.89
Sonne dysentery 004.3
Soor 112.0
Sore
   Delhi 085.1
   desert (*see also* Ulcer, skin) 707.9
   eye 379.99
   Lahore 085.1
   mouth 528.9
      canker 528.2
      due to dentures 528.9
   muscle 729.1
   Naga (*see also* Ulcer, skin) 707.9
   oriental 085.1
   pressure 707.0
      with gangrene 707.0 *[785.4]*
   skin NEC 709.9
   soft 099.0
   throat 462
      with influenza, flu, or grippe 487.1
      acute 462
      chronic 472.1
      clergyman's 784.49
      coxsackie (virus) 074.0
      diphtheritic 032.0
      epidemic 034.0
      gangrenous 462
      herpetic 054.79
      influenzal 487.1
      malignant 462
      purulent 462
      putrid 462
      septic 034.0

Sore —*continued*
      streptococcal (ulcerative) 034.0
      ulcerated 462
      viral NEC 462
         Coxsackie 074.0
   tropical (*see also* Ulcer, skin) 707.9
   veldt (*see also* Ulcer, skin) 707.9
Sotos' syndrome (cerebral gigantism) 253.0
Sounds
   friction, pleural 786.7
   succussion, chest 786.7
South African cardiomyopathy syndrome 425.2
South American
   blastomycosis 116.1
   trypanosomiasis—*see* Trypanosomiasis
Southeast Asian hemorrhagic fever 065.4
Spacing, teeth, abnormal 524.3
Spade-like hand (congenital) 754.89
Spading nail 703.8
   congenital 757.5
Spanemia 285.9
Spanish collar 605
Sparganosis 123.5
Spasm, spastic, spasticity (*see also* condition)
   781.0
   accommodation 367.53
   ampulla of Vater (*see also* Disease, gallbladder)
      576.8
   anus, ani (sphincter) (reflex) 564.6
      psychogenic 306.4
   artery NEC 443.9
      basilar 435.0
      carotid 435.8
      cerebral 435.9
         specified artery NEC 435.8
      retinal (*see also* Occlusion, retinal, artery)
         362.30
      vertebral 435.1
      vertebrobasilar 435.3
   Bell's 351.0
   bladder (sphincter, external or internal) 596.8
   bowel 564.1
      psychogenic 306.4
   bronchus, bronchiole 519.1
   cardia 530.0
   cardiac—*see* Angina
   carpopedal (*see also* Tetany) 781.7
   cecum 564.1
      psychogenic 306.4
   cerebral (arteries) (vascular) 435.9
      specified artery NEC 435.8
   cerebrovascular 435.9
   cervix, complicating delivery 661.4
      affecting fetus or newborn 763.7
   ciliary body (of accommodation) 367.53
   colon 564.1
      psychogenic 306.4
   common duct (*see also* Disease, biliary) 576.8
   compulsive 307.22
   conjugate 378.82
   convergence 378.84
   coronary (artery)—*see* Angina
   diaphragm (reflex) 786.8
      psychogenic 306.1
   duodenum, duodenal (bulb) 564.8
   esophagus (diffuse) 530.5
      psychogenic 306.4
   facial 351.8
   fallopian tube 620.8
   gait 781.2
   gastrointestinal (tract) 536.8

Spasm, spastic, spasticity— *continued*
  psychogenic 306.4
  glottis 478.75
    hysterical 300.11
    psychogenic 306.1
      specified as conversion reaction 300.11
    reflex through recurrent laryngeal nerve
      478.75
  habit 307.20
    chronic 307.22
    transient of childhood 307.21
  heart—*see* Angina
  hourglass—*see* Contraction, hourglass
  hysterical 300.11
  infantile (*see also* Epilepsy) 345.6
  internal oblique, eye 378.51
  intestinal 564.1
    psychogenic 306.4
  larynx, laryngeal 478.75
    hysterical 300.11
    psychogenic 306.1
      specified as conversion reaction 300.11
  levator palpebrae superioris 333.81
  lightning (*see also* Epilepsy) 345.6
  mobile 781.0
  muscle 728.85
    back 724.8
    psychogenic 306.0
  nerve, trigeminal 350.1
  nervous 306.0
  nodding 307.3
    infantile (*see also* Epilepsy) 345.6
  occupational 300.89
  oculogyric 378.87
  ophthalmic artery 362.30
  orbicularis 781.0
  perineal 625.8
  peroneo-extensor (*see also* Flat, foot) 734
  pharynx (reflex) 478.29
    hysterical 300.11
    psychogenic 306.1
      specified as conversion reaction 300.11
  pregnant uterus, complicating delivery 661.4
  psychogenic 306.0
  pylorus 537.81
    adult hypertrophic 537.0
    congenital or infantile 750.5
    psychogenic 306.4
  rectum (sphincter) 564.6
    psychogenic 306.4
  retinal artery NEC (*see also* Occlusion, retina,
    artery) 362.30
  sacroiliac 724.6
  salaam (infantile) (*see also* Epilepsy) 345.6
  saltatory 781.0
  sigmoid 564.1
    psychogenic 306.4
  sphincter of Oddi (*see also* Disease,
    gallbladder) 576.5
  stomach 536.8
    neurotic 306.4
  throat 478.29
    hysterical 300.11
    psychogenic 306.1
      specified as conversion reaction 300.11
  tic 307.20
    chronic 307.22
    transient of childhood 307.21
  tongue 529.8
  torsion 333.6
  trigeminal nerve 350.1

Spasm, spastic, spasticity— *continued*
  postherpetic 053.12
  ureter 593.89
  urethra (sphincter) 599.84
  uterus 625.8
    complicating labor 661.4
      affecting fetus or newborn 763.7
  vagina 625.1
    psychogenic 306.51
  vascular NEC 443.9
  vasomotor NEC 443.9
  vein NEC 459.89
  vesical (sphincter, external or internal) 596.8
  viscera 789.0
Spasmodic —*see* condition
Spasmophilia (*see also* Tetany) 781.7
Spasmus nutans 307.3
Spastic —*see also* Spasm
  child 343.9
Spasticity —*see also* Spasm
  cerebral, child 343.9
Speakers' throat 784.49
Specific, specified —*see* condition
Speech
  defect, disorder, disturbance, impediment NEC
    784.5
    psychogenic 307.9
  therapy V57.3
Spells 780.3
  breath-holding 786.9
Spencer's disease (epidemic vomiting) 078.82
Spens' syndrome (syncope with heart block)
  426.9
Spermatic cord —*see* condition
Spermatocele 608.1
  congenital 752.8
Spermatocystitis 608.4
Spermatocytoma (M9063/3)
  specified site—*see* Neoplasm, by site, malignant
  unspecified site 186.9
Spermatorrhea 608.89
Sperm counts V26.2
  postvasectomy V25.8
Sphacelus (*see also* Gangrene) 785.4
Sphenoidal —*see* condition
Sphenoiditis (chronic) (*see also* Sinusitis,
  sphenoidal) 473.3
Sphenopalatine ganglion neuralgia 337.0
Sphericity, increased, lens 743.36
Spherocytosis (congenital) (familial) (hereditary)
  282.0
  hemoglobin disease 287.7
  sickle-cell (disease) 282.60
Spherophakia 743.36
Sphincter —*see* condition
Sphincteritis, sphincter of Oddi (*see also*
  Cholecystitis) 576.8
Sphingolipidosis 272.7
Sphingolipodystrophy 272.7
Sphingomyelinosis 272.7
Spicule tooth 520.2
Spider
  finger 755.59
  nevus 448.1
  vascular 448.1
Spiegler-Fendt sarcoid 686.8
Spielmeyer-Stock disease 330.1
Spielmeyer-Vogt disease 330.1

Spina bifida (aperta) 741.9

Note—Use the following fifth-digit
subclassification with category 741:

0 unspecified region
1 cervical region
2 dorsal [thoracic] region
3 lumbar region

with hydrocephalus 741.0
fetal (suspected), affecting management of
    pregnancy 655.0
occulta 756.17
Spindle, Krukenberg's 371.13
Spine, spinal —see condition
Spiradenoma (eccrine) (M8403/0)—see
    Neoplasm, skin, benign
Spirillosis NEC (see also Fever, relapsing) 087.9
Spirillum minus 026.0
Spirillum obermeieri infection 087.0
Spirochetal —see condition
Spirochetosis 104.9
    arthritic, arthritica 104.9 [711.8]
    bronchopulmonary 104.8
    icterohemorrhagica 100.0
    lung 104.8
Spitting blood (see also Hemoptysis) 786.3
Splanchnomegaly 569.89
Splanchnoptosis 569.89
Spleen, splenic —see also condition
    agenesis 759.0
    flexure syndrome 569.89
    neutropenia syndrome 288.0
    sequestration syndrome 282.60
Splenectasis (see also Splenomegaly) 789.2
Splenitis (interstitial) (malignant) (nonspecific)
    289.59
    malarial (see also Malaria) 084.6
    tuberculous (see also Tuberculosis) 017.7
Splenocele 289.59
Splenomegalia —see Splenomegaly
Splenomegalic —see condition
Splenomegaly 789.2
    Bengal 789.2
    cirrhotic 289.51
    congenital 759.0
    congestive, chronic 289.51
    cryptogenic 789.2
    Egyptian 120.1
    Gaucher's (cerebroside lipidosis) 272.7
    idiopathic 789.2
    malarial (see also Malaria) 084.6
    neutropenic 288.0
    Niemann-Pick (lipid histiocytosis) 272.7
    siderotic 289.51
    syphilitic 095.8
        congenital 090.0
    tropical (Bengal) (idiopathic) 789.2
Splenopathy 289.50
Splenopneumonia —see Pneumonia
Splenoptosis 289.59
Splinter —see Injury, superficial, by site
Split, splitting
    heart sounds 427.89
    lip, congenital (see also Cleft, lip) 749.10
    nails 703.8
    urinary stream 788.61
Spoiled child reaction (see also Disturbance,
    conduct) 312.1
Spondylarthritis (see also Spondylosis) 721.90
Spondylarthrosis (see also Spondylosis) 721.90

Spondylitis 720.9
    ankylopoietica 720.0
    ankylosing (chronic) 720.0
    atrophic 720.9
        ligamentous 720.9
    chronic (traumatic) (see also Spondylosis)
        721.90
    deformans (chronic) (see also Spondylosis)
        721.90
    gonococcal 098.53
    gouty 274.0
    hypertrophic (see also Spondylosis) 721.90
    infectious NEC 720.9
    juvenile (adolescent) 720.0
    Kümmell's 721.7
    Marie-Strümpell (ankylosing) 720.0
    muscularis 720.9
    ossificans ligamentosa 721.6
    osteoarthritica (see also Spondylosis) 721.90
    posttraumatic 721.7
    proliferative 720.0
    rheumatoid 720.0
    rhizomelica 720.0
    sacroiliac NEC 720.2
    senescent (see also Spondylosis) 721.90
    senile (see also Spondylosis) 721.90
    static (see also Spondylosis) 721.90
    traumatic (chronic) (see also Spondylosis)
        721.90
    tuberculous (see also Tuberculosis) 015.0
        [720.81]
    typhosa 002.0 [720.81]
Spondyloarthrosis (see also Spondylosis) 721.90
Spondylolisthesis (congenital) (lumbosacral)
    756.12
    with disproportion (fetopelvic) 653.3
        affecting fetus or newborn 763.1
        causing obstructed labor 660.1
            affecting fetus or newborn 763.1
    acquired 738.4
    degenerative 738.4
    traumatic 756.12
        acute (lumbar)—see Fracture, vertebra, lumbar
        site other than lumbosacral—see Fracture,
            vertebra, by site
Spondylolysis (congenital) 756.11
    acquired 738.4
    cervical 756.19
    lumbosacral region 756.11
        with disproportion (fetopelvic) 653.3
            affecting fetus or newborn 763.1
            causing obstructed labor 660.1
                affecting fetus or newborn 763.1
Spondylopathy
    inflammatory 720.9
        specified type NEC 720.89
    traumatic 721.7
Spondylose rhizomelique 720.0
Spondylosis 721.90
    with
        disproportion 653.3
            affecting fetus or newborn 763.1
            causing obstructed labor 660.1
                affecting fetus or newborn 763.1
        myelopathy NEC 721.91
    cervical, cervicodorsal 721.0
        with myelopathy 721.1
    inflammatory 720.9
    lumbar, lumbosacral 721.3
        with myelopathy 721.42

Spondylosis—*continued*
sacral 721.3
with myelopathy 721.42
thoracic 721.2
with myelopathy 721.41
traumatic 721.7
Sponge
divers' disease 989.5
inadvertently left in operation wound 998.4
kidney (medullary) 753.17
Spongioblastoma (M9422/3)
multiforme (M9440/3)
specified site—*see* Neoplasm, by site,
malignant
unspecified site 191.9
polare (M9423/3)
specified site—*see* Neoplasm, by site,
malignant
unspecified site 191.9
primitive polar (M9443/3)
specified site—*see* Neoplasm, by site,
malignant
unspecified site 191.9
specified site—*see* Neoplasm, by site, malignant
unspecified site 191.9
Spongiocytoma (M9400/3)
specified site—*see* Neoplasm, by site, malignant
unspecified site 191.9
Spongioneuroblastoma (M9504/3)—*see*
Neoplasm, by site, malignant
Spontaneous —*see also* condition
fracture—*see* Fracture, pathologic
Spoon nail 703.8
congenital 757.5
Sporadic —*see* condition
Sporotrichosis (bones) (cutaneous)
(disseminated) (epidermal) (lymphatic)
(lymphocutaneous) (mucous membranes)
(pulmonary) (skeletal) (visceral) 117.1
Sporotrichum schenckii infection 117.1
Spots, spotting
atrophic (skin) 701.3
Bitôt's (in the young child) 264.1
café au lait 709.09
cayenne pepper 448.1
cotton wool (retina) 362.83
de Morgan's (senile angiomas) 448.1
Fúchs' black (myopic) 360.21
intermenstrual
irregular 626.6
regular 626.5
interpalpebral 372.53
Koplik's 055.9
liver 709.09
Mongolian (pigmented) 757.33
of pregnancy 641.9
purpuric 782.7
ruby 448.1
Spotted fever —*see* Fever, spotted
Sprain, strain (joint) (ligament) (muscle)
(tendon) 848.9
abdominal wall (muscle) 848.8
Achilles tendon 845.09
acromioclavicular 840.0
ankle 845.00
and foot 845.00
anterior longitudinal, cervical 847.0
arm 840.9
upper 840.9
and shoulder 840.9

Sprain, strain—*continued*
astragalus 845.00
atlanto-axial 847.0
atlanto-occipital 847.0
atlas 847.0
axis 847.0
back (*see also* Sprain, spine) 847.9
breast bone 848.40
broad ligament—*see* Injury, internal, broad
ligament
calcaneofibular 845.02
carpal 842.01
carpometacarpal 842.11
cartilage
costal, without mention of injury to sternum
848.3
involving sternum 848.42
ear 848.8
knee 844.9
with current tear (*see also* Tear, meniscus)
836.2
semilunar (knee) 844.8
with current tear (*see also* Tear, meniscus)
836.2
septal, nose 848.0
thyroid region 848.2
xiphoid 848.49
cervical, cervicodorsal, cervicothoracic 847.0
chondrocostal, without mention of injury to
sternum 848.3
involving sternum 848.42
chondrosternal 848.42
chronic (joint)—*see* Derangement, joint
clavicle 840.9
coccyx 847.4
collar bone 840.9
collateral, knee (medial) (tibial) 844.1
lateral (fibular) 844.0
recurrent or old 717.89
lateral 717.81
medial 717.82
coracoacromial 840.8
coracoclavicular 840.1
coracohumeral 840.2
coracoid (process) 840.9
coronary, knee 844.8
costal cartilage, without mention of injury to
sternum 848.3
involving sternum 848.42
cricoarytenoid articulation 848.2
cricothyroid articulation 848.2
cruciate
knee 844.2
old 717.89
anterior 717.83
posterior 717.84
deltoid
ankle 845.01
shoulder 840.8
dorsal (spine) 847.1
ear cartilage 848.8
elbow 841.9
and forearm 841.9
specified site NEC 841.8
femur (proximal end) 843.9
distal end 844.9
fibula (proximal end) 844.9
distal end 845.00
fibulocalcaneal 845.02
finger(s) 842.10

Sprain, strain—*continued*
foot 845.10
  and ankle 845.00
forearm 841.9
  and elbow 841.9
  specified site NEC 841.8
glenoid (shoulder) 840.8
hand 842.10
hip 843.9
  and thigh 843.9
humerus (proximal end) 840.9
  distal end 841.9
iliofemoral 843.0
infraspinatus 840.3
innominate
  acetabulum 843.9
  pubic junction 848.5
  sacral junction 846.1
internal
  collateral, ankle 845.01
  semilunar cartilage 844.8
    with current tear (*see also* Tear, meniscus)
      836.2
    old 717.5
interphalangeal
  finger 842.13
  toe 845.13
ischiocapsular 843.1
jaw (cartilage) (meniscus) 848.1
  old 524.69
knee 844.9
  and leg 844.9
  old 717.5
    collateral
      lateral 717.81
      medial 717.82
    cruciate
      anterior 717.83
      posterior 717.84
late effect—*see* Late, effects (of), sprain
lateral collateral, knee 844.0
  old 717.81
leg 844.9
  and knee 844.9
ligamentum teres femoris 843.8
low back 846.9
lumbar (spine) 847.2
lumbosacral 846.0
  chronic or old 724.6
mandible 848.1
  old 524.69
maxilla 848.1
medial collateral, knee 844.1
  old 717.82
meniscus
  jaw 848.1
    old 524.69
  knee 844.8
    with current tear (*see also* Tear, meniscus)
      836.2
    old 717.5
  mandible 848.1
    old 524.69
  specified site NEC 848.8
metacarpal 842.10
  distal 842.12
  proximal 842.11
metacarpophalangeal 842.12
metatarsal 845.10
metatarsophalangeal 845.12

Sprain, strain—*continued*
midcarpal 842.19
midtarsal 845.19
multiple sites, except fingers alone or toes alone
  848.8
neck 847.0
nose (septal cartilage) 848.0
occiput from atlas 847.0
old—*see* Derangement, joint
orbicular, hip 843.8
patella(r) 844.8
  old 717.89
pelvis 848.5
phalanx
  finger 842.10
  toe 845.10
radiocarpal 842.02
radiohumeral 841.2
radioulnar 841.9
  distal 842.09
radius, radial (proximal end) 841.9
  and ulna 841.9
    distal 842.09
  collateral 841.0
  distal end 842.00
recurrent—*see* Sprain, by site
rib (cage), without mention of injury to sternum
  848.3
  involving sternum 848.42
rotator cuff (capsule) 840.4
round ligament—*see also* Injury, internal, round
  ligament
  femur 843.8
sacral (spine) 847.3
sacrococcygeal 847.3
sacroiliac (region) 846.9
  chronic or old 724.6
  ligament 846.1
  specified site NEC 846.8
sacrospinatus 846.2
sacrospinous 846.2
sacrotuberous 846.3
scaphoid bone, ankle 845.00
scapula(r) 840.9
semilunar cartilage (knee) 844.8
  with current tear (*see also* Tear, meniscus)
    836.2
  old 717.5
septal cartilage (nose) 848.0
shoulder 840.9
  and arm, upper 840.9
  blade 840.9
specified site NEC 848.8
spine 847.9
  cervical 847.0
  coccyx 847.4
  dorsal 847.1
  lumbar 847.2
  lumbosacral 846.0
    chronic or old 724.6
  sacral 847.3
  sacroiliac (*see also* Sprain, sacroiliac) 846.9
    chronic or old 724.6
  thoracic 847.1
sternoclavicular 848.41
sternum 848.40
subglenoid 840.8
subscapularis 840.5
supraspinatus 840.6

Sprain, strain—*continued*
  symphysis
    jaw 848.1
      old 524.69
    mandibular 848.1
      old 524.69
    pubis 848.5
  talofibular 845.09
  tarsal 845.10
  tarsometatarsal 845.11
  temporomandibular 848.1
    old 524.69
  teres
    ligamentum femoris 843.8
    major or minor 840.8
  thigh (proximal end) 843.9
    and hip 843.9
    distal end 844.9
  thoracic (spine) 847.1
  thorax 848.8
  thumb 842.10
  thyroid cartilage or region 848.2
  tibia (proximal end) 844.9
    distal end 845.00
  tibiofibular
    distal 845.03
    superior 844.3
  toe(s) 845.10
  trachea 848.8
  trapezoid 840.8
  ulna, ulnar (proximal end) 841.9
    collateral 841.1
    distal end 842.00
  ulnohumeral 841.3
  vertebrae (*see also* Sprain, spine) 847.9
    cervical, cervicodorsal, cervicothoracic 847.0
  wrist (cuneiform) (scaphoid) (semilunar) 842.00
  xiphoid cartilage 848.49
Sprengel's deformity (congenital) 755.52
Spring fever 309.23
Sprue 579.1
  celiac 579.0
  idiopathic 579.0
  meaning thrush 112.0
  nontropical 579.0
  tropical 579.1
Spur —*see also* Exostosis
  bone 726.91
    calcaneal 726.73
  calcaneal 726.73
  iliac crest 726.5
  nose (septum) 478.1
    bone 726.91
  septal 478.1
Spuria placenta —*see* Placenta, abnormal
Spurway's syndrome (brittle bones and blue
    sclera) 756.51
Sputum, abnormal (amount) (color) (excessive)
    (odor) (purulent) 786.4
  bloody 786.3
Squamous —*see also* condition
  cell metaplasia
    bladder 596.8
    cervix—*see* condition
  epithelium in
    cervical canal (congenital) 752.49
    uterine mucosa (congenital) 752.3
  metaplasia
    bladder 596.8
    cervix—*see* condition
Squashed nose 738.0
  congenital 754.0

Squeeze, divers' 993.3
Squint (*see also* Strabismus) 378.9
  accommodative (*see also* Esotropia) 378.00
  concomitant (*see also* Heterotropia) 378.30
Stab —*see also* Wound, open, by site
  internal organs—*see* Injury, internal, by site,
    with open wound
Staggering gait 781.2
  hysterical 300.11
Staghorn calculus 592.0
Stähl's
  ear 744.29
  pigment line (cornea) 371.11
Stähli's pigment lines (cornea) 371.11
Stain
  port wine 757.32
  tooth, teeth (hard tissues) 521.7
    due to
      accretions 523.6
      deposits (betel) (black) (green) (materia
        alba) (orange) (tobacco) 523.6
      metals (copper) (silver) 521.7
      nicotine 523.6
      pulpal bleeding 521.7
      tobacco 523.6
Stammering 307.0
Standstill
  atrial 426.6
  auricular 426.6
  cardiac (*see also* Arrest, cardiac) 427.5
  sinoatrial 426.6
  sinus 426.6
  ventricular (*see also* Arrest, cardiac) 427.5
Stannosis 503
Stanton's disease (melioidosis) 025
Staphylitis (acute) (catarrhal) (chronic)
    (gangrenous) (membranous) (suppurative)
    (ulcerative) 528.3
Staphylococcemia 038.1
Staphylococcus, staphylococcal —*see* condition
Staphyloderma (skin) 686.0
Staphyloma 379.11
  anterior, localized 379.14
  ciliary 379.11
  cornea 371.73
  equatorial 379.13
  posterior 379.12
  posticum 379.12
  ring 379.15
  sclera NEC 379.11
Starch eating 307.52
Stargardt's disease 362.75
Starvation (inanition) (due to lack of food) 994.2
  edema 262
  voluntary NEC 307.1
Stasis
  bile (duct) (*see also* Disease, biliary) 576.8
  bronchus (*see also* Bronchitis) 490
  cardiac (*see also* Failure, heart, congestive)
    428.0
  cecum 564.8
  colon 564.8
  dermatitis (*see also* Varix, with stasis
    dermatitis) 454.1
  duodenal 536.8
  eczema (*see also* Varix, with stasis dermatitis)
    454.1
  foot 991.4
  gastric 536.3
  ileocecal coil 564.8

Stasis—*continued*
  ileum 564.8
  intestinal 564.8
  jejunum 564.8
  kidney 586
  liver 571.9
    cirrhotic—*see* Cirrhosis, liver
  lymphatic 457.8
  pneumonia 514
  portal 571.9
  pulmonary 514
  rectal 564.8
  renal 586
    tubular 584.5
  stomach 536.3
  ulcer
    with varicose veins 454.0
    without varicose veins 459.81
  urine NEC (*see also* Retention, urine) 788.20
  venous 459.81
State
  affective and paranoid, mixed, organic
      psychotic 294.8
  agitated 307.9
    acute reaction to stress 308.2
  anxiety (neurotic) (*see also* Anxiety) 300.00
    specified type NEC 300.09
  apprehension (*see also* Anxiety) 300.00
    specified type NEC 300.09
  climacteric, female 627.2
    following induced menopause 627.4
  clouded
    epileptic (*see also* Epilepsy) 345.9
    paroxysmal (idiopathic) (*see also* Epilepsy)
        345.9
  compulsive (mixed) (with obsession) 300.3
  confusional 298.9
    acute 293.0
      with
        arteriosclerotic dementia 290.41
        presenile brain disease 290.11
        senility 290.3
      alcoholic 291.0
      drug-induced 292.81
    epileptic 293.0
    postoperative 293.9
    reactive (emotional stress) (psychological
        trauma) 298.2
    subacute 293.1
  constitutional psychopathic 301.9
  convulsive (*see also* Convulsions) 780.3
  depressive NEC 311
    induced by drug 292.84
    neurotic 300.4
  dissociative 300.15
  hallucinatory 780.1
    induced by drug 292.12
  hyperdynamic beta-adrenergic circulatory
      429.82
  locked-in 344.81
  menopausal 627.2
    artificial 627.4
    following induced menopause 627.4
  neurotic NEC 300.9
    with depersonalization episode 300.6
  obsessional 300.3
  oneiroid (*see also* Schizophrenia) 295.4
  panic 300.01
  paranoid 297.9
    alcohol-induced 291.5
    arteriosclerotic 290.42

State—*continued*
  climacteric 297.2
  drug-induced 292.11
  in
    presenile brain disease 290.12
    senile brain disease 290.20
  involutional 297.2
  menopausal 297.2
  senile 290.20
  simple 297.0
  postleukotomy 310.0
  pregnant (*see also* Pregnancy) V22.2
  psychogenic, twilight 298.2
  psychotic, organic (*see also* Psychosis, organic)
      294.9
    mixed paranoid and affective 294.8
    senile or presenile NEC 290.9
    transient NEC 293.9
      with
        anxiety 293.84
        delusions 293.81
        depression 293.83
        hallucinations 293.82
  residual schizophrenic (*see also* Schizophrenia)
      295.6
  tension (*see also* Anxiety) 300.9
  transient organic psychotic 293.9
    anxiety type 293.84
    depressive type 293.83
    hallucinatory type 293.83
    paranoid type 293.81
    specified type NEC 293.89
  twilight
    epileptic 293.0
    psychogenic 298.2
  vegetative (persistent) 780.03
Status (post)
  absence
    epileptic (*see also* Epilepsy) 345.2
    of organ, acquired (postsurgical)—*see*
        Absence, by site, acquired
  anastomosis of intestine (for bypass) V45.3
  angioplasty, percutaneous transluminal coronary
      V45.82
  anginosus 413.9
  ankle prosthesis V43.66
  aortocoronary bypass or shunt V45.81
  arthrodesis V45.4
  artificially induced condition NEC V45.89
  artificial opening (of) V44.9
    gastrointestinal tract NEC V44.4
    specified site NEC V44.8
    urinary tract NEC V44.6
    vagina V44.7
  asthmaticus (*see also* Asthma) 493.9
  breast implant removal V45.83
  cardiac
    device (in situ) V45.00
      defibrillator, automatic implantable V45.02
      pacemaker V45.01
        fitting or adjustment V53.3
      carotid sinus V45.09
        fitting or adjustment V53.3
  carotid sinus stimulator V45.09
  cataract extraction V45.6
  chemotherapy V66.2
  colostomy V44.3
  contraceptive device V45.59
    intrauterine V45.51
    subdermal V45.52

Status (post)—*continued*

convulsivus idiopathicus (*see also* Epilepsy)
  345.3
coronary artery bypass or shunt V45.81
cystostomy V44.5
defibrillator, automatic implantable cardiac
  V45.02
dialysis V45.1
donor V59.9
drug therapy or regimen V67.59
  high-risk medication NEC V67.51
elbow prosthesis V43.62
enterostomy V44.4
epileptic, epilepticus (absence) (grand mal) (*see
  also* Epilepsy) 345.3
  focal motor 345.7
  partial 345.7
  petit mal 345.2
  psychomotor 345.7
  temporal lobe 345.7
eye (adnexa) surgery V45.6
filtering bleb (eye) (postglaucoma) V45.6
  with rupture or complication 997.99
  postcataract extraction (complication) 997.99
finger joint prosthesis V43.69
gastrostomy V44.1
grand mal 345.3
heart valve prosthesis V43.3
hip prosthesis (joint) (partial) (total) V43.64
ileostomy V44.2
intestinal bypass V45.3
intrauterine contraceptive device V45.51
jejunostomy V44.4
knee joint prosthesis V43.65
lacunaris 437.8
lacunosis 437.8
lymphaticus 254.8
malignant neoplasm, ablated or excised—*see*
  History, malignant neoplasm
marmoratus 333.7
nephrostomy V44.6
neuropacemaker NEC V45.89
  brain V45.89
  carotid sinus V45.09
  neurologic NEC V45.89
organ replacement
  by artificial or mechanical device or
    prosthesis of
    artery V43.4
    bladder V43.5
    blood vessel V43.4
    breast V43.82
    eye globe V43.0
    heart V43.2
      valve V43.3
    intestine V43.89
    joint V43.60
      ankle V43.66
      elbow V43.62
      finger V43.69
      hip (partial) (total) V43.64
      knee V43.65
      shoulder V43.61
      specified NEC 43.69
      wrist V43.63
    kidney V43.89
    larynx V43.81
    lens V43.1
    limb(s) V43.7
    liver V43.89
    lung V43.89

Status (post)—*continued*

    organ NEC V43.89
    pancreas V43.89
    tissue NEC V43.89
    vein V43.4
  by organ transplant (heterologous)
    (homologous)—*see* Status, transplant
pacemaker
  brain V45.89
  cardiac V45.01
  carotid sinus V45.09
  neurologic NEC V45.89
  specified site NEC V45.89
percutaneous transluminal coronary angioplasty
  V45.82
petit mal 345.2
postcommotio cerebri 310.2
postoperative NEC V45.89
postpartum NEC V24.2
  care immediately following delivery V24.0
  routine follow-up V24.2
postsurgical NEC V45.89
renal dialysis V45.1
reversed jejunal transposition (for bypass) V45.3
shoulder prosthesis V43.61
shunt
  aortocoronary bypass V45.81
  arteriovenous (for dialysis) V45.1
  cerebrospinal fluid V45.2
  vascular NEC V45.89
    aortocoronary (bypass) V45.81
  ventricular (communicating) (for drainage)
    V45.2
subdermal contraceptive device V45.52
thymicolymphaticus 254.8
thymicus 254.8
thymolymphaticus 254.8
tracheostomy V44.0
transplant
  blood vessel V42.8
  bone V42.4
    marrow V42.8
  cornea V42.5
  heart V42.1
    valve V42.2
  intestine V42.8
  kidney V42.0
  liver V42.7
  lung V42.6
  organ V42.9
    specified site NEC V42.8
  pancreas V42.8
  skin V42.3
  tissue V42.9
    specified type NEC V42.8
  vessel, blood V42.8
ureterostomy V44.6
urethrostomy V44.6
vagina, artificial V44.7
vascular shunt NEC V45.89
  aortocoronary (bypass) V45.81
wrist prosthesis V43.63
Stave fracture —*see* Fracture, metacarpus,
  metacarpal bone(s)
Steal
subclavian artery 435.2
vertebral artery 435.1
Stealing, solitary, child problem (*see also*
  Disturbance, conduct) 312.1
Steam burn —*see* Burn, by site
Steatocystoma multiplex 706.2

Steatoma (infected) 706.2
  eyelid (cystic) 374.84
    infected 373.13
Steatorrhea (chronic) 579.8
  with lacteal obstruction 579.2
  idiopathic 579.0
    adult 579.0
    infantile 579.0
  pancreatic 579.4
  primary 579.0
  secondary 579.8
  specified cause NEC 579.8
  tropical 579.1
Steatosis 272.8
  heart (*see also* Degeneration, myocardial) 429.1
  kidney 593.89
  liver 571.8
Stein's syndrome (polycystic ovary) 256.4
Stein-Leventhal syndrome (polycystic ovary) 256.4
Steinbrocker's syndrome (*see also* Neuropathy, peripheral, autonomic) 337.9
Steinert's disease 359.2
Stenocardia (*see also* Angina) 413.9
Stenocephaly 756.0
Stenosis (cicatricial)—*see also* Stricture
  ampulla of Vater 576.2
    with calculus, cholelithiasis, or stones—*see* Choledocholithiasis
  anus, anal (canal) (sphincter) 569.2
    congenital 751.2
  aorta (ascending) 747.22
    arch 747.10
    arteriosclerotic 440.0
    calcified 440.0
  aortic (valve) 424.1
    with
      mitral (valve)
        insufficiency or incompetence 396.2
        stenosis or obstruction 396.0
    atypical 396.0
    congenital 746.3
    rheumatic 395.0
      with
        insufficiency, incompetency or regurgitation 395.2
          with mitral (valve) disease 396.8
        mitral (valve)
          disease (stenosis) 396.0
          insufficiency or incompetence 396.2
          stenosis or obstruction 396.0
    specified cause, except rheumatic 424.1
    syphilitic 093.22
  aqueduct of Sylvius (congenital) 742.3
    with spina bifida (*see also* Spina bifida) 741.0
    acquired 331.4
  artery NEC 447.1
    basilar—*see* Narrowing, artery, basilar
    carotid (common) (internal)—*see* Narrowing, artery, carotid
    celiac 447.4
    cerebral 437.0
      due to
        embolism (*see also* Embolism, brain) 434.1
        thrombus (*see also* Thrombosis, brain) 434.0
    precerebral—*see* Narrowing, artery, precerebral
    pulmonary (congenital) 747.3
      acquired 417.8

Stenosis—*continued*
  renal 440.1
  vertebral—*see* Narrowing, artery, vertebral
  bile duct or biliary passage (*see also* Obstruction, biliary) 576.2
    congenital 751.61
  bladder neck (acquired) 596.0
    congenital 753.6
  brain 348.8
  bronchus 519.1
    syphilitic 095.8
  cardia (stomach) 537.89
    congenital 750.7
  cardiovascular (*see also* Disease, cardiovascular) 429.2
  carotid artery—*see* Narrowing, artery, carotid
  cervix, cervical (canal) 622.4
    congenital 752.49
    in pregnancy or childbirth 654.6
      affecting fetus or newborn 763.8
      causing obstructed labor 660.2
        affecting fetus or newborn 763.1
  colon (*see also* Obstruction, intestine) 560.9
    congenital 751.2
  colostomy 569.69
  common bile duct (*see also* Obstruction, biliary) 576.2
    congenital 751.61
  coronary (artery) —*see* Arteriosclerosis, coronary
  cystic duct (*see also* Obstruction, gallbladder) 575.2
    congenital 751.61
  due to (presence of) any device, implant, or graft classifiable to 996.0-996.5—*see* Complications, due to (presence of) any device, implant, or graft classified to 996.0-996.5 NEC
  duodenum 537.3
    congenital 751.1
  ejaculatory duct NEC 608.89
  endocervical os—*see* Stenosis, cervix
  enterostomy 569.69
  esophagus 530.3
    congenital 750.3
    syphilitic 095.8
      congenital 090.5
  external ear canal 380.50
    secondary to
      inflammation 380.53
      surgery 380.52
      trauma 380.51
  gallbladder (*see also* Obstruction, gallbladder) 575.2
  glottis 478.74
  heart valve (acquired)—*see also* Endocarditis
    congenital NEC 746.89
      aortic 746.3
      mitral 746.5
      pulmonary 746.02
      tricuspid 746.1
  hepatic duct (*see also* Obstruction, biliary) 576.2
  hymen 623.3
  hypertrophic subaortic (idiopathic) 425.1
  infundibulum cardiac 746.83
  intestine (*see also* Obstruction, intestine) 560.9
    congenital (small) 751.1
      large 751.2
  lacrimal
    canaliculi 375.53
    duct 375.56

Stenosis—*continued*
   congenital 743.65
   punctum 375.52
     congenital 743.65
   sac 375.54
     congenital 743.65
   lacrimonasal duct 375.56
     congenital 743.65
     neonatal 375.55
   larynx 478.74
     congenital 748.3
     syphilitic 095.8
      congenital 090.5
   mitral (valve) (chronic) (inactive) 394.0
     with
      aortic (valve)
       disease (insufficiency) 396.1
       insufficiency or incompetence 396.1
       stenosis or obstruction 396.0
      incompetency, insufficiency or regurgitation 394.2
       with aortic valve disease 396.8
     active or acute 391.1
      with chorea (acute) (rheumatic) (Sydenham's) 392.0
     congenital 746.5
     specified cause, except rheumatic 424.0
     syphilitic 093.21
   myocardium, myocardial (*see also* Degeneration, myocardial) 429.1
   hypertrophic subaortic (idiopathic) 425.1
   nares (anterior) (posterior) 478.1
     congenital 748.0
   nasal duct 375.56
     congenital 743.65
   nasolacrimal duct 375.56
     congenital 743.65
     neonatal 375.55
   organ or site, congenital NEC—*see* Atresia
   papilla of Vater 576.2
     with calculus, cholelithiasis, or stones—*see* Choledocholithiasis
   pulmonary (artery) (congenital) 747.3
     with ventricular septal defect, dextraposition of aorta and hypertrophy of right ventricle 745.2
     acquired 417.8
     infundibular 746.83
     in tetralogy of Fallot 745.2
     subvalvular 746.83
     valve (*see also* Endocarditis, pulmonary) 424.3
      congenital 746.02
     vein 747.49
      acquired 417.8
     vessel NEC 417.8
   pulmonic (congenital) 746.02
     infundibular 746.83
     subvalvular 746.83
   pylorus (hypertrophic) 537.0
     adult 537.0
     congenital 750.5
     infantile 750.5
   rectum (sphincter) (*see also* Stricture, rectum) 569.2
   renal artery 440.1
   salivary duct (any) 527.8
   sphincter of Oddi (*see also* Obstruction, biliary) 576.2
   spinal 724.00
     cervical 723.0
     lumbar, lumbosacral 724.02

Stenosis—*continued*
   nerve (root) NEC 724.9
     specified region NEC 724.09
     thoracic, thoracolumbar 724.01
   stomach, hourglass 537.6
   subaortic 746.81
     hypertrophic (idiopathic) 425.1
   supra (valvular)-aortic 747.22
   trachea 519.1
     congenital 748.3
     syphilitic 095.8
     tuberculous (*see also* Tuberculosis) 012.8
   tracheostomy 519.0
   tricuspid (valve) (*see also* Endocarditis, tricuspid) 397.0
     congenital 746.1
     nonrheumatic 424.2
   tubal 628.2
   ureter (*see also* Stricture, ureter) 593.3
     congenital 753.29
   urethra (*see also* Stricture, urethra) 598.9
   vagina 623.2
     congenital 752.49
     in pregnancy or childbirth 654.7
      affecting fetus or newborn 763.8
      causing obstructed labor 660.2
       affecting fetus or newborn 763.1
   valve (cardiac) (heart) (*see also* Endocarditis) 424.90
     congenital NEC 746.89
      aortic 746.3
      mitral 746.5
      pulmonary 746.02
      tricuspid 746.1
      urethra 753.6
   valvular (*see also* Endocarditis) 424.90
     congenital NEC 746.89
     urethra 753.6
   vascular graft or shunt 996.1
     atherosclerosis —*see* Arteriosclerosis, extremities
     embolism 996.74
     occlusion NEC 996.74
     thrombus 996.74
   vena cava (inferior) (superior) 459.2
     congenital 747.49
   ventricular shunt 996.2
   vulva 624.8
Stercolith (*see also* Fecalith) 560.39
   appendix 543.9
Stercoraceous, stercoral ulcer 569.82
   anus or rectum 569.41
Stereopsis, defective
   with fusion 368.33
   without fusion 368.32
Stereotypes NEC 307.3
Sterility
   female—*see* Infertility, female
   male (*see also* Infertility, male) 606.9
Sterilization, admission for V25.2
Sternalgia (*see also* Angina) 413.9
Sternopagus 759.4
Sternum bifidum 756.3
Sternutation 784.9
Steroid
   effects (adverse) (iatrogenic)
     cushingoid
      correct substance properly administered 255.0
      overdose or wrong substance given or taken 962.0

Steroid—*continued*
  diabetes
    correct substance properly administered
      251.8
    overdose or wrong substance given or taken
      962.0
  due to
    correct substance properly administered
      255.8
    overdose or wrong substance given or taken
      962.0
  fever
    correct substance properly administered
      780.6
    overdose or wrong substance given or taken
      962.0
  withdrawal
    correct substance properly administered
      255.4
    overdose or wrong substance given or taken
      962.0
  responder 365.03
Stevens-Johnson disease or syndrome
  (erythema multiforme exudativum) 695.1
Stewart-Morel syndrome (hyperostosis frontalis
  interna) 733.3
Sticker's disease (erythema infectiosum) 057.0
Sticky eye 372.03
Stieda's disease (calcification, knee joint) 726.62
Stiff
  back 724.8
  neck (*see also* Torticollis) 723.5
Stiff-man syndrome 333.91
Stiffness, joint NEC 719.50
  ankle 719.57
  back 724.8
  elbow 719.52
  finger 719.54
  hip 719.55
  knee 719.56
  multiple sites 719.59
  sacroiliac 724.6
  shoulder 719.51
  specified site NEC 719.58
  spine 724.9
  surgical fusion V45.4
  wrist 719.53
Stigmata, congenital syphilis 090.5
Still's disease or syndrome 714.30
Still-Felty syndrome (rheumatoid arthritis with
  splenomegaly and leukopenia) 714.1
Stillbirth, stillborn NEC 779.9
Stiller's disease (asthenia) 780.7
Stilling-Türk-Duane syndrome (ocular
  retraction syndrome) 378.71
Stimulation, ovary 256.1
Sting (animal) (bee) (fish) (insect) (jellyfish)
  (Portuguese man-o-war) (wasp) (venomous)
  989.5
  anaphylactic shock or reaction 989.5
  plant 692.6
Stippled epiphyses 756.59
Stitch
  abscess 998.59
  burst (in operation wound) 998.3
  in back 724.5
Stojano's (subcostal) syndrome 098.86
Stokes' disease (exophthalmic goiter) 242.0
Stokes-Adams syndrome (syncope with heart
  block) 426.9
Stokvis' (-Talma) disease (enterogenous
  cyanosis) 289.7

Stomach —*see* condition
Stoma malfunction
  colostomy 569.69
  cystostomy 997.5
  enterostomy 569.69
  gastrostomy 997.4
  ileostomy 569.69
  nephrostomy 997.5
  tracheostomy 519.0
  ureterostomy 997.5
Stomatitis 528.0
  angular 528.5
    due to dietary or vitamin deficiency 266.0
  aphthous 528.2
  candidal 112.0
  catarrhal 528.0
  denture 528.9
  diphtheritic (membranous) 032.0
  due to
    dietary deficiency 266.0
    thrush 112.0
    vitamin deficiency 266.0
  epidemic 078.4
  epizootic 078.4
  follicular 528.0
  gangrenous 528.1
  herpetic 054.2
  herpetiformis 528.2
  malignant 528.0
  membranous acute 528.0
  monilial 112.0
  mycotic 112.0
  necrotic 528.1
    ulcerative 101
  necrotizing ulcerative 101
  parasitic 112.0
  septic 528.0
  spirochetal 101
  suppurative (acute) 528.0
  ulcerative 528.0
    necrotizing 101
  ulceromembranous 101
  vesicular 528.0
    with exanthem 074.3
  Vincent's 101
Stomatocytosis 282.8
Stomatomycosis 112.0
Stomatorrhagia 528.9
Stone (s)—*see also* Calculus
  bladder 594.1
    diverticulum 594.0
  cystine 270.0
  heart syndrome (*see also* Failure, ventricular,
    left) 428.1
  kidney 592.0
  prostate 602.0
  pulp (dental) 522.2
  renal 592.0
  salivary duct or gland (any) 527.5
  ureter 592.1
  urethra (impacted) 594.2
  urinary (duct) (impacted) (passage) 592.9
    bladder 594.1
      diverticulum 594.0
    lower tract NEC 594.9
    specified site 594.8
  xanthine 277.2
Stonecutters' lung 502
  tuberculous (*see also* Tuberculosis) 011.4

Stonemasons'
  asthma, disease, or lung 502
    tuberculous (*see also* Tuberculosis) 011.4
  phthisis (*see also* Tuberculosis) 011.4
Stoppage
  bowel (*see also* Obstruction, intestine) 560.9
  heart (*see also* Arrest, cardiac) 427.5
  intestine (*see also* Obstruction, intestine) 560.9
  urine NEC (*see also* Retention, urine) 788.20
Storm, thyroid (apathetic) (*see also*
    Thyrotoxicosis) 242.9
Strabismus (alternating) (congenital)
    (nonparalytic) 378.9
  concomitant (*see also* Heterotropia) 378.30
    convergent (*see also* Esotropia) 378.00
    divergent (*see also* Exotropia) 378.10
  convergent (*see also* Esotropia) 378.00
  divergent (*see also* Exotropia) 378.10
  due to adhesions, scars—*see* Strabismus,
    mechanical
  in neuromuscular disorder NEC 378.73
    intermittent 378.20
      vertical 378.31
  latent 378.40
    convergent (esophoria) 378.41
    divergent (exophoria) 378.42
    vertical 378.43
  mechanical 378.60
    due to
      Brown's tendon sheath syndrome 378.61
      specified musculofascial disorder NEC
        378.62
  paralytic 378.50
    third or oculomotor nerve (partial) 378.51
      total 378.52
    fourth or trochlear nerve 378.53
    sixth or abducens nerve 378.54
  specified type NEC 378.73
  vertical (hypertropia) 378.31
Strain —*see also* Sprain, by site
  eye NEC 368.13
  heart—*see* Disease, heart
  meaning gonorrhea—*see* Gonorrhea
  physical NEC V62.89
  postural 729.9
  psychological NEC V62.89
Strands
  conjunctiva 372.62
  vitreous humor 379.25
Strangulation, strangulated 994.7
  appendix 543.9
  asphyxiation or suffocation by 994.7
  bladder neck 596.0
  bowel—*see* Strangulation, intestine
  colon—*see* Strangulation, intestine
  cord (umbilical)—*see* Compression, umbilical
    cord
  due to birth injury 767.8
  food or foreign body (*see also* Asphyxia, food)
    933.1
  hemorrhoids 455.8
    external 455.5
    internal 455.2
  hernia—*see also* Hernia, by site, with
    obstruction
    gangrenous—*see* Hernia, by site, with
      gangrene
  intestine (large) (small) 560.2
    with hernia—*see also* Hernia, by site, with
      obstruction

Strangulation, strangulated—*continued*
    gangrenous—*see* Hernia, by site, with
      gangrene
    congenital (small) 751.1
      large 751.2
    mesentery 560.2
    mucus (*see also* Asphyxia, mucus) 933.1
      newborn 770.1
    omentum 560.2
    organ or site, congenital NEC—*see* Atresia
    ovary 620.8
      due to hernia 620.4
    penis 607.89
      foreign body 939.3
    rupture (*see also* Hernia, by site, with
      obstruction) 552.9
      gangrenous (*see also* Hernia, by site, with
        gangrene) 551.9
    stomach, due to hernia (*see also* Hernia, by site,
      with obstruction) 552.9
      with gangrene (*see also* Hernia, by site, with
        gangrene) 551.9
    umbilical cord—*see* Compression, umbilical
      cord
    vesicourethral orifice 596.0
Strangury 788.1
Strawberry
  gallbladder (*see also* Disease, gallbladder) 575.6
  mark 757.32
  tongue (red) (white) 529.3
Straw itch 133.8
Streak, ovarian 752.0
Strephosymbolia 315.01
  secondary to organic lesion 784.69
Streptobacillary fever 026.1
Streptobacillus moniliformis 026.1
Streptococcemia 038.0
Streptococcicosis —*see* Infection, streptococcal
Streptococcus, streptococcal —*see* condition
Streptoderma 686.0
Streptomycosis —*see* Actinomycosis
Streptothricosis —*see* Actinomycosis
Streptothrix —*see* Actinomycosis
Streptotrichosis —*see* Actinomycosis
Stress
  fracture—*see* Fracture, pathologic
  polycythemia 289.0
  reaction (gross) (*see also* Reaction, stress,
    acute) 308.9
Stretching, nerve —*see* Injury, nerve, by site
Striae (albicantes) (atrophicae) (cutis distensae)
    (distensae) 701.3
Striations of nails 703.8
Stricture (*see also* Stenosis) 799.8
  ampulla of Vater 576.2
    with calculus, cholelithiasis, or stones—*see*
      Choledocholithiasis
  anus (sphincter) 569.2
    congenital 751.2
    infantile 751.2
  aorta (ascending) 747.22
    arch 747.10
    arteriosclerotic 440.0
    calcified 440.0
  aortic (valve) (*see also* Stenosis, aortic) 424.1
    congenital 746.3
  aqueduct of Sylvius (congenital) 742.3
    with spina bifida (*see also* Spina bifida) 741.0
    acquired 331.4

Stricture—*continued*
  artery 447.1
    basilar—*see* Narrowing, artery, basilar
    carotid (common) (internal)—*see* Narrowing,
        artery, carotid
    celiac 447.4
    cerebral 437.0
      congenital 747.81
      due to
        embolism (*see also* Embolism, brain)
            434.1
        thrombus (*see also* Thrombosis, brain)
            434.0
    congenital (peripheral) 747.60
      cerebral 747.81
      coronary 746.85
      gastrointestinal 747.61
      lower limb 747.64
      renal 747.62
      retinal 743.58
      specified NEC 747.69
      spinal 747.82
      umbilical 747.5
      upper limb 747.63
    coronary —*see* Arteriosclerosis, coronary
      congenital 746.85
    precerebral—*see* Narrowing, artery,
        precerebral NEC
    pulmonary (congenital) 747.3
      acquired 417.8
    renal 440.1
    vertebral—*see* Narrowing, artery, vertebral
  auditory canal (congenital) (external) 744.02
    acquired (*see also* Stricture, ear canal,
        acquired) 380.50
  bile duct or passage (any) (postoperative) (*see
      also* Obstruction, biliary) 576.2
    congenital 751.61
  bladder 596.8
    congenital 753.6
    neck 596.0
      congenital 753.6
  bowel (*see also* Obstruction, intestine) 560.9
  brain 348.8
  bronchus 519.1
    syphilitic 095.8
  cardia (stomach) 537.89
    congenital 750.7
  cardiac—*see also* Disease, heart
    orifice (stomach) 537.89
  cardiovascular (*see also* Disease,
      cardiovascular) 429.2
  carotid artery—*see* Narrowing, artery, carotid
  cecum (*see also* Obstruction, intestine) 560.9
  cervix, cervical (canal) 622.4
    congenital 752.49
    in pregnancy or childbirth 654.6
      affecting fetus or newborn 763.8
      causing obstructed labor 660.2
        affecting fetus or newborn 763.1
  colon (*see also* Obstruction, intestine) 560.9
    congenital 751.2
  colostomy 569.69
  common bile duct (*see also* Obstruction, biliary)
      576.2
    congenital 751.61
  coronary (artery) —*see* Arteriosclerosis,
      coronary
    congenital 746.85—
  cystic duct (*see also* Obstruction, gallbladder)
      575.2
    congenital 751.61

Stricture—*continued*
  cystostomy 997.5
  digestive organs NEC, congenital 751.8
  duodenum 537.3
    congenital 751.1
  ear canal (external) (congenital) 744.02
    acquired 380.50
      secondary to
        inflammation 380.53
        surgery 380.52
        trauma 380.51
  ejaculatory duct 608.85
  enterostomy 569.69
  esophagus (corrosive) (peptic) 530.3
    congenital 750.3
    syphilitic 095.8
      congenital 090.5
  Eustachian tube (*see also* Obstruction,
      Eustachian tube) 381.60
    congenital 744.24
  fallopian tube 628.2
    gonococcal (chronic) 098.37
      acute 098.17
    tuberculous (*see also* Tuberculosis) 016.6
  gallbladder (*see also* Obstruction, gallbladder)
      575.2
    congenital 751.69
  glottis 478.74
  heart—*see also* Disease, heart
    congenital NEC 746.89
    valve—*see also* Endocarditis
      congenital NEC 746.89
        aortic 746.3
        mitral 746.5
        pulmonary 746.02
        tricuspid 746.1
  hepatic duct (*see also* Obstruction, biliary) 576.2
  hourglass, of stomach 537.6
  hymen 623.3
  hypopharynx 478.29
  intestine (*see also* Obstruction, intestine) 560.9
    congenital (small) 751.1
      large 751.2
    ischemic 557.1
  lacrimal
    canaliculi 375.53
      congenital 743.65
    punctum 375.52
      congenital 743.65
    sac 375.54
      congenital 743.65
  lacrimonasal duct 375.56
    congenital 743.65
    neonatal 375.55
  larynx 478.79
    congenital 748.3
    syphilitic 095.8
      congenital 090.5
  lung 518.89
  meatus
    ear (congenital) 744.02
      acquired (*see also* Stricture, ear canal,
          acquired) 380.50
    osseous (congenital) (ear) 744.03
      acquired (*see also* Stricture, ear canal,
          acquired) 380.50
    urinarius (*see also* Stricture, urethra) 598.9
      congenital 753.6
  mitral (valve) (*see also* Stenosis, mitral) 394.0
    congenital 746.5
    specified cause, except rheumatic 424.0

Stricture—*continued*
  myocardium, myocardial (*see also*
    Degeneration, myocardial) 429.1
    hypertrophic subaortic (idiopathic) 425.1
  nares (anterior) (posterior) 478.1
    congenital 748.0
  nasal duct 375.56
    congenital 743.65
    neonatal 375.55
  nasolacrimal duct 375.56
    congenital 743.65
    neonatal 375.55
  nasopharynx 478.29
    syphilitic 095.8
  nephrostomy 997.5
  nose 478.1
    congenital 748.0
  nostril (anterior) (posterior) 478.1
    congenital 748.0
  organ or site, congenital NEC—*see* Atresia
  osseous meatus (congenital) (ear) 744.03
    acquired (*see also* Stricture, ear canal,
      acquired) 380.50
  os uteri (*see also* Stricture, cervix) 622.4
  oviduct—*see* Stricture, fallopian tube
  pelviureteric junction 593.3
  pharynx (dilation) 478.29
  prostate 602.8
  pulmonary, pulmonic
    artery (congenital) 747.3
      acquired 417.8
      noncongenital 417.8
    infundibulum (congenital) 746.83
    valve (*see also* Endocarditis, pulmonary) 424.3
      congenital 746.02
    vein (congenital) 747.49
      acquired 417.8
    vessel NEC 417.8
  punctum lacrimale 375.52
    congenital 743.65
  pylorus (hypertrophic) 537.0
    adult 537.0
    congenital 750.5
    infantile 750.5
  rectosigmoid 569.89
  rectum (sphincter) 569.2
    congenital 751.2
    due to
      chemical burn 947.3
      irradiation 569.2
      lymphogranuloma venereum 099.1
    gonococcal 098.7
    inflammatory 099.1
    syphilitic 095.8
    tuberculous (*see also* Tuberculosis) 014.8
  renal artery 440.1
  salivary duct or gland (any) 527.8
  sigmoid (flexure) (*see also* Obstruction,
    intestine) 560.9
  spermatic cord 608.85
  stoma (following) (of)
    colostomy 569.69
    cystostomy 997.5
    enterostomy 569.69
    gastrostomy 997.4
    ileostomy 569.69
    nephrostomy 997.5
    tracheostomy 519.0
    ureterostomy 997.5
  stomach 537.89
    congenital 750.7

Stricture—*continued*
  hourglass 537.6
  subaortic 746.81
    hypertrophic (acquired) (idiopathic) 425.1
  subglottic 478.74
  syphilitic NEC 095.8
  tendon (sheath) 727.81
  trachea 519.1
    congenital 748.3
    syphilitic 095.8
    tuberculous (*see also* Tuberculosis) 012.8
  tracheostomy 519.0
  tricuspid (valve) (*see also* Endocarditis,
    tricuspid) 397.0
    congenital 746.1
    nonrheumatic 424.2
  tunica vaginalis 608.85
  ureter (postoperative) 593.3
    congenital 753.29
    tuberculous (*see also* Tuberculosis) 016.2
  ureteropelvic junction 593.3
    congenital 753.21
  ureterovesical orifice 593.3
    congenital 753.22
  urethra (anterior) (meatal) (organic) (posterior)
    (spasmodic) 598.9
    associated with schistosomiasis (*see also*
      Schistosomiasis) 120.9 *[598.01]*
    congenital (valvular) 753.6
    due to
      infection 598.00
        syphilis 095.8 *[598.01]*
      trauma 598.1
    gonococcal 098.2 *[598.01]*
    gonorrheal 098.2 *[598.01]*
    infective 598.00
    late effect of injury 598.1
    postcatheterization 598.2
    postobstetric 598.1
    postoperative 598.2
    specified cause NEC 598.8
    syphilitic 095.8 *[598.01]*
    traumatic 598.1
    valvular, congenital 753.6
  urinary meatus (*see also* Stricture, urethra) 598.9
    congenital 753.6
  uterus, uterine 621.5
    os (external) (internal)—*see* Stricture, cervix
  vagina (outlet) 623.2
    congenital 752.49
  valve (cardiac) (heart) (*see also* Endocarditis)
    424.90
    congenital (cardiac) (heart) NEC 746.89
      aortic 746.3
      mitral 746.5
      pulmonary 746.02
      tricuspid 746.1
      urethra 753.6
  valvular (*see also* Endocarditis) 424.90
  vascular graft or shunt 996.1
    atherosclerosis —*see* Arteriosclerosis,
      extremities
    embolism 996.74
    occlusion NEC 996.74
    thrombus 996.74
  vas deferens 608.85
    congenital 752.8
  vein 459.2
  vena cava (inferior) (superior) NEC 459.2
    congenital 747.49

Stricture—*continued*
  ventricular shunt 996.2
  vesicourethral orifice 596.0
    congenital 753.6
  vulva (acquired) 624.8
Stridor 786.1
  congenital (larynx) 748.3
Stridulous —*see* condition
Strippling of nails 703.8
Stroke (*see also* Disease, cerebrovascular, acute)
    436
  apoplectic (*see also* Disease, cerebrovascular,
    acute) 436
  brain (*see also* Disease, cerebrovascular, acute)
    436
  epileptic—*see* Epilepsy
  healed or old—*see also* category 438
    without residuals V12.59
  heart—*see* Disease, heart
  heat 992.0
  iatrogenic 997.02
  in evolution 435.9
  late effect—*see* category 438
  lightning 994.0
  paralytic (*see also* Disease, cerebrovascular,
    acute) 436
  postoperative 997.02
  progressive 435.9
Stromatosis, endometrial (M8931/1) 236.0
Strong pulse 785.9
Strongyloides stercoralis infestation 127.2
Strongyloidiasis 127.2
Strongyloidosis 127.2
Strongylus (gibsoni) infestation 127.7
Strophulus (newborn) 779.8
  pruriginosus 698.2
Struck by lightning 994.0
Struma (*see also* Goiter) 240.9
  fibrosa 245.3
  Hashimoto (struma lymphomatosa) 245.2
  lymphomatosa 245.2
  nodosa (simplex) 241.9
    endemic 241.9
    multinodular 241.1
    sporadic 241.9
    toxic or with hyperthyroidism 242.3
      multinodular 242.2
      uninodular 242.1
    toxicosa 242.3
      multinodular 242.2
      uninodular 242.1
    uninodular 241.0
  ovarii (M9090/0) 220
    and carcinoid (M9091/1) 236.2
    malignant (M9090/3) 183.0
  Riedel's (ligneous thyroiditis) 245.3
  scrofulous (*see also* Tuberculosis) 017.2
  tuberculous (*see also* Tuberculosis) 017.2
    abscess 017.2
    adenitis 017.2
    lymphangitis 017.2
    ulcer 017.2
Strumipriva cachexia (*see also*
  Hypothyroidism) 244.9
Strümpell-Marie disease or spine (ankylosing
  spondylitis) 720.0
Strümpell-Westphal pseudosclerosis
  (hepatolenticular degeneration) 275.1
Stuart's disease (congenital factor X deficiency)
  (*see also* Defect, coagulation) 286.3

Stuart-Prower factor deficiency (congenital
  factor X deficiency) (*see also* Defect,
  coagulation) 286.3
Students' elbow 727.2
Stuffy nose 478.1
Stump —*see also* Amputation
  cervix, cervical (healed) 622.8
Stupor 780.09
  catatonic (*see also* Schizophrenia) 295.2
  circular (*see also* Psychosis, manic-depressive,
    circular) 296.7
  manic 296.89
  manic-depressive (*see also* Psychosis, affective)
    296.89
  mental (anergic) (delusional) 298.9
  psychogenic 298.8
  reaction to exceptional stress (transient) 308.2
  traumatic NEC—*see also* Injury, intracranial
    with spinal (cord)
      lesion—*see* Injury, spinal, by site
      shock—*see* Injury, spinal, by site
Sturge (-Weber) (-Dimitri) disease or syndrome
  (encephalocutaneous angiomatosis) 759.6
Sturge-Kalischer-Weber syndrome
  (encephalocutaneous angiomatosis) 759.6
Stuttering 307.0
Sty, stye 373.11
  external 373.11
  internal 373.12
  meibomian 373.12
Subacidity, gastric 536.8
  psychogenic 306.4
Subacute —*see* condition
Subarachnoid —*see* condition
Subclavian steal syndrome 435.2
Subcortical —*see* condition
Subcostal syndrome 098.86
  nerve compression 354.8
Subcutaneous, subcuticular —*see* condition
Subdelirium 293.1
Subdural —*see* condition
Subendocardium —*see* condition
Subependymoma (M9383/1) 237.5
Suberosis 495.3
Subglossitis —*see* Glossitis
Subhemophilia 286.0
Subinvolution (uterus) 621.1
  breast (postlactational) (postpartum) 611.8
  chronic 621.1
  puerperal, postpartum 674.8
Sublingual —*see* condition
Sublinguitis 527.2
Subluxation —*see also* Dislocation, by site
  congenital NEC—*see also* Malposition,
    congenital
    hip (unilateral) 754.32
      with dislocation of other hip 754.35
      bilateral 754.33
    joint
      lower limb 755.69
      shoulder 755.59
      upper limb 755.59
    lower limb (joint) 755.69
    shoulder (joint) 755.59
    upper limb (joint) 755.59
  lens 379.32
    anterior 379.33
    posterior 379.34
  rotary, cervical region of spine—*see* Fracture,
    vertebra, cervical
Submaxillary —*see* condition
Submersion (fatal) (nonfatal) 994.1

Submissiveness (undue), in child 313.0
Submucous —*see* condition
Subnormal, subnormality
  accommodation (*see also* Disorder,
      accommodation) 367.9
  mental (*see also* Retardation, mental) 319
    mild 317
    moderate 318.0
    profound 318.2
    severe 318.1
  temperature (accidental) 991.6
    not associated with low environmental
        temperature 780.9
Subphrenic —*see* condition
Subscapular nerve —*see* condition
Subseptus uterus 752.3
Subsiding appendicitis 542
Substernal thyroid (*see also* Goiter) 240.9
  congenital 759.2
Substitution disorder 300.11
Subtentorial —*see* condition
Subtertian
  fever 084.0
  malaria (fever) 084.0
Subthyroidism (acquired) (*see also*
    Hypothyroidism) 244.9
  congenital 243
Succenturiata placenta —*see* Placenta, abnormal
Succussion sounds, chest 786.7
Sucking thumb, child 307.9
Sudamen 705.1
Sudamina 705.1
Sudanese kala-azar 085.0
Sudden
  death, cause unknown (less than 24 hours) 798.1
    during childbirth 669.9
    infant 798.0
    puerperal, postpartum 674.9
  hearing loss NEC 388.2
  heart failure (*see also* Failure, heart) 428.9
  infant death syndrome 798.0
Sudeck's atrophy, disease, or syndrome 733.7
SUDS (Sudden unexplained death) 798.2
Suffocation (*see also* Asphyxia) 799.0
  by
    bed clothes 994.7
    bunny bag 994.7
    cave-in 994.7
    constriction 994.7
    drowning 994.1
    inhalation
      food or foreign body (*see also* Asphyxia,
          food or foreign body) 933.1
      oil or gasoline (*see also* Asphyxia, food or
          foreign body) 933.1
    overlying 994.7
    plastic bag 994.7
    pressure 994.7
    strangulation 994.7
  during birth 768.1
  mechanical 994.7
Sugar
  blood
    high 790.6
    low 251.2
  in urine 791.5
Suicide, suicidal (attempted)
  by poisoning—*see* Table of drugs and chemicals
  risk 300.9
  tendencies 300.9
  trauma NEC (*see also* nature and site of injury)
      959.9

Suipestifer infection (*see also* Infection,
    Salmonella) 003.9
Sulfatidosis 330.0
Sulfhemoglobinemia, sulphemoglobinemia
    (acquired) (congenital) 289.7
Sumatran mite fever 081.2
Summer —*see* condition
Sunburn 692.71
  dermatitis 692.71
Sunken
  acetabulum 718.85
  fontanels 756.0
Sunstroke 992.0
Superfecundation 651.9
  with fetal loss and retention of one or more
      fetus(es) 651.6
Superfetation 651.9
  with fetal loss and retention of one or more
      fetus(es) 651.6
Supernumerary (congenital)
  aortic cusps 746.89
  auditory ossicles 744.04
  bone 756.9
  breast 757.6
  carpal bones 755.56
  cusps, heart valve NEC 746.89
    mitral 746.5
    pulmonary 746.09
  digit(s) 755.00
    finger 755.01
    toe 755.02
  ear (lobule) 744.1
  fallopian tube 752.19
  finger 755.01
  hymen 752.49
  kidney 753.3
  lacrimal glands 743.64
  lacrimonasal duct 743.65
  lobule (ear) 744.1
  mitral cusps 746.5
  muscle 756.82
  nipples 757.6
  organ or site NEC—*see* Accessory
  ossicles, auditory 744.04
  ovary 752.0
  oviduct 752.19
  pulmonic cusps 746.09
  rib 756.3
    cervical or first 756.2
      syndrome 756.2
  roots (of teeth) 520.2
  spinal vertebra 756.19
  spleen 759.0
  tarsal bones 755.67
  teeth 520.1
    causing crowding 524.3
  testis 752.8
  thumb 755.01
  toe 755.02
  uterus 752.2
  vagina 752.49
  vertebra 756.19
Supervision (of)
  contraceptive method previously prescribed
      V25.40
    intrauterine device V25.42
    oral contraceptive (pill) V25.41
    specified type NEC V25.49
    subdermal implantable contraceptive V25.43
  dietary (for) V65.3
    allergy (food) V65.3

Supervision—*continued*
  colitis V65.3
  diabetes mellitus V65.3
  food allergy intolerance V65.3
  gastritis V65.3
  hypercholesterolemia V65.3
  hypoglycemia V65.3
  intolerance (food) V65.3
  obesity V65.3
  specified NEC V65.3
  lactation V24.1
  pregnancy—*see* Pregnancy, supervision of
Supplemental teeth 520.1
  causing crowding 524.3
Suppression
  binocular vision 368.31
  lactation 676.5
  menstruation 626.8
  ovarian secretion 256.3
  renal 586
  urinary secretion 788.5
  urine 788.5
Suppuration, suppurative —*see also* condition
  accessory sinus (chronic) (*see also* Sinusitis)
    473.9
  adrenal gland 255.8
  antrum (chronic) (*see also* Sinusitis, maxillary)
    473.0
  bladder (*see also* Cystitis) 595.89
  bowel 569.89
  brain 324.0
    late effect 326
  breast 611.0
    puerperal, postpartum 675.1
  dental periosteum 526.5
  diffuse (skin) 686.0
  ear (middle) (*see also* Otitis media) 382.4
    external (*see also* Otitis, externa) 380.10
    internal 386.33
  ethmoidal (sinus) (chronic) (*see also* Sinusitis,
    ethmoidal) 473.2
  fallopian tube (*see also* Salpingo-oophoritis)
    614.2
  frontal (sinus) (chronic) (*see also* Sinusitis,
    frontal) 473.1
  gallbladder (*see also* Cholecystitis, acute) 575.0
  gum 523.3
  hernial sac—*see* Hernia, by site
  intestine 569.89
  joint (*see also* Arthritis, suppurative) 711.0
  labyrinthine 386.33
  lung 513.0
  mammary gland 611.0
    puerperal, postpartum 675.1
  maxilla, maxillary 526.4
    sinus (chronic) (*see also* Sinusitis, maxillary)
    473.0
  muscle 728.0
  nasal sinus (chronic) (*see also* Sinusitis) 473.9
  pancreas 577.0
  parotid gland 527.2
  pelvis, pelvic
    female (*see also* Disease, pelvis,
      inflammatory) 614.4
      acute 614.3
    male (*see also* Peritonitis) 567.2
  pericranial (*see also* Osteomyelitis) 730.2
  salivary duct or gland (any) 527.2
  sinus (nasal) (*see also* Sinusitis) 473.9
  sphenoidal (sinus) (chronic) (*see also* Sinusitis,
    sphenoidal) 473.3
  thymus (gland) 254.1

Suppuration, suppurative—*continued*
  thyroid (gland) 245.0
  tonsil 474.8
  uterus (*see also* Endometritis) 615.9
  vagina 616.10
  wound—*see also* Wound, open, by site,
    complicated
    dislocation—*see* Dislocation, by site,
      compound
    fracture—*see* Fracture, by site, open
    scratch or other superficial injury—*see* Injury,
      superficial, by site
Suprapubic drainage 596.8
Suprarenal (gland)—*see* condition
Suprascapular nerve —*see* condition
Suprasellar —*see* condition
Supraspinatus syndrome 726.10
Surfer knots 919.8
  infected 919.9
Surgery
  cosmetic NEC V50.1
    following healed injury or operation V51
    hair transplant V50.0
  elective V50.9
    breast augmentation reduction V50.1
    circumcision, ritual or routine (in absence of
      medical indication) V50.2
    cosmetic NEC V50.1
    ear piercing V50.3
    face-lift V50.1
    following healed injury or operation V51
    hair transplant V50.0
  not done because of
    contraindication V64.1
    patient's decision V64.2
    specified reason NEC V64.3
  plastic
    breast augmentation or reduction V50.1
    cosmetic V50.1
    face-lift V50.1
    following healed injury or operation V51
    repair of scarred tissue (following healed
      injury or operation) V51
    specified type NEC V50.8
  previous, in pregnancy or childbirth
    cervix 654.6
      affecting fetus or newborn 763.8
      causing obstructed labor 660.2
        affecting fetus or newborn 763.1
    pelvic soft tissues NEC 654.9
      affecting fetus or newborn 763.8
      causing obstructed labor 660.2
        affecting fetus or newborn 763.1
    perineum or vulva 654.8
    uterus NEC 654.9
      affecting fetus or newborn 763.8
      causing obstructed labor 660.2
        affecting fetus or newborn 763.1
      due to previous cesarean delivery 654.2
    vagina 654.7
Surgical
  abortion—*see* Abortion, legal
  emphysema 998.81
  kidney (*see also* Pyelitis) 590.80
  operation NEC 799.9
  procedures, complication or misadventure—*see*
    Complications, surgical procedure
  shock 998.0
Suspected condition, ruled out (*see also*
  Observation, suspected) V71.9
  specified condition NEC V71.8

Suspended uterus, in pregnancy or childbirth 654.4
  affecting fetus or newborn 763.8
  causing obstructed labor 660.2
    affecting fetus or newborn 763.1
Sutton's disease 709.09
Sutton and Gull's disease (arteriolar
  nephrosclerosis) (*see also* Hypertension,
  kidney) 403.90
Suture
  burst (in operation wound) 998.3
  inadvertently left in operation wound 998.4
  removal V58.3
  Shirodkar, in pregnancy (with or without
    cervical incompetence) 654.5
Swab inadvertently left in operation wound
  998.4
Swallowed, swallowing
  difficulty (*see also* Dysphagia) 787.2
  foreign body NEC (*see also* Foreign body) 938
Swamp fever 100.89
Swan neck hand (intrinsic) 736.09
Sweat (s), sweating
  disease or sickness 078.2
  excessive 780.8
  fetid 705.89
  fever 078.2
  gland disease 705.9
    specified type NEC 705.89
  miliary 078.2
  night 780.8
Sweeley-Klionsky disease (angiokeratoma
  corporis diffusum) 272.7
Sweet's syndrome (acute febrile neutrophilic
  dermatosis) 695.89
Swelling
  abdominal (not referable to specific organ) 789.3
  adrenal gland, cloudy 255.8
  ankle 719.07
  anus 787.99
  arm 729.81
  breast 611.72
  Calabar 125.2
  cervical gland 785.6
  cheek 784.2
  chest 786.6
  ear 388.8
  epigastric 789.3
  extremity (lower) (upper) 729.81
  eye 379.92
  female genital organ 625.8
  finger 729.81
  foot 729.81
  glands 785.6
  gum 784.2
  hand 729.81
  head 784.2
  inflammatory—*see* Inflammation
  joint (*see also* Effusion, joint) 719.0
    tuberculous—*see* Tuberculosis, joint
  kidney, cloudy 593.89
  leg 729.81
  limb 729.81
  liver 573.8
  lung 786.6
  lymph nodes 785.6
  mediastinal 786.6
  mouth 784.2
  muscle (limb) 729.81
  neck 784.2

Swelling— *continued*
  nose or sinus 784.2
  palate 784.2
  pelvis 789.3
  penis 607.83
  perineum 625.8
  rectum 787.99
  scrotum 608.86
  skin 782.2
  splenic (*see also* Splenomegaly) 789.2
  substernal 786.6
  superficial, localized (skin) 782.2
  testicle 608.86
  throat 784.2
  toe 729.81
  tongue 784.2
  tubular (*see also* Disease, renal) 593.9
  umbilicus 789.3
  uterus 625.8
  vagina 625.8
  vulva 625.8
  wandering, due to Gnathostoma (spinigerum)
    128.1
  white—*see* Tuberculosis, arthritis
Swift's disease 985.0
Swimmers'
  ear (acute) 380.12
  itch 120.3
Swimming in the head 780.4
Swollen —*see also* Swelling
  glands 785.6
Swyer-James syndrome (unilateral hyperlucent
  lung) 492.8
Swyer's syndrome (XY pure gonadal
  dysgenesis) 752.7
Sycosis 704.8
  barbae (not parasitic) 704.8
  contagiosa 110.0
  lupoid 704.8
  mycotic 110.0
  parasitic 110.0
  vulgaris 704.8
Sydenham's chorea —*see* Chorea, Sydenham's
Sylvatic yellow fever 060.0
Sylvest's disease (epidemic pleurodynia) 074.1
Symblepharon 372.63
  congenital 743.62
Symonds' syndrome 348.2
Sympathetic —*see* condition
Sympatheticotonia (*see also* Neuropathy,
  peripheral, autonomic) 337.9
Sympathicoblastoma (M9500/3)
  specified site—*see* Neoplasm, by site, malignant
  unspecified site 194.0
Sympathicogonioma (M9500/3)—*see*
  Sympathicoblastoma
Sympathoblastoma (M9500/3)—*see*
  Sympathicoblastoma
Sympathogonioma (M9500/3)—*see*
  Sympathicoblastoma
Symphalangy (*see also* Syndactylism) 755.10
Symptoms, specified (general) NEC 780.9
  abdomen NEC 789.9
  bone NEC 733.90
  breast NEC 611.79
  cardiac NEC 785.9
  cardiovascular NEC 785.9
  chest NEC 786.9
  development NEC 783.9
  digestive system NEC 787.99

Symptoms, specified—*continued*
eye NEC 379.99
gastrointestinal tract NEC 787.99
genital organs NEC
female 625.9
male 608.9
head and neck NEC 784.9
heart NEC 785.9
joint NEC 719.60
ankle 719.67
elbow 719.62
foot 719.67
hand 719.64
hip 719.65
knee 719.66
multiple sites 719.69
pelvic region 719.65
shoulder (region) 719.61
specified site NEC 719.68
wrist 719.63
larynx NEC 784.9
limbs NEC 729.89
lymphatic system NEC 785.9
menopausal 627.2
metabolism NEC 783.9
mouth NEC 528.9
muscle NEC 728.9
musculoskeletal NEC 781.9
limbs NEC 729.89
nervous system NEC 781.9
neurotic NEC 300.9
nutrition, metabolism, and development NEC
783.9
pelvis NEC 789.9
female 625.9
peritoneum NEC 789.9
respiratory system NEC 786.9
skin and integument NEC 782.9
subcutaneous tissue NEC 782.9
throat NEC 784.9
tonsil NEC 784.9
urinary system NEC 788.9
vascular NEC 785.9
Sympus 759.89
Synarthrosis 719.80
ankle 719.87
elbow 719.82
foot 719.87
hand 719.84
hip 719.85
knee 719.86
multiple sites 719.89
pelvic region 719.85
shoulder (region) 719.81
specified site NEC 719.88
wrist 719.83
Syncephalus 759.4
Synchondrosis 756.9
abnormal (congenital) 756.9
ischiopubic (van Neck's) 732.1
Synchysis (senile) (vitreous humor) 379.21
scintillans 379.22
Syncope (near) (pre-) 780.2
anginosa 413.9
bradycardia 427.89
cardiac 780.2
carotid sinus 337.0
complicating delivery 669.2
due to lumbar puncture 349.0
fatal 798.1

Syncope—*continued*
heart 780.2
heat 992.1
laryngeal 786.2
tussive 786.2
vasoconstriction 780.2
vasodepressor 780.2
vasomotor 780.2
vasovagal 780.2
Syncytial infarct —*see* Placenta, abnormal
Syndactylism, syndactyly (multiple sites) 755.10
fingers (without fusion of bone) 755.11
with fusion of bone 755.12
toes (without fusion of bone) 755.13
with fusion of bone 755.14
Syndrome —*see also* Disease
abdominal
acute 789.0
migraine 346.2
muscle deficiency 756.7
Abercrombie's (amyloid degeneration) 277.3
abnormal innervation 374.43
abstinence
alcohol 291.81
drug 292.0
Abt-Letterer-Siwe (acute histiocytosis X)
(M9722/3) 202.5
Achard-Thiers (adrenogenital) 255.2
acid pulmonary aspiration 997.3
obstetric (Mendelson's) 668.0
acquired immune deficiency 042
acquired immunodeficiency 042
acrocephalosyndactylism 755.55
acute abdominal 789.0
Adair-Dighton (brittle bones and blue sclera,
deafness) 756.51
Adams-Stokes (-Morgagni) (syncope with heart
block) 426.9
addisonian 255.4
Adie (-Holmes) (pupil) 379.46
adiposogenital 253.8
adrenal
hemorrhage 036.3
meningococcic 036.3
adrenocortical 255.3
adrenogenital (acquired) (congenital) 255.2
feminizing 255.2
iatrogenic 760.79
virilism (acquired) (congenital) 255.2
affective organic NEC 293.89
drug-induced 292.84
afferent loop NEC 537.89
African macroglobulinemia 273.3
Ahumada-Del Castillo (nonpuerperal
galactorrhea and amenorrhea) 253.1
air blast concussion—*see* Injury, internal, by site
Albright (-Martin) (pseudohypoparathyroidism)
275.4
Albright-McCune-Sternberg (osteitis fibrosa
disseminata) 756.59
alcohol withdrawal 291.81
Alder's (leukocyte granulation anomaly) 288.2
Aldrich (-Wiskott) (eczema-thrombocytopenia)
279.12
Alibert-Bazin (mycosis, fungoides) (M9700/3)
202.1
Alice in Wonderland 293.89
Allen-Masters 620.6
Alligator baby (ichthyosis congenita) 757.1

Syndrome—*continued*
  Alport's (hereditary hematuria-nephropathy-
    deafness) 759.89
  Alvarez (transient cerebral ischemia) 435.9
  alveolar capillary block 516.3
  Alzheimer's 331.0
    with dementia—*see* Alzheimer's, dementia
  amnestic (confabulatory) 294.0
    alcoholic 291.1
    drug-induced 292.83
    posttraumatic 294.0
  amotivational 292.89
  amyostatic 275.1
  amyotrophic lateral sclerosis 335.20
  angina (*see also* Angina) 413.9
  ankyloglossia superior 750.0
  anterior
    chest wall 786.52
    compartment (tibial) 958.8
    spinal artery 433.8
      compression 721.1
    tibial (compartment) 958.8
  antibody deficiency 279.00
    agammaglobulinemic 279.00
    congenital 279.04
    hypogammaglobulinemic 279.00
  antimongolism 758.3
  Anton (-Babinski) (hemiasomatognosia) 307.9
  anxiety (*see also* Anxiety) 300.00
  aortic
    arch 446.7
    bifurcation (occlusion) 444.0
    ring 747.21
  Apert's (acrocephalosyndactyly) 755.55
  Apert-Gallais (adrenogenital) 255.2
  aphasia-apraxia-alexia 784.69
  "approximate answers" 300.16
  arcuate ligament (-celiac axis) 447.4
  arcus aortae 446.7
  arc-welders' 370.24
  argentaffin, argintaffinoma 259.2
  Argonz-Del Castillo (nonpuerperal galactorrhea
    and amenorrhea) 253.1
  Argyll Robertson's (syphilitic) 094.89
    nonsyphilitic 379.45
  arm-shoulder (*see also* Neuropathy, peripheral,
    autonomic) 337.9
  Arnold-Chiari (*see also* Spina bifida) 741.0
    type I 348.4
    type II 741.0
    type III 742.0
    type IV 742.2
  Arrillaga-Ayerza (pulmonary artery sclerosis
    with pulmonary hypertension) 416.0
  arteriomesenteric duodenum occlusion 537.89
  arteriovenous steal 996.73
  arteritis, young female (obliterative
    brachiocephalic) 446.7
  aseptic meningitis—*see* Meningitis, aseptic
  Asherman's 621.5
  asphyctic (*see also* Anxiety) 300.00
  aspiration, of newborn, massive or meconium
    770.1
  ataxia-telangiectasia 334.8
  Audry's (acropachyderma) 757.39
  auriculotemporal 350.8
  autosomal—*see also* Abnormal, autosomes NEC
    deletion 758.3
  Avellis' 344.89
  Axenfeld's 743.44

Syndrome—*continued*
  Ayerza (-Arrillaga) (pulmonary artery sclerosis
    with pulmonary hypertension) 416.0
  Baader's (erythema multiforme exudativum)
    695.1
  Baastrup's 721.5
  Babinski (-Vaquez) (cardiovascular syphilis)
    093.89
  Babinski-Fröhlich (adiposogenital dystrophy)
    253.8
  Babinski-Nageotte 344.89
  Bagratuni's (temporal arteritis) 446.5
  Bakwin-Krida (craniometaphyseal dysplasia)
    756.89
  Balint's (psychic paralysis of visual
    disorientation) 368.16
  Ballantyne (-Runge) (postmaturity) 766.2
  ballooning posterior leaflet 424.0
  Banti's—*see* Cirrhosis, liver
  Bard-Pic's (carcinoma, head of pancreas) 157.0
  Bardet-Biedl (obesity, polydactyly, and mental
    retardation) 759.89
  Barlow's (mitral valve prolapse) 424.0
  Barlow (-Möller) (infantile scurvy) 267
  Baron Munchausen's 301.51
  Barré-Guillain 357.0
  Barré-Liéou (posterior cervical sympathetic)
    723.2
  Barrett's (chronic peptic ulcer of esophagus)
    530.2
  Bársony-Polgár (corkscrew esophagus) 530.5
  Bársony-Teschendorf (corkscrew esophagus)
    530.5
  Bartter's (secondary hyperaldosteronism with
    juxtaglomerular hyperplasia) 255.1
  Basedow's (exophthalmic goiter) 242.0
  basilar artery 435.0
  basofrontal 377.04
  Bassen-Kornzweig (abetalipoproteinemia) 272.5
  Batten-Steinert 359.2
  battered
    adult 995.81
    baby or child 995.54
    spouse 995.81
  Baumgarten-Cruveilhier (cirrhosis of liver)
    571.5
  Bearn-Kunkel (-Slater) (lupoid hepatitis) 571.49
  Beau's (*see also* Degeneration, myocardial)
    429.1
  Bechterew-Strümpell-Marie (ankylosing
    spondylitis) 720.0
  Beck's (anterior spinal artery occlusion) 433.8
  Beckwith (-Wiedemann) 759.89
  Behçet's 136.1
  Bekhterev-Strümpell-Marie (ankylosing
    spondylitis) 720.0
  Benedikt's 344.89
  Béquez César (-Steinbrinck-Chédiak-Higashi)
    (congenital gigantism of peroxidase
    granules) 288.2
  Bernard-Horner (*see also* Neuropathy,
    peripheral, autonomic) 337.9
  Bernard-Sergent (acute adrenocortical
    insufficiency) 255.4
  Bernhardt-Roth 355.1
  Bernheim's (*see also* Failure, heart, congestive)
    428.0
  Bertolotti's (sacralization of fifth lumbar
    vertebra) 756.15
  Besnier-Boeck-Schaumann (sarcoidosis) 135

Syndrome—*continued*

cervical (root) (spine) NEC 723.8
  disc 722.71
  posterior, sympathetic 723.2
  rib 353.0
  sympathetic paralysis 337.0
  traumatic (acute) NEC 847.0
cervicobrachial (diffuse) 723.3
cervicocranial 723.2
cervicodorsal outlet 353.2
Céstan's 344.89
Céstan (-Raymond) 433.8
Céstan-Chenais 344.89
chancriform 114.1
Charcot's (intermittent claudication) 443.9
  angina cruris 443.9
  due to atherosclerosis 440.21
Charcot-Marie-Tooth 356.1
Charcot-Weiss-Baker 337.0
Cheadle (-Möller) (-Barlow) (infantile scurvy)
  267
Chédiak-Higashi (-Steinbrinck) (congenital
  gigantism of peroxidase granules) 288.2
chest wall 786.52
Chiari's (hepatic vein thrombosis) 453.0
Chiari-Frommel 676.6
chiasmatic 368.41
Chilaiditi's (subphrenic displacement, colon)
  751.4
chondroectodermal dysplasia 756.55
chorea-athetosis-agitans 275.1
Christian's (chronic histiocytosis X) 277.8
chromosome 4 short arm deletion 758.3
Clarke-Hadfield (pancreatic infantilism) 577.8
Claude's 352.6
Claude Bernard-Horner (*see also* Neuropathy,
  peripheral, autonomic) 337.9
Clérambault's
  automatism 348.8
  erotomania 297.8
Clifford's (postmaturity) 766.2
climacteric 627.2
Clouston's (hidrotic ectodermal dysplasia)
  757.31
clumsiness 315.4
Cockayne's (microencephaly and dwarfism)
  759.89
Cockayne-Weber (epidermolysis bullosa) 757.39
Cogan's (nonsyphilitic interstitial keratitis)
  370.52
cold injury (newborn) 778.2
Collet (-Sicard) 352.6
combined immunity deficiency 279.2
compartment(al) (anterior) (deep) (posterior)
  (tibial) 958.8
compression 958.5
  cauda equina 344.60
    with neurogenic bladder 344.61
concussion 310.2
congenital
  affecting more than one system 759.7
    specified type NEC 759.89
  facial diplegia 352.6
  muscular hypertrophy-cerebral 759.89
congestion-fibrosis (pelvic) 625.5
conjunctivourethrosynovial 099.3
Conn (-Louis) (primary aldosteronism) 255.1
Conradi (-Hünermann) (chondrodysplasia
  calcificans congenita) 756.59
conus medullaris 336.8
Cooke-Apert-Gallais (adrenogenital) 255.2

Syndrome—*continued*

Cornelia de Lange's (Amsterdam dwarf, mental
  retardation, and brachycephaly) 759.8
coronary insufficiency or intermediate 411.1
cor pulmonale 416.9
corticosexual 255.2
Costen's (complex) 524.60
costochondral junction 733.6
costoclavicular 353.0
costovertebral 253.0
Cotard's (paranoia) 297.1
craniovertebral 723.2
Creutzfeldt-Jakob 046.1
  with dementia 046.1 *[294.1]*
crib death 798.0
cricopharyngeal 787.2
cri-du-chat 758.3
Crigler-Najjar (congenital hyperbilirubinemia)
  277.4
crocodile tears 351.8
Cronkhite-Canada 211.3
croup 464.4
CRST (cutaneous systemic sclerosis) 710.1
crush 958.5
crushed lung (*see also* Injury, internal, lung)
  861.20
Cruveilhier-Baumgarten (cirrhosis of liver)
  571.5
cubital tunnel 354.2
Cuiffini-Pancoast (M8010/3) (carcinoma,
  pulmonary apex) 162.3
Curschmann (-Batten) (-Steinert) 359.2
Cushing's (iatrogenic) (idiopathic) (pituitary
  basophilism) (pituitary-dependent) 255.0
  overdose or wrong substance given or taken
    962.0
Cyriax's (slipping rib) 733.99
cystic duct stump 576.0
Da Costa's (neurocirculatory asthenia) 306.2
Dameshek's (erythroblastic anemia) 282.4
Dana-Putnam (subacute combined sclerosis
  with pernicious anemia) 281.0 *[336.2]*
Danbolt (-Closs) (acrodermatitis enteropathica)
  686.8
Dandy-Walker (atresia, foramen of Magendie)
  742.3
  with spina bifida (*see also* Spina bifida) 741.0
Danlos' 756.83
Davies-Colley (slipping rib) 733.99
dead fetus 641.3
defeminization 255.2
defibrination (*see also* Fibrinolysis) 286.6
Degos' 447.8
Deiters' nucleus 386.19
Déjérine-Roussy 348.8
Déjérine-Thomas 333.0
de Lange's (Amsterdam dwarf, mental
  retardation, and brachycephaly) (Cornelia)
  759.89
Del Castillo's (germinal aplasia) 606.0
deletion chromosomes 758.3
delusional
  induced by drug 292.11
dementia-aphonia, of childhood (*see also*
  Psychosis, childhood) 299.1
demyelinating NEC 341.9
denial visual hallucination 307.9
depersonalization 300.6
Dercum's (adiposis dolorosa) 272.8
de Toni-Fanconi (-Debré) (cystinosis) 270.0
diabetes-dwarfism-obesity (juvenile) 258.1

Syndrome—*continued*

diabetes mellitus-hypertension-nephrosis 250.4 *[581.81]*

diabetes mellitus in newborn infant 775.1

diabetes-nephrosis 250.4 *[581.81]*

diabetic amyotrophy 250.6 *[358.1]*

Diamond-Blackfan (congenital hypoplastic anemia) 284.0

Diamond-Gardener (autoerythrocyte sensitization) 287.2

DIC (diffuse or disseminated intravascular coagulopathy) (*see also* Fibrinolysis) 286.6

diencephalohypophyseal NEC 253.8

diffuse cervicobrachial 723.3

diffuse obstructive pulmonary 496

DiGeorge's (thymic hypoplasia) 279.11

Dighton's 756.51

Di Guglielmo's (erythremic myelosis) (M9841/3) 207.0

disc—*see* Displacement, intervertebral disc

discogenic—*see* Displacement, intervertebral disc

disequilibrium 276.9

disseminated platelet thrombosis 446.6

Ditthomska 307.81

Doan-Wiseman (primary splenic neutropenia) 288.0

Döhle body-panmyelopathic 288.2

Donohue's (leprechaunism) 259.8

dorsolateral medullary (*see also* Disease, cerebrovascular, acute) 436

double whammy 360.81

Down's (mongolism) 758.0

Dresbach's (elliptocytosis) 282.1

Dressler's (postmyocardial infarction) 411.0

hemoglobinuria 283.2

drug withdrawal, infant, of dependent mother 779.5

dry skin 701.1

eye 375.15

Duane's (retraction) 378.71

Duane-Stilling-Türk (ocular retraction syndrome) 378.71

Dubin-Johnson (constitutional hyperbilirubinemia) 277.4

Dubin-Sprinz (constitutional hyperbilirubinemia) 277.4

Duchenne's 335.22

due to abnormality

autosomal NEC (*see also* Abnormal, autosomes NEC) 758.5

13 758.1

18 758.2

21 or 22 758.0

D₁ 758.1

E₃ 758.2

G 758.0

chromosomal 758.89

sex 758.81

dumping 564.2

nonsurgical 536.8

Duplay's 726.2

Dupré's (meningism) 781.6

Dyke-Young (acquired macrocytic hemolytic anemia) 283.9

dyspraxia 315.4

dystocia, dystrophia 654.9

Syndrome—*continued*

Eales' 362.18

Eaton-Lambert (*see also* Neoplasm, by site, malignant) 199.1 *[358.1]*

Ebstein's (downward displacement, tricuspid valve into right ventricle) 746.2

ectopic ACTH secretion 255.0

eczema-thrombocytopenia 279.12

Eddowes' (brittle bones and blue sclera) 756.51

Edwards' 758.2

efferent loop 537.89

effort (aviators') (psychogenic) 306.2

Ehlers-Danlos 756.83

Eisenmenger's (ventricular septal defect) 745.4

Ekbom's (restless legs) 333.99

Ekman's (brittle bones and blue sclera) 756.51

electric feet 266.2

Ellison-Zollinger (gastric hypersecretion with pancreatic islet cell tumor) 251.5

Ellis-van Creveld (chondroectodermal dysplasia) 756.55

embryonic fixation 270.2

empty sella (turcica) 253.8

endocrine-hypertensive 255.3

Engel-von Recklinghausen (osteitis fibrosa cystica) 252.0

enteroarticular 099.3

entrapment—*see* Neuropathy, entrapment

eosinophilia myalgia 710.5

epidemic vomiting 078.82

Epstein's—*see* Nephrosis

Erb (-Oppenheim) -Goldflam 358.0

Erdheim's (acromegalic macrospondylitis) 253.0

Erlacher-Blount (tibia vara) 732.4

erythrocyte fragmentation 283.19

Evans' (thrombocytopenic purpura) 287.3

excess cortisol, iatrogenic 255.0

exhaustion 300.5

extrapyramidal 333.90

eyelid-malar-mandible 756.0

eye retraction 378.71

Faber's (achlorhydric anemia) 280.9

Fabry (-Anderson) (angiokeratoma corporis diffusum) 272.7

facet 724.8

Fallot's 745.2

falx (*see also* Hemorrhage, brain) 431

familial eczema-thrombocytopenia 279.12

Fanconi's (anemia) (congenital pancytopenia) 284.0

Fanconi (-de Toni) (-Debré) (cystinosis) 270.0

Farber (-Uzman) (disseminated lipogranulomatosis) 272.8

fatigue NEC 300.5

chronic 780.7

faulty bowel habit (idiopathic megacolon) 564.7

FDH (focal dermal hypoplasia) 757.39

fecal reservoir 560.39

Feil-Klippel (brevicollis) 756.16

Felty's (rheumatoid arthritis with splenomegaly and leukopenia) 714.1

fertile eunuch 257.2

fetal alcohol 760.71

late effect 760.71

fibrillation-flutter 427.32

fibrositis (periarticular) 729.0

Fiedler's (acute isolated myocarditis) 422.91

Fiessinger-Leroy (-Reiter) 099.3

Fiessinger-Rendu (erythema multiforme exudativum) 695.1

first arch 756.0

Syndrome—*continued*
  Fisher's 357.0
  Fitz's (acute hemorrhagic pancreatitis) 577.0
  Fitz-Hugh and Curtis (gonococcal peritonitis) 098.86
  Flajani (-Basedow) (exophthalmic goiter) 242.0
  floppy
    infant 781.9
    valve (mitral) 424.0
  flush 259.2
  Foix-Alajouanine 336.1
  Fong's (hereditary osteo-onychodysplasia) 756.89
  foramen magnum 348.4
  Forbes-Albright (nonpuerperal amenorrhea and lactation associated with pituitary tumor) 253.1
  Foster-Kennedy 377.04
  Foville's (peduncular) 344.89
  Fragile X 759.83
  Franceschetti's (mandibulofacial dysostosis) 756.0
  Fraser's 759.89
  Freeman-Sheldon 759.89
  Frey's (auriculotemporal) 350.8
  Friderichsen-Waterhouse 036.3
  Friedrich-Erb-Arnold (acropachyderma) 757.39
  Fröhlich's (adiposogenital dystrophy) 253.8
  Froin's 336.8
  Frommel-Chiari 676.6
  frontal lobe 310.0
  Fuller Albright's (osteitis fibrosa disseminata) 756.59
  functional
    bowel 564.9
    prepubertal castrate 752.8
  Gaisböck's (polycythemia hypertonica) 289.0
  ganglion (basal, brain) 333.90
    geniculi 351.1
  Ganser's, hysterical 300.16
  Gardner-Diamond (autoerythrocyte sensitization) 287.2
  gastroesophageal junction 530.0
  gastroesophageal laceration-hemorrhage 530.7
  gastrojejunal loop obstruction 537.89
  Gayet-Wernicke's (superior hemorrhagic polioencephalitis) 265.1
  Gee-Herter-Heubner (nontropical sprue) 579.0
  Gélineau's 347
  genito-anorectal 099.1
  Gerhardt's (vocal cord paralysis) 478.30
  Gerstmann's (finger agnosia) 784.69
  Gilbert's 277.4
  Gilford (-Hutchinson) (progeria) 259.8
  Gilles de la Tourette's 307.23
  Gillespie's (dysplasia oculodentodigitalis) 759.89
  Glénard's (enteroptosis) 569.89
  Glinski-Simmonds (pituitary cachexia) 253.2
  glucuronyl transferase 277.4
  glue ear 381.20
  Goldberg (-Maxwell) (-Morris) (testicular feminization) 257.8
  Goldenhar's (oculoauriculovertebral dysplasia) 756.0
  Goldflam-Erb 358.0
  Goltz-Gorlin (dermal hypoplasia) 757.39
  Goodpasture's (pneumorenal) 446.21
  Gopalan's (burning feet) 266.2
  Gorlin-Chaudhry-Moss 759.89

Syndrome—*continued*
  Gougerot (-Houwer) -Sjögren (keratoconjunctivitis sicca) 710.2
  Gougerot-Blum (pigmented purpuric lichenoid dermatitis) 709.1
  Gougerot-Carteaud (confluent reticulate papillomatosis) 701.8
  Gouley's (constrictive pericarditis) 423.2
  Gowers' (vasovagal attack) 780.2
  Gowers-Paton-Kennedy 377.04
  Gradenigo's 383.02
  Gray or grey (chloramphenicol) (newborn) 779.4
  Greig's (hypertelorism) 756.0
  Gubler-Millard 344.89
  Guérin-Stern (arthrogryposis multiplex congenita) 754.89
  Guillain-Barré (-Strohl) 357.0
  Gunn's (jaw-winking syndrome) 742.8
  Günther's (congenital erythropoietic porphyria) 277.1
  gustatory sweating 350.8
  H$_3$O 759.81
  Hadfield-Clarke (pancreatic infantilism) 577.8
  Haglund-Läwen-Fründ 717.89
  hairless women 257.8
  Hallermann-Streiff 756.0
  Hallervorden-Spatz 333.0
  Hamman's (spontaneous mediastinal emphysema) 518.1
  Hamman-Rich (diffuse interstitial pulmonary fibrosis) 516.3
  Hand-Schüller-Christian (chronic histiocytosis X) 277.8
  hand-foot 282.61
  Hanot-Chauffard (-Troisier) (bronze diabetes) 275.0
  Harada's 363.22
  Hare's (M8010/3) (carcinoma, pulmonary apex) 162.3
  Harkavy's 446.0
  harlequin color change 779.8
  Harris' (organic hyperinsulinism) 251.1
  Hart's (pellagra-cerebellar ataxia-renal aminoaciduria) 270.0
  Hayem-Faber (achlorhydric anemia) 280.9
  Hayem-Widal (acquired hemolytic jaundice) 283.9
  Heberden's (angina pectoris) 413.9
  Hedinger's (malignant carcinoid) 259.2
  Hegglin's 288.2
  Heller's (infantile psychosis) (*see also* Psychosis, childhood) 299.1
  H.E.L.L.P. 642.5
  hemolytic-uremic (adult) (child) 283.11
  Hench-Rosenberg (palindromic arthritis) (*see also* Rheumatism, palindromic) 719.3
  Henoch-Schönlein (allergic purpura) 287.0
  hepatic flexure 569.89
  hepatorenal 572.4
    due to a procedure 997.4
    following delivery 674.8
  hepatourologic 572.4
  Herrick's (hemoglobin S disease) 282.61
  Herter (-Gee) (nontropical sprue) 579.0
  Heubner-Herter (nontropical sprue) 579.0
  Heyd's (hepatorenal) 572.4
  HHHO 759.81
  Hilger's 337.0
  Hoffa (-Kastert) (liposynovitis prepatellaris) 272.8
  Hoffmann's 244.9 *[359.5]*

Syndrome—*continued*
  Hoffmann-Bouveret (paroxysmal tachycardia)
      427.2
  Hoffmann-Werdnig 335.0
  Holländer-Simons (progressive lipodystrophy)
      272.6
  Holmes' (visual disorientation) 368.16
  Holmes-Adie 379.46
  Hoppe-Goldflam 358.0
  Horner's (*see also* Neuropathy, peripheral,
      autonomic) 337.9
    traumatic—*see* Injury, nerve, cervical
      sympathetic
  hospital addiction 301.51
  Hunt's (herpetic geniculate ganglionitis) 053.11
    dyssynergia cerebellaris myoclonica 334.2
  Hunter (-Hurler) (mucopolysaccharidosis II)
      277.5
  hunterian glossitis 529.4
  Hurler (-Hunter) (mucopolysaccharidosis II)
      277.5
  Hutchinson's incisors or teeth 090.5
  Hutchinson-Boeck (sarcoidosis) 135
  Hutchinson-Gilford (progeria) 259.8
  hydralazine
    correct substance properly administered 695.4
    overdose or wrong substance given or taken
      972.6
  hydraulic concussion (abdomen) (*see also*
      Injury, internal, abdomen) 868.00
  hyperabduction 447.8
  hyperactive bowel 564.1
  hyperaldosteronism with hypokalemic alkalosis
      (Bartter's) 255.1
  hypercalcemic 275.4
  hypercoagulation NEC 289.8
  hypereosinophilic (idiopathic) 288.3
  hyperkalemic 276.7
  hyperkinetic—*see also* Hyperkinesia
    heart 429.82
  hyperlipemia-hemolytic anemia-icterus 571.1
  hypermobility 728.5
  hypernatremia 276.0
  hyperosmolarity 276.0
  hypersomnia-bulimia 349.89
  hypersplenic 289.4
  hypersympathetic (*see also* Neuropathy,
      peripheral, autonomic) 337.9
  hypertransfusion, newborn 776.4
  hyperventilation, psychogenic 306.1
  hyperviscosity (of serum) NEC 273.3
    polycythemic 289.0
    sclerothymic 282.8
  hypoglycemic (familial) (neonatal) 251.2
    functional 251.1
  hypokalemic 276.8
  hypophyseal 253.8
  hypophyseothalamic 253.8
  hypopituitarism 253.2
  hypoplastic left heart 746.7
  hypopotassemia 276.8
  hyposmolality 276.1
  hypotension, maternal 669.2
  hypotonia-hypomentia-hypogonadism-obesity
      759.81
  ICF (intravascular coagulation-fibrinolysis) (*see
      also* Fibrinolysis) 286.6
  idiopathic cardiorespiratory distress, newborn
      769
  idiopathic nephrotic (infantile) 581.9

Syndrome—*continued*
  Imerslund (-Gräsbeck) (anemia due to familial
      selective vitamin B$_{12}$ malabsorption) 281.1
  immobility (paraplegic) 728.3
  immunity deficiency, combined 279.2
  impending coronary 411.1
  impingement
    shoulder 726.2
    vertebral bodies 724.4
  inappropriate secretion of antidiuretic hormone
      (ADH) 253.6
  incomplete
    mandibulofacial 756.0
  infant
    death, sudden (SIDS) 798.0
    Hercules 255.2
    of diabetic mother 775.0
    shaken 995.55
  infantilism 253.3
  inferior vena cava 459.2
  influenza-like 487.1
  inspissated bile, newborn 774.4
  intermediate coronary (artery) 411.1
  internal carotid artery (*see also* Occlusion,
      artery, carotid) 433.1
  interspinous ligament 724.8
  intestinal
    carcinoid 259.2
    gas 787.3
    knot 560.2
  intravascular
    coagulation-fibrinolysis (ICF) (*see also*
      Fibrinolysis) 286.6
    coagulopathy (*see also* Fibrinolysis) 286.6
  inverted Marfan's 759.89
  IRDS (idiopathic respiratory distress, newborn)
      769
  irritable
    bowel 564.1
    heart 306.2
    weakness 300.5
  ischemic bowel (transient) 557.9
    chronic 557.1
    due to mesenteric artery insufficiency 557.1
  Itsenko-Cushing (pituitary basophilism) 255.0
  IVC (intravascular coagulopathy) (*see also*
      Fibrinolysis) 286.6
  Ivemark's (asplenia with congenital heart
      disease) 759.0
  Jaccoud's 714.4
  Jackson's 344.89
  Jadassohn-Lewandowski (pachyonychia
      congenita) 757.5
  Jaffe-Lichtenstein (-Uehlinger) 252.0
  Jahnke's (encephalocutaneous angiomatosis)
      759.6
  Jakob-Creutzfeldt 046.1
    with dementia 046.1 *[294.1]*
  Jaksch's (pseudoleukemia infantum) 285.8
  Jaksch-Hayem (-Luzet) (pseudoleukemia
      infantum) 285.8
  jaw-winking 742.8
  jejunal 564.2
  jet lag 307.45
  Jeune's (asphyxiating thoracic dystrophy of
      newborn) 756.4
  Job's (chronic granulomatous disease) 288.1
  Jordan's 288.2
  Joseph-Diamond-Blackfan (congenital
      hypoplastic anemia) 284.0
  jugular foramen 352.6

Syndrome—*continued*
nephrotic (*see also* Nephrosis) 581.9
  diabetic 250.4 *[581.81]*
Netherton's (ichthyosiform erythroderma) 757.1
neurocutaneous 759.6
neuroleptic malignant 333.92
Nezelof's (pure alymphocytosis) 279.13
Niemann-Pick (lipid histiocytosis) 272.7
Nonne-Milroy-Meige (chronic hereditary
    edema) 757.0
nonsense 300.16
Noonan's 759.89
Nothnagel's
  ophthalmoplegia-cerebellar ataxia 378.52
  vasomotor acroparesthesia 443.89
nucleus ambiguous-hypoglossal 352.6
OAV (oculoauriculovertebral dysplasia) 756.0
obsessional 300.3
oculocutaneous 364.24
oculomotor 378.81
oculourethroarticular 099.3
Ogilvie's (sympathicotonic colon obstruction)
    560.89
ophthalmoplegia-cerebellar ataxia 378.52
Oppenheim-Urbach (necrobiosis lipoidica
    diabeticorum) 250.8 *[709.3]*
oral-facial-digital 759.89
organic
  affective NEC 293.83
    drug-induced 292.84
  anxiety 293.84
  delusional 293.81
    alcohol-induced 291.5
    drug-induced 292.11
    due to or associated with
      arteriosclerosis 290.42
      presenile brain disease 290.12
      senility 290.20
  depressive 293.83
    drug-induced 292.84
    due to or associated with
      arteriosclerosis 290.43
      presenile brain disease 290.13
      senile brain disease 290.21
  hallucinosis 293.82
    drug-induced 292.84
organic affective 293.83
  induced by drug 292.84
organic personality 310.1
  induced by drug 292.89
Ormond's 593.4
orodigitofacial 759.89
orthostatic hypotensive-dysautonomic-
    dyskinetic 333.0
Osler-Weber-Rendu (familial hemorrhagic
    telangiectasia) 448.0
osteodermopathic hyperostosis 757.39
osteoporosis-osteomalacia 268.2
Österreicher-Turner (hereditary
    osteo-onychodysplasia) 756.89
Ostrum-Furst 756.59
otolith 386.19
otopalatodigital 759.89
outlet (thoracic) 353.0
ovarian vein 593.4
Owren's (*see also* Defect, coagulation) 286.3
OX 758.6
pacemaker 429.4
Paget-Schroetter (intermittent venous
    claudication) 453.8
pain—*see* Pain

Syndrome—*continued*
painful
  apicocostal vertebral (M8010/3) 162.3
  arc 726.19
  bruising 287.2
  feet 266.2
Pancoast's (carcinoma, pulmonary apex)
    (M8010/3) 162.3
panhypopituitary (postpartum) 253.2
papillary muscle 429.81
  with myocardial infarction 410.8
Papillon-Léage and Psaume (orodigitofacial
    dysostosis) 759.89
parabiotic (transfusion)
  donor (twin) 772.0
  recipient (twin) 776.4
paralysis agitans 332.0
paralytic 344.9
  specified type NEC 344.89
Paraneoplastic —*see* condition
Parinaud's (paralysis of conjugate upward gaze)
    378.81
  oculoglandular 372.02
Parkes Weber and Dimitri (encephalocutaneous
    angiomatosis) 759.6
Parkinson's (*see also* Parkinsonism) 332.0
parkinsonian (*see also* Parkinsonism) 332.0
Parry's (exophthalmic goiter) 242.0
Parry-Romberg 349.89
Parsonage-Aldren-Turner 353.5
Parsonage-Turner 353.5
Patau's (trisomy D₁) 758.1
Paterson (-Brown) (-Kelly) (sideropenic
    dysphagia) 280.8
Payr's (splenic flexure syndrome) 569.89
pectoral girdle 447.8
pectoralis minor 447.8
Pelger-Huët (hereditary hyposegmentation)
    288.2
pellagra-cerebellar ataxia-renal aminoaciduria
    270.0
Pellegrini-Stieda 726.62
pellagroid 265.2
Pellizzi's (pineal) 259.8
pelvic congestion (-fibrosis) 625.5
Pendred's (familial goiter with deaf-mutism) 243
Penfield's (*see also* Epilepsy) 345.5
Penta X 758.81
peptic ulcer—*see* Ulcer, peptic 533.9
perabduction 447.8
periodic 277.3
periurethral fibrosis 593.4
persistent fetal circulation 747.9
Petges-Cléjat (poikilodermatomyositis) 710.3
Peutz-Jeghers 759.6
phantom limb 353.6
pharyngeal pouch 279.11
Pick's (pericardial pseudocirrhosis of liver)
    423.2
  heart 423.2
  liver 423.2
Pick-Herxheimer (diffuse idiopathic cutaneous
    atrophy) 701.8
Pickwickian (cardiopulmonary obesity) 278.8
PIE (pulmonary infiltration with eosinophilia)
    518.3
Pierre Marie-Bamberger (hypertrophic
    pulmonary osteoarthropathy) 731.2
Pierre Mauriac's (diabetes-dwarfism-obesity)
    258.1
Pierre Robin 756.0

Syndrome—*continued*
  pigment dispersion, iris 364.53
  pineal 259.8
  pink puffer 492.8
  pituitary 253.0
  placental
    dysfunction 762.2
    insufficiency 762.2
    transfusion 762.3
  plantar fascia 728.71
  Plummer-Vinson (sideropenic dysphagia) 280.8
  pluricarential of infancy 260
  plurideficiency of infancy 260
  pluriglandular (compensatory) 258.8
  polycarential of infancy 260
  polyglandular 258.8
  polysplenia 759.0
  pontine 433.8
  popliteal
    artery entrapment 447.8
    web 756.89
  postartificial menopause 627.4
  postcardiotomy 429.4
  postcholecystectomy 576.0
  postcommissurotomy 429.4
  postconcussional 310.2
  postcontusional 310.2
  postencephalitic 310.8
  posterior
    cervical sympathetic 723.2
    fossa compression 348.4
    inferior cerebellar artery (*see also* Disease,
      cerebrovascular, acute) 436
  postgastrectomy (dumping) 564.2
  post-gastric surgery 564.2
  posthepatitis 780.7
  postherpetic (neuralgia) (zoster) 053.19
    geniculate ganglion 053.11
    ophthalmica 053.19
  postimmunization—*see* Complications,
    vaccination
  postinfarction 411.0
  postinfluenza (asthenia) 780.7
  postirradiation 990
  postlaminectomy 722.80
    cervical, cervicothoracic 722.81
    lumbar, lumbosacral 722.83
    thoracic, thoracolumbar 722.82
  postleukotomy 310.0
  postlobotomy 310.0
  postmastectomy lymphedema 457.0
  postmature (of newborn) 766.2
  postmyocardial infarction 411.0
  postoperative NEC 998.9
    blind loop 579.2
  postpartum panhypopituitary 253.2
  postperfusion NEC 999.8
    bone marrow 996.85
  postpericardiotomy 429.4
  postphlebitic 459.1
  postpolio (myelitis) 138
  postvagotomy 564.2
  postvalvulotomy 429.4
  postviral (asthenia) NEC 780.7
  Potain's (gastrectasis with dyspepsia) 536.1
  potassium intoxication 276.7
  Potter's 753.0
  Prader (-Labhart) -Willi (-Fanconi) 759.81
  preinfarction 411.1
  preleukemic 238.7
  premature senility 259.8

Syndrome—*continued*
  premenstrual 625.4
  premenstrual tension 625.4
  pre ulcer 536.9
  Prinzmetal-Massumi (anterior chest wall
    syndrome) 786.52
  Profichet's 729.9
  progeria 259.8
  progressive pallidal degeneration 333.0
  prolonged gestation 766.2
  prune belly 756.7
  prurigo-asthma 691.8
  pseudocarpal tunnel (sublimis) 354.0
  pseudohermaphroditism-virilism-hirsutism 255.2
  pseudoparalytica 358.0
  pseudo-Turner's 759.89
  psycho-organic 293.9
    acute 293.0
    anxiety type 293.84
    depressive type 293.83
    hallucinatory type 293.82
    nonpsychotic severity 310.1
      specified focal (partial) NEC 310.8
    paranoid type 293.81
    specified type NEC 293.89
    subacute 293.1
  pterygolymphangiectasia 758.6
  ptosis-epicanthus 270.2
  pulmonary
    arteriosclerosis 416.0
    hypoperfusion (idiopathic) 769
    renal (hemorrhagic) 446.21
  pulseless 446.7
  Putnam-Dana (subacute combined sclerosis
    with pernicious anemia) 281.0 *[336.2]*
  pyloroduodenal 537.89
  pyramidopallidonigral 332.0
  pyriformis 355.0
  Q-T interval prolongation 794.31
  radicular NEC 729.2
    lower limbs 724.4
    upper limbs 723.4
    newborn 767.4
  Raeder-Harbitz (pulseless disease) 446.7
  Ramsay Hunt's
    dyssynergia cerebellaris myoclonica 334.2
    herpetic geniculate ganglionitis 053.11
  rapid time-zone change 307.45
  Raymond (-Céstan) 433.8
  Raynaud's (paroxysmal digital cyanosis) 443.0
  RDS (respiratory distress syndrome, newborn)
    769
  Refsum's (heredopathia atactica
    polyneuritiformis) 356.3
  Reichmann's (gastrosuccorrhea) 536.8
  Reifenstein's (hereditary familial
    hypogonadism, male) 257.2
  Reilly's (*see also* Neuropathy, peripheral,
    autonomic) 337.9
  Reiter's 099.3
  renal glomerulohyalinosis-diabetic 250.4
    [581.81]
  Rendu-Osler-Weber (familial hemorrhagic
    telangiectasia) 448.0
  renofacial (congenital biliary fibroangiomatosis)
    753.0
  Rénon-Delille 253.8
  respiratory distress (idiopathic) (newborn) 769
    adult (following shock, surgery, or trauma)
      518.5
      specified NEC 518.82

Syndrome—*continued*
restless leg 333.99
retraction (Duane's) 378.71
retroperitoneal fibrosis 593.4
Rett's 330.8
Reye's 331.81
Reye-Sheehan (postpartum pituitary necrosis)
    253.2
Riddoch's (visual disorientation) 368.16
Ridley's (*see also* Failure, ventricular, left)
    428.1
Rieger's (mesodermal dysgenesis, anterior
    ocular segment) 743.44
Rietti-Greppi-Micheli (thalassemia minor) 282.4
right ventricular obstruction—*see* Failure heart,
    congestive
Riley-Day (familial dysautonomia) 742.8
Robin's 756.0
Rokitansky-Kuster-Hauser (congenital absence,
    vagina) 752.49
Romano-Ward (prolonged Q-T interval) 794.31
Romberg's 349.89
Rosen-Castleman-Liebow (pulmonary
    proteinosis) 516.0
rotator cuff, shoulder 726.10
Roth's 355.1
Rothmund's (congenital poikiloderma) 757.33
Rotor's (idiopathic hyperbilirubinemia) 277.4
Roussy-Lévy 334.3
Roy (-Jutras) (acropachyderma) 757.39
rubella (congenital) 771.0
Rubinstein-Taybi's (brachydactylia, short
    stature, and mental retardation) 759.89
Rud's (mental deficiency, epilepsy, and
    infantilism) 759.89
Ruiter-Pompen (-Wyers) (angiokeratoma
    corporis diffusum) 272.7
Runge's (postmaturity) 766.2
Russell (-Silver) (congenital hemihypertrophy
    and short stature) 759.89
Rytand-Lipsitch (complete atrioventricular
    block) 426.0
sacralization-scoliosis-sciatica 756.15
sacroiliac 724.6
Saenger's 379.46
salt
    depletion (*see also* Disease, renal) 593.9
        due to heat NEC 992.8
            causing heat exhaustion or prostration
            992.4
    low (*see also* Disease, renal) 593.9
salt-losing (*see also* Disease, renal) 593.9
Sanfilippo's (mucopolysaccharidosis III) 277.5
Scaglietti-Dagnini (acromegalic
    macrospondylitis) 253.0
scalded skin 695.1
scalenus anticus (anterior) 353.0
scapulocostal 354.8
scapuloperoneal 359.1
scapulovertebral 723.4
Schaumann's (sarcoidosis) 135
Scheie's (mucopolysaccharidosis IS) 277.5
Scheuthauer-Marie-Sainton (cleidocranialis
    dysostosis) 755.59
Schirmer's (encephalocutaneous angiomatosis)
    759.6
schizophrenic, of childhood NEC (*see also*
    Psychosis, childhood) 299.9

Syndrome—*continued*
Schmidt's
    sphallo-pharyngo-laryngeal hemiplegia 352.6
    thyroid-adrenocortical insufficiency 258.1
    vagoaccessory 352.6
Schneider's 047.9
Scholte's (malignant carcinoid) 259.2
Scholz (-Bielschowsky-Henneberg) 330.0
Schroeder's (endocrine-hypertensive) 255.3
Schüller-Christian (chronic histiocytosis X)
    277.8
Schultz's (agranulocytosis) 288.0
Schwartz (-Jampel) 756.89
Schwartz-Bartter (inappropriate secretion of
    antidiuretic hormone) 253.6
Scimitar (anomalous venous drainage, right
    lung to inferior vena cave) 747.49
sclerocystic ovary 256.4
sea-blue histiocyte 272.7
Seabright-Bantam (pseudohypoparathyroidism)
    275.4
Seckel's 759.89
Secretan's (posttraumatic edema) 782.3
secretoinhibitor (keratoconjunctivitis sicca)
    710.2
Seeligmann's (ichthyosis congenita) 757.1
Senear-Usher (pemphigus erythematosus) 694.4
senilism 259.8
serotonin 333.99
serous meningitis 348.2
Sertoli cell (germinal aplasia) 606.0
sex chromosome mosaic 758.81
Sézary's (reticulosis) (M9701/3) 202.2
shaken infant 995.55
Shaver's (bauxite pneumoconiosis) 503
Sheehan's (postpartum pituitary necrosis) 253.2
shock (traumatic) 958.4
    kidney 584.5
        following crush injury 958.5
    lung 518.5
    neurogenic 308.9
    psychic 308.9
short
    bowel 579.3
    P-R interval 426.81
shoulder-arm (*see also* Neuropathy, peripheral,
    autonomic) 337.9
shoulder-girdle 723.4
shoulder-hand (*see also* Neuropathy, peripheral,
    autonomic) 337.9
Shwachman's 288.0
Shy-Drager (orthostatic hypotension with
    multisystem degeneration) 333.0
Sicard's 352.6
sicca (keratoconjunctivitis) 710.2
sick
    cell 276.1
    cilia 759.81
    sinus 427.81
sideropenic 280.8
Siemens'
    ectodermal dysplasia 757.31
    keratosis follicularis spinulosa (decalvans)
        757.39
Silfverskiöld's (osteochondrodystrophy,
    extremities) 756.50
Silver's (congenital hemihypertrophy and short
    stature) 759.89
Silvestroni-Bianco (thalassemia minima) 282.4
Simons' (progressive lipodystrophy) 272.6
sinus tarsi 355.5

Syndrome—*continued*
sinusitis-bronchiectasis-situs inversus 759.3
Sipple's (medullary thyroid
    carcinoma-pheochromocytoma) 193
Sjögren (-Gougerot) (keratoconjunctivitis sicca)
    710.2
    with lung involvement 710.2 *[517.8]*
Sjögren-Larsson (ichthyosis congenita) 757.1
Slocumb's 255.3
Sluder's 337.0
Smith-Lemli-Opitz (cerebrohepatorenal
    syndrome) 759.89
smokers' 305.1
Sneddon-Wilkinson (subcorneal pustular
    dermatosis) 694.1
Sotos' (cerebral gigantism) 253.0
South African cardiomyopathy 425.2
spasmodic
    upward movement, eyes(s) 378.82
    winking 307.20
Spens' (syncope with heart block) 426.9
spherophakia-brachymorphia 759.89
spinal cord injury—*see also* Injury, spinal, by
    site
    with fracture, vertebra—*see* Fracture,
        vertebra, by site, with spinal cord injury
    cervical—*see* Injury, spinal, cervical
    fluid malabsorption (acquired) 331.3
splenic
    agenesis 759.0
    flexure 569.89
    neutropenia 288.0
    sequestration 282.60
Spurway's (brittle bones and blue sclera) 756.51
staphylococcal scalded skin 695.1
Stein's (polycystic ovary) 256.4
Stein-Leventhal (polycystic ovary) 256.4
Steinbrocker's (*see also* Neuropathy, peripheral,
    autonomic) 337.9
Stevens-Johnson (erythema multiforme
    exudativum) 695.1
Stewart-Morel (hyperostosis frontalis interna)
    733.3
stiff-man 333.91
Still's (juvenile rheumatoid arthritis) 714.30
Still-Felty (rheumatoid arthritis with
    splenomegaly and leukopenia) 714.1
Stilling-Türk-Duane (ocular retraction
    syndrome) 378.71
Stojano's (subcostal) 098.86
Stokes (-Adams) (syncope with heart block)
    426.9
Stokvis-Talma (enterogenous cyanosis) 289.7
stone heart (*see also* Failure, ventricular, left)
    428.1
straight-back 756.19
stroke (*see also* Disease, cerebrovascular, acute)
    436
    little 435.9
Sturge-Kalischer-Weber (encephalotrigeminal
    angiomatosis) 759.6
Sturge-Weber (-Dimitri) (encephalocutaneous
    angiomatosis) 759.6
subclavian-carotid obstruction (chronic) 446.7
subclavian steal 435.2
subcoracoid-pectoralis minor 447.8
subcostal 098.86
    nerve compression 354.8
subperiosteal hematoma 267
subphrenic interposition 751.4
sudden infant death (SIDS) 798.0

Syndrome—*continued*
Sudeck's 733.7
Sudeck-Leriche 733.7
superior
    cerebellar artery (*see also* Disease,
        cerebrovascular, acute) 436
    mesenteric artery 557.1
    pulmonary sulcus (tumor) (M8010/3) 162.3
    vena cava 459.2
suprarenal cortical 255.3
supraspinatus 726.10
swallowed blood 777.3
sweat retention 705.1
Sweet's (acute febrile neutrophilic dermatosis)
    695.89
Swyer-James (unilateral hyperlucent lung) 492.8
Swyer's (XY pure gonadal dysgenesis) 752.7
Symonds' 348.2
sympathetic
    cervical paralysis 337.0
    pelvic 625.5
syndactylic oxycephaly 755.55
syphilitic-cardiovascular 093.89
systemic fibrosclerosing 710.8
systolic click (-murmur) 785.2
Tabagism 305.1
tachycardia-bradycardia 427.81
Takayasu (-Onishi) (pulseless disease) 446.7
Tapia's 352.6
tarsal tunnel 355.5
Taussig-Bing (transposition, aorta and
    overriding pulmonary artery) 745.11
Taybi's (otopalatodigital) 759.89
Taylor's 625.5
teething 520.7
tegmental 344.89
telangiectasis-pigmentation-cataract 757.33
temporal 383.02
    lobectomy behavior 310.0
temporomandibular joint-pain-dysfunction
    [TMJ] NEC 524.60
    specified NEC 524.69
Terry's 362.21
testicular feminization 257.8
testis, nonvirilizing 257.8
tethered (spinal) cord 742.59
thalamic 348.8
Thibierge-Weissenbach (cutaneous systemic
    sclerosis) 710.1
Thiele 724.6
thoracic outlet (compression) 353.0
thoracogenous rheumatic (hypertrophic
    pulmonary osteoarthropathy) 731.2
Thorn's (*see also* Disease, renal) 593.9
Thorson-Biörck (malignant carcinoid) 259.2
thrombopenia-hemangioma 287.3
thyroid-adrenocortical insufficiency 258.1
Tietze's 733.6
time-zone (rapid) 307.45
Tobias' (carcinoma, pulmonary apex)
    (M8010/3) 162.3
toilet seat 926.0
Tolosa-Hunt 378.55
Toni-Fanconi (cystinosis) 270.0
Touraine's (hereditary osteo-onychodysplasia)
    756.89
Touraine-Solente-Golé (acropachyderma)
    757.39
toxic
    oil 710.5
    shock 040.89

Syndrome—*continued*
transfusion
  fetal-maternal 772.0
  twin
    donor (infant) 772.0
    recipient (infant) 776.4
Treacher Collins' (incomplete mandibulofacial dysostosis) 756.0
trigeminal plate 259.8
triple X female 758.81
trisomy NEC 758.5
  13 or D₁ 758.1
  16-18 or E 758.2
  18 or E₃ 758.2
  20 758.5
  21 or G (mongolism) 758.0
  22 or G (mongolism) 758.0
  G 758.0
Troisier-Hanot-Chauffard (bronze diabetes) 275.0
tropical wet feet 991.4
Trousseau's (thrombophlebitis migrans visceral cancer) 453.1
Türk's (ocular retraction syndrome) 378.71
Turner's 758.6
Turner-Varny 758.6
twin-to-twin transfusion 762.3
  recipient twin 776.4
Uehlinger's (acropachyderma) 757.39
Ullrich (-Bonnevie) (-Turner) 758.6
Ullrich-Feichtiger 759.89
underwater blast injury (abdominal) (*see also* Injury, internal, abdomen) 868.00
universal joint, cervix 620.6
Unverricht (-Lundborg) 333.2
Unverricht-Wagner (dermatomyositis) 710.3
upward gaze 378.81
Urbach-Oppenheim (necrobiosis lipoidica diabeticorum) 250.8 *[709.3]*
Urbach-Wiethe (lipoid proteinosis) 272.8
uremia, chronic 585
urethral 597.81
urethro-oculoarticular 099.3
urethro-oculosynovial 099.3
urohepatic 572.4
uveocutaneous 364.24
uveomeningeal, uveomeningitis 363.22
vagohypoglossal 352.6
vagovagal 780.2
van Buchem's (hyperostosis corticalis) 733.3
van der Hoeve's (brittle bones and blue sclera, deafness) 756.51
van der Hoeve-Halbertsma-Waardenburg (ptosis-epicanthus) 270.2
van der Hoeve-Waardenburg-Gualdi (ptosis-epicanthus) 270.2
van Neck-Odelberg (juvenile osteochondrosis) 732.1
vanishing twin 651.33
vascular splanchnic 557.0
vasomotor 443.9
vasovagal 780.2
VATER 759.89
vena cava (inferior) (superior) (obstruction) 459.2
Verbiest's (claudicatio intermittens spinalis) 435.1
Vernet's 352.6
vertebral
  artery 435.1
    compression 721.1

Syndrome—*continued*
  lumbar 724.4
  steal 435.1
vertebrogenic (pain) 724.5
vertiginous NEC 386.9
video display tube 723.8
Villaret's 352.6
Vinson-Plummer (sideropenic dysphagia) 280.8
virilizing adrenocortical hyperplasia, congenital 255.2
virus, viral 079.99
visceral larval migrans 128.0
visual disorientation 368.16
vitamin B₆ deficiency 266.1
vitreous touch 997.99
Vogt's (corpus striatum) 333.7
Vogt-Koyanagi 364.24
Volkmann's 958.6
von Bechterew-Strümpell (ankylosing spondylitis) 720.0
von Graefe's 378.72
von Hippel-Lindau (angiomatosis retinocerebellosa) 759.6
von Schroetter's (intermittent venous claudication) 453.8
von Willebrand (-Jürgens) (angiohemophilia) 286.4
Waardenburg-Klein (ptosis epicanthus) 270.2
Wagner (-Unverricht) (dermatomyositis) 710.3
Waldenström's (macroglobulinemia) 273.3
Waldenström-Kjellberg (sideropenic dysphagia) 280.8
Wallenberg's (posterior inferior cerebellar artery) (*see also* Disease, cerebrovascular, acute) 436
Waterhouse (-Friderichsen) 036.3
water retention 276.6
Weber's 344.89
Weber-Christian (nodular nonsuppurative panniculitis) 729.30
Weber-Cockayne (epidermolysis bullosa) 757.39
Weber-Dimitri (encephalocutaneous angiomatosis) 759.6
Weber-Gubler 344.89
Weber-Leyden 344.89
Weber-Osler (familial hemorrhagic telangiectasia) 448.0
Wegener's (necrotizing respiratory granulomatosis) 446.4
Weill-Marchesani (brachymorphism and ectopia lentis) 759.89
Weingarten's (tropical eosinophilia) 518.3
Weiss-Baker (carotid sinus syncope) 337.0
Weissenbach-Thibierge (cutaneous systemic sclerosis) 710.1
Werdnig-Hoffmann 335.0
Werlhof-Wichmann (*see also* Purpura, thrombocytopenic) 287.3
Wermer's (polyendocrine adenomatosis) 258.0
Werner's (progeria adultorum) 259.8
Wernicke's (nonalcoholic) (superior hemorrhagic polioencephalitis) 265.1
Wernicke-Korsakoff (nonalcoholic) 294.0
  alcoholic 291.1
Westphal-Strümpell (hepatolenticular degeneration) 275.1
wet
  brain (alcoholic) 303.9
  feet (maceration) (tropical) 991.4
  lung
    adult 518.5

Syndrome—*continued*
  newborn 770.6
  whiplash 847.0
  Whipple's (intestinal lipodystrophy) 040.2
  "whistling face" (craniocarpotarsal dystrophy)
    759.89
  Widal (-Abrami) (acquired hemolytic jaundice)
    283.9
  Wilkie's 557.1
  Wilkinson-Sneddon (subcorneal pustular
    dermatosis) 694.1
  Willan-Plumbe (psoriasis) 696.1
  Willebrand (-Jürgens) (angiohemophilia) 286.4
  Willi-Prader (hypogenital dystrophy with
    diabetic tendency) 759.81
  Wilson's (hepatolenticular degeneration) 275.1
  Wilson-Mikity 770.7
  Wiskott-Aldrich (eczema-thrombocytopenia)
    279.12
  withdrawal
    alcohol 291.81
    drug 292.0
    infant of dependent mother 779.5
  Woakes' (ethmoiditis) 471.1
  Wolff-Parkinson-White (anomalous
    atrioventricular excitation) 426.7
  Wright's (hyperabduction) 447.8
  X 413.9
  xiphoidalgia 733.99
  XO 758.6
  XXX 758.81
  XXXXY 758.81
  XXY 758.7
  yellow vernix (placental dysfunction) 762.2
  Zahorsky's 074.0
  Zieve's (jaundice, hyperlipemia and hemolytic
    anemia) 571.1
  Zollinger-Ellison (gastric hypersecretion with
    pancreatic islet cell tumor) 251.5
  Zuelzer-Ogden (nutritional megaloblastic
    anemia) 281.2
Synechia (iris) (pupil) 364.70
  anterior 364.72
    peripheral 364.73
  intrauterine (traumatic) 621.5
  posterior 364.71
  vulvae, congenital 752.49
Synesthesia (*see also* Disturbance, sensation)
  782.0
Synodontia 520.2
Synophthalmus 759.89
Synorchidism 752.8
Synorchism 752.8
Synostosis (congenital) 756.59
  astragaloscaphoid 755.67
  radioulnar 755.53
  talonavicular (bar) 755.67
  tarsal 755.67
Synovial —*see* condition
Synovioma (M9040/3)—*see also* Neoplasm,
  connective tissue, malignant
  benign (M9040/3)—*see* Neoplasm, connective
    tissue, benign
Synoviosarcoma (M9040/3)—*see* Neoplasm,
  connective tissue, malignant
Synovitis 727.00
  chronic crepitant, wrist 727.2
  due to crystals—*see* Arthritis, due to crystals
  gonococcal 098.51
  gouty 274.0

Synovitis—*continued*
  syphilitic 095.7
    congenital 090.0
  traumatic, current—*see* Sprain, by site
  tuberculous—*see* Tuberculosis, synovitis
  villonodular 719.20
    ankle 719.27
    elbow 719.22
    foot 719.27
    hand 719.24
    hip 719.25
    knee 719.26
    multiple sites 719.29
    pelvic region 719.25
    shoulder (region) 719.21
    specified site NEC 719.28
    wrist 719.23
Syphilide 091.3
  congenital 090.0
  newborn 090.0
  tubercular 095.8
    congenital 090.0
Syphilis, syphilitic (acquired) 097.9
  with lung involvement 095.1
  abdomen (late) 095.2
  acoustic nerve 094.86
  adenopathy (secondary) 091.4
  adrenal (gland) 095.8
    with cortical hypofunction 095.8
  age under 2 years NEC (*see also* Syphilis,
    congenital) 090.9
    acquired 097.9
  alopecia (secondary) 091.82
  anemia 095.8
  aneurysm (artery) (ruptured) 093.89
    aorta 093.0
    central nervous system 094.89
    congenital 090.5
  anus 095.8
    primary 091.1
    secondary 091.3
  aorta, aortic (arch) (abdominal) (insufficiency)
    (pulmonary) (regurgitation) (stenosis)
    (thoracic) 093.89
    aneurysm 093.0
  arachnoid (adhesive) 094.2
  artery 093.89
    cerebral 094.89
    spinal 094.89
  arthropathy (neurogenic) (tabetic) 094.0 *[713.5]*
  asymptomatic—*see* Syphilis, latent
  ataxia, locomotor (progressive) 094.0
  atrophoderma maculatum 091.3
  auricular fibrillation 093.89
  Bell's palsy 094.89
  bladder 095.8
  bone 095.5
    secondary 091.61
  brain 094.89
  breast 095.8
  bronchus 095.8
  bubo 091.0
  bulbar palsy 094.89
  bursa (late) 095.7
  cardiac decompensation 093.89
  cardiovascular (early) (late) (primary)
    (secondary) (tertiary) 093.9
    specified type and site NEC 093.89
  causing death under 2 years of age (*see also*
    Syphilis, congenital) 090.9
    stated to be acquired NEC 097.9

Syphilis, syphilitic—*continued*
  central nervous system (any site) (early) (late)
    (latent) (primary) (recurrent) (relapse)
    (secondary) (tertiary) 094.9
    with
      ataxia 094.0
      paralysis, general 094.1
        juvenile 090.40
      paresis (general) 094.1
        juvenile 090.40
      tabes (dorsalis) 094.0
        juvenile 090.40
      taboparesis 094.1
        juvenile 090.40
    aneurysm (ruptured) 094.87
    congenital 090.40
    juvenile 090.40
    remission in (sustained) 094.9
    serology doubtful, negative, or positive 094.9
    specified nature or site NEC 094.89
    vascular 094.89
  cerebral 094.89
    meningovascular 094.2
    nerves 094.89
    sclerosis 094.89
    thrombosis 094.89
  cerebrospinal 094.89
    tabetic 094.0
  cerebrovascular 094.89
  cervix 095.8
  chancre (multiple) 091.0
    extragenital 091.2
    Rollet's 091.0
  Charcot's joint 094.0 *[713.5]*
  choked disc 094.89 *[377.00]*
  chorioretinitis 091.51
    congenital 090.0 *[363.13]*
    late 094.83
  choroiditis 091.51
    congenital 090.0 *[363.13]*
    late 094.83
    prenatal 090.0 *[363.13]*
  choroidoretinitis (secondary) 091.51
    congenital 090.0 *[363.13]*
    late 094.83
  ciliary body (secondary) 091.52
    late 095.8 *[364.11]*
  colon (late) 095.8
  combined sclerosis 094.89
  complicating pregnancy, childbirth or
    puerperium 647.0
    affecting fetus or newborn 760.2
  condyloma (latum) 091.3
  congenital 090.9
    with
      encephalitis 090.41
      paresis (general) 090.40
      tabes (dorsalis) 090.40
      taboparesis 090.40
    chorioretinitis, choroiditis 090.0 *[363.13]*
    early or less than 2 years after birth NEC 090.2
      with manifestations 090.0
      latent (without manifestations) 090.1
        negative spinal fluid test 090.1
        serology, positive 090.1
      symptomatic 090.0
    interstitial keratitis 090.3
    juvenile neurosyphilis 090.40

Syphilis, syphilitic—*continued*
  late or 2 years or more after birth NEC 090.7
    chorioretinitis, choroiditis 090.5 *[363.13]*
    interstitial keratitis 090.3
    juvenile neurosyphilis NEC 090.40
    latent (without manifestations) 090.6
      negative spinal fluid test 090.6
      serology, positive 090.6
    symptomatic or with manifestations NEC
      090.5
      interstitial keratitis 090.3
  conjugal 097.9
    tabes 094.0
  conjunctiva 095.8 *[372.10]*
  contact V01.6
  cord, bladder 094.0
  cornea, late 095.8 *[370.59]*
  coronary (artery) 093.89
    sclerosis 093.89
  coryza 095.8
    congenital 090.0
  cranial nerve 094.89
  cutaneous—*see* Syphilis, skin
  dacryocystitis 095.8
  degeneration, spinal cord 094.89
  d'emblée 095.8
  dementia 094.89
    paralytica 094.1
    juvenilis 090.40
  destruction of bone 095.5
  dilatation, aorta 093.0
  due to blood transfusion 097.9
  dura mater 094.89
  ear 095.8
    inner 095.8
      nerve (eighth) 094.86
      neurorecurrence 094.86
  early NEC 091.0
    cardiovascular 093.9
    central nervous system 094.9
      paresis 094.1
      tabes 094.0
    latent (without manifestations) (less than 2
      years after infection) 092.9
    negative spinal fluid test 092.9
    serological relapse following treatment 092.0
    serology positive 092.9
    paresis 094.1
    relapse (treated, untreated) 091.7
    skin 091.3
    symptomatic NEC 091.89
      extragenital chancre 091.2
      primary, except extragenital chancre 091.0
      secondary (*see also* Syphilis, secondary)
        091.3
        relapse (treated, untreated) 091.7
      tabes 094.0
      ulcer 091.3
  eighth nerve 094.86
  endemic, nonvenereal 104.0
  endocarditis 093.20
    aortic 093.22
    mitral 093.21
    pulmonary 093.24
    tricuspid 093.23
  epididymis (late) 095.8
  epiglottis 095.8
  epiphysitis (congenital) 090.0
  esophagus 095.8
  Eustachian tube 095.8

Syphilis, syphilitic—*continued*
- exposure to V01.6
- eye 095.8 *[363.13]*
  - neuromuscular mechanism 094.85
- eyelid 095.8 *[373.5]*
  - with gumma 095.8 *[373.5]*
  - ptosis 094.89
- fallopian tube 095.8
- fracture 095.5
- gallbladder (late) 095.8
- gastric 095.8
  - crisis 094.0
  - polyposis 095.8
- general 097.9
  - paralysis 094.1
    - juvenile 090.40
- genital (primary) 091.0
- glaucoma 095.8
- gumma (late) NEC 095.9
  - cardiovascular system 093.9
  - central nervous system 094.9
  - congenital 090.5
  - heart or artery 093.89
- heart 093.89
  - block 093.89
  - decompensation 093.89
  - disease 093.89
  - failure 093.89
  - valve (*see also* Syphilis, endocarditis) 093.20
- hemianesthesia 094.89
- hemianopsia 095.8
- hemiparesis 094.89
- hemiplegia 094.89
- hepatic artery 093.89
- hepatitis 095.3
- hepatomegaly 095.3
  - congenital 090.0
- hereditaria tarda (*see also* Syphilis, congenital, late) 090.7
- hereditary (*see also* Syphilis, congenital) 090.9
  - interstitial keratitis 090.3
- Hutchinson's teeth 090.5
- hyalitis 095.8
- inactive—*see* Syphilis, latent
- infantum NEC (*see also* Syphilis, congenital) 090.9
- inherited—*see* Syphilis, congenital
- internal ear 095.8
- intestine (late) 095.8
- iris, iritis (secondary) 091.52
  - late 095.8 *[364.11]*
- joint (late) 095.8
- keratitis (congenital) (early) (interstitial) (late) (parenchymatous) (punctata profunda) 090.3
- kidney 095.4
- lacrimal apparatus 095.8
- laryngeal paralysis 095.8
- larynx 095.8
- late 097.0
  - cardiovascular 093.9
  - central nervous system 094.9
  - latent or 2 years or more after infection (without manifestations) 096
    - negative spinal fluid test 096
    - serology positive 096
  - paresis 094.1
  - specified site NEC 095.8
  - symptomatic or with symptoms 095.9
  - tabes 094.0

Syphilis, syphilitic—*continued*
- latent 097.1
  - central nervous system 094.9
  - date of infection unspecified 097.1
  - early or less than 2 years after infection 092.9
  - late or 2 years or more after infection 096
  - serology
    - doubtful
      - follow-up of latent syphilis 097.1
        - central nervous system 094.9
        - date of infection unspecified 097.1
        - early or less than 2 years after infection 092.9
        - late or 2 years or more after infection 096
    - positive, only finding 097.1
      - date of infection unspecified 097.1
      - early or less than 2 years after infection 097.1
      - late or 2 years or more after infection 097.1
- lens 095.8
- leukoderma 091.3
  - late 095.8
- lienis 095.8
- lip 091.3
  - chancre 091.2
  - late 095.8
  - primary 091.2
- Lissauer's paralysis 094.1
- liver 095.3
  - secondary 091.62
- locomotor ataxia 094.0
- lung 095.1
- lymphadenitis (secondary) 091.4
- lymph gland (early) (secondary) 091.4
  - late 095.8
- macular atrophy of skin 091.3
  - striated 095.8
- maternal, affecting fetus or newborn 760.2
  - manifest syphilis in newborn—*see* Syphilis, congenital
- mediastinum (late) 095.8
- meninges (adhesive) (basilar) (brain) (spinal cord) 094.2
- meningitis 094.2
  - acute 091.81
  - congenital 090.42
- meningoencephalitis 094.2
- meningovascular 094.2
  - congenital 090.49
- mesarteritis 093.89
  - brain 094.89
  - spine 094.89
- middle ear 095.8
- mitral stenosis 093.21
- monoplegia 094.89
- mouth (secondary) 091.3
  - late 095.8
- mucocutaneous 091.3
  - late 095.8
- mucous
  - membrane 091.3
    - late 095.8
  - patches 091.3
    - congenital 090.0
- mulberry molars 090.5
- muscle 095.6
- myocardium 093.82
- myositis 095.6
- nasal sinus 095.8
- neonatorum NEC (*see also* Syphilis, congenital) 090.9

Syphilis, syphilitic—*continued*
  nerve palsy (any cranial nerve) 094.89
  nervous system, central 094.9
  neuritis 095.8
    acoustic nerve 094.86
  neurorecidive of retina 094.83
  neuroretinitis 094.85
  newborn (*see also* Syphilis, congenital) 090.9
  nodular superficial 095.8
  nonvenereal, endemic 104.0
  nose 095.8
    saddle back deformity 090.5
    septum 095.8
      perforated 095.8
  occlusive arterial disease 093.89
  ophthalmic 095.8 *[363.13]*
  ophthalmoplegia 094.89
  optic nerve (atrophy) (neuritis) (papilla) 094.84
  orbit (late) 095.8
  orchitis 095.8
  organic 097.9
  osseous (late) 095.5
  osteochondritis (congenital) 090.0
  osteoporosis 095.5
  ovary 095.8
  oviduct 095.8
  palate 095.8
    gumma 095.8
    perforated 090.5
  pancreas (late) 095.8
  pancreatitis 095.8
  paralysis 094.89
    general 094.1
    juvenile 090.40
  paraplegia 094.89
  paresis (general) 094.1
    juvenile 090.40
  paresthesia 094.89
  Parkinson's disease or syndrome 094.82
  paroxysmal tachycardia 093.89
  pemphigus (congenital) 090.0
  penis 091.0
    chancre 091.0
    late 095.8
  pericardium 093.81
  perichondritis, larynx 095.8
  periosteum 095.5
    congenital 090.0
    early 091.61
    secondary 091.61
  peripheral nerve 095.8
  petrous bone (late) 095.5
  pharynx 095.8
    secondary 091.3
  pituitary (gland) 095.8
  placenta 095.8
  pleura (late) 095.8
  pneumonia, white 090.0
  pontine (lesion) 094.89
  portal vein 093.89
  primary NEC 091.2
    anal 091.1
    and secondary (*see also* Syphilis, secondary) 091.9
    cardiovascular 093.9
    central nervous system 094.9
    extragenital chancre NEC 091.2
    fingers 091.2
    genital 091.0
    lip 091.2
    specified site NEC 091.2

Syphilis, syphilitic—*continued*
  tonsils 091.2
  prostate 095.8
  psychosis (intracranial gumma) 094.89
  ptosis (eyelid) 094.89
  pulmonary (late) 095.1
    artery 093.89
  pulmonum 095.1
  pyelonephritis 095.4
  recently acquired, symptomatic NEC 091.89
  rectum 095.8
  respiratory tract 095.8
  retina
    late 094.83
    neurorecidive 094.83
  retrobulbar neuritis 094.85
  salpingitis 095.8
  sclera (late) 095.0
  sclerosis
    cerebral 094.89
    coronary 093.89
    multiple 094.89
    subacute 094.89
  scotoma (central) 095.8
  scrotum 095.8
  secondary (and primary) 091.9
    adenopathy 091.4
    anus 091.3
    bone 091.61
    cardiovascular 093.9
    central nervous system 094.9
    chorioretinitis, choroiditis 091.51
    hepatitis 091.62
    liver 091.62
    lymphadenitis 091.4
    meningitis, acute 091.81
    mouth 091.3
    mucous membranes 091.3
    periosteum 091.61
    periostitis 091.61
    pharynx 091.3
    relapse (treated) (untreated) 091.7
    skin 091.3
    specified form NEC 091.89
    tonsil 091.3
    ulcer 091.3
    viscera 091.69
    vulva 091.3
  seminal vesicle (late) 095.8
  seronegative
    with signs or symptoms—*see* Syphilis, by site
      and stage
  seropositive
    with signs or symptoms—*see* Syphilis, by site
      and stage
    follow-up of latent syphilis—*see* Syphilis,
      latent
    only finding—*see* Syphilis, latent
  seventh nerve (paralysis) 094.89
  sinus 095.8
  sinusitis 095.8
  skeletal system 095.5
  skin (early) (secondary) (with ulceration) 091.3
    late or tertiary 095.8
  small intestine 095.8
  spastic spinal paralysis 094.0
  spermatic cord (late) 095.8
  spinal (cord) 094.89
    with
      paresis 094.1
      tabes 094.0

Syphilis, syphilitic—*continued*
  spleen 095.8
  splenomegaly 095.8
  spondylitis 095.5
  staphyloma 095.8
  stigmata (congenital) 090.5
  stomach 095.8
  synovium (late) 095.7
  tabes dorsalis (early) (late) 094.0
    juvenile 090.40
  tabetic type 094.0
    juvenile 090.40
  taboparesis 094.1
    juvenile 090.40
  tachycardia 093.89
  tendon (late) 095.7
  tertiary 097.0
    with symptoms 095.8
    cardiovascular 093.9
    central nervous system 094.9
    multiple NEC 095.8
    specified site NEC 095.8
  testis 095.8
  thorax 095.8
  throat 095.8
  thymus (gland) 095.8
  thyroid (late) 095.8
  tongue 095.8
  tonsil (lingual) 095.8
    primary 091.2
    secondary 091.3
  trachea 095.8
  tricuspid valve 093.23
  tumor, brain 094.89
  tunica vaginalis (late) 095.8
  ulcer (any site) (early) (secondary) 091.3
    late 095.9
    perforating 095.9
      foot 094.0
  urethra (stricture) 095.8
  urogenital 095.8
  uterus 095.8
  uveal tract (secondary) 091.50
    late 095.8 *[363.13]*
  uveitis (secondary) 091.50
    late 095.8 *[363.13]*
  uvula (late) 095.8
    perforated 095.8
  vagina 091.0
    late 095.8
  valvulitis NEC 093.20
  vascular 093.89
    brain or cerebral 094.89
  vein 093.89
    cerebral 094.89
  ventriculi 095.8
  vesicae urinariae 095.8
  viscera (abdominal) 095.2
    secondary 091.69
  vitreous (hemorrhage) (opacities) 095.8
  vulva 091.0
    late 095.8
    secondary 091.3
Syphiloma 095.9
  cardiovascular system 093.9
  central nervous system 094.9
  circulatory system 093.9
  congenital 090.5
Syphilophobia 300.29

Syringadenoma (M8400/0)—*see also*
  Neoplasm, skin, benign
  papillary (M8406/0)—*see* Neoplasm, skin,
    benign
Syringobulbia 336.0
Syringocarcinoma (M8400/3)—*see* Neoplasm,
  skin, malignant
Syringocystadenoma (M8400/0)—*see also*
  Neoplasm, skin, benign
  papillary (M8406/0)—*see* Neoplasm, skin,
    benign
Syringocystoma (M8407/0)—*see* Neoplasm,
  skin, benign
Syringoma (M8407/0)—*see also* Neoplasm,
  skin, benign
  chondroid (M8940/0)—*see* Neoplasm, by site,
    benign
Syringomyelia 336.0
Syringomyelitis 323.9
  late effect—*see* category 326
Syringomyelocele (*see also* Spina bifida) 741.9
Syringopontia 336.0
System, systemic —*see also* condition
  disease, combined—*see* Degeneration,
    combined
  fibrosclerosing syndrome 710.8
  lupus erythematosus 710.0
    inhibitor 286.5

T

Tab —*see* Tag
Tabacism 989.8
Tabacosis 989.8
Tabardillo 080
  flea-borne 081.0
  louse-borne 080
Tabes, tabetic
  with
    central nervous system syphilis 094.0
    Charcot's joint 094.0 *[713.5]*
    cord bladder 094.0
    crisis, viscera (any) 094.0
    paralysis, general 094.1
    paresis (general) 094.1
    perforating ulcer 094.0
  arthropathy 094.0 *[713.5]*
  bladder 094.0
  bone 094.0
  cerebrospinal 094.0
  congenital 090.40
  conjugal 094.0
  dorsalis 094.0
    neurosyphilis 094.0
  early 094.0
  juvenile 090.40
  latent 094.0
  mesenterica (*see also* Tuberculosis) 014.8
  paralysis insane, general 094.1
  peripheral (nonsyphilitic) 799.8
  spasmodic 094.0
    not dorsal or dorsalis 343.9
  syphilis (cerebrospinal) 094.0
Taboparalysis 094.1
Taboparesis (remission) 094.1
  with
    Charcot's joint 094.1 *[713.5]*
    cord bladder 094.1
    perforating ulcer 094.1
  juvenile 090.40
Tachyalimentation 579.3
Tachyarrhythmia, tachyrhythmia —*see also*
  Tachycardia
  paroxysmal with sinus bradycardia 427.81
Tachycardia 785.0
  atrial 427.89
  auricular 427.89
  nodal 427.89
    nonparoxysmal atrioventricular 426.89
  nonparoxysmal atrioventricular (nodal) 426.89
  paroxysmal 427.2
    with sinus bradycardia 427.81
    atrial (PAT) 427.0
      psychogenic 316 *[427.0]*
    atrioventricular (AV) 427.0
      psychogenic 316 *[427.0]*
    essential 427.2
    junctional 427.0
    nodal 427.0
    psychogenic 316 *[427.2]*
      atrial 316 *[427.0]*
      supraventricular 316 *[427.0]*
      ventricular 316 *[427.1]*
    supraventricular 427.0
      psychogenic 316 *[427.0]*
    ventricular 427.1
      psychogenic 316 *[427.1]*
  postoperative 997.1

Tachycardia— *continued*
  psychogenic 306.2
  sick sinus 427.81
  sinoauricular 427.89
  sinus 427.89
  supraventricular 427.89
  ventricular (paroxysmal) 427.1
    psychogenic 316 *[427.1]*
Tachypnea 786.09
  hysterical 300.11
  newborn (idiopathic) (transitory) 770.6
  psychogenic 306.1
  transitory, of newborn 770.6
Taenia (infection) (infestation) (*see also*
  Infestation, taenia) 123.3
  diminuta 123.6
  echinococcal infestation (*see also*
    Echinococcus) 122.9
  nana 123.6
  saginata infestation 123.2
  solium (intestinal form) 123.0
    larval form 123.1
Taeniasis (intestine) (*see also* Infestation,
  Taenia) 123.3
  saginata 123.2
  solium 123.0
Taenzer's disease 757.4
Tag (hypertrophied skin) (infected) 701.9
  adenoid 474.8
  anus 455.9
  endocardial (*see also* Endocarditis) 424.90
  hemorrhoidal 455.9
  hymen 623.8
  perineal 624.8
  preauricular 744.1
  rectum 455.9
  sentinel 455.9
  skin 701.9
    accessory 757.39
    anus 455.9
    congenital 757.39
    preauricular 744.1
    rectum 455.9
  tonsil 474.8
  urethra, urethral 599.84
  vulva 624.8
Tahyna fever 062.5
Takayasu (-Onishi) disease or syndrome
  (pulseless disease) 446.7
Talc granuloma 728.82
Talcosis 502
Talipes (congenital) 754.70
  acquired NEC 736.79
    planus 734
  asymmetric 754.79
    acquired 736.79
  calcaneovalgus 754.62
    acquired 736.76
  calcaneovarus 754.59
    acquired 736.76
  calcaneus 754.79
    acquired 736.76
  cavovarus 754.59
    acquired 736.75
  cavus 754.71
    acquired 736.73
  equinovalgus 754.69
    acquired 736.72

Talipes—*continued*
  equinovarus 754.51
    acquired 736.71
  equinus 754.79
    acquired, NEC 736.72
  percavus 754.71
    acquired 736.73
  planovalgus 754.69
    acquired 736.79
  planus (acquired) (any degree) 734
    congenital 754.61
    due to rickets 268.1
  valgus 754.60
    acquired 736.79
  varus 754.50
    acquired 736.79
Talma's disease 728.85
Tamponade heart (Rose's) (*see also*
    Pericarditis) 423.9
Tanapox 078.89
Tangier disease (familial high-density
    lipoprotein deficiency) 272.5
Tank ear 380.12
Tantrum (childhood) (*see also* Disturbance,
    conduct) 312.1
Tapeworm (infection) (infestation) (*see also*
    Infestation, tapeworm) 123.9
Tapia's syndrome 352.6
Tarantism 297.8
Target-oval cell anemia 282.4
Tarlov's cyst 355.9
Tarral-Besnier disease (pityriasis rubra pilaris)
    696.4
Tarsalgia 729.2
Tarsal tunnel syndrome 355.5
Tarsitis (eyelid) 373.00
  syphilitic 095.8 *[373.00]*
  tuberculous (*see also* Tuberculosis) 017.0
    [373.4]
Tartar (teeth) 523.6
Tattoo (mark) 709.09
Taurodontism 520.2
Taussig-Bing defect, heart, or syndrome
    (transposition, aorta and overriding pulmonary
    artery) 745.11
Tay's choroiditis 363.41
Tay-Sachs
  amaurotic familial idiocy 330.1
  disease 330.1
Taybi's syndrome (otopalatodigital) 759.89
Taylor's
  disease (diffuse idiopathic cutaneous atrophy)
    701.8
  syndrome 625.5
Tear, torn (traumatic)—*see also* Wound, open,
    by site
  anus, anal (sphincter) 863.89
    with open wound in cavity 863.99
    complicating delivery 664.2
      with mucosa 664.3
    nontraumatic, nonpuerperal 565.0
  articular cartilage, old (*see also* Disorder,
    cartilage, articular) 718.0
  bladder
    with
      abortion—*see* Abortion, by type, with
        damage to pelvic organs
      ectopic pregnancy (*see also* categories
        633.0-633.9) 639.2
      molar pregnancy (*see also* categories
        630-632) 639.2

Tear, torn— *continued*
    following
      abortion 639.2
      ectopic or molar pregnancy 639.2
    obstetrical trauma 665.5
  bowel
    with
      abortion—*see* Abortion, by type, with
        damage to pelvic organs
      ectopic pregnancy (*see also* categories
        633.0-633.9) 639.2
      molar pregnancy (*see also* categories
        630-632) 639.2
    following
      abortion 639.2
      ectopic or molar pregnancy 639.2
    obstetrical trauma 665.5
  broad ligament
    with
      abortion—*see* Abortion, by type, with
        damage to pelvic organs
      ectopic pregnancy (*see also* categories
        633.0-633.9) 639.2
      molar pregnancy (*see also* categories
        630-632) 639.2
    following
      abortion 639.2
      ectopic or molar pregnancy 639.2
    obstetrical trauma 665.6
  bucket handle (knee) (meniscus)—*see* Tear,
    meniscus
  capsule
    joint—*see* Sprain, by site
    spleen—*see* Laceration, spleen, capsule
  cartilage—*see also* Sprain, by site
    articular, old (*see also* Disorder, cartilage,
      articular) 718.0
    knee—*see* Tear, meniscus
    semilunar (knee) (current injury)—*see* Tear,
      meniscus
  cervix
    with
      abortion—*see* Abortion, by type, with
        damage to pelvic organs
      ectopic pregnancy (*see also* categories
        633.0-633.9) 639.2
      molar pregnancy (*see also* categories
        630-632) 639.2
    following
      abortion 639.2
      ectopic or molar pregnancy 639.2
    obstetrical trauma (current) 665.3
    old 622.3
  internal organ (abdomen, chest, or pelvis)—*see*
    Injury, internal, by site
  ligament—*see also* Sprain, by site
    with open wound—*see* Wound, open by site
  meniscus (knee) (current injury) 836.2
    bucket handle 836.0
      old 717.0
    lateral 836.1
      anterior horn 836.1
        old 717.42
      bucket handle 836.1
        old 717.41
      old 717.40
      posterior horn 836.1
        old 717.43
      specified site NEC 836.1
        old 717.49

Tear, torn—*continued*
  medial 836.0
    anterior horn 836.0
      old 717.1
    bucket handle 836.0
      old 717.0
    old 717.3
    posterior horn 836.0
      old 717.2
    old NEC 717.5
  site other than knee—*see* Sprain, by site
  muscle—*see also* Sprain, by site
    with open wound—*see* Wound, open by site
  pelvic
    floor, complicating delivery 664.1
    organ NEC
      with
        abortion—*see* Abortion, by type, with
          damage to pelvic organs
        ectopic pregnancy (*see also* categories
          633.0-633.9) 639.2
        molar pregnancy (*see also* categories
          630-632) 639.2
      following
        abortion 639.2
        ectopic or molar pregnancy 639.2
      obstetrical trauma 665.5
    perineum—*see also* Laceration, perineum
      obstetrical trauma 665.5
    periurethral tissue
      with
        abortion—*see* Abortion, by type, with
          damage to pelvic organs
        ectopic pregnancy (*see also* categories
          633.0-633.9) 639.2
        molar pregnancy (*see also* categories
          630-632) 639.2
      following
        abortion 639.2
        ectopic or molar pregnancy 639.2
      obstetrical trauma 665.5
    rectovaginal septum—*see* Laceration,
      rectovaginal septum
  retina, retinal (recent) (with detachment) 361.00
    without detachment 361.30
    dialysis (juvenile) (with detachment) 361.04
    giant (with detachment) 361.03
    horseshoe (without detachment) 361.32
    multiple (with detachment) 361.02
      without detachment 361.33
    old
      delimited (partial) 361.06
      partial 361.06
      total or subtotal 361.07
    partial (without detachment)
      giant 361.03
      multiple defects 361.02
      old (delimited) 361.06
      single defect 361.01
    round hole (without detachment) 361.31
    single defect (with detachment) 361.01
    total or subtotal (recent) 361.05
      old 361.07
  rotator cuff 840.4
    current injury 840.4
  semilunar cartilage, knee (*see also* Tear,
    meniscus) 836.2
    old 717.5
  tendon—*see also* Sprain, by site
    with open wound—*see* Wound, open by site
  tentorial, at birth 767.0

Tear, torn—*continued*
  umbilical cord
    affecting fetus or newborn 772.0
    complicating delivery 663.8
  urethra
    with
      abortion—*see* Abortion, by type, with
        damage to pelvic organs
      ectopic pregnancy (*see also* categories
        633.0-633.9) 639.2
      molar pregnancy (*see also* categories
        630-632) 639.2
    following
      abortion 639.2
      ectopic or molar pregnancy 639.2
    obstetrical trauma 665.5
  uterus—*see* Injury, internal, uterus
  vagina—*see* Laceration, vagina
  vessel, from catheter 998.2
  vulva, complicating delivery 664.0
Tear stone 375.57
Teeth, tooth —*see also* condition
  grinding 306.8
Teething 520.7
  syndrome 520.7
Tegmental syndrome 344.89
Telangiectasia, telangiectasis (verrucous) 448.9
  ataxic (cerebellar) 334.8
  familial 448.0
  hemorrhagic, hereditary (congenital) (senile)
    448.0
  hereditary hemorrhagic 448.0
  retina 362.15
  spider 448.1
Telecanthus (congenital) 743.63
Telescoped bowel or intestine (*see also*
  Intussusception) 560.0
Teletherapy, adverse effect NEC 990
Telogen effluvium 704.02
Temperature
  body, high (of unknown origin) (*see also*
    Pyrexia) 780.6
  cold, trauma from 991.9
    newborn 778.2
    specified effect NEC 991.8
  high
    body (of unknown origin) (*see also* Pyrexia)
      780.6
    trauma from—*see* Heat
Temper tantrum (childhood) (*see also*
  Disturbance, conduct) 312.1
Temple —*see* condition
Temporal —*see also* condition
  lobe syndrome 310.0
**Temporomandibular joint-pain-dysfunction
  syndrome** 524.60
Temporosphenoidal —*see* condition
Tendency
  bleeding (*see also* Defect, coagulation) 286.9
  homosexual, ego-dystonic 302.0
  paranoid 301.0
  suicide 300.9
Tenderness
  abdominal (generalized) (localized) 789.6
  rebound 789.6
  skin 782.0
Tendinitis, tendonitis (*see also* Tenosynovitis)
  726.90
  Achilles 726.71
  adhesive 726.90
    shoulder 726.0

Tendinitis, tendonitis—*continued*
  calcific 727.82
    shoulder 726.11
  gluteal 726.5
  patellar 726.64
  peroneal 726.79
  pes anserinus 726.61
  psoas 726.5
  tibialis (anterior) (posterior) 726.72
  trochanteric 726.5
Tendon —*see* condition
Tendosynovitis —*see* Tenosynovitis
Tendovaginitis —*see* Tenosynovitis
Tenesmus 787.99
  rectal 787.99
  vesical 788.9
Tenia —*see* Taenia
Teniasis —*see* Taeniasis
Tennis elbow 726.32
Tenonitis —*see also* Tenosynovitis
  eye (capsule) 376.04
Tenontosynovitis —*see* Tenosynovitis
Tenontothecitis —*see* Tenosynovitis
Tenophyte 727.9
Tenosynovitis 727.00
  adhesive 726.90
    shoulder 726.0
  ankle 727.06
  bicipital (calcifying) 726.12
  buttock 727.09
  due to crystals—*see* Arthritis, due to crystals
  elbow 727.09
  finger 727.05
  foot 727.06
  gonococcal 098.51
  hand 727.05
  hip 727.09
  knee 727.09
  radial styloid 727.04
  shoulder 726.10
    adhesive 726.0
  spine 720.1
  supraspinatus 726.10
  toe 727.06
  tuberculous—*see* Tuberculosis, tenosynovitis
  wrist 727.05
Tenovaginitis —*see* Tenosynovitis
Tension
  arterial, high (*see also* Hypertension) 401.9
    without diagnosis of hypertension 796.2
  headache 307.81
  intraocular (elevated) 365.00
  nervous 799.2
  ocular (elevated) 365.00
  pneumothorax 512.0
    iatrogenic 512.1
    postoperative 512.1
    spontaneous 512.0
  premenstrual 625.4
  state 300.9
Tentorium —*see* condition
Teratencephalus 759.89
Teratism 759.7
Teratoblastoma (malignant) (M9080/3)—*see*
  Neoplasm, by site, malignant
Teratocarcinoma (M9081/3)—*see also*
  Neoplasm, by site, malignant
  liver 155.0

Teratoma (solid) (M9080/1)—*see also*
  Neoplasm, by site, uncertain behavior
  adult (cystic) (M9080/0)—*see* Neoplasm, by
    site, benign
  and embryonal carcinoma, mixed
    (M9081/3)—*see* Neoplasm, by site,
    malignant
  benign (M9080/0)—*see* Neoplasm, by site,
    benign
  combined with choriocarcinoma
    (M9101/3)—*see* Neoplasm, by site,
    malignant
  cystic (adult) (M9080/0)—*see* Neoplasm, by
    site, benign
  differentiated type (M9080/0)—*see* Neoplasm,
    by site, benign
  embryonal (M9080/3)—*see also* Neoplasm, by
    site, malignant
    liver 155.0
  fetal
    sacral, causing fetopelvic disproportion 653.7
  immature (M9080/3)—*see* Neoplasm, by site,
    malignant
  liver (M9080/3) 155.0
    adult, benign, cystic, differentiated type or
      mature (M9080/0) 211.5
  malignant (M9080/3)—*see also* Neoplasm, by
    site, malignant
    anaplastic type (M9082/3)—*see* Neoplasm, by
      site, malignant
    intermediate type (M9083/3)—*see* Neoplasm,
      by site, malignant
    liver (M9080/3) 155.0
    trophoblastic (M9102/3)
      specified site—*see* Neoplasm, by site,
        malignant
      unspecified site 186.9
    undifferentiated type (M9082/3)—*see*
      Neoplasm, by site, malignant
  mature (M9080/0)—*see* Neoplasm, by site,
    benign
  ovary (M9080/0) 220
    embryonal, immature, or malignant
      (M9080/3) 183.0
  suprasellar (M9080/3)—*see* Neoplasm, by site,
    malignant
  testis (M9080/3) 186.9
    adult, benign, cystic, differentiated type or
      mature (M9080/0) 222.0
    undescended 186.0
Terminal care V66.7
Termination
  anomalous—*see also* Malposition, congenital
    portal vein 747.49
    right pulmonary vein 747.42
  pregnancy (legal) (therapeutic) (*see* Abortion,
    legal) 635.9
    fetus NEC 779.6
    illegal (*see also* Abortion, illegal) 636.9
Ternidens diminutus infestation 127.7
Terrors, night (child) 307.46
Terry's syndrome 362.21
Tertiary —*see* condition
Tessellated fundus, retina (tigroid) 362.89
Test(s)
  AIDS virus V72.6
  allergen V72.7
  bacterial disease NEC (*see also* Screening, by
    name of disease) V74.9
  basal metabolic rate V72.6
  blood-alcohol V70.4

Test(s)—*continued*
  blood-drug V70.4
  developmental, infant or child V20.2
  Dick V74.8
  fertility V26.2
  hearing V72.1
  HIV V72.6
  human immunodeficiency virus V72.6
  Kveim V82.8
  laboratory V72.6
    for medicolegal reason V70.4
  Mantoux (for tuberculosis) V74.1
  mycotic organism V75.4
  parasitic agent NEC V75.8
  pregnancy
    positive V22.1
      first pregnancy V22.0
    unconfirmed V72.4
  preoperative V72.84
    cardiovascular V72.81
    respiratory V72.82
    specified NEC V72.83
  sarcoidosis V82.8
  Schick V74.3
  Schultz-Charlton V74.8
  skin, diagnostic
    allergy V72.7
    bacterial agent NEC (*see also* Screening, by
      name of disease) V74.9
    Dick V74.8
    hypersensitivity V72.7
    Kveim V82.8
    Mantoux V74.1
    mycotic organism V75.4
    parasitic agent NEC V75.8
    sarcoidosis V82.8
    Schick V74.3
    Schultz-Charlton V74.8
    tuberculin V74.1
  specified type NEC V72.85
  tuberculin V74.1
  vision V72.0
  Wassermann
    positive (*see also* Serology for syphilis,
      positive) 097.1
    false 795.6
Testicle, testicular, testis —*see also* condition
  feminization (syndrome) 257.8
Tetanus, tetanic (cephalic) (convulsions) 037
  with
    abortion—*see* Abortion, by type, with sepsis
    ectopic pregnancy (*see also* categories
      633.0-633.9) 639.0
    molar pregnancy (*see* categories 630-632)
      639.0
  following
    abortion 639.0
    ectopic or molar pregnancy 639.0
  inoculation V03.7
    reaction (due to serum)—*see* Complications,
      vaccination
  neonatorum 771.3
  puerperal, postpartum, childbirth 670
Tetany, tetanic 781.7
  alkalosis 276.3
  associated with rickets 268.0
  convulsions 781.7
    hysterical 300.11
  functional (hysterical) 300.11
  hyperkinetic 781.7
    hysterical 300.11

Tetany, tetanic—*continued*
  hyperpnea 786.01
    hysterical 300.11
    psychogenic 306.1
  hyperventilation 786.01
    hysterical 300.11
    psychogenic 306.1
  hypocalcemic, neonatal 775.4
  hysterical 300.11
  neonatal 775.4
  parathyroid (gland) 252.1
  parathyroprival 252.1
  postoperative 252.1
  postthyroidectomy 252.1
  pseudotetany 781.7
    hysterical 300.11
  psychogenic 306.1
    specified as conversion reaction 300.11
Tetralogy of Fallot 745.2
Tetraplegia —*see* Quadriplegia
Thailand hemorrhagic fever 065.4
Thalassanemia 282.4
Thalassemia (alpha) (beta) (disease) (Hb-C)
  (Hb-D) (Hb-E) (Hb-H) (Hb-I) (Hb-S) (high
  fetal gene) (high fetal hemoglobin)
  (intermedia) (major) (minima) (minor)
  (mixed) (sickle-cell) (trait) (with other
  hemoglobinopathy) 282.4
Thalassemic variants 282.4
Thaysen-Gee disease (nontropical sprue) 579.0
Thecoma (M8600/0) 220
  malignant (M8600/3) 183.0
Thelarche, precocious 259.1
Thelitis 611.0
  puerperal, postpartum 675.0
Therapeutic —*see* condition
Therapy V57.9
  blood transfusion, without reported diagnosis
    V58.2
  breathing V57.0
  chemotherapy V58.1
    fluoride V07.31
    prophylactic NEC V07.39
  dialysis (intermittent) (treatment)
    extracorporeal V56.0
    peritoneal V56.8
    renal V56.0
    specified type NEC V56.8
  exercise NEC V57.1
    breathing V57.0
  extracorporeal dialysis (renal) V56.0
  fluoride prophylaxis V07.31
  hemodialysis V56.0
  occupational V57.21
  orthoptic V57.4
  orthotic V57.81
  peritoneal dialysis V56.8
  physical NEC V57.1
  postmenopausal hormone replacement V07.4
  radiation V58.0
  speech V57.3
  vocational V57.22
Thermalgesia 782.0
Thermalgia 782.0
Thermanalgesia 782.0
Thermanesthesia 782.0
Thermic —*see* condition
Thermography (abnormal) 793.9
  breast 793.8
Thermoplegia 992.0

Thesaurismosis
  amyloid 277.3
  bilirubin 277.4
  calcium 275.4
  cystine 270.0
  glycogen (*see also* Disease, glycogen storage)
    271.0
  kerasin 272.7
  lipoid 272.7
  melanin 255.4
  phosphatide 272.7
  urate 274.9
Thiaminic deficiency 265.1
  with beriberi 265.0
Thibierge-Weissenbach syndrome (cutaneous
  systemic sclerosis) 710.1
Thickening
  bone 733.99
    extremity 733.99
  breast 611.79
  hymen 623.3
  larynx 478.79
  nail 703.8
    congenital 757.5
  periosteal 733.99
  pleura (*see also* Pleurisy) 511.0
  skin 782.8
  subepiglottic 478.79
  tongue 529.8
  valve, heart—*see* Endocarditis
Thiele syndrome 724.6
Thigh —*see* condition
Thinning vertebra (*see also* Osteoporosis)
  733.00
Thirst, excessive 783.5
  due to deprivation of water 994.3
Thomsen's disease 359.2
Thomson's disease (congenital poikiloderma)
  757.33
Thoracic —*see also* condition
  kidney 753.3
  outlet syndrome 353.0
  stomach—*see* Hernia, diaphragm
Thoracogastroschisis (congenital) 759.89
Thoracopagus 759.4
Thoracoschisis 756.3
Thorax —*see* condition
Thorn's syndrome (*see also* Disease, renal)
  593.9
Thornwaldt's, Tornwaldt's
  bursitis (pharyngeal) 478.29
  cyst 478.26
  disease (pharyngeal bursitis) 478.29
Thorson-Biörck syndrome (malignant
  carcinoid) 259.2
Threadworm (infection) (infestation) 127.4
Threatened
  abortion or miscarriage 640.0
    with subsequent abortion (*see also* Abortion,
      spontaneous) 634.9
    affecting fetus 762.1
  labor 644.1
    affecting fetus or newborn 761.8
    premature 644.0
  miscarriage 640.0
    affecting fetus 762.1
  premature
    delivery 644.2
      affecting fetus or newborn 761.8
    labor 644.0
      before 22 completed weeks gestation 640.0
Three-day fever 066.0

Threshers' lung 495.0
Thrix annulata (congenital) 757.4
Throat —*see* condition
Thrombasthenia (Glanzmann's) (hemorrhagic)
  (hereditary) 287.1
Thromboangiitis 443.1
  obliterans (general) 443.1
    cerebral 437.1
    vessels
      brain 437.1
      spinal cord 437.1
Thromboarteritis —*see* Arteritis
Thromboasthenia (Glanzmann's) (hemorrhagic)
  (hereditary) 287.1
Thrombocytasthenia (Glanzmann's) 287.1
Thrombocythemia (essential) (hemorrhagic)
  (primary) (M9962/1) 238.7
  idiopathic (M9962/1) 238.7
Thrombocytopathy (dystrophic) (granulopenic)
  287.1
Thrombocytopenia, thrombocytopenic 287.5
  with giant hemangioma 287.3
  amegakaryocytic, congenital 287.3
  congenital 287.3
  cyclic 287.3
  dilutional 287.4
  due to
    drugs 287.4
    extracorporeal circulation of blood 287.4
    massive blood transfusion 287.4
    platelet alloimmunization 287.4
  essential 287.3
  hereditary 287.3
  Kasabach-Merritt 287.3
  neonatal, transitory 776.1
    due to
      exchange transfusion 776.1
      idiopathic maternal thrombocytopenia 776.1
      isoimmunization 776.1
  primary 287.3
  puerperal, postpartum 666.3
  purpura (*see also* Purpura, thrombocytopenic)
    287.3
    thrombotic 446.6
  secondary 287.4
  sex-linked 287.3
Thrombocytosis, essential 289.9
Thromboembolism —*see* Embolism
Thrombopathy (Bernard-Soulier) 287.1
  constitutional 286.4
  Willebrand-Jürgens (angiohemophilia) 286.4
Thrombopenia (*see also* Thrombocytopenia)
  287.5
Thrombophlebitis 451.9
  antecubital vein 451.82
  antepartum (superficial) 671.2
    affecting fetus or newborn 760.3
    deep 671.3
  arm 451.89
    deep 451.83
    superficial 451.82
  breast, superficial 451.89
  cavernous (venous) sinus—*see*
    Thrombophlebitis, intracranial venous sinus
  cephalic vein 451.82
  cerebral (sinus) (vein) 325
    late effect—*see* category 326
    nonpyogenic 437.6
      in pregnancy or puerperium 671.5
    late effect—*see* category 438

Thrombophlebitis—*continued*
  due to implanted device—*see* Complications,
    due to (presence of) any device, implant, or
    graft classified to 996.0-996.5 NEC
  during or resulting from a procedure NEC 997.2
  femoral 451.11
  femoropopliteal 451.19
  following infusion, perfusion, or transfusion
    999.2
  hepatic (vein) 451.89
  idiopathic, recurrent 453.1
  iliac vein 451.81
  iliofemoral 451.11
  intracranial venous sinus (any) 325
    late effect—*see* category 326
    nonpyogenic 437.6
      in pregnancy or puerperium 671.5
      late effect—*see* category 438
  jugular vein 451.89
  lateral (venous) sinus—*see* Thrombophlebitis,
    intracranial venous sinus
  leg 451.2
    deep (vessels) 451.19
      femoral vein 451.11
      specified vessel NEC 451.19
    superficial (vessels) 451.0
      femoral vein 451.11
  longitudinal (venous) sinus—*see*
    Thrombophlebitis, intracranial venous sinus
  lower extremity 451.2
    deep (vessels) 451.19
      femoral vein 451.11
      specified vessel NEC 451.19
    superficial (vessels) 451.0
  migrans, migrating 453.1
  pelvic
    with
      abortion—*see* Abortion, by type, with sepsis
      ectopic pregnancy (*see also* categories
        633.0-633.9) 639.0
      molar pregnancy (*see also* categories
        630-632) 639.0
    following
      abortion 639.0
      ectopic or molar pregnancy 639.0
    puerperal 671.4
  popliteal vein 451.19
  portal (vein) 572.1
  postoperative 997.2
  pregnancy (superficial) 671.2
    affecting fetus or newborn 760.3
    deep 671.3
  puerperal, postpartum, childbirth (extremities)
    (superficial) 671.2
    deep 671.4
    pelvic 671.4
    specified site NEC 671.5
  radial vein 451.83
  saphenous (greater) (lesser) 451.0
  sinus (intracranial)—*see* Thrombophlebitis,
    intracranial venous sinus
  specified site NEC 451.89
  tibial vein 451.19
Thrombosis, thrombotic (marantic) (multiple)
    (progressive) (septic) (vein) (vessel) 453.9
  with childbirth or during the puerperium—*see*
    Thrombosis, puerperal, postpartum
  antepartum—*see* Thrombosis, pregnancy

Thrombosis, thrombotic—*continued*
  aorta, aortic 444.1
    abdominal 444.0
    bifurcation 444.0
    saddle 444.0
    terminal 444.0
    thoracic 444.1
    valve—*see* Endocarditis, aortic
  apoplexy (*see also* Thrombosis, brain) 434.0
    late effect—*see* category 438
  appendix, septic—*see* Appendicitis, acute
  arteriolar-capillary platelet, disseminated 446.6
  artery, arteries (postinfectional) 444.9
    auditory, internal 433.8
    basilar (*see also* Occlusion, artery, basilar)
      433.0
    carotid (common) (internal) (*see also*
      Occlusion, artery, carotid) 433.1
      with other precerebral artery 433.3
    cerebellar (anterior inferior) (posterior
      inferior) (superior) 433.8
    cerebral (*see also* Thrombosis, brain) 434.0
    choroidal (anterior) 433.8
    communicating posterior 433.8
    coronary (*see also* Infarct, myocardium) 410.9
      due to syphilis 093.89
      healed or specified as old 412
      without myocardial infarction 411.81
    extremities 444.22
      lower 444.22
      upper 444.21
    femoral 444.22
    hepatic 444.89
    hypophyseal 433.8
    meningeal, anterior or posterior 433.8
    mesenteric (with gangrene) 557.0
    ophthalmic (*see also* Occlusion, retina) 362.30
    pontine 433.8
    popliteal 444.22
    precerebral—*see* Occlusion, artery,
      precerebral NEC
    pulmonary 415.19
      iatrogenic 415.11
      postoperative 415.11
    renal 593.81
    retinal (*see also* Occlusion, retina) 362.30
    specified site NEC 444.89
    spinal, anterior or posterior 433.8
    traumatic (complication) (early) (*see also*
      Injury, blood vessel, by site) 904.9
    vertebral (*see also* Occlusion, artery,
      vertebral) 433.2
      with other precerebral artery 433.3
  atrial (endocardial) 424.90
    due to syphilis 093.89
  auricular (*see also* Infarct, myocardium) 410.9
  axillary (vein) 453.8
  basilar (artery) (*see also* Occlusion, artery,
    basilar) 433.0
  bland NEC 453.9
  brain (artery) (stem) 434.0
    due to syphilis 094.89
    iatrogenic 997.02
    late effect—*see* category 438
    postoperative 997.02
    puerperal, postpartum, childbirth 674.0
    sinus (*see also* Thrombosis, intracranial
      venous sinus) 325
  capillary 448.9
    arteriolar, generalized 446.6

Thrombosis, thrombotic—*continued*
  cardiac (*see also* Infarct, myocardium) 410.9
    due to syphilis 093.89
    healed or specified as old 412
    valve—*see* Endocarditis
  carotid (artery) (common) (internal) (*see also*
      Occlusion, artery, carotid) 433.1
    with other precerebral artery 433.3
  cavernous sinus (venous)—*see* Thrombosis,
      intracranial venous sinus
  cerebellar artery (anterior inferior) (posterior
      inferior) (superior) 433.8
    late effect—*see* category 438
  cerebral (arteries) (*see also* Thrombosis, brain)
      434.0
    late effect—*see* category 438
  coronary (artery) (*see also* Infarct, myocardium)
      410.9
    due to syphilis 093.89
    healed or specified as old 412
    without myocardial infarction 411.81
  corpus cavernosum 607.82
  cortical (*see also* Thrombosis, brain) 434.0
  due to (presence of) any device, implant, or
      graft classifiable to 996.0-996.5—*see*
      Complications, due to (presence of) any
      device, implant, or graft classified to
      996.0-996.5 NEC
  effort 453.8
  endocardial—*see* Infarct, myocardium
  eye (*see also* Occlusion, retina) 362.30
  femoral (vein) (deep) 453.8
    with inflammation or phlebitis 451.11
    artery 444.22
  genital organ, male 608.83
  heart (chamber) (*see also* Infarct, myocardium)
      410.9
  hepatic (vein) 453.0
    artery 444.89
    infectional or septic 572.1
  iliac (vein) 453.8
    with inflammation or phlebitis 451.81
    artery (common) (external) (internal) 444.81
  inflammation, vein—*see* Thrombophlebitis
  internal carotid artery (*see also* Occlusion,
      artery, carotid) 433.1
    with other precerebral artery 433.3
  intestine (with gangrene) 557.0
  intracranial (*see also* Thrombosis, brain) 434.0
    venous sinus (any) 325
      nonpyogenic origin 437.6
      in pregnancy or puerperium 671.5
  intramural (*see also* Infarct, myocardium) 410.9
    without
      cardiac condition 429.89
      coronary artery disease 429.89
      myocardial infarction 429.89
    healed or specified as old 412
  jugular (bulb) 453.8
  kidney 593.81
    artery 593.81
  lateral sinus (venous)—*see* Thrombosis,
      intracranial venous sinus
  leg 453.8
    with inflammation or phlebitis—*see*
      Thrombophlebitis
    deep (vessels) 453.8
    superficial (vessels) 453.8
  liver (venous) 453.0
    artery 444.89
    infectional or septic 572.1

Thrombosis, thrombotic— *continued*
  portal vein 452
  longitudinal sinus (venous)—*see* Thrombosis,
      intracranial venous sinus
  lower extremity—*see* Thrombosis, leg
  lung 415.19
    iatrogenic 415.11
    postoperative 415.11
  marantic, dural sinus 437.6
  meninges (brain) (*see also* Thrombosis, brain)
      434.0
  mesenteric (artery) (with gangrene) 557.0
    vein (inferior) (superior) 557.0
  mitral—*see* Insufficiency, mitral
  mural (heart chamber) (*see also* Infarct,
      myocardium) 410.9
    without
      cardiac condition 429.89
      coronary artery disease 429.89
      myocardial infarction 429.89
    due to syphilis 093.89
    following myocardial infarction 429.79
    healed or specified as old 412
  omentum (with gangrene) 557.0
  ophthalmic (artery) (*see also* Occlusion, retina)
      362.30
  pampiniform plexus (male) 608.83
    female 620.8
  parietal (*see also* Infarct, myocardium) 410.9
  penis, penile 607.82
  peripheral arteries 444.22
    lower 444.22
    upper 444.21
  platelet 446.6
  portal 452
    due to syphilis 093.89
    infectional or septic 572.1
  precerebral artery—*see also* Occlusion, artery,
      precerebral NEC
  pregnancy 671.9
    deep (vein) 671.3
    superficial (vein) 671.2
  puerperal, postpartum, childbirth 671.9
    brain (artery) 674.0
      venous 671.5
    cardiac 674.8
    cerebral (artery) 674.0
      venous 671.5
    deep (vein) 671.4
    intracranial sinus (nonpyogenic) (venous)
      671.5
    pelvic 671.4
    pulmonary (artery) 673.2
    specified site NEC 671.5
    superficial 671.2
  pulmonary (artery) (vein) 415.19
    iatrogenic 415.11
    postoperative 415.11
  radial vein 451.83
  renal (artery) 593.81
    vein 453.3
  resulting from presence of shunt or other
      internal prosthetic device—*see*
      Complications, due to (presence of) any
      device, implant, or graft classified to
      996.0-996.5 NEC
  retina, retinal (artery) 362.30
    arterial branch 362.32
    central 362.31
    partial 362.33

Note—Use the following fifth-digit
subclassification with category 242:

0 without mention of thyrotoxic crisis or storm
1 with mention of thyrotoxic crisis or storm

Tic —*continued*
  psychogenic 307.20
    compulsive 307.22
  salaam 781.0
  spasm 307.20
    chronic (motor or vocal) 307.22
    transient of childhood 307.21
Tick (-borne) fever NEC 066.1
  American mountain 066.1
  Colorado 066.1
  hemorrhagic NEC 065.3
    Crimean 065.0
    Kyasanur Forest 065.2
    Omsk 065.1
  mountain 066.1
  nonexanthematous 066.1
Tick-bite fever NEC 066.1
  African 087.1
  Colorado (virus) 066.1
  Rocky Mountain 082.0
Tick paralysis 989.5
Tics and spasms, compulsive 307.22
Tietze's disease or syndrome 733.6
Tight, tightness
  anus 564.8
  chest 786.59
  fascia (lata) 728.9
  foreskin (congenital) 605
  hymen 623.3
  introitus (acquired) (congenital) 623.3
  rectal sphincter 564.8
  tendon 727.81
    Achilles (heel) 727.81
  urethral sphincter 598.9
Tilting vertebra 737.9
Timidity, child 313.21
Tinea (intersecta) (tarsi) 110.9
  amiantacea 110.0
  asbestina 110.0
  barbae 110.0
  beard 110.0
  black dot 110.0
  blanca 111.2
  capitis 110.0
  corporis 110.5
  cruris 110.3
  decalvans 704.09
  flava 111.0
  foot 110.4
  furfuracea 111.0
  imbricata (Tokelau) 110.5
  lepothrix 039.0
  manuum 110.2
  microsporic (*see also* Dermatophytosis) 110.9
  nigra 111.1
  nodosa 111.2
  pedis 110.4
  scalp 110.0
  specified site NEC 110.8
  sycosis 110.0
  tonsurans 110.0
  trichophytic (*see also* Dermatophytosis) 110.9
  unguium 110.1
  versicolor 111.0
Tingling sensation (*see also* Disturbance, sensation) 782.0
Tin-miners' lung 503
Tinnitus (aurium) 388.30
  audible 388.32
  objective 388.32
  subjective 388.31

Tipping pelvis 738.6
  with disproportion (fetopelvic) 653.0
    affecting fetus or newborn 763.1
  causing obstructed labor 660.1
    affecting fetus or newborn 763.1
Tiredness 780.7
Tissue —*see* condition
Tobacco
  abuse (affecting health) NEC (*see also* Abuse, drugs, nondependent) 305.1
  heart 989.8
Tobias' syndrome (carcinoma, pulmonary apex) (M8010/3) 162.3
Tocopherol deficiency 269.1
Todd's
  cirrhosis—*see* Cirrhosis, biliary
  paralysis (postepileptic transitory paralysis) 344.89
Toe —*see* condition
Toilet, artificial opening (*see also* Attention to, artificial, opening) V55.9
Tokelau ringworm 110.5
Tollwut 071
Tolosa-Hunt syndrome 378.55
Tommaselli's disease
  correct substance properly administered 599.7
  overdose or wrong substance given or taken 961.4
Tongue —*see also* condition
  worms 134.1
Tongue tie 750.0
Toni-Fanconi syndrome (cystinosis) 270.0
Tonic pupil 379.46
Tonsil —*see* condition
Tonsillitis (acute) (catarrhal) (croupous) (follicular) (gangrenous) (infective) (lacunar) (lingual) (malignant) (membranous) (phlegmonous) (pneumococcal) (pseudomembranous) (purulent) (septic) (staphylococcal) (subacute) (suppurative) (toxic) (ulcerative) (vesicular) (viral) 463
  with influenza, flu, or grippe 487.1
  chronic 474.0
  diphtheritic (membranous) 032.0
  hypertrophic 474.0
  influenzal 487.1
  parenchymatous 475
  streptococcal 034.0
  tuberculous (*see also* Tuberculosis) 012.8
  Vincent's 101
Tonsillopharyngitis 465.8
Tooth, teeth —*see* condition
Toothache 525.9
Topagnosis 782.0
Tophi (gouty) 274.0
  ear 274.81
  heart 274.82
  specified site NEC 274.82
Torn —*see* Tear, torn
Tornwaldt's bursitis (disease) (pharyngeal bursitis) 478.29
  cyst 478.26
Torpid liver 573.9
Torsion
  accessory tube 620.5
  adnexa (female) 620.5
  aorta (congenital) 747.29
    acquired 447.1
  appendix epididymis 608.2

Torsion—*continued*
  bile duct 576.8
    with calculus, choledocholithiasis or
        stones—*see* Choledocholithiasis
    congenital 751.69
  bowel, colon, or intestine 560.2
  cervix (*see also* Malposition, uterus) 621.6
  duodenum 537.3
  dystonia—*see* Dystonia, torsion
  epididymis 608.2
    appendix 608.2
  fallopian tube 620.5
  gallbladder (*see also* Disease, gallbladder) 575.8
    congenital 751.69
  gastric 537.89
  hydatid of Morgagni (female) 620.5
  kidney (pedicle) 593.89
  Meckel's diverticulum (congenital) 751.0
  mesentery 560.2
  omentum 560.2
  organ or site, congenital NEC—*see* Anomaly,
      specified type NEC
  ovary (pedicle) 620.5
    congenital 752.0
  oviduct 620.5
  penis 607.89
    congenital 752.69
  renal 593.89
  spasm—*see* Dystonia, torsion
  spermatic cord 608.2
  spleen 289.59
  testicle, testis 608.2
  tibia 736.89
  umbilical cord—*see* Compression, umbilical
      cord
  uterus (*see also* Malposition, uterus) 621.6
Torticollis (intermittent) (spastic) 723.5
  congenital 754.1
    sternomastoid 754.1
  due to birth injury 767.8
  hysterical 300.11
  psychogenic 306.0
    specified as conversion reaction 300.11
  rheumatic 723.5
  rheumatoid 714.0
  spasmodic 333.83
  traumatic, current NEC 847.0
Tortuous
  artery 447.1
  fallopian tube 752.19
  organ or site, congenital NEC—*see* Distortion
  renal vessel, congenital 747.62
  retina vessel (congenital) 743.58
    acquired 362.17
  ureter 593.4
  urethra 599.84
  vein—*see* Varicose, vein
Torula, torular (infection) 117.5
  histolytica 117.5
  lung 117.5
Torulosis 117.5
Torus
  mandibularis 526.81
  palatinus 526.81
Touch, vitreous 997.99
Touraine's syndrome (hereditary
      osteo-onychodysplasia) 756.89
Touraine-Solente-Golé syndrome
      (acropachyderma) 757.39
Tourette's disease (motor-verbal tic) 307.23
Tower skull 756.0
  with exophthalmos 756.0

Toxemia 799.8
  with
    abortion—*see* Abortion, by type, with toxemia
  bacterial—*see* Septicemia
  biliary (*see also* Disease, biliary) 576.8
  burn—*see* Burn, by site
  congenital NEC 779.8
  eclamptic 642.6
    with pre-existing hypertension 642.7
  erysipelatous (*see also* Erysipelas) 035
  fatigue 799.8
  fetus or newborn NEC 779.8
  food (*see also* Poisoning, food) 005.9
  gastric 537.89
  gastrointestinal 558.2
  intestinal 558.2
  kidney (*see also* Disease, renal) 593.9
  lung 518.89
  malarial NEC (*see also* Malaria) 084.6
  maternal (of pregnancy), affecting fetus or
      newborn 760.0
  myocardial—*see* Myocarditis, toxic
  of pregnancy (mild) (pre-eclamptic) 642.4
    with
      convulsions 642.6
      pre-existing hypertension 642.7
    affecting fetus or newborn 760.0
    severe 642.5
  pre-eclamptic—*see* Toxemia, of pregnancy
  puerperal, postpartum—*see* Toxemia, of
      pregnancy
  pulmonary 518.89
  renal (*see also* Disease, renal) 593.9
  septic (*see also* Septicemia) 038.9
  small intestine 558.2
  staphylococcal 038.1
    due to food 005.0
  stasis 799.8
  stomach 537.89
  uremic (*see also* Uremia) 586
  urinary 586
Toxemica cerebropathia psychica
      (nonalcoholic) 294.0
  alcoholic 291.1
Toxic (poisoning)—*see also* condition
  from drug or poison—*see* Table of drugs and
      chemicals
  oil syndrome 710.5
  shock syndrome 040.89
  thyroid (gland) (*see also* Thyrotoxicosis) 242.9
Toxicemia —*see* Toxemia
Toxicity
  fava bean 282.2
  from drug or poison—*see* Table of drugs and
      chemicals
Toxicosis (*see also* Toxemia) 799.8
  capillary, hemorrhagic 287.0
Toxinfection 799.8
  gastrointestinal 558.2
Toxocariasis 128.0
Toxoplasma infection, generalized 130.9
Toxoplasmosis (acquired) 130.9
  with pneumonia 130.4
  congenital, active 771.2
  disseminated (multisystemic) 130.8
  maternal
    with suspected damage to fetus affecting
        management of pregnancy 655.4
    affecting fetus or newborn 760.2
      manifest toxoplasmosis in fetus or newborn
          771.2
  multiple sites 130.8

Toxoplasmosis—*continued*
  multisystemic disseminated 130.8
  specified site NEC 130.7
Trabeculation, bladder 596.8
Trachea —*see* condition
Tracheitis (acute) (catarrhal) (infantile)
  (membranous) (plastic) (pneumococcal)
  (septic) (suppurative) (viral) 464.10
  with
    bronchitis 490
      acute or subacute 466.0
      chronic 491.8
      tuberculosis—*see* Tuberculosis, pulmonary
    laryngitis (acute) 464.20
      with obstruction 464.21
      chronic 476.1
      tuberculous (*see also* Tuberculosis, larynx)
        012.3
    obstruction 464.11
  chronic 491.8
    with
      bronchitis (chronic) 491.8
      laryngitis (chronic) 476.1
    due to external agent—*see* Condition,
      respiratory, chronic, due to
  diphtheritic (membranous) 032.3
    due to external agent—*see* Inflammation,
      respiratory, upper, due to
  edematous 464.11
  influenzal 487.1
  streptococcal 034.0
  syphilitic 095.8
  tuberculous (*see also* Tuberculosis) 012.8
Trachelitis (nonvenereal) (*see also* Cervicitis)
  616.0
  trichomonal 131.09
Tracheobronchial —*see* condition
Tracheobronchitis (*see also* Bronchitis) 490
  acute or subacute 466.0
    with bronchospasm or obstruction 466.0
  chronic 491.8
  influenzal 487.1
  senile 491.8
Tracheobronchomegaly (congenital) 748.3
Tracheobronchopneumonitis —*see* Pneumonia,
  broncho
Tracheocele (external) (internal) 519.1
  congenital 748.3
Tracheomalacia 519.1
  congenital 748.3
Tracheopharyngitis (acute) 465.8
  chronic 478.9
    due to external agent—*see* Condition,
      respiratory, chronic, due to
    due to external agent—*see* Inflammation,
      respiratory, upper, due to
Tracheostenosis 519.1
  congenital 748.3
Tracheostomy
  attention to V55.0
  complication 519.0
  hemorrhage 519.0
  malfunctioning 519.0
  obstruction 519.0
  sepsis 519.0
  status V44.0
  stenosis 519.0
Trachoma, trachomatous 076.9
  active (stage) 076.1
  contraction of conjunctiva 076.1
  dubium 076.0

Trachoma, trachomatous—*continued*
  healed or late effect 139.1
  initial (stage) 076.0
  Türck's (chronic catarrhal laryngitis) 476.0
Trachyphonia 784.49
Training
  orthoptic V57.4
  orthotic V57.81
Train sickness 994.6
Trait
  hemoglobin
    abnormal NEC 282.7
      with thalassemia 282.4
    C (*see also* Disease, hemoglobin, C) 282.7
      with elliptocytosis 282.7
    S (Hb-S) 282.5
  Lepore 282.4
    with other abnormal hemoglobin NEC 282.4
  paranoid 301.0
  sickle-cell 282.5
    with
      elliptocytosis 282.5
      spherocytosis 282.5
Traits, paranoid 301.0
Tramp V60.0
Trance 780.09
  hysterical 300.13
Transaminasemia 790.4
Transfusion, blood
  donor V59.01
    stem cells V59.02
  incompatible 999.6
  reaction or complication—*see* Complications,
    transfusion
  syndrome
    fetomaternal 772.0
    twin-to-twin
      blood loss (donor twin) 772.0
      recipient twin 776.4
  without reported diagnosis V58.2
Transient —*see also* condition
  alteration of awareness 780.02
  blindness 368.12
  deafness (ischemic) 388.02
  global amnesia 437.7
  person (homeless) NEC V60.0
Transitional, lumbosacral joint of vertebra
  756.19
Translocation
  autosomes NEC 758.5
    13-15 758.1
    16-18 758.2
    21 or 22 758.0
    balanced in normal individual 758.4
    D_1 758.1
    E_3 758.2
    G 758.0
  balanced autosomal in normal individual 758.4
  chromosomes NEC 758.89
  Down's syndrome 758.0
Translucency, iris 364.53
Transmission of chemical substances through
  the placenta
  (affecting fetus or newborn) 760.70
  alcohol 760.71
  anti-infective agents 760.74
  cocaine 760.75
  "crack" 760.75
  diethylstilbestrol [DES] 760.76
  hallucinogenic agents 760.73
  medicinal agents NEC 760.79

Transmission—*continued*
  narcotics 760.72
  obstetric anesthetic or analgesic drug 763.5
  specified agent NEC 760.79
  suspected, affecting management of pregnancy
    655.5
Transplant (ed)
  bone V42.4
    marrow V42.8
  complication NEC—*see also* Complications,
    due to (presence of) any device, implant, or
    graft classified to 996.0-996.5 NEC
  bone marrow 996.85
  corneal graft NEC 996.79
    infection or inflammation 996.69
    reaction 996.51
    rejection 996.51
  organ (failure) (immune or nonimmune cause)
    (infection) (rejection) 996.80
    bone marrow 996.85
    heart 996.83
    intestines 996.89
    kidney 996.81
    liver 996.82
    lung 996.84
    pancreas 996.86
    specified NEC 996.89
  skin NEC 996.79
    infection or inflammation 996.69
    rejection 996.52
  cornea V42.5
  hair V50.0
  heart V42.1
    valve V42.2
  intestine V42.8
  kidney V42.0
  liver V42.7
  lung V42.6
  organ V42.9
    specified NEC V42.8
  pancreas V42.8
  skin V42.3
  tissue V42.9
    specified NEC V42.8
Transplants, ovarian, endometrial 617.1
Transposed —*see* Transposition
Transposition (congenital)—*see also*
    Malposition, congenital
  abdominal viscera 759.3
  aorta (dextra) 745.11
  appendix 751.5
  arterial trunk 745.10
  colon 751.5
  great vessels (complete) 745.10
    both originating from right ventricle 745.11
    corrected 745.12
    double outlet right ventricle 745.11
    incomplete 745.11
    partial 745.11
    specified type NEC 745.19
  heart 746.87
    with complete transposition of viscera 759.3
  intestine (large) (small) 751.5
  pulmonary veins 747.49
  reversed jejunal (for bypass) (status) V45.3
  stomach 750.7
    with general transposition of viscera 759.3
  teeth, tooth 524.3
  vessels (complete) 745.10
    partial 745.11
  viscera (abdominal) (thoracic) 759.3

Trans-sexualism 302.50
  with
    asexual history 302.51
    heterosexual history 302.53
    homosexual history 302.52
Transverse —*see also* condition
  arrest (deep), in labor 660.3
    affecting fetus or newborn 763.1
  lie 652.3
    before labor, affecting fetus or newborn 761.7
    causing obstructed labor 660.0
      affecting fetus or newborn 763.1
    during labor, affecting fetus or newborn 763.1
Transvestism, transvestitism (transvestic
    fetishism) 302.3
Trapped placenta (with hemorrhage) 666.0
  without hemorrhage 667.0
Trauma, traumatism (*see also* Injury, by site)
    959.9
  birth—*see* Birth, injury NEC
  causing hemorrhage of pregnancy or delivery
    641.8
  complicating
    abortion—*see* Abortion, by type, with damage
      to pelvic organs
    ectopic pregnancy (*see also* categories
      633.0-633.9) 639.2
    molar pregnancy (*see also* categories
      630-632) 639.2
  during delivery NEC 665.9
  following
    abortion 639.2
    ectopic or molar pregnancy 639.2
  maternal, during pregnancy, affecting fetus or
    newborn 760.5
  neuroma—*see* Injury, nerve, by site
  previous major, affecting management of
    pregnancy, childbirth, or puerperium V23.8
  psychic (current)—*see also* Reaction,
    adjustment
    previous (history) V15.49
  psychologic, previous (affecting health) V15.49
  transient paralysis—*see* Injury, nerve, by site
Traumatic —*see* condition
Treacher Collins' syndrome (incomplete facial
    dysostosis) 756.0
Treitz's hernia —*see* Hernia, Treitz's
Trematode infestation NEC 121.9
Trematodiasis NEC 121.9
Trembles 988.8
Trembling paralysis (*see also* Parkinsonism)
    332.0
Tremor 781.0
  essential (benign) 333.1
  familial 333.1
  flapping (liver) 572.8
  hereditary 333.1
  hysterical 300.11
  intention 333.1
  mercurial 985.0
  muscle 728.85
  Parkinson's (*see also* Parkinsonism) 332.0
  psychogenic 306.0
    specified as conversion reaction 300.11
  senilis 797
  specified type NEC 333.1
Trench
  fever 083.1
  foot 991.4
  mouth 101
  nephritis—*see* Nephritis, acute

Treponema pallidum infection (see also
    Syphilis) 097.9
Treponematosis 102.9
  due to
    T. pallidum—see Syphilis
    T. pertenue (yaws) (see also Yaws) 102.9
Triad
  Kartagener's 759.3
  Reiter's (complete) (incomplete) 099.3
  Saint's (see also Hernia, diaphragm) 553.3
Trichiasis 704.2
  cicatricial 704.2
  eyelid 374.05
    with entropion (see also Entropion) 374.00
Trichinella spiralis (infection) (infestation) 124
Trichinelliasis 124
Trichinellosis 124
Trichiniasis 124
Trichinosis 124
Trichobezoar 938
  intestine 936
  stomach 935.2
Trichocephaliasis 127.3
Trichocephalosis 127.3
Trichocephalus infestation 127.3
Trichoclasis 704.2
Trichoepithelioma (M8100/0)—see also
    Neoplasm, skin, benign
  breast 217
  genital organ NEC—see Neoplasm, by site,
    benign
  malignant (M8100/3)—see Neoplasm, skin,
    malignant
Trichofolliculoma (M8101/0)—see Neoplasm,
    skin, benign
Tricholemmoma (M8102/0)—see Neoplasm,
    skin, benign
Trichomatosis 704.2
Trichomoniasis 131.9
  bladder 131.09
  cervix 131.09
  intestinal 007.3
  prostate 131.03
  seminal vesicle 131.09
  specified site NEC 131.8
  urethra 131.02
  urogenitalis 131.00
  vagina 131.01
  vulva 131.01
  vulvovaginal 131.01
Trichomycosis 039.0
  axillaris 039.0
  nodosa 111.2
  nodularis 111.2
  rubra 039.0
Trichonocardiosis (axillaris) (palmellina) 039.0
Trichonodosis 704.2
Trichophytid, trichophyton infection (see also
    Dermatophytosis) 110.9
Trichophytide —see Dermatophytosis
Trichophytobezoar 938
  intestine 936
  stomach 935.2
Trichophytosis —see Dermatophytosis
Trichoptilosis 704.2
Trichorrhexis (nodosa) 704.2
Trichosporosis nodosa 111.2
Trichostasis spinulosa (congenital) 757.4
Trichostrongyliasis (small intestine) 127.6
Trichostrongylosis 127.6
Trichostrongylus (instabilis) infection 127.6
Trichotillomania 312.39

Trichromat, anomalous (congenital) 368.59
Trichromatopsia, anomalous (congenital)
    368.59
Trichuriasis 127.3
Trichuris trichiuria (any site) (infection)
    (infestation) 127.3
Tricuspid (valve)—see condition
Trifid —see also Accessory
  kidney (pelvis) 753.3
  tongue 750.13
Trigeminal neuralgia (see also Neuralgia,
    trigeminal) 350.1
Trigeminoencephaloangiomatosis 759.6
Trigeminy 427.89
  postoperative 997.1
Trigger finger (acquired) 727.03
  congenital 756.89
Trigonitis (bladder) (chronic)
    (pseudomembranous) 595.3
  tuberculous (see also Tuberculosis) 016.1
Trigonocephaly 756.0
Trihexosidosis 272.7
Trilobate placenta —see Placenta, abnormal
Trilocular heart 745.8
Tripartita placenta —see Placenta, abnormal
Triple —see also Accessory
  kidneys 753.3
  uteri 752.2
  X female 758.81
Triplegia 344.89
  congenital or infantile 343.8
Triplet
  affected by maternal complications of
    pregnancy 761.5
  healthy liveborn—see Newborn, multiple
  pregnancy (complicating delivery) NEC 651.1
    with fetal loss and retention of one or more
      fetus(es) 651.4
Triplex placenta —see Placenta, abnormal
Triplication —see Accessory
Trismus 781.0
  neonatorum 771.3
  newborn 771.3
Trisomy (syndrome) NEC 758.5
  13 (partial) 758.1
  16-18 758.2
  18 (partial) 758.2
  21 (partial) 758.0
  22 758.0
  autosomes NEC 758.5
  D_1 758.1
  E_3 758.2
  G (group) 758.0
  group D_1 758.1
  group E 758.2
  group G 758.0
Tritanomaly 368.53
Tritanopia 368.53
Troisier-Hanot-Chauffard syndrome (bronze
    diabetes) 275.0
Trombidiosis 133.8
Trophedema (hereditary) 757.0
  congenital 757.0
Trophoblastic disease (see also Hydatidiform
    mole) 630
  previous, affecting management of pregnancy
    V23.1
Tropholymphedema 757.0

Trophoneurosis NEC 356.9
  arm NEC 354.9
  disseminated 710.1
  facial 349.89
  leg NEC 355.8
  lower extremity NEC 355.8
  upper extremity NEC 354.9
Tropical —*see also* condition
  maceration feet (syndrome) 991.4
  wet foot (syndrome) 991.4
Trouble —*see also* Disease
  bowel 569.9
  heart—*see* Disease, heart
  intestine 569.9
  kidney (*see also* Disease, renal) 593.9
  nervous 799.2
  sinus (*see also* Sinusitis) 473.9
Trousseau's syndrome (thrombophlebitis
  migrans) 453.1
Truancy, childhood —*see also* Disturbance,
  conduct
  socialized 312.2
  undersocialized, unsocialized 312.1
Truncus
  arteriosus (persistent) 745.0
  common 745.0
  communis 745.0
Trunk —*see* condition
Trychophytide —*see* Dermatophytosis
Trypanosoma infestation —*see*
  Trypanosomiasis
Trypanosomiasis 086.9
  with meningoencephalitis 086.9 *[323.2]*
  African 086.5
    due to Trypanosoma 086.5
      gambiense 086.3
      rhodesiense 086.4
  American 086.2
    with
      heart involvement 086.0
      other organ involvement 086.1
    without mention of organ involvement 086.2
  Brazilian—*see* Trypanosomiasis, American
  Chagas'—*see* Trypanosomiasis, American
  due to Trypanosoma
    cruzi—*see* Trypanosomiasis, American
    gambiense 086.3
    rhodesiense 086.4
  gambiensis, Gambian 086.3
  North American—*see* Trypanosomiasis,
    American
  rhodesiensis, Rhodesian 086.4
  South American—*see* Trypanosomiasis,
    American
T-shaped incisors 520.2
Tsutsugamushi fever 081.2
Tube, tubal, tubular —*see also* condition
  ligation, admission for V25.2
Tubercle —*see also* Tuberculosis
  brain, solitary 013.2
  Darwin's 744.29
  epithelioid noncaseating 135
  Ghon, primary infection 010.0
Tuberculid, tuberculide (indurating) (lichenoid)
  (miliary) (papulonecrotic) (primary) (skin)
  (subcutaneous) (*see also* Tuberculosis) 017.0
Tuberculoma —*see also* Tuberculosis
  brain (any part) 013.2
  meninges (cerebral) (spinal) 013.1
  spinal cord 013.4

Tuberculosis, tubercular, tuberculous
  (calcification) (calcified) (caseous)
  (chromogenic acid-fast bacilli) (congenital)
  (degeneration) (disease) (fibrocaseous)
  (fistula) (gangrene) (interstitial) (isolated
  circumscribed lesions) (necrosis)
  (parenchymatous) (ulcerative) 011.9

> Note—Use the following fifth-digit
> subclassification with categories 010-018:
>
> 0 *unspecified*
> 1 *bacteriological or histological examination
>   not done*
> 2 *bacteriological or histological examination
>   unknown (at present)*
> 3 *tubercle bacilli found (in sputum) by
>   microscopy*
> 4 *tubercle bacilli not found (in sputum) by
>   microscopy, but found by bacterial culture*
> 5 *tubercle bacilli not found by bacteriological
>   examination, but tuberculosis confirmed
>   histologically*
> 6 *tubercle bacilli not found by bacteriological or
>   histological examination, but tuberculosis
>   confirmed by other methods [inoculation of
>   animals]*
>
> For tuberculous conditions specified as late
> effects or sequelae, see category 137.

  abdomen 014.8
    lymph gland 014.8
  abscess 011.9
    arm 017.9
    bone (*see also* Osteomyelitis, due to,
      tuberculosis) 015.9 *[730.8]*
      hip 015.1 *[730.85]*
      knee 015.2 *[730.86]*
      sacrum 015.0 *[730.88]*
      specified site NEC 015.7 *[730.88]*
      spinal 015.0 *[730.88]*
      vertebra 015.0 *[730.88]*
    brain 013.3
    breast 017.9
    Cowper's gland 016.5
    dura (mater) 013.8
      brain 013.3
      spinal cord 013.5
    epidural 013.8
      brain 013.3
      spinal cord 013.5
    frontal sinus—*see* Tuberculosis, sinus
    genital organs NEC 016.9
      female 016.7
      male 016.5
    genitourinary NEC 016.9
    gland (lymphatic)—*see* Tuberculosis, lymph
      gland
    hip 015.1
    iliopsoas 015.0 *[730.88]*
    intestine 014.8
    ischiorectal 014.8
    joint 015.9
      hip 015.1
      knee 015.2
      specified joint NEC 015.8
      vertebral 015.0 *[730.88]*
    kidney 016.0 *[590.81]*
    knee 015.2
    lumbar 015.0 *[730.88]*

Tuberculosis, tubercular, tuberculous—*cont.*
  lung 011.2
    primary, progressive 010.8
  meninges (cerebral) (spinal) 013.0
  pelvic 016.9
    female 016.7
    male 016.5
  perianal 014.8
    fistula 014.8
  perinephritic 016.0 *[590.81]*
  perineum 017.9
  perirectal 014.8
  psoas 015.0 *[730.88]*
  rectum 014.8
  retropharyngeal 012.8
  sacrum 015.0 *[730.88]*
  scrofulous 017.2
  scrotum 016.5
  skin 017.0
    primary 017.0
  spinal cord 013.5
  spine or vertebra (column) 015.0 *[730.88]*
  strumous 017.2
  subdiaphragmatic 014.8
  testis 016.5
  thigh 017.9
  urinary 016.3
    kidney 016.0 *[590.81]*
  uterus 016.7
 accessory sinus—*see* Tuberculosis, sinus
 Addison's disease 017.6
 adenitis (*see also* Tuberculosis, lymph gland)
   017.2
 adenoids 012.8
 adenopathy (*see also* Tuberculosis, lymph
   gland) 017.2
  tracheobronchial 012.1
    primary progressive 010.8
 adherent pericardium 017.9 *[420.0]*
 adnexa (uteri) 016.7
 adrenal (capsule) (gland) 017.6
 air passage NEC 012.8
 alimentary canal 014.8
 anemia 017.9
 ankle (joint) 015.8
  bone 015.5 *[730.87]*
 anus 014.8
 apex (*see also* Tuberculosis, pulmonary) 011.9
 apical (*see also* Tuberculosis, pulmonary) 011.9
 appendicitis 014.8
 appendix 014.8
 arachnoid 013.0
 artery 017.9
 arthritis (chronic) (synovial) 015.9 *[711.40]*
  ankle 015.8 *[730.87]*
  hip 015.1 *[711.45]*
  knee 015.2 *[711.46]*
  specified site NEC 015.8 *[711.48]*
  spine or vertebra (column) 015.0 *[720.81]*
  wrist 015.8 *[730.83]*
 articular—*see* Tuberculosis, joint
 ascites 014.0
 asthma (*see also* Tuberculosis, pulmonary)
   011.9
 axilla, axillary 017.2
  gland 017.2
 bilateral (*see also* Tuberculosis, pulmonary)
   011.9
 bladder 016.1

Tuberculosis, tubercular, tuberculous—*cont.*
  bone (*see also* Osteomyelitis, due to,
    tuberculosis) 015.9 *[730.8]*
  hip 015.1 *[730.85]*
  knee 015.2 *[730.86]*
  limb NEC 015.5 *[730.88]*
  sacrum 015.0 *[730.88]*
  specified site NEC 015.7 *[730.88]*
  spinal or vertebral column 015.0 *[730.88]*
 bowel 014.8
  miliary 018.9
 brain 013.2
 breast 017.9
 broad ligament 016.7
 bronchi, bronchial, bronchus 011.3
  ectasia, ectasis 011.5
  fistula 011.3
    primary, progressive 010.8
  gland 012.1
    primary, progressive 010.8
  isolated 012.2
  lymph gland or node 012.1
    primary, progressive 010.8
 bronchiectasis 011.5
 bronchitis 011.3
 bronchopleural 012.0
 bronchopneumonia, bronchopneumonic 011.6
 bronchorrhagia 011.3
 bronchotracheal 011.3
  isolated 012.2
 bronchus—*see* Tuberculosis, bronchi
 bronze disease (Addison's) 017.6
 buccal cavity 017.9
 bulbourethral gland 016.5
 bursa (*see also* Tuberculosis, joint) 015.9
 cachexia NEC (*see also* Tuberculosis,
   pulmonary) 011.9
 cardiomyopathy 017.9 *[425.8]*
 caries (*see also* Tuberculosis, bone) 015.9
   [730.8]
 cartilage (*see also* Tuberculosis, bone) 015.9
   [730.8]
  intervertebral 015.0 *[730.88]*
 catarrhal (*see also* Tuberculosis, pulmonary)
   011.9
 cecum 014.8
 cellular tissue (primary) 017.0
 cellulitis (primary) 017.0
 central nervous system 013.9
  specified site NEC 013.8
 cerebellum (current) 013.2
 cerebral (current) 013.2
  meninges 013.0
 cerebrospinal 013.6
  meninges 013.0
 cerebrum (current) 013.2
 cervical 017.2
  gland 017.2
  lymph nodes 017.2
 cervicitis (uteri) 016.7
 cervix 016.7
 chest (*see also* Tuberculosis, pulmonary) 011.9
 childhood type or first infection 010.0
 choroid 017.3 *[363.13]*
 choroiditis 017.3 *[363.13]*
 ciliary body 017.3 *[364.11]*
 colitis 014.8
 colliers' 011.4
 colliquativa (primary) 017.0
 colon 014.8
  ulceration 014.8

Tuberculosis, tubercular, tuberculous—*cont.*
  complex, primary 010.0
  complicating pregnancy, childbirth, or
      puerperium 647.3
    affecting fetus or newborn 760.2
  congenital 771.2
  conjunctiva 017.3 *[370.31]*
  connective tissue 017.9
    bone—*see* Tuberculosis, bone
  contact V01.1
  converter (tuberculin skin test) (without disease)
      795.5
  cornea (ulcer) 017.3 *[370.31]*
  Cowper's gland 016.5
  coxae 015.1 *[730.85]*
  coxalgia 015.1 *[730.85]*
  cul-de-sac of Douglas 014.8
  curvature, spine 015.0 *[737.40]*
  cutis (colliquativa) (primary) 017.0
  cyst, ovary 016.6
  cystitis 016.1
  dacryocystitis 017.3 *[375.32]*
  dactylitis 015.5
  diarrhea 014.8
  diffuse (*see also* Tuberculosis, miliary) 018.9
    lung—*see* Tuberculosis, pulmonary
    meninges 013.0
  digestive tract 014.8
  disseminated (*see also* Tuberculosis, miliary)
      018.9
    meninges 013.0
  duodenum 014.8
  dura (mater) 013.9
    abscess 013.8
      cerebral 013.3
      spinal 013.5
  dysentery 014.8
  ear (inner) (middle) 017.4
    bone 015.6
    external (primary) 017.0
    skin (primary) 017.0
  elbow 015.8
  emphysema—*see* Tuberculosis, pulmonary
  empyema 012.0
  encephalitis 013.6
  endarteritis 017.9
  endocarditis (any valve) 017.9 *[424.91]*
  endocardium (any valve) 017.9 *[424.91]*
  endocrine glands NEC 017.9
  endometrium 016.7
  enteric, enterica 014.8
  enteritis 014.8
  enterocolitis 014.8
  epididymis 016.4
  epididymitis 016.4
  epidural abscess 013.8
    brain 013.3
    spinal cord 013.5
  epiglottis 012.3
  episcleritis 017.3 *[379.00]*
  erythema (induratum) (nodosum) (primary)
      017.1
  esophagus 017.8
  Eustachian tube 017.4
  exposure to V01.1
  exudative 012.0
    primary, progressive 010.1
  eye 017.3
    glaucoma 017.3 *[365.62]*
  eyelid (primary) 017.0
    lupus 017.0 *[373.4]*

Tuberculosis, tubercular, tuberculous—*cont.*
  fallopian tube 016.6
  fascia 017.9
  fauces 012.8
  finger 017.9
  first infection 010.0
  fistula, perirectal 014.8
  Florida 011.6
  foot 017.9
  funnel pelvis 137.3
  gallbladder 017.9
  galloping (*see also* Tuberculosis, pulmonary)
      011.9
  ganglionic 015.9
  gastritis 017.9
  gastrocolic fistula 014.8
  gastroenteritis 014.8
  gastrointestinal tract 014.8
  general, generalized 018.9
    acute 018.0
    chronic 018.8
  genital organs NEC 016.9
    female 016.7
    male 016.5
  genitourinary NEC 016.9
  genu 015.2
  glandulae suprarenalis 017.6
  glandular, general 017.2
  glottis 012.3
  grinders' 011.4
  groin 017.2
  gum 017.9
  hand 017.9
  heart 017.9 *[425.8]*
  hematogenous—*see* Tuberculosis, miliary
  hemoptysis (*see also* Tuberculosis, pulmonary)
      011.9
  hemorrhage NEC (*see also* Tuberculosis,
      pulmonary) 011.9
  hemothorax 012.0
  hepatitis 017.9
  hilar lymph nodes 012.1
    primary, progressive 010.8
  hip (disease) (joint) 015.1
    bone 015.1 *[730.85]*
  hydrocephalus 013.8
  hydropneumothorax 012.0
  hydrothorax 012.0
  hypoadrenalism 017.6
  hypopharynx 012.8
  ileocecal (hyperplastic) 014.8
  ileocolitis 014.8
  ileum 014.8
  iliac spine (superior) 015.0 *[730.88]*
  incipient NEC (*see also* Tuberculosis,
      pulmonary) 011.9
  indurativa (primary) 017.1
  infantile 010.0
  infection NEC 011.9
    without clinical manifestation 010.0
  infraclavicular gland 017.2
  inguinal gland 017.2
  inguinalis 017.2
  intestine (any part) 014.8
  iris 017.3 *[364.11]*
  iritis 017.3 *[364.11]*
  ischiorectal 014.8
  jaw 015.7 *[730.88]*
  jejunum 014.8

Tuberculosis, tubercular, tuberculous—*cont.*
joint 015.9
  hip 015.1
  knee 015.2
  specified site NEC 015.8
  vertebral 015.0 *[730.88]*
keratitis 017.3 *[370.31]*
  interstitial 017.3 *[370.59]*
keratoconjunctivitis 017.3 *[370.31]*
kidney 016.0
knee (joint) 015.2
kyphoscoliosis 015.0 *[737.43]*
kyphosis 015.0 *[737.41]*
lacrimal apparatus, gland 017.3
laryngitis 012.3
larynx 012.3
leptomeninges, leptomeningitis (cerebral)
  (spinal) 013.0
lichenoides (primary) 017.0
linguae 017.9
lip 017.9
liver 017.9
lordosis 015.0 *[737.42]*
lung—*see* Tuberculosis, pulmonary
luposa 017.0
  eyelid 017.0 *[373.4]*
lymphadenitis—*see* Tuberculosis, lymph gland
lymphangitis—*see* Tuberculosis, lymph gland
lymphatic (gland) (vessel)—*see* Tuberculosis,
  lymph gland
lymph gland or node (peripheral) 017.2
  abdomen 014.8
  bronchial 012.1
    primary, progressive 010.8
  cervical 017.2
  hilar 012.1
    primary, progressive 010.8
  intrathoracic 012.1
    primary, progressive 010.8
  mediastinal 012.1
    primary, progressive 010.8
  mesenteric 014.8
  peripheral 017.2
  retroperitoneal 014.8
  tracheobronchial 012.1
    primary, progressive 010.8
malignant NEC (*see also* Tuberculosis,
  pulmonary) 011.9
mammary gland 017.9
marasmus NEC (*see also* Tuberculosis,
  pulmonary) 011.9
mastoiditis 015.6
maternal, affecting fetus or newborn 760.2
mediastinal (lymph) gland or node 012.1
  primary, progressive 010.8
mediastinitis 012.8
  primary, progressive 010.8
mediastinopericarditis 017.9 *[420.0]*
mediastinum 012.8
  primary, progressive 010.8
medulla 013.9
  brain 013.2
  spinal cord 013.4
melanosis, Addisonian 017.6
membrane, brain 013.0
meninges (cerebral) (spinal) 013.0
meningitis (basilar) (brain) (cerebral)
  (cerebrospinal) (spinal) 013.0
meningoencephalitis 013.0
mesentery, mesenteric 014.8
  lymph gland or node 014.8

Tuberculosis, tubercular, tuberculous—*cont.*
miliary (any site) 018.9
  acute 018.0
  chronic 018.8
  specified type NEC 018.8
millstone makers' 011.4
miners' 011.4
moulders' 011.4
mouth 017.9
multiple 018.9
  acute 018.0
  chronic 018.8
muscle 017.9
myelitis 013.6
myocarditis 017.9 *[422.0]*
myocardium 017.9 *[422.0]*
nasal (passage) (sinus) 012.8
nasopharynx 012.8
neck gland 017.2
nephritis 016.0 *[583.81]*
nerve 017.9
nose (septum) 012.8
ocular 017.3
old NEC 137.0
  without residuals V12.01
omentum 014.8
oophoritis (acute) (chronic) 016.6
optic 017.3 *[377.39]*
  nerve trunk 017.3 *[377.39]*
  papilla, papillae 017.3 *[377.39]*
orbit 017.3
orchitis 016.5 *[608.81]*
organ, specified NEC 017.9
orificialis (primary) 017.0
osseous (*see also* Tuberculosis, bone) 015.9
  [730.8]
osteitis (*see also* Tuberculosis, bone) 015.9
  [730.8]
osteomyelitis (*see also* Tuberculosis, bone)
  015.9 *[730.8]*
otitis (media) 017.4
ovaritis (acute) (chronic) 016.6
ovary (acute) (chronic) 016.6
oviducts (acute) (chronic) 016.6
pachymeningitis 013.0
palate (soft) 017.9
pancreas 017.9
papulonecrotic (primary) 017.0
parathyroid glands 017.9
paronychia (primary) 017.0
parotid gland or region 017.9
pelvic organ NEC 016.9
  female 016.7
  male 016.5
pelvis (bony) 015.7 *[730.85]*
penis 016.5
peribronchitis 011.3
pericarditis 017.9 *[420.0]*
pericardium 017.9 *[420.0]*
perichondritis, larynx 012.3
perineum 017.9
periostitis (*see also* Tuberculosis, bone) 015.9
  [730.8]
periphlebitis 017.9
  eye vessel 017.3 *[362.18]*
  retina 017.3 *[362.18]*
perirectal fistula 014.8
peritoneal gland 014.8
peritoneum 014.0
peritonitis 014.0

Tuberculosis, tubercular, tuberculous—*cont.*
pernicious NEC (*see also* Tuberculosis,
pulmonary) 011.9
pharyngitis 012.8
pharynx 012.8
phlyctenulosis (conjunctiva) 017.3 *[370.31]*
phthisis NEC (*see also* Tuberculosis,
pulmonary) 011.9
pituitary gland 017.9
placenta 016.7
pleura, pleural, pleurisy, pleuritis (fibrinous)
(obliterative) (purulent) (simple plastic)
(with effusion) 012.0
primary, progressive 010.1
pneumonia, pneumonic 011.6
pneumothorax 011.7
polyserositis 018.9
acute 018.0
chronic 018.8
potters' 011.4
prepuce 016.5
primary 010.9
complex 010.0
complicated 010.8
with pleurisy or effusion 010.1
progressive 010.8
with pleurisy or effusion 010.1
skin 017.0
proctitis 014.8
prostate 016.5 *[601.4]*
prostatitis 016.5 *[601.4]*
pulmonaris (*see also* Tuberculosis, pulmonary)
011.9
pulmonary (artery) (incipient) (malignant)
(multiple round foci) (pernicious)
(reinfection stage) 011.9
cavitated or with cavitation 011.2
primary, progressive 010.8
childhood type or first infection 010.0
chromogenic acid-fast bacilli 795.3
fibrosis or fibrotic 011.4
infiltrative 011.0
primary, progressive 010.9
nodular 011.1
specified NEC 011.8
sputum positive only 795.3
status following surgical collapse of lung
NEC 011.9
pyelitis 016.0 *[590.81]*
pyelonephritis 016.0 *[590.81]*
pyemia—*see* Tuberculosis, miliary
pyonephrosis 016.0
pyopneumothorax 012.0
pyothorax 012.0
rectum (with abscess) 014.8
fistula 014.8
reinfection stage (*see also* Tuberculosis,
pulmonary) 011.9
renal 016.0
renis 016.0
reproductive organ 016.7
respiratory NEC (*see also* Tuberculosis,
pulmonary) 011.9
specified site NEC 012.8
retina 017.3 *[363.13]*
retroperitoneal (lymph gland or node) 014.8
gland 014.8
retropharyngeal abscess 012.8
rheumatism 015.9
rhinitis 012.8
sacroiliac (joint) 015.8

Tuberculosis, tubercular, tuberculous—*cont.*
sacrum 015.0 *[730.88]*
salivary gland 017.9
salpingitis (acute) (chronic) 016.6
sandblasters' 011.4
sclera 017.3 *[379.09]*
scoliosis 015.0 *[737.43]*
scrofulous 017.2
scrotum 016.5
seminal tract or vesicle 016.5 *[608.81]*
senile NEC (*see also* Tuberculosis, pulmonary)
011.9
septic NEC (*see also* Tuberculosis, miliary)
018.9
shoulder 015.8
blade 015.7 *[730.8]*
sigmoid 014.8
sinus (accessory) (nasal) 012.8
bone 015.7 *[730.88]*
epididymis 016.4
skeletal NEC (*see also* Osteomyelitis, due to
tuberculosis) 015.9 *[730.8]*
skin (any site) (primary) 017.0
small intestine 014.8
soft palate 017.9
spermatic cord 016.5
spinal
column 015.0 *[730.88]*
cord 013.4
disease 015.0 *[730.88]*
medulla 013.4
membrane 013.0
meninges 013.0
spine 015.0 *[730.88]*
spleen 017.7
splenitis 017.7
spondylitis 015.0 *[720.81]*
spontaneous pneumothorax—*see* Tuberculosis,
pulmonary
sternoclavicular joint 015.8
stomach 017.9
stonemasons' 011.4
struma 017.2
subcutaneous tissue (cellular) (primary) 017.0
subcutis (primary) 017.0
subdeltoid bursa 017.9
submaxillary 017.9
region 017.9
supraclavicular gland 017.2
suprarenal (capsule) (gland) 017.6
swelling, joint (*see also* Tuberculosis, joint)
015.9
symphysis pubis 015.7 *[730.88]*
synovitis 015.9 *[727.01]*
hip 015.1 *[727.01]*
knee 015.2 *[727.01]*
specified site NEC 015.8 *[727.01]*
spine or vertebra 015.0 *[727.01]*
systemic—*see* Tuberculosis, miliary
tarsitis (eyelid) 017.0 *[373.4]*
ankle (bone) 015.5 *[730.87]*
tendon (sheath)—*see* Tuberculosis,
tenosynovitis
tenosynovitis 015.9 *[727.01]*
hip 015.1 *[727.01]*
knee 015.2 *[727.01]*
specified site NEC 015.8 *[727.01]*
spine or vertebra 015.0 *[727.01]*
testis 016.5 *[608.81]*
throat 012.8
thymus gland 017.9

Tuberculosis, tubercular, tuberculous—*cont.*
thyroid gland 017.5
toe 017.9
tongue 017.9
tonsil (lingual) 012.8
tonsillitis 012.8
trachea, tracheal 012.8
  gland 012.1
    primary, progressive 010.8
  isolated 012.2
tracheobronchial 011.3
  glandular 012.1
    primary, progressive 010.8
  isolated 012.2
  lymph gland or node 012.1
    primary, progressive 010.8
tubal 016.6
tunica vaginalis 016.5
typhlitis 014.8
ulcer (primary) (skin) 017.0
  bowel or intestine 014.8
  specified site NEC—*see* Tuberculosis, by site
unspecified site—*see* Tuberculosis, pulmonary
ureter 016.2
urethra, urethral 016.3
urinary organ or tract 016.3
  kidney 016.0
uterus 016.7
uveal tract 017.3 *[363.13]*
uvula 017.9
vaccination, prophylactic (against) V03.2
vagina 016.7
vas deferens 016.5
vein 017.9
verruca (primary) 017.0
verrucosa (cutis) (primary) 017.0
vertebra (column) 015.0 *[730.88]*
vesiculitis 016.5 *[608.81]*
viscera NEC 014.8
vulva 016.7 *[616.51]*
wrist (joint) 015.8
  bone 015.5 *[730.83]*
Tuberculum
auriculae 744.29
occlusal 520.2
paramolare 520.2
Tuberous sclerosis (brain) 759.5
Tubo-ovarian —*see* condition
Tuboplasty, after previous sterilization V26.0
Tubotympanitis 381.10
Tularemia 021.9
with
  conjunctivitis 021.3
  pneumonia 021.2
bronchopneumonic 021.2
conjunctivitis 021.3
cryptogenic 021.1
disseminated 021.8
enteric 021.1
generalized 021.8
glandular 021.8
intestinal 021.1
oculoglandular 021.3
ophthalmic 021.3
pneumonia 021.2
pulmonary 021.2
specified NEC 021.8
typhoidal 021.1
ulceroglandular 021.0
vaccination, prophylactic (against) V03.4
Tularensis conjunctivitis 021.3

Tumefaction —*see also* Swelling
liver (*see also* Hypertrophy, liver) 789.1
Tumor (M8000/1)—*see also* Neoplasm, by site,
  unspecified nature
Abrikossov's (M9580/0)—*see also* Neoplasm,
  connective tissue, benign
  malignant (M9580/3)—*see* Neoplasm,
    connective tissue, malignant
acinar cell (M8550/1)—*see* Neoplasm, by site,
  uncertain behavior
acinic cell (M8550/1)—*see* Neoplasm, by site,
  uncertain behavior
adenomatoid (M9054/0)—*see also* Neoplasm,
  by site, benign
  odontogenic (M9300/0) 213.1
  upper jaw (bone) 213.0
adnexal (skin) (M8390/0)—*see* Neoplasm, skin,
  benign
adrenal
  cortical (benign) (M8370/0) 227.0
  malignant (M8370/3) 194.0
  rest (M8671/0)—*see* Neoplasm, by site,
    benign
alpha cell (M8152/0)
  malignant (M8152/3)
    pancreas 157.4
    specified site NEC—*see* Neoplasm, by site,
      malignant
    unspecified site 157.4
  pancreas 211.7
  specified site NEC—*see* Neoplasm, by site,
    benign
  unspecified site 211.7
aneurysmal (*see also* Aneurysm) 442.9
aortic body (M8691/1) 237.3
  malignant (M8691/3) 194.6
argentaffin (M8241/1)—*see* Neoplasm, by site,
  uncertain behavior
basal cell (M8090/1)—*see also* Neoplasm, skin,
  uncertain behavior
benign (M8000/0)—*see* Neoplasm, by site,
  benign
beta cell (M8151/0)
  malignant (M8151/3)
    pancreas 157.4
    specified site—*see* Neoplasm, by site,
      malignant
    unspecified site 157.4
  pancreas 211.7
  specified site NEC—*see* Neoplasm, by site,
    benign
  unspecified site 211.7
blood—*see* Hematoma
brenner (M9000/0) 220
  borderline malignancy (M9000/1) 236.2
  malignant (M9000/3) 183.0
  proliferating (M9000/1) 236.2
Brooke's (M8100/0)—*see* Neoplasm, skin,
  benign
brown fat (M8880/0)—*see* Lipoma, by site
Burkitt's (M9750/3) 200.2
calcifying epithelial odontogenic (M9340/0)
  213.1
  upper jaw (bone) 213.0
carcinoid (M8240/1)—*see* Carcinoid
carotid body (M8692/1) 237.3
  malignant (M8692/3) 194.5
Castleman's (mediastinal lymph node
  hyperplasia) 785.6
cells (M8001/1)—*see also* Neoplasm, by site,
  unspecified nature

Tumor—*continued*

benign (M8001/0)—*see* Neoplasm, by site, benign

malignant (M8001/3)—*see* Neoplasm, by site, malignant

uncertain whether benign or malignant (M8001/1)—*see* Neoplasm, by site, uncertain nature

cervix

in pregnancy or childbirth 654.6

affecting fetus or newborn 763.8

causing obstructed labor 660.2

affecting fetus or newborn 763.1

chondromatous giant cell (M9230/0)—*see* Neoplasm, bone, benign

chromaffin (M8700/0)—*see also* Neoplasm, by site, benign

malignant (M8700/3)—*see* Neoplasm, by site, malignant

Cock's peculiar 706.2

Codman's (benign chondroblastoma) (M9230/0)—*see* Neoplasm, bone, benign

dentigerous, mixed (M9282/0) 213.1

upper jaw (bone) 213.0

dermoid (M9084/0)—*see* Neoplasm, by site, benign

with malignant transformation (M9084/3) 183.0

desmoid (extra-abdominal) (M8821/1)—*see also* Neoplasm, connective tissue, uncertain behavior

abdominal (M8822/1)—*see* Neoplasm, connective tissue, uncertain behavior

embryonal (mixed) (M9080/1)—*see also* Neoplasm, by site, uncertain behavior

liver (M9080/3) 155.0

endodermal sinus (M9071/3)

specified site—*see* Neoplasm, by site, malignant

unspecified site

female 183.0

male 186.9

epithelial

benign (M8010/0)—*see* Neoplasm, by site, benign

malignant (M8010/3)—*see* Neoplasm, by site, malignant

Ewing's (M9260/3)—*see* Neoplasm, bone, malignant

fatty—*see* Lipoma

fetal, causing disproportion 653.7

causing obstructed labor 660.1

fibroid (M8890/0)—*see* Leiomyoma

G cell (M8153/1)

malignant (M8153/3)

pancreas 157.4

specified site NEC—*see* Neoplasm, by site, malignant

unspecified site 157.4

specified site—*see* Neoplasm, by site, uncertain behavior

unspecified site 235.5

giant cell (type) (M8003/1)—*see also* Neoplasm, by site, unspecified nature

bone (M9250/1) 238.0

malignant (M9250/3)—*see* Neoplasm, bone, malignant

chondromatous (M9230/0)—*see* Neoplasm, bone, benign

malignant (M8003/3)—*see* Neoplasm, by site, malignant

Tumor—*continued*

peripheral (gingiva) 523.8

soft parts (M9251/1)—*see also* Neoplasm, connective tissue, uncertain behavior

malignant (M9251/3)—*see* Neoplasm, connective tissue, malignant

tendon sheath 727.02

glomus (M8711/0)—*see also* Hemangioma, by site

jugulare (M8690/1) 237.3

malignant (M8690/3) 194.6

gonadal stromal (M8590/1)—*see* Neoplasm, by site, uncertain behavior

granular cell (M9580/0)—*see also* Neoplasm, connective tissue, benign

malignant (M9580/3)—*see* Neoplasm, connective tissue, malignant

granulosa cell (M8620/1) 236.2

malignant (M8620/3) 183.0

granulosa cell-theca cell (M8621/1) 236.2

malignant (M8621/3) 183.0

Grawitz's (hypernephroma) (M8312/3) 189.0

hazard-crile (M8350/3) 193

hemorrhoidal—*see* Hemorrhoids

hilar cell (M8660/0) 220

hurthle cell (benign) (M8290/0) 226

malignant (M8290/3) 193

hydatid (*see also* Echinococcus) 122.9

hypernephroid (M8311/1)—*see also* Neoplasm, by site, uncertain behavior

interstitial cell (M8650/1)—*see also* Neoplasm, by site, uncertain behavior

benign (M8650/0)—*see* Neoplasm, by site, benign

malignant (M8650/3)—*see* Neoplasm, by site, malignant

islet cell (M8150/0)

malignant (M8150/3)

pancreas 157.4

specified site—*see* Neoplasm, by site, malignant

unspecified site 157.4

pancreas 211.7

specified site NEC—*see* Neoplasm, by site, benign

unspecified site 211.7

juxtaglomerular (M8361/1) 236.91

Krukenberg's (M8490/6) 198.6

Leydig cell (M8650/1)

benign (M8650/0)

specified site—*see* Neoplasm, by site, benign

unspecified site

female 220

male 220.0

malignant (M8650/3)

specified site—*see* Neoplasm, by site, malignant

unspecified site

female 183.0

male 186.9

specified site—*see* Neoplasm, by site, uncertain behavior

unspecified site

female 236.2

male 236.4

lipid cell, ovary (M8670/0) 220

lipoid cell, ovary (M8670/0) 220

lymphomatous, benign (M9590/0)—*see also* Neoplasm, by site, benign

Tumor—*continued*

Malherbe's (M8110/0)—*see* Neoplasm, skin, benign

malignant (M8000/3)—*see also* Neoplasm, by site, malignant

    fusiform cell (type) (M8004/3)—*see* Neoplasm, by site, malignant

    giant cell (type) (M8003/3)—*see* Neoplasm, by site, malignant

    mixed NEC (M8940/3)—*see* Neoplasm, by site, malignant

    small cell (type) (M8002/3)—*see* Neoplasm, by site, malignant

    spindle cell (type) (M8004/3)—*see* Neoplasm, by site, malignant

mast cell (M9740/1) 238.5

    malignant (M9740/3) 202.6

melanotic, neuroectodermal (M9363/0)—*see* Neoplasm, by site, benign

mesenchymal

    malignant (M8800/3)—*see* Neoplasm, connective tissue, malignant

    mixed (M8990/1)—*see* Neoplasm, connective tissue, uncertain behavior

mesodermal, mixed (M8951/3)—*see also* Neoplasm, by site, malignant

    liver 155.0

mesonephric (M9110/1)—*see also* Neoplasm, by site, uncertain behavior

    malignant (M9110/3)—*see* Neoplasm, by site, malignant

metastatic

    from specified site (M8000/3)—*see* Neoplasm, by site, malignant

    to specified site (M8000/6)—*see* Neoplasm, by site, malignant, secondary

mixed NEC (M8940/0)—*see also* Neoplasm, by site, benign

    malignant (M8940/3)—*see* Neoplasm, by site, malignant

mucocarcinoid, malignant (M8243/3)—*see* Neoplasm, by site, malignant

mucoepidermoid (M8430/1)—*see* Neoplasm, by site, uncertain behavior

Mullerian, mixed (M8950/3)—*see* Neoplasm, by site, malignant

myoepithelial (M8982/0)—*see* Neoplasm, by site, benign

neurogenic olfactory (M9520/3) 160.0

nonencapsulated sclerosing (M8350/3) 193

odontogenic (M9270/1) 238.0

    adenomatoid (M9300/0) 213.1

      upper jaw (bone) 213.0

    benign (M9270/0) 213.1

      upper jaw (bone) 213.0

    calcifying epithelial (M9340/0) 213.1

      upper jaw (bone) 213.0

    malignant (M9270/3) 170.1

      upper jaw (bone) 170.0

    squamous (M9312/0) 213.1

      upper jaw (bone) 213.0

ovarian stromal (M8590/1) 236.2

ovary

    in pregnancy or childbirth 654.4

      affecting fetus or newborn 763.8

      causing obstructed labor 660.2

        affecting fetus or newborn 763.1

pacinian (M9507/0)—*see* Neoplasm, skin, benign

Pancoast's (M8010/3) 162.3

papillary—*see* Papilloma

Tumor—*continued*

pelvic, in pregnancy or childbirth 654.9

    affecting fetus or newborn 763.8

    causing obstructed labor 660.2

      affecting fetus or newborn 763.1

phantom 300.11

plasma cell (M9731/1) 238.6

    benign (M9731/0)—*see* Neoplasm, by site, benign

    malignant (M9731/3) 203.8

polyvesicular vitelline (M9071/3)

    specified site—*see* Neoplasm, by site, malignant

    unspecified site

      female 183.0

      male 186.9

Pott's puffy (*see also* Osteomyelitis) 730.2

Rathke's pouch (M9350/1) 237.0

regaud's (M8082/3)—*see* Neoplasm, nasopharynx, malignant

rete cell (M8140/0) 222.0

retinal anlage (M9363/0)—*see* Neoplasm, by site, benign

Rokitansky's 620.2

salivary gland type, mixed (M8940/0)—*see also* Neoplasm, by site, benign

    malignant (M8940/3)—*see* Neoplasm, by site, malignant

Sampson's 617.1

Schloffer's (*see also* Peritonitis) 567.2

Schmincke (M8082/3)—*see* Neoplasm, nasopharynx, malignant

sebaceous (*see also* Cyst, sebaceous) 706.2

secondary (M8000/6)—*see* Neoplasm, by site, secondary

Sertoli cell (M8640/0)

    with lipid storage (M8641/0)

      specified site—*see* Neoplasm, by site, benign

      unspecified site

        female 220

        male 222.0

    specified site—*see* Neoplasm, by site, benign

    unspecified site

      female 220

      male 222.0

Sertoli-Leydig cell (M8631/0)

    specified site—*see* Neoplasm, by site, benign

    unspecified site

      female 220

      male 222.0

sex cord (-stromal) (M8590/1)—*see* Neoplasm, by site, uncertain behavior

skin appendage (M8390/0)—*see* Neoplasm, skin, benign

soft tissue

    benign (M8800/0)—*see* Neoplasm, connective tissue, benign

    malignant (M8800/3)—*see* Neoplasm, connective tissue, malignant

sternomastoid 754.1

superior sulcus (lung) (pulmonary) (syndrome) (M8010/3) 162.3

suprasulcus (M8010/3) 162.3

sweat gland (M8400/1)—*see also* Neoplasm, skin, uncertain behavior

    benign (M8400/0)—*see* Neoplasm, skin, benign

    malignant (M8400/3)—*see* Neoplasm, skin, malignant

Tumor—*continued*
   syphilitic brain 094.89
      congenital 090.49
   testicular stromal (M8590/1) 236.4
   theca cell (M8600/0) 220
   theca cell-granulosa cell (M8621/1) 236.2
   theca-lutein (M8610/0) 220
   turban (M8200/0) 216.4
   uterus
      in pregnancy or childbirth 654.1
         affecting fetus or newborn 763.8
         causing obstructed labor 660.2
            affecting fetus or newborn 763.1
   vagina
      in pregnancy or childbirth 654.7
         affecting fetus or newborn 763.8
         causing obstructed labor 660.2
            affecting fetus or newborn 763.1
   varicose (*see also* Varicose, vein) 454.9
   von Recklinghausen's (M9540/1) 237.71
   vulva
      in pregnancy or childbirth 654.8
         affecting fetus or newborn 763.8
         causing obstructed labor 660.2
            affecting fetus or newborn 763.1
   Warthin's (salivary gland) (M8561/0) 210.2
   white—*see also* Tuberculosis, arthritis
   White-Darier 757.39
   Wilms' (nephroblastoma) (M8960/3) 189.0
   yolk sac (M9071/3)
      specified site—*see* Neoplasm, by site,
         malignant
      unspecified site
         female 183.0
         male 186.9
Tumorlet (M8040/1)—*see* Neoplasm, by site,
   uncertain behavior
Tungiasis 134.1
Tunica vasculosa lentis 743.39
Tunnel vision 368.45
Turban tumor (M8200/0) 216.4
Türck's trachoma (chronic catarrhal laryngitis)
   476.0
Türk's syndrome (ocular retraction syndrome)
   378.71
Turner's
   hypoplasia (tooth) 520.4
   syndrome 758.6
   tooth 520.4
Turner-Kieser syndrome (hereditary
   osteo-onychodysplasia) 756.89
Turner-Varny syndrome 758.6
Turricephaly 756.0
Tussis convulsiva (*see also* Whooping cough)
   033.9   .
Twin
   affected by maternal complications of
      pregnancy 761.5
   conjoined 759.4
   healthy liveborn—*see* Newborn, twin
   pregnancy (complicating delivery) NEC 651.0
      with fetal loss and retention of one fetus 651.3
Twinning, teeth 520.2
Twist, twisted
   bowel, colon, or intestine 560.2
   hair (congenital) 757.4
   mesentery 560.2
   omentum 560.2
   organ or site, congenital NEC—*see* Anomaly,
      specified type NEC

Twist, twisted—*continued*
   ovarian pedicle 620.5
      congenital 752.0
   umbilical cord—*see* Compression, umbilical
      cord
Twitch 781.0
Tylosis 700
   buccalis 528.6
   gingiva 523.8
   linguae 528.6
   palmaris et plantaris 757.39
Tympanism 787.3
Tympanites (abdominal) (intestine) 787.3
Tympanitis —*see* Myringitis
Tympanosclerosis 385.00
   involving
      combined sites NEC 385.09
         with tympanic membrane 385.03
      tympanic membrane 385.01
         with ossicles 385.02
            and middle ear 385.03
Tympanum —*see* condition
Tympany
   abdomen 787.3
   chest 786.7
Typhlitis (*see also* Appendicitis) 541
Typhoenteritis 002.0
Typhogastric fever 002.0
Typhoid (abortive) (ambulant) (any site) (fever)
   (hemorrhagic) (infection) (intermittent)
   (malignant) (rheumatic) 002.0
   with pneumonia 002.0 *[484.8]*
   abdominal 002.0
   carrier (suspected) of V02.1
   cholecystitis (current) 002.0
   clinical (Widal and blood test negative) 002.0
   endocarditis 002.0 *[421.1]*
   inoculation reaction—*see* Complications,
      vaccination
   meningitis 002.0 *[320.7]*
   mesenteric lymph nodes 002.0
   myocarditis 002.0 *[422.0]*
   osteomyelitis (*see also* Osteomyelitis, due to,
      typhoid) 002.0 *[730.8]*
   perichondritis, larynx 002.0 *[478.71]*
   pneumonia 002.0 *[484.8]*
   spine 002.0 *[720.81]*
   ulcer (perforating) 002.0
   vaccination, prophylactic (against) V03.1
   Widal negative 002.0
Typhomalaria (fever) (*see also* Malaria) 084.6
Typhomania 002.0
Typhoperitonitis 002.0
Typhus (fever) 081.9
   abdominal, abdominalis 002.0
   African tick 082.1
   amarillic (*see also* Fever, Yellow) 060.9
   brain 081.9
   cerebral 081.9
   classical 080
   endemic (flea-borne) 081.0
   epidemic (louse-borne) 080
   exanthematic NEC 080
   exanthematicus SAI 080
      brillii SAI 081.1
      Mexicanus SAI 081.0
      pediculo vestimenti causa 080
      typhus murinus 081.0
   flea-borne 081.0
   Indian tick 082.1

Typhus—*continued*
  Kenya tick 082.1
  louse-borne 080
  Mexican 081.0
    flea-borne 081.0
    louse-borne 080
    tabardillo 080
  mite-borne 081.2
  murine 081.0
  North Asian tick-borne 082.2
  petechial 081.9
  Queensland tick 082.3
  rat 081.0
  recrudescent 081.1
  recurrent (*see also* Fever, relapsing) 087.9
  São Paulo 082.0
  scrub (China) (India) (Malaya) (New Guinea)
    081.2
  shop (of Malaya) 081.0
  Siberian tick 082.2
  tick-borne NEC 082.9
  tropical 081.2
  vaccination, prophylactic (against) V05.8
Tyrosinosis (Medes) (Sakai) 270.2
Tyrosinuria 270.2
Tyrosyluria 270.2

U

Uehlinger's syndrome (acropachyderma) 757.39
Uhl's anomaly or disease (hypoplasia of
  myocardium, right ventricle) 746.84
Ulcer, ulcerated, ulcerating ulceration,
  ulcerative 707.9
  with gangrene 707.9 *[785.4]*
  abdomen (wall) *(see also* Ulcer, skin) 707.8
  ala, nose 478.1
  alveolar process 526.5
  amebic (intestine) 006.9
    skin 006.6
  anastomotic—*see* Ulcer, gastrojejunal
  anorectal 569.41
  antral—*see* Ulcer, stomach
  anus (sphincter) (solitary) 569.41
    varicose—*see* Varicose, ulcer, anus
  aphthous (oral) (recurrent) 528.2
    genital organ(s)
      female 616.8
      male 608.89
    mouth 528.2
  arm *(see also* Ulcer, skin) 707.8
  arteriosclerotic plaque—*see* Arteriosclerosis, by
    site
  artery NEC 447.2
    without rupture 447.8
  atrophic NEC—*see* Ulcer, skin
  Barrett's (chronic peptic ulcer of esophagus)
    530.2
  bile duct 576.8
  bladder (solitary) (sphincter) 596.8
    bilharzial *(see also* Schistosomiasis) 120.9
      [595.4]
    submucosal *(see also* Cystitis) 595.1
    tuberculous *(see also* Tuberculosis) 016.1
  bleeding NEC—*see* Ulcer, peptic, with
    hemorrhage
  bone 730.9
  bowel *(see also* Ulcer, intestine) 569.82
  breast 611.0
  bronchitis 491.8
  bronchus 519.1
  buccal (cavity) (traumatic) 528.9
  burn (acute)—*see* Ulcer, duodenum
  Buruli 031.1
  buttock *(see also* Ulcer, skin) 707.8
    decubitus *(see also* Ulcer, decubitus) 707.0
  cancerous (M8000/3)—*see* Neoplasm, by site,
    malignant
  cardia—*see* Ulcer, stomach
  cardio-esophageal (peptic) 530.2
  cecum *(see also* Ulcer, intestine) 569.82
  cervix (uteri) (trophic) 622.0
    with mention of cervicitis 616.0
  chancroidal 099.0
  chest (wall) *(see also* Ulcer, skin) 707.8
  Chiclero 085.4
  chin (pyogenic) *(see also* Ulcer, skin) 707.8
  chronic (cause unknown)—*see also* Ulcer, skin
    penis 607.89
  Cochin-China 085.1
  colitis —*see* Colitis, ulcerative
  colon *(see also* Ulcer, intestine) 569.82
  conjunctiva (acute) (postinfectional) 372.00

Ulcer, ulcerated, ulcerating—*continued*
  cornea (infectional) 370.00
    with perforation 370.06
    annular 370.02
    catarrhal 370.01
    central 370.03
    dendritic 054.42
    marginal 370.01
    mycotic 370.05
    phlyctenular, tuberculous *(see also*
      Tuberculosis) 017.3 *[370.31]*
    ring 370.02
    rodent 370.07
    serpent, serpiginous 370.04
    superficial marginal 370.01
    tuberculous *(see also* Tuberculosis) 017.3
      [370.31]
  corpus cavernosum (chronic) 607.89
  crural—*see* Ulcer, lower extremity
  Curling's—*see* Ulcer, duodenum
  Cushing's—*see* Ulcer, peptic
  cystitis (interstitial) 595.1
  decubitus (any site) 707.0
    with gangrene 707.0 *[785.4]*
  dendritic 054.42
  diabetes, diabetic (mellitus) 250.8 *[707.9]*
    lower limb 250.8 *[707.1]*
    specified site NEC 250.8 *[707.8]*
  Dieulafoy's—*see* Ulcer, stomach
  due to
    infection NEC—*see* Ulcer, skin
    radiation, radium—*see* Ulcer, by site
    trophic disturbance (any region)—*see* Ulcer,
      skin
    x-ray—*see* Ulcer, by site
  duodenum, duodenal (eroded) (peptic) 532.9

> Note—Use the following fifth-digit
> subclassification with categories 531-534:
>
> *0 without mention of obstruction*
> *1 with obstruction*

    with
      hemorrhage (chronic) 532.4
        and perforation 532.6
      perforation (chronic) 532.5
        and hemorrhage 532.6
    acute 532.3
      with
        hemorrhage 532.0
          and perforation 532.2
        perforation 532.1
          and hemorrhage 532.2
    bleeding (recurrent)—*see* Ulcer, duodenum,
      with hemorrhage
    chronic 532.7
      with
        hemorrhage 532.4
          and perforation 532.6
        perforation 532.5
          and hemorrhage 532.6
    penetrating—*see* Ulcer, duodenum, with
      perforation
    perforating—*see* Ulcer, duodenum, with
      perforation
  dysenteric NEC 009.0
  elusive 595.1

Ulcer, ulcerated, ulcerating—*continued*
  endocarditis (any valve) (acute) (chronic)
    (subacute) 421.0
  enteritis —*see* Colitis, ulcerative
  enterocolitis 556.0
  epiglottis 478.79
  esophagus (peptic) 530.2
    due to ingestion
      aspirin 530.2
      chemicals 530.2
      medicinal agents 530.2
    fungal 530.2
    infectional 530.2
    varicose (*see also* Varix, esophagus) 456.1
      bleeding (*see also* Varix, esophagus,
        bleeding) 456.0
  eye NEC 360.00
    dendritic 054.42
  eyelid (region) 373.01
  face (*see also* Ulcer, skin) 707.8
  fauces 478.29
  Fenwick (-Hunner) (solitary) (*see also* Cystitis)
    595.1
  fistulous NEC—*see* Ulcer, skin
  foot (indolent) (*see also* Ulcer, lower extremity)
    707.1
    perforating 707.1
      leprous 030.1
      syphilitic 094.0
    trophic 707.1
    varicose 454.0
      inflamed or infected 454.2
  frambesial, initial or primary 102.0
  gallbladder or duct 575.8
  gall duct 576.8
  gangrenous (*see also* Gangrene) 785.4
  gastric—*see* Ulcer, stomach
  gastrocolic—*see* Ulcer, gastrojejunal
  gastroduodenal—*see* Ulcer, peptic
  gastroesophageal—*see* Ulcer, stomach
  gastrohepatic—*see* Ulcer, stomach
  gastrointestinal—*see* Ulcer, gastrojejunal
  gastrojejunal (eroded) (peptic) 534.9

Note—Use the following fifth-digit
subclassification with categories 531-534:

0 *without mention of obstruction*
1 *with obstruction*

---

    with
      hemorrhage (chronic) 534.4
        and perforation 534.6
      perforation 534.5
        and hemorrhage 534.6
    acute 534.3
      with
        hemorrhage 534.0
          and perforation 534.2
        perforation 534.1
          and hemorrhage 534.2
    bleeding (recurrent)—*see* Ulcer, gastrojejunal,
      with hemorrhage
    chronic 534.7
      with
        hemorrhage 534.4
          and perforation 534.6
        perforation 534.5
          and hemorrhage 534.6
    penetrating—*see* Ulcer, gastrojejunal, with
      perforation

Ulcer, ulcerated, ulcerating—*continued*
    perforating—*see* Ulcer, gastrojejunal, with
      perforation
  gastrojejunocolic—*see* Ulcer, gastrojejunal
  genital organ
    female 629.8
    male 608.89
  gingiva 523.8
  gingivitis 523.1
  glottis 478.79
  granuloma of pudenda 099.2
  groin (*see also* Ulcer, skin) 707.8
  gum 523.8
  gumma, due to yaws 102.4
  hand (*see also* Ulcer, skin) 707.8
  hard palate 528.9
  heel (*see also* Ulcer, lower extremity) 707.1
    decubitus (*see also* Ulcer, decubitus) 707.0
  hemorrhoids 455.8
    external 455.5
    internal 455.2
  hip (*see also* Ulcer, skin) 707.8
    decubitus (*see also* Ulcer, decubitus) 707.0
  Hunner's 595.1
  hypopharynx 478.29
  hypopyon (chronic) (subacute) 370.04
  hypostaticum—*see* Ulcer, varicose
  ileocolitis 556.1
  ileum (*see also* Ulcer, intestine) 569.82
  intestine, intestinal 569.82
    with perforation 569.83
    amebic 006.9
    duodenal—*see* Ulcer, duodenum
    granulocytopenic (with hemorrhage) 288.0
    marginal 569.82
    perforating 569.83
    small, primary 569.82
    stercoraceous 569.82
    stercoral 569.82
    tuberculous (*see also* Tuberculosis) 014.8
    typhoid (fever) 002.0
    varicose 456.8
  ischemic 707.9
    lower extremity (*see also* Ulcer, lower
      extremity) 707.1
  jejunum, jejunal—*see* Ulcer, gastrojejunal
  keratitis (*see also* Ulcer, cornea) 370.00
  knee—*see* Ulcer, lower extremity
  labium (majus) (minus) 616.50
  laryngitis (*see also* Laryngitis) 464.0
  larynx (aphthous) (contact) 478.79
    diphtheritic 032.3
  leg—*see* Ulcer, lower extremity
  lip 528.5
  Lipschütz's 616.50
  lower extremity (atrophic) (chronic)
    (neurogenic) (perforating) (pyogenic)
    (trophic) (tropical) 707.1
    with gangrene 707.1 *[785.4]*
      arteriosclerotic 440.24
    arteriosclerotic 440.23
      with gangrene 440.24
    decubitus 707.0
      with gangrene 707.0 *[785.4]*
    varicose 454.0
      inflamed or infected 454.2
  luetic—*see* Ulcer, syphilitic
  lung 518.89
    tuberculous (*see also* Tuberculosis) 011.2
  malignant (M8000/3)—*see* Neoplasm, by site,
    malignant

Ulcer, ulcerated, ulcerating—*continued*
  marginal NEC—*see* Ulcer, gastrojejunal
  meatus (urinarius) 597.89
  Meckel's diverticulum 751.0
  Meleney's (chronic undermining) 686.0
  Mooren's (cornea) 370.07
  mouth (traumatic) 528.9
  mycobacterial (skin) 031.1
  nasopharynx 478.29
  navel cord (newborn) 771.4
  neck (*see also* Ulcer, skin) 707.8
    uterus 622.0
  neurogenic NEC—*see* Ulcer, skin
  nose, nasal (infectional) (passage) 478.1
    septum 478.1
      varicose 456.8
    skin—*see* Ulcer, skin
    spirochetal NEC 104.8
  oral mucosa (traumatic) 528.9
  palate (soft) 528.9
  penetrating NEC—*see* Ulcer, peptic, with
    perforation
  penis (chronic) 607.89
  peptic (site unspecified) 533.9

Note—Use the following fifth-digit subclassification with categories 531-534:
0 without mention of obstruction
1 with obstruction

    with
      hemorrhage 533.4
        and perforation 533.6
      perforation (chronic) 533.5
        and hemorrhage 533.6
    acute 533.3
      with
        hemorrhage 533.0
          and perforation 533.2
        perforation 533.1
          and hemorrhage 533.2
    bleeding (recurrent)—*see* Ulcer, peptic, with
      hemorrhage
    chronic 533.7
      with
        hemorrhage 533.4
          and perforation 533.6
        perforation 533.5
          and hemorrhage 533.6
    penetrating—*see* Ulcer, peptic, with
      perforation
    perforating NEC (*see also* Ulcer, peptic, with
      perforation) 533.5
    skin 707.9
  perineum (*see also* Ulcer, skin) 707.8
  peritonsillar 474.8
  phagedenic (tropical) NEC—*see* Ulcer, skin
  pharynx 478.29
  phlebitis—*see* Phlebitis
  plaster (*see also* Ulcer, decubitus) 707.0
  popliteal space—*see* Ulcer, lower extremity
  postpyloric—*see* Ulcer, duodenum
  prepuce 607.89
  prepyloric—*see* Ulcer, stomach
  pressure (*see also* Ulcer, decubitus) 707.0
  primary of intestine 569.82
    with perforation 569.83
  proctitis 556.2
    with ulcerative sigmoiditis 556.3
  prostate 601.8
  pseudopeptic—*see* Ulcer, peptic

Ulcer, ulcerated, ulcerating—*continued*
  pyloric—*see* Ulcer, stomach
  rectosigmoid 569.82
    with perforation 569.83
  rectum (sphincter) (solitary) 569.41
    stercoraceous, stercoral 569.41
    varicose—*see* Varicose, ulcer, anus
  retina (*see also* Chorioretinitis) 363.20
  rodent (M8090/3)—*see also* Neoplasm, skin,
    malignant
    cornea 370.07
  round—*see* Ulcer, stomach
  sacrum (region) (*see also* Ulcer, skin) 707.8
  Saemisch's 370.04
  scalp (*see also* Ulcer, skin) 707.8
  sclera 379.09
  scrofulous (*see also* Tuberculosis) 017.2
  scrotum 608.89
    tuberculous (*see also* Tuberculosis) 016.5
    varicose 456.4
  seminal vesicle 608.89
  sigmoid 569.82
    with perforation 569.83
  skin (atrophic) (chronic) (neurogenic)
    (non-healing) (perforating) (pyogenic)
    (trophic) 707.9
    with gangrene 707.9 *[785.4]*
    amebic 006.6
    decubitus 707.0
      with gangrene 707.0 *[785.4]*
    in granulocytopenia 288.0
    lower extremity (*see also* Ulcer, lower
      extremity) 707.1
      with gangrene 707.1 *[785.4]*
        arteriosclerotic 440.24
      arteriosclerotic 440.23
        with gangrene 440.24
    mycobacterial 031.1
    syphilitic (early) (secondary) 091.3
    tuberculous (primary) (*see also* Tuberculosis)
      017.0
    varicose—*see* Ulcer, varicose
  sloughing NEC—*see* Ulcer, skin
  soft palate 528.9
  solitary, anus or rectum (sphincter) 569.41
  sore throat 462
    streptococcal 034.0
  spermatic cord 608.89
  spine (tuberculous) 015.0 *[730.88]*
  stasis (leg) (venous) 454.0
    inflamed or infected 454.2
  stercoral, stercoraceous 569.82
    with perforation 569.83
    anus or rectum 569.41
  stoma, stomal—*see* Ulcer, gastrojejunal
  stomach (eroded) (peptic) (round) 531.9

Note—Use the following fifth-digit subclassification with categories 531-534:
0 without mention of obstruction
1 with obstruction

    with
      hemorrhage 531.4
        and perforation 531.6
      perforation (chronic) 531.5
        and hemorrhage 531.6
    acute 531.3
      with
        hemorrhage 531.0
          and perforation 531.2

Ulcer, ulcerated, ulcerating—*continued*
  perforation 531.1
    and hemorrhage 531.2
  bleeding (recurrent)—*see* Ulcer, stomach,
    with hemorrhage
  chronic 531.7
    with
      hemorrhage 531.4
        and perforation 531.6
      perforation 531.5
        and hemorrhage 531.6
  penetrating—*see* Ulcer, stomach, with
    perforation
  perforating—*see* Ulcer, stomach, with
    perforation
  stomatitis 528.0
  stress—*see* Ulcer, peptic
  strumous (tuberculous) (*see also* Tuberculosis)
    017.2
  submental (*see also* Ulcer, skin) 707.8
  submucosal, bladder 595.1
  syphilitic (any site) (early) (secondary) 091.3
    late 095.9
    perforating 095.9
    foot 094.0
  testis 608.89
  thigh—*see* Ulcer, lower extremity
  throat 478.29
    diphtheritic 032.0
  toe—*see* Ulcer, lower extremity
  tongue (traumatic) 529.0
  tonsil 474.8
    diphtheritic 032.0
  trachea 519.1
  trophic—*see* Ulcer, skin
  tropical NEC (*see also* Ulcer, skin) 707.9
  tuberculous—*see* Tuberculosis, ulcer
  tunica vaginalis 608.89
  turbinate 730.9
  typhoid (fever) 002.0
    perforating 002.0
  umbilicus (newborn) 771.4
  unspecified site NEC—*see* Ulcer, skin
  urethra (meatus) (*see also* Urethritis) 597.89
  uterus 621.8
    cervix 622.0
      with mention of cervicitis 616.0
    neck 622.0
      with mention of cervicitis 616.0
  vagina 616.8
  valve, heart 421.0
  varicose (lower extremity, any part) 454.0
    anus—*see* Varicose, ulcer, anus
    broad ligament 456.5
    esophagus (*see also* Varix, esophagus) 456.1
      bleeding (*see also* Varix, esophagus,
        bleeding) 456.0
    inflamed or infected 454.2
    nasal septum 456.8
    perineum 456.6
    rectum—*see* Varicose, ulcer, anus
    scrotum 456.4
    specified site NEC 456.8
    sublingual 456.3
    vulva 456.6
  vas deferens 608.89
  vesical (*see also* Ulcer, bladder) 596.8
  vulva (acute) (infectional) 616.50
    Behçet's syndrome 136.1 *[616.51]*
    herpetic 054.12
    tuberculous 016.7 *[616.51]*

Ulcer, ulcerated, ulcerating—*continued*
  vulvobuccal, recurring 616.50
  x-ray—*see* Ulcer, by site
  yaws 102.4
Ulcerosa scarlatina 034.1
Ulcus —*see also* Ulcer
  cutis tuberculosum (*see also* Tuberculosis) 017.0
  duodeni—*see* Ulcer, duodenum
  durum 091.0
    extragenital 091.2
  gastrojejunale—*see* Ulcer, gastrojejunal
  hypostaticum—*see* Ulcer, varicose
  molle (cutis) (skin) 099.0
  serpens cornea (pneumococcal) 370.04
  ventriculi—*see* Ulcer, stomach
Ulegyria 742.4
Ulerythema
  acneiforma 701.8
  centrifugum 695.4
  ophryogenes 757.4
Ullrich (-Bonnevie) (-Turner) syndrome 758.6
Ullrich-Feichtiger syndrome 759.89
Ulnar —*see* condition
Ulorrhagia 523.8
Ulorrhea 523.8
Umbilicus, umbilical —*see also* condition
  cord necrosis, affecting fetus or newborn 762.6
Unavailability of medical facilities (at) V63.9
  due to
    investigation by social service agency V63.8
    lack of services at home V63.1
    remoteness from facility V63.0
    waiting list V63.2
      home V63.1
      outpatient clinic V63.0
    specified reason NEC V63.8
Uncinaria americana infestation 126.1
Uncinariasis (*see also* Ancylostomiasis) 126.9
Unconscious, unconsciousness 780.09
Underdevelopment —*see also* Undeveloped
  sexual 259.0
Undernourishment 269.9
Undernutrition 269.9
Under observation —*see* Observation
Underweight 783.4
  for gestational age—*see* Light-for-dates
Underwood's disease (sclerema neonatorum)
  778.1
Undescended —*see also* Malposition, congenital
  cecum 751.4
  colon 751.4
  testis 752.51
Undetermined diagnosis or cause 799.9
Undeveloped, undevelopment —*see also*
  Hypoplasia
  brain (congenital) 742.1
  cerebral (congenital) 742.1
  fetus or newborn 764.9
  heart 746.89
  lung 748.5
  testis 257.2
  uterus 259.0
Undiagnosed (disease) 799.9
Undulant fever (*see also* Brucellosis) 023.9
Unemployment, anxiety concerning V62.0
Unequal leg (acquired) (length) 736.81
  congenital 755.30
Unerupted teeth, tooth 520.6
Unextracted dental root 525.3
Unguis incarnatus 703.0
Unicornis uterus 752.3
Unicorporeus uterus 752.3

Uniformis uterus 752.3
Unilateral —*see also* condition
  development, breast 611.8
  organ or site, congenital NEC—*see* Agenesis
  vagina 752.49
Unilateralis uterus 752.3
Unilocular heart 745.8
Uninhibited (neurogenic) bladder 596.54
  with cauda equina syndrome 344.61
  neurogenic—*see* Neurogenic, bladder 596.54
Union, abnormal —*see also* Fusion
  divided tendon 727.89
  larynx and trachea 748.3
Universal
  joint, cervix 620.6
  mesentery 751.4
Unknown
  cause of death 799.9
  diagnosis 799.9
Unna's disease (seborrheic dermatitis) 690.10
Unresponsiveness, adrenocorticotropin
  (ACTH) 255.4
Unsoundness of mind (*see also* Psychosis) 298.9
Unspecified cause of death 799.9
Unstable
  back NEC 724.9
  colon 569.89
  joint—*see* Instability, joint
  lie 652.0
    affecting fetus or newborn (before labor) 761.7
    causing obstructed labor 660.0
      affecting fetus or newborn 763.1
  lumbosacral joint (congenital) 756.19
    acquired 724.6
  sacroiliac 724.6
  spine NEC 724.9
Untruthfulness, child problem (*see also*
  Disturbance, conduct) 312.0
Unverricht (-Lundborg) disease, syndrome, or
  epilepsy 333.2
Unverricht-Wagner syndrome
  (dermatomyositis) 710.3
Upper respiratory —*see* condition
Upset
  gastric 536.8
    psychogenic 306.4
  gastrointestinal 536.8
    psychogenic 306.4
    virus (*see also* Enteritis, viral) 008.8
  intestinal (large) (small) 564.9
    psychogenic 306.4
  menstruation 626.9
  mental 300.9
  stomach 536.8
    psychogenic 306.4
Urachus —*see also* condition
  patent 753.7
  persistent 753.7
Uratic arthritis 274.0
Urbach's lipoid proteinosis 272.8
Urbach-Oppenheim disease or syndrome
  (necrobiosis lipoidica diabeticorum) 250.8
  [709.3]
Urbach-Wiethe disease or syndrome (lipoid
  proteinosis) 272.8
Urban yellow fever 060.1
Urea, blood, high —*see* Uremia

Uremia, uremic (absorption) (amaurosis)
  (amblyopia) (aphasia) (apoplexy) (coma)
  (delirium) (dementia) (dropsy) (dyspnea)
  (fever) (intoxication) (mania) (paralysis)
  (poisoning) (toxemia) (vomiting) 586
  with
    abortion—*see* Abortion, by type, with renal
      failure
    ectopic pregnancy (*see also* categories
      633.0-633.9) 639.3
    hypertension (*see also* Hypertension, kidney)
      403.91
    molar pregnancy (*see also* categories
      630-632) 639.3
  chronic 585
  complicating
    abortion 639.3
    ectopic or molar pregnancy 639.3
    hypertension (*see also* Hypertension, kidney)
      403.91
    labor and delivery 669.3
  congenital 779.8
  extrarenal 788.9
  hypertensive (chronic) (*see also* Hypertension,
    kidney) 403.91
  maternal NEC, affecting fetus or newborn 760.1
  neuropathy 585 *[357.4]*
  pericarditis 585 *[420.0]*
  prerenal 788.9
  pyelitic (*see also* Pyelitis) 590.80
Ureter, ureteral —*see* condition
Ureteralgia 788.0
Ureterectasis 593.89
Ureteritis 593.89
  cystica 590.3
  due to calculus 592.1
  gonococcal (acute) 098.19
    chronic or duration of 2 months or over 098.39
  nonspecific 593.89
Ureterocele (acquired) 593.89
  congenital 753.23
Ureterolith 592.1
Ureterolithiasis 592.1
Ureterostomy status V44.6
  with complication 997.5
Urethra, urethral —*see* condition
Urethralgia 788.9
Urethritis (abacterial) (acute) (allergic) (anterior)
  (chronic) (nonvenereal) (posterior) (recurrent)
  (simple) (subacute) (ulcerative)
  (undifferentiated) 597.80
  diplococcal (acute) 098.0
    chronic or duration of 2 months or over 098.2
  due to Trichomonas (vaginalis) 131.02
  gonococcal (acute) 098.0
    chronic or duration of 2 months or over 098.2
  nongonococcal (sexually transmitted) 099.40
    Chlamydia trachomatis 099.41
    Reiter's 099.3
    specified organism NEC 099.49
  nonspecific (sexually transmitted) (*see also*
    Urethritis, nongonococcal) 099.40
  not sexually transmitted 597.80
  Reiter's 099.3
  trichomonal or due to Trichomonas (vaginalis)
    131.02
  tuberculous (*see also* Tuberculosis) 016.3
  venereal NEC (*see also* Urethritis,
    nongonococcal) 099.40

Urethrocele
  female 618.0
    with uterine prolapse 618.4
      complete 618.3
      incomplete 618.2
  male 599.5
Urethrolithiasis 594.2
Urethro-oculoarticular syndrome 099.3
Urethro-oculosynovial syndrome 099.3
Urethrorectal —*see* condition
Urethrorrhagia 599.84
Urethrorrhea 788.7
Urethrostomy status V44.6
  with complication 997.5
Urethrotrigonitis 595.3
Urethrovaginal —*see* condition
Urhidrosis, uridrosis 705.89
Uric acid
  diathesis 274.9
  in blood 790.6
Uricacidemia 790.6
Uricemia 790.6
Uricosuria 791.9
Urination
  frequent 788.41
  painful 788.1
Urine, urinary —*see also* condition
  abnormality NEC 788.69
  blood in (*see also* Hematuria) 599.7
  discharge, excessive 788.42
  enuresis 788.30
    nonorganic origin 307.6
  extravasation 788.8
  frequency 788.41
  incontinence 788.30
    active 788.30
    female 788.30
      stress 625.6
        and urge 788.33
    male 788.30
      stress 788.32
        and urge 788.33
    mixed (stress and urge) 788.33
    neurogenic 788.39
    nonorganic origin 307.6
    stress (female) 625.6
      male NEC 788.32
  intermittent stream 788.61
  pus in 599.0
  retention or stasis NEC 788.20
    bladder, incomplete emptying 788.21
    psychogenic 306.53
    specified NEC 788.29
  secretion
    deficient 788.5
    excessive 788.42
    frequency 788.41
  stream
    intermittent 788.61
    slowing 788.62
    splitting 788.61
    weak 788.62
Urinemia —*see* Uremia
Urinoma NEC 599.9
  bladder 596.8
  kidney 593.89
  renal 593.89
  ureter 593.89
  urethra 599.84
Uroarthritis, infectious 099.3
Urodialysis 788.5
Urolithiasis 592.9

Uronephrosis 593.89
Uropathy 599.9
  obstructive 599.6
Urosepsis 599.0
Urticaria 708.9
  with angioneurotic edema 995.1
    hereditary 277.6
  allergic 708.0
  cholinergic 708.5
  chronic 708.8
  cold, familial 708.2
  dermatographic 708.3
  due to
    cold or heat 708.2
    drugs 708.0
    food 708.0
    inhalants 708.0
    plants 708.8
    serum 999.5
  factitial 708.3
  giant 995.1
    hereditary 277.6
  gigantea 995.1
    hereditary 277.6
  idiopathic 708.1
  larynx 995.1
    hereditary 277.6
  neonatorum 778.8
  nonallergic 708.1
  papulosa (Hebra) 698.2
  perstans hemorrhagica 757.39
  pigmentosa 757.33
  recurrent periodic 708.8
  serum 999.5
  solare 692.72
  specified type NEC 708.8
  thermal (cold) (heat) 708.2
  vibratory 708.4
Urticarioides acarodermatitis 133.9
Use of
  nonprescribed drugs (*see also* Abuse, drugs, nondependent) 305.9
  patent medicines (*see also* Abuse, drugs, nondependent) 305.9
Usher-Senear disease (pemphigus erythematosus) 694.4
Uta 085.5
Uteromegaly 621.2
Uterovaginal —*see* condition
Uterovesical —*see* condition
Uterus —*see* condition
Utriculitis (utriculus prostaticus) 597.89
Uveal —*see* condition
Uveitis (anterior) (*see also* Iridocyclitis) 364.3
  acute or subacute 364.00
    due to or associated with
      gonococcal infection 098.41
      herpes (simplex) 054.44
        zoster 053.22
    primary 364.01
    recurrent 364.02
    secondary (noninfectious) 364.04
      infectious 364.03
  allergic 360.11
  chronic 364.10
    due to or associated with
      sarcoidosis 135 *[364.11]*
      tuberculosis (*see also* Tuberculosis) 017.3 *[364.11]*
  due to
    operation 360.11

Uveitis—*continued*
    toxoplasmosis (acquired) 130.2
      congenital (active) 771.2
    granulomatous 364.10
    heterochromic 364.21
    lens-induced 364.23
    nongranulomatous 364.00
    posterior 363.20
      disseminated—*see* Chorioretinitis,
        disseminated
      focal—*see* Chorioretinitis, focal
    recurrent 364.02
    sympathetic 360.11
    syphilitic (secondary) 091.50
      congenital 090.0 *[363.13]*
      late 095.8 *[363.13]*
    tuberculous (*see also* Tuberculosis) 017.3
      [364.11]
Uveoencephalitis 363.22
Uveokeratitis (*see also* Iridocyclitis) 364.3
Uveoparotid fever 135
Uveoparotitis 135
Uvula —*see* condition
Uvulitis (acute) (catarrhal) (chronic)
    (gangrenous) (membranous) (suppurative)
    (ulcerative) 528.3

V

Vaccination
complication or reaction—*see* Complications,
   vaccination
not done (contraindicated) V64.0
   because of patient's decision V64.2
prophylactic (against) V05.9
   arthropod-borne viral
      disease NEC V05.1
      encephalitis V05.0
   chickenpox V05.4
   cholera (alone) V03.0
      with typhoid-paratyphoid (cholera + TAB)
         V06.0
   common cold V04.7
   diphtheria (alone) V03.5
      with
         poliomyelitis (DTP + polio) V06.3
         tetanus V06.5
            -pertussis combined [DTP] V06.1
         typhoid-paratyphoid (DTP + TAB) V06.2
   disease (single) NEC V05.9
      bacterial NEC V03.9
         specified type NEC V03.89
      combinations NEC V06.9
         specified type NEC V06.8
      specified type NEC V05.8
   encephalitis, viral, arthropod-borne V05.0
   Hemophilus influenzae, type B [Hib] V03.81
   hepatitis, viral V05.3
   influenza V04.8
      with
         Streptococcus pneumoniae
            [pneumococcus] V06.6
   lileishmaniasis V05.2
   measles (alone) V04.2
      with mumps-rubella (MMR) V06.4
   mumps (alone) V04.6
      with measles and rubella (MMR) V06.4
   pertussis alone V03.6
   plague V03.3
   poliomyelitis V04.0
      with diphtheria-tetanus-pertussis (DTP +
         polio) V06.3
   rabies V04.5
   rubella (alone) V04.3
      with measles and mumps (MMR) V06.4
   smallpox V04.1
   Streptococcus pneumoniae [pneumococcus]
      V03.82
      with
         influenza V06.6
   tetanus toxoid (alone) V03.7
      with diphtheria [Td] V06.5
         with
            pertussis (DTP) V06.1
               with poliomyelitis (DTP + polio)
                  V06.3
   tuberculosis (BCG) V03.2
   tularemia V03.4
   typhoid-paratyphoid (TAB) (alone) V03.1
      with diphtheria-tetanus-pertussis (TAB +
         DTP) V06.2
   varicella V05.4
   viral
      encephalitis, arthropod-borne V05.0
      hepatitis V05.3
   yellow fever V04.4

Vaccinia (generalized) 999.0
   congenital 771.2
   conjunctiva 999.3
   eyelids 999.0 *[373.5]*
   localized 999.3
   nose 999.3
   not from vaccination 051.0
      eyelid 051.0 *[373.5]*
   sine vaccinatione 051.0
   without vaccination 051.0
Vacuum
   extraction of fetus or newborn 763.3
   in sinus (accessory) (nasal) (*see also* Sinusitis)
      473.9
Vagabond V60.0
Vagabondage V60.0
Vagabonds' disease 132.1
Vagina, vaginal —*see* condition
Vaginalitis (tunica) 608.4
Vaginismus (reflex) 625.1
   functional 306.51
   hysterical 300.11
   psychogenic 306.51
Vaginitis (acute) (chronic) (circumscribed)
      (diffuse) (emphysematous) (Hemophilus
      vaginalis) (nonspecific) (nonvenereal)
      (ulcerative) 616.10
   with
      abortion—*see* Abortion, by type, with sepsis
      ectopic pregnancy (*see also* categories
         633.0-633.9) 639.0
      molar pregnancy (*see also* categories
         630-632) 639.0
   adhesive, congenital 752.49
   atrophic, postmenopausal 627.3
   bacterial 616.10
   blennorrhagic (acute) 098.0
      chronic or duration of 2 months or over 098.2
   candidal 112.1
   chlamydial 099.53
   complicating pregnancy or puerperium 646.6
      affecting fetus or newborn 760.8
   congenital (adhesive) 752.49
   due to
      C. albicans 112.1
      Trichomonas (vaginalis) 131.01
   following
      abortion 639.0
      ectopic or molar pregnancy 639.0
   gonococcal (acute) 098.0
      chronic or duration of 2 months or over 098.2
   granuloma 099.2
   Monilia 112.1
   mycotic 112.1
   pinworm 127.4 *[616.11]*
   postirradiation 616.10
   postmenopausal atrophic 627.3
   senile (atrophic) 627.3
   syphilitic (early) 091.0
      late 095.8
   trichomonal 131.01
   tuberculous (*see also* Tuberculosis) 016.7
   venereal NEC 099.8
Vaginosis —*see* Vaginitis
Vagotonia 352.3
Vagrancy V60.0
Vallecula —*see* condition
Valley fever 114.0

Valsuani's disease (progressive pernicious anemia, puerperal) 648.2
Valve, valvular (formation)—*see also* condition
cerebral ventricle (communicating) in situ V45.2
cervix, internal os 752.49
colon 751.5
congenital NEC—*see* Atresia
formation, congenital NEC—*see* Atresia
heart defect—*see* Anomaly, heart, valve
ureter 753.29
  pelvic junction 753.21
  vesical orifice 753.22
urethra 753.6
Valvulitis (chronic) (*see also* Endocarditis) 424.90
rheumatic (chronic) (inactive) (with chorea) 397.9
  active or acute (aortic) (mitral) (pulmonary) (tricuspid) 391.1
syphilitic NEC 093.20
  aortic 093.22
  mitral 093.21
  pulmonary 093.24
  tricuspid 093.23
Valvulopathy —*see* Endocarditis
van Bogaert's leukoencephalitis (sclerosing) (subacute) 046.2
van Bogaert-Nijssen (-Peiffer) disease 330.0
van Buchem's syndrome (hyperostosis corticalis) 733.3
van Creveld-von Gierke disease (glycogenosis I) 271.0
van den Bergh's disease (enterogenous cyanosis) 289.7
van der Hoeve's syndrome (brittle bones and blue sclera, deafness) 756.51
van der Hoeve-Halbertsma-Waardenburg syndrome (ptosis-epicanthus) 270.2
van der Hoeve-Waardenburg-Gualdi syndrome (ptosis epicanthus) 270.2
Vanillism 692.89
Vanishing lung 492.0
Vanishing twin 651.33
van Neck (-Odelberg) disease or syndrome (juvenile osteochondrosis) 732.1
Vapor asphyxia or suffocation NEC 987.9
specified agent—*see* Table of drugs and chemicals
Vaquez's disease (M9950/1) 238.4
Vaquez-Osler disease (polycythemia vera) (M9950/1) 238.4
Variance, lethal ball, prosthetic heart valve 996.02
Variants, thalassemic 282.4
Variations in hair color 704.3
Varicella 052.9
with
  complication 052.8
    specified NEC 052.7
  pneumonia 052.1
vaccination and inoculation (prophylactic) V05.4
Varices —*see* Varix
Varicocele (scrotum) (thrombosed) 456.4
ovary 456.5
perineum 456.6
spermatic cord (ulcerated) 456.4

Varicose
aneurysm (ruptured) (*see also* Aneurysm) 442.9
dermatitis (lower extremity)—*see* Varicose, vein, inflamed or infected
eczema—*see* Varicose, vein
phlebitis—*see* Varicose, vein, inflamed or infected
placental vessel—*see* Placenta, abnormal
tumor—*see* Varicose, vein
ulcer (lower extremity, any part) 454.0
  anus 455.8
    external 455.5
    internal 455.2
  esophagus (*see also* Varix, esophagus) 456.1
    bleeding (*see also* Varix, esophagus, bleeding) 456.0
  inflamed or infected 454.2
  nasal septum 456.8
  perineum 456.6
  rectum—*see* Varicose, ulcer, anus
  scrotum 456.4
  specified site NEC 456.8
vein (lower extremity) (ruptured) (*see also* Varix) 454.9
  with
    inflammation or infection 454.1
      ulcerated 454.2
    stasis dermatitis 454.1
      with ulcer 454.2
    ulcer 454.0
      inflamed or infected 454.2
  anus—*see* Hemorrhoids
  broad ligament 456.5
  congenital (peripheral) NEC 747.60
    gastrointestinal 747.61
    lower limb 747.64
    renal 747.62
    specified NEC 747.69
    upper limb 747.63
  esophagus (ulcerated) (*see also* Varix, esophagus) 456.1
    bleeding (*see also* Varix, esophagus, bleeding) 456.0
  inflamed or infected 454.1
    with ulcer 454.2
  in pregnancy or puerperium 671.0
    vulva or perineum 671.1
  nasal septum (with ulcer) 456.8
  pelvis 456.5
  perineum 456.6
    in pregnancy, childbirth, or puerperium 671.1
  rectum—*see* Hemorrhoids
  scrotum (ulcerated) 456.4
  specified site NEC 456.8
  sublingual 456.3
  ulcerated 454.0
    inflamed or infected 454.2
  umbilical cord, affecting fetus or newborn 762.6
  urethra 456.8
  vulva 456.6
    in pregnancy, childbirth, or puerperium 671.1
  vessel—*see also* Varix
    placenta—*see* Placenta, abnormal
Varicosis, varicosities, varicosity (*see also* Varix) 454.9

Variola 050.9
  hemorrhagic (pustular) 050.0
  major 050.0
  minor 050.1
  modified 050.2
Varioloid 050.2
Variolosa, purpura 050.0
Varix (lower extremity) (ruptured) 454.9
  with
    inflammation or infection 454.1
      with ulcer 454.2
    stasis dermatitis 454.1
      with ulcer 454.2
    ulcer 454.0
      with inflammation or infection 454.2
  aneurysmal (*see also* Aneurysm) 442.9
  anus—*see* Hemorrhoids
  arteriovenous (congenital) (peripheral) NEC
    747.60
    gastrointestinal 747.61
    lower limb 747.64
    renal 747.62
    specified NEC 747.69
    spinal 747.82
    upper limb 747.63
  bladder 456.5
  broad ligament 456.5
  congenital (peripheral) NEC 747.60
  esophagus (ulcerated) 456.1
    bleeding 456.0
      in
        cirrhosis of liver 571.5 *[456.20]*
        portal hypertension 572.3 *[456.20]*
    congenital 747.69
    in
      cirrhosis of liver 571.5 *[456.21]*
        with bleeding 571.5 *[456.20]*
      portal hypertension 572.3 *[456.21]*
        with bleeding 572.3 *[456.20]*
  inflamed or infected 454.1
    ulcerated 454.2
  in pregnancy or puerperium 671.0
    perineum 671.1
    vulva 671.1
  labia (majora) 456.6
  orbit 456.8
    congenital 747.69
  ovary 456.5
  papillary 448.1
  pelvis 456.5
  perineum 456.6
    in pregnancy or puerperium 671.1
  pharynx 456.8
  placenta—*see* Placenta, abnormal
  rectum—*see* Hemorrhoids
  renal papilla 456.8
  retina 362.17
  scrotum (ulcerated) 456.4
  sigmoid colon 456.8
  specified site NEC 456.8
  spinal (cord) (vessels) 456.8
  spleen, splenic (vein) (with phlebolith) 456.8
  sublingual 456.3
  ulcerated 454.0
    inflamed or infected 454.2
  umbilical cord, affecting fetus or newborn 762.6
  uterine ligament 456.5
  vocal cord 456.8
  vulva 456.6
    in pregnancy, childbirth, or puerperium 671.1

Vasa previa 663.5
  affecting fetus or newborn 762.6
  hemorrhage from, affecting fetus or newborn
    772.0
Vascular —*see also* condition
  loop on papilla (optic) 743.51
  sheathing, retina 362.13
  spasm 443.9
  spider 448.1
Vascularity, pulmonary, congenital 747.3
Vascularization
  choroid 362.16
  cornea 370.60
    deep 370.63
    localized 370.61
  retina 362.16
  subretinal 362.16
Vasculitis 447.6
  allergic 287.0
  cryoglobulinemic 273.2
  disseminated 447.6
  kidney 447.8
  nodular 695.2
  retinal 362.10
  rheumatic—*see* Fever, rheumatic
Vas deferens —*see* condition
Vas deferentitis 608.4
Vasectomy, admission for V25.2
Vasitis 608.4
  nodosa 608.4
  scrotum 608.4
  spermatic cord 608.4
  testis 608.4
  tuberculous (*see also* Tuberculosis) 016.5
  tunica vaginalis 608.4
  vas deferens 608.4
Vasodilation 443.9
Vasomotor —*see* condition
Vasoplasty, after previous sterilization V26.0
Vasoplegia, splanchnic (*see also* Neuropathy,
  peripheral, autonomic) 337.9
Vasospasm 443.9
  cerebral (artery) 435.9
    with transient neurologic deficit 435.9
  nerve
    arm NEC 354.9
    autonomic 337.9
    brachial plexus 353.0
    cervical plexus 353.2
    leg NEC 355.8
    lower extremity NEC 355.8
    peripheral NEC 355.9
    spinal NEC 355.9
    sympathetic 337.9
    upper extremity NEC 354.9
  peripheral NEC 443.9
  retina (artery) (*see also* Occlusion, retinal,
    artery) 362.30
Vasospastic —*see* condition
Vasovagal attack (paroxysmal) 780.2
  psychogenic 306.2
Vater's ampulla —*see* condition
VATER syndrome 759.89
Vegetation, vegetative
  adenoid (nasal fossa) 474.2
  consciousness (persistent) 780.03
  endocarditis (acute) (any valve) (chronic)
    (subacute) 421.0
  heart (mycotic) (valve) 421.0
  state (persistent) 780.03

Veil
Jackson's 751.4
over face (causing asphyxia) 768.9
Vein, venous —*see* condition
Veldt sore (*see also* Ulcer, skin) 707.9
Velpeau's hernia —*see* Hernia, femoral
Venereal
balanitis NEC 099.8
bubo 099.1
disease 099.9
specified nature or type NEC 099.8
granuloma inguinale 099.2
lymphogranuloma (Durand-Nicolas-Favre), any
site 099.1
salpingitis 098.37
urethritis (*see also* Urethritis, nongonococcal)
099.40
vaginitis NEC 099.8
warts 078.19
Vengefulness, in child (*see also* Disturbance,
conduct) 312.0
Venofibrosis 459.89
Venom, venomous
bite or sting (animal or insect) 989.5
poisoning 989.5
Venous —*see* condition
Ventouse delivery NEC 669.5
affecting fetus or newborn 763.3
Ventral —*see* condition
Ventricle, ventricular —*see also* condition
escape 427.69
standstill (*see also* Arrest, cardiac) 427.5
Ventriculitis, cerebral (*see also* Meningitis)
322.9
Ventriculostomy status V45.2
Verbiest's syndrome (claudicatio intermittens
spinalis) 435.1
Vernet's syndrome 352.6
Verneuil's disease (syphilitic bursitis) 095.7
Verruca (filiformis) 078.10
acuminata (any site) 078.11
necrogenica (primary) (*see also* Tuberculosis)
017.0
peruana 088.0
peruviana 088.0
plana (juvenilis) 078.19
plantaris 078.19
seborrheica 702.19
inflamed 702.11
senilis 702.0
tuberculosa (primary) (*see also* Tuberculosis)
017.0
venereal 078.19
viral NEC 078.10
Verrucosities (*see also* Verruca) 078.10
Verrucous endocarditis (acute) (any valve)
(chronic) (subacute) 710.0 *[424.91]*
nonbacterial 710.0 *[424.91]*
Verruga
peruana 088.0
peruviana 088.0
Verse's disease (calcinosis intervertebralis)
275.4 *[722.90]*
Version
before labor, affecting fetus or newborn 761.7
cephalic (correcting previous malposition) 652.1
affecting fetus or newborn 763.1
cervix (*see also* Malposition, uterus) 621.6
uterus (postinfectional) (postpartal, old) (*see
also* Malposition, uterus) 621.6
forward—*see* Anteversion, uterus
lateral—*see* Lateroversion, uterus

Vertebra, vertebral —*see* condition
Vertigo 780.4
auditory 386.19
aural 386.19
benign paroxysmal positional 386.11
central origin 386.2
cerebral 386.2
Dix and Hallpike (epidemic) 386.12
endemic paralytic 078.81
epidemic 078.81
Dix and Hallpike 386.12
Gerlier's 078.81
Pedersen's 386.12
vestibular neuronitis 386.12
epileptic—*see* Epilepsy
Gerlier's (epidemic) 078.81
hysterical 300.11
labyrinthine 386.10
laryngeal 786.2
malignant positional 386.2
Ménière's (*see also* Disease, Ménière's) 386.00
menopausal 627.2
otogenic 386.19
paralytic 078.81
paroxysmal positional, benign 386.11
Pedersen's (epidemic) 386.12
peripheral 386.10
specified type NEC 386.19
positional
benign paroxysmal 386.11
malignant 386.2
Verumontanitis (chronic) (*see also* Urethritis)
597.89
Vesania (*see also* Psychosis) 298.9
Vesical —*see* condition
Vesicle
cutaneous 709.8
seminal—*see* condition
skin 709.8
Vesicocolic —*see* condition
Vesicoperineal —*see* condition
Vesicorectal —*see* condition
Vesicourethrorectal —*see* condition
Vesicovaginal —*see* condition
Vesicular —*see* condition
Vesiculitis (seminal) 608.0
amebic 006.8
gonorrheal (acute) 098.14
chronic or duration of 2 months or over 098.34
trichomonal 131.09
tuberculous (*see also* Tuberculosis) 016.5
[608.81]
Vestibulitis (ear) (*see also* Labyrinthitis) 386.30
nose (external) 478.1
vulvar 616.10
Vestibulopathy, acute peripheral (recurrent)
386.12
Vestige, vestigial —*see also* Persistence
branchial 744.41
structures in vitreous 743.51
Vibriosis NEC 027.9
Vidal's disease (lichen simplex chronicus) 698.3
Video display tube syndrome 723.8
Vienna type encephalitis 049.8
Villaret's syndrome 352.6
Villous —*see* condition

Vincent's
  angina 101
  bronchitis 101
  disease 101
  gingivitis 101
  infection (any site) 101
  laryngitis 101
  stomatitis 101
  tonsillitis 101
Vinson-Plummer syndrome (sideropenic
  dysphagia) 280.8
Viosterol deficiency (*see also* Deficiency,
  calciferol) 268.9
Virchow's disease 733.99
Viremia 790.8
Virilism (adrenal) (female) NEC 255.2
  with
    3-beta-hydroxysteroid dehydrogenase defect
     255.2
    11-hydroxylase defect 255.2
    21-hydroxylase defect 255.2
    adrenal
     hyperplasia 255.2
     insufficiency (congenital) 255.2
    cortical hyperfunction 255.2
Virilization (female) (suprarenal) (*see also*
  Virilism) 255.2
  isosexual 256.4
Virulent bubo 099.0
Virus, viral —*see also* condition
  infection NEC (*see also* Infection, viral) 079.99
  septicemia 079.99
Viscera, visceral —*see* condition
Visceroptosis 569.89
Visible peristalsis 787.4
Vision, visual
  binocular, suppression 368.31
  blurred, blurring 368.8
    hysterical 300.11
  defect, defective (*see also* Impaired, vision)
    369.9
  disorientation (syndrome) 368.16
  disturbance NEC (*see also* Disturbance, vision)
    368.9
    hysterical 300.11
  examination V72.0
  field, limitation 368.40
  fusion, with defective steropsis 368.33
  hallucinations 368.16
  halos 368.16
  loss 369.9
    both eyes (*see also* Blindness, both eyes) 369.3
    complete (*see also* Blindness, both eyes)
     369.00
    one eye 369.8
    sudden 368.16
  low (both eyes) 369.20
    one eye (other eye normal) (*see also* Impaired,
     vision) 369.70
     blindness, other eye 369.10
  perception, simultaneous without fusion 368.32
  tunnel 368.45
Vitality, lack or want of 780.7
  newborn 779.8
Vitamin deficiency NEC (*see also* Deficiency,
  vitamin) 269.2
Vitelline duct, persistent 751.0
Vitiligo 709.01
  due to pinta (carate) 103.2
  eyelid 374.53
  vulva 624.8

Vitium cordis —*see* Disease, heart
Vitreous —*see also* condition
  touch syndrome 997.99
Vocal cord —*see* condition
Vocational rehabilitation V57.22
Vogt's (Cecile) disease or syndrome 333.7
Vogt-Koyanagi syndrome 364.24
Vogt-Spielmeyer disease (amaurotic familial
  idiocy) 330.1
Voice
  change (*see also* Dysphonia) 784.49
  loss (*see also* Aphonia) 784.41
Volhard-Fahr disease (malignant
  nephrosclerosis) 403.00
Volhynian fever 083.1
Volkmann's ischemic contracture or paralysis
  (complicating trauma) 958.6
Voluntary starvation 307.1
Volvulus (bowel) (colon) (intestine) 560.2
  with
    hernia—*see also* Hernia, by site, with
     obstruction
     gangrenous—*see* Hernia, by site, with
      gangrene
    perforation 560.2
  congenital 751.5
  duodenum 537.3
  fallopian tube 620.5
  oviduct 620.5
  stomach (due to absence of gastrocolic
    ligament) 537.89
Vomiting 787.03
  with nausea 787.01
  allergic 535.4
  asphyxia 933.1
  bilious (cause unknown) 787.0
    following gastrointestinal surgery 564.3
  blood (*see also* Hematemesis) 578.0
  causing asphyxia, choking, or suffocation (*see*
    also Asphyxia, food) 933.1
  cyclical 536.2
    psychogenic 306.4
  epidemic 078.82
  fecal matter 569.89
  following gastrointestinal surgery 564.3
  functional 536.8
    psychogenic 306.4
  habit 536.2
  hysterical 300.11
  nervous 306.4
  neurotic 306.4
  newborn 779.3
  of or complicating pregnancy 643.9
    due to
     organic disease 643.8
     specific cause NEC 643.8
    early—*see* Hyperemesis, gravidarum
    late (after 22 completed weeks of gestation)
     643.2
  pernicious or persistent 536.2
    complicating pregnancy—*see* Hyperemesis,
     gravidarum
    psychogenic 306.4
  physiological 787.0
  psychic 306.4
  psychogenic 307.54
  stercoral 569.89
  uncontrollable 536.2
    psychogenic 306.4
  uremic—*see* Uremia
  winter 078.82

von Bechterew (-Strumpell) disease or syndrome (ankylosing spondylitis) 720.0
von Bezold's abscess 383.01
von Economo's disease (encephalitis lethargica) 049.8
von Eulenburg's disease (congenital paramyotonia) 359.2
von Gierke's disease (glycogenosis I) 271.0
von Gies' joint 095.8
von Graefe's disease or syndrome 378.72
von Hippel (-Lindau) disease or syndrome (retinocerebral angiomatosis) 759.6
von Jaksch's anemia or disease (pseudoleukemia infantum) 285.8
von Recklinghausen's
  disease or syndrome (nerves) (skin) (M9540/1) 237.71
  bones (osteitis fibrosa cystica) 252.0
  tumor (M9540/1) 237.71
von Recklinghausen-Applebaum disease (hemochromatosis) 275.0
von Schroetter's syndrome (intermittent venous claudication) 453.8
von Willebrand (-Jürgens) (-Minot) disease or syndrome (angiohemophilia) 286.4
von Zambusch's disease (lichen sclerosus et atrophicus) 701.0
Voorhoeve's disease or dyschondroplasia 756.4
Vossius' ring 921.3
  late effect 366.21
Voyeurism 302.82
Vrolik's disease (osteogenesis imperfecta) 756.51
Vulva —*see* condition
Vulvismus 625.1
Vulvitis (acute) (allergic) (aphthous) (chronic) (gangrenous) (hypertrophic) (intertriginous) 616.10
  with
    abortion—*see* Abortion, by type, with sepsis
    ectopic pregnancy (*see also* categories 633.0-633.9) 639.0
    molar pregnancy (*see also* categories 630-632) 639.0
  adhesive, congenital 752.49
  blennorrhagic (acute) 098.0
    chronic or duration of 2 months or over 098.2
  chlamydial 099.53
  complicating pregnancy or puerperium 646.6
  due to Ducrey's bacillus 099.0
  following
    abortion 639.0
    ectopic or molar pregnancy 639.0
  gonococcal (acute) 098.0
    chronic or duration of 2 months or over 098.2
  herpetic 054.11
  leukoplakic 624.0
  monilial 112.1
  puerperal, postpartum, childbirth 646.6
  syphilitic (early) 091.0
    late 095.8
  trichomonal 131.01
Vulvodynia 625.9
Vulvorectal —*see* condition
Vulvovaginitis (*see also* Vulvitis) 616.10
  amebic 006.8
  chlamydial 099.53
  gonococcal (acute) 098.0
    chronic or duration of 2 months or over 098.2
  herpetic 054.11
  monilial 112.1
  trichomonal (Trichomonas vaginalis) 131.01

W

Waardenburg's syndrome 756.89
  meaning ptosis-epicanthus 270.2
Waardenburg-Klein syndrome
  (ptosis-epicanthus) 270.2
Wagner's disease (colloid milium) 709.3
Wagner (-Unverricht) syndrome
  (dermatomyositis) 710.3
Waiting list, person on V63.2
  undergoing social agency investigation V63.8
Wakefulness disorder (*see also* Hypersomnia)
  780.54
  nonorganic origin 307.43
Waldenström's
  disease (osteochondrosis, capital femoral) 732.1
  hepatitis (lupoid hepatitis) 571.49
  hypergammaglobulinemia 273.0
  macroglobulinemia 273.3
  purpura, hypergammaglobulinemic 273.0
  syndrome (macroglobulinemia) 273.3
Waldenström-Kjellberg syndrome (sideropenic
  dysphagia) 280.8
Walking
  difficulty 719.7
    psychogenic 307.9
  sleep 307.46
    hysterical 300.13
Wall, abdominal —*see* condition
Wallenberg's syndrome (posterior inferior
  cerebellar artery) (*see also* Disease,
  cerebrovascular, acute) 436
Wallgren's
  disease (obstruction of splenic vein with
    collateral circulation) 459.89
  meningitis (*see also* Meningitis, aseptic) 047.9
Wandering
  acetabulum 736.39
  gallbladder 751.69
  kidney, congenital 753.3
  organ or site, congenital NEC—*see*
    Malposition, congenital
  pacemaker (atrial) (heart) 427.89
  spleen 289.59
Wardrop's disease (with lymphangitis) 681.9
  finger 681.02
  toe 681.11
War neurosis 300.16
Wart (common) (digitate) (filiform) (infectious)
  (juvenile) (plantar) (viral) 078.10
  external genital organs (venereal) 078.19
  fig 078.19
  Hassall-Henle's (of cornea) 371.41
  Henle's (of cornea) 371.41
  juvenile 078.19
  moist 078.10
  Peruvian 088.0
  plantar 078.19
  prosector (*see also* Tuberculosis) 017.0
  seborrheic 702.19
    inflamed 702.11
  senile 702.0
  specified NEC 078.19
  syphilitic 091.3
  tuberculous (*see also* Tuberculosis) 017.0
  venereal (female) (male) 078.19
Warthin's tumor (salivary gland) (M8561/0)
  210.2
Washerwoman's itch 692.4

Wassilieff's disease (leptospiral jaundice) 100.0
Wasting
  disease 799.4
    due to malnutrition 261
  extreme (due to malnutrition) 261
  muscular NEC 728.2
  palsy, paralysis 335.21
Water
  clefts 366.12
  deprivation of 994.3
  in joint (*see also* Effusion, joint) 719.0
  intoxication 276.6
  itch 120.3
  lack of 994.3
  loading 276.6
  on
    brain—*see* Hydrocephalus
    chest 511.8
  poisoning 276.6
Waterbrash 787.1
Water-hammer pulse (*see also* Insufficiency,
  aortic) 424.1
Waterhouse (-Friderichsen) disease or syndrome
  036.3
Water-losing nephritis 588.8
Wax in ear 380.4
Waxy
  degeneration, any site 277.3
  disease 277.3
  kidney 277.3 *[583.81]*
  liver (large) 277.3
  spleen 277.3
Weak, weakness (generalized) 780.7
  arches (acquired) 734
    congenital 754.61
  bladder sphincter 596.59
  congenital 779.8
  eye muscle—*see* Strabismus
  foot (double)—*see* Weak, arches
  heart, cardiac (*see also* Failure, heart) 428.9
    congenital 746.9
  mind 317
  muscle 728.9
  myocardium (*see also* Failure, heart) 428.9
  newborn 779.8
  pelvic fundus 618.8
  pulse 785.9
  senile 797
  valvular—*see* Endocarditis
Wear, worn, tooth, teeth (approximal) (hard
  tissues) (interproximal) (occlusal) 521.1
Weather, weathered
  effects of
    cold NEC 991.9
      specified effect NEC 991.8
    hot (*see also* Heat) 992.9
  skin 692.74
Web, webbed (congenital)—*see also* Anomaly,
  specified type NEC
  canthus 743.63
  digits (*see also* Syndactylism) 755.10
  esophagus 750.3
  fingers (*see also* Syndactylism, fingers) 755.11
  larynx (glottic) (subglottic) 748.2
  neck (pterygium colli) 744.5
  Paterson-Kelly (sideropenic dysphagia) 280.8
  popliteal syndrome 756.89
  toes (*see also* Syndactylism, toes) 755.13

WX YZ

Withdrawal symptoms, syndrome
alcohol 291.81
  delirium (acute) 291.0
    chronic 291.1
    newborn 760.71
drug or narcotic 292.0
newborn, infant of dependent mother 779.5
steroid NEC
  correct substance properly administered 255.4
  overdose or wrong substance given or taken
    962.0
Withdrawing reaction, child or adolescent
313.22
Witts' anemia (achlorhydric anemia) 280.9
Witzelsucht 301.9
Woakes' syndrome (ethmoiditis) 471.1
Wohlfart-Kugelberg-Welander disease 335.11
Woillez's disease (acute idiopathic pulmonary
  congestion) 518.5
Wolff-Parkinson-White syndrome (anomalous
  atrioventricular excitation) 426.7
Wolhynian fever 083.1
Wolman's disease (primary familial
  xanthomatosis) 272.7
Wood asthma 495.8
Woolly, wooly hair (congenital) (nevus) 757.4
Wool-sorters' disease 022.1
Word
blindness (congenital) (developmental) 315.01
  secondary to organic lesion 784.61
deafness (secondary to organic lesion) 784.69
  developmental 315.31
Worm (s) (colic) (fever) (infection) (infestation)
  (*see also* Infestation) 128.9
guinea 125.7
in intestine NEC 127.9
Worm-eaten soles 102.3
Worn out (*see also* Exhaustion) 780.7
"Worried well" V65.5
Wound, open (by cutting or piercing instrument)
  (by firearms) (cut) (dissection) (incised)
  (laceration) (penetration) (perforating)
  (puncture) (with initial hemorrhage, not
  internal) 879.8

Note—For fracture with open wound, see
Fracture. For laceration, traumatic rupture, tear
or penetrating wound of internal organs, such as
heart, lung, liver, kidney, pelvic organs, etc.,
whether or not accompanied by open wound or
fracture in the same region, see Injury, internal.
For contused wound, see Contusion. For crush
injury, see Crush. For abrasion, insect bite
(nonvenomous), blister, or scratch, see Injury,
superficial.

Complicated includes wounds with:
  delayed healing
  delayed treatment
  foreign body
  primary infection

For late effect of open wound, see Late, effect,
wound, open, by site.

abdomen, abdominal (external) (muscle) 879.2
  complicated 879.3
  wall (anterior) 879.2
    complicated 879.3
    lateral 879.4
      complicated 879.5

Wound, open—*continued*
alveolar (process) 873.62
  complicated 873.72
ankle 891.0
  with tendon involvement 891.2
  complicated 891.1
anterior chamber, eye (*see also* Wound, open,
  intraocular) 871.9
anus 879.6
  complicated 879.7
arm 884.0
  with tendon involvement 884.2
  complicated 884.1
forearm 881.00
  with tendon involvement 881.20
  complicated 881.10
multiple sites—*see* Wound, open, multiple,
  upper limb
upper 880.03
  with tendon involvement 880.23
  complicated 880.13
multiple sites (with axillary or shoulder
  regions) 880.09
  with tendon involvement 880.29
  complicated 880.19
artery—*see* Injury, blood vessel, by site
auditory
canal (external) (meatus) 872.02
  complicated 872.12
ossicles (incus) (malleus) (stapes) 872.62
  complicated 872.72
auricle, ear 872.01
  complicated 872.11
axilla 880.02
  with tendon involvement 880.22
  complicated 880.12
  with tendon involvement 880.29
involving other sites of upper arm 880.09
  complicated 880.19
back 876.0
  complicated 876.1
bladder—*see* Injury, internal, bladder
blood vessel—*see* Injury, blood vessel, by site
brain—*see* Injury, intracranial, with open
  intracranial wound
breast 879.0
  complicated 879.1
brow 873.42
  complicated 873.52
buccal mucosa 873.61
  complicated 873.71
buttock 877.0
  complicated 877.1
calf 891.0
  with tendon involvement 891.2
  complicated 891.1
canaliculus lacrimalis 870.8
  with laceration of eyelid 870.2
canthus, eye 870.8
  laceration—*see* Laceration, eyelid
cavernous sinus—*see* Injury, intracranial
cerebellum—*see* Injury, intracranial
cervical esophagus 874.4
  complicated 874.5
cervix—*see* Injury, internal, cervix
cheek(s) (external) 873.41
  complicated 873.51
  internal 873.61
    complicated 873.71
chest (wall) (external) 875.0
  complicated 875.1

Wound, open—*continued*
intracranial—*see* Injury, intracranial, with open
    intracranial wound
intraocular 871.9
  with
    partial loss (of intraocular tissue) 871.2
    prolapse or exposure (of intraocular tissue)
      871.1
  laceration (*see also* Laceration, eyeball) 871.4
  penetrating 871.7
    with foreign body (nonmagnetic) 871.6
      magnetic 871.5
  without prolapse (of intraocular tissue) 871.0
iris (*see also* Wound, open, eyeball) 871.9
jaw (fracture not involved) 873.44
  with fracture—*see* Fracture, jaw
  complicated 873.54
knee 891.0
  with tendon involvement 891.2
  complicated 891.1
labium (majus) (minus) 878.4
  complicated 878.5
lacrimal apparatus, gland, or sac 870.8
  with laceration of eyelid 870.2
larynx 874.01
  with trachea 874.00
    complicated 874.10
  complicated 874.11
leg (multiple) 891.0
  with tendon involvement 891.2
  complicated 891.1
  lower 891.0
    with tendon involvement 891.2
    complicated 891.1
  thigh 890.0
    with tendon involvement 890.2
    complicated 890.1
  upper 890.0
    with tendon involvement 890.2
    complicated 890.1
lens (eye) (alone) (*see also* Cataract, traumatic)
    366.20
  with involvement of other eye structures—*see*
    Wound, open, eyeball
limb
  lower (multiple) NEC 894.0
    with tendon involvement 894.2
    complicated 894.1
  upper (multiple) NEC 884.0
    with tendon involvement 884.2
    complicated 884.1
lip 873.43
  complicated 873.53
loin 876.0
  complicated 876.1
lumbar region 876.0
  complicated 876.1
malar region 873.41
  complicated 873.51
mastoid region 873.49
  complicated 873.59
mediastinum—*see* Injury, internal, mediastinum
midthoracic region 875.0
  complicated 875.1
mouth 873.60
  complicated 873.70
  floor 873.64
    complicated 873.74
  multiple sites 873.69
    complicated 873.79

wound, open—*continued*
specified site NEC 873.69
  complicated 873.79
multiple, unspecified site(s) 879.8

> Note—Multiple open wounds of sites
> classifiable to the same four-digit category
> should be classified to that category unless they
> are in different limbs.
>
> Multiple open wounds of sites classifiable to
> different four-digit categories, or to different
> limbs, should be coded separately.

  complicated 879.9
  lower limb(s) (one or both) (sites classifiable
    to more than one three-digit category in
    890 to 893) 894.0
    with tendon involvement 894.2
    complicated 894.1
  upper limb(s) (one or both) (sites classifiable
    to more than one three-digit category in
    880 to 883) 884.0
    with tendon involvement 884.2
    complicated 884.1
muscle—*see* Sprain, by site
nail
  finger(s) 883.0
    complicated 883.1
  thumb 883.0
    complicated 883.1
  toe(s) 893.0
    complicated 893.1
nape (neck) 874.8
  complicated 874.9
  specified part NEC 874.8
    complicated 874.9
nasal—*see also* Wound, open, nose
  cavity 873.22
    complicated 873.32
  septum 873.21
    complicated 873.31
  sinuses 873.23
    complicated 873.33
nasopharynx 873.22
  complicated 873.32
neck 874.8
  complicated 874.9
  nape 874.8
    complicated 874.9
  specified part NEC 874.8
    complicated 874.9
nerve—*see* Injury, nerve, by site
non-healing surgical 998.83
nose 873.20
  complicated 873.30
  multiple sites 873.29
    complicated 873.39
  septum 873.21
    complicated 873.31
  sinuses 873.23
    complicated 873.33
occipital region—*see* Wound, open, scalp
ocular NEC 871.9
  adnexa 870.9
    specified region NEC 870.8
  laceration (*see also* Laceration, ocular) 871.4
  muscle (extraocular) 870.3
    with foreign body 870.4
    eyelid 870.1
  intraocular—*see* Wound, open, eyeball

Wound, open—*continued*

penetrating (*see also* Penetrating wound, ocular) 871.7

orbit 870.8

penetrating 870.3

with foreign body 870.4

orbital region 870.9

ovary—*see* Injury, internal, pelvic organs

palate 873.65

complicated 873.75

palm 882.0

with tendon involvement 882.2

complicated 882.1

parathyroid (gland) 874.2

complicated 874.3

parietal region—*see* Wound, open, scalp

pelvic floor or region 879.6

complicated 879.7

penis 878.0

complicated 878.1

perineum 879.6

complicated 879.7

periocular area 870.8

laceration of skin 870.0

pharynx 874.4

complicated 874.5

pinna 872.01

complicated 872.11

popliteal space 891.0

with tendon involvement 891.2

complicated 891.1

prepuce 878.0

complicated 878.1

pubic region 879.2

complicated 879.3

pudenda 878.8

complicated 878.9

rectovaginal septum 878.8

complicated 878.9

sacral region 877.0

complicated 877.1

sacroiliac region 877.0

complicated 877.1

salivary (ducts) (glands) 873.69

complicated 873.79

scalp 873.0

complicated 873.1

scalpel, fetus or newborn 767.8

scapular region 880.01

with tendon involvement 880.21

complicated 880.11

involving other sites of upper arm 880.09

with tendon involvement 880.29

complicated 880.19

sclera (*see also* Wound, open, intraocular) 871.9

scrotum 878.2

complicated 878.3

seminal vesicle—*see* Injury, internal, pelvic organs

shin 891.0

with tendon involvement 891.2

complicated 891.1

shoulder 880.00

with tendon involvement 880.20

complicated 880.10

involving other sites of upper arm 880.09

with tendon involvement 880.29

complicated 880.19

skin NEC 879.8

complicated 879.9

Wound, open—*continued*

skull—*see also* Injury, intracranial, with open intracranial wound

with skull fracture—*see* Fracture, skull

spermatic cord (scrotal) 878.2

complicated 878.3

pelvic region—*see* Injury, internal, spermatic cord

spinal cord—*see* Injury, spinal

sternal region 875.0

complicated 875.1

subconjunctival—*see* Wound, open, intraocular

subcutaneous NEC 879.8

complicated 879.9

submaxillary region 873.44

complicated 873.54

submental region 873.44

complicated 873.54

subungual

finger(s) (thumb)—*see* Wound, open, finger

toe(s)—*see* Wound, open, toe

supraclavicular region 874.8

complicated 874.9

supraorbital 873.42

complicated 873.52

surgical, non-healing 998.83

temple 873.49

complicated 873.59

temporal region 873.49

complicated 873.59

testis 878.2

complicated 878.3

thigh 890.0

with tendon involvement 890.2

complicated 890.1

thorax, thoracic (external) 875.0

complicated 875.1

throat 874.8

complicated 874.9

thumb (nail) (subungual) 883.0

with tendon involvement 883.2

complicated 883.1

thyroid (gland) 874.2

complicated 874.3

toe(s) (nail) (subungual) 893.0

with tendon involvement 893.2

complicated 893.1

tongue 873.64

complicated 873.74

tonsil—*see* Wound, open, neck

trachea (cervical region) 874.02

with larynx 874.00

complicated 874.10

complicated 874.12

intrathoracic—*see* Injury, internal, trachea

trunk (multiple) NEC 879.6

complicated 879.7

specified site NEC 879.6

complicated 879.7

tunica vaginalis 878.2

complicated 878.3

tympanic membrane 872.61

complicated 872.71

tympanum 872.61

complicated 872.71

umbilical region 879.2

complicated 879.3

ureter—*see* Injury, internal, ureter

urethra—*see* Injury, internal, urethra

uterus—*see* Injury, internal, uterus

Wound, open—*continued*
  uvula 873.69
    complicated 873.79
  vagina 878.6
    complicated 878.7
  vas deferens—*see* Injury, internal, vas deferens
  vitreous (humor) 871.2
  vulva 878.4
    complicated 878.5
  wrist 881.02
    with tendon involvement 881.22
    complicated 881.12
Wright's syndrome (hyperabduction) 447.8
  pneumonia 390 *[517.1]*
Wringer injury —*see* Crush injury, by site
Wrinkling of skin 701.8
Wrist —*see also* condition
  drop (acquired) 736.05
Wrong drug (given in error) NEC 977.9
  specified drug or substance—*see* Table of drugs
    and chemicals
Wry neck —*see also* Torticollis
  congenital 754.1
Wuchereria infestation 125.0
  bancrofti 125.0
  Brugia malayi 125.1
  malayi 125.1
Wuchereriasis 125.0
Wuchereriosis 125.0
Wuchernde struma langhans (M8332/3) 193

X

Xanthelasma 272.2
  eyelid 272.2 *[374.51]*
  palpebrarum 272.2 *[374.51]*
Xanthelasmatosis (essential) 272.2
Xanthelasmoidea 757.33
Xanthine stones 277.2
Xanthinuria 277.2
Xanthofibroma (M8831/0)—*see* Neoplasm,
  connective tissue, benign
Xanthoma (s), xanthomatosis 272.2
  with
    hyperlipoproteinemia
      type I 272.3
      type III 272.2
      type IV 272.1
      type V 272.3
  bone 272.7
  craniohypophyseal 277.8
  cutaneotendinous 272.7
  diabeticorum 250.8 *[272.2]*
  disseminatum 272.7
  eruptive 272.2
  eyelid 272.2 *[374.51]*
  familial 272.7
  hereditary 272.7
  hypercholesterinemic 272.0
  hypercholesterolemic 272.0
  hyperlipemic 272.4
  hyperlipidemic 272.4
  infantile 272.7
  joint 272.7
  juvenile 272.7
  multiple 272.7
  multiplex 272.7
  primary familial 272.7
  tendon (sheath) 272.7
  tuberosum 272.2
  tuberous 272.2
  tubo-eruptive 272.2
Xanthosis 709.09
  surgical 998.81
Xenophobia 300.29
Xeroderma (congenital) 757.39
  acquired 701.1
    eyelid 373.33
  eyelid 373.33
  pigmentosum 757.33
  vitamin A deficiency 264.8
Xerophthalmia 372.53
  vitamin A deficiency 264.7
Xerosis
  conjunctiva 372.53
    with Bitôt's spot 372.53
      vitamin A deficiency 264.1
    vitamin A deficiency 264.0
  cornea 371.40
    with corneal ulceration 370.00
      vitamin A deficiency 264.3
    vitamin A deficiency 264.2
  cutis 706.8
  skin 706.8
Xerostomia 527.7
Xiphodynia 733.90
Xiphoidalgia 733.90
Xiphoiditis 733.99
Xiphopagus 759.4
XO syndrome 758.6

X-ray
  effects, adverse, NEC 990
  of chest
    for suspected tuberculosis V71.2
    routine V72.5
XXX syndrome 758.81
XXXXY syndrome 758.81
XXY syndrome 758.7
Xyloketosuria 271.8
Xylosuria 271.8
Xylulosuria 271.8
XYY syndrome 758.81

Y

Yawning 786.09
  psychogenic 306.1
Yaws 102.9
  bone or joint lesions 102.6
  butter 102.1
  chancre 102.0
  cutaneous, less than five years after infection
      102.2
  early (cutaneous) (macular) (maculopapular)
      (micropapular) (papular) 102.2
    frambeside 102.2
    skin lesions NEC 102.2
  eyelid 102.9 *[373.4]*
  ganglion 102.6
  gangosis, gangosa 102.5
  gumma, gummata 102.4
    bone 102.6
  gummatous
    frambeside 102.4
    osteitis 102.6
    periostitis 102.6
  hydrarthrosis 102.6
  hyperkeratosis (early) (late) (palmar) (plantar)
      102.3
  initial lesions 102.0
  joint lesions 102.6
  juxta-articular nodules 102.7
  late nodular (ulcerated) 102.4
  latent (without clinical manifestations) (with
      positive serology) 102.8
  mother 102.0
  mucosal 102.7
  multiple papillomata 102.1
  nodular, late (ulcerated) 102.4
  osteitis 102.6
  papilloma, papillomata (palmar) (plantar) 102.1
  periostitis (hypertrophic) 102.6
  ulcers 102.4
  wet crab 102.1
Yeast infection (*see also* Candidiasis) 112.9
Yellow
  atrophy (liver) 570
    chronic 571.8
    resulting from administration of blood,
        plasma, serum, or other biological
        substance (within 8 months of
        administration)—*see* Hepatitis, viral
  fever—*see* Fever, yellow
  jack (*see also* Fever, yellow) 060.9
  jaundice (*see also* Jaundice) 782.4
Yersinia septica 027.8

Z

Zagari's disease (xerostomia) 527.7
Zahorsky's disease (exanthema subitum) 057.8
  syndrome (herpangina) 074.0
Zenker's diverticulum (esophagus) 530.6
Ziehen-Oppenheim disease 333.6
Zieve's syndrome (jaundice, hyperlipemia, and
  hemolytic anemia) 571.1
Zika fever 066.3
Zollinger-Ellison syndrome (gastric
  hypersecretion with pancreatic islet cell
  tumor) 251.5
Zona (*see also* Herpes, zoster) 053.9
Zoophilia (erotica) 302.1
Zoophobia 300.29
Zoster (herpes) (*see also* Herpes, zoster) 053.9
Zuelzer (-Ogden) anemia or syndrome
  (nutritional megaloblastic anemia) 281.2
Zygodactyly (*see also* Syndactylism) 755.10
Zygomycosis 117.7
Zymotic —*see* condition

SECTION 2

ALPHABETIC INDEX TO POISONING AND EXTERNAL CAUSES OF ADVERSE EFFECTS OF DRUGS AND OTHER CHEMICAL SUBSTANCES

TABLE OF DRUGS AND CHEMICALS

This table contains a classification of drugs and other chemical substances to identify poisoning states and external causes of adverse effects.

Each of the listed substances in the table is assigned a code according to the poisoning classification (960–989). These codes are used when there is a statement of poisoning, overdose, wrong substance given or taken, or intoxication.

The table also contains a listing of external causes of adverse effects. An adverse effect is a pathologic manifestation due to ingestion or exposure to drugs or other chemical substances (e.g., dermatitis, hypersensitivity reaction, aspirin gastritis). The adverse effect is to be identified by the appropriate code found in Section 1, Index to Diseases and Injuries. An external cause code can then be used to identify the circumstances involved. The table headings pertaining to external causes are defined below:

> **Accidental poisoning (E850–E869)**—accidental overdose of drug, wrong substance given or taken, drug taken inadvertently, accidents in the usage of drugs and biologicals in medical and surgical procedures, and to show external causes of poisonings classifiable to 980–989.

> **Therapeutic use (E930–E949)**—a correct substance properly administered in therapeutic or prophylactic dosage as the external cause of adverse effects.

> **Suicide attempt (E950–E952)**—instances in which self–inflicted injuries or poisonings are involved.

> **Assault (E961–E962)**—injury or poisoning inflicted by another person with the intent to injure or kill.

> **Undetermined (E980–E982)**—to be used when the intent of the poisoning or injury cannot be determined whether it was intentional or accidental.

The American Hospital Formulary Service list numbers are included in the table to help classify new drugs not identified in the table by name. The AHFS list numbers are keyed to the continually revised American Hospital Formulary Service (AHFS).* These listings are found in the table under the main term **Drug**.

Excluded from the table are radium and other radioactive substances. The classification of adverse effects and complications pertaining to these substances will be found in Section 1, Index to Diseases and Injuries, and Section 3, Index to External Causes of Injuries.

Although certain substances are indexed with one or more subentries, the majority are listed according to one use or state. It is recognized that many substances may be used in various ways, in medicine and in industry, and may cause adverse effects whatever the state of the agent (solid, liquid, or fumes arising from a liquid). In cases in which the reported data indicates a use or state not in the table, or which is clearly different from the one listed, an attempt should be made to classify the substance in the form which most nearly expresses the reported facts.

*American Hospital Formulary Service, 2 vol. (Washington, DC: American Society of Hospital Pharmacists, 1959-)

Substance	Poisoning	External Cause (E-Code)				
		Accident	Therapeutic Use	Suicide Attempt	Assault	Undetermined
1–propanol	980.3	E860.4	—	E950.9	E962.1	E980.9
2–propanol	980.2	E860.3	—	E950.9	E962.1	E980.9
2, 4–D (dichlorophenoxyacetic acid)	989.4	E863.5	—	E950.6	E962.1	E980.7
2, 4–toluene diisocyanate	983.0	E864.0	—	E950.7	E962.1	E980.6
2, 4, 5–T (trichlorophenoxyacetic acid)	989.2	E863.5	—	E950.6	E962.1	E980.7
14–hydroxydihydromorphinone	965.09	E850.2	E935.2	E950.0	E962.0	E980.0
ABOB	961.7	E857	E931.7	E950.4	E962.0	E980.4
Abrus (seed)	988.2	E865.3	—	E950.9	E962.1	E980.9
Absinthe	980.0	E860.1	—	E950.9	E962.1	E980.9
beverage	980.0	E860.0	—	E950.9	E962.1	E980.9
Acenocoumarin, acenocoumarol	964.2	E858.2	E934.2	E950.4	E962.0	E980.4
Acepromazine	969.1	E853.0	E939.1	E950.3	E962.0	E980.3
Acetal	982.8	E862.4	—	E950.9	E962.1	E980.9
Acetaldehyde (vapor)	987.8	E869.8	—	E952.8	E962.2	E982.8
liquid	989.89	E866.8	—	E950.9	E962.1	E980.9
Acetaminophen	965.4	E850.4	E935.4	E950.0	E962.0	E980.0
Acetaminosalol	965.1	E850.3	E935.3	E950.0	E962.0	E980.0
Acetanilid(e)	965.4	E850.4	E935.4	E950.0	E962.0	E980.0
Acetarsol, acetarsone	961.1	E857	E931.1	E950.4	E962.0	E980.4
Acetazolamide	974.2	E858.5	E944.2	E950.4	E962.0	E980.4
Acetic						
acid	983.1	E864.1	—	E950.7	E962.1	E980.6
with sodium acetate (ointment)	976.3	E858.7	E946.3	E950.4	E962.0	E980.4
irrigating solution	974.5	E858.5	E944.5	E950.4	E962.0	E980.4
lotion	976.2	E858.7	E946.2	E950.4	E962.0	E980.4
anhydride	983.1	E864.1	—	E950.7	E962.1	E980.6
ether (vapor)	982.8	E862.4	—	E950.9	E962.1	E980.9
Acetohexamide	962.3	E858.0	E932.3	E950.4	E962.0	E980.4
Acetomenaphthone	964.3	E858.2	E934.3	E950.4	E962.0	E980.4
Acetomorphine	965.01	E850.0	E935.0	E950.0	E962.0	E980.0
Acetone (oils) (vapor)	982.8	E862.4	—	E950.9	E962.1	E980.9
Acetophenazine (maleate)	969.1	E853.0	E939.1	E950.3	E962.0	E980.3
Acetophenetidin	965.4	E850.4	E935.4	E950.0	E962.0	E980.0
Acetophenone	982.0	E862.4	—	E950.9	E962.1	E980.9
Acetorphine	965.09	E850.2	E935.2	E950.0	E962.0	E980.0
Acetosulfone (sodium)	961.8	E857	E931.8	E950.4	E962.0	E980.4
Acetrizoate (sodium)	977.8	E858.8	E947.8	E950.4	E962.0	E980.4
Acetylcarbromal	967.3	E852.2	E937.3	E950.2	E962.0	E980.2
Acetylcholine (chloride)	971.0	E855.3	E941.0	E950.4	E962.0	E980.4
Acetylcysteine	975.5	E858.6	E945.5	E950.4	E962.0	E980.4
Acetyldigitoxin	972.1	E858.3	E942.1	E950.4	E962.0	E980.4
Acetyldihydrocodeine	965.09	E850.2	E935.2	E950.0	E962.0	E980.0
Acetyldihydrocodeinone	965.09	E850.2	E935.2	E950.0	E962.0	E980.0
Acetylene (gas) (industrial)	987.1	E868.1	—	E951.8	E962.2	E981.8
incomplete combustion of — *see* Carbon monoxide, fuel, utility						
tetrachloride (vapor)	982.3	E862.4	—	E950.9	E962.1	E980.9
Acetyliodosalicylic acid	965.1	E850.3	E935.3	E950.0	E962.0	E980.0
Acetylphenylhydrazine	965.8	E850.8	E935.8	E950.0	E962.0	E980.0
Acetylsalicylic acid	965.1	E850.3	E935.3	E950.0	E962.0	E980.0
Achromycin	960.4	E856	E930.4	E950.4	E962.0	E980.4
ophthalmic preparation	976.5	E858.7	E946.5	E950.4	E962.0	E980.4
topical NEC	976.0	E858.7	E946.0	E950.4	E962.0	E980.4
Acidifying agents	963.2	E858.1	E933.2	E950.4	E962.0	E980.4
Acids (corrosive) NEC	983.1	E864.1	—	E950.7	E962.1	E980.6
Aconite (wild)	988.2	E865.4	—	E950.9	E962.1	E980.9
Aconitine (liniment)	976.8	E858.7	E946.8	E950.4	E962.0	E980.4

Substance	Poisoning	External Cause (E-Code)				
		Accident	Therapeutic Use	Suicide Attempt	Assault	Undetermined
Aconitum ferox	988.2	E865.4	—	E950.9	E962.1	E980.9
Acridine	983.0	E864.0	—	E950.7	E962.1	E980.6
vapor	987.8	E869.8	—	E952.8	E962.2	E982.8
Acriflavine	961.9	E857	E931.9	E950.4	E962.0	E980.4
Acrisorcin	976.0	E858.7	E946.0	E950.4	E962.0	E980.4
Acrolein (gas)	987.8	E869.8	—	E952.8	E962.2	E982.8
liquid	989.89	E866.8	—	E950.9	E962.1	E980.9
Actaea spicata	988.2	E865.4	—	E950.9	E962.1	E980.9
Acterol	961.5	E857	E931.5	E950.4	E962.0	E980.4
ACTH	962.4	E858.0	E932.4	E950.4	E962.0	E980.4
Acthar	962.4	E858.0	E932.4	E950.4	E962.0	E980.4
Actinomycin (C) (D)	960.7	E856	E930.7	E950.4	E962.0	E980.4
Adalin (acetyl)	967.3	E852.2	E937.3	E950.2	E962.0	E980.2
Adenosine (phosphate)	977.8	E858.8	E947.8	E950.4	E962.0	E980.4
Adhesives	989.89	E866.6	—	E950.9	E962.1	E980.9
ADH	962.5	E858.0	E932.5	E950.4	E962.0	E980.4
Adicillin	960.0	E856	E930.0	E950.4	E962.0	E980.4
Adiphenine	975.1	E855.6	E945.1	E950.4	E962.0	E980.4
Adjunct, pharmaceutical	977.4	E858.8	E947.4	E950.4	E962.0	E980.4
Adrenal (extract, cortex or medulla) (glucocorticoids) (hormones) (mineralocorticoids)	962.0	E858.0	E932.0	E950.4	E962.0	E980.4
ENT agent	976.6	E858.7	E946.6	E950.4	E962.0	E980.4
ophthalmic preparation	976.5	E858.7	E946.5	E950.4	E962.0	E980.4
topical NEC	976.0	E858.7	E946.0	E950.4	E962.0	E980.4
Adrenalin	971.2	E855.5	E941.2	E950.4	E962.0	E980.4
Adrenergic blocking agents	971.3	E855.6	E941.3	E950.4	E962.0	E980.4
Adrenergics	971.2	E855.5	E941.2	E950.4	E962.0	E980.4
Adrenochrome (derivatives)	972.8	E858.3	E942.8	E950.4	E962.0	E980.4
Adrenocorticotropic hormone	962.4	E858.0	E932.4	E950.4	E962.0	E980.4
Adrenocorticotropin	962.4	E858.0	E932.4	E950.4	E962.0	E980.4
Adriamycin	960.7	E856	E930.7	E950.4	E962.0	E980.4
Aerosol spray — see Sprays						
Aerosporin	960.8	E856	E930.8	E950.4	E962.0	E980.4
ENT agent	976.6	E858.7	E946.6	E950.4	E962.0	E980.4
ophthalmic preparation	976.5	E858.7	E946.5	E950.4	E962.0	E980.4
topical NEC	976.0	E858.7	E946.0	E950.4	E962.0	E980.4
Aethusa cynapium	988.2	E865.4	—	E950.9	E962.1	E980.9
Afghanistan black	969.6	E854.1	E939.6	E950.3	E962.0	E980.3
Aflatoxin	989.7	E865.9	—	E950.9	E962.1	E980.9
African boxwood	988.2	E865.4	—	E950.9	E962.1	E980.9
Agar (–agar)	973.3	E858.4	E943.3	E950.4	E962.0	E980.4
Agricultural agent NEC	989.89	E863.9	—	E950.6	E962.1	E980.7
Agrypnal	967.0	E851	E937.0	E950.1	E962.0	E980.1
Air contaminant(s), source or type not specified	987.9	E869.9	—	E952.9	E962.2	E982.9
specified type — see specific substance						
Akee	988.2	E865.4	—	E950.9	E962.1	E980.9
Akrinol	976.0	E858.7	E946.0	E950.4	E962.0	E980.4
Alantolactone	961.6	E857	E931.6	E950.4	E962.0	E980.4
Albamycin	960.8	E856	E930.8	E950.4	E962.0	E980.4
Albumin (normal human serum)	964.7	E858.2	E934.7	E950.4	E962.0	E980.4
Alcohol	980.9	E860.9	—	E950.9	E962.1	E980.9
absolute	980.0	E860.1	—	E950.9	E962.1	E980.9
beverage	980.0	E860.0	E947.8	E950.9	E962.1	E980.9
amyl	980.3	E860.4	—	E950.9	E962.1	E980.9
antifreeze	980.1	E860.2	—	E950.9	E962.1	E980.9

Substance	Poisoning	Accident	External Cause (E-Code)			
			Therapeutic Use	Suicide Attempt	Assault	Undetermined
butyl	980.3	E860.4	—	E950.9	E962.1	E980.9
dehydrated	980.0	E860.1	—	E950.9	E862.1	E980.9
beverage	980.0	E860.0	E947.8	E950.9	E962.1	E980.9
denatured	980.0	E860.1	—	E950.9	E962.1	E980.9
deterrents	977.3	E858.8	E947.3	E950.4	E962.0	E980.4
diagnostic (gastric function)	977.8	E858.8	E947.8	E950.4	E962.0	E980.4
ethyl	980.0	E860.1	—	E950.9	E962.1	E980.9
beverage	980.0	E860.0	E947.8	E950.9	E962.1	E980.9
grain	980.0	E860.1	—	E950.9	E962.1	E980.9
beverage	980.0	E860.0	E947.8	E950.9	E962.1	E980.9
industrial	980.9	E860.9	—	E950.9	E962.1	E980.9
isopropyl	980.2	E860.3	—	E950.9	E962.1	E980.9
methyl	980.1	E860.2	—	E950.9	E962.1	E980.9
preparation for consumption	980.0	E860.0	E947.8	E950.9	E962.1	E980.9
propyl	980.3	E860.4	—	E950.9	E962.1	E980.9
secondary	980.2	E860.3	—	E950.9	E962.1	E980.9
radiator	980.1	E860.2	—	E950.9	E962.1	E980.9
rubbing	980.2	E860.3	—	E950.9	E962.1	E980.9
specified type NEC	980.8	E860.8	—	E950.9	E962.1	E980.9
surgical	980.9	E860.9	—	E950.9	E962.1	E980.9
vapor (from any type of alcohol)	987.8	E869.8	—	E952.8	E962.2	E982.8
wood	980.1	E860.2	—	E950.9	E962.1	E980.9
Alcuronium chloride	975.2	E858.6	E945.2	E950.4	E962.0	E980.4
Aldactone	974.4	E858.5	E944.4	E950.4	E962.0	E980.4
Aldicarb	989.3	E863.2	—	E950.6	E962.1	E980.7
Aldomet	972.6	E858.3	E942.6	E950.4	E962.0	E980.4
Aldosterone	962.0	E858.0	E932.0	E950.4	E962.0	E980.4
Aldrin (dust)	989.2	E863.0	—	E950.6	E962.1	E980.7
Algeldrate	973.0	E858.4	E943.0	E950.4	E962.0	E980.4
Alidase	963.4	E858.1	E933.4	E950.4	E962.0	E980.4
Aliphatic thiocyanates	989.0	E866.8	—	E950.9	E962.1	E980.9
Alkaline antiseptic solution (aromatic)	976.6	E858.7	E946.6	E950.4	E962.0	E980.4
Alkalinizing agents (medicinal)	963.3	E858.1	E933.3	E950.4	E962.0	E980.4
Alkalis, caustic	983.2	E864.2	—	E950.7	E962.1	E980.6
Alkalizing agents (medicinal)	963.3	E858.1	E933.3	E950.4	E962.0	E980.4
Alka–seltzer	965.1	E850.3	E935.3	E950.0	E962.0	E980.0
Alkavervir	972.6	E858.3	E942.6	E950.4	E962.0	E980.4
Allegron	969.0	E854.0	E939.0	E950.3	E962.0	E980.3
Alleve see Naproxen						
Allobarbital, allobarbitone	967.0	E851	E937.0	E950.1	E962.0	E980.1
Allopurinol	974.7	E858.5	E944.7	E950.4	E962.0	E980.4
Allylestrenol	962.2	E858.0	E932.2	E950.4	E962.0	E980.4
Allylisopropylacetylurea	967.8	E852.8	E937.8	E950.2	E962.0	E980.2
Allylisopropylmalonylurea	967.0	E851	E937.0	E950.1	E962.0	E980.1
Allyltribromide	967.3	E852.2	E937.3	E950.2	E962.0	E980.2
Aloe, aloes, aloin	973.1	E858.4	E943.1	E950.4	E962.0	E980.4
Aloxidone	966.0	E855.0	E936.0	E950.4	E962.0	E980.4
Aloxiprin	965.1	E850.3	E935.3	E950.0	E962.0	E980.0
Alpha amylase	963.4	E858.1	E933.4	E950.4	E962.0	E980.4
Alphaprodine (hydrochloride)	965.09	E850.2	E935.2	E950.0	E962.0	E980.0
Alpha tocopherol	963.5	E858.1	E933.5	E950.4	E962.0	E980.4
Alseroxylon	972.6	E858.3	E942.6	E950.4	E962.0	E980.4
Alum (ammonium) (potassium)	983.2	E864.2	—	E950.7	E962.1	E980.6
medicinal (astringent) NEC	976.2	E858.7	E946.2	E950.4	E962.0	E980.4
Aluminium, aluminum (gel) (hydroxide)	973.0	E858.4	E943.0	E950.4	E962.0	E980.4
acetate solution	976.2	E858.7	E946.2	E950.4	E962.0	E980.4
aspirin	965.1	E850.3	E935.3	E950.0	E962.0	E980.0

Substance	Poisoning	External Cause (E-Code)				
		Accident	Therapeutic Use	Suicide Attempt	Assault	Undetermined
carbonate	973.0	E858.4	E943.0	E950.4	E962.0	E980.4
glycinate	973.0	E858.4	E943.0	E950.4	E962.0	E980.4
nicotinate	972.2	E858.3	E942.2	E950.4	E962.0	E980.4
ointment (surgical) (topical)	976.3	E858.7	E946.3	E950.4	E962.0	E980.4
phosphate	973.0	E858.4	E943.0	E950.4	E962.0	E980.4
subacetate	976.2	E858.7	E946.2	E950.4	E962.0	E980.4
topical NEC	976.3	E858.7	E946.3	E950.4	E962.0	E980.4
Alurate	967.0	E851	E937.0	E950.1	E962.0	E980.1
Alverine (citrate)	975.1	E858.6	E945.1	E950.4	E962.0	E980.4
Alvodine	965.09	E850.2	E935.2	E950.0	E962.0	E980.0
Amanita phalloides	988.1	E865.5	—	E950.9	E962.1	E980.9
Amantadine (hydrochloride)	966.4	E855.0	E936.4	E950.4	E962.0	E980.4
Ambazone	961.9	E857	E931.9	E950.4	E962.0	E980.4
Ambenonium	971.0	E855.3	E941.0	E950.4	E962.0	E980.4
Ambutonium bromide	971.1	E855.4	E941.1	E950.4	E962.0	E980.4
Ametazole	977.8	E858.8	E947.8	E950.4	E962.0	E980.4
Amethocaine (infiltration) (topical)	968.5	E855.2	E938.5	E950.4	E962.0	E980.4
nerve block (peripheral) (plexus)	968.6	E855.2	E938.6	E950.4	E962.0	E980.4
spinal	968.7	E855.2	E938.7	E950.4	E962.0	E980.4
Amethopterin	963.1	E858.1	E933.1	E950.4	E962.0	E980.4
Amfepramone	977.0	E858.8	E947.0	E950.4	E962.0	E980.4
Amidon	965.02	E850.1	E935.1	E950.0	E962.0	E980.0
Amidopyrine	965.5	E850.5	E935.5	E950.0	E962.0	E980.0
Aminacrine	976.0	E858.7	E946.0	E950.4	E962.0	E980.4
Aminitrozole	961.5	E857	E931.5	E950.4	E962.0	E980.4
Aminoacetic acid	974.5	E858.5	E944.5	E950.4	E962.0	E980.4
Amino acids	974.5	E858.5	E944.5	E950.4	E962.0	E980.4
Aminocaproic acid	964.4	E858.2	E934.4	E950.4	E962.0	E980.4
Aminoethylisothiourium	963.8	E858.1	E933.8	E950.4	E962.0	E980.4
Aminoglutethimide	966.3	E855.0	E936.3	E950.4	E962.0	E980.4
Aminometradine	974.3	E858.5	E944.3	E950.4	E962.0	E980.4
Aminopentamide	971.1	E855.4	E941.1	E950.4	E962.0	E980.4
Aminophenazone	965.5	E850.5	E935.5	E950.0	E962.0	E980.0
Aminophenol	983.0	E864.0	—	E950.7	E962.1	E980.6
Aminophenylpyridone	969.5	E853.8	E939.5	E950.3	E962.0	E980.3
Aminophyllin	975.7	E858.6	E945.7	E950.4	E962.0	E980.4
Aminopterin	963.1	E858.1	E933.1	E950.4	E962.0	E980.4
Aminopyrine	965.5	E850.5	E935.5	E950.0	E962.0	E980.0
Aminosalicylic acid	961.8	E857	E931.8	E950.4	E962.0	E980.4
Amiphenazole	970.1	E854.3	E940.1	E950.4	E962.0	E980.4
Amiquinsin	972.6	E858.3	E942.6	E950.4	E962.0	E980.4
Amisometradine	974.3	E858.5	E944.3	E950.4	E962.0	E980.4
Amitriptyline	969.0	E854.0	E939.0	E950.3	E962.0	E980.3
Ammonia (fumes) (gas) (vapor)	987.8	E869.8	—	E952.8	E962.2	E982.8
liquid (household) NEC	983.2	E861.4	—	E950.7	E962.1	E980.6
spirit, aromatic	970.8	E854.3	E940.8	E950.4	E962.0	E980.4
Ammoniated mercury	976.0	E858.7	E946.0	E950.4	E962.0	E980.4
Ammonium						
carbonate	983.2	E864.2	—	E950.7	E962.1	E980.6
chloride (acidifying agent)	963.2	E858.1	E933.2	E950.4	E962.0	E980.4
expectorant	975.5	E858.6	E945.5	E950.4	E962.0	E980.4
compounds (household) NEC	983.2	E861.4	—	E950.7	E962.1	E980.6
fumes (any usage)	987.8	E869.8	—	E952.8	E962.2	E982.8
industrial	983.2	E864.2	—	E950.7	E962.1	E980.6
ichthyosulfonate	976.4	E858.7	E946.4	E950.4	E962.0	E980.4
mandelate	961.9	E857	E931.9	E950.4	E962.0	E980.4
Amobarbital	967.0	E851	E937.0	E950.1	E962.0	E980.1

Substance	Poisoning	External Cause (E-Code)				
		Accident	Therapeutic Use	Suicide Attempt	Assault	Undetermined
Amodiaquin(e)	961.4	E857	E931.4	E950.4	E962.0	E980.4
Amopyroquin(e)	961.4	E857	E931.4	E950.4	E962.0	E980.4
Amphenidone	969.5	E853.8	E939.5	E950.3	E962.0	E980.3
Amphetamine	969.7	E854.2	E939.7	E950.3	E962.0	E980.3
Amphomycin	960.8	E856	E930.8	E950.4	E962.0	E980.4
Amphotericin B	960.1	E856	E930.1	E950.4	E962.0	E980.4
topical	976.0	E858.7	E946.0	E950.4	E962.0	E980.4
Ampicillin	960.0	E856	E930.0	E950.4	E962.0	E980.4
Amprotropine	971.1	E855.4	E941.1	E950.4	E962.0	E980.4
Amygdalin	977.8	E858.8	E947.8	E950.4	E962.0	E980.4
Amyl						
acetate (vapor)	982.8	E862.4	—	E950.9	E962.1	E980.9
alcohol	980.3	E860.4	—	E950.9	E962.1	E980.9
nitrite (medicinal)	972.4	E858.3	E942.4	E950.4	E962.0	E980.4
Amylase (alpha)	963.4	E858.1	E933.4	E950.4	E962.0	E980.4
Amylene hydrate	980.8	E860.8	—	E950.9	E962.1	E980.9
Amylobarbitone	967.0	E851	E937.0	E950.1	E962.0	E980.1
Amylocaine	968.9	E855.2	E938.9	E950.4	E962.0	E980.4
infiltration (subcutaneous)	968.5	E855.2	E938.5	E950.4	E962.0	E980.4
nerve block (peripheral) (plexus)	968.6	E855.2	E938.6	E950.4	E962.0	E980.4
spinal	968.7	E855.2	E938.7	E950.4	E962.0	E980.4
topical (surface)	968.5	E855.2	E938.5	E950.4	E962.0	E980.4
Amytal (sodium)	967.0	E851	E937.0	E950.1	E962.0	E980.1
Analeptics	970.0	E854.3	E940.0	E950.4	E962.0	E980.4
Analgesics	965.9	E850.9	E935.9	E950.0	E962.0	E980.0
aromatic NEC	965.4	E850.4	E935.4	E950.0	E962.0	E980.0
non–narcotic NEC	965.7	E850.7	E935.7	E950.0	E962.0	E980.0
specified NEC	965.8	E850.8	E935.8	E950.0	E962.0	E980.0
Anamirta cocculus	988.2	E865.3	—	E950.9	E962.1	E980.9
Ancillin	960.0	E856	E930.0	E950.4	E962.0	E980.4
Androgens (anabolic congeners)	962.1	E858.0	E932.1	E950.4	E962.0	E980.4
Androstalone	962.1	E858.0	E932.1	E950.4	E962.0	E980.4
Androsterone	962.1	E858.0	E932.1	E950.4	E962.0	E980.4
Anemone pulsatilla	988.2	E865.4	—	E950.9	E962.1	E980.9
Anesthesia, anesthetic (general) NEC	968.4	E855.1	E938.4	E950.4	E962.0	E980.4
block (nerve) (plexus)	968.6	E855.2	E938.6	E950.4	E962.0	E980.4
gaseous NEC	968.2	E855.1	E938.2	E950.4	E962.0	E980.4
halogenated hydrocarbon derivatives NEC	968.2	E855.1	E938.2	E950.4	E962.0	E980.4
infiltration (intradermal) (subcutaneous) (submucosal)	968.5	E855.2	E938.5	E950.4	E962.0	E980.4
intravenous	968.3	E855.1	E938.3	E950.4	E962.0	E980.4
local NEC	968.9	E855.2	E938.9	E950.4	E962.0	E980.4
nerve blocking (peripheral) (plexus)	968.6	E855.2	E938.6	E950.4	E962.0	E980.4
rectal NEC	968.3	E855.1	E938.3	E950.4	E962.0	E980.4
spinal	968.7	E855.2	E938.7	E950.4	E962.0	E980.4
surface	968.5	E855.2	E938.5	E950.4	E962.0	E980.4
topical	968.5	E855.2	E938.5	E950.4	E962.0	E980.4
Aneurine	963.5	E858.1	E933.5	E950.4	E962.0	E980.4
Angio–Conray	977.8	E858.8	E947.8	E950.4	E962.0	E980.4
Angininesee Glyceryl trinitrate						
Angiotensin	971.2	E855.5	E941.2	E950.4	E962.0	E980.4
Anhydrohydroxyprogesterone	962.2	E858.0	E932.2	E950.4	E962.0	E980.4
Anhydron	974.3	E858.5	E944.3	E950.4	E962.0	E980.4
Anileridine	965.09	E850.2	E935.2	E950.0	E962.0	E980.0
Aniline (dye) (liquid)	983.0	E864.0	—	E950.7	E962.1	E980.6
analgesic	965.4	E850.4	E935.4	E950.0	E962.0	E980.0

1234

Substance	Poisoning	External Cause (E-Code)				
		Accident	Therapeutic Use	Suicide Attempt	Assault	Undetermined
derivatives, therapeutic NEC	965.4	E850.4	E935.4	E950.0	E962.0	E980.0
vapor	987.8	E869.8	—	E952.8	E962.2	E982.8
Anisindione	964.2	E858.2	E934.2	E950.4	E962.0	E980.4
Anisotropine	971.1	E855.4	E941.1	E950.4	E962.0	E980.4
Anorexic agents	977.0	E858.8	E947.0	E950.4	E962.0	E980.4
Ant (bite) (sting)	989.5	E905.5	—	E950.9	E962.1	E980.9
Antabuse	977.3	E858.8	E947.3	E950.4	E962.0	E980.4
Antacids	973.0	E858.4	E943.0	E950.4	E962.0	E980.4
Antazoline	963.0	E858.1	E933.0	E950.4	E962.0	E980.4
Anthelmintics	961.6	E857	E931.6	E950.4	E962.0	E980.4
Anthralin	976.4	E858.7	E946.4	E950.4	E962.0	E980.4
Anthramycin	960.7	E856	E930.7	E950.4	E962.0	E980.4
Antiadrenergics	971.3	E855.6	E941.3	E950.4	E962.0	E980.4
Antiallergic agents	963.0	E858.1	E933.0	E950.4	E962.0	E980.4
Antianemic agents NEC	964.1	E858.2	E934.1	E950.4	E962.0	E980.4
Antiaris toxicaria	988.2	E865.4	—	E950.9	E962.1	E980.9
Antiarteriosclerotic agents	972.2	E858.3	E942.2	E950.4	E962.0	E980.4
Antiasthmatics	975.7	E858.6	E945.7	E950.4	E962.0	E980.4
Antibiotics	960.9	E856	E930.9	E950.4	E962.0	E980.4
antifungal	960.1	E856	E930.1	E950.4	E962.0	E980.4
antimycobacterial	960.6	E856	E930.6	E950.4	E962.0	E980.4
antineoplastic	960.7	E856	E930.7	E950.4	E962.0	E980.4
cephalosporin (group)	960.5	E856	E930.5	E950.4	E962.0	E980.4
chloramphenicol (group)	960.2	E856	E930.2	E950.4	E962.0	E980.4
macrolides	960.3	E856	E930.3	E950.4	E962.0	E980.4
specified NEC	960.8	E856	E930.8	E950.4	E962.0	E980.4
tetracycline (group)	960.4	E856	E930.4	E950.4	E962.0	E980.4
Anticancer agents NEC	963.1	E858.1	E933.1	E950.4	E962.0	E980.4
antibiotics	960.7	E856	E930.7	E950.4	E962.0	E980.4
Anticholinergics	971.1	E855.4	E941.1	E950.4	E962.0	E980.4
Anticholinesterase (organophosphorus) (reversible)	971.0	E855.3	E941.0	E950.4	E962.0	E980.4
Anticoagulants	964.2	E858.2	E934.2	E950.4	E962.0	E980.4
antagonists	964.5	E858.2	E934.5	E950.4	E962.0	E980.4
Anti–common cold agents NEC	975.6	E858.6	E945.6	E950.4	E962.0	E980.4
Anticonvulsants NEC	966.3	E855.0	E936.3	E950.4	E962.0	E980.4
Antidepressants	969.0	E854.0	E939.0	E950.3	E962.0	E980.3
Antidiabetic agents	962.3	E858.0	E932.3	E950.4	E962.0	E980.4
Antidiarrheal agents	973.5	E858.4	E943.5	E950.4	E962.0	E980.4
Antidiuretic hormone	962.5	E858.0	E932.5	E950.4	E962.0	E980.4
Antidotes NEC	977.2	E858.8	E947.2	E950.4	E962.0	E980.4
Antiemetic agents	963.0	E858.1	E933.0	E950.4	E962.0	E980.4
Antiepilepsy agent NEC	966.3	E855.0	E936.3	E950.4	E962.0	E980.4
Antifertility pills	962.2	E858.0	E932.2	E950.4	E962.0	E980.4
Antiflatulents	973.8	E858.4	E943.8	E950.4	E962.0	E980.4
Antifreeze	989.89	E866.8	—	E950.9	E962.1	E980.9
alcohol	980.1	E860.2	—	E950.9	E962.1	E980.9
ethylene glycol	982.8	E862.4	—	E950.9	E962.1	E980.9
Antifungals (nonmedicinal) (sprays)	989.4	E863.6	—	E950.6	E962.1	E980.7
medicinal NEC	961.9	E857	E931.9	E950.4	E962.0	E980.4
antibiotic	960.1	E856	E930.1	E950.4	E962.0	E980.4
topical	976.0	E858.7	E946.0	E950.4	E962.0	E980.4
Antigastric secretion agents	973.0	E858.4	E943.0	E950.4	E962.0	E980.4
Antihelmintics	961.6	E857	E931.6	E950.4	E962.0	E980.4
Antihemophilic factor (human)	964.7	E858.2	E934.7	E950.4	E962.0	E980.4
Antihistamine	963.0	E858.1	E933.0	E950.4	E962.0	E980.4
Antihypertensive agents NEC	972.6	E858.3	E942.6	E950.4	E962.0	E980.4

1235

Substance	Poisoning	External Cause (E-Code)				
		Accident	Therapeutic Use	Suicide Attempt	Assault	Undetermined
Anti–infectives NEC	961.9	E857	E931.9	E950.4	E962.0	E980.4
antibiotics	960.9	E856	E930.9	E950.4	E962.0	E980.4
specified NEC	960.8	E856	E930.8	E950.4	E962.0	E980.4
antihelmintic	961.6	E857	E931.6	E950.4	E962.0	E980.4
antimalarial	961.4	E857	E931.4	E950.4	E962.0	E980.4
antimycobacterial NEC	961.8	E857	E931.8	E950.4	E962.0	E980.4
antibiotics	960.6	E856	E930.6	E950.4	E962.0	E980.4
antiprotozoal NEC	961.5	E857	E931.5	E950.4	E962.0	E980.4
blood	961.4	E857	E931.4	E950.4	E962.0	E980.4
antiviral	961.7	E857	E931.7	E950.4	E962.0	E980.4
arsenical	961.1	E857	E931.1	E950.4	E962.0	E980.4
ENT agents	976.6	E858.7	E946.6	E950.4	E962.0	E980.4
heavy metals NEC	961.2	E857	E931.2	E950.4	E962.0	E980.4
local	976.0	E858.7	E946.0	E950.4	E962.0	E980.4
ophthalmic preparation	976.5	E858.7	E946.5	E950.4	E962.0	E980.4
topical NEC	976.0	E858.7	E946.0	E950.4	E962.0	E980.4
Anti–inflammatory agents (topical)	976.0	E858.7	E946.0	E950.4	E962.0	E980.4
Antiknock (tetraethyl lead)	984.1	E862.1	—	E950.9	E962.1	E980.9
Antilipemics	972.2	E858.3	E942.2	E950.4	E962.0	E980.4
Antimalarials	961.4	E857	E931.4	E950.4	E962.0	E980.4
Antimony (compounds) (vapor) NEC	985.4	E866.2	—	E950.9	E962.1	E980.9
anti–infectives	961.2	E857	E931.2	E950.4	E962.0	E980.4
pesticides (vapor)	985.4	E863.4	—	E950.6	E962.2	E980.7
potassium tartrate	961.2	E857	E931.2	E950.4	E962.0	E980.4
tartrated	961.2	E857	E931.2	E950.4	E962.0	E980.4
Antimuscarinic agents	971.1	E855.4	E941.1	E950.4	E962.0	E980.4
Antimycobacterials NEC	961.8	E857	E931.8	E950.4	E962.0	E980.4
antibiotics	960.6	E856	E930.6	E950.4	E962.0	E980.4
Antineoplastic agents	963.1	E858.1	E933.1	E950.4	E962.0	E980.4
antibiotics	960.7	E856	E930.7	E950.4	E962.0	E980.4
Anti–Parkinsonism agents	966.4	E855.0	E936.4	E950.4	E962.0	E980.4
Antiphlogistics	965.6	E850.6	E935.6	E950.0	E962.0	E980.0
Antiprotozoals NEC	961.5	E857	E931.5	E950.4	E962.0	E980.4
blood	961.4	E857	E931.4	E950.4	E962.0	E980.4
Antipruritics (local)	976.1	E858.7	E946.1	E950.4	E962.0	E980.4
Antipsychotic agents NEC	969.3	E853.8	E939.3	E950.3	E962.0	E980.3
Antipyretics	965.9	E850.9	E935.9	E950.0	E962.0	E980.0
specified NEC	965.8	E850.8	E935.8	E950.0	E962.0	E980.0
Antipyrine	965.5	E850.5	E935.5	E950.0	E962.0	E980.0
Antirabies serum (equine)	979.9	E858.8	E949.9	E950.4	E962.0	E980.4
Antirheumatics	965.6	E850.6	E935.6	E950.0	E962.0	E980.0
Antiseborrheics	976.4	E858.7	E946.4	E950.4	E962.0	E980.4
Antiseptics (external) (medicinal)	976.0	E858.7	E946.0	E950.4	E962.0	E980.4
Antistine	963.0	E858.1	E933.0	E950.4	E962.0	E980.4
Antithyroid agents	962.8	E858.0	E932.8	E950.4	E962.0	E980.4
Antitoxin, any	979.9	E858.8	E949.9	E950.4	E962.0	E980.4
Antituberculars	961.8	E857	E931.8	E950.4	E962.0	E980.4
antibiotics	960.6	E856	E930.6	E950.4	E962.0	E980.4
Antitussives	975.4	E858.6	E945.5	E950.4	E962.0	E980.4
Antivaricose agents (sclerosing)	972.7	E858.3	E942.7	E950.4	E962.0	E980.4
Antivenin (crotaline) (spider–bite)	979.9	E858.8	E949.9	E950.4	E962.0	E980.4
Antivert	963.0	E858.1	E933.0	E950.4	E962.0	E980.4
Antivirals NEC	961.7	E857	E931.7	E950.4	E962.0	E980.4
Ant poisons — see Pesticides						
Antrol	989.4	E863.4	—	E950.6	E962.1	E980.7
fungicide	989.4	E863.6	—	E950.6	E962.1	E980.7
Apomorphine hydrochloride (emetic)	973.6	E858.4	E943.6	E950.4	E962.0	E980.4

Substance	Poisoning	External Cause (E-Code)				
		Accident	Therapeutic Use	Suicide Attempt	Assault	Undetermined
Appetite depressants, central	977.0	E858.8	E947.0	E950.4	E962.0	E980.4
Apresoline	972.6	E858.3	E942.6	E950.4	E962.0	E980.4
Aprobarbital, aprobarbitone	967.0	E851	E937.0	E950.1	E962.0	E980.1
Apronalide	967.8	E852.8	E937.8	E950.2	E962.0	E980.2
Aqua fortis	983.1	E864.1	—	E950.7	E962.1	E980.6
Arachis oil (topical)	976.3	E858.7	E946.3	E950.4	E962.0	E980.4
cathartic	973.2	E858.4	E943.2	E950.4	E962.0	E980.4
Aralen	961.4	E857	E931.4	E950.4	E962.0	E980.4
Arginine salts	974.5	E858.5	E944.5	E950.4	E962.0	E980.4
Argyrol	976.0	E858.7	E946.0	E950.4	E962.0	E980.4
ENT agent	976.6	E858.7	E946.6	E950.4	E962.0	E980.4
ophthalmic preparation	976.5	E858.7	E946.5	E950.4	E962.0	E980.4
Aristocort	962.0	E858.0	E932.0	E950.4	E962.0	E980.4
ENT agent	976.6	E858.7	E946.6	E950.4	E962.0	E980.4
ophthalmic preparation	976.5	E858.7	E946.5	E950.4	E962.0	E980.4
topical NEC	976.0	E858.7	E946.0	E950.4	E962.0	E980.4
Aromatics, corrosive	983.0	E864.0	—	E950.7	E962.1	E980.6
disinfectants	983.0	E861.4	—	E950.7	E962.1	E980.6
Arsenate of lead (insecticide)	985.1	E863.4	—	E950.8	E962.1	E980.8
herbicide	985.1	E863.5	—	E950.8	E962.1	E980.8
Arsenic, arsenicals (compounds) (dust) (fumes) (vapor) NEC	985.1	E866.3	—	E950.8	E962.1	E980.8
anti–infectives	961.1	E857	E931.1	E950.4	E962.0	E980.4
pesticide (dust) (fumes)	985.1	E863.4	—	E950.8	E962.1	E980.8
Arsine (gas)	985.1	E866.3	—	E950.8	E962.1	E980.8
Arsphenamine (silver)	961.1	E857	E931.1	E950.4	E962.0	E980.4
Arsthinol	961.1	E857	E931.1	E950.4	E962.0	E980.4
Artane	971.1	E855.4	E941.1	E950.4	E962.0	E980.4
Arthropod (venomous) NEC	989.5	E905.5	—	E950.9	E962.1	E980.9
Asbestos	989.81	E866.8	—	E950.9	E962.1	E980.9
Ascaridole	961.6	E857	E931.6	E950.4	E962.0	E980.4
Ascorbic acid	963.5	E858.1	E933.5	E950.4	E962.0	E980.4
Asiaticoside	976.0	E858.7	E946.0	E950.4	E962.0	E980.4
Aspidium (oleoresin)	961.6	E857	E931.6	E950.4	E962.0	E980.4
Aspirin	965.1	E850.3	E935.3	E950.0	E962.0	E980.0
Astringents (local)	976.2	E858.7	E946.2	E950.4	E962.0	E980.4
Atabrine	961.3	E857	E931.3	E950.4	E962.0	E980.4
Ataractics	969.5	E853.8	E939.5	E950.3	E962.0	E980.3
Atonia drug, intestinal	973.3	E858.4	E943.3	E950.4	E962.0	E980.4
Atophan	974.7	E858.5	E944.7	E950.4	E962.0	E980.4
Atropine	971.1	E855.4	E941.1	E950.4	E962.0	E980.4
Attapulgite	973.5	E858.4	E943.5	E950.4	E962.0	E980.4
Attenuvax	979.4	E858.8	E949.4	E950.4	E962.0	E980.4
Aureomycin	960.4	E856	E930.4	E950.4	E962.0	E980.4
ophthalmic preparation	976.5	E858.7	E946.5	E950.4	E962.0	E980.4
topical NEC	976.0	E858.7	E946.0	E950.4	E962.0	E980.4
Aurothioglucose	965.6	E850.6	E935.6	E950.0	E962.0	E980.0
Aurothioglycanide	965.6	E850.6	E935.6	E950.0	E962.0	E980.0
Aurothiomalate	965.6	E850.6	E935.6	E950.0	E962.0	E980.0
Automobile fuel	981	E862.1	—	E950.9	E962.1	E980.9
Autonomic nervous system agents NEC	971.9	E855.9	E941.9	E950.4	E962.0	E980.4
Avlosulfon	961.8	E857	E931.8	E950.4	E962.0	E980.4
Avomine	967.8	E852.8	E937.8	E950.2	E962.0	E980.2
Azacyclonol	969.5	E853.8	E939.5	E950.3	E962.0	E980.3
Azapetine	971.3	E855.6	E941.3	E950.4	E962.0	E980.4
Azaribine	963.1	E858.1	E933.1	E950.4	E962.0	E980.4
Azaserine	960.7	E856	E930.7	E950.4	E962.0	E980.4

Substance	Poisoning	Accident	Therapeutic Use	Suicide Attempt	Assault	Undetermined
Azathioprine	963.1	E858.1	E933.1	E950.4	E962.0	E980.4
Azosulfamide	961.0	E857	E931.0	E950.4	E962.0	E980.4
Azulfidine	961.0	E857	E931.0	E950.4	E962.0	E980.4
Azuresin	977.8	E858.8	E947.8	E950.4	E962.0	E980.4
Bacimycin	976.0	E858.7	E946.0	E950.4	E962.0	E980.4
ophthalmic preparation	976.5	E858.7	E946.5	E950.4	E962.0	E980.4
Bacitracin	960.8	E856	E930.8	E950.4	E962.0	E980.4
ENT agent	976.6	E858.7	E946.6	E950.4	E962.0	E980.4
ophthalmic preparation	976.5	E858.7	E946.5	E950.4	E962.0	E980.4
topical NEC	976.0	E858.7	E946.0	E950.4	E962.0	E980.4
Baking soda	963.3	E858.1	E933.3	E950.4	E962.0	E980.4
BAL	963.8	E858.1	E933.8	E950.4	E962.0	E980.4
Bamethan (sulfate)	972.5	E858.3	E942.5	E950.4	E962.0	E980.4
Bamipine	963.0	E858.1	E933.0	E950.4	E962.0	E980.4
Baneberry	988.2	E865.4	—	E950.9	E962.1	E980.9
Banewort	988.2	E865.4	—	E950.9	E962.1	E980.9
Barbenyl	967.0	E851	E937.0	E950.1	E962.0	E980.1
Barbital, barbitone	967.0	E851	E937.0	E950.1	E962.0	E980.1
Barbiturates, barbituric acid	967.0	E851	E937.0	E950.1	E962.0	E980.1
anesthetic (intravenous)	968.3	E855.1	E938.3	E950.4	E962.0	E980.4
Barium (carbonate) (chloride) (sulfate)	985.8	E866.4	—	E950.9	E962.1	E980.9
diagnostic agent	977.8	E858.8	E947.8	E950.4	E962.0	E980.4
pesticide	985.8	E863.4	—	E950.6	E962.1	E980.7
rodenticide	985.8	E863.7	—	E950.6	E962.1	E980.7
Barrier cream	976.3	E858.7	E946.3	E950.4	E962.0	E980.4
Battery acid or fluid	983.1	E864.1	—	E950.7	E962.1	E980.6
Bay rum	980.8	E860.8	—	E950.9	E962.1	E980.9
BCG vaccine	978.0	E858.8	E948.0	E950.4	E962.0	E980.4
Bearsfoot	988.2	E865.4	—	E950.9	E962.1	E980.9
Beclamide	966.3	E855.0	E936.3	E950.4	E962.0	E980.4
Bee (sting) (venom)	989.5	E905.3	—	E950.9	E962.1	E980.9
Belladonna (alkaloids)	971.1	E855.4	E941.1	E950.4	E962.0	E980.4
Bemegride	970.0	E854.3	E940.0	E950.4	E962.0	E980.4
Benactyzine	969.8	E855.8	E939.8	E950.3	E962.0	E980.3
Benadryl	963.0	E858.1	E933.0	E950.4	E962.0	E980.4
Bendrofluazide	974.3	E858.5	E944.3	E950.4	E962.0	E980.4
Bendroflumethiazide	974.3	E858.5	E944.3	E950.4	E962.0	E980.4
Benemid	974.7	E858.5	E944.7	E950.4	E962.0	E980.4
Benethamine penicillin G	960.0	E856	E930.0	E950.4	E962.0	E980.4
Benisone	976.0	E858.7	E946.0	E950.4	E962.0	E980.4
Benoquin	976.8	E858.7	E946.8	E950.4	E962.0	E980.4
Benoxinate	968.5	E855.2	E938.5	E950.4	E962.0	E980.4
Bentonite	976.3	E858.7	E946.3	E950.4	E962.0	E980.4
Benzalkonium (chloride)	976.0	E858.7	E946.0	E950.4	E962.0	E980.4
ophthalmic preparation	976.5	E858.7	E946.5	E950.4	E962.0	E980.4
Benzamidosalicylate (calcium)	961.8	E857	E931.8	E950.4	E962.0	E980.4
Benzathine penicillin	960.0	E856	E930.0	E950.4	E962.0	E980.4
Benzcarbimine	963.1	E858.1	E933.1	E950.4	E962.0	E980.4
Benzedrex	971.2	E855.5	E941.2	E950.4	E962.0	E980.4
Benzedrine (amphetamine)	969.7	E854.2	E939.7	E950.3	E962.0	E980.3
Benzene (acetyl) (dimethyl) (methyl) (solvent) (vapor)	982.0	E862.4	—	E950.9	E962.1	E980.9
hexachloride (gamma) (insecticide) (vapor)	989.2	E863.0	—	E950.6	E962.1	E980.7
Benzethonium	976.0	E858.7	E946.0	E950.4	E962.0	E980.4
Benzhexol (chloride)	966.4	E855.0	E936.4	E950.4	E962.0	E980.4
Benzilonium	971.1	E855.4	E941.1	E950.4	E962.0	E980.4

Substance	Poisoning	Accident	Therapeutic Use	Suicide Attempt	Assault	Undetermined
				External Cause (E-Code)		

Benzin(e) — *see* Ligroin

Substance	Poisoning	Accident	Therapeutic Use	Suicide Attempt	Assault	Undetermined
Benziodarone	972.4	E858.3	E942.4	E950.4	E962.0	E980.4
Benzocaine	968.5	E855.2	E938.5	E950.4	E962.0	E980.4
Benzodiapin	969.4	E853.2	E939.4	E950.3	E962.0	E980.3
Benzodiazepines (tranquilizers) NEC	969.4	E853.2	E939.4	E950.3	E962.0	E980.3
Benzoic acid (with salicylic acid) (anti–infective)	976.0	E858.7	E946.0	E950.4	E962.0	E980.4
Benzoin	976.3	E858.7	E946.3	E950.4	E962.0	E980.4
Benzol (vapor)	982.0	E862.4	—	E950.9	E962.1	E980.9
Benzomorphan	965.09	E850.2	E935.2	E950.0	E962.0	E980.0
Benzonatate	975.4	E858.6	E945.4	E950.4	E962.0	E980.4
Benzothiadiazides	974.3	E858.5	E944.3	E950.4	E962.0	E980.4
Benzoylpas	961.8	E857	E931.8	E950.4	E962.0	E980.4
Benzperidol	969.5	E853.8	E939.5	E950.3	E962.0	E980.3
Benzphetamine	977.0	E858.8	E947.0	E950.4	E962.0	E980.4
Benzpyrinium	971.0	E855.3	E941.0	E950.4	E962.0	E980.4
Benzquinamide	963.0	E858.1	E933.0	E950.4	E962.0	E980.4
Benzthiazide	974.3	E858.5	E944.3	E950.4	E962.0	E980.4
Benztropine	971.1	E855.4	E941.1	E950.4	E962.0	E980.4
Benzyl						
acetate	982.8	E862.4	—	E950.9	E962.1	E980.9
benzoate (anti–infective)	976.0	E858.7	E946.0	E950.4	E962.0	E980.4
morphine	965.09	E850.2	E935.2	E950.0	E962.0	E980.0
penicillin	960.0	E856	E930.0	E950.4	E962.0	E980.4
Bephenium hydroxynapthoate	961.6	E857	E931.6	E950.4	E962.0	E980.4
Bergamot oil	989.89	E866.8	—	E950.9	E962.1	E980.9
Berries, poisonous	988.2	E865.3	—	E950.9	E962.1	E980.9
Beryllium (compounds) (fumes)	985.3	E866.4	—	E950.9	E962.1	E980.9
Beta–carotene	976.3	E858.7	E946.3	E950.4	E962.0	E980.4
Beta–Chlor	967.1	E852.0	E937.1	E950.2	E962.0	E980.2
Betamethasone	962.0	E858.0	E932.0	E950.4	E962.0	E980.4
topical	976.0	E858.7	E946.0	E950.4	E962.0	E980.4
Betazole	977.8	E858.8	E947.8	E950.4	E962.0	E980.4
Bethanechol	971.0	E855.3	E941.0	E950.4	E962.0	E980.4
Bethanidine	972.6	E858.3	E942.6	E950.4	E962.0	E980.4
Betula oil	976.3	E858.7	E946.3	E950.4	E962.0	E980.4
Bhang	969.6	E854.1	E939.6	E950.3	E962.0	E980.3
Bialamicol	961.5	E857	E931.5	E950.4	E962.0	E980.4
Bichloride of mercury — *see* Mercury, chloride						
Bichromates (calcium) (crystals) (potassium) (sodium)	983.9	E864.3	—	E950.7	E962.1	E980.6
fumes	987.8	E869.8	—	E952.8	E962.2	E982.8
Biguanide derivatives, oral	962.3	E858.0	E932.3	E950.4	E962.0	E980.4
Biligrafin	977.8	E858.8	E947.8	E950.4	E962.0	E980.4
Bilopaque	977.8	E858.8	E947.8	E950.4	E962.0	E980.4
Bioflavonoids	972.8	E858.3	E942.8	E950.4	E962.0	E980.4
Biological substance NEC	979.9	E858.8	E949.9	E950.4	E962.0	E980.4
Biperiden	966.4	E855.0	E936.4	E950.4	E962.0	E980.4
Bisacodyl	973.1	E858.4	E943.1	E950.4	E962.0	E980.4
Bishydroxycoumarin	964.2	E858.2	E934.2	E950.4	E962.0	E980.4
Bismarsen	961.1	E857	E931.1	E950.4	E962.0	E980.4
Bismuth (compounds) NEC	985.8	E866.4	—	E950.9	E962.1	E980.9
anti–infectives	961.2	E857	E931.2	E950.4	E962.0	E980.4
subcarbonate	973.5	E858.4	E943.5	E950.4	E962.0	E980.4
sulfarsphenamine	961.1	E857	E931.1	E950.4	E962.0	E980.4
Bithionol	961.6	E857	E931.6	E950.4	E962.0	E980.4

Substance	Poisoning	Accident	External Cause (E-Code)			
			Therapeutic Use	Suicide Attempt	Assault	Undetermined
Bitter almond oil	989.0	E866.8	—	E950.9	E962.1	E980.9
Bittersweet	988.2	E865.4	—	E950.9	E962.1	E980.9
Black						
flag	989.4	E863.4	—	E950.6	E962.1	E980.7
henbane	988.2	E865.4	—	E950.9	E962.1	E980.9
leaf (40)	989.4	E863.4	—	E950.6	E962.1	E980.7
widow spider (bite)	989.5	E905.1	—	E950.9	E962.1	E980.9
antivenin	979.9	E858.8	E949.9	E950.4	E962.0	E980.4
Blast furnace gas (carbon monoxide from)	986	E868.8	—	E952.1	E962.2	E982.1
Bleach NEC	983.9	E864.3	—	E950.7	E962.1	E980.6
Bleaching solutions	983.9	E864.3	—	E950.7	E962.1	E980.6
Bleomycin (sulfate)	960.7	E856	E930.7	E950.4	E962.0	E980.4
Blockain	968.9	E855.2	E938.9	E950.4	E962.0	E980.4
infiltration (subcutaneous)	968.5	E855.2	E938.5	E950.4	E962.0	E980.4
nerve block (peripheral) (plexus)	968.6	E855.2	E938.6	E950.4	E962.0	E980.4
topical (surface)	968.5	E855.2	E938.5	E950.4	E962.0	E980.4
Blood (derivatives) (natural) (plasma)						
(whole)	964.7	E858.2	E934.7	E950.4	E962.0	E980.4
affecting agent	964.9	E858.2	E934.9	E950.4	E962.0	E980.4
specified NEC	964.8	E858.2	E934.8	E950.4	E962.0	E980.4
substitute (macromolecular)	964.8	E858.2	E934.8	E950.4	E962.0	E980.4
Blue velvet	965.09	E850.2	E935.2	E950.0	E962.0	E980.0
Bone meal	989.89	E866.5	—	E950.9	E962.1	E980.9
Bonine	963.0	E858.1	E933.0	E950.4	E962.0	E980.4
Boracic acid	976.0	E858.7	E946.0	E950.4	E962.0	E980.4
ENT agent	976.6	E858.7	E946.6	E950.4	E962.0	E980.4
ophthalmic preparation	976.5	E858.7	E946.5	E950.4	E962.0	E980.4
Borate (cleanser) (sodium)	989.6	E861.3	—	E950.9	E962.1	E980.9
Borax (cleanser)	989.6	E861.3	—	E950.9	E962.1	E980.9
Boric acid	976.0	E858.7	E946.0	E950.4	E962.0	E980.4
ENT agent	976.6	E858.7	E946.6	E950.4	E962.0	E980.4
ophthalmic preparation	976.5	E858.7	E946.5	E950.4	E962.0	E980.4
Boron hydride NEC	989.89	E866.8	—	E950.9	E962.1	E980.9
fumes or gas	987.8	E869.8	—	E952.8	E962.2	E982.8
Brake fluid vapor	987.8	E869.8	—	E952.8	E962.2	E982.8
Brass (compounds) (fumes)	985.8	E866.4	—	E950.9	E962.1	E980.9
Brasso	981	E861.3	—	E950.9	E962.1	E980.9
Bretylium (tosylate)	972.6	E858.3	E942.6	E950.4	E962.0	E980.4
Brevital (sodium)	968.3	E855.1	E938.3	E950.4	E962.0	E980.4
British antilewisite	963.8	E858.1	E933.8	E950.4	E962.0	E980.4
Bromal (hydrate)	967.3	E852.2	E937.3	E950.2	E962.0	E980.2
Bromelains	963.4	E858.1	E933.4	E950.4	E962.0	E980.4
Bromides NEC	967.3	E852.2	E937.3	E950.2	E962.0	E980.2
Bromine (vapor)	987.8	E869.8	—	E952.8	E962.2	E982.8
compounds (medicinal)	967.3	E852.2	E937.3	E950.2	E962.0	E980.2
Bromisovalum	967.3	E852.2	E937.3	E950.2	E962.0	E980.2
Bromobenzyl cyanide	987.5	E869.3	—	E952.8	E962.2	E982.8
Bromodiphenhydramine	963.0	E858.1	E933.0	E950.4	E962.0	E980.4
Bromoform	967.3	E852.2	E937.3	E950.2	E962.0	E980.2
Bromophenol blue reagent	977.8	E858.8	E947.8	E950.4	E962.0	E980.4
Bromosalicylhydroxamic acid	961.8	E857	E931.8	E950.4	E962.0	E980.4
Bromo–seltzer	965.4	E850.4	E935.4	E950.0	E962.0	E980.0
Brompheniramine	963.0	E858.1	E933.0	E950.4	E962.0	E980.4
Bromural	967.3	E852.2	E937.3	E950.2	E962.0	E980.2
Brown spider (bite) (venom)	989.5	E905.1	—	E950.9	E962.1	E980.9
Brucia	988.2	E865.3	—	E950.9	E962.1	E980.9
Brucine	989.1	E863.7	—	E950.6	E962.1	E980.7

Substance	Poisoning	External Cause (E-Code)				
		Accident	Therapeutic Use	Suicide Attempt	Assault	Undetermined
Brunswick green — *see* Copper						
Bruten — *see* Ibuperofen						
Bryonia (alba) (dioica)	988.2	E865.4	—	E950.9	E962.1	E980.9
Buclizine	969.5	E853.8	E939.5	E950.3	E962.0	E980.3
Bufferin	965.1	E850.3	E935.3	E950.0	E962.0	E980.0
Bufotenine	969.6	E854.1	E939.6	E950.3	E962.0	E980.3
Buphenine	971.2	E855.5	E941.2	E950.4	E962.0	E980.4
Bupivacaine	968.9	E855.2	E938.9	E950.4	E962.0	E980.4
infiltration (subcutaneous)	968.5	E855.2	E938.5	E950.4	E962.0	E980.4
nerve block (peripheral) (plexus)	968.6	E855.2	E938.6	E950.4	E962.0	E980.4
Busulfan	963.1	E858.1	E933.1	E950.4	E962.0	E980.4
Butabarbital (sodium)	967.0	E851	E937.0	E950.1	E962.0	E980.1
Butabarbitone	967.0	E851	E937.0	E950.1	E962.0	E980.1
Butabarpal	967.0	E851	E937.0	E950.1	E962.0	E980.1
Butacaine	968.5	E855.2	E938.5	E950.4	E962.0	E980.4
Butallylonal	967.0	E851	E937.0	E950.1	E962.0	E980.1
Butane (distributed in mobile container)	987.0	E868.0	—	E951.1	E962.2	E981.1
distributed through pipes	987.0	E867	—	E951.0	E962.2	E981.0
incomplete combustion of — *see* Carbon monoxide, butane						
Butanol	980.3	E860.4	—	E950.9	E962.1	E980.9
Butanone	982.8	E862.4	—	E950.9	E962.1	E980.9
Butaperazine	969.1	E853.0	E939.1	E950.3	E962.0	E980.3
Butazolidin	965.5	E850.5	E935.5	E950.0	E962.0	E980.0
Butethal	967.0	E851	E937.0	E950.1	E962.0	E980.1
Butethamate	971.1	E855.4	E941.1	E950.4	E962.0	E980.4
Buthalitone (sodium)	968.3	E855.1	E938.3	E950.4	E962.0	E980.4
Butisol (sodium)	967.0	E851	E937.0	E950.1	E962.0	E980.1
Butobarbital, butobarbitone	967.0	E851	E937.0	E950.1	E962.0	E980.1
Butriptyline	969.0	E854.0	E939.0	E950.3	E962.0	E980.3
Buttercups	988.2	E865.4	—	E950.9	E962.1	E980.9
Butter of antimony — *see* Antimony						
Butyl						
acetate (secondary)	982.8	E862.4	—	E950.9	E962.1	E980.9
alcohol	980.3	E860.4	—	E950.9	E962.1	E980.9
carbinol	980.8	E860.8	—	E950.9	E962.1	E980.9
carbitol	982.8	E862.4	—	E950.9	E962.1	E980.9
cellosolve	982.8	E862.4	—	E950.9	E962.1	E980.9
chloral (hydrate)	967.1	E852.0	E937.1	E950.2	E962.0	E980.2
formate	982.8	E862.4	—	E950.9	E962.1	E980.9
scopolammonium bromide	971.1	E855.4	E941.1	E950.4	E962.0	E980.4
Butyn	968.5	E855.2	E938.5	E950.4	E962.0	E980.4
Butyrophenone (–based tranquilizers)	969.2	E853.1	E939.2	E950.3	E962.0	E980.3
Cacodyl, cacodylic acid — *see* Arsenic						
Cactinomycin	960.7	E856	E930.7	E950.4	E962.0	E980.4
Cade oil	976.4	E858.7	E946.4	E950.4	E962.0	E980.4
Cadmium (chloride) (compounds) (dust) (fumes) (oxide)	985.5	E866.4	—	E950.9	E962.1	E980.9
sulfide (medicinal) NEC	976.4	E858.7	E946.4	E950.4	E962.0	E980.4
Caffeine	969.7	E854.2	E939.7	E950.3	E962.0	E980.3
Calabar bean	988.2	E865.4	—	E950.9	E962.1	E980.9
Caladium seguinium	988.2	E865.4	—	E950.9	E962.1	E980.9
Calamine (liniment) (lotion)	976.3	E858.7	E946.3	E950.4	E962.0	E980.4
Calciferol	963.5	E858.1	E933.5	E950.4	E962.0	E980.4
Calcium (salts) NEC	974.5	E858.5	E944.5	E950.4	E962.0	E980.4
acetylsalicylate	965.1	E850.3	E935.3	E950.0	E962.0	E980.0
benzamidosalicylate	961.8	E857	E931.8	E950.4	E962.0	E980.4

Substance	Poisoning	Accident	Therapeutic Use	Suicide Attempt	Assault	Undetermined
			External Cause (E-Code)			
carbaspirin 965.1	E850.3	E935.3	E950.0	E962.0		E980.0
carbamide (citrated) 977.3	E858.8	E947.3	E950.4	E962.0		E980.4
carbonate (antacid) 973.0	E858.4	E943.0	E950.4	E962.0		E980.4
cyanide (citrated) 977.3	E858.8	E947.3	E950.4	E962.0		E980.4
dioctyl sulfosuccinate 973.2	E858.4	E943.2	E950.4	E962.0		E980.4
disodium edathamil 963.8	E858.1	E933.8	E950.4	E962.0		E980.4
disodium edetate 963.8	E858.1	E933.8	E950.4	E962.0		E980.4
EDTA 963.8	E858.1	E933.8	E950.4	E962.0		E980.4
hydrate, hydroxide 983.2	E864.2	—	E950.7	E962.1		E980.6
mandelate 961.9	E857	E931.9	E950.4	E962.0		E980.4
oxide 983.2	E864.2	—	E950.7	E962.1		E980.6
Calomel — *see* Mercury, chloride						
Caloric agents NEC 974.5	E858.5	E944.5	E950.4	E962.0		E980.4
Calusterone 963.1	E858.1	E933.1	E950.4	E962.0		E980.4
Camoquin 961.4	E857	E931.4	E950.4	E962.0		E980.4
Camphor (oil) 976.1	E858.7	E946.1	E950.4	E962.0		E980.4
Candeptin 976.0	E858.7	E946.0	E950.4	E962.0		E980.4
Candicidin 976.0	E858.7	E946.0	E950.4	E962.0		E980.4
Cannabinols 969.6	E854.1	E939.6	E950.3	E962.0		E980.3
Cannabis (derivatives) (indica) (sativa) 969.6	E854.1	E939.6	E950.3	E962.0		E980.3
Canned heat 980.1	E860.2	—	E950.9	E962.1		E980.9
Cantharides, cantharidin, cantharis 976.8	E858.7	E946.8	E950.4	E962.0		E980.4
Capillary agents 972.8	E858.3	E942.8	E950.4	E962.0		E980.4
Capreomycin 960.6	E856	E930.6	E950.4	E962.0		E980.4
Captodiame, captodiamine 969.5	E853.8	E939.5	E950.3	E962.0		E980.3
Caramiphen (hydrochloride) 971.1	E855.4	E941.1	E950.4	E962.0		E980.4
Carbachol 971.0	E855.3	E941.0	E950.4	E962.0		E980.4
Carbacrylamine resins 974.5	E858.5	E944.5	E950.4	E962.0		E980.4
Carbamate (sedative) 967.8	E852.8	E937.8	E950.2	E962.0		E980.2
herbicide 989.3	E863.5	—	E950.6	E962.1		E980.7
insecticide 989.3	E863.2	—	E950.6	E962.1		E980.7
Carbamazepine 966.3	E855.0	E936.3	E950.4	E962.0		E980.4
Carbamic esters 967.8	E852.8	E937.8	E950.2	E962.0		E980.2
Carbamide 974.4	E858.5	E944.4	E950.4	E962.0		E980.4
topical 976.8	E858.7	E946.8	E950.4	E962.0		E980.4
Carbamylcholine chloride 971.0	E855.3	E941.0	E950.4	E962.0		E980.4
Carbarsone 961.1	E857	E931.1	E950.4	E962.0		E980.4
Carbaryl 989.3	E863.2	—	E950.6	E962.1		E980.7
Carbaspirin 965.1	E850.3	E935.3	E950.0	E962.0		E980.0
Carbazochrome 972.8	E858.3	E942.8	E950.4	E962.0		E980.4
Carbenicillin 960.0	E856	E930.0	E950.4	E962.0		E980.4
Carbenoxolone 973.8	E858.4	E943.8	E950.4	E962.0		E980.4
Carbetapentane 975.4	E858.6	E945.4	E950.4	E962.0		E980.4
Carbimazole 962.8	E858.0	E932.8	E950.4	E962.0		E980.4
Carbinol 980.1	E860.2	—	E950.9	E962.1		E980.9
Carbinoxamine 963.0	E858.1	E933.0	E950.4	E962.0		E980.4
Carbitol 982.8	E862.4	—	E950.9	E962.1		E980.9
Carbocaine 968.9	E855.2	E938.9	E950.4	E962.0		E980.4
infiltration (subcutaneous) 968.5	E855.2	E938.5	E950.4	E962.0		E980.4
nerve block (peripheral) (plexus) 968.6	E855.2	E938.6	E950.4	E962.0		E980.4
topical (surface) 968.5	E855.2	E938.5	E950.4	E962.0		E980.4
Carbol–fuchsin solution 976.0	E858.7	E946.0	E950.4	E962.0		E980.4
Carbolic acid (*see also* Phenol) 983.0	E864.0	—	E950.7	E962.1		E980.6
Carbomycin 960.8	E856	E930.8	E950.4	E962.0		E980.4
Carbon						
bisulfide (liquid) (vapor) 982.2	E862.4	—	E950.9	E962.1		E980.9
dioxide (gas) 987.8	E869.8	—	E952.8	E962.2		E982.8

Substance	Poisoning	Accident	Therapeutic Use	Suicide Attempt	Assault	Undetermined
External Cause (E-Code)						

Substance	Poisoning	Accident	Therapeutic Use	Suicide Attempt	Assault	Undetermined
disulfide (liquid) (vapor)	982.2	E862.4	—	E950.9	E962.1	E980.9
monoxide (from incomplete combustion of) (in) NEC	986	E868.9	—	E952.1	E962.2	E982.1
blast furnace gas	986	E868.8	—	E952.1	E962.2	E982.1
butane (distributed in mobile container)	986	E868.0	—	E951.1	E962.2	E981.1
distributed through pipes	986	E867	—	E951.0	E962.2	E981.0
charcoal fumes	986	E868.3	—	E952.1	E962.2	E982.1
coal						
gas (piped)	986	E867	—	E951.0	E962.2	E981.0
solid (in domestic stoves, fireplaces)	986	E868.3	—	E952.1	E962.2	E982.1
coke (in domestic stoves, fireplaces)	986	E868.3	—	E952.1	E962.2	E982.1
exhaust gas (motor) not in transit	986	E868.2	—	E952.0	E962.2	E982.0
combustion engine, any not in watercraft	986	E868.2	—	E952.0	E962.2	E982.0
farm tractor, not in transit	986	E868.2	—	E952.0	E962.2	E982.0
gas engine	986	E868.2	—	E952.0	E962.2	E982.0
motor pump	986	E868.2	—	E952.0	E962.2	E982.0
motor vehicle, not in transit	986	E868.2	—	E952.0	E962.2	E982.0
fuel (in domestic use)	986	E868.3	—	E952.1	E962.2	E982.1
gas (piped)	986	E867	—	E951.0	E962.2	E981.0
in mobile container	986	E868.0	—	E951.1	E962.2	E981.1
utility	986	E868.1	—	E951.8	E962.2	E981.1
in mobile container	986	E868.0	—	E951.1	E962.2	E981.1
piped (natural)	986	E867	—	E951.0	E962.2	E981.0
illuminating gas	986	E868.1	—	E951.8	E962.2	E981.8
industrial fuels or gases, any	986	E868.8	—	E952.1	E962.2	E982.1
kerosene (in domestic stoves, fireplaces)	986	E868.3	—	E952.1	E962.2	E982.1
kiln gas or vapor	986	E868.8	—	E952.1	E962.2	E982.1
motor exhaust gas, not in transit	986	E868.2	—	E952.0	E962.2	E982.0
piped gas (manufactured) (natural)	986	E867	—	E951.0	E962.2	E981.0
producer gas	986	E868.8	—	E952.1	E962.2	E982.1
propane (distributed in mobile container)	986	E868.0	—	E951.1	E962.2	E981.1
distributed through pipes	986	E867	—	E951.0	E962.2	E981.0
specified source NEC	986	E868.8	—	E952.1	E962.2	E982.1
stove gas	986	E868.1	—	E951.8	E962.2	E981.8
piped	986	E867	—	E951.0	E962.2	E981.0
utility gas	986	E868.1	—	E951.8	E962.2	E981.8
piped	986	E867	—	E951.0	E962.2	E981.0
water gas	986	E868.1	—	E951.8	E962.2	E981.8
wood (in domestic stoves, fireplaces)	986	E868.3	—	E952.1	E962.2	E982.1
tetrachloride (vapor) NEC	987.8	E869.8	—	E952.8	E962.2	E982.8
liquid (cleansing agent) NEC	982.1	E861.3	—	E950.9	E962.1	E980.9
solvent	982.1	E862.4	—	E950.9	E962.1	E980.9
Carbonic acid (gas)	987.8	E869.8	—	E952.8	E962.2	E982.8
anhydrase inhibitors	974.2	E858.5	E944.2	E950.4	E962.0	E980.4
Carbowax	976.3	E858.7	E946.3	E950.4	E962.0	E980.4
Carbrital	967.0	E851	E937.0	E950.1	E962.0	E980.1
Carbromal (derivatives)	967.3	E852.2	E937.3	E950.2	E962.0	E980.2
Cardiac						
depressants	972.0	E858.3	E942.0	E950.4	E962.0	E980.4
rhythm regulators	972.0	E858.3	E942.0	E950.4	E962.0	E980.4
Cardiografin	977.8	E858.8	E947.8	E950.4	E962.0	E980.4
Cardio–green	977.8	E858.8	E947.8	E950.4	E962.0	E980.4

Substance	Poisoning	External Cause (E-Code)				
		Accident	Therapeutic Use	Suicide Attempt	Assault	Undetermined
Cardiotonic glycosides	972.1	E858.3	E942.1	E950.4	E962.0	E980.4
Cardiovascular agents NEC	972.9	E858.3	E942.9	E950.4	E962.0	E980.4
Cardrase	974.2	E858.5	E944.2	E950.4	E962.0	E980.4
Carfusin	976.0	E858.7	E946.0	E950.4	E962.0	E980.4
Carisoprodol	968.0	E855.1	E938.0	E950.4	E962.0	E980.4
Carmustine	963.1	E858.1	E933.1	E950.4	E962.0	E980.4
Carotene	963.5	E858.1	E933.5	E950.4	E962.0	E980.4
Carphenazine (maleate)	969.1	E853.0	E939.1	E950.3	E962.0	E980.3
Carter's Little Pills	973.1	E858.4	E943.1	E950.4	E962.0	E980.4
Cascara (sagrada)	973.1	E858.4	E943.1	E950.4	E962.0	E980.4
Cassava	988.2	E865.4	—	E950.9	E962.1	E980.9
Castellani's paint	976.0	E858.7	E946.0	E950.4	E962.0	E980.4
Castor						
bean	988.2	E865.3	—	E950.9	E962.1	E980.9
oil	973.1	E858.4	E943.1	E950.4	E962.0	E980.4
Caterpillar (sting)	989.5	E905.5	—	E950.9	E962.1	E980.9
Catha (edulis)	970.8	E854.3	E940.8	E950.4	E962.0	E980.4
Cathartics NEC	973.3	E858.4	E943.3	E950.4	E962.0	E980.4
contact	973.1	E858.4	E943.1	E950.4	E962.0	E980.4
emollient	973.2	E858.4	E943.2	E950.4	E962.0	E980.4
intestinal irritants	973.1	E858.4	E943.1	E950.4	E962.0	E980.4
saline	973.3	E858.4	E943.3	E950.4	E962.0	E980.4
Cathomycin	960.8	E856	E930.8	E950.4	E962.0	E980.4
Caustic(s)	983.9	E864.4	—	E950.7	E962.1	E980.6
alkali	983.2	E864.2	—	E950.7	E962.1	E980.6
hydroxide	983.2	E864.2	—	E950.7	E962.1	E980.6
potash	983.2	E864.2	—	E950.7	E962.1	E980.6
soda	983.2	E864.2	—	E950.7	E962.1	E980.6
specified NEC	983.9	E864.3	—	E950.7	E962.1	E980.6
Ceepryn	976.0	E858.7	E946.0	E950.4	E962.0	E980.4
ENT agent	976.6	E858.7	E946.6	E950.4	E962.0	E980.4
lozenges	976.6	E858.7	E946.6	E950.4	E962.0	E980.4
Celestone	962.0	E858.0	E932.0	E950.4	E962.0	E980.4
topical	976.0	E858.7	E946.0	E950.4	E962.0	E980.4
Cellosolve	982.8	E862.4	—	E950.9	E962.1	E980.9
Cell stimulants and proliferants	976.8	E858.7	E946.8	E950.4	E962.0	E980.4
Cellulose derivatives, cathartic	973.3	E858.4	E943.3	E950.4	E962.0	E980.4
nitrates (topical)	976.3	E858.7	E946.3	E950.4	E962.0	E980.4
Centipede (bite)	989.5	E905.4	—	E950.9	E962.1	E980.9
Central nervous system						
depressants	968.4	E855.1	E938.4	E950.4	E962.0	E980.4
anesthetic (general) NEC	968.4	E855.1	E938.4	E950.4	E962.0	E980.4
gases NEC	968.2	E855.1	E938.2	E950.4	E962.0	E980.4
intravenous	968.3	E855.1	E938.3	E950.4	E962.0	E980.4
barbiturates	967.0	E851	E937.0	E950.1	E962.0	E980.1
bromides	967.3	E852.2	E937.3	E950.2	E962.0	E980.2
cannabis sativa	969.6	E854.1	E939.6	E950.3	E962.0	E980.3
chloral hydrate	967.1	E852.0	E937.1	E950.2	E962.0	E980.2
hallucinogenics	969.6	E854.1	E939.6	E950.3	E962.0	E980.3
hypnotics	967.9	E852.9	E937.9	E950.2	E962.0	E980.2
specified NEC	967.8	E852.8	E937.8	E950.2	E962.0	E980.2
muscle relaxants	968.0	E855.1	E938.0	E950.4	E962.0	E980.4
paraldehyde	967.2	E852.1	E937.2	E950.2	E962.0	E980.2
sedatives	967.9	E852.9	E937.9	E950.2	E962.0	E980.2
mixed NEC	967.6	E852.5	E937.6	E950.2	E962.0	E980.2
specified NEC	967.8	E852.8	E937.8	E950.2	E962.0	E980.2
muscle–tone depressants	968.0	E855.1	E938.0	E950.4	E962.0	E980.4

Substance	External Cause (E-Code)					
	Poisoning	Accident	Therapeutic Use	Suicide Attempt	Assault	Undetermined
stimulants	970.9	E854.3	E940.9	E950.4	E962.0	E980.4
amphetamines	969.7	E854.2	E939.7	E950.3	E962.0	E980.3
analeptics	970.0	E854.3	E940.0	E950.4	E962.0	E980.4
antidepressants	969.0	E854.0	E939.0	E950.3	E962.0	E980.3
opiate antagonists	970.1	E854.3	E940.0	E950.4	E962.0	E980.4
specified NEC	970.8	E854.3	E940.8	E950.4	E962.0	E980.4
Cephalexin	960.5	E856	E930.5	E950.4	E962.0	E980.4
Cephaloglycin	960.5	E856	E930.5	E950.4	E962.0	E980.4
Cephaloridine	960.5	E856	E930.5	E950.4	E962.0	E980.4
Cephalosporins NEC	960.5	E856	E930.5	E950.4	E962.0	E980.4
N (adicillin)	960.0	E856	E930.0	E950.4	E962.0	E980.4
Cephalothin (sodium)	960.5	E856	E930.5	E950.4	E962.0	E980.4
Cerbera (odallam)	988.2	E865.4	—	E950.9	E962.1	E980.9
Cerberin	972.1	E858.3	E942.1	E950.4	E962.0	E980.4
Cerebral stimulants	970.9	E854.3	E940.9	E950.4	E962.0	E980.4
psychotherapeutic	969.7	E854.2	E939.7	E950.3	E962.0	E980.3
specified NEC	970.8	E854.3	E940.8	E950.4	E962.0	E980.4
Cetalkonium (chloride)	976.0	E858.7	E946.0	E950.4	E962.0	E980.4
Cetoxime	963.0	E858.1	E933.0	E950.4	E962.0	E980.4
Cetrimide	976.2	E858.7	E946.2	E950.4	E962.0	E980.4
Cetylpyridinium	976.0	E858.7	E946.0	E950.4	E962.0	E980.4
ENT agent	976.6	E858.7	E946.6	E950.4	E962.0	E980.4
lozenges	976.6	E858.7	E946.6	E950.4	E962.0	E980.4
Cevadilla — *see* Sabadilla						
Cevitamic acid	963.5	E858.1	E933.5	E950.4	E962.0	E980.4
Chalk, precipitated	973.0	E858.4	E943.0	E950.4	E962.0	E980.4
Charcoal						
fumes (carbon monoxide)	986	E868.3	—	E952.1	E962.2	E982.1
industrial	986	E868.8	—	E952.1	E962.2	E982.1
medicinal (activated)	973.0	E858.4	E943.0	E950.4	E962.0	E980.4
Chelating agents NEC	977.2	E858.8	E947.2	E950.4	E962.0	E980.4
Chelidonium majus	988.2	E865.4	—	E950.9	E962.1	E980.9
Chemical substance	989.9	E866.9	—	E950.9	E962.1	E980.9
specified NEC	989.89	E866.8	—	E950.9	E962.1	E980.9
Chenopodium (oil)	961.6	E857	E931.6	E950.4	E962.0	E980.4
Cherry laurel	988.2	E865.4	—	E950.9	E962.1	E980.9
Chiniofon	961.3	E857	E931.3	E950.4	E962.0	E980.4
Chlophedianol	975.4	E858.6	E945.4	E950.4	E962.0	E980.4
Chloral (betaine) (formamide) (hydrate)	967.1	E852.0	E937.1	E950.2	E962.0	E980.2
Chloralamide	967.1	E852.0	E937.1	E950.2	E962.0	E980.2
Chlorambucil	963.1	E858.1	E933.1	E950.4	E962.0	E980.4
Chloramphenicol	960.2	E856	E930.2	E950.4	E962.0	E980.4
ENT agent	976.6	E858.7	E946.6	E950.4	E962.0	E980.4
ophthalmic preparation	976.5	E858.7	E946.5	E950.4	E962.0	E980.4
topical NEC	976.0	E858.7	E946.0	E950.4	E962.0	E980.4
Chlorate(s) (potassium) (sodium) NEC	983.9	E864.3	—	E950.7	E962.1	E980.6
herbicides	989.4	E863.5	—	E950.6	E962.1	E980.7
Chlorcyclizine	963.0	E858.1	E933.0	E950.4	E962.0	E980.4
Chlordan(e) (dust)	989.2	E863.0	—	E950.6	E962.1	E980.7
Chlordantoin	976.0	E858.7	E946.0	E950.4	E962.0	E980.4
Chlordiazepoxide	969.4	E853.2	E939.4	E950.3	E962.0	E980.3
Chloresium	976.8	E858.7	E946.8	E950.4	E962.0	E980.4
Chlorethiazol	967.1	E852.0	E937.1	E950.2	E962.0	E980.2
Chlorethyl — *see* Ethyl, chloride						
Chloretone	967.1	E852.0	E937.1	E950.2	E962.0	E980.2
Chlorex	982.3	E862.4	—	E950.9	E962.1	E980.9
Chlorhexadol	967.1	E852.0	E937.1	E950.2	E962.0	E980.2

Substance	Poisoning	External Cause (E-Code)				
		Accident	Therapeutic Use	Suicide Attempt	Assault	Undetermined
Chlorhexidine (hydrochloride) 976.0		E858.7	E946.0	E950.4	E962.0	E980.4
Chlorhydroxyquinolin 976.0		E858.7	E946.0	E950.4	E962.0	E980.4
Chloride of lime (bleach) 983.9		E864.3	—	E950.7	E962.1	E980.6
Chlorinated						
camphene 989.2		E863.0	—	E950.6	E962.1	E980.7
diphenyl 989.89		E866.8	—	E950.9	E962.1	E980.9
hydrocarbons NEC 989.2		E863.0	—	E950.6	E962.1	E980.7
solvent 982.3		E862.4	—	E950.9	E962.1	E980.9
lime (bleach) 983.9		E864.3	—	E950.7	E962.1	E980.6
naphthalene — see Naphthalene						
pesticides NEC 989.2		E863.0	—	E950.6	E962.1	E980.7
soda — see Sodium, hypochlorite						
Chlorine (fumes) (gas) 987.6		E869.8	—	E952.8	E962.2	E982.8
bleach 983.9		E864.3	—	E950.7	E962.1	E980.6
compounds NEC 983.9		E864.3	—	E950.7	E962.1	E980.6
disinfectant 983.9		E861.4	—	E950.7	E962.1	E980.6
releasing agents NEC 983.9		E864.3	—	E950.7	E962.1	E980.6
Chlorisondamine 972.3		E858.3	E942.3	E950.4	E962.0	E980.4
Chlormadinone 962.2		E858.0	E932.2	E950.4	E962.0	E980.4
Chlormerodrin 974.0		E858.5	E944.0	E950.4	E962.0	E980.4
Chlormethiazole 967.1		E852.0	E937.1	E950.2	E962.0	E980.2
Chlormethylenecycline 960.4		E856	E930.4	E950.4	E962.0	E980.4
Chlormezanone 969.5		E853.8	E939.5	E950.3	E962.0	E980.3
Chloroacetophenone 987.5		E869.3	—	E952.8	E962.2	E982.8
Chloroaniline 983.0		E864.0	—	E950.7	E962.1	E980.6
Chlorobenzene, chlorobenzol 982.0		E862.4	—	E950.9	E962.1	E980.9
Chlorobutanol 967.1		E852.0	E937.1	E950.2	E962.0	E980.2
Chlorodinitrobenzene 983.0		E864.0	—	E950.7	E962.1	E980.6
dust or vapor 987.8		E869.8	—	E952.8	E962.2	E982.8
Chloroethane — see Ethyl, chloride						
Chloroform (fumes) (vapor) 987.8		E869.8	—	E952.8	E962.2	E982.8
anesthetic (gas) 968.2		E855.1	E938.2	E950.4	E962.0	E980.4
liquid NEC 968.4		E855.1	E938.4	E950.4	E962.0	E980.4
solvent 982.3		E862.4	—	E950.9	E962.1	E980.9
Chloroguanide 961.4		E857	E931.4	E950.4	E962.0	E980.4
Chloromycetin 960.2		E856	E930.2	E950.4	E962.0	E980.4
ENT agent 976.6		E858.7	E946.6	E950.4	E962.0	E980.4
ophthalmic preparation 976.5		E858.7	E946.5	E950.4	E962.0	E980.4
otic solution 976.6		E858.7	E946.6	E950.4	E962.0	E980.4
topical NEC 976.0		E858.7	E946.0	E950.4	E962.0	E980.4
Chloronitrobenzene 983.0		E864.0	—	E950.7	E962.1	E980.6
dust or vapor 987.8		E869.8	—	E952.8	E962.2	E982.8
Chlorophenol 983.0		E864.0	—	E950.7	E962.1	E980.6
Chlorophenothane 989.2		E863.0	—	E950.6	E962.1	E980.7
Chlorophyll (derivatives) 976.8		E858.7	E946.8	E950.4	E962.0	E980.4
Chloropicrin (fumes) 987.8		E869.8	—	E952.8	E962.2	E982.8
fumigant 989.4		E863.8	—	E950.6	E962.1	E980.7
fungicide 989.4		E863.6	—	E950.6	E962.1	E980.7
pesticide (fumes) 989.4		E863.4	—	E950.6	E962.1	E980.7
Chloroprocaine 968.9		E855.2	E938.9	E950.4	E962.0	E980.4
infiltration (subcutaneous) 968.5		E855.2	E938.5	E950.4	E962.0	E980.4
nerve block (peripheral) (plexus) 968.6		E855.2	E938.6	E950.4	E962.0	E980.4
Chloroptic 976.5		E858.7	E946.5	E950.4	E962.0	E980.4
Chloropurine 963.1		E858.1	E933.1	E950.4	E962.0	E980.4
Chloroquine (hydrochloride) (phosphate) . . . 961.4		E857	E931.4	E950.4	E962.0	E980.4
Chlorothen 963.0		E858.1	E933.0	E950.4	E962.0	E980.4
Chlorothiazide 974.3		E858.5	E944.3	E950.4	E962.0	E980.4

Substance	Poisoning	External Cause (E-Code)				
		Accident	Therapeutic Use	Suicide Attempt	Assault	Undetermined
Chlorotrianisene	962.2	E858.0	E932.2	E950.4	E962.0	E980.4
Chlorovinyldichloroarsine	985.1	E866.3	—	E950.8	E962.1	E980.8
Chloroxylenol	976.0	E858.7	E946.0	E950.4	E962.0	E980.4
Chlorphenesin (carbamate)	968.0	E855.1	E938.0	E950.4	E962.0	E980.4
topical (antifungal)	976.0	E858.7	E946.0	E950.4	E962.0	E980.4
Chlorpheniramine	963.0	E858.1	E933.0	E950.4	E962.0	E980.4
Chlorphenoxamine	966.4	E855.0	E936.4	E950.4	E962.0	E980.4
Chlorphentermine	977.0	E858.8	E947.0	E950.4	E962.0	E980.4
Chlorproguanil	961.4	E857	E931.4	E950.4	E962.0	E980.4
Chlorpromazine	969.1	E853.0	E939.1	E950.3	E962.0	E980.3
Chlorpropamide	962.3	E858.0	E932.3	E950.4	E962.0	E980.4
Chlorprothixene	969.3	E853.8	E939.3	E950.3	E962.0	E980.3
Chlorquinaldol	976.0	E858.7	E946.0	E950.4	E962.0	E980.4
Chlortetracycline	960.4	E856	E930.4	E950.4	E962.0	E980.4
Chlorthalidone	974.4	E858.5	E944.4	E950.4	E962.0	E980.4
Chlortrianisene	962.2	E858.0	E932.2	E950.4	E962.0	E980.4
Chlor–Trimeton	963.0	E858.1	E933.0	E950.4	E962.0	E980.4
Chlorzoxazone	968.0	E855.1	E938.0	E950.4	E962.0	E980.4
Choke damp	987.8	E869.8	—	E952.8	E962.2	E982.8
Cholebrine	977.8	E858.8	E947.8	E950.4	E962.0	E980.4
Cholera vaccine	978.2	E858.8	E948.2	E950.4	E962.0	E980.4
Cholesterol–lowering agents	972.2	E858.3	E942.2	E950.4	E962.0	E980.4
Cholestyramine (resin)	972.2	E858.3	E942.2	E950.4	E962.0	E980.4
Cholic acid	973.4	E858.4	E943.4	E950.4	E962.0	E980.4
Choline						
dihydrogen citrate	977.1	E858.8	E947.1	E950.4	E962.0	E980.4
salicylate	965.1	E850.3	E935.3	E950.0	E962.0	E980.0
theophyllinate	974.1	E858.5	E944.1	E950.4	E962.0	E980.4
Cholinergics	971.0	E855.3	E941.0	E950.4	E962.0	E980.4
Cholografin	977.8	E858.8	E947.8	E950.4	E962.0	E980.4
Chorionic gonadotropin	962.4	E858.0	E932.4	E950.4	E962.0	E980.4
Chromates	983.9	E864.3	—	E950.7	E962.1	E980.6
dust or mist	987.8	E869.8	—	E952.8	E962.2	E982.8
lead	984.0	E866.0	—	E950.9	E962.1	E980.9
paint	984.0	E861.5	—	E950.9	E962.1	E980.9
Chromic acid	983.9	E864.3	—	E950.7	E962.1	E980.6
dust or mist	987.8	E869.8	—	E952.8	E962.2	E982.8
Chromium	985.6	E866.4	—	E950.9	E962.1	E980.9
compounds — see Chromates						
Chromonar	972.4	E858.3	E942.4	E950.4	E962.0	E980.4
Chromyl chloride	983.9	E864.3	—	E950.7	E962.1	E980.6
Chrysarobin (ointment)	976.4	E858.7	E946.4	E950.4	E962.0	E980.4
Chrysazin	973.1	E858.4	E943.1	E950.4	E962.0	E980.4
Chymar	963.4	E858.1	E933.4	E950.4	E962.0	E980.4
ophthalmic preparation	976.5	E858.7	E946.5	E950.4	E962.0	E980.4
Chymotrypsin	963.4	E858.1	E933.4	E950.4	E962.0	E980.4
ophthalmic preparation	976.5	E858.7	E946.5	E950.4	E962.0	E980.4
Cicuta maculata or virosa	988.2	E865.4	—	E950.9	E962.1	E980.9
Cigarette lighter fluid	981	E862.1	—	E950.9	E962.1	E980.9
Cinchocaine (spinal)	968.7	E855.2	E938.7	E950.4	E962.0	E980.4
topical (surface)	968.5	E855.2	E938.5	E950.4	E962.0	E980.4
Cinchona	961.4	E857	E931.4	E950.4	E962.0	E980.4
Cinchonine alkaloids	961.4	E857	E931.4	E950.4	E962.0	E980.4
Cinchophen	974.7	E858.5	E944.7	E950.4	E962.0	E980.4
Cinnarizine	963.0	E858.1	E933.0	E950.4	E962.0	E980.4
Citanest	968.9	E855.2	E938.9	E950.4	E962.0	E980.4
infiltration (subcutaneous)	968.5	E855.2	E938.5	E950.4	E962.0	E980.4

Substance	Poisoning	Accident	Therapeutic Use	Suicide Attempt	Assault	Undetermined
			External Cause (E-Code)			
nerve block (peripheral) (plexus)	968.6	E855.2	E938.6	E950.4	E962.0	E980.4
Citric acid	989.89	E866.8	—	E950.9	E962.1	E980.9
Citrovorum factor	964.1	E858.2	E934.1	E950.4	E962.0	E980.4
Claviceps purpurea	988.2	E865.4	—	E950.9	E962.1	E980.9
Cleaner, cleansing agent NEC	989.89	E861.3	—	E950.9	E962.1	E980.9
of paint or varnish	982.8	E862.9	—	E950.9	E962.1	E980.9
Clematis vitalba	988.2	E865.4	—	E950.9	E962.1	E980.9
Clemizole	963.0	E858.1	E933.0	E950.4	E962.0	E980.4
penicillin	960.0	E856	E930.0	E950.4	E962.0	E980.4
Clidinium	971.1	E855.4	E941.1	E950.4	E962.0	E980.4
Clindamycin	960.8	E856	E930.8	E950.4	E962.0	E980.4
Cliradon	965.09	E850.2	E935.2	E950.0	E962.0	E980.0
Clocortolone	962.0	E858.0	E932.0	E950.4	E962.0	E980.4
Clofedanol	975.4	E858.6	E945.4	E950.4	E962.0	E980.4
Clofibrate	972.2	E858.3	E942.2	E950.4	E962.0	E980.4
Clomethiazole	967.1	E852.0	E937.1	E950.2	E962.0	E980.2
Clomiphene	977.8	E858.8	E947.8	E950.4	E962.0	E980.4
Clonazepam	969.4	E853.2	E939.4	E950.3	E962.0	E980.3
Clonidine	972.6	E858.3	E942.6	E950.4	E962.0	E980.4
Clopamide	974.3	E858.5	E944.3	E950.4	E962.0	E980.4
Clorazepate	969.4	E853.2	E939.4	E950.3	E962.0	E980.3
Clorexolone	974.4	E858.5	E944.4	E950.4	E962.0	E980.4
Clorox (bleach)	983.9	E864.3	—	E950.7	E962.1	E980.6
Clortermine	977.0	E858.8	E947.0	E950.4	E962.0	E980.4
Clotrimazole	976.0	E858.7	E946.0	E950.4	E962.0	E980.4
Cloxacillin	960.0	E856	E930.0	E950.4	E962.0	E980.4
Coagulants NEC	964.5	E858.2	E934.5	E950.4	E962.0	E980.4
Coal (carbon monoxide from) — *see also* Carbon, monoxide, coal						
oil — *see* Kerosene						
tar NEC	983.0	E864.0	—	E950.7	E962.1	E980.6
fumes	987.8	E869.8	—	E952.8	E962.2	E982.8
medicinal (ointment)	976.4	E858.7	E946.4	E950.4	E962.0	E980.4
analgesics NEC	965.5	E850.5	E935.5	E950.0	E962.0	E980.0
naphtha (solvent)	981	E862.0	—	E950.9	E962.1	E980.9
Cobalt (fumes) (industrial)	985.8	E866.4	—	E950.9	E962.1	E980.9
Cobra (venom)	989.5	E905.0	—	E950.9	E962.1	E980.9
Coca (leaf)	970.8	E854.3	E940.8	E950.4	E962.0	E980.4
Cocaine (hydrochloride) (salt)	968.5	E855.2	E938.5	E950.4	E962.0	E980.4
Coccidioidin	977.8	E858.8	E947.8	E950.4	E962.0	E980.4
Cocculus indicus	988.2	E865.3	—	E950.9	E962.1	E980.9
Cochineal	989.89	E866.8	—	E950.9	E962.1	E980.9
medicinal products	977.4	E858.8	E947.4	E950.4	E962.0	E980.4
Codeine	965.09	E850.2	E935.2	E950.0	E962.0	E980.0
Coffee	989.89	E866.8	—	E950.9	E962.1	E980.9
Cogentin	971.1	E855.4	E941.1	E950.4	E962.0	E980.4
Coke fumes or gas (carbon monoxide)	986	E868.3	—	E952.1	E962.2	E982.1
industrial use	986	E868.8	—	E952.1	E962.2	E982.1
Colace	973.2	E858.4	E943.2	E950.4	E962.0	E980.4
Colchicine	974.7	E858.5	E944.7	E950.4	E962.0	E980.4
Colchicum	988.2	E865.3	—	E950.9	E962.1	E980.9
Cold cream	976.3	E858.7	E946.3	E950.4	E962.0	E980.4
Colestipol	972.2	E858.3	E942.2	E950.4	E962.0	E980.4
Colistimethate	960.8	E856	E930.8	E950.4	E962.0	E980.4
Colistin	960.8	E856	E930.8	E950.4	E962.0	E980.4
Collagen	977.8	E866.8	E947.8	E950.9	E962.1	E980.9
Collagenase	976.8	E858.7	E946.8	E950.4	E962.0	E980.4

Substance	Poisoning	External Cause (E-Code)				
		Accident	Therapeutic Use	Suicide Attempt	Assault	Undetermined
Collodion (flexible)	976.3	E858.7	E946.3	E950.4	E962.0	E980.4
Colocynth	973.1	E858.4	E943.1	E950.4	E962.0	E980.4
Coloring matter — *see* Dye(s)						
Combustion gas — *see* Carbon, monoxide						
Compazine	969.1	E853.0	E939.1	E950.3	E962.0	E980.3
Compound						
42 (warfarin)	989.4	E863.7	—	E950.6	E962.1	E980.7
269 (endrin)	989.2	E863.0	—	E950.6	E962.1	E980.7
497 (dieldrin)	989.2	E863.0	—	E950.6	E962.1	E980.7
1080 (sodium fluoroacetate)	989.4	E863.7	—	E950.6	E962.1	E980.7
3422 (parathion)	989.3	E863.1	—	E950.6	E962.1	E980.7
3911 (phorate)	989.3	E863.1	—	E950.6	E962.1	E980.7
3956 (toxaphene)	989.2	E863.0	—	E950.6	E962.1	E980.7
4049 (malathion)	989.3	E863.1	—	E950.6	E962.1	E980.7
4124 (dicapthon)	989.4	E863.4	—	E950.6	E962.1	E980.7
E (cortisone)	962.0	E858.0	E932.0	E950.4	E962.0	E980.4
F (hydrocortisone)	962.0	E858.0	E932.0	E950.4	E962.0	E980.4
Congo red	977.8	E858.8	E947.8	E950.4	E962.0	E980.4
Coniine, conine	965.7	E850.7	E935.7	E950.0	E962.0	E980.0
Conium (maculatum)	988.2	E865.4	—	E950.9	E962.1	E980.9
Conjugated estrogens (equine)	962.2	E858.0	E932.2	E950.4	E962.0	E980.4
Contac	975.6	E858.6	E945.6	E950.4	E962.0	E980.4
Contact lens solution	976.5	E858.7	E946.5	E950.4	E962.0	E980.4
Contraceptives (oral)	962.2	E858.0	E932.2	E950.4	E962.0	E980.4
vaginal	976.8	E858.7	E946.8	E950.4	E962.0	E980.4
Contrast media (roentgenographic)	977.8	E858.8	E947.8	E950.4	E962.0	E980.4
Convallaria majalis	988.2	E865.4	—	E950.9	E962.1	E980.9
Copper (dust) (fumes) (salts) NEC	985.8	E866.4	—	E950.9	E962.1	E980.9
arsenate, arsenite	985.1	E866.3	—	E950.8	E962.1	E980.8
insecticide	985.1	E863.4	—	E950.8	E962.1	E980.8
emetic	973.6	E858.4	E943.6	E950.4	E962.0	E980.4
fungicide	985.8	E863.6	—	E950.6	E962.1	E980.7
insecticide	985.8	E863.4	—	E950.6	E962.1	E980.7
oleate	976.0	E858.7	E946.0	E950.4	E962.0	E980.4
sulfate	983.9	E864.3	—	E950.7	E962.1	E980.6
fungicide	983.9	E863.6	—	E950.7	E962.1	E980.6
cupric	973.6	E858.4	E943.6	E950.4	E962.0	E980.4
cuprous	983.9	E864.3	—	E950.7	E962.1	E980.6
Copperhead snake (bite) (venom)	989.5	E905.0	—	E950.9	E962.1	E980.9
Coral (sting)	989.5	E905.6	—	E950.9	E962.1	E980.9
snake (bite) (venom)	989.5	E905.0	—	E950.9	E962.1	E980.9
Cordran	976.0	E858.7	E946.0	E950.4	E962.0	E980.4
Corn cures	976.4	E858.7	E946.4	E950.4	E962.0	E980.4
Cornhusker's lotion	976.3	E858.7	E946.3	E950.4	E962.0	E980.4
Corn starch	976.3	E858.7	E946.3	E950.4	E962.0	E980.4
Corrosive	983.9	E864.4	—	E950.7	E962.1	E980.6
acids NEC	983.1	E864.1	—	E950.7	E962.1	E980.6
aromatics	983.0	E864.0	—	E950.7	E962.1	E980.6
disinfectant	983.0	E861.4	—	E950.7	E962.1	E980.6
fumes NEC	987.9	E869.9	—	E952.9	E962.2	E982.9
specified NEC	983.9	E864.3	—	E950.7	E962.1	E980.6
sublimate — *see* Mercury, chloride						
Cortate	962.0	E858.0	E932.0	E950.4	E962.0	E980.4
Cort–Dome	962.0	E858.0	E932.0	E950.4	E962.0	E980.4
ENT agent	976.6	E858.7	E946.6	E950.4	E962.0	E980.4
ophthalmic preparation	976.5	E858.7	E946.5	E950.4	E962.0	E980.4
topical NEC	976.0	E858.7	E946.0	E950.4	E962.0	E980.4

Substance	Poisoning	External Cause (E-Code)				
		Accident	Therapeutic Use	Suicide Attempt	Assault	Undetermined
Cortef	962.0	E858.0	E932.0	E950.4	E962.0	E980.4
ENT agent	976.6	E858.7	E946.6	E950.4	E962.0	E980.4
ophthalmic preparation	976.5	E858.7	E946.5	E950.4	E962.0	E980.4
topical NEC	976.0	E858.7	E946.0	E950.4	E962.0	E980.4
Corticosteroids (fluorinated)	962.0	E858.0	E932.0	E950.4	E962.0	E980.4
ENT agent	976.6	E858.7	E946.6	E950.4	E962.0	E980.4
ophthalmic preparation	976.5	E858.7	E946.5	E950.4	E962.0	E980.4
topical NEC	976.0	E858.7	E946.0	E950.4	E962.0	E980.4
Corticotropin	962.4	E858.0	E932.4	E950.4	E962.0	E980.4
Cortisol	962.0	E858.0	E932.0	E950.4	E962.0	E980.4
ENT agent	976.6	E858.7	E946.6	E950.4	E962.0	E980.4
ophthalmic preparation	976.5	E858.7	E946.5	E950.4	E962.0	E980.4
topical NEC	976.0	E858.7	E946.0	E950.4	E962.0	E980.4
Cortisone derivatives (acetate)	962.0	E858.0	E932.0	E950.4	E962.0	E980.4
ENT agent	976.6	E858.7	E946.6	E950.4	E962.0	E980.4
ophthalmic preparation	976.5	E858.7	E946.5	E950.4	E962.0	E980.4
topical NEC	976.0	E858.7	E946.0	E950.4	E962.0	E980.4
Cortogen	962.0	E858.0	E932.0	E950.4	E962.0	E980.4
ENT agent	976.6	E858.7	E946.6	E950.4	E962.0	E980.4
ophthalmic preparation	976.5	E858.7	E946.5	E950.4	E962.0	E980.4
Cortone	962.0	E858.0	E932.0	E950.4	E962.0	E980.4
ENT agent	976.6	E858.7	E946.6	E950.4	E962.0	E980.4
ophthalmic preparation	976.5	E858.7	E946.5	E950.4	E962.0	E980.4
Cortril	962.0	E858.0	E932.0	E950.4	E962.0	E980.4
ENT agent	976.6	E858.7	E946.6	E950.4	E962.0	E980.4
ophthalmic preparation	976.5	E858.7	E946.5	E950.4	E962.0	E980.4
topical NEC	976.0	E858.7	E946.0	E950.4	E962.0	E980.4
Cosmetics	989.89	E866.7	—	E950.9	E962.1	E980.9
Cosyntropin	977.8	E858.8	E947.8	E950.4	E962.0	E980.4
Cotarnine	964.5	E858.2	E934.5	E950.4	E962.0	E980.4
Cottonseed oil	976.3	E858.7	E946.3	E950.4	E962.0	E980.4
Cough mixtures (antitussives)	975.4	E858.6	E945.4	E950.4	E962.0	E980.4
containing opiates	965.09	E850.2	E935.2	E950.0	E962.0	E980.0
expectorants	975.5	E858.6	E945.5	E950.4	E962.0	E980.4
Coumadin	964.2	E858.2	E934.2	E950.4	E962.0	E980.4
rodenticide	989.4	E863.7	—	E950.6	E962.1	E980.7
Coumarin	964.2	E858.2	E934.2	E950.4	E962.0	E980.4
Coumetarol	964.2	E858.2	E934.2	E950.4	E962.0	E980.4
Cowbane	988.2	E865.4	—	E950.9	E962.1	E980.9
Cozyme	963.5	E858.1	E933.5	E950.4	E962.0	E980.4
Creolin	983.0	E864.0	—	E950.7	E962.1	E980.6
disinfectant	983.0	E861.4	—	E950.7	E962.1	E980.6
Creosol (compound)	983.0	E864.0	—	E950.7	E962.1	E980.6
Creosote (beechwood) (coal tar)	983.0	E864.0	—	E950.7	E962.1	E980.6
medicinal (expectorant)	975.5	E858.6	E945.5	E950.4	E962.0	E980.4
syrup	975.5	E858.6	E945.5	E950.4	E962.0	E980.4
Cresol	983.0	E864.0	—	E950.7	E962.1	E980.6
disinfectant	983.0	E861.4	—	E950.7	E962.1	E980.6
Cresylic acid	983.0	E864.0	—	E950.7	E962.1	E980.6
Cropropamide	965.7	E850.7	E935.7	E950.0	E962.0	E980.0
with crotethamide	970.0	E854.3	E940.0	E950.4	E962.0	E980.4
Crotamiton	976.0	E858.7	E946.0	E950.4	E962.0	E980.4
Crotethamide	965.7	E850.7	E935.7	E950.0	E962.0	E980.0
with cropropamide	970.0	E854.3	E940.0	E950.4	E962.0	E980.4
Croton (oil)	973.1	E858.4	E943.1	E950.4	E962.0	E980.4
chloral	967.1	E852.0	E937.1	E950.2	E962.0	E980.2
Crude oil	981	E862.1	—	E950.9	E962.1	E980.9

Substance	Poisoning	Accident	Therapeutic Use	Suicide Attempt	Assault	Undetermined
Cryogenine	965.8	E850.8	E935.8	E950.0	E962.0	E980.0
Cryolite (pesticide)	989.4	E863.4	—	E950.6	E962.1	E980.7
Cryptenamine	972.6	E858.3	E942.6	E950.4	E962.0	E980.4
Crystal violet	976.0	E858.7	E946.0	E950.4	E962.0	E980.4
Cuckoopint	988.2	E865.4	—	E950.9	E962.1	E980.9
Cumetharol	964.2	E858.2	E934.2	E950.4	E962.0	E980.4
Cupric sulfate	973.6	E858.4	E943.6	E950.4	E962.0	E980.4
Cuprous sulfate	983.9	E864.3	—	E950.7	E962.1	E980.6
Curare, curarine	975.2	E858.6	E945.2	E950.4	E962.0	E980.4
Cyanic acid — *see* Cyanide(s)						
Cyanide(s) (compounds) (hydrogen)						
(potassium) (sodium) NEC	989.0	E866.8	—	E950.9	E962.1	E980.9
dust or gas (inhalation) NEC	987.7	E869.8	—	E952.8	E962.2	E982.8
fumigant	989.0	E863.8	—	E950.6	E962.1	E980.7
mercuric — *see* Mercury						
pesticide (dust) (fumes)	989.0	E863.4	—	E950.6	E962.1	E980.7
Cyanocobalamin	964.1	E858.2	E934.1	E950.4	E962.0	E980.4
Cyanogen (chloride) (gas) NEC	987.8	E869.8	—	E952.8	E962.2	E982.8
Cyclaine	968.5	E855.2	E938.5	E950.4	E962.0	E980.4
Cyclamen europaeum	988.2	E865.4	—	E950.9	E962.1	E980.9
Cyclandelate	972.5	E858.3	E942.5	E950.4	E962.0	E980.4
Cyclazocine	965.09	E850.2	E935.2	E950.0	E962.0	E980.0
Cyclizine	963.0	E858.1	E933.0	E950.4	E962.0	E980.4
Cyclobarbital, cyclobarbitone	967.0	E851	E937.0	E950.1	E962.0	E980.1
Cycloguanil	961.4	E857	E931.4	E950.4	E962.0	E980.4
Cyclohexane	982.0	E862.4	—	E950.9	E962.1	E980.9
Cyclohexanol	980.8	E860.8	—	E950.9	E962.1	E980.9
Cyclohexanone	982.8	E862.4	—	E950.9	E962.1	E980.9
Cyclomethycaine	968.5	E855.2	E938.5	E950.4	E962.0	E980.4
Cyclopentamine	971.2	E855.5	E941.2	E950.4	E962.0	E980.4
Cyclopenthiazide	974.3	E858.5	E944.3	E950.4	E962.0	E980.4
Cyclopentolate	971.1	E855.4	E941.1	E950.4	E962.0	E980.4
Cyclophosphamide	963.1	E858.1	E933.1	E950.4	E962.0	E980.4
Cyclopropane	968.2	E855.1	E938.2	E950.4	E962.0	E980.4
Cycloserine	960.6	E856	E930.6	E950.4	E962.0	E980.4
Cyclothiazide	974.3	E858.5	E944.3	E950.4	E962.0	E980.4
Cycrimine	966.4	E855.0	E936.4	E950.4	E962.0	E980.4
Cymarin	972.1	E858.3	E942.1	E950.4	E962.0	E980.4
Cyproheptadine	963.0	E858.1	E933.0	E950.4	E962.0	E980.4
Cyprolidol	969.0	E854.0	E939.0	E950.3	E962.0	E980.3
Cytarabine	963.1	E858.1	E933.1	E950.4	E962.0	E980.4
Cytisus						
laburnum	988.2	E865.4	—	E950.9	E962.1	E980.9
scoparius	988.2	E865.4	—	E950.9	E962.1	E980.9
Cytomel	962.7	E858.0	E932.7	E950.4	E962.0	E980.4
Cytosine (antineoplastic)	963.1	E858.1	E933.1	E950.4	E962.0	E980.4
Cytoxan	963.1	E858.1	E933.1	E950.4	E962.0	E980.4
Dacarbazine	963.1	E858.1	E933.1	E950.4	E962.0	E980.4
Dactinomycin	960.7	E856	E930.7	E950.4	E962.0	E980.4
DADPS	961.8	E857	E931.8	E950.4	E962.0	E980.4
Dakin's solution (external)	976.0	E858.7	E946.0	E950.4	E962.0	E980.4
Dalmane	969.4	E853.2	E939.4	E950.3	E962.0	E980.3
DAM	977.2	E858.8	E947.2	E950.4	E962.0	E980.4
Danilone	964.2	E858.2	E934.2	E950.4	E962.0	E980.4
Danthron	973.1	E858.4	E943.1	E950.4	E962.0	E980.4
Dantrolene	975.2	E858.6	E945.2	E950.4	E962.0	E980.4
Daphne (gnidium) (mezereum)	988.2	E865.4	—	E950.9	E962.1	E980.9

Substance	Poisoning	External Cause (E-Code)				
		Accident	Therapeutic Use	Suicide Attempt	Assault	Undetermined
berry	988.2	E865.3	—	E950.9	E962.1	E980.9
Dapsone	961.8	E857	E931.8	E950.4	E962.0	E980.4
Daraprim	961.4	E857	E931.4	E950.4	E962.0	E980.4
Darnel	988.2	E865.3	—	E950.9	E962.1	E980.9
Darvon	965.8	E850.8	E935.8	E950.0	E962.0	E980.0
Daunorubicin	960.7	E856	E930.7	E950.4	E962.0	E980.4
DBI	962.3	E858.0	E932.3	E950.4	E962.0	E980.4
D–Con (rodenticide)	989.4	E863.7	—	E950.6	E962.1	E980.7
DDS	961.8	E857	E931.8	E950.4	E962.0	E980.4
DDT	989.2	E863.0	—	E950.6	E962.1	E980.7
Deadly nightshade	988.2	E865.4	—	E950.9	E962.1	E980.9
berry	988.2	E865.3	—	E950.9	E962.1	E980.9
Deanol	969.7	E854.2	E939.7	E950.3	E962.0	E980.3
Debrisoquine	972.6	E858.3	E942.6	E950.4	E962.0	E980.4
Decaborane	989.89	E866.8	—	E950.9	E962.1	E980.9
fumes	987.8	E869.8	—	E952.8	E962.2	E982.8
Decadron	962.0	E858.0	E932.0	E950.4	E962.0	E980.4
ENT agent	976.6	E858.7	E946.6	E950.4	E962.0	E980.4
ophthalmic preparation	976.5	E858.7	E946.5	E950.4	E962.0	E980.4
topical NEC	976.0	E858.7	E946.0	E950.4	E962.0	E980.4
Decahydronaphthalene	982.0	E862.4	—	E950.9	E962.1	E980.9
Decalin	982.0	E862.4	—	E950.9	E962.1	E980.9
Decamethonium	975.2	E858.6	E945.2	E950.4	E962.0	E980.4
Decholin	973.4	E858.4	E943.4	E950.4	E962.0	E980.4
sodium (diagnostic)	977.8	E858.8	E947.8	E950.4	E962.0	E980.4
Declomycin	960.4	E856	E930.4	E950.4	E962.0	E980.4
Deferoxamine	963.8	E858.1	E933.8	E950.4	E962.0	E980.4
Dehydrocholic acid	973.4	E858.4	E943.4	E950.4	E962.0	E980.4
DeKalin	982.0	E862.4	—	E950.9	E962.1	E980.9
Delalutin	962.2	E858.0	E932.2	E950.4	E962.0	E980.4
Delphinium	988.2	E865.3	—	E950.9	E962.1	E980.9
Deltasone	962.0	E858.0	E932.0	E950.4	E962.0	E980.4
Delta	962.0	E858.0	E932.0	E950.4	E962.0	E980.4
Delvinal	967.0	E851	E937.0	E950.1	E962.0	E980.1
Demecarium (bromide)	971.0	E855.3	E941.0	E950.4	E962.0	E980.4
Demeclocycline	960.4	E856	E930.4	E950.4	E962.0	E980.4
Demecolcine	963.1	E858.1	E933.1	E950.4	E962.0	E980.4
Demelanizing agents	976.8	E858.7	E946.8	E950.4	E962.0	E980.4
Demerol	965.09	E850.2	E935.2	E950.0	E962.0	E980.0
Demethylchlortetracycline	960.4	E856	E930.4	E950.4	E962.0	E980.4
Demethyltetracycline	960.4	E856	E930.4	E950.4	E962.0	E980.4
Demeton	989.3	E863.1	—	E950.6	E962.1	E980.7
Demulcents	976.3	E858.7	E946.3	E950.4	E962.0	E980.4
Demulen	962.2	E858.0	E932.2	E950.4	E962.0	E980.4
Denatured alcohol	980.0	E860.1	—	E950.9	E962.1	E980.9
Dendrid	976.5	E858.7	E946.5	E950.4	E962.0	E980.4
Dental agents, topical	976.7	E858.7	E946.7	E950.4	E962.0	E980.4
Deodorant spray (feminine hygiene)	976.8	E858.7	E946.8	E950.4	E962.0	E980.4
Deoxyribonuclease	963.4	E858.1	E933.4	E950.4	E962.0	E980.4
Depressants						
appetite, central	977.0	E858.8	E947.0	E950.4	E962.0	E980.4
cardiac	972.0	E858.3	E942.0	E950.4	E962.0	E980.4
central nervous system (anesthetic)	968.4	E855.1	E938.4	E950.4	E962.0	E980.4
psychotherapeutic	969.5	E853.9	E939.5	E950.3	E962.0	E980.3
Dequalinium	976.0	E858.7	E946.0	E950.4	E962.0	E980.4
Dermolate	976.2	E858.7	E946.2	E950.4	E962.0	E980.4
DES	962.2	E858.0	E932.2	E950.4	E962.0	E980.4

Substance	Poisoning	External Cause (E-Code)				
		Accident	Therapeutic Use	Suicide Attempt	Assault	Undetermined
Desenex	976.0	E858.7	E946.0	E950.4	E962.0	E980.4
Deserpidine	972.6	E858.3	E942.6	E950.4	E962.0	E980.4
Desipramine	969.0	E854.0	E939.0	E950.3	E962.0	E980.3
Deslanoside	972.1	E858.3	E942.1	E950.4	E962.0	E980.4
Desocodeine	965.09	E850.2	E935.2	E950.0	E962.0	E980.0
Desomorphine	965.09	E850.2	E935.2	E950.0	E962.0	E980.0
Desonide	976.0	E858.7	E946.0	E950.4	E962.0	E980.4
Desoxycorticosterone derivatives	962.0	E858.0	E932.0	E950.4	E962.0	E980.4
Desoxyephedrine	969.7	E854.2	E939.7	E950.3	E962.0	E980.3
DET	969.6	E854.1	E939.6	E950.3	E962.0	E980.3
Detergents (ingested) (synthetic)	989.6	E861.0	—	E950.9	E962.1	E980.9
external medication	976.2	E858.7	E946.2	E950.4	E962.0	E980.4
Deterrent, alcohol	977.3	E858.8	E947.3	E950.4	E962.0	E980.4
Detrothyronine	962.7	E858.0	E932.7	E950.4	E962.0	E980.4
Dettol (external medication)	976.0	E858.7	E946.0	E950.4	E962.0	E980.4
Dexamethasone	962.0	E858.0	E932.0	E950.4	E962.0	E980.4
ENT agent	976.6	E858.7	E946.6	E950.4	E962.0	E980.4
ophthalmic preparation	976.5	E858.7	E946.5	E950.4	E962.0	E980.4
topical NEC	976.0	E858.7	E946.0	E950.4	E962.0	E980.4
Dexamphetamine	969.7	E854.2	E939.7	E950.3	E962.0	E980.3
Dexedrine	969.7	E854.2	E939.7	E950.3	E962.0	E980.3
Dexpanthenol	963.5	E858.1	E933.5	E950.4	E962.0	E980.4
Dextran	964.8	E858.2	E934.8	E950.4	E962.0	E980.4
Dextriferron	964.0	E858.2	E934.0	E950.4	E962.0	E980.4
Dextroamphetamine	969.7	E854.2	E939.7	E950.3	E962.0	E980.3
Dextro calcium pantothenate	963.5	E858.1	E933.5	E950.4	E962.0	E980.4
Dextromethorphan	975.4	E858.6	E945.4	E950.4	E962.0	E980.4
Dextromoramide	965.09	E850.2	E935.2	E950.0	E962.0	E980.0
Dextro pantothenyl alcohol	963.5	E858.1	E933.5	E950.4	E962.0	E980.4
topical	976.8	E858.7	E946.8	E950.4	E962.0	E980.4
Dextropropoxyphene (hydrochloride)	965.8	E850.8	E935.8	E950.0	E962.0	E980.0
Dextrorphan	965.09	E850.2	E935.2	E950.0	E962.0	E980.0
Dextrose NEC	974.5	E858.5	E944.5	E950.4	E962.0	E980.4
Dextrothyroxin	962.7	E858.0	E932.7	E950.4	E962.0	E980.4
DFP	971.0	E855.3	E941.0	E950.4	E962.0	E980.4
DHE–45	972.9	E858.3	E942.9	E950.4	E962.0	E980.4
Diabinese	962.3	E858.0	E932.3	E950.4	E962.0	E980.4
Diacetyl monoxime	977.2	E858.8	E947.2	E950.4	E962.0	E980.4
Diacetylmorphine	965.01	E850.0	E935.0	E950.0	E962.0	E980.0
Diagnostic agents	977.8	E858.8	E947.8	E950.4	E962.0	E980.4
Dial (soap)	976.2	E858.7	E946.2	E950.4	E962.0	E980.4
sedative	967.0	E851	E937.0	E950.1	E962.0	E980.1
Diallylbarbituric acid	967.0	E851	E937.0	E950.1	E962.0	E980.1
Diaminodiphenylsulfone	961.8	E857	E931.8	E950.4	E962.0	E980.4
Diamorphine	965.01	E850.0	E935.0	E950.0	E962.0	E980.0
Diamox	974.2	E858.5	E944.2	E950.4	E962.0	E980.4
Diamthazole	976.0	E858.7	E946.0	E950.4	E962.0	E980.4
Diaphenylsulfone	961.8	E857	E931.8	E950.4	E962.0	E980.4
Diasone (sodium)	961.8	E857	E931.8	E950.4	E962.0	E980.4
Diazepam	969.4	E853.2	E939.4	E950.3	E962.0	E980.3
Diazinon	989.3	E863.1	—	E950.6	E962.1	E980.7
Diazomethane (gas)	987.8	E869.8	—	E952.8	E962.2	E982.8
Diazoxide	972.5	E858.3	E942.5	E950.4	E962.0	E980.4
Dibenamine	971.3	E855.6	E941.3	E950.4	E962.0	E980.4
Dibenzheptropine	963.0	E858.1	E933.0	E950.4	E962.0	E980.4
Dibenzyline	971.3	E855.6	E941.3	E950.4	E962.0	E980.4
Diborane (gas)	987.8	E869.8	—	E952.8	E962.2	E982.8

Substance	Poisoning	Accident	Therapeutic Use	Suicide Attempt	Assault	Undetermined
			External Cause (E-Code)			
Dibromomannitol 963.1	E858.1	E933.1	E950.4	E962.0	E980.4	
Dibucaine (spinal) 968.7	E855.2	E938.7	E950.4	E962.0	E980.4	
topical (surface) 968.5	E855.2	E938.5	E950.4	E962.0	E980.4	
Dibunate sodium 975.4	E858.6	E945.4	E950.4	E962.0	E980.4	
Dibutoline 971.1	E855.4	E941.1	E950.4	E962.0	E980.4	
Dicapthon 989.4	E863.4	—	E950.6	E962.1	E980.7	
Dichloralphenazone 967.1	E852.0	E937.1	E950.2	E962.0	E980.2	
Dichlorodifluoromethane 987.4	E869.2	—	E952.8	E962.2	E982.8	
Dichloroethane 982.3	E862.4	—	E950.9	E962.1	E980.9	
Dichloroethylene 982.3	E862.4	—	E950.9	E962.1	E980.9	
Dichloroethyl sulfide 987.8	E869.8	—	E952.8	E962.2	E982.8	
Dichlorohydrin 982.3	E862.4	—	E950.9	E962.1	E980.9	
Dichloromethane (solvent) (vapor) 982.3	E862.4	—	E950.9	E962.1	E980.9	
Dichlorophen(e) 961.6	E857	E931.6	E950.4	E962.0	E980.4	
Dichlorphenamide 974.2	E858.5	E944.2	E950.4	E962.0	E980.4	
Dichlorvos 989.3	E863.1	—	E950.6	E962.1	E980.7	
Diclofenac sodium 956.6	E850.6	E935.6	E950.0	E962.0	E980.0	
Dicoumarin, dicumarol 964.2	E858.2	E934.2	E950.4	E962.0	E980.4	
Dicyanogen (gas) 987.8	E869.8	—	E952.8	E962.2	E982.8	
Dicyclomine 971.1	E855.4	E941.1	E950.4	E962.0	E980.4	
Dieldrin (vapor) 989.2	E863.0	—	E950.6	E962.1	E980.7	
Dienestrol 962.2	E858.0	E932.2	E950.4	E962.0	E980.4	
Dietetics 977.0	E858.8	E947.0	E950.4	E962.0	E980.4	
Diethazine 966.4	E855.0	E936.4	E950.4	E962.0	E980.4	
Diethyl						
barbituric acid 967.0	E851	E937.0	E950.1	E962.0	E980.1	
carbamazine 961.6	E857	E931.6	E950.4	E962.0	E980.4	
carbinol 980.8	E860.8	—	E950.9	E962.1	E980.9	
carbonate 982.8	E862.4	—	E950.9	E962.1	E980.9	
ether (vapor) — *see* Ether(s)						
propion 977.0	E858.8	E947.0	E950.4	E962.0	E980.4	
stilbestrol 962.2	E858.0	E932.2	E950.4	E962.0	E980.4	
Diethylene						
dioxide 982.8	E862.4	—	E950.9	E962.1	E980.9	
glycol (monoacetate) (monoethyl ether) . . 982.8	E862.4	—	E950.9	E962.1	E980.9	
Diethylsulfone–diethylmethane 967.8	E852.8	E937.8	E950.2	E962.0	E980.2	
Difencloxazine 965.09	E850.2	E935.2	E950.0	E962.0	E980.0	
Diffusin 963.4	E858.1	E933.4	E950.4	E962.0	E980.4	
Diflos 971.0	E855.3	E941.0	E950.4	E962.0	E980.4	
Digestants 973.4	E858.4	E943.4	E950.4	E962.0	E980.4	
Digitalin(e) 972.1	E858.3	E942.1	E950.4	E962.0	E980.4	
Digitalis glycosides 972.1	E858.3	E942.1	E950.4	E962.0	E980.4	
Digitoxin 972.1	E858.3	E942.1	E950.4	E962.0	E980.4	
Digoxin 972.1	E858.3	E942.1	E950.4	E962.0	E980.4	
Dihydrocodeine 965.09	E850.2	E935.2	E950.0	E962.0	E980.0	
Dihydrocodeinone 965.09	E850.2	E935.2	E950.0	E962.0	E980.0	
Dihydroergocristine 972.9	E858.3	E942.9	E950.4	E962.0	E980.4	
Dihydroergotamine 972.9	E858.3	E942.9	E950.4	E962.0	E980.4	
Dihydroergotoxine 972.9	E858.3	E942.9	E950.4	E962.0	E980.4	
Dihydrohydroxycodeinone 965.09	E850.2	E935.2	E950.0	E962.0	E980.0	
Dihydrohydroxymorphinone 965.09	E850.2	E935.2	E950.0	E962.0	E980.0	
Dihydroisocodeine 965.09	E850.2	E935.2	E950.0	E962.0	E980.0	
Dihydromorphine 965.09	E850.2	E935.2	E950.0	E962.0	E980.0	
Dihydromorphinone 965.09	E850.2	E935.2	E950.0	E962.0	E980.0	
Dihydrostreptomycin 960.6	E856	E930.6	E950.4	E962.0	E980.4	
Dihydrotachysterol 962.6	E858.0	E932.6	E950.4	E962.0	E980.4	
Dihydroxyanthraquinone 973.1	E858.4	E943.1	E950.4	E962.0	E980.4	

Substance	Poisoning	External Cause (E-Code)				
		Accident	Therapeutic Use	Suicide Attempt	Assault	Undetermined
Dihydroxycodeinone	965.09	E850.2	E935.2	E950.0	E962.0	E980.0
Diiodohydroxyquin	961.3	E857	E931.3	E950.4	E962.0	E980.4
topical	976.0	E858.7	E946.0	E950.4	E962.0	E980.4
Diiodohydroxyquinoline	961.3	E857	E931.3	E950.4	E962.0	E980.4
Dilantin	966.1	E855.0	E936.1	E950.4	E962.0	E980.4
Dilaudid	965.09	E850.2	E935.2	E950.0	E962.0	E980.0
Diloxanide	961.5	E857	E931.5	E950.4	E962.0	E980.4
Dimefline	970.0	E854.3	E940.0	E950.4	E962.0	E980.4
Dimenhydrinate	963.0	E858.1	E933.0	E950.4	E962.0	E980.4
Dimercaprol	963.8	E858.1	E933.8	E950.4	E962.0	E980.4
Dimercaptopropanol	963.8	E858.1	E933.8	E950.4	E962.0	E980.4
Dimetane	963.0	E858.1	E933.0	E950.4	E962.0	E980.4
Dimethicone	976.3	E858.7	E946.3	E950.4	E962.0	E980.4
Dimethindene	963.0	E858.1	E933.0	E950.4	E962.0	E980.4
Dimethisoquin	968.5	E855.2	E938.5	E950.4	E962.0	E980.4
Dimethisterone	962.2	E858.0	E932.2	E950.4	E962.0	E980.4
Dimethoxanate	975.4	E858.6	E945.4	E950.4	E962.0	E980.4
Dimethyl						
arsine, arsinic acid — *see* Arsenic						
carbinol	980.2	E860.3	—	E950.9	E962.1	E980.9
diguanide	962.3	E858.0	E932.3	E950.4	E962.0	E980.4
ketone	982.8	E862.4	—	E950.9	E962.1	E980.9
vapor	987.8	E869.8	—	E952.8	E962.2	E982.8
meperidine	965.09	E850.2	E935.2	E950.0	E962.0	E980.0
parathion	989.3	E863.1	—	E950.6	E962.1	E980.7
polysiloxane	973.8	E858.4	E943.8	E950.4	E962.0	E980.4
sulfate (fumes)	987.8	E869.8	—	E952.8	E962.2	E982.8
liquid	983.9	E864.3	—	E950.7	E962.1	E980.6
sulfoxide NEC	982.8	E862.4	—	E950.9	E962.1	E980.9
medicinal	976.4	E858.7	E946.4	E950.4	E962.0	E980.4
triptamine	969.6	E854.1	E939.6	E950.3	E962.0	E980.3
tubocurarine	975.2	E858.6	E945.2	E950.4	E962.0	E980.4
Dindevan	964.2	E858.2	E934.2	E950.4	E962.0	E980.4
Dinitro (–ortho–) cresol (herbicide) (spray)	989.4	E863.5	—	E950.6	E962.1	E980.7
insecticide	989.4	E863.4	—	E950.6	E962.1	E980.7
Dinitrobenzene	983.0	E864.0	—	E950.7	E962.1	E980.6
vapor	987.8	E869.8	—	E952.8	E962.2	E982.8
Dinitro–orthocresol (herbicide)	989.4	E863.5	—	E950.6	E962.1	E980.7
insecticide	989.4	E863.4	—	E950.6	E962.1	E980.7
Dinitrophenol (herbicide) (spray)	989.4	E863.5	—	E950.6	E962.1	E980.7
insecticide	989.4	E863.4	—	E950.6	E962.1	E980.7
Dinoprost	975.0	E858.6	E945.0	E950.4	E962.0	E980.4
Dioctyl sulfosuccinate (calcium) (sodium)	973.2	E858.4	E943.2	E950.4	E962.0	E980.4
Diodoquin	961.3	E857	E931.3	E950.4	E962.0	E980.4
Dione derivatives NEC	966.3	E855.0	E936.3	E950.4	E962.0	E980.4
Dionin	965.09	E850.2	E935.2	E950.0	E962.0	E980.0
Dioxane	982.8	E862.4	—	E950.9	E962.1	E980.9
Dioxin — *see* herbicide						
Dioxyline	972.5	E858.3	E942.5	E950.4	E962.0	E980.4
Dipentene	982.8	E862.4	—	E950.9	E962.1	E980.9
Diphemanil	971.1	E855.4	E941.1	E950.4	E962.0	E980.4
Diphenadione	964.2	E858.2	E934.2	E950.4	E962.0	E980.4
Diphenhydramine	963.0	E858.1	E933.0	E950.4	E962.0	E980.4
Diphenidol	963.0	E858.1	E933.0	E950.4	E962.0	E980.4
Diphenoxylate	973.5	E858.4	E943.5	E950.4	E962.0	E980.4
Diphenylchloroarsine	985.1	E866.3	—	E950.8	E962.1	E980.8
Diphenylhydantoin (sodium)	966.1	E855.0	E936.1	E950.4	E962.0	E980.4

Substance	Poisoning	External Cause (E-Code)				
		Accident	Therapeutic Use	Suicide Attempt	Assault	Undetermined
Diphenylpyraline	963.0	E858.1	E933.0	E950.4	E962.0	E980.4
Diphtheria						
antitoxin	979.9	E858.8	E949.9	E950.4	E962.0	E980.4
toxoid	978.5	E858.8	E948.5	E950.4	E962.0	E980.4
with tetanus toxoid	978.9	E858.8	E948.9	E950.4	E962.0	E980.4
with pertussis component	978.6	E858.8	E948.6	E950.4	E962.0	E980.4
vaccine	978.5	E858.8	E948.5	E950.4	E962.0	E980.4
Dipipanone	965.09	E850.2	E935.2	E950.0	E962.0	E980.0
Diplovax	979.5	E858.8	E949.5	E950.4	E962.0	E980.4
Diprophylline	975.1	E858.6	E945.1	E950.4	E962.0	E980.4
Dipyridamole	972.4	E858.3	E942.4	E950.4	E962.0	E980.4
Dipyrone	965.5	E850.5	E935.5	E950.0	E962.0	E980.0
Diquat	989.4	E863.5	—	E950.6	E962.1	E980.7
Disinfectant NEC	983.9	E861.4	—	E950.7	E962.1	E980.6
alkaline	983.2	E861.4	—	E950.7	E962.1	E980.6
aromatic	983.0	E861.4	—	E950.7	E962.1	E980.6
Disipal	966.4	E855.0	E936.4	E950.4	E962.0	E980.4
Disodium edetate	963.8	E858.1	E933.8	E950.4	E962.0	E980.4
Disulfamide	974.4	E858.5	E944.4	E950.4	E962.0	E980.4
Disulfanilamide	961.0	E857	E931.0	E950.4	E962.0	E980.4
Disulfiram	977.3	E858.8	E947.3	E950.4	E962.0	E980.4
Dithiazanine	961.6	E857	E931.6	E950.4	E962.0	E980.4
Dithioglycerol	963.8	E858.1	E933.8	E950.4	E962.0	E980.4
Dithranol	976.4	E858.7	E946.4	E950.4	E962.0	E980.4
Diucardin	974.3	E858.5	E944.3	E950.4	E962.0	E980.4
Diupres	974.3	E858.5	E944.3	E950.4	E962.0	E980.4
Diuretics NEC	974.4	E858.5	E944.4	E950.4	E962.0	E980.4
carbonic acid anhydrase inhibitors	974.2	E858.5	E944.2	E950.4	E962.0	E980.4
mercurial	974.0	E858.5	E944.0	E950.4	E962.0	E980.4
osmotic	974.4	E858.5	E944.4	E950.4	E962.0	E980.4
purine derivatives	974.1	E858.5	E944.1	E950.4	E962.0	E980.4
saluretic	974.3	E858.5	E944.3	E950.4	E962.0	E980.4
Diuril	974.3	E858.5	E944.3	E950.4	E962.0	E980.4
Divinyl ether	968.2	E855.1	E938.2	E950.4	E962.0	E980.4
D–lysergic acid diethylamide	969.6	E854.1	E939.6	E950.3	E962.0	E980.3
DMCT	960.4	E856	E930.4	E950.4	E962.0	E980.4
DMSO	982.8	E862.4	—	E950.9	E962.1	E980.9
DMT	969.6	E854.1	E939.6	E950.3	E962.0	E980.3
DNOC	989.4	E863.5	—	E950.6	E962.1	E980.7
DOCA	962.0	E858.0	E932.0	E950.4	E962.0	E980.4
Dolophine	965.02	E850.1	E935.1	E950.0	E962.0	E980.0
Doloxene	965.8	E850.8	E935.8	E950.0	E962.0	E980.0
DOM	969.6	E854.1	E939.6	E950.3	E962.0	E980.3
Domestic gas — see Gas, utility						
Domiphen (bromide) (lozenges)	976.6	E858.7	E946.6	E950.4	E962.0	E980.4
Dopa (levo)	966.4	E855.0	E936.4	E950.4	E962.0	E980.4
Dopamine	971.2	E855.5	E941.2	E950.4	E962.0	E980.4
Doriden	967.5	E852.4	E937.5	E950.2	E962.0	E980.2
Dormiral	967.0	E851	E937.0	E950.1	E962.0	E980.1
Dormison	967.8	E852.8	E937.8	E950.2	E962.0	E980.2
Dornase	963.4	E858.1	E933.4	E950.4	E962.0	E980.4
Dorsacaine	968.5	E855.2	E938.5	E950.4	E962.0	E980.4
Dothiepin hydrochloride	969.0	E854.0	E939.0	E950.3	E962.0	E980.3
Doxapram	970.0	E854.3	E940.0	E950.4	E962.0	E980.4
Doxepin	969.0	E854.0	E939.0	E950.3	E962.0	E980.3
Doxorubicin	960.7	E856	E930.7	E950.4	E962.0	E980.4
Doxycycline	960.4	E856	E930.4	E950.4	E962.0	E980.4

Substance	Poisoning	External Cause (E-Code)				
		Accident	Therapeutic Use	Suicide Attempt	Assault	Undetermined
Doxylamine	963.0	E858.1	E933.0	E950.4	E962.0	E980.4
Dramamine	963.0	E858.1	E933.0	E950.4	E962.0	E980.4
Drano (drain cleaner)	983.2	E864.2	—	E950.7	E962.1	E980.6
Dromoran	965.09	E850.2	E935.2	E950.0	E962.0	E980.0
Dromostanolone	962.1	E858.0	E932.1	E950.4	E962.0	E980.4
Droperidol	969.2	E853.1	E939.2	E950.3	E962.0	E980.3
Drug	977.9	E858.9	E947.9	E950.5	E962.0	E980.5
specified NEC	977.8	E858.8	E947.8	E950.4	E962.0	E980.4
AHFS List						
4:00 antihistamine drugs	963.0	E858.1	E933.0	E950.4	E962.0	E980.4
8:04 amebacides	961.5	E857	E931.5	E950.4	E962.0	E980.4
arsenical anti–infectives	961.1	E857	E931.1	E950.4	E962.0	E980.4
quinoline derivatives	961.3	E857	E931.3	E950.4	E962.0	E980.4
8:08 anthelmintics	961.6	E857	E931.6	E950.4	E962.0	E980.4
quinoline derivatives	961.3	E857	E931.3	E950.4	E962.0	E980.4
8:12.04 antifungal antibiotics	960.1	E856	E930.1	E950.4	E962.0	E980.4
8:12.06 cephalosporins	960.5	E856	E930.5	E950.4	E962.0	E980.4
8:12.08 chloramphenicol	960.2	E856	E930.2	E950.4	E962.0	E980.4
8:12.12 erythromycins	960.3	E856	E930.3	E950.4	E962.0	E980.4
8:12.16 penicillins	960.0	E856	E930.0	E950.4	E962.0	E980.4
8:12.20 streptomycins	960.6	E856	E930.6	E950.4	E962.0	E980.4
8:12.24 tetracyclines	960.4	E856	E930.4	E950.4	E962.0	E980.4
8:12.28 other antibiotics	960.8	E856	E930.8	E950.4	E962.0	E980.4
antimycobacterial	960.6	E856	E930.6	E950.4	E962.0	E980.4
macrolides	960.3	E856	E930.3	E950.4	E962.0	E980.4
8:16 antituberculars	961.8	E857	E931.8	E950.4	E962.0	E980.4
antibiotics	960.6	E856	E930.6	E950.4	E962.0	E980.4
8:18 antivirals	961.7	E857	E931.7	E950.4	E962.0	E980.4
8:20 plasmodicides (antimalarials)	961.4	E857	E931.4	E950.4	E962.0	E980.4
8:24 sulfonamides	961.0	E857	E931.0	E950.4	E962.0	E980.4
8:26 sulfones	961.8	E857	E931.8	E950.4	E962.0	E980.4
8:28 treponemicides	961.2	E857	E931.2	E950.4	E962.0	E980.4
8:32 trichomonacides	961.5	E857	E931.5	E950.4	E962.0	E980.4
quinoline derivatives	961.3	E857	E931.3	E950.4	E962.0	E980.4
nitrofuran derivatives	961.9	E857	E931.9	E950.4	E962.0	E980.4
8:36 urinary germicides	961.9	E857	E931.9	E950.4	E962.0	E980.4
quinoline derivatives	961.3	E857	E931.3	E950.4	E962.0	E980.4
8:40 other anti–infectives	961.9	E857	E931.9	E950.4	E962.0	E980.4
10:00 antineoplastic agents	963.1	E858.1	E933.1	E950.4	E962.0	E980.4
antibiotics	960.7	E856	E930.7	E950.4	E962.0	E980.4
progestogens	962.2	E858.0	E932.2	E950.4	E962.0	E980.4
12:04 parasympathomimetic (cholinergic) agents	971.0	E855.3	E941.0	E950.4	E962.0	E980.4
12:08 parasympatholytic (cholinergic –blocking) agents	971.1	E855.4	E941.1	E950.4	E962.0	E980.4
12:12 Sympathomimetic (adrenergic) agents	971.2	E855.5	E941.2	E950.4	E962.0	E980.4
12:16 sympatholytic (adrenergic– blocking) agents	971.3	E855.6	E941.3	E950.4	E962.0	E980.4
12:20 skeletal muscle relaxants						
central nervous system muscle-tone depressants	968.0	E855.1	E938.0	E950.4	E962.0	E980.4
myoneural blocking agents	975.2	E858.6	E945.2	E950.4	E962.0	E980.4
16:00 blood derivatives	964.7	E858.2	E934.7	E950.4	E962.0	E980.4
20:04 antianemia drugs	964.1	E858.2	E934.1	E950.4	E962.0	E980.4
20:04.04 iron preparations	964.0	E858.2	E934.0	E950.4	E962.0	E980.4
20:04.08 liver and stomach preparations	964.1	E858.2	E934.1	E950.4	E962.0	E980.4

Substance	Poisoning	External Cause (E-Code)				
		Accident	Therapeutic Use	Suicide Attempt	Assault	Undetermined
20:12.04 anticoagulants	964.2	E858.2	E934.2	E950.4	E962.0	E980.4
20:12.08 antiheparin agents	964.5	E858.2	E934.5	E950.4	E962.0	E980.4
20:12.12 coagulants	964.5	E858.2	E934.5	E950.4	E962.0	E980.4
20:12.16 hemostatics NEC	964.5	E858.2	E934.5	E950.4	E962.0	E980.4
capillary active drugs	972.8	E858.3	E942.8	E950.4	E962.0	E980.4
24:04 cardiac drugs	972.9	E858.3	E942.9	E950.4	E962.0	E980.4
cardiotonic agents	972.1	E858.3	E942.1	E950.4	E962.0	E980.4
rhythm regulators	972.0	E858.3	E942.0	E950.4	E962.0	E980.4
24:06 antilipemic agents	972.2	E858.3	E942.2	E950.4	E962.0	E980.4
thyroid derivatives	962.7	E858.0	E932.7	E950.4	E962.0	E980.4
24:08 hypotensive agents	972.6	E858.3	E942.6	E950.4	E962.0	E980.4
adrenergic blocking agents	971.3	E855.6	E941.3	E950.4	E962.0	E980.4
ganglion blocking agents	972.3	E858.3	E942.3	E950.4	E962.0	E980.4
vasodilators	972.5	E858.3	E942.5	E950.4	E962.0	E980.4
24:12 vasodilating agents NEC	972.5	E858.3	E942.5	E950.4	E962.0	E980.4
coronary	972.4	E858.3	E942.4	E950.4	E962.0	E980.4
nicotinic acid derivatives	972.2	E858.3	E942.2	E950.4	E962.0	E980.4
24:16 sclerosing agents	972.7	E858.3	E942.7	E950.4	E962.0	E980.4
28:04 general anesthetics	968.4	E855.1	E938.4	E950.4	E962.0	E980.4
gaseous anesthetics	968.2	E855.1	E938.2	E950.4	E962.0	E980.4
halothane	968.1	E855.1	E938.1	E950.4	E962.0	E980.4
intravenous anesthetics	968.3	E855.1	E938.3	E950.4	E962.0	E980.4
28:08 analgesics and antipyretics	965.9	E850.9	E935.9	E950.0	E962.0	E980.0
antirheumatics	965.6	E850.6	E935.6	E950.0	E962.0	E980.0
aromatic analgesics	965.4	E850.4	E935.4	E950.0	E962.0	E980.0
non–narcotic NEC	965.7	E850.7	E935.7	E950.0	E962.0	E980.0
opium alkaloids	965.00	E850.2	E935.2	E950.0	E962.0	E980.0
heroin	965.01	E850.0	E935.0	E950.0	E962.0	E980.0
methadone	965.02	E850.1	E935.1	E950.0	E962.0	E980.0
specified type NEC	965.09	E850.2	E935.2	E950.0	E962.0	E980.0
pyrazole derivatives	965.5	E850.5	E935.5	E950.0	E962.0	E980.0
salicylates	965.1	E850.3	E935.3	E950.0	E962.0	E980.0
specified NEC	965.8	E850.8	E935.8	E950.0	E962.0	E980.0
28:10 narcotic antagonists	970.1	E854.3	E940.1	E950.4	E962.0	E980.4
28:12 anticonvulsants	966.3	E855.0	E936.3	E950.4	E962.0	E980.4
barbiturates	967.0	E851	E937.0	E950.1	E962.0	E980.1
benzodiazepine–based tranquilizers	969.4	E853.4	E939.4	E950.3	E962.0	E980.3
bromides	967.3	E852.2	E937.3	E950.2	E962.0	E980.2
hydantoin derivatives	966.1	E855.0	E936.1	E950.4	E962.0	E980.4
oxazolidine (derivatives)	966.0	E855.0	E936.0	E950.4	E962.0	E980.4
succinimides	966.2	E855.0	E936.2	E950.4	E962.0	E980.4
28:16.04 antidepressants	969.0	E854.0	E939.0	E950.3	E962.0	E980.3
28:16.08 tranquilizers	969.5	E853.9	E939.5	E950.3	E962.0	E980.3
benzodiazepine–based	969.4	E853.2	E939.4	E950.3	E962.0	E980.3
butyrophenone–based	969.2	E853.1	E939.2	E950.3	E962.0	E980.3
major NEC	969.3	E853.8	E939.3	E950.3	E962.0	E980.3
phenothiazine–based	969.1	E853.0	E939.1	E950.3	E962.0	E980.3
28:16.12 other psychotherapeutic agents	969.8	E855.8	E939.8	E950.3	E962.0	E980.3
28:20 respiratory and cerebral stimulants	970.9	E854.3	E940.9	E950.4	E962.0	E980.4
analeptics	970.0	E854.3	E940.0	E950.4	E962.0	E980.4
anorexigenic agents	977.0	E858.8	E947.0	E950.4	E962.0	E980.4
psychostimulants	969.7	E854.2	E939.7	E950.3	E962.0	E980.3
specified NEC	970.8	E854.3	E940.8	E950.4	E962.0	E980.4
28:24 sedatives and hypnotics	967.9	E852.9	E937.9	E950.2	E962.0	E980.2
barbiturates	967.0	E851	E937.0	E950.1	E962.0	E980.1
benzodiazepine–based tranquilizers	969.4	E853.2	E939.4	E950.3	E962.0	E980.3

Substance			External Cause (E-Code)			
	Poisoning	Accident	Therapeutic Use	Suicide Attempt	Assault	Undetermined
chloral hydrate (group) 967.1	E852.0	E937.1	E950.2	E962.0	E980.2	
glutethamide group 967.5	E852.4	E937.5	E950.2	E962.0	E980.2	
intravenous anesthetics 968.3	E855.1	E938.3	E950.4	E962.0	E980.4	
methaqualone (compounds) 967.4	E852.3	E937.4	E950.2	E962.0	E980.2	
paraldehyde 967.2	E852.1	E937.2	E950.2	E962.0	E980.2	
phenothiazine–based tranquilizers . . . 969.1	E853.0	E939.1	E950.3	E962.0	E980.3	
specified NEC 967.8	E852.8	E937.8	E950.2	E962.0	E980.2	
thiobarbiturates 968.3	E855.1	E938.3	E950.4	E962.0	E980.4	
tranquilizer NEC 969.5	E853.9	E939.5	E950.3	E962.0	E980.3	
36:04 to 36:88 diagnostic agents 977.8	E858.8	E947.8	E950.4	E962.0	E980.4	
40:00 electrolyte, caloric, and water						
balance agents NEC 974.5	E858.5	E944.5	E950.4	E962.0	E980.4	
40:04 acidifying agents 963.2	E858.1	E933.2	E950.4	E962.0	E980.4	
40:08 alkalinizing agents 963.3	E858.1	E933.3	E950.4	E962.0	E980.4	
40:10 ammonia detoxicants 974.5	E858.5	E944.5	E950.4	E962.0	E980.4	
40:12 replacement solutions 974.5	E858.5	E944.5	E950.4	E962.0	E980.4	
plasma expanders 964.8	E858.2	E934.8	E950.4	E962.0	E980.4	
40:16 sodium–removing resins 974.5	E858.5	E944.5	E950.4	E962.0	E980.4	
40:18 potassium–removing resins 974.5	E858.5	E944.5	E950.4	E962.0	E980.4	
40:20 caloric agents 974.5	E858.5	E944.5	E950.4	E962.0	E980.4	
40:24 salt and sugar substitutes 974.5	E858.5	E944.5	E950.4	E962.0	E980.4	
40:28 diuretics NEC 974.4	E858.5	E944.4	E950.4	E962.0	E980.4	
carbonic acid anhydrase inhibitors . . 974.2	E858.5	E944.2	E950.4	E962.0	E980.4	
mercurials 974.0	E858.5	E944.0	E950.4	E962.0	E980.4	
purine derivatives 974.1	E858.5	E944.1	E950.4	E962.0	E980.4	
saluretics 974.3	E858.5	E944.3	E950.4	E962.0	E980.4	
thiazides 974.3	E858.5	E944.3	E950.4	E962.1	E980.4	
40:36 irrigating solutions 974.5	E858.5	E944.5	E950.4	E962.0	E980.4	
40:40 uricosuric agents 974.7	E858.5	E944.7	E950.4	E962.0	E980.4	
44:00 enzymes 963.4	E858.1	E933.4	E950.4	E962.0	E980.4	
fibrinolysis–affecting agents 964.4	E858.2	E934.4	E950.4	E962.0	E980.4	
gastric agents 973.4	E858.4	E943.4	E950.4	E962.0	E980.4	
48:00 expectorants and cough preparations						
antihistamine agents 963.0	E858.1	E933.0	E950.4	E962.0	E980.4	
antitussives 975.4	E858.6	E945.4	E950.4	E962.0	E980.4	
codeine derivatives 965.09	E850.2	E935.2	E950.0	E962.0	E980.0	
expectorants 975.5	E858.6	E945.5	E950.4	E962.0	E980.4	
narcotic agents NEC 965.09	E850.2	E935.2	E950.0	E962.0	E980.0	
52:04 anti–infectives (EENT)						
ENT agent 976.6	E858.7	E946.6	E950.4	E962.0	E980.4	
ophthalmic preparation 976.5	E858.7	E946.5	E950.4	E962.0	E980.4	
52:04.04 antibiotics (EENT)						
ENT agent 976.6	E858.7	E946.6	E950.4	E962.0	E980.4	
ophthalmic preparation 976.5	E858.7	E946.5	E950.4	E962.0	E980.4	
52:04.06 antivirals (EENT)						
ENT agent 976.6	E858.7	E946.6	E950.4	E962.0	E980.4	
ophthalmic preparation 976.5	E858.7	E946.5	E950.4	E962.0	E980.4	
52:04.08 sulfonamides (EENT)						
ENT agent 976.6	E858.7	E946.6	E950.4	E962.0	E980.4	
ophthalmic preparation 976.5	E858.7	E946.5	E950.4	E962.0	E980.4	
52:04.12 miscellaneous anti–infectives (EENT)						
ENT agent 976.6	E858.7	E946.6	E950.4	E962.0	E980.4	
ophthalmic preparation 976.5	E858.7	E946.5	E950.4	E962.0	E980.4	
52:08 anti–inflammatory agents (EENT)						
ENT agent 976.6	E858.7	E946.6	E950.4	E962.0	E980.4	
ophthalmic preparation 976.5	E858.7	E946.5	E950.4	E962.0	E980.4	
52:10 carbonic anhydrase inhibitors 974.2	E858.5	E944.2	E950.4	E962.0	E980.4	

Substance	Poisoning	External Cause (E-Code)				
		Accident	Therapeutic Use	Suicide Attempt	Assault	Undetermined
52:12 contact lens solutions	976.5	E858.7	E946.5	E950.4	E962.0	E980.4
52:16 local anesthetics (EENT)	968.5	E855.2	E938.5	E950.4	E962.0	E980.4
52:20 miotics	971.0	E855.3	E941.0	E950.4	E962.0	E980.4
52:24 mydriatics						
adrenergics	971.2	E855.5	E941.2	E950.4	E962.0	E980.4
anticholinergics	971.1	E855.4	E941.1	E950.4	E962.0	E980.4
antimuscarinics	971.1	E855.4	E941.1	E950.4	E962.0	E980.4
parasympatholytics	971.1	E855.4	E941.1	E950.4	E962.0	E980.4
spasmolytics	971.1	E855.4	E941.1	E950.4	E962.0	E980.4
sympathomimetics	971.2	E855.5	E941.2	E950.4	E962.0	E980.4
52:28 mouth washes and gargles	976.6	E858.7	E946.6	E950.4	E962.0	E980.4
52:32 vasoconstrictors (EENT)	971.2	E855.5	E941.2	E950.4	E962.0	E980.4
52:36 unclassified agents (EENT)						
ENT agent	976.6	E858.7	E946.6	E950.4	E962.0	E980.4
ophthalmic preparation	976.5	E858.7	E946.5	E950.4	E962.0	E980.4
56:04 antacids and adsorbents	973.0	E858.4	E943.0	E950.4	E962.0	E980.4
56:08 Antidiarrhea agents	973.5	E858.4	E943.5	E950.4	E962.0	E980.4
56:10 antiflatulents	973.8	E858.4	E943.8	E950.4	E962.0	E980.4
56:12 cathartics NEC	973.3	E858.4	E943.3	E950.4	E962.0	E980.4
emollients	973.2	E858.4	E943.2	E950.4	E962.0	E980.4
irritants	973.1	E858.4	E943.1	E950.4	E962.0	E980.4
56:16 digestants	973.4	E858.4	E943.4	E950.4	E962.0	E980.4
56:20 emetics and antiemetics						
antiemetics	963.0	E858.1	E933.0	E950.4	E962.0	E980.4
emetics	973.6	E858.4	E943.6	E950.4	E962.0	E980.4
56:24 lipotropic agents	977.1	E858.8	E947.1	E950.4	E962.0	E980.4
56:40 miscellaneous G.I. drugs	973.8	E858.4	E943.8	E950.4	E962.0	E980.4
60:00 gold compounds	965.6	E850.6	E935.6	E950.0	E962.0	E980.0
64:00 heavy metal antagonists	963.8	E858.1	E933.8	E950.4	E962.0	E980.4
68:04 adrenals	962.0	E858.0	E932.0	E950.4	E962.0	E980.4
68:08 androgens	962.1	E858.0	E932.1	E950.4	E962.0	E980.4
68:12 contraceptives, oral	962.2	E858.0	E932.2	E950.4	E962.0	E980.4
68:16 estrogens	962.2	E858.0	E932.2	E950.4	E962.0	E980.4
68:18 gonadotropins	962.4	E858.0	E932.4	E950.4	E962.0	E980.4
68:20 insulins and antidiabetic agents	962.3	E858.0	E932.3	E950.4	E962.0	E980.4
68:20.08 insulins	962.3	E858.0	E932.3	E950.4	E962.0	E980.4
68:24 parathyroid	962.6	E858.0	E932.6	E950.4	E962.0	E980.4
68:28 pituitary (posterior)	962.5	E858.0	E932.5	E950.4	E962.0	E980.4
anterior	962.4	E858.0	E932.4	E950.4	E962.0	E980.4
68:32 progestogens	962.2	E858.0	E932.2	E950.4	E962.0	E980.4
68:34 other corpus luteum hormones						
NEC	962.2	E858.0	E932.2	E950.4	E962.0	E980.4
68:36 thyroid and antithyroid						
antithyroid	962.8	E858.0	E932.8	E950.4	E962.0	E980.4
thyroid (derivatives)	962.7	E858.0	E932.7	E950.4	E962.0	E980.4
72:00 local anesthetics NEC	968.9	E855.2	E938.9	E950.4	E962.0	E980.4
topical (surface)	968.5	E855.2	E938.5	E950.4	E962.0	E980.4
infiltration (intradermal)						
(subcutaneous) (submucosal)	968.5	E855.2	E938.5	E950.4	E962.0	E980.4
nerve blocking (peripheral) (plexus)						
(regional)	968.6	E855.2	E938.6	E950.4	E962.0	E980.4
spinal	968.7	E855.2	E938.7	E950.4	E962.0	E980.4
76:00 oxytocics	975.0	E858.6	E945.0	E950.4	E962.0	E980.4
78:00 radioactive agents	990	—	—	—	—	—
80:04 serums NEC	979.9	E858.8	E949.9	E950.4	E962.0	E980.4
immune gamma globulin (human)	964.6	E858.2	E934.6	E950.4	E962.0	E980.4
80:08 toxoids NEC	978.8	E858.8	E948.8	E950.4	E962.0	E980.4

Substance	Poisoning	Accident	Therapeutic Use	Suicide Attempt	Assault	Undetermined
			External Cause (E-Code)			
diphtheria	978.5	E858.8	E948.5	E950.4	E962.0	E980.4
and tetanus	978.9	E858.8	E948.9	E950.4	E962.0	E980.4
with pertussis component	978.6	E858.8	E948.6	E950.4	E962.0	E980.4
tetanus	978.4	E858.8	E948.4	E950.4	E962.0	E980.4
and diphtheria	978.9	E858.8	E948.9	E950.4	E962.0	E980.4
with pertussis component	978.6	E858.8	E948.6	E950.4	E962.0	E980.4
80:12 vaccines	979.9	E858.8	E949.9	E950.4	E962.0	E980.4
bacterial NEC	978.8	E858.8	E948.8	E950.4	E962.0	E980.4
with						
other bacterial components	978.9	E858.8	E948.9	E950.4	E962.0	E980.4
pertussis component	978.6	E858.8	E948.6	E950.4	E962.0	E980.4
viral and rickettsial						
components	979.7	E858.8	E949.7	E950.4	E962.0	E980.4
rickettsial NEC	979.6	E858.8	E949.6	E950.4	E962.0	E980.4
with						
bacterial component	979.7	E858.8	E949.7	E950.4	E962.0	E980.4
pertussis component	978.6	E858.8	E948.6	E950.4	E962.0	E980.4
viral component	979.7	E858.8	E949.7	E950.4	E962.0	E980.4
viral NEC	979.6	E858.8	E949.6	E950.4	E962.0	E980.4
with						
bacterial component	979.7	E858.8	E949.7	E950.4	E962.0	E980.4
pertussis component	978.6	E858.8	E948.6	E950.4	E962.0	E980.4
rickettsial component	979.7	E858.8	E949.7	E950.4	E962.0	E980.4
84:04.04 antibiotics (skin and mucous membrane)	976.0	E858.7	E946.0	E950.4	E962.0	E980.4
84:04.08 fungicides (skin and mucous membrane)	976.0	E858.7	E946.0	E950.4	E962.0	E980.4
84:04.12 scabicides and pediculicides (skin and mucous membrane)	976.0	E858.7	E946.0	E950.4	E962.0	E980.4
84:04.16 miscellaneous local anti–infectives (skin and mucous membrane)	976.0	E858.7	E946.0	E950.4	E962.0	E980.4
84:06 anti–inflammatory agents (skin and mucous membrane)	976.0	E858.7	E946.0	E950.4	E962.0	E980.4
84:08 antipruritics and local anesthetics						
antipruritics	976.1	E858.7	E946.1	E950.4	E962.0	E980.4
local anesthetics	968.5	E855.2	E938.5	E950.4	E962.0	E980.4
84:12 astringents	976.2	E858.7	E946.2	E950.4	E962.0	E980.4
84:16 cell stimulants and proliferants	976.8	E858.7	E946.8	E950.4	E962.0	E980.4
84:20 detergents	976.2	E858.7	E946.2	E950.4	E962.0	E980.4
84:24 emollients, demulcents, and protectants	976.3	E858.7	E946.3	E950.4	E962.0	E980.4
84:28 keratolytic agents	976.4	E858.7	E946.4	E950.4	E962.0	E980.4
84:32 keratoplastic agents	976.4	E858.7	E946.4	E950.4	E962.0	E980.4
84:36 miscellaneous agents (skin and mucous membrane)	976.8	E858.7	E946.8	E950.4	E962.0	E980.4
86:00 spasmolytic agents	975.1	E858.6	E945.1	E950.4	E962.0	E980.4
antiasthmatics	975.7	E858.6	E945.7	E950.4	E962.0	E980.4
papaverine	972.5	E858.3	E942.5	E950.4	E962.0	E980.4
theophylline	974.1	E858.5	E944.1	E950.4	E962.0	E980.4
88:04 vitamin A	963.5	E858.1	E933.5	E950.4	E962.0	E980.4
88:08 vitamin B complex	963.5	E858.1	E933.5	E950.4	E962.0	E980.4
hematopoietic vitamin	964.1	E858.2	E934.1	E950.4	E962.0	E980.4
nicotinic acid derivatives	972.2	E858.3	E942.2	E950.4	E962.0	E980.4
88:12 vitamin C	963.5	E858.1	E933.5	E950.4	E962.0	E980.4
88:16 vitamin D	963.5	E858.1	E933.5	E950.4	E962.0	E980.4
88:20 vitamin E	963.5	E858.1	E933.5	E950.4	E962.0	E980.4

Substance	Poisoning	Accident	Therapeutic Use	Suicide Attempt	Assault	Undetermined
			External Cause (E-Code)			
88:24 vitamin K activity	964.3	E858.2	E934.3	E950.4	E962.0	E980.4
88:28 multivitamin preparations	963.5	E858.1	E933.5	E950.4	E962.0	E980.4
92:00 unclassified therapeutic agents	977.8	E858.8	E947.8	E950.4	E962.0	E980.4
Duboisine	971.1	E855.4	E941.1	E950.4	E962.0	E980.4
Dulcolax	973.1	E858.4	E943.1	E950.4	E962.0	E980.4
Duponol (C) (EP)	976.2	E858.7	E946.2	E950.4	E962.0	E980.4
Durabolin	962.1	E858.0	E932.1	E950.4	E962.0	E980.4
Dyclone	968.5	E855.2	E938.5	E950.4	E962.0	E980.4
Dyclonine	968.5	E855.2	E938.5	E950.4	E962.0	E980.4
Dydrogesterone	962.2	E858.0	E932.2	E950.4	E962.0	E980.4
Dyes NEC	989.89	E866.8	—	E950.9	E962.1	E980.9
diagnostic agents	977.8	E858.8	E947.8	E950.4	E962.0	E980.4
pharmaceutical NEC	977.4	E858.8	E947.4	E950.4	E962.0	E980.4
Dyfols	971.0	E855.3	E941.0	E950.4	E962.0	E980.4
Dymelor	962.3	E858.0	E932.3	E950.4	E962.0	E980.4
Dynamite	989.89	E866.8	—	E950.9	E962.1	E980.9
fumes	987.8	E869.8	—	E952.8	E962.2	E982.8
Dyphylline	975.1	E858.6	E945.1	E950.4	E962.0	E980.4
Ear preparations	976.6	E858.7	E946.6	E950.4	E962.0	E980.4
Echothiopate, ecothiopate	971.0	E855.3	E941.0	E950.4	E962.0	E980.4
Ectylurea	967.8	E852.8	E937.8	E950.2	E962.0	E980.2
Edathamil disodium	963.8	E858.1	E933.8	E950.4	E962.0	E980.4
Edecrin	974.4	E858.5	E944.4	E950.4	E962.0	E980.4
Edetate, disodium (calcium)	963.8	E858.1	E933.8	E950.4	E962.0	E980.4
Edrophonium	971.0	E855.3	E941.0	E950.4	E962.0	E980.4
Elase	976.8	E858.7	E946.8	E950.4	E962.0	E980.4
Elaterium	973.1	E858.4	E943.1	E950.4	E962.0	E980.4
Elder	988.2	E865.4	—	E950.9	E962.1	E980.9
berry (unripe)	988.2	E865.3	—	E950.9	E962.1	E980.9
Electrolytes NEC	974.5	E858.5	E944.5	E950.4	E962.0	E980.4
Electrolytic agent NEC	974.5	E858.5	E944.5	E950.4	E962.0	E980.4
Embramine	963.0	E858.1	E933.0	E950.4	E962.0	E980.4
Emetics	973.6	E858.4	E943.6	E950.4	E962.0	E980.4
Emetine (hydrochloride)	961.5	E857	E931.5	E950.4	E962.0	E980.4
Emollients	976.3	E858.7	E946.3	E950.4	E962.0	E980.4
Emylcamate	969.5	E853.8	E939.5	E950.3	E962.0	E980.3
Encyprate	969.0	E854.0	E939.0	E950.3	E962.0	E980.3
Endocaine	968.5	E855.2	E938.5	E950.4	E962.0	E980.4
Endrin	989.2	E863.0	—	E950.6	E962.1	E980.7
Enflurane	968.2	E855.1	E938.2	E950.4	E962.0	E980.4
Enovid	962.2	E858.0	E932.2	E950.4	E962.0	E980.4
ENT preparations (anti–infectives)	976.6	E858.7	E946.6	E950.4	E962.0	E980.4
Enzodase	963.4	E858.1	E933.4	E950.4	E962.0	E980.4
Enzymes NEC	963.4	E858.1	E933.4	E950.4	E962.0	E980.4
Epanutin	966.1	E855.0	E936.1	E950.4	E962.0	E980.4
Ephedra (tincture)	971.2	E855.5	E941.2	E950.4	E962.0	E980.4
Ephedrine	971.2	E855.5	E941.2	E950.4	E962.0	E980.4
Epiestriol	962.2	E858.0	E932.2	E950.4	E962.0	E980.4
Epilim — see Sodium valproate						
Epinephrine	971.2	E855.5	E941.2	E950.4	E962.0	E980.4
Epsom salt	973.3	E858.4	E943.3	E950.4	E962.0	E980.4
Equanil	969.5	E853.8	E939.5	E950.3	E962.0	E980.3
Equisetum (diuretic)	974.4	E858.5	E944.4	E950.4	E962.0	E980.4
Ergometrine	975.0	E858.6	E945.0	E950.4	E962.0	E980.4
Ergonovine	975.0	E858.6	E945.0	E950.4	E962.0	E980.4
Ergot NEC	988.2	E865.4	—	E950.9	E962.1	E980.9
medicinal (alkaloids)	975.0	E858.6	E945.0	E950.4	E962.0	E980.4

Substance	Poisoning	External Cause (E-Code)				
		Accident	Therapeutic Use	Suicide Attempt	Assault	Undetermined
Ergotamine (tartrate) (for migraine) NEC . . .	972.9	E858.3	E942.9	E950.4	E962.0	E980.4
Ergotrate	975.0	E858.6	E945.0	E950.4	E962.0	E980.4
Erythrityl tetranitrate	972.4	E858.3	E942.4	E950.4	E962.0	E980.4
Erythrol tetranitrate	972.4	E858.3	E942.4	E950.4	E962.0	E980.4
Erythromycin	960.3	E856	E930.3	E950.4	E962.0	E980.4
ophthalmic preparation	976.5	E858.7	E946.5	E950.4	E962.0	E980.4
topical NEC	976.0	E858.7	E946.0	E950.4	E962.0	E980.4
Eserine	971.0	E855.3	E941.0	E950.4	E962.0	E980.4
Eskabarb	967.0	E851	E937.0	E950.1	E962.0	E980.1
Eskalith	969.8	E855.8	E939.8	E950.3	E962.0	E980.3
Estradiol (cypionate) (dipropionate)						
(valerate)	962.2	E858.0	E932.2	E950.4	E962.0	E980.4
Estriol	962.2	E858.0	E932.2	E950.4	E962.0	E980.4
Estrogens (with progestogens)	962.2	E858.0	E932.2	E950.4	E962.0	E980.4
Estrone	962.2	E858.0	E932.2	E950.4	E962.0	E980.4
Etafedrine	971.2	E855.5	E941.2	E950.4	E962.0	E980.4
Ethacrynate sodium	974.4	E858.5	E944.4	E950.4	E962.0	E980.4
Ethacrynic acid	974.4	E858.5	E944.4	E950.4	E962.0	E980.4
Ethambutol	961.8	E857	E931.8	E950.4	E962.0	E980.4
Ethamide	974.2	E858.5	E944.2	E950.4	E962.0	E980.4
Ethamivan	970.0	E854.3	E940.0	E950.4	E962.0	E980.4
Ethamsylate	964.5	E858.2	E934.5	E950.4	E962.0	E980.4
Ethanol	980.0	E860.1	—	E950.9	E962.1	E980.9
beverage	980.0	E860.0	—	E950.9	E962.1	E980.9
Ethchlorvynol	967.8	E852.8	E937.8	E950.2	E962.0	E980.2
Ethebenecid	974.7	E858.5	E944.7	E950.4	E962.0	E980.4
Ether(s) (diethyl) (ethyl) (vapor)	987.8	E869.8	—	E952.8	E962.2	E982.8
anesthetic	968.2	E855.1	E938.2	E950.4	E962.0	E980.4
petroleum — see Ligroin						
solvent	982.8	E862.4	—	E950.9	E962.1	E980.9
Ethidine chloride (vapor)	987.8	E869.8	—	E952.8	E962.2	E982.8
liquid (solvent)	982.3	E862.4	—	E950.9	E962.1	E980.9
Ethinamate	967.8	E852.8	E937.8	E950.2	E962.0	E980.2
Ethinylestradiol	962.2	E858.0	E932.2	E950.4	E962.0	E980.4
Ethionamide	961.8	E857	E931.8	E950.4	E962.0	E980.4
Ethisterone	962.2	E858.0	E932.2	E950.4	E962.0	E980.4
Ethobral	967.0	E851	E937.0	E950.1	E962.0	E980.1
Ethocaine (infiltration) (topical)	968.5	E855.2	E938.5	E950.4	E962.0	E980.4
nerve block (peripheral) (plexus)	968.6	E855.2	E938.6	E950.4	E962.0	E980.4
spinal	968.7	E855.2	E938.7	E950.4	E962.0	E980.4
Ethoheptazine (citrate)	965.7	E850.7	E935.7	E950.0	E962.0	E980.0
Ethopropazine	966.4	E855.0	E936.4	E950.4	E962.0	E980.4
Ethosuximide	966.2	E855.0	E936.2	E950.4	E962.0	E980.4
Ethotoin	966.1	E855.0	E936.1	E950.4	E962.0	E980.4
Ethoxazene	961.9	E857	E931.9	E950.4	E962.0	E980.4
Ethoxzolamide	974.2	E858.5	E944.2	E950.4	E962.0	E980.4
Ethyl						
acetate (vapor)	982.8	E862.4	—	E950.9	E962.1	E980.9
alcohol	980.0	E860.1	—	E950.9	E962.1	E980.9
beverage	980.0	E860.0	—	E950.9	E962.1	E980.9
aldehyde (vapor)	987.8	E869.8	—	E952.8	E962.2	E982.8
liquid	989.89	E866.8	—	E950.9	E962.1	E980.9
aminobenzoate	968.5	E855.2	E938.5	E950.4	E962.0	E980.4
biscoumacetate	964.2	E858.2	E934.2	E950.4	E962.0	E980.4
bromide (anesthetic)	968.2	E855.1	E938.2	E950.4	E962.0	E980.4
carbamate (antineoplastic)	963.1	E858.1	E933.1	E950.4	E962.0	E980.4
carbinol	980.3	E860.4	—	E950.9	E962.1	E980.9

Substance	Poisoning	Accident	Therapeutic Use	Suicide Attempt	Assault	Undetermined
			External Cause (E-Code)			
chaulmoograte 961.8	E857	E931.8	E950.4	E962.0	E980.4
chloride (vapor) 987.8	E869.8	—	E952.8	E962.2	E982.8
anesthetic (local) 968.5	E855.2	E938.5	E950.4	E962.0	E980.4
inhaled 968.2	E855.1	E938.2	E950.4	E962.0	E980.4
solvent 982.3	E862.4	—	E950.9	E962.1	E980.9
estranol 962.1	E858.0	E932.1	E950.4	E962.0	E980.4
ether — *see* Ether(s)					
formate (solvent) NEC 982.8	E862.4	—	E950.9	E962.1	E980.9
iodoacetate 987.5	E869.3	—	E952.8	E962.2	E982.8
lactate (solvent) NEC 982.8	E862.4	—	E950.9	E962.1	E980.9
methylcarbinol 980.8	E860.8	—	E950.9	E962.1	E980.9
morphine 965.09	E850.2	E935.2	E950.0	E962.0	E980.0
Ethylene (gas) 987.1	E869.8	—	E952.8	E962.2	E982.8
anesthetic (general) 968.2	E855.1	E938.2	E950.4	E962.0	E980.4
chlorohydrin (vapor) 982.3	E862.4	—	E950.9	E962.1	E980.9
dichloride (vapor) 982.3	E862.4	—	E950.9	E962.1	E980.9
glycol(s) (any) (vapor) 982.8	E862.4	—	E950.9	E962.1	E980.9
Ethylidene					
chloride NEC 982.3	E862.4	—	E950.9	E962.1	E980.9
diethyl ether 982.8	E862.4	—	E950.9	E962.1	E980.9
Ethynodiol 962.2	E858.0	E932.2	E950.4	E962.0	E980.4
Etidocaine................. 968.9	E855.2	E938.9	E950.4	E962.0	E980.4
infiltration (subcutaneous) 968.5	E855.2	E938.5	E950.4	E962.0	E980.4
nerve (peripheral) (plexus) 968.6	E855.2	E938.6	E950.4	E962.0	E980.4
Etilfen 967.0	E851	E937.0	E950.1	E962.0	E980.1
Etomide 965.7	E850.7	E935.7	E950.0	E962.0	E980.0
Etorphine 965.09	E850.2	E935.2	E950.0	E962.0	E980.0
Etoval 967.0	E851	E937.0	E950.1	E962.0	E980.1
Etryptamine 969.0	E854.0	E939.0	E950.3	E962.0	E980.3
Eucaine 968.5	E855.2	E938.5	E950.4	E962.0	E980.4
Eucalyptus (oil) NEC 975.5	E858.6	E945.5	E950.4	E962.0	E980.4
Eucatropine................ 971.1	E855.4	E941.1	E950.4	E962.0	E980.4
Eucodal 965.09	E850.2	E935.2	E950.0	E962.0	E980.0
Euneryl 967.0	E851	E937.0	E950.1	E962.0	E980.1
Euphthalmine 971.1	E855.4	E941.1	E950.4	E962.0	E980.4
Eurax 976.0	E858.7	E946.0	E950.4	E962.0	E980.4
Euresol 976.4	E858.7	E946.4	E950.4	E962.0	E980.4
Euthroid 962.7	E858.0	E932.7	E950.4	E962.0	E980.4
Evans blue 977.8	E858.8	E947.8	E950.4	E962.0	E980.4
Evipal 967.0	E851	E937.0	E950.1	E962.0	E980.1
sodium 968.3	E855.1	E938.3	E950.4	E962.0	E980.4
Evipan 967.0	E851	E937.0	E950.1	E962.0	E980.1
sodium 968.3	E855.1	E938.3	E950.4	E962.0	E980.4
Exalgin 965.4	E850.4	E935.4	E950.0	E962.0	E980.0
Excipients, pharmaceutical 977.4	E858.8	E947.4	E950.4	E962.0	E980.4
Exhaust gas — *see* Carbon, monoxide					
Ex–Lax (phenolphthalein) 973.1	E858.4	E943.1	E950.4	E962.0	E980.4
Expectorants 975.5	E858.6	E945.5	E950.4	E962.0	E980.4
External medications (skin) (mucous					
membrane)................ 976.9	E858.7	E946.9	E950.4	E962.0	E980.4
dental agent 976.7	E858.7	E946.7	E950.4	E962.0	E980.4
ENT agent 976.6	E858.7	E946.6	E950.4	E962.0	E980.4
ophthalmic preparation 976.5	E858.7	E946.5	E950.4	E962.0	E980.4
specified NEC 976.8	E858.7	E946.8	E950.4	E962.0	E980.4
Eye agents (anti–infective)......... 976.5	E858.7	E946.5	E950.4	E962.0	E980.4
Factor IX complex (human) 964.5	E858.2	E934.5	E950.4	E962.0	E980.4
Fecal softeners 973.2	E858.4	E943.2	E950.4	E962.0	E980.4

Substance	Poisoning	External Cause (E-Code)				
		Accident	Therapeutic Use	Suicide Attempt	Assault	Undetermined
Fenbutrazate	977.0	E858.8	E947.0	E950.4	E962.0	E980.4
Fencamfamin	970.8	E854.3	E940.8	E950.4	E962.0	E980.4
Fenfluramine	977.0	E858.8	E947.0	E950.4	E962.0	E980.4
Fenoprofen	965.6	E850.6	E935.6	E950.0	E962.0	E980.0
Fentanyl	965.09	E850.2	E935.2	E950.0	E962.0	E980.0
Fentazin	969.1	E853.0	E939.1	E950.3	E962.0	E980.3
Fenticlor, fentichlor	976.0	E858.7	E946.0	E950.4	E962.0	E980.4
Fer de lance (bite) (venom)	989.5	E905.0	—	E950.9	E962.1	E980.9
Ferric — *see* Iron						
Ferrocholinate	964.0	E858.2	E934.0	E950.4	E962.0	E980.4
Ferrous fumerate, gluconate, lactate, salt NEC, sulfate (medicinal)	964.0	E858.2	E934.0	E950.4	E962.0	E980.4
Ferrum — *see* Iron						
Fertilizers NEC	989.89	E866.5	—	E950.9	E962.1	E980.4
with herbicide mixture	989.4	E863.5	—	E950.6	E962.1	E980.7
Fibrinogen (human)	964.7	E858.2	E934.7	E950.4	E962.0	E980.4
Fibrinolysin	964.4	E858.2	E934.4	E950.4	E962.0	E980.4
Fibrinolysis–affecting agents	964.4	E858.2	E934.4	E950.4	E962.0	E980.4
Filix mas	961.6	E857	E931.6	E950.4	E962.0	E980.4
Fiorinal	965.1	E850.3	E935.3	E950.0	E962.0	E980.0
Fire damp	987.1	E869.8	—	E952.8	E962.2	E982.8
Fish, nonbacterial or noxious	988.0	E865.2	—	E950.9	E962.1	E980.9
shell	988.0	E865.1	—	E950.9	E962.1	E980.9
Flagyl	961.5	E857	E931.5	E950.4	E962.0	E980.4
Flavoxate	975.1	E858.6	E945.1	E950.4	E962.0	E980.4
Flaxedil	975.2	E858.6	E945.2	E950.4	E962.0	E980.4
Flaxseed (medicinal)	976.3	E858.7	E946.3	E950.4	E962.0	E980.4
Florantyrone	973.4	E858.4	E943.4	E950.4	E962.0	E980.4
Floraquin	961.3	E857	E931.3	E950.4	E962.0	E980.4
Florinef	962.0	E858.0	E932.0	E950.4	E962.0	E980.4
ENT agent	976.6	E858.7	E946.6	E950.4	E962.0	E980.4
ophthalmic preparation	976.5	E858.7	E946.5	E950.4	E962.0	E980.4
topical NEC	976.0	E858.7	E946.0	E950.4	E962.0	E980.4
Flowers of sulfur	976.4	E858.7	E946.4	E950.4	E962.0	E980.4
Floxuridine	963.1	E858.1	E933.1	E950.4	E962.0	E980.4
Flucytosine	961.9	E857	E931.9	E950.4	E962.0	E980.4
Fludrocortisone	962.0	E858.0	E932.0	E950.4	E962.0	E980.4
ENT agent	976.6	E858.7	E946.6	E950.4	E962.0	E980.4
ophthalmic preparation	976.5	E858.7	E946.5	E950.4	E962.0	E980.4
topical NEC	976.0	E858.7	E946.0	E950.4	E962.0	E980.4
Flumethasone	976.0	E858.7	E946.0	E950.4	E962.0	E980.4
Flumethiazide	974.3	E858.5	E944.3	E950.4	E962.0	E980.4
Flumidin	961.7	E857	E931.7	E950.4	E962.0	E980.4
Fluocinolone	976.0	E858.7	E946.0	E950.4	E962.0	E980.4
Fluocortolone	962.0	E858.0	E932.0	E950.4	E962.0	E980.4
Fluohydrocortisone	962.0	E858.0	E932.0	E950.4	E962.0	E980.4
ENT agent	976.6	E858.7	E946.6	E950.4	E962.0	E980.4
ophthalmic preparation	976.5	E858.7	E946.5	E950.4	E962.0	E980.4
topical NEC	976.0	E858.7	E946.0	E950.4	E962.0	E980.4
Fluonid	976.0	E858.7	E946.0	E950.4	E962.0	E980.4
Fluopromazine	969.1	E853.0	E939.1	E950.3	E962.0	E980.3
Fluoracetate	989.4	E863.7	—	E950.6	E962.1	E980.7
Fluorescein (sodium)	977.8	E858.8	E947.8	E950.4	E962.0	E980.4
Fluoride(s) (pesticides) (sodium) NEC	989.4	E863.4	—	E950.6	E962.1	E980.7
hydrogen — *see* Hydrofluoric acid						
medicinal	976.7	E858.7	E946.7	E950.4	E962.0	E980.4
not pesticide NEC	983.9	E864.4	—	E950.7	E962.1	E980.6

Substance	Poisoning	External Cause (E-Code)				
		Accident	Therapeutic Use	Suicide Attempt	Assault	Undetermined
stannous	976.7	E858.7	E946.7	E950.4	E962.0	E980.4
Fluorinated corticosteroids	962.0	E858.0	E932.0	E950.4	E962.0	E980.4
Fluorine (compounds) (gas)	987.8	E869.8	—	E952.8	E962.2	E982.8
salt — see Fluoride(s)						
Fluoristan	976.7	E858.7	E946.7	E950.4	E962.0	E980.4
Fluoroacetate	989.4	E863.7	—	E950.6	E962.1	E980.7
Fluorodeoxyuridine	963.1	E858.1	E933.1	E950.4	E962.0	E980.4
Fluorometholone (topical) NEC	976.0	E858.7	E946.0	E950.4	E962.0	E980.4
ophthalmic preparation	976.5	E858.7	E946.5	E950.4	E962.0	E980.4
Fluorouracil	963.1	E858.1	E933.1	E950.4	E962.0	E980.4
Fluothane	968.1	E855.1	E938.1	E950.4	E962.0	E980.4
Fluoxetine hydrochloride	969.0	E854.0	E939.0	E950.3	E962.0	E980.3
Fluoxymesterone	962.1	E858.0	E932.1	E950.4	E962.0	E980.4
Fluphenazine	969.1	E853.0	E939.1	E950.3	E962.0	E980.3
Fluprednisolone	962.0	E858.0	E932.0	E950.4	E962.0	E980.4
Flurandrenolide	976.0	E858.7	E946.0	E950.4	E962.0	E980.4
Flurazepam (hydrochloride)	969.4	E853.2	E939.4	E950.3	E962.0	E980.3
Flurobate	976.0	E858.7	E946.0	E950.4	E962.0	E980.4
Flurothyl	969.8	E855.8	E939.8	E950.3	E962.0	E980.3
Fluroxene	968.2	E855.1	E938.2	E950.4	E962.0	E980.4
Folacin	964.1	E858.2	E934.1	E950.4	E962.0	E980.4
Folic acid	964.1	E858.2	E934.1	E950.4	E962.0	E980.4
Follicle stimulating hormone	962.4	E858.0	E932.4	E950.4	E962.0	E980.4
Food, foodstuffs, nonbacterial or noxious	988.9	E865.9	—	E950.9	E962.1	E980.9
berries, seeds	988.2	E865.3	—	E950.9	E962.1	E980.9
fish	988.0	E865.2	—	E950.9	E962.1	E980.9
mushrooms	988.1	E865.5	—	E950.9	E962.1	E980.9
plants	988.2	E865.9	—	E950.9	E962.1	E980.9
specified type NEC	988.2	E865.4	—	E950.9	E962.1	E980.9
shellfish	988.0	E865.1	—	E950.9	E962.1	E980.9
specified NEC	988.8	E865.8	—	E950.9	E962.1	E980.9
Fool's parsley	988.2	E865.4	—	E950.9	E962.1	E980.9
Formaldehyde (solution)	989.89	E861.4	—	E950.9	E962.1	E980.9
fungicide	989.4	E863.6	—	E950.6	E962.1	E980.7
gas or vapor	987.8	E869.8	—	E952.8	E962.2	E982.8
Formalin	989.89	E861.4	—	E950.9	E962.1	E980.9
fungicide	989.4	E863.6	—	E950.6	E962.1	E980.7
vapor	987.8	E869.8	—	E952.8	E962.2	E982.8
Formic acid	983.1	E864.1	—	E950.7	E962.1	E980.6
vapor	987.8	E869.8	—	E952.8	E962.2	E982.8
Fowler's solution	985.1	E866.3	—	E950.8	E962.1	E980.8
Foxglove	988.2	E865.4	—	E950.9	E962.1	E980.9
Fox green	977.8	E858.8	E947.8	E950.4	E962.0	E980.4
Framycetin	960.8	E856	E930.8	E950.4	E962.0	E980.4
Frangula (extract)	973.1	E858.4	E943.1	E950.4	E962.0	E980.4
Frei antigen	977.8	E858.8	E947.8	E950.4	E962.0	E980.4
Freons	987.4	E869.2	—	E952.8	E962.2	E982.8
Fructose	974.5	E858.5	E944.5	E950.4	E962.0	E980.4
Frusemide	974.4	E858.5	E944.4	E950.4	E962.0	E980.4
FSH	962.4	E858.0	E932.4	E950.4	E962.0	E980.4
Fuel						
automobile	981	E862.1	—	E950.9	E962.1	E980.9
exhaust gas, not in transit	986	E868.2	—	E952.0	E962.2	E982.0
vapor NEC	987.1	E869.8	—	E952.8	E962.2	E982.8
gas (domestic use) — see also Carbon, monoxide, fuel						
utility	987.1	E868.1	—	E951.8	E962.2	E981.8

Substance	Poisoning	External Cause (E-Code)				
		Accident	Therapeutic Use	Suicide Attempt	Assault	Undetermined
incomplete combustion of — *see* Carbon, monoxide, fuel, utility						
in mobile container	987.0	E868.0	—	E951.1	E962.2	E981.1
piped (natural)	987.1	E867	—	E951.0	E962.2	E981.0
industrial, incomplete combustion	986	E868.3	—	E952.1	E962.2	E982.1
Fugillin	960.8	E856	E930.8	E950.4	E962.0	E980.4
Fulminate of mercury	985.0	E866.1	—	E950.9	E962.1	E980.9
Fulvicin	960.1	E856	E930.1	E950.4	E962.0	E980.4
Fumadil	960.8	E856	E930.8	E950.4	E962.0	E980.4
Fumagillin	960.8	E856	E930.8	E950.4	E962.0	E980.4
Fumes (from)	987.9	E869.9	—	E952.9	E962.2	E982.9
carbon monoxide — *see* Carbon, monoxide						
charcoal (domestic use)	986	E868.3	—	E952.1	E962.2	E982.1
chloroform — *see* Chloroform						
coke (in domestic stoves, fireplaces)	986	E868.3	—	E952.1	E962.2	E982.1
corrosive NEC	987.8	E869.8	—	E952.8	E962.2	E982.8
ether — *see* Ether(s)						
freons	987.4	E869.2	—	E952.8	E962.2	E982.8
hydrocarbons	987.1	E869.8	—	E952.8	E962.2	E982.8
petroleum (liquefied)	987.0	E868.0	—	E951.1	E962.2	E981.1
distributed through pipes (pure or mixed with air)	987.0	E867	—	E951.0	E962.2	E981.0
lead — *see* Lead						
metals — *see* specified metal						
nitrogen dioxide	987.2	E869.0	—	E952.8	E962.2	E982.8
pesticides — *see* Pesticides						
petroleum (liquefied)	987.0	E868.0	—	E951.1	E962.2	E981.1
distributed through pipes (pure or mixed with air)	987.0	E867	—	E951.0	E962.2	E981.0
polyester	987.8	E869.8	—	E952.8	E962.2	E982.8
specified source, other (see also substance specified)	987.8	E869.8	—	E952.8	E962.2	E982.8
sulfur dioxide	987.3	E869.1	—	E952.8	E962.2	E982.8
Fumigants	989.4	E863.8	—	E950.6	E962.1	E980.7
Fungi, noxious, used as food	988.1	E865.5	—	E950.9	E962.1	E980.9
Fungicides (*see also* Antifungals)	989.4	E863.6	—	E950.6	E962.1	E980.7
Fungizone	960.1	E856	E930.1	E950.4	E962.0	E980.4
topical	976.0	E858.7	E946.0	E950.4	E962.0	E980.4
Furacin	976.0	E858.7	E946.0	E950.4	E962.0	E980.4
Furadantin	961.9	E857	E931.9	E950.4	E962.0	E980.4
Furazolidone	961.9	E857	E931.9	E950.4	E962.0	E980.4
Furnace (coal burning) (domestic), gas from	986	E868.3	—	E952.1	E962.2	E982.1
industrial	986	E868.8	—	E952.1	E962.2	E982.1
Furniture polish	989.89	E861.2	—	E950.9	E962.1	E980.9
Furosemide	974.4	E858.5	E944.4	E950.4	E962.0	E980.4
Furoxone	961.9	E857	E931.9	E950.4	E962.0	E980.4
Fusel oil (amyl) (butyl) (propyl)	980.3	E860.4	—	E950.9	E962.1	E980.9
Fusidic acid	960.8	E856	E930.8	E950.4	E962.0	E980.4
Gallamine	975.2	E858.6	E945.2	E950.4	E962.0	E980.4
Gallotannic acid	976.2	E858.7	E946.2	E950.4	E962.0	E980.4
Gamboge	973.1	E858.4	E943.1	E950.4	E962.0	E980.4
Gamimune	964.6	E858.2	E934.6	E950.4	E962.0	E980.4
Gamma–benzene hexachloride (vapor)	989.2	E863.0	—	E950.6	E962.1	E980.7
Gamma globulin	964.6	E858.2	E934.6	E950.4	E962.0	E980.4
Gamulin	964.6	E858.2	E934.6	E950.4	E962.0	E980.4
Ganglionic blocking agents	972.3	E858.3	E942.3	E950.4	E962.0	E980.4

Substance	Poisoning	Accident	Therapeutic Use	Suicide Attempt	Assault	Undetermined
			External Cause (E-Code)			
Ganja	969.6	E854.1	E939.6	E950.3	E962.0	E980.3
Garamycin	960.8	E856	E930.8	E950.4	E962.0	E980.4
ophthalmic preparation	976.5	E858.7	E946.5	E950.4	E962.0	E980.4
topical NEC	976.0	E858.7	E946.0	E950.4	E962.0	E980.4
Gardenal	967.0	E851	E937.0	E950.1	E962.0	E980.1
Gardepanyl	967.0	E851	E937.0	E950.1	E962.0	E980.1
Gas	987.9	E869.9	—	E952.9	E962.2	E982.9
acetylene	987.1	E868.1	—	E951.8	E962.2	E981.8
incomplete combustion of — see Carbon, monoxide, fuel, utility						
air contaminants, source or type not specified	987.9	E869.9	—	E952.9	E962.2	E982.9
anesthetic (general) NEC	968.2	E855.1	E938.2	E950.4	E962.0	E980.4
blast furnace	986	E868.8	—	E952.1	E962.2	E982.1
butane — see Butane						
carbon monoxide — see Carbon, monoxide						
chlorine	987.6	E869.8	—	E952.8	E962.2	E982.8
coal — see Carbon, monoxide, coal						
cyanide	987.7	E869.8	—	E952.8	E962.2	E982.8
dicyanogen	987.8	E869.8	—	E952.8	E962.2	E982.8
domestic — see Gas, utility						
exhaust — see Carbon, monoxide, exhaust gas						
from wood– or coal–burning stove or fireplace	986	E868.3	—	E952.1	E962.2	E982.1
fuel (domestic use) — see also Carbon, monoxide, fuel						
industrial use	986	E868.8	—	E952.1	E962.2	E982.1
utility	987.1	E868.1	—	E951.8	E962.2	E981.8
incomplete combustion of — see Carbon, monoxide, fuel, utility						
in mobile container	987.0	E868.0	—	E951.1	E962.2	E981.1
piped (natural)	987.1	E867	—	E951.0	E962.2	E981.0
garage	986	E868.2	—	E952.0	E962.2	E982.0
hydrocarbon NEC	987.1	E869.8	—	E952.8	E962.2	E982.8
incomplete combustion of — see Carbon, monoxide, fuel, utility						
liquefied (mobile container)	987.0	E868.0	—	E951.1	E962.2	E981.1
piped	987.0	E867	—	E951.0	E962.2	E981.0
hydrocyanic acid	987.7	E869.8	—	E952.8	E962.2	E982.8
illuminating — see Gas, utility						
incomplete combustion, any — see Carbon, monoxide						
kiln	986	E868.8	—	E952.1	E962.2	E982.1
lacrimogenic	987.5	E869.3	—	E952.8	E962.2	E982.8
marsh	987.1	E869.8	—	E952.8	E962.2	E982.8
motor exhaust, not in transit	986	E868.8	—	E952.1	E962.2	E982.1
mustard — see Mustard, gas						
natural	987.1	E867	—	E951.0	E962.2	E981.0
nerve (war)	987.9	E869.9	—	E952.9	E962.2	E982.9
oils	981	E862.1	—	E950.9	E962.1	E980.9
petroleum (liquefied) (distributed in mobile containers)	987.0	E868.0	—	E951.1	E962.2	E981.1
piped (pure or mixed with air)	987.0	E867	—	E951.1	E962.2	E981.1
piped (manufactured) (natural) NEC	987.1	E867	—	E951.0	E962.2	E981.0
producer	986	E868.8	—	E952.1	E962.2	E982.1
propane — see Propane						
refrigerant (freon)	987.4	E869.2	—	E952.8	E962.2	E982.8

Substance	External Cause (E-Code)					
	Poisoning	Accident	Therapeutic Use	Suicide Attempt	Assault	Undetermined
not freon	987.9	E869.9	—	E952.9	E962.2	E982.9
sewer	987.8	E869.8	—	E952.8	E962.2	E982.8
specified source NEC (*see also* substance specified)	987.8	E869.8	—	E952.8	E962.2	E982.8
stove — *see* Gas, utility						
tear	987.5	E869.3	—	E952.8	E962.2	E982.8
utility (for cooking, heating, or lighting) (piped) NEC	987.1	E868.1	—	E951.8	E962.2	E981.8
incomplete combustion of — *see* Carbon, monoxide, fuel, utility						
in mobile container	987.0	E868.0	—	E951.1	E962.2	E981.1
piped (natural)	987.1	E867	—	E951.0	E962.2	E981.0
water	987.1	E868.1	—	E951.8	E962.2	E981.8
incomplete combustion of — *see* Carbon, monoxide, fuel, utility						
Gaseous substance — *see* Gas						
Gasoline, gasolene	981	E862.1	—	E950.9	E962.1	E980.9
vapor	987.1	E869.8	—	E952.8	E962.2	E982.8
Gastric enzymes	973.4	E858.4	E943.4	E950.4	E962.0	E980.4
Gastrografin	977.8	E858.8	E947.8	E950.4	E962.0	E980.4
Gastrointestinal agents	973.9	E858.4	E943.9	E950.4	E962.0	E980.4
specified NEC	973.8	E858.4	E943.8	E950.4	E962.0	E980.4
Gaultheria procumbens	988.2	E865.4	—	E950.9	E962.1	E980.9
Gelatin (intravenous)	964.8	E858.2	E934.8	E950.4	E962.0	E980.4
absorbable (sponge)	964.5	E858.2	E934.5	E950.4	E962.0	E980.4
Gelfilm	976.8	E858.7	E946.8	E950.4	E962.0	E980.4
Gelfoam	964.5	E858.2	E934.5	E950.4	E962.0	E980.4
Gelsemine	970.8	E854.3	E940.8	E950.4	E962.0	E980.4
Gelsemium (sempervirens)	988.2	E865.4	—	E950.9	E962.1	E980.9
Gemonil	967.0	E851	E937.0	E950.1	E962.0	E980.1
Gentamicin	960.8	E856	E930.8	E950.4	E962.0	E980.4
ophthalmic preparation	976.5	E858.7	E946.5	E950.4	E962.0	E980.4
topical NEC	976.0	E858.7	E946.0	E950.4	E962.0	E980.4
Gentian violet	976.0	E858.7	E946.0	E950.4	E962.0	E980.4
Gexane	976.0	E858.7	E946.0	E950.4	E962.0	E980.4
Gila monster (venom)	989.5	E905.0	—	E950.9	E962.1	E980.9
Ginger, Jamaica	989.89	E866.8	—	E950.9	E962.1	E980.9
Gitalin	972.1	E858.3	E942.1	E950.4	E962.0	E980.4
Gitoxin	972.1	E858.3	E942.1	E950.4	E962.0	E980.4
Glandular extract (medicinal) NEC	977.9	E858.9	E947.9	E950.5	E962.0	E980.5
Glaucarubin	961.5	E857	E931.5	E950.4	E962.0	E980.4
Globin zinc insulin	962.3	E858.0	E932.3	E950.4	E962.0	E980.4
Glucagon	962.3	E858.0	E932.3	E950.4	E962.0	E980.4
Glucochloral	967.1	E852.0	E937.1	E950.2	E962.0	E980.2
Glucocorticoids	962.0	E858.0	E932.0	E950.4	E962.0	E980.4
Glucose	974.5	E858.5	E944.5	E950.4	E962.0	E980.4
oxidase reagent	977.8	E858.8	E947.8	E950.4	E962.0	E980.4
Glucosulfone sodium	961.8	E857	E931.8	E950.4	E962.0	E980.4
Glue(s)	989.89	E866.6	—	E950.9	E962.1	E980.9
Glutamic acid (hydrochloride)	973.4	E858.4	E943.4	E950.4	E962.0	E980.4
Glutathione	963.8	E858.1	E933.8	E950.4	E962.0	E980.4
Glutethimide (group)	967.5	E852.4	E937.5	E950.2	E962.0	E980.2
Glycerin (lotion)	976.3	E858.7	E946.3	E950.4	E962.0	E980.4
Glycerol (topical)	976.3	E858.7	E946.3	E950.4	E962.0	E980.4
Glyceryl						
guaiacolate	975.5	E858.6	E945.5	E950.4	E962.0	E980.4
triacetate (topical)	976.0	E858.7	E946.0	E950.4	E962.0	E980.4

Substance	Poisoning	External Cause (E-Code)				
		Accident	Therapeutic Use	Suicide Attempt	Assault	Undetermined
trinitrate	972.4	E858.3	E942.4	E950.4	E962.0	E980.4
Glycine	974.5	E858.5	E944.5	E950.4	E962.0	E980.4
Glycobiarsol	961.1	E857	E931.1	E950.4	E962.0	E980.4
Glycols (ether)	982.8	E862.4	—	E950.9	E962.1	E980.9
Glycopyrrolate	971.1	E855.4	E941.1	E950.4	E962.0	E980.4
Glymidine	962.3	E858.0	E932.3	E950.4	E962.0	E980.4
Gold (compounds) (salts)	965.6	E850.6	E935.6	E950.0	E962.0	E980.0
Golden sulfide of antimony	985.4	E866.2	—	E950.9	E962.1	E980.9
Goldylocks	988.2	E865.4	—	E950.9	E962.1	E980.9
Gonadal tissue extract	962.9	E858.0	E932.9	E950.4	E962.0	E980.4
female	962.2	E858.0	E932.2	E950.4	E962.0	E980.4
male	962.1	E858.0	E932.1	E950.4	E962.0	E980.4
Gonadotropin	962.4	E858.0	E932.4	E950.4	E962.0	E980.4
Grain alcohol	980.0	E860.1	—	E950.9	E962.1	E980.9
beverage	980.0	E860.0	—	E950.9	E962.1	E980.9
Gramicidin	960.8	E856	E930.8	E950.4	E962.0	E980.4
Gratiola officinalis	988.2	E865.4	—	E950.9	E962.1	E980.9
Grease	989.89	E866.8	—	E950.9	E962.1	E980.9
Green hellebore	988.2	E865.4	—	E950.9	E962.1	E980.9
Green soap	976.2	E858.7	E946.2	E950.4	E962.0	E980.4
Grifulvin	960.1	E856	E930.1	E950.4	E962.0	E980.4
Griseofulvin	960.1	E856	E930.1	E950.4	E962.0	E980.4
Growth hormone	962.4	E858.0	E932.4	E950.4	E962.0	E980.4
Guaiacol	975.5	E858.6	E945.5	E950.4	E962.0	E980.4
Guaiac reagent	977.8	E858.8	E947.8	E950.4	E962.0	E980.4
Guaifenesin	975.5	E858.6	E945.5	E950.4	E962.0	E980.4
Guaiphenesin	975.5	E858.6	E945.5	E950.4	E962.0	E980.4
Guanatol	961.4	E857	E931.4	E950.4	E962.0	E980.4
Guanethidine	972.6	E858.3	E942.6	E950.4	E962.0	E980.4
Guano	989.89	E866.5	—	E950.9	E962.1	E980.9
Guanochlor	972.6	E858.3	E942.6	E950.4	E962.0	E980.4
Guanoctine	972.6	E858.3	E942.6	E950.4	E962.0	E980.4
Guanoxan	972.6	E858.3	E942.6	E950.4	E962.0	E980.4
Hair treatment agent NEC	976.4	E858.7	E946.4	E950.4	E962.0	E980.4
Halcinonide	976.0	E858.7	E946.0	E950.4	E962.0	E980.4
Halethazole	976.0	E858.7	E946.0	E950.4	E962.0	E980.4
Hallucinogens	969.6	E854.1	E939.6	E950.3	E962.0	E980.3
Haloperidol	969.2	E853.1	E939.2	E950.3	E962.0	E980.3
Haloprogin	976.0	E858.7	E946.0	E950.4	E962.0	E980.4
Halotex	976.0	E858.7	E946.0	E950.4	E962.0	E980.4
Halothane	968.1	E855.1	E938.1	E950.4	E962.0	E980.4
Halquinols	976.0	E858.7	E946.0	E950.4	E962.0	E980.4
Harmonyl	972.6	E858.3	E942.6	E950.4	E962.0	E980.4
Hartmann's solution	974.5	E858.5	E944.5	E950.4	E962.0	E980.4
Hashish	969.6	E854.1	E939.6	E950.3	E962.0	E980.3
Hawaiian wood rose seeds	969.6	E854.1	E939.6	E950.3	E962.0	E980.3
Headache cures, drugs, powders NEC	977.9	E858.9	E947.9	E950.5	E962.0	E980.9
Heavenly Blue (morning glory)	969.6	E854.1	E939.6	E950.3	E962.0	E980.3
Heavy metal antagonists	963.8	E858.1	E933.8	E950.4	E962.0	E980.4
anti–infectives	961.2	E857	E931.2	E950.4	E962.0	E980.4
Hedaquinium	976.0	E858.7	E946.0	E950.4	E962.0	E980.4
Hedge hyssop	988.2	E865.4	—	E950.9	E962.1	E980.9
Heet	976.8	E858.7	E946.8	E950.4	E962.0	E980.4
Helenin	961.6	E857	E931.6	E950.4	E962.0	E980.4
Hellebore (black) (green) (white)	988.2	E865.4	—	E950.9	E962.1	E980.9
Hemlock	988.2	E865.4	—	E950.9	E962.1	E980.9

Substance	Poisoning	External Cause (E-Code)				
		Accident	Therapeutic Use	Suicide Attempt	Assault	Undetermined
Hemostatics	964.5	E858.2	E934.5	E950.4	E962.0	E980.4
capillary active drugs	972.8	E858.3	E942.8	E950.4	E962.0	E980.4
Henbane	988.2	E865.4	—	E950.9	E962.1	E980.9
Heparin (sodium)	964.2	E858.2	E934.2	E950.4	E962.0	E980.4
Heptabarbital, heptabarbitone	967.0	E851	E937.0	E950.1	E962.0	E980.1
Heptachlor	989.2	E863.0	—	E950.6	E962.1	E980.7
Heptalgin	965.09	E850.2	E935.2	E950.0	E962.0	E980.0
Herbicides	989.4	E863.5	—	E950.6	E962.1	E980.7
Heroin	965.01	E850.0	E935.0	E950.0	E962.0	E980.0
Herplex	976.5	E858.7	E946.5	E950.4	E962.0	E980.4
HES	964.8	E858.2	E934.8	E950.4	E962.0	E980.4
Hetastarch	964.8	E858.2	E934.8	E950.4	E962.0	E980.4
Hexachlorocyclohexane	989.2	E863.0	—	E950.6	E962.1	E980.7
Hexachlorophene	976.2	E858.7	E946.2	E950.4	E962.0	E980.4
Hexadimethrine (bromide)	964.5	E858.2	E934.5	E950.4	E962.0	E980.4
Hexafluorenium	975.2	E858.6	E945.2	E950.4	E962.0	E980.4
Hexa–germ	976.2	E858.7	E946.2	E950.4	E962.0	E980.4
Hexahydrophenol	980.8	E860.8	—	E950.9	E962.1	E980.9
Hexalin	980.8	E860.8	—	E950.9	E962.1	E980.9
Hexamethonium	972.3	E858.3	E942.3	E950.4	E962.0	E980.4
Hexamethyleneamine	961.9	E857	E931.9	E950.4	E962.0	E980.4
Hexamine	961.9	E857	E931.9	E950.4	E962.0	E980.4
Hexanone	982.8	E862.4	—	E950.9	E962.1	E980.9
Hexapropymate	967.8	E852.8	E937.8	E950.2	E962.0	E980.2
Hexestrol	962.2	E858.0	E932.2	E950.4	E962.0	E980.4
Hexethal (sodium)	967.0	E851	E937.0	E950.1	E962.0	E980.1
Hexetidine	976.0	E858.7	E946.0	E950.4	E962.0	E980.4
Hexobarbital, hexobarbitone	967.0	E851	E937.0	E950.1	E962.0	E980.1
sodium (anesthetic)	968.3	E855.1	E938.3	E950.4	E962.0	E980.4
soluble	968.3	E855.1	E938.3	E950.4	E962.0	E980.4
Hexocyclium	971.1	E855.4	E941.1	E950.4	E962.0	E980.4
Hexoestrol	962.2	E858.0	E932.2	E950.4	E962.0	E980.4
Hexone	982.8	E862.4	—	E950.9	E962.1	E980.9
Hexylcaine	968.5	E855.2	E938.5	E950.4	E962.0	E980.4
Hexylresorcinol	961.6	E857	E931.6	E950.4	E962.0	E980.4
Hinkle's pills	973.1	E858.4	E943.1	E950.4	E962.0	E980.4
Histalog	977.8	E858.8	E947.8	E950.4	E962.0	E980.4
Histamine (phosphate)	972.5	E858.3	E942.5	E950.4	E962.0	E980.4
Histoplasmin	977.8	E858.8	E947.8	E950.4	E962.0	E980.4
Holly berries	988.2	E865.3	—	E950.9	E962.1	E980.9
Homatropine	971.1	E855.4	E941.1	E950.4	E962.0	E980.4
Homo–tet	964.6	E858.2	E934.6	E950.4	E962.0	E980.4
Hormones (synthetic substitute) NEC	962.9	E858.0	E932.9	E950.4	E962.0	E980.4
adrenal cortical steroids	962.0	E858.0	E932.0	E950.4	E962.0	E980.4
antidiabetic agents	962.3	E858.0	E932.3	E950.4	E962.0	E980.4
follicle stimulating	962.4	E858.0	E932.4	E950.4	E962.0	E980.4
gonadotropic	962.4	E858.0	E932.4	E950.4	E962.0	E980.4
growth	962.4	E858.0	E932.4	E950.4	E962.0	E980.4
ovarian (substitutes)	962.2	E858.0	E932.2	E950.4	E962.0	E980.4
parathyroid (derivatives)	962.6	E858.0	E932.6	E950.4	E962.0	E980.4
pituitary (posterior)	962.5	E858.0	E932.5	E950.4	E962.0	E980.4
anterior	962.4	E858.0	E932.4	E950.4	E962.0	E980.4
thyroid (derivative)	962.7	E858.0	E932.7	E950.4	E962.0	E980.4
Hornet (sting)	989.5	E905.3	—	E950.9	E962.1	E980.9
Horticulture agent NEC	989.4	E863.9	—	E950.6	E962.1	E980.7
Hyaluronidase	963.4	E858.1	E933.4	E950.4	E962.0	E980.4
Hyazyme	963.4	E858.1	E933.4	E950.4	E962.0	E980.4

Substance	External Cause (E-Code)					
	Poisoning	Accident	Therapeutic Use	Suicide Attempt	Assault	Undetermined
Hycodan	965.09	E850.2	E935.2	E950.0	E962.0	E980.0
Hydantoin derivatives	966.1	E855.0	E936.1	E950.4	E962.0	E980.4
Hydeltra	962.0	E858.0	E932.0	E950.4	E962.0	E980.4
Hydergine	971.3	E855.6	E941.3	E950.4	E962.0	E980.4
Hydrabamine penicillin	960.0	E856	E930.0	E950.4	E962.0	E980.4
Hydralazine, hydrallazine	972.6	E858.3	E942.6	E950.4	E962.0	E980.4
Hydrargaphen	976.0	E858.7	E946.0	E950.4	E962.0	E980.4
Hydrazine	983.9	E864.3	—	E950.7	E962.1	E980.6
Hydriodic acid	975.5	E858.6	E945.5	E950.4	E962.0	E980.4
Hydrocarbon gas	987.1	E869.8	—	E952.8	E962.2	E982.8
incomplete combustion of — see Carbon, monoxide, fuel, utility						
liquefied (mobile container)	987.0	E868.0	—	E951.1	E962.2	E981.1
piped (natural)	987.0	E867	—	E951.0	E962.2	E981.0
Hydrochloric acid (liquid)	983.1	E864.1	—	E950.7	E962.1	E980.6
medicinal	973.4	E858.4	E943.4	E950.4	E962.0	E980.4
vapor	987.8	E869.8	—	E952.8	E962.2	E982.8
Hydrochlorothiazide	974.3	E858.5	E944.3	E950.4	E962.0	E980.4
Hydrocodone	965.09	E850.2	E935.2	E950.0	E962.0	E980.0
Hydrocortisone	962.0	E858.0	E932.0	E950.4	E962.0	E980.4
ENT agent	976.6	E858.7	E946.6	E950.4	E962.0	E980.4
ophthalmic preparation	976.5	E858.7	E946.5	E950.4	E962.0	E980.4
topical NEC	976.0	E858.7	E946.0	E950.4	E962.0	E980.4
Hydrocortone	962.0	E858.0	E932.0	E950.4	E962.0	E980.4
ENT agent	976.6	E858.7	E946.6	E950.4	E962.0	E980.4
ophthalmic preparation	976.5	E858.7	E946.5	E950.4	E962.0	E980.4
topical NEC	976.0	E858.7	E946.0	E950.4	E962.0	E980.4
Hydrocyanic acid — see Cyanide(s)						
Hydroflumethiazide	974.3	E858.5	E944.3	E950.4	E962.0	E980.4
Hydrofluoric acid (liquid)	983.1	E864.1	—	E950.7	E962.1	E980.6
vapor	987.8	E869.8	—	E952.8	E962.2	E982.8
Hydrogen	987.8	E869.8	—	E952.8	E962.2	E982.8
arsenide	985.1	E866.3	—	E950.8	E962.1	E980.8
arseniureted	985.1	E866.3	—	E950.8	E962.1	E980.8
cyanide (salts)	989.0	E866.8	—	E950.9	E962.1	E980.9
gas	987.7	E869.8	—	E952.8	E962.2	E982.8
fluoride (liquid)	983.1	E864.1	—	E950.7	E962.1	E980.6
vapor	987.8	E869.8	—	E952.8	E962.2	E982.8
peroxide (solution)	976.6	E858.7	E946.6	E950.4	E962.0	E980.4
phosphureted	987.8	E869.8	—	E952.8	E962.2	E982.8
sulfide (gas)	987.8	E869.8	—	E952.8	E962.2	E982.8
arseniureted	985.1	E866.3	—	E950.8	E962.1	E980.8
sulfureted	987.8	E869.8	—	E952.8	E962.2	E982.8
Hydromorphinol	965.09	E850.2	E935.2	E950.0	E962.0	E980.0
Hydromorphinone	965.09	E850.2	E935.2	E950.0	E962.0	E980.0
Hydromorphone	965.09	E850.2	E935.2	E950.0	E962.0	E980.0
Hydromox	974.3	E858.5	E944.3	E950.4	E962.0	E980.4
Hydrophilic lotion	976.3	E858.7	E946.3	E950.4	E962.0	E980.4
Hydroquinone	983.0	E864.0	—	E950.7	E962.1	E980.6
vapor	987.8	E869.8	—	E952.8	E962.2	E982.8
Hydrosulfuric acid (gas)	987.8	E869.8	—	E952.8	E962.2	E982.8
Hydrous wool fat (lotion)	976.3	E858.7	E946.3	E950.4	E962.0	E980.4
Hydroxide, caustic	983.2	E864.2	—	E950.7	E962.1	E980.6
Hydroxocobalamin	964.1	E858.2	E934.1	E950.4	E962.0	E980.4
Hydroxyamphetamine	971.2	E855.5	E941.2	E950.4	E962.0	E980.4
Hydroxychloroquine	961.4	E857	E931.4	E950.4	E962.0	E980.4
Hydroxydihydrocodeinone	965.09	E850.2	E935.2	E950.0	E962.0	E980.0

Substance	Poisoning	External Cause (E-Code)				
		Accident	Therapeutic Use	Suicide Attempt	Assault	Undetermined
Hydroxyethyl starch	964.8	E858.2	E934.8	E950.4	E962.0	E980.4
Hydroxyphenamate	969.5	E853.8	E939.5	E950.3	E962.0	E980.3
Hydroxyphenylbutazone	965.5	E850.5	E935.5	E950.0	E962.0	E980.0
Hydroxyprogesterone	962.2	E858.0	E932.2	E950.4	E962.0	E980.4
Hydroxyquinoline derivatives	961.3	E857	E931.3	E950.4	E962.0	E980.4
Hydroxystilbamidine	961.5	E857	E931.5	E950.4	E962.0	E980.4
Hydroxyurea	963.1	E858.1	E933.1	E950.4	E962.0	E980.4
Hydroxyzine	969.5	E853.8	E939.5	E950.3	E962.0	E980.3
Hyoscine (hydrobromide)	971.1	E855.4	E941.1	E950.4	E962.0	E980.4
Hyoscyamine	971.1	E855.4	E941.1	E950.4	E962.0	E980.4
Hyoscyamus (albus) (niger)	988.2	E865.4	—	E950.9	E962.1	E980.9
Hypaque	977.8	E858.8	E947.8	E950.4	E962.0	E980.4
Hypertussis	964.6	E858.2	E934.6	E950.4	E962.0	E980.4
Hypnotics NEC	967.9	E852.9	E937.9	E950.2	E962.0	E980.2
Hypochlorites — *see* Sodium, hypochlorite						
Hypotensive agents NEC	972.6	E858.3	E942.6	E950.4	E962.0	E980.4
Ibufenac	965.6	E850.6	E935.6	E950.0	E962.0	E980.0
Ibuprofen	965.6	E850.6	E935.6	E950.0	E962.0	E980.0
ICG	977.8	E858.8	E947.8	E950.4	E962.0	E980.4
Ichthammol	976.4	E858.7	E946.4	E950.4	E962.0	E980.4
Ichthyol	976.4	E858.7	E946.4	E950.4	E962.0	E980.4
Idoxuridine	976.5	E858.7	E946.5	E950.4	E962.0	E980.4
IDU	976.5	E858.7	E946.5	E950.4	E962.0	E980.4
Iletin	962.3	E858.0	E932.3	E950.4	E962.0	E980.4
Ilex	988.2	E865.4	—	E950.9	E962.1	E980.9
Illuminating gas — *see* Gas, utility						
Ilopan	963.5	E858.1	E933.5	E950.4	E962.0	E980.4
Ilotycin	960.3	E856	E930.3	E950.4	E962.0	E980.4
ophthalmic preparation	976.5	E858.7	E946.5	E950.4	E962.0	E980.4
topical NEC	976.0	E858.7	E946.0	E950.4	E962.0	E980.4
Imipramine	969.0	E854.0	E939.0	E950.3	E962.0	E980.3
Immu–G	964.6	E858.2	E934.6	E950.4	E962.0	E980.4
Immuglobin	964.6	E858.2	E934.6	E950.4	E962.0	E980.4
Immune serum globulin	964.6	E858.2	E934.6	E950.4	E962.0	E980.4
Immunosuppressive agents	963.1	E858.1	E933.1	E950.4	E962.0	E980.4
Immu–tetanus	964.6	E858.2	E934.6	E950.4	E962.0	E980.4
Indandione (derivatives)	964.2	E858.2	E934.2	E950.4	E962.0	E980.4
Inderal	972.0	E858.3	E942.0	E950.4	E962.0	E980.4
Indian						
hemp	969.6	E854.1	E939.6	E950.3	E962.0	E980.3
tobacco	988.2	E865.4	—	E950.9	E962.1	E980.9
Indigo carmine	977.8	E858.8	E947.8	E950.4	E962.0	E980.4
Indocin	965.6	E850.6	E935.6	E950.0	E962.0	E980.0
Indocyanine green	977.8	E858.8	E947.8	E950.4	E962.0	E980.4
Indomethacin	965.6	E850.6	E935.6	E950.0	E962.0	E980.0
Industrial						
alcohol	980.9	E860.9	—	E950.9	E962.1	E980.9
fumes	987.8	E869.8	—	E952.8	E962.2	E982.8
solvents (fumes) (vapors)	982.8	E862.9	—	E950.9	E962.1	E980.9
Influenza vaccine	979.6	E858.8	E949.6	E950.4	E962.0	E982.8
Ingested substances NEC	989.9	E866.9	—	E950.9	E962.1	E980.9
INH (isoniazid)	961.8	E857	E931.8	E950.4	E962.0	E980.4
Inhalation, gas (noxious) — *see* Gas						
Ink	989.89	E866.8	—	E950.9	E962.1	E980.9
Innovar	967.6	E852.5	E937.6	E950.2	E962.0	E980.2
Inositol niacinate	972.2	E858.3	E942.2	E950.4	E962.0	E980.4
Inproquone	963.1	E858.1	E933.1	E950.4	E962.0	E980.4

Substance	Poisoning	External Cause (E-Code)				
		Accident	Therapeutic Use	Suicide Attempt	Assault	Undetermined
Insect (sting), venomous	989.5	E905.5	—	E950.9	E962.1	E980.9
Insecticides (*see also* Pesticides)	989.4	E863.4	—	E950.6	E962.1	E980.7
chlorinated	989.2	E863.0	—	E950.6	E962.1	E980.7
mixtures	989.4	E863.3	—	E950.6	E962.1	E980.7
organochlorine (compounds)	989.2	E863.0	—	E950.6	E962.1	E980.7
organophosphorus (compounds)	989.3	E863.1	—	E950.6	E962.1	E980.7
Insular tissue extract	962.3	E858.0	E932.3	E950.4	E962.0	E980.4
Insulin (amorphous) (globin) (isophane) (Lente) (NPH) (protamine) (Semilente) (Ultralente) (zinc)	962.3	E858.0	E932.3	E950.4	E962.0	E980.4
Intranarcon	968.3	E855.1	E938.3	E950.4	E962.0	E980.4
Inulin	977.8	E858.8	E947.8	E950.4	E962.0	E980.4
Invert sugar	974.5	E858.5	E944.5	E950.4	E962.0	E980.4
Inza—*see* Naproxen						
Iodide NEC (*see also* Iodine)	976.0	E858.7	E946.0	E950.4	E962.0	E980.4
mercury (ointment)	976.0	E858.7	E946.0	E950.4	E962.0	E980.4
methylate	976.0	E858.7	E946.0	E950.4	E962.0	E980.4
potassium (expectorant) NEC	975.5	E858.6	E945.5	E950.4	E962.0	E980.4
Iodinated glycerol	975.5	E858.6	E945.5	E950.4	E962.0	E980.4
Iodine (antiseptic, external) (tincture) NEC	976.0	E858.7	E946.0	E950.4	E962.0	E980.4
diagnostic	977.8	E858.8	E947.8	E950.4	E962.0	E980.4
for thyroid conditions (antithyroid)	962.8	E858.0	E932.8	E950.4	E962.0	E980.4
vapor	987.8	E869.8	—	E952.8	E962.2	E982.8
Iodized oil	977.8	E858.8	E947.8	E950.4	E962.0	E980.4
Iodobismitol	961.2	E857	E931.2	E950.4	E962.0	E980.4
Iodochlorhydroxyquin	961.3	E857	E931.3	E950.4	E962.0	E980.4
topical	976.0	E858.7	E946.0	E950.4	E962.0	E980.4
Iodoform	976.0	E858.7	E946.0	E950.4	E962.0	E980.4
Iodopanoic acid	977.8	E858.8	E947.8	E950.4	E962.0	E980.4
Iodophthalein	977.8	E858.8	E947.8	E950.4	E962.0	E980.4
Ion exchange resins	974.5	E858.5	E944.5	E950.4	E962.0	E980.4
Iopanoic acid	977.8	E858.8	E947.8	E950.4	E962.0	E980.4
Iophendylate	977.8	E858.8	E947.8	E950.4	E962.0	E980.4
Iothiouracil	962.8	E858.0	E932.8	E950.4	E962.0	E980.4
Ipecac	973.6	E858.4	E943.6	E950.4	E962.0	E980.4
Ipecacuanha	973.6	E858.4	E943.6	E950.4	E962.0	E980.4
Ipodate	977.8	E858.8	E947.8	E950.4	E962.0	E980.4
Ipral	967.0	E851	E937.0	E950.1	E962.0	E980.1
Iproniazid	969.0	E854.0	E939.0	E950.3	E962.0	E980.3
Iron (compounds) (medicinal) (preparations)	964.0	E858.2	E934.0	E950.4	E962.0	E980.4
dextran	964.0	E858.2	E934.0	E950.4	E962.0	E980.4
nonmedicinal (dust) (fumes) NEC	985.8	E866.4	—	E950.9	E962.1	E980.9
Irritant drug	977.9	E858.9	E947.9	E950.5	E962.0	E980.5
Ismelin	972.6	E858.3	E942.6	E950.4	E962.0	E980.4
Isoamyl nitrite	972.4	E858.3	E942.4	E950.4	E962.0	E980.4
Isobutyl acetate	982.8	E862.4	—	E950.9	E962.1	E980.9
Isocarboxazid	969.0	E854.0	E939.0	E950.3	E962.0	E980.3
Isoephedrine	971.2	E855.5	E941.2	E950.4	E962.0	E980.4
Isoetharine	971.2	E855.5	E941.2	E950.4	E962.0	E980.4
Isofluorophate	971.0	E855.3	E941.0	E950.4	E962.0	E980.4
Isoniazid (INH)	961.8	E857	E931.8	E950.4	E962.0	E980.4
Isopentaquine	961.4	E857	E931.4	E950.4	E962.0	E980.4
Isophane insulin	962.3	E858.0	E932.3	E950.4	E962.0	E980.4
Isopregnenone	962.2	E858.0	E932.2	E950.4	E962.0	E980.4
Isoprenaline	971.2	E855.5	E941.2	E950.4	E962.0	E980.4

Substance	Poisoning	External Cause (E-Code)				
		Accident	Therapeutic Use	Suicide Attempt	Assault	Undetermined
Isopropamide	971.1	E855.4	E941.1	E950.4	E962.0	E980.4
Isopropanol	980.2	E860.3	—	E950.9	E962.1	E980.9
topical (germicide)	976.0	E858.7	E946.0	E950.4	E962.0	E980.4
Isopropyl						
acetate	982.8	E862.4	—	E950.9	E962.1	E980.9
alcohol	980.2	E860.3	—	E950.9	E962.1	E980.9
topical (germicide)	976.0	E858.7	E946.0	E950.4	E962.0	E980.4
ether	982.8	E862.4	—	E950.9	E962.1	E980.9
Isoproterenol	971.2	E855.5	E941.2	E950.4	E962.0	E980.4
Isosorbide dinitrate	972.4	E858.3	E942.4	E950.4	E962.0	E980.4
Isothipendyl	963.0	E858.1	E933.0	E950.4	E962.0	E980.4
Isoxazolyl penicillin	960.0	E856	E930.0	E950.4	E962.0	E980.4
Isoxsuprine hydrochloride	972.5	E858.3	E942.5	E950.4	E962.0	E980.4
I–thyroxine sodium	962.7	E858.0	E932.7	E950.4	E962.0	E980.4
Jaborandi (pilocarpus) (extract)	971.0	E855.3	E941.0	E950.4	E962.0	E980.4
Jalap	973.1	E858.4	E943.1	E950.4	E962.0	E980.4
Jamaica						
dogwood (bark)	965.7	E850.7	E935.7	E950.0	E962.0	E980.0
ginger	989.89	E866.8	—	E950.9	E962.1	E980.9
Jatropha	988.2	E865.4	—	E950.9	E962.1	E980.9
curcas	988.2	E865.3	—	E950.9	E962.1	E980.9
Jectofer	964.0	E858.2	E934.0	E950.4	E962.0	E980.4
Jellyfish (sting)	989.5	E905.6	—	E950.9	E962.1	E980.9
Jequirity (bean)	988.2	E865.3	—	E950.9	E962.1	E980.9
Jimson weed	988.2	E865.4	—	E950.9	E962.1	E980.9
seeds	988.2	E865.3	—	E950.9	E962.1	E980.9
Juniper tar (oil) (ointment)	976.4	E858.7	E946.4	E950.4	E962.0	E980.4
Kallikrein	972.5	E858.3	E942.5	E950.4	E962.0	E980.4
Kanamycin	960.6	E856	E930.6	E950.4	E962.0	E980.4
Kantrex	960.6	E856	E930.6	E950.4	E962.0	E980.4
Kaolin	973.5	E858.4	E943.5	E950.4	E962.0	E980.4
Karaya (gum)	973.3	E858.4	E943.3	E950.4	E962.0	E980.4
Kemithal	968.3	E855.1	E938.3	E950.4	E962.0	E980.4
Kenacort	962.0	E858.0	E932.0	E950.4	E962.0	E980.4
Keratolytics	976.4	E858.7	E946.4	E950.4	E962.0	E980.4
Keratoplastics	976.4	E858.7	E946.4	E950.4	E962.0	E980.4
Kerosene, kerosine (fuel) (solvent) NEC	981	E862.1	—	E950.9	E962.1	E980.9
insecticide	981	E863.4	—	E950.6	E962.1	E980.7
vapor	987.1	E869.8	—	E952.8	E962.2	E982.8
Ketamine	968.3	E855.1	E938.3	E950.4	E962.0	E980.4
Ketobemidone	965.09	E850.2	E935.2	E950.0	E962.0	E980.0
Ketols	982.8	E862.4	—	E950.9	E962.1	E980.9
Ketone oils	982.8	E862.4	—	E950.9	E962.1	E980.9
Kiln gas or vapor (carbon monoxide)	986	E868.8	—	E952.1	E962.2	E982.1
Konsyl	973.3	E858.4	E943.3	E950.4	E962.0	E980.4
Kosam seed	988.2	E865.3	—	E950.9	E962.1	E980.9
Krait (venom)	989.5	E905.0	—	E950.9	E962.1	E980.9
Kwell (insecticide)	989.2	E863.0	—	E950.6	E962.1	E980.7
anti–infective (topical)	976.0	E858.7	E946.0	E950.4	E962.0	E980.4
Laburnum (flowers) (seeds)	988.2	E865.3	—	E950.9	E962.1	E980.9
leaves	988.2	E865.4	—	E950.9	E962.1	E980.9
Lacquers	989.89	E861.6	—	E950.9	E962.1	E980.9
Lacrimogenic gas	987.5	E869.3	—	E952.8	E962.2	E982.8
Lactic acid	983.1	E864.1	—	E950.7	E962.1	E980.6
Lactobacillus acidophilus	973.5	E858.4	E943.5	E950.4	E962.0	E980.4
Lactoflavin	963.5	E858.1	E933.5	E950.4	E962.0	E980.4
Lactuca (virosa) (extract)	967.8	E852.8	E937.8	E950.2	E962.0	E980.2

Substance	Poisoning	External Cause (E-Code)				
		Accident	Therapeutic Use	Suicide Attempt	Assault	Undetermined
Lactucarium	967.8	E852.8	E937.8	E950.2	E962.0	E980.2
Laevulose	974.5	E858.5	E944.5	E950.4	E962.0	E980.4
Lanatoside(C)	972.1	E858.3	E942.1	E950.4	E962.0	E980.4
Lanolin (lotion)	976.3	E858.7	E946.3	E950.4	E962.0	E980.4
Largactil	969.1	E853.0	E939.1	E950.3	E962.0	E980.3
Larkspur	988.2	E865.3	—	E950.9	E962.1	E980.9
Laroxyl	969.0	E854.0	E939.0	E950.3	E962.0	E980.3
Lasix	974.4	E858.5	E944.4	E950.4	E962.0	E980.4
Latex	989.82	E866.8	—	E950.9	E962.1	E980.9
Lathyrus (seed)	988.2	E865.3	—	E950.9	E962.1	E980.9
Laudanum	965.09	E850.2	E935.2	E950.0	E962.0	E980.0
Laudexium	975.2	E858.6	E945.2	E950.4	E962.0	E980.4
Laurel, black or cherry	988.2	E865.4	—	E950.9	E962.1	E980.9
Laurolinium	976.0	E858.7	E946.0	E950.4	E962.0	E980.4
Lauryl sulfoacetate	976.2	E858.7	E946.2	E950.4	E962.0	E980.4
Laxatives NEC	973.3	E858.4	E943.3	E950.4	E962.0	E980.4
emollient	973.2	E858.4	E943.2	E950.4	E962.0	E980.4
L–dopa	966.4	E855.0	E936.4	E950.4	E962.0	E980.4
L Tryptophan—*see* amino acid						
Lead (dust) (fumes) (vapor) NEC	984.9	E866.0	—	E950.9	E962.1	E980.9
acetate (dust)	984.1	E866.0	—	E950.9	E962.1	E980.9
anti–infectives	961.2	E857	E931.2	E950.4	E962.0	E980.4
antiknock compound (tetraethyl)	984.1	E862.1	—	E950.9	E962.1	E980.9
arsenate, arsenite (dust) (insecticide) (vapor)	985.1	E863.4	—	E950.8	E962.1	E980.8
herbicide	985.1	E863.5	—	E950.8	E962.1	E980.8
carbonate	984.0	E866.0	—	E950.9	E962.1	E980.9
paint	984.0	E861.5	—	E950.9	E962.1	E980.9
chromate	984.0	E866.0	—	E950.9	E962.1	E980.9
paint	984.0	E861.5	—	E950.9	E962.1	E980.9
dioxide	984.0	E866.0	—	E950.9	E962.1	E980.9
inorganic (compound)	984.0	E866.0	—	E950.9	E962.1	E980.9
paint	984.0	E861.5	—	E950.9	E962.1	E980.9
iodine	984.0	E866.0	—	E950.9	E962.1	E980.9
pigment (paint)	984.0	E861.5	—	E950.9	E962.1	E980.9
monoxide (dust)	984.0	E866.0	—	E950.9	E962.1	E980.9
paint	984.0	E861.5	—	E950.9	E962.1	E980.9
organic	984.1	E866.0	—	E950.9	E962.1	E980.9
oxide	984.0	E866.0	—	E950.9	E962.1	E980.9
paint	984.0	E861.5	—	E950.9	E962.1	E980.9
paint	984.0	E861.5	—	E950.9	E962.1	E980.9
salts	984.0	E866.0	—	E950.9	E962.1	E980.9
specified compound NEC	984.8	E866.0	—	E950.9	E962.1	E980.9
tetra–ethyl	984.1	E862.1	—	E950.9	E962.1	E980.9
Lebanese red	969.6	E854.1	E939.6	E950.3	E962.0	E980.3
Lente Iletin (insulin)	962.3	E858.0	E932.3	E950.4	E962.0	E980.4
Leptazol	970.0	E854.3	E940.0	E950.4	E962.0	E980.4
Leritine	965.09	E850.2	E935.2	E950.0	E962.0	E980.0
Letter	962.7	E858.0	E932.7	E950.4	E962.0	E980.4
Lettuce opium	967.8	E852.8	E937.8	E950.2	E962.0	E980.2
Leucovorin (factor)	964.1	E858.2	E934.1	E950.4	E962.0	E980.4
Leukeran	963.1	E858.1	E933.1	E950.4	E962.0	E980.4
Levallorphan	970.1	E854.3	E940.1	E950.4	E962.0	E980.4
Levanil	967.8	E852.8	E937.8	E950.2	E962.0	E980.2
Levarterenol	971.2	E855.5	E941.2	E950.4	E962.0	E980.4
Levodopa	966.4	E855.0	E936.4	E950.4	E962.0	E980.4
Levo–dromoran	965.09	E850.2	E935.2	E950.0	E962.0	E980.0

Substance	External Cause (E-Code)				
	Poisoning	Accident	Therapeutic Use	Suicide Attempt	Assault	Undetermined

Substance	Poisoning	Accident	Therapeutic Use	Suicide Attempt	Assault	Undetermined
Levoid	962.7	E858.0	E932.7	E950.4	E962.0	E980.4
Levo–iso–methadone	965.02	E850.1	E935.1	E950.0	E962.0	E980.0
Levomepromazine	967.8	E852.8	E937.8	E950.2	E962.0	E980.2
Levoprome	967.8	E852.8	E937.8	E950.2	E962.0	E980.2
Levopropoxyphene	975.4	E858.6	E945.4	E950.4	E962.0	E980.4
Levorphan, levophanol	965.09	E850.2	E935.2	E950.0	E962.0	E980.0
Levothyroxine (sodium)	962.7	E858.0	E932.7	E950.4	E962.0	E980.4
Levsin	971.1	E855.4	E941.1	E950.4	E962.0	E980.4
Levulose	974.5	E858.5	E944.5	E950.4	E962.0	E980.4
Lewisite (gas)	985.1	E866.3	—	E950.8	E962.1	E980.8
Librium	969.4	E853.2	E939.4	E950.3	E962.0	E980.3
Lidex	976.0	E858.7	E946.0	E950.4	E962.0	E980.4
Lidocaine (infiltration) (topical)	968.5	E855.2	E938.5	E950.4	E962.0	E980.4
nerve block (peripheral) (plexus)	968.6	E855.2	E938.6	E950.4	E962.0	E980.4
spinal	968.7	E855.2	E938.7	E950.4	E962.0	E980.4
Lighter fluid	981	E862.1	—	E950.9	E962.1	E980.9
Lignocaine (infiltration) (topical)	968.5	E855.2	E938.5	E950.4	E962.0	E980.4
nerve block (peripheral) (plexus)	968.6	E855.2	E938.6	E950.4	E962.0	E980.4
spinal	968.7	E855.2	E938.7	E950.4	E962.0	E980.4
Ligroin(e) (solvent)	981	E862.0	—	E950.9	E962.1	E980.9
vapor	987.1	E869.8	—	E952.8	E962.2	E982.8
Ligustrum vulgare	988.2	E865.3	—	E950.9	E962.1	E980.9
Lily of the valley	988.2	E865.4	—	E950.9	E962.1	E980.9
Lime (chloride)	983.2	E864.2	—	E950.7	E962.1	E980.6
solution, sulferated	976.4	E858.7	E946.4	E950.4	E962.0	E980.4
Limonene	982.8	E862.4	—	E950.9	E962.1	E980.9
Lincomycin	960.8	E856	E930.8	E950.4	E962.0	E980.4
Lindane (insecticide) (vapor)	989.2	E863.0	—	E950.6	E962.1	E980.7
anti–infective (topical)	976.0	E858.7	E946.0	E950.4	E962.0	E980.4
Liniments NEC	976.9	E858.7	E946.9	E950.4	E962.0	E980.4
Linoleic acid	972.2	E858.3	E942.2	E950.4	E962.0	E980.4
Liothyronine	962.7	E858.0	E932.7	E950.4	E962.0	E980.4
Liotrix	962.7	E858.0	E932.7	E950.4	E962.0	E980.4
Lipancreatin	973.4	E858.4	E943.4	E950.4	E962.0	E980.4
Lipo–Lutin	962.2	E858.0	E932.2	E950.4	E962.0	E980.4
Lipotropic agents	977.1	E858.8	E947.1	E950.4	E962.0	E980.4
Liquefied petroleum gases	987.0	E868.0	—	E951.1	E962.2	E981.1
piped (pure or mixed with air)	987.0	E867	—	E951.0	E962.2	E981.0
Liquid petrolatum	973.2	E858.4	E943.2	E950.4	E962.0	E980.4
substance	989.9	E866.9	—	E950.9	E962.1	E980.9
specified NEC	989.89	E866.8	—	E950.9	E962.1	E980.9
Lirugen	979.4	E858.8	E949.4	E950.4	E962.0	E980.4
Lithane	969.8	E855.8	E939.8	E950.3	E962.0	E980.3
Lithium	985.8	E866.4	—	E950.9	E962.1	E980.9
carbonate	969.8	E855.8	E939.8	E950.3	E962.0	E980.3
Lithonate	969.8	E855.8	E939.8	E950.3	E962.0	E980.3
Liver (extract) (injection) (preparations)	964.1	E858.2	E934.1	E950.4	E962.0	E980.4
Lizard (bite) (venom)	989.5	E905.0	—	E950.9	E962.1	E980.9
LMD	964.8	E858.2	E934.8	E950.4	E962.0	E980.4
Lobelia	988.2	E865.4	—	E950.9	E962.1	E980.9
Lobeline	970.0	E854.3	E940.0	E950.4	E962.0	E980.4
Locorten	976.0	E858.7	E946.0	E950.4	E962.0	E980.4
Lolium temulentum	988.2	E865.3	—	E950.9	E962.1	E980.9
Lomotil	973.5	E858.4	E943.5	E950.4	E962.0	E980.4
Lomustine	963.1	E858.1	E933.1	E950.4	E962.0	E980.4
Lophophora williamsii	969.6	E854.1	E939.6	E950.3	E962.0	E980.3
Lorazepam	969.4	E853.2	E939.4	E950.3	E962.0	E980.3

Substance	Poisoning	Accident	Therapeutic Use	Suicide Attempt	Assault	Undetermined
			External Cause (E-Code)			
Lotions NEC	976.9	E858.7	E946.9	E950.4	E962.0	E980.4
Lotusate	967.0	E851	E937.0	E950.1	E962.0	E980.1
Lowila	976.2	E858.7	E946.2	E950.4	E962.0	E980.4
Loxapine	969.3	E853.8	E939.3	E950.3	E962.0	E980.3
Lozenges (throat)	976.6	E858.7	E946.6	E950.4	E962.0	E980.4
LSD (25)	969.6	E854.1	E939.6	E950.3	E962.0	E980.3
Lubricating oil NEC	981	E862.2	—	E950.9	E962.1	E980.9
Lucanthone	961.6	E857	E931.6	E950.4	E962.0	E980.4
Luminal	967.0	E851	E937.0	E950.1	E962.0	E980.1
Lung irritant (gas) NEC	987.9	E869.9	—	E952.9	E962.2	E982.9
Lutocylol	962.2	E858.0	E932.2	E950.4	E962.0	E980.4
Lutromone	962.2	E858.0	E932.2	E950.4	E962.0	E980.4
Lututrin	975.0	E858.6	E945.0	E950.4	E962.0	E980.4
Lye (concentrated)	983.2	E864.2	—	E950.7	E962.1	E980.6
Lygranum (skin test)	977.8	E858.8	E947.8	E950.4	E962.0	E980.4
Lymecycline	960.4	E856	E930.4	E950.4	E962.0	E980.4
Lymphogranuloma venereum antigen	977.8	E858.8	E947.8	E950.4	E962.0	E980.4
Lynestrenol	962.2	E858.0	E932.2	E950.4	E962.0	E980.4
Lyovac Sodium Edecrin	974.4	E858.5	E944.4	E950.4	E962.0	E980.4
Lypressin	962.5	E858.0	E932.5	E950.4	E962.0	E980.4
Lysergic acid (amide) (diethylamide)	969.6	E854.1	E939.6	E950.3	E962.0	E980.3
Lysergide	969.6	E854.1	E939.6	E950.3	E962.0	E980.3
Lysine vasopressin	962.5	E858.0	E932.5	E950.4	E962.0	E980.4
Lysol	983.0	E864.0	—	E950.7	E962.1	E980.6
Lytta (vitatta)	976.8	E858.7	E946.8	E950.4	E962.0	E980.4
Mace	987.5	E869.3	—	E952.8	E962.2	E982.8
Macrolides (antibiotics)	960.3	E856	E930.3	E950.4	E962.0	E980.4
Mafenide	976.0	E858.7	E946.0	E950.4	E962.0	E980.4
Magaldrate	973.0	E858.4	E943.0	E950.4	E962.0	E980.4
Magic mushroom	969.6	E854.1	E939.6	E950.3	E962.0	E980.3
Magnamycin	960.8	E856	E930.8	E950.4	E962.0	E980.4
Magnesia magma	973.0	E858.4	E943.0	E950.4	E962.0	E980.4
Magnesium (compounds) (fumes) NEC	985.8	E866.4	—	E950.9	E962.1	E980.9
antacid	973.0	E858.4	E943.0	E950.4	E962.0	E980.4
carbonate	973.0	E858.4	E943.0	E950.4	E962.0	E980.4
cathartic	973.3	E858.4	E943.3	E950.4	E962.0	E980.4
citrate	973.3	E858.4	E943.3	E950.4	E962.0	E980.4
hydroxide	973.0	E858.4	E943.0	E950.4	E962.0	E980.4
oxide	973.0	E858.4	E943.0	E950.4	E962.0	E980.4
sulfate (oral)	973.3	E858.4	E943.3	E950.4	E962.0	E980.4
intravenous	966.3	E855.0	E936.3	E950.4	E962.0	E980.4
trisilicate	973.0	E858.4	E943.0	E950.4	E962.0	E980.4
Malathion (insecticide)	989.3	E863.1	—	E950.6	E962.1	E980.7
Male fern (oleoresin)	961.6	E857	E931.6	E950.4	E962.0	E980.4
Mandelic acid	961.9	E857	E931.9	E950.4	E962.0	E980.4
Manganese compounds (fumes) NEC	985.2	E866.4	—	E950.9	E962.1	E980.9
Mannitol (diuretic) (medicinal) NEC	974.4	E858.5	E944.4	E950.4	E962.0	E980.4
hexanitrate	972.4	E858.3	E942.4	E950.4	E962.0	E980.4
mustard	963.1	E858.1	E933.1	E950.4	E962.0	E980.4
Mannomustine	963.1	E858.1	E933.1	E950.4	E962.0	E980.4
MAO inhibitors	969.0	E854.0	E939.0	E950.3	E962.0	E980.3
Mapharsen	961.1	E857	E931.1	E950.4	E962.0	E980.4
Marcaine	968.9	E855.2	E938.9	E950.4	E962.0	E980.4
infiltration (subcutaneous)	968.5	E855.2	E938.5	E950.4	E962.0	E980.4
nerve block (peripheral) (plexus)	968.6	E855.2	E938.6	E950.4	E962.0	E980.4
Marezine	963.0	E858.1	E933.0	E950.4	E962.0	E980.4
Marihuana, marijuana (derivatives)	969.6	E854.1	E939.6	E950.3	E962.0	E980.3

Substance	Poisoning	External Cause (E-Code)				
		Accident	Therapeutic Use	Suicide Attempt	Assault	Undetermined
Marine animals or plants (sting)	989.5	E905.6	—	E950.9	E962.1	E980.9
Marplan	969.0	E854.0	E939.0	E950.3	E962.0	E980.3
Marsh gas	987.1	E869.8	—	E952.8	E962.2	E982.8
Marsilid	969.0	E854.0	E939.0	E950.3	E962.0	E980.3
Matulane	963.1	E858.1	E933.1	E950.4	E962.0	E980.4
Mazindol	977.0	E858.8	E947.0	E950.4	E962.0	E980.4
Meadow saffron	988.2	E865.3	—	E950.9	E962.1	E980.9
Measles vaccine	979.4	E858.8	E949.4	E950.4	E962.0	E980.4
Meat, noxious or nonbacterial	988.8	E865.0	—	E950.9	E962.1	E980.9
Mebanazine	969.0	E854.0	E939.0	E950.3	E962.0	E980.3
Mebaral	967.0	E851	E937.0	E950.1	E962.0	E980.1
Mebendazole	961.6	E857	E931.6	E950.4	E962.0	E980.4
Mebeverine	975.1	E858.6	E945.1	E950.4	E962.0	E980.4
Mebhydroline	963.0	E858.1	E933.0	E950.4	E962.0	E980.4
Mebrophenhydramine	963.0	E858.1	E933.0	E950.4	E962.0	E980.4
Mebutamate	969.5	E853.8	E939.5	E950.3	E962.0	E980.3
Mecamylamine (chloride)	972.3	E858.3	E942.3	E950.4	E962.0	E980.4
Mechlorethamine hydrochloride	963.1	E858.1	E933.1	E950.4	E962.0	E980.4
Meclizene (hydrochloride)	963.0	E858.1	E933.0	E950.4	E962.0	E980.4
Meclofenoxate	970.0	E854.3	E940.0	E950.4	E962.0	E980.4
Meclozine (hydrochloride)	963.0	E858.1	E933.0	E950.4	E962.0	E980.4
Medazepam	969.4	E853.2	E939.4	E950.3	E962.0	E980.3
Medicine, medicinal substance	977.9	E858.9	E947.9	E950.5	E962.0	E980.5
specified NEC	977.8	E858.8	E947.8	E950.4	E962.0	E980.4
Medinal	967.0	E851	E937.0	E950.1	E962.0	E980.1
Medomin	967.0	E851	E937.0	E950.1	E962.0	E980.1
Medroxyprogesterone	962.2	E858.0	E932.2	E950.4	E962.0	E980.4
Medrysone	976.5	E858.7	E946.5	E950.4	E962.0	E980.4
Mefenamic acid	965.7	E850.7	E935.7	E950.0	E962.0	E980.0
Megahallucinogen	969.6	E854.1	E939.6	E950.3	E962.0	E980.3
Megestrol	962.2	E858.0	E932.2	E950.4	E962.0	E980.4
Meglumine	977.8	E858.8	E947.8	E950.4	E962.0	E980.4
Meladinin	976.3	E858.7	E946.3	E950.4	E962.0	E980.4
Melanizing agents	976.3	E858.7	E946.3	E950.4	E962.0	E980.4
Melarsoprol	961.1	E857	E931.1	E950.4	E962.0	E980.4
Melia azedarach	988.2	E865.3	—	E950.9	E962.1	E980.9
Mellaril	969.1	E853.0	E939.1	E950.3	E962.0	E980.3
Meloxine	976.3	E858.7	E946.3	E950.4	E962.0	E980.4
Melphalan	963.1	E858.1	E933.1	E950.4	E962.0	E980.4
Menadiol sodium diphosphate	964.3	E858.2	E934.3	E950.4	E962.0	E980.4
Menadione (sodium bisulfate)	964.3	E858.2	E934.3	E950.4	E962.0	E980.4
Menaphthone	964.3	E858.2	E934.3	E950.4	E962.0	E980.4
Meningococcal vaccine	978.8	E858.8	E948.8	E950.4	E962.0	E980.4
Menningovax–C	978.8	E858.8	E948.8	E950.4	E962.0	E980.4
Menotropins	962.4	E858.0	E932.4	E950.4	E962.0	E980.4
Menthol NEC	976.1	E858.7	E946.1	E950.4	E962.0	E980.4
Mepacrine	961.3	E857	E931.3	E950.4	E962.0	E980.4
Meparfynol	967.8	E852.8	E937.8	E950.2	E962.0	E980.2
Mepazine	969.1	E853.0	E939.1	E950.3	E962.0	E980.3
Mepenzolate	971.1	E855.4	E941.1	E950.4	E962.0	E980.4
Meperidine	965.09	E850.2	E935.2	E950.0	E962.0	E980.0
Mephenamin(e)	966.4	E855.0	E936.4	E950.4	E962.0	E980.4
Mephenesin (carbamate)	968.0	E855.1	E938.0	E950.4	E962.0	E980.4
Mephenoxalone	969.5	E853.8	E939.5	E950.3	E962.0	E980.3
Mephentermine	971.2	E855.5	E941.2	E950.4	E962.0	E980.4
Mephenytoin	966.1	E855.0	E936.1	E950.4	E962.0	E980.4
Mephobarbital	967.0	E851	E937.0	E950.1	E962.0	E980.1

Substance	Poisoning	External Cause (E-Code)				
		Accident	Therapeutic Use	Suicide Attempt	Assault	Undetermined
Mepiperphenidol	971.1	E855.4	E941.1	E950.4	E962.0	E980.4
Mepivacaine	968.9	E855.2	E938.9	E950.4	E962.0	E980.4
infiltration (subcutaneous)	968.5	E855.2	E938.5	E950.4	E962.0	E980.4
nerve block (peripheral) (plexus)	968.6	E855.2	E938.6	E950.4	E962.0	E980.4
topical (surface)	968.5	E855.2	E938.5	E950.4	E962.0	E980.4
Meprednisone	962.0	E858.0	E932.0	E950.4	E962.0	E980.4
Meprobam	969.5	E853.8	E939.5	E950.3	E962.0	E980.3
Meprobamate	969.5	E853.8	E939.5	E950.3	E962.0	E980.3
Mepyramine (maleate)	963.0	E858.1	E933.0	E950.4	E962.0	E980.4
Meralluride	974.0	E858.5	E944.0	E950.4	E962.0	E980.4
Merbaphen	974.0	E858.5	E944.0	E950.4	E962.0	E980.4
Merbromin	976.0	E858.7	E946.0	E950.4	E962.0	E980.4
Mercaptomerin	974.0	E858.5	E944.0	E950.4	E962.0	E980.4
Mercaptopurine	963.1	E858.1	E933.1	E950.4	E962.0	E980.4
Mercumatilin	974.0	E858.5	E944.0	E950.4	E962.0	E980.4
Mercuramide	974.0	E858.5	E944.0	E950.4	E962.0	E980.4
Mercuranin	976.0	E858.7	E946.0	E950.4	E962.0	E980.4
Mercurochrome	976.0	E858.7	E946.0	E950.4	E962.0	E980.4
Mercury, mercuric, mercurous (compounds) (cyanide) (fumes) (nonmedicinal) (vapor) NEC	985.0	E866.1	—	E950.9	E962.1	E980.9
ammoniated	976.0	E858.7	E946.0	E950.4	E962.0	E980.4
anti–infective	961.2	E857	E931.2	E950.4	E962.0	E980.4
topical	976.0	E858.7	E946.0	E950.4	E962.0	E980.4
chloride (antiseptic) NEC	976.0	E858.7	E946.0	E950.4	E962.0	E980.4
fungicide	985.0	E863.6	—	E950.6	E962.1	E980.7
diuretic compounds	974.0	E858.5	E944.0	E950.4	E962.0	E980.4
fungicide	985.0	E863.6	—	E950.6	E962.1	E980.7
organic (fungicide)	985.0	E863.6	—	E950.6	E962.1	E980.7
Merethoxylline	974.0	E858.5	E944.0	E950.4	E962.0	E980.4
Mersalyl	974.0	E858.5	E944.0	E950.4	E962.0	E980.4
Merthiolate (topical)	976.0	E858.7	E946.0	E950.4	E962.0	E980.4
ophthalmic preparation	976.5	E858.7	E946.5	E950.4	E962.0	E980.4
Meruvax	979.4	E858.8	E949.4	E950.4	E962.0	E980.4
Mescal buttons	969.6	E854.1	E939.6	E950.3	E962.0	E980.3
Mescaline (salts)	969.6	E854.1	E939.6	E950.3	E962.0	E980.3
Mesoridazine besylate	969.1	E853.0	E939.1	E950.3	E962.0	E980.3
Mestanolone	962.1	E858.0	E932.1	E950.4	E962.0	E980.4
Mestranol	962.2	E858.0	E932.2	E950.4	E962.0	E980.4
Metacresylacetate	976.0	E858.7	E946.0	E950.4	E962.0	E980.4
Metaldehyde (snail killer) NEC	989.4	E863.4	—	E950.6	E962.1	E980.7
Metals (heavy) (nonmedicinal) NEC	985.9	E866.4	—	E950.9	E962.1	E980.9
dust, fumes, or vapor NEC	985.9	E866.4	—	E950.9	E962.1	E980.9
light NEC	985.9	E866.4	—	E950.9	E962.1	E980.9
dust, fumes, or vapor NEC	985.9	E866.4	—	E950.9	E962.1	E980.9
pesticides (dust) (vapor)	985.9	E863.4	—	E950.6	E962.1	E980.7
Metamucil	973.3	E858.4	E943.3	E950.4	E962.0	E980.4
Metaphen	976.0	E858.7	E946.0	E950.4	E962.0	E980.4
Metaproterenol	975.1	E858.6	E945.1	E950.4	E962.0	E980.4
Metaraminol	972.8	E853.3	E942.8	E950.4	E962.0	E980.4
Metaxalone	968.0	E855.1	E938.0	E950.4	E962.0	E980.4
Metformin	962.3	E858.0	E932.3	E950.4	E962.0	E980.4
Methacycline	960.4	E856	E930.4	E950.4	E962.0	E980.4
Methadone	965.02	E850.1	E935.1	E950.0	E962.0	E980.0
Methallenestril	962.2	E858.0	E932.2	E950.4	E962.0	E980.4
Methamphetamine	969.7	E854.2	E939.7	E950.3	E962.0	E980.3
Methandienone	962.1	E858.0	E932.1	E950.4	E962.0	E980.4

Substance	Poisoning	External Cause (E-Code)				
		Accident	Therapeutic Use	Suicide Attempt	Assault	Undetermined
Methandriol	962.1	E858.0	E932.1	E950.4	E962.0	E980.4
Methandrostenolone	962.1	E858.0	E932.1	E950.4	E962.0	E980.4
Methane gas	987.1	E869.8	—	E952.8	E962.2	E982.8
Methanol	980.1	E860.2	—	E950.9	E962.1	E980.9
vapor	987.8	E869.8	—	E952.8	E962.2	E982.8
Methantheline	971.1	E855.4	E941.1	E950.4	E962.0	E980.4
Methaphenilene	963.0	E858.1	E933.0	E950.4	E962.0	E980.4
Methapyrilene	963.0	E858.1	E933.0	E950.4	E962.0	E980.4
Methaqualone (compounds)	967.4	E852.3	E937.4	E950.2	E962.0	E980.2
Metharbital, metharbitone	967.0	E851	E937.0	E950.1	E962.0	E980.1
Methazolamide	974.2	E858.5	E944.2	E950.4	E962.0	E980.4
Methdilazine	963.0	E858.1	E933.0	E950.4	E962.0	E980.4
Methedrine	969.7	E854.2	E939.7	E950.3	E962.0	E980.3
Methenamine (mandelate)	961.9	E857	E931.9	E950.4	E962.0	E980.4
Methenolone	962.1	E858.0	E932.1	E950.4	E962.0	E980.4
Methergine	975.0	E858.6	E945.0	E950.4	E962.0	E980.4
Methiacil	962.8	E858.0	E932.8	E950.4	E962.0	E980.4
Methicillin (sodium)	960.0	E856	E930.0	E950.4	E962.0	E980.4
Methimazole	962.8	E858.0	E932.8	E950.4	E962.0	E980.4
Methionine	977.1	E858.8	E947.1	E950.4	E962.0	E980.4
Methisazone	961.7	E857	E931.7	E950.4	E962.0	E980.4
Methitural	967.0	E851	E937.0	E950.1	E962.0	E980.1
Methixene	971.1	E855.4	E941.1	E950.4	E962.0	E980.4
Methobarbital, methobarbitone	967.0	E851	E937.0	E950.1	E962.0	E980.1
Methocarbamol	968.0	E855.1	E938.0	E950.4	E962.0	E980.4
Methohexital, methohexitone (sodium)	968.3	E855.1	E938.3	E950.4	E962.0	E980.4
Methoin	966.1	E855.0	E936.1	E950.4	E962.0	E980.4
Methopholine	965.7	E850.7	E935.7	E950.0	E962.0	E980.0
Methorate	975.4	E858.6	E945.4	E950.4	E962.0	E980.4
Methoserpidine	972.6	E858.3	E942.6	E950.4	E962.0	E980.4
Methotrexate	963.1	E858.1	E933.1	E950.4	E962.0	E980.4
Methotrimeprazine	967.8	E852.8	E937.8	E950.2	E962.0	E980.2
Methoxa–Dome	976.3	E858.7	E946.3	E950.4	E962.0	E980.4
Methoxamine	971.2	E855.5	E941.2	E950.4	E962.0	E980.4
Methoxsalen	976.3	E858.7	E946.3	E950.4	E962.0	E980.4
Methoxybenzyl penicillin	960.0	E856	E930.0	E950.4	E962.0	E980.4
Methoxychlor	989.2	E863.0	—	E950.6	E962.1	E980.7
Methoxyflurane	968.2	E855.1	E938.2	E950.4	E962.0	E980.4
Methoxyphenamine	971.2	E855.5	E941.2	E950.4	E962.0	E980.4
Methoxypromazine	969.1	E853.0	E939.1	E950.3	E962.0	E980.3
Methoxypsoralen	976.3	E858.7	E946.3	E950.4	E962.0	E980.4
Methscopolamine (bromide)	971.1	E855.4	E941.1	E950.4	E962.0	E980.4
Methsuximide	966.2	E855.0	E936.2	E950.4	E962.0	E980.4
Methyclothiazide	974.3	E858.5	E944.3	E950.4	E962.0	E980.4
Methyl						
acetate	982.8	E862.4	—	E950.9	E962.1	E980.9
acetone	982.8	E862.4	—	E950.9	E962.1	E980.9
alcohol	980.1	E860.2	—	E950.9	E962.1	E980.9
amphetamine	969.7	E854.2	E939.7	E950.3	E962.0	E980.3
androstanolone	962.1	E858.0	E932.1	E950.4	E962.0	E980.4
atropine	971.1	E855.4	E941.1	E950.4	E962.0	E980.4
benzene	982.0	E862.4	—	E950.9	E962.1	E980.9
bromide (gas)	987.8	E869.8	—	E952.8	E962.2	E982.8
fumigant	987.8	E863.8	—	E950.6	E962.2	E980.7
butanol	980.8	E860.8	—	E950.9	E962.1	E980.9
carbinol	980.1	E860.2	—	E950.9	E962.1	E980.9
cellosolve	982.8	E862.4	—	E950.9	E962.1	E980.9

Substance	Poisoning	Accident	External Cause (E-Code)			
			Therapeutic Use	Suicide Attempt	Assault	Undetermined
cellulose 973.3	E858.4	E943.3	E950.4	E962.0	E980.4
chloride (gas) 987.8	E869.8	—	E952.8	E962.2	E982.8
cyclohexane 982.8	E862.4	—	E950.9	E962.1	E980.9
cyclohexanone 982.8	E862.4	—	E950.9	E962.1	E980.9
dihydromorphinone 965.09	E850.2	E935.2	E950.0	E962.0	E980.0
ergometrine 975.0	E858.6	E945.0	E950.4	E962.0	E980.4
ergonovine 975.0	E858.6	E945.0	E950.4	E962.0	E980.4
ethyl ketone 982.8	E862.4	—	E950.9	E962.1	E980.9
hydrazine 983.9	E864.3	—	E950.7	E962.1	E980.6
isobutyl ketone 982.8	E862.4	—	E950.9	E962.1	E980.9
morphine NEC 965.09	E850.2	E935.2	E950.0	E962.0	E980.0
parafynol 967.8	E852.8	E937.8	E950.2	E962.0	E980.2
parathion 989.3	E863.1	—	E950.6	E962.1	E980.7
pentynol NEC 967.8	E852.8	E937.8	E950.2	E962.0	E980.2
peridol 969.2	E853.1	E939.2	E950.3	E962.0	E980.3
phenidate 969.7	E854.2	E939.7	E950.3	E962.0	E980.3
prednisolone 962.0	E858.0	E932.0	E950.4	E962.0	E980.4
ENT agent 976.6	E858.7	E946.6	E950.4	E962.0	E980.4
ophthalmic preparation 976.5	E858.7	E946.5	E950.4	E962.0	E980.4
topical NEC 976.0	E858.7	E946.0	E950.4	E962.0	E980.4
propylcarbinol 980.8	E860.8	—	E950.9	E962.1	E980.9
rosaniline NEC 976.0	E858.7	E946.0	E950.4	E962.0	E980.4
salicylate NEC 976.3	E858.7	E946.3	E950.4	E962.0	E980.4
sulfate (fumes) 987.8	E869.8	—	E952.8	E962.2	E982.8
liquid 983.9	E864.3	—	E950.7	E962.1	E980.6
sulfonal 967.8	E852.8	E937.8	E950.2	E962.0	E980.2
testosterone 962.1	E858.0	E932.1	E950.4	E962.0	E980.4
thiouracil 962.8	E858.0	E932.8	E950.4	E962.0	E980.4
Methylated spirit 980.0	E860.1	—	E950.9	E962.1	E980.9
Methyldopa 972.6	E858.3	E942.6	E950.4	E962.0	E980.4
Methylene					
blue 961.9	E857	E931.9	E950.4	E962.0	E980.4
chloride or dichloride (solvent) NEC . . . 982.3	E862.4	—	E950.9	E962.1	E980.9
Methylhexabital 967.0	E851	E937.0	E950.1	E962.0	E980.1
Methylparaben (ophthalmic) 976.5	E858.7	E946.5	E950.4	E962.0	E980.4
Methyprylon 967.5	E852.4	E937.5	E950.2	E962.0	E980.2
Methysergide 971.3	E855.6	E941.3	E950.4	E962.0	E980.4
Metoclopramide 963.0	E858.1	E933.0	E950.4	E962.0	E980.4
Metofoline 965.7	E850.7	E935.7	E950.0	E962.0	E980.0
Metopon 965.09	E850.2	E935.2	E950.0	E962.0	E980.0
Metronidazole 961.5	E857	E931.5	E950.4	E962.0	E980.4
Metycaine 968.9	E855.2	E938.9	E950.4	E962.0	E980.4
infiltration (subcutaneous) 968.5	E855.2	E938.5	E950.4	E962.0	E980.4
nerve block (peripheral) (plexus) 968.6	E855.2	E938.6	E950.4	E962.0	E980.4
topical (surface) 968.5	E855.2	E938.5	E950.4	E962.0	E980.4
Metyrapone 977.8	E858.8	E947.8	E950.4	E962.0	E980.4
Mevinphos 989.3	E863.1	—	E950.6	E962.1	E980.7
Mezereon (berries) 988.2	E865.3	—	E950.9	E962.1	E980.9
Micatin 976.0	E858.7	E946.0	E950.4	E962.0	E980.4
Miconazole 976.0	E858.7	E946.0	E950.4	E962.0	E980.4
Midol 965.1	E850.3	E935.3	E950.0	E962.0	E980.0
Milk of magnesia 973.0	E858.4	E943.0	E950.4	E962.0	E980.4
Millipede (tropical) (venomous) 989.5	E905.4	—	E950.9	E962.1	E980.9
Miltown 969.5	E853.8	E939.5	E950.3	E962.0	E980.3
Mineral					
oil (medicinal) 973.2	E858.4	E943.2	E950.4	E962.0	E980.4
nonmedicinal 981	E862.1	—	E950.9	E962.1	E980.9

Substance	Poisoning	External Cause (E-Code)				
		Accident	Therapeutic Use	Suicide Attempt	Assault	Undetermined
topical	976.3	E858.7	E946.3	E950.4	E962.0	E980.4
salts NEC	974.6	E858.5	E944.6	E950.4	E962.0	E980.4
spirits	981	E862.0	—	E950.9	E962.1	E980.9
Minocycline	960.4	E856	E930.4	E950.4	E962.0	E980.4
Mithramycin (antineoplastic)	960.7	E856	E930.7	E950.4	E962.0	E980.4
Mitobronitol	963.1	E858.1	E933.1	E950.4	E962.0	E980.4
Mitomycin (antineoplastic)	960.7	E856	E930.7	E950.4	E962.0	E980.4
Mitotane	963.1	E858.1	E933.1	E950.4	E962.0	E980.4
Moderil	972.6	E858.3	E942.6	E950.4	E962.0	E980.4
Mogadon—*see* Nitrazepam						
Molindone	969.3	E853.8	E939.3	E950.3	E962.0	E980.3
Monistat	976.0	E858.7	E946.0	E950.4	E962.0	E980.4
Monkshood	988.2	E865.4	—	E950.9	E962.1	E980.9
Monoamine oxidase inhibitors	969.0	E854.0	E939.0	E950.3	E962.0	E980.3
Monochlorobenzene	982.0	E862.4	—	E950.9	E962.1	E980.9
Monosodium glutamate	989.89	E866.8	—	E950.9	E962.1	E980.9
Monoxide, carbon — *see* Carbon, monoxide						
Moperone	969.2	E853.1	E939.2	E950.3	E962.0	E980.3
Morning glory seeds	969.6	E854.1	E939.6	E950.3	E962.0	E980.3
Moroxydine (hydrochloride)	961.7	E857	E931.7	E950.4	E962.0	E980.4
Morphazinamide	961.8	E857	E931.8	E950.4	E962.0	E980.4
Morphinans	965.09	E850.2	E935.2	E950.0	E962.0	E980.0
Morphine NEC	965.09	E850.2	E935.2	E950.0	E962.0	E980.0
antagonists	970.1	E854.3	E940.1	E950.4	E962.0	E980.4
Morpholinylethylmorphine	965.09	E850.2	E935.2	E950.0	E962.0	E980.0
Morrhuate sodium	972.7	E858.3	E942.7	E950.4	E962.0	E980.4
Moth balls (*see also* Pesticides)	989.4	E863.4	—	E950.6	E962.1	E980.7
naphthalene	983.0	E863.4	—	E950.7	E962.1	E980.6
Motor exhaust gas — *see* Carbon, monoxide, exhaust gas						
Mouth wash	976.6	E858.7	E946.6	E950.4	E962.0	E980.4
Mucolytic agent	975.5	E858.6	E945.5	E950.4	E962.0	E980.4
Mucomyst	975.5	E858.6	E945.5	E950.4	E962.0	E980.4
Mucous membrane agents (external)	976.9	E858.7	E946.9	E950.4	E962.0	E980.4
specified NEC	976.8	E858.7	E946.8	E950.4	E962.0	E980.4
Mumps						
immune globulin (human)	964.6	E858.2	E934.6	E950.4	E962.0	E980.4
skin test antigen	977.8	E858.8	E947.8	E950.4	E962.0	E980.4
vaccine	979.6	E858.8	E949.6	E950.4	E962.0	E980.4
Mumpsvax	979.6	E858.8	E949.6	E950.4	E962.0	E980.4
Muriatic acid — *see* Hydrochloric acid						
Muscarine	971.0	E855.3	E941.0	E950.4	E962.0	E980.4
Muscle affecting agents NEC	975.3	E858.6	E945.3	E950.4	E962.0	E980.4
oxytocic	975.0	E858.6	E945.0	E950.4	E962.0	E980.4
relaxants	975.3	E858.6	E945.3	E950.4	E962.0	E980.4
central nervous system	968.0	E855.1	E938.0	E950.4	E962.0	E980.4
skeletal	975.2	E858.6	E945.2	E950.4	E962.0	E980.4
smooth	975.1	E858.6	E945.1	E950.4	E962.0	E980.4
Mushrooms, noxious	988.1	E865.5	—	E950.9	E962.1	E980.9
Mussel, noxious	988.0	E865.1	—	E950.9	E962.1	E980.9
Mustard (emetic)	973.6	E858.4	E943.6	E950.4	E962.0	E980.4
gas	987.8	E869.8	—	E952.8	E962.2	E982.8
nitrogen	963.1	E858.1	E933.1	E950.4	E962.0	E980.4
Mustine	963.1	E858.1	E933.1	E950.4	E962.0	E980.4
M–vac	979.4	E858.8	E949.4	E950.4	E962.0	E980.4
Mycifradin	960.8	E856	E930.8	E950.4	E962.0	E980.4
topical	976.0	E858.7	E946.0	E950.4	E962.0	E980.4

Substance	Poisoning	External Cause (E-Code)				
		Accident	Therapeutic Use	Suicide Attempt	Assault	Undetermined
Mycitracin 960.8	E856	E930.8	E950.4	E962.0	E980.4
ophthalmic preparation 976.5	E858.7	E946.5	E950.4	E962.0	E980.4
Mycostatin 960.1	E856	E930.1	E950.4	E962.0	E980.4
topical 976.0	E858.7	E946.0	E950.4	E962.0	E980.4
Mydriacyl 971.1	E855.4	E941.1	E950.4	E962.0	E980.4
Myelobromal 963.1	E858.1	E933.1	E950.4	E962.0	E980.4
Myleran 963.1	E858.1	E933.1	E950.4	E962.0	E980.4
Myochrysin(e) 965.6	E850.6	E935.6	E950.0	E962.0	E980.0
Myoneural blocking agents 975.2	E858.6	E945.2	E950.4	E962.0	E980.4
Myristica fragrans 988.2	E865.3	—	E950.9	E962.1	E980.9
Myristicin 988.2	E865.3	—	E950.9	E962.1	E980.9
Mysoline 966.3	E855.0	E936.3	E950.4	E962.0	E980.4
Nafcillin (sodium) 960.0	E856	E930.0	E950.4	E962.0	E980.4
Nail polish remover 982.8	E862.4	—	E950.9	E962.1	E980.9
Nalidixic acid 961.9	E857	E931.9	E950.4	E962.0	E980.4
Nalorphine 970.1	E854.3	E940.1	E950.4	E962.0	E980.4
Naloxone 970.1	E854.3	E940.1	E950.4	E962.0	E980.4
Nandrolone (decanoate) (phenproprioate) . . . 962.1	E858.0	E932.1	E950.4	E962.0	E980.4
Naphazoline 971.2	E855.5	E941.2	E950.4	E962.0	E980.4
Naphtha (painter's) (petroleum) 981	E862.0	—	E950.9	E962.1	E980.9
solvent 981	E862.0	—	E950.9	E962.1	E980.9
vapor 987.1	E869.8	—	E952.8	E962.2	E982.8
Naphthalene (chlorinated) 983.0	E864.0	—	E950.7	E962.1	E980.6
insecticide or moth repellent 983.0	E863.4	—	E950.7	E962.1	E980.6
vapor 987.8	E869.8	—	E952.8	E962.2	E982.8
Naphthol 983.0	E864.0	—	E950.7	E962.1	E980.6
Naphthylamine 983.0	E864.0	—	E950.7	E962.1	E980.6
Naprosyn—see Naproxen					
Naproxen 965.6	E850.6	E935.6	E950.0	E962.0	E980.0
Narcotic (drug) 967.9	E852.9	E937.9	E950.2	E962.0	E980.2
analgesic NEC 965.8	E850.8	E935.8	E950.0	E962.0	E980.0
antagonist 970.1	E854.3	E940.1	E950.4	E962.0	E980.4
specified NEC 967.8	E852.8	E937.8	E950.2	E962.0	E980.2
Narcotine 975.4	E858.6	E945.4	E950.4	E962.0	E980.4
Nardil 969.0	E854.0	E939.0	E950.3	E962.0	E980.3
Natrium cyanide — see Cyanide(s)					
Natural					
blood (product) 964.7	E858.2	E934.7	E950.4	E962.0	E980.4
gas (piped) 987.1	E867	—	E951.0	E962.2	E981.0
incomplete combustion 986	E867	—	E951.0	E962.2	E981.0
Nealbarbital, nealbarbitone 967.0	E851	E937.0	E950.1	E962.0	E980.1
Nectadon 975.4	E858.6	E945.4	E950.4	E962.0	E980.4
Nematocyst (sting) 989.5	E905.6	—	E950.9	E962.1	E980.9
Nembutal 967.0	E851	E937.0	E950.1	E962.0	E980.1
Neoarsphenamine 961.1	E857	E931.1	E950.4	E962.0	E980.4
Neocinchophen 974.7	E858.5	E944.7	E950.4	E962.0	E980.4
Neomycin 960.8	E856	E930.8	E950.4	E962.0	E980.4
ENT agent 976.6	E858.7	E946.6	E950.4	E962.0	E980.4
ophthalmic preparation 976.5	E858.7	E946.5	E950.4	E962.0	E980.4
topical NEC 976.0	E858.7	E946.0	E950.4	E962.0	E980.4
Neonal 967.0	E851	E937.0	E950.1	E962.0	E980.1
Neoprontosil 961.0	E857	E931.0	E950.4	E962.0	E980.4
Neosalvarsan 961.1	E857	E931.1	E950.4	E962.0	E980.4
Neosilversalvarsan 961.1	E857	E931.1	E950.4	E962.0	E980.4
Neosporin 960.8	E856	E930.8	E950.4	E962.0	E980.4
ENT agent 976.6	E858.7	E946.6	E950.4	E962.0	E980.4
ophthalmic preparation 976.5	E858.7	E946.5	E950.4	E962.0	E980.4

Substance	Poisoning	External Cause (E-Code)				
		Accident	Therapeutic Use	Suicide Attempt	Assault	Undetermined
topical NEC	976.0	E858.7	E946.0	E950.4	E962.0	E980.4
Neostigmine	971.0	E855.3	E941.0	E950.4	E962.0	E980.4
Neraval	967.0	E851	E937.0	E950.1	E962.0	E980.1
Neravan	967.0	E851	E937.0	E950.1	E962.0	E980.1
Nerium oleander	988.2	E865.4	—	E950.9	E962.1	E980.9
Nerve gases (war)	987.9	E869.9	—	E952.9	E962.2	E982.9
Nesacaine	968.9	E855.2	E938.9	E950.4	E962.0	E980.4
infiltration (subcutaneous)	968.5	E855.2	E938.5	E950.4	E962.0	E980.4
nerve block (peripheral) (plexus)	968.6	E855.2	E938.6	E950.4	E962.0	E980.4
Neurobarb	967.0	E851	E937.0	E950.1	E962.0	E980.1
Neuroleptics NEC	969.3	E853.8	E939.3	E950.3	E962.0	E980.3
Neutral spirits	980.0	E860.1	—	E950.9	E962.1	E980.9
beverage	980.0	E860.0	—	E950.9	E962.1	E980.9
Niacin, niacinamide	972.2	E858.3	E942.2	E950.4	E962.0	E980.4
Nialamide	969.0	E854.0	E939.0	E950.3	E962.0	E980.3
Nickle (carbonyl) (compounds) (fumes) (tetracarbonyl) (vapor)	985.8	E866.4	—	E950.9	E962.1	E980.9
Niclosamide	961.6	E857	E931.6	E950.4	E962.0	E980.4
Nicomorphine	965.09	E850.2	E935.2	E950.0	E962.0	E980.0
Nicotinamide	972.2	E858.3	E942.2	E950.4	E962.0	E980.4
Nicotine (insecticide) (spray) (sulfate) NEC	989.4	E863.4	—	E950.6	E962.1	E980.7
not insecticide	989.89	E866.8	—	E950.9	E962.1	E980.9
Nicotinic acid (derivatives)	972.2	E858.3	E942.2	E950.4	E962.0	E980.4
Nicotinyl alcohol	972.2	E858.3	E942.2	E950.4	E962.0	E980.4
Nicoumalone	964.2	E858.2	E934.2	E950.4	E962.0	E980.4
Nifenazone	965.5	E850.5	E935.5	E950.0	E962.0	E980.0
Nifuraldezone	961.9	E857	E931.9	E950.4	E962.0	E980.4
Nightshade (deadly)	988.2	E865.4	—	E950.9	E962.1	E980.9
Nikethamide	970.0	E854.3	E940.0	E950.4	E962.0	E980.4
Nilstat	960.1	E856	E930.1	E950.4	E962.0	E980.4
topical	976.0	E858.7	E946.0	E950.4	E962.0	E980.4
Niridazole	961.6	E857	E931.6	E950.4	E962.0	E980.4
Nisentil	965.09	E850.2	E935.2	E950.0	E962.0	E980.0
Nitrates	972.4	E858.3	E942.4	E950.4	E962.0	E980.4
Nitrazepam	969.4	E853.2	E939.4	E950.3	E962.0	E980.3
Nitric						
acid (liquid)	983.1	E864.1	—	E950.7	E962.1	E980.6
vapor	987.8	E869.8	—	E952.8	E962.2	E982.8
oxide (gas)	987.2	E869.0	—	E952.8	E962.2	E982.8
Nitrite, amyl (medicinal) (vapor)	972.4	E858.3	E942.4	E950.4	E962.0	E980.4
Nitroaniline	983.0	E864.0	—	E950.7	E962.1	E980.6
vapor	987.8	E869.8	—	E952.8	E962.2	E982.8
Nitrobenzene, nitrobenzol	983.0	E864.0	—	E950.7	E962.1	E980.6
vapor	987.8	E869.8	—	E952.8	E962.2	E982.8
Nitrocellulose	976.3	E858.7	E946.3	E950.4	E962.0	E980.4
Nitrofuran derivatives	961.9	E857	E931.9	E950.4	E962.0	E980.4
Nitrofurantoin	961.9	E857	E931.9	E950.4	E962.0	E980.4
Nitrofurazone	976.0	E858.7	E946.0	E950.4	E962.0	E980.4
Nitrogen (dioxide) (gas) (oxide)	987.2	E869.0	—	E952.8	E962.2	E982.8
mustard (antineoplastic)	963.1	E858.1	E933.1	E950.4	E962.0	E980.4
Nitroglycerin, nitroglycerol (medicinal)	972.4	E858.3	E942.4	E950.4	E962.0	E980.4
nonmedicinal	989.89	E866.8	—	E950.9	E962.1	E980.9
fumes	987.8	E869.8	—	E952.8	E962.2	E982.8
Nitrohydrochloric acid	983.1	E864.1	—	E950.7	E962.1	E980.6
Nitromersol	976.0	E858.7	E946.0	E950.4	E962.0	E980.4
Nitronaphthalene	983.0	E864.0	—	E950.7	E962.2	E980.6
Nitrophenol	983.0	E864.0	—	E950.7	E962.2	E980.6

Substance	External Cause (E-Code)					
	Poisoning	Accident	Therapeutic Use	Suicide Attempt	Assault	Undetermined
Nitrothiazol	961.6	E857	E931.6	E950.4	E962.0	E980.4
Nitrotoluene, nitrotoluol	983.0	E864.0	—	E950.7	E962.1	E980.6
vapor	987.8	E869.8	—	E952.8	E962.2	E982.8
Nitrous	968.2	E855.1	E938.2	E950.4	E962.0	E980.4
acid (liquid)	983.1	E864.1	—	E950.7	E962.1	E980.6
fumes	987.2	E869.0	—	E952.8	E962.2	E982.8
oxide (anesthetic) NEC	968.2	E855.1	E938.2	E950.4	E962.0	E980.4
Nitrozone	976.0	E858.7	E946.0	E950.4	E962.0	E980.4
Noctec	967.1	E852.0	E937.1	E950.2	E962.0	E980.2
Noludar	967.5	E852.4	E937.5	E950.2	E962.0	E980.2
Noptil	967.0	E851	E937.0	E950.1	E962.0	E980.1
Noradrenalin	971.2	E855.5	E941.2	E950.4	E962.0	E980.4
Noramidopyrine	965.5	E850.5	E935.5	E950.0	E962.0	E980.0
Norepinephrine	971.2	E855.5	E941.2	E950.4	E962.0	E980.4
Norethandrolone	962.1	E858.0	E932.1	E950.4	E962.0	E980.4
Norethindrone	962.2	E858.0	E932.2	E950.4	E962.0	E980.4
Norethisterone	962.2	E858.0	E932.2	E950.4	E962.0	E980.4
Norethynodrel	962.2	E858.0	E932.2	E950.4	E962.0	E980.4
Norlestrin	962.2	E858.0	E932.2	E950.4	E962.0	E980.4
Norlutin	962.2	E858.0	E932.2	E950.4	E962.0	E980.4
Normison—*see* Benzodiazepines						
Normorphine	965.09	E850.2	E935.2	E950.0	E962.0	E980.0
Nortriptyline	969.0	E854.0	E939.0	E950.3	E962.0	E980.3
Noscapine	975.4	E858.6	E945.4	E950.4	E962.0	E980.4
Nose preparations	976.6	E858.7	E946.6	E950.4	E962.0	E980.4
Novobiocin	960.8	E856	E930.8	E950.4	E962.0	E980.4
Novocain (infiltration) (topical)	968.5	E855.2	E938.5	E950.4	E962.0	E980.4
nerve block (peripheral) (plexus)	968.6	E855.2	E938.6	E950.4	E962.0	E980.4
spinal	968.7	E855.2	E938.7	E950.4	E962.0	E980.4
Noxythiolin	961.9	E857	E931.9	E950.4	E962.0	E980.4
NPH Iletin (insulin)	962.3	E858.0	E932.3	E950.4	E962.0	E980.4
Numorphan	965.09	E850.2	E935.2	E950.0	E962.0	E980.0
Nunol	967.0	E851	E937.0	E950.1	E962.0	E980.1
Nupercaine (spinal anesthetic)	968.7	E855.2	E938.7	E950.4	E962.0	E980.4
topical (surface)	968.5	E855.2	E938.5	E950.4	E962.0	E980.4
Nutmeg oil (liniment)	976.3	E858.7	E946.3	E950.4	E962.0	E980.4
Nux vomica	989.1	E863.7	—	E950.6	E962.1	E980.7
Nydrazid	961.8	E857	E931.8	E950.4	E962.0	E980.4
Nylidrin	971.2	E855.5	E941.2	E950.4	E962.0	E980.4
Nystatin	960.1	E856	E930.1	E950.4	E962.0	E980.4
topical	976.0	E858.7	E946.0	E950.4	E962.0	E980.4
Nytol	963.0	E858.1	E933.0	E950.4	E962.0	E980.4
Oblivion	967.8	E852.8	E937.8	E950.2	E962.0	E980.2
Octyl nitrite	972.4	E858.3	E942.4	E950.4	E962.0	E980.4
Oestradiol (cypionate) (dipropionate) (valerate)	962.2	E858.0	E932.2	E950.4	E962.0	E980.4
Oestriol	962.2	E858.0	E932.2	E950.4	E962.0	E980.4
Oestrone	962.2	E858.0	E932.2	E950.4	E962.0	E980.4
Oil (of) NEC	989.89	E866.8	—	E950.9	E962.1	E980.9
bitter almond	989.0	E866.8	—	E950.9	E962.1	E980.9
camphor	976.1	E858.7	E946.1	E950.4	E962.0	E980.4
colors	989.89	E861.6	—	E950.9	E962.1	E980.9
fumes	987.8	E869.8	—	E952.8	E962.2	E982.8
lubricating	981	E862.2	—	E950.9	E962.1	E980.9
specified source, other — *see* substance specified						
vitriol (liquid)	983.1	E864.1	—	E950.7	E962.1	E980.6

Substance	External Cause (E-Code)					
	Poisoning	Accident	Therapeutic Use	Suicide Attempt	Assault	Undetermined
fumes	987.8	E869.8	—	E952.8	E962.2	E982.8
wintergreen (bitter) NEC	976.3	E858.7	E946.3	E950.4	E962.0	E980.4
Ointments NEC	976.9	E858.7	E946.9	E950.4	E962.0	E980.4
Oleander	988.2	E865.4	—	E950.9	E962.1	E980.9
Oleandomycin	960.3	E856	E930.3	E950.4	E962.0	E980.4
Oleovitamin A	963.5	E858.1	E933.5	E950.4	E962.0	E980.4
Oleum ricini	973.1	E858.4	E943.1	E950.4	E962.0	E980.4
Olive oil (medicinal) NEC	973.2	E858.4	E943.2	E950.4	E962.0	E980.4
OMPA	989.3	E863.1	—	E950.6	E962.1	E980.7
Oncovin	963.1	E858.1	E933.1	E950.4	E962.0	E980.4
Ophthaine	968.5	E855.2	E938.5	E950.4	E962.0	E980.4
Ophthetic	968.5	E855.2	E938.5	E950.4	E962.0	E980.4
Opiates, opioids, opium NEC	965.00	E850.2	E935.2	E950.0	E962.0	E980.0
antagonists	970.1	E854.3	E940.1	E950.4	E962.0	E980.4
Oracon	962.2	E858.0	E932.2	E950.4	E962.0	E980.4
Oragrafin	977.8	E858.8	E947.8	E950.4	E962.0	E980.4
Oral contraceptives	962.2	E858.0	E932.2	E950.4	E962.0	E980.4
Orclprenaline	975.1	E858.6	E945.1	E950.4	E962.0	E980.4
Organidin	975.5	E858.6	E945.5	E950.4	E962.0	E980.4
Organophosphates	989.3	E863.1	—	E950.6	E962.1	E980.7
Orimune	979.5	E858.8	E949.5	E950.4	E962.0	E980.4
Orinase	962.3	E858.0	E932.3	E950.4	E962.0	E980.4
Orphenadrine	966.4	E855.0	E936.4	E950.4	E962.0	E980.4
Ortal (sodium)	967.0	E851	E937.0	E950.1	E962.0	E980.1
Orthoboric acid	976.0	E858.7	E946.0	E950.4	E962.0	E980.4
ENT agent	976.6	E858.7	E946.6	E950.4	E962.0	E980.4
ophthalmic preparation	976.5	E858.7	E946.5	E950.4	E962.0	E980.4
Orthocaine	968.5	E855.2	E938.5	E950.4	E962.0	E980.4
Ortho–Novum	962.2	E858.0	E932.2	E950.4	E962.0	E980.4
Orthotolidine (reagent)	977.8	E858.8	E947.8	E950.4	E962.0	E980.4
Osmic acid (liquid)	983.1	E864.1	—	E950.7	E962.1	E980.6
fumes	987.8	E869.8	—	E952.8	E962.2	E982.8
Osmotic diuretics	974.4	E858.5	E944.4	E950.4	E962.0	E980.4
Ouabain	972.1	E858.3	E942.1	E950.4	E962.0	E980.4
Ovarian hormones (synthetic substitutes)	962.2	E858.0	E932.2	E950.4	E962.0	E980.4
Ovral	962.2	E858.0	E932.2	E950.4	E962.0	E980.4
Ovulation suppressants	962.2	E858.0	E932.2	E950.4	E962.0	E980.4
Ovulen	962.2	E858.0	E932.2	E950.4	E962.0	E980.4
Oxacillin (sodium)	960.0	E856	E930.0	E950.4	E962.0	E980.4
Oxalic acid	983.1	E864.1	—	E950.7	E962.1	E980.6
Oxanamide	969.5	E853.8	E939.5	E950.3	E962.0	E980.3
Oxandrolone	962.1	E858.0	E932.1	E950.4	E962.0	E980.4
Oxazepam	969.4	E853.2	E939.4	E950.3	E962.0	E980.3
Oxazolidine derivatives	966.0	E855.0	E936.0	E950.4	E962.0	E980.4
Ox bile extract	973.4	E858.4	E943.4	E950.4	E962.0	E980.4
Oxedrine	971.2	E855.5	E941.2	E950.4	E962.0	E980.4
Oxeladin	975.4	E858.6	E945.4	E950.4	E962.0	E980.4
Oxethazaine NEC	968.5	E855.2	E938.5	E950.4	E962.0	E980.4
Oxidizing agents NEC	983.9	E864.3	—	E950.7	E962.1	E980.6
Oxolinic acid	961.3	E857	E931.3	E950.4	E962.0	E980.4
Oxophenarsine	961.1	E857	E931.1	E950.4	E962.0	E980.4
Oxsoralen	976.3	E858.7	E946.3	E950.4	E962.0	E980.4
Oxtriphylline	975.7	E858.6	E945.7	E950.4	E962.0	E980.4
Oxybuprocaine	968.5	E855.2	E938.5	E950.4	E962.0	E980.4
Oxybutynin	975.1	E858.6	E945.1	E950.4	E962.0	E980.4
Oxycodone	965.09	E850.2	E935.2	E950.0	E962.0	E980.0
Oxygen	987.8	E869.8	—	E952.8	E962.2	E982.8

Substance	Poisoning	External Cause (E-Code)				
		Accident	Therapeutic Use	Suicide Attempt	Assault	Undetermined
Oxylone	976.0	E858.7	E946.0	E950.4	E962.0	E980.4
ophthalmic preparation	976.5	E858.7	E946.5	E950.4	E962.0	E980.4
Oxymesterone	962.1	E858.0	E932.1	E950.4	E962.0	E980.4
Oxymetazoline	971.2	E855.5	E941.2	E950.4	E962.0	E980.4
Oxymetholone	962.1	E858.0	E932.1	E950.4	E962.0	E980.4
Oxymorphone	965.09	E850.2	E935.2	E950.0	E962.0	E980.0
Oxypertine	969.0	E854.0	E939.0	E950.3	E962.0	E980.3
Oxyphenbutazone	965.5	E850.5	E935.5	E950.0	E962.0	E980.0
Oxyphencyclimine	971.1	E855.4	E941.1	E950.4	E962.0	E980.4
Oxyphenisatin	973.1	E858.4	E943.1	E950.4	E962.0	E980.4
Oxyphenonium	971.1	E855.4	E941.1	E950.4	E962.0	E980.4
Oxyquinoline	961.3	E857	E931.3	E950.4	E962.0	E980.4
Oxytetracycline	960.4	E856	E930.4	E950.4	E962.0	E980.4
Oxytocics	975.0	E858.6	E945.0	E950.4	E962.0	E980.4
Oxytocin	975.0	E858.6	E945.0	E950.4	E962.0	E980.4
Ozone	987.8	E869.8	—	E952.8	E962.2	E982.8
PABA	976.3	E858.7	E946.3	E950.4	E962.0	E980.4
Packed red cells	964.7	E858.2	E934.7	E950.4	E962.0	E980.4
Paint NEC	989.89	E861.6	—	E950.9	E962.1	E980.9
cleaner	982.8	E862.9	—	E950.9	E962.1	E980.9
fumes NEC	987.8	E869.8	—	E952.8	E962.1	E982.8
lead (fumes)	984.0	E861.5	—	E950.9	E962.1	E980.9
solvent NEC	982.8	E862.9	—	E950.9	E962.1	E980.9
stripper	982.8	E862.9	—	E950.9	E962.1	E980.9
Palfium	965.09	E850.2	E935.2	E950.0	E962.0	E980.0
Paludrine	961.4	E857	E931.4	E950.4	E962.0	E980.4
PAM	977.2	E855.8	E947.2	E950.4	E962.0	E980.4
Pamaquine (naphthoate)	961.4	E857	E931.4	E950.4	E962.0	E980.4
Pamprin	965.1	E850.3	E935.3	E950.0	E962.0	E980.0
Panadol	965.4	E850.4	E935.4	E950.0	E962.0	E980.0
Pancreatic dornase (mucolytic)	963.4	E858.1	E933.4	E950.4	E962.0	E980.4
Pancreatin	973.4	E858.4	E943.4	E950.4	E962.0	E980.4
Pancrelipase	973.4	E858.4	E943.4	E950.4	E962.0	E980.4
Pangamic acid	963.5	E858.1	E933.5	E950.4	E962.0	E980.4
Panthenol	963.5	E858.1	E933.5	E950.4	E962.0	E980.4
topical	976.8	E858.7	E946.8	E950.4	E962.0	E980.4
Pantopaque	977.8	E858.8	E947.8	E950.4	E962.0	E980.4
Pantopon	965.00	E850.2	E935.2	E950.0	E962.0	E980.0
Pantothenic acid	963.5	E858.1	E933.5	E950.4	E962.0	E980.4
Panwarfin	964.2	E858.2	E934.2	E950.4	E962.0	E980.4
Papain	973.4	E858.4	E943.4	E950.4	E962.0	E980.4
Papaverine	972.5	E858.3	E942.5	E950.4	E962.0	E980.4
Para–aminobenzoic acid	976.3	E858.7	E946.3	E950.4	E962.0	E980.4
Para–aminophenol derivatives	965.4	E850.4	E935.4	E950.0	E962.0	E980.0
Para–aminosalicylic acid (derivatives)	961.8	E857	E931.8	E950.4	E962.0	E980.4
Paracetaldehyde (medicinal)	967.2	E852.1	E937.2	E950.2	E962.0	E980.2
Paracetamol	965.4	E850.4	E935.4	E950.0	E962.0	E980.0
Paracodin	965.09	E850.2	E935.2	E950.0	E962.0	E980.0
Paradione	966.0	E855.0	E936.0	E950.4	E962.0	E980.4
Paraffin(s) (wax)	981	E862.3	—	E950.9	E962.1	E980.9
liquid (medicinal)	973.2	E858.4	E943.2	E950.4	E962.0	E980.4
nonmedicinal (oil)	981	E962.1	—	E950.9	E962.1	E980.9
Paraldehyde (medicinal)	967.2	E852.1	E937.2	E950.2	E962.0	E980.2
Paramethadione	966.0	E855.0	E936.0	E950.4	E962.0	E980.4
Paramethasone	962.0	E858.0	E932.0	E950.4	E962.0	E980.4
Paraquat	989.4	E863.5	—	E950.6	E962.1	E980.7
Parasympatholytics	971.1	E855.4	E941.1	E950.4	E962.0	E980.4

Substance	Poisoning	External Cause (E-Code)				
		Accident	Therapeutic Use	Suicide Attempt	Assault	Undetermined
Parasympathomimetics	971.0	E855.3	E941.0	E950.4	E962.0	E980.4
Parathion	989.3	E863.1	—	E950.6	E962.1	E980.7
Parathormone	962.6	E858.0	E932.6	E950.4	E962.0	E980.4
Parathyroid (derivatives)	962.6	E858.0	E932.6	E950.4	E962.0	E980.4
Paratyphoid vaccine	978.1	E858.8	E948.1	E950.4	E962.0	E980.4
Paredrine	971.2	E855.5	E941.2	E950.4	E962.0	E980.4
Paregoric	965.00	E850.2	E935.2	E950.0	E962.0	E980.0
Pargyline	972.3	E858.3	E942.3	E950.4	E962.0	E980.4
Paris green	985.1	E866.3	—	E950.8	E962.1	E980.8
insecticide	985.1	E863.4	—	E950.8	E962.1	E980.8
Parnate	969.0	E854.0	E939.0	E950.3	E962.0	E980.3
Paromomycin	960.8	E856	E930.8	E950.4	E962.0	E980.4
Paroxypropione	963.1	E858.1	E933.1	E950.4	E962.0	E980.4
Parzone	965.09	E850.2	E935.2	E950.0	E962.0	E980.0
PAS	961.8	E857	E931.8	E950.4	E962.0	E980.4
PCBs	981	E862.3	—	E950.9	E962.1	E980.9
PCP (pentachlorophenol)	989.4	E863.6	—	E950.6	E962.1	E980.7
herbicide	989.4	E863.5	—	E950.6	E962.1	E980.7
insecticide	989.4	E863.4	—	E950.6	E962.1	E980.7
phencyclidine	968.3	E855.1	E938.3	E950.4	E962.0	E980.4
Peach kernel oil (emulsion)	973.2	E858.4	E943.2	E950.4	E962.0	E980.4
Peanut oil (emulsion) NEC	973.2	E858.4	E943.2	E950.4	E962.0	E980.4
topical	976.3	E858.7	E946.3	E950.4	E962.0	E980.4
Pearly Gates (morning glory seeds)	969.6	E854.1	E939.6	E950.3	E962.0	E980.3
Pecazine	969.1	E853.0	E939.1	E950.3	E962.0	E980.3
Pecilocin	960.1	E856	E930.1	E950.4	E962.0	E980.4
Pectin (with kaolin) NEC	973.5	E858.4	E943.5	E950.4	E962.0	E980.4
Pelletierine tannate	961.6	E857	E931.6	E950.4	E962.0	E980.4
Pemoline	969.7	E854.2	E939.7	E950.3	E962.0	E980.3
Pempidine	972.3	E858.3	E942.3	E950.4	E962.0	E980.4
Penamecillin	960.0	E856	E930.0	E950.4	E962.0	E980.4
Penethamate hydriodide	960.0	E856	E930.0	E950.4	E962.0	E980.4
Penicillamine	963.8	E858.1	E933.8	E950.4	E962.0	E980.4
Penicillin (any type)	960.0	E856	E930.0	E950.4	E962.0	E980.4
Penicillinase	963.4	E858.1	E933.4	E950.4	E962.0	E980.4
Pentachlorophenol (fungicide)	989.4	E863.6	—	E950.6	E962.1	E980.7
herbicide	989.4	E863.5	—	E950.6	E962.1	E980.7
insecticide	989.4	E863.4	—	E950.6	E962.1	E980.7
Pentaerythritol	972.4	E858.3	E942.4	E950.4	E962.0	E980.4
chloral	967.1	E852.0	E937.1	E950.2	E962.0	E980.2
tetranitrate NEC	972.4	E858.3	E942.4	E950.4	E962.0	E980.4
Pentagastrin	977.8	E858.8	E947.8	E950.4	E962.0	E980.4
Pentalin	982.3	E862.4	—	E950.9	E962.1	E980.9
Pentamethonium (bromide)	972.3	E858.3	E942.3	E950.4	E962.0	E980.4
Pentamidine	961.5	E857	E931.5	E950.4	E962.0	E980.4
Pentanol	980.8	E860.8	—	E950.9	E962.1	E980.9
Pentaquine	961.4	E857	E931.4	E950.4	E962.0	E980.4
Pentazocine	965.8	E850.8	E935.8	E950.0	E962.0	E980.0
Penthienate	971.1	E855.4	E941.1	E950.4	E962.0	E980.4
Pentobarbital, pentobarbitone (sodium)	967.0	E851	E937.0	E950.1	E962.0	E980.1
Pentolinium (tartrate)	972.3	E858.3	E942.3	E950.4	E962.0	E980.4
Pentothal	968.3	E855.1	E938.3	E950.4	E962.0	E980.4
Pentylenetetrazol	970.0	E854.3	E940.0	E950.4	E962.0	E980.4
Pentylsalicylamide	961.8	E857	E931.8	E950.4	E962.0	E980.4
Pepsin	973.4	E858.4	E943.4	E950.4	E962.0	E980.4
Peptavlon	977.8	E858.8	E947.8	E950.4	E962.0	E980.4
Percaine (spinal)	968.7	E855.2	E938.7	E950.4	E962.0	E980.4

Substance	Poisoning	External Cause (E-Code)				
		Accident	Therapeutic Use	Suicide Attempt	Assault	Undetermined
topical (surface)	968.5	E855.2	E938.5	E950.4	E962.0	E980.4
Perchloroethylene (vapor)	982.3	E862.4	—	E950.9	E962.1	E980.9
medicinal	961.6	E857	E931.6	E950.4	E962.0	E980.4
Percodan	965.09	E850.2	E935.2	E950.0	E962.0	E980.0
Percogesic	965.09	E850.2	E935.2	E950.0	E962.0	E980.0
Percorten	962.0	E858.0	E932.0	E950.4	E962.0	E980.4
Pergonal	962.4	E858.0	E932.4	E950.4	E962.0	E980.4
Perhexiline	972.4	E858.3	E942.4	E950.4	E962.0	E980.4
Periactin	963.0	E858.1	E933.0	E950.4	E962.0	E980.4
Periclor	967.1	E852.0	E937.1	E950.2	E962.0	E980.2
Pericyazine	969.1	E853.0	E939.1	E950.3	E962.0	E980.3
Peritrate	972.4	E858.3	E942.4	E950.4	E962.0	E980.4
Permanganates NEC	983.9	E864.3	—	E950.7	E962.1	E980.6
potassium (topical)	976.0	E858.7	E946.0	E950.4	E962.0	E980.4
Pernocton	967.0	E851	E937.0	E950.1	E962.0	E980.1
Pernoston	967.0	E851	E937.0	E950.1	E962.0	E980.1
Peronin(e)	965.09	E850.2	E935.2	E950.0	E962.0	E980.0
Perphenazine	969.1	E853.0	E939.1	E950.3	E962.0	E980.3
Pertofrane	969.0	E854	E939.0	E950.3	E962.0	E980.3
Pertussis						
immune serum (human)	964.6	E858.2	E934.6	E950.4	E962.0	E980.4
vaccine (with diphtheria toxoid) (with						
tetanus toxoid)	978.6	E858.8	E948.6	E950.4	E962.0	E980.4
Peruvian balsam	976.8	E858.7	E946.8	E950.4	E962.0	E980.4
Pesticides (dust) (fumes) (vapor)	989.4	E863.4	—	E950.6	E962.1	E980.7
arsenic	985.1	E863.4	—	E950.8	E962.1	E980.8
chlorinated	989.2	E863.0	—	E950.6	E962.1	E980.7
cyanide	989.0	E863.4	—	E950.6	E962.1	E980.7
kerosene	981	E863.4	—	E950.6	E962.1	E980.7
mixture (of compounds)	989.4	E863.3	—	E950.6	E962.1	E980.7
naphthalene	983.0	E863.4	—	E950.7	E962.1	E980.6
organochlorine (compounds)	989.2	E863.0	—	E950.6	E962.1	E980.7
petroleum (distillate) (products)						
NEC	981	E863.4	—	E950.6	E962.1	E980.7
specified ingredient NEC	989.4	E863.4	—	E950.6	E962.1	E980.7
strychnine	989.1	E863.4	—	E950.6	E962.1	E980.7
thallium	985.8	E863.7	—	E950.6	E962.1	E980.7
Pethidine (hydrochloride)	965.09	E850.2	E935.2	E950.0	E962.0	E980.0
Petrichloral	967.1	E852.0	E937.1	E950.2	E962.0	E980.2
Petrol	981	E862.1	—	E950.9	E962.1	E980.9
vapor	987.1	E869.8	—	E952.8	E962.2	E982.8
Petrolatum (jelly) (ointment)	976.3	E858.7	E946.3	E950.4	E962.0	E980.4
hydrophilic	976.3	E858.7	E946.3	E950.4	E962.0	E980.4
liquid	973.2	E858.4	E943.2	E950.4	E962.0	E980.4
topical	976.3	E858.7	E946.3	E950.4	E962.0	E980.4
nonmedicinal	981	E862.1	—	E950.9	E962.1	E980.9
Petroleum (cleaners) (fuels) (products)						
NEC	981	E862.1	—	E950.9	E962.1	E980.9
benzin(e) — see Ligroin						
ether — see Ligroin						
jelly — see Petrolatum						
naphtha — see Ligroin						
pesticide	981	E863.4	—	E950.6	E962.1	E980.7
solids	981	E862.3	—	E950.9	E962.1	E980.9
solvents	981	E862.0	—	E950.9	E962.1	E980.9
vapor	987.1	E869.8	—	E952.8	E962.2	E982.8
Peyote	969.6	E854.1	E939.6	E950.3	E962.0	E980.3

Substance	Poisoning	External Cause (E-Code)				
		Accident	Therapeutic Use	Suicide Attempt	Assault	Undetermined
Phanodorm, phanodorn	967.0	E851	E937.0	E950.1	E962.0	E980.1
Phanquinone, phanquone	961.5	E857	E931.5	E950.4	E962.0	E980.4
Pharmaceutical excipient or adjunct	977.4	E858.8	E947.4	E950.4	E962.0	E980.4
Phenacemide	966.3	E855.0	E936.3	E950.4	E962.0	E980.4
Phenacetin	965.4	E850.4	E935.4	E950.0	E962.0	E980.0
Phenadoxone	965.09	E850.2	E935.2	E950.0	E962.0	E980.0
Phenaglycodol	969.5	E853.8	E939.5	E950.3	E962.0	E980.3
Phenantoin	966.1	E855.0	E936.1	E950.4	E962.0	E980.4
Phenaphthazine reagent	977.8	E858.8	E947.8	E950.4	E962.0	E980.4
Phenazocine	965.09	E850.2	E935.2	E950.0	E962.0	E980.0
Phenazone	965.5	E850.5	E935.5	E950.0	E962.0	E980.0
Phenazopyridine	976.1	E858.7	E946.1	E950.4	E962.0	E980.4
Phenbenicillin	960.0	E856	E930.0	E950.4	E962.0	E980.4
Phenbutrazate	977.0	E858.8	E947.0	E950.4	E962.0	E980.4
Phencyclidine	968.3	E855.1	E938.3	E950.4	E962.0	E980.4
Phendimetrazine	977.0	E858.8	E947.0	E950.4	E962.0	E980.4
Phenelzine	969.0	E854.0	E939.0	E950.3	E962.0	E980.3
Phenergan	967.8	E852.8	E937.8	E950.2	E962.0	E980.2
Phenethicillin (potassium)	960.0	E856	E930.0	E950.4	E962.0	E980.4
Phenetsal	965.1	E850.3	E935.3	E950.0	E962.0	E980.0
Pheneturide	966.3	E855.0	E936.3	E950.4	E962.0	E980.4
Phenformin	962.3	E858.0	E932.3	E950.4	E962.0	E980.4
Phenglutarimide	971.1	E855.4	E941.1	E950.4	E962.0	E980.4
Phenicarbazide	965.8	E850.8	E935.8	E950.0	E962.0	E980.0
Phenindamine (tartrate)	963.0	E858.1	E933.0	E950.4	E962.0	E980.4
Phenindione	964.2	E858.2	E934.2	E950.4	E962.0	E980.4
Pheniprazine	969.0	E854.0	E939.0	E950.3	E962.0	E980.3
Pheniramine (maleate)	963.0	E858.1	E933.0	E950.4	E962.0	E980.4
Phenmetrazine	977.0	E858.8	E947.0	E950.4	E962.0	E980.4
Phenobal	967.0	E851	E937.0	E950.1	E962.0	E980.1
Phenobarbital	967.0	E851	E937.0	E950.1	E962.0	E980.1
Phenobarbitone	967.0	E851	E937.0	E950.1	E962.0	E980.1
Phenoctide	976.0	E858.7	E946.0	E950.4	E962.0	E980.4
Phenol (derivatives) NEC	983.0	E864.0	—	E950.7	E962.1	E980.6
disinfectant	983.0	E864.0	—	E950.7	E962.1	E980.6
pesticide	989.4	E863.4	—	E950.6	E962.1	E980.7
red	977.8	E858.8	E947.8	E950.4	E962.0	E980.4
Phenolphthalein	973.1	E858.4	E943.1	E950.4	E962.0	E980.4
Phenolsulfonphthalein	977.8	E858.8	E947.8	E950.4	E962.0	E980.4
Phenomorphan	965.09	E850.2	E935.2	E950.0	E962.0	E980.0
Phenonyl	967.0	E851	E937.0	E950.1	E962.0	E980.1
Phenoperidine	965.09	E850.2	E935.2	E950.0	E962.0	E980.0
Phenoquin	974.7	E858.5	E944.7	E950.4	E962.0	E980.4
Phenothiazines (tranquilizers) NEC	969.1	E853.0	E939.1	E950.3	E962.0	E980.3
insecticide	989.3	E863.4	—	E950.6	E962.1	E980.7
Phenoxybenzamine	971.3	E855.6	E941.3	E950.4	E962.0	E980.4
Phenoxymethyl penicillin	960.0	E856	E930.0	E950.4	E962.0	E980.4
Phenprocoumon	964.2	E858.2	E934.2	E950.4	E962.0	E980.4
Phensuximide	966.2	E855.0	E936.2	E950.4	E962.0	E980.4
Phentermine	977.0	E858.8	E947.0	E950.4	E962.0	E980.4
Phentolamine	971.3	E855.6	E941.3	E950.4	E962.0	E980.4
Phenyl						
butazone	965.5	E850.5	E935.5	E950.0	E962.0	E980.0
enediamine	983.0	E864.0	—	E950.7	E962.1	E980.6
hydrazine	983.0	E864.0	—	E950.7	E962.1	E980.6
antineoplastic	963.1	E858.1	E933.1	E950.4	E962.0	E980.4
mercuric compounds — *see* Mercury						

Substance	Poisoning	Accident	Therapeutic Use	Suicide Attempt	Assault	Undetermined
salicylate	976.3	E858.7	E946.3	E950.4	E962.0	E980.4
Phenylephrin	971.2	E855.5	E941.2	E950.4	E962.0	E980.4
Phenylethybiguanide	962.3	E858.0	E932.3	E950.4	E962.0	E980.4
Phenylpropanolamine	971.2	E855.5	E941.2	E950.4	E962.0	E980.4
Phenylsulfthion	989.3	E863.1	—	E950.6	E962.1	E980.7
Phenyramidol, phenyramidon	965.7	E850.7	E935.7	E950.0	E962.0	E980.0
Phenytoin	966.1	E855.0	E936.1	E950.4	E962.0	E980.4
pHisoHex	976.2	E858.7	E946.2	E950.4	E962.0	E980.4
Pholcodine	965.09	E850.2	E935.2	E950.0	E962.0	E980.0
Phorate	989.3	E863.1	—	E950.6	E962.1	E980.7
Phosdrin	989.3	E863.1	—	E950.6	E962.1	E980.7
Phosgene (gas)	987.8	E869.8	—	E952.8	E962.2	E982.8
Phosphate (tricresyl)	989.89	E866.8	—	E950.9	E962.1	E980.9
organic	989.3	E863.1	—	E950.6	E962.1	E980.7
solvent	982.8	E862.4	—	E950.9	E926.1	E980.9
Phosphine	987.8	E869.8	—	E952.8	E962.2	E982.8
fumigant	987.8	E863.8	—	E950.6	E962.2	E980.7
Phospholine	971.0	E855.3	E941.0	E950.4	E962.0	E980.4
Phosphoric acid	983.1	E864.1	—	E950.7	E962.1	E980.6
Phosphorus (compounds) NEC	983.9	E864.3	—	E950.7	E962.1	E980.6
rodenticide	983.9	E863.7	—	E950.7	E962.1	E980.6
Phthalimidogluarimide	967.8	E852.8	E937.8	E950.2	E962.0	E980.2
Phthalylsulfathiazole	961.0	E857	E931.0	E950.4	E962.0	E980.4
Phylloquinone	964.3	E858.2	E934.3	E950.4	E962.0	E980.4
Physeptone	965.02	E850.1	E935.1	E950.0	E962.0	E980.0
Physostigma venenosum	988.2	E865.4	—	E950.9	E962.1	E980.9
Physostigmine	971.0	E855.3	E941.0	E950.4	E962.0	E980.4
Phytolacca decandra	988.2	E865.4	—	E950.9	E962.1	E980.9
Phytomenadione	964.3	E858.2	E934.3	E950.4	E962.0	E980.4
Phytonadione	964.3	E858.2	E934.3	E950.4	E962.0	E980.4
Picric (acid)	983.0	E864.0	—	E950.7	E962.1	E980.6
Picrotoxin	970.0	E854.3	E940.0	E950.4	E962.0	E980.4
Pilocarpine	971.0	E855.3	E941.0	E950.4	E962.0	E980.4
Pilocarpus (jaborandi) extract	971.0	E855.3	E941.0	E950.4	E962.0	E980.4
Pimaricin	960.1	E856	E930.1	E950.4	E962.0	E980.4
Piminodine	965.09	E850.2	E935.2	E950.0	E962.0	E980.0
Pine oil, pinesol (disinfectant)	983.9	E861.4	—	E950.7	E962.1	E980.6
Pinkroot	961.6	E857	E931.6	E950.4	E962.0	E980.4
Pipadone	965.09	E850.2	E935.2	E950.0	E962.0	E980.0
Pipamazine	963.0	E858.1	E933.0	E950.4	E962.0	E980.4
Pipazethate	975.4	E858.6	E945.4	E950.4	E962.0	E980.4
Pipenzolate	971.1	E855.4	E941.1	E950.4	E962.0	E980.4
Piperacetazine	969.1	E853.0	E939.1	E950.3	E962.0	E980.3
Piperazine NEC	961.6	E857	E931.6	E950.4	E962.0	E980.4
estrone sulfate	962.2	E858.0	E932.2	E950.4	E962.0	E980.4
Piper cubeba	988.2	E865.4	—	E950.9	E962.1	E980.9
Piperidione	975.4	E858.6	E945.4	E950.4	E962.0	E980.4
Piperidolate	971.1	E855.4	E941.1	E950.4	E962.0	E980.4
Piperocaine	968.9	E855.2	E938.9	E950.4	E962.0	E980.4
infiltration (subcutaneous)	968.5	E855.2	E938.5	E950.4	E962.0	E980.4
nerve block (peripheral) (plexus)	968.6	E855.2	E938.6	E950.4	E962.0	E980.4
topical (surface)	968.5	E855.2	E938.5	E950.4	E962.0	E980.4
Pipobroman	963.1	E858.1	E933.1	E950.4	E962.0	E980.4
Pipradrol	970.8	E854.3	E940.8	E950.4	E962.0	E980.4
Piscidia (bark) (erythrina)	965.7	E850.7	E935.7	E950.0	E962.0	E980.0
Pitch	983.0	E864.0	—	E950.7	E962.1	E980.6
Pitkin's solution	968.7	E855.2	E938.7	E950.4	E962.0	E980.4

Substance	Poisoning	Accident	Therapeutic Use	Suicide Attempt	Assault	Undetermined
			External Cause (E-Code)			
Pitocin	975.0	E858.6	E945.0	E950.4	E962.0	E980.4
Pitressin (tannate)	962.5	E858.0	E932.5	E950.4	E962.0	E980.4
Pituitary extracts (posterior)	962.5	E858.0	E932.5	E950.4	E962.0	E980.4
anterior	962.4	E858.0	E932.4	E950.4	E962.0	E980.4
Pituitrin	962.5	E858.0	E932.5	E950.4	E962.0	E980.4
Placental extract	962.9	E858.0	E932.9	E950.4	E962.0	E980.4
Placidyl	967.8	E852.8	E937.8	E950.2	E962.0	E980.2
Plague vaccine	978.3	E858.8	E948.3	E950.4	E962.0	E980.4
Plant foods or fertilizers NEC	989.89	E866.5	—	E950.9	E962.1	E980.9
mixed with herbicides	989.4	E863.5	—	E950.6	E962.1	E980.7
Plants, noxious, used as food	988.2	E865.9	—	E950.9	E962.1	E980.9
berries and seeds	988.2	E865.3	—	E950.9	E962.1	E980.9
specified type NEC	988.2	E865.4	—	E950.9	E962.1	E980.9
Plasma (blood)	964.7	E858.2	E934.7	E950.4	E962.0	E980.4
expanders	964.8	E858.2	E934.8	E950.4	E962.0	E980.4
Plasmanate	964.7	E858.2	E934.7	E950.4	E962.0	E980.4
Plegicil	969.1	E853.0	E939.1	E950.3	E962.0	E980.3
Podophyllin	976.4	E858.7	E946.4	E950.4	E962.0	E980.4
Podophyllum resin	976.4	E858.7	E946.4	E950.4	E962.0	E980.4
Poison NEC	989.9	E866.9	—	E950.9	E962.1	E980.9
Poisonous berries	988.2	E865.3	—	E950.9	E962.1	E980.9
Pokeweed (any part)	988.2	E865.4	—	E950.9	E962.1	E980.9
Poldine	971.1	E855.4	E941.1	E950.4	E962.0	E980.4
Poliomyelitis vaccine	979.5	E858.8	E949.5	E950.4	E962.0	E980.4
Poliovirus vaccine	979.5	E858.8	E949.5	E950.4	E962.0	E980.4
Polish (car) (floor) (furniture) (metal)						
(silver)	989.89	E861.2	—	E950.9	E962.1	E980.9
abrasive	989.89	E861.3	—	E950.9	E962.1	E980.9
porcelain	989.89	E861.3	—	E950.9	E962.1	E980.9
Poloxalkol	973.2	E858.4	E943.2	E950.4	E962.0	E980.4
Polyaminostyrene resins	974.5	E858.5	E944.5	E950.4	E962.0	E980.4
Polychlorinated biphenyl—*see* PCBs						
Polycycline	960.4	E856	E930.4	E950.4	E962.0	E980.4
Polyester resin hardener	982.8	E862.4	—	E950.9	E962.1	E980.9
fumes	987.8	E869.8	—	E952.8	E962.2	E982.8
Polyestradiol (phosphate)	962.2	E858.0	E932.2	E950.4	E962.0	E980.4
Polyethanolamine alkyl sulfate	976.2	E858.7	E946.2	E950.4	E962.0	E980.4
Polyethylene glycol	976.3	E858.7	E946.3	E950.4	E962.0	E980.4
Polyferose	964.0	E858.2	E934.0	E950.4	E962.0	E980.4
Polymyxin B	960.8	E856	E930.8	E950.4	E962.0	E980.4
ENT agent	976.6	E858.7	E946.6	E950.4	E962.0	E980.4
ophthalmic preparation	976.5	E858.7	E946.5	E950.4	E962.0	E980.4
topical NEC	976.0	E858.7	E946.0	E950.4	E962.0	E980.4
Polynoxylin(e)	976.0	E858.7	E946.0	E950.4	E962.0	E980.4
Polyoxymethyleneurea	976.0	E858.7	E946.0	E950.4	E962.0	E980.4
Polytetrafluoroethylene (inhaled)	987.8	E869.8	—	E952.8	E962.2	E982.8
Polythiazide	974.3	E858.5	E944.3	E950.4	E962.0	E980.4
Polyvinylpyrrolidone	964.8	E858.2	E934.8	E950.4	E962.0	E980.4
Pontocaine (hydrochloride) (infiltration)						
(topical)	968.5	E855.2	E938.5	E950.4	E962.0	E980.4
nerve block (peripheral) (plexus)	968.6	E855.2	E938.6	E950.4	E962.0	E980.4
spinal	968.7	E855.2	E938.7	E950.4	E962.0	E980.4
Pot	969.6	E854.1	E939.6	E950.3	E962.0	E980.3
Potash (caustic)	983.2	E864.2	—	E950.7	E962.1	E980.6
Potassic saline injection (lactated)	974.5	E858.5	E944.5	E950.4	E962.0	E980.4
Potassium (salts) NEC	974.5	E858.5	E944.5	E950.4	E962.0	E980.4
aminosalicylate	961.8	E857	E931.8	E950.4	E962.0	E980.4

Substance	Poisoning	External Cause (E-Code)				
		Accident	Therapeutic Use	Suicide Attempt	Assault	Undetermined
arsenite (solution)	985.1	E866.3	—	E950.8	E962.1	E980.8
bichromate	983.9	E864.3	—	E950.7	E962.1	E980.6
bisulfate	983.9	E864.3	—	E950.7	E962.1	E980.6
bromide (medicinal) NEC	967.3	E852.2	E937.3	E950.2	E962.0	E980.2
carbonate	983.2	E864.2	—	E950.7	E962.1	E980.6
chlorate NEC	983.9	E864.3	—	E950.7	E962.1	E980.6
cyanide — *see* Cyanide						
hydroxide	983.2	E864.2	—	E950.7	E962.1	E980.6
iodide (expectorant) NEC	975.5	E858.6	E945.5	E950.4	E962.0	E980.4
nitrate	989.89	E866.8	—	E950.9	E962.1	E980.9
oxalate	983.9	E864.3	—	E950.7	E962.1	E980.6
perchlorate NEC	977.8	E858.8	E947.8	E950.4	E962.0	E980.4
antithyroid	962.8	E858.0	E932.8	E950.4	E962.0	E980.4
permanganate	976.0	E858.7	E946.0	E950.4	E962.0	E980.4
nonmedicinal	983.9	E864.3	—	E950.7	E962.1	E980.6
Povidone–iodine (anti–infective) NEC	976.0	E858.7	E946.0	E950.4	E962.0	E980.4
Practolol	972.0	E858.3	E942.0	E950.4	E962.0	E980.4
Pralidoxime (chloride)	977.2	E858.8	E947.2	E950.4	E962.0	E980.4
Pramoxine	968.5	E855.2	E938.5	E950.4	E962.0	E980.4
Prazosin	972.6	E858.3	E942.6	E950.4	E962.0	E980.4
Prednisolone	962.0	E858.0	E932.0	E950.4	E962.0	E980.4
ENT agent	976.6	E858.7	E946.6	E950.4	E962.0	E980.4
ophthalmic preparation	976.5	E858.7	E946.5	E950.4	E962.0	E980.4
topical NEC	976.0	E858.7	E946.0	E950.4	E962.0	E980.4
Prednisone	962.0	E858.0	E932.0	E950.4	E962.0	E980.4
Pregnanediol	962.2	E858.0	E932.2	E950.4	E962.0	E980.4
Pregneninolone	962.2	E858.0	E932.2	E950.4	E962.0	E980.4
Preludin	977.0	E858.8	E947.0	E950.4	E962.0	E980.4
Premarin	962.2	E858.0	E932.2	E950.4	E962.0	E980.4
Prenylamine	972.4	E858.3	E942.4	E950.4	E962.0	E980.4
Preparation H	976.8	E858.7	E946.8	E950.4	E962.0	E980.4
Preservatives	989.89	E866.8	—	E950.9	E962.1	E980.9
Pride of China	988.2	E865.3	—	E950.9	E962.1	E980.9
Prilocaine	968.9	E855.2	E938.9	E950.4	E962.0	E980.4
infiltration (subcutaneous)	968.5	E855.2	E938.5	E950.4	E962.0	E980.4
nerve block (peripheral) (plexus)	968.6	E855.2	E938.6	E950.4	E962.0	E980.4
Primaquine	961.4	E857	E931.4	E950.4	E962.0	E980.4
Primidone	966.3	E855.0	E936.3	E950.4	E962.0	E980.4
Primula (veris)	988.2	E865.4	—	E950.9	E962.1	E980.9
Prinadol	965.09	E850.2	E935.2	E950.0	E962.0	E980.0
Priscol, Priscoline	971.3	E855.6	E941.3	E950.4	E962.0	E980.4
Privet	988.2	E865.4	—	E950.9	E962.1	E980.9
Privine	971.2	E855.5	E941.2	E950.4	E962.0	E980.4
Pro–Banthine	971.1	E855.4	E941.1	E950.4	E962.0	E980.4
Probarbital	967.0	E851	E937.0	E950.1	E962.0	E980.1
Probenecid	974.7	E858.5	E944.7	E950.4	E962.0	E980.4
Procainamide (hydrochloride)	972.0	E858.3	E942.0	E950.4	E962.0	E980.4
Procaine (hydrochloride) (infiltration) (topical)	968.5	E855.2	E938.5	E950.4	E962.0	E980.4
nerve block (peripheral) (plexus)	968.6	E855.2	E938.6	E950.4	E962.0	E980.4
penicillin G	960.0	E856	E930.0	E950.4	E962.0	E980.4
spinal	968.7	E855.2	E938.7	E950.4	E962.0	E980.4
Procalmidol	969.5	E853.8	E939.5	E950.3	E962.0	E980.3
Procarbazine	963.1	E858.1	E933.1	E950.4	E962.0	E980.4
Prochlorperazine	969.1	E853.0	E939.1	E950.3	E962.0	E980.3
Procyclidine	966.4	E855.0	E936.4	E950.4	E962.0	E980.4
Producer gas	986	E868.8	—	E952.1	E962.2	E982.1

Substance	Poisoning	External Cause (E-Code)				
		Accident	Therapeutic Use	Suicide Attempt	Assault	Undetermined
Profenamine	966.4	E855.0	E936.4	E950.4	E962.0	E980.4
Profenil	975.1	E858.6	E945.1	E950.4	E962.0	E980.4
Progesterones	962.2	E858.0	E932.2	E950.4	E962.0	E980.4
Progestin	962.2	E858.0	E932.2	E950.4	E962.0	E980.4
Progestogens (with estrogens)	962.2	E858.0	E932.2	E950.4	E962.0	E980.4
Progestone	962.2	E858.0	E932.2	E950.4	E962.0	E980.4
Proguanil	961.4	E857	E931.4	E950.4	E962.0	E980.4
Prolactin	962.4	E858.0	E932.4	E950.4	E962.0	E980.4
Proloid	962.7	E858.0	E932.7	E950.4	E962.0	E980.4
Proluton	962.2	E858.0	E932.2	E950.4	E962.0	E980.4
Promacetin	961.8	E857	E931.8	E950.4	E962.0	E980.4
Promazine	969.1	E853.0	E939.1	E950.3	E962.0	E980.3
Promedol	965.09	E850.2	E935.2	E950.0	E962.0	E980.0
Promethazine	967.8	E852.8	E937.8	E950.2	E962.0	E980.2
Promin	961.8	E857	E931.8	E950.4	E962.0	E980.4
Pronestyl (hydrochloride)	972.0	E858.3	E942.0	E950.4	E962.0	E980.4
Pronetalol, pronethalol	972.0	E858.3	E942.0	E950.4	E962.0	E980.4
Prontosil	961.0	E857	E931.0	E950.4	E962.0	E980.4
Propamidine isethionate	961.5	E857	E931.5	E950.4	E962.0	E980.4
Propanal (medicinal)	967.8	E852.8	E937.8	E950.2	E962.0	E980.2
Propane (gas) (distributed in mobile container)	987.0	E868.0	—	E951.1	E962.2	E981.1
distributed through pipes	987.0	E867	—	E951.0	E962.2	E981.0
incomplete combustion of – *see* Carbon monoxide, Propane						
Propanidid	968.3	E855.1	E938.3	E950.4	E962.0	E980.4
Propanol	980.3	E860.4	—	E950.9	E962.1	E980.9
Propantheline	971.1	E855.4	E941.1	E950.4	E962.0	E980.4
Proparacaine	968.5	E855.2	E938.5	E950.4	E962.0	E980.4
Propatyl nitrate	972.4	E858.3	E942.4	E950.4	E962.0	E980.4
Propicillin	960.0	E856	E930.0	E950.4	E962.0	E980.4
Propiolactone (vapor)	987.8	E869.8	—	E952.8	E962.2	E982.8
Propiomazine	967.8	E852.8	E937.8	E950.2	E962.0	E980.2
Propionaldehyde (medicinal)	967.8	E852.8	E937.8	E950.2	E962.0	E980.2
Propionate compound	976.0	E858.7	E946.0	E950.4	E962.0	E980.4
Propion gel	976.0	E858.7	E946.0	E950.4	E962.0	E980.4
Propitocaine	968.9	E855.2	E938.9	E950.4	E962.0	E980.4
infiltration (subcutaneous)	968.5	E855.2	E938.5	E950.4	E962.0	E980.4
nerve block (peripheral) (plexus)	968.6	E855.2	E938.6	E950.4	E962.0	E980.4
Propoxur	989.3	E863.2	—	E950.6	E962.1	E980.7
Propoxycaine	968.9	E855.2	E938.9	E950.4	E962.0	E980.4
infiltration (subcutaneous)	968.5	E855.2	E938.5	E950.4	E962.0	E980.4
nerve block (peripheral) (plexus)	968.6	E855.2	E938.6	E950.4	E962.0	E980.4
topical (surface)	968.5	E855.2	E938.5	E950.4	E962.0	E980.4
Propoxyphene (hydrochloride)	965.8	E850.8	E935.8	E950.0	E962.0	E980.0
Propranolol	972.0	E858.3	E942.0	E950.4	E962.0	E980.4
Propyl						
alcohol	980.3	E860.4	—	E950.9	E962.1	E980.9
carbinol	980.3	E860.4	—	E950.9	E962.1	E980.9
hexadrine	971.2	E855.5	E941.2	E950.4	E962.0	E980.4
iodone	977.8	E858.8	E947.8	E950.4	E962.0	E980.4
thiouracil	962.8	E858.0	E932.8	E950.4	E962.0	E980.4
Propylene	987.1	E869.8	—	E952.8	E962.2	E982.8
Propylparaben (ophthalmic)	976.5	E858.7	E946.5	E950.4	E962.0	E980.4
Proscillaridin	972.1	E858.3	E942.1	E950.4	E962.0	E980.4
Prostaglandins	975.0	E858.6	E945.0	E950.4	E962.0	E980.4
Prostigmin	971.0	E855.3	E941.0	E950.4	E962.0	E980.4

Substance	Poisoning	External Cause (E-Code)				
		Accident	Therapeutic Use	Suicide Attempt	Assault	Undetermined
Protamine (sulfate)	964.5	E858.2	E934.5	E950.4	E962.0	E980.4
zinc insulin	962.3	E858.0	E932.3	E950.4	E962.0	E980.4
Protectants (topical)	976.3	E858.7	E946.3	E950.4	E962.0	E980.4
Protein hydrolysate	974.5	E858.5	E944.5	E950.4	E962.0	E980.4
Prothiaden—*see* Dothiepin hydrochloride						
Prothionamide	961.8	E857	E931.8	E950.4	E962.0	E980.4
Prothipendyl	969.5	E853.8	E939.5	E950.3	E962.0	E980.3
Protokylol	971.2	E855.5	E941.2	E950.4	E962.0	E980.4
Protopam	977.2	E858.8	E947.2	E950.4	E962.0	E980.4
Protoveratrine(s) (A) (B)	972.6	E858.3	E942.6	E950.4	E962.0	E980.4
Protriptyline	969.0	E854.0	E939.0	E950.3	E962.0	E980.3
Provera	962.2	E858.0	E932.2	E950.4	E962.0	E980.4
Provitamin A	963.5	E858.1	E933.5	E950.4	E962.0	E980.4
Proxymetacaine	968.5	E855.2	E938.5	E950.4	E962.0	E980.4
Proxyphylline	975.1	E858.6	E945.1	E950.4	E962.0	E980.4
Prozac—*see* Fluoxetine hydrochloride						
Prunus						
laurocerasus	988.2	E865.4	—	E950.9	E962.1	E980.9
virginiana	988.2	E865.4	—	E950.9	E962.1	E980.9
Prussic acid	989.0	E866.8	—	E950.9	E962.1	E980.9
vapor	987.7	E869.8	—	E952.8	E962.2	E982.8
Pseudoephedrine	971.2	E855.5	E941.2	E950.4	E962.0	E980.4
Psilocin	969.6	E854.1	E939.6	E950.3	E962.0	E980.3
Psilocybin	969.6	E854.1	E939.6	E950.3	E962.0	E980.3
PSP	977.8	E858.8	E947.8	E950.4	E962.0	E980.4
Psychedelic agents	969.6	E854.1	E939.6	E950.3	E962.0	E980.3
Psychodysleptics	969.6	E854.1	E939.6	E950.3	E962.0	E980.3
Psychostimulants	969.7	E854.2	E939.7	E950.3	E962.0	E980.3
Psychotherapeutic agents	969.9	E855.9	E939.9	E950.3	E962.0	E980.3
antidepressants	969.0	E854.0	E939.0	E950.3	E962.0	E980.3
specified NEC	969.8	E855.8	E939.8	E950.3	E962.0	E980.3
tranquilizers NEC	969.5	E853.9	E939.5	E950.3	E962.0	E980.3
Psychotomimetic agents	969.6	E854.1	E939.6	E950.3	E962.0	E980.3
Psychotropic agents	969.9	E854.8	E939.9	E950.3	E962.0	E980.3
specified NEC	969.8	E854.8	E939.8	E950.3	E962.0	E980.3
Psyllium	973.3	E858.4	E943.3	E950.4	E962.0	E980.4
Pteroylglutamic acid	964.1	E858.2	E934.1	E950.4	E962.0	E980.4
Pteroyltriglutamate	963.1	E858.1	E933.1	E950.4	E962.0	E980.4
PTFE	987.8	E869.8	—	E952.8	E962.2	E982.8
Pulsatilla	988.2	E865.4	—	E950.9	E962.1	E980.9
Purex (bleach)	983.9	E864.3	—	E950.7	E962.1	E980.6
Purine diuretics	974.1	E858.5	E944.1	E950.4	E962.0	E980.4
Purinethol	963.1	E858.1	E933.1	E950.4	E962.0	E980.4
PVP	964.8	E858.2	E934.8	E950.4	E962.0	E980.4
Pyrabital	965.7	E850.7	E935.7	E950.0	E962.0	E980.0
Pyramidon	965.5	E850.5	E935.5	E950.0	E962.0	E980.0
Pyrantel (pamoate)	961.6	E857	E931.6	E950.4	E962.0	E980.4
Pyrathiazine	963.0	E858.1	E933.0	E950.4	E962.0	E980.4
Pyrazinamide	961.8	E857	E931.8	E950.4	E962.0	E980.4
Pyrazinoic acid (amide)	961.8	E857	E931.8	E950.4	E962.0	E980.4
Pyrazole (derivatives)	965.5	E850.5	E935.5	E950.0	E962.0	E980.0
Pyrazolone (analgesics)	965.5	E850.5	E935.5	E950.0	E962.0	E980.0
Pyrethrins, pyrethrum	989.4	E863.4	—	E950.6	E962.1	E980.7
Pyribenzamine	963.0	E858.1	E933.0	E950.4	E962.0	E980.4
Pyridine (liquid) (vapor)	982.0	E862.4	—	E950.9	E962.1	E980.9
aldoxime chloride	977.2	E858.8	E947.2	E950.4	E962.0	E980.4
Pyridium	976.1	E858.7	E946.1	E950.4	E962.0	E980.4

Substance	Poisoning	External Cause (E-Code)				
		Accident	Therapeutic Use	Suicide Attempt	Assault	Undetermined
Pyridostigmine	971.0	E855.3	E941.0	E950.4	E962.0	E980.4
Pyridoxine	963.5	E858.1	E933.5	E950.4	E962.0	E980.4
Pyrilamine	963.0	E858.1	E933.0	E950.4	E962.0	E980.4
Pyrimethamine	961.4	E857	E931.4	E950.4	E962.0	E980.4
Pyrogallic acid	983.0	E864.0	—	E950.7	E962.1	E980.6
Pyroxylin	976.3	E858.7	E946.3	E950.4	E962.0	E980.4
Pyrrobutamine	963.0	E858.1	E933.0	E950.4	E962.0	E980.4
Pyrrocaine	968.5	E855.2	E938.5	E950.4	E962.0	E980.4
Pyrvinium (pamoate)	961.6	E857	E931.6	E950.4	E962.0	E980.4
PZI	962.3	E858.0	E932.3	E950.4	E962.0	E980.4
Quaalude	967.4	E852.3	E937.4	E950.2	E962.0	E980.2
Quaternary ammonium derivatives	971.1	E855.4	E941.1	E950.4	E962.0	E980.4
Quicklime	983.2	E864.2	—	E950.7	E962.1	E980.6
Quinacrine	961.3	E857	E931.3	E950.4	E962.0	E980.4
Quinaglute	972.0	E858.3	E942.0	E950.4	E962.0	E980.4
Quinalbarbitone	967.0	E851	E937.0	E950.1	E962.0	E980.1
Quinestradiol	962.2	E858.0	E932.2	E950.4	E962.0	E980.4
Quinethazone	974.3	E858.5	E944.3	E950.4	E962.0	E980.4
Quinidine (gluconate) (polygalacturonate) (salts) (sulfate)	972.0	E858.3	E942.0	E950.4	E962.0	E980.4
Quinine	961.4	E857	E931.4	E950.4	E962.0	E980.4
Quiniobine	961.3	E857	E931.3	E950.4	E962.0	E980.4
Quinolines	961.3	E857	E931.3	E950.4	E962.0	E980.4
Quotane	968.5	E855.2	E938.5	E950.4	E962.0	E980.4
Rabies						
immune globulin (human)	964.6	E858.2	E934.6	E950.4	E962.0	E980.4
vaccine	979.1	E858.8	E949.1	E950.4	E962.0	E980.4
Racemoramide	965.09	E850.2	E935.2	E950.0	E962.0	E980.0
Racemorphan	965.09	E850.2	E935.2	E950.0	E962.0	E980.0
Radiator alcohol	980.1	E860.2	—	E950.9	E962.1	E980.9
Radio–opaque (drugs) (materials)	977.8	E858.8	E947.8	E950.4	E962.0	E980.4
Ranunculus	988.2	E865.4	—	E950.9	E962.1	E980.9
Rat poison	989.4	E863.7	—	E950.6	E962.1	E980.7
Rattlesnake (venom)	989.5	E905.0	—	E950.9	E962.1	E980.9
Raudixin	972.6	E858.3	E942.6	E950.4	E962.0	E980.4
Rautensin	972.6	E858.3	E942.6	E950.4	E962.0	E980.4
Rautina	972.6	E858.3	E942.6	E950.4	E962.0	E980.4
Rautotal	972.6	E858.3	E942.6	E950.4	E962.0	E980.4
Rauwiloid	972.6	E858.3	E942.6	E950.4	E962.0	E980.4
Rauwoldin	972.6	E858.3	E942.6	E950.4	E962.0	E980.4
Rauwolfia (alkaloids)	972.6	E858.3	E942.6	E950.4	E962.0	E980.4
Realgar	985.1	E866.3	—	E950.8	E962.1	E980.8
Red cells, packed	964.7	E858.2	E934.7	E950.4	E962.0	E980.4
Reducing agents, industrial NEC	983.9	E864.3	—	E950.7	E962.1	E980.6
Refrigerant gas (freon)	987.4	E869.2	—	E952.8	E962.2	E982.8
not freon	987.9	E869.9	—	E952.9	E962.2	E982.9
Regroton	974.4	E858.5	E944.4	E950.4	E962.0	E980.4
Rela	968.0	E855.1	E938.0	E950.4	E962.0	E980.4
Relaxants, skeletal muscle (autonomic)	975.2	E858.6	E945.2	E950.4	E962.0	E980.4
central nervous system	968.0	E855.1	E938.0	E950.4	E962.0	E980.4
Renese	974.3	E858.5	E944.3	E950.4	E962.0	E980.4
Renografin	977.8	E858.8	E947.8	E950.4	E962.0	E980.4
Replacement solutions	974.5	E858.5	E944.5	E950.4	E962.0	E980.4
Rescinnamine	972.6	E858.3	E942.6	E950.4	E962.0	E980.4
Reserpine	972.6	E858.3	E942.6	E950.4	E962.0	E980.4
Resorcin, resorcinol	976.4	E858.7	E946.4	E950.4	E962.0	E980.4
Respaire	975.5	E858.6	E945.5	E950.4	E962.0	E980.4

Substance	Poisoning	Accident	Therapeutic Use	Suicide Attempt	Assault	Undetermined
			External Cause (E-Code)			
Respiratory agents NEC	975.8	E858.6	E945.8	E950.4	E962.0	E980.4
Retinoic acid	976.8	E858.7	E946.8	E950.4	E962.0	E980.4
Retinol	963.5	E858.1	E933.5	E950.4	E962.0	E980.4
Rh₀ (D) immune globulin (human)	964.6	E858.2	E934.6	E950.4	E962.0	E980.4
Rhodine	965.1	E850.3	E935.3	E950.0	E962.0	E980.0
RhoGAM	964.6	E858.2	E934.6	E950.4	E962.0	E980.4
Riboflavin	963.5	E858.1	E933.5	E950.4	E962.0	E980.4
Ricin	989.89	E866.8	—	E950.9	E962.1	E980.9
Ricinus communis	988.2	E865.3	—	E950.9	E962.1	E980.9
Rickettsial vaccine NEC	979.6	E858.8	E949.6	E950.4	E962.0	E980.4
with viral and bacterial vaccine	979.7	E858.8	E949.7	E950.4	E962.0	E980.4
Rifampin	960.6	E856	E930.6	E950.4	E962.0	E980.4
Rimifon	961.8	E857	E931.8	E950.4	E962.0	E980.4
Ringer's injection (lactated)	974.5	E858.5	E944.5	E950.4	E962.0	E980.4
Ristocetin	960.8	E856	E930.8	E950.4	E962.0	E980.4
Ritalin	969.7	E854.2	E939.7	E950.3	E962.0	E980.3
Roach killers — *see* Pesticides						
Rocky Mountain spotted fever vaccine	979.6	E858.8	E949.6	E950.4	E962.0	E980.4
Rodenticides	989.4	E863.7	—	E950.6	E962.1	E980.7
Rolaids	973.0	E858.4	E943.0	E950.4	E962.0	E980.4
Rolitetracycline	960.4	E856	E930.4	E950.4	E962.0	E980.4
Romilar	975.4	E858.6	E945.4	E950.4	E962.0	E980.4
Rose water ointment	976.3	E858.7	E946.3	E950.4	E962.0	E980.4
Rotenone	989.4	E863.7	—	E950.6	E962.1	E980.7
Rotoxamine	963.0	E858.1	E933.0	E950.4	E962.0	E980.4
Rough–on–rats	989.4	E863.7	—	E950.6	E962.1	E980.7
Rubbing alcohol	980.2	E860.3	—	E950.9	E962.1	E980.9
Rubella virus vaccine	979.4	E858.8	E949.4	E950.4	E962.0	E980.4
Rubelogen	979.4	E858.8	E949.4	E950.4	E962.0	E980.4
Rubeovax	979.4	E858.8	E949.4	E950.4	E962.0	E980.4
Rubidomycin	960.7	E856	E930.7	E950.4	E962.0	E980.4
Rue	988.2	E965.4	—	E950.9	E962.1	E980.9
Ruta	988.2	E865.4	—	E950.9	E962.1	E980.9
Sabadilla (medicinal)	976.0	E858.7	E946.0	E950.4	E962.0	E980.4
pesticide	989.4	E863.4	—	E950.6	E962.1	E980.7
Sabin oral vaccine	979.5	E858.8	E949.5	E950.4	E962.0	E980.4
Saccharated iron oxide	964.0	E858.2	E934.0	E950.4	E962.0	E980.4
Saccharin	974.5	E858.5	E944.5	E950.4	E962.0	E980.4
Safflower oil	972.2	E858.3	E942.2	E950.4	E962.0	E980.4
Salbutamol sulfate	975.7	E858.6	E945.7	E950.4	E962.0	E980.4
Salicylamide	965.1	E850.3	E935.3	E950.0	E962.0	E980.0
Salicylate(s)	965.1	E850.3	E935.3	E950.0	E962.0	E980.0
methyl	976.3	E858.7	E946.3	E950.4	E962.0	E980.4
theobromine calcium	974.1	E858.5	E944.1	E950.4	E962.0	E980.4
Salicylazosulfapyridine	961.0	E857	E931.0	E950.4	E962.0	E980.4
Salicylhydroxamic acid	976.0	E858.7	E946.0	E950.4	E962.0	E980.4
Salicylic acid (keratolytic) NEC	976.4	E858.7	E946.4	E950.4	E962.0	E980.4
congeners	965.1	E850.3	E935.3	E950.0	E962.0	E980.0
salts	965.1	E850.3	E935.3	E950.0	E962.0	E980.0
Saliniazid	961.8	E857	E931.8	E950.4	E962.0	E980.4
Salol	976.3	E858.7	E946.3	E950.4	E962.0	E980.4
Salt (substitute) NEC	974.5	E858.5	E944.5	E950.4	E962.0	E980.4
Saluretics	974.3	E858.5	E944.3	E950.4	E962.0	E980.4
Saluron	974.3	E858.5	E944.3	E950.4	E962.0	E980.4
Salvarsan 606 (neosilver) (silver)	961.1	E857	E931.1	E950.4	E962.0	E980.4
Sambucus canadensis	988.2	E865.4	—	E950.9	E962.1	E980.9
berry	988.2	E865.3	—	E950.9	E962.1	E980.9

Substance	Poisoning	External Cause (E-Code)				
		Accident	Therapeutic Use	Suicide Attempt	Assault	Undetermined
Sandril	972.6	E858.3	E942.6	E950.4	E962.0	E980.4
Sanguinaria canadensis	988.2	E865.4	—	E950.9	E962.1	E980.9
Saniflush (cleaner)	983.9	E861.3	—	E950.7	E962.1	E980.6
Santonin	961.6	E857	E931.6	E950.4	E962.0	E980.4
Santyl	976.8	E858.7	E946.8	E950.4	E962.0	E980.4
Sarkomycin	960.7	E856	E930.7	E950.4	E962.0	E980.4
Saroten	969.0	E854.0	E939.0	E950.3	E962.0	E980.3
Saturnine – see Lead						
Savln (oll)	976.4	E858.7	E946.4	E950.4	E962.0	E980.4
Scammony	973.1	E858.4	E943.1	E950.4	E962.0	E980.4
Scarlet red	976.8	E858.7	E946.8	E950.4	E962.0	E980.4
Scheele's green	985.1	E866.3	—	E950.8	E962.1	E980.8
insecticide	985.1	E863.4	—	E950.8	E962.1	E980.8
Schradan	989.3	E863.1	—	E950.6	E962.1	E980.7
Schweinfurt (h) green	985.1	E866.3	—	E950.8	E962.1	E980.8
insecticide	985.1	E863.4	—	E950.8	E962.1	E980.8
Scilla — see Squill						
Sclerosing agents	972.7	E858.3	E942.7	E950.4	E962.0	E980.4
Scopolamine	971.1	E855.4	E941.1	E950.4	E962.0	E980.4
Scouring powder	989.89	E861.3	—	E950.9	E962.1	E980.9
Sea						
anemone (sting)	989.5	E905.6	—	E950.9	E962.1	E980.9
cucumber (sting)	989.5	E905.6	—	E950.9	E962.1	E980.9
snake (bite) (venom)	989.5	E905.0	—	E950.9	E962.1	E980.9
urchin spine (puncture)	989.5	E905.6	—	E950.9	E962.1	E980.9
Secbutabarbital	967.0	E851	E937.0	E950.1	E962.0	E980.1
Secbutabaritone	967.0	E851	E937.0	E950.1	E962.0	E980.1
Secobarbital	967.0	E851	E937.0	E950.1	E962.0	E980.1
Seconal	967.0	E851	E937.0	E950.1	E962.0	E980.1
Secretin	977.8	E858.8	E947.8	E950.4	E962.0	E980.4
Sedatives, nonbarbiturate	967.9	E852.9	E937.9	E950.2	E962.0	E980.2
specified NEC	967.8	E852.8	E937.8	E950.2	E962.0	E980.2
Sedormid	967.8	E852.8	E937.8	E950.2	E962.0	E980.2
Seed (plant)	988.2	E865.3	—	E950.9	E962.1	E980.9
disinfectant or dressing	989.89	E866.5	—	E950.9	E962.1	E980.9
Selenium (fumes) NEC	985.8	E866.4	—	E950.9	E962.1	E980.9
disulfide or sulfide	976.4	E858.7	E946.4	E950.4	E962.0	E980.4
Selsun	976.4	E858.7	E946.4	E950.4	E962.0	E980.4
Senna	973.1	E858.4	E943.1	E950.4	E962.0	E980.4
Septisol	976.2	E858.7	E946.2	E950.4	E962.0	E980.4
Serax	969.4	E853.2	E939.4	E950.3	E962.0	E980.3
Serenesil	967.8	E852.8	E937.8	E950.2	E962.0	E980.2
Serenium (hydrochloride)	961.9	E857	E931.9	E950.4	E962.0	E980.4
Serepax—see Oxazepam						
Sernyl	968.3	E855.1	E938.3	E950.4	E962.0	E980.4
Serotonin	977.8	E858.8	E947.8	E950.4	E962.0	E980.4
Serpasil	972.6	E858.3	E942.6	E950.4	E962.0	E980.4
Sewer gas	987.8	E869.8	—	E952.8	E962.2	E982.8
Shampoo	989.6	E861.0	—	E950.9	E962.1	E980.9
Shellfish, nonbacterial or noxious	988.0	E865.1	—	E950.9	E962.1	E980.9
Silicones NEC	989.83	E866.8	E947.8	E950.9	E962.1	E980.9
Silvadene	976.0	E858.7	E946.0	E950.4	E962.0	E980.4
Silver (compound) (medicinal) NEC	976.0	E858.7	E946.0	E950.4	E962.0	E980.4
anti–infectives	976.0	E858.7	E946.0	E950.4	E962.0	E980.4
arsphenamine	961.1	E857	E931.1	E950.4	E962.0	E980.4
nitrate	976.0	E858.7	E946.0	E950.4	E962.0	E980.4
ophthalmic preparation	976.5	E858.7	E946.5	E950.4	E962.0	E980.4

Substance	Poisoning	External Cause (E-Code)				
		Accident	Therapeutic Use	Suicide Attempt	Assault	Undetermined
toughened (keratolytic)	976.4	E858.7	E946.4	E950.4	E962.0	E980.4
nonmedicinal (dust)	985.8	E866.4	—	E950.9	E962.1	E980.9
protein (mild) (strong)	976.0	E858.7	E946.0	E950.4	E962.0	E980.4
salvarsan	961.1	E857	E931.1	E950.4	E962.0	E980.4
Simethicone	973.8	E858.4	E943.8	E950.4	E962.0	E980.4
Sinequan	969.0	E854.0	E939.0	E950.3	E962.0	E980.3
Singoserp	972.6	E858.3	E942.6	E950.4	E962.0	E980.4
Sintrom	964.2	E858.2	E934.2	E950.4	E962.0	E980.4
Sitosterols	972.2	E858.3	E942.2	E950.4	E962.0	E980.4
Skeletal muscle relaxants	975.2	E858.6	E945.2	E950.4	E962.0	E980.4
Skin						
agents (external)	976.9	E858.7	E946.9	E950.4	E962.0	E980.4
specified NEC	976.8	E858.7	E946.8	E950.4	E962.0	E980.4
test antigen	977.8	E858.8	E947.8	E950.4	E962.0	E980.4
Sleep–eze	963.0	E858.1	E933.0	E950.4	E962.0	E980.4
Sleeping draught (drug) (pill) (tablet)	967.9	E852.9	E937.9	E950.2	E962.0	E980.2
Smallpox vaccine	979.0	E858.8	E949.0	E950.4	E962.0	E980.4
Smelter fumes NEC	985.9	E866.4	—	E950.9	E962.1	E980.9
Smog	987.3	E869.1	—	E952.8	E962.2	E982.8
Smoke NEC	987.9	E869.9	—	E952.9	E962.2	E982.9
Smooth muscle relaxant	975.1	E858.6	E945.1	E950.4	E962.0	E980.4
Snail killer	989.4	E863.4	—	E950.6	E962.1	E980.7
Snake (bite) (venom)	989.5	E905.0	—	E950.9	E962.1	E980.9
Snuff	989.89	E866.8	—	E950.9	E962.1	E980.9
Soap (powder) (product)	989.6	E861.1	—	E950.9	E962.1	E980.9
medicinal, soft	976.2	E858.7	E946.2	E950.4	E962.0	E980.4
Soda (caustic)	983.2	E864.2	—	E950.7	E962.1	E980.6
bicarb	963.3	E858.1	E933.3	E950.4	E962.0	E980.4
chlorinated — *see* Sodium, hypochlorite						
Sodium						
acetosulfone	961.8	E857	E931.8	E950.4	E962.0	E980.4
acetrizoate	977.8	E858.8	E947.8	E950.4	E962.0	E980.4
amytal	967.0	E851	E937.0	E950.1	E962.0	E980.1
arsenate — *see* Arsenic						
bicarbonate	963.3	E858.1	E933.3	E950.4	E962.0	E980.4
bichromate	983.9	E864.3	—	E950.7	E962.1	E980.6
biphosphate	963.2	E858.1	E933.2	E950.4	E962.0	E980.4
bisulfate	983.9	E864.3	—	E950.7	E962.1	E980.6
borate (cleanser)	989.6	E861.3	—	E950.9	E962.1	E980.9
bromide NEC	967.3	E852.2	E937.3	E950.2	E962.0	E980.2
cacodylate (nonmedicinal) NEC	978.8	E858.8	E948.8	E950.4	E962.0	E980.4
anti–infective	961.1	E857	E931.1	E950.4	E962.0	E980.4
herbicide	989.4	E863.5	—	E950.6	E962.1	E980.7
calcium edetate	963.8	E858.1	E933.8	E950.4	E962.0	E980.4
carbonate NEC	983.2	E864.2	—	E950.7	E962.1	E980.6
chlorate NEC	983.9	E864.3	—	E950.7	E962.1	E980.6
herbicide	983.9	E863.5	—	E950.7	E962.1	E980.6
chloride NEC	974.5	E858.5	E944.5	E950.4	E962.0	E980.4
chromate	983.9	E864.3	—	E950.7	E962.1	E980.6
citrate	963.3	E858.1	E933.3	E950.4	E962.0	E980.4
cyanide — *see* Cyanide(s)						
cyclamate	974.5	E858.5	E944.5	E950.4	E962.0	E980.4
diatrizoate	977.8	E858.8	E947.8	E950.4	E962.0	E980.4
dibunate	975.4	E858.6	E945.4	E950.4	E962.0	E980.4
dioctyl sulfosuccinate	973.2	E858.4	E943.2	E950.4	E962.0	E980.4
edetate	963.8	E858.1	E933.8	E950.4	E962.0	E980.4
ethacrynate	974.4	E858.5	E944.4	E950.4	E962.0	E980.4

Substance	Poisoning	External Cause (E-Code)				
		Accident	Therapeutic Use	Suicide Attempt	Assault	Undetermined
fluoracetate (dust) (rodenticide)	989.4	E863.7	—	E950.6	E962.1	E980.7
fluoride — *see* Fluoride(s)						
free salt	974.5	E858.5	E944.5	E950.4	E962.0	E980.4
glucosulfone	961.8	E857	E931.8	E950.4	E962.0	E980.4
hydroxide	983.2	E864.2	—	E950.7	E962.1	E980.6
hypochlorite (bleach) NEC	983.9	E864.3	—	E950.7	E962.1	E980.6
disinfectant	983.9	E861.4	—	E950.7	E962.1	E980.6
medicinal (anti–infective) (external)	976.0	E858.7	E946.0	E950.4	E962.0	E980.4
vapor	987.8	E869.8	—	E952.8	E962.2	E982.8
hyposulfite	976.0	E858.7	E946.0	E950.4	E962.0	E980.4
indigotindisulfonate	977.8	E858.8	E947.8	E950.4	E962.0	E980.4
iodide	977.8	E858.8	E947.8	E950.4	E962.0	E980.4
iothalamate	977.8	E858.8	E947.8	E950.4	E962.0	E980.4
iron edetate	964.0	E858.2	E934.0	E950.4	E962.0	E980.4
lactate	963.3	E858.1	E933.3	E950.4	E962.0	E980.4
lauryl sulfate	976.2	E858.7	E946.2	E950.4	E962.0	E980.4
L–triiodothyronine	962.7	E858.0	E932.7	E950.4	E962.0	E980.4
metrizoate	977.8	E858.8	E947.8	E950.4	E962.0	E980.4
monofluoracetate (dust) (rodenticide)	989.4	E863.7	—	E950.6	E962.1	E980.7
morrhuate	972.7	E858.3	E942.7	E950.4	E962.0	E980.4
nafcillin	960.0	E856	E930.0	E950.4	E962.0	E980.4
nitrate (oxidizing agent)	983.9	E864.3	—	E950.7	E962.1	E980.6
nitrite (medicinal)	972.4	E858.3	E942.4	E950.4	E962.0	E980.4
nitroferricyanide	972.6	E858.3	E942.6	E950.4	E962.0	E980.4
nitroprusside	972.6	E858.3	E942.6	E950.4	E962.0	E980.4
para–aminohippurate	977.8	E858.8	E947.8	E950.4	E962.0	E980.4
perborate (non-medicinal) NEC	989.89	E866.8	—	E950.9	E962.1	E980.9
medicinal	976.6	E858.7	E946.6	E950.4	E962.0	E980.4
soap	989.6	E861.1	—	E950.9	E962.1	E980.9
percarbonate — *see* Sodium, perborate						
phosphate	973.3	E858.4	E943.3	E950.4	E962.0	E980.4
polystyrene sulfonate	974.5	E858.5	E944.5	E950.4	E962.0	E980.4
propionate	976.0	E858.7	E946.0	E950.4	E962.0	E980.4
psylliate	972.7	E858.3	E942.7	E950.4	E962.0	E980.4
removing resins	974.5	E858.5	E944.5	E950.4	E962.0	E980.4
salicylate	965.1	E850.3	E935.3	E950.0	E962.0	E980.0
sulfate	973.3	E858.4	E943.3	E950.4	E962.0	E980.4
sulfoxone	961.8	E857	E931.8	E950.4	E962.0	E980.4
tetradecyl sulfate	972.7	E858.3	E942.7	E950.4	E962.0	E980.4
thiopental	968.3	E855.1	E938.3	E950.4	E962.0	E980.4
thiosalicylate	965.1	E850.3	E935.3	E950.0	E962.0	E980.0
thiosulfate	976.0	E858.7	E946.0	E950.4	E962.0	E980.4
tolbutamide	977.8	E858.8	E947.8	E950.4	E962.0	E980.4
tyropanoate	977.8	E858.8	E947.8	E950.4	E962.0	E980.4
valproate	966.3	E855.0	E936.3	E950.4	E962.0	E980.4
Solanine	977.8	E858.8	E947.8	E950.4	E962.0	E980.4
Solanum dulcamara	988.2	E865.4	—	E950.9	E962.1	E980.9
Solapsone	961.8	E857	E931.8	E950.4	E962.0	E980.4
Solasulfone	961.8	E857	E931.8	E950.4	E962.0	E980.4
Soldering fluid	983.1	E864.1	—	E950.7	E962.1	E980.6
Solid substance	989.9	E866.9	—	E950.9	E962.1	E980.9
specified NEC	989.9	E866.8	—	E950.9	E962.1	E980.9
Solvents, industrial	982.8	E862.9	—	E950.9	E962.1	E980.9
naphtha	981	E862.0	—	E950.9	E962.1	E980.9
petroleum	981	E862.0	—	E950.9	E962.1	E980.9
specified NEC	982.8	E862.4	—	E950.9	E962.1	E980.9
Soma	968.0	E855.1	E938.0	E950.4	E962.0	E980.4

Substance	Poisoning	External Cause (E-Code)				
		Accident	Therapeutic Use	Suicide Attempt	Assault	Undetermined
Somatotropin	962.4	E858.0	E932.4	E950.4	E962.0	E980.4
Sominex	963.0	E858.1	E933.0	E950.4	E962.0	E980.4
Somnos	967.1	E852.0	E937.1	E950.2	E962.0	E980.2
Somonal	967.0	E851	E937.0	E950.1	E962.0	E980.1
Soneryl	967.0	E851	E937.0	E950.1	E962.0	E980.1
Soothing syrup	977.9	E858.9	E947.9	E950.5	E962.0	E980.5
Sopor	967.4	E852.3	E937.4	E950.2	E962.0	E980.2
Soporific drug	967.9	E852.9	E937.9	E950.2	E962.0	E980.2
specified type NEC	967.8	E852.8	E937.8	E950.2	E962.0	E980.2
Sorbitol NEC	977.4	E858.8	E947.4	E950.4	E962.0	E980.4
Sotradecol	972.7	E858.3	E942.7	E950.4	E962.0	E980.4
Spacoline	975.1	E858.6	E945.1	E950.4	E962.0	E980.4
Spanish fly	976.8	E858.7	E946.8	E950.4	E962.0	E980.4
Sparine	969.1	E853.0	E939.1	E950.3	E962.0	E980.3
Sparteine	975.0	E858.6	E945.0	E950.4	E962.0	E980.4
Spasmolytics	975.1	E858.6	E945.1	E950.4	E962.0	E980.4
anticholinergics	971.1	E855.4	E941.1	E950.4	E962.0	E980.4
Spectinomycin	960.8	E856	E930.8	E950.4	E962.0	E980.4
Speed	969.7	E854.2	E939.7	E950.3	E962.0	E980.3
Spermicides	976.8	E858.7	E946.8	E950.4	E962.0	E980.4
Spider (bite) (venom)	989.5	E905.1	—	E950.9	E962.1	E980.9
antivenin	979.9	E858.8	E949.9	E950.4	E962.0	E980.4
Spigelia (root)	961.6	E857	E931.6	E950.4	E962.0	E980.4
Spiperone	969.2	E853.1	E939.2	E950.3	E962.0	E980.3
Spiramycin	960.3	E856	E930.3	E950.4	E962.0	E980.4
Spirilene	969.5	E853.8	E939.5	E950.3	E962.0	E980.3
Spirit(s) (neutral) NEC	980.0	E860.1	—	E950.9	E962.1	E980.9
beverage	980.0	E860.0	—	E950.9	E962.1	E980.9
industrial	980.9	E860.9	—	E950.9	E962.1	E980.9
mineral	981	E862.0	—	E950.9	E962.1	E980.9
of salt — *see* Hydrochloric acid						
surgical	980.9	E860.9	—	E950.9	E962.1	E980.9
Spironolactone	974.4	E858.5	E944.4	E950.4	E962.0	E980.4
Sponge, absorbable (gelatin)	964.5	E858.2	E934.5	E950.4	E962.0	E980.4
Sporostacin	976.0	E858.7	E946.0	E950.4	E962.0	E980.4
Sprays (aerosol)	989.89	E866.8	—	E950.9	E962.1	E980.9
cosmetic	989.89	E866.7	—	E950.9	E962.1	E980.9
medicinal NEC	977.9	E858.9	E947.9	E950.5	E962.0	E980.5
pesticides — *see* Pesticides						
specified content — *see* substance						
specified						
Spurge flax	988.2	E865.4	—	E950.9	E962.1	E980.9
Spurges	988.2	E865.4	—	E950.9	E962.1	E980.9
Squill (expectorant) NEC	975.5	E858.6	E945.5	E950.4	E962.0	E980.4
rat poison	989.4	E863.7	—	E950.6	E962.1	E980.7
Squirting cucumber (cathartic)	973.1	E858.4	E943.1	E950.4	E962.0	E980.4
Stains	989.89	E866.8	—	E950.9	E962.1	E980.9
Stannous — *see also* Tin						
fluoride	976.7	E858.7	E946.7	E950.4	E962.0	E980.4
Stanolone	962.1	E858.0	E932.1	E950.4	E962.0	E980.4
Stanozolol	962.1	E853.0	E932.1	E950.4	E962.0	E980.4
Staphisagria or stavesacre (pediculicide)	976.0	E858.7	E946.0	E950.4	E962.0	E980.4
Stelazine	969.1	E853.0	E939.1	E950.3	E962.0	E980.3
Stemetil	969.1	E853.0	E939.1	E950.3	E962.0	E980.3
Sterculia (cathartic) (gum)	973.3	E858.4	E943.3	E950.4	E962.0	E980.4
Sternutator gas	987.8	E869.8	—	E952.8	E962.2	E982.8
Steroids NEC	962.0	E858.0	E932.0	E950.4	E962.0	E980.4

Substance	Poisoning	Accident	Therapeutic Use	Suicide Attempt	Assault	Undetermined
			External Cause (E-Code)			
ENT agent	976.6	E858.7	E946.6	E950.4	E962.0	E980.4
ophthalmic preparation	976.5	E858.7	E946.5	E950.4	E962.0	E980.4
topical NEC	976.0	E858.7	E946.0	E950.4	E962.0	E980.4
Stibine	985.8	E866.4	—	E950.9	E962.1	E980.9
Stibophen	961.2	E857	E931.2	E950.4	E962.0	E980.4
Stilbamide, stilbamidine	961.5	E857	E931.5	E950.4	E962.0	E980.4
Stilbestrol	962.2	E858.0	E932.2	E950.4	E962.0	E980.4
Stimulants (central nervous system)	970.9	E854.3	E940.9	E950.4	E962.0	E980.4
analeptics	970.0	E854.3	E940.0	E950.4	E962.0	E980.4
opiate antagonist	970.1	E854.3	E940.1	E950.4	E962.0	E980.4
psychotherapeutic NEC	969.0	E854.0	E939.0	E950.3	E962.0	E980.3
specified NEC	970.8	E854.3	E940.8	E950.4	E962.0	E980.4
Storage batteries (acid) (cells)	983.1	E864.1	—	E950.7	E962.1	E980.6
Stovaine	968.9	E855.2	E938.9	E950.4	E962.0	E980.4
infiltration (subcutaneous)	968.5	E855.2	E938.5	E950.4	E962.0	E980.4
nerve block (peripheral) (plexus)	968.6	E855.2	E938.6	E950.5	E962.0	E980.4
spinal	968.7	E855.2	E938.7	E950.4	E962.0	E980.4
topical (surface)	968.5	E855.2	E938.5	E950.4	E962.0	E980.4
Stovarsal	961.1	E857	E931.1	E950.4	E962.0	E980.4
Stove gas — see Gas, utility						
Stoxil	976.5	E858.7	E946.5	E950.4	E962.0	E980.4
STP	969.6	E854.1	E939.6	E950.3	E962.0	E980.3
Stramonium (medicinal) NEC	971.1	E855.4	E941.1	E950.4	E962.0	E980.4
natural state	988.2	E865.4	—	E950.9	E962.1	E980.9
Streptodornase	964.4	E858.2	E934.4	E950.4	E962.0	E980.4
Streptoduocin	960.6	E856	E930.6	E950.4	E962.0	E980.4
Streptokinase	964.4	E858.2	E934.4	E950.4	E962.0	E980.4
Streptomycin	960.6	E856	E930.6	E950.4	E962.0	E980.4
Streptozocin	960.7	E856	E930.7	E950.4	E962.0	E980.4
Stripper (paint) (solvent)	982.8	E862.9	—	E950.9	E962.1	E980.9
Strobane	989.2	E863.0	—	E950.6	E962.1	E980.7
Strophanthin	972.1	E858.3	E942.1	E950.4	E962.0	E980.4
Strophanthus hispidus or kombe	988.2	E865.4	—	E950.9	E962.1	E980.9
Strychnine (rodenticide) (salts)	989.1	E863.7	—	E950.6	E962.1	E980.7
medicinal NEC	970.8	E854.3	E940.8	E950.4	E962.0	E980.4
Strychnos (ignatii) — see Strychnine						
Styramate	968.0	E855.1	E938.0	E950.4	E962.0	E980.4
Styrene	983.0	E864.0	—	E950.7	E962.1	E980.6
Succinimide (anticonvulsant)	966.2	E855.0	E936.2	E950.4	E962.0	E980.4
mercuric — see Mercury						
Succinylcholine	975.2	E858.6	E945.2	E950.4	E962.0	E980.4
Succinylsulfathiazole	961.0	E857	E931.0	E950.4	E962.0	E980.4
Sucrose	974.5	E858.5	E944.5	E950.4	E962.0	E980.4
Sulfacetamide	961.0	E857	E931.0	E950.4	E962.0	E980.4
ophthalmic preparation	976.5	E858.7	E946.5	E950.4	E962.0	E980.4
Sulfachlorpyridazine	961.0	E857	E931.0	E950.4	E962.0	E980.4
Sulfacytine	961.0	E857	E931.0	E950.4	E962.0	E980.4
Sulfadiazine	961.0	E857	E931.0	E950.4	E962.0	E980.4
silver (topical)	976.0	E858.7	E946.0	E950.4	E962.0	E980.4
Sulfadimethoxine	961.0	E857	E931.0	E950.4	E962.0	E980.4
Sulfadimidine	961.0	E857	E931.0	E950.4	E962.0	E980.4
Sulfaethidole	961.0	E857	E931.0	E950.4	E962.0	E980.4
Sulfafurazole	961.0	E857	E931.0	E950.4	E962.0	E980.4
Sulfaguanidine	961.0	E857	E931.0	E950.4	E962.0	E980.4
Sulfamerazine	961.0	E857	E931.0	E950.4	E962.0	E980.4
Sulfameter	961.0	E857	E931.0	E950.4	E962.0	E980.4
Sulfamethizole	961.0	E857	E931.0	E950.4	E962.0	E980.4

Substance	Poisoning	Accident	Therapeutic Use	Suicide Attempt	Assault	Undetermined
			External Cause (E-Code)			
Sulfamethoxazole	961.0	E857	E931.0	E950.4	E962.0	E980.4
Sulfamethoxydiazine	961.0	E857	E931.0	E950.4	E962.0	E980.4
Sulfamethoxypyridazine	961.0	E857	E931.0	E950.4	E962.0	E980.4
Sulfamethylthiazole	961.0	E857	E931.0	E950.4	E962.0	E980.4
Sulfamylon	976.0	E858.7	E946.0	E950.4	E962.0	E980.4
Sulfan blue (diagnostic dye)	977.8	E858.8	E947.8	E950.4	E962.0	E980.4
Sulfanilamide	961.0	E857	E931.0	E950.4	E962.0	E980.4
Sulfanilylguanidine	961.0	E857	E931.0	E950.4	E962.0	E980.4
Sulfaphenazole	961.0	E857	E931.0	E950.4	E962.0	E980.4
Sulfaphenylthiazole	961.0	E857	E931.0	E950.4	E962.0	E980.4
Sulfaproxyline	961.0	E857	E931.0	E950.4	E962.0	E980.4
Sulfapyridine	961.0	E857	E931.0	E950.4	E962.0	E980.4
Sulfapyrimidine	961.0	E857	E931.0	E950.4	E962.0	E980.4
Sulfarsphenamine	961.1	E857	E931.1	E950.4	E962.0	E980.4
Sulfasalazine	961.0	E857	E931.0	E950.4	E962.0	E980.4
Sulfasomizole	961.0	E857	E931.0	E950.4	E962.0	E980.4
Sulfasuxidine	961.0	E857	E931.0	E950.4	E962.0	E980.4
Sulfinpyrazone	974.7	E858.5	E944.7	E950.4	E962.0	E980.4
Sulfisoxazole	961.0	E857	E931.0	E950.4	E962.0	E980.4
ophthalmic preparation	976.5	E858.7	E946.5	E950.4	E962.0	E980.4
Sulfomyxin	960.8	E856	E930.8	E950.4	E962.0	E980.4
Sulfonal	967.8	E852.8	E937.8	E950.2	E962.0	E980.2
Sulfonamides (mixtures)	961.0	E857	E931.0	E950.4	E962.0	E980.4
Sulfones	961.8	E857	E931.8	E950.4	E962.0	E980.4
Sulfonethylmethane	967.8	E852.8	E937.8	E950.2	E962.0	E980.2
Sulfonmethane	967.8	E852.8	E937.8	E950.2	E962.0	E980.2
Sulfonphthal, sulfonphthol	977.8	E858.8	E947.8	E950.4	E962.0	E980.4
Sulfonylurea derivatives, oral	962.3	E858.0	E932.3	E950.4	E962.0	E980.4
Sulfoxone	961.8	E857	E931.8	E950.4	E962.0	E980.4
Sulfur, sulfureted, sulfuric, sulfurous, sulfuryl (compounds) NEC	989.89	E866.8	—	E950.9	E962.1	E980.9
acid	983.1	E864.1	—	E950.7	E962.1	E980.6
dioxide	987.3	E869.1	—	E952.8	E962.2	E982.8
ether — *see* Ether(s)						
hydrogen	987.8	E869.8	—	E952.8	E962.2	E982.8
medicinal (keratolytic) (ointment) NEC	976.4	E858.7	E946.4	E950.4	E962.0	E980.4
pesticide (vapor)	989.4	E863.4	—	E950.6	E962.1	E980.7
vapor NEC	987.8	E869.8	—	E952.8	E962.2	E982.8
Sulkowitch's reagent	977.8	E858.8	E947.8	E950.4	E962.0	E980.4
Sulph — *see also* Sulf–						
Sulphadione	961.8	E857	E931.8	E950.4	E962.0	E980.4
Sulthiame, sultiame	966.3	E855.0	E936.3	E950.4	E962.0	E980.4
Superinone	975.5	E858.6	E945.5	E950.4	E962.0	E980.4
Suramin	961.5	E857	E931.5	E950.4	E962.0	E980.4
Surfacaine	968.5	E855.2	E938.5	E950.4	E962.0	E980.4
Surital	968.3	E855.1	E938.3	E950.4	E962.0	E980.4
Sutilains	976.8	E858.7	E946.8	E950.4	E962.0	E980.4
Suxamethoniam (bromide) (chloride) (iodide)	975.2	E858.6	E945.2	E950.4	E962.0	E980.4
Suxethonium (bromide)	975.2	E858.6	E945.2	E950.4	E962.0	E980.4
Sweet oil (birch)	976.3	E858.7	E946.3	E950.4	E962.0	E980.4
Sym–dichloroethyl ether	982.3	E862.4	—	E950.9	E962.1	E980.9
Sympatholytics	971.3	E855.6	E941.3	E950.4	E962.0	E980.4
Sympathomimetics	971.2	E855.5	E941.2	E950.4	E962.0	E980.4
Synalar	976.0	E858.7	E946.0	E950.4	E962.0	E980.4
Synthroid	962.7	E858.0	E932.7	E950.4	E962.0	E980.4
Syntocinon	975.0	E858.6	E945.0	E950.4	E962.0	E950.4

Substance	Poisoning	External Cause (E-Code)				
		Accident	Therapeutic Use	Suicide Attempt	Assault	Undetermined
Syrosingopine	972.6	E858.3	E942.6	E950.4	E962.0	E980.4
Systemic agents (primarily)	963.9	E858.1	E933.9	E950.4	E962.0	E980.4
specified NEC	963.8	E858.1	E933.8	E950.4	E962.0	E980.4
Tablets (see also specified substance)	977.9	E858.9	E947.9	E950.5	E962.0	E980.5
Tace	962.2	E858.0	E932.2	E950.4	E962.0	E980.4
Tacrine	971.0	E855.3	E941.0	E950.4	E962.0	E980.4
Talbutal	967.0	E851	E937.0	E950.1	E962.0	E980.1
Talc	976.3	E858.7	E946.3	E950.4	E962.0	E980.4
Talcum	976.3	E858.7	E946.3	E950.4	E962.0	E980.4
Tandearil, tanderil	965.5	E850.5	E935.5	E950.0	E962.0	E980.0
Tannic acid	983.1	E864.1	—	E950.7	E962.1	E980.6
medicinal (astringent)	976.2	E858.7	E946.2	E950.4	E962.0	E980.4
Tannin — see Tannic acid						
Tansy	988.2	E865.4	—	E950.9	E962.1	E980.9
TAO	960.3	E856	E930.3	E950.4	E962.0	E980.4
Tapazole	962.8	E858.0	E932.8	E950.4	E962.0	E980.4
Tar NEC	983.0	E864.0	—	E950.7	E962.1	E980.6
camphor — see Naphthalene						
fumes	987.8	E869.8	—	E952.8	E962.2	E982.8
Taractan	969.3	E853.8	E939.3	E950.3	E962.0	E980.3
Tarantula (venomous)	989.5	E905.1	—	E950.9	E962.1	E980.9
Tartar emetic (anti–infective)	961.2	E857	E931.2	E950.4	E962.0	E980.4
Tartaric acid	983.1	E864.1	—	E950.7	E962.1	E980.6
Tartrated antimony (anti–infective)	961.2	E857	E931.2	E950.4	E962.0	E980.4
TCA — see Trichloroacetic acid						
TDI	983.0	E864.0	—	E950.7	E962.1	E980.6
vapor	987.8	E869.8	—	E952.8	E962.2	E982.8
Tear gas	987.5	E869.3	—	E952.8	E962.2	E982.8
Teclothiazide	974.3	E858.5	E944.3	E950.4	E962.0	E980.4
Tegretol	966.3	E855.0	E936.3	E950.4	E962.0	E980.4
Telepaque	977.8	E858.8	E947.8	E950.4	E962.0	E980.4
Tellurium	985.8	E866.4	—	E950.9	E962.1	E980.9
fumes	985.8	E866.4	—	E950.9	E962.1	E980.9
TEM	963.1	E858.1	E933.1	E950.4	E962.0	E980.4
Temazepan—see Benzodiazepines						
TEPA	963.1	E858.1	E933.1	E950.4	E962.0	E980.4
TEPP	989.3	E863.1	—	E950.6	E962.1	E980.7
Terbutaline	971.2	E855.5	E941.2	E950.4	E962.0	E980.4
Teroxalene	961.6	E857	E931.6	E950.4	E962.0	E980.4
Terpin hydrate	975.5	E858.6	E945.5	E950.4	E962.0	E980.4
Terramycin	960.4	E856	E930.4	E950.4	E962.0	E980.4
Tessalon	975.4	E858.6	E945.4	E950.4	E962.0	E980.4
Testosterone	962.1	E858.0	E932.1	E950.4	E962.0	E980.4
Tetanus (vaccine)	978.4	E858.8	E948.4	E950.4	E962.0	E980.4
antitoxin	979.9	E858.8	E949.9	E950.4	E962.0	E980.4
immune globulin (human)	964.6	E858.2	E934.6	E950.4	E962.0	E980.4
toxoid	978.4	E858.8	E948.4	E950.4	E962.0	E980.4
with diphtheria toxoid	978.9	E858.8	E948.9	E950.4	E962.0	E980.4
with pertussis	978.6	E858.8	E948.6	E950.4	E962.0	E980.4
Tetrabenazine	969.5	E853.8	E939.5	E950.3	E962.0	E980.3
Tetracaine (infiltration) (topical)	968.5	E855.2	E938.5	E950.4	E962.0	E980.4
nerve block (peripheral) (plexus)	968.6	E855.2	E938.6	E950.4	E962.0	E980.4
spinal	968.7	E855.2	E938.7	E950.4	E962.0	E980.4
Tetrachlorethylene—see Tetrachloroethylene						
Tetrachlormethiazide	974.3	E858.5	E944.3	E950.4	E962.0	E980.4
Tetrachloroethane (liquid) (vapor)	982.3	E862.4	—	E950.9	E962.1	E980.9
paint or varnish	982.3	E861.6	—	E950.9	E962.1	E980.9

1305

Substance	Poisoning	External Cause (E-Code)				
		Accident	Therapeutic Use	Suicide Attempt	Assault	Undetermined
Tetrachloroethylene (liquid) (vapor)	982.3	E862.4	—	E950.9	E962.1	E980.9
medicinal	961.6	E857	E931.6	E950.4	E962.0	E980.4
Tetrachloromethane — *see* Carbon, tetrachloride						
Tetracycline	960.4	E856	E930.4	E950.4	E962.0	E980.4
ophthalmic preparation	976.5	E858.7	E946.5	E950.4	E962.0	E980.4
topical NEC	976.0	E858.7	E946.0	E950.4	E962.0	E980.4
Tetraethylammonium chloride	972.3	E858.3	E942.3	E950.4	E962.0	E980.4
Tetraethyl lead (antiknock compound)	984.1	E862.1	—	E950.9	E962.1	E980.9
Tetraethyl pyrophosphate	989.3	E863.1	—	E950.6	E962.1	E980.7
Tetraethylthiuram disulfide	977.3	E858.8	E947.3	E950.4	E962.0	E980.4
Tetrahydroaminoacridine	971.0	E855.3	E941.0	E950.4	E962.0	E980.4
Tetrahydrocannabinol	969.6	E854.1	E939.6	E950.3	E962.0	E980.3
Tetrahydronaphthalene	982.0	E862.4	—	E950.9	E962.1	E980.9
Tetrahydrozoline	971.2	E855.5	E941.2	E950.4	E962.0	E980.4
Tetralin	982.0	E862.4	—	E950.9	E962.1	E980.9
Tetramethylthiuram (disulfide) NEC	989.4	E863.6	—	E950.6	E962.1	E980.7
medicinal	976.2	E858.7	E946.2	E950.4	E962.0	E980.4
Tetronal	967.8	E852.8	E937.8	E950.2	E962.0	E980.2
Tetryl	983.0	E864.0	—	E950.7	E962.1	E980.6
Thalidomide	967.8	E852.8	E937.8	E950.2	E962.0	E980.2
Thallium (compounds) (dust) NEC	985.8	E866.4	—	E950.9	E962.1	E980.9
pesticide (rodenticide)	985.8	E863.7	—	E950.6	E962.1	E980.7
THC	969.6	E854.1	E939.6	E950.3	E962.0	E980.3
Thebacon	965.09	E850.2	E935.2	E950.0	E962.0	E980.0
Thebaine	965.09	E850.2	E935.2	E950.0	E962.0	E980.0
Theobromine (calcium salicylate)	974.1	E858.5	E944.1	E950.4	E962.0	E980.4
Theophylline (diuretic)	974.1	E858.5	E944.1	E950.4	E962.0	E980.4
ethylenediamine	975.7	E858.6	E945.7	E950.4	E962.0	E980.4
Thiabendazole	961.6	E857	E931.6	E950.4	E962.0	E980.4
Thialbarbital, thialbarbitone	968.3	E855.1	E938.3	E950.4	E962.0	E980.4
Thiamine	963.5	E858.1	E933.5	E950.4	E962.0	E980.4
Thiamylal (sodium)	968.3	E855.1	E938.3	E950.4	E962.0	E980.4
Thiazesim	969.0	E854.0	E939.0	E950.3	E962.0	E980.3
Thiazides (diuretics)	974.3	E858.5	E944.3	E950.4	E962.0	E980.4
Thiethylperazine	963.0	E858.1	E933.0	E950.4	E962.0	E980.4
Thimerosal (topical)	976.0	E858.7	E946.0	E950.4	E962.0	E980.4
ophthalmic preparation	976.5	E858.7	E946.5	E950.4	E962.0	E980.4
Thioacetazone	961.8	E857	E931.8	E950.4	E962.0	E980.4
Thiobarbiturates	968.3	E855.1	E938.3	E950.4	E962.0	E980.4
Thiobismol	961.2	E857	E931.2	E950.4	E962.0	E980.4
Thiocarbamide	962.8	E858.0	E932.8	E950.4	E962.0	E980.4
Thiocarbarsone	961.1	E857	E931.1	E950.4	E962.0	E980.4
Thiocarlide	961.8	E857	E931.8	E950.4	E962.0	E980.4
Thioguanine	963.1	E858.1	E933.1	E950.4	E962.0	E980.4
Thiomercaptomerin	974.0	E858.5	E944.0	E950.4	E962.0	E980.4
Thiomerin	974.0	E858.5	E944.0	E950.4	E962.0	E980.4
Thiopental, thiopentone (sodium)	968.3	E855.1	E938.3	E950.4	E962.0	E980.4
Thiopropazate	969.1	E853.0	E939.1	E950.3	E962.0	E980.3
Thioproperazine	969.1	E853.0	E939.1	E950.3	E962.0	E980.3
Thioridazine	969.1	E853.0	E939.1	E950.3	E962.0	E980.3
Thio–TEPA, thiotepa	963.1	E858.1	E933.1	E950.4	E962.0	E980.4
Thiothixene	969.3	E853.8	E939.3	E950.3	E962.0	E980.3
Thiouracil	962.8	E858.0	E932.8	E950.4	E962.0	E980.4
Thiourea	962.8	E858.0	E932.8	E950.4	E962.0	E980.4
Thiphenamil	971.1	E855.4	E941.1	E950.4	E962.0	E980.4
Thiram NEC	989.4	E863.6	—	E950.6	E962.1	E980.7

Substance	Poisoning	External Cause (E-Code)				
		Accident	Therapeutic Use	Suicide Attempt	Assault	Undetermined
medicinal	976.2	E858.7	E946.2	E950.4	E962.0	E980.4
Thonzylamine	963.0	E858.1	E933.0	E950.4	E962.0	E980.4
Thorazine	969.1	E853.0	E939.1	E950.3	E962.0	E980.3
Thornapple	988.2	E865.4	—	E950.9	E962.1	E980.9
Throat preparation (lozenges) NEC	976.6	E858.7	E946.6	E950.4	E962.0	E980.4
Thrombin	964.5	E858.2	E934.5	E950.4	E962.0	E980.4
Thrombolysin	964.4	E858.2	E934.4	E950.4	E962.0	E980.4
Thymol	983.0	E864.0	—	E950.7	E962.1	E980.6
Thymus extract	962.9	E858.0	E932.9	E950.4	E962.0	E980.4
Thyroglobulin	962.7	E858.0	E932.7	E950.4	E962.0	E980.4
Thyroid (derivatives) (extract)	962.7	E858.0	E932.7	E950.4	E962.0	E980.4
Thyrolar	962.7	E858.0	E932.7	E950.4	E962.0	E980.4
Thyrothrophin, thyrotropin	977.8	E858.8	E947.8	E950.4	E962.0	E980.4
Thyroxin(e)	962.7	E858.0	E932.7	E950.4	E962.0	E980.4
Tigan	963.0	E858.1	E933.0	E950.4	E962.0	E980.4
Tigloidine	968.0	E855.1	E938.0	E950.4	E962.0	E980.4
Tin (chloride) (dust) (oxide) NEC	985.8	E866.4	—	E950.9	E962.1	E980.9
anti-infectives	961.2	E857	E931.2	E950.4	E962.0	E980.4
Tinactin	976.0	E858.7	E946.0	E950.4	E962.0	E980.4
Tincture, iodine — *see* Iodine						
Tindal	969.1	E853.0	E939.1	E950.3	E962.0	E980.3
Titanium (compounds) (vapor)	985.8	E866.4	—	E950.9	E962.1	E980.9
ointment	976.3	E858.7	E946.3	E950.4	E962.0	E980.4
Titroid	962.7	E858.0	E932.7	E950.4	E962.0	E980.4
TMTD — *see* Tetramethylthiuram disulfide						
TNT	989.89	E866.8	—	E950.9	E962.1	E980.9
fumes	987.8	E869.8	—	E952.8	E962.2	E982.8
Toadstool	988.1	E865.5	—	E950.9	E962.1	E980.9
Tobacco NEC	989.84	E866.8	—	E950.9	E962.1	E980.9
Indian	988.2	E865.4	—	E950.9	E962.1	E980.9
smoke, second-hand	987.8	E869.4	—	—	—	—
Tocopherol	963.5	E858.1	E933.5	E950.4	E962.0	E980.4
Tocosamine	975.0	E858.6	E945.0	E950.4	E962.0	E980.4
Tofranil	969.0	E854.0	E939.0	E950.3	E962.0	E980.3
Toilet deodorizer	989.8	E866.8	—	E950.9	E962.1	E980.9
Tolazamide	962.3	E858.0	E932.3	E950.4	E962.0	E980.4
Tolazoline	971.3	E855.6	E941.3	E950.4	E962.0	E980.4
Tolbutamide	962.3	E858.0	E932.3	E950.4	E962.0	E980.4
sodium	977.8	E858.8	E947.8	E950.4	E962.0	E980.4
Tolmetin	965.6	E856.0	E935.6	E950.0	E962.0	E980.0
Tolnaftate	976.0	E858.7	E946.0	E950.4	E962.0	E980.4
Tolpropamine	976.1	E858.7	E946.1	E950.4	E962.0	E980.4
Tolserol	968.0	E855.1	E938.0	E950.4	E962.0	E980.4
Toluene (liquid) (vapor)	982.0	E862.4	—	E950.9	E962.1	E980.9
diisocyanate	983.0	E864.0	—	E950.7	E962.1	E980.6
Toluidine	983.0	E864.0	—	E950.7	E962.1	E980.6
vapor	987.8	E869.8	—	E952.8	E962.2	E982.8
Toluol (liquid) (vapor)	982.0	E862.4	—	E950.9	E962.1	E980.9
Tolylene–2,4–diisocyanate	983.0	E864.0	—	E950.7	E962.1	E980.6
Tonics, cardiac	972.1	E858.3	E942.1	E950.4	E962.0	E980.4
Toxaphene (dust) (spray)	989.2	E863.0	—	E950.6	E962.1	E980.7
Toxoids NEC	978.8	E858.8	E948.8	E950.4	E962.0	E980.4
Tractor fuel NEC	981	E862.1	—	E950.9	E962.1	E980.9
Tragacanth	973.3	E858.4	E943.3	E950.4	E962.0	E980.4
Tramazoline	971.2	E855.5	E941.2	E950.4	E962.0	E980.4
Tranquilizers	969.5	E853.9	E939.5	E950.3	E962.0	E980.3
benzodiazepine–based	969.4	E853.2	E939.4	E950.3	E962.0	E980.3

Substance	Poisoning	External Cause (E-Code)				
		Accident	Therapeutic Use	Suicide Attempt	Assault	Undetermined
butyrophenone–based	969.2	E853.1	E939.2	E950.3	E962.0	E980.3
major NEC	969.3	E853.8	E939.3	E950.3	E962.0	E980.3
phenothiazine–based	969.1	E853.0	E939.1	E950.3	E962.0	E980.3
specified NEC	969.5	E853.8	E939.5	E950.3	E962.0	E980.3
Trantoin	961.9	E857	E931.9	E950.4	E962.0	E980.4
Tranxene	969.4	E853.2	E939.4	E950.3	E962.0	E980.3
Tranylcypromine (sulfate)	969.0	E854.0	E939.0	E950.3	E962.0	E980.3
Trasentine	975.1	E858.6	E945.1	E950.4	E962.0	E980.4
Travert	974.5	E858.5	E944.5	E950.4	E962.0	E980.4
Trecator	961.8	E857	E931.8	E950.4	E962.0	E980.4
Tretinoin	976.8	E858.7	E946.8	E950.4	E962.0	E980.4
Triacetin	976.0	E858.7	E946.0	E950.4	E962.0	E980.4
Triacetyloleandomycin	960.3	E856	E930.3	E950.4	E962.0	E980.4
Triamcinolone	962.0	E858.0	E932.0	E950.4	E962.0	E980.4
ENT agent	976.6	E858.7	E946.6	E950.4	E962.0	E980.4
ophthalmic preparation	976.5	E858.7	E946.5	E950.4	E962.0	E980.4
topical NEC	976.0	E858.7	E946.0	E950.4	E962.0	E980.4
Triamterene	974.4	E858.5	E944.4	E950.4	E962.0	E980.4
Triaziquone	963.1	E858.1	E933.1	E950.4	E962.0	E980.4
Tribromacetaldehyde	967.3	E852.2	E937.3	E950.2	E962.0	E980.2
Tribromoethanol	968.2	E855.1	E938.2	E950.4	E962.0	E980.4
Tribromomethane	967.3	E852.2	E937.3	E950.2	E962.0	E980.2
Trichlorethane	982.3	E862.4	—	E950.9	E962.1	E980.9
Trichlormethiazide	974.3	E858.5	E944.3	E950.4	E962.0	E980.4
Trichloroacetic acid	983.1	E864.1	—	E950.7	E962.1	E980.6
medicinal (keratolytic)	976.4	E858.7	E946.4	E950.4	E962.0	E980.4
Trichloroethanol	967.1	E852.0	E937.1	E950.2	E962.0	E980.2
Trichloroethylene (liquid) (vapor)	982.3	E862.4	—	E950.9	E962.1	E980.9
anesthetic (gas)	968.2	E855.1	E938.2	E950.4	E962.0	E980.4
Trichloroethyl phosphate	967.1	E852.0	E937.1	E950.2	E962.0	E980.2
Trichlorofluoromethane NEC	987.4	E869.2	—	E952.8	E962.2	E982.8
Trichlorotriethylamine	963.1	E858.1	E933.1	E950.4	E962.0	E980.4
Trichomonacides NEC	961.5	E857	E931.5	E950.4	E962.0	E980.4
Trichomycin	960.1	E856	E930.1	E950.4	E962.0	E980.4
Triclofos	967.1	E852.0	E937.1	E950.2	E962.0	E980.2
Tricresyl phosphate	989.89	E866.8	—	E950.9	E962.1	E980.9
solvent	982.8	E862.4	—	E950.9	E962.1	E980.9
Tricyclamol	966.4	E855.0	E936.4	E950.4	E962.0	E980.4
Tridesilon	976.0	E858.7	E946.0	E950.4	E962.0	E980.4
Tridihexethyl	971.1	E855.4	E941.1	E950.4	E962.0	E980.4
Tridione	966.0	E855.0	E936.0	E950.4	E962.0	E980.4
Triethanolamine NEC	983.2	E864.2	—	E950.7	E962.1	E980.6
detergent	983.2	E861.0	—	E950.7	E962.1	E980.6
trinitrate	972.4	E858.3	E942.4	E950.4	E962.0	E980.4
Triethanomelamine	963.1	E858.1	E933.1	E950.4	E962.0	E980.4
Triethylene melamine	963.1	E858.1	E933.1	E950.4	E962.0	E980.4
Triethylenephosphoramide	963.1	E858.1	E933.1	E950.4	E962.0	E980.4
Triethylenethiophosphoramide	963.1	E858.1	E933.1	E950.4	E962.0	E980.4
Trifluoperazine	969.1	E853.0	E939.1	E950.3	E962.0	E980.3
Trifluperidol	969.2	E853.1	E939.2	E950.3	E962.0	E980.3
Triflupromazine	969.1	E853.0	E939.1	E950.3	E962.0	E980.3
Trihexyphenidyl	971.1	E855.4	E941.1	E950.4	E962.0	E980.4
Triiodothyronine	962.7	E858.0	E932.7	E950.4	E962.0	E980.4
Trilene	968.2	E855.1	E938.2	E950.4	E962.0	E980.4
Trimeprazine	963.0	E858.1	E933.0	E950.4	E962.0	E980.4
Trimetazidine	972.4	E858.3	E942.4	E950.4	E962.0	E980.4
Trimethadione	966.0	E855.0	E936.0	E950.4	E962.0	E980.4

Substance	Poisoning	External Cause (E-Code)				
		Accident	Therapeutic Use	Suicide Attempt	Assault	Undetermined
Trimethaphan	972.3	E858.3	E942.3	E950.4	E962.0	E980.4
Trimethidinium	972.3	E858.3	E942.3	E950.4	E962.0	E980.4
Trimethobenzamide	963.0	E858.1	E933.0	E950.4	E962.0	E980.4
Trimethylcarbinol	980.8	E860.8	—	E950.9	E962.1	E980.9
Trimethylpsoralen	976.3	E858.7	E946.3	E950.4	E962.0	E980.4
Trimeton	963.0	E858.1	E933.0	E950.4	E962.0	E980.4
Trimipramine	969.0	E854.0	E939.0	E950.3	E962.0	E980.3
Trimustine	963.1	E858.1	E933.1	E950.4	E962.0	E980.4
Trinitrin	972.4	E858.3	E942.4	E950.4	E962.0	E980.4
Trinitrophenol	983.0	E864.0	—	E950.7	E962.1	E980.6
Trinitrotoluene	989.89	E866.8	—	E950.9	E962.1	E980.9
fumes	987.8	E869.8	—	E952.8	E962.2	E982.8
Trional	967.8	E852.8	E937.8	E950.2	E962.0	E980.2
Trioxide of arsenic — see Arsenic						
Trioxsalen	976.3	E858.7	E946.3	E950.4	E962.0	E980.4
Tripelennamine	963.0	E858.1	E933.0	E950.4	E962.0	E980.4
Triperidol	969.2	E853.1	E939.2	E950.3	E962.0	E980.3
Triprolidine	963.0	E858.1	E933.0	E950.4	E962.0	E980.4
Trisoralen	976.3	E858.7	E946.3	E950.4	E962.0	E980.4
Troleandomycin	960.3	E856	E930.3	E950.4	E962.0	E980.4
Trolnitrate (phosphate)	972.4	E858.3	E942.4	E950.4	E962.0	E980.4
Trometamol	963.3	E858.1	E933.3	E950.4	E962.0	E980.4
Tromethamine	963.3	E858.1	E933.3	E950.4	E962.0	E980.4
Tronothane	968.5	E855.2	E938.5	E950.4	E962.0	E980.4
Tropicamide	971.1	E855.4	E941.1	E950.4	E962.0	E980.4
Troxidone	966.0	E855.0	E936.0	E950.4	E962.0	E980.4
Tryparsamide	961.1	E857	E931.1	E950.4	E962.0	E980.4
Trypsin	963.4	E858.1	E933.4	E950.4	E962.0	E980.4
Tryptizol	969.0	E854.0	E939.0	E950.3	E962.0	E980.3
Tuaminoheptane	971.2	E855.5	E941.2	E950.4	E962.0	E980.4
Tuberculin (old)	977.8	E858.8	E947.8	E950.4	E962.0	E980.4
Tubocurare	975.2	E858.6	E945.2	E950.4	E962.0	E980.4
Tubocurarine	975.2	E858.6	E945.2	E950.4	E962.0	E980.4
Turkish green	969.6	E854.1	E939.6	E950.3	E962.0	E980.3
Turpentine (spirits of) (liquid) (vapor)	982.8	E862.4	—	E950.9	E962.1	E980.9
Tybamate	969.5	E853.8	E939.5	E950.3	E962.0	E980.3
Tyloxapol	975.5	E858.6	E945.5	E950.4	E962.0	E980.4
Tymazoline	971.2	E855.5	E941.2	E950.4	E962.0	E980.4
Typhoid vaccine	978.1	E858.8	E948.1	E950.4	E962.0	E980.4
Typhus vaccine	979.2	E858.8	E949.2	E950.4	E962.0	E980.4
Tyrothricin	976.0	E858.7	E946.0	E950.4	E962.0	E980.4
ENT agent	976.6	E858.7	E946.6	E950.4	E962.0	E980.4
ophthalmic preparation	976.5	E858.7	E946.5	E950.4	E962.0	E980.4
Undecenoic acid	976.0	E858.7	E946.0	E950.4	E962.0	E980.4
Undecylenic acid	976.0	E858.7	E946.0	E950.4	E962.0	E980.4
Unna's boot	976.3	E858.7	E946.3	E950.4	E962.0	E980.4
Uracil mustard	963.1	E858.1	E933.1	E950.4	E962.0	E980.4
Uramustine	963.1	E858.1	E933.1	E950.4	E962.0	E980.4
Urari	975.2	E858.6	E945.2	E950.4	E962.0	E980.4
Urea	974.4	E858.5	E944.4	E950.4	E962.0	E980.4
topical	976.8	E858.7	E946.8	E950.4	E962.0	E980.4
Urethan(e) (antineoplastic)	963.1	E858.1	E933.1	E950.4	E962.0	E980.4
Urginea (maritima) (scilla) — see Squill						
Uric acid metabolism agents NEC	974.7	E858.5	E944.7	E950.4	E962.0	E980.4
Urokinase	964.4	E858.2	E934.4	E950.4	E962.0	E980.4
Urokon	977.8	E858.8	E947.8	E950.4	E962.0	E980.4
Urotropin	961.9	E857	E931.9	E950.4	E962.0	E980.4

Substance	Poisoning	Accident	Therapeutic Use	Suicide Attempt	Assault	Undetermined
				External Cause (E-Code)		

Substance	Poisoning	Accident	Therapeutic Use	Suicide Attempt	Assault	Undetermined
Urtica	988.2	E865.4	—	E950.9	E962.1	E980.9
Utility gas — *see* Gas, utility						
Vaccine NEC	979.9	E858.8	E949.9	E950.4	E962.0	E980.4
bacterial NEC	978.8	E858.8	E948.8	E950.4	E962.0	E980.4
with						
other bacterial component	978.9	E858.8	E948.9	E950.4	E962.0	E980.4
pertussis component	978.6	E858.8	E948.6	E950.4	E962.0	E980.4
viral–rickettsial component	979.7	E858.8	E949.7	E950.4	E962.0	E980.4
mixed NEC	978.9	E858.8	E948.9	E950.4	E962.0	E980.4
BCG	978.0	E858.8	E948.0	E950.4	E962.0	E980.4
cholera	978.2	E858.8	E948.2	E950.4	E962.0	E980.4
diphtheria	978.5	E858.8	E948.5	E950.4	E962.0	E980.4
influenza	979.6	E858.8	E949.6	E950.4	E962.0	E980.4
measles	979.4	E858.8	E949.4	E950.4	E962.0	E980.4
meningococcal	978.8	E858.8	E948.8	E950.4	E962.0	E980.4
mumps	979.6	E858.8	E949.6	E950.4	E962.0	E980.4
paratyphoid	978.1	E858.8	E948.1	E950.4	E962.0	E980.4
pertussis (with diphtheria toxoid) (with tetanus toxoid)	978.6	E858.8	E948.6	E950.4	E962.0	E980.4
plague	978.3	E858.8	E948.3	E950.4	E962.0	E980.4
poliomyelitis	979.5	E858.8	E949.5	E950.4	E962.0	E980.4
poliovirus	979.5	E858.8	E949.5	E950.4	E962.0	E980.4
rabies	979.1	E858.8	E949.1	E950.4	E962.0	E980.4
rickettsial NEC	979.6	E858.8	E949.6	E950.4	E962.0	E980.4
with						
bacterial component	979.7	E858.8	E949.7	E950.4	E962.0	E980.4
pertussis component	978.6	E858.8	E948.6	E950.4	E962.0	E980.4
viral component	979.7	E858.8	E949.7	E950.4	E962.0	E980.4
Rocky mountain spotted fever	979.6	E858.8	E949.6	E950.4	E962.0	E980.4
rubella virus	979.4	E858.8	E949.4	E950.4	E962.0	E980.4
sabin oral	979.5	E858.8	E949.5	E950.4	E962.0	E980.4
smallpox	979.0	E858.8	E949.0	E950.4	E962.0	E980.4
tetanus	978.4	E858.8	E948.4	E950.4	E962.0	E980.4
typhoid	978.1	E858.8	E948.1	E950.4	E962.0	E980.4
typhus	979.2	E858.8	E949.2	E950.4	E962.0	E980.4
viral NEC	979.6	E858.8	E949.6	E950.4	E962.0	E980.4
with						
bacterial component	979.7	E858.8	E949.7	E950.4	E962.0	E980.4
pertussis component	978.6	E858.8	E948.6	E950.4	E962.0	E980.4
rickettsial component	979.7	E858.8	E949.7	E950.4	E962.0	E980.4
yellow fever	979.3	E858.8	E949.3	E950.4	E962.0	E980.4
Vaccinia immune globulin (human)	964.6	E858.2	E934.6	E950.4	E962.0	E980.4
Vaginal contraceptives	976.8	E858.7	E946.8	E950.4	E962.0	E980.4
Valethamate	971.1	E855.4	E941.1	E950.4	E962.0	E980.4
Valisone	976.0	E858.7	E946.0	E950.4	E962.0	E980.4
Valium	969.4	E853.2	E939.4	E950.3	E962.0	E980.3
Valmid	967.8	E852.8	E937.8	E950.2	E962.0	E980.2
Vanadium	985.8	E866.4	—	E950.9	E962.1	E980.9
Vancomycin	960.8	E856	E930.8	E950.4	E962.0	E980.4
Vapor (*see also* Gas)	987.9	E869.9	—	E952.9	E962.2	E982.9
kiln (carbon monoxide)	986	E868.8	—	E952.1	E962.2	E982.1
lead — *see* Lead						
specified source NEC (*see also* specific substance)	987.8	E869.8	—	E952.8	E962.2	E982.8
Varidase	964.4	E858.2	E934.4	E950.4	E962.0	E980.4
Varnish	989.89	E861.6	—	E950.9	E962.1	E980.9

Substance	Poisoning	Accident	External Cause (E-Code)			
			Therapeutic Use	Suicide Attempt	Assault	Undetermined
cleaner	982.8	E862.9	—	E950.9	E962.1	E980.9
Vaseline	976.3	E858.7	E946.3	E950.4	E962.0	E980.4
Vasodilan	972.5	E858.3	E942.5	E950.4	E962.0	E980.4
Vasodilators NEC	972.5	E858.3	E942.5	E950.4	E962.0	E980.4
coronary	972.4	E858.3	E942.4	E950.4	E962.0	E980.4
Vasopressin	962.5	E858.0	E932.5	E950.4	E962.0	E980.4
Vasopressor drugs	962.5	E858.0	E932.5	E950.4	E962.0	E980.4
Venom, venomous (bite) (sting)	989.5	E905.9	—	E950.9	E962.1	E980.9
arthropod NEC	989.5	E905.5	—	E950.9	E962.1	E980.9
bee	989.5	E905.3	—	E950.9	E962.1	E980.9
centipede	989.5	E905.4	—	E950.9	E962.1	E980.9
hornet	989.5	E905.3	—	E950.9	E962.1	E980.9
lizard	989.5	E905.0	—	E950.9	E962.1	E980.9
marine animals or plants	989.5	E905.6	—	E950.9	E962.1	E980.9
millipede (topical)	989.5	E905.4	—	E950.9	E962.1	E980.9
plant NEC	989.5	E905.7	—	E950.9	E962.1	E980.9
marine	989.5	E905.6	—	E950.9	E962.1	E980.9
scorpion	989.5	E905.2	—	E950.9	E962.1	E980.9
snake	989.5	E905.0	—	E950.9	E962.1	E980.9
specified NEC	989.5	E905.8	—	E950.9	E962.1	E980.9
spider	989.5	E905.1	—	E950.9	E962.1	E980.9
wasp	989.5	E905.3	—	E950.9	E962.1	E980.9
Ventolin—*see* Salbutamol sulfate						
Veramon	967.0	E851	E937.0	E950.1	E962.0	E980.1
Veratrum						
album	988.2	E865.4	—	E950.9	E962.1	E980.9
alkaloids	972.6	E858.3	E942.6	E950.4	E962.0	E980.4
viride	988.2	E865.4	—	E950.9	E962.1	E980.9
Verdigris (*see also* Copper)	985.8	E866.4	—	E950.9	E962.1	E980.9
Veronal	967.0	E851	E937.0	E950.1	E962.0	E980.1
Veroxil	961.6	E857	E931.6	E950.4	E962.0	E980.4
Versidyne	965.7	E850.7	E935.7	E950.0	E962.0	E980.0
Vienna						
green	985.1	E866.3	—	E950.8	E962.1	E980.8
insecticide	985.1	E863.4	—	E950.6	E962.1	E980.7
red	989.89	E866.8	—	E950.9	E962.1	E980.9
pharmaceutical dye	977.4	E858.8	E947.4	E950.4	E962.0	E980.4
Vinbarbital, vinbarbitone	967.0	E851	E937.0	E950.1	E962.0	E980.1
Vinblastine	963.1	E858.1	E933.1	E950.4	E962.0	E980.4
Vincristine	963.1	E858.1	E933.1	E950.4	E962.0	E980.4
Vinesthene, vinethene	968.2	E855.1	E938.2	E950.4	E962.0	E980.4
Vinyl						
bital	967.0	E851	E937.0	E950.1	E962.0	E980.1
ether	968.2	E855.1	E938.2	E950.4	E962.0	E980.4
Vioform	961.3	E857	E931.3	E950.4	E962.0	E980.4
topical	976.0	E858.7	E946.0	E950.4	E962.0	E980.4
Viomycin	960.6	E856	E930.6	E950.4	E962.0	E980.4
Viosterol	963.5	E858.1	E933.5	E950.4	E962.0	E980.4
Viper (venom)	989.5	E905.0	—	E950.9	E962.1	E980.9
Viprynium (embonate)	961.6	E857	E931.6	E950.4	E962.0	E980.4
Virugon	961.7	E857	E931.7	E950.4	E962.0	E980.4
Visine	976.5	E858.7	E946.5	E950.4	E962.0	E980.4
Vitamins NEC	963.5	E858.1	E933.5	E950.4	E962.0	E980.4
B$_{12}$	964.1	E858.2	E934.1	E950.4	E962.0	E980.4
hematopoietic	964.1	E858.2	E934.1	E950.4	E962.0	E980.4
K	964.3	E858.2	E934.3	E950.4	E962.0	E980.4
Vleminckx's solution	976.4	E858.7	E946.4	E950.4	E962.0	E980.4

Substance	External Cause (E-Code)					
	Poisoning	Accident	Therapeutic Use	Suicide Attempt	Assault	Undetermined
Voltaren—*see* Diclofenac sodium						
Warfarin (potassium) (sodium)	964.2	E858.2	E934.2	E950.4	E962.0	E980.4
rodenticide	989.4	E863.7	—	E950.6	E962.1	E980.7
Wasp (sting)	989.5	E905.3	—	E950.9	E962.1	E980.9
Water						
balance agents NEC	974.5	E858.5	E944.5	E950.4	E962.0	E980.4
gas	987.1	E868.1	—	E951.8	E962.2	E981.8
incomplete combustion of — *see* Carbon, monoxide, fuel, utility						
hemlock	988.2	E865.4	—	E950.9	E962.1	E980.9
moccasin (venom)	989.5	E905.0	—	E950.9	E962.1	E980.9
Wax (paraffin) (petroleum)	981	E862.3	—	E950.9	E962.1	E980.9
automobile	989.89	E861.2	—	E950.9	E962.1	E980.9
floor	981	E862.0	—	E950.9	E962.1	E980.9
Weed killers NEC	989.4	E863.5	—	E950.6	E962.1	E980.7
Welldorm	967.1	E852.0	E937.1	E950.2	E962.0	E980.2
White						
arsenic — *see* Arsenic						
hellebore	988.2	E865.4	—	E950.9	E962.1	E980.9
lotion (keratolytic)	976.4	E858.7	E946.4	E950.4	E962.0	E980.4
spirit	981	E862.0	—	E950.9	E962.1	E980.9
Whitewashes	989.89	E861.6	—	E950.9	E962.1	E980.9
Whole blood	964.7	E858.2	E934.7	E950.4	E962.0	E980.4
Wild						
black cherry	988.2	E865.4	—	E950.9	E962.1	E980.9
poisonous plants NEC	988.2	E865.4	—	E950.9	E962.1	E980.9
Window cleaning fluid	989.89	E861.3	—	E950.9	E962.1	E980.9
Wintergreen (oil)	976.3	E858.7	E946.3	E950.4	E962.0	E980.4
Witch hazel	976.2	E858.7	E946.2	E950.4	E962.0	E980.4
Wood						
alcohol	980.1	E860.2	—	E950.9	E962.1	E980.9
spirit	980.1	E860.2	—	E950.9	E962.1	E980.9
Woorali	975.2	E858.6	E945.2	E950.4	E962.0	E980.4
Wormseed, American	961.6	E857	E931.6	E950.4	E962.0	E980.4
Xanthine diuretics	974.1	E858.5	E944.1	E950.4	E962.0	E980.4
Xanthocillin	960.0	E856	E930.0	E950.4	E962.0	E980.4
Xanthotoxin	976.3	E858.7	E946.3	E950.4	E962.0	E980.4
Xylene (liquid) (vapor)	982.0	E862.4	—	E950.9	E962.1	E980.9
Xylocaine (infiltration) (topical)	968.5	E855.2	E938.5	E950.4	E962.0	E980.4
nerve block (peripheral) (plexus)	968.6	E855.2	E938.6	E950.4	E962.0	E980.4
spinal	968.7	E855.2	E938.7	E950.4	E962.0	E980.4
Xylol (liquid) (vapor)	982.0	E862.4	—	E950.9	E962.1	E980.9
Xylometazoline	971.2	E855.5	E941.2	E950.4	E962.0	E980.4
Yellow						
fever vaccine	979.3	E858.8	E949.3	E950.4	E962.0	E980.4
jasmine	988.2	E865.4	—	E950.9	E962.1	E980.9
Yew	988.2	E865.4	—	E950.9	E962.1	E980.9
Zactane	965.7	E850.7	E935.7	E950.0	E962.0	E980.0
Zaroxolyn	974.3	E858.5	E944.3	E950.4	E962.0	E980.4
Zephiran (topical)	976.0	E858.7	E946.0	E950.4	E962.0	E980.4
ophthalmic preparation	976.5	E858.7	E946.5	E950.4	E962.0	E980.4
Zerone	980.1	E860.2	—	E950.9	E962.1	E980.9
Zinc (compounds) (fumes) (salts) (vapor) NEC	985.8	E866.4	—	E950.9	E962.1	E980.9
anti–infectives	976.0	E858.7	E946.0	E950.4	E962.0	E980.4
antivaricose	972.7	E858.3	E942.7	E950.4	E962.0	E980.4
bacitracin	976.0	E858.7	E946.0	E950.4	E962.0	E980.4

Substance	External Cause (E-Code)					
	Poisoning	Accident	Therapeutic Use	Suicide Attempt	Assault	Undetermined
chloride	976.2	E858.7	E946.2	E950.4	E962.0	E980.4
gelatin	976.3	E858.7	E946.3	E950.4	E962.0	E980.4
oxide	976.3	E858.7	E946.3	E950.4	E962.0	E980.4
peroxide	976.0	E858.7	E946.0	E950.4	E962.0	E980.4
pesticides	985.8	E863.4	—	E950.6	E962.1	E980.7
phosphide (rodenticide)	985.8	E863.7	—	E950.6	E962.1	E980.7
stearate	976.3	E858.7	E946.3	E950.4	E962.0	E980.4
sulfate (antivaricose)	972.7	E858.3	E942.7	E950.4	E962.0	E980.4
ENT agent	976.6	E858.7	E946.6	E950.4	E962.0	E980.4
ophthalmic solution	976.5	E858.7	E946.5	E950.4	E962.0	E980.4
topical NEC	976.0	E858.7	E946.0	E950.4	E962.0	E980.4
undecylenate	976.0	E858.7	E946.0	E950.4	E962.0	E980.4
Zoxazolamine	968.0	E855.1	E938.0	E950.4	E962.0	E980.4
Zygadenus (venenosus)	988.2	E865.4	—	E950.9	E962.1	E980.9

Substance		Poisoning	Accident	External Cause (E-Code)			
				Therapeutic Use	Suicide Attempt	Assault	Undetermined

SECTION 3

ALPHABETIC INDEX TO EXTERNAL CAUSES
OF INJURY AND POISONING (E CODE)

This section contains the index to the codes which classify environmental events, circumstances, and other conditions as the cause of injury and other adverse effects. Where a code from the section Supplementary Classification of External Causes of Injury and Poisoning (E800-E998) is applicable, it is intended that the E code shall be used in addition to a code form the main body of the classification, Chapters 1-17.

The alphabetic index to the E codes is organized by main terms which describe the *accident, circumstance, event,* or specific *agent* which caused the injury or other adverse effect.

> *Note—Transport accidents (E800-E848) include accidents involving:*
> *aircraft and space craft (E840-E845)*
> *watercraft (E830-E838)*
> *motor vehicle (E810-E825)*
> *railway (E800-E807)*
> *other road vehicles (E826-E829)*

> *For definitions and examples related to transport accidents—see Volume 1, pages 477-491.*

> *The fourth-digit subdivisions for use with categories E800-E848 to identify the injured person are found on pages 1343-1348.*

> *For identifying the place in which an accident or poisoning occurred (circumstances classifiable to categories E850-E869 and E880-E928)— see the listing in this section under "Accident, occurring."*

See the Table of Drugs and Chemicals (Section 2 of this volume) for identifying the specific agent involved in drug overdose or a wrong substance given or taken in error, and for intoxication or poisoning by a drug or other chemical substance.

The specific adverse effect, reaction, or localized toxic effect to a correct drug or substance properly administered in therapeutic or prophylactic dosage should be classified according to the nature of the adverse effect (e.g.: allergy, dermatitis, tachycardia) listed in Section 1 of this volume.

A

Abandonment
  causing exposure to weather conditions—*see*
    Exposure
  child, with intent to injure or kill E968.4
  helpless person, infant, newborn E904.0
    with intent to injure or kill E968.4
Abortion, criminal, injury to child E968.8
Abuse, (alleged) (suspected)
  adult
    by
      child E967.4
      ex-partner E967.3
      ex-spouse E967.3
      father E967.0
      grandchild E967.7
      grandparent E967.6
      mother E967.2
      non-related caregiver E967.8
      other relative E967.7
      other specified person(s) E967.1
      partner E967.3
      sibling E967.5
      spouse E967.3
      stepfather E967.0
      stepmother E967.2
      unspecified person E967.9
  child
    by
      child E967.4
      ex-partner E967.3
      ex-spouse E967.3
      father E967.0
      grandchild E967.7
      grandparent E967.6
      mother E967.2
      non-related caregiver E967.8
      other relative E967.7
      other specified person(s) E967.1
      partner E967.3
      sibling E967.5
      spouse E967.3
      stepfather E967.0
      stepmother E967.2
      unspecified person E967.9
Accident (to) E928.9
  aircraft (in transit) (powered) E841
    at landing, take-off E840
    due to, caused by cataclysm—*see*
      categories E908, E909
    late effect of E929.1
    unpowered (*see also* Collision, aircraft,
      unpowered) E842
    while alighting, boarding E843
  amphibious vehicle
    on
      land—*see* Accident, motor vehicle
      water—*see* Accident, watercraft
  animal, ridden NEC E828
  animal-drawn vehicle NEC E827
  balloon (*see also* Collision, aircraft,
    unpowered) E842
  caused by, due to
    abrasive wheel (metalworking) E919.3
    animal NEC E906.9
      being ridden (in sport or transport) E828
    avalanche NEC E909.2
    band saw E919.4
    bench saw E919.4

Accident—*continued*
  bore, earth-drilling or mining (land)
    (seabed) E919.1
  bulldozer E919.7
  cataclysmic
    earth surface movement or eruption E909.9
    storm E908.9
  chain
    hoist E919.2
      agricultural operations E919.0
      mining operations E919.1
    saw E920.1
  circular saw E919.4
  cold (excessive) (*see also* Cold, exposure
    to) E901.9
  combine E919.0
  conflagration—*see* Conflagration
  corrosive liquid, substance NEC E924.1
  cotton gin E919.8
  crane E919.2
    agricultural operations E919.0
    mining operations E919.1
  cutting or piercing instrument (*see also*
    Cut) E920.9
  dairy equipment E919.8
  derrick E919.2
    agricultural operations E919.0
    mining operations E919.1
  drill E920.1
    earth (land) (seabed) E919.1
    hand (powered) E920.1
      not powered E920.4
    metalworking E919.3
    woodworking E919.4
  earth(-)
    drilling machine E919.1
    moving machine E919.7
    scraping machine E919.7
  electric
    current (*see also* Electric shock) E925.9
    motor—*see also* Accident, machine, by
      type of machine
    current (of)—*see* Electric shock
  elevator (building) (grain) E919.2
    agricultural operations E919.0
    mining operations E919.1
  environmental factors NEC E928.9
  excavating machine E919.7
  explosive material (*see also* Explosion)
    E923.9
  farm machine E919.0
  fire, flames—*see also* Fire
    conflagration—*see* Conflagration
  firearm missile—*see* Shooting
  forging (metalworking) machine E919.3
  forklift (truck) E919.2
    agricultural operations E919.0
    mining operations E919.1
  gas turbine E919.5
  harvester E919.0
  hay derrick, mower, or rake E919.0
  heat (excessive) (*see also* Heat) E900.9
  hoist (*see also* Accident, caused by, due
    to, lift) E919.2
    chain—*see* Accident, caused by, due to,
      chain
    shaft E919.1

Accident—*continued*
hot
  liquid E924.0
    caustic or corrosive E924.1
    object (not producing fire or flames)
      E924.8
  substance E924.9
    caustic or corrosive E924.1
    liquid (metal) NEC E924.0
    specified type NEC E924.8
ignition—*see* Ignition
internal combustion engine E919.5
landslide NEC E909.2
lathe (metalworking) E919.3
  turnings E920.8
  woodworking E919.4
lift, lifting (appliances) E919.2
  agricultural operations E919.0
  mining operations E919.1
  shaft E919.1
lightning NEC E907
machine, machinery—*see also* Accident,
  machine
drilling, metal E919.3
manufacturing, for manufacture of
  beverages E919.8
  clothing E919.8
  foodstuffs E919.8
  paper E919.8
  textiles E919.8
milling, metal E919.3
moulding E919.4
power press, metal E919.3
printing E919.8
rolling mill, metal E919.3
sawing, metal E919.3
specified type NEC E919.8
spinning E919.8
weaving E919.8
natural factor NEC E928.9
overhead plane E919.4
plane E920.4
  overhead E919.4
powered
  hand tool NEC E920.1
  saw E919.4
    hand E920.1
printing machine E919.8
pulley (block) E919.2
  agricultural operations E919.0
  mining operations E919.1
  transmission E919.6
radial saw E919.4
radiation—*see* Radiation
reaper E919.0
road scraper E919.7
  when in transport under its own
    power—*see* categories E810—E825
roller coaster E919.8
sander E919.4
saw E920.4
  band E919.4
  bench E919.4
  chain E920.1
  circular E919.4
  hand E920.4
    powered E920.1
  powered, except hand E919.4
  radial E919.4
sawing machine, metal E919.3

Accident—*continued*
shaft
  hoist E919.1
  lift E919.1
  transmission E919.6
shears E920.4
  hand E920.4
    powered E920.1
  mechanical E919.3
shovel E920.4
  steam E919.7
spinning machine E919.8
steam—*see also* Burning, steam
  engine E919.5
  shovel E919.7
thresher E919.0
thunderbolt NEC E907
tractor E919.0
  when in transport under its own
    power—*see* categories E810-E825
transmission belt, cable, chain, gear,
  pinion, pulley, shaft E919.6
turbine (gas) (water driven) E919.5
under-cutter E919.1
weaving machine E919.8
winch E919.2
  agricultural operations E919.0
  mining operations E919.1
diving E883.0
  with insufficient air supply E913.2
glider (hang) (*see also* Collision, aircraft,
  unpowered) E842
hovercraft
  on
    land—*see* Accident, motor vehicle
    water—*see* Accident, watercraft
ice yacht (*see also* Accident, vehicle NEC)
  E848
in
  medical, surgical procedure
    as, or due to misadventure—*see*
      Misadventure
    causing an abnormal reaction or later
      complication without mention of
      misadventure—*see* Reaction, abnormal
kite carrying a person (*see also* Collision,
  aircraft, unpowered) E842
land yacht (*see also* Accident, vehicle NEC)
  E848
late effect of—*see* Late effect
launching pad E845
machine, machinery (*see also* Accident,
  caused by, due to, by specific type of
  machine) E919.9
  agricultural including animal-powered
    E919.0
  earth-drilling E919.1
  earth moving or scraping E919.7
  excavating E919.7
  involving transport under own power on
    highway or transport vehicle—*see*
    categories E810-E825, E840-E845
  lifting (appliances) E919.2
  metalworking E919.3
  mining E919.1
  prime movers, except electric motors
    E919.5
    electric motors—*see* Accident, machine,
      by specific type of machine
  recreational E919.8
  specified type NEC E919.8

Accident—*continued*
  fire (*see also* Explosion, railway engine)
    E803
  hitting by, being struck by
    object falling in, on, from, rolling stock,
      train, vehicle E806
    rolling stock, train, vehicle E805
    overturning, railway rolling stock, train,
      vehicle (*see also* Derailment, railway)
      E802
    running off rails, railway (*see also*
      Derailment, railway) E802
    specified circumstances NEC E806
    train or vehicle hit by
      avalanche E909
      falling object (earth, rock, tree) E806
        due to cataclysm—*see* categories
          E908, E909
      landslide E909
  ski(ing) E885
    jump E884.9
    lift or tow (with chair or gondola) E847
  snow vehicle, motor driven (not on public
    highway) E820
    on public highway—*see* categories
      E810-E819
  spacecraft E845
  specified cause NEC E928.8
  street car E829
  traffic NEC E819
  vehicle NEC (with pedestrian) E848
    battery powered
      airport passenger vehicle E846
      truck (baggage) (mail) E846
    powered commercial or industrial (with
      other vehicle or object within
      commercial or industrial premises)
      E846
  watercraft E838
    with
      drowning or submersion resulting from
        accident other than to watercraft E832
        accident to watercraft E830
      injury, except drowning or submersion,
        resulting from
        accident other than to watercraft—*see*
          categories E833-E838
        accident to watercraft E831
    due to, caused by cataclysm—*see*
      categories E908, E909
  machinery E836
Acid throwing E961
Acosta syndrome E902.0
Aeroneurosis E902.1
Aero-otitis media —*see* Effects of, air pressure
Aerosinusitis —*see* Effects of, air pressure
After-effect, late —*see* Late effect
Air
  blast in war operations E933
  embolism (traumatic) NEC E928.9
    in
      infusion or transfusion E874.1
      perfusion E874.2
  sickness E903
Alpine sickness E902.0
Altitude sickness —*see* Effects of, air pressure
Anaphylactic shock, anaphylaxis (*see also*
  Table of drugs and chemicals) E947.9
  due to bite or sting (venomous)—*see* Bite,
    venomous
Andes disease E902.0

Apoplexy
  heat—*see* Heat
Arachnidism E905.1
Arson E968.0
Asphyxia, asphyxiation
  by
    chemical in war operations E997.2
    explosion—*see* Explosion
    food (bone) (regurgitated food) (seed)
      E911
    foreign object, except food E912
    fumes in war operations E997.2
    gas—*see also* Table of drugs and
      chemicals
      in war operations E997.2
      legal
        execution E978
        intervention (tear) E972
      tear E972
    mechanical means (*see also* Suffocation)
      E913.9
  from
    conflagration—*see* Conflagration
    fire—*see also* Fire
      in war operations E990.9
    ignition—*see* Ignition
Aspiration
  foreign body—*see* Foreign body, aspiration
  mucus, not of newborn (with asphyxia,
    obstruction respiratory passage,
    suffocation) E912
  phlegm (with asphyxia, obstruction respiratory
    passage, suffocation) E912
  vomitus (with asphyxia, obstruction
    respiratory passage, suffocation) (*see also*
    Foreign body, aspiration, food) E911
Assassination (attempt) (*see also* Assault)
  E968.9
Assault (homicidal) (by) (in) E968.9
  acid E961
    swallowed E962.1
  bite (of human being) E968.8
  bomb ((placed in) car or house) E965.8
    antipersonnel E965.5
    letter E965.7
    petrol E965.7
  brawl (hand) (fists) (foot) E960.0
  burning, burns (by fire) E968.0
    acid E961
      swallowed E962.1
    caustic, corrosive substance E961
      swallowed E962.1
    chemical from swallowing caustic,
      corrosive substance NEC E962.1
    hot liquid E968.3
    scalding E968.3
    vitriol E961
      swallowed E962.1
  caustic, corrosive substance E961
    swallowed E962.1
  cut, any part of body E966
  dagger E966
  drowning E964
  explosive(s) E965.9
    bomb (*see also* Assault, bomb) E965.8
    dynamite E965.8
  fight (hand) (fists) (foot) E960.0
    with weapon E968.9
      blunt or thrown E968.2
      cutting or piercing E966
      firearm—*see* Shooting, homicide

Assault—*continued*
  fire E968.0
  firearm(s)—*see* Shooting, homicide
  garrotting E963
  gunshot (wound)—*see* Shooting, homicide
  hanging E963
  injury NEC E968.9
    to child due to criminal abortion E968.8
  knife E966
  late effect of E969
  ligature E963
  poisoning E962.9
    drugs or medicinals E962.0
    gas(es) or vapors, except drugs and
        medicinals E962.2
    solid or liquid substances, except drugs
        and medicinals E962.1
  puncture, any part of body E966
  pushing
    before moving object, train, vehicle
        E968.8
    from high place E968.1
  rape E960.1
  scalding E968.3
  shooting—*see* Shooting, homicide
  sodomy E960.1
  stab, any part of body E966
  strangulation E963
  submersion E964
  suffocation E963
  transport vehicle E968.5
  violence NEC E968.9
  vitriol E961
    swallowed E962.1
  weapon E968.9
    blunt or thrown E968.2
    cutting or piercing E966
    firearm—*see* Shooting, homicide
  wound E968.9
    cutting E966
    gunshot—*see* Shooting, homicide
    knife E966
    piercing E966
    puncture E966
    stab E966
Attack by animal NEC E906.9
Avalanche E909.2
  falling on or hitting
    motor vehicle (in motion) (on public
        highway) E909.2
    railway train E909.2
Aviators' disease E902.1

B

**Barotitis, barodontalgia, barosinusitis,
    barotrauma** (otitic) (sinus)—*see* Effects of,
    air pressure
Battered
  baby or child (syndrome)—*see* Abuse, child
  person other than baby or child—*see* Assault
Bayonet wound (*see also* Cut, by bayonet)
    E920.3
  in
    legal intervention E974
    war operations E995
Bean in nose E912
Bed set on fire NEC E898.0
Beheading (by guillotine)
  homicide E966
  legal execution E978

Bending, injury in E927
Bends E902.0
Bite
  animal (nonvenomous) NEC E906.5
    venomous NEC E905.9
  arthropod (nonvenomous) NEC E906.4
    venomous—*see* Sting
  black widow spider E905.1
  cat E906.3
  centipede E905.4
  cobra E905.0
  copperhead snake E905.0
  coral snake E905.0
  dog E906.0
  fer de lance E905.0
  gila monster E905.0
  human being E968.8
  insect (nonvenomous) E906.4
    venomous—*see* Sting
  krait E905.0
  late effect of—*see* Late effect
  lizard E906.2
    venomous E905.0
  mamba E905.0
  marine animal
    nonvenomous E906.3
      snake E906.2
    venomous E905.6
      snake E905.0
  millipede E906.4
    venomous E905.4
  moray eel E906.3
  rat E906.1
  rattlesnake E905.0
  rodent, except rat E906.3
  serpent—*see* Bite, snake
  shark E906.3
  snake (venomous) E905.0
    nonvenomous E906.2
    sea E905.0
  spider E905.1
    nonvenomous E906.4
  tarantula (venomous) E905.1
  venomous NEC E905.9
    by specific animal—*see* category E905
  viper E905.0
  water moccasin E905.0
Blast (air) in war operations E993
  from nuclear explosion E996
  underwater E992
Blizzard E908.3
Blow E928.9
  by law-enforcing agent, police (on duty) E975
    with blunt object (baton) (nightstick)
        (stave) (truncheon) E973
Blowing up (*see also* Explosion) E923.9
Brawl (hand) (fists) (foot) E960.0
Breakage (accidental)
  cable of cable car not on rails E847
  ladder (causing fall) E881.0
  part (any) of
    animal-drawn vehicle E827
    ladder (causing fall) E881.0
    motor vehicle
      in motion (on public highway) E818
        not on public highway E825
    nonmotor road vehicle, except
        animal-drawn vehicle or pedal cycle
        E829
    off-road type motor vehicle (not on
        public highway) NEC E821

Breakage—*continued*
  on public highway E818
  pedal cycle E826
  scaffolding (causing fall) E881.1
  snow vehicle, motor-driven (not on public
      highway) E820
    on public highway E818
  vehicle NEC—*see* Accident, vehicle
Broken
  glass, injury by E920.8
  power line (causing electric shock) E925.1
Bumping against, into (accidentally)
  object (moving) (projected) (stationary) E917.9
    with fall E888
    caused by crowd (with fall) E917.1
    in
      running water E917.2
      sports E917.0
  person(s) E917.9
    with fall E886.9
      in sports E886.0
    as, or caused by, a crowd (with fall)
        E917.1
      in sports E917.0
        with fall E886.0
Burning, burns (accidental) (by) (from) (on)
    E899
  acid (any kind) E924.1
    swallowed—*see* Table of drugs and
        chemicals
  bedclothes (*see also* Fire, specified NEC)
      E898.0
  blowlamp (*see also* Fire, specified NEC)
      E898.1
  blowtorch (*see also* Fire, specified NEC)
      E898.1
  boat, ship, watercraft—*see* categories E830,
      E831, E837
  bonfire (controlled) E897
    uncontrolled E892
  candle (*see also* Fire, specified NEC) E898.1
  caustic liquid, substance E924.1
    swallowed—*see* Table of drugs and
        chemicals
  chemical E924.1
    from swallowing caustic, corrosive
        substance—*see* Table of drugs and
        chemicals
    in war operations E997.2
  cigar(s) or cigarette(s) (*see also* Fire,
      specified NEC) E898.1
  clothes, clothing, nightdress—*see* Ignition,
      clothes
    with conflagration—*see* Conflagration
  conflagration—*see* Conflagration
  corrosive liquid, substance E924.1
    swallowed—*see* Table of drugs and
        chemicals
  electric current (*see also* Electric shock)
      E925.9
  fire, flames (*see also* Fire) E899
  flare, Verey pistol E922.8
  heat
    from appliance (electrical) E924.8
    in local application or packing during
        medical or surgical procedure E873.5
  homicide (attempt) (*see also* Assault, burning)
      E968.0
  hot
    liquid E924.0
      caustic or corrosive E924.1

Burning, burns—*continued*
  object (not producing fire or flames)
      E924.8
  substance E924.9
    caustic or corrosive E924.1
    liquid (metal) NEC E924.0
    specified type NEC E924.8
  tap water E924.2
  ignition—*see also* Ignition
    clothes, clothing, nightdress—*see also*
        Ignition, clothes
      with conflagration—*see* Conflagration
  highly inflammable material (benzine)
      (fat) (gasoline) (kerosine) (paraffin)
      (petrol) E894
  inflicted by other person
    stated as
      homicidal, intentional (*see also* Assault,
          burning) E968.0
      undetermined whether accidental or
          intentional (*see also* Burn, stated as
          undetermined whether accidental or
          intentional) E988.1
  internal, from swallowed caustic, corrosive
      liquid, substance—*see* Table of drugs and
      chemicals
  in war operations (from fire-producing device
      or conventional weapon) E990.9
    from nuclear explosion E996
    petrol bomb E990.0
  lamp (*see also* Fire, specified NEC) E898.1
  late effect of NEC E929.4
  lighter (cigar) (cigarette) (*see also* Fire,
      specified NEC) E898.1
  lightning E907
  liquid (boiling) (hot) (molten) E924.0
    caustic, corrosive (external) E924.1
      swallowed—*see* Table of drugs and
          chemicals
  local application of externally applied
      substance in medical or surgical care
      E873.5
  machinery—*see* Accident, machine
  matches (*see also* Fire, specified NEC) E898.1
  medicament, externally applied E873.5
  metal, molten E924.0
  object (hot) E924.8
    producing fire or flames—*see* Fire
  pipe (smoking) (*see also* Fire, specified NEC)
      E898.1
  radiation—*see* Radiation
  railway engine, locomotive, train (*see also*
      Explosion, railway engine) E803
  self-inflicted (unspecified whether accidental
      or intentional) E988.1
    caustic or corrosive substance NEC
        E988.7
    stated as intentional, purposeful E958.1
      caustic or corrosive substance NEC E958.7
    stated as undetermined whether accidental or
        intentional E988.1
      caustic or corrosive substance NEC
          E988.7
  steam E924.0
    pipe E924.8
  substance (hot) E924.9
    boiling or molten E924.0
    caustic, corrosive (external) E924.1
      swallowed—*see* Table of drugs and
          chemicals

Burning, burns—*continued*
  suicidal (attempt) NEC E958.1
    caustic substance E958.7
    late effect of E959
  therapeutic misadventure
    overdose of radiation E873.2
  torch, welding (*see also* Fire, specified NEC)
    E898.1
  trash fire (*see also* Burning, bonfire) E897
  vapor E924.0
  vitriol E924.1
  x-rays E926.3
    in medical, surgical procedure—*see*
      Misadventure, failure, in dosage,
      radiation
Butted by animal E906.8

C

Cachexia, lead or saturnine E866.0
  from pesticide NEC (*see also* Table of drugs
    and chemicals) E863.4
Caisson disease E902.2
Capital punishment (any means) E978
Car sickness E903
Casualty (not due to war) NEC E928.9
  war (*see also* War operations) E995
Cat
  bite E906.3
  scratch E906.8
Cataclysmic (any injury)
  earth surface movement or eruption E909.9
    specified type NEC E909.8
  storm or flood resulting from storm E908.9
    specified type NEC E909.8
Catching fire —*see* Ignition
Caught
  between
    objects (moving) (stationary and moving)
      E918
      and machinery—*see* Accident, machine
  by cable car, not on rails E847
  in
    machinery (moving parts of)—*see*
      Accident, machine
    object E918
Cave-in (causing asphyxia, suffocation (by
  pressure)) (*see also* Suffocation, due to,
  cave-in) E913.3
  with injury other than asphyxia or suffocation
    E916
    with asphyxia or suffocation (*see also*
      Suffocation, due to, cave-in) E913.3
  struck or crushed by E916
    with asphyxia or suffocation (*see also*
      Suffocation, due to, cave-in) E913.3
Change(s) in air pressure—*see also* Effects of,
  air pressure
  sudden, in aircraft (ascent) (descent) (causing
    aeroneurosis or aviators' disease) E902.1
Chilblains E901.0
  due to manmade conditions E901.1
Choking (on) (any object except food or
  vomitus) E912
  apple E911
  bone E911
  food, any type (regurgitated) E911
  mucus or phlegm E912
  seed E911
Civil insurrection —*see* War operations

Cloudburst E908.8
Cold, exposure to (accidental) (excessive)
  (extreme) (place) E901.9
  causing chilblains or immersion foot E901.0
  due to
    manmade conditions E901.1
    specified cause NEC E901.8
    weather (conditions) E901.0
  late effect of NEC E929.5
  self-inflicted (undetermined whether
    accidental or intentional) E988.3
    suicidal E958.3
  suicide E958.3
Colic, lead, painters', or saturnine —*see*
  category E866
Collapse
  building E916
    burning E891.8
      private E890.8
  dam E909.3
  due to heat—*see* Heat
  machinery—*see* Accident, machine
  man-made structure E909.3
  postoperative NEC E878.9
  structure, burning NEC E891.8
Collision (accidental)

> Note—In the case of collisions between
> different types of vehicles, persons and objects,
> priority in classification is in the following order:
>
>   *Aircraft*
>   *Watercraft*
>   *Motor vehicle*
>   *Railway vehicle*
>   *Pedal Cycle*
>   *Animal-drawn vehicle*
>   *Animal being ridden*
>   *Streetcar or other nonmotor road vehicle*
>   *Other vehicle*
>   *Pedestrian or person using pedestrian*
>   *conveyance*
>   *Object (except where falling from or set in*
>   *motion by vehicle etc. listed above)*
>
> In the listing below, the combinations are listed
> only under the vehicle etc. having priority. For
> definitions, see Volume 1, page 477.

  aircraft (with object or vehicle) (fixed)
    (movable) (moving) E841
    with
      person (while landing, taking off) (without
        accident to aircraft) E844
      powered (in transit) (with unpowered
        aircraft) E841
      while landing, taking off E840
      unpowered E842
      while landing, taking off E840
  animal being ridden (in sport or transport)
    E828
    and
      animal (being ridden) (herded)
        (unattended) E828
      nonmotor road vehicle, except pedal cycle
        or animal-drawn vehicle E828
      object (fallen) (fixed) (movable) (moving)
        not falling from or set in motion by
        vehicle of higher priority E828
      pedestrian (conveyance or vehicle) E828

Collision—*continued*
animal-drawn vehicle E827
  and
    animal (being ridden) (herded)
      (unattended) E827
    nonmotor road vehicle, except pedal cycle
      E827
    object (fallen) (fixed) (movable) (moving)
      not falling from or set in motion by
      vehicle of higher priority E827
    pedestrian (conveyance or vehicle) E827
    streetcar E827
motor vehicle (on public highway) (traffic
    accident) E812
  after leaving, running off, public highway
    (without antecedent collision) (without
    re-entry) E816
  with antecedent collision on public
    highway—*see* categories E810-E815
  with re-entrance collision with another
    motor vehicle E811
  and
    abutment (bridge) (overpass) E815
    animal (herded) (unattended) E815
      carrying person, property E813
    animal-drawn vehicle E813
    another motor vehicle (abandoned)
      (disabled) (parked) (stalled) (stopped)
      E812
      with, involving re-entrance (on same
        roadway) (across median strip) E811
    any object, person, or vehicle off the
      public highway resulting from a
      noncollision motor vehicle nontraffic
      accident E816
    avalanche, fallen or not moving E815
      falling E909
    boundary fence E815
    culvert E815
    fallen
      stone E815
      tree E815
    falling E909.2
    guard post or guard rail E815
    inter-highway divider E815
    landslide, fallen or not moving E815
      moving E909
    machinery (road) E815
    moving E909.2
    nonmotor road vehicle NEC E813
    object (any object, person, or vehicle off
      the public highway resulting from a
      noncollision motor vehicle nontraffic
      accident) E815
      off, normally not on, public highway
        resulting from a noncollision motor
        vehicle traffic accident E816
    pedal cycle E813
    pedestrian (conveyance) E814
    person (using pedestrian conveyance) E814
    post or pole (lamp) (light) (signal)
      (telephone) (utility) E815
    railway rolling stock, train, vehicle E810
    safety island E815
    street car E813
    traffic signal, sign, or marker (temporary)
      E815
    tree E815
    tricycle E813
    wall of cut made for road E815

Collision—*continued*
  due to cataclysm—*see* categories E908,
    E909
  not on public highway, nontraffic accident
    E822
  and
    animal (carrying person, property)
      (herded) (unattended) E822
    animal-drawn vehicle E822
    another motor vehicle (moving), except
      off-road motor vehicle E822
      stationary E823
    avalanche, fallen, not moving E823
      moving E909
    landslide, fallen, not moving E823
      moving E909
    nonmotor vehicle (moving) E822
      stationary E823
    object (fallen) (normally) (fixed)
      (movable but not in motion)
      (stationary) E823
      moving, except when falling from, set
        in motion by, aircraft or cataclysm
        E822
    pedal cycle (moving) E822
      stationary E823
    pedestrian (conveyance) E822
    person (using pedestrian conveyance)
      E822
    railway rolling stock, train, vehicle
      (moving) E822
      stationary E823
    road vehicle (any) (moving) E822
      stationary E823
    tricycle (moving) E822
      stationary E823
    moving E909.2
  off-road type motor vehicle (not on public
    highway) E821
  and
    animal (being ridden) (-drawn vehicle)
      E821
    another off-road motor vehicle, except
      snow vehicle E821
    other motor vehicle, not on public
      highway E821
    other object or vehicle NEC, fixed or
      movable, not set in motion by aircraft,
      motor vehicle on highway, or snow
      vehicle, motor-driven E821
    pedal cycle E821
    pedestrian (conveyance) E821
    railway train E821
  on public highway—*see* Collision, motor
    vehicle
  pedal cycle E826
  and
    animal (carrying person, property)
      (herded) (unherded) E826
    animal-drawn vehicle E826
    another pedal cycle E826
    nonmotor road vehicle E826
    object (fallen) (fixed) (movable) (moving)
      not falling from or set in motion by
      aircraft, motor vehicle, or railway train
      NEC E826
    pedestrian (conveyance) E826
    person (using pedestrian conveyance) E826
    street car E826

Collision—*continued*
pedestrian(s) (conveyance) E917.9
  with fall E886.9
    in sports E886.0
  and
    crowd, human stampede (with fall) E917.1
    machinery—*see* Accident, machine
    object (fallen) (moving) (projected)
      (stationary) not falling from or set in
      motion by any vehicle classifiable to
      E800-E848 E917.9
    with fall E888
    caused by a crowd E917.1
    in
      running water E917.2
        with drowning or submersion—*see*
          Submersion
      sports E917.0
    vehicle, nonmotor, nonroad E848
  in
    running water E917.2
      with drowning or submersion—*see*
        Submersion
    sports E917.0
      with fall E886.0
person(s) (using pedestrian conveyance) (*see*
  also Collision, pedestrian) E917.9
railway (rolling stock) (train) (vehicle) (with
  (subsequent) derailment, explosion, fall or
  fire) E800
  with antecedent derailment E802
  and
    animal (carrying person) (herded)
      (unattended) E801
    another railway train or vehicle E800
    buffers E801
    fallen tree on railway E801
    farm machinery, nonmotor (in transport)
      (stationary) E801
    gates E801
    nonmotor vehicle E801
    object (fallen) (fixed) (movable) (moving)
      not falling from, set in motion by,
      aircraft or motor vehicle NEC E801
    pedal cycle E801
    pedestrian (conveyance) E805
    person (using pedestrian conveyance) E805
    platform E801
    rock on railway E801
    street car E801
snow vehicle, motor-driven (not on public
  highway) E820
  and
    animal (being ridden) (-drawn vehicle)
      E820
    another off-road motor vehicle E820
    other motor vehicle, not on public
      highway E820
    other object or vehicle NEC, fixed or
      movable, not set in motion by aircraft
      or motor vehicle on highway E820
    pedal cycle E820
    pedestrian (conveyance) E820
    railway train E820
  on public highway—*see* Collision, motor
    vehicle
street car(s) E829
  and
    animal, herded, not being ridden,
      unattended E829
    nonmotor road vehicle NEC E829

Collision—*continued*
  object (fallen) (fixed) (movable) (moving)
    not falling from or set in motion by
    aircraft, animal-drawn vehicle, animal
    being ridden, motor vehicle, pedal
    cycle, or railway train E829
  pedestrian (conveyance) E829
  person (using pedestrian conveyance) E829
vehicle
  animal-drawn—*see* Collision,
    animal-drawn vehicle
  motor—*see* Collision, motor vehicle
  nonmotor
    nonroad E848
    and
      another nonmotor, nonroad vehicle
        E848
      object (fallen) (fixed) (movable)
        (moving) not falling from or set in
        motion by aircraft, animal-drawn
        vehicle, animal being ridden,
        motor vehicle, nonmotor road
        vehicle, pedal cycle, railway train,
        or streetcar E848
    road, except animal being ridden,
      animal-drawn vehicle, or pedal cycle
      E829
    and
      animal, herded, not being ridden,
        unattended E829
      another nonmotor road vehicle, except
        animal being ridden, animal-drawn
        vehicle, or pedal cycle E829
      object (fallen) (fixed) (movable)
        (moving) not falling from or set in
        motion by, aircraft, animal-drawn
        vehicle, animal being ridden,
        motor vehicle, pedal cycle, or
        railway train E829
      pedestrian (conveyance) E829
      person (using pedestrian conveyance)
        E829
      vehicle, nonmotor, nonroad E829
  watercraft E838
    and
      person swimming or water skiing E838
    causing
      drowning, submersion E830
      injury except drowning, submersion E831
Combustion, spontaneous —*see* Ignition
Complication of medical or surgical
  procedure or treatment
  as an abnormal reaction—*see* Reaction,
    abnormal
  delayed, without mention of
    misadventure—*see* Reaction, abnormal
  due to misadventure—*see* Misadventure
Compression
  divers' squeeze E902.2
  trachea by
    food E911
    foreign body, except food E912
Conflagration
  building or structure, except private dwelling
    (barn) (church) (convalescent or
    residential home) (factory) (farm
    outbuilding) (hospital) (hotel) (institution)
    (educational) (dormitory) (residential)
    (school) (shop) (store) (theatre) E891.9

Conflagration—*continued*
  with or causing (injury due to)
    accident or injury NEC E891.9
      specified circumstance NEC E891.8
    burns, burning E891.3
    carbon monoxide E891.2
    fumes E891.2
      polyvinylchloride (PVC) or similar
        material E891.1
    smoke E891.2
  causing explosion E891.0
  not in building or structure E892
  private dwelling (apartment) (boarding house)
    (camping place) (caravan) (farmhouse)
    (home (private)) (house) (lodging house)
    (private garage) (rooming house)
    (tenement) E890.9
  with or causing (injury due to)
    accident or injury NEC E890.9
      specified circumstance NEC E890.8
    burns, burning E890.3
    carbon monoxide E890.2
    fumes E890.2
      polyvinylchloride (PVC) or similar
        material E890.1
    smoke E890.2
  causing explosion E890.0
Contact with
  dry ice E901.1
  liquid air, hydrogen, nitrogen E901.1
Cramp(s)
  Heat—*see* Heat
  swimmers (*see also* category E910) E910.2
    not in recreation or sport E910.3
Cranking (car) (truck) (bus) (engine), injury
  by E917.9
Crash
  aircraft (in transit) (powered) E841
    at landing, take-off E840
    in war operations E994
    on runway NEC E840
    stated as
      homicidal E968.8
      suicidal E958.6
      undetermined whether accidental or
        intentional E988.6
    unpowered E842
  glider E842
  motor vehicle—*see also* Accident, motor
    vehicle
    homicidal E968.8
    suicidal E958.5
    undetermined whether accidental or
      intentional E988.5
Crushed (accidentally) E928.9
  between
    boat(s), ship(s), watercraft (and dock or
      pier) (without accident to watercraft)
      E838
      after accident to, or collision, watercraft
        E831
    objects (moving) (stationary and moving)
      E918
  by
    avalanche NEC E909.2
    boat, ship, watercraft after accident to,
      collision, watercraft E831
    cave-in E916
      with asphyxiation or suffocation (*see also*
        Suffocation, due to, cave-in) E913.3
    crowd, human stampede E917.1

Crushed—*continued*
  falling
    aircraft (*see also* Accident, aircraft) E841
      in war operations E994
    earth, material E916
      with asphyxiation or suffocation (*see*
        also Suffocation, due to, cave-in)
        E913.3
    object E916
      on ship, watercraft E838
      while loading, unloading watercraft E838
  landslide NEC E909.2
  lifeboat after abandoning ship E831
  machinery—*see* Accident, machine
  railway rolling stock, train, vehicle (part
    of) E805
  street car E829
  vehicle NEC—*see* Accident, vehicle NEC
  in
    machinery—*see* Accident, machine
    object E918
    transport accident—*see* categories
      E800-E848
  late effect of NEC E929.9
Cut, cutting (any part of body) (accidental)
  E920.9
  by
    arrow E920.8
    axe E920.4
    bayonet (*see also* Bayonet wound) E920.3
    blender E920.2
    broken glass E920.8
    can opener E920.4
      powered E920.2
    chisel E920.4
    circular saw E919.4
    cutting or piercing instrument—*see also*
      category E920
    late effect of E929.8
    dagger E920.3
    dart E920.8
    drill—*see* Accident, caused by drill
    edge of stiff paper E920.8
    electric
      beater E920.2
      fan E920.2
      knife E920.2
      mixer E920.2
    fork E920.4
    garden fork E920.4
    hand saw or tool (not powered) E920.4
      powered E920.1
    hedge clipper E920.4
      powered E920.1
    hoe E920.4
    ice pick E920.4
    knife E920.3
      electric E920.2
    lathe turnings E920.8
    lawn mower E920.4
      powered E920.0
      riding E919.8
    machine—*see* Accident, machine
    meat
      grinder E919.8
      slicer E919.8
    nails E920.8
    needle E920.4
      hypodermic E920.5
    object, edged, pointed, sharp—*see*
      category E920

Cut, cutting—*continued*
    paper cutter E920.4
    piercing instrument—*see also* category
      E920
      late effect of E929.8
    pitchfork E920.4
    powered
      can opener E920.2
      garden cultivator E920.1
        riding E919.8
      hand saw E920.1
      hand tool NEC E920.1
      hedge clipper E920.1
      household appliance or implement E920.2
      lawn mower (hand) E920.0
        riding E919.8
      rivet gun E920.1
      staple gun E920.1
    rake E920.4
    saw
      circular E919.4
      hand E920.4
    scissors E920.4
    screwdriver E920.4
    sewing machine (electric) (powered)
      E920.2
      not powered E920.4
    shears E920.4
    shovel E920.4
    spade E920.4
    splinters E920.8
    sword E920.3
    tin can lid E920.8
    wood slivers E920.8
    homicide (attempt) E966
    inflicted by other person
      stated as
        intentional, homicidal E966
        undetermined whether accidental or
          intentional E986
    late effect of NEC E929.8
    legal
      execution E978
      intervention E974
    self-inflicted (unspecified whether accidental
      or intentional) E986
      stated as intentional, purposeful E956
    stated as undetermined whether accidental or
      intentional E986
    suicidal (attempt) E956
    war operations E995
Cyclone E908.1

D

Death due to injury occurring one year or
    more previous —*see* Late effect
Decapitation (accidental circumstances) NEC
    E928.9
    homicidal E966
    legal execution (by guillotine) E978
Deprivation —*see also* Privation
    homicidal intent E968.4
Derailment (accidental)
    railway (rolling stock) (train) (vehicle) (with
      subsequent collision) E802
      with
        collision (antecedent) (*see also* Collision,
          railway) E800

Derailment (accidental)—*continued*
      explosion (subsequent) (without antecedent
        collision) E802
      antecedent collision E803
      fall (without collision (antecedent)) E802
      fire (without collision (antecedent)) E802
    street car E829
Descent
    parachute (voluntary) (without accident to
      aircraft) E844
      due to accident to aircraft—*see* categories
        E840-E842
Desertion
    child, with intent to injure or kill E968.4
    helpless person, infant, newborn E904.0
      with intent to injure or kill E968.4
Destitution —*see* Privation
Disability, late effect or sequela of injury
    —*see* Late effect
Disease
    Andes E902.0
    aviators' E902.1
    caisson E902.2
    range E902.0
Divers' disease, palsy, paralysis, squeeze
    E902.0
Dog bite E906.0
Dragged by
    cable car (not on rails) E847
      on rails E829
    motor vehicle (on highway) E814
      not on highway, nontraffic accident E825
    street car E829
Drinking poison (accidental) —*see* Table of
    drugs and chemicals
Drowning —*see* Submersion
Dust in eye E914

E

Earth falling (on) (with asphyxia or
    suffocation (by pressure)) (*see also*
    Suffocation, due to, cave-in) E913.3
    as, or due to, a cataclysm (involving any
      transport vehicle)—*see* categories E908,
      E909
    not due to cataclysmic action E913.3
      motor vehicle (in motion) (on public
        highway) E818
        not on public highway E825
      nonmotor road vehicle NEC E829
      pedal cycle E826
      railway rolling stock, train, vehicle E806
      street car E829
      struck or crushed by E916
        with asphyxiation or suffocation E913.3
        with injury other than asphyxia,
          suffocation E916
Earthquake (any injury) E909.0
Effect(s) (adverse) of
    air pressure E902.9
      at high altitude E902.9
      in aircraft E902.1
      residence or prolonged visit (causing
        conditions classifiable to E902.0)
        E902.0
      due to
        diving E902.2
        specified cause NEC E902.8
      in aircraft E902.1

Effect(s)...—*continued*
  cold, excessive (exposure to) (*see also* Cold,
    exposure to) E901.9
  heat (excessive) (*see also* Heat) E900.9
  hot
    place—*see* Heat
    weather E900.0
  insulation—*see* Heat
  late—*see* Late effect of
  motion E903
  nuclear explosion or weapon in war
    operations (blast) (fireball) (heat)
    (radiation) (direct) (secondary) E996
  radiation—*see* Radiation
  travel E903
Electric shock, electrocution (accidental)
  (from exposed wire, faulty appliance, high
  voltage cable, live rail, open socket) (by)
  (in) E925.9
  appliance or wiring
    domestic E925.0
    factory E925.2
    farm (building) E925.8
      house E925.0
    home E925.0
    industrial (conductor) (control apparatus)
      (transformer) E925.2
    outdoors E925.8
    public building E925.8
    residential institution E925.8
    school E925.8
    specified place NEC E925.8
  caused by other person
    stated as
      intentional, homicidal E968.8
      undetermined whether accidental or
        intentional E988.4
  electric power generating plant, distribution
    station E925.1
  homicidal (attempt) E968.8
  legal execution E978
  lightning E907
  machinery E925.9
    domestic E925.0
    factory E925.2
    farm E925.8
    home E925.0
  misadventure in medical or surgical procedure
    in electroshock therapy E873.4
  self-inflicted (undetermined whether
    accidental or intentional) E988.4
    stated as intentional E958.4
  stated as undetermined whether accidental or
    intentional E988.4
  suicidal (attempt) E958.4
  transmission line E925.1
Electrocution —*see* Electric shock
Embolism
  air (traumatic) NEC—*see* Air, embolism
Encephalitis
  lead or saturnine E866.0
  from pesticide NEC E863.4
Entanglement
  in
    bedclothes, causing suffocation E913.0
    wheel of pedal cycle E826
Entry of foreign body, material, any —*see*
  Foreign body
Execution, legal (any method) E978

Exhaustion
  cold—*see* Cold, exposure to
  due to excessive exertion E927
  heat—*see* Heat
Explosion (accidental) (in) (of) (on) E923.9
  acetylene E923.2
  aerosol can E921.8
  aircraft (in transit) (powered) E841
    at landing, take-off E840
    in war operations E994
    unpowered E842
  air tank (compressed) (in machinery) E921.1
  anesthetic gas in operating theatre E923.2
  automobile tire NEC E921.8
    causing transport accident—*see* categories
      E810-E825
  blasting (cap) (materials) E923.1
  boiler (machinery), not on transport vehicle
    E921.0
    steamship—*see* Explosion, watercraft
  bomb E923.8
    in war operations E993
      after cessation of hostilities E998
      atom, hydrogen or nuclear E996
      injury by fragments from E991.9
        antipersonnel bomb E991.3
  butane E923.2
  caused by
    other person
      stated as
        intentional, homicidal—*see* Assault,
          explosive
        undetermined whether accidental or
          homicidal E985.5
  coal gas E923.2
  detonator E923.1
  dynamite E923.1
  explosive (material) NEC E923.9
    gas(es) E923.2
    missile E923.8
      in war operations E993
        injury by fragments from E991.9
          antipersonnel bomb E991.3
    used in blasting operations E923.1
  fire-damp E923.2
  fireworks E923.0
  gas E923.2
    cylinder (in machinery) E921.1
    pressure tank (in machinery) E921.1
  gasoline (fumes) (tank) not in moving motor
    vehicle E923.2
  grain store (military) (munitions) E923.8
  grenade E923.8
    in war operations E993
      injury by fragments from E991.9
  homicide (attempt)—*see* Assault, explosive
  hot water heater, tank (in machinery) E921.0
  in mine (of explosive gases) NEC E923.2
  late effect of NEC E929.8
  machinery—*see also* Accident, machine
    pressure vessel—*see* Explosion, pressure
      vessel
  methane E923.2
  missile E923.8
    in war operations E993
      injury by fragments from E991.9
  motor vehicle (part of)
    in motion (on public highway) E818
    not on public highway E825
  munitions (dump) (factory) E923.8
    in war operations E993

Explosion—*continued*
of mine E923.8
  in war operations
    after cessation of hostilities E998
    at sea or in harbor E992
    land E993
      after cessation of hostilities E998
      injury by fragments from E991.9
    marine E992
own weapons in war operations E993
  injury by fragments from E991.9
    antipersonnel bomb E991.3
pressure
  cooker E921.8
  gas tank (in machinery) E921.1
  vessel (in machinery) E921.9
    on transport vehicle—*see* categories
      E800-E848
    specified type NEC E921.8
propane E923.2
railway engine, locomotive, train (boiler)
  (with subsequent collision, derailment,
  fall) E803
  with
    collision (antecedent) (*see also* Collision,
      railway) E800
    derailment (antecedent) E802
    fire (without antecedent collision or
      derailment) E803
secondary fire resulting from—*see* Fire
self-inflicted (unspecified whether accidental
  or intentional) E985.5
  stated as intentional, purposeful E955.5
shell (artillery) E923.8
  in war operations E993
    injury by fragments from E991.9
stated as undetermined whether caused
  accidentally or purposely inflicted E985.5
steam or water lines (in machinery) E921.0
suicide (attempted) E955.5
torpedo E923.8
  in war operations E992
transport accident—*see* categories E800-E848
war operations—*see* War operations, explosion
watercraft (boiler) E837
  causing drowning, submersion (after
    jumping from watercraft) E830
Exposure (weather) (conditions) (rain) (wind)
  E904.3
with homicidal intent E968.4
excessive E904.3
  cold (*see also* Cold, exposure to) E901.9
    self-inflicted—*see* Cold, exposure to,
      self-inflicted
  heat (*see also* Heat) E900.9
helpless person, infant, newborn due to
  abandonment or neglect E904.0
noise E928.1
prolonged in deep-freeze unit or refrigerator
  E901.1
radiation—*see* Radiation
resulting from transport accident—*see*
  categories E800-E848
smoke from, due to
  fire —*see* Fire
tobacco, second-hand E869.4
vibration E928.2

F

Fall, falling (accidental) E888
building E916
  burning E891.8
    private E890.8
down
  escalator E880.0
  ladder E881.0
    in boat, ship, watercraft E833
  staircase E880.9
  stairs, steps—*see* Fall, from, stairs
earth (with asphyxia or suffocation (by
  pressure)) (*see also* Earth, falling) E913.3
from, off
  aircraft (at landing, take-off) (in-transit)
    (while alighting, boarding) E843
    resulting from accident to aircraft—*see*
      categories E840-E842
  animal (in sport or transport) E828
  animal-drawn vehicle E827
  balcony E882
  bed E884.4
  bicycle E826
  boat, ship, watercraft (into water) E832
    after accident to, collision, fire on E830
      and subsequently struck by (part of)
        boat E831
    and subsequently struck by (part of) boat
      E838
    burning, crushed, sinking E830
      and subsequently struck by (part of)
        boat E831
  bridge E882
  building E882
    burning E891.8
      private E890.8
  bunk in boat, ship, watercraft E834
    due to accident to watercraft E831
  cable car (not on rails) E847
    on rails E829
  car—*see* Fall from motor vehicle
  chair E884.2
  cliff E884.1
  commode E884.6
  curb (sidewalk) E880.1
  elevation aboard ship E834
    due to accident to ship E831
  embankment E884.9
  escalator E880.0
  flagpole E882
  furniture NEC E884.5
  gangplank (into water) (*see also* Fall,
    from, boat) E832
    to deck, dock E834
  hammock on ship E834
    due to accident to watercraft E831
  haystack E884.9
  high place NEC E884.9
    stated as undetermined whether accidental
      or intentional—*see* Jumping, from,
      high place
  horse (in sport or transport) E828
  ladder E881.0
    in boat, ship, watercraft E833
      due to accident to watercraft E831
  machinery—*see also* accident, machine
    not in operation E884.9
  motor vehicle (in motion) (on public
    highway) E818
    not on public highway E825

Fall, falling—*continued*
    stationary, except while alighting,
        boarding, entering, leaving E884.9
    while alighting, boarding, entering,
        leaving E824
    stationary, except while alighting,
        boarding, entering, leaving E884.9
    while alighting, boarding, entering,
        leaving, except off-road type motor
        vehicle E817
        off-road type—*see* Fall, from, off-road
          type motor vehicle
    nonmotor road vehicle (while alighting,
        boarding) NEC E829
    stationary, except while alighting,
        boarding, entering, leaving E884.9
    off road type motor vehicle (not on
        public highway) NEC E821
    on public highway E818
        while alighting, boarding, entering,
          leaving E817
    snow vehicle—*see* Fall from snow
        vehicle, motor-driven
  one
    deck to another on ship E834
        due to accident to ship E831
    level to another NEC E884.9
        boat, ship, or watercraft E834
          due to accident to watercraft E831
  pedal cycle E826
  playground equipment E884.0
  railway rolling stock, train, vehicle (while
    alighting, boarding) E804
    with
        collision (*see also* Collision, railway)
          E800
        derailment (*see also* Derailment,
          railway) E802
        explosion (*see also* Explosion. railway
          engine) E803
  rigging (aboard ship) E834
    due to accident to watercraft E831
  scaffolding E881.1
  sidewalk (curb) E880.1
    moving E885
  snow vehicle, motor-driven (not on public
    highway) E820
    on public highway E818
        while alighting, boarding, entering,
          leaving E817
  stairs, steps E880.9
    boat, ship, watercraft E833
        due to accident to watercraft E831
    motor bus, motor vehicle—*see* Fall, from,
        motor vehicle, while alighting, boarding
    street car E829
  stationary vehicle NEC E884.9
  stepladder E881.0
  street car (while boarding, alighting) E829
    stationary, except while boarding or
        alighting E884.9
  structure NEC E882
    burning E891.8
  table E884.9
  toilet E884.6
  tower E882
  tree E884.9
  turret E882
  vehicle NEC—*see also* Accident, vehicle
    NEC
    stationary E884.9

Fall, falling—*continued*
  viaduct E882
  wall E882
  wheelchair E884.3
  window E882
  in, on
    aircraft (at landing, take-off) (in-transit)
      E843
      resulting from accident to aircraft—*see*
        categories E840-E842
    boat, ship, watercraft E835
      due to accident to watercraft E831
      one level to another NEC E834
      on ladder, stairs E833
    cutting or piercing instrument or
      machine—*see* Cut
    deck (of boat, ship, watercraft) E835
      due to accident to watercraft E831
    escalator E880.0
    gangplank E835
    glass, broken E920.8
    knife—*see* Cut, knife
    ladder E881.0
      in boat, ship, watercraft E833
      due to accident to watercraft E831
    object, edged, pointed or sharp—*see* Cut
    pitchfork E920.4
    railway rolling stock, train, vehicle (while
      alighting, boarding) E804
      with
        collision (*see also* Collision, railway)
          E800
        derailment (*see also* Derailment,
          railway) E802
        explosion (*see also* Explosion, railway
          engine) E803
    scaffolding E881.1
    scissors E920.4
    staircase, stairs, steps (*see also* Fall,
      from, stairs) E880.9
    street car E829
    water transport (*see also* Fall, in, boat)
      E835
  into
    cavity E883.9
    dock E883.9
      from boat, ship, watercraft (*see also* Fall,
        from, boat) E832
    hold (of ship) E834
      due to accident to watercraft E831
    hole E883.9
    manhole E883.2
    moving part of machinery—*see* Accident,
      machine
    opening in surface NEC E883.9
    pit E883.9
    quarry E883.9
    shaft E883.9
    storm drain E883.2
    tank E883.9
    water (with drowning or submersion)
      E910.9
    well E883.1
  late effect of NEC E929.3
  object (*see also* Hit by, object, falling) E916
  over
    animal E885
    cliff E884.1
    embankment E884.9
    small object E885
  overboard (*see also* Fall, from, boat) E832

Fall, falling—*continued*
rock E916
same level NEC E888
  aircraft (any kind) E843
    resulting from accident to aircraft—*see*
      categories E840-E842
  boat, ship, watercraft E835
    due to accident to, collision, watercraft
      E831
  from
    collision, pushing, shoving, by or with
      other person(s) E886.9
      as, or caused by, a crowd E917.1
      in sports E886.0
    slipping, stumbling, tripping E885
snowslide E916
  as avalanche E909.2
stone E916
through
  hatch (on ship) E834
    due to accident to watercraft E831
  roof E882
  window E882
timber E916
while alighting from, boarding, entering,
  leaving
  aircraft (any kind) E843
  motor bus, motor vehicle—*see* Fall, from,
    motor vehicle, while alighting,
    boarding
  nonmotor road vehicle NEC E829
  railway train E804
  street car E829
Fallen on by
animal (horse) (not being ridden) E906.8
being ridden (in sport or transport) E828
Fell or jumped from high place, so stated
  —*see* Jumping, from, high place
Felo-de-se (*see also* Suicide) E958.9
Fever
heat—*see* Heat
thermic—*see* Heat
Fight (hand) (fist) (foot) (*see also* Assault,
  fight) E960.0
Fire (accidental) (caused by great heat from
  appliance (electrical), hot object or hot
  substance) (secondary, resulting from
  explosion) E899
conflagration—*see* Conflagration
controlled, normal (in brazier, fireplace,
  furnace, or stove) (charcoal) (coal) (coke)
  (electric) (gas) (wood)
  bonfire E897
  brazier, not in building or structure E897
  in building or structure, except private
    dwelling (barn) (church) (convalescent
    or residential home) (factory) (farm
    outbuilding) (hospital) (hotel)
    (institution (educational) (dormitory)
    (residential)) (private garage) (school)
    (shop) (store) (theatre) E896
  in private dwelling (apartment) (boarding
    house) (camping place) (caravan)
    (farmhouse) (home (private)) (house)
    (lodging house) (rooming house)
    (tenement) E895
  not in building or structure E897
  trash E897
forest (uncontrolled) E892
grass (uncontrolled) E892
hay (uncontrolled) E892

Fire —*continued*
homicide (attempt) E968.0
late effect of E969
in, of, on, starting in
  aircraft (in transit) (powered) E841
    at landing, take-off E840
    stationary E892
    unpowered (balloon) (glider) E842
  balloon E842
  boat, ship, watercraft—*see* categories
    E830, E831, E837
  building or structure, except private
    dwelling (barn) (church) (convalescent
    or residential home) (factory) (farm
    outbuilding) (hospital) (hotel)
    (institution (educational) (dormitory)
    (residential)) (school) (shop) (store)
    (theatre) (*see also* Conflagration,
    building or structure, except private
    dwelling) E891.9
  forest (uncontrolled) E892
  glider E842
  grass (uncontrolled) E892
  hay (uncontrolled) E892
  lumber (uncontrolled) E892
  machinery—*see* Accident, machine
  mine (uncontrolled) E892
  motor vehicle (in motion) (on public
    highway) E818
    not on public highway E825
    stationary E892
  prairie (uncontrolled) E892
  private dwelling (apartment) (boarding
    house) (camping place) (caravan)
    (farmhouse) (home (private)) (house)
    (lodging house) (private garage)
    (rooming house) (tenement) (*see also*
    Conflagration, private dwelling) E890.9
  railway rolling stock, train, vehicle (*see*
    also Explosion, railway engine) E803
    stationary E892
  room NEC E898.1
  street car (in motion) E829
    stationary E892
  transport vehicle, stationary NEC E892
  tunnel (uncontrolled) E892
  war operations (by fire-producing device
    or conventional weapon) E990.9
    from nuclear explosion E996
    petrol bomb E990.0
late effect of NEC E929.4
lumber (uncontrolled) E892
mine (uncontrolled) E892
prairie (uncontrolled) E892
self-inflicted (unspecified whether accidental
  or intentional) E988.1
  stated as intentional, purposeful E958.1
specified NEC E898.1
with
  conflagration—*see* Conflagration
  ignition (of)
    clothing—*see* Ignition, clothes
    highly inflammable material (benzine)
      (fat) (gasoline) (kerosene) (paraffin)
      (petrol) E894
started by other person
  stated as
    with intent to injure or kill E968.0
    undetermined whether or not with intent
      to injure or kill E988.1

Fire —*continued*
  suicide (attempted) E958.1
    late effect of E959
  tunnel (uncontrolled) E892
Fireball effects from nuclear explosion in war
  operations E996
Fireworks (explosion) E923.0
Flash burns from explosion (*see also*
  Explosion) E923.9
Flood (any injury) (resulting from storm)
  E908.2
  caused by collapse of dam or manmade
    structure E909.3
Forced landing (aircraft) E840
Foreign body, object or material (entrance
  into (accidental))
  air passage (causing injury) E915
    with asphyxia, obstruction, suffocation
      E912
      food or vomitus E911
    nose (with asphyxia, obstruction,
      suffocation) E912
      causing injury without asphyxia,
        obstruction, suffocation E915
  alimentary canal (causing injury) (with
    obstruction) E915
    with asphyxia, obstruction respiratory
      passage, suffocation E912
      food E911
    mouth E915
      with asphyxia, obstruction, suffocation
        E912
        food E911
    pharynx E915
      with asphyxia, obstruction, suffocation
        E912
        food E911
  aspiration (with asphyxia, obstruction
    respiratory passage, suffocation) E912
    causing injury without asphyxia,
      obstruction respiratory passage,
      suffocation E915
    food (regurgitated) (vomited) E911
      causing injury without asphyxia,
        obstruction respiratory passage,
        suffocation E915
    mucus (not of newborn) E912
    phlegm E912
  bladder (causing injury or obstruction) E915
  bronchus, bronchi—*see* Foreign body, air
    passages
  conjunctival sac E914
  digestive system—*see* Foreign body,
    alimentary canal
  ear (causing injury or obstruction) E915
  esophagus (causing injury or obstruction) (*see
    also* Foreign body, alimentary canal) E915
  eye (any part) E914
  eyelid E914
  hairball (stomach) (with obstruction) E915
  ingestion—*see* Foreign body, alimentary canal
  inhalation—*see* Foreign body, aspiration
  intestine (causing injury or obstruction) E915
  iris E914
  lacrimal apparatus E914
  larynx—*see* Foreign body, air passage
  late effect of NEC E929.8
  lung—*see* Foreign body, air passage
  mouth—*see* Foreign body, alimentary canal,
    mouth

Foreign body...—*continued*
  nasal passage—*see* Foreign body, air passage,
    nose
  nose—*see* Foreign body, air passage, nose
  ocular muscle E914
  operation wound (left in)—*see* Misadventure,
    foreign object
  orbit E914
  pharynx—*see* Foreign body, alimentary canal,
    pharynx
  rectum (causing injury or obstruction) E915
  stomach (hairball) (causing injury or
    obstruction) E915
  tear ducts or glands E914
  trachea—*see* Foreign body, air passage
  urethra (causing injury or obstruction) E915
  vagina (causing injury or obstruction) E915
Found dead, injured
  from exposure (to)—*see* Exposure
  on
    public highway E819
    railway right of way E807
Fracture (circumstances unknown or
  unspecified) E887
  due to specified external means—*see* manner
    of accident
  late effect of NEC E929.3
  occurring in water transport NEC E835
Freezing —*see* Cold, exposure to
Frostbite E901.0
  due to manmade conditions E901.1
Frozen —*see* Cold, exposure to

G

Garrotting, homicidal (attempted) E963
Gored E906.8
Gunshot wound (*see also* Shooting) E922.9

H

Hailstones, injury by E904.3
Hairball (stomach) (with obstruction) E915
Hanged himself (*see also* Hanging,
  self-inflicted) E983.0
Hang gliding E842
Hanging (accidental) E913.8
  caused by other person
    in accidental circumstances E913.8
    stated as
      intentional, homicidal E963
      undetermined whether accidental or
        intentional E983.0
  homicide (attempt) E963
  in bed or cradle E913.0
  legal execution E978
  self-inflicted (unspecified whether accidental
    or intentional) E983.0
    in accidental circumstances E913.8
    stated as intentional, purposeful E953.0
    stated as undetermined whether accidental or
      intentional E983.0
  suicidal (attempt) E953.0

Heat (apoplexy) (collapse) (cramps) (effects of) (excessive) (exhaustion) (fever) (prostration) (stroke) E900.9
- due to
  - manmade conditions (listed in E900.1, except boat, ship, watercraft) E900.1
  - weather (conditions) E900.0
- from
  - electric heating apparatus causing burning E924.8
  - nuclear explosion in war operations E996
- generated in, boiler, engine, evaporator, fire room of boat, ship, watercraft E838
- inappropriate in local application or packing in medical or surgical procedure E873.5
- late effect of NEC E989

Hemorrhage
- delayed following medical or surgical treatment without mention of misadventure—*see* Reaction, abnormal
- during medical or surgical treatment as misadventure—*see* Misadventure, cut

High
- altitude, effects E902.9
- level of radioactivity, effects—*see* Radiation
- pressure effects—*see also* Effects of, air pressure
  - from rapid descent in water (causing caisson or divers' disease, palsy, or paralysis) E902.2
- temperature, effects—*see* Heat

Hit, hitting (accidental) by
- aircraft (propeller) (without accident to aircraft) E844
  - unpowered E842
- avalanche E909.2
- being thrown against object in or part of motor vehicle (in motion) (on public highway) E818
  - not on public highway E825
  - nonmotor road vehicle NEC E829
  - street car E829
- boat, ship, watercraft
  - after fall from watercraft E838
  - damaged, involved in accident E831
  - while swimming, water skiing E838
- bullet (*see also* Shooting) E922.9
  - from air gun E917.9
  - in war operations E991.2
    - rubber E991.0
- flare, Very pistol (*see also* Shooting) E922.8
- hailstones E904.3
- landslide E909.2
- law-enforcing agent (on duty) E975
  - with blunt object (baton) (night stick) (stave) (truncheon) E973
- machine—*see* Accident, machine
- missile
  - firearm (*see also* Shooting) E922.9
  - in war operations—*see* War operations, missile
- motor vehicle (on public highway) (traffic accident) E814
  - not on public highway, nontraffic accident E822
- nonmotor road vehicle NEC E829

Hit, hitting—*continued*
- object
  - falling E916
    - from, in, on
      - aircraft E844
        - due to accident to aircraft—*see* categories E840-E842
        - unpowered E842
      - boat, ship, watercraft E838
        - due to accident to watercraft E831
      - building E916
        - burning E891.8
          - private E890.8
      - cataclysmic
        - earth surface movement or eruption E909.9
        - storm E908.9
      - cave-in E916
        - with asphyxiation or suffocation (*see also* Suffocation, due to, cave-in) E913.3
      - earthquake E909.0
      - motor vehicle (in motion) (on public highway) E818
        - not on public highway E825
        - stationary E916
      - nonmotor road vehicle NEC E829
      - pedal cycle E826
      - railway rolling stock, train, vehicle E806
      - street car E829
      - structure, burning NEC E891.8
      - vehicle, stationary E916
  - moving NEC—*see* Striking against, object
  - projected NEC—*see* Striking against, object
  - set in motion by
    - compressed air or gas, spring, striking, throwing—*see* Striking against, object
    - explosion—*see* Explosion
  - thrown into, on, or towards
    - motor vehicle (in motion) (on public highway) E818
    - not on public highway E825
    - nonmotor road vehicle NEC E829
    - pedal cycle E826
    - street car E829
- off-road type motor vehicle (not on public highway) E821
  - on public highway E814
- other person(s) E917.9
  - with blunt or thrown object E917.9
    - in sports E917.0
    - intentionally, homicidal E968.2
  - as, or caused by, a crowd (with fall) E917.1
  - in sports E917.0
- pedal cycle E826
- police (on duty) E975
  - with blunt object (baton) (nightstick) (stave) (truncheon) E973
- railway, rolling stock, train, vehicle (part of) E805
- shot—*see* Shooting
- snow vehicle, motor-driven (not on public highway) E820
  - on public highway E814
- street car E829
- vehicle NEC—*see* Accident, vehicle NEC

Homicide, homicidal (attempt) (justifiable) (*see also* Assault) E968.9
Hot
liquid, object, substance, accident caused by—*see also* Accident, caused by, hot, by type of substance
late effect of E929.8
place, effects—*see* Heat
weather, effects E900.0
Humidity, causing problem E904.3
Hunger E904.1
resulting from
abandonment or neglect E904.0
transport accident—*see* categories E800-E848
Hurricane (any injury) E908.0
Hypobarism, hypobaropathy —*see* Effects of, air pressure
Hypothermia —*see* Cold, exposure to

I

Ictus
caloris—*see* Heat
solaris E900.0
Ignition (accidental)
anesthetic gas in operating theatre E923.2
bedclothes
with
conflagration—*see* Conflagration
ignition (of)
clothing—*see* Ignition, clothes
highly inflammable material (benzine) (fat) (gasoline) (kerosene) (paraffin) (petrol) E894
benzine E894
clothes, clothing (from controlled fire) (in building) E893.9
with conflagration—*see* Conflagration
from
bonfire E893.2
highly inflammable material E894
sources or material as listed in E893.8
trash fire E893.2
uncontrolled fire—*see* Conflagration
in
private dwelling E893.0
specified building or structure, except private dwelling E893.1
not in building or structure E893.2
explosive material—*see* Explosion
fat E894
gasoline E894
kerosene E894
material
explosive—*see* Explosion
highly inflammable E894
with conflagration—*see* Conflagration
with explosion E923.2
nightdress—*see* Ignition, clothes
paraffin E894
petrol E894
Immersion —*see* Submersion
Implantation of quills of porcupine E906.8
Inanition (from) E904.9
hunger—*see* Lack of, food
resulting from homicidal intent E968.4
thirst—*see* Lack of, water
Inattention after, at birth E904.0
homicidal, infanticidal intent E968.4

Infanticide (*see also* Assault)
Ingestion
foreign body (causing injury) (with obstruction)—*see* Foreign body, alimentary canal
poisonous substance NEC—*see* Table of drugs and chemicals
Inhalation
excessively cold substance, manmade E901.1
foreign body—*see* Foreign body, aspiration
liquid air, hydrogen, nitrogen E901.1
mucus, not of newborn (with asphyxia, obstruction respiratory passage, suffocation) E912
phlegm (with asphyxia, obstruction respiratory passage, suffocation) E912
poisonous gas—*see* Table of drugs and chemicals
smoke from, due to
fire —*see* Fire
tobacco, second-hand E869.4
vomitus (with asphyxia, obstruction respiratory passage, suffocation) E911
Injury, injured (accidental(ly)) NEC E928.9
by, caused by, from
air rifle (B-B gun) E917.9
animal (not being ridden) NEC E906.9
being ridden (in sport or transport) E828
assault (*see also* Assault) E968.9
avalanche E909.2
bayonet (*see also* Bayonet wound) E920.3
being thrown against some part of, or object in
motor vehicle (in motion) (on public highway) E818
not on public highway E825
nonmotor road vehicle NEC E829
off-road motor vehicle NEC E821
railway train E806
snow vehicle, motor-driven E820
street car E829
bending E927
broken glass E920.8
bullet—*see* Shooting
cave-in (*see also* Suffocation, due to, cave-in) E913.3
earth surface movement or eruption E909.9
storm E908.9
without asphyxiation or suffocation E916
cloudburst E908.8
cutting or piercing instrument (*see also* Cut) E920.9
cyclone E908.1
earthquake E909.0
electric current (*see also* Electric shock) E925.9
explosion (*see also* Explosion) E923.9
fire—*see* Fire
flare, Very pistol E922.8
flood E908.2
foreign body—*see* Foreign body
hailstones E904.3
hurricane E908.0
landslide E909.2
law-enforcing agent, police, in course of legal intervention—*see* Legal intervention
lightning E907
live rail or live wire—*see* Electric shock
machinery—*see also* Accident, machine
aircraft, without accident to aircraft E844

Injury, injured—*continued*
- boat, ship, watercraft (deck) (engine room) (galley) (laundry) (loading) E836
- missile
  - explosive E923.8
  - firearm—*see* Shooting
  - in war operations—*see* War operations, missile
- moving part of motor vehicle (in motion) (on public highway) E818
  - not on public highway, nontraffic accident E825
  - while alighting, boarding, entering, leaving—*see* Fall, from, motor vehicle, while alighting, boarding
- nail E920.8
- needle (sewing) E920.4
  - hypodermic E920.5
- noise E928.1
- object
  - fallen on
    - motor vehicle (in motion) (on public highway) E818
    - not on public highway E825
  - falling—*see* Hit by, object, falling
- radiation—*see* Radiation
- railway rolling stock, train, vehicle (part of) E805
  - door or window E806
- rotating propeller, aircraft E844
- rough landing of off-road type motor vehicle (after leaving ground or rough terrain) E821
  - snow vehicle E820
- saber (*see also* Wound, saber) E920.3
- shot—*see* Shooting
- sound waves E928.1
- splinter or sliver, wood E920.8
- straining E927
- street car (door) E829
- suicide (attempt) E958.9
- sword E920.3
- third rail—*see* Electric shock
- thunderbolt E907
- tidal wave E909.4
  - caused by storm E908.0
- tornado E908.1
- torrential rain E908.2
- twisting E927
- vehicle NEC—*see* Accident, vehicle NEC
- vibration E928.2
- volcanic eruption E909.1
- weapon burst, in war operations E993
- weightlessness (in spacecraft, real or simulated) E928.0
- wood splinter or sliver E920.8
- due to
  - civil insurrection—*see* War operations
    - occurring after cessation of hostilities E998
  - war operations—*see* War operations
    - occurring after cessation of hostilities E998
- homicidal (*see also* Assault) E968.9
- in, on
  - civil insurrection—*see* War operations
  - fight E960.0
  - parachute descent (voluntary) (without accident to aircraft) E844
    - with accident to aircraft—*see* categories E840-E842

Injury, injured—*continued*
- public highway E819
- railway right of way E807
- war operations—*see* War operations
- inflicted (by)
  - in course of arrest (attempted), suppression of disturbance, maintenance of order, by law-enforcing agents—*see* Legal intervention
  - law-enforcing agent (on duty)—*see* Legal intervention
  - other person
    - stated as
      - accidental E928.9
      - homicidal, intentional—*see* Assault
      - undetermined whether accidental or intentional—*see* Injury, stated as undetermined
  - police (on duty)—*see* Legal intervention
- late effect of E929.9
- purposely (inflicted) by other person(s)—*see* Assault
- self-inflicted (unspecified whether accidental or intentional) E988.9
  - stated as
    - accidental E928.9
    - intentionally, purposely E958.9
- specified cause NEC E928.8
- stated as
  - undetermined whether accidentally or purposely inflicted (by) E988.9
  - cut (any part of body) E986
  - cutting or piercing instrument (classifiable to E920) E986
  - drowning E984
  - explosive(s) (missile) E985.5
  - falling from high place E987.9
    - manmade structure, except residential E987.1
    - natural site E987.2
    - residential premises E987.0
  - hanging E983.0
  - knife E986
  - late effect of E989
  - puncture (any part of body) E986
  - shooting—*see* Shooting, stated as undetermined whether accidental or intentional
  - specified means NEC E988.8
  - stab (any part of body) E986
  - strangulation—*see* Suffocation, stated as undetermined whether accidental or intentional
  - submersion E984
  - suffocation—*see* Suffocation, stated as undetermined whether accidental or intentional
- to child due to criminal abortion E968.8

Insufficient nourishment —*see also* Lack of, food
- homicidal intent E968.4

Insulation, effects —*see* Heat

Interruption of respiration by
- food lodged in esophagus E911
- foreign body, except food, in esophagus E912

Intervention, legal —*see* Legal intervention

Intoxication, drug or poison —*see* Table of drugs and chemicals

Irradiation —*see* Radiation

J

Jammed (accidentally)
between objects (moving) (stationary and moving) E918
in object E918
Jumped or fell from high place, so stated
—see Jumping, from, high place, stated as in undetermined circumstances
Jumping
before train, vehicle or other moving object (unspecified whether accidental or intentional) E988.0
stated as
intentional, purposeful E958.0
suicidal (attempt) E958.0
from
aircraft
by parachute (voluntarily) (without accident to aircraft) E844
due to accident to aircraft—*see* categories E840-E842
boat, ship, watercraft (into water)
after accident to, fire on, watercraft E830
and subsequently struck by (part of) boat E831
burning, crushed, sinking E830
and subsequently struck by (part of) boat E831
voluntarily, without accident (to boat) with injury other than drowning or submersion E883.0
building
burning E891.8
private E890.8
cable car (not on rails) E847
on rails E829
high place
in accidental circumstances or in sport—*see* categories E880-E884
stated as
with intent to injure self E957.9
man-made structures NEC E957.1
natural sites E957.2
residential premises E957.0
in undetermined circumstances E987.9
man-made structures NEC E987.1
natural sites E987.2
residential premises E987.0
suicidal (attempt) E957.9
man-made structures NEC E957.1
natural sites E957.1
residential premises E957.0
motor vehicle (in motion) (on public highway)—*see* Fall, from, motor vehicle
nonmotor road vehicle NEC E829
street car E829
structure, burning NEC E891.8
into water
with injury other than drowning or submersion E883.0
drowning or submersion—*see* Submersion
from, off, watercraft—*see* Jumping, from, boat
Justifiable homicide *—see* Assault

K

Kicked by
animal E906.8
person(s) (accidentally) E917.9
with intent to injure or kill E960.0
as, or caused by a crowd (with fall) E917.1
in fight E960.0
in sports (with fall) E917.0
Kicking against
object (moving) (projected) (stationary) E917.9
in sports E917.0
person—*see* Striking against, person
Killed, killing (accidentally) NEC (*see also* Injury) E928.9
in
action—*see* War operations
brawl, fight (hand) (fists) (foot) E960.0
by weapon—*see also* Assault
cutting, piercing E966
firearm—*see* Shooting, homicide
self
stated as
accident E928.9
suicide—*see* Suicide
unspecified whether accidental or suicidal E988.9
Knocked down (accidentally) (by) NEC E928.9
animal (not being ridden) E906.8
being ridden (in sport or transport) E828
blast from explosion (*see also* Explosion) E923.9
crowd, human stampede E917.1
late effect of—*see* Late effect
person (accidentally) E917.9
in brawl, fight E960.0
in sports E917.0
transport vehicle—*see* vehicle involved under Hit by
while boxing E917.0

L

Laceration NEC E928.9
Lack of
air (refrigerator or closed place), suffocation by E913.2
care (helpless person) (infant) (newborn) E904.0
homicidal intent E968.4
food except as result of transport accident E904.1
helpless person, infant, newborn due to abandonment or neglect E904.0
water except as result of transport accident E904.2
helpless person, infant, newborn due to abandonment or neglect E904.0
Landslide E909.2
falling on, hitting
motor vehicle (any) (in motion) (on or off public highway) E909.2
railway rolling stock, train, vehicle E909.2
Late effect of
accident NEC (accident classifiable to E928.9) E929.9
specified NEC (accident classifiable to E910-E928.8) E929.8
assault E969

Late effect of—*continued*

fall, accidental (accident classifiable to E880-E888) E929.3

fire, accident caused by (accident classifiable to E890-E899) E929.4

homicide, attempt (any means) E969

injury undetermined whether accidentally or purposely inflicted (injury classifiable to E980-E988) E989

legal intervention (injury classifiable to E970-E976) E977

medical or surgical procedure, test or therapy as, or resulting in, or from

    abnormal or delayed reaction or complication—*see* Reaction, abnormal

    misadventure—*see* Misadventure

motor vehicle accident (accident classifiable to E810-E825) E929.0

natural or environmental factor, accident due to (accident classifiable to E900-E909) E929.5

poisoning, accidental (accident classifiable to E850-E858, E860-E869) E929.2

suicide, attempt (any means) E959

transport accident NEC (accident classifiable to E800-E807, E826-E838, E840-E848) E929.1

war operations, injury due to (injury classifiable to E990-E998) E999

Launching pad accident E845

Legal

execution, any method E978

intervention (by) (injury from) E976

    baton E973

    bayonet E974

    blow E975

    blunt object (baton) (nightstick) (stave) (truncheon) E973

    cutting or piercing instrument E974

    dynamite E971

    execution, any method E973

    explosive(s) (shell) E971

    firearms(s) E970

    gas (asphyxiation) (poisoning) (tear) E972

    grenade E971

    late effect of E977

    machine gun E970

    manhandling E975

    mortar bomb E971

    nightstick E973

    revolver E970

    rifle E970

    specified means NEC E975

    stabbing E974

    stave E973

    truncheon E973

Lifting, injury in E927

Lightning (shock) (stroke) (struck by) E907

Liquid (noncorrosive) in eye E914

corrosive E924.1

Loss of control

motor vehicle (on public highway) (without antecedent collision) E816

    with

        antecedent collision on public highway—*see* Collision, motor vehicle

      involving any object, person or vehicle not on public highway E816

    on public highway—*see* Collision, motor vehicle

Loss of control—*continued*

not on public highway, nontraffic accident E825

    with antecedent collision—*see* Collision, motor vehicle, not on public highway

off-road type motor vehicle (not on public highway) E821

    on public highway—*see* Loss of control, motor vehicle

snow vehicle, motor-driven (not on public highway) E820

    on public highway—*see* Loss of control, motor vehicle

Lost at sea E832

with accident to watercraft E830

in war operations E995

Low

pressure, effects—*see* Effects of, air pressure

temperature, effects—*see* Cold, exposure to

Lying before train, vehicle or other moving object (unspecified whether accidental or intentional) E988.0

stated as intentional, purposeful, suicidal (attempt) E958.0

Lynching (*see also* Assault) E968.9

M

Malfunction, atomic power plant in water transport E838

Mangled (accidentally) NEC E928.9

Manhandling (in brawl, fight) E960.0

legal intervention E975

Manslaughter (nonaccidental)—*see* Assault

Marble in nose E912

Mauled by animal E906.8

Medical procedure, complication of

delayed or as an abnormal reaction without mention of misadventure—*see* Reaction, abnormal

due to or as a result of misadventure—*see* Misadventure

Minamata disease E865.2

Misadventure(s) to patient(s) during surgical or medical care E876.9

contaminated blood, fluid, drug or biological substance (presence of agents and toxins as listed in E875) E875.9

    administered (by) NEC E875.9

        infusion E875.0

        injection E875.1

        specified means NEC E875.2

        transfusion E875.0

        vaccination E875.1

cut, cutting, puncture, perforation or hemorrhage (accidental) (inadvertent) (inappropriate) (during) E870.9

    aspiration of fluid or tissue (by puncture or catheterization, except heart) E870.5

    biopsy E870.8

        needle (aspirating) E870.5

    blood sampling E870.5

    catheterization E870.5

        heart E870.6

    dialysis (kidney) E870.2

    endoscopic examination E870.4

    enema E870.7

    infusion E870.1

    injection E870.3

    lumbar puncture E870.5

Misadventures—*continued*
- needle biopsy E870.5
- paracentesis, abdominal E870.5
- perfusion E870.2
- specified procedure NEC E870.8
- surgical operation E870.0
- thoracentesis E870.5
- transfusion E870.1
- vaccination E870.3
- excessive amount of blood or other fluid during transfusion or infusion E873.0
- failure
  - in dosage E873.9
    - electroshock therapy E873.4
    - inappropriate temperature (too hot or too cold) in local application and packing E873.5
    - infusion
      - excessive amount of fluid E873.0
      - incorrect dilution of fluid E873.1
    - insulin-shock therapy E873.4
    - nonadministration of necessary drug or medicinal E873.6
    - overdose—*see also* Overdose
      - radiation, in therapy E873.2
    - radiation
      - inadvertent exposure of patient (receiving radiation for test or therapy) E873.3
      - not receiving radiation for test or therapy—*see* Radiation
      - overdose E873.2
    - specified procedure NEC 873.8
    - transfusion
      - excessive amount of blood E873.0
  - mechanical, of instrument or apparatus (during procedure) E874.9
    - aspiration of fluid or tissue (by puncture or catheterization, except of heart) E874.4
    - biopsy E874.8
      - needle (aspirating) E874.4
    - blood sampling E874.4
    - catheterization E874.4
      - heart E874.5
    - dialysis (kidney) E874.2
    - endoscopic examination E874.3
    - enema E874.8
    - infusion E874.1
    - injection E874.8
    - lumbar puncture E874.4
    - needle biopsy E874.4
    - paracentesis, abdominal E874.4
    - perfusion E874.2
    - specified procedure NEC E874.8
    - surgical operation E874.0
    - thoracentesis E874.4
    - transfusion E874.1
    - vaccination E874.8
  - sterile precautions (during procedure) E872.9
    - aspiration of fluid or tissue (by puncture or catheterization, except heart) E872.5
    - biopsy E872.8
      - needle (aspirating) E872.5
    - blood sampling E872.5
    - catheterization E872.5
      - heart E872.6
    - dialysis (kidney) E872.2
    - endoscopic examination E872.4
    - enema E872.8

Misadventures—*continued*
- infusion E872.1
- injection E872.3
- lumbar puncture E872.5
- needle biopsy E872.5
- paracentesis, abdominal E872.5
- perfusion E872.2
- removal of catheter or packing E872.8
- specified procedure NEC E872.8
- surgical operation E872.0
- thoracentesis E872.5
- transfusion E872.1
- vaccination E872.3
- suture or ligature during surgical procedure E876.2
- to introduce or to remove tube or instrument E876.4
  - foreign object left in body—*see* Misadventure, foreign object
- foreign object left in body (during procedure) E871.9
  - aspiration of fluid or tissue (by puncture or catheterization, except heart) E871.5
  - biopsy E871.8
    - needle (aspirating) E871.5
  - blood sampling E871.5
  - catheterization E871.5
    - heart E871.6
  - dialysis (kidney) E871.2
  - endoscopic examination E871.4
  - enema E871.8
  - infusion E871.1
  - injection E871.3
  - lumbar puncture E871.5
  - needle biopsy E871.5
  - paracentesis, abdominal E871.5
  - perfusion E871.2
  - removal of catheter or packing E871.7
  - specified procedure NEC E871.8
  - surgical operation E871.0
  - thoracentesis E871.5
  - transfusion E871.1
  - vaccination E871.3
- hemorrhage—*see* Misadventure, cut
- inadvertent exposure of patient to radiation (being received for test or therapy) E873.3
- inappropriate
  - operation performed E876.5
  - temperature (too hot or too cold) in local application or packing E873.5
- infusion—*see also* Misadventure, by specific type, infusion
  - excessive amount of fluid E873.0
  - incorrect dilution of fluid E873.1
  - wrong fluid E876.1
- mismatched blood in transfusion E876.0
- nonadministration of necessary drug or medicinal E873.6
- overdose—*see also* Overdose
  - radiation, in therapy E873.2
- perforation—*see* Misadventure, cut
- performance of inappropriate operation E876.5
- puncture—*see* Misadventure, cut
- specified type NEC E876.8
  - failure
    - suture or ligature during surgical operation E876.2
    - to introduce or to remove tube or instrument E876.4
  - foreign object left in body E871.9
  - infusion of wrong fluid E876.1

Misadventures—*continued*
   performance of inappropriate operation
     E876.5
   transfusion of mismatched blood E876.0
   wrong
     fluid in infusion E876.1
     placement of endotracheal tube during
       anesthetic procedure E876.3
   transfusion—*see also* Misadventure, by
     specific type, transfusion
     excessive amount of blood E873.0
     mismatched blood E876.0
   wrong
     drug given in error—*see* Table of drugs
       and chemicals
     fluid in infusion E876.1
     placement of endotracheal tube during
       anesthetic procedure E876.3
Motion (effects) E903
   sickness E903
Mountain sickness E902.0
**Mucus aspiration or inhalation, not of
   newborn** (with asphyxia, obstruction
   respiratory passage, suffocation) E912
Mudslide of cataclysmic nature E909.2
Murder (attempt) (*see also* Assault) E968.9

N

Nail, injury by E920.8
Needlestick (sewing needle) E920.4
   hypodermic E920.5
Neglect —*see also* Privation
   criminal E968.4
   homicidal intent E968.4
Noise (causing injury) (pollution) E928.1

O

Object
   falling
     from, in, on, hitting
       aircraft E844
         due to accident to aircraft—*see*
           categories E840-E842
       machinery—*see also* Accident, machine
       not in operation E916
       motor vehicle (in motion) (on public
         highway) E818
         not on public highway E825
         stationary E916
       nonmotor road vehicle NEC E829
       pedal cycle E826
       person E916
       railway rolling stock, train, vehicle E806
       street car E829
       watercraft E838
         due to accident to watercraft E831
   set in motion by
     accidental explosion of pressure
       vessel—*see* category E921
     firearm—*see* category E922
     machine(ry)—*see* Accident, machine
     transport vehicle—*see* categories
       E800-E848
   thrown from, in, on, towards
     aircraft E844
     cable car (not on rails) E847
       on rails E829

Object—*continued*
   motor vehicle (in motion) (on public
     highway) E818
     not on public highway E825
   nonmotor road vehicle NEC E829
   pedal cycle E826
   street car E829
   vehicle NEC—*see* Accident, vehicle NEC
Obstruction
   air passages, larynx, respiratory passages
     by
       external means NEC—*see* Suffocation
       food, any type (regurgitated) (vomited)
         E911
       material or object, except food E912
       mucus E912
       phlegm E912
       vomitus E911
   digestive tract, except mouth or pharynx
     by
       food, any type E915
       foreign body (any) E915
   esophagus
     food E911
     foreign body, except food E912
     without asphyxia or obstruction of
       respiratory passage E915
   mouth or pharynx
     by
       food, any type E911
       material or object, except food E912
   respiration—*see* Obstruction, air passages
Oil in eye E914
Overdose
   anesthetic (drug)—*see* Table of drugs and
     chemicals
   drug—*see* Table of drugs and chemicals
Overexertion (lifting) (pulling) (pushing) E927
Overexposure (accidental) (to)
   cold (*see also* Cold, exposure to) E901.9
     due to manmade conditions E901.1
   heat (*see also* Heat) E900.9
   radiation—*see* Radiation
   radioactivity—*see* Radiation
   sun, except sunburn E900.0
   weather—*see* Exposure
   wind—*see* Exposure
Overheated (*see also* Heat) E900.9
Overlaid E913.0
Overturning (accidental)
   animal-drawn vehicle E827
   boat, ship, watercraft
     causing
       drowning, submersion E830
       injury except drowning, submersion E831
   machinery—*see* Accident, machine
   motor vehicle (*see also* Loss of control,
     motor vehicle) E816
     with antecedent collision on public
       highway—*see* Collision, motor vehicle
     not on public highway, nontraffic accident
       E825
       with antecedent collision—*see* Collision,
         motor vehicle, not on public highway
   nonmotor road vehicle NEC E829
   off-road type motor vehicle—*see* Loss of
     control, off-road type motor vehicle
   pedal cycle E826
   railway rolling stock, train, vehicle (*see also*
     Derailment, railway) E802
   street car E829
   vehicle NEC—*see* Accident, vehicle NEC

P

Palsy, divers' E902.2
Parachuting (voluntary) (without accident to
aircraft) E844
due to accident to aircraft—*see* categories
E840-E842
Paralysis
divers' E902.2
lead or saturnine E866.0
from pesticide NEC E863.4
Pecked by bird E906.8
Phlegm aspiration or inhalation (with
asphyxia, obstruction respiratory passage,
suffocation) E912
Piercing (*see also* Cut) E920.9
Pinched
between objects (moving) (stationary and
moving) E918
in object E918
Pinned under
machine(ry)—*see* Accident, machine
Place of occurrence of accident —*see*
Accident (to), occurring (at) (in)
Plumbism E866.0
from insecticide NEC E863.4
Poisoning (accidental) (by)—*see also* Table of
drugs and chemicals
carbon monoxide
generated by
aircraft in transit E844
motor vehicle
in motion (on public highway) E818
not on public highway E825
watercraft (in transit) (not in transit) E838
caused by injection of poisons or toxins into
or through skin by plant thorns, spines, or
other mechanism E905.7
marine or sea plants E905.6
fumes or smoke due to
conflagration—*see* Conflagration
explosion or fire—*see* Fire
ignition—*see* Ignition
gas
in legal intervention E972
legal execution, by E978
on watercraft E838
used as anesthetic—*see* Table of drugs
and chemicals
in war operations E997.2
late effect of—*see* Late effect
legal
execution E978
intervention
by gas E972
**Pressure, external, causing asphyxia,
suffocation** (*see also* Suffocation) E913.9
Privation E904.9
food (*see also* Lack of, food) E904.1
helpless person, infant, newborn due to
abandonment or neglect E904.0
late effect of NEC E929.5
resulting from transport accident—*see*
categories E800-E848
water (*see also* Lack of, water) E904.2
**Projected objects, striking against or struck
by** —*see* Striking against, object

Prolonged stay in
high altitude (causing conditions as listed in
E902.0) E902.0
weightless environment E928.0
Prostration
heat—*see* Heat
Pulling, injury in E927
Puncture, puncturing (*see also* Cut) E920.9
by
plant thorns or spines E920.8
toxic reaction E905.7
marine or sea plants E905.6
sea-urchin spine E905.6
Pushing (injury in) (overexertion) E927
by other person(s) (accidental) E917.9
as, or caused by, a crowd, human
stampede (with fall) E917.1
before moving vehicle or object
stated as
intentional, homicidal E968.8
undetermined whether accidental or
intentional E988.8
from
high place
in accidental circumstances—*see*
categories E880-E884
stated as
intentional, homicidal E968.1
undetermined whether accidental or
intentional E987.9
man-made structure, except
residential E987.1
natural site E987.2
residential E987.0
motor vehicle (*see also* Fall, from, motor
vehicle) E818
stated as
intentional, homicidal E968.8
undetermined whether accidental or
intentional E988.8
in sports E917.0
with fall E886.0
with fall E886.9
in sports E886.0

R

Radiation (exposure to) E926.9
abnormal reaction to medical test or therapy
E879.2
arc lamps E926.2
atomic power plant (malfunction) NEC E926.9
in water transport E838
electromagnetic, ionizing E926.3
gamma rays E926.3
in
war operations (from or following nuclear
explosion) (direct) (secondary) E996
laser(s) E997.0
water transport E838
inadvertent exposure of patient (receiving test
or therapy) E873.3
infrared (heaters and lamps) E926.1
excessive heat E900.1
ionized, ionizing (particles, artificially
accelerated) E926.8
electromagnetic E926.3
isotopes, radioactive—*see* Radiation,
radioactive isotopes

Radiation—*continued*
  laser(s) E926.4
    in war operations E997.0
    misadventure in medical care—*see*
      Misadventure, failure, in dosage,
      radiation
  late effect of NEC E929.8
    excessive heat from—*see* Heat
  light sources (visible) (ultraviolet) E926.2
  misadventure in medical or surgical
    procedure—*see* Misadventure, failure, in
    dosage, radiation
  overdose (in medical or surgical procedure)
    E873.2
  radar E926.0
  radioactive isotopes E926.5
    atomic power plant malfunction E926.5
    in water transport E838
    misadventure in medical or surgical
      treatment—*see* Misadventure, failure,
      in dosage, radiation
  radiobiologicals—*see* Radiation, radioactive
    isotopes
  radiofrequency E926.0
  radiopharmaceuticals—*see* Radiation,
    radioactive isotopes
  radium NEC E926.9
  sun E926.2
    excessive heat from E900.0
  welding arc or torch E926.2
    excessive heat from E900.1
  x-rays (hard) (soft) E926.3
    misadventure in medical or surgical
      treatment—*see* Misadventure, failure,
      in dosage, radiation
Rape E960.1
Reaction —abnormal to or following(medical
  or surgical procedure) E879.9
  amputation (of limbs) E878.5
  anastomosis (arteriovenous) (blood vessel)
    (gastrojejunal) (skin) (tendon) (natural,
    artificial material, tissue) E878.2
    external stoma, creation of E878.3
  aspiration (of fluid) E879.4
    tissue E879.8
  biopsy E879.8
  blood
    sampling E879.7
    transfusion
      procedure E879.8
  bypass—*see* Reaction, abnormal, anastomosis
  catheterization
    cardiac E879.0
    urinary E879.6
  colostomy E878.3
  cystostomy E878.3
  dialysis (kidney) E879.1
  drugs or biologicals—*see* Table of drugs and
    chemicals
  duodenostomy E878.3
  electroshock therapy E879.3
  formation of external stoma E878.3
  gastrostomy E878.3
  graft—*see* Reaction, abnormal, anastomosis
  hypothermia E879.8
  implant, implantation (of)
    artificial
      internal device (cardiac pacemaker)
        (electrodes in brain) (heart valve
        prosthesis) (orthopedic) E878.1

Reaction—*continued*
  material or tissue (for anastomosis or
    bypass) E878.2
    with creation of external stoma E878.3
  natural tissues (for anastomosis or
    bypass) E878.2
    as transplantion—*see* Reaction, abnormal,
      transplant
    with creation of external stoma E878.3
  infusion
    procedure E879.8
  injection
    procedure E879.8
  insertion of gastric or duodenal sound E879.5
  insulin-shock therapy E879.3
  lumbar puncture E879.4
  perfusion E879.1
  procedures other than surgical operation (*see*
    also Reaction, abnormal, by specific type
    of procedure) E879.9
    specified procedure NEC E879.8
  radiological procedure or therapy E879.2
  removal of organ (partial) (total) NEC E878.6
    with
      anastomosis, bypass or graft E878.2
      formation of external stoma E878.3
      implant of artificial internal device E878.1
      transplant(ation)
        partial organ E878.4
        whole organ E878.0
  sampling
    blood E879.7
    fluid NEC E879.4
    tissue E879.8
  shock therapy E879.3
  surgical operation (*see also* Reaction,
    abnormal, by specified type of operation)
    E878.9
    restorative NEC E878.4
      with
        anastomosis, bypass or graft E878.2
        formation of external stoma E878.3
        implant(ation)—*see* Reaction, abnormal,
          implant
        transplant(ation)—*see* Reaction,
          abnormal, transplant
    specified operation NEC E878.8
  thoracentesis E879.4
  transfusion
    procedure E879.8
  transplant, transplantation (heart) (kidney)
    (liver) E878.0
    partial organ E878.4
  ureterostomy E878.3
  vaccination E879.8
Reduction in
  atmospheric pressure—*see also* Effects of, air
    pressure
    while surfacing from
      deep water diving causing caisson or
        divers' disease, palsy or paralysis
        E902.2
      underground E902.8
Residual (effect)—*see* Late effect
Rock falling on or hitting (accidentally)
  motor vehicle (in motion) (on public
    highway) E818
    not on public highway E825
  nonmotor road vehicle NEC E829
  pedal cycle E826
  person E916
  railway rolling stock, train, vehicle E806

Running off, away
  animal (being ridden) (in sport or transport)
      E828
    not being ridden E906.8
  animal-drawn vehicle E827
  rails, railway (*see also* Derailment) E802
  roadway
    motor vehicle (without antecedent
        collision) E816
      nontraffic accident E825
        with antecedent collision—*see* Collision,
            motor vehicle, not on public highway
    with
      antecedent collision—*see* Collision motor
          vehicle
      subsequent collision
        involving any object, person or vehicle
          not on public highway E816
          on public highway E811
    nonmotor road vehicle NEC E829
    pedal cycle E826
Run over (accidentally) (by)
  animal (not being ridden) E906.8
    being ridden (in sport or transport) E828
  animal-drawn vehicle E827
  machinery—*see* Accident, machine
  motor vehicle (on public highway)—*see* Hit
      by, motor vehicle
  nonmotor road vehicle NEC E829
  railway train E805
  street car E829
  vehicle NEC E848

S

Saturnism E866.0
  from insecticide NEC E863.4
Scald, scalding (accidental) (by) (from) (in)
    E924.0
  acid—*see* Scald, caustic
  boiling tap water E924.2
  caustic or corrosive liquid, substance E924.1
    swallowed—*see* Table of drugs and
        chemicals
  homicide (attempt)—*see* Assault, burning
  inflicted by other person
    stated as
      intentional or homicidal E968.3
      undetermined whether accidental or
          intentional E988.2
  late effect of NEC E929.8
  liquid (boiling) (hot) E924.0
  local application of externally applied
      substance in medical or surgical care
      E873.5
  molten metal E924.0
  self-inflicted (unspecified whether accidental
      or intentional) E988.2
    stated as intentional, purposeful E958.2
    stated as undetermined whether accidental or
        intentional E988.2
  steam E924.0
  tap water (boiling) E924.2
  transport accident—*see* categories E800-E848
  vapor E924.0
Scratch, cat E906.8
Sea
  sickness E903
Self-mutilation —*see* Suicide

Shock
  anaphylactic (*see also* Table of drugs and
      chemicals) E947.9
  due to
    bite (venomous)—*see* Bite, venomous NEC
    sting—*see* Sting
  electric (*see also* Electric shock) E925.9
  from electric appliance or current (*see also*
      Electric shock) E925.9
Shooting, shot (accidental(ly)) E922.9
  hand gun (pistol) (revolver) E922.0
  himself (*see also* Shooting, self-inflicted)
      E985.4
    hand gun (pistol) (revolver) E985.0
    military firearm, except hand gun E985.3
      hand gun (pistol) (revolver) E985.0
    rifle (hunting) E985.2
      military E985.3
    shotgun (automatic) E985.1
    specified firearm NEC E985.4
    Verey pistol E985.4
  homicide (attempt) E965.4
    hand gun (pistol) (revolver) E965.0
    military firearm, except hand gun E965.3
      hand gun (pistol) (revolver) E965.0
    rifle (hunting) E965.2
      military E965.3
    shotgun (automatic) E965.1
    specified firearm NEC E965.4
    Verey pistol E965.4
  inflicted by other person
    in accidental circumstances E922.9
      hand gun (pistol) (revolver) E922.0
      military firearm, except hand gun E922.3
        hand gun (pistol) (revolver) E922.0
      rifle (hunting) E922.2
        military E922.3
      shotgun (automatic) E922.1
      specified firearm NEC E922.8
      Verey pistol E922.8
    stated as
      intentional, homicidal E965.4
        hand gun (pistol) (revolver) E965.0
        military firearm, except hand gun E965.3
          hand gun (pistol) (revolver) E965.0
        rifle (hunting) E965.2
          military E965.3
        shotgun (automatic) E965.1
        specified firearm E965.4
        Verey pistol E965.4
      undetermined whether accidental or
          intentional E985.4
        hand gun (pistol) (revolver) E985.0
        military firearm, except hand gun E985.3
          hand gun (pistol) (revolver) E985.0
        rifle (hunting) E985.2
        shotgun (automatic) E985.1
        specified firearm NEC E985.4
        Verey pistol E985.4
  in war operations—*see* War operations,
      shooting
  legal
    execution E978
    intervention E970
  military firearm, except hand gun E922.3
    hand gun (pistol) (revolver) E922.0
  rifle (hunting) 922.2
    military E922.3

Shooting, shot—*continued*
self-inflicted (unspecified whether accidental
  or intentional) E985.4
  hand gun (pistol) (revolver) E985.0
  military firearm, except hand gun E985.3
    hand gun (pistol) (revolver) E985.0
  rifle (hunting) E985.2
    military E985.3
  shotgun (automatic) E985.1
  specified firearm NEC E985.4
  stated as
    accidental E922.9
      hand gun (pistol) (revolver) E922.0
      military firearm, except hand gun E922.3
        hand gun (pistol) (revolver) E922.0
      rifle (hunting) E922.2
        military E922.3
      shotgun (automatic) E922.1
      specified firearm NEC E922.8
      Verey pistol E922.8
    intentional, purposeful E955.4
      hand gun (pistol) (revolver) E955.0
      military firearm, except hand gun E955.3
        hand gun (pistol) (revolver) E955.0
      rifle (hunting) E955.2
        military E955.3
      shotgun (automatic) E955.1
      specified firearm NEC E955.4
      Verey pistol E955.4
shotgun (automatic) E922.1
specified firearm NEC E922.8
stated as undetermined whether accidental or
  intentional E985.4
  hand gun (pistol) (revolver) E985.0
  military firearm, except hand gun E985.3
    hand gun (pistol) (revolver) E985.0
  rifle (hunting) E985.2
    military E985.3
  shotgun (automatic) E985.1
  specified firearm NEC E985.4
  Verey pistol E985.4
suicidal (attempt) E955.4
  hand gun (pistol) (revolver) E955.0
  military firearm, except hand gun E955.3
    hand gun (pistol) (revolver) E955.0
  rifle (hunting) E955.2
    military E955.3
  shotgun (automatic) E955.1
  specified firearm NEC E955.4
  Verey pistol E955.4
Verey pistol E922.8
Shoving (accidentally) by other person (*see
  also* Pushing by other person) E917.9
Sickness
air E903
alpine E902.0
car E903
motion E903
mountain E902.0
sea E903
travel E903
Sinking (accidental)
boat, ship, watercraft (causing drowning,
  submersion) E830
  causing injury except drowning,
    submersion E831
Siriasis E900.0
Skydiving E844
Slashed wrists (*see also* Cut, self-inflicted)
  E986

Slipping (accidental)
on
  deck (of boat, ship, watercraft) (icy)
    (oily) (wet) E835
  ice E885
  ladder of ship E833
    due to accident to watercraft E831
  mud E885
  oil E885
  snow E885
  stairs of ship E833
    due to accident to watercraft E831
  surface
    slippery E885
    wet E885
Sliver, wood, injury by E920.8
Smothering, smothered (*see also* Suffocation)
  E913.9
Sodomy (assault) E960.1
Solid substance in eye (any part) or adnexa
  E914
Sound waves (causing injury) E928.1
Splinter, injury by E920.8
Stab, stabbing E966
accidental—*see* Cut
Starvation E904.1
helpless person, infant, newborn—*see* Lack of
  food
homicidal intent E968.4
late effect of NEC E929.5
resulting from accident connected with
  transport—*see* categories E800-E848
Stepped on
by
  animal (not being ridden) E906.8
    being ridden (in sport or transport) E828
  crowd E917.1
  person E917.9
    in sports E917.0
in sports E917.0
Stepping on
object (moving) (projected) (stationary) E917.9
  with fall E888
  in sports E917.0
person E917.9
  by crowd E917.1
  in sports E917.0
Sting E905.9
ant E905.5
bee E905.3
caterpillar E905.5
coral E905.6
hornet E905.3
insect NEC E905.5
jelly fish E905.6
marine animal or plant E905.6
nematocysts E905.6
scorpion E905.2
sea anemone E905.6
sea cucumber E905.6
wasp E905.3
yellow jacket E905.3
Storm E908.9
specified type NEC E908.8
Straining, injury in E927
Strangling —*see* Suffocation
Strangulation —*see* Suffocation
Strenuous movements (in recreational or other
  activities) E927

Striking against
  bottom (when jumping or diving into water)
      E883.0
  object (moving) (projected) (stationary) E917.9
      with fall E888
      caused by crowd (with fall) E917.1
      in
          running water E917.2
              with drowning or submersion—*see*
                  Submersion
          sports E917.0
      person(s) E917.9
          with fall E886.9
              in sports E886.0
          as, or caused by, a crowd E917.1
              in sports E917.0
                  with fall E886.0
Stroke
  heat—*see* Heat
  lightning E907
Struck by —*see also* Hit by
  lightning E907
  thunderbolt E907
Stumbling over animal, carpet, curb, rug or
      (small) object (with fall) E885
      without fall—*see* Striking against, object
Submersion (accidental) E910.8
  boat, ship, watercraft (causing drowning,
      submersion) E830
      causing injury except drowning,
          submersion E831
  by other person
      in accidental circumstances—*see* category
          E910
      intentional, homicidal E964
      stated as undetermined whether accidental
          or intentional E984
  due to
      accident
          machinery—*see* Accident, machine
          to boat, ship, watercraft E830
          transport—*see* categories E800-E848
      avalanche E909.2
      cataclysmic
          earth surface movement or eruption E909.9
          storm E908.9
      cloudburst E908.8
      cyclone E908.1
      fall
          from
              boat, ship, watercraft (not involved in
                  accident) E832
                  burning, crushed E830
                  involved in accident, collision E830
              gangplank (into water) E832
              overboard NEC E832
      flood E908.2
      hurricane E908.0
      jumping into water E910.8
          from boat, ship, watercraft
              burning, crushed, sinking E830
              involved in accident, collision E830
              not involved in accident, for swim
                  E910.2
          in recreational activity (without diving
              equipment) E910.2
              with or using diving equipment E910.1
          to rescue another person E910.3
      homicide (attempt) E964

Submersion—*continued*
  in
      bathtub E910.4
      specified activity, not sport, transport or
          recreational E910.3
      sport or recreational activity (without
          diving equipment) E910.2
          with or using diving equipment E910.1
          water skiing E910.0
      swimming pool NEC E910.8
      war operations E995
      water transport E832
          due to accident to boat, ship, watercraft
              E830
  landslide E909.2
      overturning boat, ship, watercraft E909.2
      sinking boat, ship, watercraft E909.2
      submersion boat, ship, watercraft E909.2
  tidal wave E909.4
      caused by storm E908.0
  torrential rain E908.2
  late effect of NEC E929.8
  quenching tank E910.8
  self-inflicted (unspecified whether accidental
      or intentional) E984
      in accidental circumstances—*see* category
          E910
      stated as intentional, purposeful E954
  stated as undetermined whether accidental or
      intentional E984
  suicidal (attempted) E954
  while
      attempting rescue of another person
          E910.3
      engaged in
          marine salvage E910.3
          underwater construction or repairs E910.3
      fishing, not from boat E910.2
      hunting, not from boat E910.2
      ice skating E910.2
      pearl diving E910.3
      placing fishing nets E910.3
      playing in water E910.2
      scuba diving E910.1
          nonrecreational E910.3
      skin diving E910.1
      snorkel diving E910.2
      spear fishing underwater E910.1
      surfboarding E910.2
      swimming (swimming pool) E910.2
      wading (in water) E910.2
      water skiing E910.0
Sucked
  into
      jet (aircraft) E844
Suffocation (accidental) (by external means)
      (by pressure) (mechanical) E913.9
  caused by other person
      in accidental circumstances—*see* category
          E913
      stated as
          intentional, homicidal E963
          undetermined whether accidental or
              intentional E983.9
          by, in
              hanging E983.0
              plastic bag E983.1
              specified means NEC E983.3

Suffocation—*continued*
due to, by
  avalanche E909.2
  bedclothes E913.0
  bib E913.0
  blanket E913.0
  cave-in E913.3
    caused by cataclysmic earth surface
      movement or eruption E909.9
  conflagration—*see* Conflagration
  explosion—*see* Explosion
  falling earth, other substance E913.3
  fire—*see* Fire
  food, any type (ingestion) (inhalation)
    (regurgitated) (vomited) E911
  foreign body, except food (ingestion)
    (inhalation) E912
  ignition—*see* Ignition
  landslide E909.2
  machine(ry)—*see* Accident, machine
  material, object except food, ingested, inhaled E912
    nose or mouth, ingested, inhaled E912
  mucus (aspiration) (inhalation), not of
    newborn E912
  phlegm (aspiration) (inhalation) E912
  pillow E913.0
  plastic bag—*see* Suffocation, in, plastic
    bag
  sheet (plastic) E913.0
  specified means NEC E913.8
  vomitus (aspiration) (inhalation) E911
homicidal (attempt) E963
in
  airtight enclosed place E913.2
  baby carriage E913.0
  bed E913.0
  closed place E913.2
  cot, cradle E913.0
  perambulator E913.0
  plastic bag (in accidental circumstances)
    E913.1
    homicidal, purposely inflicted by other
      person E963
    self-inflicted (unspecified whether
      accidental or intentional) E983.1
      in accidental circumstances E913.1
      intentional, suicidal E953.1
    stated as undetermined whether
      accidentally or purposely inflicted
      E983.1
    suicidal, purposely self-inflicted E953.1
  refrigerator E913.2
self-inflicted—*see also* Suffocation, stated as
  undetermined whether accidental or
  intentional E953.9
  in accidental circumstances—*see* category
    E913
  stated as intentional, purposeful—*see*
    Suicide, suffocation
stated as undetermined whether accidental or
  intentional E983.9
  by, in
    hanging E983.0
    plastic bag E983.1
    specified means NEC E983.8
suicidal—*see* Suicide, suffocation

Suicide, suicidal (attempted) (by) E958.9
  burning, burns E958.1
  caustic substance E958.7
    poisoning E950.7
    swallowed E950.7
  cold, extreme E958.3
  cut (any part of body) E956
  cutting or piercing instrument (classifiable to
    E920) E956
  drowning E954
  electrocution E958.4
  explosive(s) (classifiable to E923) E955.5
  fire E958.1
  firearm (classifiable to E922)—*see* Shooting,
    suicidal
  hanging E953.0
  jumping
    before moving object, train, vehicle
      E958.0
    from high place—*see* Jumping, from,
      high place, stated as, suicidal
  knife E956
  late effect of E959
  motor vehicle, crashing of E958.5
  poisoning—*see* Table of drugs and chemicals
  puncture (any part of body) E956
  scald E958.2
  shooting—*see* Shooting, suicidal
  specified means NEC E958.8
  stab (any part of body) E956
  strangulation—*see* Suicide, suffocation
  submersion E954
  suffocation E953.9
    by, in
      hanging E953.0
      plastic bag E953.1
      specified means NEC E953.8
  wound NEC E958.9
Sunburn E926.2
Sunstroke E900.0
Supersonic waves (causing injury) E928.1
Surgical procedure, complication of
  delayed or as an abnormal reaction without
    mention of misadventure—*see* Reaction,
    abnormal
  due to or as a result of misadventure—*see*
    Misadventure
Swallowed, swallowing
  foreign body—*see* Foreign body, alimentary
    canal
  poison—*see* Table of drugs and chemicals
  substance
    caustic—*see* Table of drugs and chemicals
    corrosive—*see* Table of drugs and
      chemicals
    poisonous—*see* Table of drugs and
      chemicals
Swimmers cramp (*see also* category E910)
  E910.2
  not in recreation or sport E910.3
Syndrome, battered
  baby or child—*see* Abuse, child
  wife—*see* Assault

T

Tackle in sport E886.0
Thermic fever E900.9
Thermoplegia E900.9
Thirst —*see also* Lack of water
  resulting from accident connected with
     transport—*see* categories E800-E848
Thrown (accidently)
  against object in or part of vehicle
    by motion of vehicle
      aircraft E844
      boat, ship, watercraft E838
      motor vehicle (on public highway) E818
        not on public highway E825
        off-road type (not on public highway)
          E821
          on public highway E818
        snow vehicle E820
          on public highway E818
      nonmotor road vehicle NEC E829
      railway rolling stock, train, vehicle E806
      street car E829
  from
    animal (being ridden) (in sport or
      transport) E828
    high place, homicide (attempt) E968.1
    machinery—*see* Accident, machine
    vehicle NEC—*see* Accident, vehicle NEC
  off—*see* Thrown, from
  overboard (by motion of boat, ship,
    watercraft) E832
    by accident to boat, ship, watercraft E830
Thunderbolt NEC E907
Tidal wave (any injury) E909.4
  caused by storm E908.0
Took
  overdose of drug—*see* Table of drugs and
    chemicals
  poison—*see* Table of drugs and chemicals
Tornado (any injury) E908.1
Torrential rain (any injury) E908.2
Traffic accident NEC E819
Trampled by animal E906.8
  being ridden (in sport or transport) E828
Trapped (accidentally)
  between
    objects (moving) (stationary and moving)
      E918
  by
    door of
      elevator E918
      motor vehicle (on public highway) (while
        alighting, boarding)—*see* Fall, from,
        motor vehicle, while alighting
      railway train (underground) E806
      street car E829
      subway train E806
    in object E918
Travel (effects) E903
  sickness E903
Tree
  falling on or hitting E916
    motor vehicle (in motion) (on public
      highway) E818
      not on public highway E825
    nonmotor road vehicle NEC E829
    pedal cycle E826
    person E916
    railway rolling stock, train, vehicle E806
    street car E829

Trench foot E901.0
Tripping over animal, carpet, curb, rug, or
  small object (with fall) E885
  without fall—*see* Striking against, object
Tsunami E909.4
Twisting, injury in E927

V

Violence, nonaccidental (*see also* Assault)
  E968.9
Volcanic eruption (any injury) E909.1
Vomitus in air passages (with asphyxia,
  obstruction or suffocation) E911

W

War operations (during hostilities) (injury)
  (by) (in) E995
  after cessation of hostilities, injury due to
    E998
  air blast E993
  aircraft burned, destroyed, exploded, shot
    down E994
  asphyxia from
    chemical E997.2
    fire, conflagration (caused by
      fire-producing device or conventional
      weapon) E990.9
      from nuclear explosion E996
      petrol bomb E990.0
    fumes E997.2
    gas E997.2
  battle wound NEC E995
  bayonet E995
  biological warfare agents E997.1
  blast (air) (effects) E993
    from nuclear explosion E996
    underwater E992
  bomb (mortar) (explosion) E993
    after cessation of hostilities E998
    fragments, injury by E991.9
      antipersonnel E991.3
  bullet(s) (from carbine, machine gun, pistol,
    rifle, shotgun) E991.2
    rubber E991.0
  burn from
    chemical E997.2
    fire, conflagration (caused by
      fire-producing device or conventional
      weapon) E990.9
      from nuclear explosion E996
      petrol bomb E990.0
    gas E997.2
  burning aircraft E994
  chemical E997.2
  chlorine E997.2
  conventional warfare, specified form NEC
    E995
  crushing by falling aircraft E994
  depth charge E992
  destruction of aircraft E994
  disability as sequela one year or more after
    injury E999
  drowning E995
  effect (direct) (secondary) nuclear weapon
    E996
  explosion (artillery shell) (breech block)
    (cannon shell) E993

RAILWAY ACCIDENTS (E800–E807)

The following fourth–digit subdivisions are for use with categories E800–E807 to identify the injured person.

.0 Railway employee

Any person who by virtue of his employment in connection with a railway, whether by the railway company or not, is at increased risk of involvement in a railway accident, such as:

catering staff on train	postal staff on train
driver	railway fireman
guard	shunter
porter	sleeping car attendant

.1 Passenger on railway

Any authorized person traveling on a train, except a railway employee

Excludes: intending passenger waiting at station (.8)
unauthorized rider on railway vehicle (.8)

.2 Pedestrian

See definition (r), Vol. 1, page 479

.3 Pedal cyclist

See definition (p), Vol. 1, page 479

.8 Other specified person

Intending passenger waiting at station

Unauthorized rider on railway vehicle

.9 Unspecified person

MOTOR VEHICLE TRAFFIC AND NONTRAFFIC ACCIDENTS
(E810–825)

The following fourth–digit subdivisions are for use with categories E810–E819 and E820–E825 to identify the injured person:

.0 Driver of motor vehicle other than motorcycle

   See definition (l), Vol. 1, page 479

.1 Passenger in motor vehicle other than motorcycle

   See definition (l), Vol. 1, page 479

.2 Motorcyclist

   See definition (l), Vol. 1, page 479

.3 Passenger on motorcycle

   See definition (l), Vol. 1, page 479

.4 Occupant of streetcar

.5 Rider of animal; occupant of animal–drawn vehicle

.6 Pedal cyclist

   See definition (p), Vol. 1, page 479

.7 Pedestrian

   See definition (r), Vol. 1, page 479

.8 Other specified person

   Occupant of vehicle other than above

   Person in railway train involved in accident

   Unauthorized rider of motor vehicle

.9 Unspecified person

OTHER ROAD VEHICLE ACCIDENTS (E826–E829)

(animal–drawn vehicle, streetcar, pedal cycle, and other nonmotor road vehicle accidents)

The following fourth–digit subdivisions are for use with categories E826–E829 to identify the injured person:

.0 Pedestrian

   See definition (r), Vol. 1, page 479

.1 Pedal cyclist (does not apply to codes E827, E828, E829)

   See definition (p), Vol. 1, page 479

.2 Rider of animal (does not apply to code E829)

.3 Occupant of animal–drawn vehicle (does not apply to codes E828, E829)

.4 Occupant of streetcar

.8 Other specified person

.9 Unspecified person

WATER TRANSPORT ACCIDENTS (E830–E838)

The following fourth–digit subdivisions are for use with categories E830–E838 to identify the injured person:

.0 Occupant of small boat, unpowered

.1 Occupant of small boat, powered

See definition (t), Vol. 1, page 479

Excludes: water skier (.4)

.2 Occupant of other watercraft — crew

Persons:

engaged in operation of watercraft

providing passenger services [cabin attendants, ship's physician, catering personnel]

working on ship during voyage in other capacity [musician in band, operators of shops and beauty parlors]

.3 Occupant of other watercraft — other than crew

Passenger

Occupant of lifeboat, other than crew, after abandoning ship

.4 Water skier

.5 Swimmer

.6 Dockers, stevedores

Longshoreman employed on the dock in loading and unloading ships

.8 Other specified person

Immigration and custom officials on board ship

Person:

accompanying passenger or member of crew

visiting boat

Pilot (guiding ship into port)

.9 Unspecified person

AIR AND SPACE TRANSPORT ACCIDENTS (E840–E845)

The following fourth–digit subdivisions are for use with categories E840–E845 to identify the injured person:

.0 Occupant of spacecraft

.1 Occupant of military aircraft, any

Crew	in military aircraft [air force] [army]
Passenger (civilian) (military)	[national guard] [navy]
Troops	

Excludes: occupants of aircraft operated under jurisdiction of police departments (.5) parachutist (.7).

.2 Crew of commercial aircraft (powered) in surface to surface transport

.3 Other occupant of commercial aircraft (powered) in surface to surface transport

Flight personnel:

not part of crew
on familiarization flight

Passenger on aircraft (powered) NOS

.4 Occupant of commercial aircraft (powered) in surface to air transport

Occupant [crew] [passenger] of aircraft (powered) engaged in activities, such as:

aerial spraying (crops) (fire retardants)
air drops of emergency supplies
air drops of parachutists, except from military craft
crop dusting
lowering of construction material [bridge or telephone pole]
sky writing

.5 Occupant of other powered aircraft

Occupant [crew] [passenger] of aircraft (powered) engaged in activities, such as:

aerobatic flying
aircraft racing
rescue operation
storm surveillance
traffic surveillance

Occupant of private plane NOS

.6 Occupant of unpowered aircraft, except parachutist

Occupant of aircraft classifiable to E842

.7 Parachutist (military) (other)

Person making voluntary descent

Excludes: person making descent after accident to aircraft (.1–.6)

.8 Ground crew, airline employee

Persons employed at airfields (civil) (military) or launching pads, not occupants of aircraft

.9 Other person

005.8 Other bacterial food poisoning
Description deleted

005.89 Other bacterial food poisoning
Description added

079.6 Respiratory syncytial virus (RSV)
New code

250 Diabetes mellitus
Exclusion revised

250.8 Diabetes with other specified manifestations
Exclusion deleted

290 Senile and presenile organic psychotic conditions
"Use additional code" revised

290.1 Presenile dementia
Description revised

291.0 Alcohol withdrawal delirium
Exclusion added

291.8 Other specified alcoholic psychosis
Description deleted

291.81 Alcohol withdrawal
New code

291.89 Other
New code

293 Transient organic psychotic conditions
"Use additional code" deleted; "Code first" added

293.84 Organic anxiety syndrome
New code

294.1 Dementia in conditions classified elsewhere
"Code first" revised

300.7 Hypochondriasis
Description revised

300.81 Somatization disorder
Description revised

300.82 Undifferentiated somatoform disorder
New code

315.31 Developmental language disorder
Description revised

315.32 Receptive language disorder (mixed)
New code

349.1 Nervous system complications from surgically implanted device
Exclusion revised

380.13 Other acute infections of external ear
Description revised

414.00 Of unspecified type of vessel, native or graft
Code revised

414.04 Of artery bypass graft
New code

414.05 Of unspecified type of bypass graft
New code

437.3 Cerebral aneurysm, nonruptured
Description added; Exclusion added

440.8 Of other specified arteries
Exclusion revised

442 Other aneurysm
Exclusion revised

442.81 Artery of neck
Description revised; Exclusion added

442.89 Other
Exclusion revised

444.89 Other
Exclusion revised

447.6 Arteritis, unspecified
Exclusion revised

453.8 Of other specified veins
Exclusion revised

459.81 Venous (peripheral) insufficiency, unspecified
"Use additional code" added

466.11 Acute bronchiolitis due to respiratory syncytial virus (RSV)
New code

466.19 Acute bronchiolitis due to other infectious organisms
New code

474.1 Hypertrophy of tonsils and adenoids
Exclusion added

483.1 Chlamydia
New code

485 Bronchopneumonia, organism unspecified
Exclusion revised

569.0 Anal and rectal polyp
Description added; Exclusion added

574.6 Calculus of gallbladder and bile duct with acute cholecystitis
New code

574.7 Calculus of gallbladder and bile duct with other cholecystitis
New code

574.8 Calculus of gallbladder and bile duct with acute and chronic cholecystitis
New code

574.9 Calculus of gallbladder and bile duct without cholecystitis
New code

575.0 Acute cholecystitis
Exclusion revised

575.1 Other cholecystitis
Exclusion revised

575.10 Cholecystitis, unspecified
New code

575.11 Chronic cholecystitis
New code

575.12 Acute and chronic cholecystitis
New code

591 Hydronephrosis
Exclusion revised

593.5 Hydroureter
Exclusion revised

599.0 Urinary tract infection, site not specified
Exclusion added

625.4 Premenstrual tension syndromes
Description revised

630-677 COMPLICATIONS OF PREGNANCY, CHILDBIRTH, AND THE PUERPERIUM
Category revised

648.9 Other current conditions classifiable elsewhere
Description revised

686.8 Other specified local infections of skin and subcutaneous tissue
Exclusion revised

691.8 Other atopic dermatitis and related conditions
Description revised

706.3 Seborrhea
Exclusion revised

707 Chronic ulcer of skin
Inclusion added; Exclusion revised

752.5 Undescended and retractile testicle
Code revised; Description deleted

752.51 Undescended testis
Code added

752.52 Retractile testis
New code

752.6 Hypospadias and epispadias and other penile anomalies
Code revised; Description deleted

752.61 Hypospadias
Code added

752.62 Epispadias
New code

752.63 Congenital chordee
New code

752.64 Micropenis
New code

752.65 Hidden penis
New code

752.69 Other penile anomalies
New code

752.8 Other specified anomalies of genital organs
Description revised; Exclusion revised

753.2 Obstructive defects of renal pelvis and ureter
Description deleted

753.20 Unspecified obstructive defect of renal pelvis and ureter
New code

753.21 Congenital obstruction of ureteropelvic junction
New code

753.22 Congenital obstruction of ureterovesical junction
New code

753.23 Congenital ureterocele
New code

753.29 Other
New code

758.8 Other conditions due to chromosome anomalies
Code revised; Description deleted

758.81 Other conditions due to sex chromosome anomalies
New code

758.89 Other
New code

780.6 Fever
Description revised

783.1 Abnormal weight gain
Exclusion revised

785.4 Gangrene
"Code first" added; Exclusion added

788.3 Urinary incontinence
"Code first" added

800-999 INJURY AND POISONING
"Use E code(s)" added

800-804 FRACTURE OF SKULL
Fifth-digit subclassification revised

844 Sprains and strains of knee and leg
Exclusion deleted

850-854 INTRACRANIAL INJURY, EXCLUDING THOSE WITH SKULL FRACTURE
Exclusion revised; Fifth-digit subclassification revised

854 Intracranial injury of other and unspecified nature
Exclusion added

922.3 Back
Description deleted

922.31 Back
New code

922.32 Buttock
New code

922.33 Interscapular region
New code

989.81 Asbestos
Exclusion added

995 Certain adverse effects not elsewhere classified
Note deleted

995.5 Child maltreatment syndrome
Description deleted; "Use additional code(s)" added; "Use additional E code" added

995.50 Child abuse, unspecified
New code

995.51 Child emotional/psychological abuse
New code

995.52 Child neglect (nutritional)
New code

995.53 Child sexual abuse
New code

995.54 Child physical abuse
New code

995.55 Shaken infant syndrome
New code

995.59 Other child abuse and neglect
New code

995.80 Adult maltreatment, unspecified
New code

995.81 Adult physical abuse
Code revised; Description revised; "Use additional code" added

995.82 Adult emotional/psychological abuse
Code added

995.83 **Adult sexual abuse**
Code added

995.84 **Adult neglect (nutritional)**
New code

995.85 **Other adult abuse and neglect**
New code

997.6 **Amputation stump complication**
Code revised; Description deleted; Exclusion revised

997.62 **Infection (chronic)**
"Use additional code" added

998.1 **Hemorrhage or hematoma or seroma complicating a procedure**
Code revised; Description deleted; Exclusion revised

998.11 **Hemorrhage complicating a procedure**
New code

998.12 **Hematoma complicating a procedure**
New code

998.13 **Seroma complicating a procedure**
New code

998.5 **Postoperative infection**
Description deleted; "Use additional code" deleted

998.51 **Infected postoperative seroma**
New code

998.59 **Other postoperative infection**
New code

998.83 **Non-healing surgical wound**
New code

999.3 **Other infection**
Exclusion revised

V15.41 **History of physical abuse**
New code

V15.42 **History of emotional abuse**
New code

V15.49 **Other**
New code

V41.7 **Problems with sexual function**
Exclusion revised

V55 **Attention to artificial openings**
Inclusion revised; Exclusion revised

V58 **Encounter for other and unspecified procedures and aftercare**
Exclusion revised

V58.0 **Radiotherapy**
Exclusion revised

V58.82 **Fitting and adjustment of non-vascular catheter NEC**
Exclusion revised

V61.1 **Counseling for marital and partner problems**
Code revised; Description deleted

V61.10 **Counseling for marital and partner problems, unspecified**
New code

V61.11 **Counseling for victim of spousal and partner abuse**
New code

V61.12 **Counseling for perpetrator of spousal and partner abuse**
New code

V61.20 **Counseling for parent-child problem, unspecified**
Code revised

V61.21 **Counseling for victim of child abuse**
Code revised; Exclusion revised

V61.22 **Counseling for perpetrator of parental child abuse**
New code

V62 **Other psychosocial circumstances**
Exclusion revised

V62.83 **Counseling for perpetrator of physical/sexual abuse**
New code

V66 **Convalescence and palliative care**
Code revised

V66.7 **Encounter for palliative care**
New code

V67.4 **Following treatment of healed fracture**
Code revised; Exclusion added

E849 **Place of occurrence**
Description revised

E908 **Cataclysmic storms, and floods resulting from storms**
Exclusion revised

E916 **Struck accidentally by falling object**
"Code first" added; Exclusion deleted

E967 **Child and adult battering and other maltreatment**
Code revised

E967.0 **By father or stepfather**
Code revised

E967.2 **By mother or stepmother**
New code

E967.3 **By spouse or partner**
New code

E967.4 **By child**
New code

E967.5 **By sibling**
New code

E967.6 **By grandparent**
New code

E967.7 **By other relative**
New code

E967.8 **By non-related caregiver**
New code

E980-89 **INJURY UNDETERMINED WHETHER ACCIDENTALLY OR PURPOSELY INFLICTED**
Note revised

PROCEDURES: TABULAR LIST
AND
ALPHABETIC INDEX
VOLUME 3

1. **OPERATIONS ON THE NERVOUS SYSTEM (01-05)**

01 **Incision and excision of skull, brain, and cerebral meninges**

   01.0 **Cranial puncture**

      01.01 **Cisternal puncture**
Cisternal tap

> Excludes: pneumocisternogram (87.02)

      01.02 **Ventriculopuncture through previously implanted catheter**
Puncture of ventricular shunt tubing

      01.09 **Other cranial puncture**
Aspiration of
  subarachnoid space
  subdural space
Cranial aspiration NOS
Puncture of anterior fontanel
Subdural tap (through fontanel)

   01.1 **Diagnostic procedures on skull, brain, and cerebral meninges**

      01.11 **Closed [percutaneous] [needle] biopsy of cerebral meninges**
Burr hole approach

      01.12 **Open biopsy of cerebral meninges**

      01.13 **Closed [percutaneous] [needle] biopsy of brain**
Burr hole approach
Stereotactic method

      01.14 **Open biopsy of brain**

      01.15 **Biopsy of skull**

      01.18 **Other diagnostic procedures on brain and cerebral meninges**

> Excludes: cerebral:
>   arteriography (88.41)
>   thermography (88.81)
> contrast radiogram of brain (87.01-87.02)
> echoencephalogram (88.71)
> electroencephalogram (89.14)
> microscopic examination of specimen from nervous system and of
>   spinal fluid (90.01-90.09)
> neurologic examination (89.13)
> phlebography of head and neck (88.61)
> pneumoencephalogram (87.01)
> radioisotope scan:
>   cerebral (92.11)
>   head NEC (92.12)
> tomography of head:
>   C.A.T. scan (87.03)
>   other (87.04)

      01.19 **Other diagnostic procedures on skull**

> Excludes: transillumination of skull (89.16)
> x-ray of skull (87.17)

   01.2 **Craniotomy and craniectomy**

> Excludes: decompression of skull fracture (02.02)
> exploration of orbit (16.01-16.09)
> that as operative approach—omit code

      01.21 **Incision and drainage of cranial sinus**

      01.22 **Removal of intracranial neurostimulator**

> Excludes: removal with synchronous replacement (02.93)

      01.23 **Reopening of craniotomy site**

	Valid O.R. procedure		Non-O.R. procedure		Nonspecific O.R. procedure		Noncovered O.R. procedure

01.24 Other craniotomy
Cranial:
  decompression
  exploration
  trephination
Craniotomy NOS
Craniotomy with removal of:
  epidural abscess
  extradural hematoma
  foreign body of skull

| *Excludes:* | *removal of foreign body with incision into brain (01.39)* |

01.25 Other craniectomy
Debridement of skull NOS
Sequestrectomy of skull

| *Excludes:* | *debridement of compound fracture of skull (02.02)* |
| | *strip craniectomy (02.01)* |

01.3 Incision of brain and cerebral meninges

01.31 Incision of cerebral meninges
Drainage of:
  intracranial hygroma
  subarachnoid abscess (cerebral)
  subdural empyema

01.32 Lobotomy and tractotomy
Division of:
  brain tissue
  cerebral tracts
Percutaneous (radio frequency) cingulotomy

01.39 Other incision of brain
Amygdalohippocampotomy
Drainage of intracerebral hematoma
Incision of brain NOS

| *Excludes:* | *division of cortical adhesions (02.91)* |

01.4 Operations on thalamus and globus pallidus

01.41 Operations on thalamus
Chemothalamectomy
Thalamotomy

01.42 Operations on globus pallidus
Pallidoansectomy
Pallidotomy

01.5 Other excision or destruction of brain and meninges

01.51 Excision of lesion or tissue of cerebral meninges
Decortication ⎤
Resection   ⎬ of (cerebral) meninges
Stripping of subdural ⎦
  membrane

| *Excludes:* | *biopsy of cerebral meninges (01.11-01.12)* |

01.52 Hemispherectomy

01.53 Lobectomy of brain

01.59 Other excision or destruction of lesion or tissue of brain
Curettage of brain
Debridement of brain
Marsupialization of brain cyst
Transtemporal (mastoid) excision of brain tumor

| *Excludes:* | *biopsy of brain (01.13-01.14)* |
| | *that by stereotactic radiosurgery (92.3)* |

01.6 Excision of lesion of skull
Removal of granulation tissue of cranium

| *Excludes:* | *biopsy of skull (01.15)* |
| | *sequestrectomy (01.25)* |

02 Other operations on skull, brain, and cerebral meninges

● Code new
  to this edition

▲ Revision of
  existing code

④ ⑤ Fourth or fifth
    digit required

02.0   Cranioplasty

> Excludes: *that with synchronous repair of encephalocele (02.12)*

02.01   Opening of cranial suture
Linear craniectomy
Strip craniectomy

02.02   Elevation of skull fracture fragments
Debridement of compound fracture of skull
Decompression of skull fracture
Reduction of skull fracture

> *Code also any synchronous debridement of brain (01.59)*

> Excludes: *debridement of skull NOS (01.25)*
> *removal of granulation tissue of cranium (01.6)*

02.03   Formation of cranial bone flap
Repair of skull with flap

02.04   Bone graft to skull
Pericranial graft (autogenous) (heterogenous)

02.05   Insertion of skull plate
Replacement of skull plate

02.06   Other cranial osteoplasty
Repair of skull NOS
Revision of bone flap of skull

02.07   Removal of skull plate

> Excludes: *removal with synchronous*
> *replacement (02.05)*

02.1   Repair of cerebral meninges

> Excludes: *marsupialization of cerebral lesion (01.59)*

02.11   Simple suture of dura mater of brain

02.12   Other repair of cerebral meninges
Closure of fistula of cerebrospinal fluid
Dural graft
Repair of encephalocele including synchronous cranioplasty
Repair of meninges NOS
Subdural patch

02.13   Ligation of meningeal vessel
Ligation of:
longitudinal sinus
middle meningeal artery

02.14   Choroid plexectomy
Cauterization of choroid plexus

02.2   Ventriculostomy
Anastomosis of ventricle to:
cervical subarachnoid space
cisterna magna
Insertion of Holter valve
Ventriculocisternal intubation

02.3   Extracranial ventricular shunt
Includes: that with insertion of valve

02.31   Ventricular shunt to structure in head and neck
Ventricle to nasopharynx shunt
Ventriculomastoid anastomosis

02.32   Ventricular shunt to circulatory system
Ventriculoatrial anastomosis
Ventriculocaval shunt

02.33   Ventricular shunt to thoracic cavity
Ventriculopleural anastomosis

02.34   Ventricular shunt to abdominal cavity and organs
Ventriculocholecystostomy
Ventriculoperitoneostomy

02.35   Ventricular shunt to urinary system
Ventricle to ureter shunt

Valid O.R. procedure	Non-O.R. procedure	Nonspecific O.R. procedure	Noncovered O.R. procedure

02.39 **Other operations to establish drainage of ventricle**
Ventricle to bone marrow shunt
Ventricular shunt to extracranial site NEC

02.4 **Revision, removal, and irrigation of ventricular shunt**

> Excludes: *revision of distal catheter of ventricular shunt (54.95)*

02.41 **Irrigation of ventricular shunt**

02.42 **Replacement of ventricular shunt**
Reinsertion of Holter valve
Replacement of ventricular catheter
Revision of ventriculoperitoneal shunt at ventricular site

02.43 **Removal of ventricular shunt**

02.9 **Other operations on skull, brain, and cerebral meninges**

> Excludes: *operations on:*
> *pineal gland (07.17, 07.51-07.59)*
> *pituitary gland [hypophysis] (07.13-07.15, 07.61-07.79)*

02.91 **Lysis of cortical adhesions**

02.92 **Repair of brain**

02.93 **Implantation of intracranial neurostimulator**
Implantation, insertion, placement, or replacement of intracranial:
brain pacemaker [neuropacemaker]
depth electrodes
electroencephalographic receiver
epidural pegs
foramen ovale electrodes
intracranial electrostimulator
subdural grids
subdural strips

02.94 **Insertion or replacement of skull tongs or halo traction device**

02.95 **Removal of skull tongs or halo traction device**

02.96 **Insertion of sphenoidal electrodes**

02.99 **Other**

> Excludes: *chemical shock therapy (94.24)*
> *electroshock therapy:*
> *subconvulsive (94.26)*
> *other (94.27)*

03 **Operations on spinal cord and spinal canal structures**

03.0 **Exploration and decompression of spinal canal structures**

03.01 **Removal of foreign body from spinal canal**

03.02 **Reopening of laminectomy site**

03.09 **Other exploration and decompression of spinal canal**
Decompression:
laminectomy
laminotomy
Exploration of spinal nerve root
Foraminotomy

> Excludes: *drainage of spinal fluid by anastomosis (03.71-03.79)*
> *laminectomy with excision of intervertebral disc (80.51)*
> *spinal tap (03.31)*
> *that as operative approach—omit code*

03.1 **Division of intraspinal nerve root**
Rhizotomy

03.2 **Chordotomy**

03.21 **Percutaneous chordotomy**
Stereotactic chordotomy

03.29 **Other chordotomy**
Chordotomy NOS
Tractotomy (one-stage) (two-stage) of spinal cord
Transection of spinal cord tracts

03.3 **Diagnostic procedures on spinal cord and spinal canal structures**

● Code new   ▲ Revision of   ④ ⑤ Fourth or fifth
to this edition   existing code   digit required

03.31   Spinal tap
Lumbar puncture for removal of dye

> Excludes: lumbar puncture for injection of dye [myelogram] (87.21)

03.32   Biopsy of spinal cord or spinal meninges

03.39   Other diagnostic procedures on spinal cord and spinal canal structures

> Excludes: microscopic examination of specimen from nervous system or of spinal
> fluid (90.01-90.09)
> x-ray of spine (87.21-87.29)

03.4   Excision or destruction of lesion of spinal cord or spinal meninges

Curettage
Debridement
Marsupialization of cyst   } of spinal cord or spinal meninges
Resection

> Excludes: biopsy of spinal cord or meninges (03.32)

03.5   Plastic operations on spinal cord structures

03.51   Repair of spinal meningocele
Repair of meningocele NOS

03.52   Repair of spinal myelomeningocele

03.53   Repair of vertebral fracture
Elevation of spinal bone fragments
Reduction of fracture of vertebrae
Removal of bony spicules from spinal canal

03.59   Other repair and plastic operations on spinal cord structures
Repair of:
 diastematomyelia
 spina bifida NOS
 spinal cord NOS
 spinal meninges NOS
 vertebral arch defect

03.6   Lysis of adhesions of spinal cord and nerve roots

03.7   Shunt of spinal theca
Includes: that with valve

03.71   Spinal subarachnoid-peritoneal shunt

03.72   Spinal subarachnoid-ureteral shunt

03.79   Other shunt of spinal theca
Lumbar-subarachnoid shunt NOS
Pleurothecal anastomosis
Salpingothecal anastomosis

03.8   Injection of destructive agent into spinal canal

03.9   Other operations on spinal cord and spinal canal structures

**03.90   Insertion of catheter into spinal canal for infusion of therapeutic or palliative
substances**
Insertion of catheter into epidural, subarachnoid, or subdural space of spine with
intermittent or continuous infusion of drug (with creation of any reservoir)

> Code also any implantation of infusion pump (86.06)

03.91   Injection of anesthetic into spinal canal for analgesia

> Excludes: that for operative anesthesia—omit code

03.92   Injection of other agent into spinal canal
Intrathecal injection of steroid
Subarachnoid perfusion of refrigerated saline

> Excludes: injection of:
> contrast material for myelogram (87.21)
> destructive agent into spinal canal (03.8)

03.93   Insertion or replacement of spinal neurostimulator

03.94   Removal of spinal neurostimulator

03.95   Spinal blood patch

03.96   Percutaneous denervation of facet

03.97   Revision of spinal thecal shunt

03.98   Removal of spinal thecal shunt

| | Valid O.R. procedure | | Non-O.R. procedure | | Nonspecific O.R. procedure | | Noncovered O.R. procedure |

03.99　**Other**

04　Operations on cranial and peripheral nerves

04.0　**Incision, division, and excision of cranial and peripheral nerves**

> Excludes: *opticociliary neurectomy (12.79)*
> *sympathetic ganglionectomy (05.21-05.29)*

04.01　**Excision of acoustic neuroma**
That by craniotomy

> Excludes: *that by stereotactic radiosurgery (92.3)*

04.02　**Division of trigeminal nerve**
Retrogasserian neurotomy

04.03　**Division or crushing of other cranial and peripheral nerves**

> Excludes: *that of:*
> *glossopharyngeal nerve (29.92)*
> *laryngeal nerve (31.91)*
> *nerves to adrenal glands (07.42)*
> *phrenic nerve for collapse of lung (33.31)*
> *vagus nerve (44.00-44.03)*

04.04　**Other incision of cranial and peripheral nerves**

04.05　**Gasserian ganglionectomy**

04.06　**Other cranial or peripheral ganglionectomy**

> Excludes: *sympathetic ganglionectomy (05.21-05.29)*

04.07　**Other excision or avulsion of cranial and peripheral nerves**
Curettage
Debridement ⎫ of peripheral nerve
Resection ⎭
Excision of peripheral neuroma [Morton's]

> Excludes: *biopsy of cranial or peripheral nerve (04.11-04.12)*

04.1　**Diagnostic procedures on peripheral nervous system**

04.11　**Closed [percutaneous] [needle] biopsy of cranial or peripheral nerve or ganglion**

04.12　**Open biopsy of cranial or peripheral nerve or ganglion**

04.19　**Other diagnostic procedures on cranial and peripheral nerves and ganglia**

> Excludes: *microscopic examination of specimen from nervous system (90.01-90.09)*
> *neurologic examination (89.13)*

04.2　**Destruction of cranial and peripheral nerves**
Destruction of cranial or peripheral nerves by:
cryoanalgesia
injection of neurolytic agent
radiofrequency

04.3　**Suture of cranial and peripheral nerves**

04.4　**Lysis of adhesions and decompression of cranial and peripheral nerves**

04.41　**Decompression of trigeminal nerve root**

04.42　**Other cranial nerve decompression**

04.43　**Release of carpal tunnel**

04.44　**Release of tarsal tunnel**

04.49　**Other peripheral nerve or ganglion decompression or lysis of adhesions**
Peripheral nerve neurolysis NOS

04.5　**Cranial or peripheral nerve graft**

04.6　**Transposition of cranial and peripheral nerves**
Nerve transplantation

04.7　**Other cranial or peripheral neuroplasty**

04.71　**Hypoglossal-facial anastomosis**

04.72　**Accessory-facial anastomosis**

04.73　**Accessory-hypoglossal anastomosis**

04.74　**Other anastomosis of cranial or peripheral nerve**

04.75　**Revision of previous repair of cranial and peripheral nerves**

● Code new　　　　▲ Revision of　　　④ ⑤ Fourth or fifth
to this edition　　　existing code　　　　digit required

04.76 Repair of old traumatic injury of cranial and peripheral nerves

04.79 Other neuroplasty

04.8 Injection into peripheral nerve

Excludes: *destruction of nerve (by injection of neurolytic agent) (04.2)*

04.80 Peripheral nerve injection, not otherwise specified

04.81 Injection of anesthetic into peripheral nerve for analgesia

Excludes: *that for operative anesthesia—omit code*

04.89 Injection of other agent, except neurolytic

Excludes: *injection of neurolytic agent (04.2)*

04.9 Other operations on cranial and peripheral nerves

04.91 Neurectasis

04.92 Implantation or replacement of peripheral neurostimulator

04.93 Removal of peripheral neurostimulator

04.99 Other

05 Operations on sympathetic nerves or ganglia

Excludes: *paracervical uterine denervation (69.3)*

05.0 Division of sympathetic nerve or ganglion

Excludes: *that of nerves to adrenal glands (07.42)*

05.1 Diagnostic procedures on sympathetic nerves or ganglia

05.11 Biopsy of sympathetic nerve or ganglion

05.19 Other diagnostic procedures on sympathetic nerves or ganglia

05.2 Sympathectomy

05.21 Sphenopalatine ganglionectomy

05.22 Cervical sympathectomy

05.23 Lumber sympathectomy

05.25 Periarterial sympathectomy

05.24 Presacral sympathectomy

05.29 Other sympathectomy and ganglionectomy
Excision or avulsion of sympathetic nerve NOS
Sympathetic ganglionectomy NOS

Excludes: *biopsy of sympathetic nerve or ganglion (05.11)*
opticociliary neurectomy (12.79)
periarterial sympathectomy (05.25)
tympanosympathectomy (20.91)

05.3 Injection into sympathetic nerve or ganglion

Excludes: *injection of ciliary sympathetic ganglion (12.79)*

05.31 Injection of anesthetic into sympathetic nerve for analgesia

05.32 Injection of neurolytic agent into sympathetic nerve

05.39 Other injection into sympathetic nerve or ganglion

05.8 Other operations on sympathetic nerves or ganglion

05.81 Repair of sympathetic nerve or ganglion

05.89 Other

05.9 Other operations on nervous system

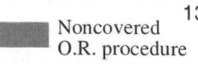

Valid O.R. procedure   Non-O.R. procedure   Nonspecific O.R. procedure   Noncovered O.R. procedure

● Code new
to this edition

▲ Revision of
existing code

④ ⑤ Fourth or fifth
digit required

2. OPERATIONS ON THE ENDOCRINE SYSTEM (06-07)

06 Operations on thyroid and parathyroid glands
Includes: incidental resection of hyoid bone

06.0 Incision of thyroid field

Excludes: *division of isthmus (06.91)*

06.01 Aspiration of thyroid field
Percutaneous or needle drainage of thyroid field

Excludes: *aspiration biopsy of thyroid (06.11)*
drainage by incision (06.09)
postoperative aspiration of field (06.02)

06.02 Reopening of wound of thyroid field
Reopening of wound of thyroid field for:
control of (postoperative) hemorrhage
examination
exploration
removal of hematoma

06.09 Other Incision of thyroid field
Drainage of hematoma
Drainage of thyroglossal tract
Exploration:
neck
thyroid (field) } by incision
Removal of foreign body
Thyroidotomy NOS

Excludes: *postoperative exploration (06.02)*
removal of hematoma by aspiration (06.01)

06.1 Diagnostic procedures on thyroid and parathyroid glands

06.11 Closed [percutaneous] [needle] biopsy of thyroid gland
Aspiration biopsy of thyroid

06.12 Open biopsy of thyroid gland

06.13 Biopsy of parathyroid gland

06.19 Other diagnostic procedures on thyroid and parathyroid glands

Excludes: *radioisotope scan of:*
parathyroid (92.13)
thyroid (92.01)
soft tissue x-ray of thyroid field (87.09)

06.2 Unilateral thyroid lobectomy
Complete removal of one lobe of thyroid (with removal of isthmus or portion of other lobe)
Hemithyroidectomy

Excludes: *partial substernal thyroidectomy (06.51)*

06.3 Other partial thyroidectomy

06.31 Excision of lesion of thyroid

Excludes: *biopsy of thyroid (06.11-06.12)*

06.39 Other
Isthmectomy
Partial thyroidectomy NOS
Excludes: *partial substernal thyroidectomy (06.51)*

06.4 Complete thyroidectomy

Excludes: *complete substernal thyroidectomy (06.52)*
that with laryngectomy (30.3-30.4)

06.5 Substernal thyroidectomy

06.50 Substernal thyroidectomy, not otherwise specified

06.51 Partial substernal thyroidectomy

06.52 Complete substernal thyroidectomy

	Valid O.R. procedure		Non-O.R. procedure		Nonspecific O.R. procedure		Noncovered O.R. procedure

06.6 **Excision of lingual thyroid**
Excision of thyroid by:
   submental route
   transoral route

06.7 **Excision of thyroglossal duct or tract**

06.8 **Parathyroidectomy**

  06.81 **Complete parathyroidectomy**

  06.89 **Other parathyroidectomy**
    Parathyroidectomy NOS
    Partial parathyroidectomy
    | Excludes: | biopsy of parathyroid (06.13)

06.9 **Other operations on thyroid (region) and parathyroid**

  06.91 **Division of thyroid isthmus**
    Transection of thyroid isthmus

  06.92 **Ligation of thyroid vessels**

  06.93 **Suture of thyroid gland**

  06.94 **Thyroid tissue reimplantation**
    Autotransplantation of thyroid tissue

  06.95 **Parathyroid tissue reimplantation**
    Autotransplantation of parathyroid tissue

  06.98 **Other operations on thyroid glands**

  06.99 **Other operations on parathyroid glands**

07 **Operations on other endocrine glands**
Includes: operations on:
    adrenal glands
    pineal gland
    pituitary gland
    thymus

| Excludes: | *operations on:*
    aortic and carotid bodies (39.8)
    ovaries (65.0-65.99)
    pancreas (52.01-52.99)
    testes (62.0-62.99)

07.0 **Exploration of adrenal field**
    | Excludes: | *incision of adrenal (gland) (07.41)*

  07.00 **Exploration of adrenal field, not otherwise specified**

  07.01 **Unilateral exploration of adrenal field**

  07.02 **Bilateral exploration of adrenal field**

07.1 **Diagnostic procedures on adrenal glands, pituitary gland, pineal gland, and thymus**

  07.11 **Closed [percutaneous] [needle] biopsy of adrenal gland**

  07.12 **Open biopsy of adrenal gland**

  07.13 **Biopsy of pituitary gland, transfrontal approach**

  07.14 **Biopsy of pituitary gland, transsphenoidal approach**

  07.15 **Biopsy of pituitary gland, unspecified approach**

  07.16 **Biopsy of thymus**

  07.17 **Biopsy of pineal gland**

  07.19 **Other diagnostic procedures on adrenal glands, pituitary gland, pineal gland, and thymus**
    | Excludes: | *microscopic examination of specimen from endocrine gland*
      (90.11-90.19)
      radioisotope scan of pituitary gland (92.11)

07.2 **Partial adrenalectomy**

  07.21 **Excision of lesion of adrenal gland**
    | Excludes: | *biopsy of adrenal gland (07.11-07.12)*

  07.22 **Unilateral adrenalectomy**
    Adrenalectomy NOS
    | Excludes: | *excision of remaining adrenal gland (07.3)*

● Code new
  to this edition
▲ Revision of
  existing code
④ ⑤ Fourth or fifth
  digit required

07.29 **Other partial adrenalectomy**
Partial adrenalectomy NOS

07.3 **Bilateral adrenalectomy**
Excision of remaining adrenal gland

> Excludes: bilateral partial adrenalectomy (07.29)

07.4 **Other operations on adrenal glands, nerves, and vessels**

07.41 **Incision of adrenal gland**
Adrenalotomy (with drainage)

07.42 **Division of nerves to adrenal glands**

07.43 **Ligation of adrenal vessels**

07.44 **Repair of adrenal gland**

07.45 **Reimplantation of adrenal tissue**
Autotransplantation of adrenal tissue

07.49 **Other**

07.5 **Operations on pineal gland**

07.51 **Exploration of pineal field**

> Excludes: that with incision of pineal gland (07.52)

07.52 **Incision of pineal gland**

07.53 **Partial excision of pineal gland**

> Excludes: biopsy of pineal gland (07.17)

07.54 **Total excision of pineal gland**
Pinealectomy (complete) (total)

07.59 **Other operations on pineal gland**

07.6 **Hypophysectomy**

07.61 **Partial excision of pituitary gland, transfrontal approach**
Cryohypophysectomy,
  partial
Division of hypophyseal
  stalk
Excision of lesion of   } transfrontal approach
  pituitary [hypophysis]
Hypophysectomy, subtotal
Infundibulectomy,
  hypophyseal

> Excludes: biopsy of pituitary gland, transfrontal approach (07.13)

07.62 **Partial excision of pituitary gland, transsphenoidal approach**

> Excludes: biopsy of pituitary gland, transsphenoidal approach (07.14)

07.63 **Partial excision of pituitary gland, unspecified approach**

> Excludes: biopsy of pituitary gland NOS (07.15)

07.64 **Total excision of pituitary gland, transfrontal approach**
Ablation of pituitary by
  implantation (stron-   } transfrontal approach
  tium-yttrium) (Y)
Cryohypophysectomy,
  complete

07.65 **Total excision of pituitary gland, transsphenoidal approach**

07.68 **Total excision of pituitary gland, other specified approach**

07.69 **Total excision of pituitary gland, unspecified approach**
Hypophysectomy NOS
Pituitectomy NOS

07.7 **Other operations on hypophysis**

07.71 **Exploration of pituitary fossa**

> Excludes: exploration with incision of pituitary gland (07.72)

 Valid O.R.
procedure

 Non-O.R.
procedure

 Nonspecific
O.R. procedure

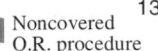 Noncovered
O.R. procedure

07.72 **Incision of pituitary gland**
Aspiration of:
craniobuccal pouch
craniopharyngioma
hypophysis
pituitary gland
Rathke's pouch

07.79 **Other**
Insertion of pack into sella turcica

07.8 **Thymectomy**

07.80 **Thymectomy, not otherwise specified**

07.81 **Partial excision of thymus**

Excludes: *biopsy of thymus (07.16)*

07.82 **Total excision of thymus**

07.9 **Other operations on thymus**

07.91 **Exploration of thymus field**

Excludes: *exploration with incision of thymus (07.92)*

07.92 **Incision of thymus**

07.93 **Repair of thymus**

07.94 **Transplantation of thymus**

07.99 **Other**
Thymopexy

● Code new
to this edition
▲ Revision of
existing code
④ ⑤ Fourth or fifth
digit required

3. OPERATIONS ON THE EYE (08-16)

08 Operations on eyelids
    Includes: operations on the eyebrow

    08.0 Incision of eyelid

        08.01 Incision of lid margin

        08.02 Severing of blepharorrhaphy

        08.09 Other incision of eyelid

    08.1 Diagnostic procedures on eyelid

        08.11 Biopsy of eyelid

        08.19 Other diagnostic procedures on eyelid

    08.2 Excision or destruction of lesion or tissue of eyelid
        Code also any synchronous reconstruction (08.61-08.74)
        Excludes: *biopsy of eyelid (08.11)*

        08.20 Removal of lesion of eyelid, not otherwise specified
               Removal of meibomian gland NOS

        08.21 Excision of chalazion

        08.22 Excision of other minor lesion of eyelid
               Excision of:
                 verruca
                 wart

        08.23 Excision of major lesion of eyelid, partial-thickness
               Excision involving one-fourth or more of lid margin, partial-thickness

        08.24 Excision of major lesion of eyelid, full-thickness
               Excision involving one-fourth or more of lid margin, full-thickness
               Wedge resection of eyelid

        08.25 Destruction of lesion of eyelid

    08.3 Repair of blepharoptosis and lid retraction

        08.31 Repair of blepharoptosis by frontalis muscle technique with suture

        08.32 Repair of blepharoptosis by frontalis muscle technique with fascial sling

        08.33 Repair of blepharoptosis by resection or advancement of levator muscle or
               aponeurosis

        08.34 Repair of blepharoptosis by other levator muscle techniques

        08.35 Repair of blepharoptosis by tarsal technique

        08.36 Repair of blepharoptosis by other techniques
               Correction of eyelid ptosis NOS
               Orbicularis oculi muscle sling for correction of blepharoptosis

        08.37 Reduction of overcorrection of ptosis

        08.38 Correction of lid retraction

    08.4 Repair of entropion or ectropion

        08.41 Repair of entropion or ectropion by thermocauterization

        08.42 Repair of entropion or ectropion by suture technique

        08.43 Repair of entropion or ectropion with wedge resection

        08.44 Repair of entropion or ectropion with lid reconstruction

        08.49 Other repair of entropion or ectropion

    08.5 Other adjustment of lid position

        08.51 Canthotomy
               Enlargement of palpebral fissure

        08.52 Blepharorrhaphy
               Canthorrhaphy
               Tarsorrhaphy

        08.59 Other
               Canthoplasty NOS
               Repair of epicanthal fold

    08.6 Reconstruction of eyelid with flaps or grafts
        Excludes: *that associated with repair of entropion and ectropion (08.44)*

	Valid O.R. procedure		Non-O.R. procedure		Nonspecific O.R. procedure		Noncovered O.R. procedure

08.61 Reconstruction of eyelid with skin flap or graft

08.62 Reconstruction of eyelid with mucous membrane flap or graft

08.63 Reconstruction of eyelid with hair follicle graft

08.64 Reconstruction of eyelid with tarsoconjunctival flap
Transfer of tarsoconjunctival flap from opposing lid

08.69 Other reconstruction of eyelid with flap or graft

08.7 **Other reconstruction of eyelid**

Excludes: *that associated with repair of entropion and ectropion (08.44)*

08.70 Reconstruction of eyelid, not otherwise specified

08.71 Reconstruction of eyelid involving lid margin, partial-thickness

08.72 Other reconstruction of eyelid, partial-thickness

08.73 Reconstruction of eyelid involving lid margin, full-thickness

08.74 Other reconstruction of eyelid, full-thickness

08.8 **Other repair of eyelid**

08.81 Linear repair of laceration of eyelid or eyebrow

08.82 Repair of laceration involving lid margin, partial-thickness

08.83 Other repair of laceration of eyelid, partial-thickness

08.84 Repair of laceration involving lid margin, full-thickness

08.85 Other repair of laceration of eyelid, full-thickness

08.86 Lower eyelid rhytidectomy

08.87 Upper eyelid rhytidectomy

08.89 Other eyelid repair

08.9 **Other operations on eyelids**

08.91 Electrosurgical epilation of eyelid

08.92 Cryosurgical epilation of eyelid

08.93 Other epilation of eyelid

08.99 Other

09 **Operations on lacrimal system**

09.0 **Incision of lacrimal gland**
Incision of lacrimal cyst (with drainage)

09.1 **Diagnostic procedures on lacrimal system**

09.11 Biopsy of lacrimal gland

09.12 Biopsy of lacrimal sac

09.19 Other diagnostic procedures on lacrimal system

Excludes: *contrast dacryocystogram (87.05)*
soft tissue x-ray of nasolacrimal duct (87.09)

09.2 **Excision of lesion or tissue of lacrimal gland**

09.20 Excision of lacrimal gland, not otherwise specified

09.21 Excision of lesion of lacrimal gland

Excludes: *biopsy of lacrimal gland (09.11)*

09.22 Other partial dacryoadenectomy

Excludes: *biopsy of lacrimal gland (09.11)*

09.23 Total dacryoadenectomy

09.3 **Other operations on lacrimal gland**

09.4 **Manipulation of lacrimal passage**
Includes: removal of calculus
that with dilation

Excludes: *contrast dacryocystogram (87.05)*

09.41 Probing of lacrimal punctum

09.42 Probing of lacrimal canaliculi

09.43 Probing of nasolacrimal duct

Excludes: *that with insertion of tube or stent (09.44)*

● Code new
to this edition

▲ Revision of
existing code

④ ⑤ Fourth or fifth
digit required

09.44 Intubation of nasolacrimal duct
Insertion of stent into nasolacrimal duct

09.49 Other manipulation of lacrimal passage

09.5 Incision of lacrimal sac and passages

09.51 Incision of lacrimal punctum

09.52 Incision of lacrimal canaliculi

09.53 Incision of lacrimal sac

09.59 Other incision of lacrimal passages
Incision (and drainage) of nasolacrimal duct NOS

09.6 Excision of lacrimal sac and passage

> Excludes: biopsy of lacrimal sac (09.12)

09.7 Repair of canaliculus and punctum

> Excludes: repair of eyelid (08.81-08.89)

09.71 Correction of everted punctum

09.72 Other repair of punctum

09.73 Repair of canaliculus

09.8 Fistulization of lacrimal tract to nasal cavity

09.81 Dacryocystorhinostomy [DCR]

09.82 Conjunctivocystorhinostomy
Conjunctivodacryocystorhinostomy [CDCR]

> Excludes: that with insertion of tube or stent (09.83)

09.83 Conjunctivorhinostomy with insertion of tube or stent

09.9 Other operations on lacrimal system

09.91 Obliteration of lacrimal punctum

09.99 Other

10 Operations on conjunctiva

10.0 Removal of embedded foreign body from conjunctiva by incision

> Excludes: removal of:
> embedded foreign body without incision (98.22)
> superficial foreign body (98.21)

10.1 Other incision of conjunctiva

10.2 Diagnostic procedures on conjunctiva

10.21 Biopsy of conjunctiva

10.29 Other diagnostic procedures on conjunctiva

10.3 Excision or destruction of lesion or tissue of conjunctiva

10.31 Excision of lesion or tissue of conjunctiva
Excision of ring of conjunctiva around cornea

> Excludes: biopsy of conjunctiva (10.21)

10.32 Destruction of lesion of conjunctiva

> Excludes: excision of lesion (10.31)
> thermocauterization for entropion (08.41)

10.33 Other destructive procedures on conjunctiva
Removal of trachoma follicles

10.4 Conjunctivoplasty

10.41 Repair of symblepharon with free graft

10.42 Reconstruction of conjunctival cul-de-sac with free graft

> Excludes: revision of enucleation socket with graft (16.63)

10.43 Other reconstruction of conjunctival cul-de-sac

> Excludes: revision of enucleation socket (16.64)

10.44 Other free graft to conjunctiva

10.49 Other conjunctivoplasty

> Excludes: repair of cornea with conjunctival flap (11.53)

 Valid O.R. procedure   Non-O.R. procedure   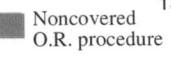 Nonspecific O.R. procedure   Noncovered O.R. procedure

10.5 **Lysis of adhesions of conjunctiva and eyelid**
Division of symblepharon (with insertion of conformer)

10.6 **Repair of laceration of conjunctiva**

> *Excludes:* *that with repair of sclera (12.81)*

10.9 **Other operations on conjunctiva**

10.91 Subconjunctival injection

10.99 Other

11 Operations on cornea

11.0 **Magnetic removal of embedded foreign body from cornea**

> *Excludes:* *that with incision (11.1)*

11.1 **Incision of cornea**
Incision of cornea for removal of foreign body

11.2 **Diagnostic procedures on cornea**

11.21 Scraping of cornea for smear or culture

11.22 Biopsy of cornea

11.29 Other diagnostic procedures on cornea

11.3 **Excision of pterygium**

11.31 Transposition of pterygium

11.32 Excision of pterygium with corneal graft

11.39 Other excision of pterygium

11.4 **Excision or destruction of tissue or other lesion of cornea**

11.41 Mechanical removal of corneal epithelium
That by chemocauterization

> *Excludes:* *that for smear or culture (11.21)*

11.42 Thermocauterization of corneal lesion

11.43 Cryotherapy of corneal lesion

11.49 Other removal or destruction of corneal lesion
Excision of cornea NOS

> *Excludes:* *biopsy of cornea (11.22)*

11.5 **Repair of cornea**

11.51 Suture of corneal laceration

11.52 Repair of postoperative wound dehiscence of cornea

11.53 Repair of corneal laceration or wound with conjunctival flop

11.59 Other repair of cornea

11.6 **Corneal transplant**

> *Excludes:* *excision of pterygium with corneal graft (11.32)*

11.60 Corneal transplant, not otherwise specified
Keratoplasty NOS

11.61 Lamellar keratoplasty with autograft

11.62 Other lamellar keratoplasty

11.63 Penetrating keratoplasty with autograft
Perforating keratoplasty with autograft

11.64 Other penetrating keratoplasty
Perforating keratoplasty (with homograft)

11.69 Other corneal transplant

11.7 **Other reconstructive and refractive surgery on cornea**

11.71 Keratomileusis

11.72 Keratophakia

11.73 Keratoprosthesis

11.74 Thermokeratoplasty

11.75 Radial keratotomy

11.76 Epikeratophakia

11.79 Other

● Code new
to this edition

▲ Revision of
existing code

④ ⑤ Fourth or fifth
digit required

11.9 Other operations on cornea

 11.91 Tattooing of cornea

 11.92 Removal of artificial implant from cornea

 11.99 Other

12 Operation on iris, ciliary body, sclera, and anterior chamber

 Excludes: *operations on cornea (11.0-11.99)*

12.0 Removal of intraocular foreign body from anterior segment of eye

 12.00 Removal of intraocular foreign body from anterior segment of eye, not otherwise specified

 12.01 Removal of intraocular foreign body from anterior segment of eye with use of magnet

 12.02 Removal of intraocular foreign body from anterior segment of eye without use of magnet

12.1 Iridotomy and simple iridectomy

 Excludes: *iridectomy associated with:*
  cataract extraction (13.11-13.69)
  removal of lesion (12.41-12.42)
  scleral fistulization (12.61-12.69)

 12.11 Iridotomy with transfixion

 12.12 Other iridotomy
  Corectomy
  Discission of iris
  Iridotomy NOS

 12.13 Excision of prolapsed iris

 12.14 Other iridectomy
  iridectomy (basal) (peripheral) (total)

12.2 Diagnostic procedures on iris, ciliary body, sclera, and anterior chamber

 12.21 Diagnostic aspiration of anterior chamber of eye

 12.22 Biopsy of iris

 12.29 Other diagnostic procedures on iris, ciliary body, sclera, and anterior chamber

12.3 Iridoplasty and coreoplasty

 12.31 Lysis of goniosynechiae
  Lysis of goniosynechiae by injection of air or liquid

 12.32 Lysis of other anterior synechiae
  Lysis of anterior synechiae:
   NOS
   by injection of air or liquid

 12.33 Lysis of posterior synechiae
  Lysis of iris adhesions NOS

 12.34 Lysis of corneovitreal adhesions

 12.35 Coreoplasty
  Needling of pupillary membrane

 12.39 Other iridoplasty

12.4 Excision or destruction of lesion of iris and ciliary body

 12.40 Removal of lesion of anterior segment of eye, not otherwise specified

 12.41 Destruction of lesion of iris, nonexcisional
  Destruction of lesion of iris by:
   cauterization
   cryotherapy
   photocoagulation

 12.42 Excision of lesion of iris
  Excludes: *biopsy of iris (12.22)*

 12.43 Destruction of lesion of ciliary body, nonexcisional

 12.44 Excision of lesion of ciliary body

12.5 Facilitation of intraocular circulation

 12.51 Goniopuncture without goniotomy

 12.52 Goniotomy without goniopuncture

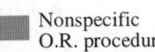

| Valid O.R. procedure | Non-O.R. procedure | Nonspecific O.R. procedure | Noncovered O.R. procedure |

12.53 Goniotomy with goniopuncture

12.54 Trabeculotomy ab externo

12.55 Cyclodialysis

12.59 Other facilitation of intraocular circulation

12.6 Scleral fistulization

> Excludes: exploratory sclerotomy (12.89)

12.61 Trephination of sclera with iridectomy

12.62 Thermocauterization of sclera with iridectomy

12.63 Iridencleisis and iridotasis

12.64 Trabeculectomy ab externo

12.65 Other scleral fistulization with iridectomy

12.66 Postoperative revision of scleral fistulization procedure
Revision of filtering bleb

> Excludes: repair of fistula (12.82)

12.69 Other fistulizing procedure

12.7 Other procedures for relief of elevated intraocular pressure

12.71 Cyclodiathermy

12.72 Cyclocryotherapy

12.73 Cyclophotocoagulation

12.74 Diminution of ciliary body, not otherwise specified

12.79 Other glaucoma procedures

12.8 Operations on sclera

> Excludes: those associated with:
>   retinal reattachment (14.41-14.59)
>   scleral fistulization (12.61-12.69)

12.81 Suture of laceration of sclera
Suture of sclera with synchronous repair of conjunctiva

12.82 Repair of scleral fistula

> Excludes: postoperative revision of scleral fistulization procedure (12.66)

12.83 Revision of operative wound of anterior segment, not elsewhere classified

> Excludes: postoperative revision of scleral fistulization procedure (12.66)

12.84 Excision or destruction of lesion of sclera

12.85 Repair of scleral staphyloma with graft

12.86 Other repair of scleral staphyloma

12.87 Scleral reinforcement with graft

12.88 Other scleral reinforcement

12.89 Other operations on sclera
Exploratory sclerotomy

12.9 Other operations on iris, ciliary body, and anterior chamber

12.91 Therapeutic evacuation of anterior chamber
Paracentesis of anterior chamber

> Excludes: diagnostic aspiration (12.21)

12.92 Injection into anterior chamber
Injection of:
   air
   liquid   } into anterior chamber
   medication

12.93 Removal or destruction of epithelial downgrowth from anterior chamber

> Excludes: that with iridectomy (12.41-12.42)

12.97 Other operations on iris

12.98 Other operations on ciliary body

12.99 Other operations on anterior chamber

● Code new
to this edition

▲ Revision of
existing code

④ ⑤ Fourth or fifth
digit required

13   Operations on lens

13.0   Removal of foreign body from lens

> Excludes: *removal of pseudophakos (13.8)*

13.00 Removal of foreign body from lens, not otherwise specified

13.01 Removal of foreign body from lens with use of magnet

13.02 Removal of foreign body from lens without use of magnet

13.1   Intracapsular extraction of lens

> *Code also any synchronous insertion of pseudophakos (13.71)*

13.11 Intracapsular extraction of lens by temporal inferior route

13.19 Other intracapsular extraction of lens
> Cataract extraction NOS
> Cryoextraction of lens
> Erysiphake extraction of cataract
> Extraction of lens NOS

13.2   Extracapsular extraction of lens by linear extraction technique

13.3   Extracapsular extraction of lens by simple aspiration (and irrigation) technique
> Irrigation of traumatic cataract

13.4   Extracapsular extraction of lens by fragmentation and aspiration technique

13.41 Phacoemulsification and aspiration of cataract

13.42 Mechanical phacofragmentation and aspiration of cataract by posterior route
> *Code also any synchronous vitrectomy (14.74)*

13.43 Mechanical phacofragmentation and other aspiration of cataract

13.5   Other extracapsular extraction of lens

> *Code also any synchronous insertion of pseudophakos (13.71)*

13.51 Extracapsular extraction of lens by temporal inferior route

13.59 Other extracapsular extraction of lens

13.6   Other cataract extraction

> *Code also any synchronous insertion of pseudophakos (13.71)*

13.64 Discission of secondary membrane [after cataract)

13.65 Excision of secondary membrane [after cataract)
> Capsulectomy

13.66 Mechanical fragmentation of secondary membrane [after cataract]

13.69 Other cataract extraction

13.7   Insertion of prosthetic lens [pseudophakos]

13.70 Insertion of pseudophakos, not otherwise specified

13.71 Insertion of intraocular lens prosthesis at time of cataract extraction, one-stage
> *Code also synchronous extraction of cataract (13.11-13.69)*

13.72 Secondary insertion of intraocular lens prosthesis

13.8   Removal of implanted lens
> Removal of pseudophakos

13.9   Other operations on lens

14   Operations on retina, choroid, vitreous, and posterior chamber

14.0   Removal of foreign body from posterior segment of eye

> Excludes: *removal of surgically implanted material (14.6)*

14.00 Removal of foreign body from posterior segment of eye, not otherwise specified

14.01 Removal of foreign body from posterior segment of eye with use of magnet

14.02 Removal of foreign body from posterior segment of eye without use of magnet

14.1   Diagnostic procedures on retina, choroid, vitreous, and posterior chamber

14.11 Diagnostic aspiration of vitreous

14.19 Other diagnostic procedures on retina, choroid, vitreous, and posterior chamber

| | Valid O.R. procedure | | Non-O.R. procedure | | Nonspecific O.R. procedure | | Noncovered O.R. procedure |

14.2   Destruction of lesion of retina and choroid
Includes: destruction of chorioretinopathy or isolated chorioretinal lesion

> Excludes: that for repair of retina (14.31-14.59)

14.21 Destruction of chorioretinal lesion by diathermy

14.22 Destruction of chorioretinal lesion by cryotherapy

14.23 Destruction of chorioretinal lesion by xenon arc photocoagulation

14.24 Destruction of chorioretinal lesion by laser photocoagulation

14.25 Destruction of chorioretinal lesion by photocoagulation of unspecified type

14.26 Destruction of chorioretinal lesion by radiation therapy

14.27 Destruction of chorioretinal lesion by implantation of radiation source

14.29 Other destruction of chorioretinal lesion
Destruction of lesion of retina and choroid NOS

14.3   Repair of retinal tear
Includes: repair of retinal defect

> Excludes: repair of retinal detachment (14.41-14.59)

14.31 Repair of retinal tear by diathermy

14.32 Repair of retinal tear by cryotherapy

14.33 Repair of retinal tear by xenon arc photocoagulation

14.34 Repair of retinal tear by laser photocoagulation

14.35 Repair of retinal tear by photocoagulation of unspecified type

14.39 Other repair of retinal tear

14.4   Repair of retinal detachment with sclera buckling and implant

14.41 Scleral buckling with implant

14.49 Other scleral buckling
Scleral buckling with:
  air tamponade
  resection of sclera
  vitrectomy

14.5   Other repair of retinal detachment
Includes: that with drainage

14.51 Repair of retinal detachment with diathermy

14.52 Repair of retinal detachment with cryotherapy

14.53 Repair of retinal detachment with xenon arc photocoagulation

14.54 Repair of retinal detachment with laser photocoagulation

14.55 Repair of retinal detachment with photocoagulation of unspecified type

14.59 Other

14.6   Removal of surgically implanted material from posterior segment of eye

14.7   Operations on vitreous

14.71 Removal of vitreous, anterior approach
Open sky technique
Removal of vitreous, anterior approach (with replacement)

14.72 Other removal of vitreous
Aspiration of vitreous by posterior sclerotomy

14.73 Mechanical vitrectomy by anterior approach

14.74 Other mechanical vitrectomy

14.75 Injection of vitreous substitute

> Excludes: that associated with removal (14.71-14.72)

14.79 Other operations on vitreous

14.9   Other operations on retina, choroid, and posterior chamber

15   Operations on extraocular muscles

15.0   Diagnostic procedures on extraocular muscles or tendons

15.01 Biopsy of extraocular muscle or tendon

15.09 Other diagnostic procedures on extraocular muscles and tendons

● Code new
to this edition

▲ Revision of
existing code

④ ⑤ Fourth or fifth
digit required

15.1 Operations on one extraocular muscle involving temporary detachment from globe

> **15.11** Recession of one extraocular muscle
>
> **15.12** Advancement of one extraocular muscle
>
> **15.13** Resection of one extraocular muscle
>
> **15.19** Other operations on one extraocular muscle involving temporary detachment from globe
>
>> Excludes: transposition of muscle (15.5)

15.2 Other operations on one extraocular muscle

> **15.21** Lengthening procedure on one extraocular muscle
>
> **15.22** Shortening procedure on one extraocular muscle
>
> **15.29** Other

15.3 Operations on two or more extraocular muscles involving temporary detachment from globe, one or both eyes

15.4 Other operations on two or more extraocular muscles, one or both eyes

15.5 Transposition of extraocular muscles

> Excludes: that for correction of ptosis (08.31-08.36)

15.6 Revision of extraocular muscle surgery

15.7 Repair of injury of extraocular muscle
> Freeing of entrapped extraocular muscle
> Lysis of adhesions of extraocular muscle
> Repair of laceration of extraocular muscle, tendon, or Tenon's capsule

15.9 Other operations on extraocular muscles and tendon

16 Operations on orbit and eyeball

> Excludes: reduction of fracture of orbit (76.78-76.79)

16.0 Orbitotomy

> **16.01** Orbitotomy with bone flap
> Orbitotomy with lateral approach
>
> **16.02** Orbitotomy with insertion of orbital implant
>
>> Excludes: that with bone flap (16.01)
>
> **16.09** Other orbitotomy

16.1 Removal of penetrating foreign body from eye, not otherwise specified

> Excludes: removal of nonpenetrating foreign body (98.21)

16.2 Diagnostic procedures on orbit and eyeball

> **16.21** Ophthalmoscopy
>
> **16.22** Diagnostic aspiration of orbit
>
> **16.23** Biopsy of eyeball and orbit
>
> **16.29** Other diagnostic procedures on orbit and eyeball
>
>> Excludes: examination of form and structure of eye (95.11-95.16)
>> general and subjective eye examination (95.01-95.09)
>> microscopic examination of specimen from eye (90.21-90.29)
>> objective functional tests of eye (95.21-95.26)
>> ocular thermography (88.82)
>> tonometry (89.11)
>> X-ray of orbit (87.14, 87.16)

16.3 Evisceration of eyeball

> **16.31** Removal of ocular contents with synchronous implant into scleral shell
>
> **16.39** Other evisceration of eyeball

16.4 Enucleation of eyeball

> **16.41** Enucleation of eyeball with synchronous implant into Tenon's capsule with attachment of muscles
> Integrated implant of eyeball
>
> **16.42** Enucleation of eyeball with other synchronous implant
>
> **16.49** Other enucleation of eyeball
> Removal of eyeball NOS

16.5 Exenteration of orbital contents

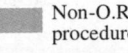 Valid O.R. procedure Non-O.R. procedure 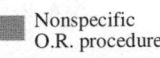 Nonspecific O.R. procedure Noncovered O.R. procedure

16.51 Exenteration of orbit with removal of adjacent structures
Radical orbitomaxillectomy

16.52 Exenteration of orbit with therapeutic removal of orbital bone

16.59 Other exenteration of orbit
Evisceration of orbit NOS
Exenteration of orbit with temporalis muscle transplant

16.6 **Secondary procedures after removal of eyeball**

> Excludes: *that with synchronous:*
> *enucleation of eyeball (16.41-1642)*
> *evisceration of eyeball (16.31)*

16.61 Secondary insertion of ocular implant

16.62 Revision and reinsertion of ocular implant

16.63 Revision of enucleation socket with graft

16.64 Other revision of enucleation socket

16.65 Secondary graft to exenteration cavity

16.66 Other revision of exenteration cavity

16.69 Other secondary procedures after removal of eyeball

16.7 **Removal of ocular or orbital implant**

16.71 Removal of ocular implant

16.72 Removal of orbital implant

16.8 **Repair of injury of eyeball and orbit**

16.81 Repair of wound of orbit

> Excludes: *reduction of orbital fracture (76.78-76.79)*
> *repair of extraocular muscles (15.7)*

16.82 Repair of rupture of eyeball
Repair of multiple structures of eye

> Excludes: *repair of laceration of:*
> *cornea (11.51-11.59)*
> *sclera (12.81)*

16.89 Other repair of injury of eyeball or orbit

16.9 **Other operations on orbit and eyeball**

> Excludes: *irrigation of eye (96.51)*
> *prescription and fitting of low vision aids (95.31-95.33)*
> *removal of:*
> *eye prosthesis NEC (97.31)*
> *nonpenetrating foreign body from eye without incision (98.21)*

16.91 Retrobulbar injection of therapeutic agent

> Excludes: *injection of radiographic contrast material (87.14)*
> *opticociliary injection (12.79)*

16.92 Excision of lesion of orbit

> Excludes: *biopsy of orbit (16.23)*

16.93 Excision of lesion of eye, unspecified structure

> Excludes: *biopsy of eye NOS (16.23)*

16.98 Other operations on orbit

16.99 Other operations on eyeball

● Code new
to this edition

▲ Revision of
existing code

④ ⑤ Fourth or fifth
digit required

4.   OPERATIONS ON THE EAR (18-20)

18   Operations on external ear
Includes: operations on:
external auditory canal
skin and cartilage of:
auricle
meatus

18.0   Incision of external ear

> Excludes: removal of intraluminal foreign body (98.11)

18.01 Piercing of ear lobe
Piercing of pinna

18.02 Incision of external auditory canal

18.09 Other incision of external ear

18.1   Diagnostic procedures on external ear

18.11 Otoscopy

18.12 Biopsy of external ear

18.19 Other diagnostic procedures on external ear

> Excludes: microscopic examination of specimen from ear (90.31-90.39)

18.2   Excision or destruction of lesion of external ear

18.21 Excision of preauricular sinus
Radical excision of preauricular sinus or cyst

> Excludes: excision of preauricular remnant [appendage] (18.29)

18.29 Excision or destruction of other lesion of external ear
Cauterization
Coagulation
Cryosurgery
Curettage   } of external car
Electrocoagulation
Enucleation
Excision of:
exostosis of external auditory canal
preauricular remnant [appendage]
Partial excision of ear

> Excludes: biopsy of external ear (18.12)
> radical excision of lesion (18.31)
> removal of cerumen (96.52)

18.3   Other excision of external ear

> Excludes: biopsy of external ear (18.12)

18.31 Radical excision of lesion of external ear

> Excludes: radical excision of preauricular sinus (18.21)

18.39 Other
Amputation of external ear

> Excludes: excision of lesion (18.21-18.29, 18.31)

18.4   Suture of laceration of external ear

18.5   Surgical correction of prominent ear
Ear:
pinning
setback

18.6   Reconstruction of external auditory canal
Canaloplasty of external auditory meatus
Construction [reconstruction] of external meatus of ear:
osseous portion
skin-lined portion (with skin graft)

18.7   Other plastic repair of external ear

18.71 Construction of auricle of ear
Prosthetic appliance for absent ear
Reconstruction:
auricle
ear

Valid O.R.   Non-O.R.   Nonspecific   Noncovered
procedure   procedure   O.R. procedure   O.R. procedure

18.72 Reattachment of amputated ear

18.79 Other plastic repair of external ear
Otoplasty NOS
Postauricular skin graft
Repair of lop ear

18.9 Other operations on external ear

Excludes:	irrigation of ear (96.52)
	packing of external auditory canal (96.11)
	removal of:
	cerumen (96.52)
	foreign body (without incision) (98.11)

19 Reconstructive operations on middle ear

19.0 Stapes mobilization

Division, otosclerotic: Remobilization of stapes
    material   Stapediolysis
    process   Transcrural stapes mobilization

Excludes:	that with synchronous stapedectomy (19.11-19.19)

19.1 Stapedectomy

Excludes:	revision of previous stapedectomy (19.21-19.29)
	stapes mobilization only (19.0)

19.11 Stapedectomy with incus replacement
Stapedectomy with incus:
homograft
prosthesis

19.19 Other stapedectomy

19.2 Revision of stapedectomy

19.21 Revision of stapedectomy with incus replacement

19.29 Other revision of stapedectomy

19.3 Other operations on ossicular chain
Incudectomy NOS
Ossiculectomy NOS
Reconstruction of ossicles, second stage

19.4 Myringoplasty
Epitympanic, type I
Myringoplasty by:
cauterization
graft
Tympanoplasty (type I)

19.5 Other tympanoplasty

19.52 Type II tympanoplasty
Closure of perforation with graft against incus or malleus

19.53 Type III tympanoplasty
Graft placed in contact with mobile and intact stapes

19.54 Type IV tympanoplasty
Mobile footplate left exposed with air pocket between round window and graft

19.55 Type V tympanoplasty
Fenestra in horizontal semicircular canal covered by graft

19.6 Revision of tympanoplasty

19.9 Other repair of middle ear
Closure of mastoid fistula
Mastoid myoplasty
Obliteration of tympanomastoid cavity

20 Other operations on middle and inner ear

20.0 Myringotomy

20.01 Myringotomy with insertion of tube
Myringostomy

20.09 Other myringotomy
Aspiration of middle ear NOS

20.1 Removal of tympanostomy tube

20.2 Incision of mastoid and middle ear

● Code new
to this edition

▲ Revision of
existing code

④ ⑤ Fourth or fifth
digit required

20.21 **Incision of mastoid**

20.22 **Incision of petrous pyramid air cells**

20.23 **Incision of middle ear**
Atticotomy
Division of tympanum
Lysis of adhesions of middle ear

> Excludes: divisions of otosclerotic process (19.0)
> stapediolysis (19.0)
> that with stapedectomy (19.11-19.19)

20.3 **Diagnostic procedures on middle and inner ear**

20.31 **Electrocochleography**

20.32 **Biopsy of middle and inner ear**

20.39 **Other diagnostic procedures on middle and inner ear**

> Excludes: auditory and vestibular function tests (89.13, 95.41-95.49)
> microscopic examination of specimen from ear (90.31-90.39)

20.4 **Mastoidectomy**
Code also any:
skin graft (18.79)
tympanoplasty (19.4-19.55)

> Excludes: that with implantation of cochlear prosthetic device (20.96-20.98)

20.41 **Simple mastoidectomy**

20.42 **Radical mastoidectomy**

20.49 **Other mastoidectomy**
Atticoantrotomy
Mastoidectomy:
NOS
modified radical

20.5 **Other exclsion of middle ear**

> Excludes: that with synchronous mastoidectomy (20.41-20.49)

20.51 **Excision of lesion of middle ear**

> Excludes: biopsy of middle ear (20.32)

20.59 **Other**
Apicectomy of petrous pyramid
Tympanectomy

20.6 **Fenestration of inner ear**

20.61 **Fenestration of inner ear(initial)**
Fenestration of:
labyrinth
semicircular canals   } with graft (skin) (vein)
vestibule

> Excludes: that with tympanoplasty type V (19.55)

20.62 **Revision of fenestration of inner ear**

20.7 **Incision, excision, and destruction of inner ear**

20.71 **Endolymphatic shunt**

20.72 **Injection into inner ear**
Destruction by injection (alcohol):
inner ear
semicircular canals
vestibule

20.79 **Other incision, excision and destruction of inner ear**
Decompression of labyrinth
Drainage of inner ear
Fistulization:
endolymphatic sac
labyrinth
Incision of endolymphatic sac
Labyrinthectomy (transtympanic)
Opening of bony labyrinth
Perilymphatic tap

> Excludes: biopsy of inner ear (20.32)

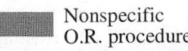 Valid O.R. procedure   Non-O.R. procedure   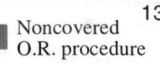 Nonspecific O.R. procedure   Noncovered O.R. procedure

20.8   **Operations on Eustachian tube**
    Catheterization
    Inflation
    Injection (Teflon paste)
    Insufflation (boric acid-salicylic acid) } of Eustachian tube
    Intubation
    Politzerization

20.9   **Other operations on inner and middle ear**

  20.91   **Tympanosympathectomy**

  20.92   **Revision of mastoidectomy**

  20.93   **Repair of oval and round windows**
    Closure of fistula:
      oval window
      perilymph
      round window

  20.94   **Injection of tympanum**

  20.95   **Implantation of electromagnetic bearing device**
    Bone conduction hearing device

> | *Excludes:* | *cochlear prosthetic device (20.96-20.98)*

  20.96   **Implantation or replacement of cochlear prosthetic device, not otherwise specified**
    Implantation of receiver (within skull) and insertion of electrode(s) in the cochlea
    Includes: mastoidectomy

> | *Excludes:* | *electromagnetic hearing device (20.95)*

  20.97   **Implantation or replacement of cochlear prosthetic device, single channel**
    Implantation of receiver (within skull) and insertion of electrode in the cochlea
    Includes: mastoidectomy

> | *Excludes:* | *electromagnetic hearing device (20.95)*

  20.98   **Implantation or replacement of cochlear prosthetic device, multiple channel**
    Implantation of receiver (within skull) and insertion of electrodes in the cochlea
    Includes: mastoidectomy

> | *Excludes:* | *electromagnetic hearing device (20.95)*

  20.99   **Other operations on middle and inner ear**
    Repair or removal of cochlear prosthetic device (receiver) (electrode)

> | *Excludes:* | *adjustment (external components) of cochlear prosthetic device (95.49)*
> | | *fitting of hearing aid (95.48)*

● Code new
  to this edition
▲ Revision of
  existing code
④ ⑤ Fourth or fifth
  digit required

5.   OPERATIONS ON THE NOSE, MOUTH, AND PHARYNX (21-29)

21   Operation on nose
Includes: operations on:
                    bone   }
                    skin   }   of nose

   21.0   Control of epistaxis

      21.00   Control of epistaxis, not otherwise specified

      21.01   Control of epistaxis by anterior nasal packing

      21.02   Control of epistaxis by posterior (and anterior) packing

      21.03   Control of epistaxis by cauterization (and packing)

      21.04   Control of epistaxis by ligation of ethmoidal arteries

      21.05   Control of epistaxis by (transantral) ligation of the maxillary artery

      21.06   Control of epistaxis by ligation of the external carotid artery

      21.07   Control of epistaxis by excision of nasal mucosa and skin grafting on septum and lateral nasal wall

      21.09   Control of epistaxis by other means

   21.1   Incision of nose
Chondrotomy
Incision of skin of nose
Nasal septotomy

   21.2   Diagnostic procedures on nose

      21.21   Rhinoscopy

      21.22   Biopsy of nose

      21.29   Other diagnostic procedures on nose

            | Excludes: | *microscopic examination of specimen from nose (90.31-90.39)* |

               nasal:
                  function study (89.12)
                  x-ray (87.16)
               rhinomanometry (89.12)

   21.3   Local excision or destruction of lesion of nose

      | Excludes: | *biopsy of nose (21.22)* |
               nasal fistulectomy (21.82)

      21.30   Excision or destruction of nose, not otherwise specified

      21.31   Local excision or destruction of intranasal lesion
           Nasal polypectomy

      21.32   Local excision or destruction of other lesion of nose

   21.4   Resection of nose
Amputation of nose

   21.5   Submucous resection of nasal septum

   21.6   Turbinectomy

      21.61   Turbinectomy by diathermy or cryosurgery

      21.62   Fracture of the turbinates

      21.69   Other turbinectomy

         | Excludes: | *turbinectomy associated with sinusectomy (22.31-22.39, 22.42. 22.60-22.64)* |

   21.7   Reduction of nasal fracture

      21.71   Closed reduction of nasal fracture

      21.72   Open reduction of nasal fracture

   21.8   Repair and plastic operations on the nose

      21.81   Suture of laceration of nose

      21.82   Closure of nasal fistula
           Nasolabial   }
           Nasopharyngeal   }   fistulectomy
           Oronasal   }

| 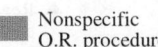 Valid O.R. procedure | Non-O.R. procedure | 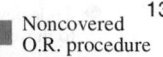 Nonspecific O.R. procedure | Noncovered O.R. procedure |

21.83 **Total nasal reconstruction**
Reconstruction of nose with:
arm flap
forehead flap

21.84 **Revision rhinoplasty**
Rhinoseptoplasty
Twisted nose rhinoplasty

21.85 **Augmentation rhinoplasty**
Augmentation rhinoplasty with:
graft
synthetic implant

21.86 **Limited rhinoplasty**
Plastic repair of nasolabial flaps
Tip rhinoplasty

21.87 **Other rhinoplasty**
Rhinoplasty NOS

21.88 **Other septoplasty**
Crushing of nasal septum
Repair of septal perforation

Excludes: *septoplasty associated with submucous resection of septum (21.5)*

21.89 **Other repair and plastic operations on nose**
Reattachment of amputated nose

21.9 **Other operations on nose**

21.91 **Lysis of adhesions of nose**
Posterior nasal scrub

21.99 **Other**

Excludes: *dilation of frontonasal duct (96.21)*
irrigation of nasal passages (96.53)
removal of:
intraluminal foreign body without incision (98.12)
nasal packing (97.32)
replacement of nasal packing (97.21)

22 **Operations on nasal sinuses**

22.0 **Aspiration and lavage of nasal sinus**

22.00 **Aspiration and lavage of nasal sinus, not otherwise specified**

22.01 **Puncture of nasal sinus for aspiration or lavage**

22.02 **Aspiration or lavage of nasal sinus through natural ostium**

22.1 **Diagnostic procedures on nasal sinus**

22.11 **Closed [endoscopic] [needle] biopsy of nasal sinus**

22.12 **Open biopsy of nasal sinus**

22.19 **Other diagnostic procedures on nasal sinuses**
Endoscopy without biopsy

Excludes: *transillumination of sinus (89.35)*
x-ray of sinus (87.15-87.16)

22.2 **Intranasal antrotomy**

Excludes: *antrotomy with external approach (22.31-22.39)*

22.3 **External maxillary antrotomy**

22.31 **Radical maxillary antrotomy**
Removal of lining membrane of maxillary sinus using Caldwell-Luc approach

22.39 **Other external maxillary antrotomy**
Exploration of maxillary antrum with Caldwell-Luc approach

22.4 **Frontal sinusotomy and sinusectomy**

22.41 **Frontal sinusotomy**

22.42 **Frontal sinusectomy**
Excision of lesion of frontal sinus
Obliteration of frontal sinus (with fat)

Excludes: *biopsy of nasal sinus (22.11-22.12)*

22.5 **Other nasal sinusotomy**

● Code new
to this edition

▲ Revision of
existing code

④ ⑤ Fourth or fifth
digit required

22.50　Sinusotomy, not otherwise specified

22.51　Ethmoidotomy

22.52　Sphenoidotomy

22.53　Incision of multiple nasal sinuses

22.6　Other nasal sinusectomy
　Includes: that with incidental turbinectomy

　Excludes:　biopsy of nasal sinus (22.11-22.12)

22.60　Sinusectomy, not otherwise specified

22.61　Excision of lesion of maxillary sinus with Caldwell-Luc approach

22.62　Excision of lesion of maxillary sinus with other approach

22.63　Ethmoidectomy

22.64　Sphenoidectomy

22.7　Repair of nasal sinus

22.71　Closure of nasal sinus fist
　Repair of oro-antral fistula

22.79　Other repair of nasal sinus
　Reconstruction of frontonasal duct
　Repair of bone of accessory sinus

22.9　Other operations on nasal sinuses
　Exteriorization of maxillary sinus
　Fistulization of sinus

　Excludes:　dilation of frontonasal duct (96.21)

23　Removal and restoration of teeth

23.0　Forceps extraction of tooth

23.01　Extraction of deciduous tooth

23.09　Extraction of other tooth
　Extraction of tooth NOS

23.1　Surgical removal of tooth

23.11　Removal of residual root

23.19　Other surgical extraction of tooth
　Odontectomy NOS
　Removal of impacted tooth
　Tooth extraction with elevation of mucoperiosteal flap

23.2　Restoration of tooth by filling

23.3　Restoration of tooth by inlay

23.4　Other dental restoration

23.41　Application of crown

23.42　Insertion of fixed bridge

23.43　Insertion of removable bridge

23.49　Other

23.5　Implantation of tooth

23.6　Prosthetic dental implant
　Endosseous dental implant

23.7　Apicoectomy and root canal therapy

23.70　Root canal not otherwise specified

23.71　Root canal therapy with irrigation

23.72　Root canal therapy with apicoectomy

23.73　Apicoectomy

24　Other operations on teeth, gums, and alveoli

24.0　Incision of gum or alveolar bone
　Apical alveolotomy

24.1　Diagnostic procedures on teeth, gums, and alveoli

24.11　Biopsy of gum

24.12　Biopsy of alveoli

Valid O.R. procedure　　Non-O.R. procedure　　Nonspecific O.R. procedure　　Noncovered O.R. procedure

24.19 Other diagnostic procedures on teeth, gums, and alveoli

> Excludes: *dental:*
> *examination (89.31)*
> *x-ray:*
> *full-mouth (87.11)*
> *other (87.12)*
> *microscopic examination of dental specimen (90.81-90.89)*

24.2 Gingivoplasty
Gingivoplasty with bone or soft tissue graft

24.3 Other operations on gum

24.31 Excision of lesion or tissue of gum

> Excludes: *biopsy of gum (24.11)*
> *excision of odontogenic lesion (24.4)*

24.32 Suture of laceration of gum

24.39 Other

24.4 Excision of dental lesion of jaw
Excision of odontogenic lesion

24.5 Alveoloplasty
Alveolectomy (interradicular) (intraseptal) (radical) (simple) (with graft or implant)

> Excludes: *biopsy of alveolus (24.12)*
> *en bloc resection of alveolar process and palate (27.32)*

24.6 Exposure of tooth

24.7 Application of orthodontic appliance
Application, insertion, or fitting of:
  arch bars
  orthodontic obturator
  orthodontic wiring
  periodontal splint

> Excludes: *nonorthodontic dental wiring (93.55)*

24.8 Other orthodontic operation
Closure of diastema (alveolar) (dental)
Occlusal adjustment
Removal of arch bars
Repair of dental arch

> Excludes: *removal of nonorthodontic wiring (97.33)*

24.9 Other dental operations

24.91 Extension or deepening of buccolabial or lingual sulcus

24.99 Other

> Excludes: *dental:*
> *debridement (96.54)*
> *examination (89.31)*
> *prophylaxis (96.54)*
> *scaling and polishing (96.54)*
> *wiring (93.55)*
> *fitting of dental appliance [denture] (99.97)*
> *microscopic examination of dental specimen (90.81-90.89)*
> *removal of dental:*
> *packing (97.34)*
> *prosthesis (97.35)*
> *wiring (97.33)*
> *replacement of dental packing (97.22)*

25 Operations on tongue

25.0 Diagnostic procedures on tongue

25.01 Closed [needle] biopsy of tongue

25.02 Open biopsy of tongue
Wedge biopsy

25.09 Other diagnostic procedures on tongue

● Code new
to this edition
▲ Revision of
existing code
④ ⑤ Fourth or fifth
digit required

25.1 Excision or destruction of lesion or tissue of tongue

> Excludes: biopsy of tongue (25.01-25.02)
> frenumectomy:
> labial (27.41)
> lingual (25.92)

25.2 Partial glossectomy

25.3 Complete glossectomy

Glossectomy NOS

Code also any neck dissection (40.40-40.42)

25.4 Radical glossectomy

Code also any:
neck dissection (40.40-40.42)
tracheostomy (31.1-31.29)

25.5 Repair of tongue and glossoplasty

25.51 Suture of laceration of tongue

25.59 Other repair and plastic operations on tongue

Fascial sling of tongue
Fusion of tongue (to lip)
Graft of mucosa or skin to tongue

> Excludes: lysis of adhesions of tongue (25.93)

25.9 Other operations on tongue

25.91 Lingual frenotomy

> Excludes: labial frenotomy (27.91)

25.92 Lingual frenectomy

> Excludes: labial frenectomy (27.41)

25.93 Lysis of adhesions of tongue

25.94 Other glossotomy

25.99 Other

26 Operations on salivary glands and ducts

Includes: operations on:
lesser salivary
parotid
sublingual } gland and duct
submaxillary

Code also any neck dissection (40.40-40.42)

26.0 Incision of salivary gland or duct

26.1 Diagnostic procedures on salivary glands and ducts

26.11 Closed [needle] biopsy of salivary gland or duct

26.12 Open biopsy of salivary gland or duct

26.19 Other diagnostic procedures on salivary glands and ducts

> Excludes: x-ray of salivary gland (87.09)

26.2 Excision of lesion of salivary gland

26.21 Marsupialization of salivary gland cyst

26.29 Other excision of salivary gland lesion

> Excludes: biopsy of salivary gland (26.11-26.12)
> salivary fistulectomy (26.42)

26.3 Sialoadenectomy

26.30 Sialoadenectomy, not otherwise specified

26.31 Partial sialoadenectomy

26.32 Complete sialoadenectomy

En bloc excision of salivary gland lesion
Radical sialoadenectomy

26.4 Repair of salivary gland or duct

26.41 Suture of laceration of salivary gland

26.42 Closure of salivary fistula

 Valid O.R.
procedure

 Non-O.R.
procedure

 Nonspecific
O.R. procedure

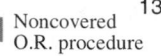 Noncovered
O.R. procedure

26.49 **Other repair and plastic operations on salivary gland or duct**
Fistulization of salivary gland
Plastic repair of salivary gland or duct NOS
Transplantation of salivary duct opening

26.9 **Other operations on salivary gland or duct**

26.91 **Probing of salivary duct**

26.99 **Other**

27 **Other operations on mouth and face**
Includes: operations on:
lips
palate
soft tissue of face and mouth, except tongue and gingiva

Excludes   *operations on:*
gingiva (24.0-24.99)
tongue (25.01-25.99)

27.0 **Drainage of face and floor of mouth**
Drainage of:
facial region (abscess)
fascial compartment of face
Ludwig's angina

Excludes: *drainage of thyroglossal tract (06.09)*

27.1 **Incision of palate**

27.2 **Diagnostic procedures on oral cavity**

27.21 **Biopsy of bony palate**

27.22 **Biopsy of uvula and soft palate**

27.23 **Biopsy of lip**

27.24 **Biopsy of mouth, unspecified structure**

27.29 **Other diagnostic procedures on oral cavity**

Excludes: *soft tissue x-ray (87.09)*

27.3 **Excision of lesion or tissue of bony palate**

27.31 **Local excision or destruction of lesion or tissue of bony palate**
Local excision or destruction of palate by:
cautery
chemotherapy
cryotherapy

Excludes: *biopsy of bony palate (27.21)*

27.32 **Wide excision or destruction of lesion or tissue of bony palate**
En bloc resection of alveolar process and palate

27.4 **Excision of other parts of mouth**

27.41 **Labial frenectomy**

Excludes: *division of labial frenum (27.91)*

27.42 **Wide excision of lesion of lip**

27.43 **Other excision of lesion or tissue of lip**

27.49 **Other excision of mouth**

Excludes: *biopsy of mouth NOS (27.24)*
excision of lesion of:
palate (27.31-27.32)
tongue (25.1)
uvula (27.72)
fistulectomy of mouth (27.53)
frenectomy of:
lip (27.41)
tongue (25.92)

27.5 **Plastic repair of mouth**

Excludes: *palatoplasty (27.61-27.69)*

27.51 **Suture of laceration of lip**

27.52 **Suture of laceration of other part of mouth**

● Code new
to this edition   ▲ Revision of
existing code   ④ ⑤ Fourth or fifth
digit required

27.53 **Closure of fistula of mouth**

> *Excludes:* | *fistulectomy:*
> *nasolabial (21.82)*
> *oro-antral (22.71)*
> *oronasal (21.82)*

27.54 **Repair of cleft lip**

27.55 **Full-thickness skin graft to lip and mouth**

27.56 **Other skin graft to lip and mouth**

27.57 **Attachment of pedicle or flap graft to lip and mouth**

27.59 **Other plastic repair of mouth**

27.6 **Palatoplasty**

27.61 **Suture of laceration of palate**

27.62 **Correction of cleft palate**

Correction of cleft palate by push-back operation

> *Excludes:* | *revision of cleft palate repair (27.63)*

27.63 **Revision of cleft palate repair**

Secondary:
attachment of pharyngeal flap
lengthening of palate

27.69 **Other plastic repair of palate**

> *Excludes:* | *fistulectomy of mouth (27.53)*

27.7 **Operations on uvula**

27.71 **Incision of uvula**

27.72 **Excision of uvula**

> *Excludes:* | *biopsy of uvula (27.22)*

27.73 **Repair of uvula**

> *Excludes:* | *that with synchronous cleft palate repair (27.62)*
> *uranostaphylorrhaphy (27.62)*

27.79 **Other operations on uvula**

27.9 **Other operations on mouth and face**

27.91 **Labial frenotomy**

Division of labial frenum

> *Excludes:* | *lingual frenotomy (25.91)*

27.92 **Incision of mouth, unspecified structure**

> *Excludes:* | *incision of:*
> *gum (24.0)*
> *palate (27.1)*
> *salivary gland or duct (26.0)*
> *tongue (25.94)*
> *uvula (27.71)*

27.99 **Other operations on oral cavity**

Graft of buccal sulcus

> *Excludes:* | *removal of:*
> *intraluminal foreign body (98.01)*
> *penetrating foreign body from mouth without incision (98.22)*

28 **Operations on tonsils and adenoids**

28.0 **Incision and drainage of tonsil and peritonsillar structures**

Drainage (oral) (transcervical) of:
parapharyngeal
peritonsillar } abscess
retropharyngeal
tonsillar

28.1 **Diagnostic procedures on tonsils and adenoids**

28.11 **Biopsy of tonsils and adenoids**

28.19 **Other diagnostic procedures on tonsils and adenoids**

> *Excludes:* | *soft tissue x-ray (87.09)*

| | Valid O.R. procedure | | Non-O.R. procedure | | Nonspecific O.R. procedure | | Noncovered O.R. procedure |

28.2	**Tonsillectomy without adenoidectomy**
28.3	**Tonsillectomy with adenoidectomy**
28.4	**Excision of tonsil tag**
28.5	**Excision of lingual tonsil**
28.6	**Adenoidectomy without tonsillectomy** Excision of adenoid tag
28.7	**Control of hemorrhage after tonsillectomy and adenoidectomy**
28.9	**Other operations on tonsils and adenoids**

    28.91 **Removal of foreign body from tonsil and adenoid by incision**

         Excludes: *that without incision (98.13)*

    28.92 **Excision of lesion of tonsil and adenoid**

         Excludes: *biopsy of tonsil and adenoid (28.11)*

    28.99 **Other**

29   **Operation on pharynx**
    Includes: operations on:
             hypopharynx
             nasopharynx
             oropharynx
             pharyngeal pouch
             pyriform sinus

29.0   **Pharyngotomy**
    Drainage of pharyngeal bursa

     Excludes: *incision and drainage of retropharyngeal abscess (28.0)*
                  removal of foreign body (without incision) (98.13)

29.1   **Diagnostic procedures on pharynx**

    29.11 **Pharyngoscopy**

    29.12 **Pharyngeal biopsy**
         Biopsy of supraglottic mass

    29.19 **Other diagnostic procedures on pharynx**

         Excludes: *x-ray of nasopharynx:*
                    contrast (87.06)
                    other (87.09)

29.2   **Excision of branchial cleft cyst or vestige**

     Excludes: *branchial cleft fistulectomy (29.52)*

29.3   **Excision or destruction of lesion or tissue of pharynx**

    29.31 **Cricopharyngeal myotomy**

         Excludes   *that with pharyngeal diverticulectomy (29.32)*

    29.32 **Pharyngeal diverticulectomy**

    29.33 **Pharyngectomy (partial)**

         Excludes   *laryngopharyngectomy (30.3)*

    29.39 **Other excision or destruction of lesion or tissue of pharynx**

29.4   **Plastic operation on pharynx**
    Correction of nasopharyngeal atresia

     Excludes: *pharyngoplasty associated with cleft palate repair (27.62-27.63)*

29.5   **Other repair of pharynx**

    29.51 **Suture of laceration of pharynx**

    29.52 **Closure of branchial cleft fistula**

    29.53 **Closure of other fistula of pharynx**
         Pharyngoesophageal fistulectomy

    29.54 **Lysis of pharyngeal adhesions**

    29.59 **Other**

29.9   **Other operations on pharynx**

    29.91 **Dilation of pharynx**
         Dilation of nasopharynx

    29.92 **Division of glossopharyngeal nerve**

   ●   Code new   ▲   Revision of   ④ ⑤   Fourth or fifth
            to this edition   existing code   digit required

29.99 **Other**

> *Excludes:* insertion of radium into pharynx and nasopharynx (92.27)
> removal of intraluminal foreign body (98.13)

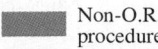 Valid O.R.
procedure

Non-O.R.
procedure

Nonspecific
O.R. procedure

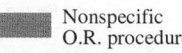 Noncovered
O.R. procedure

● Code new
to this edition   ▲ Revision of
existing code   ④ ⑤ Fourth or fifth
digit required

6. OPERATIONS ON THE RESPIRATORY SYSTEM (30-34)

30 Excision of larynx

30.0 Excision or destruction of lesion or tissue of larynx

30.01 Marsupialization of laryngeal cyst

30.09 Other excision or destruction of lesion or tissue of larynx
Stripping of vocal cords

> *Excludes:* *biopsy of larynx (31.43)*
> *laryngeal fistulectomy (31.62)*
> *laryngotracheal fistulectomy (31.62)*

30.1 Hemilaryngectomy

30.2 Other partial laryngectomy

30.21 Epiglottidectomy

30.22 Vocal cordectomy
Excision of vocal cords

30.29 Other partial laryngectomy
Excision of laryngeal cartilage

30.3 Complete laryngectomy
Block dissection of larynx (with thyroidectomy) (with synchronous tracheostomy)
Laryngopharyngectomy

> *Excludes:* *that with radical neck dissection (30.4)*

30.4 Radical laryngectomy
Complete [total] laryngectomy with radical neck dissection (with thyroidectomy) (with synchronous tracheostomy)

31 Other operations on larynx and trachea

31.0 Injection of larynx
Injection of inert material into larynx or vocal cords

31.1 Temporary tracheostomy
Tracheotomy for assistance in breathing

31.2 Permanent tracheostomy

31.21 Mediastinal tracheostomy

31.29 Other permanent tracheostomy

> *Excludes:* *that with laryngectomy (30.3-30.4)*

31.3 Other incision of larynx or trachea

> *Excludes:* *that for assistance in breathing (31.1-31.29)*

31.4 Diagnostic procedures on larynx and trachea

31.41 Tracheoscopy through artificial stoma

> *Excludes:* *that with biopsy (31.43-31.44)*

31.42 Laryngoscopy and other tracheoscopy

> *Excludes:* *that with biopsy (31.43-31.44)*

31.43 Closed [endoscopic] biopsy of larynx

31.44 Closed [endoscopic] biopsy of trachea

31.45 Open biopsy of larynx or trachea

31.48 Other diagnostic procedures on larynx

> *Excludes:* *contrast laryngogram (87.07)*
> *microscopic examination of specimen from larynx (90.31-90.39)*
> *soft tissue x-ray of larynx NEC (87.09)*

31.49 Other diagnostic procedures on trachea

> *Excludes:* *microscopic examination of specimen from trachea (90.41-90.49)*
> *x-ray of trachea (87.49)*

31.5 Local excision or destruction of lesion or tissue of trachea

> *Excludes:* *biopsy of trachea (31.44-31.45)*
> *laryngotracheal fistulectomy (31.62)*
> *tracheoesophageal fistulectomy (31.73)*

31.6 Repair of larynx

31.61 Suture of laceration of larynx

 Valid O.R. procedure 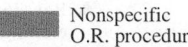 Non-O.R. procedure   Nonspecific O.R. procedure 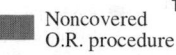 Noncovered O.R. procedure

31.62 **Closure of fistula of larynx**
Laryngotracheal fistulectomy
Take-down of laryngostomy

31.63 **Revision of laryngostomy**

31.64 **Repair of laryngeal fracture**

31.69 **Other repair of larynx**
Arytenoidopexy
Graft of larynx
Transposition of vocal cords

Excludes: construction of artificial larynx (31.75)

31.7 **Repair and plastic operations on trachea**

31.71 **Suture of laceration of trachea**

31.72 **Closure of external fistula of trachea**
Closure of tracheotomy

31.73 **Closure of other fistula of trachea**
Tracheoesophageal fistulectomy

Excludes: laryngotracheal fistulectomy (31.62)

31.74 **Revision of tracheostomy**

31.75 **Reconstruction of trachea and construction of artificial larynx**
Tracheoplasty with artificial larynx

31.79 **Other repair and plastic operations on trachea**

31.9 **Other operations on larynx and trachea**

31.91 **Division of laryngeal nerve**

31.92 **Lysis of adhesions of trachea or larynx**

31.93 **Replacement of laryngeal or tracheal stent**

31.94 **Injection of locally-acting therapeutic substance into trachea**

31.95 **Tracheoesophageal fistulization**

31.98 **Other operations on larynx**
Dilation
Division of congenital web } of larynx
Removal of keel or stent

Excludes: removal of intraluminal foreign body from larynx without incision (98.14)

31.99 **Other operations on trachea**

Excludes: removal of:
intraluminal foreign body from trachea without incision (98.15)
tracheostomy tube (97.37)
replacement of tracheostomy tube (97.23)
tracheostomy toilette (96.35)

32 **Excision of lung and bronchus**
Includes: rib resection
sternotomy
sternum-splitting incision } as operative approach
thoracotomy

Code also any synchronous bronchoplasty (33.48)

32.0 **Local excision or destruction of lesion or tissue of bronchus**

Excludes: biopsy of bronchus (33.24-33.25)
bronchial fistulectomy (33.42)

32.01 **Endoscopic excision or destruction of lesion or tissue of bronchus**

32.09 **Other local excision or destruction of lesion or tissue of bronchus**

Excludes: that by endoscopic approach (32.01)

32.1 **Other excision of bronchus**
Resection (wide sleeve) of bronchus

Excludes: radical dissection [excision] of bronchus (32.6)

32.2 **Local excision or destruction of lesion or tissue of lung**

32.21 **Plication of emphysematous bleb**

● Code new
to this edition
▲ Revision of
existing code
④ ⑤ Fourth or fifth
digit required

32.22   **Lung volume reduction surgery**

32.28   **Endoscopic excision or destruction of lesion or tissue of lung**

> *Excludes:*   *biopsy of lung (33.26-33.27)*

32.29   **Other local excision or destruction of lesion or tissue of lung**
Resection of lung:
  NOS
  wedge

> *Excludes:*   *biopsy of lung (33.26-33.27)*
>   *that by endoscopic approach (32.28)*
>   *wide excision of lesion of lung (32.3)*

32.3   **Segmental resection of lung**
Partial lobectomy

32.4   **Lobectomy of lung**
Lobectomy with segmental resection of adjacent lobes of lung

> *Excludes:*   *that with radical dissection [excision] of thoracic structures (32.6)*

32.5   **Complete pneumonectomy**
Excision of lung NOS
Pneumonectomy (with mediastinal dissection)

32.6   **Radical dissection of thoracic structures**
Block [en bloc] dissection of bronchus, lobe of lung, brachial plexus, intercostal structure, ribs (transverse process), and sympathetic nerves

32.9   **Other excision of lung**

> *Excludes:*   *biopsy of lung and bronchus (33.24-33.27)*
>   *pulmonary decortication (34.51)*

33   **Other operations on lung and bronchus**
Includes: rib resection
              sternotomy
              sternum-splitting incision   } as operative approach
              thoracotomy

33.0   **Incision of bronchus**

33.1   **Incision of lung**

> *Excludes:*   *puncture of lung (33.93)*

33.2   **Diagnostic procedures on lung and bronchus**

33.21   **Bronchoscopy through artificial stoma**

> *Excludes:*   *that with biopsy (33.24, 33.27)*

33.22   **Fiber-optic bronchoscopy**

> *Excludes:*   *that with biopsy (33.24. 33.27)*

33.23   **Other bronchoscopy**

> *Excludes:*   *that for:*
>   *aspiration (96.05)*
>   *biopsy (33.24, 33.27)*

33.24   **Closed [endoscopic] biopsy of bronchus**
Bronchoscopy (fiberoptic) (rigid) with:
  brush biopsy of "lung"
  brushing or washing for specimen collection
  excision (bite) biopsy

> *Excludes:*   *closed biopsy of lung, other than brush biopsy of "lung" (33.26, 33.27)*

33.25   **Open biopsy of bronchus**

> *Excludes:*   *open biopsy of lung (33.28)*

33.26   **Closed [percutaneous] [needle] biopsy of lung**

> *Excludes:*   *endoscopic biopsy of lung (33.27)*

33.27   **Closed endoscopic biopsy of lung**
Fiberoptic (flexible) bronchoscopy with fluoroscopic guidance with biopsy
Transbronchial lung biopsy

> *Excludes:*   *brush biopsy of "lung" (33.24)*
>   *percutaneous biopsy of lung (33.26)*

33.28   **Open biopsy of lung**

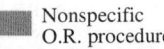

  Valid O.R.   Non-O.R.   Nonspecific   Noncovered
  procedure   procedure   O.R. procedure   O.R. procedure

33.29 Other diagnostic procedures on lung and bronchus

> Excludes: contrast bronchogram:
>> endotracheal (87.31)
>> other (87.32)
>> lung scan (92.15)
>> magnetic resonance imaging (88.92)
>> microscopic examination of specimen from bronchus or lung
>>> (90.41-90.49)
>> routine chest x-ray (87.44)
>> ultrasonography of lung (88.73)
>> vital capacity determination (89.37)
>> x-ray of bronchus or lung NOS (87.49)

33.3 Surgical collapse of lung

33.31 Destruction of phrenic nerve for collapse of lung

33.32 Artificial pneumothorax for collapse of lung
Thoracotomy for collapse of lung

33.33 Pneumoperitoneum for collapse of lung

33.34 Thoracoplasty

33.39 Other surgical collapse of lung
Collapse of lung NOS

33.4 Repair and plastic operation on lung and bronchus

33.41 Suture of laceration of bronchus

33.42 Closure of bronchial fistula
Closure of bronchostomy
Fistulectomy:
bronchocutaneous
bronchoesophageal
bronchovisceral

> Excludes: closure of fistula:
>> bronchomediastinal (34.73)
>> bronchopleural (34.73)
>> bronchopleuromediastinal (34.73)

33.43 Closure of laceration of lung

33.48 Other repair and plastic operation on bronchus

33.49 Other repair ad plastic operations on lung

> Excludes: closure of pleural fistula (34.73)

33.5 Lung transplant

> Code also cardiopulmonary bypass [extracorporeal circulation] [heart-lung machine]
> 39.61

> Excludes: Combined heart-lung transplantation (33.6)

33.50 Lung transplantation, not otherwise specified

33.51 Unilateral lung transplantation

33.52 Bilateral lung transplantation
Double-lung transplantation
En bloc transplantation

33.6 Combined heart-lung transplantation

> Code also cardiopulmonary bypass [extracorporeal circulation] [heart-lung machine]
> (39.61)

33.9 Other operations on lung and bronchus

33.91 Bronchial dilation

33.92 Ligation of bronchus

33.93 Puncture of lung

> Excludes: needle biopsy (33.26)

33.98 Other operations on bronchus

> Excludes: bronchial lavage (96.56)
>> removal of intraluminal foreign body from bronchus without incision
>>> (98.15)

33.99 Other operations on lung

● Code new
to this edition

▲ Revision of
existing code

④ ⑤ Fourth or fifth
digit required

> **Excludes:** *other continuous mechanical ventilation (96.70-96.72)*
> *respiratory therapy (93.90-93.99)*

34 **Operations on chest wall, pleura, mediastinum, and diaphragm**

> **Excludes:** *operations on breast (85.0-85.99)*

34.0 **Incision of chest wall and pleura**

> **Excludes:** *that as operative approach—omit code*

34.01 **Incision of chest wall**
Extrapleural drainage

> **Excludes:** *incision of pleura (34.09)*

34.02 **Exploratory thoracotomy**

34.03 **Reopening of recent thoracotomy site**

34.04 **Insertion of intercostal catheter for drainage**
Closed chest drainage

34.05 **Creation of pleuroperitoneal shunt**

34.09 **Other incision of pleura**
Creation of pleural window for drainage
Intercostal stab
Open chest drainage

> **Excludes:** *thoracoscopy (34.21)*
> *thoracotomy for collapse of lung (33.32)*

34.1 **Incision of mediastinum**

> **Excludes:** *mediastinoscopy (34.22)*
> *mediastinotomy associated with pneumonectomy (32.5)*

34.2 **Diagnostic procedures on chest wall, pleura, mediastinum, and diaphragm**

34.21 **Transpleural thoracoscopy**

34.22 **Mediastinoscopy**
Code also any lymph node biopsy (40.11)

34.23 **Biopsy of chest wall**

34.24 **Pleural biopsy**

34.25 **Closed [percutaneous] [needle] biopsy of mediastinum**

34.26 **Open biopsy of mediastinum**

34.27 **Biopsy of diaphragm**

34.28 **Other diagnostic procedures on chest wall, pleura, and diaphragm**

> **Excludes:** *angiocardiography (88.50-88.58)*
> *aortography (88.42)*
> *arteriography of:*
> *intrathoracic vessels NEC (88.44)*
> *pulmonary arteries (88.43)*
> *microscopic examination of specimen from chest wall. pleura, and*
> *diaphragm (90.41-90.49)*
> *phlebography of:*
> *intrathoracic vessels NEC (88.63)*
> *pulmonary veins (88.62)*
> *radiological examinations of thorax:*
> *C.A.T. scan (87.41)*
> *diaphragmatic x-ray (87.49)*
> *intrathoracic lymphangiogram (87.34)*
> *routine chest x-ray (87.44)*
> *sinogram of chest wall (87.38)*
> *soft tissue x-ray of chest wall NEC (87.39)*
> *tomogram of thorax NEC (87. 42)*
> *ultrasonography of thorax (88.73)*

34.29 **Other diagnostic procedures on mediastinum**

> **Excludes:** *mediastinal:*
> *pneumogram (87.33)*
> *x-ray NEC (87.49)*

34.3 **Excision or destruction of lesion or tissue of mediastinum**

> **Excludes:** *biopsy or mediastinum (34.25-34.26)*
> *mediastinal fistulectomy (34.73)*

	Valid O.R. procedure		Non-O.R. procedure		Nonspecific O.R. procedure		Noncovered O.R. procedure

34.4 **Excision or destruction of lesion of chest wall**
Excision of lesion of chest wall NOS (with excision of ribs)

> Excludes: *biopsy of chest wall (34.23)*
> *costectomy not incidental to thoracic procedure (77. 91)*
> *excision of lesion of:*
> *breast (85.20-85.25)*
> *cartilage (80.89)*
> *skin (86.2-86.3)*
> *fistulectomy (34. 73)*

34.5 **Pleurectomy**

34.51 **Decortication of lung**

34.59 **Other excision of pleura**
Excision of pleural lesion

> Excludes: *biopsy of pleura (34.24)*
> *pleural fistulectomy (34.73)*

34.6 **Scarification of pleura**
Pleurosclerosis

> Excludes: *injection of sclerosing agent (34.92)*

34.7 **Repair of chest wall**

34.71 **Suture of laceration of chest wall**

> Excludes: *suture of skin and subcutaneous tissue alone (86.59)*

34.72 **Closure of thoracostomy**

34.73 **Closure of other fistula of thorax**
Closure of:
bronchopleural ⎫
bronchopleurocutaneous ⎬ fistula
bronchopleuromediastinal ⎭

34.74 **Repair of pectus deformity**
Repair of:
pectus carinatum ⎫
pectus excavatum ⎬ (with implant)

34.79 **Other repair of chest wall**
Repair of chest wall NOS

34.8 **Operations on diaphragm**

34.81 **Excision of lesion or tissue of diaphragm**

> Excludes: *biopsy of diaphragm (34.27)*

34.82 **Suture of laceration of diaphragm**

34.83 **Closure of fistula of diaphragm**
Thoracicoabdominal ⎫
Thoracicogastric ⎬ fistulectomy
Thoracicointestinal ⎭

34.84 **Other repair of diaphragm**

> Excludes: *repair of diaphragmatic hernia (53.7-53.82)*

34.85 **Implantation of diaphragmatic pacemaker**

34.89 **Other operations on diaphragm**

34.9 **Other operations on thorax**

34.91 **Thoracentesis**

34.92 **Injection into thoracic cavity**
Chemical pleurodesis
Injection of cytotoxic agent or tetracycline
Requires additional code for any cancer chemotherapeutic substance (99.25)

> Excludes: *that for collapse of lung (33.32)*

34.93 **Repair of pleura**

34.99 **Other**

> Excludes: *removal of:*
> *mediastinal drain (97.42)*
> *sutures (97.43)*
> *thoracotomy tube (97.41)*

● Code new
   to this edition
▲ Revision of
   existing code
④ ⑤ Fourth or fifth
   digit required

7. OPERATIONS ON THE CARDIOVASCULAR SYSTEM (35-39)

35 Operations on valves and septa of heart

Includes: sternotomy (median)
(transverse)
thoracotomy
} as operative approach

Code also cardiopulmonary bypass [extracorporeal circulation] [heart-lung machine] (39.61)

35.0 Closed heart valvotomy

Excludes: *percutaneous (balloon) valvuloplasty (35.96)*

35.00 Closed heart valvotomy, unspecified valve

35.01 Closed heart valvotomy, aortic valve

35.02 Closed heart valvotomy, mitral valve

35.03 Closed heart valvotomy, pulmonary valve

35.04 Closed heart valvotomy, tricuspid valve

35.1 Open heart valvuloplasty without replacement

Includes: open heart valvotomy

Excludes: *that associated with repair of:*
endocardial cushion defect (35.54, 35.63, 35.73)
percutaneous (balloon) valvuloplasty (35.96)
valvular defect associated with atrial and ventricular septal defects (35.54, 35.63, 35.73)

Code also cardiopulmonary bypass, if performed [extracorporeal circulation] [heart-lung machine] (39.61)

35.10 Open heart valvuloplasty without replacement, unspecified valve

35.11 Open beard valvuloplasty of aortic valve without replacement

35.12 Open heart valvuloplasty of mitral valve without replacement

35.13 Open heart valvuloplasty of pulmonary valve without replacement

35.14 Open heart valvuloplasty of tricuspid valve without replacement

35.2 Replacement of heart valve

Includes: excision of heart valve with replacement

Code also cardiopulmonary bypass [extracorporeal circulation] [heart-lung machine] (39.61)

Excludes: *that associated with repair of:*
endocardial cushion defect (35.54, 35.63, 35.73)
valvular defect associated with atrial and ventricular septal defects (35.54, 35.63, 35.73)

35.20 Replacement of unspecified heart valve
Repair of unspecified heart valve with tissue graft or prosthetic implant

35.21 Replacement of aortic valve with tissue graft
Repair of aortic valve with tissue graft (autograft) (heterograft) (homograft)

35.22 Other replacement of aortic valve
Repair of aortic valve with replacement:
NOS
prosthetic (partial) (synthetic) (total)

35.23 Replacement of mitral valve with tissue graft
Repair of mitral valve with tissue graft (autograft) (heterograft) (homograft)

35.24 Other replacement of mitral valve
Repair of mitral valve with replacement:
NOS
prosthetic (partial) (synthetic) (total)

35.25 Replacement of pulmonary valve with tissue graft
Repair of pulmonary valve with tissue graft (autograft) (heterograft) (homograft)

35.26 Other replacement of pulmonary valve
Repair of pulmonary valve with replacement:
NOS
prosthetic (partial) (synthetic) (total)

35.27 Replacement of tricuspid valve with tissue graft
Repair of tricuspid valve with tissue graft (autograft) (heterograft) (homograft)

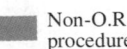 Valid O.R. procedure   Non-O.R. procedure   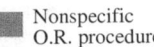 Nonspecific O.R. procedure   Noncovered O.R. procedure

35.28 **Other replacement of tricuspid valve**
Repair of tricuspid valve with replacement:
NOS
prosthetic (partial) (synthetic) (total)

35.3 **Operations on structures adjacent to heart valves**
Code also cardiopulmonary bypass [extracorporeal circulation] [heart-lung machine]
(39.61)

35.31 **Operations on papillary muscle**
Division
Reattachment } of papillary muscle
Repair

35.32 **Operations on chordae tendineae**
Division
Repair } of chordae tendineae

35.33 **Annuloplasty**
Plication of annulus

35.34 **Infundibulectomy**
Right ventricular infundibulectomy

35.35 **Operations on trabeculae carneae cordis**
Division
Excision } of trabeculae carneae cordis
Excision of aortic subvalvular ring

35.39 **Operations on other structures adjacent to valves of heart**
Repair of sinus of Valsalva (aneurysm)

35.4 **Production of septal defect in heart**

35.41 **Enlargement of existing atrial septal defect**
Rashkind procedure
Septostomy (atrial) (balloon)

35.42 **Creation of septal defect in heart**
Blalock-Hanlon operation

35.5 **Repair of atrial and ventricular septa with prosthesis**
Includes: repair of septa with synthetic implant of patch
Code also cardiopulmonary bypass [extracorporeal circulation] [heart-lung machine)
(39.61)

35.50 **Repair of unspecified septal defect of heart with prosthesis**
Excludes: *that associated with repair of:*
endocardial cushion defect (35.54)
septal defect associated with valvular defect (35.54)

35.51 **Repair of atrial septal defect with prosthesis, open technique**
Atrioseptoplasty
Correction of atrial septal
defect
Repair: } with prosthesis
foramen ovale (patent)
ostium secundum defect

Excludes: *that associated with repair of:*
atrial septal defect associated with valvular and ventricular septal
defects (35.54)
endocardial cushion defect (35.54)

35.52 **Repair of atrial septal defect with prosthesis, closed technique**
Insertion of atrial septal umbrella [King-Mills]

35.53 **Repair of ventricular septal defect with prosthesis**
Correction of ventricular
septal defect } with prosthesis
Repair of supracristal defect

Excludes: *that associated with repair of:*
endocardial cushion defect (35.54)
ventricular defect associated with valvular and atrial septal defects
(35.54)

35.54 **Repair of endocardial cushion defect with prosthesis**
Repair:

● Code new
to this edition

▲ Revision of
existing code

④ ⑤ Fourth or fifth
digit required

atrioventricular canal
ostium primum defect
valvular defect associated
  with Atrial and
  ventricular Septal defects } with prosthesis (grafted to septa)

> Excludes: *repair of isolated:*
>   *atrial septal defect (35.51-35.52)*
>   *valvular defect (35.20, 35.22, 35.24, 35.26. 35.28)*
>   *ventricular septal defect (35.53)*

35.6 Repair of atrial and ventricular septa with tissue graft

Code also cardiopulmonary bypass [extracorporeal circulation] [heart-lung machine]
(39.61)

35.60 Repair of unspecified septal defect of heart with tissue graft

> Excludes: *that associated with repair of:*
>   *endocardial cushion defect (35.63)*
>   *septal defect associated with valvular, defect (33.63)*

35.61 Repair of atrial septal defect with tissue graft
Atrioseptoplasty
Correction of atrial septal
  defect
Repair; } with tissue graft
  foramen ovale (patent)
  ostium secundum defect

> Excludes: *that associated with repair of:*
>   *atrial septal defect associated with valvular and ventricular septal*
>   *defects (35.63)*
>   *endocardial cushion defect (35.63)*

35.62 Repair of ventricular septal defect with tissue graft
Correction of ventricular
  septal defect } with tissue graft
Repair of supracristal defect

> Excludes: *that associated with repair of:*
>   *endocardial cushion defect (35.63)*
>   *ventricular defect associated with valvular and atrial septal defects*
>   *(35.63)*

35.63 Repair of endocardial cushion defect with tissue graft
Repair of:
  atrioventricular canal
  ostium primum defect } with tissue graft
  valvular defect associated with
    atrial and ventricular septal
    defects

> Excludes: *repair of isolated*
>   *atrial septal defect (35.61)*
>   *valvular defect (35.20-35.21. 35.23, 35.25. 35.27)*
>   *ventricular, septal defect (35.62)*

35.7 Other and unspecified repair of atrial and ventricular septa

Code also cardiopulmonary bypass [extracorporeal circulation] [heart-lung machine]
(39.61)

35.70 Other and unspecified repair of unspecified septal defect of heart
Repair of septal defect NOS

> Excludes: *that associated with repair of:*
>   *endocardial cushion defect (35.73)*
>   *septal defect associated with valvular defect (35.73)*

35.71 Other and unspecified repair of atrial septal defect
Repair NOS:
  atrial septum
  foramen ovale (patent)
  ostium secundum defect

> Excludes: *that associated with repair of:*
>   *atrial septal defect associated with valvular and ventricular septal*
>   *defects (35.73)*
>   *endocardial cushion defect (35.73)*

 Valid O.R.
procedure

 Non-O.R.
procedure

 Nonspecific
O.R. procedure

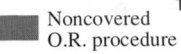 Noncovered
O.R. procedure

35.72 Other and unspecified repair of ventricular septal defect
Repair NOS:
supracristal defect
ventricular septum

Excludes: *that associated with repair of:*
endocardial cushion defect (35.73)
ventricular septal defect associated with valvular and atrial septal
defects (35.73)

35.73 Other and unspecified repair of endocardial cushion defect
Repair NOS:
atrioventricular canal
ostium primum defect
valvular defect associated with atrial and ventricular septal defects

Excludes: *repair of isolated:*
atrial septal defect (35.71)
valvular defect (35.20, 35.22, 35.24, 35.26, 35.28)
ventricular septal defect (35.72)

35.8   Total repair of certain congenital cardiac anomalies
Note: For partial repair of defect [e.g. repair of atrial septal defect in tetralogy of Fallot]—
code to specific procedure

35.81 Total repair of tetralogy of Fallot
One-stage total correction of tetralogy of Fallot with or without:
commissurotomy of pulmonary valve
infundibulectomy
outflow tract prosthesis
patch graft of outflow tract
prosthetic tube for pulmonary artery
repair of ventricular septal defect (with prosthesis)
take-down of previous systemic-pulmonary artery anastomosis

35.82 Total repair of total anomalous pulmonary venous connection
One-stage total correction of total anomalous pulmonary venous connection with or
without:
anastomosis between (horizontal) common pulmonary trunk and posterior wall of
left atrium (side-to-side)
enlargement of foramen ovale
incision [excision] of common wall between posterior left atrium and coronary sinus and roofing of resultant defect with patch graft (synthetic)
ligation of venous connection (descending anomalous vein) (to left innominate
vein) (to superior vena cava)
repair of atrial septal defect (with prosthesis)

35.83 Total repair of truncus arteriosus
One-stage total correction of truncus arteriosus with or without:
construction (with aortic homograft) (with prosthesis) of a pulmonary artery
placed from right ventricle to arteries supplying the lung
ligation of connections between aorta and pulmonary artery
repair of ventricular septal defect (with prosthesis)

35.84 Total correction of transposition of great vessels, not elsewhere classified
Arterial switch operation [Jatene]
Total correction of transposition of great arteries at the arterial level by switching
the great arteries, including the left or both coronary arteries, implanted in the
wall of the pulmonary artery

Excludes: *baffle operation [Mustard] [Senning] (35.91)*
creation of shunt between right ventricle and pulmonary artery
[Rastelli] (35.92)

35.9   Other operations on valves and septa of heart
Code also cardiopulmonary bypass, if performed [extracorporeal circulation] [heart-lung
machine) (39.61)

35.91 Interatrial transposition of venous return
Baffle:
atrial
interatrial
Mustard's operation
Resection of atrial septum and insertion of patch to direct systemic venous return to
tricuspid valve and pulmonary venous return to mitral valve

● Code new
  to this edition
▲ Revision of
  existing code
④ ⑤ Fourth or fifth
  digit required

35.92 Creation of conduit between right ventricle and pulmonary artery
Creation of shunt between right ventricle and (distal) pulmonary artery

> Excludes: *that associated with total repair of truncus arteriosus (35.83)*

35.93 Creation of conduit between left ventricle and aorta
Creation of apicoaortic shunt
Shunt between apex of left ventricle and aorta

35.94 Creation of conduit between atrium and pulmonary artery
Fontan procedure

35.95 Revision of corrective procedure on heart
Replacement of prosthetic heart valve poppet
Resuture or prosthesis of:
  septum
  valve

> Excludes: *complete revision—code to specific procedure*
> *replacement of prosthesis or graft of:*
>   *septum (35.50-35.63)*
>   *valve (35.20-35.28)*

35.96 Percutaneous valvuloplasty
Percutaneous balloon valvuloplasty

35.98 Other operations on septa of heart

35.99 Other operations on valves of heart

36 Operations on vessels of heart
Includes: sternotomy (median)
    (transverse)   } as operative approach
  thoracotomy

Code also cardiopulmonary bypass, if performed [extracorporeal circulation] [heart-lung machine] (39.61)

36.0 Removal of coronary artery obstruction and insertion of stent(s)

36.01 Single vessel percutaneous transluminal coronary angioplasty [PTCA] or coronary atherectomy without mention of thrombolytic agent

Code also any insertion of coronary stent(s) (36.06)
Balloon angioplasty of coronary artery
Coronary atherectomy
Percutaneous coronary angioplasty NOS
PTCA NOS

> Excludes: *multiple vessel percutaneous transluminal coronary angioplasty [PTCA] or coronary atherectomy performed during the same operation (36.05)*

36.02 Single vessel percutaneous transluminal coronary angioplasty [PTCA] or coronary atherectomy with mention of thrombolytic agent

Code also any insertion of coronary stent(s) 36.06
Balloon angioplasty of coronary artery with infusion of thrombolytic agent
  [streptokinase]
Coronary Atherectomy

> Excludes: *multiple vessel percutaneous transluminal coronary angioplasty [PTCA] or coronary atherectomy performed during the same operation (36.05)*
> *single vessel [PTCA] or coronary atherectomy without mention of thrombolytic agent (36.01)*

36.03 Open chest coronary artery angioplasty

Code also any insertion of coronary stent(s) 36.06
Coronary (artery):
  endarterectomy (with patch graft)
  thromboendarterectomy (with patch graft)
Open surgery for direct relief of coronary artery obstruction

> Excludes: *that with coronary artery bypass graft (36.10-36.19)*

36.04 Intracoronary artery thrombolytic infusion
That by direct coronary artery injection, infusion, or catheterization
  enzyme infusion
  platelet inhibitor

> Excludes: *that administered intravenously [IV infusion] (99.29)*
> *that associated with any procedure in 36.02, 36.03*

 Valid O.R.
procedure

 Non-O.R.
procedure

 Nonspecific
O.R. procedure

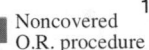 Noncovered
O.R. procedure

36.05 **Multiple vessel percutaneous transluminal coronary angioplasty [PTCA] or coronary atherectomy performed during the same operation, with or without mention of thrombolytic agent**

Balloon angioplasty of multiple coronary arteries

Coronary Atherectomy

Code also any intracoronary artery thrombolytic infusion (36.04)

Code also any insertion of coronary artery stent(s) (36.06)

Excludes:	single vessel PTCA or coronary atherectomy without mention of thrombolytic agent (36.01)
	with mention of thrombolytic agent (36.02)

36.06 **Insertion of coronary artery stent(s)**

Stent graft

Code also any open chest coronary artery angioplasty (36.03)

Code also any percutaneous transluminal coronary angioplasty [PTCA] or coronary atherectomy (36.01, 36.02, 36.05)

36.09 **Other removal of coronary artery obstruction**

Coronary angioplasty NOS

Excludes:	that by open angioplasty (36.03)
	that by percutaneous transluminal coronary angioplasty [PTCA] or coronary atherectomy (36.01-36.02, 36.05)

36.1 **Bypass anastomosis for heart revascularization**

Code also cardiopulmonary bypass [extracorporeal circulation] [heart-lung machine] (39.61)

36.10 **Aortocoronary bypass for heart revascularization, not otherwise specified**

Direct revascularization:
    cardiac
    coronary ⎫
    heart muscle ⎬ with catheter stent, prosthesis, or vein graft
    myocardial ⎭

Heart revascularization NOS

36.11 **Aortocoronary bypass of one coronary artery**

36.12 **Aortocoronary bypass of two coronary arteries**

36.13 **Aortocoronary bypass of three coronary arteries**

36.14 **Aortocoronary bypass of four or more coronary arteries**

36.15 **Single internal mammary-coronary artery bypass**

Anastomosis (single):
    mammary artery to coronary artery
    thoracic artery to coronary artery

36.16 **Double internal mammary-coronary artery bypass**

Anastomosis, double:
    mammary artery to coronary artery
    thoracic artery to coronary artery

● **36.17** **Abdominal - coronary artery bypass**

Anastomosis:
    gastroepiploic artery to coronary artery

36.19 **Other bypass anastomosis for heart revascularization**

36.2 **Heart revascularization by arterial implant**

Implantation of:
    aortic branches [ascending aortic branches] into heart muscle
    blood vessels into myocardium
    internal mammary artery [internal thoracic artery] into:
        heart muscle
        myocardium
        ventricle
        ventricular wall
Indirect heart revascularization NOS

36.3 **Other heart revascularization**

Abrasion of epicardium
Cardio-omentopexy
Intrapericardial poudrage
Myocardial graft:
    mediastinal fat
    omentum
    pectoral muscles

● Code new to this edition	▲ Revision of existing code	④ ⑤ Fourth or fifth digit required

36.9 **Other operations on vessels of heart**

Code also cardiopulmonary bypass [extracorporeal circulation] [heart-lung machine] (39.61)

36.91 **Repair of aneurysm of coronary vessel**

36.99 **Other operations on vessel of heart**
Exploration
Incision } of coronary artery
Ligation
Repair of arteriovenous fistula

37 Other operations on heart and pericardium

37.0 **Pericardiocentesis**

37.1 **Cardiotomy and pericardiotomy**

Code also cardiopulmonary bypass [extracorporeal circulation] [heart-lung machine] (39.61)

37.10 **Incision of heart, not otherwise specified**
Cardiolysis NOS

37.11 **Cardiotomy**
Incision of:
atrium
endocardium
myocardium
ventricle

37.12 **Pericardiotomy**
Pericardial window operation
Pericardiolysis
Pericardiotomy

37.2 **Diagnostic procedures on heart and pericardium**

37.21 **Right heart cardiac catheterization**
Cardiac catheterization NOS
| Excludes: | that with catheterization of left heart (37.23) |

37.22 **Left heart cardiac catheterization**
| Excludes: | that with catheterization of right heart (37.23) |

37.23 **Combined right and left heart cardiac catheterization**

37.24 **Biopsy of pericardium**

37.25 **Biopsy of heart**

37.26 **Cardiac electrophysiologic stimulation and recording studies**
Electrophysiologic studies (EPS)
Programmed electrical stimulation
Code also any concomitant procedure
| Excludes: | His bundle recording (37.29) |

37.27 **Cardiac mapping**
Code also any concomitant procedure
| Excludes: | electrocardiogram (89.52) |
| | His bundle recording (37.29) |

37.29 **Other diagnostic procedures on heart and pericardium**
Excludes:	angiocardiography (88.50-88.58)
	cardiac function tests (89.41-89.69)
	cardiovascular radioisotopic scan and function study (92.05)
	coronary arteriography (88.55-88.57)
	diagnostic pericardiocentesis (37.0)
	diagnostic ultrasound of heart (88.72)
	x-ray of heart (87.49)

37.3 **Pericardiectomy and excision of lesion of heart**
Code also cardiopulmonary bypass [extracorporeal circulation] [heart-lung machine] (39.61)

37.31 **Pericardiectomy**
Excision of:
adhesions of pericardium
constricting scar of: epicardium
pericardium

 Valid O.R. procedure   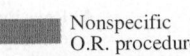 Non-O.R. procedure   Nonspecific O.R. procedure   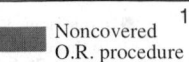 Noncovered O.R. procedure

37.32 Excision of aneurysm of heart

37.33 Excision or destruction of other lesion or tissue of heart

> *Excludes:* *catheter ablation of lesion or tissues of heart (37.34)*

37.34 Catheter ablation of lesion or tissue of heart
Cryoablation
Electrocurrent ⎱ of lesion or tissues of heart
Resection ⎰

37.4 Repair of heart and pericardium

37.5 Heart transplantation

> *Excludes:* *combined heart-lung transplantation (33.6)*

37.6 Implantation of heart assist system

37.61 Implant of pulsation balloon

37.62 Implant of other heart assist system
Insertion of:
centrifugal pump
heart assist system, not specified as pulsatile
heart assist system, NOS
heart pump

37.63 Replacement and repair of heart assist system

37.64 Removal of heart assist system

> *Excludes:* *that with replacement of implant (37.63)*

37.65 Implant of an external, pulsatile heart assist system
Note: Device not implantable (outside the body but connected to heart) with external circulation and pump

> *Excludes:* *implant of pulsation balloon (37.61)*

37.66 Implant of an implantable, pulsatile heart assist system
Note: Device directly connected to the heart and implanted in the upper left quadrant of peritoneal cavity
Transportable, implantable heart assist system

> *Excludes:* *Implant of pulsation balloon (37.61)*

37.7 Insertion, revision, replacement, and removal of pacemaker leads; insertion of temporary pacemaker system; or revision of pocket
Code also any insertion and replacement of pacemaker device (37.80-37.87)

37.70 Initial insertion of lead [electrode], not otherwise specified

> *Excludes:* *insertion of temporary transvenous pacemaker system (37.78)*
> *replacement of atrial and/or ventricular lead(s) (37.76)*

37.71 Initial insertion of transvenous lead [electrode] into ventricle

> *Excludes:* *insertion of temporary transvenous pacemaker system (37.78)*
> *replacement of atrial and/or ventricular lead(s) (37.76)*

37.72 Initial insertion of transvenous leads [electrodes] into atrium and ventricle

> *Excludes:* *insertion of temporary transvenous pacemaker system (37.78)*
> *replacement of atrial and/or ventricular lead(s) (37.76)*

37.73 Initial insertion of transvenous lead [electrode] into atrium

> *Excludes:* *insertion of temporary transvenous pacemaker system (37.78)*
> *replacement of atrial and/or ventricular lead(s) (37.76)*

37.74 Insertion or replacement of epicardial lead [electrode] into epicardium
Insertion or replacement of epicardial lead by:
sternotomy
thoracotomy

> *Excludes:* *replacement of atrial and/or ventricular lead(s) (37.76)*

37.75 Revision of lead [electrode]
Repair of electrode [removal with re-insertion]
Repositioning of lead [electrode]
Revision of lead NOS

> *Excludes:* *repositioning of temporary transvenous pacemaker system—omit code*

● Code new
to this edition   ▲ Revision of
existing code   ④ ⑤ Fourth or fifth
digit required

37.76 **Replacement of transvenous atrial and/or ventricular lead(s) [electrode]**
Removal or abandonment of existing transvenous or epicardial lead(s) with transvenous lead(s) replacement

> *Excludes:* *replacement of epicardial lead [electrode] (37.74)*

37.77 **Removal of lead(s) [electrode] without replacement**
Removal:
epicardial lead (transthoracic approach)
transvenous lead(s)

> *Excludes:* *removal of temporary transvenous pacemaker system—omit code*
> *that with replacement of:*
> *atrial and/or ventricular lead(s) [electrode] (37.76)*
> *epicardial lead [electrode] (37.74)*

37.78 **Insertion of temporary transvenous pacemaker system**

> *Excludes:* *intraoperative cardiac pacemaker (39.64)*

37.79 **Revision or relocation of pacemaker pocket**
Debridement and reforming pocket (skin and subcutaneous tissue)
Relocation of pocket [creation of new pocket]

37.8 **Insertion, replacement, removal and revision of pacemaker device**
Code also any lead insertion, lead replacement, lead removal and/or lead revision (37.70-37.77)

37.80 **Insertion of permanent pacemaker, initial or replacement, type of device not specified**

37.81 **Initial insertion of single-chamber device, not specified as rate responsive**

> *Excludes:* *replacement of existing pacemaker device (37.85-37.87)*

37.82 **Initial insertion of a single-chamber device, rate responsive**
Rate responsive to physiologic stimuli other than atrial rate

> *Excludes:* *replacement of existing pacemaker device (37.85-37.87)*

37.83 **Initial insertion of dual-chamber device**
Atrial ventricular sequential device

> *Excludes:* *replacement of existing pacemaker device (37.85-37.87)*

37.85 **Replacement of any type pacemaker device with single-chamber device, not specified as rate responsive**

37.86 **Replacement of any type pacemaker device with single-chamber device, rate responsive**
Rate responsive to physiologic stimuli other than atrial rate

37.87 **Replacement of any type pacemaker device with dual-chamber device**
Atrial ventricular sequential device

37.89 **Revision or removal of pacemaker device**
Repair of pacemaker device

> *Excludes:* *removal of temporary transvenous pacemaker system—omit code*
> *replacement of existing pacemaker device (37.85-37.87)*

37.9 **Other operations on heart and pericardium**

37.91 **Open chest cardiac massage**

> *Excludes:* *closed chest cardiac massage (99.63)*

37.92 **Injection of therapeutic substance into heart**

37.93 **Injection of therapeutic substance into pericardium**

37.94 **Implantation or replacement of automatic cardioverter/defibrillator, total system [AICD]**
Implantation of defibrillator with leads (epicardial patches), formation of pocket (abdominal fascia) (subcutaneous), any transvenous leads, intraoperative procedures for evaluation of lead signals, and obtaining defibrillator thresholds measurements
Techniques:
lateral thoracotomy
medial sternotomy
subxiphoid procedure
Code also extracorporeal circulation, if performed (39.61)
Code also any concomitant procedure [e.g., coronary bypass) (36.00-36.19)

37.95 **Implantation of automatic cardioverter/defibrillator lead(s) only**

1417

 Valid O.R.
procedure

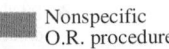 Non-O.R.
procedure

Nonspecific
O.R. procedure

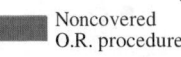 Noncovered
O.R. procedure

37.96 Implantation of automatic cardioverter/defibrillator pulse generator only

37.97 Replacement of automatic cardioverter/defibrillator lead(s) only

37.98 Replacement of automatic cardioverter/defibrillator pulse generator only

37.99 Other

Removal of cardioverter/defibrillator pulse generator only without replacement
Repositioning of lead(s) (sensing) (pacing)[electrode]
Repositioning of pulse generator
Revision of cardioverter/defibrillator (automatic) pocket

Excludes: *cardiac retraining (93.36)*
conversion of cardiac rhythm (99.60-99.69)

38 **Incision, excision, and occlusion of vessels**

Code also cardiopulmonary bypass [extracorporeal circulation] [heart-lung machine] (39.61)

Excludes: *that of coronary vessels (36.01-36.99)*

The following fourth-digit subclassification is for use with appropriate categories in sections 38.0, 38.1, 38.3, 38.5, 38.6, 38.8 and 38.9, which are marked with a symbol ④ to identify the site. Valid fourth digits are in [brackets] under each code.

0 unspecified site
1 intracranial vessels
Cerebral (anterior) (middle)
Circle of Willis
Posterior communicating artery
2 other vessels of head and neck
Carotid artery (common) (external) (internal)
Jugular vein (external) (internal)
3 upper limb vessels
Axillary   Radial
Brachial   Ulnar
4 aorta
5 other thoracic vessels
Innominate   Subclavian
Pulmonary (artery) (vein)   Vena cava, superior
6 abdominal arteries
Celiac   Mesenteric
Gastric   Renal
Hepatic   Splenic
Iliac   Umbilical

Excludes: *abdominal aorta (4)*
7 abdominal veins
Iliac   Splenic
Portal   Vena cava(inferior)
Renal
8 lower limb arteries
Femoral (common) (superficial)
Popliteal
Tibial
9 lower limb veins
Femoral   Saphenous
Popliteal   Tibial

④ **38.0** **Incision of vessels**
[0-9] Embolectomy
Thrombectomy

Excludes: *puncture or catheterization of any:*
artery (38.91, 38.98)
vein (38.92-38.95, 38.99)

④ **38.1** **Endarterectomy**
[0-6,8] Endarterectomy with:
embolectomy
patch graft
temporary bypass during procedure
thrombectomy

38.2 **Diagnostic procedures on blood vessels**

38.21 Biopsy of blood vessel

38.22 Percutaneous angioscopy

Excludes: *angioscopy of eye (95.12)*

● Code new
to this edition
▲ Revision of
existing code
④ ⑤ Fourth or fifth
digit required

38.29 **Other diagnostic procedures on blood vessels**

Excludes: *blood vessel thermography (88.86)*
circulatory monitoring (89.61-89.69)
contrast:
angiocardiography (88.50-88.58)
arteriography (88.40-88.49)
phlebography (88.60-88.67)
impedance phlebography (88.68)
peripheral vascular ultrasonography (88.77)
plethysmogram (89.58)

④ **38.3** **Resection of vessel with anastomosis**
[0-9]   Angiectomy
Excision of:
aneurysm (arteriovenous)   } with anastomosis
blood vessel (lesion)

④ **38.4** **Resection of vessel with replacement**
[0-9]   Angiectomy
Excision of
aneurysm (arteriovenous) or   } with replacement
blood vessel (lesion)

Requires the use of one of the following fourth-digit subclassifications to identify site:
0 unspecified site
1 intracranial vessels
Cerebral (anterior) (middle)
Circle of Willis
Posterior communicating artery
2 other vessels of head and neck
Carotid artery (common) (external) (internal)
Jugular vein (external) (internal)
3 upper limb vessels
Axillary   Radial
Brachial   Ulnar
4 aorta, abdominal
Code also any thoracic vessel involvement (thoracoabdominal procedure) (38.45)
5 thoracic vessel
Aorta (thoracic)   Subclavian
Innominate   Vena cava (superior)
Pulmonary (artery) (vein)
Code also any abdominal aorta involvement (thoracoabdominal procedure) (38.44)
6 abdominal arteries
Celiac   Mesenteric
Gastric   Renal
Hepatic   Splenic
Iliac   Umbilical

Excludes: *abdominal aorta (4)*
7 abdominal veins
Iliac   Splenic
Portal   Vena cava (inferior)
Renal
8 lower limb arteries
Femoral (common) (superficial)
Tibial
9 lower limb veins
Femoral   Saphenous
Popliteal   Tibial

④ **38.5** **Ligation and stripping of varicose veins**
[0-3,5,7,9]

Excludes: *ligation of varices:*
esophageal (42.91)
gastric (44.91)

④ **38.6** **Other excision of vessels**
[0-9]   Excision of blood vessel (lesion) NOS

Excludes: *excision of vessel for aortocoronary bypass (36.10-36.14)*
excision with:
anastomosis (38.30-38.39)
graft replacement (38.40-38.49)
implant (38.40-38.49)

Valid O.R.
procedure

Non-O.R.
procedure

Nonspecific
O.R. procedure

Noncovered
O.R. procedure

38.7 **Interruption of vena cava**
Insertion of implant or sieve in vena cava
Ligation of vena cava (inferior) (superior)
Plication of vena cava

④ **38.8** **Other surgical occlusion of vessels**
[0-9]
Clamping
Division
Ligation
Occlusion
} of blood vessel

Excludes: *adrenal vessels (07.43)*
esophageal varices (42.91)
gastric or duodenal vessel for ulcer (44.40-44.49)
gastric varices (44.91)
meningeal vessel (02.13)
spermatic vein for varicocele (63. 1)
surgical occlusion of vena cava (38.7)
that for chemoembolization (99.25)
that for control of (postoperative) hemorrhage:
anus (49.95)
bladder (57.93)
following vascular procedure (39.41)
nose (21.00-21.09)
prostate (60.94)
tonsil (28.7)
thyroid vessel (06.92)

38.9 **Puncture of vessel**

Excludes: *that for circulatory monitoring (89.61-89.69)*

38.91 **Arterial catheterization**

38.92 **Umbilical vein catheterization**

38.93 **Venous catheterization, not elsewhere classified**

Excludes: *that for cardiac catheterization (37.21-37.23)*
that for renal dialysis (38.95)

38.94 **Venous cutdown**

38.95 **Venous catheterization for renal dialysis**

Excludes: *insertion of totally implantable vascular access device [VAD] 86.07*

38.98 **Other puncture of artery**

Excludes: *that for:*
coronary arteriography (88.55-88.57)
arteriography (88.40-88.49)

38.99 **Other puncture of vein**
Phlebotomy

Excludes: *that for:*
angiography (88.60-88.69)
extracorporeal circulation (39.61, 50.92)
injection or infusion of:
sclerosing solution (39.92)
therapeutic or prophylactic substance (99.11-99.29)
perfusion (39.96-39.97)
phlebography (88.60-88.69)
transfusion (99.01-99.09)

39 **Other operations on vessels**

Excludes: *those on coronary vessels (36.0-36.99)*

39.0 **Systemic to pulmonary artery shunt**
Descending aorta-pulmonary artery
Left to right
Subclavian-pulmonary
} anastomosis (graft)

Code also cardiopulmonary bypass [extracorporeal circulation] [heart-lung machine]
(39.61)

● Code new
to this edition
▲ Revision of
existing code
④ ⑤ Fourth or fifth
digit required

39.1 **Intra-abdominal venous shunt**
Anastomosis:
mesocaval
portacaval
portal vein to inferior vena cava
splenic and renal veins
transjugular intrahepatic portosystemic shunt (TIPS)

Excludes: *peritoneovenous shunt (54.94)*

39.2 **Other shunt or vascular bypass**

39.21 **Caval-pulmonary artery anastomosis**
Code also cardiopulmonary bypass (39.61)

39.22 **Aorta-subclavian-carotid bypass**
Bypass (arterial):
aorta to carotid and brachial
aorta to subclavian and carotid
carotid to subclavian

39.23 **Other intrathoracic vascular shunt or bypass**
Intrathoracic (arterial) bypass graft NOS

Excludes: *coronary artery bypass (36.10-36.19)*

39.24 **Aorta-renal bypass**

39.25 **Aorta-iliac-femoral bypass**
Bypass:
aortofemoral
aortoiliac
aortoiliac to popliteal
aortopopliteal
iliofemoral [iliac-femoral]

39.26 **Other intra-abdominal vascular shunt or bypass**
Bypass:
aortoceliac
aortic-superior mesenteric
common hepatic-common iliac-renal
Intra-abdominal arterial bypass graft NOS

Excludes: *peritoneovenous shunt (54.94)*

39.27 **Arteriovenostomy for regal dialysis**
Anastomosis for renal dialysis
Formation of (peripheral) arteriovenous fistula for renal (kidney] dialysis
Code also any renal dialysis (39.95)

39.28 **Extracranial-intracranial (EC-IC) vascular bypass**

39.29 **Other (peripheral) vascular shunt or bypass**
Bypass (graft):
axillary-brachial
axillary-femoral [axillofemoral] (superficial)
brachial
femoral-femoral
femoroperoneal
femoropopliteal (arteries)
femorotibial (anterior) (posterior)
popliteal
vascular NOS

Excludes: *peritoneovenous shunt (54.94)*

39.3 **Suture of vessel**
Repair of laceration of blood vessel

Excludes: *suture of aneurysm (39.52)*
that for control of hemorrhage (postoperative):
anus (49.95)
bladder (57.93)
following vascular procedure (39.41)
nose (21.00-21.09)
prostate (60.94)
tonsil (28.7)

39.30 **Suture of unspecified blood vessel**

39.31 **Suture of artery**

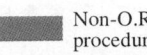 Valid O.R.
procedure

Non-O.R.
procedure

Nonspecific
O.R. procedure

 Noncovered
O.R. procedure

39.32 Suture of vein

39.4 **Revision of vascular procedure**

39.41 Control of hemorrhage following vascular surgery

> *Excludes:* *that for control of hemorrhage (postoperative):*
> *anus (49.95)*
> *bladder (57.93)*
> *nose (21.00-21.09)*
> *prostate (60.94)*
> *tonsil (28.7)*

39.42 Revision of arteriovenous shunt for renal dialysis
Conversion of renal dialysis:
end-to-end anastomosis to end-to-side
end-to-side anastomosis to end-to-end
vessel-to-vessel cannula to arteriovenous shunt
Removal of old arteriovenous shunt and creation of new shunt

> *Excludes:* *replacement of vessel-to-vessel cannula (39.94)*

39.43 Removal of arteriovenous shunt for renal dialysis

> *Excludes:* *that with replacement [revision] of shunt (39.42)*

39.49 Other revision of vascular procedure
Declotting (graft)
Revision of:
anastomosis of blood vessel
vascular procedure (previous)

39.5 **Other repair of vessels**

▲ **39.50** Angioplasty or atherectomy of non-coronary vessel
Percutaneous transluminal angioplasty (PTA) of non-coronary vessel:
Head and neck arteries:
basilar
carotid
vertebral
Lower extremity vessels
Mesenteric artery
Renal artery
Upper extremity vessels

> *Code also any injection or infusion of thrombolytic agent (99.29)*

> *Code also any insertion of non-coronary stent(s) or stent graft(s) (39.90)*

39.51 Clipping of aneurysm

> *Excludes:* *clipping of arteriovenous fistula (39.53)*

39.52 Other repair of aneurysm
Repair of aneurysm by:
coagulation
electrocoagulation
filipuncture
methyl methacrylate
suture
wiring
wrapping

> *Excludes:* *re-entry operation (aorta) (39.54)*
> *that with:*
> *graft replacement (38.40-38.49)*
> *resection (38.30-38.49, 38.60-38.69)*

39.53 Repair of arteriovenous fistula
Embolization of carotid cavernous fistula
Repair of arteriovenous fistula by:
clipping
coagulation
ligation and division

> *Excludes:* *repair of arteriovenous shunt for renal dialysis (39.42)*
> *that with:*
> *graft replacement (38.40-38.49)*
> *resection (38.30-38.49, 38.60-38.69)*

| ● Code new to this edition | ▲ Revision of existing code | ④ ⑤ Fourth or fifth digit required |

39.54 **Re-entry operation (aorta)**
Fenestration of dissecting aneurysm of thoracic aorta

Code also cardiopulmonary bypass [extracorporeal circulation] [heart-lung machine] (39.61)

39.55 **Reimplantation of aberrant renal vessel**

39.56 **Repair of blood vessel with tissue patch graft**

Excludes: *that with resection (38.40-38.49)*

39.57 **Repair of blood vessel with synthetic patch graft**

Excludes: *that with resection (38.40-38.49)*

39.58 **Repair of blood vessel with unspecified type of patch graft**

Excludes: *that with resection (38.40-38.49)*

39.59 **Other repair of vessel**
Aorticopulmonary window operation
Arterioplasty NOS
Construction of venous valves (peripheral)
Plication of vein (peripheral)
Reimplantation of artery

Code also cardiopulmonary bypass [extracorporeal circulation] [heart-lung machine) (39.61)

Excludes: *interruption of the vena cava (38.7)*
reimplantation of renal artery (39.55)
that with:
  graft (39.56-39.58)
  resection (38.30-38.49, 38.60-38.69)

39.6 **Extracorporeal circulation and procedures auxiliary to heart surgery**

39.61 **Extracorporeal circulation auxiliary to open heart surgery**
Artificial heart and lung
Cardiopulmonary bypass
Pump oxygenator

Excludes: *extracorporeal hepatic assistance (50.92)*
extracorporeal membrane oxygenation [ECMO] (39.65)
hemodialysis (39.95)
percutaneous cardiopulmonary bypass (39.66)

39.62 **Hypothermia (systemic) incidental to open heart surgery**

39.63 **Cardioplegia**
Arrest:
  anoxic
  circulatory

39.64 **Intraoperative cardiac pacemaker**
Temporary pacemaker used during and immediately following cardiac surgery

39.65 **Extracorporeal membrane oxygenation (ECMO)**

Excludes: *extracorporeal circulation auxiliary to open heart surgery (39.61)*
percutaneous cardiopulmonary bypass (39.66)

39.66 **Percutaneous cardiopulmonary bypass**
Closed chest

Excludes: *extracorporeal circulation auxiliary to open heart surgery (39.61)*
extracorporeal hepatic assistance (50.92)
extracorporeal membrane oxygenation [ECMO] (39.65)
hemodialysis (39.95)

39.8 **Operations on carotid body and other vascular bodies**
Chemodectomy   Glomectomy, carotid
Denervation of: Implantation into carotid body:
  aortic body   electronic stimulator
  carotid body   pacemaker

Excludes: *excision of glomus jugulare (20.51)*

39.9 **Other operations on vessels**

Valid O.R. procedure   Non-O.R. procedure   Nonspecific O.R. procedure   Noncovered O.R. procedure

● **39.90** **Insertion of non-coronary artery stent or stents**
Endovascular recanalization techniques
Stent graft(s)

Code also any non-coronary angioplasty or atherectomy (39.50)

39.91 **Freeing of vessel**
Dissection and freeing of adherent tissue:
artery-vein-nerve bundle
vascular bundle

39.92 **Injection of sclerosing agent into vein**

Excludes: *injection:*
esophageal varices (42.33)
hemorrhoids (49.42)

39.93 **Insertion of vessel-to-vessel cannula**
Formation of:
arteriovenous:
fistula
shunt
} by external cannula

Code also any renal dialysis (39.95)

39.94 **Replacement of vessel-to-vessel cannula**
Revision of vessel-to-vessel cannula

39.95 **Hemodialysis**
Artificial kidney   Hemofiltration
Hemodiafiltration   Renal dialysis

Excludes: *peritoneal dialysis (54.98)*

39.96 **Total body perfusion**

Code also substance perfused (99.21-99.29)

39.97 **Other perfusion**
Perfusion NOS
Perfusion, local [regional] of:
carotid artery
coronary artery
head
lower limb
neck
upper limb

Code also substance perfused (99.21-99.29)

Excludes: *perfusion of:*
kidney (55.95)
large intestine (46.96)
liver (50.93)
small intestine (46.95)

39.98 **Control of hemorrhage, not otherwise specified**
Angiotripsy
Control of postoperative hemorrhage NOS
Venotripsy

Excludes: *control of hemorrhage (postoperative):*
anus (49.95)
bladder (57.93)
following vascular procedure (39.41)
nose (21.00-21.09)
prostate (60.94)
tonsil (28.7)
that by:
ligation (38.80-38.89)
suture (39.30-39.32)

39.99 **Other operations on vessels**

Excludes: *injection or infusion of therapeutic or prophylactic substance*
(99.11-99.29)
transfusion of blood and blood components (99.01-99.09)

● Code new
to this edition

▲ Revision of
existing code

④ ⑤ Fourth or fifth
digit required

8. OPERATIONS ON THE HEMIC AND LYMPHATIC SYSTEM (40-41)

40 Operations on lymphatic system

40.0 Incision of lymphatic structures

40.1 Diagnostic procedures on lymphatic structures

40.11 Biopsy of lymphatic structure

40.19 Other diagnostic procedures on lymphatic structures

> *Excludes:* lymphangiogram
> abdominal (88.04)
> cervical (87.08)
> intrathoracic (87.34)
> lower limb (88.36)
> upper limb (88.34)
> microscopic examination of specimen (90.71-90.79)
> radioisotope scan (92.16)
> thermography (88.89)

40.2 Simple excision of lymphatic structure

> *Excludes:* biopsy of lymphatic structure (40.11)

40.21 Excision of deep cervical lymph node

40.22 Excision of internal mammary lymph node

40.23 Excision of axillary lymph node

40.24 Excision of inguinal lymph mode

40.29 Simple excision of other lymphatic structure
Excision of:
cystic hygroma
lymphangioma
Simple lymphadenectomy

40.3 Regional lymph node excision
Extended regional lymph node excision
Regional lymph node excision with excision of lymphatic drainage area including skin, subcutaneous tissue, and fat

40.4 Radical excision of cervical lymph nodes
Resection of cervical lymph nodes down to muscle and deep fascia

> *Excludes:* that associated with radical laryngectomy (30.4)

40.40 Radical neck dissection, not otherwise specified

40.41 Radical neck dissection, unilateral

40.42 Radical neck dissection, bilateral

40.5 Radical excision of other lymph nodes

> *Excludes:* that associated with radical mastectomy (85.45-85.48)

40.50 Radical excision of lymph nodes, not otherwise specified
Radical (lymph) node dissection NOS

40.51 Radical excision of axillary lymph nodes

40.52 Radical excision of periaortic lymph nodes

40.53 Radical excision of iliac lymph nodes

40.54 Radical groin dissection

40.59 Radical excision of other lymph nodes

> *Excludes:* radical neck dissection (40.40-40.42)

40.6 Operations on thoracic duct

40.61 Cannulation of thoracic duct

40.62 Fistulization of thoracic duct

40.63 Closure of fistula of thoracic duct

40.64 Ligation of thoracic duct

40.69 Other operations on thoracic duct

 Valid O.R. procedure

 Non-O.R. procedure

 Nonspecific O.R. procedure

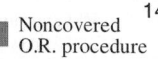 Noncovered O.R. procedure

40.9 **Other operations on lymphatic structures**
Anastomosis
Dilation
Ligation
Obliteration   of peripheral lymphatics
Reconstruction
Repair
Transplantation
Correction of lymphedema of limb, NOS

> *Excludes:*   *reduction of elephantiasis of scrotum (61.3)*

41 **Operations on bone marrow and spleen**

     41.0 **Bone marrow or hematopoietic stem cell transplant**

> *Excludes:*   *aspiration of bone marrow from donor (41.91)*

       41.00 **Bone marrow transplant, not otherwise specified**

       41.01 **Autologous bone marrow transplant**
With extracorporeal purging of malignant cells from marrow
Autograft of bone marrow NOS

       41.02 **Allogeneic bone marrow transplant with purging**
Allograft of bone marrow with in vitro removal (purging) of T-cells

       41.03 **Allogeneic bone marrow transplant without purging**
Allograft of bone marrow NOS

       41.04 **Autologous hematopoietic stem cell transplant**

     41.1 **Puncture of spleen**

> *Excludes:*   *aspiration biopsy of spleen (41.32)*

     41.2 **Splenotomy**

     41.3 **Diagnostic procedures on bone marrow and spleen**

       41.31 **Biopsy of bone marrow**

       41.32 **Closed [aspiration] [percutaneous] biopsy of spleen**
Needle biopsy of spleen

       41.33 **Open biopsy of spleen**

       41.38 **Other diagnostic procedures on bone marrow**

> *Excludes:*   *microscopic examination of specimen from bone marrow (90.61-90.69)*
> *radioisotope scan (92.05)*

       41.39 **Other diagnostic procedures on spleen**

> *Excludes:*   *microscopic examination of specimen from spleen (90.61-90.69)*
> *radioisotope scan (92.05)*

     41.4 **Excision or destruction of lesion or tissue of spleen**

> *Excludes:*   *excision of accessory spleen (41.93)*

       41.41 **Marsupialization of splenic cyst**

       41.42 **Excision of lesion or tissue of spleen**

> *Excludes:*   *biopsy of spleen (41.32-41.33)*

       41.43 **Partial splenectomy**

     41.5 **Total splenectomy**
Splenectomy NOS

     41.9 **Other operations on spleen and bone marrow**

       41.91 **Aspiration of bone marrow from donor for transplant**

> *Excludes:*   *biopsy of bone marrow (41.31)*

       41.92 **Injection into bone marrow**

> *Excludes:*   *bone marrow transplant (41.00-41.03)*

       41.93 **Excision of accessory spleen**

       41.94 **Transplantation of spleen**

       41.95 **Repair and plastic operations on spleen**

       41.98 **Other operations on bone marrow**

       41.99 **Other operations on spleen**

● Code new   ▲ Revision of   ④ ⑤ Fourth or fifth
   to this edition   existing code   digit required

9. OPERATIONS ON THE DIGESTIVE SYSTEM (42-54)

42 Operations on esophagus

42.0 Esophagotomy

42.01 Incision of esophageal web

42.09 Other incision of esophagus
Esophagotomy NOS
Excludes: *esophagomyotomy (42.7)*
esophagostomy (42.10-42.19)

42.1 Esophagostomy

42.10 Esophagostomy, not otherwise specified

42.11 Cervical esophagostomy

42.12 Exteriorization of esophageal pouch

42.19 Other external fistulization of esophagus
Thoracic esophagostomy
Code also any resection (42.40-42.42)

42.2 Diagnostic procedures on esophagus

42.21 Operative esophagoscopy by incision

42.22 Esophagoscopy through artificial stoma
Excludes: *that with biopsy (42.24)*

42.23 Other esophagoscopy
Excludes: *that with biopsy (42.24)*

42.24 Closed [endoscopic] biopsy of esophagus
Brushing or washing for specimen collection
Esophagoscopy with biopsy
Suction biopsy of the esophagus
Excludes: *esophagogastroduodenoscopy [EGD] with closed biopsy (45.16)*

42.25 Open biopsy of esophagus

42.29 Other diagnostic procedures on esophagus
Excludes: *barium swallow (87.61)*
esophageal manometry (89.32)
microscopic examination of specimen from esophagus (90.81-90.89)

42.3 Local excision or destruction of lesion or tissue of esophagus

42.31 Local excision of esophageal diverticulum

42.32 Local excision of other lesion or tissue of esophagus
Excludes: *biopsy of esophagus (42.24-42.25)*
esophageal fistulectomy (42.84)

42.33 Endoscopic excision or destruction of lesion or tissue of esophagus
Ablation of esophageal
neoplasm
Control of esophageal
bleeding
Esophageal polypectomy } by endoscopic approach
Esophageal varices
Injection of esophageal
varices
Excludes: *biopsy of esophagus (42.24-42.25)*
fistulectomy (42.84)
open ligation of esophageal varices (42.91)

42.39 Other destruction of lesion or tissue of esophagus
Excludes: *that by endoscopic approach (42.33)*

42.4 Excision of esophagus
Excludes: *esophagogastrectomy NOS (43.99)*

42.40 Esophagectomy, not otherwise specified

42.41 Partial esophagectomy
Code also any synchronous:
anastomosis other than end-to-end (42.51-42.69)

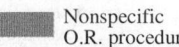

| Valid O.R. procedure | Non-O.R. procedure | Nonspecific O.R. procedure | Noncovered O.R. procedure |

esophagostomy (42.10-42.19)
gastrostomy (43.11-43.19)

42.42 Total esophagectomy

Code also any synchronous:
gastrostomy (43.11-43.19)
interposition or anastomosis other than end-to-end (42.51-42.69)

Excludes: *esophagogastrectomy (43.99)*

42.5 Intrathoracic anastomosis of esophagus

Code also any synchronous:
esophagectomy (42.40-42.42)
gastrostomy (43.1)

42.51 Intrathoracic esophagoesophagostomy

42.52 Intrathoracic esophagogastrostomy

42.53 Intrathoracic esophageal anastomosis with interposition of small bowel

42.54 Other intrathoracic esophagoenterostomy
Anastomosis of esophagus to intestinal segment NOS

42.55 Intrathoracic esophageal anastomosis with interposition of colon

42.56 Other intrathoracic esophagocolostomy
Esophagocolostomy NOS

42.58 Intrathoracic esophageal anastomosis with other interposition
Construction of artificial esophagus
Retrosternal formation of reversed gastric tube

42.59 Other intrathoracic anastomosis of esophagus

42.6 Antesternal anastomosis of esophagus

Code also any synchronous:
esophagectomy (42.40-42.42)
gastrostomy (43.1)

42.61 Antesternal esophagoesophagostomy

42.62 Antesternal esophagogastrostomy

42.63 Antesternal esophageal anastomosis with interposition of small bowel

42.64 Other antesternal esophagoenterostomy
Antethoracic:
esophagoenterostomy
esophagoileostomy
esophagojejunostomy

42.65 Antesternal esophageal anastomosis with interposition of colon

42.66 Other antesternal esophagocolostomy
Antethoracic esophagocolostomy

42.68 Other antesternal esophageal anastomosis with interposition

42.69 Other antesternal anastomosis of esophagus

42.7 Esophagomyotomy

42.8 Other repair of esophagus

42.81 Insertion of permanent tube into esophagus

42.82 Suture of laceration of esophagus

42.83 Closure of esophagostomy

42.84 Repair of esophageal fistula, not elsewhere classified

Excludes: *repair of fistula:*
bronchoesophageal (33.42)
esophagopleurocutaneous (34.73)
pharyngoesophageal (29.53)
tracheoesophageal (31.73)

42.85 Repair of esophageal stricture

42.86 Production of subcutaneous tunnel without esophageal anastomosis

● Code new
to this edition

▲ Revision of
existing code

④ ⑤ Fourth or fifth
digit required

42.87 Other graft of esophagus

> *Excludes:* *antesternal esophageal anastomosis with interposition of:*
>> *colon (42.65)*
>> *small bowel (42.63)*
>
>> *antesternal esophageal anastomosis with other interposition (42.68)*
>> *intrathoracic esophageal anastomosis with interposition of:*
>>> *colon (42.55)*
>>> *small bowel (42.53)*
>>
>>> *intrathoracic esophageal anastomosis with other interposition (42.58)*

42.89 Other repair of esophagus

42.9 Other operations on esophagus

42.91 Ligation of esophageal varices

> *Excludes:* *that by endoscopic approach (42.33)*

42.92 Dilation of esophagus
Dilation of cardiac sphincter

> *Excludes:* *intubation of esophagus (96.03, 96.06-96.08)*

42.99 Other

> *Excludes:* *insertion of Sengstaken tube (96.06)*
> *intubation of esophagus (96.03, 96.06-96.08)*
> *removal of intraluminal foreign body from esophagus without incision (98.02)*
> *tamponade of esophagus (96.06)*

43 Incision and excision of stomach

43.0 Gastrotomy

> *Excludes:* *gastrostomy (43.11-43.19)*
> *that for control of hemorrhage (44.49)*

43.1 Gastrostomy

43.11 Percutaneous [endoscopic] gastrostomy [PEG]
Percutaneous transabdominal gastrostomy

43.19 Other gastrostomy

> *Excludes:* *percutaneous [endoscopic] gastrostomy [PEG] (43.11)*

43.3 Pyloromyotomy

43.4 Local excision or destruction of lesion or tissue of stomach

43.41 Endoscopic excision or destruction of lesion or tissue of stomach
Gastric polypectomy by endoscopic approach
Gastric varices by endoscopic approach

> *Excludes:* *biopsy of stomach (44.14-44.15)*
> *control of hemorrhage (44.43)*
> *open ligation of gastric varices (44.91)*

43.42 Local excision of other lesion or tissue of stomach

> *Excludes:* *biopsy of stomach (44.14-44.15)*
> *gastric fistulectomy (44.62-44.63)*
> *partial gastrectomy (43.5-43.89)*

43.49 Other destruction of lesion or tissue of stomach

> *Excludes:* *that by endoscopic approach (43.41)*

43.5 Partial gastrectomy with anastomosis to esophagus
Proximal gastrectomy

43.6 Partial gastrectomy with anastomosis to duodenum
Billroth I operation
Distal gastrectomy
Gastropylorectomy

43.7 Partial gastrectomy with anastomosis to jejunum
Billroth II operation

43.8 Other partial gastrectomy

43.81 Partial gastrectomy with jejunal transposition
Henley jejunal transposition operation
Code also any synchronous intestinal resection (45.51)

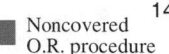

| | Valid O.R. procedure | | Non-O.R. procedure | | Nonspecific O.R. procedure | | Noncovered O.R. procedure |

43.89 **Other**
Partial gastrectomy with bypass gastrogastrostomy
Sleeve resection of stomach

43.9 **Total gastrectomy**

43.91 **Total gastrectomy with intestinal interposition**

43.99 **Other total gastrectomy**
Complete gastroduodenectomy
Esophagoduodenostomy with complete gastrectomy
Esophagogastrectomy NOS
Esophagojejunostomy with complete gastrectomy
Radical gastrectomy

44 **Other operations on stomach**

44.0 **Vagotomy**

44.00 **Vagotomy, not otherwise specified**
Division of vagus nerve NOS

44.01 **Truncal vagotomy**

44.02 **Highly selective vagotomy**
Parietal cell vagotomy
Selective proximal vagotomy

44.03 **Other selective vagotomy**

44.1 **Diagnostic procedures on stomach**

44.11 **Transabdominal gastroscopy**
Intraoperative gastroscopy
Excludes: *that with biopsy (44.14)*

44.12 **Gastroscopy through artificial stoma**
Excludes: *that with biopsy (44.14)*

44.13 **Other gastroscopy**
Excludes: *that with biopsy (44.14)*

44.14 **Closed [endoscopic] biopsy of stomach**
Brushing or washing for specimen collection
Excludes: *esophagogastroduodenoscopy [EGD] with closed biopsy (45.16)*

44.15 **Open biopsy of stomach**

44.19 **Other diagnostic procedures on stomach**
Excludes: *gastric lavage (96.33)*
microscopic examination of specimen from stomach (90.81-90.89)
upper GI series (87.62)

44.2 **Pyloroplasty**

44.21 **Dilation of pylorus by incision**

44.22 **Endoscopic dilation of pylorus**
Dilation with balloon endoscope
Endoscopic dilation of gastrojejunostomy site

44.29 **Other pyloroplasty**
Pyloroplasty NOS
Revision of pylorus

44.3 **Gastroenterostomy without gastrectomy**

44.31 **High gastric bypass**
Printen and Mason gastric bypass

44.39 **Other gastroenterostomy**
Bypass:
gastroduodenostomy
gastroenterostomy
gastrogastrostomy
Gastrojejunostomy without gastrectomy NOS

44.4 **Control of hemorrhage and suture of ulcer of stomach or duodenum**

44.40 **Suture of peptic ulcer, not otherwise specified**

44.41 **Suture of gastric ulcer site**
Excludes: *ligation of gastric varices (44.91)*

44.42 **Suture of duodenal ulcer site**

● Code new
to this edition
▲ Revision of
existing code
④ ⑤ Fourth or fifth
digit required

44.43   **Endoscopic control of gastric or duodenal bleeding**

44.44   **Transcatheter embolization for gastric or duodenal bleeding**

> Excludes: *surgical occlusion of abdominal vessels (38.86-38.87)*

44.49   **Other control of hemorrhage of stomach or duodenum**
That with gastrotomy

44.5   Revision of gastric anastomosis
Closure of:
gastric anastomosis
gastroduodenostomy
gastrojejunostomy
Pantaloon operation

44.6   **Other repair of stomach**

44.61   **Suture of laceration of stomach**

> Excludes: *that of ulcer site(44.41)*

44.62   **Closure of gastrostomy**

44.63   **Closure of other gastric fistula**
Closure of:
gastrocolic fistula
gastrojejunocolic fistula

44.64   **Gastropexy**

44.65   **Esophagogastroplasty**
Belsey operation
Esophagus and stomach cardioplasty

44.66   **Other procedures for creation of esophagogastric sphincteric competence**
Fundoplication
Gastric cardioplasty
Nissen's fundoplication
Restoration of cardio-esophageal angle

44.69   **Other**
Inversion of gastric diverticulum
Repair of stomach NOS

44.9   **Other operations on stomach**

44.91   **Ligation of gastric varices**

> Excludes: *that by endoscopic approach (43.41)*

44.92   **Intraoperative manipulation of stomach**
Reduction of gastric volvulus

44.93   **Insertion of gastric bubble [balloon]**

44.94   **Removal of gastric bubble [balloon]**

44.99   **Other**

> Excludes: *change of gastrostomy tube (97.02)*
> *dilation of cardiac sphincter (42.92)*
> *gastric:*
> *cooling (96.31)*
> *freezing (96.32)*
> *gavage (96.35)*
> *hypothermia (96.31)*
> *lavage (96.33)*
> *insertion of nasogastric tube (96.07)*
> *irrigation of gastrostomy (96.36)*
> *irrigation of nasogastric tube (96.34)*
> *removal of:*
> *gastrostomy tube (97.51)*
> *intraluminal foreign body from stomach without incision (98.03)*
> *replacement of:*
> *gastrostomy tube (97.02)*
> *(naso-)gastric tube (97.01)*

45   **Incision, excision, and anastomosis of intestine**

45.0   **Enterotomy**

> Excludes: *duodenocholedochotomy (51.41-51.42, 51.51)*
> *that for destruction of lesion (45.30-45.34)*
> *that of exteriorized intestine (46.14, 46.24, 46.31)*

 Valid O.R.
procedure

 Non-O.R.
procedure

 Nonspecific
O.R. procedure

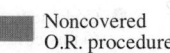 Noncovered
O.R. procedure

45.00 Incision of intestine, not otherwise specified

45.01 Incision of duodenum

45.02 Other incision of small intestine

45.03 incision of large intestine

> Excludes: proctotomy (48.0)

45.1 Diagnostic procedures on small intestine

Code also any laparotomy (54.11-54.19)

45.11 Transabdominal endoscopy of small intestine

Intraoperative endoscopy of small intestine

> Excludes: that with biopsy (45.14)

45.12 Endoscopy of small intestine through artificial stoma

> Excludes: that with biopsy (45.14)

45.13 Other endoscopy of small intestine

Esophagogastroduodenoscopy [EGD]

> Excludes: that with biopsy (45.14, 45.16)

45.14 Closed [endoscopic] biopsy of small intestine

Brushing or washing for specimen collection

> Excludes: esophagogastroduodenoscopy [EGD] with closed biopsy (45.16)

45.15 Open biopsy of small intestine

45.16 Esophagogastroduodenoscopy [EGD] with closed biopsy

Biopsy of one or more sites involving esophagus, stomach, and/or duodenum

45.19 Other diagnostic procedures on small intestine

> Excludes: microscopic examination of specimen from small intestine (90.91-90.99)
> radioisotope scan (92.04)
> ultrasonography (88.74)
> x-ray (87.61-87.69)

45.2 Diagnostic procedures on large intestine

Code also any laparotomy (54.11-54.19)

45.21 Transabdominal endoscopy of large intestine

Intraoperative endoscopy of large intestine

> Excludes: that with biopsy (45.25)

45.22 Endoscopy of large intestine through artificial stoma

> Excludes: that with biopsy (45.25)

45.23 Colonoscopy

Flexible fiberoptic colonoscopy

> Excludes: endoscopy of large intestine through artificial stoma (45.22)
> flexible sigmoidoscopy (45.24)
> rigid proctosigmoidoscopy (48.23)
> transabdominal endoscopy of large intestine (45.21)

45.24 Flexible sigmoidoscopy

Endoscopy of descending colon

> Excludes: rigid proctosigmoidoscopy (48.23)

45.25 Closed [endoscopic] biopsy of large intestine

Biopsy, closed, of unspecified intestinal site

Brushing or washing for specimen collection

Colonoscopy with biopsy

> Excludes: proctosigmoidoscopy with biopsy (48.24)

45.26 Open biopsy of large intestine

45.27 Intestinal biopsy, site unspecified

45.28 Other diagnostic procedures on large intestine

45.29 Other diagnostic procedures on intestine, site unspecified

> Excludes: microscopic examination of specimen (90.91-90.99)
> scan and radioisotope function study (92.04)
> ultrasonography (88.74)
> x-ray (87.61-87.69)

● Code new
to this edition

▲ Revision of
existing code

④ ⑤ Fourth or fifth
digit required

45.3   Local excision or destruction of lesion or tissue of small intestine

45.30   Endoscopic excision or destruction of lesion of duodenum

> Excludes: *biopsy of duodenum (45.14-45.15)*
> *control of hemorrhage (44.43)*
> *fistulectomy (46.72)*

45.31   Other local excision of lesion of duodenum

> Excludes: *biopsy of duodenum (45.14-45.15)*
> *fistulectomy (46.72)*
> *multiple segmental resection (45.61)*
> *that by endoscopic approach (45.30)*

45.32   Other destruction of lesion of duodenum

> Excludes: *that by endoscopic approach (45.30)*

45.33   Local excision of lesion or tissue of small intestine, except duodenum
Excision of redundant mucosa of ileostomy

> Excludes: *biopsy of small intestine (45.14-45.15)*
> *fistulectomy (46.74)*
> *multiple segmental resection (45.61)*

45.34   Other destruction of lesion of small intestine, except duodenum

45.4   Local excision or destruction of lesion or tissue of large intestine

45.41   Excision of lesion or tissue of large intestine
Excision of redundant mucosa of colostomy

> Excludes: *biopsy of large intestine (45.25-45.27)*
> *endoscopic polypectomy of large intestine (45.42)*
> *fistulectomy (46.76)*
> *multiple segmental resection (45.71)*
> *that by endoscopic approach (45.42-45.43)*

45.42   Endoscopic polypectomy of large intestine

> Excludes: *that by open approach (45.41)*

45.43   Endoscopic destruction of other lesion or tissue of large intestine
Endoscopic ablation of tumor of large intestine
Endoscopic control of colonic bleeding

> Excludes: *endoscopic polypectomy of large intestine (45.42)*

45.49   Other destruction of lesion of large intestine

> Excludes: *that by endoscopic approach (45.43)*

45.5   Isolation of intestinal segment

> *Code also any synchronous:*
> anastomosis other than end-to-end (45.90-45.94)
> enterostomy (46.10-46.39)

45.50   Isolation of intestinal segment not otherwise specified
Isolation of intestinal pedicle flap
Reversal of intestinal segment

45.51   Isolation of segment of small intestine
Isolation of ileal loop
Resection of small intestine for interposition

45.52   Isolation of segment of large intestine
Resection of colon for interposition

45.6   Other excision of small intestine

> *Code also any synchronous:*
> anastomosis other than end-to-end (45.90-45.93, 45.95)
> colostomy (46.10-46.13)
> enterostomy (46.10-46.39)

> Excludes: *cecectomy (45.72)*
> *enterocolectomy (45.79)*
> *gastroduodenectomy (43.6-43.99)*
> *ileocolectomy (45.73)*
> *pancreatoduodenectomy (52.51-52.7)*

45.61   Multiple segmental resection of small intestine
Segmental resection for multiple traumatic lesions of small intestine

---

1433

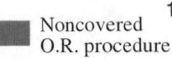

45.62 **Other partial resection of small intestine**
Duodenectomy   Jejunectomy
Ileectomy

> | Excludes: | duodenectomy with synchronous pancreatectomy (52.51-52.7) |
> | | resection of cecum and terminal ileum (45.72) |

45.63 **Total removal of small intestine**

45.7 **Partial excision of large intestine**

Code also any synchronous:
anastomosis other than end-to-end (45.92-45.94)
enterostomy (46.10-46.39)

45.71 **Multiple segmental resection of large intestine**
Segmental resection for multiple traumatic lesions of large intestine

45.72 **Cecectomy**
Resection of cecum and terminal ileum

45.73 **Right hemicolectomy**
Ileocolectomy
Right radical colectomy

45.74 **Resection of transverse colon**

45.75 **Left hemicolectomy**

> | Excludes: | proctosigmoidectomy (48.41-48.69) |
> | | second stage Mikulicz operation (46.04) |

45.76 **Sigmoidectomy**

45.79 **Other partial excision of large intestine**
Enterocolectomy NEC

45.8 **Total intra-abdominal colectomy**
Excision of cecum, colon, and sigmoid

> | Excludes: | coloproctectomy (48.41-48.69) |

45.9 **Intestinal anastomosis**

Code also any synchronous resection (45.31-45.8, 48.41-48.69)

> | Excludes: | end-to-end anastomosis – omit code |

45.90 **Intestinal anastomosis, not otherwise specified**

45.91 **Small-to-small intestinal anastomosis**

45.92 **Anastomosis of small intestine to rectal stump**
Hampton procedure

45.93 **Other small-to-large intestinal anastomosis**

45.94 **Large-to-large intestinal anastomosis**

> | Excludes: | rectorectostomy (48.74) |

45.95 **Anastomosis to anus**
Formation of endorectal ileal pouch (J-pouch) (H-pouch) (S-pouch) with
anastomosis of small intestine to anus

46 **Other operations on intestine**

46.0 **Exteriorization of intestine**
Includes: loop enterostomy
multiple stage resection of intestine

46.01 **Exteriorization of small intestine**
Loop ileostomy

46.02 **Resection of exteriorized segment of small intestine**

46.03 **Exteriorization of large intestine**
Exteriorization of intestine NOS
First stage Mikulicz exteriorization of intestine
Loop colostomy

46.04 **Resection of exteriorized segment of large intestine**
Resection of exteriorized segment of intestine NOS
Second stage Mikulicz operation

46.1 **Colostomy**

Code also any synchronous resection (45.49, 45.71-45.79, 45.8)

> | Excludes: | loop colostomy (46.03) |
> | | that with synchronous anterior rectal resection (48.62) |

● Code new
to this edition   ▲ Revision of
existing code   ④ ⑤ Fourth or fifth
digit required

46.10 Colostomy, not otherwise specified

46.11 Temporary colostomy

46.13 Other permanent colostomy

46.14 Delayed opening of colostomy

46.2 **Ileostomy**

Code also any synchronous resection (45.34, 45.61-45.63)

> Excludes: *loop ileostomy (46.01)*

46.20 Ileostomy, not otherwise specified

46.21 Temporary ileostomy

46.22 Continent ileostomy

46.23 Other permanent ileostomy

46.24 Delayed opening of ileostomy

46.3 **Other enterostomy**

Code also any synchronous resection (45.61-45.8)

46.31 Delayed opening of other enterostomy

46.32 Percutaneous [endoscopic] jejunostomy [PEJ]
Endoscopic conversion of gastrostomy to jejunostomy

46.39 **Other**
Duodenostomy
Feeding enterostomy

46.4 **Revision of intestinal stoma**

46.40 Revision of intestinal stoma, not otherwise specified
Plastic enlargement of intestinal stoma
Reconstruction of stoma of intestine
Release of scar tissue of intestinal stoma

> Excludes: *excision of redundant mucosa (45.41)*

46.41 Revision of stoma of small intestine

> Excludes: *excision of redundant mucosa (45.33)*

46.42 Repair of pericolostomy hernia

46.43 Other revision of stoma of large intestine

> Excludes: *excision of redundant mucosa (45.41)*

46.5 **Closure of intestinal stoma**

Code also any synchronous resection (45.34, 45.49, 45.61-45.8)

46.50 Closure of intestinal stoma, not otherwise specified

46.51 Closure of stoma of small intestine

46.52 Closure of stoma of large intestine
Closure or take-down of:
cecostomy
colostomy
sigmoidostomy

46.6 **Fixation of intestine**

46.60 Fixation of intestine, not otherwise specified
Fixation of intestine to abdominal wall

46.61 Fixation of small intestine to abdominal wall
Ileopexy

46.62 Other fixation of small intestine
Noble plication of small intestine
Plication of jejunum

46.63 Fixation of large intestine to abdominal wall
Cecocoloplicopexy
Sigmoidopexy (Moschowitz)

46.64 Other fixation of large intestine
Cecofixation
Colofixation

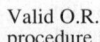 Valid O.R.
procedure

Non-O.R.
procedure

Nonspecific
O.R. procedure

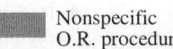 Noncovered
O.R. procedure

46.7 Other repair of intestine

> Excludes: closure of:
> ulcer of duodenum (44.42)
> vesicoenteric fistula (57.83)

46.71 Suture of laceration of duodenum

46.72 Closure of fistula of duodenum

46.73 Suture of laceration of small intestine, except duodenum

46.74 Closure of fistula of small intestine, except duodenum

> Excludes: closure of:
> artificial stoma (46.51)
> vaginal fistula (70.74)
> repair of gastrojejunocolic fistula (44.63)

46.75 Suture of laceration of large intestine

46.76 Closure of fistula of large intestine

> Excludes: closure of:
> gastrocolic fistula (44.63)
> rectal fistula (48.73)
> sigmoidovesical fistula (57.83)
> stoma (46.52)
> vaginal fistula (70.72-70.73)
> vesicocolic fistula (57.83)
> vesicosigmoidovaginal fistula (57.83)

46.79 Other repair of intestine

46.8 Dilation and manipulation of intestine

46.80 Intra-abdominal manipulation of intestine, not otherwise specified
Correction of intestinal malrotation
Reduction of:
intestinal torsion
intestinal volvulus
intussusception

46.81 Intra-abdominal manipulation of small intestine

46.82 Intra-abdominal manipulation of large intestine

46.85 Dilation of intestine
Dilation (balloon) of duodenum
Dilation (balloon) of jejunum
Endoscopic dilation (balloon) of large intestine
That through rectum or colostomy

46.9 Other operations on intestines

46.91 Myotomy of sigmoid colon

46.92 Myotomy of other parts of colon

46.93 Revision of anastomosis of small intestine

46.94 Revision of anastomosis of large intestine

46.95 Local perfusion of small intestine
Code also substance perfused (99.21-99.29)

46.96 Local perfusion of large intestine
Code also substance perfused (99.21-99.29)

46.99 Other
Ileoentectropy

> Excludes: diagnostic procedures on intestine (45.11-45.29)
> dilation of enterostomy stoma (96.24)
> intestinal intubation (96.08)
> removal of:
> intraluminal foreign body from intestine without incision (98.04)
> intraluminal foreign body from small intestine without incision (98.03)
> tube from large intestine (97.53)
> tube from small intestine (97.52)
> replacement of:
> large intestine tube or enterostomy device (97.04)
> small intestine tube or enterostomy device (97.03)

● Code new
to this edition

▲ Revision of
existing code

④ ⑤ Fourth or fifth
digit required

47   Operations on appendix
Includes: appendiceal stump

47.0   Appendectomy

Excludes: incidental appendectomy, so described (47.11, 47.19)

● **47.01   Laparoscopic appendectomy**
● **47.09   Other appendectomy**

47.1   Incidental appendectomy

● **47.11   Laparoscopic incidental appendectomy**
● **47.19   Other incidental appendectomy**

47.2   Drainage of appendiceal abscess

Excludes: that with appendectomy (47.0)

47.9   Other operations on appendix

47.91   Appendicostomy

47.92   Closure of appendiceal fistula

47.99   Other
Anastomosis of appendix

Excludes: diagnostic procedures on appendix (45.21-45.29)

48   Operations on rectum, rectosigmoid, and perirectal tissue

48.0   Proctotomy
Decompression of imperforate anus
Panas' operation [linear proctotomy]

Excludes: incision of perirectal tissue (48.81)

48.1   Proctostomy

48.2   Diagnostic procedures on rectum, rectosigmoid, and perirectal tissue

48.21   Transabdominal proctosigmoidoscopy
Intraoperative proctosigmoidoscopy

Excludes: that with biopsy (48.24)

48.22   Proctosigmoidoscopy through artificial stoma

Excludes: that with biopsy (48.24)

48.23   Rigid proctosigmoidoscopy

Excludes: flexible sigmoidoscopy (45.24)

48.24   Closed [endoscopic] biopsy of rectum
Brushing or washing for specimen collection
Proctosigmoidoscopy with biopsy

48.25   Open biopsy of rectum

48.26   Biopsy of perirectal tissue

48.29   Other diagnostic procedures on rectum, rectosigmoid and perirectal tissue

Excludes: digital examination of rectum (89.34)
lower GI series (87.64)
microscopic examination of specimen from rectum (90.91-90.99)

48.3   Local excision or destruction of lesion or tissue of rectum

48.31   Radical electrocoagulation of rectal lesion or tissue

48.32   Other electrocoagulation of rectal lesion or tissue

48.33   Destruction of rectal lesion or tissue by laser

48.34   Destruction of rectal lesion or tissue by cryosurgery

48.35   Local excision of rectal lesion or tissue

Excludes: biopsy of rectum (48.24-48.25)
[endoscopic] polypectomy of rectum (48.36)
excision of perirectal tissue (48.82)
hemorrhoidectomy (49.46)
rectal fistulectomy (48.73)

48.36   [Endoscopic] polypectomy of rectum

48.4   Pull-through resection of rectum
Code also any synchronous anastomosis other than end-to-end (45.90, 45.92-45.95)

Valid O.R.
procedure

Non-O.R.
procedure

Nonspecific
O.R. procedure

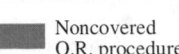
Noncovered
O.R. procedure

48.41 **Soave submucosal resection of rectum**
Endorectal pull-through operation

48.49 **Other pull-through resection of rectum**
Abdominoperineal pull-through
Altemeier operation
Swenson proctectomy

Excludes: *Duhamel abdominoperineal pull-through (48.65)*

48.5 **Abdominoperineal resection of rectum**
Combined abdominoendorectal resection
Complete proctectomy

Code also any synchronous anastomosis other than end-to-end (45.90, 45.92-45.95)

Excludes: *Duhamel abdominoperineal pull-through (48.65)*
that as part of pelvic exenteration (68.8)

48.6 **Other resection of rectum**
Code also any synchronous anastomosis other than end-to-end (45.90, 45.92-45.95)

48.61 **Transsacral rectosigmoidectomy**

48.62 **Anterior resection of rectum with synchronous colostomy**

48.63 **Other anterior resection of rectum**

Excludes: *that with synchronous colostomy (48.62)*

48.64 **Posterior resection of rectum**

48.65 **Duhamel resection of rectum**
Duhamel abdominoperineal pull-through

48.69 **Other**
Partial proctectomy
Rectal resection NOS

48.7 **Repair of rectum**

Excludes: *repair of:*
current obstetric laceration (75.62)
vaginal rectocele (70.50, 70.52)

48.71 **Suture of laceration of rectum**

48.72 **Closure of proctostomy**

48.73 **Closure of other rectal fistula**

Excludes: *fistulectomy:*
perirectal (48.93)
rectourethral (58.43)
rectovaginal (70.73)
rectovesical (57.83)
rectovesicovaginal (57.83)

48.74 **Rectorectostomy**
Rectal anastomosis NOS

48.75 **Abdominal proctopexy**
Frickman procedure
Ripstein repair of rectal prolapse

48.76 **Other proctopexy**
Delorme repair of prolapsed rectum
Proctosigmoidopexy
Puborectalis sling operation

Excludes: *manual reduction of rectal prolapse (96.26)*

48.79 **Other repair of rectum**
Repair of old obstetric laceration of rectum

Excludes: *anastomosis to:*
large intestine (45.94)
small intestine (45.92-45.93)
repair of:
current obstetrical laceration (75.62)
vaginal rectocele (70.50, 70.52)

48.8 **Incision or excision of perirectal tissue or lesion**
Includes: pelvirectal tissue
rectovaginal septum

● Code new
to this edition

▲ Revision of
existing code

④ ⑤ Fourth or fifth
digit required

48.81 Incision of perirectal tissue
Incision of rectovaginal septum

48.82 Excision of perirectal tissue

> Excludes: *perirectal biopsy (48.26)*
> *perirectofistulectomy (48.93)*
> *rectal fistulectomy (48.73)*

48.9 Other operations on rectum and perirectal tissue

48.91 Incision of rectal stricture

48.92 Anorectal myectomy

48.93 Repair of perirectal fistula

> Excludes: *that opening into rectum (48.73)*

48.99 Other

> Excludes: *digital examination of rectum (89.34)*
> *dilation of rectum (96.22)*
> *insertion of rectal tube (96.09)*
> *irrigation of rectum (96.38-96.39)*
> *manual reduction of rectal prolapse (96.26)*
> *proctoclysis (96.37)*
> *rectal massage (99.93)*
> *rectal packing (96.19)*
> *removal of:*
> *   impacted feces (96.38)*
> *   intraluminal foreign body from rectum without incision (98.05)*
> *   rectal packing (97.59)*
> *transanal enema (96.39)*

49 Operations on anus

49.0 Incision or excision of perianal tissue

49.01 Incision of perianal abscess

49.02 Other incision of perianal tissue
Undercutting of perianal tissue

> Excludes: *anal fistulotomy (49.11)*

49.03 Excision of perianal skin tags

49.04 Other excision of perianal tissue

> Excludes: *anal fistulectomy (49.12)*
> *biopsy of perianal tissue (49.22)*

49.1 Incision or excision of anal fistula

> Excludes: *closure of anal fistula (49.73)*

49.11 Anal fistulotomy

49.12 Anal fistulectomy

49.2 Diagnostic procedures on anus and perianal tissue

49.21 Anoscopy

49.22 Biopsy of perianal tissue

49.23 Biopsy of anus

49.29 Other diagnostic procedures on anus and perianal tissue

> Excludes: *microscopic examination of specimen from anus (90.91-90.99)*

49.3 Local excision or destruction of other lesion or tissue of anus
Anal cryptotomy
Cauterization of lesion of anus

> Excludes: *biopsy of anus (49.23)*
> *control of (postoperative) hemorrhage of anus (49.95)*
> *hemorrhoidectomy (49.46)*

49.31 Endoscopic excision or destruction of lesion or tissue of anus

49.39 Other local excision or destruction of lesion or tissue of anus

> Excludes: *that by endoscopic approach (49.31)*

49.4 Procedures on hemorrhoids

49.41 Reduction of hemorrhoids

 Valid O.R. procedure

 Non-O.R. procedure

 Nonspecific O.R. procedure

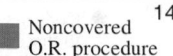 Noncovered O.R. procedure

49.42 Injection of hemorrhoids

49.43 Cauterization of hemorrhoids
Clamp and cautery of hemorrhoids

49.44 Destruction of hemorrhoids by cryotherapy

49.45 Ligation of hemorrhoids

49.46 Excision of hemorrhoids
Hemorrhoidectomy NOS

49.47 Evacuation of thrombosed hemorrhoids

49.49 Other procedures on hemorrhoids
Lord procedure

49.5 Division of anal sphincter

49.51 Left lateral anal sphincterotomy

49.52 Posterior anal sphincterotomy

49.59 Other anal sphincterotomy
Division of sphincter NOS

49.6 Excision of anus

49.7 Repair of anus

Excludes: *repair of current obstetric laceration (75.62)*

49.71 Suture of laceration of anus

49.72 Anal cerclage

49.73 Closure of anal fistula

Excludes: *excision of anal fistula (49.12)*

49.74 Gracilis muscle transplant for anal incontinence

49.79 Other repair of anal sphincter
Repair of old obstetric laceration of anus

Excludes: *anoplasty with synchronous*
hemorrhoidectomy (49.46)
repair of current obstetric laceration (75.62)

49.9 Other operations on anus

Excludes: *dilation of anus (sphincter) (96.23)*

49.91 Incision of anal septum

49.92 Insertion of subcutaneous electrical anal stimulator

49.93 Other incision of anus
Removal of:
foreign body from anus with incision
seton from anus

Excludes: *anal fistulotomy (49.11)*
removal of intraluminal foreign body without incision (98.05)

49.94 Reduction of anal prolapse

Excludes: *manual reduction of rectal prolapse (96.26)*

49.95 Control of (postoperative) hemorrhage of anus

49.99 Other

50 Operations on liver

50.0 Hepatotomy
Incision of abscess of liver
Removal of gallstones from liver
Stromeyer-Little operation

50.1 Diagnostic procedures on liver

50.11 Closed (percutaneous) [needle] biopsy of liver
Diagnostic aspiration of liver

50.12 Open biopsy of liver
Wedge biopsy

50.19 Other diagnostic procedures on liver

Excludes: *liver scan and radioisotope function study (92.02)*
microscopic examination of specimen from liver (91.01-91.09)

● Code new
to this edition

▲ Revision of
existing code

④ ⑤ Fourth or fifth
digit required

50.2   Local excision or destruction of liver tissue or lesion

    50.21   Marsupialization of lesion of liver

    50.22   Partial hepatectomy
        Wedge resection of liver

        | Excludes: | *biopsy of liver, (50.11-50.12)*
                     hepatic lobectomy (50.3)

    50.29   Other destruction of lesion of liver
        Cauterization
        Enucleation   } of hepatic lesion
        Evacuation

        | Excludes: | *percutaneous aspiration of lesion (50.91)*

50.3   Lobectomy of liver
    Total hepatic lobectomy with partial excision of other lobe

50.4   Total hepatectomy

50.5   Liver transplant

    50.51   Auxiliary liver transplant
        Auxiliary hepatic transplantation leaving patient's own liver in situ

    50.59   Other transplant of liver

50.6   Repair of liver

    50.61   Closure of laceration of liver

    50.69   Other repair of liver
        Hepatopexy

50.9   Other operations on liver

    | Excludes: | *lysis of adhesions (54.5)*

    50.91   Percutaneous aspiration of liver

        | Excludes: | *percutaneous biopsy (50.11)*

    50.92   Extracorporeal hepatic assistance

    50.93   Localized perfusion of liver

    50.94   Other injection of therapeutic substance into liver

    50.99   Other

51   Operations on gallbladder and biliary tract
    Includes: operations on:
           ampulla of Vater
           common bile duct
           cystic duct
           hepatic duct
           intrahepatic bile duct
           sphincter of Oddi

51.0   Cholecystotomy and cholecystostomy

    51.01   Percutaneous aspiration of gallbladder

        | Excludes: | *needle biopsy (51.12)*

    51.02   Trocar cholecystostomy

    51.03   Other cholecystostomy

    51.04   Other cholecystotomy
        Cholelithotomy NOS

51.1   Diagnostic procedures on biliary tract

    | Excludes: | *that for endoscopic procedures classifiable to 51.64, 51.84-51.88, 52.14,*
               52.21, 52.93-52.94, 52.97-52.98

    51.10   Endoscopic retrograde cholangiopancreatography [ERCP]

        | Excludes: | *endoscopic retrograde:*
               cholangiography [ERC] (51.11)
               pancreatography [ERP] (52.13)

    51.11   Endoscopic retrograde cholangiography [ERC]

        | Excludes: | *endoscopic retrograde:*
               cholangiopancreatography [ERCP] (51.10)
               pancreatography [ERP] (52.13)

| Valid O.R. procedure | Non-O.R. procedure | Nonspecific O.R. procedure | Noncovered O.R. procedure |

51.12 Percutaneous biopsy of gallbladder or bile ducts
Needle biopsy of gallbladder

51.13 Open biopsy of gallbladder or bile ducts

51.14 Other closed [endoscopic] biopsy of biliary duct or sphincter of Oddi
Brushing or washing for specimen collection
Closed biopsy of biliary duct or sphincter of Oddi by procedures classifiable to
51.10-51.11, 52.13

51.15 Pressure measurement of sphincter of Oddi
Pressure measurement of sphincter by procedures classifiable to 51.10-51.11, 52.13

51.19 Other diagnostic procedures on biliary tract
Excludes: *biliary tract x-ray (87.51-87.59)*
microscopic examination of specimen from biliary tract (91.01-91.09)

51.2   Cholecystectomy

● **51.21 Other partial cholecystectomy**
Revision of prior cholecystectomy
Excludes: *that by laparoscope (51.24)*

51.22 Cholecystectomy
Excludes: *laparoscopic cholecystectomy (51.23)*

51.23 Laparoscopic cholecystectomy
That by laser

● **51.24 Laparoscopic partial cholecystectomy**

51.3   Anastomosis of gallbladder or bile duct
Excludes: *resection with end-to-end anastomosis (51.61-51.69)*

51.31 Anastomosis of gallbladder to hepatic ducts

51.32 Anastomosis of gallbladder to intestine

51.33 Anastomosis of gallbladder to pancreas

51.34 Anastomosis of gallbladder to stomach

51.35 Other gallbladder anastomosis
Gallbladder anastomosis NOS

51.36 Choledochoenterostomy

51.37 Anastomosis of hepatic duct to gastrointestinal tract

51.39 Other bile duct anastomosis
Anastomosis of bile duct NOS
Anastomosis of unspecified bile duct to:
intestine
liver
pancreas
stomach

51.4   Incision of bile duct for relief of obstruction

51.41 Common duct exploration for removal of calculus
Excludes: *percutaneous extraction (51.96)*

51.42 Common duct exploration for relief of other obstruction

51.43 Insertion of choledochohepatic tube for decompression
Hepatocholedochostomy

51.49 Incision of other bile ducts for relief of obstruction

51.5   Other incision of bile duct
Excludes: *that for relief of obstruction (51.41-51.49)*

51.51 Exploration of common duct
Incision of common bile duct

51.59 Incision of other bile duct

51.6   Local excision or destruction of lesion or tissue of biliary ducts and sphincter of Oddi
Code also anastomosis other than end-to-end (51.31, 51.36-51.39)
Excludes: *biopsy of bile duct (51.12-51.13)*

51.61 Excision of cystic duct remnant

51.62 Excision of ampulla of Vater (with reimplantation of common duct)

● Code new   ▲ Revision of   ④ ⑤ Fourth or fifth
to this edition   existing code   digit required

51.63 **Other excision of common duct**
Choledochectomy

Excludes: *fistulectomy (51.72)*

51.64 **Endoscopic excision or destruction of lesion of biliary ducts or sphincter of Oddi**
Excision or destruction of lesion of biliary duct by procedures classifiable to
51.10-51.11, 52.13

51.69 **Excision of other bile duct**
Excision of lesion of bile duct NOS

Excludes: *fistulectomy (51.79)*

51.7 **Repair of bile ducts**

51.71 **Simple suture of common bile duct**

51.72 **Choledochoplasty**
Repair of fistula of common bile duct

51.79 **Repair of other bile ducts**
Closure of artificial opening of bile duct NOS
Suture of bile duct NOS

Excludes: *operative removal of prosthetic device (51.95)*

51.8 **Other operations on biliary ducts and sphincter of Oddi**

51.81 **Dilation of sphincter of Oddi**
Dilation of ampulla of Vater

Excludes: *that by endoscopic approach (51.84)*

51.82 **Pancreatic sphincterotomy**
Incision of pancreatic sphincter
Transduodenal ampullary sphincterotomy

Excludes: *that by endoscopic approach (51.85)*

51.83 **Pancreatic sphincteroplasty**

51.84 **Endoscopic dilation of ampulla and biliary duct**
Dilation of ampulla and biliary duct by procedures classifiable to 51.10-51.11, 52.13

51.85 **Endoscopic sphincterotomy and papillotomy**
Sphincterotomy and papillotomy by procedures classifiable to 51.10-51.11, 52.13

51.86 **Endoscopic insertion of nasobiliary drainage tube**
Insertion of nasobiliary tube by procedures classifiable to 51.10-51.11, 52.13

51.87 **Endoscopic insertion of stent (tube) into bile duct**
Endoprosthesis of bile duct
Insertion of stent into bile duct by procedures classifiable to 51.10-51.11, 52.13

Excludes: *nasobiliary drainage tube (51.86)*
replacement of stent (tube) (97.05)

51.88 **Endoscopic removal of stone(s) from biliary tract**
Removal of biliary tract stone(s) by procedures classifiable to 51.10-51.11, 52.13

Excludes: *percutaneous extraction of common duct stones (51.96)*

51.89 **Other operations on sphincter of Oddi**

51.9 **Other operations on biliary tract**

51.91 **Repair of laceration of gallbladder**

51.92 **Closure of cholecystostomy**

51.93 **Closure of other biliary fistula**
Cholecystogastroenteric fistulectomy

51.94 **Revision of anastomosis of biliary tract**

51.95 **Removal of prosthetic device from bile duct**

Excludes: *nonoperative removal (97.55)*

51.96 **Percutaneous extraction of common duct stones**

| | Valid O.R. procedure | | Non-O.R. procedure |

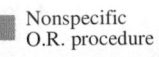

| | Nonspecific O.R. procedure | | Noncovered O.R. procedure |

51.98 Other percutaneous procedures on biliary tract
Percutaneous biliary endoscopy via existing T-tube or other tract for:
dilation of biliary duct stricture
exploration (postoperative)
removal of stone(s) except common duct stone
Percutaneous transhepatic biliary drainage

> Excludes: *percutaneous aspiration of gallbladder (51.01)*
> *percutaneous biopsy and/or collection of specimen by brushing or washing (51.12)*
> *percutaneous removal of common duct stone(s) (51.96)*

51.99 Other
Insertion or replacement of biliary tract prosthesis

> Excludes: *biopsy of gallbladder (51.12-51.13)*
> *irrigation of cholecystostomy and other biliary tube (96.41)*
> *lysis of peritoneal adhesions (54.5)*
> *nonoperative removal of:*
> *cholecystostomy tube (97.54)*
> *tube from biliary tract or liver (97.55)*

52 Operations on pancreas
Includes: operations on pancreatic duct

52.0 Pancreatotomy

52.01 Drainage of pancreatic cyst by catheter

52.09 Other pancreatotomy
Pancreatolithotomy

> Excludes: *drainage by anastomosis (52.4, 52.96)*
> *incision of pancreatic sphincter (51.82)*
> *marsupialization of cyst (52.3)*

52.1 Diagnostic procedures on pancreas

52.11 Closed [aspiration] [needle] [percutaneous] biopsy of pancreas

52.12 Open biopsy of pancreas

52.13 Endoscopic retrograde pancreatography [EPR]

> Excludes: *endoscopic retrograde:*
> *cholangiography [ERC] (51.11)*
> *cholangiopancreatography [ERCP] (51.10)*
> *that for procedures classifiable to 51.14-51.15, 51.64, 51.84-51.88, 52.14, 52.21, 52.92-52.94, 52.97-52.98*

52.14 Closed [endoscopic] biopsy of pancreatic duct
Closed biopsy of pancreatic duct by procedures classifiable to 51.10-51.11, 52.13

52.19 Other diagnostic procedure on pancreas

> Excludes: *contrast pancreatogram (87.66)*
> *endoscopic retrograde pancreatography [ERP] (52.13))*
> *microscopic examination of specimen from pancreas (91.01-91.09)*

52.2 Local excision or destruction of pancreas and pancreatic duct

> Excludes: *biopsy of pancreas (52.11-52.12, 52.14)*
> *pancreatic fistulectomy (52.95)*

52.21 Endoscopic excision or destruction of lesion or tissue of pancreatic duct
Excision or destruction of lesion or tissue of pancreatic duct by procedures classifiable to 51.10-51.11, 52.13

52.22 Other excision or destruction of lesion or tissue of pancreas or pancreatic duct

52.3 Marsupialization of pancreatic cyst

> Excludes: *drainage of cyst by catheter (52.01)*

52.4 Internal drainage of pancreatic cyst
Pancreaticocystoduodenostomy
Pancreaticocystogastrostomy
Pancreaticocystojejunostomy

52.5 Partial pancreatectomy

> Excludes: *pancreatic fistulectomy (52.95)*

52.51 Proximal pancreatectomy
Excision of head of pancreas (with part of body)
Proximal pancreatectomy with synchronous duodenectomy

● Code new
to this edition

▲ Revision of
existing code

④ ⑤ Fourth or fifth
digit required

52.52 Distal pancreatectomy
  Excision of tail of pancreas (with part of body)

52.53 Radical subtotal pancreatectomy

52.59 Other partial pancreatectomy

52.6 Total pancreatectomy
  Pancreatectomy with synchronous duodenectomy

52.7 Radical pancreaticoduodenectomy
  One-stage pancreaticoduodenal resection with choledochojejunal anastomosis,
    pancreaticojejunal anastomosis, and gastrojejunostomy
  Two-stage pancreaticoduodenal resection (first stage) (second stage)
  Radical resection of the pancreas
  Whipple procedure

  | Excludes: | radical subtotal pancreatectomy (52.53)

52.8 Transplant of pancreas

52.80 Pancreatic transplant, not otherwise specified

52.81 Reimplantation of pancreatic tissue

52.82 Homotransplant of pancreas

52.83 Heterotransplant of pancreas

● **52.84 Autotransplantation of cells of Islets of Langerhans**
  Homotransplantation of islet cells of pancreas

● **52.85 Allotransplantation of cells of Islets of Langerhans**
  Heterotransplantation of islet cells of pancreas

● **52.86 Transplantation of cells of Islets of Langerhans, not otherwise specified**

52.9 Other operations on pancreas

52.92 Cannulation of pancreatic duct

  | Excludes: | that by endoscopic approach (52.93)

52.93 Endoscopic insertion of stent (tube) into pancreatic duct
  Insertion of cannula or stent into pancreatic duct by procedures classifiable to
    51.10-51.11, 52.13

  | Excludes: | endoscopic insertion of nasopancreatic drainage tube (52.97)
            replacement of stent (tube) (97.05)

52.94 Endoscopic removal of stone(s) from pancreatic duct
  Removal of stone(s) from pancreatic duct by procedures classifiable to 51.10-51.11,
    52.13

52.95 Other repair of pancreas
  Fistulectomy ⎫
  Simple suture ⎬ of pancreas

  | Excludes: | anastomosis to:
            bile duct (51.39)
            gallbladder (51.33)

52.96 Anastomosis of pancreas
  Anastomosis of pancreas (duct) to:
    intestine
    jejunum
    stomach

  | Excludes: | anastomosis to:
            bile duct (51.39)
            gallbladder (51.33)

52.97 Endoscopic insertion of nasopancreatic drainage tube
  Insertion of nasopancreatic drainage tube by procedures classifiable to 51.10-51.11,
    52.13

  | Excludes: | drainage of pancreatic cyst by catheter (52.01)
            replacement of stent (tube) (97.05)

52.98 Endoscopic dilation of pancreatic duct
  Dilation of Wirsung's duct by procedures classifiable to 51.10-51.11,52.13

52.99 Other
  Dilation of pancreatic ⎫
    [Wirsung's] duct ⎪
  Repair of pancreatic ⎬ by open approach
    [Wirsung's] duct ⎭

  | Excludes: | irrigation of pancreatic tube (96.42)
            removal of pancreatic tube (97.56)

 Valid O.R.
procedure

 Non-O.R.
procedure

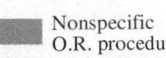 Nonspecific
O.R. procedure

Noncovered
O.R. procedure

53   Repair of hernia
Includes: hernioplasty
herniorrhaphy
herniotomy

Excludes: *manual reduction of hernia (96.27)*

53.0   **Unilateral repair of inguinal hernia**

53.00 **Unilateral repair of inguinal hernia, not otherwise specified**
Inguinal herniorrhaphy NOS

53.01 **Repair of direct inguinal hernia**

53.02 **Repair of indirect inguinal hernia**

53.03 **Repair of direct inguinal hernia with graft or prosthesis**

53.04 **Repair of indirect inguinal hernia with graft or prosthesis**

53.05 **Repair of inguinal hernia with graft or prosthesis, not otherwise specified**

53.1   **Bilateral repair of inguinal hernia**

53.10 **Bilateral repair of inguinal hernia, not otherwise specified**

53.11 **Bilateral repair of direct inguinal hernia**

53.12 **Bilateral repair of indirect inguinal hernia**

53.13 **Bilateral repair of inguinal hernia, one direct and one indirect**

53.14 **Bilateral repair of direct inguinal hernia with graft or prosthesis**

53.15 **Bilateral repair of indirect inguinal hernia with graft or prosthesis**

53.16 **Bilateral repair of inguinal hernia, one direct and one indirect, with graft or prosthesis**

53.17 **Bilateral inguinal hernia repair with graft or prosthesis, not otherwise specified**

53.2   **Unilateral repair of femoral hernia**

53.21 **Unilateral repair of femoral hernia with graft or prosthesis**

53.29 **Other unilateral femoral herniorrhaphy**

53.3   **Bilateral repair of femoral hernia**

53.31 **Bilateral repair of femoral hernia with graft or prosthesis**

53.39 **Other bilateral femoral herniorrhaphy**

53.4   **Repair of umbilical hernia**

Excludes: *repair of gastroschisis (54.71)*

53.41 **Repair of umbilical hernia with prosthesis**

53.49 **Other umbilical herniorrhaphy**

53.5   **Repair of other hernia of anterior abdominal wall (without graft or prosthesis)**

53.51 **Incisional hernia repair**

53.59 **Repair of other hernia of anterior abdominal wall**
Repair of hernia:
epigastric
hypogastric
spigelian
ventral

53.6   **Repair of other hernia of anterior abdominal wall with graft or prosthesis**

53.61 **Incisional hernia repair with prosthesis**

53.69 **Repair of other hernia of anterior abdominal wall with prosthesis**

53.7   **Repair of diaphragmatic hernia, abdominal approach**

53.8   **Repair of diaphragmatic hernia, thoracic approach**

53.80 **Repair of diaphragmatic hernia with thoracic approach, not otherwise specified**
Thoracoabdominal repair of diaphragmatic hernia

53.81 **Plication of the diaphragm**

53.82 **Repair of parasternal hernia**

● Code new   ▲ Revision of   ④ ⑤ Fourth or fifth
to this edition   existing code   digit required

53.9 **Other hernia repair**
Repair of hernia:
ischiatic   omental
ischiorectal   retroperitoneal
lumbar   sciatic
obturator

Excludes: *relief of strangulated hernia with exteriorization of intestine (46.01, 46.03)*
repair of pericolostomy hernia (46.42)
repair of vaginal enterocele (70.92)

54 **Other operations on abdominal region**
Includes: operations on:
epigastric region   male pelvic cavity
flank   mesentery
groin region   omentum
hypochondrium   peritoneum
inguinal region   retroperitoneal tissue space
loin region

Excludes: *female pelvic cavity (69.01- 70.92)*
hernia repair (53.00-53.9)
obliteration of cul-de-sac (70.92)
retroperitoneal tissue dissection (59.00-59.09)
skin and subcutaneous tissue of abdominal wall (86.01-86.99)

54.0 **Incision of abdominal wall**
Drainage of:
abdominal wall
extraperitoneal abscess
retroperitoneal abscess

Excludes: *incision of peritoneum (54.95)*
laparotomy (54.11-54.19)

54.1 **Laparotomy**

54.11 **Exploratory laparotomy**

Excludes: *exploration incidental to intra-abdominal surgery—omit code*

54.12 **Reopening of recent laparotomy site**
Reopening of recent laparotomy site for:
control of hemorrhage
exploration
incision of hematoma

54.19 **Other laparotomy**
Drainage of intraperitoneal abscess or hematoma

Excludes: *culdocentesis (70.0)*
drainage of appendiceal abscess (47.2)
exploration incidental to intra-abdominal surgery—omit code
Ladd operation (54.95)
removal of foreign body (54.92)

54.2 **Diagnostic procedures of abdominal region**

54.21 **Laparoscopy**
Peritoneoscopy

Excludes: *laparoscopic cholecystectomy (51.23)*
that incidental to destruction of fallopian tubes (66.21-66.29)

54.22 **Biopsy or abdominal wall or umbilicus**

54.23 **Biopsy of peritoneum**
Biopsy of:
mesentery
omentum
peritoneal implant

54.24 **Closed [percutaneous] [needle] biopsy of intra-abdominal mass**

Excludes: *that of:*
fallopian tube (66.11)
ovary (65.11)
peritoneum (54.23)
uterine ligaments (68.15)
uterus (68.16)

| Valid O.R. procedure | Non-O.R. procedure | Nonspecific O.R. procedure | Noncovered O.R. procedure |

54.25 Peritoneal lavage
Diagnostic peritoneal lavage

> | Excludes: | peritoneal dialysis (54.98)

54.29 Other diagnostic procedures on abdominal region

> | Excludes: | abdominal lymphangiogram (88.04)
> abdominal x-ray NEC (88.19)
> angiocardiography of venae cavae (88.51)
> C.A.T. scan of abdomen (88.01)
> contrast x-ray of abdominal cavity (88.11-88.15)
> intra-abdominal arteriography NEC (88.47)
> microscopic examination of peritoneal and retroperitoneal specimen (91.11-91.19)
> phlebography of:
>   intra-abdominal vessels NEC (88.65)
>   portal venous system (88.64)
> sinogram of abdominal wall (88.03)
> soft tissue x-ray of abdominal wall NEC (88.09)
> tomography of abdomen NEC(88.02)
> ultrasonography of abdomen and retroperitoneum (88.76)

54.3 Excision or destruction of lesion or tissue of abdominal wall or umbilicus
Debridement of abdominal wall
Omphalectomy

> | Excludes: | biopsy of abdominal wall or umbilicus (54.22)
> size reduction operation (86.83)
> that of skin of abdominal wall (86.22, 86.26, 86.3)

54.4 Excision or destruction of peritoneal tissue
Excision of:
appendices epiploicae
falciform ligament
gastrocolic ligament
lesion of:
  mesentery
  omentum
  peritoneum
presacral lesion NOS
retroperitoneal lesion NOS

> | Excludes: | biopsy of peritoneum (54.23)
> endometrectomy of cul-de-sac (70.32)

54.5 Lysis of peritoneal adhesions
Freeing of adhesions of:
biliary tract
intestines
liver
pelvic peritoneum
peritoneum
spleen
uterus

> | Excludes: | lysis of adhesions of:
>   bladder (59.11)
>   fallopian tube and ovary (65.81, 65.89)
>   kidney (59.02)
>   ureter (59.01-59.02)

● **54.51 Laparoscopic lysis of peritoneal adhesions**

● **54.59 Other lysis of peritoneal adhesions**

54.6 Suture of abdominal wall and peritoneum

54.61 Reclosure of postoperative disruption of abdominal wall

54.62 Delayed closure of granulating abdomen wound
Tertiary subcutaneous wound closure

54.63 Other suture of abdominal wall
Suture of laceration of abdominal wall

> | Excludes: | closure of operative wound—omit code

● Code new
to this edition

▲ Revision of
existing code

④ ⑤ Fourth or fifth
digit required

54.64 **Suture of peritoneum**
Secondary suture of peritoneum

> [Excludes:] *closure of operative wound—omit code*

54.7 Other repair of abdominal wall and peritoneum

54.71 **Repair of gastroschisis**

54.72 **Other repair of abdominal wall**

54.73 **Other repair of peritoneum**
Suture of gastrocolic ligament

54.74 **Other repair of omentum**
Epiplorrhaphy
Graft of omentum
Omentopexy
Reduction of torsion of omentum

> [Excludes:] *cardio-omentopexy (36.3)*

54.75 **Other repair of mesentery**
Mesenteric plication
Mesenteropexy

54.9 Other operations of abdominal region

> [Excludes:] *removal of ectopic pregnancy (69.11, 74.3)*

54.91 **Percutaneous abdominal drainage**
Paracentesis

> [Excludes:] *creation of cutaneoperitoneal fistula (54.93)*

54.92 **Removal of foreign body from peritoneal cavity**

54.93 **Creation of cutaneoperitoneal fistula**

54.94 **Creation of peritoneovascular shunt**
Peritoneovenous shunt

54.95 **Incision of peritoneum**
Ladd operation
Revision of distal catheter of ventricular shunt
Revision of ventriculoperitoneal shunt at peritoneal site

> [Excludes:] *that incidental to laparotomy (54.11-54.19)*

54.96 **Injection of air into peritoneal cavity**
Pneumoperitoneum

> [Excludes:] *that for:*
> *collapse of lung (33.33)*
> *radiography (88.12-88.13, 88.15)*

54.97 **Injection of locally-acting therapeutic substance into peritoneal cavity**

> [Excludes:] *peritoneal dialysis (54.98)*

54.98 **Peritoneal dialysis**

> [Excludes:] *peritoneal lavage (diagnostic) (54.25)*

54.99 **Other**

> [Excludes:] *removal of:*
> *abdominal wall sutures (97.83)*
> *peritoneal drainage device (97.82)*
> *retroperitoneal drainage device (97.81)*

	Valid O.R. procedure		Non-O.R. procedure		Nonspecific O.R. procedure		Noncovered O.R. procedure

● Code new
to this edition

▲ Revision of
existing code

④ ⑤ Fourth or fifth
digit required

10. OPERATIONS ON THE URINARY SYSTEM (55-59)

55   Operations on kidney
Includes: operations on renal pelvis

> | Excludes: | *perirenal tissue (59.00-59.09, 59.21-59.29, 59.91-59.92)*

55.0   Nephrotomy and nephrostomy

> | Excludes: | *drainage by:*
> *anastomosis (55.86)*
> *aspiration (55.92)*
> *incision of kidney pelvis (55.11-55.12)*

55.01   Nephrotomy
Evacuation of renal cyst
Exploration of kidney
Nephrolithotomy

55.02   Nephrostomy

55.03   Percutaneous nephrostomy without fragmentation
Nephrostolithotomy, percutaneous (nephroscopic)
Percutaneous removal of kidney stone(s) by:
  basket extraction
  forceps extraction (nephroscopic)
Pyelostolithotomy, percutaneous (nephroscopic)
With placement of catheter down ureter

> | Excludes: | *percutaneous removal by fragmentation (55.04)*
> *repeat nephroscopic removal during current episode (55.92)*

55.04   Percutaneous nephrostomy with fragmentation
Percutaneous nephrostomy with disruption of kidney stone by ultrasonic energy and
  extraction (suction) through endoscope
With placement of catheter down ureter
With fluoroscopic guidance

> | Excludes: | *repeat fragmentation during current episode (59.95)*

55.1   Pyelotomy and pyelostomy

> | Excludes: | *drainage by anastomosis (55.86)*
> *percutaneous pyelostolithotomy (55.03)*
> *removal of calculus without incision (56.0)*

55.11   Pyelotomy
Exploration of renal pelvis
Pyelolithotomy

55.12   Pyelostomy
Insertion of drainage tube into renal pelvis

55.2   Diagnostic procedures on kidney

55.21   Nephroscopy

55.22   Pyeloscopy

55.23   Closed [percutaneous] [needle] biopsy of kidney
Endoscopic biopsy via existing nephrostomy, nephrotomy, pyelostomy, or
  pyelotomy

55.24   Open biopsy of kidney

55.29   Other diagnostic procedures on kidney

> | Excludes: | *microscopic examination of specimen from kidney (91.21-91.29)*
> *pyelogram:*
> *intravenous (87.73)*
> *percutaneous (87.75)*
> *retrograde (87.74)*
> *radioisotope scan (92.03)*
> *renal arteriography (88.45)*
> *tomography:*
> *C.A.T. scan (87.71)*
> *other (87.72)*

55.3   Local excision or destruction of lesion or tissue of kidney

55.31   Marsupialization of kidney lesion

1451

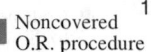

| | Valid O.R. procedure | | Non-O.R. procedure | | Nonspecific O.R. procedure | | Noncovered O.R. procedure |

55.39 **Other local destruction or excision of renal lesion or tissue**
Obliteration of calyceal diverticulum

Excludes: *biopsy of kidney (55.23-55.24)*
partial nephrectomy (55.4)
percutaneous aspiration of kidney (55.92)
wedge resection of kidney (55.4)

55.4 **Partial nephrectomy**
Calycectomy
Wedge resection of kidney

Code also any synchronous resection of ureter (56.40-56.42)

55.5 **Complete nephrectomy**

Code also any synchronous excision of:
bladder segment (57.6)
lymph nodes (40.3, 40.52-40.59)

55.51 **Nephroureterectomy**
Nephroureterectomy with bladder cuff
Total nephrectomy (unilateral)

Excludes: *removal of transplanted kidney (55.53)*

55.52 **Nephrectomy of remaining kidney**
Removal of solitary kidney

Excludes: *removal of transplanted kidney (55.53)*

55.53 **Removal of transplanted or rejected kidney**

55.54 **Bilateral nephrectomy**

Excludes: *complete nephrectomy NOS (55.51)*

55.6 **Transplant of kidney**

55.61 **Renal autotransplantation**

55.69 **Other kidney transplantation**

55.7 **Nephropexy**
Fixation or suspension of movable [floating] kidney

55.8 **Other repair of kidney**

55.81 **Suture of laceration of kidney**

55.82 **Closure of nephrostomy and pyelostomy**

55.83 **Closure of other fistula of kidney**

55.84 **Reduction of torsion of renal pedicle**

55.85 **Symphysiotomy for horseshoe kidney**

55.86 **Anastomosis of kidney**
Nephropyeloureterostomy
Pyeloureterovesical anastomosis
Ureterocalyceal anastomosis

Excludes: *nephrocystanastomosis NOS (56.73)*

55.87 **Correction of ureteropelvic junction**

55.89 **Other**

55.9 **Other operations on kidney**

Excludes: *lysis of perirenal adhesions (59.02)*

55.91 **Decapsulation of kidney**
Capsulectomy ⎫
Decortication ⎬ of kidney

55.92 **Percutaneous aspiration of kidney (pelvis)**
Aspiration of renal cyst
Renipuncture

Excludes: *percutaneous biopsy of kidney (55.23)*

55.93 **Replacement of nephrostomy tube**

55.94 **Replacement of pyelostomy tube**

55.95 **Local perfusion of kidney**

55.96 **Other Injection of therapeutic substance into kidney**
Injection into renal cyst

● Code new
to this edition

▲ Revision of
existing code

④ ⑤ Fourth or fifth
digit required

55.97 Implantation or replacement of mechanical kidney

55.98 Removal of mechanical kidney

55.99 Other

> Excludes: *removal of pyelostomy or nephrostomy tube (97.61)*

56 **Operations on ureter**

56.0 **Transurethral removal of obstruction from ureter and renal pelvis**

Removal of:
blood clot
calculus } from ureter or renal pelvis without incision
foreign body

> Excludes: *that by incision (55.11, 56.2)*
> *transurethral insertion of ureteral stent for passage of calculus (59.8)*

56.1 **Ureteral meatotomy**

56.2 **Ureterotomy**

Incision of ureter for:
drainage
exploration
removal of calculus

> Excludes: *cutting of ureterovesical orifice (56.1)*
> *removal of calculus without incision (56.0)*
> *transurethral insertion of ureteral stent for passage of calculus (59.8)*
> *urinary diversion (56.51-56.79)*

56.3 **Diagnostic procedures on ureter**

56.31 **Ureteroscopy**

56.32 **Closed percutaneous biopsy of ureter**

> Excludes: *endoscopic biopsy of ureter (56.33)*

56.33 **Closed endoscopic biopsy of ureter**

Cystourethroscopy with ureteral biopsy
Transurethral biopsy of ureter
Ureteral endoscopy with biopsy through ureterotomy
Ureteroscopy with biopsy

> Excludes: *percutaneous biopsy of ureter (56.32)*

56.34 **Open biopsy of ureter**

56.35 **Endoscopy (cystoscopy) (looposcopy) of ileal conduit**

56.39 **Other diagnostic procedures on ureter**

> Excludes: *microscopic examination of specimen from ureter (91.21-91.29)*

56.4 **Ureterectomy**

Code also anastomosis other than end-to-end (56.51-56.79)

> Excludes: *fistulectomy (56.84)*
> *nephroureterectomy (55.51-55.54)*

56.40 **Ureterectomy, not otherwise specified**

56.41 **Partial ureterectomy**

Excision of lesion of ureter
Shortening of ureter with reimplantation

> Excludes: *biopsy of ureter (56.32-56.34)*

56.42 **Total ureterectomy**

56.5 **Cutaneous uretero-ileostomy**

56.51 **Formation of cutaneous uretero-ileostomy**

Construction of ileal conduit
External ureteral ileostomy
Formation of open ileal bladder
Ileal loop operation
Ileoureterostomy (Bricker's) (ileal bladder)
Transplantation of ureter into ileum with external diversion

> Excludes: *closed ileal bladder (57.87)*
> *replacement of ureteral defect by ileal segment (56.89)*

56.52 **Revision of cutaneous uretero-ileostomy**

56.6 **Other external urinary diversion**

	Valid O.R. procedure		Non-O.R. procedure		Nonspecific O.R. procedure		Noncovered O.R. procedure

56.61 **Formation of other cutaneous ureterostomy**
Anastomosis of ureter to skin
Ureterostomy NOS

56.62 **Revision of other cutaneous ureterostomy**
Revision of ureterostomy stoma

Excludes: *nonoperative removal of ureterostomy tube (97.62)*

56.7 **Other anastomosis or bypass of ureter**

Excludes: *ureteropyelostomy (55.86)*

56.71 **Urinary diversion to intestine**
Anastomosis of ureter to intestine
Internal urinary diversion NOS

Code also any synchronous colostomy (46.10-46.13)

Excludes: *external ureteral ileostomy (56.51)*

56.72 **Revision of ureterointestinal anastomosis**

Excludes: *revision of external ureteral ileostomy (56.52)*

56.73 **Nephrocystanastomosis, not otherwise specified**

56.74 **Ureteroneocystostomy**
Replacement of ureter with bladder flap
Ureterovesical anastomosis

56.75 **Transureteroureterostomy**

Excludes: *ureteroureterostomy associated with partial resection (56.41)*

56.79 **Other**

56.8 **Repair of ureter**

56.81 **Lysis of intraluminal adhesions of ureter**

Excludes: *lysis of periureteral adhesions (59.01-59.02)*
ureterolysis (59.01-59.02)

56.82 **Suture of laceration of ureter**

56.83 **Closure of ureterostomy**

56.84 **Closure of other fistula of ureter**

56.85 **Ureteropexy**

56.86 **Removal of ligature from ureter**

56.89 **Other repair of ureter**
Graft of ureter
Replacement of ureter with ileal segment implanted into bladder
Ureteroplication

56.9 **Other operations on ureter**

56.91 **Dilation of ureteral meatus**

56.92 **Implantation of electronic ureteral stimulator**

56.93 **Replacement of electronic ureteral stimulator**

56.94 **Removal of electronic ureteral stimulator**

Excludes: *that with synchronous replacement (56.93)*

56.95 **Ligation of ureter**

56.99 **Other**

Excludes: *removal of ureterostomy tube and ureteral catheter (97.62)*
ureteral catheterization (59.8)

57 **Operations on urinary bladder**

Excludes: *perivesical tissue (59.11-59.29, 59.91-59.92)*
ureterovesical orifice (56.0-56.99)

57.0 **Transurethral clearance of bladder**
Drainage of bladder without incision
Removal of:
  blood clots
  calculus   } from bladder without incision
  foreign body

Excludes: *that by incision (57.19)*

● Code new
to this edition   ▲ Revision of
existing code   ④ ⑤ Fourth or fifth
digit required

57.1   **Cystotomy and cystostomy**

> | Excludes: | cystotomy and cystostomy as operative approach—omit code

57.11   **Percutaneous aspiration of bladder**

57.12   **Lysis of intraluminal adhesion with incision into bladder**

> | Excludes: | transurethral lysis of intraluminal adhesions (57.41)

57.17   **Percutaneous cystostomy**
Closed cystostomy
Percutaneous suprapubic cystostomy

> | Excludes: | removal of cystostomy tube (97.63)
> replacement of cystostomy tube (59.94)

57.18   **Other suprapubic cystostomy**

> | Excludes | percutaneous cystostomy (57.17)
> removal of cystostomy tube (97.63)
> replacement of cystostomy tube (59.94)

57.19   **Other cystotomy**
Cystolithotomy

> | Excludes: | percutaneous cystostomy (57.17)
> suprapubic cystostomy (57.18)

57.2   **Vesicostomy**

> | Excludes: | percutaneous cystostomy (57.17)
> suprapubic cystostomy (57.18)

57.21   **Vesicostomy**
Creation of permanent opening from bladder to skin using a bladder flap

57.22   **Revision or closure of vesicostomy**

> | Excludes: | closure of cystostomy (57.82)

57.3   **Diagnostic procedures on bladder**

57.31   **Cystoscopy through artificial stoma**

57.32   **Other cystoscopy**
Transurethral cystoscopy

> | Excludes: | cystourethroscopy with ureteral biopsy (56.33)
> retrograde pyelogram (87.74)
> that for control of hemorrhage (postoperative):
> bladder (57.93)
> prostate (60.94)

57.33   **Closed [transurethral] biopsy of bladder**

57.34   **Open biopsy of bladder**

57.39   **Other diagnostic procedures on bladder**

> | Excludes: | cystogram NEC (87.77)
> microscopic examination of specimen from bladder (91.31-91.39)
> retrograde cystourethrogram (87.76)

57.4   **Transurethral excision or destruction of bladder tissue**

57.41   **Transurethral lysis of intraluminal adhesions**

57.49   **Other transurethral excision or destruction of lesion or tissue of bladder**
Endoscopic resection of bladder lesion

> | Excludes: | transurethral biopsy of bladder (57.33)
> transurethral fistulectomy (57.83-57.84)

57.5   **Other excision or destruction of bladder tissue**

> | Excludes: | that with transurethral approach (57.41-57.49)

57.51   **Excision of urachus**
Excision of urachal sinus of bladder

> | Excludes: | excision of urachal cyst of abdominal wall (54.3)

57.59   **Open excision or destruction of other lesion or tissue of bladder**
Endometrectomy of bladder
Suprapubic excision of bladder lesion

> | Excludes: | biopsy of bladder (57.33-57.34)
> fistulectomy of bladder (57.83-57.84)

| | Valid O.R. procedure | | Non-O.R. procedure | | Nonspecific O.R. procedure | | Noncovered O.R. procedure |

57.6**Partial cystectomy**
Excision of bladder dome
Trigonectomy
Wedge resection of bladder

57.7**Total cystectomy**
Includes: total cystectomy with urethrectomy

57.71**Radical cystectomy**
Pelvic exenteration in male
Removal of bladder, prostate, seminal vesicles, and fat
Removal of bladder, urethra, and fat in a female
Code also any:
lymph node dissection (40.3, 40.5)
urinary diversion (56.51-56.79)
*Excludes:**that as part of pelvic exenteration in female (68.8)*

57.79**Other total cystectomy**

57.8**Other repair of urinary bladder**
*Excludes:**repair of:*
current obstetric laceration (75.61)
cystocele (70.50-70.51)
that for stress incontinence (59.3-59.79)

57.81**Suture of laceration of bladder**

57.82**Closure of cystostomy**

57.83**Repair of fistula involving bladder and intestine**
Rectovesicovaginal
Vesicosigmoidovaginal } fistulectomy

57.84**Repair of other fistula of bladder**
Cervicovesical
Urethroperineovesical
Uterovesical } fistulectomy
Vaginovesical
*Excludes:**vesicoureterovaginal fistulectomy (56.84)*

57.85**Cystourethroplasty and plastic repair of bladder neck**
Plication of sphincter of urinary bladder
V-Y plasty of bladder neck

57.86**Repair of bladder exstrophy**

57.87**Reconstruction of urinary bladder**
Anastomosis of bladder with isolated segment of ileum
Augmentation of bladder
Replacement of bladder with ileum or sigmoid [closed ileal bladder]
Code also resection of intestine (45.50-45.52)

57.88**Other anastomosis of bladder**
Anastomosis of bladder to intestine NOS
Cystocolic anastomosis
*Excludes:**formation of closed ileal bladder (5787)*

57.89**Other repair of bladder**
Bladder suspension, not elsewhere classified
Cystopexy NOS
Repair of old obstetric laceration of bladder
*Excludes:**repair of current obstetric laceration (75.61)*

57.9**Other operations on bladder**

57.91**Sphincterotomy of bladder**
Division of bladder neck

57.92**Dilation of bladder neck**

57.93**Control of (postoperative) hemorrhage of bladder**

57.94**Insertion of indwelling urinary catheter**

57.95**Replacement of indwelling urinary catheter**

57.96**Implantation of electronic bladder stimulator**

57.97**Replacement of electronic bladder stimulator**

● Code new to this edition ▲ Revision of existing code ④ ⑤ Fourth or fifth digit required

57.98 Removal of electronic bladder stimulator

> _Excludes:_ _that with synchronous replacement (57.97)_

57.99 Other

> _Excludes:_ _irrigation of:_
> _cystostomy (96.47)_
> _other indwelling urinary catheter (96.48)_
> _lysis of external adhesions (59.11)_
> _removal of:_
> _cystostomy tube (97.63)_
> _other urinary drainage device (97.64)_
> _therapeutic distention of bladder (96.25)_

58 Operations on urethra

Includes: operations on:
bulbourethral gland [Cowper's gland]
periurethral tissue

58.0 Urethrotomy

Excision of urethral septum
Formation of urethrovaginal fistula
Perineal urethrostomy
Removal of calculus from urethra by incision

> _Excludes:_ _drainage of bulbourethral gland or periurethral tissue (58.91)_
> _internal urethral meatotomy (58.5)_
> _removal of urethral calculus without incision (58.6)_

58.1 Urethral meatotomy

> _Excludes:_ _internal urethral meatotomy (58.5)_

58.2 Diagnostic procedures on urethra

58.21 Perineal urethroscopy

58.22 Other urethroscopy

58.23 Biopsy of urethra

58.24 Biopsy of periurethral tissue

58.29 Other diagnostic procedures on urethra and periurethral tissue

> _Excludes:_ _microscopic examination of specimen from urethra (91.31-91.39)_
> _retrograde cystourethrogram (87.76)_
> _urethral pressure profile (89.25)_
> _urethral sphincter electromyogram (89.23)_

58.3 Excision or destruction of lesion or tissue of urethra

> _Excludes:_ _biopsy of urethra (58.23)_
> _excision of bulbourethral gland (58.92)_
> _fistulectomy (58.43)_
> _urethrectomy as part of:_
> _complete cystectomy (57.79)_
> _pelvic evisceration (68.8)_
> _radical cystectomy (57.71)_

58.31 Endoscopic excision or destruction of lesion or tissue of urethra
Fulguration of urethral lesion

58.39 Other local excision or destruction of lesion or tissue of urethra
Excision of:
congenital valve
lesion } of urethra
stricture
Urethrectomy

> _Excludes:_ _that by endoscopic approach (58.31)_

58.4 Repair of urethra

> _Excludes:_ _repair of current obstetric laceration (75.61)_

58.41 Suture of laceration of urethra

58.42 Closure of urethrostomy

58.43 Closure of other fistula of urethra

> _Excludes:_ _repair of urethroperineovesical fistula (57.84)_

 Valid O.R. procedure
 Non-O.R. procedure
 Nonspecific O.R. procedure
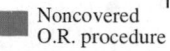 Noncovered O.R. procedure

58.44 **Reanastomosis of urethra**
Anastomosis of urethra

58.45 **Repair of hypospadias or epispadias**

58.46 **Other reconstruction of urethra**
Urethral construction

58.47 **Urethral meatoplasty**

58.49 **Other repair of urethra**
Benenenti rotation of bulbous urethra
Repair of old obstetric laceration of urethra
Urethral plication

Excludes: *repair of:*
current obstetric laceration (75.61)
urethrocele (70.50-70.51)

58.5 **Release of urethral stricture**
Cutting of urethra] sphincter
Internal urethral meatotomy
Urethrolysis

58.6 **Dilation of urethra**
Dilation of urethrovesical junction
Passage of sounds through urethra
Removal of calculus from urethra without incision

Excludes: *urethral calibration (89.29)*

58.9 **Other operations on urethra and periurethral tissue**

58.91 **Incision of periurethral tissue**
Drainage of bulbourethral gland

58.92 **Excision of periurethral tissue**

Excludes: *biopsy of periurethral tissue (58.24)*
lysis of periurethral adhesions (59.11-59.12)

58.93 **Implantation of artificial urinary sphincter [AUS]**
Placement of inflatable:
bladder sphincter
urethral sphincter
Removal with replacement of sphincter device [AUS]
With pump and/or reservoir

58.99 **Other**
Removal of inflatable urinary sphincter without replacement
Repair of inflatable sphincter pump and/or reservoir
Surgical correction of hydraulic pressure of inflatable sphincter device

Excludes: *removal of:*
intraluminal foreign body from urethra without incision (98.19)
urethral stent (97.65)

59 **Other operations on urinary tract**

59.0 **Dissection of retroperitoneal tissue**

59.00 **Retroperitoneal dissection, not otherwise specified**

59.02 **Other lysis of perirenal or periureteral adhesions**

Excludes: *that by laparoscope (59.03)*

● **59.03** **Laparoscopic lysis of perirenal or periureteral adhesions**

59.09 **Other incision of perirenal or periureteral tissue**
Exploration of perinephric area
Incision of perirenal abscess

59.1 **Incision of perivesical tissue**

▲ **59.11** **Other lysis of perivesical adhesions**

● **59.12** **Laparoscopic lysis of perivesical adhesions**

59.19 **Other incision of perivesical tissue**
Exploration of perivesical tissue
Incision of hematoma of space of Retzius
Retropubic exploration

59.2 **Diagnostic procedures on perirenal and perivesical tissue**

59.21 **Biopsy of perirenal or perivesical tissue**

● Code new
to this edition
▲ Revision of
existing code
④ ⑤ Fourth or fifth
digit required

59.29 **Other diagnostic procedures on perirenal tissue, perivesical tissue, and retroperitoneum**

> *Excludes:* *microscopic examination of specimen from:*
> *perirenal tissue (91.21-91.29)*
> *perivesical tissue (91.31-91.39)*
> *retroperitoneum NEC (91.11-91.19)*
> *retroperitoneal x-ray (88.14-88.16)*

59.3 **Plication of urethrovesical junction**
Kelly-Kennedy operation on urethra
Kelly-Stoeckel urethral plication

59.4 **Suprapubic sling operation**
Goebel-Frangenheim-Stoeckel urethrovesical suspension
Millin-Read urethrovesical suspension
Oxford operation for urinary incontinence
Urethrocystopexy by suprapubic suspension

59.5 **Retropubic urethral suspension**
Marshall-Marchetti-Krantz operation
Suture of periurethral tissue to symphysis pubis
Urethral suspension NOS

59.6 **Paraurethral suspension**
Pereyra paraurethral suspension
Periurethral suspension

59.7 **Other repair of urinary stress incontinence**

59.71 **Levator muscle operation for urethrovesical suspension**
Cystourethropexy with levator muscle sling
Gracilis muscle transplant for urethrovesical suspension
Pubococcygeal sling

59.72 **Injection of implant into urethra and/or bladder neck**
Collagen implant
Endoscopic injection of implant
Fat implant
Polytef implant

59.79 **Other**
Anterior urethropexy
Augmentation urethroplasty
Repair of stress incontinence NOS
Tudor "rabbit ear" urethropexy

59.8 **Ureteral catheterization**
Drainage of kidney by catheter
Insertion of ureteral stent
Ureterovesical orifice dilation

> *Code also any synchronous ureterotomy (56.2)*

> *Excludes:* *that for:*
> *retrograde pyelogram (87.74)*
> *transurethral removal of calculus or clot from ureter and renal pelvis (56.0)*

59.9 **Other operations on urinary system**

> *Excludes:* *nonoperative removal of therapeutic device (97.61-97.69)*

59.91 **Excision of perirenal or perivesical tissue**

> *Excludes:* *biopsy of perirenal or perivesical tissue (59.21)*

59.92 **Other operations on perirenal or perivesical tissue**

59.93 **Replacement of ureterostomy tube**
Change of ureterostomy tube
Reinsertion of ureterostomy tube

> *Excludes:* *nonoperative removal of ureterostomy tube (97.62)*

59.94 **Replacement of cystostomy tube**

> *Excludes:* *nonoperative removal of cystostomy tube (97.63)*

59.95 **Ultrasonic fragmentation of urinary stones**
Shattered urinary stones

> *Excludes:* *percutaneous nephrostomy with fragmentation (55.04)*
> *shockwave disintegration (98.51)*

 Valid O.R. procedure

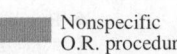 Non-O.R. procedure

Nonspecific O.R. procedure

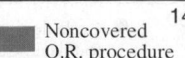 Noncovered O.R. procedure

59.99 Other

> | Excludes: | *instillation of medication into urinary tract (96.49)*
> *irrigation of urinary tract (96.45-96.48)*

● Code new
to this edition

▲ Revision of
existing code

④ ⑤ Fourth or fifth
digit required

11. OPERATIONS ON THE MALE GENITAL ORGANS (60-64)

60 Operations on prostate and seminal vesicles
Includes: operations on periprostatic tissue

> *Excludes:*   *that associated with radical cystectomy (57.71)*

60.0 Incision of prostate
Drainage of prostatic abscess
Prostatolithotomy

> *Excludes:*   *drainage of periprostatic tissue only (60.81)*

60.1 Diagnostic procedures on prostate and seminal vesicles

60.11 Closed [percutaneous] [needle] biopsy of prostate
Approach:
  transrectal
  transurethral
Punch biopsy

60.12 Open biopsy of prostate

60.13 Closed [percutaneous] biopsy of seminal vesicles
Needle biopsy of seminal vesicles

60.14 Open biopsy of seminal vesicles

60.15 Biopsy of periprostatic tissue

60.18 Other diagnostic procedures on prostate and periprostatic tissue

> *Excludes:*   *microscopic examination of specimen from prostate (91.31-91.39)*
> *x-ray of prostate (87.92)*

60.19 Other diagnostic procedures on seminal vesicles

> *Excludes:*   *microscopic examination of specimen from seminal vesicles*
> *(91.31-91.39)*
> *x-ray:*
> *contrast seminal vesiculogram (87.91)*
> *other (87.92)*

60.2 Transurethral prostatectomy

> *Excludes:*   *local excision of lesion of prostate (60.61)*

60.21 Transurethral (ultrasound) guided laser induced prostatectomy (TULIP)
Ablation (contact) (noncontact) by laser

60.29 Other transurethral prostatectomy
Excision of median bar by transurethral approach
Transurethral electrovaporization of prostate (TEVAP)
Transurethral enucleative procedure
Transurethral prostatectomy NOS
Transurethral resection of prostate (TURP)

60.3 Suprapubic prostatectomy
Transvesical prostatectomy

> *Excludes:*   *local excision of lesion of prostate (60.61)*
> *radical prostatectomy (60.5)*

60.4 Retropubic prostatectomy

> *Excludes:*   *local excision of lesion of prostate (60.61)*
> *radical prostatectomy (60.5)*

60.5 Radical prostatectomy
Prostatovesiculectomy
Radical prostatectomy by any approach

> *Excludes:*   *cystoprostatectomy (57.71)*

60.6 Other prostatectomy

60.61 Local excision of lesion of prostate
Excision of prostatic lesion by any approach

> *Excludes:*   *biopsy of prostate (60.11-60 12)*

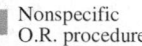

| | Valid O.R. procedure | | Non-O.R. procedure | | Nonspecific O.R. procedure | | Noncovered O.R. procedure |

60.62 **Perineal prostatectomy**
Cryoablation of prostate
Cryoprostatectomy
Cryosurgery of prostate
Radical cryosurgical ablation of prostate (RCSA)

Excludes: local excision of lesion of prostate (60.61)

60.69 **Other**

60.7 **Operations on seminal vesicles**

60.71 **Percutaneous aspiration of seminal vesicle**

Excludes: needle biopsy of seminal vesicle (60.13)

60.72 **Incision of seminal vesicle**

60.73 **Excision of seminal vesicle**
Excision of Mullerian duct cyst
Spermatocystectomy

Excludes: biopsy of seminal vesicle (60.13-60.14)
prostatovesiculectomy (60.5)

60.79 **Other operations on seminal vesicles**

60.8 **Incision or excision of periprostatic tissue**

60.81 **Incision of periprostatic tissue**
Drainage of periprostatic abscess

60.82 **Excision of periprostatic tissue**
Excision of lesion of periprostatic tissue

Excludes: biopsy of periprostatic tissue (60.15)

60.9 **Other operations on prostate**

60.91 **Percutaneous aspiration of prostate**

Excludes: needle biopsy of prostate (60.11)

60.92 **Injection into prostate**

60.93 **Repair of prostate**

60.94 **Control of (postoperative) hemorrhage of prostate**
Coagulation of prostatic bed
Cystoscopy for control of prostate hemorrhage

60.95 **Transurethral balloon dilation of the prostatic urethra**

60.99 **Other**

Excludes: prostatic massage (99.94)

61 **Operations on scrotum and tunica vaginalis**

61.0 **Incision and drainage of scrotum and tunica vaginalis**

Excludes: percutaneous aspiration of hydrocele (61.91)

61.1 **Diagnostic procedures on scrotum and tunica vaginalis**

61.11 **Biopsy of scrotum or tunica vaginalis**

61.19 **Other diagnostic procedures on scrotum and tunica vaginalis**

61.2 **Excision of hydrocele (of tunica vaginalis)**
Bottle repair of hydrocele of tunica vaginalis

Excludes: percutaneous aspiration of hydrocele (61.91)

61.3 **Excision or destruction of lesion or tissue of scrotum**
Fulguration of lesion ⎤
Reduction of elephantiasis ⎬ of scrotum
Partial scrotectomy ⎦

Excludes: biopsy of scrotum (61.11)
scrotal fistulectomy (61.42)

61.4 **Repair of scrotum and tunica vaginalis**

61.41 **Suture of laceration of scrotum and tunica vaginalis**

61.42 **Repair of scrotal fistula**

61.49 **Other repair of scrotum and tunica vaginalis**
Reconstruction with rotational or pedicle flaps

61.9 **Other operations on scrotum and tunica vaginalis**

● Code new
to this edition ▲ Revision of
existing code ④ ⑤ Fourth or fifth
digit required

61.91 Percutaneous aspiration of tunics vaginalis
Aspiration of hydrocele of tunica vaginalis

61.92 Excision of lesion of tunica vaginalis other than hydrocele
Excision of hematocele of tunica vaginalis

61.99 Other

> Excludes: *removal of foreign body from scrotum without incision (98.24)*

62 Operations on testes

62.0 Incision of testis

62.1 Diagnostic procedures on testes

62.11 Closed [percutaneous] [needle] biopsy of testis

62.12 Open biopsy or testis

62.19 Other diagnostic procedures on testes

62.2 Excision or destruction of testicular lesion
Excision of appendix testis
Excision of cyst of Morgagni in the male

> Excludes: *biopsy of testis (62.11-62.12)*

62.3 Unilateral orchiectomy
Orchidectomy (with epididymectomy) NOS

62.4 Bilateral orchiectomy
Male castration
Radical bilateral orchiectomy (with epididymectomy)
Code also any synchronous lymph node dissection (40.3, 40.5)

62.41 Removal of both testes at same operative episode
Bilateral orchidectomy NOS

62.42 Removal of remaining testis
Removal of solitary testis

62.5 Orchiopexy
Mobilization and replacement of testis in scrotum
Orchiopexy with detorsion of testis
Torek (-Bevan) operation (orchidopexy) (first stage) (second stage)
Transplantation to and fixation of testis in scrotum

62.6 Repair of testes

> Excludes: *reduction of torsion (63.52)*

62.61 Suture of laceration of testis

62.69 Other repair of testis
Testicular graft

62.7 Insertion of testicular prosthesis

62.9 Other operations on testis

62.91 Aspiration of testis

> Excludes: *percutaneous biopsy of testis (62.11)*

62.92 Injection of therapeutic substance into testis

62.99 Other

63 Operations on spermatic cord, epididymis, and vas deferens

63.0 Diagnostic procedures on spermatic cord, epididymis and vas deferens

63.01 Biopsy of spermatic cord, epididymis, or vas deferens

63.09 Other diagnostic procedures on spermatic cord, epididymis, and vas deferens

> Excludes: *contrast epididymogram (87.93)*
> *contrast vasogram (87.94)*
> *other x-ray of epididymis and vas deferens (87.95)*

63.1 Excision of varicocele and hydrocele of spermatic cord
High ligation of spermatic vein
Hydrocelectomy of canal of Nuck

63.2 Excision of cyst of epididymis
Spermatocelectomy

63.3 Excision of other lesion or tissue of spermatic cord and epididymis
Excision of appendix epididymis

> Excludes: *biopsy of spermatic cord or epididymis (63.01)*

 Valid O.R.
procedure

 Non-O.R.
procedure

Nonspecific
O.R. procedure

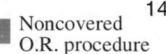 Noncovered
O.R. procedure

63.4 Epididymectomy

> Excludes: that synchronous with orchiectomy (62.3-62.42)

63.5 Repair of spermatic cord and epididymis

63.51 Suture of laceration of spermatic cord and epididymis

63.52 Reduction of torsion of testis or spermatic cord

> Excludes: that associated with orchiopexy (62.5)

63.53 Transplantation of spermatic cord

63.59 Other repair of spermatic cord and epididymis

63.6 Vasotomy

Vasostomy

63.7 Vasectomy and ligation of vas deferens

63.70 Male sterilization procedure not otherwise specified

63.71 Ligation of vas deferens

Crushing of vas deferens
Division of vas deferens

63.72 Ligation of spermatic cord

63.73 Vasectomy

63.8 Repair of vas deferens and epididymis

63.81 Suture of laceration of vas deferens and epididymis

63.82 Reconstruction of surgically divided vas deferens

63.83 Epididymovasostomy

63.84 Removal of ligature from vas deferens

63.85 Removal of valve from vas deferens

63.89 Other repair of vas deferens and epididymis

63.9 Other operations on spermatic cord, epididymis and vas deferens

63.91 Aspiration of spermatocele

63.92 Epididymotomy

63.93 Incision of spermatic cord

63.94 Lysis of adhesions of spermatic cord

63.95 Insertion of valve in vas deferens

63.99 Other

64 Operations on penis

Includes: operations on:
corpora cavernosa
glans penis
prepuce

64.0 Circumcision

64.1 Diagnostic procedures on the penis

64.11 Biopsy of penis

64.19 Other diagnostic procedures on penis

64.2 Local excision or destruction of lesion of penis

> Excludes: biopsy of penis (64.11)

64.3 Amputation of penis

64.4 Repair and plastic operation on penis

64.41 Suture of laceration of penis

64.42 Release of chordee

64.43 Construction of penis

64.44 Reconstruction of penis

64.45 Replantation of penis

Reattachment of amputated penis

64.49 Other repair of penis

> Excludes: repair of epispadias and hypospadias (58.45)

64.5 Operations for sex transformation, not otherwise classified.

● Code new to this edition	▲ Revision of existing code	④ ⑤ Fourth or fifth digit required

64.9   **Other operations on male genital organs**

   64.91   **Dorsal or lateral slit of prepuce**

   64.92   **Incision of penis**

   64.93   **Division of penile adhesions**

   64.94   **Fitting of external prosthesis of penis**
        Penile prosthesis NOS

   64.95   **insertion or replacement of non-inflatable penile prosthesis**
        Insertion of semi-rigid rod prosthesis into shaft of penis

> | *Excludes:* | *external penile prosthesis (64.94)*
> | *inflatable penile prosthesis (64.97)*
> | *plastic repair, penis (64.43-64.49)*
> | *that associated with:*
> | *construction (64.43)*
> | *reconstruction (64.44)*

   64.96   **Removal of internal prosthesis of penis**
        Removal without replacement of non-inflatable or inflatable penile prosthesis

   64.97   **Insertion or replacement or inflatable penile prosthesis**
        Insertion of cylinders into shaft of penis and placement of pump and reservoir

> | *Excludes:* | *external penile prosthesis (64.94)*
> | *non-inflatable penile prosthesis (64.95)*
> | *plastic repair, penis (64.43-64.49)*

   64.98   **Other operations on penis**
        Corpora cavernosa-corpus spongiosum shunt
        Corpora-saphenous shunt
        Irrigation of corpus cavernosum

> | *Excludes:* | *removal of foreign body:*
> | *intraluminal (98.19)*
> | *without incision (98.24)*
> | *stretching of foreskin (99.95)*

   64.99   **Other**

> | *Excludes:* | *collection of sperm for artificial insemination (99.96)*

 Valid O.R. procedure   Non-O.R. procedure   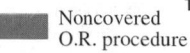 Nonspecific O.R. procedure   Noncovered O.R. procedure

● Code new
　to this edition

▲ Revision of
　existing code

④ ⑤ Fourth or fifth
　　 digit required

12. OPERATIONS ON THE FEMALE GENITAL ORGANS (65-71)

65 Operations on ovary

65.0 Oophorotomy
Salpingo-oophorotomy

- **65.01 Laparoscopic oophorotomy**
- **65.09 Other oophorotomy**

65.1 Diagnostic procedures on ovaries

65.11 Aspiration biopsy of ovary

65.12 Other biopsy of ovary

- **65.13 Laparoscopic biopsy of ovary**
- **65.14 Other laparoscopic diagnostic procedures on ovaries**

65.19 Other diagnostic procedure on ovaries

> Excludes: *microscopic examination of specimen from ovary (91.41-91-49)*

65.2 Local excision or destruction of ovarian lesion or tissue

65.21 Marsupialization of ovarian cyst

> Excludes: *that by laparoscope (65.23)*

65.22 Wedge resection of ovary

> Excludes: *that by laparoscope (65.24)*

- **65.23 Laparoscopic marsupialization of ovarian cyst**
- **65.24 Laparoscopic wedge resection of ovary**
- **65.25 Other laparoscopic local excision or destruction of ovary**

65.29 Other local excision or destruction of ovary
Bisection
Cauterization } of ovary
Partial excision

> Excludes: *biopsy of ovary (65.11-65.13)*
> *that by laparoscope (65.25)*

65.3 Unilateral oophorectomy

- **65.31 Laparoscopic unilateral oophorectomy**
- **65.39 Other unilateral oophorectomy**

> Excludes: *that by laparoscope (65.31)*

65.4 Unilateral salpingo-oophorectomy

- **65.41 Laparoscopic unilateral salpingo-oophorectomy**
- **65.49 Other unilateral salpingo-oophorectomy**

65.5 Bilateral oophorectomy

- ▲ **65.51 Other removal of both ovaries at same operative episode**
Female castration

> Excludes: *that by laparoscope (65.53)*

- ▲ **65.52 Other removal of remaining ovary**
Removal of solitary ovary

> Excludes: *that by laparoscope (65.54)*

- **65.53 Laparoscopic removal of both ovaries at same operative episode**
- **65.54 Laparoscopic removal of remaining ovary**

65.6 Bilateral salpingo-oophorectomy

- ▲ **65.61 Other removal of both ovaries and tubes at same operative episode**

> Excludes: *that by laparoscope (65.63)*

- ▲ **65.62 Other removal of remaining ovary and tube**
Removal of solitary ovary and tube

> Excludes: *that by laparoscope (65.64)*

- **65.63 Laparoscopic removal of both ovaries and tubes at same operative episode**
- **65.64 Laparoscopic removal of remaining ovary and tube**

| | Valid O.R.
procedure | | Non-O.R.
procedure | | Nonspecific
O.R. procedure | | Noncovered
O.R. procedure |

65.7   Repair of ovary
> Excludes: *salpingo-oophorostomy (66.72)*

▲ **65.71   Other simple suture of ovary**
> Excludes: *that by laparoscope (65.74)*

▲ **65.72   Other reimplantation of ovary**
> Excludes: *that by laparoscope (65.75)*

▲ **65.73   Other salpingo-oophoroplasty**
> Excludes: *that by laparoscope (65.76)*

● **65.74   Laparoscopic simple suture of ovary**

● **65.75   Laparoscopic reimplantation of ovary**

● **65.76   Laparoscopic salpingo-oophoroplasty**

65.79   Other repair of ovary
Oophoropexy

65.8   Lysis of adhesions of ovary and fallopian tube

● **65.81   Laparoscopic lysis of adhesions of ovary and fallopian tube**

● **65.89   Other lysis of adhesions of ovary and fallopian tube**
> Excludes: *that by laparoscope (65.81)*

65.9   Other operations on ovary

65.91   Aspiration of ovary
> Excludes: *aspiration biopsy of ovary (65.11)*

65.92   Transplantation of ovary
> Excludes: *reimplantation of ovary (65.72, 65.75)*

65.93   Manual rupture of ovarian cyst

65.94   Ovarian denervation

65.95   Release of torsion of ovary

65.99   Other

66   Operations on fallopian tubes

66.0   Salpingotomy and salpingostomy

66.01   Salpingotomy

66.02   Salpingostomy

66.1   Diagnostic procedures on fallopian tubes

66.11   Biopsy of fallopian tube

66.19   Other diagnostic procedures on fallopian tubes
> Excludes: *microscopic examination of specimen from fallopian tubes*
> *(91.41-91.49)*
> *radiography of fallopian tubes (87.82-87.83, 87.85)*
> *Rubin's test (66.8)*

66.2   Bilateral endoscopic destruction or occlusion of fallopian tubes
Includes: bilateral endoscopic destruction or occlusion of fallopian tubes by:
          culdoscopy
          endoscopy
          hysteroscopy
          laparoscopy
          peritoneoscopy
    endoscopic destruction of solitary fallopian tube

66.21   Bilateral endoscopic ligation and crushing of fallopian tubes

66.22   Bilateral endoscopic ligation and division of fallopian tubes

66.29   Other bilateral endoscopic destruction or occlusion of fallopian tubes

66.3   Other bilateral destruction or occlusion of fallopian tubes
Includes: destruction of solitary fallopian tube
> Excludes: *endoscopic destruction or occlusion of fallopian tubes (66.21-66.29)*

66.31   Other bilateral ligation and crushing of fallopian tubes

66.32   Other bilateral ligation and division of fallopian tubes
Pomeroy operation

● Code new   ▲ Revision of   ④ ⑤ Fourth or fifth
      to this edition   existing code   digit required

66.39 Other bilateral destruction or occlusion of fallopian tubes
Female sterilization operation NOS

66.4 Total unilateral salpingectomy

66.5 Total bilateral salpingectomy

> Excludes: bilateral partial salpingectomy for sterilization (66.39)
> that with oophorectomy (65.61-65.64)

66.51 Removal of both fallopian tubes at same operative episode

66.52 Removal of remaining fallopian tube
Removal of solitary fallopian tube

66.6 Other salpingectomy
Includes: salpingectomy by:
cauterization
coagulation
electrocoagulation
excision

> Excludes: fistulectomy (66.73)

66.61 Excision or destruction of lesion of fallopian tube

> Excludes: biopsy of fallopian tube (66.11)

66.62 Salpingectomy with removal of tubal pregnancy
Code also any synchronous oophorectomy (65.31, 65.39)

66.63 Bilateral partial salpingectomy, not otherwise specified

66.69 Other partial salpingectomy

66.7 Repair of fallopian tube

66.71 Simple suture of fallopian tube

66.72 Salpingo-oophorostomy

66.73 Salpingo-salpingostomy

66.74 Salpingo-uterostomy

66.79 Other repair of fallopian tube
Graft of fallopian tube
Reopening of divided fallopian tube
Salpingoplasty

66.8 Insufflation of fallopian tube
Insufflation of fallopian tube with:
air
dye
gas
saline
Rubin's test

> Excludes: insufflation of therapeutic agent (66.95)
> that for hysterosalpingography (87.82-87.83)

66.9 Other operations on fallopian tubes

66.91 Aspiration of fallopian tube

66.92 Unilateral destruction or occlusion of fallopian tube

> Excludes: that of solitary tube (66.21-66.39)

66.93 Implantation or replacement of prosthesis of fallopian tube

66.94 Removal of prosthesis of fallopian tube

66.95 Insufflation of therapeutic agent into fallopian tubes

66.96 Dilation of fallopian tube

66.97 Burying of fimbriae in uterine wall

66.99 Other

> Excludes: lysis of adhesions of ovary and tube (65.81, 65.89)

67 Operations on cervix

67.0 Dilation of cervical canal

> Excludes: dilation and curettage (69.01-69.09)
> that for induction of labor (73.1)

67.1 Diagnostic procedures on cervix

	Valid O.R. procedure		Non-O.R. procedure		Nonspecific O.R. procedure		Noncovered O.R. procedure

67.11 **Endocervical biopsy**

> *Excludes:* conization of cervix (67.2)

67.12 **Other cervical biopsy**
Punch biopsy of cervix NOS

> *Excludes:* conization of cervix (67.2)

67.19 **Other diagnostic procedures on cervix**

> *Excludes:* microscopic examination of specimen from cervix (91.41-91.49)

67.2 **Conization of cervix**

> *Excludes:* that by:
>> cryosurgery (67.33)
>> electrosurgery (67.32)

67.3 **Other excision or destruction of lesion or tissue of cervix**

67.31 **Marsupialization of cervical cyst**

67.32 **Destruction of lesion of cervix by cauterization**
Electroconization of cervix

67.33 **Destruction of lesion of cervix by cryosurgery**
Cryoconization of cervix

67.39 **Other excision or destruction of lesion or tissue of cervix**

> *Excludes:* biopsy of cervix (67.11-67.12)
> cervical fistulectomy (67.62)
> conization of cervix (67.2)

67.4 **Amputation of cervix**
Cervicectomy with synchronous colporrhaphy

67.5 **Repair of internal cervical os**
Cerclage of isthmus uteri
Shirodkar operation

67.6 **Other repair of cervix**

> *Excludes:* repair of current obstetric laceration (75.51)

67.61 **Suture of laceration of cervix**

67.62 **Repair of fistula of cervix**
Cervicosigmoidal fistulectomy

> *Excludes:* fistulectomy:
>> cervicovesical (57.84)
>> ureterocervical (56.84)
>> vesicocervicovaginal (57.84)

67.69 **Other repair of cervix**
Repair of old obstetric laceration of cervix

68 **Other incision and excision of uterus**

68.0 **Hysterotomy**
Hysterotomy with removal of hydatidiform mole

> *Excludes:* hysterotomy for termination of pregnancy (74.91)

68.1 **Diagnostic procedures on uterus and supporting structures**

68.11 **Digital examination of uterus**

> *Excludes:* pelvic examination, so described (89.26)
> postpartal manual exploration of uterine cavity (75.7)

68.12 **Hysteroscopy**

> *Excludes:* that with biopsy (68.16)

68.13 **Open biopsy of uterus**

> *Excludes:* closed biopsy of uterus (68.16)

68.14 **Open biopsy of uterine ligaments**

> *Excludes:* closed biopsy of uterine ligaments (68.15)

68.15 **Closed biopsy of uterine ligaments**
Endoscopic (laparoscopy) biopsy of uterine adnexa, except ovary and fallopian tube

● Code new
to this edition

▲ Revision of
existing code

④ ⑤ Fourth or fifth
digit required

68.16 Closed biopsy of uterus
Endoscopic (laparoscopy) (hysteroscopy) biopsy of uterus

Excludes: *open biopsy of uterus (68.13)*

68.19 Other diagnostic procedures on uterus and supporting structures

Excludes: *diagnostic:*
aspiration curettage (69.59)
dilation and curettage (69.09)
microscopic examination of specimen from uterus (91.41-91.49)
pelvic examination (89.26)
radioisotope scan of:
placenta (92.17)
uterus (92.19)
ultrasonography of uterus (88.78-88.79)
x-ray of uterus (87.81-87.89)

68.2 Excision or destruction of lesion or tissue of uterus

68.21 Division of endometrial synechiae
Lysis of intraluminal uterine adhesions

68.22 Incision or excision of congenital septum of uterus

● **68.23 Endometrial ablation**
Dilation and curettage
Hysteroscopic endometrial ablation

68.29 Other excision or destruction of lesion of uterus
Uterine myomectomy

Excludes: *biopsy of uterus (68.13)*
uterine fistulectomy (69.42)

68.3 Subtotal abdominal hysterectomy
Supracervical hysterectomy

68.4 Total abdominal hysterectomy
Hysterectomy:
extended
Code also any synchronous removal of tubes and ovaries (65.3-65.6)

68.5 Vaginal hysterectomy
Code also any synchronous:
removal of tubes and ovaries (65.31-65.64)
repair of cystocele or rectocele (70.50-70.52)
repair of pelvic floor (70.79)

● **68.51 Laparoscopically assisted vaginal hysterectomy (LAVH)**

● **68.59 Other vaginal hysterectomy**

Excludes: *laparoscopically assisted vaginal hysterectomy (LAVH) (68.51)*
radical vaginal hysterectomy (68.7)

68.6 Radical abdominal hysterectomy
Modified radical hysterectomy
Wertheim's operation
Code also any synchronous:
lymph gland dissection (40.3, 40.5)
removal of tubes and ovaries (65.61-65.64)

Excludes: *pelvic evisceration (68.8)*

68.7 Radical vaginal hysterectomy
Schauta operation
Code also any synchronous:
lymph gland dissection (40.3, 40.5)
removal of tubes and ovaries (65.61-65.62)

68.8 Pelvic evisceration
Removal of ovaries, tubes, uterus, vagina, bladder and urethra (with removal of sigmoid colon and rectum)
Code also any synchronous:
colostomy (46.12-46.13)
lymph gland dissection (40.3, 40.5)
urinary diversion (56.51-56.79)

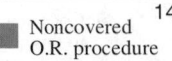

| | Valid O.R. procedure | | Non-O.R. procedure | | Nonspecific O.R. procedure | | Noncovered O.R. procedure |

68.9 **Other and unspecified hysterectomy**
Hysterectomy NOS

> Excludes: *abdominal hysterectomy, any approach (68.3, 68.4, 68.6)*
> *vaginal hysterectomy, any approach (68.51, 68.59, 68.7)*

69 **Other operations on uterus and supporting structures**

69.0 **Dilation and curettage of uterus**

> Excludes: *aspiration curettage of uterus (69.51-69.59)*

69.01 **Dilation and curettage for termination of pregnancy**

69.02 **Dilation and curettage following delivery or abortion**

69.09 **Other dilation and curettage**
Diagnostic D and C

69.1 **Excision or destruction of lesion or tissue of uterus and supporting structures**

69.19 **Other excision or destruction of uterus and supporting structures**

> Excludes: *biopsy of uterine ligament (68.14)*

69.2 **Repair of uterine supporting structures**

69.21 **Interposition operation**
Watkins procedure

69.22 **Other uterine suspension**
Hysteropexy
Manchester operation
Plication of uterine ligament

69.23 **Vaginal repair of chronic inversion of uterus**

69.29 **Other repair of uterus and supporting structures**

69.3 **Paracervical uterine denervation**

69.4 **Uterine repair**

> Excludes: *repair of current obstetric laceration (75.50-75.52)*

69.41 **Suture of laceration of uterus**

69.42 **Closure of fistula of uterus**

> Excludes: *uterovesical fistulectomy (57.84)*

69.49 **Other repair of uterus**
Repair of old obstetric laceration of uterus

69.5 **Aspiration curettage of uterus**

> Excludes: *menstrual extraction (69.6)*

69.51 **Aspiration curettage of uterus for termination of pregnancy**
Therapeutic abortion NOS

69.52 **Aspiration curettage following delivery or abortion**

69.59 **Other aspiration curettage of uterus**

69.6 **Menstrual extraction or regulation**

69.7 **Insertion of intrauterine contraceptive device**

69.9 **Other operations on uterus, cervix, and supporting structures**

> Excludes: *obstetric dilation or incision of cervix (73.1, 73.93)*

69.91 **Insertion of therapeutic device into uterus**

> Excludes: *insertion of:*
> *intrauterine contraceptive device (69.7)*
> *laminaria (69.93)*
> *obstetric insertion of bag, bougie, or pack (73.1)*

69.92 **Artificial insemination**

69.93 **Insertion of laminaria**

69.94 **Manual replacement of inverted uterus**

> Excludes: *that in immediate postpartal period (75.94)*

69.95 **Incision of cervix**

> Excludes: *that to assist delivery (73.93)*

69.96 **Removal of cerclage material from cervix**

● Code new
to this edition

▲ Revision of
existing code

④ ⑤ Fourth or fifth
digit required

69.97 Removal of other penetrating foreign body from cervix

> Excludes: removal of intraluminal foreign body
> from cervix (98.16)

69.98 Other operations on supporting structures of uterus

> Excludes: biopsy of uterine ligament (68.14)

69.99 Other operations on cervix and uterus

> Excludes: removal of:
> foreign body (98.16)
> intrauterine contraceptive device (97.71)
> obstetric bag, bougie, or pack (97.72)
> packing (97.72)

70 Operations on vagina and cul-de-sac

70.0 Culdocentesis

70.1 Incision of vagina and cul-de-sac

70.11 Hymenotomy

70.12 Culdotomy

70.13 Lysis of intraluminal adhesion of vagina

70.14 Other vaginotomy
Division of vaginal septum
Drainage of hematoma of vaginal cuff

70.2 Diagnostic procedures on vagina and cul-de-sac

70.21 Vaginoscopy

70.22 Culdoscopy

70.23 Biopsy of cul-de-sac

70.24 Vaginal biopsy

70.29 Other diagnostic procedures on vagina and cul-de-sac

70.3 Local excision or destruction of vagina and cul-de-sac

70.31 Hymenectomy

70.32 Excision or destruction of lesion of cul-de-sac
Endometrectomy of cul-de-sac

> Excludes: biopsy of cul-de-sac (70.23)

70.33 Excision or destruction of lesion of vagina

> Excludes: biopsy of vagina (70.24)
> vaginal fistulectomy (70.72-70.75)

70.4 Obliteration and total excision of vagina
Vaginectomy

> Excludes: obliteration of vaginal vault (70.8)

70.5 Repair of cystocele and rectocele

70.50 Repair of cystocele and rectocele

70.51 Repair of cystocele
Anterior colporrhaphy (with urethrocele repair)

70.52 Repair of rectocele
Posterior colporrhaphy

70.6 Vaginal construction and reconstruction

70.61 Vaginal construction

70.62 Vaginal reconstruction

70.7 Other repair of vagina

> Excludes: lysis of intraluminal adhesions (70.13)
> repair of current obstetric laceration (75.69)
> that associated with cervical amputation (67.4)

70.71 Suture of laceration of vagina

70.72 Repair of colovaginal fistula

70.73 Repair of rectovaginal fistula

70.74 Repair of other vaginoenteric fistula

 Valid O.R.
procedure

 Non-O.R.
procedure

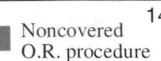 Nonspecific
O.R. procedure

Noncovered
O.R. procedure

70.75 Repair of other fistula of vagina

> Excludes: *repair of fistula:*
> *rectovesicovaginal (57.83)*
> *ureterovaginal (56.84)*
> *urethrovaginal (58.43)*
> *uterovaginal (69.42)*
> *vesicocervicovaginal (57.84)*
> *vesicosigmoidovaginal (57.83)*
> *vesicoureterovaginal (56.84)*
> *vesicovaginal (57.84)*

70.76 Hymenorrhaphy

70.77 Vaginal suspension and fixation

70.79 Other repair of vagina
Colpoperineoplasty
Repair of old obstetric laceration of vagina

70.8 Obliteration of vaginal vault
LeFort operation

70.9 Other operations on vagina and cul-de-sac

70.91 Other operations on vagina

> Excludes: *insertion of:*
> *diaphragm (96.17)*
> *mold (96.15)*
> *pack (96.14)*
> *pessary (96.18)*
> *suppository (96.49)*
> *removal of:*
> *diaphragm (97.73)*
> *foreign body (98.17)*
> *pack (97.75)*
> *pessary (97.74)*
> *replacement of:*
> *diaphragm (97.24)*
> *pack (97.26)*
> *pessary (97.25)*
> *vaginal dilation (96.16)*
> *vaginal douche (96.44)*

70.92 Other operations on cul-de-sac
Obliteration of cul-de-sac
Repair of vaginal enterocele

71 Operations on vulva and perineum

71.0 Incision of vulva and perineum

71.01 Lysis of vulvar adhesions

71.09 Other incision of vulva and perineum
Enlargement of introitus NOS

> Excludes: *removal of foreign body without*
> *incision (98.23)*

71.1 Diagnostic procedures on vulva

71.11 Biopsy of vulva

71.19 Other diagnostic procedures on vulva

71.2 Operations on Bartholin's gland

71.21 Percutaneous aspiration of Bartholin's gland (cyst)

71.22 Incision of Bartholin's gland (cyst)

71.23 Marsupialization of Bartholin's gland (cyst)

71.24 Excision or other destruction of Bartholin's gland (cyst)

71.29 Other operations on Bartholin's gland

71.3 Other local excision or destruction of vulva and perineum
Division of Skene's gland

> Excludes: *biopsy of vulva (71.11)*
> *vulvar fistulectomy (71.72)*

● Code new
to this edition

▲ Revision of
existing code

④ ⑤ Fourth or fifth
digit required

71.4 **Operations on clitoris**
Amputation of clitoris
Clitoridotomy
Female circumcision

71.5 **Radical vulvectomy**
Code also any synchronous lymph gland dissection (40.3, 40.5)

71.6 **Other vulvectomy**

71.61 **Unilateral vulvectomy**

71.62 **Bilateral vulvectomy**
Vulvectomy NOS

71.7 **Repair of vulva and perineum**
Excludes: *repair of current obstetric laceration (75.69)*

71.71 **Suture of laceration of vulva or perineum**

71.72 **Repair of fistula of vulva or perineum**
Excludes: *repair of fistula:*
urethroperineal (58.43)
urethroperineovesical (57.84)
vaginoperineal (70.75)

71.79 **Other repair of vulva and perineum**
Repair of old obstetric laceration of vulva or perineum

71.8 **Other operations on vulva**
Excludes: *removal of:*
foreign body without incision (98.23)
packing (97.75)
replacement of packing (97.26)

71.9 **Other operations on female genital organs**

 Valid O.R. procedure   Non-O.R. procedure   Nonspecific O.R. procedure   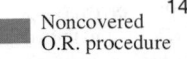 Noncovered O.R. procedure

● Code new
to this edition

▲ Revision of
existing code

④ ⑤ Fourth or fifth
digit required

13. OBSTETRICAL PROCEDURES (72-75)

72 Forceps, vacuum, and breech delivery

72.0 Low forceps operation
Outlet forceps operation

72.1 Low forceps operation with episiotomy
Outlet forceps operation with episiotomy

72.2 Mid forceps operation

72.21 Mid forceps operation with episiotomy

72.29 Other mid forceps operation

72.3 High forceps operation

72.31 High forceps operation with episiotomy

72.39 Other high forceps operation

72.4 Forceps rotation of fetal head
DeLee maneuver
Key-in-lock rotation
Kielland rotation
Scanzoni's maneuver
Code also any associated forceps extraction (72.0-72.39)

72.5 Breech extraction

72.51 Partial breech extraction with forceps to aftercoming head

72.52 Other partial breech extraction

72.53 Total breech extraction with forceps to aftercoming head

72.54 Other total breech extraction

72.6 Forceps application to aftercoming head
Piper forceps operation

Excludes:	*partial breech extraction with forceps to aftercoming head (72.51)*
	total breech extraction with forceps to aftercoming head (72.53)

72.7 Vacuum extraction
Includes: Malström's extraction

72.71 Vacuum extraction with episiotomy

72.79 Other vacuum extraction

72.8 Other specified instrumental delivery

72.9 Unspecified instrumental delivery

73 Other procedures inducing or assisting delivery

73.0 Artificial rupture of membranes

73.01 Induction of labor by artificial rupture of membranes
Surgical induction NOS

Excludes:	*artificial rupture of membranes after onset of labor (73.09)*

73.09 Other artificial rupture of membranes
Artificial rupture of membranes at time of delivery

73.1 Other surgical induction of labor
Induction by cervical dilation

Excludes:	*injection for abortion (75.0)*
	insertion of suppository for abortion (96.49)

73.2 Internal and combined version and extraction

73.21 Internal and combined version without extraction
Version NOS

73.22 Internal and combined version with extraction

73.3 Failed forceps
Application of forceps without delivery
Trial forceps

73.4 Medical induction of labor

Excludes:	*medication to augment active labor—omit code*

73.5 Manually assisted delivery

73.51 Manual rotation of fetal head

1477

 Valid O.R. procedure   Non-O.R. procedure   Nonspecific O.R. procedure   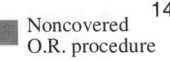 Noncovered O.R. procedure

73.59 Other manually assisted delivery
Assisted spontaneous delivery
Crede maneuver

73.6 Episiotomy
Episioproctotomy
Episiotomy with subsequent episiorrhaphy

| Excludes: | that with:
high forceps (72.31)
low forceps (72.1)
mid forceps (72.21)
outlet forceps (72.1)
vacuum extraction (72.71)

73.8 Operations on fetus to facilitate delivery
Clavicotomy on fetus
Destruction of fetus
Needling of hydrocephalic head

73.9 Other operations assisting delivery

73.91 External version

73.92 Replacement of prolapsed umbilical cord

73.93 Incision of cervix to assist delivery
Dührssen's incisions

73.94 Pubiotomy to assist delivery
Obstetrical symphysiotomy

73.99 Other

| Excludes: | dilation of cervix obstetrical, to induce labor (73.1)
insertion of bag or bougie to induce labor (73.1)
removal of cerclage material (69.96)

74 Cesarean section and removal of fetus
Code also any synchronous:
hysterectomy (68.3-68.4, 68.6, 68.8)
myomectomy (68.29)
sterilization (66.31-66.39, 66.63)

74.0 Classical cesarean section
Transperitoneal classical cesarean section

74.1 Low cervical cesarean section
Lower uterine segment cesarean section

74.2 Extraperitoneal cesarean section
Supravesical cesarean section

74.3 Removal of extratubal ectopic pregnancy
Removal of:
ectopic abdominal pregnancy
fetus from peritoneal or extraperitoneal cavity following uterine or tubal rupture

| Excludes: | that by salpingostomy (66.02)
that by salpingotomy (66.01)
that with synchronous salpingectomy (66.62)

74.4 Cesarean section of other specified type
Peritoneal exclusion cesarean section
Transperitoneal cesarean section NOS
Vaginal cesarean section

74.9 Cesarian section of unspecified type

74.91 Hysterotomy to terminate pregnancy
Therapeutic abortion by hysterotomy

74.99 Other cesarean section of unspecified type
Cesarean section NOS
Obstetrical abdominouterotomy
Obstetrical hysterotomy

● Code new
to this edition

▲ Revision of
existing code

④ ⑤ Fourth or fifth
digit required

75   Other obstetric operations

75.0   Intra-amniotic injection for abortion
Injection of:
   prostaglandin
   saline   } for induction of abortion
Termination of pregnancy by intrauterine injection

> **Excludes:** *insertion of prostaglandin suppository for abortion (96.49)*

75.1   Diagnostic amniocentesis

75.2   Intrauterine transfusion
Exchange transfusion in utero
Insertion of catheter into abdomen of fetus for transfusion
Code also any hysterotomy approach (68.0)

75.3   Other intrauterine operations on fetus and amnion
Code also any hysterotomy approach (68.0)

   75.31   Amnioscopy
   Fetoscopy
   Laparoamnioscopy

   75.32   Fetal EKG (scalp)

   75.33   Fetal blood sampling and biopsy

   75.34   Fetal monitoring not otherwise specified

   75.35   Other diagnostic procedures on fetus and amnion
   Intrauterine pressure determination

   > **Excludes:** *amniocentesis (75.1)*
   > *diagnostic procedures on gravid uterus*
   > *and placenta (87.81, 88.46, 88.78, 92.17)*

   75.36   Correction of fetal defect

75.4   Manual removal of retained placenta

> **Excludes:** *aspiration curettage (69.52)*
> *dilation and curettage (69.02)*

75.5   Repair of current obstetric laceration of uterus

   75.50   Repair of current obstetric laceration of uterus not otherwise specified

   75.51   Repair of current obstetric laceration of cervix

   75.52   Repair of current obstetric laceration of corpus uteri

75.6   Repair of other current obstetric laceration

   75.61   Repair of current obstetric laceration of bladder and urethra

   75.62   Repair of current obstetric laceration of rectum and sphincter ani

   75.69   Repair of other current obstetric laceration
   Episioperineorrhaphy
   Repair of:
      pelvic floor
      perineum
      vagina
      vulva
   Secondary repair of episiotomy

   > **Excludes:** *repair of routine episiotomy (73.6)*

75.7   Manual exploration of uterine cavity, postpartum

75.8   Obstetric tamponade of uterus or vagina

> **Excludes:** *antepartum tamponade (73.1)*

75.9   Other obstetric operations

   75.91   Evacuation of obstetrical incision hematoma of perineum
   Evacuation of hematoma of:
      episiotomy
      perineorrhaphy

   75.92   Evacuation of other hematoma of vulva or vagina

   75.93   Surgical correction of inverted uterus
   Spinelli operation

   > **Excludes:** *vaginal repair of chronic inversion of uterus (69.23)*

 Valid O.R.
procedure

 Non-O.R.
procedure

 Nonspecific
O.R. procedure

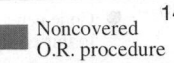 Noncovered
O.R. procedure

75.94 Manual replacement of inverted uterus

75.99 Other

● Code new
to this edition

▲ Revision of
existing code

④ ⑤ Fourth or fifth
digit required

14. OPERATIONS ON THE MUSCULOSKELETAL SYSTEM (76-84)

76 Operations on facial bones and joints

> **Excludes:** *accessory sinuses (22.00-22.9)*
> *nasal bones (21.00-21.99)*
> *skull (01.01-02.99)*

76.0 Incision of facial bone without division

76.01 Sequestrectomy of facial bone
Removal of necrotic bone chip from facial bone

76.09 Other incision of facial bone
Reopening of osteotomy site of facial bone

> **Excludes:** *osteotomy associated with orthognathic surgery (76.61-76.69)*
> *removal of internal fixation device (76.97)*

76.1 Diagnostic procedures on facial bones and joints

76.11 Biopsy of facial bone

76.19 Other diagnostic procedures on facial bones and joints

> **Excludes:** *contrast arthrogram of temporomandibular joint (87.13)*
> *other x-ray (87.11-87.12 87.14-87.16)*

76.2 Local excision or destruction of lesion of facial bone

> **Excludes:** *biopsy of facial bone (76.11)*
> *excision of odontogenic lesion (24.4)*

76.3 Partial ostectomy of facial bone

76.31 Partial mandibulectomy
Hemimandibulectomy

> **Excludes:** *that associated with temporomandibular arthroplasty (76.5)*

76.39 Partial ostectomy of other facial bone
Hemimaxillectomy (with bone graft or prosthesis)

76.4 Excision and reconstruction of facial bones

76.41 Total mandibulectomy with synchronous reconstruction

76.42 Other total mandibulectomy

76.43 Other reconstruction of mandible

> **Excludes:** *genioplasty (76.67-76.68)*
> *that with synchronous total mandibulectomy (76.41)*

76.44 Total ostectomy of other facial bone with synchronous reconstruction

76.45 Other total ostectomy of other facial bone

76.46 Other reconstruction of other facial bone

> **Excludes:** *that with synchronous total ostectomy (76.44)*

76.5 Temporomandibular arthroplasty

76.6 Other facial bone repair and orthognathic surgery

Code also any synchronous:
bone graft (76.91)
synthetic implant (76.92)

> **Excludes:** *reconstruction of facial bones (76.41-76.46)*

76.61 Closed osteoplasty [osteotomy] of mandibular ramus
Gigli saw osteotomy

76.62 Open osteoplasty [osteotomy] of mandibular ramus

76.63 Osteoplasty [osteotomy] of body of mandible

76.64 Other orthognathic surgery on mandible
Mandibular osteoplasty NOS
Segmental or subapical osteotomy

76.65 Segmental osteoplasty [osteotomy] of maxilla
Maxillary osteoplasty NOS

76.66 Total osteoplasty [osteotomy] of maxilla

76.67 Reduction genioplasty
Reduction mentoplasty

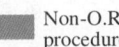 Valid O.R.
procedure

Non-O.R.
procedure

Nonspecific
O.R. procedure

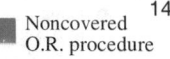 Noncovered
O.R. procedure

76.68 **Augmentation genioplasty**
Mentoplasty:
NOS
with graft or implant

76.69 **Other facial bone repair**
Osteoplasty of facial bone NOS

76.7 **Reduction of facial fracture**
Includes: internal fixation

Code also any synchronous:
bone graft (76.91)
synthetic implant (76.92)

Excludes: *that of nasal bones (21.71-21.72)*

76.70 **Reduction of facial fracture, not otherwise specified**

76.71 **Closed reduction of malar and zygomatic fracture**

76.72 **Open reduction of malar and zygomatic fracture**

76.73 **Closed reduction of maxillary fracture**

76.74 **Open reduction of maxillary fracture**

76.75 **Closed reduction of mandibular fracture**

76.76 **Open reduction of mandibular fracture**

76.77 **Open reduction of alveolar fracture**
Reduction of alveolar fracture with stabilization of teeth

76.78 **Other closed reduction of facial fracture**
Closed reduction of orbital fracture

Excludes: *nasal bone (21.71)*

76.79 **Other open reduction of facial fracture**
Open reduction of orbit rim or wall

Excludes: *nasal bone (21.72)*

76.9 **Other operations on facial bones and joints**

76.91 **Bone graft to facial bone**
Autogenous
Bone bank   } graft to facial bone
Heterogenous

76.92 **Insertion of synthetic implant in facial bone**
Alloplastic implant to facial bone

76.93 **Closed reduction of temporomandibular dislocation**

76.94 **Open reduction of temporomandibular dislocation**

76.95 **Other manipulation of temporomandibular joint**

76.96 **Injection of therapeutic substance into temporomandibular joint**

76.97 **Removal of internal fixation device from facial bone**

Excludes: *removal of:*
dental wiring (97.33)
external mandibular fixation device NEC (97.36)

76.99 **Other**

77 **Incision, excision, and division of other bones**

Excludes: *laminectomy for decompression (03.09)*
operations on:
accessory sinuses (22.00-22.9)
ear ossicles (19.0-19.55)
facial bones (76.01-76.99)
joint structures (80.00-81.99)
mastoid (19.9-20.99)
nasal bones (21.00-21.99)
skull (01.01-02.99)

● Code new
to this edition
▲ Revision of
existing code
④ ⑤ Fourth or fifth
digit required

The following fourth-digit subclassification is for use with appropriate categories in section 77, marked with a symbol to identify the site. Valid fourth-digit categories are in [brackets] under each code.

    0 unspecified site
    1 scapula, clavicle, and thorax [ribs and sternum]
    2 humerus
    3 radius and ulna
    4 carpals and metacarpals
    5 femur
    6 patella
    7 tibia and fibula
    8 tarsals and metatarsals
    9 other
        Pelvic bones
        Phalanges (of foot) (of hand)
        Vertebrae

④ **77.0** **Sequestrectomy**
[0-9]

④ **77.1** **Other incision of bone without division**
[0-9]   Reopening of osteotomy site
    | Excludes: | *aspiration of bone marrow (41.31,41.91)* |
        removal of internal fixation device (78.60-78.69)

④ **77.2** **Wedge osteotomy**
[0-9] | Excludes: | *that for hallux valgus (77.51)* |

④ **77.3** **Other division of bone**
[0-9]   Osteoarthrotomy
    | Excludes: | *clavicotomy of fetus (73.8)* |
        laminotomy or incision of vertebra (03.01-03.09)
        pubiotomy to assist delivery (73.94)
        sternotomy incidental to thoracic operation—omit code

④ **77.4** **Biopsy of bone**
[0-9]

77.5 **Excision and repair of bunion and other toe deformities**

    77.51 **Bunionectomy with soft tissue correction and osteotomy of the first metatarsal**

    77.52 **Bunionectomy with soft tissue correction and arthrodesis**

    77.53 **Other bunionectomy with soft tissue correction**

    77.54 **Excision or correction of bunionette**
        That with osteotomy

    77.56 **Repair of hammer toe**
        Fusion
        Phalangectomy (partial)   } of hammer toe
        Filleting

    77.57 **Repair of claw toe**
        Fusion
        Phalangectomy (partial)
        Capsulotomy   } of claw toe
        Tendon lengthening

    77.58 **Other excision, fusion, and repair of toes**
        Cockup toe repair
        Overlapping toe repair
        That with use of prosthetic materials

    77.59 **Other bunionectomy**
        Resection of hallux valgus joint with insertion of prosthesis

④ **77.6** **Local excision of lesion or tissue of bone**
[0-9] | Excludes: | *biopsy of bone (77.40-77.49)* |
        debridement of compound fracture (79.60-79.69)

④ **77.7** **Excision of bone for graft**
[0-9]

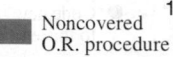

| | Valid O.R. procedure | | Non-O.R. procedure | | Nonspecific O.R. procedure | | Noncovered O.R. procedure |

④ **77.8** **Other partial ostectomy**
[0-9]   Condylectomy

Excludes:	amputation (84.00-84.19,84.91)

       arthrectomy (80.90-80.99)
       excision of bone ends associated with:
         arthrodesis (81.00-81.29)
         arthroplasty (81.51-81.59, 81.71-81.81, 81.84)
       excision of cartilage (80.5-80.6, 80.80-80.99)
       excision of head of femur with synchronous replacement (81.51-81.53)
       hemilaminectomy (03.01-03.09)
       laminectomy (03.01-03.09)
       ostectomy for hallux valgus (77.51-77.59)
       partial amputation:
         finger (84.01)
         thumb (84.02)
         toe (84.11)
       resection of ribs incidental to thoracic operation—omit code
       that incidental to other operation—omit code

④ **77.9** **Total ostectomy**
[0-9]

Excludes:	amputation of limb (84.00-84.19, 84.91)

       that incidental to other operation—omit code

78 **Other operations on bones, except facial bones**

Excludes:	operations on:

       accessory sinuses (22.00-22.9)
       facial bones (76.01-76.99)
       joint structures (80.00-81.99)
       nasal bones (21.00-21.99)
       skull (01.01-02.99)

The following fourth-digit subclassification is for use with Categories in section 78 to identify the site. Valid fourth-digit categories are in [brackets] under each code.

    0 **unspecified site**
    1 **scapula, clavicle, and thorax (ribs and sternum]**
    2 **humerus**
    3 **radius and ulna**
    4 **carpals and metacarpals**
    5 **femur**
    6 **patella**
    7 **tibia and fibulas**
    8 **tarsals and metatarsals**
    9 **other**
       Pelvic bones
       Phalanges (of foot) (of hand)
       Vertebrae

④ **78.0** **Bone graft**
[0-9]   Bone:
    bank graft
    graft (autogenous) (heterogenous)
  That with debridement of bone graft site (removal of sclerosed, fibrous, or necrotic bone or tissue)
  Transplantation of bone

  Code also any excision of bone for graft (77.70-77.79)

Excludes:	that for bone lengthening (78.30-78.39)

④ **78.1** **Application of external fixation device**
[0-9]   Minifixator with insertion of pins/wires/screws into bone

Excludes:	other immobilization, pressure, and attention to wound (93.51-93.59)

④ **78.2** **Limb shortening procedures**
[0,2-5,7-9] Epiphyseal stapling
  Open epiphysiodesis
  Percutaneous epiphysiodesis
  Resection/osteotomy

④ **78.3** **Limb lengthening procedures**
[0,2-5,7-9] Bone graft with or without internal fixation devices or osteotomy
  Distraction technique with or without corticotomy/osteotomy

  Code also any application of an external fixation device (78.10-78.19)

● Code new
    to this edition   ▲ Revision of
    existing code   ④ ⑤ Fourth or fifth
    digit required

④ **78.4** **Other repair or plastic operations on bone**
[0-9] Other operation on bone NEC
Repair of malunion or nonunion fracture NEC

> *Excludes:* *application of external fixation device (78.10-78.19)*
> *limb lengthening procedures (78.30-78.39)*
> *limb shortening procedures (78.20-78.29)*
> *osteotomy (77.3)*
> *reconstruction of thumb (82.61-82.69)*
> *repair of pectus deformity (34.74)*
> *repair with bone graft (78.00-78.09)*

④ **78.5** **Internal fixation of bone without fracture reduction**
[0-9] Internal fixation of bone (prophylactic)
Reinsertion of internal fixation device
Revision of displaced or broken fixation device

> *Excludes:* *arthroplasty and arthrodesis (81.00-81.87)*
> *bone graft (78.00-78.09)*
> *limb shortening procedures (78.20-78.29)*
> *that for fracture reduction (79.10-79.19, 79.30-79.59)*

④ **78.6** **Removal of implanted devices from bone**
[0-9] External fixator device (invasive)
Internal fixation device
Removal of bone growth stimulator (invasive)

> *Excludes:* *removal of cast, splint, and traction device (Kirschner wire) (Steinmann pin)*
> *(97.88)*
> *removal of skull tongs or halo traction device (02.95)*

④ **78.7** **Osteoclasis**
[0-9]

④ **78.8** **Diagnostic procedures on bone, not elsewhere classified**
[0-9]
> *Excludes:* *biopsy of bone (77.40-77.49)*
> *magnetic resonance imaging (88.94)*
> *microscopic examination of specimen from*
> *bone (91.51-91.59)*
> *radioisotope scan (92.14)*
> *skeletal x-ray (87.21-87.29, 87.43, 88.21-88.33)*
> *thermography (88.83)*

④ **78.9** **Insertion of bone growth stimulator**
(0-9) Insertion of:
bone stimulator (electrical) to aid bone healing
osteogenic electrodes for bone growth stimulation
totally implanted device (invasive)

> *Excludes:* *non-invasive (transcutaneous) (surface) stimulator (99.86)*

79 **Reduction of fracture and dislocation**
Includes: application of cast or splint
reduction with insertion of traction device (Kirschner wire) (Steinmann pin)

Code also any application of external fixation device (78.10-78.19)

> *Excludes:* *external fixation alone for immobilization of fracture (93.51-93.56,93.59)*
> *internal fixation without reduction of fracture (78.50-78.59)*
> *operations on:*
> *facial bones (76.70-76.79)*
> *nasal bones (21.71-21.72)*
> *orbit (76.78-76.79)*
> *skull (02.02)*
> *vertebrae (03.53)*
> *removal of cast or splint (97.88)*
> *replacement of cast or splint (97.11-97.14)*
> *traction alone for reduction of fracture (93.41-93.46)*

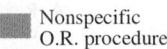 Valid O.R.
procedure

Non-O.R.
procedure

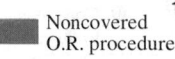 Nonspecific
O.R. procedure

Noncovered
O.R. procedure

The following fourth-digit subclassification is for use with appropriate categories in section 79, marked with a symbol to identify the site. Valid fourth-digit codes are in [brackets] under each code.

    0 unspecified site
    1 humerus
    2 radius and ulna
        Arm NOS
    3 carpals and metacarpals
        Hand NOS
    4 phalanges of hand
    5 femur
    6 tibia and fibula
        Leg NOS
    7 tarsals and metatarsals
        Foot NOS
    8 phalanges of foot
    9 other specified bone

④ **79.0** **Closed reduction of fracture without internal fixation**
[0-9] | Excludes: | that for separation of epiphysis (79.40-79.49)

④ **79.1** **Closed reduction of fracture with internal fixation**
[0-9] | Excludes: | that for separation of epiphysis (79.40-79.49)

④ **79.2** **Open reduction of fracture without internal fixation**
[0-9] | Excludes: | that for separation of epiphysis (79.50-79.59)

④ **79.3** **Open reduction of fracture with internal fixation**
[0-9] | Excludes: | that for separation of epiphysis (79.50-79.59)

④ **79.4** **Closed reduction of separated epiphysis**
[0-2,5,6,9] Reduction with or without internal fixation

④ **79.5** **Open reduction of separated epiphysis**
[0-2,5,6,9] Reduction with or without internal fixation

④ **79.6** **Debridement of open fracture site**
[0-9]   Debridement of compound fracture

79.7 **Closed reduction of dislocation**
   Includes: closed reduction (with external traction device)

   | Excludes: | closed reduction of dislocation of temporomandibular joint (76.93)

   79.70 Closed reduction of dislocation of unspecified site

   79.71 Closed reduction of dislocation of shoulder

   79.72 Closed reduction of dislocation of elbow

   79.73 Closed reduction of dislocation of wrist

   79.74 Closed reduction of dislocation of hand and finger

   79.75 Closed reduction of dislocation of hip

   79.76 Closed reduction of dislocation of knee

   79.77 Closed reduction of dislocation of ankle

   79.78 Closed reduction of dislocation of foot and toe

   79.79 Closed reduction of dislocation of other specified sites

79.8 **Open reduction of dislocation**
   Includes: open reduction (with internal and external fixation devices)

   | Excludes: | open reduction of dislocation of temporomandibular joint (76.94)

   79.80 Open reduction of dislocation of unspecified site

   79.81 Open reduction of dislocation of shoulder

   79.82 Open reduction of dislocation of elbow

   79.83 Open reduction of dislocation of wrist

   79.84 Open reduction of dislocation of hand and finger

   79.85 Open reduction of dislocation of hip

   79.86 Open reduction of dislocation of knee

   79.87 Open reduction of dislocation of ankle

   79.88 Open reduction of dislocation of foot and toe

● Code new
   to this edition

▲ Revision of
   existing code

④ ⑤ Fourth or fifth
   digit required

79.89 Open reduction or dislocation of other specified sites

④ **79.9** Unspecified operation on bone injury
[0-9]

80 **Incision and excision of joint structures**
Includes: operations on:
capsule of joint
cartilage
condyle
ligament
meniscus
synovial membrane

Excludes: *cartilage of:*
ear (18.01-18.9)
nose (21.00-21.99)
temporomandibular joint (76.01-76.99)

The following fourth-digit subclassification is for use with appropriate categories in section 80, that are marked with a symbol to identify the site:
0 unspecified site
1 shoulder
2 elbow
3 wrist
4 hand and finger
5 hip
6 knee
7 ankle
8 foot and toe
9 other specified sites
Spine

④ **80.0** **Arthrotomy for removal of prosthesis**

④ **80.1** **Other arthrotomy**
Arthrostomy

Excludes: *that for:*
arthrography (88.32)
arthroscopy (80.20-80.29)
injection of drug (81.92)
operative approach—omit code

④ **80.2** **Arthroscopy**

④ **80.3** **Biopsy of joint structure**
Aspiration biopsy

④ **80.4** **Division of joint capsule, ligament, or cartilage**
Goldner clubfoot release
Heyman-Herndon(-Strong) correction of metatarsus varus
Release of:
adherent or constrictive joint capsule
joint
ligament

Excludes: *symphysiotomy to assist delivery (73.94)*
that for:
carpal tunnel syndrome (04.43)
tarsal tunnel syndrome (04.44)

80.5 **Excision or destruction of intervertebral disc**

80.50 **Excision or destruction of intervertebral disc, unspecified**
Unspecified as to excision or destruction

Valid O.R.
procedure

Non-O.R.
procedure

Nonspecific
O.R. procedure

Noncovered
O.R. procedure

80.51 Excision of intervertebral disc
Diskectomy
Levels:
cervical
lumbar (lumbosacral)
thoracic
Removal of herniated nucleus pulposus
That by laminotomy or hemilaminectomy
That with decompression of spinal nerve root at same level
Requires additional code for any concomitant decompression of spinal nerve root at different level from excision site

Code also any concurrent spinal fusion (81.00-81.09)

Excludes: *intervertebral chemonucleolysis (80.52)*
laminectomy for exploration of intraspinal canal (03.09)
laminotomy for decompression of spinal nerve root only (03.09)

80.52 Intervertebral chemonucleolysis
Injection of proteolytic enzyme into intervertebral space (chymopapain)
With aspiration of disc fragments
With diskography

Excludes: *injection of anesthetic substance (03.91)*
injection of other substances (03.92)

80.59 Other destruction of intervertebral disc
Destruction NEC
That by laser

80.6 Excision of semilunar cartilage of knee
Excision of meniscus of knee

④ **80.7 Synovectomy**
Complete or partial resection of synovial membrane

Excludes: *excision of Baker's cyst (83.39)*

④ **80.8 Other local excision or destruction of lesion of joint**

④ **80.9 Other excision of joint**

Excludes: *cheilectomy of joint (77.80-77.89)*
excision of bone ends (77.80-77.89)

81 Repair and plastic operations on joint structures

81.0 Spinal fusion
Includes: arthrodesis of spine with:
bone graft
internal fixation

81.00 Spinal fusion, not otherwise specified

81.01 Atlas-axis spinal fusion
Craniocervical fusion
C1-C2 fusion ⎫ by anterior transoral or posterior technique
Occiput-C2 fusion ⎭

Excludes: *that for pseudoarthrosis (81.09)*

81.02 Other cervical fusion, anterior technique
Arthrodesis of C2 level or below:
anterior (interbody) technique
anterolateral technique

Excludes: *that for pseudarthrosis (81.09)*

81.03 Other cervical fusion, posterior technique
Arthrodesis of C2 level or below:
posterior (interbody) technique
posterolateral technique

Excludes: *that for pseudarthrosis (81.09)*

81.04 Dorsal and dorsolumbar fusion, anterior technique
Arthrodesis of thoracic or thoracolumbar region:
anterior (interbody) technique
anterolateral technique

Excludes: *that for pseudarthrosis (81.09)*

● Code new to this edition   ▲ Revision of existing code   ④ ⑤ Fourth or fifth digit required

81.05 Dorsal and dorsolumbar fusion, posterior technique
Arthrodesis of thoracic or thoracolumbar region:
posterior (interbody) technique
posterolateral technique

> Excludes: that for pseudarthrosis (81.09)

81.06 Lumbar and lumbosacral fusion, anterior technique
Arthrodesis of lumbar or lumbosacral region:
anterior (interbody) technique
anterolateral technique

> Excludes: that for pseudarthrosis (81.09)

81.07 Lumbar and lumbosacral fusion, lateral transverse process technique

> Excludes: that for pseudarthrosis (81.09)

81.08 Lumbar and lumbosacral fusion, posterior technique
Arthrodesis of lumbar or lumbosacral region:
posterior (interbody) technique
posterolateral technique

81.09 Refusion of spine, any level or technique
Correction of pseudarthrosis of spine

81.1 Arthrodesis of foot and ankle
Includes: arthrodesis of foot and ankle with:
bone graft
external fixation device

81.11 Ankle fusion
Tibiotalar fusion

81.12 Triple arthrodesis
Talus to calcaneus and calcaneus to cuboid and navicular

81.13 Subtalar fusion

81.14 Midtarsal fusion

81.15 Tarsometatarsal fusion

81.16 Metatarsophalangeal fusion

81.17 Other fusion of foot

81.2 Arthrodesis of other joint
Includes: arthrodesis with:
bone graft
external fixation device
excision of bone ends and compression

81.20 Arthrodesis of unspecified joint

81.21 Arthrodesis of hip

81.22 Arthrodesis of knee

81.23 Arthrodesis of shoulder

81.24 Arthrodesis of elbow

81.25 Carporadial fusion

81.26 Metacarpocarpal fusion

81.27 Metacarpophalangeal fusion

81.28 Interphalangeal fusion

81.29 Arthrodesis of other specified joints

81.4 Other repair of joint of lower extremity
Includes: arthroplasty of lower extremity with:
external traction or fixation
graft of bone chips or cartilage
internal fixation device

81.40 Repair of hip, not elsewhere classified

81.42 Five-in-one repair of knee
Medial meniscectomy, medial collateral ligament repair, vastus medialis
advancement, semitendinosus advancement, and pes anserinus transfer

81.43 Triad knee repair
Medial meniscectomy with repair of the anterior cruciate ligament and the medial
collateral ligament
O'Donoghue procedure

81.44 **Patellar stabilization**
Roux-Goldthwait operation for recurrent dislocation of patella

81.45 **Other repair of the cruciate ligaments**

81.46 **Other repair of the collateral ligaments**

81.47 **Other repair of knee**

81.49 **Other repair of ankle**

81.5 **Joint replacement of lower extremity**
Includes: arthroplasty of lower extremity with:
external traction or fixation
graft of bone (chips) or cartilage
internal fixation device or prosthesis

81.51 **Total hip replacement**
Replacement of both femoral head and acetabulum by prosthesis
Total reconstruction of hip

81.52 **Partial hip replacement**
Bipolar endoprosthesis

81.53 **Revision of hip replacement**
Partial
Total

81.54 **Total knee replacement**
Bicompartmental
Tricompartmental
Unicompartmental (hemijoint)

81.55 **Revision of knee replacement**

Excludes: arthrodesis of knee (81.22)

81.56 **Total ankle replacement**

81.57 **Replacement of joint of foot and toe**

81.59 **Revision of joint replacement of lower extremity, not elsewhere classified**

81.7 **Arthroplasty and repair of hand, fingers, and wrist**
Includes: arthroplasty of hand and finger with:
external traction or fixation
graft of bone (chips) or cartilage
internal fixation device or prosthesis

Excludes: operations on muscle, tendon, and fascia of hand (82.01-82.99)

81.71 **Arthroplasty of metacarpophalangeal and interphalangeal joint with implant**

81.72 **Arthroplasty of metacarpophalangeal and interphalangeal joint without implant**

81.73 **Total wrist replacement**

81.74 **Arthroplasty of carpocarpal or carpometacarpal joint with implant**

81.75 **Arthroplasty of carpocarpal or carpometacarpal joint without implant**

81.79 **Other repair of hand, fingers, and wrist**

81.8 **Arthroplasty and repair of shoulder and elbow**
Includes: arthroplasty of upper limb NEC with:
external traction or fixation
graft of bone (chips) or cartilage
internal fixation device or prosthesis

81.80 **Total shoulder replacement**

81.81 **Partial shoulder replacement**

81.82 **Repair of recurrent dislocation of shoulder**

81.83 **Other repair of shoulder**
Revision of arthroplasty of shoulder

81.84 **Total elbow replacement**

81.85 **Other repair of elbow**

● Code new
to this edition

▲ Revision of
existing code

④ ⑤ Fourth or fifth
digit required

81.9   Other operations on joint structures

81.91   Arthrocentesis
Joint aspiration

> *Excludes:* *that for:*
> *arthrography (88.32)*
> *biopsy of joint structure (80.30-80.39)*
> *injection of drug (81.92)*

81.92   Injection of therapeutic substance into joint or ligament

81.93   Suture of capsule or ligament of upper extremity

> *Excludes:* *that associated with arthroplasty (81.71-81.75, 81.80-81.81, 81.84)*

81.94   Suture of capsule or ligament of ankle and foot

> *Excludes:* *that associated with arthroplasty (81.56-81.59)*

81.95   Suture of capsule or ligament of other lower extremity

> *Excludes:* *that associated with arthroplasty (81.51-81.55, 81.59)*

81.96   Other repair of joint

81.97   Revision of joint replacement of upper extremity
partial
total

81.98   Other diagnostic procedures on joint structures

> *Excludes:* *arthroscopy (80.20-80.29)*
> *biopsy of joint structure (80.30-80.39)*
> *microscopic examination of specimen from joint (91.51-91.59)*
> *thermography (88.83)*
> *x-ray (87.21-87.29, 88.21-88.33)*

81.99   Other

82   Operations on muscle, tendon, and fascia of hand
Includes: operations on:
aponeurosis
synovial membrane (tendon sheath)
tendon sheath

82.0   Incision of muscle, tendon, fascia, and bursa of hand

82.01   Exploration of tendon sheath of hand
Incision of
Removal of rice bodies in   } tendon sheath of hand

> *Excludes:* *division of tendon (82.11)*

82.02   Myotomy of hand

> *Excludes:* *myotomy for division (82.19)*

82.03   Bursotomy of hand

82.04   Incision and drainage of palmar or thenar space

82.09   Other incision of soft tissue of hand

> *Excludes:* *incision of skin and subcutaneous tissue alone (86.01-86.09)*

82.1   Division of muscle, tendon, and fascia of hand

82.11   Tenotomy of hand
Division of tendon of hand

82.12   Fasciotomy of hand
Division of fascia of hand

82.19   Other division of soft tissue of hand
Division of muscle of hand

82.2   Excision of lesion of muscle, tendon, and fascia of hand

82.21   Excision of lesion of tendon sheath of hand
Ganglionectomy of tendon sheath (wrist)

82.22   Excision of lesion of muscle of hand

82.29   Excision of other lesion of soft tissue of hand

> *Excludes:* *excision of lesion of skin and subcutaneous tissue (86.21-86.3)*

| | Valid O.R. procedure | | Non-O.R. procedure | | Nonspecific O.R. procedure | | Bilateral procedure |

82.3   Other excision of soft tissue of hand
Code also any skin graft (86.61-86.62, 86.73)

Excludes: *excision of skin and subcutaneous tissue (86.21-86.3)*

82.31 Bursectomy of hand

82.32 Excision of tendon of hand for graft

82.33 Other tenonectomy of hand
Tenosynovectomy of hand

Excludes: *excision of lesion of:*
            tendon (82.29)
            sheath (82.21)

82.34 Excision of muscle or fascia of hand for graft

82.35 Other fasciectomy of hand
Release of Dupuytren's contracture

Excludes: *excision of lesion of fascia (82.29)*

82.36 Other myectomy of hand

Excludes: *excision of lesion of muscle (82.22)*

82.39 Other excision of soft tissue of hand

Excludes: *excision of skin (86.21-86.3)*
            excision of soft tissue lesion (82.29)

82.4   Suture of muscle, tendon, and fascia of hand

82.41 Suture of tendon sheath of hand

82.42 Delayed suture of flexor tendon of hand

82.43 Delayed suture of other tendon of hand

82.44 Other suture of flexor tendon of hand

Excludes: *delayed suture of flexor tendon of hand (82.42)*

82.45 Other suture of other tendon of hand

Excludes: *delayed suture of other tendon of hand (82.43)*

82.46 Suture of muscle or fascia of hand

82.5   Transplantation of muscle and tendon of hand

82.51 Advancement of tendon of hand

82.52 Recession of tendon of hand

82.53 Reattachment of tendon of hand

82.54 Reattachment of muscle of hand

82.55 Other change in hand muscle or tendon length

82.56 Other hand tendon transfer or transplantation

Excludes: *pollicization of thumb (82.61)*
            transfer of finger, except thumb (82.81)

82.57 Other hand tendon transposition

82.58 Other hand muscle transfer or transplantation

82.59 Other hand muscle transposition

82.6   Reconstruction of thumb
Includes: digital transfer to act as thumb
Code also any amputation for digital transfer (84.01, 84.11)

82.61 Pollicization operation carrying over nerves and blood supply

82.69 Other reconstruction of thumb
"Cocked-hat" procedure [skin flap and bone]
Grafts:
  bone
  skin (pedicle)   } to thumb

82.7   Plastic operation on hand with graft or implant

82.71 Tendon pulley reconstruction
Reconstruction for opponensplasty

82.72 Plastic operation on hand with graft of muscle or fascia

● Code new
  to this edition
▲ Revision of
  existing code
④ ⑤ Fourth or fifth
    digit required

82.79 **Plastic operation on hand with other graft or implant**
Tendon graft to hand

82.8 **Other plastic operations on hand**

82.81 **Transfer of finger, except thumb**
Excludes: *pollicization of thumb (82.61)*

82.82 **Repair of cleft hand**

82.83 **Repair of macrodactyly**

82.84 **Repair of mallet finger**

82.85 **Other tenodesis of hand**
Tendon fixation of hand NOS

82.86 **Other tenoplasty of hand**
Myotenoplasty of hand

82.89 **Other plastic operations on hand**
Plication of fascia
Repair of fascial hernia
Excludes: *that with graft or implant (82.71-82.79)*

82.9 **Other operations on muscle, tendon, and fascia of hand**
Excludes: *diagnostic procedures on soft tissue of hand (83.21-83.29)*

82.91 **Lysis of adhesions of hand**
Freeing of adhesions of fascia, muscle, and tendon of hand
Excludes: *decompression of carpal tunnel (04.43)*
that by stretching or manipulation only (93.26)

82.92 **Aspiration of bursa of hand**

82.93 **Aspiration of other soft tissue of hand**
Excludes: *skin and subcutaneous tissue (86.01)*

82.94 **Injection of therapeutic substance into bursa of hand**

82.95 **Injection of therapeutic substance into tendon of hand**

82.96 **Other injection of locally-acting therapeutic substance into soft tissue of hand**
Excludes: *subcutaneous or intramuscular injection (99.11-99.29)*

82.99 **Other operations on muscle, tendon, and fascia of hand**

83 **Operations on muscle, tendon, fascia, and bursa, except hand**
Includes: operations on:
aponeurosis
synovial membrane of bursa and tendon sheaths
tendon sheaths

Excludes: *diaphragm (34.81-34.89)*
hand (82.01-82.99)
muscles of eye (15.01-15.9).

83.0 **Incision of muscle, tendon, fascia, and bursa**

83.01 **Exploration of tendon sheath**
Incision of tendon sheath
Removal of rice bodies from tendon sheath

83.02 **Myotomy**
Excludes: *cricopharyngeal myotomy (29.31)*

83.03 **Bursotomy**
Removal of calcareous deposit of bursa
Excludes: *aspiration of bursa (percutaneous) (83.94)*

83.09 **Other incision of soft tissue**
Incision of fascia
Excludes: *incision of skin and subcutaneous tissue alone (86.01-86.09)*

83.1 **Division of muscle, tendon, and fascia**

83.11 **Achillotenotomy**

83.12 **Adductor tenotomy of hip**

 Valid O.R.
procedure

 Non-O.R.
procedure

 Nonspecific
O.R. procedure

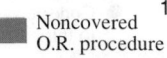 Noncovered
O.R. procedure

83.13 **Other tenotomy**
Aponeurotomy
Division of tendon
Tendon release
Tendon transection
Tenotomy for thoracic outlet decompression

83.14 **Fasciotomy**
Division of fascia
Division of iliotibial band
Fascia stripping
Release of Volkmann's contracture by fasciotomy

83.19 **Other division of soft tissue**
Division of muscle
Muscle release
Myotomy for thoracic outlet decompression
Myotomy with division
Scalenotomy
Transection of muscle

83.2 **Diagnostic procedures on muscle, tendon, fascia, and bursa, including that of hand**

83.21 **Biopsy of soft tissue**

Excludes: *biopsy of chest wall (34.23)*
biopsy of skin and subcutaneous tissue (86.11)

83.29 **Other diagnostic procedures on muscle, tendon, fascia, and bursa, including that of hand**

Excludes: *microscopic examination of specimen (91.51-91.59)*
soft tissue x-ray (87.09, 87.38-87.39, 88.09, 88.35, 88.37)
thermography of muscle (88.84)

83.3 **Excision of lesion of muscle, tendon, fascia, and bursa**

Excludes: *biopsy of soft tissue (83.21)*

83.31 **Excision of lesion of tendon sheath**
Excision of ganglion of tendon sheath, except of hand

83.32 **Excision of lesion of muscle**
Excision of:
heterotopic bone
muscle scar for release of Volkmann's contracture
myositis ossificans

83.39 **Excision of lesion of other soft tissue**
Excision of Baker's cyst

Excludes: *bursectomy (83.5)*
excision of lesion of skin and subcutaneous tissue (86.3)
synovectomy (80.70-80.79)

83.4 **Other excision of muscle, tendon, and fascia**

83.41 **Excision of tendon for graft**

83.42 **Other tenonectomy**
Excision of:
aponeurosis
tendon sheath
Tenosynovectomy

83.43 **Excision of muscle or fascia for graft**

83.44 **Other fasciectomy**

83.45 **Other myectomy**
Debridement of muscle NOS
Scalenectomy

83.49 **Other excision of soft tissue**

83.5 **Bursectomy**

83.6 **Suture of muscle, tendon, and fascia**

83.61 **Suture of tendon sheath**

83.62 **Delayed suture of tendon**

83.63 **Rotator cuff repair**

● Code new
to this edition
▲ Revision of
existing code
④ ⑤ Fourth or fifth
digit required

83.64 **Other suture of tendon**
Achillorrhaphy
Aponeurorrhaphy
Excludes: *delayed suture of tendon (83.62)*

83.65 **Other suture of muscle or fascia**
Repair of diastasis recti

83.7 **Reconstruction of muscle and tendon**
Excludes: *reconstruction of muscle and tendon associated with arthroplasty*

83.71 **Advancement of tendon**

83.72 **Recession of tendon**

83.73 **Reattachment of tendon**

83.74 **Reattachment of muscle**

83.75 **Tendon transfer or transplantation**

83.76 **Other tendon transposition**

83.77 **Muscle transfer or transplantation**
Release of Volkmann's contracture by muscle transplantation

83.79 **Other muscle transposition**

83.8 **Other plastic operations on muscle, tendon, and fascia**
Excludes: *plastic operations on muscle, tendon, and fascia associated with arthroplasty*

83.81 **Tendon graft**

83.82 **Graft of muscle or fascia**

83.83 **Tendon pulley reconstruction**

83.84 **Release of clubfoot, not elsewhere classified**
Evans operation on clubfoot

83.85 **Other change in muscle or tendon length**
Hamstring lengthening
Heel cord shortening
Plastic achillotenotomy
Tendon plication

83.86 **Quadricepsplasty**

83.87 **Other plastic operations on muscle**
Musculoplasty
Myoplasty

83.88 **Other plastic operations on tendon**
Myotenoplasty
Tendon fixation
Tenodesis
Tenoplasty

83.89 **Other plastic operations on fascia**
Fascia lengthening
Fascioplasty
Plication of fascia

83.9 **Other operations on muscle, tendon, fascia, and bursa**
Excludes: *nonoperative:*
manipulation (93.25-93.29)
stretching (93.27-93.29)

83.91 **Lysis of adhesions of muscle, tendon, fascia, and bursa**
Excludes: *that for tarsal tunnel syndrome (04.44)*

83.92 **Insertion or replacement of skeletal muscle stimulator**

83.93 **Removal of skeletal muscle stimulator**

83.94 **Aspiration of bursa**

83.95 **Aspiration of other soft tissue**
Excludes: *that of skin and subcutaneous tissue (86.01)*

83.96 **Injection of therapeutic substance into bursa**

83.97 **Injection of therapeutic substance into tendon**

	Valid O.R. procedure		Non-O.R. procedure		Nonspecific O.R. procedure		Noncovered O.R. procedure

83.98 **Injection of locally-acting therapeutic substance into other soft tissue**

> *Excludes:* *subcutaneous or intramuscular injection (99.11-99.29)*

83.99 **Other operations on muscle, tendon, fascia and bursa**
Suture of bursa

84 **Other procedures on musculoskeletal system**

84.0 **Amputation of upper limb**

> *Excludes:* *revision of amputation stump (84.3)*

84.00 **Upper limb amputation, not otherwise specified**
Closed flap amputation ⎤
Kineplastic amputation ⎥
Open or guillotine ⎥ of upper limb NOS
  amputation ⎥
Revision of current ⎥
  traumatic amputation ⎦

84.01 **Amputation and disarticulation of finger**

> *Excludes:* *ligation of supernumerary finger (86.26)*

84.02 **Amputation and disarticulation of thumb**

84.03 **Amputation through hand**
Amputation through carpals

84.04 **Disarticulation of wrist**

84.05 **Amputation through forearm**
Forearm amputation

84.06 **Disarticulation of elbow**

84.07 **Amputation through humerus**
Upper arm amputation

84.08 **Disarticulation of shoulder**

84.09 **Interthoracoscapular amputation**
Forequarter amputation

84.1 **Amputation of lower limb**

> *Excludes:* *revision of amputation stump (84.3)*

84.10 **Lower limb amputation, not otherwise specified**
Closed flap amputation ⎤
Kineplastic amputation ⎥
Open or guillotine ⎥ of lower limb NOS
  amputation ⎥
Revision of current ⎥
  traumatic amputation ⎦

84.11 **Amputation of toe**
Amputation through metatarsophalangeal joint
Disarticulation of toe

> *Excludes:* *ligation of supernumerary toe (86.26)*

84.12 **Amputation through foot**
Amputation of forefoot
Amputation through middle of foot
Chopart's amputation
Midtarsal amputation
Transmetatarsal amputation

84.13 **Disarticulation of ankle**

84.14 **Amputation of ankle through malleoli of tibia and fibula**

84.15 **Other amputation below knee**
Amputation of leg through tibia and fibula NOS

84.16 **Disarticulation of knee**
Batch, Spitler, and McFaddin amputation
Mazet amputation
S.P. Roger's amputation

● Code new
  to this edition

▲ Revision of
  existing code

④ ⑤ Fourth or fifth
   digit required

84.17 **Amputation above knee**
Amputation of leg through femur
Amputation of thigh
Conversion of below-knee amputation into above-knee amputation
Supracondylar above-knee amputation

84.18 **Disarticulation of hip**

84.19 **Abdominopelvic amputation**
Hemipelvectomy
Hindquarter amputation

84.2 **Reattachment of extremity**

84.21 **Thumb reattachment**

84.22 **Finger reattachment**

84.23 **Forearm, wrist, or hand reattachment**

84.24 **Upper arm reattachment**
Reattachment or arm NOS

84.25 **Toe reattachment**

84.26 **Foot reattachment**

84.27 **Lower leg or ankle reattachment**
Reattachment of leg NOS

84.28 **Thigh reattachment**

84.29 **Other reattachment**

84.3 **Revision of amputation stump**
Reamputation ⎫
Secondary closure ⎬ of stump
Trimming ⎭

> **Excludes:** *revision of current traumatic amputation [revision by further amputation of current injury] (84.00-84.19, 84.91)*

84.4 **Implantation or fitting of prosthetic limb device**

84.40 **Implantation or fitting of prosthetic limb device not otherwise specified**

84.41 **Fitting of prosthesis of upper arm and shoulder**

84.42 **Fitting of prosthesis of lower arm and hand**

84.43 **Fitting of prosthesis of arm, not otherwise specified**

84.44 **Implantation of prosthetic device of arm**

84.45 **Fitting of prosthesis above knee**

84.46 **Fitting of prosthesis below knee**

84.47 **Fitting of prosthesis of leg, not otherwise specified**

84.48 **Implantation of prosthetic device of leg**

84.9 **Other operations on musculoskeletal system**

> **Excludes:** *nonoperative manipulation (93.25-93.29)*

84.91 **Amputation, not otherwise specified**

84.92 **Separation of equal conjoined twins**

84.93 **Separation of unequal conjoined twins**
Separation of conjoined twins NOS

84.99 **Other**

 Valid O.R. procedure

 Non-O.R. procedure

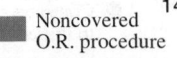 Nonspecific O.R. procedure

Noncovered O.R. procedure

● Code new
   to this edition
▲ Revision of
   existing code
④ ⑤ Fourth or fifth
   digit required

15. OPERATIONS ON THE INTEGUMENTARY SYSTEM (85-86)

85 **Operations on the breast**

Includes: operations on the skin and subcutaneous tissue of:
breast
previous mastectomy site } female or male
revision of previous mastectomy site

85.0 **Mastotomy**
Incision of breast (skin)
Mammotomy

Excludes: *aspiration of breast (85.91)*
removal of implant (85.94)

85.1 **Diagnostic procedures on breast**

85.11 **Closed [percutaneous] [needle] biopsy of breast**

85.12 **Open biopsy of breast**

85.19 **Other diagnostic procedures on breast**

Excludes: *mammary ductogram (87.35)*
mammography NEC (87.37)
manual examination (89.36)
microscopic examination of specimen (91.61-91.69)
thermography (88.85)
ultrasonography (88.73)
xerography (87.36)

85.2 **Excision or destruction of breast tissue**

Excludes: *mastectomy (85.41-85.48)*
reduction mammoplasty (85.31-85.32)

85.20 **Excision or destruction of breast tissue, not otherwise specified**

85.21 **Local excision of lesion of breast**
Lumpectomy
Removal of area of fibrosis from breast

Excludes: *biopsy of breast (85.11-8.5.12)*

85.22 **Resection of quadrant of breast**

85.23 **Subtotal mastectomy**

Excludes: *quadrant resection (85.22)*

85.24 **Excision of ectopic breast tissue**
Excision of accessory nipple

85.25 **Excision of nipple**

Excludes: *excision of accessory nipple (85.24)*

85.3 **Reduction mammoplasty and subcutaneous mammectomy**

85.31 **Unilateral reduction mammoplasty**
Unilateral:
amputative mammoplasty
size reduction mammoplasty

85.32 **Bilateral reduction mammoplasty**
Amputative mammoplasty
Reduction mammoplasty (for gynecomastia)

85.33 **Unilateral subcutaneous mammectomy with synchronous implant**

Excludes: *that without synchronous implant (85.34)*

85.34 **Other unilateral subcutaneous mammectomy**
Removal of breast tissue with preservation of skin and nipple
Subcutaneous mammectomy NOS

85.35 **Bilateral subcutaneous mammectomy with synchronous implant**

Excludes: *that without synchronous implant (85.36)*

85.36 **Other bilateral subcutaneous mammectomy**

Valid O.R. procedure   Non-O.R. procedure   Nonspecific O.R. procedure   Noncovered O.R. procedure

85.4   Mastectomy

85.41   **Unilateral simple mastectomy**
Mastectomy:
NOS
complete

85.42   **Bilateral simple mastectomy**
Bilateral complete mastectomy

85.43   **Unilateral extended simple mastectomy**
Extended simple mastectomy NOS
Modified radical mastectomy
Simple mastectomy with excision of regional lymph nodes

85.44   **Bilateral extended simple mastectomy**

85.45   **Unilateral radical mastectomy**
Excision of breast, pectoral muscles, and regional
   lymph nodes [axillary, clavicular, supraclavicular]
Radical mastectomy NOS

85.46   **Bilateral radical mastectomy**

85.47   **Unilateral extended radical mastectomy**
Excision of breast, muscles, and lymph nodes [axillary, clavicular, supraclavicular,
   internal mammary, and mediastinal]
Extended radical mastectomy NOS

85.48   **Bilateral extended radical mastectomy**

85.5   Augmentation mammoplasty

> Excludes: *that associated with subcutaneous mammectomy (85.33, 85.35)*

85.50   **Augmentation mammoplasty, not otherwise specified**

85.51   **Unilateral injection into breast for augmentation**

85.52   **Bilateral injection into breast for augmentation**
Injection into breast for augmentation NOS

85.53   **Unilateral breast implant**

85.54   **Bilateral breast implant**
Breast implant NOS

85.6   Mastopexy

85.7   Total reconstruction of breast

85.8   Other repair and plastic operations on breast

> Excludes: *that for:*
> *augmentation (85.50-85.54)*
> *reconstruction (85.7)*
> *reduction (85.31-85.32)*

85.81   **Suture of laceration of breast**

85.82   **Split-thickness graft to breast**

85.83   **Full-thickness graft to breast**

85.84   **Pedicle graft to breast**

85.85   **Muscle flap graft to breast**

85.86   **Transposition of nipple**

85.87   **Other repair or reconstruction of nipple**

85.89   **Other mammoplasty**

85.9   Other operations on the breast

85.91   **Aspiration of breast**

> Excludes: *percutaneous biopsy of breast (85.11)*

85.92   **Injection of therapeutic agent into breast**

> Excludes: *that for augmentation of breast (85.51-85.52)*

85.93   **Revision of implant of breast**

85.94   **Removal of implant of breast**

85.95   **Insertion of breast tissue expander**
Insertion (soft tissue) of tissue expander (one or more) under muscle or platysma to
   develop skin flaps for donor use

85.96   **Removal of breast tissue expander(s)**

● Code new
   to this edition   ▲ Revision of
   existing code   ④ ⑤ Fourth or fifth
   digit required

85.99 Other

86 **Operations on skin and subcutaneous tissue**

Includes: operations on:
- hair follicles
- male perineum
- nails
- sebaceous glands
- subcutaneous fat pads
- sudoriferous glands
- superficial fossae

Excludes: *those on skin of:*
- *anus (49.01-49.99)*
- *breast (mastectomy site) (85.0-85.99)*
- *ear (18.01-18.9)*
- *eyebrow (08.01-08.99)*
- *eyelid (08.01-08.99)*
- *female perineum (71.01-71.9)*
- *lips (27.0-27.99)*
- *nose (21.00-21.99)*
- *penis (64.0-64.99)*
- *scrotum (61.0-61.99)*
- *vulva (71.01-71.9)*

86.0 **Incision of skin and subcutaneous tissue**

86.01 **Aspiration of skin and subcutaneous tissue**

Aspiration of:
- abscess
- hematoma   } of nail, skin, or subcutaneous tissue
- seroma

86.02 **Injection or tattooing of skin lesion or defect**

- Injection
- Insertion   } of filling material
- Pigmenting of skin

86.03 **Incision of pilonidal sinus or cyst**

Excludes: *marsupialization (86.21)*

86.04 **Other incision with drainage of skin and subcutaneous tissue**

Excludes: *drainage of:*
- *fascial compartments of face and mouth (27.0)*
- *palmar or thenar space (82.04)*
- *pilonidal sinus or cyst (86.03)*

86.05 **Incision with removal of foreign body from skin and subcutaneous tissue**

Removal of tissue expander(s) from skin or soft tissue other than breast tissue

Excludes: *removal of foreign body without incision (98.20-98.29)*

86.06 **Insertion of totally implantable infusion pump**

Code also any associated catheterization

Excludes: *insertion of totally implantable vascular access device (86.07)*

86.07 **Insertion of totally implantable vascular access device [VAD]**

Totally implanted port

Excludes: *insertion of totally implantable infusion pump (86.06)*

86.09 **Other incision of skin and subcutaneous tissue**

Exploration:
- sinus tract, skin
- superficial fossa

Undercutting of hair follicle

Excludes: *that of fascial compartments of face and mouth (27.0)*

86.1 **Diagnostic procedures on skin and subcutaneous tissue**

86.11 **Biopsy of skin and subcutaneous tissue**

86.19 **Other diagnostic procedures on skin and subcutaneous tissue**

Excludes: *microscopic examination of specimen from skin and subcutaneous tissue (91.61-91.79)*

 Valid O.R. procedure   Non-O.R. procedure   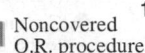 Nonspecific O.R. procedure   Noncovered O.R. procedure

86.2   Excision or destruction of lesion or tissue of skin and subcutaneous tissue

86.21 Excision of pilonidal cyst or sinus
Marsupialization of cyst

Excludes: incision of pilonidal cyst or sinus (86.03)

86.22 Excisional debridement of wound, infection, or burn
Removal by excision of:
devitalized tissue
necrosis
slough

Excludes: debridement of:
abdominal all (wound) (54.3)
bone (77.60-77.69)
muscle (83.45) of hand (82.36)
nail (bed) (fold) (86.27)
nonexcisional debridement of wound, infection, or burn (86.28)
open fracture site (79.60-79.69)
pedicle or flap graft (86.75)

86.23 Removal of nail, nailbed, or nail fold

86.24 Chemosurgery of skin
Chemical peel of skin

86.25 Dermabrasion
That with laser

Excludes: dermabrasion of wound to remove embedded debris (86.28)

86.26 Ligation of dermal appendage

Excludes: excision of preauricular appendage (18.29)

86.27 Debridement of nail, nail bed, or nail fold
Removal of:
necrosis
slough

Excludes: removal of nail, nail bed, or nail fold (86.23)

86.28 Nonexcisional debridement of wound, infection, or burn
Debridement NOS
Removal of devitalized tissue, necrosis, and slough by such methods as:
brushing
irrigation (under pressure)
scrubbing
washing

86.3   Other local excision or destruction of lesion or tissue of skin and subcutaneous tissue
Destruction of skin by:
cauterization
cryosurgery
fulguration
laser beam
That with Z-plasty

Excludes: adipectomy (86.83)
biopsy of skin (86.11)
wide or radical excision of skin (86.4)
Z-plasty without excision (86.84)

86.4   Radical excision of skin lesion
Wide excision of skin lesion involving underlying or adjacent structure
Code also any lymph node dissection (40.3-40.5)

86.5   Suture of skin and subcutaneous tissue

86.51 Replantation of scalp

86.59 Suture of skin and subcutaneous tissue of other sites

86.6   Free skin graft
Includes: excision of skin for autogenous graft

Excludes: construction or reconstruction of:
penis (64.43-64.44)
trachea (31.75)
vagina (70.61-70.62)

● Code new
to this edition   ▲ Revision of
existing code   ④ ⑤ Fourth or fifth
digit required

86.60 Free skin graft, not otherwise specified

86.61 Full-thickness skin graft to hand

> Excludes: heterograft (86.65)
> homograft (86.66)

86.62 Other skin graft to hand

> Excludes: heterograft (86.65)
> homograft (86.66)

86.63 Full-thickness skin graft to other sites

> Excludes: heterograft (86.65)
> homograft (86.66)

86.64 Hair transplant

> Excludes: hair follicle transplant to eyebrow or eyelash (08.63)

86.65 Heterograft to skin
Pigskin graft
Porcine graft

86.66 Homograft to skin
Graft to skin of:
amnionic membrane } from donor
skin

86.69 Other skin graft to other sites

> Excludes: heterograft (86.65)
> homograft (86.66)

86.7 Pedicle grafts or flaps

> Excludes: construction or reconstruction of:
> penis (64.43-64.44)
> trachea (31.75)
> vagina (70.61-70.62)

86.70 Pedicle or flap graft, not otherwise specified

86.71 Cutting and preparation of pedicle grafts or flaps
Elevation of pedicle from its bed
Flap design and raising
Partial cutting of pedicle or tube
Pedicle delay

> Excludes: pollicization or digital transfer (82.61, 82.81)
> revision of pedicle (86.75)

86.72 Advancement of pedicle graft

86.73 Attachment of pedicle or flap graft to hand

> Excludes: pollicization or digital transfer (82.61, 82.81)

86.74 Attachment of pedicle or flap graft to other sites
Attachment by: Attachment by:
advanced flap   rotating flap
double pedicled flap   sliding flop
pedicle graft   tube graft

86.75 Revision of pedicle or flap graft
Debridement } of pedicle or flap graft
Defatting

86.8 Other repair and reconstruction of skin and subcutaneous tissue

86.81 Repair for facial weakness

86.82 Facial rhytidectomy
Face lift

> Excludes: rhytidectomy of eyelid (08.86-08.87)

86.83 Size reduction plastic operation
Reduction of adipose tissue of:
abdominal wall (pendulous)
arms (batwing)
buttock
thighs (trochanteric lipomatosis)

> Excludes: breast (85.31-85.32)

Valid O.R. procedure   Non-O.R. procedure   Nonspecific O.R. procedure   Noncovered O.R. procedure

86.84 Relaxation of scar or web contracture of skin
Z-plasty of skin

> | Excludes: | Z-plasty with excision of lesion (86.3)

86.85 Correction of syndactyly

86.86 Onychoplasty

86.89 Other repair and reconstruction of skin and subcutaneous tissue

> | Excludes: | mentoplasty (76.67-76.68)

86.9 Other operations on skin and subcutaneous tissue

86.91 Excision of skin for graft
Excision of skin with closure of donor site

> | Excludes: | that with graft at same operative episode (86.60-86.69)

86.92 Electrolysis and other epilation of skin

> | Excludes: | epilation of eyelid (08.91-08.93)

86.93 Insertion of tissue expander
Insertion (subcutaneous) (soft tissue) of expander (one or more) in scalp (subgaleal space), face, neck, trunk except breast, and upper and lower extremities for development of skin flaps for donor use

> | Excludes: | flap graft preparation (86.71)
> tissue expander, breast (85.95)

86.99 Other

> | Excludes: | removal of sutures from:
> abdomen (97.83)
> head and neck (97.38)
> thorax (97.43)
> trunk NEC (97.84)
> wound catheter:
> irrigation (96.58)
> replacement (97.15)

● Code new
to this edition

▲ Revision of
existing code

④ ⑤ Fourth or fifth
digit required

16. MISCELLANEOUS DIAGNOSTIC AND THERAPEUTIC PROCEDURES (87-99)

87 Diagnostic Radiology

87.0 Soft tissue x-ray of face, head, and neck

> Excludes: angiography (88.40-88.68)

87.01 Pneumoencephalogram

87.02 Other contrast radiogram of brain and skull
Pneumocisternogram
Pneumoventriculogram
Posterior fossa myelogram

87.03 Computerized axial tomography of bead
C.A.T. scan of head

87.04 Other tomography of bead

87.05 Contrast dacryocystogram

87.06 Contrast radiogram of nasopharynx

87.07 Contrast laryngogram

87.08 Cervical lymphangiogram

87.09 Other soft tissue x-ray of face, head, and neck
Noncontrast x-ray of:
adenoid
larynx
nasolacrimal duct
nasopharynx
salivary gland
thyroid region
uvula

> Excludes: x-ray study of eye (95.14)

87.1 Other x-ray of face, head, and neck

> Excludes: angiography (88.40-88.68)

87.11 Full-mouth x-ray of teeth

87.12 Other dental x-ray
Orthodontic cephalogram or cephalometrics
Panorex examination of mandible
Root canal x-ray

87.13 Temporomandibular contrast arthrogram

87.14 Contrast radiogram of orbit

87.15 Contrast radiogram of sinus

87.16 Other x-ray of facial bones
X-ray of:
frontal area
mandible
maxilla
nasal sinuses
nose
orbit
supraorbital area
symphysis menti
zygomaticomaxillary complex

87.17 Other x-ray of skull
Lateral projection
Sagittal projection } of skull
Tangential projection

87.2 X-ray of spine

87.21 Contrast myelogram

87.22 Other x-ray of cervical spine

87.23 Other x-ray of thoracic spine

87.24 Other x-ray of lumbosacral spine
Sacrococcygeal x-ray

87.29 Other x-ray of spine
Spinal x-ray NOS

 Valid O.R. procedure

 Non-O.R. procedure

Nonspecific O.R. procedure

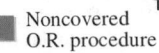 Noncovered O.R. procedure

87.3   Soft tissue x-ray of thorax

> *Excludes:* angiocardiography *(88.50-88.58)*
> angiography *(88.40-88.68)*

87.31   Endotracheal bronchogram

87.32   Other contrast bronchogram
Transcricoid bronchogram

87.33   Mediastinal pneumogram

87.34   Intrathoracic lymphangiogram

87.35   Contrast radiogram of mammary ducts

87.36   Xerography of breast

87.37   Other mammography

87.38   Sinogram of chest wall
Fistulogram of chest wall

87.39   Other soft tissue x-ray of chest wall

87.4   Other x-ray of thorax

> *Excludes:* angiocardiography *(88.50-88.58)*
> angiography *(88.40-88.68)*

87.41   Computerized axial tomography of thorax
C.A.T. scan
Crystal linea scan of x-ray
  beam
Electronic substraction   } of thorax
Photoelectric response
Tomography with use of
  computer, x-rays, and
  camera

87.42   Other tomography of thorax
Cardiac tomogram

87.43   X-ray of ribs, sternum, and clavicle
Examination for:
  cervical rib
  fracture

87.44   Routine chest x-ray, so described
X-ray of chest NOS

87.49   Other chest x-ray
X-ray of:
  bronchus NOS
  diaphragm NOS
  heart NOS
  lung NOS
  mediastinum NOS
  trachea NOS

87.5   Biliary tract x-ray

87.51   Percutaneous hepatic cholangiogram

87.52   Intravenous cholangiogram

87.53   Intraoperative cholangiogram

87.54   Other cholangiogram

87.59   Other biliary tract x-ray
Cholecystogram

87.6   Other x-ray of digestive system

87.61   Barium swallow

87.62   Upper GI series

87.63   Small bowel series

87.64   Lower GI series

87.65   Other x-ray of intestine

87.66   Contrast pancreatogram

87.69   Other digestive tract x-ray

87.7   X-ray of urinary system

> *Excludes:* angiography of renal vessels *(88.45, 88.65)*

● Code new
to this edition

▲ Revision of
existing code

④ ⑤ Fourth or fifth
digit required

87.71 Computerized axial tomography of kidney
C.A.T. scan of kidney

87.72 Other nephrotomogram

87.73 Intravenous pyelogram
Diuretic infusion pyelogram

87.74 Retrograde pyelogram

87.75 Percutaneous pyelogram

87.76 Retrograde cystourethrogram

87.77 Other cystogram

87.78 Ileal conduitogram

87.79 Other x-ray of the urinary system
KUB x-ray

87.8 X-ray of female genital organs

87.81 X-ray of gravid uterus
Intrauterine cephalometry by x-ray

87.82 Gas contrast hysterosalpingogram

87.83 Opaque dye contrast hysterosalpingogram

87.84 Percutaneous hysterogram

87.85 Other x-ray of fallopian tubes and uterus

87.89 Other x-ray of female genital organs

87.9 X-ray of male genital organs

87.91 Contrast seminal vesiculogram

87.92 Other x-ray of prostate and seminal vesicles

87.93 Contrast epididymogram

87.94 Contrast vasogram

87.95 Other x-ray of epididymis and vas deferens

87.99 Other x-ray of male genital organs

88 Other diagnostic radiology and related techniques

88.0 Soft tissue x-ray of abdomen

Excludes: *angiography (88.40-88.68)*

88.01 Computerized axial tomography of abdomen
C.A.T. scan of abdomen

Excludes: *C.A.T. scan of kidney (87.71)*

88.02 Other abdomen tomography

Excludes: *nephrotomogram (87.72)*

88.03 Sinogram of abdominal will
Fistulogram of abdominal wall

88.04 Abdominal lymphangiogram

88.09 Other soft tissue x-ray of abdominal wall

88.1 Other x-ray of abdomen

88.11 Pelvic opaque dye contrast radiography

88.12 Pelvic gas contrast radiography
Pelvic pneumoperitoneum

88.13 Other peritoneal pneumogram

88.14 Retroperitoneal fistulogram

88.15 Retroperitoneal pneumogram

88.16 Other retroperitoneal x-ray

88.19 Other x-ray of abdomen
Flat plate of abdomen

88.2 Skeletal x-ray of extremities and pelvis

Excludes: *contrast radiogram of joint (88.32)*

88.21 Skeletal x-ray of shoulder and upper arm

88.22 Skeletal x-ray of elbow and forearm

88.23 Skeletal x-ray of wrist and hand

	Valid O.R. procedure		Non-O.R. procedure		Nonspecific O.R. procedure		Noncovered O.R. procedure

88.24 Skeletal x-ray of upper limb, not otherwise specified

88.25 Pelvimetry

88.26 Other skeletal x-ray of pelvis and hip

88.27 Skeletal x-ray of thigh, knee, and lower leg

88.28 Skeletal x-ray of ankle and foot

88.29 Skeletal x-ray of lower limb, not otherwise specified

88.3 Other x-ray

88.31 Skeletal series
X-ray of whole skeleton

88.32 Contrast arthrogram

> Excludes: *that of temporomandibular joint (87.13)*

88.33 Other skeletal x-ray

> Excludes: *skeletal x-ray of:*
> *extremities and pelvis (88.21-88.29)*
> *face, head, and neck (87.11-87.17)*
> *spine (87.21-87.29)*
> *thorax (87.43)*

88.34 Lymphangiogram of upper limb

88.35 Other soft tissue x-ray of upper limb

88.36 Lymphangiogram of lower limb

88.37 Other soft tissue x-ray of lower limb

> Excludes: *femoral angiography (88.48, 88.66)*

88.38 Other computerized axial tomography
C.A.T. scan NOS

> Excludes: *C.A.T. scan of:*
> *abdomen (88.01)*
> *head (87.03)*
> *kidney (87.71)*
> *thorax (87.41)*

88.39 X-ray, other and unspecified

88.4 Arteriography using contrast material
Includes: angiography of arteries
arterial puncture for injection of contrast material
radiography of arteries (by fluoroscopy)
retrograde arteriography
Note: The fourth-digit subclassification identifies the site to be viewed, not the site of injection.

> Excludes: *arteriography using:*
> *radioisotopes or radionuclides (92.01-92.19)*
> *ultrasound (88.71-88.79)*
> *fluorescein angiography of eye (95.12)*

88.40 Arteriography using contrast material, unspecified site

88.41 Arteriography of cerebral arteries
Angiography of:
basilar artery
carotid (internal)
posterior cerebral circulation
vertebral artery

88.42 Aortography
Arteriography of aorta and aortic arch

88.43 Arteriography of pulmonary arteries

88.44 Arteriography of other intrathoracic vessels

> Excludes: *angiocardiography (88.50-88.58)*
> *arteriography of coronary arteries (88.55-88.57)*

88.45 Arteriography of renal arteries

88.46 Arteriography of placenta
Placentogram using contrast material

88.47 Arteriography of other intra-abdominal arteries

88.48 Arteriography of femoral and other lower extremity arteries

● Code new
to this edition

▲ Revision of
existing code

④ ⑤ Fourth or fifth
digit required

88.49 Arteriography of other specified sites

88.5 Angiocardiography using contrast material

Includes: arterial puncture and insertion of arterial catheter for injection of contrast
material
cineangiocardiography
selective angiocardiography

Code also synchronous cardiac catheterization (37.21-37.23)

Excludes: *angiography of pulmonary vessels (88.43, 88.62)*

88.50 Angiocardiography, not otherwise specified

88.51 Angiocardiography of venae cavae
Interior vena cavography
Phlebography of vena cava (inferior) (superior)

88.52 Angiocardiography of right heart structures
Angiocardiography of:
pulmonary valve
right atrium
right ventricle (outflow tract)

Excludes: *that combined with left heart angiocardiography (88.54)*

88.53 Angiocardiography of left heart structures
Angiocardiography of:
aortic valve
left atrium
left ventricle (outflow tract)

Excludes: *that combined with right heart angiocardiography (88.54)*

88.54 Combined right and left heart angiocardiography

88.55 Coronary arteriography using a single catheter
Coronary arteriography by Sones technique
Direct selective coronary arteriography using a single catheter

88.56 Coronary arteriography using two catheters
Coronary arteriography by:
Judkins technique
Ricketts and Abrams technique
Direct selective coronary arteriography using two catheters

88.57 Other and unspecified coronary arteriography
Coronary arteriography NOS

88.58 Negative-contrast cardiac roentgenography
Cardiac roentgenography with injection of carbon dioxide

88.6 Phlebography
Includes: angiography of veins
radiography of veins (by fluoroscopy)
retrograde phlebography
venipuncture for injection of contrast material
venography using contrast material

Note: The fourth-digit subclassification (88.60-88.67) identifies the site to be viewed, not
the site of injection.

Excludes: *angiography using:*
radioisotopes or radionuclides (92.01-92.19)
ultrasound (88.71-88.79)
fluorescein angiography of eye (95.12)

88.60 Phlebography using contrast material, unspecified site

88.61 Phlebography of veins of head and neck using contrast material

88.62 Phlebography of pulmonary veins using contrast material

88.63 Phlebography of other intrathoracic veins using contrast material

88.64 Phlebography of the portal venous system using contrast material
Splenoportogram (by splenic arteriography)

88.65 Phlebography of other intra-abdominal veins using contrast material

88.66 Phlebography of femoral and other lower extremity veins using contrast material

88.67 Phlebography of other specified sites using contrast material

88.68 Impedance phlebography

1509

| Valid O.R. | Non-O.R. | Nonspecific | Noncovered |
| procedure | procedure | O.R. procedure | O.R. procedure |

88.7 Diagnostic ultrasound
  Includes: echography
       ultrasonic angiography
       ultrasonography

  88.71 Diagnostic ultrasound of head and neck
      Determination of midline shift of brain
      Echoencephalography
      Excludes: eye (95.13)

  88.72 Diagnostic ultrasound of heart
      Echocardiography

  88.73 Diagnostic ultrasound of other sites of thorax
      Aortic arch
      Breast   } ultrasonography
      Lung

  88.74 Diagnostic ultrasound of digestive system

  88.75 Diagnostic ultrasound of urinary system

  88.76 Diagnostic ultrasound of abdomen and retroperitoneum

  88.77 Diagnostic ultrasound of peripheral vascular system
      Deep vein thrombosis ultrasonic scanning

  88.78 Diagnostic ultrasound of gravid uterus
      Intrauterine cephalometry:
        echo
        ultrasonic
      Placental localization by ultrasound

  88.79 Other diagnostic ultrasound
      Ultrasonography of:
        multiple sites
        nongravid uterus
        total body

88.8 Thermography

  88.81 Cerebral thermography

  88.82 Ocular thermography

  88.83 Bone thermography
      Osteoarticular thermography

  88.84 Muscle thermography

  88.85 Breast thermography

  88.86 Blood vessel thermography
      Deep vein thermography

  88.89 Thermography of other sites
      Lymph gland thermography
      Thermography NOS

88.9 Other diagnostic imaging

  88.90 Diagnostic imaging, not elsewhere classified

  88.91 Magnetic resonance imaging of brain and brain stem

  88.92 Magnetic resonance imaging of chest and myocardium
      For evaluation of hilar and mediastinal lymphadenopathy

  88.93 Magnetic resonance imaging of spinal canal
      Levels:
        cervical
        lumbar (lumbosacral)
        thoracic
      Spinal cord
      Spine

  88.94 Magnetic resonance imaging of musculoskeletal
      Bone marrow blood supply
      Extremities (upper) (lower)

  88.95 Magnetic resonance imaging of pelvis, prostate, and bladder

  88.97 Magnetic resonance imaging of other and unspecified sites
      abdomen   neck
      face   eye orbit

● Code new   ▲ Revision of   ④ ⑤ Fourth or fifth
    to this edition   existing code   digit required

88.98 Bone mineral density studies
Dual photon absorptiometry
Quantitative computed tomography (CT) studies
Radiographic densitometry
Single photon absorptiometry

89 Interview, evaluation, consultation, and examination

89.0 Diagnostic interview, consultation, and evaluation

> *Excludes:* psychiatric diagnostic interview (94.11-94.19)

89.01 Interview and evaluation, described as brief
Abbreviated history and evaluation

89.02 Interview and evaluation, described as limited
Interval history and evaluation

89.03 Interview and evaluation, described as comprehensive
History and evaluation of new problem

89.04 Other interview and evaluation

89.05 Diagnostic interview and evaluation, not otherwise specified

89.06 Consultation, described as limited
Consultation on a single organ system

89.07 Consultation, described as comprehensive

89.08 Other consultation

89.09 Consultation, not otherwise specified

89.1 Anatomic and physiologic measurements and manual examinations—nervous system and sense organs

> *Excludes:* ear examination (95.41-95.49)
> eye examination (95.01-95.26)
> the listed procedures when done as part of a general physical examination (89.7)

89.10 Intracarotid amobarbital test
Wada test

89.11 Tonometry

89.12 Nasal function study
Rhinomanometry

89.13 Neurologic examination

89.14 Electroencephalogram

> *Excludes:* that with polysomnogram (89.17)

89.15 Other nonoperative neurologic function tests

89.16 Transillumination of newborn skull

89.17 Polysomnogram
Sleep recording

89.18 Other sleep disorder function tests
Multiple sloop latency test [MSLT]

89.19 Video and radio-telemetered electroencephalographic monitoring
Radiographic }
Video   } EEG monitoring

89.2 Anatomic and physiologic measurements and manual examinations—genitourinary system

> *Excludes:* the listed procedures when done as part of a general physical examination (89.7)

89.21 Urinary manometry
Manometry through:
indwelling urethral catheter
nephrostomy
pyelostomy
ureterostomy

89.22 Cystometrogram

89.23 Urethral sphincter electromyogram

89.24 Uroflowmetry [UFR]

89.25 Urethral pressure profile [UPP]

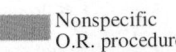 Valid O.R. procedure   Non-O.R. procedure   Nonspecific O.R. procedure   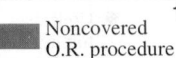 Noncovered O.R. procedure

89.26 Gynecological examination
Pelvic examination

89.29 Other nonoperative genitourinary system measurements
Bioassay of urine
Renal clearance
Urine chemistry

89.3 Other anatomic and physiologic measurements and manual examinations

> Excludes: the listed procedures when done as part of a general physical examination (89.7)

89.31 Dental examination
Oral mucosal survey
Periodontal survey

89.32 Esophageal manometry

89.33 Digital examination of enterostomy stoma
Digital examination of colostomy stoma

89.34 Digital examination of rectum

89.35 Transillumination of nasal sinuses

89.36 Manual examination of breast

89.37 Vital capacity determination

89.38 Other nonoperative respiratory measurements
Plethysmography for measurement of respiratory function
Thoracic impedance plethysmography

89.39 Other nonoperative measurements and examinations
Basal metabolic rate [BMR]
14 C-Urea breath test
Gastric:
  analysis
  function NEC

> Excludes: body measurements (93.07)
> cardiac tests (89.41-89.69)
> fundus photography (95.11)
> limb length measurement (93.06)

89.4 Cardiac stress tests and pacemaker checks

89.41 Cardiovascular stress test using treadmill

89.42 Masters' two-step stress test

89.43 Cardiovascular stress test using bicycle ergometer

89.44 Other cardiovascular stress test
Thallium stress test with or without transesophageal pacing

89.45 Artificial pacemaker rate check
Artificial pacemaker function check NOS

89.46 Artificial pacemaker artifact wave form check

89.47 Artificial pacemaker electrode impedance check

89.48 Artificial pacemaker voltage or amperage threshold check

89.5 Other nonoperative cardiac and vascular diagnostic procedures

> Excludes: fetal EKG (75.32)

89.50 Ambulatory cardiac monitoring
Analog devices [Holter-type]

89.51 Rhythm electrocardiogram
Rhythm EKG (with one to three leads)

89.52 Electrocardiogram
ECG NOS
EKG (with 12 or more leads)

89.53 Vectorcardiogram (with ECG)

89.54 Electrographic monitoring
Telemetry

> Excludes: ambulatory cardiac monitoring (89.50)
> electrographic monitoring during surgery—omit code

89.55 Phonocardiogram with ECG lead

● Code new
  to this edition
▲ Revision of
  existing code
④ ⑤ Fourth or fifth
  digit required

89.56 Carotid pulse tracing with ECG lead
> Excludes: *oculoplethysmography (89.58)*

89.57 Apexcardiogram (with ECG lead)

89.58 Plethysmogram
> Excludes: *plethysmography (for):*
> *measurement of respiratory function (89.38)*
> *thoracic impedance (89.38)*

89.59 Other nonoperative cardiac and vascular measurements

89.6 Circulatory monitoring
> Excludes: *electrocardiographic monitoring during surgery—omit code*

89.61 Systemic arterial pressure monitoring

89.62 Central venous pressure monitoring

89.63 Pulmonary artery pressure monitoring
> Excludes: *pulmonary artery wedge monitoring (89.64)*

89.64 Pulmonary artery wedge monitoring
Pulmonary capillary wedge [PCW] monitoring
Swan-Ganz catheterization

89.65 Measurement of systemic arterial blood gases

89.66 Measurement of mixed venous blood gases

89.67 Monitoring of cardiac output by oxygen consumption technique
Fick method

89.68 Monitoring of cardiac output by other technique
Cardiac output monitor by thermodilution indicator

89.69 Monitoring of coronary blood flow
Coronary blood flow monitoring by coincidence counting technique

89.7 General physical examination

89.8 Autopsy

90 Microscopic examination—I
The following fourth-digit subclassification is for use with categories in section 90 to identify type of examination:
  1 bacterial smear
  2 culture
  3 culture and sensitivity
  4 parasitology
  5 toxicology
  6 cell block and Papanicolaou smear
  9 other microscopic examination

④ **90.0 Microscopic examination of specimen from nervous system and of spinal fluid**

④ **90.1 Microscopic examination of specimen from endocrine gland, not elsewhere classified**

④ **90.2 Microscopic examination of specimen from eye**

④ **90.3 Microscopic examination of specimen from ear, nose, throat, and larynx**

④ **90.4 Microscopic examination of specimen from trachea, bronchus, pleura, lung, and other thoracic specimen, and of sputum**

④ **90.5 Microscopic examination of blood**

① **90.6 Microscopic examination of specimen from spleen and of bone marrow**

④ **90.7 Microscopic examination of specimen from lymph node and of lymph**

④ **90.8 Microscopic examination of specimen from upper gastrointestinal tract and of vomitus**

④ **90.9 Microscopic examination of specimen from lower gastrointestinal tract and of stool**

91 Microscopic examination—II
The following fourth-digit subclassification is for use with categories in section 91 to identify type of examination:
  1 bacterial smear
  2 culture
  3 culture and sensitivity
  4 parasitology
  5 toxicology
  6 cell block and Papanicolaou smear
  9 other microscopic examination

 Valid O.R. procedure   Non-O.R. procedure   Nonspecific O.R. procedure   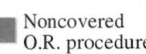 Noncovered O.R. procedure

④ **91.0** **Microscopic examination of specimen from liver, biliary trace and pancreas**

④ **91.1** **Microscopic examination of peritoneal and retroperitoneal specimen**

④ **91.2** **Microscopic examination of specimen from kidney, ureter, perirenal and periureteral tissue**

④ **91.3** **Microscopic examination of specimen from bladder, urethra, prostate, seminal vesicle, perivesical tissue, and of urine and semen**

④ **91.4** **Microscopic examination of specimen from female genital tract**
　　Amnionic sac
　　Fetus

④ **91.5** **Microscopic examination of specimen from musculoskeletal system and of joint fluid**
　　Microscopic examination of:
　　　bone　　　　　ligament
　　　bursa　　　　　muscle
　　　cartilage　　　synovial membrane
　　　fascia　　　　　tendon

④ **91.6** **Microscopic examination of specimen from skin and other integument**
　　Microscopic examination of:
　　　hair
　　　nails
　　　skin

　　| Excludes: | *mucous membrane—code to organ site that of operative wound (91.70-91.79)*

④ **91.7** **Microscopic examination of specimen from operative wound**

④ **91.8** **Microscopic examination of specimen from other site**

④ **91.9** **Microscopic examination of specimen from unspecified site**

92 **Nuclear Medicine**

　　92.0 **Radioisotope scan and function study**

　　　　92.01 **Thyroid scan and radioisotope function studies**
　　　　　　Iodine-131 uptake
　　　　　　Protein-bound iodine
　　　　　　Radio-iodine uptake

　　　　92.02 **Liver scan and radioisotope function study**

　　　　92.03 **Renal scan and radioisotope function study**
　　　　　　Renal clearance study

　　　　92.04 **Gastrointestinal scan and radioisotope function study**
　　　　　　Radio-cobalt B_{12} Schilling test
　　　　　　Radio-iodinated triolein study

　　　　92.05 **Cardiovascular and hematopoietic scan and radioisotope function study**
　　　　　　Bone marrow
　　　　　　Cardiac output
　　　　　　Circulation time　　　　　　scan or function study
　　　　　　Radionuclide cardiac
　　　　　　　　ventriculogram
　　　　　　Spleen

　　　　92.09 **Other radioisotope function studies**

　　92.1 **Other radioisotope scan**

　　　　92.11 **Cerebral scan**
　　　　　　Pituitary

　　　　92.12 **Scan of other sites of head**
　　　　　　| Excludes: | *eye (95.16)*

　　　　92.13 **Parathyroid scan**

　　　　92.14 **Bone scan**

　　　　92.15 **Pulmonary scan**

　　　　92.16 **Scan of lymphatic system**

　　　　92.17 **Placental scan**

　　　　92.18 **Total body scan**

　　　　92.19 **Stan of other sites**

　● Code new　　　　▲ Revision of　　　④ ⑤ Fourth or fifth
　　　　to this edition　　　　existing code　　　　digit required

92.2 Therapeutic radiology and nuclear medicine

> Excludes: that for:
>> ablation of pituitary gland (07.64-07.69)
>> destruction of chorioretinal lesion (14.26-14.27)

92.21 Superficial radiation
Contact radiation [up to 150 KVP]

92.22 Orthovoltage radiation
Deep radiation [200-300 KVP]

92.23 Radioisotopic teleradiotherapy
Teleradiotherapy using:
cobalt-60
iodine-125
radioactive cesium

92.24 Teleradiotherapy using photons
Megavoltage NOS
Supervoltage NOS
Use of:
Betatron
linear accelerator

92.25 Teleradiotherapy using electrons
Beta particles

92.26 Teleradiotherapy of other particulate radiation
Neutrons   Protons NOS

92.27 Implantation or insertion of radioactive elements
Code also incision of site

92.28 Injection or instillation of radioisotopes
Intracavitary
Intravenous   } injection or instillation

92.29 Other radiotherapeutic procedure

92.3 Stereotactic radiosurgery
Gamma irradiation (multisource)
Linear accelerator (single source)
Particle beam radiation (cyclotron)
Stereotactic multisource photon radiosurgery
Code also stereotactic head frame application (93.59)

93 Physical therapy, respiratory therapy, rehabilitation, and related procedures

93.0 Diagnostic physical therapy

93.01 Functional evaluation

93.02 Orthotic evaluation

93.03 Prosthetic evaluation

93.04 Manual testing of muscle function

93.05 Range of motion testing

93.06 Measurement of limb length

93.07 Body measurement
Girth measurement
Measurement of skull circumference

93.08 Electromyography

> Excludes: eye EMG (95.25)
>> that with polysomnogram (89.17)
>> urethral sphincter EMG (89.23)

93.09 Other diagnostic physical therapy procedure

93.1 Physical therapy exercises

93.11 Assisting exercise

> Excludes: assisted exercise in pool (93.31)

93.12 Other active musculoskeletal exercise

93.13 Resistive exercise

93.14 Training in joint movements

93.15 Mobilization of spine

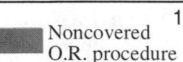

Valid O.R.
procedure

Non-O.R.
procedure

Nonspecific
O.R. procedure

Noncovered
O.R. procedure

93.16 **Mobilization of other joints**
Excludes: *manipulation of temporomandibular joint (76.95)*

93.17 **Other passive musculoskeletal exercise**

93.18 **Breathing exercise**

93.19 **Exercise, not elsewhere classified**

93.2 **Other physical therapy musculoskeletal manipulation**

93.21 **Manual and mechanical traction**
Excludes: *skeletal traction (93.43-93.44)*
skin traction (93.45-93.46)
spinal traction (93.41-93.42)

93.22 **Ambulation and pit training**

93.23 **Fitting of orthotic device**

93.24 **Training in use of prosthetic or orthotic device**
Training in crutch walking

93.25 **Forced extension of limb**

93.26 **Manual rupture of joint adhesions**

93.27 **Stretching of muscle or tendon**

93.28 **Stretching of fascia**

93.29 **Other forcible correction of deformity**

93.3 **Other physical therapy therapeutic procedures**

93.31 **Assisted exercise in pool**

93.32 **Whirlpool treatment**

93.33 **Other hydrotherapy**

93.34 **Diathermy**

93.35 **Other heat therapy**
Acupuncture with smouldering moxa
Hot packs
Hyperthermia NEC
Infrared irradiation
Moxibustion
Paraffin bath
Excludes: *hyperthermia for treatment of cancer (99.85)*

93.36 **Cardiac retraining**

93.37 **Prenatal training**
Training for natural childbirth

93.38 **Combined physical therapy without mention of the components**

93.39 **Other physical therapy**

93.4 **Skeletal traction and other traction**

93.41 **Spinal traction using skull device**
Traction using:
caliper tongs
Crutchfield tongs
halo device
Vinke tongs
Excludes: *insertion of tongs or halo traction device (02.94)*

93.42 **Other spinal traction**
Cotrel's traction
Excludes: *cervical collar (93.52)*

93.43 **Intermittent skeletal traction**

93.44 **Other skeletal traction**
Bryant's
Dunlop's } traction
Lyman Smith
Russell's

93.45 **Thomas' splint traction**

● Code new
to this edition

▲ Revision of
existing code

④ ⑤ Fourth or fifth
digit required

93.46 Other skin traction of limbs
Adhesive tape traction
Boot traction
Buck's traction
Gallows traction

93.5 Other immobilization, pressure, and attention to wound

> *Excludes:* *wound cleansing (96.58-96.59)*

93.51 Application of plaster jacket

> *Excludes:* *Minerva jacket (93.52)*

93.52 Application of neck support
Application of:
  cervical collar
  Minerva jacket
  molded neck support

93.53 Application of other cast

93.54 Application of splint
Plaster splint   Tray splint

> *Excludes:* *periodontal splint (24.7)*

93.55 Dental wiring

> *Excludes:* *that for orthodontia (24.7)*

93.56 Application of pressure dressing
Application of:
  Gibney bandage
  Robert Jones' bandage
  Shanz dressing

93.57 Application of other wound dressing

93.58 Application of pressure trousers
Application of:
  anti-shock trousers
  MAST trousers
  vasopneumatic device

93.59 Other immobilization, pressure, and attention to wound
Elastic stockings
Electronic gaiter
Intermittent pressure device
Oxygenation of wound (hyperbaric)
Stereotactic head frame application
Velpeau dressing

93.6 Osteopathic manipulative treatment

93.61 Osteopathic manipulative treatment for general mobilization
General articulatory treatment

93.62 Osteopathic manipulative treatment using high-velocity low-amplitude forces
Thrusting forces

93.63 Osteopathic manipulative treatment using low-velocity high-amplitude forces
Springing forces

93.64 Osteopathic manipulative treatment using isotonic, isometric forces

93.65 Osteopathic manipulative treatment using indirect forces

93.66 Osteopathic manipulative treatment to move tissue fluids
Lymphatic pump

93.67 Other specified osteopathic manipulative treatment

93.7 Speech and reading rehabilitation and rehabilitation of the blind

93.71 Dyslexia training

93.72 Dysphasia training

93.73 Esophageal speech training

93.74 Speech defect training

93.75 Other speech training and therapy

93.76 Training in use of lead dog for the blind

93.77 Training in braille or Moon

93.78 Other rehabilitation for the blind

 Valid O.R.
procedure
 Non-O.R.
procedure
 Nonspecific
O.R. procedure
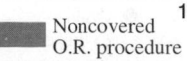 Noncovered
O.R. procedure

93.8 Other rehabilitation therapy

   93.81 Recreation therapy
      Diversional therapy
      Play therapy

      | Excludes: | *play psychotherapy (94.36)*

   93.82 Educational therapy
      Education of bed-bound children
      Special schooling for the handicapped

   93.83 Occupational therapy
      Daily living activities therapy

      | Excludes: | *training in activities of daily living for the blind (93.78)*

   93.84 Music therapy

   93.85 Vocational rehabilitation
      Sheltered employment
      Vocational:
        assessment
        retraining
        training

   93.89 Rehabilitation, not elsewhere classified

93.9 Respiratory therapy

      | Excludes: | *insertion of airway (96.01-96.05)*
                  other continuous mechanical ventilation (96.70-96.72)

   93.90 Continuous positive airway pressure [CPAP]

   93.91 Intermittent positive pressure breathing [IPPB]

   93.93 Nonmechanical methods of resuscitation
      Artificial respiration
      Manual resuscitation
      Mouth-to-mouth resuscitation

   93.94 Respiratory medication administered by nebulizer
      Mist therapy

   93.95 Hyperbaric oxygenation

      | Excludes: | *oxygenation of wound (93.59)*

   93.96 Other oxygen enrichment
      Catalytic oxygen therapy
      Cytoreductive effect
      Oxygenators
      Oxygen therapy

      | Excludes: | *oxygenation of wound (93.59)*

   93.97 Decompression chamber

   93.98 Other control of atmospheric pressure and composition
      Antigen-free air conditioning
      Helium therapy

   93.99 Other respiratory procedures
      Continuous negative pressure ventilation [CNP]
      Postural drainage

94 Procedures related to the psyche

94.0 Psychologic evaluation and testing

   94.01 Administration of intelligence test
      Administration of:
        Stanford-Binet
        Wechsler Adult Intelligence Scale
        Wechsler Intelligence Scale for Children

   94.02 Administration of psychologic test
      Administration of:
        Bender Visual - Motor Gestalt Test
        Benton Visual Retention Test
        Minnesota Multiphasic Personality Inventory
        Wechsler Memory Scale

   94.03 Character analysis

   94.08 Other psychologic evaluation and testing

● Code new   ▲ Revision of   ④ ⑤ Fourth or fifth
    to this edition   existing code   digit required

94.09 Psychologic mental status determination, not otherwise specified

94.1 Psychiatric interviews, consultations, and evaluations

94.11 Psychiatric mental status determination
Clinical psychiatric mental status determination
Evaluation for criminal responsibility
Evaluation for testimentary capacity
Medicolegal mental status determination
Mental status determination NOS

94.12 Routine psychiatric visit, not otherwise specified

94.13 Psychiatric commitment evaluation
Pre-commitment interview

94.19 Other psychiatric interview and evaluation
Follow-up psychiatric interview NOS

94.2 Psychiatric somatotherapy

94.21 Narcoanalysis
Narcosynthesis

94.22 Lithium therapy

94.23 Neuroleptic therapy

94.24 Chemical shock therapy

94.25 Other psychiatric drug therapy

94.26 Subconvulsive electroshock therapy

94.27 Other electroshock therapy
Electroconvulsive therapy (ECT)
EST

94.29 Other psychiatric somatotherapy

94.3 Individual psychotherapy

94.31 Psychoanalysis

94.32 Hypnotherapy
Hypnodrome
Hypnosis

94.33 Behavior therapy
Aversion therapy
Behavior modification
Desensitization therapy
Extinction therapy
Relaxation training
Token economy

94.34 Individual therapy for psychosexual dysfunction

> *Excludes:*   *that performed in group setting (94.41)*

94.35 Crisis intervention

94.36 Play psychotherapy

94.37 Exploratory verbal psychotherapy

94.38 Supportive verbal psychotherapy

94.39 Other individual psychotherapy
Biofeedback

94.4 Psychotherapy and counselling

94.41 Group therapy for psychosexual dysfunction

94.42 Family therapy

94.43 Psychodrama

94.44 Other group therapy

94.45 Drug addiction counselling

94.46 Alcoholism counselling

94.49 Other counselling

94.5 Referral for psychologic rehabilitation

94.51 Referral for psychotherapy

 Valid O.R. procedure
 Non-O.R. procedure
 Nonspecific O.R. procedure
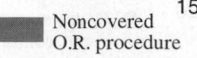 Noncovered O.R. procedure

94.52 Referral for psychiatric aftercare
That in:
halfway house
outpatient (clinic) facility

94.53 Referral for alcoholism rehabilitation

94.54 Referral for drug addiction rehabilitation

94.55 Referral for vocational rehabilitation

94.59 Referral for other psychologic rehabilitation

94.6 Alcohol and drug rehabilitation and detoxification

94.61 Alcohol rehabilitation

94.62 Alcohol detoxification

94.63 Alcohol rehabilitation and detoxification

94.64 Drug rehabilitation

94.65 Drug detoxification

94.66 Drug rehabilitation and detoxification

94.67 Combined alcohol and drug rehabilitation

94.68 Combined alcohol and drug detoxification

94.69 Combined alcohol and drug rehabilitation and detoxification

95 Ophthalmologic and otologic diagnosis and treatment

95.0 General and subjective eye examination

95.01 Limited eye examination
Eye examination with prescription of spectacles

95.02 Comprehensive eye examination
Eye examination covering all aspects of the visual system

95.03 Extended ophthalmologic work-up
Examination (for):
glaucoma
neuro-ophthalmology
retinal disease

95.04 Eye examination under anesthesia
Code also type of examination

95.05 Visual field study

95.06 Color vision study

95.07 Dark adaptation study

95.09 Eye examination, not otherwise specified
Vision check NOS

95.1 Examinations of form and structure of eye

95.11 Fundus photography

95.12 Fluorescein angiography or angioscopy of eye

95.13 Ultrasound study of eye

95.14 X-ray study of eye

95.15 Ocular motility study

95.16 P^{32} and other tracer studies of eye

95.2 Objective functional tests of eye

> Excludes: *that with polysomnogram (89.17)*

95.21 Electroretinogram [ERG]

95.22 Electro-oculogram [EOG]

95.23 Visual evoked potential [VEP]

95.24 Electronystagmogram [ENG]

95.25 Electromyogram of eye [EMG]

95.26 Tonography, provocative tests, and other glaucoma testing

95.3 Special vision services

95.31 Fitting and dispensing of spectacles

95.32 Prescription, fitting, and dispensing of contact lens

95.33 Dispensing of other low vision aids

● Code new
to this edition   ▲ Revision of
existing code   ④ ⑤ Fourth or fifth
digit required

95.34 Ocular prosthetics

95.35 Orthoptic training

95.36 Ophthalmologic counselling and instruction
Counselling in:
   adaptation to visual loss
   use of low vision aids

95.4 Nonoperative procedures related to hearing

95.41 Audiometry
Békésy 5-tone audiometry
Impedance audiometry
Stapedial reflex response
Subjective audiometry
Tympanogram

95.42 Clinical test of hearing
Tuning fork test
Whispered speech test

95.43 Audiological evaluation
Audiological evaluation by:
   Barany noise machine
   blindfold test
   delayed feedback
   masking
   Weber lateralization

95.44 Clinical vestibular function tests
Thermal test of vestibular function

95.45 Rotation tests
Barany chair

95.46 Other auditory and vestibular function tests

95.47 Hearing examination, not otherwise specified

95.48 Fitting of hearing aid
> Excludes: *implantation of electromagnetic hearing device (20.95)*

95.49 Other nonoperative procedures related to hearing
Adjustment (external components) of cochlear prosthetic device

96 Nonoperative intubation and irrigation

96.0 Nonoperative intubation of gastrointestinal and respiratory tracts

96.01 Insertion of nasopharyngeal airway

96.02 Insertion of oropharyngeal airway

96.03 Insertion of esophageal obturator airway

96.04 Insertion of endotracheal tube

96.05 Other intubation of respiratory tract

96.06 Insertion of Sengstaken tube
Esophageal tamponade

96.07 Insertion of other (naso-)gastric tube
Intubation for decompression
> Excludes: *that for enteral infusion of nutritional substances (96.6)*

96.08 Insertion of (naso-)intestinal tube
Miller-Abbott tube (for decompression)

96.09 Insertion of rectal tube
Replacement of rectal tube

96.1 Other nonoperative insertion
> Excludes: *nasolacrimal intubation (09.44)*

96.11 Packing of external auditory canal

96.14 Vaginal packing

96.15 Insertion of vaginal mold

96.16 Other vaginal dilation

96.17 Insertion of vaginal diaphragm

96.18 Insertion of other vaginal pessary

96.19 Rectal packing

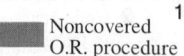

| Valid O.R. procedure | Non-O.R. procedure | Nonspecific O.R. procedure | Noncovered O.R. procedure |

96.2 Nonoperative dilation and manipulation

    96.21 Dilation of frontonasal duct

    96.22 Dilation of rectum

    96.23 Dilation of anal sphincter

    96.24 Dilation and manipulation of enterostomy stoma

    96.25 Therapeutic distention of bladder
        Intermittent distention of bladder

    96.26 Manual reduction of rectal prolapse

    96.27 Manual reduction of hernia

    96.28 Manual reduction of enterostomy prolapse

96.3 Nonoperative alimentary tract irrigation, cleaning, and local instillation

    96.31 Gastric cooling
        Gastric hypothermia

    96.32 Gastric freezing

    96.33 Gastric lavage

    96.34 Other irrigation of (naso-)gastric tube

    96.35 Gastric gavage

    96.36 Irrigation of gastrostomy or enterostomy

    96.37 Proctoclysis

    96.38 Removal of impacted feces
        Removal of impaction:
          by flushing
          manually

    96.39 Other transanal enema
        Rectal irrigation

96.4 Nonoperative irrigation, cleaning, and local instillation of other digestive and genitourinary organs

    96.41 Irrigation of cholecystostomy and other biliary tube

    96.42 Irrigation of pancreatic tube

    96.43 Digestive tract instillation, except gastric gavage

    96.44 Vaginal douche

    96.45 Irrigation of nephrostomy and pyelostomy

    96.46 Irrigation of ureterostomy and ureteral catheter

    96.47 Irrigation of cystostomy

    96.48 Irrigation of other indwelling urinary catheter

    96.49 Other genitourinary instillation
        Insertion of prostaglandin suppository

96.5 Other nonoperative irrigation and cleaning

    96.51 Irrigation of eye
        Irrigation of cornea

        | Excludes: | *irrigation with removal of foreign body (98.21)* |

    96.52 Irrigation of ear
        Irrigation with removal of cerumen

    96.53 Irrigation of nasal passages

    96.54 Dental scaling, polishing, and debridement
        Dental prophylaxis
        Plaque removal

    96.55 Tracheostomy toilette

    96.56 Other lavage of bronchus and trachea

    96.57 Irrigation of vascular catheter

    96.58 Irrigation of wound catheter

    96.59 Other irrigation of wound
        Wound cleaning NOS

        | Excludes: | *debridement (86.22, 86.27-86.28)* |

96.6 Enteral infusion of concentrated nutritional substances

● Code new to this edition   ▲ Revision of existing code   ④ ⑤ Fourth or fifth digit required

96.7   Other continuous mechanical ventilation

Includes: Endotracheal respiratory assistance
Intermittent mandatory ventilation [IMV]
Positive end expiratory pressure [PEEP]
Pressure support ventilation [PSV]
That by tracheostomy
Weaning of an intubated (endotracheal tube) patient

Excludes: *bi-level airway pressure (93.90)*
continuous negative pressure ventilation [CNP] (iron lung) (cuirass) (93.99)
continuous positive airway pressure [CPAP] (93.90)
intermittent positive pressure breathing [IPPB] (93.91)
that by face mask (93.90-93.99)
that by nasal cannula (93.90-93.99)
that by nasal catheter (93.90-93.99)

Code also any associated:
endotracheal tube insertion (96.04)
tracheostomy (31.1-31.29)

Note: Endotracheal Intubation

To calculate the number of hours (duration) of continuous mechanical ventilation during a hospitalization, begin the count from the start of the (endotracheal) intubation. The duration ends with (endotracheal) extubation.

If the patient is intubated prior to admission, begin counting the duration from the time of admission. If a patient is transferred (discharged) while intubated, the duration would end at the time of transfer (discharge).

For patients who begin on (endotracheal) intubation and subsequently have a tracheostomy performed for mechanical ventilation, the duration begins with the (endotracheal) intubation and ends when the mechanical ventilation is turned off (after the weaning period).

Tracheostomy

To calculate the number of hours of continuous mechanical ventilation during a hospitalization, begin counting the duration when mechanical ventilation is started. The duration ends when the mechanical ventilator is turned off (after the weaning period).

If a patient has received a tracheostomy prior to admission and is on mechanical ventilation at the time of admission, begin counting the duration from the time of admission. If a patient is transferred (discharged) while still on mechanical ventilation via tracheostomy, the duration would end at the time of the transfer (discharge).

96.70   Continuous mechanical ventilation of unspecified duration
Mechanical ventilation NOS

96.71   Continuous mechanical ventilation for less than 96 consecutive hours

96.72   Continuous mechanical ventilation for 96 consecutive hours or more

97   Replacement and removal of therapeutic appliances

97.0   Nonoperative replacement of gastrointestinal appliance

97.01   Replacement of (naso-)gastric or esophagostomy tube

97.02   Replacement of gastrostomy tube

97.03   Replacement of tube or enterostomy device of small intestine

97.04   Replacement of tube or enterostomy device of large intestine

97.05   Replacement of stent (tube) in biliary or pancreatic duct

97.1   Nonoperative replacement of musculoskeletal and integumentary system appliance

97.11   Replacement of cast on upper limb

97.12   Replacement of cast on lower limb

97.13   Replacement of other cast

97.14   Replacement of other device for musculoskeletal immobilization

97.15   Replacement of wound catheter

97.16   Replacement of wound packing or drain

Excludes: *repacking of:*
dental wound (97.22)
vulvar wound (97.26)

97.2   Other nonoperative replacement

97.21   Replacement of nasal packing

 Valid O.R.
procedure

 Non-O.R.
procedure

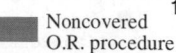 Nonspecific
O.R. procedure

Noncovered
O.R. procedure

97.22 Replacement of dental packing

97.23 Replacement of tracheostomy tube

97.24 Replacement and refitting of vaginal diaphragm

97.25 Replacement of other vaginal pessary

97.26 Replacement of vaginal or vulvar packing or drain

97.29 Other nonoperative replacements

97.3 Nonoperative removal of therapeutic device from head and neck

97.31 Removal of eye prosthesis

> Excludes: removal of ocular implant (16.71)
> removal of orbital implant (16.72)

97.32 Removal of nasal packing

97.33 Removal of dental wiring

97.34 Removal of dental packing

97.35 Removal of dental prosthesis

97.36 Removal of other external mandibular fixation device

97.37 Removal of tracheostomy tube

97.38 Removal of sutures from head and neck

97.39 Removal of other therapeutic device from head and neck

> Excludes: removal of skull tongs (02.94)

97.4 Nonoperative removal of therapeutic device from thorax

97.41 Removal of thoracotomy tube or pleural cavity drain

97.42 Removal of mediastinal drain

97.43 Removal of sutures from thorax

97.49 Removal of other device from thorax

97.5 Nonoperative removal of therapeutic device from digestive system

97.51 Removal of gastrostomy tube

97.52 Removal of tube from small intestine

97.53 Removal of tube from large intestine or appendix

97.54 Removal of cholecystostomy tube

97.55 Removal of T-tube, other bile duct tube, or liver tube

97.56 Removal of pancreatic tube or drain

97.59 Removal of other device from digestive system
Removal of rectal packing

97.6 Nonoperative removal of therapeutic device from urinary system

97.61 Removal of pyelostomy and nephrostomy tube

97.62 Removal of ureterostomy tube and ureteral catheter

97.63 Removal of cystostomy tube

97.64 Removal of other urinary drainage device
Removal of indwelling urinary catheter

97.65 Removal of urethral stent

97.69 Removal of other device from urinary system

97.7 Nonoperative removal of therapeutic device from genital system

97.71 Removal of intrauterine contraceptive device

97.72 Removal of intrauterine pack

97.73 Removal of vaginal diaphragm

97.74 Removal of other vaginal pessary

97.75 Removal of vaginal or vulva packing

97.79 Removal of other device from genital tract
Removal of sutures

97.8 Other nonoperative removal of therapeutic device

97.81 Removal of retroperitoneal drainage device

97.82 Removal of peritoneal drainage device

97.83 Removal of abdominal wall sutures

● Code new
to this edition

▲ Revision of
existing code

④ ⑤ Fourth or fifth
digit required

97.84 Removal of sutures from trunk, not elsewhere classified

97.85 Removal of packing from trunk, not elsewhere classified

97.86 Removal of other device from abdomen

97.87 Removal of other device from trunk

97.88 Removal of external immobilization device

Removal of:
    brace
    cast
    splint

97.89 Removal of other therapeutic device

98 **Nonoperative removal of foreign body or calculus**

98.0 **Removal of intraluminal foreign body from digestive system without incision**

> *Excludes:* *removal of therapeutic device (97.51-97.59)*

98.01 Removal of intraluminal foreign body from mouth without incision

98.02 Removal of intraluminal foreign body from esophagus without incision

98.03 Removal of intraluminal foreign body from stomach and small intestine without incision

98.04 Removal of intraluminal foreign body from large intestine without incision

98.05 Removal of intraluminal foreign body from rectum and anus without incision

98.1 **Removal of intraluminal foreign body from other sites without incision**

> *Excludes:* *removal of therapeutic device (97.31-97.49, 97.61-97.89)*

98.11 Removal of intraluminal foreign body from ear without incision

98.12 Removal of intraluminal foreign body from nose without incision

98.13 Removal of intraluminal foreign body from pharynx without incision

98.14 Removal of intraluminal foreign body from larynx without incision

98.15 Removal of intraluminal foreign body from trachea and bronchus without incision

98.16 Removal of intraluminal foreign body from uterus without incision

> *Excludes:* *removal of intrauterine contraceptive device (97.71)*

98.17 Removal of intraluminal foreign body from vagina without incision

98.18 Removal of intraluminal foreign body from artificial stoma without incision

98.19 Removal of intraluminal foreign body from urethra without incision

98.2 **Removal of other foreign body without incision**

> *Excludes:* *removal of intraluminal foreign body (98.01-98.19)*

98.20 Removal of foreign body, not otherwise specified

98.21 Removal of superficial foreign body from eye without incision

98.22 Removal of other foreign body without incision from head and neck

Removal of embedded foreign body from eyelid or conjunctiva without incision

98.23 Removal of foreign body from vulva without incision

98.24 Removal of foreign body from scrotum or penis without incision

98.25 Removal of other foreign body without incision from trunk except scrotum, penis, or vulva

98.26 Removal of foreign body from hand without incision

98.27 Removal of foreign body without incision from upper limb, except hand

98.28 Removal of foreign body from foot without incision

98.29 Removal of foreign body without incision from lower limb, except foot

98.5 **Extracorporeal shockwave lithotripsy [ESWL]**

Lithotriptor tank procedure
Disintegration of stones by extracorporeal induced shockwaves
That with insertion of stent

98.51 Extracorporeal shockwave lithotripsy [ESWL] of the kidney, ureter and/or bladder

98.52 Extracorporeal shockwave lithotripsy [ESWL] of the gallbladder and/or bile duct

98.59 Extracorporeal shockwave lithotripsy of other sites

 Valid O.R. procedure   Non-O.R. procedure   Nonspecific O.R. procedure   Noncovered O.R. procedure

99   Other nonoperative procedures

99.0   Transfusion of blood and blood components
Use additional code for that done via catheter or cutdown (38.92-38.94)

99.00   Perioperative autologous transfusion of whole blood or blood components
Intraoperative blood collection
Postoperative blood collection
Salvage

99.01   Exchange transfusion
Transfusion:
exsanguination
replacement

99.02   Transfusion of previously collected autologous blood
Blood component

99.03   Other transfusion of whole blood
Transfusion:
NOS
blood NOS
hemodilution

99.04   Transfusion of packed cells

99.05   Transfusion of platelets
Transfusion of thrombocytes

99.06   Transfusion of coagulation factors
Transfusion of antihemophilic factor

99.07   Transfusion of other serum
Transfusion of plasma

> Excludes: injection [transfusion] of:
> antivenin (99.16)
> gamma globulin (99.14)

99.08   Transfusion of blood expander
Transfusion of Dextran

99.09   Transfusion of other substance
Transfusion of:
blood surrogate
granulocytes

> Excludes: transplantation [transfusion] of bone marrow (41.0)

99.1   Injection or Infusion of therapeutic or prophylactic substance
Includes: injection or infusion given:
hypodermically
intramuscularly   } acting locally or systemically
intravenously

99.11   Injection of Rh immune globulin
Injection of:
Anti-D (Rhesus) globulin
RhoGAM

99.12   Immunization for allergy
Desensitization

99.13   Immunization for autoimmune disease

99.14   Injection of gamma globulin
Injection of immune sera

99.15   Parenteral infusion of concentrated nutritional substances
Hyperalimentation
Peripheral parenteral nutrition [PPN]
Total parenteral nutrition [TPN]

99.16   Injection of antidote
Injection of:
antivenin
heavy metal antagonist

99.17   Injection of insulin

99.18   Injection or infusion of electrolytes

99.19   Injection of anticoagulant

● Code new
to this edition   ▲ Revision of
existing code   ④ ⑤ Fourth or fifth
digit required

99.2 **Injection or infusion of other therapeutic or prophylactic substance**

Includes: injection or infusion given:

> hypodermically
> intramuscularly
> intravenously } acting locally or systemically

Use additional code for:

injection (into):
- breast (85.92)
- bursa (82.94, 83.96)
- intraperitoneal (cavity) (54.97)
- intrathecal (03.92)
- joint (76.96, 81.92)
- kidney (55.96)
- liver (50.94)
- orbit (16.91)
- other sites—see Alphabetic Index

perfusion:
- NOS (39.97)
- intestine (46.95, 46.96)
- kidney (55.95)
- liver (50.93)
- total body (39.96)

99.21 **Injection of antibiotic**

99.22 **Injection of other anti-infective**

99.23 **Injection of steroid**
Injection of cortisone
Subdermal implantation of progesterone

99.24 **Injection of other hormone**

99.25 **Injection or infusion of cancer chemotherapeutic substance**
Chemoembolization
Injection or infusion of antineoplastic agent

> Excludes: *immunotherapy, antineoplastic (99.28)*
> *injection or infusion of biological response modifier [BRM] as an antineoplastic agent (99.28)*
> *injection of radioisotopes (92.28)*

99.26 **Injection of tranquilizer**

99.27 **Iontophoresis**

99.28 **Injection or infusion of biological response modifier [BRM] as an antineoplastic agent**
Immunotherapy, antineoplastic

99.29 **Injection or infusion of other therapeutic or prophylactic substance**

> Excludes: *immunization (99.31-99.59)*
> *injection of sclerosing agent into:*
> *esophageal varices (42.33)*
> *hemorrhoids (49.42)*
> *veins (39.92)*

99.3 **Prophylactic vaccination and inoculation against certain bacterial diseases**

99.31 **Vaccination against cholera**

99.32 **Vaccination against typhoid and paratyphoid fever**
Administration of TAB vaccine

99.33 **Vaccination against tuberculosis**
Administration of BCG vaccine

99.34 **Vaccination against plague**

99.35 **Vaccination against tularemia**

99.36 **Administration of diphtheria toxoid**

> Excludes: *administration of:*
> *diphtheria antitoxin (99.58)*
> *diphtheria-tetanus-pertussis combined (99.39)*

99.37 **Vaccination against pertussis**

> Excludes: *administration of diphtheria-tetanus-pertussis, combined (99.39)*

 Valid O.R. procedure

 Non-O.R. procedure

 Nonspecific O.R. procedure

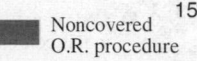 Noncovered O.R. procedure

99.38 **Administration of tetanus toxoid**

> *Excludes:* *administration of:*
> *diphtheria-tetanus-pertussis combined (99.39)*
> *tetanus antitoxin (99.56)*

99.39 **Administration of diphtheria-tetanus-pertussis, combined**

99.4 **Prophylactic vaccination and inoculation against certain viral diseases**

99.41 **Administration of poliomyelitis vaccine**

99.42 **Vaccination against smallpox**

99.43 **Vaccination against yellow fever**

99.44 **Vaccination against rabies**

99.45 **Vaccination against measles**

> *Excludes:* *administration of measles-mumps-rubella vaccine (99.48)*

99.46 **Vaccination against mumps**

> *Excludes:* *administration of measles-mumps-rubella vaccine (99.48)*

99.47 **Vaccination against rubella**

> *Excludes:* *administration of measles-mumps-rubella vaccine (99.48)*

99.48 **Administration of measles-mumps-rubella vaccine**

99.5 **Other vaccination and inoculation**

99.51 **Prophylactic vaccination against the common cold**

99.52 **Prophylactic vaccination against influenza**

99.53 **Prophylactic vaccination against arthropod-borne viral encephalitis**

99.54 **Prophylactic vaccination against other arthropod-borne viral diseases**

99.55 **Prophylactic administration of vaccine against other disease**
Vaccination against:
anthrax
brucellosis
Rocky Mountain spotted fever
Staphylococcus
Streptococcus
typhus

99.56 **Administration of tetanus antitoxin**

99.57 **Administration of botulism antitoxin**

99.58 **Administration of other antitoxins**
Administration of:
diphtheria antitoxin
gas gangrene antitoxin
scarlet fever antitoxin

99.59 **Other vaccination and inoculation**
Vaccination NOS

> *Excludes:* *injection of:*
> *gamma globulin (99.14)*
> *Rh immune globulin (99.11)*
> *immunization for:*
> *allergy (99.12)*
> *autoimmune disease (99.13)*

99.6 **Conversion of cardiac rhythm**

> *Excludes:* *open chest cardiac:*
> *electric stimulation (37.91)*
> *massage (37.91)*

99.60 **Cardiopulmonary resuscitation, not otherwise specified**

99.61 **Atrial cardioversion**

99.62 **Other electric countershock of heart**
Cardioversion:
NOS
external
Conversion to sinus rhythm
Defibrillation
External electrode stimulation

● Code new
to this edition

▲ Revision of
existing code

④ ⑤ Fourth or fifth
digit required

99.63 **Closed chest cardiac massage**
Cardiac massage NOS
Manual external cardiac massage

99.64 **Carotid sinus stimulation**

99.69 **Other conversion of cardiac rhythm**

99.7 **Therapeutic apheresis**

99.71 **Therapeutic plasmapheresis**

99.72 **Therapeutic leukopheresis**
Therapeutic leukocytapheresis

99.73 **Therapeutic erythrocytapheresis**
Therapeutic erythropheresis

99.74 **Therapeutic plateletpheresis**

99.79 **Other**
Apheresis (harvest) of stem cells

99.8 **Miscellaneous physical procedures**

99.81 **Hypothermia (central) (local)**

> *Excludes:* *gastric cooling (96.31)*
> *gastric freezing (96.32)*
> *that incidental to open heart surgery (39.62)*

99.82 **Ultraviolet light therapy**
Actinotherapy

99.83 **Other phototherapy**
Phototherapy of the newborn

> *Excludes:* *extracorporeal photochemotherapy (99.88)*
> *photocoagulation of retinal lesion (14.23-14.25, 14.33-14.35,*
> *14.53-14.55)*

99.84 **Isolation**
Isolation after contact with infectious disease
Protection of individual from his surroundings
Protection of surroundings from individual

99.85 **Hyperthermia for treatment of cancer**
Hyperthermia (adjunct therapy) induced by microwave, ultrasound, low energy
radiofrequency, probes (interstitial), or other means in the treatment of cancer
Code also any concurrent chemotherapy or radiation therapy

99.86 **Non-invasive placement of bone growth stimulator**
Transcutaneous (surface) placement of pads or patches for stimulation to aid bone
healing

> *Excludes:* *insertion of invasive or semi-invasive bone growth stimulators (device)*
> *(percutaneous electrodes) (78.90-78.99)*

99.88 **Therapeutic photopheresis**
Extracorporeal photochemotherapy
Extracorporeal photopheresis

> *Excludes:* *other phototherapy (99.83)*
> *ultraviolet light therapy (99.82)*

99.9 **Other miscellaneous procedures**

99.91 **Acupuncture for anesthesia**

99.92 **Other acupuncture**

> *Excludes:* *that with smouldering moxa (93.35)*

99.93 **Rectal massage (for levator spasm)**

99.94 **Prostatic massage**

99.95 **Stretching of foreskin**

99.96 **Collection of sperm for artificial insemination**

99.97 **Fitting of denture**

99.98 **Extraction of milk from lactating breast**

99.99 **Other**

 Valid O.R.
procedure   Non-O.R.
procedure   Nonspecific
O.R. procedure   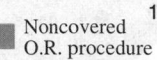 Noncovered
O.R. procedure

● Code new
to this edition

▲ Revision of
existing code

④ ⑤ Fourth or fifth
digit required

A

Abbe operation
construction of vagina 70.61
intestinal anastomosis—*see* Anastomosis
intestine
Abdominocentesis 54.91
Abdominohysterectomy 68.4
Abdominoplasty 86.83
Abdominoscopy 54.21
Abdominouterotomy 68.0
obstetrical 74.99
Abduction, arytenoid 31.69
Ablation
biliary ducts (lesion) by ERCP 51.64
endometrial (hysteroscopic) 68.23
inner ear (cryosurgery) (ultrasound) 20.79
by injection 20.72
lesion
esophagus 42.39
endoscopic 42.33
heart (ventricular) 37.33
by cardiac catheter 37.34
intestine
large 45.49
endoscopic 45.43
large intestine 45.49
endoscopic 45.43
pituitary 07.69
by
Cobalt-60 92.3
implantation (strontium-yttrium) (Y) NEC
07.68
transfrontal approach 07.64
transsphenoidal approach 07.65
proton beam (Bragg peak) 92.3
prostate
by
cryoablation 60.62
radical cryosurgical ablation (RCSA) 60.62
Abortion, therapeutic 69.51
by
aspiration curettage 69.51
dilation and curettage 69.01
hysterectomy—*see* Hysterectomy
hysterotomy 74.91
insertion
laminaria 69.93
prostaglandin suppository 96.49
intra-amniotic injection (saline) 75.0
Abrasion
corneal epithelium 11.41
for smear or culture 11.21
epicardial surface 36.3
pleural 34.6
skin 86.25
Abscission, cornea 11.49
Absorptiometry
photon (dual) (single) 88.98
Aburel operation (intra-amniotic injection for
abortion) 75.0
Accouchement forcé 73.99
Acetabulectomy 77.85
Acetabuloplasty NEC 81.40
with prosthetic implant 81.52
Achillorrhaphy 83.64
delayed 83.62
Achillotenotomy 83.11
plastic 83.85
Achillotomy 83.11
plastic 83.85

Acid peel, skin 86.24
Acromionectomy 77.81
Acromioplasty 81.83
for recurrent dislocation of shoulder 81.82
partial replacement 81.81
total replacement 81.80
Actinotherapy 99.82
Activities of daily living (ADL)
therapy 93.83
training for the blind 93.78
Acupuncture 99.92
with smouldering moxa 93.35
for anesthesia 99.91
Adams operation
advancement of round ligament 69.22
crushing of nasal septum 21.88
excision of palmar fascia 82.35
Adenectomy —*see also* Excision, by site
prostate NEC 60.69
retropubic 60.4
Adenoidectomy (without tonsillectomy) 28.6
with tonsillectomy 28.3
Adhesiolysis —*see also* Lysis, adhesions
for collapse of lung 33.39
middle ear 20.23
Adipectomy 86.83
Adjustment
cardiac pacemaker program
(reprogramming)—*omit code*
cochlear prosthetic device (external
components) 95.49
dental 99.97
occlusal 24.8
spectacles 95.31
Administration (of)—*see also* Injection
antitoxins NEC 99.58
botulism 99.57
diphtheria 99.58
gas gangrene 99.58
scarlet fever 99.58
tetanus 99.56
Bender Visual-Motor Gestalt test 94.02
Benton Visual Retention test 94.02.
intelligence test or scale (Stanford-Binet)
(Wechsler) (adult) (children) 94.01
Minnesota Multiphasic Personality Inventory
(MMPI) 94.02
MMPI (Minnesota Multiphasic Personality
Inventory) 94.02
psychologic test 94.02
Stanford-Binet test 94.01
toxoid
diphtheria 99.36
with tetanus and pertussis, combined (DTP)
99.39
tetanus 99.38
with diphtheria and pertussis, combined
(DTP) 99.39
vaccine—*see also* Vaccination
BCG 99.33
measles-mumps-rubella (MMR) 99.48
poliomyelitis 99.41
TAB 99.32
Wechsler
Intelligence Scale (adult) (children) 94.01
Memory Scale 94.02
Adrenalectomy (unilateral) 07.22
with partial removal of remaining gland 07.29

Amputation—*continued*

shoulder (disarticulation) 84.08

Sorondo-Ferré (hindquarter) 84.19

S.P. Rogers (knee disarticulation) 84.16

supracondylar, above-knee 84.17

supramalleolar, foot 84.14

Syme's (ankle amputation through malleoli of tibia and fibula) 84.14

thigh 84.17

thumb 84.02

toe (through metatarsophalangeal joint) 84.11

transcarpal 84.03

transmetatarsal 84.12

upper limb NEC (*see also* Amputation, arm) 84.00

wrist (disarticulation) 84.04

Amygdalohippocampotomy 01.39

Amygdalotomy 01.39

Analysis

character 94.03

gastric 89.39

psychologic 94.31

transactional

group 94.44

individual 94.39

Anastomosis

abdominal artery to coronary artery 36.17

accessory-facial nerve 04.72

accessory-hypoglossal nerve 04.73

anus (with formation of endorectal ileal pouch) 45.95

aorta (descending)—pulmonary (artery) 39.0

aorta-renal artery 39.24

aorta-subclavian artery 39.22

aortoceliac 39.26

aorto(ilio)femoral 39.25

aortomesenteric 39.26

appendix 47.99

arteriovenous NEC 39.29

for renal dialysis 39.27

artery (suture of distal to proximal end) 39.31

with

bypass graft 39.29

extracranial-intracranial [EC-IC] 39.28

excision or resection of vessel—*see*

Arteriectomy, with anastomosis, by site

revision 39.49

bile ducts 51.39

bladder NEC 57.88

with

isolated segment of intestine 57.87 *[45.50]*

colon (sigmoid) 57.87 *[45.52]*

ileum 57.87 *[45.51]*

open loop of ileum 57.87 *[45.51]*

to intestine 57.88

ileum 57.87 *[45.51]*

bowel—(*see also* Anastomosis, intestine) 45.90

bronchotracheal 33.48

bronchus 33.48

carotid-subclavian artery 39.22

caval-mesenteric vein 39.1

caval-pulmonary artery 39.21

cervicoesophageal 42.59

colohypopharyngeal (intrathoracic) 42.55

antesternal or antethoracic 42.65

common bile duct 51.39

common pulmonary trunk and left atrium (posterior wall) 35.82

cystic bile duct 51.39

cystocolic 57.88

epididymis to vas deferens 63.83

Anastomosis—*continued*

esophagocolic (intrathoracic) NEC 42.56

with interposition 42.55

antesternal or antethoracic NEC 42.66

with interposition 42.65

esophagocologastric (intrathoracic) 42.55

antesternal or antethoracic 42.65

esophagoduodenal (intrathoracic) NEC 42.54

with interposition 42.53

esophagoenteric (intrathoracic) NEC *see also*

Anastomosis, esophagus to intestinal segment) 42.54

antesternal or antethoracic NEC (*see also*

Anastomosis, esophagus, antesternal, to intestinal segment) 42.64

esophagoesophageal (intrathoracic) 42.51

antesternal or antethoracic 42.61

esophagogastric (intrathoracic) 42.52

antesternal or antethoracic 42.62

esophagus (intrapleural) (intrathoracic) (retrosternal) NEC 42.59

with

gastrectomy (partial) 43.5

complete or total 43.99

interposition (of) NEC 42.58

colon 42.55

jejunum 42.53

small bowel 42.53

antesternal or antethoracic NEC 42.69

with

interposition (of) NEC 42.68

colon 42.65

jejunal loop 42.63

small bowel 42.63

rubber tube 42.68

to intestinal segment NEC 42.64

with interposition 42.68

colon NEC 42.66

with interposition 42.65

small bowel NEC 42.64

with interposition 42.63

to intestinal segment (intrathoracic) NEC 42.54

with interposition 42.58

antesternal or antethoracic NEC 42.64

with interposition 42.68

colon (intrathoracic) NEC 42.56

with interposition 42.55

antesternal or antethoracic 42.66

with interposition 42.65

small bowel NEC 42.54

with interposition 42.53

antesternal or antethoracic 42.64

with interposition 42.63

facial-accessory nerve 04.72

facial-hypoglossal nerve 04.71

fallopian tube 66.73

gallbladder 51.35

to

hepatic ducts 51.31

intestine 51.32

pancreas 51.33

stomach 51.34

gastroepiploic artery (to)

coronary artery 36.17

hepatic duct 51.39

hypoglossal-accessory nerve 04.73

hypoglossal-facial nerve 04.71

ileal loop to bladder 57.87 *[45.51]*

ileoanal 45.95

ileorectal 45.93

Aneurysmectomy—*continued*
  thoracic NEC 38.65
  upper limb (artery) (vein) 38.63
  ventricle (myocardium) 37.32
Aneurysmoplasty —*see* Aneurysmorrhaphy
Aneurysmorrhaphy NEC 39.52
  by or with
    anastomosis—*see* Aneurysmectomy, with
      anastomosis, by site
Aneurysmorrhaphy—*continued*
  clipping 39.51
  coagulation 39.52
  electrocoagulation 39.52
  excision or resection—*see also*
    Aneurysmectomy, by site
    with
      anastomosis—*see* Aneurysmectomy, with
        anastomosis, by site
      graft replacement—*see* Aneurysmectomy,
        with graft replacement, by site
  filipuncture 39.52
  graft replacement—*see* Aneurysmectomy,
    with graft replacement, by site
  methyl methacrylate 39.52
  suture 39.52
  wiring 39.52
  wrapping 39.52
  Matas' 39.52
Aneurysmotomy —*see* Aneurysmectomy
Angiectomy
  with
    anastomosis 38.30
      abdominal
        artery 38.36
        vein 38.37
      aorta (arch) (ascending) (descending) 38.34
      head and neck NEC 38.32
      intracranial NEC 38.31
      lower limb
        artery 38.38
        vein 38.39
      thoracic vessel NEC 38.35
      upper limb (artery) (vein) 38.33
    graft replacement (interposition) 38.40
      abdominal
        aorta 38.44
        artery 38.46
        vein 38.47
      aorta (arch) (ascending) (descending
        thoracic)
        abdominal 38.44
        thoracic 38.45
        thoracoabdominal 38.45 *[38.44]*
      head and neck NEC 38.42
      intracranial NEC 38.41
      lower limb
        artery 38.48
        vein 38.49
      thoracic vessel NEC 38.45
      upper limb (artery) (vein) 38.43
Angiocardiography (selective) 88.50
  carbon dioxide (negative contrast) 88.58
  combined right and left heart 88.54
  left heart (aortic valve) (atrium) (ventricle)
    (ventricular outflow tract) 88.53
    combined with right heart 88.54
  right heart (atrium) (pulmonary valve)
    (ventricle) (ventricular outflow tract) 88.52
    combined with left heart 88.54
  vena cava (inferior) (superior) 88.51

Angiography (arterial) (*see also* Arteriography)
  88.40
  by radioisotope—*see* Scan, radioisotope, by site
  by ultrasound—*see* Ultrasonography, by site
  basilar 88.41
  brachial 88.49
  carotid (internal) 88.41
  celiac 88.47
  cerebral (posterior circulation) 88.41
  coronary NEC 88.57
  eye (fluorescein) 95.12
  femoral 88.48
  heart 88.50
  intra-abdominal NEC 88.47
  intracranial 88.41
  intrathoracic vessels NEC 88.44
  lower extremity NEC 88.48
  neck 88.41
  placenta 88.46
  pulmonary 88.43
  renal 88.45
  specified artery NEC 88.49
  transfemoral 88.48
  upper extremity NEC 88.49
  veins—*see* Phlebography
  vertebral 88.41
Angioplasty (laser) —*see also* Repair, blood
  vessel
  balloon (percutaneous transluminal) NEC 39.50
    coronary artery (single vessel) 36.01
      with thrombolytic agent infusion 36.02
      multiple vessels 36.05
    other sites (femoropopliteal) (iliac)
      (non-coronary) (renal) (vertebral) 39.50
  coronary 36.09
    open chest approach 36.03
    percutaneous transluminal (balloon) (single
      vessel) 36.01
      with thrombolytic agent infusion 36.02
      multiple vessels 36.05
  percutaneous transluminal (balloon)(single
    vessel) 39.50
    basilar 39.50
    carotid 39.50
    coronary (balloon) (single vessel) 36.01
      with thrombolytic agent infusion 36.02
      multiple vessels 36.05
    femoropopliteal 39.50
    head and neck 39.50
    iliac 39.50
    lower extremity NOS 39.50
    mesenteric 39.50
    renal 39.50
    upper extremity NOS 39.50
    vertebral 39.50
  specified site NEC 39.50
Angiorrhaphy 39.30
  artery 39.31
  vein 39.32
Angioscopy, percutaneous 38.22
  eye (fluorescein) 95.12
Angiotomy 38.00
  abdominal
    artery 38.06
    vein 38.07
  aorta (arch) (ascending) (descending) 38.04
  head and neck NEC 38.02
  intracranial NEC 38.01
  lower limb
    artery 38.08
    vein 38.09

Angiotomy—*continued*
thoracic NEC 38.05
upper limb (artery) (vein) 38.03
Angiotripsy 39.98
Ankylosis, production of —*see* Arthrodesis
Annuloplasty (heart) (posteromedial) 35.33
Anoplasty 49.79
with hemorrhoidectomy 49.46
Anoscopy 49.21
Antibiogram —*see* Examination, microscopic
Antiembolic filter, vena cava 38.7
Antiphobic treatment 94.39
Antrectomy
mastoid 20.49
maxillary 22.39
radical 22.31
pyloric 43.6
Antrostomy —*see* Antrotomy
Antrotomy (exploratory) (nasal sinus) 22.2
Caldwell-Luc (maxillary sinus) 22.39
with removal of membrane lining 22.31
intranasal 22.2
with external approach (Caldwell-Luc) 22.39
radical 22.31
maxillary (simple) 22.2
with Caldwell-Luc approach 22.39
with removal of membrane lining 22.31
external (Caldwell-Luc approach) 22.39
with removal of membrane lining 22.31
radical (with removal of membrane lining) 22.31
Antrum window operation —*see* Antrotomy,
maxillary
Aorticopulmonary window operation 39.59
Aortogram, aortography (abdominal)
(retrograde) (selective) (translumbar) 88.42
Aortoplasty (aortic valve) (gusset type) 35.11
Aortotomy 38.04
Apexcardiogram (with ECG lead) 89.57
Apheresis, therapeutic —*see category* 99.7
Apicectomy
lung 32.3
petrous pyramid 20.59
tooth (root) 23.73
with root canal therapy 23.72
Apicoectomy 23.73
with root canal therapy 23.72
Apicolysis (lung) 33.39
Apicostomy, alveolar 24.0
Aponeurectomy 83.42
hand 82.33
Aponeurorrhaphy (*see also* Suture, tendon)
83.64
hand (*see also* Suture, tendon, hand) 82.45
Aponeurotomy 83.13
hand 82.11
Appendectomy (with drainage) 47.09
incidental 47.19
laparoscopic 47.11
laparoscopic 47.01
Appendicectomy (with drainage) 47.09
incidental 47.19
laparoscopic 47.11
laparoscopic 47.01
Appendicocecostomy 47.91
Appendicoenterostomy 47.91
Appendicolysis 54.59
with appendectomy 47.01, 47.09
laparoscopic 54.51
Appendicostomy 47.91
closure 47.92
Appendicotomy 47.2

Application
anti-shock trousers 93.58
arch bars (orthodontic) 24.7
for immobilization (fracture) 93.55
Barton's tongs (skull) (with synchronous
skeletal traction) 02.94
bone growth stimulator (surface)
(transcutaneous) 99.86
Bryant's traction 93.44
with reduction of fracture or dislocation—*see*
Reduction, fracture and Reduction,
dislocation
Buck's traction 93.46
caliper tongs (skull) (with synchronous skeletal
traction) 02.94
cast (fiberglass) (plaster) (plastic) NEC 93.53
with reduction of fracture or dislocation—*see*
Reduction, fracture and Reduction,
dislocation
spica 93.51
cervical collar 93.52
with reduction of fracture or dislocation—*see*
Reduction, fracture and Reduction,
dislocation
clamp, cerebral aneurysm (Crutchfield)
(Silverstone) 39.51
croupette, croup tent 93.94
crown (artificial) 23.41
Crutchfield tongs (skull) (with synchronous
skeletal traction) 02.94
Dunlop's traction 93.44
with reduction of fracture or dislocation—*see*
Reduction, fracture and Reduction,
dislocation
elastic stockings 93.59
electronic gaiter 93.59
external fixation device (bone) 78.10
carpal, metacarpal 78.14
clavicle 78.11
femur 78.15
fibula 78.17
humerus 78.12
patella 78.16
pelvic 78.19
phalanges (foot) (hand) 78.19
radius 78.13
scapula 78.11
specified site NEC 78.19
tarsal, metatarsal 78.18
thorax (ribs) (sternum) 78.11
tibia 78.17
ulna 78.13
vertebrae 78.19
forceps, with delivery—*see* Delivery, forceps
graft—*see* Graft
gravity (G.) suit 93.59
intermittent pressure device 93.59
Jewett extension brace 93.59
Jobst pumping unit (reduction of edema) 93.59
Lyman Smith traction 93.44
with reduction of fracture or dislocation—*see*
Reduction, fracture and Reduction,
dislocation
MAST (military anti-shock trousers) 93.58
Minerva jacket 93.52
minifixator device (bone)—*see category* 78.1
neck support (molded) 93.52
obturator (orthodontic) 24.7
orthodontic appliance (obturator) (wiring) 24.7
pelvic sling 93.44

Application—*continued*
  with reduction of fracture or dislocation—*see*
      Reduction, fracture and Reduction,
      dislocation
  peridontal splint (orthodontic) 24.7
  plaster jacket 93.51
    Minerva 93.52
  pressure
    dressing (bandage) (Gibney) (Robert Jones')
      (Shanz) 93.56
    trousers (anti-shock) (MAST) 93.58
  prosthesis for missing ear 18.71
  Russell's traction 93.44
    with reduction of fracture or dislocation—*see*
      Reduction, fracture and Reduction,
      dislocation
  splint, for immobilization (plaster) (pneumatic)
    (tray) 93.54
    with fracture reduction—*see* Reduction,
      fracture
  stereotactic head frame 93.59
  Thomas collar 93.52
    with reduction of fracture or dislocation—*see*
      Reduction, fracture and Reduction,
      dislocation
  traction
    with reduction of fracture or dislocation—*see*
      Reduction, fracture and Reduction,
      dislocation
    adhesive tape (skin) 93.46
    boot 93.46
    Bryant's 93.44
    Buck's 93.46
    Cotrel's 93.42
    Dunlop's 93.44
    gallows 93.46
    Lyman Smith 93.44
    Russell's 93.44
    skeletal NEC 93.44
    intermittent 93.43
    skin, limbs NEC 93.46
    spinal NEC 93.42
      with skull device (halo) (caliper)
        (Crutchfield) (Gardner-Wells) (Vinke)
        (tongs) 93.41
        with synchronous insertion 02.94
    Thomas' splint 93.45
  Unna's paste boot 93.53
  vasopneumatic device 93.58
  Velpeau dressing 93.59
  Vinke tongs (skull) (with synchronous skeletal
    traction) 02.94
  wound dressing 93.57
Arc lamp —*see* Photocoagulation
Arrest
  bone growth (epiphyseal) 78.20
    by stapling—*see* Stapling, epiphyseal plate
    femur 78.25
    fibula 78.27
    humerus 78.22
    radius 78.23
    tibia 78.27
    ulna 78.23
  cardiac, induced (anoxic) (circulatory) 39.63
  circulatory, induced (anoxic) 39.63
  hemorrhage—*see* Control, hemorrhage
Arslan operation (fenestration of inner ear) 20.61
Arteriectomy 38.60
  with
    anastomosis 38.30
      abdominal 38.36

Arteriectomy—*continued*
    aorta (arch) (ascending) (descending) 38.34
    head and neck NEC 38.32
    intracranial NEC 38.31
    lower limb 38.38
    thoracic NEC 38.35
    upper limb 38.33
  graft replacement (interposition) 38.40
    abdominal
      aorta 38.44
    aorta (arch) (ascending) (descending
      thoracic)
      abdominal 38.44
      thoracic 38.45
      thoracoabdominal 38.45 *[38.44]*
    head and neck NEC 38.42
    intracranial NEC 38.41
    lower limb 38.48
    thoracic NEC 38.45
    upper limb 38.43
  abdominal 38.66
  aorta (arch) (ascending) (descending) 38.64
  head and neck NEC 38.62
  intracranial NEC 38.61
  lower limb 38.68
  thoracic NEC 38.65
  upper limb 38.63
Arteriography (contrast) (fluoroscopic)
  (retrograde) 88.40
  by
    radioisotope—*see* Scan, radioisotope
    ultrasound (Doppler)—*see* Ultrasonography,
      by site
  aorta (arch) (ascending) (descending) 88.42
  basilar 88.41
  brachial 88.49
  carotid (internal) 88.41
  cerebral (posterior circulation) 88.41
  coronary (direct) (selective) NEC 88.57
    double catheter technique (Judkins) (Ricketts
      and Abrams) 88.56
    single catheter technique (Sones) 88.55
  Doppler (ultrasonic)—*see* Ultrasonography, by
    site
  femoral 88.48
  head and neck 88.41
  intra-abdominal NEC 88.47
  intrathoracic NEC 88.44
  lower extremity 88.48
  placenta 88.46
  pulmonary 88.43
  radioisotope—*see* Scan, radioisotope
  renal 88.45
  specified site NEC 88.49
  superior mesenteric artery 88.47
  transfemoral 88.48
  ultrasound—*see* Ultrasonography, by site
  upper extremity 88.49
Arterioplasty —*see* Repair, artery
Arteriorrhaphy 39.31
Arteriotomy 38.00
  abdominal 38.06
  aorta (arch) (ascending) (descending) 38.04
  head and neck NEC 38.02
  intracranial NEC 38.01
  lower limb 38.08
  thoracic NEC 38.05
  upper limb 38.03
Arteriovenostomy 39.29
  for renal dialysis 39.27

Artificial
insemination 69.92
kidney 39.95
rupture of membranes 73.09
Arytenoidectomy 30.29
Arytenoidopexy 31.69
Asai operation (larynx) 31.75
Aspiration
abscess—*see* Aspiration, by site
anterior chamber, eye (therapeutic) 12.91
   diagnostic 12.21
aqueous (eye) (humor) (therapeutic) 12.91
   diagnostic 12.21
ascites 54.91
Bartholin's gland (cyst) (percutaneous) 71.21
biopsy—*see* Biopsy, by site
bladder (catheter) 57.0
   percutaneous (needle) 57.11
bone marrow (for biopsy) 41.31
   from donor for transplant 41.91
   stem cell 99.79
branchial cleft cyst 29.0
breast 85.91
bronchus 96.05
   with lavage 96.56
bursa (percutaneous) 83.94
   hand 82.92
calculus, bladder 57.0
cataract 13.3
   with
      phacoemulsification 13.41
      phacofragmentation 13.43
         posterior route 13.42
chest 34.91
cisternal 01.01
cranial (puncture) 01.09
craniobuccal pouch 07.72
craniopharyngioma 07.72
cul-de-sac (abscess) 70.0
curettage, uterus 69.59
   after abortion or delivery 69.52
   diagnostic 69.59
   to terminate pregnancy 69.51
cyst—*see* Aspiration, by site
diverticulum, pharynx 29.0
endotracheal 96.04
   with lavage 96.56
extradural 01.09
eye (anterior chamber) (therapeutic) 12.91
   diagnostic 12.21
fallopian tube 66.91
fascia 83.95
   hand 82.93
gallbladder (percutaneous) 51.01
hematoma—*see also* Aspiration, by site
   obstetrical 75.92
      incisional 75.91
hydrocele, tunica vaginalis 61.91
hygroma—*see* Aspiration, by site
hyphema 12.91
hypophysis 07.72
intracranial space (epidural) (extradural)
      (subarachnoid) (subdural) (ventricular) 01.09
   through previously implanted catheter or
      reservoir (Ommaya) (Rickham) 01.02
joint 81.91
   for arthrography—*see* Arthrogram
kidney (cyst) (pelvis) (percutaneous)
      (therapeutic) 55.92
   diagnostic 55.23
liver (percutaneous) 50.91

Aspiration—*continued*
lung (percutaneous) (puncture) (needle) (trocar)
      33.93
middle ear 20.09
   with intubation 20.01
muscle 83.95
   hand 82.93
nail 86.01
nasal sinus 22.00
   by puncture 22.01
   through natural ostium 22.02
nasotracheal 96.04
   with lavage 96.56
orbit, diagnostic 16.22
ovary 65.91
percutaneous—*see* Aspiration, by site
pericardium (wound) 37.0
pituitary gland 07.72
pleural cavity 34.91
prostate (percutaneous) 60.91
Rathke's pouch 07.72
seminal vesicles 60.71
seroma—*see* Aspiration, by site
skin 86.01
soft tissue NEC 83.95
   hand 82.93
spermatocele 63.91
spinal (puncture) 03.31
spleen (cyst) 41.1
stem cell 99.79
subarachnoid space (cerebral) 01.09
subcutaneous tissue 86.01
subdural space (cerebral) 01.09
tendon 83.95
   hand 82.93
testis 62.91
thymus 07.92
thyroid (field) (gland) 06.01
   postoperative 06.02
trachea 96.04
   with lavage 96.56
   percutaneous 31.99
tunica vaginalis (hydrocele) (percutaneous)
      61.91
vitreous (and replacement) 14.72
   diagnostic 14.11
Assessment
fitness to testify 94.11
mental status 94.11
nutritional status 89.39
personality 94.03
temperament 94.02
vocational 93.85
Assistance
cardiac—(*see also* Resuscitation, cardiac
      extracorporeal circulation) 39.61
endotracheal respiratory—*see* category 96.7
hepatic, extracorporeal 50.92
respiratory (endotracheal) (mechanical)—*see*
      ventilation, mechanical
respiratory (mechanical) (endotracheal) NEC
      93.92
Astragalectomy 77.98
Asymmetrogammagram —*see* Scan,
   radioisotope
Atherectomy
coronary—*see* angioplasty
peripheral 39.50
Atriocommissuropexy (mitral valve) 35.12

Atrioplasty NEC 37.99
  combined with repair of valvular and ventricular
    septal defects—*see* Repair, endocardial
    cushion defect
  septum (heart) NEC 35.71
Atrioseptopexy (*see also* Repair, atrial septal
    defect) 35.71
Atrioseptoplasty (*see also* Repair, atrial
    septal defect) 35.71
Atrioseptostomy (balloon) 35.41
Atriotomy 37.11
Atrioventriculostomy (cerebral-heart) 02.32
Attachment
  eye muscle
    orbicularis oculi to eyebrow 08.36
    rectus to frontalis 15.9
  pedicle (flap) graft 86.74
    hand 86.73
    lip 27.57
    mouth 27.57
  pharyngeal flap (for cleft palate repair) 27.62
    secondary or subsequent 27.63
  retina—*see* Reattachment, retina
Atticoantrostomy (ear) 20.49
Atticoantrotomy (ear) 20.49
Atticotomy (ear) 20.23
Audiometry (Békésy 5-tone) (impedance)
    (stapedial reflex response) (subjective) 95.41
Augmentation
  bladder 57.87
  breast—*see* Mammoplasty, augmentation
  buttock ("fanny-lift") 86.89
  chin 76.68
  genioplasty 76.68
  mammoplasty—*see* Mammoplasty,
    augmentation
  outflow tract (pulmonary valve) (gusset
    type) 35.26
    in total repair of tetralogy or Fallot 35.81
  vocal cord(s) 31.0
Auriculectomy 18.39
Autograft —*see* Graft
Autologous —*see* Blood, transfusion
Autopsy 89.8
Autotransfusion (whole blood)—*see* Blood,
    transfusion
Autotransplant, autotransplantation —*see also*
    Reimplantation
  adrenal tissue (heterotopic) (orthotopic) 07.45
  kidney 55.61
  lung —*see* Transplant, transplantation, lung
  ovary 65.72
    laparoscopic 65.75
  pancreatic tissue 52.81
  parathyroid tissue (heterotopic) (orthotopic)
    06.95
  thyroid tissue (heterotopic) (orthotopic) 06.94
  tooth 23.5
Avulsion, nerve (cranial) (peripheral) NEC 04.07
  acoustic 04.01
  phrenic 33.31
  sympathetic 05.29
Azygography 88.63

B

Bacterial smear —*see* Examination, microscopic
Baffes operation (interatrial transposition of venous return) 35.91
Baffle, atrial or interatrial 35.91
Balanoplasty 64.49
Baldy-Webster operation (uterine suspension) 69.22
Ballistocardiography 89.59
Balloon
    angioplasty—*see* Angioplasty, balloon
    dilation of pylorus 44.22
    pump, intra-aortic 37.61
    systostomy (atrial) 35.41
    valvuloplasty, percutaneous 35.96
Ball operation
    herniorrhaphy—*see* Repair, hernia, inguinal
    undercutting 49.02
Bandage 93.57
    elastic 93.56
Banding, pulmonary artery 38.85
Bankhart operation (capsular repair into glenoid, for shoulder dislocation) 81.82
Bardenheurer operation (ligation of innominate artery) 38.85
Barium swallow 87.61
Barkan operation (goniotomy) 12.52
    with goniopuncture 12.53
Barr operation (transfer of tibialis posterior tendon) 83.75
Barsky operation (closure of cleft hand) 82.82
Basal metabolic rate 89.39
Basiotripsy 73.8
Bassett operation (vulvectomy with inguinal lymph node dissection) 71.5 [40.3]
Bassini operation —*see* Repair, hernia, inguinal
Batch-Spittler-McFaddin operation (knee disarticulation) 84.16
Beck operation
    aorta-coronary sinus shunt 36.3
    epicardial poudrage 36.3
Beck-Jianu operation (permanent gastrostomy) 43.19
Behavior modification 94.33
Bell-Beuttner operation (subtotal abdominal hysterectomy) 68.3
Belsey operation (esophagogastric sphincter) 44.65
Benenenti operation (rotation of bulbous urethra) 58.49
Berke operation (levator resection of eyelid) 08.33
Bicuspidization of heart valve 35.10
    aortic 35.11
    mitral 35.12
Bicycle dynamometer 93.01
Biesenberger operation (size reduction of breast, bilateral) 85.32
    unilateral 85.31
Bifurcation, bone (*see also* Osteotomy) 77.30
Bigelow operation (litholapaxy) 57.0
Bililite therapy (ultraviolet) 99.82
Billroth I operation (partial gastrectomy with gastroduodenostomy) 43.6
Billroth II operation (partial gastrectomy with gastrojejunostomy) 43.7
Binnie operation (hepatopexy) 50.69
Biofeedback, psychotherapy 94.39

Biopsy
    abdominal wall 54.22
    adenoid 28.11
    adrenal gland NEC 07.11
        closed 07.11
        open 07.12
        percutaneous (aspiration) (needle) 07.11
    alveolus 24.12
    anus 49.23
    appendix 45.26
    artery (any site) 38.21
    aspiration—*see* Biopsy, by site
    bile ducts 51.14
        closed (endoscopic) 51.14
        open 51.13
        percutaneous (needle) 51.12
    bladder 57.33
        closed 57.33
        open 57.34
        transurethral 57.33
    blood vessel (any site) 38.21
    bone 77.40
        carpal, metacarpal 77.44
        clavicle 77.41
        facial 76.11
        femur 77.45
        fibula 77.47
        humerus 77.42
        marrow 41.31
        patella 77.46
        pelvic 77.49
        phalanges (foot) (hand) 77.49
        radius 77.43
        scapula 77.41
        specified site NEC 77.49
        tarsal, metatarsal 77.48
        thorax (ribs) (sternum) 77.41
        tibia 77.47
        ulna 77.43
        vertebrae 77.49
    bowel—*see* Biopsy, intestine
    brain NEC 01.13
        closed 01.13
        open 01.14
        percutaneous (needle) 01.13
    breast 85.11
        blind 85.11
        closed 85.11
        open 85.12
        percutaneous (needle) (Vimm-Silverman) 85.11
    bronchus NEC 33.24
        brush 33.24
        closed (endoscopic) 33.24
        washings 33.24
        open 33.25
    bursa 83.21
    cardioesophageal (junction) 44.14
        closed (endoscopic) 44.14
        open 44.15
    cecum 45.25
        brush 45.25
        closed (endoscopic) 45.25
        open 45.26
    cerebral meninges NEC 01.11
        closed 01.11
        open 01.12
        percutaneous (needle) 01.11

Block—*continued*
  breast
    bilateral 85.46
    unilateral 85.45
  bronchus 32.6
  larynx 30.3
  lymph nodes 40.50
  neck 40.40
  vulva 71.5
  epidural, spinal—*see* Injection, spinal
  gasserian ganglion 04.81
  intercostal nerves 04.81
  intrathecal—*see* Injection, spinal
  nerve (cranial) (peripheral) NEC 04.81
  paravertebral stellate ganglion 05.31
  peripheral nerve 04.81
  spinal nerve root (intrathecal)—*see* Injection,
    spinal
  stellate (ganglion) 05.31
  subarachnoid, spinal—*see* Injection, spinal
  sympathetic nerve 05.31
  trigeminal nerve 04.81
Blood
  flow study, Doppler-type (ultrasound)—*see*
    Ultrasonography
  patch, spine (epidural) 03.95
  transfusion
    antihemophilic factor 99.06
    autologous
      collected prior to surgery 99.02
      intraoperative 99.00
      perioperative 99.00
      postoperative 99.00
      previously collected 99.02
      salvage 99.00
    blood expander 99.08
    blood surrogate 99.09
    coagulation factors 99.06
    exchange 99.01
    granulocytes 99.09
    hemodilution 99.03
    other substance 99.09
    packed cells 99.04
    plasma 99.07
    platelets 99.05
    serum, other 99.07
    thrombocytes 99.05
Blount operation
  femoral shortening (with blade plate) 78.25
    by epiphyseal stapling 78.25
Boari operation (bladder flap) 56.74
Bobb operation (cholelithotomy) 51.04
Bone
  age studies 88.33
  mineral density study 88.98
Bonney operation (abdominal hysterectomy)
  68.4
Borthen operation (iridotasis) 12.63
Boot operation
  plantar dissection 80.48
  radiocarpal fusion 81.26
Bosworth operation
  arthroplasty for acromioclavicular separation
    81.83
  fusion of posterior lumbar and lumbosacral
    spine 81.08
    for pseudarthrosis 81.09
  resection of radial head ligaments (for tennis
    elbow) 80.92
  shelf procedure, hip 81.40
Bottle repair of hydrocele, tunics vaginalis 61.2

Boyd operation (hip disarticulation) 84.18
Brauer operation (cardiolysis) 37.10
Breech extraction —*see* Extraction, breech
Bricker operation (ileoureterostomy) 56.51
Brisement (force) 93.26
Bristow operation (repair of shoulder
  dislocation) 81.82
Brock operation (pulmonary valvotomy) 35.03
Brockman operation (soft tissue release for
  clubfoot) 83.84
Bronchogram, bronchography 87.32
  endotracheal 87.31
  transcricoid 87.32
Bronchoplasty 33.48
Bronchorrhaphy 33.41
Bronchoscopy NEC 33.23
  with biopsy 33.24
    lung 33.27
      brush 33.24
  fiberoptic 33.22
    with biopsy 33.24
      lung 33.27
        brush 33.24
  through tracheostomy 33.21
    with biopsy 33.24
      lung 33.27
        brush 33.24
Bronchospirometry 89.38
Bronchostomy 33.0
  closure 33.42
Bronchotomy 33.0
Browne (Denis) operation (hypospadias repair)
  58.45
Brunschwig operation (temporary gastrostomy)
  43.19
Buckling, scleral 14.49
  with
    air tamponade 14.49
    implant (silicone) (vitreous) 14.41
    resection of sclera 14.49
    vitrectomy 14.49
    vitreous implant (silicone) 14.41
Bunionectomy (radical) 77.59
  with
    arthrodesis 77.52
    osteotomy of first metatarsal 77.51
    resection of joint with prosthetic implant 77.59
    soft tissue correction NEC 77.53
Bunnell operation (tendon transfer) 82.56
Burgess operation (amputation of ankle) 84.14
Burn dressing 93.57
Burr holes 01.24
Bursectomy 83.5
  hand 82.31
Bursocentesis 83.94
  hand 82.92
Bursotomy 83.03
  hand 82.03
Burying of fimbriae in uterine wall 66.97
Bypass
  abdominal-coronary artery 36.17
  aortocoronary (catheter stent) (with prosthesis)
    (with saphenous graft) (with vein graft)
    36.10
    one coronary vessel 36.11
    two coronary vessels 36.12
    three coronary vessels 36.13
    four coronary vessels 36.14

Bypass—*continued*
  arterial (graft) (mandril grown graft) (vein graft)
      NEC 39.29
    carotid-cerebral 39.28
    carotid-vertebral 39.28
    extracranial-intracranial [EC-IC] 39.28
    intra-abdominal NEC 39.26
    intrathoracic NEC 39.23
    peripheral NEC 39.29
  cardiopulmonary 39.61
    open 39.61
    percutaneous (closed) 39.66
  carotid-cerebral 39.28
  carotid-vertebral 39.28
  coronary (sec also Bypass, aortocoronary) 36.10
  extracranial-intracranial [EC-IC] 39.28
  gastric 44.39
    high 44.31
    Printen and Mason 44.31
  gastroduodenostomy (Jaboulay's) 44.39
  gastroenterostomy 44.39
  gastroepiploic-coronary artery 36.17
  gastrogastrostomy 44.39
  heart-lung (complete) (partial) 39.61
    open 39.61
    percutaneous (closed) 39.66
  high gastric 44.31
  ileo-jejunal 45.91
  internal mammary-coronary artery (single) 36.15
    double vessel 36.16
  jejunal-ileum 45.91
  radial-coronary artery 36.19
  pulmonary 39.61
    open 39.61
    percutaneous (closed) 39.66
  shunt
    intestine
      large-to-large 45.94
      small-to-large 45.93
      small-to-small 45.91
    stomach 44.39
      high gastric 44.31
  terminal ileum 45.93
  vascular (arterial) (graft) (mandril grown graft)
      (vein graft) NEC 39.29
    aorta-carotid-brachial 39.22
    aorta-iliac-femoral 39.25
    aorta-renal 39.24
    aorta-subclavian-carotid 39.22
    aortic-superior mesenteric 39.26
    aortocarotid 39.22
    aortoceliac 39.26
    aortocoronary (*see also* Bypass,
        aortocoronary) 36.10
    aortofemoral 39.25
    aortofemoral-popliteal 39.25
    aortoiliac 39.25
      to popliteal 39.25
    aortoiliofemoral 39.25
    aortomesenteric 39.26
    aortopopliteal 39.25
    aortorenal 39.24
    aortosubclavian 39.22
    axillary-brachial 39.29
    axillary-femoral (superficial) 39.29
    axillofemoral (superficial) 39.29
    carotid to subclavian artery 39.22
    carotid-cerebral 39.28
    carotid-vertebral 39.28
    common hepatic-common iliac-renal 39.26

Bypass—*continued*
    coronary (*see also* Bypass, aortocoronary)
        36.10
    extracranial-intracranial [EC-IC] 39.28
    femoral-femoral 39.29
    femoroperoneal 39.29
    femoropopliteal (reversed saphenous vein)
        (saphenous) 39.29
    femorotibial (anterior) (posterior) 39.29
    iliofemoral 39.25
    ilioiliac 39.26
    internal mammary-coronary artery (single)
        36.15
      double vessel 36.16
    intra-abdominal (arterial) NEC 39.26
      venous NEC 39.1
    intrathoracic NEC 39.23
    peripheral artery NEC 39.29
    popliteal-tibial 39.29
    renal artery 39.24
    splenorenal (venous) 39.1
      arterial 39.26
    subclavian-axillary 39.29
    subclavian-carotid 39.22
    subclavian-subclavian 39.22
    Y graft to renal arteries 39.24

C

Caldwell operation (sulcus extension) 24.91
Caldwell-Luc operation (maxillary sinusotomy) 22.39
  with removal of membrane lining 22.31
Calibration, urethra 89.29
Calicectomy (renal) 55.4
Callander operation (knee disarticulation) 84.16
Caloric test, vestibular function 95.44
Calycectomy (renal) 55.4
Calyco-ileoneocystostomy 55.86
Calycotomy (renal) 55.11
Campbell operation
  bone block, ankle 81.11
  fasciotomy (iliac crest) 83.14
  reconstruction of anterior cruciate
    ligament 81.45
Campimetry 95.05
Canaliculodacryocystorhinostomy 09.81
Canaliculoplasty 09.73
Canaliculorhinostomy 09.81
Canaloplasty, external auditory meatus 18.6
Cannulation —*see also* Insertion, catheter
  ampulla of Vater 51.99
  antrum 22.01
  arteriovenous 39.93
  artery 38.91
  caval-mesenteric vein 39.1
  cisterna chyli 40.61
  Eustachian tube 20.8
  lacrimal apparatus 09.42
  lymphatic duct, left (thoracic) 40.61
  nasal sinus (by puncture) 22.01
    through natural ostium 22.02
  pancreatic duct 52.92
    by retrograde endoscopy (ERP) 52.93
  renoportal 39.1
  sinus (nasal) (by puncture) 22.01
    through natural ostium 22.02
  splenorenal (venous) 39.1
    arterial 39.26
  thoracic duct (cervical approach) (thoracic
    approach) 40.61
Cannulization —*see* Cannulation
Canthocystostomy 09.82
Canthoplasty 08.59
Canthorrhaphy 08.52
  division or severing 08.02
Canthotomy 08.51
Capsulectomy
  joint (*see also* Arthrectomy) 80.90
  kidney 55.91
  lens 13.65
    with extraction of lens 13.51
  ovary 65.29
    laparoscopic 65.25
Capsulo-iridectomy 13.65
Capsuloplasty —*see* Arthroplasty
Capsulorrhaphy 81.96
  with arthroplasty—*see* Arthroplasty
  ankle 81.94
  foot 81.94
  lower extremity NEC 81.95
  upper extremity 81.93

Capsulotomy
  joint (*see also* Division, joint capsule) 80.40
    for claw toe repair 77.57
  lens 13.64
    with
      discission of lens 13.2
      removal of foreign body 13.02
      by magnet extraction 13.01
Cardiac
  mapping 37.27
  massage (external) (closed chest) 99.63
    open chest 37.91
  retraining 93.36
Cardiectomy (stomach) 43.5
Cardiocentesis 37.0
Cardiography (*see also* Angiocardiography) 88.50
Cardiolysis 37.10
Cardiomyopexy 36.3
Cardiomyotomy 42.7
Cardio-omentopexy 36.3
Cardiopericardiopexy 36.3
Cardioplasty (stomach and esophagus) 44.65
  stomach alone 44.66
Cardioplegia 39.63
Cardiopneumopexy 36.3
Cardiorrhaphy 37.4
Cardioschisis 37.12
Cardiosplenopexy 36.3
Cardiotomy (exploratory) 37.11
Cardiovalvulotomy —*see* Valvulotomy, heart
Cardioversion (external) 99.62
  atrial 99.61
Carotid pulse tracing with ECG lead 89.56
Carpectomy (partial) 77.84
  total 77.94
Carroll and Taber arthroplasty (proximal
  interphalangeal joint) 81.72
Casting (for immobilization) NEC 93.53
  with fracture-reduction—*see* Reduction, fracture
Castration
  female (oophorectomy, bilateral) 65.51
    laparoscopic 65.53
  male 62.41
C.A.T. (computerized axial tomography) (*see
  also* Scan, C.A.T.) 88.38
Catheterization —*see also* Insertion, catheter
  arteriovenous 39.93
  artery 38.91
  bladder, indwelling 57.94
    percutaneous (cystostomy) 57.17
    suprapubic NEC 57.18
  bronchus 96.05
    with lavage 96.56
  cardiac (right) 37.21
    combined left and right 37.23
    left 37.22
      combined with right heart 37.23
    right 37.21
      combined with left heart 37.23
  central venous NEC 38.93
    peripherally inserted central catheter (PICC)
    38.93
  Eustachian tube 20.8
  heart (right) 37.21
    combined left and right 37.23
    left 37.22
      combined with right heart 37.23

Change —*see also* Replacement
  cast NEC 97.13
    lower limb 97.12
    upper limb 97.11
  cystostomy catheter or tube 59.94
  gastrostomy tube 97.02
  length
    bone—*see either category* 78.2 Shortening,
      bone *or category* 78.3 Lengthening, bone
    muscle 83.85
      hand 82.55
    tendon 83.85
      hand 82.55
  nephrostomy catheter or tube 55.93
  pyelostomy catheter or tube 55.94
  tracheostomy tube 97.23
  ureterostomy catheter or tube 59.93
  urethra] catheter, indwelling 57.95
Character analysis, psychologic 94.03
Charles operation (correction of lymphedema)
  40.9
Charnley operation (compression arthrodesis)
  ankle 81.11
  hip 81.21
  knee 81.22
Cheatle-Henry operation —*see* Repair, hernia,
  femoral
Check
  pacemaker, artificial (cardiac) (function) (rate)
    89.45
    amperage threshold 89.48
    artifact wave form 89.46
    electrode impedance 89.47
    voltage threshold 89.48
  vision NEC 95.09
Cheiloplasty 27.59
Cheilorrhaphy 27.51
Cheilostomatoplasty 27.59
Cheilotomy 27.0
Chemical peel, skin 86.24
Chemocauterization —*see also* Destruction,
  lesion, by site
  corneal epithelium 11.41
  palate 27.31
Chemodectomy 39.8
Chemoembolization 99.25
Chemolysis
  nerve (peripheral) 04.2
  spinal canal structure 03.8
Chemoneurolysis 04.2
Chemonucleolysis (nucleus pulposus) 80.52
Chemopallidectomy 01.42
Chemopeel (skin) 86.24
Chemosurgery
  esophagus 42.39
    endoscopic 42.33
  Mohs' 86.24
  skin (superficial) 86.24
  stomach 43.49
    endoscopic 43.41
Chemothalamectomy 01.41
Chemotherapy
  Antabuse 94.25
  for cancer NEC 99.25
  lithium 94.22
  methadone 94.25
  palate (bony) 27.31
Chevalier-Jackson operation (partial
  laryngectomy) 30.29
Child operation (radical subtotal
  pancreatectomy) 52.53
Cholangiocholangiostomy 51.39

Cholangiocholecystocholedochectomy 51.22
Cholangio-enterostomy 51.39
Cholangiogastrostomy 51.39
Cholangiogram 87.54
  endoscopic retrograde (ERC) 51.11
  intraoperative 87.53
  intravenous 87.52
  percutaneous hepatic 87.51
  transhepatic 87.53
Cholangiography (*see also* Cholangiogram)
  87.54
Cholangiojejunostomy (intrahepatic) 51.39
Cholangiopancreatography
  endoscopic retrograde 51.10
Cholangiostomy 51.59
Cholangiotomy 51.59
Cholecystectomy (total) 51.22
  laparoscopic 51.23
  partial 51.21
    laparoscopic 51.24
Cholecystenterorrhaphy 51.91
Cholecystocecostomy 51.32
Cholecystocholangiogram 87.59
Cholecystocolostomy 51.32
Cholecystoduodenostomy 51.32
Cholecystoenterostomy (Winiwater) 51.32
Cholecystogastrostomy 51.34
Cholecystogram 87.59
Cholecystoileostomy 51.32
Cholecystojejunostomy (Roux-en-Y) (with
  jejunojejunostomy) 51.32
Cholecystopancreatostomy 51.33
Cholecystopexy 51.99
Cholecystorrhaphy 51.91
Cholecystostomy NEC 51.03
  by trocar 51.02
Cholecystotomy 51.04
Choledochectomy 51.63
Choledochoduodenostomy 51.36
Choledochoenterostomy 51.36
Choledochojejunostomy 51.36
Choledocholithotomy 51.41
  endoscopic 51.88
Choledocholithotripsy 51.41
  endoscopic 51.88
Choledochopancreatostomy 51.39
Choledochoplasty 51.72
Choledochorrhaphy 51.71
Choledochoscopy 51.11
Choledochostomy 51.51
Choledochotomy 51.51
Cholelithotomy 51.04
Chondrectomy 80.90
  ankle 80.97
  elbow 80.92
  foot and toe 80.98
  hand and finger 80.94
  hip 80.95
  intervertebral cartilage *see category* 80.5
  knee (semilunar cartilage) 80.6
  nasal (submucous) 21.5
  semilunar cartilage (knee) 80.6
  shoulder 80.91
  specified site NEC 80.99
  spine *see category* 80.5
  wrist 80.93
Chondroplasty —*see* Arthroplasty
Chondrosternoplasty (for pectus excavatum
  repair) 34.74
Chondrotomy (*see also* Division, cartilage) 80.40
  nasal 21.1
Chopart operation (midtarsal amputation) 84.12

Closure—*continued*
vesicorectal 57.83
vesicosigmoidal 57.83
vesicosigmoidovaginal 57.83
vesicoureteral 56.84
vesicoureterovaginal 56.84
vesicourethral 57.84
vesicourethrorectal 57.83
vesicouterine 57.84
vesicovaginal 57.84
vulva 71.72
vulvorectal 48.73
foramen ovale (patent) 35.71
with
prosthesis (open heart technique) 35.51
closed heart technique 35.52
tissue graft 35.61
gastroduodenostomy 44.5
gastrojejunostomy 44.5
gastrostomy 44.62
ileostomy 46.51
jejunostomy 46.51
laceration—*see also* Suture, by site
liver 50.61
laparotomy, delayed 54.62
meningocele (spinal) 03.51
cerebral 02.12
myelomeningocele 03.52
nephrostomy 55.82
palmar cleft 82.82
patent ductus arteriosus 38.85
pelviostomy 55.82
peptic ulcer (bleeding) (perforated) 44.40
perforation
ear drum (*see also* Tympanoplasty) 19.4
esophagus 42.82
nasal septum 21.88
tympanic membrane (*see also*
Tympanoplasty) 19.4
proctostomy 48.72
punctum, lacrimal (papilla) 09.91
pyelostomy 55.82
rectostomy 48.72
septum defect (heart) (*see also* Repair, heart,
septum) 35.70
sigmoidostomy 46.52
skin (V-Y type) 86.59
stoma
bile duct 51.79
bladder 57.82
bronchus 33.42
common duct 51.72
esophagus 42.83
gallbladder 51.92
hepatic duct 51.79
intestine 46.50
large 46.52
small 46.51
kidney 55.82
larynx 31.62
rectum 48.72
stomach 44.62
thorax 34.72
trachea 31.72
ureter 56.83
urethra 58.42
thoracostomy 34.72
tracheostomy 31.72

Closure—*continued*
ulcer (bleeding) (peptic) (perforated) 44.40
duodenum 44.42
gastric 44.41
intestine (perforated) 46.79
skin 86.59
stomach 44.41
ureterostomy 56.83
urethrostomy 58.42
vagina 70.8
vesicostomy 57.82
wound—*see also* Suture, by site
with graft—*see* Graft
Coagulation, electrocoagulation —*see also*
Destruction, lesion, by site
aneurysm (cerebral) (peripheral vessel) 39.52
arteriovenous fistula 39.53
brain tissue (incremental) (radio frequency)
01.59
broad ligament 69.19
cervix 67.32
ear
external 18.29
inner 20.79
middle 20.51
fallopian tube 66.61
gasserian ganglion 04.05
nose, for epistaxis (with packing) 21.03
ovary 65.29
laparoscopic 65.25
pharynx (by diathermy) 29.39
prostatic bed 60.94
rectum (polyp) 48.32
radical 48.31
retina (for)
destruction of lesion 14.21
reattachment 14.51
repair of tear 14.31
round ligament 69.19
semicircular canals 20.79
spinal cord (lesion) 03.4
urethrovesical junction, transurethral 57.49
uterosacral ligament 69.19
uterus 68.29
vagina 70.33
vulva 71.3
Coating, aneurysm of brain 39.52
Cobalt-60 therapy (treatment) 92.23
Coccygectomy (partial) 77.89
total 77.99
Coccygotomy 77.39
"Cocked hat" procedure (metacarpal
lengthening and transfer of local flap) 82.69
Cockett operation (varicose vein) 38.5
lower limb 38.59
upper limb 38.53
Cody tack (perforation of footplate) 19.0
Coffey operation (uterine suspension) (Meig's
modification) 69.22
Cole operation (anterior tarsal wedge osteotomy)
77.28
Colectomy (partial) (segmental) (subtotal) 45.79
cecum (with terminal ileum) 45.72
left (Hartmann) (lower) (radical) 45.75
multiple segmental 45.71
right (radical) 45.73
sigmoid 45.76
terminal ileum with cecum 45.72
total 45.8
transverse 45.74

Collapse, lung, surgical 33.39
by
destruction of phrenic nerve 33.31
pneumoperitoneum 33.33
pneumothorax, artificially-induced 33.32
thoracoplasty 33.34
Collection, sperm for artificial insemination
99.96
Collis-Nissen operation (hiatal hernia repair
with esophagogastroplasty) 53.80
Colocentesis 45.03
Colocolostomy 45.94
proximal to distal segment 45.79
Colocystoplasty 57.87 *[45.52]*
Colofixation 46.64
Coloileotomy 45.00
Colonna operation
adductor tenotomy (first stage) 83.12
hip arthroplasty (second stage) 81.40
reconstruction of hip (second stage) 81.40
Colonoscopy 45.23
with biopsy 45.25
rectum 48.24
fiberoptic (flexible) 45.23
intraoperative 45.21
through stoma (artificial) 45.22
transabdominal 45.21
Colopexy 46.63
Coloplication 46.64
Coloproctostomy 45.94
Colorectosigmoidostomy 45.94
Colorectostomy 45.94
Colorrhaphy 46.75
Coloscopy —*see* Colonoscopy
Colosigmoidostomy 45.94
Colostomy (ileo-ascending) (ileotransverse)
(perineal) (transverse) 46.10
with anterior rectal resection 48.62
delayed opening 46.14
loop 46.03
permanent (magnetic) 46.13
temporary 46.11
Colotomy 45.03
Colpectomy 70.4
Colpoceliocentesis 70.0
Colpocentesis 70.0
Colpocleisis (complete) (partial) 70.8
Colpohysterectomy 68.59
laparoscopically assisted (LAVH) 68.51
Colpoperineoplasty 70.79
with repair of urethrocele 70.50
Colpoperineorrhaphy 70.71
following delivery 75.69
Colpopexy 70.77
Colpoplasty 70.79
Colpopoiesis 70.61
Colporrhaphy 70.71
anterior (cystocele repair) 70.51
for repair of
cystocele 70.51
with rectocele 70.50
enterocele 70.92
rectocele 70.52
with cystocele 70.50
urethrocele 70.51
posterior (rectocele repair) 70.52
Colposcopy 70.21
Colpotomy 70.14
for pelvic peritoneal drainage 70.12
Commando operation (radical glossectomy) 25.4

Commissurotomy
closed heart technique-*see* Valvulotomy, heart
open heart technique—*see* Valvuloplasty, heart
Compression, trigeminal nerve 04.02
Conchectomy 21.69
Conchotomy 21.1
Conduction study, nerve 89.15
Conduitogram, ileum 87.78
Condylectomy —*see category* 77.8
mandible 76.5
Condylotomy NEC (*see also* Division, joint
capsule) 80.40
mandible (open) 76.62
closed 76.61
Conization
cervix (knife) (sharp) (biopsy) 67.2
by
cryosurgery 67.33
electroconization 67.32
Conjunctivocystorhinostomy 09.82
with insertion of tube or stent 09.83
Conjunctivodacryocystorhinostomy (CDCR)
09.82
with insertion of tube or stent 09.83
Conjunctivodacryocystostomy 09.82
with insertion of tube or stent 09.83
Conjunctivoplasty 10.49
Conjunctivorhinostomy 09.82
with insertion of tube or stent 09.83
Constriction of globe, for scleral buckling (*see
also* Buckling, scleral) 14.49
Construction
auricle, ear (with graft) (with implant) 18.71
ear
auricle (with graft) (with implant) 18.71
meatus (osseous) (skin-lined) 18.6
endorectal ileal pouch (J-pouch) (H-pouch)
(S-pouch) (with anastomosis to anus) 45.95
esophagus, artificial—*see* Anastomosis,
esophagus
ileal bladder (open) 56.51
closed 57.87 *[45.51]*
ileal conduit 56.51
larynx, artificial 31.75
patent meatus (ear) 18.6
penis (rib graft) (skin graft) (myocutaneous
flap) 64.43
pharyngeal valve, artificial 31.75
urethra 58.46
vagina, artificial 70.61
venous valves (peripheral) 39.59
Consultation 89.09
comprehensive 89.07
limited (single organ system) 89.06
specified type NEC 89.08
Continuous positive airway pressure (CPAP)
93.90
Control
atmospheric pressure and composition NEC
93.98
antigen-free air conditioning 93.98
decompression chamber 93.97
mountain sanatorium 93.98

Control—*continued*
  epistaxis 21.00
    by
      cauterization (and packing) 21.03
      coagulation (with packing) 21.03
      electrocoagulation (with packing) 21.03
      excision of nasal mucosa with grafting 21.07
      ligation of artery 21.09
        ethmoidal 21.04
        external carotid 21.06
        maxillary (transantral) 21.05
        packing (nasal) (anterior) 21.01
          posterior (and anterior) 21.02
        specified means NEC 21.09
  hemorrhage 39.98
    abdominal cavity 54.19
    adenoids (postoperative) 28.7
    anus (postoperative) 49.95
    bladder (postoperative) 57.93
    chest 34.09
    colon 45.49
      endoscopic 45.43
    duodenum (ulcer) 44.49
      by
        embolization (transcatheter) 44.44
        suture (ligation) 44.42
      endoscopic 44.43
    esophagus 42.39
      endoscopic 42.33
    gastric (ulcer) 44.49
      by
        embolization (transcatheter) 44.44
        suture (ligation) 44.41
      endoscopic 44.43
    intrapleural 34.09
      postoperative (recurrent) 34.03
    laparotomy site 54.12
    nose (*see also* Control, epistaxis) 21.00
    peptic (ulcer) 44.49
      by
        embolization (transcatheter) 44.44
        suture (ligation) 44.40
      endoscopic 44.43
    pleura, pleural cavity 34.09
      postoperative (recurrent) 34.03
    postoperative NEC 39.98
    postvascular surgery 39.41
    prostate 60.94
    specified site NEC 39.98
    stomach (*see* Control, hemorrhage, gastric)
    thorax NEC 34.09
      postoperative (recurrent) 34.03
    thyroid (postoperative) 06.02
    tonsils (postoperative) 28.7
Conversion
  anastomosis—*see* Revision, anastomosis
  cardiac rhythm NEC 99.69
    to sinus rhythm 99.62
  gastrostomy to jejunostomy
    (endoscopic) 46.32
  obstetrical position—*see* Version
Cooling, gastric 96.31
Cordectomy, vocal 30.22
Cordopexy, vocal 31.69
Cordotomy
  spinal (bilateral) NEC 03.29
    percutaneous 03.21
  vocal 31.3
Corectomy 12.12
Corelysis 12.35
Coreoplasty 12.35
Corneoconjunctivoplasty 11.53

Correction —*see also* Repair
  atresia
    esophageal 42.85
      by magnetic forces 42.99
    external meatus (ear) 18.6
    nasopharynx, nasopharyngeal 29.4
    rectum 48.0
    tricuspid 35.94
  atrial septal defect (*see also* Repair, atrial septal
      defect) 35.71
    combined with repair of valvular and
      ventricular septal defects—*see* Repair,
      endocardial cushion defect
  blepharoptosis (*see also* Repair, blepharoptosis)
      08.36
  bunionette (with osteotomy) 77.54
  chordee 64.42
  claw toe 77.57
  cleft
    lip 27.54
    palate 27.62
  clubfoot NEC 83.84
  coarctation of aorta
    with
      anastomosis 38.34
      graft replacement 38.44
  cornea NEC 11.59
    refractive NEC 11.79
      epikeratophakia 11.76
      keratomeleusis 11.71
      keratophakia 11.72
      radial keratotomy 11.75
  esophageal atresia 42.85
    by magnetic forces 42.99
  everted lacrimal punctum 09.71
  eyelid
    ptosis (*see also* Repair, blepharoptosis) 08.36
    retraction 08.38
  fetal defect 75.36
  forcible, of musculoskeletal deformity
      NEC 93.29
  hammer toe 77.56
  hydraulic pressure, open surgery (for) penile
      prosthesis, inflatable 64.99
    urinary sphincter, artificial 58.99
  intestinal malrotation 46.80
    large 46.82
    small 46.81
  inverted uterus—*see* Repair, inverted uterus
  lymphedema (of limb) 40.9
    excision with graft 40.9
    obliteration of lymphatics 40.9
    transplantation of autogenous lymphatics 40.9
  nasopharyngeal atresia 29.4
  overlapping toes 77.58
  palate (cleft) 27.62
  prognathism NEC 76.64
  prominent ear 18.5
  punctum (everted) 09.71
  spinal pseudarthrosis 81.09
  syndactyly 86.85
  tetralogy of Fallot
    one-stage 35.81
    partial—*see specific procedure*
    total 35.81
  total anomalous pulmonary venous connection
    one-stage 35.82
    partial—*see specific procedure*
    total 35.82
  transposition, great arteries, total 35.84
  tricuspid atresia 35.94

Correction—*continued*
truncus arteriosus
one-stage 35.83
partial—*see specific procedure*
total 35.83
ureteropelvic junction 55.87
ventricular septal defect (*see also* Repair,
ventricular septal defect) 35.72
combined with repair of valvular and atrial
septal defects—*see* Repair, endocardial
cushion defect
Costectomy 77.91
with lung excision—*see* Excision, lung
associated with thoracic operation—*omit code*
Costochondrectomy 77.91
associated with thoracic operation—*omit code*
Costosternoplasty (pectus excavatum repair)
34.74
Costotomy 77.31
Costotransversectomy 77.91
associated with thoracic operation—*omit code*
Counseling (for) NEC 94.49
alcoholism 94.46
drug addiction 94.45
employers 94.49
family (medical) (social) 94.49
marriage 94.49
ophthalmologic (with instruction) 95.36
pastoral 94.49
Countershock, cardiac NEC 99.62
Coventry Operation (tibial wedge osteotomy)
77.27
CPAP (continuous positive airway pressure)
93.90
Craniectomy 01.25
linear (opening of cranial suture) 02.01
reopening of site 01.23
strip (opening of cranial suture) 02.01
Cranioclasis, fetal 73.8
Cranioplasty 02.06
with synchronous repair of encephalocele 02.12
Craniotomy 01.24
as operative approach—*omit code*
fetal 73.8
for decompression of fracture 02.02
reopening of site 01.23
Craterization, bone (*see also* Excision, lesion,
bone) 77.60
Crawford operation (tarso-frontalis sling of
eyelid) 08.32
Creation —*see also* Formation
cardiac pacemaker pocket
with initial insertion of pacemaker—*omit code*
new site (skin) (subcutaneous) 37.79
conduit
ileal (urinary) 56.51
left ventricle and aorta 35.93
right atrium and pulmonary artery 35.94
right ventricle and pulmonary (distal) artery
35.92
in repair of
pulmonary artery atresia 35.92
transposition of great vessels 35.92
truncus arteriosus 35.83
endorectal ileal pouch (J-pouch) (H-pouch)
(S-pouch) (with anastomosis to anus) 45.95
esophagogastric sphincteric competence NEC
44.66
Hartmann pouch—*see* Colectomy, by site
interatrial fistula 35.42
pericardial window 37.12

Creation—*continued*
pleural window, for drainage 34.09
shunt—*see also* Shunt
arteriovenous fistula, for dialysis 39.93
left-to-right (systemic to pulmonary
circulation) 39.0
subcutaneous tunnel for esophageal anastomosis
42.86
with anastomosis—*see* Anastomosis,
esophagus, antesternal
syndactyly (finger) (toe) 86.89
tracheoesophageal fistula 31.95
window
pericardial 37.12
pleura, for drainage 34.09
Credé maneuver 73.59
Cricoidectomy 30.29
Cricothyreotomy (for assistance in breathing)
31.1
Cricothyroidectomy 30.29
Cricothyrostomy 31.1
Cricothyrotomy (for assistance in breathing) 31.1
Cricotomy (for assistance in breathing) 31.1
Cricotracheotomy (for assistance in breathing)
31.1
Crisis Intervention 94.35
Croupette, croup tent 93.94
Crown, dental (ceramic) (gold) 23.41
Crushing
bone—*see category* 78.4
calculus
bile (hepatic) passage 51.49
endoscopic 51.88
bladder (urinary) 57.0
pancreatic duct 52.09
endoscopic 52.94
fallopian tube (*see also* Ligation, fallopian tube)
66.39
ganglion—*see* Crushing, nerve
hemorrhoids 49.45
nasal septum 21.88
nerve (cranial) (peripheral) NEC 04.03
acoustic 04.01
auditory 04.01
phrenic 04.03
for collapse of lung 33.31
sympathetic 05.0
trigeminal 04.02
vestibular 04.01
vas deferens 63.71
Cryoablation —*see* Ablation
Cryoanalgesia
nerve (cranial) (peripheral) 04.2
Cryoconization, cervix 67.33
Cryodestruction —*see* Destruction, lesion, by
site
Cryoextraction, lens (*see also* Extraction,
cataract, intracapsular) 13.19
Cryohypophysectomy (complete) (total) (*see
also* Hypophysectomy) 07.69
Cryoleucotomy 01.32
Cryopexy, retinal —*see* Cryotherapy, retina
Cryoprostatectomy 60.62
Cryoretinopexy (for)
reattachment 14.52
repair of tear or defect 14.32
Cryosurgery —*see* Cryotherapy
Cryothalamectomy 01.41
Cryotherapy —*see also* Destruction, lesion, by
site
bladder 57.59

D

Decompression—*continued*
  thoracic outlet
    by
      myotomy (division of scalenus anticus
        muscle) 83.19
      tenotomy 83.13
    trigeminal (nerve root) 04.41
Decortication
  arterial 05.25
  brain 01.51
  cerebral meninges 01.51
  heart 37.31
  kidney 55.91
  lung (partial) (total) 34.51
  nasal turbinates—*see* Turbinectomy
  nose 21.89
  ovary 65.29
    laparoscopic 65.25
  periarterial 05.25
  pericardium 37.31
  ventricle, heart (complete) 37.31
Deepening
  alveolar ridge 24.5
  buccolabial sulcus 24.91
  lingual sulcus 24.91
Defatting, flap or pedicle graft 86.75
Defibrillation, electric (external) (internal) 99.62
de Grandmont operation (tarsectomy) 08.35
Delaying of pedicle graft 86.71
Delivery (with)
  assisted spontaneous 73.59
  breech extraction (assisted) 72.52
    partial 72.52
      with forceps to aftercoming head 72.51
    total 72.54
      with forceps to aftercoming head 72.53
    unassisted (spontaneous delivery)—*omit code*
  cesarean section—*see* Cesarean section
  Credé maneuver 73.59
  De Lee maneuver 72.4
  forceps 72.9
    application to aftercoming head (Piper) 72.6
      with breech extraction
        partial 72.51
        total 72.53
    Barton's 72.4
    failed 73.3
    high 72.39
      with episiotomy 72.31
    low (outlet) 72.0
      with episiotomy 72.1
    mid 72.29
      with episiotomy 72.21
    outlet (low) 72.0
      with episiotomy 72.1
    rotation of fetal head 72.4
    trial 73.3
  instrumental NEC 72.9
    specified NEC 72.8
  key-in-lock rotation 72.4
  Kielland rotation 72.4
  Malström's extraction 72.79
    with episiotomy 72.71
  manually assisted (spontaneous) 73.59
  spontaneous (unassisted) 73.59
    assisted 73.59
  vacuum extraction 72.79
    with episiotomy 72.71

Delorme operation
  pericardiectomy 37.31
  proctopexy 48.76
  repair of prolapsed rectum 48.76
  thoracoplasty 33.34
Denervation
  aortic body 39.8
  carotid body 39.8
  facet, percutaneous (radio frequency) 03.96
  ovarian 65.94
  paracervical uterine 69.3
  uterosacral 69.3
Denker operation (radical maxillary antrotomy)
  22.31
Dennis-Barco operation —*see* Repair, hernia,
  femoral
Denonvillier operation (limited rhinoplasty)
  21.86
Densitometry, bone (serial)
  (radiographic) 88.98
Depilation, skin 86.92
Derlacki operation (tympanoplasty) 19.4
Dermabrasion (laser) 86.25
  for wound debridement 86.28
Derotation —*see* Reduction, torsion
Desensitization
  allergy 99.12
  psychologic 94.33
Desmotomy (*see also* Division, ligament) 80.40
Destruction
  breast 85.20
  chorioretinopathy (*see also* Destruction, lesion,
    choroid) 14.29
  ciliary body 12.74
  epithelial downgrowth, anterior chamber 12.93
  fallopian tube 66.39
    with
      crushing (and ligation) 66.31
        by endoscopy laparoscopy) 66.21
      division (and ligation) 66.32
        by endoscopy (culdoscopy)
          (hysteroscopy) (laparoscopy)
          (peritoneoscopy) 66.22
    ligation 66.39
      with
        crushing 66.31
          by endoscopy (laparoscopy) 66.21
        division 66.32
          by endoscopy (culdoscopy)
            (hysteroscopy) (laparoscopy)
            (peritoneoscopy) 66.22
    unilateral 66.92
  fetus 73.8
  hemorrhoids 49.49
    by
      cryotherapy 49.44
      sclerotherapy 49.42
  inner ear NEC 20.79
    by injection 20.72
  intervertebral disc NOS 80.50
    by injection 80.52
    by other specified method 80.59
    herniated (nucleus pulposus) 80.51
  lacrimal sac 09.6
  lesion (local)
    anus 49.39
      endoscopic 49.31
    Bartholin's gland 71.24
      by
        aspiration 71.21
        excision 71.24

Destruction—*continued*
    incision 71.22
      marsupialization 71.23
  biliary ducts 51.69
    endoscopic 51.64
  bladder 57.59
    transurethral 57.49
  bone—*see* Excision, lesion, bone
  bowel—*see* Destruction, lesion, intestine
  brain (transtemporal approach) NEC 01.59
    by stereotactic radiosurgery 92.3
  breast NEC 85.20
  bronchus NEC 32.09
    endoscopic 32.01
  cerebral NEC 01.59
    meninges 01.51
  cervix 67.39
    by
      cauterization 67.32
      cryosurgery, cryoconization 67.33
      electroconization 67.32
  choroid 14.29
    by
      cryotherapy 14.22
      diathermy 14.21
      implantation of radiation source 14.27
      photocoagulation 14.25
        laser 14.24
        xenon arc 14.23
      radiation therapy 14.26
  ciliary body (nonexcisional) 12.43
    by excision 12.44
  conjunctiva 10.32
    by excision 10.31
  cornea NEC 11.49
    by
      cryotherapy 11.43
      electrocauterization 11.42
      thermocauterization 11.42
  cul-de-sac 70.32
  duodenum NEC 45.32
    by excision 45.31
      endoscopic 45.30
    endoscopic 45.30
  esophagus (chemosurgery) (cryosurgery)
    (electroresection) (fulguration) NEC 42.39
    by excision 42.32
      endoscopic 42.33
    endoscopic 42.33
  eye NEC 16.93
  eyebrow 08.25
  eyelid 08.25
    excisional—*see* Excision, lesion, eyelid
  heart 37.33
    by catheter ablation 37.34
  intestine (large) 45.49
    by excision 45.41
      endoscopic 45.43
        polypectomy 45.42
    endoscopic 45.43
      polypectomy 45.42
    small 45.34
      by excision 45.33
  intranasal 21.31
  iris (nonexcisional) NEC 12.41
    by excision 12.42
  kidney 55.39
    by marsupialization 55.31
  lacrimal sac 09.6
  larynx 30.09
  liver 50.29

Destruction—*continued*
  lung 32.29
    endoscopic 32.28
  meninges (cerebral) 01.51
    spinal 03.4
  nerve (peripheral) 04.07
    sympathetic 05.29
  nose 21.30
    intranasal 21.31
    specified NEC 21.32
  ovary
    by aspiration 65.91
    by excision 65.29
      laparoscopic 65.25
    cyst by rupture (manual) 65.93
  palate (bony) (local) 27.31
    wide 27.32
  pancreas 52.22
    by marsupialization 52.3
      endoscopic 52.21
  pancreatic duct 52.22
    endoscopic 52.21
  penis 64.2
  pharynx (excisional) 29.39
  pituitary gland
    by stereotactic radiosurgery 92.3
  rectum (local) 48.32
    by
      cryosurgery 48.34
      electrocoagulation 48.32
      excision 48.35
      fulguration 48.32
      laser (Argon) 48.33
    polyp 48.36
    radical 48.31
  retina 14.29
    by
      cryotherapy 14.22
      diathermy 14.21
      implantation of radiation source 14.27
      photocoagulation 14.25
        laser 14.24
        xenon arc 14.23
      radiation therapy 14.26
  salivary gland NEC 26.29
    by marsupialization 26.21
  sclera 12.84
  scrotum 61.3
  skin NEC 86.3
  sphincter of Oddi 51.69
    endoscopic 51.64
  spinal cord (meninges) 03.4
  spleen 41.42
    by marsupialization 41.41
  stomach NEC 43.49
    by excision 43.42
      endoscopic 43.41
    endoscopic 43.41
  subcutaneous tissue NEC 86.3
  testis 62.2
  tongue 25.1
  urethra (excisional) 58.39
    endoscopic 58.31
  uterus 68.29
  nerve (cranial) (peripheral) (by cryoanalgesia)
    (by radio frequency) 04.2
  sympathetic, by injection of neurolytic agent
    05.32
  neuroma 04.07
    acoustic
      by craniotomy 04.01

Destruction—*continued*
    by radiosurgery 04.07
    cranial 04.07
    Morton's 04.07
    peripheral
      Morton's 04.07
  neuroma
    acoustic 04.01
    by stereotactic radiosurgery 92.3
  semicircular canals, by injection 20.72
  vestibule, by injection 20.72
Detachment, uterosacral ligaments 69.3
Determination
  mental status (clinical) (medicolegal)
    (psychiatric) NEC 94.11
    psychologic NEC 94.09
  vital capacity (pulmonary) 89.37
Detorsion
  intestine (twisted) (volvulus) 46.80
    large 46.82
      endoscopic (balloon) 46.85
    small 46.81
  kidney 55.84
  ovary 65.95
  spermatic cord 63.52
    with orchiopexy 62.5
  testis 63.52
    with orchiopexy 62.5
  volvulus 46.80
    endoscopic (balloon) 46.85
Detoxification therapy 94.25
  alcohol 94.62
    with rehabilitation 94.63
    combined alcohol and drug 94.68
      with rehabilitation 94.69
  drug 94.65
    with rehabilitation 94.66
    combined alcohol and drug 94.68
      with rehabilitation 94.69
Devascularization, stomach 44.99
Dewebbing
  esophagus 42.01
  syndactyly (fingers) (toes) 86.85
Dextrorotation —*see* Reduction, torsion
Dialysis
  hemodiafiltration, hemofiltration
    (extracorporeal) 39.95
  kidney (extracorporeal) 39.95
  peritoneal 54.98
  renal (extracorporeal) 39.95
Diaphanoscopy
  nasal sinuses 89.35
  skull (newborn) 89.16
Diaphysectomy —*see category* 77.8
Diathermy 93.34
  choroid—*see* Diathermy, retina
  nasal turbinates 21.61
  retina
    for
      destruction of lesion 14.21
      reattachment 14.51
      repair of tear 14.31
  surgical—*see* Destruction, lesion, by site
  turbinates (nasal) 21.61
Dickson operation (fascial transplant) 83.82
Dickson-Diveley operation (tendon transfer and
  arthrodesis to correct claw toe) 77.57
Dieffenbach operation (hip disarticulation) 84.18
Dilation
  achalasia 42.92

Dilation—*continued*
  ampulla of Vater 51.81
    endoscopic 51.84
  anus, anal (sphincter) 96.23
  biliary duct
    endoscopic 51.84
    pancreatic duct 52.99
      endoscopic 52.98
    percutaneous (endoscopy) 51.98
    sphincter
      of Oddi 51.81
        endoscopic 51.84
      pancreatic 51.82
        endoscopic 51.85
  bladder 96.25
    neck 57.92
  bronchus 33.91
  cervix (canal) 67.0
    obstetrical 73.1
    to assist delivery 73.1
  choanae (nasopharynx) 29.91
  colon, (endoscopic) (balloon) 46.85
  colostomy stoma 96.24
  duodenum,(endoscopic) (balloon) 46.85
  endoscopic—*see* Dilation, by site
  enterostomy stoma 96.24
  esophagus (by bougie) (by sound) 42.92
  fallopian tube 66.96
  foreskin (newborn) 99.95
  frontonasal duct 96.21
  gastrojejunostomy site, endoscopic 44.22
  heart valve—*see* Valvulotomy, heart
  ileostomy stoma 96.24
  ileum (endoscopic) (balloon) 46.85
  intestinal stoma (artificial) 96.24
  intestine (endoscopic) (balloon) 46.85
  jejunum (endoscopic) (balloon) 46.85
  lacrimal
    duct 09.42
    punctum 09.41
  larynx 31.98
  lymphatic structure(s) (peripheral) 40.9
  nares 21.99
  nasolacrimal duct (retrograde) 09.43
    with insertion of tube or stent 09.44
  nasopharynx 29.91
  pancreatic duct 52.99
    endoscopic 52.98
  pharynx 29.91
  prostatic urethra (transurethral) (balloon) 60.95
  punctum, lacrimal papilla 09.41
  pylorus
    by incision 44.21
    endoscopic 44.22
  rectum 96.22
  salivary duct 26.91
  sphenoid ostia 22.52
  sphincter
    anal 96.23
    cardiac 42.92
    of Oddi 51.81
      endoscopic 51.84
    pancreatic 51.82
      endoscopic 51.85
    pylorus (endoscopic) 44.22
    by incision 44.21
  Stenson's duct 26.91
  trachea 31.99
  ureter 59.8
    meatus 56.91
  ureterovesical orifice 59.8

Dilation—*continued*
  urethra 58.6
    prostatic (transurethral))balloon) 60.95
  urethrovesical junction 58.6
  vagina (instrumental) (manual) NEC 96.16
  vesical neck 57.92
  Wharton's duct 26.91
  Wirsung's duct 52.99
    endoscopic 52.98
Dilation and curettage, uterus (diagnostic) 69.09
  after
    abortion 69.02
    delivery 69.02
  to terminate pregnancy 69.01
Diminution, ciliary body 12.74
Disarticulation 84.91
  ankle 84.13
  elbow 84.06
  finger, except thumb 84.01
    thumb 84.02
  hip 84.18
  knee 84.16
  shoulder 84.08
  thumb 84.02
  toe 84.11
  wrist 84.04
Discission
  capsular membrane 13.64
  cataract (Wheeler knife) (Ziegler knife) 13.2
    congenital 13.69
    secondary membrane 13.64
  iris 12.12
  lens (capsule) (Wheeler knife) (Ziegler knife)
      (with capsulotomy) 13.2
  orbitomaxillary, radical 16.51
  pupillary 13.2
  secondary membrane (after cataract) 13.64
  vitreous strands (posterior approach) 14.74
    anterior approach 14.73
Discogram, diskogram 87.21
Discolysis (by injection) 80.52
Diskectomy, intervertebral 80.51
  herniated (nucleus pulposus) 80.51
    percutaneous 80.59
Dispensing (with fitting)
  contact lens 95.32
  low vision aids NEC 95.33
  spectacles 95.31
Dissection —*see also* Excision
  aneurysm 38.60
  artery-vein-nerve bundle 39.91
  branchial cleft fistula or sinus 29.52
  bronchus 32.1
  femoral hernia 53.29
  groin, radical 40.54
  larynx block (en bloc) 30.3
  mediastinum with pneumonectomy 32.5
  neck, radical 40.40
    with laryngectomy 30.4
    bilateral 40.42
    unilateral 40.41
  orbital fibrous bands 16.92
  pterygium (with reposition) 11.31
  radical neck—*see* Dissection, neck, radical
  retroperitoneal NEC 59.00
  thoracic structures (block) (en bloc) (radical)
      (brachial plexus, bronchus, lobe of lung,
      ribs, and sympathetic nerves) 32.6
  vascular bundle 39.91
Distention, bladder (therapeutic) (intermittent) 96.25

Diversion, urinary
  cutaneous 56.61
  ileal conduit 56.51
  internal NEC 56.71
  ureter to
    intestine 56.71
    skin 56.61
  uretero-ileostomy 56.51
Diversional therapy 93.81
Diverticulectomy
  bladder (suprapubic) 57.59
    transurethral approach 57.49
  duodenum 45.31
    endoscopic 45.30
  esophagus 42.31
    endoscopic 42.33
  esophagomyotomy 42.7
  hypopharyngeal (by cricopharyngeal myotomy) 29.32
  intestine
    large 45.41
      endoscopic 45.43
    small 45.33
  kidney 55.39
  Meckel's 45.33
  pharyngeal (by cricopharyngeal myotomy) 29.32
  pharyngoesophageal (by cricopharyngeal myotomy) 29.32
  stomach 43.42
    endoscopic 43.41
  urethra 58.39
    endoscopic 58.31
Division
  Achilles tendon 83.11
  adductor tendon (hip) 83.12
  adhesions—*see* Lysis, adhesions
  angle of mandible (open) 76.62
    closed 76.61
  anterior synechiae 12.32
  aponeurosis 83.13
  arcuate ligament (spine)—omit
  arteriovenous fistula (with ligation) 39.53
  artery (with ligation) 38.80
    abdominal 38.86
    aorta (arch) (ascending) (descending) 38.84
    head and neck NEC 38.82
    intracranial NEC 38.81
    lower limb 38.88
    thoracic NEC 38.85
    upper limb 38.83
  bladder neck 57.91
  blepharorrhaphy 08.02
  blood vessels, cornea 10.1
  bone (*see also* Osteotomy) 77.30
  brain tissue 01.32
    cortical adhesions 02.91
  canaliculus 09.52
  canthorrhaphy 08.02
  cartilage 80.40
    ankle 80.47
    elbow 80.42
    foot and toe 80.48
    hand and finger 80.44
    hip 80.45
    knee 80.46
    shoulder 80.41
    specified site NEC 80.49
    spine 80.49
    wrist 80.43
  cerebral tracts 01.32
  chordae tendineae 35.32

Division—*continued*

common wall between posterior left atrium and
   coronary sinus (with roofing of resultant
   defect with patch graft) 35.82
congenital web
  larynx 31.98
  pharynx 29.54
endometrial synechiae 68.21
fallopian tube—*see* Ligation, fallopian tube
fascia 83.14
  hand 82.12
frenulum, frenum
  labial 27.91
  lingual 25.91
  tongue 25.91
ganglion, sympathetic 05.0
glossopharyngeal nerve 29.92
goniosynechiae 12.31
hypophyseal stalk (*see also* Hypophysectomy,
  partial) 07.63
iliotibial band 83.14
isthmus
  horseshoe kidney 55.85
  thyroid 06.91
joint capsule 80.40
  ankle 80.47
  elbow 80.42
  foot and toe 80.48
  hand and finger 80.44
  hip 80.45
  knee 80.46
  shoulder 80.41
  specified site NEC 80.49
  wrist 80.43
labial frenum 27.91
lacrimal ductules 09.0
laryngeal nerve (external) (recurrent) (superior)
  31.91
ligament 80.40
  ankle 80.47
  arcuate (spine)—*omit code*
  canthal 08.36
  elbow 80.42
  foot and toe 80.48
  hand and finger 80.44
  hip 80.45
  knee 80.46
  palpebrae 08.36
  shoulder 80.41
  specified site NEC 80.49
  spine 80.49
    arcuate—*omit code*
    flavum—*omit code*
  uterosacral 69.3
  wrist 80.43
ligamentum flavum (spine)—*omit code*
meninges (cerebral) 01.31
muscle 83.19
  hand 82.19
nasolacrimal duct stricture (with drainage) 09.59
nerve (cranial) (peripheral) NEC 04.03
  acoustic 04.01
  adrenal gland 07.42
  auditory 04.01
  glossopharyngeal 29.92
  lacrimal branch 05.0
  laryngeal (external) (recurrent) (superior)
    31.91
  vestibular 04.01
phrenic 04.03
  for collapse of lung 33.31

Division—*continued*

root, spinal or intraspinal 03.1
sympathetic 05.0
tracts
  cerebral 01.32
  spinal cord 03.29
    percutaneous 03.21
  trigeminal 04.02
  vagus (*see also* Vagotomy) 44.00
  vestibular 04.01
otosclerotic process or material, middle ear 19.0
papillary muscle (heart) 35.31
patent ductus arteriosus 38.85
penile adhesions 64.93
posterior synechiae 12.33
pylorus (with wedge resection) 43.3
rectum (stricture) 48.91
scalenus anticus muscle 83.19
Skene's gland 71.3
soft tissue NEC 83.19
  hand 82.19
sphincter
  anal (external) (internal) 49.59
    left lateral 49.51
    posterior 49.52
  cardiac 42.7
  of Oddi 51.82
    endoscopic 51.85
  pancreatic 51.82
    endoscopic 51.85
spinal
  cord tracts 03.29
    percutaneous 03.21
  nerve root 03.1
symblepharon (with insertion of conformer) 10.5
synechiae
  endometrial 68.21
  iris (posterior) 12.33
    anterior 12.32
tarsorrhaphy 08.02
tendon 83.13
  Achilles 83.11
  adductor (hip) 83.12
  hand 82.11
trabeculae carneae cordis (heart) 35.35
tympanum 20.23
uterosacral ligaments 69.3
vaginal septum 70.14
vas deferens 63.71
vein (with ligation) 38.80
  abdominal 38.87
  head and neck NEC 38.82
  intracranial NEC 38.81
  lower limb 38.89
    varicose 38.59
  thoracic NEC 38.85
  upper limb 38.83
  varicose 38.50
    abdominal 38.57
    head and neck NEC 38.52
    intracranial NEC 38.51
    lower limb 38.59
    thoracic NEC 38.55
    upper limb 39.53
vitreous, cicatricial bands (posterior approach)
  14.74
  anterior approach 14.73
Doleris operation (shortening of round
  ligaments) 69.22
D'Ombrain operation (excision of pterygium
  with corneal graft) 11.32
Domestic tasks therapy 93.83

Dopplergram, Doppler flow mapping —*see also* Ultrasonography
  aortic arch 88.73
  head and neck 88.71
  heart 88.72
  thorax NEC 88.73
Dorrance operation (push-back operation for cleft palate) 27.62
Dotter operation (transluminal angioplasty) 39.59
Douche, vagina 96.44
Douglas operation (suture of tongue to lip for micrognathia) 25.59
Doyle operation (paracervical uterine denervation) 69.3
Drainage
  by
    anastomosis—*see* Anastomosis
    aspiration—*see* Aspiration
    incision—*see* Incision
  abdomen 54.19
    percutaneous 54.91
  abscess—*see also* Drainage, by site and Incision, by site
    appendix 47.2
      with appendectomy 47.09
        laparoscopic 47.01
    parapharyngeal (oral) (transcervical) 28.0
    peritonsillar (oral) (transcervical) 28.0
    retropharyngeal (oral) (transcervical) 28.0
    thyroid (field) (gland) 06.09
      percutaneous (needle) 06.01
      postoperative 06.02
    tonsil, tonsillar (oral) (transcervical) 28.0
  antecubital fossa 86.04
  appendix 47.91
    with appendectomy 47.09
      laparoscopic 47.01
    abscess 47.2
      with appendectomy 47.09
        laparoscopic 47.01
  axilla 86.04
  bladder (without incision) 57.0
    by indwelling catheter 57.94
      percutaneous suprapubic (closed) 57.17
      suprapubic NEC 57.18
  buccal space 27.0
  bursa 83.03
    by aspiration 83.94
      hand 82.92
    hand 82.03
      by aspiration 82.92
    radial 82.03
    ulnar 82.03
  cerebrum, cerebral (meninges) (ventricle) (incision) (trephination) 01.39
    by
      anastomosis—*see* Shunt, ventricular
      aspiration 01.09
      through previously implanted catheter 01.02
  chest (closed) 34.04
    open (by incision) 34.09
  crania] sinus (incision) (trephination) 01.21
    by aspiration 01.09
  cul-de-sac 70.12
    by aspiration 70.0
  cyst—*see also* Drainage, by site and incision, by site
    pancreas (by catheter) 52.01
      by marsupialization 52.3
      internal (anastomosis) 52.4

Drainage—*continued*
  pilonidal 86.03
  spleen, splenic (by marsupialization) 41.41
  duodenum (tube) 46.39
    by incision 45.01
  ear
    external 18.09
    inner 20.79
    middle (by myringotomy) 20.09
      with intubation 20.01
  epidural space, cerebral (incision) (trephination) 01.24
    by aspiration 01.09
  extradural space, cerebral (incision) (trephination) 01.24
    by aspiration 01.09
  extraperitoneal 54.0
  facial region 27.0
  fascial compartments, head and neck 27.0
  fetal hydrocephalic head (needling) (trocar) 73.8
  gallbladder 51.04
    by
      anastomosis 51.35
      aspiration 51.01
      incision 51.04
  groin region (abdominal wall) (inguinal) 54.0
    skin 86.04
    subcutaneous tissue 86.04
  hematoma—*see* Drainage, by site and Incision, by site
  hydrocephalic head (needling) (trocar) 73.8
  hypochondrium 54.0
    intra-abdominal 54.19
  iliac fossa 54.0
  infratemporal fossa 27.0
  intracranial space (epidural) (extradural) (incision) (trephination) 01.24
    by aspiration 01.09
    subarachnoid or subdural (incision) (trephination) 01.31
      by aspiration 01.09
  intraperitoneal 54.19
  kidney (by incision) 55.01
    by
      anastomosis 55.86
      catheter 59.8
    pelvis (by incision) 55.11
  liver 50.0
    by aspiration 50.91
  Ludwig's angina 27.0
  lung (by incision) 33.1
    by punch (needle) (trocar) 33.93
  midpalmar space 82.04
  mouth floor 27.0
  mucocele, nasal sinus 22.00
    by puncture 22.01
    through natural ostium 22.02
  omentum 54.19
    percutaneous 54.91
  ovary (aspiration) 65.91
    by incision 65.09
      laparoscopic 65.01
  palmar space (middle) 82.04
  pancreas (by catheter) 52.01
    by anastomosis 52.96
  parapharyngeal 28.0
  paronychia 86.04
  parotid space 27.0
  pelvic peritoneum (female) 70.12
    male 54.19
  pericardium 37.0

Drainage—*continued*
  perigastric 54.19
    percutaneous 54.91
  perineum
    female 71.09
    male 86.04
  perisplenic tissue 54.19
    percutaneous 54.91
  peritoneum 54.19
    pelvic (female) 70.12
    percutaneous 54.91
  peritonsillar 28.0
  pharyngeal space, lateral 27.0
  pilonidal cyst or sinus 86.03
  pleura (closed) 34.04
    open (by incision) 34.09
  popliteal space 86.04
  postural 93.99
  postzygomatic space 27.0
  pseudocyst, pancreas 52.3
    by anastomosis 52.4
  pterygopalatine fossa 27.0
  retropharyngeal 28.0
  scrotum 61.0
  skin 86.04
  spinal (canal) (cord) 03.09
    by anastomosis—*see* Shunt, spinal
    diagnostic 03.31
  spleen 41.2
    cyst (by marsupialization) 41.41
  subarachnoid space, cerebral (incision)
      (trephination) 01.31
    by aspiration 01.09
  subcutaneous tissue 86.04
  subdiaphragmatic 54.91
    percutaneous 54.91
  subdural space, cerebral (incision)
      (trephination) 01.31
    by aspiration 01.09
  subhepatic space 54.19
    percutaneous 54.91
  sublingual space 27.0
  submental space 27.0
  subphrenic space 54.19
    percutaneous 54.91
  supraclavicular fossa 86.04
  temporal pouches 27.0
  tendon (sheath) 83.01
    hand 82.01
  thenar space 82.04
  thorax (closed) 34.04
    open (by incision) 34.09
  thyroglossal tract (by incision) 06.09
    by aspiration 06.01
  thyroid (field) (gland) (by incision) 06.09
    by aspiration 06.01
    postoperative 06.02
  tonsil 28.0
  tunica vaginalis 61.0
  ureter (by catheter) 59.8
    by
      anastomosis NEC (*see also* Anastomosis,
        ureter) 56.79
      incision 56.2
  ventricle (cerebral) (incision) NEC 02.39
    by
      anastomosis—*see* Shunt, ventricular
      aspiration 01.09
        through previously implanted catheter
          01.02
  vertebral column 03.09
Drawing test 94.08

Dressing
  burn 93.57
  ulcer 93.56
  wound 93.57
Drilling, bone (*see also* Incision, bone) 77.10
Ductogram, mammary 87.35
Duhamel operation (abdominoperineal
    pull-through) 48.65
Dührssen's
  incisions (cervix, to assist delivery) 73.93
  operation (vaginofixation of uterus) 69.22
Dunn operation (triple arthrodesis) 81.12
Duodenectomy 45.62
  with
    gastrectomy—*see* Gastrectomy
    pancreatectomy—*see* Pancreatectomy
Duodenocholedochotomy 51.51
Duodenoduodenostomy 45.91
  proximal to distal segment 45.62
Duodenoileostomy 45.91
Duodenojejunostomy 45.91
Duodenorrhaphy 46.71
Duodenoscopy 45.13
  through stoma (artificial) 45.12
  transabdominal (operative) 45.11
Duodenostomy 46.39
Duodenotomy 45.01
Dupuytren operation
  fasciectomy 82.35
  fasciotomy 82.12
    with excision 82.35
  shoulder disarticulation 84.08
Duraplasty 02.12
Durham (Caldwell) operation (transfer of biceps
    femoris tendon) 83.75
DuToit and Roux operation (staple
    capsulorrhaphy of shoulder) 81.82
DuVries operation (tenoplasty) 83.88
Dwyer operation
  fasciotomy 83.14
  soft tissue release NEC 83.84
  wedge osteotomy, calcaneus 77.28

E

Eagleton operation (extrapetrosal drainage)
  20.22
ECG —*see* Electrocardiogram
Echocardiography 88.72
  transesophageal 88.72 *[42.23]*
  monitoring (Doppler) (ultrasound) 89.68
Echoencephalography 88.71
Echography —*see* Ultrasonography
Echogynography 88.79
Echoplacentogram 88.78
ECMO (extracorporeal membrane oxygenation)
  39.65
Eden-Hybinette operation (glenoid bone block)
  78.01
Educational therapy (bed-bound children)
  (handicapped) 93.82
EEG (electroencephalogram) 89.14
  monitoring (radiographic) (video) 89.19
Effler operation (heart) 36.2
Effleurage 93.39
EGD (esophagogastroduodenoscopy) 45.13
  with closed biopsy 45.16
Eggers operation
  tendon release (patellar retinacula) 83.13
  tendon transfer (biceps femoris tendon)
    (hamstring tendon) 83.75
EKG (*see also* Electrocardiogram) 89.52
Elastic hosiery 93.59
Electrocardiogram (with 12 or more leads) 89.52
  with vectorcardiogram 89.53
  fetal (scalp), intrauterine 75.32
  rhythm (with one to three leads) 89.51
Electrocautery —*see also* Cauterization
  cervix 67.32
  corneal lesion (ulcer) 11.42
  esophagus 42.39
  endoscopic 42.33
Electrocoagulation —*see also* Destruction,
  lesion, by site
  aneurysm (cerebral) (peripheral vessels) 39.52
  cervix 67.32
  cystoscopic 57.49
  ear
    external 18.29
    inner 20.79
    middle 20.51
  fallopian tube (lesion) 66.61
    for tubal ligation—*see* Ligation, fallopian tube
  gasserian ganglion 04.02
  nasal turbinates 21.61
  nose, for epistaxis (with packing) 21.03
  ovary 65.29
    laparoscopic 65.25
  prostatic bed 60.94
  rectum (polyp) 48.32
    radical 48.31
  retina (for)
    destruction of lesion 14.21
    reattachment 14.51
    repair of tear 14.31
  round ligament 69.19
  semicircular canals 20.79
  urethrovesical junction, transurethral 57.49
  uterine ligament 69.19
  uterosacral ligament 69.19
  uterus 68.29

Electrocoagulation—*continued*
  vagina 70.33
  vulva 71.3
Electrocochleography 20.31
Electroconization, cervix 67.32
Electroconvulsive therapy (ECT) 94.27
Electroencephalogram (EEG) 89.14
  monitoring (radiographic) (video) 89.19
Electrogastrogram 44.19
Electrokeratotomy 11.49
Electrolysis
  ciliary body 12.71
  hair follicle 86.92
  retina (for)
    destruction of lesion 14.21
    reattachment 14.51
    repair of tear 14.31
  skin 86.92
  subcutaneous tissue 86.92
Electromyogram, electromyography (EMG)
  muscle) 93.08
  eye 95.25
  urethral sphincter 89.23
Electronarcosis 94.29
Electronic gaiter 93.59
Electronystagmogram (ENG) 95.24
Electrooculogram (EOG) 95.22
Electroresection —*see also* Destruction, lesion,
  by site
  bladder neck (transurethral) 57.49
  esophagus 42.39
    endoscopic 42.33
  prostate (transurethral) 60.29
  stomach 43.49
    endoscopic 43.41
Electroretinogram (ERG) 95.21
Electroshock therapy (EST) 94.27
  subconvulsive 94.26
Elevation
  bone fragments (fractured)
    orbit 76.79
    sinus (nasal)
      frontal 22.79
      maxillary 22.79
    skull (with debridement) 02.02
    spinal 03.53
  pedicle graft 86.71
Elliot operation (scleral trephination with
  iridectomy) 12.61
Ellis Jones operation (repair of peroneal tendon)
  83.88
Ellison operation (reinforcement of collateral
  ligament) 81.44
Elmslie-Cholmeley operation (tarsal wedge
  osteotomy) 77.28
Eloesser operation (thoracoplasty) 33.34
Elongation —*see* Lengthening
Embolectomy 38.00
  with endarterectomy—*see* Endarterectomy
  abdominal
    artery 38.06
    vein 38.07
  aorta (arch) (ascending) (descending) 38.04
  head and neck NEC 38.02
  intracranial NEC 38.01
  lower limb
    artery 38.08

Enlargement—*continued*
  orbit (eye) 16.64
  palpebral fissure 08.51
  punctum 09.41
  sinus tract (skin) 86.89
Enterectomy NEC 45.63
Enteroanastomosis
  large-to-large intestine 45.94
  small-to-large intestine 45.93
  small-to-small intestine 45.91
Enterocelectomy 53.9
  female 70.92
  vaginal 70.92
Enterocentesis 45.00
  duodenum 45.01
  large intestine 45.03
  small intestine NEC 45.02
Enterocholecystostomy 51.32
Enteroclysis (small bowel) 96.43
Enterocolectomy NEC 45.79
Enterocolostomy 45.93
Enteroentectropy 46.99
Enteroenterostomy 45.90
  small-to-large intestine 45.93
  small-to-small intestine 45.91
Enterogastrostomy 44.39
Enterolithotomy 45.00
Enterolysis 54.59
  laparoscopic 54.51
Enteropancreatostomy 52.96
Enterorrhaphy 46.79
  large intestine 46.75
  small intestine 46.73
Enterostomy NEC 46.39
  cecum (*see also* Colostomy) 46.10
  colon (transverse) (*see also* Colostomy) 46.10
    loop 46.03
  delayed opening 46.31
  duodenum 46.39
    loop 46.01
  feeding NEC 46.39
    percutaneous (endoscopic) 46.32
  ileum (Brooke) (Dragstedt) 46.20
    loop 46.01
  jejunum (feeding) 46.39
    loop 46.01
    percutaneous (endoscopic) 46.32
  sigmoid colon (*see also* Colostomy) 46.10
    loop 46.03
  transverse colon (*see also* Colostomy) 46.10
    loop 46.03
Enterotomy 45.00
  large intestine 45.03
  small intestine 45.02
Enucleation —*see also* Excision, lesion, by site
  cyst
    broad ligament 69.19
    dental 24.4
    liver 50.29
    ovarian 65.29
      laparoscopic 65.25
    parotid gland 26.29
    salivary gland 26.29
    skin 86.3
    subcutaneous tissue 86.3
  eyeball 16.49
    with implant (into Tenon's capsule) 16.42
      with attachment of muscles 16.41
EOG (electro-oculogram) 95.22
Epicardiectomy 36.3

Epididymectomy 63.4
  with orchidectomy (unilateral) 62.3
    bilateral 62.41
Epididymogram 87.93
Epididymoplasty 63.59
Epididymorrhaphy 63.81
Epididymotomy 63.92
Epididymovasostomy 63.83
Epiglottidectomy 30.21
Epikeratophakia 11.76
Epilation
  eyebrow (forceps) 08.93
    cryosurgical 08.92
    electrosurgical 08.91
  eyelid (forceps) NEC 08.93
    cryosurgical 08.92
    electrosurgical 08.91
  skin 86.92
Epiphysiodesis (*see also* Arrest, bone growth)-
  see category 78.2
Epiphysiolysis (*see also* Arrest, bone growth)-
  see 78.2
Epiploectomy 54.4
Epiplopexy 54.74
Epiplorrhaphy 54.74
Episioperineoplasty 71.79
Episioperineorrhaphy 71.71
  obstetrical 75.69
Episioplasty 71.79
Episioproctotomy 73.6
Episiorrhaphy 71.71
  following routine episiotomy—*see* Episiotomy
  for obstetrical laceration 75.69
Episiotomy (with subsequent episiorrhaphy) 73.6
  high forceps 72.31
  low forceps 72.1
  mid forceps 72.21
  nonobstetrical 71.09
  outlet forceps 72.1
EPS (electrophysiologic stimulation) 37.26
Equalization, leg
  lengthening—*see* category 78.3
  shortening—*see* category 78.2
Equilibration (occlusal) 24.8
Equiloudness balance 95.43
ERC (endoscopic) retrograde cholangiography
  51.11
ERCP (endoscopic retrograde
  cholangiopancreatography) 51.10
  cannulation of pancreatic duct 52.93
ERG (electroretinogram) 95.21
ERP (endoscopic retrograde pancreatography)
  52.13
Eruption, tooth, surgical 24.6
Erythrocytapheresis, therapeutic 99.73
Escharectomy 86.22
Escharotomy 86.22
Esophageal voice training (postlaryngectomy)
  93.73
Esophagectomy 42.40
  abdominothoracocervical (combined)
    (synchronous) 42.42
  partial or subtotal 42.41
  total 42.42
Esophagocologastrostomy (intrathoracic) 42.55
  antesternal or antethoracic 42.65
Esophagocolostomy (intrathoracic) NEC 42.56
  with interposition of Colon 42.55
  antesternal or antethoracic NEC 42.66
    with interposition of colon 42.65

Esophagoduodenostomy (intrathoracic) NEC 42.54
  with
    complete gastrectomy 43.99
    interposition of small bowel 42.53
Esophagoenterostomy (intrathoracic) NEC (see also Anastomosis, esophagus, to intestinal segment) 42.54
  antesternal or antethoracic (see also Anastomosis, esophagus, antesternal, to intestinal segment) 42.64
Esophagoesophagostomy (intrathoracic) 42.51
  antesternal or antethoracic 42.61
Esophagogastrectomy 43.99
Esophagogastroduodenoscopy (EGD) 45.13
  with closed biopsy 45.16
  through stoma (artificial) 45.12
  transabdominal (operative) 45.11
Esophagogastromyotomy 42.7
Esophagogastropexy 44.65
Esophagogastroplasty 44.65
Esophagogastroscopy NEC 44.13
  through stoma (artificial) 44.12
  transabdominal (operative) 44.11
Esophagogastrostomy (intrathoracic) 42.52
  with partial gastrectomy 43.5
  antesternal or antethoracic 42.62
Esophagoileostomy (intrathoracic) NEC 42.54
  with interposition of small bowel 42.53
  antesternal or antethoracic NEC 42.64
    with interposition of small bowel 42.63
Esophagojejunostomy (intrathoracic) NEC 42.54
  with
    complete gastrectomy 43.99
    interposition of small bowel 42.53
  antesternal or antethoracic NEC 42.64
    with interposition of small bowel 42.63
Esophagomyotomy 42.7
Esophagoplasty NEC 42.89
Esophagorrhaphy 42.82
Esophagoscopy NEC 42.23
  with closed biopsy 42.24
  by incision (operative) 42.21
  through stoma (artificial) 42.22
  transabdominal (operative) 42.21
Esophagostomy 42.10
  cervical 42.11
  thoracic 42.19
Esophagotomy NEC 42.09
Estes operation (ovary) 65.72
  laparoscopic 65.75
Estlander operation (thoracoplasty) 33.34
ESWL (extracorporeal shock wave lithotripsy) NEC 98.59
  bile duct 98.52
  bladder 98.51
  gallbladder 98.52
  kidney 98.51
  Kock pouch (urinary diversion) 98.51
  renal pelvis 98.51
  specified site NEC 98.59
  ureter 98.51
Ethmoidectomy 22.63
Ethmoidotomy 22.51
Evacuation
  abscess—see Drainage, by site
  anterior chamber (eye) (aqueous) (hyphema) 12.91

Evacuation—continued
  cyst—see also Excision, lesion, by site
    breast 85.91
    kidney 55.01
    liver 50.29
  hematoma—see also Incision, hematoma
    obstetrical 75.92
    incisional 75.91
  hemorrhoids (thrombosed) 49.47
  pelvic blood clot (by incision) 54.19
    by
      culdocentesis 70.0
      culdoscopy 70.22
  retained placenta
    with curettage 69.02
    manual 75.4
  streptothrix from lacrimal duct 09.42
Evaluation (of)
  audiological 95.43
  criminal responsibility, psychiatric 94.11
  functional (physical therapy) 93.01
  hearing NEC 95.49
  orthotic (for brace fitting) 93.02
  prosthetic (for artificial limb fitting) 93.03
  psychiatric NEC 94.19
    commitment 94.13
  psychologic NEC 94.08
  testimentary capacity, psychiatric 94.11
Evans operation (release of clubfoot) 83.84
Evisceration
  eyeball 16.39
    with implant (into scleral shell) 16.31
  ocular contents 16.39
    with implant (into scleral shell) 16.31
  orbit (see also Exenteration, orbit) 16.59
  pelvic (anterior) (posterior) (partial) (total) (female) 68.8
    male 57.71
Evulsion
  nail (bed) (fold) 86.23
  skin 86.3
  subcutaneous tissue 86.3
Examination (for)
  breast
    manual 89.36
    radiographic NEC 87.37
    thermographic 88.85
    ultrasonic 88.73
  cervical rib (by x-ray) 87.43
  colostomy stoma (digital) 89.33
  dental (oral mucosa) (peridontal) 89.31
    radiographic NEC 87.12
  enterostomy stoma (digital) 89.33
  eye 95.09
    color vision 95.06
    comprehensive 95.02
    dark adaptation 95.07
    limited (with prescription of spectacles) 95.01
    under anesthesia 95.04
  fetus, intrauterine 75.35
  general physical 89.7
  glaucoma 95.03
  gynecological 89.26
  hearing 95.47

Examination—*continued*
microscopic (specimen) (of) 91.9

Note—Use the following fourth-digit
subclassification with categories 90-91 to
identify type of examination:

1   *bacterial smear*
2   *culture*
3   *culture and sensitivity*
4   *parasitology*
5   *toxicology*
6   *cell block and Papanicolaou smear*
9   *other microscopic examination*

---

adenoid 90.3
adrenal gland 90.1
amnion 91.4
anus 90.9
appendix 90.9
bile ducts 91.0
bladder 91.3
blood 90.5
bone 91.5
    marrow 90.6
brain 90.0
breast 91.6
bronchus 90.4
bursa 91.5
cartilage 91.5
cervix 91.4
chest wall 90.4
chorion 91.4
colon 90.9
cul-de-sac 91.1
dental 90.8
diaphragm 90.4
duodenum 90.8
ear 90.3
endocrine gland NEC 90.1
esophagus 90.8
eye 90.2
fallopian tube 91.4
fascia 91.5
female genital tract 91.4
fetus 91.4
gallbladder 91.0
hair 91.6
ileum 90.9
jejunum 90.9
joint fluid 91.5
kidney 91.2
large intestine 90.9
larynx 90.3
ligament 91.5
liver 91.0
lung 90.4
lymph (node) 90.7
meninges 90.0
mesentery 91.1
mouth 90.8
muscle 91.5
musculoskeletal system 91.5
nails 91.6
nerve 90.0
nervous system 90.0
nose 90.3
omentum 91.1
operative wound 91.7
ovary 91.4
pancreas 91.0
parathyroid gland 90.1

Examination—*continued*
penis 91.3
perirenal tissue 91.2
peritoneum (fluid) 91.1
periureteral tissue 91.2
perivesical (tissue) 91.3
pharynx 90.3
pineal gland 90.1
pituitary gland 90.1
placenta 91.4
pleura (fluid) 90.4
prostate 91.3
rectum 90.9
retroperitoneum 91.1
semen 91.3
seminal vesicle 91.3
sigmoid 90.9
skin 91.6
small intestine 90.9
specified site NEC 91.8
spinal fluid 90.0
spleen 90.6
sputum 90.4
stomach 90.8
stool 90.9
synovial membrane 91.5
tendon 91.5
thorax NEC 90.4
throat 90.3
thymus 90.1
thyroid gland 90.1
tonsil 90.3
trachea 90.4
ureter 91.2
urethra 91.3
urine 91.3
uterus 91.4
vagina 91.4
vas deferens 91.3
vomitus 90.8
vulva 91.4
neurologic 89.13
neuro-ophthalmology 95.03
ophthalmoscopic 16.21
panorex, mandible 87.12
pelvic (manual) 89.26
    instrumental (by pelvimeter) 88.25
    pelvimetric 88.25
physical, general 89.7
postmortem 89.8
rectum (digital) 89.34
    endoscopic 48.23
        through stoma (artificial) 48.22
        transabdominal 48.21
retinal disease 95.03
specified type (manual) NEC 89.39
thyroid field, postoperative 06.02
uterus (digital) 68.11
    endoscopic 68.12
vagina 89.26
    endoscopic 70.21
visual field 95.05
Exchange transfusion 99.01
intrauterine 75.2
Excision
aberrant tissue—*see* Excision, lesion, by site of
    tissue origin
abscess—*see* Excision, lesion, by site
accessory tissue—*see also* Excision, lesion, by
    site of tissue origin

Excision—*continued*

lung 32.29
  endoscopic 32.28
  spleen 41.93
adenoids (tag) 28.6
  with tonsillectomy 28.3
adenoma—*see* Excision, lesion, by site
adrenal gland *(see also* Adrenalectomy) 07.22
ampulla of Vater (with reimplantation of
    common duct) 51.62
anal papilla 49.39
  endoscopic 49.31
aneurysm (arteriovenous) *(see also*
    Aneurysmectomy) 38.60
  coronary artery 36.91
  heart 37.32
  myocardium 37.32
  sinus of Valsalva 35.39
  ventricle (heart) 37.32
anus (complete) (partial) 49.6
aortic subvalvular ring 35.35
apocrine gland 86.3
aponeurosis 83.42
  hand 82.33
appendiceal stump 47.01-47.09
appendices epiploicae 54.4
appendix *(see also* Appendectomy) 47.01, 47.09
  epididymis 63.3
  testis 62.2
arcuate ligament (spine)—*omit code*
arteriovenous fistula *(see also*
    Aneurysmectomy) 38.60
artery *(see also* Arteriectomy) 38.60
Baker's cyst, knee 83.39
Bartholin's gland 71.24
basal ganglion 01.59
bile duct 51.69
  endoscopic 51.64
bladder—*see also* Cystectomy
bleb (emphysematous), lung 32.29
  endoscopic 32.28
blood vessel *(see also* Angiectomy) 38.60
bone (ends) (partial), except facial—*see
    category* 77.8
  facial NEC 76.39
    total 76.45
      with reconstruction 76.44
  for graft (autograft) (homograft)—*see
    category* 77.7
  fragments (chips) *(see also* Incision, bone)
      77.10
  joint *(see also* Arthrotomy) 80.10
  necrotic *(see also* Sequestrectomy, bone)
      77.00
  heterotopic, from
    muscle 83.32
      hand 82.22
    skin 86.3
    tendon 83.31
      hand 82.21
  mandible 76.31
    with arthrodesis—*see* Arthrodesis
    total 76.42
      with reconstruction 76.41
  spur—*see* Excision, lesion, bone
  total, except facial—*see category* 77.9
    facial NEC 76.45
      with reconstruction 76.44
    mandible 76.42
      with reconstruction 76.41

Excision—*continued*

brain 01.59
  hemisphere 01.52
  lobe 01.53
branchial cleft cyst or vestige 29.2
breast *(see also* Mastectomy) 85.41
  aberrant tissue 85.24
  accessory 85.24
  ectopic 85.24
  nipple 85.25
    accessory 85.24
  segmental 85.23
  supernumerary 85.24
  wedge 85.21
broad ligament 69.19
bronchogenic cyst 32.09
  endoscopic 32.01
bronchus (wide sleeve) NEC 32.1
buccal mucosa 27.49
bulbourethral gland 58.92
bulbous tuberosities (mandible) (maxilla)
    (fibrous) (osseous) 24.31
bunion *(see also* Bunionectomy) 77.59
bunionette (with osteotomy) 77.54
bursa 83.5
  hand 82.31
canal of Nuck 69.19
cardioma 37.33
carotid body (lesion) (partial) (total) 39.8
cartilage *(see also* Chondrectomy) 80.90
  intervertebral *see category* 80.5
  knee (semilunar) 80.6
  larynx 30.29
  nasal (submucous) 21.5
caruncle, urethra 58.39
  endoscopic 58.31
cataract *(see also* Extraction, cataract) 13.19
  secondary membrane (after cataract) 13.65
cervical
  rib 77.91
  stump 67.4
cervix (stump) NEC 67.4
  cold (knife) 67.2
  conization 67.2
  cryoconization 67.33
  electroconization 67.32
chalazion (multiple) (single) 08.21
cholesteatoma—*see* Excision, lesion, by site
choroid plexus 02.14
cicatrix (skin) 86.3
cilia base 08.20
ciliary body, prolapsed 12.98
clavicle (head) (partial) 77.81
  total (complete) 77.91
clitoris 71.4
coarctation of aorta (end-to-end anastomosis)
    38.64
  with
    graft replacement (interposition)
      abdominal 38.44
      thoracic 38.45
      thoracoabdominal 38.45 *[38.44]*
  common
    duct 51.63
    wall between posterior and coronary sinus
      (with roofing of resultant defect with
      patch graft) 35.82
condyle—*see category* 77.8
  mandible 76.5
conjunctival ring 10.31

Excision—*continued*
  cornea 11.49
    epithelium (with chemocauterization) 11.41
      for smear or culture 11.21
  costal cartilage 80.99
  cul-de-sac (Douglas) 70.92
  cusp, heart valve 35.10
    aortic 35.11
    mitral 35.12
    tricuspid 35.14
  cyst—*see also* Excision, lesion, by site
    apical (tooth) 23.73
      with root canal therapy 23.72
    Baker's (popliteal) 83.39
    breast 85.21
    broad ligament 69.19
    bronchogenic 32.09
      endoscopic 32.01
    cervix 67.39
    dental 24.4
    dentigerous 24.4
    epididymis 63.2
    fallopian tube 66.61
    Gartner's duct 70.33
    hand 82.29
    labia 71.3
    lung 32.29
      endoscopic 32.28
    mesonephric duct 69.19
    Morgagni
      female 66.61
      male 62.2
    mullerian duct 60.73
    nasolabial 27.49
    nasopalatine 27.31
      by wide excision 27.32
    ovary 65.29
      laparoscopic 65.25
    parovarian 69.19
    pericardium 37.31
    periodontal (apical) (lateral) 24.4
    popliteal (Baker's), knee 83.39
    radicular 24.4
    spleen 41.42
    synovial (membrane) 83.39
    thyroglossal (with resection of hyoid bone)
      06.7
    urachal (bladder) 57.51
      abdominal wall 54.3
    vagina (Gartner's duct) 70.33
  cystic
    duct remnant 51.61
    hygroma 40.29
  dentinoma 24.4
  diaphragm 34.81
  disc, intervertebral NOS 80.50
    herniated (nucleus pulposus) 80.51
    other specified (diskectomy) 80.51
  diverticulum
    ampulla of Vater 51.62
    anus 49.39
      endoscopic 49.31
    bladder 57.59
      transurethral 57.49
    duodenum 45.31
      endoscopic 45.30
    esophagus (local) 42.31
      endoscopic 42.33
    hypopharyngeal (by cricopharyngeal
      myotomy) 29.32

Excision—*continued*
  intestine
    large 45.41
      endoscopic 45.43
    small NEC 45.33
    Meckel's 45.33
    pharyngeal (by cricopharyngeal myotomy)
      29.32
    pharyngoesophageal (by cricopharyngeal
      myotomy) 29.32
    stomach 43.42
      endoscopic 43.41
    urethra 58.39
      endoscopic 58.31
    ventricle, heart 37.33
  duct
    mullerian 69.19
    paramesonephric 69.19
    thyroglossal (with resection of hyoid bone)
      06.7
  ear, external (complete) NEC 18.39
    partial 18.29
    radical 18.31
  ectopic
    abdominal fetus 74.3
    tissue—*see also* Excision, lesion, by site of
      tissue origin
      bone, from muscle 83.32
      breast 85.24
      lung 32.29
        endoscopic 32.28
      spleen 41.93
  empyema pocket, lung 34.09
  epididymis 63.4
  epiglottis 30.21
  epithelial downgrowth, anterior chamber (eye)
    12.93
  epulis (gingiva) 24.31
  esophagus (*see also* Esophagectomy) 42.40
  exostosis (*see also* Excision, lesion, bone) 77.60
    auditory canal, external 18.29
    facial bone 76.2
    first metatarsal (hallux valgus repair)—*see*
      Bunionectomy
  eye 16.49
    with implant (into Tenon's capsule) 16.42
    with attachment of muscles 16.41
  eyelid 08.20
    redundant skin 08.86
  falciform ligament 54.4
  fallopian tube—*see* Salpingectomy
  fascia 83.44
    for graft 83.43
      hand 82.34
    hand 82.35
      for graft 82.34
  fat pad NEC 86.3
    knee (infrapatellar) (prepatellar) 86.3
    scalene 40.21
  fibroadenoma, breast 85.21
  fissure, anus 49.39
    endoscopic 49.31
  fistula—*see also* Fistulectomy
    anal 49.12
    arteriovenous (*see also* Aneurysmectomy)
      38.60
    ileorectal 46.74
    lacrimal
      gland 09.21
      sac 09.6
    rectal 48.73

Excision—*continued*

    vesicovaginal 57.84
  frenulum, frenum
    labial (lip) 27.41
    lingual (tongue) 25.92
  ganglion (hand) (tendon sheath) (wrist) 82.21
    gasserian 04.05
    site other than hand or nerve 83.31
    sympathetic nerve 05.29
    trigeminal nerve 04.05
  gastrocolic ligament 54.4
  gingiva 24.31
  glomus jugulare tumor 20.51
  goiter—*see* Thyroidectomy
  gum 24.31
  hamartoma, mammary 85.21
  hallux valgus—*see also* Bunionectomy with
    prosthetic implant 77.59
  hematocele, tunica vaginalis 61.92
  hematoma—*see* Drainage, by site
  hemorrhoids (external) (internal) (tag) 49.46
  heterotopic bone, from
    muscle 83.32
      hand 82.22
    skin 86.3
    tendon 83.31
      hand 82.21
  hydatid of Morgagni
    female 66.61
    male 62.2
  hydatid cyst, liver 50.29
  hydrocele
    canal of Nuck (female) 69.19
    male 63.1
    round ligament 69.19
    spermatic cord 63.1
    tunica vaginalis 61.2
  hygroma, cystic 40.29
  hymen (tag) 70.31
  hymeno-urethral fusion 70.31
  intervertebral disc--*see* Excision, disc,
    intervertebral (NOS) 80.50
  intestine (*see also* Resection, intestine) 45.8
    for interposition 45.50
      large 45.52
      small 45.51
    large (total) 45.8
      for interposition 45.52
      local 45.41
        endoscopic 45.43
      segmental 45.79
        multiple 45.71
    small (total) 45.63
      for interposition 45.51
      local 45.33
      partial 45.62
      segmental 45.62
        multiple 45.61
  intraductal papilloma 85.21
  iris prolapse 12.13
  joint (*see also* Arthrectomy) 80.90
  keloid (scar), skin 86.3
  labia—*see* Vulvectomy
  lacrimal
    gland 09.20
      partial 09.22
      total 09.23
    passage 09.6
    sac 09.6

Excision—*continued*

  lesion (local)
    abdominal wall 54.3
    accessory sinus—*see* Excision, lesion, nasal
      sinus
    adenoids 28.92
    adrenal gland(s) 07.21
    alveolus 24.4
    ampulla of Vater 51.62
    anterior chamber (eye) NEC 12.40
    anus 49.39
      endoscopic 49.31
    apocrine gland 86.3
    artery 38.60
      abdominal 38.66
      aorta (arch) (ascending) (descending
        thoracic) 38.64
        with end-to-end anastomosis 38.45
          abdominal 38.44
          thoracic 38.45
          thoracoabdominal 38.45 *[38.44]*
        with interposition graft replacement 38.45
          abdominal 38.44
          thoracic 38.45
          thoracoabdominal 38.45 *[38.44]*
      head and neck NEC 38.62
      intracranial NEC 38.61
      lower limb 38.68
      thoracic NEC 38.65
      upper limb 38.63
    atrium 37.33
    auditory canal or meatus, external 18.29
      radical 18.31
    auricle, ear 18.29
      radical 18.31
    biliary ducts 51.69
      endoscopic 51.64
    bladder (transurethral) 57.49
      open 57.59
      suprapubic 57.59
    blood vessel 38.60
      abdominal
        artery 38.66
        vein 38.67
      aorta (arch) (ascending) (descending) 38.64
      head and neck NEC 38.62
      intracranial NEC 38.61
      lower limb
        artery 38.68
        vein 38.69
      thoracic NEC 38.65
      upper limb (artery) (vein) 38.63
    bone 77.60
      carpal, metacarpal 77.64
      clavicle 77.61
      facial 76.2
      femur 77.65
      fibula 77.67
      humerus 77.62
      jaw 76.2
        dental 24.4
      patella 77.66
      pelvic 77.69
      phalanges (foot) (hand) 77.69
      radius 77.63
      scapula 77.61
      skull 01.6
      specified site NEC 77.69
      tarsal, metatarsal 77.68
      thorax (ribs) (sternum) 77.61
      tibia 77.67

Excision—*continued*
  wart—*see also* Excision, lesion, by site
    eyelid 08.22
  wolffian duct 69.19
  xanthoma (tendon sheath, hand) 82.21
    site other than hand 83.31
Excisional biopsy —*see* Biopsy
Exclusion, pyloric 44.39
Exenteration
  ethmoid air cells 22.63
  orbit 16.59
    with
      removal of adjacent structures 16.51
      temporalis muscle transplant 16.59
      therapeutic removal of bone 16.52
  pelvic (organs) (female) 68.8
    male 57.71
  petrous pyramid air cells 20.59
Exercise (physical therapy) NEC 93.19
  active musculoskeletal NEC 93.12
  assisting 93.11
    in pool 93.31
  breathing 93.18
  musculoskeletal
    active NEC 93.12
    passive NEC 93.17
  neurologic 89.13
  passive musculoskeletal NEC 93.17
  resistive 93.13
Exfoliation, skin, by chemical 86.24
Exostectomy (*see also* Excision, lesion, bone) 77.60
  first metatarsal (hallux valgus repair)—*see* Bunionectomy
  hallux valgus repair (with wedge osteotomy)—*see* Bunionectomy
Expiratory flow rate 89.38
Exploration —*see also* Incision
  abdomen 54.11
  abdominal wall 54.0
  adrenal (gland) 07.41
    field 07.00
      bilateral 07.02
      unilateral 07.01
  artery 38.00
    abdominal 38.06
    aorta (arch) (ascending) (descending) 38.04
    head and neck NEC 38.02
    intracranial NEC 38.01
    lower limb 38.08
    thoracic NEC 38.05
    upper limb 38.03
  auditory canal, external 18.02
  axilla 86.09
  bile duct(s) 51.59
    common duct 51.51
      endoscopic 51.11
      for relief of obstruction 51.42
        endoscopic 51.84
      for removal of calculus 51.41
        endoscopic 51.88
    for relief of obstruction 51.49
      endoscopic 51.84
  bladder (by incision) 57.19
    endoscopic 57.32
    through stoma (artificial) 57.31
  bone (*see also* Incision, bone) 77.10
  brain (tissue) 01.39
  breast 85.0
  bronchus 33.0
    endoscopic—*see* Bronchoscopy

Exploration—*continued*
  bursa 83.03
    hand 82.03
  carotid body 39.8
  carpal tunnel 04.43
  choroid 14.9
  ciliary body 12.44
  colon 45.03
  common bile duct 51.51
    endoscopic 51.11
    for
      relief of obstruction 51.42
        endoscopic 51.84
      removal of calculus 51.41
        endoscopic 51.88
  coronary artery 36.99
  cranium 01.24
  cul-de-sac 70.12
    endoscopic 70.22
  disc space 03.09
  duodenum 45.01
  endoscopic—*see* Endoscopy, by site
  epididymis 63.92
  esophagus (by incision) NEC 42.09
    endoscopic—*see* Esophagoscopy
  ethmoid sinus 22.51
  eyelid 08.09
  fallopian tube 66.01
  fascia 83.09
    hand 82.09
  flank 54.0
  fossa (superficial) NEC 86.09
    pituitary 07.71
  frontal sinus 22.41
  frontonasal duct 96.21
  gallbladder 51.04
  groin (region) (abdominal wall) (inguinal) 54.0
    skin and subcutaneous tissue 86.09
  heart 37.11
  hepatic duct 51.59
  hypophysis 07.72
  ileum 45.02
  inguinal canal (groin) 54.0
  intestine (by incision) NEC 45.00
    large 45.03
    small 45.02
  intrathoracic 34.02
  jejunum 45.02
  joint structures (*see also* Arthrotomy) 80.10
  kidney 55.01
    pelvis 55.11
  labia 71.09
  lacrimal
    gland 09.0
    sac 09.53
  laparotomy site 54.12
  larynx (by incision) 31.3
    endoscopic 31.42
  liver 50.0
  lung (by incision) 33.1
  lymphatic structure(s) (channel) (node) (vessel) 40.0
  mastoid 20.21
  maxillary antrum or sinus (Caldwell-Luc approach) 22.39
  mediastinum 34.1
    endoscopic 34.22
  middle ear (transtympanic) 20.23
  muscle 83.02
    hand 82.02
  neck (*see also* Exploration, thyroid) 06.09

Extraction—*continued*
cataract 13.19
  after cataract (by)
    capsulectomy 13.65
    capsulotomy 13.64
    discission 13.64
    excision 13.65
    iridocapsulectomy 13.65
    mechanical fragmentation 13.66
    needling 13.64
    phacofragmentation (mechanical) 13.66
  aspiration (simple) (with irrigation) 13.3
  cryoextraction (intracapsular approach) 13.19
    temporal inferior route (in presence of
      fistulization bleb) 13.11
  curette evacuation (extracapsular approach)
    13.2
  emulsification (and aspiration) 13.41
  erysiphake (intracapsular approach) 13.19
    temporal inferior route (in presence of
      fistulization bleb) 13.11
  extracapsular approach (with iridectomy)
    NEC 13.59
    by temporal inferior route (in presence of
      fistulization bleb) 13.51
    aspiration (simple) (with irrigation) 13.3
    curette evacuation 13.2
    emulsification (and aspiration) 13.41
    linear extraction 13.2
    mechanical fragmentation with aspiration by
      posterior route 13.42
      specified route NEC 13.43
    phacoemulsification (ultrasonic) (with
      aspiration) 13.41
    phacofragmentation (mechanical)
      with aspiration by
        posterior route 13.42
        specified route NEC 13.43
      ultrasonic (with aspiration) 13.41
    rotoextraction (mechanical) with aspiration
      by
      posterior route 13.42
      specified route NEC 13.43
  intracapsular (combined) (simple) (with
    iridectomy) (with suction) (with
    zonulolysis) 13.19
    by temporal inferior route (in presence of
      fistulization bleb) 13.11
  linear extraction (extracapsular approach) 13.2
  phacoemulsification (and aspiration) 13.41
  phacofragmentation (mechanical)
    with aspiration by
      posterior route 13.42
      specified route NEC 13.43
    ultrasonic 13.41
  rotoextraction (mechanical)
    with aspiration by
      posterior route 13.42
      specified route NEC 13.43
  secondary membranous (after cataract) (by)
    capsulectomy 13.65
    capsulotomy 13.64
    discission 13.64
    excision 13.65
    iridocapsulectomy 13.65
    mechanical fragmentation 13.66
    needling 13.64
    phacofragmentation (mechanical) 13.66
common duct stones (percutaneous) (through
  sinus tract) (with basket) 51.96
foreign body—*see* Removal, foreign body

Extraction—*continued*
kidney stone(s), percutaneous 55.03
  with fragmentation procedure 55.04
lens (eye) (*see also* Extraction, cataract) 13.19
Malström's 72.79
  with episiotomy 72.71
menstrual, menses 69.6
milk from lactating breast (manual) (pump)
  99.98
tooth (by forceps) (multiple) (single) NEC 23.09
  with mucoperiosteal flap elevation 23.19
  deciduous 23.01
  surgical NEC (*see also* Removal, tooth,
    surgical) 23.19
vacuum, fetus 72.79
  with episiotomy 72.71
vitreous (*see also* Removal, vitreous) 14.72

F

Face lift 86.82
Facetectomy 77.89
Facilitation, Intraocular circulation NEC 12.59
Failed (trial) forceps 73.3
Family
  counselling (medical) (social) 94.49
  therapy 94.42
Farabeuf operation (ischiopubiotomy) 77.39
Fasanella-Servatt operation
  (blepharoptosis repair) 08.35
Fasciaplasty —*see* Fascioplasty
Fascia sling operation —*see* Operation, sling
Fasciectomy 83.44
  for graft 83.43
    hand 82.34
  hand 82.35
    for graft 82.34
  palmar (release of Dupuytren's contracture)
    82.35
Fasciodesis 83.89
  hand 82.89
Fascioplasty (*see also* Repair, fascia) 83.89
  hand (*see also* Repair, fascia, hand) 82.89
Fasciorrhaphy —*see* Suture, fascia
Fasciotomy 83.14
  Dupuytren's 82.12
    with excision 82.35
  Dwyer 83.14
  hand 82.12
  Ober-Yount 83.14
  orbital (*see also* Orbitotomy) 16.09
  palmar (release of Dupuytren's
    contracture) 82.12
    with excision 82.35
Fenestration
  aneurysm (dissecting), thoracic aorta 39.54
  aortic aneurysm 39.54
  cardiac valve 35.10
  chest wall 34.01
  ear
    inner (with graft) 20.61
      revision 20.62
    tympanic 19.55
  labyrinth (with graft) 20.61
  Lempert's (endaural) 19.9
  operation (aorta) 39.54
  oval window, ear canal 19.55
  palate 27.1
  pericardium 37.12
  semicircular canals (with graft) 20.61
  stapes foot plate (with vein graft) 19.19
    with incus replacement 19.11
  tympanic membrane 19.55
  vestibule (with graft) 20.61
Ferguson operation (hernia repair) 53.00
Fetography 87.81
Fetoscopy 75.31
Fiberoscopy —*see* Endoscopy, by site
Fibroidectomy, uterine 68.29
Fick operation (perforation of foot plate) 19.0
Filipuncture (aneurysm) (cerebral) 39.52
Filleting
  hammer toe 77.56
  pancreas 52.3
Filling, tooth (amalgam) (plastic) (silicate) 23.2
  root canal (*see also* Therapy, root canal) 23.70

Fimbriectomy (*see also* Salpingectomy, partial)
  66.69
  Uchida (with tubal ligation) 66.32
Finney operation (pyloroplasty) 44.29
Fissurectomy, anal 49.39
  endoscopic 49.31
  skin (subcutaneous tissue) 49.04
Fistulectomy —*see also* Closure, fistula, by site
  abdominothoracic 34.83
  abdominouterine 69.42
  anus 49.12
  appendix 47.92
  bile duct 51.79
  biliary tract NEC 51.79
  bladder (transurethral approach) 57.84
  bone (*see also* Excision, lesion, bone) 77.60
  branchial cleft 29.52
  bronchocutaneous 33.42
  bronchoesophageal 33.42
  bronchomediastinal 34.73
  bronchopleural 34.73
  bronchopleurocutaneous 34.73
  bronchopleuromediastinal 34.73
  bronchovisceral 33.42
  cervicosigmoidal 67.62
  cholecystogastroenteric 51.93
  cornea 11.49
  diaphragm 34.83
  enterouterine 69.42
  esophagopleurocutaneous 34.73
  esophagus NEC 42.84
  fallopian tube 66.73
  gallbladder 51.93
  gastric NEC 44.63
  hepatic duct 51.79
  hepatopleural 34.73
  hepatopulmonary 34.73
  intestine
    large 46.76
    small 46.74
  intestinouterine 69.42
  joint (*see also* Excision, lesion, joint) 80.80
  lacrimal
    gland 09.21
    sac 09.6
  laryngotracheal 31.62
  larynx 31.62
  mediastinocutaneous 34.73
  mouth NEC 27.53
  nasal 21.82
    sinus 22.71
  nasolabial 21.82
  nasopharyngeal 21.82
  oroantral 22.71
  oronasal 21.82
  pancreas 52.95
  perineorectal 71.72
  perineosigmoidal 71.72
  perirectal, not opening into rectum 48.93
  pharyngoesophageal 29.53
  pharynx NEC 29.53
  pleura 34.73
  rectolabial 71.72
  rectourethral 58.43
  rectouterine 69.42
  rectovaginal 70.73
  rectovesical 57.83
  rectovulvar 71.72

Fistulectomy—*continued*
  rectum 48.73
  salivary (duct) (gland) 26.42
  scrotum 61.42
  skin 86.3
  stomach NEC 44.63
  subcutaneous tissue 86.3
  thoracoabdominal 34.83
  thoracogastric 34.83
  thoracointestinal 34.83
  thorax NEC 34.73
  trachea NEC 31.73
  tracheoesophageal 31.73
  ureter 56.84
  urethra 58.43
  uteroenteric 69.42
  uterointestinal 69.42
  uterorectal 69.42
  uterovaginal 69.42
  vagina 70.75
  vesicosigmoidovaginal 57.83
  vocal cords 31.62
  vulvorectal 71.72
Fistulization
  appendix 47.91
  arteriovenous 39.27
  cisterna chyli 40.62
  endolymphatic sac (for decompression) 20.79
  esophagus, external 42.10
    cervical 42.11
    specified technique NEC 42.19
  interatrial 35.41
  labyrinth (for decompression) 20.79
  lacrimal sac into nasal cavity 09.81
  larynx 31.29
  lymphatic duct, left (thoracic) 40.62
  orbit 16.09
  peritoneal 54.93
  salivary gland 26.49
  sclera 12.69
    by trephination 12.61
    with iridectomy 12.65
  sinus, nasal NEC 22.9
  subarachnoid space 02.2
  thoracic duct 40.62
  trachea 31.29
  tracheoesophageal 31.95
  urethrovaginal 58.0
  ventricle, cerebral (*see also* Shunt, ventricular)
    02.2
Fistulogram
  abdominal wall 88.03
  chest wall 87.38
  retroperitoneum 88.14
Fistulotomy, anal 49.11
Fitting
  arch bars (orthodontic) 24.7
    for immobilization (fracture) 93.55
  artificial limb 84.40
  contact lens 95.32
  denture (total) 99.97
    bridge (fixed) 23.42
      removable 23.43
    partial (fixed) 23.42
      removable 23.43
  hearing aid 95.48
  obturator (orthodontic) 24.7
  ocular prosthetics 95.34
  orthodontic
    appliance 24.7
    obturator 24.7

Fitting—*continued*
  wiring 24.7
  orthotic device 93.23
  periodontal splint (orthodontic) 24.7
  prosthesis, prosthetic device
    above knee 84.45
    arm 84.43
      lower (and hand) 84.42
      upper (and shoulder) 84.41
    below knee 84.46
    hand (and lower arm) 84.42
    leg 84.47
      above knee 84.45
      below knee 84.46
    limb NEC 84.40
    ocular 95.34
    penis (external) 64.94
    shoulder (and upper arm) 84.41
  spectacles 95.31
Five-in-one repair, knee 81.42
Fixation
  bone
    external, without reduction 93.59
      with fracture reduction—*see* Reduction,
        fracture
      cast immobilization NEC 93.53
      splint 93.54
      traction (skeletal) NEC 93.44
        intermittent 93.43
    internal (without fracture-reduction) 78.50
      with fracture-reduction—*see* Reduction,
        fracture
      carpal, metacarpal 78.54
      clavicle 78.51
      femur 78.55
      fibula 78.57
      humerus 78.52
      patella 78.56
      pelvic 78.59
      phalanges (foot) (hand) 78.59
      radius 78.53
      scapula 78.51
      specified site NEC 78.59
      tarsal, metatarsal 78.58
      thorax (ribs) (sternum) 78.51
      tibia 78.57
      ulna 78.53
      vertebrae 78.59
  breast (pendulous) 85.6
  cardinal ligaments 69.22
  duodenum 46.62
    to abdominal wall 46.61
  external (without manipulation for reduction)
    93.59
    with fracture-reduction—*see* Reduction,
      fracture
    cast immobilization NEC 93.53
    pressure dressing 93.56
    splint 93.54
    traction (skeletal) NEC 93.44
      intermittent 93.43
  hip 81.40
  ileum 46.62
    to abdominal wall 46.61
  internal
    with fracture-reduction—*see* Reduction,
      fracture
    without fracture-reduction—*see* Fixation,
      bone, internal
  intestine 46.60

Fox operation (entropion repair with wedge
resection) 08.43
Fracture, surgical (*see also* Osteoclasis) 78.70
turbinates (nasal) 21.62
Fragmentation
lithotriptor—*see* Lithotripsy
mechanical
cataract (with aspiration) 13.43
posterior route 13.42
secondary membrane 13.66
secondary membrane (after cataract) 13.66
ultrasonic
cataract (with aspiration) 13.41
stones, urinary 59.95
percutaneous nephrostomy 55.04
Franco operation (suprapubic cystotomy) 57.18
Frank operation 43.19
Frazier (Spiller) operation (subtemporal
trigeminal rhizotomy) 04.02
Fredet-Ramstedt operation (pyloromyotomy)
(with wedge resection) 43.3
Freeing
adhesions—*see* Lysis, adhesions
anterior synechiae (with injection of air or
liquid) 12.32
artery-vein-nerve bundle 39.91
extraocular muscle, entrapped 15.7
goniosynechiae (with injection of air or liquid)
12.31
intestinal segment for interposition 45.50
large 45.52
small 45.51
posterior synechiae 12.33
synechiae (posterior) 12.33
anterior (with injection of air or liquid) 12.32
vascular bundle 39.91
vessel 39.91
Freezing
gastric 96.32
prostate 60.62
Frenckner operation (intrapetrosal drainage)
20.22
Frenectomy
labial 27.41
lingual 25.92
lip 27.41
maxillary 27.41
tongue 25.92
Frenotomy
labial 27.91
lingual 25.91
Frenulumectomy —*see* Frenectomy
Frickman operation (abdominal proctopexy)
48.75
Frommel operation (shortening of uterosacral
ligaments) 69.22
Fulguration —*see also* Electrocoagulation *and*
Destruction, lesion, by site
adenoid fossa 28.7
anus 49.39
endoscopic 49.31
bladder (transurethral) 57.49
suprapubic 57.59
choroid 14.21
duodenum 45.32
endoscopic 45.30
esophagus 42.39
endoscopic 42.33
large intestine 45.49
endoscopic 45.43
polypectomy 45.42

Fulguration—*continued*
penis 64.2
perineum, female 71.3
prostate, transurethral 60.29
rectum 48.32
radical 48.31
retina 14.21
scrotum 61.3
Skene's gland 71.3
skin 86.3
small intestine NEC 45.34
duodenum 45.32
endoscopic 45.30
stomach 43.49
endoscopic 43.41
subcutaneous tissue 86.3
tonsillar fossa 28.7
urethra 58.39
endoscopic 58.31
vulva 71.3
Function
study—*see also* Scan, radioisotope
gastric 89.39
muscle 93.08
ocular 95.25
nasal 89.12
pulmonary—*see categories* 89.37-89.38
renal 92.03
thyroid 92.01
urethral sphincter 89.23
Fundectomy, uterine 68.3
Fundoplication (esophageal) (Nissen's) 44.66
Fundusectomy, gastric 43.89
Fusion
atlas-axis (spine) 81.01
for pseudarthrosis 81.09
bone (*see also* Osteoplasty) 78.40
cervical (spine) (C2 level or below) NEC 81.02
anterior (interbody), anterolateral technique
81.02
C1-C2 level (anterior interbody)
(anterolateral) 81.01
for pseudarthrosis 81.09
occiput-C2 81.01
posterior (interbody), posterolateral technique
81.03
claw toe 77.57
craniocervical 81.01
for pseudarthrosis 81.09
dorsal, dorsolumbar NEC 81.05
anterior (interbody) anterolateral technique
81.04
for pseudarthrosis 81.09
for pseudarthrosis 81.09
posterior (interbody) posterolateral technique
81.05
for pseudarthrosis 81.09
epiphyseal-diaphyseal (*see also* Arrest, bone
growth) 78.20
epiphysiodesis (*see also* Arrest, bone growth)
78.20
hammer toe 77.56
joint (with bone graft) (*see also* Arthrodesis)
81.20
ankle 81.11
claw toe 77.57
foot NEC 81.17
hammer toe 77.56
hip 81.21
interphalangeal, ringer 81.28
ischiofemoral 81.21

G

Gait training 93.22
Galeaplasty 86.89
Galvanoionization 99.27
Games
competitive 94.39
organized 93.89
Gamma irradiation, stereotactic 92.3
Ganglionectomy
gasserian 04.05
lumbar sympathetic 05.23
nerve (cranial) (peripheral) NEC 04.06
sympathetic 05.29
sphenopalatine (Meckel's) 05.21
tendon sheath (wrist) 82.21
site other than hand 83.31
trigeminal 04.05
Ganglionotomy, trigeminal (radio frequency)
04.02
Gant operation (wedge osteotomy of trochanter)
77.25
Garceau operation (tibial tendon transfer) 83.75
Gardner operation (spinal meningocele repair)
03.51
Gas endarterectomy 38.10
abdominal 38.16
aorta (arch) (ascending) (descending) 38.14
coronary artery 36.09
head and neck NEC 38.12
intracranial NEC 38.11
lower limb 38.18
thoracic NEC 38.15
upper limb 38.13
Gastrectomy (partial) (subtotal) NEC 43.89
with
anastomosis (to) NEC 43.89
duodenum 43.6
esophagus 43.5
gastrogastric 43.89
jejunum 43.7
esophagogastrostomy 43.5
gastroduodenostomy (bypass) 43.6
gastroenterostomy (bypass) 43.7
gastrogastrostomy (bypass) 43.89
gastrojejunostomy (bypass) 43.7
jejunal transposition 43.81
complete NEC 43.99
with intestinal interposition 43.91
distal 43.6
Hofmeister 43.7
Polya 43.7
proximal 43.5
radical NEC 43.99
with intestinal interposition 43.91
total NEC 43.99
with intestinal interposition 43.91
Gastrocamera 44.19
Gastroduodenectomy —*see* Gastrectomy
Gastroduodenoscopy 45.13
through stoma (artificial) 45.12
transabdominal (operative) 45.11
Gastroduodenostomy (bypass) (Jaboulay's)
44.39
with partial gastrectomy 43.6
Gastroenterostomy (bypass) NEC 44.39
with partial gastrectomy 43.7
Gastrogastrostomy (bypass) 44.39
with partial gastrectomy 43.89
Gastrojejunostomy (bypass) 44.39
with partial gastrectomy 43.7

Gastrolysis 54.59
laparoscopic 54.51
Gastropexy 44.64
Gastroplasty NEC 44.69
Gastroplication 44.69
Gastropylorectomy 43.6
Gastrorrhaphy 44.61
Gastroscopy NEC 44.13
through stoma (artificial) 44.12
transabdominal (operative) 44.11
Gastrostomy (Brunschwig's) (decompression)
(fine caliber tube) (Kader) (permanent)
(Stamm) (Stamm-Kader) (temporary) (tube)
(Witzel) 43.19
Beck-Jianu 43.19
Frank's 43.19
Janeway 43.19
percutaneous (endoscopic) (PEG) 43.11
Spivack's 43.19
Ssabanejew-Frank 43.19
Gastrotomy 43.0
for control of hemorrhage 44.49
Gavage, gastric 96.35
Gelman operation (release of clubfoot) 83.84
Genioplasty (augmentation) (with graft) (with
implant) 76.68
reduction 76.67
Ghormley operation (hip fusion) 81.21
Gifford operation
destruction of lacrimal sac 09.6
keratotomy (delimiting) 11.1
radial (refractive) 11.75
Gill operation
arthrodesis of shoulder 81.23
laminectomy 03.09
Gill-Stein operation (carporadial arthrodesis)
81.25
Gilliam operation (uterine suspension) 69.22
Gingivectomy 24.31
Gingivoplasty (with bone graft) (with soft tissue
graft) 24.2
Girdlestone operation
laminectomy with spinal fusion 81.00
muscle transfer for claw toe repair 77.57
resection of femoral head and neck 77.85
Girdlestone-Taylor operation (muscle transfer
for claw toe repair) 77.57
Glenn operation (anastomosis of superior vena
cava to right pulmonary artery) 39.21
Glenoplasty, shoulder 81.83
with
partial replacement 81.81
total replacement 81.80
for recurrent dislocation 81.82
Glomectomy
carotid 39.8
jugulare 20.51
Glossectomy (complete) (total) 25.3
partial or subtotal 25.2
radical 25.4
Glossopexy 25.59
Glossoplasty NEC 25.59
Glossorrhaphy 25.51
Glossotomy NEC 25.94
for tongue tic 25.91
Goebel-Frangenheim-Stoeckel operation
(urethrovesical suspension) 59.4

H

Hagner operation (epididymotomy) 63.92
Halsted operation —*see* Repair, hernia, inguinal
Hampton operation (anastomosis small intestine to rectal stump) 45.92
Hanging hip operation (muscle release) 83.19
Harelip operation 27.54
Harrison-Richardson operation (vaginal suspension) 70.77
Hartmann resection (of intestine) (with pouch)—*see* Colectomy, by site
Harvesting
bone marrow 41.91
stem cells 99.79
Hauser operation
achillotenotomy 83.11
bunionectomy with adductor tendon transfer 77.53
stabilization of patella 81.44
Heaney operation (vaginal hysterectomy) 68.59
laparoscopically assisted (LAVH) 68.51
Hearing aid (with battery replacement) 95.49
Hearing test 95.47
Hegar operation (perineorrhaphy) 71.79
Heine operation (cyclodialysis) 12.55
Heineke-Mikulicz operation (pyloroplasty) 44.29
Heller operation (esophagomyotomy) 42.7
Hellstöm operation (transplantation of aberrant renal vessel) 39.55
Hemicolectomy
left 45.75
right (extended) 45.73
Hemicystectomy 57.6
Hemigastrectomy —*see* Gastrectomy
Hemiglossectomy 25.2
Hemilaminectomy (decompression) (exploration) 03.09
Hemilaryngectomy (anterior) (lateral) (vertical) 30.1
Hemimandibulectomy 76.31
Hemimastectomy (radical) 85.23
Hemimaxillectomy (with bone graft) (with prosthesis) 76.39
Heminephrectomy 55.4
Hemipelvectomy 84.19
Hemispherectomy (cerebral) 01.52
Hemithyroidectomy (with removal of isthmus) (with removal of portion of remaining lobe) 06.2
Hemodiafiltration (extracorporeal) 39.95
Hemodialysis (extracorporeal) 39.95
Hemodilution 99.03
Hemofiltration (extracorporeal) 39.95
Hemorrhage control —*see* Control, hemorrhage
Hemorrhoidectomy 49.46
by
cautery, cauterization 49.43
crushing 49.45
cryotherapy, cryosurgery 49.44
excision 49.46
injection 49.42
ligation 49.45
Hemostasis —*see* Control, hemorrhage
Henley operation (jejunal transposition) 43.81
Hepatectomy (complete) (total) 50.4
partial or subtotal 50.22
Hepatic assistance, extracorporeal 50.92
Hepaticocholangiojejunostomy 51.37
Hepaticocystoduodenostomy 51.37

Hepaticodochotomy 51.59
Hepaticoduodenostomy 51.37
Hepaticojejunostomy 51.37
Hepaticolithectomy 51.49
endoscopic 51.88
Hepaticolithotomy 51.49
endoscopic 51.88
Hepaticostomy 51.59
Hepaticotomy 51.59
Hepatocholangiocystoduodenostomy 51.37
Hepatocholedochostomy 51.43
endoscopic 51.87
Hepatoduodenostomy 50.69
Hepatogastrostomy 50.69
Hepatojejunostomy 50.69
Hepatolithotomy
hepatic duct 51.49
liver 50.0
Hepatopexy 50.69
Hepatorrhaphy 50.61
Hepatostomy (external) (internal) 50.69
Hepatotomy (with packing) 50.0
Hernioplasty —*see* Repair, hernia
Herniorrhaphy —*see* Repair, hernia
Herniotomy —*see* Repair, hernia
Heterograft —*see* Graft
Heterotransplant, heterotransplantation —*see* Transplant
Hey operation (amputation of foot) 84.12
Hey-Groves operation (reconstruction of anterior cruciate ligament) 81.45
Heyman operation (soft tissue release for clubfoot) 83.84
Heyman-Herndon (Strong) **operation** (correction of metatarsus varus) 80.48
Hibbs operation (lumbar spinal fusion)—*see* Fusion, lumbar
Higgins operation —*see* Repair, hernia, femoral
High forceps delivery 72.39
with episiotomy 72.31
Hill-Allison operation (hiatal hernia repair, transpleural approach) 53.80
Hinging, mitral valve 35.12
His bundle recording 37.29
Hitchcock operation (anchoring tendon of biceps) 83.88
Hofmeister operation (gastrectomy) 43.7
Hoke operation
midtarsal fusion 81.14
triple arthrodesis 81.12
Holth operation
iridencleisis 12.63
sclerectomy 12.65
Homan operation (correction of lymphedema) 40.9
Homograft —*see* Graft
Homotransplant, homotransplantation —*see* Transplant
Hosiery, elastic 93.59
Hutch operation (ureteroneocystostomy) 56.74
Hybinette-Eden operation (glenoid bone block) 78.01
Hydrocelectomy
canal of Nuck (female) 69.19
male 63.1
round ligament 69.19
spermatic cord 63.1
tunica vaginalis 61.2

I

ICCE (intracapsular cataract extraction) 13.19
Ileal
  bladder
    closed 57.87 *[45.51]*
    open (ileoureterostomy) 56.51
  conduit (ileoureterostomy) 56.51
Ileocecostomy 45.93
Ileocolectomy 45.73
Ileocolostomy 45.93
Ileocolotomy 45.00
Ileocystoplasty (isolated segment anastomosis)
    (open loop) 57.87 *[45.51]*
Ileoduodenotomy 45.01
Ileoectomy (partial) 45.62
  with cecectomy 45.72
Ileoentectropy 46.99
Ileoesophagostomy 42.54
Ileoileostomy 45.91
  proximal to distal segment 45.62
Ileoloopogram 87.78
Ileopancreatostomy 52.96
Ileopexy 46.61
Ileoproctostomy 45.93
Ileorectostomy 45.93
Ileorrhaphy 46.73
Ileoscopy 45.13
  through stoma (artificial) 45.12
  transabdominal (operative) 45.11
Ileosigmoidostomy 45.93
Ileostomy 46.20
  continent (permanent) 46.22
  delayed opening 46.24
  Hendon (temporary) 46.21
  loop 46.01
  Paul (temporary) 46.21
  permanent 46.23
    continent 46.22
  repair 46.41
  revision 46.41
  tangential (temporary) 46.21
  temporary 46.21
  transplantation to new site 46.23
  tube (temporary) 46.21
  ureteral
    external 56.51
    internal 56.71
Ileotomy 45.02
Ileotransversostomy 45.93
Ileoureterostomy (Bricker's) (ileal bladder)
    56.51
Imaging (diagnostic)
  diagnostic, not elsewhere classified 88.90
  magnetic resonance (nuclear), (proton) NEC
    88.97
    abdomen 88.97
    bladder (urinary) 88.95
    bone marrow blood supply 88.94
    brain (brain stem) 88.91
    chest (hilar) (mediastinal) 88.92
    extremity (upper) (lower) 88.94
    eye orbit 88.97
    face 88.97
    head NEC 88.97
    musculoskeletal 88.94
    myocardium 88.92
    neck 88.97
    orbit of eye 88.97

Imaging—*continued*
    prostate 88.95
    specified site NEC 88.97
    spinal canal (cord) (spine) 88.93
Immobilization (by)
  with fracture-reduction—*see* Reduction, fracture
  bandage 93.53
  bone 93.53
  cast NEC 93.53
    with reduction of fracture or dislocation—*see*
      Reduction, fracture, *and* Reduction,
      dislocation
  device NEC 93.59
  pressure dressing 93.56
  splint (plaster) (tray) 93.54
    with reduction of fracture or dislocation—*see*
      Reduction, fracture, *and* Reduction,
      dislocation
  stereotactic head frame 93.59
Immunization —*see also* Vaccination
  allergy 99.12
  autoimmune disease 99.13
  BCG 99.33
  brucellosis 99.55
  cholera 99.31
  diphtheria 99.36
  DPT 99.39
  epidemic parotitis 99.46
  German measles 99.47
  Hemophilus influenzae 99.52
  influenza 99.52
  measles 99.45
  meningococcus 99.55
  mumps 99.46
  pertussis 99.37
  plague 99.34
  poliomyelitis 99.41
  rabies 99.44
  rubella 99.47
  salmonella 99.55
  smallpox 99.42
  staphylococcus 99.55
  TAB 99.32
  tetanus 99.38
  triple vaccine 99.48
  tuberculosis 99.33
  tularemia 99.35
  typhoid-paratyphoid 99.32
  typhus 99.55
  viral NEC 99.55
  whooping cough 99.37
  yellow fever 99.43
Immunotherapy, antineoplastic 99.28
  C-Parvum 99.28
  Interferon 99.28
  Interleukin-2 99.28
  Levamisole 99.28
  Thymosin 99.28
Implant, implantation
  abdominal artery to coronary artery 36.17
  artery
    aortic branches to heart muscle 36.2
    mammary to ventricular wall (Vineberg) 36.2
  baffle, atrial or interatrial 35.91
  biliary fistulous tract into stomach or intestine
    51.39
  bipolar endoprosthesis (femoral head) 81.52
  bladder sphincter, artificial (inflatable) 58.93

Implant, implantation—*continued*
  blood vessels to myocardium 36.2
  bone growth stimulator (invasive)
      (percutaneous) (semi-invasive)—*see
      category* 78.9
  breast (for augmentation) (bilateral) 85.54
    unilateral 85.53
  cardioverter/defibrillator, automatic 37.94
    leads only (patch electrodes) (sensing)
        (pacing) 37.95
    pulse generator only 37.96
    total system 37.94
  chest wall (mesh) (silastic) 34.79
  chin (polyethylene) (silastic) 76.68
  cochlea (electrode) 20.96
    prosthetic device (electrode and receiver)
        20.96
      channel (single) 20.97
        multiple 20.98
      electrode only 20.99
      internal coil only 20.99
  cornea 11.73
  custodis eye 14.41
  dental (endosseous) (prosthetic) 23.6
  device, vascular access 86.07
  diaphragmatic pacemaker 34.85
  electrode(s)
    brain 02.93
      depth 02.93
      foramen ovale 02.93
      sphenoidal 02.96
    cardiac (initial) (transvenous) 37.70
      atrium (initial) 37.73
        replacement 37.76
      atrium and ventricle (initial) 37.72
        replacement 37.76
      epicardium (sternotomy or thoracotomy
          approach) 37.74
      temporary transvenous pacemaker system
          37.78
        during and immediately following cardiac
            surgery 39.64
      ventricle (initial) 37.71
        replacement 37.76
    depth 02.93
    foramen ovale 02.93
    heart (*see also* Implant, electrode(s), cardiac)
        37.70
    intracranial 02.93
    osteogenic (invasive) for bone growth
        stimulation—*see* category 78.9
    peripheral nerve 04.92
    sphenoidal 02.96
    spine 03.93
  electroencephalographic receiver
    brain 02.93
    intracranial 02.93
  electronic stimulator
    anus (subcutaneous) 49.92
    bladder 57.96
    bone growth stimulator (invasive)
        (percutaneous) (semi-invasive) 78.9
    brain 02.93
    carotid sinus 39.8
    cochlear 20.96
      channel (single) 20.97
        multiple 20.98
    intracranial 02.93
    peripheral nerve 04.92
    phrenic nerve 34.85
    skeletal muscle 83.92

Implant, implantation—*continued*
    spine 03.93
    ureter 56.92
  electrostimulator—*see* Implant, electronic
      stimulator, by site
  endoprosthesis
    bile duct 51.87
    femoral head (bipolar) 81.52
    pancreatic duct 52.93
  endosseous (dental) 23.6
  epidural pegs 02.93
  epikeratoprosthesis 11.73
  estradiol (pellet) 99.23
  eye (Iowa type) 16.61
    integrated 16.41
  facial bone, synthetic (alloplastic) 76.92
  fallopian tube (Mulligan hood) (silastic tube)
      (stent) 66.93
    into uterus 66.74
  gastroepiploic artery to coronary artery 36.17
  half-heart 37.62
  hearing device, electromagnetic 20.95
  heart
    artificial 37.62
    assist system NEC 37.62
      external (pulsatile) 37.65
      implantable (pulsatile) 37.66
      non-pulsatile 37.62
    auxiliary ventricle 37.62
    pacemaker (*see also* Implant, pacemaker,
        cardiac) 37.80
    valve(s)
      prosthesis or synthetic device (partial)
          (synthetic) (total) 35.20
        aortic 35.22
        mitral 35.24
        pulmonary 35.26
        tricuspid 35.28
      tissue graft 35.20
        aortic 35.21
        mitral 35.23
        pulmonary 35.25
        tricuspid 35.27
  inert material
    breast (for augmentation) (bilateral) 85.54
      unilateral 85.53
    larynx 31.0
    nose 21.85
    orbit (eye socket) 16.69
      reinsertion 16.62
    scleral shell (cup) (with evisceration of
        eyeball) 16.31
      reinsertion 16.62
    Tenon's capsule (with enucleation of eyeball)
        16.42
      with attachment of muscles 16.41
      reinsertion 16.62
    urethra 59.79
    vocal cord(s) 31.0
  infusion pump 86.06
  joint (prosthesis) (silastic) (Swanson type) NEC
      81.96
    ankle (total) 81.56
      revision 81.59
    carpocarpal, carpometacarpal 81.74
    elbow (total) 81.84
      revision 81.97
    extremity (bioelectric) (cineplastic)
        (kineplastic) 84.40
      lower 84.48
        revision 81.59

Implant, implantation—*continued*	**Incision**—*continued*

Implant, implantation—*continued*	Incision—*continued*

Implant, implantation—*continued*

Rickham reservoir 02.2
silicone
  breast (bilateral) 85.54
    unilateral 85.53
  skin (for filling of defect) 86.02
    for augmentation NEC 86.89
stimoceiver
  brain 02.93
  intracranial 02.93
  peripheral nerve 04.92
  spine 03.93
subdural
  grids 02.93
  strips 02.93
Swanson prosthesis (joint) (silastic) NEC 81.96
  carpocarpal, carpometacarpal 81.74
  finger 81.71
  hand (metacarpophalangeal) (interphalangeal)
    81.71
  interphalangeal 81.71
  knee (partial) (total) 81.54
    revision 81.55
  metacarpophalangeal 81.71
  toe 81.57
    for hallux valgus repair 77.59
  wrist (partial) 81.74
    total 81.73
systemic arteries into myocardium (Vineberg
    type operation) 36.2
testicular prosthesis (bilateral) (unilateral) 62.7
tissue expander (skin) NEC 86.93
  breast 85.95
tissue mandril (for vascular graft) 39.99
  with
    blood vessel repair 39.56
    vascular bypass or shunt—*see* Bypass,
      vascular
tooth (bud) (germ) 23.5
  prosthetic 23.6
umbrella, vena cava 38.7
ureters into
  bladder 56.74
  intestine 56.71
    external diversion 56.51
  skin 56.61
urethan sphincter, artificial (inflatable) 58.93
urethra
  for repair of urinary stress incontinence
    collagen 59.72
    fat 59.72
    polytef 59.72
urinary sphincter, artificial (inflatable) 58.93
vascular access device 86.07
vitreous (silicone) 14.75
  for retinal reattachment 14.41
    with buckling 14.41
vocal cord(s) (paraglottic) 31.98
Implosion (psychologic desensitization) 94.33
Incision (and drainage)
  with
    exploration—*see* Exploration
    removal of foreign body—*see* Removal,
      foreign body
  abdominal wall 54.0
    as operative approach—*omit code*

Incision—*continued*

abscess—*see also* Incision, by site
  appendix 47.2
    with appendectomy 47.09
      laparoscopic 47.01
  extraperitoneal 54.0
  ischiorectal 49.01
  lip 27.0
  omental 54.19
  perianal 49.01
  perigastric 54.19
  perisplenic 54.19
  peritoneal NEC 54.19
    pelvic (female) 70.12
  retroperitoneal 54.0
  sclera 12.89
  skin 86.04
  subcutaneous tissue 86.04
  subdiaphragmatic 54.19
  subhepatic 54.19
  subphrenic 54.19
  vas deferens 63.6
adrenal gland 07.41
alveolus, alveolar bone 24.0
antecubital fossa 86.09
anus NEC 49.93
  fistula 49.11
  septum 49.91
appendix 47.2
artery 38.00
  abdominal 38.06
  aorta (arch) (ascending) (descending) 38.04
  head and neck NEC 38.02
  intracranial NEC 38.01
  lower limb 38.08
  thoracic NEC 38.05
  upper limb 38.03
atrium (heart) 37.11
auditory canal or meatus, external 18.02
auricle 18.09
axilla 86.09
Bartholin's gland or cyst 71.22
bile duct (with T or Y tube insertion)
    NEC 51.59
  common (exploratory) 51.51
    for
      relief of obstruction NEC 51.42
      removal of calculus 51.41
    for
      exploration 51.59
      relief of obstruction 51.49
bladder 57.19
  neck (transurethral) 57.91
  percutaneous suprapubic (closed) 57.17
  suprapubic NEC 57.18
blood vessel (*see also* Angiotomy) 38.00
bone 77.10
  alveolus, alveolar 24.0
  carpals, metacarpals 77.14
  clavicle 77.11
  facial 76.09
  femur 77.15
  fibula 77.17
  humerus 77.12
  patella 77.16
  pelvic 77.19
  phalanges (foot) (hand) 77.19
  radius 77.13
  scapula 77.11
  skull 01.24
  specified site NEC 77.19

Incision—*continued*
   tarsals, metatarsals 77.18
   thorax (ribs) (sternum) 77.11
   tibia 77.17
   ulna 77.13
   vertebrae 77.19
  brain 01.39
   cortical adhesions 02.91
  breast (skin) 85.0
   with removal of tissue expander 85.96
  bronchus 33.0
  buccal space 27.0
  bulbourethral gland 58.91
  bursa 83.03
   hand 82.03
   pharynx 29.0
  carotid body 39.8
  cerebral (meninges) 01.39
   epidural or extradural space 01.24
   subarachnoid or subdural space 01.31
  cerebrum 01.39
  cervix 69.95
   to
    assist delivery 73.93
    replace inverted uterus 75.93
  chalazion 08.09
   with removal of capsule 08.21
  cheek 86.09
  chest wall (for extrapleural drainage) (for
   removal of foreign body) 34.01
   as operative approach—*omit code*
  common bile duct (for exploration) 51.51
   for
    relief of obstruction 51.42
    removal of calculus 51.41
  common wall between posterior left atrium and
   coronary sinus (with roofing of resultant
   defect with patch graft) 35.82
  conjunctiva 10.1
  cornea 11.1
   radial (refractive) 11.75
  cranial sinus 01.21
  craniobuccal pouch 07.72
  cul-de-sac 70.12
  cyst
   dentigerous 24.0
   radicular (apical) (periapical) 24.0
  Dührssen's (cervix, to assist delivery) 73.93
  duodenum 45.01
  ear
   external 18.09
   inner 20.79
   middle 20.23
  endocardium 37.11
  endolymphatic sac 20.79
  epididymis 63.92
  epidural space, cerebral 01.24
  epigastric region 54.0
   intra-abdominal 54.19
  esophagus, esophageal NEC 42.09
   web 42.01
  exploratory—*see* Exploration
  extradural space (cerebral) 01.24
  extrapleural 34.01
  eyebrow 08.09
  eyelid 08.09
   margin (trichiasis) 08.01
  face 86.09
  fallopian tube 66.01

Incision—*continued*
  fascia 83.09
   with division 83.14
    hand 82.12
   hand 82.09
    with division 82.12
  fascial compartments, head and neck 27.0
  fistula, anal 49.11
  flank 54.0
  furuncle—*see* Incision, by site
  gallbladder 51.04
  gingiva 24.0
  gluteal 86.09
  groin region (abdominal wall) (inguinal) 54.0
   skin 86.09
   subcutaneous tissue 86.09
  gum 24.0
  hair follicles 86.09
  heart 37.10
   valve—*see* Valvulotomy
  hematoma—*see also* Incision, by site
   axilla 86.04
   broad ligament 69.98
   ear 18.09
   episiotomy site 75.91
   fossa (superficial) NEC 86.04
   groin region (abdominal wall) (inguinal) 54.0
    skin 86.04
    subcutaneous tissue 86.04
   laparotomy site 54.12
   mediastinum 34.1
   perineum (female) 71.09
    male 86.04
   popliteal space 86.04
   scrotum 61.0
   skin 86.04
   space of Retzius 59.19
   subcutaneous tissue 86.04
   vagina (cuff) 70.14
    episiotomy site 75.91
    obstetrical NEC 75.92
  hepatic ducts 51.59
  hordeolum 08.09
  hygroma—*see also* Incision, by site
   cystic 40.0
  hymen 70.11
  hypochondrium 54.0
   intra-abdominal 54.19
  hypophysis 07.72
  iliac fossa 54.0
  infratemporal fossa 27.0
  ingrown nail 86.09
  intestine 45.00
   large 45.03
   small 45.02
  intracerebral 01.39
  intracranial (epidural space) (extradural space)
   01.24
   subarachnoid or subdural space 01.31
  intraperitoneal 54.19
  ischiorectal tissue 49.02
   abscess 49.01
  joint structures (*see also* Arthrotomy) 80.10
  kidney 55.01
   pelvis 55.11
  labia 71.09
  lacrimal
   canaliculus 09.52
   gland 09.0
   passage NEC 09.59

Incision—*continued*
  thyroid (field) (gland) NEC 06.09
    postoperative 06.02
  tongue NEC 25.94
    for tongue tic 25.91
  tonsil 28.0
  trachea NEC 31.3
  tunica vaginalis 61.0
  umbilicus 54.0
  urachal cyst 54.0
  ureter 56.2
  urethra 58.0
  uterus (corpus) 68.0
    cervix 69.95
    for termination of pregnancy 74.91
    septum (congenital) 68.22
  uvula 27.71
  vagina (cull) (septum) (stenosis) 70.14
    for
      incisional hematoma (episiotomy) 75.91
      obstetrical hematoma NEC 75.92
      pelvic abscess 70.12
  vas deferens 63.6
  vein 38.00
    abdominal 38.07
    head and neck NEC 38.02
    intracranial NEC 38.01
    lower limb 38.09
    thoracic NEC 38.05
    upper limb 38.03
  vertebral column 03.09
  vulva 71.09
    obstetrical 75.92
  web, esophageal 42.01
Incudectomy NEC 19.3
  with
    stapedectomy (*see also* Stapedectomy) 19.19
    tympanoplasty—*see* Tympanoplasty
Incudopexy 19.19
Incudostapediopexy 19.19
  with incus replacement 19.11
Indentation, sclera, for buckling (*see also*
    Buckling, scleral) 14.49
Indicator dilution flow measurement 89.68
Induction
  abortion
    by
      D and C 69.01
      insertion of prostaglandin suppository 96.49
      intra-amniotic injection (prostaglandin)
        (saline) 75.0
  labor
    medical 73.4
    surgical 73.01
      intra- and extra-amniotic injection 73.1
      stripping of membranes 73.1
Inflation
  belt wrap 93.99
  Eustachian tube 20.8
  fallopian tube 66.8
    with injection of therapeutic agent 66.95
Infolding sclera, for buckling (*see also*
    Buckling, scleral) 14.49
Infraction, turbinates (nasal) 21.62
Infundibulectomy
  hypophyseal (*see also* Hypophysectomy,
    partial) 07.63
  ventricle (heart) (right) 35.34
    in total repair of tetralogy of Fallot 35.81

Infusion, (intra-arterial) (intravenous)
  antineoplastic agent (chemotherapeutic) 99.25
    biological response modifier [BRM] 99.28
  biological response modifier [BRM],
    antineoplastic agent 99.28
  cancer chemotherapy agent NEC 99.25
  electrolytes 99.18
  enzymes, thrombolytic (streptokinase) (tissue
      plasminogen activator) (TPA) (urokinase)
    direct coronary artery 36.04
    intravenous 99.29
  hormone substance NEC 99.24
  nutritional substance (*see* Nutrition)
  platelet inhibitor
    direct coronary artery 36.04
    intravenous 99.29
  prophylactic substance NEC 99.29
  therapeutic substance NEC 99.29
  thrombolytic agent (enzyme) (platelet inhibitor)
      (streptokinase) 99.29
    with percutaneous transluminal angioplasty
      coronary (single vessel) 36.02
        multiple vessels 36.05
      non-coronary vessel(s) 39.50
      specified site NEC 39.50
    direct intracoronary artery 36.04
Injection (into) (hypodermically)
    (intramuscularly) (intravenously) (acting
    locally or systemically)
  Actinomycin D, for cancer chemotherapy 99.25
  alcohol
    nerve—*see* Injection, nerve
    spinal 03.8
  anterior chamber, eye (air) (liquid) (medication)
    12.92
  antibiotic 99.21
  anticoagulant 99.19
  anti-D (Rhesus) globulin 99.11
  antidote NEC 99.16
  anti-infective NEC 99.22
  antineoplastic agent (chemotherapeutic) NEC
    99.25
    biological response modifier [BRM] 99.28
  antivenin 99.16
  BCG
    for chemotherapy 99.25
    vaccine 99.33
  biological response modifier [BRM],
    antineoplastic agent 99.28
  bone marrow 41.92
    transplant—*see* Transplant, bone, marrow
  breast (therapeutic agent) 85.92
    inert material (silicone) (bilateral) 85.52
      unilateral 85.51
  bursa (therapeutic agent) 83.96
    hand 82.94
  cancer chemotherapeutic agent 99.25
  caudal—*see* Injection, spinal
  cortisone 99.23
  costochondral junction 81.92
  dinoprost-tromethine, intra-amniotic 75.0
  ear, with alcohol 20.72
  electrolytes 99.18
  enzymes, thrombolytic (streptokinase) (tissue
      plasminogen activator) (TPA) (urokinase)
    direct coronary artery 36.04
    intravenous 99.29
  epidural, spinal—*see* Injection, spinal
  esophageal varices or blood vessel
      (endoscopic)(sclerosing agent) 42.33
  Eustachian tube (inert material) 20.8

Insertion—*continued*

arch bars (orthodontic) 24.7
  for immobilization (fracture) 93.55
atrial septal umbrella 35.52
Austin-Moore prosthesis 81.52
baffle, heart (atrial) (interatrial) (intra-atrial)
  35.91
bag, cervix (nonobstetrical) 67.0
  after delivery or abortion 75.8
  to assist delivery or induce labor 73.1
Baker's (tube) (for stenting) 46.85
balloon
  gastric 44.93
  heart (pulsation-type) (Kantrowitz) 37.61
  intestine (for decompression) (for dilation)
    46.85
Barton's tongs (skull) (with synchronous
  skeletal traction) 02.94
bipolar endoprosthesis (femoral head) 81.52
bladder sphincter, artificial (inflatable) 58.93
Blakemore-Sengstaken tube 96.06
bone growth stimulator (invasive)
  (percutaneous) (semi-invasive)—*see*
  category 78.9
bougie, cervix, nonobstetrical 67.0
  to assist delivery or induce labor 73.1
breast implant (for augmentation) (bilateral)
  85.54
  unilateral 85.53
bridge (dental) (fixed) 23.42
  removable 23.43
bubble (balloon), stomach 44.93
caliper tongs (skull) (with synchronous skeletal
  traction) 02.94
cannula
  Allen-Brown 39.93
  for extracorporeal membrane oxygenation
    (ECMO)—*omit code*
  nasal sinus (by puncture) 22.01
    through natural ostium 22.02
  pancreatic duct 52.92
    endoscopic 52.93
  vessel to vessel 39.93
catheter
  abdomen of fetus, for intrauterine transfusion
    75.2
  anterior chamber (eye), for permanent
    drainage (glaucoma) 12.79
  artery 38.91
  bile duct(s) 51.59
    common 51.51
      endoscopic 51.87
    endoscopic 51.87
  bladder, indwelling 57.94
    suprapubic 57.18
      percutaneous (closed) 57.17
  bronchus 96.05
    with lavage 96.56
  central venous NEC 38.93
    for
      hemodialysis 38.95
      pressure monitoring 89.62
    peripherally inserted central catheter (PICC)
      38.93
  chest 34.04
  esophagus (nonoperative) 96.06
    permanent tube 42.81
  intercostal (with water seal), for drainage
    34.04

Insertion—*continued*

spinal canal space (epidural) (subarachnoid)
  (subdural) for infusion of therapeutic or
  palliative substances 03.90
Swan-Ganz (pulmonary) 89.64
transtracheal for oxygenation 31.99
vein NEC 38.93
  for renal dialysis 38.95
chest tube 34.04
choledochohepatic tube (for decompression)
  51.43
  endoscopic 51.87
cochlear prosthetic device-*see* Implant, cochlea,
  prosthetic device
contraceptive device (intrauterine) 69.7
cordis cannula 54.98
coronary (artery)
  stent(s) (stent graft) 36.06
Crosby-Cooney button 54.98
Crutchfield tongs (skull) (with
  synchronous skeletal traction) 02.94
Davidson button 54.98
denture (total) 99.97
device, vascular access 86.07
diaphragm, vagina 96.17
drainage tube
  kidney 55.02
    pelvis 55.12
  renal pelvis 55.12
elbow prosthesis (total) 81.84
  revision 81.97
electrode(s)
  bone growth stimulator (invasive)
    (percutaneous) (semi-invasive)—*see*
    category 78.9
  brain 02.93
    depth 02.93
    foramen ovale 02.93
    sphenoidal 02.96
  depth 02.93
  foramen ovale 02.93
  heart (initial) (transvenous) 37.70
    atrium (initial) 37.73
      replacement 37.76
    atrium and ventricle (initial) 37.72
      replacement 37.76
    epicardium (sternotomy or thoracotomy
      approach) 37.74
    temporary transvenous pacemaker system
      37.78
      during and immediately following cardiac
        surgery 39.64
    ventricle (initial) 37.71
      replacement 37.76
  intracranial 02.93
  osteogenic (for bone growth stimulation)—*see*
    category 78.9
  peripheral nerve 04.92
  sphenoidal 02.96
  spine 03.93
electroencephalographic receiver—*see* Implant,
  electroencephalographic receiver, by site
electronic stimulator—*see* Implant, electronic
  stimulator, by site
electrostimulator—*see* Implant, electronic
  stimulator, by site
endoprosthesis
  bile duct 51.87
  femoral head (bipolar) 81.52
  pancreatic duct 52.93
epidural pegs 02.93

Insertion—*continued*
  port, vascular access 86.07
  prostaglandin suppository (for abortion) 96.49
  prosthesis, prosthetic device
    acetabulum (partial) 81.52
      revision 81.53
    ankle (total) 81.56
    arm (bioelectric) (cineplastic) (kineplastic)
      84.44
    biliary tract 51.99
    breast (bilateral) 85.54
      unilateral 85.53
    chin (polyethylene) (silastic) 76.68
    elbow (total) 81.84
      revision 81.97
    extremity (bioelectric) (cineplastic)
      (kineplastic) 84.40
      lower 84.48
      upper 84.44
    fallopian tube 66.93
    femoral head (Austin-Moore) (bipolar)
      (Eicher) (Thompson) 81.52
    hip (partial) 81.52
      revision 81.53
      total 81.51
        revision 81.53
    joint—*see* Arthroplasty
    knee (partial) (total) 81.54
      revision 81.55
    leg (bioelectric) (cineplastic) (kineplastic)
      84.48
    ocular (secondary) 16.61
      with orbital exenteration 16.42
    outflow tract (gusset type) (heart)
      in
        pulmonary valvuloplasty 35.26
        total repair of tetralogy of Fallot 35.81
    penile (non-inflatable) (internal) 64.95
      inflatable (internal) 64.97
      with
        construction 64.43
        reconstruction 64.44
    Rosen (for urinary incontinence) 59.79
    Shoulder
      partial 81.81
      revision 81.97
      total 81.80
    testicular (bilateral) (unilateral) 62.7
    toe 81.57
      for hallux valgus repair 77.59
  pseudophakos (*see also* Insertion, lens) 13.70
  pump, infusion 86.06
  radioactive isotope 92.27
  radium 92.27
  radon seeds 92.27
  Reuter bobbin (with intubation) 20.01
  Rickham, reservoir 02.2
  Rosen prosthesis (for urinary incontinence)
    59.79
  Scribner shunt 39.93
  Sengstaken-Blakemore tube 96.06
  sieve, vena cava 38.7
  skeletal muscle stimulator 83.92
  skull
    plate 02.05
    stereotactic frame 93.59
    tongs (Barton) (caliper) (Garder Wells)
      (Vinke) (with synchronous skeletal
      traction) 02.94
  sphenoidal electrodes 02.96
  Spitz-Holter valve 02.2

Insertion—*continued*
  Steinmann pin 93.44
    with reduction of fracture or dislocation—*see*
      Reduction, fracture *and* Reduction,
      dislocation
  stent(s) (stent graft)
    bile duct 51.43
      endoscopic 51.87
    coronary (artery) 36.06
    esophagus (endoscopic) (fluoroscopic) 42.81
    non-coronary vessel 39.90
      with angioplasty or atherectomy 39.50
    pancreatic duct 52.92
      endoscopic 52.93
    peripheral vessel —*see* non-coronary vessel
  stimoceiver—*see* Implant, stimoceiver, by site
  stimulator for bone growth—*see category* 78.9
  subdural
    grids 02.93
    strips 02.93
  suppository
    prostaglandin (for abortion) 96.49
    vagina 96.49
  Swan-Ganz catheter (pulmonary) 89.64
  tampon
    esophagus 96.06
    uterus 69.91
    vagina 96.14
      after delivery or abortion 75.8
  testicular prosthesis (bilateral) (unilateral) 62.7
  tissue expander (skin) NEC 86.93
    breast 85.95
  tissue mandril (peripheral vessel) (Dacron)
    (Spark's type) 39.99
    with
      blood vessel repair 39.56
      vascular bypass or shunt—*see* Bypass,
        vascular
  tongs, skull (with synchronous skeletal traction)
    02.94
  totally implanted device for bone growth
    (invasive)—*see category* 78.9
  tube—*see also* Catheterization *and* Intubation
    bile duct 51.43
      endoscopic 51.87
    endotracheal 96.04
    esophagus (nonoperative) (Sengstaken) 96.06
      permanent (silicone) (Souttar) 42.81
    feeding
      esophageal 42.81
      gastric 96.6
      nasogastric 96.6
    gastric
      by gastrostomy—*see category* 43.1
      for
        decompression, intestinal 96.07
        feeding 96.6
    Miller-Abbott (for intestinal decompression)
      96.08
    nasobiliary (drainage) 51.86
    nasogastric (for intestinal decompression)
      NEC 96.07
    nasopancreatic drainage (endoscopic) 52.97
    pancreatic duct 52.92
      endoscopic 52.93
    rectum 96.09
    stomach (nasogastric) (for intestinal
      decompression) NEC 96.07
      for feeding 96.6
  umbrella device
    atrial septum (King-Nos) 35.52

Insertion—*continued*
    vena cava (Mobitz-Uddin) 38.7
    ureteral stent (transurethral) 59.8
      with ureterotomy 59.8 *[56.2]*
    urinary sphincter, artificial (AUS) (inflatable)
      58.93
    vaginal mold 96.15
    valve
      Holter 02.2
      Hufnagel—*see* Replacement, heart valve
      pharyngeal (artificial) 31.75
      Spitz-Holter 02.2
      vas deferens 63.95
    vascular access device 86.07
    vena cava sieve or umbrella 38.7
    Vinke tongs (skull) (with synchronous skeletal
      traction) 02.94
Instillation
    bladder 96.49
    digestive tract, except gastric gavage 96.43
    genitourinary NEC 96.49
    radioisotope (intracavitary) (intravenous) 92.28
Insufflation
    Eustachian tube 20.8
    fallopian tube (air) (dye) (gas) (saline) 66.8
      for radiography—*see* Hysterosalpingography
      therapeutic substance 66.95
    lumbar retroperitoneal, bilateral 88.15
Intercricothyroidotomy (for assistance in
    breathing) 31.1
Intermittent positive pressure breathing
    (IPPB) 93.91
Interposition operation
    esophageal reconstruction (intrathoracic)
      (retrosternal) NEC (*see also* Anastomosis,
      esophagus, with, interposition) 42.58
    antesternal or antethoracic NEC (*see also*
      Anastomosis, esophagus, antesternal,
      with, interposition) 42.68
    uterine suspension 69.21
Interruption
    vena cava (inferior) (superior) 38.7
Interview (evaluation) (diagnostic)
    medical, except psychiatric 89.05
      brief (abbreviated history) 89.01
      comprehensive (history and evaluation of new
        problem) 89.03
      limited (interval history) 89.02
      specified type NEC 89.04
    psychiatric NEC 94.19
      follow-up 94.19
      initial 94.19
      pre-commitment 94.13
Intimectomy 38.10
    abdominal 38.16
    aorta (arch) (ascending) (descending) 38.14
    head and neck NEC 38.12
    intracranial NEC 38.11
    lower limb 38.18
    thoracic NEC 38.15
    upper limb 38.13
Introduction
    orthodontic appliance 24.7
    therapeutic substance (acting locally or
      systemically) NEC 99.29
      bursa 83.96
        hand 82.94
      fascia 83.98
        hand 82.96
      heart 37.92

Introduction—*continued*
    joint 81.92
      temporomandibular 76.96
    ligament (joint) 81.92
    pericardium 37.93
    soft tissue NEC 83.98
      hand 82.96
    tendon 83.97
      hand 82.95
    vein 39.92
Intubation —*see also* Catheterization *and*
    Insertion
    bile duct(s) 51.59
      common 51.51
        endoscopic 51.87
      endoscopic 51.87
    esophagus (nonoperative) (Sengstaken) 96.06
      permanent tube (silicone) (Souttar) 42.81
    Eustachian tube 20.8
    intestine (for decompression) 96.08
    lacrimal for
      dilation 09.42
      tear drainage, intranasal 09.81
    larynx 96.05
    nasobiliary (drainage) 51.86
    nasogastric
      for
        decompression, intestinal 96.07
        feeding 96.6
    nasolacrimal (duct) (with irrigation) 09.44
    nasopancreatic drainage (endoscopic) 52.97
    respiratory tract NEC 96.05
    small intestine (Miller-Abbott) 96.08
    stomach (nasogastric) (for intestinal
      decompression) NEC 96.07
      for feeding 96.6
    trachea 96.04
    ventriculocisternal 02.2
Invagination, diverticulum
    gastric 44.69
    pharynx 29.59
    stomach 44.69
Inversion
    appendix 47.99
    diverticulum
      gastric 44.69
      intestine
        large 45.49
          endoscopic 45.43
        small 45.34
      stomach 44.69
    tunica vaginalis 61.49
Ionization, medical 99.27
Iontherapy 99.27
Iontophoresis 99.27
Iridectomy (basal) (buttonhole) (optical)
    (peripheral) (total) 12.14
    with
      capsulectomy 13.65
      cataract extraction—*see* Extraction, cataract
      filtering operation (for glaucoma) NEC
        12.65
      scleral
        fistulization 12.65
        thermocauterization 12.62
        trephination 12.61
Iridencleisis 12.63
Iridesis 12.63
Irido-capsulectomy 13.65
Iridocyclectomy 12.44
Iridocystectomy 12.42
Iridodesis 12.63

Iridoplasty NEC 12.39
Iridosclerectomy 12.65
Iridosclerotomy 12.69
Iridotasis 12.63
Iridotomy 12.12
  by photocoagulation 12.12
Iridotomy—*continued*
  with transfixion 12.11
  for iris bombé 12.11
  specified type NEC 12.12
Iron lung 93.99
Irradiation
  gamma, stereotactic 92.3
Irrigation
  anterior chamber (eye) 12.91
  bronchus NEC 96.56
  canaliculus 09.42
  catheter
    ureter 96.46
    urinary, indwelling NEC 96.48
    vascular 96.57
    ventricular 02.41
    wound 96.58
  cholecystostomy 96.41
  cornea 96.51
    with removal of foreign body 98.21
  corpus cavernosum 64.98
  cystostomy 96.47
  ear (removal of cerumen) 96.52
  enterostomy 96.36
  eye 96.51
    with removal of foreign body 98.21
  gastrostomy 96.36
  lacrimal
    canaliculi 09.42
    punctum 09.41
  muscle 83.02
    hand 82.02
  nasal
    passages 96.53
    sinus 22.00
  nasolacrimal duct 09.43
    with insertion of tube or stent 09.44
  nephrostomy 96.45
  peritoneal 54.25
  pyelostomy 96.45
  rectal 96.39
  stomach 96.33
  tendon (sheath) 83.01
    hand 82.01
  trachea NEC 96.56
  traumatic cataract 13.3
  tube
    biliary NEC 96.41
    nasogastric NEC 96.34
    pancreatic 96.42
  ureterostomy 96.46
  ventricular shunt 02.41
  wound (cleaning) NEC 96.59
Irving operation (tubal ligation) 66.32
Irwin operation (*see also* Osteotomy) 77.30
Ischiectomy (partial) 77.89
  total 77.99
Ischiopubiotomy 77.39
Isolation
  after contact with infectious disease 99.84
  ileal loop 45.51
  intestinal segment or pedicle nap
    large 45.52
    small 45.51
Isthmectomy, thyroid (*see also* Thyroidectomy,
  partial) 06.39

J

Jaboulay operation (gastroduodenostomy) 44.39
Janeway operation (permanent gastrostomy)
  43.19
Jatene operation (arterial switch) 35.84
Jejunectomy 45.62
Jejunocecostomy 45.93
Jejunocholecystostomy 51.32
Jejunocolostomy 45.93
Jejunoileostomy 45.91
Jejunojejunostomy 45.91
Jejunopexy 46.61
Jejunorrhaphy 46.73
Jejunostomy (feeding) 46.39
  delayed opening 46.31
  loop 46.01
  percutaneous (endoscopic) (PEJ) 46.32
  revision 46.41
Jejunotomy 45.02
Johanson operation (urethral reconstruction)
  58.46
Jones operation
  claw toe (transfer of extensor hallucis longus
    tendon) 77.57
    modified (with arthrodesis) 77.57
  dacryocystorhinostomy 09.81
  hammer toe (interphalangeal fusion) 77.56
  modified (tendon transfer with arthrodesis)
    77.57
  repair of peroneal tendon 83.88
Joplin operation (exostectomy with tendon
  transfer) 77.53

K

Kader operation (temporary gastrostomy) 43.19
Kaufman operation (for urinary stress
  incontinence) 59.79
Kazanjiian operation (buccal vestibular sulcus
  extension) 24.91
Kehr operation (hepatopexy) 50.69
Keller operation (bunionectomy) 77.59
Kelly (Kennedy) **operation** (urethrovesical
  plication) 59.3
Kelly-Stoeckel operation (urethrovesical
  plication) 59.3
Kelotomy 53.9
Keratectomy (complete) (partial) (superficial)
  11.49
  for pterygium 11.39
    with corneal graft 11.32
Keratocentesis (for hyphema) 12.91
Keratomeleusis 11.71
Keratophakia 11.72
Keratoplasty (tectonic) (with autograft) (with
  homograft) 11.60
  lamellar (nonpenetrating) (with homograft)
    11.62
    with autograft 11.61
  penetrating (full-thickness) (with homograft)
    11.64
    with autograft 11.63
  perforating—*see* Keratoplasty, penetrating
  refractive 11.71
  specified type NEC 11.69
Keratoprosthesis 11.73

Keratotomy (delimiting) (posterior) 11.1
  radial (refractive) 11.75
Kerr operation (low cervical cesarean section)
  74.1
Kessler operation (arthroplasty, carpometacarpal
  joint) 81.74
Kidner operation (excision of accessory
  navicular bone) (with tendon transfer) 77.98
Killian operation (frontal sinusotomy) 22.41
Kineplasty —*see* Cineplasty
King-Steelquist operation (hindquarter
  amputation) 84.19
Kirk operation (amputation through thigh) 84.17
Kock pouch operation
  bowel anastomosis—*omit code*
  continent ileostomy 46.22
  cutaneous uretero-ileostomy 56.51
  ESWL (extracorporeal shockwave lithotripsy)
    98.51
  removal, calculus 57.19
  revision, cutaneous uretero-ileostomy 56.52
  urinary diversion procedure 56.51
Kondoleon operation (correction of
  lymphedema) 40.9
Krause operation (sympathetic denervation)
  05.29
Kroener operation (partial salpingectomy) 66.69
Kroenlein operation (lateral orbitotomy) 16.01
Krönig operation (low cervical cesarean section)
  74.1
Krukenberg operation (reconstruction of
  below-elbow amputation) 82.89
Kuhnt-Szymanowski operation (ectropion
  repair with lid reconstruction) 08.44

L

Labbe operation (gastrotomy) 43.0
Labiectomy (bilateral) 71.62
  unilateral 71.61
Labyrinthectomy (transtympanic) 20.79
Labyrinthotomy (transtympanic) 20.79
Ladd operation (mobilization of intestine) 54.95
Lagrange operation (iridosclerectomy) 12.65
Lambrinudi operation (triple arthrodesis) 81.12
Laminectomy (decompression) (for exploration)
  03.09
  as operative approach—*omit code*
  with
    excision of herniated intervertebral disc
      (nucleus pulposus) 80.51
    excision of other intraspinal lesion (tumor)
      03.4
  reopening of site 03.02
Laminography —*see* Radiography
Laminotomy (decompression) (for exploration)
  03.09
  as operative approach—*omit code*
  reopening of site 03.02
Langenbeck operation (cleft palate repair) 27.62
Laparoamnioscopy 75.31
Laparorrhaphy 54.63
Laparoscopy 54.21
  with
    biopsy (intra-abdominal) 54.24
      uterine ligaments 68.15
      uterus 68.16
    destruction of fallopian tubes—*see*
      Destruction, fallopian tube
Laparotomy NEC 54.19
  as operative approach—*omit code*
  exploratory (pelvic) 54.11
  reopening of recent operative site (for control of
    hemorrhage) (for exploration) (for incision
    of hematoma) 54.12
Laparotrachelotomy 74.1
Lapidus operation (bunionectomy with
  metatarsal osteotomy) 77.51
Larry operation (shoulder disarticulation) 84.08
Laryngectomy
  with radical neck dissection (with synchronous
    thyroidectomy) (with synchronous
    tracheostomy) 30.4
  complete (with partial laryngectomy) (with
    synchronous tracheostomy) 30.3
    with radical neck dissection (with
      synchronous thyroidectomy) (with
      synchronous tracheostomy) 30.4
  frontolateral partial (extended) 30.29
  glottosupraglottic partial 30.29
  lateral partial 30.29
  partial (frontolateral) (glottosupraglottic)
    (lateral) (submucous) (supraglottic)
    (vertical) 30.29
  radical (with synchronous thyroidectomy) (with
    synchronous tracheostomy) 30.4
  submucous (partial) 30.29
  supraglottic partial 30.29
  total (with partial pharyngectomy) (with
    synchronous tracheostomy) 30.3
    with radical neck dissection (with
      synchronous thyroidectomy) (with
      synchronous tracheostomy) 30.4
  vertical partial 30.29
  wide field 30.3

Laryngocentesis 31.3
Laryngoesophagectomy 30.4
Laryngofissure 30.29
Laryngogram 87.09
  contrast 87.07
Laryngopharyngectomy (with synchronous
  tracheostomy) 30.3
  radical (with synchronous thyroidectomy) 30.4
Laryngopharyngoesophagectomy (with
  synchronous tracheostomy) 30.3
  with radical neck dissection (with synchronous
    thyroidectomy) 30.4
Laryngoplasty 31.69
Laryngorrhaphy 31.61
Laryngoscopy (suspension) (through artificial
  stoma) 31.42
Laryngostomy (permanent) 31.29
  revision 31.63
  temporary (emergency) 31.1
Laryngotomy 31.3
Laryngotracheobronchoscopy 33.23
  with biopsy 33.24
Laryngotracheoscopy 31.42
Laryngotracheostomy (permanent) 31.29
  temporary (emergency) 31.1
Laryngotracheotomy (temporary) 31.1
  permanent 31.29
Laser —*see also* Coagulation, Destruction, *and*
  Photocoagulation by site
  angioplasty, percutaneous transluminal 39.59
  coronary—*see* angioplasty, coronary
Lash operation (internal cervical os repair) 67.5
Latzko operation
  cesarean section 74.2
  colpocleisis 70.4
Lavage
  antral 22.00
  bronchus NEC 96.56
  endotracheal 96.56
  gastric 96.33
  nasal sinus(es) 22.00
    by puncture 22.01
    through natural ostium 22.02
  peritoneal (diagnostic) 54.25
  trachea NEC 96.56
Leadbetter operation (urethral reconstruction)
  58.46
Leadbetter-Politano operation
  (ureteroneocystostomy) 56.74
Le Fort operation (colpocleisis) 70.8
LeMesurier operation (cleft lip repair) 27.54
Lengthening
  bone (with bone graft) 78.30
    femur 78.35
    for reconstruction of thumb 82.69
    specified site NEC (*see also category* 78.3)
      78.39
    tibia 78.37
    ulna 78.33
  extraocular muscle NEC 15.21
    multiple (two or more muscles) 15.4
  fascia 83.89
    hand 82.89
  hamstring NEC 83.85
  heel cord 83.85

Lengthening—*continued*
  leg
    femur 78.35
    tibia 78.37
  levator palpebrae muscle 08.38
  muscle 83.85
    extraocular 15.21
      multiple (two or more muscles) 15.4
    hand 82.55
  palate 27.62
    secondary or subsequent 27.63
  tendon 83.85
    for claw toe repair 77.57
    hand 82.55
Leriche operation (periarterial sympathectomy)
  05.25
Leucotomy, leukotomy 01.32
Leukopheresis, therapeutic 99.72
Lid suture operation (blepharoptosis) 08.31
Ligation
  adrenal vessel (artery) (vein) 07.43
  aneurysm 39.52
  appendages, dermal 86.26
  arteriovenous fistula 39.53
    coronary artery 36.99
  artery 38.80
    abdominal 38.86
    adrenal 07.43
    aorta (arch) (ascending) (descending) 38.84
    coronary (anomalous) 36.99
    ethmoidal 21.04
    external carotid 21.06
    for control of epistaxis—*see* Control, epistaxis
    head and neck NEC 38.82
    intracranial NEC 38.81
    lower limb 38.88
    maxillary (transantral) 21.05
    middle meningeal 02.13
    thoracic NEC 38.85
    thyroid 06.92
    upper limb 38.83
  atrium, heart 37.99
  auricle, heart 37.99
  bleeding vessel—*see* Control, hemorrhage
  blood vessel 38.80
    abdominal
      artery 38.86
      vein 38.87
    adrenal 07.43
    aorta (arch) (ascending) (descending) 38.84
    esophagus 42.91
      endoscopic 42.33
    head and neck NEC 38.82
    intracranial NEC 38.81
    lower limb
      artery 38.88
      vein 38.89
    meningeal (artery) (longitudinal sinus) 02.13
    thoracic NEC 38.85
    thyroid 06.92
    upper limb (artery) (vein) 38.83
  bronchus 33.92
  cisterna chyli 40.64
  coronary
    artery (anomalous) 36.99
    sinus 36.3
  dermal appendage 86.26
  ductus arteriosus, patent 38.85
  esophageal vessel 42.91
    endoscopic 42.33
  ethmoidal artery 21.04

Ligation—*continued*
  external carotid artery 21.06
  fallopian tube (bilateral) (remaining)
      (solitary) 66.39
    by endoscopy (culdoscopy) (hysteroscopy)
        (laparoscopy) (peritoneoscopy) 66.29
    with
      crushing 66.31
        by endoscopy (laparoscopy) 66.21
      division 66.32
        by endoscopy (culdoscopy) (laparoscopy)
            (peritoneoscopy) 66.22
      Falope ring 66.39
        by endoscopy (laparoscopy) 66.29
    unilateral 66.92
  fistula, arteriovenous 39.53
    coronary artery 36.99
  gastric
    artery 38.86
    varices 44.91
      endoscopic 43.41
  hemorrhoids 49.45
  longitudinal sinus (superior) 02.13
  lymphatic (channel) (peripheral) 40.9
    thoracic duct 40.64
  maxillary artery 21.05
  meningeal vessel 02.13
  spermatic
    cord 63.72
      varicocele 63.1
    vein (high) 63.1
  splenic vessels 38.86
  subclavian artery 38.85
  superior longitudinal sinus 02.13
  supernumerary digit 86.26
  thoracic duct 40.64
  thyroid vessel (artery) (vein) 06.92
  toes (supernumerary) 86.26
  tooth 93.55
    impacted 24.6
  ulcer (peptic) (base) (bed) (bleeding vessel)
      44.40
    duodenal 44.42
    gastric 44.41
  ureter 56.95
  varices
    esophageal 42.91
      endoscopic 42.33
    gastric 44.91
      endoscopic 43.41
    peripheral vein (lower limb) 38.59
      upper limb 38.53
  varicocele 63.1
  vas deferens 63.71
  vein 38.80
    abdominal 38.87
    adrenal 07.43
    head and neck NEC 38.82
    intracranial NEC 38.81
    lower limb 38.89
    spermatic, high 63.1
    thoracic NEC 38.85
    thyroid 06.92
    upper limb 38.83
    varicose 38.50
      abdominal 38.57
      esophagus 42.91
        endoscopic 42.33
      gastric 44.91
        endoscopic 43.41

Ligation—*continued*
    head and neck NEC 38.52
    intracranial NEC 38.51
    lower limb 38.59
    stomach 44.91
    thoracic NEC 38.55
    upper limb 38.53
  vena cava, inferior 38.7
  venous connection between anomalous
    vein to
    left innominate vein 35.82
    superior vena cava 35.82
  wart 86.26
Light coagulation *see* Photocoagulation
Lindholm operation (repair of ruptured tendon)
  83.88
Lingulectomy, lung 32.3
Linton operation (varicose vein) 38.59
Lipectomy (subcutaneous tissue) (abdominal)
  (submental) 86.83
Lip reading training 95.49
Lip shave 27.43
Lisfranc operation
  foot amputation 84.12
  shoulder disarticulation 84.08
Litholapaxy, bladder 57.0
  by incision 57.19
Lithotomy
  bile passage 51.49
  bladder (urinary) 57.19
  common duct 51.41
    percutaneous 51.96
  gallbladder 51.04
  hepatic duct 51.49
  kidney 55.01
    percutaneous 55.03
  ureter 56.2
Lithotripsy
  bile duct NEC 51.49
    extracorporeal shockwave (ESWL) 98.52
  bladder 57.0
    extracorporeal shockwave (ESWL) 98.51
    with ultrasonic fragmentation 57.0 *[59.95]*
  extracorporeal shockwave (ESWL) NEC 98.59
    bile duct 98.52
    bladder (urinary) 98.51
    gallbladder 98.52
    kidney 98.51
    Kock pouch 98.51
    renal pelvis 98.51
    specified site NEC 98.59
    ureter 98.51
  gallbladder NEC 51.04
    endoscopic 51.88
    extracorporeal shockwave (ESWL) 98.52
  kidney 56.0
    extracorporeal shock wave (EWSL) 98.51
    percutaneous nephrostomy with fragmentation
      (laser) (ultrasound) 55.04
  renal pelvis 56.0
    extracorporeal shock wave (EWSL) 98.51
    percutaneous nephrostomy with fragmentation
      (laser) (ultrasound) 55.04
  ureter 56.0
    extracorporeal shockwave (ESWL) 98.51
Littlewood operation (forequarter amputation)
  84.09
Lloyd-Davies operation (abdominoperineal
  resection) 48.5

Lobectomy
  brain 01.53
    partial 01.59
  liver (with partial excision of adjacent lobes)
    50.3
  lung (complete) 32.4
    partial 32.3
    segmental (with resection of adjacent lobes)
      32.4
  thyroid (total) (unilateral) (with removal of
    isthmus) (with removal of portion of
    remaining lobe) 06.2
    partial (*see also* Thyroidectomy, partial) 06.39
    substernal 06.51
    subtotal (*see also* Thyroidectomy, partial)
      06.39
Lobotomy, brain 01.32
Localization, placenta 88.78
  by RISA injection 92.17
Longmire operation (bile duct anastomosis)
  51.39
Loop ileal stoma (*see also* Ileostomy) 46.01
Loopogram 87.78
Looposcopy (ileal conduit) 56.35
Lord operation
  dilation of anal canal for hemorrhoids 49.49
  hemorrhoidectomy 49.49
  orchidopexy 62.5
Lower GI series (x-ray) 87.64
Lucas and Murray operation (knee arthrodesis
  with place) 81.22
Lumpectomy
  breast 85.21
  specified site—*see* Excision, lesion, by site
Lymphadenectomy (simple) (*see also* Excision,
  lymph, node) 40.29
Lymphadenotomy 40.0
Lymphangiectomy (radical) (*see also* Excision,
  lymph, node, by site, radical) 40,50
Lymphangiogram
  abdominal 88.04
  cervical 87.08
  intrathoracic 87.34
  lower limb 88.36
  pelvic 88.04
  upper limb 88.34
Lymphangioplasty 40.9
Lymphangiorrhaphy 40.9
Lymphangiotomy 40.0
Lymphaticostomy 40.9
  thoracic duct 40.62
Lysis
  adhesions
    abdominal 54.59
      laparoscopic 54.51
    appendiceal 54.59
      laparoscopic 54.51
    artery-vein-nerve bundle 39.91
    biliary tract 54.59
      laparoscopic 54.51
    bladder (neck) (intraluminal) 57.12
      external 59.11
        laparoscopic 59.12
      transurethral 57.41
    blood vessels 39.91
    bone—*see category* 78.4
    bursa 83.91
      by stretching or manipulation 93.28
      hand 82.91
    cartilage of joint 93.26
    chest wall 33.99

Lysis—*continued*
   choanae (nasopharynx) 29.54
   conjunctiva 10.5
   corneovitreal 12.34
   cortical (brain) 02.91
   ear, middle 20.23
   Eustachian tube 20.8
   extraocular muscle 15.7
   extrauterine 54.59
     laparoscopic 54.51
   eyelid 08.09
     and conjunctiva 10.5
   eye muscle 15.7
   fallopian tube 65.89
     laparoscopic 65.81
   fascia 83.91
     hand 82.91
       by stretching or manipulation 93.26
   gallbladder 54.59
     laparoscopic 54.51
   ganglion (peripheral) NEC 04.49
     cranial NEC 04.42
   hand 82.91
     by stretching or manipulation 93.26
   heart 37.10
   intestines 54.59
     laparoscopic 54.51
   iris (posterior) 12.33
     anterior 12.32
   joint (capsule) (structure) (*see also* Division,
     joint capsule) 80.40
   kidney 59.02
     laparoscopic 59.03
   labia (vulva) 71.01
   larynx 31.92
   liver 54.59
     laparoscopic 54.51
   lung (for collapse of lung) 33.39
   mediastinum 34.99
   meninges (spinal) 03.6
     cortical 02.91
   middle ear 20.23
   muscle 83.91
     by stretching or manipulation 93.27
     extraocular 15.7
     hand 82.91
       by stretching or manipulation 93.26
   nasopharynx 29.54
   nerve (peripheral) NEC 04.49
     cranial NEC 04.42
     roots, spinal 03.6
     trigeminal 04.41
   nose, nasal 21.91
   ocular muscle 15.7
   ovary 65.89
     laparoscopic 65.81
   pelvic 54.59
     laparoscopic 54.51
   penile 64.93
   pericardium 37.12
   perineal (female) 71.01
   peripheral vessels 39.91
   perirectal 48.81
   perirenal 59.02
     laparoscopic 59.03
   peritoneum (pelvic) 54.59
     laparoscopic 54.51
   periureteral 59.02
     laparoscopic 59.03
   perivesical 59.11
     laparoscopic 59.12

Lysis—*continued*
   pharynx 29.54
   pleura (for collapse of lung) 33.39
   spermatic cord 63.94
   spinal (cord) (meninges) (nerve roots) 03.6
   spleen 54.59
     laparoscopic 54.51
   tendon 83.91
     by stretching or manipulation 93.27
     hand 82.91
       by stretching or manipulation 93.26
   thorax 34.99
   tongue 25.93
   trachea 31.92
   tubo-ovarian 65.89
     laparoscopic 65.81
   ureter 59.02
     with freeing or repositioning of ureter 59.02
     intraluminal 56.81
     laparoscopic 59.03
   urethra (intraluminal) 58.5
   uterus 54.59
     intraluminal 68.21
     laparoscopic 54.51
     peritoneal 54.59
       laparoscopic 54.51
   vagina (intraluminal) 70.13
   vitreous (posterior approach) 14.74
     anterior approach 14.73
   vulva 71.01
goniosynechiae (with injection of air or
     liquid) 12.31
synechiae (posterior) 12.33
   anterior (with injection of air or liquid) 12.32

M

Madlener operation (tubal ligation) 66.31
Magnet extraction
  foreign body
    anterior chamber, eye 12.01
    choroid 14.01
    ciliary body 12.01
    conjunctiva 98.22
    cornea 11.0
    eye, eyeball NEC 98.21
      anterior segment 12.01
      posterior segment 14.01
    intraocular (anterior segment) 12.01
    iris 12.01
    lens 13.01
    orbit 98.21
    retina 14.01
    sclera 12.01
    vitreous 14.01
Magnetic resonance imaging (nuclear) *see*
  Imaging, magnetic resonance
Magnuson (Stack) operation (arthroplasty for
  recurrent shoulder dislocation) 81.82
Malleostapediopexy 19.19
  with incus replacement 19.11
Malström's vacuum extraction 72.79
  with episiotomy 72.71
Mammaplasty —*see* Mammoplasty
Mammectomy —*see also* Mastectomy
  subcutaneous (unilateral) 85.34
    with synchronous implant 85.33
    bilateral 85.36
      with synchronous implant 85.35
Mammilliplasty 85.87
Mammography NEC 87.37
Mammoplasty 85.89
  with
    full-thickness graft 85.83
    muscle flap 85.85
    pedicle graft 85.84
    split-thickness graft 85.82
  amputative (reduction) (bilateral) 85.32
    unilateral 85.31
  augmentation 85.50
    with
      breast implant (bilateral) 85.54
        unilateral 85.53
      injection into breast (bilateral) 85.52
        unilateral 85.51
  reduction (bilateral) 85.32
    unilateral 85.31
  revision 85.89
  size reduction (gynecomastia) (bilateral) 85.32
    unilateral 85.31
Mammotomy 85.0
Manchester (Donald) (Fothergill) operation
  (uterine suspension) 69.22
Mandibulectomy (partial) 76.31
  total 76.42
    with reconstruction 76.41
Maneuver (method)
  Bracht 72.52
  Credé 73.59
  De Lee (key-in-lock) 72.4
  Kristeller 72.54
  Lovset's (extraction of arms
    in breech birth) 72.52
  Mauriceau (Smellie-Veit) 72.52

Maneuver—*continued*
  Pinard (total breech extraction) 72.54
  Prague 72.52
  Ritgen 73.59
  Scanzoni (rotation) 72.4
  Van Hoorn 72.52
  Wigand-Martin 72.52
Manipulation
  with reduction of fracture or dislocation—*see*
    Reduction, fracture *and* Reduction,
    dislocation
  enterostomy stoma (with dilation) 96.24
  intestine (intra-abdominal) 46.80
    large 46.82
    small 46.81
  joint
    adhesions 93.26
      temporomandibular 76.95
    dislocation—*see* Reduction, dislocation
  lacrimal passage (tract) NEC 09.49
  muscle structures 93.27
  musculoskeletal (physical therapy) NEC 93.29
  nasal septum, displaced 21.88
  osteopathic NEC 93.67
    for general mobilization (general articulation)
      93.61
    high-velocity, low-amplitude forces
      (thrusting) 93.62
    indirect forces 93.65
    isotonic, isometric forces 93.64
    low-velocity, high-amplitude forces
      (springing) 93.63
    to move tissue fluids 93.66
  rectum 96.22
  salivary duct 26.91
  stomach, intraoperative 44.92
  temporomandibular joint NEC 76.95
  ureteral calculus by catheter 56.0
  uterus NEC 69.98
    gravid 75.99
    inverted
      manual replacement (following delivery)
        75.94
      surgical—*see* Repair, inverted uterus
Manometry
  esophageal 89.32
  spinal fluid 89.15
  urinary 89.21
Manual arts therapy 93.81
Mapping
  cardiac (electrophysiologic) 37.27
    doppler (flow) 88.72
  electrocardiogram only 89.52
Marckwald operation (cervical os repair) 67.5
Marshall-Marchetti (Krantz) operation
  (retropubic urethral suspension) 59.5
Marsupialization —*see also* Destruction, lesion,
  by site
  cyst
    Bartholin's 71.23
    brain 01.59
    cervical (nabothian) 67.31
    dental 24.4
    dentigerous 24.4
    kidney 55.31
    larynx 30.01
    liver 50.21

Mechanical ventilation —*see* Ventilation
Mediastinectomy 34.3
Mediastinoscopy (transpleural) 34.22
Mediastinotomy 34.1
  with pneumonectomy 32.5
Meloplasty, facial 86.82
Meningeorrhaphy (cerebral) 02.12
  spinal NEC 03.59
    for
      meningocele 03.51
      myelomeningocele 03.52
Meniscectomy (knee) NEC 80.6
  acromioclavicular 80.91
  sternoclavicular 80.91
  temporomandibular (joint) 76.5
  wrist 80.93
Menstrual extraction or regulation 69.6
Mentoplasty (augmentation) (with graft) (with
    implant) 76.68
  reduction 76.67
Mesenterectomy 54.4
Mesenteriopexy 54.75
Mesenteriplication 54.75
Mesocoloplication 54.75
Mesopexy 54.75
Metatarsectomy 77.98
Metroplasty 69.49
Mid forceps delivery 72.29
Mikulicz operation (exteriorization of intestine)
    (first stage) 46.03
  second stage 46.04
Miles operation (proctectomy) 48.5
Military anti-shock trousers (MAST) 93.58
Millard operation (cheiloplasty) 27.54
Miller operation
  midtarsal arthrodesis 81.14
  urethrovesical suspension 59.4
Millin-Read operation (urethrovesical
    suspension) 59.4
Mist therapy 93.94
Mitchell operation (hallux valgus repair) 77.51
Mobilization
  joint NEC 93.16
  mandible 76.95
  neostrophingic (mitral valve) 35.12
  spine 93.15
  stapes (transcrural) 19.0
  testis in scrotum 62.5
Mohs operation (chemosurgical excision of
    skin) 86.24
Molegraphy 87.81
Monitoring
  cardiac output (by)
    ambulatory (ACM) 89.50
    electrographic 89.54
      during surgery—*omit code*
    Fick method 89.67
    Holter-type device 89.50
    indicator dilution technique 89.68
    oxygen consumption technique 89.67
    specified technique NEC 89.68
    telemetry (cardiac) 89.54
    thermodilution indicator 89.68
    transesophageal (Doppler) (ultrasound) 89.68
  central venous pressure 89.62
  circulatory NEC 89.69
  coronary blood flow (coincidence counting
      technique) 89.69
  electroencephalographic 89.19
    radio-telemetered 89.19
    video 89.19
  fetus (fetal heart)

Monitoring—*continued*
  antepartum
    nonstress (fetal activity acceleration
        determinations) 75.35
    oxytocin challenge (contraction stress test)
        75.35
    ultrasonography (early pregnancy)
        (Doppler) 88.78
  intrapartum (during labor) (extrauterine)
      (external) 75.34
    auscultatory (stethoscopy)—*omit code*
    internal (with contraction measurements)
        (ECG) 75.32
    intrauterine (direct) (ECG) 75.32
    phonocardiographic (extrauterine) 75.34
    pulsed ultrasound (Doppler) 88.78
  Holter-type device (cardiac) 89.50
  intracranial pressure 01.18
  pulmonary artery
    pressure 89.63
    wedge 89.64
  sleep (recording)—*see categories* 89.17-89.18
  systemic arterial pressure 89.61
  telemetry (cardiac) 89.54
  transesophageal cardiac output (Doppler) 89.68
  ventricular pressure (cardiac) 89.62
Moore operation (arthroplasty) 81.52
Moschowitz
  enterocele repair 70.92
  herniorrhaphy—*see* Repair, hernia, femoral
  sigmoidopexy 46.63
Mountain resort sanitarium 93.98
Mouth-to-mouth resuscitation 93.93
Moxibustion 93.35
MRI —*see* Imaging, magnetic resonance
Muller operation (banding of pulmonary artery)
    38.85
Multiple sleep latency test (MSLT) 89.18
Mumford operation (partial claviculectomy)
    77.81
Musculoplasty (*see also* Repair, muscle) 83.87
  hand (*see also* Repair, muscle, hand) 82.89
Music therapy 93.84
Mustard operation (interatrial transposition of
    venous return) 35.91
Myectomy 83.45
  anorectal 48.92
  eye muscle 15.13
    multiple 15.3
  for graft 83.43
    hand 82.34
  hand 82.36
    for graft 82.34
  levator palpebrae 08.33
  rectal 48.92
Myelogram, myelography (air) (gas) 87.21
  posterior fossa 87.02
Myelotomy
  spine, spinal (cord) (tract) (one-stage)
      (two-stage) 03.29
    percutaneous 03.21
Myocardiectomy (infarcted area) 37.33
Myocardiotomy 37.11
Myoclasis 83.99
  hand 82.99
Myomectomy (uterine) 68.29
  broad ligament 69.19
Myoplasty (*see also* Repair, muscle) 83.87
  hand (*see also* Repair, muscle, hand) 82.89
  mastoid 19.9
Myorrhaphy 83.65
  hand 82.46

N

Nailing, Intramedullary 79.30
  femur 79.35
  fibula 79.36
  humerus 79.31
  radius 79.32
  tibia 79.36
  ulna 79.32
Narcoanalysis 94.21
Narcosynthesis 94.21
Narrowing, palpebral fissure 08.51
Nasopharyngogram 87.09
  contrast 87.06
Necropsy 89.8
Needleoscopy (fetus) 75.31
Needling
  Bartholin's gland (cyst) 71.21
  cataract (secondary) 13.64
  fallopian tube 66.91
  hydrocephalic head 73.8
  lens (capsule) 13.2
  pupillary membrane (iris) 12.35
Nephrectomy (complete) (total) (unilateral) 55.51
  bilateral 55.54
  partial (wedge) 55.4
  remaining or solitary kidney 55.52
  removal transplanted kidney 55.53
Nephrocolopexy 55.7
Nephrocystanastomosis NEC 56.73
Nephrolithotomy 55.01
Nephrolysis 59.02
  laparoscopic 59.03
Nephropexy 55.7
Nephroplasty 55.89
Nephropyeloplasty 55.87
Nephropyeloureterostomy 55.86
Nephrorrhaphy 55.81
Nephroscopy 55.21
Nephrostolithotomy, percutaneous 55.03
Nephrostomy (with drainage tube) 55.02
  closure 55.82
  percutaneous 55.03
   with fragmentation (ultrasound) 55.04
Nephrotomogram, nephrotomography NEC 87.72
Nephrotomy 55.01
Nephroureterectomy (with bladder cuff) 55.51
Nephroureterocystectomy 55.51 [57.79]
Nerve block (cranial) (peripheral) NEC (see also Block, by site) 04.81
Neurectasis (cranial) (peripheral) 04.91
Neurectomy (cranial) (infraorbital) (occipital) (peripheral) (spinal) NEC 04.07
  gastric (vagus) (see also Vagotomy) 44.00
  opticociliary 12.79
  paracervical 05.22
  presacral 05.24
  retrogasserian 04.07
  sympathetic—see Sympathectomy
  trigeminal 04.07
  tympanic 20.91
Neurexeresis NEC 04.07
Neuroanastomosis (cranial) (peripheral) NEC 04.74
  accessory-facial 04.72
  accessory-hypoglossal 04.73
  hypoglossal-facial 04.71

Neurolysis (peripheral nerve) NEC 04.49
  carpal tunnel 04.43
  crania] nerve NEC 04.42
  spinal (cord) (nerve roots) 03.6
  tarsal tunnel 04.44
  trigeminal nerve 04.41
Neuroplasty (cranial) (peripheral) NEC 04.79
  of old injury (delayed repair) 04.76
  revision 04.75
Neurorrhaphy (cranial) (peripheral) 04.3
Neurotomy (cranial) (peripheral) (spinal) NEC 04.04
  acoustic 04.01
  glossopharyngeal 29.92
  lacrimal branch 05.0
  retrogasserian 04.02
  sympathetic 05.0
  vestibular 04.01
Neurotripsy (peripheral) NEC 04.03
  trigeminal 04.02
Nicola operation (tenodesis for recurrent dislocation of shoulder) 81.82
Nissen operation (fundoplication of stomach) 44.66
Noble operation (plication of small intestine) 46.62
Norman Miller operation (vaginopexy) 70.77
Norton operation (extraperitoneal cesarean section) 74.2
Nuclear magnetic resonance imaging
  —see Imaging, magnetic resonance
Nutrition, concentration substances
  enteral infusion (of) 96.6
  parenteral, total 99.15
   peripheral 99.15

O

Ober (Yount) operation (gluteal-iliotibial fasciotomy) 83.14
Obliteration
  bone cavity (*see also* Osteoplasty) 78.40
  calyceal diverticulum 55.39
  canaliculi 09.6
  cerebrospinal fistula 02.12
  cul-de-sac 70.92
  frontal sinus (with fat) 22.42
  lacrimal punctum 09.91
  lumbar pseudomeningocele 03.51
  lymphatic structure(s) (peripheral) 40.9
  maxillary sinus 22.31
  meningocele (sacral) 03.51
  pelvic 68.8
  pleural cavity 34.6
  sacral meningocele 03.51
  Skene's gland 71.3
  tympanomastoid cavity 19.9
  vagina, vaginal (partial) (total) 70.4
  vault 70.8
Occlusal molds (dental) 89.31
Occlusion
  artery—*see* Ligation, artery
  fallopian tube—*see* Ligation, fallopian tube
  patent ductus arteriosus (PDA) 38.85
  vein—*see* Ligation, vein
  vena cava (surgical) 38.7
Occupational therapy 93.83
O'Donoghue operation (triad knee repair) 81.43
Odontectomy NEC (*see also* Removal, tooth, surgical) 23.19
Oleothorax 33.39
Olshausen operation (uterine suspension) 69.22
Omentectomy 54.4
Omentofixation 54.74
Omentopexy 54.74
Omentoplasty 54.74
Omentorrhaphy 54.74
Omentotomy 54.19
Omphalectomy 54.3
Onychectomy 86.23
Onychoplasty 86.86
Onychotomy 86.09
  with drainage 86.04
Oophorectomy (unilateral) 65.39
  with salpingectomy 65.49
    laparoscopic 65.41
  bilateral (same operative episode) 65.51
    laparoscopic 65.53
    with salpingectomy 65.61
      laparoscopic 65.63
  laparoscopic 65.31
  partial 65.29
    laparoscopic 65.25
    wedge 65.22
      that by laparoscope 65.24
  remaining ovary 65.52
    laparoscopic 65.54
    with tube 65.62
      laparoscopic 65.64
Oophorocystectomy 65.29
  laparoscopic 65.25
Oophoropexy 65.79
Oophoroplasty 65.79
Oophororrhaphy 65.71
  laparoscopic 65.74
Oophorostomy 65.09
  laparoscopic 65.01

Oophorotomy 65.09
  laparoscopic 65.01
Opening
  bony labyrinth (ear) 20.79
  cranial suture 02.01
  heart valve
    closed heart technique—*see* Valvulotomy, by site
    open heart technique—*see* Valvuloplasty, by site
  spinal dura 03.09
Operation
  Abbe
    construction of vagina 70.61
    intestinal anastomosis—*see* Anastomosis, intestine
  abdominal (region) NEC 54.99
  abdominoperineal NEC 48.5
  Aburel (intra-amniotic injection for abortion) 75.0
  Adams
    advancement of round ligament 69.22
    crushing of nasal septum 21.88
    excision of palmar fascia 82.35
  adenoids NEC 28.99
  adrenal (gland) (nerve) (vessel) NEC 07.49
  Albee
    bone peg, femoral neck 78.05
    graft for slipping patella 78.06
    sliding inlay graft, tibia 78.07
  Albert (arthrodesis, knee) 81.22
  Aldridge (Studdiford) (urethral sling) 59.5
  Alexander
    prostatectomy
      perineal 60.62
      suprapubic 60.3
    shortening of round ligaments of uterus 69.22
  Alexander-Adams (shortening of round ligaments of uterus) 69.22
  Almoor (extrapetrosal drainage) 20.22
  Altemeier (perineal rectal pull-through) 48.49
  Ammon (dacryocystotomy) 09.53
  Anderson (tibial lengthening) 78.37
  Anel (dilation of lacrimal duct) 09.42
  anterior chamber (eye) NEC 12.99
  anti-incontinence NEC 59.79
  antrum window (nasal sinus) 22.2
    with Caldwell-Luc approach 22.39
  anus NEC 49.99
  aortic body NEC 39.8
  aorticopulmonary window 39.59
  appendix NEC 47.99
  Arslan (fenestration of inner ear) 20.61
  artery NEC 39.99
  Asai (larynx) 31.75
  Baffes (interatrial transposition of venous return) 35.91
  Baldy-Webster (uterine suspension) 69.22
  Ball
    herniorrhaphy—*see* Repair, hernia, inguinal
    undercutting 49.02
  Bankhart (capsular repair into glenoid, for shoulder dislocation) 81.82
  Bardenheuer (ligation of innominate artery) 38.85
  Barkan (goniotomy) 12.52
    with goniopuncture 12.53
  Barr (transfer of tibialis posterior tendon) 83.75

Operation— *continued*

Barsky (closure of cleft hand) 82.82

Bassett (vulvectomy with inguinal lymph node dissection) 71.5 *[40.3]*

Bassini (herniorrhaphy)—*see* Repair, hernia, inguinal

Batch-Spittler-McFaddin (knee disarticulation) 84.16

Beck I (epicardial poudrage) 36.3

Beck II (aorta-coronary sinus shunt) 36.3

Beck-Jianu (permanent gastrostomy) 43.19

Bell-Beuttner (subtotal abdominal hysterectomy) 68.3

Belsey (esophagogastric sphincter) 44.65

Benenenti (rotation of bulbous urethra) 58.49

Berke (levator resection eyelid) 08.33

Biesenberger (size reduction of breast, bilateral) 85.32

unilateral 85.31

Bigelow (litholapaxy) 57.0

biliary (duct) (tract) NEC 51.99

Billroth I (partial gastrectomy with gastroduodenostomy) 43.6

Billroth II (partial gastrectomy with gastrojejunostomy) 43.7

Binnie (hepatopexy) 50.69

Bischoff (ureteroneocystostomy) 56.74

bisection hysterectomy 68.3

Bishoff (spinal myelotomy) 03.29

bladder NEC 57.99

flap 56.74

Blalock (systemic-pulmonary anastomosis) 39.0

Blalock-Hanlon (creation of atrial septal defect) 35.42

Blalock-Taussig (subclavian-pulmonary anastomosis) 39.0

Blascovic (resection and advancement of levator palpebrae superioris) 08.33

blood vessel NEC 39.99

Blount

femoral shortening (with blade plate) 78.25

by epiphyseal stapling 78.25

Boari (bladder flap) 56.74

Bobb (cholelithotomy) 51.04

bone NEC—*see category* 78.4

facial 76.99

injury NEC—*see category* 79.9

marrow NEC 41.98

skull NEC 02.99

Bonney (abdominal hysterectomy) 68.4

Borthen (iridotasis) 12.63

Bost

plantar dissection 80.48

radiocarpal fusion 81.26

Bosworth

arthroplasty for acromioclavicular separation 81.83

fusion of posterior lumbar spine 81.08

for pseudarthrosis 81.09

resection of radial head ligaments (for tennis elbow) 80.92

shelf procedure, hip 81.40

bottle (repair of hydrocele of tunica vaginalis) 61.2

Boyd (hip disarticulation) 84.18

brain NEC 02.99

Brauer (cardiolysis) 37.10

breast NEC 85.99

Bricker (ileoureterostomy) 56.51

Bristow (repair of shoulder dislocation) 81.82

Brock (pulmonary valvulotomy) 35.03

Operation— *continued*

Brockman (soft tissue release for clubfoot) 83.84

bronchus NEC 33.98

Browne (Denis) (hypospadias repair) 58.45

Brunschwig (temporary gastrostomy) 43.19

buccal cavity NEC 27.99

Bunnell (tendon transfer) 82.56

Burgess (amputation of ankle) 84.14

bursa NEC 83.99

hand 82.99

bypass—*see* Bypass

Caldwell (sulcus extension) 24.91

Caldwell-Luc (maxillary sinusotomy) 22.39

with removal of membrane lining 22.31

Callander (knee disarticulation) 84.16

Campbell

bone block, ankle 81.11

fasciotomy (iliac crest) 83.14

reconstruction of anterior cruciate ligaments 81.45

canthus NEC 08.99

cardiac NEC 37.99

septum NEC 35.98

valve NEC 35.99

carotid body or gland NEC 39.8

Carroll and Taber (arthroplasty proximal interphalangeal joint) 81.72

Cattell (herniorrhaphy) 53.51

Cecil (urethral reconstruction) 58.46

cecum NEC 46.99

cerebral (meninges) NEC 02.99

cervix NEC 69.99

Chandler (hip fusion) 81.21

Charles (correction of lymphedema) 40.9

Charnley (compression arthrodesis)

ankle 81.11

hip 81.21

knee 81.22

Cheatle-Henry—*see* Repair, hernia, femoral

chest cavity NEC 34.99

Chevalier-Jackson (partial laryngectomy) 30.29

Child (radical subtotal pancreatectomy) 52.53

Chopart (midtarsal amputation) 84.12

chordae tendineae NEC 35.32

choroid NEC 14.9

ciliary body NEC 12.98

cisterna chyli NEC 40.69

Clagett (closure of chest wall following open flap drainage) 34.72

Clayton (resection of metatarsal heads and bases of phalanges) 77.88

clitoris NEC 71.4

cocked hat (metacarpal lengthening and transfer of local flap) 82.69

Cockett (varicose vein)

lower limb 38.59

upper limb 38.53

Cody tack (perforation of footplate) 19.0

Coffey (uterine suspension) (Meigs' modification) 69.22

Cole (anterior tarsal wedge osteotomy) 77.28

Collis-Nissen (hiatal hernia repair) 53.80

colon NEC 46.99

Colonna

adductor tenotomy (first stage) 83.12

hip arthroplasty (second stage) 81.40

reconstruction of hip (second stage) 81.40

commando (radical glossectomy) 25.4

conjunctive NEC 10.99

destructive NEC 10.33

cornea NEC 11.99

Operation—*continued*
 Coventry (tibial wedge osteotomy) 77.27
 Crawford (tarso-frontalis sling of eyelid) 08.32
 cul-de-sac NEC 70.92
 Culp-Deweerd (spiral flap pyeloplasty) 55.87
 Culp-Scardino (ureteral flap pyeloplasty) 55.87
 Curtis (interphalangeal joint arthroplasty) 81.72
 cystocele NEC 70.51
 Dahlman (excision of esophageal diverticulum) 42.31
 Dana (posterior rhizotomy) 03.1
 Danforth (fetal) 73.8
 Darrach (ulnar resection) 77.83
 Davis (intubated ureterotomy) 56.2
 de Grandmont (tarsectomy) 08.35
 Delorme
  pericardiectomy 37.31
  proctopexy 48.76
  repair of prolapsed rectum 48.76
  thoracoplasty 33.34
 Denker (radical maxillary antrotomy) 22.31
 Dennis-Varco (herniorrhaphy)—*see* Repair, hernia, femoral
 Denonvillier (limited rhinoplasty) 21.86
 dental NEC 24.99
  orthodontic NEC 24.8
 Derlacki (tympanoplasty) 19.4
 diaphragm NEC 34.89
 Dickson (fascial transplant) 83.82
 Dickson-Diveley (tendon transfer and arthrodesis to correct claw toe) 77.57
 Dieffenbach (hip disarticulation) 84.18
 digestive tract NEC 46.99
 Doleris (shortening of round ligaments) 69.22
 D'Ombrain (excision of pterygium with corneal graft) 11.32
 Dorrance (push-back operation for cleft palate) 27.62
 Dotter (transluminal angioplasty) 39.59
 Douglas (suture of tongue to lip for micrognathia) 25.59
 Doyle (paracervical uterine denervation) 69.3
 Duhamel (abdominoperineal pull-through) 48.65
 Duhrssen (vaginofixation of uterus) 69.22
 Dunn (triple arthrodesis) 81.12
 duodenum NEC 46.99
 Dupuytren
  fasciectomy 82.35
  fasciotomy 82.12
   with excision 82.35
  shoulder disarticulation 84.08
 Durham (Caldwell) (transfer of biceps femoris tendon) 83.75
 DuToit and Roux (staple capsulorrhaphy of shoulder) 81.82
 DuVries (tenoplasty) 83.88
 Dwyer
  fasciotomy 83.14
  soft tissue release NEC 83.84
  wedge osteotomy, calcaneus 77.28
 Eagleton (extrapetrosal drainage) 20.22
 ear (external) NEC 18.9
  middle or inner NEC 20.99
 Eden-Hybinette (glenoid bone block) 78.01
 Effler (heart) 36.2
 Eggers
  tendon release (patellar retinacula) 83.13
  tendon transfer (biceps femoris tendon) (hamstring tendon) 83.75
 Elliot (scleral trephination with iridectomy) 12.61

Operation—*continued*
 Ellis Jones (repair of peroneal tendon) 83.88
 Ellison (reinforcement of collateral ligament) 81.44
 Elmslie-Cholmeley (tarsal wedge osteotomy) 77.28
 Eloesser (thoracoplasty) 33.34
 Emmet (cervix) 67.61
 endorectal pull-through 48.41
 epididymis NEC 63.99
 esophagus NEC 42.99
 Estes (ovary) 65.72
  laparoscopic 65.75
 Estlander (thoracoplasty) 33.34
 Evans (release of clubfoot) 83.84
 extraocular muscle NEC 15.9
  multiple (two or more muscles) 15.4
   with temporary detachment from globe 15.3
  revision 15.6
  single 15.29
   with temporary detachment from globe 15.19
 eyeball NEC 16.99
 eyelid(s) NEC 08.99
 face NEC 27.99
 facial bone or joint NEC 76.99
 fallopian tube NEC 66.99
 Farabeuf (ischiopubiotomy) 77.39
 Fasanella-Servatt (blepharoptosis repair) 08.35
 fascia NEC 83.99
  hand 82.99
 female (genital organs) NEC 71.9
  hysterectomy NEC 68.9
 fenestration (aorta) 39.54
 Ferguson (hernia repair) 53.00
 Fick (perforation of footplate) 19.0
 filtering (for glaucoma) 12.79
  with iridectomy 12.65
 Finney (pyloroplasty) 44.2
 fistulizing, sclera NEC 12.69
 Foley (pyeloplasty) 55.87
 Fontan (creation of conduit between right atrium and pulmonary artery) 35.94
 Fothergill (Donald) (uterine suspension) 69.22
 Fowler
  arthroplasty of metacarpophalangeal joint 81.72
  release (mallet finger repair) 82.84
  tenodesis (hand) 82.85
  thoracoplasty 33.34
 Fox (entropion repair with wedge resection) 08.43
 Franco (suprapubic cystotomy) 57.19
 Frank (permanent gastrostomy) 43.19
 Frazier (Spiller) (subtemporal trigeminal rhizotomy) 04.02
 Fredet-Ramstedt (pyloromyotomy) (with wedge resection) 43.3
 Frenckner (intrapetrosal drainage) 20.22
 Frickman (abdominal proctopexy) 48.75
 Frommel (shortening of uterosacral ligaments) 69.22
 Gabriel (abdominoperineal resection of rectum) 48.5
 gallbladder NEC 51.99
 ganglia NEC 04.99
  sympathetic 05.89
 Gant (wedge osteotomy of trochanter) 77.25
 Garceau (tibial tendon transfer) 83.75
 Gardner (spinal meningocele repair) 03.51
 gastric NEC 44.99
 Gelman (release of clubfoot) 83.84

Operation—*continued*

genital organ NEC

female 71.9

male 64.99

Ghormley (hip fusion) 81.21

Gifford

destruction of lacrimal sac 09.6

keratotomy (delimiting) 11.1

Gill

arthrodesis of shoulder 81.23

laminectomy 03.09

Gill-Stein (carporadial arthrodesis) 81.25

Gilliam (uterine suspension) 69.22

Girdlestone

laminectomy with spinal fusion 81.00

muscle transfer for claw toe 77.57

resection of femoral head and neck 77.85

Girdlestone-Taylor (muscle transfer for claw toe repair) 77.57

glaucoma NEC 12.79

Glenn (anastomosis of superior vena cava to right pulmonary artery) 39.21

globus pallidus NEC 01.42

Goebel-Frangenheim-Stoeckel (urethrovesical suspension) 59.4

Goldner (clubfoot release) 80.48

Goldthwait

ankle stabilization 81.11

patella stabilization 81.44

tendon transfer for patella dislocation 81.44

Goodall-Power (vagina) 70.4

Gordon-Taylor (hindquarter amputation) 84.19

Graber-Duvernay (drilling femoral head) 77.15

Green (scapulopexy) 78.41

Grice (subtalar arthrodesis) 81.13

Gritti-Stokes (knee disarticulation) 84.16

Gross (herniorrhaphy) 53.49

gum NEC 24.39

Guyon (amputation of ankle) 84.13

Hagner (epididymotomy) 63.92

Halsted—*see* Repair, hernia, inguinal

Hampton (anastomosis small intestine to rectal stump) 45.92

hanging hip (muscle release) 83.19

harelip 27.54

Harrison-Richardson (vaginal suspension) 70.77

Hartmann—*see* Colectomy, by site

Hauser

achillotenotomy 83.11

bunionectomy with adductor tendon transfer 77.53

stabilization of patella 81.44

Heaney (vaginal hysterectomy) 68.59

laparoscopically assisted (LAVH) 68.51

heart NEC 37.99

valve NEC 35.99

adjacent structure NEC 35.39

Hegar (perineorrhaphy) 71.79

Heine (cyclodialysis) 12.55

Heineke-Mikulicz (pyloroplasty) 44.2

Heller (esophagomyotomy) 42.7

Hellstrom (transplantation of aberrant renal vessel) 39.55

hemorrhoids NEC 49.49

Henley jejunal transposition) 43.81

hepatic NEC 50.99

hernia—*see* Repair, hernia

Hey (amputation of foot) 84.12

Hey-Groves (reconstruction of anterior cruciate ligament) 81.45

Operation—*continued*

Heyman (soft tissue release for clubfoot) 83.84

Heyman-Herndon (Strong) (correction of metatarsus varus) 80.48

Hibbs (lumbar spinal fusion)—*see* Fusion, lumbar

Higgins—*see* Repair, hernia, femoral

Hill-Allison (hiatal hernia repair, transpleural approach) 53.80

Hitchcock (anchoring tendon of biceps) 83.88

Hofmeister (gastrectomy) 43.7

Hoke

midtarsal fusion 81.14

triple arthrodesis 81.12

Holth

iridencleisis 12.63

sclerectomy 12.65

Homan (correction of lymphedema) 40.9

Hutch (ureteroneocystostomy) 56.74

Hybinette-eden (glenoid bone block) 78.01

hymen NEC 70.91

hypopharynx NEC 29.99

hypophysis NEC 07.79

ileal loop 56.51

ileum NEC 46.99

intestine NEC 46.99

iris NEC 12.97

inclusion 12.63

Irving (tubal ligation) 66.32

Irwin (*see also* Osteotomy) 77.30

Jaboulay (gastroduodenostomy) 44.39

Janeway (permanent gastrostomy) 43.19

Jatene (arterial switch) 35.84

jejunum NEC 46.99

Johanson (urethral reconstruction) 58.46

joint (capsule) (ligament) (structure) NEC 81.99

facial NEC 76.99

Jones

claw toe (transfer of extensor hallucis longus tendon) 77.57

modified (with arthrodesis) 77.57

dacryocystorhinostomy 09.81

hammer toe (interphalangeal fusion) 77.56

modified (tendon transfer with arthrodesis) 77.57

repair of peroneal tendon 83.88

Joplin (exostectomy with tendon transfer) 77.53

Kader (temporary gastrostomy) 43.19

Kaufman (for urinary stress incontinence) 59.79

Kazanjiian (buccal vestibular sulcus extension) 24.91

Kehr (hepatopexy) 50.69

Keller (bunionectomy) 77.59

Kelly (Kennedy) (urethrovesical plication) 59.3

Kelly-Stoeckel (urethrovesical plication) 59.3

Kerr (cesarean section) 74.1

Kessler (arthroplasty, carpometacarpal joint) 81.74

Kidner (excision of accessory navicular bone) (with tendon transfer) 77.98

kidney NEC 55.99

Killian (frontal sinusotomy) 22.41

King-Steelquist (hindquarter amputation) 84.19

Kirk (amputation through thigh) 84.17

Kock pouch

bowel anastomosis —*omit code*

continent ileostomy 46.22

cutaneous uretero-ileostomy 56.51

ESWL (extracorporeal shockwave lithotripsy) 98.51

removal, calculus 57.19

Operation—*continued*

revision, cutaneous uretero-ileostomy 56.52
   urinary diversion procedure 56.51
Kondoleon (correction of lymphedema) 40.9
Krause (sympathetic denervation) 05.29
Kroener (partial salpingectomy) 66.69
Kroenlein (lateral orbitotomy) 16.01
Kronig (low cervical cesarean section) 74.1
Krukenberg (reconstruction of below-elbow
   amputation) 82.89
Kuhnt-Szymanowski (ectropion repair with lid
   reconstruction) 08.44
Labbe (gastrotomy) 43.0
labia NEC 71.8
lacrimal
   gland 09.3
   system NEC 09.99
Ladd (mobilization of intestine) 54.95
Lagrange (iridosclerectomy) 12.65
Lambrinudi (triple arthrodesis) 81.12
Langenbeck (cleft palate repair) 27.62
Lapidus (bunionectomy with metatarsal
   osteotomy) 77.51
Larry (shoulder disarticulation) 84.08
larynx NEC 31.98
Lash (internal cervical Os repair) 67.5
Latzko
   cesarean section, extraperitoneal 74.2
   colpocleisis 70.8
Leadbetter (urethral reconstruction) 58.46
Leadbetter-Politano (ureteroneocystostomy)
   56.74
Le Fort (colpocleisis) 70.8
LeMesurier (cleft lip repair) 27.54
lens NEC 13.9
Leriche (periarterial sympathectomy) 05.25
levator muscle sling
   eyelid ptosis repair 08.33
   urethrovesical suspension 59.71
   urinary stress incontinence 59.71
lid suture (blepharoptosis) 08.31
ligament NEC 81.99
   broad NEC 69.98
   round NEC 69.98
   uterine NEC 69.98
Lindholm (repair of ruptured tendon) 83.88
Linton (varicose vein) 38.59
lip NEC 27.99
Lisfranc
   foot amputation 84.12
   shoulder disarticulation 84.08
Littlewood (forequarter amputation) 84.09
liver NEC 50.99
Lloyd-Davies (abdominoperineal resection) 48.5
Longmire (bile duct anastomosis) 51.39
Lord
   dilation of anal canal for hemorrhoids 49.49
   hemorrhoidectomy 49.49
   orchidopexy 62.5
Lucas and Murray (knee arthrodesis with plate)
   81.22
lung NEC 33.99
lung volume reduction 32.22
lymphatic structure(s) NEC 40.9
   duct, left (thoracic) NEC 40.69
Madlener (tubal ligation) 66.31
Magnuson (Stack) (arthroplasty for recurrent
   shoulder dislocation) 81.82
male genital organs NEC 64.99
Manchester (Donald) (Fothergill), (uterine
   suspension) 69.22

Operation—*continued*

mandible NEC 76.99
   orthognathic 76.64
Marckwald (cervical os repair) 67.5
Marshall-Marchetti (Krantz) (retropubic
   urethral suspension) 59.5
Matas (aneurysmorrhaphy) 39.52
Mayo
   bunionectomy 77.59
   herniorrhaphy 53.49
   vaginal hysterectomy 68.59
      laparoscopically assisted (LAVH) 68.51
Mazet (knee disarticulation) 84.16
McBride (bunionectomy with soft tissue
   correction) 77.53
McBurney—*see* Repair, hernia, inguinal
McCall (enterocele repair) 70.92
McCauley (release of clubfoot) 83.84
McDonald (encirclement suture, cervix) 67.5
McIndoe (vaginal construction) 70.61
McKeever (fusion of first metatarsophalangeal
   joint for hallux valgus repair) 77.52
McKissock (breast reduction) 85.33
McReynolds (transposition of pterygium) 11.31
McVay
   femoral hernia—*see* Repair, hernia, femoral
   inguinal hernia—*see* Repair, hernia, inguinal
meninges (spinal) NEC 03.99
   cerebral NEC 02.99
mesentery NEC 54.99
Mikulicz (exteriorization of intestine) (first
   stage) 46.03
   second stage 46.04
Miles (complete proctectomy) 48.5
Millard (cheiloplasty) 27.54
Miller
   midtarsal arthrodesis 81.14
   urethrovesical suspension 59.4
Millin-Read (urethrovesical suspension) 59.4
Mitchell (hallux valgus repair) 77.51
Mohs (chemosurgical excision of skin) 86.24
Moore (arthroplasty) 81.52
Moschowitz
   enterocele repair 70.92
   herniorrhaphy—*see* Repair, hernia, femoral
   sigmoidopexy 46.63
mouth NEC 27.99
Muller (banding of pulmonary artery) 38.85
Mumford (partial claviculectomy) 77.81
muscle NEC 83.99
   extraocular—*see* Operation, extraocular
   hand NEC 82.99
   papillary heart NEC 35.31
musculoskeletal system NEC 84.99
Mustard (interatrial transposition of venous
   return) 35.91
nail (finger) (toe) NEC 86.99
nasal sinus NEC 22.9
nasopharynx NEC 29.99
nerve (cranial) (peripheral) NEC 04.99
   adrenal NEC 07.49
   sympathetic NEC 05.89
nervous system NEC 05.9
Nicola (tenodesis for recurrent dislocation of
   shoulder) 81.82
nipple NEC 85.99
Nissen (fundoplication of stomach) 44.66
Noble (plication of small intestine) 46.62
node (lymph) NEC 40.9
Norman Miller (vaginopexy) 70.77
Norton (extraperitoneal cesarean operation) 74.2

Operation—*continued*
  nose, nasal NEC 21.99
    sinus NEC 22.9
  Ober (Yount) (gluteal-iliotibial fasciotomy) 83.14
  obstetric NEC 75.99
  ocular NEC 16.99
    muscle—*see* Operation, extraocular muscle
  O'Donoghue (triad knee repair) 81.43
  Olshausen (uterine suspension) 69.22
  omentum NEC 54.99
  ophthalmologic NEC 16.99
  oral cavity NEC 27.99
  orbicularis muscle sling 08.36
  orbit NEC 16.98
  oropharynx NEC 29.99
  orthodontic NEC 24.8
  orthognathic NEC 76.69
  Oscar Miller (midtarsal arthrodesis) 81.14
  Osmond-Clark (soft tissue release with peroneus brevis tendon transfer) 83.75
  ovary NEC 65.99
  Oxford (for urinary incontinence) 59.4
  palate NEC 27.99
  palpebral ligament sling 08.36
  Panas (linear proctotomy) 48.0
  Pancoast (division of trigeminal nerve at foramen ovale) 04.02
  pancreas NEC 52.99
  pantaloon (revision of gastric anastomosis) 44.5
  papillary muscle (heart) NEC 35.31
  Paquin (ureteroneocystostomy) 56.74
  parathyroid gland(s) NEC 06.99
  parotid gland or duct NEC 26.99
  Partsch (marsupialization of dental cyst) 24.4
  Pattee (auditory canal) 18.6
  Peet (splanchnic resection) 05.29
  Pemberton
    osteotomy of ilium 77.39
    rectum (mobilization and fixation for prolapse repair) 48.76
  penis NEC 64.98
  Pereyra (paraurethral suspension) 59.6
  pericardium NEC 37.99
  perineum (female) NEC 71.8
    male NEC 86.99
  perirectal tissue NEC 48.99
  perirenal tissue NEC 59.92
  peritoneum NEC 54.99
  periurethral tissue NEC 58.99
  perivesical tissue NEC 59.92
  pharyngeal flap (cleft palate repair) 27.62
    secondary or subsequent 27.63
  pharynx, pharyngeal (pouch) NEC 29.99
  pineal gland NEC 07.59
  Pinsker (obliteration of nasoseptal telangiectasia) 21.07
  Piper (forceps) 72.6
  Pirogoff (ankle amputation through malleoli of tibia and fibula) 84.14
  pituitary gland NEC 07.79
  plastic—*see* Repair, by site
  pleural cavity NEC 34.99
  Politano-Leadbetter (ureteroneocystostomy) 56.74
  pollicization (with nerves and blood supply) 82.61
  Polya (gastrectomy) 43.7
  Pomeroy (ligation and division of fallopian tubes) 66.32

Operation—*continued*
  Poncet
    lengthening of Achilles tendon 83.85
    urethrostomy, perineal 58.0
  Porro (cesarean section) 74.99
  posterior chamber (eye) NEC 14.9
  Potts-Smith (descending aorta-left pulmonary artery anastomosis) 39.0
  Printen and Mason (high gastric bypass) 44.31
  prostate NEC (*see also* Prostatectomy) 60.69
    specified type 60.99
  pterygium 11.39
    with corneal graft 11.32
  Puestow (pancreaticojejunostomy) 52.96
  pull-through NEC 48.49
  pulmonary NEC 33.99
  push-back (cleft palate repair) 27.62
  Putti-Platt (capsulorrhaphy of shoulder for recurrent dislocation) 81.82
  pyloric exclusion 44.39
  pyriform sinus NEC 29.99
  "rabbit ear" (anterior urethropexy) (Tudor) 59.79
  Ramadier (intrapetrosal drainage) 20.22
  Ramstedt (pyloromyotomy) (with wedge resection) 43.3
  Rankin
    exteriorization of intestine 46.03
    proctectomy (complete) 48.5
  Rashkind (balloon septostomy) 35.41
  Rastelli (creation of conduit between right ventricle and pulmonary artery) 35.92
    in repair of
      pulmonary artery atresia 35.92
      transposition of great vessels 35.92
      truncus arteriosus 35.83
  Raz-Pereyra procedure (bladder neck suspension) 59.79
  rectal NEC 48.99
  rectocele NEC 70.52
  re-entry (aorta) 39.54
  renal NEC 55.99
  respiratory (tract) NEC 33.99
  retina NEC 14.9
  Ripstein (repair of rectal prolapse) 48.75
  Rodney Smith (radical subtotal pancreatectomy) 52.53
  Roux-en-Y
    bile duct 51.36
    cholecystojejunostomy 51.32
    esophagus (intrathoracic) 42.54
    pancreaticojejunostomy 52.96
  Roux-Goldthwait (repair of patellar dislocation) 81.44
  Roux-Herzen-Judine (jejunal loop interposition) 42.63
  Ruiz-Mora (proximal phalangectomy for hammer toe) 77.99
  Russe (bone graft of scaphoid) 78.04
  Saemisch (corneal section) 11.1
  salivary gland or duct NEC 26.99
  Salter (innominate osteotomy) 77.39
  Sauer-Bacon (abdominoperineal resection) 48.5
  Schanz (femoral osteotomy) 77.35
  Schauta (Amreich) (radical vaginal hysterectomy) 68.7
  Schede (thoracoplasty) 33.34
  Scheie
    cautery of sclera 12.62
    sclerostomy 12.62
  Schlatter (total gastrectomy) 43.99
  Schroeder (endocervical excision) 67.39

Operation—*continued*
  tongue NEC 25.99
    flap, palate 27.62
    tie 25.91
  tonsil NEC 28.99
  Torek (Bevan) (orchidopexy) (first stage)
    (second stage) 62.5
  Torkildsen (ventriculocisternal shunt) 02.2
  Torpin (cul-de-sac resection) 70.92
  Toti (dacryocystorhinostomy) 09.81
  Touchas 86.83
  Touroff (ligation of subclavian artery) 38.85
  trabeculae corneae cordis (heart) NEC 35.35
  trachea NEC 31.99
  Trauner (lingual sulcus extension) 24.91
  truncus arteriosus NEC 35.83
  Tsuge (macrodactyly repair) 82.83
  Tudor "rabbit ear" (anterior urethropexy) 59.79
  Tuffier
    apicolysis of lung 33.39
    vaginal hysterectomy 68.59
      laparoscopically assisted (LAVH) 68.51
  tunica vaginalis NEC 61.99
  Turco (release of joint capsules in clubfoot)
    80.48
  Uchida (tubal ligation with or without
    fimbriectomy) 66.32
  umbilicus NEC 54.99
  urachus NEC 57.51
  Urban (mastectomy) (unilateral) 85.47
    bilateral 85.48
  ureter NEC 56.99
  urethra NEC 58.99
  urinary system NEC 59.99
  uterus NEC 69.99
    supporting structures NEC 69.98
  uvula NEC 27.79
  vagina NEC 70.91
  vascular NEC 39.99
  vas deferens NEC 63.99
    ligation NEC 63.71
  vein NEC 39.99
  vena cava sieve 38.7
  vertebra NEC 78.49
  vesical (bladder) NEC 57.99
  vessel NEC 39.99
    cardiac NEC 36.99
  Vicq d'Azyr (larynx) 31.1
  Vidal (varicocele ligation) 63.1
  Vineberg (implantation of mammary artery into
    ventricle) 36.2
  vitreous NEC 14.79
  vocal cord NEC 31.98
  von Kraske (proctectomy) 48.64
  Voss (hanging hip operation) 83.19
  Vulpius (Compere) (lengthening of
    gastrocnemius muscle) 83.85
  vulva NEC 71.8
  Ward-Mayo (vaginal hysterectomy) 68.59
    laparoscopically assisted (LAVH) 68.51
  Wardill (cleft palate) 27.62
  Waters (extraperitoneal cesarean section) 74.2
  Waterston (aorta-right pulmonary artery
    anastomosis) 39.0
  Watkins (Wertheim) (uterus interposition) 69.21
  Watson-Jones
    hip arthrodesis 81.21
    reconstruction of lateral ligaments, ankle 81.49
    shoulder arthrodesis (extra-articular) 81.23
    tenoplasty 83.88

Operation—*continued*
  Weir
    appendicostomy 47.91
    correction of nostrils 21.86
  Wertheim (radical hysterectomy) 68.6
  West (dacryocystorhinostomy) 09.81
  Wheeler
    entropion repair 08.44
    halving procedure (eyelid) 08.24
  Whipple (radical pancreaticoduodenectomy)
    52.7
    Child modification (radical subtotal
      pancreatectomy) 52.53
    Rodney Smith modification (radical subtotal
      pancreatectomy) 52.53
  While (lengthening of tendo calcaneus by
    incomplete tenotomy) 83.11
  Whitehead
    glossectomy, radical 25.4
    hemorrhoidectomy 49.46
  Whitman
    foot stabilization (talectomy) 77.98
    hip reconstruction 81.40
    repair of serratus anterior muscle 83.87
    talectomy 77.98
    trochanter wedge osteotomy 77.25
  Wier (entropion repair) 08.44
  Williams-Richardson (vaginal construction)
    70.61
  Wilms (thoracoplasty) 33.34
  Wilson (angulation osteotomy for hallux
    valgus) 77.51
  window
    antrum (nasal sinus)—*see* Antrotomy,
      maxillary
    aorticopulmonary 39.59
    bone cortex (*see also* Incision, bone) 77.10
      facial 76.09
    nasoantral—*see* Antrotomy, maxillary
    pericardium 37.12
    pleural 34.09
  Winiwarter (cholecystoenterostomy) 51.32
  Witzel (temporary gastrostomy) 43.19
  Woodward (release of high riding scapula) 81.83
  Young
    epispadias repair 58.45
    tendon transfer (anterior tibialis) (repair of flat
      foot) 83.75
  Yount (division of iliotibial band) 83.14
  Zancolli
    capsuloplasty 81.72
    tendon transfer (biceps) 82.56
  Ziegler (iridectomy) 12.14
Operculectomy 24.6
Ophthalmectomy 16.49
    with implant (into Tenon's capsule) 16.42
      with attachment of muscles 16.41
Ophthalmoscopy 16.21
Opponensplasty (hand) 82.56
Orbitomaxillectomy, radical 16.51
Orbitotomy (anterior) (frontal) (temporofrontal)
    (transfrontal) NEC 16.09
    with
      bone flap 16.01
      insertion of implant 16.02
    Kroenlein (lateral) 16.01
    lateral 16.01
Orchidectomy (with epididymectomy)
    (unilateral) 62.3
    bilateral (radical) 62.41
    remaining or solitary testis 62.42
Orchidopexy 62.5

Orchidoplasty 62.69
Orchidorrhaphy 62.61
Orchidotomy 62.0
Orchiectomy (with epididymectomy) (unilateral)
    62.3
  bilateral (radical) 62.41
  remaining or solitary testis 62.42
Orchiopexy 62.5
Orchioplasty 62.69
Orthoroentgenography —*see* Radiography
Oscar Miller operation (midtarsal arthrodesis)
    81.14
Osmond-Clark operation (soft tissue release
    with peroneus brevis tendon transfer) 83.75
Ossiculectomy NEC 19.3
  with
    stapedectomy (*see also* Stapedectomy) 19.19
    stapes mobilization 19.0
    tympanoplasty 19.53
      revision 19.6
Ossiculotomy NEC 19.3
Ostectomy (partial), except facial—*see also*
    category 77.8
  facial NEC 76.39
    total 76.45
      with reconstruction 76.44
  first metatarsal head—*see* Bunionectomy
  for graft (autograft) (homograft)—*see also*
      category 77.7
    mandible 76.31
      total 76.42
        with reconstruction 76.41
  total, except facial—*see also category* 77.9
    facial NEC 76.45
      with reconstruction 76.44
    mandible 76.42
      with reconstruction 76.41
Osteoarthrotomy (*see also* Osteotomy) 77.30
Osteoclasis 78.70
  carpal, metacarpal 78.74
  clavicle 78.71
  ear 20.79
  femur 78.75
  fibula 78.77
  humerus 78.72
  patella 78.76
  pelvic 78.79
  phalanges (foot) (hand) 78.79
  radius 78.73
  scapula 78.71
  specified site NEC 78.79
  tarsal, metatarsal 78.78
  thorax (ribs) (sternum) 78.71
  tibia 78.77
  ulna 78.73
  vertebrae 78.79
Osteolysis —*see category* 78.4
Osteopathic manipulation (*see also*
    Manipulation, osteopathic) 93.67
Osteoplasty NEC—*see category* 78.4
  with bone graft—*see* Graft, bone
  for
    bone lengthening—*see* Lengthening, bone
    bone shortening—*see* Shortening, bone
    repair of malunion or nonunion of
        fracture—*see* Repair, fracture, malunion
        or nonunion
  carpal, metacarpal 78.44
  clavicle 78.41

Osteoplasty—*continued*
  cranium NEC 02.06
    with
      flap (bone) 02.03
      graft (bone) 02.04
  facial bone NEC 76.69
  femur 78.45
  fibula 78.47
  humerus 78.42
  mandible, mandibular NEC 76.64
    body 76.63
    ramus (open) 76.62
      closed 76.61
  maxilla (segmental) 76.65
    total 76.66
  nasal bones 21.89
  patella 78.46
  pelvic 78.49
  phalanges (foot) (hand) 78.49
  radius 78.43
  scapula 78.41
  skull NEC 02.06
    with
      flap (bone) 02.03
      graft (bone) 02.04
  specified site NEC 78.49
  tarsal, metatarsal 78.48
  thorax (ribs) (sternum) 78.41
  tibia 78.47
  ulna 78.43
  vertebrae 78.49
Osteorrhaphy (*see also* Osteoplasty) 78.40
Osteosynthesis (fracture) —*see* Reduction,
    fracture
Osteotomy (adduction) (angulation) (block)
    (derotational) (displacement) (partial)
    (rotational) 77.30
  carpals, metacarpals 77.34
    wedge 77.24
  clavicle 77.31
    wedge 77.21
  facial bone NEC 76.69
  femur 77.35
    wedge 77.25
  fibula 77.37
    wedge 77.27
  humerus 77.32
    wedge 77.22
  mandible (segmental) (subapical) 76.64
    angle (open) 76.62
      closed 76.61
    body 76.63
    Gigli saw 76.61
    ramus (open) 76.62
      closed 76.61
  maxilla (segmental) 76.65
    total 76.66
  metatarsal 77.38
    wedge 77.28
    for hallux valgus repair 77.51
  patella 77.36
    wedge 77.26
  pelvic 77.39
    wedge 77.29
  phalanges (foot) (hand) 77.39
    for repair of
      bunion—*see* Bunionectomy
      bunionette 77.54
      hallux valgus—*see* Bunionectomy

Osteotomy—*continued*
 wedge 77.29
  for repair of
   bunion—*see* Bunionectomy
   bunionette 77.54
   hallux valgus—*see* Bunionectomy
 radius 77.33
  wedge 77.23
 scapula 77.31
  wedge 77.21
 specified site NEC 77.39
  wedge 77.29
 tarsal 77.38
  wedge 77.28
 thorax (ribs) (sternum) 77.31
  wedge 77.21
 tibia 77.37
  wedge 77.27
 toe 77.39
  for repair of
   bunion—*see* Bunionectomy
   bunionette 77.54
   hallux valgus—*see* Bunionectomy
  wedge 77.29
   for repair of
    bunion—*see* bunionectomy
    bunionette 77.54
    hallux valgus—*see* Bunionectomy
 ulna 77.33
  wedge 77.23
 vertebrae 77.39
  wedge 77.29
Otonecrectomy (inner ear) 20.79
Otoplasty (external) 18.79
 auditory canal or meatus 18.6
 auricle 18.79
 cartilage 18.79
  reconstruction 18.71
 prominent or protruding 18.5
Otoscopy 18.11
Outfolding, sclera, for buckling (*see also*
 Buckling, scleral) 14.49
Outfracture, turbinates (nasal) 21.62
Output and clearance, circulatory 92.05
Overdistension, bladder (therapeutic) 96.25
Overlapping, sclera, for buckling (*see also*
 Buckling, scleral) 14.49
Oversewing
 pleural bleb 32.21
 ulcer crater (peptic) 44.40
  duodenum 44.42
  stomach 44.41
Oxford operation (for urinary incontinence) 59.4
Oxygenation 93.96
 extracorporeal membrane (ECMO) 39.65
 hyperbaric 93.95
  wound 93.59
Oxygen therapy (catalytic) (pump) 93.96
 hyperbaric 93.95

P

Photocoagulation—*continued*
   reattachment 14.55
   repair of tear or defect 14.35
  laser (beam)
   for
    destruction of lesion 14.24
    reattachment 14.54
    repair of tear or defect 14.34
  xenon arc
   for
    destruction of lesion 14.23
    reattachment 14.53
    repair of tear or defect 14.33
Photography 89.39
  fundus 95.11
Photopheresis, therapeutic 99.88
Phototherapy NEC 99.83
  newborn 99.83
  ultraviolet 99.82
Phrenemphraxis 04.03
  for collapse of lung 33.31
Phrenicectomy 04.03
  for collapse of lung 33.31
Phrenicoexeresis 04.03
  for collapse of lung 33.31
Phrenicotomy 04.03
  for collapse of lung 33.31
Phrenicotripsy 04.03
  for collapse of lung 33.31
Phrenoplasty 34.84
Physical medicine —*see* Therapy, physical
Physical therapy —*see* Therapy, physical
Physiotherapy, chest 93.99
PICC (peripherally inserted central catheter) 38.93
Piercing ear, external (pinna) 18.01
Pigmenting, skin 86.02
Pilojection (aneurysm) (Gallagher) 39.52
Pinealectomy (complete) (total) 07.54
  partial 07.53
Pinealotomy (with drainage) 07.52
Pinning
  bone—*see* Fixation, bone, internal
  ear 18.5
Pinsker operation (obliteration of nasoseptal telangiectasia) 21.07
Piper operation (forceps) 72.6
Pirogoff operation (ankle amputation through malleoli of tibia and fibula) 84.14
Pituitectomy (complete) (total) (*see also* Hypophysectomy) 07.69
Placentogram, placentography 88.46
  with radioisotope (RISA) 92.17
Planing, skin 86.25
Plantation, tooth (bud) (germ) 23.5
  prosthetic 23.6
Plasma exchange 99.07
Plasmapheresis, therapeutic 99.71
Plastic repair —*see* Repair, by site
Plasty —*see also* Repair, by site
  bladder neck (V-Y) 57.85
  skin (without graft) 86.89
  subcutaneous tissue 86.89
Plateletpheresis, therapeutic 99.74
Play
  psychotherapy 94.36
  therapy 93.81
Pleating
  eye muscle 15.22
   multiple (two or more muscles) 15.4
  sclera, for buckling (*see also* Buckling, scleral) 14.49

Plethysmogram (carotid) 89.58
  air-filled (pneumatic) 89.58
  capacitance 89.58
  cerebral 89.58
  differential 89.58
  oculoplethysmogram 89.58
  photoelectric 89.58
  regional 89.58
  respiratory function measurement (body) 89.38
  segmental 89.58
  strain-gauge 89.58
  thoracic impedance 89.38
  venous occlusion 89.58
  water-filled 89.58
Pleurectomy NEC 34.59
Pleurocentesis 34.91
Pleurodesis 34.6
  chemical 34.92
   with cancer chemotherapy substance 34.92 *[99.25]*
   tetracycline 34.92 *[99.21]*
Pleurolysis (for collapse of lung) 33.39
Pleuropexy 34.99
Pleurosclerosis 34.6
  chemical 34.92
   with cancer chemotherapy substance 34.92 *[99.25]*
   tetracycline 34.92 *[99.21]*
Pleurotomy 34.09
Plexectomy
  choroid 02.14
  hypogastric 05.24
Plication
  annulus, heart valve 35.33
  bleb (emphysematous), lung 32.21
  broad ligament 69.22
  diaphragm (for hernia repair) (thoracic approach) (thoracoabdominal approach) 53.81
  eye muscle (oblique) (rectus) 15.22
   multiple (two or more muscles) 15.4
  fascia 83.89
  hand 82.89
  inferior vena cava 38.7
  intestine (jejunum) (Noble) 46.62
  Kelly (Stoeckel) (urethrovesical junction) 59.3
  levator, for blepharoptosis 08.34
  ligament (*see also* Arthroplasty) 81.96
   broad 69.22
   round 69.22
   uterosacral 69.22
  mesentery 54.75
  round ligament 69.22
  sphincter, urinary bladder 57.85
  stomach 44.69
  superior vena cava 38.7
  tendon 83.85
   hand 82.55
  tricuspid valve (with repositioning) 35.14
  ureter 56.89
  urethra 58.49
  urethrovesical junction 59.3
  vein (peripheral) 39.59
  vena cava (inferior) (superior) 38.7
  ventricle (heart) 37.99
Plicotomy, tympanum 20.23
Plombage, lung 33.39
Pneumocentesis 33.93
Pneumocisternogram 87.02
Pneumoencephalogram 87.01

Pneumogram, pneumography
  extraperitoneal 88.15
  mediastinal 87.33
  orbit 87.14
  pelvic 88.13
  peritoneum NEC 88.13
  presacral 88.15
  retroperitoneum 88.15
Pneumogynecography 87.82
Pneumomediastinography 87.33
Pneumonectomy (complete) (extended) (radical)
    (standard) (total) (with mediastinal dissection)
    32.5
  partial
    complete excision, one lobe 32.4
    resection (wedge), one lobe 32.3
Pneumonolysis (for collapse of lung) 33.39
Pneumonotomy (with exploration) 33.1
Pneumoperitoneum (surgically-induced) 54.96
  for collapse of lung 33.33
  pelvic 88.12
Pneumothorax (artificial) (surgical) 33.32
  intrapleural 33.32
Pneumoventriculogram 87.02
Politano-Leadbetter operation
    (ureteroneocystostomy) 56.74
Politzerization, Eustachian tube 20.8
Pollicization (with carry over of nerves and
    blood supply) 82.61
Polya operation (gastrectomy) 43.7
Polypectomy —*see also* Excision, lesion, by site
  esophageal 42.32
    endoscopic 42.33
  gastric (endoscopic) 43.41
  large intestine (colon) 45.42
  nasal 21.31
  rectum (endoscopic) 48.36
Polysomnogram 89.17
Pomeroy operation (ligation and division of
    fallopian tubes) 66.32
Poncet operation
  lengthening of Achilles tendon 83.85
  urethrostomy, perineal 58.0
Porro operation (cesarean section) 74.99
Positrocephalogram 92.11
Positron emission tomography (PET) —*see*
    Scan, radioisotope
Postmortem examination 89.8
Potts-Smith operation (descending aorta-left
    pulmonary artery anastomosis) 39.0
Poudrage
  intrapericardial 36.3
  pleural 34.6
PPN (peripheral parenteral nutrition) 99.15
Preparation (cutting), pedicle (flap) graft 86.71
Preputiotomy 64.91
Prescription for glasses 95.31
Pressure support
  ventilation [PSV]—*see* category 96.7
Printen and Mason operation (high gastric
    bypass) 44.31
Probing
  canaliculus, lacrimal (with irrigation) 09.42
  lacrimal
    canaliculi 09.42
    punctum (with irrigation) 09.41
  nasolacrimal duct (with irrigation) 09.43
    with insertion of tube or stent 09.44
  salivary duct (for dilation of duct) (for removal
      of calculus) 26.91
    with incision 26.0

Procedure —*see also* specific procedure
  diagnostic NEC
    abdomen (region) 54.29
    adenoid 28.19
    adrenal gland 07.19
    alveolus 24.19
    amnion 75.35
    anterior chamber, eye 12.29
    anus 49.29
    appendix 45.28
    biliary tract 51.19
    bladder 57.39
    blood vessel (any site) 38.29
    bone 78.80
      carpal, metacarpal 78.84
      clavicle 78.81
      facial 76.19
      femur 78.85
      fibula 78.87
      humerus 78.82
      marrow 41.38
      patella 78.86
      pelvic 78.89
      phalanges (foot) (hand) 78.89
      radius 78.83
      scapula 78.81
      specified site NEC 78.89
      tarsal, metatarsal 78.88
      thorax (ribs) (sternum) 78.81
      tibia 78.87
      ulna 78.83
      vertebrae 78.89
    brain 01.18
    breast 85.19
    bronchus 33.29
    buccal 27.24
    bursa 83.29
    canthus 08.19
    cecum 45.28
    cerebral meninges 01.18
    cervix 67.19
    chest wall 34.28
    choroid 14.19
    ciliary body 12.29
    clitoris 71.19
    colon 45.28
    conjunctiva 10.29
    cornea 11.29
    cul-de-sac 70.29
    dental 24.19
    diaphragm 34.28
    duodenum 45.19
    ear
      external 18.19
      inner and middle 20.39
    epididymis 63.09
    esophagus 42.29
    Eustachian tube 20.39
    extraocular muscle or tendon 15.09
    eye 16.29
      anterior chamber 12.29
      posterior chamber 14.19
    eyeball 16.29
    eyelid 08.19
    fallopian tube 66.19
    fascia (any site) 83.29
    fetus 75.35
    gallbladder 51.19
    ganglion (cranial) (peripheral) 04.19
      sympathetic 05.19
    gastric 44.19

Proctosigmoidoscopy (rigid) 48.23
  with biopsy 48.24
  flexible 45.24
  through stoma (artificial) 48.22
  transabdominal approach 48.21
Proctostomy 48.1
Proctotomy (decompression) (linear) 48.0
Production —*see also* Formation
  atrial septal defect 35.42
  subcutaneous tunnel for esophageal
    anastomosis 42.86
    with anastomosis—*see* Anastomosis,
      esophagus, antesternal
Prognathic recession 76.64
Prophylaxis, dental (scaling) (polishing) 96.54
Prostatectomy (complete) (partial) NEC 60.69
  loop 60.29
  perineal 60.62
  radical (any approach) 60.5
  retropubic (punch) (transcapsular) 60.4
  suprapubic (punch) (transvesical) 60.3
  transcapsular NEC 60.69
    retropubic 60.4
  transperineal 60.62
  transurethral 60.29
    ablation (contact) (noncontact) by laser 60.21
    electrovaporization 60.29
    enucleative 60.29
    resection of prostate (TURP) 60.29
    ultrasound guided laser induced (TULIP)
      60.21
  transvesical punch (suprapubic) 60.3
Prostatocystotomy 60.0
Prostatolithotomy 60.0
Prostatotomy (perineal) 60.0
Prostatovesiculectomy 60.5
Protection (of)
  individual from his surroundings 99.84
  surroundings from individual 99.84
Psychoanalysis 94.31
Psychodrama 94.43
Psychotherapy NEC 94.39
  biofeedback 94.39
  exploratory verbal 94.37
  group 94.44
    for psychosexual dysfunctions 94.41
  play 94.36
  psychosexual dysfunctions 94.34
  supportive verbal 94.38
PTCA (percutaneous transluminal coronary
  angioplasty)—*see* Angioplasty, balloon,
  coronary
Ptyalectasis 26.91
Ptyalithotomy 26.0
Ptyalolithotomy 26.0
Pubiotomy 77.39
  assisting delivery 73.94
Pubococcygeoplasty 59.71
Puestow operation (pancreaticojejunostomy)
  52.96
Pull-through
  abdomino-anal 48.49
  abdominoperineal 48.49
    Duhamel type 48.65
  endorectal 48.41
Pulmowrap 93.99
Pulpectomy (*see also* Therapy, root canal) 23.70
Pulpotomy (*see also* Therapy, root canal) 23.70
Pump-oxygenator for extracorporeal circulation
  39.61
  percutaneous 39.66

Punch
  operation
    bladder neck, transurethral 57.49
    prostate—*see* Prostatectomy
  resection, vocal cords 30.22
Puncture
  antrum (nasal) (bilateral) (unilateral) 22.01
  artery NEC 38.98
    for
      arteriography (*see also* Arteriography) 88.40
      coronary arteriography (*see also*
        Arteriography, coronary) 88.57
  bladder, suprapubic (for drainage) NEC 57.18
    needle 57.11
    percutaneous (suprapubic) 57.17
  bursa 83.94
    hand 82.92
  cisternal 01.01
    with contrast media 87.02
  cranial 01.09
    with contrast media 87.02
  craniobuccal pouch 07.72
  craniopharyngioma 07.72
  fallopian tube 66.91
  fontanel, anterior 01.09
  heart 37.0
    for intracardiac injection 37.92
  hypophysis 07.72
  iris 12.12
  joint 81.91
  kidney (percutaneous) 55.92
  larynx 31.98
  lumbar (diagnostic) (removal of dye) 03.31
  lung (for aspiration) 33.93
  nasal sinus 22.01
  pericardium 37.0
  pituitary gland 07.72
  pleural cavity 34.91
  Rathke's pouch 07.72
  spinal 03.31
  spleen 41.1
    for biopsy 41.32
  sternal (for bone marrow biopsy) 41.31
    donor for bone marrow transplant 41.91
  vein NEC 38.99
    for
      phlebography (*see also* Phlebography) 88.60
      transfusion—*see* Transfusion
  ventricular shunt tubing 01.02
Pupillotomy 12.35
Push-back operation (cleft palate repair) 27.62
Putti-Platt operation (capsulorrhaphy of
  shoulder for recurrent dislocation) 81.82
Pyelogram (intravenous) 87.73
  infusion (continuous) (diuretic) 87.73
  percutaneous 87.75
  retrograde 87.74
Pyeloileostomy 56.71
Pyelolithotomy 55.11
Pyeloplasty 55.87
Pyelorrhaphy 55.81
Pyeloscopy 55.22
Pyelostolithotomy, percutaneous 55.03
Pyelostomy 55.12
  closure 55.82
Pyelotomy 55.11
Pyeloureteroplasty 55.87
Pylorectomy 43.6
Pyloroduodenotomy —*see category* 44.2
Pyloromyotomy (Ramstedt) (with wedge
  resection) 43.3

Pyloroplasty (Finney) (Heineke-Mikulicz) 44.29
   dilation, endoscopic 44.22
     by incision 44.21
   not elsewhere classified 44.29
   revision 44.29
Pylorostomy —*see* Gastrostomy

Q-R

Quadrant resection of breast 85.22
Quadricepsplasty (Thompson) 83.86
Quarantine 99.84
Quenuthoracoplasty 77.31
Quotient, respiratory 89.38

Rachicentesis 03.31
Rachitomy 03.09
Radiation therapy —*see also* Therapy, radiation
   teleradiotheraphy—*see* Teleradiotherapy
Radical neck dissection —*see* Dissection, neck
Radicotomy 03.1
Radiculectomy 03.1
Radiculotomy 03.1
Radiography (diagnostic) NEC 88.39
  abdomen, abdominal (flat plate) NEC 88.19
    wall (soft tissue) NEC 88.09
  adenoid 87.09
  ankle (skeletal) 88.28
    soft tissue 88.37
  bone survey 88.31
  bronchus 87.49
  chest (routine) 87.44
    wall NEC 87.39
  clavicle 87.43
  contrast (air) (gas) (radio-opaque substance)
     NEC
    abdominal wall 88.03
    arteries (by fluoroscopy)—*see* Arteriography
    bile ducts NEC 87.54
    bladder NEC 87.77
    brain 87.02
    breast 87.35
    bronchus NEC (transcricoid) 87.32
      endotracheal 87.31
    epididymis 87.93
    esophagus 87.61
    fallopian tubes
      gas 87.82
      opaque dye 87.83
    fistula (sinus tract)—*see also* Radiography,
      contrast, by site
      abdominal wall 88.03
      chest wall 87.38
    gallbladder NEC 87.59
    intervertebral disc(s) 87.21
    joints 88.32
    larynx 87.07
    lymph—*see* Lymphangiogram
    mammary ducts 87.35
    mediastinum 87.33
    nasal sinuses 87.15
    nasolacrimal ducts 87.05
    nasopharynx 87.06
    orbit 87.14
    pancreas 87.66
    pelvis
      gas 88.12
      opaque dye 88.11
    peritoneum NEC 88.13
    retroperitoneum NEC 88.15
    seminal vesicles 87.91
    sinus tract—*see also* Radiography, contrast,
      by site
      abdominal wall 88.03
      chest wall 87.38
      nose 87.15
    skull 87.02
    spinal disc(s) 87.21
    trachea 87.32
    uterus
      gas 87.82
      opaque dye 87.83

Radiography—*continued*
    vas deferens 87.94
    veins (by fluoroscopy)—*see* Phlebography
    vena cava (inferior) (superior) 88.51
  dental NEC 87.12
  diaphragm 87.49
  digestive tract NEC 87.69
    barium swallow 87.61
    lower GI series 87.64
    small bowel series 87.63
    upper GI series 87.62
  elbow (skeletal) 88.22
    soft tissue 88.35
  epididymis NEC 87.95
  esophagus 87.69
    barium-swallow 87.61
  eye 95.14
  face, head, and neck 87.09
  facial bones 87.16
  fallopian tubes 87.85
  foot 88.28
  forearm (skeletal) 88.22
    soft tissue 88.35
  frontal area, facial 87.16
  genital organs
    female NEC 87.89
    male NEC 87.99
  hand (skeletal) 88.23
    soft tissue 88.35
  head NEC 87.09
  heart 87.49
  hip (skeletal) 88.26
    soft tissue 88.37
  intestine NEC 87.65
  kidney-ureter-bladder (KUB) 87.79
  knee (skeletal) 88.27
    soft tissue 88.37
  KUB (kidney-ureter-bladder) 87.79
  larynx 87.09
  lower leg (skeletal) 88.27
    soft tissue 88.37
  lower limb (skeletal) NEC 88.29
    soft tissue NEC 88.37
  lung 87.49
  mandible 87.16
  maxilla 87.16
  mediastinum 87.49
  nasal sinuses 87.16
  nasolacrimal duct 87.09
  nasopharynx 87.09
  neck NEC 87.09
  nose 87.16
  orbit 87.16
  pelvis (skeletal) 88.26
    pelvimetry 88.25
    soft tissue 88.19
  prostate NEC 87.92
  retroperitoneum NEC 88.16
  ribs 87.43
  root canal 87.12
  salivary gland 87.09
  seminal vesicles NEC 87.92
  shoulder (skeletal) 88.21
    soft tissue 88.35
  skeletal NEC 88.33
    series (whole or complete) 88.31
  skull (lateral, sagittal or tangential projection) NEC 87.17
  spine NEC 87.29
    cervical 87.22
    lumbosacral 87.24

Radiography—*continued*
    sacrococcygeal 87.24
    thoracic 87.23
  sternum 87.43
  supraorbital area 87.16
  symphysis menti 87.16
  teeth NEC 87.12
    full-mouth 87.11
  thigh (skeletal) 88.27
    soft tissue 88.37
  thyroid region 87.09
  tonsils and adenoids 87.09
  trachea 87.49
  ultrasonic—*see* Ultrasonography
  upper arm (skeletal) 88.21
    soft tissue 88.35
  upper limb (skeletal) NEC 88.24
    soft tissue NEC 88.35
  urinary system NEC 87.79
  uterus NEC 87.85
    gravid 87.81
  uvula 87.09
  vas deferens NEC 87.95
  wrist 88.23
  zygomaticomaxillary complex 87.16
Radioisotope
  scanning—*see* Scan, radioisotope
  therapy—*see* Therapy, radioisotope
Radiology
  diagnostic—*see* Radiography
  therapeutic—*see* Therapy, radiation
Radiosurgery, stereotactic 92.3
Raising, pedicle graft 86.71
Ramadier operation (intrapetrosal drainage) 20.22
Ramisection (sympathetic) 05.0
Ramstedt operation (pyeloromyotomy) (with wedge resection) 43.3
Range of motion testing 93.05
Rankin operation
  exteriorization of intestine 46.03
  proctectomy (complete) 48.5
Rashkind operation (balloon septostomy) 35.41
Rastelli operation (creation of conduit between right ventricle and pulmonary artery) 35.92
  in repair of
    pulmonary artery atresia 35.92
    transposition of great vessels 35.92
    truncus arteriosus 35.83
Raz-Pereyra procedure (Bladder neck suspension) 59.79
RCSA (radical cryosurgical ablation) of prostate 60.62
Readjustment —*see* Adjustment
Reamputation, stump 84.3
Reanastomosis —*see* Anastomosis
Reattachment
  amputated ear 18.72
  ankle 84.27
  arm (upper) NEC 84.24
  choroid and retina NEC 14.59
    by
      cryotherapy 14.52
      diathermy 14.51
      electrocoagulation 14.51
      photocoagulation 14.55
        laser 14.54
        xenon arc 14.53
  ear (amputated) 18.72
  extremity 84.29
    ankle 84.27

Reattachment—*continued*
  arm (upper) NEC 84.24
  fingers, except thumb 84.22
    thumb 84.21
  foot 84.26
  forearm 84.23
  hand 84.23
  leg (lower) NEC 84.27
    thigh 84.28
    thumb 84.21
    toe 84.25
    wrist 84.23
  finger 84.22
    thumb 84.21
  foot 84.26
  forearm 84.23
  hand 84.23
  joint capsule (*see also* Arthroplasty) 81.96
  leg (lower) NEC 84.27
  ligament—*see also* Arthroplasty
    uterosacral 69.22
  muscle 83.74
    hand 82.54
    papillary (heart) 35.31
  nerve (peripheral) 04.79
  nose (amputated) 21.89
  papillary muscle (heart) 35.31
  penis (amputated) 64.45
  retina (and choroid) NEC 14.59
    by
      cryotherapy 14.52
      diathermy 14.51
      electrocoagulation 14.51
      photocoagulation 14.55
        laser 14.54
        xenon arc 14.53
  tendon (to tendon) 83.73
    hand 82.53
    to skeletal attachment 83.88
      hand 82.85
  thigh 84.28
  thumb 84.21
  toe 84.25
  tooth 23.5
  uterosacral ligament(s) 69.22
  vessels (peripheral) 39.59
    renal, aberrant 39.55
  wrist 84.23
Recession
  extraocular muscle 15.11
    multiple (two or more muscles) (with
      advancement or resection) 15.3
  gastrocnemius tendon (Strayer operation) 83.72
  levator palpebrae (superioris) muscle 08.38
  prognathic jaw 76.64
  tendon 83.72
    hand 82.52
Reclosure —*see also* Closure
  disrupted abdominal wall (postoperative) 54.61
Reconstruction (plastic)—*see also* Construction
  and Repair, by site
  alveolus, alveolar (process) (ridge) (with graft
    or implant) 24.5
  artery (graft)—*see* Graft, artery
  artificial stoma, intestine 46.40
  auditory canal (external) 18.6
  auricle (ear) 18.71
  bladder 57.87
    with
      ileum 57.87 *[45,51]*
      sigmoid 57.87 *[45.52]*

Reconstruction—*continued*
  bone, except facial (*see also* Osteoplasty) 78.40
    facial NEC 76.46
      with total ostectomy 76.44
    mandible 76.43
      with total mandibulectomy 76.41
  breast, total 85.7
  bronchus 33.48
  canthus (lateral) 08.59
  cardiac annulus 35.33
  chest wall (mesh) (silastic) 34.79
  cleft lip 27.54
  conjunctival cul-de-sac 10.43
    with graft (buccal mucous membrane) (free)
      10.42
  cornea NEC 11.79
  diaphragm 34.84
  ear (external) (auricle) 18.71
    external auditory canal 18.6
    meatus (new) (osseous skin-lined) 18.6
    ossicles 19.3
    prominent or protruding 18.5
  eyebrow 08.70
  eyelid 08.70
    with graft or flap 08.69
      hair follicle 08.63
      mucous membrane 08.62
      skin 08.61
      tarsoconjunctival (one-stage) (two-stage)
        08.64
    full-thickness 08.74
      involving lid margin 08.73
    partial-thickness 08.72
      involving lid margin 08.71
  eye socket 16.64
    with graft 16.63
  fallopian tube 66.79
  foot and toes (with fixation device) 81.57
    with prosthetic implant 81.57
  frontonasal duct 22.79
  hip (total) (with prosthesis) 81.51
  intraoral 27.59
  joint—*see* Arthroplasty
  lymphatic (by transplantation) 40.9
  mandible 76.43
    with total mandibulectomy 76.41
  mastoid cavity 19.9
  mouth 27.59
  nipple NEC 85.87
  nose (total) (with arm flap) (with forehead flap)
    21.83
  ossicles (graft) (prosthesis) NEC 19.3
    with
      stapedectomy 19.19
      tympanoplasty 19.53
  pelvic floor 71.79
  penis (rib graft) (skin graft)
    (myocutaneous flap) 64.44
  pharynx 29.4
  scrotum (with pedicle flap) (with rotational flap)
    61.49
  skin (plastic) (without graft) NEC 86.89
    with graft—*see* Graft, skin
  subcutaneous tissue (plastic) (without skin
    graft) NEC 86.89
    with graft—*see* Graft, skin
  tendon pulley (with graft) (with local tissue)
    83.83
    for opponensplasty 82.71
    hand 82.71

Removal—*continued*
calcareous deposit
  bursa 83.03
    hand 82.03
  tendon, intratendinous 83.39
    hand 82.29
calcification, heart valve leaflets—*see*
  Valvuloplasty, heart
calculus
  bile duct (by incision) 51.49
    endoscopic 51.88
    percutaneous 51.98
  bladder (by incision) 57.19
    without incision 57.0
  common duct (by incision) 51.41
    endoscopic 51.88
    percutaneous 51.96
  gallbladder 51.04
  kidney (by incision) 55.01
    without incision 56.0
    percutaneous 55.03
      with fragmentation (ultrasound) 55.04
  renal pelvis (by incision) 55.11
    percutaneous nephrostomy 55.03
      with fragmentation (ultrasound) 55.04
    transurethral 56.0
  lacrimal
    canaliculi 09.42
      by incision 09.52
    gland 09.3
      by incision 09.0
    passage(s) 09.49
      by incision 09.59
    punctum 09.41
      by incision 09.51
    sac 09.49
      by incision 09.53
  pancreatic duct (by incision) 52.09
    endoscopic 52.94
  perirenal tissue 59.09
  pharynx 29.39
  prostate 60.0
  salivary gland (by incision) 26.0
    by probe 26.91
  ureter (by incision) 56.2
    without incision 56.0
  urethra (by incision) 58.0
    without incision 58.6
caliper tongs (skull) 02.95
cannula
  for extracorporeal membrane oxygenation
    (ECMO)—*omit code*
cardiac pacemaker (device) (initial) (permanent)
    37.89
  with replacement
    dual-chamber device 37.87
    single-chamber device 37.85
      rate responsive 37.86
cardioverter/defibrillator pulse generator
  without replacement 37.99
cast 97.88
  with reapplication 97.13
    lower limb 97.12
    upper limb 97.11
catheter (indwelling)—*see also* Removal, tube
  bladder 97.64
  middle ear (tympanum) 20.1
  ureter 97.62
  urinary 97.64
  ventricular (cerebral) 02.43
    with synchronous replacement 02.42

Removal—*continued*
cerclage material, cervix 69.96
cerumen, ear 96.52
corneal epithelium 11.41
  for smear or culture 11.21
coronary artery obstruction (thrombus) 36.09
  direct intracoronary artery infusion 36.04
  open chest approach 36.03
  percutaneous transluminal (balloon) (single
    vessel) 36.01
    with thrombolytic agent infusion 36.02
  multiple vessels 36.05
Crutchfield tongs (skull) 02.95
  with synchronous replacement 02.94
cyst—*see also* Excision, lesion, by site
  dental 24.4
  lung 32.29
    endoscopic 32.28
cystic duct remnant 51.61
decidua (by)
  aspiration curettage 69.52
  curettage (D and C) 69.02
  manual 75.4
dental wiring (immobilization device) 97.33
  orthodontic 24.8
device (therapeutic) NEC 97.89
  abdomen NEC 97.86
  digestive system NEC 97.59
  drainage—*see* Removal, tube
  for musculoskeletal immobilization NEC 97.88
  fixation device external 97.88
    mandibular NEC 97.36
    minifixator (bone) *see category* 78.6
  genital tract NEC 97.79
  head and neck NEC 97.39
  intrauterine contraceptive 97.71
  minifixator—*see* category 78.6
  thorax NEC 97.49
  trunk NEC 97.87
  urinary system NEC 97.69
diaphragm, vagina 97.73
drainage device—*see* Removal, tube
dye, spinal canal 03.31
ectopic fetus (from) 66.02
  abdominal cavity 74.3
  extraperitoneal (intraligamentous) 74.3
  fallopian tube (by salpingostomy) 66.02
    by salpingotomy 66.01
    with salpingectomy 66.62
  intraligamentous 74.3
  ovarian 74.3
  peritoneal (following uterine or tubal rupture)
    74.3
  site NEC 74.3
  tubal (by salpingostomy) 66.02
    by salpingotomy 66.01
    with salpingectomy 66.62
electrodes
  bone growth stimulator—*see category* 78.6
  brain 01.22
    depth 01.22
      with synchronous replacement 02.93
    foramen ovale 01.22
      with synchronous replacement 02.93
    sphenoidal—*omit code*
      with synchronous replacement 02.96
  cardiac pacemaker (atrial) (transvenous)
    (ventricular) 37.77
    with replacement 37.76
  depth 01.22
    with synchronous replacement 02.93

Removal—*continued*
  epicardial (myocardial) 37.77
    with replacement (by)
      atrial and/or ventricular lead(s)
        (electrode) 37.76
      epicardial lead 37.74
  epidural pegs 01.22
    with synchronous replacement 02.93
  foramen ovale 01.22
    with synchronous replacement 02.93
  intracranial 01.22
    with synchronous replacement 02.93
  peripheral nerve 04.93
    with synchronous replacement 04.92
  sphenoidal—*omit code*
    with synchronous replacement 02.96
  spinal 03.94
    with synchronous replacement 03.93
  temporary transvenous pacemaker
    system—*omit code*
  electroencephalographic receiver (brain)
    (intracranial) 01.22
  with synchronous replacement 02.93
  electronic
    stimulator
      bladder 57.98
      bone 78.6
      brain 01.22
        with synchronous replacement 02.93
      intracranial 01.22
        with synchronous replacement 02.93
      peripheral nerve 04.93
        with synchronous replacement 04.92
      skeletal muscle 83.93
        with synchronous replacement 83.92
      spinal 03.94
        with synchronous replacement 03.93
      ureter 56.94
  electrostimulator—*see* Removal, electronic,
    stimulator, by site
  embolus 38.00
    with endarterectomy—*see* Endarterectomy
    abdominal
      artery 38.06
      vein 38.07
    aorta (arch) (ascending) (descending) 38.04
    arteriovenous shunt or cannula 39.49
    bovine graft 39.49
    head and neck vessel NEC 38.02
    intracranial vessel NEC 38.01
    lower limb
      artery 38.08
      vein 38.09
    pulmonary (artery) (vein) 38.05
    thoracic vessel NEC 38.05
    upper limb (artery) (vein) 38.03
  embryo—*see* Removal, ectopic fetus
  encircling tube, eye (episcleral) 14.6
  epithelial downgrowth, anterior chamber 12.93
  external fixation device 97.88
    mandibular NEC 97.36
    minifixator (bone)—*see category* 78.6
  extrauterine embryo—*see* Removal, ectopic
    fetus
  eyeball 16.49
    with implant 16.42
      with attachment of muscles 16.41
  fallopian tube—*see* Salpingectomy
  feces (impacted) (by flushing) (manual) 96.38
  fetus, ectopic—*see* Removal, ectopic fetus
  fingers, supernumerary 86.26

Removal—*continued*
  fixation device
    external 97.88
      mandibular NEC 97.36
      minifixator (bone)—*see category* 78.6
    internal 78.60
      carpal, metacarpal 78.64
      clavicle 78.61
      facial (bone) 76.97
      femur 78.65
      fibula 78.67
      humerus 78.62
      patella 78.66
      pelvic 78.69
      phalanges—(foot) (hand) 78.69
      radius 78.63
      scapula 78.61
      specified site NEC 78.69
      tarsal metatarsal 78.68
      thorax (ribs) (sternum) 78.61
      tibia 78.67
      ulna 78.63
      vertebrae 78.69
  foreign body NEC (*see also* Incision, by site)
    98.20
    abdominal (cavity) 54.92
      wall 54.0
    adenoid 98.13
      by incision 28.91
    alveolus, alveolar bone 98.22
      by incision 24.0
    antecubital fossa 98.27
      by incision 86.05
    anterior chamber 12.00
      by incision 12.02
        with use of magnet 12.01
    anus (intraluminal) 98.05
      by incision 49.93
    artificial stoma (intraluminal) 98.18
    auditory canal, external 18.02
    axilla 98.27
      by incision 86.05
    bladder (without incision) 57.0
      by incision 57.19
    bone, except fixation device (*see also*
      Incision, bone) 77.10
      alveolus, alveolar 98.22
        by incision 24.0
    brain 01.39
      without incision into brain 01.24
    breast 85.0
    bronchus (intraluminal) 98.15
      by incision 33.0
    bursa 83.03
      hand 82.03
    canthus 98.22
      by incision 08.51
    cerebral meninges 01.31
    cervix (intraluminal) NEC 98.16
      penetrating 69.97
    choroid (by incision) 14.00
      with use of magnet 14.01
      without use of magnet 14.02
    ciliary body (by incision) 12.00
      with use of magnet 12.01
      without use of magnet 12.02
    conjunctiva (by magnet) 98.22
      by incision 10.0
    cornea 98.21
      by incision 11.1
      by magnet 11.0

Removal—*continued*
  duodenum 98.03
    by incision 45.01
  ear (intraluminal) 98.11
    with incision 18.09
  epididymis 63.92
  esophagus (intraluminal) 98.02
    by incision 42.09
  extrapleural (by incision) 34.01
  eye, eyeball (by magnet) 98.21
    anterior segment (by incision) 12.00
      with use of magnet 12.01
      without use of magnet 12.02
    posterior segment (by incision) 14.00
      with use of magnet 14.01
      without use of magnet 14.02
    superficial 98.21
  eyelid 98.22
    by incision 08.09
  fallopian tube
    by salpingostomy 66.02
    by salpingotomy 66.01
  fascia 83.09
    hand 82.09
  foot 98.28
  gall bladder 51.04
  groin region (abdominal wall) (inguinal) 54.0
  gum 98.22
    by incision 24.0
  hand 98.26
  head and neck NEC 98.22
  heart 37.11
  internal fixation, device—*see* Removal,
      fixation device, internal
  intestine
    by incision 45.00
    large (intraluminal) 98.04
      by incision 45.03
    small (intraluminal) 98.03
      by incision 45.02
  intraocular (by incision) 12.00
    with use of magnet 12.01
    without use of magnet 12.02
  iris (by incision) 12.00
    with use of magnet 12.01
    without use of magnet 12.02
  joint structure (*see also* Arthrotomy) 80.10
  kidney (transurethral) (by endoscopy) 56.0
    by incision 55.01
    pelvis (transurethral) 56.0
      by incision 55.11
  labia 98.23
    by incision 71.09
  lacrimal
    canaliculi 09.42
      by incision 09.52
    gland 09.3
      by incision 09.0
    passage(s) 09.49
      by incision 09.59
    punctum 09.41
      by incision 09.51
    sac 09.49
      by incision 09.53
  large intestine (intraluminal) 98.04
    by incision 45.03
  larynx (intraluminal) 98.14
    by incision 31.3
  lens 13.00
    by incision 13.02
    with use of magnet 13.01

Removal—*continued*
  liver 50.0
  lower limb, except foot 98.29
    foot 98.28
  lung 33.1
  mediastinum 34.1
  meninges (cerebral) 01.31
    spinal 03.01
  mouth (intraluminal) 98.01
    by incision 27.92
  muscle 83.02
    hand 82.02
  nasal sinus 22.50
    antrum 22.2
      with Caldwell-Luc approach 22.39
    ethmoid 22.51
    frontal 22.41
    maxillary 22.2
      with Caldwell-Luc approach 22.39
    sphenoid 22.52
  nerve (cranial) (peripheral) NEC 04.04
    root 03.01
  nose (intraluminal) 98.12
    by incision 21.1
  oral cavity (intraluminal) 98.01
    by incision 27.92
  orbit (by magnet) 98.21
    by incision 16.1
  palate (penetrating) 98.22
    by incision 27.1
  pancreas 52.09
  penis 98.24
    by incision 64.92
  pericardium 37.12
  perineum (female) 98.23
    by incision 71.09
    male 98.25
      by incision 86.05
  perirenal tissue 59.09
  peritoneal cavity 54.92
  perivesical tissue 59.19
  pharynx (intraluminal) 98.13
    by pharyngotomy 29.0
  pleura (by incision) 34.09
  popliteal space 98.29
    by incision 86.05
  rectum (intraluminal) 98.05
    by incision 48.0
  renal pelvis (transurethral) 56.0
    by incision 56.1
  retina (by incision) 14.00
    with use of magnet 14.01
    without use of magnet 14.02
  retroperitoneum 54.92
  sclera (by incision) 12.00
    with use of magnet 12.01
    without use of magnet 12.02
  scrotum 98.24
    by incision 61.0
  sinus (nasal) 22.50
    antrum 22.2
      with Caldwell-Luc approach 22.39
    ethmoid 22.51
    frontal 22.41
    maxillary 22.2
      with Caldwell-Luc approach 22.39
    sphenoid 22.52
  skin NEC 98.20
    by incision 86.05
  skull 01.24
    with incision into brain 01.39

Removal—*continued*

small intestine (intraluminal) 98.03
  by incision 45.02
soft tissue NEC 83.09
  hand 82.09
spermatic cord 63.93
spinal (canal) (cord) (meninges) 03.01
stomach (intraluminal) 98.03
  bubble (balloon) 44.94
  by incision 43.0
subconjunctival (by magnet) 98.22
  by incision 10.0
subcutaneous tissue NEC 98.20
  by incision 86.05
supraclavicular fossa 98.27
  by incision 86.05
tendon (sheath) 83.01
  hand 82.01
testis 62.0
thorax (by incision) 34.09
thyroid (field) (gland) (by incision) 06.09
tonsil 98.13
  by incision 28.91
trachea (intraluminal) 98.15
  by incision 31.3
trunk NEC 98.25
tunica vaginalis 98.24
upper limb, except hand 98.27
  hand 98.26
ureter (transurethral) 56.0
  by incision 56.2
urethra (intraluminal) 98.19
  by incision 58.0
uterus (intraluminal) 98.16
vagina (intraluminal) 98.17
  by incision 70.14
vas deferens 63.6
vitreous (by incision) 14.00
  with use of magnet 14.01
  without use of magnet 14.02
vulva 98.23
  by incision 71.09
gallstones
  bile duct (by incision) NEC 51.49
    endoscopic 51.88
  common duct (by incision) 51.41
    endoscopic 51.88
    percutaneous 51.96
  duodenum 45.01
  gallbladder 51.04
  hepatic ducts 51.49
    endoscopic 51.88
  intestine 45.00
    large 45.03
    small NEC 45.02
  liver 50.0
Gardner Wells tongs (skull) 02.95
  with synchronous replacement 02.94
gastric bubble (balloon) 44.94
granulation tissue—*see also* Excision, lesion, by
  site
  with repair—*see* Repair, by site
  cranial 01.6
  skull 01.6
halo traction device (skull) 02.95
  with synchronous replacement 02.94
heart assist system 37.64
  with replacement 37.63
hematoma—*see* Drainage, by site
Hoffman minifixator device (bone)—*see*
  category 78.6

Removal—*continued*

hydatidiform mole 68.0
impacted
  feces (rectum) (by flushing) (manual) 96.38
  tooth 23.19
    from nasal sinus (maxillary) 22.61
implant
  breast 85.94
  cochlear prosthetic device 20.99
  cornea 11.92
  lens (prosthetic) 13.8
  middle ear NEC 20.99
  ocular 16.71
    posterior segment 14.6
  orbit 16.72
  retina 14.6
  tympanum 20.1
internal fixation device—*see* Removal, fixation
    device, internal
intrauterine contraceptive device (IUD) 97.71
joint (structure) NOS 80.90
  ankle 80.97
  elbow 80.92
  foot and toe 80.98
  hand and finger 80.94
  hip 80.95
  knee 80.96
  other specified sites 80.99
  shoulder 80.91
  spine 80.99
  toe 80.98
  wrist 80.93
Kantrowitz heart pump 37.64
keel (tantalum plate), larynx 31.98
kidney—*see also* Nephrectomy
  mechanical 55.98
  transplanted or rejected 55.53
laminaria (tent), uterus 97.79
leads (cardiac)—*see* Removal, electrodes,
    cardiac pacemaker
lesion—*see* Excision, lesion, by site
ligamentum flavum (spine)—*omit code*
ligature
  fallopian tube 66.79
  ureter 56.86
  vas deferens 63.84
loose body
  bone—*see* Sequestrectomy, bone
  joint 80.10
  mesh (surgical)—*see* Removal, foreign body,
    by site
lymph node—*see* Excision, lymph, node
minifixator device (bone)—*see category* 78.6
  external fixation device 97.88
Mulligan hood, fallopian tube 66.94
  with synchronous replacement 66.93
muscle stimulator (skeletal) 83.93
  with replacement 83.92
myringotomy device or tube 20.1
nail (bed) (fold) 86.23
  internal fixation device—*see* Removal,
    fixation device, internal
necrosis
  skin 86.28
    excisional 86.22
neuropacemaker
  brain 01.22
    with synchronous replacement 02.93
  intracranial 01.22
    with synchronous replacement 02.93

Removal—*continued*
  peripheral nerve 04.93
    with synchronous replacement 04.92
  spinal 03.94
    with synchronous replacement 03.93
  neurostimulator
    brain 01.22
      with synchronous replacement 02.93
    intracranial 01.22
      with synchronous replacement 02.93
    peripheral nerve 04.93
      with synchronous replacement 04.92
    spinal 03.94
      with synchronous replacement 03.93
  nonabsorbable surgical material NEC—*see*
    Removal, foreign body, by site
  odontoma (tooth) 24.4
  orbital implant 16.72
  osteocartilaginous loose body, joint structures
    (*see also* Arthrotomy) 80.10
  outer attic wall (middle ear) 20.59
  ovo-testis (unilateral) 62.3
    bilateral 62.41
  pacemaker
    brain (intracranial) 01.22
      with synchronous replacement 02.93
    cardiac (device) (initial) (permanent)
      37.89
      with replacement
        dual-chamber device 37.87
        single-chamber device 37.85
          rate responsive 37.86
    electrodes (atrial) (transvenous)
      (ventricular) 37.77
      with replacement 37.76
    epicardium (myocardium) 37.77
      with replacement (by)
        atrial and/or ventricular lead(s)
          (electrode) 37.76
        epicardial lead 37.74
    temporary transvenous pacemaker
      system—*omit code*
  intracranial 01.22
    with synchronous replacement 02.93
  neural
    brain 01.22
      with synchronous replacement 02.93
    peripheral nerve 04.93
      with synchronous replacement 4.92
    spine 03.94
      with synchronous replacement 03.93
    spinal 03.94
      with synchronous replacement 03.93
  pack, packing
    dental 97.34
    intrauterine 97.72
    nasal 97.32
    rectum 97.59
    trunk NEC 97.85
    vagina 97.75
    vulva 97.75
  pantopaque dye, spinal canal 03.31
  patella (complete) 77.96
    partial 77.86
  pectus deformity implant device 34.01
  pelvic viscera, en masse (female) 68.8
    male 57.71
  pessary, vagina NEC 97.74
  pharynx (partial) 29.33
  phlebolith—*see* Removal, embolus

Removal—*continued*
  placenta (by)
    aspiration curettage 69.52
    D and C 69.02
    manual 75.4
  plaque, dental 96.54
  plate, skull 02.07
    with synchronous replacement 02.05
  polyp—*see also* Excision, lesion, by site
    esophageal 42.32
      endoscopic 42.33
    gastric (endoscopic) 43.41
    intestine 45.41
      endoscopic 45.42
    nasal 21.31
  prosthesis
    bile duct 51.95
      nonoperative 97.55
    cochlear prosthetic device 20.99
    dental 97.35
    eye 97.31
    facial bone 76.99
    fallopian tue 66.94
      with synchronous replacement 66.93
    joint structures 80.00
      ankle 80.07
      elbow 80.02
      foot and toe 80.08
      hand and finger 80.04
      hip 80.05
      knee 80.06
      shoulder 80.01
      specified site NEC 80.09
      spine 80.09
      wrist 80.03
    lens 13.8
    penis (internal) without replacement 64.96
    Rosen (urethra) 59.99
    testicular, by incision 62.0
    urinary sphincter, artificial 58.99
      with replacement 58.93
  pseudophakos 13.8
  pterygium 11.39
    with corneal graft 11.32
  pulse generator
    cardiac pacemaker 37.86
    cardioverter/defibrillator 37.99
  pump assist device, heart 37.64
    with replacement 37.63
  radioactive material—*see* Removal, foreign
    body, by site
  redundant skin, eyelid 08.86
  rejected organ
    kidney 55.53
    testis 62.42
  reservoir, ventricular (Ommaya) (Rickham)
    02.43
    with synchronous replacement 02.42
  retained placenta (by)
    aspiration curettage 69.52
    D and C 69.02
    manual 75.4
  retinal implant 14.6
  rhinolith 21.31
  rice bodies, tendon sheaths 83.01
    hand 82.01
  Roger-Anderson minifixator device (bone) *see*
    category 78.6
  root, residual (tooth) (buried) (retained) 23.11
  Rosen prosthesis (urethra) 59.99
  Scribner shunt 39.43

Removal—*continued*
  scleral buckle or implant 14.6
  secondary membranous cataract (with
      iridectomy) 13.65
  secundines (by)
    aspiration curettage 69.52
    D and C 69.02
    manual 75.4
  sequestrum—*see* Sequestrectomy
  seton, anus 49.93
  Shepard's tube (ear) 20.1
  Shirodkar suture, cervix 69.96
  shunt
    arteriovenous 39.43
      with creation of new shunt 39.42
    lumbar-subarachnoid NEC 03.98
    pleurothecal 03.98
    salpingothecal 03.98
    spinal (thecal) NEC 03.98
    subarachnoid-peritoneal 03.98
    subarachnoid-ureteral 03.98
  silastic tubes
    ear 20.1
    fallopian tubes 66.94
      with synchronous replacement 66.93
  skin
    necrosis or slough 86.28
      excisional 86.22
    superficial layer (by dermabrasion) 86.25
  skull tongs 02.95
    with synchronous replacement 02.94
  splint 97.88
  stent
    larynx 31.98
    ureteral 97.62
    urethral 97.65
  stimoceiver (brain) (intracranial) 01.22
    with synchronous replacement 02.93
  subdural
    grids 01.22
    strips 01.22
  supernumerary digit(s) 86.26
  suture(s) NEC 97.89
    abdominal wall 97.83
    by incision—*see* Incision, by site
    genital tract 97.79
    head and neck 97.38
    thorax 97.43
    trunk NEC 97.84
  symblepharon—*see* Repair, symblepharon
  temporary transvenous pacemaker
      system—*omit code*
  testis (unilateral) 62.3
    bilateral 62.41
    remaining or solitary 62.42
  thrombus 38.00
    with endarterectomy—*see* Endarterectomy
    abdominal
      artery 38.06
      vein 38.07
    aorta (arch) (ascending) (descending) 38.04
    arteriovenous shunt or cannula 39.49
    bovine graft 39.49
    coronary artery 36.09
    head and neck vessel NEC 38.02
    intracranial vessel NEC 38.01
    lower limb
      artery 38.08
      vein 38.09
    pulmonary (artery) (vein) 38.05
    thoracic vessel NEC 38.05

Removal—*continued*
    upper limb (artery) (vein) 38.0
  tissue expander (skin) NEC 86.05
    breast 85.96
  toes, supernumerary 86.26
  tongs, skull 02.95
    with synchronous replacement 02.94
  tonsil tag 28.4
  tooth (by forceps) (multiple) (single NEC 23.09
    deciduous 23.01
    surgical NEC 23.19
      impacted 23.19
      residual root 23.11
      root apex 23.73
        with root canal therapy 23.72
  trachoma follicles 10.33
  T-tube (bile duct) 97.55
  tube
    appendix 97.53
    bile duct (T-tube) NEC 97.55
    cholecystostomy 97.54
    cystostomy 97.63
    ear (button) 20.1
    gastrostomy 97.51
    large intestine 97.53
    liver 97.55
    mediastinum 97.42
    nephrostomy 97.61
    pancreas 97.56
    peritoneum 97.82
    pleural cavity 97.41
    pyelostomy 97.61
    retroperitoneum 97.81
    small intestine 97.52
    thoracotomy 97.41
    tracheostomy 97.37
    tympanostomy 20.1
    tympanum 20.1
    ureterostomy 97.62
  ureteral splint (stent) 97.62
  urethral sphincter, artificial 58.99
    with replacement 58.93
  urinary sphincter, artificial 58.99
    with replacement 58.93
  utricle 20.79
  valve
    vas deferens 63.85
    ventricular (cerebral) 02.43
  vascular graft or prosthesis 39.49
  ventricular shunt or reservoir 02.43
    with synchronous replacement 02.42
  Vinke tongs (skull) 02.95
    with synchronous replacement 02.94
  vitreous (with replacement) 14.72
    anterior approach (partial) 14.71
    open sky technique 14.71
  Wagner-Brooker minifixator device
      (bone)—*see category* 78.6
  wiring, dental (immobilization device) 97.33
    orthodontic 24.8
Renipuncture (percutaneous) 55.92
Renogram 92.03
Renotransplantation NEC 55.69
Reopening —*see also* Incision, by site
  blepharorrhaphy 08.02
  canthorrhaphy 08.02
  cilia base 08.71
  craniotomy or craniectomy site 01.23
  fallopian tube (divided) 66.79
  iris in anterior chambers 12.97
  laminectomy or laminotomy site 03.02

Reopening—*continued*
laparotomy site 54.12
osteotomy site (*see also* Incision, bone) 77.10
facial bone 76.09
tarsorrhaphy 08.02
thoracotomy site (for control of hemorrhage)
(for examination) (for exploration) 34.03
thyroid field wound (for control of hemorrhage)
(for examination) (for exploration) (for
removal of hematoma) 06.02

Repacking —*see* Replacement, pack, by site

Repair
abdominal wall 54.72
adrenal gland 07.44
alveolus, alveolar (process) (ridge) (with graft)
(with implant) 24.5
anal sphincter 49.79
laceration (by suture) 49.71
obstetric (current) 75.62
old 49.79
aneurysm (false) (true) 39.52
by or with
clipping 39.51
coagulation 39.52
electrocoagulation 39.52
excision or resection of vessel—*see also*
Aneurysmectomy, by site
with
anastomosis—*see* Aneurysmectomy,
with anastomosis, by site
graft replacement—*see*
Aneurysmectomy, with graft
replacement, by site
filipuncture 39.52
graft replacement—*see* Aneurysmectomy,
with graft replacement, by site
ligation 39.52
methyl methacrylate 39.52
occlusion 39.52
suture 39.52
trapping 39.52
wiring 39.52
wrapping (gauze) (methyl methacrylate)
(plastic) 39.52
coronary artery 36.91
sinus of Valsalva 35.39
thoracic aorta (dissecting), by fenestration
39.54
anomalous pulmonary venous connection (total)
one-stage 35.82
partial—*see* specific procedure
total 35.82
anus 49.79
laceration (by suture) 49.71
obstetric (current) 75.62
old 49.79
aorta 39.31
aorticopulmonary window 39.59
arteriovenous fistula 39.53
by or with
clipping 39.53
coagulation 39.53
division 39.53
excision or resection—*see also*
Aneurysmectomy, by site
with
anastomosis—*see* Aneurysmectomy,
with anastomosis, by site
graft replacement—*see*
Aneurysmectomy, with graft
replacement, by site

Repair—*continued*
ligation 39.53
coronary artery 36.99
occlusion 39.53
suture 39.53
artery NEC 39.59
by
non-coronary percutaneous transluminal
angioplasty or atherectomy
basilar 39.50
carotid 39.50
femoropopliteal 39.50
head and neck NOS 39.50
iliac 39.50
lower extremity NOS 39.50
mesenteric 39.50
renal 39.50
upper extremity NOS 39.50
vertebral 39.50
coronary NEC 36.99
by angioplasty—*see* Angioplasty, coronary
by atherectomy—*see* Angioplasty, coronary
with
patch graft 39.58
with excision or resection of vessel—*see*
Arteriectomy, with graft replacement,
by site
synthetic (Dacron) (Teflon) 39.57
tissue (vein) (autogenous) (homograft)
39.56
suture 39.31
artificial opening—*see* Repair, stoma
atrial septal defect 35.71
with
prosthesis (open heart technique) 35.51
closed heart technique 35.52
tissue graft 35.61
combined with repair of valvular and
ventricular septal defects—*see* Repair,
endocardial cushion defect
in total repair of total anomalous pulmonary
venous connection 35.82
atrioventricular canal defect (any type) 35.73
with
prosthesis 35.54
tissue graft 35.63
bifid digit (finger) 82.89
bile duct NEC 51.79
laceration (by suture) NEC 51.79
common bile duct 51.71
bladder NEC 57.89
exstrophy 57.86
for stress incontinence—*see* Repair, stress
incontinence
laceration (by suture) 57.81
obstetric (current) 75.61
old 57.89
neck 57.85
blepharophimosis 08.59
blepharoptosis 08.36
by
frontalis muscle technique (with)
fascial sling 08.32
suture 08.31
levator muscle technique 08.34
with resection or advancement 08.33
orbicularis oculi muscle sling 08.36
tarsal technique 08.35
blood vessel NEC 39.59
with
patch graft 39.58

Repair—*continued*
  with excision or resection—*see*
    Angiectomy, with graft replacement
  synthetic (Dacron) (Teflon) 39.57
  tissue (vein) (autogenous) (homograft)
    39.56
  resection—*see* Angiectomy
  suture 39.30
  coronary artery NEC 36.99
    by angioplasty—*see* Angioplasty, coronary
    by atherectomy—*see* Angioplasty, coronary
  peripheral vessel NEC 39.59
    by angioplasty 39.50
    by atherectomy 39.50
  bone NEC (*see also* Osteoplasty) —*see*
    category 78.4
  accessory sinus 22.79
  by synostosis technique—*see* Arthrodesis
  cranium NEC 02.06
    with
      flap (bone) 02.03
      graft (bone) 02.04
  for malunion, nonunion, or delayed union of
    fracture—*see* Repair, fracture, malunion
    or nonunion
  nasal 21.89
  skull NEC 02.06
    with
      flap (bone) 02.03
      graft (bone) 02.04
  bottle, hydrocele of tunica vaginalis 61.2
  brain (trauma) NEC 02.92
  breast (plastic) (*see also* Mammoplasty) 85.89
  broad ligament 69.29
  bronchus NEC 33.48
    laceration (by suture) 33.41
  bunionette (with osteotomy) 77.54
  canaliculus, lacrimal 09.73
  canthus (lateral) 08.59
  cardiac pacemaker NEC 37.89
    electrode (s) (lead) NEC 37.75
  cardioverter/defibrillator (automatic) pocket
    (skin) (subcutaneous) 37.99
  cerebral meninges 02.12
  cervix 67.69
    internal os 67.5
    laceration (by suture) 67.61
      obstetric (current) 75.51
      old 67.69
  chest wall (mesh) (silastic) NEC 34.79
  chordae tendineae 35.32
  choroid NEC 14.9
    with retinal repair—*see* Repair, retina
  cisterna chyli 40.69
  claw toe 77.57
  cleft
    hand 82.82
    laryngotracheal 31.69
    lip 27.54
    palate 27.62
      secondary or subsequent 27.63
  coarctation of aorta—*see* Excision, coarctation
    of aorta
  cochlear prosthetic device 20.99
    external components only 95.49
  cockup toe 77.58
  colostomy 46.43

Repair—*continued*
  conjunctiva NEC 10.49
    with scleral repair 12.81
    laceration 10.6
      with repair of sclera 12.81
    late effect of trachoma 10.49
  cornea NEC 11.59
    with
      conjunctiva flap 11.53
      transplant—*see* Keratoplasty
    postoperative dehiscence 11.52
  coronary artery NEC 36.99
    by angioplasty—*see* Angioplasty, coronary
    by atherectomy—*see* Angioplasty, coronary
  cranium NEC 02.06
    with
      flap (bone) 02.03
      graft (bone) 02.04
  cusp, valve—*see* Repair, heart, valve
  cystocele 70.51
    and rectocele 70.50
  dental arch 24.8
  diaphragm NEC 34.84
  diastasis recti 83.65
  diastematomyelia 03.59
  ear (external) 18.79
    auditory canal or meatus 18.6
    auricle NEC 18.79
    cartilage NEC 18.79
    laceration (by suture) 18.4
    lop ear 18.79
    middle NEC 19.9
    prominent or protruding 18.5
  ectropion 08.49
    by or with
      lid reconstruction 08.44
      suture (technique) 08.42
      thermocauterization 08.41
      wedge resection 08.43
  encephalocele (cerebral) 02.12
  endocardial cushion defect 35.73
    with
      prosthesis (grafted to septa) 35.54
      tissue graft 35.63
  enterocele (female) 70.92
    male 53.9
  enterostomy 46.40
  entropion 08.49
    by or with
      lid reconstruction 08.44
      suture (technique) 08.42
      thermocauterization 08.41
      wedge resection 08.43
  epicanthus (fold) 08.59
  epididymis (and spermatic cord) NEC 63.59
    with vas deferens 63.89
  epiglottis 31.69
  episiotomy
    routine following delivery—*see* Episiotomy
    secondary 75.69
  epispadias 58.45
  esophagus, esophageal NEC 42.89
    fistula NEC 42.84
    stricture 42.85
  exstrophy of bladder 57.86
  eye, eyeball 16.89
    multiple structures 16.82
    rupture 16.82
    socket 16.64
      with graft 16.63

Repair—*continued*

    Sofield type procedure—*see* categories
      77.3 *[78.5]*
    synostosis technique—*see* Arthrodesis
  vertebra 03.53
  funnel chest (with implant) 34.74
  gallbladder 51.91
  gastroschisis 54.71
  great vessels NEC 39.59
    laceration (by suture) 39.30
      artery 39.31
      vein 39.32
  hallux valgus NEC 77.59
    resection of joint with prosthetic implant 77.59
  hammer toe 77.56
  hand 82.89
    with graft or implant 82.79
      fascia 82.72
      muscle 82.72
      tendon 82.79
  heart 37.4
    assist system 37.63
    septum 35.70
      with
        prosthesis 35.50
        tissue graft 35.60
      atrial 35.71
        with
          prosthesis (open heart technique) 35.51
            closed heart technique 35.52
          tissue graft 35.61
        combined with repair of valvular and
          ventricular septal defects—*see* Repair,
          endocardial cushion defect
        in total repair of
          tetralogy of Fallot 35.81
          total anomalous pulmonary venous
            connection 35.82
          truncus arteriosus 35.83
      combined with repair of valvular
        defect—*see* Repair, endocardial cushion
        defect
      ventricular 35.72
        with
          prosthesis 35.53
          tissue graft 35.62
        combined with repair of valvular and atrial
          septal defects—*see* Repair,
          endocardial cushion defect
        in total repair of
          tetralogy of Fallot 35.81
          total anomalous pulmonary venous
            connection 35.82
          truncus arteriosus 35.83
    valve (cusps) (open heart technique) 35.10
      with prosthesis or tissue graft 35.20
      aortic (without replacement) 35.11
        with
          prosthesis 35.22
          tissue graft 35.21
        combined with repair of atrial and
          ventricular septal defects—*see* Repair,
          endocardial cushion defect
      mitral (without replacement) 35.12
        with
          prosthesis 35.24
          tissue graft 35.23

Repair—*continued*

  pulmonary (without replacement) 35.13
    with
      prosthesis 35.26
        in total repair of tetralogy of Fallot
          35.81
      tissue graft 35.25
  tricuspid (without replacement) 35.14
    with
      prosthesis 35.28
      tissue graft 35.27
  hepatic duct 51.79
  hernia NEC 53.9
    anterior abdominal wall NEC 53.59
      with prosthesis or graft 53.69
    colostomy 46.42
    crural 53.29
    cul-de-sac (Douglas') 70.92
    diaphragmatic
      abdominal approach 53.7
      thoracic, thoracoabdominal approach 53.80
    epigastric 53.59
      with prosthesis or graft 53.69
    esophageal hiatus
      abdominal approach 53.7
      thoracic, thoracoabdominal approach 53.80
    fascia 83.89
      hand 82.89
    femoral (unilateral) 53.29
      with prosthesis or graft 53.21
      bilateral 53.39
        with prosthesis or graft 53.31
    Ferguson 53.00
    Halsted 53.00
    Hill-Allison (hiatal hernia repair, transpleural
      approach) 53.80
    hypogastric 53.59
      with prosthesis or graft 53.69
    incisional 53.51
      with prosthesis or graft 53.61
    inguinal (unilateral) 53.00
      with prosthesis or graft 53.05
      bilateral 53.10
        with prosthesis or graft 53.17
        direct 53.11
          with prosthesis or graft 53.14
        direct and indirect 53.13
          with prosthesis or graft 53.16
        indirect 53.12
          with prosthesis or graft 53.15
      direct (unilateral) 53.01
        with prosthesis or graft 53.03
        and indirect (unilateral) 53.01
          with prosthesis or graft 53.03
          bilateral 53.13
            with prosthesis or graft 53.16
        bilateral 53.11
          with prosthesis or graft 53.14
      indirect (unilateral) 53.02
        with prosthesis or graft 53.04
        and direct (unilateral) 53.01
          with prosthesis or graft 53.03
          bilateral 53.13
            with prosthesis or graft 53.16
        bilateral 53.12
          with prosthesis or graft 53.15
    internal 53.9
    ischiatic 53.9
    ischiorectal 53.9
    lumbar 53.9
    manual 96.27

Repair—*continued*
  obturator 53.9
  omental 53.9
  paraesophageal 53.7
  parahiatal 53.7
  paraileostomy 46.41
  parasternal 53.82
  paraumbilical 53.49
    with prosthesis 53.41
  pericolostomy 46.42
  perineal (enterocele) 53.9
  preperitoneal 53.29
  pudendal 53.9
  retroperitoneal 53.9
  sciatic 53.9
  scrotal—*see* Repair, hernia, inguinal
  spigelian 53.59
    with prosthesis or graft 53.69
  umbilical 53.49
    with prosthesis 53.41
  uveal 12.39
  ventral 53.59
    incisional 53.51
      with prosthesis or graft 53.61
  hydrocele
    round ligament 69.19
    spermatic cord 63.1
    tunica vaginalis 61.2
  hymen 70.76
  hypospadias 58.45
  ileostomy 46.41
  ingrown toenail 86.23
  intestine, intestinal NEC 46.79
    fistula—*see* Closure, fistula, intestine
    laceration
      large intestine 46.75
      small intestine NEC 46.73
    stoma—*see* Repair, stoma
  inverted uterus NEC 69.29
    manual
      nonobstetric 69.94
      obstetric 75.94
    obstetrical
      manual 75.94
      surgical 75.93
    vaginal approach 69.23
  iris (rupture) NEC 12.39
  jejunostomy 46.41
  joint (capsule) (cartilage) NEC (*see also*
    Arthroplasty) 81.96
  kidney NEC 55.89
  knee (joint) NEC 81.47
    collateral ligaments 81.46
    cruciate ligaments 81.45
    five-in-one 81.42
    triad 81.43
  labia—*see* Repair, vulva
  laceration—*see* Suture, by site
  lacrimal system NEC 09.99
    canaliculus 09.73
    punctum 09.72
      for eversion 09.71
  laryngostomy 31.62
  laryngotracheal cleft 31.69
  larynx 31.69
    fracture 31.64
    laceration 31.61
  leads (cardiac) NEC 37.75

Repair—*continued*
  ligament (*see also* Arthroplasty) 81.96
    broad 69.29
    collateral, knee NEC 81.46
    cruciate, knee NEC 81.45
    round 69.29
    uterine 69.29
  lip NEC 27.59
    cleft 27.54
    laceration (by suture) 27.51
  liver NEC 50.69
    laceration 50.61
  lop ear 18.79
  lung NEC 33.49
  lymphatic (channel) (peripheral) NEC 40.9
    duct, left (thoracic) NEC 40.69
  macrodactyly 82.83
  mallet finger 82.84
  mandibular ridge 76.64
  mastoid (antrum) (cavity) 19.9
  meninges (cerebral) NEC 02.12
    spinal NEC 03.59
      meningocele 03.51
      myelomeningocele 03.52
  meningocele (spinal) 03.51
    cranial 02.12
  mesentery 54.75
  mouth NEC 27.59
    laceration NEC 27.52
  muscle NEC 83.87
    by
      graft or implant (fascia) (muscle) 83.82
        hand 82.72
      tendon 83.81
        hand 82.79
      suture (direct) 83.65
        hand 82.46
      transfer or transplantation (muscle) 83.77
        hand 82.58
    hand 82.89
      by
        graft or implant NEC 82.79
          fascia 82.72
        suture (direct) 82.46
        transfer or transplantation (muscle) 82.58
  musculotendinous cuff, shoulder 83.63
  myelomeningocele 03.52
  nasal
    septum (perforation) NEC 21.88
    sinus NEC 22.79
      fistula 22.71
  nasolabial flaps (plastic) 21.86
  nasopharyngeal atresia 29.4
  nerve (cranial) (peripheral) NEC 04.79
    old injury 04.76
    revision 04.75
    sympathetic 05.81
  nipple NEC 85.87
  nose (external) (internal) (plastic) NEC (*see
    also* Rhinoplasty) 21.89
    laceration (by suture) 21.81
  notched lip 27.59
  omentum 54.74
  omphalocele 53.49
    with prosthesis 53.41
  orbit 16.89
    wound 16.81

Repair—*continued*
  ostium
    primum defect 35.73
      with prosthesis 35.54
      with tissue graft 35.63
    secundum defect 35.71
      with
        prosthesis (open heart technique) 35.51
          closed heart technique 35.52
        tissue graft 35.61
  ovary 65.79
    with tube 65.73
      laparoscopic 65.76
  overlapping toe 77.58
  pacemaker
    cardiac
      device (permanent) 37.89
      electrode(s) (lead) NEC 37.75
      pocket (skin) (subcutaneous) 37.79
  palate NEC 27.69
    cleft 27.62
      secondary or subsequent 27.63
    laceration (by suture) 27.61
  pancreas NEC 52.95
    Wirsung's duct 52.99
  papillary muscle (heart) 35.31
  patent ductus arteriosus 38.85
  pectus deformity (chest) (carinatum)
    (excavatum) 34.74
  pelvic floor NEC 70.79
    obstetric laceration (current) 75.69
      old 70.79
  penis NEC 64.49
    for epispadias or hypospadias 58.45
    inflatable prosthesis 64.99
    laceration 64.41
  pericardium 37.4
  perineum (female) 71.79
    laceration (by suture) 71.71
      obstetric (current) 75.69
        old 71.79
    male NEC 86.89
      laceration (by suture) 86.59
  peritoneum NEC 54.73
    by suture 54.64
  pharynx NEC 29.59
    laceration (by suture) 29.51
    plastic 29.4
  pleura NEC 34.93
  postcataract wound dehiscence 11.52
    with conjunctival flap 11.53
  pouch of Douglas 70.52
  primum ostium defect 35.73
    with
      prosthesis 35.54
      tissue graft 35.63
  prostate 60.93
  ptosis, eyelid—*see* Repair, blepharoptosis
  punctum, lacrimal NEC 09.72
    for correction of eversion 09.71
  quadriceps (mechanism) 83.86
  rectocele (posterior colporrhaphy) 70.52
    and cystocele 70.50
  rectum NEC 48.79
    laceration (by suture) 48.71
    prolapse NEC 48.76
      abdominal approach 48.75
  retina, retinal
    detachment 14.59

Repair—*continued*
  by
    cryotherapy 14.52
    diathermy 14.51
    photocoagulation 14.55
      laser 14.54
      xenon arc 14.53
    scleral buckling (*see also* Buckling,
      scleral) 14.49
  tear or defect 14.39
    by
      cryotherapy 14.32
      diathermy 14.31
      photocoagulation 14.35
        laser 14.34
        xenon arc 14.33
  retroperitoneal tissue 54.73
  rotator cuff (suture) 83.63
  round ligament 69.29
  ruptured tendon NEC 83.88
    hand 82.86
  salivary gland or duct NEC 26.49
  sclera, scleral 12.89
    fistula 12.82
    staphyloma NEC 12.86
      with graft 12.85
  scrotum 61.49
  sinus
    nasal NEC 22.79
    of Valsalva (aneurysm) 35.39
  skin (plastic) (without graft) 86.89
    laceration (by suture) 86.59
  skull NEC 02.06
    with
      flap (bone) 02.03
      graft (bone) 02.04
  spermatic cord NEC 63.59
    laceration (by suture) 63.51
  sphincter ani 49.79
    laceration (by suture) 49.71
      obstetric (current) 75.62
        old 49.79
  spina bifida NEC 03.59
    meningocele 03.51
    myelomeningocele 03.52
  spinal (cord) (meninges) (structures) NEC 03.59
    meningocele 03.51
    myelomeningocele 03.52
  spleen 41.95
  sternal defect 78.41
  stoma
    bile duct 51.79
    bladder 57.22
    bronchus 33.42
    common duct 51.72
    esophagus 42.89
    gallbladder 51.99
    hepatic duct 51.79
    intestine 46.40
      large 46.43
      small 46.41
    kidney 55.89
    larynx 31.63
    rectum 48.79
    stomach 44.69
    thorax 34.79
    trachea 31.74
    ureter 56.62
    urethra 58.49
  stomach NEC 44.69
    laceration (by suture) 44.61

Repair—*continued*

stress incontinence (urinary) NEC 59.79
  by
    anterior urethropexy 59.79
    cystourethropexy (with levator muscle
        sling) 59.71
    injection of implant (collagen) (fat) (polytef)
        59.72
    paraurethral suspension (Pereyra) 59.6
    periurethral suspension 59.6
    plication of urethrovesical junction 59.3
    pubococcygeal sling 59.71
    retropubic urethral suspension 59.5
    suprapubic sling 59.4
    urethrovesical suspension 59.4
    gracilis muscle transplant 59.71
    levator muscle sling 59.71
subcutaneous tissue (plastic) (without skin
    graft) 86.89
  laceration (by suture) 86.59
supracristal defect (heart) 35.72
  with
    prosthesis 35.53
    tissue graft 35.62
symblepharon NEC 10.49
  by division (with insertion of conformer)˙ 10.5
  with free graft 10.41
syndactyly 86.85
synovial membrane, joint—*see* Arthroplasty
telecanthus 08.59
tendon 83.88
  by or with
    arthroplasty—*see* Arthroplasty
    graft or implant (tendon) 83.81
      fascia 83.82
        hand 82.72
      hand 82.79
      muscle 83.82
        hand 82.72
    suture (direct) (immediate) (primary) (*see
        also* Suture, tendon) 83.64
      hand 82.45
    transfer or transplantation (tendon) 83.75
      hand 82.56
  hand 82.86
    by
      graft or implant (tendon) 82.79
      suture (direct) (immediate) (primary) (*see
          also* Suture, tendon, hand) 82.45
      transfer or transplantation (tendon) 82.56
  rotator cuff (direct suture) 83.63
  ruptured NEC 83.88
    hand 82.86
  sheath (direct suture) 83.61
    hand 82.41
testis NEC 62.69
tetralogy of Fallot
  partial—*see* specific procedure
  total (one-stage) 35.81
thoracic duct NEC 40.69
thoracostomy 34.72
thymus (gland) 07.93
tongue NEC 25.59
tooth NEC 23.2
  by
    crown (artificial) 23.41
    filling (amalgam) (plastic) (silicate) 23.2
    inlay 23.3
total anomalous pulmonary venous
    connection
  partial—*see* specific procedure

Repair—*continued*

  total (one-stage) 35.82
trachea NEC 31.79
  laceration (by suture) 31.71
tricuspid atresia 35.94
truncus arteriosus
  partial—*see* specific procedure
  total (one-stage) 35.83
tunica vaginalis 61.49
  laceration (by suture) 61.41
tympanum—*see* Tympanoplasty
ureter NEC 56.89
  laceration (by suture) 56.82
ureterocele 56.89
urethra NEC 58.49
  laceration (by suture) 58.41
    obstetric (current) 75.61
    old 58.49
  meatus 58.47
urethrocele (anterior colporrhaphy) (female)
    70.51
  and rectocele 70.50
urinary sphincter, artificial (component) 58.99
urinary stress incontinence—*see* Repair, stress
    incontinence
uterus, uterine 69.49
  inversion—*see* Repair, inverted uterus
  laceration (by suture) 69.41
    obstetric (current) 75.50
    old 69.49
  ligaments 69.29
    by
      interposition 69.21
      plication 69.22
uvula 27.73
  with synchronous cleft palate repair 27.62
vagina, vaginal (cuff) (wall) NEC 70.79
  anterior 70.51
    with posterior repair 70.50
  cystocele 70.51
    and rectocele 70.50
  enterocele 70.92
  laceration (by suture) 70.71
    obstetric (current) 75.69
    old 70.79
  posterior 70.52
    with anterior repair 70.50
  rectocele 70.52
    and cystocele 70.50
  urethrocele 70.51
    and rectocele 70.50
varicocele 63.1
vas deferens 63.89
  by
    anastomosis 63.82
      to epididymis 63.83
    reconstruction 63.82
  laceration (by suture) 63.81
vein NEC 39.59
  with
    patch graft 39.58
      with excision or resection of vessel—*see*
          Phlebectomy, with graft replacement,
          by site
    synthetic (Dacron) (Teflon) 39.57
    tissue (vein) (autogenous) (homograft)
        39.56
  suture 39.32

Repair—*continued*
  ventricular septal defect 35.72
    with
      prosthesis 35.53
        in total repair of tetralogy of Fallot 35.81
      tissue graft 35.62
      combined with repair of valvular and atrial
        septal defects—*see* Repair, endocardial
        cushion defect
      in total repair of
        tetralogy of Fallot 35.81
        truncus arteriosus 35.83
  vertebral arch defect (spina bifida) 03.59
  vulva NEC 71.79
    laceration (by suture) 71.71
    obstetric (current) 75.69
      old 71.79
  Wirsung's duct 52.99
  wound (skin) (without graft) 86.59
    abdominal wall 54.63
      dehiscence 54.61
    postcataract dehiscence (corneal) 11.52
Replacement
  acetabulum (with prosthesis) 81.52
  ankle, total 81.56
    revision 81.59
  aortic valve (with prosthesis) 35.22
    with tissue graft 35.21
  artery—*see* Graft, artery
  bag—*see* Replacement, pack or bag
  Barton's tongs (skull) 02.94
  bladder
    with
      ileal loop 57.87 *[45.51]*
      sigmoid 57.87 *[45.52]*
    sphincter, artificial 58.93
  caliper tongs (skull) 02.94
  cannula
    arteriovenous shunt 39.94
    pancreatic duct 97.05
    vessel-to-vessel (arteriovenous) 39.94
  cardioverter/defibrillator (total system) 37.94
    leads only (electrodes) (sensing) (pacing)
      37.97
    pulse generator only 37.98
  cast NEC 97.13
    lower limb 97.12
    upper limb 97.11
  catheter
    bladder (indwelling) 57.95
    cystostomy 59.94
    ventricular shunt (cerebral) 02.42
    wound 97.15
  Crutchfield tongs (skull) 02.94
  cystostomy tube (catheter) 59.94
  diaphragm, vagina 97.24
  drain—*see also* Replacement, tube
    vagina 97.26
    vulva 97.26
    wound, musculoskeletal or skin 97.16
  ear (prosthetic) 18.71
  elbow (joint), total 81.84
  electrode(s)—*see* Implant, electrode or lead, by
    site or name of device
    brain
      depth 02.93
      foramen ovale 02.93
      sphenoidal 02.96
    depth 02.93
    foramen ovale 02.93
    sphenoidal 02.96

Replacement— *continued*
  electroencephalographic receiver (brain)
    (intracranial) 02.93
  electronic
    cardioverter/defibrillator—*see* Replacement,
      cardioverter/defibrillator
    leads (electrodes) —*see* Replacement,
      pacemaker, electrodes, cardiac
    stimulator—*see also* Implant, electronic
      stimulator, by site
      bladder 57.97
      muscle (skeletal) 83.92
      ureter 56.93
  electrostimulator—*see* Implant, electronic
    stimulator, by site
  enterostomy device (tube)
    large intestine 97.04
    small intestine 97.03
  epidural pegs 02.93
  femoral head, by prosthesis 81.52
    revision 81.53
  Gardner Wells tongs (skull) 02.94
  graft—*see* Graft
  halo traction device (skull) 02.94
  Harrington rod (with refusion of spine) 81.09
  heart
    artificial 37.63
    valve (with prosthesis) (with tissue graft)
      35.20
      aortic (with prosthesis) 35.22
        with tissue graft 35.21
      mitral (with prosthesis) 35.24
        with tissue graft 35.23
      poppet (prosthetic) 35.95
      pulmonary (with prosthesis) 35.26
        with tissue graft 35.25
        in total repair of tetralogy of Fallot 35.81
      tricuspid (with prosthesis) 35.28
        with tissue graft 35.27
  hip (partial) (with fixation device) (with
    prosthesis) (with traction) 81.52
    acetabulum 81.52
      revision 81.53
    femoral head 81.52
      revision 81.53
    total 81.51
      revision 81.53
  inverted uterus—*see* Repair, inverted uterus
  iris NEC 12.39
  kidney, mechanical 55.97
  knee, (bicompartmental) (hemijoint) (partial)
    (total) (tricompartmental)
    (unicompartmental) 81.54
    revision 81.55
  laryngeal stent 31.93
  leads (electrode) (s)—*see* Replacement,
    pacemaker, electrode(s), cardiac
  mechanical kidney 55.97
  mitral valve (with prosthesis) 35.24
    with tissue graft 35.23
  Mulligan hood, fallopian tube 66.93
  muscle stimulator (skeletal) 83.92
  nephrostomy tube 55.93
  neuropacemaker—*see* Implant,
    neuropacemaker, by site
  neurostimulator—*see also* Implant,
    neurostimulator, by site
    peripheral nerve 04.92
    skeletal muscle 83.92

Replacement—*continued*
  pacemaker
    brain 02.93
    cardiac device (initial) (permanent)
      dual-chamber device 37.87
      single-chamber device 37.85
      rate responsive 37.86
    electrode(s), cardiac (atrial) (transvenous)
      (ventricular) 37.76
      epicardium (myocardium) 37.74
    intracranial 02.93
    neural
      brain 02.93
      intracranial 02.93
      peripheral nerve 04.92
      spine 03.93
    spine 03.93
    temporary transvenous pacemaker system
      37.78
  pack or bag
    nose 97.21
    teeth, tooth 97.22
    vagina 97.26
    vulva 97.26
    wound 97.16
  pessary, vagina NEC 97.25
  prosthesis
    acetabulum 81.53
    arm (bioelectric) (cineplastic) (kineplastic)
      84.44
    biliary tract 51.99
    cochlear 20.96
    channel (single) 20.97
      multiple 20.98
    elbow 81.97
    extremity (bioelectric) (cineplastic)
      (kineplastic) 84.40
      lower 84.48
      upper 84.44
    fallopian tube (Mulligan hood) (stent) 66.93
    femur 81.53
    knee 81.55
    leg (bioelectric) (cineplastic) (kineplastic)
      84.48
    penis (non-inflatable) (internal) 64.95
      inflatable (internal) 64.97
    shoulder NEC 81.83
      partial 81.81
      total 81.80
    urinary sphincter, artificial 58.93
  pulmonary valve (with prosthesis) 35.26
    with tissue graft 35.25
    in total repair tetrology of Fallot 35.81
  pyelostomy tube 55.94
  rectal tube 96.09
  shoulder NEC 81.83
    partial 81.81
    total 81.80
  skull
    plate 02.05
    tongs 02.94
  specified appliance or device NEC 97.29
  stent
    bile duct 97.05
    fallopian tube 66.93
    larynx 31.93
    pancreatic duct 97.05
    trachea 31.93
  stimoceiver—*see* Implant, stimoceiver, by site

Replacement—*continued*
  subdural
    grids 02.93
    strips 02.93
  testis in scrotum 62.5
  tongs, skull 02.94
  tracheal stent 31.93
  tricuspid valve (with prosthesis) 35.28
    with tissue graft 35.27
  tube
    bile duct 97.05
    bladder 57.95
    cystostomy 59.94
    esophagostomy 97.01
    gastrostomy 97.02
    large intestine 97.04
    nasogastric 97.01
    nephrostomy 55.93
    pancreatic duct 97.05
    pyelostomy 55.94
    rectal 96.09
    small intestine 97.03
    tracheostomy 97.23
    ureterostomy 59.93
    ventricular (cerebral) 02.42
  umbilical cord, prolapsed 73.92
  ureter (with)
    bladder flap 56.74
    ileal segment implanted into bladder 56.89
      [45.51]
  ureterostomy tube 59.93
  urethral sphincter, artificial 58.93
  urinary sphincter, artificial 58.93
  valve
    heart—*see also* Replacement, heart valve
      poppet (prosthetic) 35.95
    ventricular (cerebral) 02.42
  ventricular shunt (catheter) (valve) 02.42
  Vinke tongs (skull) 02.94
  vitreous (silicone) 14.75
    for retinal reattachment 14.59
Replant, replantation —*see also* Reattachment
  extremity—*see* Reattachment, extremity
  penis 64.45
  scalp, 86.51
  tooth 23.5
Reposition
  cardiac pacemaker
    electrode(s) (atrial) (transvenous) (ventricular)
      37.75
    pocket 37.79
  cardioverter/defibrillator
    lead(s) (sensing) (pacing) (epicardial patch)
      37.99
    pocket 37.99
    pulse generator 37.99
  cilia base 08.71
  iris 12.39
  renal vessel, aberrant 39.55
  thyroid tissue 06.94
  tricuspid valve (with plication) 35.14
Resection —*see also* Excision, by site
  abdominoendorectal (combined) 48.5
  abdominoperineal (rectum) 48.5
    pull-through (Altmeier) (Swenson) NEC 48.49
      Duhamel type 48.65
  alveolar process and palate (en bloc) 27.32
  aneurysm—*see* Aneurysmectomy
  aortic valve (for subvalvular stenosis) 35.11
  artery—*see* Arteriectomy

Resection—*continued*
bile duct NEC 51.69
  common duct NEC 51.63
bladder (partial) (segmental) (transvesical)
  (wedge) 57.6
  complete or total 57.79
  lesion NEC 57.59
    transurethral approach 57.49
  neck 57.59
    transurethral approach 57.49
blood vessel—*see* Angiectomy
brain 01.59
  by
    stereotactic radiosurgery 92.3
  hemisphere 01.52
  lobe 01.53
breast—*see also* Mastectomy
  quadrant 85.22
  segmental 85.23
broad ligament 69.19
bronchus (sleeve) (wide sleeve) 32.1
block (en bloc) (with radical dissection of
  brachial plexus, bronchus, lobe of lung, ribs,
  and sympathetic nerves) 32.6
bursa 83.5
  hand 82.31
cecum (and terminal ileum) 45.72
cerebral meninges 01.51
chest wall 34.4
clavicle 77.81
clitoris 71.4
colon (partial) (segmental) 45.79
  ascending (cecum and terminal ileum) 45.72
  cecum (and terminal ileum) 45.72
  complete 45.8
  descending (sigmoid) 45.76
  for interposition 45.52
  Hartmann 45.75
  hepatic flexure 45.73
  left radical (hemicolon) 45.75
  multiple segmental 45.71
  right radical (hemicolon) (ileocolectomy)
    45.73
  segmental NEC 45.79
    multiple 45.71
  sigmoid 45.76
  splenic flexure 45.75
  total 45.8
  transverse 45.74
conjunctiva, for pterygium 11.39
  corneal graft 11.32
cornual (fallopian tube) (unilateral) 66.69
  bilateral 66.63
diaphragm 34.81
endaural 20.79
endorectal (pull-through) (Soave) 48.41
  combined abdominal 48.5
esophagus (partial) (subtotal) (*see also*
  Esophagectomy) 42.41
  total 42.42
exteriorized intestine—*see* Resection, intestine,
  exteriorized
fascia 83.44
  for graft 83.43
    hand 82.34
  hand 82.35
    for graft 82.34
gallbladder (total) 51.22
gastric (partial) (sleeve) (subtotal) NEC (*see*
  also Gastrectomy) 43.89
  with anastomosis NEC 43.89

Resection—*continued*
  esophagogastric 43.5
  gastroduodenal 43.6
  gastrogastric 43.89
  gastrojejunal 43.7
  complete or total NEC 43.99
    with intestinal interposition 43.91
  radical NEC 43.99
    with intestinal interposition 43.91
  wedge 43.42
  endoscopic 43.41
hallux valgus (joint)—*see also* Bunionectomy
  with prosthetic implant 77.59
hepatic
  duct 51.69
  flexure (colon) 45.73
infundibula, heart (right) 35.34
intestine (partial) NEC 45.79
  cecum (with terminal ileum) 45.72
  exteriorized (large intestine) 46.04
    small intestine 46.02
  for interposition 45.50
    large intestine 45.52
    small intestine 45.51
  hepatic flexure 45.73
  ileum 45.62
    with cecum 45.72
  large (partial) (segmental) NEC 45.79
    for interposition 45.52
    multiple segmental 45.71
    total 45.8
  left hemicolon 45.75
  multiple segmental (large intestine) 45.71
    small intestine 45.61
  right hemicolon 45.73
  segmental (large intestine) 45.79
    multiple 45.71
    small intestine 45.62
      multiple 45.61
  sigmoid 45.76
  small (partial) (segmental) NEC 45.62
    for interposition 45.51
    multiple segmental 45.61
    total 45.63
  total
    large intestine 45.8
    small intestine 45.63
joint structure NEC (*see also* Arthrectomy)
  80.90
kidney (segmental) (wedge) 55.4
larynx—*see also* Laryngectomy
  submucous 30.29
lesion—*see* Excision, lesion, by site
levator palpebrae muscle 08.33
ligament (*see also* Arthrectomy) 80.90
  broad 69.19
  round 69.19
  uterine 69.19
lip (wedge) 27.43
liver (partial) (wedge) 50.22
  lobe (total) 50.3
  total 50.4
lung (wedge) NEC 32.29
  endoscopic 32.28
  segmental (any part) 32.3
  volume reduction 32.22
meninges (cerebral) 01.51
  spinal 03.4
mesentery 54.4

Resection—*continued*
muscle 83.45
  extraocular 15.13
    with
      advancement or recession of other eye
        muscle 15.3
      suture of original insertion 15.13
    levator palpebrae 08.33
    Müller's for blepharoptosis 08.35
    orbicularis oculi 08.20
    tarsal, for blepharoptosis 08.35
    for graft 83.43
      hand 82.34
    hand 82.36
      for graft 82.34
    ocular—*see* Resection, muscle, extraocular
myocardium 37.33
nasal septum (submucous) 21.5
nerve (cranial) (peripheral) NEC 04.07
  phrenic 04.03
    for collapse of lung 33.31
  sympathetic 05.29
  vagus—*see* Vagotomy
nose (complete) (extended) (partial)
    (radical) 21.4
omentum 54.4
orbitomaxillary, radical 16.51
ovary—(*see also* Oophorectomy
  wedge 65.22
    laparoscopic 65.24
palate (bony) (local) 27.31
  by wide excision 27.32
  soft 27.49
pancreas (total) (with synchronous
    duodenectomy) 52.6
  partial NEC 52.59
    distal (tail) (with part of body) 52.52
    proximal (head) (with part or body) (with
      synchronous duodenectomy) 52.51
    radical subtotal 52.53
  radical (one-stage) (two-stage) 52.7
  subtotal 52.53
pancreaticoduodenal (*see also* Pancreatectomy)
    52.6
pelvic viscera (en masse) (female) 68.8
  male 57.71
penis 64.3
pericardium (partial) (for)
  chronic constrictive pericarditis 37.31
  drainage 37.12
  removal of adhesions 37.31
peritoneum 54.4
pharynx (partial) 29.33
phrenic nerve 04.03
  for collapse of lung 33.31
prostate—*see also* Prostatectomy
  transurethral (punch) 60.29
pterygium 11.39
radial head 77.83
rectosigmoid (*see also* Resection, rectum) 48.69
rectum (partial) NEC 48.69
  with
    pelvic exenteration 68.8
    transsacral sigmoidectomy 48.61
  abdominoendorectal (combined) 48.5
  abdominoperineal 48.5
    pull-through NEC 48.49
      Duhamel type 48.65
  anterior 48.63
    with colostomy (synchronous) 48.62
  Duhamel 48.65

Resection—*continued*
  endorectal 48.41
    combined abdominal 48.5
  posterior 48.64
  pull-through NEC 48.49
    endorectal 48.41
  submucosal (Soave) 48.41
    combined abdominal 48.5
rib (transaxillary) 77.91
  as operative approach—*omit code*
  incidental to thoracic operation—*omit code*
right ventricle (heart), for infundibular
    stenosis 35.34
root (tooth) (apex) 23.73
  with root canal therapy 23.72
  residual or retained 23.11
round ligament 69.19
sclera 12.65
  with scleral buckling (*see also* Buckling,
    scleral) 14.49
  lamellar (for retinal reattachment) 14.49
    with implant 14.41
scrotum 61.3
soft tissue NEC 83.49
  hand 82.39
sphincter of Oddi 51.89
spinal cord (meninges) 03.4
splanchnic 05.29
splenic flexure (colon) 45.75
sternum 77.81
stomach (partial) (sleeve) (subtotal) NEC (*see
    also* Gastrectomy) 43.89
  with anastomosis NEC 43.89
    esophagogastric 43.5
    gastroduodenal 43.6
    gastrogastric 43.89
    gastrojejunal 43.7
  complete or total NEC 43.99
    with intestinal interposition 43.91
  fundus 43.89
  radical NEC 43.99
    with intestinal interposition 43.91
  wedge 43.42
    endoscopic 43.41
submucous
  larynx 30.29
  nasal septum 21.5
  vocal cords 30.22
synovial membrane (complete) (partial) (*see
    also* Synovectomy) 80.70
tarsolevator 08.33
tendon 83.42
  hand 82.33
thoracic structures (block) (en bloc) (radical)
    (brachial plexus, bronchus, lobes of lung,
    ribs, and sympathetic nerves) 32.6
thorax 34.4
tongue 25.2
  wedge 25.1
tooth root 23.73
  with root canal therapy 23.72
  apex (abscess) 23.73
    with root canal therapy 23.72
  residual or retained 23.11
trachea 31.5
transurethral
  bladder NEC 57.49
  prostate 60.29
transverse colon 45.74
turbinates—*see* Turbinectomy

Resection—*continued*
ureter (partial) 56.41
total 56.42
uterus—*see* Hysterectomy
vein—*see* Phlebectomy
ventricle (heart) (left) 35.34
vesical neck 57.59
transurethral 57.49
vocal cords (punch) 30.22
Respirator, volume-controlled (Bennett)
(Byrd)—*see* Ventilation
Restoration
cardioesophageal angle 44.66
dental NEC 23.49
by
application of crown (artificial) 23.41
insertion of bridge (fixed) 23.42
removable 23.43
extremity—*see* Reattachment, extremity
eyebrow 08.70
with graft 08.63
eye socket 16.64
with graft 16.63
tooth NEC 23.2
by
crown (artificial) 23.41
filling (amalgam) (plastic) (silicate) 23.2
inlay 23.3
Resuscitation
artificial respiration 93.93
cardiac 99.60
cardioversion 99.62
atrial 99.61
defibrillation 99.62
external massage 99.63
open chest 37.91
intracardiac injection 37.92
cardiopulmonary 99.60
endotracheal intubation 96.04
manual 93.93
mouth-to-mouth 93.93
pulmonary 93.93
Resuture
abdominal wall 54.61
cardiac septum prosthesis 35.95
chest wall 34.71
heart valve prosthesis (poppet) 35.95
wound (skin and subcutaneous tissue) (without
graft) NEC 86.59
Retinaculotomy NEC (*see also* Division,
ligament) 80.40
carpal tunnel (flexor) 04.43
Retraining
cardiac 93.36
vocational 93.85
Retrogasserian neurotomy 04.02
Revascularization
cardiac (heart muscle) (myocardium) (direct)
36.10
with
bypass anastomosis
abdominal artery to coronary artery 36.17
aortocoronary (catheter stent) (homograft)
(prosthesis) (saphenous vein graft)
36.10
one coronary vessel 36.11
two coronary vessels 36.12
three coronary vessels 36.13
four coronary vessels 36.14
gastroepiploic artery to coronary artery
36.17

Revascularization—*continued*
internal mammary-coronary artery (single
vessel) 36.15
double vessel 36.16
radial artery 36.19
specified type NEC 36.19
thoracic artery-coronary artery (single
vessel) 36.15
double vessel 36.16
implantation of artery into heart (muscle)
(myocardium) (ventricle) 36.2
indirect 36.2
specified type NEC 36.3
Reversal, intestinal segment 45.50
large 45.52
small 45.51
Revision
amputation stump 84.3
current traumatic—*see* Amputation
anastomosis
biliary tract 51.94
blood vessel 39.49
gastric, gastrointestinal (with jejunal
interposition) 44.5
intestine (large) 46.94
small 46.93
pleurothecal 03.97
pyelointestinal 56.72
salpingothecal 03.97
subarachnoid-peritoneal 03.97
subarachnoid-ureteral 03.97
ureterointestinal 56.72
ankle replacement (prosthesis) 81.59
anterior segment (eye) wound (operative) NEC
12.83
arteriovenous shunt (cannula) (for dialysis)
39.42
arthroplasty—*see* Arthroplasty
bone flap, skull 02.06
breast implant 85.93
bronchostomy 33.42
cannula, vessel-to-vessel (arteriovenous) 39.94
canthus, lateral 08.59
cardiac pacemaker
device (permanent) 37.89
electrode(s) (atrial) (transvenous) (ventricular)
37.75
pocket 37.79
cardioverter/defibrillator (automatic) pocket
37.99
cholecystostomy 51.99
cleft palate repair 27.63
colostomy 46.43
conduit, urinary 56.52
cystostomy (stoma) 57.22
elbow replacement (prosthesis) 81.97
enterostomy (stoma) 46.40
large intestine 46.43
small intestine 46.41
enucleation socket 16.64
with graft 16.63
esophagostomy 42.83
exenteration cavity 16.66
with secondary graft 16.65
extraocular muscle surgery 15.6
fenestration, inner ear 20.62
filtering bleb 12.66
fixation device (broken) (displaced) (*see also*
Fixation, bone, internal) 78.50
flap or pedicle graft (skin) 86.75
foot replacement (prosthesis) 81.59

Revision—*continued*
gastric anastomosis (with jejunal interposition) 44.5
gastroduodenostomy (with jejunal interposition) 44.5
gastrointestinal anastomosis (with jejunal interposition) 44.5
gastrojejunostomy 44.5
gastrostomy 44.69
hand replacement (prosthesis) 81.97
heart procedure NEC 35.95
hip replacement (acetabulum) (femoral head) (partial) (total) 81.53
Holter (Spitz) valve 02.42
ileal conduit 56.52
ileostomy 46.41
jejunoileal bypass 46.93
jejunostomy 46.41
joint replacement 81.59
    acetabulum 81.53
    ankle 81.59
    elbow 81.97
    femoral head 81.53
    foot 81.59
    hand 81.97
    hip (partial) (total) 81.53
    knee 81.55
    lower extremity NEC 81.59
    toe 81.59
    upper extremity 81.97
    wrist 81.97
knee replacement (prosthesis) 81.55
laryngostomy 31.63
lateral canthus 08.59
mallet finger 82.84
mastoid antrum 19.9
mastoidectomy 20.92
nephrostomy 55.89
neuroplasty 04.75
ocular implant 16.62
orbital implant 16.62
previous mastectomy site—*see categories* 85.0-85.99
proctostomy 48.79
prosthesis
    acetabulum
        hip 81.53
    ankle 81.59
    breast 85.93
    elbow 81.97
    femoral head 81.53
    foot 81.59
    hand 81.97
    heart valve (poppet) 35.95
    hip (partial) (total) 81.53
    knee 81.55
    lower extremity NEC 81.59
    shoulder 81.97
    toe 81.59
    upper extremity 81.97
    wrist 81.97
ptosis overcorrection 08.37
pyelostomy 55.12
pyloroplasty 44.29
rhinoplasty 21.84
scar
    skin 86.84
        with excision 86.3
scleral fistulization 12.66
shoulder replacement (prosthesis) 81.97

Revision—*continued*
shunt
    arteriovenous (cannula) (for dialysis) 39.42
    lumbar-subarachnoid NEC 03.97
    peritoneojugular 54.99
    pleurothecal 03.97
    salpingothecal 03.97
    spinal (thecal) NEC 03.97
    subarachnoid-peritoneal 03.97
    subarachnoid-ureteral 03.97
    ventricular (cerebral) 02.42
    ventriculoperitoneal
        at peritoneal site 54.95
        at ventricular site 02.42
stapedectomy NEC 19.29
    with incus replacement (homograft) (prosthesis) 19.21
stoma
    bile duct 51.79
    bladder (vesicostomy) 57.22
    bronchus 33.42
    common duct 51.72
    esophagus 42.89
    gallbladder 51.99
    hepatic duct 51.79
    intestine 46.40
        large 46.43
        small 46.41
    kidney 55.89
    larynx 31.63
    rectum 48.79
    stomach 44.69
    thorax 34.79
    trachea 31.74
    ureter 56.62
    urethra 58.4
tack operation 20.79
toe replacement (prosthesis) 81.59
tracheostomy 31.74
tympanoplasty 19.6
uretero-ileostomy, cutaneous 56.52
ureterostomy (cutaneous) (stoma) NEC 56.62
    ileal 56.52
urethrostomy 58.49
urinary conduit 56.52
vascular procedure (previous) NEC 39.49
ventricular shunt (cerebral) 02.42
vesicostomy stoma 57.22
wrist replacement (prosthesis) 81.97
Rhinectomy 21.4
Rhinocheiloplasty 27.59
    cleft lip 27.54
Rhinomanometry 89.12
Rhinoplasty (external) (internal) NEC 21.87
    augmentation (with graft) (with synthetic implant) 21.85
    limited 21.86
    revision 21.84
    tip 21.86
    twisted nose 21.84
Rhinorrhaphy (external) (internal) 21.81
    for epistaxis 21.09
Rhinoscopy 21.21
Rhinoseptoplasty 21.84
Rhinotomy 21.1
Rhizotomy (radio frequency) (spinal) 03.1
    acoustic 04.01
    trigeminal 04.02
Rhytidectomy (facial) 86.82
    eyelid
        lower 08.86
        upper 08.87

Rhytidoplasty (facial) 86.82
Ripstein operation (repair of prolapsed rectum)
    48.75
Rodney Smith operation (radical subtotal
    pancreatectomy) 52.53
Roentgenography —*see also* Radiography
    cardiac, negative contrast 88.58
Rolling of conjunctiva 10.33
Root
    canal (tooth) (therapy) 23.70
        with
            apicoectomy 23.72
            irrigation 23.71
    resection (tooth) (apex) 23.73
        with root canal therapy 23.72
        residual or retained 23.11
Rotation of fetal head
    forceps (instrumental) (Kielland) (Scanzoni)
        (key-in-lock) 72.4
    manual 73.51
Routine
    chest x-ray 87.44
    psychiatric visit 94.12
Roux-en-Y operation
    bile duct 51.36
    cholecystojejunostomy 51.32
    esophagus (intrathoracic) 42.54
    pancreaticojejunostomy 52.96
Roux-Goldthwait operation (repair of recurrent
    patellar dislocation) 81.44
Roux-Herzen-Judine operation (jejunal loop
    interposition) 42.63
Rubin test (insufflation of fallopian tube) 66.8
Ruiz-Mora operation (proximal phalangectomy
    for hammer toe) 77.99
Rupture
    esophageal web 42.01
    joint adhesions, manual 93.26
    membranes, artificial 73.09
        for surgical induction of labor 73.01
    ovarian cyst, manual 65.93
Russe operation (bone graft of scaphoid) 78.04

S

Sacculotomy (lack) 20.79
Sacrectomy (partial) 77.89
  total 77.99
Saemisch operation (corneal section) 11.1
Salpingectomy (bilateral) (total) (transvaginal)
  66.51
  with oophorectomy 65.61
    laparoscopic 65.63
  partial (unilateral) 66.69
    with removal of tubal pregnancy 66.62
    bilateral 66.63
      for sterilization 66.39
      by endoscopy 66.29
  remaining or solitary tube 66.52
    with ovary 65.62
      laparoscopic 65.64
  unilateral (total) 66.4
    with
      oophorectomy 65.49
        laparoscopic 65.41
      removal of tubal pregnancy 66.62
      partial 66.69
Salpingography 87.85
Salpingohysterostomy 66.74
Salpingo-oophorectomy (unilateral) 65.49
  that by laparoscope 65.41
  bilateral (same operative episode) 65.61
    laparoscopic 65.63
  remaining or solitary tube and ovary 65.62
    laparoscopic 65.64
Salpingo-oophoroplasty 65.73
  laparoscopic 65.76
Salpingo-oophororrhaphy 65.79
Salpingo-oophorostomy 66.72
Salpingo-oophorotomy 65.09
  laparoscopic 65.01
Salpingoplasty 66.79
Salpingorrhaphy 66.71
Salpingosalpingostomy 66.73
Salpingostomy (for removal of non-ruptured
  ectopic pregnancy) 66.02
Salpingotomy 66.01
Salpingo-uterostomy 66.74
Salter operation (innominate osteotomy) 77.39
Salvage (autologous blood) (intraoperative)
  (perioperative) (postoperative) 99.00
Sampling, blood for genetic determination of
  fetus 75.33
Sandpapering (skin) 86.25
Saucerization
  bone (see also Excision, lesion, bone) 77.60
  rectum 48.99
Sauer-Bacon operation (abdominoperineal
  resection) 48.5
Scalenectomy 83.45
Scalenotomy 83.19
Scaling and polishing, dental 96.54
Scan, scanning
  C.A.T. (computerized axial tomography) 88.38
    abdomen 88.01
    bone 88.38
      mineral density 88.98
    brain 87.03
    head 87.03
    kidney 87.71
    skeletal 88.38
      mineral density 88.98
    thorax 87.41

Scan, scanning—continued
  computerized axial tomography (C.A.T.) (see
    also Scan, C.A.T.) 88.38
  C.T.—see Scan, C.A.T.
  gallium—see Scan, radioisotope
  liver 92.02
  positron emission tomography (PET)—see
    Scan, radioisotope
  radioisotope
    adrenal 92.09
    bone 92.14
      marrow 92.05
    bowel 92.04
    cardiac output 92.05
    cardiovascular 92.05
    cerebral 92.11
    circulation time 92.05
    eye 95.16
    gastrointestinal 92.04
    head NEC 92.12
    hematopoietic 92.05
    intestine 92.04
    iodine-131 92.01
    kidney 92.03
    liver 92.02
    lung 92.15
    lymphatic system 92.16
    myocardial infarction 92.05
    pancreatic 92.04
    parathyroid 92.13
    pituitary 92.11
    placenta 92.17
    protein-bound iodine 92.01
    pulmonary 92.15
    radio-iodine uptake 92.01
    renal 92.03
    specified site NEC 92.19
    spleen 92.05
    thyroid 92.01
    total body 92.18
    uterus 92.19
  renal 92.03
  thermal—see Thermography
Scapulectomy (partial) 77.81
  total 77.91
Scapulopexy 78.41
Scarification
  conjunctiva 10.33
  nasal veins (with packing) 21.03
  pericardium 36.3
  pleura 34.6
    chemical 34.92
      with cancer chemotherapy substance 34.92
        [99.25]
    tetracycline 34.92 [99.21]
Schanz operation (femoral osteotomy) 77.35
Schauta (Amreich) operation (radical vaginal
  hysterectomy) 68.7
Schede operation (thoracoplasty) 33.34
Scheie operation
  cautery of sclera 12.62
  sclerostomy 12.62
Schlatter operation (total gastrectomy) 43.99
Schroeder operation (endocervical excision)
  67.39
Schuchardt operation (nonobstetrical
  episiotomy) 71.09
Schwartze operation (simple mastoidectomy)
  20.41

Splinting
dental (for immobilization) 93.55
 orthodontic 24.7
musculoskeletal 93.54
ureteral 56.2
Splitting —*see also* Division
canaliculus 09.52
lacrimal papilla 09.51
spinal cord tracts 03.29
 percutaneous 03.21
tendon sheath 83.01
 hand 82.01
Spondylosyndesis (*see also* Fusion, spinal) 81.00
S.P. Rogers operation (knee disarticulation) 84.16
Ssabanejew-Frank operation (permanent gastrostomy) 43.19
Stab, intercostal 34.09
Stabilization, joint —*see also* Arthrodesis
patella (for recurrent dislocation) 81.44
Stacke operation (simple mastoidectomy) 20.41
Stallard operation
 (conjunctivocystorhinostomy) 09.82
with insertion of tube or stent 09.83
Stamm (Kader) operation (temporary gastrostomy) 43.19
Stapedectomy 19.19
with incus replacement (homograft) (prosthesis) 19.11
revision 19.29
 with incus replacement 19.21
Stapediolysis 19.0
Stapling
artery 39.31
blebs, lung (emphysematous) 32.21
diaphysis (*see also* Stapling, epiphyseal plate) 78.20
epiphyseal plate 78.20
 femur 78.25
 fibula 78.27
 humerus 78.22
 radius 78.23
 specified site NEC 78.29
 tibia 78.27
 ulna 78.23
gastric varices 44.91
graft—*see* Graft
vein 39.32
Steinberg operation 44.5
Steindler operation
fascia stripping (for cavus deformity) 83.14
flexorplasty (elbow) 83.77
muscle transfer 83.77
Stereotactic head frame application 93.59
Stereotactic radiosurgery 92.3
Sterilization
female (*see also* specific operation) 66.39
male NEC (*see also* Ligation, vas deferens) 63.70
Sternotomy 77.31
as operative approach—*omit code*
for bone marrow biopsy 41.31
Stewart operation (renal plication with pyeloplasty) 55.87
Stimulation (electronic) —*see also* Implant, electronic stimulator
bone growth (percutaneous)—*see category* 78.9
 transcutaneous (surface) 99.86
cardiac (external) 99.62
 internal 37.91
carotid sinus 99.64

Stimulation (electronic)— *continued*
electrophysiologic, cardiac 37.26
nerve, peripheral or spinal cord, transcutaneous 93.39
Stitch, Kelly-Stoeckel (urethra) 59.3
Stomatoplasty 27.59
Stomatorrhaphy 27.52
Stone operation (anoplasty) 49.79
Strassman operation (metroplasty) 69.49
Strayer operation (gastrocnemius recession) 83.72
Stretching
eyelid (with elongation) 08.71
fascia 93.28
foreskin 99.95
iris 12.63
muscle 93.27
nerve (cranial) (peripheral) 04.91
tendon 93.27
Stripping
bone (*see also* Incision, bone) 77.10
carotid sinus 39.8
cranial suture 02.01
fascia 83.14
 hand 82.12
membranes for surgical induction of labor 73.1
meninges (cerebral) 01.51
 spinal 03.4
saphenous vein, varicose 38.59
subdural membrane (cerebral) 01.51
 spinal 03.4
varicose veins (lower limb) 38.59
 upper limb 38.53
vocal cords 30.09
Stromeyer-Little operation (hepatotomy) 50.0
Strong operation (unbridling of celiac artery axis) 39.91
Stryker frame 93.59
Study
bone mineral density 88.98
bundle of His 37.29
color vision 95.06
conduction, nerve (median) 89.15
dark adaptation, eye 95.07
electrophysiologic stimulation and recording, cardiac 37.26
function—*see also* Function, study
 radioisotope—*see* Scan, radioisotope
lacrimal flow (radiographic) 87.05
ocular motility 95.15
pulmonary function—*see categories* 89.37-89.38
radiographic—*see* Radiography
radio-iodinated triolein 92.04
renal clearance 92.03
spirometer 89.37
tracer—*see also* Scan, radioisotope
 eye (P^{32}) 95.16
ultrasonic—*see* Ultrasonography
visual field 95.05
xenon flow NEC 92.19
 cardiovascular 92.05
 pulmonary 92.15
Sturmdorf operation (conization of cervix) 67.2
Submucous resection
larynx 30.29
nasal septum 21.5
Summerskill operation
 (dacryocystorhinostomy by intubation) 09.81
Surmay operation (jejunostomy) 46.39

Suture—*continued*
  sphincter ani 75.62
  urethra 75.61
  uterus 75.50
  vagina 75.69
  vulva 75.69
  omentum 54.64
  ovary 65.71
    laparoscopic 65.74
  palate 27.61
    cleft 27.62
  palpebral fissure 08.59
  pancreas 52.95
  pelvic floor 71.71
    obstetric laceration (current) 75.69
  penis 64.41
  peptic ulcer (bleeding) (perforated) 44.40
  pericardium 37.4
  perineum (female) 71.71
    after delivery 75.69
      episiotomy repair—*see* Episiotomy
    male 86.59
  periosteum 78.20
    carpal, metacarpal 78.24
    femur 78.25
    fibula 78.27
    humerus 78.22
    pelvic 78.29
    phalanxes (foot) (hand) 78.29
    radius 78.23
    specified site NEC 78.29
    tarsal metatarsal 78.28
    tibia 78.27
    ulna 78.23
    vertebrae 78.29
  peritoneum 54.64
  periurethral tissue to symphysis pubis 59.5
  pharynx 29.51
  pleura 34.93
  rectum 48.71
    obstetric laceration (current) 75.62
  retina (for reattachment) 14.59
  sacrouterine ligament 69.29
  salivary gland 26.41
  scalp 86.59
    replantation 86.51
  sclera (with repair of conjunctive) 12.81
  scrotum (skin) 61.41
  secondary
    abdominal wall 54.61
    episiotomy 75.69
    peritoneum 54.64
  sigmoid 46.75
  skin (mucous membrane) (without graft) 86.59
    with graft—*see* Graft, skin
    breast 85.81
    ear 18.4
    eyebrow 08.81
    eyelid 08.81
    nose 21.81
    penis 64.41
    scalp 86.59
      replantation 86.51
    scrotum 61.41
    vulva 71.71
    specified site NEC—*see* Repair, by site
  spermatic cord 63.51
  sphincter ani 49.71
    obstetric laceration (current) 75.62
    old 49.79
  spinal meninges 03.59

Suture—*continued*
  spleen 41.95
  stomach 44.61
    ulcer (bleeding) (perforated) 44.41
      endoscopic 44.43
  subcutaneous tissue (without skin graft) 86.59
    with graft—*see* Graft, skin
  tendon (direct) (immediate) (primary) 83.64
    delayed (secondary) 83.62
      hand NEC 82.43
      flexors 82.42
    hand NEC 82.45
      delayed (secondary) 82.43
      flexors 82.44
      delayed (secondary) 82.42
    ocular 15.7
    rotator cuff 83.63
    sheath 83.61
      hand 82.41
    supraspinatus (rotator cuff repair) 83.63
    to skeletal attachment 83.88
      hand 82.85
  Tenon's capsule 15.7
  testis 62.61
  thymus 07.93
  thyroid gland 06.93
  tongue 25.51
  tonsillar fossa 28.7
  trachea 31.71
  tunics vaginalis 61.41
  ulcer (bleeding) (perforated) (peptic) 44.40
    duodenum 44.42
      endoscopic 44.43
    gastric 44.41
      endoscopic 44.43
    intestine 46.79
    skin 86.59
    stomach 44.41
      endoscopic 44.43
  ureter 56.82
  urethra 58.41
    obstetric laceration (current) 75.61
  uterosacral ligament 69.29
  uterus 69.41
    obstetric laceration (current) 75.50
    old 69.49
  uvula 27.73
  vagina 70.71
    obstetric laceration (current) 75.69
    old 70.79
  vas deferens 63.81
  vein 39.32
  vulva 71.71
    obstetric laceration (current) 75.69
    old 71.79
Suture-ligation —*see also* Ligation
  blood vessel—*see* Ligation, blood vessel
Sweep, anterior iris 12.97
Swenson operation
  bladder reconstruction 57.87
  proctectomy 48.49
Swinney operation (urethral reconstruction) 58.46
Switch, switching
  coronary arteries 35.84
  great arteries, total 35.84
Syme operation
  ankle amputation through malleoli of tibia and fibula 84.14
  urethrotomy, external 58.0

Sympathectomy NEC 05.29
  cervical 05.22
  cervicothoracic 05.22
  lumbar 05.23
  periarterial 05.25
  presacral 05.24
  renal 05.29
  thoracolumbar 05.23
  tympanum 20.91
Sympatheticotripsy 05.0
Symphysiotomy 77.39
  assisting delivery (obstetrical) 73.94
  kidney (horseshoe) 55.85
Symphysis, pleural 34.6
Synchondrotomy (*see also* Division, cartilage)
  80.40
Syndactylization 86.89
Syndesmotomy (*see also* Division, ligament)
  80.40
Synechiotomy
  endometrium 68.21
  iris (posterior) 12.33
    anterior 12.32
Synovectomy (joint) (complete) (partial) 80.70
  ankle 80.77
  elbow 80.72
  foot and toe 80.78
  hand and finger 80.74
  hip 80.75
  knee 80.76
  shoulder 80.71
  specified site NEC 80.79
  spine 80.79
  tendon sheath 83.42
    hand 82.33
  wrist 80.73
Syringing
  lacrimal duct or sac 09.43
  nasolacrimal duct 09.43
    with
      dilation 09.43
      insertion of tube or stent 09.44

T

Taarnhoj operation (trigeminal nerve root decompression) 04.41
Tack operation (sacculotomy) 20.79
Take-down
  anastomosis
    arterial 39.49
    blood vessel 39.49
    gastric, gastrointestinal 44.5
    intestine 46.93
    stomach 44.5
    vascular 39.49
    ventricular 02.43
  arterial bypass 39.49
  arteriovenous shunt 39.43
    with creation of new shunt 39.42
  cecostomy 46.52
  colostomy 46.52
  duodenostomy 46.51
  enterostomy 46.50
  esophagostomy 42.83
  gastroduodenostomy 44.5
  gastrojejunostomy 44.5
  ileostomy 46.51
  intestinal stoma 46.50
    large 46.52
    small 46.51
  jejunoileal bypass 46.93
  jejunostomy 46.51
  laryngostomy 31.62
  sigmoidostomy 46.52
  stoma
    bile duct 51.79
    bladder 57.82
    bronchus 33.42
    common duct 51.72
    esophagus 42.83
    gall bladder 51.92
    hepatic duct 51.79
    intestine 46.50
      large 46.52
      small 46.51
    kidney 55.82
    larynx 31.62
    rectum 48.72
    stomach 44.62
    thorax 34.72
    trachea 31.72
    ureter 56.83
    urethra 58.42
  systemic-pulmonary artery anastomosis 39.49
    in total repair of tetralogy of Fallot 35.81
  tracheostomy 31.72
  vascular anastomosis or bypass 39.49
  ventricular shunt (cerebral) 02.43
Talectomy 77.98
Talma-Morison operation (omentopexy) 54.74
Tamponade
  esophageal 96.06
  intrauterine (nonobstetric) 69.91
    after delivery or abortion 75.8
    antepartum 73.1
  vagina 96.14
    after delivery or abortion 75.8
    antepartum 73.1
Tanner operation (devascularization of stomach) 44.99

Tap
  abdomen 54.91
  chest 34.91
  cisternal 01.01
  crania] 01.09
  joint 81.91
  lumbar (diagnostic) (removal of dye) 03.31
  perilymphatic 20.79
  spinal (diagnostic) 03.31
  subdural (through fontanel) 01.09
  thorax 34.91
Tarsectomy 08.20
  de Grandmont 08.35
Tarsoplasty (*see also* Reconstruction, eyelid) 08.70
Tarsorrhaphy (lateral) 08.52
  division or severing 08.02
Tattooing
  cornea 11.91
  skin 86.02
Tautening, eyelid for entropion 08.42
Telemetry (cardiac) 89.54
Teleradiotherapy
  beta particles 92.25
  Betatron 92.24
  cobalt-60 92.23
  electrons 92.25
  iodine-125 92.23
  linear accelerator 92.24
  neutrons 92.26
  particulate radiation NEC 92.26
  photons 92.24
  protons 92.26
  radioactive cesium 92.23
  radioisotopes NEC 92.23
Temperature gradient study (*see also* Thermography) 88.89
Temperament assessment 94.02
Tendinoplasty —*see* Repair, tendon
Tendinosuture (immediate) (primary) (*see also* Suture, tendon) 83.64
  hand (*see also* Suture, tendon, hand) 82.45
Tendolysis 83.91
  hand 82.91
Tendoplasty *see* Repair, tendon
Tenectomy 83.39
  eye 15.13
    levator palpebrae 08.33
    multiple (two or more tendons) 15.3
  hand 82.29
  levator palpebrae 08.33
  tendon sheath 83.31
    hand 82.21
Tenodesis (tendon fixation to skeletal attachment) 83.88
  Fowler 82.85
  hand 82.85
Tenolysis 83.91
  hand 82.91
Tenomyoplasty (*see also* Repair, tendon) 83.88
  hand (*see also* Repair, tendon, hand) 82.86
Tenomyotomy —*see* Tenonectomy
Tenonectomy 83.42
  for graft 83.41
    hand 82.32
  hand 82.33
    for graft 82.32
Tenontomyoplasty —*see* Repair, tendon
Tenontoplasty —*see* Repair, tendon

Therapy—*continued*

individual, psychiatric NEC 94.39
  for psychosexual dysfunction 94.34
industrial 93.89
infrared irradiation 93.35
inhalation NEC 93.96
insulin shock 94.24
intermittent positive pressure breathing (IPPB) 93.91
IPPB (intermittent positive pressure breathing) 93.91
lithium 94.22
manipulative, osteopathic (*see also* Manipulation, osteopathic) 93.67
manual arts 93.81
methadone 94.25
mist (inhalation) 93.94
music 93.84
nebulizer 93.94
neuroleptic 94.23
occupational 93.83
oxygen 93.96
  catalytic 93.96
  hyperbaric 93.95
    wound 93.59
  wound (hyperbaric) 93.59
paraffin bath 93.35
physical NEC 93.39
  combined (without mention of components) 93.38
  diagnostic NEC 93.09
play 93.81
  psychotherapeutic 94.36
positive and expiratory pressure—*see* category 96.7
psychiatric NEC 94.39
  drug NEC 94.25
  lithium 94.22
radiation 92.29
  contact (150 KVP or less) 92.21
  deep (200-300 KVP) 92.22
  high voltage (200-300 KVP) 92.22
  low voltage (150 KVP or less) 92.21
  megavoltage 92.24
  orthovoltage 92.22
  particle source NEC 92.26
  photon 92.24
  radioisotope (teleradiotherapy) 92.23
  retinal lesion 14.26
  superficial (150 KVP or less) 92.21
  supervoltage 92.24
radioisotope, radioisotopic NEC 92.29
  implantation or insertion 92.27
  injection or instillation 92.28
  teleradiotherapy 92.23
radium (radon) 92.23
recreational 93.81
rehabilitation NEC 93.89
respiratory NEC 93.99
  bi-level airway pressure 93.90
  continuous positive airway pressure [CPAP] 93.90
  endotracheal respiratory assistance—*see* category 96.7
  intermittent mandatory ventilation [IMV]—*see* category 96.7
  intermittent positive pressure breathing [IPPB] 93.91
  negative pressure (continuous) [CNP] 93.99

Therapy—*continued*

  other continuous (unspecified duration) 96.70
    for less than 96 consecutive hours 96.71
    for 96 consecutive hours or more 96.72
  positive and expiratory pressure [PEEP]—*see* category 96.7
  pressure support ventilation [PSV]—*see* category 96.7
root canal 23.70
  with
    apicoectomy 23.72
    irrigation 23.71
shock
  chemical 94.24
  electric 94.27
    subconvulsive 94.26
  insulin 94.24
speech 93.75
  for correction of defect 93.74
ultrasound 93.35
  hyperthermia for cancer treatment 99.85
ultraviolet light 99.82
Thermocautery —*see* Cauterization
Thermography 88.89
blood vessel 88.86
bone 88.83
breast 88.85
cerebral 88.81
eye 88.82
lymph gland 88.89
muscle 88.84
ocular 88.82
osteoarticular 88.83
specified site NEC 88.89
vein, deep 88.86
Thermokeratoplasty 11.74
Thermosclerectomy 12.62
Thermotherapy (hot packs) (paraffin bath) NEC 93.35
Thiersch operation
anus 49.79
skin graft 86.69
  hand 86.62
Thompson operation
cleft lip repair 27.54
correction of lymphedema 40.9
quadricepsplasty 83.86
thumb apposition with bone graft 82.69
Thoracectomy 34.09
for lung collapse 33.34
Thoracentesis 34.91
Thoracocentesis 34.91
Thoracolysis (for collapse of lung) 33.39
Thoracoplasty (anterior) (extrapleural) (paravertebral) (posterolateral) (complete) (partial) 33.34
Thoracoscopy, transpleural (for exploration) 34.21
Thoracostomy 34.09
for lung collapse 33.32
Thoracotomy (with drainage) 34.09
exploratory 34.02
Three-snip operation, punctum 09.51
Thrombectomy 38.00
with endarterectomy—*see* Endarterectomy
abdominal
  artery 38.06
  vein 38.07
aorta (arch) (ascending) (descending) 38.04
bovine graft 39.49

Thrombectomy—*continued*
  coronary artery 36.09
  head and neck vessel NEC 38.02
  intracranial vessel NEC 38.01
  lower limb
    artery 38.08
    vein 38.09
  pulmonary vessel 38.05
  thoracic vessel NEC 38.05
  upper limb (artery) (vein) 38.03
Thromboendarterectomy 38.10
  abdominal 38.16
  aorta (arch) (ascending) (descending) 38.14
  coronary artery 36.09
    open chest approach 36.03
  head and neck NEC 38.12
  intracranial NEC 38.11
  lower limb 38.18
  thoracic NEC 38.15
  upper limb 38.13
Thymectomy 07.80
  partial 07.81
  total 07.82
Thymopexy 07.99
Thyrochondrotomy 31.3
Thyrocricoidectomy 30.29
Thyrocricotomy (for assistance in breathing)
  31.1
Thyroidectomy NEC 06.39
  by mediastinotomy (*see also* Thyroidectomy,
    substernal) 06.50
  with laryngectomy—*see* Laryngectomy
  complete or total 06.4
    substernal (by mediastinotomy) (transsternal
      route) 06.52
    transoral route (lingual) 06.6
  lingual (complete) (partial) (subtotal) (total) 06.6
  partial or subtotal NEC 06.39
    with complete removal of remaining lobe 06.2
    submental route (lingual) 06.6
    substernal (by mediastinotomy) (transsternal
      route) 06.51
  remaining tissue 06.4
  submental route (lingual) 06.6
  substernal (by mediastinotomy)
    (transsternal route) 06.50
    complete or total 06.52
    partial or subtotal 06.51
  transoral route (lingual) 06.6
  transsternal route (*see also* Thyroidectomy,
    substernal) 06.50
  unilateral (with removal of isthmus) (with
    removal of portion of other lobe) 06.2
Thyroidorrhaphy 06.93
Thyroidotomy (field) (gland) NEC 06.09
  postoperative 06.02
Thyrotomy 31.3
  with tantalum plate 31.69
Toilette
  skin—*see* Debridement, skin or subcutaneous
    tissue
  tracheostomy 96.55
Token economy (behavior therapy) 94.33
Tomkins operation (metroplasty) 69.49
Tomography —*see also* Radiography
  abdomen NEC 88.02
  cardiac 87.42

Tomography—*continued*
  computerized axial NEC 88.38
    abdomen 88.01
    bone 88.38
      quantitative 88.98
    brain 87.03
    head 87.03
    kidney 87.71
    skeletal 88.38
      quantitative 88.98
    thorax 87.41
  head NEC 87.04
  kidney NEC 87.72
  lung 87.42
  thorax NEC 87.42
Tongue tie operation 25.91
Tonography 95.26
Tonometry 89.11
Tonsillectomy 28.2
  with adenoidectomy 28.3
Tonsillotomy 28.0
Topectomy 01.32
Torek (Bevan) operation (orchidopexy) (first
  stage) (second stage) 62.5
Torkildsen operation (ventriculocisternal shunt)
  02.2
Torpin operation (cul-de-sac resection) 70.92
Toti operation (dacryocystorhinostomy) 09.81
Touchas operation 86.83
Touroff operation (ligation of subclavian artery)
  38.85
Toxicology —*see* Examination, microscopic
TPN (total parenteral nutrition) 99.15
Trabeculectomy ab externo 12.64
Trabeculodialysis 12.59
Trabeculotomy ab externo 12.54
Trachelectomy 67.4
Trachelopexy 69.22
Tracheloplasty 67.69
Trachelorrhaphy (Emmet) (suture) 67.61
  obstetrical 75.51
Trachelotomy 69.95
  obstetrical 73.93
Tracheocricotomy (for assistance breathing) 31.1
Tracheofissure 31.1
Tracheography 87.32
Tracheolaryngotomy (emergency) 31.1
  permanent opening 31.29
Tracheoplasty 31.79
  with artificial larynx 31.75
Tracheorrhaphy 31.71
Tracheoscopy NEC 31.42
  through tracheotomy (stoma) 31.41
Tracheostomy (emergency) (temporary) (for
  assistance in breathing) 31.1
  mediastinal 31.21
  permanent NEC 31.29
  revision 31.74
Tracheotomy (emergency) (temporary) (for
  assistance in breathing) 31.1
  permanent 31.29
Tracing, carotid pulse with ECG lead 89.56
Traction
  with reduction of fracture or dislocation—*see*
    Reduction, fracture *and* Reduction,
    dislocation
  adhesive tape (skin) 93.46
  boot 93.46
  Bryant's (skeletal) 93.44
  Buck's 93.46

U

V

Vaccination (prophylactic) (against) 99.59
  anthrax 99.55
  brucellosis 99.55
  cholera 99.31
  common cold 99.51
  disease NEC 99.55
    arthropod-borne viral NEC 99.54
  encephalitis, arthropod-borne viral 99.53
  German measles 99.47
  hydrophobia 99.44
  infectious parotitis 99.46
  influenza 99.52
  measles 99.45
  mumps 99.46
  paratyphoid fever 99.32
  pertussis 99.37
  plague 99.34
  poliomyelitis 99.41
  rabies 99.44
  Rocky Mountain spotted fever 99.55
  rubella 99.47
  rubeola 99.45
  smallpox 99.42
  Staphylococcus 99.55
  Streptococcus 99.55
  tuberculosis 99.33
  tularemia 99.35
  typhoid 99.32
  typhus 99.55
  undulant fever 99.55
  yellow fever 99.43
Vacuum extraction, fetal head 72.79
  with episiotomy 72.71
Vagectomy (subdiaphragmatic) (*see also* Vagotomy) 44.00
Vaginal douche 96.44
Vaginectomy 70.4
Vaginofixation 70.77
Vaginoperineotomy 70.14
Vaginoplasty 70.79
Vaginorrhaphy 70.71
  obstetrical 75.69
Vaginoscopy 70.21
Vaginotomy 70.14
  for
    culdocentesis 70.0
    pelvic abscess 70.12
Vagotomy (gastric) 44.00
  parietal cell 44.02
  selective NEC 44.03
    highly 44.02
    Holle's 44.02
    proximal 44.02
  truncal 44.01
Valvotomy —*see* Valvulotomy
Valvulectomy, heart —*see* Valvuloplasty, heart
Valvuloplasty
  heart (open heart technique) (without valve replacement) 35.10
    with prosthesis or tissue graft—*see* Replacement, heart, valve, by site
  aortic valve 35.11
    percutaneous (balloon) 35.96
  combined with repair of atrial and ventricular septal defects—*see* Repair, endocardial cushion defect
  mitral valve 35.12

Valvuloplasty—*continued*
  percutaneous (balloon) 35.96
  pulmonary valve 35.13
    in total repair of tetralogy of Fallot 35.81
    percutaneous (balloon) 35.96
  tricuspid valve 35.14
Valvulotomy
  heart (closed heart technique) (transatrial) (transventricular) 35.00
  aortic valve 35.01
  mitral valve 35.02
  open heart technique—*see* Valvuloplasty, heart
  pulmonary valve 35.03
    in total repair of tetralogy of Fallot 35.81
  tricuspid valve 35.04
Varicocelectomy, spermatic cord 63.1
Varicotomy, peripheral vessels (lower limb) 38.59
  upper limb 38.53
Vascularization —*see* Revascularization
Vasectomy (complete) (partial) 63.73
Vasogram 87.94
Vasoligation 63.71
  gastric 38.86
Vasorrhaphy 63.81
Vasostomy 63.6
Vasotomy 63.6
Vasotripsy 63.71
Vasovasostomy 63.82
Vectorcardiogram (VCG) (with ECG) 89.53
Venectomy —*see* Phlebectomy
Venipuncture NEC 38.99
  for injection of contrast material—*see* Phlebography
Venography —*see* Phlebography
Venorrhaphy 39.32
Venotomy 38.00
  abdominal 38.07
  head and neck NEC 38.02
  intracranial NEC 38.01
  lower limb 38.09
  thoracic NEC 38.05
  upper limb 38.03
Venotripsy 39.98
Venovenostomy 39.29
Ventilation,
  bi-level airway pressure 93.90
  continuous positive airway pressure [CPAP] 93.90
  endotracheal respiratory assistance—*see category* 96.7
  intermittent positive airway pressure breathing [IPPB] 93.91
  mechanical
    endotracheal respiratory assistance—*see category* 96.7
    intermittent mandatory ventilation [IMV]—*see category* 96.7
    other continuous (unspecified duration) 96.70
      for less than 96 consecutive hours 96.71
      for 96 consecutive hours or more 96.72
    positive and expiratory pressure [PEEP]—*see category* 96.7
    pressure support ventilation [PSV]—*see category* 96.7
  negative pressure (continuous) [CNP] 93.99
Ventriculocholecystostomy 02.34
Ventriculocisternostomy 02.2

W

Wada test (hemispheric function) 89.10
Ward-Mayo operation (vaginal hysterectomy)
68.59
laparoscopically assisted (LAVH) 68.51
Washing —*see* Lavage *and* Irrigation
Waterston operation (aorta-right pulmonary
artery anastomosis) 39.0
Watkins (Wertheim) **operation** (uterus
interposition) 69.21
Watson-Jones operation
hip arthrodesis 81.21
reconstruction of lateral ligaments, ankle 81.49
shoulder arthrodesis (extra-articular) 81.23
tenoplasty 83.88
Webbing (syndactylization) 86.89
Weir operation
appendicostomy 47.91
correction of nostrils 21.86
Wertheim operation (radical hysterectomy) 68.6
West operation (dacryocystorhinostomy) 09.81
Wheeler operation
entropion repair 08.44
halving procedure (eyelid) 08.24
Whipple operation (radical
pancreaticoduodenectomy) 52.7
Child modification (radical subtotal
pancreatectomy) 52.53
Rodney Smith modification (radical subtotal
pancreatectomy) 52.53
White operation (lengthening of tendon
calcaneus by incomplete tenotomy) 83.11
Whitehead operation
glossectomy, radical 25.4
hemorrhoidectomy 49.46
Whitman operation
foot stabilization (talectomy) 77.98
hip reconstruction 81.40
repair of serratus anterior muscle 83.87
talectomy 77.98
trochanter wedge osteotomy 77.25
Wier operation (entropion repair) 08.44
Williams-Richardson operation (vaginal
construction) 70.61
Wilms operation (thoracoplasty) 33.34
Wilson operation (angulation osteotomy for
hallux valgus) 77.51
Window operation
antrum (nasal sinus)—*see* Antrotomy, maxillary
aorticopulmonary 39.59
bone cortex (*see also* Incision, bone) 77.10
facial 76.09
nasoantral—*see* Antrotomy, maxillary
pericardium 37.12
pleura 34.09
Winiwarter operation (cholecystoenterostomy)
51.32
Wiring
aneurysm 39.52
dental (for immobilization) 93.55
with fracture-reduction—*see* Reduction,
fracture
orthodontic 24.7
Wirsungojejunostomy 52.96
Witzel operation (temporary gastrostomy) 43.19
Woodward operation (release of high riding
scapula) 81.83
Wrapping, aneurysm (gauze) (methyl
methacrylate) (plastic) 39.52

X

Xenograft 86.65
Xerography, breast 87.36
Xeromammogmphy 87.36
Xiphoidectomy 77.81
X-ray
chest (routine) 87.44
wail NEC 87.39
contrast—*see* Radiography, contrast
diagnostic—*see* Radiography
injection of radio-opaque substance—*see*
Radiography, contrast
skeletal series, whole or complete 88.31
therapeutic—*see* Therapy, radiation

Y

Young operation
epispadias repair 58.45
tendon transfer (anterior tibialis) (repair of flat
foot) 83.75
Yount operation (division of iliotibial band)
83.14

Z

Zancolli operation
capsuloplasty 81.72
tendon transfer (biceps) 82.56
Ziegler operation (iridectomy) 12.14
Zonulolysis (with lens extraction) (*see also*
Extraction, cataract, intracapsular) 13.19
Z-plasty
epicanthus 08.59
eyelid (*see also* Reconstruction, eyelid) 08.70
hypopharynx 29.4
skin (scar) (web contracture) 86.84
with excision of lesion 86.3

36.17 Abdominal - coronary artery bypass
New code

37.99 Other
Inclusion term added

**39.50 Angioplasty or atherectomy of
non-coronary vessel**
Inclusion term deleted, Code also added

**39.90 Insertion of non-coronary artery stent
or stents**
New code

47.0 Appendectomy
New category

47.01 Laparoscopic appendectomy
New code

47.09 Other appendectomy
New code

47.1 Incidental appendectomy
New category

47.11 Laparoscopic incidental appendectomy
New code

47.19 Other incidental appendectomy
New code

51.21 Other partial cholecystectomy
New code

51.24 Laparoscopic partial cholecystectomy
New code

**52.84 Autotransplantation of cells of Islets of
Langerhans**
New code

**52.85 Allotransplantation of cells of Islets of
Langerhans**
New code

**52.86 Transplantation of cells of Islets of
Langerhans, not otherwise specified**
New code

54.5 Lysis of peritoneal adhesions
New category

**54.51 Laparoscopic lysis of peritoneal
adhesions**
New code

54.59 Other lysis of peritoneal adhesions
New code

58.92 Excision of periurethral tissue
Exclusion term added

**59.01 Ureterolysis with freeing or
repositioning of ureter for
retroperitoneal fibrosis**
Code deleted

**59.02 Other lysis of perirenal or periureteral
adhesions**
Exclusion term added

**59.03 Laparoscopic lysis of perirenal or
periureteral adhesions**
New code

59.11 Other lysis of perivesical adhesions
Code title revised

**59.12 Laparoscopic lysis of perivesical
adhesions**
New code

60.29 Other transurethral prostatectomy
Inclusion term added

65.0 Oophorotomy
New category

65.01 Laparoscopic oophorotomy
New code

65.09 Other oophorotomy
New code

65.13 Laparoscopic biopsy of ovary
New code

**65.14 Other laparoscopic diagnostic
procedures on ovaries**
New code

65.21 Marsupialization of ovarian cyst
Exclusion term added

65.22 Wedge resection of ovary
Exclusion term added

**65.23 Laparoscopic marsupialization of
ovarian cyst**
New code

65.24 Laparoscopic wedge resection of ovary
New code

**65.25 Other laparoscopic local excision or
destruction of ovary**
New code

**65.29 Other local excision or destruction of
ovary**
Exclusion term added

65.3 Unilateral oophorectomy
New category

65.31 Laparoscopic unilateral oophorectomy
New code

65.39 Other unilateral oophorectomy
New code

65.4 Unilateral salpingo-oophorectomy
New category

**65.41 Laparoscopic unilateral
salpingo-oophorectomy**
New code

65.49 Other unilateral salpingo-oophorectomy
New code

**65.51 Other removal of both ovaries at same
operative episode**
Code title revised, Exclusion term added

65.52 Other removal of remaining ovary
Code title revised, Exclusion term added

**65.53 Laparoscopic removal of both ovaries
at same operative episode**
New code

**65.54 Laparoscopic removal of remaining
ovary**
New code

**65.61 Other removal of both ovaries and
tubes at same operative episode**
Code title revised, Exclusion term added

65.62 Other removal of remaining ovary and tube
Code title revised, Exclusion term added

65.63 Laparoscopic removal of both ovaries and tubes at same operative episode
New code

65.64 Laparoscopic removal of remaining ovary and tube
New code

65.71 Other simple suture of ovary
Code title revised, Exclusion term added

65.72 Other reimplantation of ovary
Code title revised, Exclusion term added

65.73 Other salpingo-oophoroplasty
Code title revised, Exclusion term added

65.74 Laparoscopic simple suture of ovary
New code

65.75 Laparoscopic reimplantation of ovary
New code

65.76 Laparoscopic salpingo-oophoroplasty
New code

65.8 Lysis of adhesions of ovary and fallopian tube
New category

65.81 Laparoscopic lysis of adhesions of ovary and fallopian tube
New code

65.89 Other lysis of adhesions of ovary and fallopian tube
New code

65.92 Transplantation of ovary
Exclusion codes added

66.5 Total bilateral salpingectomy
Exclusion codes changed

66.62 Salpingectomy with removal of tubal pregnancy
Exclusion codes changed

66.69 Other
Exclusion codes changed

68.23 Endometrial ablation
New code

68.5 Vaginal hysterectomy
New category

68.51 Laparoscopically assisted vaginal hysterectomy (LAVH)
New code

68.59 Other vaginal hysterectomy
New code

68.6 Radical abdominal hysterectomy
Code also code changed

68.9 Other and unspecified hysterectomy
Exclusion codes changed

80.51 Excision of intervertebral disc
Code also added